McKinney's®
New York
Rules of Court

Volume III – Local Civil

2012 Edition

WEST®

A Thomson Reuters business

D1473653

Mat #41034690

ISBN: 978-0-314-94055-1

ADDITIONAL INFORMATION OR
RESEARCH ASSISTANCE

For additional information or research assistance call the West reference attorneys at 1–800–REF–ATTY (1–800–733–2889). Contact West's editorial department directly with your questions and suggestions by e-mail at west.editor@thomson.com.

Visit West's home page at west.thomson.com.

PREFACE

This edition of *McKinney's New York Rules of Court, Volume III – Local Civil, 2012* replaces the 2011 edition. It provides in convenient form court rules governing local civil practice in New York courts in the First, Second, Third, Fifth, Seventh, Eighth, Ninth, Tenth, Eleventh, Twelfth, and Thirteenth Judicial Districts, as well as rules for the Commercial Courts, Court of Claims, and Housing Courts. Rules for Albany, Bronx, Dutchess, Erie, Kings, Monroe, Nassau, New York, Onondaga, Orange, Putnam, Richmond, Rockland, Queens, Suffolk and Westchester counties are included. This volume is current with amendments received through September 1, 2011.

THE PUBLISHER

October 2011

WestlawNext™

THE NEXT GENERATION OF ONLINE RESEARCH

WestlawNext is the world's most advanced legal research system. By leveraging more than a century of information and legal analysis from Westlaw, this easy-to-use system not only helps you find the information you need quickly, but offers time-saving tools to organize and annotate your research online. As with Westlaw.com, WestlawNext includes the editorial enhancements (e.g., case headnotes, topics, key numbers) that make it a perfect complement to West print resources.

- FIND ANYTHING by entering citations, descriptive terms, or Boolean terms and connectors into the WestSearch™ box at the top of every page.

- USE KEYCITE® to determine whether a case, statute, regulation, or administrative decision is good law.

- BROWSE DATABASES right from the home page.

- SAVE DOCUMENTS to folders and add notes and highlighting online.

SIGN ON: next.westlaw.com
LEARN MORE: West.Thomson.com/WestlawNext
FOR HELP: 1–800–WESTLAW (1–800–937–8529)

*

TABLE OF CONTENTS

LOCAL CIVIL COURTS

TABLE OF CONTENTS

TABLE OF CONTENTS

TABLE OF CONTENTS

McKINNEY'S NEW YORK RULES OF COURT

LOCAL RULES OF COURT

FIRST JUDICIAL DISTRICT — NEW YORK COUNTY

Westlaw Electronic Research

These rules may be searched electronically on Westlaw® *in the NY–RULES database; updates to these rules may be found on* Westlaw *in NY–RULESUP-DATES. For search tips and a summary of database content, consult the* Westlaw *Scope Screens for each database.*

Form

26. Article 78 Proceeding, Order Transferring to Appellate Division (Substantial Evidence (CPLR 7804(g))).
27. Assessment of Damages (Inquest), Order Directing.
28. Attachment, Order of.
29. Consolidation, Order Directing (Transfer From Other County).
30. Consolidation, Order Directing (Two or More NY County Actions).
31. Dismiss Complaint on Default, Order Granting Motion to.
32. Dismiss Complaint, Order Granting Motion to.
33. Dismissing Defense, Order.
34. Dismissing Some Causes of Action, Order.
35. Dismissing With Leave to Replead, Order.
36. Ejectment, Order and Judgment.
37. Enforcement Order, Downward Modification of Maintenance.
38. Framed Issue Hearing (Uninsured Motorist), Order Directing.
39. Intervention, Order Granting.
40. Joint Trial, Order Directing.
41. Pendente Lite Relief, Including Maintenance, Child Support, Custody, Injunctive Relief, Counsel Fees, etc.
42. Preliminary Injunction.
43. Reference to Determining -- Long Account, Order of.

Form

44. Reference to Hear and Report, Order Directing.
45. Resettling Order, Order.
46. Sealing Order.
47. Security for Costs, Order Directing.
48. Seizure, Order of (On Notice).
49. Severance of Claim for Counsel Fees, Order Directing.
50. Standard Format, Long Form Order.
51. Stay of Action and Severance Pending Outcome of Bankruptcy Proceeding.
52. Stay of Action Pending Outcome of Other Action or Arbitration Proceeding.
53. Substitution of Plaintiff, Order for.
54. Summary Judgment Dismissing Complaint, Order Granting.
55. Summary Judgment in Lieu of Complaint, Order Denying.
56. Summary Judgment On the Complaint On Default, Order Granting.
57. Summary Judgment On the Complaint, Order Granting.
58. Summary Judgment, Partial, Order Granting.
59. Turn-Over Order and Judgment.
60. Venue, Change of: from New York County.
61. Venue, Change of: to NY County.
62. Withdraw as Counsel, Order on Motion to.
63. Withdraw as Counsel, Order on Motion To, With Order of Reference re Retaining Lien.

NEW YORK COUNTY
COURTHOUSE PROCEDURES
COMMENCEMENT OF CASES

Procedure I. Commencement of Cases

A. Starting a Case

To commence an action or special proceeding, a summons and complaint or summons with notice in an action, or a petition in a special proceeding shall be filed with the County Clerk in Room 141B, 60 Centre Street. CPLR 304. The filing party obtains an index number by (i) completing an index number purchase sheet (see Forms on this site); and (ii) paying to the County Clerk's cashier a fee of $ 210 (absent a poor person order). All fees must be paid by cash, certified check (payable to the County Clerk), credit card (Visa or Mastercard), or U.S. postal money order. The checks of attorneys within New York State bearing "Attorney at Law" or "Esquire" and the attorney's address and phone number will be accepted. Checks from outside New York must be certified. The County Clerk will issue a receipt, which the applicant will need to show when proceeding to court.

To make a filing that commences a case, the attorney must deliver the summons and complaint, summons with notice or petition to the County Clerk in Room 141B together with the index number fee. At the time of filing, the original and a copy of these papers will be date stamped by the Clerk, who shall file the original and maintain a record of the date of filing and who shall immediately return the copy to the filing party. CPLR 304.

When the matter commenced is a special proceeding or a motion/action pursuant to CPLR 3213, the filing attorney should file the original papers with the County Clerk and a duplicate original with the Motion Support Office (Room 119). D. Siegel, NEW YORK PRACTICE 96 (4th ed. 2005).

In electronically filed cases (in New York County, tort, tax certiorari and commercial cases can be so filed and certain commercial cases must be so filed (Uniform Rule 202.5-bb)), documents can be filed online and the filing fee can be paid for by credit card on-line.

A Request for Judicial Intervention ("RJI") is purchased in the County Clerk's cashier's office, Room 160 (cost $ 95). The filer of an RJI may seek an assignment only (e.g., so that a Justice might be available for rulings if difficulties were to arise during an impending deposition) or judicial action, principally with regard to a request for a preliminary conference; a motion on notice or petition and notice of petition; an order to show cause; or a note of issue (cost $ 30, $ 125 with RJI). Rule 202.6 of the Uniform Rules for the Trial Courts.

The filer of an RJI must check off a box identifying the case type, which brings about a random assignment of the case by computer to a Justice handling cases of that type. Random assignment of course ensures fairness. The filer must also designate a Differentiated Case Management ("DCM") track ("expedite", "standard" or "complex") (Rule 202.19 of the Uniform Rules for the Trial Courts) and provide information on service in matrimonial cases.

B. Related Cases

In an effort to conserve judicial resources and avoid inconsistent rulings, the filing counsel must check off whether a related case exists. If the new case is designated as related, it will automatically be assigned to the Justice who was assigned the earlier case provided that the latter has not already been disposed of. If the earlier case has been disposed of, the Clerk will assign the case at random; the filing attorney is, however, free to argue to the Justice to whom the case is assigned that the matter ought to be assigned to the Justice who had handled the earlier case due to considerations of judicial efficiency and the like. If a party believes that such a related-case designation and resulting assignment were made in error, or that the filing party incorrectly failed to designate the case as related, the issue should be raised before the assigned Justice, who may send the matter to the back office for a random reassignment or a transfer if the complaint is justified. If further review is required, it occurs before the Administrative Judge. The policy of the court is that one Justice may not order the transfer of a case directly to another particular Justice except (i) pursuant to procedures governing related cases or (ii) in the case of motions to reargue or renew (CPLR 2221) or (iii) with the permission of the Administrative Judge.

C. Assignment of Cases

When an RJI is presented in a back office, the case is "initialized" by data entry personnel, that is, the caption, index number and attorney appearance(s) are recorded in the Civil Case Information System computer, the court's computer system. An assignment is made by the computer, and the intervention requested is set in motion.

It may happen that an RJI has been filed but has not yet been processed and another party to the case may wish to bring on an order to show cause immediately. In most instances the County Clerk's computer will show whether an RJI has been purchased. So will the Supreme Court Records On-Line Library ("Scroll"), the case data and document repository available on this website. The office that receives the proposed order to show cause will try to locate the pending RJI in the other back office and cause it immediately to be processed by that other office so that the case can be assigned to a Justice to whom the order to show cause may be referred; or the receiving office will seek from the party presenting the order to show cause a copy of the RJI, which should have been served upon that party. This will permit the back office handling the proposed order to show cause to ascertain that an RJI has indeed been filed (though not yet processed) and to assign the case in accordance with the designations on the RJI. The party who first filed the RJI has the right to have the case processed in accordance with the designation made on the RJI by that party. If, in the view of another party, the RJI has not properly been completed, that party may raise this issue with the assigned Justice. Clerks cannot alter the RJI as filed nor can they direct another attorney to do so.

D. Commercial Division Assignments

Pursuant to procedures that became effective on January 17, 2006, a party filing an RJI who wishes to have the case assigned to the Commercial Division must designate the case as a "Commercial" one on the RJI and must submit together with the RJI a Statement in Support of Assignment to Commercial Division and a copy of the pleadings. Uniform Rule 202.70(d). The Statement form is available on the Commercial Division website (www.nycourts.gov/comdiv under "Operational Info" on the New York County home page). If the filer submits an RJI without the Statement and pleadings, the case will be assigned at random as a General Assignment case (i.e., not to the Division), although the Clerk may inform the filer that this will be done and allow the filer an opportunity to return with the missing Statement and pleadings.

E. Anonymous Captions/Filing Under Seal

A party may sometimes wish to obtain an order permitting a case to proceed under an anonymous caption, or to file initiating papers under seal pending a ruling by a Justice. For information, click here.[1]

March 2011

1 http://www.nycourts.gov/supctmanh/litigation_functions.htm

MOTIONS/PROCEEDINGS ON NOTICE

Procedure II. Motions and Special Proceedings by Notice of Motion/Petition

Motions made by notice of motion and petitions and notices of petition in special proceedings are processed by the Motion Support Office (Room 119) and are to be made returnable in the Motion Support Office Courtroom (Room 130) on any business day of the week at 9:30 AM. There are some differences in electronically-filed cases, which are explained in the Protocol on Courthouse Procedures in E-Filed Cases on this website (under "E Filing").

A. Intake and Processing of Motions/Special Proceedings

Papers to be Filed to Calendar Motions/Petitions: Effective March 15, 2011, an attorney seeking to calendar a motion/petition on notice shall present to the Motion Support Office (Room 119) only the following: (i) the original notice of motion/petition, proof of service thereof, and any annexed Rule 202.7 affirmation/affidavit, together with (ii) one photocopy of the foregoing documents, which is used to scan the documents into the Supreme Court Records On-Line Library ("Scroll "). Affidavits or affirmations in support of the motion and a memorandum of law will not be accepted at that time, but shall instead be submitted in the Motion Support Office Courtroom (Room 130) on the final return date. Proof of service of the affirmations, affidavits, and memorandum, if separate from the proof of service of the notice of motion/petition, etc., may be submitted with the former documents. An attorney whose office is located outside the County of New York may submit to the Motion Support Office by mail or express delivery service the notice of motion/petition, proof of service, and 202.7 affirmation/affidavit and the photocopy thereof, together with the motion fee ($45) in the form of a money order or attorney's check made payable to the New York County Clerk (personal checks are not accepted), provided that the package arrives within the time set forth in the next paragraph.

Time to File: The original notice of motion/petition, proof of service, and affirmation of good faith shall be presented to the Motion Support Office no later than five business days before the original return date, but no earlier than 30 days prior to that date. Any such submission that is presented more than 30 days prior to the return date will not be accepted at that time.

RJI, Proof of Payment of Index Number Fee, Required Papers in Commercial Division Cases, Court Computer, Sequence Numbers: In an unassigned case, counsel must submit an RJI and exhibit an index number receipt as proof that an index number fee was paid. If the filer is a party to a case in which someone else purchased the index number, a receipt showing that the purchase has been made can be obtained from a computer terminal in the County Clerk's Office. If the party submitting the RJI wishes to have a matter assigned to the Commercial Division, the RJI must be marked to show that the case is a commercial one and it must be accompanied by a signed statement in support of the Commercial Division assignment (this form is available on the New York County pages of the Commercial Division website (www.nycourts.gov/comdiv)) and a copy of the pleadings (Uniform Rule 202.70(d)). If the case is designated a commercial matter on the RJI but the required documents are not included, the Motion Support Office will assign the case as a non-Commercial Division matter. The RJI shall be marked to reflect the existence of any "related case" as explained on the "Commencement of Cases" page under "Courthouse Procedures" on this site. Motion Support will process the RJI and, via computer, randomly assign an unassigned case. Once the fee for the motion/petition, if required (see below), has been paid, Motion Support will record the motion/petition and the return date in the court's Civil Case Information System ("CCIS") computer, and give the motion/petition an identifying number (a "sequence number," such as "Seq. No. 2"), which will also be recorded in the computer. The next motion/petition presented to the court in that matter will be assigned the next sequence number in numerical order. Cross-motions are not assigned sequence numbers, i.e., they are treated as appendages to the main motion for processing purposes.

In special proceedings and with regard to motions pursuant to CPLR 3213, counsel should file the original petition and a summons and the original motion papers with the County Clerk to commence the case. CPLR 304. A duplicate original of the petition, the original notice of petition, and an original affidavit of service in a special proceeding, and a duplicate original of the 3213 papers and an original affidavit of service in any such motion-action shall be filed with the Motion Support Office.

Review of Papers for Form: When papers have been submitted to the Motion Support Office in the manner described above for the purpose of calendaring a motion/petition, the staff will review the papers for form (e.g., to be sure that proof of service has been filed, that the motion/petition has been made returnable in the Motion Support Office Courtroom (Room 130) on a business day at 9:30 AM). If any defects in the papers have been found, the staff will note those defects for counsel. The papers will not be "rejected" (CPLR 2102(c)) except as permitted in e-filed cases and as allowed by Uniform Rule 202.5(d). Defects noted by the clerk but not corrected by counsel may be brought to the attention of the assigned Justice.

Filing Fee on Motions and Cross-Motions:

1). Filing Fee on Motions Required

A motion fee must be paid on motions made in writing by notice of motion, order to show cause or ex parte after the commencement of an action. For this purpose, the term "action" shall mean any application to the court that requires the assignment of an index number, regardless of whether a formal pleading is filed. Applications or motions that commence an action and for which an index number fee must be paid require no motion fee. Thus, for example, an application commencing an Article 78 or other special proceeding or a motion pursuant to CPLR 3213 would not require a motion fee because this application or motion requires an index number fee. An ex parte application for pre-action disclosure (CPLR 3102(c)) would likewise not require payment of the motion fee. However, any motions made after the initial applications in these situations would require payment of the motion fee. A motion that is the initial application in a case commenced by the filing of a summons and complaint would require a motion fee since the filing of the summons and complaint rather than the application itself would require the purchase of an index number. Uncontested matrimonial matters do not require payment of the motion fee.

The fee must be paid on written cross-motions filed in opposition to motions on which a fee is required and also in opposition to applications or petitions for which a motion fee is not required.

The fee must be paid on post-judgment motions and cross-motions made in writing.

2). Procedures for Fee Payment for Motions/Cross Motions

Attorneys making motions by notice of motion should present the papers to the Motion Support Office (Room 119, 60 Centre Street) in the first instance as described above. The staff of that office will inspect the papers for form as noted above. This review will be conducted prior to the payment of the motion fee in order to ensure that fees are not paid with respect to motions that are defective (e.g., motions lacking proof of service or noticed for the wrong date). The filer shall then carry the papers to the Cashier of the County Clerk in Room 160 on the first floor of the 60 Centre Street courthouse and pay the $ 45 fee (except where in a proper case the papers and fee are submitted by mail or express delivery service). When the fee is paid, the County Clerk will place on the front of the notice of motion proof of payment in the form of a cashier's receipt stamp. The filer should then return to the Motion Support Office and deliver the papers.

The same process should be followed with cross-motions except that, after preliminary review in Room 119 and the obtaining of the cashier's receipt stamp, the papers should be delivered to the Motion Support Office Courtroom (Room 130) on the final return date. The Motion Support Office will accept the cross-motion bearing the cashier's receipt stamp even if the call of the calendar has concluded in Room 130 provided that the papers are submitted the same day as the call (and also, of course, that the papers were timely served and are in compliance with the procedures of the Courtroom).

The staff in court Parts on motions returnable in the Part will likewise accept cross-motions on the call of the calendar in the Part only if they bear proof of payment of the fee in the form of the cashier's receipt stamp.

Attorneys in electronically-filed cases can pay motion and cross-motion fees on-line using a Visa or Mastercard credit or bank card.

Subsequent Papers on Motions Returnable in Room 130: Cross-motions, papers in opposition, and reply papers on motions/petitions on notice returnable in Room 130 in a hard copy case shall be submitted to the Motion Support Office Courtroom (Room 130) on the final return date of the motion/petition and will not be accepted until that date.

Documents in E-Filed Cases: Documents in electronically filed cases in which a motion/petition on notice is made returnable in the Motion Support Office Courtroom (Room 130) may be e-filed at any time, as at present, except that the moving papers should be e-filed at least eight days prior to the return date to allow the staff time to process and calendar the motion. Unless the Justice assigned dispenses with such copies, attorneys must submit working copies of documents on the motion/petition in the Courtroom on the final return date, including copies of all opposition and reply documents, to each of which a copy of the Confirmation Notice shall be firmly affixed as the back page facing out. See the Protocol on E-Filing posted on the "E-Filing" page of this site.

B. Motions Made in More Than One Case on a Single Set of Papers

On occasion, attorneys may wish to make a motion in more than one case on a single set of papers. In such cases, by definition consolidation will not have been directed since consolidation signifies the combination of more than one case into a single one with a single caption and index number and ending in a single judgment. If more than one case is consolidated for joint trial, on the other hand, the cases remain separate, will end in separate judgments and are merely tried together. Where counsel seeks to make a motion affecting more than one case using a single set of papers, the moving papers should bear only one caption and index number, that of the case in which the motion is being made, which may be the principal case of the group involved. Counsel should not place a series of captions and index numbers on the single set of moving papers since this may lead to confusion and court staff will be unable to determine under which case to record the motion in the court's computer and in which file to place the papers.

The court is eager to minimize burdens on counsel whenever possible. Therefore, the court will not require counsel to file multiple sets of the same motion papers, including possibly numerous and lengthy affidavits, affirmations and briefs. Instead, the moving party should file one set of papers in the main case or some other single case using the caption for that case and its index number. Obviously, the moving attorney must be counsel of record in the case in which the motion is being made. If that counsel or any other wishes to make the identical motion in a related case, counsel should submit a notice of motion in the related case bearing only the caption and index number for that related case, and should attach thereto an affirmation/affidavit in which counsel refers to and adopts the motion papers and arguments made in the first case. This process of incorporation in separate, very brief motion papers should be repeated in each related case in which a party wishes to make the identical motion. This method will achieve efficiency for all concerned while maintaining an orderly and accurate process and record and sound record keeping.

The Motion Support Office (Room 119) will reject motions made with multiple captions and require resubmission in accordance with the procedure outlined here.

C. Return Date Submission Procedure—Room 130

Place of Return and Return Date: All motions/proceedings brought on by notice of motion or notice of petition, in both assigned and unassigned cases, shall be made returnable in the Motion Support Office Courtroom (Room 130) on any business day at 9:30 A.M.

Motion Calendars: The Motion Support Office prepares various calendars for the motions that appear in the Motion Support Office Courtroom daily. There is a Submission Calendar published separately for Commercial Division motions/petitions and for motions/petitions in electronically-filed cases.

The Courtroom also maintains a "Three–Day Submission" calendar, used when a party or parties seek an adjournment but fail to comply with the Courtroom's procedures. The case may be put over for three days to allow compliance with those procedures, as described further below.

Advance Publication of Room 130 Calendars: Two days prior to the return date, the New York Law Journal will publish, in alphabetical order, the calendars of all motions returnable in the Courtroom on that date. This information is also available from the court's Supreme Court Records On-Line Library ("Scroll") and from private information services.

Basic Procedures in Room 130—Collection of Papers: The purpose of the Room 130 procedures is to achieve an easy and efficient means for attorneys to submit and the court to collect all opposition, cross-

moving and reply papers in connection with motions on the calendar. Each day in the Motion Support Office Courtroom, commencing at 9:30 A.M., all motions returnable that day will be "called" for the submission of these papers, which must be handed up at this "call" or, as described below, immediately before. Because hundreds of motions appear on the Room 130 calendars every day, motion papers (other than the initial papers as described above) cannot be accepted on any day prior to the return date. Courtesy copies are not accepted, but working copies are required by certain Justices (e.g., all Commercial Division Justices, unless otherwise directed in a specific case) in e-filed cases.

Given the purpose of the Room 130 procedure, the substance of motions will not be addressed at the submission "call." No Judge is present. To the extent possible, motions submitted in Room 130 will be decided "on the papers." If argument is directed, it will take place on an announced date shortly after the day of submission. Attorneys are not required to be present in Room 130. Indeed, attorneys are encouraged to use service or clerks to deliver papers, or to agree among themselves to have one of them deliver papers for all parties by service or a clerk. Counsel for the movant need not appear to "take a default" on any motion or for any other reason. Motions will be submitted, not marked off, in the absence of the movant. Opposing counsel similarly need not appear in person in order to avoid suffering a default. Delivery of papers by service or a clerk will suffice. The court's goal is to be able to collect papers on motions in an orderly fashion but without any attorney having to make an appearance in Room 130 at any time.

Applications, Adjournments, Submission of Late Papers—Procedures for Notice to Counsel:

Once a motion is made, counsel for all parties are strongly encouraged to agree upon a briefing schedule and submit a stipulation of adjournment reflecting that schedule using service or a clerk. Where a briefing schedule has not been agreed upon, the movant can avoid the need to attend simply to see if anyone will hand up opposing papers by demanding papers as provided by CPLR 2214(b). To protect movants against the submission of late opposition papers or cross-motions, the Motion Support Office will screen motions in which such papers are submitted without a response (reply or opposition respectively) to ensure that proper time to respond has been afforded and it will sua sponte adjourn for one week cases in which such time has not been given.

The court has established procedures to ensure that no attorney need feel compelled to attend the "call" out of fear that another party to the case will appear and make an unexpected application.

Adjournments by Stipulation: Specifically, a party seeking an adjournment must contact all other parties in an effort to obtain consent and demonstrate that

that was done. Adjournments are allowed in Room 130 in response to written stipulations. No more than three adjournments for a total of no more than 60 days are allowed except with the permission of the assigned Justice (Rule 202.8(e)(1) of the Uniform Rules for the Trial Courts), given by means of a so-ordered stipulation.

Adjournments by Affidavit/Affirmation of Consent: If all parties consent to an adjournment as allowed by these rules but a written stipulation cannot be obtained in time for submission, the applicant for the adjournment on consent may submit an affidavit or affirmation reciting that such consent was obtained. That document must state the reason for the adjournment request, how consent was obtained from all parties, when it was obtained, and the name of each attorney who gave oral consent. The affidavit/affirmation must have been served before the date on which the request for adjournment is made.

Adjournments by E–Mail: Parties seeking an adjournment on consent in compliance with the procedures outlined here may do so by e-mail. Counsel who wish to avail themselves of this procedure must submit the stipulation or affidavit/affirmation in PDF format as an attachment to an e-mail message sent to the following e-mail address: NYMOTCAL@courts. state.ny.us. Any such message may be sent up to 5 P.M. of the day before the return date of the motion to which it relates. In addition to the caption and the index number, each submission must identify the date on which the motion is then returnable. The party filing the paper must retain the original paper for 60 days in case any issue should later be raised about the PDF copy submitted.

Due to the volume of matters on the Room 130 calendar each day, it will not be possible for court staff to respond to every e-submission to indicate whether it has been granted or not. However, counsel should understand that requests for adjournment by stipulation or on consent recorded in an affidavit/affirmation of counsel will be granted if the request complies with the procedures of the Courtroom, including that with such adjournment there be no more than three adjournments for a total of no more than 60 days. Further, if there is a reason why a particular request by stipulation or on consent that is in compliance with Rule 202.8(e)(1) cannot be granted, counsel will be informed by e-mail; if such e-mail response is transmitted the day before or the day of the calendar in question, the matter will be adjourned by court staff to the three-day calendar for clarification. Counsel may confirm the outcome of a request by consulting the "Motion Support Calendars" link on the home page of this site. The dispositions of each day's Room 130 calendars are posted on the website at 3 P.M. in the afternoon of the same day.

Applications for Adjournment Not on Consent: If consent was not obtained from all parties prior to the return date, any party making an application for adjournment must submit an affidavit or affirmation in support of the application, reciting the reason for the requested adjournment and a description of the efforts made to obtain such consent, including the date when a contact was initiated or attempted, the means used, and the person contacted (if consent was refused) or for whom a message was left (if no contact was made). Furthermore, an applicant must, by phone, fax, e-mail, or mail transmitted with adequate lead time, advise all parties who have not consented that an application will be made, and the affidavit or affirmation must provide specifics on this as well. Applications for adjournments that are not properly supported will not be entertained. Rather, the matter will be adjourned for three days to permit compliance. These matters will then appear on the Three-Day Submission calendar. If there is no compliance, the Clerk of the Motion Support Office will mark the case submitted and refer it to the assigned Justice.

Submitting Papers Prior to the "Call": For the convenience of counsel, between 9:00 A.M. and 9:30 A.M. each day, in advance of the "call", Room 130 accepts (1) written stipulations; (2) affidavits/affirmations reciting the required details as to an adjournment on consent; (3) stipulations, letters or other writings withdrawing motions; and (4) final papers or complete sets of papers on motions. For motions in which these items are handed in before the "call", no one need remain to answer the "call." Counsel/parties must advise the court, either between 9:00 A.M. and 9:30 A.M. or at the "call", of all motions or cases that have been resolved by counsel/parties themselves and all motions that the movant no longer wishes to pursue. If such resolution occurs subsequent to the "call", the assigned Justice must be advised as soon as possible, by written notice sent to the Part, so that the court does not do unnecessary work.

D. Scheduling of Oral Argument/Appearances

Pursuant to request of some Justices, motions submitted in Room 130 will automatically be scheduled for a set argument date in the Part. Other Justices determine on a case-by-case basis whether to accept a particular substantive motion on submission, to require oral argument or to hold a conference. Counsel who wish oral argument must so request conspicuously on the front of their papers. See Uniform Rule 202.8(d). If argument is directed, notice will be given in Room 130 if service or counsel answer the "call"; the appearing party is expected to give notice to all parties and an announcement to this effect is made in Room 130. Where no one appears in Room 130, notice by mail will be sent by the court. If no notice of the one sort or the other is provided, counsel should understand that the motion has been taken on submission for decision on the papers. The results of the "call" are also published. See Section E.

In order that mail notice can be given, all attorneys should confirm that their names, addresses and phone numbers are correctly recorded in the court's computer, which can be done by consulting the Supreme Court Records On-Line Library ("Scroll") on this website. If any error exists, it can be corrected by submitting a form to the Trial Support Office (Room 158).

E. Publication of the Results of the Submission Calendar

The results of the submission process for all motions "called" in the Motion Support Office Courtroom are posted daily on the court's website (see "Motion Support Calendars"). Each posting generally occurs late in the same day on which the "call" took place. Calendars are also published in the New York Law Journal two days after each return date. This information identifies all motions that were marked submitted and automatically scheduled for argument/appearance, together with the Part and the date set down for argument/appearance; all motions that were marked submitted and sent on to the assigned Justices in cases assigned to Justices who do not automatically schedule argument or appearance; all motions that were marked "submitted on default"; all motions that were adjourned and the adjourned date; and all motions that were marked "withdrawn." The Supreme Court Records On-Line Library ("Scroll") will also reveal such information (with a brief time lag from entry of the data into the court's computer system).

F. Post–Submission Procedures in Motion Support

1) *Decisions: Issuance, Processing, Access to Copies With Entry Stamp, and Public Information*

All decisions on motions and orders are delivered to Motion Support, which records in the court computer that a decision has been issued, the date thereof and whether the case has been disposed of, and makes similar notations as to long form orders. Decisions (other than those in matrimonial and Article 81 cases and cases under seal or decisions as to which the Justice directs otherwise) are posted on the Supreme Court Records On-Line Library ("Scroll") on this website within a few business hours after recordation of data in the court's computer. Except as to decisions that call for settlement of an order or judgment, the decisions as posted generally bear the County Clerk's entry stamp so that counsel may serve a notice of entry promptly and without having to make a trip to the courthouse to retrieve a copy of the decision with entry stamp. The court system offers a service, known as "E Track" (at www.nycourts.gov under "E Courts"), that tracks, and provides notice of activity in, at no charge, cases identified and listed by the subscribing attorney. The New York Law Journal also daily publishes notice of issuance of orders and decisions and the text of selected decisions. Counsel should not contact Chambers for information about decisions and orders.

2) *The Settlement of Long Form Orders*

Although the court strongly favors the use of short form orders and judgments, there are instances when settlement of an order or judgment is appropriate. When a Justice directs in a decision that a long form order or judgment be settled, that decision is recorded in the court's computer system by Motion Support and the motion file with decision is held in the Order Section of the Motion Support Office in Room 119. The settlement process takes place there. (There are a few exceptions. Orders in cases under Article 81 of the Mental Hygiene Law and orders for receivership and other fiduciary accountings are to be settled in the Guardianship and Fiduciary Support Office (Room 148) because of the special expertise required to review them. Orders in Commercial Division cases are to be settled in the Commercial Division Office (Room 119A)).

A proposed long form order or judgment in compliance with Rule 202.48 of the Uniform Rules for the Trial Courts must be presented to the relevant back office, together with a notice of settlement which bears a settlement date, the date on which the order is to be ready for formal presentation to the Justice. This date and time must be at 9:30 A.M. no sooner than either five days from personal service of the proposed order or ten days from service by mail. Proof of timely service on the other parties must accompany the proposed order. If an order or judgment is submitted late (later than 60 days from signing and filing of the decision) and the proponent can show good cause for this tardiness, an affidavit or affirmation justifying the delay should be annexed to the proposed order, together with proof of service thereof. If persuaded, the Justice will consider the proposed order despite its untimeliness.

Any proposed counter-order or counter-judgment must be accompanied by a copy marked to indicate all respects in which it differs from the proposal to which it responds (Uniform Rule 202.48 (c) (2), as amended Sept. 1, 2007) and must bear an affidavit of service and have been timely served pursuant to the Rule. When the time to present a counter-order or counter-judgment has expired, the Order Section staff will review a submission. No appearance is required of any party and the settlement date is not the day on which the papers will actually be presented to the Justice. If there are defects, the submission will be returned to the party who presented it. Once the submission has been reviewed and found proper in form, it will be sent to Chambers. Formal changes will be made by the staff directly on the order/judgment.

The settlement process is expedited and simplified in e-filed cases. See the Protocol cited above.

Sometimes a decision will state "Submit Order." The submitting party should prepare a long form order and make it returnable to the Justice without notice. Counsel should deliver the proposed order to the Order Section of the appropriate back office.

Proposed orders or judgments that did not arise out of a formal motion (e.g., out of a conference or trial) should be submitted to the Part of the assigned Justice.

February 9, 2011

EX PARTE APPLICATIONS

Procedure III. Ex Parte Applications

All ex parte applications are to be submitted to the Ex Parte Office (Room 315) except in Commercial Division cases, in which the applications should be submitted to the Commercial Division Support Office (Room 148). The following discussion concerns non–Division cases only. Attorneys who submit proposed orders to show cause or ex parte orders in electronically filed cases can save themselves labor and expedite processing of the papers.For information, click here.

A. Orders to Show Cause

Proposed orders to show cause ("OSC") must be submitted to Room 315 in the first instance. The Ex Parte Office records the proposed OSC in the court's computer system, as well as the names of the attorneys for the movant and other attorneys, if known, and assigns the case if previously unassigned.

The Ex Parte Office also reviews proposed OSC's for form, in a process similar to the initial examination of motions on notice by the Motion Support Office, prior to fee payment. All ex parte motions must comply with CPLR 2217(b). CPLR 6313(a) precludes the *ex parte* issuance of a temporary restraining order ("TRO") against a public officer, board, or municipal corporation of the State (which includes New York City) to restrain the performance of statutory duties. If an applicant seeks such relief, advance notice to the Corporation Counsel's Office, the Office of the Attorney General, or agency counsel if the municipality is so represented is required.

Further, Uniform Rule 202.7 was amended recently to provide for notice except under certain circumstances. Specifically, pursuant to Uniform Rule 202.7 (f), upon an application for an order to show cause that seeks a temporary restraining order, the application must contain an affirmation demonstrating that there will be significant prejudice to the party seeking the restraining order by the giving of notice. In the absence of such prejudice, the affirmation must demonstrate that a good faith effort has been made to notify the party against whom the restraining order is sought of the time, date and place that the application will be made sufficient to permit the party an opportunity to appear in response to the application. It is the practice of this court that the applicant must notify the party against whom the restraining order is sought of the time and date that the application will be submitted to the Ex Parte Office. Further, counsel shall advise the adversary that he or she will inform the adversary of the place, date and precise time when the Justice will entertain the application. Once the papers have been submitted to the Ex Parte Office, applying counsel shall contact the Part of the Justice in question to determine when and where it will be convenient for the Justice to entertain the application. Counsel shall then promptly notify the adversary. Counsel shall not appear in the courtroom of the assigned justice without having first made such an inquiry.

If the papers are satisfactory, staff in Room 315 will mark them so indicating. The attorney seeking to present the proposed OSC shall then proceed to the County Clerk's cashier's office in Room 160, pay the $ 45 fee, receive a cashier's receipt stamp on the OSC, and return to Room 315 to submit it.

A proposed OSC not of an emergency nature is reviewed expeditiously. The clerks will advise the attorney who presents such an OSC of any defects therein. If an OSC cannot be processed within a short time, the presenting attorney should return as instructed or send a clerk to Ex Parte in order to deliver the papers to the assigned Justice. If the proposed OSC requests immediate attention because of an emergency, an affidavit or affirmation is required explaining the nature of the claimed emergency. The Ex Parte Office will attend to the matter immediately and will ask counsel to remain. If oral argument of a motion brought on by OSC is sought, counsel must so indicate on the front of the proposed order. See Rule 202.8 (d) of the Uniform Rules for the Trial Courts. Should the proposed OSC be signed, the Justice decides whether argument is appropriate and, if so, will indicate as much in the OSC. If the OSC contains a TRO or oral argument is directed, the motion should be made returnable directly in the IAS Part, usually on the customary argument day. Whether a motion brought on by OSC is made returnable in the Motion Support Office Courtroom (Room 130) or directly in the IAS Part, the movant is responsible for providing proof of service on the return date.

Once the OSC has been signed, the papers must be delivered to the Motion Support Office for further processing to ensure that the OSC appears on the proper motion calendar for the return date just fixed.

During absences of Justices, OSC's are handled by Ex Parte Justices.

Sometimes a party must submit an OSC to a Justice outside of normal court hours. There are two problems that may arise from applications entertained by Justices outside of normal court hours. First, the existence of the application may never be recorded in the court computer. Second, parties may be concerned about the potential risk of judge-shopping. To avoid these problems, all such applications should be made returnable before the assigned Justice or, if there is none, in the Ex Parte Office for random assignment (not before the Justice who signs the OSC unless he or she is the already-assigned Justice). The papers should be delivered to Ex Parte as soon as possible after the application has been signed.

B. Infant's, Incompetent's and Wrongful Death Compromise Orders

Court approval is required when an action commenced by an infant or an incompetent or an action for wrongful death is settled. The approval will take the form of a compromise order. If an action is pending before the court (an RJI was obtained), the proposed order and accompanying affidavits should be submitted to the Ex Parte Office for review. Upon completion of the review, the Office will forward the papers to the Justice assigned to the case. If an action was commenced but no RJI was filed, the papers should be submitted to the Ex Parte Office along with an RJI so that the matter may be assigned to a Justice. If no action was commenced, an RJI is not required; the papers will be submitted to an Ex Parte Justice through the Ex Parte Office.

C. Other *Ex Parte* Applications and Related Applications on Notice

Ex parte applications in addition to OSCs are filed in the Ex Parte Office. Depending on their nature, these are either referred to an Ex Parte Justice or entered into the court's computer and assigned to a Justice except where made in a previously-assigned action, in which event the application will be submitted to the assigned Justice. The following is a detailed summary of key ex parte applications processed by the Ex Parte Office and related applications on notice. (Applications for poor person status involving the self-represented are handled by the Office for the Self–Represented (Room 116)).

Anonymous Caption Order

Bars anyone but the parties and counsel from access to the papers and proceedings in a case and accords the case a caption of "Anonymous v. Anonymous." Should be sought by order to show cause in which the applicant is accorded in a TRO, pending a hearing on the motion, the right to obtain an index number and file an RJI using the Anonymous caption, and access to the file is restricted to the parties, counsel and court personnel.

Attachment, Ex Parte Orders

By order of attachment a party secures identified property against removal or dissipation to provide either security for an eventual money judgment or

court jurisdiction over the case premised upon the presence of property in New York. The class of cases in which such an order may be granted is listed in CPLR 6201. The order may be granted ex parte, including before service of a summons. CPLR 6211.

An ex parte order may be sought without the need to file an RJI. The papers must contain a statement that no prior application for the relief in question was made or, if one was, what the new facts are that justify granting the relief now. CPLR 2217(b). The plaintiff must also state whether any other provisional remedy has been sought or obtained in the case. CPLR 6001. If there is any possible doubt about the matter, the applicant must provide a detailed explanation of the jurisdictional nexus to New York. If the matter is brought pursuant to CPLR 6201(1), the moving papers should contain either a certificate as to the foreign and unqualified status of any corporate defendant, or an affirmation of counsel reciting that he or she spoke by phone with a representative of the Secretary of State or the Banking Department where a bank is involved and learned that the defendant is neither a New York corporation nor qualified to do business here, or, if the defendant is an individual, the source of knowledge that the defendant is a nondomiciliary residing without the state.

Further, the moving papers must show that the case is one within CPLR 6201. The papers must contain evidentiary proof of the claims being asserted and that the plaintiff will succeed on the merits; and a showing that the amount demanded exceeds all counterclaims known to plaintiff. The proposed order must specify the amount to be secured by the order of attachment, including interest, costs and sheriff's fees and expenses.

The plaintiff must post an attachment bond, unless other security is adequate. For example, an applicant bank may issue a certified check (payable to the Clerk). Personal checks are not acceptable. The sheriff will levy upon the amount in issue, plus 14%, plus $ 400, to cover interest, poundage fees, and levy fees. The bond should be 5 % of the above total for each defendant, plus 5% for the sheriff (up to $ 50,000.)

Where an order is obtained ex parte (except one based upon CPLR 6201(1)), it must provide that the applicant, within five days after levy on the property, shall move on such notice as the court shall direct to confirm the attachment. In a case in which the order is based on CPLR 6201(1), a garnishee's statement must be served and the plaintiff shall move within ten days after levy to confirm the order. CPLR 6211.

Attachment, by Motion on Notice

On a motion on notice by order to show cause, the court may grant a TRO without notice prohibiting the transfer of assets by a garnishee (CPLR 6214(b)). The order of attachment must contain the provisions set out in CPLR 6211(a).

The moving papers must satisfy CPLR 6212(a) and provide for an undertaking for the TRO (generally 5% of amount to be restrained).

Commission; Letters Rogatory

Where deposition is sought of an out-of-state witness who may not or will not appear voluntarily, the deposing party must obtain a commission from our court. This is a document formally seeking cooperation of the court system of the other state. It is necessary since an order of the courts of this state may have no force in another jurisdiction. The parties may jointly agree to appoint an officer in the other state who would, if necessary, make an application to compel the testimony. D. Siegel, NEW YORK PRACTICE Sec. 360, at 589–90 (4th ed. 2005). The authority in the other state should issue an order there that will bind the witness and require his or her appearance. CPLR 3108. A commission to take testimony on oral questions is sometimes referred to as an "open commission" and one to take testimony on written questions is sometimes referred to as a "sealed commission."

If all parties to the New York action are in accord about the need for the deposition, they should sign a stipulation, in which event the deposing party may proceed ex parte. The deposing party should submit to the Ex Parte Office a proposed order, a proposed commission, the stipulation, and a verified petition or in a pending case an affidavit/affirmation. In the affidavit/ affirmation, the applicant should describe the nature of the action, the name and home or business address of the witness, and the nature of the testimony sought and why it is material and necessary. The papers should contain a statement regarding prior, similar applications (CPLR 2217(b)).

The commission should be signed with the full signature of the Justice (not merely initials) since it is intended to be operative in the other state and should be in a form to pass muster there with the least possible difficulty. In the alternative, the court may direct the County Clerk to issue the commission and the applying party would obtain the commission from the Clerk by presenting the signed order.

The letter rogatory is a similar, somewhat more complex device used to obtain testimony in a foreign country. D. Siegel, *supra*. A letter is granted on motion or stipulation. If the request is granted, an order is initialed by the court and, as with the commission, the letter is signed with a full signature. The court will not direct the County Clerk to issue and sign the letter inasmuch as that may render the letter ineffective in a foreign jurisdiction expecting to see the signature of a judge on such a document.

Contempt (Civil)

Such a motion must of course be on notice. An order to show cause must contain the statutory warnings that the purpose of the hearing is to punish for contempt, punishment may include imprisonment, and failure to appear may result in arrest and imprisonment. The moving papers must be served on the accused not less than 10 and no more than 30 days prior to the time set for the hearing. The application must comply with CPLR 2217(b) regarding prior, similar applications and state that the contemnor has impeded, impaired, prejudiced and defeated the rights of the applicant. In matrimonial cases, if the application is made with respect to an enforcement procedure under DRL 245, there must also be a statement that payment cannot be enforced by sequestration (DRL 243) or the giving of security, by enforcement of a judgment (DRL 244), or by an income execution or income deduction order for support enforcement. CPLR 5241 and 5242.

Default and Inquest

Upon the default of a defendant, the plaintiff may seek a default money judgment or an inquest ex parte under some circumstances. The plaintiff may apply to the County Clerk for judgment if the sum involved is certain or can by calculation be made certain. CPLR 3215(a). The default must be taken within one year or the court, absent good cause, shall instead dismiss the complaint. CPLR 3215(c). The defendant who appeared in the case is entitled to notice, or, if more than one year has elapsed since the default, even if he or she has not appeared unless the court orders otherwise. CPLR 3215(g)(1). Where an application must be made to the court, a defendant who has failed to appear may serve a written demand for, and is then entitled to, notice of any reference or assessment by a jury. CPLR 3215(g)(2). Additional notice is required when the default judgment based on nonappearance is sought against (i) a natural person in an action based on nonpayment of a contractual obligation, or (ii) a domestic or foreign corporation served pursuant to BCL 306(b). CPLR 3215(g)(3) and (4).

The moving papers must contain a copy of the summons with notice or summons and complaint with Clerk's filing stamp; a factual affidavit by the client or a complaint verified by the client; a detailed affidavit or affirmation as to the default; proof of service with Clerk's stamp; and a statement in compliance with Section 2217(b) regarding prior, similar applications.

If there are multiple defendants, the moving papers must account for all of them. If any has not been summoned, the plaintiff must provide for a severance and disposition with respect to that party (dismissal or discontinuance).

If a motion on notice for a default is granted, the order should provide, where possible, that the Clerk shall enter judgment in favor of plaintiff in the sum of $ X, plus interest (where applicable) from Y date, together with costs and disbursements. If an inquest is required, the order should provide for severance or discontinuance of other parties, and direct the Clerk of the Trial Support Office to assign the action for an inquest and assessment of damages. This directive should be on condition that plaintiff, within a set period (e.g., 60 days), upon pain of dismissal for non-compliance, serve a copy of the order on Trial Support and file a Request for Judicial Intervention (if no Justice has been assigned previously) with a note of issue and pay the proper fees. The statement of readiness is waived.

In a foreclosure matter, the order should provide, in addition to the foregoing, for deleting John Doe defendants and amending the caption and should direct an inquest to compute the amounts due plaintiff on its note and mortgage. It should direct the judicial officer on inquest to report whether the mortgaged premises can be sold in one parcel. The order should determine counsel fees due plaintiff pursuant to the mortgage and provide for the entry of a judgment of foreclosure and sale.

Discharge of Ancient Mortgage

In the case of a mortgage over 20 years old, an application may be made for a discharge pursuant to RPAPL 1931. Any such application must be brought by order to show cause. A verified petition shall set out the name, address and nature of petitioner's interest, a description of the mortgage, and an explanation as to why the mortgage should be discharged. An official search by the Register of the City of New York, an attorney admitted to practice, or a title company incorporated and authorized to transact business in New York must be presented showing the last record holder of the mortgage. The papers must also comply with CPLR 2217(b) regarding prior, similar applications.

Examination Inside New York—Foreign Action

In response to a commission, letters rogatory or order from another state, a deposition may be taken of a witness in New York, or documents produced from such a witness, and an order of this court may be obtained to ensure this result. CPLR 3102(e). Generally, the order is sought by ex parte application requiring the purchase of an index number but not an RJI. The application must be made by an attorney admitted to practice in New York who has a New York address. The petition for this relief should not use the caption from the underlying case, but rather a caption in the form used in a special proceeding (e.g., "In the Matter of the Application of Washington, Jefferson & Lincoln, P.C., Attorneys at Law, Petitioners, to Take the Deposition on Oral Questions of Aaron Burr, Respondent"). The petition should be supported by an affidavit of New York counsel, a copy of the foreign commission or other process, a proposed order, and a New York subpoena to be served with a copy of the signed order. If a notice of deposition was previously served, a copy should be included. The signing requirement of Section 130–1.1-a of Part 130 must be satisfied. The attorney's affidavit must state that it is by a New York attorney with a New York

address; set forth a basis for the application, including the nature of the action, the name and home or business address of the witness, the nature of the testimony sought and its materiality and necessity; address CPLR 2217(b); and set forth any other information required by any special circumstances. Video taping is allowed only if the commission specifically provides for it. See Uniform Rule 202.15. The order should provide for a place, date and time for the examination or for the production of documents and authorize a subpoena or subpoena duces tecum to be served on the witness. The subpoena must be served together with a copy of the order at least 20 days prior to the examination unless the court orders otherwise. CPLR 3106(b).

Examination Outside the State—New York Action

See Commission; Letters Rogatory.

Extension of Time

Pursuant to CPLR 2004, the court may extend time periods (not statutory periods of limitation), such as the time within which to answer or move against a complaint. If the time has not yet expired, the motion may be made ex parte. If the time has expired, the motion should be made on notice, and interim relief may be requested. The court now has the power to extend the deadline for effecting service of process. CPLR 306-b.

The moving papers should include a copy of the summons and complaint, and an affirmation/affidavit explaining that the case is not one pursuant to CPLR 3213 and setting forth the pertinent facts about the deadline in question. The papers should make clear whether any previous extensions were granted by stipulation or order and whether any effort was made to obtain an extension on consent. CPLR 2217(b) must be complied with as to prior, similar applications.

Foreclosure

Applications to foreclose may be made ex parte when all defendants have either defaulted or filed notices of appearances and waivers of service of further papers. In other instances, a motion on notice must be made. Where the application may be made ex parte, the procedure is as follows:

1) Application to Appoint Referee

The process begins with an application to appoint a referee to compute the sum due the plaintiff. The applicant must submit an affirmation/affidavit that recites that a notice of pendency was filed and when that was done; that the time for the defendants to appear, answer or move has expired and that no defendant has appeared or answered (except for those who have made limited appearances); and, if that is the case, that the defendants or some of them have admitted the plaintiff's right to foreclose. The moving papers should include a proposed order of reference. The designated referee must be an appointee whose name is taken from the approved fiduciary list or who has superior qualifications (see Part 36 of the Rules of the Chief Judge). The order should direct the referee to compute the amount due and determine whether the premises can be sold in a single parcel. RPAPL 1321. An ex parte application of this sort must be accompanied by the filing of an RJI (unless for some reason the matter had already been assigned, e.g., on a motion for the appointment of a receiver).

2) Motion to Confirm

The report of the referee is normally prepared by the plaintiff's counsel. It must recite the work of the referee (usually including a schedule of the documents examined and relied upon by the referee) and set forth findings of fact and conclusions of law regarding the issues referred, chiefly, the amounts of principal and interest and sums otherwise due. If testimony was taken, the transcript must be annexed to the report unless the parties stipulate to dispense with it. If the referee was appointed by ex parte order in a default situation as explained above, the application to confirm may proceed ex parte as well. In such an instance, the application will include a request for the entry of a judgment of foreclosure and sale, as explained in Item 5 below.

3) Motion to Appoint Receiver

A receiver may be appointed without notice if the mortgage contains a receivership clause. RPL 254. The plaintiff need not show that the property is inadequate security if the mortgage contains such a clause. Such a showing is dispensed with where the mortgage authorizes the appointment of a receiver of the rents and profits and provides that, upon default, rents and profits are assigned or pledged as added security.

The papers in support of the application must state the amount of the monthly rent roll and include a copy of the summons and complaint, the mortgage, note or lien and tax certificate, proof of service, a proposed order for appointment of a receiver, and a Request for Judicial Intervention (if there has not been one already). The court will appoint the receiver, who must be a person on the official fiduciary list or one with better qualifications, and there must be compliance with Parts 26 and 36 of the Rules of the Chief Judge. A bank must be designated by the court to serve as depository for the receiver's accounts.

A receiver must qualify before exercising power. This requires filing an oath and posting an undertaking. CPLR 6402–03. The court order shall specify the amount of the undertaking. As to powers, duties, and responsibilities, see CPLR 5228, RPAPL 1325 and GOL 9–101.

The receiver is entitled to a commission as fixed by the court in an amount not exceeding 5 % of amounts received and dispersed. CPLR 8004(a).

4) Termination of Receivership

The plaintiff may apply ex parte to terminate a receivership. The application must be supported by an affidavit/affirmation justifying the request, the consent of the receiver, and a proposed order, together with compliance with CPLR 2217(b) regarding prior, similar applications. The proposed order should provide that the receivership be terminated, contain a direction that the receiver surrender the premises to the owner, and direct the receiver to settle an account with all appropriate speed or within a fixed deadline.

5) Judgment of Foreclosure

The order and judgment of foreclosure usually is submitted with the ex parte application to confirm the report of the referee to compute. The papers must establish default or consent to the foreclosure. See Default and Inquest above for papers required on a motion for a default judgment.

The proposed order and judgment should be submitted with the papers. It should contain a direction that the premises be sold in the manner set forth in the referee's report and should specify clearly the amount of the plaintiff's lien with interest, costs and extra allowances (CPLR Art. 83). A blank line for costs and disbursements may be left for completion by the Clerk. The order and judgment should clearly identify the mortgagor's interest that is to be sold (fee, etc.) and any superior interests that limit the estate being sold.

The order and judgment appoints a referee to sell, who usually is the referee to compute. If a new person is appointed, there must be compliance with CPLR 4312 and Parts 26 and 36 of the Rules of the Chief Judge. The order and judgment will specify the referee's fee, the place and time of the sale, and where notice will be published. See CPLR 8003(b).

If an answer was served, the plaintiff will have to proceed by motion on notice for summary judgment and the appointment of a referee to compute. This motion is processed through the Motion Support Office (Room 119).

Letter Rogatory: See Commission; Letters Rogatory.

Mechanic's Lien, Discharge of: See Discharge of Mechanic's Lien.

Pro Hac Vice Applications

May be made to the IAS Justice on notice or ex parte. See Section 520.11 of the Rules of the Court of Appeals and Section 602.2(a) of the Rules of the Appellate Division, First Department. The applicant must submit an affirmation describing admission to the bar of some state, the length of time in practice, the location and nature of the practice and disclaiming discipline in another jurisdiction. The applicant must indicate who from the New York bar will be associated in the prosecution or defense of the matter in question. An affirmation of New York counsel must be submitted stating the purpose of the admission and compliance with CPLR 2217(b) regarding prior, similar applications. A proposed order must be submitted that sets forth the purpose of the admission. The application must include a stipulation or consent, or be made on notice.

Security for Costs

May be made ex parte. CPLR 8501. The affirmation or affidavit in support must state that the plaintiff has not been granted permission to proceed as a poor person and is not a petitioner in a habeas corpus proceeding; that the plaintiff is not a domestic or foreign corporation authorized in this state; that plaintiff is not a resident of this state; and that CPLR 8501(b) does not apply (a fiduciary is not in place). The papers must include proof of the plaintiff's non-residency, which may consist of a copy of the summons, proof from the Secretary of State where a corporation is involved, and the like.

The defendant should move on notice to the plaintiff if the amount of security requested is in excess of $ 500 or if the case is listed in CPLR 8501(b).

The papers should include a Request for Judicial Intervention if the case has not previously been assigned and a proposed order which should fix the amount of security, provide a deadline (30 days) for its posting, stay the proceeding as set forth in CPLR 8502, and provide for service on plaintiff within 10 days.

Seizure, Order of

An order to seize a chattel (replevy) may not be made ex parte except where, in addition to the basic prerequisites for such an order, the court finds that, unless such an order is granted without notice, it is probable that the chattel will be transferred, concealed, disposed of, or removed from the state, or will become substantially impaired in value. CPLR 7102(d)(3). A detailed affidavit of facts justifying the extraordinary ex parte nature of the relief sought is required (Section 7102(c)(7)), as is, of course, a statement satisfying CPLR 2217(b) regarding prior, similar applications. An order granted ex parte must provide that the plaintiff will move to confirm the seizure on such notice as the court shall direct within no more than five days after seizure. CPLR 7102(d)(4).

An application for an order of seizure must be supported by an affidavit and an undertaking. See Section 7102(c) & (e).

A TRO may be obtained on a motion brought on by OSC preventing the chattel from being removed, sold, assigned, or otherwise encumbered or disposed of. Section 7102(d)(2).

Substituted Service (CPLR 308(5))

A plaintiff may move ex parte for leave to serve a defendant in such manner as the court directs. This relief may be obtained only if service under subdivisions 1, 2 and 4 of Section 308 is impracticable.

Courts have broad discretion in ordering methods of service under 308(5) provided that they are reasonably calculated to provide notice.

The method of service proposed by the plaintiff need not be adopted and should not be if it is not reasonably calculated to provide notice. The affidavit in support must show that there is a reasonable chance that the defendant will receive notice of the action. Otherwise, publication may be necessary.

The papers required on an application of this sort include a copy of the summons with notice or summons and complaint, an affidavit/affirmation of past efforts to serve and why alternative service is required, proof of the last known address of the defendant, a proposed order, and compliance with CPLR 2217(b) regarding prior, similar applications.

Substituted Service—By Publication

A plaintiff may obtain an order ex parte for publication under certain circumstances. CPLR 316. The plaintiff must submit an affirmation/affidavit in support, an affidavit of due diligence by a process server, exhibits demonstrating the results of a search for defendant (Post Office, Surrogate's Court, Board of Elections, Department of Motor Vehicles, military (in the five branches)), notice of publication (see Rule 316 (a)), a summons and complaint or summons with notice, a proposed order in compliance with Rule 316, and a Request for Judicial Intervention (if required).

Withdrawal of Funds—Commissioner of Finance

In connection with certain proceedings in this court, funds are sometimes deposited with the Commissioner of Finance pursuant to court order. An application for release of these funds can be made ex parte if the consent of all persons who have appeared in the action is submitted as part of the application. Otherwise, the applicant should move on notice to all parties.

The applicant should obtain from the Commissioner of Finance proof of the deposit, which is called a Certificate of Deposit. In a pending action an application can be submitted or else the claimant must execute and present a verified, duly acknowledged petition setting forth the facts that substantiate the claim to the funds in question. The petition must be sworn to before a notary public and a copy of the Certificate of Deposit, the application therefor, and the receipt issued by the County Clerk when the funds were originally deposited must be submitted. The claimant must present a proposed order reciting the material submitted and containing a directive to the Commissioner of Finance of the City of New York to pay the claimant, upon service of a certified copy of the order, the sum shown on the Certificate of Deposit, plus accrued interest, less lawful fees. A certified copy of the order may be obtained after filing in the Office of the County Clerk (cost $ 8.00, payable by check to the County Clerk). This copy should be served on the Commissioner of Finance.

August 2007

EMERGENCY APPLICATIONS AFTER HOURS

Procedure IV. Emergency Applications Outside Normal Court Hours

From time to time, counsel seek to make emergency civil applications, such as a request for a temporary restraining order, in Supreme Court during the evening and on weekends and holidays, when the courthouse is closed. To address such applications, the following procedure has been established.

A central point of contact with a single toll-free telephone number and e-mail address has been created through which attorneys outside normal hours may request to appear before a Judge. The central staff, who will be available 24 hours every day of the week, will contact the Administrative Judge (or designated backup) with any request. The Administrative Judge will then determine if there is a real need for a Judge to hear the application outside of regular court hours. If so, the Administrative Judge will make the appropriate arrangements with an available trial Judge or perhaps handle the matter directly.

An attorney who wishes to make an application outside normal court hours should proceed as follows:

- The attorney should call or e-mail a central office using (800) 430–8457 or the e-mail address: emergency@nycourts.gov
- The telephone call or e-mail will be answered by staff of the Unified Court System's Division of Technology.
- The staff member will take down the essential information, including the names and telephone numbers of the attorneys and the county.
- The staff member will then contact the Administrative Judge or designated back-up to pass on the information. (In the event that Administrative Judge or back-up is not available, staff will contact the appropriate Deputy Chief Administrative Judge.) The Administrative Judge will take the information and make any further arrangements.

Please note that the staff member initially receiving the calls or e-mails will only pass on the request and the information to the Administrative Judge. The staff will not screen any calls, as any screening should be left to the Administrative Judge.

Dated: November 19, 2008

Hon. Jacqueline W. Silbermann
Administrative Judge

ASSIGNMENTS AND CASE MANAGEMENT

Procedure V. Assignments and Case Management

A. Assignments and Operation of the Parts in General

The court currently operates the following Parts: (a) Tax Certiorari and Condemnation; (b) City; (c) Transit; (d) Matrimonial; (e) Motor Vehicle; (f) Medical, Dental and Podiatric Malpractice; (g) Mass Tort; (h) Article 81 Parts; and (i) General. In addition, the court operates the Commercial Division, which handles commercial cases, and trial parts.

Justices are assigned to the various parts by the Administrative Judge. Upon the filing of an RJI, cases are identified by action type and then by an automated process assigned at random to a Justice from among those designated to handle cases of that type.

1. *The Comprehensive Civil Justice Program and Case Assignments*

In 2000, the court began implementation of the Comprehensive Civil Justice Program ("CCJP"). Under the CCJP, each case is generally assigned to an IAS Justice for its life, including for trial purposes, except for City cases. Each City case is assigned to a City Justice until a note of issue is filed, when it is reassigned to the City Waiting List in calendar number order.

The pure IAS regime is qualified as follows. If a pure IAS Justice calls in a group of cases for trial expecting that one or several will settle and the expectations are disappointed, he or she may be able to give a brief adjournment to a case and resolve the problem. Since the ability to issue firm trial dates is important to the achievement of settlements and to counsel's ability to schedule and prepare for trials, and since parties and witnesses also need to be able to depend upon the accuracy of trial dates, the Justice will not wish to grant a long adjournment. However, circumstances may arise in which even a brief adjournment is not possible (e.g., an expert witness's schedule prohibits it or there is a witness from afar). Such cases may be referred out to trial before another Justice through the Administrative Coordinating Part (Part 40) as described hereafter. Second, after a case has been pending in a pure IAS Part for a period without having advanced to trial, it will be subject to removal from the Part by the Administrative Judge for prompt trial so as to prevent serious backlogs and disparities in waiting times in the IAS Parts. Cases so removed will also proceed to trial through the

Administrative Coordinating Part. Third, some cases, with the approval of the assigned Justice, may be referred to Part 40 for trial by a Neutral Evaluation Attorney when settlement cannot be reached in the Neutral Evaluation Program.

In implementation of the CCJP, there are at present various pure IAS General Assignment Parts (handling General cases), one Motor Vehicle Part, five pure IAS Medical, Dental and Podiatric Malpractice Parts, and three pre-note City Parts and one Transit Part (for City and non–City Transit cases). To address the overflow of trial-ready cases referred to in the preceding paragraph, and to assist in trial of City cases to the extent that the City Justices are unable to accommodate all such cases ready for trial, there are a number of back-up Trial Parts. An Administrative Coordinating Judge ("ACJ") in Part 40, working with the Administrative Judge ("AJ"), coordinates referral of these trial-ready cases to a trial Justice. Pure IAS Justices refer cases to the ACJ. Except for the Motor Vehicle Justice and the AJ or ACJ, an IAS Justice will not refer a case directly to another Justice for trial as this would defeat the implementation of a major component of CCJP.

In addition, there are, as noted, Commercial Division Parts. There are also Justices assigned on a rotating basis from upstate to assist the court with the trial of ready cases. These Justices are assigned to one or more Upstate Trial Parts, located at 71 Thomas Street. A number of Justices, primarily from the Appellate Term, handle Article 81 matters and two Justices divide the large tax certiorari inventory. Finally, several Justices have been designated by the Administrative Judge to serve as part of a Center for Complex Litigation, which handles mass tort cases. The Justices so assigned are Justice Helen E. Freedman (Part 39), Justice Marcy S. Friedman (Part 57), Justice Shirley W. Kornreich (Part 54), and Justice Martin Shulman (Part 1). These Justices also maintain other assignments.

All cases seeking forfeiture of criminal proceeds or other remedy pursuant to Article 13-A of the Civil Practice Law and Rules are assigned to a single Justice (Justice Martin Shulman).

City cases are assigned in accordance with a protocol. For access to this protocol, click here. [1]

For the current arrangement of Parts and assignment of Justices thereto, click here. [2]

2. Differentiated Case Management

The CCJP also introduced the concept of Differentiated Case Management ("DCM"), whereby cases are assigned to one of three tracks upon filing of the RJI: standard, expedited and complex. Medical Malpractice and Commercial Division cases are considered complex matters unless the filing attorney designates otherwise on the RJI. All Motor Vehicle cases are treated as expedited matters upon filing. All other cases are treated as standard cases when filed.

Pursuant to Uniform Rule 202.19 (b), a preliminary conference must be held within 45 days after the RJI is filed. The Rule is interpreted to mean that if the RJI accompanies a non-discovery motion, the conference shall be held within 45 days after the decision on the motion, assuming that the decision does not dispose of the case. If the RJI accompanies a disclosure motion, the preliminary conference shall be held within 45 days. See Uniform Rule 202.8 (f). At the preliminary conference, the court will consider requests by a party to modify the DCM track.

The time within which discovery must be completed according to the Rule varies depending on the track to which a case is assigned. The deadlines are:

Expedited - Eight months from RJI

Standard - 12 months from RJI

Complex - 15 months from RJI

These deadlines also constitute pre-note standards and goals for purposes of internal tracking of case activity. Since these time frames are calculated from RJI, the court must be attentive to the early commencement of the discovery process even if the case is one in which a preliminary conference need not be held within 45 days due to the filing of a non-discovery motion at the outset of the case.

A compliance conference must be held no later than 60 days before the filing of the note of issue. Rule 202.19(b).

Within 180 days from filing of the note of issue, a pretrial conference must be held at which the court will fix a date for commencement of trial, which is to be no later than eight weeks after the conference date.

The standard and goal for cases post-note is 15 months. The court system also keeps data on the overall standards and goals (pre-note and post-note combined).

Attorneys who consult the court's Supreme Court Records On–Line Library ("Scroll") on this website [3] or the Civil Case Information System computer or who receive information from attorneys' service companies based on this data may note that the overall standards and goals deadlines are included in the computer for each applicable case in accordance with the track assignment of each case. The computer will show, for instance, a note of issue deadline for the case consistent with the track assignment of the case and in accordance with Rule 202.19. However, that deadline is only a benchmark; the actual date by which a note of issue must be filed in any particular case is the date directed by the Justice assigned, usually in a preliminary conference or compliance conference order.

In City cases, a unique set of DCM procedures are applied. See below.

Pre-note and trial procedures are set forth in the Uniform Rules of the Justices and, for Commercial Division cases, the Rules of the Commercial Division Justices, set out in Uniform Rule 202.70 (eff. date 1/17/06).

3. *The Neutral Evaluation Program*

When a note of issue is filed in a case in the General inventory (i.e., in one of the pure IAS General Assignment Parts), in a Motor Vehicle case, or in a commercial case outside the Commercial Division, the matter is promptly referred to the court's Neutral Evaluation Program (known informally as "Mediation"). These cases are conferenced by a Neutral Evaluation Attorney, a senior Court Attorney with special experience and expertise in settlements, and settlement is explored in detail.

The procedures of the Program are explained in the Program Protocol.

4. *Trial Activity*

When a case is sent out for jury selection, the attorneys will be given a jury slip and must report immediately to the Central Jury Room. A jury will be selected in accordance with Uniform Rule 202.33. There is a five-day maximum time during which a selected jury may wait for trial to begin. Time spent on telephone standby ("TCI") is included. After five days the jury must be disbanded.

5. *Placement of Cases for Trial*

Cases reach the Jury Room from the pure IAS Parts, the Motor Vehicle Part, and the Administrative Coordinating Part (Part 40). The Justice assigned to a pure IAS Part who sends a case to the Jury Room will try that case. If the IAS Justice cannot try the case, it will be sent to the Administrative Coordinating Judge. Cases processed through Part 40 will be assigned for trial in accordance with the directives of the Administrative Coordinating Judge. In this process, the Administrative Coordinating Judge will contact the Justice to whom the case had been assigned upon the filing of the RJI and offer that Justice the first opportunity to try the case. If the original IAS Justice is not available, the Administrative Coordinating Judge will assign the case to a Back-up Trial Justice or pure IAS Justice.

B. City Case Automated Differentiated Case Management

1. *City DCM - Overview*

The court operates an automated Differentiated Case Management Program for tort cases in the City Parts, i.e., those in which the City of New York is a party and in which the City is represented by the Tort Division of the Corporation Counsel's Office. Not included in this Program are special proceedings and City contract, medical malpractice, and lead paint cases. The aims of the Program are to expedite cases, minimize litigation expense, conserve the time

of counsel, promote efficiency, and permit the City Justices to concentrate the bulk of their time on the resolution of substantive issues and trial of City cases.

2. *Setting a Disclosure Schedule in City DCM Cases*

Upon the filing of a request for judicial intervention and a request for a preliminary conference, the following procedures will be utilized to schedule discovery. If the RJI is filed with a non-discovery motion, this process will be followed after disposition of the motion, assuming that the decision does not dispose of the case. If the RJI is filed with a discovery motion, the motion will be referred to the court's Case Management Office for the scheduling of a conference or the issuance of a Case Scheduling Order.

Instead of requiring that attorneys appear in court for a preliminary conference, the court will issue and transmit to the parties a Case Scheduling Order. City cases are presumed to be standard cases under the DCM regime, meaning that discovery is to be completed within 12 months from filing of the RJI. However, where the RJI is accompanied by a motion, 12 months will be allowed for discovery commencing from the time the motion is resolved, if the case remains active after the decision. The standard-form Order will contain provisions for items of discovery generally necessary in the major varieties of City case. Deadlines for the completion of the pertinent items of discovery within the overall 12-month time frame will be set forth. The Order provides that the parties may agree to adjourn various deadlines provided that all discovery due to be completed prior to the compliance conference is in fact completed by then. The Order will include an EBT date furnished by the City. Since the City will know the type of case involved at this early point and can take that into account when determining an appropriate EBT date, the expectation of the court is that the date is more likely to prove realistic than has been the case in the past under a non-automated system and to require at most only modest adjustments to suit the schedules of the parties.

The deadlines and the form of the Order were arrived at by the court after extensive consultations between representatives of the City of New York and plaintiffs' counsel on, and other members of, this court's Tort Advisory Committee. To consult a copy of this form Order, click here [4].

This Order will be transmitted by the Case Management Office to counsel by fax, e-mail or regular mail. Counsel will be afforded a period of time within which to challenge the designation of the case as a standard matter and any aspect of the discovery schedule set out in the Order. All such challenges are to be brought to the attention of the Case Management Coordinators, who are senior court clerks specially designated to serve in this role. A conference will promptly be arranged by the Coordinator to resolve any difficulty that arises. If good reason is presented for doing so, modifications will be made to the Order. However, failure to raise objections within the period fixed will result in waiver of those objections. If no objections are raised, the parties need not appear in court and the Order as framed will govern future disclosure in the case. Avoidance of an appearance in court of course saves time and money and is helpful to counsel.

Counsel are strongly advised that the deadlines set forth in the Order must be taken seriously. Failure to comply with the Order may well result in the imposition of a penalty, such as waiver of the discovery, a financial sanction, preclusion, and the like.

3. *Subsequent Disclosure Problems*

In the event any disclosure dispute arises after the discovery process begins, the party aggrieved shall promptly, prior to the deadline in question and before making a motion, inform the Case Management Coordinator of the existence of the dispute. The Case Management Coordinator will promptly schedule a conference at a convenient date and time.

Conferences about discovery problems and compliance conferences will take place before Judicial Hearing Officers, the Law Secretary of the Justice assigned to the case or Court Attorneys specially designated for this purpose. In the event that the problems raised cannot be resolved in this fashion, the matter will be referred to the assigned Justice.

The court will transmit notices to the parties during the course of discovery. The purpose of these notices is to provide reminders of critical upcoming discovery deadlines so that busy counsel do not inadvertently fall into non-compliance with the court's Order.

The Case Scheduling Order will contain a date for a compliance conference. Pursuant to Uniform Rule 202.19, a compliance conference must be conducted no later than 60 days prior to filing of the note of issue. That conference will take place in a central location for all City DCM cases (Room 103 at 80 Centre Street).

4. *Post–Note Procedures*

Immediately after the filing of the note of issue, a conference will be scheduled in all City cases before a Judicial Hearing Officer. At this conference, an examination will be made of settlement prospects. Numbers of cases settle at this stage and counsel should therefore be prepared to discuss settlement in

detail. The parties will also be called upon to review the state of discovery, which of course should have been completed by then. The court will confirm that the parties have received all discovery that was required, including that the City has in its file documents necessary to thorough settlement discussions, such as the relevant map in a slip and fall case. To the extent that any items have not been furnished by one side to the other, arrangements will be made for a very prompt completion of the disclosure process. It is important that this be done so that settlement discussions can be pursued thereafter, as discussed below, with all parties having in hand the information needed to evaluate the case and consider settlement.

As City cases pending on the City Waiting List near the top of the list, they will be referred to the Neutral Evaluation Program, described above. Attorneys for the plaintiffs will be required to bring their case file to conferences with a Neutral Evaluation Attorney so that discussions can be detailed and meaningful. Because of the great volume of cases being handled by the Corporation Counsel's Office, it is not practical for that Office to transport the case files to the court in all cases being conferenced on any given day.

C. Motor Vehicle Automated Differentiated Case Management

A similar automated approach is applied to Motor Vehicle cases, which, like the tort cases in the City Parts, tend to be homogeneous. As with the City cases, an automated Case Scheduling Order will be issued by the Case Management Office upon filing of an RJI accompanied by a request for a preliminary conference or a discovery motion, or after disposition by the court of a non-disclosure motion if the case remains active. To consult a copy of this form, click here. [4] Motor Vehicle cases are presumed to be expedited cases. Objections to the Order will be addressed by conference call or conference. Should any disclosure difficulties arise thereafter, the Case Management Office must be advised immediately, in advance of the deadline in issue and prior to motion practice. The Office will transmit periodic reminder notices. Compliance conferences will be conducted as needed to assure compliance with the Order.

September 2006

1 http://www.nycourts.gov/supctmanh/CityCases.pdf
2 http://www.nycourts.gov/supctmanh/part_assignments.htm
3 http://www.nycourts.gov/supctmanh/
4 http://www.nycourts.gov/supctmanh/preliminary_conf_forms.htm

GUARDIANSHIP CASES AND FIDUCIARY ACCOUNTINGS

Doc. 1. Administrative Order—Guardianship Proceedings

By the authority vested in me as Administrative Judge of the Supreme Court, Civil Branch, New York

County, I issue this Administrative Order and direct as follows:

1) Effective December 22, 2008, as to guardianship cases commenced in 2008 and thereafter, and matters

that were commenced prior to 2008 but in which the first annual report and examination thereof will be filed after December 22, 2008, all annual reports shall be judicially settled by the assigned court examiner in accordance with the provisions of Mental Hygiene Law ("MHL") Section 81.33(c), (d), (e) and (f), and upon filed objections, if any.

2) No later than the 31st of May of each year, the guardian shall submit an annual report for the preceding year, in accordance with MHL Section 81.31, to: a) all parties entitled to notice identified in the order of appointment in accordance with MHL Section 81.16(c); b) the assigned court examiner; and c) the Guardianship and Fiduciary Support Office of this court located at 60 Centre Street, Room 148, New York, New York 10007.

3) Court examiners shall: a) examine each annual report in accordance with MHL Section 81.32(a)(2); b) serve the proposed order with respect to each annual report and examination thereof upon all parties entitled to notice identified in the order of appointment in accordance with MHL Section 81.16(c) and the surety, if any; and c) submit each examined annual report, with notice of settlement, for judicial approval to the Guardianship and Fiduciary Support Office at the address listed above.

4) With respect to matters in which one or more annual reports were filed prior to the date of this Administrative Order, a guardian may move to settle an intermediate report pursuant to MHL Section 81.33(a). Once an intermediate report has been settled, all subsequent annual reports shall be judicially settled as provided above.

5) In all matters in which all intermediate and annual reports have been judicially settled, the final report shall contain a) a copy of the most recent order approving the intermediate and/or annual report; b) an accounting of financial management of the guardianship assets subsequent to the date of the last judicially settled report in the form prescribed by the court; c) proof of death of the incapacitated person or the guardian or proof that a guardian has been appointed in another jurisdiction, as applicable; d) an order settling the final report; and e) an order appointing a successor guardian, if applicable. The final report shall be served on all interested parties and the affidavit of service shall be filed with the final report.

6) As to all guardianship matters that were commenced prior to December 22, 2008 in which annual reports have been confirmed by the court, but have not been judicially settled and no intermediate report has been judicially settled, the procedure for filing annual and final reports that was in place prior to the date of this Administrative Order shall remain unchanged, unless modified by the court.

Dated: December 4, 2008

Hon. Jacqueline W. Silbermann

Doc. 2. Overview of Guardianship Proceedings

Whether due to advanced age, infirmity or other difficulty, individuals may cease to be able to manage their own affairs or care for themselves. Family, friends or others may wish to apply to the court for the appointment of a person or persons to provide assistance to such individuals. The person appointed is called a Guardian. The procedure by which such an application may be made is a proceeding for the appointment of a Guardian. Mental Hygiene Law Article 81 governs these cases.

Article 81 of the Mental Hygiene Law provides for the appointment by the court, upon a proper showing, of a Guardian or Guardians to meet the personal needs of an incapacitated person and/or manage his or her property.

Any interested person (as defined by Section 81.06 of the Mental Hygiene Law) over the age of 18 has the right to petition the court for a judicial directive appointing an adult Guardian for a person who, because of illness or disability, is unable to manage his or her affairs (this Guardian is called a Guardian of the property) or properly take care of himself or herself (Guardian of the person). At the application stage the person in need of assistance is known as an "alleged incapacitated person" or ("AIP"). The alleged incapacitated person has various rights and may request the court to appoint legal counsel to represent him or her; the court may make such an appointment on its own initiative. Proof must be presented to the court at a hearing establishing that the AIP is unable to manage his or her affairs or take care of himself or herself properly (that is why the subject of the proceeding is called an alleged incapacitated person). In acting on any such application, the court must also take into account the personal wishes, preferences and desires of the AIP, and afford that person the greatest possible amount of independence and self-determination and participation in all the decisions affecting the person's life.

A. Making The Application

An application for Guardianship is made to the court by filing a verified petition in the office of the County Clerk (Room 141B at 60 Centre Street, Manhattan) and then presenting an order to show cause and a copy of the verified petition and supporting papers to the court's Ex–Parte Office (Room 315 at 60 Centre Street, Manhattan). Article 81 of the Mental Hygiene Law defines the procedures to be followed, including providing notice of the application and the hearing to all interested persons.

B. Court Evaluator

In the order to show cause, the court will appoint an individual to serve as a Court Evaluator. The Court Evaluator must communicate with the alleged incapacitated person, investigate the person's circumstances, and report in a writing to the court. The Court Evaluator may be an attorney, a physician, a psychologist, an accountant, a social worker, a nurse or any other person properly trained to perform this task. Under certain circumstances, the court may decide to appoint counsel in addition to the Court Evaluator to protect the interests of the alleged incapacitated person.

C. The Hearing

In the order to show cause, a hearing on the application will be scheduled for no later than 28 days from the signing of the order to show cause. At the hearing, evidence will be presented to the court on the questions of whether or not the person is incapacitated and, if so, what may be the best and least restrictive solution to safeguard the alleged incapacitated person and his or her interests. Questions or objections may be raised at the hearing by the AIP, the AIP's attorney, family members, or other interested persons. The burden of proof rests on the petitioner to establish that a person is incapacitated within the meaning of Article 81. The court will decide the issues often at the conclusion of the hearing and in any event within seven days after the hearing.

D. Order And Judgment

After the hearing the court will issue a decision on the questions presented. If the court denies the application, it may cast the decision as an order and judgment, which would resolve the case. If it decides to grant the application, it will issue a decision setting out its findings and conclusions (that a Guardian has been found to be necessary; whether more than one Guardian is required; who the Guardian is to be; what role the Guardian or Guardians will have; any limitations on the authority thereof; and the like); the Guardianship may be unlimited in time or for a definite period and the court will make clear which. Sometimes only a Guardian of the person is needed and sometimes a Guardian of the property is required. And the court may find that the circumstances make appropriate appointment of one person in both roles or two persons, one in either role. As noted above, the court will seek the least restrictive form of intervention possible given the circumstances.

If the application is granted, the court will usually issue a relatively brief directive (called a "short form order") that will state generally the court's findings and rulings, which may also be given orally and included in the record of the proceedings. The court will normally require that a separate document, an Order and Judgment or findings of fact and order and judgement, be signed by it setting out in extensive detail the court's findings with regard to the condition of the AIP, the need for a Guardian or Guardians, the nature of the Guardianship appropriate to the situation, including a definition of the powers the Guardian(s) will have and any restrictions thereon, who the Guardian or Guardians are to be, etc. It is possible that a proposed Order and Judgment may be submitted by the petitioning party with the supporting papers and may be signed by the court, or the court may issue an Order and Judgment along with or shortly after the decision using a form prepared by it, modified as required by the circumstances of the case. The court in its decision may instead require that an Order and Judgment be "settled." This means that the petitioner must prepare a draft Order and Judgment in conformity with the court's directions in its decision and, after service on all parties involved, must submit it to the court. The "settlement" procedure is often done because it ensures that the parties served will have an opportunity to object to any aspects of the draft they find deficient, because it fails to conform to the court's findings and rulings or for other reasons, and to seek modifications. At the end of this process, the court may sign the draft, perhaps after making changes the court feels to be necessary.

If the draft Order and Judgment must be settled, the petitioner or proposed Guardian or the attorney for either must do so promptly.

The Guardian may exercise only those powers that the Guardian is authorized to exercise by the court's order and judgment. The duties of the Guardian are set out in Section 81.20 and will be detailed in the order and judgment.

Guardians must not take any compensation for themselves nor pay any legal or accounting fees without first having obtained from the assigned Justice authorization to do so.

E. Qualification Of Guardian

After the Order and Judgment appointing one or more Guardians is issued, each Guardian must complete a process called qualification. This step is necessary, but not particularly complicated. The Guardian must complete the qualification process immediately after receiving the order and judgment.

After the Justice signs the Order and Judgment appointing the Guardian, the Guardian must take certain steps to qualify fully as Guardian, that is, to become fully and formally empowered to exercise the authority and fulfill the duties set out by the Justice in the order and judgment. First, the Guardian is required to file a bond (unless a bond is dispensed with ("waived") by order of the court); that is, in essence, an insurance policy protecting the incapacitated person against any possible errors by the Guardian. The Guardian must also sign an oath and designation of Clerk. Here, the Guardian formally undertakes to carry out the duties of Guardian. The designation of the Clerk is a document that designates the Clerk of the court to receive service of legal process on behalf of the Guardian should the incapacitated person be served when the Guardian is unavailable. These papers must be filed with the County Clerk. Within five days thereafter, a commission must be issued by the County Clerk.

The commission is a legal form that formally identifies the appointed Guardian as such and as having been appointed pursuant to law and authorizes the Guardian to carry out the responsibilities required by the order and judgment. The commission constitutes proof of the legal authority of the Guardian to act as such, for example, in dealing with a bank in safeguarding funds belonging to the incapacitated person. Absent adequate legal proof of authority, a bank or other entity will not allow a stranger to exercise power over a bank account or other property of the incapacitated person. The commission is typically prepared by the Guardian or his/her attorney or the petitioner's attorney. If the commission is in proper form, it will be signed by the County Clerk. The papers necessary to receive the commission, in addition, of course, to the Order and Judgment of the court, are the bond and the oath and designation of Clerk for service of process.

F. Marshalling The Assets

One of the first tasks of a Guardian of the property is to engage in the marshalling of the assets of the incapacitated person. This means to identify and locate the assets and to take the steps needed to safeguard them. The Guardian of the property must make a list of ALL assets and properties belonging to the incapacitated person and find where they are. In order to do this, the Guardian should do such things as the following:

- Review bank statements;
- Inventory the contents of any safe deposit boxes (in the presence of a bank officer);
- Collect all assets;
- Inspect the incapacitated person's home and files;
- Determine the status of the incapacitated person's housing arrangements (rental apartment, co-operative apartment, home, etc.);
- Identify all sources of income (fixed, investment, interest, etc.) and contact former employer, government agency, bank, brokerage house, etc., as necessary;
- Review all investment records;
- Review all bills;
- Identify and review the status of all credit cards and any outstanding credit card bills;
- Seek appraisals of any real property, as needed;
- Inventory all personal valuables (e.g., fur coats, jewelry, art objects);
- Locate the incapacitated person's will.

G. Training And Education

Article 81 contains educational requirements for Guardians and Court Evaluator's. Generally, each person appointed as Guardian must, within 90 days after issuance of the commission, complete a training course, approved by the court system, that covers the duties of the Guardian, the rights of the incapacitated person, the preparation of required reports on the Guardianship, and other matters. The Office of Court Administration periodically offers classes and generates a list of those who have completed the classes. Those who complete the class are certified by the court system.

H. Court Examiners

Guardians in Article 81 matters must submit to the court certain reports on their activities, described hereafter. Court Examiners are persons appointed by the court to review the Guardian's reports for accuracy and regularity. Each Guardianship matter has a Court Examiner assigned to it. Court Examiners are attorneys and accountants with expertise in Guardianship law and fiduciary accounting who have been appointed by the Appellate Division of the Supreme Court to review the work of the Guardians and to file a report for each.

Throughout the duration of the Guardianship the Guardian must cooperate with the Court Examiner at all times and the Guardian or his/her attorney must serve copies of reports and relief applications on the Examiner. The relationship between Guardian and Examiner is not intended to be adversarial, but collaborative and supportive. However, the Examiner, if confronted with non-compliance by the Guardian, can refer the Guardian for a compliance conference before the court, recommend a reduction in Guardian compensation (if any) or similar sanction, or seek the Guardian's removal when warranted.

The court's Guardianship and Fiduciary Support Office (Room 148, 60 Centre Street, Manhattan) monitors the filing of reports by Article 81 Guardians and the reports filed by the Court Examiners.

I. Initial Report

The Guardian is required to file an Initial Report within 90 days of the issuance of the commission (Section 81.30). A required standard form of this report is available on-line. The original of the completed report is filed with the Guardianship and Fiduciary Support Office, and a copy must be sent to the Court Examiner assigned to the case. The Initial Report must include proof that the Guardian has completed the required education course and must describe the steps the Guardian has taken to fulfill his/her responsibilities. If the Guardian has been granted powers with respect to property management of the incapacitated person, the Guardian must include in the report a complete inventory of resources over which the Guardian has control, must name therein the location of a will (if any), and must set out the plan for management of the property. If the Guardian has been granted powers regarding personal needs, the Guardian must indicate the dates of visits to the incapacitated person, describe what the Guardian has done to provide for his/her ward's personal needs and set out a plan for meeting those needs. If the Guardian believes that changes are needed in the powers authorized by the court, this must be explained. If the Initial Report includes any recommendations for a change in any powers, the Guardian must apply to the court for those changes within 10 days of the filing of the report on notice to all persons entitled to notice. For further information, please see Section 81.30.

A Guardian of the property of an incapacitated person must keep meticulous records regarding all financial activity on behalf of that person and relating to the assets of that person. Such records will be necessary for the completion of the Initial Report and the Annual and Final Report's, described below.

J. Annual Report

The Guardian must also file an Annual Report (Section 81.31). This must be done by May 31st of each year covering the period ending December 31st of the previous year. The original shall be filed with the Guardianship and Fiduciary Support Office and a copy shall be sent to the Court Examiner assigned to the case, the incapacitated person, the surety (the company that issued the bond) and, if the incapacitated person is in a nursing home or other rehabilitative facility, to the director of such facility and Mental Hygiene Legal Services. The Court Examiner will review the report.

The Annual Report provides information about the status and well-being of the incapacitated person and the activities of the Guardian. The Annual Report must include a financial accounting, a social and medical summary of the condition of the incapacitated person, and a current medical report from a qualified professional who has evaluated the incapacitated person within the three months prior to the filing of the Annual Report. The Guardian should seek assistance in the preparation of the accounting schedules if needed. The Court Examiner will reject the account if it is not in proper form.

The Guardian will be examined under oath by the Examiner concerning financial and personal matters relevant to the Guardianship. The Court Examiner will reject the accounting if it is not in the proper form. The Court Examiner will require back-up documentation from the Guardian supporting the account and transactions regarding it, such as cancelled checks, brokerage statements, bank statements, bills, invoices, receipts etc., in order to complete the audit of the account. It is thus very important for the Guardian to maintain accurate records of all financial activity. In addition, the Court Examiner will request a copy of any order regarding Guardian compensation, attorney and accounting fees, the purchase or sale of any real property, or any other order pertinent to the Guardianship.

Again, Guardians must not take compensation or pay legal or accounting fees without prior court authorization. The Court Examiner will need to see a copy of any order awarding compensation or authorizing payment of professional fees, authorizing purchase or sale of real property, or otherwise involving the Guardianship.

K. Intermediate Report

Another form of report is an intermediate report. A Guardian may petition the court by notice of motion or by order to show cause for permission to submit an intermediate report. Alternatively, a court may also order a Guardian to submit such an report. A required form of such report is available on-line.

L. Final Report

When, for one of a variety of reasons, the Guardian ceases to function as such, the Guardian must file a Final Report. Section 81.33. A Guardian must submit a final account when:

- the incapacitated person dies;
- the Guardian is removed, suspended, discharged or allowed to resign;
- the Guardian dies (in which case the Final Report shall be submitted by the legal representative of the estate);
- the assets of the incapacitated person are depleted;
- the incapacitated person is placed in a nursing home by a community Guardian.

The report must be submitted in a form prescribed by the court. The required form is available on-line.

The Final Report includes a final accounting, showing in detailed schedules all income received by, and expenses incurred on behalf of, the incapacitated person, assets, and their disposition. The Final Report must cover the entire Guardianship period, from the date of appointment to the date of death or other termination. Notice must be given to all persons who would have an interest in the estate of the incapacitated person, such as heirs, creditors, the surety and any other person who should receive notice. The Guardian should bring on a motion before the court requesting that the report be approved by the Justice and filed. The court will require that a proposed order of approval be settled, that is, served upon all parties and submitted to the court. Notice procedures provide all interested persons an opportunity to raise objections if any aspect of the report and the order cause concern. The report, the accounting and the proposed settled order are closely reviewed by the Guardianship and Fiduciary Support Office. When necessary, the staff will request corrections or supplemental information as needed before sending those documents to the Justice's Chambers.

M. Informal Final Report

In lieu of the formal report just discussed, an informal Final Report may at times be used. As the name suggests, this report is shorter and less complicated than the formal one. It can be used instead of a formal report if it has been served upon all persons interested in the proceeding and each of them has signed a form consenting to and approving the report and releasing and discharging the Guardian. Section 81.34. The informal report must be filed with the court together with the executed forms of consent. An informal Final Report on consent of all parties shall be filed with the Ex Parte Office Room (315, 60 Centre Street, Manhattan). The informal report is reviewed by the Ex Parte Clerk and then sent directly to the Justice assigned.

N. Assistance To Guardians

The court's Guardianship and Fiduciary Support Office (646–386–3328, Room 148, 60 Centre Street, Manhattan) tries to answer inquiries about procedures in Guardianship cases. However, because of its many responsibilities keeping track of cases, monitoring and reviewing filings, and assisting the Justices, the Office is not in a position to answer all of the questions an individual Guardian may have. In some cases, the Guardian can consult counsel. In others, however, it may be less practical to do so because of the modest size of the assets of the incapacitated person.

Recognizing the challenges that confront a Guardian who is not an attorney in a case in which the assets are of modest extent, the court has entered into a collaboration with the New York County Lawyers' Association, which is located near the court (at 14 Vesey Street, Manhattan). The Association, in conjunction with the court, has established a program to provide assistance to non-attorney Guardians in modest cases at no fee.

In this program, attorneys will explain the powers and duties of the Guardian and help him or her to carry out those duties, including in regard to completion of the initial (90-day) report and the first Annual Report. The assistance will not extend past the filing of the first Annual Report, but by that point, the Guardian will have gained a considerable understanding of his or her role so as to be able to carry it out properly and file the required reports thereafter. Assistance will be provided on an appointment-only basis. Appointments will be scheduled on weekday evenings at the Association.

To be eligible for this program, a Guardian who is not an attorney must have been appointed in New York County as a Guardian with powers over the person and/or the property of the incapacitated person and the assets in the case must total $70,000 or less. Any such Guardian who is interested in this program should contact the Association at 212–267–6646.

O. Avoiding Guardianship

Persons who retain the capacity to manage their own affairs may take steps to avoid a Guardianship proceeding in the future. An attorney can provide detailed information about these steps and about es-

tate planning in general. Two important devices are the durable power of attorney and the health care proxy. In combination, these devices allow a person to designate someone else to look after the personal well-being of the person and to safeguard and administer his or her assets in the event that the person should thereafter become unable to do so; these documents can accomplish what the appointment of a Guardian does, but without any need to come to court.

1) *Durable Power Of Attorney*

The durable power of attorney is a document which allows a person to grant to someone else the authority to perform legal transactions on his/her behalf without having to go to court for approval. The durable power of attorney is especially beneficial since it allows the holder to perform estate planning without delay, thereby preserving assets as well as, where applicable, maximizing benefits under the Medicaid Law. The durable power of attorney can be issued prior to any disability and remains valid even if the grantor becomes disabled or incapacitated.

2) *Health Care Proxy*

A health care proxy, which also can be issued prior to any disability, is a document which allows a person to give someone else the legal authority to make health care decisions for that person should he or she become physically or mentally unable to do so.

SOME KEY TERMS DEFINED

Settle Order/Judgment

This is a directive from the Justice requiring that an order or judgment be drafted by a party to a proceeding, that it be served on all parties, and that it be filed with the court for judicial consideration and possible execution. When a settlement is directed by the court, the file is retained by the court and the proposed order or judgment and any proposed counter-order or counter-judgment (that is a competing proposal offered, served and filed by another party) should be submitted to the Guardianship and Fiduciary Support Office unless otherwise directed.

Motion

A motion is a written request for a court order. The motion should briefly state the relief sought, the supporting documents attached, and why the Justice should grant the type of relief requested.

Service and Notice

Legal papers, e.g. motions, orders, proposed orders, judgments, are served on all parties involved in the case, thus putting these persons "on notice." These papers must be served by someone over the age of 18, who is NOT a party in the case. Typically, service may be accomplished by mail or by personal delivery. Afterwards, the person who performed the service must fill out an affidavit of service and sign it before a notary as proof of service. That proof must be annexed to or submitted with papers presented to the court.

Order To Show Cause

An order to show cause is an order (that is, it is signed by a judge) directing a party to come forward with reasons ("show cause") why some stated relief should not be granted to the applicant. The proposed order to show cause is prepared by the applicant or his/her counsel. It should briefly state the relief sought, and be accompanied by an affidavit or affidavits explaining in detail the nature of the relief sought and why it should be granted. The proposed order to show cause is submitted to and reviewed for form by the Ex–Parte Office (Room 315, 60 Centre Street, Manhattan). An application to appoint a Guardian is always made by order to show cause. Once signed, the order is served on the parties to the case by an appropriate person on behalf of the applicant in the manner directed by the court in the order.

Verified Petition

A petition is a formal legal document in which the party seeking the appointment of a Guardian (the petitioner) sets out his or her claims, or requests for legal relief. A verified petition is one that includes a declaration under oath or upon penalty of perjury that the contents and statements included in the petition are true. The verification is typically located at the end of the document.

Bond

A bond is a sort of insurance policy used to protect the incapacitated person by ensuring responsible performance by the Guardian, as well as security of the person's assets. The amount of the bond is set by the Justice assigned to the case. The Guardian obtains the bond through a bonding company or surety. The bond may be referred to as a surety bond.

Community Guardian

A community Guardian is a not-for-profit corporation or a local governmental agency that has contracted with a local social services agency to provide services to incapacitated persons or other eligible individuals. For more information, please see Social Services Law § 473-c.

Mental Hygiene Legal Service

This is a State Agency that advocates for the rights of individuals who reside in treatment facilities licensed to provide services for the mentally ill, developmentally disabled or chemically dependant, as well as any other persons who might become subject to substituted decision-making either by having been made a ward of the court or by Guardianship proceeding.

Doc. 3. Outline of Filing and Other Court Procedures in Guardianship Cases

1. Application for Appointment of Guardian(s)

A. *Initial Application*

☐ Verified petition should be filed in the County Clerk's Office (Room 141B, 60 Centre Street) and an Index Number obtained (fee $ 210). Order to Show Cause and verified petition then filed in the Ex–Parte Office (Room 315, 60 Centre Street).

   ☐ If papers are approved for form, the petitioner must file a Request for Judicial Intervention with the County Clerk's Office (Room 160) (fee $95).

   ☐ Ex–Parte Clerk will record case in court's case management system and a Guardianship Justice will be randomly assigned

   ☐ OSC and petition brought to Justice assigned by applying attorney

☐ Order to Show Cause signed by Justice

   ☐ Justice appoints a Court Evaluator and/or attorney for Alleged Incapacitated Person (AIP); sets date of hearing ("return date") (which will be no later than 28 days from signing of the OSC) and date by which service (transmission of papers to interested persons) is to be made, method of service and who is to be served.

   ☐ Attorney for petitioner will "conform" a copy of OSC as signed or make a photocopy thereof, or Justice's staff may phone attorney and provide information.

   ☐ Fiduciary clerk sends "Notice of Appointment/Certification of Compliance" (UCS 872) to appointees.

B. *Hearing*

☐ Court Evaluator will submit report prior to hearing.

☐ Evidence will be presented at hearing as to incapacity of AIP, needs, assets, etc.

☐ In event court makes a finding of incapacity, the Justice may state findings orally and the court reporter will record them ("on the record") and/or the Justice will issue a brief written order ("short form order"). Typically, the Justice will direct the petitioner to "settle" an Order and Judgment setting forth particulars in full on notice to interested parties.

C. *Order and Judgment—Review and Approval*

☐ Proposed Order and Judgment must be submitted to Guardianship & Fiduciary Support Office (Room 148) by petitioner together with proof of service thereof on all interested parties.

☐ Guardianship & Fiduciary Support Office reviews proposed Order and Judgment as to form and content (proposal must conform to the Justice's findings and directives in the short form order and on the record); reviews any fee requests and makes a recommendation as to the amount of the bond; prepares a summary with recommendations for the Justice's review.

☐ Justice reviews and signs Order and Judgment (as modified, if necessary).

☐ Order and Judgment will be recorded in court's computer. Case file sent to Motion Support for entry into computer and then file is forwarded to the County Clerk for entry of judgment into County Clerk's minutes and file.

☐ Guardianship and Fiduciary Support sends copy of Order and Judgment to petitioner and assigned court examiner; the UCS 872's are sent to appointees (Guardian(s), court examiner).

2. Initial Steps After Appointment of Guardian

A. *Involvement of Court Examiner*

☐ Shortly after the Guardian's appointment, the Court Examiner will contact the Guardian to review the Guardian's duties and obligations.

☐ The Examiner, if not served by the petitioner's attorney, will typically request a copy of the order of appointment, commission, the Court Evaluator's report, the OSC and petition and other documentation relevant to the Guardianship.

B. *Initial Actions by Guardian(s)*

☐ *Qualification*—The Guardian must obtain a bond if directed by the court and file proof that that has been done, and file oath and designation of clerk and a commission with the County Clerk. The latter forms are posted on this site [1]. The County Clerk will then issue the Guardian's commission.

☐ *Initial Report*—Within 90 days of the issuance of the commission the Guardian is required to file an "Initial Report" (90-day report). A form of Initial Report is posted on this site. The original is filed with Guardianship and Fiduciary Support Office and a copy is sent to the Court Examiner assigned, who reviews same and reports to the court.

☐ The Court Examiner files a summary with recommendations and a proposed order confirming Report and approving the Examiner's fee. The Justice reviews the Report and the Examiner's review and signs the order if found proper.

C. *Subsequent Actions and Reporting Thereon by Guardian*

☐ *Annual Report*—The Guardian must carry out the duties set out in the Order and Judgment of the court. The Guardian must file an Annual Report by May 31st of each year covering the period ending December 31st of the previous year; original filed with the Guardianship Office and a copy is sent to the Court Examiner, the Incapacitated Person, the surety (the company that provided the bond (if one was directed)), and, if the IP is in a nursing home or other rehabilitative facility, to the director of the facility and Mental Hygiene Legal Services. A form of the Annual Report is posted on this site. [1]

☐ *Examination of the Annual Report*—The Examiner's report on the Annual Report is submitted to the Guardianship and Fiduciary Support Office. The report will include the following: 1) a proposed order confirming the report; 2) information on the medical and social condition of the IP; 3) a summary of events leading to the Guardian's appointment; 4) a financial summary of the accounting period; 5) any recommendations for actions to be taken by the Guardian; 6) a verified transcript of the Guardian's testimony; 7) a copy of the order and judgment appointing the Guardian and any order approving fees and commissions; 8) the Guardian's Annual Report; and 9) a recent medical evaluation. The Guardianship and Fiduciary Support Office reviews the Examiner's report, prepares a summary with recommendations, endorses fiduciary compensation forms, if any, and sends the order and papers to the Justice.

☐ If satisfied, the Justice will sign an order confirming the Examiner's report and providing for the approval of commissions and fees as found appropriate by the Justice and any change to the bond determined to be needed. The Examiner is sent a copy of the order and the original is filed with the County Clerk after all databases are updated.

☐ Final Report—A Guardian must render a Final Report when the Incapacitated Person dies and in other circumstances. A form of Final Report is posted on this site. [1]

☐ *If the Incapacitated Person is alive*, a Guardian can only move the court for discharge by an ex-parte application seeking permission to file a Final Report. A short form order is issued directing the filing of the Final Report within 45 days from the order date.

☐ When seeking to settle a Final Report upon death of the incapacitated person, the Guardian is required to file an Order to Show Cause or Notice of Motion (the latter should be returnable in the Motion Support Office Courtroom (Room 130) on any business day of the week at 9:30 AM). The motion and all papers are forwarded to the Justice. If the Justice approves the application, a short form order will be issued. The Final Report should be sent to the Guardianship Office for review. All interested parties specified in the Order and Judgment must be served with a copy and proof of such service must accompany the original filed with the Office.

☐ The Guardianship and Fiduciary Support Office will review the Report and prepare a summary with recommendations for the Justice. If it is found to be proper, the Justice will sign an order settling (approving) the Final Report and forward the file to Motion Support (Room 119), which will make a notation of such action in the court's computer. Then, the file will be forwarded to the County Clerk. Upon filing proof of compliance with the court's final order, the Guardian must seek an ex-parte order discharging the surety (the company that provided the bond) and the Guardian. Upon the submission of proof of compliance with the final order, the court will issue an order of discharge.

No. 1: 10/23/06

1 http://www.nycourts.gov/supctmanh/

Doc. 4. Outline of Court Rules on Fiduciary Appointments and the Fiduciary Clerk

In all matters under Article 81, as well as in all other matters involving fiduciaries, Parts 26 and 36 of the Rules of the Chief Judge must be scrupulously followed. Compliance with these filing requirements is monitored by the Fiduciary Clerk, who is located in the Guardianship and Fiduciary Support Office (Room 148, 60 Centre Street, Manhattan). The following is a summary of some key aspects of these provisions, but all fiduciaries should consult them closely in full.

Part 36 of the Rules of the Chief Judge applies to appointments of, among others, a guardian, guardian ad litem, law guardians, court evaluator, court examiners, and attorney for an alleged incapacitated person ("AIP"), as well as a receiver, referee, and a person designated to perform services for a guardian or receiver, such as counsel, an accountant, and an appraiser or property manager. Section 36.1. Except for some provisions thereof, Part 36 does not apply to the appointment of a guardian who is a relative of the subject of a guardianship proceeding or a person nominated as guardian by the subject of such a proceeding or proposed by a party. Section 36.1(b)(2). Appointments under Part 36 shall be made from a list established by the Chief Administrative Judge. Section 36.2 (b) (1). The Justice may, however, make a designation from outside the list upon a finding of good cause, but in such case the basis for the appointment shall be set forth in writing and filed with the Fiduciary Clerk. Section 36.2 (b)(2).

Part 36 prohibits, among others, relatives of judges, employees of the Unified Court System, and certain persons connected with a political party or involved in a candidacy for judicial office, as well as associates thereof, from being appointed. Section 36.2 (c). No receiver or guardian may be appointed as his or her own counsel, nor may a person associated with his or her law firm, absent a compelling reason. Section 36.2 (c) (8). The attorney for the AIP shall not be appointed as guardian, or counsel to the guardian, of that person. Section 36.2 (c)(9). No court evaluator shall be appointed as guardian for the AIP except under extenuating circumstances that are set forth in writing and filed with the Fiduciary Clerk. Section 36.2 (c)(10).

No person or institution is eligible to receive more than one appointment within a calendar year for which the anticipated compensation to be awarded in any calendar year exceeds $15,000. Section 36.2 (d)(1). If a person or entity has been awarded more than an aggregate of $ 50,000 during any calendar year, the person or entity shall not be eligible for compensated appointments by any court during the next calendar year. Section 36.2 (d) (2). These limitations do not apply where the appointment "is necessary to maintain continuity of representation of or service to the same person or entity in further or subsequent proceedings." Section 36.2 (d)(4).

All appointees must complete a Notice of Appointment and a Certification of Compliance (OCA forms) and submit them within 30 days to the Fiduciary Clerk. An appointee who accepts an appointment without compensation need not complete the certification of compliance. Section 36.4 (a).

If an appointee seeks compensation of more than $500, he or she must file with the Fiduciary Clerk, on a court-issued form, a statement of approval of compensation, which shall contain a confirmation to be signed by that Clerk that the appointee has filed the Notice of Appointment and Certification of Compliance. A Judge shall not approve compensation of more than $500 and no compensation shall be awarded unless the appointee has filed the Notice and Certification and the Fiduciary Clerk has confirmed the filing to the Judge. Section 36.4 (b).

If the fees to appointees under Part 36 are $5,000 or more, the Justice must provide a written explanation of the reasons therefor, which is to be filed with the Fiduciary Clerk along with the order approving compensation. Section 36.4 (b)(3).

Part 26 of the Rules of the Chief Judge requires that a Justice who has approved compensation of more than $ 500 shall file with the Office of Court Administration the week after approval a statement of compensation on a form authorized by the Chief Administrative Judge. The appointees covered by Part 26 include guardians, court evaluators and counsel for an incapacitated person, as well as guardians ad litem, referees, counsel and receivers.

A "Fiduciary Information Sheet" and fiduciary forms are available in the Guardianship and Fiduciary Support Office. For access to this sheet and forms, click here.

The Fiduciary Clerk maintains a database for tracking the filing by appointees of the required fiduciary forms. All original fiduciary forms are placed in the County Clerk's file and copies are mailed to the Office of Court Administration, where a statewide centralized database of reported appointments and approvals of compensation is maintained.

REFERENCES

Procedure VII. References and Referees

From time to time Justices refer issues to Special Referees, who are court employees, or to Judicial Hearing Officers ("JHO's") to hear and report or to hear and determine. (Subject to certain limitations, persons outside the court may be designated Referees.)

Most references are to hear and report, meaning that the JHO/Referee holds an evidentiary hearing if required and issues a report containing recommended findings and conclusions. A transcript of the hearing can be produced, but its filing may be waived by the parties. After a report has been filed, notice is to be given to the parties of the filing. The plaintiff must move to confirm or reject all or part of the report within 15 days of the giving of notice. If plaintiff fails to so move, the defendant shall do so within 30 days. CPLR 4403; Uniform Rule 202.44 (a). A referee may also be appointed to supervise disclosure. CPLR 3104.

On a reference to determine, the JHO/Referee decides the matter referred. There is nothing for the referring Justice to confirm or reject. Any appeal is taken directly to the Appellate Division from the entered order or judgment of the JHO/Referee. Because of the constitutional right to a jury trial, the court's power to order references to determine is circumscribed. CPLR 4317. The court may order such a reference on consent (with a few exceptions) or in the case of a long account, or where otherwise constitutionally permitted, i.e., issues in which references were permitted historically. The parties may also, with few limits, designate their own referee.

An order of reference must make clear the exact issue being referred and any and all constraints on the JHO/Referee.

The court, through its Special Referee Clerk (Room 119, 646–386–3028), will endeavor to identify all decisions in which a reference to a JHO/Referee is directed by a Justice and to calendar same promptly after issuance without the need for action by counsel. A box has been placed on the court's decision form ("gray sheet") so that the assigned Justice can use this means to notify the Special Referee Clerk that a reference is being directed. The Clerk will inform counsel of the issuance of the order of reference and forward a copy of an Information Sheet. However, as a safeguard to ensure against inadvertent delay, counsel must, as soon as possible after issuance of the decision (which will in most cases be posted on the court's website within hours after issuance), serve on the Special Referee Clerk a copy of the Information Sheet. The Information Sheet must be completed in full and transmitted as soon as possible to the Special Referee Clerk as directed in the Sheet. For access to a copy of the Information Sheet, click here.[1]

The matter will be placed on the Reference Calendar in the Special Referees Part (Part SRP) for some weeks after notice of the reference comes to the attention of the Special Referee Clerk and counsel will be informed of the date of the hearing. The Reference Calendar is conducted Monday through Thursday by Honorable John Bradley, JHO (Part SRP, Room 546 at 80 Centre Street, 9:30 AM). Judge Bradley assigns matters to an available JHO/Referee for a hearing. Cases are assigned to a JHO/Referee on the original hearing date in the Referees Part and the reference hearing normally commences on the original date and attorneys should therefore be prepared to proceed on that date. The hearing will be conducted in the same manner as a trial before a Justice without a jury (CPLR 4318, 4320 (a)) (the proceeding will be recorded by a court reporter, the rules of evidence apply, etc.). For the Rules of Part SRP, including procedures regarding adjournments, and a list of the JHO's/Referees, etc., click here.[2] The Rules also appear under "Special Referees Part" in the "Basic Information" section of the Rules of the Justices posted on this site.

Calendar information on cases pending in the Special Referees Part (Part SRP) and on those that have been referred therefrom to a JHO/Special Referee is recorded in the court's computer system (the Civil Case Information System) and it is reported in the Supreme Court Records On-Line Library ("SCROLL") on this website (under "Case Information"). Each JHO/Referee is assigned to a separate Part and once a case has been referred to a JHO/Referee, it will be marked in the court's records as appearing in that JHO/Referee's Part. Information about individual cases assigned to JHO's/Referees can be obtained from the court's free case-tracking service, E–Track, and is also made available to attorneys' tracking services. When the JHO's/Referee's report or decision is ready, it is transmitted to the Special Referee Clerk (Room 119) for processing. Reports and decisions issued by the JHO's/Referees are posted on the website of the court in "SCROLL" within hours after their issuance, except in matrimonial matters, Article 81 cases, sealed cases, or where the JHO/Referee directs otherwise.

September 2010

1 http://www.nycourts.gov/supctman/refpart-infosheet-10-09.pdf

2 http://www.nycourts.gov/supctman/refereesrules12-09.pdf

CONFERENCES/CAPTIONS AND TRIAL STATUS/NOTES OF ISSUE/WITHDRAWAL OF COUNSEL SUBPOENAED RECORDS

Procedure VIII. Conferences/Captions or Trial Status/Notes of Issue/Withdrawal of Counsel/Subpoenaed Records

A. Conferences

1. *Preliminary Conferences*

Preliminary conferences sought by parties pursuant to Rule 202.12 of the Uniform Rules for the Trial Courts are scheduled through the Trial Support Office (Room 158) upon filing with that office of a request for a preliminary conference with proof of service. If the case has not yet been assigned to a Justice, the party must also submit an original and one copy of an RJI with proof of service; and proof of purchase of the index number for the main action, if applicable, and payment of filing fees for all third-party actions. If the filing party wishes to have the case assigned to the Commercial Division, the preliminary conference request and RJI, marked to reflect a Commercial assignment, must be filed with the Commercial Division Support Office (Room 148) and must be accompanied by a statement in support of the requested assignment and a copy of the pleadings (Uniform Rule 202.70 (d)). The conference is to be held within 45 days of filing the RJI. Uniform Rule 202.19. Likewise, if the case has been assigned to a Justice, the party must submit proof of payment of the filing fees for any third-party action (the County Clerk's computer will issue a receipt that can be used as such proof).

The Trial Support Office will give notice by mail of the preliminary conference, which shall take place at the Justice's regularly scheduled conference time, which can be found in the Uniform Rules of the Justices. Our court's website (in the Supreme Court Records On–Line Library ("Scroll"), as well as the court system's case tracking program, "Case Trac" (at www.nycourts.gov under "E Courts" and under "CaseTrac"), also contain information on future appearances in our court.

If counsel submit, prior to the scheduled conference date, a completed preliminary conference stipulation and order form, and the court finds no problems, counsel need not appear and the court will remove the case from the conference calendar and make an entry in the court computer or mark the calendar with the future appearance date stipulated in the form. Uniform Rule 202.12(b). Under the Differentiated Case Management ("DCM") system (Uniform Rule 202.19), all disclosure must be completed within eight, 12 or 15 months in expedited, standard and complex cases, respectively. Commercial and medical malpractice cases are treated by the court as complex matters unless the filing party designates otherwise. Motor vehicle cases are categorized as expedited matters. If the stipulation and order form is not submitted, the conference shall take place.

At a preliminary conference the court will, at the request of a party or on its own, confirm or modify the DCM track selected by the party who filed the RJI, and establish a schedule within the DCM deadline for completion of pre-trial proceedings. The court will also address, to the extent appropriate, limitation of issues, addition of parties and settlement. Uniform Rule 202.12(c). Failure to comply with the terms of a preliminary conference order, and making frivolous motions, shall, in the discretion of the court, result in the imposition of costs or other sanctions on the offending party. Uniform Rule 202.12(f). Particular attention is drawn to deadlines for adding parties, completing all discovery and filing a note of issue, as these dates are important to efficient case management.

The plaintiff must file a Notice of Medical, Dental or Podiatric Malpractice Action in cases of those types within 60 days of joinder of issue or after the time for a defaulting party to appear has expired. The Notice must be accompanied by an RJI if the case is unassigned. CPLR 3406; Rule 202.56(a). The proposed Notice and RJI must be submitted to the Trial Support Office for approval (after which the RJI fee is paid in Room 160). The assigned Justice shall conduct a preliminary conference as soon as practicable after the filing of the Notice and shall schedule disclosure proceedings so as to expedite a final disposition of the matter. Rule 202.56(b).

The progress of cases in the court is governed by standards and goals, which exist both for pre-note and post-note periods. The standards and goals for DCM cases are eight, 12 or 15 months pre-note, and 15 months post-note. However, Uniform Rule 202.19 requires that a pretrial conference be held within 180 days from filing of the note of issue, with trial to occur within eight weeks from the conference.

Although Uniform Rule 202.19 sets a standard and goal for the filing of a note of issue and the court's computer automatically calculates the standard and goal therefor in each case from RJI and in accordance with the DCM track of the case for the purposes of tracking standards and goals and compliance therewith in the court, the date for filing of the note of issue set by the Justice assigned in the preliminary conference order or in any other directive is the deadline to which the parties must adhere. That deadline may be shorter than that fixed by standards and goals, or it may be longer if circumstances require. See Section 202.19 (b).

2. *Other Conferences*

Compliance and pretrial conferences are fixed by the Justice either (i) in a discovery scheduling order issued at a preliminary conference or compliance conference or (ii) in a decision on a motion. Notices are not sent by Trial Support for conferences subsequent to the preliminary conference since the parties will have attended the preliminary conference and received notice then of the future appearance or received a copy of a decision. However, individual notice is transmitted for post-note-of-issue conferences conducted in the Neutral Evaluation Program.

3. *Status Conferences*

Our court may, from time to time, schedule status conferences in the Part. With respect to the latter, Trial Support, at the request of a Justice, will mail notices to the attorneys in each of the cases in an inventory that have been selected to undergo this procedure. These notices announce that counsel must appear on a given date pursuant to a directive of the presiding Justice. Failure to respond will result in appropriate judicial action (not, however, including a markoff pursuant to CPLR 3404; see *Johnson v. Sam Minskoff & Sons*, 287 A.D.2d 233, 735 N.Y.S. 2d 503 (1st Dept. 2001) (holding that CPLR 3404 does not apply to pre-note cases)). When counsel appear, the Justice will make whatever order is required to insure future progress in the case.

B.   Orders Affecting the Caption or Trial Status

If a motion affecting the caption or the trial status of a case (e.g., a motion to correct a caption, to substitute a party, to amend, to strike a note of issue, or to obtain a preference) is granted, the prevailing attorney must serve a copy of the court's order on both the County Clerk and the Trial Support Office. Because the court issues over 30,000 decisions on motions each year and many long form orders as well, neither the County Clerk nor the court's Clerks Offices can read all decisions/orders searching for judicial directives on these matters. Counsel must bring them to the attention of the County Clerk and the relevant Clerk's Office. See CPLR 8019 (c). Both the County Clerk and Trial Support must be served with copies of orders regarding captions, etc. since each office maintains computer records on cases in our court but these records are not connected to one another.

C.   Filing of Notes of Issue

A note of issue must of course be filed in order to place a case on the calendar for trial (CPLR 3402(a)), including inquests or framed issue hearings before a Justice (but not hearings conducted by a Referee). The fees for filing a note of issue and jury demand must be paid to the County Clerk (Room 160 at 60 Centre Street) first (fees are $ 30 and $ 65 respective-

ly). The Trial Support Office manages the procedure of processing notes of issue and jury demands. A note of issue must be filed with Trial Support, accompanied by a certificate of readiness, an affirmation of counsel reciting compliance with any preliminary conference order, a copy of such order and an affidavit of service. Uniform Rule 202.21. If an attorney seeks to file a note of issue late, Trial Support will not accept it. The court, though, can authorize a late filing by endorsement on the note (a notation of "OK to file by _____" with a signature by the Justice will suffice); or the parties may seek an extension from the court by presenting a stipulation for "so ordering." In light of DCM deadlines, counsel should not assume that extensions, even by stipulation, can be had without good cause.

D.   Appearance and Withdrawal of Counsel

Attorneys who appear in cases in the court should check the court's Civil Case Information System (computerized case history system) or the attorney listings in our court's Supreme Court Records On–Line Library ("Scroll") on this website to be sure that their appearance has been recorded there since this system is the basis for notices to counsel in cases pending in the court. With regard to some matters that come before the court the staff may be unable to identify the attorneys for all parties (e.g., some orders to show cause) and it may be that not all appearances will be recorded in the court's computer. If counsel becomes aware of any gaps in the CCIS/Scroll appearance information, the Trial Support Office should be informed.

An attorney of course can withdraw from a representation without court approval upon filing a consent to change counsel. Consents to change attorneys must be filed in the Trial Support Office so that the court's computer can be modified to reflect accurately the representations in the case. Filing with the County Clerk does not suffice since, as noted, the two offices maintain separate computer systems. The County Clerk will decline to accept consents that have not been filed with Trial Support.

Absent the proper filing of a consent, an attorney will continue as attorney of record, irrespective of discord with the client or longstanding inability to contact the client, unless the attorney obtains judicial approval to withdraw. The attorney must make a motion for leave to withdraw. If the motion is granted, outgoing counsel must of course comply with all terms of the court's order. A copy of the order must be served by the attorney on both the County Clerk and the Trial Support Office so that each may modify its records.

E.   Subpoenaed Records

The Trial Support Office operates a Subpoenaed Records Section (Room 145M), which receives, logs in, and maintains all subpoenaed records. Parties may learn of the arrival of records by consulting the computer terminals in the courthouse. After trial, original records are returned to the person who submitted them and copies are destroyed. However, if the case is appealed, all records will be retained pending the outcome of the appeal; the Trial Support Office should be notified of the intent to appeal. In actions that have been transferred to Civil Court pursuant to CPLR 325 (c) or (d), the subpoenaed records will be sent to that court.

September 2006

NEUTRAL EVALUATION PROGRAM ("MEDIATION")

Procedure IX. Protocol for the Court–Annexed Neutral Evaluation Program ("Mediation")

The Supreme Court, Civil Branch, New York County operates the Court-annexed Neutral Evaluation Program ("the Program") (informally known as "Mediation"). The procedures followed in the Program are set forth below.

A. Nature of the Process

In this program, Neutral Evaluation Attorneys, specially selected staff attorneys, evaluate cases based upon informal presentations by the attorneys for the parties. The Evaluation Attorney will endeavor to facilitate a settlement between the parties. Where deemed appropriate, the Evaluation Attorney may offer opinions about the parties' chances for success on the issues presented in the case. These opinions may assist parties in their own analysis of the merits of their cases and thus help to facilitate discussion between the parties and to generate a settlement.

In general, presentations are made to the Evaluation Attorneys in sessions attended by counsel for all parties. The attorneys will then meet with an Evaluation Attorney individually. Experience has shown that counsel may be reluctant to be completely candid and expansive about their positions in the presence of the adversary. These private discussions are very helpful to the Evaluation Attorney in determining if a case can be settled.

Cases eligible for the program consist of personal injury matters, commercial cases that were not filed in or were transferred out of the Commercial Division, real estate cases, and other cases in the "General" category of the court's inventory, as well as Motor Vehicle Cases. Cases will be referred upon the filing of the note of issue, as explained below. Counsel who receive notice to attend an evaluation conference are required to do so. Many cases in which attorneys initially are skeptical about the chances for a settlement, or indeed in which they are certain that settlement is impossible, in fact come to a settlement. No settlement will be reached unless all counsel agree, and there will be no penalty if a party refuses to settle.

B. Confidentiality

Presentations or communications made by attorneys during the evaluation about the merits of their cases are confidential. The Evaluation Attorney will not communicate with the Justice to whom the case is assigned, or other persons not participants in the process, concerning any aspect of the merits of any case that goes into the Program. If a case fails to settle, the Evaluation Attorney will not inform the Justice which attorney refused to agree on a resolution. Nor will the Evaluation Attorney discuss with any counsel to any case being evaluated any information that that attorney may convey to the Evaluation Attorney in confidence without the advance permission of that attorney. Communications between the attorneys during any evaluation session or made to the Evaluation Attorney as part of the process may not be used by any party as an admission or otherwise in the case or in any other litigation. The Evaluation Attorney will not testify about any aspects of the evaluation process, whether as a witness in that case or in another case. The Evaluation Attorney will not, for instance, testify as to any alleged concessions or admissions made on behalf of any party in the process, nor as to whether any party agreed to settle a matter in general or on any particular terms.

Notwithstanding the foregoing, if a case is remanded to the assigned IAS Justice for trial or sent to the Administrative Coordinating Part for that purpose, an Evaluation Attorney may advise the Justice presiding of the amount of any final demand or settlement offer made by a party unless the demand or offer is stated to be confidential, in which event it shall not be disclosed to anyone, other than counsel for parties to the case, without the advance authorization of the attorney who made it. Further, refusal by any attorney to appear for an evaluation session is a violation of the rules of the Program and will be reported to the assigned IAS Justice for appropriate action.

C. How Cases Enter the Program

When a note of issue is filed in any Motor Vehicle case or in any case assigned to most of the General Assignment Parts, the case will be referred to the Program. All of these cases will be evaluated unless evaluation would be impractical, in which event the case will be referred back to the assigned Justice.

Upon filing of the note of issue, calendar cards are prepared and filed in the Clerk's Office. When an Evaluation Attorney requires additional cases, the Office will be so advised and will cull out the cases that have been waiting longest assigned to all of the aforesaid Parts, unless a Part is completely current.

In addition, if the conduct of a Settlement Day (see below) is appropriate and efficient, cases of a particular defendant/carrier may be selected in a single group and not in strict waiting time order. Finally, because of the disproportionately large number of cases pending in the Motor Vehicle Part, a substantial number of Motor Vehicle referrals will take place.

Attorneys for the parties will be advised by Program staff by telephone or mail of a date and time for the evaluation session. Adjournments may be obtained if the scheduled date proves inconvenient. A stipulation or letter request reflecting the consent of all parties, setting forth the reason for the adjournment, and preferably setting forth a requested adjourned date must be submitted 72 hours or more in advance of the scheduled date. Requests for adjournment by phone are not accepted.

For the convenience of the Bar, the evaluation sessions are conducted on a staggered schedule. Attorneys will be advised when to appear. The calendar published in the Law Journal will also list the precise times of each scheduled appearance. In order that the staggered schedule may work effectively for the benefit of all attorneys, it is vital that, at or before the time scheduled for each case, the attorneys on the case appear and check in with the Court Clerk in the Part. If an attorney anticipates any difficulty appearing on time, he or she should contact the opposing counsel prior to the date of the appearance and inform him or her of the problem.

The attorneys shall communicate prior to the initial conference and plaintiff's counsel shall advise the adversary of a "record demand." This expedites the process by permitting defense counsel to evaluate a case preliminarily prior to the initial conference.

The evaluation process will generally be completed within 120 days from the filing of the note of issue. However, in some cases several sessions may be required or parties may need time to consult and to reflect on issues, offers and demands. Such cases may be retained in the Program beyond 120 days where necessary to complete the process and where the assigned IAS Justice approves.

D. Settlement Days

The Program has in the past conducted settlement days involving groups of cases against particular defendants or in which insurance coverage is provided by particular carriers. Claims adjusters or other persons with full authority to settle on the part of defendant are present on these days and counsel for plaintiffs are advised that that will be the case. Experience has demonstrated that the presence at the evaluation of the decision-maker for a party can greatly assist the productivity of the process. Because the adjuster or other authorized person will be present, serious consideration can be given to a number of cases at the same time much more expeditiously and efficiently than would otherwise be possible.

E. Preparation by Counsel/Participation by Knowledgeable and Authorized Counsel

Because the evaluation process will address the merits of liability and damages issues, it is essential that parties be represented at the evaluation by an attorney who is knowledgeable about the case and fully authorized to settle it or in ready communication with the client or the client representative who can authorize settlement. Otherwise, time may be wasted, both that of counsel and of the Evaluation Attorneys. Cf. Uniform Rule for the Trial Courts 202.26 (e).

Counsel shall be prepared to present at the evaluation a copy of the pleadings, the bill of particulars, and any medical or other records necessary to an informed evaluation of the case and of the injuries claimed.

F. When Cases Fail to Reach Settlement in the Program

Cases that fail to come to settlement in the Program will be remanded to the Parts from which they came. However, in some instances, the case may instead be scheduled by the Neutral Evaluation Attorney for jury selection for a date certain; in these instances, counsel will be advised to report to the Administrative Coordinating Part (Part 40) or the Motor Vehicle Part on the selection date and the case will proceed to jury selection that day (unless the Judge presiding in the Part permits the matter to be adjourned). Counsel will be afforded an opportunity to consult their schedules before the final selection date is fixed by the Neutral Evaluation Attorney.

All trial-ready City cases will proceed through the Neutral Evaluation Program. If a City case does not come to settlement in the Program, then, in the presence of counsel, it will be assigned a date by the Evaluation Attorney on which the case will appear before the Neutral Evaluation Attorney for a Last Clear Chance Conference, which will represent the last opportunity for a settlement conference prior to jury selection. Cases scheduled for this Conference will not be adjourned, whether to accommodate further settlement talks or consideration of settlement offers, or for other reasons. Since discovery will have long since been completed, counsel should not expect to be able to ask for additional disclosure. If the case does not settle on the day of the Last Clear Chance Conference, it will appear in the Administrative Coordinating Part (Part 40) without fail 14 days later, a Monday, at which time it will be sent out for jury selection and trial. The court will conduct no settlement discussions on the date set for trial or during jury selection. Thus, counsel who receive from a Neutral Evaluation Attorney notice of a proposed date to appear for a Last Clear Chance Conference should understand that the date for jury selection and trial of their case is firmly fixed for 14 days after the date of the Last Clear Chance Conference, subject only to the possibility that the trial date might be mooted by settlement at the Conference. Adjournment of the trial date will not be permitted. Therefore, attorneys should check their calendars when the Evaluation Attorney proposes a date for the Last Clear Chance Conference. The schedule of counsel and their witnesses will be taken into account at that time. Since counsel will definitely be going to trial two weeks after that conference, if that trial date is inconvenient, they should immediately advise the Evaluation Attorney.

The Evaluation Attorney handling Last Clear Chance Conferences will schedule dates for appearances for such Conferences (and consequently for trial) using a form that explains the procedure. To consult this form, **click here.**[1]

G. Staff of the Program

The evaluations are conducted by Shelley Rossoff Olsen, Esq. (Mediation 1), Neutral Evaluation Attorney, and Michael Tempesta, Esq. (Mediation 2), Senior Neutral Evaluation Attorney.

H. Further Information

Parties with questions about any aspect of the Program should call 646–386–3689 (Mediation 1) or 646–386–3691 (Mediation 2).

Dated: March 1, 2006

HON. JACQUELINE W. SILBERMANN
ADMINISTRATIVE JUDGE

[1] http://www.nycourts.gov/supctmanh/LCCstip020408.pdf

JURY SELECTION

Procedure X. Jury Selection

A major goal of the Court is, with the cooperation of the County Clerk, to administer the jury selection process so that jurors are utilized to try cases, not as tools to induce settlements; jurors are selected quickly, but with full and fair opportunity for questioning by counsel; the time of prospective and selected jurors is conserved; and the experience of jury service is as meaningful as possible. See Uniform Rule 202.33.

The County Clerk's jury clerk will assign and reassign jury selection rooms according to the order in which cases appear for selection, the complexity of the cases and the number of attorneys and prospective jurors involved. Attorneys who are sent to select must appear in the Central Jury Room (Room 452) promptly. Attorneys directed to appear at the start of a day should be present by 9:30 AM at the latest.

The staff of the Jury Room provides jury questionnaires to counsel in advance of the voir dire process. Generally speaking, each side is allotted one hour and a half to question jurors. A JHO, or in some cases the Justice assigned to try the case, will rule on all issues that arise during selection. Attorneys may not interrupt voir dire to seek a ruling from the trial Justice without consent of the JHO. If a record needs to be made regarding a ruling of the JHO, that shall be done at the end of jury selection or as directed by the JHO.

The actual process of jury selection shall take place in accordance with Rule 202.33 and Appendix E of the Uniform Rules for the Trial Courts. All jury selections that are not being supervised by the trial Judge are to select using the struck method. In order to have non-designated alternates, the attorneys must agree.

If a juror requests confidentiality or an attorney concludes or is advised by a juror that a response may poison the panel, the attorneys may withdraw the juror from the room or to a place outside the presence of the rest of the panel for further inquiry.

If jury selection continues into the following day, the Jury Clerk will determine the presence of all necessary persons in the selection room. The voir dire will continue at 9:30 AM sharp.

All counsel are assigned selection rooms on a first-come, first-served basis. If there should be a delay in reaching a case, counsel shall remain available until told otherwise to enable the Jury Clerk to report when a selection room becomes available.

Once a jury is selected, the case will proceed promptly to a trial Justice. Attorneys and jurors may be asked to remain available until a trial Justice becomes free to take the case. The Administrative Coordinating Judge (Parts 40, 27C) may on occasion direct the jury to report the next day at a particular time to be referred to a Justice for the trial and jurors and counsel must be sure to report at the time set by the Administrative Coordinating Judge. On very rare occasion, a jury may be placed "on TCI" (telephone call-in), that is, required to telephone the County Clerk for information about when the case will commence. A jury can remain in this status for only five days. Rule of the Chief Administrative Judge 128.8 (b). If the case does not commence by that point, the jury must be disbanded. Rule 128.8 (a). Obviously, it is important for all concerned that disbandments not occur. Once the jury is selected, the Part to which a jury is to be sent will proceed with the trial shortly thereafter given the five-day time limits. Stacking of juries is prohibited. The Part will instruct a selected jury to return for the beginning of trial at the earliest possible moment and in any event no later than the five-day maximum allowed under Rule 128.8 (b).

March 2006

COUNTY CLERK LITIGATION FUNCTIONS

Procedure XI. County Clerk Litigation Functions

A. Filings Made With/Items Obtained From the County Clerk

Important litigation papers must be filed by counsel with the County Clerk. The chief among these are:

- Summons and complaint or summons with notice
- Petition (special proceedings)
- CPLR 3213 motion papers
- Proof of service of summons and complaint
- Poor person order
- Notice of appeal
- Proposed judgments for signature by the County Clerk

All of these documents must be submitted by counsel to Room 141B (in the basement). Specifically, papers commencing a case are submitted to the Cashier in that room with an index number purchase form and fee. For copies of these two forms, click here.[1] For information on fees, click here.[2] Subsequent papers for filing are submitted to the Law and Equity desk in that room except for proposed judgments for signature by the County Clerk, which are to be presented to the Judgment Clerk there. An RJI, a note of issue and a jury demand must be paid for in Room 160. The last two of these three must be filed with the Trial Support Office (Room 158).

With regard to initiating papers in special proceedings and moving papers in CPLR 3213 motion/actions:

Special Proceedings: Counsel should file the original petition with the County Clerk (Room 141B) to commence a special proceeding. The notice of petition need not be filed with the County Clerk. CPLR 304. In a special proceeding, a duplicate original of the petition, the original notice of petition (which is process, the counterpart of the summons, D. Siegel, *New York Practice* 949 (4th ed. 2005)), and an original affidavit of service shall be filed in the Motion Support Office (Room 119); these are the papers that will be forwarded to the assigned Justice for action. The petitioner may proceed by order to show cause instead of a notice of petition (CPLR 403 (d)); the proposed order should be presented to the Ex Parte Office (Room 315).

Motion/Actions under CPLR 3213: The original 3213 papers should be filed with the County Clerk (Room 141B). A duplicate original of the 3213 papers and an original affidavit of service in any such motion/action shall be filed with the Motion Support Office (Room 119); these are the papers that will be forwarded to the assigned Justice for action.

Index Numbers: When a case is being commenced, the filing party must file the initiating papers with the County Clerk and purchase an index number. Filing means the delivery of the summons with notice, summons and complaint or petition to the County Clerk (Room 141B), or any other person designated by the Clerk for this purpose, together with the filing fee. At the time of filing, the Clerk will date stamp the original and a copy, will file the original, maintaining a record of the date of the filing, and will immediately return the copy to the filing party. CPLR 304. The index number will be issued upon the filing. CPLR 306–a. The Clerk will open a County Clerk's file and create a color-coded file jacket bearing the index number assigned to the case. Papers subsequently presented for filing will be filed in this jacket. Index numbers take the form of six digits followed by a slash and the four digits of the year the case began, e.g., 340705/2005.

Certain blocks or series of index numbers are allotted to particular types of cases. At present, these are:

- 100,000 — General Assignment Cases
- 150,000 — E-Filed General Assignment Cases
- 200,000 — Tax Certiorari Cases
- 250,000 — E-Filed Tax Certiorari Cases
- 300,000 — Uncontested Matrimonial Cases
- 350,000 — Contested Matrimonial Cases
- 400,000 — No-Fee Cases
- 500,000— 510,000 — Article 81
- 570,000 — 580,000 — Appellate Term
- 590,000 — Third-Party Actions
- 600,000 — Commercial Division Cases
- 650,000 — E-filed Commercial Cases

Commencement of Cases: For information on case commencement, click here.[3]

Third-Party Actions: A defendant who wishes to proceed against a non-party must file and serve a third-party summons and complaint. This third-party action (or fourth or fifth, etc.) will be an appendage of the main action. The defendant-third-party plaintiff is required to pay a filing fee for the third-party action. CPLR 1007. The County Clerk will not add a new index number to the caption to reflect the third-party action; an index number identifies an entire case (including its appendages) and there can be only one such number per case. The third-party action will be given a separate number for record-keeping purposes, which number need not appear on court papers.

Certification, Transfers, Appeals, etc.: Certified copies of court documents may be obtained at the

Certification Window in Room 141B (cost $ 8.00), which also does exemplifications (see CPLR 4540), effects transfers of cases to Civil Court or other courts, handles subpoenaing of records on appeals, and accepts filings of notices of appeal.

Decisions and Orders/Entry: All decided motions and signed long form orders (as for judgments, see Section B below) are delivered to the Motion Support Office (Room 119) from Chambers. The issuance of decisions is recorded in the court's Civil Case Information System ("CCIS") computer. The decisions (except for those in matrimonial, Article 81 and sealed cases and those which the assigned Justice has directed not to be posted), with County Clerk entry stamp, are posted to the court's website (in the Supreme Court Records On–Line Library ("Scroll"), generally within two or three hours after the notation is made in CCIS, or overnight if the entry is made at the end of the day. All decisions, orders, and papers on motions are then delivered to the County Clerk (Room 141B). However, where a decision on a motion directs that an order be settled, the file will be retained in the Motion Support Office Order Section or the Commercial Division Support Office to await the submission of the proposed order and any counter-order. These files will not be delivered to the County Clerk until after the long form order has been signed by the Judge. However, the decisions directing settlement of an order will be posted on the court's website.

"Entry" consists of the recording of a document in the County Clerk's minutes (which are available in Scroll for most case types) and the file stamping of the document (the stamp reads "Filed" and the date). Entry gives effect to orders and judgments. Service of a copy of the decision and order or judgment with notice of entry causes the appellate clock to start to tick. "Entry" in the records of the Clerk is done as of the day on which the County Clerk stamps a document with the official stamp.

The County Clerk maintains a list of the entries (e.g., affidavit of service, order) made in the official record ("minutes") of each case. Handwritten minute books exist for cases prior to 1993 and computerized records for all cases from 1993 on. In addition to Scroll, the minutes may be accessed by means of courthouse terminals located in the County Clerk's Office (Rooms 141B, 103B, 109B, and 160).

Emergency Entries: Occasionally an emergency will arise requiring expedited entry of a document with the County Clerk (e.g., an order issued in the courtroom after a conference or argument of a critical matter), such as for purposes of an immediate appeal. Expedition can be achieved by the Part as follows: the document should be carried by a Court Officer or staff member to the Motion Support Office to assure immediate and proper recordation in the computer and, as appropriate, the posting of the document to the Supreme Court Records On–Line Library

("Scroll"). The court will accommodate counsel in emergencies.

Stipulations of Settlement/Discontinuance: All stipulations of settlement/discontinuance should be filed with the County Clerk in Room 160. A fee of $ 35 must be paid. CPLR 8020 (d). The defendant is responsible for filing the document and paying the fee. Id. The County Clerk will deliver the stipulation to the Trial Support Office after processing so that the court can mark its records (CCIS) to reflect the settlement/discontinuance. If a case is resolved at a time when a motion is *sub judice*, an attorney on the case should be sure to notify the assigned Justice as soon as possible so that the Judge does not waste time working on a motion that has been rendered moot.

B. Judgments

1) *In Special Proceedings*

Special proceedings end in judgments, as do normal civil actions. Since it is usual for the decision on the initial motion to end the proceeding, the decision on Motion Sequence No. 001 will often be a decision and judgment.

2) *In Civil Actions*

Judgments in civil actions present a more complex subject.

Judgments on Default: The County Clerk is empowered by the CPLR to enter judgments on default involving a sum that is certain or can be made so by calculation. The applicant must present to the Judgment Clerk in Room 141B a copy of the summons and complaint, a statement for judgment documenting service and the default, and an affidavit by the client as to the merit of the case and the sum certain. In cases not involving a sum certain, the Court must order the entry of judgment on ex parte application or after a motion on notice. If there is a default on the motion and the court cannot direct the Clerk to enter judgment immediately, it will direct an inquest. See CPLR 3215. A defendant who appeared is entitled to notice. A non-appearing defendant is also entitled to notice if more than one year has elapsed since the default, unless the court orders otherwise. CPLR 3215(g)(1). Where an application must be made to the court, a defendant who has failed to appear may serve a written demand for, and is then entitled to, notice of any reference or assessment by a jury. CPLR 3215(g)(2). Additional notice is required for certain default judgments. CPLR 3215(g)(3) and (4). The court must sign judgments awarding equitable relief.

Judgments after Motions: A decision on a motion will actually be a decision and order the latter portion of which may direct the Clerk to enter judgment in favor of the plaintiff for a particular sum (again, where that can be determined on papers alone) or in favor of defendant usually dismissing the case. The Clerk will then sign and enter a judgment in accordance with the order of the Court. This will happen when counsel submits to the Judgment Clerk a judgment in proper form that substantively complies with the order of the court (the court enters judgments automatically only in matrimonial cases). On some motions (e.g., to confirm a referee's report in a foreclosure action) the Justice may sign a judgment.

Sometimes the court will issue a decision on a motion on the record. To serve notice of entry, counsel should obtain a certified copy of the transcript from the Court Reporter and append it to a copy of the court's decision (gray sheet). Counsel should also cause a copy of the transcript to be placed in the County Clerk's file since it will likely not have been transcribed at the time the court signs and transmits the decision for filing.

An award of costs and disbursements will be included in the judgment where authorized and when the prevailing party presents a proper bill of costs. Where interest is awarded or provided for statutorily, the Judgment Clerk will calculate the amount of interest. It is customary, in orders signed by the Court that award costs, disbursements or interest, for the Court to direct that the Clerk calculate the amount of interest and tax or compute the costs and disbursements. Where a Justice signs a judgment, blank spaces will usually be left by the Justice for the dollar amount of interest, costs and disbursements, and for the resulting total sum, which spaces will be completed by the Clerk.

Where a cause of action contains a prayer for declaratory relief, the order of the Court on that claim must actually be an order and judgment and must declare as the judgment of the Court ("It is hereby adjudged and declared . . .") whatever the Court has found.

Post–Trial Judgments: After a jury trial, the Part Clerk will record the outcome in the minutes. Upon request, for cases of money judgments or judgments of dismissal upon a general verdict (CPLR 5016 (b)) (a general verdict is one in which the jury finds in favor of one or more parties (CPLR 4111 (a))), the Part Clerk will issue and sign an "extract" from these minutes, which lists the venue, the index number, the full title of the action (not the short-form one), the name of the Justice, the outcome of any motion affecting the caption, the verdict, and the date. The extract must account for all parties and all claims that were not submitted to the jury. Either party can then present to the Judgment Clerk in the County Clerk's Office for signature and entry a judgment dismissing the case or for a particular sum, as set forth in the extract. The Justice need never sign anything in such cases, neither an order nor the judgment itself, since the jury has provided the verdict. Extracts are not suited to complex verdicts/decisions.

Where there is a special verdict (which is one in which the jury finds the facts only, leaving it to the court to determine which party is entitled to judgment

thereon (CPLR 4111 (a))), the court shall direct entry of an appropriate judgment. CPLR 5016 (b).

When settlement is directed, it occurs in the Part or in Chambers. Where questions arise about how the judgment should be framed, it is recommended that attorneys consult with the Judgment Clerk in Room 141B or the Law Secretary of the Justice.

If the trial is non-jury, the Justice will set forth the outcome on the record or in a written decision and will usually direct that a judgment in conformity therewith be settled or submitted. Whenever equitable relief is granted, the Justice needs to sign the judgment. If equitable relief is denied, the court may direct the County Clerk to enter judgment of dismissal.

3. *Entry and Filing*

Decisions and orders are recorded in the County Clerk's minutes and filed in the County Clerk's file jacket. Counsel wishing to serve notice of entry of an order should consult the Supreme Court Records On-Line Library ("Scroll") on this court's website since most decisions and orders will be posted there, very promptly after issuance, with County Clerk entry stamp.

Executed judgments are set aside in the Law and Equity Section of Room 141B in a group referred to as "unfiled judgments." These are not entered and filed by the Clerk on his own (except in matrimonial cases). Rather, the County Clerk awaits the arrival of counsel or a representative in person at the Judgment Clerk's desk with a bill of costs to secure the calculation of any interest and entry of the judgment and to effect the preparation of a judgment roll. Documentation of contractual interest rates may have to be submitted to the Judgment Clerk. The Clerk will not enter judgment without the creation of a judgment roll, which consists of the basic papers in the case (pleadings, orders, admissions, etc.). Most of these papers may be in the County Clerk's case file, in which event the attorney seeking entry of judgment need only present those that are missing for inclusion in the judgment roll. CPLR 5017.

The court's Scroll program will contain copies of judgments in unfiled form in cases included within the ambit of Scroll and will later include a copy of each judgment as filed.

C. The County Clerk's Record Room

The County Clerk operates a Record Room (Room 103B in the basement, hours 9:00 A.M.–3:00 P.M.) for maintenance of case files in all pending matters (2001 forward). Files in old matters are archived. Case files for 1996–2000 (soon to include 2001) are located at, and may be viewed at, 31 Chambers Street (7th Floor) (hours: Tuesdays and Thursdays only from 9:00 AM to 5:00 PM). Case files for cases with index numbers for the years 1984 to 1995 are in storage off site; for access, contact the County Clerk staff. Files from 1955–1983 (soon to be followed by 1984) are on microfilm at 60 Centre Street.

1. *Sealing of Files*

Matrimonial files may not be inspected except by counsel or parties to the case. DRL § 235. In addition, the files in other cases may be sealed on an individual basis by court order. See Part 216 of the Uniform Rules of the Trial Courts, which provides that the Court shall not enter an order sealing a file in whole or in part except upon a written finding of good cause specifying the grounds, taking into account the interests of the parties and the public. A sealing order should be an order separate from other orders and a copy should be directed to be served on the County Clerk; unless the attorneys make such service and thereby bring the order to the County Clerk's particular attention (see CPLR 8019 (c)), the file will not be sealed because the County Clerk cannot read all orders that are delivered to him by court staff for filing (the court processed over 34,000 decisions on motions in 2005). This order must state who is entitled to see the sealed file. Absent clarity on this point, the Clerk will seal the file and let no one see it, including the parties and counsel in the case. Usually, attorneys will want to have the order provide for access to the sealed file by attorneys of record in the case, the parties, and persons designated in writing by the attorneys of record (e.g., paralegals).

In some instances, entire case files may be sealed. However, under Part 216, case files may be sealed in part and there may well be instances in which it would not be appropriate to seal more than a part of a case file. See *Danco Laboratories Ltd. v. Chemical Works*, 274 A.D.2d 1, 711 N.Y.S.2d 419 (1st Dept. 2000). Thus, some files in the County Clerk's Office will be sealed in their entirety while others will be sealed in part. Any sealing order entered in a case should clearly indicate whether the entire file is to be sealed; if not, the order must clearly designate the portions that are to be so treated. Further, on each occasion during the course of a case when a portion of the file is to be sealed, a separate partial sealing order must be issued.

Documents produced during discovery but not filed are, of course, subject to such protective orders as the court may issue pursuant to CPLR 3103.

A Justice can place a document in an envelope, mark his or her initials over the flap and place an endorsement on the envelope that it is to be opened only on further order of the court. However, if a sealing order pursuant to Part 216 is not issued, the County Clerk will make the file in that case available to the public. If a member of the public opens the envelope, he or she will be subject to a contempt citation.

A device that can serve as an alternative to sealing is an order of impoundment. This order directs the County Clerk to take an individual set of motion papers or discrete items of evidence and place them in the Clerk's safe. The file itself remains unsealed, but the impounded papers cannot be read. The order may be crafted by the Justice so that the papers cannot be read by anyone, including the parties, and cannot even be transmitted to the Appellate Division with the file on an appeal until the order is lifted by the Justice who signed it. Or the order may permit access to the papers by the attorneys, the clients or others. And the order can provide that when the papers are needed for an appeal, the affected party can submit an order to the Justice to lift the impoundment order. Here again, clarity is important. Clearly such an order should only be issued in unusual circumstances. Indeed, since impoundment has the same practical effect as a partial sealing order, the considerations set forth in Part 216 should be taken into account before an order of impoundment is issued.

For more information, contact the County Clerk's Office.

2. *Commencing Actions Claimed To Be Confidential*

If a party wishes to commence an action under seal or use an anonymous caption, practical problems arise. The County Clerk cannot do either without a court order. However, since the press is given access to new case filings each day, if a party files a summons and complaint and then seeks a sealing order, the confidentiality of the case can be rendered moot at the outset. A filing made in the routine way will also be listed in the County Clerk's minutes and the listing will appear in electronic attorney's services.

Sealing: Accordingly, if a party wishes to seal a file from the start, the attorney should, before any papers are filed, consult the Chief Clerk of Law and Equity (Room 141B), or the Chief Deputy County Clerk, and advise either of the desire to seal. If papers are in proper form and the index number fee is paid, the County Clerk will issue an index number but not process the filing for two or three days. This will allow the party time to file an RJI with a proposed order to show cause seeking a sealing order and a TRO sealing the file pending the decision on the request for a sealing order. As to standards governing sealing of files, see Part 216. If the TRO is granted, then that order should be promptly brought to the attention of the County Clerk's staff, who will seal the file pending the decision of the court on the main sealing request. If the attorney fails to alert senior County Clerk staff at the outset, prior to filing any papers, that sealing is sought, if, that is, the summons and complaint are simply filed in the normal manner, the information contained in the papers may be revealed before a Justice has a chance to act. Likewise, if a copy of a TRO is not promptly presented to the County Clerk, the information in question may be disclosed. The procedure described here, it should be noted, does not involve an anonymous caption. The real caption of the case will be listed in the Clerk's minutes.

If a party follows the steps outlined above and delivers to the County Clerk a summons and complaint and if the complaint contains sensitive information that the plaintiff wishes to have sealed, the plaintiff cannot be assured that the Justice to whom the case is assigned will approve the request for a TRO sealing the file pending decision on the main sealing request. Should the TRO be denied, the County Clerk will proceed to file the summons and complaint in the normal manner, meaning that those documents will be publicly accessible. It is possible that this may occur before the plaintiff has a chance to appeal the rejection of the TRO. The County Clerk will not return the documents to the plaintiff if plaintiff seeks not to proceed with the case in view of the lack of a sealing order. Since an index number will have already been issued and the documents delivered to the County Clerk for filing, the Clerk will file them.

A plaintiff may assure avoidance of disclosure of sensitive information in a complaint in the event that a TRO sealing a file is denied. The plaintiff can do this by filing a summons with notice and describing the case for sealing in the papers supporting the order to show cause. If the sealing order is denied, the plaintiff can either discontinue the action or file a complaint lacking in sensitive detail. In the alternative, the plaintiff can file a summons and a complaint lacking in sensitive detail and amend that complaint as required if the sealing application is granted.

Anonymous Caption: If a party wishes to proceed using an anonymous caption, he or she should bring on an order to show cause, with the real parties named in the caption, seeking an anonymous caption and a sealing order since presumably the applicant will not want to obtain an anonymous caption and yet leave the file open to public access. The OSC should include a TRO providing a directive that the County Clerk issue an index number under an anonymous caption and seal the file pending the return date on the order to show cause or decision thereon. Before the papers are filed with the County Clerk, they should be submitted to the Ex Parte Office or the Commercial Division Support Office. They will be presented to an Ex Parte Justice, who, if in agreement, will initial the TRO. The papers can then be presented to the County Clerk senior staff (not the normal filing window in Room 141B) for the issuance of an index number under an anonymous caption and sealing. The papers can then be filed and an RJI purchased. The back office to which the papers are submitted (the Ex Parte Office or the Commercial Division Support Office) should be informed that the papers being submitted are covered by a TRO sealing the file. The papers should be presented to the assigned Justice for further action. Normally, the matter will proceed anonymously at least until the return date on the OSC, at which time the adversary

will have an opportunity to explain why confidentiality should not be continued.

D. Appeals

Notices: Notices of appeal must be filed with the County Clerk in Room 141B. The current fee is $ 65. No personal checks are accepted. A New York State attorney's check or a postal money order made out to the New York County Clerk, or a Visa or Mastercard credit card is required.

The Notice of Appeal must be filed in duplicate. In one legal back an original Notice of Appeal with original proof of service must be filed. In a second separate back an original Notice of Appeal, a Pre-Argument Statement, and a copy of the entered order or judgment from which appeal is to be taken must be filed. An appeal can be taken from only one order or judgment. As to the content of the Pre-Argument Statement, see Section 600.17 of the Rules of the Appellate Division, First Department.

If necessary, a corrected or amended Notice of Appeal can be filed (no fee required). The submission requirements are the same as for a Notice of Appeal except that the Notice must be the corrected/amended one and shall bear on the first page a statement as to what is being corrected or amended. In addition, at the time of filing, the filer shall present the original receipt of payment showing the original number. The same procedure should be followed if the document being corrected/amended is the Pre-Argument Statement.

State and City agencies can proceed without fee. Any such agency must, however, submit a letter on original letterhead bearing the original signature of the attorney of record.

The fee for a Cross-Notice of Appeal is $ 65. An original thereof, together with proof of service and a copy of the order/judgment in question must be filed in a legal back. In a separate legal back, an original Cross-Notice must also be filed.

For appeals to the Court of Appeals, the fee is $ 65. An original Notice of Appeal, plus original proof of service, must be filed in one separate legal back. In another, an original Notice must also be filed.

Subpoenaing the File: Pursuant to the rules of the First Department, appeals can be taken on a printed record, or an original one. In the case of appeals on the original record, the record is transferred to the Appellate Division as follows (fee — $ 24.50). The appellant should deliver to the County Clerk's Record Room (Room 103B) a signed attorney's subpoena (the subpoena of a self-represented litigant must be so ordered by a Justice) specifying the file to be transferred and the destination. The subpoena must be accompanied by four copies of a form of Certificate and two copies of a Statement of Attorney, signed by counsel, as well as two Pre-Argument Statements or 5531 Statements. In the Certificate, counsel must list each paper in the file that is being subpoenaed, one by one, by type of document and date of filing with the County Clerk's Office, in conformity with the County Clerk's listing in the case minutes, which are accessible in the "Supreme Court Records On-Line Library" ("Scroll"), available on this website. If the document was not filed in the County Clerk's Office, it cannot be listed on the Certificate, but should be included in the Statement of Attorney.

Counsel should retrieve the file from the Record Room, put the papers listed on the Certificate in the order listed, and bring the file and accompanying papers to the Certification counter in Room 141B, where the papers will be reviewed. Hours: 9–11AM or 1:30–2:30 PM.

Two business days are required between service of the subpoena and delivery to the First Department.

E. Judgment Docket and Lien Section

The County Clerk records judgments, liens and notices of pendency electronically. The Section is located in Room 109B. Satisfactions of judgment are filed in this Section, not in the Law and Equity Section. Transcripts of judgment are issued and filed in this Section.

F. Depositing Money With the County Clerk

From time to time a need arises in litigation for a party to deposit money with the court. The money is deposited with the County Clerk; payment must be in cash or by certified check. But the Clerk does not hold onto this money for more than a brief time (perhaps 24–48 hours). He forwards the money to the New York City Department of Finance, which records the deposit, secures the money in an account and administers that account. When the time comes to pay that money out to someone, a court order releasing the money is required. That order must be directed to the Department of Finance, not to the County Clerk, who will no longer have possession of the funds. The Department of Finance will issue a certificate to the party seeking the money reporting on the amount of money in the account at the time of the inquiry. The order should refer to the account and the amount therein and direct the Department to release the money as the court desires, less the 2% fee of the Department.

November 2010

1 http://www.nycourts.gov/supctmanh/forms.htm

2 http://www.nycourts.gov/supctmanh/court_fees.htm

3 http://www.nycourts.gov/supctmanh/case_commencement.htm.

COURT RECORDS

Procedure XII.   County Records

The County Clerk is responsible for receiving papers initiating actions and special proceedings and maintaining the official case files of the court, which contain all papers filed with the court in each case. These files (other than older files and electronic files described below) are kept in the Supreme Court Record Room (Room 103 B, in the basement at 60 Centre Street, hours: 9 A.M. to 3 P.M.). Anyone who wishes to do so may examine the case files in that room. There are, however, two exceptions. First, by law the files in all matrimonial cases are confidential and are available only to the parties to the case or their attorneys, upon presentation of proper identification. Second, by law, a Justice of the court may, upon an adequate showing of certain circumstances (e.g., where trade secrets are involved), order that a file in a particular case be sealed in whole or in part or that a portion of the file be impounded by the County Clerk. All documents subject to such an order are confidential and may not be viewed unless the Justice in the order provides for such examination; often, an order will provide for access by all parties and their attorneys upon presentation of proper identification.

Documents in cases that have been commenced by means of the New York State Courts Electronic Filing

System ("NYSCEF") or that have been converted to e-filed status may be examined in the NYSCEF system at www.nycourts.gov/efile. There are some limits on availability of these documents (in general, some might be subject to a sealing order as described above and others may be viewable at the courthouse).

Older hard-copy files are stored as follows:

1996—2001 — 31 Chambers Street, 7th Floor

1984—1995 — In storage

1984 — Being converted to microfiche

1955—1983 — At 60 Centre Street on microfiche

1910—1954 — Files in storage

1799—1910 — 31 Chambers Street, 7th Floor

For additional information, contact County Clerk staff.

Supreme Court Record Room — 646–386–5942

County Clerk Archives, 31 Chambers Street, 7th Floor

Hours: Monday to Friday, 9 AM to 5 PM

646–386–5395

July 2009

COURT REPORTERS

Procedure XIII. Court Reporters

Senior Court Reporters are responsible for verbatim recording and transcribing of testimony in court. Senior Court Reporters record proceedings upon request of a Part, Judicial Hearing Officer or Court Attorney–Referee. Due to staff shortages, Court Reporters may not be able routinely to cover arguments on motions and may not always be immediately available if a record has to be made in a Part on a non-trial day.

Parties obtain copies of transcripts by contacting the Reporter in the Part or the main Court Reporters' Office (646–386–3050).

For information on technologically advanced capabilities offered by the Court Reporters, click here.*

Reporters rotate among the Parts according to a schedule.

  March 2006

* See Appendix to this Procedure

APPENDIX. COURTHOUSE TECHNOLOGY

A. Electronic Case Information On–line

County Clerk and court information in most cases, both those in which a Request for Judicial Intervention has been filed and those in which it has not, and many documents in such cases are available on-line (in the Supreme Court Records On–Line Library ("SCROLL")). Included in this data is information about motions, conferences and trial appearances.

The court system also operates a program that monitors developments in groups of cases designated by subscribing attorneys. The attorney identifies one, two or a number of cases and each program will promptly notify counsel, including by e-mail message, of all developments in each case as reflected in the court's computer system. This program, known as "CaseTrac," can be accessed at www.nycourts.gov (go to "E–Courts" and then to "CaseTrac").

B. Private Information Services

Various private companies make available to subscribers through electronic means the court's computer database of case histories and County Clerk data. All events in a case that are recorded in the computer can be tracked.

C. The Court's Web Pages

On this website [1] can be found the Uniform Rules of the Justices, announcements and much other information. Decisions and orders of the Justices and the Commercial Division Justices, with County Clerk entry stamp, are posted daily in Scroll. Daily calendars of the Motion Support Office Courtroom can be found here as well. In addition, the Commercial Division operates a separate website (at www.nycourts.gov/comdiv).

D. Courtroom 2000 and Other Advanced Courtrooms

The Court Reporters in this court offer some of the most sophisticated capabilities available in the State, such as e-mailing of transcripts, ASSCII disks, e-transcripts, realtime transcription in the courtroom and on the internet, CD Roms, indices of each day's proceedings, and a master index of the whole trial. Our court operates several technologically advanced courtrooms, including a pioneering Courtroom 2000 for the New Millennium. For further information, click here [2].

E. Electronic Case Filing

Commercial, tax certiorari and tort cases can be filed by means of the court's Filing by Electronic Means System. The FBEM website can be located by going to the court system's website (www.nycourts.gov), clicking on "E–Courts" and then clicking on "Electronic Filing." A *User's Manual* and *FAQ's* can be located there. For information on our court's E Filing Office and the procedures followed in e-filed cases for the submission and processing of papers, click here [3].

  September 2006

[1] http://www.nycourts.gov/supctmanh/RulesEffec9-06.pdf

[2] http://www.nycourts.gov/supctmanh/courtroom_2000.htm

[3] http://www.nycourts.gov/supctmanh/E-Filing.htm

INTERPRETERS

Procedure XIV. Interpreters

Litigants who require interpreters for simultaneous translation in depositions, to consult with counsel outside the court or for other aspects of civil cases must make their own arrangements. However, the court will provide interpreters for witnesses in trials or hearings in this court or if the court needs to communicate with a party. Such services require the authorization of the Justice presiding. The court has several Spanish–English interpreters on staff. The Trial Support Office (646–386–3160) maintains a list of interpreters for some other languages, including sign language. The qualifications of these interpreters have been reviewed by the Office of Court Administration and found satisfactory.

An attorney who seeks an interpreter in a language other than Spanish must inform the Justice presiding of the request several days in advance to afford the Justice time to consider the request. The Trial Sup-port Office needs 48 hours notice in order to be able to make necessary arrangements if approval is granted.

March 2006

MATRIMONIAL LITIGATION

Procedure XIV.   Matrimonial Litigation

CONTESTED CASES

A.   Deadlines and Processing of Papers

Motions, orders to show cause, long form orders, and disclosure orders in matrimonial cases are pro-cessed through the regular back offices of the court. As to orders of protection, see the next Section. Net Worth Statements are filed in the Trial Support Office (Room 158). Proposed findings of fact and conclu-sions of law and proposed judgments in matrimonial matters, and Qualified Domestic Relations Orders (QUADROS) are filed in the Matrimonial Support Office (Room 311).

Technically, matrimonial cases are not part of the universe of Differentiated Case Management (Uni-form Rule 202.19) matters. The deadlines set forth in Rule 202.16 of the Uniform Rules for the Trial Courts are more accelerated than the DCM standards.

Rule 202.16 was amended in July 2000 to provide that detailed items of financial disclosure must be furnished and filed with the court at least ten days prior to the preliminary conference. Previously only the Net Worth Statement was specifically required to be provided at that time.

B.   Orders of Protection

Orders of protection are critical. The court will do all that it can to ensure that, when a Justice issues such an order, it is transmitted immediately to the police liaison in Family Court for service, if police service is required, and in any case to One Police Plaza for informational purposes. In addition, this court will transmit, within 24 hours, copies of the relevant orders and essential related information to the Registry, which is run by the State Police.

Standard forms of orders of protection, both tempo-rary and permanent, are available on the Unified Court System's web site (at www.nycourts.gov). In-formation contained in the orders can be automatically fed into the Registry's electronic database. Because of the gravity of this matter, it is vital that these forms of order be used in all cases. In addition, standardized data collection forms have been issued to ensure that the needed information is included in the Registry and provided to the police. These forms must be completed whenever an order of protection is issued. Order numbers are issued by the Trial Sup-port Office upon request of the Part Clerk.

UNCONTESTED CASES

A.   Commencement of an Action

A summons and complaint or summons with notice, must be filed with the County Clerk (Room 141B). Compliance with Rule 130–1.1 of the Rules of the Chief Administrator is required. In order properly to file, the plaintiff must fill out a cover sheet and an index number purchase form; purchase an index num-ber (cost $ 210); fill the index number in on the summons and the complaint or the summons with notice and add the date the index number was pur-chased. Plaintiff will file one set of the summons and complaint or summons with notice with the Clerk. One set of these papers will be served on the defen-dant and the original papers will later be filed with the Matrimonial Support Office (Room 311).

The plaintiff must cause the summons and com-plaint or summons with notice to be served within 120 days of the date the summons and complaint were filed in the County Clerk's Office. Failure to serve the defendant on time can result in dismissal upon motion. See CPLR 306-b.

If the defendant defaults, a default judgment of divorce may be obtained. The defendant must appear or answer within 20 days of being served (30 days if service is made outside the state).

The vast majority (by a factor of roughly 15 to one) of the judgments of divorce granted in New York County are uncontested. That is, either the other spouse consents to the divorce or defaults and does not contest the lawsuit. If the defendant signs a Defendant's Affidavit of Consent providing for imme-diate placement on the calendar or waiving all applica-ble time periods, the plaintiff may proceed to place the case on the calendar for action by the court immedi-ately after service of the summons and complaint. If such a consent has not been signed, then the plaintiff must wait 40 days after the date of such service.

B.   Pursuing a Judgment

In order to obtain an uncontested divorce, the plain-tiff must present the following, properly notarized when required, to the Matrimonial Support Office (Room 311):

1) *Note of Issue:* An original and two copies with proof of index number purchase.

2) *Summons and Verified Complaint, with Proof of Service:* A verified complaint must be filed in all cases.

3) *Affidavit of Defendant:* If defendant appears and consents to the divorce.

4) *Affidavit of Regularity:* By plaintiff. States that defendant has consented to placement on the calendar, or shows the manner of service and claims a default after the proper time has elapsed, relying on the third-party affidavit of service.

5) *Affidavit as to Military Status:* This document, which states that the defendant is not in the military service, is unnecessary in cases where the defendant has signed a consent to the divorce.

6) *Plaintiff's Affidavit:* This must establish all the elements of the plaintiff's case to justify the relief requested.

7) *Affidavit of Child's Residence:* Required when there are children under the age of 18, but advisable in all cases. This information can be included in Item 5.

8) *Child Support Worksheet:* Usually necessary when there is a child of the marriage under 21.

9) *Sworn Statement as to Barriers to Remarriage (With Proof of Service):* Necessary only when the marriage had been performed in a religious ceremony or one conducted by the Ethical Culture Society. When the ground for divorce is DRL § 170(5) or (6) (separation decree or separation agreement), the defendant has made a general appearance (signed the Affidavit of Defendant or appeared by an attorney) and the marriage was performed in a religious ceremony, then both parties must execute the Removal of Barriers Affidavit or one party must execute and serve the Affidavit and waive reciprocal performance by the other.

10) *Proposed Findings of Fact and Conclusions of Law:* A proposed decision submitted to the court for its consideration and possible execution.

11) *Proposed Judgment:* A proposed form of the document that formally ends the marriage and resolves all issues between the parties.

12) *Postcard:* A stamped, self-addressed postcard containing the title of the action and the calendar and index numbers; used to notify the plaintiff of the status of the case.

13) *Part 130 Certification*

14) *Certificate of Dissolution:* Certificate reflecting dissolution.

15) *Defendant's Affidavit of Consent* (Unnecessary where defendant has defaulted)

16) *UCS - 111 (Divorce and Child Support Summary Form):* Form required only if there is child support involved (children under 21).

17) *Notice of Entry*

18) *New York State Case Registry Filing Form:* Only if there are children under 21.

These forms can be found on the Unified Court System's web site (at www.nycourts.gov).

The Clerk of the Matrimonial Support Office reviews these papers for form. If the papers are found satisfactory, the filer can place the case on the court's calendar. The applicant brings the papers to the Cashier in the County Clerk's Office for purchase of a calendar number (cost $ 125).

The papers will then be presented by the Clerk in the Matrimonial Support Office to a Justice or a Court Attorney–Referee for consideration. No RJI is filed. Cases proceed in calendar number order and are assigned in strict rotation to the next open Justice or Referee.

In some cases, a hearing may be required depending upon the circumstances revealed in the papers submitted. On occasion, the court may find that a divorce cannot be granted under the law of this State and may dismiss the action. Should the court find instances of fraud, such as apparently fraudulent signatures, further action will be taken, which may include referral of the matter to the New York County District Attorney. Signed judgments are sent to the County Clerk's Office to be entered in the minutes and placed in the permanent file in the Record Room. The defective cases are retained in Room 311. The self-addressed postcard (see above) is sent to the attorney or filer advising that the papers have been signed or are defective.

When defective papers are corrected (and a new postcard is submitted for notification purposes), the papers are resubmitted to the Judge or Court Attorney–Referee who had previously been assigned the case.

Every 30–60 days, a "Mark Off Calendar" is created. Cases that have been found defective, are more than six months old and have had no activity in the last thirty days are placed on the calendar to be marked off by a Referee. An attorney or filer may restore a marked off case within one year by compliance with a procedure sheet supplied by the Matrimonial Office. After one year, the matter is deemed to have been dismissed. CPLR § 3404.

March 2006

OFFICE FOR THE SELF–REPRESENTED

Procedure XV. The Office For the Self–Represented

A. The Basic Role of the Office; Information

Individuals who have no attorney and seek information about legal processes in the court are advised to visit the Help Center (Room 116). The staff of the Center will attempt to answer questions about court operations and procedures and make certain forms available so that inquiring persons can take legal action on their own if so inclined. The staff will not itself complete these forms and is not permitted to offer legal advice. The Center may make a quick examination of papers for formal sufficiency. This work by the Center will increase the chances that, when the self-represented person appears in a back office, the papers will be in proper form. The Center is not a point of intake of legal papers, with one exception, poor person applications, described below.

B. Poor Person Applications

The Help Center is a point of intake in one instance, with regard to poor person applications, which are applications made prior to substantive legal action. In this instance, the applicant claims to be a poor person within the meaning of Article 11 of the CPLR who would be unable to proceed with some form of legal action absent an exemption from the obligation to pay court filing fees.

Poor person applications require, in order to be successful, that the applicant submit an affidavit setting forth in detail the amount and sources of the person's income and the value of his/her property. The applicant must show an inability to pay the costs, fees and expenses to prosecute or defend the action. The affidavit should describe the nature of the action and set forth facts needed for an accurate evaluation of the merit of the contentions involved. The court may require that the applicant submit a certificate of an attorney stating that the attorney has examined the action and believes that there is merit to the applicant's position. CPLR 1101. Fees and costs are waived in cases brought by legal services attorneys. See CPLR 1101(e).

Poor person applications frequently are brought on without notice. Some, however, must be made on notice. CPLR 1101.

C. Other Applications by Self–Represented Persons

Other applications frequently made by self-represented persons include:

> Matrimonial action — see section of this website describing uncontested matrimonial matters

> Article 78 proceedings to challenge the decision/determination of an agency of New York State or New York City government (for example, termination of tenancy (New York City Housing Authority), correction of a New York City birth certificate, denial/reduction of social services benefits, decision by New York State Commission on Human Rights)

> Other Article 78 proceedings

> Application for a change of name—see also New York City Civil Court web site

> Application for extension of time

The Help Center maintains information sheets on all of the above, as well as forms for common procedures such as bringing on and answering motions.

D. Paper Flow

Poor person applications are carried by the staff of the Center to the Ex Parte Justices on a daily basis. If signed, the papers are filed in the County Clerk's Office by the staff. Orders to show cause brought by the self-represented are filed with the Ex Parte Office. After normal processing by Ex Parte, the OSC's are carried to the assigned Justices located at 60 Centre Street by the staff of the Help Center and by movants themselves in the case of Justices located in the court's satellite facilities. A copy of the order is given to the movant to facilitate conforming the signed OSC and instructions for completing the process. Other ex parte applications are filed by the self-represented directly with the Ex Parte Office (Room 315).

March 2006

SPECIAL COURTHOUSE PROCEDURES FOR E–FILED CASES

Doc. 1. Protocol on Courthouse Procedures for Electronically Filed Cases (Revised 1/31/11)

[NOTICE TO THE BAR: MANDATORY E-FILING BEGAN IN NEW YORK COUNTY SUPREME COURT IN CERTAIN COMMERCIAL CASES ON MAY 24, 2010]

Attorneys seeking information about how the New York State Courts Electronic Filing System ("NYSCEF") works are advised to consult the *User's Manual* and *FAQ's*, both available at the NYSCEF website (www.nycourts.gov/efile). What follows is an explanation of how traditional courthouse requirements for the processing of cases are applied in e-filed cases. These procedures seek to minimize the need for trips to the courthouse by counsel and inconvenience generally.

A. E–Filed Cases Generally

1) *Cases Commenced via NYSCEF*: Cases that are commenced by filing of the initial papers with the NYSCEF system are identified as e-filed cases by assignment of a special index number (i.e., cases beginning with 650,000 (commercial matters), 250,000 (tax certiorari matters), and 150,000 (tort cases)).

2) *Cases Converted to NYSCEF*: Cases originally commenced in hard-copy form but later converted to NYSCEF status will bear a regular index number initially. However, when a case is converted to that status, court staff will change the case indicator in the court's Civil Case Information System ("CCIS") computer to identify the matter as a NYSCEF case. This action will also add a suffix to the index number in CCIS (e.g., 600136/2005 E). This suffix should be used on all documents filed with the court in e-filed matters.

3) *Mandatory E–Filing*: Certain commercial cases must be commenced by filing with the County Clerk electronically through NYSCEF and all subsequent documents in such cases must be e-filed. Mandatory commercial cases consist of commercial matters of the types set forth in the rules governing mandatory e-filing (Uniform Rule 202.5–bb). See also Chapter 416 of the Laws of 2009 (posted on the "E–Filing" page of this court's website (at www.nycourts.gov/supctmanh)). A summary of the definition is attached hereto. Section 202.5–bb provides for limited exceptions to the mandatory e-filing requirement: commencement in a defined emergency, filing of subsequent documents in a defined emergency, and exemptions from e-filing. An attorney who states in writing in good faith that he or she lacks the equipment or knowledge needed to e-file and who has no staff member or employee under his or her direction who has such knowledge and equipment may opt out of participation in e-filing in a mandatory case by filing a form with the Clerk. A self-represented party may choose to opt out by filing the same form. The form is posted on the "E–Filing" page on this court's website (at www.nycourts.gov/supctmanh). An attorney may also seek an exemption from the Justice assigned to a mandatory case upon a showing of good cause.

4) *Presumptive E–Filing—Commercial Division Cases and Certain Other Parts*: Commercial Division cases commenced between June 15, 2008 and May 24, 2010 in New York County have been designated as presumptively e-filed matters. All such cases that have not been commenced electronically have been converted by court staff upon filing of the Request for

Judicial Intervention ("RJI"). See Notice to the Commercial Division Bar of the Administrative Judge, May 20, 2008 (posted on the "E–Filing" page of this court's website). (The same procedure is followed in commercial and tort cases in General Assignment Parts 12 (Feinman, J.), 35 (Edmead, J.), and 61 (Sherwood, J.)). If parties fail to consent to e-filing in these cases within a reasonable time, the court may convert them back to hard copy cases.

5) *Partially E–Filed Cases*: If one party or more than one but fewer than all consent to e-filing in a consensual case, or if, in a mandatory e-filed case, an attorney or self-represented party obtains an exemption from participating in e-filing, each participating attorney or party shall e-file all interlocutory documents to be filed with the court and such attorneys or parties shall serve one another electronically as provided in the E–Filing Rules. Non-participating parties shall file and serve and be served in hard copy format.

B. Filing of Papers Generally

1) *Mandatory E–Filed Cases; Paper Documents Not Accepted*: All mandatory e-filed cases must be commenced electronically. Unless otherwise provided by the E–Filing Rules or this Protocol, in these cases, the County Clerk will not accept commencement documents in paper form nor will the court accept subsequent documents in that form. If a party wishes to commence a case under seal or to proceed under an anonymous caption, the party should contact the Chief Deputy County Clerk or the Clerk in Charge of Law and Equity of the County Clerk's Office before filing any documents. See "Commencement of Cases" under the "Courthouse Procedures" link on this court's website.

2) *Mandatory E–Filed Cases; Exempt and Emergency Filers*: Any emergency filing made in hard copy in accordance with the Mandatory E–Filing Rules and any document filed with the court in hard copy form by an attorney or self-represented party who has opted out of participation in e-filing in accordance with the Rules must bear, as the back page facing out, a completed Notice of Hard Copy Submission—E–Filed Case (accessible on the "E–Filing" page of the court's website). Under the Rules, a filer must electronically file the documents initially filed in hard copy form within three business days of an emergency filing. The originals will be discarded after the documents have been processed; failure to e-file as required will therefore lead to an incomplete record.

3) *Consensual E–Filing; Paper Documents Not Accepted*: Unless otherwise provided by the E–Filing Rules or this Protocol, in any case that is subject to e-filing by consent of the parties, all documents required to be filed with the court must be e-filed by consenting parties. Any such document that is submitted in hard copy form will not be accepted by the Clerk.

4) *Index Numbers*: In cases commenced electronically, the County Clerk will issue an index number as soon as possible. In the event that counsel faces exigent circumstances that require the accelerated assignment of an index number, counsel may send a request for such assignment by e-mail to the County Clerk at ccnyef@courts.state.ny.us.

5) *Fees*: Court fees in NYSCEF cases may be paid via NYSCEF by a credit or bank card (Mastercard or Visa). Documents may also be filed with the NYSCEF system and the fee paid at the County Clerk's Office. In the latter case, the document is not considered to have been filed until payment of the fee has been tendered (see CPLR 304). Whenever an attorney uses the latter option, payment must be submitted within three business days. If it is not, the County Clerk will return the document to the filer. When so paying, counsel should alert the County Clerk Cashier (646–386–5932 or 5949) that the case is a NYSCEF matter.

6) *Papers Must Be Filed to the System*: Unless otherwise provided in the Rules or herein, all documents to be filed with the court in a NYSCEF case, including all documents on motions and all letters, must be filed with the NYSCEF system (except where a special exemption is granted (e.g., oversized maps)). Documents that attorneys would not ordinarily file with the court in a hard-copy case need not be filed in a NYSCEF matter.

7) *Working Copies of Documents for Judicial Review*: Unless otherwise directed by the court or as described herein, in all NYSCEF cases in which an RJI has been filed, working copies of e-filed documents that are intended for judicial review must be submitted (except with respect to hard copy emergency or exempt filings in mandatory cases). With the possible exceptions of proposed orders to show cause and supporting documents (see Section G), documents must be filed with the NYSCEF system and any required working copy must be delivered to the court thereafter. The working copies shall include exhibit tabs and backs and, for motion papers, the Motion Sequence Number. In addition, the filer of a working copy of an e-filed document must firmly bind thereto, as the back page facing out, a copy of the Confirmation Notice that was generated by NYSCEF when that document was e-filed. Working copies that are submitted without the related Confirmation Notice will not be accepted. Notwithstanding any references in this Protocol to required working copies, such copies shall not be submitted in e-filed cases in Part 12 (Feinman, J.), Part 35 (Edmead, J.), Part 52 (Kern, J.), and Part 6 (Lobis, J.) unless requested by the court in a particular case.

8) *Discarding of Working Copies*: The official record of a document in an e-filed case is the electronic record of the document stored by the Clerk (Uniform Rule 202.5–b (d) (4)). Working copies are intended only for the use of the Justice and will be discarded after the Justice has finished with them. Thus, in the event that counsel fails to e-file a document, it will not be part of the court record.

9) *Court Will Print Out and Deliver Certain Non–Voluminous Papers for Judicial Review*: To assist counsel, the relevant back office of the court will (after payment via NYSCEF of any related filing fee) print out from the NYSCEF system hard copies of certain non-voluminous documents (i.e., those up to 25 pages long) that are intended for review by a Justice and will deliver them to the relevant back office for processing and transmission to the Justice. No working copy need be delivered by counsel. See, e.g., Section F (proposed long form orders).

10) *Working Copies Not Required of E–Filed Documents Not Intended for Judicial Review*: E-filed documents intended for processing by a back office but not for review by a Justice (e.g., preliminary conference requests, notes of issue) will, after payment of any fee via NYSCEF, be processed by the relevant back office. These papers must be e-filed. Counsel does not need to appear or to submit working copies.

11) *Authorization Form—Filing Agent*: The Rules require that a firm acting as filing agent for an attorney or party to a case must file a form (accessible on the NYSCEF website) whereby the attorney or party authorizes the agent to file on the attorney or party's behalf. Only one such form need be filed for an attorney or party in any specific NYSCEF case.

C. Requests for So–Ordered Stipulations

If an attorney wishes to submit a stipulation to be "so ordered," he or she should file the document with NYSCEF, designating it on the filing menu as a "Proposed Stipulation to be So Ordered." The Clerk will print out a hard copy and forward it to the Justice assigned or transmit the document to the Justice electronically. No appearance by counsel is needed.

D. Requests for Judicial Intervention

1) *Supplement to RJI Required in Certain Hard Copy Cases*: To assist in identification of cases, in any commercial case or special proceeding involving commercial arbitration or seeking dissolution of a business, the filer of an RJI in hard copy form must file with it a completed Supplement to Request for Judicial Intervention (form available on the "E–Filing" page of this court's website). The papers will not be accepted without the Supplement.

2) *RJI in NYSCEF Cases*: An RJI in a NYSCEF case shall be submitted via NYSCEF. Once filed and paid for via NYSCEF, the RJI and any accompanying document will be forwarded to the relevant back office for random assignment of the case and processing of the document. Counsel need not appear. In the case of RJIs seeking assignment to the Commercial Division, pursuant to Uniform Rule 202.70 (d) (2), the filer must submit therewith a statement in support of the

assignment and a copy of the pleadings, which will be forwarded to the assigned Justice for review. If the RJI seeks intervention with regard to a document that is intended for review by a Justice, such as a motion, a working copy of the RJI must be submitted with the working copy of the motion and the NYSCEF Confirmation Notice.

E. Motions on Notice

1) *Motions/Petitions Returnable in Room 130*: A motion on notice or a notice of petition in a NYSCEF case, as in others, shall be made returnable in the Motion Support Office Courtroom (Room 130). The motion must be filed with NYSCEF and the motion fee paid for either via NYSCEF by credit/bank card or by the "Pay at the County Clerk's Office" option. The moving documents must be e-filed no later than eight days prior to the return date.

2) *Calendaring of Motion/Petition and Notice by Court Staff*: After a motion/petition and notice are filed with the NYSCEF system, the Motion Support Office will automatically place the motion/proceeding on the calendar of the Motion Support Office Courtroom (Room 130) for the date fixed; no appearance or other action by the filing attorney is required in order for the motion to be calendared if the motion fee is paid for via NYSCEF. Motions in e-filed cases appear on a separate calendar in the Courtroom.

3) *Adjournments on Motions/Petitions in Room 130; Appearance Can Be Avoided*: Motions that have been e-filed may be adjourned in Room 130 if an adjournment complies with any directives of the assigned Justice and the procedures of the Motion Support Office Courtroom (explained in the "Motions" section of the "Courthouse Procedures" link on the website of this court). An adjournment that so complies may be obtained by filing a stipulation of all parties with NYSCEF (designated in the filing menu as a "Stipulation to Adjourn Motion"). The Office will effectuate the adjournment without need for an appearance or any other action by the parties.

4) (a) *Working Copies on Motions in Room 130*: After papers on motions have been e-filed, working copies thereof, with Confirmation Notice firmly attached as the back page facing out, must be submitted. (Each document or group of documents that is separately bound shall bear a Confirmation Notice.) Working copies lacking the Notice will not be accepted. WORKING COPIES OF MOTION PAPERS MUST BE SUBMITTED IN THE MOTION SUPPORT OFFICE COURTROOM (ROOM 130) AS EXPLAINED HEREIN. THEY MUST NOT BE DELIVERED TO THE PART OR CHAMBERS; DOING SO WILL CAUSE ADMINISTRATIVE CONFUSION AND POSSIBLE MISPLACEMENT OF PAPERS. Working copies, including copies of the moving papers, will not be accepted in the Motion Support Office (Room 119), but shall be handed up at or before the "call" of the E–Filed Calendar in the Motion Support Office Courtroom (Room 130) on the final return date. Counsel should confer with one another regarding adjournments so that all parties are aware of what the final return date will be. Working copies should not be submitted before that date. Counsel may submit their own working copies on the final return date or agree that one party may submit the copies of all parties at that time. If the Clerk becomes aware that an attorney has failed to submit required working copies on the final return date, the motion may be placed, for one time only, on the three-day calendar to permit submission of those copies. The court will not provide direct notice to the attorney that this has occurred; attorneys should consult the listing in the Law Journal regarding disposition of the Room 130 calendar. If the working copies are not submitted on the three-day calendar, the motion will be transmitted as is to the Justice for such action as the Justice finds appropriate. Attorneys who maintain their office outside the County of New York may submit working copies on motions by mail or overnight delivery. Any such submission shall be sent in a timely manner to the Motion Support Office (Room 119) and be conspicuously marked on the outside "NYSCEF Matter;" lack of such marking may delay processing.

(b) Working Copies on OSCs Returnable in the Part; Subsequent Papers Handed up in the Part: On orders to show cause that are made returnable in the Part, working copies of e-filed opposition and (if allowed) reply papers (with backs and tabs) must be delivered to the Part. As to all such documents, and any document the court may allow a party to hand up in the courtroom on a motion/petition on notice beyond those previously submitted in Room 130, the attorney must file each document with NYSCEF and thereafter submit a working copy bearing firmly affixed thereto, as the back page facing out, a copy of the related NYSCEF Confirmation Notice. Documents lacking a copy of the related Notice will not be accepted.

5) *Exhibits*: Whenever possible, attorneys submitting exhibits in NYSCEF cases should make each exhibit a separate attachment to an affidavit/affirmation in the system (i.e., they should not be filed as a single PDF).

6) *Notification of Decisions and Orders*: After issuance of a decision and order on a motion in a NYSCEF case, the document will be processed into the NYSCEF system, which constitutes entry (Uniform Rule 202.5–b (h)), as will be reflected in a legend on the document. The NYSCEF system will immediately transmit notice of this event via e-mail, including a link to the entered document, to all participating attorneys and self-represented parties. Such transmittal does not constitute notice of entry. See Section K.

F. Long Form Orders on Motions

If the court directs that an order be settled or submitted on a motion in a NYSCEF case, the proposed order, with notice of settlement where required, and any proposed counter-order shall be filed with the court via NYSCEF. The relevant back office (the Motion Support Office Order Section (Room 119) or the Commercial Division Support Office (Room 148)) will process the documents in the customary manner. The Clerk of the back office will print out a copy of the documents and, as appropriate, may make changes on the proposed order/counter-order by hand or may contact the submitting attorney by e-mail or telephone. Once a proposed order/counter-order in final form has been arrived at, the Clerk of the back office will forward it in hard copy to the Justice. No appearance by counsel nor working copy is required. After an order/counter-order has been signed, it will be scanned, with County Clerk entry stamp, into the NYSCEF system, which will immediately transmit notice of this event via e-mail, including a link to the entered document, to all participating attorneys and self-represented parties in the case. Such transmittal does not constitute notice of entry. See Section K.

G. Orders to Show Cause

1) *Proposed Orders to Show Cause and Supporting Documents to be Filed On–Line*: Except as provided in the following paragraph, proposed orders to show cause and supporting documents in all NYSCEF cases must be submitted by filing with the NYSCEF system; original documents will not be accepted by the Clerk. Counsel must comply with Uniform Rule 202.7 (f) regarding notice of the application. See also Commercial Division Rule 20 (Uniform Rule 202.70).

2) *Permissible Submissions in Hard Copy*: If a party seeking a TRO submits an affirmation/affidavit demonstrating significant prejudice from the giving of notice (see Rules 202.7 (f) and Commercial Division Rule 20) or if in accordance with the Rules a party to a mandatory e-filed case is exempt from participation or seeks to submit documents in an emergency, the proposed order to show cause and supporting documents may be presented to the Commercial Division Support Office or the Ex Parte Office in hard copy form. The papers must be accompanied by, as the back page facing out, a completed Notice of Hard Copy Submission—E-Filed Case. A proposed order to show cause and supporting documents that must be presented to a Justice outside normal court hours shall be presented in hard copy. In all situations described in this paragraph (other than that of an exempt party), documents submitted in hard copy form must thereafter be e-filed, as set forth below.

3) *Office Review of Submissions Will be Done On–Line*: Absent unusual practical difficulties, a proposed order to show cause and supporting documents that have been filed with NYSCEF will be reviewed on-line by the Commercial Division Support Office or by the Ex Parte Office. If there are problems with the

documents, the submitting attorney will be promptly contacted by the back office by e-mail or telephone.

4) *Working Copies*: Except for instances covered by Par. (2) of this section, a working copy of a proposed order to show cause and the supporting documents with Confirmation Notice(s) must be submitted to the Commercial Division Support Office or the Ex Parte Office. A second working copy of the proposed order only, to which a Confirmation Notice shall not be attached, shall be submitted simultaneously.

5) *Hard Copy Service*: In cases in which hard copy service is made of documents that were submitted in hard copy form pursuant to Par. (2) of this section and where no party is served electronically, the filing attorney or party shall, no later than three business days after service, e-file the supporting papers (designating them in the NYSCEF document type drop-down menu on the filing screen as "Supporting Papers to OSC (After Service))," together with proof of hard copy service. Failure to do so will cause the County Clerk file to be incomplete. The Clerk will e-file the signed order to show cause after the deadline for service has passed.

6) *Declination*: If the Justice declines to sign the order to show cause, the Clerk will electronically file the declined order. If the proposed order to show cause and supporting documents were filed with the court in hard copy form, the filing attorney or party (other than an exempt party) shall file the supporting documents with NYSCEF no later than three business days after the filing by the clerk. Failure to do so will cause the County Clerk file to be incomplete.

7) *E–Service of Signed OSC and Supporting Documents*: If the court directs that the signed order to show cause and supporting documents be served electronically, a conformed copy of the signed order should be designated as "Conformed Copy of OSC" in the NYSCEF document type drop-down menu on the filing screen.

H. Procedures Regarding Service On–Line

Pursuant to the NYSCEF Rules, service of interlocutory documents is made by posting a document to the NYSCEF site, which immediately transmits an e-mail notice of the filing, including a link to the document, to all participating counsel and self-represented parties on the case. The Rules also authorize service by other methods permitted by the CPLR. If service by such a method is made, proof of service must be filed with NYSCEF.

I. Service of Orders on the County Clerk and Back Offices

If an order in a NYSCEF case requires that the County Clerk or a back office of the court take action, a copy of the order must be served on the County Clerk or the back office. This may be done by transmitting a copy of the order by e-mail to the appropriate e-mail box. The e-mail addresses are as follows:

County Clerk:
cc-nyef@courts.state.ny.us
Motion Support Office:
mso-nyef@courts.state.ny.us

Trial Support Office:
trialsupport-nyef@ courts.state.ny.us
Special Referee:
spref-nyef@ courts.state.ny.us

J. Secure Documents and Sealing of Documents

1) *Social Security Numbers*: "No person may file any document available for public inspection ... in any court of this state that contains a social security account number of any other person, unless such other person is a dependent child, or has consented to such filing, except as required by federal or state law or regulation, or by court rule." GBL 399–dd (6).

2) *Secure Documents*: Pursuant to the Rules, documents may be designated "secure" by the filing user. The effect of such designation is that the document may be viewed in the NYSCEF system only by counsel and self-represented parties to the case who have consented to NYSCEF and by the court and the County Clerk. The electronic file, however, remains open for public inspection via computer at the courthouse (unless sealed in accordance with Part 216 of the Uniform Rules for the Trial Courts).

3) *Sealing; Compliance with Part 216; Procedures*:

(a) Application for Sealing Order: In order to seal a document in a NYSCEF case, a party must proceed in accordance with Part 216 of the Uniform Rules. If a party wishes to file and maintain papers under seal and no sealing order has been issued in the case, the party must, either by motion or on submission to the court of a stipulation, obtain a court order pursuant to Part 216 directing the Clerk to seal the file in whole or in part. If the motion/stipulation is filed with the NYSCEF system, it will be open to the public until a sealing order is issued. Should this create difficulty, the applicant may wish to consider filing the motion/stipulation as a "secure" document if that is appropriate and sufficient. Or counsel may make a motion or submit a stipulation without filing it to the system until after the court has ruled on the sealing issue or has issued an order temporarily sealing the papers in question. Any such motion or stipulation submitted in hard copy form must bear, as the back page facing out, a Notice of Hard Copy Submission—E–Filed Case and be accompanied by a computer disk containing the papers in PDF format, which the County Clerk will use to e-file the documents after effectuating sealing if directed by the court. Any opposition or reply papers shall likewise be submitted in hard copy form, with said Notice, and be accompanied by a disk containing the documents in PDF format. Each disk shall be identified by the name of the case, the index number, and the name and e-mail address of the attorney submitting it. An attorney or party exempted from e-filing in a mandatory case need not submit a PDF copy.

b) Implementing Sealing Order:

(i) Sealing Existing E–File in Whole or in Part: If the court issues an order directing the sealing of a complete existing NYSCEF file or a document or documents already filed with NYSCEF, the applicant shall file with the NYSCEF system a Notification for Sealing in Electronically–Filed Case (form available on the NYSCEF website), together with a copy of the court's order. No further action by counsel is required. The County Clerk will seal the file or the document(s) in question as directed by the court, both in the NYSCEF system and, if any of the covered documents are found therein, in the hard copy file.

(ii) Sealing Document or Documents Not Yet E–Filed: If the court issues an order directing the sealing of a document that has not yet been e-filed, the document should be presented (unless the court directs otherwise) to the County Clerk in hard copy form with a copy of the court's sealing order and a disk, labeled as indicated above, bearing the document in PDF format.

4) *Previously Sealed File*: If a case that was previously sealed pursuant to court order is converted to NYSCEF status, counsel for the parties should promptly alert the County Clerk's Office (cc-nyef@ courts.state.ny.us or 646–386–5943) that an order sealing the file was issued.

K. Entry and Notice of Entry

Pursuant to the NYSCEF Rules, the Clerk shall file orders electronically and such filing shall constitute entry of the order. An e-mail message will be transmitted to all filing users on the case notifying that the order has been entered. Such notice does not constitute service of notice of entry by any party. Notice of entry is served as follows: a party shall transmit electronically to the parties to be served a notice of entry, a copy of the notification received from the court, and a copy of the order or judgment.

L. Judgments and the Judgment Roll

1) *Entry of Judgment; Procedures*: If the court in an order directs entry of judgment by the County Clerk, the party seeking entry shall submit to the County Clerk a proposed judgment with bill of costs (both of which shall be in one PDF file), and interest calculations and supporting information. It is requested that a legal back be included with these documents since the County Clerk uses the back as the location for stamps affixed upon entry. These documents should be e-filed or may be sent by e-mail outside the NYSCEF system to the following e-mail box: cc-nyef@courts.state.ny.us. The Judgment Clerk will promptly communicate with counsel by e-mail or phone in the event of any difficulties with the submission. Once the judgment is in final form, it will be printed out by the Judgment Clerk and submitted to the County Clerk for signature. When the judgment is signed, the Judgment Clerk will post it to the

system, along with the supporting information, at which time notification will be sent via e-mail to all participating parties.

2) *Default Judgment; Entry by Clerk*: If the plaintiff in a NYSCEF case seeks entry of a default judgment by the Clerk pursuant to CPLR 3215, the attorney shall pay the $ 45 motion fee and either transmit to the NYSCEF system a proposed Clerk's default judgment with bill of costs, etc., or forward these documents to the Clerk outside the NYSCEF system (to the e-mail box cc-nyef@courts.state.ny.us). The Clerk will communicate with counsel if any questions or issues arise. Where the submissions are made to NYSCEF, the Judgment Clerk will promptly enter the judgment. If the submission is made to the e-mail box outside NYSCEF, the attorney must file on the NYSCEF system the proposed Clerk's default judgment in final form with bill of costs, etc. To enter the judgment the Clerk will print out the judgment from NYSCEF, have it signed, and scan it to the system.

3) *Judgments Signed by Court*: Where the court signs the judgment, calculation of disbursements, costs and interest will be left to the County Clerk. Papers supporting such calculation may be submitted to the County Clerk in the manner described above.

4) *Entry of Judgment*: Once the County Clerk has taxed costs and disbursements and calculated interest and has in hand a signed judgment, the Clerk will stamp the judgment with the County Clerk file stamp and post the judgment to NYSCEF. This constitutes entry. The Clerk will transmit an e-mail message to all filing users notifying that the judgment has been entered. This notice does not constitute service of notice of entry by any party.

M. Notices of Appeal and Appeal Papers

1) *Notice of Appeal; Payment of Fee*: A notice of appeal shall be filed on-line in a NYSCEF case. The fee therefor must be paid by credit or bank card via NYSCEF or by means of the "Pay at the County Clerk's Office" option. Pursuant to the Rules, in the latter situation the notice will not be considered "filed" until payment of the fee is tendered to the County Clerk at the office. When paying at the Office, the filer must inform the Clerk that the case in question is an e-filed matter. No hard copy should be delivered to the County Clerk's Office.

2) *Notice of Appeal; Procedures*: The notice shall be filed together with a pre-argument statement and a copy of the judgment or order appealed from. The other participating parties to the case may be served via NYSCEF. The County Clerk will print a hard copy of any e-filed notice of appeal and include it in the County Clerk file.

3) *NYSCEF; Appellate Division*: The Appellate Division, First Department does yet not handle appeals in NYSCEF cases by electronic means, although the Court has announced its intention to move toward that goal in the near future. Counsel are advised to consult the rules of that court and to confer with the County Clerk.

ANY ATTORNEY WHO REQUIRES ASSISTANCE IN A NYSCEF CASE IS ENCOURAGED TO CONTACT THE NEW YORK COUNTY E–FILING OFFICE OR THE E–FILING RESOURCE CENTER. COMPUTER EQUIPMENT IS AVAILABLE AT THE COURTHOUSE FOR THE USE OF ATTORNEYS WHO MAY NEED TO MAKE FILINGS IN NYSCEF CASES AND WHO FROM TIME TO TIME ARE UNABLE TO MAKE THE FILINGS FROM THEIR OWN OFFICES.

Dated: January 31, 2011

ELECTRONIC FILING OFFICE
SUPREME COURT, CIVIL BRANCH
NEW YORK COUNTY
60 Centre Street, Room 119
New York, New York 10007
Phone: 646–386–3610
E–Mail: newyorkef@courts.state.ny.us

JEFFREY CARUCCI
STATEWIDE COORDINATOR OF
ELECTRONIC FILING

NEW YORK STATE COURTS
ELECTRONIC FILING
RESOURCE CENTER
60 Centre Street, Room 119 M
New York, New York 10007
646–386–3033
efile@ courts.state.ny.us

EDWARD KVARANTAN
CHRISTOPHER GIBSON
DEPUTY COORDINATORS

Doc. 2. Summary: Mandatory E–Filing Commercial Case Defined

SUMMARY: MANDATORY E–FILING COMMERCIAL CASE DEFINED[1]

Mandatory e-filing applies to certain commercial cases (not limited to Commercial Division cases). Mandatory cases are:

(a) Cases in which over $ 100,000 is in controversy (not counting punitive damages, interest, costs, disbursements, and attorney's fees), and

(b) Which are or assert the following:

(i) breach of contract, breach of fiduciary duty, fraud, misrepresentation, business tort, statutory or common law claims arising out of business dealings;

(ii) UCC cases;

(iii) commercial real estate cases;

(iv) shareholder derivative and commercial class actions;

(v) cases involving business transactions with banks or other financial entities;

(vi) internal affairs of business organizations;

(vii) accounting, actuarial or commercial legal malpractice;

(viii) environmental or commercial insurance coverage;

(ix) proceedings to dissolve corporations or other businesses; or

(x) commercial arbitration proceedings (Art. 75).

1 The full definition is available in Section 202.5–bb (a) (2) of the Uniform Rules. See also Chapter 416 of the Laws of 2009.

Doc. 3.   Notice to Commercial Practitioners: Mandatory Electronic Filing

IMPORTANT NOTICE TO COMMERCIAL PRACTITIONERS: MANDATORY ELECTRONIC FILING

Pursuant to Chapter 416 of the Laws of 2009, **mandatory electronic filing will be instituted in this Court in certain commercial cases ("mandatory commercial cases"). The commencement date for this program is May 24, 2010.** A Uniform Rule (Section 202.5–bb) has been promulgated setting forth the procedures for mandatory e-filing. The following are the key aspects of mandatory e-filing that the Court will implement in conformity with this Rule. Some other e-filing rule changes have also been made. Please consult the "E–Filing" page on this Court's website (at www.nycourts.gov/supctmanh) for access to these rules.

Any mandatory commercial case commenced on or after May 24 must be electronically filed through the New York State Courts Electronic Filing System ("NYSCEF"), as must subsequent filings therein. Mandatory commercial cases consist of certain commercial matters (not limited to Commercial Division cases) in which the amount in controversy is over $ 100,000 (exclusive of interest, costs, disbursements, counsel fees, and punitive damages). The types of cases that are subject to mandatory e-filing are cases alleging or constituting the following: (i) breach of contract, breach of fiduciary duty, fraud, misrepresentation, business tort, statutory or common law claims arising out of business dealings; (ii) UCC cases; (iii) commercial real estate cases; (iv) shareholder derivative or commercial class actions; (v) cases involving business transactions with banks or other financial entities; (vi) internal affairs of business organizations; (vii) accounting, actuarial or commercial legal malpractice; (viii) environmental or commercial insurance coverage; (ix) proceedings for dissolution of a corporation or other business; and (x) commercial arbitration proceedings.

Except to the extent that the rules provide otherwise, on and after May 24, the County Clerk and court clerks will not accept documents filed in mandatory commercial cases in hard copy form. Working copies of motion papers and other documents intended to be reviewed by a Justice must be delivered to the court unless the Justice indicates otherwise and each such document must bear a NYSCEF Confirmation Notice. This procedure applies to consensual e-filed cases as well. For procedures regarding submission of working copies and other matters, please consult the Protocol on Electronic Filing posted on the "E–Filing" page of this Court's website. To facilitate identification of mandatory commercial cases, a supplement to the RJI must be filed when an RJI and accompanying documents are presented in a commercial case in hard copy form.

The NYSCEF system offers many benefits to attorneys and their clients. There is no charge to use the system (usual court fees apply)—that is, **there is no charge to file a document, serve a document (which NYSCEF does automatically), consult the NYSCEF case file, or print documents from the system.** The NYSCEF system resembles the Federal ECF system. Thus, those familiar with the latter will be able to use the former with no formal training. Because the system is simple and easy to learn, many will find sufficient a brief review of the *User's Manual* and *FAQ's* that are available on the NYSCEF site (www.nycourts.gov/efile), or some practice using the NYSCEF "Practice System." Training, however, is available: those interested are urged to contact the NYSCEF Resource Center at efile@courts.state.ny.us or 646–386–3033. A two-credit CLE course is offered at no charge at the New York County Courthouse every week. The staff of the Resource Center can answer any other questions attorneys may have and are eager to be of assistance.

Please follow our website for additional information on this important new initiative. Thank you.

Dated: May 19, 2010

HON. SHERRY KLEIN HEITLER
Administrative Judge
JEFFREY CARUCCI
Statewide Coordinator for Electronic Filing
Unified Court System

Doc. 4.   Mandatory E–Filing Order

ADMINISTRATIVE ORDER OF THE
CHIEF ADMINISTRATIVE JUDGE OF THE COURTS

Pursuant to the authority vested in me, and in consultation with the Honorable Luis A. Gonzalez, Presiding Justice of the Appellate Division, First Department, and the Honorable A. Gail Prudenti, Presiding Justice of the Appellate Division, Second Department, I have established programs for the mandatory use of electronic means for the filing and service of documents ("e-filing"), in the manner authorized pursuant to L. 1999, c. 367, as amended by L. 2009, c. 416, and L. 2010, c. 528, in the counties, courts, actions and circumstances set forth in Appendix A attached hereto. Such programs shall be subject to section 202.5-bb and, as provided therein, section 202.5-b of the Uniform Rules for the New York State Trial Courts.

This order is effective immediately.

Dated: March 1, 2011

APPENDIX A

(March 1, 2011)

County	Authorized Mandatory E–Filing Program Courts	Implemented Mandatory E–Filing Programs (and effective date)
New York	Supreme Court	Commercial actions (5/24/2010)
Westchester	Supreme Court	Commercial actions (2/1/2011) Tort actions (3/1/ 2011)

I. For purposes of the e-filing program, the following definitions, restrictions, and conditions shall apply.[1]

1. "Commercial actions" with threshold amount in controversy requirement. "Commercial actions" shall mean actions which both (a) exceeds the threshold amount in controversy requirement set forth in sec. 2 infra; and (b) address at least one of the following claims or transactions:

(1) in matters arising out of business dealings (including but not limited to sales of assets or securities, corporate restructuring, partnership, shareholder, joint venture, and other business agreements, trade secrets; restrictive covenants; and employment agreements, not including claims that principally involve alleged discriminatory practices), claims of:

(i) breach of contract (with a threshold amount in controversy requirement in New York County and Westchester County only);

(ii) breach of fiduciary duty;

(iii) fraud, misrepresentation, business tort (including but not limited to actions involving claims of unfair competition); and

(iv) statutory and/or common law violation;

(2) transactions governed by the uniform commercial code (exclusive of those concerning individual cooperative or condominium units);

(3) transactions involving commercial real property, including Yellowstone injunctions and excluding actions for the payment of rent only;

(4) business transactions involving or arising out of dealings with commercial banks and other financial institutions;

(5) internal affairs of business organizations;

(6) malpractice by accountants or actuaries;

(7) legal malpractice arising out of representation in commercial matters;

(8) environmental insurance coverage; and

(9) commercial insurance coverage (including but not limited to directors and officers, errors and omissions, and business interruption coverage).

2. Amount in controversy requirement in certain commercial actions. The threshold amount in controversy requirement described in sec. 1(a) supra are as follows, exclusive of punitive damages, interest, costs, disbursements and counsel fees claimed:

a. New York County: $100,000.00.

b. Westchester County: $ 100,000.00.

3. "Commercial actions" without threshold amount in controversy requirement. In addition to the actions described in sec. 1 supra, "commercial actions" shall include actions that assert at least one claim arising from the following, without regard to the amount in controversy:

(1) breach of contract (outside New York County and Westchester);

(2) shareholder derivative actions;

(3) commercial class actions;

(4) dissolution of corporations, partnerships, limited liability companies, limited liability partnerships and joint ventures; and

(5) applications to stay or compel arbitration and affirm or disaffirm arbitration awards and related injunctive relief pursuant to article 75 of the civil practice law and rules involving any of the commercial issues enumerated in sec. 1 and this section.

4.   Exclusions from commercial actions. "Commercial actions" shall not include:

(1) actions to collect professional fees;

(2) actions seeking a declaratory judgment as to insurance coverage for personal injury or property damage;

(3) residential real estate disputes, including landlord-tenant matters, and commercial real estate disputes involving the payment of rent only;

(4) proceedings to enforce a judgment regardless of the nature of the underlying case;

(5) first-party insurance claims and actions by insurers to collect premiums or rescind non-commercial policies; and

(6) attorney malpractice actions except as otherwise provided in par. 1 above.

5.   Tort actions. "Tort actions" are actions that (a) seek only monetary damages; and (b) assert at least one claim (other than a commercial action claim described in pars. 1 and 3 <u>supra</u>, or a claim expressly excluded from commercial actions as described in par. 4 <u>supra</u>) that arises out of or alleges:

(1) a motor vehicle accident, product liability, injury to person or property from tortious conduct, wrongful death, mass tort, and medical, dental or podiatric malpractice;

(2) other professional malpractice;

(3) damages to persons or property from environmental conditions; or

(4) negligence, defamation, intentional infliction of emotional distress or other intentional harm.

6.   Commercial and Tort Claims in a Single Action. An action which meets both the definition of "commercial action" and "tort action" shall be treated as a tort action in Westchester County for e-filing purposes.

1 If any definition, restriction or condition set forth in this Administrative Order conflicts with L. 1999, c. 367, as amended by L. 2009, c. 416, and L. 2010, c. 528, or sections 202.5–b and 202.5–bb of the Uniform Rules of the Trial Courts, the statutory provision or Uniform Rule shall apply.

Form 1. Notice of commencement of Action
Subject to Mandatory Electronic Filing

SUPREME COURT OF THE STATE OF NEW YORK
COUNTY OF _____
---X

Plaintiff/Petitioner,

–against–

Index No. _____

Defendant/Respondent.
---X

NOTICE OF COMMENCEMENT OF ACTION
SUBJECT TO MANDATORY ELECTRONIC FILING

PLEASE TAKE NOTICE that the matter captioned above, which has been commenced by filing of the accompanying documents with the County Clerk, is subject to mandatory electronic filing pursuant to Section 202.5–bb of the Uniform Rules for the Trial Courts. This notice is being served as required by Subdivision (b) (3) of that Section.

For information about electronic filing, including access to Section 202.5–bb, consult the website of the New York State Courts Electronic Filing System ("NYSCEF") at www.nycourts.gov/efile or contact the NYSCEF Resource Center at 646–386–3033 or efile@courts.state.ny.us.

Dated: _____

_____ (Signature)

_____ (Name)

_____ (Firm Name)

_____ (Address)

_____

_____ (Phone)

_____ (E–Mail)

To: _____

_____

_____

5/17/10

Form 2. Commercial Division Request for
Judicial Intervention—Addendum

SUPREME COURT OF THE STATE OF NEW YORK

COUNTY OF _____

UCS–840C
3/2011

_____x   Index No. _____

                  Plaintiff(s)/Petitioner(s)   RJI No. (if any) _____

-against-

             Defendant(s)/Respondent(s)   **COMMERCIAL DIVISION**
                                          Request for Judicial Intervention Addendum

_____x

COMPLETE WHERE APPLICABLE [add additional pages if needed]:

Plaintiff/Petitioner's cause(s) of action [check all that apply]:

☐ Breach of contract or fiduciary duty, fraud, misrepresentation, business tort (e.g. unfair competition), or statutory and/or common law violation where the breach or violation is alleged to arise out of business dealings (e.g. sales of assets or securities; corporate restructuring; partnership, shareholder, joint venture, and other business agreements; trade secrets; restrictive covenants; and employment agreements not including claims that principally involve alleged discriminatory practices)

☐ Transactions governed by the Uniform Commercial Code (exclusive of those concerning individual cooperative or condominium units)

☐ Transactions involving commercial real property, including Yellowstone injunctions and excluding actions for the payment of rent only

☐ Shareholder derivative actions—without consideration of the monetary threshold

☐ Commercial class actions—without consideration of the monetary threshold

☐ Business transactions involving or arising out of dealings with commercial banks and other financial institutions

☐ Internal affairs of business organizations

☐ Malpractice by accountants or actuaries, and legal malpractice arising out of representation in commercial matters

☐ Environmental insurance coverage

☐ Commercial insurance coverage (e.g. directors and officers, errors and omissions, and business interruption coverage)

☐ Dissolution of corporations, partnerships, limited liability companies, limited liability partnerships and joint ventures—without consideration of the monetary threshold

☐ Applications to stay or compel arbitration and affirm or disaffirm arbitration awards and related injunctive relief pursuant to CPLR Article 75 involving any of the foregoing enumerated commercial issues—without consideration of the monetary threshold

Plaintiff/Petitioner's claim for compensatory damages [exclusive of punitive damages, interest, costs and counsel fees claimed]:

    $ _____

Plaintiff/Petitioner's claim for equitable or declaratory relief [brief description]: _____

_____

Defendant/Respondent's counterclaim(s) [brief description, including claim for monetary relief]:

_____

I REQUEST THAT THIS CASE BE ASSIGNED TO THE COMMERCIAL DIVISION. I CERTIFY THAT THE CASE MEETS THE JURISDICTIONAL REQUIREMENTS OF THE COMMERCIAL DIVISION SET FORTH IN 22 NYCRR § 202.70(a), (b) AND (c).

Dated: _____   _____
                                     SIGNATURE

                                    _____
                                     PRINT OR TYPE NAME

Form 3.   Notice of Hard Copy Submission—E–Filed Case

SUPREME COURT OF THE STATE OF NEW YORK
COUNTY OF NEW YORK

---X

                    Plaintiff/Petitioner,

                                               Index No. _____

–against –

                    Defendant/Respondent.

---X

NOTICE OF HARD COPY SUBMISSION—E–FILED CASE

(This Form Must be Annexed to Hard Copy Submissions in E–Filed Cases)

With limited exceptions, all documents in mandatory e-filed cases and e- filed cases in which consent has been given must be filed electronically; all hard copies submitted must be working copies in compliance with the E–Filing Rules. Counsel who seek to submit hard copy original documents in mandatory e-filed cases or cases subject to e-filing in which consent is being withheld must indicate the reason for hard copy submission by initialing in the relevant blank space provided below.

1.   Consensual Cases

___ In this consensual case, I am authorized to and do hereby withhold consent to e-filing on behalf of my client, a party to the case, or, if self-represented, myself.

2.   Mandatory Cases

___ I am exempt from the requirement to e-file because, in accordance with the E–Filing Rules, either I have filed with the court the exemption form required by the Rules or the court has granted my application upon good cause shown.

___ I am authorized to file this document in hard copy in this e- filed case pursuant to an emergency exception and am submitting the affirmation/affidavit required by Uniform Rule 202.5–bb (b) (2) or (c) (3).   I understand that I am required by the Rules to, and 1 shall, e-file these documents within three business days hereafter.

3.   Consensual or Mandatory Case—Sealing Application

___ I am applying for a sealing order and the need to protect sensitive information in the moving papers requires that I submit the papers in hard copy form, as permitted by the Protocol on Electronic Filing.

4.   Proposed Orders to Show Cause

___ As provided by the Protocol on Electronic Filing, I am submitting in hard copy form a proposed order to show cause and supporting papers seeking a TRO, together with an affirmation/affidavit demonstrating that there will be significant prejudice to the applicant from the giving of notice (Uniform Rule 202.7 (f)).

Dated: _____   _____ (Signature)

                                       _____ (Name)

                                       _____ (Firm Name)

                                       _____ (Address)

                                       _____

_____ (Phone)

_____ (E–Mail)

9/27/10

Form 4. Notice of Opt–Out From Participation in
Action Subject to Mandatory Electronic Filing

SUPREME COURT OF THE STATE OF NEW YORK

COUNTY OF ————————

---X

Plaintiff/Petitioner,

Index No. ——————————

–against –

Defendant/Respondent.

---X

NOTICE OF OPT–OUT FROM PARTICIPATION IN ACTION
SUBJECT TO MANDATORY ELECTRONIC FILING

Pursuant to Section 202.5–bb of the Uniform Rules for the Trial Courts, I hereby opt out of participation in electronic filing in this mandatory e-filed case.

For Attorneys:

I certify in good faith that I am unable to participate in mandatory electronic filing of documents in this case on behalf of my client, ——————————, because [place your initials in the applicable space]:

___ I lack [check off the applicable box]:

☐ the necessary computer hardware

☐ a connection to the internet

☐ a scanner or other device by which documents may be converted to an electronic format

___ I lack the knowledge regarding operation of computers and/or scanners needed to participate in electronic filing of documents in this case and no employee of mine or of my firm, office or business who is subject to my direction possesses such knowledge.

For Self–Represented Litigants:

I choose not to participate in electronic filing of documents in this case.

Dated: ————————————   ————————————— (Signature)

————————————— (Name)

————————————— (Firm Name)

————————————— (Address)

—————————————

————————————— (Phone)

5/7/10

RULES OF THE JUSTICES

Preamble

The following constitute the rules of the Justices of the Supreme Court, Civil Branch, New York County (hereinafter "the Rules" or "the Local Rules") with the exception of the Justices of the Commercial Division. A separate set of uniform rules governs cases assigned to the Commercial Division.

STRUCTURE OF THESE RULES: Immediately below is a Basic Information section that lists the Justices of the court in alphabetical order and a summary of the operational details of their Parts (e.g., motion days). Variations exist among the Parts in regard to such details. Except as so indicated, the Local Rules are uniform throughout the Supreme Court, Civil Branch, New York County (Commercial Division apart). An attorney who wishes to know the requirements followed in a particular Part should consult the main body of the Rules together with the portion of the Basic Information section that pertains to that Part. Information on the status of cases and activity therein and copies of decisions and other case documents are available in SCROLL, which is accessible through the website of this court (at www.nycourts.gov/supctmanh).

BASIC INFORMATION

Doc. 1. Basic Information

(Rooms are located at 60 Centre Street unless otherwise indicated.)[1]

HON. LUCY BILLINGS Part 46, General IAS Part, Room 103, 71 Thomas Street, Phone: 646–386–3279

Motions: Thurs., 9:30 AM

Conferences: Thurs., 2:15 PM

HON. RICHARD F. BRAUN Part 23, General IAS Part, Room 418, 60 Centre Street, Phone: 646–386–3754

Conferences: Tues., 9:30 AM (compliance conferences); 10:30 AM (preliminary conferences). **Motions**: Thurs., 9:30 AM (motions that have been adjourned in the Part); 10:30 AM (motions newly calendared in the Part). All contested motions are scheduled for argument in the Part following final submission in Room 130. Opposing papers on orders to show cause will be accepted at oral argument thereof.

HON. MATTHEW F. COOPER Part 9, Matrimonial Part, Room 289, 80 Centre Street, Phone (646) 386–3848 (646) 386–5696

Senior Law Clerk: Joshua H. Pike, Esq. (646) 386–5856 jpike@courts.state.ny.us

Assistant Law Clerk: Heather Weiner Hart, Esq. (646) 386–5853 hhart@ courts.state.ny.us

Part Clerk: (646) 386–3848 chwillia@courts.state.ny.us

GENERAL PART RULES

1. All parties and attorneys are required to be present on the return date and on every subsequent adjourned date unless directed otherwise by the court.

2. All adjournments require the prior approval of the court and must be requested no later than 1 PM of the business day immediately preceding the return date.

3. Any adjournment granted by the court must be reduced to a written stipulation prepared by counsel for the party requesting the adjournment and must be signed by the attorneys for all parties. The stipulation must include a briefing schedule for the submission of any responsive papers outstanding.

4. Motion papers, responsive papers and/or any other correspondence shall NOT be faxed or e-mailed to the court without the express permission of the court.

MOTIONS

1. Wednesday is the part's designated motion day.

2. Oral argument is required on all motions and orders to show cause unless directed otherwise by the court. If a hearing is requested or required, the parties shall be prepared to go forward on the return date of the application.

3. Opposition papers must be served and filed with the Part 9 Clerk at least seven (7) days prior to the return date or, where an adjournment has been granted, at least seven (7) days prior to the adjourn date. The Reply, if any, must be served and filed with the Part 9 Clerk at least one (1) day prior to the return date or, where an adjournment has been granted, at least one (1) day prior to the adjourn date.

4. Any cross-motion must be served and filed in the same time frame for responsive papers described above except that the original cross-motion must first be presented to the County Clerk for payment of the appropriate fee. After payment of the required fee, the original cross-motion with proof of payment must be filed with the Part 9 Clerk.

HON. LAURA DRAGER Part 31, Matrimonial IAS Part, Room 311, 71 Thomas Street, Phone: 646–386–3355

Motions & Conferences: Mon. all day and Tues. mornings

HON. CAROL EDMEAD Part 35, General IAS Part, Room 438, Phone: 646–386–3322

Motions: Tues. 9:30 A.M. and 11:30 A.M. on a staggered schedule

Discovery motions are strongly discouraged. (*See also* Rules of the Justices, New York County Supreme Court, Civil Branch (Non–Commercial Division), NYLJ, Rule 11).

Motions returnable in the Motion Submission Part Room 130 and assigned to the Part will be on submission unless the court advises the parties that oral argument is required.

Orders to show cause will be returnable in the Part. Responsive papers to orders to show cause must be delivered to the courtroom at least 4 days prior to the return date unless the court indicates otherwise. Absent an emergency, orders to show cause may not be adjourned. If the motion is adjourned, all papers are due in the Part on the Friday before the adjourned date.

In the event a motion has been resolved by withdrawal or settlement of the case, counsel are encouraged to advise the court prior to the Tuesday calendar by promptly faxing to the court a letter of withdrawal or a stipulation of settlement and discontinuance. There shall be no ex parte communications with chambers and there will be no telephone adjournments. (*See also* NYLJ, Rules 1(a), 4, 13(b), 14(a) and 14(c)).

Conferences:

(*See* NYLJ, Rule 1(a), 7(c), and 10(b)).

All preliminary conferences are scheduled for Tuesdays at 2:15 P.M.

Preliminary conferences may not be adjourned. All stipulations of adjournment are subject to court approval and must be on consent, in writing. If there is no consent, the date must be honored and counsel must appear for an oral application for an adjournment. When an order to show cause is filed prior to the scheduling of a preliminary conference, the court will hold the preliminary conference on the return date of the Order to Show Cause, except where an Order involves (1) a reference; (2) a stay of the proceedings, i.e. bankruptcy or (3) the death of a party or other substitutions. (*See also* NYLJ, Rule 7(a)).

At a compliance conference, a scheduled conference may be adjourned one time for no more than two weeks by stipulation of the parties faxed to the court by noon on the preceding Friday. Any further adjournments require the approval of the court, which will be granted only for good cause. The request for any such additional adjournment must be submitted to the court by fax no later than 4 P.M. on the preceding Friday. No adjournments will be given over the telephone. (*See also* NYLJ, Rule 1(b)).

At a pre-trial conference, counsel and their clients must appear unless the court expressly directs otherwise. (*See also* NYLJ, Rule 1(b)).

Trials:

Trials are scheduled for a date certain generally within 45 days after a conference is held following the filing of a note of issue. Trial dates scheduled by the court are firm and may only be adjourned upon application based upon an emergency. Trials are held every day of the week except Tuesdays, which is a calendar day. No adjournments will be granted if a witness is unavailable to testify unless the court concludes, in rare instances, that good cause exists. (*See also* NYLJ, Rules 20 and 21, and Pre–Trial Information Sheet available in the Part).

HON. SARALEE EVANS Part 51, Matrimonial IAS Part, Room 305, 71 Thomas Street, Phone: 646–386–3846

Motions: Tues., 9:30 AM **Conferences:** Tues, 11 AM

HON. PAUL G. FEINMAN Part 12, General IAS Part (Presumptive E–Filing Part), Room 212, Phone: 646–386–3273; Chambers Room 529, Phone 646–386–3375.

Principal Law Clerk: Ms. Julia Herd, Esq.

Assistant Law Clerk: Mr. D. Allen Zachary, Esq.

Part 12 Clerk: Mr. Michael Kasper

Preliminary Conferences: Wednesdays, commencing at 2:15 p.m., or as otherwise directed.

Compliance Conferences: Wednesdays, commencing at 2:15 p.m., or as otherwise directed.

Oral Argument on Motions: Wednesdays, staggered in ½ hour intervals commencing at 9:30 a.m. to 12:30 p.m., or as otherwise directed by order to show cause. Discovery motions will sometimes be scheduled with afternoon conferences.

1. Communications With the Part Clerk and Chambers

A. *DO NOT CALL OR WRITE CHAMBERS REGARDING SCHEDULING MATTERS AND REQUESTS FOR ADJOURNMENTS.* Any such calls will simply result in your being directed to the Part Clerk. The Law Clerks do not handle adjournments.

Adjournment requests for conferences and oral arguments scheduled in Part 12 should be made by contacting Mr. Michael Kasper, the Part 12 Clerk.

Adjournment requests for mediation dates in Mediation I and/or jury selection dates in Trial Part 40 should be made by contacting the appropriate part clerks. Justice Feinman and his Part Clerk do not administer those calendars.

Adjournment requests for matters pending in the Motion Submission Part should follow the General

Procedures for New York County found at http://www.nycourts.gov/supctmanh/motions_on_notice.htm

Do not call chambers or the Part 12 Clerk regarding adjournments in the Motion Submission Part.

B. *No ex parte communications.*

C. **DO NOT WRITE LETTERS TO THE COURT UNLESS YOU**

1. seek to withdraw a motion in whole or in part;

2. wish to advise the court that a case is settled; or

3. were granted leave to write the court at oral argument.

2. Motion Practice

A. *Page Limits*

Per Rule 14 [b] of Rules of the Justices, New York County Supreme Court Civil Branch, effective April 17, 2006 (*see*, "Rules of Justices" at http://www.nycourts.gov/supctman), memoranda of law shall not exceed 30 pages each (exclusive of table of contents and table of authorities), and affidavits/affirmations shall not exceed 25 pages each, double-spaced.

B. *E–Filing*

i. Pursuant to the joint statement of then-Administrative Judge Jacqueline W. Silbermann and Justice Feinman, effective October 31, 2008, all commercial and tort cases in Part 12 shall presumptively be e-filed. Others are also strongly encouraged to e-file.

ii. Parties shall file an E-filing Consent Form with the E–Filing Office in Room 119A at 60 Centre Street, or electronically at newyorkef@courts.state.ny.us.

iii. Unless requested by the court at oral argument or in an order to show cause, in Part 12, courtesy copies are not required in NYSCEF cases, nor in non-electronically filed cases. Indeed, courtesy copies are actively discouraged. The court only considers papers filed through the appropriate clerks.

iv. Where a party seeks to use the same set of papers to move, oppose, or reply to more than one motion, the party shall separately e-file that set of papers under each assigned motion sequence number. Failure to do so may cause the motion to appear, and be treated, as though it is unopposed or submitted on default.

v. Questions regarding e-filing should be addressed to the E-Filing Office at 646–386–3610 or at efile@courts.state.ny.us. Answers to frequently asked questions can be found at http://www.nycourts.gov/supctmanh/E-Filing.htm.

C. *Oral Argument*

i. Scheduling

After motions are submitted in the Motion Submission Part, Room 130 at 60 Centre Street, they are forwarded to the part. Motions submitted on default or with no opposition are not generally scheduled for oral argument. Other motions will be scheduled for oral argument at the discretion of Justice Feinman (*see*, 22 NYCRR 202. 8[d]). If oral argument is requested, it should have been so indicated on the notice of motion. DO NOT SEND LETTERS TO THE PART OR CHAMBERS REQUESTING ORAL ARGUMENT. If oral argument is scheduled, you will be so notified electronically.

ii. Adjournments

To adjourn oral argument on a motion, file a stipulation of adjournment no later than 5:00 p.m. of the Monday before the oral argument date. If the parties do not agree on an adjournment, they should arrange a conference call with the Part 12 Clerk, Mr. Kasper. However, parties are reminded of the importance of courteous cooperation with each other.

iii. Settlement Authority

Parties appearing on dispositive motions MUST have settlement authority. A failure to appear with settlement authority may be deemed a default.

D. DO NOT copy the court on letters exchanged between counsel. The court will not read them.

E. If a case has settled while a motion is *sub judice, please so advise the Part 12 Clerk–IMMEDIATELY!* This is an exception to the "no letter" rule set forth above at 1. C.

F. *Send NOTHING to chambers, unless previously directed to do so by the Court.* Stipulations, papers, etc. should be e-filed, or, delivered to the appropriate Clerk. The appropriate Clerk accepts documents for filing, NOT chambers. If a document has been e-filed, that is sufficient.

G. The court no longer provides courtesy copies of decisions. Counsel are notified electronically when decisions or orders are filed with the County Clerk. The entered decision will be available to counsel through the e-filing system. Even if a matter is not e-filed, decisions are scanned and posted on the internet. However, the court will send a courtesy copy of decisions in which it has marked the gray sheet "do not post."

H. Do not call chambers or the Part 12 Clerk to determine whether a decision has issued. This information is easily available through the Supreme Court Records On-Line Library (SCROLL) and, if the action is e-filed, through NYSCEF.

I. Parties are advised that the court adheres to the following rules, which may differ from the Uniform Rules:

i. CPLR 3212 summary judgment motions are to be *filed* within 60 days of *filing* the Note of Issue. Absent good cause shown for the late filing, a late motion may be summarily denied, even if the adversary has failed to raise the issue. A cross motion for summary judgment will be deemed filed on the day it is filed, and its timeliness does not relate back to the filing of the main motion.

ii. CPLR 2215 is strictly followed, that is to say, a cross motion may only be filed if it seeks relief against the moving party. If you are seeking relief against a party other than the one who made the initial motion, you should filed a separate motion, not a so-called cross motion. A party failing to comply with this rule will have their "cross motion" denied without prejudice to refiling, but with no extension of any filing deadlines. Strict adherence to this rule is designed to avoid problems with "short service" of cross motions and contributes to a more accurate tracking of parties' and third-parties' motions in multi-party litigation.

J. *No sur-replies.*

3. Preliminary and Compliance Conferences

A. *Scheduling*

Preliminary conferences may be scheduled pursuant to a RJI or a motion. Alternatively, any party in which a RJI has already been filed, may simply contact the Part 12 Clerk who will schedule one for the first available date.

Compliance conferences may be scheduled pursuant to a prior discovery order, a decision on a motion, or by any party contacting the Part 12 Clerk who will schedule a date as soon as practicable. Do not contact chambers.

Adjournments of conferences may only be done *after* the parties have spoken in a conference call with the Part 12 Clerk, Mr. Kasper, who will determine if an adjournment is reasonable and select a new conference date. Adjournments will generally only be granted when requested no later than 5:00 p.m. on the Monday prior to the scheduled conference. If granted, the parties will be asked to file a stipulation of adjournment with the court.

B. Please bring copies of all prior conference orders and stipulations to the conferences. If you have any motions pending in the Motion Submission Part, or which are *sub judice*, please bring this to the attention of the Part 12 Clerk and consult with the Justice's law clerks.

C. Attorneys attending conferences must have authority to bind the party on all issues, including conversion of the action to electronic filing. Appearances by counsel without authority may be deemed a default.

D. *Instructions Applicable to Preliminary Conference and Compliance Conference Orders*

i. Please write legibly with a black ball point pen. Press hard. Illegible orders will not be signed. You must indicate the names, addresses, and telephone numbers of all counsel appearing at the conference.

ii. Number the pages (e.g., 1 of 3, 2 of 3). At the top of page 1, please indicate whether this is the 1st, 2nd, or 3rd Compliance Order and whether the matter has already been converted to electronic filing.

iii. If it is a P.C. form, all items must be completed or marked "n/a" if not applicable.

iv. Use complete dates, including the correct year. Please remember some of the dates you are selecting may be in the next calendar year.

v. Use firm cut-off dates such as "on or before December 31, 2011." Do not use "within 45 days," etc. You are assumed to have consulted your clients, examining doctors, etc. regarding their availability for EBTs, IMEs, etc. before you pick the date. Pick a reserve date if you have any uncertainty.

vi. If this is the 2nd Compliance Conference addressing an issue, please add the following language:

"The parties have been advised that the dates contained herein will be strictly enforced and that failure to comply with this court's *orders* will result in the imposition of any appropriate sanction, including, but not limited to, monetary costs and sanctions, issue or defense preclusion, witness preclusion, and or the complete or partial striking of a pleading."

vii. Do not leave the courtroom until either the Justice or one of his law clerks has reviewed your completed forms. Copies of preliminary conference and compliance conference orders will be available electronically in e-filed matters. Copies of such orders are not scanned in matters that have not be converted to electronic filing.

viii. Consult with the Justice's law clerks regarding any issues you cannot amicably resolve. *They serve as referees appointed by him to resolve disputes.*

E. *Instructions Applicable to Preliminary Conference Order Forms only.*

[*available in the Court Room*]

F. At each compliance conference, counsel should have a complete list of any discovery previously ordered but not yet completed. Failure to address such items at the subsequent conference will be deemed a waiver of the party's right to that discovery.

5. Trial Dates

Unless otherwise directed, after a note of issue has been filed, the case will be assigned to Mediation I or Trial Part 40 by the Trial Support Office. Part 12 will no longer maintain a separate pre-trial conference calendar.

HON. MARCY S. FRIEDMAN Part 57, General IAS Part and Complex Litigation Part (E–Filing), Room 335, Phone: 646–386–3759

Chambers: Room 326, 80 Centre Street, Phone: 646–386–3760

Motions: Thurs., 9:30 AM

Preliminary Conferences: 11:00 AM unless otherwise directed by the Court. **Compliance Conferences**: 2:15 PM unless otherwise directed by the Court.

HON. IRA GAMMERMAN (JHO) (ADMINISTRATIVE COORDINATING JUDGE) Parts 40 and 27C, Room 242, Phone 646–386–3265

HON. ELLEN GESMER Part 24, Matrimonial Part, Room 210, 71 Thomas Street, Courtroom Phone: 646–386–3285; Chambers phone: 646–386–3730; Fax 212–884–8986

Law Secretary: Kristin Bebelaar

Motions and Conferences: Thursdays and Fridays, at staggered times.

Adjournments: Adjournments may be sought either by a conference call with the Law Secretary or the Part Clerk.

Motions: All applications for relief, except cross-motions, must be made by Order to Show Cause unless otherwise directed by the Court. To reduce the need for motion practice, counsel are encouraged to contact the Court by conference call prior to filing a motion.

Communication with court: Counsel and parties may not communicate with the Court by letter, email or fax, and may not send the court copies of correspondence between counsel, without prior approval by the Court.

Post-trial submissions: After trial, parties shall submit post-trial proposed findings of fact and conclusions of law, with copies on computer disk or Word Perfect formatted email attachment.

HON. JUDITH J. GISCHE, Part 10, General IAS Part, Room 232, Part Clerk/Court Room: (646) 386–3722, Fax: (212) 401–9288, Chambers: (646) 386–3723

Eileen Kaspar, Esq., Principal Court Attorney

Beth M. Kaufman, Esq., Assistant Law Clerk

Preliminary Conferences

Preliminary conferences are held each Thursday at 9:30 a.m. Cases are called when all sides have checked in and are present. Default applications will be heard after 11:00 a.m.

Motions

Orders to Show Cause are returnable directly in the Part, usually on a Thursday. Motions on notice are returnable any day in Room 130 and those motions can only be adjourned through (and in accordance with the rules of) Part 130. Once a motion is marked submitted in Part 130, oral argument, if directed by the court, will be scheduled in Part 10. Unusually large motions should be accompanied by a CD version of the hard copy. No advance permission is required to bring a motion, even discovery motions.

Decisions and Orders

The foregoing court documents are scanned and all available online at: http://iapps.courts.state.ny.us/webcivil/FCASMain

E–Filing

Part 10 is a presumptive E–Filing Part. Please see www.nycourts.gove/efile for more information.

Compliance, Status and Trial Readiness Conferences

Counsel must be prepared and have authority to discuss all aspects of a matter, including settlement, at each conference.

Adjournments

Stipulations on consent can be sent via fax to the clerk in the part (no emails accepted) at (212) 401–9288 or delivered by another means so they arrive in advance of the scheduled court appearance. All adjournments are subject to court approval; they must include: 1) the reason for the adjournment, 2) the date the case was last on, and 3) the Thursday you would like the case/motion adjourned to. If there is no consent, you must submit an affirmation of actual engagement (if applicable), or honor the scheduled date and make the application for an adjournment orally. To follow up on an adjournment, please call the clerk in the part. Stipulations in E–Filed cases must be uploaded into the system first. The stipulation can then be faxed to the number above with a confirmation notice attached.

Note of Issue

When the plaintiff is ready to file the note of issue, plaintiff <u>must</u> obtain a signed stipulation signed by all sides indicating that all discovery is complete. Plaintiff may not file the note of issue unless all discovery is complete. Once that stipulation is received by the Clerk in Part 10, the court will dispense with the next scheduled compliance conference and transfer the case to Mediation. The stip may be sent by fax or mailed.

Summary Judgment

The part adheres to the time limitations set forth in CPLR 3212, that is a timely motion for summary judgment must be made no later than 120 days after note of issue has been filed.

Trials

Trials proceed day by day until completed. Marked pleadings, proposed jury instructions and verdict sheets and a one paragraph summary of the contentions must be provided to the court electronically: ekaspar@courts.state.ny.us. Counsel should also provide the court with cell phone numbers where they can be reached in the case of an emergency.

HON. EMILY JANE GOODMAN Part 17, General IAS Part, Room 422, Phone: 646–386–3283

Law Secretary: Andrea S. Field, Esq.

Motions & Conferences: Thurs.

1. Only attorneys thoroughly familiar with the case may appear. Bring SIGNED copies of all prior decisions and orders, which can be obtained from the County Clerk file, to the conference.

2. Preliminary Conferences are held at 10:00 a.m. and Compliance Conferences are held at 10:30 a.m.

3. Attorneys who appear at discovery and compliance conferences may not leave the courtroom once they have signed in until the case is conferenced absent opposing counsel's permission.

4. While you are waiting for your case to be called, please confer with opposing counsel and draft a preliminary or compliance conference order/stipulation providing for all remaining discovery. Disputes will be resolved at the conference. Discovery orders/stipulations must set specific dates certain for all deadlines, including IMES and impleaders.

5. Compliance conferences will be held at least every three months.

6. The Judge will not sign illegible documents, and spelling counts!

7. Adjournments are permitted only with the approval of the Part Clerk or Law Clerk. This includes all conferences and all oral arguments. NO TELEPHONE CALLS to Chambers absent emergency or a previously scheduled conference call with the Law Clerk. If you need to contact Chambers, please e-mail the Law Clerk at Afield@courts.state.ny.us and copy all counsel.

8. Before inquiring about the status of any pending motion, judgment or order, please check eTrack or The New York Law Journal. Please refrain from making any status inquiry unless 60 days from submission has expired.

9. If you would like a copy of a decision, please check SCROLL, posted at www.nycourts.gov/supct manh (under "Case Information") or obtain a copy from the County Clerk.

10. We do **NOT** accept courtesy copies.

11. Absent leave of Court on good cause shown, dispositive motions must be made within 45 days after the filing of the Note of Issue.

12. Except for the delivery of an Order to Show Cause with a Temporary Restraining Order, all document deliveries or retrievals from Chambers must be done between 3 PM—4PM. Arguments in connection with any Temporary Restraining Order must be made by appointment.

Settlement Conferences. Attorneys with authority to settle must attend all Settlement Conferences and bring the client or claims adjuster when directed. At least one week prior to Conference, plaintiff must communicate a demand to defendants and defendants must respond with a counter-offer. Failure to adhere to these rules may result in sanctions.

HON. SHLOMO HAGLER Part 25, Guardianship Part, Room 623, 111 Centre Street, 646–386–5675

HON. SHERRY KLEIN HEITLER Part 30, Center for Complex Litigation, Room 543, Phone: 646–386–3291

HON. CAROL E. HUFF Part 32, Trial Part, Room 331, Phone: 646–386–3281

HON. BARBARA JAFFE City IAS Part 5 Room 307, 80 Centre Street, Phone: 386–3374 Fax: 212–374–3907 (please reference on the fax "Part 5, Attention: Judge Jaffe"). Chambers Phone: (646) 386–3727; Court Attorney: Catherine Paszkowska—cpaszko@courts.state.ny.us; Asst. Law Clerk: Mark H. Jaffe—mjaffe@courts.state.ny.us

COMPLIANCE CONFERENCES:

Conference Clerk: Yolanda Baskerville, (646) 386–3687, fax 212–374–1753

Conference Courtroom: 80 Centre Street, room 103

Procedures:

Compliance conferences are held on Tuesdays at 2 pm in room 103.

Counsel appearing at a compliance conference are expected to be familiar with the case and to have the authority to discuss all discovery issues and to settle.

Counsel must bring to each conference a list of all outstanding discovery.

Upon a party's first failure to appear for a compliance conference, the conference will be adjourned. Upon a party's failure to appear for the adjourned conference, the case will be dismissed or the answer will be stricken.

If the case has settled, the parties must promptly fax the Part Clerk to this court a stipulation of settlement and discontinuance containing all pertinent information regarding the settlement.

Adjournments:

Adjournments are strongly discouraged and must be directed to the Conference Clerk only by telephone conference no later than 4 pm on the preceding Monday.

MOTIONS:

General Procedures:

Motions will be scheduled for oral argument by the court only as needed and will be held on Tuesdays at 9:30 am in room 307.

Sur-replies are not permitted; letters and papers are not accepted after the return date unless on the consent of all parties or order of the Court. If a motion has been withdrawn or settled, the parties must promptly fax the Part Clerk a stipulation.

The Court will engage in no *ex parte* communications. Please do not call absent a previously scheduled conference call.

All summary judgment motions must be filed within 60 days after the filing of the note of issue.

Information about decisions on motions should be obtained by checking with the appropriate clerk's office, the New York Law Journal or the court's website at www.nycourts.gov/supctmanh under "case information" or www.nycourts.gov under the E-courts link. Please do not call the Part Clerk or chambers.

Discovery Motions:

Discovery motions are strongly discouraged, however, if a discovery dispute arises before the issuance of a preliminary or conference order and a party has made a formal discovery motion, a conference will be scheduled for the return date of the motion.

If a discovery dispute arises after the issuance of a preliminary or conference order, it must be directed to the Conference Clerk who will promptly schedule a resolution conference. Only after this conference is held may a discovery motion be filed.

Orders to Show Cause

Absent express permission, reply papers are not accepted on an order to show cause.

MISCELLANEOUS ORDERS:

Subpoenas will be promptly signed and the submitting party may pick up the signed order within two days after submission or call the Part Clerk to arrange for pick-up.

Other ex parte orders will be promptly signed and the submitting party may pick up the signed order within two days after submission or call the Part Clerk to arrange for pick-up.

PRE–NOTE SETTLEMENT CONFERENCES:

The court will conduct pre-note settlement conferences when requested to do so by all parties on a case. The parties must fill out and sign a conference request form which is available in the DCM Office (room 102) or from the conference clerk, Yolanda Baskerville. Once the request is submitted, the court will send the parties a letter with the date and time of the conference. The conferences will usually be held on Tuesday afternoons.

Counsel must keep in mind the following rules:

1) attorneys who appear for the conference must be knowledgeable about the case and must bring any relevant documents;

2) only attorneys with authority to settle the case may appear;

3) if an insurance company is involved, an adjuster or someone from the company authorized to enter into a settlement must appear;

4) attorneys may, but are not required to, bring their clients to the conference;

5) if a settlement is reached, the parties, through their attorneys, will be expected to sign a stipulation of settlement at the conference; and

6) all adjournment requests must be in writing, signed by all parties, and sent to the court by 5 p.m. the day before the conference.

TRIALS:

Requirements:

Upon the first appearance before this court, the parties must furnish the court with the following:

a) a list of proposed witnesses indicating on it the need for any interpreters and the language/dialect;

b) all marked pleadings and bills of particulars;

c) all prior decisions in the case;

d) any notices to admit; and

e) copies of those portions of EBTs intended for use at trial for any purpose.

Jury Trials:

Just prior to openings, the parties must furnish the court and opposing counsel with the following:

a) Proposed jury instructions:

1) if the proposed instructions are taken verbatim from the Pattern Jury Instructions, PJI numbers will suffice;

2) if a PJI instruction is not verbatim or requires a characterization or description of the evidence or the parties' contentions, the exact requested language must be submitted together with the authority for it; and

b) Proposed jury verdict sheet

The proposed instructions and verdict sheet must be emailed as an attachment in WordPerfect or Word format to cpaszko@courts.state.ny.us and to opposing counsel simultaneously. Do not assume that the email has been received until a confirmation email is sent to you. If no confirmation is received within 24 hours of the email's transmission, please call the court attorney for further instructions.

c) Parties are strongly urged to have the court stenographer pre-mark all exhibits for identification and/or in evidence if without objection. Any issues as to admissibility are best raised before trial commences or at the beginning of the day on which a party expects to offer the exhibit.

HON. DEBRA A. JAMES Part 59, General IAS Part (E–Filing), Room 1254, 111 Centre Street, Phone: 646–386–3351

Motions and Preliminary Conferences: Tuesdays, 9:30 AM and 11:00 AM

Compliance Conferences: Tuesdays, 11:00 AM

Status Conferences: Tuesdays, 2:30 PM

Pre–Trial Conferences: Tuesdays, 12 noon

Appearances by Counsel: Counsel who appear at conferences or for oral argument of a motion or other matter that is scheduled in the courtroom shall note their appearance on the calendar posted inside the courtroom. The Clerk of the Part will call each matter in the order in which all parties have so marked their appearances as present. Counsel who appear at conferences shall complete the appropriate form and submit such form to the Part Clerk prior to the matter being called. Counsel shall produce copies of all prior discovery stipulations and orders at each conference.

Motions: Contested motions, after submission to the Motion Support Office, shall be rescheduled by the Part Clerk for oral argument. Notice to the parties of such argument will be transmitted by the court.

Orders to Show Cause: Orders to Show Cause, unless directed otherwise, are returnable in the Part.

Adjournments: If the parties consent to an adjournment of a Show Cause Order, the Part Clerk, Ms. Charlotte Williams (646–386–3351) must be notified two business days before the scheduled return date. Upon approval by the court, the stipulation of adjournment shall be faxed or delivered to the court by 4 PM on the business day preceding the return date.

Disputes and Motions Concerning Discovery: If counsel are unable to resolve a discovery dispute in the manner called for by Uniform Rule 202.7, the aggrieved party shall contact Charlotte Williams, the Part Clerk promptly, within any applicable deadline, and prior to bringing a formal motion. As appropriate in the circumstances, the court may direct submission of concise letters or telephonic or in-court conference. Where a formal motion concerning discovery is brought and no preliminary conference has been conducted, the court will schedule and hold a preliminary conference on the return date of such motion.

Trials: At the pre-trial conference, the court will distribute to each party a Pre–Trial Information Sheet and Stipulation and Order that require, inter alia, a statement of undisputed facts and an estimate of required trial days, which each party must complete and submit to the court within one week before the date set for trial.

Miscellaneous: There shall be no ex parte communications with the court.

HON. DEBORAH A. KAPLAN Part 20, Matrimonial Part, Room 540, Courtroom Phone: 646–386–3300; Chambers Phone: 646–386–5567; Fax: 212–401–9037

Principal Law Clerk: Hemalee, J. Patel, Esq.

Assistant Law Clerk: Deanna Lucci, Esq.

Rules (effective March 25, 2009):

GENERAL PART RULES

All court appearances are on a staggered schedule.

All adjournments require the prior approval of the court.

All adjournments due to the actual engagement of counsel shall be granted in accordance with Part 125 of the Rules of the Chief Administrator of the Courts. Affirmations must be faxed to the Court at least one (1) day prior to the court appearance.

All parties **must** be present for all appearances and conferences unless excused by the Court.

Correspondence, whether by mail, e-mail or facsimile, between counsel is not to be copied to Chambers.

Pursuant to 22 N.Y.C.R.R. 202.16(d) a R.J.I. must be filed within the forty-five (45) days of the date of service of the summons unless an affidavit of no necessity is filed, in which event the R.J.I. must be filed within one hundred and twenty (120) days.

All papers submitted to Part 20 must include a fax number.

MOTIONS

Wednesday is designated as motion day.

Oral argument is required on all motions and orders to show cause, unless directed otherwise by the Court.

Counsel are required to file all responsive papers in Part 20. All exhibits are to be identified by tabs. Cross motions are to be filed with the Matrimonial Clerk's Office two (2) days prior to the return date.

Motions may not be adjourned on consent more than once without court approval. Counsel are directed to submit a written stipulation reflecting their consent which must include additional available dates.

Counsel are reminded that the CPLR does not provide for sur-reply papers or allow the presentation of papers or letters to the court after argument of a motion. Sur-replies, letters and the responses to such letters addressed to the substance of motions will not be considered.

Any allegations of fact submitted to the court, including allegations contained in an affidavit and/or the complaint, must be certified by counsel in the form prescribed by the Chief Administrative Judge.

ORDERS OF PROTECTION

Ex-parte requests for orders of protection must be accompanied by the Family Protection Registry Information Sheet and the litigant must be present. Motions to consolidate Family Court orders of protection actions must contain a complete copy of the Family Court file.

PRELIMINARY CONFERENCE

Preliminary Conferences will be held on Wednesdays and Thursdays, unless notified otherwise by the Court. The conference must be held within forty-five (45) days of the filing of an R.J.I. The party seeking judicial intervention is required to notify the opposing party of the Preliminary Conference date. There will be no adjournments of Preliminary Conferences without express permission from the court.

Counsel are reminded that pursuant to 22 N.Y.C.R.R. 202.16(f)(1) Net Worth affidavits are to be filed with the court ten (10) days prior to the conference date. They are to be accompanied by the attorneys' retainer statements and the parties' recent paystubs or W–2 statements.

COMPLIANCE CONFERENCE

Compliance Conferences will be held on Wednesdays and Thursdays or on a date selected by the court.

The date of the Compliance Conference shall be set at the time of the Preliminary Conference. Counsel should not wait until the date of the Compliance Conference to advise the Court of any failures to comply with Preliminary Conference directives and discovery orders. Such failure should be addressed prior to the Compliance Conference either by motion or conference call to Chambers. Failure to timely comply with the Court ordered discovery may result in the imposition of sanctions and counsel fees.

PRE–TRIAL CONFERENCE

Note of Issue shall be filed prior to the pre-trial conference and in accordance with the compliance order. At the pre-trial conference, counsel will provide the court with statements of proposed disposition, updated net worth statements with the last three years of tax returns and a child support worksheet, if applicable. Counsel shall present all motions in limine at this conference.

TRIAL

The Court is to be provided with the following pursuant to Court Order but no less than thirty (30) days prior to day of trial:

1. Marked pleadings.

2. Updated statement of net worth, statement of proposed disposition and child support worksheet, if applicable.

3. A witness list, expert reports not previously filed and any pre-trial memorandum.

4. A list of all proposed exhibits.

5. A list of documents which counsel may stipulate into evidence, such documents are to be pre-marked by counsel.

6. A written copy of any issues or facts to which the parties can stipulate in the advance of trial. Said stipulation to be read into the record at the commencement of the trial.

7. Statements of proposed disposition.

Counsel are reminded that pursuant to 22 N.Y.C.R.R. 202.16(9) all expert reports are to be exchanged and filed with the Court sixty (60) days before the date set for trial. Reply reports, if any, shall be exchanged and filed no later than thirty (30) days before said date.

Sanctions and/or costs may be imposed for failure to comply with any rules set forth herein.

Once a case has been assigned a trial date, it is presumed ready for trial. Trials will be day to day. No consent adjournments will be accepted. Failure to proceed will result in default relief being granted or the action being dismissed. In the event the action is resolved prior to the court date, counsel are expected to notify Chambers immediately.

The Court is to be provided with duplicates of all items marked into evidence.

The Court may direct one or both parties to order the transcript and allocate the costs.

All judgments of divorce must contain a form VS 140 containing the social security number of both parties. All judgments must be submitted within 60 days or the action will be deemed abandoned and dismissed. All QDROs must be submitted within 45 days of the signing of the Judgment and must be accompanied by written plan approval.

Copies of decisions and orders will be mailed to all counsel and any self-represented litigants.

Information on whether decisions have been issued or judgments or signed orders should be obtained by telephoning the Matrimonial Clerk's Office between 9–5 p.m. or by checking the New York Law Journal.

HON. JOAN M. KENNEY, Part 8, General IAS Part, Room 304, 71 Thomas St., Phone 646–386–3572

Preliminary Conferences: Thursdays, commencing at 9:30 a.m., or as otherwise directed.

Compliance Conferences: Thursdays, commencing at 10:00 a.m., or as otherwise directed.

1. Communications with the Part Clerk and Chambers

A. Adjournment requests for conferences and oral arguments scheduled in Part 8 should be made by contacting the Part Clerk. If granted, a stipulation signed by all counsel shall be sent via facsimile (212–748–4294), to the Part Clerk. Counsel seeking an adjournment of any appearance, must make the request prior to the Monday immediately preceding the scheduled appearance date. Late requests for adjournments may not be entertained by the Court.

B. Adjournment requests for motions returnable in the Motion Submission Part (Room 130—[646–386–3030]), for mediation dates in Mediation I (646–386–3689) and for jury selection dates in Trial Part 40 (646–386–3265) should be made by contacting the appropriate part clerks.

C. No *ex parte* communications except pursuant to CPLR 6313.

2. Motion Practice

A. If oral argument is scheduled after the motion is submitted in Room 130 you will be contacted.

B. Any party seeking injunctive relief must appear with an adversary when the application is presented for signature.

C. DO NOT copy the court on letters exchanged between counsel. The court will not read them. They will be discarded and unread.

D. If a case has settled while a motion is *sub judice, please so advise the Part 8 Clerk IMMEDIATELY!*

E. Stipulations, papers, etc. should always be filed or delivered to the appropriate back office or Clerk and not to chambers unless previously directed to do so by the Court.

F. All decisions are scanned and posted on the internet with the entry date. This information is easily available through the Supreme Court Records On–Line Library (SCROLL) (www.nycourts.gov/supct manh).

G. Do not call chambers or the Part 8 Clerk to determine whether a decision has been issued.

H. Parties are advised that the court adheres to the following rules:

i. CPLR 3212 summary judgment motions are to be *filed* with the motion support office within *30* days of *filing* the Note of Issue. Absent good cause shown for the late filing, a late motion will be summarily denied, even if the adversary has failed to raise the issue. A cross-motion will be deemed filed on the day it is filed, and its timeliness does not relate back to the filing of the motion-in-chief.

ii. Discovery is to continue during the pendency of CPLR 3212 motions, unless good cause is shown why discovery should be stayed.

iii. CPLR 2215 motions seeking relief by a non-moving party, requires that a cross-motion shall be made on the moving party. If the cross-movant is seeking relief against a party other than the one who made the initial motion, the cross-motion *must* be filed as a separate motion. A party failing to comply with this rule will have their "cross-motion"

denied without prejudice to re-file. Strict adherence to this rule avoids problems with "short service" of cross-motions and permits for a much more orderly and efficient administration of the part.

I. No sur-replies will be considered as part of a motion deemed submitted for decision.

3. Preliminary and Compliance Conferences

A. *Scheduling*

Preliminary conferences are scheduled by the Trial Support Office pursuant to the filing of a RJI or a motion.

Compliance conferences may be scheduled pursuant to the preliminary conference Order.

B. Please bring copies of all prior conference orders and stipulations to the conferences. If you have any motions pending in the Motion Submission Part, or are *sub judice*, please bring this to the attention of the Justice's law clerks at the next conference.

C. *Instructions Applicable to Preliminary Conference and Compliance Conference Orders*

i. Please write legibly with a black ball point pen. Press hard. Illegible orders will not be signed. You must indicate the names, addresses, and telephone numbers of all counsel appearing at the conference.

ii. Number the pages (e.g., 1 of 3, 2 of 3). At the top of page 1, please indicate whether this is the 1st, 2nd, or 3rd Compliance Order.

iii. If it is a preliminary conference form, all items must be completed or marked "n/a" if not applicable.

iv. Use complete dates, including the correct year. Please remember some of the dates you are selecting may be in the next calendar year.

v. Use firm cut-off dates such as "on or before December 31, 2009." Do not use "within 45 days," etc. You are assumed to have consulted your clients, examining doctors, etc. regarding their availability for EBTs, IMEs, etc. before you pick the date. Pick a reserve date if you have any uncertainty.

vi. If this is the 2nd Compliance Conference addressing an issue, please add the following language:

"The parties have been advised that the dates contained herein will be strictly enforced and that failure to comply with this court's *orders* will result in the imposition of any appropriate sanction, including, but not limited to, monetary costs and sanctions, issue or defense preclusion, witness preclusion, and or the complete or partial striking of a pleading."

vii. Do not leave the courtroom until either the Justice, or one of the law clerks, have reviewed the forms. Copies of such orders are not scanned.

viii. Consult with the Justice's law clerks regarding any issues you cannot amicably resolve. *They serve as referees appointed by the Court to resolve disputes.*

D. *Instructions Applicable to Preliminary Conference Order Forms only.*

The time frames here are for initial Preliminary Conference Orders only; Compliance Conference Orders should generally have a *shorter* time frame.

i. Caption: Part 8, Justice Joan M. Kenney.

ii. Appearances: Please provide, legibly, your phone number and address in addition to your name.

Item 1: (Insurance Coverage): Select a date for insurance information to be provided not later than 21days from today's date. As set forth above, for this, and all items requiring a cut-off date, use an actual date such as "on or before December 31, 2009." Do not use "within 45 days," etc.

Item 2: (Bill of Particulars): Select an actual date for the demand to be served that is within 15 days of today's date and then the bill shall be served as per CPLR.

Item 3: (Medical Records/Authorizations): Select an actual date by which authorizations shall be served and be sure that the date is within 20 days of today's date. Medical records shall be served within 75 days of today's date.

Item 4: (Physical Examinations): Exams shall be held within 45 days of the deposition. A copy of the physician's report shall be furnished to plaintiff within 30 days of the exam.

Item 5: (Depositions): The court will assume you have consulted a calendar and clients when scheduling depositions. Designate a time and place for depositions and be as specific as possible regarding whom you will produce. You must also select an actual end date after which the right to depositions may be deemed waived. This end date for depositions must be within 4 months of today's date and may not be adjourned without court approval.

Item 6: Exchange of delineated items to occur within 21 days of today's date.

Item 7: (End date for disclosure): Select a date not later than eight months from today's date. If a party is more than 70 years of age, select a date not later than four months from today's date.

Item 8: (Impleader): Select a date not later than 45 days after your last scheduled deposition.

Item 9: (Compliance Conference): Pick a Thursday date not later than six months from today's date. Please verify with the Clerk that this is an available Thursday.

Item 10: (Dispositive motions): "Summary judgment motions *must* be within *30* days of the *filing* of the note of issue." The court uses filing, not service of the note of issue to measure the timeliness of dispositive motions, so be advised accordingly. The party filing the note of issue, shall notify all other parties to the action, in writing, of the filing date within 48 hours of the filing date.

Item 11: (Note of Issue): Select a date not later than 60 days after the date selected for the end date of disclosure in item 7.

Additional Directives: Counsel should indicate that they have received a copy of the Part 8 Rules (Jan. 2010 version).

4. Trial Dates

Unless otherwise directed, after a note of issue has been filed, the case will be assigned to Mediation I Trial Part 40 by the Trial Support Office. Part 8 will no longer maintain a separate pre-trial conference calendar on the matter. However, the matter may be referred to Part 8 after jury selection

5. Settlement Authority

Parties appearing in Part 8 must have settlement authority. A failure to appear with settlement authority, may be deemed in default or "unnecessary appearance" for the purpose of evaluating an application for fees, costs or sanctions.

Attorneys attending conferences must have authority to bind the party on all issues. Appearances by counsel without authority may be deemed a default.

HON. CYNTHIA S. KERN City IAS Part 52 (E-Filing Part), Room 328, 80 Centre Street (Trial and Motion Courtroom), Phone: (646) 386–3742; DCM Courtroom, 80 Centre Street, Room 103, (646) 386–3683; DCM Clerk's Office, 80 Centre Street, Room 102; Chambers Law Clerks: Rachel Fremmer, Esq., Aeri Pang, Esq., and Yael Wilkofsky, Esq.

Oral Argument on non-Discovery Motions: Wednesdays at 9:30 a.m. in the Trial and Motions Courtroom.

DCM Compliance Conferences, and Discovery Motions: Wednesdays at 2:00 p.m. in DCM Courtroom (room 103).

1. Communications with the DCM Clerk, Part Clerk and Chambers.

A. *DO NOT CALL CHAMBERS REGARDING SCHEDULING MATTERS AND REQUESTS FOR ADJOURNMENTS.* Any such calls will simply result in your being directed to the appropriate court clerk. Judge Kern's court attorneys do not handle adjournments.

i. Adjournment requests for Wednesday morning Early Settlement Conferences should be directed to the DCM Clerk's office.

ii. Adjournment requests for Wednesday afternoon DCM compliance conferences and appearances should be made by contacting the DCM Clerk.

iii. Adjournment requests for Wednesday morning motions and other appearances scheduled in the Trial and Motion Courtroom should be made by contacting the Courtroom Part Clerk.

B. *No ex parte communications.*

2. Motion Practice

A. Motions submitted on default in Room 130 are generally not scheduled for oral argument.

B. Non-discovery motions with opposition will automatically be scheduled for oral argument in the Trial and Motion Courtroom for a Wednesday morning after the final appearance in the Submission Part in Room 130 at 60 Centre Street.

C. *You need not send courtesy copies* of motions.

D. Please do not copy the court on letters exchanged between counsel.

E. If a case has settled while a motion is *sub judice, pleased so advise the Trial and Motion Courtroom Clerk IMMEDIATELY!*

F. *Send NOTHING to chambers unless previously directed to do so by the Court.* Stipulations, papers, etc. should be sent or delivered to the appropriate Clerk.

G. Please do not call Chambers or the Part Clerk to determine whether a decision has been issued. Inquiries as to the status of motions can be obtained from the court's "Supreme Court Records On–Line Library" ("Scroll"), access to which is available at no charge under "Case Information" on the website of the court (www.nycourts.gov/supctmanh).

3. General Instructions for Completing Compliance Conference Stipulation and Order Forms

A. Please write legibly with a black ball point pen. You must indicate the names, addresses, and telephone numbers of all counsel appearing at the conference.

B. Number the pages (e.g., 1 of 3, 2 of 3). At the top of page 1, please indicate whether this is the 1st, 2nd, or 3rd Compliance Order.

C. Use firm cut-off dates such as "on or before December 31, 2009." Do not use "within 45 days," etc.

D. Do not leave the courtroom until either the Justice or one of the court attorneys have reviewed your completed forms.

4. E-filing

Part 52 is a presumptive e-filing part. The New York State Courts Electronic Filing System ("NYS-CEF") is a means for filing legal papers and for serving those papers by electronic means. The system is accessible through a website located at this address: www.nycourts.gov/efile. In order to be able to use NYSCEF to file and serve documents, an attorney for a party to a case or a self-represented party must obtain a User Identification and Password. There is no fee for use of this system and courtesy copies of papers do not need to be provided in this part. For additional information, contact the NYS-CEF Resource Center at (646) 386-3033 or efile@courts.state.ny.us.

TRIAL REQUIREMENTS

1. Prior to the start of trial, please supply the court with the following:

1. All marked pleadings and bills of particular.

2. All prior decisions in the case.

3. Any Notices to Admit.

4. Copies of transcripts of depositions intended for use at trial.

5. Proposed jury verdict sheet.

6. A list of *all* requested PJI sections from the most current volume to be included in the final charge to the jury. You may list the section by number only, if it does not call for any characterization of the evidence or the contentions of the parties. If the section does call for a characterization or description of the evidence or contentions of the parties, you must supply such description of evidence or contention in writing. If you are requesting other language, not based on the PJI, you must provide the proposed language in writing, along with the appropriate citations. Please provide copies of any cases upon which you rely for charge language.

7. Copies of cases and authorities upon which you will be relying on for *in limine* or other applications. Provide a list of citations for the court reporter.

8. Copies of any statutes or sections from the Administrative Code or other rules and regulations which are pertinent to the case.

9. A list of proposed witnesses. If a witness needs an interpreter, please indicate the language and any dialect.

2. Please stipulate to all facts and documents not in dispute prior to trial. Have agreed-upon documents, photographs and other exhibits pre-marked into evidence by the court reporter while the jury is not present.

3. It is the duty of counsel, not court personnel, to make sure all subpoenaed documents have arrived in the subpoenaed records room at 60 Centre Street. Court personnel may only retrieve records from subpoenaed records when not needed in the courtroom.

4. The court will not engage in *ex parte* communications. Any phone calls to chambers must be made with all parties present. Avoid letters and emails, but if sent they must be copied to the other parties, or they will be returned unread.

HON. SHIRLEY W. KORNREICH Part 54, General IAS Part and Complex Litigation Part (E–Filing)[also Commercial Division Part (see Commercial Division website)], Room 228, Phone: 646–386–3362

Motions: Motions are heard on Thursdays at 9:30 AM. Discovery motions a re strongly discouraged. If a discovery dispute arises after a preliminary or compliance conference order is issued, counsel should, prior to making a motion, telephone the Part Clerk, Ms. Celia Rodriguez, at 646–386–3362 to advance the date of the next conference scheduled in the order. Waiting for the next scheduled conference is not automatic "good cause" for failing to proceed with discovery orders. Similarly, counsel are cautioned that one party's non-compliance with directives of the court will not automatically excuse other parties' non-compliance.

Orders to show cause will be returnable in the Part. When an Order to Show Cause is filed prior to the scheduling of a preliminary conference, the court will hold the preliminary conference on the return date of the Order to Show Cause.

No motions may be adjourned without consent of the court. Absent emergency, requests for adjournments must be submitted to the Part at least two business days before the return date. If the motion is adjourned, all papers are due in the Part on the Monday before the adjourned date.

Counsel are reminded that the CPLR does not provide for any sur-reply papers, however denominated. Nor does the court accept reply papers on Orders to Show Cause. The submission of papers or letters after the return date is not permitted. Sur-replies and other papers or letters addressed to the substance of motions will not be read or considered. Except in cases electronically filed through the New York State Courts Electronic Filing System ("NYS-CEF"), courtesy copies should not be submitted unless specifically requested by the court. Information on whether decisions have been rendered should be obtained by checking with the appropriate clerk's office.

The court will no longer send courtesy copies of decisions to represented parties unless their case is "e-filed" through the NYSCEF System. However, the court will continue to send courtesy copies to unrepresented parties. Please do not contact the Part Clerk for a courtesy copy; the Part will *only* provide courtesy copies in the instances outlined above.

Calls to chambers inquiring about the status of a particular motion or special proceeding should not be made. However, if a motion is withdrawn or a special proceeding is settled, the parties should promptly contact the Part Clerk, Ms. Celia Rodriguez, by faxing to the Part (212–374–6360) a letter of withdrawal or a stipulation of settlement and discontinuance. If the parties are then unable to reach Ms. Rodriguez, then they may contact chambers to provide such information.

Conferences: All preliminary conferences in newly assigned cases are scheduled for Thursdays at 9:30 A.M. Preliminary conferences may not be adjourned and must be held within 30 days of the Request for Judicial Intervention. All stipulations of adjournment are subject to court approval and must be on consent, in writing. If there is no consent, the date must be honored and counsel must appear for an oral application for the adjournment.

Counsel appearing at a preliminary, compliance or status conference are expected to be familiar with the case and to have the authority to discuss all discovery issues and possible settlement. Counsel must bring

copies of all prior discovery orders to conferences. If there is a dispute as to whether discovery requests are proper or responses are sufficient, counsel should bring relevant documents and transcripts to the conference. At a compliance conference, counsel who will actually be trying the case or an attorney fully familiar with trial counsel's schedule must appear. Further, where a compliance or status conference concerns the scheduling of depositions, counsel must have with them dates on which they and/or their clients are available to appear.

Trials: Trial dates scheduled by the court are firm and may only be adjourned upon application based upon emergency. At least three days prior to any scheduled trial, counsel and pro se parties are required to serve and submit the following:

a. A witness list, any expert reports not previously provided, and any pretrial memoranda and in limine motions;

b. Proof of filing the Note of Issue; for a jury trial, at least five days before trial, counsel shall obtain from the Part Clerk a Jury Request Form.

c. Marked pleadings and the bill of particulars;

d. In a jury trial, requests to charge, contentions and a proposed verdict sheet.

If a case is settled, the parties must promptly fax to the Court a stipulation of settlement and discontinuance outlining the terms of the settlement.

HON. DORIS LING–COHAN Part 36, General IAS Part, Room 428, Phone: 646–386–3733

PART 36 General Procedural Information:

Only admitted attorneys familiar with the case may appear on matters before the Court.

Motions: All motions (except orders to show cause) shall be made returnable to: Motion Support Office, Room 130, 60 Centre Street. Oral argument will be scheduled at the Court's discretion, and will generally be held on Thursday morning at 9:30 a.m., Room 279 at 80 Centre Street, unless otherwise directed, by the Court. Parties will be notified, should oral argument be required.

Adjournments: shall be by stipulation, with Court approval, not to exceed one month, and must be requested by the parties at least two (2) days prior to the return/argument date; stipulation to be submitted to the Part Clerk, at 80 Centre Street, Room 279.

Once a motion is fully submitted in the Motion Support Office, the Court will not accept additional papers, unless by stipulation of the parties.

Motion Guidelines:

1. Any references to EBT testimony shall cite to the exact page and line numbers relied upon rather than merely attaching the entire transcript or "relevant portions"; full transcripts shall be supplied.

2. Protruding exhibit tabs shall be used to reference all exhibits.

3. On motions to renew and reargue, a separate appendix containing the original motion, and all papers submitted, with a copy of the Court's decision shall be provided. The appendix shall contain protruding exhibit tabs, as was originally provided to the Court. Such appendix shall be labeled "Appendix Containing Decision, Original Motion Papers".

4. Plastic covers shall not be provided to the Court.

5. Courtesy copies shall not be provided, unless directed by the Court.

6. Counsel is requested to ensure that any staples are not protruding.

Discovery Issues: Prior to filing a discovery related motion, if still unable to resolve discovery issues after efforts have been made as required by 22 NYCRR § 202.7(a), parties are encouraged to write a letter to the Court, with a copy to opposing counsel, requesting a conference, if a regularly scheduled conference is not imminent. In addition, all discovery issues shall be brought to the Court's attention at regularly scheduled discovery compliance conferences, or shall be considered waived.

Discovery Conferences: Discovery Compliance Conferences are generally held on Fridays (unless notified otherwise), in Room 279, at 80 Centre Street, on a staggered schedule, beginning at 9:30 a.m. Counsel appearing shall be prepared to discuss all outstanding discovery issues, as well as the facts of the case and settlement options. Parties shall advise the Court of any pending motions, and if any party is self-represented. There shall be no adjournments, unless by written stipulation, with Court approval; such stipulation shall be received at least two (2) days prior to the scheduled conference, to be delivered/mailed to: Part 36 Clerk, Room 279, 80 Centre Street, N.Y., N.Y. 10013. When a note of issue is filed, counsel shall send a courtesy copy to the Part 36 Clerk.

Dispositive Motions: Dispositive motions shall be filed within 60 days of filing a note of issue. The filing of a motion for summary judgment will not stay the discovery process, nor mediation.

Facsimiles: The Court does not accept faxes, unless prior permission has been received from the Court. Any fax received without prior Court permission will not be considered.

Letters: Do not send letters to the Court in triplicate (i.e. via regular mail, fax and hand delivery); please choose one delivery method when sending a letter to the Court.

Conference Calls: To the extent possible, please arrange conference calls between 3 and 3:30 p.m., unless otherwise directed by the Court.

HON. JOAN B. LOBIS Part 6, Medical Malpractice IAS Part (E–Filing), Room 345, Phone: 646–386–3312

Motions: Tues., 9:30 AM **Conferences:** Tues., As directed by the court

HON. JOAN A. MADDEN Part 11, General IAS Part (E–Filing), Room 351, Phone: 646–386–3314

Motions: Thurs., 9:30 AM **Conferences:** Thurs., 9:30 AM

HON. DOUGLAS MCKEON, Part 38 Medical Malpractice IAS Part, Room 408

Settlement Conferences: Third Wednesday of each month at 10 AM

Other Appearances: Every Thursday

HON. DONNA MILLS Part 58, Trial Part, Room 574, 111 Centre Street, Phone: 646–386–3347

HON. PETER MOULTON Part 40 B

HON. JEFFREY K. OING Part 48, General IAS Part, Room 412, Phone: 646–386–3298

Principal Law Clerk: Tracey A. Dunn, Esq., 646–386–5723, tdunn@courts.state.ny.us

Assistant Law Clerk: Lauren B. Jacobson, Esq., 646–386–5723, lbjacobs@courts.state.ny.us

Facsimile Telephone Number: 212–419–8462

Counsel are advised that there shall be no ex parte communications with Chambers.

GENERAL PART RULES

1. All adjournments (motions, conferences, trials) require prior court approval.

2. A court approved adjournment shall be reduced to a written stipulation prepared by the requesting counsel and must be signed by all counsel. If applicable, the stipulation shall set forth a briefing schedule.

3. Any paper and/or correspondence shall not be faxed or e-mailed to the court unless expressly permitted by the court.

MOTIONS: Friday, 9:30 a.m.

1. Motions returnable in the Motion Submission Part, Room 130, and assigned to the Part are on submission unless the court advises counsel that oral argument is required. Notice of such argument will be transmitted to counsel by the court. Courtesy copies are not to be submitted to the court.

2. Orders to Show Cause are returnable in the Part. Opposition papers to an OSC will be accepted on the return date unless otherwise directed by the court. Reply papers are not permitted, absent court approval. An OSC providing for temporary injunctive relief pending hearing of the OSC shall not be adjourned absent good cause.

3. Discovery motions are strongly discouraged. If a discovery dispute arises after the issuance of a preliminary or compliance conference order, counsel

shall telephone Chambers to seek a conference telephone call with all counsel to resolve the discovery dispute. If the issue cannot be resolved, counsel may move for appropriate relief.

4. If a motion is withdrawn or resolved, counsel shall promptly notify Chambers by facsimile.

5. A copy of a decision can be obtained from www.nycourts.gov/supctmanh under "Case Information", www.nycourts.gov under E-courts, or from the County Clerk. Please do not call the Part Clerk or Chambers.

CONFERENCES (Preliminary, Compliance, Status, Pre–Trial): Friday, 10:30 a.m.

1. All cases are heard in the order in which they are ready. All counsel must be present for the case to be deemed ready. Do not check in with the Part Clerk until all sides are present.

2. Default applications will be entertained by the court at 11:30 a.m.

3. Counsel appearing shall be familiar with the case and have the authority to discuss all discovery issues and to participate in a settlement conference.

4. Pending an appearance with the court, counsel are advised to confer with each other and draft a preliminary or compliance conference order or stipulation providing for all remaining discovery. Discovery disputes will be resolved at the conference. Discovery orders/stipulations must set forth specific dates for all deadlines, including IMEs and impleaders.

TRIALS

1. Trials are scheduled for a date certain, and are held every day of the week except Fridays.

2. For jury trials, counsel shall submit to the court at least seven (7) days prior to trial a witness list, proposed jury instructions, and a proposed verdict sheet. If the proposed jury instructions are verbatim from the Pattern Jury Instructions, providing the PJI numbers will be sufficient. If a PJI instruction is modified, exact language shall be submitted supported by appropriate authority.

3. For bench trials, counsel shall submit a witness list, proposed findings of fact, and a memorandum of law.

4. For all trials, counsel shall submit marked pleadings and a copy of the bill of particulars. If a witness needs an interpreter, counsel shall notify the court in writing seven (7) days prior to trial. Please indicate the language and dialect.

5. No adjournments will be granted if a witness is unavailable to testify unless good cause is shown.

HON. EILEEN A. RAKOWER Part 15, General IAS Part, Room 308, 80 Centre Street, 646–386–3374

HON. SALIANN SCARPULLA Part 19, General IAS Part, Room 279, 80 Centre Street, Phone:

646–386–3277, Chambers Room 283, 80 Centre Street, 646–386–3690

Motions: Weds., 9:30 AM **Pre–Trial Conferences:** Weds., 11:15 AM **Pre–Note Conferences:** Weds., 2:15 PM

Principal Law Clerks (646–386–3690): Ms. Ariella Zarfati, Esq. and Ms. Danielle Schweiloch, Esq.

1. Communications with the Part Clerk and Chambers.

A. *DO NOT CALL CHAMBERS REGARDING SCHEDULING MATTERS AND REQUESTS FOR ADJOURNMENTS.* Adjournment requests for motions and other appearances scheduled in the Courtroom should be made by contacting the Part Clerk.

B. *No ex parte communications.*

2. Motion Practice

A. Motions submitted on default in Room 130 are generally not scheduled for oral argument.

B. Non-discovery motions with opposition will automatically be scheduled for oral argument in the Trial and Motion Courtroom for a Wednesday morning after the final appearance in the Submission Part in Room 130 at 60 Centre Street.

C. *You need not send courtesy copies* of motions.

D. *Please do not* copy the court on letters exchanged between counsel.

E. If a case has settled while a motion is *sub judice, please so advise the Trial and Motion Courtroom Clerk IMMEDIATELY!*

F. *Send NOTHING to chambers, unless previously directed to do so by the Court.* Stipulations, papers, etc. should be sent or delivered to the appropriate Clerk.

G. Please do not call Chambers or the Part Clerk to determine whether a decision has issued. Inquiries as to the status of motions can be obtained from the court's "Supreme Court Records On–Line Library" ("Scroll"), access to which is available at no charge under "Case Information" on the website of the court (www.nycourts.gov/supctmanh).

3. General Instructions for Completing Compliance Conference Stipulation and Order Forms

A. Please write legibly with a black ball point pen. You must indicate the names, addresses, and telephone numbers of all counsel appearing at the conference.

B. Number the pages (e.g., 1 of 3, 2 of 3). At the top of page 1, please indicate whether this is the 1st, 2nd, or 3rd Compliance Order.

C. Use firm cut-off dates such as "on or before December 31, 2009." Do not use "within 45 days," etc.

D. If this is the 3rd Compliance Conference, please add the following language: "The parties have been advised that the dates contained herein will be strictly enforced and that failure to comply with this court's will result in the imposition of any appropriate sanction, including but not limited to monetary costs and sanctions, issue or defense preclusion, witness preclusion, and or the complete or partial striking of a pleading."

E. Do not leave the courtroom until either the Justice or one of the court attorneys have reviewed your completed forms.

Trial Requirements

1. Prior to the start of trial, please supply the court with the following:

a) All marked pleadings and bills of particulars.

b) All prior decisions in the case.

c) Any Notices to Admit.

d) Copies of transcripts of depositions intended for use at trial.

e) Proposed jury verdict sheet.

f) A list of *all* requested **PJI sections** from the most current volume to be included in the final charge to the jury. You may list the section by number only, if it does not call for any characterization of the evidence or the contentions of the parties. *If the section does call for a characterization or description of the evidence or contentions of the parties, you must supply such description of evidence or contention in writing. If you are requesting other language, not based on the PJI, you must provide the proposed language in writing, along with the appropriate citations. Please provide copies of any cases upon which you rely for charge language.*

(g) A short (one or two lines) summary of your party's claims to be used by the court as part of the preliminary instructions given to the jury before opening statements.

(h) Copies of cases and authorities upon which you will be relying on for *in limine* or other applications. Provide a list of citations for the court reporter.

i) Copies of any statutes or sections from the Administrative Code or other rules and regulations which are pertinent to the case.

j) Three copies of a list of proposed witnesses. If a witness needs an interpreter, please indicate the language and any dialect. One copy goes to the part clerk, one copy to the court reporter and one part to the Court.

2. Please stipulate to all facts and documents not in dispute prior to trial. Have agreed-upon documents, photographs and other exhibits pre-marked into evidence by the court reporter while the jury is not present.

3. Please bring copies of all exhibits for all parties and the Court.

4. It is the duty of counsel, not court personnel, to make sure all subpoenaed documents have arrived in the subpoenaed records room at 60 Centre Street. Court personnel may only retrieve records from 60 Centre when not needed in the courtroom.

5. The court will not engage in *ex parte* communications. Any phone calls to chambers must be made with all parties present. Avoid letters and e-mails, but if sent they must be copied to the other parties, or they will be returned unread.

6. If you have a medical or other condition that prevents you from standing, please bring it to the Court's attention outside the hearing of the jury so that you are not put in an awkward position in front of the jury.

HON. ALICE SCHLESINGER Part 16, Medical Malpractice IAS Part (E–Filing), Room 222, Phone: 646–386–3318

Motions: Wed., 9:30 AM (Discovery), 2 PM (Substantive) **Conferences:** Wed., 9:30 AM

HON. MARTIN SCHOENFELD Part 28, Room 609, Phone: 646–386–3232

HON. MARTIN SHULMAN, Part 1, General IAS Part and Complex Litigation Part (E–Filing), Room 325, 60 Centre Street, Phone: 646–386–5758; also Tax Certiorari and Condemnation Part (E-filing).

Motions and Conferences: Tues., on a staggered schedule. Any requests for adjournments must be made to the Part Clerk by conference call with all parties represented.

HON. GEORGE J. SILVER, Part 22 (Motor Vehicle Part), Room 136, 80 Centre Street, N.Y., N.Y 10013 Phone: 646–386–3271

DCM Clerk: 80 Centre Street, Room 102, 646–386–3682

DCM Courtroom (Mon. & Fri. AM): 80 Centre Street, Room 103, 646–386–3683; DCM Judicial Hearing Officer: Hon. William Leibovitz, JHO

Principal Court Attorney: Dennis M. Reo, Esq.

Courtroom Part 22 Clerk: 646–386–3271

Differentiated Case Managers: 646–386–3682

Oral Argument on Motions: Wednesdays at 9:30 a.m. in IAS Part 22 Courtroom, Room 136

DCM Compliance Conferences: Mondays and Fridays at 9:30 a.m. in the DCM Courtroom, Room 103

1. Communications with the DCM Clerk, Part Clerk and Chambers

A. *Scheduling Matters and Request for Adjournments:*

For all scheduling matters and requests for adjournments, please call the appropriate Court Clerk.

Do not call chambers. Neither the Justice nor his Court Attorneys handle adjournments.

- Adjournment requests for all appearances including oral arguments on motions, scheduled in Part 22 court room should be made by contacting the Part Clerk.

- Adjournment requests for Monday morning or Friday morning DCM compliance conferences or any other DCM appearance should be made by contacting the assigned DCM Case Manager. All inquiries concerning the filing of or extension of the time to file a Note of Issue should be directed to the DCM Clerk's office.

B. *No ex parte communications.* Please do not e-mail the Justice or her Court Attorneys. It is not necessary to copy the court on letters exchanged between counsel. Do not send anything directly to chambers, unless previously advised to do so by the Court. Stipulations, papers, CD–Roms, etc. should be sent or delivered to the appropriate Clerk. The Clerks accept documents for filing, where appropriate. Do not deliver opposition to motions pending in the Submission Calendar to any Clerk at 80 Centre Street.

2. Motion Practice

A. All discovery disputes should be directed to the assigned DCM Case Manager who will promptly schedule a resolution conference. Only after this conference is held shall any discovery motion be filed. The date the resolution conference occurred should be included in the good faith affirmation filed with the motion. If the Court has granted permission to a party to file a discovery motion without first scheduling a DCM resolution conference, please indicate this on the Notice of Motion and flag it by circling in red or highlighting that directive.

B. Motions submitted on default in the Submission Part, Room 130 at 60 Centre Street are generally *not* scheduled for oral argument.

C. Motions with opposition will automatically be scheduled for oral argument in the Part 22 Courtroom for Wednesday, 9:30 a.m., approximately two weeks after the final appearance in the Submission Part.

D. If a case has settled while a motion is *sub judice,* please advise the Part Clerk or chamber staff in writing immediately.

E. Except in unusual circumstances, all decisions are scanned and available on the internet and can be accessed through E–LAW or SCROLL (www.nycourts.gov/supctmanh.—click on "Case Information" on top of page). Please do not call Chambers or the Part Clerk to ask whether a decision has issued. Such inquiries are properly made to the County Clerk's office.

F. All Dispositive Motions must be made no later than 60 days after filing of the note of issue—no exception without leave of the court.

G. Do not attempt to file the note of issue if you have not completed all discovery before your deadline. You must schedule a DCM compliance conference to have the note of issue date extended to a date when all discovery is complete. This avoids unnecessary motion practice to strike the note of issue.

3. Appearances

A. Attorneys appearing for oral argument or any scheduled conference on any case must be thoroughly familiar with the case, and have authority to settle the case.

B. Parties may request an adjournment by telephoning the Part Clerk at (646) 386–3271. An adjournment by telephone must be made by conference call and only on consent of all parties.

C. An appearance for a conference or oral argument scheduled in IAS Part 22 Courtroom will be excused only if a stipulation, executed by all parties fully resolving the pending motion or settling the case, is submitted to Room 136, two days prior to the appearance date.

D. An appearance for a conference scheduled in DCM Courtroom may be excused, for good cause, by contacting the assigned DCM Case Manager in Room 102, two days prior to the appearance date.

HON. ANIL SINGH Part 61, General IAS Part, Room 320, 80 Centre Street, Phone: 646–386–3218.

HON. JANE S. SOLOMON Part 55, General IAS Part and Tax Cert and Condemnation Part (E–Filing), Room 432, Phone: 646–386–3289 **Motions**: Mon., 10 AM (unless otherwise directed. The court attempts to stagger appearances). Contested discovery motions will generally be set down for an appearance in the Part. Other contested motions will be argued as determined by the court. The Part Clerk will phone the movant and give notice of the date and time of argument. Movant must notify all parties and confirm availabilities. Because counsel are so consulted, adjournments beyond the first as of right are not freely given; except for personal emergencies, no consideration is given to requests for adjournments made after the Thursday before argument. Counsel for all parties must appear at all arguments. Absent court order, post note of issue dispositive motions shall be within 60 days thereof.

Conferences: Mon., AM or PM as set by the court. The court attempts to stagger appearances.

Orders to Show Cause: On orders to show cause returnable in the Part, originals of all subsequent papers should be delivered to the Part shortly after service. The court will attempt to review proposed orders as soon after presentation as possible. To expedite review, counsel may telephone the Part or the Law Secretary to make an appointment.

Courtroom Operations: Counsel in any case assigned to Part 55 who seek to establish or alter a discovery schedule should call the Part Clerk to arrange a conference. Written requests for conferences should be concise. Communications relating to all pending matters should be directed to the Part. Materials submitted for signature must be accompanied by a brief letter of explanation.

Expert disclosure is governed by the CPLR. Cf., Rule 11 infra.

SPECIAL REFEREES' PART (PART SRP)

RULES AND LIST OF JUDICIAL HEARING OFFICERS AND SPECIAL REFEREES

SPECIAL REFEREES' PART (Part SRP), HON. JOHN BRADLEY, JHO, Presiding

RULES GOVERNING REFERENCES

The Special Referee Assignment Calendar will be called promptly at 9:30 AM in Room 300 at 60 Centre Street, unless otherwise posted. There is no second call of the calendar.

Order of Reference; Information Sheet: Issues referred to a Special Referee are limited to those specifically set forth in the Order of Reference. Unless otherwise provided in the Order, counsel must consult and, within 15 days from the date o submit a fully completed Information Sheet to the Special Referee Clerk, Motion Support Office, Room 119, at 60 Centre Street, by fax (212–401–9186) or e-mail (spref@courts.state.ny.us). The Information Sheet is accessible on the court's website (the address of which is: www.nycourts.gov/supctmanh) at the "References" link under "Courthouse Procedures". It is vital that counsel set forth in the Information Sheet as accurately as possible the estimated length of the hearing and the number of witnesses to be called by each side; this information is required in order efficiently to assign the matter to a JHO/Special Referee. Upon receipt of the completed Information Sheet, the Special Referee Clerk will place the matter on the calendar of Part SRP for the earliest available date. Cases are assigned to a JHO/Special Referee upon their first appearance in Part SRP and the hearing will commence on the original hearing date. Therefore, all attorneys must have their witnesses and exhibits present and be ready to proceed to the hearing on the first appearance in Part SRP, subject only to the following procedures regarding adjournments.

Adjournments: One adjournment (maximum four weeks) may be obtained on consent. A copy of a stipulation of all parties must be submitted to the Special Referee Clerk *in advance of the original Part SRP appearance date*. Prior to execution of the stipulation, counsel must consult with the Special Referee Clerk and obtain an adjourned date that is an available hearing date in the Part. That date must be inserted in the stipulation. No other adjournments will be allowed except upon a showing of extraordinary circumstances (e.g., sudden illness of counsel or a witness) upon application to Judge Bradley in Part SRP. If such an application is to be made, the applying attorney must notify all other attorneys *in advance of the appearance date.*

Hearings: The hearing will be conducted in the same manner as a trial before a Justice without a jury (CPLR 4318, 4320 (a))(the proceeding will be recorded by a court reporter, the rules of evidence apply, etc.) Unless otherwise directed by the JHO/Special Referee for good cause shown, hearings shall proceed from day to day until completion. To comply with this requirement, counsel must arrange their own schedules and those of their witnesses accordingly and, if needed, adjourn the commencement date of the hearing on consent as above provided.

Restoration to Calendar: A reference may be marked off, but only where a compelling reason is shown (e.g., bankruptcy stay (general scheduling preferences of counsel do not constitute such a reason)), or in the event of no appearance by either side. If the reference is marked off due to nonappearance, a new order from the assigned Justice will be required to restore the reference to the calendar. Counsel must serve upon the Special Referee Clerk a copy of any stay order or order lifting a stay previously directed.

Mechanics of Obtaining Adjournments and Restorations: Copies of stipulations for an initial adjournment in compliance herewith may be transmitted to the Special Referee Clerk by fax (212–401–9186) or e-mail (spref@courts.state.ny.us)(counsel for a party shall retain the original stipulation); if the said adjournment is requested in compliance with these Rules, no appearance will be required in these instances. As to restorations that do not require an order of the assigned Justice, contact the Special Referee Clerk.

Communications Regarding References: Please direct all inquiries to the Special Referee Clerk, Motion Support Office, Room 119 at 646–386–3028 or by e-mail.

Judicial Hearing Officers / Special Referees:

Hon. John A.K. Bradley, JHO	Part 90R		646–386–3028 (Special Referee Clerk)
Hon. Beverly Cohen, JHO	Part 84R	80 Centre St., Room 116	646–386–3719
Hon. Phyllis Gangel–Jacob, JHO	Part 91R	Room 665	646–386–3205
Hon. William McCooe, JHO	Part 92R	Room 527	646–386–3223

Hon. Stanley L. Sklar, JHO	Part 93R	Room 564	646–386–3165
Hon. Louis Crespo, Jr.	Part 85R	71 Thomas St., Room 203	**646–386–3794**
Hon. Nicholas Figueroa	Part 95R	Room 556	646–386–3186
Hon. Lancelot B. Hewitt	Part 81/R	80 Centre St., Room 321	646–386–3680
Hon. Sue Ann Hoahng	Part 89R	80 Centre St., Room 476	646–386–3676
Hon. Edward H. Lehner	Part 94R	Room 659	646–386–3171
Hon. Steven E. Liebman	Part 86R	Room 641	**646–386–3662**
Hon. Marilyn Sugarman	Part 88R	Room 651	212–256–7839

HON. MICHAEL D. STALLMAN Part 21, Transit/City Transit Part, Room 278, 80 Centre Street, Phone: 646–386–3738

Motions & Conferences: Thursdays.

Papers: Counsel are encouraged to submit papers with a readable typeface in large print (e.g., Arial—14 point).

HON. MILTON A. TINGLING Part 44, General IAS Part, Room 321, Courtroom Clerk: 646–386–3370

HON. ROBERT E. TORRES Part 29

HON. LAURA VISITACION–LEWIS Part 26, Guardianship Part, Room 355, Phone: 646–386–3308

Motions: Thurs., 9:30 AM **Conferences:** Thurs., 2:15 PM

HON. LOTTIE E. WILKINS Part 18, Trial & Art. 81 Part, Room 104, 71 Thomas St., Phone: 646–386–3850

HON. PAUL WOOTEN, Part 7, General IAS Part, Room 341, 60 Centre Street Courtroom Phone: 646–386–3746, Facsimile: 212–374–3282

Principal Law Clerk: Lyssa M. Sampson, Esq. 646–386–3580

Assistant Law Clerk: Erin M. Gelfand, Esq. 646–386–3256

Part 7 General Information:

Only admitted attorneys familiar with the case who have the authority to discuss all discovery issues and participate in a settlement conference may appear on matters before the Court.

Motions: Oral argument on motions are at the Court's discretion and are generally scheduled on Wednesdays at 9:30 A.M. and 2:30 P.M.

Motion Guidelines:

- Motions (except Orders to Show Cause) shall be made returnable to: Motion Submission Part, Room 130, 60 Centre Street, unless directed by the Court.

- There is no check in for motions.

- The calendar will be called once, there is no second calendar call. If all parties are not present when the calendar is called, notify the part clerk when all parties are present. Oral argument will only be heard once all parties are present.

- Protruding exhibit tabs shall be used to reference all exhibits

- In the event that a motion has been resolved by withdrawal or settlement of the case, counsel must notify the court prior to the Wednesday calendar by promptly calling the Part Clerk and faxing to the Court a letter of withdrawal or a stipulation of settlement and discontinuance.

- In the event that the Note of Issue has been filed prior to a scheduled status conference, no appearance is necessary if counsel has notified the part clerk prior to the conference.

- If there is a discrepancy between the relief sought in your Notice of Motion and the relief sought in your supporting motion papers, the notice of motion is controlling.

- Courtesy copies shall not be provided, unless directed by the Court.

- A copy of a decision can be obtained from www.nycourts.gov/supctmanh under "Case Information," www.nycourts.gov under E-courts, or from the County Clerk. Please do not call the Part Clerk or Chambers.

Discovery Conferences: Conferences in pre-note cases are generally scheduled Wednesdays at 11:00 A.M and 2:30 P.M., or at such other day and time as the court may direct. Conferences on special proceedings may be directed by the Court.

Conference Guidelines:

- There is no check in for conferences.

- If appearing for a preliminary conference, use the dates provided in the Judge's Directives which are located on the same table as the blank order forms.

- Once all sides are present, counsel shall confer with each other and draft a preliminary or compliance conference order or stipulation providing for all remaining discovery, to the fullest extent possible. Place the drafted order or stipulation in the basket near the Part Clerk's desk, sit down and wait for your case to be called. Discovery disputes will be resolved at the conference.

- Do not fill in the Note of Issue date, this is to be determined by the Court.

- Discovery orders/stipulations must set forth specific dates for all deadlines.

Dispositive Motions: Dispositive motions shall be filed within 60 days of filing the note of issue. The filing of a motion for summary judgment will not stay the discovery process, nor mediation.

Adjournments: Adjournment requests for motions and other appearances scheduled in the Courtroom should be made by contacting the Part Clerk no less than two days prior to the scheduled appearance.

Discovery Issues: Prior to filing a discovery related motion, if still unable to resolve discovery issues after efforts have been made as required by 22 NYCRR § 202.7(a), parties should call the Part Clerk to schedule a conference, if a regularly scheduled conference is not imminent (*i.e.*, within 30 days).

Orders to Show Cause: Orders to Show Cause are returnable to the Part. Opposition papers to an OSC will be accepted on the return date unless otherwise directed by the Court. Reply papers are not permitted, absent court approval. An OSC providing for temporary injunctive relief pending hearing of the OSC shall not be adjourned absent good cause.

Letters: Motions made in the form of a letter will not be accepted, unless specifically directed by the Court. If directed by the Court, an affidavit of service of the letter must be attached.

Facsimile: The Court does not accept faxes, unless prior permission has been received from the Court. Any fax received without prior Court permission will not be considered.

HON. GEOFFREY D. WRIGHT Part 62, City Part, Room 122, 80 Centre Street, Phone: 646–386–3728.

HON. LOUIS B. YORK Part 2, General IAS Part, Room 205, 71 Thomas St., Phone: 646–386–3852

Argued Motions: Wed., 9:30 AM. Conferences and Discovery Motions: Wed., 2 PM

Courtroom Operations: The court will consider applications for adjournments only by telephone conference including all parties, or by stipulation with permission of the court, or by application on the return date of the motion or conference.

Listing of Parts in Order and Justices Assigned (excluding Commercial)

Part	Justice
1	Shulman
2	York
5	Jaffe
6	Lobis
7	Wooten
8	Kenney
9	Cooper
10	Gische
11	Madden
12	Feinman
15	Rakower
16	Schlesinger
17	Goodman
18	Wilkins
19	Scarpulla
20	Kaplan
21	Stallman
22	Silver
23	Braun
24	Gesmer
25	Hagler
26	Visitacion–Lewis
28	Schoenfeld
29	Torres
30	Heitler
31	Drager
32	Huff
33	Hunter
35	Edmead
36	Ling–Cohan
38	McKeon
40, 27C	Gammerman (JHO)
40 B	Moulton
44	Tingling
46	Billings
48	Oing
51	Evans
52	Kern
54	Kornreich
55	Solomon
57	Friedman
58	Mills
59	James
61	Singh
62	Wright

[1] The motion days set forth set forth in this section consist of the days on which Justices normally hear motions that have been submitted in the Motion Support Office Courtroom (Room 130) and then rescheduled for argument in the relevant Part. However, Justices may of course schedule argument on orders to show cause at other times as need requires.

RULES

In addition to the Rules that follow, procedures have been developed to simplify and expedite the submission of papers to the court in electronically-filed cases. Many documents can be submitted, processed by the court and acted upon by the assigned Justice without counsel having to make any trip to the courthouse. Counsel are advised to consult the court's Protocol on this subject (posted on the court's website at www.nycourts.gov/supctmanh). Parts II and IV of these Rules are inapplicable to condemnation and tax certiorari cases. Emergency medical hearings and proceedings under the Mental Hygiene Law have their own special rules. Part V is applicable to matrimonial cases only.

I. RULES REGARDING THE PUBLIC ACCESS ON–LINE PROJECT ("SCROLL")

Rule A–1. Information in Documents Filed with the County Clerk and the Court

Attorneys filing pleadings and other documents with the County Clerk or the Court that fall within a category of document that is, as explained in the Court's Notice to the Bar on the Public Access Project, included in the Scroll Public Access Project system or that shall hereafter be so included shall not set out in such documents social security numbers, bank account numbers, the names of minor children, dates of birth, health information concerning any individual and other similar sensitive information, or, if doing so is unavoidable, shall, to the extent practical, provide only a portion of the information (e.g., some but not all digits of an account number, initials only in place of the names of minor children). If circumstances make it unavoidable to include such information in full in a document that is or may be included in the system, the party preparing the document shall apply to the Court, in the manner set forth hereafter, for a directive restricting access to the document in the system. The following documents will not be included in the Scroll Public Access Project system: documents filed or issued by the Court in matters pursuant to the Mental Hygiene Law, matrimonial cases, and cases that are sealed by order of a Justice pursuant to Part 216 of the Uniform Rules for the Trial Courts, and other individual documents as to which the Justice assigned so directs.

Rule A–2. Application for Restriction of Access to Records

A party or person who claims that the availability of a document in the Public Access Project system may cause harm to that party or person or who seeks to limit access in compliance with Rule 1 may apply to the Court for a directive restricting access. Any such application shall be made as follows. If the case has been assigned to a Justice, a request shall be made to the Justice by letter describing the document as to which a restriction on access is sought and explaining the reasons why such a restriction is appropriate. If the case has not been assigned to a Justice, the party shall direct such a request to the Administrative Judge. The Court on its own initiative may direct that access be restricted. An interested party or person may apply by letter to remove a document from the Scroll database if, notwithstanding this notice and rules, a document is posted on the Public Access Project system that contains sensitive information access to which in this form causes harm to that party or person.

Rule A–3. Form of Restriction on Access to Records

Where the Court grants grants a request to limit access to a document in the Scroll Public Access Project system or issues a directive sua sponte, the directive shall take the form of an administrative direction to the staff of the Court that the document in question not be included in the Scroll system or, if already included therein, that it be deleted from the database. Any such directive as may be issued in a case in which documents are otherwise available in the Scroll system shall not affect the status of the County Clerk hard-copy case file, which is open to the public unless otherwise ordered by the Court pursuant to Part 216 of the Uniform Rules for the Trial Courts.

Rule A–4. Notices of Motion and Notices of Petition

Any party who files a notice of motion or notice of petition with the Court shall submit therewith to the relevant back office a photocopy of the notice (not including the supporting papers).

II. GENERAL RULES

Rule 1. Appearances by Counsel; Knowledge and Authority

Counsel who appear at preliminary conferences must have sufficient familiarity with the case and authority to be able to discuss a discovery schedule in a meaningful way and to enter into agreements with regard thereto. Counsel who appear at other conferences and at the argument of motions must be familiar with the entire case in regard to which they appear and fully authorized to enter into agreements, both substantive and procedural, on behalf of their clients.

Rule 2. Settlements and Discontinuances; Change of Counsel

(a) If an action is settled or discontinued, a stipulation shall be submitted promptly to the County Clerk with the appropriate fee (Cashier's Office, Room 160) and a copy shall be forwarded to the Part in question. If the case is otherwise disposed of, in whole or in part, counsel for the defendant affected shall immediately file a letter with the Clerk of the Part. If at the time of a settlement, discontinuance or other disposition a submitted motion is sub judice that is rendered moot, in whole or in part, by the disposition, or where a motion previously submitted is withdrawn, it is imperative that the Part be informed immediately.

(b) If counsel is changed on consent, a copy of the form shall be filed in the Trial Support Office (Room 158). Filing with the County Clerk does not suffice. Absent submission of a consent form, an attorney of record will continue as such unless a motion for leave to withdraw is granted. If such an order is issued, counsel must serve a copy on the Trial Support Office and all other counsel. A notice of appearance shall be filed by substitute counsel with the Trial Support Office and the Clerk of the Part.

Rule 3. Information on Cases

County Clerk data, case history information from the court's Civil Case Information System, and many documents from the case file of most cases in the court (e.g., pleadings, decisions, orders, notes of issue, judgments) are available on-line in the Supreme Court Records On–Line Library ("Scroll") of the County Clerk of New York County and the New York County Supreme Court, accessible on the court's website at www.nycourts.gov/supctmanh/. Decisions of the court with County Clerk entry stamp are posted in Scroll very promptly after their issuance. Information on scheduled court appearances and other case activity, including the issuance of decisions and orders, can also be obtained from Scroll, as well as from CaseTrac, the court system's case tracking and notification service, private services, courthouse terminals, or the New York Law Journal. The Clerk of the Part can also provide information about scheduling in the Part (trials, conferences, and arguments on motions in the Part). Counsel should not telephone Chambers.

Rule 4. Papers by Fax

Unless indicated otherwise by the court in a particular case or in the Basic Information section above, Justices do not accept papers by fax.

III.   CONFERENCES AND DISCOVERY

Rule 5.   Preliminary Conferences; Requests

(a) A preliminary conference will be held or, in Motor Vehicle cases and most tort cases against the City of New York, an automated Differentiated Case Management ("DCM") scheduling order issued (i) within 45 days of assignment of a case to a Justice, unless impracticable for unusual reasons; or (ii) where a Request for Judicial Intervention is accompanied by a dispositive motion, within 45 days following disposition of such motion (if the case is not mooted by that disposition). Cases will be assigned to a DCM track (see Uniform Rule 202.19(b)) upon filing. The court will afford all parties an opportunity to raise objections to the track assignment or any DCM scheduling order issued without a conference. Requests for preliminary conferences in unassigned cases should be filed with an RJI in the Trial Support Office (Room 158). In assigned cases, if the court itself does not direct a conference in a decision nor issue an order scheduling pretrial proceedings, counsel should contact the Part Clerk.

(b) The court utilizes distinct forms of preliminary conference order in General, Medical, Dental and Podiatric Malpractice, City, Matrimonial, and Motor Vehicle cases. See the website (at www.nycourts.gov/supctmanh, under "Forms") for these forms.

Rule 6.   Adjournments of Conferences

Except as otherwise provided in the Basic Information section above or in Rule 26, adjournment of conferences will be allowed only as follows. The parties may adjourn any preliminary conference once for no more than 21 days, but only by submission of a written stipulation to the Part Clerk on or before the scheduled date thereof. Appearance by counsel is not required. Further adjournment of preliminary conferences and adjournments of compliance and pretrial conferences will be allowed only with permission of the court for good cause.

Rule 7.   Consultation Prior to Preliminary and Compliance Conferences

Prior to a preliminary or compliance conference, counsel for all parties shall consult one another about, and shall make a good faith effort to reach agreement on, (i) resolution of the case, in whole or in part, and (ii) discovery and any other issues to be discussed at the conference.

Rule 8.   Discovery Schedule

Strict compliance with all discovery orders is required. See *Kihl v. Pfeffer*, 94 N.Y.2d 118 (1999). Unexcused or unjustified failure to comply with deadlines fixed by the court, including those set out in Preliminary Conference Orders, may result in an award of costs, conditional or otherwise, or the imposition of another penalty authorized by CPLR 3126. Unless otherwise provided in the Basic Information section above or in the order, no extensions of deadlines set forth in a preliminary conference, compliance conference or other discovery order shall be allowed except with permission of the court for good cause shown.

Rule 9.   Medical Authorizations

When a defendant in a personal injury action serves a demand for authorizations together with a demand for a bill of particulars, counsel for plaintiff shall serve the authorizations with the bill.

Rule 10.   Disclosure Disputes

Prior to making a discovery motion, counsel shall consult one another in a good faith effort to resolve any discovery disputes (see Uniform Rule 202.7). If a dispute is not thus resolved, the party seeking disclosure, unless otherwise directed in the Background Information section above, is advised to contact the Part Clerk promptly, and within any applicable deadline, for the purpose of arranging a conference, in court or by telephone.

Rule 11.   Expert Disclosure

Unless otherwise directed by the court in a preliminary conference order or otherwise, a party having the burden of proof shall serve a response to an expert demand pursuant to CPLR 3101(d) no later than 30 days prior to the date set by the court for trial. Within 15 days after receipt of this response any adverse party shall serve its response.

Rule 12.   Conferences Regarding Settlement of Actions by Infants and Others

Any proposed infant's compromise or other proposed settlement pursuant to CPLR 1207 shall be considered by the court at an appearance in court on the record. An attorney seeking approval of such a proposal shall serve on all parties, at least five days prior to the scheduled appearance, a Notice of Conference on Proposed Infant's [or other] Compromise. This Notice shall indicate the date, time and place of the conference. A copy of the proposed order of approval shall be annexed to the Notice unless previously served upon all parties. Said attorney shall submit to the court at the conference proof of service of such Notice.

IV.   MOTIONS

Rule 13.   Motions on Notice; Orders to Show Cause

(a) Motions brought by notice of motion shall be made returnable in the Motion Support Office Courtroom 130. Relevant procedures are explained on the court's website (see "Courthouse Procedures" at www.nycourts.gov/supctmanh). Depending upon the assigned Part, contested motions submitted in the Motion Support Office Courtroom are submitted without argument, or rescheduled for oral argument if so directed by the assigned Justice. For Justices who schedule argument on a case-by-case basis, notice of the argument date will be transmitted by the court. Counsel may ascertain how a motion submitted in Courtroom 130 was marked by consulting the court's website (under "Motion Support Calendars") or Scroll, or, on the two days immediately following the submission date, the New York Law Journal.

(b) Motions should be brought on by order to show cause only in a proper case (CPLR 2214 (d)). Unless otherwise directed in the Basic Information section above or in an order to show cause, original opposition papers on orders to show cause made returnable in the Part shall be delivered to the Part Clerk at least one business day prior to that date and reply papers should not be submitted.

Rule 14.   Motion Papers

(a) Counsel must attach to motion papers copies of all pleadings and other documents as required by the CPLR and as necessary for an informed decision on the motion. Documents in a foreign language shall be properly translated (CPLR 2101(b)). Whenever reliance is placed upon a decision or other authority not officially published or readily available to this court, a copy of the case or of pertinent portions of the authority shall be submitted with the motion papers. Courtesy copies shall not be submitted unless requested by the court, but such copies are required in electronically filed cases (see the court's Protocol for e-filed cases on the website (www.nycourts.gov/supctmanh, under "E Filing")). Exhibits should be tabbed and be legible; a typed version of any exhibit that is difficult to read should be submitted with the original. Exhibits printed on both sides of the page should be bound and tabbed on the side.

(b) Unless advance permission otherwise is granted by the court for good cause, memoranda of law shall not exceed 30 pages each (exclusive of table of contents and table of authorities) and affidavits/affirmations shall not exceed 25 pages each.

(c) The CPLR does not provide for sur-reply papers, however denominated. Papers or letters regarding a motion should not be presented to the court after submission of the motion in the Motion Support Office Courtroom (Room 130), or after argument in the Part, if any, except with the advance permission of the court. Materials presented in violation of this Rule will not be read.

Rule 15.   Oral Argument; Adjournments

(a) Calendars of motions to be argued in the Parts are published on the morning of the argument date and on the day before in the New York Law Journal under each Part. Argument information is available on a case-by-case basis in Scroll, accessible on the court's website (at www.nycourts.gov/supctmanh/).

(b) Unless provided otherwise in the Basic Information section: argument may be adjourned for good cause; there shall be only one adjournment, for no more than 14 days, unless otherwise directed by the court. A request for an adjournment shall be made prior to the scheduled date.

Rule 16. Orders

(a) A copy of any order affecting the caption of a case (e.g., amendment, substitution, correction of errors) shall be served by counsel upon the Trial Support Office (Room 158) and upon the County Clerk (Room 141B) so that the court's records and the County Clerk's records may be corrected. A copy of any order affecting the trial status of a case (e.g., striking a note of issue) shall be served on the Trial Support Office.

(b) Proposed counter-orders submitted to the court pursuant to Uniform Rule 202.48 (c) (2) shall be marked to identify all respects in which the proposal differs from the submission to which it responds.

Rule 17. Motions for Summary Judgment

Unless otherwise provided in a particular case in the preliminary conference order or other directive of the Justice assigned, a motion for summary judgment shall be made no later than 120 days after the filing of the note of issue, except with leave of court for good cause shown.

Rule 18. Neutral Evaluation Program

City cases and many other cases will be referred to the court's Neutral Evaluation Program (informally known as "Mediation") after filing of the note of issue. The procedures of this program are available on the court's website (www.nycourt.gov/supctmanh under "ADR Programs").

V. TRIALS

This section sets forth trial procedures generally applicable to cases to be tried in pure IAS Parts (i.e., not including cases scheduled for trial through the Administrative Coordinating Part (Part 40) or the City Trial Part (Part 27 C)). However, since the nature of particular cases may make departure from these rules efficient and appropriate, counsel should in every instance confirm with the court at the pre-trial conference the Justice's directive regarding applicability of these procedures to the case.

Rule 19. Pretrial Conference

In cases to be tried in IAS Parts (i.e., not including cases scheduled for trial through the Administrative Coordinating Part (Part 40) or the City Trial Part (Part 27 C)), the court will conduct a pretrial conference at which settlement will be explored and a trial date will be confirmed or a firm date set. Prior to the pretrial conference, counsel shall confer in a good faith effort to identify issues not in contention, resolve all disputed questions without need for court intervention, and settle the case. Unless otherwise directed by the court, each party must be represented at the pretrial conference by counsel having full knowledge of the case and specific authority to settle or the ability immediately to contact by telephone a person with such authority. To permit the fixing of a trial date, counsel must, prior to the conference, consult their own schedules and those of their witnesses and be prepared to furnish a realistic estimate of the trial's length and discuss a suitable trial date unless previously fixed.

Rule 20. Trial Schedule in Pure IAS Parts

(a) Insofar as possible, trials in pure IAS Parts will be scheduled at least one month in advance. As the schedules of counsel and witnesses will have been taken into account in determining the trial date, counsel will be expected to be ready to proceed at that time either to select a jury or to begin presentation of proof. Hence, once a firm trial date is set and counsel are so informed, counsel must immediately reconfirm the availability of witnesses and their own schedules. If for any reason, including trial commitments in other Parts or courts, counsel are not prepared to proceed on the scheduled date, counsel must inform the court of the difficulty within seven days of the date on which counsel were given the firm trial date. Absent extraordinary circumstances, failure of counsel to provide such notification will be deemed a waiver of any objection to the trial date.

(b) The court will endeavor, through contact with Justices in other Parts and courts, to resolve trial scheduling difficulties for counsel who notify the court in accordance with subdivision (a) of this Rule and in instances of extraordinary and unanticipated conflicts. The court will resolve such problems in accordance with Part 125 of the Rules of the Chief Administrator (Uniform Rules for the Engagement of Counsel), taking into account the need to conserve judicial trial time or the time of jurors, the demands upon trial counsel, and the importance of the clients' right to the attorney of his or her choice.

(c) The jury shall be selected in accordance with Uniform Rule 202.33.

Rule 21. Pretrial Identification of Exhibits and Deposition Testimony in Pure IAS Parts

Counsel for the parties shall consult prior to trial and attempt in good faith to agree upon the exhibits and portions of deposition testimony (with the deletion of irrelevant matter) that will be offered into evidence on the direct case without objection.

Rule 22. Marked Pleadings and Other Pre–Trial Submissions in Pure IAS Parts

In cases to be tried in IAS Parts, unless the court directs otherwise, at least ten days prior to trial or at such other time as the court may direct, counsel shall submit to the court marked pleadings, the bill of particulars, and a list of witnesses (direct case); and in a jury case, requests to charge, a proposed verdict sheet, and, as appropriate, a memorandum of law or copies of authorities addressed to any unusual jury charge requests; and, in all jury cases in which doing so will facilitate efficient presentation of proof and in all non-jury cases, pretrial memoranda. If counsel wishes the court to charge verbatim from the Pattern Jury Instructions, it is sufficient if the request cites the PJI charge by number only. All other requested charges should be written out in full.

Rule 23. Subpoenaed Records

Subpoenaed records should be directed to and may be reviewed at the Subpoenaed Records Office, 60 Centre Street, Room 145M.

VI. MATRIMONIAL RULES

The following Rules shall apply to all matrimonial cases and shall take precedence over any inconsistent Rule set forth above. Otherwise, the foregoing rules are applicable in matrimonial cases.

Rule 24. Appearances at Conferences

Counsel and client must appear at the preliminary conference, all compliance conferences and the pre-trial conference. Failure to appear may result in costs or sanctions being imposed against the defaulting party.

Rule 25. Submissions at Preliminary Conference

Each party is required to submit at the preliminary conference a properly certified net worth statement and a copy of the retainer agreement in accordance with Section 202.16 of the Uniform Rules for the Trial Courts.

Rule 26. Adjournments

No stipulations of adjournment will be honored without prior approval of the court.

Rule 27. P.E.A.C.E. Program

Except for cases in which there has been a history of orders of protection, parties with unemancipated children should be aware that the Justice may assign the parties to the P.E.A.C.E. Program.

Rule 28. Pre–Trial Conference

Unless directed otherwise, all cases scheduled for trial must appear for a pre-trial conference on a date set by the court. All motions *in limine* must be presented at this time and counsel should be prepared to discuss all evidentiary issues.

Rule 29. Mandatory Pre–Trial Submissions

At the pre-trial conference, counsel shall provide his or her adversary and the court (a) marked pleadings (if grounds are in issue), (b) proposed statement of disposition, (c) child support worksheet (if applicable), (d) updated net worth statement, (e) list of all proposed exhibits, (f) witness list, (g) any expert report not previously provided, (h) pre-trial memoranda and (i) proof of filing of the note of issue.

VII. EMINENT DOMAIN

These local rules supplement Uniform Rule § 202.61 with respect to the obtaining of Index Numbers for Claims and the Exchange and Filing of Appraisal Reports in Eminent Domain Proceedings.

Rule 30. Index Numbers for Fee Claims

Within sixty days from the expiration of the time set forth, pursuant to EDPL 503 (B), in an order of acquisition for the filing of written claims or notices of appearance, condemnor shall obtain an index number for each of the fee claims on file with the court pursuant to the said order so that the Clerk can separately maintain the claim and all further proceedings with respect thereto, and the condemnor shall notify the claimant or its attorney of record of the index number assigned to its claim.

Thereafter, papers pertaining to each claim shall be separately prepared and filed under the index number assigned to the claim. A Request for Judicial Intervention is required to initiate proceedings before the court pertaining to a claim.

Rule 31. Index Numbers for Fixture Claims

Within six months after appraisals of fixtures have been exchanged pursuant to Uniform Rule § 202.61(a)(1), condemnor shall obtain an index number for each individual claim for which an appraisal has been exchanged so that the Clerk can separately maintain the claim and all further proceedings with respect thereto, and the condemnor shall notify the claimant or its attorney of record of the index number assigned to its claim. Thereafter, papers pertaining to each claim shall be separately prepared and filed under the index number assigned to the claim. A Request for Judicial Intervention is required to initiate proceedings before the court pertaining to a claim.

Rule 32. Submission and Filing of Appraisal Reports

In all proceedings for the determination of the value of property taken pursuant to eminent domain, counsel may request that the court modify the procedure set forth in Uniform Rule § 202.61 for the exchange of appraisal reports. Within the nine-month period for filing of appraisals set forth in Rule § 202.61(a), the parties may agree by stipulation, and present same to the court for approval, to a direct exchange of appraisals without filing copies of appraisals with the court.

Thereafter, the parties may extend the date for exchange of appraisal reports set forth in the stipulation by further stipulation, without court approval, for no more than an additional nine months, provided such stipulation(s) are filed with the Clerk of the court. In such event, a copy of each exchanged appraisal shall be provided to the court upon the earlier of (i) its request or (ii) a pre-trial conference called upon the filing of a note of issue. Original appraisals shall be retained for presentation as an exhibit at trial.

Rule 33.   Index Numbers for Other Matters

If the condemnor seeks relief against a person who has not filed a claim, the condemnor shall commence a special proceeding or action as may be appropriate.

SUMMARY JURY TRIALS

Doc. 1. Statement of Summary Jury Trial Procedures

A summary jury trial is generally a binding one- to two-day jury trial that is conducted in accordance with a comprehensive Pre–Trial Order.

1. Consent of Parties: A summary jury trial requires the consent of the parties. The signatories to the relevant stipulation represent that they have the authority of their respective clients and/or insurance carriers to enter into the agreement and such agreement will be irrevocably binding upon their respective principals.

2. Stipulation: If the parties agree to a summary jury trial, the stipulation shall be signed by the attorneys and clients, capping damages at the stated policy limits or reciting any high/low parameters, and waiving any right to appeal. This stipulation shall be a part of the Pre–Trial Order and marked as a Court exhibit.

3. No right to appeal: There is no right to appeal. However, a mistrial and retrial may be permitted in the event of an inconsistent verdict that cannot be reconciled by further instruction from the Court or of prejudicial conduct, subject to the discretion of the Court. Following the determination, the parties shall not enter judgment, but shall instead exchange General Releases and Stipulations of Discontinuance.

4. Pre–Trial Service of Documentary Evidence: Any party intending to offer documentary evidence upon trial, including accident reports, medical records and lost income records, shall serve copies of such evidence upon all parties not less than two weeks before the trial date. Failure to serve documentary evidence as required may result in preclusion of that evidence at the time of trial.

5. Pre–Trial Hearing: A pre-trial hearing shall be conducted no later than 10 days before the commencement of the summary jury trial. At this hearing, objections to documentary evidence previously submitted as provided for herein shall be determined and witness lists shall be exchanged. If there is no objection, counsel shall so stipulate in writing. The need for a translator, if any, shall be made known to the Court and a provision will be placed in the Pre–Trial Order. Any issue regarding collateral sources and/or liens shall be raised at or before this hearing. Reference to Pattern Jury Instructions shall be sufficient as requests to charge. Requests to charge that deviate from the Pattern Jury Instructions must be submitted in writing prior to the pre-trial hearing. Proposed verdict sheets must be submitted at this hearing.

6. Trial Date: Summary jury trials will be placed on the trial calendar at the earliest date available. Once the date is assigned, it shall be considered a date certain.

7. Jury Selection: Jury selection shall be conducted by the Court and counsel within strict time limits.

8. Trial: Each side shall be entitled to make a ten-minute opening and closing statement and shall have one hour after the openings for presentation of its case. No more than two witnesses for each side may be called (no expert witnesses allowed).

9. No Directed Verdicts: Parties agree to waive any motions for a directed verdict, as well as any motions to set aside the verdict rendered by said jury.

For further information, please contact rmoser@ courts.state.ny.us.

Form 1. Pre–Trial Order in General Cases

SUPREME COURT OF THE STATE OF NEW YORK

COUNTY OF NEW YORK

PRESIDING: HON. _____

--X

       Plaintiff(s),

 -against-

       Defendant(s).

--X

Index No. _____

SUMMARY JURY TRIAL

PRE–TRIAL ORDER

The Court hereby orders as follows in accordance with the procedures for Summary Jury Trials in this County:

I. NATURE OF ACTION AND JURISDICTION

This is an action for personal injuries allegedly sustained by the plaintiff(s) as a result of an accident which occurred on _____. The jurisdiction of the Court is not disputed and is invoked pursuant to the Stipulation for a Summary Jury Trial entered into by and between the parties herein dated _____, which is annexed as Exhibit A.

II. EXHIBITS TO THE ORDER

The following have been submitted and are made a part of this Order:

1) Marked copies of the pleadings are annexed as Exhibit B.

2) A written statement of the stipulated or uncontested facts signed by the attorneys for the parties is annexed as Exhibit C.

3) A written waiver of claims and defenses which have been abandoned by the parties is annexed as Exhibit D.

4) A written statement as to the contested issues of fact or law is annexed as Exhibit E.

5) Separate lists of the witnesses whom the plaintiff(s) and defendant(s) will call at the trial of the action on that party's (s') case or defense are annexed as Exhibit F and Exhibit G, respectively.

6) Separate lists identifying exhibits, documents, and photographs that each party will rely upon at the trial of the action on that party's (s') case are annexed as Exhibit H and Exhibit I for plaintiff(s) and defendant(s), respectively.

7) Separate lists of the medical records or reports that each party will rely upon at trial, together with an identification of each expert and a statement of his or her field of expertise, are annexed as Exhibit J and Exhibit K for plaintiff(s) and defendant(s), respectively.

8) An itemized statement of all special damages claimed on behalf of plaintiff(s) is annexed as Exhibit L.

9) Annexed as Exhibit M is _____.

10) Additional Directives: _____

_____

Dated: _____ _____

               J.S.C.

7/24/09

EXHIBIT A

SUPREME COURT OF THE STATE OF NEW YORK
COUNTY OF NEW YORK

---X

　　　　　　　　　　　　Plaintiff(s),

　　-against-

　　　　　　　　　　　　Defendant(s).
---X

Index No. _____

SUMMARY JURY TRIAL
STIPULATION

IT IS HEREBY STIPULATED AND AGREED BY THE PARTIES AND THEIR ATTORNEYS THAT THIS MATTER SHALL BE TRANSFERRED TO THE SUMMARY JURY TRIAL PROGRAM FOR TRIAL IN ACCORDANCE WITH THE PROCEDURES THEREOF AND THAT:

1.　The signatories hereto represent that they have the authority of their respective clients and/or insurance carriers to enter into this stipulation.

2.　The jury's finding in this matter will be final and irrevocably binding and there is no right to appeal nor, except as provided in the Statement of Procedures with respect to a mistrial, any right to request the trial judge to change or modify the jury's verdict.

3.　The amount of the defendant's (s') insurance coverage is _____.

4.　[Cross out any inapplicable portion of this paragraph]:

(a) There is no right to recover any amount of money in excess of the defendant's (s') insurance policy (policies) regardless of the amount of money that the jury awards in its verdict.

OR

(b) It has been agreed between the parties that, no matter what the jury may award in its verdict, the plaintiff(s) shall receive no more than $ _____ as the highest possible award and that defendant(s) shall have to pay at least $ _____.

5.　The date that will be assigned for the Summary Jury Trial is a date certain and counsel and parties must be present on that date in order to participate in the trial.

_____
Signature

_____
Name

_____
Address

_____

_____
Phone Number(s)

Attorneys for Plaintiff(s)

_____
Client Signature

_____
Signature

_____
Name

_____
Address

_____

_____
Phone Number(s)

Attorneys for Defendant(s)

_____
Client Signature

Dated: _____

7/24/09

EXHIBIT B

PLEADINGS

EXHIBIT C

SUPREME COURT OF THE STATE OF NEW YORK
COUNTY OF NEW YORK

--X

Plaintiff(s),

   -against-

Defendant(s).
--X

Index No. _____

SUMMARY JURY TRIAL

STATEMENT OF
STIPULATED OR
UNCONTESTED FACTS

The parties to this action hereby stipulate and agree to the following uncontested facts:

1. _____
_____
_____
_____
_____
_____
_____

2. _____
_____
_____
_____
_____
_____
_____

3. _____
_____
_____
_____
_____
_____
_____

4. _____
_____
_____
_____

_____

_____.

_____   _____
Signature   Signature

_____   _____
Name   Name

_____   _____
Address   Address

_____   _____

_____   _____
Phone Number(s)   Phone Number(s)

Attorneys for Plaintiff(s)   Attorneys for Defendant(s)

Dated: _____

7/24/09

EXHIBIT D

SUPREME COURT OF THE STATE OF NEW YORK
COUNTY OF NEW YORK

---X

                         Plaintiff(s),   Index No. _____

      -against-   **SUMMARY JURY TRIAL**

                                           WAIVER OF
                  Defendant(s).   **CLAIMS AND DEFENSES**

---X

     The parties to this action hereby stipulate and agree to waive claims and defenses herein as follows:

1. _____

_____

_____

_____

_____

_____.

2. _____

_____

_____

_____

_____

3. _____.
   _____
   _____
   _____
   _____
   _____
   _____.

4. _____
   _____
   _____
   _____
   _____
   _____.

_____   _____
Signature   Signature

_____   _____
Name   Name

_____   _____
Address   Address

_____   _____
_____   _____

_____   _____
Phone Number(s)   Phone Number(s)

Attorneys for Plaintiff(s)   Attorneys for Defendant(s)

Dated: _____

7/24/09

EXHIBIT E

SUPREME COURT OF THE STATE OF NEW YORK
COUNTY OF NEW YORK

--X

                         Plaintiff(s),

       -against-

                      Defendant(s).

--X

Index No. _____

SUMMARY JURY TRIAL

STATEMENT OF
CONTESTED ISSUES OF
FACT AND LAW

    The Parties to this action hereby stipulate and agree to the following Statement of Contested Issues of Fact and Law:

1.   Was the defendant(s) negligent?

2.   What is the amount of the defendant's (s') negligence as a proximate cause of plaintiff's (s') injuries?

3.   _____.

4.   _____.

5.   _____.

_____	_____
Signature	Signature
_____	_____
Name	Name
_____	_____
Address	Address
_____	_____
_____	_____

Phone Number(s)_____   Phone Number(s)_____

   Attorneys for Plaintiff(s)   Attorneys for Defendant(s)

Dated: _____

7/24/09

EXHIBIT F

Case: _____   Index No. _____

PLAINTIFF'S (S') LIST OF WITNESSES

   Pursuant to the Pre–Trial Order in the case captioned above, the plaintiff(s) states (state) that the plaintiff(s) will call the following witnesses:

_____

_____

7/24/09

EXHIBIT G

Case: _____   Index No. _____

DEFENDANT'S (S') LIST OF WITNESSES

   Pursuant to the Pre–Trial Order in the case captioned above, the defendant(s) states (state) that the defendant(s) will call the following witnesses:

_____

_____

7/24/09

EXHIBIT H

Case: _____   Index No. _____

PLAINTIFF'S (S') LIST OF EXHIBITS, DOCUMENTS, AND PHOTOGRAPHS

   Pursuant to the Pre–Trial Order in the case captioned above, the plaintiff(s) states (state) that the following constitute the exhibits, documents, and photographs that the plaintiff(s) will rely upon at trial:

1. _____
2. _____
3. _____
4. _____
5. _____
6. _____
7. _____
8. _____
9. _____
10. _____

7/24/09

EXHIBIT I

Case: _____   Index No. _____

DEFENDANT'S (S') LIST OF EXHIBITS, DOCUMENTS, AND PHOTOGRAPHS

Pursuant to the Pre–Trial Order in the case captioned above, the defendant(s) states (state) that the following constitute the exhibits, documents, and photographs that the defendant(s) will rely upon at trial:

1. _____
2. _____
3. _____
4. _____
5. _____
6. _____
7. _____
8. _____
9. _____
10. _____

7/24/09

EXHIBIT J

Case: _____   Index No. _____

PLAINTIFF'S (S') LIST OF MEDICAL RECORDS AND REPORTS (WITH EXPERT IDENTIFICATION)

Pursuant to the Pre–Trial Order in the case captioned above, the plaintiff(s) states (state) that the following constitute (i) the medical records and reports that the plaintiff(s) will rely upon at trial and (ii) the identification of each expert required by said Order:

1. _____
2. _____

3. _____

4. _____

5. _____

6. _____

7. _____

8. _____

9. _____

10. _____

7/24/09

EXHIBIT K

Case: _____   Index No. _____

DEFENDANT'S (S') LIST OF MEDICAL RECORDS AND REPORTS
(WITH EXPERT IDENTIFICATION)

Pursuant to the Pre–Trial Order in the case captioned above, the defendant(s) states (state) that the following constitute (i) the medical records and reports that the defendant(s) will rely upon at trial and (ii) the identification of each expert required by said Order:

1. _____

2. _____

3. _____

4. _____

5. _____

6. _____

7. _____

8. _____

9. _____

10. _____

7/24/09

EXHIBIT L

Case: _____   Index No. _____

PLAINTIFF'S (S') ITEMIZED STATEMENT OF ALL
SPECIAL DAMAGES CLAIMED ON BEHALF OF
PLAINTIFF FROM THE DATE OF ACCIDENT
TO THE PRESENT

Pursuant to the Pre–Trial Order in the case captioned above, the plaintiff(s) states (state) that the following constitute all special damages claimed on behalf of plaintiff(s) from the date of the accident to the present:

1. _____

2. _____

3. _____

4. _____

5. _____

6. _____

7. _____

8. _____

9. _____

10. _____

7/24/09

Form 2. Pre–Trial Order in Motor Vehicle Cases

SUPREME COURT OF THE STATE OF NEW YORK

COUNTY OF NEW YORK

PRESIDING: HON. _____

---X

Plaintiff(s),

-against-

Defendant(s).

---X

Index No. _____

SUMMARY JURY TRIAL

PRE–TRIAL ORDER

The Court hereby orders as follows in accordance with the procedures for Summary Jury Trials in this County:

I. NATURE OF ACTION AND JURISDICTION

This is an action for personal injuries allegedly sustained by the plaintiff(s) as a result of an accident which occurred on _____. The jurisdiction of the Court is not disputed and is invoked pursuant to the Stipulation for a Summary Jury Trial entered into by and between the parties herein dated _____, which is annexed as Exhibit A.

II. EXHIBITS TO THE ORDER

The following have been submitted and are made a part of this Order:

1) Marked copies of the pleadings are annexed as Exhibit B.

2) A written statement of the stipulated or uncontested facts signed by the attorneys for the parties is annexed as Exhibit C.

3) A written waiver of claims and defenses which have been abandoned by the parties is annexed as Exhibit D.

4) A written statement as to the contested issues of fact or law is annexed as Exhibit E.

5) Separate lists of the witnesses whom the plaintiff(s) and defendant(s) will call at the trial of the action on that party's (s') case or defense are annexed as Exhibit F and Exhibit G, respectively.

6) Separate lists identifying exhibits, documents, and photographs that each party will rely upon at the trial of the action on that party's (s') case are annexed as Exhibit H and Exhibit I for plaintiff(s) and defendant(s), respectively.

7) Separate lists of the medical records or reports that each party will rely upon at trial, together with an identification of each expert and a statement of his or her field of expertise, are annexed as Exhibit J and Exhibit K for plaintiff(s) and defendant(s), respectively.

8) An itemized statement of all special damages claimed on behalf of plaintiff(s) is annexed as Exhibit L.

9) Annexed as Exhibit M is _____.

10) Additional Directives: _____

_____

Dated: _____   _____

J.S.C.

7/24/09

EXHIBIT A

SUPREME COURT OF THE STATE OF NEW YORK

COUNTY OF NEW YORK

---X

Plaintiff(s),   Index No. _____

-against-   **SUMMARY JURY TRIAL**
                                                      STIPULATION
Defendant(s).

---X

IT IS HEREBY STIPULATED AND AGREED BY THE PARTIES AND THEIR ATTORNEYS THAT THIS MATTER SHALL BE TRANSFERRED TO THE SUMMARY JURY TRIAL PROGRAM FOR TRIAL IN ACCORDANCE WITH THE PROCEDURES THEREOF AND THAT:

1. The signatories hereto represent that they have the authority of their respective clients and/or insurance carriers to enter into this stipulation.

2. The jury's finding in this matter will be final and irrevocably binding and there is no right to appeal nor, except as provided in the Statement of Procedures with respect to a mistrial, any right to request the trial judge to change or modify the jury's verdict.

3. The amount of the defendant's (s') insurance coverage is _____.

4. [Cross out any inapplicable portion of this paragraph]:

(a) There is no right to recover any amount of money in excess of the defendant's (s') insurance policy (policies) regardless of the amount of money that the jury awards in its verdict.

OR

(b) It has been agreed between the parties that, no matter what the jury may award in its verdict, the plaintiff(s) shall receive no more than $ _____ as the highest possible award and that defendant(s) shall have to pay at least $ _____.

5. The date that will be assigned for the Summary Jury Trial is a date certain and counsel and parties must be present on that date in order to participate in the trial.

_____   _____
Signature   Signature

_____   _____
Name   Name

_____   _____
Address   Address

_____   _____

_____   _____
Phone Number(s)   Phone Number(s)

Attorneys for Plaintiff(s)   Attorneys for Defendant(s)

_____   _____
Client Signature   Client Signature

Dated: _____

7/24/09

EXHIBIT B

PLEADINGS

EXHIBIT C

SUPREME COURT OF THE STATE OF NEW YORK
COUNTY OF NEW YORK

--X

                     Plaintiff(s),

      -against-

                   Defendant(s).

--X

Index No. _____

SUMMARY JURY TRIAL

**STATEMENT OF
STIPULATED OR
UNCONTESTED FACTS**

    The parties to this action hereby stipulate and agree to the following uncontested facts:

1. _____
_____
_____
_____
_____
_____
_____

2. _____
_____
_____
_____
_____
_____
_____

3. _____
_____
_____
_____
_____
_____
_____

4. _____
_____
_____
_____

_____
_____.

_____   _____
Signature   Signature

_____   _____
Name   Name

_____   _____
Address   Address

_____   _____

_____   _____
Phone Number(s)   Phone Number(s)

Attorneys for Plaintiff(s)   Attorneys for Defendant(s)

Dated: _____

                                                           7/24/09

EXHIBIT D

SUPREME COURT OF THE STATE OF NEW YORK
COUNTY OF NEW YORK

---X
                                       Index No. _____
                    Plaintiff(s),
                                       SUMMARY JURY TRIAL
        -against-
                                       WAIVER OF
                                       CLAIMS AND DEFENSES
                    Defendant(s).
---X

   The parties to this action hereby stipulate and agree to waive claims and defenses
herein as follows:

   1. _____
_____
_____
_____
_____
_____.

   2. _____
_____
_____
_____
_____

3. _____.
   _____
   _____
   _____
   _____
   _____
   _____.

4. _____
   _____
   _____
   _____
   _____
   _____
   _____
   _____.

_____	_____
Signature	Signature
_____	_____
Name	Name
_____	_____
Address	Address
_____	_____
_____	_____
Phone Number(s)	Phone Number(s)
Attorneys for Plaintiff(s)	Attorneys for Defendant(s)

Dated: _____

7/24/09

EXHIBIT E

SUPREME COURT OF THE STATE OF NEW YORK
COUNTY OF NEW YORK

---X

                    Plaintiff(s),   Index No. _____

       –against–   **SUMMARY JURY TRIAL**

                                         STATEMENT OF
                                         CONTESTED ISSUES OF
                                         FACT AND LAW—
                    Defendant(s).   **MOTOR VEHICLE CASE**
---X

The Parties to this action hereby stipulate and agree to the following Statement of Contested Issues of Fact and Law:

1. Was the defendant(s) negligent?

2. What is the amount of the defendant's (s') negligence as a proximate cause of plaintiff's (s') injuries?

3. Did the plaintiff sustain significant limitation of use of body function or system?

4. Did the plaintiff(s) sustain a permanent consequential limitation of use of body organ or member?

5. Did the plaintiff(s) sustain a non-permanent, medically-determined injury that prevents performance of usual and customary daily activities for 90 of 180 days immediately subsequent to injury?

Signature	Signature
Name	Name
Address	Address

Phone Number(s) _____   Phone Number(s) _____

    Attorneys for Plaintiff(s)   Attorneys for Defendant(s)

Dated: _____

7/24/09

EXHIBIT F

Case: _____ Index No. _____

PLAINTIFF'S (S') LIST OF WITNESSES

Pursuant to the Pre–Trial Order in the case captioned above, the plaintiff(s) states (state) that the plaintiff(s) will call the following witnesses:

_____

_____

7/24/09

EXHIBIT G

Case: _____ Index No. _____

DEFENDANT'S (S') LIST OF WITNESSES

Pursuant to the Pre–Trial Order in the case captioned above, the defendant(s) states (state) that the defendant(s) will call the following witnesses:

_____

_____

7/24/09

EXHIBIT H

Case: _____   Index No. _____

PLAINTIFF'S (S') LIST OF EXHIBITS, DOCUMENTS, AND PHOTOGRAPHS

Pursuant to the Pre–Trial Order in the case captioned above, the plaintiff(s) states (state) that the following constitute the exhibits, documents, and photographs that the plaintiff(s) will rely upon at trial:

1. _____
2. _____
3. _____
4. _____
5. _____
6. _____
7. _____
8. _____
9. _____
10. _____

7/24/09

EXHIBIT I

Case: _____   Index No. _____

DEFENDANT'S (S') LIST OF EXHIBITS, DOCUMENTS, AND PHOTOGRAPHS

Pursuant to the Pre–Trial Order in the case captioned above, the defendant(s) states (state) that the following constitute the exhibits, documents, and photographs that the defendant(s) will rely upon at trial:

1. _____
2. _____
3. _____
4. _____
5. _____
6. _____
7. _____
8. _____
9. _____
10. _____

7/24/09

EXHIBIT J

Case: _____   Index No. _____

PLAINTIFF'S (S') LIST OF MEDICAL RECORDS AND REPORTS
(WITH EXPERT IDENTIFICATION)

Pursuant to the Pre–Trial Order in the case captioned above, the plaintiff(s) states (state) that the following constitute (i) the medical records and reports that the plaintiff(s) will rely upon at trial and (ii) the identification of each expert required by said Order:

1. _____
2. _____
3. _____
4. _____
5. _____
6. _____
7. _____
8. _____
9. _____
10. _____

7/24/09

EXHIBIT K

Case: _____ Index No. _____

DEFENDANT'S (S') LIST OF MEDICAL RECORDS AND REPORTS
(WITH EXPERT IDENTIFICATION)

Pursuant to the Pre–Trial Order in the case captioned above, the defendant(s) states (state) that the following constitute (i) the medical records and reports that the defendant(s) will rely upon at trial and (ii) the identification of each expert required by said Order:

1. _____
2. _____
3. _____
4. _____
5. _____
6. _____
7. _____
8. _____
9. _____
10. _____

7/24/09

EXHIBIT L

Case: _____ Index No. _____

PLAINTIFF'S (S') ITEMIZED STATEMENT OF ALL
SPECIAL DAMAGES CLAIMED ON BEHALF OF
PLAINTIFF FROM THE DATE OF ACCIDENT
TO THE PRESENT

Pursuant to the Pre–Trial Order in the case captioned above, the plaintiff(s) states (state) that the following constitute all special damages claimed on behalf of plaintiff(s) from the date of the accident to the present:

1. _____

2. _____

3. _____

4. _____

5. _____

6. _____

7. _____

8. _____

9. _____

10. _____

7/24/09

MATRIMONIAL MEDIATION PROGRAM

Doc. 1. Statement of Procedures

MATRIMONIAL MEDIATION PROGRAM

I. OVERVIEW

Mediation is a confidential, problem-solving process in which a neutral third party — the mediator — helps disputing parties to identify issues, clarify perceptions, and explore options for a mutually acceptable outcome. Mediation often results in faster, less expensive, more durable, and less acrimonious settlement than might be the case in the normal course of litigation.

The Matrimonial Mediation Program of this Court ("the Program") provides parties a free, 90-minute initial session with a Program mediator. Program mediators have significant training and experience in family mediation and in opening paths of communication that emphasize common ground and encourage cooperation. They help divorcing parties to resolve key issues that affect their relationships with their children and the financial well-being of all family members.

Although parties are not obligated to reach agreement in mediation, the process often concludes with a written agreement, as well as improved communication between the parties. If the parties reach an agreement during mediation, the mediator may assist the parties and their counsel in drafting a written agreement. The written agreement is then returned to the referring Justice for review. Subject to the referring Justice's approval, the agreement will be incorporated in the Court's Order or Judgment of Divorce.

II. PROCEDURES

Supreme Court Justices may refer parties to the Program or parties on their own may request referral to it at any time. Cases involving child abuse or neglect (as defined in Family Court Act § 1012(e) and (f) and Social Services Law § 412), domestic violence, or a severe power imbalance between the parties are not appropriate for mediation and shall be excluded from the Program.

To begin the process, the Justice will sign an Order of Reference directing parties and their counsel to appear at an initial, free, 90-minute mediation session with a mediator from the Program's Roster of Mediators. The Order of Reference will specify the topics (e.g., child custody and visitation and/or financial issues) to be submitted to the mediation.

The Matrimonial Mediation Program Coordinator ("the Coordinator"), who is located in Room 148 in the New York County Courthouse at 60 Centre Street, New York, New York 10013, will receive the referring Justice's Order of Reference. The Coordinator will select from the Court's Roster of Mediators the next available mediator, proceeding in alphabetical order.[1]

Within five business days from receipt of the Order of Reference, the Coordinator will provide the parties with a mediator's name and contact information and send the parties an Initiation Form. The Initiation Form must be completed by the parties and returned to the Coordinator within five business days from receipt of the Form. The parties are free to select a different mediator, but if they do so, they must still return the completed Initiation Form within five business days.

Next, within five business days from receipt of the Initiation Form, the Coordinator will send to the parties and to the selected mediator a Notice of Confirmation. The parties are required to appear at the initial mediation session within 20 days after receiving a Notice of Confirmation.

At least one week before the initial mediation session, the mediator may require the parties' counsel to send the mediator a copy of the pleadings and any other information necessary for the effective negotiation of the issues involved. The mediator may also request a conference call with the parties' counsel regarding any preliminary matters.

If parties wish to extend the mediation process beyond the initial 90-minute session, they may continue that session or schedule additional sessions with the mediator, who shall be entitled from that point forward to compensation at a rate that shall not exceed $250 per hour. Parties shall complete all scheduled mediation sessions within 75 days of receiving the Notice of Confirmation.

Within five business days after the mediation's conclusion, which shall occur whenever after the initial 90-minute session one party, both parties, or the mediator decides that the mediation has ended, the mediator shall send a Mediator's Report to counsel and to the Coordinator, but not to the referring Justice. The Report shall state: (1) the date of the initial session and whether each party and counsel appeared at the initial session; (2) the dates of any subsequent scheduled sessions, but not whether parties appeared; and (3) whether the parties reached partial, complete, or no agreement on the issues. The mediator may attach to the Report any original, signed agreement and return it to the Coordinator.

Once counsel receives a copy of the Mediator's Report, counsel shall promptly contact the Part of the assigned Justice to schedule a conference concerning further proceedings in the case. The Coordinator shall report to the referring Justice whether the case settled (in whole or in part), but shall not reveal to the referring Justice the selected mediator's identity or disclose other information discussed during the mediation, except as described in Section IX.

[1] The Coordinator, however, has discretion to designate another mediator in appropriate cases.

III. ROLE OF THE MEDIATOR

The mediator's primary role is to help the parties communicate and negotiate. The mediator will not give legal advice, predict likely court outcomes, or force solutions on the parties.

At the initial mediation session, the mediator will explain that all communications are confidential (with narrow exceptions outlined below) and will not be disclosed to the Justice hearing the case or in any other judicial or administrative proceeding. The mediator will also explain that either party is free at the close of the initial session or at any time thereafter to end the mediation process and return to court.

During the mediation process, all parties are free to discuss the case as they see it and to raise particular issues of concern that they would like to address. The mediator may ask the parties clarifying questions related to the care of their children, parenting time, and allocation of property and income. The mediatory will then help the parties to develop and choose options that meet the parties' needs.

At some point in the process, either party, the party's counsel, or the mediator may suggest a caucus. Caucuses are meetings that mediators hold separately with each side in a dispute. During the caucus, the mediator may explore how each party views the dispute and the impact of any proposed solutions. The mediator will keep confidential the information discussed in caucus unless the party permits disclosure.

If the parties reach a written agreement during mediation, the parties are strongly encouraged to submit the agreement to their respective attorneys for review.

IV. THE ROLES OF PARTIES, COUNSEL, ATTORNEYS FOR THE CHILD, AND GUARDIANS AD LITEM

Experience has demonstrated that party participation — as opposed to participation exclusively by counsel — not only increases the likelihood of settlement, but also improves compliance with any agreed-upon terms and enhances the parties' overall satisfaction with the process and outcome. Accordingly, unless exempted by the mediator for good cause shown, the parties must be present during the mediation.

The presence of separate counsel for each party during mediation sessions is encouraged. Without representation by counsel, parties may risk entering into agreements with insufficient knowledge about financial, legal or other issues. If counsel for either party is discharged or withdraws for any reason during the mediation process, the case will not proceed in mediation until a substitution occurs.

If parties decide to participate in mediation without their attorneys present, they are strongly advised to consult counsel before finalizing any written agreement. Whether appearing in the mediation alongside their clients or advising clients outside of the mediation process, attorneys play a crucial role in informing parties of their legal rights and responsibilities and the consequences of proposed solutions.

For those cases in which an attorney for the child has been assigned, mediation may not commence without the appropriate attorney's or guardian's presence. If the parties and the attorney or guardian agree to proceed in mediation without the attorney or guardian present, they may do so, unless otherwise ordered by the Court.

V. THE ROLE OF THE COURT

The Program is conducted under Court auspices and pursuant to these rules. Judicial and non-judicial staff are encouraged to inform the parties of the Program's existence. If the parties wish to go to mediation but cannot afford it, the Coordinator will endeavor to assist qualifying parties to find a mediator who will take their case.

The Court welcomes the feedback of parties, counsel, and mediators after the conclusion of the proceedings. Comments should be sent to the Coordinator.

VI. THE ROSTER OF MEDIATORS

The Court has assembled a Roster of Mediators. The Roster appears on the website of this Court (www.nycourts.gov/supctmanh) and is also available in Room 148 in the Courthouse at 60 Centre Street. The prerequisites to joining the Roster are as follows:

• Completion of at least 60 hours of family mediation training in a training program sponsored or recognized by the New York State Office of Court Administration ("OCA"). [2]

• At least four years of family mediation experience, including 250 hours of face-to-face mediation with clients and a minimum of 25 custody and visitation cases, and any other mediation training or experience deemed appropriate by the Court.

Cases involving financial disputes will be referred only to those Program mediators with knowledge of, training in and experience with the financial aspects of divorce.

Continuing presence on the Court's Roster of Mediators is subject to review by the Administrative Judge of this Court. Mediators may be removed from the Roster at the discretion of the Administrative Judge.

[2] The training and qualifications guidelines for the Program exceed the minimum requirements established in Part 146 of the Rules of the Chief Administrative Judge. See www.nycourts.gov/rules/chiefadmin/146.shtml.

VII. FEES

The Program itself does not impose a fee, nor does it administer fees payable to mediators. As indicated above, parties referred to mediation pursuant to this Statement of Procedures shall not be required to compensate the mediator for services rendered before or during the initial 90-minute mediation session. Should the parties agree to continue mediation beyond the 90-minute period or schedule additional sessions with the mediator, the mediator shall be entitled to compensation for services rendered as follows: compensable services shall consist of time spent conducting any mediation that follows the initial 90-minute session, and time spent reviewing materials submitted by the parties for purposes of such subsequent mediation. The mediator's fee for such services shall not exceed $250.00 per hour. The fee arrangement must be agreed to in writing, and must include the ratio at which the fee will be divided between the parties. The parties must sign this fee agreement before commencing any additional mediation beyond the initial mediation session. Parties through their counsel are required to notify the Coordinator in the event that a total of $1000.00 or more in billable fees is paid or becomes owing to the mediator.

Mediators are encouraged to use a sliding scale to take into account the parties' financial circumstances, and may consult with the Coordinator to ensure that no one is denied access to the Program based on inability to pay.

VIII. IMMUNITY

The mediator shall be immune from suit as a result of any conduct or omission during the performance of duties in that capacity to the extent permissible under the law. The execution of the Initiation Form constitutes a waiver of any right to sue the mediator because of his or her actions in that role. Persons who, as a matter of public service, volunteer their time to assist parties in resolving their matrimonial differences should not run the risk of some sort of blame, especially when that service does not bind the parties to a particular result but instead offers them the opportunity to reach a consensual resolution to their dispute.

IX. CONFIDENTIALITY

Except as set forth below, all oral, written, or other communications made during the course of any mediation by any party, mediator or any other person present shall be immune from disclosure in any present or future judicial or administrative proceeding. Similarly, all information generated in or in connection with the mediation — including memoranda, work products or case files of a mediator — shall remain confidential and not be subject to disclosure in any present or future judicial or administrative proceeding. However, mediation will not be used as a shield with respect to otherwise discoverable documents or information produced or occurring prior to or outside the mediation.

Moreover, except as set forth below, nothing about the substance of the mediation, such as the weaknesses or strengths of the parties' cases or the relative willingness of parties to discuss settlement proposals, will be revealed to the referring Justice or any other person by the mediator or any party or attorney. Nor will any party or lawyer for a party reveal the outcome of the mediation process to the referring Justice or a member of the Justice's staff unless both sides agree to the disclosure.

Notwithstanding these confidentiality provisions, communications and information may be subject to disclosure in any present or future judicial or administrative proceeding in any of the following five circumstances:

1. *Attendance/Compliance with Rules*

Whether the parties and their counsel attended the initial mediation session will be reported to the referring Justice. The Coordinator will report any failure to comply with the rules that may be reported to the Coordinator by the mediator.

2. *Waiver*

Parties to the mediation and the mediator agree in writing to waive confidentiality. The waiver must specify the individual communication(s) or information that will be disclosed, the person or entity to whom the disclosure will be made, and the purpose of the disclosure.

3. *Written Agreement*

A writing signed by all the parties embodying a mediated agreement submitted to the court for review. Additionally, a limited report of the outcome will be sent to the referring Justice by the Coordinator. Only those signed, mediated agreements that have become court orders may be admissible in any present or future judicial or administrative proceeding.

4. *Threats of Imminent, Serious Harm*

If communications or information constitute a credible threat of serious and imminent harm, either to the speaker or another person or entity, the appropriate authorities and/or the potential victim may be notified.

5. *Allegations of Child Abuse or Neglect*

The communication or information relates to an allegation of child abuse or neglect as defined in Family Court Act § 1012(e) and (f) and Social Services Law § 412 and for which disclosure is required pursuant to Social Services Law § 413.

X. CHILD ABUSE AND NEGLECT

If an allegation of child abuse or neglect is made by any party during the mediation, the mediator will stop the mediation process and consult with each party individually for the purpose of obtaining as much information about the circumstances as possible. Mediators shall report to the referring Justice allegations of child abuse or neglect for which disclosure is required pursuant to Social Services Law § 413.

XI. DOMESTIC VIOLENCE/SEVERE POWER IMBALANCE

When an allegation of domestic violence or severe power imbalance is made by any party during the mediation, the mediator shall stop the mediation process, meet with each party individually where appropriate to learn as much as possible about the circumstances, and consult with the Coordinator (but not the assigned Justice or members of that Justice's staff) as to whether to resume the mediation process. Allegations of domestic violence will not be disclosed to the referring Justice; instead, victims will be given information regarding their rights in the form prescribed in Family Court Act § 812(5), and they will receive safety planning information.

XII. REFERRAL TO THE PROGRAM AND ONGOING LITIGATION

Cases may be referred to mediation, typically at the preliminary conference, on consent of the parties or at any time deemed appropriate by the Justice. A party who attends the initial 90-minute session complies with the Order of Reference, even if that party ultimately chooses not to proceed with mediation. Parties may move to opt out of the Program for good cause.

Referral to mediation will not stay the court proceedings in any respect. The "no stay" policy recognizes the special need for prompt action in matrimonial and family proceedings. Full discovery, emergency and *pendente lite* relief, family dynamics, and the needs of children require ongoing access to the court, as a general rule. However, parties committed to the mediation process who conclude that additional time is required to explore fully the issues pertaining to their case may request an adjournment.

XIII. AVOIDING CONFLICTS OF INTEREST

Before accepting a mediation, a mediator shall make an inquiry that is reasonable under the circumstances to determine whether there are any known facts that a reasonable individual would consider likely to affect the impartiality of the mediator, including a financial or personal interest in the outcome, and an existing or past relationship with a mediation party or foreseeable participant in the mediation. The mediator shall disclose any such known fact to the mediation parties and counsel as soon as possible before accepting a mediation. The mediator is obliged to disclose all potentially disqualifying facts to the parties and, where such facts exist, shall not serve unless the parties consent in writing. If a mediator learns of any disqualifying fact after accepting a mediation, the mediator shall disclose it as soon as practicable. If unable to function in a fair, impartial and objective manner, the mediator shall seek disqualification.

XIV. FAILURE TO COMPLY WITH ORDER OF REFERENCE AND THESE RULES

If a party or counsel fails to schedule an appearance for an initial mediation session in a timely manner or to appear at an initial scheduled session, or otherwise fails to comply with these rules, the mediator shall advise the Coordinator and may, if appropriate, recommend the imposition of sanctions. The Coordinator shall report any failure and recommendation to the referring Justice.

Dated: January 22, 2009

MATRIMONIAL MEDIATION PROGRAM
Supreme Court, Civil Branch, New York County
New York County Courthouse
60 Centre Street, Room 148
New York, New York 10007

Program Coordinator: Loren Schwartz

Phone: 212–256–7985
Email: lschwart@courts.state.ny.us

Documents may be emailed to the email address above as Word, WordPerfect, or PDF attachments.

APPELLATE TERM

Doc. 1. Appellate Term

This court hears and decides appeals from the Criminal and Civil Courts of the City of New York for New York and Bronx Counties, including appeals from the Housing Part and the Small Claims Part. The Justices of the Appellate Term are listed on the "Justices" page of this site. The Clerk's Office is located in Room 401 at 60 Centre Street (hours: 9:00 A.M. to 5:00 P.M., Monday through Friday).

The filing deadline dates for each term of the court are generally as follows:

- The appellant's records on appeal, briefs and notice of argument are to be filed approximately eight weeks before the term begins. A term usually begins on the first Monday of the month, January through June and September through December. There is no court term in July or August.

- The respondent's briefs are to be filed approximately five weeks before the term begins.

- For exact dates, consult the Clerk's Office (at (646–386–3040).

Motions to the Appellate Term are made on submission and can be noticed for any business day at 10:00 A.M. Moving and opposing papers are to be filed with the Clerk's Office on or before 10:00 A.M. on the return date. Regular motion practice is applicable. To adjourn a motion, submit a stipulation to the Clerk's Office prior to the return date. If you require an immediate stay or other relief, you must submit the application, by notice of motion format, to the Clerk's Office. The return date on the notice of motion page must be left blank. You must attach to the supporting affidavit or affirmation a copy of the notice of appeal, and the order or judgment being appealed. Advise the Court Clerk that a temporary restraining order or other immediate relief is requested. Applications pursuant to CPLR 5704 (b) are obtained by submitting a proposed order, along with a supporting affidavit and/or affirmation and copies of the underlying Civil Court papers sought to be reviewed.

Appeals in the Appellate Term, First Department, are heard on (i) a record on appeal, either the original record or five copies of a reproduced record or appendix; (ii) five copies of a brief; and (iii) a notice of argument. The only appeals heard on the original record are from Criminal Court, Small Claims Court, and civil matters where written permission has been given by a Civil Court Judge or Appellate Term Justice. Appeals heard on Reproduced Records should contain all papers in the file from summons and complaint or petition and notice of petition in landlord and tenant actions up to and including the Notice of Appeal.

Sample copies of reproduced records on appeal, briefs and notice of argument may be obtained at the Clerk's Office.

March 2006

PUBLIC ACCESS TO COURT RECORDS

Preamble

Pursuant to direction of the Chief Judge of the State of New York, the Office of Court Administration has designated courts in two counties in the State — Supreme Court, Civil Branch, New York County and the Supreme and County Courts in Broome County —

as venues for pilot programs for enhanced public access to court records. The Supreme Court, Civil Branch, New York County issues this revised Notice and Rules to inform the Bar practicing in the court of the nature of this program and to set out certain related procedural requirements.

I. NOTICE TO THE BAR

Doc. 1. Notice to the Bar

The Public Access Project in New York County Supreme Court (Civil Branch)

The public access project ("the Public Access Project") in the Supreme Court, Civil Branch, New York County ("the Court") is a joint effort by the court and the Honorable Norman Goodman, County Clerk of New York County. Since September 15, 2006, the Court and County Clerk, working together and using a software program developed by the Court called the *"Supreme Court Records On Line Library"* (or *"Scroll"*), have placed images of a variety of case documents (described below) on-line at the court's website (at www.nycourts.gov/supctmanh). *Scroll* also makes available for each case County Clerk data and Court data on case history from the Court's case tracking computer system, the Civil Case Information System ("CCIS"). This information and the documents are accessible to the Bar and the public at no charge. The case file in hard-copy form remains available for all cases in the Office of the County Clerk as at present.

Cases Available In Scroll: Most cases in the Court's inventory are available in *Scroll.* No information (neither data nor case documents) will be available in *Scroll* for cases brought under Article 81 of the Mental Hygiene Law, or other sections of that Law. *Scroll* will make available only data from the County Clerk's records and CCIS data in matrimonial cases and in cases that have been sealed; no documents will be available in such cases. Further, in any kind of case, the assigned Justice has the right to direct Court staff not to post a decision or other document in *Scroll* (a box for this purpose has been placed on the Court's standard short order form sheet). When the Justice so directs, the document will not be posted on *Scroll* on-line.

Information and Documents Available In Scroll: In the cases that are included in the Scroll Public Access Project system as just described, the following will be available:

(i) the full County Clerk case caption and the County Clerk's minutes, which list all documents in the case that have been filed with the County Clerk;

(ii) CCIS data, that is, complete case history information, including case caption, judicial assignment, comments noting changes in assignment or other developments, a history of conference appearances, a history of motion appearances, trial dates, and the like;

(iii) scanned images (exact PDF copies) of various key documents filed with the Court or the County Clerk or issued by the Court in the case.

Scroll identifies the dates from which coverage is provided for various County Clerk and Court data and documents.

Although some documents may not be posted pursuant to the direction of the assigned Justice and the scanning of some categories of document may proceed in stages as the Public Access Project develops, the Court and the County Clerk intend to scan and post in *Scroll* the following documents:

— Initial papers (summons and complaint, petition, etc.)

— Answers and other pleadings filed

— Requests for Judicial Intervention

— Notices of Motion/Petition (exclusive of supporting papers)

— Signed Orders to Show Cause (exclusive of supporting papers)

— Preliminary Conference Orders

— Compliance Conference and Other Discovery Orders

— Decisions on Motions, Orders to Show Cause, and Special Proceedings

— Long Form Orders on Motions, etc.

— Other Orders

— Notes of Issue

— Stipulations of discontinuance/settlement

— Extracts

— Judgments

Although the foregoing constitutes the plan for *Scroll,* the County Clerk and the Court cannot guarantee that all such documents will be scanned in all covered cases.

For the present, the following documents will not be included in *Scroll*: supporting papers on motions and special proceedings, hearing transcripts, disclosure documents, correspondence (except for any that may be so ordered by the Justice assigned), bills of particulars, and trial exhibits.

There will be a lag of 30 days between the time a summons and complaint or other initiating paper is filed with the County Clerk and the time it is posted in *Scroll*. Decisions on motions and other formal applications and long form orders are posted to *Scroll*, bearing the entry stamp of the County Clerk, as quickly as possible after the issuance of the decision is noted in the CCIS system (normally a matter of an hour to a few hours). Judgments in unfiled form are also posted with similar expedition. Other documents will be scanned and posted with somewhat less immediacy. Judgments in entered form will also be posted in *Scroll*.[1]

Electronically Filed Cases: Documents from cases in the court's electronic filing system may not be included in *Scroll*, but in that event can be accessed through the e-filing system (at www.nycourts.gov/efile).

Applications Regarding Documents in Scroll: Because documents posted in *Scroll* will be accessible on the Internet, the Court has issued a rule requiring attorneys filing any of the documents set forth above to avoid including therein, insofar as possible, social security numbers, bank account numbers, names of minor children, personal health information, and other sensitive information. In the event that any such information must be included in a document (e.g., a proposed judgment or order), or if another attorney representing a party to the case in question does not comply with said rule and the client of the attorney may be adversely affected as a result, counsel for the affected party or person may apply for a directive from the Justice assigned or from the Administrative Judge in an unassigned case that the document in question shall not be posted or, if already posted, shall be removed from the *Scroll* database. See below. The Court will endeavor not to include in decisions and orders issued by it any such sensitive information or will direct that a decision or order containing such information not be posted in *Scroll*.

[1] In cases outside the matrimonial inventory, a judgment is not entered by the County Clerk until an attorney on the case applies to the County Clerk in person in Room 141B in the basement of 60 Centre Street so that the judgment roll can be prepared and interest, costs and disbursements, if any, can be correctly calculated. Unfiled judgments posted in *Scroll* in non-matrimonial matters bear a stamp identifying them as such.

II. RULES REGARDING PUBLIC ACCESS TO COURT INFORMATION[1]

[1] The Rules set out here were first promulgated by Notice to the Bar dated July 7, 2006, with an effective date of Sept. 15, 2006. The Rules are included in the Rules of the Justices, Supreme Court, Civil Branch, New York County.

Rule A–1. Information in Documents Filed with the County Clerk and the Court

Attorneys filing pleadings and other documents with the County Clerk or the Court that fall within a category of document that is, as explained in the Court's Notice to the Bar on the Public Access Project, included in the *Scroll* Public Access Project system or that shall hereafter be so included shall not set out in such documents social security numbers, bank account numbers, the names of minor children, dates of birth, health information concerning any individual and other similar sensitive information, or, if doing so is unavoidable, shall, to the extent practical, provide only a portion of the information (e.g., some but not all digits of an account number, initials only in place of the names of minor children). If circumstances make it unavoidable to include such information in full in a document that is or may be included in the system, the party preparing the document shall apply to the Court, in the manner set forth hereafter, for a directive restricting access to the document in the system. The following documents will not be included in the *Scroll* Public Access Project system: documents filed or issued by the Court in matters pursuant to the Mental Hygiene Law, matrimonial cases, and cases that are sealed by order of a Justice pursuant to Part 216 of the Uniform Rules for the Trial Courts, and other individual documents as to which the Justice assigned so directs.

Rule A–2. Application for Restriction of Access to Records

A party or person who claims that the availability of a document in the Public Access Project system may cause harm to that party or person or who seeks to limit access in compliance with Rule 1 may apply to the Court for a directive restricting access. Any such application shall be made as follows. If the case has been assigned to a Justice, a request shall be made to the Justice by letter describing the document as to which a restriction on access is sought and explaining the reasons why such a restriction is appropriate. If the case has not been assigned to a Justice, the party shall direct such a request to the Administrative Judge. The Court on its own initiative may direct that access be restricted. An interested party or person may apply by letter to remove a document from the *Scroll* database if, notwithstanding this notice and rules, a document is posted on the Public Access Project system that contains sensitive information access to which in this form causes harm to that party or person.

Rule A-3.　Form of Restriction on Access to Records

Where the Court grants a request to limit access to a document in the *Scroll* Public Access Project system or issues a directive sua sponte, the directive shall take the form of an administrative direction to the staff of the Court that the document in question not be included in the *Scroll* system or, if already included therein, that it be deleted from the database. Any such directive as may be issued in a case in which documents are otherwise available in the *Scroll* system shall not affect the status of the County Clerk hard-copy case file, which is open to the public unless otherwise ordered by the Court pursuant to Part 216 of the Uniform Rules for the Trial Courts.

Rule A-4.　Notices of Motion and Notices of Petition

Any party who files a notice of motion or notice of petition with the Court shall submit therewith to the relevant back office a photocopy of the notice (not including the supporting papers).

Dated: June 18, 2007

HON. JACQUELINE W. SILBERMANN

ADMINISTRATIVE JUDGE

No. 8: 6/18/07

COURT FEES

Doc. 1. Court Fees

The following is a list of fees that must be paid in order to take the listed actions in our court or in the Office of the County Clerk of New York County. These fees must be paid to the County Clerk in one of his two Cashier's Offices (Room 160 and Room 141B in the basement, both at 60 Centre Street). The fees must be paid in cash, by Visa or Mastercard credit cards, by an attorney's check made payable to the New York County Clerk, or in the form of a U.S. postal money order made payable to the New York County Clerk. An attorney's check will be accepted if it is from a New York attorney, provided that words such as "Attorney at Law" or "Esq." appear thereon, together with the attorney's address and phone number. Other checks must be certified. Fees in cases in the court's electronic filing system may be paid by credit card on-line.

COURT FEES	
Index Number	$210
Index Number (RPAPL Art. 13 Foreclosure)	$400
Request for Judicial Intervention	$ 95
Note of Issue (no prior RJI)	$125

COURT FEES	
Note of Issue (prior RJI paid for)	$ 30
Calendar Number, Uncontested Matrimonial	$125
Jury Demand	$ 65
Filing of a Motion	$ 45
Filing of a Cross–Motion	$ 45
Filing of a Stipulation of Settlement	$ 35
Filing of a Stipulation of Discontinuance	$ 35

COUNTY CLERK FILING AND OTHER FEES	
Notice of Appeal	$ 65
Building Loan Agreement	$ 50
Notice of Pendency (lis pendens)	$ 35
Notary Commission	$ 30
Certificate of Official Character (Filing)	$ 10
Certificate of Official Character (Issuance)	$ 5
Authentication of Notary's Signature	$ 3
Mechanic's Lien	$ 30
Transcript of Judgment (Filing)	$ 25
Transcript of Judgment (Issuance)	$ 15
Certificate of Exemplification	$ 25
Business Records, Certified Copy	$ 10
Supreme Court Actions, Certified Copy	$ 8
Wage Assignments	$ 10
Affidavit of Service for Mechanic's Liens	$ 5

FORMS

FORMS TO COMMENCE ACTIONS

Form 1.   Index Purchase Cover Sheet

SUPREME COURT, CIVIL BRANCH, NEW YORK COUNTY

INDEX PURCHASE COVER SHEET

INDEX #: _____

NATURE OF ACTION OR PROCEEDING (check ONE box only and enter on Index Purchase Form)

MATRIMONIAL

[ ]   Contested - CM
[ ]   Uncontested - UM

COMMERCIAL

[ ]   Contract - CONT
[ ]   Corporate - CORP
[ ]   Insurance - INS
[ ]   Other Commercial - OC
        (Other than Contract)
[ ]   UCC (including but not
        limited to Sales, Negotiable
        Instruments etc.)

REAL PROPERTY

[ ]   Condemnation - COND
[ ]   Foreclosure - FOR
[ ]   Landlord/Tenant - ORP
[ ]   Other Real Property–ORP
[ ]   Tax Certiorari - TAX

TORTS

[ ]   Asbestos - ASB
[ ]   Breast Implant - BI
[ ]   Dental Malpractic - DM
[ ]   Medical/Podiatric Malpractice - MM
[ ]   Other Professional Malpractice - OPM
[ ]   Motor Vehicle - MV
[ ]   Negligence - OTN
[ ]   Other Tort - OT (including
        but not limited to Intentional
        Tort, Environmental, Toxic,
        Airline, Seaman, etc.)
[ ]   Products Liability - PL

SPECIAL PROCEEDINGS

[ ]   Article 75 (Arbitration) - ART 75
[ ]   Article 77 (Trusts) - ART 77
[ ]   Article 78 - ART 78
[ ]   Incompetency - INC
[ ]   Guardianship - GUARD
[ ]   Other Mental Hygiene–MHYG
[ ]   Other Special Proceeding - OSP

OTHER ACTIONS

[ ]   Election - ELEC
[ ]   Other - OTH

Check "YES" or "NO" for each of the following questions.

Is this action/proceeding against a

YES NO
[ ] [ ] Municipality: YES NO
                                           [ ] [ ] Public Authority:

(specify _____)   (specify _____)

YES NO
[ ] [ ] Does this action/proceeding seek equitable relief?
[ ] [ ] Does this action/proceeding seek recovery for personal injury?
[ ] [ ] Does this action/proceeding seek recovery for property damage?

B-383

Form 2.   Application for Index Number

46–3004R-100M92

COUNTY CLERK, NEW YORK COUNTY

INDEX NUMBER
_____

Application for INDEX NUMBER pursuant to
Section 8018, C.P.L.R.

FEE $210.00

Space below to be TYPED or PRINTED by applicant   Do not write in this space
_____

TITLE OF ACTION OR PROCEEDING   CHECK ONE

☐ COMMERCIAL ACTION   ☐ NOT COMMERCIAL ACTION

☐ CONSUMER CREDIT TRANSACTION   ☐ NOT. CONSUMER CREDIT TRANSACTION

☐ THIRD PARTY ACTION   ☐ NOT THIRD PARTY ACTION

**IF THIRD PARTY ACTION
MAIN INDEX NO.** _____

SAMPLE

Name and address of Attorney for Plaintiff or Petitioner.

Telephone No.

Name and address of Attorney for Defendant or Respondent.

Telephone No.

  A. Nature and object of action or _____

Nature of special proceeding _____

  B. Application for Index Number filed by: Plaintiff ☐ Defendant ☐

  C. Was a previous Third Party Action filed Yes ☐ No ☐

Date filed _____

COMPLETE THIS STUB

DO NOT DETACH

**INDEX NUMBER FEE
$210.00**
_____

Title of Action or Proceeding to be
TYPED or PRINTED by applicant
SUPREME COURT,
NEW YORK COUNTY
_____

Endorse This INDEX NUMBER ON All
Papers and advise your adversary of
the number assigned. Sec. 202.5,
Uniform Rules Of Trial Courts

v.
_____

_____

REQUEST FOR JUDICIAL INTERVENTION

Form 3.   Request for Judicial Intervention

REQUEST FOR JUDICIAL INTERVENTION UCS–840 (3/2011)	**For Court Clerk Use Only:**
	IAS Entry Date

Supreme_____   COURT, COUNTY OF _____

Index No: _____   Date Index Issued: _____

	Judge Assigned

CAPTION: Enter the complete case caption. Do not use et al or et ano. If more space is required, attach a caption rider sheet.

	RJI Date

Plaintiff(s)/Petitioner(s)

-against-

Defendant(s)/Respondent(s)

NATURE OF ACTION OR PROCEEDING: Check ONE box only and specify where indicated.

MATRIMONIAL

- ○ Contested
- ○ Uncontested
  NOTE: For all Matrimonial actions where the parties have children under the age of 18, complete and attach the **MATRIMONIAL RJI Addendum.**

TORTS

- ○ Asbestos
- ○ Breast Implant
- ○ Environmental: _____
  (specify)
- ○ Medical, Dental, or Podiatric Malpractice
- ○ Motor Vehicle
- ○ Products Liability: _____
  (specify)
- ○ Other Negligence: _____
  (specify)
- ○ Other Professional Malpractice: _____
  (specify)
- ○ Other Tort: _____
  (specify)

COMMERCIAL

- ○ Business Entity (including corporations, partnerships, LLCs, etc.)
- ○ Contract
- ○ Insurance (where insurer is a party, except arbitration)
- ○ UCC (including sales, negotiable instruments)
- ○ Other Commercial: _____
  (specify)

NOTE: For Commercial Division assignment requests, complete and attach the **COMMERCIAL DIV RJI Addendum.**

REAL PROPERTY: How many properties does the application include? _____

- ○ Condemnation
- ○ Foreclosure
Property Address: _____
  Street Address   City   State   Zip
  NOTE: For Foreclosure actions involving a one- to four-family, owner-occupied, residential property, or an owner-occupied condominium, complete and attach the **FORECLOSURE RJI Addendum.**
- ○ Tax Certiorari—Section: _____ Block: _____ Lot: __
- ○ Other Real Property: _____
  (specify)

OTHER MATTERS

- ○ Certificate of Incorporation/Dissolution [see **NOTE** under Commercial]
- ○ Emergency Medical Treatment
- ○ Habeas Corpus
- ○ Local Court Appeal
- ○ Mechanic's Lien
- ○ Name Change
- ○ Pistol Permit Revocation Hearing
- ○ Sale or Finance of Religious/ Not–for–Profit Property
- ○ Other: _____
  (specify)

SPECIAL PROCEEDINGS

- ○ CPLR Article 75 (Arbitration) [see **NOTE** under Commercial]
- ○ CPLR Article 78 (Body or Officer)
- ○ Election Law
- ○ MHL Article 9.60 (Kendra's Law)
- ○ MHL Article 10 (Sex Offender Confinement–Initial)
- ○ MHL Article 10 (Sex Offender Confinement–Review)
- ○ MHL Article 81 (Guardianship)
- ○ Other Mental Hygiene: _____
  (specify)
- ○ Other Special Proceeding: _____
  (specify)

STATUS OF ACTION OR PROCEEDING: Answer YES or NO for EVERY question AND enter additional information where indicated.

	YES	NO	
Has a summons and complaint or summons w/notice been filed?	○	○	If yes, date filed: _____
Is this action/proceeding being filed post–judgment?	○	○	If yes, judgment date: _____

NATURE OF JUDICIAL INTERVENTION: Check ONE box only AND enter additional information where indicated.

- ○ Infant's Compromise
- ○ Note of Issue and/or Certificate of Readiness
- ○ Notice of Medical, Dental, or Podiatric Malpractice
- ○ Notice of Motion
- ○ Notice of Petition
- ○ Order to Show Cause
- ○ Other Ex Parte Application
- ○ Poor Person Application
- ○ Request for Preliminary Conference
- ○ Residential Mortgage Foreclosure Settlement Conference
- ○ Writ of Habeas Corpus
- ○ Other (specify):

Date Issue Joined: _____

Relief Sought: _____ Return Date: _____
Relief Sought: _____ Return Date: _____
Relief Sought: _____ Return Date: _____
Relief Sought: _____

RELATED CASES: List any related actions. For Matrimonial actions, include any related criminal and/or Family Court cases. If additional space is required, complete and attach the **RJI Addendum**. If none, leave blank.

Case Title	Index/Case No.	Court	Judge (if assigned)	Relationship to Instant Case

PARTIES: If additional space is required, complete and attach the **RJI Addendum**.
For parties without an attorney, check "Un–Rep" box AND enter party address, phone number and e-mail address in "Attorneys" space.

Un–Rep	Parties:	Attorneys:		Issue Joined (Y/N):	Insurance Carrier(s):
	List parties in caption order and indicate party role(s) (e.g. defendant; 3rd–party plaintiff).	Provide name, firm name, business address, phone number and e-mail address of all attorneys that have appeared in the case.			

	Last Name	Last Name	First Name	○ YES	
□	First Name Primary Role:	Firm Name			
	Secondary Role (if any):	Street Address	City State Zip	○ NO	
		Phone	Fax e-mail		

	Last Name	Last Name	First Name	○ YES	
□	First Name Primary Role:	Firm Name			
	Secondary Role (if any):	Street Address	City State Zip	○ NO	
		Phone	Fax e-mail		

	Last Name	Last Name	First Name	○ YES	
□	First Name Primary Role:	Firm Name			
	Secondary Role (if any):	Street Address	City State Zip	○ NO	
		Phone	Fax e–mail		

	Last Name	Last Name	First Name	○ YES	
□	First Name Primary Role:	Firm Name			
	Secondary Role (if any):	Street Address	City State Zip	○ NO	
		Phone	Fax e-mail		

I AFFIRM UNDER THE PENALTY OF PERJURY THAT, TO MY KNOWLEDGE, OTHER THAN AS NOTED ABOVE, THERE ARE AND HAVE BEEN NO RELATED ACTIONS OR PROCEEDINGS, NOR HAS A REQUEST FOR JUDICIAL INTERVENTION PREVIOUSLY BEEN FILED IN THIS ACTION OR PROCEEDING.

Dated: _____   _____
                                                 SIGNATURE

_____   _____
ATTORNEY REGISTRATION NUMBER   **PRINT OR TYPE NAME**

FIRST JUDICIAL DISTRICT – NEW YORK COUNTY

Request for Judicial Intervention Addendum

UCS–840A (3/ 2011)

Supreme _____ COURT, COUNTY OF _____ Index No: _____

For use when additional space is needed to provide party or related case information.

PARTIES: For parties without an attorney, check " Un–Rep" box AND enter party address, phone number and e-mail address in " Attorneys" space.

Un–Rep	Parties:	Attorneys:					Issue Joined (Y/N):	Insurance Carrier(s):
	List parties in caption order and indicate party role(s) (e.g. defendant; 3rd–party plaintiff).	Provide name, firm name, business address, phone number and e-mail address of all attorneys that have appeared in the case.						

	Last Name	Last Name		First Name			○ YES	
☐	First Name Primary Role:	Firm Name						
	Secondary Role (if any):	Street Address	City	State	Zip		○ NO	
		Phone	Fax	e-mail				

	Last Name	Last Name		First Name			○ YES	
☐	First Name Primary Role:	Firm Name						
	Secondary Role (if any):	Street Address	City	State	Zip		○ NO	
		Phone	Fax	e-mail				

	Last Name	Last Name	First Name			○ YES	
☐	First Name Primary Role:	Firm Name					
	Secondary Role (if any):	Street Address	City	State	Zip	○ NO	
		Phone	Fax	e-mail			

	Last Name	Last Name	First Name			○ YES	
☐	First Name Primary Role:	Firm Name					
	Secondary Role (if any):	Street Address	City	State	Zip	○ NO	
		Phone	Fax	e-mail			

	Last Name	Last Name	First Name			○ YES	
☐	First Name Primary Role:	Firm Name					
	Secondary Role (if any):	Street Address	City	State	Zip	○ NO	
		Phone	Fax	e-mail			

	Last Name	Last Name	First Name			○ YES	
☐	First Name Primary Role:	Firm Name					
	Secondary Role (if any):	Street Address	City	State	Zip	○ NO	
		Phone	Fax	e-mail			

RELATED CASES: List any related actions. For Matrimonial actions, include any related criminal and/or Family Court cases.

Case Title	Index/Case No.	Court	Judge (if assigned)	Relationship to Instant Case

SUPREME COURT OF THE STATE OF NEW YORK   UCS–840C
                                                                3/2011
COUNTY OF _____

---x   Index No. _____

                    Plaintiff(s)/Petitioner(s)   RJI No. (if any) _____

-against-

                                                                     COMMERCIAL DIVISION
                    Defendant(s)/Respondent(s)   **Request for Judicial Intervention Addendum**

---x

COMPLETE WHERE APPLICABLE [add additional pages if needed]:
Plaintiff/Petitioner's cause(s) of action [check all that apply]:

☐ Breach of contract or fiduciary duty, fraud, misrepresentation, business tort (e.g. unfair competition), or statutory and/or common law violation where the breach or violation is alleged to arise out of business dealings (e.g. sales of assets or securities; corporate restructuring; partnership, shareholder, joint venture, and other business agreements; trade secrets; restrictive covenants; and employment agreements not including claims that principally involve alleged discriminatory practices)

☐ Transactions governed by the Uniform Commercial Code (exclusive of those concerning individual cooperative or condominium units)

☐ Transactions involving commercial real property, including Yellowstone injunctions and excluding actions for the payment of rent only

☐ Shareholder derivative actions — without consideration of the monetary threshold

☐ Commercial class actions — without consideration of the monetary threshold

☐ Business transactions involving or arising out of dealings with commercial banks and other financial institutions

☐ Internal affairs of business organizations

☐ Malpractice by accountants or actuaries, and legal malpractice arising out of representation in commercial matters

☐ Environmental insurance coverage

☐ Commercial insurance coverage (e.g. directors and officers, errors and omissions, and business interruption coverage)

☐ Dissolution of corporations, partnerships, limited liability companies, limited liability partnerships and joint ventures — without consideration of the monetary threshold

☐ Applications to stay or compel arbitration and affirm or disaffirm arbitration awards and related injunctive relief pursuant to CPLR Article 75 involving any of the foregoing enumerated commercial issues — without consideration of the monetary threshold

Plaintiff/Petitioner's claim for compensatory damages [exclusive of punitive damages, interest, costs and counsel fees claimed]:
    $ _____

Plaintiff/Petitioner's claim for equitable or declaratory relief [brief description]: _____

_____

Defendant/Respondent's   counterclaim(s)
[brief description, including claim for monetary relief]:

_____

I REQUEST THAT THIS CASE BE ASSIGNED TO THE COMMERCIAL DIVISION. I CERTIFY THAT THE CASE MEETS THE JURISDICTIONAL REQUIREMENTS OF THE COMMERCIAL DIVISION SET FORTH IN 22 NYCRR § 202.70(a), (b) AND (c).
Dated: _____   _____
                                          SIGNATURE

                                  _____
                                  PRINT OR TYPE NAME

                                                                UCS–840M
                                                                3/2011
MATRIMONIAL Request for Judicial Intervention Addendum

 Supreme _____ COURT, COUNTY OF _____ INDEX NO. _____

For use when there are children under the age of 18 who are subject to the matrimonial action.
Plaintiff
        Last Name: _____   First Name: _____   Date of Birth: _____

Prior Names (List any other names used, including   **Gender:** ☐ Male ☐ Female
maiden and/or former married names):
Last Name: _____   First Name: _____
Last Name: _____   First Name: _____
Last Name: _____   First Name: _____

Present Address: _____ New York _____
                 (Street Address)   (City)   (State)   (Zip)

Address History
for past 3 years: _____
                 (Street Address)   (City)   (State)   (Zip)

                 _____
                 (Street Address)   (City)   (State)   (Zip)

                 _____
                 (Street Address)   (City)   (State)   (Zip)

Defendant
Last Name: _____   First Name: _____   Date of Birth: _____

Prior Names (List any other names used, including   **Gender:** ☐ Male ☐ Female
maiden and/or former married names):
Last Name: _____   First Name: _____
Last Name: _____   First Name: _____
Last Name: _____   First Name: _____

Present Address: _____ New York _____
                 (Street Address)   (City)   (State)   (Zip)

Address History
for past 3 years: _____
                 (Street Address)   (City)   (State)   (Zip)

                 _____
                 (Street Address)   (City)   (State)   (Zip)

                 _____
                 (Street Address)   (City)   (State)   (Zip)

Children
Last Name: _____   First Name: _____   Date of Birth: _____   **Gender:** ☐ M ☐ F

Last Name: _____   First Name: _____   Date of Birth: _____   **Gender:** ☐ M ☐ F

Last Name: _____   First Name: _____   Date of Birth: _____   **Gender:** ☐ M ☐ F

Last Name: _____   First Name: _____   Date of Birth: _____   **Gender:** ☐ M ☐ F

Last Name: _____   First Name: _____   Date of Birth: _____   **Gender:** ☐ M ☐ F

PRELIMINARY CONFERENCE FORMS

Form 4.   General

SUPREME COURT OF THE STATE OF NEW YORK
COUNTY OF NEW YORK
---x

Present: Hon. _____

Justice

Plaintiff(s),   IAS PART _____

-against-   Index No. _____

DCM Track: _____

Defendant(s).

PRELIMINARY CONFERENCE
ORDER

---x

APPEARANCES:

Plaintiff(s): _____

_____

Defendant(s): _____

_____

It is hereby ORDERED that disclosure shall proceed as follows:

(1) INSURANCE COVERAGE: If not already provided, shall be furnished by _____ on or before _____.

(2) BILL OF PARTICULARS [See CPLR 3130(1)]:

   (a) Demand for a bill of particulars shall be served by _____ on or before _____.

   (b) Bill of particulars shall be served by _____ on or before _____.

   (c) A supplemental bill of particulars shall be served by _____ as to Items _____ on or before _____.

(3) MEDICAL REPORTS AND AUTHORIZATIONS:

Shall be served as follows: _____

_____

(4) PHYSICAL EXAMINATION:

   (a) Examination of _____ shall be held _____

_____

   (b) A copy of the physician's report shall be furnished to plaintiff within _____ days of the examination.

(5) DEPOSITIONS:
   Depositions of   [ ] Plaintiff(s)   [ ] Defendant(s)   [ ] All Parties

shall be held _____

_____

(6) OTHER DISCLOSURE:

119

(a) All parties, on or before _____, shall exchange names and addresses of eyewitnesses and notice witnesses, statements of opposing parties and photographs, or, if none, provide an affirmation to that effect.

(b) Authorization for plaintiff(s)' employment records for the period _____ shall be furnished on or before _____.

(c) Demand for discovery and inspection shall be served by _____ on or before _____.   The items sought shall be produced to the extent not objected to, and objections, if any, shall be stated on or before _____.

(d) Other [interrogatories, etc.] _____

_____

(7) COMPLIANCE CONFERENCE [See Uniform Rule 202.19]: Shall be held on _____.

(8) IMPLEADER: Shall be completed on or before _____.

(9) END DATE FOR ALL DISCLOSURE [See Uniform Rule 202.19]: _____.

(10) MOTIONS: Any dispositive motion(s) shall be made on or before _____

_____

(11) NOTE OF ISSUE: _____ shall file a note of issue/certificate of readiness on or before _____.

A copy of this order shall be served and filed with the note of issue/certificate of readiness, together with an affirmation or affidavit, with proof of service, showing compliance with this order. Uniform Rule 202.12 (f).

DATES SET FORTH HEREIN MAY NOT BE ADJOURNED EXCEPT WITH ADVANCE APPROVAL OF THE COURT.

SO ORDERED:

Dated: _____   _____, J.S.C.

ADDITIONAL DIRECTIVES

In addition to the directives set forth above, it is further ORDERED as follows:

_____

_____

_____

_____

SO ORDERED:

Dated: _____   _____, J.S.C.

Form 5. Motor Vehicle Cases

Supreme Court of the State of New York
New York County Courthouse
60 Centre Street
New York, New York

DIFFERENTIATED CASE MANAGEMENT PROGRAM

PRESENT: HON. MILTON TINGLING (DCM), JUSTICE   PART 22

2001

To:

Index #

_____
                    ,PLAINTIFF

                    ,DEFENDANT
_____

CASE SCHEDULING ORDER[1]

A request for a preliminary conference having been filed or the court having taken action on its own initiative,

IT IS HEREBY ORDERED that this case is designated an Expedited matter (Uniform Rule 202.19 (b)) and disclosure not already furnished shall proceed in accordance with the deadlines set forth below. However, a party claiming to be prejudiced by this order may, after consulting opposing counsel, seek a modification of the Expedited designation or the schedule by contacting Robert Berardelli, Case Management Coordinator, at the Case Management Office (by phone at 748–5310 or fax at 374–0006 or e-mail to Rberarde@courts.state.ny.us) by _____. That Office will provide an opportunity to the parties to be heard on the request by telephone or court conference and the court will take such action as is appropriate. Failure to contact the Office within the said deadline shall constitute a waiver of any objection to the designation or schedule. The parties shall not in the first instance contact the Justice assigned.

NONE OF THE DATES IN THE ORDER MAY BE EXTENDED WITHOUT ADVANCE APPROVAL BY THE COURT. All requests for extensions shall be directed to the Case Management Office in the first instance.

(1) Mandatory Notification: The attorney who receives a copy of this Order shall, within ten days from receipt, transmit a copy to counsel for all parties who have appeared in the case and to all self-represented litigants and shall, by ___, return to the Case Management Office an original by mail or a copy by fax of an affidavit of service or a letter setting forth the dates the parties were served.

(2) Insurance Information: All parties shall exchange insurance and coverage information by _____.

(3) Bill of Particulars: A demand shall be served by _____. A bill(s) shall be served by _____.

(4) Authorizations: Authorizations for medical records and for employment records for two years prior to the accident shall be served by _____.

(5) Witness and Other Information: All parties shall exchange statements of opposing parties, photographs, and the names and addresses of all fact witnesses by ___. If any of these items do not exist, the parties shall serve by that date an affirmation clearly so specifying.

121

(6) Depositions: All depositions must be completed by ___. Plaintiff shall be deposed first and defendants shall be deposed in the order in which their names appear in the caption. Within 20 days from service of a copy of this Order, the parties shall confer and agree upon a detailed schedule in compliance with this deadline. If a witness thereafter is unable to appear as scheduled, the parties shall confer and attempt to agree upon a resolution of the problem, including, if necessary, an alternative schedule or order of production. However, absent extraordinary circumstances, the failure of one defendant to appear as scheduled shall not constitute an excuse for the refusal of others to submit to deposition as scheduled and within the deadline fixed above.

(7) Demands for Documents: Demands for documents shall be served no later than 10 days after completion of depositions and shall be responded to within 20 days from service.

(8) Physical Examinations and Reports (Uniform Rule 202.17): Physical examination(s) of the plaintiff shall be completed by ___. The examining party shall notify all other parties of the identity of the examining physician at least 20 days prior to said examination. Copies of medical reports shall be served by plaintiff at least 15 days prior to said examination. A copy of the report of the examining physician shall be served on all parties within 21 days of said examination.

(9) Other Disclosure: All other disclosure shall be completed by _____.

(10) Impleader: Shall be completed by _____.

(11) Mandatory Pre–Note Settlement Conference: Will be held on _____ in Room 121 at 80 Centre Street before Senior Neutral Evaluation Attorney Michael McAllister, Esq.

(12) Note of Issue: Shall be filed on or before _____.

(13) Summary Judgment Motions: Summary judgment motions shall be made no later than 30 days after filing of the note of issue (CPLR 3212 (a)).

RESOLUTION OF DISPUTES/PENALTIES FOR NON–COMPLIANCE

If disputes arise about compliance with this Order, the parties shall promptly confer in an effort to resolve them. If that effort fails, the parties shall immediately, in advance of deadlines and prior to initiating motion practice, bring the dispute to the attention of the Case Management Office (not the assigned Justice) and shall participate in any telephonic or court conference that Office may require. Absent good cause, failure to raise discovery problems with that Office immediately, in advance of deadlines, other non-compliance with this Order, or failure to comply with any Disclosure Reminder Notice transmitted by that Office may result in the imposition of penalties upon the offending party and, where warranted, upon counsel. Such penalties may include waiver of the discovery, preclusion, dismissal, striking of an answer, costs, sanctions, and attorney's fees. Counsel should be particularly aware that penalties may be imposed in the event of the failure of a defendant to give notice of, designate a physician for, schedule, or conduct an examination of plaintiff as set forth herein, the failure of said defendant to serve a report as set forth herein, the failure of plaintiff to appear at an examination as required, and the failure of a party to schedule or attend a deposition.

TINGLING, M.A. (DCM)

J.S.C.

Jun 08, 2001

1 This is a conformed copy. The original order has been signed and has been or will be filed with the County Clerk.

Form 6.   Medical; Dental, and Podiatric Malpractice Cases

INSTRUCTIONS: PLEASE TYPE OR PRINT NEATLY MAKING SURE ALL WRITING IS CLEAR AND LEGIBLE ON EACH COPY

SUPREME COURT OF THE STATE OF NEW YORK
COUNTY OF NEW YORK

....X   IAS PART _____

_____   HON. _____

_____

Plaintiff(s)

-against-   **Preliminary Conference**
                                                 Stipulation and Order
                                                 For Medical, Dental and
(1) _____   **Podiatric Malpractice**
(2) _____   **Actions**
(3) _____
(4) _____   **INDEX NO:** _____
(5) _____
                                                 RJI DATE: _____

Defendant(s)

....X

BRIEF CASE DESCRIPTION:

_____
_____
_____

APPEARANCES:

Plaintiff: _____
Firm: _____
By: _____
Phone/Fax:* _____
E–mail:* _____
* not for service purposes

Defendant 1: _____
Firm: _____
By: _____
Phone/Fax:* _____
E–mail:* _____
* not for service purposes

Defendant 2: _____
Firm: _____
By: _____
Phone/Fax:* _____
E–mail:* _____
* not for service purposes

Defendant 3: _____
Firm: _____
By: _____
Phone/Fax:* _____
E–mail:* _____
* not for service purposes

If there are Defendants # 4 or # 5 or others in this case, please insert pages for additional parties.

THIS ACTION having come on for a Preliminary Conference pursuant to Section 202.56 of the Uniform Rules of the New York State Trial Courts in order to establish a schedule for the completion of disclosure and other related matters. The parties stipulate and it is hereby:

ORDERED that the action is entitled to a preference pursuant to CPLR 3403(a)(5), and it is further

ORDERED *that there is to be timely compliance with each of the items below within the time set forth unless the time is extended by a* **"so-ordered"** *OR* **court-approved written stipulation**.

I. INSURANCE INFORMATION

Insurance coverage information shall be provided in writing with respect to each defendant for all applicable periods within 30 (thirty) days as follows [check applicable spaces:]

___ Primary coverage, including insurance carrier, policy number(s) and policy coverage periods;

___ Excess coverage, including insurance carrier, policy number(s) and policy coverage periods; and

___ Declaration sheets.

II. BILL OF PARTICULARS

(a) A further Verified Bill of Particulars shall be served upon each defendant within 20 (twenty) days as to the following items:

_____

_____

_____

(b) Defendant(s) shall serve upon plaintiff a Verified Bill of Particulars as to the affirmative defenses and/or counterclaims in the Answer (when demanded) within 20 (twenty) days.

III. MEDICAL RECORDS AND AUTHORIZATIONS

(a) HIPAA–compliant medical authorizations, *if not already provided with the Bill of Particulars*, shall be furnished to defendant(s) within 20 (twenty) days as to the following health care providers:

_____

_____

_____

(b) Following plaintiff's deposition, plaintiff shall provide HIPAA–compliant authorizations for appropriate records within 10 (ten) days of receipt of a written request from the defendant(s).

(c) Medical records shall be furnished by the defendant(s) within 30 (thirty) days as follows [check where applicable, and identify specifically]:

1.   ___ Office records, including reports and correspondence. _____

2.   ___ Hospital chart. _____

3.   ___ Billing records. _____

4.   ___ Autopsy report. _____

5.   ___ Radiology film/report. _____

6.   ___ Curriculum vitae of defendant(s). _____

7.   ___ Hospital rules and regulations. _____

8. ___ Other. _____

_____

(d) If a medical record to be supplied by a defendant is not available, within 30 (thirty) days, an affidavit shall be supplied by defendant, or by a records custodian with personal knowledge, which shall set forth a statement concerning the customary record-keeping practices of the physician/hospital, and the date, nature and location of the search conducted, including all efforts undertaken to locate such records.

(e) If the records described in paragraph (d) above are subsequently located, they shall be promptly supplied to all parties. Any party who fails to produce such items more than 30 (thirty) days after they are located but, in any event, no later than 30 (thirty) days prior to trial shall be precluded from introducing the items into evidence, unless good cause is demonstrated.

IV. DEPOSITIONS

• All dates listed below are dates certain *and may NOT be adjourned unless the time is extended by a "so-ordered" OR court-approved written stipulation.*

• Inability to obtain medical records prior to the deposition dates *shall NOT be cause for adjournment of the deposition.* If the records subsequently obtained reveal the need for additional information, a further limited deposition may be held by agreement of the parties or by Order of the Court.

(a) Dates:

Plaintiff(s) on or before: _____

Defendant _____ on or before _____

Defendant _____ on or before _____

Defendant _____ on or before _____

Defendant _____ on or before _____

Defendant _____ on or before _____

THE DEPOSITION OF EACH DEFENDANT SHALL BE CONDUCTED ON THE DATE SET FORTH ABOVE EVEN THOUGH AN EARLIER SCHEDULED DEPOSITION OF ANOTHER DEFENDANT WAS NOT CONDUCTED.

(b) Deposition of Institutional Defendant(s):

Within 30 (thirty) days after plaintiff's deposition, plaintiff shall serve upon counsel for any institutional defendant(s) a demand for the identification of no more than 5 (five) health care providers who are referred to, or made entries, in the medical records. Within 20 (twenty) days of service of the demand, the institutional defendant(s) shall provide the full name and employment status of each of these individuals, and, if not under the institution(s)' control, the last known address of each individual. Within 5 (five) business days thereafter, plaintiff shall designate the first witness under the institution(s)' control to be deposed and the institutional defendant(s) shall produce said witness. Plaintiff shall then designate additional witnesses under defendant(s)' control for deposition within 5 (five) business days after said EBT. If the institutional defendant(s) do not voluntarily produce the additional requested witnesses within 20 (twenty) days of plaintiff's designation, plaintiff may seek an order compelling additional depositions pursuant to statute.

All of these individuals shall be deposed on or before _____.

(c) Non–Party Witness Depositions:

Plaintiff is to advise defendant(s) within 30 (thirty) days of this Preliminary Conference Order whether the following non-party witnesses will be produced for deposition voluntarily, or whether a subpoena will be necessary. If the latter, plaintiff is to provide the witnesses' last known addresses within 30 (thirty) days of this Stipulation and Order.

Name of Non–Party Witness: _____

Name of Non–Party Witness: _____

(d) Time and Place:

Plaintiff(s)' deposition(s) shall be held at _____, commencing at _____ (a.m.) (p.m).

Defendant(s)' deposition(s) shall be held as follows [List the time and place for each deposition]:

_____

_____

_____

_____

(e) Objections:

• ALL questions asked at any deposition must be answered UNLESS they (a) infringe upon a privilege, (b) bear SOLELY on the negligence of a co-defendant and NOT in any way on the potential negligence of the deponent, or (c) are palpably irrelevant.

• If a party makes an objection as to *form*, the objector shall immediately and succinctly indicate the nature of the defect so as to permit correction. In any event, the witness shall answer the question.

• Depositions shall not be interrupted for an attorney-deponent conference.

• Counsel for the deponent shall NOT engage in coaching during the deposition and shall NOT suggest answers to questions (e.g. "If you know . . ."; "If you remember . . .").

V. PHYSICAL EXAMINATIONS

Defendant(s) who wishes to conduct a physical or mental examination pursuant to CPLR 3121 shall designate in writing an examining physician or other specialist within 30 (thirty) days of plaintiff's deposition. The examination of the plaintiff must be conducted at least 30 (thirty) days before the filing of the Note of Issue.

Specialty: _____

Defendant(s) shall serve upon all parties written reports of any examining physician within 60 (sixty) days after the examination, and at least 30 (thirty) days before trial. Pursuant to CPLR 3121, plaintiff shall provide defendant(s) with a written report by any non-treating examining physician within 60 (sixty) days after an examination, and at least 60 (sixty) days before trial.

VI. OTHER DISCLOSURE*

(a) Witnesses: Parties shall exchange names and addresses of all FACT WITNESSES concerning liability and/or damages (other than expert witnesses) no later than 60 (sixty) days before trial. Parties shall also exchange adverse party statements within that same period.

(b) Photographs and Videotapes: Parties shall exchange all photographs and/or videotapes within 60 (sixty) days after their creation and/or availability but not less than 30 (thirty) days before trial absent a showing of good cause.

(c) Employment: If loss of earnings is claimed, authorizations for plaintiff's employment records (including W-2's, 1099's and/or income tax returns) for a period of __ years before the claimed malpractice and continuing to date, shall be provided within 30 (thirty) days.

(d) Collateral Sources: Plaintiff shall provide authorizations for the following collateral source providers within 30 (thirty) days:

_____

_____

_____

(e) Discovery Notices: Responses to the following outstanding Discovery and Inspection Notices shall be furnished within 30 (thirty) days:

_____

_____

_____

* This disclosure demand shall be considered ongoing and continuous. If requested items subsequently become available, they are to be supplied immediately upon receipt of the same to all parties to the action.

VII. EXPERT EXCHANGE

Plaintiff shall serve a CPLR 3101(d) expert disclosure no later than 60 (sixty) days before trial.

Defendant(s) shall serve a CPLR 3101(d) expert disclosure no later than 45 (forty-five) days before trial.

VIII. DEATH ACTIONS

In wrongful death actions, plaintiff shall provide the following when available within 30 (thirty) days. If not currently available, then within 30 (thirty) days after receipt of the document: death certificate, letters of administration or letters testamentary, marriage certificate, and authorization for the autopsy reports.

IX. ADDITIONAL DIRECTIVES

_____

_____

_____

_____

_____

_____

_____

_____

_____

_____

_____

_____

_____

_____

_____

_____

_____

_____

X. NOTE OF ISSUE: The Note of Issue and Certificate of Readiness shall be filed on or before _____.

XI. SUMMARY JUDGEMENT AND/OR OTHER DISPOSITIVE MOTIONS

Motions for Summary Judgement and/or other dispositive motions shall be made no later than **60 (sixty) days** from the filing of the Note of Issue, unless the Court directs otherwise.

XII. FURTHER DIRECTIVES: It is

ORDERED that failure to comply with the terms of this STIPULATION AND ORDER may result in sanctions as authorized by CPLR 3126, and it is further

ORDERED that a compliance conference shall be held on _____ at _____ (AM) (PM), and it is further

ORDERED that **ALL *prior* discovery** orders of this court be brought to any and all subsequent conferences.

Dated: _____

SO STIPULATED:

Plaintiff: _____   Defendant # 1 _____

Printed Name: _____   Printed Name: _____

Firm Name: _____   Firm Name: _____

Defendant # 2 _____   Defendant # 3 _____

Printed Name: _____   Printed Name: _____

Firm Name: _____   Firm Name: _____

Defendant # 4 _____   Defendant # 5 _____

Printed Name: _____   Printed Name: _____

Firm Name: _____   Firm Name: _____

SO ORDERED:

_____

JUSTICE OF THE SUPREME COURT

3/31/07

INSTRUCTIONS FOR PRELIMINARY CONFERENCE STIPULATION AND ORDER FOR MEDICAL, DENTAL AND PODIATRIC MALPRACTICE ACTIONS

Justice Sheila Abdus–Salaam	Part 13	(815–0877)	71 Thomas Street, Room 305
Justice Eileen Bransten	Part 6	(374–8340)	60 Centre Street, Room 442
Justice Joan B. Carey	Part 40 D	(374–3936)	111 Centre Street, Room 948
Justice Alice Schlesinger	Part 16	(374–4721)	60 Centre Street, Room 222
Justice Stanley L. Sklar	Part 29	(374–4732)	60 Centre Street, Room 212

General Comments: The preliminary conference form should be modified as follows:

1.   First page should be labeled "Stipulation and Order".

2.   Last page should include signature lines for the attorneys before judge's signature.

Additional General Instructions:

A short caption (i.e., names of plaintiff and the first defendant) and the index number must be written on each page of the preliminary conference order. A brief description of the case (i.e., the date of the alleged malpractice as well as the injuries alleged) must be written on the first page of the order.

Item II.   Bills of Particulars:

If the Bill of Particulars contains broad boilerplate language but sufficiently apprises defendant of plaintiff's claim, applications to strike will not be granted unless plaintiff fails to amend the Bill of Particulars within 60 days after all defendants' EBT's (see *Aksanov v. St. Luke's–Roosevelt Hosp. Ctr.*, 233 AD2d 277, 650 NYS 2d 541 (1st Dept. 1996)).

Item III.   Medical Records/Authorizations:

Authorizations shall be supplied within 30 days after the preliminary conference.

Item V.   Depositions:

Scheduling: Depositions will be scheduled in the preliminary conference order. If an extraordinary circumstance (such as sudden hospitalization) prevents one defendant's EBT from proceeding as scheduled, the remaining defendants' EBTs shall nonetheless proceed as scheduled.

At the EBT: If there is an objection as to form, the objector shall indicate what the defect is so as to permit correction. Otherwise, questions shall be answered, if reasonably relevant, unless the question would violate a privilege, would implicate a constitutional right, is palpably improper, or violates a limitation in a court order. Objections shall be stated succinctly and so as not to suggest an answer. Counsel for the deponent shall not interject suggestions like "if you know," "if you remember." Upon request of the questioner, the objector shall give a clear explanation of the claimed defect. The EBT shall not be interrupted for an attorney-deponent conference unless all parties consent. In all parts except Part 13, if counsel are unable to resolve disputes after a good faith, professional effort, they shall telephone the court. **Justice Abdus–Salaam** (Part 13) instructs counsel not to call chambers for rulings.

Item X.   Summary Judgment Motions:

Modify Order form; insert "No later than 60 days after the filing of the Note of Issue."

Item XI.   Note of Issue:

The Note of Issue, Certificate of Readiness and compliance/status conferences shall be as stated in the preliminary conference or subsequent order.

Compliance Conference:

Compliance conferences must be scheduled for no later than 60 days prior to Note of Issue date. The Court will choose a compliance conference date usually as follows.

Justice Bransten: for a Tuesday morning.

Justice Sklar: for a Thursday or on the last Friday of the month.

Justice Schlesinger: for a Wednesday morning.

Justice Abdus–Salaam: for a Thursday.

Justice Carey: for a Friday.

If you have resolved all issues within the above guidelines, please advise the court clerk when you present the Conference Order.

3/25/04

Form 7.   City Cases (Sample)

SUPREME COURT OF THE STATE OF NEW YORK
New York County
80 Centre Street, Room 102
New York, New York 10007

PRESENT: Hon _____   DCM Part
Date _____

CASE SCHEDULING ORDER - CITY CASES

Index Number: _____

C.C.T.T.No: _____

PLAINTIFF
v
DEFENDANT

A request for a preliminary conference having been filed or the court having taken action on its own initiative,

IT IS HEREBY ORDERED that this case is designated a Standard matter (Uniform Rule 202.19 (b) and disclosure not already furnished shall proceed in accordance with the deadlines set forth below. However, a party claiming to be prejudiced by this order may seek a modification of the Standard designation or the schedule by contacting the Case Management Office at phone number 646–386–3687 or by fax to 212–374–1753, within **20 DAYS FROM THE DATE OF THIS ORDER**. That Office will provide an opportunity to the parties to be heard on the request at a court conference and the court will take such action as is appropriate. Failure to contact the office before the conference date shall constitute a waiver of any objection to the designation or schedule. The parties shall not contact the Justice assigned.

1. Mandatory Notification: The attorney who receives this Order shall, within ten days from receipt, (a) transmit a copy to counsel for all parties who have appeared in the case and to all self-represented litigants and (b) return to the Case Management Office an original by mail or a copy by fax of an affidavit of service or a letter setting forth the dates the parties were served.

2. Insurance Coverage: Within 30 days from the date of this order, defendant City of New York and any other defendant represented by Corporation Counsel, shall state in writing, whether it is self-insured or covered by an insurance policy, and all defendant(s), including the City (if applicable), shall furnish to all parties evidence of primary and excess coverage and Certificate of insurance.

3. Bill of Particulars:

Any party seeking particulars (including as to affirmative defenses, if any) shall serve a demand for a bill within 21 days from the date of this order. The party receiving the demand shall serve a verified bill of particulars within 60 days from the date of this order.

This is a conformed copy. The original has been signed and filed with the County Clerk.

4. Medical Reports and Authorizations:

(a) Plaintiff(s) shall provide authorizations to obtain copies of the actual records of all treating and examining health care providers, including diagnostic tests, x-rays, MRIs, EMGs, CT Scans, for injuries specified in the bill of particulars, within 30 days from the date of this order.

(b) Plaintiff(s) shall provide an authorization for collateral source information, if any, within 30 days from the date of this order.

(c) If plaintiff is claiming a loss of income or wages, within 30 days from the date of this order, plaintiff shall provide authorizations for W-2 forms or employment records shall be provided for the year of, year before and year after the date of the alleged accident, as well as for the period of time lost from work as a result of the alleged accident, or IRS records if provided by law.

(d) If plaintiff was a student at the time of the alleged accident, within 30 days from the date of this order plaintiff shall provide an authorization for school attendance records for the period of time lost from school as a result of the alleged accident, within 30 days from the date of this order thereof.

(e) For cases alleging police assault or false arrest, plaintiff(s) shall, within 30 days from the date of this order, submit an unsealing order, to be "so ordered" by this Court, to obtain a copy of the Criminal Court File. Plaintiff(s) shall then serve the "so ordered" unsealing order upon the Criminal Court. After that Court provides plaintiff with a copy of the Criminal Court file, plaintiff shall provide a copy of the file to the Corporation Counsel within 30 days of the date of service of the unsealing order.

5. Depositions:

(a) The depositions of all parties shall take place on _____ @ _____ **AM/PM** in the Office of the Corporation Counsel, located at 52 Duane Street, 4th floor, New York, New York, 10007. **Absent prior court approval, any deposition which is not held as scheduled in this order must be immediately re-scheduled for a date which is not later than four (4) weeks after the original date.**

(b) Defendant(s)' right to a further deposition of plaintiff(s) is reserved as to any new injuries or damages claimed in any supplemental bill of particulars served by plaintiff(s) following the plaintiff's deposition.

6. Physical Examination:

(a) A physical examination of the plaintiff (s) shall be conducted within 45 days after completion of examination before trial of the plaintiff(s).

(b) A copy of the physician's report shall be furnished to plaintiff(s) within 45 after the examination.

(c) Defendant(s)' right to a further physical is reserved as to any new injuries claimed in any supplemental bill of particulars served by plaintiff(s).

7. Other Disclosure:

(a) All parties shall provide the names and addresses of any witnesses to the occurrence and notice the witnesses; accident reports; party statements; and photographs taken in the ordinary course of business and/or to be presented at trial, within 90 days from the date of this order.

(b) All parties shall supply expert witness disclosure pursuant to CPLR.

(c) All defendants other than those listed in Item 7(d) hereof shall, within 90 days from the date of this order, provide to all parties copies of maintenance and repair records for 2 years prior to and including the date of the occurrence.

(d) The City of New York and/or other defendants represented by Corporation Counsel, if any, shall provide the following Additional Disclosure to all parties within 90 days from the date of this order, subject to the date and location specified in the notice of claim [check if applicable]:

ADDITIONAL DISCLOSURE ITEM 7(d)

Cases involving allegations of police misconduct:

The City will provide the following within 90 days after receipt from plaintiff of an authorization and "so-ordered" unsealing order described in 4(e) above.

    i. Complaint Report;

ii.   Complaint Follow Up Report;

iii.   Arrest Report;

iv.   Memo Book entries for incident in question;

v.   On-line Booking Sheet;

vi.   Copies of the applicable Patrol Guide shall be made available by the City for inspection and copying within 90 days from the date of this order.

vii.   Copies of all 911 tapes, if still in existence, and of all sprint printouts for any 911 calls and radio transmissions related to the events of the action.

Inmate assault cases (Department of Correction (DOC):

i.   Department of correction incident report, subject to redaction of privileged information, including any information regarding criminal acts of other inmates and/or personal information regarding DOC employees;

ii.   Injury to inmate report (within 90 days after receipt of an authorization from plaintiff);

iii.   In camera review of redactions to be made upon request of plaintiff's attorney.

Premise liability Cases:

i.   Departmental accident/incident report from respective City agency;

ii.   For non-transitory conditions (including recurrent conditions), maintenance and repair records and written complaints regarding the condition complained of for 18 months prior to and including the date of occurrence.

iii.   For transitory conditions, maintenance records and written complaints regarding the condition complained of for one month prior to and including the date of the occurrence.

iv.   If applicable, lease and/or sublease for the City-owned building.

Board of Education Cases:

i.   Board of Education Comprehensive Accident Report for the occurrence, subject to redaction of privileged information pursuant to the Family Education and Privacy Act, 20 U.S. Code Ch 31. Extent and nature of the redaction, if questioned, are subject to motion under the statute.

ii.   Witness statements, subject to redaction of privileged information pursuant to the Family Education and Privacy Act. Extent and nature of the redaction, if questioned, are subject to motion under the statute.

iii.   For non-transitory conditions (including recurrent conditions), maintenance and repair records, written complaints and, to the extent applicable, related contracts for the situs of plaintiff's accident, regarding the condition complained of for 18 months prior to and including the date of occurrence.

iv.   For transitory conditions, maintenance records and written complaints regarding the condition complained of for three months prior to and including the date of the occurrence.

Motor vehicle accidents involving City-owned vehicles:

i. Departmental Accident Report from respective City agency.

ii. Maintenance and repair records for the department vehicle involved for one year prior to and including the date of the occurrence, if a vehicular defect is alleged in either the departmental accident report or the MV–104.

iii. Photos of damage to City vehicle.

iv. Records regarding post-accident repairs shall be supplied by the City unless determined by the court not to be relevant to an issue in the case.

Slip and Fall Cases (Department of Sanitation):

i. District Operation Log (carting book) for the period of two weeks prior to and including the date of occurrence.

ii. District Snow Operation Book for the above period of time.

iii. Snow Removal Operation Report (SR–2) and spreading or plowing operation card for the above time period, if the occurrence took place in the roadway.

Trip and Fall Cases (Department of Transportation (DOT):

i. Applications for permits and permits for 2 years prior to and including the date of occurrence;

ii. Cut forms, repair orders and repair records for 2 years prior to and including the date of occurrence;

iii. Violations issued for 2 years prior to and including the date of occurrence;

iv. A copy of the title and signature pages, and insurance declaration sheets and/or certificates, for all contracts in effect for two years prior to and including the date of occurrence.

v. Contracts and all related contract documents (i.e. progress reports) for two years prior to and including the date of occurrence will be made available for inspection and copying at either the Office of the Corporation Counsel designated by said Counsel, or the appropriate City agency, upon a mutually convenient appointment, but in no event more than 90 days hereafter or a subsequent request for same by plaintiff.

vi. Complaints made for 2 years prior to and including the date of occurrence;

vii. A copy of the most recent Big Apple Pothole and Sidewalk Protection Corporation map filed for the area in issue and, if the incident at issue occurred six months or less after the filing of the most recent such map, then the City shall also produce the last such map filed before the most recent such map for that location.

Cases involving allegations of defective traffic signals (DOT):

i. Maintenance and repair records for 30 days prior to and including date of occurrence;

ii. Complaints made for 30 days prior to and including date of occurrence;

iii. The name and address of the contractor responsible for maintenance of traffic signals on date of the occurrence.

iv. A copy of title and signature pages, and insurance declaration sheet and/or certificates, for all contracts in effect for two years prior to and including the date of the occurrence.

v. Contracts and all related contract document (i.e., progress reports) for two years prior to and including the date of occurrence will be made available for inspection and copying at either the Office of the Corporation Counsel designated by said Counsel, or the appropriate City agency, upon a mutually convenient appointment, but in no event more than 90 days hereafter or a subsequent request for same by plaintiff.

Cases involving allegation of defective traffic signs (DOT):

i. Maintenance and repair records for six months prior to and including the date of occurrence;

ii. Complaints for six months prior to and including the date of the occurrence.

(e) Surveillance videos to be provided in accordance with CPLR 3101(i).

(f) Any party who wishes to obtain prior notices of claim, pursuant to GML'50-g, may do so by contacting Lee McNeil at (212) 669–4329 to set up an appointment to search the index maintained at One Centre Street, New York, New York.

(g) The New York City Police Department no longer maintains MV-104s beyond 30 days for accidents occurring after April 15, 1995.

(h) All searches shall be conducted based upon the date and location as described in the notice of claim.

8. <u>Third-party actions/Impleader</u> shall be completed on or before _____.

9. <u>Compliance Conference</u> shall be held on _____ at **2:00 PM,** in Room 103 at 80 Centre Street, New York, NY 10013.

10. <u>Note of Issue Date</u> shall be determined at a future conference.

11. Plaintiff shall within fifteen days after the note of issue is filed and receipt of a request by defense counsel, provide to defense counsel, HIPAA compliant authorizations in order to subpoena medical records for trial. Any disputes shall promptly be brought to the attention of the case management coordinator.

12. Summary Judgment Motions shall be filed no later than 60 days after filing the note of issue.

If disputes arise about compliance with this Order, the parties shall promptly confer in an effort to resolve them. If that effort fails, the parties, or any party aggrieved, shall, in advance of deadlines and prior to initiating motion practice, bring the dispute to the attention of the Case Management Coordinator (not the assigned Justice), who will schedule a conference shortly thereafter to resolve the dispute.

All disclosure called for by this Order must be completed prior to the compliance conference.

The compliance conference will not be adjourned.

Absent good cause, failure to comply with this Order may result in the imposition of penalties upon the offending party and, where warranted, upon counsel. Such penalties may include waiver of the discovery, preclusion, dismissal, striking of an answer, costs, sanctions, and attorney's fees.

This constitutes the Order of this Court.

Date _____

_____
                              J.S.C.

Index number _____

Form 8. Matrimonial Cases

SUPREME COURT OF THE STATE OF NEW YORK
COUNTY OF NEW YORK
--X

Plaintiff,
(Husband / Wife)

Index No.: _____

-against-

Part No.: _____

Defendant.
(Husband / Wife)

--X

**PRELIMINARY CONFERENCE STIPULATION/ORDER CONTESTED
MATRIMONIAL**

PRESIDING: _____

Justice of the Supreme Court

The parties and counsel have appeared before this Court on _____ at a preliminary conference on this matter held pursuant to 22 NYCRR § 202.16.

The Court has received a copy of: Date Filed or To Be Filed

                Plaintiff   Defendant

(1) A sworn statement of net worth as of date of commencement of the action. _____ _____

(2) A signed copy of each party's attorney's retainer agreement: _____ _____

A. REQUIRED INFORMATION:

(1) Attorneys for Plaintiff: Attorneys for Defendant:

_____ _____

_____ _____

_____ _____

Phone: _____ Phone: _____

Fax: _____ Fax: _____

Email: _____ Email: _____

(2) Summons: Date Filed: _____ Date Served: _____

(3) Date of Marriage: _____

(4) Name(s) and Date(s) of Birth of Child(ren):

_____ _____

_____ _____

(5) There is ___ or is not ___ an Order of Protection issued against _____ from _____ Court. The order is dated _____ and is / is not currently outstanding. Attach copy of order.

(6) The following other orders are outstanding:

Order: _____

Court Issuing: _____

Issue Addressed: _____

Order: _____

Court Issuing: _____

Issue Addressed: _____

(7) _____ needs a translator in the _____ language.

(8)   Premarital, Marital or Separation Agreements:
       Is there a written agreement being asserted   Yes_____   No_____
       If asserted, is either party challenging such
       agreement   Yes_____   No_____
       If unknown presently, any challenge shall be asserted no later than _____.
       Nature of the agreement _____
       Date of the agreement _____
       Are there any other agreements: _____
       _____
       _____

(9) Alternate Dispute Resolution/Mediation:

The parties *are/are not* aware of the existence of alternate dispute resolution methods of resolving their matrimonial action, including, but not limited to, mediation and collaborative lawyering.

B. GROUNDS FOR DIVORCE:

The parties hereby stipulate, for purposes of trial, as follows:

1. **Grounds:** The issue of fault is resolved _____ or unresolved _____.

If the issue of grounds is resolved:

The parties agree that _____ will proceed on an uncontested basis to obtain a divorce on the grounds of _____.

If the issue of grounds is unresolved:

A Note of Issue shall be filed. Failure to file a Note of Issue prior to the grounds trial and/or failure to demand a jury in a timely fashion shall be deemed a waiver of the jury demand.

A trial of this issue shall be held on _____.

C. CUSTODY:

(a) The issue of custody is resolved _____ unresolved _____.

ORDERED: If the issues of custody, including parenting time and decision making, are resolved: The parties are to submit a stipulated parenting plan no later than _____.

(b) **Parenting Time:**

The issue of parenting time is resolved _____ unresolved _____.

ORDERED: If the issue of parenting time is resolved: The parties are to submit a stipulation reflecting the parental access schedule no later than _____.

(c) The issues relating to decision making are resolved _____ or unresolved _____.

ORDERED: If the issues relating to decision making are resolved: The parties are to submit a stipulation reflecting the decision making agreement no later than _____.

ORDERED:

(d) **As to any issue related to custody, including parenting time and decision making which is unresolved:** Each party is to serve and submit a proposed parenting plan no later than _____.

After receipt of the parenting plans, if the parties do not notify the Court that all issues related to custody are resolved, a conference shall be held on _____ at which time the Court shall determine the need for a law guardian / guardian ad litem and/or a forensic evaluation and set a schedule for resolving all issues relating to custody.

Any appointment of a law guardian / guardian ad litem or forensic evaluator shall be by separate order which shall designate the law guardian appointed, the manner of payment, source of funds for payment and each party's responsibility for such payment. The parties propose to allocate the fees of such law guardian / guardian ad litem or forensic evaluator as follows:

_____% Husband   _____% Wife

The fees shall be subject to reallocation at the time of trial.

Parent Education:
The Court: _____ has provided information as to parent education.
_____ has referred the parties to parent education.
_____ hereby orders the parties to attend parent education.
_____ has taken no action with respect to parent education.

D. STIPULATION:

The parties hereby stipulate, for purposes of trial, as to the following:

1. Grounds (per Par. B, above) is resolved _____ unresolved _____
2. Maintenance is resolved _____ unresolved _____
3. Child Support is resolved _____ unresolved _____
4. Custody (per Par. C, above) is resolved _____ unresolved _____
5. Parenting Time (per Par. C above) is resolved _____ unresolved _____
6. Equitable Distribution is resolved _____ unresolved _____
7. Other Causes of Action _____
8. Other Ancillary Relief Issues _____

The above is hereby stipulated to by the parties and so ordered by the Court.

_____   _____
Plaintiff   Defendant

_____   _____
Attorney(s) for Plaintiff   Attorney(s) for Defendant

E. *PENDENTE LITE* RELIEF:

With respect to *pendente lite* applications, the Court hereby directs or the parties stipulate that:

_____
_____
_____
_____
_____

_____

_____

_____

_____

F. DISCOVERY: THE COURT ORDERS THE FOLLOWING:

1. Preservation of Evidence:

(1) **Financial Records:** Each party shall maintain all financial records in his or her possession through the date of the entry of a judgment of divorce.

(2) **Electronic Evidence:** For the relevant periods relating to the issues in this litigation, each party shall maintain and preserve all electronic files, other data generated by and/or stored on the party's computer system(s) and storage media (i.e. hard disks, floppy disks, backup tapes), or other electronic data. Such items include, but are not limited to, e-mail and other electronic communications, word processing documents, spreadsheets, data bases, calendars, telephone logs, contact manager information, internet usage files, offline storage or information stored on removable media, information contained on laptops or other portable devices and network access information.

2. Document Production:

(1) No later than forty-five days after the date of this Order, the parties are to exchange the following records for the following periods:

Check if Needed	Time Period	
_____	_____	Federal, state and local tax returns, including all schedules, K-1's, 1099's, W-2's and similar data.
_____	_____	Credit card statements for all credit cards used by a party.
_____	_____	Joint Checking account statements, checks and register.
_____	_____	Individual Checking account statements, checks and register.
_____	_____	Brokerage Account statements.
_____	_____	Savings Account records.
_____	_____	Other: (specify) _____

Absent any specified time period definition, records are to be produced for the **three years** prior to the commencement of this action through the present. If a party does not have complete records for the time period, the party shall provide a written authorization to obtain such records directly from the source within five days of presentation. Any costs associated with the use of the authorization shall be ☐ paid by _____ **OR** ☐ reserved for the Court once the amount is determined.

No later than _____, the parties shall notify the Court of all items to be provided in forty-five days which have not been provided. Failure to comply with the scheduled discovery may result in sanctions, including the award of legal fees.

(2) No later than _____, a notice for discovery and inspection shall be served by plaintiff.

(3) No later than _____, a notice for discovery and inspection shall be served by defendant.

3. Other Discovery:

			Plaintiff	Defendant
(1)	Interrogatories	To be served no later than	_____	_____
(2)	Party Depositions	To be completed no later than	_____	_____
	3rd–Party Depositions	To be completed no later than	_____	_____
(3)	Other	_____		

Compliance with discovery demands shall be on a timely basis pursuant to the CPLR. Failure to comply may result in sanctions, including the award of legal fees.

4. **Valuation/Financial Experts and Other Experts:**

Check if experts are required to value any of the following:

(1)	Deferred Compensation	_____
(2)	Retirement assets	_____
(3)	Business interest	_____
(4)	Professional Practice	_____
(5)	License/degree	_____
(6)	Art, antiques, personal property, jewelry	_____
(7)	Separate property	_____
(8)	Residential real estate	_____
(9)	Commercial real estate	_____
(10)	Stock options, stock plans or other benefit plan	_____
(11)	Intellectual property	_____
(12)	Other	_____
	Identify: _____	

(i) The date of valuation shall be _____ for items _____ and shall be the date of commencement of this action for items _____.

Neutral Experts:

(ii) The Court shall appoint a neutral expert for items _____ listed above. Appointment of the expert shall be pursuant to a separate order which shall designate the neutral expert, what is to be valued, the manner of payment, source of funds for payment each party's responsibility for such payment.

(iii) The parties may suggest names for the Court to consider appointing. Said names shall be submitted by letter no later than _____.

(iv) The parties are not able to determine whether a neutral expert is necessary. The parties shall notify the Court no later than _____ as to whether any other neutral experts are required.

(v) The parties seek to have the fees of the neutral expert allocated ___ % to the husband and ___ % to the wife. The fees shall be subject to reallocation at trial.

Experts to be Retained by a Party:

(vi) Each party shall select his/her own expert with respect to items _____ listed above. The expert shall be identified to the other party by letter with their qualifications and retained no later than _____. If a party requires fees to retain an expert and the parties cannot agree upon the source of the funds, an application for fees shall be made no later than _____. Any expert retained by a party must represent to the party hiring such expert that he or she is available to proceed promptly with the valuation.

(vii) Expert reports are to be exchanged by _____. Absent any date specified, they are to be exchanged sixty days prior to trial. Reply reports are to be exchanged thirty days after service of an expert report.

Additional Experts:

(viii) If a net worth statement has not been served prior to this order or a party cannot identify all assets for valuation or cannot identify all issues for an expert, upon other issues such identification, the party promptly shall notify the other party as to any valuation or as to which an expert is needed. If the parties cannot agree upon a neutral expert or the retention of individual experts, either party may notify the Court for appropriate action. Timely application shall be made to the Court if assistance is necessary to implement valuation or the retention of an expert.

5. **Confidentiality/Non–Disclosure Agreement:**

(a) In the event there is a need for a Confidentiality/Non–Disclosure Agreement prior to disclosure, the party demanding same shall prepare and circulate the proposed agreement amongst the parties involved. If the parties cannot agree as to same, they shall promptly notify the Court. The failure to promptly seek a confidentiality agreement may result in the waiver of same.

(b) Plaintiff / Defendant anticipates the need for a Confidentiality Agreement as to the following issues: _____

_____

_____

_____

(c) The Confidentiality/Non–Disclosure Agreement shall be provided to opposing counsel by _____. Within ten days of receipt, opposing counsel shall provide comments. If there are no comments received within ten days, and an extension of such time has not been agreed upon by counsel, the agreement is deemed accepted and all parties are to sign it and be bound by it. If comments are received and the parties cannot resolve its terms within twenty days of receipt of the comments or it is not signed within twenty days of the later of receipt of comments or delivery of the proposed agreement as to which no comments are received in the specified time period, the Court is to be notified by the party seeking such agreement by letter with copy to opposing counsel.

G.   FURTHER ORDERS:

1. The Court orders **the parties** and **their attorneys** to appear at a compliance conference to be held on _____ at _____.

2. The Court orders a Note of Issue to be filed on or before _____. Failure to file a Note of Issue as directed herein may result in dismissal pursuant to CPLR 3216.

THE COURT ORDERS THAT THE TRIAL IN THIS MATTER BE HELD ON:

_____ at _____ am / pm

Dated:

                                           SO ORDERED:

                                         _____

                                         Justice of the Supreme Court

Form 9. Commercial Cases

SUPREME COURT OF THE STATE OF NEW YORK
COUNTY OF NEW YORK

--x

                    Plaintiff(s)

      -against-

                   Defendant(s)

--x

Present: Hon. _____
                          Justice

IAS PART _____

Index No. _____

DCM Track: _____

PRELIMINARY CONFERENCE
ORDER—COMMERCIAL CASES

APPEARANCES:

  Plaintiff(s): _____
_____
_____ .

  Defendant(s): _____
_____
_____ .

It is hereby ORDERED that disclosure shall proceed as follows:

(1) BILL OF PARTICULARS (See CPLR 3130(1)):

(a) Demand for a bill of particulars shall be served by _____ on or before _____.

(b) Bill of particulars shall be served by _____ on or before _____.

(2) DOCUMENT PRODUCTION:

(a) Demand for discovery and inspection shall be served by _____ on or before _____.

(b) Response to demand shall be served by _____ on or before _____
_____ .

(3) INTERROGATORIES:

(a) Interrogatories shall be served by _____ on or before _____.

(b) Answers to interrogatories shall be served by _____ on or before _____
_____ .

(4) DEPOSITION ON ORAL QUESTIONS:

          [ ] Plaintiff(s)   [ ] Defendant(s)   [ ] All Parties

shall be held _____
_____
_____
_____ .

(5) OTHER DISCLOSURE:

_____
_____
_____
_____

(6) If a motion relating to disclosure has raised additional disclosure issues, the parties shall: _____

_____
_____
_____

(7) IMPLEADER: Shall be completed on or before _____.

(8) END DATE FOR ALL DISCLOSURE: _____.

(9) COMPLIANCE CONFERENCE: Shall be held on _____.

(10) MOTIONS: Any dispositive motion(s) shall be made on or before _____

_____

(11) NOTE OF ISSUE: _____ shall file a note of issue/certificate of readiness on or before _____.

A copy of this order shall be served and filed with the note of issue.

THE DATES SET FORTH HEREIN MAY NOT BE ADJOURNED EXCEPT WITH APPROVAL OF THE COURT.

SO ORDERED:

        Dated: _____   _____, J.S.C.

ADDITIONAL DIRECTIVES

In addition to the directives set forth above, it is further ORDERED as follows:

_____
_____
_____
_____
_____

SO ORDERED:

        Dated: _____   _____, J.S.C.

FORMS FOR GUARDIANSHIP CASES

Form 10. Order and Judgment Appointing Guardian

At IAS Part ___ of the Supreme Court of
the State of New York, County of New
York, at the courthouse thereof, 60 Centre Street, New York, New York, on the
___ day of _____, 200 ___

Present:
   Hon. _____,
                            Justice
--X
In the Matter of the Application of

_____
                              Petitioner,

for the Appointment of a Guardian for

_____

      An Alleged Incapacitated Person.

--X

**FINDINGS OF FACT,
CONCLUSIONS OF LAW,
ORDER AND JUDGMENT
AND
SHORT FORM COMMISSION**
(To be executed by the County Clerk)

INDEX NO. _____

A petition in the above-captioned matter, verified on the ___ day of _____, 20___ by the petitioner therein named having been duly presented to this court seeking the appointment of a guardian for the Alleged Incapacitated Person pursuant to the Mental Hygiene Law, and the Court, by Order to Show Cause dated _____, 20___, having required that notice of presentation of petition be given to the Alleged Incapacitated Person and to _____ _____,
and proof of service on each of the above named persons having been duly filed; and the court having considered the petition and the proof submitted in support thereof, and a hearing having been held on _____, 200___; and upon the evidence presented at the hearing;

> Choose the applicable phrase or provision. Delete the phrase or
> provision that does not apply.

JURISDICTION AND SERVICE

In this guardianship proceeding pursuant to Article 81 of the Mental Hygiene Law ("MHL"), the Court, having been satisfied that at the commencement hereof the Alleged Incapacitated Person was a

resident of this State **_or_** nonresident of the State present in the State,

_or_ nonresident of this State, not present in the State, with property in the State (MHL § 81.18),

and having been satisfied that the Alleged Incapacitated Person was served with the order to show cause and petition by personal delivery at least 14 days prior to the return date, and that all other persons required to be served under MHL § 81.07 were timely served with the order to show cause and petition, and having appointed a/an

- Court Evaluator: _____, [Name]
- Attorney for the Alleged Incapacitated Person: _____, [Name]

HEARING

and having scheduled a hearing for this proceeding, at which time:

- the Alleged Incapacitated Person appeared personally **_or_**

- the Alleged Incapacitated Person was absent [*choose one, delete others*]

▲ because it was determined that he/she was not present in the State. *or*

▲ the Alleged Incapacitated Person appeared by counsel, who waived his/her appearance and entered a consent to the petition and the appointment of a guardian. *or*

▲ the Alleged Incapacitated Person appeared by counsel and a hearing was conducted. *or*

▲ because it was determined by clear and convincing evidence that the Alleged Incapacitated Person was completely unable to participate in the trial or no meaningful participation would result from his/her presence at the trial. [Specify reasons]: _____

_____

FINDINGS OF FACT

NEED FOR GUARDIAN

It has been established that the Alleged Incapacitated Person has the following functional limitations:

- Physical (Specify): _____
- Mental (Specify): _____

and as a result is in need of a guardian to provide for

- personal needs, including [*choose all that apply, delete others*]

▶ food   ▶ clothing   ▶ shelter   ▶ health care   ▶ safety   ▶ activities of daily living

▶ other _____)

- financial and property management, including [*choose all that apply, delete others*]

▶ collection of income   ▶ payment of bills   ▶ protection and investment of assets

▶ other _____)

It has been established

- that no other available resources exist *or*
- that other available resources appear to exist [*choose all that apply, delete others*]

▲ Power of Attorney ▲ Health Care Proxy ▲ Volunteer Service from Community Organization ▲ Other [Specify]: _____

but are insufficient, unreliable, or invalid because [*choose all that apply, delete others*]

- - the Power of Attorney or Health Care Proxy were improperly given, *or*

- - the Attorney in Fact or Health Care Agent have violated their fiduciary duties *or*

- - the Power of Attorney fails to contain powers sufficient to meet current needs *or*

- - the volunteers are not sufficiently skilled *or*

- - Other [Specify]: _____

It has been established that the powers herein granted are necessary to provide for the needs of the Alleged Incapacitated Person and that without the grant of these powers such needs would not be met.

DURATION OF GUARDIANSHIP

It has been established that the guardianship of the person is required for

- an indefinite duration *or*
- a period of [specify time] _____

the guardianship of the property is required for

- an indefinite duration *or*
- a period of [specify time] _____

CONSENT–INCAPACITY

As to the appointment of a guardian:

- It is made upon the consent of the Alleged Incapacitated Person; *or*
- It has been established by clear and convincing evidence upon the documentary proof and testimony presented that the Alleged Incapacitated Person lacks understanding and appreciation of the nature and consequences of the functional limitations set forth above and it is likely that the Alleged Incapacitated Person will suffer harm because of these functional limitations and the inability to understand adequately and appreciate the nature and consequences of such limitations.

GUARDIAN

It has been established that _____

is/are eligible for appointment as a Guardian/co–Guardian under MHL § 81.19 and is/are best suited to exercise the powers necessary to assist the Alleged Incapacitated Person, because:

- of the family relationship [specify: _____] of said person(s) with the Alleged Incapacitated Person *and/or*,
- of another relationship (e.g., friend) [specify: _____] of said person(s) with the Alleged Incapacitated Person *and/or*,
- of the nomination by the Alleged Incapacitated Person *and/or*
- of education and experience *and/or*,
- said person(s) is/are the best choice among others proposed *and/or*,
- no one was proposed and the Court had to choose from the Fiduciary List *or*,
- the person is a non-profit organization not on the list but expert in this field *or*,
- Other [Specify]: _____.

PROPERTY OF ALLEGED INCAPACITATED PERSON

It has been established that the approximate total value of the Alleged Incapacitated Person's assets (excluding real property) is $ _____, and his/her total monthly income is $ _____.

CONCLUSIONS OF LAW

The Court has jurisdiction in this proceeding as to subject matter and person. The Alleged Incapacitated

Person, _____, residing at
                        Name

_____
Address   City   State   Zip   Phone

is a person in need of the appointment of a guardian.

As set forth above, the Alleged Incapacitated Person has consented to the appointment of a Guardian *or* has been found to be an incapacitated person in accordance with MHL § 81.02.

The powers granted in this judgment are the least restrictive means of intervention consistent with the Alleged Incapacitated Person's functional limitations.

ORDER AND JUDGMENT

GUARDIANS

IT IS HEREBY ORDERED AND ADJUDGED that, for the period(s) set forth above, the following is/are appointed:

Guardian of the Property: _____

Name

_____

Address   Phone

Guardian of the Person: _____

Name

_____

Address   Phone

Co–Guardian of the Property: _____

Name

_____

Address   Phone

Co–Guardian of the Person: _____

Name

_____

Address   Phone

ORDERED AND ADJUDGED that the Guardian and Co–Guardian (if any) of the Property shall

- serve without bond *or*
- file a bond in the amount of $ _____.

ORDERED AND ADJUDGED that the said Guardian(s)/Co–Guardian(s) shall file with the Clerk of this Court, within fifteen days of the date hereof, a designation of the Clerk for service of process, in the form attached hereto, and a bond, if required, and, upon the filing thereof, the Clerk of this Court shall execute and issue a commission, in the form attached hereto, and this commission shall constitute the sole warrant of the Guardian(s)/Co–Guardian(s) to act;

ORDERED AND ADJUDGED, that, within ten days from the date hereof, the attorney for the petitioner shall serve by first class mail a copy of this document, the petition, other pertinent pleadings, and the Court Evaluator's report, if any, on the Guardian(s)/Co–Guardian(s) herein appointed and on the designated Court Examiner and affidavits of service shall be filed within five days after service with the New York County Clerk, and a copy of the commission shall be served by the attorney on the Court Examiner promptly after its issuance; further, the attorney for the petitioner shall assist the Guardian(s)/Co–Guardian(s) with the preparation of the commission, the oath and designation and the obtaining of the bond, if required, and shall assist the Guardian(s)/Co–Guardian(s) in obtaining the certified and executed commission from the Clerk of the Court;

IF THE COURT FOUND THAT A POWER OF ATTORNEY OR HEALTH CARE PROXY WAS IMPROPERLY GIVEN OR THE AGENTS HAD VIOLATED THEIR FIDUCIARY DUTIES, the

following shall be completed with the requested information and marked accordingly. Otherwise, the
following shall be left blank and mark "Y" below, indicating that the entire box does not apply.

ORDERED AND ADJUDGED that the following is/are revoked:

the   Power   of   Attorney,   executed   on   _____,   appointing
_____ as
                        Date   Name
Attorney-in–Fact.

the   Health   Care   Proxy,   executed   on   _____,   appointing
_____
                        Date   Name
Health Care Agent.

                                              [   ] This entire box does not apply.

DUTIES OF GUARDIAN(S) GENERALLY

ORDERED AND ADJUDGED, that pursuant to MHL § 81.20, the Guard-
ian(s)/Co–Guardian(s) shall:

1. Exercise only those powers that the guardian is authorized to exercise by
Court Order;

2. Exercise the utmost care and diligence when acting on behalf of the incapacitated person;

3. Exhibit the utmost degree of trust, loyalty and fidelity in relation to the
incapacitated person;

4. File initial and annual reports in accordance with Sections 81.30 and 81.31 of
the Mental Hygiene Law;

5. Visit the incapacitated person not less than four times a year or more
frequently if so specified by the court;

6. If given authority with respect to property management for the incapacitated
person, shall:

(i) Afford the incapacitated person the greatest amount of independence and self-
determination with respect to property management in light of that person's
functional level, understanding and appreciation of his/her functional limitations and
personal wishes, preferences and desires with regard to managing the activities of
daily living;

(ii) Preserve, protect and account for such property and financial resources
faithfully;

(iii) Determine whether the incapacitated person has executed a will, determine
the location of any will, and the appropriate persons to be notified in the event of the
death of the incapacitated person, and in the event of the incapacitated person's
death, notify those persons;

(iv) Use the property and financial resources and income available therefrom to
maintain and support the incapacitated person, and to make application to this Court
to maintain and support those persons dependent upon the incapacitated person;

(v) At the termination of the appointment, deliver such property to the persons
legally entitled to it, pursuant to Court Order;

(vi) File with the recording officer of the county wherein the incapacitated person
is possessed of real property an acknowledged statement to be recorded and indexed
under the name of the incapacitated person identifying the real property possessed
by the incapacitated person, and the tax map numbers of the property, and stating
the date of adjudication of incapacity of the person regarding property management,
and the name, address, and telephone number of the guardian and the guardian's
surety;

(vii) Perform all other duties required by law.

7. A Guardian who is given authority relating to the personal needs of the incapacitated person shall afford the incapacitated person the greatest amount of independence and self-determination with respect to personal needs in light of that person's functional level, understanding and appreciation of that person's functional limitations, and personal wishes, preferences and desires with regard to managing the activities of daily living.

POWERS OF GUARDIAN OF THE PROPERTY

ORDERED AND ADJUDGED that the Guardian/Co–Guardian of the Property shall have the following powers with regard to the property of the incapacitated person;

1. Marshal his/her income and assets and establish bank, brokerage and other similar accounts in the name of the Guardian and Co–Guardian (if any) for the incapacitated person, and endorse, collect, negotiate and deposit all negotiable instruments drawn to the order of the incapacitated person, including but not limited to government entitlement checks; invest funds with the same authority as a trustee pursuant to New York EPTL § 11–2.3; inventory personal belongings, and store or dispose as appropriate; and inventory any safe deposit box in the presence of a representative of the bank and in the presence of the Surety, if any, and the Guardian/Co-guardians shall promptly file an inventory of the contents of the safe deposit box with the Court and await further order as to the disposition of its contents.

2. Pay such bills as may be reasonably necessary for the maintenance and care of the incapacitated person;

3. Make gifts as specifically authorized by the court in advance;

4. Provide support for persons dependent upon him/her as follows:

Name	Address	
	Yes/No	
Relationship	Legal Obligation	Amount of Support

5. Enter into contracts subject to the following conditions: (a) contracts for the sale or purchase of assets (e.g., cars, safety equipment, etc.) and contracts for construction or repairs must be approved by the court; (b) the terms of contracts for the sale of real property must be approved by the court **prior to the closing of title** upon submission of a copy of the fully executed contract and a written appraisal of the value of the property, provided that the property is listed for sale with a New York State licensed real estate broker; and (c) ALL PURCHASES OF REAL ESTATE and COOPERATIVE APARTMENTS shall require PRIOR court approval upon proof of a PROPOSED contract of purchase and a written appraisal of the value of the property;

6. Establish an irrevocable prepaid funeral trust and a personal allowance account in accordance with Medicaid regulations from resources only and not from income.

7. Engage in Medicaid and estate planning, except that court approval is required in advance as provided in MHL § 81.21 (b) of all proposed transfers of a part of the incapacitated person's assets to or for the benefit of another person;

8. Apply for government and private benefits;

9. Prosecute and defend civil proceedings, including administrative proceedings, and settle and compromise all matters related to such proceedings.

10. Sign and file income tax returns and all other tax documents for any and all tax obligations and appear before federal, state and local taxing authorities on all claims, litigation, settlements and other matters related thereto;

11. Authorize access to or release of confidential/medical records;

12.   Apply to the court for appointment of an attorney or an accountant, or other professional (e.g. a geriatric care manager, financial adviser), pursuant to Part 36 of the Rules of the Chief Judge. If the request is for the appointment of an attorney or accountant, a name of an individual practitioner should be supplied, not a firm name. A guardian who is an attorney may not serve as his or her own attorney;

13.   Pay professional fees upon court approval, subject to the submission of an affidavit of services and pursuant to Parts 36 and 26 of the Rules of the Chief Judge;

14.   Pay the funeral expenses of the incapacitated person out of any funds remaining in the guardianship estate at death, to the extent that a prepaid funeral trust, if any, is insufficient to pay for same;

15.   Pay such bills after death if incurred prior thereto and if authority to pay same would have otherwise existed;

16.   And any other powers which the court in its discretion shall deem appropriate to meet the property management needs of the incapacitated person.

POWERS OF GUARDIAN OF THE PERSON

ORDERED AND ADJUDGED that the Guardian and Co–Guardian (if any) of the Person shall have the following powers with regard to the personal needs of the incapacitated person;

1.   Determine who shall provide personal care or assistance for him/her;

2.   Make decisions regarding social environment and other social aspects of his/her life;

3.   Determine whether he/she should travel;

4.   Determine whether he/she should possess a license to drive;

5.   Authorize access to or release of confidential/medical records;

6.   Make decisions regarding education;

7.   Apply for government and private benefits (unless a Guardian of the Property has been so empowered above);

8.   Choose the place of abode, upon further order of the Court

provided that the incapacitated person shall not be placed in a skilled nursing facility or residential care facility, as defined by Public Health Law § 2801, without further order of the court.

including placement or continued placement in a skilled nursing facility or residential care facility, as defined by Public Health Law § 2801, provided that no consent shall be given to the voluntary formal or informal admission of the incapacitated person to a mental hygiene facility under MHL Article 9 or 15 or to an alcoholism facility under MHL Article 21.

9.   Consent to or refuse generally accepted routine or major medical or dental treatment (including the power to consent to an "Order Not to Resuscitate," as a surrogate, pursuant to Public Health Law § 2965 [2][a][I]), provided that treatment decisions are made consistent with the findings of MHL § 81.15 and in accordance with the standards set forth in MHL § 81.22 (a)(8),

10.   [Other] _____

COMPENSATION OF GUARDIAN(s)

ORDERED AND ADJUDGED that

• unless an alternate plan is submitted and approved by court order, the Guardian/Co–Guardian of the Property and Person shall be compensated pursuant to Surrogate's Court Procedure Act [Specify one]

▲ § 2307

▲ § 2309

149

• the Guardian/Co–Guardians of the Person shall be compensated pursuant to a plan to be submitted and approved by court order.

ORDERED AND ADJUDGED that the Guardian/Co–Guardians shall take no commissions for any year until that year's annual account is filed, reviewed by the Court Examiner designated by the Appellate Division, and approved by the court.

FILING OF REPORTS BY GUARDIAN(s)

ORDERED AND ADJUDGED, that, pursuant to MHL § 81.30, no later than ninety days after the date on which the commission is issued, the Guardian/Co–Guardian shall file the initial report, in the form prescribed by the court, with proof of completion, if required, of the Guardian's education requirements, with the Guardianship and Fiduciary Support Office, located at New York County Supreme Court, 60 Centre Street, Room 148, New York, N.Y. 10007, and shall serve a copy of said initial report upon the designated Court Examiner by regular mail; and, in the event of the Guardian/Co–Guardian's failure to file said report in a timely manner, the Court Examiner shall PROMPTLY serve the Guardian with a demand letter by certified mail, and, upon the Guardian's failure to comply, shall move the court by order to show cause to remove the Guardian.

ORDERED AND ADJUDGED that, pursuant to MHL § 81.31, between JANUARY 1 and MAY 31 of each year, the Guardian/Co–Guardian shall file with the Guardianship and Fiduciary Support Office at the address listed above an annual report in the form prescribed by the Court and required by Section 81.31, and shall serve a copy of said report upon the designated Court Examiner by regular mail.

ORDERED AND ADJUDGED that the Guardian/Co-guardians shall serve a copy of the annual report upon all persons entitled to notice of all further proceedings.

PAYMENT OF BOND PREMIUM(s)

ORDERED AND ADJUDGED, that, if a bond has been directed herein, the guardian shall pay the bond premium(s) from the funds of the incapacitated person to the surety or its agent within 60 (sixty) days after qualifying, and it is further

ORDERED AND ADJUDGED, that the guardian of the property shall pay the renewal premium(s) from the funds of the incapacitated person to the surety or its agent within 60 (sixty) days after the bond renews, and it is further

ORDERED AND ADJUDGED, that the surety or its agent may bring a motion in this Court to collect unpaid premiums if the guardian of the property fails to pay the bond premiums timely.

DEATH OF INCAPACITATED PERSON

ORDERED AND ADJUDGED that, pursuant to MHL § 81.33, no later than sixty days after the death of the incapacitated person, the Guardian/Co–Guardian shall move for judicial settlement of a final account, in the form prescribed by the Court, on such notice that the Court shall direct and shall serve same by regular mail on all persons entitled to notice of all further proceedings.

TRANSFER OF ASSETS

ORDERED AND ADJUDGED that no portion of the Guardianship Estate shall be transferred to any person, Court or entity without prior order of the Court.

APPOINTEES - COMPLIANCE WITH STATUTE AND RULES

ORDERED AND ADJUDGED that any appointee shall comply with Section 35-a of the Judiciary Law and Parts 36 and 26 of the Rules of the Chief Judge and no fee shall be paid to such appointee until the appointee has filed the Notice of Appointment and Certification of Compliance (the Unified Court System form (UCS) No. 872) **_and_** the Statement of Approval of Compensation (the Unified Court System form (UCS) No. 875) with the Office of the Fiduciary Clerk (Room 148, 60 Centre Street, New York, New York) and said forms have been approved by the court.

COMPENSATION OF COURT EVALUATOR AND OTHERS

ORDERED AND ADJUDGED that compensation is approved for the following in the following amounts (but, in the cases of the Court Evaluator and the Court–Appointed Attorney, subject to the filing of a Statement of Approval of Compensation form (UCS form 875)):

Court Evaluator: $_____

                                                 Amount   Name   Address

Court–Appointed Attorney: $_____

                                                 Amount   Name   Address

Petitioner's Attorney $_____

                                                 Amount   Name   Address

Expert Witnesses (**Specify**): $_____

                                                 Amount   Name   Address

Other: _____ $_____

                                                 Amount   Name   Address

Compensation to the _____ shall be approved in a separate order, upon submission of affidavits of services.

OTHER PROVISIONS

ORDERED AND ADJUDGED that upon appointment of a Guardian for personal needs or property management, prior to judgment, a Notice of Pendency must be filed if real property or interest therein is or may be affected by the proceeding.

ORDERED AND ADJUDGED that the Guardian/Co–Guardians

- **shall be required**

- **shall not be required**

to complete a training program, as mandated by MHL § 81.39, no later than ninety days after issuance of the commission and obtain proof that the training was completed.

ORDERED AND ADJUDGED that the Guardian/Co–Guardian shall fully cooperate with the Court Examiner designated by the Appellate Division to examine the condition, care and finances of the incapacitated person, and this court has been advised that the designated Court Examiner is

_____

                    Name   Address

_____

                   Phone   Fax   Email

and that, in the event that there is a change of Court Examiner, the name of any designated successor Court Examiner shall be obtainable through the Guardianship and Fiduciary Support Office, 60 Centre Street, Room 148, New York, N.Y., 10007, telephone number 646–386–3328.

ORDERED AND ADJUDGED that for the purposes of Section 9–I of the Banking Law and for the purposes of Section 238 of the Banking Law, this Order shall be deemed a declaration of incompetence and no banking institution or savings bank shall impose any penalty for the repayment of a time deposit prior to maturity.

ORDERED AND ADJUDGED that the Guardian/Co-guardians may not alienate, mortgage, lease or otherwise dispose of real property without special direction of the Court obtained upon proceedings taken for that purpose as prescribed in Article 17 of the Real Property Actions and Proceedings Law, provided, however, that without instituting such proceedings, the Guardian/Co-guardians may, with the authorization of the Court, lease real property for a term not exceeding five years and may, without further authorization of the Court, lease a primary residence for the incapacitated person for a term not to exceed three years.

ORDERED AND ADJUDGED that all persons are directed and commanded to deliver to the Guardian/Co-guardians, upon demand and presentation of a certified copy of the commission, all property of the incapacitated person, of every kind and nature, which may be in their possession or under their control.

SERVICE

ORDERED AND ADJUDGED that the following shall be served with notice on all further proceedings in this matter:

Incapacitated Person   Guardian/Co–Guardian

Mental Hygiene Legal Service   Court Examiner

Other [**Specify**] _____

ORDERED AND ADJUDGED that a copy of this document shall be served on the incapacitated person in accordance with MHL § 81.16(e), and, by regular mail, upon all persons who appeared in this proceeding, within 10 days of the date hereof; affidavits of service shall be filed within five (5) days after service with the New York County Clerk.

ENTER:

_____

J.S.C.

No. 2: 12/14/06

SUPREME COURT OF THE STATE OF NEW YORK
COUNTY OF NEW YORK
--X

In the Matter of the Application of

Index No. _____

_____,

Petitioner,

for the Appointment of a Guardian for

	OATH AND DESIGNATION
	OF CLERK TO RECEIVE
	PROCESS

_____,

an Incapacitated Person.

--X

STATE OF NEW YORK   )
) ss:
COUNTY OF NEW YORK   )

I, _____ [Guardian], having been appointed Guardian for the Person and/or Property of _____ [IP], by order of Hon. _____, Justice of the Supreme Court, made in this proceeding and entered in the Office of the Clerk of the County of New York on the ___ day of _____, 20___, do depose and say:

I am a resident of the State of New York residing at _____ [Address in full]. I am a citizen of the United States, and over 21 years of age. I hereby state and swear that I will faithfully and honestly discharge my duties as Guardian of _____ [IP], an Incapacitated Person.

Further, I do hereby designate the Clerk of the County of New York, or his/her successor in office, as a person on whom may be made service of any process issuing from said Court in this proceeding or in any other proceeding which shall affect the personal needs and/or property management of said Incapacitated Person, in like manner and with like effect as if it were served personally upon me, whenever I cannot be found and served within the State of New York after diligence is used.

Dated: _____, 20___

_____
[Signature]

_____
[Name of Guardian]

_____
[Address of Guardian]

_____
[City, State]

On this ___ day of _____, 20___,
before me personally appeared the within named
_____ to me known
and known to me to be the individual(s) described in and
who executed the foregoing and acknowledged that he(she)
executed the same.

_____
Notary Public

SUPREME COURT OF THE STATE OF NEW YORK
COUNTY OF NEW YORK
---X
In the Matter of the Application of

_____,   Index No. _____
                                     Petitioner,

for the Appointment of a Guardian for

_____,
                     an Incapacitated Person.
---X

COMMISSION TO GUARDIAN(S)

THE PEOPLE OF THE STATE OF NEW YORK, TO ALL TO WHOM THESE PRESENTS SHALL COME, GREETING.

WHEREAS, an Order and Judgment (a copy of which is annexed hereto), dated _____, was issued and filed in the matter captioned above appointing the following person(s) as Guardian(s) of the incapacitated person named above:

_____

_____

and (1) a bond having been filed or waived; and (2) a designation of the Clerk to accept service of process upon each such Guardian(s) above appointed having been filed on _____, 20 ___.

NOW, THEREFORE, KNOW YE THAT WE HAVE GRANTED, GIVEN AND COMMITTED, AND DO GIVE, GRANT AND COMMIT UNTO THE ABOVE-NAMED GUARDIAN(S) THE POWERS SET FORTH ABOVE.

By the Court this ___ day of
_____, 20___

_____
Clerk of the County of New York

Form 11. Guardian's Initial (90-Day) Report and Instructions

SUPREME COURT OF THE STATE OF NEW YORK
COUNTY OF NEW YORK
--   IAS Part No. _____
IN THE MATTER OF THE APPLICATION OF

_____,   Index No. _____

                              Petitioner,

       FOR THE APPOINTMENT OF
       A GUARDIAN FOR

_____,   **INITIAL REPORT**
                                              OF GUARDIAN
           An Alleged Incapacitated Person,

_____, the Guardian in this proceeding, submits this Initial Report of Guardian pursuant to Mental Hygiene Law § 81.30 and states as follows:

1. I reside at _____. My telephone number is _____. I was appointed guardian of the person [or property or person and property] of _____ [THE INCAPACITATED PERSON] by Order and Judgment of the Honorable _____, Justice of the Supreme Court of the State of New York, dated _____. I received my commission on _____.

2. I am not related to the incapacitated person [or I am the incapacitated person's _____ [NAME RELATIONSHIP]]. The incapacitated person's date of birth is _____. I shall separately provide to the court's Guardianship and Fiduciary Support Office (60 Centre Street, Room 148) the incapacitated person's social security number.

3. I attended the guardianship training course at _____ on _____ [DATE] [or I did not attend the guardianship training course because _____]. I have attached a copy of the certificate evidencing my completion of the course.

4. The incapacitated person is currently living at the following address: _____
_____
I visited him [her] there on the following days: _____
_____
_____

5. The incapacitated person's primary diagnosis is [Set forth the diagnosis of the IP's medical condition] _____
_____
This statement is based upon [e.g., Doctor's report] _____
_____
_____

6. If the incapacitated person lives in an apartment or a house, list here the name and relationship of all other persons living with the incapacitated person: __
_____
_____

7. If the incapacitated person has home care services, describe the services here and state the number of hours a day each such service is provided: _____
_____
_____

8. The incapacitated person has a [check all that apply]:

    ☐ Will   ☐ Living Will   ☐ Health Care Proxy   ☐ Power of Attorney

If you are uncertain as to whether any one of these documents exists, please explain: _____

_____

As to each of the documents listed below, please indicate by marking "Yes," "No," or "NA" [for Not Applicable] whether you have located the document, provided a copy, or filed same with the Surrogate's Court:

	Determined Location	Provided Copy	Filed with Surr. Ct.
Will			
Living Will			
Health Care Proxy			
Power of Attorney			
Other			

Guardians of the Person Answer the Following Questions:

9. I have taken the following steps to ensure that the Incapacitated person has adequate medical, dental, mental health or other health care services [PLEASE DESCRIBE]: _____

_____

_____

10. The plan to ensure that the incapacitated person has adequate medical, dental, mental health or other health care services in the future is as follows [PLEASE DESCRIBE]: _____

_____

_____

11. I have taken the following steps to ensure that the incapacitated person has adequate social and personal services (for example, day care and recreation) [PLEASE DESCRIBE]: _____

_____

_____

12. I have applied for the following health and accident insurance and government benefits on behalf of the incapacitated person [PLEASE DESCRIBE]: _____

_____

_____

13. There is no need to modify my powers as personal needs guardian [or the following changes are necessary in my personal needs powers] [PLEASE DESCRIBE]]: _____

_____

_____

Guardians of the Property of the Incapacitated Person Fill In the Following Information

14. I have marshaled the following assets of the incapacitated person:

A.(1) Bank Accounts [list the name of the bank, account numbers and amount of money in the account before you closed the account and transferred the money to a guardianship account]:

Bank	Account Number	Amount

Bank	Account Number	Amount

(2) <u>Guardianship Bank Accounts</u> [list the name of the bank, account numbers and the amount of money currently in the guardianship bank accounts]:

Bank	Account Number	Amount

B.   <u>Safe Deposit Box</u> [if the incapacitated person has a safe deposit box, list the name and address of the bank at which it is located].

_____

_____

Have you inventoried the contents of the safe deposit box? ☐Yes ☐No. If yes, attach a list of the contents and the appraisal or the approximate value of the contents.

C.   <u>Stocks and Securities</u> [if the incapacitated person owns stocks or other securities, list here the name of the company, number of shares, the market value of each security on the date you received your commission, and the broker]:

Company Name	Number of Shares	Market Value	Brokerage

Company Name	Type of Bonds etc.	Market Value	Brokerage

Company Name	Type of Bonds etc.	Market Value	Brokerage

D. Real Estate [list the address of the property, give a description of the property [i.e. store, single family house], approximate value of the property on the date you were commissioned, and name of tenants and rental income, if any. Also, write down the date you filed a statement identifying real property with the County Clerk.]:

Address	Description	Approx. Value	Tenants	Rental Income	Statement

E. Personal Property [list any jewelry, antiques, paintings, automobiles, or other valuable property or cash and set forth the approximate value]:

Property Type	Appraised Value	Approx. Value

F. Income [set forth here all sources of income for the incapacitated person, i.e. social security, pensions, etc. and the monthly or annual amount received]:

Source of Income	Amount

G. Assets Not Yet Marshaled [list all property owned by the incapacitated person that you have not yet been able to transfer to the guardianship]: _____

15. There is no need to modify my powers as property guardian [or the following changes are necessary to my powers as property guardian [EXPLAIN]: ⎯⎯⎯⎯

⎯⎯⎯⎯⎯⎯⎯⎯⎯⎯⎯⎯⎯⎯⎯⎯⎯⎯⎯⎯⎯⎯⎯⎯⎯⎯⎯⎯⎯⎯⎯

⎯⎯⎯⎯⎯⎯⎯⎯⎯⎯⎯⎯⎯⎯⎯⎯⎯⎯⎯⎯⎯⎯⎯⎯⎯⎯⎯⎯⎯⎯⎯.

16. I ☐ *WILL*   [or] ☐ *WILL NOT* need help preparing my annual report
                    [CHECK ONE].

⎯⎯⎯⎯⎯⎯⎯⎯⎯⎯⎯⎯⎯⎯⎯⎯⎯⎯⎯⎯⎯⎯⎯⎯⎯⎯⎯⎯⎯⎯⎯

⎯⎯⎯⎯⎯⎯⎯⎯⎯⎯⎯⎯⎯⎯⎯⎯⎯⎯⎯⎯⎯⎯⎯⎯⎯⎯⎯⎯⎯⎯⎯

⎯⎯⎯⎯⎯⎯⎯⎯⎯⎯⎯⎯⎯⎯⎯⎯⎯⎯⎯⎯⎯⎯⎯⎯⎯⎯⎯⎯⎯⎯⎯

STATE OF NEW YORK   )
) ss.:
COUNTY OF NEW YORK   )

⎯⎯⎯⎯⎯⎯⎯⎯⎯⎯⎯⎯, being duly sworn, states as follows:

I am the guardian for the above-named incapacitated person, having been duly appointed by Order and Judgment of the Supreme Court of the State of New York, New York County. The foregoing Initial Report, including the account and inventory therein, contains, to the best of my knowledge and belief, an accurate statement of the facts set forth, as well as a full and true statement of all my receipts and disbursements on account of said person and of all money and other personal property of said person which have come into my hands or have been received by any other persons by my order or authority or for my use as guardian since my appointment, and of the value of all property. I do not know of any error of omission in the report to the prejudice of the incapacitated person.

⎯⎯⎯⎯⎯⎯⎯⎯⎯⎯⎯⎯⎯⎯⎯⎯⎯⎯⎯
                                              Guardian

Sworn before me this day
day of ⎯⎯⎯⎯⎯⎯, 20⎯⎯

⎯⎯⎯⎯⎯⎯⎯⎯⎯⎯⎯⎯⎯⎯⎯⎯⎯⎯⎯
Notary Public or Commissioner of Deeds

INSTRUCTIONS FOR INITIAL (90-DAY) REPORT

This is the report that you <u>must</u> file no later than ninety (90) days after you receive your commission. This report tells the court what you have done so far to help the incapacitated person.

To answer Questions 1 through 7, fill in the blanks with the requested information.

To answer Question 8, put a circle around all the documents that the incapacitated person has. If the incapacitated person does not have any of the documents, leave this blank. If you are uncertain about the existence of any document, please explain. Also, using "Yes," "No," or "NA" [for Not Applicable], please indicate as to each of the listed documents whether you have determined the location thereof, provided a copy, or filed with the Surrogate's Court (e.g., will).

If you were appointed a guardian of the person of the incapacitated person, you must answer Questions 9 through 13. If you were only appointed a guardian of the person's property, you should skip these questions.

Question 9—Tell the court what you have done so far to provide for the incapacitated person's medical, dental, mental and other health care needs. (For example: I took the incapacitated person to the eye doctor to get new glasses and to the dentist to have a tooth pulled.)

Question 10—Tell the court what you plan to do in the future to make sure that the incapacitated person has adequate medical, dental, mental health and other health care. (For example: I will bring the incapacitated person to Doctor X for an annual physical and to Doctor Y, a podiatrist, for special shoes.)

Question 11—Tell the court what you have done to make sure that, if feasible, the incapacitated person has an opportunity to be with other people, or work, attend school, or participate in other activities.

Question 12—List the government benefits and/or insurance you have applied for on behalf of the incapacitated person (Medicare, Medicaid, etc.).

Question 13—If you think you need more powers to meet the personal needs of the incapacitated person, or fewer powers, write down the changes you would like to see made and tell the court why you want them.

If the court gave you management powers over the incapacitated person's property, you must answer Question 14, sections A through G, and Question 15. If you are only a guardian of the person, you should not answer these questions.

Question 14 (A)(1)—List all the bank accounts that the incapacitated person had when you were appointed guardian, the account numbers and the amount in each account.

Question 14(A)(2)—List all of the guardianship accounts that you set up, the name of the bank where they are located, the account number and the amount of money in each account.

Question 14(B)—If the incapacitated person had a safe deposit box, provide the requested information. If the incapacitated person did not have a safe deposit box, leave this section blank.

Question 14(C)—If the incapacitated person owned shares of stock, provide a complete list of all stock, including the name of the company, the number of shares and the market value of the stock on the date you received your commission. If the incapacitated person owned bonds or other types of securities, provide information regarding the type of security and the market value on the date you received your commission. Please also provide the name of the brokerage house holding the stock, bonds, or other securities.

Question 14(D)—Provide the requested information for all real property owned by the incapacitated person.

Question 14(E)—Separately list all valuable personal property and provide an appraisal or approximate value if you do not have an appraisal. If the incapacitated person owned ordinary household furnishings and clothing, provide an approximate value for this personal property.

Question 14 (F)—List all monthly income (for example, social security, pensions and trust income) and the monthly amount the incapacitated person receives from each source.

Question 14(G)—List all of the assets that the incapacitated person owns that you have not yet transferred into guardianship accounts.

Question 15—If you think you need more power over the incapacitated person's property, or less power, write down the changes you would like to see made and tell the court why they should be made.

Question 16—If you think you will need assistance preparing the Annual Report, circle "will". If you think you can do the Annual Report on your own, circle "will not."

When you have answered all the questions, bring this report to a notary public and sign the paragraph at the end (the certification paragraph) in front of the notary and then have the report notarized.

You must then mail a copy of the report to:

Guardianship and Fiduciary Support Services

New York Supreme Court

60 Centre Street, Room 201-B

New York, NY 10007

The Court Examiner named in your appointing Order and judgment.

The Incapacitated Person

The Court Evaluator named in the appointing Order

If the incapacitated person lives in a residential facility, to the director of the facility

To Mental Hygiene Legal Services if the incapacitated person lives in a Mental Hygiene Facility

If you have any questions, please call the Guardianship and Fiduciary Support Office of the New York County Supreme Court at 646–386–3328.

Thank you.

No. 1: 10/23/06

Form 12.   Annual Report of the Guardian

SUPREME COURT OF THE STATE OF NEW YORK
COUNTY OF NEW YORK   I.A. Part _____

--x

IN THE MATTER OF THE APPLICATION OF

_____,   Index No.: _____
                                    Petitioner,

FOR THE APPOINTMENT OF A
GUARDIAN FOR   **ANNUAL REPORT**

_____,   **FOR 20** _____
          an Alleged Incapacitated Person.

--x

I, _____, residing at _____, as Guardian for _____, who was heretofore determined by this court to be an incapacitated person ("IP"), do hereby make, render and file the following Annual Report.

On the ___ day of _____, 20 ___, I was duly appointed Guardian of the above-named person by Order of the Supreme Court of New York County and have continued to act as such fiduciary since that date, giving a bond in the original sum of $ _____, [now in the sum of $ _____, pursuant to subsequent orders,] which is still in force and effect with _____, as Surety. There has been no change in the Surety thereon, and the Surety is in as good financial standing as when the bond was given. [There has been no change in the Surety thereon, other than as explained in Schedule F.]

The following is a true and full account of all receipts and disbursements for the year 20 ___.

SUMMARY

Schedule A - Principal on hand as of Date of
    Appointment or Last Annual Report $ _____

Schedule B - Changes to Principal $ _____

Schedule C - Income Received $ _____

                     Sub–Total $ _____

Schedule D - Paid Disbursements $ _____

Schedule E-1 - Balance of Cash and Securities to be
    Charged to Next Year's Account $ _____

Schedule E-2 - Real Estate $ _____

Schedule E-3 - All Other Personal Property $ _____

                   Total Estate $ _____

SCHEDULE A - PRINCIPAL ON HAND AS OF DATE OF APPOINTMENT OR LAST ANNUAL REPORT

SOURCE: Name and address   AMOUNT (i.e., number of shares)
of bank or financial institution

        TOTAL OF SCHEDULE A $ _____

SCHEDULE B - INCREASES OR DECREASES TO PRINCIPAL

(List additional property received, gain or loss on sale or liquidation of stocks or bonds, any net receipts from sale of realty (attach copy of closing statement), etc.)

SOURCE   AMOUNT

        TOTAL OF SCHEDULE B $ _____

SCHEDULE C - RECEIVED INCOME AND CASH INCREASES

(If any property listed in the last Report has been converted to cash, list here the amount received from the sale and attach an explanation. If the Guardian has used or employed the services of the IP, or if moneys have been earned by or received on behalf of the IP, state details and amounts here (See Par. 9, below)):

SOURCE   AMOUNT

TOTAL OF SCHEDULE C $ _____

SCHEDULE D - PAID DISBURSEMENTS

PAID TO   AMOUNT

TOTAL OF SCHEDULE D $ _____

SCHEDULE E-1 - BALANCE ON HAND AND OTHER PERSONAL AND REAL PROPERTY

BANK ACCOUNTS,   INVENTORY   MARKET
BROKERAGE ACCOUNTS,   VALUE   VALUE
PERSONAL PROPERTY,
SECURITIES

(List names of joint   (List values as of end of accounting period; for
owners, if any, and their   securities, list both inventory and market val-
relationship to the IP)   ues)

_____ _____ _____
_____ _____ _____
_____ _____ _____
_____ _____ _____
_____ _____ _____
_____ _____ _____
_____ _____ _____
_____ _____ _____
_____ _____ _____
_____ _____ _____

TOTAL OF SCHEDULE E-1 $ _____ $ _____

SCHEDULE E-2 - REAL ESTATE

List all real estate owned in whole or in part by the IP. State location, assessed value, current market value, amount of mortgage (if any), and the weekly or monthly rental. If property is owned jointly, give names of joint owners and their relationship to the IP.

LOCATION	ASSESSED VALUE	MARKET VALUE	MORTGAGE	RENTAL INCOME	JOINT OWNERS

TOTAL OF SCHEDULE E-2

Assessed Value: $ _____   Market Value: $ _____

Mortgages: $_____   Rental Income: $ _____

SCHEDULE E-3 - ALL OTHER PERSONAL PROPERTY

DESCRIPTION   INVENTORY/MARKET VALUE

_____
_____
_____
_____
_____
_____
_____
_____
_____
_____
_____
_____
_____
_____
_____
_____
_____
_____
_____
_____
_____
_____

TOTAL OF SCHEDULE E-3 $_____

SCHEDULE F - NAME AND ADDRESS OF SURETY

Attach a copy of the latest bond. Also, state and explain any changes in the bond, of the Surety thereon, or in the financial standing of the Surety.)

NAME AND ADDRESS   AMOUNT   BOND NUMBER
OF SURETY   OF BOND

_____   _____   _____

_____   _____   _____

AS TO THE INCAPACITATED PERSON:

1. State the age, date of birth and marital status of the Incapacitated Person.

_____
_____
_____

2. If any are living, list the name and present address of the spouse, children and siblings of the Incapacitated Person.

_____
_____
_____
_____
_____
_____

3. State the present residence address and telephone number of the Guardian.

_____

_____

4. State the present residence address and telephone number of the Incapacitated Person. If the IP does not currently reside at her/his personal home, set forth the name, address and telephone number of the facility or place at which he/she resides, and the name of the chief executive officer of the facility or the person otherwise responsible for the care of the IP.

_____

_____

_____

_____

_____

5. State whether there have been any changes in the physical or mental condition of the Incapacitated Person, and any substantial change in medication.

_____

_____

_____

_____

_____

_____

_____

6. State the date and place the Incapacitated Person was last seen by a physician and the purpose of that visit.

_____

_____

_____

_____

_____

7. Attach a statement by a physician, psychologist, nurse clinician or social worker, or other qualified person who has evaluated or examined the Incapacitated Person within the three months prior to the filing of this report, setting forth an evaluation of the Incapacitated Person's condition and the current functional level of the Incapacitated Person.

8. If the Guardian has been charged with providing for the personal needs of the Incapacitated Person:

(a) Attach a statement indicating whether the current residential setting is suitable to the current needs of the Incapacitated Person.

(b) Attach a resume of any professional medical treatment given to the Incapacitated Person during the preceding year.

(c) Attach the plan for medical, dental and mental health treatment and related services for the coming year.

(d) Attach a resume of any other information concerning the social condition of the Incapacitated Person, including the social and personal services currently utilized by the Incapacitated Person and the social skills and needs of the Incapacitated Person.

9. State whether the Guardian has used or employed the services of the Incapacitated Person, or whether moneys have been earned by or received on behalf of such Incapacitated Person. Provide details in Schedule C.

_____

_____

_____

_____

10. Attach a resume of any other pertinent facts about the care and maintenance of the Incapacitated Person, including the frequency of your visits; whether the Incapacitated Person has made a Will or executed a Power of Attorney; and any other information necessary for the proper administration of this matter.

STATE OF NEW YORK　　　)
　　　　　　　　　　　　　　) ss.:
COUNTY OF _____　)

_____, being duly sworn, says:

I am the Guardian for the above-named Incapacitated Person. The foregoing Annual Report contains, to the best of my knowledge and belief, a full and true statement of all my receipts and disbursements on account of said Incapacitated Person; and of all money and other personal property of said person which have come into my hands or have been received by any other persons by my order or authority since my appointment or since filing my last Annual Report and of the value of all such property, together with a full and true statement and account of the manner in which I have disposed of the same and of all property remaining in my hands at the time of filing this Report; also a full and true description of the amount and nature of each investment made by me since my appointment or since the filing of my last Report. I do not know of any error or omission in the Report to the prejudice of said person.

_____
Guardian

Sworn to before me this

day of _____, 20 ___

_____
Notary Public

FORMS FOR PROCEEDING FOR AN ORDER
RELEASING AND DISCHARGING GUARDIAN - ON
CONSENT

Form 13.   Petition

SUPREME COURT OF THE STATE OF NEW YORK
COUNTY OF NEW YORK
--x   Index No: _____
IN THE MATTER OF THE APPLICATION OF

_____ ,

                            Petitioner,   VERIFIED PETITION FOR
                                            ORDER RELEASING AND
                                            DISCHARGING GUARDIAN
                                            AND SURETY UPON DEATH
                                            OF INCAPACITATED
                                            PERSON AND FILING OF
                                            INSTRUMENTS APPROVING
                                            ACCOUNT

FOR THE APPOINTMENT OF A GUARDIAN
FOR

_____ ,
              An Alleged Incapacitated Person.   (Sec. 81.34 MHL)
--x

The petitioner, _____ , hereby states the following:

(1) I am the guardian of the person and the property of _____ an incapacitated person, having been appointed by Order and Judgment of this court dated _____ .   I duly filed a bond with the County Clerk of New York County pursuant to the Order and Judgment [The filing of a bond was waived by the Order and Judgment] and a commission was issued to me by the Clerk of this court on _____ .

(2) The above-named incapacitated person died at _____ [place] on _____ [Date] attached hereto as Exhibit A is a certified copy of the death certificate.   I bring on this petition in accordance with Mental Hygiene Law Section 81.34 for an order releasing and discharging me as guardian of the person and the property of _____ and filing of instruments approving the account of my actions as guardian.

(3) As provided in Section 81.16 (c) (3) of the Mental Hygiene Law, the following are the names and addresses of all persons entitled to notice:

_____
_____
_____

_____
_____
_____

_____
_____
_____

_____
_____
_____

_____
_____
_____

(4) All annual reports have been filed as required by law.

(5) I have made a full report and full disclosure in writing to all interested persons, listed in Paragraph 3 hereof, regarding all of my actions as guardian affecting the property of the incapacitated person. I annex hereto as Exhibit B an informal accounting, a copy of which has been served upon all interested persons, as shown in the proof of service attached thereto.

(6) All interested persons [including the surety, the Attorney General, and the Veteran's Administration, if involved] have executed acknowledged waivers and consents approving the accounting, consenting to commissions, attorney's fees, and all other payments, and agreeing to the release and discharge of the petitioner. These instruments are annexed to this petition as Exhibit C.

(7) All debts and taxes have been paid or none is due in that _____.

(8) The balance of the assets as set forth in the annexed accounting has been distributed to _____, personal representative of the estate of the deceased incapacitated person.

(9) No previous application for the relief sought herein was made.

WHEREFORE, the petitioner respectfully requests that the court issue the annexed order releasing and discharging the petitioner [and the surety, if any] from any further liability to the persons interested/

New York, New York.

_____

       _____
          [Name]
          Petitioner

<u>VERIFICATION</u>

STATE OF NEW YORK   )
) ss.:
COUNTY OF NEW YORK   )

_____, being duly sworn, states as follows:

I am the petitioner in the within proceeding. I have read the foregoing petition and know the contents thereof and the same are true to petitioner's own knowledge.

        _____

Sworn to before me this ____

day of _____, 20____

_____
   Notary Public

Form 14. Order Waiving Filing of Formal Account

At IAS Part ___ of the Supreme
Court of the State of New York,
held in and for the County of
New York, at the Supreme
Court Building thereof located
at 60 Centre Street, New York,
New York, on the ___ day of
_____, 20 ___.

PRESENT: HON. _____
                 Justice

---x

IN THE MATTER OF THE APPLICATION OF

_____,   Index No: _____

               Petitioner,

FOR THE APPOINTMENT OF A GUARDIAN
FOR

_____,   ORDER WAIVING
                             FILING AND JUDICIAL
                             SETTLEMENT OF A
       An Alleged Incapacitated Person.   FORMAL FINAL
                             REPORT
---x   (Sec. 81.34 MHL)

_____, the Guardian of the person and property of _____, a deceased incapacitated person, having submitted a verified petition pursuant to Section 81.34 of the Mental Hygiene Law requesting an order waiving filing and judicial settlement of a Formal Final Report, awarding him commissions in the amount of _____, releasing and discharging the Guardian and the surety from further liability to the persons interested in the property of the incapacitated person, and petitioner having submitted with such verified petition his Informal Account and the acknowledged consents of all persons interested approving the said Account,

On reading and filing the petition of _____, dated _____, the certified copy of the certificate of death of the incapacitated person, dated _____, and the duly acknowledged instruments annexed to the petition approving the report of petitioner and releasing and discharging him from further liability, and no papers having been submitted in opposition to the petition, and due deliberation having been had,

NOW THEREFORE it is,

ORDERED, that the application be and hereby is in all respects granted, and it is further

ORDERED, that the filing and judicial settlement of a formal and final account of _____, as Guardian of _____, deceased, is waived, and it is further,

ORDERED, that the Informal Account annexed to the petition is settled upon consent of the parties, and it is further,

ORDERED, that the Guardian is authorized to pay to:

1. _____ commissions in the sum of $ _____ (annex OCA form 875)

2. _____, Esq. an attorney's fee in the sum of $ _____, and it is further

ORDERED, that the balance of the estate in the sum of $ _____ be delivered to the Personal Representative of the Estate of _____, deceased, [distributees in estates less than $5,000] and a receipt therefor shall be taken, and it is further

ORDERED, that upon filing proof of compliance with the provisions of this order the Guardian may apply ex parte for an order discharging the Guardian and Surety and canceling the Surety Bond.

ENTER:

_____

J.S.C.

Form 15.   Order Discharging Guardian and Surety

At IAS Part ___ of the Supreme
Court of the State of New York,
held in and for the County of New
York, at the Courthouse thereof
located at 60 Centre, New York,
New York on the ___ day of
_____, 20 ___.

PRESENT: HON. _____

                                          Justice

---x
IN THE MATTER OF THE APPLICATION
OF

_____,   Index No: _____

                        Petitioner,

FOR THE APPOINTMENT OF A GUARDIAN
FOR
                                                         ORDER DISCHARGING
_____,   GUARDIAN AND
                                                         SURETY

            An Alleged Incapacitated Person.
---x

_____, Guardian of the person and property of _____, a deceased incapacitated person, having submitted due proof of compliance with the provisions of the Order Waiving Filing and Judicial Settlement of a Formal Final Accounting issued by this Court (Honorable _____), dated _____, and

On reading and filing the said Order, the Affidavit of _____, sworn to on the _____ day of _____, 20 ___, along with the Updated Verified Statement of _____, sworn to on the ___ day of _____, 20 ___,

NOW, on Motion of _____,

IT IS HEREBY ORDERED that the Guardian and his surety, _____, be and the same hereby are discharged from any and all further liability, accountability and responsibility with respect to all matters embraced in the Informal Account, and it is further

ORDERED, that the bond filed herein is cancelled, and it is further

ORDERED, that a copy of this Order shall be served upon the County Clerk of New York County and the surety within ___ days from the date hereof.

                                          ENTER:

                                          _____
                                                    J.S.C.

Form 16. Consent to Informal Account

SUPREME COURT OF THE STATE OF NEW YORK
COUNTY OF NEW YORK

--x   IAS Part No. _____

IN THE MATTER OF THE APPLICATION
OF

_____,   Index No: _____

Petitioner,

FOR THE APPOINTMENT OF A GUARDIAN
FOR

                                             CONSENT TO WAIVING
_____,   FORMAL ACCOUNT
                                             (Sec. 81.34 MHL)
An Alleged Incapacitated Person.

--x

   I, _____, residing at _____, and having an interest in this proceeding as _____, and being over the age of 18 years and fully competent, do appear herein and waive the filing of a formal account. I have read the petition and examined the informal account submitted by _____ as Guardian of the estate of _____, deceased, who was previously determined by this court to be an incapacitated person, and I have found this account to be true and correct in all respects. I hereby consent to the entry of an order waiving the filing of a formal account, authorizing the payment of Guardian commissions and attorney's fee as requested in said petition, and releasing and discharging the Guardian and the surety from any further liability to the persons interested without further notice.

                                                   _____

                                                      [Name]

Sworn to before me this _____

day of _____ 20___

_____
          Notary Public

Form 17.   Order to Show Cause to Settle a Final Report

At IAS Part ___ of the Supreme Court
of the State of New York, held in and for
the County of New York, at the New
York County Courthouse, located at 60
Centre Street, New York, New York, on
the ___ day of _____, 20 ___.

PRESENT: HON. _____
                        Justice

---x
IN THE MATTER OF THE APPLICATION OF

_____,   Index No: _____

                                   Petitioner,

FOR THE APPOINTMENT OF A GUARD-
IAN FOR
                                                     ORDER TO SHOW CAUSE
_____,   TO SETTLE A FINAL REPORT
                                                     AND ACCOUNTING
An Alleged Incapacitated Person.
---x

On reading and filing the annexed Final Report and Account of _____, the
Guardian [*or:* Co–Guardians, or: Special Guardian] herein, verified on the ___ day
of _____, 20 ___, and the Petition verified on the ___ day of _____, 20 ___,
from which it appears that _____, who was heretofore determined to be an
incapacitated person, is deceased, having died on _____, 20 ___, the Guardian
[*or:* Co–Guardians, or: Special Guardian] is seeking to settle the Final Account of
her/his/their proceeding as Guardian [*or:* Co–Guardians, or: Special Guardian] so as
to be discharged herein, and upon the affidavit of legal services of _____,
counsel for the Guardian, sworn to the ___ day of _____, 20 ___, attached
hereto,

LET _____ *[Financial institution]*, the surety; _____, the legal representative of the Estate of the said incapacitated person, deceased, appointed by the
Surrogate's Court; and anyone else entitled to notice herein,

SHOW CAUSE before the Justice presiding at IAS Part ___, Room ___, of this
court to be held in the County of New York at the Courthouse thereof, 60 Centre
Street, New York, New York, on the ___ day of _____, 20 ___, at _____
a.m., or as soon thereafter as counsel can be heard.

WHY an Order should not be entered herein as follows:

(1) settling the Final Report of the Guardian [*or:* Co–Guardians, or: Special
Guardian];

(2) upon settlement of the Final Report of the Guardian, approving payment of
commissions due pursuant to statute to the Guardian [*or:* Co–Guardians, or: Special
Guardian];

(3) approving reimbursement of the Guardian's [*or:* Co–Guardians, or: Special
Guardian] reasonable and necessary disbursements;

(4) approving a reasonable amount of legal fees for the legal services rendered by
_____, counsel for the Guardian [*or:* Co–Guardians, or: Special Guardian] and
for her/his/their additional and extraordinary services rendered;

(5) determining the rights and interests, if any, of _____ *[Creditor and/or
beneficiary of IP's estate]*, as relating to _____ *[Nature of asset]*;

(6) approving and authorizing the Guardian [*or:* Co–Guardians, or: Special Guardian] to hold sufficient funds on hand to pay the accountant to file the final tax return of the incapacitated person, deceased, and also to cover and pay any tax liability on the final tax return;

(7) approving and authorizing the Guardian [*or:* Co–Guardian, or: Special Guardian] to pay the funeral and burial expenses of the incapacitated person from funds from *her/his* estate;

(8) determining the rights and interest of any of the interested parties herein;

(9) authorizing transmittal of the funds and assets on hand (after payment of all approved payments) to _____, the legal representative of the Estate of _____, the deceased incapacitated person, appointed by the Surrogate's Court;

(10) discharging _____, the Guardian [*or:* Co–Guardians, or: Special Guardian] from any and all further liability and accountability for all matters contained within the Final Report and Account;

(11) that the bond be cancelled; and

(12) granting such other and further relief as the Court may deem proper and just.

Sufficient reason APPEARING therefor, it is

ORDERED that service of a copy of this Order and the Petition and the Final Report and Account and all other papers attached hereto, via certified mail or overnight delivery service on all parties required to receive Notice of this proceeding by _____, 20 __ shall be deemed good and sufficient service.

ENTER:

_____
J.S.C.

Form 18.   Find Report (Sample)

SAMPLE FORM

SUPREME COURT OF THE STATE OF NEW YORK
COUNTY OF NEW YORK   IAS Part No. _____
---X
IN THE MATTER OF THE APPLICATION OF

_____,   Index No: _____

                                                           Petitioner,

FOR THE APPOINTMENT OF A GUARDIAN FOR

_____,   FINAL REPORT
                                                           OF GUARDIAN

                        An Alleged Incapacitated Person.
---X

TO THE SUPREME COURT OF THE STATE OF NEW YORK, COUNTY OF NEW YORK:

I, John Smith of 145–21 85th Drive, Jamaica, New York, being the Guardian of the property of Jane Doe, an incapacitated person, do hereby make, render and file this Final Report, Account and inventory:

I was duly appointed as Guardian of the property of the within named incapacitated person by order of this court dated September 6th, 2004, and thereafter, pursuant to said order, did file with the County Clerk of the County of New York a bond with the Maryland Casualty Company as surety thereon, and have continuously acted as such Guardian since the date of my appointment.

That this Final Report of my proceedings as such Guardian is rendered and filed pursuant to Order of this Court made the 20th day of July, 2006.

SUMMARY STATEMENT

SCHEDULE A PRINCIPAL RECEIVED	$72,935.41
SCHEDULE A1 ADDITIONAL PRINCIPAL	$ 3,853.76
TOTAL PRINCIPAL & ADDITIONAL PRINCIPAL	$76,789.17
TOTAL INCOME	$12,784.81
TOTAL PRINCIPAL, ADDITIONAL PRINCIPAL & INCOME	$89,573.98
TOTAL DISBURSEMENTS	$44,726.67
BALANCE ON HAND	$44,873.30

SCHEDULES

SCHEDULE A
PRINCIPAL RECEIVED ON MY APPOINTMENT AS GUARDIAN

DIME SAVINGS BANK ACCOUNT # S5283650	$72,150.24
CHEMICAL BANK ACCOUNT # 104–7202	$ 1,785.17
TOTAL RECEIVED AT TIME OF APPOINTMENT	$72,935.41

SCHEDULE A1

ADDITIONAL PRINCIPAL RECEIVED IN 2006 FROM MORRIS FISHMAN	$ 3,050.00
FROM MORRIS FISHMAN, MARINE MIDLAND ACCOUNT # 016–628703	$ 803.76
TOTAL PRINCIPAL RECEIVED	$76,789.17

SCHEDULE B
INCOME RECEIVED
(Itemization of income by date is required for any accounting period not previously
examined and confirmed by court order).

2004

SOCIAL SECURITY 2 PAYMENTS AT 330.30 EACH	$ 660.60
JAMAICA SAVINGS ACCT. # 2–208174 - INTEREST	$ 228.63
CHEMICAL BANK ACCT. # 054068270 - INTEREST	$ 17.84
DIME SAVINGS BANK ACCT. # M2385757 - INTEREST	$ 766.47
TOTAL	$ 1,673.54

2005

SOCIAL SECURITY 6 PAYMENTS AT 330.30	$ 1,981.80
ADDITIONAL SOCIAL SECURITY PAYMENT	$ 50.00
SOCIAL SECURITY 6 PAYMENTS AT 357.30	$ 2,143.80
JAMAICA SAVINGS BANK - INTEREST	$ 1,331.62
DIME SAVINGS BANK - INTEREST	$ 2,034.28
CHEMICAL SAVINGS BANK - INTEREST	$ 4.83
TOTAL	$ 7,546.33

2006

SOCIAL SECURITY	$ 2,143.80
DIME SAVINGS BANK - INTEREST	$ 1,047.57
JAMAICA SAVINGS BANK - INTEREST	$ 233.49
CHEMICAL BANK - INTEREST	$ 32.08
G.H.I. REFUND	$ 108.00
TOTAL	$ 3,564.94
TOTAL INCOME	$12,784.81
TOTAL INCOME, PRINCIPAL & ADDITIONAL PRINCIPAL	$89,573.98

SCHEDULE C
DISBURSEMENTS
(Itemization of disbursements by date is required for any accounting period not
previously examined and confirmed by court order).

2004

MADELINE DAYE, CARE MAINTENANCE AND SALARY	$ 3,010.16
MADELINE DAYE, FOOD	$ 586.65
NEW YORK CITY HOUSING AUTHORITY, RENT	$ 338.80
TELEPHONE	$ 211.58
LAUNDRY	$ 19.00
UNDERWEAR	$ 8.52
COURT EVALUATOR FEE, PER COURT ORDER	$ 600.00
RICHARD DE VENUTO, LEGAL FEE AND DISBURSEMENTS PER COURT ORDER	$ 1,225.00
SOCIAL SECURITY REFUND	$ 42.71
MARYLAND CASUALTY, BOND PREMIUM	$ 353.00
BANK CHARGES	$ 4.00
TOTAL	$ 6,399.42

2005

MADELINE DAYE, CARE AND MAINTENANCE	$ 8,680.28
ZADA PALMER, CARE AND MAINTENANCE	$ 1,375.00
SYBEL MORGAN, CARE AND MAINTENANCE	$ 35.00
FOOD	$ 2,088.96
LAUNDRY	$ 144.91
TELEPHONE	$ 699.19
INTERNAL REVENUE SERVICE	$ 1,113.66
NEW YORK CITY HOUSING AUTHORITY - RENT	$ 992.00

DR. EVAN C. SCHWEITZER	$ 390.00
MEDICINES	$ 50.89
UNDERCLOTHING ETC.	$ 53.48
COURT EXAMINER FEE PER COURT ORDER	$ 270.00
JOHN SMITH, COMPENSATION PER COURT ORDER	$ 455.96
MARYLAND CASUALTY, BOND PREMIUM	$ 290.00
AX–RET REPORTING SERVICE	$ 42.85
STATE TAX COMMISSION	$ 500.00
BANK CHARGES	$ 32.00
TOTAL	$17,184.18

2006

MADELINE DAYE, CARE AND MAINTENANCE	$ 5,527.53
FEORENA BELL, CARE AND MAINTENANCE	$ 42.00
FOOD	$ 948.97
LAUNDRY	$ 85.80
TELEPHONE	$ 499.91
INTERNAL REVENUE SERVICE	$ 533.13
NEW YORK STATE INCOME TAX	$ 136.00
NEW YORK CITY INCOME TAX	$ 46.00
NEW YORK CITY HOUSING AUTHORITY, RENT	$ 435.15
DR. EVAN SCHWEITZER	$ 300.00
MEDICINES	$ 13.04
BANK CHARGES	$ 6.00
AK–RET REPORTING INC.	$ 797.05
HERZ & RYDER ESQS., LEGAL FEES PER COURT ORDER	$ 6,025.00
DOUGLAS WITSCHIEBEN ESQ., REFEREE FEE	$ 1,200.00
DUES	$ 9.00
JEFFREY PEPPER, MINUTES	$ 15.00
HERZ & RYDER ESQS., LEGAL FEES PER COURT ORDER	$ 1,057.50
GRATUITIES	$ 32.00
RABBI MORDECAI MAYER	$ 65.00
RESNICK & BUCHBINDER INS., FUNERAL DIRECTORS	$ 1,900.00
NEW YORK STATE UNEMPLOYMENT INSURANCE	$ 426.02
DR. ISSAC H. SHOHET	$ 25.00
NEW YORK TELEPHONE CO	$ 17.97
TOTAL	$27,143.07
TOTAL DISBURSEMENTS	$44,726.67

SCHEDULE D
BALANCE ON HAND

JAMAICA SAVINGS BANK ACCOUNT # 2–208174	$ 3,669.18
DIME SAVINGS BANK ACCOUNT # M2385757	$39,998.55
CHEMICAL BANK ACCOUNT	$ 1,025.85
CHEMICAL BANK CHECKING ACCOUNT	$ 179.78
TOTAL	$44,873.36

SCHEDULE E
CLAIMS AGAINST THE ESTATE

CLAIM OF THE DEPARTMENT OF SOCIAL SERVICES OF THE CITY OF NEW YORK	$ 7,589.90
REIMBURSEMENT TO GUARDIAN FOR BANK CHARGES ADVANCED OUT OF HIS OWN FUNDS	$ 26.00
COMPENSATION TO GUARDIAN - REASONABLE IN THE DISCRETION OF THE COURT	
LEGAL FEE TO HERZ & RYDER ESQS. - REASONABLE IN THE DISCRETION OF THE COURT	
MARYLAND CASUALTY CO. PREMIUM ON BOND	$ 290.00

STATE OF NEW YORK   )

) ss.:

COUNTY OF _____   )

John Smith, being duly sworn, states as follows:

I am the Guardian of the property of the within-named incapacitated person. The foregoing Final Report contains, to the best of my knowledge and belief, a full and true statement of all receipts and disbursements on account of said incapacitated person and of all money and other property of said incapacitated person which had come into my hands or had been received by any other person by my order or authority or for my use on behalf of the incapacitated person since my appointment, and of the value of such property; together with a full and true statement and account of the manner in which I have disposed of same; and of all the property remaining in my hands at the time of the filing of this Report, account and inventory; and a full and true description of the amount and nature of each investment made by me since my appointment.

I do not know of any error or omission in the Final Report to the prejudice of said incapacitated person.

_____
John Smith

Sworn to before me this

___ day of _____, 20___

_____
Notary Public

Form 19.   Order Settling and Approving a Final Report

At IAS Part ___ of the Supreme Court of the State of New York, held in and for the County of New York, at the Supreme Court Building thereof located at 60 Centre Street, New York, New York, on the ___ day of _____, 20 ___.

PRESENT: HON. _____
                                           Justice

--x
IN THE MATTER OF THE APPLICATION
OF

_____,   Index No: _____

                              Petitioner,

FOR THE APPOINTMENT OF A
GUARDIAN FOR
                                                       ORDER SETTLING
_____,   AND APPROVING
                                                       FINAL REPORT
            An Alleged Incapacitated Person.
--x

_____, having been appointed as Guardian for _____, an incapacitated person, pursuant to an Order and Judgment of this Court dated _____, 20 ___, and the incapacitated person having died on _____, 20 ___,

AND the Guardian having submitted a Final Report and Account of Guardian, verified on _____, 20 ___, and the Petition having been verified on _____, 20 ___, and an Order to Show Cause having been signed on _____, 20 ___, directing that the Final Report and Account be served on all interested parties; and same having been served and filed with proof of service on all interested parties,

AND upon the foregoing papers and upon the Affidavit of Services of _____, Esq., attorney for the Guardian, sworn to on the ___ day of _____, 20 ___, and upon the Affidavit of _____, sworn to on the ___ day of _____, 20 ___, and upon the Affidavit of _____, sworn to on the ___ day of _____, 20 ___

AND upon the written decision of the Court dated _____, 20 ___,

NOW THEREFORE IT IS HEREBY

ORDERED, that the Final Report is hereby judicially settled and approved with the following Summary Schedule:

Schedule A - Principal on hand at date of appointment (*or:* last accounting)	$_____
Schedule B - Changes to principal	$_____
Schedule C - Income Received	$_____
Sub Total	$_____
Schedule D - Paid Disbursements	$_____
Schedule E-1 Balance of cash and securities	$_____
Total Estate	$_____

and it is further

ORDERED, that the Guardian is allowed the sum of $ _____ as commissions for serving as Guardian, and the Guardian is authorized to pay same; and it is further

ORDERED, that _____, Esq. is awarded legal fees for services rendered in the sum of $ _____, plus $ _____ for disbursements, and the Guardian is authorized to pay same; and it is further

ORDERED, that the Guardian is allowed the sum of $ _____ to compensate for unpaid disbursements incurred by the Guardian, and the Guardian is authorized to pay same, and it is further

ORDERED, that the Guardian is authorized to and shall pay the funds remaining on hand after payment of the amounts approved by this Order to _____ as Executor of the Estate of the incapacitated person, deceased, and it is further

ORDERED, that outstanding bills, if any, shall be referred to the Executor of the Estate of the incapacitated person for payment, and it is further

ORDERED that, upon the submission by the Guardian of proof of compliance with all provisions of this Order, an Ex Parte Order shall be entered, discharging the Guardian and the surety from any and all further liability, accountability and responsibility with respect to all matters embraced in the Final Report and canceling the bond.

ENTER:

_____
J.S.C.

Form 20. Affidavit in Support of Discharge of Guardian and Cancellation of Bond

SUPREME COURT OF THE STATE OF NEW YORK
COUNTY OF NEW YORK
--x   IAS Part No. _____
IN THE MATTER OF THE APPLICATION OF

_____,   Index No: _____

                              Petitioner,

FOR THE APPOINTMENT OF A GUARDIAN FOR

                                                     AFFIDAVIT IN
                                                     SUPPORT OF
                                                     DISCHARGE OF
                                                     GUARDIAN AND
                                                     CANCELLATION
                                                     OF BOND

_____,
                    An Alleged Incapacitated Person.
--x

STATE OF NEW YORK   )
)   ss.:
COUNTY OF _____   )

_____, being duly sworn, deposes and says:

1. I am the Guardian in this proceeding, having been duly appointed by Order and Judgment of this Court dated the ___ day of _____, 20___.

2. I make this Affidavit in support my Motion to Discharge the Guardian and Cancel the Bond.

3. I have fully complied with all provisions of the Order Judicially Settling and Approving the Final Report in this proceeding signed by this Court on the ___ day of _____, 20___.

4. An Updated Verified Statement indicating the balance of the funds on hand at the date of the Final Report with interest that has accrued since that date and the payments made pursuant to the Order Judicially Settling and Approving the Final Report is attached as Exhibit A.

5. All required disbursements having been made, there are currently no funds held by the Guardian.

6. The Guardian requests that the Court sign the attached Order and discharge the Guardian and cancel the bond of the surety.

7. No prior application for the same or similar relief has been made.

                                        _____
                                                  Guardian

Sworn to before me this

___ day of _____, 20 ___.

_____
Notary Public

Form 21.   Order Discharging Guardian and Surety

At IAS Part ___ of the Supreme Court of the State of New York, held in and for the County of New York, at the New York County Courthouse, located at 60 Centre Street, New York, New York, on the ___ day of _____, 20 ___.

PRESENT: HON. _____
....x
                                                                        Justice

IN THE MATTER OF THE APPLICATION
OF

_____,

                                                                        Index No: _____

Petitioner,

FOR THE APPOINTMENT OF A GUARDIAN
FOR

                                                                        ORDER DISCHARGING
                                                                        GUARDIAN AND
                                                                        SURETY

_____,

An Alleged Incapacitated Person.
....x

_____, Guardian of the property [and/or: personal needs] of _____, an incapacitated person, deceased, having submitted due proof of compliance with the provisions of the Order Judicially Settling and Approving the Final Report issued by this Court (the Honorable _____, J.S.C.), dated _____, 20___,

NOW THEREFORE, on reading and filing the Order Judicially Settling and Approving the Final Report, the Affidavit of _____, the Guardian, sworn to on the ___ day of _____, 20___, [if applicable: along with the Updated Verified Statement of the Guardian sworn to on _____, 20 ___,]

NOW on Motion of _____, Esq., counsel for the Guardian,

IT IS HEREBY ORDERED that the Guardian and the surety herein be and the same hereby are discharged from any and all further liability, accountability and responsibility with respect to all matters embraced in the Final Report, and it is further

ORDERED, that the bond filed herein is canceled, and it is further

ORDERED, that a copy of this Order shall be served upon the County Clerk of New York County and the surety within ___ days from the date hereof.

                                        ENTER:

                                        _____
                                                            J.S.C.

OTHER FORMS

Form 22.   Amend, Leave to, Order Granting

At IAS Part ___ of the Supreme
Court of the State of New York,
held in and for the County of
New York, at the Courthouse
thereof, 60 Centre Street, New
York, New York on the ___ of
_____, 200___.

PRESENT: HON: _____
JUSTICE

_____
                  Plaintiff,   INDEX No. _____

- against -

                                                ORDER

                  Defendant.
_____

A motion having been made by _____ and having duly come on to be heard
on the ___ of _____, 200___, for an order _____,

NOW, on reading and filing the following papers submitted to the Court,
_____, and upon the Court's decision thereon dated _____, it is

ORDERED that the plaintiff's motion for leave to amend the complaint herein is
granted, and the amended complaint in the proposed form annexed to the moving
papers shall be deemed served upon service of a copy of this order with notice of
entry thereof; and it is further

ORDERED that the defendant have 20 days from the date of said service to serve
an answer to the amended complaint.

Dated: _____

ENTER:

_____
J.S.C.

Form 23.   Arbitration, Order and Judgment Confirming Award

At IAS Part ___ of the Supreme
Court of the State of New York, held
in and for the County of New York,
at the Courthouse thereof, 60 Centre
Street, New York, New York on the
___ of _____, 200___.

PRESENT: HON: _____
                        JUSTICE

_____

                    Petitioner,   INDEX No. _____

        - against -

                                          ORDER AND JUDGMENT

                    Respondent.

_____

    An application having been made by petitioner and having duly come on to be heard on the ___ of _____, 200___, for an order and judgment confirming an award,

    NOW, on reading and filing the following papers submitted to the Court, _____, and upon the Court's decision thereon dated _____, it is

    ORDERED that the application is granted and the award rendered in favor of petitioner and against respondent is confirmed; and it is further

    ORDERED and ADJUDGED that petitioner _____, having an address at _____, shall have judgment and recover against respondent _____, having an address at _____, in the amount of $ _____, plus interest at the rate of ___ % per annum from the date of _____, as computed by the Clerk in the amount of $ _____, together with costs and disbursements in the amount of $ _____ as taxed by the Clerk, for the total amount of $ _____, and that the petitioner have execution therefor.

    Dated: _____

                                    ENTER:

                                    _____
                                    J.S.C.

Form 24.   Article 78 Application, Judgment Denying

At IAS Part ___ of the Supreme
Court of the State of New York, held
in and for the County of New York,
at the Courthouse thereof, 60 Centre
Street, New York, New York on the
___ of _____, 200___.

PRESENT: HON: _____
                          JUSTICE

_____

                    Petitioner,   INDEX No. _____

  - against -
                                          JUDGMENT

                    Respondent.

_____

An application having been made by _____ and having duly come on to be heard on the ___ of _____, 200___, for a judgment _____,

NOW, on reading and filing the following papers submitted to the Court, _____, and upon the Court's decision thereon dated _____, it is

ADJUDGED that the application of petitioner is denied and the petition is dismissed, with costs and disbursements to respondent.

Dated: _____

                    ENTER:

                    _____
                    J.S.C.

Form 25.   Article 78 Application, Judgment Granting
(Police Officer—Reinstatement & Back Pay)

At IAS Part ___ of the Supreme Court of the State of New York, held in and for the County of New York, at the Courthouse thereof, 60 Centre Street, New York, New York on the ___ of _____, 200___.

PRESENT: HON: _____
                              JUSTICE

_____

                            Petitioner,   INDEX No. _____

- against -

                                                JUDGMENT

                            Respondent.

_____

An application having been made by petitioner and having duly come on to be heard on the ___ of _____, 200___, for a judgment _____,

NOW, on reading and filing the following papers submitted to the Court, _____, and upon the Court's decision thereon dated _____, it is

ADJUDGED that the application of petitioner is granted as follows:

(1) The determination of respondent New York City Police Department, dated _____, 200___, terminating petitioner as a probationary police officer, is vacated and annulled and petitioner is reinstated to said position with back pay from _____, 200___, the date of termination, and the balance of petitioner's probationary period shall commence to run upon said reinstatement.

(2) Petitioner, having an address at _____, do recover from respondent New York City Police Department the aforesaid back pay in the amount of $ _____, with interest at the rate of ___% from the aforesaid date of termination, plus costs and disbursements in the sum of $ _____ as taxed by the Clerk, and petitioner shall have execution therefor.

Dated: _____

                              ENTER:

                              _____
                              J.S.C.

Form 26. Article 78 Proceeding, Order Transferring to Appellate Division (Substantial Evidence (CPLR 7804(g)))

At IAS Part ___ of the Supreme Court of the State of New York, held in and for the County of New York, at the Courthouse thereof, 60 Centre Street, New York, New York on the ___ of _____, 200___.

PRESENT: HON: _____
                         JUSTICE

_____

                    Petitioner,   INDEX No. _____

    - against -

                                         ORDER

                    Respondent.

_____

An application having been made by petitioner and having duly come on to be heard on the ___ of _____, 200___, for a judgment _____,

NOW, on reading and filing the following papers submitted to the Court, _____, and upon the Court's decision thereon dated _____, it is

ORDERED that the application by petitioner seeking to vacate and annul a determination by respondent is respectfully transferred to the Appellate Division, First Department, for disposition, pursuant to CPLR 7804(g). This proceeding involves an issue as to whether a determination made as a result of a hearing held, and at which evidence was taken, pursuant to direction of law is, on the entire record, supported by substantial evidence (CPLR 7803(4)).

The Clerk is directed to transfer the file to the Appellate Division, First Department, upon service of a copy of this order with notice of entry.

Dated: _____

                              ENTER:

                              _____
                              J.S.C.

Form 27. Assessment of Damages (Inquest), Order Directing

At IAS Part ___ of the Supreme
Court of the State of New York, held
in and for the County of New York,
at the Courthouse thereof, 60 Centre
Street, New York, New York on the
___ of _____, 200___.

PRESENT: HON: _____

JUSTICE

_____

Plaintiff,

    - against -

Defendant.

INDEX No. _____

ORDER

_____

A motion having been made by plaintiff and having duly come on to be heard on the ___ of _____, 200___, for an order _____,

NOW, on reading and filing the following papers submitted to the Court, _____, and upon the Court's decision thereon dated _____, it is

ORDERED that an assessment of damages against defendant [defendants _____ and _____] is directed, and it is further

ORDERED that a copy of this order with notice of entry be served upon the Trial Support Clerk (Room 158), who is directed, upon the filing of a note of issue and a statement of readiness and the payment of proper fees, if any, to place this action on the appropriate trial calendar for the assessment hereinabove directed.

Dated: _____

ENTER:

_____

J.S.C.

Form 28. Attachment, Order of

At IAS Part ___ of the Supreme
Court of the State of New York, held
in and for the County of New York,
at the Courthouse thereof, 60 Centre
Street, New York, New York on the
___ of _____, 200___.

PRESENT: HON: _____
                         JUSTICE

_____
                    Plaintiff,   INDEX No. _____

- against -

                                                   ORDER

                    Defendant.
_____

    A motion having been made by plaintiff and having duly come on to be heard on the ___ of _____, 200___, for an order of attachment,

    NOW, on reading and filing the following papers submitted to the Court, _____, and upon the Court's decision thereon dated _____, it is

    ORDERED that the plaintiff's motion for an order of attachment is granted, and it is further

    ORDERED that the amount to be secured by this order of attachment, inclusive of probable interest, costs and Sheriff's fees and expenses, shall be $ _____, and it is further

    ORDERED that the plaintiff's undertaking be and the same is hereby fixed in the sum of $ _____ conditioned that the plaintiff shall pay to the defendant an amount not exceeding $ _____ for legal costs and damages which may be sustained by reason of the attachment, and up to and not exceeding $ _____ to the Sheriff for allowable fees, if the defendant recovers judgment or if it is decided that the plaintiff is not entitled to an attachment of the property of the defendant, and it is further

    ORDERED that the Sheriff of the City of New York, or the Sheriff of any County of the State of New York, levy within his jurisdiction on the amount held by the law firm of _____, New York, New York, in an interest bearing account of the _____ Bank, New York, New York, Account Number _____ entitled _____ for the purpose of securing and satisfying any judgment recovered by the plaintiff herein, together with interest from _____, 200___, costs, disbursements and reasonable Sheriff's fees, and that the Sheriff proceed herein in the manner and make his return within the time prescribed by law.

    Dated: _____

                              ENTER:

                              _____
                              J.S.C.

Form 29. Consolidation, Order Directing
(Transfer from Other County)

At IAS Part ___ of the Supreme
Court of the State of New York, held
in and for the County of New York,
at the Courthouse thereof, 60 Centre
Street, New York, New York on the
___ of _____, 200___.

PRESENT: HON: _____
JUSTICE

_____

<table>
<tr><td>Plaintiff,</td><td>INDEX No. _____</td></tr>
<tr><td>- against -</td><td></td></tr>
<tr><td></td><td>ORDER</td></tr>
<tr><td>Defendant.</td><td></td></tr>
</table>

_____

A motion having been made by _____ and having duly come on to be heard on the ___ of _____, 200___, for an order of consolidation,

NOW, on reading and filing the following papers submitted to the Court, _____, and upon the Court's decision thereon dated _____, it is

ORDERED that the motion is granted and the above-captioned action is consolidated in this Court with _____ vs. _____, Index No. _____ (_____ County) under New York County Index No. _____ and the consolidated action shall bear the following caption:

_____
_____

Plaintiff(s),
-against-

_____
_____

Defendant(s).

And it is further

ORDERED that the Clerk of _____ Court, _____ County, shall transfer the papers on file under Index No. _____ to the Clerk of this Court upon service of a certified copy of this order and payment of the appropriate fee, if any; and it is further

ORDERED that the pleadings in the actions hereby consolidated shall stand as the pleadings in the consolidated action; and it is further

ORDERED that upon service on the Clerk of this Court of a copy of this order with notice of entry, the Clerk shall consolidate the papers in the actions hereby consolidated and shall mark his records to reflect the consolidation, and it is further

ORDERED that a copy of this order with notice of entry shall also be served upon the Clerk of the Trial Support Office (Room 158), who is hereby directed to mark the court's records to reflect the consolidation.

Dated: _____

ENTER:

_____

J.S.C.

Form 30. Consolidation, Order Directing
(Two or More NY County Actions)

At IAS Part ___ of the Supreme
Court of the State of New York, held
in and for the County of New York,
at the Courthouse thereof, 60 Centre
Street, New York, New York on the
___ of _____, 200___.

PRESENT: HON: _____
                 JUSTICE

_____

            Plaintiff,   INDEX No. _____

- against -

                               ORDER

           Defendant.

_____

A motion having been made by _____ and having duly come on to be heard on the ___ of _____, 200___, for an order of consolidation,

NOW, on reading and filing the following papers submitted to the Court, _____, and upon the Court's decision thereon dated _____, it is

ORDERED that the motion is granted and the above-captioned action is consolidated in this Court with _____ vs. _____, Index No. _____, under Index No. _____, and the consolidated action shall bear the following caption:

_____

_____

                 Plaintiff(s),

                 -against-

_____

_____

                 Defendant(s).

And it is further

ORDERED that the pleadings in the actions hereby consolidated shall stand as the pleadings in the consolidated action; and it is further

ORDERED that upon service on the Clerk of this Court of a copy of this order with notice of entry, the Clerk shall consolidate the papers in the actions hereby consolidated and shall mark his records to reflect the consolidation, and it is further

ORDERED that a copy of this order with notice of entry shall also be served upon the Clerk of the Trial Support Office (Room 158), who is hereby directed to mark the court's records to reflect the consolidation.

Dated: _____

                 ENTER:

                 _____

                 J.S.C.

Form 31. Dismiss Complaint on Default, Order Granting Motion to

At IAS Part ___ of the Supreme
Court of the State of New York, held
in and for the County of New York,
at the Courthouse thereof, 60 Centre
Street, New York, New York on the
___ of _____, 200___.

PRESENT: HON: _____
                          JUSTICE

_____

                Plaintiff,   INDEX No. _____

        - against -

                                      ORDER

                Defendant.

_____

A motion having been made by defendant and having duly come on to be heard on
the ___ of _____, 200___, for an order dismissing the complaint,

NOW, on reading and filing the following papers submitted to the Court,
_____, and upon the Court's decision thereon dated _____, it is

ORDERED that the defendant's motion to dismiss the complaint is granted on
default, and the Clerk is directed to enter judgment in favor of defendant dismissing
the complaint in its entirety, with costs and disbursements to defendant as taxed by
the Clerk [, upon submission by affirmation of counsel of proof of service on plaintiff
of a copy of this order with notice of entry at least ___ days prior to the entry of said
judgment].

Dated: _____

                        ENTER:

                        _____

                        J.S.C.

Form 32.   Dismiss Complaint, Order Granting Motion to

At IAS Part ___ of the Supreme
Court of the State of New York, held
in and for the County of New York,
at the Courthouse thereof, 60 Centre
Street, New York, New York on the
___ of _____, 200___.

PRESENT: HON: _____
                 JUSTICE

_____

                Plaintiff,   INDEX No. _____

     - against -

                Defendant.   ORDER

_____

A motion having been made by defendant and having duly come on to be heard on the ___ of _____, 200___, for an order dismissing the complaint,

NOW, on reading and filing the following papers submitted to the Court, _____, and upon the Court's decision thereon dated _____, it is

ORDERED that the motion to dismiss is granted and the complaint is dismissed with costs and disbursements to defendant as taxed by the Clerk; and it is further

ORDERED that the Clerk is directed to enter judgment accordingly.

Dated: _____

                      ENTER:

                      _____

                      J.S.C.

Form 33. Dismissing Defense, Order

At IAS Part ___ of the Supreme
Court of the State of New York, held
in and for the County of New York,
at the Courthouse thereof, 60 Centre
Street, New York, New York on the
___ of _____, 200___.

PRESENT: HON: _____
                              JUSTICE

_____

                    Plaintiff,   INDEX No. _____

        - against -
                                              ORDER

                    Defendant.
_____

A motion having been made by plaintiff and having duly come on to be heard on
the ___ of _____, 200___, for an order dismissing an affirmative defense,

NOW, on reading and filing the following papers submitted to the Court,
_____, and upon the Court's decision thereon dated _____, it is

ORDERED that the motion is granted and the _____ affirmative defense of
defendant _____ is dismissed; and it is further

ORDERED that the action in all other respects continues.

Dated: _____

                              ENTER:

                              _____
                              J.S.C.

Form 34. Dismissing Some Causes of Action, Order

At IAS Part ___ of the Supreme
Court of the State of New York,
held in and for the County of New
York, at the Courthouse thereof, 60
Centre Street, New York, New
York on the ___ of _____,
200___.

PRESENT: HON: _____
                                    JUSTICE

_____

                    Plaintiff,   INDEX No. _____

    - against -

                                        ORDER

                    Defendant.

_____

A motion having been made by defendant and having duly come on to be heard on the ___ of _____, 200___, for an order dismissing certain causes of action,

NOW, on reading and filing the following papers submitted to the Court, _____, and upon the Court's decision thereon dated _____, it is

ORDERED that the motion to dismiss is granted and the _____, _____, and _____ cause[s] of action of the complaint is [are] severed and dismissed; and it is further

ORDERED that the remainder of the action shall continue; and it is further

ORDERED that defendant is directed to serve an answer to the complaint within 10 days after service of a copy of this order with notice of entry; and it is further

ORDERED that the Clerk is directed to enter judgment accordingly.

Dated: _____

                              ENTER:

                              _____
                              J.S.C.

Form 35. Dismissing with Leave to Replead, Order

At IAS Part ___ of the Supreme
Court of the State of New York, held
in and for the County of New York,
at the Courthouse thereof, 60 Centre
Street, New York, New York on the
___ of _____, 200___.

PRESENT: HON: _____
                          JUSTICE

_____

                    Plaintiff,   INDEX No. _____

- against -
                                        ORDER

                    Defendant.

_____

    A motion having been made by defendant and having duly come on to be heard on the ___ of _____, 200___, for an order dismissing the complaint,

    NOW, on reading and filing the following papers submitted to the Court, _____, and upon the Court's decision thereon dated _____, it is

    ORDERED that the motion to dismiss is granted and the complaint is dismissed; and it is further

    ORDERED that plaintiff is granted leave to serve an amended complaint so as to replead the _____ cause[s] of action within 20 days after service on plaintiff's attorney of a copy of this order with notice of entry. In the event that plaintiff fails to serve an amended complaint within such time, leave to replead shall be deemed denied and the action shall be deemed dismissed with prejudice.

    Dated: _____

ENTER:

_____
J.S.C.

Form 36.   Ejectment, Order and Judgment

At IAS Part ___ of the Supreme
Court of the State of New York, held
in and for the County of New York,
at the Courthouse thereof, 60 Centre
Street, New York, New York on the
___ of _____, 200___.

PRESENT: HON: _____
                          JUSTICE

_____

                        Plaintiff,   INDEX No. _____

        - against -

                                                 ORDER AND JUDGMENT

                        Defendant.

_____

A motion having been made by plaintiff and having duly come on to be heard on
the ___ of _____, 200___, for an order of ejectment,

NOW, on reading and filing the following papers submitted to the Court,
_____, and upon the Court's decision thereon dated _____, it is

ORDERED that the motion is granted, and it is further

ORDERED and ADJUDGED that plaintiff is entitled to possession of
_____, New York, New York as against defendant _____, and the Sheriff
of the City of New York, County of New York, upon receipt of a certified copy of
this Order and Judgment and payment of proper fees, is directed to place plaintiff in
possession accordingly, and it is further

ORDERED and ADJUDGED that immediately upon entry of this Order and
Judgment, plaintiff may exercise all acts of ownership and possession of _____,
New York, New York, including entry thereto, as against defendant _____, and
it is further

ORDERED that the branch of the above-entitled action relating to recovery of
damages is severed and continued.

Dated: _____

                                        ENTER:

                                        _____
                                        J.S.C.

Form 37. Enforcement Order, Downward
Modification of Maintenance

At IAS Part ___ of the Supreme
Court of the State of New York, held
in and for the County of New York,
at the Courthouse thereof, 60 Centre
Street, New York, New York on the
___ of _____, 200___.

PRESENT: HON: _____
                      JUSTICE

_____

                    Plaintiff,   INDEX No. _____

       - against -

                                         ORDER

                    Defendant.

_____

A motion having been made by plaintiff and having duly come on to be heard on the ___ of _____, 200___, for an order _____,

NOW, on reading and filing the following papers submitted to the Court, _____, and upon the Court's decision thereon dated _____, it is

ORDERED that the Clerk of the Court, upon service of a copy of this order with notice of entry, shall enter a money judgment in plaintiff's favor against defendant in the sum of $ _____, together with costs and disbursements; and it is further ORDERED that the defendant shall post security with the Clerk in the form of certified check, cash or security bond in the sum of $ _____, to assure payment of arrears and sums that may come due in the future; and it is further

ORDERED that the defendant shall so act within ___ days after service of a copy of this order with notice of entry. In the event that the defendant fails to post security as directed herein, plaintiff may, without further notice, settle an order providing for the sequestration of defendant's income and assets and the appointment of a receiver; and it is further

ORDERED that plaintiff's application to punish defendant for contempt is denied with leave to renew upon a showing that the plaintiff has been unable to effect collection of the arrears due her through the relief granted herein; and it is further

ORDERED that the defendant's application for a modification of maintenance is denied.

Dated: _____

                                    ENTER:

                                    _____
                                    J.S.C.

Form 38. Framed Issue Hearing (Uninsured Motorist), Order Directing

At IAS Part ___ of the Supreme Court of the State of New York, held in and for the County of New York, at the Courthouse thereof, 60 Centre Street, New York, New York on the ___ of _____, 200___.

PRESENT: HON: _____
          JUSTICE

_____

                Petitioner,   INDEX No. _____

- against -

                                      ORDER

                Respondent.

_____

An application having been made by petitioner and having duly come on to be heard on the ___ of _____, 200___, for a judgment staying arbitration,

NOW, on reading and filing the following papers submitted to the Court, _____, and upon the Court's decision thereon dated _____, it is

ORDERED that the application to stay arbitration is granted to the extent that a trial is directed of the preliminary issues as to coverage [cancellation of the policy; timely notification of the police, etc.], and the arbitration is stayed pending such trial, and it is further ORDERED that the Trial Support Clerk is directed to assign this matter to an appropriate Part for trial upon receipt of a copy of this order with notice of entry, the filing of a note of issue and a statement of readiness, and the payment of appropriate fees, if any, and it is further

ORDERED that a copy of this order with notice of entry be served upon the attorneys for the respondent and the arbitrator within 20 days of entry hereof, and it is further

ORDERED that _____ shall be added as a party respondent upon service upon said party respondent of a copy of this order with notice of entry together with copies of all papers previously served in the proceeding, and it is further

ORDERED that the caption of this proceeding is amended to reflect inclusion of said additional party respondent and the Clerk of this Court and the Trial Support Clerk (Room 158), upon service on each of them of a copy of this order with notice of entry, shall mark their records to reflect the amendment.

Dated: _____

                            ENTER:

                            _____
                            J.S.C.

Form 39. Intervention, Order Granting

At IAS Part ____ of the Supreme
Court of the State of New York, held
in and for the County of New York,
at the Courthouse thereof, 60 Centre
Street, New York, New York on the
____ of _____, 200____.

PRESENT: HON: _____
            JUSTICE

_____

         Plaintiff,   INDEX No. _____

- against -

                       ORDER

         Defendant.

_____

A motion having been made by _____ and having duly come on to be heard on the ____ of _____, 200____, for an order of intervention,

NOW, on reading and filing the following papers submitted to the Court, _____, and upon the Court's decision thereon dated _____, it is

ORDERED that the motion is granted, and that _____ be permitted to intervene in the above-entitled action as a party defendant; and it is further

ORDERED that the summons and complaint in the above-entitled action be amended by adding _____ thereto as a party defendant; and it is further

ORDERED that _____ be and hereby is permitted to serve his [her/its] answer upon the attorneys for the plaintiff and the defendant, or otherwise move with respect to the complaint in the above-entitled action, within 20 days from service of a copy of this order with notice of entry; and it is further

ORDERED that the attorney for the intervenor shall serve a copy of this order with notice of entry upon the Clerk of the Court and upon the Trial Support Office (Room 158), which are directed to amend their records to reflect such change in the caption herein.

Dated: _____

               ENTER:

               _____
               J.S.C.

Form 40.   Joint Trial, Order Directing

At IAS Part ___ of the Supreme Court of the State of New York, held in and for the County of New York, at the Courthouse thereof, 60 Centre Street, New York, New York on the ___ of _____, 200___.

PRESENT: HON: _____
                          JUSTICE

_____

                     Plaintiff,   INDEX No. _____

          - against -

                                                   ORDER

                     Defendant.

_____

A motion having been made by _____ and having duly come on to be heard on the ___ of _____, 200___, for an order directing a joint trial,

NOW, on reading and filing the following papers submitted to the Court, _____, and upon the Court's decision thereon dated _____, it is

ORDERED that the motion is granted and the above-captioned action shall be jointly tried with _____ v _____, Index No. _____, _____ County; and it is further

ORDERED that the Clerk of the _____ Court of _____ County, upon receipt of a certified copy of this order and upon payment of the proper fees, shall transfer to the Clerk of the Supreme Court, New York County, all of the papers on file in the action/proceeding _____ v _____, Index No. _____, and it is further

ORDERED that the Clerk of the Supreme Court, New York County, upon receipt of a copy of this order with notice of entry, shall, without further fee, assign an index number to the file transferred pursuant to this order; and it is further

ORDERED that upon payment of the appropriate calendar fees, the filing of notes of issue and statements of readiness in each of the above actions, and upon service of a copy of this order with notice of entry on the Clerk of the Trial Support Office (Room 158), said Clerk shall place the aforesaid actions upon the trial calendar for a joint trial.

Dated: _____

                                        ENTER:

                                        _____

                                        J.S.C.

Form 41. Pendente Lite Relief, including Maintenance, Child Support, Custody, Injunctive Relief, Counsel Fees, etc.

At IAS Part ___ of the Supreme Court of the State of New York, held in and for the County of New York, at the Courthouse thereof, 60 Centre Street, New York, New York on the ___ of _____, 200___.

PRESENT: HON: _____
                         JUSTICE

_____

Plaintiff,   INDEX No. _____

- against -

                                  ORDER

Defendant.

_____

A motion having been made by _____ and having duly come on to be heard on the ___ of _____, 200___, for an order _____,

NOW, on reading and filing the following papers submitted to the Court, _____, and upon the Court's decision thereon dated _____, it is

ORDERED that the plaintiff [defendant] is awarded $ _____ per week temporary maintenance which shall [shall not] be income to the plaintiff and shall [shall not] be deductible to the defendant for taxation purposes; and it is further

ORDERED that pending final determination of this action, the plaintiff [defendant] is directed to pay all rent, insurance, and utilities such as gas and electricity on the marital residence; and it is further

ORDERED that the defendant [plaintiff] is directed to pay the sum of $ _____ per week as and for interim child support; and it is further

ORDERED that the defendant [plaintiff] is directed to maintain and continue in full force and effect all presently existing policies of life, medical and dental insurance in behalf of plaintiff and the parties' children and to pay all unreimbursed, non-elective pharmaceutical, medical and dental expenses for them; and it is further

ORDERED that the award at the rate of $ _____ in addition to the award of pendente lite relief is retroactive to the original date of service of this application; retroactive sums due by reason of this award shall be paid in their entirety within 20 days after service of a copy of this order with notice of entry. Defendant [plaintiff] may take credit for sums voluntarily paid for maintenance and support for this period for which he [she] has cancelled checks or other similar proof of payment; and it is further

ORDERED that the first weekly payment hereunder shall be made ___ days after service of a copy of this order with notice of entry, and continue on a weekly basis thereafter; and it is further

ORDERED that the plaintiff [defendant] is awarded interim counsel fees in the sum of $ _____ to be paid by defendant [plaintiff] to plaintiff's [defendant's] attorney within twenty (20) days after service of this order with notice of entry. This award is made without prejudice to an application by plaintiff [defendant] for additional counsel fees, if necessary; and it is further

ORDERED that the plaintiff [defendant] is granted [denied] exclusive occupancy of the marital residence; and it is further

ORDERED that the defendant [plaintiff] may remove his [her] personalty from the marital residence on a date and at a time to be agreed to by the parties, in the presence of their respective counsel or designees. This shall take place no later than ___ days after service of a copy of this order with notice of entry. Defendant [plaintiff] shall furnish plaintiff [defendant] with a list of the personalty to be removed no later than ___ days prior to the date scheduled for removal of same; and it is further

ORDERED that the plaintiff [defendant] is awarded interim custody of the parties' minor child [children]. The parties within 20 days after service of a copy of this order with notice of entry shall settle an order fixing an appropriate schedule of interim visitation. In the event that the parties are unable to settle such an order, the matter of determining a schedule of interim visitation that shall serve the best interest of the minor child [children] is referred to a Special Referee to hear and report with recommendations on an expedited basis; pending receipt of the report, should a hearing be necessary, final determination of the matter of interim visitation is held in abeyance; and it is further

ORDERED that the matter of custody and visitation is referred to a Special Referee to hear and report with recommendations; and it is further

ORDERED, that the parties are enjoined from selling, transferring, conveying or otherwise disposing of assets pending further court order, except for ordinary and routine living and business expenses, in order to maintain the status quo for possible equitable distribution upon the plenary trial of this action. The exception for "ordinary and routine living and business expenses" contemplates that payment of these expenses be made from current income unless current income is clearly insufficient to meet the reasonable needs of the parties. The parties are cautioned that any unauthorized invasion of assets for any purpose may result in a finding of contempt if it is later found that current income was not exhausted prior to invasion of assets; and it is further

ORDERED that all relief sought in this consolidated application which is not specifically granted herein shall be deemed denied. A copy of this order with notice of entry shall be served on the Judicial Support Office (Room 311) for the purpose of obtaining a calendar date, if such a hearing on interim visitation shall become necessary.

Dated: _____

ENTER:

_____
J.S.C.

Form 42. Preliminary Injunction

At IAS Part ___ of the Supreme
Court of the State of New York, held
in and for the County of New York,
at the Courthouse thereof, 60 Centre
Street, New York, New York on the
___ of _____, 200___.

PRESENT: HON: _____
                         JUSTICE

_____

                    Plaintiff,   INDEX No. _____

        - against -

                                       ORDER

                    Defendant.

_____

A motion having been made by plaintiff and having duly come on to be heard on the ___ of _____, 200___, for an order granting a preliminary injunction,

NOW, on reading and filing the following papers submitted to the Court, _____, and upon the Court's decision thereon dated _____, and

Due deliberation having been had, and it appearing to this Court that a cause of action exists in favor of the plaintiff and against the defendant and that the plaintiff is entitled to a preliminary injunction on the ground that the defendant threatens or is about to do, or is doing or procuring or suffering to be done, an act in violation of the plaintiff's rights respecting the subject of the action and tending to render the judgment ineffectual, as set forth in the aforesaid decision [the plaintiff has demanded and would be entitled to a judgment restraining the defendant from the commission or continuance of an act, which, if committed or continued during the pendency of the action, would produce injury to the plaintiff, as set forth in the aforesaid decision], it is

ORDERED that the undertaking is fixed in the sum of $ _____ conditioned that the plaintiff, if it is finally determined that he [she/it] was not entitled to an injunction, will pay to the defendant all damages and costs which may be sustained by reason of this injunction; and it is further

ORDERED that defendant, his [her/its] agents, servants, employees and all other persons acting under the jurisdiction, supervision and/or direction of defendant, are enjoined and restrained, during the pendency of this action, from doing or suffering to be done, directly or through any attorney, agent, servant, employee or other person under the supervision or control of defendant or otherwise, any of the following acts:

_____

_____

_____

_____

_____

Dated: _____

                                   ENTER:

                                   _____
                                   J.S.C.

Form 43.   Reference to Determine—Long Account, Order of

At IAS Part ___ of the Supreme
Court of the State of New York, held
in and for the County of New York,
at the Courthouse thereof, 60 Centre
Street, New York, New York on the
___ of _____, 200___.

PRESENT: HON: _____
                        JUSTICE

_____

                        Plaintiff,   INDEX No. _____

        - against -

                                             ORDER

                        Defendant.

_____

A motion having been made by _____ and having duly come on to be heard on the ___ of _____, 200___, for an order _____,

NOW, on reading and filing the following papers submitted to the Court, _____, and upon the Court's decision thereon dated _____, it is

ORDERED that a long accounting is directed as to the following entity: _____; and it is further

ORDERED that, within 30 days after service of a copy of this order with notice of entry, the _____ shall prepare and serve, upon all other parties hereto, a long accounting, with all appropriate schedules attached, for the period commencing _____, through and including _____; and it is further

ORDERED that any formal objections to such accounting shall be served within 30 days after service of a copy of the accounting; and it is further

ORDERED that, pursuant to CPLR 4317(b), the issue of the long accounting is referred for assignment to a Special Referee to hear and determine; and it is further

ORDERED that, no later than the hearing date to be assigned, a copy of the long accounting and any formal objections shall be filed with the Special Referee to whom this long accounting is assigned; and it is further

ORDERED that this motion is held in abeyance pending the hearing and determination of the Special Referee to whom this long accounting is assigned; and it is further

ORDERED that counsel shall serve and file a copy of this order with notice of entry on the Judicial Support Office (Room 311) for the purpose of arranging a calendar date for hearing and assignment of this long accounting to a Special Referee for determination.

Dated: _____

                        ENTER:

                        _____

                        J.S.C.

Form 44. Reference to Hear and Report, Order Directing

At IAS Part ___ of the Supreme
Court of the State of New York, held
in and for the County of New York,
at the Courthouse thereof, 60 Centre
Street, New York, New York on the
___ of _____, 200___.

PRESENT: HON: _____
                                    JUSTICE

_____

                          Plaintiff,   INDEX No. _____

        - against -

                                                ORDER

                          Defendant.

_____

A motion having been made by _____ and having duly come on to be heard
on the ___ of _____, 200___, for an order _____,

NOW, on reading and filing the following papers submitted to the Court,
_____, and upon the Court's decision thereon dated _____, it is

ORDERED that the issue of _____ is referred to a Special Referee to hear
and report with recommendations, except that, in the event of and upon the filing of
a stipulation of the parties, as permitted by CPLR 4317, the Special Referee, or
another person designated by the parties to serve as referee, shall determine the
aforesaid issue; and it is further

ORDERED that this motion is held in abeyance pending receipt of the report and
recommendations of the Special Referee and a motion pursuant to CPLR 4403 or
receipt of the determination of the Special Referee or the designated referee; and it
is further

ORDERED that a copy of this order with notice of entry shall be served on the
Judicial Support Office (Room 311) to arrange a date for the reference to a Special
Referee.

Dated: _____

                                                ENTER:

                                                _____

                                                J.S.C.

Form 45.   Resettling Order, Order

At IAS Part ___ of the Supreme
Court of the State of New York, held
in and for the County of New York,
at the Courthouse thereof, 60 Centre
Street, New York, New York on the
___ of _____, 200___.

PRESENT: HON: _____
                                 JUSTICE

_____

                         Plaintiff,   INDEX No. _____

          - against -

                                              ORDER

                         Defendant.

_____

    A motion having been made by _____ and having duly come on to be heard
on the ___ of _____, 200___, for an order _____,

    NOW, on reading and filing the following papers submitted to the Court,
_____, and upon the Court's decision thereon dated _____, it is

    ORDERED that the order of this Court dated _____, 200___, is resettled as
follows:

    [Repeat the original order as entered, including the entire caption and the body
through and including the signature line, except that portion being changed.]

    Dated: _____

                         ENTER:

                         _____

                         J.S.C.

Form 46. Sealing Order

At IAS Part ___ of the Supreme
Court of the State of New York, held
in and for the County of New York,
at the Courthouse thereof, 60 Centre
Street, New York, New York on the
___ of _____, 200___.

PRESENT: HON: _____
                          JUSTICE

_____

                    Plaintiff,   INDEX No. _____

      - against -

                                            ORDER

                    Defendant.

_____

A motion having been made by _____ and having duly come on to be heard
on the ___ of _____, 200___, for an order _____,

NOW, on reading and filing the following papers submitted to the Court,
_____, and upon the Court's decision thereon dated _____, it is

ORDERED that the Clerk, upon presentation to the Clerk of a copy of this order
with notice of entry, is directed to seal the file in this action, and it is further

ORDERED that, absent further order of the court, the Clerk shall deny access to
the file to anyone except for counsel of record to any party to this case, a party, and
any representative of counsel of record to a party upon presentation to the Clerk of
written authorization from said counsel.

Dated: _____

                              ENTER: _____

                              _____
                              J.S.C.

Form 47. Security for Costs, Order Directing

At IAS Part ___ of the Supreme
Court of the State of New York, held
in and for the County of New York,
at the Courthouse thereof, 60 Centre
Street, New York, New York on the
___ of _____, 200___.

PRESENT: HON: _____
                              JUSTICE

_____

                    Plaintiff,   INDEX No. _____

        - against -

                                         ORDER

                    Defendant.

_____

A motion having been made by plaintiff and having duly come on to be heard on the ___ of _____, 200___, for an order requiring security for costs,

NOW, on reading and filing the following papers submitted to the Court, _____, and upon the Court's decision thereon dated _____, it is

ORDERED that, within 30 days from the date of service of a copy of this order with notice of entry, the plaintiff either (i) pay into the Court the sum of $500.00 to be applied to the payment of costs, if any, awarded against the plaintiff, or (ii), at his [her/its] election, file with the Clerk of this Court an undertaking with sufficient surety in a like amount to be applied to the payment of costs, if any, awarded against the plaintiff in this action, and it is further

ORDERED that, within 30 days from the date of service of a copy of this order with notice of entry, plaintiff shall serve upon the attorneys for the defendant a written notice of the payment or of the filing of such undertaking, and it is further

ORDERED that all further proceedings, except to review this order, are stayed for 30 days from the date of service of a copy of this order with notice of entry.

Dated: _____

                              ENTER:

                              _____
                              J.S.C.

Form 48.   Seizure, Order of (On Notice)

At IAS Part ___ of the Supreme
Court of the State of New York, held
in and for the County of New York,
at the Courthouse thereof, 60 Centre
Street, New York, New York on the
___ of _____, 200___.

PRESENT: HON: _____
                    JUSTICE

_____

                Plaintiff,   INDEX No. _____

       - against -

                                     ORDER

                Defendant.

_____

A motion having been made by _____ and having duly come on to be heard
on the ___ of _____, 200___, for an order of seizure, NOW, on reading and
filing the following papers submitted to the Court, _____, and upon the Court's
decision thereon dated _____, it is

ORDERED that the motion is granted; and it is further

ORDERED that the Sheriff of any county of the State of New York wherein the
chattel is found, upon service upon him or her of a certified copy of this order, the
papers on which this order was granted, and the undertaking approved by this Court
in the amount of $ _____, which is not less than twice the value of the chattel,
and payment of the proper fees, is directed to seize the chattel at issue, to wit:

_____

_____

_____

_____

and for that purpose, if the chattel is not delivered to him or her, to break open,
enter and search for the chattel in the place specified in the supporting affidavit,
namely, _____, and to hold the chattel pursuant to Article 71 of the Civil
Practice Law and Rules.

Dated: _____

                              ENTER:

                              _____

                              J.S.C.

Form 49.   Severance of Claim for Counsel Fees, Order Directing

At IAS Part ___ of the Supreme
Court of the State of New York, held
in and for the County of New York,
at the Courthouse thereof, 60 Centre
Street, New York, New York on the
___ of _____, 200___.

PRESENT: HON: _____
                              JUSTICE

_____

                Plaintiff,   INDEX No. _____

- against -

                                      ORDER

                Defendant.

_____

A motion having been made by _____ and having duly come on to be heard
on the ___ of _____, 200___, for an order _____,

NOW, on reading and filing the following papers submitted to the Court,
_____, and upon the Court's decision thereon dated _____, it is

ORDERED that that portion of the plaintiff's action that seeks the recovery of
attorney's fees is severed and an assessment thereof is directed, and it is further

ORDERED that a copy of this order with notice of entry be served upon the Trial
Support Clerk (Room 158), who is directed, upon the filing of a note of issue and a
statement of readiness and the payment of proper fees, if any, to place this action on
the appropriate trial calendar for the assessment hereinabove directed.

Dated: _____

                              ENTER:

                              _____
                              J.S.C.

Form 50.   Standard Format, Long Form Order

At IAS Part ___ of the Supreme
Court of the State of New York, held
in and for the County of New York,
at the Courthouse thereof, 60 Centre
Street, New York, New York on the
___ of _____, 200___.

PRESENT: HON: _____
                    JUSTICE

_____

              Plaintiff,   INDEX No. _____

    - against -

                                      ORDER

              Defendant.

_____

A motion having been made by _____ and having duly come on to be heard
on the ___ of _____, 200___, for an order _____,

NOW, on reading and filing the following papers submitted to the Court,
_____, and upon the Court's decision thereon dated _____, it is

ORDERED that the motion is granted, and it is further

ORDERED that _____.

Dated: _____

                    ENTER:

                    _____
                    J.S.C.

Form 51. Stay of Action and Severance Pending Outcome of Bankruptcy Proceeding

At IAS Part ___ of the Supreme Court of the State of New York, held in and for the County of New York, at the Courthouse thereof, 60 Centre Street, New York, New York on the ___ of _____, 200___.

PRESENT: HON: _____
                          JUSTICE

_____

                    Plaintiff,   INDEX No. _____

          - against -

                                             ORDER

                    Defendant.

_____

   A motion having been made by _____ and having duly come on to be heard on the ___ of _____, 200___, for an order _____,

   NOW, on reading and filing the following papers submitted to the Court, _____, and upon the Court's decision thereon dated _____, it is

   ORDERED that the action is severed as to defendant _____, and is continued as to the remaining defendants, and it is further

   ORDERED that further prosecution of and proceedings in this action are stayed as to defendant _____, except for an application to vacate or modify said stay, and it is further

   ORDERED that either party may make an application by order to show cause to vacate or modify this stay upon the final determination of, or vacatur of the stay issued by the Bankruptcy Court in, the proceeding known as _____ v. _____, pending before the United States Bankruptcy Court for _____, Docket No. _____.

   Dated: _____

                                   ENTER:

                                   _____
                                   J.S.C.

Form 52. Stay of Action Pending Outcome of
Other Action or Arbitration Proceeding

At IAS Part ___ of the Supreme
Court of the State of New York, held
in and for the County of New York,
at the Courthouse thereof, 60 Centre
Street, New York, New York on the
___ of _____, 200___.

PRESENT: HON: _____
                          JUSTICE

_____

                    Plaintiff,   INDEX No. _____

    - against -

                                                ORDER

                    Defendant.

_____

A motion having been made by _____ and having duly come on to be heard
on the ___ of _____, 200___, for an order _____,

NOW, on reading and filing the following papers submitted to the Court,
_____, and upon the Court's decision thereon dated _____, it is

ORDERED that the motion to dismiss is granted to the extent of staying further
prosecution of and proceedings in this action, except for an application to vacate or
modify said stay, and it is further

ORDERED that either party may make an application by order to show cause to
vacate or modify this stay upon the final determination of the action/proceeding
known as _____ v. _____, Index No. _____, pending before the
_____.

Dated: _____

                                         ENTER:

                                         _____
                                         J.S.C.

Form 53. Substitution of Plaintiff, Order for

At IAS Part ___ of the Supreme Court of the State of New York, held in and for the County of New York, at the Courthouse thereof, 60 Centre Street, New York, New York on the ___ of _____, 200___.

PRESENT: HON: _____
                           JUSTICE

_____

                           Plaintiff,   INDEX No. _____

    - against -

                                                 ORDER

                           Defendant.

_____

A motion having been made by _____ and having duly come on to be heard on the ___ of _____, 200___, for an order of substitution,

NOW, on reading and filing the following papers submitted to the Court, _____, and upon the Court's decision thereon dated _____, it is

ORDERED that the motion is granted, and that _____, as executor of the estate of _____, deceased, be substituted as plaintiff in the above-entitled action in the place and stead of the plaintiff, _____, without prejudice to any proceedings heretofore had herein; and it is further

ORDERED that all papers, pleadings and proceedings in the above-entitled action be amended by substituting the name of _____, as executor of the estate of _____, deceased, as plaintiff in the place and stead of said decedent, without prejudice to the proceedings heretofore had herein; and it is further

ORDERED that counsel for plaintiff shall serve a copy of this order with notice of entry upon the Clerk of the Court and upon the Trial Support Office (Room 158), which are directed to amend their records to reflect such change in the caption herein.

Dated: _____

                           ENTER:

                           _____
                           J.S.C.

Form 54. Summary Judgment Dismissing Complaint, Order Granting

At IAS Part ___ of the Supreme
Court of the State of New York, held
in and for the County of New York,
at the Courthouse thereof, 60 Centre
Street, New York, New York on the
___ of _____, 200___.

PRESENT: HON: _____
                     JUSTICE

_____

                    Plaintiff,   INDEX No. _____

        - against -

                                        ORDER

                    Defendant.

_____

A motion having been made by defendant and having duly come on to be heard on the ___ of _____, 200___, for an order granting summary judgment,

NOW, on reading and filing the following papers submitted to the Court, _____, and upon the Court's decision thereon dated _____, it is

ORDERED that defendant's motion for summary judgment is granted and the complaint is dismissed with costs and disbursements to defendant as taxed by the Clerk upon the submission of an appropriate bill of costs; and it is further

ORDERED that the Clerk is directed to enter judgment accordingly.

Dated: _____

                              ENTER:

                              _____
                              J.S.C.

Form 55. Summary Judgment in Lieu of Complaint, Order Denying

At IAS Part ___ of the Supreme
Court of the State of New York, held
in and for the County of New York,
at the Courthouse thereof, 60 Centre
Street, New York, New York on the
___ of _____, 200___.

PRESENT: HON: _____
JUSTICE

_____

Plaintiff,

- against -

Defendant.

INDEX No. _____

ORDER

A motion having been made by plaintiff and having duly come on to be heard on
the ___ of _____, 200___, for an order granting summary judgment,

NOW, on reading and filing the following papers submitted to the Court,
_____, and upon the Court's decision thereon dated _____, it is

ORDERED that the motion for summary judgment in lieu of complaint is denied;
and it is further

ORDERED that plaintiff shall serve a formal complaint upon defendant's attorney
within 20 days of service on plaintiff's counsel of a copy of this order with notice of
entry and defendant shall move against or serve an answer to the complaint within
20 days after service of the complaint.

Dated: _____

ENTER:

_____
J.S.C.

Form 56. Summary Judgment on the Complaint on Default, Order Granting

At IAS Part ___ of the Supreme Court of the State of New York, held in and for the County of New York, at the Courthouse thereof, 60 Centre Street, New York, New York on the ___ of _____, 200___.

PRESENT: HON: _____

                JUSTICE

_____

              Plaintiff,   INDEX No. _____

- against -

                                     ORDER

              Defendant.

_____

A motion having been made by plaintiff and having duly come on to be heard on the ___ of _____, 200___, for an order granting summary judgment,

NOW, on reading and filing the following papers submitted to the Court, _____, and upon the Court's decision thereon dated _____, it is

ORDERED that the plaintiff's motion for summary judgment is granted on default, and the Clerk is directed to enter judgment in favor of plaintiff and against defendant [defendants _____ and _____] in the sum of $ _____, with interest as prayed for allowable by law [at the rate of ___ % per annum from the date of _____,] until the date of entry of judgment, as calculated by the Clerk, and thereafter at the statutory rate, together with costs and disbursements as taxed by the Clerk [,upon submission by affirmation of counsel of proof of service on defendant of a copy of this order with notice of entry at least ___ days prior to the entry of said judgment].

Dated: _____

                      ENTER:

                      _____

                      J.S.C.

Form 57. Summary Judgment on the Complaint, Order Granting

At IAS Part ___ of the Supreme
Court of the State of New York, held
in and for the County of New York,
at the Courthouse thereof, 60 Centre
Street, New York, New York on the
___ of _____, 200___.

PRESENT: HON: _____
JUSTICE

_____

                    Plaintiff,   INDEX No. _____

          - against -

                                                  ORDER

                    Defendant.
_____

A motion having been made by plaintiff and having duly come on to be heard on the ___ of _____, 200___, for an order granting summary judgment,

NOW, on reading and filing the following papers submitted to the Court, _____, and upon the Court's decision thereon dated _____, it is

ORDERED that the motion is granted and the Clerk is directed to enter judgment in favor of plaintiff and against defendant [defendants _____ and _____] in the amount of $ _____, together with interest as prayed for allowable by law [at the rate of ___ % per annum from the date of _____], until the date of entry of judgment, as calculated by the Clerk, and thereafter at the statutory rate, together with costs and disbursements to be taxed by the Clerk upon submission of an appropriate bill of costs.

Dated: _____

                                        ENTER:

                                        _____
                                        J.S.C.

Form 58. Summary Judgment, Partial, Order Granting

At IAS Part ___ of the Supreme
Court of the State of New York, held
in and for the County of New York,
at the Courthouse thereof, 60 Centre
Street, New York, New York on the
___ of _____, 200___.

PRESENT: HON: _____
                    JUSTICE

_____

                    Plaintiff,   INDEX No. _____

    - against -

                                        ORDER

                    Defendant.

_____

A motion having been made by plaintiff and having duly come on to be heard on
the ___ of _____, 200___, for an order granting summary judgment,

NOW, on reading and filing the following papers submitted to the Court,
_____, and upon the Court's decision thereon dated _____, it is

ORDERED that the motion is granted to the extent of granting partial summary
judgment in favor of plaintiff and against defendant [defendants _____ and
_____] as follows:

1. Plaintiff is granted judgment on the first cause of action in the amount of
$ _____, together with interest as prayed for allowable by law [at the rate of
___ % from the date of _____,] until the entry of judgment, as calculated by the
Clerk, and thereafter at the statutory rate, together with costs and disbursements to
be taxed by the Clerk upon submission of an appropriate bill of costs, the first cause
of action is severed, and the Clerk is directed to enter judgment accordingly;

2. Defendant is [defendants _____ and _____ are] found liable to
plaintiff on the second cause of action and the issue of the amount of a judgment to
be entered thereon shall be determined at the trial herein; and

3. The action shall continue as to the second through fifth causes of action.

Dated: _____

                    ENTER:

                    _____
                    J.S.C.

Form 59.   Turn–Over Order and Judgment

At IAS Part ___ of the Supreme
Court of the State of New York, held
in and for the County of New York,
at the Courthouse thereof, 60 Centre
Street, New York, New York on the
___ of _____, 200___.

PRESENT: HON: _____
JUSTICE

_____

Petitioner,   INDEX No. _____

- against -

                                ORDER AND JUDGMENT

Respondent.

_____

    An application having been made by plaintiff and having duly come on to be heard on the ___ of _____, 200___, for a turn-over order,

    NOW, on reading and filing the following papers submitted to the Court, _____, and upon the Court's decision thereon dated _____, it is

    ORDERED that the application is granted, and it is further

    ORDERED and ADJUDGED that the _____ Bank is directed, upon receipt of a certified copy of this order and judgment, to turn over to the petitioner, _____, all funds in the account of _____, judgment debtor, to the maximum amount of $ _____, and it is further

    ADJUDGED that upon such turn-over of funds, the respondent _____ Bank shall be discharged of all liability on this account to the extent of payment made.

    Dated: _____

ENTER:

_____
J.S.C.

Form 60.   Venue, Change of: From New York County

At IAS Part ___ of the Supreme
Court of the State of New York,
held in and for the County of New
York, at the Courthouse thereof,
60 Centre Street, New York, New
York on the ___ of _____,
200___.

PRESENT: HON: _____
                          JUSTICE

_____

                Plaintiff,   INDEX No. _____

    - against -

                                    ORDER

                Defendant.

_____

A motion having been made by defendant and having duly come on to be heard on
the ___ of _____, 200___, for an order changing the venue of this matter,

NOW, on reading and filing the following papers submitted to the Court,
_____, and upon the Court's decision thereon dated _____, it is

ORDERED that the venue of this action is changed from this Court to the
Supreme Court, County of _____, and the Clerk of this Court is directed to
transfer the papers on file in this action to the Clerk of the Supreme Court, County
of _____ upon service of a copy of this order with notice of entry and payment
of appropriate fees, if any.

Dated: _____

                            ENTER:

                            _____

                            J.S.C.

Form 61.   Venue, Change of: To NY County

At IAS Part ___ of the Supreme Court of the State of New York, held in and for the County of New York, at the Courthouse thereof, 60 Centre Street, New York, New York on the ___ of _____, 200___.

PRESENT: HON: _____
                                    JUSTICE

_____

                    Plaintiff,   INDEX No. _____

        - against -

                                            ORDER

                    Defendant.

_____

A motion having been made by defendant and having duly come on to be heard on the ___ of _____, 200___, for an order changing the venue of this matter,

NOW, on reading and filing the following papers submitted to the Court, _____, and upon the Court's decision thereon dated _____, it is

ORDERED that the venue of this action is changed from the _____ Court, County of _____, to this Court and the Clerk of the _____ Court, County of _____, is directed to transfer the papers on file in this action (Index No. _____) to the Clerk of the Supreme Court, County of New York, upon service of a certified copy of this order and payment of the appropriate fee, if any, and it is further

ORDERED that the Clerk of the Supreme Court, New York County, upon receipt of a copy of this order with notice of entry, shall, without further fee, assign a New York County index number to the file(s) transferred pursuant to this order.

Dated: _____

                        ENTER:

                        _____
                        J.S.C.

Form 62.   Withdraw as Counsel, Order on Motion to

At IAS Part ___ of the Supreme Court
of the State of New York, held in and
for the County of New York, at the
Courthouse thereof, 60 Centre Street,
New York, New York on the ___ of
_____, 200___.

PRESENT: HON: _____
                                JUSTICE

_____

                    Plaintiff,   INDEX No. _____

        - against -

                                        ORDER

                    Defendant.

_____

A motion having been made by _____ and having duly come on to be heard
on the ___ of _____, 200___, for an order granting leave to withdraw,

NOW, on reading and filing the following papers submitted to the Court,
_____, and upon the Court's decision thereon dated _____, it is

ORDERED that the motion of _____, Esq. to be relieved as attorney for
_____ is granted upon the filing by movant of proof of compliance with the
following conditions; and it is further

ORDERED that said attorney serve a copy of this order with notice of entry upon
the former client at his [her/its] last known address by certified mail, return receipt
requested, and upon the attorneys for all other parties appearing herein by regular
mail; and it is further

ORDERED that together with the copy of the order with notice of entry served
upon the former client moving counsel shall forward a notice directing the former
client to appoint a substitute attorney within 30 days after service of the notice; and
it is further

ORDERED that no further proceedings may be taken against the former client
without leave of this court for a period of 30 days after service on the former client
of the aforesaid notice to appoint a substitute attorney.

Dated: _____

                            ENTER:

                            _____
                            J.S.C.

Form 63. Withdraw as Counsel, Order on Motion to, With Order of Reference re Retaining Lien

At IAS Part ___ of the Supreme Court of the State of New York, held in and for the County of New York, at the Courthouse thereof, 60 Centre Street, New York, New York on the ___ of _____, 200___.

PRESENT: HON: _____
                            JUSTICE

_____

                    Plaintiff,   INDEX No. _____

        - against -

                                              ORDER

                    Defendant.

_____

A motion having been made by _____ and having duly come on to be heard on the ___ of _____, 200___, for an order granting leave to withdraw,

NOW, on reading and filing the following papers submitted to the Court, _____, and upon the Court's decision thereon dated _____, it is

ORDERED that the motion of _____, Esq. to be relieved as attorney for _____ is granted without opposition upon filing of proof of compliance with the following conditions; and it is further

ORDERED that said attorney serve a copy of this order with notice of entry upon the former client at his [her/its] last known address by certified mail, return receipt requested, and upon the attorneys for all other parties appearing herein by regular mail; and it is further

ORDERED that together with the copy of the order with notice of entry served upon the former client moving counsel shall forward a notice directing the former client to appoint a substitute attorney within 30 days from the date of mailing the notice; and it is further

ORDERED that the issue of the reasonable value of legal services rendered and disbursements paid by counsel is severed and referred to the Judicial Support Office for assignment to a Special Referee to hear and report with recommendations (or if the parties shall so stipulate, to hear and determine). Pending receipt of the report and a motion pursuant to CPLR 4403, final determination of that branch of the motion is held in abeyance; and it is further

ORDERED that counsel shall turn over the file pertaining to this case upon the fixing of the value of his [her] services and the payment thereof (Yaron v. Yaron, 58 A.D. 2d 752) or the posting of a bond for the payment thereof.

A copy of this order with notice of entry shall be filed with the Judicial Support Office (Room 311) for the purpose of obtaining a calendar date.

Dated: _____

                                    ENTER:

                                    _____
                                    J.S.C.

SECOND JUDICIAL DISTRICT — KINGS COUNTY

Westlaw Electronic Research

These rules may be searched electronically on Westlaw® *in the NY–RULES database; updates to these rules may be found on* Westlaw *in NY–RULESUP-DATES. For search tips and a summary of database content, consult the* Westlaw *Scope Screens for each database.*

KINGS COUNTY
SUPREME COURT—CIVIL
UNIFORM CIVIL TERM RULES

The Judges of the Civil Term Supreme Court, in order to promote the efficient and impartial administration of justice, hereby adopt the following common and uniform rules:[1]

[Adopted effective January 2, 2010.]

[1] Rules pertaining to Matrimonial, Commercial and Foreclosure parts are incorporated herein. Where rules in such parts differ from general rules, specialized rules shall govern.

PART A

Papers

This rule applies to all Civil Term Parts of the Court.

Motions, orders and other filed papers shall be indexed with protruding tabs. Clerks are required to reject papers that do not have protruding exhibit tabs, except papers in matrimonial cases and papers filed by pro se litigants. Motion papers must be filed with the Motion Support Office, currently located in Room 227, or in the Ex Parte Office, currently located on the 10th floor North, or in the Foreclosure Part Office, Room 773, or in the Guardianship Office, Room 850, or in the Mental Hygiene Office, Room 479a,[1] at 360 Adams Street at least five (5) business days before the return date of the motion. Cross–motions must be filed at least two (2) days before the return date of the motion.[2]

[Adopted effective January 2, 2010.]

[1] These rules do not otherwise control the Mental Hygiene or Condemnation Parts.

[2] Room changes may be made upon appropriate notice.

PART B. PC (PRELIMINARY CONFERENCE) RULES

Rule 1

The filing/purchasing of an RJI will automatically prompt the scheduling of a preliminary conference, but the Court will accept a stipulation of adjournment if there is a dispositive motion pending.

[Adopted effective January 2, 2010.]

Rule 2

The attorneys shall, in the first instance, attempt to reach an agreement on all relevant discovery categories outlined in the consent order. Disputed matters will be adjudicated by the Court.

[Adopted effective January 2, 2010.]

Rule 3

The parties must be prepared with bills of particulars, medical reports and insurance coverage.

[Adopted January 2, 2010.]

Rule 4

Strict compliance with the PC order shall be enforced by the imposition of costs and sanctions when appropriate.

[Adopted January 2, 2010.]

Rule 5

Discovery in third party and joint actions will be expedited.

[Adopted January 2, 2010.]

Rule 6

Any motion seeking discovery related relief filed prior to the PC shall be scheduled concurrently with the PC in the Intake Part.

[Adopted January 2, 2010.]

PART C

Motions in IAS Parts

Rule 1

Motion papers, answering affidavits and reply affidavits must be served on adversaries in accordance with CPLR 2214.

[Adopted effective January 2, 2010.]

Rule 2

Irrespective of the return date indicated in the notice of motion, motions will be rescheduled by the Motion Support Office to a date designated by the assigned Judge.

[Adopted effective January 2, 2010.]

Rule 3

All motions require appearances and oral argument.

[Adopted effective January 2, 2010.]

Rule 4

Unless the Judge's Part Rules provide otherwise, motions may be adjourned twice, on consent, without appearance, for a period not to exceed sixty (60) days from the initial return date of the motion. Adjournment of motions without appearance may be done by usage of stipulation or affirmation submitted no later than the previous work day. Any subsequent adjournment shall be by personal application.

[Adopted effective January 2, 2010.]

Rule 5

No courtesy copies of motion papers are required by the Court, except as may be required for electronic filing or by the Judge's Part Rules. In tort cases against the City of New York, courtesy copies shall be supplied to the Corporation Counsel's office in Brooklyn.

[Adopted effective January 2, 2010.]

Rule 6

Post Note of Issue Summary Judgment Motion: In cases where the City of New York is a defendant and is represented by the Tort Division of the Corporation Counsel's office, summary judgment motions may be made no later than 120 days after the filing of a Note of Issue. In all other matters, including third party actions, motions for summary judgment may be made no later than 60 days after the filing of a Note of Issue. In both instances the above time limitation may only be extended by the Court upon good cause shown. See CPLR 3212(a).

[Adopted effective January 2, 2010.]

Motion Calendar Calls

Rule 7

There shall be two (2) calendar calls on motion days. The first calendar call shall be at 9:30 AM and the second calendar call shall be at 10:45 AM, unless the Judge's Part Rules provide otherwise. Defaults shall only be taken on second call. Attorneys with appear-ances elsewhere in the courthouse may advise the clerk of their whereabouts to avoid a default. Failure to so advise the clerk or appear at the default calendar call will result in a default order being entered or the motion being marked off the calendar.

[Adopted effective January 2, 2010.]

PART D. NOTE OF ISSUE

Rule 1

The filing requirement for Notes of Issue in Kings County is an original and two (2) copies.

[Adopted effective January 2, 2010.]

Rule 2

Any party objecting to the filing of a Note of Issue may move to vacate, pursuant to Uniform Rules for the NYS Trial Courts section 202.21(e).

[Adopted effective January 2, 2010.]

Rule 3

Any third party action commenced after the filing of a Note of Issue shall be subject to severance.

[Adopted effective January 2, 2010.]

Rule 4

A 90–day notice (CPLR 3216) shall permit a plaintiff to file a Note of Issue within such ninety (90) days without a Court order.

[Adopted effective January 2, 2010.]

PART E.   CENTRAL COMPLIANCE PART RULES

Compliance Conferences

Rule 1

The purpose of the compliance conference is to monitor the progress of discovery, set a deadline for filing a Note of Issue and resolve any outstanding discovery issues. Consequently, parties attending the compliance conference must be fully familiar with the case, the status of any disclosure proceedings, and any settlement negotiations. The parties attending the conference must also be prepared and authorized to enter into binding stipulations.

[Adopted effective January 2, 2010.]

Rule 2

Appearance at the compliance conference is not necessary if a Note of Issue has been served and filed with the Court prior to the compliance conference date. In such cases, a copy of the Note of Issue may be presented to the part clerk on the date of the conference or a party may notify the clerk prior thereto.

[Adopted effective January 2, 2010.]

Rule 3

There will be no adjournments of a scheduled compliance conference except in special circumstances. Special circumstances include pending dispositive motions and stays at the discretion of the presiding Judge.

[Adopted effective January 2, 2010.]

Conference Calendar Calls

Rule 4

Attorneys are required to check in with the clerk between 9:30 AM and 10 AM. Compliance conference forms are available in the courtroom and may be completed when all parties are present. Consent orders must be signed by all parties prior to review by a court attorney. When all parties are present and there is a disagreement on any issue, a court attorney will conference the case in the first instance. If the court attorney is unsuccessful in resolving the issue, the matter will be referred to the assigned Judge.

[Adopted effective January 2, 2010.]

Rule 5

There are two calendar calls: the first call is at 10:45 AM and a default call at 11:45 AM. Attorneys with appearances elsewhere in the courthouse should advise the clerk of their whereabouts to avoid a default. Failure to so advise the clerk or appear at the default calendar call will result in a default order being entered or dismissal of the action. Any order granted on default must be served on all defaulting parties within seven (7) days of the order.

[Adopted effective January 2, 2010.]

Rule 6

Cases dismissed for non-appearance may be restored by written stipulation signed by all parties or by motion.

[Adopted effective January 2, 2010.]

Motions

Rule 7

Motions which only seek discovery related relief are scheduled by the Motion Support Office in the Centralized Compliance Part on the notice date of the motion, regardless of judicial assignment. Motions are heard in the Centralized Compliance Part every day of the week. Attorneys are advised to consult the New York Law Journal or the Unified Court System's Future Court Appearance Website for the return dates and parts of motions that do not only seek discovery related relief.

[Adopted effective January 2, 2010.]

Orders

Rule 8

Any order granted on default must be served on all defaulting parties within seven (7) days of the order.

[Adopted effective January 2, 2010.]

Rule 9

If all parties who were served with the motion are present, they may enter into a consent order. The consent order must be signed by all parties. If a new Note of Issue date is required, the order should be filled out and signed by all parties leaving a space for the Note of Issue filing date to be entered by a court attorney. Consent orders are not effective until they have been reviewed by a court attorney and signed by the Judge.

[Adopted effective January 2, 2010.]

Rule 10

Motions or orders seeking transfer of lottery or structured settlement proceeds shall be placed on motion calendars.

[Adopted effective January 2, 2010.]

Adjournment of Motions

Rule 11

One adjournment, for a period not to exceed sixty (60) days from the initial return date of the motion, will be permitted on consent of all parties either by written stipulation or by appearance in Court. Any application for a further adjournment will be referred to the assigned IAS judge forthwith.

a. *Adjournment by stipulation:* Stipulations must be signed by all parties who were served with the motion.

b. *In Court Adjournment:* For the first adjournment, all parties who were served with the motion must be present and consent to the adjournment.

c. There shall be no extension of time for filing summary judgment motions after the Note of Issue except upon application to the Court.

[Adopted effective January 2, 2010.]

PART F.   GENERAL FORECLOSURE RULES

Rule 1

All foreclosure matters dealing with the same block and lot number shall be assigned to the same judge even where an earlier matter has been previously disposed.

[Adopted effective January 2, 2010.]

Rule 2

In all foreclosure proceedings, the following form orders, judgments and applications, available at the Clerk's office or online, must be utilized: the Order of Reference; the Judgement of Foreclosure and Sale; a Deficiency Judgment; the Order in a Surplus Money

Proceeding; and the Referee's Application for Additional Compensation.

[Adopted effective January 2, 2010.]

Rule 3

The Ex–Parte Clerk is authorized to reject:

• Motion papers that are not in compliance with the CPLR;

• Motion papers filed less than five (5) days before the return date of the motion;

• An application for an Order of Reference or Judgment that does not contain a statement pursuant to CPLR 3408, indicating eligibility/exemption from conference;

• A notice of sale that does not comply with Rule 12;

• An application for surplus money that does not contain a recognized title search or its equivalent as an exhibit;

[Adopted effective January 2, 2010.]

Rule 4

A proposed order must be attached to any motion submitted to the Motion Support Office. In the event that a proposed order is not submitted with the motion it must be submitted to the IAS Judge within sixty (60) days or the motion may be deemed abandoned.

[Adopted effective January 2, 2010.]

Rule 5

Each Order of Reference must have appended thereto, the history of the property by way of a chain of assignment, the date of the assignment, and a reference to the tab where that assignment is located.

[Adopted effective January 2, 2010.]

Rule 6

If opposed, motions will be adjourned by the clerk to the assigned judge's next available motion date for argument.

[Adopted effective January 2, 2010.]

Rule 7

Every affidavit for an exemption from a conference made pursuant to CPLR 3408 and RPAPL 1304 must specify the grounds for same and provide supporting documentation and affidavits from persons with direct knowledge. Where the claim is that the borrower is not living in the subject house, then an affidavit of investigation substantiating this allegation must be appended which states *inter alia* that the borrower is not living in the house and that no action by the

mortgagee or its agents procured same. This affidavit shall be included in the motion for a Judgment of Foreclosure and Sale.

[Adopted effective January 2, 2010.]

Rule 8

In addition to a conference mandated by statute, a conference will be ordered in every case when there is an appearance by the defendant owner of the equity of redemption.

[Adopted effective January 2, 2010.]

Rule 9

Within one year after the signing and entry of an Order of Reference, an application for a Judgment of Foreclosure and Sale must be made. Such period of time will be suspended by the filing a Forbearance or Settlement Agreement with the clerk of this court. Failure to comply will result in an automatic dismissal of the action.

[Adopted effective January 2, 2010.]

Rule 10

The court-appointed referee shall determine the date of the sale which is to be held at the time and place indicated in the Judgement of Foreclosure and Sale and shall notify plaintiff sufficiently in advance thereof to permit publication of the Notice of Sale in compliance with RPAPL § 231.

[Adopted effective January 2, 2010.]

Rule 11

It is the plaintiff's responsibility to arrange for publication. The costs of publication may be recouped from the proceeds of the sale.

[Adopted effective January 2, 2010.]

Rule 12

A Notice of Sale must be submitted to the Foreclosure Department at least ten (10) days prior to the date of the auction. A copy of the Notice of Sale must simultaneously be sent to the owner of the equity of redemption at both his/her last known address and the property address. An affidavit of service of such notice shall be presented to the clerk on or before the auction sale.

[Adopted effective January 2, 2010.]

Rule 13

Notices of Sale may be filed with the Clerk within one year of the entry of the Judgment of Foreclosure and Sale. Permission of the Court must be obtained for any filings made thereafter.

[Adopted effective January 2, 2010.]

Rule 14

It is the plaintiff's responsibility to notify the referee of any encumbrances in advance of the sale date.

[Adopted effective January 2, 2010.]

Rule 15

In the event plaintiff adjourns or cancels the sale, at least five (5) days notice, both written and telephonic must be given to the referee. If such notice is not timely given, plaintiff shall pay $250.00 to the referee in compensation.

[Adopted effective January 2, 2010.]

Rule 16

A legally competent representative of plaintiff authorized to act on plaintiff's behalf, must appear at the auction sale.

[Adopted effective January 2, 2010.]

Rule 17

The upset price may not be greater than the amount stated in the referee's report of sale together with CPLR judgment interest running from the filing of the Judgment of Foreclosure and Sale together with the amount represented by receipted bills for taxes. The referee appointed for the sale of the property may add judgment interest and taxes to the upset price at the time of the auction. Any additional maintenance charges or other expenses must be by separate order of the Court.

[Adopted effective January 2, 2010.]

Rule 18

All Forbearance Agreements must be filed with the Foreclosure Clerk of the Court within twenty (20) days of the execution thereof.

[Adopted effective January 2, 2010.]

PART G.   FORECLOSURE SETTLEMENT PART RULES

The purpose of this part is to preserve community housing, preserve banking funds, and to help a homeowner avoid the loss of his or her home.

Rule 1

A conference may be required by statute or mandated by appearance, reference or request.

[Adopted effective January 2, 2010.]

Rule 2

An appearing homeowner shall file a notice of appearance in the action indicating the homeowner's name, address, telephone number, cell phone number and e-mail address on a form provided by the Court, with the clerk of the Foreclosure Conference Part who shall then forward it for appropriate filing.

[Adopted effective January 2, 2010.]

Rule 3

Each appearing homeowner shall be provided with an information sheet that informs him/her of the foreclosure process.

[Adopted effective January 2, 2010.]

Rule 4

Plaintiffs' counsel must appear in the Foreclosure Conference Part with the work-out package describing potential loss mitigation options, reasonably current payoff and reinstatement figures, and with settlement authority and/ or a direct contact number where a

servicing agent with settlement authority can be reached and participate in settlement discussions before the Court.

[Adopted effective January 2, 2010.]

Rule 5

The homeowner or his/her agent shall provide to the conference part employment verification, tax, and other records as required.

[Adopted effective January 2, 2010.]

Rule 6

For cases involving servicing agents who have opted into the Home Affordable Modification Program (HAMP), counsel shall appear in the Foreclosure Conference Part with a status report regarding the outcome of the servicing agents' evaluation for HAMP modification, and specific written justification with supporting details if modification under HAMP was denied.

[Adopted effective January 2, 2010.]

Rule 7

All foreclosure cases in which the servicing agent as well as the homeowner has agreed to a trial modification, whether under HAMP or otherwise, shall be given a control date in the Foreclosure Conference Part coincident with the trial modification period.

[Adopted effective January 2, 2010.]

Rule 8

In cases where settlement cannot be reached, plaintiffs' counsel shall submit a letter to the Foreclosure Conference Part and to the IAS Part, indicating the appearance of the homeowner and the good faith basis for the termination of the settlement negotiations that may result in foreclosure which may lead to the defendant's losing his/her home, cf. CPLR 3408(a).

[Adopted effective January 2, 2010.]

Rule 9

Foreclosure cases will be marked off the Foreclosure Conference calendar if: (a) the defendant has failed to appear for two (2) scheduled settlement conferences; (b) the Court has determined that the parties would not benefit from further settlement discussions; or (c) a settlement has been reached and

the plaintiff has filed a Stipulation of Discontinuance or Forbearance Agreement with the Foreclosure Settlement Conference Part as well as the Court.

[Adopted effective January 2, 2010.]

Rule 10

Any agency or representative assisting the homeowner shall provide copies of all documents, including the completed work-out package, to the homeowner, who should bring them to the settlement conference.

[Adopted effective January 2, 2010.]

Rule 11

All parties must appear at the settlement conference until the action is settled by means of a modification or other agreement signed by all parties as well as the IAS judge or the matter is referred to the IAS part.

[Adopted effective January 2, 2010.]

PART H. AUCTION RULES

Rule 1

The Referee and all interested parties must be present at the place indicated in the Order of the Court on the published date promptly at 3:00 PM.

[Adopted effective January 2, 2010.]

Rule 2

The Terms of Sale, including any known encumbrances, must be posted outside of the courtroom no later than 2:15 PM of the day of sale.

[Adopted effective January 2, 2010.]

Rule 3

Referees shall announce any encumbrance on the property prior to bidding.

[Adopted effective January 2, 2010.]

Rule 4

Referees will accept either 1) cash; or 2) certified or bank check made payable to the Referee. No double-endorsed checks will be accepted.

[Adopted effective January 2, 2010.]

Rule 5

A successful bidder must have in his/her possession at the time of the bid the full 10% of the sum bid, in

cash or certified or bank check to be made payable to the Referee.

[Adopted effective January 2, 2010.]

Rule 6

All bidders must have proof of identification and will be required to stand and state their names and addresses on the record at the time the bid is made.

[Adopted effective January 2, 2010.]

Rule 7

No sale will be deemed final until the full 10% deposit has been paid to the Referee and a contract has been signed, which must be done in the courthouse immediately following the sale.

[Adopted effective January 2, 2010.]

Rule 8

If a successful bidder fails to immediately pay the deposit and sign the Terms of Sale, the property will be promptly returned to auction the same day.

[Adopted effective January 2, 2010.]

Rule 9

Bidders are cautioned that the failure to pay the full purchase price bid and appropriate closing costs at a closing to be scheduled within thirty (30) days following the auction may result in the forfeiture of the 10%

deposit. The consent of the Court will be required for adjournment of the closing beyond ninety (90) days.

[Adopted effective January 2, 2010.]

Rule 10

The amount of the successful bid, which will become the "purchase price," will be recorded by the court reporter.

[Adopted effective January 2, 2010.]

Rule 11

If the successful bidder defaults in concluding the transaction at the purchase price, he/she may be liable for the difference if the property is subsequently sold

at auction for a sum which is inadequate to cover all items allowed in the Final Order and Judgment.

[Adopted effective January 2, 2010.]

Rule 12

It is the responsibility of the bidder to acquaint him/herself with the property, any encumbrances thereon, and the Terms of Sale before placing a bid and to be certain that adequate funds are available to make good the bid. The failure of the successful bidder to complete the transaction under the terms bid will presumptively result in the bidder's preclusion from bidding at auction for a period of sixty (60) days.

[Adopted effective January 2, 2010.]

PART I. COMMERCIAL DIVISION RULES

General

Rule 1

The following rules are intended to supplement the Statewide Standards and Rules for the Commercial Division (Uniform Rule § 202.70), which are applicable in Kings County. Counsel are expected to comply with all Statewide Rules as well as those promulgated herein.

[Adopted effective January 2, 2010.]

Rule 2

The monetary threshold for cases in Kings County Commercial Division has been raised from $50,000.00 to $75,000.00.

[Adopted effective January 2, 2010.]

Rule 3

Any party requesting a preliminary conference must annex a copy of the pleadings to the RJI when the request is filed with the Court.

[Adopted effective January 2, 2010.]

Rule 4

Other than as expressly provided in the Rules of the Commercial Division or upon instruction of the Court, the Court will not accept or entertain letter applications for substantive relief. Unless directed by the Court, no communications are to be FAXED to Chambers other than Stipulations of Adjournment in compliance with these rules, PC Orders prepared in conformity with Rule 7, or disclosure-related communications pursuant to Rule 18.

[Adopted effective January 2, 2010.]

Rule 5

Courtesy copies should not be provided unless the Court so directs.

[Adopted effective January 2, 2010.]

Conferences

Rule 6

Preliminary Conferences. All preliminary and compliance conferences will be held on Wednesdays beginning at 9:45 AM unless otherwise directed by the Court. The conference calendar will be called after the first call of the motion calendar.

[Adopted effective January 2, 2010.]

Rule 7

Online Preliminary Conference Orders. Preliminary Conference Orders may be entered on consent of the Court and all parties by printing and filling out the Preliminary Conference Form posted on the

Kings County Commercial Division website. Following a conference call with the Court, the PC order, executed by all parties, must be faxed to Chambers two (2) business days prior to the date scheduled for the PC conference. Failure to timely comply with the procedural constraints herein will require an appearance on the scheduled date.

[Adopted effective January 2, 2010.]

Rule 8

Prior to appearing for a preliminary conference, counsel should confer with clients so that schedules can be set for discovery.

[Adopted effective January 2, 2010.]

Rule 9

Adjournment of Preliminary Conference. Adjournment of a preliminary conference may be requested by submission of a written stipulation at least two (2) business days prior to the scheduled date. Stipulations must be accompanied by a cover letter explaining the reason for the adjournment. The adjournment of a conference is at the discretion of the Court and may be permitted for good cause shown. No preliminary conference shall be adjourned more than once or for more than thirty (30) days. Fax numbers for all counsel must be provided in the cover letter or the stipulation. Any request for further adjournments will be entertained only under the most compelling circumstances and must be made via a telephone conference call with the Court in which all parties participate.

[Adopted effective January 2, 2010.]

Rule 10

Adjournments of any other conferences are permitted for good cause with the approval of the Court on written stipulation of all parties submitted at least two (2) business days prior to the scheduled date of the conference. Stipulations may be faxed to the Judge's Chambers. Fax numbers may be found on the Kings County Commercial Division website under the Judges' Part and Chambers Information.

[Adopted effective January 2, 2010.]

Motions

Rule 11

The Court will entertain motions, as scheduled in the New York Law Journal and on ECourts, on Wednesdays unless otherwise directed by the Court. Information on future court appearances is available on E–Courts (www.nycourts.gov/ecourts). All motions require appearances and oral argument. All responsive papers must be filed with the Motion Support Office or the Clerk of the Part at least two (2) business days before the scheduled date of the motion.

[Adopted effective January 2, 2010.]

Rule 12

The first call of the motion calendar will be at 9:45 AM. The second and final call will be held at 10:15 AM.

[Adopted effective January 2, 2010.]

Rule 13

An appearance by an attorney with knowledge of the case and authority to bind the party is required on all motions and conferences.

[Adopted effective January 2, 2010.]

Rule 14

Upon the argument of a dispositive motion the Court will determine whether discovery shall proceed pending decision. As a general rule, discovery is not stayed by the filing of a dispositive motion.

[Adopted effective January 2, 2010.]

Rule 15

Motions for Summary Judgement. All summary judgment motions shall be accompanied by a Statement of Material Facts as set forth in the Uniform Rules, § 202.70(g), Rule 19–a.

[Adopted effective January 2, 2010.]

Rule 16

Following argument and reservation of decision by the Court, no supplemental submissions will be accepted by letter or otherwise unless expressly authorized in advance. Uniform Rules, § 202.70(g), Rule 18.

[Adopted effective January 2, 2010.]

Rule 17

Adjournment of Motions. Dispositive motions (made pursuant to CPLR 3211, 3212 or 3213) may be adjourned only with the Court's consent. Non–dispositive motions may be adjourned by written stipulation no more than three times for a total of no more than sixty (60) days unless otherwise directed by the Court. Adjournments must be obtained at least two (2) business days in advance of the return date except in the case of an emergency. Stipulations must be accompanied by a cover letter explaining the reason for the adjournment. Fax numbers for all counsel must be provided in the cover letter or the stipulation.

[Adopted effective January 2, 2010.]

Rule 18

Disclosure Disputes. Parties must comply with the Uniform Rules, § 202.70(g), Rule 14, regarding consultation among counsel prior to contacting the Court. If counsel are unable to resolve a dispute, the party seeking Court intervention shall send a letter to the Court, of no more than two (2) pages, upon notice to all parties, describing the problem and the relief requested. Such letter may be answered within eight (8) days by letter of no more than two (2) pages, also on notice to all parties. The party requesting relief shall then contact Chambers to arrange a conference (preferably by telephone) to resolve such dispute. If no effort is made by counsel to schedule such conference, the Court will infer that the matter has been resolved and will take no action. The Court may order that a motion be made but no discovery motion will be entertained without prior compliance wit this rule.

[Adopted effective January 2, 2010.]

Rule 19

The Kings County Commercial Division will strictly enforce Uniform Rules, § 202.70(g), Rules 6 and 17 relating to the form and length of papers submitted to the Court. Unless the Court has authorized a longer brief in advance, counsel are advised that briefs and affidavits in excess of 25 and 15 pages as specified in the rules may be rejected.

[Adopted effective January 2, 2010.]

Orders to Show Cause/Temporary Restraining Orders

Rule 20

Orders to Show Cause are argued on the date indicated in the order unless otherwise adjourned with the consent of the court.

[Adopted effective January 2, 2010.]

Rule 21

Where no affidavit of prejudice has been provided pursuant to Uniform Rules, § 202.70(g)(3), Rule 20, notice of applications for Temporary Restraining Orders (TRO) contained in an Order to Show Cause must be given to opposing counsel, or parties if no attorney has previously appeared, at least six hours in advance of submission to the court and must contain a specific time and date of submission so as to afford an opportunity to appear. Proof of such notice (which may be by attorney's affirmation) must accompany the proposed Order.

[Adopted effective January 2, 2010.]

Rule 22

Contested applications for TROs will not be heard after 4:00 PM absent extraordinarily compelling circumstances. [See Uniform Rules, § 202.70(g), Rule 20. Temporary Restraining Orders]

[Adopted effective January 2, 2010.]

Trials

Rule 23

A firm trial date will be established at a final settlement conference to be held at the conclusion of discovery. The Court may direct the parties to appear at such conference.

[Adopted effective January 2, 2010.]

Rule 24

At the final settlement conference, a pre-trial conference will be scheduled in compliance with Uniform Rules, § 202.70(g), Rules 25 to 33, to be held following the filing of a Note of Issue and approximately ten (10) days in advance of the trial date. Trial counsel must appear. Pre–marked exhibits, pre-trial memoranda, requests to charge, witness lists, and in-limine applications, which are to be made by letter of no more than two (2) pages, duly served upon all parties and the Court at least eight (8) days in advance of the date of the pre-trial conference, shall be provided at the pre-trial conference as required pursuant to Uniform Rules, § 202.70(g), Rules 25 to 33. Responses to in limine applications, also in letter form of no more than two (2) pages, shall be served at least five (5) days prior to the pre-trial conference. Short and concise pre-trial memoranda are preferred, containing a statement of the facts and issues of the case and the relevant principles of law with citations to controlling authority. Counsel must confer prior to appearance at the pre-trial conference so that exhibits that are not disputed can be identified and stipulated into evidence. Failure to identify an exhibit on the pre-trial list of exhibits may result in preclusion of such exhibit at trial.

[Adopted effective January 2, 2010.]

Alternative Dispute Resolution

Rule 25

In the interest of expediting prompt resolution of disputes at a minimum expense to the litigants, a mediation program is available through the Kings County Commercial Division. Pursuant to Uniform Rules § 202.70(g) (3), the Court may direct counsel and the parties to participate in non- binding mediation. In Kings County, experienced former jurists, acting as JHOs, are available at no expense to the parties. Alternatively, Kings County has available a roster of trained practitioners willing to accept a referral from the Court for mediation, to whom litigants may be referred. Discovery continues pending mediation unless otherwise ordered by the Court. Counsel are referred to the Rules for Alternative Dispute Resolution for Kings County for more detailed information

[Adopted effective January 2, 2010.]

PART J.   UNIFORM MATRIMONIAL RULES

These rules apply to all matrimonial actions including those assigned to the Integrated Domestic Violence Parts.

ALL PAPERS IN MATRIMONIAL ACTIONS SHALL BE FILED IN THE MATRIMONIAL CLERKS OFFICE ON THE 10th FLOOR, AT 360 ADAMS STREET.

Appearances and Adjournments

Rule 1

All parties must be present at each appearance unless excused by the Court.

[Adopted effective January 2, 2010.]

Rule 2

A Notice of Appearance shall be filed in the Office of the County Clerk and the Matrimonial Office on the 10th Floor.

[Adopted effective January 2, 2010.]

Rule 3

Requests for adjournments should be made in advance by conference call to the court and include the attorney for the child. Counsel is then to prepare a stipulation including the caption and index number of the case, the appearance date, the adjourn date, and the reason for the adjournment. The stipulation shall be faxed to the chambers at least one (1) day prior to the scheduled appearance date. All adjournments are subject to final approval by the Judge.

[Adopted effective January 2, 2010.]

Rule 4

All adjournments on the grounds of engagement of counsel shall be granted only in accordance with Part 125 of the Rules of the Chief Administrator of the Courts. Affirmation must be faxed to the court at least one (1) day prior to the court appearance.

[Adopted effective January 2, 2010.]

Rule 5

Two business cards are to be submitted to the court at the first appearance.

[Adopted effective January 2, 2010.]

Rule 6

Litigants are to be advised by counsel that communication with chambers staff or the court is not permitted at any time when they are represented.

[Adopted effective January 2, 2010.]

Orders of Protection

Rule 7

Ex Parte Orders of Protection are heard the same day they are filed.

[Adopted effective January 2, 2010.]

Rule 8

Counsel are required to have their clients present, unless excused by the court.

[Adopted effective January 2, 2010.]

Automatic Order

Rule 9

Pursuant to Domestic Relations Law section 236 B (2), when serving a summons, a copy of the automatic order must also be served.

[Adopted effective January 2, 2010.]

Request for Judicial Intervention (RJI)

Rule 10

A request for a preliminary conference shall accompany the RJI and both are to be served on all parties.
[Adopted effective January 2, 2010.]

Rule 11

Both a copy of the RJI and the request for a preliminary conference shall be filed with the Kings County Clerk's office and a copy is to be brought to the Matrimonial Clerk's office.

[Adopted effective January 2, 2010.]

Ex Parte Applications

Rule 12

Any application for temporary injunctive relief shall contain an affirmation demonstrating there will be significant prejudice to the party seeking the restraining order by giving notice. In the absence of a showing of significant prejudice, an affirmation must demonstrate that a good faith effort has been made to notify the party against whom the restraining order is sought in accordance with 22 NYCRR 202.7. This rule does not apply to temporary orders of protection.
[Adopted effective January 2, 2010.]

Motions and Orders to Show Cause

Rule 13

Motions shall be made returnable only on the part's motion date(s), or they can be calendared to the part's next available motion date by the Matrimonial Clerk's Office. If the case already has a date scheduled in the future, the motion may be made returnable on that previously assigned date even if it is not a regularly scheduled motion date.

[Adopted effective January 2, 2010.]

Rule 14

Oral argument is required on all motions unless dispensed with by the Judge.

[Adopted effective January 2, 2010.]

Rule 15

All responsive papers, including cross-motions, shall be filed in the Matrimonial Clerk's Office at least two (2) days prior to the return date of the motion.

[Adopted effective January 2, 2010.]

Rule 16

All exhibits are to be tabbed.

[Adopted effective January 2, 2010.]

Rule 17

Any application related to child support shall include a child support standards act worksheet.

[Adopted effective January 2, 2010.]

Rule 18

Counsel and the parties are required to appear personally on all motions.

[Adopted effective January 2, 2010.]

Rule 19

The court does not accept courtesy copies of motion papers.

[Adopted effective January 2, 2010.]

Rule 20

Pursuant to the CPLR, after argument of an application, sur-replies, memorandum and letters addressed to the substance of the pending application will not be considered without prior permission of the court.

[Adopted effective January 2, 2010.]

Rule 21

Allegations of fact submitted to the court, including allegations contained in an affidavit or the complaint, must be certified by counsel in the form prescribed by the Chief Administrative Judge.

[Adopted effective January 2, 2010.]

Rule 22

Copies of the Family Court petition and any existing orders must be submitted with the applications to consolidate.

[Adopted effective January 2, 2010.]

Rule 23

Initial post-judgment applications shall be brought by Order to Show Cause. In the event that there is a post-judgment application pending, further applications may be made by Notice of Motion or Cross Motion.

[Adopted effective January 2, 2010.]

Rule 24

All motions for contempt must be made by Order to Show Cause in conformity with the Judiciary Law.

Preliminary Conference

Rule 25

Pursuant to 22 NYCRR. 202.16(d), an RJI shall be filed within forty-five (45) days of the date of service of the summons unless an affidavit of no necessity is filed, in which case, the RJI shall be filed within 120 days.

[Adopted effective January 2, 2010.]

Rule 26

Pursuant to 22 N.Y.C.R.R.202.16 (f) (1), net worth affidavits shall be filed with the court ten (10) days prior to the conference date, accompanied by the attorneys' retainer statements and the parties' recent pay stubs or W–2.

[Adopted effective January 2, 2010.]

Compliance Conference

Rule 27

Counsel are directed to bring to the court's attention, by way of motion or conference call, any failure to comply with discovery orders or court directions prior to the compliance conference date.

[Adopted effective January 2, 2010.]

Pre-trial Conferences

Rule 28

A Note of Issue shall be filed prior to the pre-trial conference, in accordance with the compliance conference order. A copy of the Note of Issue, showing the County Clerk's stamp, shall be filed with the Matrimonial Clerk's Office prior to the pre-trial conference.

[Adopted effective January 2, 2010.]

Rule 29

Counsel shall provide the court with statements of proposed disposition, updated net worth statements with the last three (3) years tax returns, and child support worksheets when applicable.

[Adopted effective January 2, 2010.]

Rule 30

All motions *in limine* shall be made by the time of the pre-trial conference.

[Adopted effective January 2, 2010.]

Trial

Rule 31

Chambers shall be notified by all sides immediately if the action is resolved prior to the scheduled trial date.

[Adopted effective January 2, 2010.]

Rule 32

The following, if applicable, shall be provided to the court at least one week prior to the date of trial if not previously provide at a pre-trial conference:

a. Marked pleadings;

b. Updated affidavits of net-worth, statement of proposed dispositions and child support worksheets;

c. A witness list and any pre-trial memorandum;

d. Expert reports which were served no later than thirty (30) days before trial;

e. A list of all proposed exhibits;

f. A list of documents, pre-marked by counsel, which counsel may stipulate into evidence;

g. A written copy of any issues or facts to which parties can stipulate before trial, to be read into the record at the commencement of trial.

[Adopted effective January 2, 2010.]

Rule 33

When presenting a witness with a document to be marked into evidence, a courtesy copy of that document must also be provided to the court.

[Adopted effective January 2, 2010.]

Rule 34

There will be no adjournments of the trial date without express court permission.

[Adopted effective January 2, 2010.]

Rule 35

Failure to proceed may result in a judgment of default or dismissal of the action.

[Adopted effective January 2, 2010.]

Rule 36

Copies of trial memorandum/decisions will be mailed or faxed to counsel and self-represented litigants.

[Adopted effective January 2, 2010.]

Judgments

Rule 37

All judgments shall include a completed copy of the Matrimonial Term Clerk Office's contested judgment checklist, indicating all necessary attachments.

[Adopted effective January 2, 2010.]

Rule 38

Pursuant to 22 NYCRR 202.48 proposed judgments with proof of service on all parties must be submitted for signature, unless otherwise directed by the court within sixty (60) days.

[Adopted effective January 2, 2010.]

Post Judgment Applications

Rule 39

If a contested judgment of divorce was signed within 18 months of an application to modify the issue of custody and/or visitation the application will be heard in the Supreme Court.

[Adopted effective January 2, 2010.]

JUDGES' RULES
JUSTICE RACHEL A. ADAMS

Part 5F.   Hon. Rachel A. Adams

Justice Rachel A. Adams — Part 5F

Court Attorney: Enid Langbert/Cara Ben

Courtroom: 365

Courtroom Phone: 347–296–1636

Chambers Room: 389

Chambers Phone: 347–401–9260

Chambers Fax: 212–401–9232

Motions — Tuesdays and Thursdays

Preliminary Conferences — Tuesdays and Thursdays

Compliance and Pre-trial Conferences — Tuesdays and Thursdays

Part 5F has adopted the Kings County Uniform Matrimonial Rules. All submitted motions shall be made returnable only for Tuesdays or Thursdays, unless otherwise directed by the Court.

Counsel are reminded to present two business cards when appearing before the Court.

JUSTICE JACK M. BATTAGLIA

Part 59.   Hon. Jack M. Battaglia

Calendars

Part 59 motions are heard on Fridays.

Hearings, arguments, and conferences on matters determined by the Court to require attention that cannot effectively be given on regular calendar days will be scheduled as convenient to the Court, counsel, and others affected. The Court invites counsel to contact chambers, preferably prior to the scheduled calendar date, to request a rescheduling for this purpose.

Calendar Calls

Motions

First call at 9:45 A.M.

Second call at 10:45 A.M.

Oral argument is required on all motions.

Conferences/Hearings

As scheduled

Defaults

Pursuant to Uniform Rule § 202.27, the Court has discretion in addressing a calendar default. When appropriate, among other possible sanctions, an action might be dismissed, or judgment entered, for the failure of a party to appear for a conference or hearing, or a motion denied upon the failure of a movant to appear on the return date. Vacatur of the Court's order would then require both a reasonable excuse for the nonappearance and a showing of merit. In the usual case, however, the first and only nonappearance of a movant will result in a "mark-off."

Adjournments

Motions

Disclosure-related motions will not be adjourned, unless there are extraordinary circumstances shown on application to the Court. The issues raised by the motion will be resolved by agreement or Court resolution on the return date.

Dispositive motions, including motions for dismissal or summary judgment, and other substantive motions may be adjourned once on consent of all parties, with a schedule for remaining briefing. Application for adjournment may be made before the return date by stipulation faxed to chambers, or on the calendar call on the return date.

Conferences/Hearings

Conferences and hearings will not be adjourned, except for good cause shown on application to the Court, and, unless there are extraordinary circumstances, may not be adjourned more than once. Even on adjournment, the parties will be expected to address as many open matters as possible. Application for an adjournment may be made before the scheduled conference or hearing date by fax to chambers, showing good cause or extraordinary circumstances, as the case may be, as well as issues resolved.

Note of Issue Date

A motion is generally required to extend the Note of Issue date (§ 202.21[d]), but the Court may "so order" a stipulation extending the note of issue upon application faxed to chambers, containing, at the least, the following information: the reason for the extension, which shall constitute good cause; the dates of the preliminary conference order and all compliance conference orders; a description of any disclosure that remains to be completed, and a date for completion of each item.

JUSTICE LAURA JACOBSON

Part 21. Hon. Laura Jacobson

Motions: Every other Tuesday

Appearances must be made by attorneys with knowledge of the case and the pending motions. The first call is at 9:45am and the 2nd call is at 10:30am. The judge hears applications as they are announced during the calendar call. After hearing the applications, the judge then hears all ready cases in the order in which they are marked ready. Motions can be adjourned by stipulation only on the first return date. Parties are encouraged to work out discovery motions in a short form order. All motions made pursuant to Insurance Law Section 5102 must be orally argued. Arguments on serious injury motions will be heard the following Tuesday after the motion has been fully submitted at 9:45 a.m. in Room 961.

On all other motions, all parties must be present and ready for argument. The motion will be marked off if the movant fails to appear. If any other party does not appear and an order is signed, the order must be served on non-moving parties and all parties are bound by the terms of the order. No applications will be granted over the telephone.

Trials: All parties must be present in court at 9:45am unless otherwise scheduled by the court. Prior to trial, counsel must submit to the court marked pleadings and the bill of particulars. In addition, counsel must also provide to the court copies of any deposition testimony that will be offered into evidence.

Infant Compromise hearings will be scheduled by the court. Any adjournments must be obtained through Chambers.

JUSTICE LAWRENCE KNIPEL

Part 57. Hon. Lawrence Knipel

Motions:

- First call - 9:30 a.m.

- Second call - 10:30 a.m.

- Judge is on bench for both calls.

- No check in.

- No submission. All motions require oral argument.

- Court will grant up to four adjournments on consent.

- Stipulation required for adjournments prior to calendar call. (Chambers FAX: 212/457–2666).

- Refer to wall calendar for appropriate dates.

- Proposed orders to be reviewed by part clerk prior to signature.

Trials:

- Plaintiff to provide a copy of marked pleadings prior to the start of trial.

- Exhibits and subpoenaed records are on table in front of Officers' desk.

- Judge does not require attorneys and litigants to stand during his entrance.

JUSTICE HERBERT KRAMER

Part 13. Hon. Herbert Kramer

PART 13 ADOPTS THE KINGS COUNTY UNIFORM CIVIL TERM RULES IN ALL RESPECTS EXCEPT THAT PART C SECTION 7 IS AMENDED AS FOLLOWS:

Motion Calendar Calls

7. There shall be two (2) calendar calls on motion days. The first calendar call shall be at 9:30 a.m. and the second calendar call shall be at *10:00 a.m.*

JUSTICE MARK I. PARTNOW

Part 43. Hon. Mark I. Partnow

Trials

1. The Court will conference every case when it is assigned for Trial.

2. At the initial conference, or soon thereafter, plaintiff must submit marked pleadings to the Law Secretary as well as any motions in limine.

3. Prior to the trial, each attorney shall inform the Court of any schedule conflicts and the need for an interpreter.

4. Requests to charge and proposed verdict sheets shall be made in writing and submitted to the Law Secretary.

Motions

Appearances must be made by attorneys with knowledge of the case and the pending motion. The first call is at 9:45 a.m. and the 2nd call is at 10:30 a.m. Ready cases are called in the order in which they are marked ready and oral argument is required on all ready cases. Motions can be adjourned by stipulation on the first return date. Parties are encouraged to work out discovery motions in a short form order. On all other motions, all parties must be present and ready for argument. The motion will be marked off if the movant fails to appear. If the non moving party does not appear, the motion will be granted on default, a copy of the signed short form order must be served on the non-moving parties by certified mail and all parties are bound by the terms of the order.

Inquests

1. At the time of the inquest Plaintiff shall provide the Court with a copy of Marked Pleadings and a copy of the Default Judgment.

2. Certified Medical Records or testimony of a physician is required to prove damages.

Infant Compromise

Dates for appearance shall be scheduled by Chambers.

Mental Hygiene Hearings

Hearings shall be scheduled.

JUSTICE ERIC I. PRUS

Part 5A. Hon. Eric I. Prus

Justice Eric I. Prus — Part 5A

Court Attorney: Marilyn Rothstein

Courtroom: 938

Courtroom Phone: 347–296–1646

Chambers Room: 379

Chambers Phone: 374–296–1486

Chambers Fax: 718–643–5916

Motions: Tuesdays and Wednesdays

Preliminary Conferences — Tuesdays and Wednesdays.

Compliance and Pre-trial Conferences — Thursdays.

Part 5A has adopted the Kings County Uniform Matrimonial Rules. Motion and Conference calendars will be called promptly at 9:30 AM. All submitted motions shall be made returnable only for Tuesdays or Wednesdays, unless otherwise directed by the court. All parties must be present for every appearance unless excused by the Court. Requests for adjournments must be made by conference call to the Clerk of the Part; if granted, stipulations consenting to the date agreed upon must be subsequently faxed to Chambers. Applications to consolidate existing Family Court matters must contain a copy of the Family Court petition and any existing orders.

JUSTICE FRANCOIS RIVERA

Part 52. Hon. Francois Rivera

Whenever an action involving an infant party appears in the Intake Part for a preliminary conference, the deposition of the infant may not be scheduled until this court has issued an order which finds that the infant is competent to give sworn testimony. Any party wishing to contest this procedure should set forth their position in a motion on notice to all parties who have appeared in the action. Motions are heard on Fridays. Any case previously scheduled for a Thursday will be heard on that Friday.

JUSTICE WAYNE P. SAITTA

Part 29. Hon. Wayne P. Saitta

General Motion Calendar:

• The general motions calendar is heard every Thursday.

• First call is at 9:30 a.m. Second call is at 10:45 a.m.

• Defaults may be entered on second call.

• If you must leave to another part, inform the court clerk of your whereabouts prior to leaving the courtroom.

• Exhibit tabs are required on all papers filed with the Court.

• Summary judgment motions must be made within sixty days (60) of the filing of the note of issue.

• Cross motions must be filed with Motion Support, courtesy copies filed with the court clerk, room 538, one week prior to the return date.

• Motions on the general motion calendar may be adjourned on consent of the parties (to any Part 29 motion date).

• Adjournments may be made by written stipulation prior to the motion date or at the general motion calendar call.

• Motions on the general motion calendar may be adjourned, settled or withdrawn.

• Motions on the general motion calendar may not be submitted.

• If one or more parties is ready to proceed on a motion on the general motion calendar, an application may be made to put it on the Oral Argument calendar on the next available date. No oral argument will be heard on the day of the application to place a motion on the oral argument calendar.

Oral Argument Calendar:

• The oral argument calendar is heard every Thursday.

• First call is at 10:00. Second call is at 10:45.

• Defaults may be entered on second call.

• Parties who have answered "ready" should remain in the courtroom. If you must leave to another part, inform the court clerk of your whereabouts prior to leaving the courtroom.

• Motions on the oral argument calendar are those motions which have been adjourned from the general motion calendar, Orders to Show Cause, and cross motions to motions that have been placed on the oral argument calendar.

• Cross motions must be filed with Motion Support, courtesy copies filed with the court clerk, room 538, one week prior to the return date.

• Courtesy copies of responsive papers, and of cross motions, must be filed with the court clerk, room 538, at least one week prior to the return date. Papers handed up on the date of the calendar call may not be considered.

• Adjournments for motions on the oral argument calendar are on application to the Court, even if the parties consent, and will only be granted for good cause shown.

Trials:

All parties must be present in court by 10:00 a.m. unless otherwise scheduled by the Court. Prior to trial, counsel must submit to the Court marked pleadings and the bill of particulars. In addition, counsel must provide to the Court copies of any deposition testimony that will be offered into evidence. All exhibits must be pre-marked by the clerk before trial begins.

Infant Compromise:

Hearings will be scheduled by the Court. Any adjournments must be obtained through chambers.

JUSTICE ARTHUR M. SCHACK

Part 27. Hon. Arthur M. Schack

Inquiries:

All inquiries as to case or calendar status should, in the first instance, be made to the Trial Support Office at (347) 296–1694. The only inquiries to be made directly to Chambers or the Part should be those involving the exercise of judicial discretion.

Motions:

1. All motions, including orders to show cause, are returnable every Friday at 9:45 a.m. All motions require appearances and oral argument.

2. There will be two (2) calendar calls on motion days. First call of the motion calendar will be at 9:45 a.m. Second call will be at 10:30 a.m.

3. Upon the first call of the motion calendar, any matter upon which the movant answers the call and the opposing party does not, and for which no written opposition has been submitted, will be marked second call.

4. Anyone failing to answer the second call of the calendar will have their motion marked off, if they are the movant, or the motion will be granted upon default as against the opposing party who fails to answer the calendar call.

5. In order to adjourn any matter on the motion calendar, the part requires: (1) a stipulation pre-approved as to adjourn date by the court, signed by all sides and marked final; or (2) an attorney must appear and make a formal application for an adjournment.

6. There will be no adjournments of motions which have appeared on the motion calendar two (2) previous times. If a stipulation is submitted for a matter that has already been adjourned twice, and the parties do not answer the call of the calendar, the matter will be marked off.

7. There will be no adjournments of motions related to discovery. If a stipulation is submitted for a motion related to discovery, and the parties do not answer the call of the calendar, the motion will be marked off.

8. Filing of motion and cross motions is governed by the Uniform Civil Term Rules. Pursuant to those rules, NO MOTIONS OR CROSS MOTIONS ARE TO BE SENT TO CHAMBERS NOR WILL MOTIONS OR CROSS MOTIONS BE ACCEPTED IN THE PART ON MOTION DAYS. NO COURTESY COPIES OF MOTIONS, CROSS MOTIONS OR MEMOS OF LAW ARE TO BE FILED WITH CHAMBERS.

9. No affirmations or affidavits in opposition can be served on the motion day. All parties must comply with CPLR Rule 2214 for service of motion papers.

Pre–Trial Conference:

At this conference counsel should be prepared:

a. To alert the Court as to all anticipated disputed issues of law and fact, and provide the Court with citations to all statutory and common law authority upon which counsel will rely.

b. To stipulate to undisputed facts and the admissibility of clearly admissible documents and records.

c. To alert the Court to any anticipated in limine motions or evidentiary objections which counsel believes will be made during the course of the trial.

d. To provide the Court with a copy of all prior decisions and orders which may be relevant to said in limine applications.

e. To discuss scheduling as well as the number of witnesses to be called at trial, and the estimated length of the trial.

f. To alert the Court as to any anticipated problems regarding the attendance at trial of parties, attorneys or essential witnesses, and any other practical problems which the Court should consider in scheduling.

g. To alert the Court to any anticipated requests for a jury instruction relating to missing witnesses and/or documents.

h. To alert the Court to any anticipated request for apportionment as to alleged culpable non-parties pursuant to CPLR Article 16.

Rules for Trial Counsel:

1. *Be Prepared*: Prior to jury selection, counsel is cautioned to ascertain the availability of all witnesses and subpoenaed documents. Plaintiff's counsel shall requisition the file to the Courtroom as soon as possible after assignment of the case to this part. If you have non-English speaking witnesses, or any other special needs, e.g., easels, blackboards, shadow boxes, television, subpoenaed material, etc., it is your responsibility to notify the Court Officer, in advance, so as not to delay the progress of the trial.

2. *Marked Pleadings Plus*: Plaintiff's counsel shall furnish the Court with copies of:

a. Marked pleadings as required by CPLR 4012;

b. A copy of any statutory provisions in effect at the time the cause of action arose upon which either the plaintiff or defendant relies;

c. The bill(s) of particulars;

d. All expert reports relevant to the issues;

e. If any part of a deposition is to be read into evidence (as distinguished from mere use on cross-examination) you must, well in advance, provide the Court and your adversary with the page and line number of all such testimony so that all objections can be addressed prior to use before the jury.

3. *Pre–Marked Exhibits*: All trial exhibits should be pre-marked for identification, and copies of a list of exhibits must be given to the Court before the trial actually begins. Failure to comply with this rule may result in sanctions, which may include an order precluding the offering of such exhibits at trial. See, Davis Eckert v State of New York, 70 NY2d 632 (1987).

4. *No Communication With Jurors*: In order to maintain the appearance of total impartiality, once the jury has been selected no one is to communicate in any form at any time with any juror. This includes both verbal and non-verbal communication, including, without limitation, nods, shrugs and shaking the head. Do not even say "hello" or "good morning".

5. *Check–In*: At the start of each day on trial, check in with the clerk of the Court and or the Court Officer so that (s)he will be aware of your presence.

6. *Trial Objections and Arguments*: If a lawyer wishes to make an objection, it can be accomplished by standing and saying the word, "objection", and by adding thereto up to three more words so as to state the generic grounds for the objection, such as "hearsay," "bolstering," "leading," or "asked and answered." If you believe further argument is required, ask permission to approach the bench. This request will almost always be granted. Keep in mind that you will always be given the opportunity to make a full record.

7. *Courtroom Comments and Demeanor*: All remarks should be directed to the Court. Comments should not be made to opposing counsel. Personal remarks, including name-calling and insults, to or about opposing counsel will not be tolerated. Remember do not try to "talk over" each other; only one person speaks at a time or the record of the proceeding will be incomprehensible. Simple requests (e.g., a request for a document or an exhibit), should be accomplished in a manner which does not disrupt the proceedings or your adversary. If you require a significant discussion with your adversary, such as a possible stipulation, ask for permission to approach the bench. I will grant that request, and you will have a chance to talk to each other outside the presence of the jury. In addition, no grandstanding in the presence of the jury, i.e., making demands, offers or statements that should properly be made outside the presence of the jury.

8. *Use of Proposed Exhibits*: Do not show anything, including an exhibit or proposed exhibit to a witness without first showing it to opposing counsel. If this procedure is claimed to compromise trial strategy, a pre offer ruling outside the presence of the jury should be first obtained.

9. *Examination of Witnesses*: Do not approach a witness without permission of the Court. Please allow the witness to complete his/her answer to your question before asking another question. Do not interrupt the witness in the middle of an answer, unless it's totally un-responsive in which event you should seek a ruling from the Court. Direct examination, cross, redirect and re-cross are permitted. However, the Court does not ordinarily permit re-redirect examination of a witness.

10. *Jury Charge & Verdict Sheet*: At the commencement of the trial all counsel shall submit suggested jury charges and a suggested verdict questionnaire. Amendments thereto shall be permitted at the final charging conference. If counsel relies on a Pattern Jury Instruction [PJI] without any change thereto, it should be referred to by PJI number and topic only. If any changes to the PJI are suggested, then the entire proposed charge should set forth and the changes should be highlighted or otherwise called to the Court's attention. Citations to appropriate statutory or common law authority shall be given in support of suggested non-PJI jury charges or suggested PJI modifications. In addition, unless a marshaling of the evidence is waived, Counsel should, at the final charging conference, provide the Court with the proposed facts which counsel believes should be marshaled by the Court; and the respective contentions of the parties.

JUSTICE KENNETH P. SHERMAN

Part 67. Hon. Kenneth P. Sherman
MOTIONS:

All motions for Part 67 shall be noticed and heard on Wednesday. Motions for JCP and CTRP shall follow the specific Part routine. Oral argument is required on all opposed motions. The first call on motions is at 10:00 a.m., and the second call is at 11:30 a.m. All papers must be filed in accordance with the CPLR. Answering papers shall be filed in the Motion Support office or with the Clerk of the Part.

ADJOURNMENTS & CORRESPONDENCE:

No unsolicited courtesy copies of papers shall be sent to chambers. No correspondence between attorneys shall be sent to chambers, other than stipulations signed by all parties. If the parties agree to a conference with the Court in lieu of/or to stave off further motion practice, the parties may contact chambers by conference call to schedule a meeting. No ex-parte communications will be entertained.

Motion adjournments conform to specific Part routine (JCP, CTRP).

CONFERENCES: Held according to specific Part routine or on consent of the parties in coordination with chambers staff.

INFANT COMPROMISE: Hearings will be scheduled by the Court. Any adjournments must be obtained through chambers.

JUSTICE DEBRA SILBER

Part 9. Hon. Debra Silber
Motion Calendar

Motions are heard on designated Thursdays. Oral argument is required on all motions except motions solely concerning the serious injury threshold in Insurance Law § 5102(d) may be submitted without oral argument if all parties consent to waive oral argument. Appearances must be made by attorneys with knowledge of the case and the motion to be argued.

First call is at 9:45 a.m. Second call is at 11:00 a.m.

Defaults may be entered on second call. Motions will be marked off calendar if the movant fails to appear at the second call.

Motions, other than motions concerning discovery referred from the Central Compliance Part (CCP), may be adjourned twice on consent pursuant to a stipulation of all parties. Stipulations must be signed by all parties, or their attorneys if represented, and delivered to chambers, either in person or by fax. After two adjournments, applications must be sought in person at the calendar call on the adjourned date of the motion.

Applications will be taken after the calendar call. Parties must be ready to proceed in the event the application is denied.

Discovery motions will not be adjourned except for good cause shown.

Parties are encouraged to resolve discovery motions and to present consent orders for signature listing the specific items outstanding and the dates for production.

All papers are to be filed in accordance with the CPLR.

Exhibit tabs are required on all papers filed with the Court. Affirmations, affidavits and legal memoranda must be double spaced.

Summary judgment motions must be made within sixty days (60) of the date of filing of the Note of Issue.

Cross motions must be filed with Motion Support, courtesy copies to the court clerk, room 359.

Courtesy copies of responsive papers, and of cross motions, must be filed with the court clerk in room 359 at least one week prior to the return date.

Parties who have answered ready should remain in the court room. If your case is called and you are not present, a default may be taken.

If you must leave to go to another part, inform the court clerk of your whereabouts prior to leaving the court room.

Orders to Show Cause

Proposed orders to show cause must be brought to the Ex Parte Motion Support Office for review prior to submission to the part. Required fees must be paid to the County Clerk prior to submission.

Trials

All parties must be present in court by 9:45 a.m. unless otherwise scheduled with the Court. Prior to trial, counsel must submit marked pleadings and the Bill of Particulars. In addition, counsel must also provide the Court with copies of any deposition testimony that is expected to be used during the trial. It is the responsibility of the attorneys to ensure that subpoenaed records have arrived in the Subpoenaed Record Room.

Infant Compromises

Hearings will initially be scheduled by the Court. Any adjournments must be obtained through Chambers.

Miscellaneous

The Kings County Supreme Court Uniform Civil Term Rules can be located at: http://www.nycourts.gov/courts/2jd/kings/Civil/KingsCivilSupremeRules.shtml

JUSTICE MARTIN M. SOLOMON

Part 38. Hon. Martin M. Solomon
Motions

(1) Motions shall be heard every Thursday in Room 424, in 360 Adams Street. The calendar call is at 9:45 A.M. promptly. The Second Call is at 10:45 A.M. promptly. Motions that have not been previously adjourned or appropriately answered on the call, may be marked off, or a default may be entered, as appropriate. Counsels are advised that if a motion has been marked ready on the second call and no one appears to argue the motion when it is called to be heard, default may be taken against the party that answered ready and then failed to appear.

(2) No courtesy copies of motion papers are to be filed with Chambers or the Courtroom.

(3) Motion papers, answering affidavits and reply affidavits must be served on adversaries as per CPLR 2214.

(4) All motions require appearances and oral arguments.

(5) Motions may be adjourned twice upon consent of the parties or upon application to the Court. A confirmation, in stipulation form, is to be faxed to Chambers at (718) 643–4861. Any further adjournments must be made upon application to the Court for good cause.

(6) Summary judgment motions must be made within sixty (60) days of the filing of the note of issue.

(7) Motions to either seek or enforce discovery may not be made without court approval.

(8) Proposed orders to show cause must be brought to the Ex Parte Motion Support Office for review prior to submission to the part. Fees as required by

law must be paid to the County Clerk prior to submission.

Trials

(1) *Marked Pleadings.* Prior to trial, counsel shall furnish to the Court marked pleadings pursuant to CPLR Section 4012.

(2) *Exhibits.* Counsel shall pre-mark all exhibits in the order which they intend to introduce them at trial. A list of the exhibits shall be provided to the Court prior to trial. Plaintiffs will number their exhibits and defendants will letter their exhibits. On the day of trial the exhibits and the list will be given to the Court reporter who will officially mark them before trial.

(3) *Witnesses.* Prior to trial, Counsel shall provide to the court a list of potential witnesses in order in which they intend to call them at trial, including expert witnesses, their expertise, and summary of expected trial testimony.

(4) *Motions in Limine.* Any potential evidentiary question or procedural or substantive law matter not previously adjudicated shall be brought to the Court's attention and addressed prior to trial by way of a written or oral motion *in limine*. A written memorandum of law with citations to the Official Reports is strongly encouraged; citations and copies of relevant court decisions and statutes should be furnished to the Court prior to commencement of plaintiff's case and when otherwise requested by the Court.

(5) *Depositions.* A copy of depositions intended to be used at trial should be furnished to the Court at the commencement of the trial.

(6) *Proposed Jury Charges and Verdict Sheets.* All proposed jury charges and proposed verdict sheets

shall be submitted to the Court in typed form no later than the close of plaintiff's case.

JUSTICE JEFFREY S. SUNSHINE

Part 5G.   Hon. Jeffrey S. Sunshine

Justice Jeffrey S. Sunshine—Part 5G

Court Attorney: Lara Genovesi

Courtroom: 941

Courtroom Telephone: 347–296–1654

Chambers: Room 1166

Chambers Telehone: 347–296–1527

Chambers Facsimile: 718–643–7655

Motions: Wednesday

Preliminary Conferences with an accompanying motion: Wednesday 9:30 a.m.–1:00 p.m.

Preliminary Conferences without motion, Compliance and Pre-trial Conferences: Monday 9:30 a.m.–1:00 p.m.

Part 5G has adopted the Uniform Matrimonial Rules, Supreme Court, Kings County. All submitted motions shall be made returnable only for Wednesdays, unless otherwise directed by the Court.

Applications to consolidate existing Family Court matters must contain a copy of the Family Court petition and any other orders.

Applications for adjournment must be made to Chambers via conference call with all attorneys on the line. Please have index number available. If an adjourn date is assigned, a faxed stipulation must be sent to Chambers the day prior to the scheduled appearance. All adjournments are subject to final approval by the Judge.

Counsel are reminded always to bring their clients to Court for appearances unless previously excused or unless an adjournment has been granted.

JUSTICE DELORES J. THOMAS

Part 5T.   Hon. Delores J. Thomas

Justice Delores J. Thomas — Part 5T

Court Attorneys: Susan Leibman/Jeffrey Chery

Courtroom: 924

Courtroom Telephone: 347–401–9211

Chambers: 451

Chambers Telehone: 347–296–1539

Chambers Fax: 718–643–3932

Motions: Thursday.

Preliminary Conferences with Accompanying Motion: Thursday.

Preliminary Conferences or Compliance Conference without Motion: Monday.

Part 5T has adopted the Uniform Matrimonial Rules, Supreme Court, Kings County.

Motion and Conference calendars will be called promptly at 9:30 a.m.

All parties must be present for every appearance unless excused by the Court.

Requests for adjournment must be made by conference call to Chambers with all attorneys on the line. If the request is granted, a stipulation must be faxed to Chambers at least one day prior to the scheduled appearance. All adjournments are subject to final approval by the Judge.

Applications to consolidate existing Family Court matters must contain a copy of the Family Court petition and all existing Orders.

(Revised 12/23/2010)

MATRIMONIAL FORMS
MOTION FILING GUIDELINES

Doc. 4. Motion Filing Guidelines

—— Paid R.J.I. form or previous assignment to a Matrimonial Judge.

—— Matrimonial Motions are returnable at:

Matrimonial Part 5 _____

    360 Adams St. (unless I.D.V. which is located @ 320 Jay St.)

    @ 9:30 a.m.—(unless otherwise directed)

—— Part 130 Certification.

—— Affirmations shall be signed.

—— Affidavits shall be signed and notarized.

—— Exhibits shall be tabbed.

—— Proper service pursuant to CPLR 2214 in the form of an affidavit, affirmation or admission of service.

—— Motions shall be submitted to the Matrimonial Department at least 5 days prior to return date and cross-motions should be submitted at least 2 business days before the return date for proper calendaring.

Each Matrimonial Part has a designated motion day; however the Court may direct a motion to be returnable on other than the normal part motion day to coincide with a conference or trial.

The designated motion days are as follows:

Hon. Eric I. Prus	Part 5A—Tuesday or Wednesday
Hon. Rachel A. Adams	Part 5F—Tuesday or Wednesday
Hon. Jeffrey S. Sunshine	Part 5G—Wednesday
Hon. Delores J. Thomas	Part 5T—Thursday

No courtesy copies of papers are to be filed with the courtroom or chambers. In order to insure that motions, cross-motions or opposition/reply papers are properly received and calendared, please file the above in a timely fashion.

PRELIMINARY CONFERENCE (PC) REQUEST CHECKLIST

Doc. 5. Preliminary Conference Request Requirements

PRELIMINARY CONFERENCE REQUEST REQUIREMENTS

** *Please note, paying requisite fee for RJI and filing RJI with the County Clerk's Office will not effectuate the scheduling of a Preliminary Conference in the Matrimonial Term. To effectuate the scheduling of a Preliminary Conference and subsequent notification as to PC date and Judge assigned please provide the following:*

Index # _____

Your Preliminary Conference has not been scheduled for the following reasons:

To file for a Preliminary Conference you must submit:

☐ Fully completed RJI
☐ Request for P.C. form (or *Blumberg* form T–305)

☐ RJI proof of payment
☐ Proof of Service of both Request for PC form & RJI

Resubmit all papers that were returned, in addition to the above to the 10th Floor Matrimonial Clerks Office 360 Adams St.

ORDER TO SHOW CAUSE CHECKLIST

Doc. 6. Order to Show Cause Checklist

Order to Show Cause Guideline Form

This form serves to alert you that your filing may not comport to statutes or rules and to afford you the opportunity to make corrections. It is an overview of requirements and does not cover every circumstance.

Title of Action _____ Index # _____

Please note the following:

Order to Show Cause

☐ All forms being submitted are fully completed with legible print using black ink

☐ Proper Heading (Jurat)   ☐ **Fax # on legal back**

☐ Proper "Show Cause" statement

☐ Affidavit in Support (signed - dated - notarized)

☐ Part 130 Certification

☐ Exhibit tabs on each supporting document identified and noted in the order to show cause

☐ CPLR 2217 prior or no prior application in this or any other court statement (affidavit or affirmation)

In addition

For New Actions

☐ Request for Judicial Intervention (RJI) with payment stamped by the County Clerk (RM. 189)

☐ Stamped Copy of the Summons with Notice or Summons and Complaint

☐ Simultaneous personal service of Summons clause within order to show cause when made by plaintiff, unless affidavits show previous service

For Money Requests - (Child Support, Maintenance)

☐ Net Worth Statement (signed - dated - notarized - **total net worth section completed)**

☐ Child Support Registry Form

For Counsel Fee Requests—attorney affirmation required

☐ Retainer Agreement (signed by attorney and client)

☐ Net worth Statement, if not filed previously

For Order of Protection Requests

☐ Family Offense Registry Form

☐ T.O.P. Form

For Contempt Applications

☐ Proper Warning and Notice pursuant to Judicial Law 756

☐ Copy of order or judgment that contempt application is based on and any transcript or signed agreements that would support your application

☐ Personal service on other party

For All Post–Judgment Applications (first time applications from uncontested actions require an RJI)

☐ Copy of signed Judgment

For Enforcement of Judgment and First Time Post Judgment Applications Made by Prevailing Side

☐ copy of signed Judgment with proof of service and notice of entry (prevailing party only) along with any signed agreements or transcript that would support your application

For Emergency Applications (*An attorney with knowledge of the action is required to appear*)

☐ separate Affidavit of emergency (nature of emergency explained - signed - dated - notarized)

For Modification of an existing child support order or child support arrears

☐ Updated Net Worth Statement (signed - dated - notarized)

For Up Front (ex-parte) Preliminary Injunctive Relief; Temporary Restraining Orders etc.

☐ Affirmation or affidavit includes information in compliance with UCR 202.7 (f) eff. (10/1/06)

ORDER TO SHOW CAUSE INSTRUCTIONS

Doc. 7.   Order to Show Cause Instructions

KINGS COUNTY SUPREME COURT
MATRIMONIAL TERM OFFICE—10TH FLOOR

ALL ORDERS TO SHOW CAUSE MUST INCLUDE THE FOLLOWING:

1. An **Order to Show Cause** form containing a proper heading (jurat) and some form of the following statement: "Let the plaintiff/defendant or his/her/their attorney show cause at IAS Part ___, Room ___, of this Court, to be held at the Courthouse, 360 Adams Street, Brooklyn, N.Y., on the ___ day of _____, 200___, at ___ o'clock in the ___ noon or as soon as counsel may be heard why an order should not be made . . . ."

2. A properly signed, dated and acknowledged **Affidavit in Support** containing a statement pursuant to CPLR 2217 as to whether any prior applications for the relief requested have been made. If so, describe the outcome of the prior application. If not, state that no prior applications have been made.

3. **Exhibit tabs** for each supporting paper attached to the application.

4. A **Part 130 certification.**

Additional requirements:

1. When an Order to Show Cause begins the action, you must submit a paid Request for Judicial Intervention and a copy of the Summons with Notice or Summons with Complaint. The service clause in the Order to Show Cause must also state that the Summons with Notice or Summons with Complaint will be served by personal delivery simultaneously with the Order to Show Cause.

2. When making a money request (i.e., maintenance, child support, etc.), you must provide a signed, notarized Net Worth Statement. **First time** applications for child support also require a Child Support Registry Form. When requesting the **modification of an existing child support order or child support arrears,** you must submit an updated Net Worth Statement.

3. For **counsel fee** requests, you must provide a signed retainer agreement and a net worth statement if one has not been recently filed.

4. If you are requesting an **Order of Protection**, you must submit a Family Offense Registry Form and a T.O.P. form.

5. Orders to Show Cause for **Contempt** must include a proper warning and notice pursuant to 756 of the Judiciary Law. Personal service is required on the person alleged to be in contempt. If the application is post-judgment, a copy of the judgment must be attached to the application.

6. When applying for **financial restraints on marital assets**, you must state that the restraint does not apply to daily living expenses or ordinary business expenses.

7. You must provide a copy of the judgment with any application for post-judgment relief. If you are trying to **enforce a judgment**, you must provide a copy of the judgment with proof of notice of entry and proof of service.

8. If you are bringing an **Emergency Order to Show Cause**, you must submit an Emergency Affidavit explaining the nature of the emergency.

SUBMIT YOUR COMPLETED FORMS TO THE
MATRIMONIAL TERM OFFICE—10TH FL.

OFFICE OF THE SELF–REPRESENTED

FORMS

Form 1.   Order to Show Cause (Instructions)

1.   Prepare the Order to Show Cause and Affidavit in Support. Have the Affidavit in Support notarized. Label and attach all relevant exhibits.

2.   Obtain an RJI request form from the County Clerk (RM 189), complete both sides of the forms and submit to the County Clerk with the fee ($95). If an RJI has previously been filed by either side, you do not have to purchase an RJI and you may proceed to Step 3.

3.   Bring your papers to the Ex Parte Office (RM 267). Once your papers are approved, you must return to the County Clerk and pay the filing fee ($45).*

4.   The County Clerk will stamp your papers PAID and you can then submit them in the Ex Parte Office where they will be filed and forwarded to a judge for signature.

5.   Once your papers are signed by the judge, you must make copies of them and have them served on all parties in the manner directed by the court. Be sure to come to court on the return date selected by the judge promptly at 9:00 with your affidavit of service.

* If you are filing as a poor person, you must complete the poor person request forms, available at this office and submit them with your initial papers in the Ex Parte Office.

Form 2.   Order to Show Cause

Instructions: Fill in the names of the parties and the Index Number. Complete the blank spaces next to the instructions in bold type. PRINT AND USE BLACK INK ONLY. [Other blank spaces are for Court use.]

At IAS Part ____ of the Supreme Court of the State of New York, held in and for the County of Kings at the Courthouse thereof, 360 Adams Street, Brooklyn, New York, on the ____ day of _____, 200 ____.

PRESENT: HON. _____
                         Justice of the Supreme Court

---X

_____,

[FILL IN NAME(S)]   Plaintiff(s)

                    -against-

Index No.

_____/ ____

_____,

[FILL IN NAME(S)]   Defendants(s)

---X

ORDER TO SHOW CAUSE

IN CIVIL ACTION

Upon reading and filing the affidavit of _____ **[YOUR NAME]**, sworn to on the ____ day of _____, 200____ **[DATE THE AFFIDAVIT WAS SWORN TO BEFORE A NOTARY PUBLIC]**, and upon the exhibits attached to the affidavit, and **[LIST OTHER SUPPORTING PAPERS, E.G., ADDITIONAL AFFIDAVITS, EXHIBITS]** _____.

Let the plaintiff(s)/defendant(s) **[CIRCLE ONE]** or his/her/their attorney show cause at IAS PART ____, Room ____, of this Court, to be held at the Courthouse, 360 Adams Street, Brooklyn N.Y., on the ____ day of _____, 200____, at ____ o'clock in the ____ noon or as soon as counsel may be heard why an order should not be made **[DESCRIBE THE RELIEF BEING SOUGHT]** _____
_____
_____
_____

for the reasons that **[BRIEFLY DESCRIBE THE REASONS FOR THE RELIEF YOU ARE REQUESTING]** _____
_____
_____
_____.

Sufficient cause appearing therefor, let personal service of a copy of this order, and the papers upon which this order is granted, upon the plaintiff(s)/defendant(s) on or before the ____ day of _____, 200____ be deemed good and sufficient. An affidavit or other proof of service shall be presented to this Court on the return date directed in the second paragraph of this order.

ENTER

_____
                    J.S.C.

OSC–Act–6/01

257

Form 3. Order to Show Cause TRO

Instructions: Fill in the names of the parties and the Index Number. Complete the
blank spaces next to the instructions printed in bold type. PRINT AND USE
BLACK INK ONLY. [Other blank spaces are for Court use.]

At IAS Part ____ of the Supreme Court of the
State of New York held in and for the County
of Kings at the Courthouse, thereof, 360
Adams Street, Brooklyn, N.Y., on the ____ day
of _____, 200 ___.

PRESENT: HON. _____
                                    Justice of the Supreme Court

--X

_____,
[FILL IN NAME(S)]   Plaintiff(s)

                          -against-

Index No.

_____/ _____

ORDER TO SHOW CAUSE
WITH T.R.O.
IN CIVIL ACTION

_____,
[FILL IN NAME(S)]   Defendant(s)
--X

   Upon reading and filing the affidavit of _____ [YOUR NAME]
sworn to on the ____ day of _____, 200___, [DATE THE AFFIDAVIT WAS
SWORN TO BEFORE A NOTARY PUBLIC] and upon the exhibits attached to
the affidavit, and [LIST OTHER SUPPORTING PAPERS, E.G. ADDITIONAL
AFFIDAVITS, EXHIBITS] _____
_____.

   Let the plaintiff(s)/defendant(s) [CIRCLE ONE] or his/her/their attorney show
cause at IAS Part ____, Room ____, of this Court, to be held at the Courthouse, 360
Adams Street, Brooklyn, N.Y., on the ____ day of _____, 200___, at ____ o'clock
in the ____ noon or as soon as counsel may be heard why an order should not be
made [DESCRIBE THE RELIEF BEING SOUGHT] _____
_____.

for the reasons that [BRIEFLY DESCRIBE THE REASONS FOR THE RE-
LIEF YOU ARE REQUESTING] _____
_____
_____.

   Pending the hearing of this motion it is ORDERED that _____
_____
_____
_____.

   Sufficient cause appearing therefor, let personal service of a copy of this order,
and the papers upon which this order is granted, upon the plaintiff(s) /defendant(s)
on or before the ____ day of _____, 200___ be deemed good and sufficient. An
affidavit or other proof of service shall be presented to this Court on the return date
directed in the second paragraph of this order.

ENTER

_____
                                                      J.S.C.

OSC/TRO–ACT–6/01

Form 4.   Affidavit in Opposition (Instructions)

1. Prepare the Affidavit in Opposition and have it notarized, attaching any exhibits you may want to submit, with exhibit tabs.

2. Make copies of the completed opposition papers and exhibits. Be certain to keep the original copies of your legal papers, as they will be submitted to the Court once copies have been served. **THE COURT ONLY ACCEPTS THE ORIGINAL COPIES.**

3. Have someone other than you serve the opposition papers on all parties. This must be a New York State Resident over 18 years old who is not a party to the action. The papers may be served by mail, if statutory time allows.

4. The person serving your papers must complete and notarize the affidavit of service and return it to you.

5. Bring your original copies of the opposition papers with the completed affidavit of service to the **Motion Support Office in Room 227.**

6. You must appear in court at **9:30** on the date stated in the notice of motion. You can check in the motion support office to find out in which courtroom your case will be heard on that date.

YOU MAY CHECK TO VERIFY YOUR CASE HAS NOT BEEN ADJOURNED TO A FUTURE DATE BEFORE YOU COME TO COURT. GO TO THE COURT WEBSITE AT www.nycourts.gov and go to FCAS (Future Court Appearance Site) OR CHECK IN THE MOTION SUPPORT OFFICE.

Form 5.   Affidavit in Opposition

Instructions: Fill in the names of the parties and the Index Number. Complete the blank spaces next to the instructions printed in bold type. PRINT AND USE BLACK INK ONLY. SIGN YOUR NAME BEFORE A NOTARY PUBLIC.

SUPREME COURT OF THE STATE OF NEW YORK
COUNTY OF KINGS

---X

_____,

[FILL IN NAME(S)] Plaintiff(s) /Petitioner(s)

         -against-

Index No.

_____/ ____

AFFIDAVIT

IN OPPOSITION

_____,

[FILL IN NAMES(S)] Defendant(s) /Respondent(s)

---X

STATE OF NEW YORK
COUNTY OF _____ **[COUNTY WHERE NOTARIZED]**   ss:

_____ **[YOUR NAME]**,
being duly sworn, deposes and says:

     1. I am the plaintiff/petitioner/defendant/respondent **[CIRCLE ONE]** in this action/proceeding. I make this affidavit in opposition to the motion by _____ **[NAME OF PARTY]** for an order **[STATE WHAT RE-LIEF THE OTHER SIDE ASKS FOR]** _____

_____

_____.

     2. I believe the Court should deny the motion because **[EXPLAIN YOUR REASONS. USE ADDITIONAL PAPER IF NECESSARY]** _____

_____

_____

_____.

     WHEREFORE, I respectfully request that this motion be denied.

Sworn to before me on

_____ day of _____, 200 ___

_____
        Notary Public

[SIGN YOUR NAME BEFORE A NOTARY PUBLIC]

_____
[PRINT YOUR NAME]

Aff–Opp–6/01

Form 6.   Affidavit in Support

Instructions: Fill in the names of the parties and the Ind. Number. Complete the blank spaces next to the instructions printed in bold type. PRINT AND USE BLACK INK ONLY. SIGN YOUR NAME BEFORE A NOTARY PUBLIC.

SUPREME COURT OF THE STATE OF NEW YORK
COUNTY OF KINGS
---X

_____,   Index No.

                                                          _____/ _____

                    -against-

                                                          AFFIDAVIT

_____,   **IN SUPPORT**
   [FILL IN NAME(S)]
---X

STATE OF NEW YORK
COUNTY OF _____ [COUNTY WHERE NOTARIZED]   ss:

_____ [YOUR NAME],

being duly sworn, deposes and says:

1. I am the plaintiff/defendant in this action/proceeding. I make this affidavit in support of my motion for an order [**STATE WHAT YOU WANT THE COURT'S ORDER TO PROVIDE OR GRANT YOU. THIS STATEMENT MUST ALSO BE INCLUDED IN THE NOTICE OF MOTION OR ORDER TO SHOW CAUSE.** _____

_____

_____.

2. I believe the Court should grant my motion because [**EXPLAIN YOUR REASONS. USE ADDITIONAL PAPER IF NECESSARY.**] _____

_____

_____.

3. [**IF YOU ARE MOVING BY ORDER TO SHOW CAUSE YOU MUST FILL IN THIS PARAGRAPH.**] No prior application has been made for the relief sought herein except [**LIST ALL PRIOR REQUESTS FOR THE SAME RELIEF MADE IN THIS OR ANY OTHER COURT AND THE RESULTS OF THOSE APPLICATIONS. USE ADDITIONAL PAPER IF NECESSARY. IF NO PRIOR REQUESTS HAVE BEEN MADE, STATE "None"**] _____

_____.

   WHEREFORE, I respectfully request that this motion be granted, and that I have such other and further relief as may be just and proper.

Sworn to before me on the   _____
                                             [SIGN YOUR NAME BEFORE A
_____ day of _____, 200 ___   NOTARY PUBLIC]

_____   _____
            Notary Public   [PRINT YOUR NAME]

                                                      Aff–Supp–6/01

SUMMARY JURY TRIAL PROGRAM

Preamble.   Information Sheet

Essential Features:

- A SJT is a binding one day jury trial with relaxed rules of evidence

- Medical evidence can be submitted without live medical testimony

- Hi–Low parameters can be stipulated to, ie. $0/ $25k/$50k/$250k

- No appeal

- No directed verdict

- No motion to set aside the verdict

- A date certain for trial

- Innovative method of case presentation to the jury, including direct submission to jury of medical records, reports, power point presentations, etc.

- Supreme Court Judge presides at trial

- Verdict limited to amount of insurance policy

General Rules:

- Written stipulation by attorneys required to participate

- Signed waiver of right to appeal and waiver of post trial motions

- No Findings of Fact/Conclusions of Law required

- No Judgment entered. Rather, releases and stipulations are exchanged

- Pre-marked exhibits, medical records, reports, photos, diagrams, and other physical evidence presented directly to jury

- All evidence, trial notebook and exhibits must be exchanged in advance of trial or be excluded

- Evidentiary hearing held before trial to resolve objections, redactions and other pre-trial issues, including objections to proposed exhibits

- Medical records which are not certified or affirmed are admissible on consent or by court order

- Video live/pre-recorded testimony permitted

General Procedures:

- Abbreviated jury selection

- 10 minute opening and 10 minute closing for each side

- One hour for case presentation and cross examination by each side

- Modified jury charges

- Record waived if all sides agree

Full set of rules available at The Brooklyn Bar Association, www.brooklynbar.org, at the Motion Support Office and the 11th floor Desk Officer

Rule 1.   Consent of Parties

Attorneys for all parties must sign a Stipulation, (hereinafter referred to as "Transfer Agreement") that they have the authority of their respective clients and/or insurance carriers to enter into the agreement, that the agreement is irrevocably binding upon their respective principals, and that these summary jury trial rules and procedures will be applied.

Rule 2.   Stipulation

In addition to the above, the Transfer Agreement shall contain provisions relating to the establishment, if agreed upon, of high/low damages parameters; agreement waiving any rights to appeal and such other terms as may be required by the court from time to time. The high and low parameters, if any, shall not be disclosed to the jury in a summary jury trial.

Rule 3.   No Right to Appeal

The parties shall agree to waive costs and disbursements and to waive the right to appeal from the determination of this matter. Written findings of fact and conclusions of law shall not be required. Following a jury determination, the parties shall not enter judgment but, instead, will exchange general releases and stipulations of discontinuance. Payment of any funds due shall be made in accordance with the relevant provisions of the Civil Practice Laws and Rules and applicable law.

Rule 4.   Scheduling

The Administrative Judge will establish procedures for the selection of cases for summary jury trials with the understanding that the parties must voluntarily agree to participate. The Administrative Judge will [a] advise the Jury Coordinating Part [J.C.P.] to select cases for summary jury trials from those that are marked to be sent to Civil Court pursuant to CPLR § 325(d), [b] set up a mechanism for attorneys to communicate to the court administration that they desire to explore the possibility of having a particular case resolved by the summary jury trial (hereinafter "SJT") process, and [c] create such other administrative rules relating to the selection and assignment of cases to the SJT process as are necessary. The Administrative Judge will assign, on a rotating basis, an appropriate number of judges to the pretrial conferencing and trial of SJT matters.

Summary jury trials will be placed on the calendar for trial at the earliest possible date available in the SJT part. At the first conference date the parties shall discuss settlement and if there is no settlement, discuss evidentiary matters and such other issues as the SJT judge directs. The SJT judge will then direct the parties to appear at a second conference [hereinafter second conference"] at which each party shall supply to the court and exchange with opposing counsel proposed evidentiary offerings.

The proposed evidentiary offering should preferably be presented in the form of a trial notebook with a table of contents. The court will rule on the admissibility and redaction of each of the items submitted by the parties. Only items approved and so marked by the court will be admissible upon the trial of the matter. At the second conference, the court shall set down a firm and final date for trial. This date may be adjourned for good cause shown. At any time between the second conference and the scheduled trial date, if any party desires to add evidence to the trial notebook or otherwise proposes new evidence for the trial, the parties may so stipulate and provide a copy of the exhibit and stipulation to the court. If the parties can not agree they may request a third conference prior to the trial date limited to the narrow issues concerned. The part clerk will pre-mark each exhibit. The time between the first and second conference should be two to three weeks. The time between the second conference and the trial also should be two to three weeks.

Upon determination of the evidentiary issues at the second conference the transfer agreement will be signed, irrevocably setting the case down for summary jury trial.

Rule 5. Pre-trial and Trial Submissions

a) Any party intending to offer documentary evidence at trial, including but not limited to accident reports, medical records, lost income records and portions of examinations before trial that a party intends to read to the jury as part of its direct case, shall serve copies of such documentary evidence upon all parties not less than five (5) days before the second conference. Lists of proposed trial witnesses shall be similarly served.

b) At this second conference, the SJT judge assigned to the case shall conduct a conference in the nature of an evidentiary hearing at which time objections to such documentary evidence shall be determined and witness lists finalized. Upon the completion of the judge's rulings the parties shall stipulate in writing as to the final exhibits and witness lists. Only evidence so identified and marked at the second conference shall be allowed to be exhibited or mentioned at trial.

c) The requests to charge shall list PJI section numbers. Any request to charge that deviates from the standard Pattern Jury Instructions shall be submitted to the Judge and to all adversaries at least two (2) days prior to trial.

Rule 6. Record

A summary jury trial will not be recorded by a court reporter unless requested by all parties. In the latter event, the court reporter will only record testimony.

Rule 7. Existing Offer and Demand

The parties may stipulate in the Transfer Agreement that the pre-trial offer and demand remain unaltered throughout the binding summary jury trial. Either party may elect to accept the last settlement proposal of the opponent at any time before the verdict is announced by the jury.

Rule 8. Jury Selection

Jury selection shall be conducted by counsel within the time limits agreed to and/or mandated by the judge. If the court conducts the voir dire, each side shall have ten minutes to also question potential jurors. Summary juries shall consist of no less than six jurors and one alternate unless the parties stipulate to fewer jurors. The court shall allow each side two peremptory challenges. It is anticipated that jury selection and trial will be concluded in one day. The parties may agree, or by order be directed to meet on a date certain before the trial date to select a jury in which case jury selection shall be completed on that day.

Rule 9. Time Limits

Each side shall be entitled to a ten minute opening and ten minute closing, and to one hour for presentation of its case. The court may allot more time to a party to insure full exploration of the issues, provided that a compelling reason supports the request for additional time. Unless the judge directs otherwise, the court clerk will advise counsel of the amount of time available at appropriate intervals. Unless the jury has been already selected, the trial shall begin with jury selection as early in the morning as is possible and shall continue without interruption.

Rule 10. Case Presentation upon Trial

a. Counsel may summarize the evidence, factual allegations, and reasonable inferences for the jury.

b. All materials to be submitted to the jury as part of the presentation of the case must be exchanged with opposing counsel and provided to the court and marked in accordance with these rules.

c. No more than two (2) witnesses for each side may be called upon direct and upon cross- examination. On application of a party and good cause shown at the second conference, the court may allow an increase in the number of witnesses. Plaintiff proceeds first. Plaintiff may be granted a ten (10) minute rebuttal following defendant's presentation. Time spent by counsel on direct and cross examinations counts against the party's allotted time unless the court directs otherwise.

d. In the event that other documentation or witnesses come to light after the second conference but before Jury Selection, counsel may stipulate as to the evidence to be submitted or seek permission from the court as previously indicated.

e. Jurors shall be allowed to take notes only upon consent of all parties.

Rule 11. Rules of Evidence upon Trial

a. The parties may offer such evidence as is relevant and material to the dispute, in accordance with these rules, compliance with the rules of evidence with respect to the introduction of exhibits previously marked and redacted shall not be necessary, subject to the provisions relating to documentary evidence set forth below.

b. The deposition or prior testimony of a party may be offered by any opposing party, however, a party shall not be permitted to offer his/her own deposition or prior testimony except as provided by the CPLR. This section shall apply to video depositions as well.

c. Past and future lost income may be proven by the submission of documentary evidence from the plaintiffs' employer, including but not limited to pay stubs, tax returns, W-2 and/or 1099 forms, provided that such amounts may be calculated with a reasonable degree of mathematical certainty based solely upon present income and life expectancy.

d. Non-party eyewitness testimony can only be offered by means of the deposition testimony of the non-party witness taken pursuant to the notice requirements of the CPLR or by producing that witness at trial. Affidavits are not admissible.

e. The following shall also be admissible and subject to redaction: police reports, the MV104 accident report of any party; medical records including but not limited to hospital records, ambulance records; medical records and/or reports from plaintiff's medical providers, defendant doctor's reports inclusive of no fault insurance medical exam reports; diagnostic test results including but not limited to X-rays, MRI, CT scan and EMG reports; or any other graphic, numerical, symbolic, or pictorial representation of medical or diagnostic procedure or test of plaintiff. Any other evidence so agreed upon or ordered in accordance with these rules shall also be admitted.

f. There shall be no requirement that any record referred to in these Rules be certified, affirmed or sworn to.

g. The judge may, where required, issue "so ordered" subpoenas to secure the attendance of witnesses or the production of documents.

Rule 12. Jury Verdict

Upon request by the jury, the court where appropriate shall give the jury a written copy of the jury charge for use during deliberations. Five out of six jurors must agree on the verdict unless otherwise agreed to by the parties. The verdict will be binding as rendered or limited by a high/low stipulation.

Rule 13. No Prima Facie Motions or Directed Verdicts

Parties agree to waive prima facie motions, motions for directed verdicts and motions to set aside the verdict or any judgment rendered by the jury. The trial court may not set aside any verdict or judgment entered thereon, nor shall it direct that judgment be entered in favor of a party or order a new trial as to any issues. Should the circumstances so warrant, this provision shall not preclude review by the Administrative Judge.

Rule 14. Inconsistent Verdicts

In the case of inconsistent verdicts, the trial judge shall question and instruct the jury as appropriate to resolve the inconsistency.

Rule 15. Infant Plaintiff

When the plaintiff is an infant, the court must approve any high/low damages parameters prior to trial.

Rule 16. Jury Charges

The jury shall be charged with the standard Pattern Jury Instruction Charges. However, the charges may be reduced to their essential elements.

Rule 17. High/Low Damage Parameters and Apportionment of Liability

The parties may agree to high/low damage parameter for an award to the plaintiff. In the event that the jury determines that the plaintiff bears a percentage of fault, then any monetary award shall be reduced by such percentage. In the event that such reduction results in an award to the plaintiff below the "low" parameter, the plaintiff shall recover the "low" amount. If the award of the jury is above the "high" parameter, the plaintiff's recovery is limited to that "high" amount. If the reduction of the monetary award by reason of the plaintiff's culpable conduct results in the computation of a recovery between the "low" and the "high" parameter then that sum shall be recovered by the plaintiff. For example (a) the jury awards $75,000 but finds the plaintiff 50% responsible, then the award is $37,500. With a $10,000/$30,000 "high/low" the plaintiff's recovery would be $30,000; (b) the jury awards $12,500 and finds the plaintiff 10% liable, then the award is $11,250. With a $15,000/$25,000 "high/low" the plaintiff's recovery would be $15,000; (c) the jury awards $12,500 and finds the plaintiff 10% liable, then the award is $11,250. With a $5,000/$25,000 "high/low" the plaintiff's recovery would be $11,250.

Rule 18. No Judgment entered. Releases and stipulations exchanged

Regardless of whether the parties have agreed to "high/low" parameters, after the jury verdict, if the plaintiff is entitled to damages, then the plaintiff shall provide to the defendant a general release and stipulation of discontinuance. Any award or settlement amount shall be deemed to include interest, costs and disbursements. Plaintiff shall not enter a judgment until and unless the defendant(s) fail to make payment pursuant to CPLR § 5003-a. Any judgment rendered shall be treated as a stipulation of settlement and shall not be intended to have res judicata or collateral estoppel effect.

FAMILY COURT
CUSTODY, VISITATION, AND DOMESTIC VIOLENCE PARTS

Rule I. General Rules

(A) Supplementary Petitions on Pending Matters

(1) Attorneys shall advise their clients to contact them prior to filing any supplemental petitions, motions or applications for judicial action so they may attempt to resolve problems and other non-emergency issues without court intervention. These provisions do not apply to the filing of writs or petitions alleging violations of an order of protection.

(2) Allegations of fact contained in an affidavit submitted by a person who is represented by counsel shall be certified by counsel in the form prescribed in Rule 130–1.1–a of the Chief Administrator of the Courts.

(B) Pretrial Applications

(1) Motions to correct or amend the petition or to dismiss it for facial insufficiency shall be made on notice to respondent(s) and the child's attorney within 20 days after issue is joined.

(2) Demands for bills of particulars and responses to such demands shall be made in accordance with CPLR 3042 except that demands shall be served within 20 days after issue has been joined and responses to such demands shall be served within 20 days after service of the demand.

(3) Ex parte motions for ancillary services (interpreters, investigators, social workers, etc.) under County Law § 722–c to assist counsel in the preparation of the case shall include a supporting affirmation or affidavit stating the basis for the request and the work to be done and shall be submitted to the Court with a proposed order.

(4) *Discovery and Subpoenae*

(a) Discovery may be sought by motion in accordance with Articles 4 and 31 of the CPLR.

(b) If a party or the child's attorney expects to call an expert to testify (other than the court-ordered forensic evaluator), counsel for that party shall identify such expert and disclose to opposing counsel, the child's attorney and the Court the information specified in CPLR 3101(d)(1) no less than thirty (30) days prior to the pretrial conference, except for good cause shown.

(c) All subpoenae must be in accordance with Article 23 of the CPLR.

(d) Applications for court-ordered subpoenae for health, medical, or educational records for which releases are required but refused shall be made by order to show cause.

(C) Adjournments

(1) Attorneys shall submit requests for adjournments of conferences to the court at the earliest possible time and simultaneously provide notice to the opposing counsel, the parties and the child's attorney. All parties and counsel must appear on the adjourned date unless the request for adjournment is granted.

(2) Adjournments on consent will not be entertained unless they are in writing and accompanied by a stipulation signed by all counsel, the child's attorney and any party appearing *pro se*. Counsel shall provide a copy of the written request to the Part Clerk to send to any party who has a confidential address. Such adjournments shall not exceed thirty (30) days unless otherwise permitted by the court. If no consent is given, a written request shall be submitted to the Court at least one week in advance with copies to opposing counsel, the child's attorney, and any party appearing *pro se*. No more than two (2) adjournments on consent will be permitted.

(3) Attorneys seeking adjournments based upon scheduling conflicts shall file affirmations of engagement in accordance with Section 125 of the Rules of the Chief Administrator of the Courts (22 NYCRR Subpart 125) and affirmations of nonavailability for other absences must specify the reason for the attorney's unavailability and contain a list of dates when the matter might be rescheduled. The Court will accept these affirmations by personal delivery, fax (347.401.9900) or e-mail to the judge's court attorney or part clerk. Requests for adjournments that are not in substantial compliance with the foregoing shall be denied and unexcused absences may result in fines or other sanctions as authorized by the rules.

(4) Trial dates cannot be adjourned by stipulation. Adjournments will not be granted by the Court for the trial dates unless there are exceptional circumstances.

(5) Final determination on all requests to adjourn remains with the Court.

(D) Timeliness

(1) Counsel shall appear at the appointed time on every adjourned date that is scheduled for a "time certain." Counsel shall check into each part in which s/he has a case by 8:59 am on the date of the scheduled appearance through the Family Court attorney electronic check-in program which can be accessed at: http://www.nycourts.gov/familycourtcheckin/.

(2) If counsel fails to appear for any "time certain" appearance without good cause, s/he shall be subject to the imposition of sanctions pursuant to the Rules of the Chief Administrator of the Courts (22 NYCRR Subpart 130–2). The imposition of sanctions shall be

within the discretion of the individual Judge and imposed in accordance with the Rules.

(E) Proposed Orders

(1) Proposed orders on motions shall be submitted to the court in accordance with Article 22 of the CPLR and 22 NYCRR 205.15. Counsel shall submit two copies to the Court.

Rule II.   Procedures for Cases to be Tried

Where appropriate, cases shall be referred to Court Attorney Referees for conferencing and possible settlement. When attempts to settle a case have been unsuccessful, the Court shall make a determination that a trial is necessary and shall schedule a preliminary conference as soon thereafter as the Court's calendars permit.

(A) Preliminary Conference

(1) At the Preliminary Conference, counsel for the parties and the child's attorney (if one has been assigned) shall:

(a) Specify the legal and factual issues to be resolved.

(b) Request court orders for services that may be necessary or helpful for the parties, the children, and/or the resolution of these proceedings (e.g., individual or family counseling/therapy; therapeutic visits, supervised visits, mediation, PACT program, etc.). If counsel agree on the provision of such services, proposed orders may be submitted on consent to the Court at the Preliminary Conference.

(c) Identify what information may be necessary or useful for the resolution of the matter (e.g., forensics, visitation reports, educational, medical or psychiatric records, COIs, etc.).

(2) An order specifying the legal and factual issues to be resolved, the court-ordered services that the court has determined are necessary for the proceeding, any evaluations or documents determined by the court to be necessary for the proceeding and setting a compliance conference date shall be issued at the conclusion of the preliminary conference.

(3) A compliance conference shall be scheduled within forty-five (45) days after the Preliminary Conference is held.

(B) Compliance Conference

(1) Reports from the providers of all services ordered by the Court at the Preliminary conference, including status/compliance reports from the forensic evaluator (if any) shall be reviewed and appropriate actions for the expeditious progress of the case shall be agreed upon or ordered by the Court.

(2) The status of discovery, if any, will be reviewed.

(3) Motions to compel discovery or to determine the admissibility of testimonial or documentary evidence shall be made returnable no later than 10 days before the scheduled date for the pretrial conference. All motions shall otherwise conform to the requirements of the CPLR. All responsive papers shall be filed two (2) days prior to the return date of the motion. Counsel shall be prepared for oral argument on the motion if required by the Court.

(4) Motions for summary judgment may be made but must be returnable no later than 30 days before the first scheduled trial date. Such motions shall otherwise conform to the requirements of CPLR 3212.

(5) The Case Coordinator shall send copies of the Forensic Evaluation Report to the attorneys for the parties and the attorney for the child[ren] at least 3 days prior to the Pretrial/Settlement Conference. *Pro se* litigants shall be notified by the Case Coordinator that they may review the report in court prior to or at the Pretrial/Settlement Conference. Copies of the report shall be held by the Court for use by the *pro se* litigants at trial.

(6) An order, memorializing the matters that have been discussed and specifying the actions that are required to be taken prior to trial, including compliance with any outstanding orders, completion of the forensic evaluation, if applicable, completion of discovery, and identification of the legal and factual issues that are to be tried shall be issued at the conclusion of the Compliance Conference.

(7) A pretrial conference will be scheduled within thirty (30) days after the scheduled receipt of the forensic evaluation.

(C) Pretrial Conference

(1) Before the Pretrial Conference, counsel and their clients, *pro se* litigants, and the attorney for the child[ren] shall make reasonable efforts to confer with respect to settlement of the case. If a settlement is reached, counsel shall prepare a written agreement and order, reciting the terms and conditions of the proposed settlement and submit it in advance of the conference date for the Court's review.

(2) If no settlement is reached, trial dates shall be selected and any unresolved pretrial issues shall be addressed.

Rule III.   Trial

(A) Documentary Evidence

(1) Counsel shall provide copies of all proposed exhibits which they will seek to have admitted on their case in chief to opposing counsel, the child's attorney, and any pro se litigant thirty (30) days prior to trial or as soon thereafter as the exhibit becomes available. All responsive papers shall be filed two (2) days prior to the return date of the motion. Counsel shall be prepared for oral argument on the motion if required by the Court.

(2) Counsel shall pre-mark for identification all documents, photographs, audio or video tapes or other items to be offered into evidence. Petitioner's exhib-

its shall be identified by number (e.g., "Petitioner's Ex. 1"). Respondent's exhibits shall be identified by letter (e.g., "Respondent's Ex. A"). The child's attorney's exhibits shall be identified by "CA" and Roman numerals (e.g., "CA's Ex. IV"). Counsel shall make arrangements with the Clerk to pre-mark exhibits in the court's possession.

(B) Procedures

(1) No more than thirty (30) days before trial, the parties and the attorney for the child shall exchange witness lists and provide copies to the Court. Witnesses who were unknown at the time the witness list is furnished may be added with an explanation as to why the witness was not previously identified and an offer of proof of the substance of the witness's testimony. Disclosure of expert witnesses shall be made in compliance with CPLR § 3101(d).

(2) Counsel for each party, the child's attorney (if one has been assigned) and any party appearing *pro se* shall be afforded the opportunity to make a brief opening statement, but may waive an opening statement.

(3) A written copy of any issues or facts to which the parties can stipulate before trial, to be read into the record at the commencement of trial, shall be provided to the Court at the commencement of the trial.

(4) If there is an objection to a question propounded to a witness, counsel shall state the basis for the objection succinctly. Counsel conducting the examination shall be afforded an opportunity to briefly respond to the objection. Once the Court has ruled on the objection, no further argument shall be heard, unless requested by the Court.

(5) Counsel for each party, the attorney for the child (if one has been assigned) and any party appearing *pro se* shall be afforded the right to make brief closing statements. The Court, in its discretion, may require submissions of written summations or proposed findings of fact and conclusions of law.

(6) If applicable, the attorney for the child shall confirm that the child will be appearing for the in camera interview twenty-four (24) hours prior to the date it is scheduled.

Doc. 1. Applications for Relief in Article VI and VIII Proceedings – Part 3

All motions for "non-emergency relief" filed on cases assigned to Judge McElrath should be calendared for Wednesday mornings at 11 am. The motion calendar will be called between 11 am and 1 pm. Orders to Show Cause seeking "emergency relief" should be brought to Judge McElrath's court attorney who, after consultation with the judge, will notify the motion clerk what action the Court will take with respect to the motion and provide a date and time for calendaring.

APPLICATIONS FOR RELIEF IN ARTICLE X PROCEEDINGS

Doc. 2. Applications for Non-emergency Relief in Article X Proceedings

Pursuant to CPLR 2214(c), copies of all motion papers for non-emergency relief must be furnished to the court and submitted to the clerk at the time of filing or the papers will not be accepted. All petitions alleging a violation of prior court orders and motions to extend supervision shall also be filed on the judges' motion days. Motions for non-emergency relief, return of process on violation petitions and motions to extend supervision are to be made returnable on one of the judge's motion days, allowing sufficient time for service under the CPLR. Non-emergency motions are those addressed to matters other than changes of placement, motions seeking to suspend visitation and motions addressed to the child's health or safety. Motion papers are to be filed in Room 6.97. As provided in 22 NYCRR 205.8, the papers shall be clearly addressed to the judge for whom they are intended and prominently show the nature of the papers, the title and docket number of the proceeding in which they are filed, the judge's name and the name of the attorney or party submitting them. As further provided in 22 NYCRR 205.7(d) proof of service on all parties shall be annexed to the motion papers. Pursuant to 22 NYCRR 205.8, copies of all papers for any judge which are filed in the Clerk's office shall be delivered promptly to the judge by the clerk. Counsel shall furnish copies to the Court of all answers to the petitions, and answering or reply affirmations/affidavits and briefs filed with the clerk pursuant to 22 NYCRR 205.11(b). Motions will be deemed submitted unless oral argument has been requested or directed by the Court in accordance with 22 NYCRR 205.11(d). The motion calendar will be called between 10 a.m. and 12 p.m.

Motion Day is Tuesday

Part 4   Hon. Susan S. Danoff

Motion Day is Wednesday

Part 8   Hon. Ilana Gruebel
Part 17   Hon. Emily Olshansky
Part 18   Hon. Alan Beckoff
Part 19   Hon. Daniel Turbow

Motion Day is Tuesday

Part 2   Hon. Amanda White
Part 5   Hon. Stewart Weinstein

Doc. 3. Applications for Emergency Relief in Article X Proceedings

Pursuant to CPLR 2214(c), all motion papers seeking immediate relief must be filed with the clerk in Room 6.97 together with the "emergency declaration form."[1] As provided in NYCRR § 205.8, the motion papers shall be clearly addressed to the judge for whom they are intended and prominently show the nature of the motion, the title and docket number of the proceeding in which they are filed, the judge's name and the name of the attorney or party submitting them. In accordance with FCA § 1023, counsel shall submit an acknowledgment that every reasonable effort given the circumstances has been made to notify all attorneys on the case and the parties, if pro se, in advance of the application. If the papers are complete, the clerk will deliver the motion papers promptly to the judge's court attorney for review in accordance with 22 NYCRR 205.8. After consultation with the judge, the court attorney will notify the motion clerk what action the court will take with respect to the motion. The motion calendar will be called between 10:00 am and 12:00 pm.

Motion Day is Tuesday

Part 4   Hon. Susan S. Danoff

Motion Day is Wednesday

Part 8   Hon. Ilana Gruebel
Part 17   Hon. Emily Olshansky
Part 18   Hon. Alan Beckoff
Part 19   Hon. Daniel Turbow

Motion Day is Tuesday

Part 2   Hon. Amanda White
Part 5   Hon. Stewart Weinstein

[1] Although seeking the return of children removed and included within the definition of "emergency interim relief," in instances where the case is assigned to a CP judge but is pending before a court attorney referee for permanency proceedings, all requests for a hearing pursuant to FCA § 1028 shall be by Notice of Motion and calendared on the assigned judge's motion day.

JUVENILE DELINQUENCY/PINS PROCEEDINGS

Doc. 4. Juvenile Delinquency/PINS Proceedings

A. Motions

Motions in Article III cases may be filed in accordance with FCA 315.2(3), FCA 332.2, FCA 355.2, and FCA 375.2. Motions in Article VII cases may be filed in accordance with Article 22 of the CPLR. Pursuant to CPLR 2214(c), copies of all motion papers must be furnished to the Court and submitted to the Clerk at the time of filing or the papers will not be accepted. Motion papers are to be filed in room 6.97. As provided in the 22 NYCRR 205.8, the papers shall be clearly addressed to the judge for whom they are intended and prominently show the nature of the papers, the title and docket number of the proceeding in which they are filed, the judge's name and the name of the attorney or party submitting them.

Counsel shall furnish copies to the Court of all answering and reply affidavits and briefs filed with the clerk pursuant to 22 NYCRR 205.11(b). Pursuant to 22 NYCRR 205.8, copies of all papers for any judge which are filed in the clerk's office shall be delivered promptly to the judge by the clerk.

B. Transfers

Transfers of Article III cases for disposition, authorized pursuant to FCA 302.3(4), shall be calendared before the JD intake judge on the day of receipt regardless of whether the sending court selected an adjourned date in Kings County. This will assure optimal compliance with speedy disposition and afford the JD judges a chance to review the file for completeness and make any appropriate interim orders they deem necessary.

THIRD JUDICIAL DISTRICT – ALBANY, COLUMBIA, GREENE, RENSSELAER, SCHOHARIE, SULLIVAN, ULSTER COUNTIES

Westlaw Electronic Research

These rules may be searched electronically on Westlaw® *in the NY–RULES database; updates to these rules may be found on* Westlaw *in NY–RULESUPDATES. For search tips and a summary of database content, consult the* Westlaw *Scope Screens for each database.*

Form
UCS 137–14. Consent to Submit Fee Dispute to Arbitration Pursuant to Part 137.2 (c) of the Rules of the Chief Administrator and to Waive Right to Trial *De Novo.*

Form
UCS 137–15. Consent to Submit Fee Dispute to Mediation Pursuant to Part 137 of the Rules of the Chief Administrator.

UCS 137–16. Consent to Final and Binding Arbitration in an Arbitral Forum Outside Part 137 Under 137.2 (d) of the Rules of the Chief Administrator.

DISTRICT RULES
SUPREME COURT
THIRD DISTRICT RULES

Doc. 1. Case Initiation and Assignment Process

A litigant shall first pay for an index number and a Request for Judicial Intervention in the County Clerk's Office in the county of the venue of the case and then file in the Chief Clerk's Office the Request for Judicial Intervention. The chief clerk shall assign a consecutive number to each request for judicial intervention. This will become the case identification number. The index number, the request for judicial intervention number and the assigned justice's name shall appear on all subsequent papers filed with the court. With the exception of those matters specified for Special Assignments, all contested matters will be assigned to an IAS justice. If there is any question, the clerk shall refer the matter to a justice for determination.

The District Administrative Judge will:

a) Make case assignments when judges are disqualified;

b) Reassign cases if IAS Justice will be absent for a lengthy period;

c) Assign cases to Acting Justices of the Supreme Court and Judicial Hearing Officers; and

d) Adjust assignment patterns to insure equal distribution of cases.

Doc. 2. Motion Practice

Motion Filing Fee: In general, any filing subsequent to the commencement of an action which is designated as a motion or cross-motion requires the payment of a filing fee to the County Clerk's Office prior to submission to the Supreme Court Clerk's Office for referral to the assigned judge. The fee is assessed regardless of whether an application is made by notice of motion, order to show cause or *ex parte.* No fee will be charged upon the filing of a motion for poor person status on in conjunction with an application which served to commence an action or special

proceeding. In the event a motion is received by the court unaccompanied by proof of payment to the County Clerk, the Supreme Court Clerk's Office will telephone the submitting party to advise that the application will be held pending receipt of the filing fee only until the return date of the motion. If proof of payment is not submitted to the Supreme Court Clerk's Office by the return date (*ex parte* applications will be held ten days), the papers will be returned by mail with a notification that the motion has been removed from the court's calendar and that it must be re-noticed and re-filed with the court along with the requisite filing fee. Inquiries concerning the applicability of the motion fee to a proposed filing may be directed the Supreme Court Clerk's Office.

All motions shall be returnable before the assigned justice. Supreme Court Justices are sitting at "All Purpose Terms of Court" at all times, therefore all motions, except for certain matters in Albany County as specified below, brought on by notice of motion or by order to show cause will be made returnable on any day, Monday through Friday, as chosen by the movant in compliance with the CPLR. Parties shall submit all papers in a timely fashion as required by the CPLR by delivering them or mailing them directly to the Supreme Court Clerk's office (see Section 202.8 of Uniform Rules for Supreme and County Courts [22 NYCRR 202.8]), except that motions and other applications subject to a filing fee shall first be presented to the County Clerk's Office for payment of the requisite fee and then subsequently filed with the Supreme Court Clerk's Office.

All motions made returnable in a county other than the county of the venue of the case shall be forwarded by the chief clerk of that court to the chief clerk of the county of the venue of the case to be submitted to the justice assigned to the case as herein provided except that where a motion is brought pursuant to CPLR 5221(a)(4) seeking the enforcement of a judgment (i.e., contempt of court) in a county in which the judgment debtor resides, is employed, or has a place of business, which is a county other than that where the judgment was initially entered, the motion shall be put on a county court motion calendar of the county where it was made returnable, provided an index number and RJI number have been obtained in the county of original venue. Upon determination of the application, all papers will be returned for filing to the county of original venue and the case remitted for further proceedings as may be necessary.

All motions are deemed "submitted" on the return date and no appearances are required by the parties. A party may request oral argument on a motion by indicating such request on the first page of the notice of motion, order to show cause, or answering papers in the area across from the caption of the action/proceeding. In the event oral argument is requested, the parties should not appear on the return date. At the discretion of the assigned judge and upon the granting of a request for oral argument, the parties will be notified by chambers of the scheduled time and place at which argument will be heard. Where a motion is brought on by order to show cause, the court may set forth in the order that appearances and/or oral argument are required on the return date of the motion.

An application for the issuance of an order to show cause to punish for contempt shall be made directly to the assigned justice or judge who signed the judgment or order which is the subject of the contempt application. In a situation where there is no assigned justice or judge, the chief clerk shall, upon receipt of a request for judicial intervention (if one is required), assign a justice or judge and the applicant shall then make the application directly to the assigned justice or judge. If the assigned justice or judge is unavailable, any other justice or judge may issue the order to show cause, returnable before the assigned justice or judge, at a date and time when the assigned justice or judge will be available.

A justice who signs an order to show cause which contains a stay or temporary restraining order may, if appropriate, require a hearing on short notice to determine if the stay or TRO should be continued until the return date before the assigned justice.

Prior to the submission of a notice of motion relating to disclosure or a bill of particulars, the parties must make a good faith effort to resolve the matter in question and submit an affirmation attesting to this good faith effort. The affirmation of good faith effort to resolve the issues raised by the motion shall indicate the time, place and nature of the consultation and the issues discussed and any resolutions, or shall indicate good cause why no such conferral with counsel for opposing parties was held. An assigned justice may dismiss a motion for failure to demonstrate that such effort was made with leave to renew the motion after such effort has been demonstrated.

Doc. 3. Preliminary Conference

(See Section 202.12 of Uniform Civil Rules for the Supreme and County Courts [22 NYCRR 202.12])

Doc. 4. Special Assignments

Any available Supreme Court Justice present may perform the following functions. The chief clerk's office will assist in the referral of these matters to the appropriate justice.

a) Hold Mental Health Hearings (except for Albany County);

b) Impanel Supreme Court Trial and Grand Juries and receive Grand Jury Reports;

c) Entertain Orders to Show Cause;

d) Entertain Temporary Restraining Orders;

e) Hear requests for emergency medical services;

f) Entertain Infant Settlements;

g) Entertain bail applications;

h) Handle Writs of Habeas Corpus;

i) Perform marriages;

j) Handle emergency-type matters.

In any county, during periods when no Supreme Court Trial Term is in session in that county, any county-level judge may perform such functions if permitted by law.

Doc. 5. Albany County Supreme Court— Commercial Division

The Commercial Division of the Albany County Supreme Court exercises jurisdiction over selected business and commercial disputes in which the amount at issue generally involves damage claims in a minimum amount of $25,000, as well as claims for unspecified amounts where the value of the commercial asset(s) in dispute exceeds $25,000. A separate publication promulgating the rules and criteria relating to the filing and management of Commercial Court cases in this part may be obtained from the Albany County Supreme Court Clerk's Office. Also, § 202.70 of the Uniform Civil Rules of the Supreme and County Courts sets forth statewide rules effective January 17, 2006.

Doc. 6. Albany Motion Terms

There shall be a Mental Hygiene Calendar each Thursday and a Motion Term on each Friday in the Supreme Court, Albany County. The Friday Motion Term shall include all Article 78 Proceedings involving New York State and proceedings commenced pursuant to Article 14 of the Civil Service Law (including applications for injunctive relief made pursuant to Section 209-a of the Civil Service Law). All non–State Article 78 proceedings commenced in Albany County shall be assigned at random on the "wheel" to the IAS Justices to whom Albany County cases are assigned.

Generally, parties will be granted only one adjournment for the Friday Motion Term. Requests for an adjournment of the proceeding or an extension of time in which to submit papers must be made in writing to the Supreme Court Clerk's Office for referral to the assigned judge for consideration. Upon the request and consent of all parties to an Article 78 proceeding, a petition may be "marked off" the calendar and re-noticed for a subsequent motion term. When a motion to dismiss the petition in an Article 78 is denied by the assigned judge, the matter shall be re-noticed to be heard before the same assigned judge.

Doc. 7. All Election Law Cases

All proceedings commenced pursuant to Article 16 of the Election Law shall be made returnable in the county in which the decision sought to be reviewed was made. In the event a hearing is required to determine a proceeding under the Election Law, the IAS Justice may, in the exercise of discretion, transfer the matter to a trial term in the county in which the proceeding is pending.

All orders to show cause bringing on a proceeding under the Election Law shall be made returnable within ten (10) days (or sooner if necessary) and all arguments, hearings and decisions shall be expedited to insure that appeals from the trial court can be heard in a timely fashion according to the schedule set annually by the Appellate Division, Third Department.

Doc. 8. Proceedings Under Article 81 of the Mental Hygiene Law

All applications for orders to show cause bringing on a proceeding for the appointment of a guardian pursuant to the Mental Hygiene Law shall be accompanied by a Request for Judicial Intervention and shall be made returnable before the IAS Justice assigned to that proceeding.

Doc. 9. Expert Disclosure Rule

Except as otherwise directed by the Court, a party who has the burden of proof on a claim, cause of action, damage or defense shall serve its response to an expert demand pursuant to CPLR 3101(d) on or before the filing of the Note of Issue. Such party has until the filing of the Note of Issue to serve such response regardless of how early the demand is made. Any opposing party shall serve its answering response pursuant to CPLR 3101(d) within 60 days after the filing of the Note of Issue. Any amended or supplemental expert disclosure shall be allowed only with the permission of the Court. Unless the Court directs otherwise, a party who fails to comply with this rule is precluded from offering the testimony and opinions of the expert for whom a timely response has not been given.

The statutory stay for disclosure [CPLR 3214(b)] upon the service of a dispositive motion under CPLR 3211 shall not apply to the service of these expert responses.

The word "expert" shall include, but is not limited to, any physician, dentist, chiropractor, psychiatrist, psychologist, other health care provider of any specialty, economist, engineer, architect, lawyer, accountant, appraiser, rehabilitation counselor or other person who will testify concerning his/her qualifications and give opinions concerning the issues in the case. However, "expert" shall not include a treating physician or other treating health care provider whose record(s), and report(s) have been timely provided and whose testimony is limited solely to the contents of the records or reports provided. In the event that a treating physician or other treating health care provider is intending to testify as to matters not within the contents of the records or reports provided, then disclosure as an "expert" is required.

This rule shall apply to all actions commenced after April 1, 1999 and to those commenced before that date where a Note of Issue has not been filed.

Any motion by a party to preclude, or limit expert testimony under this rule, must be made as soon as practicable but no later than forty-five (45) days after the party's receipt of the expert disclosure or the motion will be waived.

This rule does not apply to matrimonial actions.

Doc. 10. Trial Activity

1. Day Certain Assignment Process

An IAS assigned Justice shall manage all cases assigned to the point of trial readiness at which time a Note of Issue shall be filed indicating that the case is ready for trial. The Note of Issue shall be forwarded to the IAS Justice who shall set the matter down for a conference and give the matter a Day Certain. The IAS Justice shall inform the Chief Clerk that the matter has been certified to trial which letter shall also confirm the Day Certain. When any case is certified as trial ready by the IAS Justice, it shall be given a Day Certain.

In determining the particular Day Certain, the IAS Justice shall first ascertain the availability of the specific date from the Chief Clerk's Office which shall maintain a calendar for the purpose of scheduling Days Certain. In Albany County, the maximum number of days certain scheduled shall be ten (10) jury cases on Mondays, six (6) jury cases on Tuesdays and four (4) non-jury cases on Wednesdays. In Rensselaer and Ulster Counties, the maximum number of days certain shall be six (6) jury cases on Mondays, and three (3) non-jury cases on Wednesdays. In Sullivan County, the maximum number of days certain shall be four (4) jury cases on Mondays and three (3) non-jury cases on Wednesdays. In Greene County, the maximum numbers of days certain shall be four (4) jury cases on Mondays and two (2) non-jury cases on Wednesdays during each trial term. In Columbia and Schoharie Counties, the maximum number of days certain shall be four (4) jury cases on Mondays and two (2) non-jury cases on Wednesdays during each trial term.

Prior to the beginning of each Trial Term, the Chief Clerk shall prepare the Day Certain Calendar for that particular term setting forth all appropriate information including the name of the case, date of trial and attorneys representing the various parties. Said calendar shall be provided to the Part 1 Justice at least one day prior to the calendar call.

Applications for adjournment of a scheduled trial date shall be addressed to the IAS Justice until the commencement of the trial term for which the case has been set down for trial. Once a trial term has commenced, applications for adjournment of the trial of a case scheduled to be tried during that trial term shall be addressed to the Part I trial Justice only.

2. Part I Justice

The Part 1 Justice assigned to each respective county is the duty judge for that particular term. In addition to conferencing each case assigned for trial in advance of the Day Certain, the Part I Justice shall keep in close communication with the Chief Clerk and the Commissioner of Jurors so as to insure that only the necessary number of prospective jurors are called in.

Every effort should be made to have the attorneys involved consider non-jury trials, if appropriate, and the use of Judicial Hearing Officers, as available. The back-up trial justices assigned to each term will be assigned as needed to trials by the Part I Justice. Once the list of back-up trial justices assigned to that term has been exhausted, the Part I Justice shall communicate with the other Part I Justices in the district, or in the alternative the District Administrative Judge, so as to utilize every available back-up trial justice for any particular trial need in the district. Where the need arises and their schedules permit, Part I Justices are also expected to try cases on their Part I calendar. If, after all of the aforesaid options are exhausted, the Part I Justice still cannot find an available trial justice, the District Administrative Judge should be consulted so that all available resources can be considered, including but not limited to the use of available county level judges as Acting Supreme Court Justices on a case-to-case basis.

All ex parte matters, orders to show cause in unassigned cases, and other miscellaneous matters (including welcoming trial jurors) should be referred by the Chief Clerk's office to the Part I Justice.

The Part I Justice, in the event a particular case assigned a Day Certain is not ready for trial, shall either give the matter a future Day Certain or shall strike the Note of Issue and return the case to the assigned IAS Justice, whichever procedure is appropriate in the Part I Justice's opinion. Under no circumstances will a case be marked over the term without a new Day Certain. Furthermore, no case with a Day Certain shall be put over the term due to the unavailability of a Trial Justice without consultation with the District Administrative Justice. In the event the case is returned to the IAS Justice, that justice shall approve the filing of a new Note of Issue, without costs, when the case is ready for trial and shall assign a new Day Certain. If a jury fee was paid, it will not be required to be paid again.

All Preference cases shall be appropriately designated and the Preference shall be honored by the Part I Justice.

All motions made after a case has been assigned a Day Certain shall be referred to the IAS Justice unless the motion is returnable during the term in which the matter has been assigned a Day Certain, in that event the matter will be referred to the Part 1 Justice for that particular term who may entertain the motion or refer such motion to the IAS Justice. Under those circumstances, the Part I Justice shall decide whether or not to strike the Note of Issue or assign the matter a new Day Certain.

3. Jury Selection in Civil Cases

The Part I Justice assigned to each county, or a Justice or Judicial Hearing Officer designated by the Part I Justice shall preside at the commencement of the *voir dire* and determine, in his or her discretion, whether in-court supervision should continue over all or a portion of the remainder of the *voir dire*.

The Part I Justice, or a Justice or Judicial Hearing Officer designated by the Part I Justice shall determine, in his or her discretion, after consultation with the attorneys for the parties where appropriate, the period of time to be afforded each party for jury selection.

The attorneys conducting the *voir dire* shall utilize juror questionnaires furnished by the Commissioner of Jurors prior to the commencement of the *voir dire*.

All prospective jurors (six plus the agreed upon number of alternates) will be selected at random from the panel and seated in the jury box. Unless there is consent of all parties and the presiding judge to designate alternates, the jurors selected will not be designated. The attorney for plaintiff will first examine these prospective jurors followed by the attorney for defendant who will then examine them. If there are additional parties, each party will examine the potential jurors in the order they are named in the pleadings.

After the prospective jurors have been examined by counsel for all parties, counsel will advise the Clerk of the Court or the Court of any peremptory challenges on an alternating basis, in the same order as was followed for the examination. (For example, if there are two parties, plaintiff makes the first challenge, then defendant makes the second challenge, then plaintiff makes the third challenge, defendant makes the fourth challenge, etc.). If a party fails to make a peremptory challenge when it is that party's turn to do so, that party may not thereafter make a peremptory challenge as to that group of jurors.

Once a party has stated that a juror is satisfactory or has failed to exercise a peremptory challenge after having the opportunity to do so, the party cannot exercise a peremptory challenge as to that prospective juror. Challenges for cause may be made at any time.

Any seats vacated because of the exercise of peremptory challenges will then be filled, and the examination of peremptory challenge procedure will be repeated as to the newly seated prospective jurors only. The process will continue until a complete jury has been selected.

After all parties state that the jurors then seated are satisfactory, the jury will be sworn and the trial will commence.

4. Trial Rules and Special Directives

Prior to jury selection, marked pleadings, copies of the bills of particulars and the demands therefor, discovery responses and the demands therefor, and expert reports shall be presented to the Court.

Prior to jury selection, a list (without the charge) of PJI jury requests citing the section numbers and title of the PJI jury charge should be available to the Court. Other requests shall be typed on separate sheets with appropriate sources or citations. A charge conference will be held prior to summations.

Prior to jury selection, each party shall provide the Court and opposing counsel with a one-page statement of the party's contentions and a list of witnesses to be called at trial.

Experts who testify at trial must bring with them to Court their entire file and all documents considered in arriving at their opinion(s).

All motions *in limine* should be in writing and should be prepared and filed at the earliest possible time to the extent that the basis for these motions are know by a party and will arise during the trial of the action.

Exhibits should be pre-marked by the Court Reporter. Counsel shall also confer prior to trial to determine if the admission into evidence of any exhibits will be stipulated, and advise the Court of that prior to trial.

Exhibits should be pre-marked by the Court Reporter. Counsel shall also confer prior to trial to determine if the admission into evidence of any exhibits will be stipulated, and advise the Court of that prior to trial.

Trial briefs are suggested if intricate evidentiary or trial issues are anticipated.

Verdict sheets: Counsel shall cooperate to prepare an agreed verdict sheet. If that is not possible, then the parties shall submit separate proposed verdict sheets following the suggested forms in the PJI (see PJI Supplement Vol. 1B, 2:275 and 2:301). Each question shall be on a separate page.

For good cause shown, and in the interest of justice, the Court in which an action or proceeding is pending may waive compliance with any of these rules unless prohibited by doing so by Statute or a Rule of the Chief Judge.

JUDGES' RULES

JUSTICE EUGENE P. DEVINE

Doc. 1. Hon. Eugene P. Devine

Communications:

Chambers are open 8:00 a.m. to 4:00 p.m. An answering machine will take messages at other times. Scheduling of any conferences may be done with either secretary or law clerk and should be done by in writing by letter or fax. Please provide the Court with dates convenient to all counsel and a reason for the conference.

When the Judge is assigned to Part I of a Trial Term, scheduling of conferences for cases on trial calendar shall be by the Supreme Court Clerk.

Motion Practice:

Oral Argument: May be requested by contacting Chambers. Article 78 petitions may require personal appearances and oral argument unless the parties prefer to submit.

Submissions of Motion Papers, Orders and Judgments: Motions are returnable any weekday. All original papers including opposition and reply papers shall be timely served on all counsel and filed with the Supreme Court Clerk, Room 102, Albany County Courthouse, after payment of the required motion fee to the Albany County Clerk. Please do not send courtesy copies of motion papers to Chambers. Any papers filed or served late may not be considered. Sur–Reply papers are discouraged and may not be considered. Memoranda of Law should reflect brevity and specificity.

Requests to Adjourn Motions: Counsel must first ask for consent to adjourn motion from opposing counsel. If consent is granted, counsel should advise the Court in writing prior to the return date. If the parties do not consent, requesting counsel shall write the Court prior to the return date to make an adjournment request and provide a reason why such request is not on consent. Adjournments are limited to sixty (60) days per 22 NYCRR 202.8(e)(1).

If motion is one specifically scheduled by the Court, a request for adjournment shall be made to the Court only.

If a proposed order or judgment is submitted for signature with respect to an oral or written decision, the submitting party shall do so in a timely fashion. Unless otherwise directed by the Court, such order shall first be submitted for approval of its form and content to all other counsel. Once submitted for signature, it shall be (a) accompanied with a letter from the submitting counsel stating that all counsel have approved the same as to form and content, or (b) accompanied by a letter, copied to all counsel giving

them 10 days to object or they shall be deemed to have given consent.

Discovery Motions:

Discovery motions must include affirmations from all parties that an attempt was made, in good faith, to resolve any outstanding issues (See 22 NYCRR 202.7).

Orders to Show Cause:

An Order to Show Cause **must** be presented by an attorney familiar with the case. If the case is unassigned under IAS, presentment should first be attempted to the Part I Judge. For any Order to Show Cause that contains a motion for a preliminary injunction or temporary restraining order, notice must be provided to the opposing party.

Special Instructions for Matrimonial Motions and Matters:

For matrimonial motions, the parties shall request a conference with the Court to attempt to resolve any requests for pendente lite relief prior to filing a motion, if practicable. Motions for pendente lite relief shall be made no later than sixty (60) days before trial. Otherwise, matrimonial motions shall be governed by the general provisions regarding motions and/or by any scheduling order, if applicable. Appearances on non-contempt matrimonial motions will be scheduled by the Court as necessary.

Court Conferences; Requests for Adjournment:

Counsel must first contact opposing counsel to request consent for an adjournment, and if counsel consents, determine three (3) mutually convenient dates. Once consent is given, the adjournment request must be made in writing to Chambers in a reasonable time prior to the scheduled appearance. The requesting counsel shall provide three (3) proposed new dates to Chambers and a reason for the postponement. **No conference shall be deemed adjourned without Court approval.**

Preliminary Conferences:

Preliminary Conferences are scheduled pursuant to 22 NYCRR 202.12(a) and for matrimonial cases pursuant to 22 NYCRR 202.16(f).

The Court will provide all parties with a Preliminary Conference Stipulation & Order to set forth a scheduling order for all cases. The order may be completed and sent back to the Court. In that case, the order will be signed and there will be no conference. If the completed order cannot be completed by the parties, a conference may be scheduled. Prior to the preliminary conference, each party shall submit to the Court a brief summary of the case and an explanation of all issues to be discussed at the conference (See 22 NYCRR 202.12(a)).

In a contested matrimonial, a preliminary conference will be scheduled by letter. Clients must be present and counsel must file a statement of net worth and retainer agreement with the Court before the conference. All pertinent matters will be discussed at the conference in an effort to resolve and limit contested issues.

Contempt:

Upon the return date of a motion for contempt, the Court will hold a hearing at which all parties must personally appear.

Note of Issue:

If a note of issue is not timely served and filed pursuant to a scheduling order and no party has requested an extension of that order, the Court will mark the case ready for trial, direct that a note of issue be filed and schedule a final conference. No case shall be scheduled for trial unless a note of issue has been filed.

Final Conference (after discovery):

In contested matrimonials, clients must attend. In all cases, final conferences will be scheduled by letter after the filing of the note of issue. Counsel should contact their clients, witnesses and experts before this conference to determine their availability for trial.

PURSUANT TO THE UNIFORM RULES OF THE NEW YORK STATE TRIAL COURTS (§ 202. 26), ALL INSURANCE CARRIERS INVOLVED MUST HAVE A REPRESENTATIVE PRESENT WHO NOT ONLY HAS AUTHORITY TO SETTLE, BUT ALSO HAS THE ABILITY TO NEGOTIATE WITHOUT CONTACTING A SUPERIOR. THAT REPRESENTATIVE SHALL BE THE SENIOR MOST OFFICER WHO HAS PARTICIPATED IN EVALUATING THIS CASE AND WHO HAS THE "FINAL CALL" IN NEGOTIATIONS.

Counsel attending the conference **shall be familiar** with the case, have pertinent portions of the file with them and **have authority** to discuss settlement. Client(s) and a representative of any insurance carrier **shall** be requested to attend. All counsel shall confer prior to the date of the conference discuss settlement, the resolution of any trial issues, and whether the parties will agree to a Judicial Hearing Officer to preside at the trial. Counsel are encouraged to videotape any witness or expert who is unavailable for the scheduled trial. Postponement of any trial after the pre-trial conference is discouraged and will not be granted in the absence of extraordinary circum-

stances. **Appearances by telephone are not allowed.**

Trial Rules and Special Directives:

1. Marked pleadings shall be presented to the Court before jury selection. Copies of the bills of particulars, discovery responses and expert reports should be available.

Experts who testify at trial shall bring with them to Court their entire file and all documents considered in arriving at their opinion(s). Failure to do so may result in an expert's testimony being limited or stricken.

2. Jury selection shall follow the Court Rules. The modified struck system shall be followed. The Court may preside over a portion of or the entire jury selection process. Time limits on counsel may be imposed. Counsel are to confine their voir dire questions to the qualifications of the jurors.

3. Any motion in *limine* should be in writing, timely served on all counsel a reasonable time before trial.

4. Exhibits should be pre-marked by the Court Reporter. Counsel shall also confer prior to trial to determine if the admission into evidence of any exhibits will be stipulated, and advise the Court of that prior to trial.

5. Trial briefs are suggested if intricate evidentiary or trial issues are anticipated.

6. A list (without the charge) of PJI jury requests must be available to the Court prior to trial. A charge conference will be held prior to summations.

7. Counsel shall stand to object during the trial and briefly state the ground(s) for the objection.

Argument on an objection will not be taken in front of the jury. Exceptions to any ruling need not be taken.

8. Verdict sheets: Counsel shall cooperate to prepare an agreed verdict sheet. If that is not possible, then the parties shall submit separate proposed verdict sheets following the suggested forms in the PJI (See PJI Supplement Vol 1, 2:275 and 2:301). Each question shall be on a separate page.

9. Non–Jury Cases: Each party shall submit in duplicate post-trial proposed Findings of Fact and Conclusions of Law. A Memoranda of Law may also be requested.

10. Post–Trial Motions: May be presented orally or in writing.

11. CPLR Article 50–B Motions: Should be submitted in motion form with notice to all parties.

JUSTICE JOSEPH C. TERESI

Doc. 1.   Hon. Joseph C. Teresi

Communications:

Chambers are open 08:00 A.M. to 04:30 P.M. Answering machine will take messages at other times. Scheduling of any conferences may be done with either secretary or law clerk and should be done by telephoning with available dates convenient to all counsel. Letter requests for conference should give reason for a conference and available dates convenient to all counsel. Conferences are held each morning beginning at 8:15 A.M.

When the Judge is assigned to Part I of a Trial Term, scheduling of conferences for cases on trial calendar shall be by the Courtroom Clerk.

Motions at a Glance:

Pre–Motion Conference: None, except for discovery motions.

Oral argument: May be requested. Not generally held unless requested by the Court.

Article 78 motion terms do require personal appearance and oral argument unless the parties submit. A time limit for each party may be applied.

Submissions of Motion Papers, Order and Judgments:

Motions are returnable any weekday. All original papers including opposition and reply papers shall be timely served on all counsel and filed with the Supreme Court Clerk, Room 102, Albany County Courthouse, Attention: Motion Clerk., after payment of the required motion fee to the Albany County Clerk. A courtesy copy of any motion papers should not be sent to chambers prior to the return date. Any papers filed or served late may not be considered.

Sur–Reply papers are discouraged and not considered. Memoranda of law should reflect Brevity and specificity.

Requests to adjourn motions: initially, counsel shall confer to determine if adjournment is on consent. If so, a letter shall be delivered to the Motion Clerk before the return date. A copy of that letter need not be sent to chambers. If agreement is not reached, requesting counsel shall write the court prior to the return date to request an adjournment. Adjournments are limited to sixty (60) days per 22 NYCRR 202.8(c)(1).

If motion is one specifically scheduled by the Court, a request for adjournment shall be made to the Court only.

If an order or judgment is submitted for signature with respect to an oral or written decision, the submitting party shall do so in a timely fashion. Unless otherwise directed by the Court, such order shall first be submitted for approval of its form and content to all other counsel. Once submitted for signature, it shall be accompanied with a letter from the submitting counsel stating that all counsel have approved the same as to form and content. The notice of settlement procedure provided in 22 NYCRR 202.48(c) shall not be used unless directed by the Court.

Discovery Motions:

No discovery motion may be filed unless counsel personally confer, to resolve the discovery issue (See 22 NYCRR 202.7) and the motion papers show compliance with that Rule. In addition, if the case is covered by a preliminary conference order and/or stipulation, that order requires that a conference with the court must be held in an attempt to resolve the dispute. That conference shall be requested by phone for a date convenient to all counsel. Prior to the conference, each party shall deliver to the court, a short letter outlining its position in respect to the discovery dispute.

Orders to Show Cause:

An Order to Show Cause should be presented by an attorney familiar with the case. If the case is unassigned under IAS, presentment should first be attempted to the Part I Judge. If the Part I Judge is unavailable or if the case is assigned to this Court, it is preferable that presentment be made in the morning before the court begins its trial calendar. Personal presentment is requested rather than mailing to or leaving the proposed papers at chambers. For any order to show cause that contains a motion for a preliminary injunction or Temporary Restraining Order, 22 NYCRR 202.7(f) must be followed to give notice to the opposing party.

Special Instructions for Matrimonial Motions and Matters:

For matrimonial motions in cases not governed by a scheduling order, follow the general procedure for the filing of motions. If the case is governed by a scheduling order, that order will specify any motions which were requested at the time of the preliminary conference and provide a return date. If a party wishes to file a motion after the scheduling order is issued, permission of the court must be obtained.

Application for Adjournment:

Counsel shall initially contact all other counsel to determine their position in respect to any adjournment.

An adjournment of any conference may be requested by phone. The requesting counsel shall provide proposed new date(s), and a reason for the postponement.

Preliminary Conferences:

Preliminary Conferences are scheduled pursuant to 22 NYCRR 202.12(a) and for matrimonial cases pursuant to 22 NYCRR 202.16(f).

The Court does use pre-trial scheduling orders for all cases. Once the case is assigned to the court, a letter will be sent scheduling the preliminary conference. A pre-trial scheduling order (similar to that set forth in Appendix D of the Uniform Court Rules) will be used which may be completed and sent back to the court before the conference. That form is available at www.nycourts.gov/courts/3jd/. Click onto Supreme Court then click onto rules. In those cases the conference will not be held. If the form is not returned, the conference will be held and each party shall submit to the Court a short (no longer than 2 pages) summary of the case before the conference outlining the case and any issues to be discussed at the conference. See 22 NYCRR 202.16(f)

In a contested matrimonial, a preliminary conference will be scheduled by letter. Clients must be present and counsel must file a statement of net worth, and retainer agreement with the Court before the conference. A scheduling order will be issued containing a return date for any *pendente lite* motion(s). All pertinent matters will be discussed at the conference in an effort to resolve and limit contested issues.

If a note of issue is not timely served and filed pursuant to a scheduling order and no party has requested an extension of that order, the Court will mark the case ready for trial, direct that a note of issue be filed and schedule a final conference. No case shall be scheduled for trial unless a note of issue has been filed.

Final Conference (after discovery):

In contested matrimonials, clients must attend. In all cases, final conferences will be scheduled by letter after the filing of a note of issue. Counsel should contact their client(s), witnesses and experts before this conference to determine their availability for trial. The Court will attempt to schedule the trial within three (3) months of the final conference.

Counsel attending the conference shall be familiar with the case, have pertinent portions of the file with them and have authority to discuss settlement. Client(s) or a representative of the insurance carrier may be required to attend. All counsel shall confer prior to the date of the conference to discuss settlement, the resolution of any trial issues, and whether the parties will agree to a Judicial Hearing Officer to preside at the trial. Counsel are encouraged to videotape any witness or expert who is unavailable for the scheduled trial. Postponement of any trial after the pre-trial conference is discouraged and will not be granted except for extraordinary circumstances.

Trial Rules and Special Directives:

1. Marked pleadings shall be presented to the Court before jury selection. Copies of the bills of particulars, discovery responses and expert reports should be available.

Experts who testify at trial shall bring with them to Court their entire file and all documents considered in arriving at their opinion(s). Failure to do so may result in an expert's testimony being limited or stricken.

2. Jury selection shall follow the Court Rules. The modified struck system shall be followed. The Court may preside over a portion of or the entire jury selection process. Time limits on counsel may be imposed. Counsel are to confine their voir dire questions to the qualifications of the jurors.

3. Any motions in *limine* should be in writing, timely served on all counsel a reasonable time before trial.

4. Exhibits should be pre-marked by the Court Reporter. Counsel shall also confer prior to trial to determine if the admission into evidence of any exhibits will be stipulated, and advise the Court of that prior to trial. All exhibits shall be pre marked with the exhibit sticker commonly used.

5. Trial briefs are suggested if intricate evidentiary or trial issues are anticipated.

6. A list (without the charge) of PJI jury requests should be available to the Court prior to trial. Other requests shall be typed on separate sheets with appropriate sources or citations. The Court's "boilerplate" charge is available to any counsel upon request. A charge conference will be held prior to summations.

7. Counsel shall stand to object during the trial and briefly state the ground(s) for the objection.

Argument on an objection will not be taken in front of the jury. Exceptions to any ruling need not be taken.

8. Verdict sheets: Counsel shall cooperate to prepare an agreed verdict sheet. If that is not possible then the parties shall submit separate proposed verdict sheets following the suggested forms in the PJI (See PJI Supplement Vol. 1, 2:275 and 2:301) Each question shall be on a separate page.

In non-jury cases, each party shall submit in duplicate post-trial proposed findings of facts and conclusions of law. A memoranda of law may also be requested.

9. Post Trial Motions: May be presented orally or in writing.

10. CPLR Article 50-B Motions: should be submitted in motion form with notice to all parties.

App. 1. Preliminary Conference Stipulation and Order

SUPREME COURT, COUNTY OF ———————

INDIVIDUAL ASSIGNMENT PART, Justice Teresi

———————————————————

Plaintiff(s)

-against-

**PRELIMINARY CONFERENCE
STIPULATION AND ORDER**
(Sections 202.8 and 202.12 of the
Uniform Rules)
INDEX NO. ————————

Defendant(s)

———————————————————

(All items on this form must be completed unless inapplicable).

It is hereby STIPULATED and ORDERED that disclosure shall proceed as follows:

(1) Insurance Coverage: If not already provided, shall be furnished by each defendant and third-party defendant on or before ————————.

(2) Bill of Particulars:

(a) Demand for bill of particulars/interrogatories and discovery demand shall be served by ———————— on or before ————————.

(b) Bill of particulars/interrogatory answers and discovery response shall be served by ———————— on or before ————————.

(c) A supplemental bill of particulars shall be served by ———————— as to Items ———————— on or before ————————.

(3) Medical Reports and Authorizations:

Shall be served as follows: ————————————————————

————————————————————————————————————

————————————————————————————————————

————————————————————————————————————

Plaintiff shall send defendant(s) copies of all medical Records obtained within ten (10) days of receipt.

Defendant(s) may use any authorization to obtain Medical records and if it does, copies of those Records shall be supplied to plaintiff within ten (10) days of receipt.

(4) Physical Examination:

(a) Examination of ———————— shall be held ————————————

(b) A copy of the physician's report shall be furnished to plaintiff within ——— days of the examination.

(5) Depositions: Depositions of { } Plaintiff(s) { } Defendant(s) { } All Parties and non-party Witness

shall be completed by: ————————————————————

————————————————————————————————————

————————————————————————————————————

(6) Other Disclosure:

————————————————————————————————————

————————————————————————————————————

(7) End Date for All Disclosure {must be within 12 months}: _____

(8) Impleader: Shall be completed on or before _____.

A copy of this order shall be served with any third-party summons, and shall apply to any added parties. If the added party wishes a modification of this order, it must schedule a conference or submit an amended schedule signed by all parties. Any conference shall be scheduled by phoning chambers to select a date. The conference shall be held or the amended schedule submitted to the Court within thirty (30) days of service of the third-party summons.

(9) Motions: Any dispositive motion(s) shall be made <u>returnable</u> on or before _____. All motions and answering papers are to be <u>filed with</u> the Supreme Court Clerk.

(a) *Motions:* The filing of <u>any</u> motion shall follow the following procedure.

All original motion (or cross-motion) papers, including any order to show cause shall be filed with the County Supreme Court Clerk, after paying the required motion fee to the County Clerk. All answering papers shall be filed with the Supreme Court Clerk.

(10) Note of Issue: _____ shall file a note of issue/certificate of readiness on or before _____. A copy of this stipulation and order, an affirmation stating that the terms of the stipulation and order have been complied with, and an affidavit of service of the affirmation and note of issue shall be served and filed with the note of issue on or before said date.

(11) Discovery disputes or issues: If there is a discovery issue (at any time), the parties agree as follows:

To comply with 22 NYCRR 202.07 to resolve the dispute and if it cannot be resolved, then to immediately <u>telephone</u> chambers and schedule a conference on a date convenient to all counsel for the purpose of resolving any discovery dispute before filing any discovery motion. Every effort shall be made to select a date convenient to all counsel.

At the conference the Court will hear all counsel and either issue a decision, reserve decision or direct that formal motion papers be filed and served.

At least two days before the conference, each party shall deliver to the Court a statement outlining the dispute and stating its position. *It should be delivered so that the Court will have time to read it.*

(12) The final pre-trial conference shall be held at the chambers of the Hon. Joseph C. Teresi at a time to be noticed by this court, at which time counsel for each party must be present and certify to the court that:

    a. discovery has been completed

    b. settlement discussions have been unsuccessful

    c. the case is ready for trial

(13) Expert Disclosure: Except as otherwise directed by the Court, a party who has the burden of proof on a claim, cause of action, damage or defense shall serve its response to an expert demand served pursuant to CPLR 3101(d) on or before the filing of the note of issue, and sixty (60) days after receipt of that response, any opposing party shall serve its answering response pursuant to CPLR 3101(d). Any amended or supplemental expert disclosure shall be allowed only with the permission of the Court. Unless the Court directs otherwise, a party who fails to comply with this rule is precluded from offering the testimony and opinions of the expert for whom a timely response has not be given.

The word "expert" shall include, but is not limited to, any physician, dentist, chiropractor, psychiatrist, psychologist, other health care provider of any speciality, economist, engineer, architect, lawyer, accountant, appraiser, rehabilitation counselor or other person who will testify concerning his/her qualifications and give opinions concerning the issues in the case. However, "expert" shall not include a treating physician or other treating health care provider whose records(s), and report(s) have been timely provided.

Any motion to preclude, or limit expert testimony under this rule must be returnable as soon as practicable but no later than forty-five(45) days of its receipt or the motion will be waived.

(14) It is further ordered that any objections concerning the propriety of questions or other applications made during the course of the examinations provided for herein shall be immediately presented orally and ruled upon by this Court, or to a Judicial Hearing Officer designated to entertain such objections, with all attorneys physically present or by telephone conference call, at the Court's discretion.

(15) Extensions: Extensions of this stipulation are granted only if necessary. An Application may be made by (1) submitting an explanation outlining the discovery completed and outstanding together with an amended schedule on a "consent letter" showing all dates to be affected, (2) or by phoning chambers and scheduling a conference on a date convenient to all counsel. Any application must be received by the Court before the last date in the stipulation to be amended.

In extending discovery, all discovery shall be completed within twelve (12) months of the filing of the Request for Judicial intervention (RJI) form. See 22 NYCRR 202.12.

(16) Failure to comply with any of these directives may result in the imposition of costs or sanctions or other action authorized by law.

(17) In the event a note of issue is not timely filed, the Court will declare this case ready for trial and schedule a final conference. If that occurs, no extensions of any deadlines will be granted, and any discovery not requested will be deemed waived.

(18) Conferences: Any conferences requested by counsel shall be scheduled by telephoning chambers, and giving date(s) on which all counsel are available. The conference will be scheduled on a date convenient to counsel and the Court.

DATED:

_____   _____
                                    Attorney for Plaintiff(s)

                                    _____
                                    Attorney for Defendant(s)

                                    _____
                                    Attorney for Defendant(s)

Dated:
        Albany, New York

SO ORDERED!

_____

J.S.C.

ADDITIONAL DIRECTIVES

In addition to the directives set forth on the annexed pages, it is further **ORDERED** as follows:

_____

_____

_____

_____

_____

Dated:

SO ORDERED!

Joseph C. Teresi, J.S.C.

App. 2. Tax Certiorari Order

STATE OF NEW YORK
SUPREME COURT   COUNTY OF

_____

                    Petitioner(s),

  -against-   **ORDER**
                                     Index No.
                                     RJI No.

_____

                    Respondent(s)

_____

   The Petitioner(s) herein, by his/her/their/its attorney(s), _____ and Respondent(s), by his/her/their/its attorney, _____, having stipulated to the entry of an Order extending the time for the parties to file their respective appraisal reports in the above-referenced tax certiorari proceedings:

   NOW, upon motion of _____ attorney for Respondent(s), it is

   ORDERED, that his proceeding shall be dismissed without further order of this Court unless the Petitioner(s) file(s) an appraisal report and Statement of Income and Expenses in the above referenced certiorari proceeding on or before _____; and is further

   ORDERED, that in the event that the Petitioner(s) shall file the appraisal report and serve the income and expense statement within the times prescribed by this Order, the Respondent(s) file an appraisal report in the above-referenced certiorari proceeding on or before _____, and it further

   ORDERED, that upon file in their respective appraisal report, each party shall serve upon their adversaries a notice of the date of such filing.

   SO STIPULATED!

   Dated:

                                     _____
                                     Petitioner

   Dated:

                                     _____
                                     Respondent

   SO ORDERED!

   Dated: Albany, New York

                                     _____
_____   Joseph C. Teresi, J.S.C.

FORMS

NAME CHANGE

Form 1.1. Overview

Name Change Forms & Requirements

Please note: The forms below are meant to provide basic information for proceeding with a name change application. Before starting a proceeding, check with the court in your local jurisdiction.

Name Change Requirements:

1. If born in the State of New York, original or certified copy of Birth Certificate

2. Self–Addressed/Stamped Envelope

3. Original and copy of Name Change Order & Petition

4. For name changes in Supreme Court, in some counties, you may need to file a Request for Judicial Intervention form in triplicate (Original & 2 copies)

5. For name changes in Supreme Court, there is a fee of $210, made payable to the local County Clerk. The fee to file in NYC Civil Court is $65.00.

6. Notice: Civil Rights Law Sec. 62

If the petition be to change the name of an infant, notice of the time and place when and where the petition will be presented must be served, in like manner as a notice of motion upon an attorney in an action, upon (a) both parents of the infant, if they be living, unless the petition be made by one of the parents, in which case notice must be served upon the other, if he or she be living, and (b) the general guardian or guardian of the person, if there be one. But if any of the persons, required to be given notice by this section, reside without the state, then the notice required by this section must be sent by registered mail to the last known address of the person to be served. If it appears to the satisfaction of the court that a person required to be given notice by this section cannot be located with due diligence within the state, and that such person has no known address without the state, then the court may dispense with notice or require notice to be given to such persons and in such manner as the court thinks proper.

Name Change Forms:

Filing in NYC Civil Court

Name Change Petition

Name Change Order

Sample Publication Notice

Form 1.2. Petition

_____ COURT OF THE STATE OF NEW YORK

COUNTY OF _____

---x

IN THE MATTER OF THE APPLICATION OF

_____,   **PETITION
FOR A
NAME CHANGE**

Petitioner,

Index # _____

FOR LEAVE TO CHANGE _____ NAME TO:

_____
(His/Her)

_____

(Proposed New Name)

---x

TO THE _____ COURT OF THE STATE OF NEW YORK:

The Petition of _____ respectfully shows this court:

    1. The petitioner resides at No._____, in

the _____ of _____, County of _____, and has so resided for
(Street Address)

a period of ___ years and ___ months prior to the making of this application.

2. The petitioner _____ was born at _____ on the ___ day of
_____, ___ and is now ___ years of age. (Attached hereto and made a part
hereof is a copy of the petitioner's birth certificate.)

3. The Petitioner proposes to change said His/ Her name to _____.

4. The petitioner is a natural born citizen of the United States.

5. The petitioner is / is not married and has / has not been married previously.

6. The petitioner: (Check One):

___ has never been convicted of a crime.

___ has been convicted of a crime, the details of which are attached in a separate
statement, annexed hereto and made a part hereof.

7. The petitioner has never been adjudicated a bankrupt.

8. There are no judgments or liens of record and no actions pending against your
in petitioner in any court of this state or of the United States, or of any governmental subdivision thereof, or elsewhere, whether the court be of record or not. There
are no bankruptcy or insolvency proceedings, voluntary or involuntary, pending
against your petitioner in any court whatsoever or before any officer, person, body
or board having jurisdiction thereof and your petitioner has not, at any time, made
any assignments for the benefit of creditor. (If there have been, enter details
instead of previous statement).

9. There are no claims, demands, liabilities or obligations of any kind whatsoever
on a written instrument or otherwise against your infants under the only names by
which they have been known, which are the names sought herein to be abandoned,
and your infants have no creditors who may be adversely affected or prejudiced in
any way by the proposed change of name. (If there have been, enter details instead
of previous statement).

10. The petitioner is / is not responsible for child support obligations. (If there are
child support obligations, details are attached in a separate statement)

11. The petitioner is / is not responsible for spousal support obligations. (If there
are spousal support obligations, details are attached in a separate statement)

12.   The grounds of this application to change the petitioner's name are as follows: _____.

13.   No previous application has been made for the relief sought herein.

        WHEREFORE, petitioner respectfully prays for an order permitting the petitioner _____ to assume the name _____

        in place of that of _____.

                                              (Current Name)

DATED: _____, 20 ___.

                                              _____

                                                (Signature of petitioner)

        STATE OF NEW YORK   )

                                    ss.: **INDIVIDUAL VERIFICATION**

        COUNTY OF _____)

THIS IS TO CERTIFY that **I,** _____ being duly sworn deposes and says: your deponent is the Petitioner in the within action; your deponent has read the foregoing Petition and knows the contents thereof. The same is true to deponent's own knowledge, except as to the matters therein stated to be alleged on information and belief, and as to those matters deponent believes it to be true.

        Sworn to before me this

        ___ day of _____, 20 ___   _____

                                                              Petitioner

        _____
              Notary Public

Form 1.3.   Order

At a _____ Term, Part ___ of
the _____ Court of the State
of New York, held in and for the
County of _____, _____,
_____, New York on the ___
day of _____, 20 ___

PRESENT: HON. _____

--X

IN THE MATTER OF THE APPLICATION OF

_____   NAME CHANGE ORDER

FOR LEAVE TO CHANGE HIS / HER NAME TO: INDEX NO.

_____

--X

Upon reading and filing the petition of _____ verified the ___ day of
_____ 200 ___ praying for leave to change his name / her name to _____
and the court being satisfied thereby that the petition is true and that there is no
reasonable objection to the change of name proposed.

Now on motion of _____ Petitioner, it is

ORDERED that the petitioner, _____ having been born in the City of
_____, County of _____ in the State of _____ Birth certificate
_____ [Birth certificate is not available] shall be known by the name
_____ which he / she is hereby authorized to assume, and it is further

ORDERED that this order shall be entered and the papers upon which it was
granted shall be filed, prior to the publication hereinafter directed, in the office of
the Clerk of the County of _____, wherein petitioner resides, and it is further

ORDERED that at least once within sixty days after the making of this order, a
notice in substantially the following form, prescribed by article 6 of the civil rights
law of the State of New York shall be published in the _____ a newspaper
published in the said County of _____:

Notice is hereby given that an order entered by the _____ Court
_____ County, on the ___ day of _____ 200 ___, bearing Index No.
_____, a copy of which may be examined at the office of the clerk, located
at _____, _____, N.Y. grants me the right, to assume the name
_____. My present address is _____; The date of my birth is
_____; My present name is _____, and it is further

ORDERED that proof of publication as heretofore directed shall be filed in the office
of the _____ County Clerk within 90 days after the signing of this order, and it
is further

ORDERED that upon full compliance with the provisions of this order, petitioner
shall be known by the name _____ which he / she is authorized to assume, and
by no other name.

ENTER

_____

J.S.C.

Form 1.4. Notice

SAMPLE PUBLICATION NOTICE

Notice is hereby given that an order entered by the Supreme Court of Rockland County on May   , 1997, index #   , /97, copy of which may be examined at the office of the County Clerk, located in Rockland County, 11 New Hempstead Rd, New City, grants me the right affected on June   , 1997 to assume the name of Kevin Michael   . My present name is Kevin   . My address   is 137   Dr., W. Haver straw, NY. My place of   birth is Nyack, New York on May   , 1995.

REQUEST FOR JUDICIAL INTERVENTION

Form 2. Request for Judicial Intervention

REQUEST FOR JUDICIAL INTERVENTION UCS–840 (3/2011)	For Court Clerk Use Only:
	IAS Entry Date

Supreme _____ COURT, COUNTY OF _____

	Judge Assigned

Index No: _____ Date Index Issued: _____

CAPTION: Enter the complete case caption. Do not use et al or et ano. If more space is required, attach a caption rider sheet.	RJI Date

Plaintiff(s)/Petitioner(s)

-against-

Defendant(s)/Respondent(s)

NATURE OF ACTION OR PROCEEDING: Check ONE box only and specify where indicated.

MATRIMONIAL

○ Contested

○ Uncontested
   NOTE: For all Matrimonial actions where the
   parties have children under the age of 18, complete
   and attach the **MATRIMONIAL RJI Addendum.**

TORTS

○ Asbestos
○ Breast Implant

○ Environmental: _____
              (specify)

○ Medical, Dental, or Podiatric Malpractice
○ Motor Vehicle
○ Products Liability: _____
              (specify)
○ Other Negligence: _____
              (specify)
○ Other Professional Malpractice: _____
              (specify)

○ Other Tort: _____
              (specify)

OTHER MATTERS

○ Certificate of Incorporation/Dissolution [see **NOTE**
   under Commercial]
○ Emergency Medical Treatment
○ Habeas Corpus
○ Local Court Appeal
○ Mechanic's Lien
○ Name Change
○ Pistol Permit Revocation Hearing
○ Sale or Finance of Religious/ Not–for–Profit
   Property
○ Other: _____
              (specify)

COMMERCIAL

○ Business Entity (including corporations, partnerships, LLCs,
   etc.)
○ Contract
○ Insurance (where insurer is a party, except arbitration)
○ UCC (including sales, negotiable instruments)
○ Other Commercial: _____
              (specify)

NOTE: For Commercial Division assignment requests, complete and attach the **COMMERCIAL DIV RJI Addendum.**

REAL PROPERTY: How many properties does the application include? _____

○ Condemnation
○ Foreclosure
Property Address: _____
       Street Address   City   State   Zip
   NOTE: For Foreclosure actions involving a one- to
   four-family, owner-occupied, residential property, or an
   owner-occupied condominium, complete and attach the
   FORECLOSURE RJI Addendum.
○ Tax Certiorari—Section: _____ Block: _____ Lot: _____
○ Other Real Property: _____
              (specify)

SPECIAL PROCEEDINGS

○ CPLR Article 75 (Arbitration) [see **NOTE** under
   Commercial]
○ CPLR Article 78 (Body or Officer)
○ Election Law
○ MHL Article 9.60 (Kendra's Law)
○ MHL Article 10 (Sex Offender Confinement–Initial)
○ MHL Article 10 (Sex Offender Confinement–Review)
○ MHL Article 81 (Guardianship)
○ Other Mental Hygiene: _____
              (specify)

○ Other Special Proceeding: _____
              (specify)

STATUS OF ACTION OR PROCEEDING: Answer YES or NO for EVERY question AND enter additional
information where indicated.

	YES	NO	
Has a summons and complaint or summons w/notice been filed?	○	○	If yes, date filed: _____
Is this action/proceeding being filed post–judgment?	○	○	If yes, judgment date: _____

NATURE OF JUDICIAL INTERVENTION: Check ONE box only AND enter additional information where indicated.

- ○ Infant's Compromise
- ○ Note of Issue and/or Certificate of Readiness
- ○ Notice of Medical, Dental, or Podiatric Malpractice
- ○ Notice of Motion
- ○ Notice of Petition
- ○ Order to Show Cause
- ○ Other Ex Parte Application
- ○ Poor Person Application
- ○ Request for Preliminary Conference
- ○ Residential Mortgage Foreclosure Settlement Conference
- ○ Writ of Habeas Corpus
- ○ Other (specify): _____

Date Issue Joined: _____
Relief Sought: _____ Return Date: _____
Relief Sought: _____ Return Date: _____
Relief Sought: _____ Return Date: _____
Relief Sought: _____

RELATED CASES: List any related actions. For Matrimonial actions, include any related criminal and/or Family Court cases. If additional space is required, complete and attach the **RJI Addendum**. If none, leave blank.

Case Title	Index/Case No.	Court	Judge (if assigned)	Relationship to Instant Case

PARTIES: If additional space is required, complete and attach the **RJI Addendum**.
For parties without an attorney, check "Un–Rep" box AND enter party address, phone number and e-mail address in "Attorneys" space.

Un–Rep	Parties:	Attorneys:		Issue Joined (Y/N):	Insurance Carrier(s):
	List parties in caption order and indicate party role(s) (e.g. defendant; 3rd–party plaintiff).	Provide name, firm name, business address, phone number and e-mail address of all attorneys that have appeared in the case.			

	Last Name	Last Name	First Name	○ YES	
☐	First Name Primary Role:	Firm Name			
	Secondary Role (if any):	Street Address	City	State	Zip	○ NO
		Phone	Fax	e-mail	

	Last Name	Last Name	First Name	○ YES	
☐	First Name Primary Role:	Firm Name			
	Secondary Role (if any):	Street Address	City	State	Zip	○ NO
		Phone	Fax	e-mail	

	Last Name	Last Name	First Name	○ YES	
☐	First Name Primary Role:	Firm Name			
	Secondary Role (if any):	Street Address	City	State	Zip	○ NO
		Phone	Fax	e–mail	

	Last Name	Last Name	First Name	○ YES	
☐	First Name Primary Role:	Firm Name			
	Secondary Role (if any):	Street Address	City	State	Zip	○ NO
		Phone	Fax	e-mail	

I AFFIRM UNDER THE PENALTY OF PERJURY THAT, TO MY KNOWLEDGE, OTHER THAN AS NOTED ABOVE, THERE ARE AND HAVE BEEN NO RELATED ACTIONS OR PROCEEDINGS, NOR HAS A REQUEST FOR JUDICIAL INTERVENTION PREVIOUSLY BEEN FILED IN THIS ACTION OR PROCEEDING.

Dated: _____

_____
SIGNATURE

_____
ATTORNEY REGISTRATION NUMBER

_____
PRINT OR TYPE NAME

Request for Judicial Intervention Addendum

UCS–840A (3/ 2011)

Supreme _____ COURT, COUNTY OF _____ Index No: _____

For use when additional space is needed to provide party or related case information.

PARTIES: For parties without an attorney, check " Un–Rep" box AND enter party address, phone number and e-mail address in " Attorneys" space.

Un–Rep	Parties:	Attorneys:		Issue Joined (Y/N):	Insurance Carrier(s):
	List parties in caption order and indicate party role(s) (e.g. defendant; 3rd–party plaintiff).	Provide name, firm name, business address, phone number and e-mail address of all attorneys that have appeared in the case.			

Un-Rep	Parties	Attorneys		Issue Joined	Insurance Carrier
	Last Name	Last Name	First Name	○ YES	
☐	First Name / Primary Role:	Firm Name			
	Secondary Role (if any):	Street Address City State Zip		○ NO	
		Phone Fax e-mail			
	Last Name	Last Name	First Name	○ YES	
☐	First Name / Primary Role:	Firm Name			
	Secondary Role (if any):	Street Address City State Zip		○ NO	
		Phone Fax e-mail			
	Last Name	Last Name	First Name	○ YES	
☐	First Name / Primary Role:	Firm Name			
	Secondary Role (if any):	Street Address City State Zip		○ NO	
		Phone Fax e-mail			
	Last Name	Last Name	First Name	○ YES	
☐	First Name / Primary Role:	Firm Name			
	Secondary Role (if any):	Street Address City State Zip		○ NO	
		Phone Fax e-mail			
	Last Name	Last Name	First Name	○ YES	
☐	First Name / Primary Role:	Firm Name			
	Secondary Role (if any):	Street Address City State Zip		○ NO	
		Phone Fax e-mail			
	Last Name	Last Name	First Name	○ YES	
☐	First Name / Primary Role:	Firm Name			
	Secondary Role (if any):	Street Address City State Zip		○ NO	
		Phone Fax e-mail			

RELATED CASES: List any related actions. For Matrimonial actions, include any related criminal and/or Family Court cases.

Case Title	Index/Case No.	Court	Judge (if assigned)	Relationship to Instant Case

_____

_____

_____

SUPREME COURT OF THE STATE OF NEW YORK

COUNTY OF _____

- x

                    Plaintiff(s)/Petitioner(s)

-against-

                    Defendant(s)/Respondent(s)

- x

UCS–840C
3/2011

Index No. _____

RJI No. (if any) _____

COMMERCIAL DIVISION
Request for Judicial Intervention Addendum

COMPLETE WHERE APPLICABLE [add additional pages if needed]:

Plaintiff/Petitioner's cause(s) of action [check all that apply]:

☐ Breach of contract or fiduciary duty, fraud, misrepresentation, business tort (e.g. unfair competition), or statutory and/or common law violation where the breach or violation is alleged to arise out of business dealings (e.g. sales of assets or securities; corporate restructuring; partnership, shareholder, joint venture, and other business agreements; trade secrets; restrictive covenants; and employment agreements not including claims that principally involve alleged discriminatory practices)

☐ Transactions governed by the Uniform Commercial Code (exclusive of those concerning individual cooperative or condominium units)

☐ Transactions involving commercial real property, including Yellowstone injunctions and excluding actions for the payment of rent only

☐ Shareholder derivative actions — without consideration of the monetary threshold

☐ Commercial class actions — without consideration of the monetary threshold

☐ Business transactions involving or arising out of dealings with commercial banks and other financial institutions

☐ Internal affairs of business organizations

☐ Malpractice by accountants or actuaries, and legal malpractice arising out of representation in commercial matters

☐ Environmental insurance coverage

☐ Commercial insurance coverage (e.g. directors and officers, errors and omissions, and business interruption coverage)

☐ Dissolution of corporations, partnerships, limited liability companies, limited liability partnerships and joint ventures — without consideration of the monetary threshold

☐ Applications to stay or compel arbitration and affirm or disaffirm arbitration awards and related injunctive relief pursuant to CPLR Article 75 involving any of the foregoing enumerated commercial issues — without consideration of the monetary threshold

Plaintiff/Petitioner's claim for compensatory damages [exclusive of punitive damages, interest, costs and counsel fees claimed]:

     $ _____

Plaintiff/Petitioner's claim for equitable or declaratory relief [brief description]:

_____

Defendant/Respondent's counterclaim(s)
[brief description, including claim for monetary relief]:

_____

_____

I REQUEST THAT THIS CASE BE ASSIGNED TO THE COMMERCIAL DIVISION. I CERTIFY THAT THE CASE MEETS THE JURISDICTIONAL REQUIREMENTS OF THE COMMERCIAL DIVISION SET FORTH IN 22 NYCRR § 202.70(a), (b) AND (c).

Dated: _____

                              _____
                              SIGNATURE

                              _____
                              PRINT OR TYPE NAME

UCS–840M
3/2011

MATRIMONIAL Request for Judicial Intervention Addendum

Supreme _____ COURT, COUNTY OF _____ INDEX NO. _____

For use when there are children under the age of 18 who are subject to the matrimonial action.

Plaintiff

Last Name: _____ First Name: _____ Date of Birth: _____

Prior Names (List any other names used, including   **Gender:** ☐ Male ☐ Female
maiden and/or former married names):

Last Name: _____ First Name: _____
Last Name: _____ First Name: _____
Last Name: _____ First Name: _____

Present Address: _____ New York _____
                        (Street Address)   (City)   (State)   (Zip)

Address History
for past 3 years: _____
                        (Street Address)   (City)   (State)   (Zip)

_____
(Street Address)   (City)   (State)   (Zip)

_____
(Street Address)   (City)   (State)   (Zip)

Defendant

Last Name: _____ First Name: _____ Date of Birth: _____

Prior Names (List any other names used, including   **Gender:** ☐ Male ☐ Female
maiden and/or former married names):

Last Name: _____ First Name: _____
Last Name: _____ First Name: _____
Last Name: _____ First Name: _____

Present Address: _____ New York _____
                        (Street Address)   (City)   (State)   (Zip)

Address History
for past 3 years: _____
                        (Street Address)   (City)   (State)   (Zip)

_____
(Street Address)   (City)   (State)   (Zip)

_____
(Street Address)   (City)   (State)   (Zip)

Children

Last Name: _____ First Name: _____ Date of Birth: _____ Gender: ☐ M ☐ F

Last Name: _____ First Name: _____ Date of Birth: _____ Gender: ☐ M ☐ F

Last Name: _____ First Name: _____ Date of Birth: _____ Gender: ☐ M ☐ F

Last Name: _____ First Name: _____ Date of Birth: _____ Gender: ☐ M ☐ F

Last Name: _____ First Name: _____ Date of Birth: _____ Gender: ☐ M ☐ F

SMALL CLAIMS ASSESSMENT REVIEW (SCAR) PETITION

Form 3. Small Claims Assessment Review (SCAR) Petition

PART 1
GENERAL INFORMATION

SUPREME COURT, COUNTY OF _____

1. Filing # _____ Calendar # _____

2. Assessing Unit _____

3. Date of final completion and filing of assessment roll _____

   (a) Total   _____

   (b) Exempt amount   _____

   (c) Taxable assessed value (3a-3b)   _____

4. Date of filing (or mailing) petition   _____

5. Name of owner or owners of property:

Post Office Address:

Telephone #:

6. If applicable, name and address of representative of owner, if representative is filing application: (Owner must complete Designation of Representative section.)

Telephone#:

7. Description of property as it appears on the assessment roll.

Tax Map # _____ Section _____ Block _____ Lot _____

8. Location of property (street, road, highway number, and city, town or village)

_____

_____

PART II
GROUNDS FOR PETITION

A.   Assessment requested on the complaint form filed with the Board of Assessment Review

         1.   Total assessment
         2.   Exempt amount, if any   _____
         3.   Taxable assessment   _____

B.   CALCULATION OF EQUALIZED VALUE AND MAXIMUM REDUCTION IN ASSESSMENT
      1. [ ]   Property is NOT in a special assessing unit.

ASSESSED VALUE ÷ EQUALIZATION RATE = EQUALIZED VALUE

_____ _____ _____

2. [ ] Property IS in a special assessing unit.

ASSESSED VALUE ÷ CLASS ONE RATIO = EQUALIZED VALUE

_____ _____ _____

3. [ ] If the EQUALIZED VALUE exceeds $150,000, enter the ASSESSED VALUE here: _____
Multiply the ASSESSED VALUE by: × .25
Enter the result here:
The result is the maximum total assessment request reduction allowable.

C.   [ ] UNEQUAL ASSESSMENT: The total assessment is unequal because the property is assessed at a higher percentage of full (market) value than (check one).
[ ] (a) the average of all other property on the assessment roll, or
[ ] (b) the average of residential property on the assessment roll.

Full (market) value of property: $ _____

Based on one or more of the following, petitioner believes this property should be assessed at __ % of full (market) value:

1. [ ] The latest State equalization rate for the assessing unit in which the property is located (enter latest equalization rate: _____ %).

2. [ ] The latest residential assessment ratio for the assessing unit in which the property is located (enter residential assessment ratio: _____%).

3. [ ] A sample of market values of recent sales prices and assessments of comparable residential properties on which petitioner relies for objection (list parcels on a separate sheet and attach).

4. [ ] Statements of the assessor or other local official that property has been placed on the roll at _____%.

Petitioner believes the total assessment should be reduced to $ _____. This amount may not be less than the total assessment amount indicated in Section A (1), or Section B (3), whichever is greater.

D.   [ ] EXCESSIVE ASSESSMENT:

1. [ ] The total assessed value exceeds the full (market) value of the property.
Total assessed value of property: $ _____
Complainant believes the total assessment should be reduced to a full value of $ _____
Attach list of parcels upon which complainant relies for objection, if applicable.
This amount may not be less than the amount indicated in Section A (1), or Section B (3).

2. [ ] The taxable assessed value is excessive because of the denial of all or a portion of a partial exemption. Specify exemption _____ (e.g., aged, clergy, veterans, etc.).
Amount of exemption claimed: $ _____. Amount granted, if any: $ _____. This amount may not be greater than the amount indicated in A (2).
If application for exemption was filed, attach a copy of application to this petition.

E.   INFORMATION TO SUPPORT THE FULL (MARKET) VALUE CLAIMED

1. [ ] Purchase price of property $ _____
Date of purchase _____
Relationship, if any, between seller and purchaser _____

2. [ ] If property has been recently offered for sale:
When and for how long: _____
How offered:
Asking price: $

3. [ ] If property has been recently appraised:
When: _____ By Whom: _____
Purpose of appraisal:
Appraised value: $ _____

4. [ ] If buildings have been recently remodeled, constructed, or additional improvements made, state:
Year remodeled, constructed, or additions made:
Date commenced: _____ Date completed: _____
Cost: $ _____

5. [ ] Amount for which your property is insured: $ _____
Name of insurance company and policy number: _____

6. [   ] Purchase price of comparable property(ies) recently sold: $ _____

_____

PART III
LISTING OF TAXING DISTRICTS

_____

Names of Taxing Districts

1.   COUNTY:

2.   TOWN:

3.   VILLAGE:

4.   SCHOOL DISTRICT

PART IV

DESIGNATION OF REPRESENTATIVE OF FILE PETITION

_____ I, _____, as petitioner (or officer thereof) hereby designate _____ to act as my representative in any and all proceedings before the Small Claims Assessment Review of the Supreme Court in _____ County for purposes of reviewing the assessment of my real property as it appears on the ___ year assessment roll of _____ (assessing unit) _____

_____

Signature of Owner

(Or officer thereof)

_____

Date

PART V

ELIGIBILITY AND CERTIFICATION

I certify that:

(a) The owner has previously filed a complaint required for administrative review of assessments.

(b) The property is improved by a one, two or three family, owner-occupied residential structure used exclusively for residential purposes, and is not a condominium; except a condominium designated as Class 1 in Nassau County or as "homestead" Class in an approved assessing unit.

(c) The requested assessment is not lower than the assessment requested on the complaint filed with the assessor or the Board of Assessment Review.

(d) If the equalized value of the property exceeds $150,000, the requested assessment reduction does not exceed 25 percent of the assessed value.

(e) I have mailed, by certified mail, return receipt requested, or, delivered in person, within ten days after the day of filing this petition with the County Clerk, one (1) copy of this petition to the clerk of the assessing unit, or if there by no such clerk, then to the officer who performs the customary duties of that official.

(f) I have mailed by regular mail within 10 (ten) days after the filing of the Petition with the County Clerk one (1) copy of the Petition to:

(a) The clerk of the school district(s)* within which the real property is located, or if there be no clerk or the name and address cannot be obtained, then to a trustee, and

(b) The treasurer of the county in which the property is located.

I certify that all statements made on this application are true and correct to the best of my knowledge and belief, and I understand that the making of any willful false statement of material fact herein will subject me to the provisions of the Penal law relevant to the making and filing of false instruments.

_____

_____ Signature of owner or
representative

(*NOTE: You are not required to file with the Buffalo City School District, the Rochester City School District, the Syracuse City School District or the Yonders City School District.)

SURROGATE'S COURTS

SMALL ESTATE PROCEEDING

Doc. 1.   Article 13 Instructions

INSTRUCTIONS AND WORKSHEET FOR AFFI-DAVIT OF VOLUNTARY ADMINISTRATION -Complete all sections of the Article 13 Affidavit.

VOLUNTARY ADMINISTRATION or SMALL ESTATE PROCEEDING may be used when a fiduciary is needed to transfer estate assets (personal property only) and the value of the assets does not exceed $20,000 (for decedents dying on or after 8/30/96), exclusive of property set off under EPTL 5–3.1. This is a legal proceeding and you may need the assistance of a lawyer. If you do not have a lawyer, you may wish to contact the Lawyer Referral Service of your local County Bar Association for assistance in obtaining one. Court employees cannot dispense legal advice. Generally, you will file the proceeding with the Court in the County where the decedent resided at the time of his death.

ELIGIBILITY TO SERVE: You must be a named executor or alternate executor in the decedent's will, or a distributee (as that term is defined in EPTL 1–2.5 and 4–1.1) of the decedent, or a court appointed guardian of the property of an infant distributee to be eligible to serve as Voluntary Administrator. If you are not eligible to serve, or, if you are applying solely to pay a Medicaid or other public assistance claim, contact the Public Administrator/Treasurer of your County.

DEATH CERTIFICATE: A certified copy of the death certificate (with raised seal) must be filed with the affidavit. Court employees cannot make a photocopy of this document.

FILING FEE: $1.00. Please make check or money order payable to the Surrogate's Court of whatever County you are filing in.

WILL: If the decedent had a Will, the original Will must be filed with the affidavit. Make a copy for yourself, **without** removing the staples.

ENVELOPES: Submit 4 in × 9.5 in. post paid envelopes addressed to each person listed in items 6 & 7 of the affidavit, plus one return addressed envelope to mail documents to the Voluntary Administrator or the attorney.

WORKSHEET

DISTRIBUTEES:

Complete the following showing the classification of the decedent's distributees (nearest blood relatives): [Information is required only as to those classes of surviving relatives who are deemed to be distributees

as defined in EPTL 4–1.1. Indicate the number of survivors in each category.]

  A. Spouse (husband or Wife)

If "no", was the decedent divorced at time of death?

  B.1 Marital and/or adopted children.

    Number of Survivors [   ]

Descendants of predeceased marital and/or adopted children

    Number of Survivors [   ]

  B.2 Non marital children

    Number of Survivors [   ]

[Each of the above boxes must indicate either "no" or "yes". If "yes", the number of survivors in each category must be shown. If the number of survivors is unknown, insert a "?" and explain in detail in Paragraph 7. If subparagraphs a, b-1 or b-2 indicates "yes", complete item b-3, but do not answer items c through h below. If a, b-1 and b-2 all indicate "no", you must continue to complete the classifications below (in the order shown) until the answer is "yes" to ONE of the classes of distributees or the answer is "no" to ALL of the categories shown.]

  C. Father or Mother

    Number of Survivors [   ]

  D. Brothers or sisters (either whole or half-blood)

    Number of Survivors [   ]

Descendants of predeceased brothers/sisters

    Number of Survivors [   ]

  E. Grandparents

    Number of Survivors [   ]

  F. Aunts/Uncles

    Number of Survivors [   ]

  G. Descendants of predeceased aunts/uncles (1st cousins)

    Number of Survivors [   ]

  H. Children of predeceased first cousins

    Number of Survivors [   ]

EXEMPT PROPERTY:

The surviving spouse of a decedent, or if there is none, the surviving children under the age of 21 years old are entitled to claim certain property from the decedent without including it in the calculation of estate assets, and free from the claims of any creditor except for funeral expenses. This property is referred to as "exempt property", and is not included in the calculation of the value of the estate for determining if the estate may be administered as a "Small Estate". In order to determine the "exempt property", complete the following:

(A) No exemption is claimed []

or

(B) An exemption is claimed for [ ] spouse [ ] children under 21 years of age for the following classifications of property under Estates, Powers & Trusts Law Section 5–3.1 (a):

(1) Furnishings, appliances, provisions, etc. (max. exemption $10,000) $ _____

(2) Family pictures and books (max. exemption $1,000) _____

(3) Domestic animals, farm machinery, etc. (max. exemption $15,000) _____

(4) One motor vehicle (max. exemption $15,000) _____

(5) Money or other personal property (max. exemption $15,000) _____

Total exempt $ _____

A Certificate should NOT be needed for the above items. Please check with the appropriate party.

If you will need a certificate to obtain or transfer any item of exempt property, describe (i.e., HSBC Savings Account # 12345; 1997 Dodge Stratus auto, VIN # 12345678) item(s) and value below and return this form to the Court along with the Affidavit:

Item: Value:

COMPLETING THE AFFIDAVIT

CAPTION: Write the decedent's name in the caption box the same as the signature appears on the will or, if there is no will, as the name appears on the death certificate. Complete the blanks with name of the State and County in which you (affiant) reside. Do not fill in the file number, as the court will assign the number when filed. Fill in your name and address on the top lines above the numbered paragraphs.

(1) Complete the blanks.

(2) Complete date and place of death of decedent.

(3) Complete decedent's address at the time of death. Nursing homes are usually NOT considered to be a residence, so the address where the decedent lived before entering a nursing home.

(4) Check the appropriate box. If the decedent died with a will, the original will must be filed with the affidavit. Photocopies of the will are not acceptable.

(5) Read and verify.

(6) Read and verify.

(7) Complete the blanks. Write the names and addresses (with ZIP) of the decedent's distributees identified in the distributee worksheet on page 1 of these instructions and their relationship to the decedent. Include age if under 18.

(8) If decedent left a will, list the names and addresses of the beneficiaries. Please address the post paid envelopes to each of the persons who are listed as a distributee in item 6 of the affidavit and, if there is a will, to all of the persons listed in item 7 of the affidavit.

(9) List the assets for which you will require a certificate from the court, together with that item's value.

(i.e., "1997 Dodge Stratus auto, VIN #12345678 — $2,000, etc.) Do not repeat items listed above in the "Exempt Property" worksheet.

(10) Furnish the names of creditors of the deceased, how much was paid by your or others to them (for which reimbursement is sought) and how much remains unpaid. If the deceased was receiving Medicaid or other public assistance, check with the County Department of Social Services to determine the amount of the claim, if any.

(11) The Voluntary Administrator will be undertaking serious responsibilities and obligations. Please review these carefully.

(13) You will be required to file a "Report and Account" with the court detailing the administration of the estate and the disposition of assets. Be sure you or the Voluntary Administrator understand these representations. Keep records and receipts to show what you have done with the property and money that you took control of as Voluntary Administrator.

Your application to be appointed Voluntary Administrator must be accompanied by all necessary fees, postage paid envelopes addressed to all distributees listed in paragraph #6 and all the beneficiaries listed in paragraph #7, and a return addressed envelope for the court to send certificates to the Voluntary Administrator or attorney.

If the affidavit is prepared by an attorney, sign, print name, address and phone number of attorney or law firm.

If you have any questions, please call the Court at which you are filing.

Doc. 2.   Fee Schedule

The variable fee schedule applicable to proceedings listed in SCPA 2402(1) through (6) is provided in SCPA 2402(7) and reads as follows:

Value of Estate or Subject Matter Fee	Fee Rate
Less than $ 10,000	$ 45.00
10,000 but under 20,000	75.00
20,000 but under 50,000	215.00

Value of Estate or Subject Matter Fee	Fee Rate
50,000 but under 100,000	280.00
100,000 but under 250,000	420.00
250,000 but under 500,000	625.00
500,000 and over	1,250.00

Fixed Fee Proceedings

SCPA 2402(8)(a) provides a fixed fee for filing a petition to commence certain proceedings, as follows:

SCPA		Fee Rate
607	To punish respondent for contempt	$ 30.00
711	Suspend, modify, revoke letters or remove a fiduciary other than a custodian or guardian	75.00
711	Suspend, modify, revoke letters or remove a custodian or guardian	30.00
715	Application of fiduciary to resign	30.00
717	Suspend powers-fiduciary in war	30.00
1401	Compel production of will	20.00
1420	Construction of will	75.00
1421	Determination of right of election	75.00
1502	Appointment of trustee	45.00
1508	Release against state	50.00
1703	Appointment of guardian	20.00
2003	Open safe deposit box	20.00
2102	Proceedings against a fiduciary	20.00
2103	Proceedings by fiduciary to discover property	75.00
2107	Advice and directions	75.00
2108	Continue business	45.00
2114	Review corporate trustee compensation	10.00
2205	Petition to compel fiduciary to account	30.00
EPTL		
7–4.6	Appointment of successor custodian	20.00

SCPA 2402(8)(b) provides that for filing a petition to commence a proceeding for the appointment of a trustee of a lifetime trust or for the appointment of a conservator, the fee shall be the same as that which is payable in the supreme court pursuant to CPLR 8018.

Fixed Fees for Filing Papers

Fees for filing certain papers are provided in SCPA 2402(9), as follows:

SCPA		Fee Rate
502	a demand for trial by jury in any proceeding	$150.00
1410	objections to the probate of a will	150.00
	a note of issue in any proceeding	45.00
	objection or answer in any action or proceeding other than probate	75.00
2507	a will for safekeeping except that the court in any county may reduce or dispense with such a fee	45.00
	a bond, including any additional bond: less than $10,000	20.00
	a bond, including any additional bond: $10,000 and over	30.00

Fees for Certain Services

Fees for certain services are provided in SCPA 2402(10) through (15), as follows:

SCPA 2402		Fee Rate
(10)	for furnishing a transcript of a decree	$ 20.00
(11)	for a certificate of letters evidencing that the appointment of a fiduciary is still in full force & effect	6.00
(12a)	for making and certifying or comparing and certifying a copy of a will or any paper on file or recorded in his office	6.00 pg.
(12b)	Authenticating the same, additional	20.00
(13)	For searching and certifying to any record for which search is made (under 25 years)	30.00
	For searching and certifying to any record for which search is made (over 25 years)	90.00
(14a)	For producing papers, documents, books of record on file in his office under a subpoena duces tecum, for use within the county where the office of the court is situated	30.00
(14b)	For use in any other county, such fee to be paid for each day or part thereof that the messenger is detailed from the office and to be in addition to mileage fee and the necessary expenses of the messenger. The clerk of the court shall not be required to make any collection or return of the money so paid for expenses	.30
(15a)	for recording any instrument, decree or other paper which is required by law to be recorded	8.00 pg. (or part) 16.00 (minimum)
(15b)	for filing an authenticated copy of a foreign will	8.00 pg. (or part) 64.00 (minimum)
(15c)	for taxing bill of costs	15.00

Proceedings and Services for Which no Fee Shall Be Charged

SCPA 2402(16) provides that no fee shall be charged in the following instances:

(a) for filing objections of a guardian ad litem, or of a respondent in a proceeding brought pursuant to SSL 384(b);

(b) for filing a guardian's annual account;

(c) for any certificate or certified copy of a paper required to be filed with the United States Veterans Administration;

(d) for filing a petition in a proceeding for filing an additional bond, to reduce the penalty of a bond or substitute a new bond or discharge any bond when no accounting is required;

(e) in respect to the proceedings for the appointment of a fiduciary when the appointment is made solely for the purpose of collecting bounty, arrears of pay, prize money, pension dues or other dues or gratuities due from the federal or state government for services of an infant or of a decedent formerly or now in the military or naval services or to collect the proceeds of a war risk insurance policy;

(f) to or received from the state of New York or any public agency of the state or any civil subdivision or agency thereof with respect to a social services official when taking any proceeding with respect to the estate of a person who was a recipient of benefits from social services; and

(g) for the filing of a petition for an order granting funds for the maintenance or other proper needs of any infant or for any certificate or any certified copy of the order on such an application.

SCPA 2402(17) provides that the fee charged for the filing of a petition shall include the recording of any decree made in that proceeding which is required by law to be recorded and shall include the recording of any letters required by law to be recorded.

PART 137. ATTORNEY–CLIENT FEE DISPUTE RESOLUTION PROGRAM

LOCAL PROGRAM RULES AND PROCEDURES

§ 1. Policy

It is the policy of the Third Judicial District ("district") to encourage out-of-court resolution of fee disputes between attorneys and clients in a fair, impartial and efficient manner. The Administrative Judge of the Third Judicial District is designated as the Administrator of the Attorney–Client Fee Dispute Resolution program under these Rules and may delegate duties to such officers, committees, and employees as he/she may direct.

§ 2. Definitions

A. "Answer" (also referred to as "Response to Request for Fee Arbitration") means the response to the "Request for Fee Arbitration" or "Petition".

B. "Arbitrator" means the person(s) designated by the Administrative Judge or his/her designee to hear the evidence presented by the parties and make a final determination.

C. "Administrator" means the Administrative Judge (or designee) of the Third Judicial District who oversees the Program.

D. "Approval" by the Board of Governors means, where so required by Part 137, recommendation by the Board of Governors with approval of the appropriate Presiding Justice of the Appellate Division.

E. "Arbitration" means the settlement of disputes between parties by neutral third person(s) who hear both sides and render an award.

F. "Board" means the Board of Governors of the Attorney–Client Fee Dispute Resolution Program established under Part 137 of the Rules of the Chief Administrator.

G. "Client" means a person or entity who receives legal services or advice from an attorney on a fee basis in the attorney's professional capacity.

H. "District Office" means the Administrative Judges Office of the Third Judicial District.

I. "Petition" means a "Request for Fee Arbitration" requested by either the client or the attorney.

J. "Petitioner" means the party requesting the fee arbitration.

K. "Program" means the Attorney–Client Fee Dispute Resolution Program established under Part 137 and administered and implemented by the Administrative Judges Office of the Third Judicial District pursuant to the Rules and Procedures set forth herein.

L. "Respondent" means the party responding to the petition in opposition to the claim.

M. "Service" means personal service or service by certified mail.

N. "Written Instructions" means the Standard Instructions to Clients For the Resolution Of Fee Disputes Pursuant to Part 137 Of the Rules Of the Chief Administrator (Form UCS 137–3 5/02) published by the Office of Court Administration.

§ 3. The Program and Jurisdiction

A. The jurisdiction of this program will include the counties of Albany, Columbia, Greene, Rensselaer, Schoharie, Sullivan and Ulster.

B. In the event of a fee dispute between an attorney and client, where the representation has commenced on or after January 1, 2002, whether or not the attorney already has received some or all of the fee in dispute, the client may seek to resolve the dispute by arbitration pursuant to the Program.

C. Arbitration under this Program shall be mandatory for an attorney if requested by a client, and the arbitration award shall be final and binding unless de novo review is sought as further described herein.

D. Arbitration of fee disputes between attorneys and clients, shall take place through this Program. However, this Program shall not apply to any of the following:

1. Representation in criminal matters;

2. Amounts in dispute involving a sum of less that $1000 or more than $50,000, except that the district may hear disputes involving other amounts if the parties have consented;

3. Claims involving substantial legal questions, including professional malpractice or misconduct;

4. Claims against an attorney for damages or affirmative relief other than the adjustment of the fee;

5. Disputes where the fee to be paid by the client has been determined pursuant to statute or rule and allowed as of right by a court; or where the fee has been determined pursuant to a court order;

6. Disputes where no attorney's services have been rendered for more than two years;

7. Disputes where the attorney is admitted to practice in another jurisdiction and maintains no office in the State of New York, or where no material portion of the services was rendered in New York;

8. Disputes where the request for arbitration is made by a person who is not the client of the attorney or the legal representative of the client.

E. Pursuant to a written request and subsequent approval by the District Administrative Judge, the Board of Governors and the Presiding Justice of the Appellate Division, Third Judicial Department, this Program may be administered by a local bar association in accordance with all the rules and procedures set forth herein.

F. There shall be NO FEE charged to any of the parties who participate in the Attorney–Client Fee Dispute Resolution Program.

G. In the event Service becomes necessary, after having unsuccessfully attempted service by certified mail where required under these Rules and Procedures, the Petitioner must pay, in advance by check or money order made payable to the entity delegated to make such personal service the cost of such service. At the discretion of the arbitrator(s), and to the extent authorized by law, these costs may be added to the arbitrator(s) award, if previously paid by the prevailing party

H. 1. Arbitration under this Program shall be voluntary for the client unless:

(a) The client has previously consented in writing to submit fee disputes to the fee dispute resolution process by prior written agreement between the attorney and client wherein the client consented in advance to submit fee disputes to arbitration. To be valid on the part of the client, such consent must be knowing and informed. The clients consent shall be stated in a retainer agreement or other writing specifying that the client has read pursuant to Part 137, the district's approved Rules and Procedures and that the client consents to resolve fee disputes pursuant to the Program; or

(b) The attorney and client have consented in advance to submit fee disputes to arbitration that is final and binding and not subject to a trial de novo. To be valid on the part of the client, such consent must be knowing and informed and obtained in the same manner as set forth in the previous subsection of this section, except that the retainer agreement or other writing shall also state that the client understands that he/she is waiving the right to reject an arbitration award and subsequently commence a trial *de novo* in a court of competent jurisdiction.

2. Where an agreement to arbitrate exists between the attorney and client under either subsections H1 (a) or (b) of this section, those provisions of Section 137.6(a) (1) and (b) of Part 137 relating to the notice of client's right to arbitrate shall not apply and no further notice of the right to arbitrate shall be required. In such circumstance, Section 137.6 (a)(2) of Part 137 shall apply and either party may commence the dispute resolution process by filing a Peti-

tion with the Administrative Judge, together with a copy of the parties' agreement to arbitrate.

3. The attorney and client may consent in advance to final and binding arbitration in an arbitral forum other than the one created under Part 137. To be valid on the part of the client, such consent must be knowing and informed and must be obtained in a retainer agreement or other writing. Arbitration in an arbitral forum outside Part 137 shall be governed by the rules and procedures of that forum. The Board may maintain information concerning other established arbitral programs and shall provide contact information for such programs upon request.

4. Fee disputes may be referred to the District Administrative Judge by means not specifically described in Part 137, including but not limited to, attorney disciplinary authorities, bar associations, and employees, officers or judges of the courts. In those instances, the Administrative Office shall provide the client with information about the Program.

I. Upon notice of appointment, the Chairperson may contact both parties to make an effort to settle the dispute, however, the Chairperson is not authorized to provide legal advice to any of the parties involved.

§ 4. Arbitrators

The district shall establish and maintain a sufficient number of arbitrators in order to meet the Program's caseload. Attorneys and non-attorneys shall serve as arbitrators. In recruiting arbitrators, the district shall recruit arbitrators representing a wide range of law practices and a diversity of non-attorney professions and occupations representing a cross-section of the communities. The District Office shall seek the assistance of local Bar Associations in the recruitment of attorney arbitrators. Non-attorney arbitrators will be recruited by contacting established Alternative Dispute Resolution programs throughout the district as well as the Unified Court System, Office of Alternative Dispute Resolution Programs.

A. Attorney arbitrators, approved by the Board, shall be appointed to provide as broad a spectrum of the Bar as possible. For an attorney to qualify for appointment as an arbitrator, the attorney must meet the following criteria:

1. be admitted to the New York Bar for at least five years, and

2. been engaged in the practice of law for at least three years, and

3. be qualified as an arbitrator under the American Arbitration Association rules, by the Office of Court Administration or by the United States District Court through any of their arbitration programs; or

4. Have completed an district-approved arbitration training program or the equivalent.

B. Non–Attorney Arbitrators, approved by the Board, shall be appointed by the District Administrative Judge of the Third Judicial District from as broad a spectrum of the general public as possible. For a non-attorney to qualify for appointment as an arbitrator, the non-attorney must meet the following requirements:

1. be a resident of the 3rd Judicial District or work within the district.

2. be fluent in speaking, reading and writing English; and

3. have completed a district-approved arbitration training program or the equivalent.

C. The number of arbitrators assigned to hear a fee dispute matter under this Program shall depend upon the amount in dispute as follows:

1. disputes involving a sum of less than $6,000.00 shall be submitted to one attorney Arbitrator; and

2. disputes involving a sum of $6,000.00 or greater shall be submitted to a panel of three Arbitrators, which shall include at least one attorney and one non-attorney member of the public; the chairperson of all the panels shall be an attorney and all decisions on the merits shall be decided by majority rule.

D. Lists of attorney Arbitrators may be maintained under the following headings: matrimonials, litigation, real estate, business and other. Attorney Arbitrators will self-identify themselves as being within one or more of these areas and where practical, matters will be assigned to Arbitrators in order of placement on the respective lists; should there be a conflict of interest pursuant to subsection G of this section requiring the Arbitrator to be recused, the Arbitrator will remain at the top of the list for appointment in the next matter to be assigned.

E. Prospective arbitrators shall submit a summary of credentials to the District Administrative Judge which shall be kept on record.

F. All arbitrators must sign a written oath or affirmation to faithfully and fairly arbitrate all disputes that come before them, which written oath or affirmation shall be kept on file by the district.

G. All arbitrators must conduct a conflict of interest check within 3 business days of initial contact by the administrator prior to accepting a case. A person who has any personal bias regarding a party or the subject matter of a dispute, a financial interest in the subject matter of the dispute, or a close personal relationship or financial relationship with a party to the dispute shall not serve as an arbitrator. An arbitrator shall disclose any information that he or she has reason to believe may provide a basis for recusal.

H. Arbitrators shall serve as volunteers. However, Continuing Legal Education ("CLE") credits may be awarded for training and/or service as an arbitrator, subject to the rules and standards of the New York State Continuing Legal Education Board.

I. In making an award, arbitrators shall specify in a concise statement, the amount of and basis for the award.

J. Arbitrators have a duty to maintain the confidentiality of all proceedings, hearings and communications, including all papers pertaining to the arbitration conducted in accordance with Part 137 and these Rules and Procedures, except to the extent necessary in connection with ancillary legal action with respect to a fee matter. Arbitrators should refer all requests for information concerning a fee dispute to the District Office. Arbitrators shall not be competent to testify in a subsequent proceeding or trial *de novo*.

K. Arbitrators shall complete a minimum of six hours of fee dispute arbitration training approved by the Board. However, the Board may take previous arbitration training and experience under consideration in determining whether the foregoing training requirement has been met. In any case, all Arbitrators must complete a short orientation program designed to introduce them to Part 137 and these Rules and Procedures. Arbitrators may be required to undergo periodic refresher courses.

§ 5. The Fee Dispute Resolution Process

A. Where an attorney and client cannot agree as to the attorney's fee and there has been no prior written consent to arbitration as described in Section 3H above, the attorney shall serve a written notice to the client, entitled "Notice of Clients Right to Arbitrate", by certified mail or personal service. The notice shall:

1. be in a form approved by the Board of Governors;

2. contain a statement of the clients right to arbitrate;

3. advise that the client has 30 days after the notice is received or served in which to elect to resolve the fee dispute;

4. be accompanied by a copy of these Rules and Procedures;

5. be accompanied by a copy of Written Instructions; and

6. be accompanied by a copy of the petition form necessary to commence the arbitration proceeding.

B. If the attorney serves a Notice of the Clients Right to Arbitrate as described in subsection A of this section and the client does not file a Petition with the district within 30 days after the Notice was received or served, the attorney may commence an action in a court of competent jurisdiction to recover the fee and the client no longer shall have the right to request arbitration pursuant to Part 137 with respect to the fee dispute at issue.

NOTE: An attorney who institutes an action to recover a fee must allege in the complaint (i) that the client received notice under Part 137 of the client's right to pursue arbitration and did not file a timely Request for Arbitration or (ii) that the dispute is not otherwise covered by Part 137.

C. If, in the alternative event the client elects to pursue arbitration on his own initiative, the client may contact the Administrative Judges Office ("District Office") at (518) 445–7867 or the attorney with whom the client has the dispute. In the case of the latter, the attorney shall be under an obligation to refer the client to the District Office. Upon request, the District Office shall forward the Petition to the client by mail.

D. The Petitioner shall then file the Petition with the District Office.

1. Upon receipt of the Petition, the District Office shall assign a filing number to the matter.

2. The District Office shall contact the Petitioner to review the facts and circumstances supporting the Petition to insure that this is a matter within the jurisdiction of the Program. If it is determined that this is a matter not within the jurisdiction of the Program, the District Office shall inform the Petitioner.

3. If it is determined that this matter is a matter within the jurisdiction of the Program, the District Office shall mail, by certified mail, a copy of the Petition to the Respondent together with an answer form to be completed by the Respondent and returned to the District Office within 15 business days of mailing of the Petition. If service cannot be made by certified mail and personal service becomes necessary, the Petitioner will be so informed and the Petitioner will be required to pay the expense of such service in advance by cashiers check or money order, made payable to the entity making such service, as designated by the district. The cost for such personal service may be added to the Arbitrator(s) award, if previously paid by the prevailing party, at the discretion of the Arbitrators, to the extent authorized by law.

4. The Respondent shall return its Answer to the District Office, together with a signed, written statement (certification) stating that a copy of the Answer was served upon the Petitioner.

5. Once the Answer and certification have been received or, if 15 business days have elapsed since the service of the Petition and answer form without any response from the Respondent, the District Office shall designate the Arbitrator(s) who will hear the dispute and shall expeditiously schedule a hearing.

6. At least 15 days prior to the date of the hearing, the District Office shall notify the parties in writing of the date, time and place of the hearing and of the identity of the Arbitrator(s). Any subsequent re-scheduling will be a matter between the parties and the Arbitrator(s) at the discretion of the Arbitrator(s).

7. Either party may request the removal of an Arbitrator based upon the Arbitrator's personal or professional relationship to a party or party's counsel. A request for removal must be made to the District Office no later than 5 days prior to the scheduled date of the hearing. The District Office shall have the final decision concerning the removal of an Arbitrator.

8. The Petitioner may not withdraw from the process once an Answer has been submitted. If the Petitioner seeks to withdraw at anytime thereafter, the arbitration will proceed as scheduled whether or not the Petitioner appears, and a decision will be made on the basis of the evidence presented.

9. If the Respondent, without good cause, fails to respond to a petition or otherwise does not participate in the arbitration, the arbitration will proceed as scheduled and a decision will be made on the basis of the evidence presented.

10. Any party may participate in the arbitration hearing without a personal appearance by submitting to the Arbitrator(s) testimony and exhibits by written declaration under penalty of perjury.

11. Arbitrators shall have the power to:

a. compel, by subpoena, the attendance of witnesses and the production of books, papers, and documents pertaining to the proceeding;

b. administer oaths and affirmations; and

c. take and hear evidence pertaining to the proceeding.

12. The rules of evidence need not be observed at the hearing.

13. Either party, at its own expense, may be represented by counsel.

14. The burden shall be on the attorney to prove the reasonableness of the fee by a preponderance of the evidence and to present documentation of the work performed and the billing history. The client may then present his or her account of the services rendered and time expended. Witnesses may be called by the parties. The attorney shall have the right of reply. The client shall have the right of final reply.

15. Where there is more than one Arbitrator, any disputes arising among them shall be decided by the Chairperson, consistent with Part 137 of the Rules of the Chief Administrator and the minimum Standards and Guidelines of the Board of Governors.

16. Any party may provide for a stenographic or other record at the party's expense. The other party to the arbitration shall be entitled to a copy of said record upon written request and payment of the expense of duplication.

17. The arbitration award shall be issued by mail with a copy forwarded to the District Office no later than 30 days after the date of the hearing. Arbitration awards shall be in writing and shall state the amount and basis for the award. If *de novo* review has been waived pursuant to Section 3G1(b) of these Rules and Procedures, then the arbitration award shall be final and binding.

§ 6. *De Novo* Review

If *de novo* review has not been previously waived in writing, either party may seek *de novo* review of the arbitration award by commencing an action on the merits in any court of competent jurisdiction within thirty (30) days after the Notice of Arbitration Award has been mailed. Notice of commencement of such an action shall be provided to the District Office. If no action is commenced within thirty (30) days of the mailing of the Notice of Arbitration Award, the award shall become final and binding. Any party who fails to participate in the hearing shall not be entitled to seek *de novo* review absent good cause shown for such failure to participate. Arbitrators may not be called as witnesses nor shall the arbitration award be admitted in evidence at the trial *de novo*.

§ 7. Notices

Except as otherwise stated herein, all notices, correspondence and papers necessary and proper for the arbitration proceeding under this Program and for the entry of judgement of any arbitration award may be served upon any party by regular mail addressed to that party at that party's last known addresses or to the party's counsel of record.

§ 8. Correspondence

Requests for further information and correspondence relating to this Program may be sent to the Office of the Administrative Judge of the 3rd Judicial District at the following address:

District Administrative Judge's Office

Third Judicial District

40 Steuben Street

Albany, New York 12207

(518) 285–8300

§ 9. Periodic Review

The functioning of this Program shall be reviewed periodically from the reports submitted by the District Office to the Board of Governors including any recommendations or suggested changes of the Program.

§ 11.[1] Effective Date

These Rules and Procedures shall take effect immediately upon approval of the Board of Governors. These Rules and Procedures and any amendments thereto shall apply in the form in effect at the time an arbitration is initiated.

[1] So in original, no § 10.

FORMS

UCS 137–1. Notice of Client's Right to Arbitrate
a Dispute Over Attorneys Fees

The amount of $ _____ is due and owing for the provision of legal services with respect to _____. If you dispute that you owe this amount, you have the right to elect to resolve this dispute by arbitration under Part 137 of the Rules of the Chief Administrator of the Courts. To do so, you must file the attached Request for Fee Arbitration within 30 days from the receipt of this Notice, as set forth in the attached instructions. If you do not file a Request for Fee Arbitration within 30 days from the receipt of this Notice, you waive the right to resolve this dispute by arbitration under Part 137, and your attorney will be free to bring a lawsuit in court to seek payment of the fee.

Dated: _____   _____
                                  _____
                                  _____

[Attorney's name and address]

UCS 137-2. Notice of Client's Right to Arbitrate
a Dispute Over a Refund of Attorneys Fees

You claim that you are entitled to a refund in connection with legal fees you have paid the undersigned in the matter of _____. The undersigned disputes the refund that you are claiming. You have the right to elect to resolve this fee dispute by arbitration under Part 137 of the Rules of the Chief Administrator of the Courts. To do so, you must file the attached Request for Fee Arbitration within 30 days from the receipt of this Notice, as set forth in the attached instructions.

If you do not file a Request for Fee Arbitration within 30 days from the receipt of this Notice, you waive the right to resolve this dispute by arbitration under Part 137.

Dated: _____   _____
                                  _____
                                  _____
                                  [Attorney's name and address]

UCS 137–3. Standard Written Instructions and Procedures to Clients for the Resolution of Fee Disputes Pursuant to Part 137 of the Rules of the Chief Administrator

Part 137 of the Rules of the Chief Administrator of the Courts provides a procedure for the arbitration (and in some cases mediation) of fee disputes between attorneys and clients in civil matters. Your attorney can provide you with a copy of Part 137 upon request or you can download a copy at www.courts.state.ny.us/feegov. Fee disputes may involve both fees that you have already paid to your attorney and fees that your attorney claims are owed by you. If you elect to resolve your dispute by arbitration, your attorney is required to participate. Furthermore, the arbitration will be final and binding on both your attorney and you, unless either of you seeks a trial *de novo* within 30 days, which means either of you reject the arbitrator's decision by commencing an action on the merits of the fee dispute in a court of law within 30 days after the arbitrator's decision has been mailed. Fees disputes which may not be resolved under this procedure are described in Part 137.1 of the Rules of Chief Administrator of the Courts: representation in criminal matters; amounts in dispute involving a sum of less than $1000 or more than $50,000 unless the parties consent; and claims involving substantial legal questions, including professional malpractice or misconduct. Please consult Part 137.1 for additional exclusions.

Your attorney may not bring an action in court to obtain payment of a fee unless he or she first has provided written notice to you of your right to elect to resolve the dispute by arbitration under Part 137. If your attorney provides you with this notice, he or she must provide you with a copy of the written instructions and procedures of the approved local bar association-sponsored fee dispute resolution program ("Local Program") having jurisdiction over your dispute. Your attorney must also provide you with the "Request for Fee Arbitration" form and advise that you must file the Request for Fee Arbitration with the local program within 30 days of the receipt of the notice. If you do not file the Request within those 30 days, you will not be permitted to compel your attorney to resolve the dispute by arbitration, and your attorney will be free to bring a lawsuit in court to seek to obtain payment of the fee.

In order to elect to resolve a fee dispute by arbitration, you must file the attached "Request for Fee Arbitration" with the approved local program. An updated list of local programs is available at www.courts.state.ny.us/feegov or by calling (212) 428-2862. Filing of the Request for Fee Arbitration must be made with the appropriate local program for the county in which the majority of legal services were performed. Once you file the Request for Fee Arbitration, the local program will mail a copy of the request to your attorney, who must provide a response within 15 days of the mailing. You will receive at least 15 days notice in writing of the time and place of the hearing and of the identity of the arbitrator(s). The arbitrator(s) decision will be issued no later than 30 days after the date of the hearing. You may represent yourself at the hearing, or you may appear with an attorney if you wish.

Some local programs may offer mediation services in addition to arbitration. Mediation is a process by which those who have a fee dispute meet with the assistance of a trained mediator to clarify issues and explore options for a mutually acceptable resolution. Mediation provides the opportunity for your attorney and you to discuss your concerns without relinquishing control over the outcome and of achieving a result satisfactory to both of you. Participation in mediation is voluntary for your attorney and you, and it does not waive any of your rights to arbitration under these rules. If you wish to attempt to resolve your dispute through mediation, you may indicate your wish on the Request for Fee Arbitration form.

UCS 137–4a.   Client Request for Fee Arbitration

1.   Your name, address and telephone number:

Name:

Address:

Telephone Number:

2.   Name, address and office telephone number of the law firm and/or attorney who handled your matter:

Name:

Address:

Telephone Number:

3.   If your attorney filed a lawsuit on your behalf, in which county and court was the lawsuit filed?

Court: _____ County: _____

4.   On what date did your attorney first agree to handle your case?

_____, 20 _____

5.   Briefly describe the type of legal matter involved and what your attorney agreed to do in the course of representing you (attach a copy of the written retainer agreement, letter of engagement, or other papers describing the fee arrangement, if any):

6.   In the space below, indicate the date, amount and purpose of each payment you made to your attorney. Attach additional sheets if necessary.

Date   Amount   Purpose (e.g., attorney's time, out-of-pocket expenses, filing fees, etc.)

_____ $ _____ _____
_____ $ _____ _____
_____ $ _____ _____
_____ $ _____ _____

7.   How much of your attorney's fee is in dispute (attach a copy of your attorney's bill, if available): $ _____

8.   Have you received a "Notice of Client's Right to Arbitrate" from your attorney? _____. If yes, please attach a copy.

9.   Briefly describe why you believe your attorney is not entitled to the amount set forth in question 7 (use additional sheets if necessary):

10.   Indicate whether you wish to attempt to resolve this fee dispute through mediation (Participation in mediation is voluntary for your attorney and you, and it does not waive your rights to arbitration under these rules in the event that mediation is unsuccessful or the attorney refuses to participate in mediation; note that the local program with jurisdiction over your fee dispute may not offer mediation.)

The Third Judicial District does not offer mediation.

11.   I elect to resolve this fee dispute by arbitration, to be conducted pursuant to Part 137 of the Rules of the Chief Administrator [22 NYCRR] and the procedures of the Third Judicial District, copies of which I have received. I understand that the determination of the arbitrator(s) is binding upon both the lawyer and myself, unless either party rejects the arbitrator's award by commencing an action on the merits of the fee dispute (trial *de novo*) in a court of law within 30 days after the arbitrator's decision has been mailed.

Dated: _____   Signed: _____

IMPORTANT: You must file this Request for Fee Arbitration to:

District Administrative Judge

Third Judicial District Administrative Office

40 Steuben Street, Sixth Floor

Albany, NY 12207

UCS 137–5a. Attorney Response to Request for Fee Arbitration

**In the Matter of Fee Dispute
Arbitration between**

, Client

**ATTORNEY RESPONSE
TO REQUEST
FOR FEE ARBITRATION**

and

, Attorney

INSTRUCTIONS

Attached is a copy of a "Request for Fee Arbitration" by the above Client. Please complete this attorney response below and return it to the undersigned within 15 days of this mailing along with a certification that you have served the Client with the attorney response and indicating the manner of service:

1. Name, address, telephone number:

2. Set forth in narrative fashion your response to the request for fee arbitration, indicating those items in the request with which you disagree and providing a brief explanation of why you believe you are entitled to the amount of the fee that is in dispute (use additional pages if necessary):

3. ☐ I agree to attempt to resolve this fee dispute first through mediation [applicable only if client so indicates in item 10 of the request]

The Third Judicial District does not offer mediation.

Dated: _____, 20___   Signature _____

UCS 137–6. Notice of Arbitration Hearing

In the Matter of Fee Dispute
Arbitration between

, Client

    and   **NOTICE OF**
                                     ARBITRATION HEARING

, Attorney

To:

PLEASE TAKE NOTICE, that an arbitration hearing to determine the fee dispute between the above parties will be held on ————, 200 ——, at ———— (a.m.) (p.m.), at ————.

The arbitrator(s) hearing the dispute will be: ————.

You are required to bring to the hearing all evidence that you intend to introduce and to present any witnesses that you will call to testify on your behalf. If you wish a record to be made of the arbitration hearing, you may provide, at your own expense, a stenographer or tape recorder. If you have any objection to a particular arbitrator who has been designated to hear this case, you must provide your objections to the undersigned within 5 days of your receipt of this Notice.

Dated: ————, 20——   Local Program Address

                                      Signature

UCS 137-7. Arbitrator's Oath or Affirmation

I, _____, hereby agree to serve as an arbitrator pursuant to Part 137 of the Rules of the Chief Administrator and I swear or affirm that I will arbitrate all matters coming before me faithfully and fairly.

Signed: _____

Affirmed before me this ___ day
of _____, 200___.

_____
(Notary Public)

UCS 137–8. Mediator's Oath or Affirmation

I, —————, hereby agree to serve as a mediator pursuant to Part 137 of the Rules of the Chief Administrator and I swear or affirm that I will mediate all matters coming before me faithfully and fairly.

Signed: —————————————

Affirmed before me this — day
of —————————, 200—.

—————————————————
(Notary Public)

UCS 137-9.   Notice of Arbitration Award

In the Matter of Fee Dispute
Arbitration between

          , Client

  and

                                   NOTICE OF
                          ARBITRATION AWARD

          , Attorney
_____

    Attached is the determination of the arbitrator(s) who heard the fee dispute between the above parties. This determination is final and binding on the parties, unless either party rejects the arbitrator(s) decision by commencing an action on the merits of the fee dispute (trial *de novo*) in a court of law within 30 days after the arbitrator(s) decision has been mailed.

Dated: _____, 20 _____

UCS 137–10.   Notice of Final and Binding Arbitration Award

In the Matter of Fee Dispute
Arbitration between

_____

, Client

and   NOTICE OF FINAL AND
                                                      BINDING
                                              ARBITRATION AWARD

, Attorney
_____

Attached is the determination of the arbitrator(s) who heard the fee dispute between the above parties. This determination is final and binding on the parties. Article 75 of the Civil Practice Law and Rules permits review of arbitration awards on the narrow grounds set forth therein, and you are entitled to seek review of the award by the courts within 90 days of your receipt of this decision.

Dated: _____, 20____

  Third Judicial District

  40 Steuben Street

  Albany, NY 12207

UCS 137-11. Stipulation of Settlement

**In the Matter of Fee Dispute
Arbitration between**

_____

, Client

and

**STIPULATION OF
SETTLEMENT**

, Attorney

_____

A request for fee arbitration having been made and the parties having come to an agreement as to the reasonable amount of the fee due in this matter, it is hereby stipulated and agreed:

1. The AMOUNT IN DISPUTE is: $ _____

2. The TOTAL of the AMOUNT IN DISPUTE to which the attorney is entitled is (including all costs and disbursements and amounts previously paid by the client): $ _____

3. The AMOUNT of this total PREVIOUSLY PAID by the client is: $ _____

4. (a) The BALANCE DUE by the client to the attorney is: $ _____

-OR-

(b) The AMOUNT TO BE REFUNDED by the attorney is: $ _____

It is further agreed that the payment of the amount agreed shall be made within ___ days of the date of this stipulation.

_____   _____

ATTORNEY   CLIENT
(Please print names below signatures)

Dated: _____ [Give copy to each party]

UCS 137–12. Arbitration Award

**In the Matter of Fee Dispute
Arbitration between**

, Client

and   **ARBITRATION
AWARD**

, Attorney

1. The AMOUNT IN DISPUTE is: $ _____

2. The TOTAL of the AMOUNT IN DISPUTE to which the
   attorney is entitled is (including all costs and disbursements
   and amounts previously paid by the client): $ _____

3. The AMOUNT of this total PREVIOUSLY PAID by the
   client is: $ _____

4. (a) The BALANCE DUE by the client to the attorney is: $ _____

                              -OR-

   (b) The AMOUNT TO BE REFUNDED by the attorney
        is: $ _____

Statement of Reasons:
_____
_____
_____

_____   _____   _____
(Signatures of Arbitrator(s); print name below signatures)

Dated: _____   [Mail copy to each party]

UCS 137–13. Consent to Resolve Fee Dispute by Arbitration Pursuant to Part 137.2 (b) of the Rules of the Chief Administrator

[The language below may be incorporated into a retainer agreement between the parties]

The parties to this agreement, _____ ("Client"), and _____, Esq. ("Attorney"), agree that in the event a dispute should arise as to the attorney's fee for legal services, they will resolve the fee dispute by arbitration pursuant to Part 137 of the Rules of the Chief Administrator of the Courts (22 NYCRR), which provides for binding arbitration unless either party rejects the arbitration award by commencing an action on the merits of the fee dispute in a court of law (trial *de novo*) within 30 days after the arbitrator's decision has been mailed.

By signing this agreement, attorney and client indicate that they have received and read the official written instructions and procedures for both Part 137 and the Third Judicial District. Attorney and Client understand that they are not required to sign this agreement. Client understands that in the absence of this agreement, (s)he would have the right to choose whether or not to participate in this program. This agreement does not foreclose the parties' attempting to resolve this fee dispute at any time through voluntary mediation.

Attorney: _____   Client: _____

_____   _____

Date: _____   Date: _____

UCS 137-14. Consent to Submit Fee Dispute to Arbitration Pursuant to Part 137.2 (c) of the Rules of the Chief Administrator and to Waive Right to Trial *De Novo*

[The language below may be incorporated into a
retainer agreement between the parties]

The parties to this agreement, _____ ("Client"), and _____, Esq. ("Attorney"), agree that in the event a dispute should arise as to the attorney's fee for legal services, they will resolve the fee dispute by arbitration conducted pursuant to Part 137 of the Rules of the Chief Administrator of the Courts (22 NYCRR), except that they agree to be bound by the decision of the arbitrator(s) and agree to waive their rights to reject the arbitrator(s) award by commencing an action on the merits (trial *de novo*) in a court of law within 30 days after the arbitrator(s) decision has been mailed.

By signing this agreement, attorney and client acknowledge that they have received and read the official written instructions and procedures for Part 137 and the written instructions and procedures for the Third Judicial District. Attorney and Client understand that they are not required to agree to waive their right to seek a trial *de novo* under Part 137. This agreement does not foreclose the parties' attempting to resolve this fee dispute at any time through voluntary mediation.

_____   _____
Attorney   Client

(Please print names below signatures)

Dated: _____

UCS 137–15. Consent to Submit Fee Dispute to Mediation Pursuant to Part 137 of the Rules of the Chief Administrator

[The language below may be incorporated into a
retainer agreement between the parties]

The parties to this agreement, _____ ("Client"), and _____, Esq. ("Attorney"), agree to attempt to resolve their fee dispute through mediation pursuant to Part 137 of the Rules of the Chief Administrator of the Courts (22 NYCRR).

By signing this agreement, attorney and client acknowledge that they have received and read the official written instructions and procedures for both Part 137 and the _____. Attorney and Client understand that participation in mediation does not waive any of their rights to arbitration under Part 137 in the event that mediation does not result in a final settlement.

Attorney and Client further agree that all communications made during or in connection with the mediation process are confidential and shall not be disclosed in any subsequent civil or administrative proceeding, including any subsequent fee arbitration or trial de novo.

_____   _____
           Attorney   Client

(Please print names below signatures)

Dated: _____

UCS 137–16.   Consent to Final and Binding Arbitration in an Arbitral Forum Outside Part 137 Under 137.2 (d) of the Rules of the Chief Administrator

[The language below may be incorporated into a
retainer agreement between the parties]

The parties to this agreement, _____ ("Client"), and _____, Esq. ("Attorney"), agree that in the event a dispute should arise as to the attorney's fee for legal services, they will resolve the fee dispute by arbitration before an arbitral forum outside Part 137 of the Rules of the Chief Administrator of the Courts (22 NYCRR), and that the arbitration shall be governed by the rules and procedures of that forum.

By signing this agreement, attorney and client acknowledge that they have received and read the official written instructions and procedures for both Part 137 and the _____, and the client has been advised: (1) that (s)he has the right to use the fee arbitration procedures of Part 137, and; (2) that (s)he is not required to agree to arbitrate this fee dispute in an arbitral forum outside Part 137. By signing this form, Attorney and Client agree to waive their rights with regard to arbitration pursuant to Part 137, which includes the right to reject the arbitrator(s) award by commencing an action on the merits (trial de novo) in a court of law.

_____   _____
             Attorney   Client

(Please print names below signatures)

Dated: _____

FIFTH JUDICIAL DISTRICT — HERKIMER, JEFFERSON, LEWIS, ONEIDA, ONONDAGA, OSWEGO COUNTIES

Westlaw Electronic Research

These rules may be searched electronically on Westlaw® in the NY–RULES database; updates to these rules may be found on Westlaw in NY–RULESUP-DATES. For search tips and a summary of database content, consult the Westlaw Scope Screens for each database.

DISTRICT RULES

CIVIL CASE MANAGEMENT RULES

Rule I. Entry Into System

Actions and proceedings are assigned to the justices of the court upon the filing of a Request for Judicial Intervention with the Clerk of the Court (County Clerk) pursuant to 22 NYCRR 202.6.

Assignment of cases is made by the Supreme and County Court Clerk's Office. In those counties where there is more than one justice, assignments will be made pursuant to a method of random Individual Assignment System (IAS) authorized by the District Administrative Judge (DAJ). The DAJ may authorize a transfer of any action or proceeding from one justice to another according to the needs of the court and when, upon request of the assigned justice, the DAJ deems it inappropriate for the assigned justice to continue handling a particular action.

Rule II. All Purpose Justice

In each of the counties in the Fifth Judicial District, a justice will be assigned to an All Purpose Part for each term. Except as otherwise provided in these rules, the All Purpose Justice will be responsible for handling ex parte matters including name changes, default judgments, applications for attorney fees, infancy settlements, foreclosures, and mental hygiene calendars. The All Purpose Justice will take emergency applications brought by Order to Show Cause if the originally assigned justice in unavailable, as discussed in Section IV of these rules.

In Onondaga County, foreclosures and infancy settlements are assigned from the Individual Assignment System rotation. In Oneida County, foreclosures are assigned from the Individual Assignment System rotation and infancy settlements are heard by the All Purpose Justice. In Oneida County, Kendra's Law applications are heard by the All Purpose Justice. In other counties, Kendra's Law applications are assigned IAS.

Rule III. Motion Procedure

Unless excused by the assigned justice, or his/her designee, the moving party must appear on the return date of any motion or petition where oral argument is required. For those justices who do not require oral argument, the assigned justice at his/her discretion may determine that such motion be orally argued, and will so advise the parties. Please see Requirements for Oral Argument http://www.nycourts.gov/courts/5 jd/Rules_Motion_Appearances.pdf for information with respect to the judges' preferences for appearance for information with respect to the judges' preferences for appearance for oral argument. Where all parties to a motion or petition request oral argument, oral argument will be granted unless the court determines

it is not necessary. For a motion relating to disclosure or to a bill of particulars, see also Section VII (Preliminary Conferences).

All justices in the Fifth Judicial District have designated return dates for motions. These dates are set forth on the annual schedule which is distributed throughout the district. Copies are available in the Supreme and County Court Clerk's Office in each county.

All cases are required to be assigned to an Individual Assignment justice before a motion or petition may be made returnable in an action. If the case has not yet been assigned to a justice, the moving party, upon obtaining an index number from the County Clerk, will deliver the original motion papers, a Request for Judicial Intervention (RJI) with proof of payment of the filing fee, and the Motion Note of Issue in duplicate to the Supreme and County Court Clerk's Office in the county of venue, for assignment to a justice. Once the case has been assigned, counsel for the moving party will select a return date from one of that justice's available return dates. If the case is received by mail at the Supreme and County Court Clerk's Office, the assignment clerk will place the motion on the nearest available motion return date for the assigned justice. The moving party will then serve the motion papers containing the assigned justice's name and return date upon all of the parties. The Supreme and County Court Clerk's Office will submit the motion papers to the assigned justice. The moving party will deliver the affidavit of service to the assigned justice.

The answering party(ies) will serve copies of all affidavits and briefs as required by CPLR 2214 upon opposing counsel and will deliver the originals of such documents to the Supreme and County Court Clerk's Office for delivery to the assigned justice. The Court Clerk's Office will be unable to accept answering papers filed less than two business days prior to the return date of the motion without prior written approval from the assigned justice.

Stipulations made by the parties of a first adjournment of the return date of a motion must be directed to the part clerk assigned to the justice in Onondaga or Oneida Counties, and to the Chief Clerk in Herkimer, Jefferson, Lewis and Oswego Counties. Such stipulations will be effective unless the court otherwise directs; in that case, the parties will be so notified.

If the request is for a subsequent adjournment, or where all the parties do not agree to an adjournment, a request for the adjournment must be made to the assigned judge's chambers, with notice to the other party(ies). The court will notify the requesting party whether the adjournment has been granted. Stipulations or requests for adjournment will be in writing, unless the justice or the justice's designee finds that circumstances justify the stipulation or request not being made in writing.

Pursuant to CPLR 3212(a), motions for summary judgment must be filed no later than one hundred twenty (120) days after the date of filing of the Trial Note of Issue. Permission to file such motions thereafter must be obtained from the assigned justice for good cause shown.

Rule IV. Orders to Show Cause/Special Proceedings

For new cases, an index number and Request for Judicial Intervention must be purchased from the Clerk of the Court (County Clerk) prior to assignment (see Section I). Once the case is assigned, the original papers are delivered to the assigned justice for signature. After the papers are signed, copies are conformed by the filing attorney for service, the original signed order and supporting papers are filed with the County Clerk, and a certified copy of the papers are delivered to the Supreme Court Clerk's Office for data entry and delivery to the assigned justice. Please note that the Court Clerk's Office has one (1) business day to process the papers. Therefore, unless there is a situation which requires immediate attention (see below), attorneys should not expect an immediate assignment and signature.

For previously assigned cases, applicable fees are paid to the County Clerk, and the papers are processed and submitted to the assigned justice by the Supreme Court Clerk's Office.

In an emergency situation, (i.e., a temporary restraining order, temporary order of protection, emergency medical treatment, etc.), the papers will processed immediately, and forwarded to the assigned justice. If the assigned justice is unavailable, the All Purpose justice will handle the initial application. Any subsequent proceedings with respect to the case will be handled by the assigned justice.

If a return date on the Order to Show Cause is required which is earlier than the next regular motion return date for the assigned justice, the All Purpose justice will obtain an alternate date from the assigned justice's chambers.

Rule V. Preliminary Conferences

The assigned justice will schedule a preliminary conference as set forth in 22 NYCRR 202.12(a). Attorneys appearing at the conference must have full authorization to act on behalf of their clients.

At the conclusion of the conference, a scheduling order will be signed by the assigned justice.

Rule VI. Trial Rules

Trial rules for counties or individual judges within the Fifth Judicial District are available on the Fifth Judicial District website or by contacting the Chief Clerk in the county of venue.

Web links to individual rules may be found at http://www.nycourts.gov/courts/5jd/fifth.shtml. Hard copies of trial rules may be obtained at the Supreme and County Court Clerk's Offices in the Fifth Judicial District.

Rule VII. Tax Certiorari

All tax certiorari cases brought under Article 7 of the Real Property Tax Law will be assigned to a designated justice, except in Onondaga County, where they will be assigned to the Tax Certiorari Part. The calendar of cases for which a Trial Note of Issue has been filed will be called monthly. All attorneys and self represented litigants are required to be present at that time, unless excused in advance by the court. Tax certiorari calendar calls and conferences may be held by a Judicial Hearing Officer.

Rule VIII. Transfers

Once an action has been assigned to a justice, the District Administrative Judge or, in his absence, the Deputy District Administrative Judge, must approve any transfer of that action to another justice.

Please see the section on Integrated Domestic Violence Courts for specifics with respect to removal of cases to that Court.

When required, cases filed in the Fifth Judicial District may be heard by justices from courts outside the Fifth Judicial District, by Administrative Order of the Deputy Chief Administrative Judge for Courts Outside New York City.

Rule IX. Criminal Cases

Criminal cases filed in a county in the Fifth Judicial District are assigned to an Individual Assignment Judge in that county. Any transfers of cases for the purpose of trial or other disposition must be approved by the District Administrative Judge.

Rule X. Matrimonial Cases

Matrimonial actions will be assigned in the same manner as any other civil proceeding with the exception of those counties that have a Dedicated Matrimonial Part.

Rules for matrimonial actions for the Dedicated Matrimonial Parts in Onondaga and Oneida Counties may be found at http://www.nycourts.gov/courts/5jd/Rules_Matrimonial.pdf. Copies of the rules are also available at the Supreme and County Court Clerk's Office in Onondaga and Oneida Counties.

Rules for Justice McGuire may be found at http://www.nycourts.gov/courts/5jd/Rules_McGuire.pdf.

Rule XI. Asbestos Cases

A separate set of rules for asbestos cases in the Fifth Judicial District may be found on the Fifth Judicial District website http://www.nycourts.gov/courts/5jd/Rules_Asbestos.pdf. Copies may be obtained by contacting the Chief Clerk in the individual county.

Rule XII. Interpretation of Rules

Any questions which should arise with respect to the interpretation of these rules should be directed to the District Administrative Judge for the Fifth Judicial District.

Rule XIII. Specialty Parts

A. Integrated Domestic Violence Court

Cases in Onondaga County shall be eligible for the Integrated Domestic Violence part (IDV) when there are simultaneously pending:

1. (i) a criminal case involving domestic violence and (ii) a case in Supreme Court or a case in Family Court or both, in which the defendant or complaining witness in the criminal case or both is a party thereto,

2. (i) a case in Family Court and (ii) a case in Supreme Court in which a party in the case in Family Court is a party thereto, provided that there are sworn allegations of domestic violence in either case, .

3. a case which would have been IDV eligible had it been pending simultaneously with one or more earlier-filed IDV eligible cases already disposed of in an IDV Part.

4. a criminal case in the county in which the outcome thereof may affect the interests of a party to a case pending in the IDV Part in the county.

The Administrative Judge shall determine whether or not a transfer of the case to the Supreme Court, for disposition in the IDV Part thereof, would promote the administration of justice. If the Administrative Judge determines that it would, he or she may order such transfer, in which event the case shall be referred for disposition to the IDV Part, all original papers shall be sent thereto, and all further proceedings shall be conducted therein. Once a case is transferred to IDV court, it remains in IDV court.

If the Administrative Judge determines that such a transfer would not promote the administration of justice, he or she shall cause all papers and other documents in the case to be returned to the court from which they were received, where all further proceed-

ings in such case shall be conducted in accordance with law.

Notwithstanding the foregoing, where the case is a criminal case and the defendant is held by the local criminal court for the action of a grand jury empaneled by a County Court, only copies of the papers and other documents filed with such court shall be delivered to the office of the Administrative Judge; and the Administrative Judge may at any time order a transfer of the case to the Supreme Court provided he or she determines that such a transfer would promote the administration of justice. The original papers and other documents filed with the local criminal court shall be delivered to the County Court as required by section 180.30(1) of the Criminal Procedure Law.

B. Commercial Part — Onondaga County

The statewide commercial part rules may be found on the Unified Court System website at http://www.nycourts.gov and in the New York State Court Rules at 22 NYCRR 202.70.

The local rules for the commercial part may be found at http://www.nycourts.gov/courts/comdiv/onondaga.shtml.

App. A(1). Supreme Court Motions

Oral Argument and Appearance Required:

Hon. John C. Cherundolo, Acting JSC	Onondaga County
Hon. Michael E. Daley	Herkimer/Oneida County
Hon. Brian F. DeJoseph	Onondaga County
Hon. Donald A. Greenwood	Onondaga County
Hon. John W. Grow	Oneida County
Hon. Samuel D. Hester	Oneida County
Hon. Martha Walsh Hood, Acting JSC	Onondaga County
Hon. Deborah H. Karalunas	Onondaga County
Hon. James W. McCarthy, Acting JSC	Oswego County
Hon. David A. Murad, Acting JSC	Oneida County
Hon. James P. Murphy	Onondaga County
Hon. Anthony J. Paris	Onondaga County
Hon. Bernadette T. Romano	Oneida County
Hon. Norman W. Seiter, Jr.	Oswego County
Hon. Anthony F. Shaheen	Oneida County
Hon. Norman I. Siegel, Acting JSC	Oneida County
Hon. James C. Tormey	Onondaga County
Hon. Kevin G. Young	Onondaga County

All motions submitted unless oral argument directed:

Hon. Hugh A. Gilbert	Jefferson County
Hon. Joseph D. McGuire	Lewis/Jefferson County

ASBESTOS CASE MANAGEMENT RULES

Introduction

More than 200 asbestos-related actions for personal injury or wrongful death are now pending in the Fifth Judicial District. Of that number less than 5% of the claimants or decedents suffer or suffered from asbestos-related malignant diseases, and a small percentage of the remainder have sustained functionally impairing asbestosis. For the great majority of plaintiffs and decedents, however, the only clinical markers of asbestos exposure are pleural thickening or plaques that caused no discernible physical impairment.

To protect the interests of the significantly impaired, the "first in, first out" system of docket management ("FIFO") heretofore used in the Fifth Judicial District as set forth in the Amended Case Management Order (the "CMO") shall be modified to establish a (1) a "Deferred Docket" of claimants with minimal or no impairment, (2) "Active Docket" for clustering and trying cases of significantly impaired claimants who are ineligible for the Accelerated Trials under the CMO [*see also*, New York Civil Practice Law and Rules § 3407], and (3) a procedure for transferring cases from the Deferred Docket to the Active Docket.

Rule I. Amendment of CMO

To the extent that this order conflicts with any provisions of the CMO, this order supersedes those provisions, *except* that this order shall not apply to or affect any case which has already been assigned a trial date.

Rule II. Definitions

For purposes of this order:

1. A "board-certified pulmonary specialist" or "board-certified internist" means a physician currently actively licensed to practice medicine in one or more of the States of the United States who is currently actively certified by the American Board of Internal Medicine in the Subspeciality of Pulmonary Medicine (pulmonary specialist) or the American Board of Internal Medicine (internist).

2. A "currently certified B–reader" shall refer to an individual who has successfully completed the NIOSH–sponsored X–ray interpretation course and whose NIOSH–certification is up-to-date.

3. ILO grade" shall refer to the radiological ratings of the International Labor Office set forth in "Guidelines for the Use of ILO International Classification of Radiographs of Pneumoconiosis" (1980).

4. "Chest X–rays" means chest films taken in four views (PA, Lateral, Left and Right Oblique) that are graded quality 1 for reading according to the ILO criteria.

5. "Pulmonary Function Testing" shall refer to spirometry, lung volume testing and diffusing capacity testing which conform to quality criteria established by the American Thoracic Society (ATS) and is performed on equipment which meets ATS standards for technical quality and calibration, all as set forth in 20 C.F.R. 718.103 and Appendix B thereto or in the ATS guidelines in 144 American Review of Respiratory Disease 1202–18 (1991). Each subject must be tested with and without inhaled bronchodilators, with best values taken. Predicted values for spirometry and lung volumes shall be those published by Morris, CLINICAL PULMONARY FUNCTION TESTING, 2d ed., Intermountain Thoracic Society (1984).

6. "The minimum criteria for activation" shall be defined as follows:

Non–Malignant Changes Shown by Testing:

A. Chest X–rays which, in the opinion of a currently certified B–reader, show small irregular opacities of ILO grade 1/0; and pulmonary function testing that, in the opinion of a board-certified pulmonary specialist or internist, shows either:

    (i) FVC $\leq$80% of predicted value with FEV–1/FVC $\geq$65% (actual value), or

    (ii) TLC $\leq$80% of predicted value.

OR

B. Chest X–rays which, in the opinion of a currently certified B–reader, show small irregular opacities of ILO grade 1/1 or greater; and

pulmonary function testing that, in the opinion of a board-certified pulmonary specialist or internist, shows either:

    (iii) FVC $\leq$80% of predicted value with FEV–1/FVC $\geq$65% (actual value), or

    (iv) TLC $\leq$80% of predicted value

OR

C. Chest X–rays which, in the opinion of a currently certified B–reader, to a reasonable degree of medical certainty, demonstrate bilateral asbestos-related pleural thickening which has an ILO grade B2 or greater and with pulmonary function testing that, in the opinion of a board certified pulmonary specialist or internist, to a reasonable degree of medical certainty shows either:

    (i) FVC $\leq$80% of predicted value with FEV–1/FVC $\geq$68% (actual value), or

    (ii) TLC $\leq$80% of predicted value

and with a statement by a board-certified pulmonary specialist or internist that, based upon a complete review of the claimant's entire medical record, to a reasonable degree of medical certainty, the asbestos-related changes are a substantial contributing factor to the pulmonary function changes;

OR

Non–Malignant Changes Shown by Pathology:

D. In the case of a claim brought on behalf of a decedent, if representative lung tissue of the decedent is available, a report by a board-certified pathologist, stating that, to a reasonable degree of medical probability, more than one representative section of lung tissue that is unaffected by any other process (e.g., cancer or emphysema) demonstrates a pattern of peri-bronchiolar or parenchyma scarring in the presence of characteristic asbestos bodies, and that there is no other more likely explanation for the presence of the fibrosis;

OR

Diagnosis of Cancer:

E. A diagnosis of cancer, which is demonstrated by a medical report of a board-certified internist, pulmonary specialist, oncologist or pathologist showing the diagnosis as a primary cancer, which states to a reasonable degree of medical certainty that the cancer in question is caused by asbestos exposure.

Rule III.   Deferred Docket

1. The Deferred Docket consists of all actions brought by or on behalf of claimants who do not meet the minimum criteria for activation. All proceedings with respect to cases on the Deferred Docket are stayed, except for stipulations (as described below) to transfer cases to the Active Docket, as hereinafter defined, and motions for leave to amend the complaint (as described below), until further order of the Court.

2. Any case that, as of the date of this order, has been assigned a trial date is deemed to be on the Deferred Docket, unless:

A. On or before June 15, 2003:

(i) plaintiffs and (ii) Special Liaison Counsel for the defendants stipulate that the party allegedly injured from asbestos exposure satisfies the minimum criteria for activation;

B. On or before May 15, 2003:

(i) the plaintiff(s) (a) move for leave to amend the complaint so as to allege with specificity that the party injured from asbestos exposure satisfies the minimum criteria for activation and (b) annex the requisite documentation to the proposed amended complaint, and

(ii) the Court grants leave to amend the complaint. Leave to amend shall be denied if the minimum criteria for activation have not been satisfied.

C. Any case that is commenced after the date of this order is deemed to be on the Deferred Docket, unless the complaint, as initially filed and served,

alleges with specificity that the party claiming injury from asbestos exposure meets the minimum criteria for activation and annexes the requisite documentation as evidence thereof, No plaintiff may file a Request for Judicial Intervention for any Deferred Docket case commenced after the date of this order.

3. Any case that:

A. is commenced after the date of this order and initially deemed to be on the Deferred Docket.

OR

B. was commenced before the date of this order but not transferred to the Active Docket by timely stipulation or motion, under the procedures set forth above in section III(2),

shall be removed from it and placed on the "Active Docket," as described below, if

C. plaintiffs and Special Liaison Counsel for the defendants, Linda Clark, stipulate that the party allegedly injured from asbestos exposure now satisfies the minimum criteria for activation,

OR

D. (i) The plaintiff or plaintiffs (a) move for leave to amend the complaint so as to allege with specificity that the party injured from asbestos exposure meets the minimum criteria for activation and (b) annex the requisite documentation to the proposed amended complaint, and

(ii) the Court grants leave to amend the complaint. Leave to amend shall be denied and the case shall remain on the Deferred Docket if the minimum criteria for activation have not been satisfied.

Rule IV.   Active Docket

1. All cases which (A) as of the date hereof. have been assigned a trial date shall be prosecuted and tried in the manner now set forth in the CMO.

2. All other cases which are not on the Deferred Docket are deemed to be on the Active Docket. A case on the Active Docket shall be scheduled for trial strictly in FIFO order except as described below. For cases on the Active Docket, FIFO order is determined by the date that the action was commenced, except for:

A. Cases which receive a preference pursuant to New York Civil Practice Law and Rules § 3407, or

B. Is commenced after the date of this order which is initially on the Deferred Docket, and which is later placed on the Active Docket by stipulation or Order of the Court granting leave to amend the complaint, or

C. was commenced before the date of this order but not transferred to the Active Docket by timely stipulation or motion, pursuant to Section III(2), shall be determined by the date of said stipulation or Order.

Rule V. Docket Lists

On or before July 1, 2003, counsel for plaintiffs shall submit to the Court and plaintiffs' and defendants' liaison counsel, complete lists of (1) the inventory of cases on the Deferred Docket and (2) the inventory of cakes on the Active Docket, specifying for each the disease alleged and FIFO date. The lists shall be every six months thereafter.

DEDICATED MATRIMONIAL PART RULES (ONONDAGA AND ONEIDA COUNTIES)

Doc. 1. Dedicated Matrimonial Part Rules (Onondaga and Oneida Counties)

The Dedicated Matrimonial Parts will adhere to the Uniform Civil Rules for the Supreme Court and the County Court (22 NYCRR Part 202) and the Procedure for Attorneys in Domestic Relations Matters (22 NYCRR Part 1400). The Dedicated Matrimonial Part Rules supplement the Part 202 and Part 1400 rules.

A. Preliminary Conference

(1) The Preliminary Conference will be scheduled to be held within forty-five (45) days of the date of the filing of the Request for Judicial Intervention by the Court Clerk assigned to the Supreme Court Justice by the mailing of a Preliminary Conference Notice. Counsel or self-represented parties must comply with the directives contained in the Preliminary Conference Notice.

(2) The Preliminary Conference will be conducted by the Matrimonial Referee (Court Attorney-Referee); in the absence of the Matrimonial Referee, at the discretion of the Supreme Court Justice, either a Principal Law Clerk to the Supreme Court Justice or the Supreme Court Justice will conduct the Preliminary Conference.

(3) All requests for adjournment of the Preliminary Conference must be made in writing or by facsimile to the Court Clerk assigned to the Supreme Court Justice.

(a) Only one (1) adjournment of the Preliminary Conference will be permitted and the adjourned Preliminary Conference must take place within forty-five (45) days of the date of the filing of the Request for Judicial Intervention.

(b) The consent of the opposing counsel or the self-represented opposing party must be obtained prior to contacting the Court Clerk for an adjournment. In the event consent is denied, a request for adjournment may be made directly to the assigned justice upon notice to the opposing counsel or self-represented party.

(4) *Preliminary Conference Stipulation and Order*

(a) The parties and their counsel, if any, will sign a Preliminary Conference Stipulation indicating which issues, if any, have been resolved; any temporary relief agreed upon by the parties; appointing a law guardian, if necessary; and establishing the dates for completion of discovery, document exchange, a Compliance Conference, the filing of the trial note of issue, a Pre-Trial Conference and the Trial date.

(b) The Supreme Court Justice will sign the Preliminary Conference Stipulation as a "So Ordered" order.

(c) The Preliminary Conference Order may be modified for good cause shown.

B. Temporary Relief

Counsel or self-represented parties may file motions for temporary relief at any time in accordance with the provisions of the CPLR and these rules. Motions seeking emergency relief may be made returnable on a date prior to the Preliminary Conference date. All orders to show cause shall be submitted in accordance with the rules found at Section IV or these rules. Two (2) copies of all motion papers shall be submitted to the Court.

C. Compliance Conference

(1) The Compliance Conference will be conducted by the Matrimonial Referee (Court Attorney-Referee); in the absence of the Matrimonial Referee, at the discretion of the Supreme Court Justice, either a Principal Law Clerk to the Supreme Court Justice or the Supreme Court Justice will conduct the Compliance Conference.

D. Settlement Before Trial

At any time prior to trial where the matter has been resolved in its entirety, the parties may place an oral stipulation on the record before the Matrimonial Referee (Court Attorney-Referee); or in the absence of the Matrimonial Referee, at the discretion of the Supreme Court Justice, either a Principal Law Clerk to the Supreme Court Justice or the Supreme Court Justice. The parties and their counsel, if any, will be required to execute an Acknowledgment of Appearance and Adoption of Oral Stipulation form provided by the Court.

E. Trial

(1) At least ten (10) days prior to the scheduled Pre-Trial Conference, counsel or self-represented parties must submit to the Court and exchange with each other a list of known witnesses, including parties, if applicable.

(2) Trials will be conducted in accordance with the trial rules for the individual justice to whom the case is assigned. In Onondaga County, trials will be held in accordance with the General Trial Rules. See General Rules for Non Jury Trials in Onondaga County Supreme Court http://www.nycourts.gov/courts/5jd/Rules_OnonNonJuryTrial.pdf and General Rules for Jury Trials in Onondaga County Supreme Court http://www.nycourts.gov/courts/5jd/Rules_OnonJuryTrial.pdf.

F. Parties Presence Required

Unless otherwise directed by the Matrimonial Referee (Court Attorney-Referee), a Principal Law Clerk to the Supreme Court Justice or the Supreme Court Justice conducting a conference, the parties must attend any conference.

G. Judgments (Additional Language Required)

(1) For all matrimonial cases assigned to the Dedicated Matrimonial part in which the Judgment of Divorce adopts or continues, either by agreement or by default, an order of Family Court concerning custody or visitation, each judgment in such cases will contain the following provision:

All future matters concerning child support and custody or visitation are hereby referred to the appropriate Family Court. All other matters concerning this Judgment will be retained by the Supreme Court Dedicated Matrimonial Part for a period of one (1) year from the date of the signing of this Judgement of Divorce. Thereafter, all matters except equitable distribution will be referred to the appropriate Family Court.

(2) For all other matrimonial cases assigned to the Dedicated Matrimonial Part, each judgment in such cases will contain the following provision:

All future matters concerning child support are hereby referred to the appropriate Family Court. All other matters concerning this Judgment will be retained by the Supreme Court Dedicated Matrimonial part for a period of one (1) year from the date of the signing of this Judgment of Divorce. Thereafter, all matters except equitable distribution will be referred to the appropriate Family Court.

H. Post-Judgment Proceedings

It is preferred that after the execution of the Judgment of Divorce all post-judgment proceedings brought in Supreme Court be commenced by Order to Show Cause.

JUDGES' RULES
JUSTICE JOSEPH D. MCGUIRE

Doc. 1.   Motion Practice Rules

All Supreme Court actions are processed in accordance with the Uniform Rules for the New York State Trial Courts (22 NYCRR 202) and the Civil Case Management Rules of the Fifth Judicial District.

Submission. Pursuant to Uniform Rule § 202.8(d), all motions are deemed submitted unless oral argument is directed by the Court or requested by a party. If oral argument is requested, it must be clearly indicated in bold typeface in the case caption on the first page of the Notice of Motion, or in the case caption on the first page of answering papers, as the case may be.

Appearance. Personal appearance is not required or expected unless directed by the Court or if oral argument is scheduled.

Return date. Use of assigned calendar days for motions in the Fifth District calendar for Lewis and Jefferson County matters is preferred. In an exceptional circumstance, with prior Court Clerk approval, a Submitted Motion may be Noticed for a return date provided by the Court Clerk.

Oral Argument Date. The return date for a Motion noticed for oral argument shall be on a date assigned in the Fifth District calendar schedule for Lewis and Jefferson County matters, or such other date as the Court Clerk may designate in an appropriate circumstance. If the request is contained in the answering papers, the Court will hear oral argument on the next available date assigned in the District calendar schedule for Lewis and Jefferson County matters, or such other date as the Court Clerk may designate.

Orders to Show Cause. Oral argument is required on all Orders to Show Cause seeking emergency relief, with personal appearances of parties and/or counsel as specified by the Court in the Order to Show Cause. The return date for an Order to Show Cause shall be determined by the Court at the time papers are submitted for consideration and executed.

Notice of Argument. In instances when the Court wishes to hear oral argument on a Notice Motion, as permitted by Uniform rule 202.8(d), all counsel and pro se litigants shall be provided with reasonable prior notice of the date and time scheduled for such purpose at which appearances are expected.

Special Proceedings. Oral argument is required on all Article 78 proceedings, and all contempt proceedings.

Failure to Appear. Failure of any party to appear by submission of documents or for oral argument at the scheduled date and time may result in the motion being denied and otherwise marked off, or the motion being argued ex parte. A motion may be decided on default.

Adjournments. Upon consent of all counsel and pro se litigants, the Court will normally grant a first request for an adjournment of a motion or Order to Show Cause unless, in the discretion of the Court, there is a specific reason not to do so, in which instance the Court will so advise the litigants. Uniform Rule 202.8(e) is applicable to adjournment procedures. The party seeking the adjournment must obtain the consent of opposing parties and notify the Court Clerk at least twenty-four (24) hours before the return date. Confirmatory letters to all counsel are preferred. A written request for adjournment will not be entertained by the Court unless the party seeking the adjournment has first attempted to obtain consent from all other parties in the action. Parties seeking an adjournment that is not on consent must provide good cause why the adjournment should be granted.

Filing of Papers. Except with the express permission of the Court, all motion papers and Orders to Show Cause, including Notices of Motion, Notices of Petition, proposed Orders, affidavits or affirmations in support, affidavits or affirmations of good faith and memoranda of law, must be filed with the County Clerk, who will deliver them to the Court Clerk. All papers must be typewritten, double-spaced, securely bound, entirely legible and all exhibits labeled. Motion papers and related correspondence must reflect the Index Number assigned to the action.

Certification. All papers must be certified as non-frivolous and signed by counsel to the extent required by Section 130–1.1-a of the Rules of the Chief Administrator.

Papers Required in Particular Motions.

1. *Pendente Lite Relief.* In any matrimonial action seeking pendente lite relief where a party's Statement of Net Worth is annexed as an exhibit, one courtesy copy of the Statement of Net Worth must be separately provided, if not already filed with the Court. Upon disposition of the motion, all papers and exhibits are filed with the Lewis or Jefferson Clerk, and the courtesy copy of the Statement of Net Worth filed is the only such copy available for use by the Court thereafter.

2. *Motions for Summary Judgment and Similar Relief.* On any motion seeking summary judgment under CPLR 3212, dismissal of a complaint, a cross-claim or counterclaim under CPLR 3211 or 3212, or the striking of a pleading under CPLR 3124 and CPLR 3126, copies of all pleadings filed as of the date

of the motion must be provided to the Court as exhibits by the moving party.

3. *Motions to Renew or Reargue.* On any motion seeking leave to renew or reargue a prior determination under CPLR 2221, copies of all papers submitted on the prior motion, including all exhibits, must be provided to the Court by the moving party.

4. *Motions to Amend, Supplement or Correct Pleadings.* On any motion seeking to correct pleadings under CPLR 3024 or to amend or supplement pleadings under CPLR 3025, copies of all pleadings filed as of the date of the motion must be provided to the Court as exhibits by the moving party, along with the proposed amended, supplemented or corrected pleadings.

5. *Applications Seeking Injunctive Relief.* In any Order to Show Cause presented to the Court or motion which seeks a temporary restraining order or preliminary injunction or the vacatur or modification of injunctive relief, copies of the summons and complaint commencing the underlying action or proceeding, and any filed responsive pleadings, must be provided by the moving party.

6. *Discovery Motions.* All motions involving issues of discovery under CPLR Article 31 must contain an affidavit or affirmation of good faith as required by Uniform Rule 202.7.

Decisions and Orders.

1. *Written Decisions and Orders.* In certain instances, a Decision and Order may be reserved and rendered in written form following the full submission of the motion. The Decision and Order, with all supporting and opposition papers, will be filed by the Court with the County Clerk. A copy of the Decision and Order will be mailed to all counsel and pro se litigants upon filing.

2. *Oral Decisions and Orders.* With many motions, the Court will render a Decision and issue an Order orally from the Bench, or by letter to counsel. In such instances, the prevailing party shall submit an Order for Court signature, approved as to form by other parties. If there is disagreement over the contents of the proposed order, the matter shall be submitted to the Court with a Notice of Settlement on a date obtained from the Court Clerk.

3. *Notice of Entry.* It is the responsibility of the prevailing party to provide other parties with a Notice of Entry of an Order or Judgment determining a Motion or Special Proceeding, notwithstanding that an Order or Judgment may have been filed by the Court with a written Decision.

Doc. 2. Matrimonial Motion Practice Rules

Supreme Court matrimonial actions are processed in accordance with the Uniform Rules for the New York State Trial Courts (22 NYCRR 202) and the

Civil Case Management Rules of the Fifth Judicial District, Part X.

Submission. Pursuant to Uniform Rule § 202.8(d), all motions are deemed submitted unless oral argument is directed by the Court or requested by a party. If oral argument is requested, it must be clearly indicated in bold typeface in the case caption on the first page of the Notice of Motion, or in the case caption on the first page of answering papers, as the case may be.

Appearance. Personal appearance is not required, expected, or permitted unless directed by the Court or if oral argument is scheduled.

Return Date. The assigned calendar days for motions submitted to Justice McGuire for Oneida County matters are the first and third Friday of each term. A Submitted Motion that is Noticed for an improper return date is deemed submitted as of the next assigned Friday. In an exceptional circumstance, with prior Court Clerk approval, a Submitted Motion may be Noticed for a return date provided by the Court Clerk.

Orders to Show Cause. Oral argument is required on all Orders to Show Cause seeking emergency relief, with personal appearances of parties and/or counsel as specified by the Court in the Order to Show Cause. The return date for an Order to Show Cause shall be determined by the Court at the time papers are submitted for consideration and executed.

Notice of Argument. In instances when the Court wishes to hear oral argument on a Notice Motion, as permitted by Uniform rule 202.8(d), all counsel and pro se litigants shall be provided with reasonable prior notice of the date and time scheduled for such purpose at which appearances are expected.

Failure to Appear. Failure of any party to appear by submission of documents or for oral argument at the scheduled date and time may result in the motion being denied and otherwise marked off, or the motion being argued ex parte. A motion may be decided on default.

Adjournments. Upon consent of all counsel and pro se litigants, the Court will normally grant a first request for an adjournment of a motion or Order to Show Cause unless, in the discretion of the Court, there is a specific reason not to do so, in which instance the Court will so advise the litigants. Uniform Rule 202.8(e) is applicable to adjournment procedures. The party seeking the adjournment must obtain the consent of opposing parties and notify the Court Clerk at least twenty-four (24) hours before the return date. Confirmatory letters to all counsel are preferred. A written request for adjournment will not be entertained by the Court unless the party seeking the adjournment has first attempted to obtain consent from all other parties in the action. Parties seeking an adjournment that is not on consent must provide good cause why the adjournment should be granted.

JUSTICE MICHAEL L. HANUSZCZAK

Doc. 1. Matrimonial Proceeding Instructions

In addition to complying with the applicable statutes and trial court rules, please consult the Fifth Judicial District Court Rules, Supreme Court Trial Rules, and Dedicated Matrimonial Part Rules, which can be found on New York Courts website at courts. state.ny.us for other procedures and rules. The following topics contain information which is frequently requested by matrimonial attorneys.

• Automatic order

In accordance with DRL § 236B(2)(b) and Rule 202.16–a of the Uniform Rules—Trial Courts, in every matrimonial proceeding filed after 9/1/09, the plaintiff must serve a copy of the so-called "automatic order" upon the defendant simultaneous with the service of the summons. The automatic order is effective on the plaintiff as of the date of filing of the summons and is effective on the defendant as of the date of service of the summons. In general, the automatic order prohibits the dissipation of marital assets and directs that there be no changes to the coverage of health insurance, life, auto, homeowners, and other insurances. A copy of the text of the automatic order may be found in DRL § 236B(2)(b)(1,2,3,4,5) or in Appendix F of the Uniform Rules—Trial Courts or on the matrimonial forms section of courts.state.ny.us.

• Health insurance notice for the parties

Any matrimonial proceeding which was commenced on or before 10/8/09 must provide notice in accordance with DRL § 177 concerning the continued availability of health insurance after the divorce decree is signed.

Any matrimonial proceeding which was commenced after 10/9/09 must contain notice in accordance with DRL § 255 concerning the continued availability of health insurance after the divorce decree is signed. Under this statute, it is acceptable to give such warning in writing at the time of service of the summons, in the Adoption of Oral Stipulation form, or in an Opting Out Agreement.

• Motion practice (Please consult the Uniform Rules—Trial Part for additional requirements which may apply to your case.)

In accordance with Rule 202.16(e) of the Uniform Rules—Trial Courts, every paper served on another party or filed or submitted to the court (including motions) shall be signed in accordance with Subpart 130.1 regarding the certification that the information in the paper is not frivolous and is not obtained through illegal conduct.

In accordance with Rule 202.16(k) of the Uniform Rules—Trial Part, the moving papers in a motion for pendente lite child support, spousal maintenance, or counsel fees must contain a statement of net worth and, in the case of counsel fees, an attorney affidavit/affirmation stating moneys previously received or promised on behalf of the movant.

• Requirements for matrimonial proceeding when there are minor children

I. Domestic violence/child abuse finding

In accordance with the requirements of DRL § 240(1)(a), if either party makes an allegation in a sworn pleading that the other party has committed an act of domestic violence upon a party or member of the household or that the child is a victim of abuse, and such allegation is proven by a preponderance of evidence, the court must consider the effect of such domestic violence or abuse on the best interest of the child in its decision or in its consideration of any stipulation of the parties

If this review is applicable to the proceeding, the court will inform the parties and attorneys of its finding on the record during a court appearance or in writing in the order. If the parties settle the proceeding prior to making a court appearance, the person who prepares the custody order should contact the court for the finding.

Any temporary or final order of custody/parental access, including the judgment of divorce, must contain the finding. It is acceptable to place this language in the preamble section of the order or decree near the records review language. It is preferable, but not mandated, that the language also be placed in the Findings of Fact/Conclusion of Law document in the Findings section

II. Records review (when the child is under the age of 18 years)

In accordance with DRL § 240(a–1)(1), prior to issuing any temporary or permanent order of custody or parental access and/or one week prior to the preliminary conference, the court shall conduct a review of the decisions and reports in the following sources: related decisions in court proceedings initiated pursuant to Family Court Act, Article 10 (child protective proceedings); all warrants issued under the Family Court Act; reports of the statewide computerized registry of orders of protection, and reports of the sex offender registry. The court shall inform the parties and attorneys of the results of the search and shall make a finding as to the impact of the search results on custody or parental access. During the pendency of the proceeding, the court shall repeat the records review every 90 days.

The court will inform the parties and attorneys of the results of the search and make the finding as to the impact on custody on the record during a court appearance or in writing in the order. If the parties settle the proceeding prior to making a court appearance, the person who prepares the custody order should contact the court for the results of the review and the finding of impact on custody/parental access.

Any temporary or final order of custody/parental access, including the judgment of divorce, must state that the records review has been conducted and that the results were considered by the court. It is acceptable to place this language in the preamble section of the order or decree. It is preferable, but not mandated, that the language also be placed in the Findings of Fact/Conclusion of Law document in the Findings section.

III. Child support agreement (when the child is under the age of 21)

In accordance with the requirements of DRL § 240, the following elements must be included in a child support agreement which is contained in an executed, written agreement such as an Opting Out Agreement or in an on-the-record oral stipulation in Court. Be sure to include the effective date of the support obligation in the agreement, in accordance with statutory requirements.

(1) Apprise the parties of the provisions of the Child Support Standards Act (CSSA) and a pro-se party must be given a copy of the CSSA guidelines. A statement to this effect must be included in the child support agreement.

(2) If neither party is in receipt of public assistance, apprise the parties that they have the right to request the services of the Child Support Unit (CSU) for collection and enforcement of child support. If such services have been declined, so state. If support is to be payable through the CSU and it is a new account, have the payee complete an application for services and submit the application to the court with the judgment roll or directly to the CSU.

(3) The presumptively correct child support obligation under the CSSA for "basic care" must be calculated and stated in the agreement. If the parties wish to deviate from that amount, the reasons for such deviation must be stated. Effective January 31, 2010, the CSSA standard calculations applies to combined parental income up to $130,000. This amount will be revisited administratively every two years, in accordance with § 111–i(2) of the Social Services Law.

(4) Child support consists of the following elements, all of which must be contained in the agreement: (a) basic care; (b) obligation to provide health insurance for the child; and (c) child care to permit the custodial parent to work, if applicable. The agreement must specify how frequently payments are made, e.g. weekly, monthly, etc.

(a) basic care: state how this obligation is paid: (1) direct payment to the payee; (2) through the CSU via income execution; (3) through the CSU by direct payment from the payor; or (4) by income execution directly to the payee. If payable though income execution directly to payee, submit the appropriate order to the court with the judgment roll.

(b) health insurance: state which parent has the obligation to provide health insurance for the child and state how the expenditures which are not covered by health insurance are to be divided by the parties. The cost of providing health insurance is deemed to be "cash medical support" and the agreement shall state whether both parents have an obligation to contribute to the cost of the health insurance and, if so, what pro-rated dollar amount is to be credited against or added to the basic child support award.

(c) with respect to child care, it is acceptable to state the dollar amount of the obligation for child care or to state the percentage amount due from each parent.

(5) In accordance with DRL § 240–c(5)(b), if the child support is paid through the CSU, there are certain notices which must be attached to the judgment of divorce with respect to the right of an administrative adjustment of support. It is acceptable to place these notices below the caption of the decree or after the judge's signature line. The text of the notices may be found in the statute.

• Judgment roll

The following documents are required to be filed with the County Clerk as a part of the judgment roll. (CPLR 5017; 22 NYCRR 202.50) If you have already filed such a document, such as the Summons and Complaint, a signed order after motion return, or the Trial Note of Issue, with the County Clerk you are not required to provide that document to the judge for his final review.

Certificate of Dissolution (need not be submitted to the Judge for review)

Request for Judicial Intervention (RJI)

Trial Note of Issue and Certificate of Readiness with proof of service

Summons and Complaint with proof of service

Answer, if applicable

Answer and Counterclaim, if applicable

Reply, if applicable

Waiver of Answer, if applicable

DRL Section 253 Affidavit with proof of service (religious ceremony)

Affidavit of Regularity (CPLR 3215: default judgment)

Affidavit of Merits (CPLR 3215: default judgment)

UCCJEA Affidavit (DRL 75–j)

Decision of the Court, if applicable

Transcript of oral stipulation, if applicable

Opting Out Agreement, if applicable

Findings of Fact and Conclusions of Law

Judgment of Divorce

Child Support Summary Form—USC Form 111, if applicable [22 NYCRR 202.50(c)]

New York State Case Registry Filing Form, if applicable (Soc.Svs. 111–b)

ONONDAGA COUNTY
SUPREME AND COUNTY COURTS
GENERAL RULES FOR JURY TRIALS

Rule 1. Final Pre–Trial Conference

The IAS Justice will hold a final pre-trial conference in chambers at 9:30 a.m. on the trial date. Counsel must be prepared to discuss settlement, witness and exhibit lists, scheduling of witnesses, identity of expert witnesses, *voir dire*, proposed jury charges, special verdict sheet, motions *in limine*, EBT transcripts, videotaped testimony, stipulations and courtroom assignment. If an attorney does not have settlement authority, then his/her client and/or insurance adjuster must be personally present at the pre-trial conference.

Rule 2. Trial Hours

Generally, the trial will be conducted between 9:00 a.m. and 4:15 p.m. each day, with an hour break for lunch. The starting time of the trial may be delayed on the IAS Justice's motion day. The Fifth Judicial District observes summer hours from Memorial Day through Labor Day, so the schedule may be adjusted accordingly.

Rule 3. Motions *in Limine*

Motions *in limine* must be filed with the Onondaga County Clerk's Office and served on opposing counsel at least one week prior to the trial date. Opposing papers, if any, must be filed and served, no later than two business days prior to the trial date. Motions *in limine* are to be made returnable in chambers at 9:30 a.m. on the trial date.

Rule 4. Proposed Jury Charges and Special Verdict Sheets

Proposed jury charges and special verdict sheets must be delivered to chambers no later than 9:30 a.m. on the trial date. These items should, if possible, be submitted in both hard copy and electronic form. The courts in Onondaga County have Corel WordPerfect software and the electronic copy must be compatible with that software. Proposed jury charges must include the PJI section number and title and the text of the charge. If there is no applicable PJI charge, or if counsel is requesting a deviation from the PJI, then counsel must provide the text of the proposed charge with citations to relevant legal authority and a highlighted copy of all referenced authority. Counsel need not request PJI charges 1:2 through 1:41 because these form part of the Court's "boiler plate" charge. Additionally, PJI charges 1:90 (expert witness); 1:91 (interested witness); 1:94 (use of pre-trial deposition upon trial) and 1:97 (special verdicts) will

be charged when applicable, and these charges need not be requested.

Rule 5. Pleadings

Pleadings must be delivered to chambers no later than 10:00 a.m. on the Friday immediately preceding the trial date.

Rule 6. Exhibits

A list of all exhibits, except those exhibits to be used solely for credibility or rebuttal, must be served on opposing counsel and delivered to the IAS Justice no later than 10:00 a.m. on the Friday immediately preceding the trial date. The exhibit list must include a brief description of the exhibit. Counsel shall consult in good faith to agree upon the exhibits that will be offered into evidence without objection. The exhibits are to be marked immediately following the final pre-trial conference and prior to commencement of trial, subject to the availability of the assigned court reporter. Plaintiff's exhibits shall be marked with numbers and defendant's exhibits shall be marked with letters.

Rule 7. Use of EBT Transcripts and Videotaped Testimony

If counsel intends to read EBT testimony into evidence, then at least one week prior to trial counsel must provide opposing counsel and the IAS Justice with a copy of the portions of the testimony counsel intends to proffer. In addition, prior to the final pre-trial conference counsel must attempt to reach agreement with opposing counsel about the admissibility of that testimony. For those portions of the testimony upon which agreement is not reached, the party opposing admissibility must provide the IAS Justice at the final pre-trial conference with a written memorandum setting forth the legal basis for his/her objections, with citations to authority.

If counsel intends to use videotaped testimony, at least one week prior to trial counsel must provide opposing counsel and the IAS Justice with a copy of the videotape accompanied by a written transcript of the testimony counsel intends to proffer. In addition, prior to the final pre-trial conference counsel must attempt to reach agreement with opposing counsel about the admissibility of that testimony. For those portions of the testimony upon which agreement is not reached, the party opposing admissibility must provide the IAS Justice at the final pre-trial conference with a written memorandum setting forth the legal basis for his/her objections, with citations to authority.

Rule 8.   Stipulations

Be prepared to discuss possible stipulations at the final pre-trial conference.

Rule 9.   Date Certain and Scheduling of Witnesses During Trial

The trial date is a date certain. Trial adjournments will be granted ONLY upon good cause shown. Once the trial is commenced, it will proceed, without interruption, until a verdict is rendered. The Court will not inconvenience jurors by delaying the trial to accommodate witnesses. However, the Court will allow witnesses to testify out of order, as necessary.

Rule 10.   Interpreters and Other Special Trial Needs

At the earliest possible time, but no later than **three weeks** before the trial date, counsel must advise the Court if they need an interpreter or any other special trial accommodations.

THESE ARE THE GENERAL RULES FOR JURY TRIALS IN ONONDAGA COUNTY SUPREME COURT. PRIOR TO TRIAL YOU SHOULD CONSULT WITH THE CHAMBERS OF THE ASSIGNED IAS JUSTICE TO DETERMINE WHETHER HE/SHE HAS ANY SPECIAL TRIAL RULES.

GENERAL RULES FOR NON JURY TRIALS

Rule 1. Final Pre-trial Conference

The IAS Justice will hold a final pre-trial conference in chambers at 9:30 A.M. on the trial date. Counsel must be prepared to discuss settlement, witness and exhibit lists, scheduling of witnesses, identity of expert witnesses, motions in limine, EBT transcripts, videotaped testimony, proposed findings of fact and conclusions of law and stipulations. If an attorney does not have settlement authority, then his/her client and/or insurance adjuster must be personally present at the pre-trial conference.

Rule 2. Trial Hours

Generally, the trial will be conducted between 9:00 A.M. and 4:15 P.M. each day, with an hour break for lunch. The starting time of the trial may be delayed on the IAS Justice's motion day. The Fifth Judicial District observes summer hours from Memorial Day through Labor Day, so the schedule may be adjusted accordingly.

Rule 3. Motions *in Limine*

Motions *in limine* must be filed with the Onondaga County Clerk's Office and served on opposing counsel at least one week prior to the trial date. Opposing papers, if any, must be filed and served no later than two business days prior to the trial date. Motions *in limine* are to be made returnable in chambers at 9:30 A.M. on the trial date.

Rule 4. Pre-Trial Memorandum

Absent prior permission from the IAS Justice, at least one week prior to the trial date, counsel must serve on opposing counsel and deliver to the IAS Justice a pre-trial memorandum. The pre-trial memorandum should be short (i.e., generally not more than five pages in length) and provide a brief overview of the facts, law and anticipated evidentiary issues.

Rule 5. Pleadings

Pleadings must be delivered to chambers no later than 10:00 A.M. on the Friday immediately preceding the trial date.

Rule 6. Exhibits

A list of all exhibits, except those exhibits to be used solely for credibility or rebuttal, must be served on opposing counsel and delivered to the IAS Justice no later than 10:00 A.M. on the Friday immediately preceding the trial date. The exhibit list must include a brief description of each exhibit. Counsel shall consult in good faith to agree upon the exhibits that will be offered into evidence without objections. The exhibits are to be marked immediately following the final pre-trial conference and prior to commencement of trial, subject to the availability of the assigned court reporter. Plaintiff's exhibits shall be marked with numbers and defendant's exhibits shall be marked with letters.

Rule 7. Use of EBT Transcripts and Video-taped Testimony

If counsel intends to read EBT testimony into evidence, then at least one week prior to trial counsel must provide opposing counsel and the IAS Justice with a copy of the portions of the testimony counsel intends to proffer. In addition, prior to the final pre-trial conference counsel must attempt to reach agreement with opposing counsel about the admissibility of that testimony. For those portions of the testimony upon which agreement is not reached, the party opposing admissibility must provide the IAS Justice at the final pre-trial conference with a written memorandum setting forth the legal basis for his/her objections, with citations to authority.

If counsel intends to use videotaped testimony, then at least one week prior to trial counsel must provide opposing counsel and the IAS Justice with a copy of the videotape accompanied by a written transcript of the testimony counsel intends to proffer. In addition, prior to the final pre-trial conference, counsel must attempt to reach agreement with opposing counsel about the admissibility of that testimony. For those portions of the testimony upon which agreement is not reached, the party opposing admissibility must provide the IAS Justice at the final pre-trial conference with a written memorandum setting forth the legal basis for his/her objections, with citations to authority.

Rule 8. Stipulations

Be prepared to discuss possible stipulations at the pre-trial conference.

Rule 9. Date Certain and Scheduling of Witnesses During Trial

The trial date is a date certain. Trial adjournments will be granted ONLY upon good cause shown. Once the trial is commenced, it will proceed without interruption until all parties rest. However, the Court will allow witnesses to testify out of order, as necessary.

Rule 10. Interpreters and other Special Trial Needs

At the earliest possible time, but no later than **three weeks** prior to the trial date, counsel must advise the Court if they need an interpreter or any other special trial accommodations.

Rule 11. Findings of Fact and Conclusions of Law

Absent prior permission from the IAS Justice, post trial findings of fact and conclusions of law must be filed and served within 30 days of receipt of the trial transcript. These items must be submitted to the

Court in both hard copy and electronic form (either on a 3.5 computer disk, a CD in Corel WordPerfect format, or by e-mail to the IAS Justice's secretary or law clerk).

THESE ARE THE GENERAL RULES FOR NON-JURY TRIALS IN ONONDAGA COUNTY SUPREME COURT. PRIOR TO TRIAL YOU SHOULD CONSULT WITH THE CHAMBERS OF THE ASSIGNED IAS JUSTICE TO DETERMINE WHETHER HE/SHE HAS ANY SPECIAL TRIAL RULES.

FORMS

Form 1. Uncontested Divorces Additional Instructions

The Court Clerk's Office Is Prohibited From Providing Legal Advice

The Court Clerk's Office cannot assist you in the completion of these forms.

If you require assistance, seek the advice of an attorney.

You may be able to obtain assistance from

Legal Aid Society of Mid–New York	475–3127
Hiscock Legal Aid Society	422–8191
Onondaga County Bar Association	
Lawyer Referral Service	471–2690
Volunteer Lawyer Project	471–3409

The Onondaga County Bar Association's Volunteer Lawyer Project conducts a "Pro Se Divorce Workshop" each year in January, April and September. You may call 471–3409 for information on upcoming dates and eligibility.

Filing Fees

At the start. You must pay the following fees to the Onondaga County Clerk to begin your action for an uncontested divorce unless you are granted Poor Person status by the Court:

Index Number Fee	$ 210.00
Note of Issue Fee	$ 30.00
Request for Judicial Intervention Fee	$ 95.00

Please check with the Onondaga County Clerk's Office to determine how to pay the fees. The Onondaga County Clerk's Office telephone numbers are 435–2226 or 435–2227.

At the end. You must pay the following fees to the Onondaga County Clerk to finalize your action for an uncontested divorce unless you are granted Poor Person status by the Court:

Certificate of Dissolution Filing Fee	$ 5.00
Certified Copy Judgment of Divorce	
(to send to Defendant)	$ 5.00 Minimum

Forms Available On The Internet

You may obtain copies of the Uncontested Divorces Without Children Under 21 Official Forms Set or the Uniform Uncontested Divorce Packet on the Unified Court System's **CourtHelp** website at www.nycourts.gov/litigants/divorce. **Please avoid using inkjet printers to print the forms.**

Current Address Needed

Please be sure to provide the Court Clerk's Office with your **current** address and telephone number.

Additional Forms Required Or Used By Onondaga County Supreme

Matrimonial Checklist. You must complete the **Matrimonial Checklist** (*2007 Edition*) and include it with your papers when you file them with the Court Clerk's Office.

You May Request the Judicial Hearing Officer ("JHO") to Review Your Paperwork. Paperwork submitted to a justice assigned to the **Dedicated Matrimonial Part** will be reviewed as soon as that justice's calendar and trial schedule allow. Because the JHO is only responsible for reviewing uncontested matrimonial actions, paperwork submitted to the JHO may be reviewed sooner than paperwork submitted to a justice assigned to the Dedicated Matrimonial Part. If you want your paperwork reviewed by the JHO, you must sign the **Stipulation on Uncontested Matrimonial Action.**

Judgment of Divorce. The **Fifth Judicial District Civil Case Management Rules** (*Revised 10/13/05*) require that you include additional language with respect to the referral of future matters to Family Court in the Judgment of Divorce. The Court Clerk's Office has included substitute pages for either page 4 of the **Judgment of Divorce (Form A-13)** in the Uncontested Divorces Without Children Under 21 Official Forms Set or the last two (2) pages of the **Judgment of Divorce (Form UD-11)** in the Uniform Uncontested Divorce Packet. Please use the substitute pages.

Copy of Separation Agreement, Opting–Out Agreement or Family Court Order. A copy of any Separation Agreement, Opting-out Agreement or Family Court Order must be attached to the **Judgment of Divorce (Form A-13 or UD-11)** if the terms are being incorporated in the Judgment of Divorce.

Health Insurance Coverage Notification. Beginning **October 30, 2007,** you must complete this form and include it with your papers when you file them with the Court Clerk's Office.

Form UCS–111. The Form UCS–111 provided in the Uniform Uncontested Divorce Packet is not the most recent revision. Please use the **Form UCS–111** (*Revised 12/01*) provided as a separate form. **Ignore** the reference to Form UCS–113 in the Uniform Uncontested Divorce Packet on pages 10 and 33.

Application for Child Support Services. Complete this form if you want your child support payments through the Support Collection Unit.

Forms NOT Required By Onondaga County Supreme Court

You do not have to use the **Support Collection Unit Information Sheet (Form UD-8a) Postcard** or **Notice of Settlement** supplied with the Uniform Uncontested Divorce Packet.

Revised 08–27–07

Form 2. Stipulation on Uncontested Matrimonial Action

CPLR Article 43; 22 NYCRR § 202.43
Onondaga Combined Courts (Revised 02–20–07)

SUPREME COURT
STATE OF NEW YORK
COUNTY OF ONONDAGA

_____,   **STIPULATION**
(Print Your Name)   Plaintiff,   **ON**
                                            UNCONTESTED
              -vs-   **MATRIMONIAL ACTION**
                                            (Referral to Judicial Hearing Officer)

_____,
(Print Other Party's Name)   Defendant.   INDEX No.

    IT IS HEREBY stipulated and agreed that the above-captioned uncontested matrimonial action be referred to a Judicial Hearing Officer for hearing and determination.

Date: *(Print Date)* _____   _____
                                            Sign Name
                                            Attorney for Plaintiff <u>or</u>
                                            Self–Represented Plaintiff

                                            _____
                                            Sign Name
                                            Attorney for Defendant <u>or</u>
                                            Self–Represented Defendant
                                            (*If Applicable*)

The Judicial Hearing Officer (or "JHO") is a retired judge or justice who has been assigned to review uncontested matrimonial actions.

You May Request That A JHO Be Assigned To Preside Over Your Uncontested Matrimonial Action. Paperwork submitted to a justice assigned to the **Dedicated Matrimonial Part** will be reviewed as part of that justice's overall caseload, which includes trials and motions. Because the JHO is only responsible for reviewing uncontested matrimonial actions, paperwork submitted to the JHO may be reviewed sooner than paperwork submitted to a justice assigned to the Dedicated Matrimonial Part. If you want your uncontested matrimonial action assigned to a JHO, you must sign the **Stipulation on Uncontested Matrimonial Action.**

JHO Responsibility. The JHO reviews the paperwork submitted for compliance with the appropriate statutes and rules of the court. If the paperwork is in proper order, the JHO will sign the **Findings of Fact and Conclusions of Law,** the **Judgment of Divorce** and the **Qualified Medical Child Support Order** or **Income Deduction Order,** if requested. If there are any problems with the paperwork submitted, you will be contacted.

Form 3. Judgment of Divorce Forms (UD–11) Replacement Pages

_____; **OR** ☐ *Not applicable*; **and** it is further

28 ORDERED AND ADJUDGED that ☐ *Plaintiff* **OR** ☐ *Defendant* is hereby awarded exclusive occupancy of the marital residence located at _____, together with its contents until further order of the court, **OR** ☐ as follows: _____

_____; **OR** ☐ *Not applicable*; and it is further

29 ORDERED AND ADJUDGED that the Settlement Agreement entered into between the parties on the ___ day of _____, a ☐ *copy* **OR** ☐ *transcript* of which is on file with this Court and incorporated herein by reference, shall survive and shall not be merged into this judgment, and the parties are hereby directed to comply with all legally enforceable terms and conditions of said agreement as if such terms and conditions were set forth in their entirety herein; **OR** ☐ *Not applicable*; and it is further

30 ORDERED AND ADJUDGED that a separate Qualified Medical Child Support Order shall be issued simultaneously herewith **OR** ☐ *Not applicable*; and it is further

31 ORDERED AND ADJUDGED that, pursuant to the ☐ *parties' Settlement Agreement* **OR** ☐ *the court's decision*, a separate Qualified Domestic Relations Order shall be issued simultaneously herewith or as soon as practicable **OR** ☐ *Not applicable*; and it is further

32 ORDERED AND ADJUDGED that, ☐ *pursuant to this Court's direction* **OR** ☐ *pursuant to the parties' agreement*, this Court shall issue an income deduction order simultaneously herewith **OR** ☐ *Not applicable*; and it is further

33 ORDERED AND ADJUDGED that both parties are authorized to resume the use of any former surname, and it is further

34 ORDERED AND ADJUDGED that ☐ *Plaintiff* **OR** ☐ *Defendant* is authorized to resume use of the prior surname _____.

35 ORDERED AND ADJUDGED that ☐ *Plaintiff* **OR** ☐ *Defendant* shall be served with a copy of this judgment, with notice of entry, by the ☐ *Plaintiff* **OR** ☐ *Defendant*, within ___ days of such entry.

35a ORDERED AND ADJUDGED that *(If there is an existing Family Court Order for custody or visitation which is being adopted or continued by the judgment of divorce)*
☐ all future matters concerning child support and custody and visitation are hereby referred to the appropriate Family Court. All other matters concerning this Judgment will be retained by the Supreme Court Dedicated Matrimonial Part for one (1) year from the date of the signing this Judgment of Divorce. Thereafter, all matters except equitable distribution will be referred to the appropriate Family Court **OR** *(For all other cases)*
☐ all future matters concerning child support are hereby referred to the appropriate Family Court. All other matters concerning this Judgment will be retained by the Supreme Court Dedicated Matrimonial Part for one (1) year from the date of the signing of this Judgment of Divorce. Thereafter, all matters except equitable distribution will be referred to the appropriate Family Court.

39 Dated:

ENTER:

_____
J.S.C./Referee

_____
CLERK

(Form UD–11 — Rev. 5/99) (Onondaga County Revision 10/05)

Form 4.   Uncontested Matrimonial Action Checklist

2007 Edition (Revised 08/07)
(This edition must be submitted; no earlier form will be accepted.)

_____ v. _____   _____   _____
  Plaintiff   Defendant   Index Number   Attorney/Self–Represented
                                                            Litigant

The following checklist must be filled in by the Attorney or Self–Represented Litigant before the Supreme Court Clerk will accept papers as an Uncontested Matrimonial Action pursuant to 22 NYCRR § 202.21(i). The Attorney or Self–Represented Litigant must sign the completed checklist certifying compliance with these requirements.

Please submit the papers in the order listed. Forms beginning with "A" are from the Uncontested Divorces Without Children Under 21 Official Forms Set and forms beginning with "UD" are from the Uniform Uncontested Divorce Packet Forms.

If the papers are prepared by an Attorney, substantial conformity to the Uniform Uncontested Divorce Packet Forms is required (22 NYCRR § 202.21(i)(2)).

___ STIPULATION ON UNCONTESTED MATRIMONIAL ACTION (Referral to JHO) if used

___ REQUEST FOR JUDICIAL INTERVENTION (RJI) (Form A–11 or UD–13 or UCS–840 [*Revised 01/00*])

___ TRIAL NOTE OF ISSUE (Form A–10 or UD–9)

___ SUMMONS WITH NOTICE (Form A–1 or UD–1) or SUMMONS (Form UD–1a) containing

(A) ___ Venue basis

(B) ___ Index Number assigned

(C) ___ Date of Filing with County Clerk printed by County Clerk on SUMMONS WITH NOTICE (Form A–1 or UD–1) or SUMMONS (Form UD–1a)

(D) ___ Statement of nature of action (i.e., "Action for a Divorce")

(E) ___ If SUMMONS WITH NOTICE (Form A–1 or Form UD–1) was served without COMPLAINT (Form A–3 or UD–2), Statement of nature of action and full statement as to any ancillary relief requested (such as child support, custody, maintenance, equitable distribution, etc.) and specific nature thereof, including any request to incorporate any prior court orders, must be on SUMMONS WITH NOTICE (Form A–1 or UD–1)*(Attach copy(ies) of orders)*

___ COMPLAINT (Form A–3 or UD–2)

(A) ___ Statement as to required jurisdictional residence

(B) ___ Statement that Plaintiff has taken or will take all steps solely within Plaintiff's power to remove any barrier to the Defendant's remarriage following divorce, if marriage officiant is listed in DRL § 11(1)

(C) ___ Full statement of the grounds for the relief requested and, if the grounds are based on Defendant's misconduct, the nature and circumstances of such misconduct, including the date and place of each act complained of, with detail as required by CPLR 3016 (c)

(D) ___ Full statement as to any ancillary relief requested (such as child support, custody, maintenance, equitable distribution, etc.) and specific nature thereof, including any request to incorporate any prior court orders *(Attach copy(ies) of orders)*

(E) ___ Verified and jurat signed by notary public

___ AFFIDAVIT OF SERVICE (Form A–4 or UD–3) unldss AFFIDAVIT OF DEFENDANT (Form A–5 or UD–7) is provided

(A) ___ Date of Service on Defendant shown

(B) ___ Date of Filing with County Clerk printed on AFFIDAVIT OF SERVICE (Form A–4 or UD–3) by County Clerk

(C) ___ Statement of knowledge the affiant had that the person served was the Defendant and how the affiant acquired such knowledge *(Attach photograph if used)*

(D) ___ Physical description of the person served

___ AFFIDAVIT OF DEFENDANT (Form A–5 or UD–7) if signed by Defendant, admitting service of SUMMONS WITH NOTICE and/or SUMMONS and COMPLAINT. The Defendant's signature must be notarized

---

___ AFFIRMATION/AFFIDAVIT OF REGULARITY (Form A–8 or UD–5). If the default in appearing or answering occurred more than one (1) year before date of submission of the AFFIRMATION/AFFIDAVIT OF REGULARITY, an affirmation or affidavit pursuant to CPLR § 3215(c) showing sufficient cause for the delay in filing must be submitted and the CONCLUSIONS OF LAW and JUDGMENT OF DIVORCE must contain an ordering paragraph permitting the late filing

---

___ SWORN STATEMENT OF REMOVAL OF BARRIERS TO REMARRIAGE (Form A–6 or UD–4) only if marriage officiant is listed in DRL § 11(1), stating that pursuant to DRL § 253(3) and (4) that Plaintiff has taken all steps solely within his or her power to remove any barrier to the Defendant's remarriage following divorce

(A) ___ AFFIDAVIT OF SERVICE of REMOVAL OF BARRIERS STATEMENT upon Defendant (Form A–4 or UD–4a) must be attached

(B) ___ but if divorce is based upon the parties living separate and apart pursuant to a decree or judgment of separation or a written agreement of separation for a period of one or more years pursuant to DRL § 170(5) or (6), both parties must comply with DRL § 253(3) and (4) requirements

---

___ AFFIDAVIT OF PLAINTIFF (Form A–9 or UD–6) if SUMMONS WITH NOTICE (Form A–1 or UD–1) was served without COMPLAINT (Form A–3 or UD–2)

___ If there are any UNEMANCIPATED CHILDREN:

(A) ___ AFFIDAVIT OF PLAINTIFF (Form UD–6) or DRL § 76–h AFFIDAVIT (Form UCCJEA–3)

(1) ___ Certified copy of any Family Court Order of Custody or Visitation to be continued by Judgment of Divorce

(2) ___ Certified copy of any Family Court Order of Support to be continued by Judgment of Divorce

(B) ___ If AFFIDAVIT OF PLAINTIFF (Form UD–6) is not used, statement of Plaintiff pursuant to DRL § 240(1) either requesting or declining child support enforcement services and if child support is to be paid through Support Collection Unit, complete APPLICATION FOR CHILD SUPPORT SERVICES

(C) ___ SEPARATION AGREEMENT or OPTING–OUT AGREEMENT, if signed

(1) ___ Must contain provision regarding custody and

(2) ___ Must contain provision that any self-represented party has been provided with a copy of the CHILD SUPPORT STANDARDS CHART (Form LDSS 4515) prepared by the New York State Office of Temporary and Disability Assistance and

(3) ___ Must contain either a calculation of the basic child support obligation made pursuant to DRL § 240(1–b) or have a CHILD SUPPORT WORKSHEET (Form UD–8) attached or continue an existing Family Court Order of Support containing the calculations and have a certified copy of the Family Court Order of Support attached and

(4) ___ If the agreed upon child support deviates from the basic child support obligation calculated pursuant to DRL § 240(1–b), must contain a provision stating that the parties were advised of the provisions of the Child Support Standards Act or were provided with a copy of the CHILD SUPPORT STANDARDS CHART; showing the calculation of the basic child support obligation; stating that the basic child support obligation would presumptively result in the correct amount of child support to be awarded; and the reason or reasons for deviation from the basic child support obligation, and

(5) ___ Must contain a provision with respect to which party will provide health insurance for the children or whether the children will be covered by Child Health Plus and must also contain a calculation of the pro rata shares of the cost to provide health insurance, child care expenses and any uncovered health expenses for the children

(D) ___ CHILD SUPPORT WORKSHEET (Form UD–8) with Plaintiff's signature notarized if child support is sought or provided for unless a full statement complying with DRL § 240(1–b)(h) with respect to child support is incorporated in Attorney-prepared Separation Agreement or Opting-out Agreement.

Note: For STEP 10 on the CHILD SUPPORT WORKSHEET (Form UD–8), starting March 1, 2007 the self-support reserve amount is $ 13,784 and the poverty level amount is $ 10,210

(E) ___ QUALIFIED MEDICAL CHILD SUPPORT ORDER (Form UD–8b) if applicable

(F) ___ NEW YORK STATE CASE REGISTRY FILING FORM (in APPENDIX to Uniform Uncontested Divorce Packet Forms) if child support is not paid through Support Collection Unit or
APPLICATION FOR CHILD SUPPORT SERVICES (available from the Court Clerk's Office) if child support is to be paid through Support Collection Unit

___ With respect to EQUITABLE DISTRIBUTION:

(A) ___ AFFIDAVIT OF PLAINTIFF (Form A–9) or AFFIDAVIT OF PLAINTIFF (Form UD–6) with Paragraph 5 filled out completely, including the applicable statement regarding equitable distribution or

(B) ___ Affidavit of equitable distribution of marital property pursuant to DRL § 236B, including sworn waiver of equitable distribution, if applicable, and if not included in complaint or

(C) ___ OPTING–OUT AGREEMENT (Original, County Clerk certified or Attorney certified copy), or

(D) ___ SEPARATION AGREEMENT (Original, County Clerk certified or Attorney certified copy)

___ For OPTING–OUT AGREEMENT or SEPARATION AGREEMENT,

(A) ___ Sworn Statement of Plaintiff that the agreement was fair and reasonable when entered into and is not now unconscionable

(B) ___ Signed Statement pursuant to DRL § 177(1) with respect to health insurance coverage not continuing

___ HEALTH INSURANCE COVERAGE NOTIFICATION if there is no OPTING–OUT AGREEMENT or SEPARATION AGREEMENT

___ WITHDRAWAL OF ANSWER/REPLY BY STIPULATION if applicable. The CONCLUSIONS OF LAW and JUDGMENT OF DIVORCE must order withdrawal

___ FINDINGS OF FACT AND CONCLUSIONS OF LAW (Form A–12 or UD–10) or Attorney-prepared (22 NYCRR § 202.50(b) Appendix B)

(A) ___ Findings of Fact incorporating evidentiary allegations actually set forth in the Complaint and any supplemental affidavits

(B) ___ Findings regarding custody

(C) ___ Findings in compliance with DRL § 240(1–b)(c) or (h) if child support awarded, showing the calculation of the basic child support obligation and the reason or reasons for deviation from the basic child support obligation, if any

(D) ___ Conclusions of Law containing recitals providing for each aspect of relief to be ordered by the Court

___ JUDGMENT OF DIVORCE (Form A–13 or UD–11) or Attorney-prepared (22 NYCRR § 202.50(b) Appendix B)

(A) ___ Award of matrimonial relief

(B) ___ Provision regarding custody, if there are any unemancipated children, including the name(s) and date(s) of birth of the child(ren)

(C) ___ Provision in compliance with DRL § 240(1–b)(c) or (h) if child support awarded

(D) ___ Provisions in compliance with DRL §§ 240–a, 240–b and 240–c if child support awarded and child support is to be paid through the Support Collection Unit, providing the Social Security Numbers of the parties and the subject child(ren); the name and address of the employer of the party paying child support; notice of the requirement to report certain information changes to the Support Collection Unit; and notice of the right to a review and cost of living adjustment of the child support provisions

(E) ___ Copy of SEPARATION AGREEMENT or OPTING–OUT AGREEMENT attached and statement as to incorporation and merger or non-merger

(F) ___ Provision permitting either party to resume use of pre-marriage name or any other former surname

(G) ___ Family Court referral provision pursuant to Fifth Judicial District Civil Case Management Rules (*Revised 10/13/05*) added to Judgment of Divorce (*Replace either page 4 of A–13 or the last two (2) pages of UD–11 with Court-provided pages*)

(H) ___ Copy of any Family Court Order of Custody or Visitation and/or Order of Support to be continued by Judgment of Divorce

____ FORM UCS–111 (*Revised 12/01*) CHILD SUPPORT SUMMARY FORM, if there are any unemancipated children <u>and/or</u> maintenance/spousal support is award-ed

____ WRITTEN RETAINER AGREEMENT (22 NYCRR § 1400.3) <u>if</u> Attorney filing

Dated: _____   _____   _____

                       Signature of Attorney/Self–Represented   Telephone Number
                                     Litigant

Form 5. Child Support Summary Form (UCS–111)

UCS–111 (rev: 12/01)

CHILD SUPPORT SUMMARY FORM
SUPREME AND FAMILY COURT

COMPLETE FORM FOR <u>EACH BASIC CHILD SUPPORT OBLIGATION ORDER</u>[1]

A. **Court:**   ☐ Supreme   ☐ Family

B. **County:** _____

C. **Index #/Docket #:** _____

D. **Date Action Commenced:**
    _____/_____/_____

E. **Date Judgment/Order Submitted or Signed:**
    _____/_____/_____

F. **# Of Children Subject to Child Support Order:**
    _____

G. **Annual Gross Income:**

  1. Father: $ _____   Mother: $ _____

H. **Amount of Child Support Payment:**

  1. By Father: $ _____   2. By Mother: $ _____
      annually   annually

I. **Additional Child Support:**
    (Circle as many as appropriate)

         By Father: By Mother:

  1. Medical/Med. Ins.   1. Medical/Med. Ins.

  2. Child Care   2. Child Care

  3. Education   3. Education

  4. Other   4. Other

J. **Did the court make a finding that the child support award varied from the Child Support Standards Act amount? (Circle one)**
                1. Yes   2. No

K. **If answer to "J" was yes, circle court's reason(s):**

  1.   Financial resources of parents/child.

  2.   Physical/emotional health of child: special needs or aptitudes.

  3.   Child's expected standard of living had household remained intact.

  4.   Tax consequences.

  5.   Non-monetary contribution toward care and well-being of child.

  6.   Educational needs of either parent.

7.   Substantial differences in gross income of parents.

8.   Needs of other children of non-custodial parent.

9.   Extraordinary visitation expenses of non-custodial parent.

10.   Other (specify):

_____

_____

_____

L.   **Maintenance/Spousal Support: (Circle one)**

    1.   None   2.   By Father   3.   By Mother

M.   **Value of Maintenance/Spousal Support:**

    $ _____ annually

SUPREME COURT ONLY

N.   **Allocation of Property:**

    _____ % To Father   _____ % To Mother

NEW YORK STATE UNIFIED COURT SYSTEM
SUPPORT SUMMARY FORM: FAMILY & SUPREME COURT

INSTRUCTION SHEET

Prepare one report for each proposed judgment or <u>final</u> order granted pursuant to Article 4 or 5 of the Family Court Act and DRL § 240 and § 236 B(9)(b) which includes a provision for child support (including modification of order).

SUBMIT COMPLETED FORM TO:

   Office of Court Administration
   Office of Court Research
   25 Beaver Street, Room 975
   New York, New York 10004

GENERAL INSTRUCTIONS: → ALL ITEMS MUST BE ANSWERED

- If a number or amount in dollars is required and the answer is none, write 0.

- If a certain item is not applicable, write NA.

- If the information is unknown or not known to the party filling out the form, write UK.

- "mm/dd/yy" means "month/day/year".

SPECIAL INSTRUCTIONS FOR PARTICULAR ITEMS:

G.   Use gross income figures from the last complete calendar year. <u>Do not include maintenance or child support as income.</u>

H.   If the child support award is calculated weekly, multiply it by 52 for the annual amount; if biweekly, multiply it by 26, if monthly, multiply it by 12.

M.   If the maintenance award is calculated weekly, multiply it by 52 for the annual amount; if biweekly, multiply it by 26; if monthly, multiply it by 12. If the maintenance award calls for decreasing or increasing amounts (for example, a certain amount for five years and half that amount for another three years), then provide the average of the awards (total amount for all years divided by the number of years).

NOTE: THIS INFORMATION IS CONFIDENTIAL AND WILL BE USED FOR STATISTICAL PURPOSES ONLY. IT WILL NOT BE RETAINED IN THE CASE FILE.

[1] Defined by FCA 413(2) and DRL § 240(1–b)(b)(2): "Child Support" shall mean a sum to be paid pursuant to court order or decree by either or both parents or pursuant to a valid agreement between the parties for care, maintenance and education of any unemancipated child under the age of twenty-one years.

Form 6. Judgment of Divorce Form (A–13) Replacement Page
ORDERED AND ADJUDGED that:

☐ *Plaintiff*

☐ *Defendant*   is (are) hereby awarded equitable distribution of the marital property as follows:

_____

_____

_____

_____

_____

_____ ,

========== **OR** ==========

☐ *this section is not applicable,*

and it is further,

_____

_____

ORDERED AND ADJUDGED that:

A) ☐ the Settlement/Separation Agreement entered into between the parties on the

_____

day of _____ , _____ ,   ☐ *the original*
        Month   Year   ☐ *a copy*   of which is submitted herewith and
incorporated in this   ☐ *the transcript*
judgment by reference,   ☐ *shall survive and shall not be merged*   into this
                               ☐ *shall not survive and shall merge*

judgment, and the parties are hereby directed to comply with all legally enforceable terms and conditions of said agreement as if such terms and conditions were set forth in their entirety herein,

========== **OR** ==========

B) ☐ *there is no Settlement/Separation Agreement between the parties,*

_____

_____

    ORDERED AND ADJUDGED that all other matters concerning this Judgment will be retained by the Supreme Court Dedicated Matrimonial Part for one (1) year from the date of the signing of this Judgment of Divorce. Thereafter, all matters except equitable distribution will be referred to the appropriate Family Court, and it is further

_____

Page 4 of 5

(Form A–13) (Onondaga County Revision 06/06)

Form 7.   Health Insurance Coverage Notification

DRL § 177
Onondaga Combined Courts (Revised 08–27–07)

SUPREME COURT
STATE OF NEW YORK
COUNTY OF ONONDAGA _____

_____,
(Print Your Name)   Plaintiff,

         **HEALTH INSURANCE
COVERAGE NOTIFICATION**

       -vs-

         INDEX No.

_____,
(Print Other Party's Name)   Defendant.

If There Is No Opting–Out Agreement or Separation Agreement,
The Court will mail a copy of this Notice to both parties

NOTICE

Once the judgment of divorce is entered, a person may or may not be eligible to be covered under his or her former spouse's health insurance plan, depending on the terms of the plan.

If There is an Opting–Out Agreement or Separation Agreement,
The Following Must be Completed and Signed

I, *(Print Plaintiff's Name)* _____, fully understand that upon the entrance of this divorce agreement, I may no longer be allowed to receive health coverage under my former spouse's health insurance plan. I may be entitled to purchase health insurance on my own through a COBRA option, if available, otherwise I may be required to secure my own health insurance.

Date: *(Print Date)* _____   _____
                             Sign Name
                             Plaintiff

I, *(Print Defendant's Name)* _____, fully understand that upon the entrance of this divorce agreement, I may no longer be allowed to receive health coverage under my former spouse's health insurance plan. I may be entitled to purchase health insurance on my own through a COBRA option, if available, otherwise I may be required to secure my own health insurance.

Date: *(Print Date)* _____   _____
                             Sign Name
                             Defendant

SEVENTH JUDICIAL DISTRICT — CAYUGA, LIVINGSTON, MONROE, ONTARIO, SENECA, STEUBEN, WAYNE, YATES COUNTIES

Westlaw Electronic Research

These rules may be searched electronically on Westlaw® *in the NY–RULES database; updates to these rules may be found on* Westlaw *in NY–RULESUP-DATES. For search tips and a summary of database content, consult the* Westlaw *Scope Screens for each database.*

App.

F. Trial Ready Letter and Trial Preparation Memorandum.

G. Summary Trial Order.

H. Stipulation of Binding Summary Jury Trial.

ASBESTOS LITIGATION

Doc.

1. Filing of Papers.
2. Case Management Order.

App.

A. Plaintiff's Statement.

App.

B. Acknowledgement of Service.

C. Acknowledgment of Service.

D. Stipulation (JH).

E. Defendants' Alternative Standard Interrogatories.

F. Defendants' First Set of Interrogatories.

G. Plaintiffs' First Set of Interrogatories.

H. Discovery Scheduling Order.

I. Juror Questionnaire.

FORMS

UCS–840. Request for Judicial Intervention.

DISTRICT RULES
FAMILY COURT

Form 1. Petition for Support or to Modify Support

FAMILY COURT OF THE STATE OF NEW YORK COUNTY OF

Seventh Judicial District Family Court information: http:// www.nycourts.gov/courts/7jd/courts/family

In the Matter of

FILE #: _____

_____, PETITIONER   DOCKET#: _____

FIRST   M.I.   LAST   (PERSON FILING)

SS # _____ DOB _____   **PETITION FOR**

Address** _____   ☐ CHILD SUPPORT ☐ SPOUSAL SUPPORT

_____   — OR —

-AGAINST-   ☐ MODIFY FAMILY COURT ORDER OF SUPPORT

☐ MODIFY ORDER OF ANOTHER COURT SUPPORT

_____, RESPONDENT

FIRST   M.I.   LAST   (PERSON FILING AGAINST)

SS # _____ DOB _____

Address** _____

_____

** Or indicate if address ordered to be confidential pursuant to Family Court Act § 154–b(2) or Domestic Relations Law § 254. **If requesting a confidential address, you must file a confidential address application (Form GF– 21).**

THE PETITIONER STATES THE FOLLOWING:

1. Petitioner is authorized (able) to begin this proceeding because:
   - ☐ Petitioner and Respondent were married at _____ on _____
   - ☐ Petitioner and Respondent have the child(ren) named below in common
   - ☐ Other [Specify Petitioner's relationship to the child(ren) _____]

2. The (Petitioner) (Respondent) is chargeable with the support of the following (spouse)(dependents):

Spouse:	NAME	DOB		SS #		SEX	
	_____	__ / __ / __		_____		M F	

Child(ren):	NAME	DOB		SS #		SEX	LIVES WITH

_____   ___ / ___ / ___   _____   M   F   ☐ Pet ☐ Resp

_____   ___ / ___ / ___   _____   M   F   ☐ Pet ☐ Resp

_____   ___ / ___ / ___   _____   M   F   ☐ Pet ☐ Resp

_____   ___ / ___ / ___   _____   M   F   ☐ Pet ☐ Resp

3. The relationship of each party to the children named above is: (If you are a relative, state whether related to mother or father).

            Mother   Father   Other

Petitioner   ☐   ☐   _____

Respondent   ☐   ☐   _____

4. [If the mother has not been named in this petition]
Name and address of the mother is _____

    ☐   Mother is deceased

    ☐   Mother's address is confidential [pursuant to Family Court Act § 154–b(2) or Domestic Relations Law § 254]

If there HAS NOT been a support Order issued in any court, complete numbers 5–8, & 16–18

5. The father of the child(ren) in this proceeding is (name) _____
(if the children have different fathers, **please complete a separate petition for each father**)

Paternity of the children was established as follows:

    ☐   Mother and Father were married at the time of conception or birth

    ☐   An Acknowledgment of Paternity signed on _____, ___ for _____ (attach copy)

    ☐   Court Order of Filiation: Docket No. ___ (attach copy of Order if not from this Court)

    ☐   The father is deceased

    ☐   **PATERNITY HAS NOT BEEN LEGALLY ESTABLISHED**

(If the category selected does not apply to all children, explain)

_____

6. ___ Respondent, on or about _____, and thereafter, has not provided fair and reasonable support for Petitioner and the dependent(s) according to Respondent's means and earning capacity. **(Income)**

7. Respondent is unlikely to make payments in accordance with the order of support requested, because _____

8. ___ Respondent has an employer whose name and address is _____
_____ as a source of income.

If there HAS been a support Order issued in any court complete numbers 9 through 18

9. By an Order of ☐ This Family Court ☐ Another Family Court [specify] _____
☐ Supreme Court [specify] _____ Order date _____
(You MUST attach a copy of the Order if it is not from this Court)
The ☐ Petitioner ☐ Respondent was directed to pay $ _____, (weekly)(Bi-weekly)(monthly)(other _____) for the support of the following child(ren): _____

10. The ☐ Petitioner ☐ Respondent was directed to pay ___ % of any uncovered (medical) (daycare) (dental) expenses.
The ☐ Petitioner ☐ Respondent was directed to provide (medical) (dental) insurance.

11. Payments are being made ☐ through the Support Collection Unit or ☐ directly to the payee.
☐ Petitioner ☐ Respondent ☐ had ☐ did not have a prior order of support that was payable through the Support Collection Unit.

12. a. ☐ Under the terms of the (judgment)(order), the (Supreme Court)(Other Court _____) has not retained exclusive jurisdiction to modify the (judgment)(order).

    b. ☐ The other Court is a court of competent jurisdiction outside the State of New York.

13. Since the entry of that Order, there has been a change in circumstances as follows: **(state what has changed since the last Order was made)**

_____
_____
_____
_____
_____
_____

14. Because of this change in circumstances, the Order should be modified (changed) as follows: **(state how you want the Order changed)**

_____
_____
_____
_____
_____
_____

15. The Petitioner failed to make an application earlier for relief from said judgment or order directing payment prior to the accrual of arrears for the following reason(s). **(state why you did not file sooner).**

_____
_____
_____

16. Is either party paying support for a spouse or child(ren) that is/are **NOT** named in this petition?
    ☐ Yes ☐ No. If yes, (name) _____ is directed to pay $ ___ (weekly)(Bi-weekly)(monthly) through (specify Court and county) _____

17. No previous application has been made to any judge or Court, including a Native American tribunal, for the relief requested in this petition (except _____)

18. Petitioner
    ☐ has applied for child support services with the local Department of Social Services
    ☐ now applies for child support enforcement services by the filling of this petition.
    ☐ does not wish to make an application for child support services
    ☐ is not eligible for child support enforcement services. [Petitioners seeking <u>only</u> spousal support are ineligible.]

I REQUEST: ☐ **AN ORDER OF SUPPORT**
                 ☐ **THAT THE RESPONDENT BE REQUIRED TO PROVIDE ADDITIONAL COVERAGE FOR HEALTH INSURANCE OR**
                 ☐ **THAT THE (JUDGMENT)(ORDER) OF THE (FAMILY COURT) (SUPREME COURT) (OTHER COURT _____) DATED _____, ___, BE MODIFIED AS SET FORTH ABOVE AND FOR ANY OTHER APPROPRIATE RELIEF.**

     DATED: _____

                             PETITIONER-signature

_____

                             PRINT NAME

NOTE: (1) A COURT ORDER OF SUPPORT RESULTING FROM A PROCEEDING COMMENCED BY THIS APPLICATION (PETITION) SHALL BE ADJUSTED BY THE APPLICATION OF A COST OF LIVING ADJUSTMENT AT THE DIRECTION OF THE SUPPORT COLLECTION UNIT NO EARLIER THAN TWENTY–FOUR MONTHS AFTER SUCH ORDER IS ISSUED, LAST MODIFIED OR LAST ADJUSTED, UPON THE REQUEST OF ANY PARTY TO THE ORDER OR PURSUANT TO PARAGRAPH (2) BELOW. SUCH COST OF LIVING ADJUSTMENT SHALL BE ON NOTICE TO BOTH PARTIES WHO, IF THEY OBJECT TO THE COST OF LIVING ADJUSTMENT, SHALL HAVE THE RIGHT TO BE HEARD BY THE COURT AND TO PRESENT EVIDENCE WHICH THE COURT WILL CONSIDER IN ADJUSTING THE CHILD SUPPORT ORDER IN ACCORDANCE WITH SECTION FOUR HUNDRED THIRTEEN OF THE FAMILY COURT ACT, KNOWN AS THE CHILD SUPPORT STANDARDS ACT.
(2) A PARTY SEEKING SUPPORT FOR ANY CHILD(REN) RECEIVING FAMILY ASSISTANCE SHALL HAVE A CHILD SUPPORT ORDER REVIEWED AND ADJUSTED AT

THE DIRECTION OF THE SUPPORT COLLECTION UNIT NO EARLIER THAN TWEN-
TY–FOUR MONTHS AFTER SUCH ORDER IS ISSUED, LAST MODIFIED OR LAST
ADJUSTED BY THE SUPPORT COLLECTION UNIT, WITHOUT FURTHER APPLICA-
TION BY ANY PARTY. ALL PARTIES WILL RECEIVE A COPY OF THE ADJUSTED
ORDER.

**(3) WHERE ANY PARTY FAILS TO PROVIDE, AND UPDATE UPON ANY CHANGE,
THE SUPPORT COLLECTION UNIT WITH A CURRENT ADDRESS, AS REQUIRED BY
SECTION FOUR HUNDRED FORTY–THREE OF THE FAMILY COURT ACT, TO WHICH
AN ADJUSTED ORDER CAN BE SENT, THE SUPPORT OBLIGATION AMOUNT CON-
TAINED THEREIN SHALL BECOME DUE AND OWING ON THE DATE THE FIRST
PAYMENT IS DUE UNDER THE TERMS OF THE ORDER OF SUPPORT WHICH WAS
REVIEWED AND ADJUSTED OCCURRING ON OR AFTER THE EFFECTIVE DATE OF
THE ADJUSTED ORDER, REGARDLESS OF WHETHER OR NOT THE PARTY HAS
RECEIVED A COPY OF THE ADJUSTED ORDER.**

Form 2. Petition for Custody/Visitation

FAMILY COURT OF THE STATE OF NEW YORK COUNTY OF

Seventh Judicial District Family Court information: http://www.nycourts.gov/courts/7jd/courts/family

In the Matter of

FILE #: _____

_____, **PETITIONER**   DOCKET#: _____

FIRST   M.I.   LAST   (DOB)   (PERSON FILING)   **PETITION FOR**

ADDRESS:** _____

☐ CUSTODY ☐ VISITATION

_____

☐ MODIFY FAMILY COURT ORDER

–AGAINST–   ☐ MODIFY ORDER OF ANOTHER COURT

RESPONDENT 1 (PERSON FILED   RESPONDENT 2 (PERSON FILED

AGAINST) _____   AGAINST)

FIRST   M.I.   LAST   (DOB)   FIRST   M.I.   LAST   (DOB)

ADDRESS:** _____   ADDRESS:** _____

Or indicate if address ordered to be confidential pursuant to Family Court Act § 154–b(2) or Domestic Relations Law § 254. **If requesting a confidential address, you must file a confidential address application (Form GF–21).

THE PETITIONER STATES THE FOLLOWING:

1. The Relationship between the Petitioner and the Respondent is:
    - ☐ Spouse (date of marriage _____)
    - ☐ Former Spouse (date of divorce _____) Attach copy of Divorce Decree
    - ☐ Have child in common—never married
    - ☐ Petitioner is the Parent of (specify) _____
    - ☐ Other (specify) _____

2. The children who are the subjects of this proceeding are:

NAME	DOB	SEX	LIVES WITH
_____	__/__/__	M F	PET ☐ RESP 1 ☐ RESP 2 ☐
_____	__/__/__	M F	PET ☐ RESP 1 ☐ RESP 2 ☐
_____	__/__/__	M F	PET ☐ RESP 1 ☐ RESP 2 ☐
_____	__/__/__	M F	PET ☐ RESP 1 ☐ RESP 2 ☐

3. The relationship of each party to the children named above is: (If you are a relative, state whether related to mother or father).

	Mother	Father	Other
Petitioner	☐	☐	_____
Respondent 1	☐	☐	_____
Respondent 2	☐	☐	_____

Note: If a custody or visitation proceeding is pending or an order of custody or visitation has been issued by a court outside of the State of New York, including a Native American Tribunal, or if the Respondents live outside the State of New York, the custody/visitation petition for proceedings under the *Uniform Child Custody Jurisdiction and Enforcement Act* (Form UCCJEA–1) should be used instead of this form.

4. Is Petitioner ☐ Respondent ☐ on active duty, deployed or temporarily assigned to military service? ☐ No ☐ Yes (If Yes—name military branch or National Guard unit, expected dates and location of duty and how such duty is likely to affect ability to exercise custody, if at all:

_____

_____

5. List where the child/children has/have lived in the past 5 years:

CHILD'S NAME   COUNTY/STATE   DURATION (from/to)

_____

_____
_____
_____

6.   List the name(s) of the person(s) with whom each child has lived during the past 5 years:

     NAME   COUNTY/STATE   DURATION (from/to)

_____
_____
_____

IF THERE *HAS NOT* BEEN A CUSTODY OR VISITATION ORDER ISSUED IN ANY COURT, COMPLETE NUMBERS 7 AND 8, THEN SKIP TO THE INSTRUCTIONS ABOVE NUMBER 12.

7.   The father of the child(ren) in this proceeding is (name) _____
     The mother of the child(ren) in this proceeding is (name) _____
     Paternity of the children was established as follows:
     ☐ Mother and Father were married at the time of conception or birth
     ☐ An Acknowledgment of Paternity signed on _____ ___, for _____ (attach copy)
     ☐ Court Order of Filiation: Docket No. ___ (attach copy of Order if not from this Court)
     ☐ **PATERNITY HAS NOT BEEN LEGALLY ESTABLISHED**
     (If the category selected does not apply to all children, explain)

_____
_____

8.   State why it would be in the best interest of the child(ren) for you to have custody or visitation: **(IF YOU NEED ADDITIONAL SPACE, PLEASE ASK FOR A CONTINUATION SHEET.)**

_____
_____
_____
_____
_____
_____
_____

IF THERE HAS BEEN A CUSTODY OR VISITATION ORDER ISSUED IN ANY COURT, COMPLETE NUMBERS 9 THROUGH 11.

9.   By an Order of ☐ This Family Court ☐ Another Family Court [specify] _____ ☐
     Supreme Court [specify] ___ Order Date _____.
     (You must attach a copy of the Order if it is not from this Court)
     The ☐ Petitioner ☐ Respondent was given ☐ Custody ☐ Visitation as follows:
     (state what the Order is now)

_____
_____
_____
_____
_____
_____

10.   Since the entry of that Order, there has been a change in circumstances as follows: **(state what has changed** since the last Order was made)

_____
_____
_____
_____
_____
_____
_____
_____
_____
_____

11. Because of this change in circumstances, the Order should be modified (changed) as follows: **(state how you want the Order changed)**

_____
_____
_____
_____

Answer Question 12 only if you are NOT a parent to the child(ren) named in this Petition.

12. Do you know of any Neglect or Permanency Proceedings involving the Child(ren) on this petition?

☐ **Yes** ☐ **No If Yes, please ask for and fill out the Neglect Question Sheet.**

13. Are you involved in any other proceeding in any other court? ☐ Yes ☐ No If Yes, explain:

_____

A Final or Temporary **Order of Protection** has been issued ☐ against Respondent ☐ against me in the following proceeding(s) [specify criminal, matrimonial or Family Court, date of Order, next court date and status of case if available]

COURT	ORDER DATE	AGAINST	ORDER EXPIRES	NEXT COURT DATE

14. The Petitioner requests a Temporary Order of Protection [FCA 655] because:

_____

15. The subject child(ren) ☐ is(are) ☐ is(are) not Native–American child(ren) subject to the Indian Child Welfare Act of 1978 (25 U.S.C. §§ 1901–1963).

I ASK THE COURT TO ISSUE AN ORDER OF ☐ CUSTODY AND/OR ☐ VISITATION AND FOR ANY OTHER APPROPRIATE RELIEF.

DATED: _____

                                        _____
                                        PETITIONER-signature

_____

| STATE OF NEW YORK | : | VERIFICATION | PRINT NAME |
| COUNTY OF | : | | |

Petitioner, being duly sworn, states: I have read this petition and its contents are true to my own knowledge, except to matters alleged to be on information and belief and, as to those matters, I believe them to be true.
Sworn to before me on

                                        _____
                                        PETITIONER-signature

_____ 20 __

_____
(Deputy) Clerk of the Court,
Notary or Comm. Of Deeds

Form 3. Petitioner's Worksheet for Orders to Show Cause

(Attach to Petition)   Rev. 6/10

PETITIONER'S WORKSHEET—TO ACCOMPANY ORDER TO SHOW CAUSE /PETITION:

I am (or) We are seeking an immediate temporary order from the Court for the following reasons:

☐ **The Child(ren) is (are) in danger due to:**

     ☐ Lack of Supervision (insufficient food, clothing, housing, cleanliness, medical care, etc.)

     ☐ Left unattended (alone)

     ☐ Sexual abuse

     ☐ Physical harm

     ☐ Alcohol and/or substance abuse by an adult responsible for the children

     ☐ Other reasons (**List in your petition**)

     ● Do you know if anyone has contacted the Child Abuse Hotline or Social Services (DSS/DHS)? Yes ___ No ___ Caseworker's Name _____

☐ **The person who has the child(ren) is unable to keep the child(ren) because:**

     ☐ Of a child protective action

When was the referral to Social Services made? ___ Caseworker's name: _____

     ☐ Of a court order including an Order of Protection

     ☐ A problem with another person in the home

     ☐ Illness

     ☐ He/she will be leaving the home (travel, jail sentence, etc.)

     ☐ Other reasons (**List in your petition**)

☐ **There has been a threat made to take the child(ren)**

     ☐ Away from the home

     ☐ Out of New York State

     ☐ To a place where one party would be unable to have visitation

     ☐ None of the above -

(Explain and list date(s) of threats for each checked category in your petition)

☐ **If the Petitioner and Respondent lived together,**

     ● Who left most recently? _____

     ● When did he or she leave? _____

     ● With whom has the child lived since the separation? _____

☐ **The child(ren) have not been returned to a party as ordered or agreed upon.**

(Explain in your petition).

☐ **Threats have been made against the child(ren) or one of the parents**

(Explain and list date(s) of threats in your petition).

☐ **The child(ren) has (have been left with one parent (or a non-parent person) with an indication that the <u>other parent is not returning</u>.**

(Explain in your petition).

☐ **The child(ren) are in a new home and need to be enrolled in school.**

(Explain in your petition).

☐ **NONE OF THE ABOVE**

(Briefly state the reasons(s) below for your request and explain in your petition:

_____
_____

☐ **Is there a court order for custody/visitation?** Yes ___ No _____

If there is an order, please indicate **under question 9 on your petition**:

● **What court made the order.**
● **What is the date of the order.**
● **What are the terms of the order.**

        Remember to provide a full explanation of each box checked on this form in your petition.

IMMEDIATE TEMPORARY RELIEF REQUESTED (What are you requesting—Not why you want it):

(Please check provisions that you are requesting)

___ Temporary Custody

___ Temporary Physical Residence

___ Visitation Suspended

___ Visitation Arranged/Transferred by 3rd Party

___ The child(ren) shall NOT be removed from _____ County

___ The child(ren) shall NOT be removed from New York State

___ Residence of the child(ren) shall not be changed

___ Child(ren) shall be immediately returned to Petitioner

___ (Ordered) **(enter any other provisions that you are requesting)** _____
_____
_____
_____

VERIFICATION

STATE OF NEW YORK

COUNTY OF SENECA

Petitioner, being duly sworn, states: I have read this petition attachment and its contents are true to my own knowledge, except to matters alleged to be on information and belief and, as to those matters, I believe them to be true.

_____

Petitioner—Signature

_____

Petitioner—Print name

Sworn to before me on

_____, 20 ___

_____

(Deputy) Clerk of the Court
Notary or Comm. Of Deeds

Form 4. Neglect/Abuse Question Sheet

If you are NOT a parent of the child(ren) and there has been a child protective petition (neglect or abuse) or permanency hearing report filed regarding the child(ren), complete this page.

12. a. ☐ A petition was filed in [specify county] _____ County Family Court, on [specify date] _____ alleging that [specify names of respondents on that petition]: _____ neglected or abused child(ren). The petition resulted in [specify what happened in court; if the case was adjourned to be combined with this petition [1], specify the next court date]:

b. ☐ A permanency report, pursuant to Article 10-A of the Family Court Act, was filed in [specify county] _____ Family Court, on [specify date] _____, indicating a permanency plan of placement of the child(ren) with Petitioner(s). The permanency hearing was adjourned to [specify date] _____, so that the matter can be heard with this petition.[2]

c. ☐ The child's birth mother ☐ has ☐ has not consented to the award of custody to the Petitioner(s). If not, the following extraordinary circumstances support Petitioners' application to seek custody of the child(ren) [State the extraordinary circumstances]: _____

_____

_____

d. ☐ The child's legally-established birth father ☐ has ☐ has not consented to the award of custody to the Petitioner(s). If not, the following extraordinary circumstances support Petitioner's application to seek custody of the child(ren) [State the extraordinary circumstances]: _____

_____

_____

e. ☐ The child has been living with the following foster parent(s) [specify names]: _____ since [specify date] _____. The foster parent(s) ☐ has/have ☐ has/have not consented to the award of custody to the Petitioner(s).

☐ I don't know whether they have consented.

f. ☐ The local Department of Social Services [specify county]: _____ in the related ☐ child abuse or neglect or ☐ permanency proceeding, ☐ has ☐ has not consented to the award of custody to the Petitioner(s).

☐ I don't know whether the department has consented.

g. ☐ The attorney for the child(ren) [specify attorney's name]: _____ in the related ☐ child abuse or neglect or ☐ permanency proceeding, ☐ has ☐ has not consented to the award of custody to the Petitioner(s).

☐ I don't know whether he/she has consented.

[1] Pursuant to FCA § 1055–1b.

[2] Pursuant to F.C.A. § 1089–a.

Form 5. Support Information Sheet Monroe County

__ MEDICAID __ PATERNITY __ LEGAL __ CHANGE OF PAYEE

APPLICATION FOR CHILD SUPPORT SERVICES: **REQUEST DATE: _____**

(A) CLIENT	NAME (Last, First, M.I.) Relationship to Children	Social Security No. Date of Birth
	ADDRESS–Legal Residence (Street, City, State, Zip)	Telephone Number (Include Area Code)
		Home Business

(B) ABSENT Parent	NAME (Last, First, M.I.) Relationship to Applicant	Social Security No. Date of Birth
	ADDRESS–Legal Residence (Street, City, State, Zip)	Telephone Number (Include Area Code)
		Home Business
	Employer Name/Address (Current or Last Known)	Telephone Number (Include Area Code)

Place of Birth   Mother's Maiden Name   Father's Full Name   Date of Desertion

(C) CHILD(REN)	NAME (Last, First, M.I.) Date of Birth	Social Security No.

AFFIRMATION—I hereby apply pursuant to Social Services Law § 111–g and 111–h for child support services under Title IV–D of the Social Security Act as amended. I subscribe and affirm under penalty of perjury that this application is made for the sole purpose(s) of obtaining assistance in establishing paternity and/or obtaining child support from an individual who is (or may be) legally responsible for the support of dependent children; and that statements made in this application or accompanying document have been examined by me and to the best of my knowledge and belief are true and correct.

In making this application for child support services, I authorize the Child Support Enforcement Unit, its agents and employees to undertake any investigation necessary, including a review of any records that involve the child support obligation which may be on file in any County Clerk's Office, which records would otherwise be protected from disclosure by Section 235 of the Domestic Relations Law.

SIGNATURE _____ DATE _____

COMPLETE THIS SECTION FOR LEGAL SERVICES FOR MEDICAID ONLY CLIENTS

I hereby request legal services as provided by Monroe County Child Support Enforcement for legal proceedings related to establishment, enforcement or modification of a child support in Family Court for dependents in receipt of Medicaid.

SIGNATURE   DATE
X

COMPLETE THIS SECTION ONLY IF LEGAL REPRESENTATION IS REQUESTED for non–MA clients RIGHT TO RECOVERY MUST BE SIGNED IN THE PRESENCE OF A IV–D STAFF MEMBER FOR LEGAL SERVICES.

I assign to the Monroe County Department of Social Services and New York State the title to and right to receive up to 25 % of each child support payment to be received by me on behalf of children listed above until such time that DSS is reimbursed for actual costs incurred to providing the necessary services(s) requested. If child support payments are made payable through the Support Collection Unit (S.C.U.) I authorize the S.C.U. to pay the Monroe County Department of Social Services the amounts assigned above. I understand that if I do not reimburse the Monroe County Department of Social Services and New York State for these costs out of child support payments receive by me, they may initiate a civil proceeding, the total costs for which I will be responsible to pay.

X _____   _____
         Signature   Date

New York
Monroe

_____ day of _____, 200 ___. _____, to me known to be the individual described in and who executed the foregoing instrument and acknowledge that he executed the same.

X _____   _____
            Commissioner of Deeds   expires on date.

APPOINTMENT DATE _____   WITH _____
CSMS: _____   STATUS: _____
NOTES:

MONROE COUNTY
JUDGES' RULES

JUSTICE DAVID M. BARRY

Rule 1. Preliminary Conferences

Conferences will be scheduled upon one of the following events: (1) after filing of a summons with notice or summons and complaint (2) filing of an RJI; (3) filing of a Note of issue where no prior RJI has been filed requesting a pre-trial conference; or (4) at the request of counsel. The Court must be provided with a copy of all pleadings and other relevant papers at least seven (7) days prior to the conference. Counsel are also encouraged to provide a brief written statement as to the nature of their client's positions. All preliminary conferences involving Pro Se litigants will be conducted in open Court and upon the record. Questions or requests regarding pre-trial conferences should be directed to the Judge Barry's Secretary, Joan Hettis at 428–2929.

Rule 2. Motions

Special Term:

Special Term will be held each week on Wednesday at 2:00 P.M. (But for the last Wednesday of each month which may be set aside for a status calendar) unless otherwise scheduled to avoid holiday conflicts. The Court will set the return date for all Motions and Orders to Show Cause after submission. Movants must supply two copies of all motion papers. Questions or requests regarding return dates should be directed to the Law Clerk. Sharon Higginbotham, Esq. at 428–3817.

Adjournments:

Adjournments of motions will be routinely granted by the Court if they are upon the consent of all attorneys and without prejudice to the litigants. Requests for adjournments should be made at least forty-eight (48) hours in advance of the motion's return date. The Court, not counsel, will set the new return date for any motion which has been adjourned. Written confirmation of the adjourned return date must be provided to the Court and all parties. Confirmation may be faxed to the Chambers at 428–2513. Failure to provide such written confirmation will result in the motion being called on its original motion date.

Submission of papers:

Copies of any cases that are cited within the motion papers or memoranda of law must accompany same, except when the case is cited for general propositions of law.

All motion papers, including memoranda of law should be submitted to the Court at the time schedul-

ing of the motion is requested. All responsive papers and memoranda of law are to be received by the court no later than seven (7) days preceding the return date. The Court reserves the right not to consider any papers submitted after this time.

Appearances:

Appearances and oral argument are required on all motions unless excused by the Court. Counsel shall notify the Court by facsimile (428–2513) at least twenty-four (24) hours prior to the return date whenever a motion has been settled, withdrawn, or a consent order agreed upon.

Decisions:

All orders in contested matters must reference and append the transcript of the oral decision or a copy of the written decision upon which the order is based.

Orders:

In all matters, counsel shall obtain the approval of opposing counsel on all Orders. If approval cannot be obtained, then a copy of the order shall be served on opposing counsel advising that the Order is being presented to the Court for signature allowing ten (10) days to interpose objections as to the form or substance of the Order.

Rule 3. Discovery Motions

The Court requires compliance with Sec. 22 NYCRR 202.07 prior to bringing a discovery motion. Such motions must be accompanied by a separate Affidavit certifying that good faith efforts to resolve the dispute have been made. No return date will be assigned to motions that are not in compliance with this requirement.

Dispositive Motions:

Any dispositive motions, such as a summary judgment motions, must be submitted to the Court for scheduling within thirty (30) days of the filing of the Notice of Issue. Dispositive motions which are not made in compliance with this rule will not be considered by the Court pursuant to CPLR 3212 (a).

Rule 4. Pre–Note Calendar Calls

A representative with knowledge of the case, prepared to answer any questions concerning its status, must appear. Failure to answer calendar call may result in the case being stricken.

Rule 5. Note of Issue Calendar Call

A representative with knowledge of the case, prepared to answer questions concerning the length of trial and the schedules of counsel and witnesses, must appear. Counsel will be bound by the representations made at calendar call. Failure to appear may result in the Note of Issue being stricken or in the entry of a default pursuant to Sec. 22 NYCRR 202.27.

Rule 6. Matrimonial Action

The court intends to strictly adhere to the Milonas Rules contained in Sec. 22 NYCRR Sec. 202.16. Accordingly, upon the filing of a RJI the Court will schedule a preliminary conference within forty-five (45) days. The parties must attend the preliminary conference. At least (10) days prior to the preliminary conference, the Court shall be provided with copies of all pleadings, a Statement of Net Worth and if completed, a Statement of Proposed Disposition. The failure to supply the Court with these papers may result in the cancellation of the preliminary conference. At the preliminary conference, the Court will issue a scheduling order establishing a timetable for the completion of all discovery. Counsel should be prepared to stipulate in writing as to those issues which are not contested. The Court will schedule a date for trial not later than six (6) months from the date of conference. The Court will also schedule a compliance conference at which the parties also must personally attend.

Motions for temporary spousal support or child support, must be accompanied by an updated Statement of Net Worth. This includes any motion returnable prior to the preliminary conference.

Rule 7. Trials

No adjournments shall be granted for cases scheduled for trial absent an emergency and subject to the uniform rules for the engagement of counsel (22 NYCRR Part 125).

Rule 8. Motions to Withdraw as Counsel

Except in cases of substitution of counsel by consent pursuant to CPLR Sec. 321 (b) (1), motion to withdraw must be in accordance with CPLR Sec. 321 (b) (2). The notice of motion should contain an advisement to the client that he or she must be present in Court on the return date.

Rule 9. Motions for Attorneys Fees

All motions for attorneys fees shall be accompanied by an Affidavit of Attorney, a Statement of Services Rendered and a Retainer Agreement.

Rule 10. Discontinuance of Civil Actions

The attorney for the plaintiff shall file a Stipulation of Discontinuance within twenty (20) days of that discontinuance, in compliance with Sec. NYCRR 203.28.

JUSTICE DANIEL J. DOYLE

Rule 1. Applications

The Court does not accept letter applications. All applications for an order must be made by formal motion properly filed in the Monroe County Clerk's Office. Motions are generally heard by the Court every Tuesday morning at 9:30 a.m. Such motions may, at the discretion of the Court, be heard at a conference.

Discovery motions are governed by 22 NYCRR § 202.7. In addition, prior to making motions for other types of relief, counsel should consult with one another in a good faith effort to resolve such issues prior to making a motion, particularly those matters related to visitation.

All motions shall be orally argued at the place and time assigned by the Court and the parties must be present, unless otherwise directed by the Court. The Motion Calendars of the Court are published on the day of the return date in *The Daily Record* and available at http://www.nycourts.gov/courts/7jd/monroe/.

Rule 2. Motion Papers

There shall be compliance with the procedures prescribed in the court rules, DRL and the CPLR. Counsel are reminded that the CPLR does not provide for sur-reply papers, however denominated.

The Court does not accept motion papers by facsimile or electronic means unless approved, in advance, by the Court.

Counsel must use tabs when submitting papers containing exhibits and exhibits must be legible.

Rule 3. Adjournments

All adjournments are made at the discretion of the Court and may be permitted for good cause shown.

Counsel requesting an adjournment of a Preliminary Conference must contact the Matrimonial Screening Part.

Counsel requesting an adjournment of a subsequent Conference should contact Chambers via fax or e-mail no later that 48 hours before the scheduled conference, except in the case of emergency. Counsel shall indicate the position of all other counsel regarding the requested adjournment, including future dates that would be available to all counsel for rescheduling.

Adjournment of a motion is allowed on consent of all the parties and with the permission of the Court. The Court has the discretion to grant an adjournment for just cause.

The Court encourages counsel to communicate with the Court and each other by e-mail as this will effectuate timely rescheduling. Please contact Connie Giliberti cgiliber@courts.state.ny.us.

Rule 4. Correspondence by Facsimile or Other Electronic Means

Under circumstances necessitating, in the Court's discretion, expedited proceedings, the Court may correspond with counsel by facsimile or other electronic means. Counsel are required to provide the court with facsimile numbers and/or e-mail addresses to be used for service under such circumstances.

Rule 5. Compliance Rules for Matrimonial Actions

Counsel must comply with the provisions of 22 NYCRR 202.16. Note well: No motion for spousal maintenance, child support or counsel fees will be heard unless the moving papers include a statement of net worth.

Rule 6. [Counsel Compliance]

Should counsel be unable to comply with any of these court rules, counsel must seek leave of the Court in writing, explaining the reason(s) for their inability to comply, along with a specific request of alternative relief.

JUSTICE EVELYN FRAZEE

Doc. 1. Hon. Evelyn Frazee

The Court will follow the Uniform Civil Rules for the Supreme Court (22 NYCRR Part 202) as supplemented herein.

MOTIONS

Special Term:

Special Term will be held every other Thursday at 9:30 a.m. unless such date is a legal holiday or the Court otherwise reschedules. Return dates for all motions and orders to show cause will be set by the Court.

Adjournments:

In most instances, adjournments of motions will be routinely granted if they are by consent of all attorneys. A request for an adjournment should be made as soon as possible, but no later than 12:00 p.m. on the Tuesday preceding the Thursday return date. All requests regarding adjournments should be made to the Court's law clerk, Edward J. Usinger, Esq., at (585) 428-5753. If a request for an adjournment is not consented to by all parties, the Court may require oral argument by telephone in determining whether to grant an adjournment. Counsel for the party requesting the adjournment shall provide written confirmation of the adjourned return date to the Court and all parties within two (2) business days of obtaining the adjournment.

Settlement/Withdrawal:

Counsel shall advise the Court promptly when a matter is resolved or withdrawn.

Submission of Papers:

All papers must be served in compliance with CPLR 2214 and 2215. All responsive papers and memoranda of law are to be received by the Court no later than 12:00 p.m. on the Tuesday preceding the return date. Any papers submitted after this time may not be considered by the Court. For the ease of the Court in reviewing the papers, a list specifying all motion exhibits should be submitted.

Appearances:

Appearances and oral argument are required for all motions except:

(1) Counsel whose office is located outside the Monroe County and surrounding areas may request that oral argument be done by telephone. Such request must be made no later than 12:00 p.m. on the Tuesday preceding the Thursday return date and should be directed to the Court's law clerk, Edward J. Usinger, Esq. (585–428–5753);

(2) Consent orders where Court is notified in advance;

(3) Unopposed motions; and

(4) Withdrawn motions.

Decisions:

Decisions will be made in one of three ways:

(1) By oral decision from the bench without a transcript.

(2) By oral decision from the bench which is transcribed. The transcript must be appended to the order. The cost of the transcript of the decision shall be split equally between the parties unless the Court otherwise directs.

(3) By written decision after oral argument. The decision will be mailed to the Monroe County Clerk's Office for filing by the Court and a copy mailed to counsel. A copy of the written decision should be referenced in the order or judgment.

Judgments/Orders:

The original and a copy (for the Court's file) of all judgments (except mortgage foreclosures and divorces) and orders shall be submitted for cases which are not concluded by the order or judgment. Such submission should be made within twenty (20) days from the date of decision, but in no event exceeding the time requirements contained in CPLR 2219 and 22 NYCRR 210.33. Approval from opposing counsel should be sought prior to submission. If approval cannot be obtained, then opposing counsel should be served with a copy of the proposed judgment or order with written notice advising that it is being presented to the Court for signature. Thereafter, counsel shall have five (5) business days to raise an objection to the proposed judgment or order.

Return of Judgments/Orders:

All judgments and orders will be returned to the Supreme Court Clerk's Office unless counsel has submitted a self-addressed stamped envelope with sufficient postage.

CONFERENCES

Conferences will be scheduled upon one of the following events: (1) filing of a RJI; (2) filing of a Note of Issue, where no prior RJI has been filed, requesting a pretrial conference; or (3) at the request of counsel. The Court must be provided with a copy of all pleadings, a brief synopsis of the case, procedural history and relevant issues before a conference will be set.

TRIALS

Except where a trial preference has been granted or the interests of judicial economy otherwise require, the Court will endeavor to reach trial-ready cases in order based upon the filing date of the Note of Issue. Prior to trial, the Court will send counsel a letter stating the date of jury selection and the Court's rules concerning jury selection, if applicable, the date of trial and the papers (marked pleadings, requests to charge, witness lists, etc.) which the Court requires to be submitted. No adjournments will be granted for cases scheduled for trial absent an emergency or circumstances beyond the control of counsel and the parties and subject to the Uniform Rules for the engagement of counsel (22 NYCRR part 125). Applications for bifurcation will be considered in light of whether judicial economy can be achieved thereby.

Settlement:

Cases settled prior to trial should be promptly reported to the Court in conformity with Uniform Trial Court Rule 202.28. Discontinued cases should follow the same procedure.

Contacts:

Questions about the Court's procedure which are not contained in these guidelines or other inquiries should be directed as follows:

Motions, including requests for adjournments:

    Law Clerk: Edward J. Usinger, Esq.   (585) 428–5753

Status reports on pending cases, scheduling of conferences/trials:

    Court Clerk: Eileen Collins   (585) 428–2027

Status of orders:

    Secretary: Roberta Kerry-Sharick   (585) 428–2486

HONORABLE EVELYN FRAZEE

Justice Supreme Court

Telephone: (585) 428–2486

Fax: (585) 428–2698

JUSTICE THOMAS A. STANDER

I. GENERAL RULES

Rule 1. Appearances by Counsel With Knowledge and Authority

Counsel who appear in the Court must be fully familiar with the case in regard to which they appear and fully authorized to enter into agreements, both substantive and procedural, on behalf of their clients. Failure to comply with this rule will be regarded as a default and dealt with appropriately. (See Rule 12) It is important that counsel be on time for all scheduled appearances.

Rule 2. Settlements and Discontinuances

If an action is settled, discontinued, or otherwise disposed of, counsel shall immediately inform the Court by submission of a copy of the stipulation or by a letter, telephone or email. Filing a stipulation of discontinuance with the County Clerk is required by Law but does not suffice as notice to chambers.

Rule 3. Alternate Dispute Resolution (ADR)

At any stage of the matter, the Court may direct a mediator for the purpose of mediating a resolution of all or some of the issues presented in the litigation.

Rule 4. Fax and E–mail

Rule 4(a). Papers by Fax. The Court does not accept papers of any sort by fax unless approved by the Court in advance in a particular case. All papers allowed to be submitted by fax must be followed by timely submission of the originals.

Rule 4(b). Correspondence by e-mail. The Court may permit counsel to communicate with the Court and each other by e-mail. In fact, the Court, in its discretion, may require information be provided electronically. Please note that e-mail may only be used to provide information, the Court does not, and will not respond to e-mail.

Rule 5. Information on Cases

Information on scheduled Court appearances or other case activity can be obtained from the Court Clerk or Chambers. Motion Term Calendars of the Court are published on the return date in *The Daily Record* and available at www.courts.state.ny.us/courts/7jd/Monroe/calendars.shtml.

Rule 6. Answering Calendars

A Pre–Note Calendar and Note of Issue Calendar for pending actions is held at regular intervals and is published in *The Daily Record* in advance of the date of the Calendar Call. The attorney trying the case must answer the Note of Issue Calendar in person as a trial date will likely be set. A person with knowledge of the status of the case (and with the authority to agree to a Scheduling Order) must answer the Pre–Note Calendar call in person.[1]

[1] **Cases Marked Off the Calendar.** All cases that have been "marked off" or "stricken" from the Court's calendar are subject to § 3404 of the CPLR.

II. CONFERENCES

Rule 7. Conference: Requests

A Conference will generally be promptly scheduled upon a request of counsel (either by contacting chambers on a case assigned to Justice Stander or by the filing of a RJI which requests a conference). A Conference Letter may be sent by the Court scheduling the conference or following the scheduling of a conference which occurs by phone. Counsel in receipt of the Conference Letter must comply with the requirements set forth therein. Appendix A—Conference Letter

Rule 8. Conference: Agenda

At any Court conference counsel for all parties shall be prepared to discuss (i) resolution of the case, in whole or in part, (ii) discovery and any other issues to be discussed at the conference and (iii) the use of Alternate Dispute Resolution to resolve some or all of the issues in the litigation. Counsel shall make a good faith effort to reach agreement on these matters at or in advance of the conference.

Rule 9. Conference: Outstanding Motions

Counsel must be prepared to discuss at conferences any motions that have been submitted and are outstanding.

Rule 10. Submission of Information

At the Conference counsel shall provide the Court with the following: (i) a copy of all pleadings which shall show a complete caption, including the index number; (ii) the name, address, telephone and fax numbers of all counsel; (iii) a brief written statement (limited to two pages) as to their client's contentions and any anticipated matters of law in dispute; (iv) a statement as to what motions, if any, are pending; and (v) copies of any decisions previously rendered in the case.

Rule 11. Discovery Schedule

The Conference will generally result in the issuance by the Court of a Scheduling Order. Appendix B—Scheduling Order. Where appropriate, the order may also contain specific provisions for early means of disposition of the case, such as directions for submission to a mediation or Alternative Dispute Resolution Program.

Rule 12. Non–Appearance at a Conference

The failure of counsel to appear for a conference shall be dealt with by an order directing dismissal, the striking of an answer and an inquest or direction for judgment, or other appropriate sanction. See 22 NYCRR § 130–2.1 and § 202.27.

Rule 13. Adherence to Discovery Schedule

Parties shall strictly comply with discovery obligations and the dates set forth in all Scheduling Orders. Any request for an extension or amendment of the Scheduling Order must be made by a letter request to the Court on notice to opposing counsel at least ten (10) days in advance of the date to be extended and must be accompanied by a proposed Amended Scheduling Order.

Non-compliance with a Scheduling Order may have the following consequences:

if any party fails to produce documents in timely fashion, an appropriate sanction may be imposed against that party pursuant to CPLR § 3126;

if a party seeking an examination before trial fails to proceed with it on the date or by the deadline fixed, that party may be held to have waived it;

if a party fails to submit to an examination as scheduled, either that party may be precluded from introducing testimony at trial or another sanction may be imposed;

if a party seeks documents as a condition precedent to a deposition and the documents are not produced by the date fixed, the party seeking disclosure may ask the Court to intervene on penalty of waiving the deposition.

Rule 14. Disclosure/Discovery Disputes

Counsel must consult with one another in a good faith effort to resolve all disputes about disclosure. See 22 NYCRR § 202.7. If counsel are unable to resolve a disclosure dispute in this fashion, the aggrieved party may have the right to bring a formal motion to compel or for sanctions or other relief. If opposed, such motions may, at the discretion of the Court, be held in conference. Dispositive motions, such as motions for summary judgment or to dismiss, will not be entertained by the Court as cross-motions for motions for discovery.

Rule 15. Adjournments of Conferences

Counsel requesting an adjournment of a Conference should contact Chambers and indicate the position of all other counsel regarding the requested adjournment. The adjournment of conferences is at the discretion of the Court and may be permitted for good cause shown. Parties should be careful not to unnecessarily request the adjournment of a Note of Issue Pre–Trial conference as the matter may be set for trial before the adjourned date of the conference.

III. Motions

Rule 16. Motion Procedures

Rule 16(a). Form of Motion Papers. So as to facilitate the framing of a decision and order, the movant must specify, clearly and comprehensively, in the notice of motion, order to show, or in a concluding section of a memorandum of law, the exact relief counsel seeks.

• Motion papers must be submitted with the return date blank; the Court will advise movant by phone of the assigned return date.

• The motion papers should be bound in a backing, indicating the law firm name, with all submissions from a party being bound in the same color backing. Separate Affidavits shall be bound separately and should not be "buried" in exhibits or a memorandum of law.

• Motion papers shall comply with Part 130 of the Rules of the Chief Administrator, be double-spaced and contain print no smaller than ten-point, on 8 ½ × 11 inch paper, bearing margins no smaller than one inch. CPLR Rule 2101; 22 NYCRR § 202.5(a). The print size of footnotes shall be no smaller than nine-point.

• Counsel must attach copies of all pleadings and other documents as required by the CPLR and as necessary for an informed decision on the motion (especially on motions pursuant to CPLR § 3211 and § 3212).

• Counsel must use tabs when submitting papers containing exhibits and exhibits must be legible. If a document to be annexed to an affidavit or affirmation is very voluminous and only discrete portions are relevant to the motion, counsel shall attach excerpts and submit the full exhibit separately.

• If Exhibits are voluminous they should be bound separately and all parties shall, where possible, refer to the Exhibits already submitted. All exhibits shall be legible. Documents in a foreign language shall be properly translated (CPLR Rule 2101[b]).

• Whenever reliance is placed upon a decision or other authority not readily available to this Court, a copy of the case or of pertinent portions of the authority shall be submitted with the motion papers.

Rule 16(b). Proposed Orders. When appropriate, proposed orders should be submitted with motions, e.g., motions to withdraw, *pro hac vice* admissions, open commissions, etc. No proposed order should be submitted with dispositive motions.

Rule 16(c). Adjournment of Motions. Adjournment of a motion is allowed on consent of all the parties and with the permission of the Court. The Court has the discretion to grant an adjournment for just cause. Upon the granting of an adjournment of a motion the Court does not allow the filing of any additional papers without the permission of the Court. If no opposition papers have yet been submitted, or, if additional papers are specifically allowed by the Court, any such opposition papers are required to be submitted ten (10) days prior to the adjourned return date and reply papers are to be submitted seven (7) days prior to the adjourned return date.

Rule 17. Length of Papers

Unless otherwise permitted by the Court for good cause, briefs or memoranda of law are limited to 25 pages each. Affidavits and affirmations shall be reasonable in length.

Rule 18. Sur–Reply and Post–Submission Papers

Counsel are reminded that the CPLR does not provide for sur-reply papers, however denominated. Nor is the presentation of papers or letters to the Court after submission or oral argument of a motion permitted. Absent express permission in advance, such materials will be returned unread. Opposing counsel who receives a copy of materials submitted in violation of this Rule should not respond in kind.

Rule 19. Motions—Discovery, Pro Hoc Vice, Reargue/Renew

Rule 19(a). Discovery

(1) Prior to the making or filing of any non-dispositive post–RJI motions (i.e. after the assignment of the matter to Justice Stander), counsel for the moving party may, where appropriate, advise the Court on notice to opposing counsel of the issue(s) in dispute and request a conference or telephone conference. This rule shall not apply to motions to be relieved as

counsel, for pro hac vice admission or motions to reargue/renew.

(2) Upon receipt of the request, the Court may schedule a conference or telephone conference with counsel. Counsel fully familiar with the matter and with authority to bind their client must be available to participate in the conference. The unavailability of counsel for the scheduled conference, except for good cause shown, may result in granting of the application without opposition and/or the imposition of sanctions.

(3) If the matter can be resolved during the conference or telephone conference, an order consistent with such resolution may be issued and counsel will be directed to forward a letter confirming the resolution to be "so ordered".

(4) If the matter cannot be resolved, the parties will set a briefing schedule for the motion which shall be approved by the Court. Except for good cause shown, the failure to comply with the briefing schedule may result in the submission of the motion unopposed or the dismissal of the motion, as may be appropriate.

(5) Nothing herein shall be construed to bar counsel from making any motion deemed appropriate to best represent a party's rights. However, in order to permit the parties the opportunity to resolve issues before motion practice ensues and for the Court to control its calendar, in the context of the discovery and trial schedule, pre-motion conferences in accordance herewith are encouraged.

Rule 19(b). Pro Hac Vice. Pursuant to the Rules of the Court of Appeals, an attorney in good standing from another state, territory, district or foreign country may be admitted pro hac vice in the discretion of this Court (22 NYCRR § 520.11). A motion for pro hac vice admission must be made to the Court. The application shall include affidavits in support of the motion which comply with the Rules of the Supreme Court, Appellate Division, Fourth Department (22 NYCRR §§ 1022.9 and 1000.13[1]).

After such motion is submitted, if there is no opposition to the request then counsel may submit a stipulated Consent Order prior to the return date. An Order may not be granted without the affidavits required by the Court Rules. Any Order from the motion should reflect the necessary representations required by the Court Rules. A proposed form for a Pro Hac Vice Order is attached. Appendix C—Pro Hoc Vice Order.

Rule 19(c). Motions to Reargue/Renew Motions to reargue/ renew are, by order of the Court, always on submission. No appearance of counsel is required or permitted,

Rule 20. Temporary Restraining Orders

The Court will not generally issue a temporary restraining order on substantive issues unless the applicant has given notice to the opposing parties sufficient to permit them an opportunity to appear and contest the application. Therefore upon receipt of a TRO request, the Court may set a conference with both counsel as soon as possible to address the application. (This conference procedure will generally not be applied to Mental Hygiene Law applications and Article 81 proceedings.)

Rule 21. Courtesy Copies

Courtesy copies or extra copies of motion papers and memos of law should not be submitted unless requested by the Court. Submission of an "extra copy" by e-mail may be requested by the Court. The parties should be prepared to promptly comply with such a request.

Rule 22. Oral Argument

All motions shall be orally argued at the place and time assigned by the Court and noted in the motion papers, unless otherwise directed by the Court. The Motion Calendars of the Court are published on the day of the return date in *The Daily Record*. No appearance for oral argument is required when the Court approves the waiver of oral argument; the Court is notified in advance of a consent Order; it is an uncontested motion; the motion is withdrawn; or the motion is to reargue or renew a prior motion. Oral arguments of contested Motions shall be limited to seven minutes (7) per side unless otherwise directed by the Court.

Rule 23. Motion Decisions and Orders

On an unopposed motion, counsel must submit an order, with an affidavit of service of the motion, in accordance with correspondence (Fax) sent by the Court. Counsel must submit an order on any motion resolved by consent of counsel. If such orders are not timely received, the motion will be considered withdrawn, without prejudice. When the Court issues a Bench Decision on a motion, counsel will be directed attach a transcript or copy of the written Bench Decision, and reference the transcript or written Bench Decision in the Order. When the Court reserves on a motion decision, counsel must provide the Court with a copy of all memorandum of law formatted for Microsoft Word or WordPerfect and attached to an e-mail directed to the Court. No other submissions on reserved decisions will be accepted unless specifically directed by the Court. Written decisions of the Court not issued from the bench will generally be filed by the Court directly in the Monroe County Clerk's Office. Counsel is notified of these decisions electronically.

Rule 24. Blank

IV. Trials

Rule 25. Trial Procedures

Rule 25a. Trial Schedule. The Courts Trial Ready Calendar is published in the *Daily Record* on each Friday that the Court is in session. Matters will generally be tried in the order they appear on the Trial Ready Calendar but will be scheduled at the discretion of the Court. The Court does not have a backlog of cases and Counsel should be aware that their case will be tried very soon after the filing of a Note of Issue and Statement of Readiness.

Counsel will be expected to be ready to proceed either to select a jury or to begin presentation of proof upon a call from the Court scheduling a trial date. (Generally the Court will try to conference a case before scheduling the case for trial. However this is not always possible and Counsel should be aware that once they file a Note of Issue they should be prepared to go to trial.)

Once a trial date is set (either by a phone call or conference), counsel are immediately to determine the availability of witnesses. If, for any reason, counsel are not prepared to proceed on the scheduled date, the Court is to be notified within 48 hours of the date on which counsel are given the trial date or, in extraordinary circumstances, as soon as reasonably practicable. Failure of counsel to provide such notification will be deemed a waiver of any application to adjourn the trial because of the unavailability of a witness. Witnesses are to be scheduled so that all trial time is completely utilized.

Rule 25b. Trial Order. The Court will generally issue a Trial Order establishing the trial date as a date certain and setting forth the Rules of the Court specific to the Trial. Counsel is urged to read the Trial Order carefully and completely. Appendix D—Trial Order.

Rule 25c. Jury Selection. The jury shall be selected in accordance with procedures set forth in the Court's Jury Selection Process. Appendix E—Jury Selection Process.

Rule 25d. Trial Times. (The Court does not try cases on Fridays) Unless otherwise directed by the Court, trials will commence each Court day promptly at 10:00 A.M. and will proceed on a day-to-day basis until approximately 4:30–5 P.M., Monday through Thursday. The Court holds Motion Term on Friday and therefore does not start (except for Jury Selection) or continue trials on Friday (except for Jury deliberation). Failure of counsel to attend the trial at the time scheduled will constitute a waiver of the right of that attorney and his or her client to participate in the trial for the period of counsel's absence.

Rule 26. Settlement Conference

It is the Courts desire to hold a Settlement Conference (Note of Issue Conference) prior to scheduling a Trial. In preparation for the Settlement Conference, counsel shall comply with the requirements set forth in the Trial Ready Letter and Memorandum. Appendix F—Trial Ready Letter and Trial Preparation Memorandum. Counsel is advised to read the Trial Order at Appendix D prior to and in preparation for the settlement conference. Also Counsel for all parties shall furnish the Court with a realistic estimate of the length of the trial.

Rule 27. Motions *in Limine*

At least seven (7) days prior to trial, counsel shall notify opposing counsel of any intended motions *in limine* and provide opposing counsel with a copy of such motion. At least four (4) days prior to the earlier of trial or jury selection, the parties shall submit all motions in limine, and responses, except for those not reasonably anticipated in advance. No additional reply papers will be allowed. Such motions shall be on submission unless otherwise directed by the Court. The moving and opposition papers on such motions shall be no longer than 6 pages and these papers shall comply with the limitations as to print size and margins set forth in Rule 16a above.

Rule 28. Pre–Marking of Exhibits

Counsel for the parties shall consult prior to trial and shall in good faith attempt to agree upon the exhibits that will be offered into evidence without objection. With the Court Reporter, each side shall then mark its exhibits with plaintiff using numbers for its exhibits and defendant letters. If the exhibits are voluminous, the attorneys should consult with the Court's Part Clerk for another method of marking the exhibits (double and triplicate letters are strongly discouraged). The parties shall thereafter stipulate to those exhibits which may be received into evidence and the Court Reporter shall mark those items as received by stipulation.

Whenever a subject matter will reasonably require itemization, computation or illustration, counsel shall prepare such diagrams, photographs or other similar exhibits as may reasonably be necessary for a clear presentation of the subject matter.

Rule 29. Identification of Deposition Testimony

Counsel for the parties shall consult prior to trial and shall in good faith attempt to agree upon the portions of deposition testimony to be offered into evidence without objection. The parties shall delete from the testimony to be read questions and answers that are irrelevant to the point for which the testimony is offered. Prior to trial, each party shall submit to the Court a courtesy copy of any deposition testimony they intend to read at trial.

Rule 30.   Pretrial Conference

The Court will set a pretrial conference immediately prior to commencement of the jury pick or trial. Prior to the conference, counsel shall make a good faith effort to identify issues not in contention and resolve all disputed questions without need for Court intervention. At the conference, counsel shall be prepared to discuss all matters as to which there is disagreement between the parties, including those identified in Rules 27–29, evidentiary issues, witness timing issues, and the possibility of settlement. At or before the conference, the Court may require the parties to prepare a written stipulation of undisputed facts.

Rule 31.   Pre–Trial Memoranda, Exhibit Book, and P.J.I. Charge

Counsel shall submit pre-trial memoranda at the Pre–Trial Conference or at the time required by the Court's Trial Order. No memoranda in response need be submitted.

In a jury trial, counsel must, pursuant to the Trial Order, and prior to jury selection, provide the Court with case-specific paragraph references to Pattern Jury Instructions, as well as any requested jury verdict interrogatories. The failure to do so may waive your right to object to the Court's charge to the jury until after it is presented. (The Court is aware that additional or different charges may be necessary based on the developments or testimony at trial. On this basis, a supplemental request to charge will be permitted.) The PJI charge and the jury verdict sheet shall be provided to the Court in hard copy written form and attached to an e-mail directed to the Court at tstander@courts.state.ny.us (Microsoft Word or WordPerfect format).

In preparing the request to charge, counsel should be aware that the Court will use an opening charge to the jury which will include information and directions to the jury as set forth in the Pattern Jury Instructions. The Court will also generally charge paragraphs 1:20, 2:325; 1:40; 1:37; 1:38; 1:25; 1:21; 1:91; 1:22; 1:90; 1:70; when appropriate.

In a non-jury trial, counsel shall at the pre-trial conference, submit a book of trial exhibits for the Court's use.

Rule 32.   Scheduling of Witnesses/Doctors

At the pretrial conference immediately before the trial, each party shall identify in writing for the Court and the other parties the witnesses it intends to call, the order in which they shall testify and the estimated length of their testimony.

If the matter involves the testimony of a doctor or doctors, the parties must video tape the doctor's testimony in advance of trial or secure the in person testimony of the doctor. If the trial has been scheduled more that 30 days after the Note of Issue conference, the matter will NOT be adjournment because of the unavailability of a doctor.

Rule 33.   Preclusion

Except for good cause shown, no party shall present the testimony of a witness, portions of deposition testimony, or exhibits that were not identified as provided in Rules 28, 29, and 31 hereof and not identified during the course of disclosure in response to a relevant discovery demand of a party or an order of the Court.

Rule 34.   Summary Jury Trial Rules

The Court's rules for the conduct of a Summary Jury Trial are as set forth below and in the Court's Summary Jury Trial Order (Appendix G):

I.   Summary Trial Generally.

1.   Jury Selection shall generally be held on the morning or afternoon of the day before trial.

2.   The Summary Jury Trial shall commence promptly on 9:30 a.m.

3.   All parties, through their attorneys, must consent to conducting a Summary Jury Trial. Therefore, the Parties shall, prior to jury selection, stipulate to conducting the Summary Jury Trial in accordance with this Court's Summary Trial Order and Rules. Further such stipulation must be in accordance with the terms of the attached Summary Jury Trial Stipulation (Appendix H). Any other or additional terms agreed to by the parties must also be set forth in the Stipulation or in open court and approved by the Presiding Judge.

4.   Counsel is directed to conference with the Court one-half hour prior to Jury Selection and one-half hour prior to Trial.

II.   Jury Selection

1.   Counsel will conduct Jury Selection at ___ a.m./ p.m. on _____, 20 ___. Each side shall be allowed 30 minutes of questioning and Jury Selection shall be completed by ___ a.m./ p.m. The Attorneys will select six (6) jurors using the Struck Method (and two alternates). Each party is permitted two peremptory challenges.

OR

1.   The Court will conduct jury selection without counsel's participation, or, in the Court's discretion, counsel may be allowed to participate in jury selection to the extent permitted by the Court. Counsel shall submit proposed voir dire questions or concepts to the Court in advance of the trial date. The Court will select six (6) jurors using the Struck Method. (No

Alternates will be selected unless otherwise directed by the Court). Upon request and with the consent of the court, each party may be permitted one or two peremptory challenges.

III. Trial Presentation

1. Each side shall be entitled to a ten (10) minute opening and closing and ninety (90) minutes for presentation of its case. The Court may allot more time if counsel presents a compelling reason to do so. The time allotted to each side shall include the presentation of their case in chief and the cross examination of opposing witnesses. The Court Clerk will keep track of the time and remind counsel of allotted time at appropriate intervals.

2. Presentation of the case by counsel will involve a combination of witnesses, comment on admissible evidence and trial summation. No more than two witnesses for each side may be called for direct and cross-examination. Counsel may not refer to or comment on "evidence" which would not be admissible at Trial.

3. *Presentation Generally*: Attorneys may not independently testify but may comment on, and focus the attention of the Jury on admissible evidence. Counsel may quote from depositions affidavits, and verified Bills of Particular (but only the language from the most recent answers) Counsel may also use and comment on exhibits admitted into evidence. Of course, non-medical testimony may be presented by witnesses.

Medical Evidence: In presenting medical "testimony" or evidence, counsel may call a doctor to testify as one (or both) of his two witnesses or may submit medical records and comment on the medical records presented with emphasis on those portions of the record that counsel believes are relevant. Of course, opposing counsel may also comment on such record and may do so in a manner consistent with cross-examination or during his or her own case. A summary of medical records can be presented and provided to the jury for their consideration in deliberation as long as each record provide is, as stipulated by the parties or in the discretion of the Court, "fair and complete." The hearsay contents of medical records shall be redacted for records or documents received into evidence and provide to the jury, and for any summary of medical records that will be submitted to the jury.

Rules of Evidence: Clearly the rules of evidence will be liberally construed. In the interest of time, "non-essential" leading questions may be asked in the discretion of the Court.

4. Jurors will be permitted to ask questions of the attorneys following the Trial. The Court will instruct the jurors at the commencement of the Trial that they can write their questions at any point. At any regular break in the Trial, the questions will be presented to the Judge. If the Judge allows the question, the Judge will present the question to the attorneys either before or after the attorney's summation as the Judge in his discretion feels appropriate. Each attorney will be given few minutes to answer each question.

5. All counsel will submit to the Court a narrative summary statement of the case, including a summary of the evidence, no longer than one pages in length, which the Judge will use in explaining the case to the Jurors both in Jury Selection and at the commencement at the Summary Jury Trial.

IV. Jury Charge

1. All counsel must submit to the Court at least 24 hours prior to Trial a requests for charge and a proposed verdict sheet with appropriate questions to the jury. The submission shall be by e-mail (see below). The Court will then fashion a verdict sheet(s) for the jury from those submitted by counsel. There will not be a post trial charge conference.

2. In the event there are separate issues to be decided by the jury (such as liability, no fault threshold, damages, etc.) the jury will be charged, will deliberate, and will answer the question or questions on the verdict sheet on each issue. The jury shall answer questions on separate verdict sheets by and as each issue is charged seriatim.

3. The statement of the case, the summary of the evidence, requests to charge, and proposed verdict sheets must be sent to the Court by email (tstander@ courts.state.ny.us) at least 24 hours prior to the start of the Trial. Hard copies shall be provided to the Court at the start of Trial.

Justice Thomas A. Stander
New York State Supreme Court Justice

App. A. Conference Letter

Date

RE:

Index #

Dear Counsel:

The above-referenced action was assigned to Supreme Court Justice Thomas A. Stander either by the filing of an RJI or by the submission of a motion. **The Court has scheduled a preliminary conference for   , 20___ at   a.m.**

Adjournments of this conference are discouraged. If you have any questions, please contact my Chambers.

Each party, (this includes, if relevant, a representative of any insurance carrier) or a representative with binding authority to settle the matter, must be available by phone at the time of the conference.

Copies of all pleadings shall be provided to the Court at the time of the conference. A short description of the facts and the parties contention may also be provided at this time. At the conference, the Court will generally issue a Scheduling Order as well as address the use of alternative dispute resolution, will discuss the handling of further motions, and may schedule future conferences for case control. Counsel are urged to bring their personal calendar with them to this preliminary conference.

Very truly yours,

Honorable Thomas A. Stander
Supreme Court Justice

TAS/RBw

App. B. Scheduling Order

PRESENT: <u>HON. THOMAS A. STANDER</u>
——————Justice Presiding
STATE OF NEW YORK
SUPREME COURT   COUNTY OF MONROE

————————————————————

Plaintiff(s),

SCHEDULING
ORDER

- vs -

Index #

Defendant(s).

————————————————————

The Court hereby issues the following Scheduling Order in the above-entitled matter:

ORDERED, that except as set forth below, all CPLR Article 31 discovery responses shall be completed on or before the ___ day of _____, 20 ___; and it is further

ORDERED, that all Examinations Before Trial shall be completed on or before the ___ day of _____, 20 ___; and it is further

ORDERED, that the Independent Medical Examination of Plaintiff, if any, shall be completed within ninety (90) days after completion of Plaintiff's Examination Before Trial; and it is further

ORDERED, that with respect to the Independent Medical Examination the parties shall, in a timely manner, comply with the requirements of 22 NYCRR 202.17; and it is further

ORDERED, that Plaintiff shall file a Note of Issue and Certificate of Readiness on or before the ___ day of _____, 20 ___; and it is further

ORDERED, that any request for an extension or amendment of this Scheduling Order <u>must</u> be made by letter request on notice to opposing counsel at least ten (10) days in advance of the date sought to be extended and <u>must</u> be accompanied by a proposed Amended Scheduling Order along with a self-addressed, stamped envelope.

Dated:
    Rochester, New York   Hon. Thomas A. Stander
                                     Supreme Court Justice

App. C. Pro Hac Vice Order

STATE OF NEW YORK
SUPREME COURT   COUNTY OF MONROE

————————————————————

                    Plaintiff,   ORDER

        -vs-   Index #

                    Defendant.

————————————————————

Upon the Application to Admit Counsel <u>Pro Hac Vice</u>, dated _____, 20 ___, and the affidavits annexed thereto of _____, Esq., sworn to _____, 20 ___, and good cause shown, pursuant to the Rules of the Court of Appeals, Part 520, § 520.11, and there being no opposition to this motion, it is hereby

ORDERED, that the application requesting the admission of _____, Esq. pro hac vice as counsel with respect to the above entitled action is hereby GRANTED; it is further

ORDERED, that such counsel shall comply with the New York professional responsibility requirements and disciplinary rules and shall be subject to the jurisdiction of the New York Courts for any violation; it is further

ORDERED, that _____, Esq. is hereby authorized to appear and participate before this Court in this action on behalf of _____; and it is further

ORDERED, that [out of town atty] shall be associated with [NY firm & atty] _____, _____, Esq. of counsel; [NY firm] shall be the attorney of record in this matter.

Dated: ENTER:

                              ———————————————————
                              Hon. Thomas A. Stander
                              Supreme Court Justice

App. D. Trial Order

PRESENT: **THE HONORABLE THOMAS A. STANDER**
            Justice of the Supreme Court

SUPREME COURT
STATE OF NEW YORK   MONROE COUNTY

————————————————————

                                        JURY
                                   TRIAL ORDER

        -against-

                                        Index #

————————————————————

The parties having indicated their readiness for a trial by jury, it is now hereby **ORDERED:**

1. Trial Date:

That selection of the Jury in the above-captioned matter shall be held on Friday the ___ day of _____, 20___ at 10:00 a.m.

Trial of this matter shall commence at 10:00 a.m. on Monday, the ___ day of _____, 20___.

When a matter has been set for trial pursuant to a Trial Order, it is for all purposes a DAY CERTAIN and will not be adjourned or postponed without the written consent of the Court.

Counsel is advised to report to Justice Stander's Chambers (Room 420, Hall of Justice, Rochester, New York) for a **Pre-trial Conference**, one-half hour prior to the start of jury selection/trial. The purpose of the conference is to give the parties a final opportunity to settle the matter, to set the trial schedule and to discuss any scheduling problems, to review any anticipated evidentiary problems, and to entertain any pre-trial applications.

Please be advised that the Court holds Special Term on Fridays and, therefore, does not start (except for jury selection) or continue trials on Friday.

Parties are advised that it is not necessary to answer any calendar calls on the status of the case up to and through the date of trial unless the matter has settled.

2. Pleading/Prior Orders

Four (4) days prior to jury selection, a copy of all pleadings, including a copy of the Complaint and Answer, the Demand and Bill of Particulars, and any other relevant discovery and/or trial-related orders of the Court shall be submitted by Plaintiff.

3. Witnesses/ Doctors Testimony

If not disclosed previously, **four (4) days prior to jury selection**, each party shall provide the Court and opposing counsel, a **list of all witnesses** whom the party expects to call. The list shall identify those whom the party expects to call in person and those who shall be called through deposition. A courtesy copy of such deposition testimony for the Court is required. As to any experts, the witness list shall also provide the information required by CPLR § 3101(d).

If the matter involves the **testimony of a doctor or doctors**, the parties must video tape the doctor's testimony in advance of trial or secure the in person testimony of the doctor. If the trial has been scheduled more that 30 days after the Note of Issue conference, the matter will NOT be adjourned because of the unavailability of a doctor.

4. Exhibits:

OPTIONAL: [On the ___ day of _____ 20___ at _____ a.m./p.m. and prior to the start of trial,] *OR* [**Prior to, or immediately following Jury Selection,**] the parties shall, with the Court Reporter, mark all exhibits for identification (numbers for plaintiff; letters for defendant); and shall, at the time of trial, submit to the Court a list of all such exhibits. All parties are herein ordered to consult with each other and, to the extent possible, enter into a stipulation governing the authenticity and admissibility of exhibits.

Whenever a subject matter will reasonably require itemization, computation or illustration, counsel may prepare such diagrams, photographs or other similar exhibits as may reasonably be necessary for a clear presentation of the subject matter. The week before trial, counsel should make known to the Court any requests for special equipment (e.g., blackboard, shadow box, easel, markers, audio-video equipment.) The Court will not be responsible for equipment not timely requested.

If the parties can agree on facts or matters not in dispute, they should submit an appropriate stipulation to the Court at the time of trial.

5. Trial Memorandum of Law:

Four (4) days prior to jury selection, each party shall submit a trial **memorandum of law**. The memorandum shall be brief (less than five [5] pages unless otherwise allowed by the Court) but comprehensive, and must address each question of law that the party expects to arise at trial including, but not limited to, the elements of proof necessary for each cause of action. Each party shall provide opposing counsel a copy of the Trial Memorandum. An answer or reply memorandum is not required but is permissible.

6. Requests to Charge:

Four (4) days prior to jury selection, counsel must provide the Court with case-specific paragraph references to **Pattern Jury Instructions**, as well as any requested jury verdict **interrogatories**. The PJI charge and the jury verdict sheet shall be provided to the Court in written form and attached to an e-mail addressed to tstander@courts.state.ny.us (Microsoft Word or WordPerfect format).

Your failure to provide these items may waive your right to object to the Court's charge to the jury until after it is presented. (The Court is aware that additional or different charges may be necessary based on the developments or testimony at trial. On this basis, supplemental requests to charge will be permitted.)

In preparing the request to charge, counsel should be aware that the Court will use an opening charge to the jury which will include information and directions to the jury as set forth in the Pattern Jury Instructions. The Court will generally charge, either in the opening or closing charge, paragraphs 1:20; 1:21; 1:22; 1:24; 1:25; 1:27; 1:36; 1:37; 1:38; 1:39; 1:40; 1:41; 1:90; 1:91 and 1:97; when appropriate. You do not need to formally request that these paragraphs be charged.

7. Jury Questionnaire:

Generally Jury Questionnaires will, to the extent the Commissioner of Jurors has provided them to the jury panel, be used by the Court in the selection of the jury. These questionnaires will be provided just before jury selection unless Counsel has requested a longer period of review well in advance of trial. Also, upon prior application to the Court at least 10 days prior to jury selection, or upon the Court's own initiative, prospective jurors may be asked to complete a more detailed questionnaire supplied by the Court after consultation with the trial attorney.

8. Jury Selection/Time Limitation:

Except as set forth below, the Voir Dire will generally not be judicially supervised. The Court will commence the jury selection process with an introduction of the attorneys and the case to the jury pool. The identity of the parties and the list of possible witnesses may be made known to the Jury. The Jury pool will be advised that the Court Clerk is the Court's representative and that any questions regarding attorneys or jurors conduct should be reported to the Clerk. **Each side will be limited to 45 minutes** of questioning during Voir Dire unless the Court has specifically, in the presence of all counsel, set other time limitations.

9. Jury Selection Process: Struck Method / Non–Designated Alternates:

Unless otherwise ordered by the Court, the Jury shall be selected by the Voir Dire procedures known as the "Struck Method". Under the Struck Method, the panel selected is large enough so that the number of cause-free prospective jurors is equal to the ultimate jury size desired (including alternates), plus the total number of peremptories that can be exercised by all parties. The attorneys then exercise their peremptory challenges by alternately striking names from a list of jurors until the number of jurors left equals six plus the number of alternates. If there are still too many jurors after everyone has exercised peremptories, the first eight names seated are selected to sit as the jury. The alternates will not be designated unless counsel has objected to non-designated alternates prior to jury selection. At the conclusion of the trial, and after the jury charge, six jurors will be randomly selected to deliberate. Any remaining juror(s) will be considered alternates and, at the discretion of the Court, be dismissed. A detailed description of the Struck Method Rules **is enclosed** for your review.

10. Limitations of Opening and Closing:

Counsel is advised that the Court will impose **a time limit of 15 minutes on each attorney for their opening and closing statements to the Jury**. Upon request, the time limit may be modified at the Pre–Trial Conference. The time limits will be strictly adhered to.

11. Motions—in limine; Summary Judgment:

Unless otherwise specifically ordered by the Court, counsel shall, at least seven (7) days prior to trial, notify opposing counsel of any intended motions *in limine* and provide opposing counsel with a copy of such motion. At least four (4) days prior to the earlier of trial or jury selection, the parties shall submit all motions *in limine*, and responses. No additional reply papers will be allowed. Such motions shall be on submission unless otherwise directed by the Court. The moving and opposition papers on such motions shall be no longer than 6 pages and these papers shall comply with the limitations as to print size and margins set forth in Rule 16a of the Court's Rules.

Unless otherwise specifically ordered by the Court, summary judgment motions may not be made more than thirty (30) days after the filing of the note of issue, except with leave of the Court on good cause shown

(Optional)

12. Conference Date:

A conference on the matter will be held on _____, 200 ___ at _____ a.m. for the Court to review counsel's compliance with this Order, to discuss trial schedule and, possible settlement. Trial counsel must attend this conference.

Dated:

Rochester, New York

_____

Thomas A. Stander, J.S.C.

App. E.   Jury Selection Process

THOMAS A. STANDER

SUPREME COURT JUSTICE

JURY SELECTION

STRUCK METHOD/NON–DESIGNATED ALTERNATES

(1) Unless otherwise ordered by the Court, selection of jurors shall be made from an initial panel of prospective jurors, who shall be seated randomly and who shall maintain the order of seating throughout the voir dire.

(2) Counsel first shall ask questions generally to the prospective jurors as a group to determine whether any prospective juror has knowledge of the subject matter, the parties, their attorneys or the prospective witnesses. A response from a juror that requires further elaboration may be the subject of further questioning of that juror by the Court (or, in the Court's discretion, by counsel) on an individual basis. Counsel may exercise challenges for cause at this time or in the event of newly discovered information, after questioning as set forth in (3) below.

(3) After the general questioning has been completed by the Court, in an action with one Plaintiff and one Defendant, counsel for the Plaintiff initially shall question the prospective jurors, followed by questioning by Defendant's counsel. Each counsel may be permitted to ask follow-up questions on newly revealed information. In cases with multiple parties, questioning shall be undertaken by counsel in the order in which the parties' names appear in the caption.

A challenge for cause shall be made by counsel to any party as soon as the reason therefor becomes apparent. At the end of the period, all challenges for cause to any prospective juror on the panel must have been exercised by respective counsel.

(4) After challenges for cause are exercised, the number of prospective jurors remaining shall be counted. If that number is less than the total number of jurors to be selected (including alternates) plus the maximum number of peremptory challenges allowed by the Court for all parties (such sum shall be referred to as the "jury panel number"), then additional prospective jurors shall be added until the number of prospective jurors not subject to challenge for cause equals the "jury panel number". Counsel for each party then shall question each replacement juror pursuant to the procedure set forth in paragraph 3.

(5) After all prospective jurors in the panel have been questioned, and all challenges for cause have been made, counsel for each party, one at a time beginning with counsel for the Plaintiff, shall then exercise allowable peremptory challenges by alternately striking a single juror's name from a list or ballot passed back and forth between or among counsel until all challenges are exhausted or waived. In cases with multiple Plaintiffs and/or Defendants, peremptory challenges shall be exercised by counsel in the order in which the parties' names appear in the caption, unless following that order would, in the opinion of the Court, unduly favor a side. In that event, the Court, after consulting with the parties, shall specify the order in which the peremptory challenges shall be exercised in a manner that shall balance the interests of the parties.

An attorney who waives a challenge may not thereafter exercise a peremptory challenge. Any *Batson* or other objections shall be resolved by the Court before any of the struck jurors are dismissed.

(6) After all preemptory challenges have been made, the trial jurors (including non-designated alternates) then shall be selected in the order in which they have been seated from those prospective jurors remaining on the panel.

The Juror shall then be sworn and excused until the start of trial.

App. F. Trial Ready Letter and Trial Preparation Memorandum

TRIAL READY LETTER

Date

RE:

Index #

Case #

Dear Counsel:

A Note of Issue and Statement of Readiness has been filed on this case. When the Note of Issue is filed on a matter, this Court requires the parties and their attorneys to attend a Settlement Conference. **A Settlement Conference of this matter has been scheduled for   , 20__ at   am.** Adjournment of this conference is strongly discouraged.

The purpose of the Settlement Conference is to clarify the issues and provide an opportunity for settlement. Please note that you and your clients (including the insurance adjuster with authority) **are required to be present in person** at this Settlement Conference. (see attached Memorandum) Failure of attendance in person by any of the foregoing will result in a default of the offending party under § 202.27 of the Uniform Rules.

If a disposition of the matter does not result from the Settlement Conference, a TRIAL ORDER may be issued at that time setting the date of trial. Please be prepared to set a trial date at the time of the conference. Where a Trial Order is not issued, the case will be held on the Trial Ready.

In order to facilitate the trial of cases, this Court maintains a Trial Ready Calendar for those matters that have not settled at conference and which have not been given a trial date or TRIAL ORDER. [The Trial Ready Calendar is published each Friday that Court is in session in the Daily Record.] Each matter on the Trial Ready Calendar is considered ready for trial and is expected to proceed to trial upon reasonable notice from the Court Clerk. Therefore, counsel is urged to immediately take any necessary steps to prepare for trial.

Please read carefully the attached **Settlement Conference and Trial Preparation Memorandum** regarding your responsibilities in preparing for the conference and trial.

If you have any questions concerning the Court's procedures, please call my Chambers.

Very truly yours,

Thomas A. Stander
Supreme Court Justice

TAS/RBw

Enclosure

JUSTICE STANDER—SETTLEMENT CON-
FERENCE AND TRIAL PREPARA-
TION MEMORANDUM

*The following information is provided to you for
your review when your case has been set for a Settlement Conference.*

The purpose of the Settlement Conference is to
clarify the issues, discuss trial procedure, and to provide an opportunity for settlement. Each counsel is
encouraged to provide a brief (2 page) written statement as to the nature of their client's contentions with
an indication of their demands/offer to date.

The Settlement Conference shall be attended by at
least one of the attorneys who will conduct the trial
for each of the parties and any pro se litigants. (See
NYCRR 202.27) The parties (this includes, if relevant,
the representative of any insurance carrier) to the
action *must* also be at the Conference in person
(insurance carrier can be readily available by telephone) for the purpose of settling the matter, as well
as for consultation on availability for trial. Only with
the Court's prior approval may the client be available
by phone and not be present in person.

If the matter does not settle at the Conference, a
trial date may be set at this Conference or, as is
discussed in the accompanying letter, at a later date
upon a call from the Court Clerk. In setting a trial
date counsel is advised that if they are involved in
the "actual engagement" in another Court on the
scheduled trial date, the Uniform Rules for the Engagement of Counsel will govern any requested trial
postponements, and the Court reserves the right to
receive an affidavit or affirmation, as provided by
those rules. (McKinney's Revised 1986 NY Rules of
Court, § 125.1).

Though the Court will generally issue a Trial Order
with detailed instructions regarding trial preparation,
Counsel is advised that when a matter has been *set for
trial* the following is required:

Once the matter has been scheduled for trial, counsel is advised to **report to Justice Stander's Chambers** (Room 420) one-half hour prior to the start of
trial (i.e., 9:30 a.m. for a 10:00 a.m. trial; 1:30 p.m. for
a 2:00 p.m. trial). The purpose of this *Pre–Trial
Conference* is to set the trial schedule and discuss any
scheduling problems, anticipated evidentiary problems, or pre-trial applications. The Pre–Trial Conference shall be attended by all trial counsel, their clients
and any unrepresented (pro se) parties.

Unless otherwise ordered by the Court in the Trial
Order, counsel must provide the Court with 1) case-
specific paragraph references to **Pattern Jury Instructions**, as well as any requested jury verdict
interrogatories at the Pre–Trial Conference; 2) **Pre–
Trial Memorandums of Law** and the case pleading;
3) a stipulation to the introduction of evidence not in
dispute. All exhibits to be presented at trial shall be
pre-marked with the Court Reporter.

Please be advised that the Court holds Motion Term
on **Fridays** and, therefore, does not start or continue
trials on Friday (except for jury selection).

App. G.   Summary Trial Order

STATE OF NEW YORK
SUPREME COURT   COUNTY OF MONROE

Plaintiff,	**SUMMARY**
	TRIAL ORDER
vs.	Index #
Defendants.	

HON. THOMAS A. STANDER

It is ORDERED, that following a stipulation by the
parties in chambers, a **SUMMARY JURY TRIAL** of
the issues of liability and damages is hereby scheduled
as a Day Certain Trial before the **Honorable Thomas
A. Stander**, at the Hall of Justice, 99 Exchange Boulevard, Rochester, New York 14614. The trial shall be
conducted in accordance with this Order. It is therefore:

ORDERED, that:

I.   Summary Trial Generally.

1.   Jury Selection shall be held on ____, 20 ___ at
a.m./ p.m.

2.   The Summary Jury Trial shall commence
promptly on ____, 20 ___ at ___ a.m./p.m.

3.   The Parties shall, prior to trial, familiarize
themselves with the Courts Rules for the conduct of a
Summary Jury Trial, and shall enter into the Stipulation for Binding Summary Jury Trial in the form
attached hereto. The Parties shall, prior to trial and
in writing or in open court, also stipulate to any other
terms agreed to by the parties.

4.   Counsel is directed to conference with the Court
one-half hour prior to Jury Selection and one-half
hour prior to Trial.

II.   Jury Selection

1.   Counsel will conduct Jury Selection at ___ a.m./
p.m. on ___, 20___. Each side shall be allowed 30
minutes of questioning and Jury Selection shall be
completed by **3:30 p.m.** The Attorneys will select six
(6) jurors using the Struck Method (and two alternates). Each party is permitted two peremptory challenges.

OR

2.   The Court will conduct jury selection without
counsel's participation, or, in the Court's discretion,
counsel may be allowed to participate in jury selection
to the extent permitted by the court. Counsel shall
submit proposed voir dire questions or concepts to the
court in advance of the trial date. The court will

select six (6) jurors using the Struck Method. (No Alternates will be selected unless otherwise directed by the Court). Upon request and with the consent of the court, each party may be permitted one or two peremptory challenges.

III. Trial Presentation

1. Each side shall be entitled to a ten (10) minute opening and closing and ninety (90) minutes for presentation of its case. The Court may allot more time if counsel presents a compelling reason to do so. The time allotted to each side shall include the presentation of their case in chief and the cross examination of opposing witnesses. The court clerk will keep track of the time and remind counsel of allotted time at appropriate intervals.

2. Presentation of the case by counsel will involve a combination of witnesses, comment on admissible evidence and trial summation. No more than two witnesses for each side may be called for direct and cross-examination. Counsel may not refer to or comment on "evidence" which would not be admissible at Trial.

3. Counsel may quote from depositions and may use exhibits, affidavits and video tapes. In presenting medical "testimony" or evidence, counsel may call a doctor to testify as one of his two witnesses or may submit medical records and comment on the medical records presented with emphasis on those portions of the record that counsel believes are relevant. Of course, opposing counsel may also comment on such record and may do so in a manner consistent with cross-examination or during his or her own case. The hearsay contents of medical records shall be redacted and counsel shall, before Trial, agree on the medical document or documents that will be submitted to the jury.

4. Jurors will be permitted to ask questions of the attorneys following the Trial. The Court will instruct the jurors at the commencement of the Trial that they can write their questions at any point. At any regular break in the Trial, the questions will be presented to the Judge. If the Judge allows the question, the Judge will present the question to the attorneys either before or after the attorney's summation as the Judge in his discretion feels appropriate. Each attorney will be given few minutes to answer each question.

5. All counsel will submit to the Court a narrative summary statement of the case, including a summary of the evidence, no longer than two pages in length, which the Judge will use in explaining the case to the Jurors both in Jury Selection and at the commencement at the Summary Jury Trial.

IV. Jury Charge

1. All counsel must submit to the Court at least 24 hours prior to Trial a requests for charge and a proposed verdict sheet with appropriate questions to the jury. The submission shall be by e-mail (see below). The Court will then fashion a verdict sheet(s) for the jury from those submitted by counsel. There will not be a post trial charge conference.

2. In the event there are separate issues to be decided by the jury (such as liability, no fault threshold, damages, etc.) the jury will be charged, will deliberate, and will answer the question or questions on the verdict sheet on each issue. The jury shall answer questions on separate verdict sheets by and as each issue is charged seriatim.

3. The statement of the case, the summary of the evidence, requests to charge, and proposed verdict sheets must be sent to the Court by email (tstander@courts.state.ny.us) at least 24 hours prior to the start of the Trial. Hard copies shall be provided to the Court at the start of Trial.

DATED:

Rochester, New York

HON. THOMAS A. STANDER
SUPREME COURT JUSTICE

App. H. Stipulation of Binding Summary Jury Trial

SUPREME COURT
STATE OF NEW YORK   MONROE COUNTY

Plaintiff,	**STIPULATION OF BINDING SUMMARY JURY TRIAL**
vs.	
	Index # Case #
Defendants.	

IT IS HEREBY STIPULATED AND AGREED that this action shall be resolved by submission to a Summary Jury Trial in accordance with the Court's Rules for Summary Jury Trials and the Summary Jury Trial Order of this Court and that all parties shall be bound by the Summary Jury Trial verdict, [except that the Plaintiff shall recover no less than $ _____, and no more than $ _____].

IT IS ALSO STIPULATED AND AGREED that the right to move to set aside the verdict, or to appeal, is limited to instances in which the rights of a party were significantly prejudiced by 1) corruption, fraud or misconduct in procuring the award; 2) a miscalculation of figures or a mistake in the description of any person, thing or property referred to in the award; 3) the award being imperfect in a matter of form, not affecting the merits of the controversy; or 4) an error of law that occurred during the course of the trial. **All other rights of appeal are waived.**

_____   _____   Dated:
Plaintiff(s)   Defendant(s)
                                                        Rochester, New York
_____   _____
Attorney for Plaintiff   Attorney for Defendant

ASBESTOS LITIGATION

Doc. 1. Filing of Papers

Whenever a paper is required to be filed in an individual case, as provided by the Case Management Order, such paper should be filed in the Office of the Clerk of the County in which the action is pending.

The following constitutes the address of the County Clerk for each of the 8 counties in the Seventh Judicial District.

CAYUGA COUNTY:

Susan Dwyer
Cayuga County Clerk
160 Genesee Street
Auburn, NY 13021–3424
Tel: 315–253–1271

LIVINGSTON COUNTY:

James Culbertson
Livingston County Clerk
The Courthouse
2 Court Street
Geneseo, NY 14454–1030
Tel: 585–243–7010

MONROE COUNTY:

Cheryl Dinolfo
Monroe County Clerk
County Office Building
Rochester, NY 14614
Tel: 585–428–5152

ONTARIO COUNTY:

John H. Cooley
Ontario County Clerk
County Municipal Building
20 Ontario Street
Canandaigua, NY 14424
Tel: 585–396–4200

SENECA COUNTY:

Tina Lotz
Seneca County Clerk
1 DiPronio Drive
Waterloo, NY 13165–1681
Tel: 315–539–1771

STEUBEN COUNTY:

Judith M. Hunter
Steuben County Clerk
3 East Pulteney Square
Bath, NY 14310
Tel: 607–776–9631 ext. 3210

WAYNE COUNTY:

Michael Jankowski
Wayne County Clerk
9 Pearl Street
Lyons, NY 14489–1138
Tel: 315–946–7470

YATES COUNTY:

Julie Betts
Yates County Clerk
110 Court Street
Penn Yan, NY 14527–1176
Tel: 315–536–5120

Doc. 2. Case Management Order

SUPREME COURT OF THE STATE OF NEW YORK

In RE: SEVENTH JUDICIAL DISTRICT ASBESTOS LITIGATION

This Document Relates To: All Cases

Master Index No: 2001–012718

SEVENTH JUDICIAL DISTRICT ASBESTOS LITIGATION

(7 JDAL)

CASE MANAGEMENT ORDER

Date: March 21, 2003

I. Applicability of This Order

This Order applies to procedures involving all personal injury and wrongful death cases, based upon claims of exposure to asbestos, whether commenced prior to this order and currently pending, or hereafter commenced in the Supreme Court, State of New York, Seventh Judicial District, comprising the Counties of Monroe, Livingston, Ontario, Wayne, Cayuga, Seneca, Yates and Steuben, except as otherwise directed by the Court upon motion and for cause shown. This order supersedes all previous case management orders and amendments in regard to such litigation.

Pursuant to separate orders, all cases, now pending or hereinafter filed, will be assigned to one or more Supreme Court Justices, to be designated, therein.

A copy of this Case Management Order, as well as other material pertaining to the Seventh Judicial District Asbestos Litigation, including the trial calendar, is available on the Monroe County Supreme Court website: http://www.nycourts.gov/courts/7jd/monroe/asbestos/.

II. Purpose and Objectives

It is in the interests of justice to encourage and bring about the fair, expeditious, and least expensive resolution of these cases. This Case Management Order (CMO) is established in an effort to achieve this goal by allowing the parties to obtain necessary documents and information without imposing undue burdens, and to permit the parties to evaluate these cases, reach early settlements, and frame the issues in order to prepare unsettled cases for trial. The essential elements of the CMO include to the extent feasible:

11. Automatic assignment of all pending and hereafter commenced asbestos litigation in each of the counties of the Seventh Judicial District to one designated Part of Supreme Court.

12. Standardization of discovery in order that parties may obtain the necessary information to evaluate cases for settlement or to prepare them for trial at minimum expense.

13. Scheduling and conducting pre-trial conferences within 60 days of the filing of a Request for Judicial Intervention (RJI) to resolve pretrial management problems, establish discovery schedules, set a trial Day Certain pursuant 22 NYCRR § 125.1(g), appoint Liaison Counsel(s) on behalf of Defendants, and obtain consent for utilization of one of the panel of available JHO's provided herein to preside over motions and trials.

14. Consider settlement opportunities including the grouping of cases and any other orders as necessary to avoid duplication, contain costs and expedite disposition through settlement or trial.

III.   Index Numbers and Filing Procedures

A.   Files

A master file, known as Seventh Judicial District Asbestos Litigation ("7 JDAL") Master File, has been established in the Office of the County Clerk of Monroe County for all asbestos cases commenced in the Seventh Judicial District and designated as Monroe County Index No. 2001–012718. Entries in the 7 JDAL Master File shall be applicable to each personal injury and wrongful death case, commenced in the Seventh Judicial District, which is governed by this Order or any amendment thereof.

The original of this Order shall be filed by the County Clerk in the 7 JDAL Master File, and a copy shall be provided to each of the County Clerk's Offices in the remaining seven Counties in the Seventh Judicial District, and a copy shall be deemed to be part of the Record of each and every case commenced in the Seventh Judicial District.

A separate file shall also be maintained under a Separate Index Number in the County, venued by the Plaintiff(s), for each individual action and each individual Plaintiff in the applicable County Clerk's Office,

and entries shall be made therein in accordance with this Order.

Copies of all papers filed under the Master Index Number and in the respective County Clerk's offices must also be submitted to the Supreme Court Justice designated to receive all assignments under this Order.

B.   Captions of Cases

Every document filed in these coordinated actions, which has general application to all cases, shall bear a caption as follows:

SUPREME COURT OF THE STATE OF NEW YORK

SEVENTH JUDICIAL DISTRICT

In RE: SEVENTH JUDICIAL DISTRICT ASBESTOS LITIGATION

This Document Applies to: Master File

Index No. 2001–012718

C.   Filing of Papers

1. Whenever a paper has general application to all cases, such as a Notice of Filing of Bankruptcy by a named Defendant, the caption shall bear Index No. 2001–012718 and the Monroe County Clerk shall file such a paper in the 7 JDAL Master File. Any document so filed shall be deemed to have been filed in each case to which this Order applies, and shall constitute part of the record of each such file.

2. Whenever a paper, such as a Plaintiff's Initial Fact Sheet ("PIFS") or a motion, is applicable only to an individual case, the attorney submitting such paper for filing shall supply to the Clerk of the County in which the action is venued a cover sheet containing the caption, name, and Index Number to which the paper is applicable. The County Clerk shall file such paper in the individual file for the action under the appropriate Index Number. The Monroe County Clerk shall NOT file such paper in the 7 JDAL Master File.

3. Whenever a paper is filed that is applicable to two or more, but less than all of these coordinated actions, the captions shall state the case names and separate Index Numbers of the actions to which that paper is applicable. The Clerk of the counties, in which the actions so identified are venued, shall file a copy of the paper in each separate file under the index numbers so identified. It is the responsibility of the attorney submitting such paper for filing to supply a cover sheet containing the captions, titles, and index numbers of all actions to which the paper is applicable and to supply the appropriate County Clerks with sufficient copies of the paper to facilitate compliance with the directives of this paragraph.

4. When a paper is filed that requires some action by the Court, such as an RJI, Notice of Motion, Request for a Pre–Trial conference, or a Note of Issue

and Certificate of Readiness, the attorney submitting such paper to the appropriate County Clerk shall be responsible for serving a copy to all counsel of record and forward a copy to the Court.

5. Following the filing and service of the Complaint and the appearance by or on behalf of defense counsel, but in no event more than ninety (90) days from the filing of the Complaint, Counsel for the Plaintiff(s) shall cause to be filed an RJI in the office of the appropriate County Clerk, where the case is venued, requesting a Preliminary Conference. In addition, counsel for the Plaintiff(s) shall submit to the Court a copy of said RJI, together with a list of the Defendants' counsel, including mailing address, telephone, fax, and e-mail address, by e-mail or on a disk, in a format which may be converted to Word Perfect. Plaintiff(s)' counsel shall have the obligation to update said disk within thirty (30) days of any change. Counsel for each Plaintiff and Defendant shall be obligated to identify trial counsel within 14 days of the trial date, as provided in the scheduling order issued in each case, and to so advise the designated Supreme Court Justice, accordingly, including trial counsel's phone number, fax, and e-mail address.

6. Following receipt of the RJI, together with the required information for Defendants' counsel, Chambers of the designated Supreme Court Justice, shall notify all counsel of record of a date and time for a Preliminary Conference, which will be scheduled, within sixty (60) days, at the Hall of Justice, Rochester, New York.

7. In addition to the foregoing, all counsel representing Plaintiffs shall file with the Court, and serve Liaison Counsel, a current chronological list of each and every personal injury and wrongful death case pending and subject of this Case Management Order. The list shall include the name, date of birth, and trade of the Plaintiff, or decedent, as well as filing date of the action. The list shall be updated on a monthly basis.

IV. Judicial Hearing Officers

The Civil Practice Law and Rules and the applicable Uniform Court Rules, together with the express provisions of this Order, shall govern all cases, based upon claims of exposure to asbestos, in the Seventh Judicial District.

Consistent with the objectives of this CMO and in order to expedite the processing of these claims, a panel of Judicial Hearing Officers shall be available for assignment to rule on motions and preside over jury trials. Failure, at the Preliminary Conference, on the part of any party to object to the assignment of a JHO from this panel to hear and determine any part of the case will be deemed a consent pursuant to CPLR Section 4317(a). Following the Preliminary Conference, and absent objection by a party, counsel for the Plaintiff(s) and Liaison Counsel for the Defendants shall execute a Stipulation, as required by

CPLR 4317, and in a form annexed hereto and contained in Appendix "D." The Stipulation shall be filed in the Office of the Clerk of the County, in which the case has been venued, under the Index Number for that case, and a copy provided to the Court. Thereafter, an Order will be issued appointing a specific Judicial Hearing Officer to preside over issues in the case. The panel of Judicial Hearing Officers will be contained in a separate Court Order, which will be filed in the Master File.

V. Pleadings

A. Plaintiff's Statement:

A Plaintiff's Initial Fact Statement ("PIFS"), annexed hereto as Appendix "A," shall be submitted to the Court and be included with the Complaint or served upon the Defendants within sixty (60) days after filing of the Complaint or sixty (60) days from the date of this Order, whichever date is later. If the PIFS is not attached to the Complaint, the original PIFS shall be filed by counsel in the office of the County Clerk of the County in which the action is venued under the Index Number of the action to which it applies. The PIFS shall include the Plaintiff's specific work site(s) at which it is claimed that injurious asbestos exposure occurred. In a case of alleged derivative exposure, the PIFS shall include the specific work site(s) of the person(s) through whom Plaintiff was exposed, to the extent known. In no event are the PIFS intended to limit proof and are not admissible for any purpose.

If at any time after the filing of the PIFS, but before service of Plaintiff's Answer to Standard Interrogatories, Plaintiff's claimed asbestos-related illness changes from a non-malignancy to a malignancy, the PIFS shall be amended accordingly. All such amendments must be filed and served, as hereinbefore set forth, within sixty (60) days of notification to Plaintiff's counsel of such change in claimed illness.

B. Standardized Pleadings:

1. Plaintiff's counsel may file in the 7 JDAL Master File and serve on Defendants, a Complaint, or set of Complaints, containing standard allegations generally applicable to all claims of a similar nature. Thereafter, counsel may file and serve a short form Complaint which incorporates by reference all of the allegations contained in the appropriate standard Complaint.

2. Regardless of whether or not Plaintiff has elected to serve and file a Standard Complaint, any Defendant may file in the 7 JDAL Master File and serve on Plaintiff(s)' and other Defendants' counsel a standard Answer with affirmative defenses. When such standard answer has been filed, a Defendant may within 60 days of service of the Complaint, serve an Acknowledgment of Service, in a form annexed hereto, and contained in Appendix "B," incorporating a standard answer by reference. All Defendants to which any

cross claim has been asserted will be deemed to have denied all material allegations contained in the cross claim. Nothing herein shall preclude a Defendant from filing an individual answer, which may be served within 60 days of service of the Complaint.

3. Third–Party Plaintiff(s)' counsel may file in the 7 JDAL Master File and serve on Third–Party Defendants a Third–Party Complaint or set of Third–Party Complaints containing standard allegations generally applicable to all Third–Party claims of a similar nature. Thereafter, Third–Party Plaintiffs may file and serve short form Third–Party Complaints that incorporate by reference all of the allegations contained in the appropriate standard Third–Party Complaint.

4. A Third–Party Defendant may file, in the 7 JDAL Master File and serve on Third–Party Plaintiff(s), a Standard Answer to a Third–Party Complaint with affirmative defenses. When a Standard Answer to a Third–Party Complaint has been filed, a Third–Party Defendant may serve a Third–Party Plaintiff in an action with an Acknowledgment of Service of Third–Party Complaint, in a form annexed hereto and contained in Appendix "C." Upon service of an Acknowledgment of Service of a Third–Party Complaint, a Third–Party Defendant will be deemed to have denied all material allegations contained in the Third–Party Complaint, except as stated in such Acknowledgment, and to have raised each affirmative defense contained in its Standard Answer to Third–Party Complaint, except as stated in such Acknowledgment. Nothing herein shall preclude a Third–Party Defendant from filing an individual answer, if it so chooses.

C. Amendments/Substitution Following Death of Plaintiff

Upon the death of an injured Plaintiff, and prior to the date set for filing the Note of Issue, the personal representative of the deceased injured Plaintiff may be substituted as Plaintiff, without leave of the Court, if said personal representative submits to the Court and serves upon all attorneys of record in the pending action:

1. The date and place of the deceased injured Plaintiff's death;

2. The name and address of the deceased injured Plaintiff's personal representative;

3. A copy of the death certificate for the deceased injured Plaintiff;

4. A copy of the Surrogate's certification of the appointment of the personal representative; and

5. A proposed Order of Substitution.

Prior to the date set for filing the Note of Issue, a substituted Plaintiff may, without leave of Court, amend the original Complaint to add a claim of wrongful death. Service of such amendments on counsel who has appeared for a Defendant shall be considered

service on that Defendant. Defendants may answer as set forth in this Order.

A substituted Plaintiff seeking to amend a Complaint to add claims, based upon wrongful death, must support the enlargement of the Complaint, to include such cause of action, with medical documentation including: the certificate of death; and an autopsy report or hospital admission/discharge summary or a report prepared and signed by a physician supporting the allegation of a connection between the alleged injurious exposure to asbestos and the death. No presumption regarding causation is created by such enlargement of a Complaint. The issue of the connection between the alleged injurious exposure to asbestos, if any, and the death shall be preserved for the trier of fact or for the Court upon motion. A Defendant who served an Acknowledgment of Service or answer in the original action is not required to serve an answer to the amended Complaint as all new material allegations contained in the amended Complaint will be deemed denied by any such Defendant.

D. Other Amendments to Pleadings

Amendments to the pleadings, other than those set forth in Section V(C) of this Order shall be made in compliance with CPLR Section 3025. The parties are encouraged to consent to amendments where appropriate based upon New York State's recognition that leave to amend is to be freely granted.

VI. Liaison Counsel

A. Appointment of Plaintiffs' Liaison Counsel and Defendants' Liaison Counsel to act on behalf of Plaintiffs' counsel and Defendants' counsel, respectively, after appropriate consultation where necessary, will facilitate communication between the Court and counsel, minimize duplication of effort, and provide for the efficient progress and control of this litigation.

B. Subject to the right of any party to present individual positions or divergent positions or to take individual actions, Liaison Counsel are vested by the Court with the following responsibilities and duties:

1. Coordinating the conduct of discovery procedures, including but not limited to coordination of the preparation of joint written interrogatories, joint requests to admit, and joint requests for the production of documents, where applicable;

2. Coordinating the examination of witnesses in depositions;

3. Calling meetings of counsel for Plaintiffs' counsel and Defendants' counsel, respectively, for the purpose of proposing joint actions, including but not limited to responses to questions and suggestions of the Court or of adversaries with regard to orders, schedules, briefs, and stipulations of the facts.

4. Draft and consent to proposed scheduling and other orders, and agree upon stipulations.

C. Liaison Counsel are authorized to receive orders, notices, correspondence and telephone calls from the Court regarding general case management issues on behalf of all Defendants, and receive medical authorizations from counsel for Plaintiffs. Liaison Counsel shall be responsible for notifying all Defense counsel of all communications received from the Court and to send medical records received from counsel for Plaintiff(s) to any counsel for a Defendant upon request for same. Liaison Counsel is not responsible for obtaining medical records from other Defendants, and further, may not be used by any party for service and/or distribution of papers, orders, notices or correspondence to other counsel.

D. Notwithstanding the appointment of Liaison Counsel, each counsel shall have the right to participate in all proceedings before the Court as fully as such counsel deems necessary.

E. Liaison Counsel shall not have the right to bind any party except Liaison Counsel's own respective clients as to any matter without the consent of counsel for any other party.

F. Subject to approval of the Court, Plaintiffs' Liaison Counsel and Defendants' Liaison Counsel shall be reimbursed periodically, by counsel for Plaintiffs and Defendants, respectively, for necessary and reasonable disbursements actually incurred in performing their responsibilities pursuant to this Order. Liaison Counsel shall keep records of such disbursements in reasonable detail for examination by counsel. Liaison Counsel shall be paid, respectively, by each Plaintiff or Defense law firm on an equitable basis to be agreed upon by the parties or fixed by the Court with each Plaintiff and Defense law firm having to pay a proportionate share of the disbursements incurred by its respective Liaison Counsel in representing its interest. Liaison Counsels' invoices for services as Liaison Counsel pursuant to this Order shall be due and payable when submitted. Interest shall be computed at the rate applicable to judgments starting thirty (30) days after the date of their submission.

G. In the event that the client of Liaison Counsel ceases to be a party, because of settlement, discontinuance, dismissal or otherwise, counsel may be relieved of further responsibility as liaison upon application to the Court, or arranging for substitute Liaison Counsel.

VII. Standard Consolidated Discovery

A. Interrogatories and Document Requests:

Standard Interrogatories and Requests for Production of Documents shall be used as set forth herein. The Court on its own motion hereby permits the use of interrogatories in addition to depositions pursuant to CPLR § 3130.

1. *Defendants' Interrogatories and Document Requests:*

a. A standard set of interrogatories to Plaintiff(s) has been filed in the 7 JDAL Master File. These standard interrogatories, captioned "Defendants' First Set of Interrogatories and Request for Production of Documents" ("Defendants' Standard Interrogatories"), are annexed hereto and contained in Appendix "F." An alternative, short form, standard set of interrogatories have also been filed in the 7 JDAL Master File. These alternative, standard interrogatories, captioned "Defendants' Short Form, First Set of Interrogatories and Requests Production of Documents" ("Defendants' Alternative Standard Interrogatories") are annexed hereto and contained in Appendix "E."

b. Unless otherwise directed by the Court, upon request by a Defendant, Plaintiff(s) may respond to either "Defendants' Standard Interrogatories" or "Defendants' Alternative Standard Interrogatories." Plaintiff(s) shall serve responses to such Interrogatories ("Plaintiffs' Answers to Standard Interrogatories") upon all Defendants in an action and in accordance with the applicable discovery and trial submission schedule for that action. Such Interrogatories shall be answered in full, unless appropriate objections are stated in lieu of an answer. "Plaintiffs' Answers to Standard Interrogatories" shall be verified by the individual injured Plaintiff(s) or Plaintiff estate representative. In the event that Plaintiff(s) has responded to "Defendants' Alternative Standard Interrogatories," and upon receipt of same, any Defendant may specifically make a written request, to the Court, that Plaintiff(s) also respond to "Defendants' Standard Interrogatories."

c. Defendant may serve supplemental, non-repetitive interrogatories and requests for production of documents ("Defendant's Supplemental Interrogatories") in accordance with the applicable discovery and trial submission schedule for an action.

d. Copies of any records obtained by a Defendant pursuant to authorization of a Plaintiff, other than those records which are obtained through a mutually agreed upon records retrieval service, shall be made available to Plaintiff's counsel by notice of receipt mailed to Plaintiff's counsel within ten (10) days of Defendant's receipt of such records.

2. *Plaintiffs' Interrogatories and Document Requests:*

a. Plaintiffs' standard set of general liability interrogatories have been filed in the 7 JDAL Master File. These standard interrogatories, captioned "Plaintiffs' First Standard Set of Liability Interrogatories and Request for Production of Documents" ("Plaintiffs' Standard Interrogatories"), are annexed hereto and contained in Appendix "G." In the event that a Plaintiff's counsel commences an action against a Defendant not previously a party, said Plaintiff's counsel will serve Plaintiffs' Standard Interrogatories on such Defendant.

b. Each Defendant shall file a single set of responses to "Plaintiffs' Standard Interrogatories" ("Defendants' Answers to Standard Interrogatories") and shall give notice of the filing to, or serve same on, Plaintiff's counsel in accordance with the applicable discovery schedule in each individual action. In the event that a Plaintiff's counsel commences an action against a Defendant not previously a party, and fails to serve Plaintiffs' Standard Interrogatories, such Defendant is not required to file and serve responses to Plaintiffs' Standard Interrogatories.

c. A Plaintiff may serve supplemental, non-repetitive interrogatories and requests for production of documents ("Plaintiffs' Supplemental Interrogatories") in accordance with the applicable discovery and trial submission schedule for an action.

d. A Plaintiff may serve non-duplicative, standard product identification interrogatories with respect to particular work sites ("Plaintiffs' Standard Product Identification/Work Site Interrogatories") in accordance with the applicable discovery and trial submission schedule for an action.

B. General Guidelines Regarding Document Requests:

1. A party requesting discovery and inspection of documents shall specify a reasonable time, place, and manner for making the inspection. The request will describe each item with reasonable particularity.

2. Responses to requests for discovery and inspection of documents should be, to the extent practicable, in such form as will make clear the request to which the document is responsive.

3. Any response that a document cannot be located, shall state with reasonable particularity the efforts made to obtain the requested document.

4. Counsel are to exercise good faith in making requests for and in responding to requests to production of documents.

5. Counsel are to exercise their best efforts to resolve, on an informal basis, disputes arising out of the document requests and responses and objections thereto.

C. General Guidelines Regarding Discovery:

1. Disputes with regard to discovery shall be called immediately to the attention of the Court for resolution and, unless otherwise directed by the Court, shall not be relied upon by any party, as a justification for not adhering to any applicable discovery and trial submission schedule.

2. Objections to discovery based on privilege shall clearly identify the privilege claimed and shall provide sufficient information concerning (i) the basis for the claim of privilege to establish, prima facie, the validity of the claim, and (ii) the privileged information to permit identification of the information or document

as to which privilege is claimed. If not so identified, the privilege shall be deemed waived. The parties shall negotiate in an effort to preserve the confidentiality of trade secrets.

3. Any objection to discovery based on burdensomeness shall describe the burden with reasonable particularity. Any objection to the time, place, or manner of production shall state a reasonable alternative as a counterproposal.

4. Any response that information cannot be determined, shall state with reasonable particularity, the efforts made to obtain the requested information.

5. Any notice and/or motion for discovery served upon a non-party shall be served contemporaneously upon all parties to the action.

VIII. Medical Examinations of Plaintiff(s)

Physical examinations of Plaintiff(s) shall be conducted in accordance with the CPLR and applicable case law. Counsel for Plaintiff(s) shall provide Liaison Counsel with original, or duplicate original, authorizations for Plaintiff(s)' medical records.

IX. Depositions

A. General Guidelines:

1. All depositions of parties shall be held in the Seventh Judicial District unless otherwise ordered by the Court or agreed to by the parties, and coordinated with Liaison Counsel.

2. All counsel shall avoid unnecessary and repetitive questioning of witnesses.

3. Unless all parties otherwise agree, all objections, except as to the form of the question, shall be reserved for determination by the trial judge.

4. All counsel may attend any deposition.

5. Counsel may notice any deposition to apply to more than one case and shall use best efforts to insure that depositions are noticed to apply to all appropriate cases. Nothing in this provision shall be deemed to prohibit a party from moving to limit the use of deposition testimony based upon good cause shown.

6. All depositions shall be conducted with due regard for the physical and emotional condition, health, and disability of the deponent.

7. In the event that a notice for a discovery deposition is not served, but such deposition is scheduled by agreement of counsel or order of the Court, any such deposition of an injured Plaintiff, Plaintiff's spouse or personal representative will be deemed to have been noticed for or scheduled by Defendant's counsel and any such depositions of a Defendant will be deemed to have been noticed for or scheduled by Plaintiff's counsel.

8. Deposition testimony may be used only against those parties which received actual written notification of the deposition stating the date, time and location of

the deposition. Said notification must be served in compliance with the CPLR, this Order, or other court order and, in any event, unless good cause is shown, must be served no later than three (3) business days prior to the scheduled date of the deposition.

B. Depositions of Plaintiff(s)

1. Depositions of injured Plaintiff(s) will be scheduled by Liaison Counsel when preparing discovery and trial submission schedules for actions scheduled for trial. In all actions, the rights of Defendants and Third Party Defendants to depose Plaintiff's spouse, personal representative, and distributees of a decedent at any time prior to jury selection are reserved. Such a deposition may be requested, noticed for, and/or scheduled by any defense counsel.

2. Questioning of the injured Plaintiff by defense counsel shall begin with interrogation by Defendants' Liaison Counsel, followed by interrogation by other defense counsel in an order agreed to by defense counsel or as decided by Defendants' Liaison Counsel when such an agreement cannot be reached.

3. Questioning a Plaintiff's spouse, personal representative and distributees of a decedent shall begin with interrogation by the defense counsel who requested, noticed, and/or scheduled the deposition, followed by interrogation by other defense counsel in an order agreed to by defense counsel or as decided by Defendants' Liaison Counsel when such an agreement cannot be reached. If the above deponent is a present or former officer or employee of a Defendant, such Defendant shall question first, followed by other defense counsel in the order described in Section IX (B)(2) of this Order.

C. Depositions of Defendants and Non–Party Witnesses

1. Depositions of Defendants and non-party witnesses will be noticed for, and/or scheduled, by the party seeking the deposition during the period of time provided in the applicable discovery and trial submission schedule for the action.

2. The parties shall make every effort to use depositions as well as other discovery obtained from Defendants in other actions in New York State and other jurisdictions for all purposes as if taken in each action in these cases in accordance with this Order.

3. Any Plaintiff may serve notice of intent to take non-repetitive depositions of Defendants' representatives pertaining to issues which were not covered or not adequately covered by prior depositions of that Defendant. All corporate depositions shall be noticed at a time and place convenient to the parties and witnesses, taking into account the expense to the parties and the health of the Defendants' witnesses.

4. Questioning by Plaintiff's counsel shall begin with interrogation by the Plaintiff's counsel, who noticed the deposition, followed by other Plaintiffs' counsel in the order of their appearance in this litigation

and defense counsel in the order described in Section IX (B)(2) of this Order. If the above deponent is a present or former officer or employee of a Defendant, questioning by a defense counsel shall begin with counsel for such Defendant, followed by other defense counsel in the order described in Section IX (B)(2) of this Order.

D. Stenographers' Fees

1. Unless otherwise agreed, when a deposition of a party to an action is taken at the request of any other party, the cost of the stenographer's appearance, the preparation of the transcript, and the party deponent's copy of the transcript shall be divided equally among all counsel who appear at the deposition, other than counsel for the party-deponent. Each party, other than the party-deponent, who requests a copy of the transcript shall bear the cost of that copy.

2. Unless otherwise agreed, when a party elects to take his, her, or its own testimony, that party shall bear the cost of the stenographer's appearance and the preparation of the transcript. Any party who requests a copy of the transcript shall bear the cost of that copy.

3. Unless otherwise agreed, when a deposition of a non-party is taken, the cost of the stenographer's appearance, the preparation of the transcript, and the non-party's copy of the transcript will be divided equally among all counsel who appear at the deposition, other than counsel for the non-party. Any party, other than the non-party's counsel, who requests a copy of the transcript shall bear the cost of that copy.

E. Videotaped Depositions

1. For the purpose of this section, the term videotaped depositions shall include videotaped trial testimony.

2. Any party, upon service of a proper notice of deposition, may videotape the depositions for any use permitted by the CPLR. All videotape depositions shall be conducted in accordance with 22 NYCRR 202.15, with the exceptions and stipulations set forth below:

  a. If the party noticing for or scheduling a deposition wants the deposition to be videotaped, that party shall so advise all parties either in its notice of the deposition or by letter;

  b. The video technician may not be an employee of any party or any party's counsel.

  c. The videotaped deposition shall be taken before a person authorized by statute who will swear the deponent and make a stenographic record of the proceedings;

  d. At the beginning of the deposition, the video technician will state, on camera, in addition to that required by Uniform Rule Section 202.15(d)(1): the title and venue of the action; the name of the deponent; and the name of the officer before whom the deposition is being taken.

3. Unless otherwise agreed to by counsel, video-taped depositions of deponents who have not been previously deposed in the pending action and who are not terminally ill may not be taken sooner than fifteen (15) days after completion of that witness' non-video-taped discovery deposition. Upon agreement of all counsel, this provision may be waived.

4. A videotape deposition of a terminally ill Plain-tiff, who has previously submitted to a discovery depo-sition, and whose availability for trial may reasonably be doubted, may be promptly taken on notice and without further order of the Court provided that Plaintiff serves on all parties: a medical affidavit executed by a treating physician specifying Plaintiff's present diagnosis and prognosis and indicating any prescribed medication which would in any way affect Plaintiff's mental faculties and ability to understand and respond to questioning; and all other documents, requested by defense counsel, including, but not limit-ed to, supplemental responses to Defendants' Stan-dard Interrogatories and all new medical records and reports in the possession of Plaintiff and Plaintiff's counsel. Plaintiff's counsel should confer with Defen-dants' Liaison Counsel to schedule the deposition with reasonable notice, giving due consideration to Plain-tiff's medical condition. If notice of the deposition is given seven (7) days or less prior to the date when the deposition is to be taken, notice must be served by facsimile. In no event shall the taking of the video-tape deposition be delayed more than ten (10) days from the date of receipt of Plaintiff's counsel certifica-tion and notice to take the videotape deposition, ex-cept with agreement of Plaintiff's counsel, or by order of the Court. Plaintiff's counsel shall permit Defen-dants to take a further discovery deposition for the purposes of obtaining non-repetitive testimony off-camera at Defendants' expense prior to the videotape deposition.

5. Unless all counsel agree otherwise or unless the Court on motion directs otherwise, only one camera may be used and the camera will record the witness' head and shoulders view only, with the exception that, at the request of questioning counsel, the camera may record a close-up of a deposition exhibit or other exhibit, including demonstrative exhibits, while the witness is being questioned concerning the exhibit.

6. All objections to questions and testimony given, at a videotaped deposition, except as to the form of the question, are preserved until the time of trial.

7. The cost of the videotape, as a material, and the cost of recording the deposition on videotape will be borne by the party noticing the videotaped deposition; that party shall have ownership of the videotape.

X. Expedited Discovery and Trials for *In Extremis* Plaintiffs

A. When an injured Plaintiff is *in extremis*, Plain-tiff's counsel may make application to the Court for an Order providing for a jury selection date and an expedited discovery and trial submission schedule, in accordance with CPLR Rule 3407. Any such applica-tion shall be served on all parties and/or prospective parties and in addition to the requirements of CPLR Rule 3407, shall include and/or be accompanied by:

1. A medical affidavit executed by a treating phy-sician specifying the injured Plaintiff's present diagno-sis and prognosis and indicating any prescribed medi-cation which would in any way affect the injured Plaintiff's mental faculties and ability to understand and respond to questioning.

2. A copy of the summons and complaint and any amended and/or supplemental summonses and com-plaints.

3. Plaintiff's responses to Defendants' Standard Interrogatories and to any supplemental interrogato-ries previously served;

4. All medical records and reports in the posses-sion of Plaintiff and Plaintiff's counsel; and

5. All other documents in Plaintiff's or Plaintiff's counsel's possession relating to taxes, workers' com-pensation and social security

B. In the event that Plaintiff's counsel seeks to conduct videotaped trial testimony of the injured Plaintiff, Plaintiff's counsel will permit Defendants to conduct a discovery deposition prior to the videotaped trial testimony.

C. Plaintiff may not conduct videotaped trial testi-mony of an *in extremis* injured Plaintiff unless the materials set forth in Section X(A) have been provided to all defense counsel and defense counsel have com-pleted their discovery deposition.

D. The parties will make a good faith effort to schedule the *in extremis* discovery deposition and videotaped trial testimony at mutually agreeable times and locations. All parties are encouraged to act rea-sonably concerning the scheduling.

XI. Motion Practice

A. General Provisions

Unless otherwise directed by the Court, all motions shall be made returnable in Monroe County.

B. Discovery Motions:

Parties will make a good faith effort to resolve all discovery disputes without the need for Court inter-vention. However, when a dispute cannot be resolved by the parties, a motion may be brought pursuant to the applicable provisions of the CPLR.

C. Accelerated Judgment:

Each party, at any time, has a right to seek or oppose an accelerated judgment pursuant to CPLR Sections 3211 and/or 3212. However, in an effort to avoid unnecessary motion practice and to streamline the conclusion of these cases, the Court hereby adopts the following process:

1. At any time, Plaintiff's counsel may notify a Defendant that, upon the review of a particular action, it appears unlikely that Plaintiff will be able to produce any evidence of Defendant's presence at a job site and/or identification of products containing asbestos manufactured, supplied or applied by that particular Defendant. Upon receipt of such notification, such Defendant may prepare and serve on Plaintiff's and co–Defendants' counsel a proposed order dismissing Plaintiffs' claims and all cross-claims, giving notice to all parties of Defendant's intention to enter said order. If no party serves written objection to such proposed order within twenty (20) days of its service, the Defendant may submit the proposed order to the Court, with copies to all parties. If, within twenty (20) days of service of a proposed order and notice pursuant to this paragraph, any co–Defendant advises in writing that it intends to pursue in good faith its cross-claims against the submitting Defendant, that co–Defendant's cross claims and reflecting the revised caption, or may move for other or different relief.

2. Unless otherwise specified in the scheduling order, at any time after Plaintiff's service of Responses to Defendants' Standard Interrogatories and Requests for Production of Documents, or at any time after the date for Plaintiff's disclosure of job site and/or Product Identification, pursuant to a scheduling order, whichever is later, a Defendant may, in good faith, serve upon the Plaintiff a statement in writing that there is no evidence that the Defendant was present at any of the job sites identified by Plaintiff ("Job site Identification Letter") and/or that there is no evidence of product identification ("Product Identification Letter"). When a Product Identification Letter and/or "Job site Identification Letter" is served, Plaintiff shall within 30 days, respond by:

a. Advising the Defendant of the identities of co-worker(s) or other witness(es) who will testify concerning job site and/or product identification or specifying documents that will evidence job site and/or product identification, and in doing so, Plaintiff will not be precluded from presenting additional witnesses or documents at the time of trial so long as such witnesses or documents have been identified as required by the CPLR and/or this Order; or

b. By advising the Defendant that no evidence of job site and/or product identification will be forthcoming, in which case, defendant may proceed to enter an order in accordance with Section XI(C)(1) of this Order.

3. In the event that a Plaintiff responds by advising Defendant of identities of co-workers and/or other

witnesses, the Plaintiff must refer the Defendant to prior testimony substantiating job site and/or product identification or provide sworn affidavit(s) of the designated witnesses stating: (a) the job sites and the time period's, affiant was at the job sites; and (b) a summary of the anticipated testimony regarding the identification of products and the circumstances of injured Plaintiff's/decedent's exposure to the product.

4. If Plaintiff fails to respond to Defendant's demand for job site and/or product identification, such Defendant is entitled to submit to the Court, on notice, an order dismissing Plaintiff's complaint against that Defendant. Plaintiff retains the right to be heard in opposition to the signing and entry of such an order by the Court, and also retains their right to oppose an accelerated judgment pursuant to CPLR Sections 3211 and 3212, or both.

5. If, based upon Plaintiff's response to its Job site and/or Product Identification Letter, a Defendant desires to depose co-workers and/or other witnesses, such Defendant shall advise Plaintiff's counsel in writing. Noticing and/or scheduling of the depositions will proceed in accordance with Section IX of this Order.

6. When a Plaintiff discontinues an action against a Defendant, such Defendant may proceed in either of the following manners:

a. Such Defendant may serve written notice of the discontinuance upon all parties to the action and a proposed order dismissing all claims and cross-claims against it, giving notice to all parties of Defendant's intention to enter said order. If no party serves written objection to such proposed order within twenty (20)days of its service, the Defendant may submit the proposed order to the Court, with copies to all parties. If, within twenty (20) days of service of said proposed order and notice, a co–Defendant serves a written objection to dismissal on the ground that it intends to pursue in good faith its cross-claims against the Defendant obtaining the discontinuance, the Defendant's cross-claims may be converted to third-party claims in accordance with Section 1007 of the CPLR. The Defendant obtaining the discontinuance may then submit to the Court a revised order dismissing all claims and all cross-claims except those of the objecting co–Defendant and reflecting the revised caption, or may move the Court for other or different relief.

b. In the alternative, such Defendant may move for an order dismissing all claims and cross-claims against it in the action. The return date of such motion shall be at least twenty (20) days following service of said motion unless, by Order to Show Cause, the Court permits a shorter notice period. If no party serves written objection to such dismissal within twenty (20) days following service of such motion, or within such other time period as the Court may set, the motion will be granted and the moving Defendant may submit to the Court, with copies to all parties, an order dismissing all claims and cross-claims against it and deleting it from the action. If any party to the action serves written objection to such motion for dismissal within the applicable time period, the Court shall hear the motion and issue such order as is just.

XII. Scheduling of Trials and Discovery

At the Preliminary Conference, the Court will, issue Orders setting forth dates for filing of Notes of Issue and trials in actions pending in the 7 JDAL in accordance with this Order. For the purpose of this section of this Order, the term "injured Plaintiff" is meant to refer to the individual who was allegedly injured by reason of exposure to asbestos and, when the Plaintiff is a personal or estate representative, is meant to refer to the decedent.

A. Trial Dates:

The Court will issue individual trial dates for asbestos actions pending in the 7 JDAL. The Court may group for discovery and trial purposes: (1) actions of injured Plaintiffs, who were the direct employees of a legal entity at a plant site in the Seventh Judicial District (2) the action of an injured Plaintiff who alleges injurious exposure to asbestos by reason of kinship or cohabitation with the action of a related person who also has an action pending in the 7 JDAL; and (3) other cases which under the circumstances would warrant discovery and/or trial grouping. Nothing in this Case Management Order shall be construed to prevent the Court from consolidating two or more actions in groups for trial. Nothing in this Case Management Order shall be construed to prevent the Court from directing the removal or severance of one or more Plaintiffs from a group for a trial.

B. Procedure for Scheduling Trial Dates:

At the Preliminary Conference, the Court will set a day certain trial date for each case or group of cases. In the event of a severance of one or more cases within a group, the cases with the earliest Index Numbers, together with other cases continued to be joined in the same group, will first proceed to trial, followed by the severed cases, in an order based upon the same procedure, unless otherwise ordered by the Court.

C. Schedule:

Following the Preliminary Conference, Liaison Counsel will meet and confer in order to develop a proposed Scheduling Order for each action assigned a trial date. Unless otherwise agreed upon, the Discovery and Trial Submission Schedule will be in the form and contain dates as set forth in Appendix H.

XIII. Pretrial Submissions

A. Pretrial submissions shall be served in accordance with the applicable discovery and trial submission schedule. Pretrial submissions include a list of all expert witnesses, fact witnesses and all exhibits that the parties intend to use at trial. Counsel shall have an opportunity to designate additional witnesses and exhibits in response to their adversaries' designations as set forth in the discovery and trial submission schedule or at some later time for good cause shown.

B. The trial judge shall make such further orders, deemed appropriate, for submission of proposed *voir dire*, requests for jury charges or other submissions. Additionally, the trial court shall direct a schedule for objections to exhibits or proposed deposition testimony, as necessary and as the Court so chooses.

C. Plaintiff's counsel shall deliver seventy (70) copies of the completed juror questionnaire (attached as Appendix I) to the appropriate county's Jury Commissioner no later than the Thursday before the commencement of jury selection.

XIV. Settlements

If Plaintiff(s) and Defendant(s) stipulate to discontinue the action, the parties' counsel shall sign a Stipulation of Discontinuance, provide all parties with 20 days notice, thereof, and forward same to the Court, with an Order approving same, and providing that said discontinuance/dismissal is on the merits and applies to any and all cross-claims or counterclaims.

Any settlement of a wrongful death case will be subject to the approval of this Part, and shall be submitted to the designated Supreme Court Justice and no other Court or Judge. EPTL § 5-4.6, as interpreted by the Court of Appeals, in *Pollincina v. Misericordia Hospital*, (82 NY2d 332 [1993]), requires the "Court to evaluate and resolve the fairness and reasonableness of the settlement, including the amount to be paid, the manner in which the payment obligation is amortized and the parties' arrangements for payment of costs and attorney's fees." Accordingly, within 60 days of resolution of all claims, in a pending wrongful death action, Plaintiff's counsel must submit a proposed order for approval of the settlement, including an allowance for attorney's fees and expenses. The papers, submitted in support of such application, should include an affidavit from the personal representative, consenting to the compromise on behalf of the distributees. In lieu of an affidavit, a personal representative may be produced, in person, for purposes of examination by the Court. In addition, an affirmation from counsel should be submitted, setting forth the time expended and other bases for the requested amount of attorney's fees and an itemized list of expenses. Further, the application should contain the specific amounts to be contributed by each Defendant, who has participated in the settlement, and the reasons for agreeing to accept such amounts. If a settlement has been reached with a Defendant for a total amount, which encompasses other, unrelated claims, Plaintiff's counsel must set forth the manner and method used in the allocation of such amount among the respective cases. In the event that monies have been paid by a Defendant, such amounts are to be retained in an interest bearing trust account, maintained by Plaintiff's counsel for the benefit of the distributees, and thereafter, disbursed only after approval by the Court, and in accordance with the Order.

If claims against one or more, but not all, Defendants are resolved by settlement, approval by the Court, as required herein, will be withheld until final resolution of all claims. Alternatively, the parties may request approval of settlement of one or more such claims as well as permission to disburse monies already or to be paid, prior to resolution of all claims, but only upon compliance with the foregoing requirements relating to approval following resolution of all claims. In such circumstances, the affirmation, submitted by Plaintiff's counsel, should indicate the reasons for such request and, insofar as possible, an estimate of anticipated future proceeds.

An application, made pursuant to this section, may request issuance of an order approving the total amount of a settlement without an allocation between wrongful death and other types of claims. In such event, and upon approval, the Court will refer the matter to the appropriate Surrogate's Court for purposes of making such allocation and directing distribution of the proceeds. Alternatively, Plaintiff(s) may request that the entire proceeds, or a portion, thereof, be allocated to the wrongful death claim. In such event, and upon approval, the Court may make a determination concerning the proper allocation for the wrongful death claim, and after making an allowance for payment of counsel fees and disbursements, direct a distribution of the net proceeds. Any portion of the settlement, which has not been allocated to the wrongful death claim, will be referred to the appropriate Surrogate's Court for approval and distribution.

An action, which has been resolved by settlement, following the filing of a Note of Issue and Certificate of Readiness, will remain on the trial calendar until compliance with the requirements of this section. Nevertheless, a case may be marked "Off" the calendar, and subject to restoration to the trial calendar, if counsel submits an application for, and the Court

grants, preliminary approval of a settlement, pending a formal application for approval in compliance with the requirements of this section. Such application for preliminary approval must include a statement from Plaintiff's counsel, certifying that the personal representative has consented to the compromise, the specific amounts to be contributed by each Defendant, and a brief statement of the reasons for compromise of such amounts.

Upon the entry of any order, approving a settlement of a wrongful death claim under this section, counsel for Plaintiff(s) shall give written notice, thereof, to all counsel of record for Defendants who have agreed to pay monetary amounts in consideration of resolution of the claim.

XV. Miscellaneous

The Court recognizes that cooperation among counsel and parties is essential for the orderly and expeditious resolution of this litigation. The communication of information among the Plaintiff's counsel, among defense counsel, and among Defendants shall not be deemed a waiver of the attorney-client privilege, the protection afforded by the attorney work-product doctrine, or any other privilege to which a party may be entitled. Any cooperative efforts described above shall not, in any way, be used against any of the parties, shall not constitute evidence of conspiracy, concerted action, or any wrongful conduct, and shall not be communicated to the jury. The exchange of information or documents by counsel will not, by itself, render such information or documents privileged.

The failure to comply with any provision contained in this Order, or subsequent Scheduling Order, either upon a party's motion or the Court's own motion, may result in a case being marked Off the calendar, preclusion, dismissal, the imposition of costs or sanctions, or other appropriate remedy.

SO ORDERED.

Hon. Ann Marie Taddeo
Supreme Court Judge

App. A. Plaintiff's Statement

SUPREME COURT OF THE STATE OF NEW YORK
SEVENTH JUDICIAL DISTRICT
. . . .

In re SEVENTH JUDICIAL DISTRICT
       ASBESTOS LITIGATION
. . . .

This document applies to:
(Title of Case)
                                                      Index No. _____
                                                      County _____
. . . .

PLAINTIFF'S STATEMENT

PLEASE STATE:

Nature of Action: Personal Injury   _____
                         In Extremis   _____

                         Wrongful Death   _____
                         Date of Death   _____
                         Cause of Death   _____

As to Plaintiff/Decedent:

1. Full Name and Social Security Number:

2. Date of Birth:

3. Most Recent Address:

4. State whether there has been use of tobacco products, including the smoking of cigarettes, and if so, the time period:

As to alleged Asbestos Exposure:

5. Indicate which of the following types of activities resulted in Plaintiff/Decedent's alleged exposure to asbestos:

A. Insulating Trade:

B. Boiler Trade:

C. Construction Trade:

D. Plant Worker:

E. Brake Lining or Friction Worker:

F. Non–Occupational (describe):

G. Other (describe):

6. Primary work sites(s) (Plants, Departments, etc.):

7. Date of First Exposure:

8. Date of Last Exposure:

9. Asbestos containing products to which plaintiff/decedent was allegedly exposed:

10. Nature of alleges asbestos related illness and date of diagnosis:

Date of Diagnosis

Asbestosis   _____

Lung Cancer   _____

Mesothelioma   _____

Pleural Changes   _____

Other (identify)   _____

Dated:

Attorney:

Law Firm:

Address:

Telephone:

E-mail address:

Fax Number:

App. B.   Acknowledgement of Service

SUPREME COURT OF THE STATE OF NEW YORK
SEVENTH JUDICIAL DISTRICT
....

In re SEVENTH JUDICIAL DISTRICT
       ASBESTOS LITIGATION
....

This document applies to:
(Title of Case

                                    Index No. _____
                                      County _____

....

ACKNOWLEDGMENT OF SERVICE

Defendant _____, by its attorneys _____, acknowledges receipt of a summons and complaint in this action.

Pursuant to 7 JDAL Case Management Order, Section V, B-2, the Defendant hereby answers the complaint in this action and refers Plaintiff(s) to its standard answer filed in the 7 JDAL on _____ and raises each of the affirmative defenses and cross-claims contained therein.

                       Respectfully submitted,

                       Defendant _____

                       By its Attorneys:

                       _____

                       (Typed name of signator)

                       Name, address, telephone, fax and e-mail of Attorney for Defendant

Dated:

App. C. Acknowledgment of Service

SUPREME COURT OF THE STATE OF NEW YORK
SEVENTH JUDICIAL DISTRICT
....

In re SEVENTH JUDICIAL DISTRICT
      ASBESTOS LITIGATION
....

This document applies to:
(Title of Case)

Index No. _____
County _____

....

ACKNOWLEDGMENT OF SERVICE

Defendant _____, by its attorneys _____, acknowledges receipt of a summons and complaint in this action.

Pursuant to 7 JDAL Case Management Order, Section V, B-3, the third-party Defendant hereby answers the third-party complaint in this action and refers third-party Plaintiff(s) to its standard answer filed in the 7 JDAL on _____ and raises each of the affirmative defenses and cross-claims contained therein.

Respectfully submitted,

Third–Party Defendant _____

By its Attorneys:

_____

(Typed name of signator)

Name, address, telephone, fax and e-mail of Attorney for Defendant

Dated:

App. D.   Stipulation (JH)

SUPREME COURT OF THE STATE OF NEW YORK
SEVENTH JUDICIAL DISTRICT
. . . .

In re   SEVENTH JUDICIAL DISTRICT
       ASBESTOS LITIGATION

. . . .

This document applies to:
(Title of Case)

. . . .

STIPULATION

Index No. _____
County _____

    The Court having issued an Order, directing all parties to appear at a preliminary conference, as required by **22 NYCRR 212(b)**, and

    A preliminary conference having been held at the Conference Room, Fifth Floor, Hall of Justice, Rochester, New York, at which time the parties agreed upon liaison counsel to represent the interests of all Defendants, and further, agreed that a Judicial Hearing Officer may be designated to preside over all issues, including trial of this action, it is hereby

    STIPULATED by and between the parties, that a Judicial Hearing Officer may be designated as a Referee to preside over all issues, including trial of this action, pursuant to CPLR § 4317(a).

Dated:

_____   _____
Attorney for Plaintiff(s)   Liaison Counsel for Defendants

App. E.   Defendants' Alternative Standard Interrogatories

SUPREME COURT OF THE STATE OF NEW YORK
SEVENTH JUDICIAL DISTRICT
....

In RE: SEVENTH JUDICIAL DISTRICT ASBESTOS LITIGATION

....

This Document Relates To: Index No. _____
(Title of Case)   County _____

....

SEVENTH JUDICIAL DISTRICT ASBESTOS LITIGATION

(7 JDAL)

DEFENDANTS' ALTERNATIVE STANDARD INTERROGATORIES

PART A

INTERROGATORY NO. 1

Please provide the following information pertaining to the Plaintiff:

a.   Full name and all other names by which you have been known;

b.   Address;

c.   Social Security No.;

d.   Branch of military service, Military Service No., and dates of military service;

e.   Age;

f.   Height;

g.   Weight;

h.   Date of birth;

i.   Place of birth;

j.   Marital status and, if married, date of marriage;

k.   Name of spouse; and

l.   Spouse's age and date of birth.

ANSWER

| 1

INTERROGATORY NO. 2

If the plaintiff is an estate representative, please provide the following information:

a.   Decedent's date of death;

b.   Decedent's age at death;

c.   Cause of decedent's death;

d.   Date of birth of decedent's surviving spouse; and

e.   If there is no surviving spouse, names and dates of birth of next-of-kin; and

f.   Name and address of estate representative and relationship to decedent.

ANSWER

| 2

INTERROGATORY NO. 3

Please provide the following information pertaining to the plaintiff's children, parents and siblings:

a. Names and dates of birth;

b. Current condition of each one's health. If any individual is deceased, please state the age, date and cause of death for that individual.

ANSWER

| 3

INTERROGATORY NO. 4

Set forth the name and address of the doctor or physician who first diagnosed your illness and/or physical abnormality as being asbestos related and set forth the date when this diagnosis was made.

ANSWER

| 4

INTERROGATORY NO. 5

When was the last time you saw a doctor for evaluation or treatment of the injuries which you allege in the complaint? Please state the name and address of the doctor seen and any treatment provided.

ANSWER

| 5

INTERROGATORY NO. 6

If you are still treating with or consulting with any doctor(s), for whatever reason, please state as to each doctor:

a. The name and address of the doctor;

b. The date of your last visit/consult;

c. The nature of your last visit;

d. The date of your next scheduled visit/consult; and

e. Any treatment or medication provided.

ANSWER

| 6

INTERROGATORY NO. 7

As to each doctor or other health care professional who you have consulted with during your life for any reason, please set forth the following:

ANSWER

Physicians Name and Address	Approximate date(s) of Treatment or Examination	Reason for Consultation	Chest X-ray PFT or Biopsy Performed? (Yes/No; please specify)

INTERROGATORY NO. 8

As to each hospital in which you have been a patient during your life, please set forth the following:

ANSWER

Name and Address of Hospital	Date of Admission	Reason for Hospitalization	Chest X-ray PFT or Biopsy Performed? (Yes/No; please specify)

INTERROGATORY NO. 9

As to each address at which you have resided during your life, please set forth the following:

ANSWER

Address	Dates of Residence	Type of Heating System	Asbestos Use or Exposure? (Yes/No; please describe and identify products)

PART B

INTERROGATORY NO. 1

Are you currently employed?

ANSWER

| 1

INTERROGATORY NO. 2

If you are currently employed, please state what your job is and who you are employed by, how many hours per week you work, the amount of your current wage/salary, and any union affiliation.

ANSWER

| 2

INTERROGATORY NO. 3

If you are retired, please state:

a. The date of your retirement;

b. The reason for your retirement;

c. The name and address of your last employer;

d. Your last place of employment;

e. The job/position you held at the time of your retirement;

f. Your wage/salary at the time of your retirement; and

g. Your union affiliation at the time of your retirement.

ANSWER

| 3

INTERROGATORY NO. 4

Do you claim that you have lost wages as a result of the injuries alleged in your complaint?

ANSWER

| 4

INTERROGATORY NO. 5

If the answer to Interrogatory No. 4 is yes, please set forth the following:

a. The dollar amount of wages which you claim have been lost to date;

b. How you calculated the above number;

c. State in inclusive dates during which you claim that you were unable to work as a result of the injuries alleged in your complaint;

d. State the name and address of your employer and your wage/salary at the time you became unable to work as a result of the injuries alleged in the complaint; and

e. State the amount of gross income reported by you on your Federal income tax returns for the three years preceding the date on which you claim that you were unable to work as a result of the injuries alleged in the complaint.

ANSWER

| 5

INTERROGATORY NO. 6

If plaintiff's spouse is claiming damages for loss of consortium, society, affection, services, or sexual enjoyment as a result of injuries alleged in your complaint, please set forth in complete detail all facts on which this claim is based, including a complete description of the loss suffered.

ANSWER

| 6

INTERROGATORY NO. 7

If you have been a member of any union(s), please state as to each union:

a. The name, address and local number of the union;

b. The inclusive dates of your membership;

c. Any union offices held by you and the dates you held such offices.

ANSWER

| 7

INTERROGATORY No. 8

Are there any persons who have been partially or totally dependent upon you for financial support and/or assistance during the last ten years?

ANSWER

| 8

INTERROGATORY No. 9

If the answer to Interrogatory No. 8 is yes, please state the names, addresses, sex, age, current condition of health and relationship of each such person and state the amounts that you contributed during the last ten years to the support of each.

ANSWER

| 9

INTERROGATORY No. 10

State, in the form of an itemized list, the amount of monetary damages, if any, other than lost wages, which you contend that you have incurred as a result of the injuries which are alleged in the complaint, including (but not limited to) hospital charges, medical charges, medicines, funeral expenses, etc. and set forth as to each charge, the person or entity to whom payment was made, and the date that such payments were made.

ANSWER

| 10

INTERROGATORY No. 11

State whether or not you smoke or smoked cigarettes, cigars, a pipe, or any other tobacco substance from birth to the present time, and if yes, state the following:

a. The inclusive dates during which you smoked;

b. The number of cigarettes, cigars, or pipes full of tobacco, smoked per day during that period of time (if it varies, state the quantity for each given period of time); and

c. The brand of cigarettes smoked and whether they were filtered or non-filtered.

ANSWER

| 11

INTERROGATORY No. 12

Were you ever advised by any physician to stop smoking or using tobacco products? If your answer is yes, identify each physician who gave any such advice, the dates on which the advice was given, and also state what you did in response to that advice.

ANSWER

| 12

INTERROGATORY No. 13

Does your spouse or any member of your household smoke now or have they ever in the past? If so, answer the above Interrogatory No. 11(a)—(c) as they apply to your spouse or other household member.

ANSWER

| 13

INTERROGATORY No. 14

State whether or not you have consumed alcoholic beverages? If yes, state the following:

a. The type of alcoholic beverages consumed;

b. The period of time during which you consumed alcoholic beverages;

c. On a daily basis, how many drinks do you have;

d. How does your present pattern of drinking differ, if at all, from your past pattern; and

e. Whether you have been treated for any illness or disease related to your consumption of alcoholic beverages.

ANSWER

| 14

INTERROGATORY No. 15

Have you ever made a claim for health or accident insurance benefits, social security disability benefits, state of federal benefits for disabilities, workers' compensation claims, Longshoremen and Harbor Workers Act claims, unemployment compensation insurance benefits, or early payment from any public or private pensions due to disability or your medical condition?

ANSWER

| 15

INTERROGATORY No. 16

If the answer to Interrogatory No. 15 is yes, set forth the following:

a. Date of the claim(s);

b. The name and nature of the entity with which the claim was made;

c. The injury for which each claim was filed;

d. Any identifying number, such as a docket number, for each claim;

e. The employer at the time of injury; and

f. The outcome of the claim.

ANSWER

| 16

INTERROGATORY No. 17

Have you ever testified at any Workers' Compensation hearing or courtroom proceeding?

ANSWER

| 17

INTERROGATORY No. 18

If your answer to Interrogatory No. 17 is yes, please indicate the following:

a. The name of the case in which you testified;

b. The nature of your testimony;

c. The date of your testimony; and

d. Place where you testified.

ANSWER

| 18

INTERROGATORY No. 19

State all injuries and physical abnormalities for which you are claiming compensation in this lawsuit.

ANSWER

| 19

INTERROGATORY No. 20

Describe any pain, incapacity, inability to act or work, or disability alleged to have resulted from the injuries and physical abnormalities you sustained.

ANSWER

| 20

INTERROGATORY No. 21

Set forth, to the best of your ability, the date when you first complained of any symptoms which you now believe to be related to the disease or injury alleged in this lawsuit and describe the nature of your complaints.

ANSWER

| 21

INTERROGATORY No. 22

As to each and every employer you have had from the time you were first employed to the present, set forth the following:

a. Please provide the product identification on Chart A from your personal knowledge only.

b. Please provide the product identification on Chart B from sources other than your own personal knowledge.

ANSWER

Please refer to Charts A and B at the end of these interrogatory responses.

INTERROGATORY No. 23

Have you ever seen any warning labels on packages or containers of asbestos products? If your answer is yes, please state:

a. The type of product;

b. The name of the manufacturer;

c. Where you saw the warning labels;

d. On what occasion did you see the warning label; and

e. The wording of the warning label.

ANSWER

| 23

INTERROGATORY No. 24

State whether you had available for use during any period of your employment, respirators, masks or other dust inhalation inhibitors or protective gear. If so, please state:

    a. Which items were available;

    b. The period of time during which said items were available;

    c. What instructions were given with regard to the use of each of said items;

    d. Did plaintiff use any respirators, masks or other dust inhibitors or protective gear and, if so:

    1. Describe and identify the equipment by manufacturer, trade or brand name; and

    2. State the period of time plaintiff used such equipment.

ANSWER

| 24

INTERROGATORY No. 25

Did you at any time receive or learn about any publication, warning, order, directive, requirement, or recommendation, whether written or oral, which advised or warned of the possible harmful effects to, or inhalation of, asbestos materials and/or asbestos-containing products? If so, please state:

    a. The nature and exact wording of such warning, recommendation, etc.;

    b. The complete identity of each source of such warning, recommendation, etc.;

    c. The date, time, place, manner and circumstances when such warning, recommendation, etc., was given; and

    d. The identity of each witness to your reception of such advice, warning, recommendation, etc.

ANSWER

| 25

INTERROGATORY No. 26

State whether you have ever seen or received any information, instruction, direction, warning, or directive from any source whatsoever, concerning alleged dangers of exposure to asbestos materials and/or asbestos-containing products, and if so, identify:

    a. Each such warning, directive, notification, direction, instruction or information;

    b. The means by which such was given to you;

    c. The source and the date on which it was received by you; and

    d. Your response or reaction, including any complaints made or changes in work habits.

ANSWER

| 26

INTERROGATORY No. 27

If you have ever been exposed to, used, inhaled or ingested any of the following substances on a regular basis or at work, indicate which substance and, if so, state the date(s), place(s), and circumstances thereof:

    (a) Acids;

    (b) Aluminum;

(c) Arsenic;

(d) Barium;

(e) Beryllium;

(f) Butanol;

(g) Cadmium;

(h) Carborundum;

(i) Chloreothylene;

(j) Chlorine;

(k) Chromate;

(l) Chromite;

(m) Chromium;

(n) Coal dust [coal];

(o) Coal tar;

(p) Cotton dust;

(q) Epoxy;

(r) Ethanol;

(s) Grinding dust;

(t) Iron;

(u) Isocyanates;

(v) Isopropanol;

(w) Lead;

(x) Live chickens;

(y) Manganese;

(z) Nickel;

(aa) Nitrogen dioxide;

(bb) Nuclear radiation;

(cc) Ozone;

(dd) Petroleum distillates;

(ee) Phosgene;

(ff) Radiation;

(gg) Silica;

(hh) Titanium;

(ii) Toluene;

(jj) Welding smoke or fumes;

(kk) Xylene;

(ll) Zinc

ANSWER

| 27

INTERROGATORY No. 28

If you contend you were exposed to asbestos or asbestos-containing products at any time other than in the scope of your employment or as set forth in response to Interrogatory No. 9 in Part A and/or Interrogatory No. 22 in Part B, state for each such exposure(i.e. alleged exposure during military service, self-employment, or non-residential/no-employment premises exposure and/or bystander exposure, etc):

a. The date, location and circumstances; and

b. The type of product and the name of the manufacturer, distributor, and/or miner.

ANSWER

| 28

INTERROGATORY No. 29

If you allege that any defendant violated or was negligent in following any trade standard, safety standard, statute, rule, regulation, or ordinance, identify each defendant against whom this claim is made and with respect to each such defendant provide the name and a citation for each trade standard, safety standard, statute, rule, regulation, or ordinance at issue and state how and in what manner the defendant committed the violation or was otherwise negligent.

ANSWER

| 29

INTERROGATORY No. 30

If you contend that you are entitled to punitive damages against any defendant, identify each defendant against whom you are seeking punitive damages and with respect to each such defendant, state the basis for your contention.

ANSWER

| 30

II. REQUESTS TO PRODUCE

1. Copies of all documents identified in your answers to the standard interrogatories by defendants to plaintiffs, Part A and Part B.

2. Copies of all notes or records kept by you and prepared by you during the course of your employment, which relate to the dates on which you worked for particular employers or at particular job locations, the products you or others used at such job sites or while employed by such employers.

3. All documents of which you have ever become aware relating in any way to warnings, potential health hazards, instructions or precautions regarding the use or handling of, or exposure to, asbestos, asbestos-containing products and/or asbestos-containing materials.

4. All photographs of the Plaintiff at work or in work clothes and all photographs of all photographs of products or conditions complained of in the Plaintiff's place of employment.

5. If you are claiming that you have lost wages as a result of the injuries alleged in your complaint, your income tax returns for the past three years.

6. If you are claiming that you have incurred medical expenses as a result of the injuries alleged in your complaint, copies of all itemized bills covering all such expenses.

7. Copies of all reports, correspondence and records from each doctor or hospital where or by whom you have been seen or treated at any time.

8. If your answer to Interrogatory No. 19 is yes, produce all documents in your possession or in the possession of your attorney which relate to this claim or its outcome, including, but not limited to, the application, supporting physicians reports, supporting medical records, transcripts of hearings, or copies of depositions taken regarding said claim.

9. Copies of all applications for disability claims or disability pensions made by you during the course of your lifetime.

10. All boxes, containers or wrappers that allegedly contained the asbestos or asbestos-containing products which are the subject of Plaintiff's complaint and which are in the Plaintiff's possession.

Dated:

    | ATTNAME

State of New York   )
)
) ss.
County of Monroe   )

_____, being duly sworn, deposes and says that | he is the plaintiff in this action; that | he has read the foregoing Answers to Defendants' Interrogatories and knows the contents thereof; that the same is true to the knowledge of deponent, except as to the matters therein stated to be alleged on information and belief, and that as to those matters | he believes it to be true.

_____

Sworn to before me this ___ day of _____, 2002

NOTARY PUBLIC

State of New York   )
)
) ss.
County of Monroe   )

_____, being duly sworn, deposes and says that | he is the | EXAD of the estate of | _____, plaintiff in this action; that | he has read the foregoing Answers to Defendants' Interrogatories and knows the contents thereof; that the same is true to the knowledge of deponent, except as to the matters therein stated to be alleged on information and belief, and that as to those matters | he believes it to be true.

_____

Sworn to before me this ___ day of _____, 2002

NOTARY PUBLIC

App. F. Defendants' First Set of Interrogatories

SUPREME COURT OF THE STATE OF NEW YORK
SEVENTH JUDICIAL DISTRICT

....

In RE: SEVENTH JUDICIAL DISTRICT ASBESTOS LITIGATION

....

This Document Applies to: Index No. _____
(Title of Case)   County _____

....

DEFENDANTS' FIRST SET OF INTERROGATORIES AND REQUEST
FOR PRODUCTION OF DOCUMENTS (revised)

Pursuant to Rule 3130 of the Civil Practice Law and Rules of New York State and Seventh Judicial District Asbestos Litigation Case Management Order, dated October 26, 2001, defendants propound the following interrogatories to the plaintiffs, to be answered under oath and in accordance with the Civil Practice Law and Rules and said Case Management Order.

These interrogatories are continuing in nature and require you to file supplementary responses in accordance with the Civil Practice Law and Rules if you obtain further or different information after your initial responses and before trial, including in such supplemental responses, the date upon and the manner in which such further or different information came to your attention.

EXPLANATION AND DEFINITIONS

For the convenience of the plaintiffs and to prevent the need for duplicative answers, this document concurrently propounds interrogatories and requests for production of documents. The documents to be produced are in each instance identified by responses to the interrogatories.

The terms used in these interrogatories and document requests and listed below are defined as follows:

A. "Decedent," "the decedent," or "your decedent" means the decedent and all persons acting on his or her behalf.

B. "Defendants," unless otherwise specified, means any defendant named as a party to this action as well as any predecessors in interest to any named defendants, and all other subsidiaries or divisions of any named defendants.

C. "Document" or "documents," means any writing of any kind, including originals and all nonidentical copies (whether different from the originals by reason of any notation made on such copies otherwise), as well as, without limitation, correspondence, memoranda, notes, calendars, diaries, statistics, letters, telegrams, minutes, contracts, reports, studies, checks, invoices, statements, receipts, returns, warranties, guarantees, summaries, pamphlets, books, prospectuses, intra office and interoffice communications, offers, notations of any sort of conversations, telephone calls, meetings or other communications, bulletins, magazines, publications, printed matter, photographs, motion pictures, video tapes, audio tapes, computer printouts, teletypes, telefax, invoices, work sheets, tapes, tape recordings, transcripts, graphic or audio records or representations of any kind, x-rays, and all drafts, alterations, modifications, changes and amendments of any of the foregoing, of which you have knowledge or which are now or were formerly in your actual or constructive possession, custody or control.

D. "He" means he and/or she; "him" means him and/or her; "his" means his and/or hers.

E. "Health Care Institution" means any entity providing health care services, including hospitals, laboratories, nursing homes, clinics and convalescent homes.

F. "Identify," "identity" and "identification";

(1) When used to refer to an entity other than a natural person, mean to state its full name, the present or last known address of its principal office or place of doing business, and the type of entity (e.g., corporation, partnership, unincorporated association);

(2) When used to refer to a natural person, mean to state the following:

(a) The person's full name and present or last known home address, home telephone number, business address and business telephone number;

(b) The person's present title and employer or other business affiliation;

(c) The person's home address, home telephone number, business address and business telephone number at the time of the actions at which each interrogatory is directed; and

(d) The person's employer and title at the time of the actions at which each interrogatory is directed.

(3) When used to refer to a document, mean to state the following:

(a) The subject of the document;

(b) The title of the document;

(c) The type of document (e.g., letter, memorandum, telegraph, chart);

(d) The date of the document, or, if the specific date thereof is unknown, the month and year or other best approximation of such date;

(e) The identity of the person, or persons, who wrote, contributed to, prepared or originated such document; and

(f) The present or last known location and custodian of the document.

G. "Injured plaintiff" means a plaintiff who is asserting a claim for recovery of damages for his own personal injuries.

H. "Medical condition" means any condition or conditions for which a claim is being made, including any asbestos- related disease, any preexisting condition, or any condition brought about by an asbestos-related disease, including, but not limited to physical or mental illness, disease, injury, symptom, complaint or adverse reaction.

I. "Person" means any natural person, firm, corporation, partnership, proprietorship, joint venture, organization, group of natural persons, or other association separately identifiable, whether or not such association or entity has a separate juristic existence in its own right.

J. "Photograph" or "photographs" means any photographic prints, photographic slides, motion pictures or videotapes in your actual or constructive possession, custody or control.

K. "Physician" includes physicians, nurses, laboratory or other hospital personnel and other health care providers or practitioners of health care, including psychologists, social workers and counselors.

L. "Possession," "custody," or "control" includes the joint or several possession, custody or control, not only by the person, or persons, to whom these interrogatories and requests are addressed, but also the joint or several possession, custody or control by each or any other person acting or purporting to act on behalf of the person, whether as employee, attorney, accountant, agent, sponsor, spokesperson, or otherwise.

M. "Relates to" means supports, evidences, describes, mentions, refers to, contradicts or comprises.

INSTRUCTIONS

A. In the event that an action involves two named plaintiffs and each plaintiff is asserting a claim for recovery of damages for his own personal injuries, a separate set of responses to these interrogatories and document requests should be served for each plaintiff.

B. In the event that an action is sued by a representative of a decedent's estate and that representative is asserting a claim for recovery of damages for his own personal injuries, separate sets of responses to these interrogatories and document requests should be served for the decedent and for the representative of decedent's estate.

C. With respect to each interrogatory, in addition to supplying the information asked for and identifying the specific documents referred to, identify all documents which were referred to in preparing the answer thereto.

D. If any document identified in an answer to an interrogatory was, but is no longer, in your possession or subject to your custody or control, or was known to you, but is no longer in existence, state what disposition was made of it or what became of it.

E. If any document is withheld from production hereunder on the basis of a claim of privilege or otherwise, identify each such document and the grounds upon which its production is being withheld.

F. The following releases and authorizations should be signed by the plaintiff or a person with proper authority and returned with the responses to these interrogatories:

(a) A release in the form annexed hereto as Exhibit A for defendants to obtain a record of injured plaintiff's/decedent's tax records from the Internal Revenue Service and employment and earnings history from the Social Security Administration;

(b) A release in the form annexed hereto as Exhibit B for each workers' compensation claim file referred to in the responses to these interrogatories;

(c) Authorizations in the form annexed hereto as Exhibit C to obtain injured plaintiff's/decedent's employment records from each employer identified or referred to in the responses to these interrogatories;

(d) Medical records' authorizations in the form annexed hereto as Exhibit D to obtain injured plaintiff's/decedent's medical records from each physician, health care institution, and pharmacy identified or referred to in the responses to these interrogatories.

(e) If applicable, a release in the form annexed as Exhibit E to obtain injured plaintiff's/decedent's military service records; and

(f) A release in the form annexed as Exhibit F to obtain injured plaintiff's/decedent's school records.

G. You are requested to furnish all information in your possession and all information available to you, not merely such information as you know of your own personal knowledge but also all knowledge that is available to you, your representatives, attorneys and agents, by reason of inquiry, including inquiry of their representatives. Where a response to the following interrogatories sets forth information that is not based upon your own personal knowledge, but rather upon the knowledge of your representatives, attorneys and agents, you should so indicate in your response to that interrogatory.

INTERROGATORIES

PERSONAL BACKGROUND OF PLAINTIFF AS REPRESENTATIVE OF DECEDENT'S ESTATE

1. If you represent decedent's estate, state the following for yourself:

(a) Full name and all other names by which you have been known;

(b) Relationship to the decedent;

(c) Date and place of birth;

(d) Address;

(e) Social security number;

(f) Present marital status and, if applicable, name of present spouse and date of marriage; and

(g) Dates of all prior marriages, spouses' names, and dates of termination of marriages.

PERSONAL BACKGROUND OF INJURED PLAINTIFF/DECEDENT

2. State the following for injured plaintiff/decedent:

(a) Full name and all other names by which injured plaintiff/decedent has been known;

(b) Date and place of birth;

(c) Whether injured plaintiff/decedent was an adopted child and, if adopted, state date of adoption;

(d) Present age; or date and place of death;

(e) Present marital status and, if applicable, name of present spouse and date of marriage, or marital status at the time of death, and if applicable, the name of spouse at the time of death and date of marriage;

(f) Dates of all prior marriages, spouses' names, and dates of termination of marriages;

(g) Present home address, or home address at time of death; and

(h) Social Security number.

3. State the following with regard to injured plaintiff's/decedent's father, mother, and each sibling:

(a) Name, relationship and date of birth;

(b) Current address (if deceased, state last known address);

(c) Current condition of each one's health, including any specific medical problems;

(d) If either of injured plaintiff's/decedent's parents is deceased, please state for each deceased parent:

(i) Specific medical problems;

(ii) Date and place of death;

(iii) Cause of death.

(e) If injured plaintiff's/decedent's grandparent, aunt, uncle, great-aunt, great-uncle or first cousin has had any respiratory illness (other than common colds), cardiac problem, or any cancer, state as to each:

(i) Name, relationship and date of birth;

(ii) Current address (if deceased, state last known address); and

(iii) The specific respiratory illness, cardiac problem, or cancer the individual had or has.

4. State the following with regard to each of injured plaintiff's/decedent's children:

(a) Name;

(b) Date of birth;

(c) Sex;

(d) Current address (if deceased, state the last known address);

(e) Whether a natural child or adopted child and, if adopted, state date of adoption;

(f) Current state of health, including a statement of specific medical problems;

(g) If any of injured plaintiff's/decedent's children are deceased, state for each deceased child:

(i) Specific medical problems;

420

(ii) Date and place of death; and

(iii) Cause of death.

5. List all injured plaintiff's/decedent's residences, the dates injured plaintiff/decedent resided at each, and with respect to each state:

(a) Whether such residence contained asbestos insulation;

(b) Whether any improvements were made to the residence (i.e., insulation, rewiring, etc.);

(c) The type of fuel used for heating;

(d) The type of fuel used for cooking; and

(e) Whether injured plaintiff/decedent ever changed residence for health reasons and, if so, the residence left and the health reason for leaving.

6. Identify each member of the injured plaintiff's/decedent's household in the last five years, or during the last five years prior to death, and also state as to each:

(a) His age, occupation, and relationship to the injured plaintiff/decedent; and

(b) The portion of the last 12 months, or the last 12 months of the decedent's life, during which he was a member of the household.

7. List injured plaintiff's/decedent's hobbies or the major leisure activities in which he engaged during the last twenty years, or the last twenty years of his life. If the injured plaintiff/decedent did not have hobbies or participate in leisure activities, describe how he spent his leisure time.

8. Did injured plaintiff/decedent or his spouse ever file for divorce against the other?

If your answer is yes, state the date of suit, its disposition, and the date of disposition.

9. Were injured plaintiff/decedent and his spouse ever separated for any period more than 48 hours because of a marital disagreement?

If your answer is yes, indicate every such incident, stating the reason for the separation and the length of time of each separation.

10. Was injured plaintiff/decedent ever a party to or a witness in any lawsuit, court or administrative proceeding?

If your answer is yes, state:

(a) Whether injured plaintiff/decedent was a party or a witness and, if a party, whether he was a plaintiff or a defendant;

(b) The title of the lawsuit or proceeding, the court or agency in which it was brought, and the docket number;

(c) The nature of the charges or claims and, if injured plaintiff/decedent was a witness, the substance of his testimony;

(d) The disposition of the case; and

(e) Identify all insurance carriers or administrative agencies that either made payment or declined to make payment with respect to each such lawsuit or claim.

11. Has injured plaintiff/decedent ever applied and been rejected for a life insurance, medical insurance, or disability insurance policy?

If your answer is yes, state with regard to each such event:

(a) The identity of the insurer to whom such application was made;

(b) The date of such application;

(c) The identity of any Physician conducting a physical examination with regard to such application and the date thereof;

(d) The reason for such rejection; and

(e) Produce all documentation of said application and rejection.

EMPLOYMENT HISTORY

12. Have you or anyone on your behalf requested from the Social Security Administration a listing of all of the injured plaintiff's/decedent's employers and dates of employment? If your answer is yes, attach a copy of such listing to your responses to these interrogatories. If not available, execute and provide a release in the form annexed as Exhibit A.

13. Identify each and every employer that injured plaintiff/decedent had from the time he was first employed to the present, or to the time of his death, including any and all military service, and as to each, state:

(a) The period of time injured plaintiff/decedent worked for each such employer;

(b) Each position/job title which injured plaintiff/decedent held with each such employer and the dates each such position/job title was held by injured plaintiff/decedent;

(c) The nature of the work performed;

(d) The location(s) of injured plaintiff's/decedent's particular job site(s);

(e) The nature of the materials or products injured plaintiff/decedent worked with; and

(f) Whether said activity involved working in the presence of dust, pollutants, or toxic substances and, if so:

(i) Identify by name or type said dust, pollutants, or toxic substances;

(ii) State whether any suction device, fan, or other ventilation system was present at the job site; and

(iii) State whether the employer or any governmental agency or union took air samplings at the job site and, if so, identify the persons who took the air samplings, the dates such samplings were taken and the persons presently having possession or control of any documents relating to such air samplings.

14. If injured plaintiff/decedent was self-employed at any time, identify each such business, and as to each, state:

(a) The period during which injured plaintiff/ decedent was self-employed;

(b) The nature of the work performed;

(c) The location(s) of injured plaintiff's/ decedent's particular job site(s);

(d) The nature of the materials or products injured plaintiff/decedent worked with; and

(e) Whether said activity involved working in the presence of dust, pollutants, or toxic substances and, if so:

(i) Identify by name or type said dust, pollutants, or toxic substances;

(ii) State whether any suction device, fan, or other ventilation system was present at the job site; and

(iii) State whether the employer, any governmental agency, any union or any other person took air samplings at any job site at which injured plaintiff/decedent worked, and,

(iv) if so, identify the person(s) who took the air samples, the dates such air samples were taken and the persons presently having possession or control of any documents relating to such air samples.

15. Did injured plaintiff/decedent ever lose a job, change jobs or change his position with an employer for health reasons?

If your answer is yes, state as to each such event:

(a) The employer and job position which injured plaintiff/decedent left;

(b) The date of such event;

(c) The health reason for such event; and

(d) The new employer and/or job position which injured plaintiff/decedent next assumed.

16. Are you aware of, have you ever seen, or do you or your attorney possess or have access to any photographs, charts, drawings, diagrams or other graphic representations depicting work conditions at work sites where you claim injured plaintiff/ decedent was exposed to asbestos materials and/or asbestos- containing products?

If your answer is yes, with respect to each:

(a) Identify each such photograph or other document, including a statement as to which views, scenes or objects it purports to depict, the person who took or prepared each such photograph or other document, and the date taken or prepared;

(b) State whether the photograph or other document was prepared on your behalf or on behalf of other persons allegedly exposed to asbestos or as a result of circumstances relating to this or any other lawsuit; and

(c) Attach a copy.

17. During the period of time for which you claim injured plaintiff/decedent was exposed to asbestos materials and/or asbestos-containing products, did injured plaintiff/ decedent share a household with any other person(s) who worked or was employed outside the household?

If your answer is yes, identify:

(a) Each such other person;

(b) The period(s) of time each such other person shared such household;

(c) The period(s) of time each such other person worked or was so employed;

(d) The nature of each job held or job title for each such other person in each such period of time; and

(e) Each and every employer of each such other person in each such period of time.

TOXIC EXPOSURES

18. Was injured plaintiff/decedent ever exposed to, or did injured plaintiff/decedent ever use, inhale or ingest any of the following substances on a regular basis or at work?

If your answer is yes, state the date(s), place(s), and circumstances thereof:

(a) Acids;

(b) Aluminum;

(c) Ammonia;

(d) Arsenic;

(e) Barium;

(f) Berylium;

(g) Butanol;

(h) Cadmium;

(i) Carborundum;

(j) Chloroethylene;

(k) Chlorine;

(l) Chromate;

(m) Chromite;

(n) Chromium;

(o) Coal and/or coal dust;

(p) Coal tar;

(q) Cotton dust;

(r) Creosote;

(s) Epoxy;

(t) Ethanol;

(u) Formaldehyde;

(v) Grinding dust;

(w) Iron;

(x) Isocyanates;

(y) Isopropanol;

(z) Lead;

(aa) Live chickens;

(bb) Manganese;

(cc) Nickel;

(dd) Nitrogen dioxide;

(ee) Nuclear radiation;

(ff) Ozone;

(gg) Petroleum distillates;

(hh) Phosgene;

(ii) Radiation;

(jj) Silica;

(kk) Titanium

(ll) Toluene;

(mm) Welding smoke or fumes;

(nn) Zylene; or

(oo) Zinc.

19. From the time of his birth to the present or to the time of his death, did injured plaintiff/decedent ever use cigarettes, cigars, pipes, smokeless tobacco, or any other tobacco substance?

If your answer is yes, state the following:

(a) The brand and type of tobacco product(s) used (e.g., filter, non-filter, chewing tobacco);

(b) The period(s) during which he used each such product;

(c) The amount of the product used per day, during each period of time (e.g., two packs of cigarettes per day for two years);

(d) Whether injured plaintiff/decedent was ever told that he was suffering from any disease or illness contributed to or caused by use of tobacco, and if so identify each person who gave injured plaintiff/decedent any such advice, the dates on which the advice was given, and state exactly what, if anything, injured plaintiff/decedent did in response to that advice;

(e) Whether the injured plaintiff/decedent was ever advised that use of tobacco products could adversely affect his health, and if so, identify each person who gave injured plaintiff/decedent any such advice, the dates on which the advice was given, and state exactly what, if anything, injured plaintiff/decedent did in response to that advice; and

(f) Whether injured plaintiff/decedent was ever advised to stop using tobacco products, and if so, identify each person who gave injured plaintiff/decedent any such advice, the dates on which the advice was given, and state exactly what, if anything, injured plaintiff/decedent did in response to that advice.

20. For each spouse and member of injured plaintiff's/decedent's household, from injured plaintiff's/decedent's birth until the present or until his death, state whether each individual ever used cigarettes, cigars, pipes, smokeless tobacco, or any other tobacco substance, and if so, state the following for each:

(a) The brand and type of tobacco product(s) used (e.g., filter, non-filter, chewing tobacco);

(b) The period(s) during which he used each such product; and

(c) Whether he was ever told by a doctor that he is or was suffering from any disease or illness caused or contributed to by his use of tobacco, and if so, when and by whom.

21. If injured plaintiff/decedent ever worked in an office or other enclosed space, state whether injured plaintiff/decedent shared a room with anyone who used or smoked cigarettes, cigars or pipes.

22. Did injured plaintiff/decedent consume alcoholic beverages?

If your answer is yes, state the following:

(a) The type of alcoholic beverages consumed;

(b) The periods during which injured plaintiff/decedent consumed each such alcoholic beverage;

(c) The amount of such beverage injured plaintiff/ decedent consumed each day during each period of use; and

(d) Whether injured plaintiff/decedent was ever treated for any illness or disease related to his consumption of alcoholic beverages or was ever advised to reduce his consumption.

23. Did injured plaintiff/decedent ever take any prescription medication, any nonprescription medication, or any other drugs for the treatment of respiratory problems, cardiac problems, gastrointestinal problems, cancer, or any chronic health condition or illness?

If your answer is yes, state for each:

(a) The medication or drug taken;

(b) The amount of medication or drug taken and the period over which it was taken;

(c) The reason for taking the medication or drug; and

(d) If the medication was prescribed:

(i) Identify the person prescribing the medication;

(ii) Identify the pharmacy filling the prescription; and

(iii) Produce any document reflecting the prescribing, filing, or payment of any prescription medication.

PRODUCT INFORMATION

24. State with regard to each asbestos material and/or asbestos-containing product to which injured plaintiff/decedent allegedly has ever been exposed, or which the injured plaintiff/ decedent allegedly has ever used, ingested or inhaled:

(a) The kind or type of material or product, using its generic name (e.g., asbestos block, asbestos cement, asbestos cloth, brake linings);

(b) The trade name, brand name and trade symbol;

(c) The name of the manufacturer, distributor(s), and miner(s) of such material or product;

(d) The color, dimensions, shape, form, texture, weight, appearance and flexibility of each material or product;

(e) The appearance of the package or container, indicating the manner of packaging, size, dimensions, color and weight;

(f) The name, logo, label, numerical and alphabetical markings and other markings or words, including warnings, on the material product, package and/or container;

(g) The dates of injured plaintiff's/decedent's exposure to each material or product;

(h) The exact location(s) at which injured plaintiff/decedent was working, indicating each job site, ship, building and place where injured plaintiff/decedent was exposed to, used, ingested or inhaled each material or product, and for each:

(i) State the dates of the exposure;

(ii) Identify injured plaintiff's/decedent's employer at the time of exposure; and

(iii) Describe injured plaintiff's/decedent's activities and duties at the time of exposure.

(i) Whether or not you contend that exposure to such material or product caused injured plaintiff's/decedent's injuries or damages;

(j) The identity of all sources of information stated in response to sub-parts (a) through (i) (including your personal knowledge, witnesses and documents); and for each source state the material and/or product identified and the factual basis of the identification.

25. If you contend that injured plaintiff/decedent was exposed to, used, ingested or inhaled asbestos materials and/or asbestos-containing products at any time other than in the scope of his employment, state for each such exposure:

(a) The date, location and circumstances;

(b) The type of material or product, using its generic name (e.g., asbestos block, asbestos cement, asbestos cloth, brake linings);

(c) The trade name, brand name and trade symbol;

(d) The name of the manufacturer, distributors, and miners of such material or product;

(e) The color, dimensions, shape, form, texture, weight, appearance and flexibility of each material or product;

(f) The appearance of the package or container, indicating the manner of packaging, size, dimensions, color and weight;

(g) The name, logo, label, numerical and alphabetical markings and other markings or words, including warnings, on the material, product, package and/or container; and

(h) The identity of all sources of information stated in response to sub-parts (a) through (g) (including your personal knowledge, witnesses and documents); and for each source state the material or product identified and the factual basis of the identification.

26. Are you aware of, or have you ever seen, or do you possess or have access to any photographs of asbestos materials or asbestos-containing products or any cartons, containers, labels or wrappers of any asbestos materials or asbestos-containing products which you claim injured plaintiff/decedent actually applied or was exposed to?

If your answer is yes, state:

(a) The identity of each such photograph or other document, including a statement as to which objects it purports to depict, the person who took or prepared each such photograph or other document, and the date taken or prepared;

(b) Whether each such photograph or other document was prepared on your behalf or on behalf of other persons allegedly exposed to asbestos or as a result of circumstances relating to this or any other lawsuit; and

(c) Attach a copy.

26A. Have you or has injured plaintiff/decedent ever identified an asbestos material or asbestos-containing product or any cartons, containers, labels or wrappers of any asbestos materials or asbestos-containing products, which you claim injured plaintiff/decedent actually applied, or was exposed to, from a photograph displayed to you or injured plaintiff/decedent, by your attorney?

If your answer is yes, state:

(a) The identity of each such photograph or other document, including a statement as to which objects it purports to depict, the person who took or prepared each such photograph or other document, and the date taken or prepared;

(b) Whether each such photograph or other document was prepared on your behalf or on behalf of other persons allegedly exposed to asbestos or as a result of circumstances relating to this or any other lawsuit; and

(c) Attach a copy.

27. Other than those persons identified in your answers to interrogatories 24 through 26, identify anyone with knowledge of asbestos products to which injured plaintiff/decedent may have been exposed, and as to each such person:

(a) Identify the person's employer at the time of the alleged asbestos exposure;

(b) State the nature of the person's work;

(c) Identify the particular job site(s) where the person worked; and

(d) State the person's dates of employment.

28. Identify by date, vendee (e.g., Government Services Administration, United States Navy, Brooklyn Navy Shipyard or private entity or individual), vendee representative, and vendor representative, if any, all invoices, bills, statements, and any other writings or records, which you contend evidence the sale of any products containing asbestos to any of the places of employment at which you claim that injured plaintiff/decedent was exposed to asbestos. In addition, identify the present custodian of each item.

CLAIMS AGAINST DEFENDANTS

29. State separately as to each defendant:

(a) Each and every alleged act or omission constituting negligence;

(b) The identity of all persons allegedly acting or omitting to act on behalf of the defendant; and

(c) How and in what manner such act or omission caused or contributed to injured plaintiff's/decedent's injury.

30. If you contend that the inhalation of asbestos dust and/or asbestos-containing particles is highly dangerous and the proximate cause of any disease, state:

(i) The diseases allegedly caused;

(ii) The basis for the contention; and

(iii) The date(s) on which it allegedly became well established or well known that the inhalation of asbestos dust and/or asbestos-containing particles is highly dangerous and the proximate cause of the diseases listed in response to sub-part (i).

31. If you contend that any defendant violated or was negligent in following any trade standards, safety standards, statutes, rules, regulations or ordinances for the mining, design, production, or manufacturing process or use for asbestos or any asbestos-containing product, identify such defendants and state with respect to each defendant:

(a) The name and citation of each standard, statute, rule, or regulation, which you contend the defendant violated and the date of each such violation; and

(b) The manner in which the defendant violated or was negligent in following the standard, statute, rule, or regulation described in subpart (a) of this interrogatory.

32. If you contend that any defendant knew or should have known that the asbestos present in asbestos-containing products allegedly mined, manufactured, distributed and/or sold by such defendant was inherently dangerous, defective, ultra-hazardous, unsound for use, or otherwise harmful, identify such defendants and with respect to each defendant:

(a) Identify the persons acting on its behalf who allegedly had actual knowledge that the asbestos contained in any product of such defendant was inherently dangerous, defective, ultra-hazardous, unsound for use or otherwise harmful;

(b) State the substance and date of the actual knowledge possessed by each person identified in sub-part (a) above;

(c) Identify all documents which support each contention, giving a summary of the substantive contents of each or, alternatively, attach such documents hereto; and

(d) State the complete factual basis for any contention that such defendant should have known of the alleged dangers of asbestos or asbestos-containing products.

33. If you contend that any defendant failed to properly warn or instruct injured plaintiff/decedent as to the dangers of asbestos or asbestos-containing products, identify such defendants and with respect to each defendant:

(a) Identify the product(s); and

(b) Describe the exact danger or hazardous condition or use of said product(s) about which you contend such defendant should have warned or instructed injured plaintiff/decedent.

34. If you contend that any defendant's negligence consisted of the use of an improper or unsuitable design for asbestos or asbestos-containing products, identify such defendants and with respect to each defendant describe how its design was improper or unsuitable for the product.

35. If you contend that injured plaintiff's/decedent's medical condition(s) was due to any defendant's negligence in the mining, manufacture or assembly of any asbestos and/or asbestos-containing product, identify each such defendant and each such asbestos and/or asbestos-containing product and with respect to each defendant and each product:

(a) State each act which such defendant did or failed to do in the manufacture or assembly of such product which caused or contributed to injured plaintiff's/decedent's medical condition(s);

(b) Describe the defect or defective condition in the product which you contend was caused by such defendant's conduct as described in subpart (a) of this interrogatory; and

(c) Describe what you contend such defendant should have done, or should have refrained from doing, in the mining, manufacture or assembly of the product.

36. If you contend that injured plaintiff's/decedent's injuries or damages were in any way due to any defendant's negligence in the testing or inspection of asbestos or any asbestos- containing product, identify each such defendant and each such asbestos and/or asbestos-containing product and with respect to each defendant and each product:

(a) State each act which such defendant did or failed to do in the testing or inspection of the product which caused injured plaintiff's/decedent's medical condition(s);

(b) Describe the defect or defective condition in the product, which you contend was caused by such defendant's conduct as described in subpart (a) of this interrogatory; and

(c) Describe what you contend such defendant should have done, or should have refrained from doing, in the testing or inspection of the product.

37. If you contend that any defendant stated, advertised, or otherwise represented to injured plaintiff/decedent or to any other purchaser or user that there were no health hazards associated with asbestos and/or asbestos-containing products, identify each such defendant and with respect to each defendant state:

(a) The content of each such statement, advertisement or representation;

(b) The date, place and manner of such acts;

(c) All facts which support each such contention; and

(d) The identity of all persons involved in such contentions.

38. If you contend that asbestos or any asbestos-containing product failed to satisfy any express warranty or other representation of any defendant concerning potential uses or standards of performance, or that asbestos or any asbestos-containing product was unfit for its intended use, identify each such product and defendant and with respect to each product and defendant:

(a) State the content and source of all representations or warranties which allegedly were not fulfilled;

(b) State all the facts which you contend prove the existence of the warranties or representations as described in subpart (a);

(c) Describe the manner in which the product did not conform to the above-described warranties or representations;

(d) State the date(s) on which injured plaintiff/ decedent gave notice of said breach(es) of warranty or misrepresentation(s);

(e) State to whom and in what manner injured plaintiff/decedent gave notice of said breach(es) of warranty or misrepresentation(s);

(f) State how long after injured plaintiff/ decedent was exposed to, used, ingested or inhaled the product did injured plaintiff/decedent give notice of said breach(es) of warranty or misrepresentation(s); and

(g) If injured plaintiff/decedent did not give notice of said breach(es) of warranty or misrepresentation(s), state why said notice was not given, whether you contend that each defendant was not prejudiced by lack of notice or lack of timely notice, and the facts upon which you rely in support of that contention.

39. If you contend that asbestos or any asbestos- containing product failed to satisfy any implied warranty or other representation of any defendant concerning potential uses or standards of performance, or that asbestos or any asbestos-containing product was unfit for its intended use, identify each such product and defendant and with respect to each product and defendant:

(a) Describe the manner in which the product did not conform to the above-described warranties or representations;

(b) Explain how injured plaintiff/decedent relied upon the warranties or representations; and

(c) State in what manner each defendant's breach of any or all warranties or misrepresentations as alleged contributed to or caused injured plaintiff's/decedent's injuries or damages, giving full details as to how the proper fitness or quality of the product would have prevented injured plaintiff's/ decedent's injuries or damages.

40. If you contend that asbestos or any asbestos- containing product was inherently dangerous when put into normal or foreseeable use or operation, identify each such product and defendant and describe the alleged inherent danger or hazard in the product.

41. If you contend that any defendant conspired to deprive the public, injured plaintiff/decedent and others similarly situated of relevant medical and scientific data, or actively defrauded the public, injured plaintiff/decedent and others similarly situated, by the solicitation of favorable scientific and medical data, or otherwise, identify each defendant against whom such claim is made and state:

(a) The date, place and manner of such acts;

(b) The medical and scientific data of which the public was deprived or which was solicited;

(c) All facts which support each such contention; and

(d) The identity of all persons involved in such contentions.

42. If you contend that any defendant acted in concert to deprive injured plaintiff/decedent, the public and others similarly situated, or to actively defraud injured plaintiff/ decedent, the public and others similarly situated, identify each defendant against whom such claim is made and state:

(a) The date, place and manner of such acts;

(b) All facts which support each such contention; and

(c) The identity of all persons involved in such contentions.

43. If you contend that intentional conduct of any defendant is actionable, identify each such defendant and with respect to each defendant state:

(a) The intentional conduct;

(b) The date, place and manner of such acts;

(c) All facts which support such contention; and

(d) The identity of all persons involved in such contentions.

44. If you contend that any defendant intentionally suppressed and/or concealed by affirmative act material facts as to health hazards associated with the purchase of, use of, and/or exposure to asbestos or any asbestos-containing product, identify each such defendant and state as to each:

(a) The date, place and manner of such affirmative acts;

(b) The material facts suppressed or concealed;

(c) All facts which support each such contention; and

(d) The identity of all persons involved in such acts.

45. If you are asserting claims based upon market share or percentage of injured plaintiff's/decedent's total alleged contact or exposure to asbestos or materials containing asbestos:

(a) State the market share or percentage which you attribute to each individual or entity which you claim was a manufacturer or supplier of asbestos or materials containing asbestos;

(b) Indicate or identify:

(i) The manner of and the factors relied upon in making each such percentage calculation;

(ii) The individuals assisting you or otherwise involved in calculating the above percentages;

(iii) All documents, writings or other records, if any, relied upon in your calculation and the present location and identity of the present custodian of each such document, writing or other records; and

(c) If you are unable to attribute such percentages, state all efforts you have made to ascertain such percentages.

46. If you contend that you are entitled to punitive damages against any defendant, identify each such defendant and with respect to each defendant state the basis for this contention.

WARNINGS AND SAFETY PRACTICES

47. List all publications which injured plaintiff/decedent regularly received or read.

48. Did injured plaintiff/decedent regularly receive or read "The Asbestos Worker"?

49. Did injured plaintiff/decedent at any time receive or learn about any advice, publication, warning, order, directive, requirement, or recommendation, whether written or oral, which advised or warned of the possible harmful effects of exposure to, or inhalation of, asbestos, or asbestos-containing products?

If your answer is yes, state:

(a) The nature and exact wording of such advice, warning, recommendation, etc.;

(b) The identity of each source of such advice, warning, recommendation, etc.;

(c) The date, time, place, manner and circumstances when each such advice, warning, recommendation, etc., was given; and

(d) The identity of each witness to decedent's receipt of such advice, warning, recommendation, etc.

50. Was injured plaintiff/decedent ever a member of any labor union?

If your answer is yes, state:

(a) The identity of each local, national and international union;

(b) The inclusive dates of injured plaintiff's/decedent's membership; and

(c) Any position(s) injured plaintiff/decedent held with each such union, and the dates during which he held such positions.

51. Did injured plaintiff/decedent receive any newspapers, newsletters, or other publications from any labor union? If your answer is yes, state whether such publications ever discussed the subject of worker exposure to asbestos, and if so:

(a) Identify the publication; and

(b) State the date(s) that such publication discussed the subject of asbestos and the nature of said discussion.

52. Did injured plaintiff/decedent ever attend any international, national, regional or local union meetings, seminars, conferences, or conventions where the subject of occupational health, and, in particular, exposure to asbestos, was discussed?

If your answer is yes:

(a) Identify such meeting, seminar, conference or convention and state the date(s) and place held;

(b) State the reason and/or official capacity for injured plaintiff/decedent attending;

(c) Identify the speaker(s);

(d) Summarize the information presented concerning exposure to asbestos; and

(e) Identify any persons with whom injured plaintiff/decedent discussed the information presented.

53. Was injured plaintiff/decedent ever informed by any employer or by any person in an official capacity in his local or international union of any possible hazards associated with exposure to asbestos dust or fiber?

If your answer is yes, state:

(a) The identity and official capacity of the individual or individuals who furnished injured plaintiff/ decedent with such information;

(b) The date and place such information was furnished;

(c) The manner in which such information was communicated;

(d) The nature of such information; and

(e) What action, if any, injured plaintiff/ decedent took in response to such information.

54. Did injured plaintiff/decedent ever see any warning labels on packages or containers of asbestos products?

If your answer is yes, state:

(a) The type of product using its generic name;

(b) The trade name, brand name and trade symbol;

(c) The name of the manufacturer, distributors and miners of such product;

(d) The appearance of the package or container, indicating the manner of packaging, size, dimensions, color and weight;

(e) The name, logo, label, numerical and alphabetical markings or words on the package or container;

(f) When and where injured plaintiff/decedent saw the labels; and

(g) The nature of the warnings.

55. Did injured plaintiff/decedent ever see or receive any information, instruction, direction, warning, or directive, from any source whatsoever, concerning alleged dangers of exposure to asbestos materials or asbestos-containing products?

If your answer is yes, identify:

(a) Each such warning, directive, notification, direction, instruction, or information;

(b) The means by which such was given to injured plaintiff/decedent;

(c) The source and the date on which it was received by injured plaintiff/decedent; and

(d) Injured plaintiff's/decedent's response or reaction, including any complaints made or changes in work habits.

56. Did injured plaintiff/decedent have available for use during any period of his employment, respirators or masks or other dust inhalation inhibitor or protective gear?

If your answer is yes, state:

(a) The period of time during which said items were available;

(b) What instructions were given with regard to the use of each of said items;

(c) Whether injured plaintiff/decedent used said items and the dates of his use;

(d) That percentage of time during which injured plaintiff/decedent was exposed to asbestos materials or asbestos- containing products, injured plaintiff/decedent used said items; and

(e) Whether injured plaintiff/decedent ever requested said items, and if so, when, where and to whom the request was made, and the response to the request.

57. Did anyone, at any time, suggest, recommend or require that injured plaintiff/decedent use a respirator or mask or other dust inhalation inhibitor or protective gear when he used or was exposed to asbestos materials or asbestos-containing products or dust?

If your answer is yes, state:

(a) The identity of the person or entity making such suggestion, recommendation or requirement;

(b) The date on which each such suggestion, recommendation or requirement was made;

(c) The substance of each such suggestion, recommendation or requirement; and

(d) What action, if any, injured plaintiff/ decedent took in response to each suggestion, recommendation or requirement.

MEDICAL INFORMATION

58. For every Physician by whom injured plaintiff/decedent has ever been treated or examined or with whom injured plaintiff/decedent consulted, state the following:

(a) The identity of the Physician;

(b) Dates of treatment, examination or consultation; and

(c) The nature of such treatment, examination or consultation.

59. For every Health Care Institution in which injured plaintiff/decedent has ever been admitted, treated, tested or examined, whether as an in-patient or as an out patient, state:

(a) The identity of the Health Care Institution;

(b) The date of and nature of each admission, treatment, test or examination; and

(c) The diagnosis at each admission, treatment, test or examination.

60. For each and every medical condition which you contend is directly or indirectly related to injured plaintiff's/ decedent's exposure to asbestos or asbestos-containing products, state:

(a) The nature and description of such medical condition;

(b) The disease, disability or physical condition to which said medical condition is related and the nature and extent of such relationship;

(c) The date on which injured plaintiff/decedent first exhibited signs of the medical condition;

(d) The date upon which each medical condition was first reported to a Physician;

(e) The identity of each Physician to whom said medical condition was reported;

(f) Any physical change in injured plaintiff's/decedent's appearance occasioned by such medical condition;

(g) Each part of injured plaintiff's/decedent's body, which you contend had been thus affected;

(h) Whether you claim that such medical condition caused injured plaintiff/decedent to suffer a disability and, if so, when injured plaintiff/decedent first suffered such a disability; and

(i) The date each such medical condition ceased to affect injured plaintiff/decedent.

61. State the date that injured plaintiff/decedent first noticed, if ever, each of the following symptoms or complaints:

(a) Shortness of breath;

(b) Crackling noises in the lungs;

(c) Coughing;

(d) Clubbing or swelling of the fingers;

(e) Discoloration of the skin;

(f) Wheezing;

(g) Chest pain;

(h) Abdominal swelling;

(i) Weight loss;

(j) Respiratory discomfort or pain; and

(k) Sputum production.

62. State when injured plaintiff/decedent was first diagnosed as suffering from an asbestos-related medical condition and include in your answer:

(a) The date of such diagnosis;

(b) The identity of the diagnosing Physician, and state whether said Physician made positive findings of:

(i) Fibrosis;

(ii) Pleural plaques;

(iii) Calcification;

(iv) Dysphea;

(v) Emphysema;

(vi) Tuberculosis; or

(vii) Disease grade (i.e., 1, 2, 3, 4) pneumonia.

(c) The identity of any Health Care Institution or Physician involved in any part of such diagnosis;

(d) The identity of every person, including injured plaintiff's/decedent's relatives, employer, or anyone acting on his behalf, to whom such diagnosis was made known, including the date, time and place, and the identity of anyone witnessing said revelation;

(e) Whether injured plaintiff/decedent continued to engage in any activity or occupation where he was exposed to asbestos materials after he was informed of such diagnosis;

(f) The course of treatment or therapy prescribed, including any medication, as a result of such diagnosis, and the identity of each prescribing Physician;

(g) Whether injured plaintiff/decedent followed the treatment, medication or therapy regimen prescribed by each of the said Physicians for the treatment of said diagnosed medical condition; and

(h) The identity of every Physician subsequently affirming or making the same diagnosis.

63. Did any of the Physicians identified in response to Interrogatory 62 inform injured plaintiff/decedent at any time that his asbestos-related medical condition may have been caused by factors other than exposure to asbestos or asbestos-containing products?

If your answer is yes, state:

(a) The other factors or reasons involved;

(b) The identity of the Physicians so informing injured plaintiff/decedent;

(c) The dates that said Physicians so informed injured plaintiff/decedent; and

(d) State whether any such factors or reasons were excluded as possible sources or causes of the medical condition.

64. State the following with regard to injured plaintiff's/decedent's medical condition:

(a) The identity of each Physician who treated, examined or consulted with injured plaintiff/decedent, the dates of said treatment, examination or consultation and any diagnosis made and the date of diagnosis;

(b) The identity of each Health Care Institution in which injured plaintiff/decedent was confined, treated or examined, stating the inclusive dates of any hospitalization and/or the dates of any out-patient treatment, the diagnosis made, the date of diagnosis, and the nature of the treatment; and

(c) If the injured plaintiff/decedent is presently under a Physician's care for his medical condition(s), or was at the time of his death, state:

(i) The identity of each Physician;

(ii) Any drugs or treatments prescribed by each Physician; and

(iii) The dates of injured plaintiff's/ decedent's visits or treatments.

65. If injured plaintiff/decedent ever had any medical symptoms, complaints, injuries, illnesses, accidents or operations or any medical complaints, injuries, illnesses or accidents requiring medical attention, other than those related to his asbestos-related medical condition(s), state with regard to each:

(a) Its nature and the dates thereof;

(b) The identity of each Physician who treated, examined, or consulted with injured plaintiff/decedent in each such instance, the dates of said treatment, examination or consultation and any diagnosis made;

(c) The identity of each Health Care Institution in which injured plaintiff/decedent was confined, treated or examined, stating the inclusive dates of any hospitalization or the dates of any out-patient treatment, the diagnosis made, the date of diagnosis, and the nature of the treatment; and

(d) The nature and extent of any permanent disabilities or residual effects.

66. If injured plaintiff/decedent ever underwent any periodic, pre-employment, employment-related, insurance-related, armed forces or national guard medical or physical examinations, state as to each such examination:

(a) The entity (including, but not limited to, any employer, union or insurance company) who offered, required, or sponsored such examination;

(b) The dates and locations of each such examination;

(c) The identity of the Physician under whose supervision each examination was conducted; and

(d) The nature and results of each such examination.

67. State any disease, injury or preexisting condition of health which you contend contributed to, or may have contributed to, injured plaintiff's/decedent's medical condition(s).

68. If you contend that injured plaintiff's/decedent's medical condition caused, or contributed to, the aggravation of any preexisting physical, nervous or mental condition, identify the preexisting condition and state the date injured plaintiff/decedent first became aware that his medical condition had caused, or contributed to, an aggravation of any preexisting condition.

69. Describe any pain, incapacity, inability to lead a normal life, inability to work, or disability (including retirement) alleged to have resulted from injured plaintiff's/decedent's medical condition, including the date and basis therefor.

70. If you or your attorney has any medical reports from any persons or institution that ever treated or examined injured plaintiff/decedent at any time, provide copies of all of the reports.

If you object to the production of copies of any reports, state for each report:

(a) The identity of the report; and

(b) The reason it was prepared.

71. Did injured plaintiff/decedent ever have any biopsies or tissue samples taken?

If your answer is yes, state for each such procedure:

(a) The identity of each Physician performing such procedures;

(b) The date and place of such procedures; and

(c) The results, conclusions, and/or diagnoses arising from such procedures, and the dates on which injured plaintiff/decedent was advised of same.

72. Were any pathology slides made from any of injured plaintiff's/decedent's tissue samples at any time?

If your answer is yes, for each set of slides made, state:

(a) The identity of the Physician obtaining the tissue sample, the identity of the Health Care Institution where the tissue sample was obtained, and the date the tissue sample was obtained;

(b) The identity of the Physician preparing the pathology slides, the identity of the Health Care Institution where the slides were prepared, and the date the slides were prepared;

(c) The identity of all Physicians who have analyzed the pathology slides, the identity of the Health Care Institution where the analysis was done, and the date of the analysis;

(d) The results of said analysis;

(e) The conclusions and/or diagnoses arising from analysis of the pathology slides, and the dates on which injured plaintiff/decedent was advised of the results;

(f) The current location of said slides; and

(g) Provide appropriate authorization to view and/or obtain and make photographic reproductions of said slides.

73.   Did injured plaintiff/decedent ever have any chest, lung, or other respiratory system X–rays taken?

If your answer is yes, state for each set of X–rays:

(a) If applicable, the identity of the Physician ordering said x-rays;

(b) The identity of the place where said x-rays were taken and the date;

(c) The reason said x-rays were taken;

(d) The identity of all Physicians who have read, analyzed, or interpreted said x-rays;

(e) The results of said x-rays;

(f) The conclusions and/or diagnoses arising from such procedure, and the dates on which injured plaintiff/decedent was advised of the results;

(g) The location of all said x-ray films; and

(h) Provide appropriate authorization to view or obtain and make photographic reproduction of said X–rays.

74.   Did injured plaintiff/decedent ever have any pulmonary function tests conducted?

If your answer is yes, state for each such test:

(a) If applicable, the identity of the Physician ordering said test;

(b) The identity of the place where said test was conducted and the date;

(c) The reason said test was conducted;

(d) The identity of all Physicians who analyzed or interpreted said test;

(e) The results of said test;

(f) The conclusions and/or diagnoses arising from such test, and the dates on which injured plaintiff/decedent was advised of the results; and

(g) The identity of the person who advised injured plaintiff/decedent of the results.

75.   Did injured plaintiff/decedent ever consult with or was he ever seen professionally by a psychiatrist, psychologist or counselor?

If your answer is yes, state:

(a) The date of such consultation or visit; and

(b) If said consultation or visit occurred within the last ten years, or within ten years prior to decedent's death:

(i) The identity of the psychiatrist, psychologist or counselor; and

(ii) The reason for the consultation or visit.

76. If injured plaintiff/decedent was ever unable to work for more than one week due to a medical condition, describe for each such condition:

(a) The nature of the condition;

(b) The identity of injured plaintiff's/decedent's treating Physician; and

(c) The dates of and length of time injured plaintiff/decedent was ill, disabled, or out of work.

77. Did injured plaintiff/decedent ever make any claim for, or receive any, health or accident insurance benefits, social security benefits, state or federal benefits for disabilities, workers' compensation benefits, veterans' benefits, tort claims or suits, Federal Employers Liability Act claims or suits, Longshoremen and Harbor Workers Act claims or suits, unemployment compensation insurance benefits, or early payment from any public, or private pensions due to disability or his medical condition?

If your answer is yes, state:

(a) The date and place where each such claim was made;

(b) The identity of the entity with which the claim was made;

(c) Any identifying number, such as a docket number, for each claim;

(d) The defendant, agency, insurer, employer or other entity to or against whom the claim was made;

(e) The nature of the claim; and

(f) The result of such claim, including any amount received by way of settlement, judgment or award upon the claim.

78. Was a death certificate prepared after the death of the decedent?

If the answer is yes, attach a copy to your responses to these interrogatories.

To the extent the death certificate does not so indicate, state:

(a) Whether it was filed;

(b) The identity of the office in which it was filed;

(c) The identity of the person listed on the certificate as the informant;

(d) The relationship of the person listed as the informant to or connection with the decedent;

(e) The identity and professional specialty of each Physician furnishing the information appearing on the death certificate;

(f) The immediate cause of death; and

(g) The exact time, date and place of death.

79. Was an autopsy performed on the body of the decedent?

If the answer is yes, state for each autopsy:

(a) The identity and official capacity of each person authorizing or ordering the autopsy;

(b) The relationship to or connection with the decedent of each person authorizing or ordering the autopsy;

(c) Why the autopsy was ordered;

(d) The identity and professional specialty of each person performing the autopsy;

(e) The date, time and place the autopsy was performed;

(f) The cause of death shown by the autopsy;

(g) The identity and occupation of each person having custody of the report of the results of the autopsy; and

(h) Attach a copy of each autopsy report to your responses to these interrogatories or execute and provide appropriate authorizations to examine and obtain photocopies of said autopsy reports.

DAMAGES

80. State, in the form of an itemized list, all special damages alleged in this lawsuit including, but not limited to, Physician services, Health Care Institution expenses, Ambulance expenses, X–rays, diagnostic tests, prescription drugs, physiotherapy, psychiatric services, and lost wages, and identify the person or organization to whom each item of expense was paid or due, and by whom each item of expense was paid.

If there is any lien on the damages the plaintiff is claiming, identify the lienholder and state the total amount of lien.

81. If you are making a claim for loss of earnings or impairment of earning power because of injured plaintiff's/ decedent's medical condition, state:

(a) The identity of injured plaintiff's/decedent's employer, job classification and monthly or weekly rate of pay at the time of the onset of his medical condition;

(b) Whether injured plaintiff/decedent had more than one employer during the three-year period prior to the date of the onset of his medical condition, and if your answer is yes, identify each such employer, other than the one stated above, and injured plaintiff's/decedent's job classification, monthly or weekly rate of pay, and inclusive dates of such employment during the three-year period;

(c) Injured plaintiff's/decedent's total earnings for the period of three years prior to the onset of his medical condition;

(d) The inclusive dates during which you allege that injured plaintiff/decedent was unable to work as a result of his medical condition and the total amount of pay you claim he lost because of this absence;

(e) The date on which injured plaintiff/decedent started work again; and

(f) The name and address of each employer for whom injured plaintiff/decedent worked, with inclusive dates of employment and indicating whether retired, each job classification injured plaintiff/decedent held and each monthly or weekly rate of pay which he received, from the date he first started working again after the onset of his medical condition through the present time, or to the time of death.

82. Do you claim damages for loss of consortium, society, affection, services, or sexual enjoyment?

If your answer is yes, set forth all facts on which this claim is based, including a complete description of the loss suffered. As to the alleged lost services, additionally provide:

(a) The duration of the loss of any service; and

(b) The cost, if any, incurred to obtain substitute services.

83. State fully and in detail the annual earnings for the past ten years, or the ten years prior to death, for injured plaintiff/decedent and injured plaintiff's/decedent's spouse.

84. Do you have access to injured plaintiff's/ decedent's W-2 forms and income tax returns for the last ten years or the ten years prior to death?

If your answer is yes, attach copies to your responses to these interrogatories.

If not available, execute and provide a release in form acceptable to the Internal Revenue Service to obtain copies of said tax records.

85. Itemize the expenses incurred in connection with the funeral, burial, cremation or other means of attending to the decedent's remains.

86. Did the decedent die testate?

If your answer is yes, state:

(a) The date the will and each codicil were executed;

(b) Details of any attempts to revoke or invalidate the will;

(c) Whether the will has been filed for probate and, if so, the date and place;

(d) The identity of each executor named in the will;

(e) Whether the estate is still in probate;

(f) The identity of and relationship to the decedent of each beneficiary named in the will and the bequest or devise made to each;

(g) The identity of each attorney of record to the probate of the will; and

(h) Attach a copy of each will and codicil to your responses to these interrogatories.

87.　Has there been a contest of the will of the decedent?

If your answer is yes, state:

(a) The identity of and relationship to the decedent of each person contesting the will;

(b) The date the contest was filed;

(c) The name of the court and the title and file number of the contest;

(d) The grounds for contesting the will; and

(e) How and when the contest was determined by the court.

88.　Did the decedent die intestate?

If your answer is yes, state:

(a) Whether there is necessity for administration of the decedent's estate;

(b) Whether an application for administration has been filed and, if so, the date, name of the court, and the title of proceeding and file number;

(c) The identity of each duly qualified and appointed administrator of the estate;

(d) Whether the estate is still being administered;

(e) Whether any Letters of Administration (general or special) were ever issued in connection with the decedent's estate, and if so, attach copies of such Letters to your responses to the interrogatories;

(f) The date on which Letters of Administration were issued to said administrator;

(g) The court, name of the Judge and the clerk issuing said Letters of Administration;

(h) Whether there were any limitations or restrictions placed on said Letters of Administration, and if so, the nature of those limitations or restrictions;

(i) Whether any court has issued Letters of Administration and subsequently suspended, modified or revoked them and, if so, set forth the circumstances;

(j) Whether Letters of Administration or Letters Testamentary have ever been issued to any persons other than those identified in (c), above and if so, set forth the circumstances;

(k) Whether there were any objections filed to any application for Letters of Administration, and if so, set forth the circumstances; and

(l) Whether any bond was posted in order to qualify as administrator, and if so, attach a copy to your responses to these interrogatories.

89.　Has there been a proceeding to determine the heirs of the decedent's estate?

If your answer is yes, state:

(a) The name of the court and the title of the proceeding and file number;

(b) The date of commencement of the proceeding;

(c) The date the order adjudicating heirship was rendered;

(d) Whether there has been an appeal from such order;

(e) Whether such order has ever been altered, amended or reversed; and

(f) The identity of and relationship to decedent and extent of right to inherit from the decedent of each heir as determined by this proceeding.

90. If you are suing on behalf of the decedent or the decedent's estate or if you are the personal representative of the decedent, attach copies of the papers which authorize you to maintain this action.

91. If it is claimed that any damages are owing to any person or entity on account of loss of an inheritance as a result of decedent's alleged exposure to asbestos or asbestos-containing products:

(a) State the decedent's net worth at the time of death;

(b) List all real and personal property owned by the decedent at the time of the decedent's death and where the same was located (clothing and personal effects need not be included); and

(c) Indicate all bank savings accounts maintained in the name of the decedent, indicating with respect to each:

(i) The identity of the bank;

(ii) The account number; and

(iii) The amount in the account at the time of the decedent's death.

92. Has an estate tax return been filed by the decedent's estate?

If your answer is yes:

(a) State the identity of the person or firm that prepared the return; and

(b) Identify the present custodian of the return.

93. Do you have or have access to the decedent's estate tax return?

If your answer is yes, attach a copy to your response to these interrogatories.

If not available, execute and provide a release in form acceptable to the Internal Revenue Service to obtain a copy of said tax record.

94. During the last five years of the decedent's life, did anyone other than the decedent contribute to the decedent's support?

If your answer is yes, state as to each:

(a) His identity and relationship to or connection with the decedent;

(b) The amount of each contribution, specifying whether in money, services, gifts or other forms; and

(c) The annual amount of such contributions.

95. During the last five years of the decedent's life, did anyone other than the decedent contribute to the support of any of the decedent's immediate family?

If your answer is yes, state as to each:

(a) The identity and relationship of each relative receiving such support;

(b) The identity of each person, other than the decedent, who contributed to each relative's support;

(c) The amount of each contribution, specifying whether in money, services, gifts, or other forms; and

(d) The annual amount of such contributions.

96. During the last ten years of his life, did the decedent contribute money or other tangible benefits to any of his children, spouses, former spouse(s), or parents?

If your answer is yes, state for each such person:

(a) His identity and relationship to decedent;

(b) The date and place of birth;

(c) The date of each contribution;

(d) The reason for each contribution;

(e) The amount or value of each contribution;

(f) A description of anything of value the decedent received in exchange for such contribution; and

(g) The years for which decedent claimed this person as a dependent for income tax purposes.

97. During the last ten years of his life, did decedent ever contribute to the support of persons other than his children, spouse, former spouse (s) or parents?

If your answer is yes, state for each such person:

(a) His identity and relationship to decedent;

(b) The date and place of birth;

(c) The date of each contribution;

(d) The reason for each contribution;

(e) The amount or value of each contribution;

(f) A description of anything of value decedent received in exchange for such contribution; and

(g) The years for which decedent claimed this person as a dependent for income tax purposes.

98. Did the decedent perform services for any of his children, spouses, former spouse(s) or parents?

If your answer is yes, state for each person:

(a) The identity and relationship to the decedent of the person for whom the service was performed;

(b) A description of each service performed for such person;

(c) The total time spent by the decedent performing the service per year and the frequency with which he performed such service;

(d) The date the decedent last performed each such service;

(e) The compensation, if any, the decedent received for performing each service;

(f) The identity and relationship to the decedent of each person or agency compensating the decedent for each service;

(g) The total cost to such person of getting others to perform each service performed by the decedent; and

(h) The identity and occupation of each person performing each such service since the decedent's death.

MISCELLANEOUS

99. Identify and give the substance of all written statements, recordings, or videotapes which relate to the facts of this lawsuit and the alleged damages given by you, injured plaintiff/decedent or any witness.

100. Have you or did injured plaintiff/decedent have any written or oral communication with any defendant?

If your answer is yes, state with respect to each defendant:

(a) Whether you were and/or the injured plaintiff/ decedent was a party to such communication;

(b) The sum and substance of each such communication;

(c) The date and exact location of each;

(d) Whether such communication was written or oral, and if written, annex a copy of same to your response to these interrogatories;

(e) The identity of or if not known, a description of such defendant or its employees, agents and/or servants with whom the communication was had; and

(f) The identity of or if not known, a description of each witness to each such oral communication.

101.   Have you or did injured plaintiff/decedent give or send to any defendant or have you or did the injured plaintiff/ decedent receive from any defendant any written communication?

If your answer is yes:

(a) State as to each:

(i) The identity of the person who gave or sent such communication;

(ii) The identity of the person who received such communication;

(iii) The date of such communication;

(iv) The sum and substance of such communication; and

(v) The identity of the present custodian of such communication; and

(b) Annex a copy of each such communication to your response to these interrogatories.

102.   Have you, did injured plaintiff/decedent, or has anyone acting on behalf of you or injured plaintiff/decedent obtained any statements, either written or record-ed, from any defendant or from any person in the employ of any defendant with respect to the occurrences alleged in the complaint?

If your answer is yes:

(a) State as to each:

(i) Who obtained such statement;

(ii) The identity of the person from whom such statement was obtained;

(iii) The date such statement was obtained;

(iv) The sum and substance of such statement;

(v) The identity of the present custodian of such statement; or

(b) Annex a copy of each such communication to your response to these interrogatories.

103.   State separately as to each defendant the identity of and, if known, the social security numbers of all potential witnesses who may give testimony concerning injured plaintiff's/ decedent's alleged exposure to and/or the manufacture and sale of asbestos materials and asbestos-containing products.

104.   Identify all persons, except experts, on whose testimony plaintiff intends to rely at trial.

105.   With regard to each person whom the plaintiff expects to call as an expert witness at trial, provide a copy of the witness' curriculum vitae or a summary of the witness' qualifications and state for each such expert witness:

(a) His identity;

(b) The subject matter on which such expert is to testify;

(c) The substance of all facts and opinions regarding which such expert is to testify;

(d) A summary of the grounds for each opinion of such expert;

(e) Whether the facts and opinions listed in (c) above are contained in a written report, memorandum or transcript;

(f) Whether such expert intends to base his testimony on any book, treatise, article, study, or any other document, and if so, identify all such documents; and

(g) Whether the witness has testified at trial or by deposition in other asbestos-related personal injury or wrongful death cases, and if so, state for each such case:

    (i) The name and docket number;

    (ii) The court in which each such case is or was pending; and

    (iii) The identity of the party for whom the witness testified.

106. Identify all persons, other than your attorneys, who provided you with any information used in answering these interrogatories, and state the particular information each person supplied.

REQUEST FOR PRODUCTION OF DOCUMENTS

Pursuant to Rule 3120 of the Civil Practice Law and Rules of New York State, the defendants request that plaintiffs produce for inspection and copying at such time as the responses to the interrogatories herein are filed, the following documents for discovery, inspection and copying:

1. All documents identified in your responses to these interrogatories.

2. All documents relating to injured plaintiff's/ decedent's job qualifications and professional licenses held.

3. All documents relating to injured plaintiff's/decedent's employment.

4. All documents relating to injured plaintiff's/ decedent's membership in any labor trade association or professional organization.

5. All documents relating to injured plaintiff's/ decedent's military or foreign service, including and not limited to personnel records, discharge papers, military occupational specialty qualifications, promotions, reductions or disciplinary actions.

6. All documents relating to any claim or demand ever made by injured plaintiff/decedent for damages, compensation or other benefits allegedly resulting from any illness or injury, including but not limited to workers' Compensation Board records, social security disability claim records, federal or state employment compensation claim records, social disability records, pension claim records or any other health or accident insurance claim records.

7. All documents, relating to the subject matter of this lawsuit, of which you have ever become aware, relating in any way to meetings, correspondence, statements or other communications of or from any manufacturer or supplier of asbestos, asbestos-containing products and/or asbestos-containing materials or from their agents or representatives.

8. All documents, relating to the subject matter of this lawsuit, of which you have ever become aware, relating in any way to meetings, correspondence or other communications of or from any trade association, labor union, employer or governmental agency, of or from any of their agents or representatives, relating to the subjects of occupational health and exposure to asbestos, asbestos-containing products and/or asbestos-containing materials.

9. All documents prepared by or on behalf of the plaintiff or decedent, prior to this litigation, in any way relating to the documents requested in item Nos. 5 and 6, above, of this request for production.

10. All documents relating in any way to injured plaintiff's/decedent's exposure or possible exposure to asbestos, asbestos-containing products and/or asbestos-containing materials.

11. All documents relating in any way to injured plaintiff's/decedent's exposures to substances identified in Interrogatory 18.

12. All documents relating in any way to any asbestos, asbestos-containing products and/or asbestos-containing materials manufactured, distributed and/or supplied by any person or entity or by any of the named defendants herein to which you claim injured plaintiff/decedent applied or was exposed.

13. All documents, of which you have ever become aware, relating, in any way, to warnings, potential health hazards, instructions or precautions regarding the use or

handling of, or exposure to, asbestos, asbestos-containing products, and/or asbestos-containing materials.

14.   All applications prepared or submitted by or on behalf of injured plaintiff/decedent for life insurance, medical insurance, health and accident insurance, and/or disability insurance.

15.   All statements, recorded interviews, films, videotapes, reports, questionnaires, forms or other documents made, submitted, compiled, prepared or filled out by, on behalf of, or under the direction of, plaintiff or decedent relating in any way to exposure or alleged exposure to asbestos, asbestos-containing products and/or asbestos-containing materials or any other issues relating to this lawsuit, except that information prepared by, for, or at the request of plaintiff's counsel must be identified (including the date made), but need not be produced without an Order by the Court, provided that written or recorded communication between plaintiff and counsel, made after an attorney-client relationship has been established need not be produced or identified.

16.   All documents relating to injured plaintiff's/decedent's first knowledge, notice or awareness about the alleged adverse effects of exposure to asbestos, asbestos-containing products and/or asbestos-containing materials.

17.   All records relating to comments, complaints, suggestions, or proposals made to injured plaintiff's/decedent's employer or injured plaintiff's/decedent's union, by injured plaintiff/decedent or by other employees or union members regarding asbestos exposure.

18.   All written, recorded, filmed, transcribed or videotaped statements of all parties and nonparty declarants pertaining to the subject of this lawsuit, except as to nonparty declarants that information prepared by, for, or at the request of plaintiff's counsel must be identified (including the date made), but need not be produced without an Order by the Court, provided that written or recorded communication between plaintiff and counsel, made after an attorney-client relationship has been established need not be produced or identified.

19.   All photographs of injured plaintiff/decedent at work or in work clothes and all photographs of all products or conditions complained of in injured plaintiff's/decedent's place of employment.

20.   Copies of all itemized bills covering all the special damages and losses and expenses claimed in this matter.

21.   Copies of all reports, correspondence and records from any doctor who has examined injured plaintiff/decedent, any hospital where injured plaintiff/decedent was treated either as an in-patient or as an out-patient, except for any reports, records, correspondence, or communications issued by any consulting physicians who have been retained or specially employed in anticipation of litigation or preparation for trial and who are not expected to be called as a witness at trial.

22.   All tissue specimens, tissue slides, and X–ray films pertaining to injured plaintiff/decedent.

23.   Copies of injured plaintiff's/decedent's income tax records for the last ten years, or for ten years prior to his death, as well as any other documents including economic loss reports, upon which plaintiff relies in support of his claims. If loss of earnings or earning capacity is alleged or claimed to have occurred before the current year, include copies of the income tax returns of injured plaintiff/decedent from ten years prior to the claimed loss and up to the current tax year, or the year of death.

24.   Any asbestos materials and/or asbestos-containing products of the type to which injured plaintiff/decedent allegedly was exposed, and which plaintiff has in his possession, custody or control.

25.   All photographs, charts, drawings, diagrams or other graphic representations depicting work conditions and sites where injured plaintiff/decedent was allegedly exposed to asbestos or asbestos-containing products.

26. All boxes, containers or wrappers that allegedly contained the asbestos materials and/or asbestos-containing products which are the subject of plaintiff's complaint and which are in the plaintiff's or plaintiff's attorney's possession, custody or control.

27. All labels, tags, or warnings on the boxes, containers or wrappers which allegedly contained asbestos materials and/or asbestos-containing products, which are the subject of plaintiffs' complaint and which are in plaintiff's or plaintiff's attorney's possession, custody or control.

28. All invoices, bills, statements and any other writings or records, which plaintiff contends evidence the sale of any products containing asbestos to the place of injured plaintiff's/decedent's employment at which injured plaintiff/ decedent was allegedly exposed to asbestos.

29. Any written advice, publication, warning, order, directive, requirement, or recommendation, which advised or warned of the possible harmful effects of exposure to or inhalation of asbestos materials and/or asbestos-containing products in the possession, custody or control of the plaintiff which came into the possession, custody or control of the injured plaintiff/ decedent during alleged period of exposure.

30. Any accident or incident reports which relate to the facts, circumstances or incidents which form the basis of plaintiff's complaint.

31. Any written statements given by the plaintiff or the decedent which relate to facts, circumstances, incidents, injuries or damages which form the basis of plaintiffs' complaint, including but not limited to statements made to any police or law enforcement officers, insurance company representatives, state or federal agents, or representatives or employees of other companies.

DATED:

    ATTY NAME, ETC.

TO:

EXHIBIT A

AUTHORIZATION

TO: INTERNAL REVENUE SERVICE and SOCIAL SECURITY ADMINISTRATION

RE: (Name of injured plaintiff/decedent)

Social Security Number: _____

Date of Birth: _____

This will authorize you to permit _____ and/or the bearer of this authorization to inspect and obtain copies of the following documents relating to _____:

(a) Any and all income tax returns, including all W-2 forms and schedules, filed either individually, jointly, or on behalf of an Estate;

(b) Any and all records of employment history; and

(c) Any and all records of earnings history.

Dated: _____

    (Signature)

    Name and, -if applicable,

    identity of signator

STATE OF   )
COUNTY OF   ) ss:

On the ___ day of _____, 19__, before me personally came appeared _____, to me known and known to me to be the individual described in and who executed the foregoing instrument, and who duly acknowledged to me that he executed the same.

_____

Notary Public, State of

Qualified in _____ County

My Commission Expires _____

EXHIBIT B

AUTHORIZATION

TO: WORKERS' COMPENSATION BOARD

RE: <u>(Name of injured plaintiff/decedent)</u>

Social Security Number: _____

Date of Birth: _____

This will authorize you to permit _____ and/or the bearer of this authorization to inspect and obtain copies of all documents and records relating to any and all Workers' Compensation claims made by or on behalf of _____ including but not limited to the records of the above Workers' Compensation claims.

Dated: _____

   (Signature)

Name and, if applicable,

identity of signator

STATE OF   )

COUNTY OF   ) ss:

On the ___ day of _____, 19 ___, before me personally came and appeared _____, to me known and known to me to be the individual described in and who executed the foregoing instrument, and who duly acknowledged to me that he executed the same.

_____

Notary Public, State of

Qualified in _____ County

My Commission Expires _____

EXHIBIT C

AUTHORIZATION

TO: <u>(NAME OF EMPLOYER)</u>

  <u>(Address)</u>

RE: <u>(Name of injured plaintiff/decedent)</u>

Social Security Number: _____

Date of Birth: _____

This will authorize you to permit _____ and/or the bearer of this authorization to inspect and obtain copies of any and all records relating to your employment of _____, including but not limited to all personnel and medical records.

Dated: _____

   <u>(Signature)</u> Name and, if applicable,

identity of signator

STATE OF   )

COUNTY OF   ) ss:

On the ___ day of _____, 19 ___, before me personally came and appeared _____, to me known and known-to me to be the individual described in and who executed the foregoing instrument, and who duly acknowledged to me that he executed the same.

_____

Notary public, State of

Qualified in _____ County

My Commission Expires _____

EXHIBIT D

AUTHORIZATION

TO: (NAME OF PHYSICIAN or HEALTH CARE INSTITUTION)

(Address)

RE: (Name of injured plaintiff/decedent)

Date of Birth: _____

Date(s) of Treatment and/or Admissions:

_____

_____

This will authorize you to permit _____ and/or the bearer of this authorization to inspect and obtain copies of the following documents relating to _____

_____:

(a) Hospital records, including x-rays, treatment and prognosis, pathology material, pathology slides, and tissue block;

(b) Medical records, including x-rays, treatment and prognosis, pathology material, pathology slides and tissue block;

(c) Medical Examiners and Autopsy reports; and

(d) Pharmacy records.

Dated: _____

(Signature)

Name and, if applicable,

identity of signator

STATE OF   )

COUNTY OF   ) ss:

On the ___ day of _____, 19, before me personally came and appeared _____, to me known and known to me to be the individual described in and who executed the foregoing instrument, and who duly acknowledged to me that he executed the same.

_____

Notary Public, State of

Qualified in _____ County My Commission Expires _____

EXHIBIT E

AUTHORIZATION

TO: (NAME OF MILITARY SERVICE)

RE: (Name of injured plaintiff/decedent)

Military Identification Number: _____

Dates of Military Service: _____

Social Security Number: _____

Date of Birth: _____

Place of Birth: _____

This will authorize you to permit _____ and/or the bearer of this authorization to inspect and obtain copies of any and all records relating to the military service of _____, including personnel records, medical records, discharge papers, military occupational specialty qualifications, promotions or reductions, and disciplinary actions.

Dated: _____

(Signature)

Name and, if applicable,

identity of signator

STATE OF   )
COUNTY OF   ) ss:

On the __ day of _____, 19 __, before me personally came and appeared _____, to me known and known to me to be the individual described in and who executed the foregoing instrument, and who duly acknowledged to me that he executed the same.

_____

Notary Public, State of

Qualified in _____ County

My Commission Expires _____

EXHIBIT F

AUTHORIZATION

TO: (NAME OF SCHOOL DISTRICT OR EDUCATIONAL INSTITUTION)

(Address)

RE: (Name of injured plaintiff/decedent)

Date of Birth: _____

This will authorize you to permit _____ and/or the bearer of this authorization to inspect and obtain copies of any and all school records, including medical records, of _____.

Dated: _____

(Signature)

Name and, if applicable,

identity of signator

STATE OF   )
COUNTY OF   ) ss:

On the __ day of _____, 19 __, before me personally came and appeared _____, to me known and known to me to be the individual described in and who executed the foregoing instrument, and who duly acknowledged to me that he executed the same.

_____

Notary Public, State of

Qualified in _____ County

My Commission Expires _____

App. G. Plaintiffs' First Set of Interrogatories

SUPREME COURT OF THE STATE OF NEW YORK
SEVENTH JUDICIAL DISTRICT
....

In RE: SEVENTH JUDICIAL DISTRICT ASBESTOS LITIGATION

....

This Document Relates To: Index No. _____
(Title of Case)   County _____

....

SEVENTH JUDICIAL DISTRICT ASBESTOS LITIGATION

(7 JDAL)

PLAINTIFFS' FIRST STANDARD SET OF ASBESTOS LITIGATION LIABILITY INTERROGATORIES AND REQUEST FOR PRODUCTION OF DOCUMENTS

All plaintiff's, pursuant to the Civil Practice Law and Rules and the Case Management Order of this Court, propound the following interrogatories to each and every defendant, to be answered under oath, and request that each defendant produce the documents requested herein. These interrogatories are continuing in character and require you to file supplementary answers if you obtain further or different information after your initial answers and before trial, including in such supplemental answers, the date upon and the manner in which such further or different information came to your attention. (For further instructions and definitions see Appendix A).

I. General Liability Interrogatories

Q1. State the full name, address, telephone number and position of the corporate officer answering these interrogatories.

Q2. Have any documents and records of the defendant been used or referred to, in connection with the preparation of or answers to these interrogatories? If so, for each document referred to, state the following:

    a. The number of the question and its sub-part;

    b. The identity and title of the document;

    c. The name and location of the file in which the document was found;

    d. The name and location of the file in which the document is presently located;

    e. The originator of the document.

Q3. State the names of each person who was spoken to or who provided information to assist in answering these interrogatories and for each person state the following:

    a. The number of each question and its subpart for which such personnel provided information;

    b. For each question identified in a., state the name, title and position description of the personnel supplying information;

    c. the present location and address of the personnel supplying information;

    d. the contents of the information provided.

Q4. Please state in which state or states of the United States or what foreign countries your business is incorporated and where its principal place of business is located.

Q5. Please state whether:

    a. Your company is authorized to do business in: New York

    b. Your company does business in: New York

Q6. State the full and complete legal name under which your company or any predecessor is now doing business and has done business at all times from the date when it began mining, processing, manufacturing and/or selling asbestos products or thermal insulation products and materials up until the present time.

Q7. Have you ever acquired, by way of a consolidation, merger, purchase of assets, or otherwise, any company which manufactured or sold, processed, designed, distributed, or contracted to supply any asbestos-containing products? If so, as to each such acquisition:

    a. State the name and state of incorporation of the company which was acquired;

    b. State the reasons for the acquisition;

    c. State the date of the acquisition;

    d. State the terms of the acquisition, including but not limited to the consideration paid (e.g., amount of stock, cash, etc.) if any;

    e. Identify all of the company's assets which were acquired (e.g., plants, machinery, stock in trade, trademarks, patents, goodwill, etc.);

    f. Identify all of the company liabilities which were assumed by you in the acquisition;

    g. Identify all of the company's asbestos-containing product lines;

    h. Identify each asbestos-containing product line of the acquired company which you continued to manufacture after the acquisition;

    i. State the number of employees of the acquired company which were retained by you after the acquisition;

    j. State the names of the directors, officers, and major stockholders of your company and the acquired company at the time of the acquisition and the names of the directors, officers, and major stockholders of your company and, if it continued to exist, of the acquired company, after the acquisition;

    k. State the total number of shares of the acquired company which you held before and after the acquisition;

    l. Identify and produce a copy of the agreement between you and the acquired company, the pertinent minutes of your Board of Directors and all other related documents.

Q8. State the names and positions of all corporate officers or officials having the responsibility for creating, directing or setting the policy of your firm with regard to the mining, manufacturing, processing, design, refining, supply, distribution, sale and/or packaging of asbestos products since 1930.

Q9. Have you or any of your predecessors or subsidiaries ever mined, manufactured, designed, supplied, processed, refined, sold or distributed asbestos or asbestos- containing products? If so, for each such product, complete an "Asbestos Product Information Sheet, Attachment I.

Q10. If your company ever manufactured or sold any of the following types cf. asbestos products, please describe how they are cut, shaped, mixed and applied on the job:

    a. asbestos cement mixes;

    b. asbestos pipe covering;

    c. asbestos bricks or blocks;

    d. asbestos sheeting, boards or marinite;

    e. asbestos insulation used to protect against extremes of heat as well as cold;

    f. asbestos insulation in loose form which may be blown into homes or buildings;

    g. asbestos applied in spray form;

    h. asbestos tape, cloth, yarn, thread or tape;

    i. asbestos felt or blanket;

    j. asbestos paper;

    k. asbestos gaskets; giving particular reference as to whether or not the materials have to be sawed or cut on the job, blown into confined areas, or mixed with water into a cement or paste.

Q11. Please state if there is any way known to you that the products listed in questions 9 and 10 can be used, applied or installed without the worker involved inhaling any asbestos dust or fibers.

Q12. Is it possible to distinguish the asbestos products listed by you in Answers 9 and 10 from those manufactured or distributed by a competitor?

    a. If so, please describe how you contend your product can be distinguished and identify each of your products by trade and generic name.

    b. If there are products which, in your opinion, cannot be distinguished from products of a similar kind manufactured by a competitor, please state the name of each such similar product, who manufactured it, as well as the trade name of the product manufactured by your competitor.

Q13. For each asbestos product listed by you in Answers 9 and 10, state whether the product could be used interchangeably with products of other manufacturers, distributors, or sellers, and if so, please identify such product(s) and manufacturer(s).

Q14. For each asbestos product listed by you in Answers 9 and 10, state the names and addresses of each customer within the State of New York, the product, by year and complete a Work site/Purchase Sales Information Sheet (Attachment II) for each purchaser or work site.

Q15. For each asbestos product, state the total dollar, linear feet and/or number of pounds:

    a. Sold in New York State;

    b. Sold in the United States.

Q16. Identify for the period from 1935 to 1980, each distributor, dealer, wholesaler and contractor who sold, distributed or used your asbestos-containing products in the City of Rochester and within a 200 mile radius of the City of Rochester. For each such distributor, dealer, whole saler and contractor, state:

    a. The name, last known address and person with whom you did business;

    b. The years of your relationship with the distributor, dealer, wholesaler and contractor;

    c. Whether there was a written agreement. If so, identify it (or them) by date, title, signatories and present location;

    d. Whether the relationship was exclusive, i.e., whether the distributor was not allowed to carry competing brands of some or all of the relevant products. If exclusive as to any particular product, identify that product;

    e. The annual volume in pounds and linear feet and dollar amount of each type of asbestos product sold;

    f. The names and ultimate recipients of the asbestos products sold to or through each dealer, distributor, wholesaler, sales agent and contractor.

Q17. Identify each of your sales personnel responsible from 1935 to 1980 for (1) sales of asbestos products in the City of Rochester and within a 200 mile radius of the City of Rochester. For each such person, state the years of such employment, the last known addresses and whether he is still your employee.

Q18. Did you at any time manufacture asbestos-containing products which were sold to another manufacturer for resale by that company under its own name? If so:

    a. Identify each manufacturer to whom such sales were made and the date of such sales;

    b. Identify the product or products involved in each such agreement;

    c. If such sales were made pursuant to an agreement, identify the dates that each such agreement was in effect and produce a copy of the agreement.

Q19. Did you ever purchase asbestos-containing products of any other manufacturer for distribution or sale under your name or trademark? If so:

    a. Identify each manufacturer from whom such products were purchased;

    b. Identify the name of each product purchased;

    c. Identify the dates of each such purchase and distribution.

    d. Produce a copy of each purchase agreement;

Q20. Did you ever enter into distribution or licensing agreements with any manufacturer of asbestos-containing products? If so:

    a. Identify each manufacturer with whom such agreement was entered into;

    b. State the dates, products and geographical areas involved;

    c. Produce a copy of each such agreement;

Q21. State whether you ever sold any of your products containing asbestos fibers or any raw asbestos fiber to any of the companies named as co-defendants in this suit. If so:

    a. Identify each individual, including their job classification, who currently has possession of such knowledge, either by documents of records.

    b. Identify "each co-defendant to whom your products have been sold.

    c. State the dates of each such sale and the amount and kind of materials sold.

Q22. For the period 1928 to the present, state the address of each miner, manufacturer or processor of asbestos or asbestos fibers used in your products and for each such miner, manufacturer or processor state:

    a. The date, amounts and delivery point for each shipment of asbestos you received;

    b. The products in which the asbestos was used.

Q23. With respect to each asbestos product (including loose asbestos fiber) you manufactured, refined, processed, sold or delivered, state whether you claim any caution, warning, caveat or other statement about health involved in using the product and/or dust generated by the product was ever given to purchasers of the product or directed to users of the product. If so, state separately for each product:

    a. The precise wording of each caution or set of instructions;

    b. The exact date you claim each caution was first used;

    c. The inclusive dates you contend any warning was affixed to each of your asbestos-containing products;

    d. Whether the wording has been altered since its first appearance, and if so, when and how amended;

    e. Specifically what prompted you to first affix such caution, warning, caveat, statement or explanation, and what prompted the amendments, (i.e., if medical reports were relied upon, identify such reports).

    f. The name, title and present address of the author of each such warning and/or instructions;

g. Whether the warning and instructions were physically attached to the product itself when sold and/or delivered by you, and if so, the method of attachment;

h. Whether you have a copy-of the warning and/or instructions in your possession at the present time, and if so, where it is located;

i. Whether any studies, evaluations or analyses of any potential hazards of your asbestos product were conducted by you prior to your use of each warning and/or instructions. If so, identify the study by date, author, title and file number and state its present location;

j. The exact date you decided to use the warning, caution and/or instructions;

k. The method used to distribute the warning, caution and/or instructions to persons who are likely to use the product.

Q24. State whether you ever specifically informed the purchaser or user of your asbestos-containing products that the use of those products or exposure to asbestos dust could cause cancer, asbestosis or other serious diseases. If so:

a. State the date(s) you so informed the purchaser or users.

b. Identify and produce the documents containing this information.

Q25. State whether any of your distributors, dealers, contractors and/or customers were provided with any warnings, cautions, caveats or instructions regarding the use of your asbestos-containing products. If so, please state:

a. By whom and when these instructions were first made;

b. Whether the instructions were written or oral; if written, attach a copy; if oral, state the contents thereof;

c. Whether your company carried out follow-up inspections to ascertain whether such instructions were adhered to and if so, please state when, where and by whom such inspections were made and the results of each such inspection;

d. The date the warnings, cautions, caveats or instructions were communicated to the distributors, dealers, contractors and/or customers;

e. The identity of the person who received the instructions;

f. Whether any industrial psychologist or human factor engineers were consulted prior to utilizing such warning, caution and/or instruction and, if so, identify who was consulted;

g. Where the warnings, cautions, and/or instructions were located on the product or packaging.

Q26. State the first time any officers of your Company discussed putting a warning or caution on an asbestos-containing product, and as to that first discussion, state:

a. The names of the persons who were involved in the discussion and the date and place of the discussion;

b. The identity and location of all documents memorializing the discussion;

c. The alleged substance of the discussion;

d. What action, if any, the Company took as a result of the discussion.

Q27. Do you know of any facts or documents to support a claim that you provided any warnings, instructions or information as to the dangers of asbestos inhalation to any insulator, construction worker, building trades worker or other user of your asbestos products in New York State, prior to 1972? If so, for each such alleged warning:

a. Describe in detail each such warning, instruction or information given;

b. State the exact date of each such warning;

c. State whether such warning, instruction or information was oral or written;

d. If oral, identify the substance of the warning, instruction or information given and the date and name of the person to whom given;

e. If written or printed, attach a copy of each warning, instruction and information, identify it by date given, title and reference number and state the matter and location whereby it was transmitted to users of the product.

Q28. Do you claim that you ever recommended to purchasers or users of the asbestos-containing products you manufactured, processed, mined, distributed, or sold, that respirators, protective masks and/or protective safeguards be worn while working with, installing or removing your asbestos-containing product? If so, state separately for each product:

a. The date or dates when each such recommendation was made;

b. Who made the recommendation;

c. When and precisely to whom the recommendations were made;

d. If oral, the manner and substance of the recommendation;

e. If written, identify the document by title, date, file designation and author of each such recommendation and the location and present custodian of each such recommendation.

Q29. Did you at any time recommend that your employees use respirators, protective masks or other precautionary safeguards when working with asbestos-containing materials? If so, state:

a. When and precisely to whom the recommendations were made;

b. Whether you ever supplied respirators and/or face masks to your employees, and if so, the date when first supplied and whether you are supplying them now;

c. From what specific source you have obtained such respirators and face masks (state address of company and dates obtained).

Q30. Have you stopped producing, distributing and/or selling or has asbestos been eliminated from any of the asbestos products listed in Answers 9 or 10? If so, state for each product:

a. The reason and date you stopped producing the product, or eliminated asbestos;

b. The names and titles of each person who recommended and who authorized or directed the action;

c. Whether any studies were conducted before you directed that production and sale of the product be stopped, or asbestos eliminated from the product, and if so, identify each study by date, author, title and subject matter and attach a copy.

Q31. Have any officers or employees of defendant ever discussed or evaluated whether sales of your asbestos products would be damaged if the public learned of the health hazards associated with asbestos exposure? If so, state the dates and names of participants of each such meeting and identify all documents relating to such meetings.

Q32. At the time of the development of, and sale of each of your asbestos products did you attempt to determine whether the product complied with any allegedly applicable safety standards, orders or rules, regulations or design requirements promulgated by any professional society, association, or government body?

a. If you did not, please state the reasons for not conducting such an analysis and identify the name of the person deciding not to conduct the analysis;

b. If you did, identify the safety standards, safety orders, rules, regulations, which you claim you considered by naming the title, number, page and date of the regulation, and identifying the place where a copy of said regulation can be obtained.

Q33. For each asbestos-containing product, identify and produce all promotional and/or advertising material used by you with regard to the sale and/or promotion and distribution of such products.

Q34. Identify and produce pictures and descriptions of each product.

Q35. Were any brochures, writings, or other materials made available to distributors, dealers, contractors, ultimate users, or the general public concerning the design, manufacture, use, quality and/or properties of the asbestos products referred to in Answers 9 and 10. If so, for each such brochure or other material:

a. State the purpose of each brochure and give the name, present address, telephone number of the person responsible for the preparation and acceptance of the material for distribution on behalf of the company;

b. Identify the brochure or material by author, date and present location and custodian, and attach copies of each.

Q36. Have you at any time since 1930 bought from, sold to, delivered or supplied any asbestos products to any other defendant in this action or to any other manufacturer listed in Attachment III. If so:

a. Identify the products involved by name and description;

b. List the dates, quantity and price of each sale and the names of the persons who placed or accepted the order;

c. Were any warnings regarding the health hazards of the product given or received and if so identify the warning by description, date, to whom it was given and by whom received, and if oral state the substance, and if written identify the document and state its present location.

Q37. With respect to any product manufactured by you which does not contain asbestos, have you ever included a warning with the product indicating that it may in some way be harmful to human beings? If so, for each such non-asbestos' containing product state:

a. The name of the product, its intended use or purpose, and the chemical composition or ingredients of the product;

b. The manner in which it is thought that the product may cause harm to human beings;

c. The size, color and contents of each warning;

d. The date warning was first given to the public;

e. The names, addresses and titles of the people responsible for or participating in the decision to provide the warning; and

f. Identify every document which related to the making of the decision to provide a warning.

Q38. Were any of the asbestos-containing products sold by you to private persons or companies (i.e., non-military or non-government sales) the same products you sold to the government pursuant to military or federal specifications? If so, please state:

a. Your name or designation for the product;

b. The military or federal specification you claim is applicable;

c. The person or company to whom sold and the date and amount sold.

Q39. Do you claim that you did anything prior to 1972 to notify users of asbestos-containing products of the possible dangers of inhalation of asbestos dust and fibers? If so, explain in detail what you did, whom you notified, and give the dates.

Q40. Had you at any time prior to 1973 performed, participated in or financed any tests, studies, investigations of analyses to determine the asbestos level produced when your asbestos products were used, installed or removed from a prior installation?

Q41. Had you at any time prior to 1973 performed, participated in or financed any tests, studies, investigations of analyses to determine the effects of your product on workers using or working with any of your asbestos products?

Q42. Had you, at any time prior to 1973 performed, participated in or financed any tests, studies, investigations or analyses which had the purpose to prevent, minimize or eliminate inhalation or ingestion or both of asbestos dust or fibers by those using or exposed to your asbestos products?

Q43. Had you at any time prior to 1973 performed, funded or participated in any investigation, study, test or analysis concerning asbestos-related diseases, asbestosis, pulmonary diseases or cancer?

Q44. Had you, at any time prior to 1973 performed, participated in or financed any tests, studies, investigations or analyses to determine the effects of inhalation of asbestos dust or fibers on anyone using or being exposed to asbestos products manufactured by your company?

Q45. Have you ever performed, participated in or financed any studies to determine whether any type of respirator and/or protective mask would either eliminate or reduce asbestos inhalation to safe levels?

Q46. Have you ever undertaken or financed any tests or studies to determine whether any type of ventilator or ventilating system would eliminate or decrease the number of airborne asbestos fibers in confined spaces?

Q47. For each study identified in response to Questions 38–44, state:

a. The subject matter, title, date and names of the persons who conducted and/or authored the study;

b. The reason for the study;

c. The date the study was completed;

d. If the results were disseminated, where and to whom, and if published the name and identity of the publication;

e. The results of each study, and the data and assumptions relied on;

f. If in writing, identify it by date, title, identification number, present location and custodian and attach a copy.

Q48. State whether you took any action as a result of any of the studies listed in answer to interrogatories 38, 39, 40, 41, 42, 43 and 44. If so:

a. Describe the date and, action taken;

b. Identify who authorized or directed the action;

c. Why was the action taken;

d. Identify all documents discussing the study, the action considered and the action taken by date, title, subject, author and present custodian and produce the documents;

e. If you have not taken any action state in detail, why not;

f. If you have not given any consideration to taking such actions, state in detail the reasons why.

Q49. From the year 1920 to date, have you supported by gift, grant, direct cash or property payment any kind of medical research concerning asbestos? If so, state:

a. The date or dates of such support;

b. The dollar amount paid or contributed;

c. The identity of the persons and/or organizations carrying out the research study;

d. The title, name or other identification of each such study;

e. Identify and produce all documents relating to each such study.

Q50. Have you, at any time prior to 1975, conducted, financed, or had conducted for you any asbestos inspection or made any dust count in any facility where your asbestos products were used? whether or not you have conducted such inspections or tests, state whether you ever considered doing so and for each such occasion when such consideration was given, state the date, form and results of each such consideration and:

    a. If the consideration occurred at a meeting, identify all individuals attending the meeting.

    b. Identify and produce any records of such considerations.

Q51. Have you, at any time prior to 1975, conducted, financed, or had conducted for you any asbestos inspection or made any dust count in any of your plants which are or were engaged in the manufacture of asbestos products? If so state the date, place and people involved in each such inspection or test and identify all records.

Q52. Does your company recognize that workers in the following trades were foreseeable users of your asbestos products? If so, when did you come to such a recognition?

    a. Pipe Laggers;

    b. Pipe Fitters;

    c. Welders;

    d. Burners;

    e. Sheet-metal Workers;

    f. Tapers;

    q. Chippers;

    h. Plasterers;

    i. Riggers;

    j. Grinders;

    k. Inspectors;

    l. Shipwrights;

    m. Painters;

    n. Boiler makers;

    o. Insulators;

    p. Custodians;

    q. Planners;

    r. Testers;

    s. Teachers

Q53. Does your company recognize that the types of trades listed in Question 50 would be exposed to asbestos in the course of working on jobs where other trades would be using asbestos products?

Q54. Does your company recognize that it was foreseeable that people working in the same area where your asbestos products were being used or installed would inhale and/or ingest asbestos fibers from your products?

Q55. Does your company recognize that it was foreseeable that tradesmen listed in Question 50 would inhale and/or ingest asbestos fibers from your asbestos products?

Q56. Do you contend that any respirators or other breathing devices would prevent inhalation of the asbestos dust and fibers released from your product? If so, state:

    a. When the respirator was sold;

    b. Give the derailed description of such respirator or other breathing device;

c.   The basis of your claim that it will prevent the inhalation of such dust and fibers;

d.   Identify any relevant tests performed by date, title, author and number.

e.   The first date you reached the conclusion.

Q57.   From the year 1930 to the present, identify:

a.   The name of each physician in your employ and/or the employ of your subdivision or contract unit;

b.   The current and/or last known address for each such individual;

c.   The dates of employment of each such individual;

d.   The job duties and/or responsibilities for each such individual identified;

e.   The duration of each such individual's employment, the office address or duty assignment location held by each such individual, and the dates associated with each such assignment.

Q58.   Have you, at any time since 1930, maintained any office or department dealing with medical research? If so, state:

a.   The name and location of such department; and

b.   The name, address and title of each person who has been in charge of the department.

Q59.   From the year 1930 to the present, state:

a.   The address of each medical library maintained by you or your subdivisions and/or contract units;

b.   When each such library came into existence;

c.   The custodian of each such library facility records, such as individual's dates of employment and last known address or current address.

Q60.   For each facility identified in response to the two preceding interrogatories, state the name or title of each medical journal or periodical subscribed to and the inclusive dates of each such subscription.

Q61.   Other than the medical library facilities referenced in the immediately preceding interrogatories, state the identity of each medical library, from 1930 to date, in which you held a membership, or funded by way of contribution, gift, grant, or any other direct cash or property payments.

Q62.   State the names and addresses of all professional, trade, industrial, safety, hygiene, or health associations and research foundations or organizations you have been a member of since 1930, indicating for each association:

a.   The inclusive dates of your membership;

b.   The names of your employees who attended meetings and the dates and designations of such meetings;

c.   The positions held by any of your employees;

d.   The location of all minutes, digests, reports and documents received or concerning such association.

Q63.   When did you first learn that there were health hazards associated with the use and/or fabrication of asbestos-containing products? State the date, source, nature and extent of such information.

Q64.   Have you knowledge of any deaths or cases of lung disease or lung impairment prior to 1975 among your employees engaged in the manufacture or use of asbestos products which are attributable to, or were alleged to be caused by, the inhalation of asbestos dust or fibers? If so, please give the name and address of each such employee, identify all medical records possessed in relation to the employee, and state whether reports of occupational disease were furnished to any bureau, branch or governmental body of the relevant state; attach copies of the latter.

Q65. If any of your employees or officers have testified at trial or by deposition in any litigation or before any congressional Committee or administrative agency concerning asbestos exposure, pulmonary or asbestos-related diseases or industrial hygiene relating to asbestos use, state:

a. The name, address and title of each person who testified;

b. The date, location and forum of such testimony;

c. Whether the defendant has a copy of such testimony;

d. Whether the defendant will voluntarily produce a copy of such testimony.

Q66. Have you or any employee or agent of yours ever communicated with an agency or department of the United States concerning specifications and/or standards for any asbestos product or thermal insulation product? If so, state separately for each product or set of specifications:

a. Identify each such product and its military or federal specification or standard;

b. The intended purpose or use for the product so specified;

c. The date, time and place of each communication including;

(1) The name of each of your agents or employees who participated in each communication;

(2) The names, titles, and agencies of each individual with whom such communication was had;

(3) The subject of the communication;

(4) Whether any notes, minutes or memoranda in any form were recorded of such communication or of any meetings between you and the agency;

(5) Whether any documents were submitted to the agency;

(6) If (4) or (5) is answered in the affirmative, state the name and location of the custodian of such records.

Q67. Does your company recognize that:

a. Asbestos causes asbestosis;

b. Asbestos exposure leads to an individual contracting asbestosis;

c. There is a correlation between exposure to asbestos and the occurrence of asbestosis;

d. Asbestos causes lung cancer;

e. There is a correlation between asbestos exposure and the occurrence of lung cancer;

f. Asbestos contributes to the development of gastrointestinal cancer;

g. That a portion of inhaled asbestos fibers remains in the lungs after being inhaled into the human body and is not destroyed;

h. That symptoms of asbestosis and other asbestos- induced lung diseases or cancers may not manifest themselves until many years after the asbestos was inhaled into the body;

i. Prolonged use of asbestos material can cause or contribute to various occupational diseases, including asbestosis, mesothelioma, cancer and other lung and respiratory diseases;

j. The use of asbestos insulating products listed in Answer (10) is dangerous and harmful to human health;

k. There is a connection between the inhalation of asbestos dust and fibers and the disease mesothelioma?

If your answer to any part of this question is "Yes",

(i) State when and how you first learned this knowledge.

(ii) State whether the knowledge was obtained by the attendance at any conference, lecture, convention, or meeting, and, if so, identify such event, the person attending and identify and produce the documents obtained from that meeting.

(iii) State whether the knowledge was obtained from a medical or scientific study or any other published works and, if so, identify the same.

(iv) State whether the knowledge was otherwise obtained and, if so, identify the manner of receipt of the document or communication.

(v) State what, if anything, you have done to notify the public or users of your products.

If your answer is that your products are not harmful, then explain what facts and tests were made upon which you base such conclusion.

Q68.   Have any workers' compensation claims based on asbestosis, mesothelioma, lung cancer, other cancers, asbestos induced diseases, or lung diseases been filed against you? If so, for each claim state:

a.   The date, place filed, reference numbers and outcome of each claim;

b.   Whether you advised your workers' compensation carrier of the claims;

c.   The location and custodian of all records of claims and correspondence with your compensation carrier.

Q69.   Have you as part of your business ever employed any steam plant operators, boiler repair workers, insulators or had a division or unit which installed insulation materials on a contract by contract basis (e.g., a "contract unit")? If so, state:

a.   The location where such persons or unit was based;

b.   The names of the operators or managers of the contract units;

c.   Whether there existed rules, regulations and/or work practices which were to be followed by such employees;

d.   Were such employees ever required to wear respirators? If so, state:

(1) Whether the requirement was by written regulation or oral direction;

(2) The names of the people in your firm originating such a requirement and/or in charge of enforcing it;

(3) The date the requirement was imposed for the first time.

e.   Have such former employees ever filed workers' compensation claims due to lung or coronary illness?

If so, for each such claim, state the date, jurisdiction and docket number and outcome of the claims.

Q70.   State the total number of employees of yours or your contract unit receiving benefits under any Occupation Disease or Workers' Compensation statute for asbestosis, mesothelioma, bronchogenic carcinoma and/or cancer of the stomach, colon or rectum for each year, from the date that you first manufactured, distributed or sold any asbestos-containing products until the present time.

Q71.   State by year the total dollar amount, paid out by you, your contract unit and/or your insurance carrier as a result of claims under any Occupational Disease or Workers' Compensation statute for asbestosis, mesothelioma, bronchogenic carcinoma and/or cancer of the stomach, colon or rectum.

Q72.   Identify any action, other than workers' compensation claims, brought against you by claimants injured as a result of exposure to asbestos and asbestos-containing products prior to 1970, stating the court in which the action was brought, the date of filing, case style, and case number.

Q73.   For each calendar year for the period 1928 to the present, state:

a.   The total pound volume of asbestos mined by your company;

b.   The total pound volume of asbestos purchased by your company;

c. The total pound volume of asbestos used by your company in its manufacturing processes;

d. The total pound volume of asbestos sold by your company;

e. The total pound volume of asbestos acquired by your company in any manner other than mining or purchase, and identify the manner of acquisition for each year.

f. The total dollar value of asbestos mined by your company;

g. The total dollar value of asbestos purchased by your company;

h. The total dollar value of asbestos used by your company in its manufacturing process;

i. The total dollar value of asbestos sold by your company;

j. The total dollar value of all asbestos products sold by you;

k. The total number of pounds or linear feet of each asbestos product sold by you and the dollar value of such sales;

l. The percentage of sales by dollar value and by linear foot and weight of your asbestos to all asbestos sold in the United States;

m. The percentage of sales by dollar value and by linear foot and weight of your asbestos to all asbestos-containing materials sold in the United States.

Q74. Did you in any way assist or participate in:

a. The Metropolitan Life Insurance Company studies of asbestos conducted from 1929–1950;

b. The Trudeau Foundation Saranac Lake studies from 1929–1960;

c. The Quebec Asbestos Mining Association study of asbestos and Health between 1940 and 1970?

If so, state what role or action you took and identify all documents relevant to such activities by name, date, title, file number and present location.

Q75. Has your firm ever been cited or admonished by any government agency (federal, state or local) for dust levels in excess of any threshold limit value (TLV) or other predetermined number? If so, please state:

a. The date(s) of citation and/or admonishment and the dust and TLV or number involved, and the government agency which cited or admonished you.

b. The means of identifying any document related to such an occurrence;

c. Any action taken by you and/or the agency involved.

Q76. State whether from 1930 to date you promulgated any rules, written or oral for the handling of asbestos or asbestos products by your own employees. If so, state

a. When such rules were promulgated;

b. The substance of the rules, if oral, and the name, address and title of the person who disseminated them;

c. If in writing, either attach a copy of the rules or identify the written rules by date, title, identification number, present location and the name and address of the custodian thereof;

d. Whether any such material was provided to any users of your asbestos products and, if so, when and to whom.

Q77. Have any of your employees been reassigned to other duties because of pulmonary or coronary health problems?

If so, please state for each such reassignment:

a. The date and reason for reassignment;

b. The jobs prior to and after reassignment;

    c. The age and health problem of the person reassigned.

Q78. Prior to 1972, were your employees ever subject to periodic medical examinations? If so, please identify any medical examination programs offered or sponsored by you or your insurance carrier for employees handling or otherwise exposed to asbestos and asbestos-containing products. With respect to each such program, state:

    a. The manner of communication with employees about such program;

    b. Whether the examination was mandatory or optional.

    c. What percentage of workers permitted to undergo such examination actually participated;

    d. What percentage of workers were found to have asbestosis or mesothelioma or bronchogenic carcinoma.

Q79. If, prior to 1972, your employees were ever subject to periodic medical examination, please state:

    a. Whether the examinations were performed by your firm, its agents or employees or by outside personnel either private or governmental; if by outside personnel, identify the individual, firm or agency;

    b. Whether the examinations were performed as a result of an internal corporate decision or to comply with some governmental rule;

    c. Whether any person was rejected for employment as a result of such examination. If so, state the date and reason for such rejection;

    d. Whether any employee was reassigned, terminated or pensioned as the result of such examination and the date and reason for each such occurrence.

Q80. Have you ever removed or had removed any asbestos insulation or other asbestos-containing material from any building, plant or facility which you owned, operated, leased or maintained? If so identify the building, plant or facility; state the date the asbestos material was removed and who removed the asbestos, and identify all documents relating to or referring to the removal.

Q81. Was the monitoring of dust levels required by any government regulation or rule or any government, agency, or insurance company? If so, state the substance of the rule, the source imposing it and the date it was first imposed.

Q82. Do you agree that the possibility of exposure to asbestos dust and fibers extends not only to workers actually handling the asbestos products but also to:

    a. Other workers in the area where the asbestos products are being used;

    b. Members of the families of workers.

If your answer to either subpart is "yes", state what your knowledge is and:

    (i) State when and how you first learned this knowledge.

    (ii) State whether the knowledge was obtained by the attendance at any conference, lecture, convention, or meeting, and if so, identify such event, person attending and identify and produce the documents obtained from that meeting.

    (iii) State whether the knowledge was obtained from a medical or scientific study of any other published works and, if so, identify the same.

    (iv) State whether the knowledge was otherwise obtained and, if so, identify the manner of receipt of the document or communication.

Q83. Does your company have a record or document "retention" policy, plan or program? If so, please describe such plan. If the plan is different for separate categories of records, please describe the plan for each-category. Please include in the descriptions the following:

    a. The name and title of the custodian of the records;

    b. The length of time for which records are retained;

c. The titles and names of the personnel responsible for the removal and destruction of any records, pursuant to any such plans from 1935 to the present.

d. The titles and names of the personnel responsible for determining the policy or plan from 1935 to the present.

Q84. Have you destroyed any documents, records or writings pertaining to:

a. Health hazards of asbestos;

b. Workmen's Compensation claims, arising out of asbestosis, lung cancer, mesothelioma, cor pulmonale, pneumoconiosis, or pulmonary fibrosis;

c. Placing warning labels on your products;

d. Hazardous conditions in your plants or factories;

e. Funding of studies about health hazards of asbestos;

f. Lawsuits arising out of injuries alleged to have been caused by asbestos.

g. Sales of asbestos products; and/or

h. Purchases of raw asbestos.

Q85. Have you ever had a division or subsidiary engaged in the business of abating, removing or encapsulating asbestos materials? If so, state:

a. The name of the unit and the names of all personnel involved;

b. The location where such persons or units were based;

c. The dates such persons or units functioned;

d. The sites where such abatement, repair, encapsulation or removal occurred.

Q86. Identify and produce all Minutes of each meeting of the Board of Directors or of any committee of the Board at which meeting the hazards of asbestos exposure, and/or the possible application of warning labels on asbestos-containing products were discussed.

Q87. If there is any person whom the defendant expects to call as an expert witness at trial, please provide a copy of the witness' curriculum vitae, or summary of the witness' qualifications if there is no vitae, and please state for each such expert witness:

a. The person's identity, giving name, profession or occupation and address;

b. The subject matter on which each such expert is to testify;

c. The substance of all facts and opinions regarding which each such expert is to testify;

d. A summary of the grounds for each opinion of each such expert;

e. Whether the facts and opinions listed in (c) above are contained in a written report, memorandum or transcript and if they are, produce the same pursuant to the Request for Production of Documents attached hereto;

f. If the opinion of any expert listed above is based in whole or in part on any code or regulation, governmental or otherwise, identify said code or regulation and specifically set forth the section relied upon;

g. Whether each such expert intends to base his or her testimony on any book, treatise article, study, or any other document, and, if so, identify all such documents; and

h. Whether the witness has testified at trial or by deposition in other asbestos-related personal injury or wrongful death cases, and if so, state for each such case:

(1) the name and docket number;

(2) the court in which each such case was pending; and

(3) the party for whom the witness testified.

Q88. Identify the name and address of each non-expert witness whom you intend to call at trial, and specifically set forth the nature and substance of the matters to which each such person will testify and summarize the facts to which such person will testify.

Q89. Identify and produce each exhibit that you intend to rely upon at trial.

Q90. Identify all persons, other than your attorneys, who provided you with any information used in answering these interrogatories, and state the particular information each person supplied.

Q91. At any time prior to 1972, did you learn of any recommended levels of asbestos proposed by The American Conference of Governmental and, Industrial Hygienists (ACGIH)? If so, state

a. The exact date you first learned of any ACGIH recommended levels;

b. How did you first learn of it?

c. Which of your employees or agents first learned of it;

d. The steps or action you took to advise your sales personnel of the recommendation;

e. The steps or action you took to advise your customers, dealers, distributors and contractors of the ACGIH recommendation;

f. Any comment you filed or submitted to ACGIH;

g. Identify all documents related to ACGIH.

Q92. Do you contend that there is a minimum safe threshold level of exposure to asbestos below which there is no risk in developing mesothelioma or lung cancer? If so, specify the minimum safe threshold level of exposure for each disease, the date you claim the threshold was arrived at, and the precise basis for your contention.

Q93. Do you contend that there is any difference between chrysotile fiber, amosite fiber, crocidolite fiber, and/or tremolite fiber in the development of (a) mesothelioma; and (b) lung cancer? If so, explain in detail your contention as to the distinction between or among fiber types in the development of each disease and the medical authority you rely on.

Q94. Identify all divisions, subsidiaries or affiliated companies of the defendant and all prior names or predecessors of the defendant and:

a. State the current address and state of incorporation of each entity.

b. State whether each entity is an active business.

c. For each such entity and the defendant state whether they did or presently do engage in any phase of:

(i) The mining of asbestos material;

(ii) The processing and/or refining of asbestos material;

(iii) The manufacture and/or design of asbestos products; and/or

(iv) The sale, supply and/or distribution of asbestos products.

d. State the period of time during which each entity and the defendant was in existence and identify the nature and extent of each entity's and the defendant's function during the period of time it was in existence.

Q95. State for any asbestos-containing insulation product manufactured or distributed by you whether:

a. The cement changed colors when water was applied;

b. Describe the appearance of said cement after it was properly applied; that is, whether it was rough or smooth, its consistency and color.

Q96. State whether any pipe covering, block, or insulating cloth has any distinctive markings, design, or weaving, and describe same in detail.

Q97. State when you first became aware that warnings or instructions, if any, were placed on the asbestos-containing products distributed by the co-defendants or other companies and identify and produce all documents relating thereto.

Q98.   Identify and produce any and all labeling or re-labeling agreements in existence since 1925 between you and any other person, including the co-defendants.

Q99.   State whether you ever imposed or considered any restriction or limitation on the intended use, frequency of use and/or likely use of the asbestos products referred to in Attachment I.   If so, state separately for each product:

a.   The verbatim content of each restriction or limitation, indicating to which product the restriction or limitation is applied.

b.   Whether the restriction or limitation was imposed and, if so, the date it was first imposed and the reason for imposing the restriction or limitation.

c.   The identify of each document, by date, author, title and location, which sets forth the reason for the restriction or limitation.

d.   The person responsible for imposing the restriction or limitation.

e.   How the limitation or restriction was communicated to purchasers of the product, and, if in writing, identify and produce the communication.

f.   Whether the restriction or limitation was simply considered and not imposed and, if so, the reason why it was not imposed.

Q100.   State whether you had, as part of your processing, distribution and sales of asbestos materials and products, a system of quality control inspections or safety inspections.   If so:

a.   State when the system was initiated.

b.   Identify who was responsible for initiating and overseeing the system.

c.   Describe, in detail, the system used.

d.   Identify and produce all documents describing the inspection system.

e.   State whether any asbestos products were rejected during the inspection process and, if so, identify the product and state what the reasons were for any such rejection.

Q101.   State whether, since 1925, the asbestos products listed in your Attachment I were the subject of any type of advertisement, regardless of media, issued on your behalf.   If so, state for each product:

a.   The subject matter of the advertisement;

b.   The media in which the advertisement was placed;

c.   When the advertisement(s) was so placed;

d.   The geographic area(s) the advertisement was used in;

e.   Whether any photographs or diagrams were included in the copy of the advertisement;

f.   Where the advertisement was published; broadcast or made public;

g.   The identity of the advertisement and attach copies of all advertisements; and

h.   Whether anyone, besides you, was involved in the preparation of the copy for the advertisement, and, if so, identify such other person.

Q102.   State whether you are still manufacturing, selling or distributing any asbestos-containing products.   If so, give the brand names of each such product.

Q103.   For each year during the period 1925 to date identify the source or sources from which you obtained raw asbestos fiber.

Q104.   State whether any warnings, cautions, caveats or directions accompanied the raw asbestos fiber referred to in your response to Interrogatory No. 103 and:

a.   Identify the nature and extent of said warnings, cautions, caveats or directions accompanying said fiber.

b. State the date said warnings, cautions, caveats or directions first appeared on the mined asbestos fiber.

c. Identify and produce the warning, cautions, caveats or directions.

Q105. State whether it is your claim that the asbestos products listed in your Attachment I are not harmful. If that is your claim, describe, in detail, the basis of your claim and identify and produce any and all tests of your asbestos products upon which you base your claim.

Q106. State whether you directed to be performed, sponsored, financed or received the results of any studies or tests performed by the Saranac Lake Laboratory or the Trudeau Foundation relating to asbestos exposure and its effect on human life. If so:

a. Identify all documents summarizing findings or results of those studies or tests which you have in your possession or control.

b. Identify all communications; oral or written, between you and Saranac personnel.

c. Identify all documents relating to Saranac studies received, or submitted by you, either directly, through associated or predecessor companies, through other companies, or through any trade associations, organizations or entities.

d. Identify all recommendations or findings of such studies relating to:

(i) adequacy or inadequacy of the threshold limit values; and/or

(ii) the substitution of materials other than asbestos to be used in insulation process.

e. State where the documents and/or communications identified in your response to this Interrogatory are presently maintained.

Q107. For every policy of liability insurance insuring you against losses as a result of claims for bodily injury or death as a result of the use of and/or exposure to your asbestos products from 1935 to the present, state:

a. The name of each insurer;

b. Each policy number;

c. The term of each policy;

d. The amount of the coverage;

e. Whether each policy provides for primary or excess coverage and if excess, the limits;

f. The deductible, if any, for each policy;

g. The basis of coverage for each, e.g., claims made, occurrence;

h. The identity of the person having possession of each policy; and

i. If the policy is involved in litigation concerning coverage of asbestos claims, identify the litigation by style, civil action, index or court number, and by subject matter.

Q108. State whether you ever received any reports or communications from your workers' compensation insurance carrier or products liability insurance carrier with regard to the hazards incidental to the use of and/or exposure to asbestos-containing products. If so:

a. Identify who has possession of such reports.

b. State the location of such reports and describe, in detail, the contents of such reports and/or communications.

c. Identify, for each such report, the respective insurance company; the agents signing such correspondence and state the date of such notice or report.

d. State the date(s) you received the reports or communications.

Q109. State whether any of the co-defendants named in this litigation ever furnished you with any information, including medical information, concerning the connection between asbestos dust exposure and the contracting of pulmonary diseases, including asbestosis and cancer. If so:

a. State what information was furnished and describe in detail, how the information was furnished.

b. Identify who furnished that information and who received that information.

c. State when that information was furnished.

d. Identify and produce all documents relating thereto.

Q110. State whether, at any time since 1930, you and any other person, including any co-defendants in this action, exchanged results of research tests, medical studies or experiments regarding the connection between asbestos exposure and the contracting of pulmonary diseases, including lung cancer and asbestosis. If so:

a. State when this interchange took place.

b. Identify who participated in these interchanges.

c. Describe, in detail, the content of these interchanges or studies.

d. Identify and product all documents relating thereto.

Q111. State whether anyone ever made any recommendations and/or suggestions to you pertaining to the risks and hazards associated with the manufacturing, use of, and/or exposure to products containing asbestos. If so:

a. State when and where such recommendations or suggestions were made.

b. Identify who made such recommendations or suggestions.

c. Identify to whom these recommendations or suggestions were made.

d. Describe, in detail, the substance of the recommendations or suggestions.

e. State what action you took as the result of those recommendations or suggestions.

Q112. Identify all records of your purchase of raw asbestos, including invoices, shipping records, and computer records and:

a. Identify the location of each record.

b. Identify the custodian of each record.

c. State the geographical distribution or areas covered by such records.

d. State the time period covered by each record.

e. State whether an index or summary or each record exists.

f. Describe the format or matter by which the records are organized.

Q113. Identify each index, summary, card catalog, computer listing, outline, or other listing of records stored or retained by you pursuant to any record retention policy or otherwise, and:

a. State the location of each index, summary, card catalog, computer listing, outline or other listing of the records.

b. Identify the custodian of each record.

c. State the time period covered by each index, summary, card catalog, computer listing, outline or other listing of the records.

d. Identify the documents covered by each index, summary, card catalog, computer listing, outline or other listing of the records.

Q114. For each asbestos-containing product that you manufactured, set forth the supplier of the raw asbestos fiber used for that product and:

a. Identify any pertinent trademark that was applicable to the product during any time of its sale.

b.   Identify the label on the packaging of that particular product for each year of its manufacture.

c.   Identify all sales brochures, specification sheets, performance data or other promotional materials, as well as any and all installation materials, data or brochures which would have accompanied or been distributed in connection with the installation, application or use of each of the products listed above.

d.   Describe, in detail, the advertised use of the product.

e.   Identify the individuals having custody of all documents or copies thereof referred to in answer to this Interrogatory, and state where the documents are located.

Q115.   State whether you were and/or are a member of the Industrial Hygiene Foundation, the Asbestos Textile Institute, the Magnesia Insulation Manufacturer's Association and/or the Quebec Asbestos Mining Association. If so, for each such membership:

a.   State the inclusive dates of your membership;

b.   Identify employees, offices and/or agents who attended meetings of the foregoing associations, the dates of attendance, and the designations of such meetings.

c.   Identify and produce copies of all minutes, digests, reports and documents received concerning such association.

Q116.   Identify all persons and/or entities which were employed, retained, consulted, or otherwise engaged by you who functioned as a physician, biological scientist, industrial hygienist, occupational health specialist, industrial hygiene organization, or health organization whose duties related to asbestos or occupational diseases and state:

a.   Their dates of employment;

b.   Their duties and responsibilities;

c.   The location, identifying titles or code, and custodians or all reports or memoranda written by each;

d.   Their professional specialization;

e.   The reason for hiring them; and

f.   The identity of the persons in your firm responsible for hiring such person.

Q117.   Identify every person of whom you are aware who may have information or knowledge which is material to the subject matter of this lawsuit or which may lead to the discovery of information material to the subject matter of this lawsuit.

II.   REQUEST FOR PRODUCTION OF DOCUMENTS

Pursuant to Article 31 of the Civil Practice Law and Rules, the plaintiffs request that each defendant produce for inspection and copying, the documents and things identified below. The documents and things identified herein shall be produced for inspection and copying at such time as the answers to the interrogatories herein are filed.

You are hereby requested to produce the following documents and things:

(1) All documents identified in your answers to these interrogatories.

(2) All records of sales and deliveries of your asbestos-containing products to any company or work site in the City of Rochester or within 200 miles of the City of Rochester.

(3) All computer printouts and analyses of sales and delivery of your asbestos-containing products to any companies or work sites in the State of New York.

(4) All records showing the amount and dollar value of each asbestos-containing product you manufactured and sold.

(5) All documents showing your share of the market, by volume and by dollars of sales, for each asbestos-containing product, for each type of asbestos-containing product (e.g., pipe covering, cement, acoustical material, etc.) and for all asbestos-containing products you sold and manufactured.

(6) All research reports prepared by or for you or which you received concerning the following aspects of any asbestos-containing products you manufactured or sold:

(a) The health hazards of the product;

(b) The amount of asbestos released by the product when used;

(c) The capability of the product to comply with industry standards, state or federal regulations or other limits;

(d) Efforts to reduce or eliminate asbestos from the products;

(e) The aerodynamic nature of the products;

(f) The friability or durability of the product;

(g) The ability of the product to resist deterioration or water damage.

(7) Organizational Charts for the years 1940, 1945, 1950, 1955, 1960, 1965, 1970, 1975 and the present.

(8) All rules, regulations, manuals, standards, procedures and instructions to salesmen and other documents dealing with:

(a) Sales of asbestos-containing products;

(b) Health hazards of asbestos products you were selling; and

(c) Communication with customers re: health hazards of asbestos.

(9) All licensing, sales, dealer, distributor and contractor agreements with any firm located in New York, or any such agreements with any firm outside of New York, which involved the sale of asbestos-containing materials within New York.

(10) Photographs of each of your asbestos-containing products and other packages in which they were shipped.

(11) All documents in your possession relating in any way to meetings, correspondence, statements or other communications to or from any manufacturer or supplier of asbestos, asbestos-containing products and/or asbestos- containing materials or from their agents or representatives or trade associations concerning the health effects of asbestos.

(12) All documents in your possession or which you have ever become aware of, relating in any way to meetings, correspondence or other communications of or from any type of association, labor union, employer or governmental agency or from any of their agents or representatives, regarding the subjects of occupational health and exposure to asbestos-containing products and/or asbestos-containing materials.

(13) All documents prepared by or on behalf of the defendant, prior to this litigation, in any way relating to the documents requested in item Nos. 11 and 12 above, of this request for production.

(14) All documents relating in any way to the exposure or possible exposure to asbestos, asbestos-containing products and/or asbestos-containing materials by workers at:

(a) Shipyards;

(b) Insulating trades;

(c) Boiler trades;

(d) Construction trades;

(e) Plants manufacturing or using asbestos;

(f) Brake lining or friction material;

(g) Seamen

(h) Railroads;

(i) Non-occupational and/or neighborhood exposures.

(15) All documents relating in any way to the health effects of asbestos, asbestos-containing products and/or asbestos-containing materials manufactured, distributed, sold and/or supplied by any person or entity or by any of the named defendants herein.

(16) All documents prepared, reviewed, issued or commented on by you relating in any way to warnings, potential health hazards, instructions, or precautions regarding the use or handling of, or exposure to asbestos, asbestos-containing, products, and/or asbestos-containing materials.

(17) All statements, recorded interviews, films, videotapes, reports, question-naires, forms or other documents made, submitted, compiled, prepared or filled out by, on behalf of, or under the direction of defendant relating in any way to exposure or alleged exposure to asbestos, asbestos-containing products and/or asbestos-containing materials or any other issues relating to these lawsuits, except that information prepared by, for, or at the request of defendant's counsel must be identified (including the date made), but need not be produced without an order by the Court, provided that written or recorded communication between plaintiff and counsel, made after an attorney-client relationship has been established need not be produced or identified.

(18) All documents relating to defendant's first knowledge, notice or awareness about the alleged adverse effects of exposure to asbestos, asbestos-containing products and/or asbestos-containing materials.

(19) All records relating to comments, complaints, suggestions, or proposals made by your employees, by your customers, dealers, distributors or contractors or by yourself regarding the health effects of asbestos exposure.

(20) All written, recorded, filmed, transcribed or videotaped statements of all parties and non-party declarants pertaining to the subject of these lawsuits, except that information prepared by, for, or at the request of plaintiff's counsel must be identified (including the date made), but need not be produced without an order by the Court, provided that written or recorded communication between plaintiff and counsel, made after an attorney-client relationship has been established need not be produced or identified.

(21) All photographs of people working with, using or being exposed to your asbestos-containing materials.

(22) Copies of all reports, correspondence and records which relate to the subject matter of these cases from any expert who is expected to testify at trial, either with respect to issues such as state-of-the-art, standards, threshold limits, government or military specification, industrial hygiene, ship or railroad design or construction, warnings, friability of defendants' products, health hazards involving defendants' products, general medical issues relating to asbestos diseases and their causes or with particular reference to any individual plaintiff's case, or both.

(23) All documents submitted to any federal, state or local government or agency in connection with that body's efforts to establish standards, specifications or levels of ambient or occupational exposure to asbestos or asbestos from your products.

(24) Any asbestos and/or asbestos-containing products of the type manufactured by defendant and which the defendant has in his possession, custody or control.

(25) All boxes, containers or wrappers that defendant used to package or ship its asbestos or asbestos-containing products.

(26) All labels, tags, or warnings which defendant alleges it placed on the boxes, containers or wrappers which contained defendants' asbestos or asbestos-contain-ing products.

(27) Any customer, contractor, dealer or distributor complaint relating to defendant's asbestos products and any incident or accident reports defendant received relating to the health hazards of its asbestos products.

(28) Any written statements obtained by the defendant which relate to facts, circumstances, incidents, injuries or damages which form the basis of the complaint of each plaintiff including but not limited to statements made to any police or law officers, insurance company representatives, state or federal agents, or representative of plaintiff's employers or of other companies.

(29) All records and documents including tax returns, compensation claims, disability claims, social security claims, hospital and medical records, x-rays, pathology material, photographs, statements, reports and other documents relating to the claim of each plaintiff other than documents provided to you by the particular plaintiff's counsel.

(30) All communications with or concerning the American Conference of Government and Industrial Hygienists.

(31) All documents received by you or in your possession relating to or concerning the Quebec Asbestos Mining Association (QAMA).

(32) All documents marked as exhibits in any insurance coverage litigation between you and any liability insurance carrier.

(33) All documents produced by you in the litigation with your liability insurance carrier.

(34) All documents marked as exhibits in any indemnity or liability litigation between you and the U.S. Government.

(35) All documents produced by you in the litigation with the U.S. Government.

(36) Any and all records of this defendant, including all subsidiaries, divisions, and predecessor entities of the defendant, which refer, reflect or relate to the shipment, receipt, transfer, purchase, sale or distribution of any asbestos or asbestos-containing product in the State of New York, including, but not limited to, invoices, bills of lading, freight bills, shipping orders, or other documents of transfer.

(37) A sample of each product catalog ever used by the defendant, including all subsidiaries, divisions, and predecessor entities of the defendant, which contains information about or concerns about asbestos or any asbestos-containing product. This includes by explanation but not by limitation, pamphlets, binders, sales brochures and dealer brochures.

(38) All records which reflect the dissemination by this defendant, including all subsidiaries, divisions, and predecessor entities of the defendant, of the literature referred to in the immediately preceding request, to distributors, consumers, contractors, subcontractors, unions, and other persons and entities to whom dissemination was made.

(39) All bulletins disseminated by this defendant, including all such subsidiaries, divisions, and predecessor entities of the defendant, to consumers, contractors, and unions relating to any advice given concerning the use of asbestos or any asbestos-containing product.

(40) All records, including, but not limited to, all correspondence, agreements, memoranda, minutes, guidelines, and test results, reflecting any study or tests concerning asbestos-related diseases or the effects of the inhalation of asbestos dust in which this defendant, including all subsidiaries, divisions, and predecessor entities of the defendant, has ever participated or ever funded, in whole or in part.

(41) Any and all documents from any insurance carriers for this defendant, including all subsidiaries, divisions, and predecessor entities of the defendant, concerning the safety of workers relative to their involvement or employment with asbestos or asbestos-containing insulation products.

(42) Any and all records necessary to sufficiently reflect the dollar amount spent annually on medical research since 1930 by this defendant, including all subsidiaries, divisions, and predecessor entities of the defendant.

(43) All personnel records necessary to sufficiently reflect the employment since 1930 of all industrial hygienists by this defendant including all subsidiaries, divisions, and predecessor corporations of the defendant.

(44) A bibliography of all material contained in any and all medical libraries of this defendant, including all subsidiaries, divisions, and predecessor corporations of the defendant.

(45) All records necessary to sufficiently reflect the history of warnings and the actual warnings that were placed on asbestos or asbestos-containing products or other documents concerning the health effects of asbestos-containing products.

(46) All handouts and materials relating to any internal seminars conducted by this defendant, including all subsidiaries, divisions, and previous entities of the defendant, wherein the potential health effects of asbestos have been discussed.

(47) All records of this defendant, including all subsidiaries, divisions, and previous entities of the defendant, which reflect the performance of dust respirators in connection with fibrous dust.

(48) Any and all environmental control department manuals or similar documents of this defendant, including all subsidiaries, divisions and previous entities of the defendant.

(49) All records of this defendant, including all subsidiaries, divisions and predecessor entities of the defendant, which set forth the existence and contents of any insurance agreement which the defendant possesses with respect to any insurance business which will satisfy part or all of the judgment which may be entered in the action or to defend or indemnify or reimburse for payments made to satisfy the judgment.

(50) Any and all statements, whether signed or otherwise, of plaintiff or the agents, servants and/or employees of such party, in your possession or control, or in the possession or control of your client's representatives, and if there be no such statements, that you so advise the undersigned.

Dated: _____, New York

_____

ATTY NAME, ETC.

ATTACHMENT I

ASBESTOS PRODUCT INFORMATION SHEET:

(a) A description of the product:

_____

_____

(b) Generic Name: _____

(c) Brand Name: _____

(d) Trademark Name, Number, Registration date, and period of Trademark Use:

_____

(e) Asbestos Content by Percentage: _____

(f) Type of Asbestos: _____

(g) Mineralogical and/or constituent composition by weight of each constituent:

    (i) _____

    (ii) _____

    (iii) _____

    (iv) _____

(h) Inclusive Dates of manufacture, mining, and/or processing:

_____

(i) Inclusive Dates of sale, marketing and/or distribution:

_____

(j) Name of Manufacturer and place of manufacture:

_____
_____

(k) Did you "re-brand" or sell the product to others for resale by them under some other name? If so, for whom and when:

_____
_____

(*l*) Did you purchase the product from another manufacturer? And if so, from whom, when and under what other name was it sold:

_____
_____

(m) The color, size, shape, consistency, composition, physical characteristics and appearances of the product:

_____
_____

(n) The purpose for using asbestos as an ingredient in the product:

_____
_____

(*o*) The number and date of each patent or patent application relating to the product:

_____
_____

(p) A precise description of any logo, symbol, initials or identifying mark used in connection with the product:

_____
_____
_____

(q) The form in which it was sold (e.g., drum, carton, bag, etc.):

_____
_____

(r) A full and precise description of the package in which the product was sold including, but not limited to, type of package (e.g., bag, drum), size, color and writing thereon:

_____
_____
_____

(s) The intended use of the product: _____

_____
_____

(t) The manner of forming, shaping or molding such product to the application surface:

_____

_____

(u) The procedure for applying such product, including the type of surface to which it was meant to be applied:

_____

_____

(v) The type of bonding material, adhesive and/or other material used in the course of applying such product:

_____

_____

_____

(w) The identity and location of all records relating to the development of the product:

_____

_____

(x) The identity and location of all records relating to the product:

_____

_____

_____

(y) The identity of the Custodian of actual containers and photographs of containers of the products:

_____

_____

(z) With regard to each product, state the manner in which each such product can be distinguished from those manufactured by any other company:

_____

_____

_____

_____

(aa) The names and addresses of the people responsible for the development of the product:

_____

_____

_____

(ab) If the product continued to be produced after the deletion of asbestos, the reason why asbestos was deleted and the date the product was first commercially sold without asbestos: _____

_____

_____

(ac) If the product is no longer produced, all reasons why it was discontinued, the brand name of the replacement and the date the replacement was first sold commercially:

_____

_____

_____

(ad) The type of asbestos fiber used in each product: _____

_____

_____

_____

(ae) The temperature ranges for each product: _____

_____

(af) The specific batching requirements for each product and the time period each particular batching requirement was followed and any changes that were made:

_____

_____

_____

_____

(ag) The application for which each product was advertised or sold:

_____

_____

_____

(ah) Whether the product was a cement, pipe covering, cloth or other type of thermal insulation product:

_____

_____

(ai) The method of disbursement and sale of each asbestos- containing product:

_____

_____

_____

(aj) The identity and present location of all records dealing with the testing of the product, including those tests dealing with the use, application, durability and toxicity of the product:

_____

_____

_____

_____

(ak) Did you give any consideration to the possibility of inhalation of asbestos fibers by the users of the product and, if so, describe the factors considered, state the date, location and name of the participants of each meeting where the matter was discussed or considered, and identify all documents relating thereto:

_____

_____

_____

_____

(al) If the product was altered in chemical composition or asbestos type or content since first being marketed, state the date such product was altered, state the nature of the alteration, state the reason for the alteration, identify those individuals having knowledge of the alterations: _____

_____

_____

_____

_____

ATTACHMENT II

WORK SITE/PURCHASER SALES INFORMATION SHEET

Name of the work site or Purchaser: _____

_____

P1. Identify each product sold or delivered by generic and/or brand name and description:

_____

_____

_____

_____

P2. For each product listed state:

    a. The date, invoice and purchase numbers of each sale or delivery;

    b. The quantity and price of each such sale or delivery;

Date	Invoice Number	Number	Quantity	Amount	Price
____	____	____	____	____	$____
____	____	____	____	____	$____
____	____	____	____	____	$____
____	____	____	____	____	$____
____	____	____	____	____	$____
____	____	____	____	____	$____
____	____	____	____	____	$____
____	____	____	____	____	$____

Purchase

    c. The shipping details of each delivery including the names and departments that handled the sale and shipment.

Shipping Details	Employee Name	
____	____	____
____	____	____
____	____	____
____	____	____
____	____	____
____	____	____
____	____	____
____	____	____

Department

P3. Did you provide the purchaser with any product specifications, advertising, instructional material or technical information concerning the products sold? Yes [ ] No [ ] If so, identify the material provided by date, description, present location and custodian. _____

_____
_____
_____
_____

P4. Did you in any way alter the asbestos-containing products between the time they came into your possession and the time they were delivered? Yes [ ] No [ ] If so, state:

    a. The form the asbestos products were in when they first came into your possession

_____
_____

    b. What alteration you made to the asbestos product

_____
_____

    c. The reason for the alteration made by you before you shipped the asbestos product _____

_____
_____
_____

P5. Did you provide any warnings or information as to the dangers of asbestos inhalation when you sold, shipped, delivered or supplied each order of asbestos products to the purchasers? Yes [ ] No [ ] If so, for each shipment:

    a. Describe in detail each such warning, instruction or information given and the date and person to whom the warning was given.

_____
_____
_____

    b. If oral, identify the substance of the warning instruction or information given and the date and name of the person to whom given _____

_____
_____

    c. If written, or printed attach a copy of each warning, instruction and information, identify it by date given, title and reference number and state the manner and location whereby it was transmitted to users of the product

_____
_____
_____

P6. Specify all correspondence (other than the invoice and purchase orders) between you and the purchaser by number, date, subject matter, name and title of sender and state where such documents are presently located and the name of the custodian of such documents

_____
_____

P7. Has any officer, employee, salesman or other representative of your Company ever visited the purchaser? Yes [ ] No [ ] If so, state the date and purpose of the visit and the name and title of your employee and with whom he spoke

_____

_____

_____

P8. Were the products listed in Q9 and/or Q10 manufactured in accordance with company product specifications (whether or not they also were produced in accordance with specifications of any outside organization)? Yes [ ] No [ ] If so, please state the following:

a. The identity or designation of each of the specifications, including its number, title and date _____

_____

_____

b. The present location of the specification _____

_____

_____

c. The names and titles of the persons preparing and approving each specification and any amendments thereto.

_____

_____

_____

P9. Have you ever provided directly to workers or employees of the purchaser a warning concerning the dangers of exposure to asbestos or inhalation of asbestos as a result of the use of or exposure to your asbestos product? Yes [ ] No [ ] If so:

a. State the date of each such direct warning and to whom it was given;

b. Identify the name of your employee who communicated or provided the direct warning;

c. Identify the employee who determined to provide a warning;

d. If the warning was in writing, identify each document containing the warning, and state the content of each warning;

e. If the warning was oral, state the substance of the warning, where given and the names of the employees to whom it was given.

Date	Employee Giving Warning		
____	_____	_____	_____
____	_____	_____	_____
____	_____	Substance of Oral Warning	_____
____	_____	_____	_____
____	Identity of Written Document	_____	_____
Name of	_____	_____	_____
____	_____	_____	_____

_____   _____   _____
_____   _____   _____
_____   _____   _____
_____   _____
_____   _____
_____   _____
_____   _____
_____   _____
_____   _____

P10. Have you ever conducted, financed or made inspection of any dust counts of work areas at the purchaser's facility or at sites where the purchaser's employees worked to determine the level of asbestos dust where your asbestos products were used? Yes [ ] No [ ] If you have:

    a. Identify each inspection report and test, setting forth the date and places done and the details of each test _____

_____

_____

_____

    b. State what action, if any, you took following receipt of the test or inspection results and identify all related documents _____

_____

_____

_____

    c. Whether or not you have conducted such studies, state whether you ever considered doing so and for each such occasion when such consideration was given, state:

    i. The form of the consideration _____

_____

_____

    ii. The date of the consideration _____

_____

_____

    iii. If the consideration occurred at a meeting, the names and present business and home addresses of those attending.

_____

_____

_____

    iv. The location of any records of such considerations

_____

_____

_____

_____

ATTACHMENT III

A.P. GREEN REFRACTORIES CO. INC.

ACANDS, INC.

ARMSTRONG WORLD–INDUSTRIES, INC., successor in interest to Armstrong Cork Company

ASBESTOS CORPORATION, LTD.

ASBESTOSPRAY CORP.

ATLAS TURNER, INC.

CAPASCO LIMITED

CAPE INDUSTRIES PLC.

CAREY CANADA INC., f/k/a CAREY CANADIAN MINES, LTD.

CERTAIN–TEED CORPORATION

CHILDERS PRODUCTS COMPANY, INC.

COLLINS PACKING CO., INC.

COMBUSTION ENGINEERING, INC.

COMMERCIAL CHEMICALS, INC.

CROWN CORK & SEAL COMPANY, INC.

DRESSER INDUSTRIES, INC., individually, and as successor by merger to HARBISON–WALKER

EAGLE–PICHER INDUSTRIES, INC.

EGNEP LIMITED

EMPIRE–ACE INSULATION MFG. CORP.

FIBREBOARD CORPORATION

FLEXITALLIC GASKET CORPORATION

FOSTER WHEELER CORPORATION

GAF CORPORATION, CO., successor by merger to RUBEROID CO., and successor in interest, and alter ego of VERMONT ASBESTOS CORPORATION, VERMONT PRODUCTION COMPANY, and the VERMONT ASBESTOS CORPORATION

GARLOCK, INC.

GENERAL REFRACTORIES COMPANY

GEORGIA–PACIFIC CORPORATION

GOULDS PUMPS

H.K. PORTER COMPANY, INC.

HEDMAN RESOURCES, LTD. f/k/a HEDMAN MINES, LTD.

J.H. FRANCE REFRACTORIES CO., INC.

J.W. ROBERTS, LTD.

JOHN CRANE–HOUDAILLE, INC.

KAISER REFRACTORIES

KEENE CORPORATION, successor in interest to MUNDET CORK CORPORATION; BALDWIN–EHRET–HILL, INC.; and EHRET MAGNESIA MANUFACTURING COMPANY

MANVILLE CORPORATION

MEYERS CHEMICALS INC.

NATIONAL GYPSUM COMPANY

NICOLET, INC.

NORTH AMERICAN ASBESTOS CORPORATION

NORTH AMERICAN REFRACTORIES COMPANY

OWENS–CORNING FIBERGLASS CORPORATION

OWENS–ILLINOIS, INC.

PITTSBURGH CORNING CORPORATION, individually and as successor in interest to UNARCO INDUSTRIES, INC.

QUIGLEY CO., INC.

RAYMARK INDUSTRIES, INC., successor in interest to RAYBESTOS–MAN-HATTAN, INC.

ROCK WOOL MANUFACTURING CO.

SOUTHERN TEXTILE CORP.

SPECIAL MATERIALS, INC., a/k/a SPECIAL ASBESTOS CO., INC. SPRAY-DON CORPORATION

THE ANCHOR PACKING COMPANY

THE BABCOCK & WILCOX COMPANY

The CELOTEX CORPORATION, individually and as successor in interest to PHILIP CAREY MANUFACTURING CO., PHILIP CAREY CORPORATION, BRIGGS MANUFACTURING CO., SMITH & KANZLER CORPORATION and PANACON CORPORATION

THE FLINTKOTE COMPANY

TURNER & NEWALL, PLC., individually and as successor to KEASBEY-MATTISON CORPORATION

UNION CARBIDE CORPORATION

UNITED STATES GYPSUM COMPANY

UNITED STATES MINERAL PRODUCTS COMPANY

VERMONT ASBESTOS GROUP, INC.

W.R. GRACE & CO.

APPENDIX A

1. The word "document" is used herein in its broadest sense, and includes any original, reproduction or copy of any kind typed, recorded, graphic, printed, written or documentary materials, including without limitation correspondence, memoranda, interoffice communications, notes, diaries, contracts, documents, drawings, plans, specifications, estimates, vouchers, permits, written ordinances, minutes of meetings, invoices, billings, checks, reports, studies, telegrams, notes of telephone conversations, computer tapes and programs and notes of any and all communications and every other means of recording any tangible things, any form of communication or representation, including letters, words, pictures, sounds or symbols or combinations thereof.

2. "Identify" has the following meaning:

(a) When used in reference to a person, it means to state the person's: (1) full name; (2) present business address, or if unavailable, last known business address; (3) present home address, or if unavailable, last known home address; and (4) business or governmental affiliation and job title, or if unavailable, last known business or governmental affiliation and job title;

(b) When used in reference to a document, it means to state the type of document (e.g., letter, memorandum, telegram, chart) or some other means of identifying it, its author and originator., its date or dates, all addresses and recipients, its present location or custodian and any identifying marks, numerals, code words or letters distinguishing it from other like documents, and attach the document as an exhibit or indicate whether you will produce the document as an exhibit or indicate whether you will produce the document without a formal request. If any such document was but is no longer in your possession or subject to your control, state what disposition was made of it.

(c) When used in reference to an oral communication, it means to identify the speaker, each person spoken to and who otherwise heard the communication, the date and place of communication, whether the communication was in person or by telephone, and the substance of such communication with particularity, and to identify each document in which such communication was recorded or described or referred to.

3. "Oral Communication" means any utterance heard by another person, whether in person, by telephone or otherwise.

4. The response to all interrogatories relating to oral communications shall set forth whether or not the oral communication was by telephone or face-to-face, and also the names, present addresses, business positions, and occupations of the parties involved in said communication, and the names and addresses of any other persons present during said communications.

5. The word "representative" shall be liberally construed and shall include all agents, employees, officials, officers, executives, directors, consultants and any others who directly or indirectly represent in any manner the defendants.

6. You are requested to furnish all information in your possession and all information available to you, not merely such information as you know of your own personal knowledge, but also all knowledge that is available to you, your employees, officers and agents, by reason of inquiry including inquiry of their representatives.

7. If you are unable to answer any of the preceding interrogatories completely, answer to the extent possible, and specifically state the reason for your incomplete answer.

8. "Asbestos products" or "asbestos-containing products" are used interchangeably and include any supplies, products, materials, or equipment containing or including asbestos in whole or in mixture with other products or materials.

App. H.   Discovery Scheduling Order

STATE OF NEW YORK
SUPREME COURT SEVENTH JUDICIAL DISTRICT

....

In Re: Seventh Judicial District
        Asbestos Litigation

....

This Document Applies to:

                        Plaintiff(s),

                                              Index No. _____
  -vs-   County _____

                        Defendants.

....

DISCOVERY SCHEDULING ORDER

EVENT	DATE On or Before
1. Plaintiff(s) to respond to defendants' Seventh Judicial District asbestos litigation interrogatories and Notice to Produce; and to submit executed medical and employment authorizations, and to provide Defendants with copies of all medical records, medical reports and employment records in their possession.	_____,
2. Defendants to respond to Plaintiff(s)' Seventh Judicial District Asbestos Litigation interrogatories and Notice for Discovery and Inspection of Documents.	60 days after service _____,
3. Depositions of Plaintiff(s).	_____,
4. Last day for Defendants to file third-party actions.	_____,
5. Plaintiff(s) to make motion for consolidation and/or defendant(s) to make motion for severance.	_____,
6. Plaintiff(s) to serve expert disclosure pursuant to CPLR § 3101 and all pathology and radiology films in Plaintiff(s)' possession to be turned over to defendants	_____,
7. Plaintiff(s) to disclose job site and/or product identification witnesses.	_____,
8. Defendants to serve job site and/or product identification letters.	_____,
9. Plaintiff(s) to file Note of Issue and Certificate of Readiness for Trial, settlement demands and serve trial exhibits, witness lists and deposition designations.	_____,
10. Plaintiff(s) to respond to defendants' requests for product identification.	_____,
11. Plaintiff(s) and Defendants to serve all motions in limine and/or summary judgment motions.	_____,

12.   Defendants to serve expert disclosure pursuant to CPLR § 3101 and serve trial witness and exhibit lists.   _____,

13.   Summary judgment to be argued before the Court.   To be set by Court

14.   Depositions of non-parties, Defendants and third-party Defendants.   Up to jury selection

15.   Seventy (70) copies of the approved Juror Questionnaire to be served on the Commissioner of Jurors by Plaintiff's counsel.   _____,

16.   Jury selection, motion in limine and Trial.   _____,

ORDER signed this __ day of _____,   .

ENTER: _____

                      HON. ANN MARIE TADDEO, J.S.C.

App. I. Juror Questionnaire

STATE OF NEW YORK
SUPREME COURT COUNTY OF MONROE

JOHN DOE,

       Plaintiff,

   vs.

                            Index No. 2011–1234

A.W. CHESTERTON COMPANY, et al.,

       Defendants.

CIVIL VOIR DIRE QUESTIONNAIRE

In order to help the Court and the lawyers, please answer the following questions to the best of your ability. Allowing you, as a potential juror, to express your beliefs and experiences is the best way to make sure that everyone involved in this lawsuit is treated fairly. Many of the questions in the questionnaire will give you the opportunity to express your beliefs and experiences in private. YOUR ANSWERS ARE CONFIDENTIAL AND WILL ONLY BE USED FOR THE PURPOSES OF SELECTING THIS JURY. Questionnaires will be seen only by the attorneys and the Judge and will be destroyed upon completion of the jury selection process. Remember you are under oath. Please write your answer clearly and firmly.

BACKGROUND INFORMATION

Name: _____

Town: _____

Gender (circle) M   F   Age: _____

1. What is your current job status? (Circle all that apply)

    Working full-time   Working Part-time   Unemployed   Full- time student

          Disabled   Homemaker   Retired

2. What is your occupation and who is your employer? [If you are unemployed, retired or not currently working please list your last occupation.]

_____

_____

3. What other jobs have you had?

Job	Employer	Years Employed

4. What is your marital status? (Circle all that apply)

        Single   Divorced   Married   Widowed   Separated
    (Never Married)

5. If you are married or if you have a significant other, what is his/her occupation and who is his/her employer? [If he/she unemployed, retired or not currently working please list his/her last occupation.]

    _____

    _____

6. What other jobs has he/she had?

Job	Employer	Years Employed

7. Have you—or has anyone close to you—ever owned your own business?

                  Yes   No

If Yes, please describe the business and whether you/they still own the business:

    _____

    _____

8. Do you have children/step-children? (Circle one)

                  Yes   No

If yes, what are their ages and occupations (if applicable)?

Son / Daughter (circle)	Age	Occupation/Employer
Son / Daughter		
Son / Daughter		
Son / Daughter		
Son / Daughter		

9. What is the highest level of education you have completed? (Circle one)

      Grade School   High School   Some College

   Technical or Business   College Graduate   Post–Graduate Work
         School

10. If you have education beyond high school, what has been your primary area of study?

_____

_____

11. Have you or anyone close to you ever been a member of a union?

Yes   No

If so, who and which union? _____

_____

12. Have you or an immediate family member ever owned stock in an insurance company?

Yes   No

If so, who and which company? _____

_____

13. Have you or has anyone close to you ever worked at Eastman Kodak Company in Rochester?

Yes   No

If Yes, please who the person was and the type of work they do or did at Kodak?

_____

_____

14. Have you or has anyone close to you ever worked in a construction trade or as a machinist or mechanic or in a large industrial complex similar to Kodak?

Yes   No

If Yes, please who the person was and the type of work they do or did and where?

_____

_____

15. Have you or has anyone close to you suffered any personal traumatic event within the last year (i.e. injury, divorce, family separation, loss of job)?

Yes   No

If Yes, please, please briefly explain the circumstances?

_____

_____

ASBESTOS KNOWLEDGE AND EXPERIENCE

16. Have you or a close family member ever worked around or been exposed to asbestos or any asbestos-containing products?

   Yes   No

17. Do you know anyone who has ever been diagnosed with an asbestos- related disease, including mesothelioma?

   Yes   No

   If yes, please explain who the person is and what disease they were diagnosed with:

   _____

   _____

   _____

18. Have you, or has anyone close to you, ever suffered from difficulty breathing? (Circle all that apply)

   Yes, I have   Yes, someone close has   Yes, both   No

   If Yes, please explain and tell us if any of those conditions are permanent:

   _____

   _____

19. Have you or a close family member ever suffered from any form of cancer?

   Yes   No

   If Yes, please explain who and what form of cancer and whether the treatment was successful:

   _____

   _____

EXPERIENCE WITH AND OPINIONS ABOUT LAWSUITS

20. Have you, or has anyone close to you, ever: (Check all that apply)

	SELF	FAMILY	FRIEND
a) Sued someone for money			
b) Been sued for money			
c) Been in a situation where you could have filed a lawsuit, but chose not to.			

If Yes to any of the above, please describe the situation and how it turned out.

_____

_____

_____

21. Have you ever served on a jury before: (Check all that apply)

    _____ Yes, a grand jury
    _____ Yes, a civil trial
    _____ Yes, a criminal trial
    _____ No, I have been called for jury, but did not serve (SKIP to Q. 23)
    _____ No, I have never been called for jury duty before (SKIP to Q. 23)

If Yes, how long ago did you serve? _____

If Yes, and you served more than once, how many times have you served on a jury? _____

If Yes, did you deliberate to verdict? (Circle one)

Yes   No

If Yes, is there anything about that experience that would make it difficult for you to serve on this case? Please explain below.

_____

_____

_____

22. Do you agree or disagree with the following statement: _Most civil lawsuits (suits seeking money damages) are frivolous._ (Check one)

    _____ Strongly Agree
    _____ Tend to Agree
    _____ Tend to Disagree
    _____ Strongly Disagree
    _____ Neither Agree nor Disagree

Please explain: _____

_____

_____

23. Do you agree or disagree with the following statement: _If a person gets sick from using a product, they should be compensated regardless of whether the manufacturer knew the product could cause illness._ (Check one)

    _____ Strongly Agree
    _____ Tend to Agree
    _____ Tend to Disagree
    _____ Strongly Disagree
    _____ Neither Agree nor Disagree

Please explain: _____

_____

24. Some people just do not believe in civil lawsuits [suing someone or company for money damages]. What do you think about civil lawsuits in general?

_____

_____

_____

_____

25. Sometimes juries are asked to decide if money damages should be awarded for intangible damages like pain and suffering and loss of enjoyment of life. What do you think about the idea of awarding money for these kinds of damages?

_____

_____

_____

_____

PARTIES, ATTORNEYS AND WITNESSES

26. Are you, or is anyone close to you (family member or friend) familiar with, or in any way associated with, the following people or companies involved in this lawsuit: (Check all that apply)

	SELF	FAMILY	FRIEND
John Doe			

27. If Yes to any of the above, please describe the association.

_____

_____

28. Do you know any of the potential witnesses? (If yes, please check beside the name.)

                    _____

                    _____

                    _____

                    _____

                    _____

                    _____

Please explain how you know the person that you checked in question 28, above:

_____

_____

29. Do you know any of the attorneys or law firms involved in this case? (If yes, please check beside the name.)

   _____

   _____

   _____

If Yes, please explain how you know of one of the attorneys or law firms shown above:

_____

_____

HARDSHIPS

30. This trial could last until approximately XXX, 2011. Will you be able to serve for that period? (Circle one)

                    Yes   No

If you answered No, please explain why not: _____

_____

31. Is there anything else you would like to let us know about your ability to serve on the jury in this case? If so, please explain below:

_____

_____

32. Do you have any medical or physical condition that would make it difficult to serve on this jury? If so, please explain below:

_____

_____

33. Do you have any questions for the attorneys or the Court?

_____

_____

_____

Thank you very much for your time answering these questions. It will save time when you arrive for jury selection.

You may NOT use any internet services, such as Google, Facebook, Twitter or any others to conduct any independent research on any topic discussed in this questionnaire, which includes the law, information about any of the issues in contention, the parties, the lawyers or the court; nor may you discuss these matters with others unless ordered by the Court to do so. Please be careful to remember these rules whenever you use a computer or other personal electronic device during the time you are serving as a juror but you are not in the courtroom.

MONROE COUNTY
FORMS

Form UCS–840. Request for Judicial Intervention

REQUEST FOR JUDICIAL INTERVENTION

UCS–840 (3/2011)

For Court Clerk Use Only:
IAS Entry Date

Supreme_____ **COURT, COUNTY OF** _____

Judge Assigned

Index No: _____ **Date Index Issued:** _____

CAPTION: Enter the complete case caption. Do not use et al or et
ano. If more space is required, attach a caption rider sheet.

RJI Date

Plaintiff(s)/Petitioner(s)

-against-

Defendant(s)/Respondent(s)

NATURE OF ACTION OR PROCEEDING: Check ONE box only and specify where indicated.

MATRIMONIAL

○ Contested

○ Uncontested
 NOTE: For all Matrimonial actions where the
 parties have children under the age of 18, complete
 and attach the **MATRIMONIAL RJI Addendum.**

TORTS

○ Asbestos
○ Breast Implant

○ Environmental: _____
   (specify)

○ Medical, Dental, or Podiatric Malpractice
○ Motor Vehicle
○ Products Liability: _____
   (specify)
○ Other Negligence: _____
   (specify)
○ Other Professional Malpractice: _____
    (specify)

○ Other Tort: _____
   (specify)

OTHER MATTERS

○ Certificate of Incorporation/Dissolution [see **NOTE**
 under Commercial]
○ Emergency Medical Treatment
○ Habeas Corpus
○ Local Court Appeal
○ Mechanic's Lien
○ Name Change
○ Pistol Permit Revocation Hearing
○ Sale or Finance of Religious/ Not–for–Profit
 Property
○ Other: _____
   (specify)

COMMERCIAL

○ Business Entity (including corporations, partnerships, LLCs,
 etc.)
○ Contract
○ Insurance (where insurer is a party, except arbitration)
○ UCC (including sales, negotiable instruments)
○ Other Commercial: _____
   (specify)

NOTE: For Commercial Division assignment requests, complete and attach the **COMMERCIAL DIV RJI Addendum.**

REAL PROPERTY: How many properties does the application include? _____

○ Condemnation
○ Foreclosure
Property Address: _____
   Street Address City State Zip
 NOTE: For Foreclosure actions involving a one- to
 four-family, owner-occupied, residential property, or an
 owner-occupied condominium, complete and attach the
 FORECLOSURE RJI Addendum.
○ Tax Certiorari—Section: _____ Block: _____ Lot: __
○ Other Real Property: _____
    (specify)

SPECIAL PROCEEDINGS

○ CPLR Article 75 (Arbitration) [see **NOTE** under
 Commercial]
○ CPLR Article 78 (Body or Officer)
○ Election Law
○ MHL Article 9.60 (Kendra's Law)
○ MHL Article 10 (Sex Offender Confinement–Initial)
○ MHL Article 10 (Sex Offender Confinement–Review)
○ MHL Article 81 (Guardianship)
○ Other Mental Hygiene: _____
   (specify)

○ Other Special Proceeding: _____
   (specify)

STATUS OF ACTION OR PROCEEDING: Answer YES or NO for EVERY question AND enter additional
information where indicated.

          YES NO

Has a summons and complaint or summons w/notice been filed? ○ ○ If yes, date filed: _____

Is this action/proceeding being filed post–judgment?   ○   ○   If yes, judgment date: _____

NATURE OF JUDICIAL INTERVENTION: Check ONE box only AND enter additional information where indicated.

○ Infant's Compromise
○ Note of Issue and/or Certificate of Readiness
○ Notice of Medical, Dental, or Podiatric Malpractice   Date Issue Joined: _____
○ Notice of Motion   Relief Sought: _____   Return Date: _____
○ Notice of Petition   Relief Sought: _____   Return Date: _____
○ Order to Show Cause   Relief Sought: _____   Return Date: _____
○ Other Ex Parte Application   Relief Sought: _____
○ Poor Person Application
○ Request for Preliminary Conference
○ Residential Mortgage Foreclosure Settlement Conference
○ Writ of Habeas Corpus
○ Other (specify): _____

RELATED CASES: List any related actions.   For Matrimonial actions, include any related criminal and/or Family Court cases. If additional space is required, complete and attach the **RJI Addendum**.   If none, leave blank.

Case Title	Index/Case No.	Court	Judge (if assigned)	Relationship to Instant Case

PARTIES: If additional space is required, complete and attach the **RJI Addendum**.
For parties without an attorney, check "Un–Rep" box AND enter party address, phone number and e-mail address in "Attorneys" space.

Un–Rep	Parties:	Attorneys:		Issue Joined (Y/N):	Insurance Carrier(s):
	List parties in caption order and indicate party role(s) (e.g. defendant; 3rd–party plaintiff).	Provide name, firm name, business address, phone number and e-mail address of all attorneys that have appeared in the case.			
	Last Name	Last Name	First Name	○ YES	
☐	First Name Primary Role:	Firm Name			
	Secondary Role (if any):	Street Address City State Zip		○ NO	
		Phone Fax e-mail			
	Last Name	Last Name	First Name	○ YES	
☐	First Name Primary Role:	Firm Name			
	Secondary Role (if any):	Street Address City State Zip		○ NO	
		Phone Fax e-mail			
	Last Name	Last Name	First Name	○ YES	
☐	First Name Primary Role:	Firm Name			
	Secondary Role (if any):	Street Address City State Zip		○ NO	
		Phone Fax e-mail			
	Last Name	Last Name	First Name	○ YES	
☐	First Name Primary Role:	Firm Name			
	Secondary Role (if any):	Street Address City State Zip		○ NO	
		Phone Fax e-mail			

I AFFIRM UNDER THE PENALTY OF PERJURY THAT, TO MY KNOWLEDGE, OTHER THAN AS NOTED ABOVE, THERE ARE AND HAVE BEEN NO RELATED ACTIONS OR PROCEEDINGS, NOR HAS A REQUEST FOR JUDICIAL INTERVENTION PREVIOUSLY BEEN FILED IN THIS ACTION OR PROCEEDING.

Dated: _____   _____
                                              SIGNATURE

_____   _____
ATTORNEY REGISTRATION NUMBER   PRINT OR TYPE NAME

Request for Judicial Intervention Addendum   UCS–840A (3/ 2011)

Supreme _____ COURT, COUNTY OF _____   Index No: _____

For use when additional space is needed to provide party or related case information.

PARTIES: For parties without an attorney, check " Un–Rep" box AND enter party address, phone number and e-mail address in " Attorneys" space.

Un–Rep	Parties:	Attorneys:				Issue Joined (Y/N):	Insurance Carrier(s):
	List parties in caption order and indicate party role(s) (e.g. defendant; 3rd–party plaintiff).	Provide name, firm name, business address, phone number and e-mail address of all attorneys that have appeared in the case.					
	Last Name	Last Name		First Name		○ YES	
☐	First Name Primary Role:	Firm Name					
	Secondary Role (if any):	Street Address	City	State	Zip	○ NO	
		Phone	Fax	e-mail			
	Last Name	Last Name		First Name		○ YES	
☐	First Name Primary Role:	Firm Name					
	Secondary Role (if any):	Street Address	City	State	Zip	○ NO	
		Phone	Fax	e-mail			
	Last Name	Last Name		First Name		○ YES	
☐	First Name Primary Role:	Firm Name					
	Secondary Role (if any):	Street Address	City	State	Zip	○ NO	
		Phone	Fax	e-mail			
	Last Name	Last Name		First Name		○ YES	
☐	First Name Primary Role:	Firm Name					
	Secondary Role (if any):	Street Address	City	State	Zip	○ NO	
		Phone	Fax	e-mail			
	Last Name	Last Name		First Name		○ YES	
☐	First Name Primary Role:	Firm Name					
	Secondary Role (if any):	Street Address	City	State	Zip	○ NO	
		Phone	Fax	e-mail			
	Last Name	Last Name		First Name		○ YES	
☐	First Name Primary Role:	Firm Name					
	Secondary Role (if any):	Street Address	City	State	Zip	○ NO	
		Phone	Fax	e-mail			

RELATED CASES: List any related actions. For Matrimonial actions, include any related criminal and/or Family Court cases.

Case Title	Index/Case No.	Court	Judge (if assigned)	Relationship to Instant Case

SUPREME COURT OF THE STATE OF NEW YORK

COUNTY OF _____

--x

             Plaintiff(s)/Petitioner(s)

-against-

             Defendant(s)/Respondent(s)

--x

UCS–840C
3/2011

Index No. _____

RJI No. (if any) _____

COMMERCIAL DIVISION
Request for Judicial Intervention Addendum

COMPLETE WHERE APPLICABLE [add additional pages if needed]:
Plaintiff/Petitioner's cause(s) of action [check all that apply]:

☐ Breach of contract or fiduciary duty, fraud, misrepresentation, business tort (e.g. unfair competition), or statutory and/or common law violation where the breach or violation is alleged to arise out of business dealings (e.g. sales of assets or securities; corporate restructuring; partnership, shareholder, joint venture, and other business agreements; trade secrets; restrictive covenants; and employment agreements not including claims that principally involve alleged discriminatory practices)

☐ Transactions governed by the Uniform Commercial Code (exclusive of those concerning individual cooperative or condominium units)

☐ Transactions involving commercial real property, including Yellowstone injunctions and excluding actions for the payment of rent only

☐ Shareholder derivative actions — without consideration of the monetary threshold

☐ Commercial class actions — without consideration of the monetary threshold

☐ Business transactions involving or arising out of dealings with commercial banks and other financial institutions

☐ Internal affairs of business organizations

☐ Malpractice by accountants or actuaries, and legal malpractice arising out of representation in commercial matters

☐ Environmental insurance coverage

☐ Commercial insurance coverage (e.g. directors and officers, errors and omissions, and business interruption coverage)

☐ Dissolution of corporations, partnerships, limited liability companies, limited liability partnerships and joint ventures — without consideration of the monetary threshold

☐ Applications to stay or compel arbitration and affirm or disaffirm arbitration awards and related injunctive relief pursuant to CPLR Article 75 involving any of the foregoing enumerated commercial issues — without consideration of the monetary threshold

Plaintiff/Petitioner's claim for compensatory damages [exclusive of punitive damages, interest, costs and counsel fees claimed]:

    $ _____

Plaintiff/Petitioner's claim for equitable or declaratory relief [brief description]: _____

Defendant/Respondent's counterclaim(s) [brief description, including claim for monetary relief]: _____

I REQUEST THAT THIS CASE BE ASSIGNED TO THE COMMERCIAL DIVISION. I CERTIFY THAT THE CASE MEETS THE JURISDICTIONAL REQUIREMENTS OF THE COMMERCIAL DIVISION SET FORTH IN 22 NYCRR § 202.70(a), (b) AND (c).
Dated: _____

                            SIGNATURE

                            PRINT OR TYPE NAME

UCS–840M
3/2011

MATRIMONIAL Request for Judicial Intervention Addendum

<u>Supreme</u>   COURT, COUNTY OF _____   INDEX NO. _____

For use when there are children under the age of 18 who are subject to the matrimonial action.

Plaintiff

Last Name: _____ First Name: _____ Date of Birth: _____

Prior Names (List any other names used, including   Gender: ☐ Male ☐ Female
maiden and/or former married names):

Last Name: _____ First Name: _____
Last Name: _____ First Name: _____
Last Name: _____ First Name: _____

Present Address: _____ New York _____
     (Street Address)   (City)   (State)   (Zip)

Address History
for past 3 years: _____
     (Street Address)   (City)   (State)   (Zip)

_____
     (Street Address)   (City)   (State)   (Zip)

_____
     (Street Address)   (City)   (State)   (Zip)

Defendant

Last Name: _____ First Name: _____ Date of Birth: _____

Prior Names (List any other names used, including   Gender: ☐ Male ☐ Female
maiden and/or former married names):

Last Name: _____ First Name: _____
Last Name: _____ First Name: _____
Last Name: _____ First Name: _____

Present Address: _____ New York _____
     (Street Address)   (City)   (State)   (Zip)

Address History
for past 3 years: _____
     (Street Address)   (City)   (State)   (Zip)

_____
     (Street Address)   (City)   (State)   (Zip)

_____
     (Street Address)   (City)   (State)   (Zip)

Children

Last Name: _____ First Name: _____ Date of Birth: _____ Gender: ☐ M ☐ F

Last Name: _____ First Name: _____ Date of Birth: _____ Gender: ☐ M ☐ F

Last Name: _____ First Name: _____ Date of Birth: _____ Gender: ☐ M ☐ F

Last Name: _____ First Name: _____ Date of Birth: _____ Gender: ☐ M ☐ F

Last Name: _____ First Name: _____ Date of Birth: _____ Gender: ☐ M ☐ F

EIGHTH JUDICIAL DISTRICT — ALLEGANY, CATTARAUGUS, CHAUTAUQUA, ERIE, GENESEE, NIAGARA, ORLEANS, WYOMING COUNTIES

Westlaw Electronic Research

These rules may be searched electronically on Westlaw® in the NY–RULES database; updates to these rules may be found on Westlaw in NY–RULESUPDATES. For search tips and a summary of database content, consult the Westlaw Scope Screens for each database.

Guideline

    V.   Limits of Confidentiality.
    VI. Scope of Parent Coordinator Role.
    VII. Authority Granted to PC.
    VIII. Court Order.
    IX. Explanation of Role.
    X.   Fees and Costs.
    XI. Domestic Violence Issues.
    XII. Communications and Reports.
    XIII. Outcomes.
    XIV. Regulation.

ERIE COUNTY
E-FILING
PROTOCOL

Doc.

1. Protocols on Courthouse Procedures for Cases Filed on the New York State Electronic Filing System.

FORMS

Form

1. Commercial Division Certification.
2. Certificate Requesting Entry of Judgment.
3. Consent to E–Filing.
4. Request for Judicial Intervention.
5. Special Term Note of Issue.
6. Notice of Filing in E–Filed Case.

Form

7. Certificate Requesting Sealing of Document in E–Filed Case.
8. Notice Regarding Availability of Electronic Filing.
9. Affidavit of Service of Interlocutory Paper — E–Filed Case.

NIAGARA COUNTY
E-FILING
PROTOCOL

Doc.

1. Protocol on Procedures for Electronically Filed Cases

FORMS

Form

1. Certificate Requesting Entry of Judgment in Electronically–Filed Case.
2. Consent to FBEM.
3. Request for Judicial Intervention.
4. Special Term Motion Note of Issue.
5. Notice of Filing in E–Filing Case.
6. Request for Preliminary Conference.
7. Certificate Requesting Sealing of Document in Electronically–Filed Case.
8. Notice Regarding Availability of E–Filing.
9. Affidavit of Service of Interlocutory Paper—E–Filed Case (FBEM).

DISTRICT RULES & POLICIES
JUDGES' RULES

JUSTICE TRACEY A. BANNISTER

Doc. 1. Hon. Tracey A. Bannister

Motions:

Civil & Matrimonial: Alternating Thursdays in Part 31 at 9:30 a.m. Please call for exact dates prior to scheduling motion.

Civil and Matrimonial matters:

All original moving papers, answering papers, memoranda and special term notes of issue to be sent to chambers before 12:00 noon on the Tuesday before the motion return date. If motion papers are not timely served, motion may be adjourned by the court. TROs on notice if other attorney known. No general adjournments.

Adjournments granted with consent of parties, subject to Court's approval.

Conferences:

Civil Actions:

Preliminary conference will be held within forty-five (45) days of the Court's receipt of filed RJI. All conferences before IAS Judge or law clerk. Adjournments granted with consent of all parties, subject to Court's approval. Any IDV matters assigned to this Court will be heard in Part 31.

IAS Matrimonials:

Preliminary conferences will be scheduled upon assignment. Pleadings, discovery demands, 236B Affidavits, motions, responses, prior orders, settlement proposals, proposed stipulations or agreements should be submitted to the Court as far in advance as possible. Adjournments granted with consent of parties, subject to Court's approval, by contacting secretary.

Trials:

Trial dates considered to be "date certain" and adjournments will be granted only in the most exceptional circumstances. All motions in limine shall be made returnable prior to jury selection. Expert disclosure deadlines per court's trial order.

JUSTICE M. WILLIAM BOLLER

Doc. 2.   Hon. M. William Boller

Motions, Hearings, Pleas, Sentencings:

Fridays at 9:30 AM or as otherwise scheduled by the Court.

Cases called by order of readiness of parties. Advise Court Clerk when all parties present.

All moving papers, responding papers, etc. must be delivered to chambers at least 5 days prior to the return date. Please follow the time schedules and procedures set forth in the CPL for Demands, Motions, Responding Papers, etc.

Conferences:

Pre-trial conferences on indicted cases will be scheduled upon assignment of an indictment to the Part.

Adjournments:

Adjournments are granted by the judge, secretary or law clerk only, with notice to opposing counsel. No general adjournments will be granted; all matters must have a return date for further proceedings.

Any attorney who will be late for a scheduled appearance must notify the Court Clerk at 845–9410 prior to the scheduled time of appearance.

JUSTICE RALPH A. BONIELLO, III

Doc. 3.   Hon. Ralph A. Boniello, III

Motions:

Civil Motions and Matrimonial Motions Will Be Heard on Wednesdays at 9:30 A.M. Infant Settlements Will Be Heard at 1:30 P.M. in the Judge's Chambers. Special Term Motions are Called by the Order in Which Attorneys Check In. Kindly Report With the Court Clerk Immediately Upon Arrival. Article 81 Proceedings and Mental Hygiene Hearings Will Be Held on Wednesdays at 2:00 P.M.

Motions, Cross–Motions and Orders to Show Cause Will Not Be Scheduled Until and Unless Chambers Receives a Paid, Stamped Note of Issue Showing the Original Was Filed With the Niagara County Clerk.

Civil:

All moving papers, answering papers, reply affidavits, memoranda and paid Special Term Notes of Issue, are to be received in Chambers by 3:00 p.m. the Wednesday before the return date, notwithstanding CPLR 2214(b), any papers submitted after 3:00 p.m. on Thursday may result in an adjournment, at the Court's discretion. Affirmation of good faith required for discovery motions. Original papers with Affidavits of Service to be supplied to the Court. Oral argument required unless written consent by all attorneys to submit papers is received or the Court directs otherwise. TROs handled on a case-by-case basis. TROs must be on notice to other attorney if known or where a government entity is involved. Orders to Show Cause/TROs on a case assigned to another judge will be signed only upon prior written approval of IAS judge or his/her law clerk. Motions cannot be adjourned generally. The first adjournment can be obtained without Court permission, on consent of all counsel, by informing the court clerk at least twenty-four (24) hours prior to return date.

Matrimonial:

All moving papers, answering papers, reply affidavits, memoranda and paid Special Term Notes of Issue, are to be received in Chambers by 3:00 p.m. the wednesday before the return date, notwithstanding CPLR 2214(b), any papers submitted after 3:00 p.m. on Thursday may result in an adjournment, at the Court's discretion.

However, initial motions in matrimonial actions may be returnable at the preliminary conference, rather than matrimonial special term. In such case, the papers must be received in Chambers at least seventy-two (72) hours prior to the return date. Original papers with Affidavits of Service to be supplied to the Court. Any request for financial relief will not be considered unless a 236(b) Financial Affidavit is attached to the motion. TROs rarely granted if not mutual; if granted a quick return date is required and only where assets are in jeopardy or in extreme circumstances, supported by objective evidence (police or medical report). TROs on notice to other attorney, if known. Orders to Show Cause/TROs on a case assigned to another judge will be signed only upon prior approval of IAS judge or his/her law clerk. Oral argument required unless written consent by all attorneys to submit papers is received or the Court directs otherwise. Motions cannot be adjourned generally. The first adjournment can be obtained without Court permission on consent of all counsel by informing the court clerk at least twenty-four (24) hours prior to return date.

Late Submissions: All motion papers, including cross-motions, answering affidavits, and reply affidavits must be submitted to the Court within the time periods prescribed herein and the CPLR, unless the Court directs otherwise. Failure to comply with the filing deadline will result either an adjournment of the motion or refusal by the Court to consider the untimely submission.

Matrimonial Defaults: On submission only except for Pro Se applications which may require a hearing to be determined by the Court.

Orders:

Must be submitted within thirty (30) days. There must be an indication that the order has been sent to all opposing counsel or pro se litigant and that no objection has been received. Orders will not be signed unless opposing counsel has had an opportunity to review for at least seven (7) days. However, if no objections are received after ten (10) days, the Order will be signed without further delay.

Conferences:

Civil:

Preliminary conferences will be scheduled within 45 days of the filing of the RJI and are mandatory. At the conference, a scheduling order will be issued. Pretrial conferences will be scheduled upon completion of discovery. All conferences before IAS judge or designated Court attorney. Pleadings, including Summons, Complaint, Answer and Bill of Particulars, must be submitted seven (7) days prior to the preliminary conference. Adjournments will be granted only with consent of all attorneys and subject to Court approval.

Matrimonial:

Preliminary conferences are scheduled within 45 days of filing of the RJI and are mandatory. At the conference a scheduling order will be issued. Clients must be present. At least one (1) week prior to the preliminary conference, the Court must receive the following:

Plaintiff's counsel will be asked to produce:

1. A letter stating what issues are resolved and unresolved;
2. A 236b financial affidavit;
3. A copy of the current year W-2;
4. A copy of the signed retainer agreement;
5. A copy of the date-stamped summons;
6. A copy of the affidavit of service.

Defendant's counsel must produce:

1. A letter stating what issues are resolved and unresolved;
2. A 236b financial affidavit;
3. A copy of the current year W-2;
4. A copy of the signed retainer agreement.

Adjournments are granted by consent of the Judge's secretary, but never beyond the 45 day requirement. No adjournments will be granted on the date of the scheduled conference, except for extreme emergency and by consent of the judge.

Trials and References:

Civil:

Adjournments granted by the Judge only. Jury selection begins at 9:30 a.m. on Tuesday with trial to commence at 9:30 a.m. on Thursday. Trials will be down each Wednesday. Pleadings, list of witnesses, proposed jury charge and verdict sheets required one (1) week prior to jury selection. Charge conference by informal discussion with results placed on the record upon request. Any motions regarding the adequacy of expert disclosure are to be made within ten (10) days of receipt of such disclosure. Deadline on expert disclosure at least thirty (30) days prior to commencement of trial, unless otherwise ordered by the Court. Motions in limine must be returnable at least one (1) week prior to jury selection on a regular Special Term date.

Matrimonial:

Adjournment granted by the Judge only. References to law clerk to hear and report on divorces on stipulation for contested economic issues and post-divorce matters. References to JHOs to hear and determine or hear and report on any issue upon consent of both sides. Judgments must specifically recite the terms of custody, visitation, child support and maintenance. Complete transcript and original affidavit of appearance and adoption of oral stipulation must be submitted with judgment. Bifurcation when proof may be complex and it appears that testimony may be lengthy. The parties must file a statement of proposed disposition at least five (5) days prior to the hearing/trial.

Facsimilies: (orders, subpoenas, etc.) will not be signed as originals.

JUSTICE CHRISTOPHER J. BURNS

Doc. 4.   Hon. Christopher J. Burns

Motions:

Thursdays in Part 19 at 9:30 a.m. (Alternate)

25 Delaware Avenue - 3rd Floor

Civil:

All moving papers, answering papers, reply papers and memoranda to be received by chambers by 2 p.m. on the Tuesday preceding the return date. If papers are not timely delivered, motions will be adjourned. Oral argument expected on all cases, unless, 1) the motion is known in advance to be uncontested or 2) a letter requesting the motion be decided on the papers is received by the Court prior to the return date. Discovery motions may be subject to a conference with the Law Clerk prior to argument on the return date. Original papers must be supplied to the Court on an Order to Show Cause, on all other motions copies are acceptable. TRO's on notice to other side, if known. TROs in case assigned to other Judge upon approval of IAS Judge or his/her Law Clerk. Motions cannot be adjourned generally, and should only be adjourned upon good cause after obtaining the consent of Chambers.

Matrimonial:

All moving papers, answering papers, reply papers and memoranda to be sent to chambers by 2 p.m. on the Tuesday preceding the return date. If papers are not timely delivered, motions will be adjourned. Original papers must be supplied to the Court. TRO's on notice to other side, if known. TROs in case assigned to other Judge upon approval of IAS Judge or his/her Law Clerk. Motions cannot be adjourned generally, and should only be adjourned upon good cause after obtaining the consent of Chambers.

Conferences:

Civil:

Preliminary and Pre-trial conferences are automatically scheduled upon court's receipt of RJI or calendar note of issue, otherwise, a preliminary conference may be scheduled upon request. Conference before IAS Judge or Law Clerk. Adjournments granted upon agreement of all parties and after obtaining the consent of Chambers.

Matrimonial:

Preliminary conferences for settlement permitted and encouraged. Pleadings and 236-b affidavits in advance. Adjournments granted upon agreement of all parties and after obtaining the consent of Chambers.

Trial and References:

Civil:

Court adheres strictly to trial schedule. Papers for motion *in limine* required prior to commencement of trial. Conference with IAS Judge upon completion of jury selection. Jury Selection Forms to be submitted at least one (1) month before jury selection date. Formal Requests to Charge and proposed Verdict Sheets required prior to jury selection. Charge conference held prior to summations. Deadline on expert disclosure, without good cause shown, thirty (30) days before the scheduled commencement date of jury selection.

Matrimonial:

References to Law Clerk to hear and report on divorces on stipulation, contested economics, post-divorce arrears and post-divorce modification.

JUSTICE RUSSELL P. BUSCAGLIA

Doc. 5.   Hon. Russell P. Buscaglia

Motions:

Wednesdays at 2:00 p.m.

Cases called by order of appearance of counsel, not by Index Number. Report to Court Clerk.

All moving papers, answering papers, memoranda and special term note of issue to be sent to chambers at least five (5) days prior to the return date. Original papers not required. Discovery motions upon affirmation of good faith. TRO's on notice to opposing attorney. TRO's on cases assigned to other judges, only if prior approval by IAS judge or his or her law clerk. Motions cannot be adjourned generally and can only be adjourned by consent of all parties and with court permission.

Conferences:

Preliminary and pretrial conferences scheduled within 10 days of court's receipt of RJI or calendar note of issue. Conferences before IAS judge or law clerk. Prior to the conferences, each party must forward a letter setting forth their respective positions and any other matter that should be brought to the attention of the court. Adjournments only by consent of all parties and with court permission.

Trials and References:

Adjournments are granted by permission of the judge only. No proof taken on motion days. Pleadings and papers for motions *in limine* required one (1) day prior to beginning of trial. Conference with IAS judge upon completion of jury selection. Formal requests to charge required prior to summations. Charge conference after proof completed.

JUSTICE FRANK CARUSO

Doc. 6.   Hon. Frank Caruso

Motions:

Civil Motions will be heard on Thursdays at 9:30 A.M.

Infant settlements will be heard at 9:15 A.M. in the Judge's Chambers.

Special Term Motions are called by the order in which attorneys check in. Kindly report with the Court Clerk immediately upon arrival.

Motions, Cross–Motions and Orders to Show Cause will not be scheduled until and unless chambers receives a paid, stamped special term note of issue showing the original was filed with the Niagara County Clerk.

Civil:

All moving papers, answering papers, reply affidavits, memoranda and paid Special Term Notes of Issue, are to be received in Chambers by 3:00 p.m. the Friday before the return date, notwithstanding CPLR 2214(b), any papers submitted after 3:00 p.m. on Friday may result in an adjournment, at the Court's discretion. Affirmation of good faith required for discovery motions. Original papers with Affidavits of Service to be supplied to the Court. Oral argument required unless written consent by all attorneys to submit papers is received or the Court directs otherwise. TROs handled on a case-by-case basis. TROs must be on notice to other attorney if known or where a government entity is involved. Orders to Show Cause/TROs on a case assigned to another judge will be signed only upon prior written approval of IAS judge or his/her law clerk. Motions cannot be adjourned generally. The first adjournment can be obtained without Court permission, on consent of all counsel, by informing the court clerk at least twenty-four (24) hours prior to return date.

Late Submissions:

All motion papers, including cross-motions, answering affidavits, and reply affidavits must be submitted to the Court within the time periods prescribed herein and the CPLR, unless the Court directs otherwise. Failure to comply with the filing deadline will result

either in an adjournment of the motion or refusal by the Court to consider the untimely submission.

Orders:

Must be submitted within thirty (30) days with indication that the order has been sent out to all opposing counsel or pro se litigant and that no objection has been received. Orders will not be signed unless opposing counsel has had an opportunity to review for at least seven (7) days. However, if no objections are received after ten (10) days, the Order will be signed without further delay.

Conferences:

Civil:

Preliminary conferences will be scheduled within 45 days of the filing of the RJI and are mandatory. At the conference, a scheduling order may be issued. Pretrial conferences will be scheduled upon completion of discovery. All conferences before IAS judge or designated Court attorney. Pleadings, including Summons, Complaint, Answer and Bill of Particulars, must be submitted seven (7) days prior to the preliminary conference. Adjournments will be granted only with consent of all attorneys and subject to Court approval.

Trials and References:

Civil:

Adjournments granted by the Judge only. Pleadings, list of witnesses, proposed jury charge and verdict sheets and papers on motions *in limine* required one (1) week in advance. Deadline on expert disclosure, without good cause shown, are to be exchanged thirty (30) days before the commencement date of trial. Jury selection begins at 9:30 a.m. on Tuesday. Charge conference with the Judge after proof completed with results put on record upon request.

JUSTICE STEPHEN W. CASS

Doc. 7. Hon. Stephen W. Cass

Motions/OTSC:

Mondays, beginning at 1:30 p.m. in Judge Cass' Courtroom; scheduled at one-half hour intervals with the time scheduled by Chambers. Emergency matters may be heard at other times specifically arranged with Chambers.

Orders to Show Cause must be presented by movant's attorney to one of the Court Attorneys for review prior to scheduling and signature. To schedule a motion date and time, contact Chambers. An original and copy must be submitted to the Court for scheduling and signature. Motions and Orders to Show Cause will not be placed on the Court's calendar unless and until the required motion fee is paid to the County Clerk's Office.

All answering papers and any other moving papers must be received by chambers by Thursday at 5:00 p.m. or a least one day prior to the return date and should include an original and copy.

Requests for TRO's should be on notice to opposing counsel and the Law Guardian, if known, except for rare circumstances.

Motions/OTSC's may not be adjourned without prior Chamber and opposing counsel approval. This can be done by calling chambers and securing a rescheduled date at least 24 hours in advance of the scheduled time. Motions must be adjourned to a specific date and time, and will not be adjourned generally. The party requesting the adjournment must send written confirmation of the adjournment and the rescheduled date to all parties and the Court.

Submission of Proposed Orders/Judgments and Divorce Packets:

1. Proposed orders should be sent directly to Chambers at P.O. Box C, Mayville, New York 14757 for review by one of the Court Attorneys prior to presentation for signature.

2. Proposed orders/judgments must be submitted with indication that the order or judgment has been sent to all opposing counsel, Law Guardian or pro se litigant and no objection has been received. Orders/judgments will not be signed without proof of opportunity of opposing counsel, Law Guardian or pro se litigant to review.

3. Divorce Packets — All divorce packets, whether contested, uncontested and/or affidavit divorce packets should be sent directly to the County Clerk's Office. If the divorce is submitted on affidavit, please note the same in your cover letter.

Matrimonial Cases:

1. *Preliminary Conferences:* 22 NYCRR 202.12(b) requires that a Preliminary Conference be held within 45 days of the filing of the RJI for a matrimonial action. Remember this time frame when requesting adjournments. Financial Affidavits (236B) and Retainer Agreements MUST be submitted to Chambers at least 48 hours prior to the Preliminary Conference.

2. *Pre-Trial Conferences:* Statements of Proposed Disposition must be submitted to the Court at least 48 hours prior to the Pre-Trial Conference.

3. If a case is resolved by stipulation of the parties, the matter WILL NOT be taken off the calendar until the Court receives a signed copy of the stipulation. Since this usually occurs on the eve of trial, stipulations may be faxed directly to chambers at 753–4730.

4. When Judgments of Divorce provide for the full continuation of Family Court orders (custody/visitation or child support), the Judgment must reference the Docket number(s) and Date(s) of Family Court orders, in separate decretal paragraphs and have copies of the orders attached.

5. When an oral default is put on the record, the transcript of the default must be filed in the County Clerk's office with the record; however, DO NOT attach the default transcript to the Judgment of Divorce.

6. When a stipulation of settlement is placed on the record or if the case is settled by written stipulation of the parties, a transcript of the oral stipulation or the written stipulation MUST be attached to the judgment of divorce. Where the case has been settled by oral stipulation, the Affidavit of Appearance and Adoption of Oral Stipulation MUST ALSO be attached to the Judgment.

7. When the court has rendered a written decision or bench decision, the written decision or transcript of the bench decision MUST be attached to the Findings of Fact and Conclusions of Law; and, directives of the Court must be detailed in decretal paragraphs in the Judgment of Divorce.

8. When a divorce is settled by stipulation which is incorporated into the Judgment of Divorce, the decretal paragraphs need not specify the provisions concerning equitable distribution. However, separate decretal paragraphs must specify provisions regarding custody, visitation, child support and maintenance.

9. *CPLR 306–b:* Where service of the Summons with Notice or Summons and Complaint has not been effected within 120 days of filing with the County Clerk's Office, you must obtain the Court's permission to extend the time for service for "good cause shown". This can be done on the papers without the necessity of counsel's appearance, on ex parte notice of motion and payment of the necessary motion filed fee.

10. *UCS–111 Forms:* 202 NYCRR 202.50c requires that judgments submitted to the court shall be accompanied by a completed form.

11. *Effective Date of Child Support and/or Maintenance in Judgments and/or Orders:* Every proposed judgment of divorce or temporary order containing an order of support or maintenance MUST specify the effective date. If the parties entered into an oral stipulation placed on the record in court and the stipulation does not specify the effective date of any child support and/or maintenance orders, the effective date to be inserted in the proposed judgment or order will be the date the stipulation was placed on the record. If the matter is resolved by a written stipulation and there is no date specified in the stipulation, the effective date to be inserted in the proposed judgment or order will be effective the date the stipulation is fully signed by both parties. The best practice would be to specify the effective date in any stipulation, written or oral. If the child support and/or maintenance order is by decision of the Court, the decision will indicate the effective date and this date must be inserted in the proposed judgment. If orders are payable through the Support Enforcement Unit and the effective date is not specified in the Judgment, the Support Enforcement Unit will adhere to the dates specified in this paragraph.

12. *Prior Family Court Orders:* In some judgments, the language continues a prior Family Court order but with changes. This causes confusion in the future to have two orders in effect. In this case, attorneys should either specify that the Family Court order will continue in it's entirety or set forth a new, complete order in the Judgment and specify the effective date of the new order, and terminating the prior family court order.

13. *Direct Pay Orders or Though Support Enforcement Unit:* Any proposed judgment of divorce should state whether child support is by way of direct pay or through the Support Enforcement Unit. If the

order is by direct pay, counsel must file the necessary form with the State Case Registry in Albany, and provide the Court with a copy of the form and letter of filing. If payments are to be made through the Support Enforcement Unit, the proposed judgment must contain a provision directing the filing of a copy of the judgment with the Support Enforcement Unit.

14. *Social Security Numbers:* Every proposed Judgment of Divorce must contain the social security numbers of parties. In addition, pursuant to DRL 240–b, any proposed judgment with an order for child support, must contain the social security numbers of the minor children.

15. DRL Section 177 (health insurance notification) will be enforced. All stipulations after November 1, 2007 must contain a provision and Judgments of Divorce must contain a decretal paragraph in accordance with the statute.

Temporary Orders of Protection:

1. If one form of relief requested in an Order to Show Cause is an order of protection PRIOR to the return date of the Order to Show Cause, counsel should have the client available at the time the Court signs the Order To Show Cause to present testimony on the issue. If the Order to Show Cause seeks an order of protection upon the return date of the Order to Show Cause, counsel should have the client available on the return date to present testimony on the

issue. As a matter of course, mutual orders of protection will not be granted.

2. If there is a pending criminal charge involving the same parties and domestic violence allegations arising in any of the local courts and/or county court the divorce action may be transferred to the IDV Court. Proceedings will continue in the matrimonial court until the case is accepted and transferred.

Statement of New Worth:

1. MUST be in substantial compliance with the Statement of New Worth form contained in appendix A of the uniform rules. 22 NYCRR 202.16(b).

2. MUST complete all categories, marking "NONE", "INAPPLICABLE" or "UNKNOWN" if necessary.

3. MUST attach pay stubs (3 pay periods), W-2 statements or previous year's tax return.

Qualified Domestic Relations Orders:

1. Those QDRO's (or DRO's) submitted with the Judgment of Divorce or within one year after entry do not require a motion. However, they do require either the opposing counsel's approval (or litigant's approval if pro se) or proper notice and default, with proof provided to the Court of same. Those presented greater than one year after entry require a formal motion, on notice, to the opposing party and his/her former attorney, with proof provided to the Court. A motion fee is not required.

JUSTICE DEBORAH A. CHIMES

Doc. 8.   Hon. Deborah A. Chimes

Civil and Matrimonial:

CPLR service applies except reply motion papers are due to the Court by 12:00 p.m. on the Tuesday before special term. No fax submissions are permitted. If motion papers are not timely served, the motion may be adjourned by the Court. Adjournment of motions may be granted on consent of parties, subject to approval by the Court. Only stipulated or initialed Orders, with consent of opposing counsel, should be submitted to the Court for signature. Motions cannot be adjourned generally. Confirmation of an adjournment, with notice of rescheduled dates, must be made in writing to the Court and all parties.

Discovery motions may be subject to a conference with the Law Clerk prior to argument on the return date. Affidavits of good faith are required on all discovery motions.

TROs on notice, if other attorney known. Requests for TROs on cases assigned to another Judge will be considered only upon prior approval of the IAS Judge or his/her Law Clerk.

All other hearings scheduled by calling the Court.

Conferences:

Civil:

A preliminary conference will be held within 45 (forty-five) days of the Court's receipt of a filed RJI. Preliminary conferences will also be scheduled on request. All conferences before the IAS Judge or Law Clerk. Pleadings and a brief summary of the case in letter form are required in advance of the initial conference. Adjournments granted with the consent of all parties, subject to the Court's approval by contacting the Court's Secretary.

Matrimonial:

Preliminary conferences will be scheduled upon assignment. Pleadings, discovery demands, 236B Affidavits, motions, responses, prior Orders, settlement proposals, proposed stipulations and agreements should be submitted to the Court as far in advance as possible. Adjournments granted with consent of parties, subject to the Court's approval, by contacting Court's Secretary.

Trials and References:

Civil:

Trial dates are considered to be "date certain." Adjournments granted by Judge only. Expert disclosure deadlines per the Court's scheduling and/or trial Order. Any motions regarding the adequacy of expert disclosure are to be made within twenty (20) days of service of the expert disclosure. Motions in limine, pleadings, list of witnesses, expert disclosure are required to be filed with the Court one (1) week prior to jury selection. Motions in limine are heard at 9:15 a.m., the morning of jury selection.

Conference with the Judge upon completion of jury selection. Requests to Charge and proposed Verdict Sheets required prior to jury selection. Charge conference held prior to summations, with results placed on the record upon request.

Matrimonial:

References to Law Clerk to hear and report on divorces on stipulation, contested economics, post-divorce arrears and post-divorce modification.

JUSTICE JOHN M. CURRAN

Doc. 9.   Hon. John M. Curran

Special Term:

Alternating Thursdays starting at 9:30 a.m.

Motion papers must be received no later than one (1) week in advance of the return date, together with a special term note of issue. Answering papers and/or cross-motions must be received no later than two (2) days before the return date. Reply papers must be received by no later than noon (12:00 p.m.) on the day before the return date. Motion papers, including cross-motions, must bear the County Clerk's "Paid" stamp pursuant to CPLR § 8020(a). Please do not send motion papers by fax without prior consent of the Court.

Conferences:

Preliminary conferences are scheduled upon receipt of the filed RJI from the County Clerk. At the conference, a scheduling order will be issued. Pre-trial conferences will be set forth in the scheduling order or scheduled upon receipt of a calendar note of issue. Counsel must bring their calendars, including trial availability, to all conferences.

Adjournments:

1.   No same day adjournments permitted except in extraordinary circumstances and upon consent of the Court.

2.   Adjournments of conferences granted only with consent of all attorneys, subject to Court approval.

3.   If counsel cannot agree to an adjournment of a motion, all counsel must appear on the return date to request an adjournment which will be liberally granted in the absence of prejudice.

4.   Motions will not be adjourned generally. The first and second adjournments can be obtained without Court permission, on consent of all counsel, by informing the Court Clerk at least twenty-four (24) hours prior to the return date. Letters confirming the adjournment must be provided to all counsel and the Court.

5.   Consent of all parties required prior to requesting an adjournment of a trial.

Motions:

1.   Oral argument is anticipated but counsel may stipulate to submit on papers.

Appearance on motions by telephone will not be permitted.

2.   Orders are to be approved by all attorneys/parties prior to submission to the Court for signature, with notice to the Court of such approval. Otherwise, they are to be settled pursuant to 22 NYCRR § 202.48.

TRO's:

TRO's on a case-by-case basis. TRO's must be on notice to opposing counsel if known. TRO's for other Justices will be signed only with approval of that Justice or Justice's Law Clerk.

Trials and References:

Trial dates are provided at final pre-trial conferences conducted after the Note of Issue and Statement of Readiness has been filed. Court adheres strictly to its trial schedule and adjournments are discouraged. Marked pleadings, requests to charge, proposed verdict sheets and papers for motions in limine required one (1) week prior to beginning of jury selection or trial.

JUSTICE DIANE Y. DEVLIN

Doc. 10.   Hon. Diane Y. Devlin

Motions:

Every Thursday, Part 32 at 9:30 a.m.

Civil:

All motions, except motions *in limine*, shall be made with a first return date not less than sixty (60) days prior to any trial date. Motions made returnable within sixty (60) days of a trial date shall only be made by Order to Show Cause. Dispositive Motions

(Summary Judgment Motions) shall be made within 60 days from the filing of the Note of Issue. All moving papers, memoranda and a Special Term Note of Issue are to be delivered to the Part 32 Court Clerk not less than noon on the Friday prior to the return date of the motion. Original papers are not required. Answering papers are to be delivered to the Part 32 Court Clerk not later than Tuesday at noon. Oral arguments are required except on permission of judge or law clerk. TRO's, where possible, will require notice to the opposing attorney. TRO's on cases assigned to another Justice will only be granted upon the prior approval of the IAS Justice or his/her Law Clerk. Motions shall not be adjourned generally. Motions can only be adjourned upon consent of all parties and with notice to the Court. Orders based upon a decision of this court shall be submitted to all counsel for approval prior to submission to the court. If the parties are unable to agree to a proposed order, the proposed order and notice of settlement shall be served in accordance with Uniform Rule § 202.48 which provides for ten days mailed notice or five days notice if by personal service and made returnable before the court at 9:30 a.m. in Part 32. Proposed counter-orders shall be made returnable on the same date and time as the original proposed order.

Conferences:

Preliminary and Pre-trial conferences are scheduled upon the court's receipt of an RJI and/or Calendar Note of Issue. A scheduling order will be issued after the Uniform Rule 202.12 preliminary conference. Rule 202.12 preliminary conference may only be adjourned upon consent of all counsel and only to a date within the 45 days from the filing of the RJI. Adjournments of compliance conferences or pre-trials to a day certain will be granted upon consent of all parties. Confirmation of any adjournment together with its rescheduled date must be made in writing to all parties and to the court by counsel seeking the adjournment.

Trials:

Trial dates may only be adjourned by the Court. No testimony is taken on the court's special term day. Stays pending appeals will only be granted upon good cause shown and will generally not be granted. Lists of witnesses, lay and expert, to be called at trial must be filed with the court one month before jury selection. Jury selection form is to be completed and submitted at least one month before jury selection date. Motions *in limine* and requests to charge and proposed verdict sheet shall be submitted to the court at least one week before the jury selection date. Expert Disclosure shall be simultaneous and shall be made by all parties not less than 60 days before the jury selection date.

JUSTICE KEVIN M. DILLON

Doc. 11. Hon. Kevin M. Dillon

Motions:

Every Thursday in Part 3 — 10:00 A.M.

Motions can be made returnable every Thursday at 10:00 A.M. with the exception of Summary Judgment motions which are limited to 3 being scheduled on each Special Term date. The return date for Summary Judgment motions will be scheduled by the secretary once the motion has been filed in the Clerk's office and then received in chambers. Return dates on Summary Judgment motions will be given in the order received with the date stamp at the Clerk's office. Infant settlements, Article 81 matters and hearings are heard at 2:00 P.M. on the 1st and 3rd Thursday of the month.

All moving papers including hard copies of those filed electronically, must be received by the Court Clerk and chambers no later than ten days in advance of the return date, together with a Special Term Note of Issue. All answering papers are to be received by chambers no later than 4:00 P.M. on the Friday immediately preceding the return date, unless earlier service is required by the CPLR. Reply papers are accepted from the moving party up until 4:00 P.M. on the Monday immediately preceding the return date. No service accepted by FAX.

Affidavits of good faith are required for discovery motions. TRO's on a case-by-case basis, on notice to opposing counsel. Motions cannot be adjourned generally and can be adjourned by contacting the secretary or court clerk. Consent of opposing counsel is necessary for all adjournments unless court directs otherwise. Orders are to be initialed by both attorneys prior to submission to the court.

Conferences:

Preliminary conference scheduled upon court receipt of RJI. Pre-trial conferences scheduled upon court's receipt of calendar Note of Issue. All conferences before IAS Judge or Law Clerk. Adjournments granted with consent of parties, subject to court approval by speaking directly to the secretary or law clerk in Justice Dillon's chambers.

Trials and References:

Adjournments generally by Judge only. Any motions regarding the adequacy of expert disclosure are to be made within 10 days of receipt of such disclosure. Pleadings, expert disclosure, list of witnesses, and papers for motions in limine required one (1) week prior to jury selection. Motions in limine will be given a return date by calling the Judge's secretary.

Trials will be down every Thursday.

Requests to charge and proposed verdict sheets are to be submitted at least 1 day prior to the close of proof. Charge conference by informal discussion with results placed on the record upon request.

JUSTICE TIMOTHY J. DRURY

Doc. 12. Hon. Timothy J. Drury

Motions:

Motions heard daily at 10:00 A.M. or 2:00 P.M. Please check with Court personnel for exact dates.

Motion practice pursuant to CPLR and original papers (including affidavits of service) to be provided to the Court simultaneously. All papers must be received by the Court at least two (2) business days before the return date. Late submissions may result in an adjournment at the Court's discretion or refusal by the Court to consider the untimely submission.

Adjournments will be granted upon consent of opposing counsel. The Court may also grant an adjournment without consent if good cause is shown. This is especially true if the papers were hand delivered to opposing counsel before a weekend or before a holiday and for summary judgment motions. Counsel should keep in mind the rules of civility. Motions must be adjourned to a specific date; general adjournments will not be permitted. Requests for adjournment of motions where opposing counsel does not consent should be made by conference call to the Court.

Motions to resolve discovery disputes shall be accompanied by an affidavit of good faith attempt at resolution. Summary judgment motions must be timely made pursuant to CPLR 3212(a).

All orders must be submitted with an indication that the order has been sent to all opposing counsel or pro se litigant. Orders will not be signed without proof of opportunity of opposing counsel or pro se party to review.

All requests for TROs must comply with Uniform Rules for Trial Courts § 202.7(f). Requests for TROs on cases assigned to another judge will be considered only upon approval of the IAS judge or his/her law clerk.

Conferences:

Civil:

Pretrial conferences will be scheduled upon the Court's receipt of an RJI and/or calendar Note of Issue. Pleadings and a brief summary of the case in letter form are required in advance of the conference. Any request for an adjournment shall be made to the Judge's secretary and confirmation of all adjournments and notice of rescheduled dates must be made in writing to all parties and the Court.

Trials and References:

Adjournments are granted by permission of the Judge only. Deadlines on expert disclosure shall be set by the Judge on a case by case basis. Pleadings and list of witnesses (both expert and lay) should be sent to the Court one (1) week in advance of jury selection. Motions in limine shall be submitted prior to jury selection and heard thereafter as scheduled by the Court. Proposed requests to charge and verdict sheets shall be submitted on the first day of proof. The Court's preference is to receive these by e-mail with the requests attached. They may be supplemented upon the conclusion of proof. A charge conference by informal discussion shall be held at or near the close of proof with results put on the record upon request.

Pre-trial memoranda for matrimonial and other non-jury trials are to be served and submitted to the Court two (2) weeks before the first day of trial.

JUSTICE PAULA L. FEROLETO

Doc. 13. Hon. Paula L. Feroleto

Motions:

Most Wednesdays at 9:00 a.m. but, check with Court Clerk for exact dates.

Motion practice pursuant to CPLR and original papers (including affidavits of service) to be provided to the Court simultaneously. All papers must be received by the Court at least two (2) business days before the return date. Late submissions may result in an adjournment at the Court's discretion or refusal by the Court to consider the untimely submission.

Adjournments are granted upon consent of opposing counsel, but if counsel refuses, the Court has a liberal adjournment policy of motions made within the minimum time limits of the CPLR and will grant an adjournment upon request even if opposed. This is especially true if the papers were hand delivered to opposing counsel before a weekend or before a holiday and for summary judgment motions. Counsel should keep in mind the rules of civility. Motions must be adjourned to a specific date; general adjournments will not be permitted. Requests for adjournment of motions where opposing counsel does not consent should be made by conference call to the Court.

Motions to resolve discovery disputes shall be accompanied by an affidavit of good faith attempt at resolution. Letters between counsel are insufficient.

There must have been a conversation between counsel to attempt to resolve discovery disputes. Summary judgment motions must be timely made pursuant to CPLR 3212(a).

All orders must be submitted with an indication that the order has been sent to all opposing counsel or pro se litigant. Orders will not be signed without proof of opportunity of opposing counsel or pro se party to review.

All requests for TROs must comply with Uniform Rules for Trial Courts § 202.7(f). Requests for TROs on cases assigned to another judge will be considered only upon approval of the IAS judge or his/her law clerk except in cases where both are unavailable.

Conferences:

Civil:

Pretrial conferences will be scheduled upon the Court's receipt of an RJI and/or calendar Note of Issue. Pleadings and a brief summary of the case in letter form are required in advance of the conference. Any request for an adjournment shall be made to the Judge's secretary and confirmation of all adjournments and notice of rescheduled dates must be made in writing to all parties and the Court.

Matrimonial:

Preliminary conferences scheduled pursuant to Matrimonial Rules. One adjournment without Court permission; thereafter, prior consent of the Court required.

Trials and References:

Adjournments are granted by permission of the Judge only. Deadlines on expert disclosure shall be set by the Judge on a case by case basis. Pleadings and list of witnesses (both expert and lay) should be sent to the Court one (1) week in advance of jury selection. (Exception in medical malpractice cases for expert name disclosure.) Motions *in limine* to be submitted prior to jury selection and heard thereafter as scheduled by the Court. Proposed requests to charge and verdict sheets shall be submitted on the first day of proof. The Court's preference is to receive these by e-mail with the requests attached. They may be supplemented upon the conclusion of proof. Charge conference by informal discussion to be held at or near close of proof with results put on the record upon request.

Pre-trial memoranda for matrimonial and other non-jury trials to be served and submitted to the Court two (2) weeks before the first day of trial.

References will be made to the Law Clerk to hear and report in matrimonial actions on stipulation regarding contested economics, post-divorce arrears and post-divorce modifications. References to JHO's to hear and determine or hear and report on any issue upon consent of all parties.

Special Requirements on Policy Limits Cases:

If a case with a value in excess of the policy limits is being settled for available insurance coverage be prepared to submit an affidavit from the insured detailing their knowledge of insurance coverage, an affidavit from counsel offering the policy limits detailing their activities in ascertaining the existence of all available insurance coverage, and an affidavit from a principal with the insurance company swearing they have no knowledge of any other insurance coverage.

JUSTICE JOSEPH R. GLOWNIA

Doc. 14.   Hon. Joseph R. Glownia

Motions:

Alternate Fridays in Part 6

9:30 AM

Civil:

All moving papers, answering papers, memoranda and special term note of issue to be sent to chambers at least 48 hours prior to return date. Court requires strict adherence to CPLR 2214(b). Originals supplied to the court or filed prior to return date. Oral argument not required in all cases. TROs on notice if other attorney is known. Motions cannot be adjourned generally and can be adjourned without court permission a limited number of times by informing the law clerk or secretary.

Matrimonial:

All moving papers, answering papers, memoranda and special term note of issue to be sent to chambers at least 48 hours prior to return date. Original papers to be supplied to the court or filed prior to return date. Will not sign TROS in a case assigned to another judge, without prior approval of IAS judge or his/her law clerk. Oral argument not required in all cases. Motions cannot be adjourned generally and can be adjourned without court permission a limited number of times by informing the law clerk or secretary.

Conferences:

Civil:

Pretrial conferences scheduled upon court's receipt of calendar note of issue. Preliminary conferences upon request. All conferences before IAS judge or law clerk. Pleadings required. Adjournments flexible; court will accommodate attorneys' schedules within reason.

Matrimonial:

Preliminary conferences to settle permitted; and divorce proven without prior filing of a calendar note of issue. Court's pretrial form required. Adjournments flexible; court will accommodate attorneys' schedules within reason.

Trials and References:

Civil:

Adjournments by judge or law clerk, if judge not available. Pleadings and papers for motions *in limine*

required a reasonable period in advance. Conference with IAS judge immediately preceding jury selection. Requests to charge required as directed on a case-by-case basis.

Matrimonial:

References to law clerk to hear and report on divorces on stipulation, contested economics, contested visitation, post-divorce arrears and post-divorce modification. Court prefers not to bifurcate.

JUSTICE DEBORAH A. HAENDIGES

Doc. 15. Hon. Deborah A. Haendiges

Adjournments:

Due to our unique calendar involving matters of both civil and criminal cases and multiple necessary parties, the ADJOURNMENT REQUESTS ARE RARELY GRANTED, PLEASE REFER TO OUR STRICT ADJOURNMENT POLICY.

Procedures to Adjourn Cases Scheduled Before IDV Court:

Adjournments will not be granted in IDV Court unless the following applies:

A. *First Appearance Only:*

1. All adjournment requests must be in writing and on notice to the opposing party, and all counsel participating in any portion of the IDV Litigation still pending (Criminal, Matrimonial, and Family).

2. All adjournment requests require Court approval and three suggested dates that you and all other counsel (including the Law Guardian, D.A. or *pro se* litigants) are available.

3. Adjournment requests are to be mailed or hand delivered to the IDV Court at 25 Delaware, Buffalo, NY, 14202 or sent by fax to 716–851–3222 four business days prior to the scheduled Court date.

4. The party or attorney requesting the adjournment and the opposing parties or attorneys must call the Court at 716–845–2762 at least two business days prior to the scheduled court date to confirm whether or not the adjournment was granted. Do not assume that the adjournment will be granted. The Court is not responsible for this confirming telephone call.

5. If the adjournment is granted:

a. The Court will send reschedule notices only if the request was made by a party who is not represented by an attorney.

b. If an attorney requested the adjournment, the attorney will be required to forward a confirm-

ing letter to the Court with copies to all parties and/or attorneys (This includes the District Attorney and Law Guardian). The adjournment will not be considered in effect unless such correspondence is timely received.

B. Emergency situations will be handled on a case by case basis.

Motions:

Criminal:

Bail motions heard daily upon notice to the court and your opponent. All bail motions must be made in writing. All other motions are heard Monday through Thursday on scheduled return date of matter.

Civil:

Motions are heard Monday through Friday on scheduled return date of matter. *(Contact chambers if an order to show cause requires a dates earlier than next return date for matter.)*

All motion papers must be received to chambers 48 hours in advance of date.

Submit Special Term Note of Issue with proof of payment for Supreme Court motions. Counsel to file original and one copy of motion/order to show cause to be conformed and returned to counsel for service. Unless the court directs otherwise, ALL REQUESTS FOR TEMPORARY RELIEF (TRO's) must be upon notice to opposing counsel, if known, or after good faith attempt to discover and contact opposing counsel.

Matrimonial:

All matters require strict compliance with court rules. Scheduling orders will be issued during conferences. Proposed disposition statements must be submitted for all trials and or hearings.

Reference to Law Clerk or County Attorney Referee to hear and report on divorces upon stipulation and upon contested economics.

JUSTICE RICHARD C. KLOCH, SR.

Doc. 16.   Hon. Richard C. Kloch, Sr.

Motions:

2nd and 4th Thursdays at 9:30 a.m.

Special Term motions are not called by Index Number but by the order in which all the attorneys are present and checked in with the Court Clerk.

Civil:

All moving papers answering papers, memoranda and special term note of issue to be received by Lockport chambers at least seventy-two [72] hours prior to return date. (i.e., close of business the Monday before Special Term.) Court requires strict adherence to CPLR 2214 (b). Affirmation of good faith required for discovery motions. Original papers to be supplied to the Court. Oral argument required unless written consent by all attorneys to submit papers is received or the Court directs otherwise. TROs handled on a case-by-case basis. TROs must be on notice to other attorney if known or where a government entity is involved. Orders to show cause/ TROs on a case assigned to another judge will be signed only upon prior approval of IAS judge or law clerk. Motions cannot be adjourned generally. An adjournment can be obtained without court permission, on consent of all counsel, by informing the court clerk at least twenty-four [24] hours prior to return date. The Court follows prevailing rules that motions must be heard within 60 days. Any motion exceeding 60 days will be dismissed. Orders must be approved by opposing counsel prior to submission to the Court by initialing each page or submitting a letter indicating approval.

Conference:

Civil:

Preliminary conferences are scheduled upon filing of the RJI and assignment. At this conference a scheduling order will be issued. Pretrial conferences will be scheduled upon Court's receipt of a calendar note of issue. All conferences before IAS judge or law clerk. Pleadings required in advance of conference.

Adjournments granted only with consent of all attorneys, subject to Court approval. Adjournments granted on consent of the secretary, but never beyond the 45 day requirement.

No adjournments will be granted on date of the scheduled conference except in extreme emergency and by consent of the judge.

Trials and References:

Civil:

Adjournments by judge only. Pleadings, list of witnesses, proposed jury charge and verdict sheet and papers for motions *in limine* required two [2] weeks in advance. Jury selection begins at 9:30 a.m., Mondays, with trial to follow immediately. Conference with the IAS judge upon completion of jury selection. Counsel are required to comply with trial practice rules of Court which will be provided to attorneys.

Correspondence:

All correspondence to the Court should be sent to the Lockport chambers, not the Buffalo chambers.

JUSTICE FREDERICK J. MARSHALL

Doc. 17.   Hon. Frederick J. Marshall

Motions:

1st and 3rd Tuesday of each month, 9:30 AM

Part 33 — 50 Delaware Avenue

Civil:

Motions will be heard on the first and third Tuesday of the month. All moving papers with a Special Term note of issue must be delivered to the Court at least one week prior to the return date. All answering papers and memoranda to be sent to Chambers at least three days prior to return date. Original papers must be supplied to Court. No oral argument unless requested and papers are received by the Court as set forth above. All requests for TROs must be on notice if other attorney is known. Requests for TROs on cases assigned to another judge will be considered only upon prior approval of the IAS judge or his/her law clerk. Motions must be adjourned to a specific date and will not be adjourned generally. Motions will not be adjourned more than three (3) times without the Judge's permission, granted at least 48 hours prior to the scheduled date. Confirmation of all adjournments and notice of rescheduled dates must be made in writing to all parties and the Court. Summary judgment motions must be made within 120 days of the filing of the calendar note of issue, or on such earlier date as set by the Court. All Orders submitted for signature must be accompanied by notice to opposing counsel. Counsel shall appear on time and check in with the Clerk.

Matrimonial:

Motions and Orders to Show Cause will be heard as scheduled. All moving papers, answering papers, memoranda and special term note of issue to be sent to Chambers at least two [2] days prior to return date. Original papers must be supplied to the Court. TROs will be granted, if not mutual, where assets are in jeopardy and there is an expeditious return date. Police and/or medical record/reports are required for an Order of protection. Requests for TROs on cases assigned to another judge will be considered only upon prior approval of the IAS judge or his/her Law Clerk. Oral argument on request. Motions must be adjourned to a specific date and will not be adjourned generally. Motions will not be adjourned more than three (3) times without Court permission granted at least 48 hours prior to the scheduled date. Confirmation of all adjournments and notice of rescheduled dates must be made in writing to all parties and the Court. Counsel shall appear on time and check in with the Clerk. All Orders, including Qualified Domestic Relations Orders submitted for signature must be accompanied by notice to opposing counsel.

Conferences:

Civil:

Pretrial conferences will be scheduled upon the Court's receipt of an RJI and/or calendar note of issue. Preliminary conferences will also be scheduled on request. Counsel are to provide copies of all relevant pleadings, bills of particulars, narrative medical reports, independent medical examination reports and police reports in advance of the conference. All conferences will be held before the IAS judge or law clerk. Any request for an adjournment shall be made to the judge's secretary and confirmation of all adjournments and notice of rescheduled dates must be made in writing to all parties and the Court.

Matrimonial:

Preliminary conferences to settle permitted, with divorce proven without prior filing of a calendar note of issue. Pleadings, 236-B affidavit and settlement proposal to be delivered to Court at least 72 hours prior to conference. Request for adjournments grant-

ed only on consent of all parties and the Court. No adjournments will be granted on the date of the scheduled conference absent exigent circumstances and consent of the Judge. One week prior to the date of the final report back before trial, counsel shall deliver memoranda of law, updated 236-B affidavits, current W-2s, rulings request, proof of acquisition of calendar number and statements of proposed disposition pursuant to 22 NYCRR 202.16[h], to the Court.

Trials and References:

Civil:

Adjournments only with approval of the Judge. List of witnesses, both lay and expert must be delivered to the Court thirty [30] days before jury selection, and exchanged among counsel. Motions *in limine* to be returnable on such date as set by the Court. Requests to charge and proposed verdict sheets required prior to the close of proof. Conference with IAS judge upon completion of jury selection. Charge conference will be held at/near close of proof.

Matrimonial:

Adjournments only with the approval of the judge. References to law clerk to hear and report on divorces on stipulation, contested economics, post divorce arrears and post divorce modification. References to JHOs to hear and determine on any issue on consent. Bifurcation whenever practicable or requested. Proposed findings of fact and conclusions of law and trial briefs to be filed at least five [5] days prior to commencement of trial. Judgments should contain decretal paragraphs relating to custody, visitation, maintenance and support, where appropriate and if made pursuant to an agreement or stipulation should so reflect. Judgments must reflect whether child support is based on CSSA or if the parties have opted out.

JUSTICE JOHN A. MICHALEK

Doc. 18. Hon. John A. Michalek

Special Term:

Every other Thursday. All discovery motions are heard at 9:30 a.m. All other motions are heard according to plaintiff's name as follows:

A–O at 10:00 a.m.   P–Z at 11:00 a.m.

When Scheduling Motions—contact the Court Clerk who will assign a date and time.

Motion papers must be received no later than one (1) week in advance of the return date, together with a special term note of issue. Answering papers and/or cross-motions must be received no later than 48 hours prior to the return date. Motion papers, including cross-motions, must bear the County Clerk's "Paid" stamp pursuant to CPLR § 8020(a). Please do not

send motion papers by fax without prior consent of the Court.

Rules of the Commercial Division of the Supreme Court:

Except as noted herein, the practice in the Commercial Division, Erie County is governed by Section 202.70(g) of the Uniform Rules for the New York State Trial Courts (22 NYCRR 202.70[g]).

Conferences:

Preliminary conferences are scheduled upon receipt of the filed RJI from the County Clerk. At the conference, a scheduling order will be issued. At the preliminary conference, the Court will indicate whether or not a stay of disclosure will be employed pursuant to CPLR § 3214(b). Pre-trial conferences will be set forth in the scheduling order or scheduled upon receipt of a calendar note of issue. Counsel must bring their calendars, including trial availability, to all conferences.

Adjournments:

1. No same day adjournments permitted except in extraordinary circumstances and upon consent of the Court.

2. Adjournments of conferences granted only with consent of all attorneys, subject to Court approval.

3. If counsel cannot agree to an adjournment of a motion, all counsel must appear on the return date to request an adjournment which will be liberally granted in the absence of prejudice.

4. Motions will not be adjourned generally. The first and second adjournments can be obtained without Court permission, on consent of all counsel, by informing the Court Clerk at least twenty-four (24) hours prior to the return date. Letters confirming the adjournment must be provided to all counsel and the Court.

5. Consent of all parties required prior to requesting an adjournment of a trial will be necessary.

6. Please contact Mary Lou Enser at 845–9416 for a new Motion date.

Motions:

1. Statements of material facts for summary judgment motions are not required.

2. Oral argument is anticipated but counsel may stipulate to submit on papers. Appearance on motions by telephone will not be permitted.

3. Pre-motion conferences are to be requested by telephone contact with Chambers.

4. Orders are to be approved by all attorneys/parties prior to submission to the Court for signature, with notice to the Court of such approval. Otherwise, they are to be settled pursuant to 22 NYCRR § 202.48.

TRO's

TRO's on a case-by-case basis. TRO's must be on notice to opposing counsel if known. TRO's for other Justices will be signed only with approval of that Justice or Justice's Law Clerk.

Trials and References:

Trial dates are provided at pre-trial conferences conducted after the Note of Issue and Statement of Readiness has been filed. Court adheres strictly to its trial schedule and adjournments are discouraged. Marked pleadings, requests to charge, proposed verdict sheets and papers for motions in limine required one (1) week prior to beginning of jury selection or trial.

JUSTICE MATTHEW J. MURPHY

Doc. 19. Hon. Matthew J. Murphy

Conferences:

Preliminary conferences will be scheduled within 45 days of the filing of the RJI and are mandatory. Pleadings, including Summons, Complaint, Answer and Bill of Particulars, must be submitted seven (7) days prior to the preliminary conference. Adjournments will be granted only with consent of all attorneys and subject to Court approval. At that preliminary conference, a scheduling order will be issued. Any subsequent requests to modify the scheduling order must be presented in the form of a proposed modified scheduling order, with opposing counsel's consent indicated thereon. No modifications of the original scheduling order will be permitted unless approved by the Judge.

A compliance/settlement conference will be held 180 +/- days from filing the RJI; and a pretrial conference will be held 60 +/- days before the scheduled trial date. Pretrial conferences will be scheduled upon completion of discovery. All conferences held before IAS Judge.

A final pretrial conference will be held with the Judge approximately one week before jury selection.

Adjournments:

Adjournments are granted by the judge, secretary or law clerk only; with notice to, and consent of, opposing counsel. Such consent shall not be unreasonably withheld. If counsel cannot agree to an adjournment of a motion, all counsel must appear on the return date to request an adjournment, which will be liberally granted in the absence of prejudice.

No general adjournments will be granted; all matters must have a return date for further proceedings.

Any attorney who will be late for a scheduled appearance must notify the Court Clerk at (716) 439–7153 prior to the scheduled time of appearance.

No same day adjournments permitted except in extraordinary circumstances and upon consent of the Court.

Consent of all parties is required prior to requesting an adjournment of a trial.

Papers:

All moving papers, answering papers, reply affidavits, memoranda and paid Special Term Notes of Issue are to be received in Chambers by 3:00 p.m. at least two (2) business days before the return date, notwithstanding CPLR 2214(b). Papers submitted after such time may be rejected by the court, or the offending attorney otherwise penalized as deemed appropriate.

Original papers, with Affidavits of Service, are to be supplied to the Court. Oral argument is required unless written consent by all attorney to submit on papers is received or the Court directs otherwise. TROs handled on a case-by-case basis. TROs must be on notice to other attorney if known or where a governmental entity is involved. Motions cannot be adjourned generally.

Orders:

Must be submitted within thirty (30) days. There must be a written indication that the order has been sent to all opposing counsel or pro se litigants and that no objection has been received. Orders will not be signed unless opposing counsel has had an opportunity to review for at least seven (7) days. However, if no objections are received after ten (10) days, the Order will be signed without further delay.

Discovery:

Motions to resolve discovery disputes shall be accompanied by an affidavit of good faith attempt at resolution. Letters between counsel are insufficient. There must have been a conversation between counsel to attempt to resolve discovery disputes.

Subpoenas:

Any subpoena requesting healthcare records must be accompanied by a valid authorization and contain appropriate HIPAA language in bold on the front of the subpoena.

Such subpoenas must be made returnable only directly to the Court Chambers, and not to the attorney's office or personnel.

Motions:

Summary judgment motions must be timely made pursuant to CPLR 3212(a).

Trials:

Trial dates are considered "dates certain." Trial adjournments are granted only upon exceptional circumstances and by permission of the Judge. Pleadings, vanilla statement of facts, list of witnesses, proposed jury charges, proposed verdict sheet, and papers on motions in limine are required to be served and received in Chambers at least one (1) week in advance of jury selection.

Attorneys should present proposed jury charges and the verdict sheet in both written form and in digital form. The digital submission should be in MS Word, any version. In both instances, the digital versions should be sent to the Law Clerk, whose email address is: sshierli@courts.state.ny.us. The jury charges should be completely written out, in the format you desire the Court to read to the jury, rather than merely reciting "PJI 1:90," etc.

Each separate charge requested should begin on a separate page, rather than combining multiple charges on the same page.

Expert disclosures, without good cause shown, are to be exchanged not less than thirty (30) days before the commencement of jury selection.

Jury Selection and trial days begin at 9:30 a.m. sharp.

JUSTICE PATRICK H. NEMOYER

Doc. 20.   Hon. Patrick H. NeMoyer

Daily Motions:

Dates and times as scheduled by the Court. Please call secretary to schedule.

Civil:

All moving papers, answering papers, memoranda and special term notes of issue to be sent to chambers at least two [2] days prior to return date. Original papers not required. Oral argument required in all cases, except with permission of the Court. Discovery motions upon affirmation of good faith. TROs on notice to opposing attorney. TROs on cases assigned to other judge, only with prior approval by IAS judge or his/her law clerk. Motions cannot be adjourned generally nor can they be adjourned without the permission of the court. Consent of opposing counsel is necessary for all adjournment requests prior to contacting the Court.

Matrimonial:

All moving papers, answering papers, memoranda and special term notes of issue are to be sent to chambers as soon as possible after service on opponent, but at least two [2] days prior to return date. Original papers not required. TROs on a case-by-case basis. Oral argument not required if attorneys agree to submit. Motions cannot be adjourned generally and can only be adjourned with permission of the Court by requesting an adjournment with the secretary. Consent of opposing counsel is necessary for all adjournments, unless court directs otherwise. Information sheets are required on all motions. If motion is for omnibus relief, motion will be converted to a conference within one [1] week of return date.

Conferences:

Civil:

Pretrial conferences scheduled upon court's receipt of calendar note of issue. Conferences before IAS judge or law clerk. No papers required. Adjournment by consent of all parties after first getting permission from the Court.

Matrimonial:

Preliminary conferences to settle are permitted and encouraged; divorces proven up but no judgment signed without filing calendar note of issue.

Trials and References:

Civil:

Court adheres strictly to trial schedule; adjournments are discouraged. Consent of all parties required prior to requesting adjournments. Adjournments by secretary are possible, but not likely.

Pleadings and papers for motions *in limine* required one [1] day prior to beginning of trial. Conference with IAS judge upon completion of jury selection. Formal requests to charge required prior to summations. Charge conference held after proof is complete.

Matrimonial:

References to law clerk to hear and report on divorces on stipulation and contested economics. Default papers required in advance. Signed and granted judgments of divorce and referee's report will be held by the court pending receipt of the filed note of issue.

JUSTICE ROBERT C. NOONAN

Doc. 21. Hon. Robert C. Noonan

Calendar:

Special Term will be held on alternate Fridays, with all motions scheduled at 9:30 a.m. and conferences (including infant settlements) every 15 minutes beginning at 11:00 a.m. Compliance, settlement and pretrial conferences with the Judge will be held on Special Term dates, or other dates, as necessary, before a JHO or Court Attorney/Referee. Trials will begin the day following jury selection at 9:30 a.m.

Motions:

Unless an order to show cause is granted based upon exigencies of time, the original motion papers and appropriate fee must be filed with the County Clerk at least 16 days in advance of the return date (21 days if service is by mail) and include a 7-day demand for responding papers in the notice of motion (CPLR 2214[b]). Failure to provide sufficient time will entail adjournment of the motion. Duly demanded responding papers not timely filed will not be considered by the Court absent good cause for the delay. Affirmations of good faith are required for motions regarding discovery or particulars. Adjournment of motions cannot be more than four weeks in the aggregate without Court permission. Orders prepared by counsel should be submitted on notice to opposing counsel and will be held 7 days for comment unless approval as to form is endorsed thereon or submitted by letter from opposing counsel.

Default Matrimonial:

Shall be submitted on papers unless special circumstances require an inquest. Only one set of papers should be submitted. The pertinent statutory factors should be addressed in the party's affidavit and enumerated in the proposed findings of fact. If the parties opt out of the CSSA, the agreement and proposed judgement must comply with DRL 240(1–b)(h).

Conferences:

Conferences cannot be adjourned without permission of the Judge. A preliminary conference will be scheduled by the Court upon filing an RJI. For matrimonials, the conference must be scheduled within 45 days of filing the RJI. Any requests to modify the preliminary conference order must be presented in the form of a proposed modified preliminary conference order, with opposing counsel's consent indicated thereon. A compliance/settlement conference will be held 180+/− days from filing the RJI; and a pre-trial conference 60+/− days before the scheduled trial date. A trial conference will be held with the Judge approximately one week before jury selection in nonmatrimonial cases.

Matrimonial Stipulations:

Transcripts of oral stipulations and the Affidavit of Appearance and Adoption of Oral Stipulations must be submitted with the proposed Judgement, which must be endorsed as to form by the opposing counsel.

Trial and Hearings:

Counsel are expected to engage in vigorous efforts to reach settlement in advance of the trial date so that the County jury pool will not be unnecessarily expended. The Court will contact counsel two weeks before the trial date to ascertain the status of negotiations.

Adjournments are only with the permission of the Judge. No proof will be taken on (Special Term) Fridays except for infant settlements. Copies of pleadings, particulars, requests to charge and proposed verdict sheets, and original in limine motions, shall be filed 5 business days, and responding papers filed 2 business days, in advance of the trial conference. Requests to charge should be made by PJI number only unless significant additional language is requested (with cited authorities). Prior to jury selection, counsel are required to exchange names and addresses of witnesses, including expert witnesses. Prior to the commencement of proof, all exhibits are to be marked for identification. Jury selection shall be by the "struck method" (22NYCRR § 202.33[f][2], Appendix E[C]).

Matrimonial:

References will made to a JHO or Court Attorney/Referee to hear contested issues and post-judgment applications for modification or arrears.

JUSTICE JOHN F. O'DONNELL

Doc. 22.   Hon. John F. O'Donnell

Motions:

Every day in Part 21 — upon confirmation with chambers — 9:30 a.m.

Civil:

All moving papers, answering papers, memoranda and special term note of issue to be sent to chambers at least five [5] days prior to return date. Originals required. Oral argument not required when court determines. Motions may not be adjourned generally, but may be adjourned without court permission by informing the secretary.

Matrimonial:

All moving papers, answering papers, memoranda and special term note of issue to be sent to chambers at least five [5] days prior to return date. Original papers to be supplied to the court. Oral argument not required when court deems it unnecessary. Motions may not be adjourned generally, but may be adjourned without court permission by informing the secretary.

Conferences:

Civil:

Pretrial conferences are scheduled upon court's receipt of calendar note of issue or RJI. Conferences before law clerk or Judge. Pleadings required in advance. One adjournment without court permission; thereafter, prior written consent required.

Matrimonial:

Preliminary conferences scheduled under Matrimonial Rules. Divorces proven and marked off without filing calendar note of issue. One adjournment without court permission; thereafter, prior consent required.

JUSTICE JANICE M. ROSA

Doc. 23.   Hon. Janice M. Rosa

Motions:

Generally, alternating Tuesdays beginning at 9:00 a.m. in Part 16, 2nd Floor, 25 Delaware Avenue, scheduled at one-half hour intervals with time scheduled by Court Clerk or secretary. Emergency matters may be heard at other times specifically arranged with Chambers.

Orders to Show Cause and Motions should be filed in Part 16, 2nd Floor at 25 Delaware Avenue for review, scheduling and signature. Requests for TRO's should be on notice to opposing counsel, if known, except for certain circumstances (e.g. request for protective order). An original and one copy must be submitted to the court for scheduling and signature. The copy will be retained for court use. A Matrimonial Term Note of Issue must be included with the Order to Show Cause or Motion.

All answering papers and any other moving papers must be received by the Court at least 48 hours prior to the return date. Late submissions may result in an adjournment at the Court's discretion or refusal by the Court to consider the untimely submission.

Motions may usually be adjourned upon consent of all attorneys without prior court approval by calling chambers and securing a rescheduled date at least 24 hours before the scheduled time. Motions must be adjourned to a specific date and will not be generally adjourned. The party requesting the adjournment must send written confirmation of the adjournment and the rescheduled date to all parties and the Court. At times, the Court may not grant approval for the adjournment.

Orders:

All orders must be submitted with an indication that the order has been sent to all opposing counsel or self-represented litigant. Orders will not be signed without proof of opportunity of opposing counsel or self-represented party to review. Include an original and one copy. The copy will be retained for the court's use.

Trials:

Trial dates are considered to be "date certain". Adjournments are granted only upon exceptional circumstances and by permission of the Court. Contact the Law Clerk to discuss. Compliance with trial letter scheduling order is expected, including timely submission of Statement of Proposed Disposition. References may be made to Law Clerk to hear and report on divorces and contested financial issues, upon stipulation of counsel.

JUSTICE FRANK A. SEDITA, JR.

Doc. 24. Hon. Frank A. Sedita, Jr.

Motions:

Every other Tuesday in Part 35 at 9:30 AM

Please call Court Clerk regarding scheduling/adjourning Motions.

Civil:

All moving papers, answering papers, memoranda and Special Term Note of Issue to be received by chambers on Friday by 12:00 noon, prior to the Tuesday return date. Originals are required. Oral argument required in all cases. TROs on notice if other attorney is known, if strong showing of meritorious claim and possibility of irreparable harm. TROs on cases assigned to other judge, only if prior approval by IAS judge or his/her law clerk. Motions cannot be adjourned generally and may only be adjourned with Court permission, consent of all parties and confirmation of the adjournment with the Court Clerk in writing. Orders must be submitted in duplicate, with copies provided to all attorneys, before submission to Court.

Matrimonial:

All moving papers, memoranda, answering papers and special term note of issue to be delivered to chambers at least three [3] days prior to return date. Original papers to be supplied to the court. TROs on notice to other attorney, if possible, and on strong showing of a meritorious claim and possibility of irreparable damage. TROs in case assigned to another judge, only if prior approval by IAS judge or his/her law clerk. Oral argument required in all cases. Motions cannot be adjourned generally and can be adjourned without court permission. Orders to be submitted in duplicate.

Conferences:

Please call Secretary regarding scheduling/adjourning conferences.

Civil:

Pretrial conferences scheduled upon Court's receipt of Request for Judicial Intervention or Note of Issue. All conferences before Law Clerk. Pleadings required in advance of initial scheduling conference. Adjournments with Court permission and consent of all parties, with confirmation of the adjournment in writing to chambers, copies to all counsel.

Matrimonial:

Preliminary conferences scheduled under Matrimonial Rules effective November 30, 1993. Divorce proven and marked off without filing calendar note of issue. Papers required under matrimonial rules should be filed with the court prior to or at date of preliminary conference. Conferences held before law clerk or Judge.

Trials and References:

Civil:

Adjournments by Judge only. No proof taken on Special Term days (every other Tuesday). Requests to charge, proposed verdict sheet and list of witnesses required prior to the first day of jury selection. Charge conference by informal discussion of Court's proposed charge and counsels' requests.

Matrimonial:

References to law clerk to hear and report on divorces on stipulation, contested economics, contested visitation, post-divorce arrears and post-divorce modification. References to JHOs to hear and determine or hear and report on any issue. Copies of proposed judgments should be forwarded to opposing counsel at least three [3] days prior to submission to the court.

JUSTICE DONNA M. SIWEK

Doc. 25. Hon. Donna M. Siwek

Motions:

Civil & Matrimonial: Alternating Thursdays in Part 29 at 9:30 a.m.

Infant Settlements: contact secretary/Court Clerk to schedule

Civil, including Matrimonial:

All original moving papers, answering papers, memoranda and special term notes of issue to be sent to chambers before 12:00 noon on the Tuesday before the motion return date. No fax submissions are permitted. If motion papers are not timely served, motion may be adjourned by the court. Adherence

to CPLR 2214[b] expected. TROs on notice to the other side if other attorney known. No general adjournments. Adjournments granted with consent of parties, subject to Court's approval, by contacting secretary or court clerk. Only stipulated or initialed Orders with consent of opposing counsel should be submitted to the Court for signature. (Matrimonials only — Counsel are required to confer before oral argument to narrow issues.)

Conferences:

Civil:

Preliminary conferences must be held within forty-five (45) days of the Court's receipt of filed RJI. All conferences before IAS Judge or law clerk. Adjournments granted with consent of parties, subject to Court's approval, by contacting secretary.

IAS Matrimonials:

Preliminary conferences to settle required. Pleadings, discovery demands, 236B Affidavits, motions, responses, prior orders, settlement proposals, proposed stipulations or agreements should be submitted to the Court as far in advance as possible, but no less than 48 hours prior to conference. Adjournments granted with consent of parties, subject to Court's approval, by contacting secretary.

Trials and References:

Civil, Including Matrimonial:

Trial dates considered to be "date certain." Adjournments granted only in the most exceptional circumstances, not upon consent of counsel. All motions in limine shall be made returnable prior to jury selection. Expert disclosure deadlines per court's trial order. Summary jury trial rules available upon request.

Matrimonial:

References to law clerk to hear and report on contested economics, post-divorce arrears and post-divorce modifications. Judgments and findings of fact to be submitted on notice to opposing counsel within four weeks of prove-up or decision.

JUSTICE SHIRLEY TROUTMAN

Doc. 26. Hon. Shirley Troutman

Motions:

Motions will be heard on Tuesdays and Thursdays commencing at 9:30 a.m. and 2:00 p.m. However, counsel should contact chambers to confirm the availability of a desired date. Clients are to appear with their attorneys unless excused by the court.

A time-stamped copy of a Motion and a special term note of issue should be delivered directly to Chambers, 25 Delaware Avenue, 5th Floor, after confirming return date with chambers. Motion papers, including cross-motions, must bear the County Clerk's "Paid" stamp pursuant to CPLR § 8020(a).

An original and time-stamped copy of an Order to Show Cause and a special term note of issue, together with a time-stamped copy of an RJI showing judge assignment should be delivered directly to Chambers, 25 Delaware Avenue, 5th Floor, for review, scheduling and signature. Original will be returned upon granting. Copy will be retained for court use.

Requests for TRO's should be on notice to opposing counsel, if know, except for certain circumstances (e.g., requests for protective order).

All answering papers and any other moving papers must be received in chambers no later than 2 days prior to the return date by 4 p.m. unless otherwise specified in the case of an Order to Show Cause.

Motions cannot be adjourned generally and can be adjourned only with consent of all counsel involved and the court. The party requesting the adjournment must send written confirmation of the adjournment and the rescheduled date to all parties and the Court.

Orders:

Orders are to be initialed by all attorneys in the action prior to submission to the court.

Settlement/Discontinuance:

The parties are to provide the court with written evidence of any settlements or discontinuance of a case within 10 days of said settlement or discontinuance. Otherwise the parties will be required to appear for a report back.

JUSTICE TIMOTHY J. WALKER

Doc. 27. Hon. Timothy J. Walker

Motions:

Every Monday at 9:30 a.m.

Attorneys shall contact John Garbo prior to scheduling same.

1. Courtesy copies of all moving papers, answering papers, memoranda and special term notes of issue must be received by chambers at least five (5) days prior to the return date, and before 2:00 p.m. Reply papers and memoranda, if any, must be received at least one (1) day prior to the return date, and before 2:00 p.m., and shall not re-iterate previously filed pleadings. Cross-motions shall be governed by the CPLR, and the Court requires strict compliance with

CPLR § 2214(b). Only papers served in accordance with the provisions of these rules will be read in connection with any such motion or cross-motion. Except as noted below as to Orders to Show Cause, the originals of all papers shall be filed with the Office of the Clerk of the County in which the matter is commenced/pending. Oral argument is expected on all cases, unless a) the motion is known in advance to be uncontested or b) a letter requesting the motion be decided on the papers is received by the Court prior to the original return date. Discovery motions may be subject to a conference with the Law Clerk prior to argument on the return date. Discovery and motions for a Bill of Particulars must be accompanied by the affirmation of good faith required by 22 NYCRR

§ 202.7. Original papers must be supplied to Chambers on an Order to Show Cause; on all other motions copies are acceptable. Counsel shall refrain from citing case law in affidavits and/or affirmations.

2. Special Term Motions are called in the order in which attorneys check in. Kindly report with the Court Clerk immediately upon arrival.

3. Motions, cross-motions and orders to show cause will not be scheduled until and unless chambers receives a paid, stamped Request For Judicial Intervention and/or a special term Note of Issue showing the original papers were filed with the office of the clerk of the county in which the matter is commenced/pending.

Orders:

Must be submitted within ten (10) days with verification that the order has been served upon all opposing counsel (or pro se litigants), and that no objection has been received within three (3) days of service. Orders will not be signed without verification of opportunity of opposing counsel to review.

Conferences:

Civil:

Preliminary and Pre-trial conferences are automatically scheduled upon Court's receipt of filed RJI or calendar note of issue. Otherwise, a preliminary conference may be scheduled upon request. Prior to the initial conference, counsel shall provide the Court with copies of all pleadings, bills of particulars and a one (1) paragraph summary of the case. At the conference, a scheduling order will be issued. Counsel shall bring calendars, including trial availability, to all conferences. Conferences shall take place with the Law Clerk (or the Court, as matters dictate).

Trials and References:

Civil:

The Court adheres strictly to trial schedules. Marked pleadings, requests to charge, witness lists, proposed verdict sheets and papers for motion *in limine* required two (2) weeks prior to commencement of trial. Motions *in Limine* shall be decided prior to commencement of trial. A conference with Court will be held upon completion of jury selection. A final charging conference will be held prior to summations. Deadline on expert disclosure, without good cause shown, is thirty (30) days before the scheduled commencement date of jury selection.

Mortgage Foreclosures:

1. The caption of all Orders Appointing Referee to Compute and proposed Judgments of Foreclosure shall include the address of the property being foreclosed upon in the caption;

2. All exhibits shall be separately tabbed for easy location by the Court, including the bill of costs, the note and mortgage, and any written assignments thereof;

3. In order to receive an award of attorneys fees, the submitted copy of the mortgage shall have highlighted the language allegedly entitling the party to such an award;

4. 90–Day Pre-Foreclosure Notice — Enforcement. For actions requiring a 90-day pre-foreclosure notice pursuant to RPAPL § 1304:

(a) Plaintiff shall file proof of service of such notice and a true copy of such notice and attachments simultaneous with the filing of a summons and complaint. Failure to comply with this section shall result in the Clerk refusing to accept any papers; and

(b) Plaintiff shall bring a copy of the specialized request for judicial intervention required by Uniform Civil Rule § 202.12–a(b) (RJI), the 90-day pre-foreclosure notice, and proof of service of the 90-day pre-foreclosure notice to any settlement conference. Failure to comply with this section shall result in the dismissal of the action.

5. Documentation to Bring to Settlement Conference.

(a) Defendant homeowners are strongly encouraged to bring copies of loan documents (Note and Mortgage); closing documents (HUD–1 Settlement Statement, all documents disclosing broker fees and other closing costs); home improvement/repair contracts; list of payments and proof of payments made towards mortgage, real estate taxes, and homeowner's insurance. Defendants also are encouraged to bring copies of pay stubs and/or other documentation of income or benefits received. Defendants may not be prohibited from proceeding with the conference if they do not have documents because they were never provided, are missing, or are lost.

(b) Plaintiff shall bring the entire loan file, including the Note and Mortgage, any allonge to the Note, and subsequent assignments; copies of all loan applications, including those completed by the borrower and the lender's final copy; copies of all Good Faith Estimates and Truth in Lending disclosures; the HUD–1 Settlement Statement; a detailed payment history; and explanation of all charges; and a reinstatement figure including a breakdown of all fees, costs and other charges that are allegedly due and owing.

(c) The Court may adjourn the settlement conference if Plaintiff fails to bring the entire loan file to the conference.

6. The Court will not consider or decide any pending (or new) motions until after the settlement conference process is concluded.

7. At the initial settlement conference, if the Defendant has not filed a written answer, the Court may consider a request by Defendant to submit a late answer.

8. The Court will have the discretion to calendar a follow-up conference with the parties to track and encourage any potential resolution.

9. Adjournment of a settlement conference shall be granted for good cause shown by any party.

10. The Court shall adjourn the fist settlement conference if the Defendant homeowner is seeking an attorney and/or if the Court appoints counsel pursuant to CPLR § 1102(a). Subsequent adjournments shall be at the discretion of the Court.

11. A representative of Plaintiff (with authority) shall be available by telephone and shall be up to speed on the file.

12. Plaintiff's counsel shall have conferred with a representative of Plaintiff (with authority and up to speed on the file) prior to the initial conference (and any subsequent conference scheduled by the Court).

13. Failure to comply with this section may result in the dismissal of the action.

General Rules:

Adjournments:

1. No same day adjournments shall be permitted, except in extraordinary circumstances and only upon consent of the Court.

2. Motions shall not be adjourned generally. The first and second adjournments may be obtained without Court permission, on consent of all counsel, by informing the Court at least twenty-four (24) hours prior to the return date. Letters confirming the adjournment shall be provided to all counsel and the Court.

3. Adjournments of conferences shall be granted only with consent of all attorneys, but remain subject to Court approval.

TROs:

Issued on a case-by-case basis. TROs shall be on notice to opposing counsel, if known. TROs in cases assigned to another Judge will be granted only upon approval of that Judge or his/her Law Clerk.

Discontinuance:

In any discontinued action, the attorney for the defendant shall file a stipulation or statement of discontinuance with the appropriate County Clerk within twenty (20) days of such discontinuance and shall provide the Court with a date-stamped copy of same. If the action has been noticed for judicial activity within twenty (20) days of such discontinuance, the stipulation or statement shall be filed before the date scheduled for such activity.

JUSTICE GERALD J. WHALEN

Doc. 28. Hon. Gerald J. Whalen

Motions:

Thursdays — Part 22 — 9:30A.M.
2:00 P.M. Summary judgment motions and Infant settlements

Civil:

All moving papers, answering papers, memoranda and special term note of issue to be sent to chambers by 5:00 p.m. on Monday prior to return date. Strict adherence to CPLR 2214(b) required. Originals are required. Oral argument required on all cases, except on permission of judge or law clerk. Discovery motions on affirmation of good faith. TROs on notice if other attorney is known. TROs on cases assigned to other judge, only if prior approval by IAS judge or his/her law clerk. Motions cannot be adjourned generally. Adjournments without court permission not permitted. Orders must be approved by opposing counsel before submission. Any subpoena requesting healthcare records must be accompanied by a valid authorization and contain appropriate HIPAA language in bold on the front of the subpoena. Summary judgment motions must be made within thirty days

following filing of the note of issue. Article 81 proceedings held Fridays at 9:30 a.m.

Conferences:

Civil:

Preliminary conferences must be held within forty-five (45) days of the Court's receipt of filed RJI. All conferences before IAS Judge or law clerk. Adjournments granted with consent of parties, subject to Court's approval, by contacting secretary. Pleadings required in advance.

Trials and References:

Civil:

Adjournments by Judge only. Marked pleadings, requests to charge, proposed verdict sheets and papers for motions *in limine* required one (1) week prior to beginning of trial. Conference with IAS judge upon completion of jury selection. Requests to charge and charge conferences on case-by-case basis. E-mailing of proposed verdict sheets and requests to charge, in Word Perfect format, to Judge's law clerk is requested: jgorman@courts.state.ny.us.

JUSTICE PENNY M. WOLFGANG

Doc. 29. Hon. Penny M. Wolfgang

Motions:

Thursdays in Part 24 at 9:30 AM

Civil:

All moving papers, answering papers, memoranda and special term note of issue to be received by the court two (2) days prior to return date. Originals not required. Oral argument not required at attorneys' option. TROs on notice if other attorney is known. TROs in a case assigned to another judge, upon prior approval of IAS judge or his/her law clerk. Motions cannot be adjourned generally and cannot be adjourned without court permission.

Matrimonial:

All moving papers, answering papers, memoranda and special term note of issue to be received by the court two [2] days prior to return date. Originals not required. TROs not granted if not mutual. Will not sign TROS in a case assigned to another judge, without prior approval of IAS judge or his/her law clerk. Oral argument not required at attorneys' option. Motions cannot be adjourned generally and can be adjourned without court permission by informing the court clerk.

Conferences:

Civil:

Pretrial conferences scheduled upon court's receipt of calendar note of issue. Preliminary conferences upon request. All conferences before law clerk. Scheduling for trial does require a conference. No papers required. Adjournments handled on a case by case basis.

Matrimonial:

Preliminary conferences to settle permitted; and divorce proven without prior filing of a calendar note of issue. Adjournments handled on a case by case basis.

Trials and References:

Civil:

Pleadings and papers for motions *in limine* required on day of commencement of trial. Requests to charge required mid-trial.

Matrimonial:

References to law clerk to hear and report on divorces on stipulation, contested economics, post-divorce arrears and post-divorce modification. References to JHOs to hear and determine on any issue within jurisdiction. References to JHOs to hear and report on any issue within jurisdiction. Bifurcation where parties request or law applies.

SUPREME COURT LEGAL STAFF

Doc. 30. Supreme Court Legal Staff

Uncontested Divorces/Annulments:

All uncontested matrimonial actions will be considered on papers only. (Inquests are available if special circumstances warrant oral testimony.) After obtaining calendar number, file all required papers with the Supreme Court Calendar/Matrimonial Office (845–9301). The list of required papers is available in the Calendar/Matrimonial Office. For a status check of a particular action, call the Calendar/Matrimonial Office first before calling the Referee.

Appeals to Erie County Court:

Effective April 22, 2002, civil and criminal appeals to Erie County Court will be subject to an individual assignment system. Accordingly, with respect to matters in which a Notice of Appeal is filed with the Court on or after that date, the Chief Clerk's Office will randomly assign each such action to a Judge of the County Court. Inquiries relative to appeals taken prior to April 22, 2002 should be directed to the Court's legal staff at 845–9329.

Search Warrants:

Law enforcement authorities are to contact Michael P. Clohessy for information and instructions.

ALTERNATIVE DISPUTE RESOLUTION

PROTOCOLS

§ 1. Introduction

1.1 Title

This program is titled the 8th Judicial District Martin P. Violante Alternative Dispute Resolution ("ADR") Program. It is named in honor of Court Attorney Referee Martin P. Violante, who implemented the highly successful pilot ADR program for civil cases in the 8th Judicial District. His exceptional case settlement skills are legendary and well-respected on a statewide basis, as he generously shared his expertise with members of the Bench and Bar over the years. Marty's standard of excellence and dedication to alternative dispute resolution has inspired these protocols for ADR in civil, commercial and matrimonial cases and for parenting issues in Family Court cases.

To our knowledge, this is the first comprehensive protocol developed in the New York State courts to standardize alternative dispute resolution in civil, commercial and matrimonial cases and parenting issues in Family Court actions.

1.2 Purpose and Scope of Program

A. *Purpose*—These protocols for the 8th Judicial District Martin P. Violante ADR Program will encourage the use of ADR in civil, commercial and matrimonial cases and for parenting issues in Family Court cases, and will standardize services provided by ADR Neutrals. ADR Neutrals in this Program include ADR Court staff Neutrals, individuals on the Court's Rosters of ADR Neutrals, and non-profit agency ADR providers under contract with the Unified Court System. These protocols shall govern cases referred to the 8th Judicial District ADR Program by the Court or upon consent of the parties. This program is not intended to preclude private resolution of disputes.

These rules were developed in collaboration among the Bench, the practicing Bar and ADR practitioners.

B. *Scope*—These ADR Protocols are effective immediately and shall apply to all civil, commercial and matrimonial actions, and to parenting issues in Family Courts within the 8th Judicial District pending or commenced on and after the effective date.

C. *Program Oversight*—Hon. Sharon S. Townsend, the Administrative Judge of the 8th Judicial District shall have oversight and be responsible for operation of the ADR Program. She will consult with Daniel M. Weitz, Esq, Coordinator of the Office of Court Administration's Office of Alternative Dispute Resolution Programs and Court Improvement Programs ("OCA ADR,") Hon. Donna M. Siwek, Supervising Judge of Civil Matters, Hon. Janice M. Rosa, Supervising Judge of Matrimonial Matters, Hon. Mi-

chael F. Griffith, Supervising Judge of the Family Courts for the 8th Judicial District, and Hon. John M. Curran, the Justice assigned to the Commercial Division in Erie County.

D. *Program Administration*—The Administrative Judge of the 8th Judicial District has assigned Mary Louise Hayden, Esq. as ADR Program Administrator to supervise and manage the program. William E. Gersten, Esq. is the Civil ADR Program Administrator. Anne S. Rutland, Esq. is the Commercial ADR Program Administrator, Tracey A. Kassman, Esq. is the Matrimonial ADR Program Administrator for Matrimonial Matters and Sheila Weir Schwanekamp, Esq. is the Family Court ADR Program Administrator for parenting issues.

ADR proceedings, but not their content, will be tracked and supervised by the ADR Program Administrator, as directed by the District Administrative Judge, with the assistance of clerical support personnel. Tracking will ensure efficient case management and monitor the performance of the program with respect to: litigant satisfaction; number of cases referred; number of cases reaching full or partial agreement; the Neutrals who receive assignments and any purpose requested by OCA ADR. Information or assistance required by Neutrals or counsel may be obtained from the Program Administrators. The program will be continually monitored and periodically assessed. Suggestions and comments from Neutrals, counsel and parties are welcome and may be made to the ADR Program Administrators.

§ 2. ADR Process

2.1 Definitions

A. *Alternative Dispute Resolution* is a process, other than litigation, that parties use to resolve disputes. ADR offers the possibility of a settlement or resolution that is achieved sooner, at less expense, and with less inconvenience and acrimony than can occur in the normal course of litigation.

B. *Neutral* means an individual assigned by the Court or selected by the parties to provide ADR services. Neutrals may include Judicial Hearing Officers, Court staff and members of Court Rosters established pursuant to this protocol, as well as staff and/or volunteers assigned by agencies under contract with the Unified Court System to provide ADR services.

C. *Arbitration*

1. Voluntary Arbitration is an adversarial dispute resolution process in which one or more trained Arbitrators hears arguments, weighs evidence and renders a final and binding award after an expedited hearing. Voluntary arbitration is of-

ten conducted pursuant to a stipulated agreement. The award may be confirmed by a court and is subject to CPLR Article 75.

2. Compulsory Arbitration is a non-binding, adversarial dispute resolution process in which one or more trained Arbitrators hears arguments, weighs evidence and renders a non-binding award after an expedited hearing. Either party may reject the arbitrator's award and pursue litigation options. Compulsory arbitration in New York is governed in Part 28 of the Rules of the Chief Administrator (22 NYCRR §§ 28.1–28.16) which is incorporated herein by reference.

D. *Summary Jury Trial* is an adversarial, voluntary, dispute resolution process where a jury is asked to render a verdict on specified issues after an expedited trial. A six member jury is screened and selected by counsel or the trial Judge within strict time limits. Attorneys present their case within strict time limits. Testimony may be live or presented through deposition transcripts, affidavits or expert reports. The summary jury verdict may be binding or non-binding as agreed by the parties.

E. *Summary Bench Trial* is the same process as a summary jury trial but the Judge, or by agreement of the parties, a Judicial Hearing Officer (JHO) or a Court Attorney–Referee serves as the fact-finder.

F. *Neutral Evaluation* is a non-binding, confidential process in which a Neutral Evaluator who is a subject matter expert on the issues in controversy, advises parties of the strengths and weaknesses of their case and offers an opinion as to likely court outcomes. The Neutral Evaluator hears abbreviated informal presentations by the attorneys for the parties or by self-represented litigants. The Neutral Evaluator's opinions may assist parties in their analysis of the merits of their cases, help to facilitate discussion between the parties and aid in reaching a settlement. The neutral evaluator may endeavor to facilitate a settlement between the parties.

G. *Mediation* is a confidential, informal procedure in which a specially trained Neutral helps parties negotiate with each other. With the assistance of a Mediator, parties identify issues, clarify perceptions and explore options for a mutually acceptable outcome. The process often improves the parties' ability to communicate with each other. The process may conclude with a written agreement. Mediation has the following elements:

1. Mediators offer the opportunity to expand the settlement discussion beyond the legal issues in dispute and to focus on developing creative solutions that emphasize the parties' practical concerns.

2. Mediation places importance on self-determination by the parties. Disputants are encouraged to speak for themselves, as well as through counsel.

3. Mediation may be conducted in several multi-hour sessions and is generally less time limited than other facilitated settlement conferences.

4. Mediators do not offer their own opinions regarding likely court outcomes or the merits of the case.

There may be a request made by the parties, during the course of the mediation, for an opinion from the Mediator as to the merits of their positions. Only a qualified Neutral Evaluator can offer such opinion (*see Section 12.2*). If the Mediator is also a qualified Neutral Evaluator in the subject area, and upon full consent of the parties, the mediation may expand to include neutral evaluation concerning these issues. However, if the Mediator is not a qualified Neutral Evaluator in the specific subject area, the Mediator should not offer an opinion regarding likely court outcomes or the merits of the case.

H. *Parenting Coordination* is used in child custody matters. The parenting coordinator is a specially trained Neutral assigned by the Court to manage chronic, recurring parenting disputes under the direction of and on behalf of the Court. He or she helps parents comply with court orders by acting as an educator, mediator and counselor. The parenting coordinator assists parents in developing conflict management skills and may resolve day-to-day parenting disputes in emergency circumstances if and when parents cannot do so themselves.

I. *Case Conferencing—Settlement Conferencing* is a non-confidential process that provides effective ways of narrowing issues and resolving disputes. Cases are either Judge-referred or party-initiated for this process which is conducted by the Court's legal staff and Court staff Neutrals.

2.2 ADR Process in Specific Actions

A. *Civil and Commercial Actions*

ADR processes in civil and commercial actions include arbitration, summary trials, neutral evaluation, mediation and case conferencing–settlement conferencing.

B. *Matrimonial Actions*

ADR processes for matrimonial actions include summary trials, neutral evaluation, mediation (parenting issues only) and parenting coordination.

Rules pertaining to parenting coordination are addressed in separate guidelines developed at the direction of the Administrative Judge of the 8th Judicial District.

The Court may also employ Family Services Coordinators to conduct initial case assessments for the purpose of identifying family dynamics. This assessment will include analysis of the level of family conflict and complexity of issues involving the family in order to assist the judge in tailoring an appropriate service plan. Family Services Coordinators have knowledge of court-based and community services available to assist parents and children experiencing difficulties and may link parents and children with such services.[1]

C. *Family Court Cases*

ADR processes for parenting issues in Family Court cases include mediation, parenting coordination, and the use of Family Service Coordinators, if available. These procedures will apply to existing ADR programs to address parenting issues in Erie County Family Court but do not replace any other existing ADR program in any other Family Courts, including, but not limited to, the Permanency Mediation Project in the 8th Judicial District.

1 Family Service Coordinators are part of the Children Come First Initiative, piloted in Erie County.

§ 3. Engagement of the ADR Process

3.1. In General

Every action filed in the Eighth Judicial District shall be assessed to determine its suitability for ADR. This can occur when the RJI is filed, after referral to a Judge, or at the time a petition is filed in Family Court. Subject to the approval of the Court, a case deemed not appropriate for referral at its outset may be referred to the Program later at the request of the parties.

Parties shall attend a 2 hour initial ADR session. Counsel's attendance at the ADR sessions will be presumed unless specifically waived by counsel and parties. At the initial ADR session, the Neutral will explain the selected ADR process and will begin to outline and address issues of concern. After that session, the parties may choose to schedule additional sessions with the Neutral as they work toward resolution. If the parties, counsel, and the Neutral agree, the parties may schedule the initial session to exceed the two hour requirement.

However, the Neutral will be entitled to compensation for services beyond the initial two hour period as well as compensation for the Neutral's preparation time when the session(s) exceed the initial two hour period.

3.2 Referral By Parties' Request at the Time of Filing an RJI or Petition

Parties may agree to request referral to ADR by filing a Request for ADR—ADR Initiation Form when a Request for Judicial Intervention (RJI) or Petition in Family Court is filed. The request will be docketed by the Chief Clerk who will forward it to the ADR Program Administrator.

A. *Civil and Commercial matters*

In civil or commercial matters, the parties shall indicate on the Request for ADR—ADR Initiation Form whether they are seeking the services of a Court staff Neutral or a Court Roster Neutral to conduct the ADR session. If the parties have selected a Court Roster Neutral, they will indicate on this form the name of a mutually agreed upon Court Roster Neutral who the parties have confirmed is available to hear the matter within thirty (30) days of the filing of the RJI. The ADR Program Administrator will coordinate the assignment of the case to the Court Roster Neutral.

If the parties have requested that the ADR session be conducted by a Court staff Neutral, the ADR Program Administrator will send the request to the Civil ADR Program Administrator or the Commercial ADR Program Administrator. The Administrator will schedule an ADR session before a Court staff Neutral to be held within thirty (30) days of the filing of the RJI.

B. *Matrimonial or Family Court (parenting issue) matters*

In matrimonial and Family Court cases, the parties should indicate on the Request for ADR—ADR Initiation Form the name of the mutually agreed upon Court Roster Neutral. In matrimonial matters, the request will be reviewed at the initial preliminary conference with the Court. In Family Court cases, the request will be referred by the Chief Clerk to the Family Court ADR Program Administrator.

3.3 Referral to ADR by Court at Request of Parties

The ADR Program will also accept requests for referrals to ADR on consent from parties in any eligible case after the filing of an RJI or Petition in Family Court with approval of and on referral from the Assigned Judge.

A. *Civil and Commercial Matters*

Parties should advise the Assigned Judge, at a conference or by agreement, of their desire to participate in the ADR Program and any preference with regard to the appointment of a Court staff Neutral or a Court Roster Neutral. The Court will determine whether the matter will be referred to ADR and will assign a return date for a report back to the Court after the ADR session, not to exceed sixty (60) days from the date of the referral to ADR by the Court.

The parties shall complete either the ADR Initiation Form for Court staff Neutrals or the ADR Initiation Form for Court Roster Neutrals and forward the completed form to the ADR Program Administrator within ten (10) business days from the date of the referral to ADR. There will be no adjournment for the return of this form.

If the matter is to be heard by a Court Roster Neutral, the ADR Program Administrator will forward the ADR Initiation Form to the selected Court Roster Neutral who will hear the matter within the time line provided herein.

If the matter is to be heard by a Court staff Neutral, the ADR Program Administrator will forward the ADR Initiation Form to the Civil or Commercial ADR Program Administrator who will oversee the assignment of the matter to a Court Staff Neutral.

The same procedures in 3.2 (A) for assignment of the Neutral shall also apply to post-RJI assignments in civil and commercial matters except where there is no agreement on the neutral. In that event, the parties will submit three ranked names from the applicable Court Roster on their ADR Initiation form and the Assigned Judge will select the Court Roster Neutral.

B. *Matrimonial and Family Court matters*

The parties shall complete the ADR Initiation Form for Court Roster Neutrals and will return the form to the Court and to the respective Matrimonial or Family Court ADR Program Administrator within ten (10) business days from the date of the referral to ADR. There will be no adjournment for the return of this form. The respective ADR Program Administrator will coordinate the dissemination of the ADR Initiation Form to the assigned Neutral who will hear the matter within the time line provided herein.

The parties should indicate on the ADR Initiation Form the name of the mutually agreed upon Court Roster Neutral or submit three ranked names from the Court Roster of Neutrals.

In matrimonial matters, the Assigned Judge will oversee the selection of the Court Roster Neutral if there is no agreement.

In Family Court matters, the Family Court ADR Program Administrator will coordinate the assignment of the Court Roster Neutral. If there is no agreement, the Family Court ADR Program Administrator will select the Neutral.

3.4   Order of Reference to ADR

The Court may direct the parties to proceed to an initial ADR session by issuance of an Order of Reference to ADR. After the initial session, the parties may agree to continue with ADR or return to the Court. The Court will include in the Order of Reference to ADR a return date for a report back to the Court which will not exceed sixty (60) days from the date of issuance of said Order. The Order of Reference to ADR shall indicate time frames in which the ADR session shall be conducted. The issuance of the Order of Reference to ADR may be directed by the Court at a conference or in response to a request from any party made on notice to all other parties.

An Order of Reference to ADR will be issued by the Court and sent to the parties through their counsel and to the Civil or Commercial or Matrimonial or Family Court ADR Program Administrator. The parties must thereafter submit to the Court and to the respective Civil, Commercial, Matrimonial or Family Court ADR Program Administrator the appropriate ADR Initiation Form within ten (10) business days from the issuance of the Order of Reference to ADR.

3.5   Discovery Issues

At the discretion of the Assigned Judge or by request of the parties, a "mini discovery" order may issue prior to the issuance of an Order of Reference to ADR.

Additionally at the discretion of the Judge, the ADR option may be scheduled so as to identify the nature of the discovery required by each party. The exchange of information may be completed in the context of the ADR option.

3.6   Special Considerations

If the parties do not submit the ADR Initiation Form within ten (10) business days from the notification of the issuance of the Order of Reference to ADR, or if administrative necessity so requires, the Court shall select the Neutral. The ten (10) business day deadline is not subject to adjournment or extension.

Notwithstanding the foregoing, the parties may, by written stipulation, at the outset designate as the Neutral a person from the Court's roster or may proceed to ADR using the offices of a private ADR provider; in either instance, the parties must complete the ADR process within the deadlines set forth in these Rules.

§ 4.   Time for Engagement of ADR

4.1   Time Line When Request for ADR Filed With RJI

Upon receipt of the Request for ADR–ADR Initiation Form, the ADR Program Administrator will immediately send a confirmation of the assignment along with the Request for ADR–ADR Initiation Form to the Neutral. If the parties have selected a Court staff Neutral, the Civil or Commercial ADR Program Administrator will schedule the ADR session. Where a Court Roster Neutral is selected, the Neutral shall then contact the parties' counsel or, if the parties are self-represented, the parties themselves to schedule the initial ADR session.

At least five (5) business days before the initial session, the parties or their attorneys shall send to the Neutral the ADR Summary Form of the case (not to exceed 2 pages) and any other information necessary to the effective negotiation of the outstanding issues. The Neutral may initiate a conference call with counsel regarding any preliminary matters. All ADR sessions shall be conducted within thirty (30) days from the filing of the Request for ADR–ADR Initiation Form.

4.2   Time Line for Post–RJI Referrals to Add or Issuance of Order of Reference to Add

Upon receipt of the completed ADR Initiation Form from the parties or the Order of Reference to ADR along with the ADR Initiation Form from the Court, the Civil, Commercial, Matrimonial or Family Court ADR Program Administrator will immediately forward the form and, if one has been issued, the Order, to the Court Roster Neutral, if that is the parties' choice. If the parties have selected a Court staff Neutral, the Civil or Commercial ADR Program Administrator will schedule the ADR session. Where a Court Roster Neutral is selected, the Neutral shall contact the parties' counsel or, if the parties are self-represented, the parties directly, to schedule the initial ADR session. The initial ADR session with the Court Roster Neutral shall be conducted within 20 days from the date the Program Administrator sends the form or order to the Neutral. This deadline is to be met by parties, counsel and the Neutrals.

At least five (5) business days before the initial session, the parties or their attorneys shall send the ADR Summary Form of the case (not to exceed 2 pages) and any other information necessary to the effective negotiation of the outstanding issues to the Neutral. The Neutral may initiate a conference call with counsel regarding any preliminary matters. All ADR sessions shall be conducted within 60 days from the issuance of the Order of Reference to ADR or within sixty (60) days from the date of the Court's referral to ADR. Those deadlines and the Court report back date will be stated on the ADR Initiation Form.

A. *Family Court parenting issues*

The parties in these cases will send to the Neutral a copy of the Family Court petition and any responding papers filed by the respondent prior to the initial mediation session in lieu of the ADR Summary Form.

4.3 Presence of Counsel at ADR Proceedings

Issues regarding potential inequalities between the parties, e.g. unequal financial strength, lack of knowledge about financial issues, general inequality of business skill or knowledge, strong personalities, etc., favor the presence of counsel for each party at each ADR session. However, by agreement of the parties, ADR may proceed in the absence of counsel, unless otherwise ordered by the Court.

If, during the process, counsel for either party is discharged or withdraws for any reason, the case will not proceed in ADR until a substitution of counsel occurs or the party indicates in writing a decision to be self-represented.

§ 5. Confidentiality During the ADR Process

5.1 All written or oral communications made during the course of ADR proceedings are confidential and inadmissible in court with the exception of neutral case conferencing-settlement conferencing conducted by Court staff Neutrals. No party to an ADR proceeding shall seek to compel production of documents, notes or other writings prepared for or generated in connection with the ADR proceeding, or seek to compel the testimony of any other party or the Neutral concerning the substance of the ADR process. Documents and information otherwise discoverable under the law shall not be shielded from disclosure merely because they are submitted or referred to in the ADR proceeding.

5.2 ADR communications and information may be subject to disclosure in judicial or administrative proceedings in any of the following six circumstances:

1. Attendance by the parties and counsel at the initial ADR session will be reported to the Assigned Judge. No information regarding attendance at subsequent sessions will be revealed.

2. Disclosure of otherwise privileged communications may be made pursuant to a written waiver of confidentiality by parties and Neutral. The waiver must specify the individual communication(s) or information that will be disclosed, the person or entity to whom the disclosure will be made, and the purpose of the disclosure.

3. In civil actions, where the case has been resolved by a stipulation of settlement or a stipulation of discontinuance and execution of appropriate releases pursuant to the law, the terms of such stipulation and release are not confidential unless otherwise agreed between the parties.

4. In matrimonial and Family Court matters, where signed agreements have been incorporated into Court orders or judgments, such agreements may be admissible in any judicial or administrative proceeding.

5. If a communication is made or information is disclosed during an ADR session which presents a credible threat of serious and imminent harm to a party or to another person or entity, the appropriate authorities, the potential victim and the referring Court may be notified.

6. If the communication or information relates to an allegation of child abuse or neglect as defined in Family Court Act §§ 1012(e) and (f) and Social Services Law § 412 and for which disclosure is or may be required pursuant to Social Services Law § 413, confidentiality will not apply as to those disclosures. If an allegation of child abuse or neglect is made by any party during the ADR session, the Neutral will stop the ADR process and consult with each party individually to obtain as much information about the allegation as possible. Neutrals will report to the Assigned Judge allegations of child abuse or neglect for which disclosure is required pursuant to Social Services Law § 413, and if under a professional duty as a mandated reporter, may take independent action as required by statute.

5.3 Mediation

Nothing about the substance of the mediation proceeding, such as the weaknesses or strengths of the parties' positions or the relative willingness of parties to discuss settlement proposals will be revealed to the referring Judge or any other person by the mediator, or any party or attorney, or court personnel. No party or counsel for a party may reveal the details of the mediation process to the referring Judge or a member of his/her staff, except for an executed agreement or a stipulation of settlement pursuant to CPLR § 2104.

Notwithstanding the foregoing: the parties may include confidential information in a written settlement agreement; the Neutral and the parties may communicate with the Program Administrator about administrative details of the proceeding; and the Neutral may make reference to the services rendered by him or her in any action to collect an unpaid, authorized fee for services performed under these Rules.

§ 6. Stays

6.1 Civil and Commercial Actions

The Assigned Judge may, in his or her discretion, issue a stay of proceedings while the case is pending in ADR and shall so indicate in the Order of Reference to ADR. Upon the issuance of an Order of Reference with a stay, all proceedings over which the Court has jurisdiction other than the ADR process shall be stayed for not more than sixty (60) days.

If the matter has not been entirely resolved within the 60-day period and the parties and the Neutral believes that it would be beneficial if the ADR process were to continue, the process may go forward with approval of the Court. However, absent extraordinary circumstances, no additional stay shall be ordered.

6.2 Matrimonial and Family Court Cases

Referral to ADR in contested matrimonial and Family Court cases will not stay the Court proceeding. OCA policy in these cases recognizes the special need for prompt action in matrimonial and Family Court proceedings. As a general rule, full discovery, emergency and *pendente lite* relief, family dynamics, and the needs of children require ongoing access to the Court. However, if the parties agree that additional time is required to fully explore resolution through ADR, they may request an adjournment of a court date from the Assigned Judge, which may be granted sparingly.

§ 7. Completion of ADR Report of Disposition

7.1 Report of Disposition

The ADR session or sessions shall be concluded within thirty (30) days if initiated by a Request for ADR- ADR Initiation Form filed with an RJI or a Petition in Family Court or within sixty (60) days from the issuance of the Order of Reference to ADR or date of referral to ADR by the Court.

The Neutral shall report, by ADR Disposition Form, to the ADR Program Administrator for Civil or Commercial Matters or the Matrimonial or Family Court ADR Program Administrator as to whether the parties reached an agreement or whether the parties require judicial intervention no later than two (2) business days after the final ADR session. The "final ADR session" is the session in which the parties have either resolved the case or the parties have not reached an agreement by the end of the respective completion period.

If the ADR session had been initiated by the Request for ADR filed with the RJI or a Petition in Family Court, the Neutral shall the ADR Disposition Form to the Chief Clerk and to the ADR Program Administrator as well as to all counsel and self-represented litigants. If the matter has not been resolved after completion of the ADR Process, the Chief Clerk shall assign the matter to a Judge.

If the ADR session had been initiated by referral of the Court or by Order of Reference to ADR, the Neutral must complete and send the ADR Disposition Form to the Assigned Justice and to the Civil or Commercial or Matrimonial or Family Court ADR Program Administrator and to all counsel and self-represented litigants.

7.2 Completion of ADR Disposition Form

The ADR Disposition Form shall set forth the date of the initial ADR session, whether each party and counsel appeared at the first session, and the date of any subsequently scheduled sessions. The form shall indicate whether the parties reached agreement on some, all, or any of the issues referred to the ADR proceeding. The Neutral shall attach any stipulations or agreements executed by the parties.

7.3 Court Conference Scheduling

If the case has not resolved, or if otherwise directed by the Court, the parties and counsel shall appear before the Court on the scheduled report back conference date, designated on the ADR Initiation Form.

7.4 Special Considerations

A. *Civil and Commercial Actions*

Any settlement, in whole or in part, reached during the ADR proceeding shall be enforceable upon compliance with the applicable requirements enunciated in the CPLR.

If the case has been referred to Arbitration, the Arbitrator's Award shall be in writing, signed and affirmed by the Arbitrator within the time fixed by the agreement, or if the time is not fixed, within such time as the court orders. (See CPLR § 7507 and CPLR § 7508 regarding an award by confession).

If the case has been referred to Mediation by the Assigned Judge after Neutral Evaluation has been unsuccessful, the Mediator will follow the process outlined in 7.1–7.3 above and comply with any time limits set by the Assigned Judge.

B. *Matrimonial and Family Court Cases*

The Mediator or Neutral Evaluator shall complete the ADR Disposition Form, attach to the form any original signed agreement, and return it to the Judge, JHO or Court Attorney Referee assigned to the case. The Mediator or Neutral Evaluator shall send copies to the Matrimonial or Family Court ADR Program Administrator, counsel, and to any self-represented litigants.

If the parties voluntarily reach an agreement, the Mediator or Neutral Evaluator may assist the parties and their counsel in drafting a written agreement. Subject to review and approval of the referring Judge, the Stipulated Agreement will be incorporated in the Court's Order.

Any settlement, in whole or in part, reached during the ADR proceeding shall be effective only upon execution of a written agreement signed by all parties or their duly authorized agents. Such an agreement shall be kept confidential unless the parties agree otherwise, except that any party thereto may thereafter commence an action for violation of the agreement.

C. *All Cases*

If the case is not resolved after completion of the ADR proceeding, the Assigned Justice may determine, or the parties may stipulate, to resolve the matter by another ADR process.

§ 8. Immunity of Neutrals

8.1 Any person designated to serve as a Neutral pursuant to these Rules shall be immune from suit based upon any actions engaged in or omissions made while serving in a *pro bono* capacity. The execution of an ADR Initiation Form constitutes a waiver of any right to sue the Court Roster Neutral because of his or her actions in that *pro bono* role.

§ 9. Special Considerations Regarding Referrals to Mediation in All Cases

9.1 The following cases shall not be referred to Court mediation:

A. Child abuse or neglect (as defined in Family Court Act §§ 1012(e) and (f) and Social Services Law § 412) except that these protocols do not preclude the continuation of the Permanency Mediation Project in the Eighth Judicial District; OR

B. A pending family offense proceeding (Family Court Act Art. 8) between the parties; OR

C. A pending criminal action between the parties except for those cases covered by Judiciary Law Article 21 A; OR

D. An existing temporary or permanent stay away Order of Protection between the parties; OR

E. A severe power imbalance between the parties that precludes an individual's capacity to exercise self-determination.

§ 10. Domestic Violence

If, during the course of the ADR process, an allegation of domestic violence or severe power imbalance is made by any party, the Neutral will stop the ADR process, consult with each party individually for the purpose of obtaining as much information as possible, and determine whether the process should continue. Allegations of domestic violence which are not a matter of public record will not be disclosed to the referring Judge; instead individuals will be given information regarding their rights in the form statement prescribed in Family Court Act § 812(5) and they will also receive safety planning information.

§ 11. Neutrals

11.1 Court Roster of Neutrals

A. The Court's Roster of Neutrals includes Neutrals who have complied with the training and experience requirements set forth below and have been accepted for Court Roster Membership.

Any other individual seeking to be included on the Court's Roster of Neutrals, including, but not limited to, those who are affiliated with an organization providing ADR services pursuant to a contract with the Unified Court System, must also meet the training and experience requirements of OCA ADR and adhere to standards of conduct that may be adopted by OCA ADR. These standards of conduct for all Neutrals incorporate, but are not limited to, ethical standards adopted by recognized professional organizations.

The Court may assemble Rosters of Neutrals for specific roles and case types. To be eligible for inclusion on any roster, an individual must submit an application and document successful completion of the specific criteria outlined in Section 12. In addition, Court Roster Neutrals may be required to fulfill continuing education requirements prescribed by OCA ADR.

Pursuant to The Rules of the Chief administrator of the Courts, 22 NYCRR § 146.3(b), Neutrals shall be redesignated to the Court Roster every two years. In determining whether to redesignate any Neutral, the Neutral must show proof of compliance with the requirement that he or she attend at least six hours of additional approved training relevant to his or her respective practice areas every two years pursuant to 22 NYCRR § 146.5.

B. Acceptance to each Court Roster of Neutrals is at the discretion of the District Administrative Judge in consultation with the OCA ADR. Continuing presence on a Court Roster is subject to review by the District Administrative Judge. Court Roster Neutrals may be removed from the Court Rosters at the discretion of the District Administrative Judge in consultation with the OCA ADR.

C. To avoid conflicts of interest, upon selection every Neutral shall, as a condition to confirmation in that role, conduct a conflict check of his or her prior association with any of the parties in the matter and those of any firm of which he or she is a member or employee in compliance with ethics and standards of conduct required for that category of Neutral. If appropriate, any such conflicts review shall include a check with regard to all parties, subsidiaries, or affiliates of corporate parties.

In the event that any potentially disqualifying facts are discovered, the Neutral shall either decline the appointment or shall fully inform the parties and the Program Administrator of all relevant details. Unless all parties, after full disclosure, consent in writing to the service of that Neutral, the Neutral shall decline the appointment and another Neutral shall promptly be selected by the Program Administrator.

The Neutral shall disqualify himself or herself if he or she would not be able to participate fairly, objectively, impartially, and in accordance with the highest professional standards.

The Neutral shall always avoid an appearance of a conflict of interest.

D. Court Rosters of Neutrals will be available in the 8th Judicial District ADR Office and shall be updated periodically as necessary. The Court Roster of Neutrals for each case type, including the name of the Neutral, area of expertise, resume and a schedule of fees will be maintained by the Program Administrator for review by parties and their attorneys.

§ 12. Qualifications of Neutrals for Court Roster

12.1 Arbitrator:

To be eligible to receive a Court referral and be included on the Court's Roster of Arbitrators, an individual must submit an application and have successfully completed at least six (6) hours of training in procedural and ethical matters related to arbitration and:

1. Be an attorney in good standing, admitted to the practice of law for at least five (5) years AND have at least five (5) years of substantial experience in the specific subject area of the cases that will be referred; OR

2. Have served as a Judge, JHO, Court Attorney–Referee or Confidential Law Clerk to a Judge AND have at least five (5) years of substantial experience in the specific subject area of the cases that will be referred; OR

3. Be a "Subject Matter Expert" defined as a professional with at least five (5) years of professional experience in the specific subject area of the cases that will be referred to Arbitration.

12.2 Neutral Evaluator:

To be eligible to receive a court referral and be included on the Court's Roster of Neutral Evaluators, an individual must submit an application and have successfully completed at least six (6) hours of training in procedural and ethical matters related to neutral evaluation and must:

1. Be an attorney in good standing, admitted to the practice of law for at least five (5) years AND have at least five (5) years of substantial experience in the specific subject area of the cases that will be referred; OR

2. Have served as a Judge, JHO, Court Attorney–Referee or Confidential Law Clerk to a Judge AND have at least five (5) years of substantial experience in the specific subject area of the referred cases; OR [1]

[1] So in original.

12.3. Mediator in Civil Cases:

To be eligible to receive a Court referral and be included on the Court's Roster of Mediators—Civil Matters, other than commercial and matrimonial actions, an individual must have extensive, relevant civil litigation experience, civil matter experience or serve or have recently served as in house counsel. In addition, each candidate must submit an application with proof of successful completion of a minimum of forty (40) hours of mediation training sponsored or recognized by OCA ADR, or training that OCA ADR deems to comport substantively with its curriculum guidelines. The forty (40) hour training must include at least twenty-four (24) hours of training in mediation skills and techniques and at least sixteen (16) hours of additional training in the specific mediation techniques pertaining to the subject area of the types of cases to be referred to the applicant. The applicant must also document substantial recent experience mediating actual cases. Substantial recent experience is defined by the applicable Court.

An individual who has completed the minimum forty (40) hours of mediation training but has not completed the experiential requirements described herein, may be provisionally accepted on the Court Roster on the condition that he or she complete the experiential requirements within six (6) months of their acceptance on the Court Roster.

12.4 Mediator in Commercial Cases

To be eligible to receive a Court referral and be included on the Court's Roster of Mediators–Commercial Matters, an individual must submit an application and proof of completion of all of the requirements outlined in 12.3 above AND have extensive commercial litigation experience, commercial matter experience or serve or have recently served as in-house counsel.

12.5 Mediator in Matrimonial and Family Court Matters (Parenting issues only)

To be eligible to receive a Court referral and be included on the Court's Roster of Mediators–Parenting Issues in Matrimonial and/or Family Court Matters, an individual must have extensive, relevant legal expertise in parenting issues or extensive professional training and expertise regarding parenting issues and must submit an application and proof of successful completion of a minimum of forty (40) hours of mediation training sponsored or recognized by OCA ADR or training that OCA ADR deems to comport substantively with its curriculum guidelines. The forty (40) hour training must include at least twenty-four (24) hours of training in mediation skills and techniques and at least sixteen (16) hours of additional training in the specific mediation techniques pertaining to the subject area of the types of cases to be referred to the applicant. The applicant must also document substantial recent experience mediating actual cases. Substantial recent experience is defined as a minimum of one hundred fifty (150) hours of actual face-to-face mediation practice as either a solo or co-mediator within the last five years OR successful completion of a structured apprenticeship. Such apprenticeship must, at a minimum, include the following components:

1. Mediation or co-mediation of at least two structured role-plays. The role-plays may be conducted as part of the aforementioned training requirement provided that the apprentice is given a sufficient opportunity to: deliver an opening statement; help parties exchange information, identify negotiable issues and explore options for resolution; and draft a written agreement that incorporates the terms of the parties' resolution; AND

2. Observation by apprentice of at least one mediation session involving an actual controversy between actual parties; AND

3. Mediation or co-mediation of at least ten (10) matters involving actual controversies between parties under the direct supervision of a coach or mentor who has previously been admitted to the ADR Program Roster; AND

4. Mediation or co-mediation of at least one case as the primary mediator followed by either a debriefing session with the coach or mentor or completion of a self-evaluation instrument.

An individual who has completed the minimum twenty-four (24) hours of mediation training described above, as well as the additional twelve (16) hours of training on mediation of parenting issues, may be provisionally accepted on the Court Roster on the condition that they complete the substantial experience requirement within six (6) months of his or her acceptance on the Court Roster of Mediators.

§ 13. Compensation of Neutrals

13.1 General Information Regarding Compensation of Neutrals

A. Court staff Neutrals and individuals providing ADR services pursuant to a contract with the Unified Court System shall not receive any additional compensation for ADR services provided under this program. However, individuals affiliated with a program providing ADR services pursuant to a contract with the Unified Court System shall not be precluded from receiving reimbursement when the services provided are outside the scope of the contract.

B. Court staff Neutrals are prohibited from accepting any outside employment as a Neutral for a fee.

C. Court Roster Neutrals shall not be compensated for time spent in required ADR training sessions conducted pursuant to these rules or for time spent on the application, selection and/or appointment process.

D. Court Roster Neutrals shall not be compensated for the first two (2) hours spent in ADR. Thereafter, all time spent following the first two (2) hours by the Neutral shall be compensable in accordance with these rules.

E. After the initial ADR two hour session, the Court Roster Neutral shall be permitted to charge the fee schedule published in the list of Court Roster Neutrals.

F. If the parties continue the ADR process after the initial session, the Neutral may also charge for the preparation time expended in the case.

G. Neutrals are encouraged to use a sliding scale when appropriate or to waive fees to ensure that no one is denied access to the ADR program based on inability to pay.

H. In the event that the Neutral's fees exceed fifteen hundred dollars ($1500.00) or more, the parties through their counsel are required to notify the Civil or Commercial or Matrimonial or Family Court ADR Program Administrator who will advise the Assigned Judge or Chief Clerk where no Judge is assigned. At that point, the Court will determine whether the ADR process should continue or advise the parties and counsel to appear for a court conference to discuss the status of the matter. The respective ADR Program Administrator will coordinate the notice to parties, counsel and the Neutral.

13.2 Special Considerations:

A. *Civil and Commercial Matters*

The Court Roster Neutral's fees and expenses shall be borne equally by the parties unless otherwise agreed in writing.

B. *Matrimonial and Family Court Matters*

The Neutral's fees shall be as agreed in a written Retainer Agreement executed by the parties and the Neutral before the commencement of the ADR session. The retainer agreement shall include the ratio at which the fee will be divided between the parties.

Some Family Courts in the 8th District may have access to Neutrals who provide mediation services to court litigants pursuant to a contract with the Unified Court System. These Neutrals may also be included on the Court Roster but they shall not receive any additional compensation for ADR services provided under this program.

The Court may employ Family Services Coordinators who are court employees, they shall not receive any additional compensation for ADR services provided under this program.

Fees for parenting coordinators are addressed in specific guidelines being developed for parenting coordination in the 8th Judicial District.

§ 14. Ongoing Review

The 8th Judicial District ADR Protocols will be subject to periodic review and adjustment as the program matures and develops, including statewide oversight and application of administrative rules.

In addition, litigants will be asked to complete an evaluation form, which will seek information about their experience with the process and the Court Roster Neutral. Court staff will collect the forms, analyze the data, and continue to work on improving the program.

02-03-09

COURT ROSTERS

Form 1. Court Roster Arbitrator for Civil Matters

APPLICATION FORM AND INSTRUCTIONS

The 8th Judicial District ADR Program is assembling a Court Roster of arbitrators to handle civil matters pending before the Court.

Arbitrators will not be compensated for the first two (2) hours spent in ADR. Thereafter, arbitrators, not employed by an agency having a contract with the Office of Court Administration, will be paid at the hourly rate they have listed on the Court Roster for arbitration work. Billable time will include actual time spent in arbitration sessions and up to one-half hour of pre or post preparation time for each scheduled session. Compensation exceeding $1,500.00 is subject to prior court approval.

Arbitrators responsibilities may include:

- Coordinating with Court staff;

- Managing cases promptly and efficiently;

- Conducting arbitration in accordance with the procedural and ethical standards related to arbitrations;

- Preparing decisions and/or disposition forms in a format acceptable to the Court.

Requirements for roster membership include completion of at least six (6) hours of training in procedural and ethical matters related to arbitration and either be:

1) A lawyer admitted to the practice of law for at least five (5) years AND have at least five (5) years of substantial experience in the specific subject area of the cases that will be referred; OR

2) A Judge, JHO, Court Attorney–Referee or Confidential Law Clerk to a Judge AND have at least five (5) years of substantial experience in the specific subject area of the cases that will be referred; OR

3) A "Subject Matter Expert" defined as a professional with at least five (5) years of professional experience in the specific subject area of the cases that will be referred to arbitration.

Appointment to the Court Roster is at the discretion of the Administrative Judge of the Eighth Judicial District in consultation with the Coordinator of the Unified Court System's Office of Alternative Dispute Resolution Programs. Admission will be competitive and will be based on each applicant's training, experience, education, and availability to arbitrate. Applicants may be required to participate in an interview process before a review committee appointed by the Administrative Judge.

Arbitrators may be removed from the panel at the discretion of the Administrative Judge in consultation with the Coordinator of the Unified Court System's Office of Alternative Dispute Resolution Programs.

To be considered for the Eighth Judicial District Court Roster of Arbitrators, please complete the enclosed application and return it to:

Sheila Schwanekamp, Esq.
8th Judicial District ADR Program Administrator
One Niagara Plaza, 5th Floor
Buffalo, New York 14202

Include a copy of your resume or curriculum vitae including references along with your hourly rate. Please also indicate if you utilize a sliding fee scale in appropriate cases.

Answer all questions completely.

Inform your references that they may be contacted by the 8th District Administrative Judge's Office.

Sign and date the declaration at the end of the application.

8th JUDICIAL DISTRICT ADR PROGRAM

APPLICATION

Court Roster Arbitrator—Civil Matters

A. General Information

Name: _____

Address: _____

_____

_____

Phone: _____

Email: _____

☐ I meet the training and experience requirements outlined above and am applying to be included on the Court Roster of Arbitrators for Civil matters.

B. Education

(Please list in reverse chronological order. Attach additional pages if necessary):

School	Graduated?	Major or Type of Course	Degree earned or expected

List any professional licenses you hold:

_____

C. Arbitration Training

Please detail all arbitration training you have taken (attach additional pages if necessary):

Course	Instructor(s)	Date of Completion	Total Hours

Attach copies of certificates of completion for the above-referenced trainings. If no certificate is available, the review committee may request relevant syllabus or course materials or other documentation that will enable the committee to determine if the course meets the established requirements.

D. Arbitration Experience

How many cases have you arbitrated in the last five (5) years? _____

On a separate sheet, please provide a brief statement (one page) outlining your substantial experience in the specific subject area of cases that will be referred.

State the percentage of your practice that consists of representing:

Plaintiffs ____%   Defendants ____%

E. Professional Fee

Hourly Rate: $ _____

Sliding Fee Scale: Yes _____   No _____

Answer all questions by placing an X in the appropriate column

If you answer "YES" to any of these questions, provide details on an attached sheet

	YES	NO
A) Except for minor traffic offenses and adjudications as youthful offender, wayward minor or juvenile delinquent:		
i) Have you ever been convicted of an offense against the law?		
ii) Have you ever forfeited bail or other collateral?		
iii) Do you now have any criminal charges pending against you?		
B) Have you ever received a discharge from the Armed Forces that was other than honorable?		
C) Have you ever been dismissed from any employment for reasons other than lack of work or funds?		
D) Are you currently in violation of a court order in any state for child or spousal support?		
E) Have you ever been subject to any disciplinary action concerning your current or any past profession?		

I affirm that all statements on this application (including any attached papers) are true.

_____   _____
Signature of Applicant   Date

Form 2. Court Roster Arbitrator for Commercial Matters

APPLICATION FORM AND INSTRUCTIONS

The 8th Judicial District ADR Program is assembling a Court Roster of arbitrators to handle commercial matters pending before the Court.

Arbitrators will not be compensated for the first two (2) hours spent in ADR. Thereafter, arbitrators, not employed by an agency having a contract with the Office of Court Administration, will be paid at the hourly rate they have listed on the Court Roster for arbitration work. Billable time will include actual time spent in arbitration sessions and up to one-half hour of pre or post preparation time for each scheduled session. Compensation exceeding $1,500.00 is subject to prior court approval.

Arbitrators responsibilities may include:

- Coordinating with Court staff;
- Managing cases promptly and efficiently;
- Conducting arbitration in accordance with the procedural and ethical standards related to arbitrations;
- Preparing decisions and/or disposition forms in a format acceptable to the Court.

Requirements for roster membership include completion of at least six (6) hours of training in procedural and ethical matters related to arbitration and either be:

1) A lawyer admitted to the practice of law for at least five (5) years AND have at least five (5) years of substantial experience in the specific subject area of the cases that will be referred; OR

2) A Judge, JHO, Court Attorney–Referee or Confidential Law Clerk to a Judge AND have at least five (5) years of substantial experience in the specific subject area of the cases that will be referred; OR

3) A "Subject Matter Expert" defined as a professional with at least five (5) years of professional experience in the specific subject area of the cases that will be referred to arbitration.

Appointment to the Court Roster is at the discretion of the Administrative Judge of the Eighth Judicial District in consultation with the Coordinator of the Unified Court System's Office of Alternative Dispute Resolution Programs. Admission will be competitive and will be based on each applicant's training, experience, education, and availability to arbitrate. Applicants may be required to participate in an interview process before a review committee appointed by the Administrative Judge.

Arbitrators may be removed from the panel at the discretion of the Administrative Judge in consultation with the Coordinator of the Unified Court System's Office of Alternative Dispute Resolution Programs.

To be considered for the Eighth Judicial District Court Roster of Arbitrators, please complete the enclosed application and return it to:

Sheila Schwanekamp, Esq.
8th Judicial District ADR Program Administrator
One Niagara Plaza, 5th Floor
Buffalo, New York 14202

Include a copy of your resume or curriculum vitae including references along with your hourly rate. Please also indicate if you utilize a sliding fee scale in appropriate cases.

Answer all questions completely.

Inform your references that they may be contacted by the 8th District Administrative Judge's Office.

Sign and date the declaration at the end of the application.

8th JUDICIAL DISTRICT ADR PROGRAM

APPLICATION

Court Roster Arbitrator—Commercial Matters

A. General Information

Name: _____

Address: _____

_____

_____

Phone: _____

Email: _____

☐ I meet the training and experience requirements outlined above and am applying to be included on the Court Roster of Arbitrators for Commercial matters.

B. Education

(Please list in reverse chronological order. Attach additional pages if necessary):

School	Graduated?	Major or Type of Course	Degree earned or expected

List any professional licenses you hold:

_____

C. Arbitration Training

Please detail all arbitration training you have taken (attach additional pages if necessary):

Course	Instructor(s)	Date of Completion	Total Hours

Attach copies of certificates of completion for the above-referenced trainings. If no certificate is available, the review committee may request relevant syllabus or course materials or other documentation that will enable the committee to determine if the course meets the established requirements.

D. Arbitration Experience

How many cases have you arbitrated in the last five (5) years?   _____

On a separate sheet, please provide a brief statement (one page) outlining your substantial experience in the specific subject area of cases that will be referred.

State the percentage of your practice that consists of representing:

Plaintiffs ____%   Defendants ____%

E. Professional Fee

Hourly Rate: $ ____

537

Sliding Fee Scale: Yes _____   No _____

Answer all questions by placing an X in the appropriate column

If you answer "YES" to any of these questions, provide details on an attached sheet

	YES	NO
A) Except for minor traffic offenses and adjudications as youthful offender, wayward minor or juvenile delinquent:		
i) Have you ever been convicted of an offense against the law?		
ii) Have you ever forfeited bail or other collateral?		
iii) Do you now have any criminal charges pending against you?		
B) Have you ever received a discharge from the Armed Forces that was other than honorable?		
C) Have you ever been dismissed from any employment for reasons other than lack of work or funds?		
D) Are you currently in violation of a court order in any state for child or spousal support?		
E) Have you ever been subject to any disciplinary action concerning your current or any past profession?		

I affirm that all statements on this application (including any attached papers) are true.

_____   _____
Signature of Applicant   Date

Form 3.   Court Roster Mediator for Civil Matters

APPLICATION FORM AND INSTRUCTIONS

The 8th Judicial District ADR Program is assembling a Court Roster of paid mediators to handle civil matters (excluding commercial and matrimonial matters) pending before the Court.

Mediators will not be compensated for the first two (2) hours spent in ADR. Thereafter, mediators, not employed by an agency having a contract with the Office of Court Administration, will be paid at the hourly rate they have listed on the Court Roster for mediation work. Billable time will include actual time spent in mediation sessions and up to one-half hour of pre or post preparation time for each scheduled session.   Compensation exceeding $1,500.00 is subject to prior court approval.

Mediators' responsibilities may include:

- Coordinating with Court staff;

- Managing cases promptly and efficiently;

- Conducting mediation in accordance with the ABA, AAA and ACR Model Standards of Conduct for Mediators;

- Preparing mediation agreements and/or disposition forms in a format acceptable to the Court; and

- Mentoring apprentice and student mediators.

Requirements for court roster membership include completion of 40 hours of mediation training which includes at least 24 hours of training on mediation skills and techniques and at least 16 hours of additional training in the specific mediation techniques pertaining to the subject area of the types of cases. This training must be sponsored or recognized by the New York State Unified Court System's Office of Alternative Dispute Resolution Programs or training that the Office of Court Administration's Alternative Dispute Resolution Program deems to comport substantively with the curriculum guidelines promulgated by that office AND have extensive civil litigation experience, or serve or have recently served as in-house counsel.

Applicants must also document substantial recent experience mediating actual cases, preferably civil matters. Substantial recent experience is defined by the applicable court.

Individuals who have completed the minimum forty (40) hours of mediation training described herein may be provisionally accepted on the Court Roster on the condition they complete the experiential requirements within six (6) months of their acceptance on the Court Roster.

Appointment to the Court Roster is at the discretion of the Administrative Judge of the Eighth Judicial District in consultation with the Coordinator of the Unified Court System's Office of Alternative Dispute Resolution Programs. Admission will be competitive and will be based on each applicant's training, experience, education, and availability to mediate. Applicants may be required to participate in an interview process before a review committee appointed by the Administrative Judge. Applicants may be requested to complete additional training or experiential requirements prior to admission to the roster if, in the opinion of the review committee, the applicant's mediation training and experience does not fully prepare them for mediator status.

Pursuant to the Rules of the Chief Administrator of the Courts, 22 NYCRR 146.3b, neutrals shall be redesignated to the court roster every two years. In determining whether to redesignate any neutral, the neutral must show proof of compliance with the requirement that they attend at least six (6) hours of additional approved training relevant to their respective practice areas every two years pursuant to 22 NYCRR 146.5. Mediators may also be removed from the panel at the discretion of the Administrative Judge in consultation with the Coordinator of the Unified Court System's Office of Alternative Dispute Resolution Programs.

To be considered for the Eighth Judicial District Court Roster of Civil Mediators, please complete the enclosed application and return it to:

Mary Louise Hayden, Esq.
8th Judicial District ADR Program Administrator
92 Franklin Street
Buffalo, New York 14202

Include a copy of your resume or curriculum vitae including references along with your hourly rate. Please also indicate if you utilize a sliding fee scale in appropriate cases.

Answer all questions completely.

Inform your references that they may be contacted by the 8th District Administrative Judge's Office.

Sign and date the declaration at the end of the application.

8th JUDICIAL DISTRICT ADR PROGRAM

APPLICATION

Court Roster Mediator—Civil Matters

A. General Information

Name: _____

Address: _____

_____

_____

_____

Phone: _____

Email: _____

2) Please check one:

☐ I meet the training and experience requirements outlined above and am applying to be included on the Court Roster of Mediators for Civil Matters.

☐ I do not meet the training requirement; however, I would like my application to be filed and to be informed of further training opportunities.

B. Education

(Please list in reverse chronological order. Attach additional pages if necessary):

School	Graduated?	Major or Type of Course	Degree earned or expected

List any professional licenses you hold:
_____

C. Mediation Training

Please detail all mediation training you have taken (attach additional pages if necessary):

Course	Instructor(s)	Date of Completion	Total Hours

Attach copies of certificates of completion for the above-referenced trainings. If no certificate is available, the review committee may request relevant syllabus or course materials or other documentation that will enable the committee to determine if the course meets the established requirements.

D. Mediation Experience

How many cases have you mediated in the last five (5) years? _____

Of these, how many involved civil issues? _____

On a separate sheet, please provide a brief statement (one page) outlining your mediation experience.

State the percentage of your practice that consists of representing:

Plaintiffs ____%   Defendants ____%

Are you able to conduct mediation in a language other than English?

☐ Yes

☐ No

If yes, specify language(s) and level of proficiency:

_____

E. Professional Fee

Hourly Rate: _____

Sliding Fee Scale: Yes _____   No _____

Answer all questions by placing an X in the appropriate column

If you answer "YES" to any of these questions, provide details on an attached sheet

	YES	NO
A) Except for minor traffic offenses and adjudications as youthful offender, wayward minor or juvenile delinquent:		
i) Have you ever been convicted of an offense against the law?		
ii) Have you ever forfeited bail or other collateral?		
iii) Do you now have any criminal charges pending against you?		
B) Have you ever received a discharge from the Armed Forces that was other than honorable?		
C) Have you ever been dismissed from any employment for reasons other than lack of work or funds?		
D) Are you currently in violation of a court order in any state for child or spousal support?		
E) Have you ever been subject to any disciplinary action concerning your current or any past profession?		

I affirm that all statements on this application (including any attached papers) are true.

_____   _____
Signature of Applicant   Date

08-28-08

Form 4.   Court Roster Mediator for Commercial Matters

APPLICATION FORM AND INSTRUCTIONS

The 8th Judicial District ADR Program is assembling a Court Roster of paid mediators in commercial matters pending before the Court.

Mediators will not be compensated for the first two (2) hours spent in ADR. Thereafter, mediators who are not employed by an agency having a contract with the Office of Court Administration will be paid at an hourly rate they have listed on the Court Roster for mediation work. Billable time will include actual time spent in mediation sessions and up to one-half hour of pre or post preparation time for each scheduled session.   Compensation exceeding $1,500.00 is subject to prior court approval.

Mediators' responsibilities may include:

- Coordinating with Court staff;

- Managing cases promptly and efficiently;

- Conducting mediation in accordance with the ABA, AAA and ACR Model Standards of Conduct for Mediators;

- Preparing mediation agreements and/or disposition forms in a format acceptable to the Court; and

- Mentoring apprentice and student mediators.

Requirements for court roster membership include completion of 40 hours of mediation training which includes at least 24 hours of training on mediation skills and techniques and at least 16 hours of additional training in the specific mediation techniques pertaining to the subject area of the types of cases. This training must be sponsored or recognized by the New York State Unified Court System's Office of Alternative Dispute Resolution Programs or training that the Office of Court Administration's Alternative Dispute Resolution Program deems to comport substantively with the curriculum guidelines promulgated by that office AND have extensive commercial litigation experience, commercial matter experience or serve or have recently served as in-house counsel.

Applicants must also document substantial recent experience mediating actual cases, preferably commercial matters.   Substantial recent experience is defined by the applicable court.

Appointment to the Court Roster is at the discretion of the Administrative Judge of the Eighth Judicial District in consultation with the Coordinator of the Unified Court System's Office of Alternative Dispute Resolution Programs. Admission will be competitive and will be based on each applicant's training, experience, education, and availability to mediate. Applicants may be required to participate in an interview process before a review committee appointed by the Administrative Judge. Applicants may be requested to complete additional training or experiential requirements prior to admission to the roster if, in the opinion of the review committee, the applicant's mediation training and experience does not fully prepare them for mediator status.

Pursuant to the Rules of the Chief Administrator of the Courts, 22 NYCRR 146.3b, neutrals shall be redesignated to the court roster every two years. In determining whether to redesignate any neutral, the neutral must show proof of compliance with the requirement that they attend at least six (6) hours of additional approved training relevant to their respective practice areas every two years pursuant to 22 NYCRR 146.5. Mediators may also be removed from the panel at the discretion of the Administrative Judge in consultation with the Coordinator of the Unified Court System's Office of Alternative Dispute Resolution Programs. Mediators may also be removed from the panel at the discretion of the Administrative Judge in consultation with the Coordinator of the Unified Court System's Office of Alternative Dispute Resolution Programs.

To be considered for the Eighth Judicial District Court Roster of Civil Mediators, please complete the enclosed application and return it to:

Mary Louise Hayden, Esq.
8th Judicial District ADR Program Administrator
92 Franklin Street
Buffalo, New York 14202

Include a copy of your resume or curriculum vitae including references along with your hourly rate. Please also indicate if you utilize a sliding fee scale in appropriate cases.

Answer all questions completely.

Inform your references that they may be contacted by the 8th District Administrative Judge's Office.

Sign and date the declaration at the end of the application.

8th JUDICIAL DISTRICT ADR PROGRAM

APPLICATION

Court Roster Mediator—Commercial Matters

A. General Information

Name: _____

Address: _____

_____

_____

Phone: _____

Email: _____

2) Please check one:

☐ I meet the training and experience requirements outlined above and am applying to be included on the Court Roster of Mediators for Commercial Matters.

☐ I do not meet the training requirement; however, I would like my application to be filed and to be informed of further training opportunities.

B. Education

(Please list in reverse chronological order. Attach additional pages if necessary):

School	Graduated?	Major or Type of Course	Degree earned or expected

List any professional licenses you hold: _____

C. Mediation Training

Please detail all mediation training you have taken (attach additional pages if necessary):

Course	Instructor(s)	Date of Completion	Total Hours

Attach copies of certificates of completion for the above-referenced trainings. If no certificate is available, the review committee may request relevant syllabus or course materials or other documentation that will enable the committee to determine if the course meets the established requirements.

D. Mediation Experience

How many cases have you mediated in the last five (5) years? _____

Of these, how many involved commercial issues? _____

On a separate sheet, please provide a brief statement (one page) outlining your mediation experience.

State the percentage of your practice that consists of representing:

Plaintiffs _____%   Defendants _____%

Are you able to conduct mediation in a language other than English?

☐ Yes

☐ No

If yes, specify language(s) and level of proficiency:

_____

E. Professional Fee

Hourly Rate: _____

Sliding Fee Scale: Yes _____   No _____

Answer all questions by placing an X in the appropriate column

If you answer "YES" to any of these questions, provide details on an attached sheet

	YES	NO
A) Except for minor traffic offenses and adjudications as youthful offender, wayward minor or juvenile delinquent:		
i) Have you ever been convicted of an offense against the law?		
ii) Have you ever forfeited bail or other collateral?		
iii) Do you now have any criminal charges pending against you?		
B) Have you ever received a discharge from the Armed Forces that was other than honorable?		
C) Have you ever been dismissed from any employment for reasons other than lack of work or funds?		
D) Are you currently in violation of a court order in any state for child or spousal support?		
E) Have you ever been subject to any disciplinary action concerning your current or any past profession?		

I affirm that all statements on this application (including any attached papers) are true.

_____   _____

Signature of Applicant   Date

08/2008

Form 5.   Court Roster Mediator—Family
Court (Parenting Issue) Matters

APPLICATION FORM AND INSTRUCTIONS

The 8th Judicial District ADR Program is assembling a Court Roster of paid mediators in Family Court matters and unpaid apprentice mediators to handle parenting issues pending before the court.

Mediators will not be compensated for the first two (2) hours spent in ADR. Thereafter, mediators, not employed by an agency having a contract with the Office of Court Administration, will be paid at the hourly rate of $50.00 in Family Court matters for mediation work. Billable time will include actual time spent in mediation sessions and up to one-half hour of pre or post preparation time for each scheduled session.

Mediators' responsibilities may include:

● Coordinating with Court staff;

● Managing cases promptly and efficiently;

● Conducting mediation in accordance with the Model Standard of Conduct for Family and Divorce Mediation (www.afccnet.org/resources/resources_model_ mediation.asp);

● Preparing mediation agreements and/or disposition forms in a format acceptable to the court; and

● Mentoring apprentice and student mediators.

To be eligible to receive a Court referral and be included on the Court's Roster of Mediators- Parenting Issues in Matrimonial and/or Family Court Matters, an individual must have extensive, relevant legal expertise in parenting issues or extensive professional training and expertise regarding parenting issues. Additionally, the individual must complete 40 hours of mediation training either conducted by a trainer whom the New York State Unified Court System's Office of Alternative Dispute Resolution Programs has certified or that the Office of Court Administration's Alternative Dispute Resolution Program deems to comport substantively with the curriculum guidelines promulgated by that office. The 40 hours of training must include at least 24 hours of training in mediation skills and techniques and at least 16 hours of additional training on the specific training on mediation of child custody and parenting issue matters.

Applicants must also document substantial recent experience mediating actual cases, preferably family matters. Substantial recent experience is defined as at least 150 hours of actual face-to-face mediation practice as either a solo or co-mediator within the last five (5) years or the applicant must document successful completion of a structured apprenticeship.

Appointment to the Court Roster is at the discretion of the Administrative Judge of the Eighth Judicial District in consultation with the Coordinator of the Unified Court System's Office of Alternative Dispute Resolution Programs. Admission will be competitive and will be based on each applicant's training, experience, education, and availability to mediate. Applicants may be required to participate in an interview process before a review committee appointed by the Administrative Judge. Applicants may be requested to complete additional training or experiential requirements prior to admission to the Court Roster if, in the opinion of the review committee, the applicant's mediation training and experience does not fully prepare them for mediator status.

Individuals who have completed the training requirement but do not meet the experiential requirement may be admitted as an unpaid apprentice mediator. Before being admitted to the Court Roster as a paid mediator, an apprentice must conduct two structured roleplay mediation sessions as a co-mediator under the mentorship of a mediator previously admitted to the program roster and observation of at least one mediation session involving an actual controversy between the parties;

and mediation or co-mediation of at least ten (10) matters involving actual controversies between parties; and mediation or co-mediation of at least one case as the primary mediator followed by either a debriefing session with the coach or mentor or completion of a self-evaluation instrument.

An individual who has completed the minimum forty (40) hours of mediation training described above, may be provisionally accepted on the Court Roster on the condition that they complete all other requirements within six (6) months of their acceptance on the Court Roster of Mediators.

Pursuant to the Rules of the Chief Administrator of the Courts, 22 NYCRR 146.3b, neutrals shall be redesignated to the court roster every two years. In determining whether to redesignate any neutral, the neutral must show proof of compliance with the requirement that they attend at least six (6) hours of additional approved training relevant to their respective practice areas every two years pursuant to 22 NYCRR 146.5. Mediators may also be removed from the panel at the discretion of the Administrative Judge in consultation with the Coordinator of the Unified Court System's Office of Alternative Dispute Resolution Programs.

Mediators may be removed from the panel at the discretion of the Administrative Judge in consultation with the Coordinator of the Unified Court System's Office of Alternative Dispute Resolution Programs.

To be considered for the Eighth Judicial District Family Court's Mediator roster, please complete the enclosed application and return it to:

Mary Louise Hayden, Esq.
8th Judicial District ADR Program Administrator
92 Franklin Street
Buffalo, New York 14202

Include a copy of your resume or curriculum vitae including references along with your hourly rate. Please also indicate if you utilize a sliding fee scale in appropriate cases.

Answer all questions completely.

Inform your references that they may be contacted by the 8th District Administrative Judge's Office.

Sign and date the declaration at the end of the application.

8th JUDICIAL DISTRICT ADR PROGRAM

APPLICATION

Court Roster Mediator—Family Court (Parenting Issue) Matters

A. General Information

Name: _____

Address: _____

_____

_____

Phone: _____

Email: _____

2) Please check one:

☐ I meet the training and experience requirements outlined above and am applying to be included on the Court Roster of Mediators.

☐ I believe that I meet the training requirement, but not the experience requirement. I am applying to be included on the roster as an unpaid apprentice mediator so that I may acquire the necessary experience to be considered for admission as a paid mediator at a future time.

☐ I do not meet the training requirement; however, I would like my application to be filed and to be informed of further training opportunities.

B. Education

(Please list in reverse chronological order. Attach additional pages if necessary):

School	Graduated?	Major or Type of Course	Degree earned or expected

List any professional licenses you hold:

C. Mediation Training

Please detail all mediation training you have taken (attach additional pages if necessary):

Course	Instructor(s)	Date of Completion	Total Hours

Attach copies of certificates of completion for the above-referenced trainings. If no certificate is available, the review committee may request relevant syllabus or course materials or other documentation that will enable the committee to determine if the course meets the established requirements.

D. Mediation Experience

How many cases have you mediated in the last five (5) years? _____

Of these, how many involved family issues? _____

On a separate sheet, please provide a brief statement (one page) outlining your mediation experience.

Are you a Volunteer Community Mediator?

☐ Yes
☐ No

If yes, with which agency or agencies? _____

Are you able to conduct mediation in a language other than English?

☐ Yes
☐ No

If yes, specify language(s) and level of proficiency:

Answer all questions by placing an X in the appropriate column

If you answer "YES" to any of these questions, provide details on an attached sheet

                                                    YES   NO

A) Except for minor traffic offenses and adjudications as youthful offender, wayward minor or juvenile delinquent:

i)	Have you ever been convicted of an offense against the law?	
ii)	Have you ever forfeited bail or other collateral?	
iii)	Do you now have any criminal charges pending against you?	

B) Have you ever received a discharge from the Armed Forces that was other than honorable?

C) Have you ever been dismissed from any employment for reasons other than lack of work or funds?

D) Are you currently in violation of a court order in any state for child or spousal support?

E) Have you ever been subject to any disciplinary action concerning your current or any past profession?

I affirm that all statements on this application (including any attached papers) are true.

_____   _____
Signature of Applicant   Date

05–06–09

Form 6.   Court Roster Mediator—Matrimonial
(Parenting Issue) Matters

APPLICATION FORM AND INSTRUCTIONS

The 8th Judicial District ADR Program is assembling a Court Roster of paid mediators in matrimonial and Family Court matters and unpaid apprentice mediators to handle parenting issues pending before the court.

Mediators will not be compensated for the first two (2) hours spent in ADR. Thereafter, mediators, not employed by an agency having a contract with the Office of Court Administration, will be paid at the hourly rate they have listed on the Court Roster for mediation work. Billable time will include actual time spent in mediation sessions and up to one-half hour of pre or post preparation time for each scheduled session. Compensation exceeding more than $1,500.00 is subject to prior court approval.

Mediators' responsibilities may include:

- Coordinating with Court staff;
- Managing cases promptly and efficiently;
- Conducting mediation in accordance with the Model Standard of Conduct for Family and Divorce Mediation (www.afccnet.org/resources/resources_model_mediation.asp);
- Preparing mediation agreements and/or disposition forms in a format acceptable to the court; and
- Mentoring apprentice and student mediators.

To be eligible to receive a Court referral and be included on the Court's Roster of Mediators- Parenting Issues in Matrimonial and/or Family Court Matters, an individual must have extensive, relevant legal expertise in parenting issues or extensive professional training and expertise regarding parenting issues. Additionally, the individual must complete 40 hours of mediation training either conducted by a trainer whom the New York State Unified Court System's Office of Alternative Dispute Resolution Programs has certified or that the Office of Court Administration's Alternative Dispute Resolution Program deems to comport substantively with the curriculum guidelines promulgated by that office. The 40 hours of training must include at least 24 hours of training in mediation skills and techniques and at least 16 hours of additional training on the specific training on mediation of child custody and parenting issue matters.

Applicants must also document substantial recent experience mediating actual cases, preferably family matters. Substantial recent experience is defined as at least 150 hours of actual face-to-face mediation practice as either a solo or co-mediator within the last five (5) years or the applicant must document successful completion of a structured apprenticeship.

Appointment to the Court Roster is at the discretion of the Administrative Judge of the Eighth Judicial District in consultation with the Coordinator of the Unified Court System's Office of Alternative Dispute Resolution Programs. Admission will be competitive and will be based on each applicant's training, experience, education, and availability to mediate. Applicants may be required to participate in an interview process before a review committee appointed by the Administrative Judge. Applicants may be requested to complete additional training or experiential requirements prior to admission to the Court Roster if, in the opinion of the review committee, the applicant's mediation training and experience does not fully prepare them for mediator status.

Individuals who have completed the training requirement but do not meet the experiential requirement may be admitted as an unpaid apprentice mediator. Before being admitted to the Court Roster as a paid mediator, an apprentice must conduct two structured roleplay mediation sessions as a co-mediator under the mentorship of a mediator previously admitted to the program roster and observation of at least one mediation session involving an actual controversy between the parties; and mediation or co-mediation of at least ten (10) matters involving actual controversies between parties; and mediation or co-mediation of at least one case as the primary mediator followed by either a debriefing session with the coach or mentor or completion of a self-evaluation instrument.

An individual who has completed the minimum forty (40) hours of mediation training described above, may be provisionally accepted on the Court Roster on the condition that they complete all other requirements within six (6) months of their acceptance on the Court Roster of Mediators.

Pursuant to the Rules of the Chief Administrator of the Courts, 22 NYCRR 146.3b, neutrals shall be redesignated to the court roster every two years. In determining whether to redesignate any neutral, the neutral must show proof of compliance with the requirement that they attend at least six (6) hours of additional approved training relevant to their respective practice areas every two years pursuant to 22 NYCRR 146.5. Mediators may also be removed from the panel at the discretion of the Administrative Judge in consultation with the Coordinator of the Unified Court System's Office of Alternative Dispute Resolution Programs.

Mediators may be removed from the panel at the discretion of the Administrative Judge in consultation with the Coordinator of the Unified Court System's Office of Alternative Dispute Resolution Programs.

To be considered for the Eighth Judicial District Matrimonial and/or Family Court's Mediator roster, please complete the enclosed application and return it to:

Mary Louise Hayden, Esq.
8th Judicial District ADR Program Administrator
92 Franklin Street
Buffalo, New York 14202

Include a copy of your resume or curriculum vitae including references along with your hourly rate. Please also indicate if you utilize a sliding fee scale in appropriate cases.

Answer all questions completely.

Inform your references that they may be contacted by the 8th District Administrative Judge's Office.

Sign and date the declaration at the end of the application.

8th JUDICIAL DISTRICT ADR PROGRAM

APPLICATION

Court Roster Mediator—Matrimonial (Parenting Issue) Matters

A. General Information

Name: _____

Address: _____

_____

_____

Phone: _____

Email: _____

2) Please check one:

☐ I meet the training and experience requirements outlined above and am applying to be included on the Court Roster of Mediators.

☐ I believe that I meet the training requirement, but not the experience requirement. I am applying to be included on the roster as an unpaid apprentice mediator so that I may acquire the necessary experience to be considered for admission as a paid mediator at a future time.

☐ I do not meet the training requirement; however, I would like my application to be filed and to be informed of further training opportunities.

B. Education

(Please list in reverse chronological order. Attach additional pages if necessary):

School	Graduated?	Major or Type of Course	Degree earned or expected

List any professional licenses you hold:

_____

C. Mediation Training

Please detail all mediation training you have taken (attach additional pages if necessary):

Course	Instructor(s)	Date of Completion	Total Hours

Attach copies of certificates of completion for the above-referenced trainings. If no certificate is available, the review committee may request relevant syllabus or course materials or other documentation that will enable the committee to determine if the course meets the established requirements.

D. Mediation Experience

How many cases have you mediated in the last five (5) years?   _____

Of these, how many involved family issues?   _____

On a separate sheet, please provide a brief statement (one page) outlining your mediation experience.

Are you a Volunteer Community Mediator?

☐ Yes

☐ No

If yes, with which agency or agencies? _____

Are you able to conduct mediation in a language other than English?

☐ Yes

☐ No

If yes, specify language(s) and level of proficiency:

_____

E. Professional Fee

Hourly Rate: _____

Sliding Fee Scale   Yes _____   No _____

_____

Answer all questions by placing an X in the appropriate column

If you answer "YES" to any of these questions, provide details on
an attached sheet

	YES	NO
A) Except for minor traffic offenses and adjudications as youthful offender, wayward minor or juvenile delinquent:		
i) Have you ever been convicted of an offense against the law?		
ii) Have you ever forfeited bail or other collateral?		
iii) Do you now have any criminal charges pending against you?		
B) Have you ever received a discharge from the Armed Forces that was other than honorable?		
C) Have you ever been dismissed from any employment for reasons other than lack of work or funds?		
D) Are you currently in violation of a court order in any state for child or spousal support?		
E) Have you ever been subject to any disciplinary action concerning your current or any past profession?		

I affirm that all statements on this application (including any attached papers) are
true.

_____   _____
        Signature of Applicant   Date

05–07–09

Form 7. Court Roster Neutral Evaluator for Civil, Commercial and Matrimonial Matters

8TH JUDICIAL DISTRICT ADR PROGRAM

COURT ROSTER NEUTRAL EVALUATOR FOR CIVIL, or COMMERCIAL or MATRIMONIAL MATTERS

APPLICATION FORM AND INSTRUCTIONS

The 8th Judicial District ADR Program is assembling a Court Roster of neutral evaluators to handle civil, commercial and matrimonial matters pending before the Court.

Neutral evaluators will not be compensated for the first two (2) hours spent in ADR. Thereafter, neutral evaluators, who are not court employees and who are not employed by an agency having a contract with the Office of Court Administration, will be paid at an hourly rate they have listed on the Court Roster for neutral evaluation work. Billable time will include actual time spent in neutral evaluation sessions and up to one-half hour of pre or post preparation time for each scheduled session. Compensation exceeding $1,500.00 is subject to prior court approval.

Neutral evaluators responsibilities may include:

- Coordinating with Court staff;

- Managing cases promptly and efficiently;

- Conducting neutral evaluations in accordance with the procedural and ethical standards related to neutral evaluation;

- Preparing agreements and/or disposition forms in a format acceptable to the Court.

Requirements for Court Roster membership include completion of at least six (6) hours of training in procedural and ethical matters related to neutral evaluation and either be:

1) A lawyer admitted to the practice of law for at least five (5) years AND have at least five (5) years of substantial experience in the specific subject area of the cases that will be referred; OR

2) A Judge, JHO, Court Attorney–Referee or Confidential Law Clerk to a Judge AND have at least five (5) years of substantial experience in the specific subject area of the cases that will be referred.

Appointment to the Court Roster is at the discretion of the Administrative Judge of the Eighth Judicial District in consultation with the Coordinator of the Unified Court System's Office of Alternative Dispute Resolution Programs. Admission will be competitive and will be based on each applicant's training, experience, education, and availability to conduct neutral evaluations. Applicants may be required to participate in an interview process before a review committee appointed by the Administrative Judge.

Pursuant to the Rules of the Chief Administrator of the Courts, 22 NYCRR 146.3b, neutrals shall be redesignated to the court roster every two years. In determining whether to redesignate any neutral, the neutral must show proof of compliance with the requirement that they attend at least six (6) hours of additional approved training relevant to their respective practice areas every two years pursuant to 22 NYCRR 146.5. Neutral evaluators may be removed from the panel at the discretion of the Administrative Judge in consultation with the Coordinator of the Unified Court System's Office of Alternative Dispute Resolution Programs.

To be considered for the Eighth Judicial District Court Roster of Arbitrators, please complete the enclosed application and return it to:

Mary Louise Hayden, Esq.
8th Judicial District ADR Program Administrator

92 Franklin Street
Buffalo, New York 14202

Include a copy of your resume or curriculum vitae with references along with your hourly rate. Please also indicate if you utilize a sliding fee scale in appropriate cases.

Answer all questions completely.

Inform your references that they may be contacted by the 8th District Administrative Judge's Office.

Sign and date the declaration at the end of the application.

8th JUDICIAL DISTRICT ADR PROGRAM

APPLICATION

Court Roster Neutral Evaluator—Civil, or Commercial, or Matrimonial Matters

A. General Information

Name: _____

Address: _____

_____

_____

Phone: _____

Email: _____

☐ I meet the training and experience requirements outlined above and are applying to be included on the Court Roster of Neutral Evaluators.

I am applying for Court Roster Neutral Evaluator for (please check all that apply)

☐ Civil Matters

☐ Commercial Matters

☐ Matrimonial Matters

B. Education

(Please list in reverse chronological order. Attach additional pages if necessary):

School	Graduated?	Major or Type of Course	Degree earned or expected

List any professional licenses you hold:

_____

C. Neutral Evaluation Training

Please detail all neutral evaluation training you have taken (attach additional pages if necessary):

Course	Instructor(s)	Date of Completion	Total Hours

Attach copies of certificates of completion for the above-referenced trainings. If no certificate is available, the review committee may request relevant syllabus or course materials or other documentation that will enable the committee to determine if the course meets the established requirements.

D. Neutral Evaluation Experience

How many cases have you conducted neutral evaluations in the last five (5) years? _____

On a separate sheet, please provide a brief statement (one page) outlining your substantial experience in the specific subject area of cases that will be referred.

State the percentage of your practice that consists of representing:

Plaintiffs ___%   Defendants ___%

E. Professional Fee

Hourly Rate: _____

Sliding Fee Scale   Yes _____   No _____

Answer all questions by placing an X in the appropriate column

If you answer "YES" to any of these questions, provide details on an attached sheet

	YES	NO
A) Except for minor traffic offenses and adjudications as youthful offender, wayward minor or juvenile delinquent:		
i) Have you ever been convicted of an offense against the law?		
ii) Have you ever forfeited bail or other collateral?		
iii) Do you now have any criminal charges pending against you?		
B) Have you ever received a discharge from the Armed Forces that was other than honorable?		
C) Have you ever been dismissed from any employment for reasons other than lack of work or funds?		
D) Are you currently in violation of a court order in any state for child or spousal support?		
E) Have you ever been subject to any disciplinary action concerning your current or any past profession?		

I affirm that all statements on this application (including any attached papers) are true.

_____   _____
Signature of Applicant   Date

08/2008

COURT ROSTER PARENTING COORDINATOR

APPLICATION FORM AND INSTRUCTIONS

Doc. 1.   Application Form and Instructions

4/25/08

The 8th Judicial District ADR Program is assembling a Court Roster of parenting coordinators in matrimonial and Family Court matters to handle high conflict parenting time matters pending before the court.

Parenting coordination is a child-focused alternative dispute resolution (ADR) process in which a mental health or legal professional with mediation training and experience assists high conflict parents to implement their parenting plan by facilitating the resolution of their disputes in a timely manner, educating parenting about children's needs. With prior approval of the parties and the court, the PC may make decisions within the scope of the court order or appointment contract.

The overall objective of parenting coordination is to assist parents in high conflict to implement their parenting plan, to monitor compliance with the details of the plan, to resolve conflicts regarding their children and the parenting plan in a timely manner, and to protect and sustain safe, healthy and meaningful parent-child relationships. Parenting coordination is a quasi-legal, mental health, alternative dispute resolution process that combines assessment, education, case management, conflict management and, upon consent, sometimes decision making functions.

Qualifications required for Court Roster membership include:

A PC shall be qualified by education and training to undertake parenting coordination and shall continue to develop professionally in the role.

A. The PC will be required to have training and experience in family mediation and professional interaction with high conflict families. The PC shall have completed the training required by then-current rules adopted by the 8th Judicial District, and as they may be amended or modified, or have sufficient years of professional experience to seek a waiver (whether temporary or conditional as determined by the ADR Administration of the 8th Judicial District) of this requirement.

B. The PC shall be a licensed mental health professional or licensed attorney with experience in an area relating to families, or a certified family mediator with a master's degree in a mental health field.

C. The PC should have extensive practical experience in the profession with high conflict or litigating parents.

D. The PC shall have completed training approved by the ADR Administration of the 8th Judicial District in the parenting coordination process, family dynamics in separation and divorce, parenting coordination techniques, domestic violence and child maltreatment, and court specific parenting coordination procedures.

E. A PC must acquire and maintain professional competence in the parenting coordination process. A PC shall regularly participate in educational activities promoting professional growth. A PC may participate in peer consultation or mentoring to receive feedback and support on cases and such professional consultation is specifically permitted.

F. A PC must decline an appointment, withdraw, or request appropriate assistance when the facts and circumstances of a case are beyond the PC's skill or expertise, particularly when elements of domestic violence surface.

G. In the first twelve (12) months after adoption of these protocols, professionals who have significant exposure with high conflict families but lack some part of the criteria noted above, may petition the District, through the Office of Court Administration's Office of ADR and Court Improvement, for waiver of a qualification.

Candidates who attend the OCA sponsored parenting coordination training agree to provide 20 pro bono hours of parenting coordination services in exchange for the free training for those families who would otherwise not be able to afford these services. After fulfilling the pro bono requirement, Parenting Coordinators will be eligible for reimbursement at the hourly rate they establish and publish in the 8th District Court Roster of Parenting Coordinators. Compensation exceeding more than $1,500.00 is subject to prior court approval.

Appointment to the Court Roster is at the discretion of the Administrative Judge of the Eighth Judicial District in consultation with the Coordinator of the Unified Court System's Office of Alternative Dispute Resolution Programs. Admission will be competitive and will be based on each applicant's training, experience, education, and availability to mediate. Applicants may be requested to complete additional training or experiential requirements prior to admission to the Court Roster if, in the opinion of the review committee, the applicant's parenting coordination training and experience does not fully prepare them for parenting coordinator status.

Parenting coordinators may be removed from the panel at the discretion of the Administrative Judge in consultation with the Coordinator of the Unified Court System's Office of Alternative Dispute Resolution Programs.

To be considered for the Eighth Judicial District Matrimonial and/or Family Court's Parenting Coordinator roster, please complete the enclosed application and return it to:

Sheila Schwanekamp

8th Judicial District ADR Program Administrator

One Niagara Plaza, 5th Floor

Buffalo, New York 14202

Include a copy of your resume or curriculum vitae.

Answer all questions completely.

Inform your references that they may be contacted by the 8th District Administrative Judge's Office.

Sign and date the declaration at the end of the application.

APPLICATION

Doc. 2.   Application

8th JUDICIAL DISTRICT ADR PROGRAM

APPLICATION FOR COURT ROSTER PARENTING COORDINATOR

A. General Information

Name: _____

Address: _____

_____

_____

Phone: _____

Email: _____

2) Please check one:

☐ I meet the training and experience requirements outlined above and am applying to be included on the Court Roster of Parenting Coordinators.

☐ I have significant exposure with high conflict families but I do not have some part of the criteria noted above. I would like my application to be considered by the Administrative Judge and the OCA ADR Office for inclusion of the Court Roster.

B. Education

(Please list in reverse chronological order. Attach additional pages if necessary):

School	Graduated?	Major or Type of Course	Degree earned or expected

List any professional licenses you hold—licensed mental health professional or attorney with experience in an area relating to families, or a certified family mediator with a master's degree in a mental health field:

C. Experience

Please detail in an attachment your extensive practical experience in the profession with high conflict or litigating parents.

D. Parenting Coordination Training

Please detail all parenting coordination training you have taken (attach additional pages if necessary):

Course	Instructor(s)	Date of Completion	Total Hours

Attach copies of certificates of completion for the above-referenced training. If no certificate is available, the review committee may request relevant syllabus or course materials or other documentation that will enable the committee to determine if the course meets the established requirements.

E. Are you able to conduct parenting coordination in a language other than English?

☐ Yes

☐ No

If yes, specify language(s) and level of proficiency:

F. Professional Fees

Hourly rate _____

Will you accept referrals on a sliding scale basis in appropriate cases?

Yes _____   No _____

Answer all questions by placing an X in the appropriate column

If you answer "YES" to any of these questions, provide details on an attached sheet

	YES NO
A) Except for minor traffic offenses and adjudications as youthful offender, wayward minor or juvenile delinquent: i) Have you ever been convicted of an offense against the law?	

    ii)   Have you ever forfeited bail or other collateral? _____

    iii)   Do you now have any criminal charges pending against you? _____

B)   Have you ever received a discharge from the Armed Forces that was other than honorable? _____

C)   Have you ever been dismissed from any employment for reasons other than lack of work or funds? _____

D)   Are you currently in violation of a court order in any state for child or spousal support? _____

I affirm that all statements on this application (including any attached papers) are true.

_____   _____
       Signature of Applicant   Date

ORDER APPOINTING PARENTING COORDINATOR

Doc. 3. Order Appointing Parenting Coordinator

PRESENT:
Hon.

        Justice

                                   ORDER APPOINTING PARENTING
                                   COORDINATOR

          Plaintiff/Petitioner,

                                     Index No:

     —against—

     Defendant/Respondent.

_____

The above referenced (action) (proceeding) was brought pursuant to _____. (Family Court Act § 6) (Domestic Relations Law § 240). The (Plaintiff) (Petitioner) _____, represented by _____ and/or the (Defendant)(Respondent) _____, represented by _____ seek an Order enforcing and/or modifying an existing custody and/or parenting time order concerning the following minor child(ren);

_____

_____

_____

The matter has come to be heard before this Court on _____, 200 ___. The Plaintiff/Petitioner and the Defendant/Respondent have appeared before this Court and have been advised by the Court of their right to counsel pursuant to Family Court Act § 261–62; and the (Plaintiff/Petitioner) and/or (Defendant/Respondent) have waived their right to counsel or do not meet the financial threshold to qualify for Court appointed counsel, and a Law Guardian, _____ having been appointed to represent the interest of the child(ren).

The Court has examined and taken inquiry into the facts and circumstances of this matter adduced through a review of the stipulation of the parties, the conferences held before this Court on _____, a hearing held before this Court on _____, and review of the submittals before this Court.

The Court takes note that the parties are engaged in high conflict litigation over the custody and visitation issues and have demonstrated a pattern of prior and ongoing acrimony and dissension potentially detrimental to their own self interests and the interests of their child(ren).

The Court finds that the utilization of a Parenting Coordinator is necessary to assist the parties/parents herein in implementing the terms of the existing parenting plan dated _____ as incorporated but not merged by the Order/Judgment dated _____ so as to reduce conflict and/or its possible detrimental impact upon the child(ren)'s welfare.

Accordingly, in attempts to mitigate against further acrimony, conflict, repeated costly court appearances and motion practice, this Court issues the following Order so as to adopt and facilitate the desired use of a Parenting Coordinator to assist the parties/parents herein in implementing the terms of the existing parenting plan dated _____ as incorporated but not merged by the Order/Judgment dated _____.

Parenting Coordinator:

The Court appoints _____ from the 8th District Court Roster of qualified parenting coordinators with offices at _____ tel. _____ to serve as the Parenting Coordinator.

A copy of this Order shall immediately be forwarded by the Court to the Parenting Coordinator upon the issuance of this Order. The parties shall thereafter contact the Parenting Coordinator within five (5) days of the issuance of this Order to engage this process.

Term:

The term of the Parenting Coordinator's service shall be for a period of __ months/ __ years from the date of this Order. The Parenting Coordinator may withdraw, resign or decline service upon written notification to the Court and both parties. In addition, the Parenting Coordinator's services may be terminated upon written agreement of both parties approved by the Court or by further Court order. Absent such resignation, agreement or order, however, the Parenting Coordinator may not be terminated by either of the parties before expiration of the term.

Fees and Compensation:

The Parenting Coordinator shall be compensated by the parties at an hourly rate established by the parenting coordinator.

The parties and Parenting Coordinator shall execute a retainer agreement concerning the fees to be paid to the parenting coordinator by the parties. In pro bono cases, the parties will each be required to pay a minimum fee of $2.00 per hour to the parenting coordinator.

Father shall pay __ % and Mother shall pay __ % of the parenting coordinator's retainer within 10 days of this order. Father shall pay __ % and Mother shall pay __ % for additional services beyond the retainer upon 5 days receipt of a written invoice.

Issues Subject to Parenting Coordination:

In order to facilitate the implementation of the court-ordered parenting plan, the Parenting Coordinator is appointed to assist the parties to resolve their conflicts in the following areas:

Check appropriate box(s) below:

☐ 1.   Minor changes or clarification of parenting time/access schedules or conditions

☐ including vacation, holidays and temporary variation from the existing parenting plan.

☐ 2.   Transitions/exchanges of the children including date, time, place, means of transportation and transporter;

☐ 3.   Health care management including medical, dental, orthodontic, and vision care;

☐ 4.   Child-rearing issues;

☐ 5. Psychotherapy or other mental health care including substance abuse assessment or counseling for the children;

☐ 6. Psychological testing or other assessment of the children and parents;

☐ 7. Education or daycare including the school choice, tutoring, summer school, participation in special education testing and programs or other major educational decisions;

☐ 8. Enrichment and extracurricular activities including camps and jobs;

☐ 9. Religious observances and education;

☐ 10. Children's travel and passports arrangements;

☐ 11. Clothing, equipment, and personal possessions of the children;

☐ 12. Communication between the parents about the children including telephone, fax, email, notes in backpacks, etc.

☐ 13. Communication by a parent with the children including telephone, cell phone, pager, fax and email when they are not in that parent's care.

☐ 14. Alteration of appearance of the children including haircuts, tattoos, ear and body piercing

☐ 15. Role of and contact with significant others and extended families;

☐ 16. Substance abuse assessment or testing for either or both parents or a child, including access to results;

☐ 17. Parenting classes for either or both parents.

☐ 18. Other

_____

_____

_____

_____

Appointments and Communications:

Each parent shall make a good faith effort to be available for appointments when requested by the Parenting Coordinator.

The Parenting Coordinator shall set a time and place to meet with each parent individually for a brief informational meeting within twenty (20) days of the signing of this Order. Each parent shall attend, or shall notify the Parenting Coordinator upon receipt of the meeting notice, of any scheduling difficulties.

During subsequent meetings, the Parenting Coordinator may meet with the parties and the children jointly or separately. The Parenting Coordinator shall determine whether appointments will be joint, separate, by telephone, or in person. Either parent may contact the Parenting Coordinator if meeting in the same room with the other parent would be uncomfortable. The Parenting Coordinator has the discretion to decide if subsequent meeting will held together or separately.

The Parenting Coordinator shall assist the parties in resolving parenting issues in this matter only after ascertaining that the parties cannot resolve the issues themselves.

Assistance provided by the Parenting Coordinator is not intended to be a "crisis service." The Parenting Coordinator should not be contacted outside of normal working hours as defined in the Parenting Coordination Agreement.

It is the responsibility of each parent to contact the Parenting Coordinator to schedule, and arrange times for meetings, and also attend appointments when scheduled by the Parenting Coordinator.

The parents, their attorneys and/or the law guardian, if any, may communicate with the Parenting Coordinator *ex parte* (without the other parent present). This applies to oral communications and any written documentation or communication submitted to the Parenting Coordinator.

The Parenting Coordinator may have *ex parte* communications with the parents, their attorneys or the law guardian, and other professionals involved in the case. This applies to both written and oral communications. The Parenting Coordinator may talk with the law guardian or each parent without the presence of either counsel.

In specific circumstances, the Parenting Coordinator may request and notify the parties and/or their attorneys that communications with the Parenting Coordinator not be *ex parte*.

The Parenting Coordinator shall not communicate with the Judge assigned to the case and/or any member of the Judge's staff except to notify the Court that he or she is not available to provide the services contemplated by the parties, which notification shall be made on notice to both parties.

The parties and/or their attorneys shall cooperate with the Parenting Coordinator and agree to follow the terms specified in this Order. The parties shall further cooperate with the Parenting Coordinator by providing any documents, papers or information requested, including the execution of releases and/or authorizations permitting the Parenting Coordinator to speak with, or receive information from, any mental health professionals, social service workers or agencies, physicians, schools or other facilities or individuals who may have information regarding the parties or their child(ren).

The Parenting Coordinator is not a substitute for having independent legal counsel or working with an independent mental health professional. Whether or not your Parenting Coordinator is an attorney or mental health professional, the Parenting Coordinator will be functioning with you solely as a Parenting Coordinator.

Both parties shall fully cooperate with completing anonymous questionnaires that are part of the parenting coordination program evaluation.

Role of Parenting Coordinator:

The primary role of the Parenting Coordinator is to assist parties to implement their court ordered parenting plan in a way that minimizes conflict and is in their child(ren)'s best interests. In the event of an unresolved parenting conflict, either party may contact the Parenting Coordinator and the Parenting Coordinator may:

Check box(s) below:

☐ Educate the parties on communication skills, principles of child development, litigation impact on children and the parties and other issues relevant to the parties' controversy and the child's(children's) needs;

☐ Facilitate the execution of and compliance with the existing child custody and parenting time agreement;

☐ Maintain communication among the parties by serving, if necessary, as a conduit of information.

☐ Recommend how a particular element or elements of the existing parenting plan or parenting schedule should be implemented, including without limitation the frequency and length of visitation, temporary changes in the parenting schedule, holiday or vacation planning, logistics of pick up and drop off, suitability of accommodation, and issues dealing with stepparents and significant others;

☐ Propose clear and detailed plans which reallocate parenting time to the parties as a means of reducing conflict but without significantly reducing actual net parenting time;

☐ Notify and remind the parties that the Parenting Coordinator is not the ally of either party, but a neutral professional whose role is to actively and specifically focus on helping parents work together for the benefit of the children;

☐ Consult with professionals, family members and others who have information about the parents or children, such as law guardians, therapists, custody evaluators, school teachers, doctors, etc. To this end, the parties agree to execute any written authorization requested by the Parent Coordinator and necessary to access such information;

☐ Determine the protocol and time of all interviews and sessions including but not limited to, the discretion to determine who attends such meetings and whether a child or children should attend with the parents or parent;

☐ Upon consent of the law guardian, interview the children privately in order to ascertain their needs as to the issues in controversy;

☐ Attorneys to give consent before any communications that the parenting coordinator has with the parties;

☐ Ensure that both parents maintain ongoing relationships with the children so long as it is safe to do so;

☐ Provide both parents with a written summary of the parenting coordinator's recommendations;

☐ If parents are still unable to reach an agreement about how to facilitate the implementation of their court-ordered parenting plan after the Parenting Coordinator has provided parents with relevant parenting information, tried to help them resolve the disagreement themselves, and offered suggestions, then the Parenting Coordinator has decision making authority on these specified issue areas:

_____

_____

☐ Other:

_____

_____

Scope of agreements:

☐ Upon consent of the parties, counsel and the Law Guardian the Parenting Coordinator will submit the agreement to the Court to be incorporated into a court order.

–Supreme Court may confirm the agreement through an Amended Court Order.

–Family Court will confirm the agreement under the same docket number used in the case from which the instant order issued.

☐ Absent consent, the decision of the Parenting Coordinator will remain in effect until otherwise changed by the parties or the Court.

CONTINUING JURISDICTION OF COURT

The parties retain their right to return to Court and the Court retains continuing jurisdiction over the case until termination of the appointment of the parenting coordinator.

The Parenting Coordinator may send a letter to the Court on notice to all parties requesting a court conference to resolve an outstanding issue or to report on the compliance of the parties.

–Supreme Court will schedule a court conference upon receipt of a letter from the Parenting Coordinator and will notify the parties of the return date. Parties will determine whether they will have counsel present for this initial court conference.

If an issue regarding contempt of an Order of the Court is raised during this court conference, a motion will be required by the Court prior to addressing this issue.

–Family Court will require the filing of a new petition by one of the parties prior to the scheduling of a court conference to address any issues raised by the parenting coordinator regarding the parties' compliance with the court order.

Confidentiality:

Communications between the parents and the Parenting Coordinator are not confidential. The parties will sign any waivers of privilege of confidentiality with any of the following in order to permit the Parenting Coordinator to communicate with law guardians, custody evaluators, screeners, assessors, any mental health professionals, social service workers or agencies, physicians, schools or other facilities or individuals who may have information regarding the parties or their child(ren). During such communications, the parties authorize and direct the Parenting Coordinator to use at the Parenting Coordinator's discretion information learned while working with the parties.

The Parenting Coordinator may be required by law to report child and domestic abuse, and threats of abuse against another person. In such cases, the Parenting Coordinator and legal counsel (or the parents themselves if not represented) shall address any safety concerns to the Court.

Waiver of Liability:

The parties and their attorneys agree that the Parenting Coordinator shall be immune from suit by any of the parties, attorneys or other participants in this case because of or based upon the Parenting Coordinator's activities as such in this matter. The Parenting Coordinator shall not be liable to the parties or counsel for any acts or omissions in his or her deliberations and recommendations. The parties and counsel agree that the Parenting Coordinators shall not be subject to subpoena for trial, deposition, or other purpose. The recommendations made by the Parenting Coordinator are made to help the parties settle their custody and parenting disputes. Accordingly, anything said by the attorneys, Parenting Coordinator, law guardians or parties in and during the course of the Parenting Coordinator's services is confidential and may not be used for trial, deposition or any other purpose.

Grievance Procedures:

Any grievance from either parent regarding the performance or actions of the Parent Coordinator shall be dealt with in the following manner:

A person with a grievance shall discuss the matter with the Parent Coordinator in person before pursuing it in any other manner.

If, after meeting with the Parenting Coordinator the parent decides to pursue a complaint, the parent must then submit a written letter detailing the complaint to the Parenting Coordinator, to the other parent, and any attorneys representing the parents and/or children. The Parenting Coordinator shall provide a written response to the parent and attorneys within thirty (30) days.

D. The Parenting Coordinator will then meet with the complaining parent and his or her attorney (if any), to discuss the matter. As noted above, the Parenting Coordinator retains the right to withdraw or decline service for any reason upon written notification to all parties.

E. If the Parenting Coordinator does not make notification that he or she is resigning, and the complaint remains unresolved after the above referenced meeting, the complaining party may file a motion with the Court for removal of the Parenting Coordinator. The motion shall proceed and be determined by the Court on the written documents submitted by both parents and the Parenting Coordinator and without appearances absent Court order.

I have read, understand and agree to the above provisions contained herein:

Plaintiff/ Petitioner: **Defendant/Respondent:**
X _____   X _____

Address   **Address**

_____   _____

Phone No.: _____   Phone No. _____
Dated: _____   Dated: _____

Attorney for Plaintiff/Petitioner: **Attorney for Defendant/ Respondent:**

_____   _____

Phone No.: _____   Phone No. _____

Attorney for child/children

_____

Phone No.: _____

So Ordered:

_____   Dated _____
_____ JSC JFC

STIPULATED ORDER APPOINTING PARENTING COORDINATOR

Doc. 4.   Stipulated Order Appointing Parenting Coordinator

PRESENT:
Hon.

                    Justice

                              STIPULATED ORDER APPOINTING
                              PARENTING COORDINATOR

          Plaintiff/Petitioner,

                              Index No:

     —*against*—

          Defendant/Respondent.

_____

     The above referenced (action) (proceeding) was brought pursuant to _____ (Family Court Act § 6) (Domestic Relations Law § 240). The (Plaintiff) (Petitioner) _____, represented by _____ and/or the (Defendant)(Respondent) _____, represented by _____ seek an Order enforcing and/or modifying an existing custody and/or parenting time order concerning the following minor child(ren);

          _____

          _____

     The matter has come to be heard before this Court on _____, 200 ___. The Plaintiff/Petitioner and the Defendant/Respondent have appeared before this Court and have been advised by the Court of their right to counsel pursuant to Family Court Act § 261–62; and the (Plaintiff/Petitioner) and/or (Defendant/Respondent) have waived their right to counsel or do not meet the financial threshold to qualify for Court appointed counsel, and a Law Guardian, _____ having been appointed to represent the interest of the child(ren).

     The Court has examined and taken inquiry into the facts and circumstances of this matter adduced through a review of the stipulation of the parties, the conferences held before this Court on _____, a hearing held before this Court on _____, and review of the submittals before this Court.

The Court takes note that the parties are engaged in high conflict litigation over the custody and visitation issues and have demonstrated a pattern of prior and ongoing acrimony and dissension potentially detrimental to their own self interests and the interests of their child(ren).

The parties agree and the Court finds that the utilization of a Parenting Coordinator is necessary to assist the parties/parents herein in implementing the terms of the existing parenting plan dated _____ as incorporated but not merged by the order/judgment dated _____ so as to reduce conflict and/or its possible detrimental impact upon the child's(ren's) welfare.

Accordingly, in attempts to mitigate against further acrimony, conflict, repeated costly court appearances and motion practice and upon consent of the parties and their attorneys, this Court issues the following Consent Order so as to adopt and facilitate the desired use of a Parenting Coordinator to assist the parties/parents herein in implementing the terms of the existing parenting plan dated _____ as incorporated but not merged by the Order/Judgment dated _____.

Parenting Coordinator:

The Court appoints _____ from the 8th District Court Roster of qualified parenting coordinators with offices at _____ tel. _____ to serve as the Parenting Coordinator.

A copy of this Order shall immediately be forwarded by the Court to the Parenting Coordinator upon the issuance of this Order. The parties shall thereafter contact the Parenting Coordinator within five (5) days of the issuance of this Order to engage this process.

Term:

The term of the Parenting Coordinator's service shall be for a period of __ months/ __ years from the date of this Order. The Parenting Coordinator may withdraw, resign or decline service upon written notification to the Court and both parties. In addition, the Parenting Coordinator's services may be terminated upon written agreement of both parties approved by the Court or by further Court order. Absent such resignation, agreement or order, however, the Parenting Coordinator may not be terminated by either of the parties before expiration of the term.

Fees and Compensation:

The Parenting Coordinator shall be compensated by the parties at an hourly rate established by the parenting coordinator.

The parties and Parenting Coordinator shall execute a retainer agreement concerning the fees to be paid to the parenting coordinator by the parties. In pro bono cases, the parties will each be required to pay a minimum fee of $2.00 per hour to the parenting coordinator.

Father shall pay __ % and Mother shall pay __ % of the parenting coordinator's retainer within 10 days of this order. Father shall pay __ % and Mother shall pay __ % for additional services beyond the retainer upon 5 days receipt of a written invoice.

Issues Subject to Parenting Coordination:

In order to facilitate the implementation of the court-ordered parenting plan, the Parenting Coordinator is appointed to assist the parties to resolve their conflicts in the following areas:

Check appropriate box(s) below:

☐ 1. Minor changes or clarification of parenting time/access schedules or conditions

☐ including vacation, holidays and temporary variation from the existing parenting plan.

☐ 2. Transitions/exchanges of the children including date, time, place, means of transportation and transporter;

☐ 3.   Health care management including medical, dental, orthodontic, and vision care;

☐ 4.   Child-rearing issues;

☐ 5.   Psychotherapy or other mental health care including substance abuse assessment or counseling for the children;

☐ 6.   Psychological testing or other assessment of the children and parents;

☐ 7.   Education or daycare including the school choice, tutoring, summer school, participation in special education testing and programs or other major educational decisions;

☐ 8.   Enrichment and extracurricular activities including camps and jobs;

☐ 9.   Religious observances and education;

☐ 10.   Children's travel and passports arrangements;

☐ 11.   Clothing, equipment, and personal possessions of the children;

☐ 12.   Communication between the parents about the children including telephone, fax, email, notes in backpacks, etc.

☐ 13.   Communication by a parent with the children including telephone, cell phone, pager, fax and email when they are not in that parent's care.

☐ 14.   Alteration of appearance of the children including haircuts, tattoos, ear and body piercing

☐ 15.   Role of and contact with significant others and extended families;

☐ 16.   Substance abuse assessment or testing for either or both parents or a child, including access to results;

☐ 17.   Parenting classes for either or both parents.

☐ 18.   Other

_____

_____

_____

_____

Appointments and Communications:

Each parent shall make a good faith effort to be available for appointments when requested by the Parenting Coordinator.

The Parenting Coordinator shall set a time and place to meet with each parent individually for a brief informational meeting within twenty (20) days of the signing of this Order. Each parent shall attend, or shall notify the Parenting Coordinator upon receipt of the meeting notice, of any scheduling difficulties.

During subsequent meetings, the Parenting Coordinator may meet with the parties and the children jointly or separately. The Parenting Coordinator shall determine whether appointments will be joint, separate, by telephone, or in person. Either parent may contact the Parenting Coordinator if meeting in the same room with the other parent would be uncomfortable. The Parenting Coordinator has the discretion to decide if subsequent meeting will held together or separately.

The Parenting Coordinator shall assist the parties in resolving parenting issues in this matter only after ascertaining that the parties cannot resolve the issues themselves.

Assistance provided by the Parenting Coordinator is not intended to be a "crisis service." The Parenting Coordinator should not be contacted outside of normal working hours as defined in the Parenting Coordination Agreement.

It is the responsibility of each parent to contact the Parenting Coordinator to schedule, and arrange times for meetings, and also attend appointments when scheduled by the Parenting Coordinator.

The parents, their attorneys and/or the law guardian, if any, may communicate with the Parenting Coordinator *ex parte* (without the other parent present). This applies to oral communications and any written documentation or communication submitted to the Parenting Coordinator.

The Parenting Coordinator may have *ex parte* communications with the parents, their attorneys or the law guardian, and other professionals involved in the case. This applies to both written and oral communications. The Parenting Coordinator may talk with the law guardian or each parent without the presence of either counsel.

In specific circumstances, the Parenting Coordinator may request and notify the parties and/or their attorneys that communications with the Parenting Coordinator not be *ex parte*.

The Parenting Coordinator shall not communicate with the Judge assigned to the case and/or any member of the Judge's staff except to notify the Court that he or she is not available to provide the services contemplated by the parties, which notification shall be made on notice to both parties.

The parties and/or their attorneys shall cooperate with the Parenting Coordinator and agree to follow the terms specified in this Order. The parties shall further cooperate with the Parenting Coordinator by providing any documents, papers or information requested, including the execution of releases and/or authorizations permitting the Parenting Coordinator to speak with, or receive information from, any mental health professionals, social service workers or agencies, physicians, schools or other facilities or individuals who may have information regarding the parties or their child(ren).

The Parenting Coordinator is not a substitute for having independent legal counsel or working with an independent mental health professional. Whether or not your Parenting Coordinator is an attorney or mental health professional, the Parenting Coordinator will be functioning with you solely as a Parenting Coordinator.

Both parties shall fully cooperate with completing anonymous questionnaires that are part of the parenting coordination program evaluation.

Role of Parenting Coordinator:

The primary role of the Parenting Coordinator is to assist parties to implement their court ordered parenting plan in a way that minimizes conflict and is in their child(ren)'s best interests. In the event of an unresolved parenting conflict, either party may contact the Parenting Coordinator and the Parenting Coordinator may:

Check box(s) below:

☐ Educate the parties on communication skills, principles of child development, litigation impact on children and the parties and other issues relevant to the parties' controversy and the child's(children's) needs;

☐ Facilitate the execution of and compliance with the existing child custody and parenting time agreement;

☐ Maintain communication among the parties by serving, if necessary, as a conduit of information.

☐ Recommend how a particular element or elements of the existing parenting plan or parenting schedule should be implemented, including without limitation the frequency and length of visitation, temporary changes in the parenting schedule, holiday or vacation planning, logistics of pick up and drop off, suitability of accommodation, and issues dealing with stepparents and significant others;

☐ Propose clear and detailed plans which reallocate parenting time to the parties as a means of reducing conflict but without significantly reducing actual net parenting time;

☐ Notify and remind the parties that the Parenting Coordinator is not the ally of either party, but a neutral professional whose role is to actively and specifically focus on helping parents work together for the benefit of the children;

☐ Consult with professionals, family members and others who have information about the parents or children, such as law guardians, therapists, custody evaluators, school teachers, doctors, etc. To this end, the parties agree to execute any written authorization requested by the Parent Coordinator and necessary to access such information;

☐ Determine the protocol and time of all interviews and sessions including but not limited to, the discretion to determine who attends such meetings and whether a child or children should attend with the parents or parent;

☐ Upon consent of the law guardian, interview the children privately in order to ascertain their needs as to the issues in controversy;

☐ Attorneys to give consent before any communications that the parenting coordinator has with the parties;

☐ Ensure that both parents maintain ongoing relationships with the children so long as it is safe to do so;

☐ Provide both parents with a written summary of the parenting coordinator's recommendations;

☐ If parents are still unable to reach an agreement about how to facilitate the implementation of their court-ordered parenting plan after the Parenting Coordinator has provided parents with relevant parenting information, tried to help them resolve the disagreement themselves, and offered suggestions, then the Parenting Coordinator has decision making authority on these specified issue areas:

_____

_____

☐ Other:

_____

_____

Scope of agreements:

☐ Upon consent of the parties, counsel, and the Law Guardian, the Parenting Coordinator will submit the agreement to the Court to be incorporated into a court order.

–Supreme Court may confirm the agreement through an Amended Court Order.

–Family Court will confirm the agreement under the same docket number used in the case from which the instant order issued.

☐ Absent consent, the decision of the Parenting Coordinator will remain in effect until otherwise changed by the parties or the Court.

CONTINUING JURISDICTION OF COURT

The parties retain their right to return to Court and the Court retains continuing jurisdiction over the case until termination of the appointment of the parenting coordinator.

The Parenting Coordinator may send a letter to the Court on notice to all parties requesting a court conference to resolve an outstanding issue or to report on the compliance of the parties.

–Supreme Court will schedule a court conference upon receipt of a letter from the Parenting Coordinator and will notify the parties of the return date. Parties will determine whether they will have counsel present for this initial court conference.

If an issue regarding contempt of an Order of the Court is raised during this court conference, a motion will be required by the Court prior to addressing this issue.

–Family Court will require the filing of a new petition by one of the parties prior to the scheduling of a court conference to address any issues raised by the parenting coordinator regarding the parties' compliance with the court order.

Confidentiality:

Communications between the parents and the Parenting Coordinator are not confidential. The parties will sign any waivers of privilege of confidentiality with any of the following in order to permit the Parenting Coordinator to communicate with law guardians, custody evaluators, screeners, assessors, any mental health professionals, social service workers or agencies, physicians, schools or other facilities or individuals who may have information regarding the parties or their child (ren). During such communications, the parties authorize and direct the Parenting Coordinator to use at the Parenting Coordinator's discretion information learned while working with the parties.

The Parenting Coordinator may be required by law to report child and domestic abuse, and threats of abuse against another person. In such cases, the Parenting Coordinator and legal counsel (or the parents themselves if not represented) shall address any safety concerns to the Court.

Waiver of Liability:

The parties and their attorneys agree that the Parenting Coordinator shall be immune from suit by any of the parties, attorneys or other participants in this case because of or based upon the Parenting Coordinator's activities as such in this matter. The Parenting Coordinator shall not be liable to the parties or counsel for any acts or omissions in his or her deliberations and recommendations. The parties and counsel agree that the Parenting Coordinators shall not be subject to subpoena for trial, deposition, or other purpose. The recommendations made by the Parenting Coordinator are made to help the parties settle their custody and parenting disputes. Accordingly, anything said by the attorneys, Parenting Coordinator, law guardians or parties in and during the course of the Parenting Coordinator's services is confidential and may not be used for trial, deposition or any other purpose.

Grievance Procedures:

Any grievance from either parent regarding the performance or actions of the Parent Coordinator shall be dealt with in the following manner:

A person with a grievance shall discuss the matter with the Parent Coordinator in person before pursuing it in any other manner.

If, after meeting with the Parenting Coordinator the parent decides to pursue a complaint, the parent must then submit a written letter detailing the complaint to the Parenting Coordinator, to the other parent, and any attorneys representing the parents and/or children. The Parenting Coordinator shall provide a written response to the parent and attorneys within thirty (30) days.

D. The Parenting Coordinator will then meet with the complaining parent and his or her attorney (if any), to discuss the matter. As noted above, the Parenting Coordinator retains the right to withdraw or decline service for any reason upon written notification to all parties.

E. If the Parenting Coordinator does not make notification that he or she is resigning, and the complaint remains unresolved after the above referenced meeting, the complaining party may file a motion with the Court for removal of the Parenting Coordinator. The motion shall proceed and be determined by the Court on the written documents submitted by both parents and the Parenting Coordinator and without appearances absent Court order.

I have read, understand and agree to the above provisions contained in this Consent Order:

Plaintiff/ Petitioner:
X _____

Defendant/Respondent:
X _____
_____

Address
_____
_____

Address
_____
_____

Phone No.: _____
Dated: _____

Phone No. _____
Dated: _____

Attorney for Plaintiff/ Petitioner:
_____

Attorney for Defendant / Respondent:
_____

Phone No.: _____

Phone No. _____

Attorney for child/children
_____
_____

Phone No.: _____

So Ordered:

_____ JSC JFC

Dated _____

GUIDELINES

Preamble

Overview and Definitions

Parenting coordination is a child-focused alternative dispute resolution (ADR) process in which a mental health or legal professional with training and experience assists high conflict parents to implement their parenting plan by facilitating the resolution of their disputes in a timely manner. With prior approval of the parties and the court, the PC may make decisions within the scope of the court order or appointment contract.

The overall objective of parenting coordination is to assist parents in high conflict to implement their parenting plan, to monitor compliance with the details of the plan, to resolve conflicts regarding their children and the parenting plan in a timely manner, and to protect and sustain safe, healthy and meaningful parent-child relationships.

Parenting Coordination is most frequently reserved for those high conflict parents who have demonstrated a sustained inability or unwillingness to make parenting decisions on their own, to comply with parenting agreements and orders, to reduce their child-related conflicts, and/or to protect their children from the impact of that conflict.

Because the Parent Coordinator ("PC") makes recommendations and/or decisions for the parties and reports to the court, the PC will be appointed by and be responsible to the court. The power and authority inherent in the role of the PC are substantial whether stipulated by the parties or assigned by the court. Therefore, the following guidelines for PC practice and programs are created, and will be reviewed and modified as necessary.

These protocols recognize the complexities of some parenting dynamics. The alternative dispute resolution process described above as central to the PC's role may be inappropriate and potentially exploited by perpetrators of domestic violence who have exhibited patterns of violence, threat, intimidation and coercive control over their co-parent. In those cases of domestic violence where one parent seeks to obtain and maintain power and control over the other, the role of the PC changes to an almost purely enforcement function. Here, the PC is likely to be dealing with a court order, the more detailed the better, rather than a mutually agreed upon parenting plan. The role of the PC then is to ensure compliance with the details of the order and to test each request for variance from its terms with an eye to protecting the custodial parent's autonomy to make decisions based on the children's best interests and guarding against manipulation by the abusing parent. Since ADR techniques in such cases may have the effect of maintaining or increasing the imbalance of power and the victim's risk of harm, protocols and procedures are included for this type of case. PCs must always routinely screen prospective cases for domestic violence and must decline to accept such cases if they do not have specialized expertise and procedures to effectively manage domestic violence cases involving an imbalance of power, control and coercion. The Court will ensure that at all times the safety of parents and children are of paramount and overriding importance.

The PC's role is not to be confused with a forensic evaluation, the practice of law, or therapy.

The *Protocols for Parenting Coordination* include different levels of guidance:

• Use of the term "may" in the *Protocols* indicates a practice that the PC should consider adopting, but from which the PC can deviate in the exercise of good professional judgment;

• Most of the *Protocols* use the term "should", which indicates that the practice described is highly desirable and should be departed from only with very strong professional reason.

• The use of the term "shall" in the *Protocols* is a higher level of guidance to the PC, indicating that the PC does not have discretion to depart from the practice described.

In creating these protocols, due consideration was given to the suggestions published by the Association of Family and Conciliation Courts (AFCC) Parenting Coordination Standards Task Force: Guidelines for Parenting Coordination (2005).

Guideline I. Education and Training

A PC shall be qualified by education and training to undertake parenting coordination and shall continue to develop professionally in the role.

A. The PC will be required to have training and experience in family mediation and professional interaction with high conflict families. The PC shall have completed the training required by then-current rules adopted by the 8th Judicial District, and as they may be amended or modified, or have sufficient years of professional experience to seek a waiver (whether temporary or conditional as determined by the ADR Administration of the 8th Judicial District) of this requirement.

B. The PC shall be a licensed mental health professional or licensed attorney with experience in an area relating to families, or a certified family mediator with a master's degree in a mental health field.

C. The PC should have extensive practical experience in the profession with high conflict or litigating parents.

D. The PC shall have completed training approved by the ADR Administration of the 8th Judicial District in the parenting coordination process, family dynamics in separation and divorce, parenting coordination techniques, domestic violence and child maltreatment, and court specific parenting coordination procedures.

E. A PC must acquire and maintain professional competence in the parenting coordination process. A PC shall regularly participate in educational activities promoting professional growth. A PC may participate in peer consultation or mentoring to receive feedback and support on cases and such professional consultation is specifically permitted.

F. A PC must decline an appointment, withdraw, or request appropriate assistance when the facts and circumstances of a case are beyond the PC's skill or expertise, particularly when elements of domestic violence surface.

G. In the first twelve (12) months after adoption of these protocols, professionals who have significant exposure with high conflict families but lack some part of the criteria noted above, may petition the District, through the Office of Court Administration's Office of ADR and Court Improvement, for waiver of a qualification.

Guideline II. Impartiality

A PC shall maintain impartiality in the process of parenting coordination. Impartiality means freedom from favoritism or bias in word, action, or appearance, and includes a commitment to assist all parties, as opposed to any one individual.

A. A PC must withdraw if the PC determines he or she cannot act in an impartial manner;

B. A PC shall neither give nor accept a gift, favor, loan or other item of value from any party having an interest in the parenting coordination process. During the parenting coordination process a PC shall not solicit or otherwise attempt to procure future professional services or positions from which the PC may profit.

C. A PC shall not coerce or improperly influence any party to make a decision.

D. A PC shall not intentionally or knowingly misrepresent or omit any material fact, law, or circumstance in the parenting coordination process.

E. A PC shall not accept any engagement, provide any service or perform any act outside the role of PC that would compromise the PC's integrity or impartiality in the parenting coordination process.

Guideline III. Conflict of Interest

A PC shall not serve in a matter that presents a clear conflict of interest.

A. A conflict of interest arises when any relationship between the PC and the participants or the subject matter of dispute compromises or appears to compromise a PC's impartiality.

B. A PC must disclose potential conflicts of interest as soon as practical after a PC becomes aware of the interest or relationship giving rise to the potential conflict.

C. After appropriate disclosure, the PC may serve with the written agreement of all parties and consent of the Court. However, if a conflict of interest clearly impairs a PC's impartiality, the PC must withdraw regardless of the express agreement of the parties.

D. During the parenting coordination process, a PC will not create a conflict of interest by providing any services to any party that are not directly related to the parenting coordination process.

E. A PC may make referrals to other professionals to work with the family, but shall avoid actual or apparent conflicts of interest by referrals. No commissions, rebates, or similar renumeration can be given or received by a PC for professional referrals.

Guideline IV. Prohibition Against Multiple Roles

A PC shall not serve in dual sequential roles.

A. A PC shall not serve in multiple roles in a case that create a professional conflict.

    1. A child's attorney or child advocate shall not become a PC in the same case.

    2. A mediator or custody evaluator, after completion of an evaluation, shall be cautious about becoming a PC in the same case afterward, even with the consent of the parties, because of the differences in the role and potential impact of the role change. However, the mediator or evaluator is not prohibited from undertaking the parenting coordinator role, but may not thereafter resume the role of mediator or custodial evaluator.

    3. A PC shall not become a custody evaluator either during or after the term of a PC's involvement with the family.

    4. A PC shall not be appointed after serving as a therapist, consultant, or coach, or serve in another mental health role to any family member.

    5. A PC shall not become a therapist, consultant, or coach or serve in any other mental health role to any family member, either during or after the term of the PC's involvement.

    6. A PC shall not become one client's lawyer, either during or after the term of the PC's involvement, nor shall one client's lawyer become the PC in that client's case.

B. A PC should attempt to facilitate resolution of issues by agreement of the parties; however, the PC does not act in a formal mediation role. An effort toward resolving an issue which may include therapeutic, mediation, educational, and negotiation skills, does not disqualify a PC from deciding an issue (when such authority has been given) that remains unresolved after efforts of facilitation are unsuccessful.

Guideline V. Limits of Confidentiality

A PC shall inform the parties of the limitation on confidentiality in the parenting coordination process. Information shall not be shared outside of the parenting coordination process except for legiti-

mate and allowed professional purposes. A PC shall maintain confidentiality regarding the sharing of information outside of the scope of the parenting coordination process, except as provided by court order or by written agreement of the parties.

A. Parenting coordination is not a confidential process, either for communications between the parties and their children and the PC, or for communications between the PC and other relevant parties to the parenting coordination process, or for communications with the court.

B. Appropriate provisions need to be included in the written agreement and/or court order for the effective waiver of all privileges and rules of evidence or professional conduct regarding confidentiality. In addition, a clear statement must be provided that the PC will not provide either party with legal advice, representation, therapy or counseling, and the parents are advised to seek any such advice from independent providers of their own choice.

C. A PC must inform the parties of the following limitation of confidentiality regarding serious matters:

    1. The PC will report suspected child abuse or neglect to child protective services whether or not a mandatory or voluntary reporter under state or federal law; and

    2. The PC will report to law enforcement or other authorities if the PC has reason to believe that any family member appears to be at a serious risk to harm himself or herself, another family member or third party.

Guideline VI. Scope of Parent Coordinator Role

A PC shall assist the parties in reducing harmful conflict and in promoting the best interests of the children consistent with the roles and functions of a PC.

A. A PC serves an assessment function. The PC should review the custody evaluation, other relevant records, interim or final court orders, information from interviews with parents and children and other collateral sources, domestic violence protection orders, (and any other applicable information involving criminal assault, domestic violence or child abuse), educational records, and analyze the impasses and issues of the family.

B. A PC serves an educational function. The PC should educate the parties about child development, divorce research, the impact of their behavior on the children, parenting skills, and communication and conflict resolution skills. The PC should coach the parties about these issues, enabling the parties to develop more constructive and productive behavior that promotes stable family relationships. A PC should empower parties to resolve future conflicts with learned appropriate skills, and to disengage from interpersonal conflict.

C. A PC serves a coordination/case management function. The PC should work with the professionals and systems involved with the family (e.g. mental health, health care, social services, education, legal) as well as with extended family, stepparents, and significant others.

D. A PC serves a conflict management function. The PC's primary role is to assist the parties to work out disagreements regarding the children with minimal or decreasing conflict. As a neutral facilitator the PC may utilize dispute resolution skills from principles and practices of negotiation, mediation and arbitration. To assist the parents in reducing conflict, the PC may monitor the faxed, emailed, or written exchanges of parent communications and suggest more productive forms of communication that limit conflict between the parents. In order to protect the parties and children in domestic violence cases involving power, control and coercion, it is imperative that a PC tailor all techniques used so as to avoid offering the opportunity for further coercion.

E. A PC may serve a decision-making function. When parents are not able to decide or resolve disputes on their own, the PC can be empowered to make decisions to the extent described in the court order, or to make reports or recommendations to the court for further consideration. PCs must communicate their decisions in a timely manner in person or by fax, email or telephone. In the event decisions are provided orally, a written version shall follow in a timely manner

F. A PC has no other role. A PC will not offer legal advice, representation, therapy or counseling.

Guideline VII. Authority Granted to PC

A PC should attempt to facilitate agreement between the parties in a timely manner on all disputes regarding their children as they arise. When parents are unable to reach agreement, and if it has been ordered by the Court, or authorized by consent, the PC will decide the disputed issues.

A. A PC may make recommendations to the parties or the Court consistent with the role and limitations described in these protocols.

B. By Court order following consent of the parties and all counsel a PC may be granted the authority to make decisions for the parties when they cannot agree, and/or the PC may be allowed to make recommendations to the parties or the court.

C. A PC shall not make determinations that substantially alter custody orders, relocation determinations, religion or child support.

D. A PC shall have only the authority that is delegated in the court order or as provided by the written consent of the parties. If so written in the

order or consent agreement, a PC may have authority to resolve some or all of the following types of issues:

1. Minor changes or clarification of parenting time/access schedules or conditions including vacation, holidays and temporary variation from the existing parenting plan;

2. Transitions/exchanges of the children including date, time, place, means of transportation and transporter;

3. Health care management including medical, dental, orthodontic, and vision care;

4. Child-rearing issues;

5. Therapy, counseling, or other mental health care for the children;

6. Psychological testing or other assessment of the children and parents;

7. Education or daycare including the school choice, tutoring, summer school, participation in special education testing and programs, or other educational decisions;

8. Enrichment and extracurricular activities including camps, sports, and jobs;

9. Religious observances and education;

10. Children's travel and passport arrangements;

11. Clothing, equipment, and personal possessions of the children;

12. Communication between the parents about the children including telephone, fax, email, notes in backpacks, etc.;

13. Communication by a parent with the children including telephone, cell phone, pager, fax and email when they are not in that parent's care;

14. Alteration of appearance of the children including haircuts, tattoos, ear and body piercing;

15. Role of and contact with significant others and extended families;

16. Substance abuse assessment or testing for either or both parents or a child, including access to results;

17. Parenting classes for either or both parents.

E. The PC should use or gather written or verbal statements of the dispute from each party, as well as other relevant sources of information. The methodology used by the PC shall be fair to both parties, and be transparent to both the court and the parties. Each party shall be given the opportunity to be heard in the process. Notice shall be given as to what is expected from the participation of the parties and the consequences of non-participation. If on party refuses to cooperate after notice, then the PC may continue to resolve the dispute.

F. When granted the authority to resolve a selected issue, the PC shall issue a written resolution of the dispute, or a verbal decision in time sensitive matters, which may be followed by a written decision. The PC or one of the attorneys for the parents or children should prepare any order needed to effectuate the implementation of the decision, and arrange for submission, signing, filing, and dissemination to all parties and counsel.

G. A PC shall and must refrain from making any decision that would alter legal custody and physical custody from one parent to the other or substantially change the parenting plan. Such major decisions are more properly within the scope of judicial authority. In limited cases, the PC may need to make a temporary suspension in the parenting plan if a parent is impaired in his or her functioning and incapable of fulfilling his or her court-ordered parenting functions until further information and assessment is obtained and the court has assumed decision-making responsibility. In such a case the PC shall immediately advise the court, counsel and the parties.

H. The PC shall notify the Attorney for the Child/Children of any anticipated substantive change to the status quo of the children, with an opportunity by the Attorney for the Child/Children to be heard by the PC before implementation when exercised by the Attorney for the Child/Children. This includes any recommendations for assessment, testing, therapy or counseling.

I. Under no circumstances shall a PC delegate any portion of the PC process to anyone else. The power provided to the PC is personal in nature and not be assumed by third parties.

Guideline VIII.   Court Order

A PC shall serve by formal order of the court and/or stipulation of the parties which shall clearly and specifically define the PC's scope of authority and responsibilities.

A. A Court order is necessary to provide the PC authority to work with the parents outside of the adversarial process, to obtain information, and to make recommendations and decisions as specified in the order.

B. In addition to the court order for the PC, a written agreement between the parties and the PC may be used to detail specific issues not contained in the court order, such as fee payments, billing practices and retainers.

C. The Court order must specify a term of service for the PC, including starting and ending dates. Parents can request that a PC continue for additional terms of service following the expiration of each term. Similarly the PC can give notice prior to the end of the term of service that the PC will not continue to serve as PC after expiration of the term.

D. A PC should not initiate services until the PC has received a fully executed and filed court order appointing the PC.

Guideline IX.   Explanation of Role

A PC must facilitate the participants' understanding of the parenting coordination process so that they can give informed consent to the process.

A. The position of the PC can be one of considerable authority and power. If applicable, it is important that parents fully understand the extent of the parental rights and power they are assigning to the PC in the form of decision-making. They should understand the limited nature of the confidentiality of the process, the professional persons with whom the PC will be authorized to consult or obtain information, and what the parents' rights are in seeking redress with the court.

B. In the first session, a PC will carefully review the nature of the PC's role with the parents, to ensure that they understand what the parenting coordination process involves. In cases of domestic violence involving power, control and coercion, the PC must hold individual sessions with the parties to convey this information.

Guideline X.   Fees and Costs

A PC shall fully disclose and explain the basis of any fees and charges to the participants.

A. All charges for parenting coordination services must be based upon the actual time expended by the PC. All fees and costs shall be appropriately assessed between the parties as directed by the court order of appointment, or as agreed upon in the PC's written fee agreement with the parties but only with the approval of the court. The court, rather than the PC, should make a determination of the appropriate ratio of payment based on the available financial data. The Court should be advised of any reasons to consider altering the original payment ratio.

B. Prior to beginning the parenting coordination process, and in writing, a PC shall explain to the parties and counsel the basis of fees and costs and the method of payment and any fees associated with postponement, cancellation and/or nonappearance, as well as any other items, and the parties' pro-rata share of the fees and costs as determined to the court order or agreed to by the parties with approval of the court. In cases of domestic violence involving power, control and coercion, the PC must hold individual sessions with the parties to convey this information.

C. Activities for which a PC may charge typically will include, but are not limited to, time spent interviewing parents, children and collateral sources of information; preparation of agreements; correspondence, decisions and reports; review of records and correspondence; telephone and electronic conversation; travel; court preparation; and appearances at court, meetings, or conferences.

D. The PC is expected to comply with any practice rules regarding fees. A PC may request a retainer or advance deposit prior to starting a case. The parties should be billed on a regular basis and notified when the retainer or advance deposit, if any, is to be replenished.

E. A PC must maintain records necessary to support the charges for services and expenses and should provide a detailed accounting of those charges to the parties, their counsel, and the court on a regular basis.

Guideline XI.   Domestic Violence Issues

A Parenting Coordinator shall and must routinely screen all cases for domestic violence.

A. The safety of parents and children shall be paramount at all times. A PC shall make ongoing efforts to stay abreast of domestic violence research, effective intervention, safety measures and other professional advances.

B. A PC shall scrupulously adhere to all protective orders.

C. A PC must decline to accept such cases if he/she does not have specialized expertise to effectively manage domestic violence cases, or any case involving an imbalance of power, control and coercion.

D. In those cases of domestic violence where one parent seeks to obtain and maintain power and control over the other, the role of the PC changes to an almost purely enforcement function. In domestic violence cases the PC's role is to ensure compliance with the details of the order and to test each request for variance from its terms with an eye to protecting the custodial parent's autonomy to make decisions based on the children's best interests and guarding against manipulation by the abusing parent.

E. In cases of domestic violence, a PC should tailor techniques used and services provided to avoid a situation where an abuser can continue the pattern of power, control and coercion.

F. In cases of domestic violence, a PC shall ensure that interviews and sessions with the parties are conducted separately, even if the parties should request joint meetings.

G. A PC should always be aware that an abused parent and the children could well be at increased risk if information is shared with the abusing parent. The PC must alert the protected parent to the disclosure in advance to enable the parent to take needed safety precautions.

H. A domestic violence situation may form the basis for a PC to recommend to the court an unequal division of fees and costs, placing more of the financial burden on the abusing parent. In such cases, the protected parent's requests for assistance by the PC

shall not form the basis for the parent to pay an increased amount of fees.

Guideline XII.   Communications and Reports

A PC will communicate with all parties, counsel, children, and the court in a manner which preserves the integrity of the parenting coordination process and considers the safety of the parents and children. The PC will have access to persons involved with family members and to documentary information necessary to fulfill the responsibilities of the assignment.

A. Because parenting coordination is a non-adversarial process designed to reduce acrimony and settle disputes efficiently, a PC may engage in ex-parte (individual) communications with each of the parties and/or their attorneys, unless prohibited in the order of appointment, PC agreement or stipulation. The PC may initiate or receive *ex-parte* oral or written communications with the parties and their attorneys, legal representatives of the children, and other parties relevant to understanding the issues. The PC will do so in an objective, balanced manner that takes into consideration the possibility or perception of bias. The PC should communicate agreements, recommendations, or decisions (if applicable) to all parties and counsel as nearly contemporaneous as practicable.

B. The PC will never communicate *ex-parte* with the judge. If written reports are provided to the parties and counsel, the PC should follow the court's rules or instructions regarding whether the court should receive a copy.

C. The PC will have access to any person involved with family members, including but not limited to, the custody evaluator, lawyers, school officials, and physical and mental health care providers. The PC shall have the authority to meet with the children (upon prior notice to the Attorney for the Child/Children), any stepparent or person acting in that role, or others the PC determines to have a significant role in contributing to or resolving the conflict. The PC should notify any such collateral sources that information obtained from them is not confidential and that it may be used in making decisions or writing reports or recommendations to or testifying in court.

D. The PC shall have access to all orders and pleadings filed in the case, as well as the custody evaluation report, school and medical records of the children, and reports of psychological testings that were generated prior to, during or after the pendency of the case. The court order will direct the parties to execute releases and consents permitting access to such data and other relevant information.

E. The PC should have initial individual and/or joint interviews with the parties. The PC may want to interview the children if the PC has the appropriate training and skills and upon prior notice to the Attorney for the Child/Children. The PC may interview any individuals who provide services to the children as needed to assess the children's needs and wishes. The communication between the parties may be in joint fact-to-face meetings, telephone conference calls, individual face-to-face or telephone meetings, email or fax. The PC will determine whether separate or joint sessions are most appropriate at any particular time. In cases of domestic violence involving power, control or coercion, the PC interviews and sessions with the parties are always to be conducted individually, even if the parties should request joint meetings.

F. The PC must be alert to the reasonable suspicion of any acts of domestic violence directed at the other parent, a current partner or the children. The PC will adhere to any protection orders, and take whatever measures may be necessary to ensure the safety of the parties, the children and others.

G. The PC must be alert to the reasonable suspicion of any substance abuse by either parent or child, as well as any psychological or psychiatric impairment of any parent or child.

H. The PC should keep notes regarding all communication with the parties, the children and other persons with whom the PC speaks about the case.

I. A PC must document in writing all resolutions agreed upon by the parties or determined by arbitration, noting the process by which the agreement or decision was made.

J. The PC must maintain records in a manner that is professional, comprehensive and inclusive of information and documents that relate to the parenting coordination process and that support decisions and recommendations by the PC.

Guideline XIII.   Outcomes

A PC will not engage in marketing practices that contain false or misleading information. A PC will ensure that any advertisements regarding qualifications, services to be rendered, or the parenting coordination process are accurate and honest. A PC will not make claims of achieving specific outcomes or promises implying favoritism for the purpose of obtaining business.

A. A PC should not promise or make claims to any parent or child to achieve a specific outcome.

B. A PC should advise the parties that they always retain the right to seek court review of any outcomes of the parent coordination process.

Guideline XIV.   Regulation

A. The ADR Administration of the 8th Judicial District shall have authority to accept and process PC applications, interview applicants, set qualifications, and from time to time offer training for PCs.

B. These protocols will be reviewed from time to time and may be modified or revised. All concerns or comments should be forwarded in writing to the ADR Administration, c/o the 8th Judicial District Office, 92 Franklin Street, Buffalo, New York 14202.

ERIE COUNTY
E–FILING
PROTOCOL

Doc. 1. Protocols on Courthouse Procedures for Cases Filed on the New York State Electronic Filing System

Attorneys seeking information concerning the New York State Electronic Filing System (otherwise known as NYSEF) are advised to consult the User's Manual and FAQs, both available on-line at the NYSEF website (www.nycourts.gov/efile).

In addition, attorneys should consult the Uniform Rules for Supreme and County Courts, at 22 NYCRR 202.5b, for rules that currently govern e-filing.

What follows is an outline of the steps that must be taken in e-filed cases to satisfy traditional courthouse requirements for the processing of cases, such as the submission of orders to show cause. To the maximum extent possible, the steps outlined here seek to integrate e-filing capabilities with normal courthouse procedures in ways that will save attorneys time, trouble and trips to the courthouse, while meeting the needs of Justices and of the Court.

A. What Cases May Be E–filed

1) All authorized cases may be commenced by e-filing; however, all parties need to consent for the action or proceeding to continue as an e-filed case.

2) Cases authorized for e-filing in Erie County at this time are Commercial Cases (as defined by 22 NYCRR 202.70); proceedings filed pursuant to Article 7 of the Real Property Tax Law (i.e., tax assessment cases, 22 NYCRR 202.59), and all tort cases.

B. Identifying E–Filed Cases

1) *Cases Commenced via NYSEF:*

Cases that are commenced by filing of the initial papers with the NYSEF system are identified as e-filed cases by assignment of an index number beginning with the number 8 (i.e., 800001–2007).

2) *Cases Converted to NYSEF:*

Cases originally commenced in hard-copy form but later converted to NYSEF status will bear a regular index number initially. When a case is converted to e-filing, the letter "E" will be placed after the index number by the County Clerk's office to designate the matter as an e-filed case (i.e., 000123–2007E). The "E" suffix must appear on all documents following the conversion of the case.

It will be the filing party's responsibility to scan all papers previously filed in hard-copy form on to the NYSEF system.

C. Summons and Complaint/Notice of Petition and Petition

1) *How Filed:*

Papers commencing an action or special proceeding may be filed on-line with NYSEF. Fees shall be paid by MasterCard or Visa, or by choosing the "Pay at the County Clerk's Office" option. However, until all parties (including the plaintiff or petitioner) have consented to e-filing, service of initiating papers must be in hard copy pursuant to the CPLR. To obtain consent of opposing parties, the commencing party should include with the papers a Notice Regarding Availability of Electronic Filing. A sample copy of the Notice Regarding Availability can be found on the Eighth Judicial District website, and is also available on the NYSEF Home Page under "Forms", as Form # EF–3. Although all filings to the system generate automatic e-mail notifications to e-mail addresses on record, such automatic e-mails do not constitute service by a party (*see infra*, section E).

2) *Consent By All is Required:*

According to 22 NYCRR 202.5b (b) (2), "[p]arties who consent to participate in [e-filing] shall promptly file with the court and serve on all parties of record a consent to [e-filing], in hard copy, in conformance with [22 NYCRR 202.5b(c)]. A party represented by an attorney who has already registered as a filing user pursuant to subdivision (d) of this section may instead file and serve the consent * * * electronically by checking the designated box and following the instructions" on page 16 of the User's Manual, which is available on the NYSEF Home Page (www.nycourts. gov/efile).

3) *Commencing Party Must Also Consent:*

The NYSEF system does not assume that the commencing party has consented to e-filing. Thus, the commencing party must also consent on line. *See* the User's Manual at page 14.

4) *Return Dates on Petitions:*

The Part Clerk will assign a return date to petitions that have been e-filed, and notify counsel by e-mail or, if no consents have yet been filed, by mail or telephone, or otherwise as per the individual Justice's Part Rules.

D. Filing of Papers Generally

1) *Fees:*

Court fees (e.g., RJI fee, motion fee) in NYSEF cases may be paid for on-line using a Visa or MasterCard. Alternatively, documents may be filed on NY-

SEF and the fee(s) paid in person at the County Clerk's Office. However, the document is not considered to have been filed until payment of the fee has been tendered (see CPLR 304; 22 NYCRR 202.5b [e] [3], [4] [i]).

2) *Papers to Be Filed to the System:*

All papers to be filed in a NYSEF case shall be filed on-line with the NYSEF system, unless a special exemption is granted (e.g., for oversized maps, photographs) or as directed by the Court. Papers that attorneys would not ordinarily file with the court in a hard-copy case need not be filed in a NYSEF matter (e.g., Notice to Produce Documents, Notice of Deposition).

3) *Signatures:*

Papers filed or served electronically shall be deemed to be signed by the signatory when the paper identifies the person as such, in compliance with 22 NYCRR 202.5b (f). Please see the specific rules regarding signing of affidavits and affirmations (see 22 NYCRR 202.5b [f] [Signatures]).

4) *Courtesy Hard Copies of Papers for Judicial Review:*

Absent request by an individual Justice, counsel should NOT provide hard copies of any documents.

E. Service On–Line

1) *Generally:*

In cases authorized for e-filing, a party may commence an action by filing the initiating papers on the NYSEF system, but until all parties (including the plaintiff or petitioner) have consented to e-filing, service of initiating papers must be in hard copy pursuant to the CPLR, along with a Notice Regarding Availability of Electronic Filing. A sample copy of a Notice Regarding Availability can be found on the Eighth Judicial District website — www.nycourts.gov/courts/8jd/Erie/efile.shtml.

2) *Interlocutory Papers:*

Once all parties have consented to e-filing a particular case, papers are served as follows. A party shall file the document on the NYSEF site. On the same day, the party shall send to all e-mail addresses of record for that case a Notice of Filing, setting forth the title of the paper filed, its sequence number on the NYSEF docket, the date and the time filed (see 22 NYCRR 202.5b [g] [2]). Electronic transmission of the Notice of Filing constitutes service on the addressees (see infra, section 3). A sample form of a Notice of Filing can be found on the Eighth Judicial District website — www.nycourts.gov/courts/8jd/Erie/efile.shtml.

3) *Proof of Service to Be Posted On–Line:*

After service of interlocutory papers by e-mail Notice of Filing, the filer shall file an Affidavit or Affirmation of service on the NYSEF system. However,

proof of service need not be served on opposing parties. A sample form of Affidavit of Service can be found on the Eighth Judicial District website — www.nycourts.gov/courts/8jd/Erie/efile.shtml.

4) *Other Methods of Service Permitted:*

The rules authorize service by other methods permitted by the CPLR (see 22 NYCRR 202.5b [g] [2]).

F. Requests for Judicial Intervention

1) *How Made:*

A Request for Judicial Intervention ("RJI") in a NYSEF case shall be filed electronically on NYSEF. When the RJI is filed and paid for, either on-line by Visa or MasterCard, or by the "Pay at the County Clerk's Office" option, the Erie County Clerk's Office will forward the RJI and any accompanying documents to the Chief Clerk's Office to be reviewed and processed. Once processed, the RJI will be randomly assigned by the Chief Clerk's Office.

2) *RJIs in Commercial Cases:*

If a party seeks assignment of a case to the Commercial Division, that party must file on-line on NYSEF the Request for Judicial Intervention and the Commercial Division Certification, indicating that the case falls within the standards for assignment of cases to the Commercial Division (see 22 NYCRR 202.70 [a], [b]). A copy of the Commercial Division Certification form can be found on the Eighth Judicial District website — www.nycourts.gov/courts/8jd/Erie/efile.shtml.

G. Motions on Notice

1) *Filing of Motions on Notice:*

A motion on notice in a NYSEF case shall be filed on-line and the motion fee paid for either on-line by MasterCard or Visa or by the "Pay at the County Clerk's Office" option. The motion will be calendared by the Part Clerk once the fee is paid. Consenting parties will be notified of the return date via e-mail.

2) *Service; Time for Service:*

With regard to service of motion papers, the moving party shall send e-mail notifications to all consenting parties' counsel of record or, in the case of consenting pro se parties, directly to the parties. CPLR 2214 (b) and 2215 apply. Proof of service shall be filed on-line.

3) *Filing of Exhibits:*

It is recommended that, whenever possible, attorneys filing exhibits in a NYSEF case make each exhibit a separate attachment to an affidavit /affirmation. In other words, each exhibit should be scanned and uploaded as a separate document, and separate from the affidavit or affirmation to which it is attached.

4) *Sequence Number for NYSEF Motions:*

As in a hard-copy case, each document/motion filed on-line in a NYSEF case is assigned an identifying number (a "Sequence Number", i.e., Seq. No. 006). In other words, the Clerk will tag each new motion, document or separate exhibit with a sequence number. Cross motions should have the same sequence number as the original motion sequence number.

5) *Cross Motions, Responses and Replies:*

Cross motions, responses and replies shall be e-filed on NYSEF. Fees shall be paid for cross motions, as for motions.

6) *Adjournments on Motions and Cross Motions:*

Please consult the rules of the IAS Justice to whom the case has been assigned.

7) *Decisions and Orders of the Court:*

When the Court signs a decision or an order in a NYSEF case, the document will be stamped "Filed" with the filing date, scanned and filed by the Part Clerk on the NYSEF system. The system will immediately transmit notice of the filing of the decision or order by e-mail to all parties who have consented on-line in the case, with a link to the document(s) so filed.

H. Proposed Orders

If the Court directs that an order be settled on a motion in a NYSEF case, the proposed order and any proposed counter-orders shall be filed in the NYSEF system, together with proof of service, and served on all counsel of record.

I. Orders to Show Cause

1) *Commercial Cases:* Proposed Orders to Show Cause and Supporting Papers to be E–Mailed to Commercial Division

Proposed Orders to Show Cause and supporting papers in a NYSEF case should not be filed with the NYSEF system until after their review by the Commercial Division. Instead, the papers should be emailed to the Commercial Division. Unless otherwise ordered, the Commercial Division will not require courtesy copies of any documents.

After review, the Court will contact counsel with further directions. Once the Order to Show Cause has been executed, the order will be stamped "Filed" by the Erie County Clerk's office, uploaded and filed to NYSEF by the Part Clerk. Thereafter, the rest of the papers will be returned to Counsel. Counsel shall thereafter file the supporting papers on the NYSEF system, and serve all counsel of record, as directed in the Order to Show Cause.

2) *Other Justices:*

In any case not assigned to the Commercial Division, please check the individual Justice's Part Rules.

J. Sealing of Documents; "Secure" Documents

1) Sealing Requires Compliance with Part 216 of the Uniform Rules of the Supreme and County Courts

As in all other cases, some or all of the documents in an e-filed case may be sealed, but only upon a written finding by the Court as required under 22 NYCRR Part 216.

2) *Secure Documents*

A "Secure" document in the NYSEF system is a document the party does not wish to be widely available on the Web, because it contains confidential information such as social security numbers, the names of minor children, bank account numbers and the like. Whenever a document is being filed, the system will prompt the filer to choose to "secure" the document due to the presence of such information. Counsel may secure documents without prior approval of the Court or opposing counsel or parties. However, the documents will still be available for on-line viewing by the court, counsel of record for the parties to the action or proceeding and to any pro se party to that action or proceeding who has registered as a consenting user. It will also be available for public inspection at the Courthouse unless otherwise sealed by the Court.

3) *Sealing; Procedures:*

If a party wishes to file and maintain papers under seal and no sealing order has been issued in the case, the party must, by motion, obtain a Court order directing the Clerk to seal the file. The Court will conduct a Part 216 analysis in deciding whether to issue such an order. If the motion is filed with the NYSEF system, it will be open to the public until a sealing order is issued. If this creates concern for the parties about the release of confidential information in the meantime, they may wish to consider filing the motion as a "secure" document if that is appropriate. Or, the motion may be filed with the system but without the attachment of any exhibits that would disclose confidential information. If the file is sealed in whole or in part, the exhibits can be filed with NYSEF after the fact. Questions should be addressed to the individual Justice's Chambers to which the case has been assigned.

4) *Execution of Sealing Order:*

If the Court issues an order directing the sealing of a NYSEF file in whole or in part, the party seeking the sealing should file with the NYSEF system a Certificate Requesting Sealing of Documents in Electronically–Filed Case, together with a copy of the Court's order. This form is available on the Eighth Judicial District website. If such a request is properly made, the County Clerk will seal the file or the document(s) in question as directed by the Court, both in the NYSEF system and, if any of the covered documents are found therein, in the hard copy file.

K. Entry of Orders and Notice of Entry

1) *Entry:*

Pursuant to 22 NYCRR 202.5b [j], "the Clerk shall file electronically orders and judgments of the court in accordance with the procedures for [e-filing], which shall constitute entry of the order or judgment." Simultaneously, the Clerk shall transmit by e-mail to the e-mail addresses of record a notification of the entry. However, these steps shall not constitute notice of entry by any party.

2) *Notice of Entry:*

Notice of entry is served by a party as follows: the party simply transmits electronically to the parties to be served the notification received from the Court, along with an express statement that the transmittal constitutes notice of entry.

L. Judgments and the Judgment Roll

1) *Entry of Judgment; Procedures*

If the Court in an order directs entry of judgment by the County Clerk, the party seeking entry shall file on the NYSEF system a proposed judgment with bill of costs, interest calculations and supporting information, together with a Certificate Requesting Entry of Judgment. The Judgment Clerk will promptly communicate with counsel by e-mail or phone in the event of any difficulties with the submission. Once the judgment is in proper form, it will be printed out by the Judgment Clerk and submitted to the County Clerk for signature. The Judgment Clerk will scan the judgment once signed and post it to the system, along with the supporting information, at which time notification will be sent via e-mail to all consenting users.

2) *Default Judgment; Entry by Clerk*

If the plaintiff in a NYSEF cases seeks entry of a default judgment by the Clerk pursuant to CPLR 3215, the attorney shall transmit to the NYSEF system a Proposed Clerk's Default Judgment with bill of costs, etc. and the Certificate Requesting Entry of Judgment. When the submissions are made to NYSEF, the Judgment Clerk will promptly accept the fee and enter the judgment or will communicate with the filer by phone or e-mail if a problem is detected. To enter the judgment, the Clerk will print out the judgment from NYSEF, have it signed and scan it to the system.

3) *Judgments Signed by Court*

In some instances, the Court itself may sign the judgment. Calculation of disbursements, costs and interest will generally be left to the County Clerk by the court. Papers supporting such calculation may be submitted to the County Clerk in the same manner as described above.

4) *Judgment Roll*

Whenever a judgment is to be entered, a judgment roll must be created by counsel or the clerk (CPLR 5017[a]). Counsel shall submit the Certificate Requesting Entry of Judgment and shall identify therein, by title of the paper, number of the paper on the NYSEF List of Papers Filed, and date filed, all e-filed documents that should form part of the judgment roll. Any documents that were filed in hard-copy form only that are to be included in the judgment roll should be scanned into the system by counsel and included in the Certificate. The County Clerk will review the Certificate on-line and, once it has been approved, sign the judgment and scan it to the NYSEF system.

5) *Entry of Judgment*

Once the County Clerk has taxed costs and disbursements and calculated interest and has in hand a signed judgment, the Clerk will stamp the judgment with the County Clerk file stamp and scan the judgment to the system. This constitutes entry. The Clerk is required to and will transmit an e-mail message to all filing users on the case notifying that the judgment has been entered. This notice does not constitute service of notice of entry by any party. As to notice of entry, *see* section K(2) above.

M. Notice of Appeal and Appeal Papers

1) *Notice of Appeal; Payment of Fee*

A notice of appeal shall be filed on-line in a NYSEF case. The fee therefore must be paid by credit card on-line or by means of the "Pay at the County Clerk's Office" option. In the latter situation, the notice will NOT be considered "filed" until payment of the fee is tendered to the Erie County Clerk at the office.

2) *Notice of Appeal; Procedures*

The notice of appeal shall be e-filed on the NYSEF system together with a copy of the judgment or order appealed from. The other parties to the case shall be served on-line in the manner described above (*see* section E[2]). Proof of service must also be filed on-line (*see* section E[3]). The County Clerk shall print a hard copy of any e-filed notice of appeal and include it in the County Clerk's file.

3) *NYSEF; Appellate Division*

At present, the Appellate Division, Fourth Department does not handle appeals in NYSEF cases by electronic means. Counsel are advised to consult the rules of the Appellate Division for its procedures (*see* www.nycourts.gov/ad4).

Dated: October 1, 2007

HON. SHARON S. TOWNSEND
ADMINISTRATIVE JUDGE
EIGHTH JUDICIAL DISTRICT
92 Franklin Street
Buffalo, NY 14202

FORMS

Form 1. Commercial Division Certification

SUPREME COURT OF THE STATE OF NEW YORK   UCS–840C
                                                          3/2011
COUNTY OF _____

_____ x   Index No. _____
                                              RJI No. (if any) _____
              Plaintiff(s)/Petitioner(s)
-against-

              Defendant(s)/Respondent(s)   **COMMERCIAL DIVISION**
_____ x   **Request for Judicial Intervention Addendum**

COMPLETE WHERE APPLICABLE [add additional pages if needed]:

Plaintiff/Petitioner's cause(s) of action [check all that apply]:

☐ Breach of contract or fiduciary duty, fraud, misrepresentation, business tort (e.g. unfair competition), or statutory and/or common law violation where the breach or violation is alleged to arise out of business dealings (e.g. sales of assets or securities; corporate restructuring; partnership, shareholder, joint venture, and other business agreements; trade secrets; restrictive covenants; and employment agreements not including claims that principally involve alleged discriminatory practices)

☐ Transactions governed by the Uniform Commercial Code (exclusive of those concerning individual cooperative or condominium units)

☐ Transactions involving commercial real property, including Yellowstone injunctions and excluding actions for the payment of rent only

☐ Shareholder derivative actions—without consideration of the monetary threshold

☐ Commercial class actions—without consideration of the monetary threshold

☐ Business transactions involving or arising out of dealings with commercial banks and other financial institutions

☐ Internal affairs of business organizations

☐ Malpractice by accountants or actuaries, and legal malpractice arising out of representation in commercial matters

☐ Environmental insurance coverage

☐ Commercial insurance coverage (e.g. directors and officers, errors and omissions, and business interruption coverage)

☐ Dissolution of corporations, partnerships, limited liability companies, limited liability partnerships and joint ventures—without consideration of the monetary threshold

☐ Applications to stay or compel arbitration and affirm or disaffirm arbitration awards and related injunctive relief pursuant to CPLR Article 75 involving any of the foregoing enumerated commercial issues—without consideration of the monetary threshold

Plaintiff/Petitioner's claim for compensatory damages [exclusive of punitive damages, interest, costs and counsel fees claimed]:

$ _____

Plaintiff/Petitioner's claim for equitable or declaratory relief [brief description]:

_____

_____

Defendant/Respondent's counterclaim(s) [brief description, including claim for monetary relief]:

_____

_____

I REQUEST THAT THIS CASE BE ASSIGNED TO THE COMMERCIAL DIVISION. I CERTIFY THAT THE CASE MEETS THE JURISDICTIONAL REQUIREMENTS OF THE COMMERCIAL DIVISION SET FORTH IN 22 NYCRR § 202.70(a), (b) AND (c).

Dated: _____   _____
                                                SIGNATURE

                                  _____
                                        PRINT OR TYPE NAME

Form 2.   Certificate Requesting Entry of Judgment

SUPREME COURT OF THE STATE OF NEW YORK

COUNTY OF ERIE

---x

Plaintiff/Petitioner,

- vs. -   Index No. _____

Defendant/Respondent.

---x

CERTIFICATE REQUESTING ENTRY OF JUDGMENT IN ELECTRONICALLY–FILED CASE

To: The County Clerk, County of Erie _____

_____, an attorney admitted to the Bar of the State of New York and counsel for _____ in the above-captioned electronically-filed case, does hereby request that judgment be entered in this case based upon the _____, dated _____ and entered on _____. Pursuant to CPLR 5017 (a), I do hereby certify that the following documents shall constitute the Judgment Roll for this Judgment. Each document is identified by title of the paper, the date filed with the NYS electronic filing system ("NYSEF"), and the number of the paper as listed on the EF List of Papers Filed.

Title of Document	Number of Paper On NYSEF List of Papers	Date Filed
1) _____	No. _____	_____
2) _____	No. _____	_____
3) _____	No. _____	_____
4) _____	No. _____	_____
5) _____	No. _____	_____
6) _____	No. _____	_____
7) _____	No. _____	_____
8) _____	No. _____	_____
9) _____	No. _____	_____
10) _____	No. _____	

The documents listed above are available on the NYSEF website and may be
downloaded and printed as needed.

Dated: _____   _____(Signature)

                                 _____(Name)
                                 _____(Firm Name)
                                 _____(Address)
                                 _____
                                 _____

                                 Attorney for _____

                                                    10/1/07

Form 3. Consent to E–Filing

SUPREME COURT OF THE STATE OF NEW YORK

COUNTY OF ERIE

---x

Plaintiff/Petitioner(s),   Index No. _____

- vs. -

CONSENT TO E–FILING*

Defendant/Respondent(s).

---x

* As provided in the NYSEF Rules, consent of the parties is required for a matter to proceed as an NYSEF case. This form must be filed with the court and served on all parties. If an attorney has previously registered as a NYSEF Filing User, consent may be filed and served by means of the NYSEF system.

    I, _____, am a party or an attorney for a party, identified below, in the above-captioned law suit, and I consent to the use of the New York State Electronic Filing System ("NYSEF") in this case. I further consent to be bound by the service and filing provisions of the NYSEF Rules (22 NYCRR § 202.5-b) and will comply with the *User's Manual* approved by the Chief Administrator of the Courts and posted on the NYSEF website (www.nycourts.gov/efile).

    I set forth in the following spaces up to three Internet e-mail addresses to be used for the purposes of service and giving notice of each filing:

_____

_____

_____

_____

Signature   Address

_____

Print or Type Name

_____

Law Firm Name   Telephone Number

Attorney for _____

10/1/07

Form 3.   Request for Judicial Intervention

<table>
<tr><td colspan="2">

REQUEST FOR JUDICIAL INTERVENTION
UCS–840 (3/2011)

</td><td>

For Court Clerk Use Only:
IAS Entry Date
_____

</td></tr>
</table>

Supreme_____ COURT, COUNTY OF _____

Index No: _____   Date Index Issued: _____

	Judge Assigned _____

CAPTION: Enter the complete case caption. Do not use et al or et ano. If more space is required, attach a caption rider sheet.

RJI Date _____

Plaintiff(s)/Petitioner(s)
_____

-against-

Defendant(s)/Respondent(s)
_____

NATURE OF ACTION OR PROCEEDING: Check ONE box only and specify where indicated.

MATRIMONIAL

- ○ Contested
- ○ Uncontested
  NOTE: For all Matrimonial actions where the parties have children under the age of 18, complete and attach the **MATRIMONIAL RJI Addendum.**

TORTS

- ○ Asbestos
- ○ Breast Implant
- ○ Environmental: _____
  (specify)
- ○ Medical, Dental, or Podiatric Malpractice
- ○ Motor Vehicle
- ○ Products Liability: _____
  (specify)
- ○ Other Negligence: _____
  (specify)
- ○ Other Professional Malpractice: _____
  (specify)
- ○ Other Tort: _____
  (specify)

COMMERCIAL

- ○ Business Entity (including corporations, partnerships, LLCs, etc.)
- ○ Contract
- ○ Insurance (where insurer is a party, except arbitration)
- ○ UCC (including sales, negotiable instruments)
- ○ Other Commercial: _____
  (specify)

NOTE: For Commercial Division assignment requests, complete and attach the **COMMERCIAL DIV RJI Addendum.**

REAL PROPERTY: How many properties does the application include? _____

- ○ Condemnation
- ○ Foreclosure
Property Address: _____
             Street Address   City   State   Zip
NOTE: For Foreclosure actions involving a one- to four-family, owner-occupied, residential property, or an owner-occupied condominium, complete and attach the **FORECLOSURE RJI Addendum.**
- ○ Tax Certiorari—Section: _____ Block: _____ Lot: __
- ○ Other Real Property: _____
  (specify)

OTHER MATTERS

- ○ Certificate of Incorporation/Dissolution [see **NOTE** under Commercial]
- ○ Emergency Medical Treatment
- ○ Habeas Corpus
- ○ Local Court Appeal
- ○ Mechanic's Lien
- ○ Name Change
- ○ Pistol Permit Revocation Hearing
- ○ Sale or Finance of Religious/ Not–for–Profit Property
- ○ Other: _____
  (specify)

SPECIAL PROCEEDINGS

- ○ CPLR Article 75 (Arbitration) [see **NOTE** under Commercial]
- ○ CPLR Article 78 (Body or Officer)
- ○ Election Law
- ○ MHL Article 9.60 (Kendra's Law)
- ○ MHL Article 10 (Sex Offender Confinement–Initial)
- ○ MHL Article 10 (Sex Offender Confinement–Review)
- ○ MHL Article 81 (Guardianship)
- ○ Other Mental Hygiene: _____
  (specify)
- ○ Other Special Proceeding: _____
  (specify)

STATUS OF ACTION OR PROCEEDING: Answer YES or NO for EVERY question AND enter additional information where indicated.

	YES	NO	
Has a summons and complaint or summons w/notice been filed?	○	○	If yes, date filed: _____
Is this action/proceeding being filed post–judgment?	○	○	If yes, judgment date: _____

NATURE OF JUDICIAL INTERVENTION: Check ONE box only AND enter additional information where indicated.

- ○ Infant's Compromise
- ○ Note of Issue and/or Certificate of Readiness
- ○ Notice of Medical, Dental, or Podiatric Malpractice
- ○ Notice of Motion

Date Issue Joined: _____

Relief Sought: _____   Return Date: _____

○ Notice of Petition   Relief Sought: _____   Return Date: _____
○ Order to Show Cause   Relief Sought: _____   Return Date: _____
○ Other Ex Parte Application   Relief Sought: _____
○ Poor Person Application
○ Request for Preliminary Conference
○ Residential Mortgage Foreclosure Settlement Conference
○ Writ of Habeas Corpus
○ Other (specify): _____

RELATED CASES: List any related actions. For Matrimonial actions, include any related criminal and/or Family
                     Court cases. If additional space is required, complete and attach the **RJI Addendum**. If none,
                     leave blank.

Case Title	Index/Case No.	Court	Judge (if assigned)	Relationship to Instant Case

PARTIES: If additional space is required, complete and attach the **RJI Addendum**.
               For parties without an attorney, check "Un–Rep" box AND enter party address, phone number and e-mail
               address in "Attorneys" space.

Un–Rep	Parties:	Attorneys:					Issue Joined (Y/N):	Insurance Carrier(s):
	List parties in caption order and indicate party role(s) (e.g. defendant; 3rd–party plaintiff).	Provide name, firm name, business address, phone number and e-mail address of all attorneys that have appeared in the case.						
	Last Name	Last Name		First Name			○ YES	
☐	First Name / Primary Role:	Firm Name						
	Secondary Role (if any):	Street Address	City	State	Zip		○ NO	
		Phone	Fax	e-mail				
	Last Name	Last Name		First Name			○ YES	
☐	First Name / Primary Role:	Firm Name						
	Secondary Role (if any):	Street Address	City	State	Zip		○ NO	
		Phone	Fax	e-mail				
	Last Name	Last Name		First Name			○ YES	
☐	First Name / Primary Role:	Firm Name						
	Secondary Role (if any):	Street Address	City	State	Zip		○ NO	
		Phone	Fax	e-mail				
	Last Name	Last Name		First Name			○ YES	
☐	First Name / Primary Role:	Firm Name						
	Secondary Role (if any):	Street Address	City	State	Zip		○ NO	
		Phone	Fax	e-mail				

**I AFFIRM UNDER THE PENALTY OF PERJURY THAT, TO MY KNOWLEDGE, OTHER THAN
AS NOTED ABOVE, THERE ARE AND HAVE BEEN NO RELATED ACTIONS OR PROCEED-
INGS, NOR HAS A REQUEST FOR JUDICIAL INTERVENTION PREVIOUSLY BEEN FILED IN
THIS ACTION OR PROCEEDING.**

Dated: _____   _____
                                              SIGNATURE

_____   _____
ATTORNEY REGISTRATION NUMBER   **PRINT OR TYPE NAME**

Request for Judicial Intervention Addendum   UCS–840A (3/ 2011)

Supreme _____   **COURT, COUNTY OF** _____   **Index No:** _____

For use when additional space is needed to provide party or related case information.

PARTIES: For parties without an attorney, check " Un–Rep" box AND enter party address, phone number and e-mail address in " Attorneys" space.

Un–Rep	Parties:	Attorneys:		Issue Joined (Y/N):	Insurance Carrier(s):
	List parties in caption order and indicate party role(s) (e.g. defendant; 3rd–party plaintiff).	Provide name, firm name, business address, phone number and e-mail address of all attorneys that have appeared in the case.			
	Last Name	Last Name	First Name	○ YES	
☐	First Name Primary Role:	Firm Name			
	Secondary Role (if any):	Street Address City	State Zip	○ NO	
		Phone Fax	e-mail		
	Last Name	Last Name	First Name	○ YES	
☐	First Name Primary Role:	Firm Name			
	Secondary Role (if any):	Street Address City	State Zip	○ NO	
		Phone Fax	e-mail		
	Last Name	Last Name	First Name	○ YES	
☐	First Name Primary Role:	Firm Name			
	Secondary Role (if any):	Street Address City	State Zip		
		Phone Fax	e-mail	○ NO	
	Last Name	Last Name	First Name	○ YES	
☐	First Name Primary Role:	Firm Name			
	Secondary Role (if any):	Street Address City	State Zip		
		Phone Fax	e-mail	○ NO	
	Last Name	Last Name	First Name	○ YES	
☐	First Name Primary Role:	Firm Name			
	Secondary Role (if any):	Street Address City	State Zip		
		Phone Fax	e-mail	○ NO	
	Last Name	Last Name	First Name	○ YES	
☐	First Name Primary Role:	Firm Name			
	Secondary Role (if any):	Street Address City	State Zip		
		Phone Fax	e-mail	○ NO	

RELATED CASES: List any related actions. For Matrimonial actions, include any related criminal and/or Family Court cases.

Case Title	Index/Case No.	Court	Judge (if assigned)	Relationship to Instant Case

SUPREME COURT OF THE STATE OF NEW YORK

COUNTY OF _____

---x

Plaintiff(s)/Petitioner(s)

-against-

Defendant(s)/Respondent(s)

---x

UCS–840C
3/2011

Index No. _____

RJI No. (if any) _____

COMMERCIAL DIVISION
Request for Judicial Intervention Addendum

COMPLETE WHERE APPLICABLE [add additional pages if needed]:

Plaintiff/Petitioner's cause(s) of action [check all that apply]:

☐ Breach of contract or fiduciary duty, fraud, misrepresentation, business tort (e.g. unfair competition), or statutory and/or common law violation where the breach or violation is alleged to arise out of business dealings (e.g. sales of assets or securities; corporate restructuring; partnership, shareholder, joint venture, and other business agreements; trade secrets; restrictive covenants; and employment agreements not including claims that principally involve alleged discriminatory practices)

☐ Transactions governed by the Uniform Commercial Code (exclusive of those concerning individual cooperative or condominium units)

☐ Transactions involving commercial real property, including Yellowstone injunctions and excluding actions for the payment of rent only

☐ Shareholder derivative actions — without consideration of the monetary threshold

☐ Commercial class actions — without consideration of the monetary threshold

☐ Business transactions involving or arising out of dealings with commercial banks and other financial institutions

☐ Internal affairs of business organizations

☐ Malpractice by accountants or actuaries, and legal malpractice arising out of representation in commercial matters

☐ Environmental insurance coverage

☐ Commercial insurance coverage (e.g. directors and officers, errors and omissions, and business interruption coverage)

☐ Dissolution of corporations, partnerships, limited liability companies, limited liability partnerships and joint ventures — without consideration of the monetary threshold

☐ Applications to stay or compel arbitration and affirm or disaffirm arbitration awards and related injunctive relief pursuant to CPLR Article 75 involving any of the foregoing enumerated commercial issues — without consideration of the monetary threshold

Plaintiff/Petitioner's claim for compensatory damages [exclusive of punitive damages, interest, costs and counsel fees claimed]:

$ _____

Plaintiff/Petitioner's claim for equitable or declaratory relief [brief description]:

_____

_____

Defendant/Respondent's counterclaim(s) [brief description, including claim for monetary relief]:

_____

_____

I REQUEST THAT THIS CASE BE ASSIGNED TO THE COMMERCIAL DIVISION. I CERTIFY THAT THE CASE MEETS THE JURISDICTIONAL REQUIREMENTS OF THE COMMERCIAL DIVISION SET FORTH IN 22 NYCRR § 202.70(a), (b) AND (c).

Dated: _____

_____
SIGNATURE

_____
PRINT OR TYPE NAME

MATRIMONIAL Request for Judicial Intervention Addendum   UCS–840M
                                                                          3/2011

Supreme _____ COURT, COUNTY OF _____ INDEX NO. _____

For use when there are children under the age of 18 who are subject to the matrimonial action.

Plaintiff

Last Name: _____ First Name: _____ Date of Birth: _____

Prior Names (List any other names used, including   Gender: ☐ Male ☐ Female
maiden and/or former married names):
Last Name: _____ First Name: _____
Last Name: _____ First Name: _____
Last Name: _____ First Name: _____

Present Address: _____ New York _____
                    (Street Address)   (City)   (State)   (Zip)
Address History
for past 3 years: _____
                    (Street Address)   (City)   (State)   (Zip)

                    _____
                    (Street Address)   (City)   (State)   (Zip)

                    _____
                    (Street Address)   (City)   (State)   (Zip)

Defendant

Last Name: _____ First Name: _____ Date of Birth: _____

Prior Names (List any other names used, including   Gender: ☐ Male ☐ Female
maiden and/or former married names):
Last Name: _____ First Name: _____
Last Name: _____ First Name: _____
Last Name: _____ First Name: _____

Present Address: _____ New York _____
                    (Street Address)   (City)   (State)   (Zip)
Address History
for past 3 years: _____
                    (Street Address)   (City)   (State)   (Zip)

                    _____
                    (Street Address)   (City)   (State)   (Zip)

                    _____
                    (Street Address)   (City)   (State)   (Zip)

Children

Last Name: _____ First Name: _____ Date of Birth: _____ Gender: ☐ M ☐ F

Last Name: _____ First Name: _____ Date of Birth: _____ Gender: ☐ M ☐ F

Last Name: _____ First Name: _____ Date of Birth: _____ Gender: ☐ M ☐ F

Last Name: _____ First Name: _____ Date of Birth: _____ Gender: ☐ M ☐ F

Last Name: _____ First Name: _____ Date of Birth: _____ Gender: ☐ M ☐ F

Form 5. Special Term Note of Issue

(This part to be typed out by party making motion and filed with
the Clerk of Special Term pursuant to Rule XVIII)

SUPREME COURT: ERIE COUNTY   Dated: ....

                                            Index No: ....

....

.................Plaintiff, ...
                                            Attorney
   -vs-   Phone: ....

....
                                            Attorney
.................Defendant,   Phone: ....
                                                            Am
Motion made by: ....   Returnable: ....Pm

Relief Sought: ....

Special Term Clerk's Use Only:
Note of Issue Received ....

Adjourned to: .... 20 ..... at .... M.
                .... 20 ..... at .... M.
                .... 20 ..... at .... M.
Papers obtained from counsel and submitted to court at time of argument:

        In support of Motion: Against Motion:

   ....

   ....

Notes made at Justice's Direction:

FOR JUSTICES USE ONLY:
DECISION:

   Date: ....

Form 6.   Notice of Filing in E–Filed Cases

SUPREME COURT OF THE STATE OF NEW YORK
COUNTY OF ERIE

---x

              Plaintiff/Petitioner(s),   Index No. _____

    - vs. -

            Defendant/Respondent(s).

---x

NOTICE OF FILING IN ELECTRONICALLY–FILED CASE

To: All E–Mail Addresses of Record in the Above–Captioned Case

PLEASE TAKE NOTICE that, pursuant to Section 202.5-b (g) of the Uniform Rules for the Trial Courts, the undersigned hereby notifies all E–Mail Addresses of Record that the undersigned filed in the electronic List of Papers Filed in this case, on the date listed below, the following documents:

Title of Paper Filed	Sequence Number of Paper on NYSEF List of Papers	Date Filed
1) _____	No. _____	_____
2) _____	No. _____	_____
3) _____	No. _____	_____
4) _____	No. _____	_____

Parties hereby notified may access the filing on the NYSEF website at the following address: www.nycourts.gov/efile

Dated: _____ _____(Filer)

                            _____(Firm Name)

                            _____(Address)

                            _____

                            _____

10/1/07

Form 7. Certificate Requesting Sealing of Document in E–Filed Case

SUPREME COURT OF THE STATE OF NEW YORK
COUNTY OF ERIE

---x

Plaintiff/Petitioner,

- vs. -   Index No. _____

Defendant/Respondent.

---x

CERTIFICATE REQUESTING SEALING OF DOCUMENT IN ELECTRONICALLY–FILED CASE

To: County Clerk, County of Erie

_____, an attorney admitted to the Bar of the State of New York and counsel for _____ in the above-captioned electronically-filed case, does hereby request that the document(s) identified below be sealed pursuant to the order of the court, a copy of which is annexed hereto. Except in instances in which the order requires sealing of the entire file, each document to be sealed is identified by title of the paper, the date filed with the NYS electronic filing system ("NYSEF"), and the sequence number of the paper as listed on the NYSEF List of Papers Filed.

Sealing of Entire File Requested _____ [Initial here] Or

Sealing of the Document(s) Identified Below Requested:

Title of Document	Number of Paper On NYSEF List of Papers	Date Filed
1) _____	No. _____	_____
2) _____	No. _____	_____
3) _____	No. _____	_____
4) _____	No. _____	_____
5) _____	No. _____	_____

Dated: _____   _____(Signature)

                            _____(Name)
                            _____(Firm Name)
                            _____(Address)
                            _____
                            _____

Attorney for _____

10/1/07

Form 8.   Notice Regarding Availability of Electronic Filing

SUPREME COURT OF THE STATE OF NEW YORK

COUNTY OF ERIE

---x

<table>
<tr><td>Plaintiff(s)/Petitioner(s),</td><td>Index No. _____</td></tr>
<tr><td>- vs. -</td><td></td></tr>
<tr><td></td><td>NOTICE REGARDING
AVAILABILITY OF
ELECTRONIC FILING</td></tr>
<tr><td>Defendant(s)/Respondent(s).</td><td></td></tr>
</table>

---x

PLEASE TAKE NOTICE that plaintiff(s)/petitioner(s) [defendant(s)/respondent(s)] in the case captioned above intend(s) that this matter proceed as an electronically-filed case in the New York State Electronic Filing System ("NYSEF") in accordance with the procedures therefor, described below. Service of papers by electronic means cannot be made upon a party unless that party consents to use of the system. Within ten days after service of this Notice, each party served must indicate whether it consents.

General Information

In New York State, actions may be commenced and cases processed by means of the NYSEF system in (1) tort, commercial, and tax certiorari cases in the Supreme Court in New York City and in Albany, Erie, Essex, Monroe, Nassau, Niagara, Onondaga, Suffolk, Sullivan and Westchester Counties; (2) any kind of case in Broome County Supreme Court designated by the Administrative Judge thereof; (3) proceedings in Erie County Surrogate's Court; and (4) claims against the State of New York in the Court of Claims.

Electronic filing offers significant benefits for attorneys and litigants, permitting papers to be filed with the County Clerk and the court and served in a simple, convenient and expeditious manner. NYSEF case documents are filed with the County Clerk and the court by filing on the NYSEF Website (at www.nycourts.gov/efile), which can be done at any time of the day or night on any day of the week. Documents are deemed filed when received by the NYSEF server (with payment if required). The use of NYSEF is governed by Section 202.5-b (Supreme Court), and 206.5 and 206.5-aa (Court of Claims) of the Uniform Rules for the Trial Courts.

Instructions

1.   Service of this Notice constitutes a statement of intent by the undersigned that the NYSEF system be used in this case. When an action or proceeding is being commenced by means of the system, this Notice must accompany service of the initiating papers.

2.   **Within ten days after service of this Notice, the party served shall file with the court and serve on all parties the attached Consent to NYSEF, or a writing declining to consent.** When this Notice is served with papers initiating a lawsuit, the Consent form must be filed and served within the stated deadline and prior to service of, or with, the responsive pleadings or motion addressed to the pleadings. If the party served is represented by an attorney who has already registered as a NYSEF Filing User, that attorney may consent electronically on the NYSEF site.

3.   Once parties agree that the case will be subject to NYSEF, each attorney, unless already registered, must **PROMPTLY** submit a Filing User Registration form (see the "Forms" section of the Website) to obtain the confidential Filing User Identification Number and Password necessary to use the system.

4. For additional information about NYSEF, see the *User's Manual* and *Frequently Asked Questions* on the Website, or contact the court in question or the NYSEF Resource Center (at 646–386–3033 or NYFBEM@courts.state.ny.us).

Dated: _____   _____(Name)

_____(Firm)

_____(Address)

_____

_____(Phone)

_____(Fax)

_____(E–Mail)

Attorney(s) for _____

10/1/07

Form 9.   Affidavit of Service of Interlocutory Paper—E–Filed Case

SUPREME COURT OF THE STATE OF NEW YORK

COUNTY OF ERIE

---x

<table>
<tr><td>

Plaintiff/Petitioner(s),

vs.-

Defendant/Respondent(s).
</td><td>

**AFFIDAVIT OF SERVICE
OF INTERLOCUTORY
PAPER—E–FILED
CASE (NYSEF)**
</td></tr>
</table>

---x   **Index No.** _____

STATE OF NEW YORK   )

COUNTY OF ERIE   )

_____, being duly sworn, deposes and says:

1) I am an attorney admitted to the practice of law in the State of New York and am counsel to _____, a party to the above-captioned matter.

2) On _____, pursuant to Section 202.5–b (g) (2) of the Uniform Rules for the Trial Courts, I served an interlocutory paper in this electronically-filed action by sending electronically to all E–Mail Addresses of Record posted on the NYS electronic filing system the attached Notice of Filing of the paper. In compliance with said Section, the Notice of Filing identified the paper by its title, the sequence number on the list of documents filed, and by the date and time filed.

Sworn to before me this ___ day

of _____, 20 ___

_____
(Signature)

_____
        Notary Public   _____ (Name)

10/1/07

NIAGARA COUNTY

E-FILING

PROTOCOL

Doc. 1. Protocol on Procedures for Electronically Filed Cases

Attorneys seeking information about how the court's filing by electronic means system (E-filing) works are advised to consult the *User's Manual* and *FAQ's*, both available on-line at the E-filing website (see "E–Courts" at www.nycourts.gov). What follows is an outline of the steps that will be used in e-filed cases to satisfy traditional courthouse requirements for the processing of cases. The steps outlined here seek, to the maximum extent possible, to integrate e-filing capabilities with normal courthouse procedures in ways that will save attorneys time, trouble and trips to the courthouse while meeting the needs of Judges and the court.

Please note: The Niagara County Clerk's Office is located in Lockport, NY which is 22 miles away from the Supreme Court Courthouse in Niagara Falls. All forms for E-filing in Niagara County are available on the 8th Judicial District Website by accessing the following link, http://www.nycourts.gov/courts/8jd/Niagara/efile.shtml.

A. Identifying E–Filed Cases:

All authorized Torts, Commercial and Tax Certiorari cases may be commenced by e-filing, however, all parties need to consent for the action to continue as an e-filing case.

1) *Cases Commenced via E–Filing*: Cases that are commenced by filing of the initial papers with the E-filing system are identified as e-filed cases by assignment of an index number prefixed with the letter "E".

2) *Cases Converted to E–Filing*: Cases originally commenced in hard-copy form but later converted to E-filing status will bear the original index number, the E prefix will be added by the Niagara County Clerk. Court staff will add the prefix in the court's data base system. Attorneys must use the prefix on all papers filed with the court in electronically-filed matters.

B. Filing of Papers Generally

1) *Fees*: Court fees (e.g., RJI fee, motion fee) in E-filed cases may be paid for on-line using a credit card. Papers may also be filed with the E-filing System and the fee may be paid at the County Clerk's Office. The paper is not considered to have been filed until payment of the fee has been tendered (see CPLR 304). Payment of fees on-line can save an attorney from having to make a trip to the County Clerk's Office in many situations.

2) *Papers to Be Filed to the System*: All papers to be filed with the court in an E-filed case shall be filed on-line with the E-filing System (except where a special exemption is granted (e.g., oversized maps, photographs) or as directed by the court). Papers that attorneys would not ordinarily file with the county clerk in a hard-copy case need not be filed in an E-filed matter.

3) *Courtesy Hard Copies of Papers for Judicial Review*:

(a) Unless otherwise directed by the court or as described below, in all cases in the court's E-filing System in which an RJI has been filed, the court requires that courtesy hard copies of motion papers and other papers *intended for review by a Justice* be submitted. These papers shall also bear the following marking conspicuously placed on the front page: "Courtesy Copy. Original Papers Filed with E-filing System." Again, filings in E-filed cases should bear the index number with the "E" prefix.

(b) On any motion or order to show cause, if the court permits any party to submit additional papers, the attorney must be sure to file those papers on line with the E-filing System as well as submitting courtesy copies to the court.

4) *Filing With the System First; Deliver Courtesy Hard Copies Thereafter*: Generally speaking, unless otherwise directed or authorized by the court, counsel should file papers with the E-filing System first and thereafter deliver any required courtesy copy to the court. Filing with the system permits counsel to serve the papers electronically pursuant to Section 202.5–b (g) of the Uniform Rules for the Trial Courts once the consent to E-filing has been filed on-line. Proof of service should be filed on-line. Thereafter, the courtesy copy of the paper can be delivered to the court with appropriate proof of service attached. As to proposed orders to show cause, see Par. F.

C. Requests for Judicial Intervention

A Request for Judicial Intervention ("RJI") in an E-filed case shall be submitted via the E-filing System. When the RJI is filed and paid for on-line, the Niagara County Clerk's Office will forward the RJI and any accompanying documents to the relevant back office (Supreme Court) for random assignment of the case and processing of the document. Notification of judge assignment and date will be sent to all consenting parties via e-mail. Counsel need not appear.

D. Motions on Notice

1) *Service*: With regard to service of motion papers, CPLR 2214 (b) applies. Proof of service shall be filed on-line.

2) *Exhibits*: It is recommended that, whenever possible, attorneys submitting exhibits to the court in E-filed cases make each exhibit a separate attachment to an affidavit/affirmation in the system.

3) *Calendaring of Motion/Petition and Notice by Court Staff*: After a motion/petition and notice are filed with the E-filing System, the Niagara County Clerk will assign an index number and e-mail the back office support staff in Supreme Court for assignment to a part and scheduling a return date for the motion/petition. Consenting parties will be notified via e-mail.

4) *Cross–Motions and Other Motion Papers to be Filed On–Line*: Cross-motions and opposition and reply papers must be submitted on-line. A fee must be paid on cross-motions and may be paid on-line.

5) *Adjournments on Motions*: Motions cannot be adjourned generally. The first adjournment can be obtained by consent of all counsel, by contacting the IAS Judge's court clerk by telephone or letter at least 24 hours prior to the return date of the motion. All other adjournments must be by consent of the court.

6) *Scanning and Transmission of Decisions*: After the court issues a decision on a motion in an E-filed case, it will obtain an entry stamp from the County Clerk and promptly scan it into the E-filing System. The system will transmit notice of this event via e-mail.

E. Long Form Orders on Motions

If the court directs that an order be settled on a motion in a E-filed case, the proposed order and any proposed counter-order shall be filed with the court on-line with proof of service. The back office support staff in Supreme Court will then print out and/or transmit the proposed order and any proposed counter-order to the Judges chambers, which will process the papers in the customary manner. The E-filing Rules provide that any paper that requires a judicial signature must be submitted in hard-copy form; this requirement will be satisfied by the printing of hard copies by the back office for the judge. No appearance by counsel is required. After an order/counter-order has been signed, the Supreme Court Clerk will scan it, with County Clerk entry stamp, into the E-filing System, which will immediately transmit notice of this event via e-mail, including a link to the entered document, to all parties who have consented on-line in the case.

F. Orders to Show Cause

1) *Proposed OSC's and Supporting Papers to be Filed On–Line; Alternative Submission by E–Mail*: Proposed orders to show cause and supporting papers in an E-filed case must be filed with the system by the applicant. Generally, it is expected that the proposed

order and supporting papers will be filed on-line prior to review by the law clerk. There may, however, be instances in which a party, because of exigent or other circumstances, does not wish to provide advance notice to the adversary of a proposed order by filing it and supporting papers with the E-filing System (which generates an e-mail message to all parties). In those cases, the proposed order to show cause and supporting papers may be submitted to the law clerk personally or by regular e-mail (i.e., outside the E-filing System). In such instances, the applicant must file the proposed order and supporting papers with the E-filing System after signature.

2) *Review of Proposed OSC's Will be Done On–Line*: Absent unusual practical difficulties, a proposed order to show cause and supporting papers will be reviewed for form on-line in the E-filing System or as an e-mail attachment outside the E-filing System by the IAS Judge's law clerk. If there are difficulties with the form of the papers, the submitting attorney will be promptly contacted by the court.

3) *Courtesy Hard Copies: Delivery by Counsel; Receipt and Review of Papers On–Line by Some Justices*: Since a proposed order to show cause requires a judicial signature and a courtesy hard copy is required of all papers intended for judicial review, a proposed order to show cause and, unless otherwise directed, the supporting papers must also be submitted to the Judge in hard copy. Thus, after the proposed order to show cause has been transmitted to the court, approved for form, and the motion fee paid, the court will print out a hard copy of the proposed order to show cause, but, in addition, courtesy hard copies of the supporting papers must be delivered by the applicant to the Court.

4) *Posting the Signed Order to Show Cause to the E–Filing Site*: In all instances, the Court Clerk will promptly post the order to the site. In the event that any supporting papers were not previously posted, counsel will be directed to make such posting.

G. Procedures Regarding Service On–Line

1) *Service; Notice of Filing; Procedure*: An interlocutory paper is served as follows. The party files it with the E-filing site. Then, on the same day, the filer must, according to the E-filing Rules (Section 202.5–b (g) (2)), send to all e-mail addresses of record a Notice of Filing, which shall set forth the title of the paper filed, the number of the paper as shown on the E-filing System docket (List of Papers Filed), and the date and time filed. The Rules provide (id.) that the electronic transmission of the Notice of Filing shall constitute service on the addressee(s).

2) *Proof of Service to be Posted On–Line*: In contrast with the Federal system, the E–Filing System Rules (Section 202.5–B (g) (2)), require that, in addition to making the electronic transmission of the Notice of Filing, the filing attorney must file proof of service on-line. That is, the fact that the filing attor-

ney served the Notice of Filing by means of the E-filing System does not suffice. Thus, the serving party must file with the E-filing System an Affidavit or Affirmation of Service which recites the electronic transmission of the Notice of Filing and to which is appended a copy of the Notice of Filing. This proof of service need not itself be served on the parties.

3) *Other Methods of Service*: The Rules authorize service by other methods permitted by the CPLR. If an attorney serves another party or parties with a paper filed with the E-filing System by mail or in person, the attorney may file an affidavit/affirmation of service on-line.

H. Sealing of Documents

1) *Sealing—Compliance with Part 216*: As with hard copy files, in order to seal a paper in an E-filed case, a party must proceed in accordance with Part 216 of the Uniform Rules for the Trial Courts.

2) *Secure Documents*: Documents may, however, be designated "secure" by the filing user without an order of the court. The effect of such designation is that the document may be viewed outside of Court in the E-filing System only by the consenting parties of record and by the court. The electronic file, however, remains open for public inspection via computer at the Niagara County Clerk's Office (unless sealed in accordance with Part 216).

3) *Sealing; Procedures*: To obtain a sealing order, a motion/stipulation can be filed with the E-filing System, but it will be open to the public unless it is filed as a "secure" document. Or, the motion/stipulation may also be filed with the system but without the attachment of any exhibits that would disclose confidential information. If the file is sealed in whole or in part, the exhibits can be filed with the E-filing System after the fact. Or the parties may make a motion or submit a stipulation without filing it to the system until after the court rules on the sealing issue if such filing would disclose confidential information.

4) *Execution of Sealing Order*: If the court issues an order directing the sealing of an electronic file in whole or in part, the party seeking the sealing should file with the E-filing System a Certificate Requesting Sealing of Document in Electronically–Filed Case, together with a copy of the court's order. If such a request is properly made, the County Clerk will seal the file or the document(s) in question as directed by the court, both in the E-filing System and, if any of the covered documents are found therein, in the hard copy file.

5) *Previously Sealed File*: If a case that was previously sealed pursuant to court order is converted to E-filing status, counsel for the parties should promptly alert the Supreme Court Clerk's Office that an order sealing the file was issued. Counsel are advised to contact Supreme Court by telephone and must submit a copy of the sealing order by posting it to the

E-filing System. Upon such submission, Supreme Court will contact the County Clerk and the e-file will be sealed.

I. Preliminary Conferences in Electronically Filed Cases

In lieu of making an appearance at a scheduled preliminary conference and with consent of the Court, all parties in an E-filing case may agree upon a discovery schedule and submit an appropriate preliminary conference form, stipulated to by all parties, including medical malpractice actions. The discovery schedule therein set forth must be in compliance with the disclosure guidelines for a case of the type in question as set forth in Uniform Rule 202.19. The stipulated form must be filed on-line with the E-filing System at least two days prior to the conference date. Counsel should contact the Court by phone (at the number listed below) to inform it of the filing so that the clerk's office can take expeditious action. The Court will promptly forward the form to the Part in question. No further action by counsel is required. The signed form will be posted on the E-filing site and counsel will be notified by e-mail. If the court perceives a problem with the contents of the form submitted, counsel will be contacted. See Uniform Rule 202.12 (b).

J. Entry and Notice of Entry

1) *Entry*: Pursuant to the E–Filing Rules (Section 202.5–b (j)), the Clerk shall file orders electronically and such filing shall constitute entry of the order. The Clerk is required to and will transmit an e-mail message to all filing users on the case notifying that the order has been entered. Such notice does not constitute service of notice of entry by any party.

2) *Notice of Entry*: Notice of entry is served by a party as follows: the party simply transmits electronically to the parties to be served the notification received from the court, along with an express statement that the transmittal constitutes notice of entry.

K. Judgments and the Judgment Roll

1) *Entry of Judgment; Procedures*: If the court in an order directs entry of judgment by the County Clerk, the party seeking entry shall submit a proposed judgment with a bill of costs, interest calculations and supporting information to the County Clerk, together with a Certificate Requesting Entry of Judgment. If the judgment is in proper form, it will be printed out by the Judgment Clerk and submitted to the County Clerk for signature. The Judgment Clerk will scan the judgment once signed and post it to the system, along with the supporting information, at which time notification will be sent via e-mail to all consenting users.

2) *Default Judgment; Entry by Clerk*: The fee for filing a default judgment is $45.00. If the plaintiff in an E-filed case seeks entry of a default judgment by the Clerk pursuant to CPLR 3215, the attorney should

transmit to the E-filing System a Clerk's Default Judgment with bill of costs, etc. and the Certificate Requesting Entry of Judgment. The Judgment Clerk will promptly enter the judgment or will communicate with the filer by phone or e-mail if a problem is detected. To enter the judgment the Clerk will print out the judgment from the E-filing System, have it signed, and scan it to the system.

3) *Judgments Signed by Court*: In some instances, the court itself may sign the judgment. See above L (1).

4) *Judgment Roll*: Counsel shall submit the Certificate Requesting Entry of Judgment and shall identify therein, by title of the paper, number of the paper on the E-filing System List of Papers Filed, and date filed, all e-filed documents that should form part of the judgment roll. Any documents that were filed in hard-copy form only, that are to be included in the judgment roll, should be scanned into the system by counsel and included in the Certificate. The County Clerk will post the Certificate on-line, once approved, and this will constitute the judgment roll.

5) *Entry of Judgment*: Once the County Clerk has taxed costs and disbursements and calculated interest and has in hand a signed judgment, the Clerk will stamp the judgment with the County Clerk file stamp and scan the judgment to the system. This constitutes entry. The Clerk is required to and will transmit an e-mail message to all filing users on the case notifying that the judgment has been entered. This notice does not constitute service of notice of entry by any party. As to notice of entry, see Par. L (2) above.

L. Notices of Appeal and Appeal Papers

1) *Notice of Appeal; Payment of Fee*: A notice of appeal shall be filed on-line in an E-filed case. The fee therefore must be paid by credit card on-line or by means of the "Pay at the County Clerk's Office" option. In the latter situation, the notice will not be considered "filed" until payment of the fee is tendered to the County Clerk at the office.

2) *Notice of Appeal: Procedures*: The notice shall be filed together with a pre-calendar statement and a copy of the judgment or order appealed from. The other parties to the case may be served on-line in the manner described above. Proof of service must also be filed on-line. The County Clerk will print a hard copy of any e-filed notice of appeal and include it in the County Clerk file.

3) *E–Filing System: Appellate Division*: At present, the Appellate Division, First Department does not handle appeals in E-filed cases by electronic means. Counsel are advised to consult the rules of that court and to confer with the County Clerk.

HON. SHARON S. TOWNSEND
ADMINISTRATIVE JUDGE

ANY ATTORNEY WHO REQUIRES ASSISTANCE IN AN ELECTRONICALLY FILED CASE IS ENCOURAGED TO CONTACT NIAGARA COUNTY SUPREME COURT AT THE NUMBER LISTED BELOW:

SUPREME COURT
ANGELO A. DELSIGNORE CIVIC BUILDING
775 THIRD STREET
NIAGARA FALLS, NY 14302
(716)278–1800

FORMS

Form 1. Certificate Requesting Entry of Judgment in Electronically–Filed Case

SUPREME COURT OF THE STATE OF NEW YORK
COUNTY OF NIAGARA
---x

Plaintiff/Petitioner,

-against-   Index No. _____

Defendant/Respondent.
---x

CERTIFICATE REQUESTING ENTRY OF JUDGMENT
IN ELECTRONICALLY–FILED CASE

To: The County Clerk, County of Niagara

_____, an attorney admitted to the Bar of the State of New York and counsel for _____ in the above-captioned electronically-filed case, does hereby request that judgment be entered in this case based upon the _____, dated _____ and entered on _____. Pursuant to CPLR 5017 (a), I do hereby certify that the following documents shall constitute the Judgment Roll for this Judgment. Each document is identified by title of the paper, the date filed with the electronic filing system ("FBEM"), and the number of the paper as listed on the FBEM List of Papers Filed.

Title of Document	Number of Paper On FBEM List of Papers	Date Filed
1) _____	No. _____	_____
2) _____	No. _____	_____
3) _____	No. _____	_____
4) _____	No. _____	_____
5) _____	No. _____	_____
6) _____	No. _____	_____
7) _____	No. _____	_____
8) _____	No. _____	_____
9) _____	No. _____	_____
10) _____	No. _____	_____

The documents listed above are available on the FBEM website and may be downloaded and printed as needed.

Dated: _____

_____ (Signature)

_____ (Name)
_____ (Firm Name)
_____ (Address)
_____
_____

Attorney for _____

7/5/06

601

Form 2.   Consent to FBEM

SUPREME COURT OF THE STATE OF NEW YORK

COUNTY OF NIAGARA

---x

Plaintiff/Petitioner(s),

Index No. _____

—against—

<u>CONSENT TO FBEM</u>

Defendant/Respondent(s).

---x

   I, _____, am a party or an attorney for a party, identified below, in the above-captioned law suit, and I consent to the use of the Filing by Electronic Means System ("FBEM") in this case. I further consent to be bound by the service and filing provisions of the FBEM Rules (22 NYCRR § 202.5–b) and will comply with the *User's Manual* approved by the Chief Administrator of the Courts and posted on the FBEM website.

   I set forth in the following spaces up to three Internet e- mail addresses to be used for the purposes of service and giving notice of each filing:

* As provided in the FBEM Rules, consent of the parties is required for a matter to proceed as a FBEM case. This form must be filed with the court and served on all parties. If an attorney has previously registered as a FBEM Filing User, consent may be filed and served by means of the FBEM system.

_____

_____

_____

_____   _____
Signature   Address

_____   _____
Print or Type Name

_____   _____
Law Firm Name   Telephone Number

Attorney for _____

Form 3.   Request for Judicial Intervention

REQUEST FOR JUDICIAL INTERVENTION
UCS–840 (3/2011)

For Court Clerk Use Only:
IAS Entry Date

Supreme_____   COURT, COUNTY OF _____

Judge Assigned

Index No: _____   Date Index Issued: _____

CAPTION: Enter the complete case caption. Do not use et al or et
ano. If more space is required, attach a caption rider sheet.

RJI Date

Plaintiff(s)/Petitioner(s)

-against-

Defendant(s)/Respondent(s)

NATURE OF ACTION OR PROCEEDING: Check ONE box only and specify where indicated.

MATRIMONIAL

○ Contested

○ Uncontested
    NOTE: For all Matrimonial actions where the
    parties have children under the age of 18, complete
    and attach the **MATRIMONIAL RJI Addendum.**

TORTS

○ Asbestos
○ Breast Implant

○ Environmental: _____
    (specify)

○ Medical, Dental, or Podiatric Malpractice
○ Motor Vehicle
○ Products Liability: _____
    (specify)
○ Other Negligence: _____
    (specify)
○ Other Professional Malpractice: _____
    (specify)

○ Other Tort: _____
    (specify)

OTHER MATTERS

○ Certificate of Incorporation/Dissolution [see **NOTE**
    under Commercial]
○ Emergency Medical Treatment
○ Habeas Corpus
○ Local Court Appeal
○ Mechanic's Lien
○ Name Change
○ Pistol Permit Revocation Hearing
○ Sale or Finance of Religious/ Not–for–Profit
    Property
○ Other: _____
    (specify)

COMMERCIAL

○ Business Entity (including corporations, partnerships, LLCs,
    etc.)
○ Contract
○ Insurance (where insurer is a party, except arbitration)
○ UCC (including sales, negotiable instruments)
○ Other Commercial: _____
    (specify)

NOTE: For Commercial Division assignment requests, complete and attach the **COMMERCIAL DIV RJI Addendum.**

REAL PROPERTY: How many properties does the application include? _____

○ Condemnation
○ Foreclosure
Property Address: _____
                    Street Address   City   State   Zip
    NOTE: For Foreclosure actions involving a one- to
    four-family, owner-occupied, residential property, or an
    owner-occupied condominium, complete and attach the
    FORECLOSURE RJI Addendum.
○ Tax Certiorari—Section: _____ Block: _____ Lot: __
○ Other Real Property: _____
                            (specify)

SPECIAL PROCEEDINGS

○ CPLR Article 75 (Arbitration) [see **NOTE** under
    Commercial]
○ CPLR Article 78 (Body or Officer)
○ Election Law
○ MHL Article 9.60 (Kendra's Law)
○ MHL Article 10 (Sex Offender Confinement–Initial)
○ MHL Article 10 (Sex Offender Confinement–Review)
○ MHL Article 81 (Guardianship)
○ Other Mental Hygiene: _____
                            (specify)

○ Other Special Proceeding: _____
                                (specify)

STATUS OF ACTION OR PROCEEDING: Answer YES or NO for EVERY question AND enter additional
information where indicated.

	YES	NO	
Has a summons and complaint or summons w/notice been filed?	○	○	If yes, date filed: _____
Is this action/proceeding being filed post–judgment?	○	○	If yes, judgment date: _____

NATURE OF JUDICIAL INTERVENTION: Check ONE box only AND enter additional information where
indicated.

○ Infant's Compromise
○ Note of Issue and/or Certificate of Readiness
○ Notice of Medical, Dental, or Podiatric Malpractice   Date Issue Joined: _____
○ Notice of Motion   Relief Sought: _____ Return Date: _____

EIGHTH JUDICIAL DISTRICT

- ○ Notice of Petition   Relief Sought: _____   Return Date: _____
- ○ Order to Show Cause   Relief Sought: _____   Return Date: _____
- ○ Other Ex Parte Application   Relief Sought: _____
- ○ Poor Person Application
- ○ Request for Preliminary Conference
- ○ Residential Mortgage Foreclosure Settlement Conference
- ○ Writ of Habeas Corpus
- ○ Other (specify): _____

RELATED CASES: List any related actions. For Matrimonial actions, include any related criminal and/or Family Court cases. If additional space is required, complete and attach the **RJI Addendum**. If none, leave blank.

Case Title	Index/Case No.	Court	Judge (if assigned)	Relationship to Instant Case

PARTIES: If additional space is required, complete and attach the **RJI Addendum**.
For parties without an attorney, check "Un–Rep" box AND enter party address, phone number and e-mail address in "Attorneys" space.

Un–Rep	Parties:	Attorneys:		Issue Joined (Y/N):	Insurance Carrier(s):
	List parties in caption order and indicate party role(s) (e.g. defendant; 3rd–party plaintiff).	Provide name, firm name, business address, phone number and e-mail address of all attorneys that have appeared in the case.			
	Last Name	**Last Name**	**First Name**	○ YES	
☐	**First Name** Primary Role:	**Firm Name**			
	Secondary Role (if any):	Street Address	City State Zip	○ NO	
		Phone Fax	e-mail		
	Last Name	**Last Name**	**First Name**	○ YES	
☐	**First Name** Primary Role:	**Firm Name**			
	Secondary Role (if any):	Street Address	City State Zip	○ NO	
		Phone Fax	e-mail		
	Last Name	**Last Name**	**First Name**	○ YES	
☐	**First Name** Primary Role:	**Firm Name**			
	Secondary Role (if any):	Street Address	City State Zip	○ NO	
		Phone Fax	e-mail		
	Last Name	**Last Name**	**First Name**	○ YES	
☐	**First Name** Primary Role:	**Firm Name**			
	Secondary Role (if any):	Street Address	City State Zip	○ NO	
		Phone Fax	e-mail		

I AFFIRM UNDER THE PENALTY OF PERJURY THAT, TO MY KNOWLEDGE, OTHER THAN AS NOTED ABOVE, THERE ARE AND HAVE BEEN NO RELATED ACTIONS OR PROCEEDINGS, NOR HAS A REQUEST FOR JUDICIAL INTERVENTION PREVIOUSLY BEEN FILED IN THIS ACTION OR PROCEEDING.

Dated: _____   _____
                          SIGNATURE

_____   _____
ATTORNEY REGISTRATION NUMBER   PRINT OR TYPE NAME

Request for Judicial Intervention Addendum   UCS–840A (3/ 2011)

<u>Supreme</u> _____ COURT, COUNTY OF _____ Index No: _____

For use when additional space is needed to provide party or related case information.

PARTIES: For parties without an attorney, check " Un–Rep" box AND enter party address, phone number and e-mail address in " Attorneys" space.

Un–Rep	Parties:	Attorneys:					Issue Joined (Y/N):	Insurance Carrier(s):
	List parties in caption order and indicate party role(s) (e.g. defendant; 3rd–party plaintiff).	Provide name, firm name, business address, phone number and e-mail address of all attorneys that have appeared in the case.						
	Last Name	Last Name		First Name			○ YES	
☐	First Name Primary Role:	Firm Name						
	Secondary Role (if any):	Street Address	City	State	Zip		○ NO	
		Phone	Fax	e-mail				
	Last Name	Last Name		First Name			○ YES	
☐	First Name Primary Role:	Firm Name						
	Secondary Role (if any):	Street Address	City	State	Zip		○ NO	
		Phone	Fax	e-mail				
	Last Name	Last Name		First Name			○ YES	
☐	First Name Primary Role:	Firm Name						
	Secondary Role (if any):	Street Address	City	State	Zip		○ NO	
		Phone	Fax	e-mail				
	Last Name	Last Name		First Name			○ YES	
☐	First Name Primary Role:	Firm Name						
	Secondary Role (if any):	Street Address	City	State	Zip		○ NO	
		Phone	Fax	e-mail				
	Last Name	Last Name		First Name			○ YES	
☐	First Name Primary Role:	Firm Name						
	Secondary Role (if any):	Street Address	City	State	Zip		○ NO	
		Phone	Fax	e-mail				
	Last Name	Last Name		First Name			○ YES	
☐	First Name Primary Role:	Firm Name						
	Secondary Role (if any):	Street Address	City	State	Zip		○ NO	
		Phone	Fax	e-mail				

RELATED CASES: List any related actions. For Matrimonial actions, include any related criminal and/or Family Court cases.

Case Title	Index/Case No.	Court	Judge (if assigned)	Relationship to Instant Case

SUPREME COURT OF THE STATE OF NEW YORK

COUNTY OF _____

---x

           Plaintiff(s)/Petitioner(s)

-against-

           Defendant(s)/Respondent(s)

---x

UCS–840C
3/2011

Index No. _____

RJI No. (if any) _____

COMMERCIAL DIVISION
Request for Judicial Intervention Addendum

COMPLETE WHERE APPLICABLE [add additional pages if needed]:
Plaintiff/Petitioner's cause(s) of action [check all that apply]:

☐ Breach of contract or fiduciary duty, fraud, misrepresentation, business tort (e.g. unfair competition), or statutory and/or common law violation where the breach or violation is alleged to arise out of business dealings (e.g. sales of assets or securities; corporate restructuring; partnership, shareholder, joint venture, and other business agreements; trade secrets; restrictive covenants; and employment agreements not including claims that principally involve alleged discriminatory practices)

☐ Transactions governed by the Uniform Commercial Code (exclusive of those concerning individual cooperative or condominium units)

☐ Transactions involving commercial real property, including Yellowstone injunctions and excluding actions for the payment of rent only

☐ Shareholder derivative actions — without consideration of the monetary threshold

☐ Commercial class actions — without consideration of the monetary threshold

☐ Business transactions involving or arising out of dealings with commercial banks and other financial institutions

☐ Internal affairs of business organizations

☐ Malpractice by accountants or actuaries, and legal malpractice arising out of representation in commercial matters

☐ Environmental insurance coverage

☐ Commercial insurance coverage (e.g. directors and officers, errors and omissions, and business interruption coverage)

☐ Dissolution of corporations, partnerships, limited liability companies, limited liability partnerships and joint ventures — without consideration of the monetary threshold

☐ Applications to stay or compel arbitration and affirm or disaffirm arbitration awards and related injunctive relief pursuant to CPLR Article 75 involving any of the foregoing enumerated commercial issues — without consideration of the monetary threshold

Plaintiff/Petitioner's claim for compensatory damages [exclusive of punitive damages, interest, costs and counsel fees claimed]:

    $ _____

Plaintiff/Petitioner's claim for equitable or declaratory relief [brief description]:

_____

_____

Defendant/Respondent's counterclaim(s)
[brief description, including claim for monetary relief]:

_____

I REQUEST THAT THIS CASE BE ASSIGNED TO THE COMMERCIAL DIVISION. I CERTIFY THAT THE CASE MEETS THE JURISDICTIONAL REQUIREMENTS OF THE COMMERCIAL DIVISION SET FORTH IN 22 NYCRR § 202.70(a), (b) AND (c).

Dated: _____

_____
                SIGNATURE

_____
                PRINT OR TYPE NAME

UCS–840M
3/2011

MATRIMONIAL Request for Judicial Intervention Addendum

Supreme   COURT, COUNTY OF _____   INDEX NO. _____

For use when there are children under the age of 18 who are subject to the matrimonial action.
Plaintiff

    Last Name: _____   First Name: _____   Date of Birth: _____

    Prior Names (List any other names used, including **Gender:** ☐ Male ☐ Female
    maiden and/or former married names):
    Last Name: _____   First Name: _____
    Last Name: _____   First Name: _____

Last Name: _____ First Name: _____

Present Address: _____ New York _____
                (Street Address)   (City)   (State)   (Zip)

**Address History
for past 3 years:** _____
                (Street Address)   (City)   (State)   (Zip)

                (Street Address)   (City)   (State)   (Zip)

                (Street Address)   (City)   (State)   (Zip)

Defendant

    Last Name: _____ **First Name:** _____ **Date of Birth:** _____

    Prior Names (List any other names used, including   **Gender:** ☐ Male ☐ Female
maiden and/or former married names):
    Last Name: _____ First Name: _____
    Last Name: _____ First Name: _____
    Last Name: _____ First Name: _____

    Present Address: _____ New York _____
                 (Street Address)   (City)   (State)   (Zip)

    **Address History
for past 3 years:** _____
                 (Street Address)   (City)   (State)   (Zip)

                 (Street Address)   (City)   (State)   (Zip)

                 (Street Address)   (City)   (State)   (Zip)

Children

    Last Name: _____ **First Name:** _____ **Date of Birth:** _____ **Gender:** ☐ M ☐ F

    Last Name: _____ **First Name:** _____ **Date of Birth:** _____ **Gender:** ☐ M ☐ F

    Last Name: _____ **First Name:** _____ **Date of Birth:** _____ **Gender:** ☐ M ☐ F

    Last Name: _____ **First Name:** _____ **Date of Birth:** _____ **Gender:** ☐ M ☐ F

    Last Name: _____ **First Name:** _____ **Date of Birth:** _____ **Gender:** ☐ M ☐ F

Form 4. Special Term Motion Note of Issue

SPECIAL TERM MOTION NOTE OF ISSUE

Dated: _____

SUPREME COURT: NIAGARA COUNTY

Index No.: _____

Honorable _____

_____
Attorneys for Plaintiffs

vs.

_____
Attorneys for Defendants

Phone: _____

Motion made by: _____   Returnable: _____

Relief Sought: _____
_____
_____
_____
_____
_____

Special Term Motion Clerk's Use Only

Note of Issue Received:

Adjourned to: _____, 20 ___ at _____ ___.m.

_____, 20 ___ at _____ ___.m.

_____, 20 ___ at _____ ___.m.

Papers obtained from counsel and submitted to court at time of argument:

In Support of Motion: **Against Motion:**

_____   _____
_____   _____
_____   _____

Notes made at Justice's direction:

For Justice's Use Only: Decision:

Form 5.   Notice of Filing in E–Filing Case

SUPREME COURT OF THE STATE OF NEW YORK
COUNTY OF NIAGARA

-- x

Plaintiff/Petitioner(s),   Index No. _____

- against -

Defendant/Respondent(s).

-- x

NOTICE OF FILING IN ELECTRONICALLY–FILED CASE

To: All E–Mail Addresses of Record in the Above–Captioned Case

PLEASE TAKE NOTICE that, pursuant to Section 202.5–b(g) of the Uniform Rules for the Trial Courts, the undersigned hereby notifies all E–Mail Addresses of Record that the undersigned filed in the electronic List of Papers Filed in this case, on the date listed below, the following documents:

Title of Paper Filed	Number of Paper On FBEM List of Papers	Date Filed
1) No. _____	No. _____	_____
2) No. _____	No. _____	_____
3) No. _____	No. _____	_____
4) No. _____	No. _____	_____

Parties hereby notified may access the filing on the FBEM website at the following address: https://iapps.courts.state.ny.us/fbem/mainframe.html.

Dated: _____   _____ (Filer)
                         _____ (Firm Name)
                         _____ (Address)
                         _____
                         _____

7/5/06

Form 6. Request for Preliminary Conference

Index No.

Request for Preliminary Conference

Plaintiff(s)	Attorney(s) for
vs.	Post Office Address & Tel. No.

Defendant(s)

Service of a copy of the within

is hereby admitted

Dated.

. . . .

Attorney(s) for

STATE OF NEW YORK, COUNTY OF   ss.:

I,   being sworn, say; I am not a party to the action, am over 18 years
of age and reside at
On   I served the within

**Service
☐ By Mail**   by depositing a true copy thereof enclosed in a post-paid wrapper, in an official
depository under the exclusive care and custody of the U.S. Postal Service within
New York State, addressed to the following person at the last known address set
forth after the name:

**Personal
☐ Service on
Individual**   by delivering a true copy thereof personally to the person named below at the
address indicated. I know the person served to be the person mentioned and
described in said papers as a party therein:

**Leaving
☐ at
residence**   by leaving a true copy thereof at the residence within this State of the person named
below at the address indicated with a person of suitable age and discretion.

Sworn to before me on   _____

The name signed must be printed beneath

Form 7. Certificate Requesting Sealing of Document
in Electronically–Filed Case

SUPREME COURT OF THE STATE OF NEW YORK
COUNTY OF NIAGARA
---x

Plaintiff/Petitioner,

-against-   Index No. _____

Defendant/Respondent.
---x

CERTIFICATE REQUESTING SEALING OF DOCUMENT
IN ELECTRONICALLY–FILED CASE

To: County Clerk, County of Niagara

_____, an attorney admitted to the Bar of the State of New York and counsel for _____ in the above-captioned electronically-filed case, does hereby request that the document(s) identified below be sealed pursuant to the order of the court, a copy of which is annexed hereto.   Except in instances in which the order requires sealing of the entire file, each document to be sealed is identified by title of the paper, the date filed with the electronic filing system ("FBEM"), and the number of the paper as listed on the FBEM List of Papers Filed.

Sealing of Entire File Requested _____ [Initial here] Or

Sealing of the Document(s) Identified Below Requested:

Title of Document	Number of Paper On FBEM List of Papers	Date Filed
1) _____	No. _____	_____
2) _____	No. _____	_____
3) _____	No. _____	_____
4) _____	No. _____	_____
5) _____	No. _____	_____

Dated: _____   _____ (Signature)

_____ (Name)
_____ (Firm Name)
_____ (Address)
_____
_____

Attorney for _____

7/5/06

611

Form 8.   Notice Regarding Availability of E–Filing

SUPREME COURT OF THE STATE OF NEW YORK

COUNTY OF NIAGARA

---x

| | |
| Plaintiff(s)/Petitioner(s), | Index No. _____ |

—against—

**NOTICE REGARDING AVAILABILITY
OF ELECTRONIC FILING**

Defendant(s)/Respondent(s).

---x

PLEASE TAKE NOTICE that plaintiff(s)/petitioner(s) [defendant(s)/respondent(s)] in the case captioned above intends that this matter proceed as an electronically-filed case in the Filing by Electronic Means System ("FBEM") in accordance with the procedures therefor, described below. Service of papers by electronic means cannot be made upon a party unless that party consents to use of the system. Promptly after service of this Notice, each party served must indicate whether it consents.

General Information

In New York State, actions may be commenced and cases processed by means of the FBEM system in (1) tort, commercial, and tax certiorari cases in the Supreme Court in New York City and in Albany, Erie, Essex, Monroe, Nassau, Niagara, Onondaga, Suffolk, Sullivan and Westchester Counties; (2) any kind of case in Broome County Supreme Court designated by the Administrative Judge thereof; (3) proceedings in Erie County Surrogate's Court; and (4) claims against the State of New York in the Court of Claims.

Electronic filing offers significant benefits for attorneys and litigants, permitting papers to be filed with the County Clerk and the court and served in a simple, convenient and expeditious manner. FBEM case documents are filed with the County Clerk and the court by filing on the FBEM Website (go to "E–Courts" at www.nycourts.gov), which can be done at any time of the day or night on any day of the week. Documents are deemed filed when received by the FBEM server (with payment if required). The use of FBEM is governed by Section 202.5–b (Supreme Court), and 206.5 and 206.5–aa (Court of Claims) of the Uniform Rules for the Trial Courts.

Instructions

1. Service of this Notice constitutes a statement of intent by the undersigned that the FBEM system be used in this case. When an action or proceeding is being commenced by means of the system, this Notice must accompany service of the initiating papers.

2. **PROMPTLY after service of this Notice, the party served shall file with the court and serve on all parties the attached Consent to FBEM, or a writing declining to consent.** When this Notice is served with papers initiating a lawsuit, the Consent form must be filed and served prior to service of, or with, the responsive pleadings or motion addressed to the pleadings. If the party served is represented by an attorney who has already registered as a FBEM Filing User, that attorney may consent electronically on the FBEM site.

3. Once parties agree that the case will be subject to FBEM, each attorney, unless already registered, must **PROMPTLY** submit a Filing User Registration form (see the "Forms" section of the Website) to obtain the

confidential Filing User Identification Number and Password necessary to use the system.

4. For additional information about FBEM, see the *User's Manual* and *Frequently Asked Questions* on the Website, or contact the court in question or the FBEM Resource Center (at 646–386–3033 or NYFBEM@courts.state. ny.us).

Dated: _____   _____ (Name)

                                    _____ (Firm)

                                    _____ (Address)

                                    _____

                                    _____ (Phone)

                                    _____ (Fax)

                                    _____ (E–Mail)

                     Attorney(s) for _____

                                        7/5/06

Form 9.   Affidavit of Service of Interlocutory
Paper—E–Filed Case (FBEM)

SUPREME COURT OF THE STATE OF NEW YORK
COUNTY OF NIAGARA
--x

Plaintiff/Petitioner(s),

- against -   Index No. _____

Defendant/Respondent(s).   **AFFIDAVIT OF SERVICE OF
                                INTERLOCUTORY PAPER—
                                E–FILED CASE (FBEM)**
--x

STATE OF NEW YORK   )
                              cc:
COUNTY OF NIAGARA   )

_____, being duly sworn, deposes and says:

1) I am an attorney admitted to the practice of law in the State of New York and am counsel to _____, a party to the above-captioned matter.

2) On _____, pursuant to Section 202.5–b (g) (2) of the Uniform Rules for the Trial Courts, I served an interlocutory paper in this electronically-filed action by sending electronically to all E–Mail Addresses of Record posted on the electronic filing system the attached Notice of Filing of the paper. In compliance with said Section, the Notice of Filing identified the paper by title, number on the list of documents filed, and the date and time filed.

Sworn to before me this _____ day

of _____, 20 _____

_____ (Signature)

_____
          Notary Public   _____ (Name)

NINTH JUDICIAL DISTRICT — DUTCHESS, ORANGE, PUTNAM, ROCKLAND, WESTCHESTER COUNTIES

Westlaw Electronic Research

These rules may be searched electronically on Westlaw® in the NY–RULES database; updates to these rules may be found on Westlaw in NY–RULESUP-DATES. For search tips and a summary of database content, consult the Westlaw Scope Screens for each database.

DISTRICT RULES

TAX CERTIORARI/CONDEMNATION

JUSTICE JOHN LA CAVA

Doc.
1. Tax Certiorari and Condemnation.

GUARDIANSHIP PART — COUNTIES OF DUTCHESS, ORANGE, AND PUTNAM

1. Guardianship Part: Dutchess, Orange and Putnam Counties.

GUARDIANSHIP ACCOUNTING PART — COUNTY OF ROCKLAND

1. Guardianship Accounting Part: Rockland County.

FORECLOSURE PART

1. Foreclosure Part.

Form
1. Request for Judicial Intervention.
2. Mortgage Foreclosure Conference Information Sheet.
3. HAMP Checklist.
4. Affirmation.

DUTCHESS COUNTY

SUPREME COURT

JUDGES' PART RULES

JUSTICE JAMES V. BRANDS

Doc.
1. Part Rules.
2. Procedures for Trial Counsel.
3. Election Rules.

JUSTICE JAMES D. PAGONES

1. Hon. James D. Pagones.

JUSTICE VALENTINO T. SAMMARCO

1. Hon. Valentino T. Sammarco.

JUSTICE CHRISTINE A. SPROAT

1. Hon. Christine A. Sproat.

JUSTICE CHARLES D. WOOD

Rule
I. Staff.
II. Communications With the Court.
III. Conferences.
IV. Motions.
V. Trials.
VI. Disposition.
VII. Mental Hygiene Law Article 81 Proceedings.

ORANGE COUNTY

JUDGES' PART RULES

JUSTICE CATHERINE M. BARTLETT

Rule
I. Communications With the Court.
II. Court Conferences and Calendar Calls.
III. Discovery and Inspection.
IV. Motions and Orders to Show Cause.
V. Decisions and Orders.
VI. Trials and Hearings.
VII. Settled and Discontinued Cases.

JUSTICE LAWRENCE H. ECKER

I. Communications with the Court.
II. Calendar Call & Conferences.
III. Motion Practice.
IV. Decisions and Orders.
V. Matrimonial Actions.
VI. Settled and Discontinued Cases.
VII. Summary Jury Trial.

JUSTICE JOHN K. McGUIRK

I. General Rules.
II. Motions.
III. Conferences.
IV. Matrimonial Actions.
V. Trial.
VI. Submission of Orders and Judgments.

JUSTICE ROBERT A. ONOFRY, A.J.S.C.

I. General Rules.
II. Motion Practice.
III. Trials.

Rule

JUSTICE ELAINE SLOBOD

I. Motions.
II. Orders to Show Cause.
III. Conferences.
IV. Trials.
V. Orders/Judgment Submission.
VI. Infant Compromise Applications and Orders.
VII. Litigation Correspondence.

PUTNAM COUNTY

SUPREME COUNTY, FAMILY AND SURROGATE'S COURT

JUDGES' PART RULES

JUSTICE FRANCIS A. NICOLAI

Rule

I. Communications With the Court.
II. Court Conferences.
III. Motions and Orders to Show Cause.
IV. Decisions and Orders.
V. Trials and Hearings.
VI. Settled and Discontinued Cases.

JUSTICE LEWIS J. LUBELL

Doc.

1. General.
2. Adjournments.
3. Conferences.
4. Discovery Matters.
5. Motions.
6. Trials.
7. Matrimonial Matters.

JUSTICE JAMES T. ROONEY

1. Hon. James T. Rooney.

JUSTICE JAMES F. REITZ

1. Hon. James F. Reitz.

ROCKLAND COUNTY

SUPREME AND COUNTY COURT

JUDGES' PART RULES

JUSTICE VICTOR J. ALFIERI

PART I. E-FILING RULES OF THE COURT

Rule

I. E-Filing Rules and Protocol.
II. Electronic Filing.
III. Working Copies.
IV. Hard Copy Submissions.
V. Scheduling.

PART II. RULES OF THE COURT

I. General Rules.
II. Communication With the Court.
III. Court Appearances.
IV. Discovery and Inspection.
V. Motions.
VI. Trials.
VII. Summary Jury Trials (SJT).

JUSTICE CHARLES APOTHEKER

Doc.

1. Hon. Charles Apotheker.

JUSTICE MARGARET GARVEY

Rule

I. Communications With the Court.
II. Court Conferences.
III. Motions and Orders to Show Cause.
IV. Decisions and Orders.
V. Trials and Hearings.
VI. Settled and Discontinued Cases.

JUSTICE LINDA S. JAMIESON

Doc.

1. Part Rules.

Form

1. Designation and Discovery Stipulation and Order—Complex Case.
2. Designation and Discovery Stipulation and Order—Expedited Case.
3. Designation and Discovery Stipulation—Standard Case.

JUSTICE WILLIAM A. KELLY

Rule

1. General.
2. E–Filing.
3. Conference and Appearances.
4. Adjournments.
5. Discovery Matters.
6. Motions.
7. Motion Adjournments.
8. Trials.
9. Settlement or Discontinuance.

JUSTICE WILLIAM K. NELSON

Doc.

1. Hon. William K. Nelson.

JUSTICE THOMAS E. WALSH

Rule

I. Communications With The Court.
II. Court Conferences and Calendar Calls.
III. Discovery and Inspection.
IV. Motions and Orders to Show Cause.
V. Decisions and Orders.
VI. Trials and Hearings.
VII. Adjournments.
VIII. Settled and Discontinued Cases.
IX. Matrimonials.
X. Article 81 Proceedings.
XI. Rules Applicable Only to Surrogate's Court.
XIII. E–Filing.
XII. Rules Applicable Only to Surrogate's Court.

JUSTICE ALFRED J. WEINER

Doc.

1. Hon. Alfred J. Weiner.

WESTCHESTER COUNTY

SUPREME AND COUNTY COURTS

JUDGES' PART RULES

JUSTICE LESTER B. ADLER

Doc.

1. Hon. Lester B. Adler.

JUSTICE ORAZIO R. BELLANTONI

1. Hon. Orazio R. Bellantoni.

Form

3. Objection Form.
4. Law Guardian Assignment Instructions.
5. Financial Disclosure Affidavit (03/05).

Doc.

1. Joint Protocols for NYSCEF Cases Filed in Westchester County.

DISTRICT RULES
TAX CERTIORARI/CONDEMNATION
JUSTICE JOHN LA CAVA

Doc. 1. Tax Certiorari and Condemnation
APPEARANCES

All appearances are to be at the Richard A. Daronco Westchester County Courthouse, 111 Dr. Martin Luther King, Jr. Blvd., White Plains, New York. Trials are held in Courtroom 1603: calendar calls and conferences are held in Room 1619.

Tax Certiorari (Article 7) Matters Generally

Article 7 (Tax Cert) petitions are to be filed with the County Clerk of the County where the index number is purchased. There are to be no appearances before this Court on the return date of the petition.

Article 7 petitions do not appear on a calendar for appearance until and unless a Request for Judicial Intervention (RJI) and a Note of Issue (NOI) are filed.

Condemnation (Eminent Domain) Matters Generally

To place a Condemnation matter on the calendar only an RJI is required. Within 30 days of the filing of a claim in a condemnation matter the claimant is directed to send a copy of the notice of claim to this part. The court will then hold a scheduling conference with counsel to determine dates for discovery, including the date for the exchange of trial appraisals. Upon the completion of discovery and the filing of a note of issue a trial date will be set.

Calendar Calls

Upon the filing of an RJI and NOI in a Tax Certiorari matter, or an RJI in a Condemnation matter, said matter will be placed on a calendar call for an initial appearance.

Calendar calls for new matters filed in Westchester County are held the 1st Thursday of each month. Calendar call listings may be viewed on the court website.

Calendar calls for new matters filed in Dutchess, Orange, Putnam and Rockland Counties are held twice a year—usually on the 2nd Thursday in April and on the 2nd Thursday in October. Attorneys are notified of calendar calls in writing by the Calendar Clerk of the particular County.

Appearances at calendar calls are not required. But, as a courtesy, you should inform your adversary if you do not intend to appear. Matters appearing on calendar calls for the first time are adjourned 60 to 90 days for a preliminary conference (PLC). However, if a matter has other companion cases already on track it will be adjourned to the same date as the other matters.

Calendar calls are held in Conference Room 1619 (behind Courtroom 1603) and commence at 2:00 p.m.

Preliminary Conference (PLC)

All conferences from the calendar call forward are called preliminary conferences (PLCs). Calendars may be viewed on the court website.

PLCs are held in Conference Room 1619 at 2:00 p.m.

Do not call, write or fax the Court regarding an adjournment of a PLC. If you are unable to attend a PLC you may advise your adversary of the adjourned date you prefer and the Clerk will, to the extent possible, accommodate your request at the time the calendar is called. If neither side appears, the PLC will be adjourned for 30 to 45 days. The new PLC date may be obtained by calling the office of the Calendar Clerk of the particular County where the matter is filed (see list of telephone numbers below) or on the court website. Allow 7 to 10 days for adjourned dates to appear on the court website.

Trial Scheduling Conference (SC)

A party may request a trial scheduling conference (SC) at any point after the first PLC. That request must be in writing and on notice to all other parties who have appeared and must be accompanied by a copy of the RJI, NOI and petition for each tax year in question. A separate request should be submitted for each individual property. The Clerk will notify the requesting party of the date and time of the SC. The requesting party will in turn notify all other parties of the SC date in writing with a copy to the Court.

The SC will yield dates for the exchange of trial appraisals (ETA), pre-trial conference (PTC), submission of pre-trial memorandum (PTM) and for trial. These dates will be *so ordered* by the court and a copy of the scheduling order will be mailed to all parties who have appeared.

SCs and PTCs are held in Conference Room 1619 and commence at 2:30 p.m. or other designated time.

Trials

Trials are held in Courtroom 1603 and commence promptly at 10:30 a.m.

Photocopies of trial exhibits and other documents are to be made outside the courthouse. All exhibits must be pre-marked prior to the commencement of trial. A list of all exhibits to be offered by each party shall be provided to the Court at the commencement of the trial. Should the exhibit list be amended during the trial, a copy of the updated or amended list shall be provided to the Court.

All witnesses, including but not limited to assessors, appraisers, experts, and fact witnesses, who maintain and/or possess a file and/or documents relevant to their testimony and/or the subject matter of the trial, hearing, or other matter before the Court, shall bring their entire and complete file and/or any and all relevant documents with them to Court on the date of their testimony and on any dates on which their testimony continues. Any party whose witness fails to appear with his or her complete file and/or any and all relevant documents as detailed above, will bear any and all costs associated with the adjournment of the trial, hearing, or other proceeding as may be necessary to secure the witness' file and/or relevant documents.

Trial appraisals, pre and post trial memoranda are to be submitted as follows: An original and two (2) copies are to be delivered to this Part on or before the ETA or PTM date, as the case may be. Each pleading is to be labeled on its face so as to distinguish which is the original and the copy. Counsel are directed to mutually exchange trial appraisals, pre and post trial memoranda, and expert reports if any, without the assistance of the Court.

Adjournment of So Ordered Dates

All court ordered discovery and trial dates are to be strictly complied with and no adjournments will be granted, except with specific permission of the Court, for good cause shown. Failure to comply may result in the imposition of sanctions,including the striking of pleadings and/or preclusion of evidence. All adjournments must be requested from Chambers at (914) 824-5417.

MOTIONS

Submission of Papers

All pleadings, i.e., petitions, RJIs, NOIs, motions, stipulations, settlement orders and judgments must be submitted to the Calendar Clerk of the County where the index number is purchased and the action is filed. Said Calendar Clerk will process the papers and send them to this part for determination. However, correspondence regarding a matter already calendared in this part should be sent directly to the Chambers of the Hon. John R. La Cava at the Westchester County Courthouse.

Should you need to contact the Calendar Clerk's office of a particular County, the telephone numbers are as follows:

Westchester:	(914) 824-5300
Rockland:	(845) 638-5387
Orange:	(845) 291-3111
Putnam:	(845) 225-3641
Dutchess:	(845) 486-2260

Motion papers are to be submitted in the following form: an original and one (1) courtesy copy. Each set of papers should be labeled on its face as to distinguish which is the original and which is the copy.

Motions are to be on submission of papers only; no appearances required. Should the Court deem oral argument necessary, the parties will be notified of the date and time by the Clerk.

Orders to show cause will be conformed by fax.

Items are not to be faxed to the Court without prior approval.

Motion Return Dates

Motions are to be made returnable on the following days for each County of filing:

Monday:	Rockland
Tuesday:	Putnam
Wednesday:	Westchester
Thursday:	Orange
Friday:	Dutchess

Adjournment of Motion Return Dates

Requests for motion adjournment are to be directed to the Clerk at (914) 824-5354.

Adjournments on consent are generally granted. Confirmation must be by letter addressed to the Court with a copy to opposing counsel.

An adjournment without consent may be granted but it must be requested in person on the motion return date. Adequate advance notice should be given to the Court and opposing counsel.

Settlement Orders, Stipulations & Judgements

Settlement orders, stipulations and/or judgments must be accompanied by a copy of the RJI (and NOI, if any) for each index number listed.

A conformed copy of an order or judgment will be sent back to the submitting party only when it is accompanied by a stamped, self-addressed envelope.

A conformed copy of an order or judgment filed with the County Clerk of Westchester County will bear a "Filed & Entered" stamp noting the date of filing and entry of the original. For other counties you will have to contact the County Clerk of the particular County for that information.

Special note re. Tax Cert Settlement/Judgment Orders: The county attorneys for the counties of Westchester, Dutchess and Orange reserve the right to review tax cert judgment orders before they are signed by the Court. The Clerk of the part will send the judgment order to the Westchester County Attorney for review. As for Dutchess and Orange counties, counsel are directed to file the original and a copy of the judgment order with the Calendar Clerk and to send an additional copy to the following:

Dutchess County: Dutchess County Attorney's Office

22 Market Street

Pougkeepsie, NY 12601

Attn.: Gail Epstein, Esq.

Orange County: Orange County Attorney's Office

255 Main Street

Goshen, NY 10924

Attn.: Matthew Nothnagle, Esq.

General information and court decisions of the Ninth Judicial District Tax Certiorari/Condemnation Part may be accessed through www.nycourts.gov courts/9jdtaxcert.shtml.

GUARDIANSHIP PART — DUTCHESS, ORANGE, AND PUTNAM COUNTIES

Doc. 1. Guardianship Part: Dutchess, Orange and Putnam Counties

1. Mental Hygiene Law Article 81 Guardianships are commenced by filing of an Order to Show Cause and Petition with a copy of the RJI. (A format for the OSC may be obtained by e-mail from mharan@courts.state.ny.us.) The back of the Order to Show Cause shall contain the Petitioner's Attorney's telephone and FAX number. Hearing dates are set by the Court.

2. All filings and correspondence must contain the assigned Index Number and, if applicable, return date.

3. No motions shall be allowed without prior permission of the Court. The CPLR is the governing procedure for all motions.

4. All orders and judgments shall be served by the movant on all counsel. Guardian(s) and Court Examiner within 10 days of the date of the decision, order and judgment.

5. Proof of service must be filed with the Court on or before the return date of all motions and petitions.

6. All adjournments require specific permission of the Court.

7. Due to statutory dictates, it is the policy of the Part that only one (1) brief adjournment of a scheduled hearing date shall be allowed. The party who obtains the adjournment must submit a letter to the court confirming the adjournment, on notice to all counsel, by FAX.

8. Discovery shall not be permitted except under unusual circumstances and with the specific permission of the Court.

9. Upon completion of the hearing, all individuals appointed by the Court shall comply with Part 36 of the Rules of the Chief Judge and file, when appropriate, a Statement of Approval of Compensation (UCS form 875—with items 1 through 14 completed) along with their affidavit of services.

10. All proposed Orders, Judgments and Referee's Reports shall follow the court forms, which may be obtained from the Part Clerk (e-mail address: www.mharan@courts.state.ny.us), and be submitted within 7 days of the hearing by Notice of Settlement. Note: The Judgment must contain the proposed Guardian's name, address and phone number.

11. Petitioner's counsel shall assist the proposed Guardian in obtaining the Commission to act as Guardian from the County Clerk. The Commission must be obtained within 15 days of the signing of the Judgment.

12. Any request for attorney's fees must be accompanied by a detailed affirmation of services and must be approved by the Court prior to any payment being made.

13. No guardianship commissions or fees for any professional services may be paid without prior court order.

GUARDIANSHIP ACCOUNTING PART — ROCKLAND COUNTY

Doc. 1. Guardianship Accounting Part: Rockland County

1. For the County of Rockland, copies of all signed Orders to Show Cause, Petitions, Judgments and Orders shall be filed with the 9th Judicial District Guardianship Accounting Part by the attorney for the moving party. Upon Judgment, petitioner's attorney must supply this Part with the following information: IP's address, date of birth and social security number/Guardian's name, address and phone number.

2. All accountings are to be filed with the county clerk in the county where the original petition was heard with a copy to the assigned court examiner. Upon submission of the assigned Court Examiner's Report, the accountings are transferred to the 9th

Judicial District Guardianship Accounting Part for approval by the Presiding Justice. Note: No compensation will be approved absent compliance with rule #9 above.

3. The filing schedule for accountings by Guardian(s) is as follows:

a. *Initial Report*—within 90 days of the signing of the Judgment.

b. *Annual Accountings*—no later than May 15th for the preceding calendar year.

c. *Final Accounting*—within 45 days of the death of the IP. Note: No estate assets may be dispersed or turned over to the Surrogates Court without prior approval of this Court.

FORECLOSURE PART

Doc. 1. Foreclosure Part

Notices to the Bar:

Please be advised that no motions are to be filed with the Special Residential Foreclosure Request for Judicial Intervention (RJI). That RJI is for the purpose of requesting a foreclosure settlement conference. Any motions filed with that RJI will be either returned or denied as the matters are not ripe. No plaintiffs' motions will be accepted for cases that are currently pending in the Special Foreclosure Part.

Please be advised that any application involving a residential foreclosure must contain a separate statement from the moving party affixed to the front of the application that the action does or does not fit the criteria for inclusion in the residential foreclosure program and that if it was in the special foreclosure program, that the case was released from the part with full authority to proceed with motion practice.

Adjournments

Adjournment Requests–Requests for adjournments must be made in writing and on consent of all sides. The request must be faxed to the Court at (914) 995–4483 and received at least two (2) business days prior to the conference. The request must state that the adjournment is on consent, and must contain the new conference date that the parties have agreed to which can only be a Tuesday, Thursday or Friday at 9:30AM. Include the index number and the title of the case. Please be advised that the law (NYCRR 202. 12–a) requires that the court must schedule the conference within 60 (sixty) days of the filing of the RJI. Please note that you will not receive a response from the court. Check e-courts to confirm if the adjournment has been granted the next business day. Do not call the Court to confirm the adjournment.

Settlements

If a case has been settled, we cannot remove the conference from the calendar until the following has been submitted to the Foreclosure Conference Part: The Notice to Discontinue and Cancel the Notice of Pendency, and a letter stating the reason for the discontinuance i.e.: short sale, loan reinstated, loan modification, loan satisfied, MHA program. This should be completed within 150 days of settlement.

Conferences

All mortgage foreclosure settlement conferences are held in Courtroom 1802. Conferences are scheduled as the requests for Judicial Intervention are received. Pursuant to the Uniform Rules of the trial Court, the initial conference must be held within sixty (60) days of the filing of the RJI.

ForeclosureConferenceWestchester@courts.state. ny.us is for the purpose of requesting an initial Foreclosure Settlement Conference on a voluntary case only. Please be advised you will not receive an e-mail response from the court for your conference. You will receive a letter in the mail from the Court with the conference date. If this e-mail address is utilized for any other purpose, you will not receive a response from the Court.

Defendant's Counsel submitting a Request for Conference Form must first check with the Westchester County Clerk's Office to determine if an RJI has been filed. If not, you must file an RJI before a conference request can be submitted.

Motions

No motions can be made by the plaintiff while the matter is in the Foreclosure Settlement Part. Any motions made by defendant while a case is pending in the Foreclosure Settlement Part will automatically be removed to an IAS Part. If plaintiff wants to make a motion, an application may be made in the Foreclosure Settlement Part for permission. Discovery is also stayed during the pendency of the case in the Foreclosure Conference Part.

All cases released from the Special Foreclosure Part will be stayed for a period of forty-five (45) days from the date of the release.

Forms

Affirmation Foreclosure

Request for Judicial Intervention Settlement Conference in Residential Foreclosure Actions

This form is only to be used for requesting a conference in a case that is eligible for a conference pursuant to CPLR 3408. No motions are to be filed with this RJI.

Mortgage Foreclosure Conference Information Sheet

This form must be completed by the plaintiff's counsel, prior to the conference, for all first time appearances.

HAMP Checklist

This is a general list of documents required by the lenders for a HAMP modification. Most of these documents are also required for internal loan modifications.

Form 1. Request for Judicial Intervention

Settlement Conference in Residential Mortgage Foreclosure Actions

SUPREME COURT, STATE OF NEW YORK, _____ County

Index No. _____ Date Index No. Issued: _____

Date of Service of Summons and Complaint: _____

PLAINTIFF(S):

    -against-

DEFENDANT(S):

For Clerk Only:

IAS entry date

Judge Assigned

RJI Date

This form requests the scheduling of the settlement conference required by Rule 3408 of the Civil Practice Law and Rules in a mortgage foreclosure action involving all of the following:
- residential property
- one to four-family owner-occupied principal dwelling or condominium

Provide the following information:

Type of loan: ☐ subprime/high-cost/nontraditional ☐ prime/ traditional/conventional ☐ open end credit plan

Property Address: Property Type: ☐ one to four-family ☐ condominium

Defendant(s) [name, address, telephone number, e-mail address]:

Attorney for Plaintiff(s) [name, address, telephone number, e-mail address]:

Attorney for Defendant(s) (if known) [name, address, telephone number, e-mail address]:

90–day notice [RPAPL § 1304(1)] mailed on [date]:
Related cases [title, index no. court, judge (if assigned), relationship to instant case]:

    I AFFIRM UNDER PENALTY OF PERJURY THAT, TO MY KNOWLEDGE, ALL THE INFORMATION CONTAINED HEREIN IS ACCURATE AND TRUE AND THAT, OTHER THAN AS NOTED ABOVE, THERE ARE AND HAVE BEEN NO RELATED ACTIONS OR PROCEEDINGS, NOR HAS A REQUEST FOR JUDICIAL INTERVENTION PREVIOUSLY BEEN FILED IN THIS ACTION.

Dated:

SIGNATURE

PRINT OR TYPE NAME
Address and telephone number (if different from above):

Form 2. Mortgage Foreclosure Conference Information Sheet

Title of Action: _____ Mandatory _____ Voluntary _____

Initial Conference Date: _____ Parties Present: _____

Assigned Judge: _____ Property Location: _____

FMV of Property: _____ Annual Property Taxes: _____

Amount Borrowed: _____ Interest Rate: ___ (fixed) ___ (adjustable) ____

Current Rate: _____ Note Signed: ___ Term: ___ Defaulted On: _____

Initial Payment Amount: _____ Defendants in Default? ___ (Yes) ___ (No)

Summons and Complaint Filed On: _____ Deficiency? ___ (Yes) ___ (No)

Reinstatement Amount: _____ HO in Residence? _____ Employed?

Plaintiff Counsel: _____ Defense Counsel: _____

Servicer: _____ HAMP Eligible? _____

Notes:

Form 3. HAMP Checklist

___ Last 2 years of tax returns

___ 3 months bank statements

___ 30 days pay stubs

___ Hardship Affidavit

___ Utility bill (telephone, electric, gas)

___ Year to date profit and lost statement (if self employed)

___ Award letters (Social Services, Pension, Social Security, Welfare, etc.)

Form 4.   Affirmation

SUPREME COURT OF THE STATE OF NEW YORK
COUNTY OF _____

                         Plaintiff,

                                            AFFIRMATION

v.

                                            Index No.: _____

                    Defendant(s)

                                            Mortgaged Premises:

N.B.: During and after August 2010, numerous and widespread insufficiencies in foreclosure filings in various courts around the nation were reported by major mortgage lenders and other authorities, including failure to review documents and files to establish standing and other foreclosure requisites; filing of notarized affidavits which falsely attest to such review and to other critical facts in the foreclosure process; and "robosignature" of documents.

[_____], Esq., pursuant to CPLR § 2106 and under the penalties of perjury, affirms as follows:

1. I am an attorney at law duly licensed to practice in the state of New York and am affiliated with the Law Firm of _____, the attorneys of record for Plaintiff in the above-captioned mortgage foreclosure action. As such, I am fully aware of the underlying action, as well as the proceedings had herein.

2. On [date], I communicated with the following representative or representatives of Plaintiff, who informed me that he/she/they (a) personally reviewed plaintiff's documents and records relating to this case for factual accuracy; and (b) confirmed the factual accuracy of the allegations set forth in the Complaint and any supporting affidavits or affirmations filed with the Court, as well as the accuracy of the notarizations contained in the supporting documents filed therewith.

Name   Title

_____   _____

_____   _____

_____   _____

3. Based upon my communication with [person/s specified in ¶2], as well as upon my own inspection and other reasonable inquiry under the circumstances, I affirm that, to the best of my knowledge, information, and belief, the Summons, Complaint, and other papers filed or submitted to the Court in this matter contain no false statements of fact or law. I understand my continuing obligation to amend this Affirmation in light of newly discovered material facts following its filing.

4. I am aware of my obligations under New York Rules of Professional Conduct (22 NYCRR Part 1200) and 22 NYCRR Part 130.

                                          _____

DATED:

N.B.: Counsel may augment this affirmation to provide explanatory details, and may file supplemental affirmations or affidavits for the same purpose.

[Revised 11/18/10]

SUPREME COURT OF THE STATE OF NEW YORK
COUNTY OF _____

_____

Plaintiff,

v.

Defendant(s)

AFFIDAVIT

Index No.: _____

Mortgaged Premises:

_____

_____

STATE OF NEW YORK	)	
	)	ss:
COUNTY OF _____	)	

_____, being duly sworn, deposes and says:

1. I am a _____, a representative of plaintiff in the above-captioned mortgage foreclosure action. I am authorized to execute this affidavit and am fully aware of the underlying action, as well as the papers and proceedings heretofore had herein.

2. This Affidavit is made in further support of plaintiff's counsel's affirmation pursuant to the October 2010 Administrative Order of the Chief Administrative Judge of the Courts of New York, as supplemented.

3. I have performed the following actions in order to confirm the truth and veracity of the statements made herein. This review is based upon my access to the books and records relating to this loan which are kept in the ordinary course of business.

Initial all that are applicable:

A ___ Confirmed the notice of default, if required, was properly mailed prior to commencement of foreclosure.

B ___ Reviewed the summons and complaint in this action to confirm the factual accuracy of the identity of the proper plaintiff, the defaults and the amounts claimed to be due to plaintiff as set forth therein.

C ___ Confirmed the affidavit(s) executed and submitted by plaintiff together with this application have been personally reviewed by the signatory; that the notary acknowledging the affiant's signature followed applicable law in notarizing the affiant's signature.

D ___ I am unable to confirm or deny that the underlying documents previously filed with the Court have been properly reviewed or notarized.

E ___ Inasmuch as the underlying mortgage loan has been transferred prior to commencement or during the pendency of this action, I am unable to confirm or deny that the underlying documents filed with the Court have been properly reviewed or notarized by the prior servicer.

F ___ (other) _____

_____

_____

_____

N.B.: Affiants may augment this affidavit to provide explanatory details, and may file supplemental affirmations or affidavits for the same purpose.

WHEREFORE, it is respectfully requested that the Court grant the proposed relief requested herein together with such other relief as the Court deems just and proper

_____
(Affiant)

STATE OF _____   )   SS:
COUNTY OF _____   )

On the ___ day of ___ in the year _____ before me, the undersigned, personally appeared _____, personally known to me or proved to me on the basis of satisfactory evidence to be the individual(s) whose name(s) is(are) subscribed to the within instrument and acknowledged to me that he/she/they executed the same in his/her/their capacity(ies), that by his/her/their signature(s) on the instrument, the individual(s), or the personal upon behalf of which the individual(s) acted, executed the instrument, and that such individual made such appearance before the undersigned in the.

_____

Notary Public

DUTCHESS COUNTY
SUPREME COURT
JUDGES' PART RULES
JUSTICE JAMES V. BRANDS

Doc. 1. Part Rules

Certification of Papers:

Every pleading, written motion and other paper served or filed in an action must be signed by an attorney pursuant to § 130–1.1a of the Rules of the Chief Administrator of the Courts.

Appearances:

(a) Within ten (10) days of written notification of this Part's assignment to a case, or written notification of a Preliminary Conference, whichever shall first occur, each attorney shall file a record of appearance with chambers. The record of appearance shall include the attorney's name, firm affiliation, mailing address, telephone and facsimile number as well as the party represented. The record of appearance shall also contain a written acknowledgment that counsel is familiar with these Part Rules.

(b) Pursuant to § 130–2.1 of the Rules of the Chief Administrator of the Courts, the Court may impose financial sanctions and award costs and reasonable attorney's fees against any attorney who, without good cause, fails to appear at a time and place scheduled for an appearance in any action or proceeding.

(c) Pursuant to § 202.27 of the Uniform Civil Rules for the Supreme Court, upon the default of any party in appearing at a scheduled call of a calendar or at any conference, the Court may grant judgment by default against the non-appearing party.

(d) At all scheduled appearances and conferences before the Court, only an attorney thoroughly familiar with the action and authorized to act on behalf of a party shall appear.

Preliminary Conferences:

A party may request a preliminary conference any time after issue has been joined. In any event, the Court will schedule a preliminary conference within forty-five (45) days after an RJI has been filed on a matter. A form stipulation and order shall be provided to the parties which shall establish a timetable for discovery within parameters set forth by the Court after determination as to whether a matter should be designated a "standard" or a "complex" case. If all parties sign the stipulation and return it to chambers prior to the scheduled conference, such form shall be "so ordered" by the Court and, unless the Court orders otherwise, appearances will not be required at the preliminary conference.

Once the stipulation has been "so ordered", no modifications are permitted except by written order of the Court.

Matrimonial Actions:

(a) No later than ten (10) days prior to preliminary conference in any matrimonial action, each party shall file and serve copies of the following documents:

1. retainer agreement

2. net worth statement

3. most recent paystub and income tax return

(b) Parties must be present at the preliminary conference.

(c) Any application regarding child support must be accompanied by a completed Child Support Worksheet.

Compliance Conference:

The preliminary conference order shall provide a date and time for the parties to appear at compliance conference.

(a) At the compliance conference, the Court will ensure that discovery is proceeding as scheduled.

(b) Unless a note of issue has been earlier filed, the Court shall direct a date as the deadline for filing a note of issue and certificate of readiness.

Pretrial Conference:

Within 45 days of the filing of a note of issue, the Court shall schedule a Pretrial Conference.

(a) At the pretrial conference, the Court shall establish a deadline for the exchange of expert witness information pursuant to CPLR § 3101(d)(1) which shall, in no event, be later than ninety (90) days before trial for the party bearing the burden of proof on that issue. The opposing party must serve its disclosure within forty-five (45) days of trial. Any amended or supplemental expert disclosure shall be allowed only with leave of the Court on good cause shown. The statutory stay of disclosure (CPLR 3214[d]) upon the service of a dispositive motion under CPLR 3211 shall not apply to the service of these expert responses. Unless the Court directs otherwise, a party who fails to comply with this rule is precluded from offering the testimony and opinions of the expert for whom a timely response has not been given.

(b) The Court will explore limitation of issues for trial, including referring certain issues to a referee if appropriate.

(c) The Court will schedule a date certain for trial of all outstanding issues.

(d) Counsel should be prepared to discuss settlement and should have full authority from their respective clients.

Trials:

(a) Once scheduled, a trial shall not be adjourned for any reason other than the actual engagement of counsel as provided for in § 125.1 of the Rules of the Chief Administrator of the Courts. Any application for an adjournment must be made in writing and must be supported by an affirmation of counsel establishing the requisite grounds set forth in 22 NYCRR § 125.1.

(b) Prior to the time scheduled for the trial to commence, counsel shall:

1. pre-mark all exhibits

2. file a brief concerning any unusual issue(s) counsel believes may arise at trial (motions *in limine* should be made at least 30 days before trial when possible)

3. submit a list of probable trial witnesses.

(c) The plaintiff shall file and bring to the trial a copy of each of the following:

1. marked pleadings including verified bill of particulars

(d) Counsel shall submit a verdict sheet jointly prepared by counsel. If agreement cannot be reached, then each side shall submit a proposed verdict sheet.

(e) Counsel shall submit all requests to charge by referencing the appropriate Pattern Jury Instructions (PJI) number.

(f) Jury selection. Attorneys shall employ "White's Method" of selecting the jury panel. In each round, questioning shall be conducted first by plaintiff's counsel.

(g) Refer to our trial part rules.

Motions:

(a) Motions are returnable on any day of the week. There will be no appearances unless specifically stated by the court.

(b) Original initiating motion papers should be submitted directly to the County Clerk accompanied by an affidavit/affirmation of service and the required fees. All answering and reply papers should be submitted directly to chambers. DO NOT SUBMIT COURTESY COPIES. MOTION PAPERS MUST BE BOUND TOGETHER. THE COURT WILL NOT ACCEPT LOOSE MOTION PAPERS, AFFIDAVITS, AFFIRMATIONS OR EXHIBITS

(c) Motion papers must be accompanied by proof of payment to the County Clerk of all required fees.

(d) All affirmations, affidavits and memoranda of law must contain numbered pages.

(e) All citations must be to an official state reporter, if available.

(f) All documents required to decide the application must be attached. It is not sufficient that documents may be on file with the Clerk of the Court.

(g) The Court does not accept sur-reply papers or correspondence on motions, nor any papers filed after the final submission date of the motion.

(h) Motion papers, orders and judgments must be accompanied by a stamped, self-addressed envelope. Counsel must provide an additional copy of any order and judgment submitted to conform to the original.

(i) All motions will be decided by submission and personal appearances on the return date are not required unless the Court specifically directs oral argument.

(j) Summary Judgment or other dispositive motions must be made within 60 days after filing the note of issue.

(k) Any motions seeking to exclude potential evidence shall be made in writing and shall be returnable at least 30 days in advance of trial.

(*l*) NO ADJOURNMENTS on a motion will be granted with a return date within thirty (30) days prior to the date of trial.

(m) Counsel shall immediately notify the court when it becomes unnecessary to decide a motion.

Motion *In Limine*:

Any applications addressing the preclusion of evidence, testimony or other trial related matters shall be brought to the attention of the court immediately upon counsel becoming aware of such matter to be addressed, it being the intent to avoid applications made on the eve of, or during trial of a matter. Failure to bring the matter before the court in a timely fashion may result in summary denial of such application.

Videotaping:

While the court strives for adherence to scheduled jury selection and commencement dates, the court's trial calendar is such that exact days cannot always be guaranteed. Requests for a continuance or rescheduling due to an expert's unavailability for testimony generally cannot be granted due to the large number of matters pending for trial. Counsel may use videotaping of experts when necessary.

Expert Testimony Preclusion:

1. Any motion by a party to preclude or limit expert testimony under the expert disclosure part of

this order or pursuant to CPLR 3101(d) must be made as soon as practicable.

2. Where a party's summary judgment motion is or will be based in whole or in part upon the granting of a motion directed at precluding or limiting expert testimony made pursuant to this part of this order, the motions' return date shall be the same.

Adjournments:

(a) Adjournments of scheduled trials and hearings are not permitted except as provided in 22 NYCRR § 125.1 and in accordance with the procedure set forth therein.

(b) Adjournments of motions and conferences may be requested on consent of opposing counsel. After obtaining such consent, the requesting party must fax the adjournment request to (845) 486–6497 to obtain a new date. A REQUEST TO ADJOURN A CONFERENCE MUST BE FAXED TO THIS COURT AT LEAST 24 HOURS IN ADVANCE OF THE SCHEDULED APPEARANCE. All adjournments must be confirmed in writing to the Court, by the requesting party, and a copy of the letter sent to all parties. No more than two adjournments shall be permitted on any matter unless good cause is shown upon written application made to and approved by the Court. WHEN REQUESTING AN ADJOURNMENT OF A CONFERENCE OR MOTION, THE LETTER REQUEST SHALL INCLUDE THE CURRENT DATE OF ANY MOTION RETURNABLE OR ANY CONFERENCE SCHEDULED.

Settled and Discontinued Cases:

Counsel shall immediately notify the Court of a case disposition.

Mental Hygiene Law Article 81 Proceedings:

(a) All proceedings instituted pursuant to Mental Hygiene Law § 81 *et seq.* will be returnable on a Thursday morning at a date and time to be determined by the Court.

(b) All proposed orders to show cause must conform with the requirements of MHL § 81.07.

(c) Proposed orders to show cause must contain separate decretal paragraphs for service as provided in MHL § 81.07(d)(1) and (2).

(d) Court evaluators and appointed attorneys must complete and file each of the following forms:

1. Notice of Appointment (UCS–830.1)

2. Statement of Approval of Compensation (UCS–830)

3. Certification of Compliance (UCS–830.3)

4. Affirmation of legal services.

Fiduciary Appointments:

(a) In order to be eligible for appointments to serve as a referee, court evaluator, guardian ad litem, re-

ceiver, attorney for receiver or attorney for an Alleged Incompetent Person (AIP), counsel must appear on the Part 36 list promulgated by the Office of Court Administration.

(b) In order to be eligible for appointment to serve as a law guardian, counsel must be a member of the Dutchess County Law Guardian Panel.

(c) Court evaluators and appointed attorneys must complete and file each of the following forms:

1. Notice of Appointment (UCS–830.1)

2. Statement of Approval of Compensation (UCS–830)

3. Certification of Compliance (UCS–830.3)

4. Affirmation of legal services.

Doc. 2. Procedures for Trial Counsel

1. A. Trial Readiness: Prior to jury selection, counsel is cautioned to ascertain the availability of all witnesses and subpoenaed documents. If you have non-English speaking or deaf witnesses, the court must be notified at the pre-trial conference to allow the clerk time to arrange for the presence of a New York State certified interpreter, in the event the party does not provide their own.

B. Bifurcated Trials: All trials other than Medical Malpractice and Wrongful Death are bifurcated in the Second Department. The damages portion commences with the same jury immediately following a liability verdict. Counsel should have medical testimony and any other professionals for the damages portion ready to proceed at that time.

2. Marked Pleadings Plus: Counsel shall furnish the Court with copies of:

A. Marked pleadings as required by CPLR 4012 (including the bill(s) of particular);

B. A copy of any statutory provisions in effect at the time the cause of action arose upon which either the plaintiff or defendant relies;

C. All expert reports relevant to the issues;

D. All reports, depositions and written statements which may be used to either refresh a witness' recollection and/or cross-examine the witness;

E. If any part of a deposition is to be read into evidence (as distinguished from mere use on cross-examination) you must provide the Court and your adversary with the page and line number of all such testimony so that all objections can be addressed prior to use before the jury.

3. Pre-Marked Exhibits: All trial exhibits should be pre-marked by the court reporter whenever possible, for identification, and copies of the resulting Exhibit Sheet provided to the Court.

4. Ten Days Prior to Jury Selection: Counsel should be prepared:

A. To alert the Court as to all anticipated disputed issues of law and fact, and provide the Court with citations to all statutory and common law authority upon which counsel will rely;

B. To stipulate to undisputed facts and the admissibility of clearly admissible documents and records;

C. To alert the Court to any anticipated *in limine* motions or evidentiary objections which counsel believes will be made during the course of the trial;

D. To provide the Court with a copy of all prior decisions and orders which may be relevant to said *in limine* applications;

E. To discuss scheduling as well as the number of witnesses to be called at trial, and the estimated length of the trial;

F. To alert the Court as to any anticipated problems regarding the attendance at trial of parties, attorneys or essential witnesses, and any other practical problems which the Court should consider in scheduling;

G. To alert the Court to any anticipated requests for a jury instruction relating to missing witnesses and/or documents;

H. To alert the Court to any anticipated request for apportionment as to alleged culpable non-parties pursuant to CPLR Article 16.

5. Jury Selection: THIS PART USES UNDESIGNATED ALTERNATES. There is no exception to this rule.

No Communication with Jurors: In order to maintain the appearance of total impartiality, once the jury has been selected no one is to communicate in any form at any time with any juror. This includes both verbal and non-verbal communication, including, without limitation, nods, shrugs and shaking the head. Do not even say "hello" or "good morning".

6. Trial Objections and Arguments: When making an objection, after saying the word, "objection", add only those few words necessary to state the generic grounds for the objection, such as "hearsay", "bolstering", "leading", or "asked and answered". If you believe further argument is required, ask permission to approach the bench.

7. Courtroom Demeanor: All remarks should be directed to the Court. Comments should not be made to opposing counsel. If you require a significant discussion with your adversary, such as possible stipulation, ask for permission to approach the bench, so you may have a chance to talk to each other outside the presence of the jury.

8. Use of Proposed Exhibits: Do not show anything, including an exhibit or proposed exhibit to a witness without first showing it to opposing counsel. If this procedure is claimed to compromise trial strategy, a pre offer ruling outside the presence of the jury should be first obtained.

9. Examination of Witnesses: Do not approach a witness without permission of the Court Please allow the witness to complete his/her answer to your question before asking another question. Do not interrupt the witness in the middle of an answer, unless it's totally un-responsive in which event you should seek a ruling from the Court. Direct examination, cross, redirect and re-cross are permitted.

10. Jury Charge & Verdict Sheet: At the commencement of the trial, all counsel shall submit suggested jury charges and a suggested verdict questionnaire. Amendments thereto shall be permitted at the final charging conference. If counsel relies on a Pattern Jury instruction [PJI] without any change thereto, it should be referred to by PJI number and and topic only. If any changes to the PJI are suggested, then the entire proposed charge should be set forth and the changes should be highlighted or otherwise called to the Court's attention. Citations to appropriate statutory or common law authority shall be given in support of suggested non–PJI jury charges or suggested PJI modification.

11. Post trial interview with jurors: Any contact or discussion with jurors after a verdict is rendered may be conducted outside this part, not in the jury room or adjacent to it.

Doc. 3.　Election Rules

(1) Orders to Show Cause to validate or invalidate designating or nominating petitions will be made returnable no later than five (5) days after the last day to statutorily commence such proceedings. A copy of these rules shall be attached to the original and each copy of the Order to Show Cause.

(2) The calendar call on the return date must be answered by counsel or the litigant(s), (self represented) who shall provide the Part Clerk with their addresses and telephone numbers. Non-lawyer "representatives" of the parties are not permitted to answer the calendar call. Proof of service of the Orders to Show Cause, as well as any interposed Counterclaims or Answers, shall be filed with the Part Clerk at or before the initial appearance.

(3) On or before the return date and time:

(A) a written offer of proof in any matter alleging a question of residency of a candidate shall be filed with the court clerk and served on the opposing party;

(B) specifications of objections or bills of particulars not previously served and/or filed with the Board of Elections shall be filed with the court clerk and served on the opposing party;

(C) a complete written offer of proof in all matters alleging fraud including identification of witness to be called, their names and addresses, volume, page and line together with status of each (candidate, signatory, notary, expert, subscribing witness, etc.) shall be filed with the court clerk and served on all opposing parties.

FAILURE TO COMPLY WITH SECTION A, B, OR C OF THIS PARAGRAPH SHALL BE DEEMED A WAIVER, AND FURTHER PROOF MAY BE PRECLUDED, EXCEPTING THE TESTIMONY OF A WITNESS THE COURT DETERMINES COULD NOT BE IDENTIFIED BEFORE THE RETURN DATE.

JUSTICE JAMES D. PAGONES

Doc. 1. Hon. James D. Pagones

Certification of Papers:

Every pleading, written motion and other paper served or filed in an action must be signed by an attorney pursuant to § 130–1.1a of the Rules of the Chief Administrator of the Courts.

Appearances:

(a) Within ten (10) days of written notification of this Part's assignment to a case, or written notification of a Preliminary Conference, whichever shall first occur, each attorney shall file a record of appearance with chambers. The record of appearance shall include the attorney's name, firm affiliation, mailing address, telephone and facsimile number as well as the party represented. The record of appearance shall also contain a written acknowledgment that counsel is familiar with these Part Rules.

(b) Pursuant to § 130–2.1 of the Rules of the Chief Administrator of the Courts, the Court may impose financial sanctions and award costs and reasonable attorney's fees against any attorney who, without good cause, fails to appear at a time and place scheduled for an appearance in any action or proceeding.

(c) Pursuant to § 202.27 of the Uniform Civil Rules for the Supreme Court, upon the default of any party in appearing at a scheduled call of a calendar or at any conference, the Court may grant judgment by default against the non-appearing party.

(d) At all scheduled appearances and conferences before the Court, only an attorney thoroughly familiar with the action and authorized to act on behalf of a party shall appear.

Preliminary Conferences:

A party may request a preliminary conference any time after issue has been joined. In any event, the Court will schedule a preliminary conference within forty-five (45) days after an RJI has been filed on a matter. A form stipulation and order shall be provided to the parties which shall establish a timetable for discovery within parameters set forth by the Court after determination as to whether a matter should be designated a "standard" or a "complex" case. If all parties sign the stipulation and return it to chambers prior to the scheduled conference, the stipulation shall be "so ordered" by the Court and, unless the Court orders otherwise, appearances will not be required at the preliminary conference.

Once the stipulation has been "so ordered", no modifications are permitted except by written order of the Court.

Matrimonial Actions:

(a) No later than ten (10) days prior to a preliminary conference in any matrimonial action, each party shall file and serve copies of the following documents:

1. retainer agreement
2. net worth statement
3. most recent paystub, income tax return and W–2

(b) Parties must be present at the preliminary conference.

(c) All pendente lite applications must be in writing and any application regarding child support must be accompanied by a completed Child Support Worksheet.

Compliance Conference:

The preliminary conference order shall provide a date and time for the parties to appear at a compliance conference.

(a) At the compliance conference, the Court will ensure that discovery is proceeding as scheduled.

(b) Unless a note of issue has been earlier filed, the Court shall direct a date as the deadline for filing a note of issue and certificate of readiness.

Pretrial Conference:

Within 45 days of the filing of a note of issue, the Court shall schedule a Pretrial Conference.

(a) The plaintiff shall file, no later than five (5) days prior to the Pretrial Conference a copy of each of the following:

1. marked pleadings
2. verified bill of particulars
3. any medical reports and records

(b) At the pretrial conference, the Court shall establish a deadline for the exchange of expert witness information pursuant to CPLR § 3101(d)(1) which shall, in no event, be later than ninety (90) days before trial for the party bearing the burden of proof on that issue. The opposing party must serve its disclosure within forty-five (45) days of trial.

(c) The Court will explore limitation of issues for trial, including referring certain issues to a referee if appropriate.

(d) The Court will schedule a date certain for trial of all outstanding issues.

(e) Counsel should be prepared to discuss settlement and should have full authority from their respective clients.

Trials:

(a) Once scheduled, a trial shall not be adjourned for any reason other than the actual engagement of counsel as provided for in § 125.1 of the Rules of the Chief Administrator of the Courts. Any application for an adjournment must be made in writing and must be supported by an affirmation of counsel establishing the requisite grounds set forth in 22 NYCRR § 125.1.

(b) *Matrimonial Actions Only:*

1. Expert Witnesses: At least ninety (90) days prior to the trial date set forth below, each party shall serve and file with the court a written report of each expert witness whom the party expects to call at trial and, at least sixty (60) days prior to the trial date set forth below, each party shall serve and file with the court any reply report. If a party intends that a written report shall substitute at trial for direct testimony, that party shall so advise the other party and the court at least ten (10) days prior to trial.

2. Witnesses (Other Than Expert): At least ten (10) days prior to trial, each side shall submit to the court and the other side a list of all other witnesses (except impeachment or rebuttal witnesses) whom that side intends to call at trial, specifying, where applicable, those whose depositions will be used.

3. Statement of Proposed Disposition: At least ten (10) days prior to trial, each side shall submit to the court and the other side a statement of proposed disposition. 22 NYCRR § 202.16(h).

4. Exhibits: The parties shall consult and work out a stipulation governing the authenticity and admissibility of all trial exhibits concerning which the parties can agree, which exhibits shall be pre-marked before the case is called for trial. Ten (10) days prior to trial, the parties shall submit to the Part a list or lists of: (I) all exhibits stipulated to be admissible, (ii) plaintiff's proposed additional exhibits, and (iii) defendant's proposed additional exhibits.

(c) All Other Supreme Court Actions:

No later than 72 hours prior to the time scheduled for the trial to commence, counsel shall:

1. pre-mark all exhibits and shall submit an exhibit list on a form to be provided by the Court.

2. file a brief concerning any unusual issue(s) counsel believes may arise at trial

3. submit a list of probable trial witnesses.

(d) Counsel shall submit with the exhibit list a verdict sheet jointly prepared by counsel. If agreement cannot be reached, then each side shall submit a proposed verdict sheet.

(e) Counsel shall submit all requests to charge by referencing the appropriate Pattern Jury Instructions (PJI) number.

(f) *Jury selection.* Attorneys shall employ "White's Method" of selecting the jury panel. In each round, questioning shall be conducted first by plaintiff's counsel.

Motions:

(a) Motions are returnable on any day of the week.

(b) Original motion papers should be submitted directly to chambers accompanied by an affidavit/affirmation of service. No courtesy copies are necessary.

(c) Motion papers must be accompanied by proof of payment to the County Clerk of all required fees.

(d) All affirmations, affidavits and memoranda of law must contain numbered pages.

(e) All citations must be to an official state reporter, if available.

(f) All documents required to decide the application must be attached. It is not sufficient that documents may be on file with the Clerk of the Court.

(g) The Court does not accept sur-reply papers or correspondence filed after the submission of the motion.

(h) Motion papers, orders and judgments must be accompanied by a stamped, self-addressed envelope. Counsel must provide an additional copy of any order and judgment submitted to conform to the original.

(i) All motions will be decided by submission and personal appearances on the return date are not required unless the Court specifically directs oral argument.

(j) Motions for summary judgment may not be filed later than one hundred and twenty (120) days after the note of issue is filed.

ADJOURNMENTS:

(a) Adjournments of scheduled trials and hearings are not permitted except as provided in 22 NYCRR § 125.1 and in accordance with the procedure set forth therein.

(b) Adjournments of motions and conferences may be obtained on consent of opposing counsel. After obtaining such consent, the requesting party must contact the Court's calendar clerk, Claudette Vatore 431–1725 to obtain a new date. All adjournments must be confirmed in writing to the Court, by the requesting party, and a copy of the letter sent to all parties. No more than two adjournments shall be permitted on any matter unless written application is made to and approved by the Court. *Adjournments are only granted with leave of the Court.*

SETTLED AND DISCONTINUED CASES:

Counsel shall immediately notify the Court of a case disposition. Following the initial notification, counsel shall submit a copy of the stipulation of discontinuance to chambers so that the matter may be marked off the calendar.

FIDUCIARY APPOINTMENTS:

(a) In order to be eligible for appointments to serve as a referee, court evaluator, guardian ad litem, receiver, attorney for receiver or attorney for an Alleged Incompetent Person (AIP), counsel must appear on the Part 36 list promulgated by the Office of Court Administration.

(b) In order to be eligible for appointment to serve as attorney for a child (*f/k/a* law guardian) counsel must be a member of the Dutchess County Law Guardian Panel.

JUSTICE VALENTINO T. SAMMARCO

Doc. 1. Hon. Valentino T. Sammarco

This part handles contested and uncontested matrimonial actions.

Attention of the Bar is directed to the Uniform Rules for Matrimonial Actions (§ 202.16).

Once the action is assigned to Judge Sammarco, all papers submitted to the Court shall be filed with Chambers, at 50 Market Street, Poughkeepsie, New York 12601 and shall include the Index Number and shall be marked "Supreme Court Action" on the envelope.

Any application for *ex parte* "emergency relief" must be accompanied by a written certification of counsel as to the efforts, if any, which have been made to give written or oral notice to the opposing party, or that party's attorney, if represented, and the attorney for the child(ren), if any, or a statement supporting a claim that notice should not be required. Except in an extreme emergency, an *ex parte* application will not be entertained, absent notice to the opposing party, or counsel, if represented, and the attorney for child(ren), if any.

Counsel are encouraged to request conferences with the Court prior to filing motion papers to allow the Court an opportunity to resolve the matter before the motion is made. It is hoped that this policy will eliminate excessive motion practice.

Sur-replies will not be considered unless the Court grants permission. Papers, including letters sent after the submission of the motion, will not be considered on the motion.

Motions and preliminary conferences may be adjourned only with the consent of the Court and the opposing party or counsel. All requests must be in writing. However, in exceptional circumstances, the Court will entertain applications by telephone for adjournments *ex parte*.

Copies of correspondence between counsel shall not be sent to the Court. Such copies will be disregarded and not placed in the Court file.

If an attorney is assigned to represent the child(ren), copies of all correspondence, motions, proposed orders and any other documents filed with the Court involving issue(s) with respect to the child(ren), must also be provided to their attorney.

All case citations must be made to the Official Reporters.

Proposed orders and motions, including a motion for a default judgment, must be submitted with proof of service on the opposing counsel or party, if unrepresented, and the attorney for the child(ren).

A stamped self-addressed envelope must be submitted with all motions and orders/judgments and a copy of the order/judgment if a conformed copy is requested.

JUSTICE CHRISTINE A. SPROAT

Doc. 1. Hon. Christine A. Sproat

Motions

After a case has been assigned to a part, prior to making any motion, movant shall notify the Court in writing, with a copy to all parties, setting forth the relief sought and the basis for that relief. The Court will then schedule a conference call with counsel or a Court conference date. This procedure does not preclude the moving party from making a motion, but provides the Court with an opportunity to resolve the

dispute giving rise to the motion without the need for a formal written application. Failing resolution of the dispute, or if the Court, in its discretion does not schedule the call or conference within ten days of mailing, then the party seeking the relief may proceed with the motion.

All motions are returnable on Friday except by order of the Court. Original Motions or Cross–Motions with the appropriate fee should be mailed to the Dutchess County Clerk's Office with a cover letter requesting that the original papers be forwarded to

Justice Sproat. All answering and reply papers should be forwarded directly to Chambers. No courtesy copies are necessary.

Summary judgment motions must be made within 120 days of the filing of the note of issue unless otherwise authorized by the Court for good cause shown.

Cases cited in support of or in opposition to the motion must include the cite to an official state reporter if available. All documents needed to reach a decision on the motion shall be attached to the motion papers. It is not sufficient that copies of such documents may be on file with the Dutchess County Clerk.

If new issues are raised in the reply, or if there has been a change in the law while the motion is pending, counsel are to advise chambers, in writing, of the request to submit additional affidavits or memoranda.

Appearances are not required unless directed by the court. Oral argument may be requested by noting "Oral Argument Requested" immediately over the index number on the Notice of Motion.

If the Court, in its discretion, requires such argument, the movant's attorney will be so advised and will be required to notify all parties.

Self-addressed, stamped envelopes must be provided by all parties with all motions and opposition papers.

Adjournments on motions:

a) on consent—the parties must seek consent of all other parties for an adjournment of a motion. The clerk of the part is to be advised by telephone, followed by a letter, that the motion is adjourned on consent. A copy of the letter is to be sent to all the parties. No more than three adjournments, for an aggregate period of sixty (60) days, without prior permission of the Court, will be granted. The cooperation of counsel is urged.

b) opposed—in the event a party cannot obtain the consent of the other parties, the party seeking an adjournment must notify the other parties that an oral request, by telephone, will be made for a one week adjournment for good cause. If the Court grants a one week adjournment, such good cause should be detailed in a letter to the Court and a copy of that letter must be sent to all other parties confirming the adjournment.

Discovery

Counsel must consult with one another in a good faith effort to resolve all disclosure disputes. See Uniform Rule 202.7. If counsel are unable to resolve a disclosure dispute in this manner, the procedures set forth above must be followed before any formal motion may be made.

Conferences

Conferences are scheduled for 9:30 a.m. unless otherwise directed by the Court.

Parties will be expected to abide by the provisions of the Preliminary Conference Stipulation and Order issued by this part. Failure to do so may result in sanctions.

Preliminary Conferences—After a case is assigned, a conference will be held within 45 days. The attorney who filed the RJI will receive notice of the scheduled date and time with directions to notify opposing counsel of same. Appearances are required in all Matrimonial, Medical/Dental Malpractice, and Product Liability actions. In all other actions, a Preliminary Conference Stipulation and Order will be included with the assignment notification. The attorneys are encouraged to complete the document and mail it back for the Court's signature, unless they are unable to agree, in which case they are to appear at the conference.

Compliance/Settlement Conferences—Counsel must come prepared to discuss settlement at the Compliance/Settlement Conference.

Pre–Trial Conference—Will occur after the filing of the Note of Issue as required in the Preliminary Conference Stipulation and Order. A trial date will be set at the Pre–Trial Conference.

Adjournment of Conferences

Must be approved by the Court even if it is on consent. Counsel must check with the clerk of the part regarding the adjourned date and send a confirming letter, stating the reason for the adjournment, to the Court and all other parties.

Trial

When the attorneys appear to begin selecting a jury or to begin a bench trial, they shall provide the Court with:

a) marked pleadings.

b) an exhibit list. Material to be used on cross-examination need not be listed. The attorneys are to pre-mark their exhibits. Only those received in evidence will be marked by the reporter. The reporter is to be provided with an exhibit list.

c) request for charges. The charge will be drawn from the Pattern Jury Instructions (PJI). A complete list of requested charges is to be submitted. Unless counsel seeks a deviation from the pattern charge or additions to the pattern charge, only the PJI numbers need be submitted. Where deviations or additions are requested, the full text of such requests must be submitted, together with any supporting legal precedents. All submissions must be served on opposing counsel.

d) verdict sheet. Counsel shall jointly prepare a verdict sheet and present it to the Court in a typed final form for presentation to the jury. If agreement cannot be reached, then each side shall present a proposed verdict sheet. If it is feasible, such proposals shall also be submitted on a computer disc in a format convertible to Word Perfect 8.0.

e) IN MATRIMONIAL ACTIONS: a statement of proposed disposition and an updated Statement of Net Worth, if circumstances have changed. Both must be exchanged at least 10 days prior to the trial date.

General

Orders/judgments must have at least one line of text on the signature page. Each must be submitted with a self-addressed, stamped envelope and a copy if a conformed copy is requested.

Counsel who appear must be fully familiar with the case and have authority to enter into any agreement, either substantive or procedural, on behalf of their clients. Counsel must be on time for all scheduled appearances and must bring sufficient material to allow meaningful discussion of unresolved issues to each Court appearance. Sanctions may be imposed for failure to comply with this rule.

Faxes—will not be accepted except in an emergency and its receipt has been authorized by chambers.

If an action is settled, discontinued, or otherwise disposed of, counsel shall immediately inform the Court by submission of a copy of the stipulation or other document evidencing the disposition.

JUSTICE CHARLES D. WOOD

Rule I. Staff

Michael V. Curti, Principal Law Clerk

Milena Schieb, Part Clerk

Barbara Seelbach, Secretary

Rule II. Communications With the Court

A. Correspondence. Correspondence to the Court must reflect the title and index number of the action, the return date and time of any pending motion and the trial date, if one has been established. Copies of all correspondence to the Court shall be provided to counsel for all other parties by the same means and at the same time as the correspondence is sent to the Court. Copies of correspondence between counsel shall not be provided to the Court unless the Court has so directed or the correspondence requests judicial action.

B. Telephone Calls. Telephone calls regarding conferences, trials and all non-emergency matters other than motions shall be directed to the part clerk. Telephone calls regarding motions shall be directed to Justice Wood's secretary. Telephone calls to Justice Wood's principal law clerk are permitted where provided by these rules and in the case of emergency situations requiring immediate attention that cannot otherwise be obtained by correspondence.

C. Faxes. The fax number for chambers is noted above. Any correspondence to the Court may be submitted by fax, provided that a copy of the correspondence identical to that faxed to the Court is simultaneously faxed or delivered to all counsel. It is not necessary to mail a copy of the faxed correspondence to the Court. Copies of papers that must otherwise be filed in original form with the clerk of the Court, such as judgments, motions, opposition papers and replies, will not be accepted by fax. Faxed documents will not be signed by the Court. Counsel are encouraged to avoid faxes to chambers that exceed three pages in length.

D. E-mail. Although the Court is equipped with e-mail, communications will not yet be accepted by such means.

E. Ex Parte Communications. Ex parte communications are strictly prohibited except upon the consent of all counsel or with respect to scheduling matters or the presentation of orders to show cause for signature.

F. Substitutions of Counsel. Notices of substitution of counsel shall be filed with the part clerk, in addition to any other filing that is required. A "substitution of counsel" to a pro se litigant is a withdrawal of counsel that may be accomplished only in accordance with CPLR 321.

Rule III. Conferences

A. General Rules.

1. *Attendance of Parties and Counsel required.* The attendance of all counsel and parties, if self represented, is expected, unless such appearances are dispensed with by the Court on prior request made on notice to counsel, or pursuant to the Court Rules. The calendar will be called promptly at the scheduled time and the parties and counsel are expected to be prompt. To the extent possible, cases will be heard in the order in which all counsel and parties appear. Attorneys and self represented parties must check in with the part clerk immediately upon arriving. Appearances in other Court parts will be accommodated, provided that counsel first checks in with the part clerk and advises the part clerk where he or she can be reached.

2. *Translators.* Counsel should advise the part clerk not later than two days prior to any conference at which the services of a foreign language translator will be required for any party (or any special services will be required for any hearing-impaired party).

3. *Counsel to be Familiar with Action.* Counsel who appear must be fully familiar with the action on

which they appear and must be authorized to enter
into both substantive and procedural agreements on
behalf of their clients. Attorneys appearing "of counsel" to any attorney of record are held to the same
standard. Any failure to comply with this rule may be
considered by the Court to be a default in appearing
for the conference.

4. *Transcripts.* Parties may be required to purchase a copy of the transcript of conferences conducted in open Court, the cost of which will be divided
equally between the parties unless otherwise agreed
to by the parties or directed by the Court.

B. Preliminary Conferences.

1. *Preliminary Conferences (Non Matrimonial
Cases).* A party may request a preliminary conference any time after issue has been joined. The Court
will schedule a preliminary conference within forty-
five (45) days after the request for judicial intervention has been filed. A form stipulation and order will
be provided to the parties which shall establish a
timetable for discovery within parameters set forth by
the Court after determination as to whether a matter
should be designated an "expedited" "standard" or
"complex" case. If all parties sign the stipulation and
return it to chambers prior to the scheduled conference, such form shall be "so ordered" by the Court
subject to the Court's review and approval, and unless
the Court orders otherwise, appearances will not be
required at the preliminary conference.

Once the stipulation has been "so ordered," no
modifications are permitted except by written order of
the Court.

2. *Preliminary Conferences (Matrimonial Cases).*
No later than ten (10) days prior to preliminary
conference in any matrimonial action, each party shall
file and serve copies of the following documents: 1)
Retainer agreement; 2) Net worth statement; 3)
Most recent pay stub and income tax return. Parties
must be present at all preliminary conferences.

3. *Adjournment of Preliminary Conference.*
Each party will be permitted one adjournment of the
preliminary conference. The preliminary conference
will not be permitted to be adjourned for more that a
total of 30 days from the date on which it is initially
scheduled. No further adjournments will be permitted. Deadlines for the completion of discovery will be
established without regard to the date on which the
preliminary conference is held.

**C. Compliance Conferences, Pre–Trial Confer-
ence, Charging Conference.**

1. *Compliance Conference.* The preliminary conference order shall provide a date and time for the
parties to appear at a compliance conference. The
purpose of the compliance conference is to report to
the Court on the progress of pre-trial discovery and to
address any issues that have arisen with respect to
discovery. The Court may modify the discovery

schedule at the compliance conference if the litigation
or interest of justice so require and may impose
appropriate sanctions against any party or counsel
responsible for a non excusable failure to comply with
the discovery schedule. The parties are cautioned
that any adjournment of the compliance conference
will not excuse a failure to provide discovery or failure
to adhere to the preliminary conference order and
that discovery shall proceed during the period of any
adjournment. The parties are cautioned to arrive on
time for the compliance conference. Defaulting or
late arriving counsel, in the absence of an adequate
excuse, may be subject to sanctions and/or costs.
Counsel who repeatedly fail to appear or arrive late to
compliance conferences may summarily be subject to
sanctions and/or costs.

2. *Pre–Trial Conference.* Within 45 days of the
filing of a Note of Issue, the Court will schedule a
Pretrial Conference. The Court will schedule a date
certain for trial of all outstanding issues. All counsel
appearing before the Court should be prepared to
discuss settlement and should have full authority for
their representative clients.

3. *Charging Conference.* Within two weeks prior
to trial, the Court will schedule a charging conference.
With regard to jury trials, the parties shall submit
their proposed charges from the Pattern Jury Instructions, Civil, Second Edition (hereinafter "PJI"). The
proposed charges must include the appropriate reference number contained denoting where the charge
may be found within the PJI. At the charging conference, the Court will also entertain any special jury
instructions. Such special jury instructions must be
in writing. At the charging conference, the parties
shall also exchange and be prepared to discuss proposed verdict sheets.

4. *Conference Adjournments.* A compliance conference or pre-trial conference may be adjourned
once, for a period not to exceed two weeks, by stipulation of the parties faxed to the part clerk by noon on
the second Court day preceding the scheduled conference. The Court is reluctant to grant any further
adjournments or any adjournments for longer than
two weeks, even if on consent, but will entertain
requests for such adjournments if made in writing and
faxed to the part clerk not later than noon on the
second Court day preceding the scheduled conference,
accompanied by a statement setting forth (I) good
cause why the adjournment is sought (including, if the
adjournment is sought by reason of the engagement of
counsel, an affirmation of engagement in accordance
with part 125 of the Rules of the Chief Administrator)
(ii) whether the adversary party and any court-appointed attorney (if any), consents or objects to the
application, and (iii) a proposed date, agreeable to all
parties, to which the adjournment is sought in the
event that the adjournment is granted. All such
communications must be copied to all counsel. The
Court may, in the exercise of discretion, permit or

refuse a conference adjournment in any instance. No request for an adjournment will be accepted. Counsel will be advised of the Court's determination by telephone or by return fax. If the adjournment is granted, the party requesting the adjournment shall notify all counsel in writing, including Court appointed attorneys (if any), if one has been appointed. Charging Conferences may not be adjourned, absent a settlement.

5. *Failure to Appear at a Scheduled Conference.* The failure of any counsel or any party to appear for a scheduled conference may be treated by the Court as a default and shall be dealt within a manner permitted by the Uniform Rules by awarding reasonable attorney's fees to the appearing party from a non-appearing party or counsel whose presence was not excused by the Court.

Rule IV.   Motions

A.   General Rules. Motions may be made returnable on Fridays. Any motion returnable on another day of the week will be automatically adjourned by the Court to the next succeeding Friday that the Court is in session. The return date for an order to show cause shall be determined by the Court. Motion papers must be accompanied by proof of payment to the County Clerk of all required fees. All affirmations, affidavits and memoranda of law must contain numbered pages. All citations must be to an official state reporter, if available. All documents required to decide the application must be attached. It is not sufficient that the documents may be on file with the Clerk of the Court. The Court does not accept surreply papers or correspondence on motions, nor any papers filed after the final submission date of the motion. Motion papers, orders and judgments must be accompanied by a stamped, self-addressed envelope. Counsel must provide an additional copy of any order and judgment submitted to conform to the original. All motions will be decided by submission. Personal appearances on the return date are not required unless the Court specifically directs oral argument. Summary Judgment or other dispositive motions must be made within 60 days after filing the note of issue. Any motions seeking to exclude potential evidence shall be made in writing and shall be returnable at least 30 days in advance of trial. NO ADJOURNMENTS on a motion will be granted with a return date within thirty (30) days prior to the date of trial. Counsel shall immediately notify the Court when it becomes unnecessary to decide a motion.

B.   Orders to Show Cause. Orders to show cause submitted for signature shall be presented to the office of the calendar clerk or as may be otherwise required by that office. Proposed orders to show cause may be rejected where the relief requested can be sought by notice of motion. A conformed copy of the order will be faxed to counsel for the moving party when signed. All inquiries concerning orders to show cause that have been submitted for signature should be directed to Justice Wood's secretary. Except in cases of exigent circumstances, no phone call regarding the status of an order to show cause should be made until 48 hours have elapsed from the time of submission. When the Court declines to sign an order to show cause, counsel will be so notified.

C.   Requests from Temporary Orders of Protection. If the proposed order to show cause contains a request for a temporary order of protection, counsel should so advise the part clerk upon presentation of the proposed order to the office of the calendar clerk and should be prepared to be present, with his or her client, for an *ex parte* hearing at such time as the Court will direct during the 24 hours after presentation of the proposed order.

D.   Discovery Disputes. No motion regarding discovery may be made without the prior approval of the Court. Pursuant to § 202.7 of the Uniform Rules, counsel must consult with each other in a good faith effort to resolve any dispute regarding discovery or compliance with discovery deadlines before requesting that the issue be resolved by the Court. In the event that counsel are unable to resolve such a dispute in this fashion, the party seeking relief from the demand or deadline, or to compel compliance shall immediately advise the Court of the dispute by faxing a letter not exceeding two pages in length. A copy of the letter shall be faxed to opposing counsel contemporaneously with the fax to the Court. Any response, by letter also not exceeding two pages in length, shall be made by fax, with a copy to opposing counsel, within 48 hours. Upon reviewing the submissions, the Court will schedule a telephone conference, a Court conference, or grant permission to make a written motion and set a briefing schedule therefor. Any such request shall be made within a reasonable time after the cause for the dispute arose. The failure to do so may result in the objection being deemed waived or the request being deemed abandoned and discovery being deemed complete as of the date on which discovery is required to be complete.

E.   Filing of Papers Applicable to All Motions. All papers must be typewritten, double-spaced, securely bound with no sharp edges, entirely legible and bearing original signatures. All exhibits must be labeled with tab markings. Motion papers and all related correspondence must reflect the index number assigned to the action, the return date of any other pending motion and the trial date, if one has been established. Unless the Court orders, or a statute or the Uniform Rules require, otherwise, the filing of a motion does not relieve any party from attending any previously-scheduled conference or Court appearance, regardless of the nature of the relief sought, or from complying with any discovery deadline. Where the return date of a motion is adjourned, all answering affidavits, replies or other papers with respect to the motion will be required to be served on dates bearing the same relationship to the adjourned return date as the original service dates bore to the original return date, unless the Court orders or the parties agree otherwise. All moving papers, opposition papers and replies shall be filed with the Court not later than noon on the Friday preceding the return date of the motion.

F. Specific Requirements for Particular Motions.

1. *Motions for Leave to Renew or Reargue.* Any motion pursuant to CPLR 2221 seeking leave to renew or reargue shall be accompanied by copies of all papers submitted on the prior motion, including all exhibits. Failure to comply with this requirement shall result in the denial of the motion.

2. *Motions for Leave to Amend, Supplement or Correct Pleadings.* Any motion for leave to correct pleadings, pursuant to CPLR 3024, or to amend or supplement pleadings, pursuant to CPLR 3025, shall be accompanied by copies of all pleadings filed as of the date of the motion and the proposed amended, supplemented or corrected pleading. Failure to comply with this requirement shall result in the denial of the application.

3. *Post–Judgment Motions.* Any application for post-judgment relief must be by order to show cause. The proposed order to show cause should provide for service on the opposing party in the manner required for the commencement of a special proceeding, and shall not provide for service on the opposing party's prior attorney unless the supporting papers establish that such attorney has the authority to accept such service. Any post-judgment motion involving custody or visitation shall provide for the reappointment of and service upon any previously appointed attorney for the child.

4. *Motions for Leave to Withdraw as Counsel.* No appearance will be required on a motion pursuant to CPLR 321 for leave to withdraw as counsel if the motion papers are accompanied by an affidavit of the client attesting to his or her consent to the withdrawal and the opposing party does not object to leave being granted.

5. *Cross Motions.* Cross motions seeking no relief other than the denial of the relief requested in the motion will not be recognized as motions with respect to which a reply may be submitted.

6. *Child Support Applications.* Any application regarding child support must be accompanied by a completed Child Support Worksheet.

G. Motion Adjournments.

1. *On Consent.* Motions may be adjourned on consent no more than two times and for no longer than a total of 45 days. Counsel seeking the adjournment must notify Justice Wood's secretary of the requested adjournment date by facsimile not later than noon on the second Court day before the return

date. The Court will then assign an adjourned date, giving due consideration to any specific date that has been agreed upon by counsel. No telephone requests for adjournments will be accepted. Counsel will be advised of the Court's determination by telephone or by return fax. Counsel seeking the adjournment will then be responsible to give notice of the adjourned date to all other counsel, including any Court appointed attorneys (if any), by facsimile.

2. *Without Consent.* A request for adjournment of a motion return date with respect to which consent has been refused shall be made by facsimile to Justice Wood's secretary not later than noon on the second Court day preceding the return dates. No adjournment request will be granted by the Court unless the party requesting the adjournment can show good cause for the adjournment. If the adjournment is granted, the Court will assign an adjourned date and Counsel seeking the adjournment will be responsible to give notice of the adjourned date to all other Counsel, including the law guardian, by facsimile.

H. Reply Papers. Reply papers shall not set forth new factual claims, legal arguments or requests for relief that were not within the scope of the papers that initiated the motion or the opposition papers.

Rule V. Trials

A. Trial Dates.

1. *Trial Dates are Firm.* Trial dates established by the Court are to be considered firm, subject only to minor adjustments based upon the Court's availability. Counsel should be prepared to commence the trial at the scheduled time on the scheduled date. Counsel should check with the part clerk after 2:00 p.m. on the business day prior to the scheduled trial date to verify that the Court will be available to commence the trial as scheduled.

2. *Adjournment of Trial Dates.* Requests for adjournment of a trial date shall be made to the part clerk. Adjournments of trial dates will not be granted except upon a showing of unusual and unanticipated circumstances. As required by § 202.32 of the Uniform Rules, adjournments requested by reason of the engagement of counsel must be accompanied by the affidavit required by part 125 of the Rules of the Chief Administrator. Anticipation that the matter will settle is not considered a legitimate basis for adjournment. No adjournment will be granted within the three days prior to the scheduled trial date except upon exigent circumstances.

B. Trial Preparation.

1. *Exchange of Expert Reports.* Not later than 60 days prior to the scheduled trial date, counsel shall each provide to opposing counsel a copy of any report by an expert whom counsel expects to call to trial. Any report that was received by counsel within 60 days of the scheduled trial date shall be provided to

opposing counsel within 10 days of its receipt by counsel.

2. *Trial Notebook.* Not later than five days prior to the scheduled trial date, counsel shall each submit a trial notebook, which shall consist of: (a) marked pleadings in accordance with CPLR Rule 4012; (b) the joint statement of the relevant facts that are not in dispute; (c) the list of witnesses whom the party expect to call at trial, stating the address of each witness and the general subject matter as to which each identified witness is expected to testify; (d) the list of all exhibits to be offered by such party in the form required by the Court (which may be obtained from the part clerk) (e) copies of the exhibits intended to be offered by counsel, pre-marked, with the plaintiff's exhibits numbered sequentially and the defendant's exhibits lettered sequentially; (f) in matrimonial actions, the updated net worth statement and statement of proposed disposition submitted at the settlement conference; (g) all expert reports, including reports of financial and psychological experts and appraisals; and (h) any other information that the Court has determined to be appropriate in the action. The Court may, in its discretion, relieve counsel from all or part of the trial notebook requirements upon a showing that the issues to be tried are sufficiently narrow that the trial notebook is not necessary or that the interests of justice otherwise justify such relief. Such a request will be entertained only at the pre-trial conference.

3. *Evidentiary Objections.* Not later than one day prior to the scheduled trial date, each counsel shall provide to the other and submit to the Court a statement setting forth any objection to the exhibits identified in the list provided by opposing counsel and the specific basis therefor. Any exhibit as to which no objection is identified shall be admitted into evidence on consent. The failure to submit such a statement of objections on a timely basis may be deemed to be consent to the admission of all of the exhibits included in the trial notebook submitted by the opposing party.

C. Witnesses.

1. *Identification.* Any witness not identified in the witness list provided to opposing counsel, other than an impeachment or rebuttal witness, shall not be permitted to testify unless an adequate explanation is provided for the failure to identify such witness prior to trial.

2. *Scheduling.* Parties, fact witnesses and expert witnesses should be advised of the scheduled dates at the time they are set. Absent unanticipated, exigent circumstances, last minute claims of unavailability will not be recognized where the trial dates have been long established. All witnesses should be on one-hour phone call notice so that their waiting time in Court is minimized. Professional witnesses, such as doctors, nurses and social workers, and witnesses who are public employees, such as teachers, counselors and police officers, will be permitted to testify out of order to accommodate their employment schedules. School teachers should be scheduled after 3:00 p.m. so that it is not necessary for their employers to provide substitutes.

3. *Subpoenas.* Subpoenas duces tecum shall be made returnable to the part at 9:30 a.m. on the third Court day prior to commencement of trial. The part clerk will allow all counsel and pro se litigants to inspect the subpoenaed material prior to the trial in a manner that will ensure its evidentiary integrity.

4. *Translators.* Counsel should advise the part clerk one week prior to trial if the services of a foreign language translator will be required for any party or witness, or any special services are required for any hearing-impaired party or witness.

D. Exhibits. An exhibit not identified in the exhibit list provided to opposing counsel, other than an exhibit offered for the purpose of impeachment or rebuttal, shall not be admitted into evidence unless an adequate explanation is provided for the failure to identify such exhibit prior to the trial. In addition to the copies of exhibits provided in the trial notebook, each party shall provide at trial one additional set of exhibits which will be used when counsel wishes to publish an exhibit to a witness.

E. Transcripts and Post-trial Briefs. Unless the Court directs otherwise, the parties will obtain and provide to the Court, on or before the date set by the Court at the conclusion of the trial, a copy of the trial transcript and each party will submit a post-trial brief with respect to the issues raised at the trial, setting forth specific references to the relevant portions of the transcript and the documents in evidence and citing applicable law.

Rule VI. Disposition

A. Discontinuance. Counsel shall notify the Court immediately upon the discontinuance of an action. A copy of the notice or stipulation of discontinuance shall be submitted to the part clerk at the same time as it is filed with the County Clerk. No action shall be considered discontinued until the part clerk receives a copy of the notice or stipulation of discontinuance.

B. Settlement

1. *Notification of Court.* On any date that the case appears on the calendar and the parties are present, a stipulation of settlement may be placed on the record and "so ordered" by the Court. If an action is settled out of Court, counsel shall immediately inform the part clerk. Upon placing a stipulation on the record in open Court or receiving written confirmation that a stipulation of settlement has been executed by all parties, the action will be marked "settled" and placed on the judgment submission calendar.

2. *Pending Conferences and Motions.* Until an action is marked settled, counsel will be responsible for responding to all pending motions and counsel and the parties will be expect to attend all scheduled Court appearances. Once the action is marked settled, all pending motions will be deemed withdrawn, unless explicit provision is made for their continuance, and all pending Court appearances will be vacated.

Rule VII. Mental Hygiene Law Article 81 Proceedings

1. **Proceedings.** All proceedings instituted pursuant to the Mental Hygiene Law § 81 *et seq.* will be returnable on a Thursday morning at a date and time to be determined by the Court.

2. **Orders to Show Cause.** All proposed orders to show cause must conform with the requirements of Mental Hygiene Law § 81.07. Proposed orders to show cause must contain separate decretal paragraphs for service as provided in Mental Hygiene Law § 81.07 (d)(1) and (2).

3. **Forms.** Court evaluators and appointed attorneys must complete and file each of the following forms: 1) Notice of Appointment (UCS–830.1); 2) Statement of Approval of Compensation (UCS–830); 3) Certification of Compliance (UCS–830.3); 4) Affirmation of Legal Services.

February 2010

ORANGE COUNTY
JUDGES' PART RULES
JUSTICE CATHERINE M. BARTLETT

Rule I. Communications With the Court

A. Correspondences. All correspondences to the Court shall be copied to all adversaries and must reflect the Index Number of the matter to which it relates. Correspondences between attorneys and/or pro se litigants shall not be copied to the Court unless there is some specific judicial purpose to be served by transmitting copies to the Court.

B. Telephone Calls. A serious effort should be made to limit telephone calls to the Court staff to situations requiring immediate attention that cannot otherwise be addressed by correspondence.

C. Faxes. The fax number to be used for all matters (including Chambers) is (845) 291–2106. Neither Chambers nor the clerk will accept faxed copies of papers that must otherwise be filed in original form with the Office of the Clerk (such as objections, petitions, proofs of service, motions, opposition to motions, replies, proposed Orders, and documents to be "So Ordered"). All faxes must be faxed simultaneously to all other parties and the original document must be sent to the Court via regular mail. Counsel are not permitted, without prior approval, to send facsimile transmissions to Chambers that exceed five (5) pages in length.

D. Ex Parte Communications. Ex parte communications are prohibited except where an Order to Show Cause is submitted for signature, or, with the prior consent of all parties during settlement negotiations at the Courthouse.

E. Court Papers. All submissions bearing the caption of the matter must be signed by counsel as required by *Section 130–1.1a* of the Rules of the Chief Administrator. In any instance where a 'service list' is required on a legal document, the service list must set forth not only the name, address and phone number of the submitting party or attorney but must also identify the party or person represented by that attorney and the person or party represented by the other persons named in that service list. All filings are to be made at the Supreme Court Civil window, except for opposition and reply papers on motions which are to be directed to chambers.

Rule II. Court Conferences and Calendar Calls

A. General Rules. Appearances at the calendar call are required by attorneys in all matters. All calendar calls are conducted in court before Judge Bartlett Monday through Friday, promptly at 9:30 a.m. Detailed settlement discussions in any matter may be conducted in Chambers when permitted by law, appropriate, advisable and permitted by the Court. **Counsel must be fully familiar with the matter(s) on which they appear and must be authorized to enter into both substantive and procedural agreements on behalf of their clients.** Counsel must be on time for all scheduled appearances and must bring sufficient material to allow meaningful discussion of unresolved issues to each Court appearance. Attorneys appearing "of counsel" to an attorney of record, and parties appearing pro se, are held to the same requirements. Pursuant to § 130–2.1 of the Rules of the Chief Administrator of the Courts, the Court may impose financial sanctions and award costs and reasonable attorney's fees against any attorney who, without good cause, fails to appear at a time and place scheduled for an appearance in any action or proceeding. Pursuant to § 202.27 of the Uniform Civil Rules for the Supreme Court, upon the default of any party in appearing at a scheduled call of a calendar or at any scheduled conference, the Court may grant judgment by default against the non-appearing party.

B. Preliminary Conferences. Appearances at the Preliminary Conference are mandatory. Counsel are expected to have propounded preliminary discovery demands and to have responded to outstanding discovery requests and demands for bills of particulars prior to attending the conference. Parties will be expected to abide by all provisions of the preliminary conference order issued and the failure to do so may result in sanctions against the recalcitrant party. Preliminary Conferences shall be scheduled and then conducted: (1) after a Request For Judicial Intervention ("RJI") is filed with the Office of the Clerk in accordance with *Uniform Rule 202.12(a)*, or, (2) upon a specific directive by the Court. Preliminary Conferences will ordinarily result in a scheduling order which will address all aspects of anticipated pretrial discovery, and which will set forth a date on which a Compliance Conference will later be conducted, or, the dates by which a Note of Issue is to be filed, and or, the date by which an order framing issues is to be filed. Discovery may be expedited in third party actions, joint actions and consolidated actions to avoid undue delay. All counsel and pro se litigants are expected to adhere to the Court's discovery schedule and deadlines, and non-compliance shall be excused only if explained by extenuating circumstances.

C. Compliance Conferences in Civil Matters. The purpose of the Compliance Conference is for counsel and pro se litigants to report to the Court that pre-trial discovery has been completed, to enable the Court to direct a date on which a Note of Issue or order framing issues shall be filed, and to schedule dates for mediation, a pre-trial conference, and trial. Parties are not permitted to file a Note of Issue in any action unless permission to do so is granted by the Court at the Compliance Conference. Motions to strike Notes of Issue are discouraged as matters of outstanding discovery, if any, shall be raised, discussed and resolved at the Compliance Conference. The Court may issue a further discovery schedule at the Compliance Conference if circumstances or the interests of justice require. Any such additional discovery is likely to be based on an expedited schedule. The Court may, where appropriate, impose appropriate sanctions against any party or counsel responsible for a non-excusable failure to complete pretrial discovery by the date of the Compliance Conference. Counsel must be prepared to discuss meaningful settlement at the compliance/settlement conference. Therefore, any counsel in attendance must have full authority to settle the matter and resolve any discovery disputes at that time, including per diem or covering counsel. Counsel's failure to be present at the time of a conference or to be prepared to resolve any matters raised at said conference may be subject to sanctions by the Court.

D. Pre-trial Conferences. Failure to appear at a Trial Readiness Conference may result in sanctions, including striking the pleadings. A formal motion for relief from the sanctions for such default will be required. A note of issue must be filed within twenty (20) days of the Trial Readiness Conference. Sanctions, including the striking of pleadings, may be imposed for failure to do so. The Court's intent is to promote and encourage well considered settlements, where they are agreeable to and in the best interests of the parties, prior to trial or the seating of a jury panel. In furtherance of this objective (a) The Court will conduct a Pre-trial Conference with all counsel and pro se litigants on a date approximately thirty (30) days prior to the trial, fact finding or hearing date. Pre-trial Conference and trial dates that have been scheduled during a Pre-trial Conference should be viewed by parties and counsel as firm dates, (b) Counsel attending Pre-trial Conferences shall be fully familiar with the facts and issues of the matter and shall be authorized to discuss and to enter into binding settlements, agreements and stipulations with respect to: (1) the factual, legal and evidentiary issues presented by the litigation, (2) settlement demands and offers, (3) unique or unusual issues likely to present themselves at trial, (4) witness scheduling, as well trial attorneys' vacation schedule, (5) likely duration of the trial and requests for adjournments of the trial date, and (6) applications for relief from part or all of the Trial Notebook requirements set forth in Section VI D(8) hereof, (c) The actual parties in any litigation, or in actions involving insurance carriers, an authorized claims representative, must be available for the Pre-trial Conference either in person or, by telephone for the purpose of direct contact with the attorneys engaged in settlement discussions, (d) The Court will make itself available to be of assistance to the parties in settling litigated matters prior to trial. In the event a Pre-trial Conference does not result in a settlement of an action or proceeding, the Court will favorably entertain any request by the parties, on consent, for an additional Pre-trial Conference prior to the date of trial, but any such additional conference will not delay the trial schedule. The Court will not permit settlement discussions to delay the proceedings once the jury panel is seated for selection.

E. Adjournments. As a matter of general practice requests for adjournments of conferences, fact findings, hearings and trials are discouraged. Applications for such adjournments must be made in writing actually received by the Court (by letter or facsimile) at least twenty-four (24) hours in advance of the last scheduled conference, and must address: (1) good cause why an adjournment is sought, (2) whether the adverse party (parties) consent or object to the application, and (3) may, at the option of the sender, suggest an approximate time period or an exact date for which the adjournment is sought. All such communications must be copied to all counsel and *pro se* litigants in accordance with Section I above. All requests for adjournments of a trial, fact finding or hearing submitted after the scheduling of the trial, fact finding or hearing or the pre-trial conference, will not be entertained except upon extra-ordinary good cause shown.

F. Non–Appearance at Scheduled Conferences. The failure of any attorney or pro se litigant to appear for a scheduled conference may be treated as a default and may, when appropriate, result in the dismissal of a Complaint or Petition, the striking of an Answer or objections, or by other appropriate remedy authorized by *Uniform Rule 202.27*.

G. Substitution/withdrawal. (i) In any matter in court all Substitutions of Counsel must be in writing, signed by the client, the incoming and the outgoing attorney, and, filed with the Court and served on all other parties in accordance with the CPLR before the outgoing attorney is relieved and discharged from the matter. (ii) In any matter in court where an attorney wants to be relieved and discharged, or, where a client wants to discharge an attorney, and where there is no incoming attorney, a motion for that relief must be made by Order to Show Cause on notice to the client and all other parties. In such event the moving attorney will remain the attorney of record until the court decides the motion and relieves and discharges the moving attorney.

Rule III. Discovery and Inspection

A. General Rules. 1) Every attorney shall exert a continuing effort to work cooperatively and courteously with all adverse attorneys towards the goal of completing all discovery expeditiously, efficiently and in the spirit of avoiding unnecessary motion practice and court intervention. See uniform Rule 202.7. Any discovery related motions will automatically be converted to a conference at which time the matter will be resolved. Counsel are advised that the failure to cooperate in discovery may subject them to sanctions. 2) Once a discovery schedule has been set by the court the dates and deadlines set forth therein shall be adhered to.

Rule IV.   Motions and Orders to Show Cause

A. Prerequisite. Prior to the filing of any motion (including motions regarding discovery and disclosure and except motions to be relieved and discharged as an attorney), the potential movant must notify the court in writing (one page maximum length), with a copy to all parties, setting forth the relief sought and the basis for the requested relief. The Court will then schedule a conference the purpose of which will be to hear and try to resolve the issues to be addressed in the motion without the necessity of a written application. Where this conference does not resolve the dispute the party seeking the relief may proceed with the motion.

B.   General Rules. All motions and oppositions to motions must be accompanied by a stamped, self-addressed envelope. No courtesy copies of motions are to be submitted. All motions must reflect the name of the Court to which the motion is addressed and the index, file or docket number. The Court will entertain motions brought by Notice of Motion on a submission basis, at 9:30 a.m. on any day the Court is in session, and appearances are not required except where notified by the Court. All Orders to Show Cause, REQUIRE A PERSONAL APPEARANCE BY THE PARTIES on the return date. All Orders to Show Cause shall be submitted with original signatures affixed to the supporting affidavits and affirmations, shall include one proposed Order affixed to the supporting papers, and shall include a separate duplicate proposed Order. The return date for an Order to Show Cause will be determined by the Court when the papers are submitted for consideration. There shall be no oral argument heard on any noticed motion unless otherwise directed by the Court. All counsel and pro se litigants will be given reasonable notice of the date for such oral argument. Oral argument may be requested by noting "Oral Argument Requested" immediately over the index number on the Notice of motion. If the Court, in its discretion, requires such an argument, the movant's attorney will be so advised and will be required to notify all parties. The failure of a party to appear for oral argument when directed to will result in the waiver of that party's opportunity to offer oral argument in connection with the motion. All Orders to Show Cause shall include a provision that the method of service selected by the Court will be sufficient only if proof of such service is filed with the Court prior to the return date of the Order to Show Cause. Strict compliance by counsel with the CPLR will be required as to all motions. Appropriate timeframes for proper notice and reply must be adhered to by all parties or else the non-compliant party's papers will not be considered.

C. Filing of Papers Applicable To All Motions. Except with the express permission of the Court, all motion papers and Orders to Show Cause, including Notices of Motion, proposed Orders, affidavits or affirmations in support, affidavits or affirmations of good faith and memoranda of law, must contain both the telephone and facsimile numbers of counsel and be typewritten, doubled-spaced, securely bound, entirely legible, and all exhibits labeled with exhibit tabs. The service list on all motions must also include the identity of the party represented by each attorney identified in that service list. The Court may refuse to accept any such paper that does not conform to the foregoing. Motion papers and all related correspondence must reflect the Index Number assigned to the matter. The filing of a motion does not relieve any party from attending any previously scheduled conference or court appearance, regardless of the nature of the relief sought in the motion. All filings are to be made at the Supreme Court Civil window, except for opposition and reply papers on motions which are to be directed to chambers.

D. Supporting Documents. All documents required to decide the application must be included in the moving papers. It is not sufficient that those documents are on file with the Court Clerk. All motions to renew or reargue must contain as exhibits a complete copy of all papers filed on the motion sought to be reargued as well as a complete copy of any decision and order of the Court pertaining to same. Failure to do so will result in a denial of the application.

E. Adjournments. Upon consent of all counsel and pro se litigants, the Court will ordinarily grant no more than two (2) adjournments of a motion or Order to Show Cause, and will be done so only with the consent of the Court. The party seeking the adjournment must obtain the consent of adversary parties and notify the appropriate Clerk of the requested adjournment date at least twenty-four (24) hours before the return date. The Court will then assign a new date for the motion or Order to Show Cause. In assigning an adjourned date, the Court will give due consideration to any specific date agreed upon by all parties. Motion adjournments should be confirmed to the Court and all adversary parties in writing, in accordance with Section I of these Individual Rules. All non-consented requests for adjournments require Court approval, obtained at least twenty-four (24) hours before the return date. No adjournment request will be entertained by the Court unless the party seeking the adjournment has first attempted to obtain consent from all other parties in the action. Parties seeking a non-consented to adjournment must provide good cause as to why the adjournment should be granted, in accordance with the communication requirements set forth in Section I of these Individual Rules. The application for a non-consented adjournment must be made in person on the return date of the motion. The requesting party must advise al other parties that the application will be made and must do so in writing with a copy of said letter to be provided to the Court on the return date. Any party wishing to be head in opposition to the adjournment must appear at that time.

F. Reply Papers. Reply papers shall not set forth new factual claims, legal arguments or requests for relief that were not within the scope of the papers that initiated the motion.

G. Sur–Reply Papers. The *CPLR* does not recognize the existence of Sur–Reply papers, however denominated, and accordingly, the Court will not consider any post-Reply papers or materials absent a party receiving express permission from the Court in advance. Post–Reply materials received in violation of this rule will be returned, unread, to the Office of the County Clerk for filing. Opposing counsel who receives a copy of post–Reply materials submitted in violation of this rule should not respond in kind. If new issues are raised in the reply, or if there has been a change in the law while the motion is pending, counsel are to notify chambers, in writing, of the request to submit additional affidavits or memoranda. Other papers including letters which are sent after the submission of the motion (other than as previously indicated), will not be considered.

H. Summary Judgment. Summary Judgment motions must be made no later than sixty (60) days from the date of the filing of the Note of Issue or the motion will not be entertained.

I. Motions for temporary injunctive relief, including stays and temporary restraining orders: If a party's motion papers establish, *prima facie*, that "... immediate and irreparable injury, loss or damage will result" unless the other party is restrained before the hearing and determination of a motion for a preliminary junction, the matter will then be scheduled in accordance with 22 NYCRR 202.7(f) unless the moving party demonstrates there will be significant prejudice by the giving of notice.

COUNSEL SHALL IMMEDIATELY NOTIFY THE COURT WHEN IT BECOMES UNNECESSARY TO DECIDE A MOTION. FAILURE TO DO SO MAY RESULT IN SANCTIONS.

Rule V. Decisions and Orders

In certain instances, the Court may render a Decision and issue an Order orally from the Bench. In such instances a transcript of the Decision and Order, the cost of which shall be born equally by the parties, shall be purchased by the plaintiff or petitioner and then served on all other parties and submitted to the

court so the same can be executed by the Court and filed with the Office of the Orange County Clerk. Indigent parties may be excused from having to pay their share for the cost of the transcripts of such decisions and orders whereupon the other parties will pay their proportionate share of the total cost of the transcript.

Rule VI. Trials and Hearings

A. Trial Dates. Scheduled trial and hearing dates shall be adhered to except for the most extraordinary good cause shown and accordingly it is expected that clients, fact witnesses, physicians, experts and others will be timely advised of scheduled dates to avoid last minute unavailability. The parties and their attorneys are encouraged to videotape the trial testimony of witnesses who are likely to be unavailable at trial in accordance with the applicable statutes and uniform rules, at the producing party's expense. All such videotaping should be conducted between the date of the Pre-trial Conference and the date of the trial. In scheduling and conducting trials, the Court shall endeavor to accommodate bona fide special preferences to the extent recognized by *CPLR Rule 3403* and *Uniform Rules 202.24* and *202.25*.

B. Subpoenas. When subpoenas are directed to documents of libraries, hospitals, and municipal corporations and their departments and bureaus, the subpoena must be "So Ordered" by the Court pursuant to *CPLR Section 2306* and *2307*, and, the subpoena duces tecum must be served on the intended recipient at least three days before the time fixed for the production of the documents, unless such notice is waived by the Court due to emergency circumstances as permitted by *CPLR Section 2307*. Motions for "So Ordered" subpoenas should be filed with the County Clerk. No "So Ordered" subpoena seeking documents from municipalities shall be issued without the party's compliance with the CPLR's motion practice requirements. The Court's issuance of a "So Ordered" subpoena does not constitute a ruling as to the admissibility of the subpoenaed materials. All subpoena for materials protected by HIPPA shall refer to and annex a duly executed HIPPA compliant authorization.

C. Interpreters. In the event that any party requires the services of a translator for foreign languages or services for the hearing impaired during a trial or hearing, the party shall notify the Court, and the Clerk of the Court in which the matter is pending, of the need for same no later than at the Pretrial Conference so that timely and appropriate arrangements can be made.

D. Pre–Trial Requirements

a. *Trial Notebook.* No later than five (5) business days prior to the scheduled trial date, counsel shall each provide to the other (one copy) and submit to the Court (two copies) a trial notebook which shall consist of:

1) marked pleadings in accordance with CPLR 4012;

2) statement of the relevant facts stating separately those that are not in dispute and those that are;

3) pre-trial memorandum of addressing any known or anticipated disputed legal issues that must be determined by the court;

4) a list of all potential witnesses for each party;

5) a list of all exhibits to be offered into evidence at trial by each party with a brief description of each exhibit;

6) preliminary requests to charge. The charges will be drawn from the Pattern Jury Instructions (PJI). A complete list of requested charges is to be submitted simultaneously with service on all adversaries. Unless counsel seek a deviation from the pattern charge, or additions to the pattern charge, only the PJI numbers need be submitted. Where deviations or additions are requested, the full text of such requests must be submitted in writing together with any supporting authority. A charge conference will be held between the Court and the parties in order to finalize any of the proposed jury charges. Said conference will be held at an appropriate time during the course of the trial.

7) In jury trials a proposed joint verdict sheet is to be typed in final form for presentation to the jury. Such proposals shall also be submitted on a computer disc in a format convertible to Word Perfect 8.0. If agreement cannot be reached on a joint submission, then each side shall present a proposed verdict sheet, along with a written explanation as to why agreement on the verdict sheet was not reached.

8) The court may, in its discretion and for good cause shown, relieve counsel from all or part of the trial notebook requirements upon a showing that the issues to be tried are sufficiently narrow that the trial notebook is not necessary or that the interest of justice otherwise justifies such relief. Such a request will be entertained only at the pre-trial conference.

b. *Evidentiary Objections.* Not later than one business day prior to the scheduled trial date each counsel shall provide to the other and submit to the court a statement setting forth the factual basis and authority for any objection to the introduction into evidence of the exhibits identified in the list provided by opposing counsel. The failure to submit such a statement of objections on a timely basis may be deemed to be consent to the admission of all or one of the exhibits included in the trial notebook submitted by the opposing party.

c. *Witnesses.* A witness not identified in the witness list provided to opposing counsel either in discovery or in the trial notebook, other than an impeach-ment or rebuttal witness, may not be permitted to testify unless an adequate explanation is provided for the failure to identify such witness prior to trial. Parties, fact witnesses and expert witnesses should be advised of the scheduled dates at the time the dates are set. Absent unanticipated, exigent circumstances, last minute claims of unavailability will not be accommodated where the trial dates have been previously set. All witnesses should be on one-hour phone call notice so that their waiting time in court is minimized. Professional witnesses, such as doctors, nurses and social workers, and witnesses who are public employees, such as teachers, counselors and police officers, will be permitted to testify out of order to accommodate their employment schedules. School teachers should be scheduled after 3:00 p.m. so that it is not necessary for their employers to provide substitutes.

d. *Exhibits.* Any exhibit not identified in the exhibit list provided to opposing counsel, other than an exhibit offered for the purpose of impeachment or rebuttal, may not be admitted into evidence unless an adequate explanation is provided for the failure to identify such exhibit prior to trial. Exhibits marked into evidence at trial will not be returned until the final conclusion of the matter. Exhibits marked for identification will be retained by the offering attorney during trial, unless taken into evidence.

E. Settlement. The court is available for a settlement conference at any time prior to the scheduled trial date. If the matter is not settled prior to the scheduled trial date, the trial will commence as scheduled. Settlement negotiations may not be entertained by the court on the scheduled trial date prior to commencement of the trial. If the matter is settled outside the presence of the court, counsel shall advise the part clerk immediately. Proceedings requiring the presence of the jury will not be delayed by settlement discussions once the jury panel has been drawn by the jury commissioner.

F. Motions *in limine*. All motions *in limine* must be delivered to the Part Clerk or and served upon adversary counsel(s) not later than seven (7) business days prior to the scheduled date of the trial or hearing, except as to issues that cannot be reasonable anticipated prior to trial. Unless otherwise directed by the Court, motions *in limine* and opposition papers to such motions shall not exceed ten (10) pages in length.

G. Identification of Trial Counsel. Whenever a matter is to be tried by an attorney other than the attorney of record, trial counsel shall be identified in a writing, filed with the Court on notice to all parties, no later than fifteen (15) days from the date of the Pre-trial Conference. See *Uniform Rule 202.31.* The court may waive this rule only in instances where the attorney of record is unexpectedly engaged in an unrelated trial and the late retention of trial counsel permits the trial before the Court to proceed without adjournment.

H.   Pre–Voir Dire Conference. Immediately prior to jury selection the Court will conduct a conference [See *Uniform Rule 202.33(b)*] in order to set time limits on jury selection, to hear and determine arguments concerning the number of peremptory challenges, to discuss trial stipulations, to hear and determine last minute arguments on motions *in limine*, to discuss scheduling and to address any other appropriate trial-related issue.

J.   Jury Selection. Juries shall be selected by the parties outside the presence of the Court in accordance with "Whites Rules" found in *Appendix "E"* of the *Uniform Rules for the New York Trial Courts*. The Court will impose time limits for jury selection as authorized by *Uniform Rule 202.33(d)*. Such time limits will vary based upon the nature and complexity of the particular matter. The Court will be available to resolve disputes that arise during jury selection, including but not limited to disputes involving challenges for cause as contemplated by *CPLR Section 4108*. Peremptory challenges will ordinarily be pooled between multiple plaintiffs on the one hand and between multiple defendants on the other, and generally, each side shall be entitled to three (3) peremptory challenges for regular jurors per panel and one (1) peremptory challenge for each alternate juror per panel. However, pursuant to *CPLR Section 4109*, the number of peremptory challenges may be adjusted by the court in certain matters in the discretion of the court and in the interests of justice. The jury selec-

tion process will not be delayed by settlement negotiations once the jury panel is seated.

K.   Bifurcation. Trials of personal injury actions involving issues of both liability and damages shall be bifurcated in accordance with *Uniform Rule 202.42* and all subdivisions thereof. Trials on damages will commence immediately upon completion of the trials on liability.

L.   Non-jury Trials. Unless the Court directs otherwise, the parties may obtain and provide to the Court, at the party's expense, on or before the date set by the Court at the conclusion of the trial, a copy of the trial transcript and each party may submit a post-trial brief with respect to the issues raised at the trial, setting forth specific references to the relevant portions of the transcript and the documents in evidence and citing the applicable law. Along with the submission of the post-trial briefs, counsel may also present the Court with proposed findings of fact and a proposed disposition.

Rule VII.   Settled and Discontinued Cases

Counsel shall immediately notify the Court of a settled or discontinued matter. Following the initial notification counsel shall file a fully executed duplicate original stipulation of discontinuance with the County Clerk and the Part Clerk.

April, 2010

JUSTICE LAWRENCE H. ECKER

Rule I.   Communications with the Court

A.   Correspondence: Correspondence to the Court shall, without exception, be copied to all adversary counsel and self-represented parties. Correspondence between counsel and/or self-represented parties shall not be copied to the Court unless there is some specific judicial purpose to be served by transmitting copies to the Court.

B.   Telephone Calls: Telephone calls to the Court staff are permitted only in necessary or emergency situations requiring immediate attention that cannot otherwise be attained by correspondence. Counsel should contact the Court's Principal Court Attorney or Assistant Law Clerk for advice concerning any issues or problems not addressed herein, or when the Court's intervention may be helpful in facilitating settlement of the matter.

C.   Fax transmissions: The Court does not accept motion papers or other papers of any kind by fax transmission unless otherwise requested or approved by the Court in advance in a particular case. Copies of letters requesting or confirming an adjournment of a motion or conference may be sent to the Court by

fax. However, the original of all correspondence must be mailed to the Part Clerk.

Rule II.   Calendar Call & Conferences

A.   General Rules: The Court shall call its calendar in Courtroom 2 at 9:30 a.m. or as soon thereafter as possible. Counsel and self-represented parties are expected to appear for all court appearances on time and must be fully familiar with the action on which they appear. Counsel must be authorized to discuss all factual and legal issues presented by the litigation, and settlement demands or offers. Represented parties need not appear for conferences unless directed to do so by the Court. However, counsel must appear with their clients for all conferences in matrimonial actions, unless such appearances are dispensed with by the Court on prior request on notice to the adversary and any attorneys for children.

B.   Preliminary Conference: The Court will schedule a Preliminary Conference within 45 days after a Request for Judicial Intervention (RJI) has been filed on a matter. The Part Clerk will forward to the party filing the RJI a letter setting forth the date on which the Preliminary Conference will be conducted, and directing that the recipient advise all other parties of the Preliminary Conference date.

At the Preliminary Conference, the Court will issue a Preliminary Conference Stipulation and Order (PCSO) which shall include the date by which all disclosure must be completed, and the dates for a Compliance Conference and a Trial Readiness Conference. A form stipulation and order shall be provided to the parties which shall establish a timetable for discovery within parameters set forth by the Court after determination whether a matter should be designated a "standard" or complex" case. All counsel and pro se litigants are expected to take most seriously the Court's discovery schedule and deadlines, and non-compliance shall only be excused if explained by extenuating circumstances. No modifications are permitted except by order of the Court.

Counsel are generally referred to Uniform Rule 202.12(c) for the conduct of the Preliminary Conference and the matters to be considered. Counsel in medical, dental and podiatric malpractice actions are referred to Uniform Rule 202.56(b) and counsel in matrimonial actions are referred to Uniform Rule 202.16 and D.R.L. § 236(B)(4) for other specific requirements in such cases.

C. Compliance Conference: The Court shall conduct a Compliance Conference approximately two weeks after the date by which disclosure was to be completed as directed in the PCSO. At the Compliance Conference, the Court will ensure that discovery is proceeding as scheduled, and be informed regarding settlement discussions.

D. Trial Readiness Conference: The Court shall conduct a Trial Readiness Conference approximately 30 days after the Compliance Conference. Counsel attending a Trial Readiness Conference must be fully familiar with the action and authorized to discuss all factual and legal issues presented by the litigation, settlement demands or offers, witness scheduling, and trial procedure—including for example, whether any party or witness will require a translator or accommodation for a physical challenge. Counsel must also be authorized to enter into settlements on terms agreeable to the parties and to the Court. The Court will explore limitation of issues for trial.

If the matter is ready for trial and a note of issue has not been filed, the Court shall direct a note of issue be filed within 20 days.

E. Pre–Selection Conference: A Pre–Selection Conference with all counsel and self-represented parties shall be conducted on the Monday of the week preceding the week during which the trial date is scheduled. On or before the Pre–Selection Conference, counsel and self-represented parties shall provide the Court and opposing counsel or self-represented party with a Trial Notebook, consisting of a binder containing the following:

(1) Marked pleadings in accordance with C.P.L.R. Rule 4012, including copies of any exhibits incorporated by reference in the pleadings.

(2) A list of probable trial witnesses;

(3) Marked copies of all documentary or photographic evidence, including but not limited to accident reports, medical records, and lost income records which the party expects to offer at trial, but excluding previously exchanged transcripts of examinations before trial;

(4) Memoranda of law concerning any procedural, evidentiary, or other legal issue which the Court may need to determine;

(5) *Requests to charge.* A complete list of requested charges, drawn from the Pattern Jury Instructions (PJI), must be submitted; a list of the PJI numbers of all charges requested is sufficient. However, if deviations from or additions to the PJI are requested, the full text of such requests must be submitted, together with any supporting legal precedents. In addition, such proposals shall be submitted in a format convertible to Word Perfect and submitted to the Court's principal court attorney at dsteinberg@courts.state.ny.us.

(6) A proposed verdict sheet, jointly prepared by all parties, typewritten and in final form for presentation to the jury. If agreement cannot be reached prior to the Pre–Selection Conference, each party shall present a proposed verdict sheet which shall be served upon all the parties. In addition, the proposed verdict sheet(s) shall be submitted in a format convertible to Word Perfect and emailed to the Court's Principal Court Attorney at dsteinberg@courts.state.ny.us.

Failure to submit a complete Trial Notebook on or before the Pre–Selection Conference date, or to establish a reasonable excuse for such failure, may constitute grounds for a motion to preclude evidence and/or to strike pleadings.

F. Adjournment of Conferences: An application to adjourn a conference must be made in writing or by fax actually received by the Court at least twenty-four (24) hours in advance of the scheduled conference, and must set forth: 1) good cause why an adjournment is sought, 2) whether the adversary party(ies) consent(s) or object(s) to the application, and 3) may, at the option of the sender, suggest an approximate time period or an exact date for which the adjournment is sought. All such communications must be copied to all counsel and self-represented parties.

(1) *On Consent*—After telephone approval by the Part Clerk, a conference may be adjourned on consent.

(2) *Opposed*—If your adversary (ies) will not consent to an adjournment, you should fax a short letter request to the Court with a copy to all interested parties. The opposing counsel or self-represented party shall succinctly provide their reasons for object-

ing in a reply fax. No further communication will be permitted.

Rule III. Motion Practice

A. General Rules: 1. Written applications by Notice of Motion may be made returnable at 9:30 a.m. on any Monday the Court is in session. During weeks in which Monday is a court holiday, written motions may be made returnable on Tuesday.

2. The return date for an Order to Show Cause shall be determined by the Court at the time papers are submitted for consideration and executed.

3. Orders to Show Cause must include the submitting attorney's fax number.

4. There shall be no oral argument heard on any motions or Orders to Show Cause unless directed by the Court.

5. Except by permission of the Court otherwise, all motion papers and Orders to Show Cause must be typewritten, double-spaced, securely bound and entirely legible. All exhibits must be legible and labeled with external tab markings.

6. Use official citations.

7. Deposition transcripts included as exhibits must be single, front-faced pages only.

8. Courtesy copies are not to be submitted, except for motions in limine.

B. Orders to Show Cause—Temporary Restraining Orders: Unless there are extremely unusual circumstances in which significant prejudice will ensue as set forth in a supporting affidavit, opposing counsel shall be advised by telephone or fax that an Order to Show Cause containing a Temporary Restraining Order is being presented to the Court. If there has been no appearance by opposing counsel, the adverse party shall be provided with notice as provided by Uniform Rule 202.7(f).

C. Summary Judgment Motions: All summary judgment motions must be made within sixty (60) days of filing of the Note of Issue.

D. Adjournment of Motion:

(1) *On consent*—Upon consent of all counsel and self-represented parties, the Court may grant an adjournment of a motion or Order to Show Cause; however, no more than three (3) adjournments of any single motion or cross-motion will be permitted. The party seeking the adjournment must obtain the consent of adversary parties and notify the Court's Principal Court Attorney of the requested adjourned date at least twenty four (24) hours before the return date.

(2) *Opposed*—If your adversary will not consent to an adjournment, you should fax a short letter request to the Court with a copy to all counsel or self-represented parties. The opposing counsel or self-represented party shall succinctly provide their rea-

sons for objecting in a reply fax. No further communication will be permitted.

(3) Motion adjournments should be confirmed in writing to the Court and all adversary parties.

E. Discovery related Motions:. In lieu of discovery motion practice, it is the policy of the Court to make itself and its staff available to resolve any disputes related to pretrial discovery. Therefore, unless authorized by the Court, no discovery motion shall be made by any party. Instead, if a dispute arises which relates to pretrial discovery, counsel for the aggrieved party or the aggrieved self-represented party shall immediately seek a telephone conference with the Court's Principal Court Attorney. If the dispute cannot be resolved with his assistance, a conference shall be promptly scheduled.

F. Motions in limine: Written motions for the Court's consideration in limine in any matter must be made returnable on no less than seven (7) days notice to adversary counsel and/or self-represented parties, and made returnable on the Monday of the week prior to the week the trial date is scheduled.

Rule IV. Decisions and Orders

(1) All orders or judgments, including counter-orders and judgments, submitted for signature on notice will be returned unsigned unless an Affidavit of Service and Notice of Settlement for a date designated in accordance with Uniform Rule 202.48 have been included.

(2) Do not fax proposed orders or judgments.

(3) The parties are responsible to obtain copies of all written Orders and Decisions. Courtesy copies will be furnished only when Chambers are provided with a stamped, self-addressed envelope.

Rule V. Matrimonial Actions

1. Counsel shall be familiar with and comply with the provisions of Uniform Rule 202.16. Prior to the preliminary conference, the parties shall file and exchange those documents set forth in Uniform Rule 202.16 (f)(1), including nets worth statements, paycheck stubs, W-2 statements, tax returns and statements of accounts.

2. Counsel should inform their clients of the automatic orders created by DRL Section 236 Part B (2)(b) as soon as the attorney-client relationship is formed.

3. Parties shall appear at all matrimonial conferences unless otherwise directed by the Court.

4. **Matrimonial Pendente Lite Motions:** There shall be appearances by both parties and counsel on the return date of all pendente lite motions. The Court shall conduct either a preliminary conference or conference on the motion, as appropriate. In the event a Bench Decision is issued on the motion, a copy of the transcript will be ordered by the Court, the cost

of which shall be shared by the parties unless otherwise ordered.

5. In matrimonial actions, updated net worth statements (with the latest available supporting documents, such as income tax returns, W–2's, brokerage statements, and retirement plan statements), statements of proposed disposition as required by Uniform Rule 202.16(h), and any forensic reports, appraisals and evaluations shall be provided in the Trial Notebook filed no later than ten (10) days prior to trial.

Rule VI. Settled and Discontinued Cases

Counsel shall immediately notify the Court of a case disposition. Following the initial notification, counsel shall submit a copy of the stipulation of discontinuance to chambers so that the matter may be marked off the calendar.

Rule VII. Summary Jury Trial

A summary jury trial ("SJT") is a one-day or two-day proceeding that combines the flexibility and cost-effectiveness of arbitration with the structure of a conventional trial. The rules of evidence are relaxed but not eliminated. The trial is conducted in accordance with a comprehensive Pre–Trial Order in which the jury decides issues of fact and renders a binding verdict just as a jury would in a traditional trial.

Upon request, the Court will provide the Rules Governing Summary Jury Trials and a Proposed Waiver.

JUSTICE JOHN K. McGUIRK

Rule I. General Rules

Appearances

Counsel who appear, whether of counsel or otherwise, must be familiar with the case and have authority to enter agreements for their clients. Parties whose counsel are unfamiliar with the case or without authority may be considered in default and subject to appropriate sanctions.

Settlements and Discontinuances

Counsel shall submit a stipulation or letter to the court if an action is settled or discontinued.

Fax

The court does not accept papers or letters by fax without prior permission from chambers.

Rule II. Motions

Return Date

Motions may be made returnable at 9:00 a.m. on any day the court is in session. The court will set the return date on orders to show cause.

Adjournments

The court will usually grant the adjournment of a motion's return date if the parties consent. An attorney seeking an adjournment must first seek the consent of opposing counsel.

If consent is obtained, the attorney must notify the part clerk of the proposed adjourned date at least 48 hours before the return date. The court will then assign an adjourned date giving consideration to the date chosen by the parties.

If consent is not obtained, the attorney may seek court approval directing the request to the part clerk at least 48 hours before the return date.

Appearances

No appearances are required on motions and no oral argument will be heard unless directed by the court. This rule does not apply to motions for *pendente lite* relief in matrimonial actions.

Papers

Papers shall be typewritten and exhibits labeled and marked with tabs. Exhibits must be legible.

All motion papers submitted in opposition or in reply, or their transmittal letter, shall state the return date of the motion.

Do not submit courtesy copies.

Reply papers shall not contain new factual assertions or legal arguments unless they directly respond to arguments made in the opposition papers. Such assertions will not be considered by the court in rendering its decision.

The court will not consider sur-reply papers or papers submitted after the return date without the permission of the court. Such papers will be filed with the County Clerk unread.

Discovery Motions

A motion shall be the last resort in resolving discovery disputes.

Counsel must first try to resolve a discovery dispute without court intervention. If counsel are unsuccessful, then they shall contact the court's law clerk and try to resolve the issue through a conference call or other mutually acceptable means. If the issue remains unresolved a court conference will be scheduled. At the conclusion of the conference the court will issue an order on the record and direct one party to submit a proposed written order. A copy of the transcript, the cost of which shall be paid as directed by the court, shall be attached to the proposed order. The court may order sanctions authorized by CPLR 3126 for a wilful failure to disclose information which ought to have been disclosed.

If, notwithstanding this rule, a party makes a written discovery motion, the court may deem it a request for a conference and schedule a conference.

Summary Judgment or Dismissal Motions

Copies of the pleadings shall be attached to a motion seeking summary judgment or dismissal of the complaint. Failure to comply will result in denial of the motion unless the pleadings are attached to other papers submitted with the motion.

Summary Judgment motions must be filed and served no later than 60 days after the filing of the note of issue

Motions to Renew or Reargue

A party moving to renew or reargue must attach copies of the papers submitted in connection with the underlying motion to the motion to renew or reargue. Failure to comply will result in denial of the motion.

Requests for Temporary Restraining Orders

Copies of the summons and complaint shall be attached to any motion seeking a temporary restraining order.

Rule III.   Conferences

Preliminary Conferences

A discovery order shall be issued either in writing or on the record at the conclusion of a preliminary conference.

A compliance conference shall be scheduled at the conclusion of the preliminary conference.

Compliance Conference

The court will review the status of discovery at the compliance conference.

The court may issue a further order compelling discovery, or it may issue an order imposing sanctions pursuant to CPLR 3126 for a failure to obey a prior discovery order or for a willful failure to disclose information which ought to have been disclosed.

At the conclusion of the compliance conference the court will schedule a further compliance conference or a trial readiness conference.

Trial Readiness Conference

At the trial readiness conference the court will review whether the matter is ready for trial. If a note of issue has been filed then the court will schedule a trial date and pretrial conference which will be approximately one month before the trial date. If the matter is ready for trial and a note of issue has not been filed the court will direct a note of issue be filed within twenty (20) days and schedule a further trial readiness conference.

Pretrial Conference

At the pretrial conference all counsel must be present prepared to make a good faith demand and a good faith offer. Counsel must have authority to negotiate and settle the matter. A party represented by an attorney without authority to negotiate and settle the matter may be considered in default and the court may issue appropriate orders pursuant to CPLR 3215 and 22 NYCRR 202.27.

Rule IV.   Matrimonial Actions

Counsel shall be familiar with and shall comply with the provisions of 22 NYCRR 202.16. Prior to the preliminary conference the parties shall file and exchange those documents set forth in 22 NYCRR 202.16(f)(1) including net worth statements, paycheck stubs, W–2 statements, tax returns and statements of account.

Parties shall appear at all matrimonial conferences unless otherwise directed by the court.

Each party must file a statement of proposed disposition (22 NYCRR 202.16[h]) no later than 10 days prior to trial.

Counsel and parties are required to appear on the return date of motions seeking *pendente lite* relief.

Rule V.   Trial

Submissions Prior to Trial

Prior to the commencement of trial counsel shall submit:

1.   Marked pleadings

2.   A concise statement of disputed facts and the contention of the parties.

3.   An exhibit list. Exhibits other than those to be used for cross examination shall be pre-marked. The court reporter will mark only those exhibits received into evidence. Counsel shall provide the court reporter with a copy of the exhibit list. Counsel shall indicate which exhibits are admissible by stipulation.

4.   Request to charge. Counsel for each party shall submit a complete list of requests to charge. Unless counsel seeks a deviation from the Pattern Jury Instructions (PJI) counsel shall only submit a list of the numbers of the pattern instructions requested. If counsel requests a charge which differs from the pattern instruction counsel must submit the full text of the requested charge, the authority for the requested charge and a copy of the case(s) on which the requested charge is based.

5.   Verdict Sheet. Counsel shall consult on the preparation of the verdict sheet. If counsel agree on a verdict sheet they shall submit a copy which will be submitted to the jury. If counsel cannot agree then counsel for each party shall submit a proposed verdict sheet.

Motions *in Limine*

Motions *in limine*, except those which could not reasonably be anticipated, shall be delivered to the court and served on opposing counsel at least seven (7) days before trial.

Rule VI. Submission of Orders and Judgments

An order or judgment shall be submitted with an affidavit of service and noticed for settlement on a date which complies with 22 NYCRR 202.48.

JUSTICE ROBERT A. ONOFRY, A.J.S.C.

Rule I. General Rules

Communications with the Court:

Correspondence: All correspondence to the Court shall be copied to all adversaries and must reflect the Index Number of the matter to which it reflects. Correspondence between attorneys and/or *pro se* litigants shall not be copied to the Court unless there is some specific judicial purpose to be served by transmitting copies to the Court.

Faxes: The fax number to be used for all matters (including Chambers) is (845) 291–2543. Neither Chambers nor the clerk will accept faxed copies of papers that must otherwise be filed in original form with the Office of the Clerk (such as objections, petitions, proofs of service, motions, opposition to motions, replies, proposed orders and documents to be "So Ordered"). All faxes must be faxed simultaneously to all other parties and the original document must be sent to the Court via regular mail. Counsel are not permitted, without prior approval, to send facsimile transmissions to Chambers that exceed five (5) pages in length.

Court Conferences and Calendar Call:

Effective AUGUST 1, 2011, this Court (Judge Onofry) shall call its Supreme Court calendar each day at the Orange County Surrogate's Courthouse located at 30 Park Place, Goshen, New York at 9:00 a.m. or as soon thereafter as possible.

Detailed settlement conferences in any matter may be conducted in Chambers when permitted by law, appropriate, advisable and permitted by the Court. Counsel must be fully familiar with the matter(s) on which they appear and must be authorized to enter into both substantive and procedural agreements on behalf of their clients. Counsel must be on time for all scheduled appearances and must bring sufficient material to allow meaningful discussion of unresolved issues to each Court appearance. Attorneys appearing "of counsel" to an attorney of record, and parties appearing *pro se*, are held to the same requirements.

Adjournments: As a matter of general practice requests for adjournments of conferences, fact findings, hearing and trials are discouraged. Applications for such adjournments must be made in writing actually received by the Court (by letter or facsimile) not less than forty-eight (48) hours in advance of the scheduled conference and must address: (1) good cause why an adjournment is sought, (2) whether the adverse party (parties) consent or object to the application, and (3) may, at the option of the sender, suggest an approximate time period or an exact date for which the adjournment is sought. All such communications must be copied to all counsel and *pro se* litigants in accordance with the correspondence rules above. All requests for adjournments of a trial, fact finding or hearing submitted after the scheduling of the trial, fact finding or hearing or the pre-trial conference, will not be entertained except upon good cause shown.

Rule II. Motion Practice

Motion Calendar and Appearances: All motions/proceedings brought on by notice of motion or notice of petition shall be made returnable before the Court on any Thursday the Court is in session at 9:00 a.m. Appearances are not required on motions unless oral argument is requested in writing. Along with filing with the Clerk, a copy of all motions, opposition, cross-moving and reply papers are to be sent to the Judge's chambers at 30 Park Place, Goshen, New York 10924.

Time for Filing and Serving Summary Judgment Motions: Summary judgment motions shall be filed with the Court and served upon all adverse parties no later than one hundred twenty (120) days after the filing of the Note of Issue. If an application to extend the time to make such a motion is granted by the Court, the moving party must so state in its motion papers or risk being held to the one hundred twenty (120) day requirement.

No Stay of Discovery: There shall be no stay of pretrial discovery resulting from the filing of a motion made pursuant to CPLR 3211 or 3212 unless otherwise ordered by the Court.

Discovery Motions: It is the policy of this Court to make itself and its staff available to resolve any disputes related to pretrial discovery. Therefore, no discovery motion shall be made by any party unless authorized by the Court after the discovery dispute has been first conferenced by the Judge's Law Clerk and the Judge and such dispute has not been resolved. Instead, if a pre-trial discovery dispute arises, counsel for the aggrieved party or the aggrieved self-represented party shall immediately notify the Court and a conference will be scheduled.

COUNSEL SHALL IMMEDIATELY NOTIFY THE COURT WHEN IT BECOMES UNNECES-

SARY TO DECIDE A MOTION. FAILURE TO DO SO MAY RESULT IN SANCTIONS.

Submission of Orders and Judgments: An order or judgment shall be submitted with an affidavit of service and noticed for settlement on a date which complies with 22 NYCRR 202.48.

A conformed copy of an order or judgment will be sent back to the submitting party ONLY WHEN IT IS ACCOMPANIED BY A STAMPED, SELF–ADDRESSED ENVELOPE.

Rule III. Trials

Pretrial Settlement Conference: At the pretrial conference all counsel must be present and prepared to make a good faith demand and a good faith offer. Counsel are expected to be vested with the requisite authority to negotiate and settle the matter. All parties and insurance carriers are to either be present or available by telephone. A party represented by an attorney without authority to negotiate and settle the matter may be considered in default and the Court may issue appropriate orders pursuant to CPLR 3215 and 22 NYCRR 202.27.

Jury Charges: In all jury trials, a complete list of requests to charge shall be submitted to the Court immediately preceding the commencement of trial, with copies to be provided to all other counsel and self-represented parties. If a requested charge is drawn from current Pattern Jury Instructions (PJI), the PJI number need only be submitted. Where deviations from, or additions to, the PJI are requested, the full text of such requests must be submitted in writing, together with any supporting legal precedent. In addition, such proposals shall be submitted in a format convertible to Word Perfect and submitted to the Court's Law Clerk at abbrady@courts.state.ny.us.

Verdict Sheet: The parties shall jointly prepare and submit a verdict sheet to the Court. If agreement cannot be reached, each party shall present a proposed verdict sheet which shall be served upon all other parties. The proposed verdict sheet shall be in a final typewritten form which may be given to the jury. In addition, the proposed verdict sheet(s) shall be submitted in a format convertible to Word Perfect and emailed to the Court's Law Clerk at abbrady@courts.state.ny.us.

Post–Trial Submissions: Motions brought by a party after jury trial pursuant to CPLR 4403 or CPLR 4404 must be supported by a copy of the trial transcript.

Unless otherwise directed by the Court, in accordance with the schedule set by the Court at the conclusion of a bench-trial or hearing, the parties shall jointly submit a trial transcript, and each party shall prepare and submit a post-trial memorandum. The post-trial memorandum shall also be submitted electronically to abbrady@courts.state.ny.us.

In all matrimonial actions, each party shall also submit proposed Findings of Fact and Conclusions of Law and a proposed Judgment of Divorce. Factual arguments set forth in the memorandum shall be supported by citations to the trial transcript, and legal arguments shall be supported by citations to relevant statutes and/or case law. In their post-trial submissions following a trial of equitable distribution issues, the parties shall identify each item of property as either separate or marital, and shall state the value of each item of property. They should also identify all of the parties' outstanding debts as either separate or marital and shall state the amount of each debt. All assertions as to the separate or marital status of each item of property and each outstanding debt, and the value of each item of property and the amount of each debt, shall be supported by citations to the final transcript.

Settled and Discontinued Cases: Counsel shall immediately notify the Court of a settled or discontinued matter. Following the initial notification counsel shall file a fully executed duplicate original stipulation of discontinuance with the County Clerk and the Part Clerk.

Matrimonial Actions: Counsel shall be familiar with and shall comply with the provisions of 22 NYCRR 202.16. Prior to the preliminary conference the parties shall file and exchange those documents set forth in 22 NYCRR 202.16(f)(1) including net worth statements, paycheck stubs, W–2 statements, tax returns and statements of account.

Each party must file a statement of proposed disposition (22 NYCRR 202.16(h)) no later than ten (10) days prior to trial.

Counsel and parties are required to appear on the return date of motions seeking *pendente lite* relief.

JUSTICE ELAINE SLOBOD, J.S.C.

Rule I. Motions

A. General

(1) Notice of Motion may be made returnable any day at 9:15 AM. NO APPEARANCES ARE REQUIRED EXCEPT ON MATRIMONIAL MOTIONS and MOTIONS BROUGHT ON BY ORDER TO SHOW CAUSE when the Court has issued a TRO which will expire on the return date.

(2) Use official citations.

(3) No courtesy copies of motions are to be submitted.

(4) Motion papers are to be securely bound. Papers that are not securely bound run the risk of being lost. Attorneys are requested to instruct clerical staff not to overload paper fasteners and to check the condition of papers before the papers leave the attorneys' office.

(5) Exhibits should be tabbed. Please do not use exhibit sheets.

(6) Appearances are not required except on matrimonial motions. Oral arguments may be requested by noting "Oral Argument Requested" immediately over the Index Number on the Notice of Motion. If the Court, in its discretion, requires such argument, the movant's attorney will be so advised and will be required to notify all parties.

(7) Self-addressed, stamped envelopes must be submitted with all motions. Orders/Judgments must also have self-addressed, stamped envelopes and a copy if a conformed copy is requested.

(8) Do not send opposing or reply papers to the County Clerk. They should be forwarded directly to Judge Slobod showing the motion return date at the top of the first page.

(9) The court will not consider sur-reply papers or papers submitted after the return date without prior permission of the court.

(10) A party moving to renew or reargue must attach copies of the papers submitted in connection with the underlying motion to the motion to renew or reargue.

B. Submission of Orders and Judgments Based Upon Rulings in Open Court. Proposed orders and judgments based upon rulings in open court must be supported by a copy of the stenographic minutes reflecting the ruling upon which the proposed order or judgment is based.

C. Summary Judgment. Summary judgment motions must be made no later than 60 days from the date of the filing of the Note of Issue or the motion will be denied.

D. Discovery Matters

(1) Counsel must consult with one another in a "good faith" effort to resolve all disclosure disputes. See Uniform Rule 202.7. A pro forma letter to your adversary does not constitute "good faith." Discovery issues which cannot be resolved may be discussed at the next scheduled court conference or by motion. The service of a motion does not, in and of itself, stay any scheduling order. The making of a motion may result in a conference.

Simple discovery disputes, i.e., the scheduling of depositions, IMEs and the like may be addressed by letter faxed to the court and fax copied to all counsel. Substantive disputes, i.e., the application of privilege, should be addressed by a letter faxed to the court requesting an immediate conference or by written motion.

E. Adjournments of Motions

(1) Standards and Goals—No adjournments of a motion in a case in which the trial note of issue is filed and that is over or within 3 months of going over standards and goals will be permitted without prior written approval of the Court.

(2) Other than Standards and Goals

(a) On Consent—The Clerk of the Part is to be advised by telephone, followed by a timely fax or letter, that the motion is adjourned on consent to a date no later than 21 days from the current return date. The combination of consent adjournments shall not exceed 45 days from the original return date. Any further adjournment will require an appearance. A copy of the letter is to be sent to all parties.

(b) Opposed—If your adversary will not consent to an adjournment, you should fax a short letter request to the Court with a copy to all interested counsel. Opposing counsel shall succinctly provide their reasons for objecting in a reply fax. No further communications will be permitted.

(c) Please show the index number and the current return date in your letter.

Rule II. Orders to Show Cause

Temporary Restraining Orders. Unless there are extremely unusual circumstances which are recited in a supporting affidavit, opposing counsel shall be advised by phone or fax that an Order to Show Cause containing a TRO is being presented to the Court and a good faith effort must be made to do so or a demonstration of significant prejudice must be made.

If there has been no appearance by opposing counsel, the adverse party shall be provided with notice as directed by the rules (Rule 202.7(f)).

Counsel are reminded that, if the summons and complaint have not already been served, copies must be served with the Order to Show Cause. Therefore, to obtain personal jurisdiction in the action being commenced, personal service of the Order to Show Cause will be required unless supporting papers justify service under CPLR 308(5).

Rule III. Conferences

A. Preliminary Conference

(1) Appearances at the preliminary conference are mandatory.

(2) Only an attorney familiar with the case and prepared to discuss and consent to the terms of a Preliminary Conference Order shall appear.

B. Compliance/Settlement Conference. Counsel must be prepared to discuss all procedural and substantive issues, as well as engage in meaningful settlement negotiations at the compliance/settlement conference.

C. Trial Readiness Conference. Failure to appear at a trial readiness conference may result in sanctions, including striking the pleadings. A formal motion for relief from the sanctions for such default will be required.

D. Adjournment of Conferences

(1) *Standards and Goals*—No adjournments of a conference in a case in which the trial note of issue has been filed and which is over or within 3 months of going over standards and goals will be permitted without prior written approval of the Court.

(2) *Other than Standards and Goals*

(a) On Consent—After telephone approval by the Part Clerk (291–4511), a conference may be adjourned on consent to a date no later than 15 days from the current scheduled date. There may be a second adjournment on consent, however, no combination of adjournments on consent shall exceed 30 days from the original conference date.

A letter or fax confirming any adjournment shall be sent to the Part Clerk and all counsel.

(b) Opposed—If your adversary will not consent to an adjournment, you should fax a short letter request to the Court with a copy to all interested counsel. Opposing counsel shall succinctly provide their reasons for objecting in a reply fax. No further communications will be permitted.

(c) Please show the index number and current conference date in your letter.

MATRIMONIAL ACTIONS

Counsel shall be familiar with and shall comply with the provisions of 22 NYCRR 202.16. Prior to the preliminary conference, the parties shall file and exchange those documents set forth in 22 NYCRR 202.16(f)(1) including net worth statements, paycheck stubs, W–2 statements, tax returns and statements of account.

Counsel should inform their clients of the automatic orders created by Domestic Relations Law §236 Part B(2)(b) as soon as the attorney-client relationship is formed.

Parties shall appear at all matrimonial conferences unless otherwise directed by the court.

Each party must file a statement of proposed disposition (22 NYCRR 202.16[h]) no later than 3 days prior to trial.

Counsel and parties are required to appear on the return date of motions seeking pendente lite relief.

Rule IV.   Trials

A. Pleadings and Exhibits. Prior to the commencement of a trial, counsel shall provide the Court with:

(1) marked pleadings.

(2) an exhibit list. The attorneys are to pre-mark their exhibits. Only those received in evidence will be marked by the reporter. The reporter is to be provided with an exhibit list.

B. Motions in Limine. Shall be made returnable at least 15 days before the trial date.

C. Requests to Charge. Shall be submitted to the Court as directed at a conference immediately preceding trial. The charge will be drawn from the Pattern Jury Instructions (PJI). A complete list of requested charges is to be submitted. Unless counsel seek a deviation from the pattern charge or additions to the pattern charge, only the PJI numbers and heading need be listed.

Where deviations or additions are requested, the full text of such requests must be submitted, together with any supporting legal precedents.

D. Verdict Sheet. Counsel shall jointly prepare a verdict sheet. The verdict sheet is to be typed and in final form for presentation to the jury. If agreement cannot be reached, then each side shall present a proposed verdict sheet. If it is feasible, such proposals shall also be submitted on a computer disc in a format convertible to Word Perfect X3.

Verdict sheets should provide signature lines for each juror as to each question and after the last question, a line for the foreperson.

E. Identification of Deposition Testimony. Counsel for the parties shall consult prior to trial and shall in good faith attempt to agree upon the portions of deposition testimony to be offered into evidence without objection. The parties shall delete from the testimony to be read questions and answers that are irrelevant to the point for which the testimony is offered. Each party shall prepare a list of testimony to be offered by it as to which objection has not been made and, identified separately and clearly, a list of testimony as to which objection has been made.

At least five days prior to trial, each party shall submit its list to the Court and other counsel, together with a copy of the portions of testimony as to which objections has been made. The Court will rule upon the objections at the earliest possible time after consultation with counsel.

F. Scheduling. As a general rule all trials will begin at about 10:00 A.M. immediately following the conference calendar call.

Rule V.   Orders/Judgment Submission

A. All orders or judgments, including counter-orders and judgments, submitted for signature on notice will be returned unsigned unless an affidavit of service of same and Notice of Settlement for a date designated in accordance with 22 NYCRR 202.48 have been included.

B. Do not fax proposed orders or judgments.

C. (1) If a counter-order contains only a very minor change, the cover letter should clearly identify that change by page and paragraph.

(2) All other proposed changes to an adversary's original order should be highlighted in a duplicate sample copy of the proposed counter-order, and a brief explanation of counsel should accompany the counter-order.

(3) A copy of any relevant transcript should accompany the counter-order.

(4) Counsel who submitted the original order may submit a short response to the counter-order within 3 business days of receipt of same.

Rule VI. Infant Compromise Applications and Orders

A. Attorneys should not seek reimbursement for disbursements for overhead expenses such as the cost of postage, in -house photocopies, legal research, phone, fax, etc.

B. The amount of insurance coverage shall be stated in counsel's affirmation and, when relevant, a statement that an asset search was conducted on the defendants.

C. Every proposed order shall provide that:

(1) "___% of the attorney's fees approved herein shall be held in escrow until the Court has been advised that [the infant's funds have been deposited in the bank designated] and/or [the policy required by the structured settlement has actually been purchased]."

(2) The bank may issue checks without court order each year for Federal and New York State taxes owed by the infant upon receipt of copies of tax returns. The bank may also in each year issue a check to a CPA or licensed tax preparer for up to $___ upon submission of an invoice for that amount.

(3) ___% of said deposit shall be placed in the highest yielding certificate of deposit providing these funds shall be available without penalty when the infant attains the age of 18 years. The balance shall be kept in a regular passbook account.

Rule VII. Litigation Correspondence

Copies of correspondence between or among counsel should not be sent to the Court for informational purposes.

DATED: March 2011

PUTNAM COUNTY
SUPREME, COUNTY, FAMILY AND SURROGATE'S COURT
JUDGES' PART RULES
JUSTICE FRANCIS A. NICOLAI

Rule I. Communications With the Court

A. Correspondence. Correspondence to the Court shall, without exception, be copied to all adversary counsel(s) and pro se litigants. Correspondence between counsel(s) and/or pro se litigants shall not be copied to the Court unless there is some specific judicial purpose to be served by transmitting copies to the Court.

B. Telephone Calls. Telephone calls to the Court staff are permitted only in necessary or emergency situations requiring immediate attention that cannot otherwise be attained by correspondence.

Rule II. Court Conferences

A. General Rules. All conferences with the Court are conducted at 9:30 a.m. sharp weekdays in the Putnam County Courthouse, unless otherwise directed. Counsels and pro se litigants are expected to appear for all conferences on time and must be fully familiar with the action(s) on which they appear. Attorneys are to appear with their clients for all conferences in matrimonial actions, unless such appearances are dispensed with by the Court on prior request on notice to the adversary and any law guardians.

B. Preliminary Conferences. Preliminary Conferences shall be conducted 1) after a written Request For Judicial Intervention ("RJI") is duly filed with the Office of the Clerk in accordance with Uniform Rule 202.12(a), or 2) after an appropriate notice is filed in medical malpractice actions pursuant to Uniform Rule 202.56, or 3) after an appropriate notice is filed in matrimonial actions pursuant to Uniform Rule 202.16, or 4) upon a specific directive by the Court. Matrimonial actions will be conducted in accordance with uniform Rule 202.16 and DRL Section 236(B)(4). Preliminary Conferences of medical, dental and podiatric malpractice actions will be conducted in accordance with Uniform Rule 202.56(b). All counsels and pro se litigants are expected to take most seriously the Court's discovery schedule and deadlines, and non-compliance shall only be excused if explained by extenuating circumstances.

C. Compliance Conferences. The purpose of the Compliance Conference is for counsels and pro se litigants to report to the Court that pre-trial discovery has been completed, to enable the Court to direct a date on which a Note of Issue shall be filed and to schedule dates for a Pre–Trial Conference and trial. Settlement discussions may also take place. Parties are not permitted to file a Note of Issue in any action unless permission to do so is granted by the Court at the Compliance Conference.

D. Pre–Trial Conferences. The Court shall conduct a Pre–Trial Conference with all counsel and pro se litigants on a date that shall ordinarily be within thirty (30) days preceding the trial date. It is expected that counsels attending Pre–Trial Conferences shall be fully familiar with the action and be authorized to discuss 1) all factual and legal issues presented by the litigation, 2) settlement demands or offers, 3) trial procedure and witness scheduling, and 4) that counsels also be authorized to enter into settlements on terms agreeable to the parties and to the Court.

E. Adjournments. Applications for adjournments must be made in writing *actually received* by the Court at least twenty-four (24) hours in advance of the scheduled conference, and must address 1) good cause why an adjournment is sought, 2) whether the adversary party(ies) consent or object to the application, and 3) may, at the option of the sender, suggest an approximate time period or an exact date for which the adjournment is sought. All such communications must be copied to all counsel(s) and pro se litigants.

Rule III. Motions and Orders to Show Cause

A. General Rules. The Court will entertain motions on submission, whether brought by Notice of Motion or by Order to Show Cause, for 9:30 a.m. on any Friday the Court is in session. The return date for an Order To Show Cause shall of course be determined by the Court at the time papers are submitted for consideration and executed. There shall be no oral argument heard on any motions unless directed by the Court in a given instance. In the unusual instance when the Court wishes to hear oral argument on a motion, as permitted by Uniform Rule 202.8(d), all counsels and pro se litigants shall be provided with reasonable prior notice of the date and time scheduled for such purpose at which parties are expected to appear in Court.

All summary judgment motions must be made within 60 days of filing of the Note of Issue.

B. Filing of Papers Applicable To All Motions. Except with the expressed permission of the Court, all motion papers and Orders to Show Cause, must be typewritten, double-spaced, securely bound, entirely legible and all exhibits labeled with tab markings. Deposition transcripts included as exhibits must be single, front-faced pages only. The Court may refuse to accept any such paper which does not conform to the foregoing. Courtesy copies are not to be submitted.

C. Motion Adjournments. Upon consent of all counsels and pro se litigants, the Court typically will grant an adjournment of a motion or Order to Show Cause; however, no more than three adjournments of any single motion will be permitted. The party seeking the adjournment must obtain the consent of adversary parties and notify the Part Clerk of the requested adjourned date at least twenty-four (24) hours before the return date. Motion adjournments should be confirmed in writing to the Court and all adversary parties.

D. Discovery–Related Motions. Counsel must consult with one another in a good faith effort to resolve all disclosure disputes. No formal motion regarding discovery may be filed absent a statement that counsel has spoken with Ms. Florio regarding the issue(s) presenting and that her efforts to resolve the issue(s) were unavailing. Motions which do not include a statement that Ms. Florio had been contacted and that her efforts could not resolve the discovery dispute will be summarily denied.

* * * * * * IMPORTANT * * * * * *

Rule IV. Decisions and Orders

A. The parties are responsible to obtain copies of all written Orders, Motions and Decisions. Courtesy copies will be furnished only when Chambers is provided with a stamped, self-addressed envelope.

Parties who do NOT furnish stamped, self-addressed envelopes will nevertheless be BOUND BY ALL DATES, OBLIGATIONS & APPEARANCES directed in Orders, Motions and Decisions.

Rule V. Trials and Hearings

A. Prior to commencement of a trial, counsel shall provide the Court with:

1) marked pleadings in accordance with CPLR Rule 4012;

2) pre-trial memoranda of law as to any known disputed legal issues that must be determined by the Court;

3) a list of witnesses for each party;

4) requests to charge. The charge will be drawn from the Pattern Jury Instructions (PJI). A complete list of requested charges is to be submitted. Unless counsel seek a deviation from the pattern charge or additions to the pattern charge, only the PJI numbers need be submitted. Where deviations or additions are requested, the full text of such requests must be submitted, together with any supporting legal precedents.

5) verdict sheet. Counsel shall jointly prepare a verdict sheet. The verdict sheet is to be typed and in final form for presentation to the jury. If agreement cannot be reached, then each side shall present a proposed verdict sheet. If it is feasible, such proposals shall also be submitted on a computer disc in the format convertible to Word Perfect 8.0

6) in matrimonial actions, updated net worth statements (with the latest available supporting documents such as income tax returns, W–2's, brokerage statements, retirement plan statements), statements of proposed disposition as required by uniform Rule 202.16(h), and any forensic reports, appraisals and evaluations.

B. Motion in Limine. Any motions for the Courts's consideration *in limine* must be delivered to the Part Clerk and served upon adversary counsel(s) not later than seven (7) days prior to the scheduled date of the trial, except as to issues that cannot be reasonably anticipated prior to trial.

Rule VI. Settled and Discontinued Cases

Counsel shall immediately notify the Court of a case disposition. Following the initial notification, counsel shall submit a copy of the stipulation of discontinuance to chambers so that the matter may be marked off the calendar.

Ms. Florio shall be contacted for advice concerning any issues or problems not addressed or resolved by the foregoing.

JUSTICE LEWIS J. LUBELL

Rule 1. General

Counsel who appear must be fully familiar with the case and have authority to enter into any agreement, either substantive or procedural, on behalf of their clients. Counsel must be on time for all scheduled appearances and must bring sufficient material to allow meaningful discussion of unresolved issues to each Court appearance. Sanctions may be imposed for failure to comply with this rule including, but not limited to, an adjournment of the conference with an

award of counsel fees against the offending attorney/party.

Faxes and letters addressing anything other than procedural issues, such as, but not limited to adjournments, will not be considered by the Court absent prior Court approval.

Any relief sought by way of letter application, facsimile transmission or e-mail or not otherwise properly contained in a motion on notice or order to show cause, is deemed denied without any further action by the Court.

If an action is settled, discontinued, or otherwise disposed, counsel shall immediately inform the Court by submission of a copy of the stipulation or other document evidencing the disposition. In addition, counsel must advised the Court about the existence of any open motions.

Rule 2. Adjournments

All adjournments, on consent or otherwise, whether for a conference, motion, or any other purpose or matter, must first be approved by the Court. Counsel are directed to contact the Part Clerk for approval of any agreed upon consent or opposed contested adjournments.

Rule 3. Conferences

ALL CONFERENCES WILL BE CALLED ON MONDAY MORNINGS PROMPTLY AT 9:30 A.M. UNLESS OTHERWISE SCHEDULED

Preliminary Conference. The attorneys are to provide the Court with a copy of the marked pleadings and bills of particulars and are to be prepared to advise the Court with regard to any outstanding motions. Appearances at the Preliminary Conference are mandatory. Only counsel fully prepared to discuss the matter including facts, issues of liability and defenses of the case should appear.

Compliance/Settlement Conference. Counsel are to be fully knowledgeable as to the status of the case. Counsel are to be prepared to delineate compliance or lack thereof with all discovery matters. Counsel must be prepared to discuss settlement at the compliance/settlement conference and have authority to enter into stipulations, including stipulations of settlement, or settle the matter.

Failure to appear at a Trial Readiness Conference may result in sanctions, including the striking of the Note of Issue and/or the pleadings. A formal motion for relief from any the sanctions for such default will be required.

A Note of Issue note of issue must be filed within twenty (20) days of the Final Trial Readiness Conference. Sanctions, including the striking of pleadings, may be imposed for failure to do so.

Rule 4. Discovery Matters

Counsel must consult with one another in a good faith effort to resolve all disclosure disputes. See Uniform Rule 202.7. If counsel are unable to resolve a disclosure dispute in this manner, they may raise the issue at the next scheduled court appearance, if scheduled to take place within 45 days or less. Alternatively, counsel may ask that the case be advanced for purposes of resolving the issue.

All discovery motions will be orally argued on the return date. At the Court's discretion, the motions will be resolved at the bench or by written decision after argument.

Prior to making a discovery motion, counsel are directed to contact the court for a conference. In the event that a motion is necessary, all discovery motions will be orally argued on the return date. At the Court's discretion, the motions will be resolved at the bench by conference or by written decision after argument.

Prior to making a discovery motion, counsel are directed to contact the court for a conference. In the event that a motion is necessary, all discovery motions will be orally argued on the return date. At the Court's discretion, the motions will be resolved at the bench by conference or by written decision after argument.

Rule 5. Motions

Motions will be returnable on Mondays at 9:30 AM, except by order of the Court. Papers not received by the Court by noon of the return date may not, in the Court's discretion, be considered by the Court. No courtesy copies of motions are to be submitted. Notice of Motion, affidavits and exhibits with exhibit tabs, if applicable, should be assembled in that order in one blue back unless the exhibits are voluminous. The failure to properly tab exhibits may result in the rejection of the submission. Unbound motions are subject to rejection as well.

Unless otherwise advised by the Court, appearances are required on discovery motions, orders to show cause, and contempt motions. Please call chambers if there is any uncertainty about an appearance.

Unless otherwise advised by the Court, appearances are not required on the return date of any other motion. However, oral argument may be requested by noting Oral Argument Requested immediately over the index number on the Notice of Motion. If the Court, in its discretion, desires such argument, either by counsels' request or on its own directive, the movant's attorney will be so advised and will be required to notify all parties. A request for the requesting of oral argument should not be construed by counsel as an automatic granting of same.

Sur-replies will not be considered, unless the Court otherwise directs. If new issues are raised in the reply, or if there has been a change in the law while the motion is pending, counsel are to advise chambers, in writing, of the request to submit additional affidavits or memoranda. Other papers, including letters which are sent after the submission of the motion, will not be considered.

Any objection to the filing of a Sur-reply should be made to the Court by way of letter addressing the procedural transgression and not the merits of any issue raised.

The Court does not permit litigation by way of letter correspondence/application to the Court or by way of being copied with letter correspondence by and between counsel, from one attorney to the other. Any such submission should be considered by counsel as having been denied filed without further action or consideration of the Court.

Post–Note of Issue Motions must be made within 60 days of the service of the Note of Issue.

Self-addressed, stamped envelopes must be provided by all parties with all motions. Orders/judgments must also have self-addressed, stamped envelopes and a copy, if a conformed copy is requested.

Rule 6.   Trials

On the date of scheduled jury selection of a trial, counsel shall provide the Court with: a) marked pleadings, and an exhibit list; b) contentions on one typed page, single spaced; and c) proposed requests to charge. Material to be used on cross-examination need not be listed on the exhibit list. Only those received in evidence will be marked by the reporter. The reporter is to be provided with an exhibit list.

Requests to charge will be drawn from the Pattern Jury Instructions (PJI). A complete list of requested charges is to be submitted via e-mail to llubell@courts.state.ny.us, notwithstanding the standard charges given by the Court. Unless counsel seek a deviation from the pattern charge or additions to the pattern charge, only the PJI numbers and section title need be submitted. Where deviations or additions are requested, the full text of such requests must be submitted, together with any supporting legal precedents. All submissions must be served on opposition counsel. Final charges will be formalized at a charge conference during the course of the trial.

Verdict Sheet. Counsel shall jointly prepare a proposed verdict sheet. The verdict sheet is to be typed and in final form for presentation to the jury. If agreement cannot be reached, then each side shall present a proposed verdict sheet. If it is feasible, such proposals shall also be submitted via e-mail to llubell@courts.state.ny.us such as is compatible on a computer disc in a format convertible to with Word Perfect 12.0. The final verdict sheet will be formalized during a charge conference to be held during the course of the trial after the conclusion of the plaintiff(s) case.

Rule 7.   Matrimonial Matters

(All of the above rules are applicable to the extent they apply procedurally and/or substantively.)

Litigants must appear at all conferences and proceedings unless earlier excused by the court.

PRELIMINARY CONFERENCE

All sides shall have exchanged Statements of Net Worth no later than two weeks prior to the conference. Counsel shall provide the court with courtesy copies of Statements of Net Worth, Statements of Client's Rights and Retainers at the time of the conference. Pendente Lite applications, to the extent necessary, should be made as soon as practicable after the conference. If grounds are contested, the court is to be advised at the Preliminary Conference. Attorneys for the child(ren), and forensics, evaluators and appraisers, etc will be appointed assigned at the preliminary conference, if appropriate, necessary as well as appraisers.

STATUS/COMPLIANCE/TRIAL READY CONFERENCE

Counsel should be fully prepared to apprise the court of the status of discovery and any other issues which may be extant at the time of the conference. Substantive applications are to be brought via Order to Show Cause and not through oral application or written/faxed letters to the court.

PRE–TRIAL CONFERENCE

Counsel should have all issues framed for trial. Counsel will provide to the Court a Statement of Proposed Disposition as well as a witness list with a one line statement of the context of each witness' testimony. All pre-trial disclosure including, but not limited to 3101(d) disclosure, will be governed by the NYCRR and the DRL.

JUSTICE JAMES T. ROONEY

Doc. 1.   Hon. James T. Rooney

Motions

Prior to making any motion, the movant should write the Court, with a copy to all parties, specifying the relief sought and the basis for that relief. The Court will then schedule either a conference or a conference call with counsel. This procedure does not preclude the moving party from making a motion, but rather, provides the Court with an opportunity to resolve the dispute without the need for a formal written application. Failing resolution of the issue in this manner, the party seeking the relief may proceed with a motion.

All motions and orders to show cause must be filed with the Office of the County Clerk with the appropriate filing fee. All motions will be limited to twenty (20) pages unless prior Court approval is given. All motions will be returnable on Thursdays at 2:00 p.m., except by Order of the Court.

Appearances on the return date of motions are not required unless otherwise notified by the Court. Oral argument may be requested by noting "Oral Argument Requested" immediately over the index number on the Notice of Motion. If the Court, in its discretion, requires such argument, the movant's attorney will be so advised and will be required to notify all parties.

Sur-replies will not be considered. Papers, including letters which are sent after the submission of the motion, will not be considered.

Self-addressed, stamped envelopes must be submitted with all motions. Orders/judgments must also have self-addressed, stamped envelopes and a copy to be conformed if required.

Adjournments

Requests for adjournments must be made by fax to Chambers. Counsel must attempt to gain the consent of all parties. If applicable, an affidavit of engagement must be filed with the Court. No adjournments will be permitted unless approved by Chambers. If an adjournment is granted by Chambers, the requesting party must inform all other parties of the adjourned date and time and copy the Court on that correspondence.

Discovery Matters

Counsel must consult with one another in a good faith effort to resolve all disclosure disputes. (See Uniform Rule 202.7). If counsel are unable to resolve a disclosure dispute in this manner, the procedures set forth above regarding motion practice must be followed before a motion may be filed.

Conferences

Preliminary Conference—The attorneys should complete the Preliminary Conference Order before the conference with the Court. They also must be prepared to discuss with the Court any outstanding motions. Counsel must have full knowledge of the facts and status of the case and be prepared to engage in a meaningful conference. Appearances by counsel and parties at the Preliminary Conference are mandatory. Failure to appear at a Preliminary Conference may result in sanctions.

Compliance/Settlement Conferences—Counsel must appear with full authority to discuss settlement. Appearances at Compliance/Settlement Conferences by counsel and parties are mandatory unless otherwise ordered by the Court. Failure to appear or failure to appear with full authority/ability to discuss settlement at this conference may result in sanctions.

Failure to appear at a Trial Readiness Conference with full authority/ability to settle may result in sanctions, including striking the pleadings.

Trials

Motions—In Limine: Counsel should advise the Court in writing of any issues which they are aware of in advance of trial, which may require a ruling by the Court during the trial.

Exhibits—Prior to the commencement of a trial, counsel shall provide the Court with marked pleadings and an exhibit list.

The attorneys are to pre-mark all exhibits. The court reporter is to be provided with an exhibit list.

Requests to Charge—Requests to charge shall be submitted to the Court as directed at a conference immediately preceding trial. The charge will be drawn from the Pattern Jury Instructions (PJI). A complete list of requested charges is to be submitted. Unless counsel seeks a deviation from the pattern charge or additions to the pattern charge, only the PJI numbers need to be submitted. Where deviations or additions are requested, the full text of such requests must be submitted, with the proposed deviation or addition underlined, together with any supporting legal precedent.

Verdict Sheet—Counsel shall jointly prepare a verdict sheet. The verdict sheet is to be typed and in final form for presentation to the jury. If agreement cannot be reached, then each side shall prepare a proposed verdict sheet.

General

The Court should not be copied on correspondence between counsel.

Counsel who appear before the Court must be fully familiar with the case and have full authority to enter into any agreement, either substantive or procedural, on behalf of their clients. Counsel must be on time for all scheduled appearances and must bring the full file with them to each Court appearance.

If an action is settled, discontinued or otherwise reaches disposition, counsel shall immediately inform the Court by submission of a copy of the stipulation or other document evidencing the disposition. Where the matter is disposed of but the final stipulation has not been executed by all the necessary parties prior to a scheduled Court appearance, Chambers should be notified by letter with proof of copies to all counsel so that the Court may determine if appearances are required. This letter may be sent by fax to Chambers.

Faxes—Unless otherwise authorized by these Rules, faxes will not be accepted unless it is an emergency and the receipt has been authorized by Chambers.

E-Courts—While E-Courts can be a useful tool, it is not always accurate. In the event of a conflict between the appearance date provided by the Court and E-Courts, the parties should appear on the date provided by the Court.

E-Mail—The Court will not communicate through e-mail and encourages any correspondence to be sent by regular mail.

JUSTICE JAMES F. REITZ

Doc. 1. Hon. James F. Reitz

MOTIONS

Prior to making any motion, the movant shall write the Court, with a copy to all parties, specifying the relief sought and the basis for that relief. The Court will then schedule either a conference or a conference call with counsel. This procedure does not preclude the moving party from making a motion, but rather, provides the Court with an opportunity to resolve the dispute without the need for a formal written application. Failing resolution of the issue in this manner, the party seeking the relief may proceed with a motion.

All motions and orders to show cause must be filed with the Office of the County Clerk with the appropriate filing fee. The Court will notify counsel of the return date for the Motions.

Appearances on the return date of motions will or will not be required as noted by the Court. Oral argument may be requested by noting "Oral Argument Requested" immediately over the index number on the Notice of Motion. If the Court, in its discretion, requires such argument, the movant's attorney will be so advised and will be required to notify all parties.

If requested by counsel, the Court may consider sur-replies on a case-by-case basis. Papers, including letters which are sent after the submission of the motion, will not be considered.

Self-addressed, stamped envelopes must be submitted with all motions. Orders/judgments must also have self-addressed, stamped envelopes and a copy to be conformed if required.

ADJOURNMENTS

Requests for adjournments can be made either by telephone or fax to the Court. Counsel must attempt to gain the consent of all parties. If applicable, an affidavit of engagement must be filed with the Court. No adjournments will be permitted unless approved by the Court. If an adjournment is granted by the Court, the requesting party must inform all other parties of the adjourned date and time and copy the Court on that correspondence.

DISCOVERY MATTERS

Counsel must consult with one another in a good faith effort to resolve all disclosure disputes. (See Uniform Rule 202.7.) If counsel are unable to resolve a disclosure dispute in this manner, the procedures set forth above regarding motion practice must be followed before a motion may be filed.

CONFERENCES

Preliminary Conference—The attorneys must attempt to complete the Preliminary Conference Order before the conference date. They also must be prepared to discuss with the Court any outstanding motions. Attorneys appearing at preliminary conferences must have full authority to dispose of any outstanding discovery matters or matters involving pending motions. Personal appearances by counsel and parties at the Preliminary Conference are mandatory. Failure to appear at a Preliminary Conference may result in sanctions.

Compliance/Settlement Conferences—Counsel must appear with full authority to discuss settlement. Personal appearances at Compliance/Settlement Conferences by counsel and parties are mandatory unless otherwise ordered by the Court. Failure to so appear or failure to appear with full authority to discuss settlement at this conference may result in sanctions.

Failure to personally appear at a Trial Readiness Conference with full authority to settle may result in sanctions, including striking the pleadings.

TRIALS

Motions In Limine—Counsel should advise the Court in writing of any issues which they are aware of in advance of trial, which may require a ruling by the Court during the trial.

Exhibits—Prior to the commencement of a trial, counsel shall provide the Court with marked pleadings and an exhibit list.

The attorneys are to pre-mark all exhibits. The court reporter is to be provided with an exhibit list.

Requests to Charge—Requests to charge shall be submitted to the Court as directed at a conference immediately preceding trial. The charge will be drawn from the Pattern Jury Instructions (PJI). A complete list of requested charges is to be submitted. Unless counsel seeks a deviation from the pattern charge or additions to the pattern charge, only the PJI numbers need to be submitted. Where deviations or additions are requested, the full text of such requests must be submitted, with the proposed deviation or addition underlined, together with any supporting legal precedents.

Verdict Sheet—Counsel shall jointly prepare a verdict sheet. The verdict sheet is to be typed and in final form for presentation to the jury. If agreement cannot be reached, then each side shall prepare a proposed verdict sheet.

GENERAL

The Court should not be copied on correspondence between counsel.

Counsel who appear before the Court must be fully familiar with the case and have full authority to enter into any agreement, either substantive or procedural, on behalf of their clients. Counsel must be on time for all scheduled appearances and must bring the full file with them to each Court appearance.

Faxes—Unless otherwise authorized by these Rules, faxes will not be accepted unless it is an emergency and the receipt has been authorized by the Court.

If an action is settled, discontinued or otherwise reaches disposition, counsel shall immediately inform the Court by submission of a copy of the stipulation or other document evidencing the disposition. Where the matter is disposed of but the final stipulation has not been executed by all the necessary parties prior to a scheduled Court appearance, the Court should be notified by letter with proof of copies to all counsel so that the Court may determine if appearances are required. This letter may be sent by fax to the Court.

ROCKLAND COUNTY
SUPREME AND COUNTY COURT
JUDGES' PART RULES
JUSTICE VICTOR J. ALFIERI
PART I. E-FILING RULES OF THE COURT

Rule I. E–Filing Rules and Protocol

A. General Rules. All parties should familiarize themselves with the statewide E–Filing Rules Uniform Rule §§ 202.5–b and 202.5–bb — available at www.nycourts.gov/efile) and the Rockland County E-Filing Protocol.

B. Contact Information. General questions about e-filing should be addressed to the E–Filing Resource Center at (646) 386–3033 or efile@courts. state.ny.us. Specific questions relating to local procedures should be addressed to the Chief Clerk's Office (845) 638–5393.

Rule II. Electronic Filing

All [case type(s)] actions in Judge Alfieri's part are to be filed through the New York State Courts E-Filing system (NYSCEF). All submissions to the Court, including proposed orders, proposed judgments, and letters, must be electronically filed.

Rule III. Working Copies

A. General Rules. A court may require the submission of "working copies" of electronically filed documents. See Uniform Rule § 202.5–b(d)(4). Working copies shall be delivered to the Rockland Chief Clerk's Office.

B. Part Rule:

☐ This Part does not require working copies.

☐ This Part does not require working copies but may request working copies in specific instances.

☐ This Part requires working copies for all electronic submissions.

☐ This Part requires working copies for:
[ ] motion submissions
[ ] proposed orders to show cause
[ ] proposed orders/judgments
[ ] stipulations
[ ] transcripts
[ ] letters

C. Submission of Working Copies. All working copies submitted to this Part must include a copy of the NYSCEF Confirmation Notice firmly fastened as the front cover page of the submission and comply with other requirements set forth in the Rockland County Protocol. Working copies without the Confirmation Notice will not be accepted. Working copies are to be delivered no later than 2:00 p.m. on the first business day following the electronic filing of the document on the NYSCEF site.

Rule IV. Hard Copy Submissions

This Part will reject any hard copy submissions in e-filed cases unless those submissions bear the "Notice of Hard Copy Submission — E–Filed Case" required by Uniform Rule § 202.5–b(d)(1). The form is available at www.nycourts.gov/efile.

Rule V. Scheduling

Counsel/parties should address questions about scheduling appearances or adjourning appearances to the Part Clerk, Thomas Morrissey, at (845) 638–5490.

PART II. RULES OF THE COURT

Rule I. General Rules

A. Calendar Call. The Court shall call its calendar each day at 9:30 a.m. or as soon thereafter as possible.

B. Court Papers. All submissions bearing the caption of the action must be signed by counsel as required by 22 NYCRR § 130–1.1a. In any instance where a "service list" is required on a legal document, the service list must set forth the name, address and telephone number of the submitting party or attorney AND identify the party or person represented by that attorney and the person or party represented by the other persons named in that service list. All filings are to be made at the Supreme Court Civil window except for opposition and reply papers on motions which are to be sent directly to chambers.

C. Statutes and Rules. This Court strictly adheres to the procedural requirements set forth in the CPLR and Uniform Rules–Trial Courts, as well as all other state statutes that set forth specific procedural requirements to be followed in order to obtain the relief sought.

D. Standards and Goals. Recognizing the important public policy considerations behind the various time limitations set by statute and rule, this Court strictly adheres to those time limitations. See, 22 NYCRR § 202.12 and § 202.16.

Rule II. Communication With the Court

A. Correspondence. Copies of all correspondence to the Court shall be sent to all counsel of record and must reflect the Index Number of the case to which it relates. Copies of correspondence between attorneys and/or pro se litigants shall NOT be sent to the Court unless there is some specific judicial purpose to be served by transmitting copies to the Court.

B. Telephone Calls. Telephone calls to Court staff should be limited to those situations requiring immediate attention that cannot otherwise be addressed by correspondence.

C. Papers by Facsimile. The Court does not accept papers of any kind by fax transmission that must otherwise be filed in original form with the Office of the Clerk (e.g., petitions, proof of service, motions, opposition to motions, replies, proposed Orders, documents to be "So Ordered"). Copies of letters confirming an adjournment of a motion or a conference may be sent to the Court by facsimile. However, all faxes must be faxed simultaneously to all other parties and the original correspondence must be mailed to the Part Clerk by mail. Counsel are not permitted, without prior approval, to send facsimile transmissions to Chambers that exceed five (5) pages in length.

D. Ex Parte Communications. Ex parte communications are prohibited except where an Order to Show Cause is submitted for signature or during settlement negotiations upon the consent of all of the parties.

Rule III. Court Appearances

A. General Rules.

1. Appearances at the calendar call are required by all attorneys in all matters. Detailed settlement discussions in any matter may be conducted in Chambers when permitted. Counsel must be fully familiar with the matter(s) on which they appear and must be authorized to enter into both substantive and procedural agreements on behalf of their clients. Any agreements entered into by counsel will be binding on their respective law firm.

2. Counsel must be on time for all scheduled appearances and must bring sufficient material to allow meaningful discussion of unresolved issues to each Court appearance. Attorneys appearing "of counsel" to an attorney of record and parties appearing pro se will be held to the same requirements.

B. Adjournments. As a matter of general practice, requests for adjournments of conferences, hearings and trials are greatly discouraged. Applications for such adjournments must be made in writing and received by the Court (by letter or facsimile) at least 24 hours in advance of the scheduled proceeding to be adjourned and must set forth: (1) good cause as to why an adjournment is sought; and (2) whether the other party/parties consent or object to the adjournment. The request may also suggest an approximate time period or a new date for the adjournment. The party requesting the adjournment must notify all parties of record as to the Court's decision regarding the adjournment request.

C. Conferences.

1. *In general*: Appearances at conferences are mandatory. Failure to appear at a conference may result in sanctions, as appropriate.

2. *Matrimonial Actions*: Where a preliminary conference has been scheduled in a matrimonial action, the parties shall, prior to the conference, file and exchange the required documents as set forth in 22 NYCRR 202.16(f)(1), including the net worth statements, paycheck stubs, W–2 statements, tax returns and statements of account. Counsel shall inform their respective clients of the automatic orders set forth in Domestic Relations Law Section 236 Part B(2)(b) as soon as the attorney-client relationship is formed. The parties, as well as counsel, shall appear at all matrimonial conferences unless otherwise directed by the Court.

Rule IV. Discovery and Inspection

A. General Rules. Counsel shall exert a continuing effort to work cooperatively and courteously with all adverse counsel towards the goal of completing all discovery expeditiously and efficiently and in the spirit of avoiding unnecessary motion practice and court intervention. See, 22 NYCRR 202.7. In other words, discovery motions are strongly discouraged.

B. Motion Procedure Prior to filing a discovery-related motion, counsel for the aggrieved party or the aggrieved pro se litigant shall request a conference with the Court at which time the matter will be resolved. In the event that a discovery motion is filed, see Part Rule V(H)(3).

Rule V. Motions

A. General Rules. All motions shall be accompanied by a Notice of Motion and shall set forth a return date. See, CPLR Section 2212 and CPRL R 2214. Ex parte motions shall be accompanied by an Affidavit and shall set forth a return date. See, 22 NYCRR Section 202.7(d) and 22 NYCRR Section 202.8(a) and (b).

B. Return Dates. Motions shall be returnable every Friday at 9:30 a.m. except those Fridays that fall on a legal holiday.

C. Appearances/Oral Argument. No appearances shall be made on motion return dates EXCEPT for motions and Orders to Show Cause made in matrimonial actions or unless otherwise ordered by the Court. Oral argument may be requested by noting "Oral Argument Requested" immediately over the index number on the Notice of Motion. If the Court, in its discretion, determines that oral argument would assist the Court in rendering its decision, whether requested or not, the movant's attorney will be so advised and will be required to notify all parties of the date scheduled for oral argument.

D. Papers to Be Submitted. All motions and opposition papers must be accompanied by a stamped, self-addressed envelope. Courtesy copies of motions shall NOT be submitted. All documents required to decide the motion must be included in the moving papers. It is not sufficient to refer the Court to the County Clerk, where the documents may be on file.

E. Proposed Orders. The moving party shall submit with its motion papers a proposed Order.

F. Form of Papers. Motion papers are to be securely bound. Exhibits tabs should be used in lieu of exhibit sheets. Papers should be in clear type of no less than 12 point in size and all paragraphs, where appropriate, and pages should be properly numbered.

G. Filing. All motions, including ex parte motions and Orders to Show Cause, shall be filed with the Chief Clerk's Office, Civil Division window (upon the appropriate payment to the County Clerk). Opposition and reply papers shall be sent directly to the Part Clerk. Sur-reply papers WILL NOT BE considered absent express permission from the Court in advance. If new issues are raised in the reply, or if there has been a change in the law while the motion is pending, counsel is to advise chambers, in writing, and request to submit additional affidavits or memoranda. Other papers, including letters, which are sent after the submission of the motion, will not be considered.

H. Adjournments

1. *With Consent*: Upon consent of all counsel and pro se litigants, the Court will ordinarily grant no more than two (2) adjournments of a motion or Order to Show Cause. The party seeking the adjournment must obtain the consent of adversary parties and notify the Part Clerk of the requested adjournment date at least 24 hours before the return date. The Court will assign a new date for the motion or Order to Show Cause and in doing so, will give due consideration to any specific date agreed upon by the parties.

2. *Without Consent*: Parties requesting an adjournment without the consent of the other parties shall send a brief letter to the Court with a copy to all interested counsel at least 24 hours prior to the return date. Parties seeking a non-consented-to adjournment must provide good cause as to why the adjournment should be granted. Counsel opposing the adjournment request should submit a brief response setting forth their reasons for objecting. No further communications will be permitted.

3. *Notification*: The party seeking the adjournment request shall send a confirming letter to the Court and all parties indicating whether the request has been granted or denied.

G.* Withdrawn Motions. In the event that a motion has been resolved by a withdrawal or settlement of the case, counsel are to immediately notify the Court by faxing to Chambers a letter of withdrawal or a Stipulation of Settlement and Discontinuance.

H. Types of Motions.

1. *Summary Judgment Motions*: Motions for summary judgment shall be filed with the Court and served upon all parties no later than 60 days from the date of the filing of the Note of Issue. If an application to extend the time to make a summary judgment motion is granted by the Court, the moving party must indicate same in its motion papers. The filing of a motion made pursuant to CPLR 3211 or 3212 shall not stay pre-trial discovery unless otherwise ordered by the Court.

2. *Motions to Renew and Reargue*: All motions to renew and reargue a prior motion pursuant to CPLR 2221 must contain as exhibits all papers submitted on the prior motion, as well as a copy of the Court's decision on the prior motion. Failure to comply with this requirement shall result in the denial of the motion.

3. *Discovery–Related Motions*: All discovery-related motions will automatically be converted to a conference for resolution of the issue.

4. *Orders to Show Cause*:

a. General Rules: The filing of Orders to Show Cause in lieu of Notices of Motion are greatly discouraged. Orders to Show Cause should be filed only where required by statute, setting forth the citation to the applicable statute, or where the moving party establishes "proper cause."

b. Stays and Temporary Restraining Orders: The moving party must provide notice to all other parties pursuant to 22 NYCRR 202.7(f) unless the moving party demonstrates that there will be significant prejudice by the giving of such prior notice. The Court may schedule a conference to determine whether such temporary relief should be granted. Following the conference, the Court shall render a determination only on the request for temporary relief.

c. Matrimonial Motions/OTSC for Pendente Lite Relief: There shall be appearances by both parties and counsel on the return date of all pendente lite motions/OTSC. The Court will conduct a preliminary conference, where appropriate, or a conference on the OTSC. Counsel shall have all exchanges and submissions made prior to the return date and counsel shall be prepared for oral argument on each issue. The Court may, in its discretion, decide the motion/OTSC from the bench on the return date. Counsel shall order a copy of the transcript, the cost to be shared equally by the parties (with a re-allocation to be determined at a later date if necessary), and provide a copy to the Court. Counsel are encouraged to submit a proposed order to the Court, on notice, with a copy of the transcript attached thereto, for the Court's signature.

I. Motion Decisions and Orders.

1. *Proposed Orders*: The moving party shall submit a proposed Order with the Notice of Motion and supporting papers at the time of filing.

2. *Written Decisions*: Where appropriate, the Court will utilize the proposed Order submitted by the moving party. Otherwise, a written Decision and Order will be issued by the Court. A copy of the decision shall be sent to all counsel and parties who have submitted a self-addressed stamped envelope.

3. *Bench Decisions*: In certain instances, the Court will render a decision from the bench. Any party seeking a written order of a decision rendered from the bench shall submit to the Court a proposed Order with a copy of the transcript attached thereto. Where a decision from the bench is rendered in matrimonial actions, a copy of the transcript will be ordered by the Court, the cost of which shall be split between the parties unless otherwise ordered by the Court.

* So in original.

Rule VI. Trials

A. Trial Dates. Trial dates shall be strictly adhered to and adjournments will rarely be granted except in the most extraordinary instances where good cause has been shown.

B. Scheduling. Once a trial date has been scheduled, clients, fact witnesses, physicians, experts and others are to be timely advised of scheduled dates to avoid last minute claims of unavailability. The parties and their attorneys are encouraged to videotape trial testimony of witnesses who are likely to be unavailable at trial. Videotaping shall be conducted in accordance with the applicable statutes and uniform rules at the producing party's expense and shall occur between the pre-trial conference date and the trial date. In addition, the Court shall endeavor to accommodate bona fide special preferences to the extent recognized by CPLR Rule 3403 and Uniform Rules 202.24 and 202.25.

C. Subpoenas.

1. *In General.* All counsel are reminded that they may sign trial subpoenas duces tecum and subpoenas ad testificatum as officers of the Court pursuant to CPLR Section 2302.

2. *"So Ordered" Subpoenas.* Subpoenas seeking documents in the possession of libraries, hospitals, and municipal corporations and their departments and bureaus must be "So Ordered" by the Court pursuant to CPLR Section 2306 and 2307. Subpoenas for docu-

ments possessed by libraries, hospitals and municipal corporations may only be "So Ordered" upon by notice of motion served upon the intended recipients of the subpoenas with at least one (1) day's notice pursuant to CPLR Section 2307. "So Ordered" subpoenas must then be served upon the intended recipient at least twenty-four (24) hours before the time fixed for the production of documents, unless such notice is waived by the Court due to emergency circumstances as permitted by CPLR Section 2307. [Motions for "So Ordered" subpoenas should be delivered to the Part Clerk at the courthouse, and will be addressed by the Court promptly when time sensitive.] The Court's issuance of a "So Ordered" subpoena does not constitute a ruling as to the admissibility of the subpoenaed materials.

3. *Medical Records.* All subpoenas for materials protected by HIPPA shall refer to and annex a duly executed HIPPA compliant authorization.

4. *Cover Letter.* A cover letter shall accompany all subpoenas submitted to the Court to be "So Ordered" setting forth any information about the action that may assist the Court.

D. Interpreters. In the event that any party requires the services of an interpreter during trial for foreign languages or services for the hearing impaired, the Court is to be notified of same no later than the Pretrial Conference so that appropriate arrangements can be made by the Court in advance of the trial date.

E. Pre–Trial Requirements. At least five (5) days prior to the commencement of trial, counsel shall provide the following to the Court: marked pleadings, a list of names of witnesses with a one-line summary of their anticipated testimony (including expert witnesses in accordance with the CPLR), an exhibit list, a proposed verdict sheet, and requested jury charges referring to the section number of the Pattern Jury Instructions (PJI).

F. Motions in Limine. Motions in limine must be delivered to the Part Clerk and served upon all counsel of record no later than seven (7) business days prior to the scheduled date of the trial, except as to issues that cannot be reasonably anticipated prior to trial. Unless otherwise directed by the Court, motions in limine and opposition papers to such motions shall not exceed ten (10) pages in length. If more than one motion in limine is contemplated by a party, each such motion shall be separately bound and is subject to a separate page limit.

Rule VII. Summary Jury Trials (SJT)

A. In General. Summary jury trials are highly encouraged. The summary jury trial is a prompt, inexpensive method of resolving disputes before a jury in a one-day trial. Some other features of the summary jury trial are: (i) There are specific time limits for each stage of the jury trial, e.g., jury selection (two hours), opening statements (ten minutes), case presentation per party (one hour); (ii) Expert reports are read to the jury instead of live testimony of expensive expert witnesses; (iii) Medical records need not be certified; and (iv) Recognized medical or other scientific or technical treatises are read to the jury.

B. Request for an SJT. Submit a written request for an SJT to the Court with copies to all counsel and/or pro se parties of record.

JUSTICE CHARLES APOTHEKER

Doc. 1. Hon. Charles Apotheker

E–Filing Rules and Protocol

All parties should familiarize themselves with the statewide E–Filing Rules (Uniform Rule §§ 202.5–b and 202.5–bb — available at www.nycourts.gov/efile) and the Rockland County E–Filing Protocol.

General questions about e-filing should be addressed to the E–Filing Resource Center at (646) 386–3033 or efile@courts.state.ny.us.

Specific questions relating to local procedures should be addressed to the Chief Clerk's Office (845) 483–8310.

Electronic Filing

All civil actions approved for e-filing in Judge Apotheker's part are to be filed through the New York State Courts E–Filing system (NYSCEF). All submissions to the Court, including proposed orders, proposed judgments, and letters, must be electronically filed.

Working Copies

A court may require the submission of "working copies" of electronically filed documents. See Uniform Rule § 202.5–b(d)(4).

Working copies shall be delivered to the Rockland Chief Clerk's Office.

[ ] This Part does not require working copies.

[ ] This Part does not require working copies but may request working copies in specific instances.

[X] This Part requires 1 working copy for all electronic submissions.

[ ] This Part requires working copies for:

   [ ] motion submissions

   [ ] proposed orders to show cause

   [ ] proposed orders/judgments

   [ ] stipulations

   [ ] transcripts

   [ ] letters

All working copies submitted to this Part <u>must</u> include a copy of the NYSCEF Confirmation Notice firmly fastened to the front cover page of the submission and comply with other requirements set forth in the Rockland County Protocol. Working copies without the Confirmation Notice will not be accepted.

Working copies are to be delivered no later than 3:00 p.m. on the first business day following the electronic filing of the document on the NYSCEF site.

Hard Copy Submissions

Part will reject any hard copy submissions in e-filed cases unless those submissions bear the Notice of Hard Copy Submission — E–Filed Case required by Uniform Rule § 202.5–b(d)(1). The form is available at www.nycourts.gov/efile.

Scheduling

Counsel/parties should address questions about scheduling appearances or adjourning appearances to the Part Clerk, Senior Court Clerk Robert Rolle, at (845) 483–8350.

JUSTICE MARGARET GARVEY

Rule I. Communications With The Court

  A. Correspondence. Correspondence to the Court shall, without exception, be copied to all adversary counsel(s) and *pro se* litigants and must reflect the Index Number of the action to which it relates. Correspondence between counsel(s) and/or *pro se* litigants shall not be copied to the Court unless there is some judicial purpose to be served by transmitting copies to the Court.

  B. Telephone Calls. Telephone calls to the Court staff are permitted only in necessary or emergency situations requiring immediate attention that cannot otherwise be attained by correspondence.

  C. Faxes. The fax number to Chambers is noted above. Chambers will not accept faxed copies of papers that must otherwise be electronically filed or filed in original form with the Office of the Clerk (such as motions, oppositions to motions, replies, proposed Orders, and documents to be "So Ordered"). Faxes will be accepted of any correspondence intended for the Court so long as copies are simultaneously faxed or delivered to all adversary parties, an so long as the sender transmits the same document(s) intended for the Court via regular mail. Counsel are not permitted, without prior approval, to send facsimile transmissions to Chambers that exceed five (5) pages in length.

D. *Ex Parte* Communications. *Ex parte* communications are strictly prohibited except: 1) in the limited permissible context involving the presentation of Orders to Show Cause for signature, or 2) with the consent of all parties during settlement negotiations at the Courthouse, or 3) in the unusual circumstance where oral argument is required by the Court on a motion and a party fails to appear at the scheduled date and time, argument may be heard by the adversary party/parties in attendance in open court. Inappropriate ex parte communications will be returned to the sender, unread.

E. Court Papers. All pleadings, motions, Orders to Show Cause, opposition papers, replies, memoranda of law and other submissions must be signed by counsel to the extent required by Section 130–1.1a of the Rules of the Chief Administrator.

F. E–Filing. All parties should familiarize themselves with the statewide E–Filing Rules (Uniform Rule 202.5–b and 202.5–bb, available at www.nycourts.gov/efile and the Rockland County E–Filing protocol. General questions about e-filing should be addressed to the E–Filing Resource Center at (646) 386–3033 or efile@courts.state.ny.us. Specific questions relating to local procedures should be addressed to the Chief Clerk's Office at (845) 638–5393. All actions specified by the Chief Administrator of the Courts, except those specifically excluded pursuant to Uniform Rule 202.5–bb, in Justice Garvey's Part are to be filed through the New York State Courts E–Filing system (NYSCEF). All submissions to the Court, including proposed Orders, proposed judgments, and letters, must be electronically filed. Subpoenas duces tecum and Subpoenas Ad Testificatum should still be presented to the Court in paper form for signature for upcoming trials.

G. Working Copies. This Court requires working copies on all submissions or electronically filed documents pursuant to Uniform Rule 202.5–b(d)(4) and such working copies shall be sent directly to Chambers—not to the Clerk's office. All working copies submitted must include a copy of the NYSCEF Confirmation Notice firmly fastened as the back cover page of the submission and comply with other requirements set forth in the Rockland County Protocol. Working copies without the Confirmation Notice will not be accepted. Working copies are to be delivered directly to Chambers no later than 12:00 p.m. on the first business day following the electronic filing of the document on the NYSCEF site, except in tax certiorari cases**.

** In tax certiorari cases, working copies of any previously filed documents, for instance a Notice of Petition, shall be delivered directly to Chambers at the time of the filing of the RJI. Once the RJI is filed, for all subsequent filings, working copies shall be delivered directly to Chambers no later than 12:00 p.m. on the first business day following the electronic filing of the document on the NYSCEF site.

H. Hard Copy Submissions. The Court will reject any hard copy submissions in e-filed cases unless those submissions bear the Notice of Hard Copy Submission—E–Filed Case required by Uniform Rule 202.5–b(d)(1). The form is available at www.nycourts.gov/efile.

Rule II. Court Conferences

A. General Rules. All conferences with the Court are conducted in public before Justice Garvey at 9:15 a.m. sharp weekdays in Courtroom #2 of the Rockland County Courthouse, unless otherwise directed. Matrimonial conferences and detailed settlement discussions of any litigation may be conducted in Chambers when permitted by law and when otherwise appropriate and advisable. Counsel and *pro se* litigants are expected to appear for all conferences on time. Counsel must be fully familiar with the action(s) on which they appear and must be authorized to enter into both substantive and procedural agreements on behalf of their clients. Attorneys appearing "of counsel" to an attorney of record, and parties appearing *pro se*, are held to the same requirements. A failure to comply with this rule may be deemed by the Court as a default and dealt with appropriately. Attorneys are expected to appear with their clients for all conferences in matrimonial actions, unless such appearances are dispensed with by the Court on prior request, noticed to the adversary and any law guardians.

B. Preliminary Conferences. Preliminary Conferences shall be conducted: (1) after a written Request For Judicial Intervention ("RJI") is duly filed with the Office of the Clerk in accordance with Uniform Rule 202.12(a), or (2) after an appropriate notice is filed in medical malpractice actions pursuant to Uniform Rule 202.56, or (3) after an appropriate notice is filed in matrimonial actions pursuant to Uniform Rule 202.16, or (4) upon a specific directive by the Court. Preliminary Conferences will ordinarily result in the issuance by the Court on the same day of a reasonable and complete scheduling Order, which shall address all aspects of anticipated pretrial discovery, and which shall set forth a date on which a Compliance Conference will later be conducted. Discovery may be expedited in third party actions, joint actions and consolidated actions to avoid undue delay in the completion of discovery overall. Preliminary Conferences of matrimonial actions will be conducted in accordance with Uniform Rule 202.16 and DRL Section 236(B)(4), by which the parties are required, *inter alia*, to submit at the conference copies of counsels' retainer agreements and certified copies of the parties' net worth statements (including copies of their most recent three years of federal and state income tax returns, latest W–2 forms and pay stubs, bank and investment statements and other relevant supporting documentation). Preliminary Conferences of medical, dental, and podiatric malpractice actions will be conducted in accordance with Uniform Rule

202.56(b). All counsel and *pro se* litigants are expected to take most seriously the Court's discovery schedule and deadlines, and non-compliance shall only be excused if explained by extenuating circumstances.

C. Compliance Conferences. The purpose of the Compliance Conference is for counsel and *pro se* litigants to report to the Court that pre-trial discovery has been completed, to enable the Court to direct a date on which a Note of Issue shall be filed and to schedule dates for Mediation, a Pre-trial Conference, and trial. Parties are not permitted to file a Note of Issue in any action unless permission to do so is granted by the Court at the Compliance Conference. Motions to strike Notes of Issue are discouraged, as matters of outstanding discovery, if any, are expected to be raised, discussed and resolved at the Compliance Conference. The Court reserves the right to set forth at the Compliance Conferences a further discovery schedule if the litigation or the interests of justice so require, though parties are warned that any additional permissible discovery may be subject to an expedited schedule. The Court also reserves the right to impose appropriate sanction against any party or counsel responsible for a non-excusable failure to complete pretrial discovery by the date of the Compliance Conference.

D. Pre-trial Conference. The Court shall conduct a Pre-trial Conference with all counsel and *pro se* litigants on a date that shall ordinarily be within thirty (30) days of the trial date. Pre-trial Conference and trial dates that are scheduled during a Compliance Conference should be viewed by the parties and counsel as firm dates. It is expected that counsel attending Pre-trial Conferences shall be fully familiar with the action and be authorized to discuss: (1) all factual and legal issues presented by the litigation, (2) settlement demands or offers, (3) trial procedure and witness scheduling, and (4) that counsel also be authorized to enter into settlements on terms agreeable to the parties and to the Court. The actual parties in any litigation, or in actions involving insurance carriers and authorized claims representative, must be available for the Pre-trial Conference either in person or, if prior permission granted by the Court, by telephone for the purpose of direct contact with the Court in settlement discussions. The Court endeavors to be of assistance to parties in settling litigations prior to trial. In the event a Pre-trial Conference does not result in a settlement of an action, the Court will favorably entertain any later request by the parties, on consent, for the conduct of an additional Pre-trial Conference prior to the date of trial, but shall not allow any such additional conference to delay the trial schedule.

E. Adjournments. As a matter of general practice, adjournments will not be granted for conferences (Preliminary, Compliance, Mediation, Pre-trial) or trials. Applications for adjournments must be made in writing actually received by the Court (by letter or facsimile) at least twenty-four (24) hours in advance of the scheduled conference, and must address: (1) good cause why an adjournment is sought, (2) whether the adverse party (parties) consent or object to the application, and (3) may, at the option of the sender, suggest an approximate time period, or an exact date, for which the adjournment is sought. All such communications must be copied to all counsel and pro se litigants in accordance with Section I of these Part Rules. The Court may, in the exercise of sound discretion, permit or refuse a conference adjournment in any given instance.

F. Non–Appearance at Scheduled Conferences. The failure of any counsel or *pro se* litigant to appear for Preliminary, Compliance, or Pre-trial Conferences may, with notice, be treated by the Court as a default and shall be dealt with by an Order directing the dismissal of a Complaint or Petition, the striking of any Answer, and the conduct of an inquest, or by other appropriate remedy authorized by Uniform Rule 202.27.

Rule III. Motions and Orders to Show Cause

Prior to making any motion (including motions regarding Discovery/Disclosure issues), the potential movant (or counsel) must notify the court in writing (two page maximum length), with a copy to all parties, setting forth the relief sought and the basis for that relief. The Court will then schedule either a conference call with counsel, or an in-court conference date. This procedure does not preclude the moving party from making a motion, but provides the Court with an opportunity to resolve the dispute giving rise to the motion without the need for a formal written application. Failing resolution of the dispute, the party seeking the relief may proceed with the motion.

A. General Rules. The Court will entertain motions on submission, whether brought by Notice of Motion or by Order to Show Cause, for 9:15 a.m. on any Friday the Court is in session. The return date for an Order to Show Cause shall, of course, be determined by the Court at the time papers are submitted for consideration and executed. There shall be no motion calendar called by the Court, and no oral argument heard on any motions unless directed by the Court in a given instance. In the unusual instance when the Court wishes to hear oral argument on a motion, as permitted by Uniform Rule 202.8(d), all counsel and *pro se* litigants shall be provided with reasonable prior notice of the date and time scheduled for such purpose at which the parties are expected to appear in Court. The failure of a moving party to appear for oral argument at the scheduled date and time may result in the motion being denied and otherwise marked off, while the failure of appearance by an opposing party may result in the motion being argued *ex parte* and then decided either on the merits or granted on default.

B. Filing of Papers Applicable To All Motions. Except with the express permission of the Court, all motion papers and Orders to Show Cause, including Notices of Motion, proposed Orders, affidavits or affirmations in support, affidavits or affirmations of good faith and memoranda of law, must contain by the telephone and facsimile numbers of counsel and be typewritten, double-spaced, securely bound if submitted in paper form, entirely legible, and all exhibits labeled with exhibit tabs if submitted in paper form. The Court may refuse to accept any such paper which does not conform to the foregoing. Motion papers and all related correspondence must reflect the Index Number assigned to the action. Courtesy copies and/or working copies are neither requested, nor expected. The filing of a motion does not relieve any party from attending any previously scheduled conferences, or court appearances, regardless of the nature of the relief sought in the motion.

C. Electronically Filed Submissions. This Court requires working copies of electronically filed submissions. Counsel must attach each exhibit as a separate exhibit in submissions filed with exhibits. In lieu of exhibit tabs as used in paper submissions, the first page of each separately attached exhibit should be a blank page with the exhibit number or letter in bold letters centered on the page. Counsel should label submissions accurately and clearly in the Electronic Filing system.

D. Supporting Documents. All documents required to decide the application must be included in the moving papers. It is not sufficient that those documents are on file with the County Clerk. Compliance with this rule is particularly important on motions brought pursuant to CPLR § 2221.

E. Motion Adjournments. Upon consent of all counsel and pro se litigants, the Court will typically grant an adjournment of a motion or Order to Show Cause, however, no more than three adjournments of any single motion will be permitted. The party seeking the adjournment must obtain the consent of the adversary parties and notify the Part Clerk of the requested adjournment date at least twenty-four (24) hours before the return date. The Court will then assign a new date for the motion or Order to Show Cause. In assigning an adjourn date, the Court shall give due consideration to any specific date agreed upon by all parties. Motion adjournments should be confirmed to the Court and all adversary parties in writing, in accordance with Section I of these Part Rules. All non-consented requests for adjournments require Court approval, obtained at least twenty-four (24) hours before the return date. No adjournment request will be entertained by the Court unless the party seeking the adjournment has first attempted to obtain consent from all the other parties in the action. Parties seeking a non-consented to adjournment must provide good cause as to why the adjournment should be granted, in accordance with the communication

requirements set forth in Section I of these Part Rules.

F. Reply Papers. Reply papers shall not set forth new factual claims, legal arguments, expert affidavits, or requests for relief that were not within the scope of the papers that initiated the motion.

G. Sur–Reply Papers. The CPLR does not recognize the existence of Sur–Reply Papers, however denominated, and accordingly, this Court will not consider any post-Reply papers or materials absent a party receiving express permission from the Court in advance. Post–Reply materials received in violation of the rule will be returned, unread, to the Office of the Rockland County Clerk for filing. Opposing counsel who receives a copy of post-Reply materials submitted in violation of this rule should not respond in kind.

H. Summary Judgment Motions. Summary Judgment motions must be made no later than sixty (60) days from the date of the filing of the Note of Issue.

Rule IV. Decisions and Orders

A. Written Decisions and Orders. In most instances, a Decision and Order will be rendered in written form following the full submission of the motion, or Order to Show Cause. The Decision and Order, with all supporting and opposition papers, will be filed by the Court with the Office of the Rockland County Clerk. A copy of the Decision and Order will be mailed to all counsel and *pro se* litigants after filing. If counsel has provided a facsimile number with the motion as required by these Part Rules, the Decision and Order will also be faxed to counsel.

B. Oral Decisions and Orders. In certain instances, the Court may render a Decision and issue an Order orally from the Bench. In such instances, a transcript of the Decision and Order, paid for by the parties and provided to the Court, will be executed or "so ordered" by the Court and filed with the Office of the Rockland County Clerk.

Rule V. Trials and Hearings

A. Trial Dates. Trial dates provided by the Court should be deemed firm in every action, and accordingly, it is expected that clients, fact witnesses, physicians, experts and others be timely advised of scheduled dates to avoid last minute claims of unavailability. Counsel is again reminded of the "Sixty Day Rule," pursuant to Uniform Rule 125.1(g) regarding applications for adjournments. If a date for trial of an action or proceeding has been scheduled for two months in advance, counsel previously designated as trial counsel must appear on that date, or if engaged elsewhere or has a scheduling conflict, must produce substitute trial counsel. Videotaped trial testimony can be arranged with the Court at the producing party's expense, to be conducted between the date of the Pre-trial Conference and the date of the trial, to accommodate serious, prejudicial and unavoidable scheduling difficulties that might arise without delaying the scheduled trial itself. In scheduling and conducting trials, the Court shall endeavor to accommodate bona fide special preferences to the extent recognized by CPLR § 3403 and Uniform Rules 202.24 and 202.25.

B. Subpoenas. All counsel are reminded that they may sign trial subpoenas duces tecum and subpoenas ad testificatum as officers of the Court pursuant to CPLR § 2302, except when subpoenas are directed to documents of libraries, hospitals, and municipal corporations and their departments and bureaus, in which cases they must be "So Ordered" by the Court pursuant to CPLR §§ 2306 and 2307. Subpoenas for documents possessed by libraries, hospitals and municipal corporations may only be "So Ordered" upon motion served upon the intended recipients of the subpoena with at least one (1) day's notice pursuant to CPLR § 2307. "So Ordered" subpoenas must then be served upon intended recipient at least twenty-four (24) hours before the time fixed for the production of the documents, unless such notice is waived by the Court due to emergency circumstances as permitted by CPLR § 2307. Motions for "So Ordered" subpoenas should be delivered to the Part Clerk at the Courthouse in paper form, and will be addressed by the Court promptly when time sensitive. Subpoenas will be "So Ordered" if they appear on their face to relate to evidence that is at least minimally material and relevant to the action, and benefits of the doubt shall ordinarily be resolved in favor of the party seeking the "So Ordered" subpoena. The Court's issuance of "So Ordered" subpoenas should not be viewed by parties as collateral estoppel on the issue of admissibility at trial of the documents to which such subpoenas relate.

C. Interpreters. In the event that any party requires the services of a translator during trial for foreign languages or services for the hearing impaired, the Court is to be notified of same no later than the Pre-trial Conference so that appropriate arrangements can be made by the Court in advance of the trial date.

D. Pre–Trial Requirements.

Trial Notebooks

No later than five (5) business days prior to the scheduled trial date, counsel shall each provide to the other and submit to the Court a trial notebook which shall consist of:

1. marked pleadings in accordance with CPLR § 4012

2. The joint statement of the relevant facts that are not in dispute

3. Pre-trial memoranda of law as to any known disputed legal issues that must be determined by the court

4. A list of witnesses for each party

5. A list of all exhibits to be offered by each party

6. Copies of the exhibits intended to be offered by counsel, pre-marked with plaintiff's exhibits numbered sequentially and defendant's exhibits lettered sequentially

7. Requests to Charge—The charge will be drawn from the Pattern Jury Instructions (PJI). A complete list of requested charges is to be submitted. Unless counsel seeks a deviation from the pattern charge, or additions to the pattern charge, only the PJI numbers need to be submitted. Where deviations or additions are requested, the full test of such requests must be submitted in writing and on computer disk in Word Perfect 8.0 format, together with any supporting legal precedent. Additionally, if the PJI calls for incorporation of a statute, counsel must submit the full charge including the text of the statute with proposed or agreed upon edits.

8. Verdict Sheet—Counsel shall jointly prepare a verdict sheet. The verdict sheet is to be typed in final form for presentation to the jury. If agreement cannot be reached, then each side shall present a proposed verdict sheet, along with a written explanation as to why agreement on the verdict sheet cannot be reached. If it is feasible, such proposals shall also be submitted on a computer disk in Word Perfect 8.0.

9. In Matrimonial Actions—updated net worth statements, statements of proposed dispositions as required by Uniform Rule 202.16(h) and any forensic reports, appraisals and evaluations.

The court may in its discretion relieve counsel from all or part of the trial notebook requirements upon a showing that the issues to be tried are sufficiently narrow that the trial notebook is not necessary or that the interest of justice otherwise justify such relief. Such a request will be entertained only at the pre-trial conference. Failure to submit a trial notebook five (5) business days prior to the date of trial may result in the Court, on it's own motion, or on motion of opposing counsel, striking the pleadings of the party who failed to submit the trial notebook in accordance with these Part Rules.

Evidentiary Objections. Not later than one (1) business day prior to the scheduled trial date, each counsel shall provide to the other and submit to the court a statement setting forth any objection to the exhibits identified in the list provided by opposing counsel and the specific basis therefor. Any exhibit as to which no objection is identified shall be admitted into evidence on consent. The failure to submit such a statement of objections on a timely basis may be deemed to be consent to the admission of all of the exhibits included in the trial notebook submitted by the opposing party.

Witnesses. Any witness not identified in the witness list provided to opposing counsel, other than an impeachment or rebuttal witness, shall not be permitted to testify unless an adequate explanation is provided for the failure to identify such witness prior to trial. Parties, fact witnesses and expert witnesses should be advised of the scheduled dates at the time they are set. Absent unanticipated, exigent circumstances, last minute claims of unavailability will not be recognized where trial dates have been previously set. All witnesses should be on one-hour phone call notice so that their waiting time in court is minimized. Professional witnesses, such as doctors, nurses, and social workers, and witnesses who are public employees, such as teachers, counselors and police officers, will be permitted to testify out of order to accommodate their employment schedules. School teachers should be scheduled after 3:00 p.m. so that it is not necessary for the employers to provide substitutes.

Exhibits. Any exhibit not identified in the exhibit list provided to opposing counsel, other than an exhibit offered for the purpose of impeachment or rebuttal, shall not be admitted into evidence unless an adequate explanation is provided for the failure to identify such exhibit prior to trial. In addition to the copies of exhibits provided in the trial notebook, each party shall provide at trial one additional set of exhibits which will be used when counsel wishes to publish an exhibit to a witness.

Settlement. The court is available for a settlement conference at any time prior to the scheduled trial date. If the matter is not settled prior to the trial date, the trial will commence as scheduled. Settlement negotiations will not be entertained on the scheduled trial date prior to the commencement of the trial. If the matter is settled outside the presence of the court, counsel shall advise the part clerk immediately so that another matter may be scheduled in its place.

Motions in Limine. Any motions for the Court's consideration *in limine* must be electronically filed and working copies must be delivered directly to Chambers, as well as served upon adversary counsel(s) not later than seven business days prior to the scheduled date of the trial, except as to issues that cannot be reasonably anticipated prior to trial. Unless otherwise directed by the Court, motions *in limine* and opposition papers to such motion shall not exceed ten (10) pages in length. If more than one motion *in limine* is contemplated by a party, each such motion shall be separately bound and is subject to a separate page limit.

Identification of Trial Counsel. Attorneys are reminded that if a trial is to be argued by counsel other than the attorney of record, Uniform Rule 202.31 requires that the trial counsel be identified in writing to the Court and to all parties not later than fifteen (15) days from the date of the Pre-trial Conference, with such writing signed by both the attorney of record and the incoming trial counsel. This rule will be waived by the Court in any instance when the attorney of record is engaged in an unrelated trial and the retention of trial counsel allows the parties to proceed with the trial by Justice Garvey without adjournment.

*Pre-*Voir Dire *Conference.* Immediately prior to the commencement of jury selection, the Court shall conduct with all the attorneys and pro se litigants a pre-*voir dire* conference as required by the Uniform Rule 202.33(b). The purpose of the conference shall be to: set time limits upon jury selection and to determine limits upon peremptory challenges; discuss trial stipulations; argue and/or decide motions *in limine*; further discuss potential full, or partial, settlements; discuss scheduling; and address other appropriate trial-related issues.

Jury Selection. Juries shall be selected by the parties outside the presence of the Court in accordance with "White Rules", a copy of which comprises Appendix E of the Uniform Rules for the New York Trial Courts. The Court shall impose upon parties in all actions time limits on a Panel-to-Panel basis for the conduct of jury selection, as authorized by Uniform Rule 202.33(d). And such time limits may vary in the exercise of court discretion based upon the nature and complexity of given actions. The Court shall be available to resolve any conflicts that arise between parties during the jury selection process, including but not limited to disputes over challenges for cause as contemplated by CPLR § 4108. Peremptory challenges shall be pooled between multiple plaintiffs on the one hand and between multiple defendants on the other, and generally, each side shall be entitled, per panel, to three (3) peremptory challenges for regular jurors and one (1) peremptory challenges for each alternate juror. However, pursuant to CPLR § 4109, the number of peremptory challenges may be adjusted by the court in certain actions in the exercise of sound discretion and in the interests of justice.

Bifurcation. The trials of personal injury actions involving issues of both liability and damages shall be bifurcated in accordance with Uniform Rule 202.42 and all subdivisions thereof. Jury selection, opening statements and the presentation of evidence shall be governed accordingly. Trials on damages will commence immediately upon completion of the trials on liability.

Non-jury Trials. Transcripts and Post–Trial Briefs. Unless the Court directs otherwise, the parties will obtain and provide to the Court, on or before the date set by the Court at the conclusion of the trial, a copy of the trial transcript and each party will submit a post-trial brief with respect to the issues raised at the trial, setting forth specific references to the relevant portions of the transcript and the documents in evidence and citing the applicable law. Along with the submission of the post-trial briefs, counsel will also present the Court with a computer disk, in Word Perfect 8.0 format, containing a proposed findings of fact and a proposed disposition.

Rule VI. Settled and Discontinued Cases

Counsel shall immediately notify the Court of a case disposition. Following the initial notification, counsel shall submit a copy of the stipulation of discontinuance to chambers so that the matter may be marked off the calendar.

JUSTICE LINDA S. JAMIESON

Doc. 1. Part Rules

E–Filing Rules and Protocol

All parties should familiarize themselves with the statewide E-Filing Rules (Uniform Rule §§ 202.5–b and 202.5–bb—available at www.nycourts.gov/efile) and the Rockland County E–Filing Protocol.

General questions about e-filing should be addressed to the E–Filing Resource Center at 646–386–3033 or efile@courts.state.ny.us

Specific questions relating to local procedures should be addressed to the Chief Clerk's Office (845) 483-8310.

Electronic Filing

All non-exempt actions in Justice Jamieson's Part are to be filed through the New York State Courts E–Filing system (NYSCEF). All submissions to the Court, including proposed orders, proposed judgments, and letters, must be electronically filed. Note that trial exhibits should not be electronically filed, but must be submitted to the Court in a tabbed binder, as set forth below.

Working Copies

A court may require the submission of "working copies" of electronically filed documents. See Uniform Rule § 202.5–b(d)(4).

Working copies shall be delivered to the Rockland Chief Clerk's Office.

[ ] This Part does not require working copies.

[ ] This Part does not require working copies but may request working copies in specific instances.

[ ] This Part requires working copies for all electronic submissions.

[•] This Part requires working copies for:

[•] motion submissions

[•] proposed orders to show cause

[•] proposed orders/judgments

[•] stipulations to be so-ordered

[•] transcripts to be so-ordered

[ ] letters

All working copies submitted to this Part *must* include a copy of the NYSCEF Confirmation Notice firmly fastened as the front cover page of the submission and comply with other requirements set forth in the Rockland County Protocol. Working copies without the Confirmation Notice will not be accepted.

Working copies are to be delivered no later than 2:00 p.m. on the first business day following the electronic filing of the document on the NYSCEF site.

Hard Copy Submissions

This Part will reject any hard copy submissions in e-filed cases unless those submissions bear the Notice of Hard Copy Submission — E–Filed Case required by Uniform Rule § 202.5–b(d)(1). The form is available at www.nycourts.gov/efile.

Note that any documents that counsel wish to have sent back must be accompanied by a self-addressed, stamped envelope.

Scheduling and Letters to the Court

Counsel/parties should address questions about scheduling appearances or adjourning appearances to the Part Clerk, Carole Slattery, (including the case name, index number, date of next appearance and the post office and email addresses and phone and fax numbers of all counsel). All letters, on any subject, to the Court must be (1) copied to all counsel; (2) contain email addresses for all counsel; and (3) state the next appearance date. Letters not complying with these rules will be disregarded.

A. *Appearances*

Adjournments of appearances are not granted unless (1) there is an affirmation of prior engagement in full compliance with 22 NYCRR § 125.1, and it must include the date the conflicting appearance was scheduled; or (2) there are exceptional circumstances.

Adjournment requests made less than two Court days before a schedule set by the Court will not be considered absent exceptional circumstances. In matrimonial actions, the Court does not cancel appearances where the parties have signed a stipulation of settlement but have not yet submitted the appropriate divorce papers.

Do not telephone the Court to determine the status of an adjournment request; the Court will respond as soon as possible. If you do not receive a response, it means the adjournment was not granted. Note that the party requesting the adjournment is responsible for notifying all parties of the status of the adjournment.

B. *Motions*

(1) On consent: If the motion is adjourned on consent, send a letter to the Part Clerk, copied to all

parties. No more than two adjournments will be allowed without the Court's permission.

(2) Without consent: If a party does not consent to the requested adjournment, send a letter to the Part Clerk indicating the reason for the adjournment request, and the reason for the refusal.

Under no circumstances may parties represented by counsel contact the Court. Counsel must be discharged, and a Consent to Change Attorneys filed, or a motion to be relieved must have been made and granted, before counsel is relieved.

Ex parte communications are strictly prohibited except upon consent of all counsel, or with respect to scheduling matters or the presentation of Orders to Show Cause for signature.

Submission of Papers

All counter-orders and counter-judgments must be submitted with a cover letter and a "red-lined" copy highlighting the language which differs from that of the originally submitted order or judgment. See 22 NYCRR § 202.48.

All proposed orders or other documents for the Judge's signature must include a signature line with the Honorable Linda S. Jamieson pre-printed.

Proposed orders must include any transcript or other evidence that the Judge has directed the submission of such order.

For matrimonial actions, judgment documents must be submitted within 60 days of the date an action is marked settled or a decision is rendered, unless otherwise directed by the Court. Failure to submit judgment documents within 60 days (absent permission of the Court) will result in the action being deemed abandoned pursuant to 22 NYCRR § 202.48 and may be the subject of a conditional order of dismissal establishing a date on which the action will be dismissed as abandoned unless papers are received.

Discontinuing an Action

If an action is settled, discontinued, or otherwise disposed, counsel shall immediately provide written confirmation of the settlement to the Clerk of the Part. Counsel shall also advise the Court if there are any outstanding motions or scheduled conferences, hearings or trial dates. As soon as is practicable, counsel shall provide the Court with a fully executed stipulation or other document evidencing the disposition. The failure to abide by these requirements may result in the imposition of sanctions. Note that in matrimonial actions, unless all papers necessary to obtain a divorce have been submitted to the Court prior to the scheduled date, all parties and counsel must appear.

Motion Practice

A. Papers must be received by the Court on or before the date and time set forth in the Order to Show Cause or return date in the Notice of Motion in order to be considered. Late papers will be rejected unless good cause is shown and there is no prejudice caused by the delay.

Motions are on submission, unless the Court specifically requests oral argument.

B. The Court does NOT hold motions in abeyance. Motions must be formally withdrawn by letter.

C. The index number shall be clearly shown to the right of the caption of the matter on all litigation papers. The next scheduled appearance date, if any, must also be listed. All other papers and related correspondence must include the same.

D. Reply papers are to respond to issues raised in opposition to the motion. New issues raised in reply papers shall not be considered without specific permission from the Court. Cross-motions which seek only the denial of the relief in the original motion will not be recognized as motions with respect to which a reply may be submitted.

Sur-replies shall not be considered without specific permission from the Court. Permission is granted only upon a showing of exceptional circumstances.

F. On motions pursuant to CPLR § 2221, movant must submit copies of all papers on the prior motion. Failure to comply with this provision shall result in the automatic denial of the motion unless another party submits the papers to the Court.

G. Letters sent to the Court following submission of motions will not be considered.

H. No motions regarding discovery shall be made without first contacting the Court. All motions, whether discovery or otherwise, must provide proof that the parties or counsel have attempted to resolve the issue before making the motion.

I. All cited authorities that are not available on Westlaw must be submitted to the Court.

J. Affidavits of service must be filed at least two days before the return date unless the Court indicates a different date in an Order to Show Cause. The Court will deny any motion where it has received neither opposition nor an affidavit of service.

K. Motions for summary judgment shall be accompanied by a Statement of Undisputed Facts. A motion for summary judgment which lacks this Statement may be rejected.

L. Orders to Show Cause. In addition to the motion rules, the following provisions are applicable to orders to show cause:

If a requested order has specific urgency, counsel should make the Clerk aware of the issue. The Court will use every effort to address all orders as soon as is practical after their receipt. If a proposed order to show cause contains a request for a temporary order of protection or other emergency ex parte relief, counsel should advise the Part Clerk and should be prepared, with his or her client, for a hearing at such time as the Court will direct. Counsel should not appear without permission from the Court.

If an order to show cause requests temporary relief, counsel must comply with the provisions of 22 NYCRR § 202.7(f). If counsel has complied with this provision, the order to show cause must clearly specify such, either in a separate affirmation clearly marked with a tab, or an accompanying letter to the Court. Failure to comply with this section will result in all temporary relief being struck. Note that compliance with this section does not ensure that temporary relief will be granted.

Discovery Matters

A. Counsel must consult with one another in a good faith effort to resolve all disclosure disputes. See Uniform Rule 202.7. If problems exist regarding discovery that cannot be resolved, they should be brought to the Court's attention immediately (but no later than the date specified for completion of discovery) via a short letter. Any response to that letter must be made within 48 hours. Upon reviewing the submissions, the Court will determine the appropriate course of action.

B. Parties are also expected to abide by the provisions of the Preliminary Conference Order and Stipulation. Failure to do so may result in the imposition of costs or sanctions.

C. The Court will not allow discovery after the dates set forth in the Preliminary Conference Order without good cause shown for noncompliance.

D. Subpoenaed documents may only be reviewed after prior arrangements have been made with the Part Clerk.

E. Rulings will not be given over the telephone regarding disputes which may arise during an Examination Before Trial. Counsel should hold the specific issue in abeyance and continue with the balance of the Examination Before Trial if it is possible to do so.

Appearances

Counsel who appear in Court must be fully familiar with the case and have authority to enter into any agreement, either substantive or procedural, on behalf of their clients. Counsel and their clients must be on time for all scheduled appearances. Sanctions may be imposed for failure to comply with this rule. Note that in matrimonial actions, clients must come to every appearance, unless previously excused by the Court.

Interpreters and Special Services: No later than one week prior to the date for any scheduled court appearance, counsel shall advise the Part Clerk if the services of a foreign language interpreter are required for any party or witness, or if any special services are required for any party or witness who is hearing-impaired or who suffers from any other disability.

Preliminary Conference

A. *Civil Actions*: The preliminary conference will be held in accordance with, and attorneys must be prepared to comply with, 22 NYCRR § 202.12. In addition, attorneys must be prepared to advise the Court as to any outstanding motions and any other issues they expect to require the Court's involvement.

B. *Matrimonial Actions*: The preliminary conference will be held in accordance with, and attorneys must be prepared to comply with, 22 NYCRR § 202.16(f). In addition, attorneys must be prepared to advise the Court as to any outstanding motions and any other issues they expect to require the Court's involvement. The parties will be expected to comply with DRL § 236–B(4).

Trial Readiness/Settlement Conference— Counsel must be prepared to discuss the potential for settlement of the case at the trial readiness/settlement conference. Counsel should be prepared to place upon the record or provide a written stipulation as to all matters that are resolved.

A Note of Issue must be filed within 20 days of the Trial Readiness conference, and a file-stamped copy submitted to the Part Clerk. Sanctions, including the striking of pleadings or dismissal of the action, may be imposed for failure to do so.

Pre–Trial/Settlement Conference—Counsel must be fully prepared to discuss settlement. Sanctions may be imposed upon counsel who are not prepared for the conference. In the event counsel believe that there are no prospects to settle the case, they should be prepared to explain their reasoning.

At the Pre–Trial Conference, counsel should bring with them:

1) an exhibit list. The attorneys are to pre-mark their exhibits. Only those items which are received in evidence will be marked by the reporter. The reporter is to be provided with an exhibit list. Copies of all exhibits intended to be offered must be presented to the Court in a notebook with a table of contents, with the plaintiff's exhibits numbered and the defendant's exhibits lettered in the order in which they are generally intended to be used. Counsel must be prepared to argue to the Court any exhibits that are not agreed upon;

2) a list of witnesses, including the address of each witness and the general subject matter of his or her testimony;

3) a joint statement of the relevant facts that are not in dispute;

4) in matrimonial actions, a joint statement of proposed disposition. To the extent that the parties disagree on any item, the plaintiff's position should be set out first, followed by the defendant's position.

The Court will NOT accept separate statements of proposed disposition;

5) in matrimonial actions, a child support worksheet if applicable;

6) in matrimonial actions, updated statements of net worth;

7) proof of filing of the Note of Issue;

8) marked pleadings.

Note that expert reports must comply with CPLR § 3101 and, if applicable, 22 NYCRR § 202.16(g). Failure to exchange and file the reports not later than 60 days prior to the trial date (and replies not later than 30 days before the trial date) may, in the Court's discretion, preclude the use of the expert.

Trial

At least five business days prior to jury selection, counsel must submit to the Court any motions in limine, requests to charge and a joint proposed verdict sheet. Counsel must indicate to the Court all requests to charge that are in dispute. Requests to charge shall come from the Pattern Jury Instructions. When counsel requests deviations or additions to the Pattern Charge, the full text of such request must be submitted, with any supporting legal precedent.

If counsel cannot agree on the proposed verdict sheet, each side may submit its own proposed verdict sheet, indicating with a cover letter the disputed issues.

For all bench trials, counsel must submit, within 30 days (or as otherwise set by the Court) a post-trial memorandum, with separate sections for each cause of action. All references to exhibits or testimony must be cited with specificity, and all such documents must be attached. Replies will be due 10 days thereafter, unless the Court otherwise directs.

Form 1. Designation and Discovery Stipulation and Order—Complex Case

SUPREME COURT OF THE STATE OF NEW YORK
COUNTY OF ROCKLAND
PRESENT: HON. LINDA S. JAMIESON
---X

Plaintiff(s)

—against—   Index No.

Defendant(s).
---X

This case has been assigned to the Hon. Linda S. Jamieson and has been designated a complex case. Disclosure must be completed within fifteen months of the date of the filing of the RJI.

A. DISCOVERY SCHEDULE

1. Insurance Coverage: If not already provided, shall be furnished on or before _____.

The following information must be provided:

Name of Primary Carrier:

Amount of Coverage:

Name of Excess Carrier(s):

Amount of Coverage:

Self–Insured: ( )Yes   ( )No

2. Bill of Particulars:

   (a) Demand for Bill of Particulars shall be served on or before _____ (within two[2] weeks).

   (b) Bill of Particulars shall be served on or before _____, but within thirty (30) days of receipt of demand. Defendant to serve Bill of Particulars as to any affirmative defenses within thirty (30) days of receipt of a demand.

   (c) A Supplemental Bill of Particulars shall be served by _____ as to Items _____ on or before _____.

3. Authorizations: Medical, Hospital, Other:

( ) Have been furnished.

( ) Plaintiff shall provide all necessary doctor and hospital authorizations to defendant(s) within twenty (20) days of the date of this order and not later than _____. Defendant shall request all records within fifteen (15) days of receipt of authorizations, not later than _____.

( )Plaintiff shall provide all employment records or tax returns for years _____, no later than _____.

4. Examination before Trial:

( )Have been completed/waived.

( )Ordered to commence on _____ at the offices of _____.

( )All partied are to be deposed.

( )Plaintiff(s) are to be deposed.

( )Defendant(s) are to be deposed.

Said examinations shall continue from day to day until completed. The priority of examination shall be governed by previously served notices, if any.

5. Physical Examinations/Doctors Reports:

( )Physical and/or psychiatric examinations are to be completed no later than _____ (within thirty[30] days of completion of Examination before Trial) and doctor's reports of such examinations shall be exchanged not later than forty-five (45) days after the physical.

6. Third Party Actions/Impleader:

Third party actions, if any, shall be commenced not later than thirty (30) days after the Examination before Trial or the date of this order, whichever is later.

7. Other Discovery:

(a) _____ shall provide to _____, not later than _____, the following items: _____

_____

_____

_____.

(b) All parties, on or before _____, shall exchange names and addresses of all witnesses, statements of opposing parties and photographs, or, if none, provide an affirmation to that effect.

(c) Demand for discovery and inspection shall be served by (plaintiff)/(defendant) on or before _____. The items sought shall be produced to the extent not objected to, and objections, if any, shall be stated within ten (10) days of service of the demand.

B. **END DATE FOR ALL DISCLOSURE:** _____.

FAILURE TO COMPLY WITH THE TERMS OF THIS ORDER MAY RESULT IN SANCTIONS, WHICH MAY INCLUDE COSTS INCURRED BY THE OTHER PARTY, AND ANY OTHER SANCTION AUTHORIZED BY LAW, INCLUDING BUT NOT LIMITED TO CONTEMPT, DISMISSAL, STRIKING OF PLEADINGS.

NO ADJOURNMENTS OF ANY TIME DIRECTIVE ABOVE SHALL BE HAD WITHOUT THE PERMISSION OF THE COURT TO WHICH THIS CASE IS ASSIGNED.

THIS ORDER SUPERSEDES THE STATUTORY STAY IN CPLR 3214 FOR DISPOSITIVE MOTIONS MADE PURSUANT TO CPLR 3211, 3212, OR 3213. UNLESS OTHERWISE ORDERED BY THE COURT ALL PRETRIAL DISCOVERY SHALL CONTINUE NOTWITHSTANDING THE FILING OF A DISPOSITIVE MOTION.

Attorney for Plaintiff(s)   Attorney for Defendant(s)
Office Phone: _____   Office Phone: _____
Cell Phone: Cell Phone:
Fax Number: Fax Number:

Dated: New City, New York
        _____, 2011   SO ORDERED:

                                 _____
                                 HON. LINDA S. JAMIESON, J.S.C.

Form 2. Designation and Discovery Stipulation and Order—Expedited Case

SUPREME COURT OF THE STATE OF NEW YORK
COUNTY OF ROCKLAND
PRESENT: HON. LINDA S. JAMIESON
--X

Plaintiff(s)

—against—   Index No.

Defendant(s).
--X

This case has been assigned to the Hon. Linda S. Jamieson and has been designated a expedited case. Disclosure must be completed within eight months of the date of the filing of the RJI.

A. DISCOVERY SCHEDULE

1. Insurance Coverage: If not already provided, shall be furnished on or before _____.

The following information must be provided:

Name of Primary Carrier:

Amount of Coverage:

Name of Excess Carrier(s):

Amount of Coverage:

Self–Insured: ( )Yes   ( )No

2. Bill of Particulars:

   (a) Demand for Bill of Particulars shall be served on or before _____ (within two[2] weeks).

   (b) Bill of Particulars shall be served on or before _____, but within thirty (30) days of receipt of demand. Defendant to serve Bill of Particulars as to any affirmative defenses within thirty (30) days of receipt of a demand.

   (c) A Supplemental Bill of Particulars shall be served by _____ as to Items _____ on or before _____.

3. Authorizations: Medical, Hospital, Other:

( ) Have been furnished.

( ) Plaintiff shall provide all necessary doctor and hospital authorizations to defendant(s) within twenty (20) days of the date of this order and not later than _____. Defendant shall request all records within fifteen (15) days of receipt of authorizations, not later than _____.

( )Plaintiff shall provide all employment records or tax returns for years _____, no later than _____.

4. Examination before Trial:

( )Have been completed/waived.

( )Ordered to commence on _____ at the offices of _____.

( )All partied are to be deposed.

( )Plaintiff(s) are to be deposed.

( )Defendant(s) are to be deposed.

Said examinations shall continue from day to day until completed. The priority of examination shall be governed by previously served notices, if any.

5. Physical Examinations/Doctors Reports:

( )Physical and/or psychiatric examinations are to be completed no later than _____ (within thirty [30] days of completion of Examination before Trial) and doctor's reports of such examinations shall be exchanged not later than forty-five (45) days after the physical.

6. Third Party Actions/Impleader:

Third party actions, if any, shall be commenced not later than thirty (30) days after the Examination before Trial or the date of this order, whichever is later.

7. Other Discovery:

(a) _____ shall provide to _____, not later than _____, the following items: _____

_____

_____

_____.

(b) All parties, on or before _____, shall exchange names and addresses of all witnesses, statements of opposing parties and photographs, or, if none, provide an affirmation to that effect.

(c) Demand for discovery and inspection shall be served by (plaintiff)/(defendant) on or before _____. The items sought shall be produced to the extent not objected to, and objections, if any, shall be stated within ten (10) days of service of the demand.

B. END DATE FOR ALL DISCLOSURE: _____.

FAILURE TO COMPLY WITH THE TERMS OF THIS ORDER MAY RESULT IN SANCTIONS, WHICH MAY INCLUDE COSTS INCURRED BY THE OTHER PARTY, AND ANY OTHER SANCTION AUTHORIZED BY LAW, INCLUDING BUT NOT LIMITED TO CONTEMPT, DISMISSAL, STRIKING OF PLEADINGS.

NO ADJOURNMENTS OF ANY TIME DIRECTIVE ABOVE SHALL BE HAD WITHOUT THE PERMISSION OF THE COURT TO WHICH THIS CASE IS ASSIGNED.

THIS ORDER SUPERSEDES THE STATUTORY STAY IN CPLR 3214 FOR DISPOSITIVE MOTIONS MADE PURSUANT TO CPLR 3211, 3212, OR 3213. UNLESS OTHERWISE ORDERED BY THE COURT ALL PRETRIAL DISCOVERY SHALL CONTINUE NOTWITHSTANDING THE FILING OF A DISPOSITIVE MOTION.

_____
Attorney for Plaintiff(s)
Office Number:
Cell Number:
Fax Number:

_____
Attorney for Defendant(s)
Office Number:
Cell Number:
Fax Number:

Dated: New City, New York
              _____, 2011

SO ORDERED:

_____
HON. LINDA S. JAMIESON, J.S.C.

Form 3. Designation and Discovery Stipulation—Standard Case

SUPREME COURT OF THE STATE OF NEW YORK
COUNTY OF ROCKLAND
PRESENT: HON. LINDA S. JAMIESON
--X

Plaintiff(s)

—against—   Index No.

Defendant(s).
--X

This case has been assigned to the Hon. Linda S. Jamieson and has been designated a standard case. Disclosure must be completed within twelve months of the date of the filing of the RJI.

A. DISCOVERY SCHEDULE

1. Insurance Coverage: If not already provided, shall be furnished on or before _____.

The following information must be provided:

Name of Primary Carrier:

Amount of Coverage:

Name of Excess Carrier(s):

Amount of Coverage:

  Self–Insured: ( )Yes   ( )No

2. Bill of Particulars:

(a) Demand for Bill of Particulars shall be served on or before _____ (within two[2] weeks).

(b) Bill of Particulars shall be served on or before _____, but within thirty (30) days of receipt of demand. Defendant to serve Bill of Particulars as to any affirmative defenses within thirty (30) days of receipt of a demand.

(c) A Supplemental Bill of Particulars shall be served by _____ as to Items _____ on or before _____.

3. Authorizations: Medical, Hospital, Other:

( ) Have been furnished.

( ) Plaintiff shall provide all necessary doctor and hospital authorizations to defendant(s) within twenty (20) days of the date of this order and not later than _____. Defendant shall request all records within fifteen (15) days of receipt of authorizations, not later than _____.

( )Plaintiff shall provide all employment records or tax returns for years _____, no later than _____.

4. Examination before Trial:

( )Have been completed/waived.

( )Ordered to commence on _____ at the offices of _____.

( )All partied are to be deposed.

( )Plaintiff(s) are to be deposed.

( )Defendant(s) are to be deposed.

Said examinations shall continue from day to day until completed. The priority of examination shall be governed by previously served notices, if any.

5. Physical Examinations/Doctors Reports:

( )Physical and/or psychiatric examinations are to be completed no later than _____ (within thirty [30] days of completion of Examination before Trial) and doctor's reports of such examinations shall be exchanged not later than forty-five (45) days after the physical.

6. Third Party Actions/Impleader:

Third party actions, if any, shall be commenced not later than thirty (30) days after the Examination before Trial or the date of this order, whichever is later.

7. Other Discovery:

(a) _____ shall provide to _____, not later than _____, the following items: _____

_____

_____

_____.

(b) All parties, on or before _____, shall exchange names and addresses of all witnesses, statements of opposing parties and photographs, or, if none, provide an affirmation to that effect.

(c) Demand for discovery and inspection shall be served by (plaintiff)/(defendant) on or before _____. The items sought shall be produced to the extent not objected to, and objections, if any, shall be stated within ten (10) days of service of the demand.

B. **END DATE FOR ALL DISCLOSURE:** _____.

FAILURE TO COMPLY WITH THE TERMS OF THIS ORDER MAY RESULT IN SANCTIONS, WHICH MAY INCLUDE COSTS INCURRED BY THE OTHER PARTY, AND ANY OTHER SANCTION AUTHORIZED BY LAW, INCLUDING BUT NOT LIMITED TO CONTEMPT, DISMISSAL, STRIKING OF PLEADINGS.

NO ADJOURNMENTS OF ANY TIME DIRECTIVE ABOVE SHALL BE HAD WITHOUT THE PERMISSION OF THE COURT TO WHICH THIS CASE IS ASSIGNED.

THIS ORDER SUPERSEDES THE STATUTORY STAY IN CPLR 3214 FOR DISPOSITIVE MOTIONS MADE PURSUANT TO CPLR 3211, 3212, OR 3213. UNLESS OTHERWISE ORDERED BY THE COURT ALL PRETRIAL DISCOVERY SHALL CONTINUE NOTWITHSTANDING THE FILING OF A DISPOSITIVE MOTION.

_____   _____
Attorney for Plaintiff(s)   Attorney for Defendant(s)
Office Number: Office Number:
Cell Number: Cell Number:
Fax Number: Fax Number:

Dated: New City, New York
         _____, 2011   SO ORDERED:

                                         _____
                                         HON. LINDA S. JAMIESON, J.S.C.

JUSTICE WILLIAM A. KELLY

Rule 1. General

Counsel who appear, including those who appear "of counsel," must be fully familiar with the case and able to discuss the case in detail. Any counsel who appears must have authority to enter into any agreement, either substantive or procedural, on behalf of their clients. Counsel must be on time for all scheduled appearances and must bring sufficient material to allow meaningful discussion of unresolved issues to each Court appearance. Sanctions may be imposed for failure to comply with this rule.

There shall be no *ex parte* communications with the Court or Court personnel.

Rule 2. E–Filing

All parties should familiarize themselves with the statewide E-Filing Rules (Uniform Rule §§ 202.5–b and 202.5–bb — available at www.nycourts.gov/efile) and the Rockland County E–Filing Protocol. General questions about e-filing should be addressed to the E-Filing Resource Center at 646–386–3033 or efile@courts.state.ny.us. Specific questions relating to local procedures should be addressed to the Chief Clerk's Office (845) 638–5393.

In all case required to be filed through the New York State Courts E-Filing system (NYSCEF), submissions to the Court, including proposed orders, proposed judgments, and letters, must be electronically filed.

This Part requires working copies for: motion submissions, proposed orders to show cause, proposed orders/judgments, stipulations, transcripts and letters directed to the Court.

All working copies submitted to this Part must include a copy of the NYSCEF Confirmation Notice firmly fastened as the cover page of the submission and comply with other requirements set forth in the Rockland County Protocol. Working copies without the Confirmation Notice will not be accepted.

Working copies are to be delivered no later than 12:00 p.m. on the first business day following the electronic filing of the document on the NYSCEF site.

Hard Copy Submissions

Part will reject any hard copy submissions in e-filed cases unless those submissions bear the Notice of Hard Copy Submission — E-Filed Case required by Uniform Rule § 202.5–b(d)(1). The form is available at www.nycourts.gov/efile.

Rule 3. Conferences and Appearances

Conferences—Counsel must be prepared to discuss settlement at the compliance/settlement conference. It is expected that discovery Orders issued at the preliminary conference will be complied with. Failure to comply with the Order may result in a waiver of further discovery. Additional time to complete discovery will only be granted upon a showing of good cause for failure to complete discovery as previously ordered,

The parties and counsel must appear at matrimonial conferences. In Matrimonial Cases, Net Worth Statements are to be filed with the Court at least 3 days prior to the conference. Upon arrival at the preliminary conference, prior to having the case called, each side must complete a stipulation, provided by the Court, detailing the issues that have been resolved and those that remain open. If the grounds for divorce are not resolved at the preliminary conference, the matter will be set down for an immediate trial on grounds.

Rule 4. Adjournments

Requests for adjournments, other than an adjournment of a motion, whether on consent or not, must be faxed to the Court Clerk at least 5 business days prior to the scheduled appearance. The fax must set forth the reasons for the request. The parties will be advised by the Clerk, no later than two days before the case is scheduled appearance, whether the request is granted.

THE PARTIES MAY NOT CONTACT CHAMBERS REGARDING AN ADJOURNMENT OR CONCERNING FUTURE APPEARANCES.

Rule 5. Discovery Matters

Discovery motions are discouraged. No discovery motion should be made prior to a preliminary conference having been conducted. Where a discovery motion is brought and no preliminary conference has been conducted, the Court shall schedule and hold a preliminary conference on the return date of such motion.

Counsel must consult with one another in a good faith effort to resolve all disclosure disputes. See Uniform Rule 202.7. If counsel are unable to resolve a disclosure dispute in the matter, before any formal motion may be made, the procedures set forth below must be followed.

Rule 6. Motions

ALL MOTIONS ARE ON SUBMISSION, UNLESS OTHERWISE DIRECTED BY THE COURT. APPEARANCES ARE NOT REQUIRED ON THE MOTION RETURN DATE.

Motions for summary judgment must be filed no more than 30 days after the filing of the note of issue and made returnable no more than 45 days after the filing of the note of issue.

Oral argument may be requested by noting "Oral Argument Requested" immediately over the index number on the Notice of Motion. If the Court, in its discretion, requires such argument, the movant's attorney will be so advised and will be required to notify all parties.

Sur-replies will not be considered, unless the Court otherwise directs. If new issues are raised in the reply, or if there has been a change in the law while the motion is pending, counsel are to advise chambers, in writing, of the request to submit additional affidavits or memoranda. Other papers, including letters which are sent after the submission of the motion, will not be considered.

Self-addressed, stamped envelopes must be provided by all parties with all motions. Order/judgments must also have self-addressed, stamped envelopes and a copy if a conformed copy is requested. In the event a party fails to include a self-addressed, stamped envelope, the Court's Order will not be mailed to counsel.

In the event a motion has been resolved by a withdrawal or settlement of the case, counsel are to advise the Court by promptly faxing to the Court a letter of withdrawal or a Stipulation of Settlement or Discontinuance.

Orders to Show Cause

Upon the issuance of an Order to Show Cause, a copy of the Order will be faxed to counsel for the movant. If a further copy to be conformed is not included, the Court will not copy or otherwise supply a conformed copy.

Unless a TRO is included in the Order to Show Cause, APPEARANCES ARE NOT REQUIRED.

Upon an application for an Order to Show Cause seeking a temporary restraining order or other emergency relief, the application shall contain, in addition to the other information required by this section, an affirmation demonstrating there will be significant prejudice to the party seeking the restraining order by the giving of the notice. In the absence of a showing of significant prejudice, the affirmation must demonstrate that a good faith effort has been made to notify the party against whom the temporary restraining order is sought of the time, date, and place that the application will be made in a manner sufficient to permit the party an opportunity to appear in response to the application. Failure to comply with the above requirements will result in the striking of any temporary relief from the proposed Order.

Proof of service shall be submitted to the Court prior to the return date of the motion. Failure to submit proof of service will result in denial of the motion.

Rule 7. Motion Adjournments

THE PARTIES MAY NOT CALL CHAMBERS REGARDING AN ADJOURNMENT.

Requests for adjournments, whether on consent or not, must be faxed to the Court Clerk at least 5 business days prior to the return date of the motion appearance. The fax must set forth the reasons for the requested adjournment.

When an adjournment is on consent, unless the parties are informed otherwise, it may be presumed that the request is granted. However, no more than two adjournments, aggregating a total of 60 days, will be granted.

Failure to follow this procedure will result in a forfeiture of the right to submit papers. Counsel should therefore retain the written confirmation that the fax was timely received by the Court.

The parties may not adjourn a motion past a scheduled trial date. Even upon consent of the parties, the scheduled trial date will not be adjourned because of a pending motion.

Rule 8. Trials

Trials are scheduled to proceed day by day until completed.

A. Subpoenas. All counsel are reminded that they may sign trial subpoenas duces tecum and subpoenas ad testificatum as officers of the Court pursuant to CPLR Section 2302, except when subpoenas are directed to documents of libraries, hospitals, and municipal corporations and their departments and bureaus, in which cases they must be "So Ordered" by the Court pursuant to CPLR Section 2306 and 2307.

The Court will not "So Order" a subpoena unless it is required as described above. Subpoenas submitted for signature will be ignored if the Court's Order is not required.

The Courts issuance of "So Ordered" subpoenas should not be viewed by parties as collateral estoppel on the issue of admissibility at trial of the documents to which such subpoenas relate.

B. Interpreters. In the event that any party requires the services of a translator during trial for foreign languages or services for the hearing impaired, the Court is to be notified of same no later than the Pretrial Conference so that appropriate arrangements can be made by the Court in advance of the trial date.

C. Pre-Trial Requirements.

Trial notebook

No later than five (5) business days prior to the scheduled trial date, counsel shall each provide to the other and submit to the Court a trial notebook which shall consist of:

1) marked pleadings in accordance with CPLR Rule 4012;

2) the joint statement of the relevant facts that are not in dispute;

3) pre-trial memorandum of law as to any known disputed legal issues that must be determined by the court. Counsel to annex copies of any cases on which he relies;

4) a list of witnesses for each party;

5) a list of all exhibits to be offered by each party;

6) copies of the exhibits intended to be offered by counsel, pre-marked with plaintiff's exhibits numbered sequentially and defendant's exhibits lettered sequently;

7) requests to charge. The charge will be drawn from the Pattern Jury Instructions (PJI). A complete list of requested charges is to be submitted. Unless counsel seek a deviation from the pattern charge, or additions to the pattern charge, only the PJI numbers need be submitted. Where deviations or additions are requested, the full text of such requests must be submitted (in writing and on computer disk in Word Perfect format), together with any supporting legal precedent(s). Additionally, to the extent that a requested pattern charge requires a factual statement or a statement of contentions, the text of the statement must be submitted (in writing and on computer disk in Word Perfect format).

8) verdict sheet. Counsel shall jointly prepare a verdict sheet. The verdict sheet is to be typed in final form for presentation to the jury. If agreement cannot be reached, then each side shall present a proposed verdict sheet, along with a written explanation as to why agreement on the verdict sheet was not reached. If it is feasible, such proposals shall also be submitted on a computer disk in the format convertible to Word Perfect 8.0.

9) in matrimonial actions, updated net worth statements, statements of proposed dispositions as required by Rule 202.16(h) and any forensic reports, appraisals and evaluations.

Parties who appear for trial without having timely submitted a trial notebook will be subject to sanctions.

The Trial Notebook shall not be filed electronically.

The court may in its discretion relieve counsel from all or part of the trial notebook requirements upon a showing that the issues to be tried are sufficiently narrow that the trial notebook is not necessary or that the interest of justice otherwise justifies such relief.

Such a request will be entertained only at the pre-trial conference.

D. Depositions

No later than five (5) business days prior to the scheduled trial date, counsel shall each provide to the other and submit to the Court a detailed list, including line and page numbers, of any deposition testimony they intend to offer at trial. Not later than one day prior to the scheduled trial date, each counsel shall provide to the other and submit to the court a detailed list of objections to opposing counsel's proffer.

E. Evidentiary Objections.

Not later than one day prior to the scheduled trial date, each counsel shall provide to the other and submit to the court a statement setting forth any objection to the exhibits identified in the list provided by opposing counsel and the specific basis therefor. Any exhibit as to which no objection is identified shall be admitted into evidence on consent. The failure to submit such a statement of objections on a timely basis may be deemed to be consent to the admission of all of the exhibits included in the trial notebook submitted by the opposing party.

F. Witnesses.

Any witness not identified in the witness list provided to opposing counsel, other than an impeachment or rebuttal witness, shall not be permitted to testify unless an adequate explanation is provided for the failure to identify such witness prior to trial. Parties, fact witnesses and expert witnesses should be advised of the scheduled dates at the time they are set. Absent unanticipated, exigent circumstances, last minute claims of unavailability will not be recognized where the trial dates have been previously set. All witnesses should be on one-hour phone call notice so that their waiting time in court is minimized.

G. Exhibits.

Any exhibit not identified in the exhibit list provided to opposing counsel, other than an exhibit offered for the purpose of impeachment or rebuttal, shall not be admitted into evidence unless an adequate explanation is provided for the failure to identify such exhibit prior to trial. In addition to the copies of exhibits provided in the trial notebook, each party shall provide at trial one additional set of exhibits which will be used when counsel wishes to publish an exhibit to a witness.

Rule 9. Settlement or Discontinuance

If an action is settled, discontinued, or otherwise disposed, counsel shall immediately inform the Court by submission of a copy of the stipulation or other document evidencing the disposition.

JUSTICE WILLIAM K. NELSON

Doc. 1. Hon. William K. Nelson

Motions

After a case has been assigned to a part, prior to making any motion, with the exception of dispositive motions made after the note of issue is filed, movant shall notify the Court in writing, with a copy to all parties, setting forth the relief sought and the basis for that relief. The Court will schedule a conference call with counsel or a Court conference date. This procedure does not preclude the moving party from making a motion, but provides the Court with an opportunity to resolve the dispute giving rise to the motion without the need for a formal written application. Failing resolution of the dispute, or if the Court, in its discretion does not schedule the call or conference within ten days of mailing, then the party seeking the relief may proceed with the motion. Motions will be returnable on Friday, except by order of the Court. No courtesy copies of motions are to be submitted.

Appearances are not required. Oral argument may be requested by noting "Oral Argument Requested" immediately over the index number on the Notice of Motion.

If the Court, in its discretion, requires such argument, the movant's attorney will be so advised and will be required to notify all parties.

Sur-replys will not be considered, unless the Court otherwise directs. If new issues are raised in the reply, or if there has been a change in the law while the motion is pending, counsel are to advise chambers, in writing of the request to submit additional affidavits or memoranda. Other papers including letters which are sent after the submission of the motion, will not be considered.

Self-addressed, stamped envelopes must be provided by all parties with all motions. Orders/judgments must also have self-addressed, stamped envelopes and a copy, if a conformed copy is requested.

Adjournments

a) *On consent*—The clerk of the part is to be advised by telephone, followed by a letter, that the motion is adjourned on consent. A copy of the letter is to be sent to all parties. No more than three adjournments, for an aggregate period of sixty (60) days, without prior permission of the Court, will be granted. The co-operation of counsel is urged.

b) *Opposed*—The application must be made in person on the return date of the motion. The requesting party must advise all other parties that the application will be made. Any party wishing to be heard in opposition to the adjournment must appear.

Discovery Matters

Counsel must consult with one another in a good faith effort to resolve all disclosure disputes. See Uniform Rule 202.7. If counsel are unable to resolve a disclosure dispute in this manner, before any formal motion may be made, the procedures set forth above must be followed.

Conferences

Preliminary Conference—The attorneys are to provide the Court with a copy of the marked pleadings and are to be prepared to advise the Court with regard to any outstanding motions. Appearances at the Preliminary Conference are mandatory.

Compliance/Settlement Conference—Counsel must be prepared to discuss settlement at the compliance/settlement conference.

Failure to appear at a Trial Readiness Conference may result in sanctions, including striking the pleadings. A formal motion for relief from the sanctions for such default will be required.

A note of issue must be filed within twenty (20) days of the Trial Readiness Conference. Sanctions, including the striking of pleadings, may be imposed for failure to do so.

Trials

Prior to the commencement of a trial, counsel shall provide the Court with:

a) marked pleadings, and

b) an exhibit list. Material to be used on cross-examination need not be listed. The attorneys are to pre-mark their exhibits. Only those received in evidence will be marked by the reporter. The reporter is to be provided with an exhibit list.

Requests to charge shall be submitted to the Court as directed at a conference immediately preceding trial. The charge will be drawn from the Pattern Jury Instructions (PJI). A complete list of requested charges is to be submitted. Unless counsel seek a deviation from the pattern charge or additions to the pattern charge, only the PJI numbers need be submitted. Where deviations or additions are requested, the full text of such requests must be submitted, together with any supporting legal precedents. All submissions must be served on opposing counsel.

Verdict sheet—Counsel shall jointly prepare a verdict sheet. The verdict sheet is to be typed and in final form for presentation to the jury. If agreement cannot be reached, then each side shall present a proposed verdict sheet. If it is feasible, such proposals shall also be submitted on a computer disc in a format convertible to Word Perfect 8.0.

General

Counsel who appear must be fully familiar with the case and have authority to enter into any agreement, either substantive or procedural, on behalf of their clients. Counsel must be on time for all scheduled appearances and must bring sufficient material to allow meaningful discussion of unresolved issues to each Court appearance. Sanctions may be imposed

for failure to comply with this rule. Faxes will not be accepted except in an emergency and if the receipt has been authorized by chambers.

If an action is settled, discontinued, or otherwise disposed, counsel shall immediately inform the Court by submission of a copy of the stipulation or other document evidencing the disposition.

JUSTICE THOMAS E. WALSH

Rule I. Communications With The Court

A. Correspondences. All correspondences to the Court and Clerk shall be copied to all adversaries and must include the Index Number or Surrogates' File Number. Correspondences between attorneys and/or pro se litigants shall not be copied to the Court unless otherwise directed or where there is some specific judicial purpose to be served by transmitting copies to the Court. All correspondences and phone calls to the Clerk of the Court in a Supreme Court matter shall be addressed the Supreme Court Part Clerk and all correspondences and phone calls in a Surrogate's Court matter shall be addressed to the Chief Surrogate's Court Clerk.

B. Faxes. The fax number to be used for all Surrogates' matters is (845) 638–5632 and the fax number for all other matters (including Chambers) is (845) 638–5944. Neither Chambers nor the clerk will accept faxed copies of papers that must otherwise be filed in original form (such as objections, petitions, proofs of service, motions, opposition to motions, replies, proposed Orders, and documents to be "So Ordered"). All faxes must be faxed simultaneously to all other parties and the original document must be sent to the Court via regular mail. Counsel are not permitted, without prior approval, to send facsimile transmissions to Chambers that exceed five (5) pages in length.

C. Ex Parte Communications. Ex parte communications are prohibited except where an Order to Show Cause is submitted for signature, or, with the prior consent of all parties during settlement negotiations at the Courthouse.

D. Court Papers. All submissions bearing the caption of the matter must be signed by counsel [See Rules of the Chief Administrator Section 130–1.1a]. In any instance where a 'service list' is required on a legal document, the list must set forth not only the name, address and phone number of the submitting party or attorney but must also identify the party or person represented by that attorney and the person or party represented by the other persons named in that service list. All Surrogates' Court filings are to be made at the office of the Surrogate's Court clerk, and all Supreme Court filings are to be made at the Supreme Court Civil window.

Rule II. Court Conferences and Calendar Calls

[Text of subsec. A effective until January 1, 2012.]

A. General Rules. Appearances at the calendar call are required by attorneys in all matters. All calendar calls are conducted before Judge Walsh in the Surrogates' Courtroom of the Rockland County Courthouse Monday through Friday, except Surrogate matters which shall be called on Tuesdays, at 9:30 a.m., unless otherwise directed. Settlement discussions may be conducted in Chambers. All counsel, and pro se litigants, must be fully familiar with the matter(s) on which they appear and must be authorized to enter into both substantive and procedural agreements on behalf of their clients.

[Text of subsec. A effective January 1, 2012.]

A. General Rules. Appearances at the calendar call are required by attorneys in all matters. All calendar calls are conducted before Judge Walsh in the Surrogates' Courtroom of the Rockland County Courthouse Monday through Friday, except Surrogate matters which shall be called on Tuesdays at 9:30 a.m., unless otherwise directed. All counsel, and pro se litigants, must be fully familiar with the matter on which they appear and be authorized to enter into substantive and procedural agreements on behalf of their clients.

B. Preliminary Conferences. Preliminary Conferences shall be scheduled and then conducted: (1) in civil matters after a Request For Judicial Intervention ("RJI") is filed in accordance with *Uniform Rule 202.12(a)*, or, (2) upon a specific directive by the Court, or, (3) once the Surrogate has obtained jurisdiction and objections to probate are filed. Preliminary Conferences will ordinarily result in an order addressing all aspects of anticipated pretrial discovery and scheduling a Compliance Conference or the dates by which a Note of Issue, Order Framing Issues or Statement of Issues is to be filed. Discovery may be expedited in third party actions, joint actions and consolidated actions to avoid undue delay.

C. Compliance Conferences in Civil Matters. The purpose of the Compliance Conference is for counsel, and pro se litigants, to report to the Court that pre-trial discovery has been completed, to enable the Court to direct a date by which a Note of Issue or

Order Framing issues shall be filed, and to schedule dates for motions, a pre-trial conference, and trial. Parties are not permitted to file a Note of Issue in any action or proceeding unless permission to do so is granted by the Court at the Compliance Conference. Motions to strike Notes of Issue are discouraged as matters of outstanding discovery, if any, shall be raised, discussed and resolved at the Compliance Conference. The Court may issue a further discovery schedule at the Compliance Conference if circumstances or the interests of justice require. Any such additional discovery is likely to be based on an expedited schedule.

[Text of subsec. D effective until January 1, 2012.]

D. Pre-trial Conferences. The Court will conduct a Pre-trial Conference with all counsel and pro se litigants prior to the trial. Trial dates scheduled during a Pre-trial Conference should be viewed by parties and counsel as firm dates. Counsel attending Pre-trial Conferences shall be fully familiar with the facts and issues of the matter and shall be authorized to discuss and to enter into binding settlements, agreements and stipulations with respect to: (1) the factual, legal and evidentiary issues presented by the litigation, (2) settlement demands and offers, (3) unique or unusual issues likely to present themselves at trial, (4) witness scheduling, as well trial attorneys' vacation schedule, (5) likely duration of the trial and requests for adjournments of the trial date, and (6) applications for relief from part or all of the Trial Notebook requirements set forth in section VI(D)(A) hereof. The parties in any litigation, or in actions involving insurance carriers an authorized claims representative, must be available for the Pre-trial Conference either in person or by telephone for the purpose of direct contact with the attorneys engaged in settlement discussions. The Court will, on consent, conduct an additional Pre-trial Conference prior to the trial, but any such additional conference will not delay the trial as then scheduled. Settlement discussions will not delay the proceedings once the jury panel is seated for selection. Counsel shall notify all clients, witnesses and experts, in writing, of the trial date within three (3) business days of the pre-trial conference [See *Part VI(E)(b)* hereof].

[Text of subsec. D effective January 1, 2012.]

D. Pre-trial Conferences. The Court will conduct a Pre-trial Conference with all counsel and pro se litigants prior to the trial. Trial dates scheduled during a Pre-trial Conference should be viewed by parties and counsel as firm dates. Counsel attending Pre-trial Conferences shall be fully familiar with the facts and issues of the matter and shall be authorized to discuss and to enter into binding settlements, agreements and stipulations with respect to: (1) the factual, legal and evidentiary issues presented by the litigation, (2) settlement demands and offers, (3) unique or unusual issues likely to present themselves

at trial, (4) witness scheduling, as well trial attorneys' vacation schedule, (5) likely duration of the trial and requests for adjournments of the trial date, and (6) applications for relief from part or all of the Trial Notebook requirements set forth in section VI(D)(A) hereof. The parties in any litigation, or in actions involving insurance carriers an authorized claims representative, must be available for the Pre-trial Conference in person if directed, or by telephone, for the purpose of direct contact with the attorneys engaged in settlement discussions [See 22 NYCRR §202.26(e)]. The Court will conduct an additional Pre-trial Conference, but no such additional conference will delay the trial as then scheduled or once the jury panel is seated for selection. Counsel shall notify all clients, witnesses and experts, in writing, of the trial date within three (3) business days of the pre -trial conference [See Part VI(E)(b) hereof].

E. Non-Appearance at Scheduled Conferences. The failure of any attorney or pro se litigant to appear for a scheduled conference may be treated as a default and may, when appropriate, result in the dismissal of a Complaint or Petition, the striking of an Answer or objections, or by other appropriate remedy authorized by *Uniform Rule 202.27.*

F. Substitution/Withdrawal. (i) In any matter in court all Substitutions of Counsel must be in writing, signed by the client, the incoming and the outgoing attorney, and, filed with the Court and served on all other parties in accordance with the CPLR before the outgoing attorney is relieved and discharged from the matter. (ii) In any matter in court where an attorney wants to be relieved and discharged, or, where a client wants to discharge an attorney, and where there is no incoming attorney, a motion for that relief must be made by Order to Show Cause on notice to the client and all other parties. In such event the moving attorney will remain the attorney of record until the court decides the motion and relieves and discharges the moving attorney.

Rule III. Discovery and Inspection

[Text effective until January 1, 2012.]

A. General Rules. Every attorney shall exert a continuing effort to work co-operatively and courteously with all adverse attorneys towards the goal of completing all discovery expeditiously, efficiently and in the spirit of avoiding unnecessary motion practice and court intervention. Once a discovery schedule has been set by the court the dates and deadlines set forth therein shall be adhered to.

[Text effective January 1, 2012.]

A. General Rules. Every attorney shall exert a continuing effort to work co-operatively and courteously with all adverse attorneys towards the goal of completing all discovery expeditiously, efficiently and in the spirit of avoiding unnecessary motion practice and court intervention. Once a discovery schedule has been set by the court the dates and deadlines set forth therein shall be adhered to. All CPLR § 3101(d) expert witness disclosure shall be completed by no later than thirty (30) days prior to trial, except that on application on notice and for good cause shown, the Court may shorten this requirement. All objections to Expert witness disclosure must be served within five (5) days of receipt of the disclosure.

Rule IV. Motions and Orders to Show Cause

[Text effective until January 1, 2012.]

A. Prerequisite. Prior to the filing of any motion regarding discovery and disclosure the potential movant must notify the court in writing (one page maximum length), with a copy to all parties, setting forth the relief sought and the basis for the requested relief. The Court will then schedule a conference the purpose of which will be to hear and resolve the issues to be addressed in the motion without the necessity of a written application. Only where this conference does not resolve the dispute may the party seeking the relief proceed with the motion.

B. General Rules. All motions and oppositions to motions must be accompanied by a stamped, self-addressed envelope. The Court will entertain motions at 9:30 a.m. on any Friday, or in the case of a Surrogates' proceeding on any Tuesday, when the Court is in session. All Orders to Show Cause shall be submitted with original signatures affixed to the supporting affidavits and affirmations, shall include one proposed Order affixed to the supporting papers. The return date for an Order to Show Cause will be determined by the Court when the papers are submitted for consideration. There shall be no oral argument on any motion unless otherwise directed by the Court. The failure of a party to appear for oral argument when directed to will result in the waiver of that party's opportunity to offer oral argument in connection with the motion. All Orders to Show Cause shall include a provision that the method of service selected by the Court will be sufficient only if proof of such service is filed with the Court prior to the return date of the Order to Show Cause.

C. Filing of Papers Applicable to All Motions. The service list on all motions must include the identity of the party represented by each attorney identified in that service list. Motion papers must reflect the Index Number or Surrogates' File Number. The filing of a motion does not relieve any party from attending any previously scheduled conference or court appearance, regardless of the nature of the relief sought in the motion.

D. Supporting Documents. All documents required to decide the application must be included in the moving papers. It is not sufficient that those documents are on file with the Court Clerk. All motions to re-argue and renew shall include a copy of the prior decision and the entire prior motion, with its exhibits, if any.

E. Reply Papers. Reply papers shall not set forth new factual claims, legal arguments or requests for relief that were not within the scope of the papers that initiated the motion.

F. Sur-Reply Papers. Neither the CPLR nor the SCPA recognizes the existence of Sur-Reply papers, however denominated, and accordingly, the Court will not consider any post-Reply papers or materials absent a party receiving express permission from the Court in advance. Post-Reply materials received in violation of this rule will be returned, unread, to the Office of the Rockland County or Surrogate's Clerk for filing. Opposing counsel who receives a copy of post-Reply materials submitted in violation of this rule should not respond in kind.

G. Summary Judgment. Summary Judgment motions must be made no later than sixty (60) days from the date of the filing of the Note of Issue or Order Framing Issues.

Rule IV. Motions and Orders to Show Cause

[Text effective January 1, 2012.]

A. Prerequisite. Prior to the filing of any motion the potential movant must notify the court in writing (one page maximum length), with a copy to all parties, setting forth the relief sought and the basis for the requested relief. The Court will then schedule a conference the purpose of which will be to hear and resolve the issues to be addressed in the motion without the necessity of a written application. Only where this conference does not resolve the dispute may the party seeking the relief proceed with the motion.

All motions shall contain an "affirmation in support" executed by the movant's attorney which shall recite the details of the compliance with this paragraph. Failure to comply with this paragraph will result in a denial of the motion and or appropriate sanctions.

B. General Rules. All motions and oppositions to motions must be accompanied by a stamped, self-addressed envelope. The Court will entertain motions at 9:30 a.m. on any Friday, or in the case of a Surrogates' proceeding on any Tuesday, when the Court is in session. All Orders to Show Cause shall be submitted with original signatures affixed to the supporting affidavits and affirmations, shall include one proposed Order affixed to the supporting papers. There shall be no oral argument on any motion unless otherwise directed by the Court. The failure of a party to appear for oral argument when directed to will result in the waiver of that party's opportunity to offer oral argument in connection with the motion. All Orders to Show Cause shall include a provision that the method of service selected by the Court will be sufficient only if proof of such service is filed with the Court prior to the return date of the Order to Show Cause.

C. Filing of Papers Applicable to All Motions. The service list on all motions must include the identity of the party represented by each attorney identified in that service list. Motion papers must reflect the Index Number or Surrogates' File Number. The filing of a motion does not relieve any party from attending any previously scheduled conference or court appearance, regardless of the nature of the relief sought in the motion.

D. Supporting Documents. All documents required to decide the application must be included in the moving papers. It is not sufficient that those documents are on file with the Court Clerk. All motions to re-argue and renew shall include a copy of the prior decision and the entire prior motion, with its exhibits, if any.

E. Reply Papers. Reply papers shall not set forth new factual claims, legal arguments or requests for relief that were not within the scope of the papers that initiated the motion.

F. Sur-Reply Papers. Neither the CPLR nor the SCPA recognizes the existence of Sur-Reply papers, however denominated, and accordingly, the Court will not consider any post-Reply papers or materials absent a party receiving express permission from the Court in advance. Post-Reply materials received in violation of this rule will be returned, unread, to the Office of the Rockland County or Surrogate's Clerk for filing. Opposing counsel who receives a copy of post-Reply materials submitted in violation of this rule should not respond in kind.

G. Summary Judgment. Summary Judgment motions must be made no later than sixty (60) days from the date of the filing of the Note of Issue or Order Framing Issues. All such motions must be fully submitted by no later than ninety (90) days from the date of the filing of the Note of Issue and under no circumstances may they be fully submitted beyond one hundred and twenty (120) days from the filing of the Note of Issue.

Rule V.   Decisions and Orders

In certain instances, the Court may render a Decision and issue an Order orally from the Bench. In such instances a transcript of the Decision and Order, the cost of which shall be born equally by the parties, shall be purchased by the plaintiff or petitioner and then served on all other parties and submitted to the court so the same can be executed by the Court and filed with the Office of the Rockland County Clerk or Surrogates' Clerk. Indigent parties may be excused from having to pay their share for the cost of the transcripts of such decisions and orders whereupon the other parties will pay their proportionate share of the total cost of the transcript.

Rule VI.   Trials and Hearings

A. Trial Dates. Scheduled trial and hearing dates shall be adhered to except for the most extra-ordinary good cause shown and accordingly it is expected that clients, witnesses, experts and others will be timely advised of scheduled dates pursuant to Part II, Subdivision (D) hereof. The parties and their attorneys are encouraged to videotape the trial testimony of witnesses who are likely to be unavailable at trial in accordance with the applicable statutes and uniform rules, at the producing party's expense. All such videotaping should be conducted between the date of the Pre-trial Conference and the date of the trial. In scheduling and conducting trials, the Court shall endeavor to accommodate bona fide special preferences to the extent recognized by *CPLR Rule 3403* and *Uniform Rules 202.24* and *202.25.*

B. Subpoenas. When a Subpoena Duces Tecum is sought for a library, hospital or municipal corporation, or their departments and bureaus, the subpoena must be "So Ordered" on notice in accordance with *CPLR §2306* and *§2307*, and, the subpoena must be served on the intended recipient at least three days before the time fixed for the production of the documents, unless such notice is waived by the recipient of the subpoena or dispensed with by the Court. The Court's issuance of a "So Ordered" subpoena does not constitute a ruling as to the admissibility of the subpoenaed materials. All subpoena for materials protected by HIPPA shall refer to and annex a duly executed HIPPA compliant authorization.

C. Interpreters. In the event that any party or witness requires the services of a translator for foreign languages or services for the hearing impaired during a court appearance, conference, hearing or trial, the party shall notify, in writing, the Court, and the Clerk of the Court in which the matter is pending, of the need for same no later than three weeks prior to the court appearance, conference, hearing or trial.

D. E.B.T. Transcripts. Copies of E.B.T. transcripts that will be read or used for cross examination at trial shall be provided to the Court just before their use at trial.

E. Pre-Trial Requirements

a. *Trial Notebook.* No later than five (5) business days prior to the scheduled trial date, counsel shall each provide to the other (one copy) and submit to the Court (two copies) a trial notebook which shall consist of:

1) Marked pleadings in accordance with *CPLR §4012*;

2) Statement of the relevant facts stating separately those that are not in dispute and those that are;

3) Pre-trial memorandum of law addressing any known or anticipated disputed legal issues that must be determined by the court;

4) A list of all potential witnesses for each party;

5) A **list** of all exhibits to be offered into evidence at trial by each party with a brief description of each exhibit...do **not** submit copies of the exhibits;

6) Preliminary requests to charge. The charges will be drawn from the Pattern Jury Instructions (PJI). If no deviation from the pattern charge is sought only the PJI numbers need be submitted. Where deviations or additions are requested, the full text of such requests must be submitted in writing together with any supporting authority.

7) In jury trials a proposed verdict sheet typed in final form for presentation to the jury. If agreement cannot be reached on a joint submission, then each side shall present a proposed verdict sheet, along with a written explanation as to why agreement on the verdict sheet was not reached.

8) All motions In Limine and or for Preclusion. Each shall set forth the factual basis and authority for the objected to exhibits or testimony. All opposition shall be filed no later than the first day of jury selection or openings in a non-jury trial.

9) The court may, in its discretion and for good cause shown, relieve counsel from all or part of the trial notebook requirements upon a showing that the issues to be tried are sufficiently narrow that the trial notebook is not necessary or that the interest of justice otherwise justifies such relief. Such requests will be entertained only at the pretrial conference.

b. *Witnesses.* A witness not identified in the witness list provided to opposing counsel either in discovery or in the trial notebook, other than an impeachment or rebuttal witness, may not be permitted to testify unless an adequate explanation is provided for the failure to identify such witness prior to trial. Parties, witnesses and experts shall be advised of the scheduled dates in writing within three (3) business days of the day on which the trial dates are set [See *Part II (D)* hereof].

c. *Exhibits.* Any exhibit not identified in the exhibit list provided to opposing counsel, other than an exhibit offered for the purpose of impeachment or rebuttal, may not be admitted into evidence unless an adequate explanation is provided for the failure to identify such exhibit prior to trial. Exhibits marked into evidence at trial will not be returned until the final conclusion of the matter. Exhibits marked for identification will be retained by the offering attorney during trial, unless taken into evidence.

F. Identification of Trial Counsel. Whenever a matter is to be tried by an attorney other than the attorney of record, trial counsel shall be identified in a writing, filed with the Court on notice to all parties, no later than fifteen (15) days from the date fo the pretrial conference [See *Uniform Rule 202.31*]. The court may waive this rule only in instances where the

attorney of record is unexpectedly engaged in an unrelated trial and the late retention of trial counsel permits the trial before Judge Walsh to proceed without adjournment.

G. Pre-Voir Dire Conference. Immediately prior to jury selection the Court will conduct a conference [See *Uniform Rule 202.33(b)*] in order to set time limits on jury selection, to hear and determine arguments concerning the number of peremptory challenges, to discuss trial stipulations, to hear and determine last minute arguments on motions In Limine, to discuss scheduling and to address any other appropriate trial related issues.

H. Jury Selection. Juries shall be selected by the parties outside the presence of the Court in accordance with "Whites Rules" found in *Appendix "E"* of the *Uniform Rules for the New York Trial Courts*. The Court may impose time limits for jury selection as authorized by *Uniform Rule 202.33 (d)*. Peremptory challenges will ordinarily be pooled between multiple plaintiffs on the one hand and between multiple defendants on the other, and generally, each side shall be entitled to three (3) peremptory challenges for regular jurors per panel and one (1) peremptory challenge for each alternate juror per panel. However, pursuant to *CPLR Section 4109*, the number of peremptory challenges may be adjusted by the Court in certain matters in the discretion of the Court and in the interest o justice. The jury selection process will not be delayed by settlement negotiations once the jury panel is seated.

I. Bifurcation. Trials of personal injury actions involving issues of both liability and damages shall be bifurcated in accordance with *Uniform Rule 202.42* and all subdivisions thereof. Trials on damages will commence immediately upon the completion of the trial on liability.

J. Non-Jury Trials. Unless the Court directs otherwise, the parties may obtain and provide to the Court, at the party's expense, at the conclusion of the trial, a copy of the trial transcript, and each party may submit a post-trial brief with respect to the issues raised at the trial, setting forth specific references to the relevant portions of the transcript and the documents in evidence and citing the applicable law. Along with the submission of the post-trial briefs, counsel may also present the Court with proposed findings of fact and proposed disposition.

Rule VII.   Adjournments

[Text effective until January 1, 2012.]

All applications for adjournments of conferences, court appearances, hearings, trials and motions **shall** be made in writing actually received by the appropriate Clerk. No request for adjournment will be entertained unless the party seeking the adjournment has first attempted to obtain consent from all other parties. The application must be made immediately upon receipt of knowledge of the event or reason giving rise to the need for the adjournment. All requests shall state: good cause for the adjournment; whether the adverse party(ies) consent(s) to the adjournment; and may, at the option of the requesting party, suggest a date for the adjournment. The attorney receiving the adjournment **shall** immediately advise all other parties and pro-se litigants in writing of the adjourned date with a copy to the Court.

[Text effective January 1, 2012.]

All applications for adjournments of conferences, court appearances, hearings, trials and motions **shall** be made in writing actually received by the appropriate Clerk. No request for adjournment will be entertained unless the party seeking the adjournment has first attempted to obtain consent from all other parties. The application must be made immediately upon receipt of knowledge of the event or reason giving rise to the need for the adjournment. All requests shall state: good cause for the adjournment; whether the adverse party(ies) consent(s) to the adjournment; and may, at the option of the requesting party, suggest a date for the adjournment. The attorney receiving the adjournment **shall** immediately advise all other parties and pro se litigants in writing of the adjourned date with a copy to the Court. Under no circumstances will there by any adjournments for greater than twenty-eight (28) days without a court appearance by all attorneys.

Rule VIII.　Settled and Discontinued Cases

Counsel shall immediately notify the Court in writing of a settled or discontinued matter. Following the initial notification counsel shall file a fully executed duplicate original Stipulation of Discontinuance or Settlement with the appropriate Court Clerk. Court appearances and jury proceedings scheduled prior to the settlement or discontinuance are not excused or delayed until the fully executed Stipulation is received by the Court.

Rule IX.　Matrimonials

A motion for a default Judgment of Divorce is required in all un-contested Matrimonial Actions unless the submitted papers include, among the other documents otherwise required by Statute or Rule: (i) an acknowledged affidavit from the defaulting party admitting service of the Summons & Complaint and consenting to all of the relief requested, or, (ii) an acknowledged Stipulation of Settlement executed by the defaulting party addressing all of the relief requested; and, (iii) a proposed Findings of Fact and Judgment.

Rule X.　Article 81 Proceedings

All Court Evaluator's reports shall be filed with the Court no later than noon of the day before the scheduled hearing date.

Rule XI.　Rules Applicable Only to Surrogate's Court

[Text effective until January 1, 2012.]

1. Whenever a citation is served in an Accounting Proceeding a copy of the accounting shall be served on all parties, including waiving parties, with the Citation, and the Citation and affidavit of service shall recite that a copy of the accounting was served with the Citation.

2. If, in a probate proceeding, a beneficiary, attorney or draftsman has a fiduciary or confidential relationship with the testator/testatrix, an affidavit explaining the circumstances of the making the bequest and the drafting of the Will must be filed with the petition.

3. The clerk will not take a deposition or the testimony of any attesting witness in a probate proceeding unless the time to file objections limited in *SCPA 1410* has expired.

Rule XIII *.　E–Filing

[Text effective January 1, 2012.]

Counsel for all parties should familiarize themselves with the statewide E-Filing Rules (Uniform Rule §§ 202.5–b and 202.5–bb) available at www.nycourts.gov/efile) and the Rockland County E–Filing Protocol. General questions about e-filing should be addressed to the E–Filing Resource Center at (646) 386–3033 or efile@courts.state.ny.us. Specific questions relating to local procedures should be addressed to the Chief Clerk's Office (845) 638–5393.

Electronic Filing: All Supreme actions and proceedings in Judge Thomas E. Walsh II's Part [60] are to be filed through the New York State Courts E-Filing system (NYSCEF). All submissions to the Court, including proposed orders, proposed judgments, and letters, must be electronically filed.

Working Copies: One working copy is required in addition to the submission of working copies of electronically filed documents. See Uniform Rule § 202.5–b(d)(4). Working copies shall be delivered to the Rockland Chief Clerk's Office.

[ ] This Part does not require working copies.

[ ] This Part does not require working copies but may request working copies in specific instances.

[ ] This Part requires working copies for all electronic submissions. [X] This Part requires working copies for:

[X] motion submissions

[X] proposed orders to show cause

[X] proposed orders/judgments [X]

stipulations to be "so ordered" [ ]

transcripts [X] letters

* So in original.

Rule XII *. Rules Applicable Only to Surrogate's Court

[Text effective January 1, 2012.]

1. Whenever a citation is served in an Accounting Proceeding a copy of the accounting shall be served on all parties, including waiving parties, with the Citation, and the Citation and affidavit of service shall recite that a copy of the accounting was served with the Citation.

2. If, in a probate proceeding, a beneficiary, attorney or draftsman has a fiduciary or confidential relationship with the testator/testatrix, an affidavit explaining the circumstances of the making the bequest and the drafting of the Will must be filed with the petition.

3. The clerk will not take a deposition or the testimony of any attesting witness in a probate proceeding unless the time to file objections limited in SCPA 1410 has expired.

* So in original.

JUSTICE ALFRED J. WEINER

Doc. 1. Hon. Alfred J. Weiner

Motions

General Information. Motions shall be made returnable at the Rockland County Courthouse on Fridays at 9:30 a.m. Motion papers are to be submitted to the Office of the Supreme Court Clerk (2nd Floor). The provisions of the Civil Practice Law and Rules will apply. Appearances on motions are not required nor are courtesy copies. Oral argument may be requested by a written communication to the Court setting forth the reason(s) why oral argument is necessary. If the Court, in its discretion, allows such argument movant's attorney will be so advised and will be required to notify all parties.

Exhibits annexed to all motions are to be separated by tabs to permit easy identification of the exhibit. Telephone and facsimile numbers shall be included on all papers submitted to the Court. Self-addressed, stamped envelopes must be provided by all parties with all motions.

Prior to making any discovery related motion, movant shall notify the Court in writing, with a copy to all parties, setting forth the relief sought and the basis for that relief. The Court may schedule a conference call with counsel or a court conference date. This procedure does not preclude the moving party from making such motion, but provides the Court with an opportunity to resolve the dispute giving rise to the motion without the need for a formal written application. Failing resolution of the dispute or if the Court, in its discretion, does not schedule the call or conference within ten days of mailing, then the party seeking the relief may proceed with the motion.

Sur-replys will not be considered unless the Court otherwise directs. If new issues are raised in the reply or if there has been a change in the law while the motion is pending, counsel are to advise chambers in writing of the request to submit additional affidavits or memoranda. Other papers, including letters which are sent after the submission of the motion, will not be considered.

Discovery Motions: Counsel must consult with one another in a good faith effort to resolve all disclosure disputes. See Uniform Rule 202.7. If counsel are unable to resolve a disclosure dispute, the procedures previously set forth must be followed before any formal motion may be made.

Summary Judgment Motions: All motions for summary judgment must be made within sixty (60) days of the filing of the Note of Issue unless otherwise ordered by the Court (the "motion period") or the motion will not be entertained. Counsel may seek an extension of the motion period through the submission of a letter to the Court with a copy to opposing counsel setting forth good cause why additional time is needed. The Court will then determine whether an extension of the motion period is warranted.

Motions for temporary injunctive relief, including stays and temporary restraining orders: If a party's motion papers establish, prima facie, that "...immediate and irreparable injury, loss or damage will result" unless the other party is restrained before the hearing and determination of a motion for a preliminary junction, the matter will then be scheduled in accordance with 22 NYCRR 202.7(f) unless the moving party demonstrates there will be significant prejudice by the giving of notice.

Motions adjournments

a) On Consent – The clerk of the part is to be advised by telephone followed by a letter advising that the motion is adjourned on consent. A copy of the letter is to be sent to all parties. No more than three (3) adjournments for an aggregate period of sixty (60) days will be granted without prior permission of the Court.

b) Opposed – Absent agreement by the parties, a request by any party for an adjournment shall be submitted in writing, upon notice to the other party, to the Part Clerk on or before the return date. The court will notify the requesting party whether the adjournment has been granted.

E-FILING

E–Filing Rules and Protocol: All parties should familiarize themselves with the statewide E–Filing Rules (Uniform Rule §§ 202.5–b and 202.5–bb – available at www.nycourts.gov/efile) and the Rockland County E–Filing Protocol. General questions about e-filing should be addressed to the E–Filing Resource Center at 646–386–3033 or efile@courts.state.ny.us

Specific questions relating to local procedures should be addressed to the Chief Clerk's Office at 845–483–8320.

Electronic Filing: All Supreme Court actions or proceedings subject to either voluntary or mandatory E–Filing in Judge Weiner's part are to be filed through the New York State Courts E–Filing system (NYSCEF). All submissions to the Court, including proposed orders, proposed judgments, and letters, must be electronically filed.

Working Copies: This Part requires working copies for all electronic submissions. See Uniform Rule § 202.5–b(d)(4). Working copies shall be delivered to the Rockland Chief Clerk's Office.

All working copies submitted to this Part must include a copy of the NYSCEF Confirmation Notice firmly fastened as the front cover page of the submission and comply with other requirements set forth in the Rockland County Protocol. Working copies without the Confirmation Notice will not be accepted.

Working copies are to be delivered no later than 5:00 p.m. on the first business day following the electronic filing of the document on the NYSCEF site.

Hard Copy Submissions: Part will reject any hard copy submissions in e-filed cases unless those submissions bear the Notice of Hard Copy Submission — E–Filed Case required by Uniform Rule § 202.5–b(d)(1). The form is available at ww.nycourts.gov/efile.

Conferences

Preliminary Conference – Appearances at the Preliminary Conference are mandatory and counsel must be prepared to discuss the facts of the case, prepare a discovery schedule and, if appropriate, discuss settlement. In Matrimonial Cases the provisions of 22 NYCRR 202.16(f) shall also apply. The attorneys shall advise the Court of any outstanding motions.

Pre-Trial Conference – All discovery must be completed and the Note of Issue and Certificate of Readiness must be filed prior to the conference. Counsel must be prepared to discuss settlement at the conference.

Trials

Prior to the commencement of a trial, counsel shall provide the Court with marked pleadings. Attorneys are to pre-mark their exhibits and provide the Court and the court reporter with an exhibit list. Only those exhibits received in evidence will be marked by the reporter.

Requests to charge shall be submitted to the Court immediately preceding trial. The charge will be drawn from Pattern Jury instructions (PJI). Only the PJI numbers along with the PJI heading need be submitted. If counsel seeks a deviation from the pattern charge or additions to it, the full text of such requests must be submitted, together with any supporting legal precedents. All submissions must be served upon opposing counsel.

Verdict sheet – Counsel shall jointly prepare a proposed verdict sheet. The verdict sheet is to be typed and in final form for presentation to the jury. If agreement cannot be reached, then each party shall present a proposed verdict sheet.

General

Counsel who appear must be familiar with the case and have authority to enter into any agreement, either substantive or procedural, on behalf of their clients. Counsel must be on time for all scheduled appearances and must bring sufficient material to allow meaningful discussion of unresolved issues to each court appearance.

If an action is settled, discontinued or otherwise disposed, counsel shall immediately inform the Court by submission of a copy of the stipulation or other document evidencing the disposition.

If a conformed copy of an order or judgment is requested, a stamped self-addressed envelope must be included with a copy of the order or judgment to be conformed.

No facsimile transmissions to the Court shall exceed five pages in length. The original of all correspondence must be mailed to the Part Clerk.

Counsel/parties should address questions about scheduling appearances or adjourning appearances to the Part Clerk, James Loures, at 845–483–8338.

Copies of correspondence between parties are not to be sent to the Court unless specifically requested by the Court.

WESTCHESTER COUNTY
SUPREME AND COUNTY COURTS
JUDGES' PART RULES
JUSTICE LESTER B. ADLER

Doc. 1. Hon. Lester B. Adler

E-Filing Rules and Protocol

All parties should familiarize themselves with the statewide E-Filing Rules (Uniform Rule §§ 202.5–b and 202.5–bb—available at www.nycourts.gov/efile) and the Westchester County E-Filing Protocol available at http://www.courts.state.ny.us/courts/9jd/efile/WestchesterCountyJointProtocols.pdf

General questions about e-filing should be addressed to the E–Filing Resource Center at 646–386–3033 or efile@courts.state.ny.us

Specific questions relating to local procedures should be addressed to **the Civil Calendar Office (914) 824–5300.**

Electronic Filing

All Civil actions in Judge Lester B. Adler's Part are to be filed through the New York State Courts E–Filing system (NYSCEF). All submissions to the Court, including proposed orders, proposed judgments, and letters, must be electronically filed.

Working Copies

A court may require the submission of "working copies" of electronically filed documents. See Uniform Rule § 202.5–b(d)(4).

[ ] This Part does not require working copies.

[ ] This Part does not require working copies but may request working copies in specific instances.

[ ] This Part requires working copies for all electronic submissions.

[X] This Part requires working copies for:

    [X] motion submissions

    [X] proposed orders to show cause

    [X] proposed orders/judgments

    [ ] stipulations

    [ ] transcripts

    [ ] letters

[ ] Working copies shall be delivered to:

[X] Chambers [For access, please call: 914–824–5386]

[ ] Part Clerk [specific types listed here]

[ ] [Other office] [specific types listed here]

All working copies submitted to this Part must include a copy of the NYSCEF Confirmation Notice firmly fastened as the back cover page of the submission and comply with other requirements set forth in the Westchester County Protocol. Working copies without the Confirmation Notice will not be accepted.

Working copies are to be delivered no later than 5:00 p.m. on the first business day following the electronic filing of the document on the NYSCEF site.

Hard Copy Submissions

Part will reject any hard copy submissions in e-filed cases unless those submissions bear the Notice of Hard Copy Submission—E–Filed Case required by Uniform Rule § 202.5–b(d)(1). The form is available at www.nycourts.gov/efile.

Scheduling

Counsel/parties should address questions about scheduling appearances or adjourning appearances to the Part Clerk, Jeff Wizwer, at (914) 824–5371. Do not contact Chambers regarding such issues. All requests for adjournments must be made with the consent of all opposing counsel and, if approved by the Court, confirmed by a signed Stipulation of all counsel.

1. Counsel may call the Part Clerk with respect to the scheduling of appearances and with respect to adjournment applications.

2. Counsel may call Chambers and/or the Part Clerk to arrange for a telephone conference with the Court or with the Law Clerk.

3. Counsel may not contact Chambers without all opposing counsel on the phone, except for the purpose of facilitating a conference call.

Motions

Motions are to be returnable on Monday at 9:30 a.m. motions made returnable at any other time, absent prior permission of the Court, will be adjourned by the Part Clerk to the next available Monday.

Adjournments are governed by Part Rules.

Motions are submitted without oral argument, unless otherwise directed by the Court.

Reply papers are not permitted, unless: (a) the right of reply is obtained by service of a notice of motion in accordance with CPLR 2214[b]; or (b) expressly permitted by the Court. Sur-reply papers are not permitted absent prior permission of the Court. Any unauthorized papers will not be read.

A copy of all stipulations discontinuing an action where a motion remains pending must be submitted to the Court.

All papers must comply with the applicable provisions of the CPLR and with the Part Rules. In addition, the font size of text and footnotes must be no smaller than 12 point. Papers which do not comply may be rejected.

All exhibits shall be separately tabbed. In the event that multiple affidavits or affirmations are submitted in support of a motion under the same legal back, each such exhibit shall be accompanied by a clearly discernible side or bottom tab containing the last name of the affiant.

JUSTICE ORAZIO R. BELLANTONI

Doc. 1. Hon. Orazio R. Bellantoni

Motions

Motions are returnable on Wednesday, except by order of this Court. Permission is not necessary to make a motion.

Appearances are not required. Oral argument may be requested by noting "Oral Argument Requested" immediately over the index number on the Notice of Motion. If this Court, in its discretion, requires such argument, the movant's attorney will be so advised and will be required to notify all parties.

Sur-replies will not be considered, unless this Court otherwise directs. Other papers including letters which are sent after the submission of the motion, will not be considered.

Adjournments

a) On Consent—The clerk of this Part is to be advised by telephone, followed by a letter, that the motion is adjourned on consent. No more than two adjournments on consent will be allowed, unless granted by the Court.

b) Opposed—The application must be made on or before the return date of the motion. The requesting party must advise all other parties of the application. No appearances are required unless directed by the Court.

Trials

Prior to the commencement of a trial, counsel shall provide the court with marked pleadings.

Requests to charge shall be submitted to this Court as directed at a conference immediately preceding trial. The charge will be drawn from the Pattern Jury Instructions (PJI). A complete list of requested charges is to be submitted. Unless counsel seek a deviation from the pattern charge or additions to the pattern charge, only the PJI numbers and topic need be submitted. Where deviations or additions are requested, the full text of such requests must be submitted, together with any supporting legal precedents.

Verdict sheet—Counsel shall jointly prepare a verdict sheet. The verdict sheet is to be typed and in final form for presentation to the jury. If agreement cannot be reached, then each side shall present a proposed verdict sheet. If it is feasible, such proposals shall also be submitted on a computer disc in format convertible to Word Perfect 8.0.

General

Counsel who appear must be fully familiar with the case and have authority to enter into any agreement, either substantive or procedural, on behalf of their clients. Counsel should make every effort to be on time for all scheduled appearances.

Faxes

Faxes to chambers are permitted only if copies are simultaneously faxed or delivered to all counsel. The fax number is 914–995–4010.

If an action is settled, discontinued, or otherwise disposed, counsel shall immediately inform the Court by submission of a copy of the stipulation or other document evidencing the disposition.

E–Filing Rules and Protocol

All parties should familiarize themselves with the statewide E–Filing Rules (Uniform Rule §§ 202.5–b and 202.5–bb—available at www.nycourts.gov/efile) and the Westchester County E–Filing Protocol available at http://www.courts.state.ny.us/courts/9jd/efile/WestchesterCountyJointProtocols.pdf General questions about e-filing should be addressed to the E–Filing Resource Center at 646–386–3033 or efile@courts.state.ny.us

Specific questions relating to local procedures should be addressed to the Civil Calendar Office 914–824–5300.

Electronic Filing

All documents in mandatory e-filed cases, except documents subject to the opt-out provision of Section 202.5–bb of the Uniform Rules for the New York State Trial Courts, or documents subject to e-filing in which consent is being withheld, are to be filed through the New York State Courts E–Filing System (NYSCEF). All submissions to the Court, including proposed orders, proposed judgments, and letters, must be electronically filed.

Working Copies

This Part requires the submission of "working copies" of all electronically filed documents. See Uniform Rule § 202.5–b(d)(4). Working copies are to be delivered to the Part Clerk, Jude Badaracco, Courtroom 1203.

All working copies submitted to this Part <u>must</u> include a copy of the NYSCEF Confirmation Notice firmly fastened to the front cover page of the submission and comply with all the other requirements set forth in the Westchester County Protocol. Working copies without the Confirmation Notice will not be accepted.

Working copies are to be delivered no later than 4:00 p.m. on the first business day following the electronic filing of the document on the NYSCEF site.

Notice of E–Filing

Within 24 hours of e-filing a motion, a courtesy copy of said motion shall be sent to all counsel so that they can be aware of said e-filing.

Hard Copy Submissions

This Part will reject any hard copy submissions in e-filed cases unless those submissions bear the Notice of Hard Copy Submission—E–Filed Case required by Uniform Rule § 202.5–b(d)(1). The form is available at www.nycourts.gov/efile.

Scheduling

Counsel/parties should address questions about scheduling appearances or adjourning appearances to the Part Clerk, Jude Badaracco, at 914–824–5368.

JUSTICE NICHOLAS COLABELLA

Doc. 1. Hon. Nicholas Colabella

E–Filing Rules and Protocol

All parties should familiarize themselves with the statewide E–Filing Rules (Uniform Rule §§ 202.5–b and 202.5–bb—available at www.nycourts.gov/efile) and the Westchester County E–Filing Protocol available at http://www.courts.state.ny.us/courts/9jd/efile/WestchesterCountyJointProtocols.pdf.

General questions about e-filing should be addressed to the E–Filing Resource Center at 646–386–3033 or efile@courts.state.ny.us

Specific questions relating to local procedures should be addressed to the Civil Calendar Office (914) 824–5300.

Electronic Filing

All actions in Judge Colabella's IAS Part [NC] are to be filed through the New York State Courts E–Filing system (NYSCEF). All submissions to the Court, including proposed orders, proposed judgments, and letters, must be electronically filed.

Working Copies

A court may require the submission of "working copies" of electronically filed documents. See Uniform Rule § 202.5–b(d)(4).

[ ] This Part does not require working copies.

[ ] This Part does not require working copies but may request working copies in specific instances.

[x] This Part requires working copies for all electronic submissions.

[x] This Part requires working copies for:

    [x] motion submissions

    [x] proposed orders to show cause

    [x] proposed orders/judgments

    [x] stipulations

    [x] transcripts

    [x] letters

[x] Working copies shall be mailed to the Part Clerk or delivered to:

    [X] 12th Floor Lobby Drop Off Basket

All working copies submitted to this Part must include a copy of the NYSCEF Confirmation Notice firmly fastened as the back cover page of the submission and comply with other requirements set forth in the Westchester County Protocol. Working copies without the Confirmation Notice will not be accepted.

Working copies are to be delivered no later than 10:00 a.m. on the first business day following the electronic filing of the document on the NYSCEF site.

Hard Copy Submissions

Part will reject any hard copy submissions in e-filed cases unless those submissions bear the Notice of Hard Copy Submission—E–Filed Case required by Uniform Rule § 202.5–b(d)(1). The form is available at www.nycourts.gov/efile.

Part Procedure

Counsel/parties should address questions about Part Procedure to the Part Clerk, Jude Badaracco, at 914–824–5281.

Motions

Unless an exception is made by the Court, motions are returnable in the Part, rm 1200, on Fridays, at 9:30 a.m. Motions made on any other day will be adjourned by the Court to the next regular motion calendar. Courtesy copies of motions are not required. Sur-replies will not be considered without prior permission of the Court. No papers will be considered after the return date of the motion.

Appearances are not required. Oral argument may be requested by noting "Oral Argument Requested" immediately over the index number on the Notice of Motion. If the Court, in its discretion, requires such argument, the movant's attorney will be so advised and will be required to notify all parties.

Adjournments

No adjournments of motions will be considered without prior notice to the other party that an adjournment is being sought. Applications to adjourn shall be made to the Part Clerk, Jude Badaracco, at 914–824–5281 by telephone or in writing. The party seeking an adjournment shall advise the Court whether the application is consented to or opposed. If the application is opposed, the party in opposition may request an opportunity to be heard by conference call or in person.

Adjournments of motions are subject to Court approval. If an adjournment is approved, it shall be confirmed in writing with a copy of the letter sent to all parties. Absent good cause, motions will not be adjourned for periods longer than two weeks or granted more than two adjournments.

General

Counsel who appear at conferences or otherwise must be fully familiar with the case and have authority to enter into any agreement, either substantive or procedural, on behalf of their clients.

Faxes

Faxes will not be accepted without prior permission of the Court.

Settlements & Discontinuances

If an action is settled, discontinued, or otherwise disposed, counsel shall immediately inform the Court by submission of a copy of the stipulation or other document evidencing the disposition.

JUSTICE ROBERT DIBELLA

Doc. 1. Hon. Robert Dibella

Commencing on February 1, 2008, the Civil Part of this Court shall be conducted pursuant to the following information, practices, rules and procedures:

Counsel must be fully familiar with the Uniform Civil Rules for the Supreme Court, 22 NYCRR Part 202.

Pleadings:

Within ten (10) business days of notification of assignment to this part, Plaintiff's counsel and counsel for the third party Plaintiffs must furnish a set of marked pleadings; a copy of the Bill of Particulars must also be furnished at that time or within ten (10) days of service.

Motions:

Prior to making any motion, with the exception of dispositive motions made after the Note of Issue is filed, movant shall notify the Court in writing, with a copy to all parties, setting forth the relief sought and the basis for the relief. The Court shall then schedule a conference call with counsel or a Court conference date. This procedure does not preclude the moving party from making a motion, but it provides the Court with an opportunity to resolve the dispute giving rise to the motion without the need for a formal written application. Failing resolution of the dispute, the party seeking relief may proceed with the motion.

Unless an exemption is made by the Court, motions are returnable in the Part, Room 302, on Fridays at 9:30 am. Motions made on any other day will be adjourned by the Court to the next regular motion calendar. Courtesy copies of motions are not required. Sur-replies will not be considered without prior permission of the Court. No papers will be considered after the return date of the motion.

Appearances are not required. Oral argument may be requested by noting "Oral Argument Requested" immediately over the index number on the Notice of Motion. If the Court, in its discretion, requires such argument, the movant's attorney will be so advised and will be required to notify all parties.

Self-addressed, stamped envelopes must be submitted with all motions for a return decision. Orders and Judgments must also have self-addressed, stamped envelopes and a copy to be conformed if one is requested.

Adjournments:

Requests to adjourn any motion date must be made either in person on the return date of the motion or via a conference telephone call with all interested parties and the Court. The requesting party must advise all parties that the application will be made. Any party wishing to be heard in opposition to the adjournment must participate.

Discovery:

Counsel must consult with one another in a good faith effort to resolve all disclosure disputes before seeking judicial intervention. See Uniform Rule 202.7. If counsel are unable to resolve a disclosure dispute in this manner, before any formal motion is made, the procedures set forth above for filing motions must be followed. In addition, if the proposed resolution of any discovery dispute would alter the timing provisions set forth in the Preliminary Conference Order, counsel must obtain prior Court approval for the change.

Conferences:

Be sure to diary the dates of the Interim Conference, Compliance Conference, Settlement, and Trial Readiness as no further notice will be given. Conferences are held in the courtroom promptly at 9:30 am.

Adjournments of Interim Compliance Conference: contact Carolyn Carpenito, Part Clerk, at 914-824-5449 at least 48 hours in advance of conference date. If you have any problems, contact Chambers at 914-824-5407. If you believe you have a legal reason in the case for not coming to the conference, such as a pretrial matter pending or a dispositive motion pending, you must still appear for the conference.

Failure to appear or notify the Court that you cannot appear at the conference may result in an adverse order pursuant to 22 NYCRR 202.27. A formal motion for relief from your default may then be required.

Note of Issue cannot be filed until you have a Compliance Conference. If the case is not settled at that time, the Court will sign a Trial Readiness Order and then you can file the Note of Issue. The signed Trial Readiness Order must be filed with the Calendar Clerk within twenty (20) days or the case will be marked off the calendar.

Trials:

Prior to the commencement of a trial, counsel shall provide the Court with:

—marked pleadings

—an exhibit list

(material to be used on cross-examination need not be listed. The attorneys are to pre-mark their exhibits. Only those received into evidence will be marked by the reporter. The reporter is to be provided with an exhibit list.)

Requests to charge shall be submitted to the Court as directed. The charge will be drawn from the Pattern Jury Instructions (PJI). A complete list of requested charges is to be submitted.

Unless counsel seek a deviation from the pattern charge or additions to the pattern charge, only the PJI numbers need to be submitted. Where deviations or additions are requested, the full text of such requests must be submitted together with any supporting legal precedents. All submissions must be served upon opposing counsel.

The verdict sheet is to be prepared jointly by counsel. The verdict sheet is to be typed and in final form for presentation to the jury. If agreement cannot be reached, then each side shall present a proposed verdict sheet. If it is feasible, such proposals shall also be submitted on a computer disc in a format convertible to Word Perfect 12.0.

General:

Counsel who appear must be fully familiar with the case and have authority to enter into any agreement, either substantive or procedural, on behalf of their clients. Counsel must be on time for all scheduled appearances and must bring the full file with them to each Court appearance.

Faxes:

Faxes will not be accepted unless it is an emergency and the receipt has been authorized by Chambers.

Settlements:

If an action is settled, discontinued, or otherwise disposed, counsel shall immediately inform the Court by submission of a copy of the stipulation or other document evidencing the disposition.

JUSTICE WILLIAM J. GIACOMO

Rule I. General Rules

A. Compliance Conferences. Please note this Part no longer conducts compliance conferences. See Westchester Supreme Court Differentiated Case Management Protocol Part Rules effective September 14, 2009. Please contact Carolyn Carpenito, Room 800, at 914-824-5344 or ComplianceWestchester@courts.state.ny.us.

B. Settlement Conferences. Please note this Part no longer conducts settlement conferences. See Westchester Supreme Court Differentiated Case Management Protocol Part Rules effective September 14, 2009. Please contact Robert Arena, Room 1201, at 914-824-5339.

C. Appearances by Counsel With Knowledge and Authority. All counsel who appear before the Court must be familiar with the case and be fully

authorized to enter into agreements as to both substantive and procedural matters on behalf of their clients. Attorneys appearing of counsel to the attorneys of record and self-represented parties shall be held to the same requirements. Failure to comply with this rule may be regarded as a default and dealt with appropriately. All counsel and self-represented parties must be on time for all scheduled appearances.

D. Settlements and Discontinuances. If an action is settled, discontinued or disposed of in any other manner by the parties, counsel shall immediately inform the Court by letter and by filing a Stipulation of Discontinuance or Stipulation of Settlement with the Part Clerk. The Court shall not mark any matter as settled unless it has received a copy of a Stipulation of Discontinuance or Stipulation of Settlement, the original of which has been filed with the County Clerk.

E. Papers by Fax. The Court does not accept papers of any kind by fax transmission unless otherwise requested by the Court in advance in a particular case. Copies of letters confirming an adjournment of a motion or a conference may be sent to the Court by fax at its chambers. However, the original of all correspondence must be mailed to the Part Clerk. Any authorized fax transmission directed to the Part Clerk shall be faxed only to the telephone number: (914) 995–4182. All faxes shall be limited to 5 pages.

F. Conduct of Parties and Counsel. It is expected that all parties and counsel shall conduct themselves appropriately in all in-court and out-of-court proceedings and in their communications with each other and the Court. PERSONAL ATTACKS UPON PARTIES OR COUNSEL SHALL NOT BE TOLERATED AND SHALL RESULT IN THE IMPOSITION OF SANCTIONS AS DETERMINED BY THE COURT TO BE WARRANTED UNDER THE PARTICULAR CIRCUMSTANCES.

G. Ex Parte Communications. Ex parte communications are strictly prohibited except upon the consent of all counsel, or with respect to scheduling matters or the presentation of orders to show cause for signature.

H. Communications With Represented Parties. Counsel are directed to inform their clients that under no circumstances shall any member of the Court's staff engage in any conversation or exchange any communication with a represented party. If a represented party communicates with any member of the Court's staff, all counsel shall be informed of the communication and, if it is in writing, shall be sent a copy of that writing.

Rule II. Motion Practice Rules

A. Motion Calendar and Appearances. All motions/proceedings brought on by notice of motion or notice of petition shall be made returnable before the Court on any Monday the Court is in session at 9:30 A.M. There will be a Motion Calendar called by the Court. The purpose of the Motion Calendar call is to achieve an easy and efficient means for attorneys to submit and the Court to collect all opposition, cross-moving and reply papers in connection with motions on the calendar. During the Motion Calendar call, commencing at 9:30 A.M., all motions returnable that day will be "called" for the submission of these papers. These papers may either be submitted by mail or in person and received by the Court prior to the "call" or must be handed up at this "call". If opposition, cross-moving and reply papers are not submitted before or at the submission "call," the opportunity to do so will be lost (unless an adjournment is arranged or court permission is obtained).

To the extent possible, motions will be decided "on the papers." If argument is directed, it will take place on an announced date shortly after the day of submission. Counsel for the movant need not appear to "take a default" on any motion or for any other reason. Motions will be submitted, not marked off, in the absence of the movant. Opposing counsel similarly need not appear in person in order to avoid suffering a default. Delivery of papers by mail, service or a clerk will suffice.

B. Applications, Adjournments, Submission of Late Papers. To protect movants against the submission of late opposition papers or cross-motions, the Court will sua sponte adjourn for one week cases in which appropriate time has not been given. Parties seeking an adjournment must follow the direction delineated below in order to adjourn a motion. Unless the Part Clerk, the Court's Secretary or the Court's Law Clerk has conveyed the Court's approval of an adjournment, no motion shall be considered to have been adjourned.

C. Adjournments by Stipulation. A party seeking an adjournment must contact all other parties in an effort to obtain consent and demonstrate that that was done. No more than three adjournments for a total of no more than 60 days are allowed except with the permission of the Court (Rule 202.8(e)(1) of the Uniform Rules for the Trial Courts), given by means of a so-ordered stipulation.

D. Adjournments by Affidavit/Affirmation of Consent. If all parties consent to an adjournment as allowed by these rules but a written stipulation cannot be obtained in time for submission, the applicant for the adjournment on consent may submit an affidavit or affirmation reciting that such consent was obtained. That document must state the reason for the adjournment request, how consent was obtained from all parties, when it was obtained, and the name of each attorney who gave oral consent. The affidavit/affirmation must be received by the Court before the date on which the request for adjournment is made or application may be made by counsel at the Motion Calendar call.

E. Applications for Adjournment Not on Consent. If consent was not obtained from all parties prior to the return date, any party making an application for adjournment at the Motion Calendar must appear at the Motion Calendar call and put on the record before the Court the reason for the requested adjournment and a description of the efforts made to obtain such consent, including the date when a contact was initiated or attempted, the means used, and the person contacted (if consent was refused) or for whom a message was left (if no contact was made). Furthermore, an applicant must, by phone, fax, e-mail, or mail transmitted with adequate lead time, advise all parties who have not consented that an application will be made at the Motion Calendar call. Applications for adjournments that are not properly supported will not be entertained. If there is no compliance, the Part Clerk will mark the motion submitted.

F. Orders to Show Cause. Orders to show cause submitted for signature shall be presented to the office of the calendar clerk, after the payment of any required fee at the County Clerk's Office. If the order to show cause is signed by the Court, a copy of it shall be sent by fax to counsel for the moving party. If appearances are required on the return date of the motion, the Court shall so indicate in the order to show cause. Otherwise, no appearances shall be required and no oral argument shall be heard on the return date of the motion.

G. Requests for Temporary Restraining Orders. When an order to show cause is to be presented to the Court which seeks a temporary restraining order, counsel for the moving party must first communicate by telephone or fax transmission with counsel for all adverse parties, and with any unrepresented adverse parties, to advise such counsel or parties that a request for a temporary restraining order shall be made to the Court and that such counsel or parties have the right to be heard on the application. A conference on the request for a temporary restraining order shall be conducted by the Court at 9:30 a.m. on the first day that the Court is in session following the day on which the order to show cause is presented. Following the conference, either by way of a bench decision or a written decision, the Court shall render its determination only on the request for a temporary restraining order. No request for a temporary restraining order shall be considered without a conference unless the moving party demonstrates to the Court that conducting such a conference will clearly cause the moving party irreparable injury.

H. Communications Regarding Motions. All communications regarding motions, including requests for adjournments and questions concerning the status of motions, shall be directed to the Court's Secretary. Only in the absence of the Court's Secretary shall any communication regarding a motion be directed to the Part Clerk or the Law Clerk.

I. Time for Filing and Serving Summary Judgment Motions. Summary judgment motions shall be filed with the Court and served upon all adverse parties no later than thirty (30) days after the filing of the Note of Issue.

J. No Stay of Discovery. There shall be **no stay of pretrial discovery** resulting from the filing of a motion made pursuant to CPLR 3211 or 3212 unless otherwise ordered by the Court.

K. Form of Papers. Except with the express permission of the Court, all motion papers submitted to the Court, including Orders to Show Cause, must be typewritten and all exhibits must be labeled with tab markings and entirely legible. Motion papers and all correspondence must indicate the index number assigned to the action. Courtesy copies of papers shall not be submitted to Chambers.

L. Papers Required on Particular Motions.

1. *Dispositive Motions.* On any motion seeking summary judgment, dismissal of a complaint, cross-claim or counterclaim, or the striking of a pleading, copies of all pleadings filed as of the date of filing of the motion must be provided to the Court by the moving party. The failure to comply with this requirement shall result in the denial of the motion unless the pleadings are provided to the Court by another party.

2. *Motions for Leave to Renew or Reargue.* On any motion seeking leave to renew or reargue a prior motion, the moving party shall submit copies of all papers submitted on the prior motion. The failure to comply with this requirement shall result in the denial of the motion unless the papers on the prior motion are submitted to the Court by another party.

3. *Motions for Leave to Amend, Supplement or Correct Pleadings.* On any motion for leave to amend, supplement or correct a pleading, in addition to the proposed amended, supplemental or corrected pleading, the moving party shall submit copies of all pleadings filed as of the date of the motion. The failure to comply with this requirement shall result in the denial of the motion unless copies of the prior pleadings are submitted to the Court by another party.

4. *Motions for Injunctive Relief.* When an order to show cause is to be presented to the Court which seeks a temporary restraining order or a preliminary injunction, copies of the summons and complaint commencing the underlying action must be provided to the Court by the moving party. No order to show cause seeking such relief will be considered by the Court if the moving party fails to comply with this requirement.

5. *Default Motions.* On any motion for a default judgment, proof must be presented that a military-status investigation of all defendants who are persons has been conducted after the time for each such defendant to appear or answer, as applicable, has transpired. In addition, to be sufficient, the military-status investigation must include, at a minimum, a search conducted through the Department of Defense, which may be performed through that agency's internet site, www.dmdc.osd.mil/scra/owa/home.

M. Discovery Motions. Please note this Part no longer conducts compliance conferences or handles discovery motion. Those matters are handled in the Compliance Part, room 800. See Westchester Supreme Court Differentiated Case Management Protocol Par Rules effective September 14, 2009.

N. Reply Papers. Counsel and self-represented parties shall not set forth factual claims or legal arguments in reply papers which were not set forth in the papers initiating the motion or cross-motion. New factual claims and legal arguments which are not directly in response to factual claims or legal arguments offered in opposition to a motion or cross-motion shall not be considered by the Court in its determination of a motion or cross-motion.

O. Sur–Reply and Post–Submission Papers. Counsel and the parties are reminded that the CPLR does not provide for the submission of sur-reply papers, however denominated, or the presentation of papers or letters to the Court after the return date of a motion. Nor is motion practice by correspondence permitted. Absent express permission obtained in advance from the Court, such materials shall be filed with the County Clerk unread. Any opposing counsel and self-represented party who receives a copy of such materials submitted in violation of this rule shall not respond in kind.

P. Length of Papers. Absent express permission obtained in advance from the Court, which shall be granted only upon a showing of good cause, briefs or memoranda of law shall be limited to 30 pages each, and affirmations and affidavits shall be limited to 25 pages each. Papers submitted to the Court in violation of this rule may not be considered by the Court in deciding the motion, without prior notice to the party who submitted the papers.

Q. Settled Motions. In the event that the parties settle a motion or part of a motion in advance of the motion return date, they shall immediately inform the Court in writing. Any failure to inform the Court of a settlement which results in the needless expenditure of court resources in the issuance of a decision on a motion may result in the imposition of sanctions against counsel for all parties to the action and any self-represented parties.

R. Motion Decisions and Orders.

1. *Written Decisions.* In most instances, a written Decision and Order will be issued by the Court following the submission of the motion. The Decision and Order, with supporting papers, will be filed in the Westchester County Clerk's Office by the Court. A copy of the Decision and Order shall be sent to all counsel and self-represented parties that have submitted a self addressed, stamped envelope after filing with the County Clerk.

2. *Bench Decisions.* In certain instances, the Court will render a decision from the bench. Any party seeking a written order shall submit to the Court a proposed order supported by a copy of the transcript of the proceeding at which the bench decision was rendered. The signed order will be filed in the Westchester County Clerk's Office by the Court.

S. E–Filing Rules and Protocol.

All parties should familiarize themselves with the statewide E–Filing Rules (Uniform Rule §§ 202.5–b and 202.5–bb—available at www.nycourts.gov/efile) and the Westchester County E–Filing Protocol available at http://www.courts.state.ny.us/courts/9jd/efile/WestchesterCountyJointProtocols.pdf.

General questions about e-filing should be addressed to the E–Filing Resource Center at 646–386–3033 or efile@courts.state.ny.us.

Specific questions relating to local procedures should be addressed to the Civil Calendar Office (914) 824–5300.

1. *Electronic Filing.* All actions required to be filed electronically are to be filed through the New York State Courts E–Filing system (NYSCEF). All submissions to the Court, including proposed orders, proposed judgments, and letters, must be electronically filed.

2. *Working Copies.* A court may require the submission of "working copies" of electronically filed documents. See Uniform Rule § 202.5–b(d)(4).

This Part requires working copies for:

    [x] motion submissions
    [x] proposed orders to show cause
    [ ] proposed orders/judgments
    [ ] stipulations
    [x] transcripts
    [ ] letters

Working copies shall be delivered to the Part Clerk - Selene Jackson, Courtroom 1402.

All working copies submitted to this Part must include a copy of the NYSCEF Confirmation Notice firmly fastened as the front cover page of the submission and comply with other requirements set forth in the Westchester County Protocol. Working copies without the Confirmation Notice will not be accepted.

Working copies are to be delivered no later than noon on the first business day following the electronic filing of the document on the NYSCEF site.

3. *Hard Copy Submissions.* This Part will reject any hard copy submissions in e-filed cases unless those submissions bear the Notice of Hard Copy Submission—E–Filed Case required by Uniform Rule § 202.5–b(d)(1). The form is available at www.nycourts.gov/efile.

4. *Scheduling.* Counsel/parties should address questions about scheduling appearances on the motion, if any, or adjourning appearances to the Part Clerk, Selene Jackson, at 914–824–5349.

Rule III. Trial Practice Rules

A. Trial Preparation. Prior to the commencement of the trial or hearing, counsel shall ascertain the availability of all witnesses and subpoenaed documents. Plaintiff's counsel shall request that the Part Clerk requisition the County Clerk file in the case to the courtroom as soon as possible after the assignment of the case to this Court. In addition, counsel for any party or any self-represented party who has issued subpoenas for the production of records shall request that the Part Clerk requisition all subpoenaed documents from the file room.

B. Interpreters and Special Services. Upon reporting to the Court for a trial or a hearing, counsel and any self-represented party shall immediately advise the Part Clerk if the services of a foreign language interpreter are required for any party or witness, or if any special services are required for any party or witness who is hearing-impaired or who suffers from any other disability. Similarly, the Part Clerk shall be immediately informed if there is a need for an easel, blackboard, shadow box, television or any other trial aid.

C. Pleadings and Submissions Due Immediately Upon Appearance. Immediately upon being assigned to this Court for a trial or hearing, counsel for each party, including the Law Guardian, if any, and any self-represented party, shall report to the Part Clerk, or in her absence, the Law Clerk. At that time, counsel for each party and each self-represented party shall submit the following to the Court:

1. A statement of the estimated length of trial.

2. Marked pleadings and all bills of particulars.

3. A list of all witnesses who may be called at trial, including any known, potential rebuttal witnesses.

4. A list of all exhibits the party expects to use at trial, indicating whether such exhibits are stipulated for admission into evidence or are marked only for identification.

5. A written stipulation governing all facts that are not in dispute.

6. In all matrimonial actions, an updated net worth statement and a statement of proposed disposition.

7. A copy of any statutory provisions in effect at the time the cause of action arose, upon which any party to the action relies.

8. All expert witness reports relevant to the issues.

9. All reports, transcripts of examinations before trial and written statements which may be used either to refresh a witness' recollection or for cross-examination.

D. Marking of Exhibits. After filing the above-listed submissions with the Court, counsel shall meet with the assigned Official Stenographer to pre-mark all exhibits for identification. Any exhibits whose admission is agreed to by the parties shall be pre-marked for admission.

E. Conference. Immediately prior to the commencement of the trial, the Court shall conduct a brief conference with all counsel and self-represented parties, to discuss preliminary matters. At this conference, all counsel and self-represented parties shall be prepared to:

1. Advise the Court as to all anticipated disputed issues of law and fact, and provide the Court with citations to all statutory and common-law authority upon which they will rely.

2. Stipulate to undisputed facts and the admission of clearly-admissible documents, records and other exhibits.

3. Alert the Court to any anticipated in limine motions or evidentiary objections which they believe will be made during the trial.

4. Provide the Court with a copy of all prior decisions and orders which may be relevant to any in limine applications or objections.

5. Discuss scheduling, as well as the number of witnesses to be called at trial, any anticipated problems regarding the attendance at trial of any party, attorney or witnesses, and any other practical problems which the Court should consider in scheduling.

6. Alert the Court as to any anticipated requests for a jury instruction relating to missing witnesses or evidence.

7. Alert the Court as to any anticipated request pursuant to CPLR Article 16 for apportionment as to an allegedly culpable non-party.

8. Supply a proposed verdict sheet and request to charge.

F. Copies of Transcripts. If any part of a transcript of an examination before trial or other recorded proceeding will be read as evidence-in-chief, the proponent of the transcript shall provide a complete copy of it to the Court and all other counsel or self-represented parties, well in advance of the time that it shall be read, with citations to the page and line numbers for all portions to be read, so that all objections may be addressed by the Court prior to the proposed reading.

G. Copies of Exhibits. Upon the admission of an exhibit at trial, the proponent of the exhibit shall provide a complete copy of it to the Court.

H. Addressing the Court. Any counsel or self-represented party who is raising an objection, presenting an argument or otherwise addressing the Court, shall stand while doing so, or shall not be recognized by the Court. All objections shall be made by stating the word "objection", together with up to three more words identifying the generic ground for objection, such as "hearsay", "bolstering", "leading" or "asked and answered". If it is believed that argument on an objection is necessary, any counsel or self-represented party may ask permission to approach the bench. Keep in mind that any counsel or self-represented party will be given the opportunity to make a full record of his or her position.

I. Courtroom Behavior. All remarks shall be directed to the Court. Comments shall not be made to opposing counsel or self-represented parties. PERSONAL ATTACKS UPON PARTIES OR COUNSEL SHALL NOT BE TOLERATED AND SHALL RESULT IN THE IMPOSITION OF SANCTIONS AS

DETERMINED BY THE COURT TO BE WARRANTED UNDER THE PARTICULAR CIRCUMSTANCES. Do not attempt to "talk over" an adversary; only one person shall speak at a time. Simple requests, e.g., a request for a document or an exhibit, shall be accomplished in a manner which does not disrupt the proceedings or an adversary. Ask for permission to approach the bench if a significant discussion with an adversary is required, such as a proposed stipulation. There shall be no "grandstanding" in the presence of the jury, e.g., making demands, offers or statements that should properly be made outside of the presence of the jury.

J. Use of Exhibits. Do not show anything, including an exhibit or proposed exhibit, to a witness without first showing it to all opposing counsel and self-represented parties. If any counsel or self-represented party believes that this procedure will compromise his or her trial strategy, he or she shall first request a pre-offer ruling outside of the presence of the jury.

K. Summation Exhibits. Any counsel or self-represented party who intends during summation to use any type of demonstrative exhibit not marked into evidence must advise the Court and all other counsel and self-represented parties of that intention at the precharge conference. Failure to comply with this rule shall result in an order precluding the use of such exhibit during summation.

L. Examination of Witnesses. Do not approach a witness without permission of the Court. The questioning counsel or self-represented party shall allow the witness to complete his or her answer to a question before asking another question. Do not interrupt a witness in the middle of an answer unless it is totally unresponsive, in which event a ruling from the Court shall be requested.

M. Jury Charges. In all jury trials, a complete list of requests to charge shall be submitted to the Court immediately preceding the commencement of trial, with copies to be provided to all other counsel and self-represented parties. If a requested charge is drawn from the current Pattern Jury Instructions (PJI), only the PJI number need be submitted. Where deviations from, or additions to, the PJI are requested, the full text of such requests must be submitted in writing, together with any supporting legal precedents. In addition such proposals shall be submitted on a computer disc in a format convertible to Word Perfect or emailed to the Court's law clerk at tmontele@courts.state.ny.us. At the final charging conference, if marshaling of the evidence is required as to a particular jury charge, counsel and all self-represented parties shall provide the Court with the proposed facts which they believe should be presented to the jury.

N. Verdict Sheet. At the commencement of the trial, counsel for the parties and any self-represented parties shall jointly prepare a verdict sheet. If agreement cannot be reached, each party shall present a proposed verdict sheet which shall be served upon all other parties. The verdict sheet shall be in a final, typewritten form which may be given to the jury. In addition the proposed verdict sheet(s) shall be submitted on a computer disc in a format convertible Word Perfect or emailed to the Court's law clerk at tmontele@courts.state.ny.us.

O. Post–Trial Submissions. Unless otherwise directed by the Court, in accordance with the schedule set by the Court at the conclusion of a bench-trial or hearing, the parties shall jointly submit a trial transcript, and each party shall prepare and submit a post-trial memorandum. In all matrimonial actions, each party shall also submit proposed Findings of Facts and Conclusions of Law and a proposed Judgment of Divorce. Factual arguments set forth in the memorandum shall be supported by citations to the trial transcript, and legal arguments shall be supported by citations to relevant statutes or case law. In their post-trial submissions following a trial of equitable distribution issues, the parties shall identify each item of property as either separate or marital, and shall state the value of each item of property. They shall also identify all of the parties' outstanding debts as either separate or marital, and shall state the amount of each debt. All assertions as to the separate or marital status of each item of property and each outstanding debt, and the value of each item of property and the amount of each debt, shall be supported by citations to the trial transcript.

P. Check–In. At the start of each day of trial, all counsel and self-represented parties shall check in with the Part Clerk so that she will be aware of your presence.

Q. Food and Drinks. Absent permission of the Court obtained in advance, no counsel or party shall bring any beverage or food into the Courtroom. Water may be requested from the Clerk or a Court Officer during the trial, in which event only a cup of water as provided shall be permitted on the counsel table or the podium.

R. No Communication With Jurors. In order to maintain the appearance of total impartiality, once the jury has been selected no one is to communicate in any form at any time with any juror. This prohibition includes both verbal and non-verbal communication, including, without limitation, nods, shrugs and shaking the head. Do not even say "hello" or "good morning".

JUSTICE JOAN B. LEFKOWITZ

Doc. 1.   Hon. Joan B. Lefkowitz

MOTIONS

Motions are returnable at 9:30 A.M. on Fridays, except by order of this Court. Permission is not necessary to make a motion. Oral Argument is not encouraged as it is expected all contentions should be in your papers.

ADJOURNMENTS

On Consent: The Clerk of this Part is to be advised by telephone, followed by a letter that the motion is adjourned on consent. The letter may be faxed to (914) 995–4184.

Opposed: The application must be made on or before the return date of the motion. The requesting party must advise all other parties of the application. No appearances are required unless directed by the Court. Where exigent circumstances exist, an application for an adjournment may be made personally on the return date or by telephone.

TRIALS

Prior to the commencement of a trial, counsel shall provide the Court with marked pleadings and fill out forms provided by the Court and inform the Part Clerk if there are subpoenaed records.

Requests to charge shall be submitted to this Court as directed at a conference immediately preceding trial. The charge will be drawn from the Pattern Jury Instructions (PJI). A complete list of requested charges must be submitted. Unless counsel seek a deviation from the pattern charge or additions to the pattern charge, only the PJI numbers and topic need by submitted. Where deviations or additions are requested, the full text to such requests must be submitted together with any supporting law.

Verdict Sheet: Counsel shall jointly prepare a verdict sheet. If agreement cannot be reached, then each side shall present a proposed verdict sheet.

GENERAL

Counsel who appear must be fully familiar with the case and have authority to enter into any agreement, either substantive or procedural, on behalf of their clients. Counsel should be on time for all scheduled appearances.

FAXES

Faxes to Chambers are permitted only if copies are simultaneously faxed or delivered to all counsel (only as to IAS cases—not Compliance Cases) and pro se parties. The fax number is (914) 995–4184. Similarly, letters to the Court must indicate service on all parties.

SETTLEMENT/DISCONTINUANCE

If an action is settled, discontinued or otherwise disposed, counsel shall immediately inform the Court by submission of a copy of the stipulation or other document evidencing the disposition.

E–FILING RULES AND PROTOCOL

All parties should familiarize themselves with the statewide E–Filing Rules (Uniform Rule §§ 202.5–b and 202.5–bb available at www.nycourts.gov/efile) and the Westchester County E–Filing Protocol available at hp://www.courts.state.ny.us/courts/9jd/efile/WestchesterCountyJointProtocols.pdf

General questions about e-filing should be addressed to the E–Filing Resource Center at (646) 386–3033 or efile@courts.state.ny.us

Specific questions relating to local procedures should be addressed to the Civil Calendar Office at (914) 824–5300.

ELECTRONIC FILING

All documents in mandatory e-filed cases, except documents subject to the opt-out provision of Section 202.5-bb of the Uniform Rules for the New York State Trial Courts, or documents subject to e-filing in which consent is being withheld, are to be filed through the New York State Courts E-Filing Systems (NYSCEF). All submissions to the Court, including proposed orders, proposed judgments and letters, must be electronically filed.

WORKING COPIES

This Part requires the submission of "working copies" of all electronically filed documents. See Uniform Rule § 202.5–b(d)(4). Working copies are to be delivered to the Part Clerk, Robert Arena, Room 1608.

All working copies submitted to this Part must include a copy of the NYSCEF Confirmation Notice firmly fastened to the front cover page of the submission and comply with all the other requirements set forth in the Westchester County Protocol. Working copies without the Confirmation Notice will not be accepted.

Working copies are to be delivered to the Part Clerk no later than 4:00 P.M. on the first business day following the electronic filing of the document on the NYSCEF site.

NOTICE OF FILING

Within 24 hours of e-filing a motion, a courtesy copy of said filing shall be sent to all counsel so that they can be aware of said e-filing, unless for good cause shown, notice of such e-filing is withheld.

HARD COPY SUBMISSIONS

This Part will reject any hard copy submissions in e-filed cases unless those submissions bear the Notice of Hard Copy Submission—E-Filed Case required by

Uniform Rule § 202.5–b(d)(1). The form is available at www.nycourts.gov/efile.

SCHEDULING

Counsel/parties should address questions about scheduling appearances or adjournments to the Part Clerk, Robert Arena, at (914) 824–5350.

COMPLIANCE PART

No calls, faxes or correspondence should be directed to Chambers or the IAS Part Clerk relating to matters (discovery disputes, discovery motions) pending in the Compliance Part. These rules are not applicable to matters in the Compliance Part.

Questions regarding Compliance Part matters may be emailed at www.compliancewestchester@courts. state.ny.us, by fax at (914) 995–2194 or by calling the Conference Part Clerk at (914) 824–5344 or the Motion Part Clerk at (914) 824–5343.

ENVELOPES

All Working Copies that require disposition by the Court, i.e., a motion decision, order, judgment, must have attached a stamped, self-addressed envelope.

ORDERS/JUDGMENTS

A copy must be submitted for conforming.

JUSTICE RICHARD B. LIEBOWITZ

Rule I.   E–Filing Rules and Protocol

All parties should familiarize themselves with the statewide E–Filing Rules (Uniform Rules for the New York State Trial Courts §§ 202.5–b and 202.5–bb available at http://www.nycourts.gov/efile) and the Westchester County E–Filing Protocol available at-http://www.courts.state.ny.us/courts/9jd/efile/WestchesterCountyJointProtocols.pdf.

General questions about e-filing should be addressed to the E–Filing Resource Center at (646) 386–3033 or efile@courts.state.ny.us.

Specific questions relating to local procedures should be addressed to the Civil Calendar Office (914) 824–5300.

Electronic Filing

All documents filed in mandatory e-filed cases, except those documents which are subject to the "opt-out" provision of § 202.5–bb of the Uniform Rules for the State of New York State Trial Courts, or documents subject to e-filing in which consent is being withheld, are to be filed through the New York State Courts E–Filing System (NYSCEF). All submissions to the Court, including proposed orders, judgments and letters must be electronically filed.

Working Copies

[X] This Part requires working copies for all electronic submissions.

This part requires working copies for:

X motion submissions

X proposed orders to show cause

X proposed orders/judgments

X stipulations

X transcripts

X letters

Working copies shall be provided to:

[X] Part Clerk

All working copies submitted to this Part <u>must</u> include a copy of the NYSCEF Confirmation Notice firmly fastened as the [back] cover page of the submission and comply with other requirements set forth in the Westchester County Protocol. Working copies without the Confirmation Notice will not be accepted.

Working copies are to be delivered no later than [time] on the first business day following the electronic filing of the document on the NYSCEF site.

Hard Copy Submissions

This Part will reject any hard copy submissions in e-filed cases unless those submissions bear the Notice of Hard Copy Submission—E–Filed Case required by Uniform Rules for the State Trial Courts § 202.5–b(d)(1). The form is available at www.nycourts.gov/efile.

Scheduling

Counsel/parties should address questions about scheduling appearances or adjourning appearances to the Part Clerk, Frances Doyle, at (914) 824–5351.

Rule II.   General Rules

A.   Appearances by Counsel With Knowledge and Authority. All counsel who appear before the Court must be familiar with the case and be fully authorized to enter into agreements on behalf of their clients as to both substantive and procedural matters. Attorneys appearing of counsel to the attorneys of record and parties appearing pro se shall be held to the same requirements.

B.   Settlements and Discontinuances. If an action is settled, discontinued or disposed of in any other manner by the parties, counsel shall immediately inform the Court by letter and by filing a Stipulation of Discontinuance or Stipulation of Settlement with the Part Clerk. The Court shall not mark any matter as settled unless it has received a copy of a Stipulation of Discontinuance or Stipulation of Settlement, the original of which has been filed with the County Clerk.

C. So-Ordered Transcripts. The Court shall be provided with an original and two copies of transcripts to be so-ordered. One copy will be retained for the Court's file and one copy will be returned to counsel.

D. Conduct of Parties and Counsel. It is expected that all parties and counsel shall conduct themselves in an appropriate manner in all in-court and out-of-court proceedings and in their communications with each other and the Court. Personal attacks upon parties or counsel shall not be tolerated and shall result in the imposition of sanctions as determined by the court to be warranted under the particular circumstances.

E. Ex Parte Communications: Ex parte communications are strictly prohibited except upon consent of all counsel, or with respect to scheduling matters or the presentation of Orders to Show Cause for signature

F. Communications With Represented Parties. Counsel are directed to inform their clients that under no circumstances will any member of the Court's staff engage in any conversation or exchange any communication with a represented party.

Rule III. Motion Practice

A. Noticed Motions. Motions on notice shall be made returnable at 9:30 A.M. on any Thursday that the Court is in session. Any motion made returnable on any other day shall be adjourned by the Court to the next available motion day. No appearances shall be required and no oral argument shall be heard on a motion unless ordered by the Court.

B. Orders to Show Cause. Counsel and any party appearing pro se are directed to comply with the Order to Show Cause requirements specified in §202.7 of the Uniform Rules for the New York State Trial Courts, including, but not limited to, §202.7(f). If the Order to Show Cause is signed by the Court, a copy of it shall be sent either electronically or by fax to counsel for the moving party or to the pro se movant, if applicable. If appearances are required on the return date of the motion, the Court shall so indicate in the Order to Show Cause.

C. Communications Regarding Motions. All communications regarding motions, including requests for adjournments, shall be directed to the Part Clerk. Only in the absence of the Part Clerk shall any communication regarding a motion be directed to the Principal Law Clerk or to the Assistant Law Clerk.

D. Adjournments. Before requesting an adjournment of a motion, the requesting counsel or party appearing pro se shall communicate with all other counsel and any party appearing pro se, in an attempt to obtain consent for the adjournment. If the adjournment request is not on consent, the requesting counsel shall arrange for a conference call with all other counsel and the Principal Law Clerk. Whether the request is on consent or not, if an adjournment is granted, the Court shall schedule a new return date, and the requesting counsel shall send a fax transmission to the Court and all other counsel confirming the new return date. Unless the Part Clerk, the Principal Law Clerk or the Assistant Law Clerk has conveyed the Court's approval of an adjournment, no motion shall be considered to have been adjourned. Under no circumstances will the Court recognize an adjournment of a motion, if any, unless approval of the adjournment has been obtained as set forth in this rule.

E. Motions for Leave to Renew or Reargue. On any motion seeking leave to renew or reargue a prior motion, the moving party shall submit copies of all papers submitted on the prior motion. The failure to comply with this requirement shall result in the denial of the motion unless the papers on the prior motion are submitted to the Court by another party.

F. Motions for Leave to Amend, Supplement or Correct Pleadings. On any motion for leave to amend, supplement or correct a pleading, in addition to the proposed amended, supplemental or corrected pleading, the moving party shall submit copies of all pleadings filed as of the date of the motion. The failure to comply with this requirement shall result in the denial of the motion unless copies of the prior pleadings are submitted to the Court by another party.

G. Summary Judgment Motions. All motions for summary judgment in post-Note of Issue cases must be accompanied by a Trial Readiness Order and a filed Note of Issue or the motion will be denied.

H. Reply Papers. Counsel shall not set forth factual claims or legal arguments in reply papers which were not set forth in the papers initiating the motion or cross-motion. New factual claims or legal arguments offered in opposition to the motion or cross-motion shall not be considered by the Court in its determination of the motion or cross-motion.

I. Sur–Reply and Post–Submission Papers. Counsel and the parties are reminded that the Civil Practice Law and Rules does not provide for the submission of Sur-Reply papers, however denominated, or the presentation of papers or letters to the Court after the return date of a motion. Nor is motion practice by correspondence permitted. Absent express permission obtained in advance from the Court, such papers shall not be considered. Opposing counsel who receive a copy of such material submitted in violation of this rule shall not respond in kind.

JUSTICE GERALD E. LOEHR

Doc. 1. Hon. Gerald E. Loehr

E-Filing Rules and Protocol

All parties should familiarize themselves with the statewide E–Filing Rules (Uniform Rule §§ 202.5–b and 202.5–bb—available at www.nycourts.gov/efile) and the Westchester County E–Filing Protocol available at http://www.courts.state.ny.us/courts/9jd/efile/WestchesterCountyJointProtocols.pdf. General questions about e-filing should be addressed to the E–Filing Resource Center at 646–386–3033 or efile@courts.state.ny.us.

Specific questions relating to local procedures should be addressed to the Civil Calendar Office (914) 824-5300.

Electronic Filing

All commercial and tort actions in Part 103, Justice Gerald E. Loehr are to be filed through the New York State Courts E–Filing system (NYSCEF). All submissions to the Court, including proposed orders, proposed judgments, and letters, must be electronically filed.

Working Copies

See Uniform Rule § 202.5–b(d)(4).

This Part requires working copies for all electronic submissions.

Working copies shall be delivered to Chambers.

All working copies submitted to this Part must include a copy of the NYSCEF Confirmation Notice firmly fastened as the [front] cover page of the submission and comply with other requirements set forth in the Westchester County Protocol. Working copies without the Confirmation Notice will not be accepted.

Working copies are to be delivered no later than noon on the first business day following the electronic filing of the document on the NYSCEF site.

Hard Copy Submissions

Part will reject any hard copy submissions in e-filed cases unless those submissions bear the Notice of Hard Copy Submission—E-Filed Case required by Uniform Rule § 202.5–b(d)(1). The form is available at www.nycourts.gov/efile.

Commercial Division Case Rules:

No motion shall be made, except as allowed by Rule 24 of the Commercial Division Rules, without a prior conference with the Court, which conference may be obtained either by conference call or, upon obtaining permission from chambers, the submittal of a brief letter application, not exceeding 1 page in length. At the conference, the Court will set a schedule for making the motion, opposing it, and, if applicable, for reply.

Motions are to be returnable on Fridays at 9:30 a.m. Motions made returnable at any other time, absent prior permission of the Court, will be adjourned by the Part Clerk to the next available Friday.

Adjournments are governed by Rule 16(c) of the Commercial Division Rules.

Motions are submitted without oral argument, unless otherwise directed by the Court.

Reply papers are not permitted, unless: (a) the right of reply is obtained by service of a notice of motion in accordance with CPLR 2214[b]; or (b) expressly permitted by the Court.

Commercial Division Case Rules Continued:

Counsel may submit supplemental citations as allowed by Rule 18 of the Commercial Division Rules. Sur-reply papers, including reply papers in support of a cross-motion, are not permitted, absent prior permission of the Court. Any unauthorized papers will not be read and will be discarded.

All papers must comply with the applicable provisions of the CPLR and with Rules 16 and 18 of the Commercial Division Rules. In addition, the font size of text and footnotes must be no smaller than 12 point. Papers which do not comply may be rejected.

All motions for summary judgment shall be accompanied by a Statement of Undisputed Facts Pursuant to Rule 19-a of the Commercial Division Rules. A motion for summary judgment which lacks such a statement may be rejected. All opposing papers must include a response to the Statement of Undisputed Facts.

All exhibits shall be separately tabbed. In the event that multiple affidavits or affirmations are submitted in support of a motion under the same legal back, each such exhibit shall be accompanied by a clearly discernible side or bottom tab containing the last name of the affiant.

No motion papers will be sealed without a prior, or contemporaneous, application for sealing made pursuant to 22 NYCRR § 216.1

The Court generally does not stay disclosure pending determination of motions to dismiss or motions for summary judgment (made prior to completion of discovery).

Discovery Disputes:

With respect to cases already assigned to this Court at the time that a discovery dispute arises, no motion with respect to the dispute shall be made without a prior conference with the Court, which may be obtained by submission of a letter application, not exceeding one (1) page in length. Counsel must obtain permission from Chambers prior to the submission of such letter application.

Counsel are obligated to formulate a discovery plan that states the parties' views and proposals on any issues about disclosure or discovery of electronically stored information, including the form or forms in which it should be produced.

Commercial Division Case Rules Continued:

With respect to cases in which a discovery motion accompanies the Request for Judicial Intervention which leads to the assignment to this Court, no opposition papers shall be served until there has been a prior conference with the Court, which may be obtained by letter application, not exceeding one (1) page in length. The application for a discovery conference may be made by the movant or by the opposing counsel; however, the application must be made within eight (8) days of service of the motion. Counsel must obtain permission from Chambers prior the submission of a letter application. Failure to request a discovery conference may result in the denial of the motion.

The Court endeavors to resolve discovery disputes promptly, usually by conference, which may be held telephonically or in person. In the event that the dispute is not resolved, the Court will set an expedited briefing schedule. Counsel shall, prior to requesting a conference, meet in person to discuss the issues and endeavor to resolve or limit them, prior to seeking judicial intervention.

Preliminary Conferences:

Upon receipt of a letter from the Court scheduling a preliminary conference, counsel shall meet in person and shall **jointly** prepare a brief statement describing the case and the contentions of the parties. In addition, counsel shall **jointly** complete a proposed Preliminary Conference Order, on the form supplied by the Court (also available on the Court's website). Counsel are advised that, absent very unusual complexity, the Court will require that discovery be completed within six months of the assignment of the case to the Court. These submissions shall be furnished to the Court not later than 12 p.m. on the day prior to the conference. In the event that the Court does not receive the submissions, the Court will take such action as may be appropriate under the circumstances, including adjournment of the conference, requiring counsel to complete the forms at the conference, or other steps.

Commercial Division cases sent to alternate dispute resolution shall proceed in accordance with the Rules Of The Alternate Dispute Resolution Program as promulgated by Justice Alan D. Scheinkman.

For All Cases

Trials

Prior to the commencement of a trial, counsel shall provide the Court with:

a) marked pleadings, and

b) an exhibit list. Material to be used on cross-examination need not be listed. The attorneys are to pre-mark their exhibits. Only those received into evidence will be marked by the reporter.

The reporter is to be provided with an exhibit list.

Requests to charge shall be submitted to the Court as directed. The charge will be drawn from the Pattern Jury Instructions (PJI). A complete list of requested charges is to be submitted.

Unless counsel seek a deviation from the pattern charge or additions to the pattern charge, only the PJI numbers need to be submitted. Where deviations or additions are requested, the full text of such requests must be submitted, together with any supporting legal precedents. All submissions must be served upon opposing counsel.

Verdict sheet - Counsel shall jointly prepare a verdict sheet. The verdict sheet is to be typed and in final form for presentation to the jury. If agreement cannot be reached, then each side shall present a proposed verdict sheet. If it is feasible, such proposals shall also be submitted on a computer disc in a format convertible to Word Perfect 12.0.

Communications with the Court:

(a) Written correspondence: No written correspondence may be sent to the Court without prior permission. Written correspondence sent by letter, fax or any other means, without permission will not be read and will be discarded.

(b) Telephone calls:

1. Counsel may call the Part Clerk with respect to the scheduling of appearances and with respect to adjournment applications.

2. Counsel may call Chambers and/or the Part Clerk to arrange for a telephone conference with the Court or with the Law Secretary.

3. Counsel may not contact Chambers without all opposing counsel on the phone, except for the purpose of facilitating a conference call.

(c) Faxes: Faxes will not be accepted unless it is an emergency and the receipt has been authorized by Chambers.

JUSTICE J. EMMETT MURPHY

Doc. 1. Hon. J. Emmett Murphy
COMPLIANCE CONFERENCES:

This Part does not conduct compliance conferences (see Westchester Supreme Court Differentiated Case

Management Protocol Part Rules effective September 14, 2009). Please contact Carolyn Carpenito, Room 800, at (914) 824–5344 or ComplianceWestchester@ courts.state.ny.us as to matters of discovery.

SETTLEMENT CONFERENCES:

This Part does not conduct settlement conferences (see Westchester Supreme Court Differentiated Case Management Protocol Part Rules effective September 14, 2009). Please contact Robert Arena, Room 1201, at (914) 824–5339.

MOTIONS:

After a case has been assigned to this Part, prior to the bringing of any motion, with the exception of dispositive motions made after the note of issue is filed, movant shall notify the Court, in writing, with a copy to all parties, setting forth the relief sought and the basis for that relief. The Court will schedule a conference call with counsel or a Court conference date. This procedure does not preclude the moving party from making a motion, but provides the Court with an opportunity to resolve the dispute giving rise to the motion without need for a formal written application. Failing the resolution of the dispute, or if the Court in its discretion does not schedule the call or conference within ten days of mailing, then the party seeking the relief may proceed with the motion.

Motions will be returnable on Wednesdays except by order of the Court.

Appearances are not required on the return date. Oral argument may be requested by noting, "Oral Argument Requested" immediately over the index number on the Notice of Motion or Order to Show Cause.

If the Court, in its discretion, requires such oral argument, counsel for the movant will be advised and will be required to notify all parties.

Sur-replies will not be considered unless the Court directs otherwise. If new issues are raised in the reply, or if there has been a change in the law while the motion has been pending, counsel are to advise the Court, in writing, of the request to submit additional affidavits or memoranda. Other papers, including letters, which are sent after the submission date on the motion, will not be considered.

If, in advance of the motion return dates, the parties resolve any or all of the issues in dispute, movant shall immediately notify the Court Clerk in writing. An unexcused failure to inform the Court of a settlement, resulting in the expenditure of court resources, will subject the movant to sanctions.

ADJOURNMENTS:

On Consent: Mary Haran, Part Clerk is to be advised by telephone ([914]–824–5372), followed by a letter, that the motion is adjourned on consent. A copy of this letter is to be sent to all parties. No more than three adjournments, for an aggregate peri-od of sixty (60) days, will be granted by the Court without prior permission of the Court. The cooperation of counsel is urged.

Opposed: The application for an adjournment must be made in person on the return date of the motion. Any party wishing to be heard in opposition to the request for an adjournment must appear in person. Alternatively, the application for adjournment may be made via a conference telephone call with all parties and the law clerk. In either event, the requesting party must advise all other parties that the application for an adjournment will be made.

TRIALS:

Prior to the commencement of a trial, counsel shall provide the Court with:

a) Marked pleadings, and

b) An exhibit list. Material to be used on cross-examination need not be listed. The attorneys are to pre-mark their exhibits. Only those received in evidence will be marked by the reporter. The reporter is to be provided with an exhibit list.

Requests to charge:

Requests to charge shall be submitted to the Court as directed at a conference immediately preceding trial. The charge will be drawn from the Pattern Jury Instructions (PJI) to the fullest extent practicable. A complete list of requested charges is to be submitted. Unless counsel seek a deviation from the pattern charge or additions to the pattern charge, only the PJI numbers and topic headings need be submitted. Where deviations or additions are requested, the full text of such requests must be submitted, together with any supporting legal precedents. In addition, such proposals shall be submitted by e-mail to Anne Minihan, the Court's Law Clerk at aminihan@courts. state.ny.us in a format convertible to WordPerfect 8.0.

Verdict sheet:

Counsel shall jointly prepare a verdict sheet. The verdict sheet is to be typed and in final form for presentation to the jury. If agreement cannot be reached, then each side shall present a proposed verdict sheet. In addition, such proposals shall be submitted by e-mail to Anne Minihan, the Court's Law Clerk at aminihan@courts.state.ny.us in a format convertible to WordPerfect 8.0.

GENERAL:

Counsel who appear must be fully familiar with the case and have authority to enter into any agreement, either substantive or procedural, on behalf of their clients. Counsel must be on time for all scheduled appearances and must bring sufficient material to allow meaningful discussion of unresolved issues to each Court appearance. Sanctions may be imposed for failure to comply with this rule.

Submission by fax will not be accepted except in an emergency and if the receipt has been authorized by Chambers. In cases not subject to e-filing rules and protocol, copies of letters confirming an adjournment of a motion or a conference may be sent by fax to Mary Haran, Part Clerk at (914) 995–4396 with the original correspondence mailed to Court.

If an action is settled, discontinued, or otherwise disposed, counsel shall immediately inform the Court by submission of a copy of the stipulation or other document evidencing the disposition.

Counsel/parties shall address questions regarding scheduling appearances or adjourning appearances to Mary Haran, Part Clerk (914) 824–5372.

E–FILING RULES AND PROTOCOL:

Counsel for all parties shall familiarize themselves with the statewide E–Filing Rules (see Uniform Rule §§ 202.5–b and 202.5–bb, available at www.nycourts. gov/efile) and the Westchester County E–Filing Protocol available at http://www.courts.state.ny.us/courts/ 9jd/efile/WestchesterCountyJointProtocols.pdf.

General questions about e-filing should be addressed to the E–Filing Resource Center at (646) 386–3033 or efile@courts.state.ny.us.

Specific questions about local procedures should be addressed to the Civil Calendar Office at (914) 824–5300.

ELECTRONIC FILING:

All documents filed in mandatory e-filed cases, except those documents which are subject to the "opt out" provision of § 202.5–bb of the Uniform Rules for the State of New York State Trial Courts, or documents subject to e-filing in which consent is being withheld, are to be filed through the New York State Courts E–Filing System (NYSCEF). All submissions to the Court, including proposed orders, judgments and letters must be electronically filed.

WORKING COPIES:

The Court, which does not require the submission of working copies of electronically filed documents, may request the submission of working copies in specific instances (see Uniform Rule § 202.5–b[d][4]).

All working copies submitted MUST include a copy of the NYSCEF Confirmation Notice firmly fastened to the front cover page of the working copy submission and must comply with all of the other requirements set forth in the Westchester County Protocol. Working copies that do not include a NYSCEF Confirmation Notice will be rejected.

Working copies shall be delivered to Mary Haran, Part Clerk, 14th Floor no later than 12:00 noon on the first business day following the electronic filing of the document on the NYSCEF site.

HARD COPY SUBMISSION:

This Court will reject any hard copy submissions in e-filed cases unless those submissions bear the Notice of Hard Copy Submission — E–Filed Case required by Uniform Rule § 202.5–b(d)(1). The form is available at www.nycourts.gov/efile.

JUSTICE MARY H. SMITH

Rule I. Communications With the Court

A. Correspondence. Correspondence to the Court shall, without exception, be copied to all adversary counsel and pro se litigants. Correspondence between counsel and/or pro se litigants shall not be copied to the Court unless there is some specific judicial purpose to be served by transmitting copies to the Court.

B. Telephone Calls. Telephone calls to the Court staff are permitted only in necessary or emergency situations requiring immediate attention that cannot otherwise be attained by correspondence.

Rule II. E–Filing Rules and Protocol

A. E–FILING RULES AND PROTOCOL

All parties should familiarize themselves with the statewide E–Filing Rules (Uniform Rule §§ 202.5–b and 202.5–bb—available at www.nycourts.gov/efile) and the Westchester County E–Filing Protocol available at http://www.courts.state.ny.us/courts/9jd/efile/ WestchesterCountyJointProtocols.pdf.

General questions about e-filing should be addressed to the E–Filing Resource Center at 646–386–3033 or efile@courts.state.ny.us.

Specific questions relating to local procedures should be addressed to the Civil Calendar Office at (914) 824–5300.

B. ELECTRONIC FILING

All civil actions in Judge Smith's Part are to be filed through the New York State Courts E–Filing system (NYSCEF). All submissions to the Court, including proposed orders, proposed judgments, and letters, must be electronically filed.

C. WORKING COPIES

THIS PART REQUIRES THE SUBMISSION OF "WORKING COPIES" OF ELECTRONICALLY FILED DOCUMENTS. See Uniform Rule § 202.5–b(d)(4). Working copies of motions, proposed Orders to Show Cause and proposed Orders and Judgments shall be delivered to Ms. Jackson, the Part Clerk no later than 3:00 p.m. within three (3) business days following the electronic filing. UNDER NO CIR-

CUMSTANCES SHALL WORKING COPIES BE FURNISHED TO CHAMBERS VIA FACSIMILE.

This part requires working copies for:

[X] Motion submissions

[X] Proposed Orders to Show Cause

[X] Proposed orders/judgments

[ ] Stipulations

[ ] Transcripts

[ ] Letters

All working copies submitted to this Part must include a copy of the NYSCEF Confirmation Notice firmly fastened as the front cover page of the submission and comply with other requirements set forth in the Westchester County Protocol. WORKING COPIES WITHOUT THE CONFIRMATION NOTICE WILL NOT BE ACCEPTED.

D. HARD COPY SUBMISSIONS

This Part will reject any hard copy submissions in e-filed cases unless those submissions bear the Notice of Hard Copy Submission—E–Filed Case required by Uniform Rule § 202.5–b(d)(1). The form is available at www.nycourts.gov/efile.

Rule III.   Motions and Orders to Show Cause

A.   General Rules. The Court will entertain motions on submission, whether brought by Notice of Motion or by Order to Show Cause, at 9:30 a.m. on any Friday the Court is in session. The return date for an Order To Show Cause shall be determined by the Court at the time papers are submitted for consideration and executed. There shall be no oral argument heard on any motions unless directed by the Court in a given instance. In the unusual instance when the Court wishes to hear oral argument on a motion, as permitted by Uniform Rule 202.8(d), all counsel and pro se litigants shall be provided with reasonable prior notice of the date and time scheduled for such purpose at which parties are expected to appear in Court.

B. Where Temporary Restraining Orders are requested, moving counsel must submit adequate proof of compliance with 22 NYCRR 202.7(f).

C.   Working Copies of Papers Applicable to All Motions. All motion papers and Orders to Show Cause, must be typewritten, double-spaced, securely bound, entirely legible and all exhibits labeled with tab markings. Deposition transcripts included as exhibits must be single, front-faced pages only. The Court may refuse to accept any such paper which does not conform to the foregoing.

D.   Motion Adjournments. Upon consent of all counsel and pro se litigants, the Court typically will grant an adjournment of a motion or Order to Show Cause; however, no more than three adjournments of any single motion will be permitted. The party seeking the adjournment must obtain the consent of adversary parties and notify Ms. Jackson, the Part Clerk, at 914–824–5366, of the requested adjourned date at least twenty-four (24) hours before the original return date. Granted motion adjournments should be confirmed in writing to the Court and all adversary parties.

Rule IV.   Decisions and Orders

The parties are responsible to obtain copies of all written Orders, Motions and Decisions. Courtesy copies will be furnished only when Chambers is provided with a stamped, self-addressed envelope.

Rule V.   Trials and Hearings

A. Prior to commencement of a trial, counsel shall provide the Court with:

1) Marked pleadings and Bill of Particulars in accordance with CPLR Rule 4012;

2) Pre-trial memoranda of law as to any known disputed legal issues that must be determined by the Court;

3) A list of witnesses for each party;

4) Requests to charge. The charge will be drawn from the Pattern Jury Instructions (PJI). A complete list of requested charges is to be submitted. Unless counsel seek a deviation from the pattern charge or additions to the pattern charge, only the PJI numbers need be submitted. Where deviations or additions are requested, the full text of such requests must be submitted, together with any supporting legal precedents.

5) Proposed verdict sheet. Counsel shall jointly prepare a verdict sheet. The verdict sheet is to be typed and in final form for presentation to the jury. If agreement cannot be reached, then each side shall present a proposed verdict sheet.

B.   Motion *in Limine*. Any motions for the Courts's consideration *in limine* must be delivered to the Part Clerk and served upon adversary counsel not later than one (1) day prior to the scheduled date of the trial, except as to issues that cannot be reasonably anticipated prior to trial.

Rule VI.   Settled and Discontinued Cases

Counsel shall immediately notify the Court of a case disposition. Following the initial notification, counsel shall efile the stipulation of discontinuance so that the matter may be marked off the calendar.

JUSTICE BRUCE E. TOLBERT

Doc. 1. Hon. Bruce. E. Tolbert

Return Date:

Motions shall be made returnable at the Westchester County Courthouse 111 Dr. Martin Luther King Jr., Blvd. White Plains, New York on Fridays at 9:30 A.M. Motion papers are to be submitted to the Court. The Court does not accept papers of any sort by fax unless expressly indicated by the Court. The usual CPLR provisions with regard to motion practice will apply. Appearances are not required or expected, unless expressly indicated by the Court. In those instances in which a motion is brought by Order to Show Cause, the motion return date, the necessity of appearances and all other document return dates shall be determined by the Court.

Requests for Oral Argument:

Oral argument will be granted, subject to the Justice's calendar, if requested by the initiating party by prominent request made at the top right hand portion of the order to show cause or notice of motion/petition, or if so requested in the same fashion by opposing counsel or party in the responsive papers. Call the Part Clerk at least 3 days before the return date to ascertain the Court's calendar and whether oral argument will occur.

Adjournments:

Adjournments of motions is governed by 22 NYCRR 202.8(e) which provides: "(e)(1) Stipulations of adjournments of the return date made by the parties shall be in writing and shall be submitted to the assigned judge. Such stipulation shall be effective unless the court otherwise directs. No more than three stipulated adjournments for an aggregate period of 60 days shall be submitted without prior permission of the court. (2) absent agreement by the parties, a request by any party for an adjournment shall be submitted in writing, upon notice to the other party, to the assigned judge on or before the return date. The court will notify the requesting party whether the adjournment has been granted."

All Adjournment requests must be in writing directed to the Part Clerk for submission to Chambers for consideration. Where exigent circumstances exist, an application for an adjournment may be made via fax to the attention of the Law Secretary.

Papers Required on a Particular Motion:

1) On any motion seeking summary judgment dismissal of a complaint, cross-claim or counterclaim, or the striking of a pleading, copies of all pleadings filed as of the date of the motion must be provided to the Court by the moving party. The failure to comply with this requirement shall result in the denial of the motion unless the pleadings are provided to the Court by another party.

2) On any motion seeking leave to renew or reargue a prior motion, copies of all papers submitted on the prior motion must be provided to the Court by the moving party. The failure to comply with this requirement shall result in the denial of the motion unless the papers on the prior motion are provided by the Court by another party.

STAMPED, SELF-ADDRESSED ENVELOPES MUST BE ATTACHED TO EVERY MOTION AND OPPOSING PAPERS OR DECISIONS WILL NOT BE MAILED.

E-FILING RULES AND PROTOCOL

All parties should familiarize themselves with the Statewide E-Filing Rules which can be found in Uniform Rules Sections 202.5-b and 202.5-bb and found at www.nycourts.gov/efile.

The Westchester County E-Filing Protocol is available at: http://www.courts.state.ny.us/courts/9jd/efile/WestchesterCountyJointProtocols.pdf.

General questions about e-filing should be addressed to the E-Filing Resource Center at telephone number 646-386-3033 or via email at: efile@courts.state.ny.us

Specific questions relating to local procedures should be addressed to the Civil Calendar Office (914) 824-5300.

ELECTRONIC FILING

All matters in this part are to be filed through the New York State Courts E-Filing system (NYSCEF). All submissions to the Court, including motion submissions, proposed Orders to Show Cause, proposed orders and judgments, stipulations, transcripts and letters, must be electronically filed.

WORKING COPIES

This Part requires the submission of "working copies" of electronically filed documents. See Uniform Rule Section 202.5-b(d)(4). This part requires working copies for all electronic submissions including motion submissions, proposed Orders to Show Cause, proposed orders and judgments, stipulations, transcripts and letters. All working copies shall be delivered to the Part Clerk. This rule pertaining to working copies can only be modified upon this Court's approval.

DIFFERENTIATED CASE MANAGEMENT PROTOCOL

PART RULES

On September 14, 2009 Differentiated Case Management Protocol came into effect for the Westchester County Supreme Court. They are broken down into Preliminary Conference Part Rules, Compliance Part Rules, Settlement Conference Part Rules and Trial Ready Part Rules. All of these Part Rules must be reviewed, understood and followed by all counsel and litigants before this Court.

TRIALS

Prior to the commencement of a trial, counsel shall provide the Court with:

1) Marked Pleadings, and; 2) an Exhibit List: The attorneys are to pre-mark their exhibits. The reporter is to be provided with and exhibit list. Material to be used on cross-examination need not be listed.

Requests to charge shall be submitted to the Court as directed. The charge(s) will be drawn from the Pattern Jury Instructions (PJI). A complete list of requested charges is to be submitted. Unless counsel seek a deviation from the pattern charge, only the PJI numbers need be submitted. Where deviations or additions are requested, the full text of such requests must be submitted, together with any supporting legal precedents. All submissions must be served upon opposing counsel.

Verdict Sheet:

Counsel Shall jointly prepare a verdict sheet.

Which shall be submitted to the Court concurrently with the requests to charge. The verdict sheet is to be typed and in final form for presentation to the jury. If agreement cannot be reached, then each side shall present a proposed verdict sheet. If it is feasible, such proposals shall also be submitted on a computer disk in a format convertible to Word Perfect 8.0.

GENERAL

Counsel who appear must be fully familiar with the case and have authority to enter into any agreement, either substantive or procedural, on behalf of their clients. Counsel must be on time for all scheduled appearances and must bring sufficient material to allow for meaningful discussion of unresolved issues at each court appearance. Sanctions may be imposed for failure to comply with this rule.

If an action is settled, discontinued, or other wise disposed, counsel shall immediately inform the Court by submission of a copy of the stipulation or other document evidencing the disposition.

It is this Court's intention to help litigants resolve their disputes in a fair and equitable manner. Should the attorneys have need of the Court's assistance at any time a conference with all parties and counsel present in person or by telephone can be arranged through the Court's Law Clerk. Attorneys are reminded, however, that ex parte communications to the Court are prohibited by the CPLR and the Code of Professional Conduct.

JUSTICE SAM D. WALKER

Rule I. General Rules

A. Compliance Conferences. Please note this Part no longer conducts compliance conferences. See Westchester Supreme Court Differentiated Case Management Protocol Part Rules amended January 4, 2010. Please contact Caroline Carpenito, Room 800, at 914-824-5344 or ComplianceWestchester@courts. state.ny.us.

B. Settlement Conferences. Please note this Part no longer conducts settlement conferences. See Westchester Supreme Court Differentiated Case Management Protocol Part Rules amended January 4, 2010. Settlement Conferences are conducted by the Hon. Joan Lefkowitz, JSC., in Room 1601.

C. Appearances by Counsel With Knowledge and Authority. All counsel who appear before the Court must be familiar with the case and be fully authorized to enter into agreements as to both substantive and procedural matters on behalf of their clients. Attorneys appearing of counsel to the attorneys of record and self-represented parties shall be held to the same requirements. Failure to comply with this rule may be regarded as a default and dealt with appropriately. All counsel and self-represented parties must be on time for all scheduled appearances.

D. Settlements and Discontinuances. If an action is settled, discontinued or disposed of in any other manner by the parties, counsel shall immediately inform the Court by letter and by filing a Stipulation of Discontinuance or Stipulation of Settlement with the Part Clerk. The Court shall not mark any matter as settled unless it has received a copy of a Stipulation of Discontinuance or Stipulation of Settlement, the original of which has been filed with the County Clerk.

E. Papers by Fax. The Court does not accept papers of any kind by fax transmission unless otherwise requested by the Court in advance in a particular case. Copies of letters confirming an adjournment of a motion or a conference may be sent to the Court by fax at its chambers. However, the original of all correspondence must be mailed to the Part Clerk. Any authorized fax transmission directed to the Part Clerk shall be faxed only to the telephone number: (914) 995–4316. All faxes shall be limited to 5 pages.

F. Conduct of Parties and Counsel. It is expected that all parties and counsel shall conduct themselves appropriately in all in-court and out-of-court proceedings and in their communications with each other and the Court. PERSONAL ATTACKS UPON PARTIES OR COUNSEL SHALL NOT BE TOLERATED AND SHALL RESULT IN THE IMPOSITION OF SANCTIONS AS DETERMINED BY THE COURT TO BE WARRANTED UNDER THE PARTICULAR CIRCUMSTANCES.

G. **Ex Parte Communications.** Ex parte communications are strictly prohibited except upon the consent of all counsel, or with respect to scheduling matters or the presentation of orders to show cause for signature.

H. **Communications With Represented Parties.** Counsel are directed to inform their clients that under no circumstances shall any member of the Court's staff engage in any conversation or exchange any communication with a represented party. If a represented party communicates with any member of the Court's staff, all counsel shall be informed of the communication and, if it is in writing, shall be sent a copy of that writing.

I. **Scheduling.** Counsel/parties should address questions about scheduling appearances or adjourning appearances to the Part Clerk, Demary Lopez (914) 824-5167.

Rule II. Motion Practice Rules

A. **Motion Calendar and Appearances.** All motions/proceedings brought on by notice of motion or notice of petition shall be made returnable before the Court on any Wednesday the Court is in session at 9:30 A.M. There will be a Motion Calendar called by the Court. The purpose of the Motion Calendar call is to achieve an easy and efficient means for attorneys to submit and the Court to collect all opposition, cross-moving and reply papers in connection with motions on the calendar. During the Motion Calendar call, commencing at 9:30 A.M., all motions returnable that day will be "called" for the submission of these papers. These papers may either be submitted by mail or in person and received by the Court prior to the "call" or must be handed up at this "call". If opposition, cross-moving and reply papers are not submitted before or at the submission "call," the opportunity to do so will be lost (unless an adjournment is arranged or court permission is obtained).

To the extent possible, motions will be decided "on the papers." If argument is directed, it will take place on an announced date shortly after the day of submission. Counsel for the movant need not appear to "take a default" on any motion or for any other reason. Motions will be submitted, not marked off, in the absence of the movant. Opposing counsel similarly need not appear in person in order to avoid suffering a default. Delivery of papers by mail, service or a clerk will suffice.

B. **Applications, Adjournments, Submission of Late Papers.** To protect movants against the submission of late opposition papers or cross-motions, the Court will sua sponte adjourn for one week cases in which appropriate time has not been given. Parties seeking an adjournment must follow the direction delineated below in order to adjourn a motion. Unless the Part Clerk, the Court's Assistant Law Clerk or the Court's Law Clerk has conveyed the Court's approval of an adjournment, no motion shall be considered to have been adjourned.

C. **Adjournments by Stipulation.** A party seeking an adjournment must contact all other parties in an effort to obtain consent and demonstrate that that was done. No more than three adjournments for a total of no more than 60 days are allowed except with the permission of the Court (Rule 202.8(e)(1) of the Uniform Rules for the Trial Courts), given by means of a so-ordered stipulation.

D. **Adjournments by Affidavit/Affirmation of Consent.** If all parties consent to an adjournment as allowed by these rules but a written stipulation cannot be obtained in time for submission, the applicant for the adjournment on consent may submit an affidavit or affirmation reciting that such consent was obtained. That document must state the reason for the adjournment request, how consent was obtained from all parties, when it was obtained, and the name of each attorney who gave oral consent. The affidavit/affirmation must be received by the Court before the date on which the request for adjournment is made or application may be made by counsel at the Motion Calendar call.

E. **Applications for Adjournment Not on Consent.** If consent was not obtained from all parties prior to the return date, any party making an application for adjournment at the Motion Calendar must appear at the Motion Calendar call and put on the record before the Court the reason for the requested adjournment and a description of the efforts made to obtain such consent, including the date when a contact was initiated or attempted, the means used, and the person contacted (if consent was refused) or for whom a message was left (if no contact was made). Furthermore, an applicant must, by phone, fax, e-mail, or mail transmitted with adequate lead time, advise all parties who have not consented that an application will be made at the Motion Calendar call. Applications for adjournments that are not properly supported will not be entertained. If there is no compliance, the Part Clerk will mark the motion submitted.

F. **Orders to Show Cause.** Orders to show cause submitted for signature shall be presented to the office of the calendar clerk, after the payment of any required fee at the County Clerk's Office. If the order to show cause is signed by the Court, a copy of it shall be sent by fax to counsel for the moving party. If appearances are required on the return date of the motion, the Court shall so indicate in the order to show cause. Otherwise, no appearances shall be required and no oral argument shall be heard on the return date of the motion.

G. **Requests for Temporary Restraining Orders.** When an order to show cause is to be presented to the Court which seeks a temporary restraining order, counsel for the moving party must first communicate by telephone or fax transmission with counsel for all adverse parties, and with any unrepresented adverse parties, to advise such counsel or parties that a request for a temporary restraining order shall be made to the Court and that such counsel or parties have the right to be heard on the application. A conference on the request for a temporary restraining order shall be conducted by the Court at 9:30 a.m. on the first day that the Court is in session following the day on which the order to show cause is presented. Following the conference, either by way of a bench decision or a written decision, the Court shall render its determination only on the request for a temporary restraining order. No request for a temporary restraining order shall be considered without a conference unless the moving party demonstrates to the Court that conducting such a conference will clearly cause the moving party irreparable injury.

H. Communications Regarding Motions. All communications regarding motions, including requests for adjournments and questions concerning the status of motions, shall be directed to the Court's Assistant Law Clerk. Only in the absence of the Court's Assistant Law Clerk shall any communication regarding a motion be directed to the Part Clerk or the Law Clerk.

I. Time for Filing and Serving Summary Judgment Motions. Summary judgment motions shall be filed with the Court and served upon all adverse parties no later than thirty (30) days after the filing of the Note of Issue.

J. No Stay of Discovery. There shall be no stay of pretrial discovery resulting from the filing of a motion made pursuant to CPLR 3211 or 3212 unless otherwise ordered by the Court.

K. Form of Papers. Except with the express permission of the Court, all motion papers submitted to the Court, including Orders to Show Cause, must be typewritten and all exhibits must be labeled with tab markings and entirely legible. Motion papers and all correspondence must indicate the index number assigned to the action. Courtesy copies of papers shall not be submitted to Chambers.

L. Papers Required on Particular Motions.

1. *Dispositive Motions*: On any motion seeking summary judgment, dismissal of a complaint, cross-claim or counterclaim, or the striking of a pleading, copies of all pleadings filed as of the date of filing of the motion must be provided to the Court by the moving party. The failure to comply with this requirement shall result in the denial of the motion unless the pleadings are provided to the Court by another party.

2. *Motions for Leave to Renew or Reargue*: On any motion seeking leave to renew or reargue a prior motion, the moving party shall submit copies of all papers submitted on the prior motion. The failure to comply with this requirement shall result in the denial

of the motion unless the papers on the prior motion are submitted to the Court by another party.

3. *Motions for Leave to Amend, Supplement or Correct Pleadings*: On any motion for leave to amend, supplement or correct a pleading, in addition to the proposed amended, supplemental or corrected pleading, the moving party shall submit copies of all pleadings filed as of the date of the motion. The failure to comply with this requirement shall result in the denial of the motion unless copies of the prior pleadings are submitted to the Court by another party.

4. *Motions for Injunctive Relief*: When an order to show cause is to be presented to the Court which seeks a temporary restraining order or a preliminary injunction, copies of the summons and complaint commencing the underlying action must be provided to the Court by the moving party. No order to show cause seeking such relief will be considered by the Court if the moving party fails to comply with this requirement.

5. *Default Motions*: On any motion for a default judgment, proof must be presented that a military-status investigation of all defendants who are persons has been conducted after the time for each such defendant to appear or answer, as applicable, has transpired. In addition, to be sufficient, the military-status investigation must include, at a minimum, a search conducted through the Department of Defense, which may be performed through that agency's internet site, https://www.dmdc.osd.mil/appj/scra/index.jsp.

M. Reply Papers. Counsel and self-represented parties shall not set forth factual claims or legal arguments in reply papers which were not set forth in the papers initiating the motion or cross-motion. New factual claims and legal arguments which are not directly in response to factual claims or legal arguments offered in opposition to a motion or cross-motion shall not be considered by the Court in its determination of a motion or cross-motion.

N. Sur–Reply and Post–Submission Papers. Counsel and the parties are reminded that the CPLR does not provide for the submission of sur-reply papers, however denominated, or the presentation of papers or letters to the Court after the return date of a motion. Nor is motion practice by correspondence permitted. Absent express permission obtained in advance from the Court, such materials shall be filed with the County Clerk unread. Any opposing counsel and self-represented party who receives a copy of such materials submitted in violation of this rule shall not respond in kind.

O. Length of Papers. Absent express permission obtained in advance from the Court, which shall be granted only upon a showing of good cause, briefs or memoranda of law shall be limited to 30 pages each, and affirmations and affidavits shall be limited to 25 pages each. Papers submitted to the Court in violation of this rule may not be considered by the Court in deciding the motion, without prior notice to the party who submitted the papers.

P. Settled Motions. In the event that the parties settle a motion or part of a motion in advance of the motion return date, they shall immediately inform the Court in writing. Any failure to inform the Court of a settlement which results in the needless expenditure of court resources in the issuance of a decision on a motion may result in the imposition of sanctions against counsel for all parties to the action and any self-represented parties.

Q. Motion Decisions and Orders.

1. *Written Decisions*: In most instances, a written Decision and Order will be issued by the Court following the submission of the motion. The Decision and Order, with supporting papers, will be filed in the Westchester County Clerk's Office by the Court. A copy of the Decision and Order shall be sent to all counsel and self-represented parties that have submitted a self addressed, stamped envelope after filing with the County Clerk.

2. *Bench Decisions*: In certain instances, the Court will render a decision from the bench. Any party seeking a written order shall submit to the Court a proposed order supported by a copy of the transcript of the proceeding at which the bench decision was rendered. The signed order will be filed in the Westchester County Clerk's Office by the Court.

Rule III. Trial Practice Rules

A. Trial Preparation. Prior to the commencement of the trial or hearing, counsel shall ascertain the availability of all witnesses and subpoenaed documents. Plaintiff's counsel shall request that the Part Clerk requisition the County Clerk file in the case to the courtroom as soon as possible after the assignment of the case to this Court. In addition, counsel for any party or any self-represented party who has issued subpoenas for the production of records shall request that the Part Clerk requisition all subpoenaed documents from the file room.

B. Interpreters and Special Services. Upon reporting to the Court for a trial or a hearing, counsel and any self-represented party shall *immediately* advise the Part Clerk if the services of a foreign language interpreter are required for any party or witness, or if any special services are required for any party or witness who is hearing-impaired or who suffers from any other disability. Similarly, the Part Clerk shall be *immediately* informed if there is a need for an easel, blackboard, shadow box, television or any other trial aid.

C. Pleadings and Submissions Due Immediately Upon Appearance. Immediately upon being assigned to this Court for a trial or hearing, counsel for each party, including the Law Guardian, if any, and any self-represented party, shall report to the Part Clerk, or in her absence, the Law Clerk. At that time, counsel for each party and each self-represented party shall submit the following to the Court:

1. A statement of the estimated length of trial.

2. Marked pleadings and all bills of particulars.

3. A list of all witnesses who may be called at trial, including any known, potential rebuttal witnesses.

4. A list of all exhibits the party expects to use at trial, indicating whether such exhibits are stipulated for admission into evidence or are marked only for identification.

5. A written stipulation governing all facts that are not in dispute.

6. In all matrimonial actions, an updated net worth statement and a statement of proposed disposition.

7. A copy of any statutory provisions in effect at the time the cause of action arose, upon which any party to the action relies.

8. All expert witness reports relevant to the issues.

9. All reports, transcripts of examinations before trial and written statements which may be used either to refresh a witness' recollection or for cross-examination.

D. Marking of Exhibits. After filing the above-listed submissions with the Court, counsel shall meet with the assigned Official Stenographer to pre-mark all exhibits for identification. Any exhibits whose admission is agreed to by the parties shall be pre-marked for admission.

E. Conference. Immediately prior to the commencement of the trial, the Court shall conduct a brief conference with all counsel and self-represented parties, to discuss preliminary matters. At this conference, all counsel and self-represented parties shall be prepared to:

1. Advise the Court as to all anticipated disputed issues of law and fact, and provide the Court with citations to all statutory and common-law authority upon which they will rely.

2. Stipulate to undisputed facts and the admission of clearly-admissible documents, records and other exhibits.

3. Alert the Court to any anticipated *in limine* motions or evidentiary objections which they believe will be made during the trial.

4. Provide the Court with a copy of all prior decisions and orders which may be relevant to any in limine applications or objections.

5. Discuss scheduling, as well as the number of witnesses to be called at trial, any anticipated problems regarding the attendance at trial of any party, attorney or witnesses, and any other practical problems which the Court should consider in scheduling.

6. Alert the Court as to any anticipated requests for a jury instruction relating to missing witnesses or evidence.

7. Alert the Court as to any anticipated request pursuant to CPLR Article 16 for apportionment as to an allegedly culpable non-party.

8. Supply a proposed verdict sheet and request to charge.

F. Copies of Transcripts. If any part of a transcript of an examination before trial or other recorded proceeding will be read as evidence-in-chief, the proponent of the transcript shall provide a complete copy of it to the Court and all other counsel or self-represented parties, *well in advance* of the time that it shall be read, with citations to the page and line numbers for all portions to be read, so that all objections may be addressed by the Court prior to the proposed reading.

G. Copies of Exhibits. Upon the admission of an exhibit at trial, the proponent of the exhibit shall provide a complete copy of it to the Court.

H. Addressing the Court. Any counsel or self-represented party who is raising an objection, presenting an argument or otherwise addressing the Court, shall stand while doing so, or shall not be recognized by the Court. All objections shall be made by stating the word "objection", together with up to three more words identifying the generic ground for objection, such as "hearsay", "bolstering", "leading" or "asked and answered". If it is believed that argument on an objection is necessary, any counsel or self-represented party may ask permission to approach the bench. Keep in mind that any counsel or self-represented party will be given the opportunity to make a full record of his or her position.

I. Courtroom Behavior. All remarks shall be directed to the Court. Comments shall not be made to opposing counsel or self-represented parties. PERSONAL ATTACKS UPON PARTIES OR COUNSEL SHALL NOT BE TOLERATED AND SHALL RESULT IN THE IMPOSITION OF SANCTIONS AS DETERMINED BY THE COURT TO BE WARRANTED UNDER THE PARTICULAR CIRCUMSTANCES. Do not attempt to "talk over" an adversary; only one person shall speak at a time. Simple requests, e.g., a request for a document or an exhibit, shall be accomplished in a manner which does not disrupt the proceedings or an adversary. Ask for permission to approach the bench if a significant discussion with an adversary is required, such as a proposed stipulation. There shall be no "grandstanding" in the presence of the jury, e.g., making demands, offers or statements that should properly be made outside of the presence of the jury.

J. Use of Exhibits. Do not show anything, including an exhibit or proposed exhibit, to a witness without first showing it to all opposing counsel and self-

represented parties. If any counsel or self-represented party believes that this procedure will compromise his or her trial strategy, he or she shall first request a pre-offer ruling outside of the presence of the jury.

K. Summation Exhibits. Any counsel or self-represented party who intends during summation to use any type of demonstrative exhibit not marked into evidence must advise the Court and all other counsel and self-represented parties of that intention at the pre-charge conference. Failure to comply with this rule shall result in an order precluding the use of such exhibit during summation.

L. Examination of Witnesses. Do not approach a witness without permission of the Court. The questioning counsel or self-represented party shall allow the witness to complete his or her answer to a question before asking another question. Do not interrupt a witness in the middle of an answer unless it is totally unresponsive, in which event a ruling from the Court shall be requested.

M. Jury Charges. In all jury trials, a complete list of requests to charge shall be submitted to the Court immediately preceding the commencement of trial, with copies to be provided to all other counsel and self-represented parties. If a requested charge is drawn from the current Pattern Jury Instructions (PJI), only the PJI number need be submitted. Where deviations from, or additions to, the PJI are requested, the full text of such requests must be submitted in writing, together with any supporting legal precedents. In addition such proposals shall be submitted on a computer disc in a format convertible to Word Perfect or emailed to the Court's law clerk at jworthey@courts.state.ny.us. At the final charging conference, if marshaling of the evidence is required as to a particular jury charge, counsel and all self-represented parties shall provide the Court with the proposed facts which they believe should be presented to the jury.

N. Verdict Sheet. At the commencement of the trial, counsel for the parties and any self-represented parties shall jointly prepare a verdict sheet. If agreement cannot be reached, each party shall present a proposed verdict sheet which shall be served upon all other parties. The verdict sheet shall be in a final, typewritten form which may be given to the jury. In addition the proposed verdict sheet(s) shall be submitted on a computer disc in a format convertible Word Perfect or emailed to the Court's law clerk at jworthey@courts.state.ny.us.

O. Post–Trial Submissions. Unless otherwise directed by the Court, in accordance with the schedule set by the Court at the conclusion of a bench-trial or hearing, the parties shall jointly submit a trial transcript, and each party shall prepare and submit a post-trial memorandum. Factual arguments set forth in the memorandum shall be supported by citations to the trial transcript, and legal arguments shall be supported by citations to relevant statutes or case law. In their post-trial submissions following a trial of equitable distribution issues, the parties shall identify each item of property as either separate or marital, and shall state the value of each item of property. They shall also identify all of the parties' outstanding debts as either separate or marital, and shall state the amount of each debt. All assertions as to the separate or marital status of each item of property and each outstanding debt, and the value of each item of property and the amount of each debt, shall be supported by citations to the trial transcript.

P. Check–In. At the start of each day of trial, all counsel and self-represented parties shall check in with the Part Clerk so that she will be aware of your presence.

Q. Food and Drinks. Absent permission of the Court obtained in advance, no counsel or party shall bring any beverage or food into the Courtroom. Water may be requested from the Clerk or a Court Officer during the trial, in which event only a cup of water as provided shall be permitted on the counsel table or the podium.

R. No Communication With Jurors. In order to maintain the appearance of total impartiality, once the jury has been selected no one is to communicate in any form at any time with any juror. This prohibition includes both verbal and non-verbal communication, including, without limitation, nods, shrugs and shaking the head. Do not even say "hello" or "good morning".

Rule IV.   E–Filing Rules and Protocol

All parties should familiarize themselves with the statewide E–Filings Rules (Uniform Rule §§ 202.5–b and 202.5–bb—available at www.nycourts.gov/efile) and the Westchester County E–Filing Protocol available at http://www.courts.state.ny.us/courts/9jd/efile/ WestchesterCountyJointProtocols.pdf. General questions about e-filing should be addressed to the E–Filing Resource Center at 646–386–3033 or efile@ courts.state.ny.us.

[Specific questions relating to local procedures should be addressed to **the Civil Calendar Office (914) 824–5300.**]

Electronic Filing

Beginning on January 19, 2011: Tort cases (as defined in Section I(D)(3)(a) of the Westchester County Protocol and commercial cases (as defined in Section I(D)(3)(b)) may be commenced either electronically or in hard copy with conversion to NYSCEF status upon filing of the consent.

Tort actions in Justice Sam D. Walker's part are to be filed through the New York State Courts E-Filing system (NYSCEF). All submissions to the Court, including proposed orders, proposed judgments, and letters, must be electronically filed.

Working Copies

A court may require the submission of "working copies" of electronically filed documents. See Uniform Rule § 202.5–b(d)(4).

[ ] This Part does not require working copies.

[X] This Part does not require working copies but may request working copies in specific instances.

[ ] This Part requires working copies for all electronic submissions.

[ ] This Part requires working copies for:

    [ ] motion submissions

    [ ] proposed orders to show cause

    [ ] proposed orders/judgments

    [ ] stipulations

    [ ] transcripts

    [ ] letters

[X] When specifically requested by this Part, working copies of motions, exhibits, letters, transcripts, stipulations shall be delivered to the Part Clerk

All working copies submitted to this Part *must* include a copy of the NYSCEF Confirmation Notice firmly fastened as the back cover page of the submission and comply with other requirements set forth in the Westchester County Protocol. Working copies without the Confirmation Notice will not be accepted.

When requested by this Court, working copies are to be delivered no later than 10:00 AM the first business day following the request for same.

Hard Copy Submissions

Judge Walker's Part will reject any hard copy submissions in e-filed cases unless previously requested by the Part and the hard copy submissions bear the Notice of Hard Copy Submission—E–Filed Case required by Uniform Rule § 202.5–b(d)(1). The form is available at www.nycourts.gov/efile.

DIFFERENTIATED CASE MANAGEMENT

PROTOCOL

Doc. 1. Protocol

By Order of the Hon. Alan D. Scheinkman, Administrative Judge of the Ninth Judicial District, the Westchester Supreme Court Differentiated Case Management Protocol as set forth herein has been established for the handling of general civil litigation in Westchester Supreme Court. The protocol was developed in consultation with Hon. Ann Pfau, Chief Administrative Judge, Hon. A. Gail Prudenti, Presiding Justice of the Appellate Division, Second Department, and Hon. Michael V. Coccoma, Deputy Chief Administrative Judge, Courts Outside New York City, and has been revised in light of experience since September 14, 2009 and in consultation with the Bar.

The realigned protocol is designed to promote active and effective case management consistent with the guidelines set forth in the Uniform Civil Rules for the Supreme Court. The realigned protocol focuses on the use of judicial resources by concentrating the use of judges to trials and resolution of substantive motions. The protocol is implemented through a comprehensive framework designed to provide intensive case supervision throughout the civil litigation process. As part of the protocol, four component Parts operate to monitor the progress of cases from discovery to trial - a Preliminary Conference Part, a Compliance Part, a Settlement Conference Part and a Trial Ready Part. Excluded from the protocol are tax certiorari, contested matrimonial, Commercial Division, and Article 81 Mental Hygiene Law cases, which will continue to be handled in specialized parts.

The Westchester Supreme Court Differentiated Case Management Protocol took effect with the Tenth Term of 2009 on September 14, 2009. The following constitute the Rules of the Preliminary Conference Part, Compliance Part, Settlement Conference Part and the Trial Ready Part, as amended, and are effective as of May 31, 2011.

This revised protocol includes information specific to the implementation of the New York State Courts E-Filing system (hereinafter referred to as "the NYS-CEF system") in the Westchester County Supreme Court in accordance with the program established by the Chief Administrator of the Courts pursuant to Uniform Rules for the Supreme and County Courts (hereinafter "Uniform Rules") §§ 202.5-b and 202.5-bb, the Administrative Judge of the Ninth Judicial District and the Westchester County Clerk as Clerk of the Supreme and County Courts.

In any matters commenced by e-filing assigned to the DCM parts, counsel and unrepresented parties should familiarize themselves with the statewide E-Filing Rules (Uniform Rule §§ 202.5-b and 202.5-bb—available at www.nycourts.gov/efile) and the Westchester County E-Filing Protocol available at http://www.courts.state.ny.us/courts/9jd/efile/ WestchesterCountyJointProtocols.pdf. General questions about e-filing should be addressed to the E-Filing Resource Center at (646) 386-3033 or efile@ courts.state.ny.us. Questions relating to local e-filing procedures may be addressed to the Civil Calendar Office at (914) 824-5300.

PRELIMINARY CONFERENCE PART

Doc. 2. Preliminary Conference Part

I. **Preliminary Conferences in Matters Not Subject to E-Filing**

A. **Requests for Preliminary Conferences**

In accordance with 22 NYCRR § 202.12 (a), a party may request a preliminary conference at any time after service of process. The request shall state the title of the action; index number; names, addresses and telephone numbers of all attorneys appearing in the action; and the nature of the action. If the action has not been assigned to a judge, the party shall file a request for judicial intervention (RJI) together with the request for a preliminary conference. The request shall be served on all other parties.

Preliminary conferences sought by parties pursuant to 22 NYCRR § 202.12 will be scheduled through the Preliminary Conference Part (PCP) upon filing of a

request for a preliminary conference with proof of service. If the case has not yet been assigned to an IAS Justice, the party must also submit an original and one copy of an RJI with proof of service; proof of purchase of the index number for the main action, if applicable, and payment of filing fees for all third-party actions. Similarly, if the case has been assigned to an IAS Justice, the party must submit proof of payment of the filing fees for any third-party action.

Pursuant to 22 NYCRR § 202.12 (b), the preliminary conference will be held within 45 days of the filing of the RJI unless the Court orders otherwise. Any party may move to advance the date of a preliminary conference upon a showing of special circumstances (22 NYCRR § 202.12 (g)).

The PCP will give notice by mail of the preliminary conference. The preliminary conference may be adjourned once by written request of all parties submitted at least two (2) days prior to the preliminary conference. The request for an adjournment may be made to the PCP by mail, facsimile or e-mail to PreliminaryConferenceWestchester@courts.state.ny. us and shall include two (2) proposed alternative dates for rescheduling the preliminary conference, which dates shall be no later than one month following the scheduled preliminary conference. The PCP will thereupon give notice to the parties of the adjourned preliminary conference date by mail, or by e-mail if the parties so request.

The parties are cautioned to arrive on time for the preliminary conference. Defaulting or late arriving counsel, in the absence of an adequate excuse, may be subject to sanctions and/or costs. Counsel who repeatedly fail to appear or arrive late to preliminary conferences may summarily be subject to sanctions and/or costs.

Pursuant to 22 NYCRR § 202.12 (c), the matters to be addressed at the preliminary conference shall include as appropriate, the simplification and limitation of factual and legal issues; the establishment of a timetable for the completion of all disclosure proceedings; the establishment of the method and scope of any electronic discovery; the addition of other necessary parties; settlement of the action; and removal to a lower court pursuant to CPLR § 325.

Court attorney-referee(s) may conduct the preliminary conferences. At the preliminary conference, the PCP will confirm or modify the DCM track selected by the party who filed the RJI and will establish the schedule within the applicable DCM deadline for completion of pretrial proceedings. Parties are reminded of the purpose and consequence of the DCM designations and that even if they designate a case as expedited, the case will be not be expedited, unless the PCP confirms that an expedited DCM track is warranted. At the conclusion of the preliminary conference, a preliminary conference order will be issued.

B. Preliminary Conference Stipulation

Where all parties can agree upon a discovery schedule, they may submit a preliminary conference stipulation to the PCP to be "so ordered". In the event that the preliminary conference stipulation is submitted at least three (3) business days prior to the scheduled conference date and is determined to be acceptable, no appearance at the previously scheduled preliminary conference will be required.

A standard form to be used as the preliminary conference stipulation will be available in the PCP and online on the web site of the Ninth Judicial District. Parties will be permitted to submit same to the PCP by facsimile, mail or e-mail (fully executed, scanned pdf format only) to PreliminaryConference Westchester@courts.state.ny.us.

The preliminary conference stipulation submitted to be "so ordered" must be signed by all parties who have appeared in the action. If all parties are unable to come to an agreement as to the terms of the preliminary conference stipulation, the preliminary conference will be conducted as scheduled.

The preliminary conference stipulation must strictly comply with 22 NYCRR § 202.19 and provide that all disclosure be completed within 8, 12 or 15 months in expedited, standard and complex cases, respectively as set forth in 22 NYCRR § 202.19. The preliminary conference stipulation will be reviewed by the PCP to confirm that the DCM track selected by the party who filed the RJI and the schedule proposed by the parties is within the applicable DCM deadline for completion of pre-trial proceedings. The parties may agree in the preliminary conference stipulation to change the DCM track, subject to approval by the PCP.

By not later than the day prior to the scheduled preliminary conference, if the preliminary conference stipulation is acceptable and so ordered, the PCP will contact the parties to confirm the cancellation of the preliminary conference. If the proposed preliminary conference stipulation is not acceptable, the PCP will advise the parties that a preliminary conference is necessary. In the discretion of the PCP, a telephone conference with the parties may be held to address any issues with the preliminary conference stipulation that can be resolved without the necessity of a physical appearance at a preliminary conference. In the event that matters cannot be resolved without a physical appearance, the in-person preliminary conference shall proceed on the scheduled conference date.

If the preliminary conference stipulation is not submitted, or is not submitted in a timely basis to allow proper review, the preliminary conference shall take place as scheduled. Untimely submissions will be rejected by the PCP, except in exigent circumstances as determined on a discretionary basis by the PCP. It is incumbent upon the parties to ascertain that the PCP has received a timely submission of the preliminary conference stipulation and that no appearance will be required at the preliminary conference. Parties should not assume that a preliminary conference has been cancelled in the absence of verification from the PCP.

Once a preliminary conference stipulation is so-ordered, a copy will be transmitted to counsel by mail or facsimile, or if an e-mail address is designated by the parties for such purposes, by e-mail. The parties are cautioned that preliminary conference orders are to be followed and it is expected that pre-trial proceedings will be completed on time, absent good cause. Lack of diligence will not be regarded as a sufficient excuse.

These PCP rules shall apply in medical, dental and podiatric malpractice actions only to the extent that they are not inconsistent with the provisions of 22 NYCRR § 202.56. A preliminary conference will be scheduled as soon as practicable after the filing of the notice of medical, dental or podiatric action in accordance with 22NYCRR § 202.56(b). The PCP rules shall also apply where a request is filed for a preliminary conference in an action involving a terminally ill party governed by CPLR § 3407 only to the extent that they are not inconsistent with the provisions of CPLR § 3407. In such cases, the request for a preliminary conference may be filed at any time after commencement of the action and shall be accompanied by the physician's affidavit as required by CPLR § 3407 (22 NYCRR § 202.12 (*l*)).

C. Motions

No motions (including cross-motions) relating to discovery may be interposed until a preliminary conference has been held in the PCP. The parties will be expected to attend such conferences and attempt in good faith to resolve all discovery disputes. In the event that motion practice is necessary, a briefing schedule will be established by the court-attorney referee at the preliminary conference and the motion will be referred to the Compliance Part for disposition. Such motions shall be orally argued and the Compliance Part Justice may render a bench decision or a written decision, as appropriate. Motions relating to a failure to provide discovery or adhere to the preliminary conference order shall be heard in the Compliance Part (see Compliance Part Rules below). However, no such discovery motion (including a motion to dismiss predicated upon a discovery violation and including any discovery cross-motion) may be interposed until a pre-motion conference has been requested and held in the Compliance Part (see Compliance Part Rules below).

Failure to comply with the terms of a preliminary conference order, and making frivolous motions may result in the imposition of costs or other sanctions on the offending party (22 NYCRR § 202.12(f)). Motions made after the preliminary conference has been scheduled and before a pre-motion conference has been held, may be denied unless there is shown good cause why such relief is warranted before the conference is held (22 § NYCRR § 202.12(h)).

In the event that a dispositive motion accompanies the RJI rather than a request for a preliminary conference, the case will be referred to the PCP for a preliminary conference and will also be assigned to an IAS Justice. Unless otherwise directed by Order of the Court, the statutory stay in CPLR § 3214 for dispositive motions made pursuant to CPLR §§ 3211, 3212 or 3213 is superceded by this protocol. While counsel may agree to submit a preliminary conference stipulation to be so-ordered that defers discovery during the pendency of a dispositive motion, the parties are cautioned that they will be expected to complete all discovery within the designated DCM track and discovery shall not be stayed or otherwise extended due to the pendency of motions.

II. Preliminary Conference Part E–Filing Rules

A. Requests for Preliminary Conferences in E–Filed Actions

In accordance with 22 NYCRR § 202.12 (a), a party may request a preliminary conference at any time after service of process. The request shall state the title of the action; index number; names, addresses and telephone numbers of all attorneys appearing in the action; and the nature of the action. If the action has not been assigned to a judge, the party shall e-file a request for judicial intervention (RJI) together with the request for a preliminary conference.

Preliminary conferences sought by parties pursuant to 22 NYCRR § 202.12 will be scheduled through the Preliminary Conference Part (PCP) upon e-filing of a request for a preliminary conference and RJI.

Pursuant to 22 NYCRR § 202.12 (b), the preliminary conference will be held within 45 days of the filing of the RJI unless the Court orders otherwise. Any party may move to advance the date of a preliminary conference upon a showing of special circumstances (22 NYCRR § 202.12 (g)).

The PCP will give notice by e-mail of the preliminary conference. The preliminary conference may be adjourned once by written request of all parties submitted at least two (2) days prior to the preliminary conference. The request for an adjournment may be made to the PCP by e-filing or by e-mail to PreliminaryConferenceWestchester@courts.state.ny. us and shall include two (2) proposed alternative dates for rescheduling the preliminary conference, which dates shall be no later than one month following the scheduled preliminary conference. The PCP will thereupon give notice to the parties of the adjourned preliminary conference date by e-mail if the parties so request.

The parties are cautioned to arrive on time for the preliminary conference. Defaulting or late arriving counsel, in the absence of an adequate excuse, may be subject to sanctions and/or costs. Counsel who repeatedly fail to appear or arrive late to preliminary conferences may summarily be subject to sanctions and/or costs.

Pursuant to 22 NYCRR § 202.12 (c), the matters to be addressed at the preliminary conference shall include as appropriate, the simplification and limitation of factual and legal issues; the establishment of a timetable for the completion of all disclosure proceedings; the establishment of the method and scope of any electronic discovery; the addition of other necessary parties; settlement of the action; and removal to a lower court pursuant to CPLR § 325.

Court attorney-referee(s) may conduct the preliminary conferences. At the preliminary conference, the PCP will confirm or modify the DCM track selected by the party who filed the RJI and will establish the schedule within the applicable DCM deadline for completion of pre-trial proceedings. Parties are reminded of the purpose and consequence of the DCM designations and that even if they designate a case as expedited, the case will be not be expedited, unless the PCP confirms that an expedited DCM track is warranted. At the conclusion of the preliminary conference, a preliminary conference order will be issued.

B. Preliminary Conference Stipulation in E–Filed Actions

For actions subject to E-filing assigned to the PCP, in lieu of making an appearance at a scheduled preliminary conference, all parties in a NYSCEF case may agree upon a discovery schedule and submit a preliminary conference form stipulation executed by all parties available at (http://www.nycourts.gov/courts/9jd/diffCaseMgmt/PreConfForm_Rev122409.pdf) by uploading same as a "Proposed Stipulation to be So Ordered—Preliminary Conference" in the NYSCEF system at least two days prior to the conference date.

The preliminary conference stipulation submitted to be "so ordered" must be signed by all parties who have appeared in the action. If all parties are unable to come to an agreement as to the terms of the preliminary conference stipulation, the preliminary conference will be conducted as scheduled.

The preliminary conference stipulation must strictly comply with 22 NYCRR § 202.19 and provide that all disclosure be completed within 8, 12 or 15 months in expedited, standard and complex cases, respectively as set forth in 22 NYCRR § 202.19. The preliminary conference stipulation will be reviewed by the PCP to confirm that the DCM track selected by the party who filed the RJI and the schedule proposed by the parties is within the applicable DCM deadline for completion of pre-trial proceedings. The parties may agree in the preliminary conference stipulation to change the DCM track, subject to approval by the PCP.

If the preliminary conference stipulation is acceptable and so ordered, it will be uploaded to the NYSCEF site and the preliminary conference will be cancelled. If the proposed preliminary conference stipulation is not acceptable, the PCP will advise the parties that a preliminary conference is necessary. In the discretion of the PCP, a telephone conference with the parties may be held to address any issues with the preliminary conference stipulation that can be resolved without the necessity of a physical appearance at a preliminary conference. In the event that matters cannot be resolved without a physical appearance, the in-person preliminary conference shall proceed on the scheduled conference date.

If the preliminary conference stipulation is not submitted, or is not submitted in a timely basis to allow proper review, the preliminary conference shall take place as scheduled. Untimely submissions will be rejected by the PCP, except in exigent circumstances as determined on a discretionary basis by the PCP. It is incumbent upon the parties to ascertain that the PCP has received a timely submission of the preliminary

conference stipulation and that no appearance will be required at the preliminary conference. Parties should not assume that a preliminary conference has been cancelled in the absence of verification from the PCP.

The parties are cautioned that preliminary conference orders are to be followed and it is expected that pre-trial proceedings will be completed on time, absent good cause. Lack of diligence will not be regarded as a sufficient excuse.

These PCP rules shall apply in medical, dental and podiatric malpractice actions only to the extent that they are not inconsistent with the provisions of 22 NYCRR § 202.56. A preliminary conference will be scheduled as soon as practicable after the filing via NYSCEF of the notice of medical, dental or podiatric action in accordance with 22NYCRR § 202.56(b). The PCP rules shall also apply where a request is filed for a preliminary conference in an action involving a terminally ill party governed by CPLR § 3407 only to the extent that they are not inconsistent with the provisions of CPLR § 3407. In such cases, the request for a preliminary conference may be filed at any time after commencement of the action and shall be accompanied by the physician's affidavit as required by CPLR § 3407 (22 NYCRR § 202.12(l)).

C. Discovery Motions in E–Filed Actions

No motions (including cross-motions) relating to discovery may be interposed until a preliminary conference has been held in the PCP. The parties will be expected to attend such conferences and attempt in good faith to resolve all discovery disputes. In the event that motion practice is necessary, a briefing schedule will be established by the court-attorney referee at the preliminary conference and the motion will be referred to the Compliance Part for disposition. Such motions shall be orally argued and the Compliance Part Justice may render a bench decision or a written decision, as appropriate. Motions relating to a failure to provide discovery or adhere to the preliminary conference order shall be heard in the Compliance Part (see Compliance Part Rules below). However, no such discovery motion (including a motion to dismiss predicated upon a discovery violation and including any discovery cross-motion) may be interposed and e-filed until a pre-motion conference has been requested and held in the Compliance Part (see Compliance Part Rules below).

Failure to comply with the terms of a preliminary conference order, and making frivolous motions may result in the imposition of costs or other sanctions on the offending party (22 NYCRR § 202.12(f)). Motions e-filed after the preliminary conference has been scheduled and before a promotion conference has been held, may be denied unless there is shown good cause why such relief is warranted before the conference is held (22 NYCRR § 202.12(h)).

In the event that a dispositive motion is E-filed and accompanies the RJI rather than a request for a preliminary conference, the case will be referred to the PCP for a preliminary conference and will also be assigned to an IAS Justice. Unless otherwise directed by Order of the Court, the statutory stay in CPLR § 3214 for dispositive motions made pursuant to CPLR §§ 3211, 3212 or 3213 is superceded by this protocol. While counsel may agree to submit a prelimi-nary conference stipulation to be so-ordered that de-fers discovery during the pendency of a dispositive motion, the parties are cautioned that they will be expected to complete all discovery within the designat-ed DCM track and discovery shall not be stayed or otherwise extended due to the pendency of motions.

COMPLIANCE PART

Doc. 3.   Compliance Part

I.   Compliance Part Matters Not Subject to E-Filing

A.   Compliance Conferences

To assure that a case stays on its designated DCM track, a compliance conference will be scheduled ap-proximately one hundred twenty (120) days to one hundred fifty (150) days prior to the date fixed as the last day of discovery in the preliminary conference order.

The compliance conference may be adjourned once by written request of the parties submitted at least two (2) days prior to the compliance conference. The request for an adjournment may be made to the Compliance Part (CP) by mail, facsimile or e-mail to ComplianceWestchester@courts.state.ny.us, and shall include two (2) proposed alternative dates for resched-uling the compliance conference, which dates shall be no later than sixty (60) days prior to the last day of discovery set forth in the preliminary conference or-der. The CP will thereupon give notice to the parties of the adjourned compliance conference date by mail, or by e-mail if the parties so request. The parties are cautioned that any adjournment of the compliance conference will not excuse a failure to provide discov-ery or failure to adhere to the preliminary conference order and that discovery shall proceed during the period of any adjournment.

The parties are cautioned to arrive on time for the compliance conference. Defaulting or late arriving counsel, in the absence of an adequate excuse, may be subject to sanctions and/or costs. Counsel who re-peatedly fail to appear or arrive late to compliance conferences may summarily be subject to sanctions and/or costs.

Compliance conferences will be conducted by court attorney-referees who will monitor the progress of discovery to completion and assure that discovery obligations and deadlines are enforced (and, where appropriate, adjusted) on a consistent basis. The court attorney-referees may, if discovery is not complete, and under limited circumstances, extend the time to complete discovery and adjourn the compliance con-ference to a later date, but the parties are cautioned that no further adjournments may be forthcoming. Requests for modifications to discovery schedules shall be addressed to the court attorney-referee(s) at a conference. Inquiries by e-mail to the Compliance Part are restricted to scheduling matters and routine submissions only. The Compliance Part will not enter-tain requests to extend court-ordered discovery dead-lines by email or respond to discovery disputes sub-mitted by e-mail. If assistance is required in regards to a discovery issue, the parties shall request a compli-ance conference in a timely manner.

B.   Discovery Motions

Motions relating to a failure to provide discovery or failure to adhere to the preliminary conference order shall be made returnable and heard in the Compliance Part. However, no discovery or discovery compliance motion (including a motion to dismiss predicated upon a discovery violation) may be interposed until a pre-liminary conference has been held in the PCP and a pre-motion conference has been requested and held in the Compliance Part.

Pre-motion conferences may be requested by letter, transmitted to the CP by mail, facsimile or e-mail to ComplianceWestchester@courts.state.ny.us. The par-ties will be expected to attend such conferences and attempt in good faith to resolve all discovery disputes. Nothing in these rules shall be construed to prevent or limit counsel from making any motion deemed appropriate to best represent a party's interests. However, to foster the just, expeditious and inexpen-sive resolution of discovery disputes, pre-motion con-ferences shall be held in order to permit the Court the opportunity to resolve issues before motion practice ensues. In the event that motion practice is necessary, a briefing schedule will be established by the court attorney-referee(s). Failure to make a motion within the time allowed by the briefing schedule may result in a waiver of the issues that were to be raised by the motion. Failure to oppose a motion within the time allowed by the briefing schedule may result in the motion being decided without consideration of opposi-tion. All motions will be orally argued and the CP Justice may render a bench decision or a written decision, as appropriate.

Substantive motions made in the case through sum-mary judgment will be decided by the assigned IAS Justice. Substantive motions do not require a pre-motion conference and, absent a specific order to the contrary from the IAS Justice, will be submitted without oral argument. Unless otherwise accepted by the Compliance Part and a briefing schedule issued in the Compliance Part, motions to sever, amend, consolidate and with regard to spoliation of evidence are referred to the IAS Parts for disposition.

Motions to be relieved as counsel, for pro hac vice admission, or for reargument of a decision and order rendered in the Compliance Part do not require a pre-motion conference. However, motions to be relieved as counsel shall be made by Order to Show Cause returnable in the Compliance Part and shall be orally argued. The Compliance Part Motion Calendar shall be called generally every Monday at 2 p.m.

C. Note of Issue and Motions for Summary Judgment

At the conclusion of the compliance conference if discovery is complete, the CP Justice shall issue a Trial Readiness Order pursuant to which plaintiff will be ordered to serve and file a Note of Issue and Certificate of Readiness within twenty (20) days. Where all parties agree that discovery is complete and request the issuance of a Trial Readiness Order without the necessity of an appearance at a compliance conference, they may submit a signed Trial Readiness Stipulation to such effect to the CP in the form available online on the web site of the Ninth Judicial District at http://www.nycourts.gov/courts/9jd/diffCase Mgmt/TrialReadyStip_2_10_10.pdf, to be "so ordered".

The CP Justice shall establish the deadline for any post-note summary judgment motions in the Trial Readiness Order which shall provide that any motion for summary judgment by any party must be served within sixty (60) days following the filing of the Note of Issue.

The CP Justice shall set a briefing schedule for the service of papers in opposition or support of summary judgment motions in the Trial Readiness Order, which shall provide that opposition papers must be served within thirty (30) days of service of motion papers and reply papers, if any, must be served within ten (10) days following service of any opposition papers.

Failure of a party to serve and file the initiatory motion papers within the time allowed by the briefing schedule may result in a waiver of the motion for summary judgment. The Court may grant a request by a party for an adjournment of a deadline to serve and file initiatory, opposition or reply papers with respect to any summary judgment motion and accordingly, the return date of the summary judgment motion. Any request for an adjournment must be in writing submitted at least two (2) days prior to any such deadline. The time within which to make a summary judgment motion shall not be extended for more than thirty (30) days from the original deadline. The return date for a motion for summary judgment once made may not be extended more than three (3) times and such return date may not be extended for more than a total of sixty (60) days. Any request for an adjournment may be made in writing to the Com-

pliance Part (CP), to the attention of the Motion Clerk, by mail, facsimile or e-mail to Compliance Westchester@courts.state.ny.us.

Applications seeking to vacate a note of issue or to otherwise challenge readiness for trial shall be made within twenty (20) days of the service of the Note of Issue as required by 22 N.Y.C.R.R. § 202.21(e). Applications made after the twenty (20) day period has expired shall be denied except in the unusual circumstances recognized by 22 NYCRR § 202.21(d). Any such motion shall be made returnable and heard in the Compliance Part. However, no such motion shall be interposed until a pre-motion conference has been requested no less than two (2) days in advance.

Unless otherwise directed by Order of the Court, the statutory stay in CPLR § 3214 for dispositive motions made pursuant to CPLR §§ 3211, 3212 or 3213 is superceded by this protocol. While counsel may agree to defer discovery during the pendency of a dispositive motion, the parties are cautioned that they will be expected to complete all discovery within the designated DCM track and pursuant to the preliminary conference order and any compliance conference orders and that discovery shall not be stayed or otherwise extended due to the pendency of such motions.

II. Compliance Part E–Filing Rules

A. Conferences in E–Filed Actions

To assure that a case stays on its designated DCM track, a compliance conference will be scheduled approximately one hundred twenty (120) days to one hundred fifty (150) days prior to the date fixed as the last day of discovery in the preliminary conference order.

Correspondence regarding scheduling, only as expressly permitted herein, may be filed and transmitted to other parties via the NYSCEF system. A party seeking an adjournment shall do so in accordance with this protocol via the NYSCEF system by choosing the following NYSCEF document type: Correspondence (Request for Adjournment). No duplicate copies of the correspondence shall be provided to the Compliance Part by either fax or mail.

The compliance conference may be adjourned once by request of the parties submitted via the NYSCEF system at least two (2) days prior to the compliance conference. The request for an adjournment may be made to the Compliance Part (CP) through the NYSCEF system and shall include two (2) proposed alternative dates for rescheduling the compliance conference, which dates shall be no later than sixty (60) days prior to the last day of discovery set forth in the preliminary conference order. The CP will thereupon give notice to the parties of the adjourned compliance conference date by the NYSCEF system. The parties are cautioned that any adjournment of the compliance conference will not excuse a failure to provide discovery or failure to adhere to the preliminary conference order and that discovery shall proceed during the period of any adjournment.

The parties are cautioned to arrive on time for the compliance conference. Defaulting or late arriving counsel, in the absence of an adequate excuse, may be subject to sanctions and/or costs. Counsel who repeatedly fail to appear or arrive late to compliance conferences may summarily be subject to sanctions and/or costs.

Compliance conferences will be conducted by court attorney-referees who will monitor the progress of discovery to completion and assure that discovery obligations and deadlines are enforced (and, where appropriate, adjusted) on a consistent basis. The court attorney-referees may, if discovery is not complete, and under limited circumstances, extend the time to complete discovery and adjourn the compliance conference to a later date, but the parties are cautioned that no further adjournments may be forthcoming. Requests for modifications to discovery schedules shall be addressed to the court attorney-referee(s) at a conference. Inquiries submitted via the NYSCEF system to the Compliance Part are restricted to scheduling matters and routine submissions only. The Compliance Part will not entertain requests to extend court-ordered discovery deadlines by E-filed requests or respond to discovery disputes submitted via the NYSCEF system. If assistance is required in regards to a discovery issue, the parties shall request a compliance conference in a timely manner.

B. Discovery Materials in E–Filed Actions

Discovery materials are not required to be filed via NYSCEF. However, in any action subject to E-filing, parties and non-parties producing materials in response to discovery demands may enter into a stipulation authorizing the electronic filing of discovery responses and discovery materials to the degree and upon terms and conditions set forth in the stipulation. In the absence of such a stipulation, no party shall file electronically any such materials except in the form of excerpts, quotations, or selected exhibits from such materials as part of motion papers, pleadings or other filings with the court unless otherwise specified by statute, rule or part rule. The parties must comply with the requirements of GBL § 399–dd(6), regarding the redaction of social security numbers.

C. Discovery Motions in E–Filed Actions

Any party seeking to make a discovery motion shall do so in accordance with this protocol by requesting a pre-motion conference by e-filing a "Request for Pre-Motion Conference (Compliance Part)" via the NYSCEF system. The parties will be expected to attend such conferences and attempt in good faith to resolve all discovery disputes. Nothing in these rules shall be construed to prevent or limit counsel from making any motion deemed appropriate to best represent a party's interests. However, to foster the just, expeditious and inexpensive resolution of discovery disputes, pre-motion conferences shall be held in order to permit the Court the opportunity to resolve issues before motion practice ensues. In the event that motion practice is necessary, a briefing schedule will be established by the court attorney-referee(s). Failure to make a motion within the time allowed by the briefing schedule may result in a waiver of the issues that were to be raised by the motion. Failure to oppose a motion within the time Allowed by the briefing schedule may result in the motion being decided without consideration of opposition. All motions shall be made by Order to Show Cause and will be orally argued. The CP Justice may render a bench decision or a written decision, as appropriate. When e-filing a discovery motion by Order to Show Cause in the NYSCEF system, you may utilize the "Special Instructions" field to reference the Briefing Schedule in accordance with which the motion is being made.

Absent unusual practical difficulties, a proposed Order To Show Cause and supporting documents that have been filed with NYSCEF will be reviewed through the NYSCEF system by the Court. If there are problems with the documents, the submitting attorney will be promptly contacted by e-mail or telephone. If the Compliance Part Justice declines to sign the Order To Show Cause, the Clerk will electronically file the declined order.

In the NYSCEF system, each exhibit to an OTSC should be uploaded as a separate PDF file. After uploading the OTSC, please choose the document type "Exhibit", enter the appropriate number or letter, and be sure to place a check mark to the left of "Attach to main document." Any Order To Show Cause not filed in accordance with the Uniform Rules and the DCM part rules will not be addressed by the Compliance Part, however a conference will be scheduled.

Motions relating to a failure to provide discovery or failure to adhere to the preliminary conference order shall be made returnable and heard in the Compliance Part. However, no discovery or discovery compliance motion (including a motion to dismiss predicated upon a discovery violation) may be interposed until a preliminary conference has been held in the PCP and a pre-motion conference has been requested and held in the Compliance Part.

The Compliance Part does not require working copies unless otherwise directed by the Compliance Part in a particular matter. In the event that the Compliance Part requires a working copy, the working copy shall have the Confirmation Notice generated by the NYSCEF system firmly fastened thereto as a cover page. Should counsel fail to file a document required to be filed with NYSCEF, that document will not be part of the County Clerk's file and will not be reviewed by the Compliance Part.

Decisions and/or orders issued will be scanned by court staff into the NYSCEF system, which will immediately transmit notice of the event via the NYS-CEF system to all parties and a link to the decision and/or order. In the case of orders, this notice does not constitute service of notice of entry by any party.

Substantive motions made in the case through summary judgment will be decided by the assigned IAS Justice. Substantive motions do not require a pre-motion conference and, absent a specific order to the contrary from the IAS Justice, may be served and filed via NYSCEF and submitted without oral argument. Notification will be forwarded through the NYSCEF system upon the assignment of an IAS Justice. Unless otherwise accepted by the Compliance Part and a briefing schedule issued in the Compliance Part, motions to sever, amend, consolidate and with regard to spoliation of evidence are referred to the IAS Parts for disposition.

Motions to be relieved as counsel, for pro hac vice admission, or for reargument of a decision and order rendered in the Compliance Part do not require a pre-motion conference. However, motions to be relieved as counsel shall be made by Order to Show Cause returnable in the Compliance Part and shall be orally argued. The Compliance Part Motion Calendar shall be called generally every Monday at 2 p.m.

D. Note of Issue and Motions for Summary Judgment

At the conclusion of the compliance conference if discovery is complete, the CP Justice shall issue a Trial Readiness Order pursuant to which plaintiff will be ordered to serve via and file via the NYSCEF system a Note of Issue and Certificate of Readiness within twenty (20) days. Where all parties agree that discovery is complete and request the issuance of a Trial Readiness Order without the necessity of an appearance at a compliance conference, they may submit via the NYSCEF system a signed Trial Readiness Stipulation to such effect to the CP in the form available at http://www.nycourts.gov/courts/9jd/diff CaseMgmt/TrialReadyStip_2_10_10.pdf, to be "so ordered".

The CP Justice shall establish the deadline for any post-note summary judgment motions in the Trial Readiness Order which shall provide that any motion for summary judgment by any party must be made within sixty (60) days following the filing of the Note of Issue.

The CP Justice shall set a briefing schedule for the service of papers in opposition or support of summary

judgment motions in the Trial Readiness Order, which shall provide that opposition papers must be served and filed via NYSCEF within thirty (30) days of service and filing via the NYSCEF system of motion papers and reply papers, if any, must be served and filed via NYSCEF within ten (10) days following service of any opposition papers.

Failure of a party to serve and file via NYSCEF the initiatory motion papers within the time allowed by the briefing schedule may result in a waiver of the motion for summary judgment. The Court may grant a request by a party for an adjournment of a deadline to serve and file via NYSCEF initiatory, opposition or reply papers with respect to any summary judgment motion and accordingly, the return date of the summary judgment motion. Any request for an adjournment must be submitted via the NYSCEF system at least two (2) days prior to any such deadline. The time within which to make a summary judgment motion shall not be extended for more than thirty (30) days from the original deadline. The return date for a motion for summary judgment once made may not be extended more than three (3) times and such return date may not be extended for more than a total of sixty (60) days.

Applications seeking to vacate a note of issue or to otherwise challenge readiness for trial shall be made via NYSCEF within twenty (20) days of the service of the Note of Issue as required by 22 NYCRR § 202.21(e). Applications made after the twenty (20) day period has expired shall be denied except in the unusual circumstances recognized by 22 NYCRR § 202.21(d). Any such motion shall be made returnable and heard in the Compliance Part. However, no such motion shall be interposed until a pre-motion conference has been requested no less than two (2) days in advance.

Unless otherwise directed by Order of the Court, the statutory stay in CPLR § 3214 for dispositive motions made pursuant to CPLR §§ 3211, 3212 or 3213 is superceded by this protocol. While counsel may agree to defer discovery during the pendency of a dispositive motion, the parties are cautioned that they will be expected to complete all discovery within the designated DCM track and pursuant to the preliminary conference order and any compliance conference orders and that discovery shall not be stayed or otherwise extended due to the pendency of such motions.

SETTLEMENT CONFERENCE PART

Doc. 4. Settlement Conference Part

I. Settlement Conference Part Matters Not Subject to E-Filing

A. Settlement Conferences

There will be generally two (2) intensive settlement conferences held in the Settlement Conference Part to maximize the resolution of cases. Additional settlement conferences may be held at the request of the parties and in the discretion of the Settlement Conference Part to promote the just and expeditious resolution of a case through settlement.

Once a note of issue is filed, the case will be assigned to the Settlement Conference Part (SCP). Cases will be placed on the Settlement Conference Calendar for an initial settlement conference which will be scheduled, to the extent possible, ninety (90) to one hundred (120) days following the filing of the Note of Issue. Cases will not be placed on the Settlement Conference Calendar unless the time within which to move for summary judgment has expired or any pending summary judgment motion has been determined.

The SCP will give notice by mail of the first settlement conference. The first settlement conference may be adjourned no more than two (2) times by written request of the parties submitted at least two (2) days prior to the scheduled settlement conference date. The request for an adjournment may be made to the SCP by mail, facsimile or e-mail to SettlementConference Westchester@courts.state.ny.us, and shall include two (2) proposed alternative dates for rescheduling the first settlement conference, which dates shall be no later than three (3) weeks following the previously scheduled settlement conference date. The SCP will thereupon give notice to the parties of the adjourned settlement conference date by mail, or by e-mail if the parties so request.

The parties are cautioned to arrive on time for settlement conferences. Defaulting or late arriving counsel, in the absence of an adequate excuse, may be subject to sanctions and/or costs. Counsel who repeatedly fail to appear or arrive late to settlement conferences may summarily be subject to sanctions and/or costs. Attorneys attending the first settlement conference must bring a copy of all documents relevant to the issues of liability and damages, be fully familiar with every aspect of the case, and be expressly authorized to engage in meaningful settlement negotiations. Attorneys must have evaluated the case prior to the settlement conference date and be prepared to negotiate in good faith to effectuate a reasonable settlement. Absent good cause, the plaintiff(s) and defendant(s) must be reachable by phone to consent to any settlement. No answering services will be permitted. The plaintiff(s) and defendant(s) may attend such conferences with counsel.

Should counsel report that all efforts to settle the case have been previously exhausted and request that a trial date be set, they may waive the settlement conference before the Justice and appear to schedule a trial date directly with the Settlement Conference Part Clerk. Should counsel report after the first settlement conference is conducted that a second settlement conference will be futile and request that a trial date be set, a trial date will be set at the conclusion of the first conference.

Except as set forth above, at least two months before trial, the parties will be scheduled to appear at a second settlement conference in the SCP. The second settlement conference shall be calendared at the conclusion of the first settlement conference, except as set forth above.

The second settlement conference may be adjourned no more than two (2) times, by written request of all parties submitted at least two (2) days prior to the scheduled settlement conference. The request for an adjournment may be made to the SCP by e-mail to SettlementConferenceWestchester@ courts.state.ny.us, or by facsimile or mail and shall include two (2) proposed alternative dates for rescheduling the second settlement conference, which dates shall be no later than three (3) weeks following the previously scheduled second settlement conference. The SCP will thereupon give notice to the parties of the adjourned second settlement conference date by mail, or by e-mail if the parties so request. Except as set forth above, the date for trial will be fixed at the second settlement conference.

The second and final settlement conference will be the parties' last clear chance to settle the case prior to trial before the IAS Trial Judge. The parties are cautioned that there will be no further settlement conferences held or adjournments permitted on the trial date. Attorneys must have evaluated the case prior to the final settlement conference date and be prepared to negotiate in good faith to effectuate a reasonable settlement. Each attorney attending the final settlement conference must bring a complete file including the marked pleadings, medical reports and all other documents related to the issues of liability and damages. Moreover, counsel must be authorized to settle and/or make binding concessions. Absent good cause, the plaintiff(s) and defendant(s) must be reachable by phone to consent to any settlement.

B. Trial Date Scheduling

All trial dates will be no earlier than two months after the second conference. Attorneys are reminded of the rules regarding actual engagement of counsel (Section 125.1(g) of the Rules of the Chief Administrator: Attorneys designated as trial counsel must appear for trial on the scheduled trial date. If any of such attorneys is actually engaged on trial elsewhere, he or she must produce substitute trial counsel. If neither trial counsel nor substitute trial counsel is ready to try the case on the scheduled date, sanctions may be imposed). Attorneys are cautioned that the rules regarding actual engagement will be strictly enforced.

C. Summary Jury Trial Program

The Westchester County Supreme Court operates a summary jury trial program. Parties electing to proceed by summary jury trial must file a fully executed summary jury trial stipulation with the SCP thirty (30) days prior to the second settlement conference. Actions appropriate for summary jury trial shall be transferred to the Summary Jury Trial Part and calendared for trial. The untimely submission of a summary jury trial stipulation may result in the action being retained in the Settlement Conference Part and the scheduling of a conventional trial.

D. Settlement

The parties are cautioned that the all too common practice of appearing before the Court and representing that a settlement has been made will no longer be accepted. Counsel or self-represented parties must file a stipulation of discontinuance before the case is marked settled and disposed and submit a copy to the SCP stamped filed by the County Clerk indicating that the required fee was paid to the County Clerk (CPLR§ 2104, CPLR § 3217, CPLR § 8020[c]).

The parties will be permitted to submit a copy of the stamped and filed stipulation of discontinuance to the SCP by facsimile, mail or by e-mail to Settlement ConferenceWestchester@courts.state.ny.us. In the event that a copy of the stamped and filed stipulation is submitted no later than noon of the business day prior to the scheduled conference date, the parties will not be required to appear on the scheduled settlement conference date. If a stipulation of discontinuance is not submitted, or is not submitted in a timely basis, the parties must appear on the scheduled settlement conference date to report to the SCP Justice the status of any such settlement. It is incumbent upon the parties to ascertain that the SCP has received a timely submission of a stipulation and that no appearance will be required. E-mail may be used only to submit fully executed, scanned (pdf format) stipulations. In the event that the parties reach a settlement agreement on the record and require time to effectuate the filing of a stipulation of discontinuance or to address settlement related issues such as liens, the matter may be set down for an appearance in the Settlement Conference Part to ensure that discontinuance is effectuated in accordance with CPLR§ 2104, CPLR § 3217, CPLR § 8020[c]. However, the pendency of settlement negotiations will not delay, adjourn or in any way affect the scheduled trial date.

II. Settlement Conference Part E–Filing Rules

A. Settlement Conferences in E–Filed Actions

There will be generally two (2) intensive settlement conferences held in the Settlement Conference Part to maximize the resolution of cases. Additional settlement conferences may be held at the request of the parties and in the discretion of the Settlement Conference Part to promote the just and expeditious resolution of a case through settlement.

Once a note of issue is filed, the case will be assigned to the Settlement Conference Part (SCP). Cases will be placed on the Settlement Conference Calendar for an initial settlement conference which will be scheduled, to the extent possible, ninety (90) to one hundred twenty (120) days following the filing of the Note of Issue. Cases will not be placed on the Settlement Conference Calendar unless the time with-

in which to move for summary judgment has expired or any pending summary judgment motion has been determined.

The SCP will give notice by email via NYSCEF of the first settlement conference. The first settlement conference may be adjourned no more than two (2) times by written request of the parties submitted at least two (2) days prior to the scheduled settlement conference date. The request for an adjournment shall be made to the SCP via NYSCEF and shall include two (2) proposed alternative dates for rescheduling the first settlement conference, which dates shall be no later than three (3) weeks following the previously scheduled settlement conference date. The SCP will thereupon give notice by email via NYSCEF to the parties of the adjourned settlement conference date.

The parties are cautioned to arrive on time for settlement conferences. Defaulting or late arriving counsel, in the absence of an adequate excuse, may be subject to sanctions and/or costs. Counsel who repeatedly fail to appear or arrive late to settlement conferences may summarily be subject to sanctions and/or costs. Judicial Hearing Officers, IAS Justices or court attorney-referees will conduct the settlement conferences. Attorneys attending the first settlement conference must bring a copy of all documents relevant to the issues of liability and damages, be fully familiar with every aspect of the case, and be expressly authorized to engage in meaningful settlement negotiations. Attorneys must have evaluated the case prior to the settlement conference date and be prepared to negotiate in good faith to effectuate a reasonable settlement. Absent good cause, the plaintiff(s) and defendant(s) must be reachable by phone to consent to any settlement. No answering services will be permitted.

Should counsel report that all efforts to settle the case have been previously exhausted and request that a trial date be set, they may waive the settlement conference before the Justice and appear to schedule a trial date directly with the Settlement Conference Part Clerk. Should counsel report after the first settlement conference is conducted that a second settlement conference will be futile and request that a trial date be set, a trial date will be set at the conclusion of the first conference.

Except as set forth above, at least two months before trial, the parties will be scheduled to appear at a second settlement conference in the SCP. The second settlement conference shall be calendared at the conclusion of the first settlement conference, except as set forth above.

The second settlement conference may be adjourned no more than two (2) times, by request of the parties submitted at least two (2) days prior to the scheduled settlement conference. The request for an adjournment shall be made to the SCP via NYSCEF and shall include two (2) proposed alternative dates for rescheduling the second settlement conference, which dates shall be no later than three (3) weeks following the previously scheduled second settlement conference. The SCP will thereupon give notice by email via NYSCEF to the parties of the adjourned second settlement conference date. Except as set forth above, the date for trial will be fixed at the second settlement conference.

Correspondence regarding scheduling, only as expressly permitted herein, shall be filed and transmitted to other parties via the NYSCEF system. A party seeking an adjournment shall do so in accordance with this protocol via the NYSCEF system by choosing the following NYSCEF document type: Correspondence (Request for Adjournment). No duplicate copies of the correspondence shall be provided to the Settlement Conference Part by either fax or mail.

The second and final settlement conference will be the parties' last clear chance to settle the case prior to trial before the IAS Trial Judge. The parties are cautioned that there will be no further settlement conferences held or adjournments permitted on the trial date. Attorneys must have evaluated the case prior to the final settlement conference date and be prepared to negotiate in good faith to effectuate a reasonable settlement. Each attorney attending the final settlement conference must bring a complete file including the marked pleadings, medical reports and all other documents related to the issues of liability and damages. Moreover, counsel must be authorized to settle and/or make binding concessions. Absent good cause, the plaintiff(s) and defendant(s) must be reachable by phone to consent to any settlement.

B. Trial Date Scheduling in E–Filed Actions

All trial dates will be no earlier than two months after the second conference. Attorneys are reminded of the rules regarding actual engagement of counsel (Section 125.1(g) of the Rules of the Chief Administrator: Attorneys designated as trial counsel must appear for trial on the scheduled trial date. If any of such attorneys is actually engaged on trial elsewhere, he or she must produce substitute trial counsel. If neither trial counsel nor substitute trial counsel is ready to try the case on the scheduled date, sanctions may be

imposed). Attorneys are cautioned that the rules regarding actual engagement will be strictly enforced.

C. Summary Jury Trial Program in E–Filed Actions

The Westchester County Supreme Court operates a summary jury trial program. Parties electing to proceed by summary jury trial must file via NYSCEF a fully executed summary jury trial stipulation with the SCP thirty (30) days prior to the second settlement conference. Actions appropriate for summary jury trial shall be transferred to the Summary Jury Trial Part and calendared for trial. The untimely submission of a summary jury trial stipulation may result in the action being retained in the Settlement Conference Part and the scheduling of a conventional trial.

D. Settlement

The parties are cautioned that the all too common practice of appearing before the Court and representing that a settlement has been made will no longer be accepted. Counsel or self-represented parties must file a stipulation of discontinuance before the case is marked settled and disposed via NYSCEF before the case is marked settled and disposed.

In the event that a stipulation has been filed no later than noon of the business day prior to the scheduled conference date, the parties will not be required to appear on the scheduled settlement conference date. If a stipulation of discontinuance is not filed, or is not filed in a timely basis, the parties must appear on the scheduled settlement conference date to report to the SCP Justice the status of any such settlement. It is incumbent upon the parties to ascertain that the SCP has notice of the filing of a stipulation and that no appearance will be required. In the event that the parties reach a settlement agreement on the record and require time to effectuate the filing of a stipulation of discontinuance or to address settlement related issues such as liens, the matter may be set down for an appearance in the Settlement Conference Part to ensure that discontinuance is effectuated in accordance with CPLR§ 2104, CPLR § 3217, CPLR § 8020[c]. However, the pendency of settlement negotiations will not delay, adjourn or in any way affect the scheduled trial date.

TRIAL READY PART

Doc. 5. Trial Ready Part

I. Trial Ready Part Matters Not Subject to E–Filing

A. Trial Calendar

A call of the Trial Calendar will be held promptly at 9:30 a.m. in the Trial Ready Part (TRP) by the TRP Justice. Trial counsel for all parties must appear and be ready to commence trial (and, in cases in which juries have been demanded, to select a jury). No

requests for adjournments will be granted, absent unusual and exigent circumstances. Sanctions and/or costs may be imposed on counsel who are not present upon the call of the TRP Calendar. Failure to proceed may result in the striking of the case from the trial calendar, vacating the Note of Issue, dismissal of the complaint or the striking of the answer, or other remedies, including, but not limited to, those set forth in CPLR 3404 and 22 NYCRR § 202.21 and § 202.27. Counsel are cautioned that where the Note of Issue is stricken, no case will be restored to the trial calendar without the filing of a new Note of Issue.

B. Rules Regarding Actual Engagement of Counsel

Attorneys are reminded of the rules regarding actual engagement of counsel (Section 125.1(g) of the Rules of the Chief Administrator: Attorneys designated as trial counsel must appear for trial on the scheduled trial date. If any of such attorneys is actually engaged on trial elsewhere, he or she must produce substitute trial counsel. If neither trial counsel nor substitute trial counsel is ready to try the case on the scheduled date, sanctions may be imposed). Attorneys are cautioned that the rules regarding actual engagement will be strictly enforced.

C. Trial

Any cases which are not sent out for trial (or jury selection) will be deemed ready and passed to the following day or otherwise as directed by the TRP Justice. The TRP will endeavor to send all cases to jury selection, beginning with special preference cases, and then by oldest cases as determined by the date of filing of the Note of Issue. In the event that counsel fail to proceed to select a jury, or timely appear before the assigned IAS Trial Judge, the action may be dismissed or a default taken or other sanction imposed, as appropriate under the circumstances. Every effort will be made to assign the trial to the IAS Justice who had the case previously.

D. Settlement

The parties are cautioned that the all too common practice of appearing at the trial calendar and representing that a settlement has been made will no longer be accepted. Counsel or self-represented parties must file a stipulation of discontinuance before the case is marked settled and disposed and submit a copy to the TRP stamped filed by the County Clerk indicating that the required fee was paid to the County Clerk (CPLR§ 2104, CPLR § 3217, CPLR § 8020[c]).

The parties will be permitted to submit a copy of the stamped and filed stipulation of discontinuance to the TRP by facsimile, mail or by e-mail to TrialReady Westchester@courts.state.ny.us. In the event that a copy of the stamped and filed stipulation is submitted no later than noon of the business day prior to the scheduled trial date, the parties will not be required to appear on the scheduled trial date. If a stipulation of discontinuance is not submitted, or is not submitted in a timely basis, the parties must appear on the scheduled trial date to report to the TRP Justice the status of any such settlement. It is incumbent upon the parties to ascertain that the TRP has received a timely submission of a stipulation and that no appearance will be required. E-mail may be used only to submit fully executed, scanned (pdf format) stipulations. In the event that the parties reach a settlement agreement on the record and require time to effectu-

ate the filing of a stipulation of discontinuance or to address settlement related issues such as liens, the matter may be taken off the Trial Calendar and referred back to the Settlement Conference Part to ensure that discontinuance is effectuated in accordance with CPLR§ 2104, CPLR § 3217, CPLR § 8020[c].

II. Trial Ready Part E–Filing Rules

A. Trial Calendar

A call of the Trial Calendar will be held promptly at 9:30 a.m. in the Trial Ready Part (TRP) by the TRP Justice. Trial counsel for all parties must appear and be ready to commence trial (and, in cases in which juries have been demanded, to select a jury). No requests for adjournments will be granted, absent unusual and exigent circumstances. Sanctions and/or costs may be imposed on counsel who are not present upon the call of the TRP Calendar. Failure to proceed may result in the striking of the case from the trial calendar, vacating the Note of Issue, dismissal of the complaint or the striking of the answer, or other remedies, including, but not limited to, those set forth in CPLR 3404 and 22 NYCRR § 202.21 and § 202.27. Counsel are cautioned that where the Note of Issue is stricken, no case will be restored to the trial calendar without the filing of a new Note of Issue.

B. Rules Regarding Actual Engagement of Counsel

Attorneys are reminded of the rules regarding actual engagement of counsel (Section 125.1(g) of the Rules of the Chief Administrator: Attorneys designated as trial counsel must appear for trial on the scheduled trial date. If any of such attorneys is actually engaged on trial elsewhere, he or she must produce substitute trial counsel. If neither trial counsel nor substitute trial counsel is ready to try the case on the scheduled date, sanctions may be imposed). Attorneys are cautioned that the rules regarding actual engagement will be strictly enforced.

C. Trial

Any cases which are not sent out for trial (or jury selection) will be deemed ready and passed to the following day or otherwise as directed by the TRP Justice. The TRP will endeavor to send all cases to jury selection, beginning with special preference cases, and then by oldest cases as determined by the date of filing of the Note of Issue. In the event that counsel fail to proceed to select a jury, or timely appear before the assigned IAS Trial Judge, the action may be dismissed or a default taken or other sanction imposed, as appropriate under the circumstances. Every effort will be made to assign the trial to the IAS Justice who had the case previously.

D. Settlement in E–Filed Actions

The parties are cautioned that the all too common practice of appearing at the trial calendar and representing that a settlement has been made will no longer be accepted. Counsel or self-represented parties must file a stipulation of discontinuance via NYSCEF before the case is marked settled and disposed and submit a working copy to the TRP with the NYSCEF Confirmation Notice firmly fastened to the front cover page of the stipulation of discontinuance. Working copies without the Confirmation Notice will not be accepted.

The parties will be permitted to submit a working copy of the e-filed stipulation of discontinuance to the TRP by facsimile, mail or by e-mail to TrialReady Westchester@courts.state.ny.us. In the event that a working copy of the e-filed stipulation is submitted no later than noon of the business day prior to the scheduled trial date, the parties will not be required to appear on the scheduled trial date. If a stipulation of discontinuance is not filed via NYSCEF and a working copy is not submitted, or is not submitted in a timely basis, the parties must appear on the scheduled trial date to report to the TRP Justice the status of any such settlement. It is incumbent upon the parties to ascertain that the TRP has received a timely submission of the working copy and that no appearance will be required. Email may be used only to submit fully executed, scanned (pdf format) stipulations. In the event that the parties reach a settlement agreement on the record and require time to effectuate the filing of a stipulation of discontinuance or to address settlement related issues such as liens, the matter may be taken off the Trial Calendar and referred back to the Settlement Conference Part to ensure that discontinuance is effectuated in accordance with CPLR§ 2104, CPLR § 3217, CPLR § 8020[c].

E. Motions in the Trial Ready Part in E–Filed Actions

1. *Working Copies.* The Trial Ready Part requires the submission of "working copies" of all electronically filed motions and other documents. See Uniform Rule § 202.5–b(d)(4). Working copies are to be submitted to the Trial Ready Part by mail or delivery to the 12th Floor Lobby Drop Off Basket designated for such purpose.

All working copies submitted to this Part must include a copy of the NYSCEF Confirmation Notice firmly fastened to the front cover page of the submission and comply with all the other requirements set forth in the Westchester County Protocol. Working copies without the Confirmation Notice will not be accepted.

Working copies are to be delivered no later than 10 a.m. on the first business day following the electronic filing of the document on the NYSCEF site.

2. *Hard Copy Submissions.* The Trial Ready Part will reject any hard copy submissions in e-filed cases unless those submissions bear the Notice of Hard Copy Submission—E–Filed Case required by Uniform Rule § 202.5–b(d)(1). The form is available at www.nycourts.gov/efile.

FORMS

Form 1. Preliminary Conference Stipulation

If the parties submit this form 3 business days prior to the scheduled preliminary conference date, completed and executed by all parties, and the Court finds no problems, counsel need not appear. This form may be sent by mail, facsimile to (914)995–2194 or by email to PreliminaryConferenceWestchester@courts.state.ny. us. Pursuant to 22 NYCRR § 202.19, all disclosure must be completed within 8, 12 or 15 months in expedited, standard and complex cases, respectively. If this form is not properly completed and submitted in advance, the conference shall take place as scheduled.

SUPREME COURT OF THE STATE OF NEW YORK
COUNTY OF WESTCHESTER
PRELIMINARY CONFERENCE PART
---X

<table>
<tr><td>Plaintiff(s),</td><td>PRELIMINARY
CONFERENCE
STIPULATION</td></tr>
<tr><td>–against–</td><td>Index No.: _____</td></tr>
<tr><td></td><td>Date RJI Filed:
_____</td></tr>
<tr><td>Defendant(s).</td><td></td></tr>
</table>

---X

It is hereby STIPULATED by and between all parties to the within action that disclosure shall proceed and be completed as follows:

(1) Nature of Case:

a. DCM track: ☐ Standard (12 Mos.)   ☐ Complex (15 mos.)
                                                             ☐ Expedited (8 mos.)

b. Plaintiff(s) Claims:

_____

c. Defendant(s) Claims and Defenses:

_____

(2) Insurance Coverage:

If not yet provided, _____ shall disclose in writing the existence and contents of any insurance agreement as described in CPLR § 3101(f) on or before

_____.

N/A ☐ Previously provided ☐

(3) Bill of Particulars:

a. A Demand for a Bill of Particulars shall be served by _____ on or before

_____.

b. A Bill of Particulars shall be served by _____ on or before _____.

c. A Supplemental Bill of Particulars shall be served by _____ as to items _____ on or before _____.

(4) **Medical Records and authorizations:**

On or before _____, duly executed written authorizations shall be furnished by _____ for the following:

    __ Physician, and/or hospital, and/or autopsy records;

    __ Employment records for the period _____;

    __ No-fault file;

    __ Other (specify) _____

(5) Physical Examinations:

a. Examination of _____ shall be held on or before _____.

b. Pursuant to 22 NYCRR § 202.17(b), at least 20 days before such examination, _____ shall serve upon all other parties copies of the medical reports of those physicians who have previously treated or examined him/her.

c. A copy of the examining physician's report shall be furnished to all parties on _____ by _____ or within __ days of the examination.

(6) Depositions:

a. Examinations before trial shall be conducted as follows (priority shall be in accordance with CPLR§ 3106 unless otherwise agreed or ordered):

Plaintiff(s) shall appear for examination before trial at _____, on _____, at __ a.m./p.m. and shall produce all relevant books, papers, records, and other material for use at the deposition, including _____.

Defendant(s) shall appear for examination before trial at _____, on _____, at __ a.m./p.m. and shall produce all relevant books, papers, records, and other material for use at the deposition, including _____.

b. Attorneys seeking rulings on objections or making application for any other relief pertaining to the depositions shall communicate with the Preliminary Conference Part by telephone conference call for a determination and shall make no motion in the absence of a conference with the Court and a good faith effort to resolve the matter without unnecessary motion practice.

c. Once begun, a deposition shall continue until completed and shall not be adjourned without further order of the Court, unless all parties agree that the adjournment of such deposition does not delay or otherwise impede any party's ability to perform or enforce any of the terms of this Stipulation.

d. The transcript of an examination before trial shall be delivered to the party deposed within forty-five (45) days of the deposition, and shall be returned, duly executed thereafter pursuant to CPLR 3116 (a).

e. Depositions of all parties shall be completed on or before _____.

f. Depositions of all non-party witnesses shall be completed on or before _____.

(7) Other Disclosure:

a. On or before _____, all parties shall exchange names and addresses of all witnesses, and shall exchange statements of opposing parties and photographs, or if none, shall so state in writing.

b. All parties shall exchange information relating to expert witnesses in compliance with CPLR § 3101 and the governing case law.

c. Demands for Discovery and Inspection (CPLR § 3120) shall be served on or before _____.

d. All responses to Discovery and Inspection demands shall be served no later than __ after receipt of the opposing party's demands.

e. Objections to disclosure, inspection or examination shall be made in conformity with the provisions of CPLR § 3122.

f. Supplemental Demands for Discovery and Inspection may be served with respect to items as to which the demanding party could not reasonably have demanded in such party's prior Demand(s) for Discovery and Inspection, provided such Supplemental Demands are served at least twenty (20) days (or if service is by mail twenty-five [25] days) prior to the expiration of the time herein set forth for the completion of disclosure. Responses to such Supplemental Demands shall be served within the time provided by CPLR § 3120, except that objections to Supplemental Demands shall be interposed sufficiently in advance of the time hereinafter set forth for the completion of disclosure so as to permit the demanding party a reasonable time to seek, and obtain a conference with the Court with respect to such objections and to request an extension of the time to complete disclosure.

g. All demands for production of books, documents, records and other writings relevant to the issues in this case shall be deemed to include a demand for production of any photograph, audiotape, videotape, computer disk or program and e-mail.

h. All Interrogatories shall be served on or before _____. Responses shall be served in conformity with CPLR § 3133.

(8) Additional Disclosure issues:

With respect to additional disclosure issues, the parties shall comply with the following agreement: _____.

_____

_____

(9) Impleaders:

All third-party actions shall be commenced on or before _____.

Joinder of a third-party action beyond this date without leave of Court may result in a severance.

(10) Confidentiality/Non–Disclosure Agreement:

a. In the event that there is a need for a Confidentiality/Non–Disclosure Agreement prior to disclosure, the part(y) demanding same shall prepare and circulate the proposed agreement. If the parties cannot agree as to same, they shall promptly notify the Court. The failure to promptly seek a confidentiality agreement may result in a waiver of same (22 NYCRR § 216.1). Any Confidentality/Non–Disclosure Agreement will be "so ordered" or entered as an Order of the Court only upon compliance with 22 N.Y.C.R.R. § 216.1.

b. _____ anticipates the need for a Confidentiality Agreement and will prepare and circulate same on or before _____ as to the following issues: _____.

_____

[To be filled in by Court]
COMPLETION OF DISCLOSURE:
ALL DISCLOSURE SHALL BE COMPLETED ON OR BEFORE _____.
Compliance Conference: Counsel for all parties shall appear at a compliance conference which shall be held in the Compliance Part on _____.

Pursuant to 22 NYCRR § 202.28, the attorney for defendant is directed to file a stipulation or statement of discontinuance with the Court within (a) 30 days of the making of the payment required as a condition of the discontinuance; or (b) 30 days of the discontinuance in the event no payment is required as a condition of the discontinuance.

The failure of any party to perform any of the requirements contained in this Stipulation shall not excuse any other party from performing any other requirement contained herein. Failure to comply with any provision of this Stipulation may result in the imposition of costs, or sanctions, or other action authorized by law, including but not limited to contempt, dismissal and the striking of pleadings.

No adjournments of any time directive above shall be permitted without the permission of the Court. This stipulation supercedes the statutory stay in CPLR § 3214 for dispositive motions made pursuant to CPLR §§ 3211, 3212, or 3213.

The contents and provisions of the foregoing proposed stipulation are agreed to, and the parties request that the Court order same.

Dated: _____

Attorneys for Plaintiff:
(Print Name) _____
(Signature) _____
Mailing Address:

_____

_____

Phone/Facsimile Number:

_____

E-mail Address:

_____

Attorneys for Defendant:
(Print Name) _____
(Signature) _____
Mailing Address:

_____

_____

Phone/Facsimile Number:

_____

E-mail Address:

_____

* * * *

Attorneys for/or *pro se* party:
(Print Name) _____
(Signature) _____
Mailing Address:

_____

_____

Phone/Facsimile Number:

_____

E-mail Address:

_____

Attorneys for/or *pro se* party:
(Print Name) _____
(Signature) _____
Mailing Address:

_____

_____

Phone/Facsimile Number:

_____

E-mail Address:

_____

SO ORDERED:

_____

Hon. Joan B. Lefkowitz, J.S.C.

Form 2. Certification Conference Stipulation

If the parties submit this form 2 business days prior to the scheduled certification conference date, completed and executed by all parties, counsel need not appear. This form may be sent by mail, facsimile to (914) 995–4552 or by email to SettlementConferenceWestchester@ courts.state.ny.us.

SUPREME COURT OF THE STATE OF NEW YORK
COUNTY OF WESTCHESTER
SETTLEMENT CONFERENCE PART
---X

Plaintiff(s),	CERTIFICATION CONFERENCE STIPULATION
–against–	Index No.: _____
	Date RJI Filed: _____
Defendant(s).	Trial Date: _____

---X

It is hereby STIPULATED and agreed by and between all parties to the within action that this action is ready to proceed to trial without delay on the previously scheduled trial date established by the court as set forth above.

Dated: _____

Attorneys for Plaintiff: Attorneys for Defendant:

Mailing Address: Mailing Address:

Phone/Facsimile Number: Phone/Facsimile Number:

E-mail Address: E-mail Address:

Attorneys for Defendant: Attorneys for Defendant:

Mailing Address: Mailing Address:

Phone/Facsimile Number: Phone/Facsimile Number:

E-mail Address: E-mail Address:

Plaintiff (unrepresented):   Defendant (unrepresented):

Mailing Address: Mailing Address:

Phone/Facsimile Number: _____   Phone/Facsimile Number: _____

E-mail Address: _____   E-mail Address: _____

Form 3. Trial Readiness Stipulation

If the parties submit this form 2 business days prior to the scheduled compliance conference date, completed and executed by all parties, counsel need not appear. This form may be sent by mail, facsimile to (914) 995–2194 or by email to ComplianceWestchester@ courts.state.ny.us.

SUPREME COURT OF THE STATE OF NEW YORK
COUNTY OF WESTCHESTER
COMPLIANCE PART
---X

Plaintiff(s),

–against–

Defendant(s).
---X

TRIAL READINESS
STIPULATION

Index No.: _____
Date RJI Filed: _____

It is hereby STIPULATED and agreed by and between all parties to the within action that all disclosure previously ordered herein has been completed or waived, the matter is ready for trial and the parties jointly request that the Court issue a Trial Readiness Order directing plaintiff to serve and file a Note of Issue and Certificate of Readiness.

Dated: _____

Attorneys for Plaintiff:
_____

Mailing Address:
_____
_____

Phone/Facsimile Number:
_____

E-mail Address:
_____

Attorneys for Defendant:
_____

Mailing Address:
_____
_____

Phone/Facsimile Number:
_____

E-mail Address:
_____

Attorneys for Defendant:
_____

Mailing Address:
_____
_____

Phone/Facsimile Number:
_____

E-mail Address:
_____

Attorneys for Defendant:
_____

Mailing Address:
_____
_____

Phone/Facsimile Number:
_____

E-mail Address:
_____

FORECLOSURE PART

Doc. 1. Foreclosure Part

Notices to the Bar:

Please be advised that no motions are to be filed with the Special Residential Foreclosure Request for Judicial Intervention (RJI). That RJI is for the purpose of requesting a foreclosure settlement conference. Any motions filed with that RJI will be either returned or denied as the matters are not ripe. No plaintiffs' motions will be accepted for cases that are currently pending in the Special Foreclosure Part.

Please be advised that any application involving a residential foreclosure must contain a separate statement from the moving party affixed to the front of the application that the action does or does not fit the criteria for inclusion in the residential foreclosure program and that if it was in the special foreclosure program, that the case was released from the part with full authority to proceed with motion practice.

Adjournments

Adjournment Requests-Requests for adjournments must be made in writing and on consent of all sides. The request must be faxed to the Court at (914) 995–4483 and received at least two (2) business days prior to the conference. The request must state that the adjournment is on consent, and must contain the new conference date that the parties have agreed to which can only be a Tuesday, Thursday or Friday at 9:30 AM. Include the index number and the title of the case. Please be advised that the law (NYCRR 202.12–a) requires that the court must schedule the conference within 60 (sixty) days of the filing of the RJI. Please note that you will not receive a response from the court. Check e-courts to confirm if the adjournment has been granted the next business day. Do not call the Court to confirm the adjournment.

Settlements

If a case has been settled, we cannot remove the conference from the calendar until the following has been submitted to the Foreclosure Conference Part: The Notice to Discontinue and Cancel the Notice of Pendency, and a letter stating the reason for the discontinuance ie: short sale, loan reinstated, loan modification, loan satisfied, MHA program. This should be completed within 150 days of settlement.

Conferences

All mortgage foreclosure settlement conferences are held in Courtroom 1802. Conferences are scheduled as the requests for Judicial Intervention are received. Pursuant to the Uniform Rules of the trial Court, the initial conference must be held within sixty (60) days of the filing of the RJI.

ForeclosureConferenceWestchester@courts.state.ny.us is for the purpose of requesting an initial Foreclosure Settlement Conference on a voluntary case only. Please be advised you will not receive an e-mail response from the court for your conference. You will receive a letter in the mail from the Court with the conference date. If this e-mail address is utilized for any other purpose, you will not receive a response from the Court.

Defendant's Counsel submitting a Request for Conference Form must first check with the Westchester County Clerk's Office to determine if an RJI has been filed. If not, you must file an RJI before a conference request can be submitted.

Motions

No motions can be made by the plaintiff while the matter is in the Foreclosure Settlement Part. Any motions made by defendant while a case is pending in the Foreclosure Settlement Part will automatically be removed to an IAS Part. If plaintiff wants to make a motion, an application may be made in the Foreclosure Settlement Part for permission. Discovery is also stayed during the pendency of the case in the Foreclosure Conference Part.

All cases released from the Special Foreclosure Part will be stayed for a period of forty-five (45) days from the date of the release.

Forms

Affirmation Foreclosure

Request for Judicial Intervention Settlement Conference in Residential Foreclosure Actions

This form is only to be used for requesting a conference in a case that is eligible for a conference pursuant to CPLR 3408. No motions are to be filed with this RJI.

Mortgage Foreclosure Conference Information Sheet

This form must be completed by the plaintiff's counsel, prior to the conference, for all first time appearances.

HAMP Checklist

This is a general list of documents required by the lenders for a HAMP modification. Most of these documents are also required for internal loan modifications.

ENVIRONMENTAL CLAIMS PART

Rule 1. Criteria for Selection of Environmental Claims Part

The ECP may hear and determine disputes and controversies where the predominant claims involve the adjudication of potential impacts to the environment, including but not limited to, potential impacts to the land, air, water, traffic and transportation, minerals, natural resources, forest management, flora, fauna, noise, patterns of population concentrations, distribution or growth, existing community neighborhood character and human health.

A. Actions or Proceedings in which the principal claims involve the following may be Retained in the Environmental Claims Part:

(i) determinations made under, among other environmental laws, the State Environmental Quality Review Act, State Environmental Conservation Law, Urban Renewal Law, Eminent Domain and Procedure Law, New York State Historic Preservation Act, Costal Erosion Law, and the relevant governing and implementing rules and licenses based on environmental criteria;

(ii) determinations made by a local Legislative body, Planning Board, and Wetland Board or Commission, including, the approval or denial of zoning, subdivision, wetland, site plan and excavation permits, regulatory interpretations, and other land disturbance and other permits and licenses based on environmental criteria;

(iii) determinations of local Zoning Boards of Appeals;

(iv) regulatory taking and other constitutional claims challenging land use and other environmentally related laws, regulations, ordinances and determinations;

(v) determinations made under the New York City Watershed Rules and Regulations, the New York City Water Supply and Sources, and the New York State Department of Health Regulations pertaining to the protection of the water supply; or

(vi) actions involving the remediation, civil enforcement and/or cost allocation or recovery relating to the discharge, threatened discharge or regulation of those elements, wastes, materials, substances or compounds identified or regulated as hazardous or toxic under local, state or federal law, pursuant to, without limitation, New York State common law, the New York State Navigation Law, Industrial Hazardous Waste Management Act, Inactive Hazardous Waste Disposal Sites, Resource Conservation and Recovery Act, Comprehensive Environmental Response Compensation and Liability Act, Clean Water Act, Lead Based Paint Hazardous Reduction Act, National Emission Standard or Asbestos, New York State Department of Labor Industrial Code Rule 56, Insecticide, Fungicide and Rodenticide Act, and all other laws regulations, legal requirements, and statutes, as may be amended or enacted from time to time, relating to the regulation of hazardous and toxic substances and the protection of the environment;

B. The following Actions and Proceedings may be Excluded from the Environmental Claims Part:

(i) challenges to the granting or denial of area variances involving single-family, two-family or three family residences;

(ii) challenges involving easement disputes by or among single-family, two family or three family residences;

(iii) any of the aforementioned core environmental cases involving disputes or controversies by or among single-family, two-family or three family residences, except as they relate to the discharge, threatened discharge or regulation of those elements, wastes, materials, substances or compounds identified or regulated as hazardous or toxic materials as set forth in the above subparagraph (vi); provided that the ECP justice may accept such cases in the event that he or she determines in his or her discretion that the action involves exceptional or unique issues of environmental law or the resolution of the action could potentially result in significant environmental impacts;

(iv) determination of compensation under Article 5 of the Eminent Domain and Procedure Law;

(v) criminal enforcement and other criminal proceedings;

(vi) matters arising under the Occupational Safety and Health Act; or

(vii) all matters to be tried.

Rule 2. Environmental Claims Part Assignment Procedures

A. Application Procedure for Assignment to the ECP

Counsel in any action or proceeding raising substantial environmental issues, as set forth herein, may seek to have the matter adjudicated in the ECP by submitting a filed copy of an RJI together with a one page letter stating why assignment to the ECP would be appropriate. The letter, which shall be served on all parties or counsel, shall, in addition, set forth the name of the matter, its index number and a statement indicating the nature of the action and the specific basis why adjudication in the ECP would be appropriate. The Chief Clerk shall refer the letter application and RJI to the Administrative Judge for review.

Within 5 days of service of the RJI and letter application, opposing counsel or any unrepresented party may join in the application or oppose it by submitting to the Administrative Judge a one page letter, including the criteria set forth above, on notice to all adverse counsel and unrepresented parties. The determination of whether a matter is to be assigned to the ECP or to an IAS Justice is an administrative matter. The determination of the Administrative Judge or his designee with respect to the granting or denial of admission to the ECP is final and subject to no further review or appeal. Nothing, however, shall prevent the Administrative Judge or his designee from later transferring an appropriate case from the ECP to an IAS part.

B.   Consent to Change Venue

If a matter arising out of a dispute involving property or proposed development in Westchester County is not accepted into the ECP it shall remain with the IAS justice previously assigned or be given a random assignment. Where an action arises out of a dispute involving property or proposed development in Rockland, Orange, Dutchess or Putnam Counties and is denied admission to the ECP, the letter of counsel seeking admission to the ECP shall be deemed to be counsel's motion to change venue and consent to transfer the matter to the county where the proposed development or disputed property is actually located.

C.   Case Tracking

Assignment to the ECP shall by-pass the DCM Preliminary Conference Part and proceed on an expedited track.

Rule 3.   General Rules

A.   Appearances by Counsel with Knowledge and Authority

Counsel who appear in the ECP must be familiar with the case in regard to which they appear and fully authorized to enter into agreements, both substantive and procedural, on behalf of their clients. Attorneys appearing of counsel to the attorney of record, and parties appearing pro se, shall be held to the same requirement. Failure to comply with this rule may be regarded as a default and dealt with appropriately. It is important that counsel be on time for all scheduled appearances.

B.   Settlements and Discontinuances

If an action is settled, discontinued or otherwise disposed of, counsel shall immediately inform the Court by submission of a copy of the stipulation or a letter directed to the Clerk of the ECP. Filing a stipulation of discontinuance with the County Clerk shall not be sufficient.

C.   Papers by FAX

Copies of letters confirming an adjournment may be sent by fax to (914) 995–4552, Attn: Albert J. Degatano, Court Attorney Referee. No other submissions by fax will be accepted or considered unless indicated otherwise by the Court in advance in a particular case.

The original of all correspondence must be mailed to the Clerk of the ECP.

Rule 4.   Motion/Petition Practice

The Court will entertain motions/petitions on submission on each day when Court is in session. There shall be no motion/petition calendar called by the Court. There shall be no oral arguments heard on motions/petitions and no appearances shall be required unless the Court otherwise directs. Questions or problems concerning the ECP calendar should be addressed to the Clerk of the ECP.

A.   Filing of Papers

Except with the express permission of the Court, all motion/petition papers submitted to the ECP, including pleadings, opposition and reply papers, and Orders to Show Cause, must be typewritten, double-spaced, on single, front-faced letter size pages, securely bound and entirely legible, and all exhibits must be legible and labeled with tab markings. The ECP may refuse to accept or consider any such papers which do not conform to the foregoing. Motion/petition papers and all correspondence must indicate the index number assigned to the action and that the action has been assigned to the ECP. Counsel shall simultaneously submit with their motion/ petition a disc version saved in WordPerfect 8.0 or translatable into same of the affidavits, affirmations and memoranda submitted with the application. Courtesy copies should not be submitted.

B.   Requests for Temporary Restraining Orders

Applications for temporary injunctive relief, including applications for temporary restraining orders, are subject to section 202.7(f) of the Uniform Rules for Trial Courts. Therefore, any application for such relief must include "an affirmation demonstrating there will be significant prejudice to the party seeking the restraining order by the giving of notice. In the absence of a showing of significant prejudice, the affirmation must demonstrate that a good faith effort has been made to notify the party against whom the temporary restraining order is sought of the time, date and place that the application will be made in a manner sufficient to permit the party an opportunity to appear in response to the application." 22 NYCRR 202.7(f). Where the party against whom the temporary restraining order is sought is a public officer, board or municipal corporation the affirmation must also demonstrate that the applicant does not seek to restrain such party in the performance of its statutory duties in violation of section 6313(c) of the Civil Practice Laws and Rules.

C.   Motion/Petition Return Date

The moving party may select a motion/petition return date which shall be set forth in the notice of motion/petition. Motions/petitions may be made returnable at 9:30 a.m. on any day of the week on which the Court is in session. In those instances in which a motion is brought by order to show cause, the return date shall be determined by the Court.

D. Motion/Petition Adjournments

Upon the consent of all attorneys, the Court will routinely grant an adjournment of a motion/petition. The attorney seeking the adjournment must obtain the consent of opposing counsel and notify the Clerk of the ECP of the requested adjourned date at least 48 hours before the return date. The Court will then assign an adjourned date for the motion/petition. In assigning that date, the Court shall give consideration to any date agreed upon by all counsel.

All non-consensual requests to adjourn the return date require Court approval, which shall be directed to the Clerk of the ECP at least 48 hours before the return date. Prior to seeking permission from the Court, the requesting counsel must first attempt to obtain consent from all other counsel in the action.

E. Length of Papers

Unless otherwise permitted by the Court for good cause, briefs shall not exceed 70 pages and reply briefs shall not exceed 30 pages. Affidavits and affirmations shall not exceed 25 pages each. Papers submitted to the Court in violation of this rule may not be considered by the Court without notice to the submitting party in advance of the decision on the motion/petition.

F. Filing of Papers for Adjourned Motions/Petitions

If the Court, upon its own motion, adjourns the return date, no additional papers will be allowed to be submitted beyond the service dates for the original motion/petition return date, except by leave of the Court.

G. Papers Required on Particular Motions

(i) On any motion seeking summary judgment, dismissal of a complaint/petition, cross-claim or counter-claim, or the striking of a pleading, copies of all pleadings filed as of the date of the motion must be provided to the Court by the moving party. The failure to comply with this requirement shall result in the denial of the motion unless the pleadings are provided to the Court by another party.

(ii) On any motion seeking leave to renew or reargue a prior motion, copies of all papers submitted on the prior motion must be provided to the Court by the moving party. The failure to comply with this requirement shall result in the denial of the motion unless the papers on the prior motion are provided to the Court by another party.

(iii) When an order to show cause is presented to the Court which seeks a temporary restraining order

or a preliminary injunction, copies of the summons and complaint or petition commencing the underlying action must be provided to the Court by the moving party. No order to show cause seeking such relief will be considered by the Court if the moving party fails to comply with this requirement.

H. Reply Papers

Counsel shall not set forth factual claims or legal arguments in reply papers which were not set forth in the papers initiating the motion/petition.

I. Sur–Reply and Post–Submission Papers

Counsel are reminded that the CPLR does not provide for sur-reply papers, however denominated. Nor is the presentation of papers or letters to the Court after submission of a motion/petition permitted. Absent express permission in advance, such materials will be filed with the County Clerk unread. Opposing counsel who receives a copy of materials submitted in violation of this rule should not respond in kind.

J. Decisions and Orders

In most instances, a written Decision and Order will be issued following the submission of the motion/petition. This Decision and Order, with supporting papers, will be filed in the Westchester County Clerk's Office by the Court. A copy of the Decision and Order shall be sent to counsel who have submitted a self addressed envelope with first class postage affixed, after filing.

Rule 5. Ex Parte

The ECP sits "ex parte" at all times for matters assigned to it. All ex parte matters are filed with the Civil Calendar Office. The Clerk of the Supreme Court will review an ex parte application on an expedited basis to determine whether it is a ECP matter. All ex parte applications will be forwarded to the ECP, unless the ECP Judge is not available. Under these circumstances, the regular IAS Duty Judge will act in his or her place. Following review and action, if any, by the regular IAS Duty Judge, the case will be returned to the ECP.

Rule 6. Conferences

It is envisioned that preliminary, discovery and pretrial conferences will not be required for the matters selected for the ECP. However, the purpose of this Court is to help litigants resolve their disputes in a fair and equitable manner. Should the attorneys have need of the Court's services at any time, a conference with all parties present in person or by telephone can be arranged through the Clerk of the ECP. Attorneys are reminded, however, that ex parte communications to the Court are prohibited by the CPLR and the Code of Professional Conduct.

MATRIMONIAL PART

OPERATIONAL RULES

Doc. 1. Matrimonial Part Operational Rules

By Order of the Hon. Alan D. Scheinkman, Administrative Judge of the Ninth Judicial District, the operations of the Matrimonial Part of the Supreme Court, Westchester County, are revised as set forth herein, effective February 1, 2010:

These operational rules will promote active and effective matrimonial case management consistent with the requirements and guidelines set forth in the Uniform Civil Rules for the Supreme Court. The revisions focus the use of judicial resources by concentrating the use of judges to trials and resolution of substantive motions, while, at the same time, assuring intensive case supervision throughout the civil litigation process. These operational rules also establish procedures for expeditious resolution of pre-trial matrimonial disputes, which will reduce the number of motions and court appearances, conserve judicial resources, and reduce expense, delay, and emotional trauma for the parties and their children. These operational rules have been developed in consultation with the Justices presiding in the Matrimonial Part and after receiving input from the Matrimonial Bar.

A. Application. These rules shall apply to all matrimonial actions and proceedings in the Supreme Court, Westchester County, including any applications to enforce or modify matrimonial judgments.

B. Post–Judgment Part. The existing Post Judgment Part is eliminated. Each of the assigned Matrimonial Justices will preside over his or her own post-judgment matters. Post-judgment matters arising in cases which were heard by Justices other than those presently presiding in the Matrimonial Part are to be randomly assigned to the Matrimonial Part Judges. The provisions of Paragraphs 1, 2, 3, 4, and 5 of Section E, *infra*, shall not apply to the initiation of a post-judgment application in the Matrimonial Part.

C. Assignment of Court Attorney–Referees. A court attorney-referee shall be assigned to a case on a random basis and shall be designated at the same time that a Matrimonial Justice is assigned to the case, which is also done on a random basis. Once a court attorney referee is assigned to a case, she or he shall continue with that assignment.

D. Court Conferences.

1. The assigned court attorney referee shall conduct a Preliminary Conference, which shall be scheduled and conducted in accordance with 22 N.Y. C.R.R. § 202.16(subd. f). A preliminary conference may be adjourned not more than two (2) times, subject to the approval of the court attorney referee and in no event may the preliminary conference be adjourned more than thirty (30) days beyond the date originally established.

2. In each case, the attorneys for the parties (including a party not represented by counsel) shall meet in person at least two (2) days prior to the conference and review and complete a proposed preliminary conference order and submit same to the Matrimonial Part by facsimile transmitted to: (212) 457–2879 or by e-mail transmitted in WordPerfect format to: MatrimonialWestchester@nycourts.gov. The form of preliminary conference order that shall be utilized is annexed hereto.

3. The assigned court attorney-referee shall meet personally with counsel for the parties (including a party not represented by counsel) and with the parties at the Preliminary Conference and at any other conferences held by the assigned court attorney/referee. Unless agreed to by the parties personally in the presence of the assigned court attorney-referee, the parties shall be personally present throughout all conferences.

4. If all issues relating to decision-making and/or parenting time with a child have not been completely resolved by the conclusion of the Preliminary Conference, the court attorney-referee shall forthwith refer the parties to the Family Counseling and Case Analyst who shall conduct a prompt conference. The Family Counseling and Case Analyst shall confer with the parties for the purposes of developing a parenting plan. In the event that a parenting plan is agreed upon, the Family Counseling and Case Analyst shall forward the plan to the assigned court attorney-referee for inclusion as an order of the Court. In the event that no parenting plan is agreed upon, or only a partial agreement is reached, the Family Counseling and Case Analyst shall so advise the court attorney-referee.

5. Upon consent of the parties, the court attorney-referee may refer the parties to mediation or other form of alternative dispute resolution and may adjourn the preliminary conference for not more than two (2) times, for a total not to exceed sixty (60) days, pending the outcome of the mediation or alternative dispute resolution process. After a Preliminary Conference held, examinations before trial may be adjourned, upon consent, by the court-attorney referee once for a period not to exceed thirty (30) days. A protocol for mediation is separately established.

6. During the Preliminary Conference, the court attorney-referee shall ascertain whether the granting of a divorce is contested. In the event the parties agree that the granting of a divorce will not be contested, a stipulation to that effect shall be entered

into by not later than thirty (30) days following the conclusion of the Preliminary Conference. In the event that a complaint or answer has not been served, the stipulation shall provide that the parties waive and relinquish any right either may otherwise have to discontinue the action as of right. In the event that, a party opposes the granting of a divorce, then the court attorney-referee shall adjourn the Preliminary Conference and: (1) if a complaint or answer has not yet been served, the court attorney-referee shall provide a schedule for the service of all required pleadings; and (2) provide for the filing of a note of issue limited to the issue of divorce grounds, which filing date shall be no later than twenty (20) days after the service of the answer or, in the event an answer has been served, within twenty (20) days of the Preliminary Conference; and (3) notify the Supervising Clerk of the Matrimonial Part of the necessity for a trial on the issue of grounds for divorce so that such trial may be promptly scheduled. In the event that a finding is made upon trial that divorce grounds exist, then the court attorney-referee shall fix a date for the resumption of the Preliminary Conference.

7. During the Preliminary Conference, the court attorney-referee shall determine whether the case is complex, moderately complex or non-complex and fix a schedule for the completion of disclosure accordingly. The schedule shall require that all disclosure be completed and a note of issue filed within four (4) months of the Preliminary Conference in non-complex cases; that all disclosure be completed and a note of issue filed within seven (7) months of the Preliminary Conference in moderately complex cases; and that all disclosure shall be completed and a note of issue filed within eleven (11) months of the Preliminary Conference in complex cases.

(a). For purposes of this provision, a case shall be considered non-complex where the following factors predominate:

— Custody and/or parenting time is not in dispute.

— There are no allegations of domestic violence or egregious conduct.

— The parties are W–2 wage earners and have filed tax returns for the preceding three (3) years.

— Neither party owns any commercial real property or business interest, degree or license that requires valuation.

(b). For purposes of this provision, a case shall be considered moderately complex where the following factors predominate:

— Custody and/or parenting time is in dispute but forensic evaluation is not sought by either party.

— There are allegations of domestic violence or egregious conduct.

— The parties are W–2 wage earners but do not have recently filed tax returns.

— One or both parties is self-employed with less than two (2) employees.

— One or both parties owns commercial real property or a business interest, degree or license that requires valuation.

(c). For purposes of this provision, a case shall be considered complex where the following factors predominate:

— Custody and/or parenting time is in dispute and both parties seek forensic involvement.

— There are allegations of domestic violence or egregious conduct.

— One or both parties hold a license or degree or business that must be valued.

— One or both parties are self-employed in a business that has more than two (2) employees.

— Both parties seek to conduct non-party depositions.

— There are allegations that one or both parties receives substantial cash or unreported income.

— There are allegations as to the secreting of assets.

— One or both parties claims that substantial property is separate property.

— There is a dispute as to the validity and/or interpretation of a prenuptial or other marital agreement.

8. During the Preliminary Conference, the court attorney-referee shall provide appropriate direction to resolve any existing or anticipated disclosure disputes.

9. If a party or their counsel request the appointment of an attorney for the child, or request the appointment of a forensic evaluator for issues relating to a child, the party or parties making such request shall submit to the court attorney-referee, at the time the proposed preliminary conference order is submitted, a statement, no more than four (4) pages in length, setting forth the reasons why the appointment is requested and identifying the particular issues for which the appointee shall provide assistance and, in the case of a forensic evaluator for child issues, identifying the specific matters as to which evaluation is sought. In addition, the requesting party shall include: an estimate of the expense that the appointment will entail through the completion of the case, the amount to be authorized as a retainer or initial payment, and the proposed apportionment of responsibility between the parties, including the reasons therefor. The court attorney-referee shall discuss the requests at the Preliminary Conference and shall provide copies of the requests to the Family Counseling

and Case Analyst. Such statement shall be served upon all adverse parties at least two (2) days prior to the Preliminary Conference and any party opposing the application, in whole or in part, shall submit a statement, no more than four (4) pages in length, setting forth which part(s) of the application is opposed and the basis for such opposition. The Matrimonial Part Justice shall determine the application within ten (10) days of the Preliminary Conference by written order. In lieu of this procedure, a party or counsel may move, by Order to Show Cause, for such an appointment, at any time following the Preliminary Conference, provided that a pre-motion conference is held pursuant to the provisions of these Rules.

10. No attorney shall be appointed for a child nor a child forensic evaluation ordered, except upon order of the assigned Matrimonial Part Justice which shall be made either: (a) upon a motion made by Order to Show Cause pursuant to these Rules; or (b) upon evaluation of the requests made therefor by a party or parties, the parties' net worth statements and most recent tax returns, any recommendation by the assigned court attorney-referee, and any recommendation by the Family Counseling and Case Analyst.

11. Counsel (including a party not represented by counsel) may stipulate at a Preliminary or other Conference to designate a particular person or firm to conduct a property evaluation and to the allocation of the expense thereof between the parties. In the event that counsel (including any party not represented by counsel) agree upon the evaluation is necessary and as to the allocation of expenses, but cannot agree upon a person or firm to conduct the evaluation, they may submit proposed names to the court attorney-referee who shall forward them to the assigned Matrimonial Part Justice to order the designation. In the event that the parties cannot agree upon the necessity for the evaluation or upon the allocation of responsibility therefor, an application shall be made, on notice to all parties, to the assigned Matrimonial Part Justice who shall determine the application. Such application shall be made, not later than ten (10) days after the Preliminary Conference, by a statement, no more than four (4) pages in length, setting forth the reasons why the appointment is requested and identifying the specific matters as to which evaluation is sought. In addition, the requesting party shall include: an estimate of the expense that the appointment will entail through the completion of the case, the amount to be authorized as a retainer or initial payment, and the proposed apportionment of responsibility between the parties, including the reasons therefor. Such statement shall be served upon all adverse parties and any party opposing the application, in whole or in part, shall submit a statement, no more than four (4) pages in length, setting forth which part(s) of the application is opposed and the basis for such opposition, which statement shall be submitted not later than ten (10) days after the service of the application. In lieu of

this procedure, a party or counsel may move, by Order to Show Cause, for such an appointment, at any time following the Preliminary Conference, provided that a pre-motion conference is held pursuant to the provisions of these Rules.

12. At the conclusion of the Preliminary Conference, the court attorney-referee shall designate a date for a Compliance Conference, which shall be held at least ten (10) days prior to the date by which disclosure is to be completed, for the purpose of confirming that all disclosure is complete or will be completed timely. The date for the Compliance Conference shall be set in the Preliminary Conference Order and, if the date is thereafter adjourned, the adjourned date shall be set forth in an Order. The Compliance Conference may be adjourned, with the approval of the assigned court attorney/referee, no more than two (2) times and for no more than a total of thirty (30) days. Any disclosure which was not completed in conformity with the Preliminary Conference Order, such discovery may be deemed waived or appropriate sanctions imposed against a party who failed to timely provide discovery.

13. The court attorney-referee shall conduct a Certification Conference within five (5) business days of the date set for completion of discovery. In lieu of a physical appearance, counsel (including a party not represented by counsel) may transmit by e-mail (in pdf format) to: MatrimonialWestchester@nycourts. gov or by facsimile transmitted to: (212) 457–2879, a stipulation certifying that all disclosure has been completed and that the action is ready for trial. At the Certification Conference, the court attorney-referee shall confirm that all disclosure has been completed or, if not, that such disclosure has been waived and shall recommend to the assigned Matrimonial Part Justice that the action is ready for trial. No further disclosure may be ordered, except upon order of the assigned Matrimonial Part Justice, which order shall be only obtained by motion made pursuant to Order to Show Cause, in accordance with provisions of Paragraph 17 below. The date for the Certification Conference shall be set in the Preliminary Conference Order and any adjournment shall be to a date set in the Order adjourning the Compliance Conference.

14. Either party or any attorney for the child may, before the date set for the Compliance Conference, request a conference with the assigned court attorney referee, including a conference for the purpose of addressing any issues relating to disclosure. In the event that disclosure cannot be completed within the time allowed by the Preliminary Conference Order in a non-complex or moderately complex case due to unanticipated complexity, the court attorney-referee may, for good cause shown, change the track to which the case is assigned and reschedule the date for completion of disclosure, which date shall not be later than eleven (11) months from the date of the Preliminary Conference. In a complex case, if disclosure

cannot be completed despite due diligence within the time allowed by the Preliminary Conference Order, the court attorney referee may, extend the date for completion of disclosure, provided that the date for completion of disclosure shall not be extended beyond fourteen (14) months from the date of the Preliminary Conference.

15. At the conclusion of every conference, including a Preliminary Conference, the court attorney-referee shall have counsel for the parties (including any party not represented by counsel) execute a stipulation as to any issues resolved at the conference. The court attorney-referee shall issue a report to the assigned Matrimonial Part Justice as to each unresolved issue, summarizing the positions and arguments advanced by the parties and counsel, and shall also submit a recommended order as to each unresolved issue. The court attorney-referee may make recommendations to the assigned Matrimonial Part Justice as to any matters, procedural or substantive, relating to the case. Copies of the report shall be provided to counsel for the parties (including any party not represented by counsel. The assigned Matrimonial Part Justice may consider the report(s) and recommendation(s) of the court attorney-referee in making any determinations in the case, including any determination as to the awarding of counsel fees or the allocation of responsibility for any expenses, including the expenses of an attorney for the child and forensic evaluation.

16. Conferences with the court attorney-referee may be requested by written request, not to exceed two (2) pages in length, outlining the issues to be considered and the amount of time needed for the conference and setting forth the availability of counsel and the parties. Counsel for the parties (including any party not represented by counsel) shall consult with each other in person prior to requesting any conference. A request for a conference shall be transmitted to the Matrimonial Part only by facsimile to (212) 457–2879 or by e-mail (with the request contained in a letter appended in pdf format) to MatrimonialWestchester@nycourts.gov. Copies shall be served upon all adverse parties contemporaneously by e-mail and either (1) facsimile or (2) hand delivery. Any response to a conference request shall likewise not exceed two (2) pages in length and shall be transmitted to the Matrimonial Part by facsimile or by e-mail (with the response contained in a letter appended in pdf format) by 5 p.m. of the next business day following of the transmission of the request, with copies sent contemporaneously to all adverse parties by email and either (1) facsimile or (2). There shall be no reply by counsel to any such response nor any sur-reply to any unauthorized reply. All unauthorized submissions shall be rejected, not considered, and shall not be included in the court files. The court attorney-referee shall notify counsel of the action taken in response to the conference request within two

(2) business days following the transmission of the request.

17. In the event that any party objects to or disagrees with the recommended order of the court attorney-referee, such party must indicate the basis for the objection or disagreement at the Preliminary Conference or other conference and may thereafter apply, by order to show cause, to the assigned Matrimonial Part Justice to vacate or modify the recommended order. The order to show cause must be submitted for signature to the assigned Matrimonial Part Justice within ten (10) days of the issuance of the recommended order. In the event that no motion is made within such period, the Matrimonial Part Justice may issue the recommended order.

E. Motions.

1. Except in the event of an emergency which requires immediate relief from a Matrimonial Part Justice, no motions are to be made without the movant first requesting a pre-motion conference and without the holding of a pre-motion conference, unless the motion seeks to vacate or modify a recommended order.

2. A pre-motion conference is to be requested by letter application to the assigned court attorney-referee. The request shall not exceed two (2) pages in length and shall briefly enumerate the subjects to be discussed at the pre-motion conference. The request shall also contain a signed representation by the person requesting a conference that he or she personally had a conversation with opposing counsel (or party, where appropriate) and made a good faith effort to resolve the issues, which representation shall include the date and time of such conversation. A person receiving a request for a pre-motion conference may respond by submitting a written request that additional subjects be discussed, providing that such request also contain a representation by the requesting person that he or she personally had a conversation with opposing counsel (or party, where appropriate) and made a good faith effort to resolve the issues, which representation shall include the date and time of such conversation. Failure by counsel (or party, where appropriate) to make himself or herself available for a direct conversation with the person seeking a conference, or failure to make a good faith effort to resolve the issues before, during or after the pre-motion conference may be considered in connection with counsel fees and expenses related to the conference.

3. A request for a pre-motion conference shall be transmitted to the Matrimonial Part only by facsimile to (212) 457–2879 or by e-mail (with the request contained in a letter appended in pdf format) to MatrimonialWestchester@nycourts.gov, with copy sent contemporaneously to all adverse parties by facsimile and by (1) by e-mail or (2) hand delivery to all counsel. Any response to a conference request shall likewise not exceed two (2) pages in length and shall

be transmitted, by facsimile or by e-mail (with the response contained in a letter appended in pdf format) by 5 p.m. of the next business day following of the transmission of the request, with copies sent contemporaneously to all adverse parties by e-mail or by (1) facsimile or (2) hand delivery. There shall be no reply by counsel to any such response nor any sur-reply to any unauthorized reply. All unauthorized submissions shall be rejected, not considered, and shall not be included in the court files. The court attorney-referee shall notify counsel of the action taken in response to the conference request within two (2) business days following the transmission of the request.

4. The assigned court attorney-referee shall conduct the pre-motion conference, either in person, in the courthouse or by telephone conference. The procedures set forth in Section D, Paragraphs 14 and 15, shall apply to the completion of pre-motion conferences.

5. In the event that a party perceives that there an emergency which requires immediate judicial intervention, such person may submit an Order to Show Cause directly to the assigned Matrimonial Part Judge. Except with respect to applications for orders of protection, in the event that a temporary restraining order or similar relief is requested, unless the person making the motion set forth in an affidavit that significant prejudice would be suffered by him or her by giving notice to the other parties, notice shall be given to all adverse parties of the time and place when the application will be submitted. Notice shall be given sufficiently in advance to permit the adverse parties an opportunity to appear and respond to the application. A full copy of the application shall be provided to all adverse parties contemporaneously with its presentation to the assigned Justice. In the event that the assigned Justice determines that the matter is not emergent, the Justice may decline to sign the Order to Show Cause and refer the parties for a pre-motion conference. In the event that the assigned Justice issues the Order to Show Cause (either with or without any interim relief), a conference shall be held by the assigned court attorney referee at least two (2) business days prior to the return date of the Order to Show Cause.

6. Unless expressly authorized by the assigned Matrimonial Part Justice: (a) no affidavit or affirmation shall exceed 15 pages in length; (b) affirmations or affidavits of counsel shall address only those facts which are within their personal knowledge and shall not contain any citations to statutes or legal authorities; (c) any matters of law shall be addressed only in a separate memorandum of law, which may not exceed 15 pages in length; (d) the only exhibits that shall be attached to motion papers shall be those which are specifically referred into an accompanying affidavit or affirmation and only that portion of the document which is specifically referenced shall be attached as an exhibit; (e) there shall be no reply papers; and (f)

there shall be no oral argument on motions. Any unauthorized papers or submissions shall not be considered and other appropriate sanctions may be granted, including but not limited to an award of counsel fees and expenses to the party required to respond to papers submitted in violation of this provision.

7. All orders to show cause are to be presented to the assigned Matrimonial Part Justice within one hour of their presentation in the Calendar Office. In the event that the assigned justice is unavailable, then the order to show cause is to be reviewed by the assigned justice's staff and, following such review, presented to the Duty Judge. If the assigned justice's staff is not available to review the order to show cause, the Supervising Clerk of the Matrimonial Part is to be notified and will arrange to have the order to show cause reviewed by the assigned court attorney referee or, if the assigned court attorney-referee is unavailable by another court attorney-referee in the Matrimonial Part.

8. In the event that the assigned Matrimonial Justice is not available to review an order to show cause containing a request for interim relief within two (2) hours of its presentation, the order to show cause is to be brought to the Duty Judge. In the event that the Duty Judge is not available, the District Administrative Judge is to be notified forthwith by the Supervising Clerk of the Matrimonial Part.

9. Where an action or proceeding is pending in the Matrimonial Part, all applications for relief shall be brought there in accordance with the procedures set forth above. In the event that an application for relief is brought in the Family Court, in a circumstance in which a prior action has been pending (and process served) in the Matrimonial Part, the parties shall promptly notify the assigned court attorney-referee shall be promptly notified, who shall hold a conference within two (2) business days of notification to review whether the Family Court proceeding should be removed to the Matrimonial Part. Nothing contained herein shall be construed as limiting or restricting the right of any party to seek relief in Family Court. The purpose of this provision is to coordinate whether, if a proceeding is brought in Family Court, the proceeding should continue there or be removed to Supreme Court, in the interests of judicial economy and in the interest of the parties and any children of the parties.

10. All motions shall be decided within sixty (60) days of the submission of the papers in opposition or, if no such papers are submitted, within sixty (60) days of the return date.

F. Trials.

1. Upon filing of the Note of Issue (except in actions in which only the grounds for divorce is to be tried), a copy thereof is to be provided to the Part Clerk for the assigned Matrimonial Part Judge, who shall schedule the case for trial. Notice of the trial date must be given in writing at least two (2) months

prior to the first trial date. The provisions of 22 N.Y.C.R.R. § 125.1(subd. g) shall apply.

2. All matrimonial trials and hearings shall proceed day to day until conclusion.

3. The assigned Matrimonial Part Justice may, in her or his discretion, determine that issues relating to child decision-making and/or parenting time are to be bifurcated from the economic issues, with the issues relating to child decision-making and/or parenting time tried first.

4. All trials and hearings shall be conducted by the assigned Matrimonial Part Justice, except that the District Administrative Judge may, in the interests of the administration of justice, transfer or re-assign any action or proceeding scheduled for trial to another Justice for purposes of trial or hearing.

G. Rules of Conduct.

1. All attorneys and parties must be present at the time scheduled for a conference or trial. In the event that an attorney or party fails to timely appear, such lateness or failure to appear may be considered in the award of counsel fees and expenses.

2. Unless expressly authorized by the court attorney-referee or Matrimonial Part Justice to whom it is directed, or unless specifically authorized by these rules, no letter or other written communication is to be transmitted to the Matrimonial Part by any means of transmission. Attorneys shall not copy the Part on any correspondence between them. There shall be no replies to any unauthorized submissions and all unauthorized papers shall not be considered, shall be rejected, and shall not be filed in the court records.

3. Failure by counsel (or party, where appropriate) to make himself or herself available for a direct conversation with counsel (including a party not represented by counsel) or failure to make a good faith effort to resolve the issues before, during or after any conference may be considered in connection with counsel fees and expenses.

4. Violations of the provisions of these Rules may result in the imposition of appropriate sanctions, including the award of counsel fees and expenses to the non-violating parties or by the denial of counsel fees and expenses to the violating party.

5. In any order appointing any expert, the assigned Matrimonial Part Justice shall designate the name of the expert and identify the subjects to be addressed in the report and/or evaluation to be ren-

dered by the expert. The Matrimonial Part Justice shall also set a date for the completion of the report. In the event that the expert does not complete the assignment within the time set by the assigned Matrimonial Part Justice, the assigned Matrimonial Part Justice may disqualify the expert, may order a refund or return of any monies paid to the expert, may take the expert's failure to complete the assignment timely in deciding whether to appoint such expert to another matter. In no event may an expert who has not completed his or her assignment within the time set by the assigned Matrimonial Justice be granted another assignment until the expert has completed all past-due assignments. The Supervising Clerk of the Matrimonial Part shall be provided with copies of all assignment orders and shall apprise the Matrimonial Part Justices of the names of experts who have not timely completed their assignments.

H. Compensation for Attorneys for the Children and Court-appointed Experts.

1. In the order appointing an attorney for the child or appointing an expert, the Matrimonial Part Justice shall designate the name of the person or firm appointed, shall provide for an initial payment to the appointee, and shall provide for the allocation of financial responsibility as between the parties.

2. Attorneys for the children and all court-appointed experts shall submit itemized statements of their services to each parent or party at least every sixty (60) days. However, no demand shall be made upon any parent or party for any payment not authorized in an order of the assigned Matrimonial Part Justice. In the event that an attorney for a child or a court-appointed expert seeks additional interim payment(s) above the amount of the initial payment, such attorney or expert shall make application to the assigned Matrimonial Part Justice, on notice to each parent and all parties. Such application shall include an affirmation or affidavit of services, identify what, if any, additional services are required and difficulties in providing them, and provide an estimate of the amount of time and funds necessary to complete the appointment through the date of completion of disclosure. The assigned Matrimonial Part Justice shall make a determination as to the amount of any further payments and shall allocate responsibility therefore between the parents or parties. The failure to comply with this provision may result in the denial of fees and/or an order directing disgorgement of fees and such other sanction as may be appropriate.

FORMS

Form 1. Preliminary Conference Stipulation/Order
With Respect to Grounds for Divorce

SUPREME COURT OF THE STATE OF NEW YORK
COUNTY OF WESTCHESTER
--X

                                                          Index No.:

                                    Plaintiff,

–against–

                                    Defendant.
--X

PRELIMINARY CONFERENCE STIPULATION/ORDER
WITH RESPECT TO GROUNDS FOR DIVORCE

PRESIDING: _____
                        Hon
                        Justice of the Supreme Court

   The parties and counsel have appeared for a preliminary conference on this matrimonial action on _____, held pursuant to 22 NYCRR § 202.16.

A. If the issue of grounds is resolved:

   1) The parties agree that _____ proceed on an uncontested basis to obtain a divorce on the grounds of _____ and that _____ agrees not to interpose any defense or opposition to the application by _____ for a divorce.

   2) The parties hereby waive their rights, if any, under CPLR Rule 3217(a) to discontinue this matrimonial action as of right and agree that this action may be discontinued only upon court order.

   3) If the Verified Complaint/Verified Answer with Counter Claim has been served:

      a. Service of the Verified Complaint/Verified Answer with Counter Claim was admitted on _____ or is hereby admitted.

      b. _____ hereby waives a statutory time period during which he/she could serve a Verified Answer/Verified Reply; and

      c. _____ neither admits nor denies the allegations in the Verified Complaint/Verified Answer with Counterclaim; and

      d. _____ waives any applicable waiting period.

      e. The parties hereby agree *(check one)*:

      ___ that an inquest be scheduled with respect to the evidence supporting the granting the divorce, with the stipulation that, absent a court order determining the existence of extraordinary circumstances, no judgment of divorce will be granted or entered until all issues in this matrimonial action have been resolved and/or determined; or

      ___ to submit papers to obtain an uncontested default divorce at trial or, after the filing of a fully executed Stipulation of Settlement resolving all issues in this matrimonial action, to submit papers for an uncontested default divorce or for a conversion divorce.

4) If the Verified Complaint/Verified Answer with Counter Claim has not been served or must be amended to conform to the agreed upon grounds:

    a. _____ agrees to serve the Verified Complaint/Verified Answer with Counter Claim/Amended Pleading on or before _____; and

    b. On or before _____, the parties agree to submit to the Court a Stipulation signed by the parties and their counsel completing the provisions set forth in items A 1 through A 3 above.

    c. If the parties do not submit a Stipulation to the Court completing the provisions set forth in items A1 through A3 above on or before _____, they shall appear with their counsel for a Court Conference at _____ on _____.

B.   If the issue of grounds is unresolved:

1) A trial of this issue shall be held on _____, and a jury *is/is not* requested.

2) If the pleadings have not been served:

    a. Plaintiff will serve a Verified Complaint upon defendant's attorney on or before _____.

    b. Defendant will serve a Verified Answer upon plaintiff's attorney on or before _____.

    c. Plaintiff will serve, if appropriate, a Verified Reply upon defendant's attorney on or before _____.

_____   _____
Plaintiff   Defendant

_____   _____
Attorney(s) for Plaintiff   Attorney(s) for Defendant

Dated: _____

I recommend that the Court approve the foregoing stipulation:

Dated: _____   _____
                                         Court Attorney–Referee

The foregoing stipulation is approved and entered as an Order of the Court:

SO ORDERED:

Dated: _____   _____
                                         Hon.
                                         Justice of the Supreme Court

Form 2. Preliminary Conference Stipulation/Order
Contested Matrimonial

SUPREME COURT OF THE STATE OF NEW YORK
COUNTY OF WESTCHESTER

--X

                     Plaintiff,

   –against–

                     Defendant.

Index No.:

Assigned Justice:
Hon.

--X

PRELIMINARY CONFERENCE STIPULATION/ORDER
CONTESTED MATRIMONIAL

The parties and counsel appeared on _____, 2010 for a Preliminary Conference, conducted by _____, Court Attorney–Referee, pursuant to 22 NYCRR§ 202.16 and the Westchester Supreme Court Matrimonial Part Operational Rules:

The parties have filed with the Court or will file by the date indicated the following documents:

	Date Filed Plaintiff	or	To Be Filed Defendant
(1) A sworn statement of net worth as of date of commencement of the action.	_____		_____
(2) A signed copy of the retainer agreement with his/her attorney:	_____		_____

A.   BACKGROUND INFORMATION

(1)   Attorneys for Plaintiff: Attorneys for Defendant

     _____   _____

     _____   _____

     _____   _____

Phone:_____   Phone:_____

Fax: _____   Fax: _____

Email:_____   Email:_____

(2)   Summons: Date filed: _____   Date Served: _____

(3)   *Date of marriage*: _____

(4)   *Name(s) and date(s) of birth child(ren)*:

     _____   _____

_____   _____

_____   _____

(5) There is ___ or is not ___ an Order of Protection issued against _____ by _____ Court. The order is dated _____ and is/is not currently outstanding. Attach a copy of order.

(6) The following other orders are outstanding:

Order:

Court issuing:

Issue addressed:

Attach a copy of order.

(7) _____ is requesting a translator in the _____ language.

(8) *Premarital, Marital or Separation Agreements*:

  (a) State the nature of each agreement and the date of the agreement

_____

_____

_____

  (b) State whether the validity of any such agreement is disputed and, if so, by whom, and briefly state the basis for such dispute:

_____

_____

_____

  (c) If the validity of any such agreement is disputed, state whether such dispute is presently asserted in any existing pleading and, if not interposed in any existing pleading, state date by which a pleading asserting the invalidity of any such agreement will be interposed:

_____

_____

_____

B. GROUNDS FOR DIVORCE.

The issue of fault is resolved ___ or unresolved ___.

A separate Preliminary Conference Stipulation/Order With Respect to Grounds for Divorce is entered into contemporaneously herewith. (*The separate Preliminary Conference Stipulation/Order with Respect to Grounds for Divorce must be completed, whether the issue of grounds for divorce is resolved or unresolved*).

C. ISSUES WITH RESPECT TO CHILDREN:

(1) The issue of custody/decision-making is:

  resolved _____ unresolved _____.

(2) The issue of parenting time is:

  resolved _____ unresolved _____.

(3) The issues relating to decision making are resolved ___ unresolved ___.

If the issues of custody, including parenting time and decision-making, are resolved: The parties are to submit a stipulated parenting plan no later than _____.

If any issue related to custody, including parenting time and decision-making is unresolved, the parties shall be referred to the Family Counseling and Case Analyst.

The parties have ___ or have not ___ requested the appointment of an attorney for the child(ren) and/or a forensic evaluator for child issues in accordance with the provisions of the Westchester County Supreme Court Matrimonial Operational Rules.

(To be completed by the court attorney-referee where applicable:)

The undersigned court attorney-referee, having reviewed the application of _____ of _____ for the appointment of an attorney for the child(ren) and having conducted the Preliminary Conference and discussed the application with the parties and counsel, recommends that the application be determined as follows:

_____

_____

_____

_____

_____

(To be completed by the court attorney-referee where applicable:)

The undersigned court attorney-referee, having reviewed the application of _____ of _____ for the appointment of a forensic evaluator for child issues and having conducted the Preliminary Conference and discussed the application with the parties and counsel, recommends that the application be determined as follows:

_____

_____

_____

_____

D. FINANCIAL CLAIMS

    (1) Maintenance is: resolved _____ unresolved _____

    (2) Child support is: resolved _____ unresolved _____

    (3) Equitable distribution is: resolved _____ unresolved _____

    (4) Counsel fee is: resolved _____ unresolved _____

The parties agree that the following items are the separate property of Plaintiff:

_____

_____

_____

The parties agree that the following items are the separate property of Defendant:

_____

_____

_____

In addition to any items agreed as being the separate property of Plaintiff, Plaintiff claims that the following items of property are his/her separate property:

_____

_____

_____

In addition to any items agreed as being the separate property of Defendant, Defendant claims that the following items of property are his/her separate property:

_____

_____

_____

List all other causes of action and ancillary relief issues that are unresolved:

_____

_____

_____

_____

Any issues not specifically listed in this Stipulation as unresolved may not be raised in this action unless good cause is shown.

E. FINANCIAL EVALUATIONS

A. The parties stipulate that the following persons or firms shall conduct the property evaluations indicated with the parties to bear the costs thereof in accordance with the allocation set forth below. The parties further stipulate that they will fully cooperate with such stipulated evaluator(s) and provide all documents and information necessary to complete the evaluation(s). The evaluation(s) shall be completed by: _____.

Name of Evaluator	Property to be Evaluated	Allocation of Financial Responsibility

B. The parties agree that the following evaluation is necessary and agree as to the allocation of financial responsibility as set forth below but cannot agree upon a person or firm to conduct the evaluation:

Property to be Evaluated	Allocation of Financial Responsibility

As to the foregoing evaluations, the parties may submit proposed names to the court attorney-referee, by not later than _____, who shall forward them to the assigned Matrimonial Part Justice to order the designation.

C. The parties cannot agree upon the necessity for the evaluation(s) set forth below or upon the allocation of the responsibility therefor:

Property Sought to Be Evaluated	Positions of Parties as to Financial Allocation

_____

_____

_____

(*To be completed by the court attorney-referee where applicable*:) The under-signed court attorney-referee, having reviewed the parties' positions as to the referenced evaluation(s) and allocation of financial responsibility, recommends that the application as follows:

_____

_____

_____

_____

_____

_____

F. PENDENTE LITE RELIEF:

The parties stipulate as follows as to *pendente lite* support, exclusive occupancy, counsel fees and other interim issues:

_____

_____

_____

_____

(*To be completed by the court attorney-referee where applicable*:) As to the following pendente lite issues which have not been resolved by the parties, the court attorney-referee, having conducted the Preliminary Conference reports as follows as to each such issue and recommends that the Court enter the following orders:

_____

_____

_____

_____

_____

_____

G. DISCOVERY:

1. (*To be completed by the court attorney-referee*:) The undersigned court attorney-referee, having reviewed the issues and conducted a Preliminary Conference, hereby designates this action as:

___ non-complex

___ moderately complex

___ complex

Accordingly, the court-attorney directs that all disclosure be completed and a note of issue filed by _____.(*Where case is noncomplex, this date shall be within four (4) months of the Preliminary Conference; where the case is moderately complex, this date shall be within seven (7) months of the Preliminary Conference; where the case is complex, this date shall be within eleven (11) months of the Preliminary Conference*).

2. *(To be completed by the court attorney-referee:)* **The undersigned court attorney-referee hereby directs that a Compliance Conference be conducted on** _____ (this date shall be at least ten (10) days prior to the date by which disclosure is to be completed), for the purpose of confirming that all disclosure is complete or will be completed timely.

3. *Preservation of Evidence:*

(a) Financial Records: Each party shall maintain all financial records in his or her possession through the date of the entry of judgment of divorce.

(b) Electronic Evidence: For the relevant periods relating to the issues in this litigation, each party shall maintain and preserve all electronic files, other data generated by and/or stored on the party's computer system(s) and storage media (i.e. hard disks, floppy disks, backup tapes), or other electronic data. Such items include but are not limited to email and other electronic communications, word processing documents, spreadsheets, data bases, calendars, telephone logs, contact manager information, internet usage files, offline storage or information stored on removable media, information contained on laptops or other portable devices and network access information.

4. *Document Production:*

(a) The parties shall exchange the following records for the following periods by _____:

Check if needed	Time Period	
_____	_____	Federal, state and local tax returns, including all schedules, K-1's, 1099's, W-2's and similar data.
_____	_____	Credit card statements for all credit cards used by a party.
_____	_____	Joint checking account statements, checks and registers.
_____	_____	Individual checking account statements, checks and register.
_____	_____	Brokerage account statements.
_____	_____	Savings account records.
_____	_____	Other: (specify)

Absent the specification of a time period above, records are to be produced for the three years prior to the commencement of this action through the present. If a party does not have complete records for the time period, the party shall execute and deliver a written authorization to obtain such records from the source within five (5) days of presentation. Any costs associated with the use of the authorization shall, unless otherwise ordered, allocated by the Court once the amount of the expense is determined.

In the event that a party or parties fails to comply with the foregoing provision for document production, the party or parties aggrieved shall forthwith contact the court attorney-referee. Failure to produce documents may result in sanctions, including preclusion and the award/denial of legal fees, and failure to timely insist upon production may result in waiver of production.

(b) Plaintiff shall serve his/her notice for discovery and inspection by not later than ____. Defendant shall respond to said notice by not later than ____.

(c) Defendant shall serve his/her notice for discovery and inspection by not later than ____. Plaintiff shall respond to said notice by not later than ____.

5. Each party may serve a Demand for Interrogatories by not later than ___ Each party shall respond to any Demand for Interrogatories by not later than ___.

6. Examinations before trial shall be conducted as follows:

(A) Plaintiff shall appear for examination before trial on or before ___ and the examination shall be completed by ___.

(B) Defendant shall appear for examination before trial on or before ___ and the examination shall be completed by ___.

Absent express written permission of the court attorney-referee and/or the assigned Matrimonial Part Justice examinations before trial may not be conducted after the expiration of the period allowed therefor.

7. All parties shall timely comply with all discovery demands pursuant to the provisions of the CPLR. Failure to comply may result in sanctions, including preclusion and/or the award/denial of legal fees.

8. The parties stipulate as follows with respect to disclosure disputes presently existing:

_____
_____
_____
_____
_____
_____

9. (*To be completed by the court attorney-referee where applicable:*) As to the following disclosure issues which have not been resolved by the parties, the court attorney-referee, having conducted the Preliminary Conference reports as follows as to each such issue and recommends that the Court enter the following orders:

_____
_____
_____
_____
_____
_____

H. ADDITIONAL STIPULATIONS:

The parties further stipulate and agree as follows:

_____
_____
_____
_____
_____
_____

I. ADDITIONAL ISSUES

(*To be Completed by the Court Attorney–Referee*):

The following issues are unresolved. As to each unresolved issue, the positions and arguments advanced by the parties and counsel are as set forth below, as are my recommendations as to the disposition of each unresolved issue.

_____
_____
_____
_____
_____
_____
_____
_____
_____
_____
_____
_____
_____

J. CONCLUSION

The parties hereby confirm that they have agreed to the stipulations and agreements set forth above.

Dated:

_____   _____
Plaintiff   Defendant

_____   _____
Attorney(s) for Plaintiff   Attorney(s) for Defendant

I recommend that the Court approve the foregoing stipulation and further recommend the adoption of the items identified above as recommendations:

Dated: _____   _____
           White Plains, New York   Court Attorney–Referee

The stipulation of the parties is approved and entered as an Order of the Court. The recommendations of the court attorney-referee are adopted and made an Order of the Court, except that:

_____
_____
_____
_____
_____

SO ORDERED: ENTER:

Dated: _____
           White Plains, New York

                                          _____
                                          Hon.
                                          Justice of the Supreme Court

Form 3.   Trial Ready Order

SUPREME COURT OF THE STATE OF NEW YORK
COUNTY OF WESTCHESTER

---X

<table>
<tr><td>Plaintiff,</td><td>**TRIAL READY ORDER**</td></tr>
<tr><td>–against–</td><td>Index No.</td></tr>
<tr><td>Defendant.</td><td></td></tr>
</table>

---X

This matter is hereby certified ready for trial. No further discovery shall be permitted except upon a showing of compelling and unanticipated circumstances. Any application for post-note discovery must be pursued in accordance with Section E of the Matrimonial Part Rules.

Plaintiff shall serve and file a Note of Issue and Certificate of Readiness within twenty (20) days of the date of this order. A file-stamped copy must be submitted to the Supervising Part Clerk of the Matrimonial Part, within two (2) business days of filing. Sanctions, including the striking of pleadings or dismissal of the action, may be imposed for failure to timely serve and file the Note of Issue and Certificate of Readiness and/or failure to timely submit a file-stamped copy of the Supervising Part Clerk.

The trial of this action is hereby scheduled to commence on _____, 20 ___ at __ a.m. The trial shall continue on successive days until completion. As the trial date is more than two months hence, no adjournment requests will be considered (*See*, 22 NYCRR § 125.1[g]). Expert reports must furnished in accordance with 22 NYCRR 202.16(g). Failure to exchange and file the reports not later than 60 days prior to the trial date (and replies not later than 30 days before the trial date) may, in the Court's discretion, preclude the use of the expert.

A Pre–Trial Conference is hereby scheduled to be held before the undersigned on _____, 20 ___ at __ __ m. Counsel must meet in person at least two (2) business days prior to the scheduled Pre–Trial Conference. Counsel must be fully prepared to discuss settlement at the conference. Sanctions may be imposed upon counsel who are not prepared for the conference, such as the preclusion of witnesses or exhibits, and/or the making of an award of counsel fees and expenses or the denial of an award of counsel fees and expenses. In the event counsel believes that there are no prospects to settle the case, they should be prepared to explain their reasoning. At the Pre–Trial Conference, counsel must submit to the Court:

1) marked pleadings;

2) a full executed stipulation of relevant facts that are not in dispute. The Court expects that, no matter how contentious the case, there will be at least some facts that are not in dispute (*e.g.*, the date of marriage, the names and birth dates of children, the location of any residential real estate and the approximate date of acquisition, approximate cost and the approximate balance on any mortgage);

3) an exhibit list and exhibits as set forth herein. The attorneys are to pre-mark their exhibits. Only those items which are received in evidence will be marked by the reporter. Copies of all exhibits intended to be offered must be presented to the Court in a ringed notebook with a table of contents, with the plaintiff's exhibits numbered and the defendant's exhibits lettered in the order in which they are generally intended to be used. Counsel are to exchange their proposed exhibits at least seven (7) business days prior to the Pre–Trial Conference. Failure to timely submit an exhibit list and proposed exhibits may result in preclusion. Counsel must either stipulate to the admission of the exhibits to be offered by the adverse parties or state the ground of any objection to admission of any such exhibit. Counsel must

be prepared to argue to the Court at the time of the Pre–Trial Conference the admissibility of any exhibits to which objection is taken. Counsel are advised that the failure to include an exhibit in the exhibit list and exhibit exchange provided for herein may result in preclusion of that exhibit;

4) a list of witnesses, including the address of each witness, the time anticipated for the witness' direct examination, and the general subject matter of his or her testimony. The failure to identify a witness may result in the preclusion of the witness' testimony.

5) a **joint** statement of proposed disposition. To the extent that the parties disagree on any item, the plaintiff's position should be set out first, followed by the defendant's position. The Court will NOT accept separate statements of proposed disposition;

6) a child support worksheet if applicable; and

7) updated statements of net worth.

I recommend that the foregoing order be issued.

Dated: _____
      White Plains, New York

                                                _____
                                                Court Attorney–Referee

The foregoing is entered as an Order of the Court.

Dated: _____
      White Plains, New York

                                                ENTER:

                                                _____
                                                Hon.
                                                Justice of the Supreme Court

MATRIMONIAL MEDIATION PROGRAM

Rule I.   Overview

The Westchester County Supreme Court's Matrimonial Mediation Program offers parties access to qualified Mediators who meet the criteria set out in Section VII. The Court will in the near future offer parties access to qualified Neutral Evaluators, but for now the program offers mediation.

Mediation is a confidential ADR process that may result in faster, more convenient, less expensive, and less acrimonious settlement than might be the case in the normal course of litigation. In Mediation, a neutral third party—the Mediator—helps disputing parties to identify issues, clarify perceptions, and explore options for a mutually acceptable outcome. Mediators have significant training and experience in family mediation and in opening paths of communication that emphasize common ground and encourage cooperation. Mediators help parties to resolve key issues that affect their relationships with their children and the financial well-being of all family members.

Although parties are not obligated to settle in mediation, parties often emerge with a written agreement. If the parties cannot reach agreement, they return to court. Parties are strongly encouraged, but are not required, to attend the Mediation session with their own attorneys. Referral to the Program is not appropriate where only one party is represented by counsel, or in cases of domestic violence, child abuse, or severe power imbalance.

Rule II.   Definitions[1]

(a) "Neutral" shall refer to mediators.

(b) "Mediation" shall refer to a confidential dispute resolution process in which a neutral third party (the mediator) helps parties identify issues, clarify perceptions and explore options for a mutually acceptable outcome.

[1] The definitions for this Program are established in Part 146 of the Rules of the Chief Administrative Judge. See http://nycourts.gov/rules/chiefadmin/146.shtml.

Rule III.   Procedures

The assigned Matrimonial Part Justice or the assigned court attorney-referee may refer parties to the Program or parties on their own may request referral to the Program. Cases involving child abuse or neglect (as defined in Family Court Act § 1012(e) and (f) and Social Services Law § 412), domestic violence, or a severe power imbalance between the parties are not appropriate for referral to the Program. Cases will be screened to avoid inappropriate referrals.

To begin the process, the Court issues an Order of Reference. The Order of Reference specifies the topics (e.g., child custody, visitation and/or financial issues) to be submitted to the Program for resolution.

The Order shall direct parties to attend an initial, free, 90–minute session with a Mediator from the Program's Roster of Neutrals. Counsel for the parties are encouraged but not required to attend. If parties wish to continue mediation beyond the initial ninety (90) minute session, they may continue that session or schedule additional sessions. Mediators shall be entitled to compensation from the parties at a rate that shall not exceed $300 per hour, following the initial session. Payment shall be made in advance of scheduled sessions. See Section VIII.

The Order of Reference shall contain the control date set by the referring justice or court-attorney referee for the parties to appear in Court for a conference following the initial Mediation session. All pre-trial proceedings scheduled in the Preliminary Conference order shall continue, and shall not be stayed, pending additional mediation sessions, except that, if all parties request, the referring justice or court-attorney referee may extend the dates for the taking of examinations before trial, provided that, in no event, may such dates be extended beyond twenty (20) days from the date set in the Preliminary Conference Order for the completion of discovery. In no event shall the date for completion of discovery set in the Preliminary Conference Order or the date for the Compliance Conference be extended or adjourned by reason of the pendency of mediation.

The Court shall deliver the Order of Reference to the Program Coordinator ("Coordinator"), Katherine Mueller in the Westchester County Courthouse. The Coordinator shall select the next available Mediator from the Court's Roster of Neutrals, proceeding in alphabetical order.[2] The parties are free to select a different mediator, but if they do so, they must notify the Coordinator of the substitution within 5 business days. Next, the Coordinator shall send to the parties and to the selected Mediator a Notice of Confirmation. The parties are required to appear at the initial session within ten (10) days of receiving a Notice of Confirmation. At least three (3) business days prior to the initial session, the parties' counsel shall send the Mediator a copy of the pleadings, the Statements of Net Worth, and any other information necessary for the effective negotiation and resolution of the issues involved. The Mediator may request a conference call with both counsel regarding any preliminary matters.

The Mediator may give to the parties any agreements or memorandum of understating generated at the sessions.

Within five (5) business days after the conclusion of the Mediation sessions—which shall occur whenever after the initial session one party, both parties, or the Mediator decides that the process has ended—the Mediator shall send a Report ("Report of the Neutral") to the Coordinator and to counsel for the parties stating:

(1) the date of the initial session and whether each party and counsel appeared at the initial session;

(2) the dates of any subsequent scheduled sessions, but not whether parties appeared; and

(3) whether the parties reached partial, complete, or no agreement on the issues.

The Mediator shall not disclose other information discussed during the Mediation, except as described in Section X.

The Coordinator shall forward the Report of the Neutral to the referring Justice or court-attorney referee.

2 The Coordinator has discretion to designate another Neutral in appropriate cases.

Rule IV.   Role of the Neutral

The Mediator serves as a neutral facilitator of communication and helps the parties reach future-oriented solutions that meet their families' individualized needs. The Mediator can probe the parties' feelings, values, and preferences underlying their stated positions. The Mediator does not give legal advice, predict likely court outcomes, or force solutions on the parties.

At the initial session, the Mediator explains that all communications are confidential (with narrow exceptions outlined below) and will not be disclosed to the Justice hearing their case or in any other judicial or administrative proceeding. The Mediator also explains that either party is free at the close of the initial session or at any time thereafter to end the Mediation and return to court.

During the Mediation, each party relates the facts of the dispute and raises particular issues of concern. The Mediator may ask the parties clarifying questions related to the care of their children, parenting time, and allocation of property and income. The Mediator then helps the parties work collaboratively to develop and choose options that meet the parties' needs.

At some point in the process, either party, the party's counsel, or the Mediator may suggest a caucus. Caucuses are meetings that Mediators hold separately with each side in a dispute. During the caucus, the Mediator may explore how each spouse views the dispute and the impact of any proposed solutions. The Mediator keeps confidential the information discussed in caucus unless the party permits disclosure.

If the parties reach a written agreement during Mediation, the parties are strongly encouraged to submit the agreement to their respective attorneys for review.

Rule V.   The Role of Parties, Counsel, Attorneys for the Child and Guardians Ad Litem

Experience has demonstrated that party participation—as opposed to exclusive participation by counsel—not only increases the likelihood of settlement, but also improves compliance with any agreed-upon terms and enhances the parties' satisfaction. Accordingly, unless exempted by the Neutral for good cause shown, the parties must be present during the Mediation session.

The presence of separate counsel for each party at all mediation sessions is encouraged. Whether appearing alongside their clients or advising clients outside of the mediation process, attorneys play a crucial role in informing parties of their legal rights and responsibilities and the consequences of proposed solutions. Without representation by counsel, parties risk entering into agreements with insufficient knowledge about financial, legal, or other issues. If counsel for either party is discharged or withdraws for any reason, the case will not proceed in Mediation.

For those cases in which an Attorney for the Child or guardian ad litem has been assigned, Mediation may not commence without the appropriate Attorney or guardian's presence, unless the parties agree otherwise.

Rule VI.   The Role of the Court

The Program is conducted under Court auspices and pursuant to these rules. Judicial and non-judicial staff are encouraged to inform the parties of the Program's existence. If the parties wish to go to Mediation but cannot afford it, the Coordinator can assist qualifying parties to find a Mediator who may take their case for a reduced fee.

The Court welcomes the feedback of parties, counsel, and Mediators after the conclusion of the proceedings.

Rule VII.   The Roster of Neutrals

The Court has assembled a Roster of Neutrals. Mediators who wish to join the Roster must comply with the following prerequisites:[3]

● Training: Completion of at least 60 hours of family mediation training in a training program recognized by the New York State Office of Court Administration ("OCA").

● Experience: At least four years of family mediation experience, including 250 hours of face-to-face mediation with clients and a minimum of 25 custody and visitation cases, and any other mediation training or experience deemed appropriate by the Court.

●NOTE: Cases involving financial issues will be referred only to those Mediators with knowledge of, training in and experience with financial aspects of divorce. Cases involving issues relating to decision-making for a child or parenting time with a child shall be referred only those Mediators with knowledge of, training in and experience with such issues.

● Continuing Education: Pursuant to Part 146 of the Rules of the Chief Administrative Judge, all mediators must attend at least six hours of additional approved training relevant to their respective practice areas every two years. See www.nycourts.gov/rules/chiefadmin/146.shtml

The District Administrative Judge shall determine whether a person qualifies for inclusion on the Roster of Neutrals and whether a person seeking inclusion on the Roster of Neutrals has the requisite temperament, character, and discretion. Continuing presence on the Court's Roster of Neutrals is subject to review by the District Administrative Judge. Neutrals may be removed from the Roster at the discretion of the District Administrative Judge.

[3] The training and qualifications guidelines for the Program exceed the minimum requirements established in Part 146 of the Rules of the Chief Administrative Judge. See www.nycourts.gov/rules/chiefadmin/146.shtml.

Rule VIII.   Fees

The Program itself does not charge or administer fees. Parties referred to Mediation pursuant to this Statement of Procedures shall be required to compensate the Mediator for services rendered following the initial 90–minute session and for time spent reviewing materials submitted by the parties for purposes of any subsequent sessions at a rate not to exceed $300.00 per hour. The fee arrangement with the Mediator must be agreed to in writing, and must include the ratio at which the fee will be divided between the parties. The parties must sign this fee agreement before commencing any sessions for which compensation is required. Sessions shall be paid for in advance. Mediators are encouraged to work on a sliding scale to take into account the parties' financial circumstances.

Rule IX.   Immunity

Neutrals serving in this program shall be immune from suit as a result of any conduct or omission during the performance of duties in that capacity to the extent permissible by law.

Rule X.   Confidentiality

Except as set forth below, all oral, written, or other communications made during the course of the Mediation by any party, Mediator or any other person present shall be immune from disclosure in any present or future judicial or administrative proceeding. Similarly, all information generated in or in connection with the Mediation -including memoranda, work products or case files of a Mediator-shall remain confidential and not be subject to disclosure in any present or future judicial or administrative proceeding. However, Mediation will not be used as a shield with respect to otherwise discoverable documents or information

produced or occurring prior to or outside the mediation process.

Moreover, except as set forth below, nothing about the substance of the Mediation, such as the weaknesses or strengths of the parties' cases or the relative willingness of parties to discuss settlement proposals, will be revealed to the referring Justice, Court-attorney referee or any other person by the Mediator or any party or attorney. Nor will any party or attorney for a party reveal the outcome of the mediation process to the referring Justice or a member of the Justice's staff or to any Court personnel, including Court attorney-referees unless both sides agree to the disclosure.

Notwithstanding these confidentiality provisions, communications and information may be subject to disclosure in any present or future judicial or administrative proceeding in any of the following five circumstances:

1. Attendance. Whether the parties and their counsel attended the initial session will be reported to the referring Justice or Court attorney-referee.

2. Waiver. Parties to the Mediation and the Mediator agree in writing to waive confidentiality. The waiver must specify the individual communication(s) or information that will be disclosed, the person or entity to whom the disclosure will be made, and the purpose of the disclosure.

3. Written Agreement. A writing signed by all the parties embodying a negotiated agreement submitted to the Court for review. Additionally, a limited report of the outcome, as explained in **Section III**, will be sent to the referring Justice or Court attorney-referee. Only those signed agreements that have become Court orders may be admissible in any present or future judicial or administrative proceeding.

4. Threats of Imminent, Serious Harm. If communications or information constitute a credible threat of serious and imminent harm, either to the speaker or another person or entity, the appropriate authorities and/or the potential victim may be notified.

5. Allegations of Child Abuse or Neglect. The communication or information relates to an allegation of child abuse or neglect as defined in Family Court Act § 1012(e) and (f) and Social Services Law § 412 and for which disclosure is required pursuant to Social Services Law § 413.

Rule XI.   Child Abuse and Neglect

If an allegation of child abuse or neglect is made by any party during the Mediation, the Mediator will safely stop the mediation process. Mediators shall report to the referring Justice or Court attorney-referee allegations of child abuse or neglect for which disclosure is required pursuant to Social Services Law § 413.

Rule XII. Domestic Violence/Severe Power Imbalance

When an allegation of domestic violence or severe power imbalance is made by any party during the Mediation, the Mediator shall safely stop the mediation process, meet with each party individually where appropriate to learn as much as possible about the circumstances, and consult with the Coordinator (but not the assigned Justice or members of that Justice's staff or Court attorney-referee) as to whether to resume the process. Allegations of domestic violence shall not be disclosed to the referring Justice or court attorney-referee; instead, the Coordinator will give victims information regarding their rights in the form prescribed in Family Court Act § 812 (5), and they will receive additional information.

Rule XIII. Referral to the Program and On-going Litigation

Cases may be referred to Mediation at anytime including the preliminary conference (which is typically when referrals are made). A party who attends the initial session complies with the Order of Reference, even if that party ultimately chooses not to proceed with mediation.

Referral to the Program will not stay the court proceedings in any respect. The "no stay" policy recognizes the special need for prompt action in matrimonial and family proceedings. Full discovery, emergency and *pendente lite* relief, family dynamics, and the needs of children require ongoing access to the Court.

Rule XIV. Avoiding Conflicts of Interest

Before accepting a Mediation, a Mediator shall make an inquiry that is reasonable under the circumstances to determine whether there are any known facts that a reasonable individual would consider likely to affect the impartiality of the Mediator, including a financial or personal interest in the outcome, and an existing or past relationship with a party or their attorneys or foreseeable participant in the Mediation. The Mediator shall disclose any such known conflict to the parties and counsel as soon as possible before accepting a referral. If the Mediator wishes to accept a referral after discovering a potentially disqualifying fact, the Mediator is obliged to disclose the disqualifying facts to the parties and, where such facts exist, shall not serve unless the parties consent in writing. If a Mediator later learns of any disqualifying fact after accepting a case, the Mediator shall disclose it as soon as practicable. If unable to function in a fair and impartial manner, the Mediator shall seek disqualification and notify the Coordinator.

Dated: February 23, 2010

FORMS

Form 1. Order of Reference—Matrimonial Mediation Program

SUPREME COURT OF THE STATE OF NEW YORK
COUNTY OF WESTCHESTER

PRESENT: HON.
                    Justice
_____

                    Plaintiff   Index No. _____

- against -

                    Defendant   ORDER OF REFERENCE—
                                        MATRIMONIAL MEDIATION
                                        PROGRAM

_____

1. On consent of the parties/by Order of the Court (**CIRCLE ONE**) the following issues are hereby referred to the Westchester County Supreme Court, Civil Branch, Matrimonial Mediation Program and shall be conducted in accordance with the Program's STATEMENT OF PROCEDURES:

_____

_____

2. Counsel for the parties shall complete this form, and once so-ordered, the Court shall send it to the Program Coordinator, Katherine Mueller, who can be reached at 914–824–5051 or via email at kmueller@courts.state.ny.us.

3. The Program Coordinator shall designate a Mediator from the Court's Roster of Neutrals and forward this Order of Reference to the Mediator.

4. The Program Coordinator shall provide the parties' counsel and the selected Mediator with a Notice of Confirmation within five days (5) of receipt of the Order. The parties shall appear at the initial session within ten (10) days of receiving a Notice of Confirmation.

5. At least three (3) business days prior to the initial session, the parties' counsel shall send the Mediator a copy of the pleadings, the Statements of Net Worth, and any other information necessary for the effective negotiation and resolution of the issues involved.

6. Please indicate whether there are in this case:

Motions *sub judice*: Yes ___ No ___ Appeals: Yes ___ No ___ Order(s) of protection: Yes ___ No ___

7. **By signing below, the parties and/or their counsel, agree that they shall comply with the Statement of Procedures for the Matrimonial Mediation Program, including those provisions regarding confidentiality and immunity. Parties and/or their counsel further understand and agree that no attorney-client relationship exists between the Mediator and the parties, and that the Mediator may not provide legal advice to the parties.**

8. The attorneys for the parties herein are as follows:

For Plaintiff: _____   For Defendant: _____

Address: _____   Address: _____

_____   _____

Phone: _____

Phone: _____

E–Mail: _____

E–Mail: _____

9. The parties shall appear for a status conference before this court on __/__/__

_____

Signature of Plaintiff

_____

Signature of Defendant

_____

Signature of Counsel for Plaintiff

_____

Signature of Counsel for Defendant

Dated: White Plains, New York
_____, 20 ___

_____

JSC or Court–Attorney Referee

Form 2. Report of Neutral

SUPREME COURT OF THE STATE OF NEW YORK
COUNTY OF WESTCHESTER

_____

                          Plaintiff   Index No. _____

- against -

                                         REPORT OF NEUTRAL

                        Defendant

_____

This case was referred to me for Mediation by Order of _____, dated _____.

In an effort to resolve or narrow the dispute, an initial session was held on _____ (and further sessions were held on _____.)

    The result was as follows (please check one):

    ☐ The matter remains unresolved and is ready to proceed in court.

    ☐ The matter remains unresolved in part and is ready to proceed in court.

    ☐ The matter was resolved.

    ☐ The following party(ies) and/or attorney(s) failed to appear at the initial session:

_____.

    ☐ The matter is not appropriate for mediation. (If terminated due to allegations of child abuse or neglect, please specify.)

_____.

Dated: _____   _____
                                             Mediator

    NOTE: No other comment should be made as to any substantive aspect of the case, or if applicable, the reason why the Mediation failed to resolve the case.

PLEASE RETURN COMPLETED COPIES OF THIS FORM TO COUNSEL FOR THE PARTIES AND TO KATHERINE MUELLER, PROGRAM COORDINATOR:

    Supreme Court, Civil Branch, Westchester County
    Matrimonial Mediation Program
    Westchester County Courthouse
    111 Dr. Martin Luther King, Jr. Blvd.
    White Plains, New York 10601
    Email: kmueller@courts.state.ny.us

MEDICAL MALPRACTICE CONFERENCE PART

Doc. 1. Medical Malpractice Conference Part

1. Purpose:

Medical Malpractice cases involving the Westchester County Medical Center are eligible for a conference before Justice Lefkowitz where at least one plaintiff and one defendant in the litigation consent.

2. Informal Request Procedure:

Counsel for either plaintiff or defendant in a medical malpractice action involving the Westchester County Medical Center, having obtained the consent of at least one adversary, may request a conference with the Medical Malpractice Conference Part by e-mailing such request to the Part Clerk. It is suggested that the consenting parties identify the case by caption and index number, provide the Court with at least two dates they are available for a conference and include e-mail addresses or other contact information of all participants should the conference need to be adjourned. By return e-mail, the Part Clerk will advise counsel of the date, time and location of the conference. Counsel shall, in turn, advise all other counsel/parties/participants of such date, time and location.

3. Conference Days/Time:

Medical Malpractice Conferences shall take place on Wednesdays at 2:00 P.M. in Courtroom 1600, unless otherwise indicated by the Part Clerk. Upon consent of the Court, additional conferences may be scheduled.

4. Who Must Appear at the Conference:

All counsel who have consented to a conference, the consenting plaintiff, any defendant physician with a consent based insurance policy who is willing to conference but who has not yet expressed a willingness to consent to a settlement within such policy limit, the insurance claims adjuster or risk management officer for any party consenting to the conference shall appear at the conference and any subsequent conference unless the appearance of such party/participant is excused by the Court. A party or party's representative not consenting to a conference shall have a right to attend.

5. No Impact on Existing Court Orders and Directives:

Conferences may be requested at any time prior to trial, however, the request for a conference, consent thereto or participation in same shall not effect any court-ordered discovery, extend the time within which to make applications to the court or effect any scheduled court appearance or trial date.

6. Adjournments:

An adjournment request shall be granted if made by a consenting counsel on notice to all participants and the Court not less than 24 hours before the scheduled conference date and time. The conference may be rescheduled in accordance with the procedures set forth in paragraph 2.

FAMILY COURT

FORMS

Form 1. Telephonic Request Forms

FAMILY COURT OF THE STATE OF NEW YORK
WESTCHESTER COUNTY

_____

F.C.A. §§ 433, 531-a, 580–316

_____ **Petitioner,**

vs.

_____ **Respondent.**

_____

**REQUEST TO TESTIFY IN COURT
PROCEEDINGS BY TELEPHONE**

**THIS FORM MUST BE COMPLETED AND RETURNED TO THE COURT
NO LESS THAN THREE (3) DAYS BEFORE THE SCHEDULED HEARING.**

FILE #   _____

DOCKET #   _____

Unless you hear from the court denying your request for a telephone hearing, you may consider your request granted. If your hearing is scheduled in the morning, you must be available between the hours of 9:00 am 1:00 pm Eastern Standard Time. If your hearing is scheduled in the afternoon, you must be available between 1:00 pm and 5:00 pm Eastern Standard Time. You must resubmit this application via fax to 914–995–8648 if your case is forwarded to a Family Court Judge for further proceedings.

I, _____, am the (circle one) Petitioner / Respondent in the above

action. I reside at _____.

A hearing is scheduled on this matter on _____ at _____ am / pm

New York time, before Support Magistrate _____

at the **Westchester County Family Court of the State of New York, located at
111 Dr. Martin Luther King Jr. Blvd., White Plains, New York 10601.**

Pursuant to New York State Family Court Act 433, 531-a, or 580–316, I respectfully request that I be permitted to testify in this matter by telephone/audio visual/other electronic means for the following reasons:

_____

_____

_____

The telephone number that I may be reached at on the date of the hearing is: _____
THIS IS MY (CIRCLE ONE) WORK / HOME / CELL / OTHER

_____

I understand that it is my responsibility to provide the Westchester Family Court with a telephone number for the Court to use to telephone me on the scheduled court hearing date and time so that I may testify by telephone.

I further understand that I must be available to the Court to testify by telephone for up to a four (4) hour period after the time the court hearing is scheduled, and that if the Court telephones me and I do not answer the phone, the Court can proceed in my absence if I am the Respondent, and grant the relief requested in the petition; or, if I am the Petitioner, the Court may dismiss my petition if there is a failure to establish a prima facie case. I may also seek assistance from my local Child Support Enforcement Agency to arrange the telephonic hearing.

Any request for information on a case must be made in writing to:
The Office of Child Support Enforcement at 100 East First Street (3rd and 5th Floors), Mount Vernon, New York 10550, or to your local Office of Child Support Enforcement, and not to the Court.

DATE: _____

                 Telephonic Applicant

Sworn to me this   day of   200 __

_____

Please print or type name

_____

Notary Public   Home Address: _____

_____

_____

For Court Use Only

Status of Case:

FAMILY COURT OF THE STATE OF NEW YORK
WESTCHESTER COUNTY

         F.C.A. §§ 433, 531-a, 580–316

_____ **Petitioner,**

vs.

_____ **Respondent.**

REQUEST TO TESTIFY IN COURT
PROCEEDINGS BY TELEPHONE

THIS FORM MUST BE COMPLETED AND RETURNED TO THE COURT
NO LESS THAN THREE (3) DAYS BEFORE THE SCHEDULED HEARING.

         FILE # _____

         DOCKET # _____

Unless you hear from the court denying your request for a
telephone hearing, you may consider your request granted.
If your hearing is scheduled in the morning, you must be available
between the hours of 9:00 am 1:00 pm Eastern Standard Time.
If your hearing is scheduled in the afternoon, you must be available
between 1:00 pm and 5:00 pm Eastern Standard Time. You must
resubmit this application via fax to 914–231–3016 if your case is
forwarded to a Family Court Judge for further proceedings.

I, _____, am the (circle one) Petitioner / Respondent in the above

action. I reside at _____.

A hearing is scheduled on this matter on _____ at _____ am / pm

New York time, before Support Magistrate _____

at the **Yonkers Family Court of the State of New York, located at**
     53 South Broadway, 3rd Floor, Yonkers, New York 10701.

Pursuant to New York State Family Court Act 433, 531-a, or 580–316, I respectfully request that I be
permitted to testify in this matter by telephone/audio visual/other electronic means for the following reasons:

_____

_____

_____

The telephone number that I may be reached at on the date of the hearing is: _____
THIS IS MY (CIRCLE ONE) WORK / HOME / CELL / OTHER

I understand that it is my responsibility to provide the Westchester Family Court with a telephone number for the Court to use to telephone
me on the scheduled court hearing date and time so that I may testify by telephone.

I further understand that I must be available to the Court to testify by telephone for up to a four (4) hour period after the time the court hearing is scheduled, and that if the Court telephones me and I do not answer the phone, the Court can proceed in my absence if I am the Respondent, and grant the relief requested in the petition; or, if I am the Petitioner, the Court may dismiss my petition if there is a failure to establish a prima facie case. I may also seek assistance from my local Child Support Enforcement Agency to arrange the telephonic hearing.

Any request for information on a case must be made in writing to:
The Office of Child Support Enforcement at 100 East First Street (3rd and 5th Floors), Mount Vernon, New York 10550, or to your local Office of Child Support Enforcement, and not to the Court.

DATE: _____

                                       Telephonic Applicant

Sworn to me this   day of   200 ___   _____

                                          Please print or type name

_____   Home Address: _____

Notary Public

                                  For Court Use Only

Status of Case:

FAMILY COURT OF THE STATE OF NEW YORK
WESTCHESTER COUNTY   **REQUEST TO TESTIFY IN COURT**
                                            PROCEEDINGS BY TELEPHONE

       F.C.A. §§ 433, 531-a, 580–316   **THIS FORM MUST BE COMPLETED AND RETURNED TO THE COURT**
                                     NO LESS THAN THREE (3) DAYS BEFORE THE SCHEDULED HEARING.

                                    FILE # _____

_____ **Petitioner,**   DOCKET # _____

                                   Unless you hear from the court denying your request for a
                                   telephone hearing, you may consider your request granted.
vs.   *If your hearing is scheduled in the morning, you must be available*
                                 between the hours of 9:00 am 1:00 pm Eastern Standard Time.
                                 If your hearing is scheduled in the afternoon, you must be available
                                 between 1:00 pm and 5:00 pm Eastern Standard Time. You must
_____ **Respondent.**   *resubmit this application via fax to 914–813–5580 if your case is*
                                 forwarded to a Family Court Judge for further proceedings.

I, _____, am the (circle one) Petitioner / Respondent in the above

action. I reside at _____.

A hearing is scheduled on this matter on _____ at _____ am / pm

New York time, before Support Magistrate _____

at the **New Rochelle Family Court of the State of New York, located at**
    420 North Avenue, 3rd Floor, New Rochelle, New York 10801.

Pursuant to New York State Family Court Act 433, 531-a, or 580–316, I respectfully request that I be permitted to testify in this matter by telephone/audio visual/other electronic means for the following reasons:

_____

_____

_____

The telephone number that I may be reached at on the date of the hearing is: _____

THIS IS MY (CIRCLE ONE) WORK / HOME / CELL / OTHER

I understand that it is my responsibility to provide the Westchester Family Court with a telephone number for the Court to use to telephone me on the scheduled court hearing date and time so that I may testify by telephone.

I further understand that I must be available to the Court to testify by telephone for up to a four (4) hour period after the time the court hearing is scheduled, and that if the Court telephones me and I do not answer the phone, the Court can proceed in my absence if I am the Respondent, and grant the relief requested in the petition; or, if I am the Petitioner, the Court may dismiss my petition if there is a failure to establish a prima facie case. I may also seek assistance from my local Child Support Enforcement Agency to arrange the telephonic hearing.

Any request for information on a case must be made in writing to:
The Office of Child Support Enforcement at 100 East First Street (3rd and 5th Floors), Mount Vernon, New York 10550, or to your local Office of Child Support Enforcement, and not to the Court.

DATE: _____   _____
                                                      Telephonic Applicant

Sworn to me this   day of   200 __   _____
                                                      Please print or type name

_____   Home Address: _____
Notary Public
                                       _____

                                       _____

_____

For Court Use Only

Status of Case:

Form 2.   Transcript Request Form

TRANSCRIPT REQUEST FORM

_____
Petitioner

Docket# _____

vs.

File# _____

_____
Respondent

I hereby request a transcript of the Family Court hearing in the above-captioned manner which was held in this Court on _____*, before
_____

*If requesting transcript for an Appeal, a copy of the Appellate order must be attached

Requester Name _____

Address _____

_____

_____

Telephone _____

**Name & Address of Transcript Agency

_____

Identification verified by:

_____

_____
Clerk

_____

Please choose and provide the name and address of a Transcription Service that is **Reporter Deck capable (able to provide transcripts from audio tapes and compact discs) in the event the proceeding was not recorded by a court reporter. The Electronic Recording Transcription Services list may be obtained from the Court Clerk. Once this form is completed, you may fax it to 914-995-8650._

Date: _____

_____

Office Use Only

Date of Hearing:	_____	Date of Hearing:	_____
Court Reporter:	_____	Court Reporter:	_____
Electronic Reading		Electronic Reading:	
Tape#	1 2	Tape#	1 2
Range	_____ _____	Range	_____ _____

Form 3.   Objection Form

SIDE ONE   **REV 7/05**

INFORMATION CONCERNING THE FILING OF OBJECTIONS AND REBUTTAL IN A PROCEEDING BEFORE THE SUPPORT MAGISTRATE

You have received a copy of an **Order of Support** signed by a Support Magistrate, and a copy of the Support Magistrate's **findings of fact** upon which the order is based. This order must be obeyed.

* Either party has a right to file *specific written objections* to this order with the clerk of the court. Objections are reviewed by a Judge of the Family Court. Even if you file an objection, the amount ordered by the Support Magistrate must be paid until a new order is entered. (*Objections cannot be taken on an order entered on *consent*, and the respondent may not file an objection on an order entered on *default*.)

INSTRUCTIONS FOR FILING OBJECTIONS

Objections must be filed within **30 days** of the date the order was received by you *in court*, or personally served to you (or, if the order was received by mail, within **35 days** of the mailing of the order).

    1.   Complete all required case file information in caption area on <u>side two</u> of this form.

    2.   Attach a statement of your reason(s) for objection to the order. Sign and date the statement.

    3.   Attach a copy of the *order* that you are objecting to.

    4.   Have a copy of the *objection package* served on the opposing party either in person or by mail.

    (The party serving the papers must be over 18 years of age and <u>not</u> a party to the action.)

    5.   The *party who served the papers* must complete the *affidavit of service* on <u>side two</u> of this form and have his or her signature notarized.

    6.   File the *original* objection and attachments, including the *affidavit of service*, with the Court, and maintain a *copy* for your own records.

INSTRUCTIONS FOR FILING A REBUTTAL TO OBJECTION

The party that has been served with an objection has a right to file a rebuttal to the objection. A rebuttal is an answer to the objection.

    1.   Complete all required case file information in the caption area on <u>side two</u> of this form.

    2.   Attach a statement of your reason(s) for rebuttal. Sign and date the statement.

    3.   Have a *copy* of the rebuttal package served on the opposing party either in person or by mail within **13 days** of the receipt of the objections.

    (The party serving the papers must be over 18 years of age and <u>not</u> a party to the action.)

    4.   The *party who served the papers* must complete the *affidavit of service* on <u>side two</u> of this form and have his or her signature notarized.

    5.   File the *original* rebuttal, including the *affidavit of service*, with the Court, and maintain a *copy* for your own records.

INFORMATION ABOUT TRANSCRIPTS

The party filing the objection MAY be required to provide a transcript of the proceeding. This will not be necessary unless the judge requires one. If the judge requires a transcript, the party filing the objection must pay the cost for

the duplicate recording or the transcript. If the party cannot afford to pay for a duplicate recording or transcript, the clerk of the court will provide information about procedures for obtaining a duplicate recording or transcript without charge. Even if the judge does not require a transcript, either party may request a duplicate recording or transcript. The requesting party must pay the cost for such duplicate recording or transcript.

SIDE TWO

CASE CAPTION

NAMES OF PARTIES: .... VS. ....

DOCKET # .... FILE # ....

I, ... [ ] **OBJECT TO SUPPORT ORDER DATED** ....
(Enter your name)

[ ] **REBUT OBJECTIONS RECEIVED ON** ....

Attach a separate sheet of paper(s) stating your specific objection to the order (or a rebuttal to objection filed). Follow the instructions on reverse side on how to prepare and properly serve and file these papers. Failure to comply with procedure may result in your application being denied by the court.

AFFIDAVIT OF SERVICE

The party serving the papers either by mail or in person, MUST be eighteen years of age and NOT a party to the action. The party serving the papers must complete the following information, and sign the form in front of a notary public.

I, ... *being duly sworn deposes and says: I am over eighteen years of age:* **not a party to the action***: and have served a true copy of objection/rebuttal documents on the party named below who I personally know to be the same person to whom the said process is directed:*

[ ] **BY MAIL** in a sealed envelope addressed to: (Name) ....
(Address) ....
(Date of mailing) ....

[ ] **IN PERSON** by delivering to: (Name) ....
(Date) .... (Time) ....
(And place) .... of service.

Complete this section for personal service ONLY

Describe the party who was served with the papers ▶
Approximate age ....Sex ....
Approximate weight ....Height ....
Skin color ....Hair color ....
Identifying marks, if any ....

The person who served the papers must **SIGN HERE X** ....
Print name ▶ ....

Sworn to before me on ....
Notary Public of the State of New York,
appointed in and for the County of
....
Commission expires on ....

(Signature must be notarized by a notary public)

779

Form 4. Law Guardian Assignment Instructions

TERM #4 ENDING April 22, 2007

1. Law Guardians are to be assigned on a ROTATIONAL BASIS ... DO NOT SKIP ANY NAMES.

2. At the beginning of the term, it is the responsibility of each part to insure that the starting position is at the point where the last selection was made for the previous term.

3. When contacting the law guardian for assignment and you reach an answering machine, DO NOT HANG UP, leave a message and request that your call be returned as soon as possible or within a specified period of time. If the call is not returned, indicate in the column 'UNABLE TO CONTACT'—left message—no response and proceed to the next name.

4. EMERGENCY CASES—You may assign the most available attorney if you need a law guardian immediately and use an 'E' to indicate emergency assignment.

5. REMINDER—all attorneys contacted during the current term must have a comment in one of the columns ... ABSOLUTELY NO BLANKS, unless the attorney has requested not to be assigned to a particular location.

6. Please include any change of address, phone number, fax, etc. on the copy submitted to this office and the necessary correction(s) will be made prior to the preparation of the list for the next term.

Form 5. Financial Disclosure Affidavit (03/05)

Family Court of the State of New York—County of Westchester

Instructions: Complete this form **prior** to the court appearance date and have your signature **notarized**. Attach the following to this form: **ONE** (1) original and **TWO** (2) copies of this **financial affidavit form,** plus **TWO** (2) copies of your most recent **Federal Tax Return,** including **W-2 forms** and **TWO** (2) copies of **3 recent paycheck stubs** representative of your current average salary. Please keep a copy of this financial affidavit for your own records and **keep your original tax returns and pay stubs.** The court will **not** provide copies on the hearing day.

CASE FILE INFORMATION

File #:	Docket #:	S.S.#:	DOB:

Name:	[ ]Petitioner [ ]Respondent

Street Address:	Home Tel:

City, State:	ZIP:	Bus. Tel:

Enter Total Number of Dependents:

Name:	Relationship:	Address:
SS#/DOB:		
Name:	Relationship:	Address:
SS#/DOB:		
Name:	Relationship:	Address:
SS#/DOB:		

(Attach extra pages if needed)

INCOME

Employer/Company Name:	# of hours worked per week:	Check here if self employed:

Address:	❶GROSS WEEKLY SALARY/WAGES:

Deductions

Soc. Sec.:	Health Insurance:	State Tax:	❷TOTAL PAYROLL DEDUCTIONS:
Fed. Tax:	Other payroll deductions:		

Subtract box ❷ from box ❶ → ❸NET WEEKLY SALARY/WAGES:

Income from other sources

Second Job:	Pensions/Retirement Benefits:	Workers Compensation:	❹TOTAL OTHER SOURCES:
Tips:	Social Security Benefits	Veterans Benefits:	
Rents:	Unemployment:	Fellowships/Stipends/Annuities:	
Dividends:	Disability:		

Income from other household members

Specify:	$	❺TOTAL OTHER MEMBERS:
Specify:	$	

(Add lines ❸, ❹ and ❺) → ❻TOTAL WEEKLY INCOME:

Enter total taxable income declared on last Federal Tax Return:	Are you eligible for Employer-provided Health Insurance?

ASSETS

Residence Owned

Address:	
Estimated Market Value:	Mortgage Owed:

Other Real Property

Address:	
Estimated Market Value:	Mortgage Owed:

Other Property

Description:	
Estimated Market Value:	Mortgage Owed:

Bank/Brokerage Accounts

Bank Name:	Acct. #:	[ ]Checking [ ]Savings	Balance:
Bank Name:	Acct. #:	[ ]Checking [ ]Savings	Balance:
Bank Name:	Acct. #:	[ ]Checking [ ]Savings	Balance:

Vehicle(s)

Make and Model:	Year:	Value:
Make and Model:	Year:	Value:
Make and Model:	Year:	Value:

List below all assets transferred in any manner during preceding three years or length of marriage, whichever is shorter.

Description of Property:	To whom transferred:	Date of transfer:	Value:
Description of Property:	To whom transferred:	Date of transfer:	Value:

EXPENSES

Rent/Mortgage →				
Real Estate Taxes (if not included in mortgage payment) →				
Home Insurance (if not included in mortgage payment) →				

Utilities

Heat:		Electric:	Total Utilities:
Gas:		Telephone:	
Water:		Trash:	

Food

Self:	Children (incl. lunches):	Total Food:

Childcare

Child:	Provider:	Amount:	Total Childcare:
Child:	Provider:	Amount:	
Child:	Provider:	Amount:	

Clothing

Self:	Children:	Total Clothing

Laundry

Self:	Children:	Total Laundry:

Insurance

Life:	Auto:	Total Insurance:
Accident:	Other:	

Balance due on auto loan/lease:	Auto Payment →	

Transportation

Public:	Gas/Oil:	Total Transportation:
Maintenance:	Other:	

Tuition (Specify):	→
Alimony or Maintenance →	
Child Support/Previous Marriage →	

Other expenses (specify)

Health Insurance [ ] check if payroll deduction

Provider/Plan name:		Total Health Insurance:
Policy #:	Address:	

Dental Insurance [ ] check if payroll deduction

Provider/Plan name:		Total Dental Insurance:
Policy #:	Address:	

Other Insurance

Provider/Plan name:		Total Other Insurance:
Policy #:	Address:	

You may elect to list all expenses on a weekly or monthly basis, however, you must be consistent. For items paid on a monthly basis, divide by 4.3 to obtain weekly payment. For items paid on a weekly basis, multiply by 4.3 to obtain monthly payment.

Check one:
[ ] Monthly
[ ] Weekly

YOU ARE REQUIRED TO PROVIDE INFORMATION RELATING TO ALL INSURANCE PLANS AVAILABLE TO YOU FOR THE PROVISION OF INSURANCE, HEALTH CARE, DENTAL CARE, OPTICAL CARE, PRESCRIPTION DRUG AND OTHER PHARMACEUTICAL AND OTHER HEALTH-RELATED BENEFITS FOR THE CHILD(REN) FOR WHOM SUPPORT IS SOUGHT.

TOTAL EXPENSES →

LIABILITIES, LOANS & DEBTS (Attach separate sheet if necessary)

Owed to:	Date Incurred:	Monthly Payment:
Purpose:	Balance Due:	
Owed to:	Date Incurred:	Monthly Payment:
Purpose:	Balance Due:	
Owed to:	Date Incurred:	Monthly Payment:
Purpose:	Balance Due:	

TOTAL MONTHLY PAYMENTS →

VERIFICATION, SIGNATURE & NOTARIZATION

I, ..., being duly sworn, depose and say that the foregoing is an accurate statement of my net worth (assets of whatsoever kind and nature and wherever situated, and my liabilities), and statement of income from all sources and statement of assets transferred of whatsoever kind and nature and wherever situated.

X ....

Sworn to before me this .... day   (Sign your name)
of ...., 20 ....
....
Notary Public or (Deputy) Clerk of the Court

Unless the court makes a finding the non-custodial parent's share is unjust or inappropriate, the child support percentages to be applied to gross income are as follows: 17%-one child; 25%-two children; 29%-three children, 31%-four children and no less than 35% for five or more children.

Any variances to the percentages shall be based on the following factors:

1. The financial resources of the parents and of the child.

2. The physical and emotional health of the child and any special needs/aptitudes.

3. The standard of living the child would have enjoyed had the marriage or household not been dissolved.

4. The tax consequences to the parties.

5. Any non-monetary contributions the parent will make toward the care and well being of the child.

6. The educational needs of either parent.

7. A determination that the gross income of one parent is substantially less than that of the other parent.

8. The needs of the children of the non-custodial parent for whom the non-custodial parent is providing support, who are not a subject of the instant matter.

9. Provided the child is not on public assistance, extraordinary expenses incurred by the non-custodial parent in exercising visitation.

10. Any other factors the court determines are relevant in each case.

NOTE: For more complete and statutory language see the Family Court Act 413(1) and the Domestic Relations Law 236-B and 240.

IMPORTANT NOTICE—PLEASE READ CAREFULLY (03/05)

Upon your appearance on the return date of the summons you **must be prepared to proceed to conclusion of this case.** You must provide the court with proof of your income and assets.

You must provide to the court the following documents on that date:

• **Notarized original and two copies** of the enclosed financial disclosure form.

• **Two copies** of current and representative pay stubs.

• **Two copies** of your most recently filed state and federal income tax return including copy of your W-2 wage and tax statement(s).

• **Two copies** of social security, pension, unemployment, workers compensation or other award letters if applicable.

Note: you may also be required to provide past pay stubs, income tax returns, employer statements, corporate, business or partnership books, records, corporate and business income tax returns, receipts for expenses or such measures of verification as the court deems appropriate.

You have the right to bring an attorney or you may represent yourself. **Under limited circumstances**, the court may consider appointing counsel **after** the first court appearance.

You have the right, through an attorney or by yourself, to present evidence both by testimony and the submission of documentation. The Support Magistrate will decide what may be considered and entered as evidence.

You may qualify to testify by telephone, audio-visual or other electronic means [FCA433(c)].

To qualify you must either:

• Reside out of state.

• Reside in a New York State county not contiguous to Westchester County. The five counties of New York City are treated as one county for this purpose.

• Be incarcerated and not expect to be released within a reasonable period after the scheduled date.

• Prove you will suffer undue hardship by appearing in court.

If you wish to request permission to appear telephonically, you must submit form UIFSA-10, which you may obtain from any Family Court or on the Internet at www. courts.state.ny.us.

Special Notices

The Petitioner must appear as directed on the notice. If the petitioner appears late, fails to appear or fails to submit the required financial disclosure documents as directed above, the petition may be dismissed without further consideration.

The Respondent must appear as directed on the summons. If the respondent fails to appear, a warrant may be issued for his/her arrest and/or an inquest may be taken granting the relief requested. If the respondent fails to submit the required financial disclosure documents as described above, an order may be entered which excludes that information. A temporary or permanent order will be made on the return date of this petition whether or not you appear.

Child Support Orders: State Law requires the Family Court to order the non-custodial parent to pay at least twenty-five dollars ($25) per month in child support. However, if the non-custodial parent's income is below the poverty level as reported by the federal Department of Health and Human Services, that parent or his/her legal representative is allowed to tell the Family Court why (s)he should not be ordered to pay $25 per month in child support. If you wish to tell the Family Court that you should be ordered to pay less than $25 per month, you will need to tell the court that your income is below the poverty level, what your income consists of and the reasons why you think that you should be ordered to pay less than $25. The Family Court will then decide the amount of your support order.

Paternity Petitions: If a denial to the paternity allegation is entered, both parties and the child will be required to submit to genetic screening. The tests may be performed on the return date of the summons/notice. Please bring with you two forms of identification (one of which must contain a photo). You may be required to pay the cost of testing.

AVISO IMPORTANTE—POR FAVOR LEA ATENTAMENTE (03/05)

Cuando se presente en la fecha indicada en la citación, **deberá estar preparado para proceder hasta la conclusión de esta causa**. Deberá proveer a la Corte comprobantes de sus ingresos y bienes.

En esa fecha deberá proveer a la Corte los siguientes documentos:

• **Un original notarizado y dos copias** de la declaración jurada de divulgación de finanzas que se adjunta.

- **Dos copias** de talones de pago recientes y representativos de sus ingresos corrientes.

- **Dos copias** de su declaración de impuestos más recientes, tanto federales como estatales, incluyendo copias de su formulario W–2 detallando ingresos y contribuciones.

- **Dos copias** de cartas de adjudicación de seguro social, pensiones, seguro de desempleo, compensación por accidentes y enfermedades relativas a su trabajo, u otros comprobantes de ingresos recibidos.

Nota: Es posible que se le requiera presentar copias de antiguos talones de pago, declaraciones de impuestos, corroborantes de su empleador, registros o libros y declaraciones de impuestos corporativos, recibos de gastos y cualquier otro comprobante que la Corte considere necesario.

Tiene derecho a presentarse con un abogado, o puede representarse a sí mismo. En **ciertas ocasiones limitadas**, el Juez puede considerar asignarle un abogado de oficio **después** de su comparecencia inicial.

Tiene derecho, a través de un abogado o por sí mismo, a presentar evidencia tanto en forma de testimonio como a través de la entrega de documentación. El Arbitro decidirá los materiales que sean aceptables como evidencia.

Es posible que Ud. califique para testificar por teléfono, audiovisual u otro método electrónico. [FCA433(c)].

Para calificar, deberá cumplir con al menos una de las siguientes condiciones:

- Vivir fuera del Estado de New York.

- Residir en un Condado del Estado de New York que no sea lindero al Condado de Westchester. Los cinco Condados de la Ciudad de New York se cuentan como un Condado para este propósito.

- Estar encarcelado, y no esperar que se lo libere hasta pasado un período razonable después de la cita establecida.

- Probar que padecería privaciones excesivas si compareciera.

Si desea pedir autorización para presentar testimonio telefónico, deberá utilizar el formulario UIFSA-10, el cual puede obtener en cualquier Corte de Familia o por Internet en www.courts.state.ny.us.

Avisos Especiales

El Demandante no necesita comparecer. Su petición sera basada únicamente según los documentos entablados. Usted puede comparecer en persona o puede ponerse en contacto con La Unidad de Manutención Infantil **914–995–5781** para contratar un abogado privado o testificar por método electrónico. Si usted desea testificar por teléfono envie por correo o fax a **914–995–8648/8649** el formulario UIFSA-10 al tribunal. Si el demandante se presenta tarde, no se presentara, o no entregara los comprobantes de divulgación de finanzas que se indican más arriba, se podrá desestimar su petición sin más contemplaciones.

El Demandado deberá comparecer según se indique en el auto de comparecencia. Si el demandado se ausentara, podría expedirse una orden de arresto en su contra, y/o podría ordenarse una investigación otorgando lo pedido por el demandante. Si el demandado no entregara los comprobantes que se requieren más arriba, podría expedirse una orden excluyendo tal información. Independientemente de la comparecencia del demandado, se expedirá una orden permanente o temporaria el día de la audiencia.

Ordenes de Manutención Infantil: La Ley Estatal establece que el Tribunal de Familia deberá ordenar el pago de un mínimo de veinticinco dolares ($25) mensuales en concepto de manutención por parte del padre que no tenga la custodia de los menores. Sin embargo, si sus ingresos fueran inferiores al índice de pobreza según lo reporta el Departamento Federal de Salud y Servicios Humanos (Federal

Department of Health and Human Services), tal padre o su representante legal podría explicarle al Tribunal las razones por las que no debería ordenársele pagar esos $25. Si Ud. deseara pagar menos de $25 mensuales por manutención infantil, deberá explicarle al Juez que sus ingresos son inferiores al índice de pobreza, en qué consisten tales ingresos, y las razones por las que Ud. crea que debería pagar menos de $25. El Tribunal de Familia decidirá el monto final que se fijará en la orden de manutención.

Peticiones de Paternidad: Si se entablara una denegación al alegato de paternidad, ambas partes y el menor en cuestión deberán someterse a un análisis de material genético. Tal análisis podría realizarse en la fecha indicada en su citación. Por favor, traiga consigo dos identificaciones, una de las cuales deberá incluir su retrato. Se le podrá exigir el pago del costo del análisis.

UIFSA   **IMPORTANT NOTICE—PLEASE READ CAREFULLY** (08/05)

Upon your appearance on the return date of the summons you **must be prepared to proceed to conclusion of this case.** You must provide the court with proof of your income and assets.

You must provide to the court the following documents on that date:

- **Notarized original and two copies** of the enclosed financial disclosure form.

- **Two copies** of current and representative pay stubs.

- **Two copies** of your most recently filed state and federal income tax return including copies of your W-2 wage and tax statement(s).

- **Two copies** of social security, pension, unemployment, workers compensation or other award letters if applicable.

Note: you may also be required to provide past pay stubs, income tax returns, employer statements, corporate, business or partnership books, records, corporate and business income tax returns, receipts for expenses or such measures of verification as the court deems appropriate.

You have the right to bring an attorney or you may represent yourself. **Under limited circumstances**, the court may consider appointing counsel **after** the first court appearance.

You have the right, through an attorney or by yourself, to present evidence both by testimony and the submission of documentation. The Support Magistrate will decide what may be considered and entered as evidence.

You may qualify to testify by telephone, audio-visual or other electronic means [FCA433(c)].

To qualify you must either:

- Reside out of state.

- Reside in a New York State county not contiguous to Westchester County. The five counties of New York City are treated as one county for this purpose.

- Be incarcerated and not expect to be released within a reasonable period after the scheduled date.

- Prove you will suffer undue hardship by appearing in court.

If you wish to request permission to appear telephonically, you must submit form UIFSA-10, which you may obtain from any Family Court or on the Internet at www.courts.state.ny.us.

Special Notices

The Petitioner need not appear. Your petition may be based solely on the documents file! You may, however, choose to appear in person or you may contact the Support Collection Unit at (914–995–5781) to hire paid representation or you may appear electronically. If you wish to appear telephonically, mail or fax (914–995–8648/8649) UIFSA–10 to the court.

The Respondent must appear as directed on the summons. If the respondent fails to appear, a warrant may be issued for his/her arrest and/or an inquest may be taken granting the relief requested. If the respondent fails to submit the required financial disclosure documents as described above, an order may be entered which excludes that information. A temporary or permanent order will be made on the return date of this petition whether or not you appear.

Child Support Orders: State Law requires the Family Court to order the non-custodial parent to pay at least twenty-five dollars ($25) per month in child support. However, if the non-custodial parent's income is below the poverty level as reported by the federal Department of Health and Human Services, that parent or his/her legal representative is allowed to tell the Family Court why (s)he should not be ordered to pay $25 per month in child support. If you wish to tell the Family Court that you should be ordered to pay less than $25 per month, you will need to tell the court that your income is below the poverty level, what your income consists of and the reasons why you think that you should be ordered to pay less than $25. The Family Court will then decide the amount of your support order.

Paternity Petitions: If a denial to the paternity allegation is entered, both parties and the child will be required to submit to genetic screening. The tests may be performed on the return date of the summons/notice. Please bring with you two forms of identification (one of which must contain a photo). You may be required to pay the cost of testing.

E-FILING

Doc. 1. Joint Protocols for NYSCEF Cases Filed in Westchester County

I. Introduction. In implementation of the New York State Courts E–Filing system (hereinafter referred to as "the NYSCEF system") in Westchester County Supreme Court in accordance with the program established by the Chief Administrator of the Courts pursuant to Uniform Rules for the Supreme and County Courts (hereinafter "Uniform Rules") §§ 202.5–b and 202.5–bb, the Administrative Judge of the Ninth Judicial District and the Westchester County Clerk as Clerk of the Supreme and County Courts hereby promulgate local user protocols to assist users in implementing NYSCEF in practice and provide guidance with respect to local practice and procedures used to process filings, fees and court calendaring. In addition, it is suggested that users consult the User Manuals provided on-line at the NYSCEF website (www.nycourts.gov/efile) as well as any applicable part rules.

A. *Effect of Joint Protocols*: The NYSCEF system does not change the rules applicable to civil litigation. As such, the protocols promulgated herein, as well as any additions or amendments thereto, do not change applicable rules or statutes with respect to civil practice as defined by the New York State Civil Practice Law and Rules (hereinafter "CPLR"), the Uniform Rules or the Commercial Division Rules (22 NYCRR 202.70). In addition, users are encouraged to be fully familiar with the Westchester Supreme Court Differentiated Case Management Protocol (http://www. nycourts.gov/courts/9jd/diffCaseMgmt/CivilProtocols_ rev011110.pdf), the Practice Guide to the Commercial Division (http://www.nycourts.gov/courts/comdiv/ PDFs/PracticeGuideToTheCommercialDivision-Scheinkman.pdf), the Calendar Procedure for the Tax Certiorari/Condemnation Part (http://www.nycourts. gov/courts/9jd/TacCert_pdfs/Part%20Rules%20Tax %20Certiorari.pdf) and the IAS Part Rules as they apply to the action type being filed in the NYSCEF system.

B. *Official Case Record*: The official case record for any action or proceeding, and the filing or entry of documents therefore, shall be the records maintained by the Office of the Westchester County Clerk via its electronic database, online images and hard copy filings as per the constitutional authority vested as the Clerk of the Supreme and County Courts. In addition, as Clerk of the Supreme and County Courts, the Westchester County Clerk is and remains the vested constitutional official with respect to access, maintenance and retention and dissemination of court records within Westchester County.

C. *Getting Started*: Prior to utilizing the NYSCEF system, an attorney, party, or filing agent must register to become an authorized user of the NYSCEF site at www.nycourts.gov/efile. A firm acting as filing agent for an attorney or party to a case must file a form accessible at www.nycourts.gov/efile, whereby the attorney or party authorizes the agent to file on the attorney or party's behalf. Only one such form may be filed in any NYSCEF case. Any NYSCEF User shall immediately contact the NYSCEF Resource Center if they have reason to believe their user identification or password may have been compromised, and may request a new user identification or password.

D. *Cases Eligible for E–Filing*: In Westchester County, e-filing is available in certain case types on a voluntary basis but will become mandatory in certain cases at a later date. The schedule for expansion of electronic filing in Westchester County follows:

1. Voluntary Electronic Filing:

a. Presently: Cases eligible for assignment to the Commercial Division pursuant to 22 N.Y.C.R.R. 202.70 (a) and Tax Certiorari Proceedings may be commenced electronically or in hard copy with conversion to NYSCEF status upon filing of the consent. Tax certiorari filings via the NYSCEF system shall be limited to actions and proceedings commenced in Westchester County.

b. Beginning on January 19, 2011: Tort cases (as defined in Section I(D)(3)(a) below) and commercial cases (as defined in Section I(D)(3)(b) below) may be commenced either electronically or in hard copy with conversion to NYSCEF status upon filing of the consent.

c. Consenting to Electronic Filing: The procedure for obtaining consent for voluntary electronic filing is set forth in Uniform Rule §202.5-b(b)(2). In general, consent shall be obtained by stipulation or by the service of a Notice of Availability of E-Filing (Form EF-3 on the NYSCEF website) responded to by the filing of Consent to E-Filing (Form EF-6 on the NYSCEF website) by all other parties.

d. Paper Documents Not Accepted: Unless otherwise provided by the Uniform Rules or this Protocol, in any case that is subject to e-filing by consent of the parties, all documents required to be filed with the court must be electronically filed. Any such document that is submitted in hard copy form without a Notice of Hard Copy Submission – E-filed Case attached as a cover sheet will not be accepted by the Clerk.

2. Mandatory Electronic Filing: All mandatory e-filed cases must be commenced electronically beginning on the dates set forth below. Unless otherwise provided by the Uniform Rules, the County Clerk will not accept commencement documents in paper form in these cases nor will the court accept

subsequent documents in such matters in paper form. If a party wishes to commence a case under seal or under an anonymous caption, the party should contact the Office of the Chief Clerk of the Court before filing any documents.

a. Beginning on or about February 1, 2011: Cases eligible for assignment to the Commercial Division pursuant to 22 N.Y.C.R.R. 202.70 (a) must be commenced electronically.

b. Beginning on or about March 1, 2011: Tort actions (as defined in Section I(D)(3)(a) below) must be commenced electronically.

c. Beginning on or about June 1, 2011: Commercial actions (as defined in Section I(D)(3)(b) below) must be commenced electronically.

d. Exemptions from Electronic Filing in Mandatory Actions: An exemption from having to file and serve documents electronically may be claimed by an attorney or a party not represented by an attorney by filing the form prescribed by the Chief Administrator (www.nycourts.gov/efile). If an attorney or self-represented party is exempt from participation in e-filing in accordance with the Uniform Rules, any document filed with the court in hard copy form by that person must bear a completed Notice of Hard Copy Submission – E-filed Case indicating that the document is exempt from mandatory e-filing. Any emergency filing made in hard copy in accordance with the Uniform Rules must also bear a completed Notice of Hard Copy Submission – E-Filed Case. Please note that the emergency filing procedures set forth in the Uniform Rules refer to statutory deadlines and not deadlines as set by the court. Further, under the Uniform Rules, the filer must electronically file the documents initially filed in hard copy form within three business days of the emergency filing. The originals will be discarded after the documents have been processed so failure to electronically file as required will lead to an incomplete record.

e. Rejection of Hard Copy Filings: In accordance with Uniform Rule §202.5(d)(1), the County Clerk shall refuse to accept for filing hard copy papers filed in an action subject to electronic filing unless hard copy filing is permitted by the Uniform Rules and the papers bear a Notice of Hard Copy Filing Submission – E-filed Case. Equipment will be available in the 9th floor courthouse library for use by filers with hard copy submissions so that such papers can be electronically filed.

3. Action Types Defined:

a. Tort Actions Defined: For the purposes of these protocols, and subject to any amendments hereof, "tort actions" shall mean cases in which only money damages are sought and that arise out of or allege:

    i. motor vehicle accidents, product liability claims, injuries to persons or property, wrongful death, mass tort, or medical, dental or podiatric malpractice;

    ii. other professional malpractice;

    iii. damages to persons or property from environmental conditions;

    iv. a primary claim for money damages based upon negligence, defamation, intentional infliction of emotional distress or other intentional harm, or other wrong founded in tort;

    v. but excluding any actions alleging tortious interference with contract, tortious interference with pre-contractual relations, business torts, fraudulent or negligent misrepresentation, or other tortious actions listed in section 202.70(b) of the Uniform Rules.

b. Commercial Cases Defined: For the purposes of these protocols, and subject to any amendments hereof, "commercial cases" shall mean the following classes of cases provided that the amount in controversy (exclusive of punitive damages, interest, costs, disbursements and counsel fees claimed) is over $100,000, regardless of whether cases eligible hereunder are also eligible for assignment to the Commercial Division:

    i. Breach of contract (regardless of amount in controversy) or fiduciary duty, fraud, misrepresentation, business tort (including but not limited to actions involving claims of unfair competition), or statutory and/or common law violation where the breach or violation is alleged to arise out of business dealings (including but not limited to sales of assets or securities; corporate restructuring; partnership, shareholder, joint venture, and other business agreements; trade secrets; restrictive covenants; and employment agreements not including claims that principally involve alleged discriminatory practices);

    ii. Transactions governed by the uniform commercial code (exclusive of those concerning individual cooperative or condominium units);

    iii. Transactions involving commercial real property, including Yellowstone injunctions and excluding actions for the payment of rent only;

    iv. Shareholder derivative actions, without consideration of the monetary threshold;

    v. Commercial class actions, without consideration of the monetary threshold;

    vi. Business transactions involving or arising out of dealings with commercial banks and other financial institutions;

    vii. Internal affairs of business organizations;

    viii. Malpractice by accountants or actuaries, and legal malpractice arising out of representation in commercial matters;

    ix. Environmental insurance coverage;

x. Commercial insurance coverage (including but not limited to directors and officers, errors and omissions, and business interruption coverage);

xi. Dissolution of corporations, partnerships, limited liability companies, limited liability partnerships and joint ventures, without consideration of the monetary threshold; and

xii. Applications to stay or compel arbitration and affirm or disaffirm arbitration awards and related injunctive relief pursuant to article 75 of the civil practice law and rules involving any of the foregoing enumerated commercial issues, without consideration of the monetary threshold.

Provided, however, the following cases are not included:

i. Actions to collect professional fees;

ii. Actions seeking a declaratory judgment as to insurance coverage for personal injury or property damage;

iii. Residential real estate disputes, including landlord-tenant matters, and commercial real estate disputes involving the payment of rent only;

iv. Proceedings to enforce a judgment regardless of the nature of the underlying case;

v. First-party insurance claims and actions by insurers to collect premiums or rescind non-commercial policies.

II. Identifying E–Filed Cases. E-filed cases must be readily identifiable and marked as such. Whenever counsel presents papers to the Office of the Westchester County Clerk or the Court Clerk in a NYSCEF matter, counsel should alert the Clerk that the case is a NYSCEF matter. Further:

A. *When commenced via NYSCEF:* Cases that are commenced by the filing of initial papers with the NYSCEF system are identified as e-filed cases by assignment of an index number beginning with 50,000, regardless of case type. In addition, an identifying action code of "e" shall follow the index number. Upon filing of the commencement pleadings and payment of the statutory fee, the Westchester County Clerk as Clerk of the Supreme and County Courts will assign a NYSCEF designated Index Number and notify the filer via the NYSCEF system of the number assigned and filing date. Such index number must be affixed to all document submissions, filings and communications to the Westchester County Clerk as Clerk of the Supreme and County Courts and the Court.

B. *When converted to NYSCEF:* Cases originally commenced in hard-copy form but later converted to NYSCEF status consensually will retain the initially issued index number, but the County Clerk will add the identifying action code of "e" following the index number. This suffix serves only as identification and is not formally a part of the index number assigned by the County Clerk.

C. *Attorneys must put "e" on all filings:* Attorneys must use the identifying action code of "e" after the index number on all submissions filed with the court in electronically-filed matters.

III. Filing of Papers.

A. *Payment of Fees:* Payment for fee-bearing NYSCEF documents may be made online via credit card (MasterCard or Visa) at the time of submission. In addition, fee payment may be made in person at the Office of the Westchester County Clerk via credit card (American Express, Discover, MasterCard or Visa), debit card (with a MasterCard or Visa logo only), attorney's check, bank check, money order or cash. Once the NYSCEF system accepts American Express and Automated Clearing House (ACH) or electronic check debits, the option to pay at the Office of the Westchester County Clerk will no longer be available in Westchester County.

1. Effect of Payment: Pursuant to CPLR §304, a document is not filed until payment of the fee has been tendered. If payment is going to be made in the office, payment shall be made within two (2) business days from the date the document is received on the NYSCEF server. If payment is not received within two (2) business days, the document(s) will be rejected and deemed not filed.

2. Effect of Refused Payment: If for any reason or at any time the fee payment is returned or refused, the filer will be required to pay the document fee. Failure to pay or a reoccurring payment return notification will result in the filer being reported to the Court and the Unified Court System for further action.

B. *Filing a Document Where Size, Consistency or Context Prevent E–Filing:* With limited exceptions as set forth in the Uniform Rules and herein, all documents to be filed with the court in a NYSCEF case shall be filed online via the NYSCEF system. However, should the size, consistency or context of a hard copy document preclude its electronic filing, the user shall electronically file a Notice of Hard Copy Filing (www.nycourts.gov/efile). Any hard copy submitted pursuant to this section shall include, as a cover page firmly fastened thereto, a copy of the Confirmation Notice received from the NYSCEF site confirming receipt of the Notice of Hard Copy Filing. Any party may object to such hard copy filing, and the Court, in response to such objection, may, following the hard copy filing, fashion such relief as it deems appropriate pursuant to and in furtherance of the Uniform Rules and these protocols, including, but not limited to, an Order directing the filing party to file such documents online via the NYSCEF system.

C. *Social Security Numbers:* An attorney or self-represented party filing a document via the NYSCEF system must comply with the requirements of General Business Law §399-dd(6), which will often require redaction of any social security number that appears in the original document.

D. *Exhibits*: In the NYSCEF system, each exhibit should be uploaded as a separate PDF file. After uploading a primary document, please choose the document type "Exhibit", enter the appropriate number or letter, and be sure to place a check mark to the right of "Attach to main document".

E. *Errors Upon Submission*: Submission of documents which, upon examination, require correction or addition will result in notification to the filer advising that there is a problem with a document. The filer shall make the required corrections and/or additions and transmit the corrected document.

F. *Technical Failures*: When filing by electronic means is hindered by a technical failure (as set forth in Uniform Rule §202.5-b(h)(3)(i)), a party may file with the appropriate Clerk in hard copy. With the exception of deadlines that by law cannot be extended (e.g., a statute of limitations or the deadline for filing a notice of appeal), the time for filing of any document that is delayed due to technical failure of the NYSCEF system shall be extended for one day for each day on which such failure occurs, unless otherwise ordered by the court.

G. *Correspondence*: Correspondence, only as expressly permitted by part rules, must be filed and transmitted to other parties via the NYSCEF system. No duplicate copies of the correspondence shall be provided to the court by either fax or mail.

H. *Discovery Materials*: In any action subject to electronic filing, parties and non-parties producing materials in response to discovery demands may enter into a stipulation authorizing the electronic filing of discovery responses and discovery materials to the degree and upon terms and conditions set forth in the stipulation. In the absence of such a stipulation, no party shall file electronically any such materials except in the form of excerpts, quotations, or selected exhibits from such materials as part of motion papers, pleadings or other filings with the court unless otherwise specified by statute, rule or part rule.

I. *Notice of Entry*: Pursuant to the NYSCEF Rules, the Court Clerk shall file orders electronically and such filing shall constitute entry of the order. The NYSCEF system will provide notification that the order has been entered. Such notice does not constitute service of notice of entry by any party. Notice of Entry is served by a party as follows: the party shall transmit electronically to the parties to be served a notice of entry, a copy of the notification received from the court, and a copy of the order or judgment.

J. *Working Copies*: Electronically filed documents subject to review and processing by the Civil Calendar Clerk's office do not require a working copy unless otherwise directed or provided for in part rules. Any working copy without a Confirmation Notice generat-

ed by the NYSCEF system firmly fastened thereto as a cover page will not be accepted.

1. Filing Must Precede Delivery of Working Copies: Pursuant to Uniform Rule §202.5-b, any working copy submitted shall include, as a cover page firmly fastened thereto, a copy of the Confirmation Notice received from the NYSCEF site. Court staff will not screen each working copy to be sure that it is an accurate reflection of the document filed via NYSCEF. Should counsel fail to file a document with NYSCEF, that document will not be part of the County Clerk's file.

2. Format of Working Copies: Working copies must contain tabs and backs. Each document or group of documents that is separately bound must have a Confirmation Notice firmly fastened thereto as a cover page.

3. Working Copies Not Accepted by the County Clerk: Working copies are not accepted by the Office of the Westchester County Clerk for forwarding to the assigned IAS Justice, nor are they received and filed as part of the case file maintained by the Westchester County Clerk in his capacity as Clerk of the Supreme and County Courts.

4. Printing of Working Copies: Working hard copy documents, when required by the assigned IAS Justice or by rules of procedure, are not printed and provided by the Office of the Westchester County Clerk or the Civil Calendar Clerk's office.

5. Delivery of Working Copies: All working copy documents shall be delivered to the court part of the assigned IAS Justice or in the manner directed by the court. Filers must familiarize themselves with part rules to determine whether working copies are permitted. Working copies submitted by mail or overnight delivery must be conspicuously marked on the outside of the package – "Working Copy".

6. Working Copies Discarded: The official record of a document in an electronically filed case is the document filed via the NYSCEF system. Working copies are intended only for use by the Justice. The court will discard all working copies after the Justice has finished with them. Thus, in the event that counsel fails to file a document via the NYSCEF system, the document will not be part of the court record.

IV. Preliminary Conferences. For actions in the preliminary conference part, in lieu of making an appearance at a scheduled preliminary conference, all parties in a NYSCEF case may agree upon a discovery schedule and submit an appropriate preliminary conference form order stipulated to by all parties (http://www.nycourts.gov/courts/9jd/diffCaseMgmt/Pre ConfForm_Rev122409.pdf) as a Proposed Stipulation to be So Ordered – Preliminary Conference in the NYSCEF system at least two days prior to the conference date. The discovery schedule therein set forth must be in compliance with the disclosure guidelines for a case of the type in question as set forth in Uniform Rule 202.19. No further action by counsel is required. The signed preliminary conference order will be posted on the NYSCEF site, and counsel will be notified via the NYSCEF system. If the contents of the form submitted are not acceptable to the court, counsel will be contacted. See Uniform Rule 202.12(b).

V.   Requests for Judicial Intervention (RJIs). A RJI in a NYSCEF case shall be filed via the NYS-CEF system. Any attachments to an RJI, with the exception of a motion or order to show cause, shall be submitted along with the RJI as one PDF file.

A.   *Tort Actions*: In a tort action, if an RJI is accompanied by a Notice of Medical Malpractice, the filer should choose document type RJI re: Notice of Medical Malpractice and both documents should be uploaded as one PDF file in the NYSCEF system. If an RJI is accompanied by a Request for a Preliminary Conference, the filer should choose document type RJI re: PC Request and both documents should be uploaded as one PDF file in the NYSCEF system.

B.   *Commercial Division Assignments*: In the case of an RJI seeking assignment to the Commercial Division, the filer must submit, as required by the standards for assignment of cases to the Commercial Division (Uniform Rule 202.70 (d)(2)), an attorney's certification in support of the assignment (http://www. nycourts.gov/courts/comdiv/PDFs/WestchesterForm. pdf) and a copy of the pleadings. The RJI, certification in support of the assignment, and pleadings should be uploaded as one PDF file in the NYSCEF system.

C.   *Tax Certiorari Proceedings*: In the case of an RJI accompanying a petition to commence a Tax Certiorari proceeding, neither document is forwarded to the court for calendaring purposes. Said filings shall remain with the Westchester County Clerk as Clerk of the Supreme and County Courts and entered into the casebook as required by CPLR §9702(2). The filing of commencement pleadings institutes precalendaring activities as prescribed by the Uniform Rule 202.59.

VI.   Motions. Motion submission, including cross motions, shall comply with all relevant provisions of the CPLR, the Rules of the Court, the Commercial Division Rules (22 NYCRR 202.70), the Practice Guide to the Commercial Division, the Differentiated Case Management Protocol and part rules.

A.   *General*: A motion on notice or a notice of petition in a NYSCEF case shall be filed through the NYSCEF system and, except regarding a notice of petition commencing a Tax Certiorari Action, must be accompanied by a Request for Judicial Intervention if the motion is being filed upon commencement or if the matter has not yet been assigned to an IAS Justice. In addition, cross motions and opposition and reply papers must be submitted via the NYSCEF system.

1.   Tort Actions: A party seeking to make a discovery motion shall do so in accordance with the Differentiated Case Management Protocol and via the NYSCEF system by initially filing a Request for Pre-Motion Conference (Compliance Part) via the NYSCEF system. As substantive motions do not require a pre-motion conference, they may be filed via the NYSCEF system and will be referred to an IAS Justice. Notification will be forwarded through the NYSCEF system upon the assignment of an IAS Justice. Please review the Differentiated Case Management Protocol and IAS part rules for additional information about motion practice.

2.   Commercial Division: Pursuant to the Commercial Division Rules (22 NYCRR 202.70) and the Practice Guide to the Commercial Division, no motion shall be made, except as allowed by Rule 24 of the Commercial Division Rules, without a pre-motion conference with the court. Pre-motion conference requests shall be made via telephone to chambers at (914) 824-5419 rather than via the NYSCEF system. All motions for summary judgment shall be made via the NYSCEF System and shall be accompanied by the document type Statement of Material Facts pursuant to Rule 19-a of the Commercial Division Rules. No reply papers are permitted where the motion is brought by Order to Show Cause unless previously authorized by the Court. Use the "Special Instructions" field in the NYSCEF system to reference court authorization of reply papers.

B.   *Calendaring of Motion*: After a motion or notice of petition is filed with the NYSCEF system, the fee accepted by the County Clerk and the submission reviewed by court staff, the matter will be placed on the appropriate calendar.

1.   Tort Actions: When filing a discovery motion which shall be made by Order to Show Cause in the NYSCEF system, you may utilize the "Special Instructions" field to reference the Briefing Schedule in accordance with which the motion is being made. Oral argument will be heard and appearances are required. Substantive motions shall be made returnable and heard in the IAS parts in accordance with the part rules. Please refer to part rules to determine whether an appearance is required and utilize the "Special Instructions" field in the NYSCEF system to incorporate appropriate instructions.

2.   Commercial Division: When filing your motion in the NYSCEF system, enter a Friday return date. Motions made returnable at any other time, absent prior permission of the Court, will be adjourned by the Part Clerk to the next available Friday. Motions are submitted without appearances unless otherwise directed by the Court.

3.   Tax Certiorari/Condemnation Part: When filing a motion in the NYSCEF system, enter a

Wednesday return date. No appearance is required unless notified by the Clerk.

C. *Adjournments*: Motions that have been electronically filed may be adjourned only if an adjournment complies with any directives of the assigned Justice or relevant part rules. If an attorney wishes to submit a stipulation regarding an adjournment to be "so ordered", such stipulation should be filed via the NYSCEF system. Attorneys should not assume a request for an adjournment submitted by stipulation has been granted until and unless the Court approves and so-orders the same.

1. Tort Actions: A party seeking an adjournment shall do so in accordance with the Differentiated Case Management Protocol and via the NYSCEF system by choosing the following NYSCEF document type: Correspondence (Request for Adjournment).

2. Commercial Division: Adjournments are governed by Rule 16(c) of the Commercial Division Rules and the court's practice guide. In addition, pursuant to the court's practice guide, requests for adjournment of matters appearing on the Friday calendar should be made no later than 3 p.m. on Thursday. Requests for adjournments should be on consent and, if approved by the Court, confirmed by a signed stipulation by all counsel. Such stipulation must be filed via the NYSCEF system and designated as a Stipulation to Adjourn Motion.

3. Tax Certiorari/Condemnation Part: A party seeking an adjournment shall do so in accordance with part rules and via the NYSCEF system by choosing the following NYSCEF document type: Correspondence (Request for Adjournment).

D. *Exhibits*: In the NYSCEF system, each motion exhibit should be uploaded as a separate PDF file. After uploading motion papers, please choose the document type "Exhibit", enter the appropriate number or letter, and place a check mark to the left of "Attach to main document".

E. *Working Copies*: Please see Section III (J) above regarding working copies.

F. *Affidavits of Service*: All affidavits of service must be filed with the NYSCEF system in compliance with statutory requirements or pursuant to the directive of the court.

G. *Decisions*: Decisions and/or orders issued will be scanned by court staff into the NYSCEF system, which will immediately transmit notice of the event via the NYSCEF system to all parties and a link to the decision and/or order. In the case of orders, this notice does not constitute service of notice of entry by any party (See Section III (J) for more information regarding Notice of Entry).

VII. Orders to Show Cause. Proposed Orders to Show Cause (hereinafter "OTSC") shall comply with all relevant provisions of the CPLR, the Uniform Rules, Commercial Division Rule 20 (22 NYCRR 202.70), Uniform Rule 202.7(f) and the Differentiated Case Management Protocol regarding notice of the application to the opposing party. Those OTSCs in which interim relief is sought require prior notice in accordance with the aforementioned rules. Counsel must contact chambers to set up a time to be heard as to the interim relief requested.

A. *General*: Except as provided in the following paragraph, a proposed OTSC and supporting documents in a NYSCEF case must be submitted by filing with the NYSCEF system. Original documents will not be accepted by the County Clerk.

B. *Hard Copy Submission*: If a party seeking a TRO submits an affirmation/affidavit demonstrating significant prejudice from the giving of notice (see Uniform Rule 202.7(f) and Commercial Division Rule 20) or if a party seeks to submit documents in an emergency in a mandatory e-filed case in accordance with the Uniform Rules, the proposed OTSC and supporting documents may be presented to the Commercial Division Clerk in commercial cases and the Calendar Clerk's Office (9th floor) in hard copy form. The papers must have affixed thereto a completed Notice of Hard Copy Submission – E-Filed Case. A proposed OTSC and supporting documents that must be presented to a Justice outside of normal court hours shall be presented in hard copy. Documents submitted in hard copy form must thereafter be filed via the NYSCEF system pursuant to the Uniform Rules.

C. *Review*: Absent unusual practical difficulties, a proposed OTSC and supporting documents that have been filed with NYSCEF will be reviewed through the NYSCEF system by the Court. If there are problems with the documents, the submitting attorney will be promptly contacted by e-mail or telephone.

D. *Working Copies*: Counsel should consult relevant part rules to determine whether a working copy of the proposed OTSC and the supporting documents must be submitted.

E. *Hard Copy Service*: In cases in which hard copy service is made of documents that were submitted in hard copy form pursuant to paragraph VII(B) and where no party is served electronically, the filing attorney or party shall, not later than two days after service, electronically file the OTSC and the supporting papers, together with proof of hard copy service.

F. *Declination*: If the Justice declines to sign the OTSC, the Clerk will electronically file the declined order. If the proposed OTSC and supporting documents were filed with the court in hard copy form, the filing attorney or party shall file the supporting documents with NYSCEF no later than two days after the filing by the Clerk.

G. *Exhibits*: In the NYSCEF system, each exhibit to an OTSC should be uploaded as a separate PDF file. After uploading the OTSC, please choose the document type "Exhibit", enter the appropriate number or letter, and be sure to place a check mark to the left of "Attach to main document".

H. *Other*: Any OTSC not filed in accordance with the Uniform Rules and part rules will not be addressed by the part.

VIII. Sealed Documents and Secure Documents.

In order to seal a document in a NYSCEF case, a party must proceed in accordance with Part 216 of the Uniform Rules for the Trial Courts. If concerns exist with respect to confidential information in the request to the Court, the submitting party should submit the request as a secure document via the NYSCEF website.

A. *Secure Documents*: Documents may be designated as "Secure" by the filer without an order of the court. The effect of such designation is that the document may be viewed in the NYSCEF system only by counsel and self-represented parties to the case who have consented to NYSCEF and by the court and the County Clerk. The electronic file, however, remains open for public inspection at the Office of the Westchester County Clerk.

B. *Application for a Sealing Order*: If a party wishes to file and maintain papers under seal and no sealing order has been issued in the case, the party must, either by motion or on submission to the court of a stipulation, obtain a court order directing the County Clerk to seal the file. The court will conduct a Part 216 analysis in deciding whether to issue such an order. If the motion/stipulation is filed via the NYSCEF system, it will be open to the public until a sealing order is served upon the County Clerk. If this creates concern for the parties about the release of confidential information while the application is pending, they may wish to consider filing the motion/stipulation as a "secure" document (See Section VIII(A) above). Alternatively, the parties may make a motion or submit a stipulation without filing it to the NYSCEF system until the court rules on the sealing issue. Any such motion or stipulation submitted in hard copy form must bear a Notice of Hard Copy Submission – E-Filed Case and must be accompanied by a CD, DVD or other acceptable electronic storage device containing the filings in PDF format. Any opposition or reply papers shall likewise be submitted in hard copy form with such Notice, and be accompanied by a disk containing the documents in PDF format. Each such disk shall bear a label containing the name of the case, the index number, and the name and e-mail address of the attorney submitting it.

C. *Sealing Existing NYSCEF Document*: If the court issues an order directing the sealing of an existing NYSCEF file or a document or documents already filed via the NYSCEF system, the applicant shall file with the NYSCEF system a Notification for Sealing in Electronically Filed Case, a form for which

is available at www.nycourts.gov/efile, along with a copy of the order as required by CPLR §8019(c). The County Clerk will seal the file or document(s) in question as directed by the court. In addition, service should include a reference, if applicable, to any hard copy filings that may exist for the sealed case in question. Upon receipt of the notification, the Clerk shall seal the documents in question and implement a secure action code to prevent access to these documents except by the parties to the action and the court.

D. *Previously Sealed Documents in Converted Cases*: If a case that was previously sealed pursuant to court order is converted to NYSCEF status, attorneys for the parties to the action or proceeding shall notify the Westchester County Clerk as Clerk of the Supreme and County Courts of the sealing status. Notification shall consist of an e-mail in a format promulgated by the Clerk for such purposes and attached thereto shall be a copy of the original sealing order.

E. *Identifying Sealed Documents*: Further, submission of documents sealed via court order or by operation of law shall be clearly labeled as SEALED on the title page of the document submitted and, wherein applicable, be accompanied by a copy of the court order directing or permitting the sealing of same.

IX. Note of Issue.

A. *Tort Actions*: No Note of Issue may be filed via the NYSCEF system without a compliance conference at which time a trial readiness order will be issued. Alternatively, in lieu of an appearance, the parties may submit via the NYSCEF system document type: Trial Readiness Stipulation (http://www.nycourts.gov/courts/9jd/diffCaseMgmt/TrialReadyStip_2_10_10.pdf) pursuant to the Differentiated Case Management Protocol and a trial readiness order shall be issued and uploaded to the NYSCEF system.

B. *Commercial Division*: No Note of Issue may be filed via the NYSCEF system without a trial readiness conference at which a trial readiness order will be issued and uploaded to the NYSCEF system.

C. *Tax Certiorari Proceedings*: The filing of a Note of Issue in Tax Certiorari proceedings shall not occur via the NYSCEF system unless all disclosure proceedings, except as hereinafter set forth, have been completed. Any statement of income and expenses in such proceedings, as provided for pursuant to Uniform Rule §202.59 (22 NYCRR 202.59) must be served upon the respondent prior to filing of the Note of Issue. Upon service of said Note of Issue in such proceedings, the respondent may request an audit as similarly provided for in Uniform Rule §202.59. Prior to any trial of said proceedings, the Court may also require the exchange of pre-trial memoranda and/or trial property appraisals by the parties to such proceedings.

X. Consolidation or Joint Trial. Consolidation or joint trial of proceedings shall be at the discretion of the court. In the case of consolidation of tax certiorari proceedings, all pleadings containing multiple index numbers for multiple tax years shall be entered into the Clerk of the Court's casebook bearing the first year NYSCEF index number assigned unless directed otherwise by the court.

XI. Judgments.

A. *General Procedures*: In order to expedite entry, filers are advised to submit judgments through the NYSCEF system as single transactions, and not combined with any other unrelated filings or transactions.

1. Submission: A party seeking the entry of a judgment must submit a Bill of Costs, interest calculation, any necessary supporting information or a judgment roll as defined by CPLR §5017. If the entry of a judgment is based upon a Decision and Order or Stipulation of Settlement, the submission must also contain a copy of the same pursuant to CPLR §5016(c) or CPLR §3215(i) respectively. The statement for judgment must contain the addresses of the debtor(s) and creditor(s) in order to be docketed by the Clerk as required by CPLR §5018(c)(1).

2. Examination: The Judgment Clerk will examine the submission for entry. If the submission is deficient, the deficiencies will be communicated to the submitter via the NYSCEF system. Once corrected, the judgment should be resubmitted via the NYSCEF system.

3. Notification of Entry: Once the judgment is entered, notification will be sent via the NYSCEF system to the submitting party. Entry consists of both entry as defined by CPLR §5016(a) and recordation of any required statutory fee. Such notification shall not constitute service of Notice of Entry, but instead only notification of entry of the judgment. It shall be the responsibility of the submitting party to serve Notice of Entry on all parties.

B. *Entry of Default Judgments*: A party seeking the entry of a default judgment by the Clerk pursuant to CPLR §3215 shall choose the following NYSCEF document type: Clerk Default Judgment (Proposed). If the bill of costs is not included on the judgment itself, the filer must choose the Bill of Costs document type and file it as a separate document. The filing fee is forty-five dollars ($45) unless entry is predicated upon a not heretofore filed Stipulation of Settlement, in which case the fee is thirty-five dollars ($35). If the entry of the judgment is conditioned upon a previously filed Stipulation or a Decision and Order, in which case no fee is due.

C. *Judgment Signed by the Court*: As prescribed by Uniform Rule §202.5-b(d)5, a party seeking the entry of a judgment signed by the court shall choose the following NYSCEF document type: Judgment – To Court (Proposed). The judgment shall comply with statutory requirements and all necessary supporting pleadings must be filed as separate documents. A working copy of the submission should only be provided to the assigned Justice if indicated in part rules. Upon signature by the court, a copy will be forwarded to the County Clerk for taxation and interest calculation and converted into electronic format. Notification of entry will be transmitted by e-mail to the filer pursuant to Uniform Rule 202.5-b(h)3, and such notice shall not constitute service of notice of entry. Individual court part rules regarding the submission of judgments must be complied with in addition to statutory requirements and protocols.

D. *Judgments on Notice*:

1. Judgment to be Signed by the Court: Judgments submitted on Notice to the court should comply with specific direction as provided in the order directing same, or be in compliance with Uniform Rule 202.48. A party submitting a Judgment on Notice shall choose the following NYSCEF document type: Judgment – To Court (Proposed)and a working copy of the submission should only be submitted if provided in part rules.

2. Judgment Entered by the Clerk: A party submitting a Judgment on Notice to the Clerk via the NYSCEF system should choose the following document type: Judgment – To Clerk (Proposed). The Judgment on Notice must be submitted five (5) days prior to the settlement date, and must include all necessary supporting pleadings to allow entry.

3. Objections: Opposing counsel may object to the taxation of costs and disbursements by submitting the document type Objections to Taxation/Notice of Re Taxation in the NYSCEF system.

4. Entry: Upon entry by the Judgment Clerk, notification of entry shall be communicated via the NYSCEF system by the Clerk to the filer, and the in cases of objections, to objecting counsel. Notification of entry shall not constitute service of notice of entry to or for any party.

E. *Taxation Review*: A party submitting an application to the County Clerk to review taxation of costs without notice pursuant to CPLR §8403 via the NYSCEF system shall submit document type Objections to Taxation/Notice of Re Taxation within the statutory time provided. Determination of review will be communicated to both filer and opposing counsel via the NYSCEF system by the Judgment Clerk.

F. *Confession of Judgment*: Entry of judgment by confession shall adhere to statutory requirements of CPLR §3218.

1. Submission: A party seeking the entry of judgment by confession via the NYSCEF system shall choose the document types Confession of Judgment (Affidavit of Defendant) and Confession of Judgment for the statement. A statutory fee of two hundred and ten dollars ($210) for the assign-

ment of an Index Number is required, unless the affidavit is executed in conjunction with a pre-existing Westchester County action. The statement for judgment must be submitted simultaneously with the affidavit, and judgment entered immediately thereupon the filing of the affidavit.

2. Venue: Venue is properly based in Westchester County upon either the residence of the confessor at the time of execution of the affidavit, or upon express authorization as contained in the affidavit.

3. Entry: Notification will be communicated via the NYSCEF system to the filer upon entry. Such notification shall not constitute service of Notice of Entry, but instead only notification of entry of the judgment. It shall be the responsibility of the submitting party to serve Notice of Entry on all parties.

G. *Docketing Judgments in Tax Certiorari Proceedings*: In Tax Certiorari proceedings, judgments shall be docketed only in the Declaratory Judgment program as promulgated by the Westchester County Clerk as Clerk of the Supreme and County Courts to satisfy compliance with CPLR §9705(5) when said judgments do not contain provision for costs and disbursements. If judgments do contain provision for costs and disbursements, the judgments will be additionally docketed in the Monetary Judgment program as promulgated by the Westchester County Clerk as Clerk of the Supreme and County Courts to satisfy compliance with CPLR §5018. In both instances, judgments will be docketed bearing the first year NYSCEF case number assigned unless directed otherwise by the Court.

H. *Subsequent Judgment or Order*: When a previously entered judgment is affected by a subsequent order or judgment, the Clerk will make the appropriate notation to the docket entry as required by CPLR §5019(b).

1. New or Amended Judgments: In instances wherein the change to an entered judgment is the result of a new or amended judgment, the notation will be made simultaneously with the entry of the new or amended judgment, and notification of same will be transmitted via the NYSCEF system to the submitting party.

2. Order: In instances wherein the change to an entered judgment is the result of an order, notation of the docket will not be made until proper notice is given to the County Clerk pursuant to CPLR §8019(c). A party seeking the modification of a judgment by order shall choose document type CPLR 8019(c) Notification to Amend Docket which must include as part of the attached PDF file a copy of the order directing the Clerk to note the docket.

XII. Notice of Appeal and Appeal Papers. A Notice of Appeal shall be filed online in a NYSCEF case and the fee paid as set forth above. The Notice of Appeal will not be considered filed until the payment of the fee has been accepted by the Westchester County Clerk as Clerk of the Supreme and County Courts. The Notice shall be filed in conformity with existing rules, and shall contain the Request for Appellate Division Intervention (RADI) form as required by the Appellate Division. The other parties to the case may be served via the NYSCEF system in the manner described above. Proof of hard copy service must be filed via NYSCEF. At present, the Appellate Division does not handle appeals in NYSCEF cases by electronic means. As such, the appellant shall be responsible for conversion of electronic submissions to hard copy. The Office of the Westchester County Clerk will not provide hardcopies of filed documents to constitute the record. Upon disposition of the appeal, the party that prevails on appeal must upload a copy of the appellate decision in the NYSCEF system.

XIII. Other.

A. *Effect of Communication from the Office of the Westchester County Clerk*: Any and all e-mail notifications from the Westchester County Clerk as Clerk of the Supreme and County Courts shall not be construed or considered to be service of notice of entry for purposes of commencement of the statutory time to appeal or otherwise. Such communications from the Clerk shall constitute and serve only as notification of receipt or entry in a ministerial capacity.

B. *Appearances*: Electronically filed documents subject to review and processing by the Calendar Clerk's Office do not require an appearance by counsel unless otherwise directed or provided for in local rules of practice.

C. *Support*: Any attorney who requires assistance in a NYSCEF case is encouraged to contact the part with questions about individual part rules or to contact the E-filing Resource Center at 646-386-3033 with any questions about the NYSCEF system. In addition, a computer and scanner will be made available in the 9th floor courthouse law library for the use of attorneys who may need assistance in making filings in a NYSCEF case.

TENTH JUDICIAL DISTRICT — NASSAU AND SUFFOLK COUNTIES

Westlaw Electronic Research

These rules may be searched electronically on Westlaw® *in the NY–RULES database; updates to these rules may be found on* Westlaw *in NY–RULESUP-DATES. For search tips and a summary of database content, consult the* Westlaw *Scope Screens for each database.*

NASSAU COUNTY
SUPREME COURT

DEPARTMENTAL RULES AND PROCEDURES

Doc. 1. Motion Support Office

Papers to be filed in commencing an action or special proceeding in the Supreme Court should be brought to the clerk of the Supreme Court, which is the Nassau County Clerk, 240 Old Country Road, Room 108, Mineola, NY. The phone number is (516) 571-2663). Any fees to be processed shall be paid to the Nassau County Clerk. The Special Term Clerk's Office cannot process any fees, nor accept any papers to commence an action.

Motions

All inquiries regarding the assignment of an IAS Justice, return date of a motion or a hearing, trial or conference date shall be directed to the Supreme Court Calendar Office, Room 186, (516) 571-3511. The information is also available by utilizing E–Courts or the Courts Website at www.courts.state.ny.us and navigating to the Future Case Appearance System.

Adjournments of motions on consent shall be directed to the clerk of the IAS Justice assigned. A letter confirming the adjournment, with a copy sent to the adversary, should be sent to the Justice's part once the adjournment has been granted.

All papers being submitted to the court shall have the index number, return date and the name of the assigned Justice on their face. All such papers such be submitted or addressed to the Supreme Court Calendar Office in Room 186.

All counsel are directed to submit self-addressed stamped envelopes with any motion papers in order to receive a copy of the court's decision.

Motion papers shall be filed with the Supreme Court Calendar Office in Room 186 at least five (5) business days before the return date.

Conforming Orders and Judgments

Certified copies of all orders and judgments can be obtained from the County Clerk's Office for a fee. Fees are set by the office of the Nassau County Clerk. Court employees will not conform orders or judgments. A self-addressed stamped postcard may be affixed to the order or judgment for the court to mail back when it has been signed.

Proposed Orders and Judgments with Motions on Notice

When submitting a proposed order or judgment, together with a Motion on Notice, such order or judgment is to be placed under a separate legal back. The affidavit of service shall indicate that the motion was served together with such order or judgment. Orders or judgments contained.

Doc. 2. Case Management (DCM)

Preliminary Conference Rules

When requesting a preliminary conference, please include the following:

a) Receipted RJI, an original and a copy.

b) Proof of service of RJI.

c) Request for preliminary conference.

d) Proof of service of the request for preliminary conference.

e) Commercial cases must include a copy of summons and complaint.

f) Commercial cases must include letter of justification for commercial division. *Uniform Rule 202.70 (d)(2)*.

Preliminary conferences will be calendared and held within 45 days of the filing of the RJI and preliminary conference request. Uniform Rule 202.12(b), 202.19(b). Adjournments can be granted to the extent the 45 day deadline is not surpassed.

All parties noticed on the RJI will be notified of the assigned judge, date, time, and place of the conference.

All initial discovery motions and preclusion motions will be converted to a preliminary conference and the motions will be marked withdrawn.

All preliminary conferences will be conducted by Differentiated Case Managers which will result in the case being assigned to a discovery track based on the complexity of the case and the amount of judicial intervention required. Uniform Rule 202.19(2).

The preliminary conference office is located in room 186 of the Supreme Court Building. Phone 516–571–3511.

Doc. 3. Orders to Show Cause Containing Temporary Restraining Orders

Starting October 1, 2006, the party seeking a TRO must comply with UCR 202.7 as follows:

Procedure for giving notice pursuant to Section 202.7 of the Uniform Civil Rules for the Supreme and County Court:

If you are seeking a temporary restraining order (TRO), you must comply with Section 202.7 of the Uniform Civil Rules for the Supreme and County Court. This rule provides that a party seeking a TRO from the Court must make good faith efforts to notify the party against whom the TRO is sought, of the time, date and place that the application will be made in a manner sufficient to permit the opposing party an opportunity to appear in response to the application. This notice requirement may be waived by the assigned Justice upon consideration of an affirmation demonstrating that there will be significant prejudice to the party seeking the restraining order by the giving of such notice.

In actions and proceedings pending before the Nassau County Supreme Court (exclusive of guardianship, matrimonial, and commercial matters), all motions which include a request for a TRO must be filed with the TRO Clerk in Room 186 of the Supreme Court in Mineola (Differentiated Case Management/Preliminary Conference Office). The Clerk will enter the motion into the Court's computer system and upon request, provide the movant with the name of the randomly assigned IAS Justice. The original application will be forwarded to the assigned Justice for all further purposes. The movant shall retain a copy of his or her application and shall contact the chambers of the assigned Justice to obtain all further instruction as it concerns the application and TRO.

Doc. 4. Emergency Orders to Show Cause

In emergency cases, notice may be given in advance. If no Justice has been assigned and emergency conditions exist, you may give 24 hours notice that the Order to Show Cause will be submitted to a Justice of the Supreme Court. A Justice will be assigned upon the presentation of the papers with a fee paid RJI.

If there is a Justice assigned, the attorney for the movant should contact the chambers of the assigned Justice in advance to prearrange a time and date for submission.

For Commercial Cases, the Order to Show Cause should be submitted to Room 186 of the Supreme Court, but will be held there until there is compliance with UCR 202.7/Commercial Rule 20. Notice under Commercial Rule 20 shall be given as follows:

Case assigned to:	Shall be noticed for submission:
Hon. Leonard B. Austin	at 9:30 AM or 2:30 PM
Hon. Ira B. Warshawsky	between 9:30—10:30 AM or 2:30—2:30 PM
Hon. Stephen A. Bucaria	at 10:00 AM or 2:00 PM

Attorneys requesting that the action be assigned to the Commercial Division must submit, along with the Order to Show Cause and supporting papers, a copy of the pleadings, the RJI with the commercial designation marked, and a brief signed statement justifying the Commercial Division designation.

Generally, compliance with Section 202.7 may be accomplished by providing the opposing parties or their attorneys with a copy of the proposed order, and the supporting affidavits/affirmations and exhibits, and a cover letter advising them that the annexed order is being presented to the assigned Justice on a time and date certain which was previously obtained from the chambers of the assigned Justice. Nothing in the new rule precludes the assigned Justice from denying the application in its entirety or from striking the request for the TRO and filing a return date on the motion prior to entertaining argument on the TRO.

Doc. 5. Supreme Court Matrimonial

All papers to be submitted on a matrimonial action (after payment of any requisite fees), should be brought to the Matrimonial Center, 400 County Seat Drive, Mineola, NY 11501 (Clerk's Office—2nd Floor—Room 219).

Please refer to the Matrimonial Center website at www.nycourts.govcourts/10jdnassaumatrimonialindex. shtml for further information, including contact numbers, procedures and rules and searchable transmittal reports of matrimonial orders and judgments sent to the County Clerk for entry.

Orders of Protection

When an application is made for an *ex parte* order of protection, the applying party, together with counsel if so represented, shall be present in court at the time of the application, and shall remain available to give testimony if the presiding Justice determines it necessary. Notice to the other party of a hearing on the application may be required at the discretion of the court.

On all applications for an order of protection, a completed Family Protection Registry Information Sheet shall be required. An affidavit in support of such an application shall inform the court whether there has been any prior orders of protection issued between the parties and whether or not they are still in effect.

Doc. 6. Article 81 Mental Hygiene Law

Guardianships

All papers being submitted in Article 81 M.H.L. guardianship proceedings are to be delivered to the

Supreme Court, Guardianship Department, Room 152 after payment of the required fee{s}, if any. All papers submitted shall have the index number, return date and assigned Justice on the face of the paper{s}. All orders to show cause being submitted for signature shall have the attorney's fax number on the blue back and a copy will be faxed to the attorney by the Clerk's Office after the order to show cause is signed. All inquiries can be made to the Guardianship Department at (516) 571–2938 or (516) 571–2097. Any requests for adjournments shall be directed to the Justice assigned to the particular case.

Doc. 7. Court Information Center

The Court information Center in Nassau County Supreme Court officially opened on June 13, 2006. The Center was designed to assist members of the public who may require procedural and other court-related information to help them navigate the court system. The Center has in excess of 50 forms and instructional brochures for use by the public. The forms include the uncontested divorce packet, legal name change forms and the summons and complaint which litigants may use to commence a lawsuit. The staff does not complete the forms, nor are we permitted to offer legal advice.

The Court Information Center is available to all members of the public including attorneys. The Center also handles questions regarding other courts in the county including the District Court and the Family Court. The Center is located in the rear of the Law Library on the second floor of the Nassau County Supreme Court, 100 Supreme Court Drive, Mincola, NY 11501. The telephone number is (516) 571–3291.

Doc. 8. Nassau County Supreme—Civil CCP Part

Cases appearing on the DCM and CCP Calendars in the Trial Assignment Part are ready for trial. Pursuant to 22 NYCRR § 202.27, failure by counsel for a party plaintiff or a self-represented party plaintiff to appear will subject that case to dismissal. Failure by counsel for a party defendant or self-represented party defendant to appear will subject the case to an immediate inquest.

All cases appearing on the DCM Trial Calendar will be disposed pursuant to the time limits set forth in 22 NYCRR § 202.19.

Attorney service may answer the Calendar and request an adjournment, within the 22 NYCRR § 202.19 time frame, only on consent of all parties.

In all cases in which a party intends to present a motion *in limine*, that party shall so advise the Court prior to jury selection.

Doc. 9. Nassau County Foreclosure Auction Rules

1. Notice of sales must be submitted to the Clerk's Office in room 152 at least 10 days prior to the date of an auction.

2. Terms of sale must be posted outside of the Calendar Control Part (CCP) Courtroom prior to 11:15 am on the date of the auction.

3. Referees must be present at 11:15 am in the Calendar Control Part (CCP) Courtroom.

4. Referees and plaintiffs (or plaintiff's agent) must check in with the Clerk in charge upon arrival.

5. Referees must accept either: a) Cash or b) Certified check made payable to the referee. NOTE: Referees will not accept double endorsed checks.

6. Sales will not be deemed final until all scheduled auctions have been completed and the clerk announces the conclusion of business for the day.

BIDDING

1. All successful bidders must have proof of ID and state their name and address on the record. In addition, they must have 10% of the bid in either cash or certified check made payable to the referee.

2. Any successful bidder, who after the auction but prior to the transfer of the 10% deposit, decides not to finalize the sale due to new information received after the auction, must inform the referee immediately. If the transaction is not completed, the property will be placed for auction immediately thereafter.

IMPROPER BIDS

1. If any participant improperly bids on a property and causes the property to be returned to the auction calendar, the Court, in its discretion, reserves the right to bar the participant from bidding at any future auctions in Nassau County for a period to be determined by the Court.

Doc. 10. Records Retention/Destruction

Effective May 25, 2004, the following revised policies and procedures have been implemented regarding the retention/destruction of subpoenaed records.

Absent Court order, records should never be subpoenaed to the Court sooner than 45 days prior to trial. Upon disposition of a case, all subpoenaed records are to be returned to the subpoenaed records room for retention/destruction in accordance with these policies.

Plaintiff or Defendant's Verdicts – Dismissed Case – Discontinued Case

Records will be retained for thirty (30) days and then destroyed upon any verdict, non–CCP dismissal or discontinuance if not picked up by the party that issued the subpoena prior thereto. No subpoenaed records will be destroyed before (30) thirty days after the case has been disposed of by plaintiff or defendant's verdict, non–CCP dismissal or discontinuance unless otherwise ordered by Court.

Arbitration and Mediation

Records will be retained for one (1) year and then destroyed, if not picked up by the party that issued the subpoena prior thereto, unless the Court directs otherwise. On a case referred to arbitration conducted by an agency independent of the Court, counsel are advised to pick up the records to be hand delivered to the arbitrator(s) forthwith.

ADR (Alternative Dispute Resolution)

Records will be immediately turned over to the ADR Coordinator, unless the Court directs otherwise.

MOCA (Marked Off Calendar Active)

Records will be retained one (1) year from the date on which the case was marked off. If the case is not restored to the calendar within that one (1) year, the records will be destroyed if not picked up by the party that issued the subpoena prior thereto, unless the Court directs otherwise.

VNI (Vacate Note of Issue), Dismissal in CCP Part or Mistrial

Records will be retained and then destroyed one (1) year from the date on which the Note of Issue was vacated, the date the matter was dismissed by the Judge assigned to CCP or the date a mistrial was noted, unless the Court directs otherwise.

Stayed Cases

Records will be retained for one (1) year after a stay is issued and then destroyed, unless the Court directs otherwise. Counsel must furnish the Subpoenaed Records Room with a copy of the decision, order or petition (in the case of a voluntary bankruptcy) imposing the stay, as well as any dispositive order removing the stay.

Appealed Cases

Counsel must provide the subpoenaed records room with proof that an appeal has been filed as well as a copy of any dispositive order resulting from the appeal. The records shall be held for two (2) years upon the filing of an appeal, unless counsel shall provide additional proof that the appeal is still pending, prior to the expiration of the two (2) years, and that the stay remains in effect.

ANY PROVIDER'S REQUEST FOR THE RETURN OF SUBPOENAED ORIGINAL DOCUMENTS WILL CONTINUE TO BE HONORED, PROVIDED A SELF–ADDRESSED STAMPED ENVELOPE WAS ENCLOSED ALONG WITH THE SUBMISSION OF RECORDS

Doc. 11. Rules with Regard to Examination of Subpoenaed Records in The Record Room of The Supreme Court, Nassau County

Please be advised that records subpoenaed involving cases that are not on the ready day calendar of TAP I or TAP II or scheduled to be added to such calendar within 45 days of receipt or scheduled for trial or hearing before an IAS Justice, will not be accepted by the record room and will be returned to the subpoenaed party at the expense of counsel who subpoenaed such records.

The records properly received may be examined by the party's counsel and/or said counsel's authorized representative. Permission of the court must be obtained to remove records from the record room.

1) Hospital Records—

A) A party's counsel may examine the hospital records and x-rays of their own client without consent.

B) The opposing counsel must either obtain the consent of the party's counsel or Court consent.

C) No party can examine records of non-parties without Court consent.

2) Employment Records and School Records (Other than Psychological School Records)—

A) A party's counsel may examine these records of their own client without consent.

B) The opposing counsel must either obtain consent of the party's counsel or Court consent.

3) Police Records—

All parties can review these records without consent except if there is criminal involvement, a criminal court file or a district attorney's file. In the latter event consent must be obtained from the Court.

4) Psychiatric Hospital Records and Physician's Psychiatric Records and Records of Mental Hospitals—

No party can examine these records except by consent of the Court.

5) Physician's Records—

A) A party's counsel may examine these records of their own client without consent

B) The opposing counsel must either obtain consent of the party's counsel or Court consent.

C) No party can examine records of non parties without consent of the Court.

6) Social Services Records—

No party can examine these records without consent of the Court.

7) Workers Compensation—

No party can examine these records without consent of the Court.

8) Insurance Company Files and Records (Including No-Fault Files)—

No party can examine these records without consent of the Court.

9) Records of All Courts Other Than the Family Court—

No party can examine these records without consent of the Court.

10) Family Court Records—

These records are to be sealed. No party can examine these records without an order by a Family Court Judge or the consent of a Supreme Court Justice after an "in camera" review. (Family Court Act §§ 783 and 784).

JUDGES' PART RULES

JUSTICE THOMAS FEINMAN

Part 13.　Hon. Thomas Feinman

Courtroom Appearances, Conduct and Demeanor

Calendar call is at 9:30 AM. Counsel must first check in with the Clerk of the Part, who is located in the courtroom on the 4th floor.

There shall be no gum or candy chewing in Court. All cell phones shall be turned off. Proper attire is required. Counsel shall remove overcoats prior to approaching the well.

Only counsel familiar with the case, its status and history shall appear. These directives apply to per diem counsel and attorneys of counsel as well.

Communications with Court

The court will not accept any ex parte communication by telephone or letter from counsel or a self-represented party.

Telephone Calls: TELEPHONE CALLS TO CHAMBERS ARE PERMITTED BY COUNSEL ONLY. (No paralegals or secretaries.)

Faxes: Faxes to chambers are not permitted unless prior authorization is obtained. Should authorization be obtained, counsel must advise on the cover sheet who the authorization was obtained from. Should correspondence be faxed to chambers, upon authorization, copies of the correspondence shall be simultaneously faxed and mailed to all counsel.

Only correspondence, upon authorization, may be faxed to chambers. No additional papers, such as pleadings, motions, orders to show cause, or any other requests for relief and replies shall be faxed to chambers.

No excessive faxes: There shall be no more than five (5) pages faxed to chambers.

Motions

All movants shall provide the Court with self-addressed stamped envelopes for each party served with the motion.

All writs, motions, petitions, and orders to show cause are to be made returnable at 9:30 AM on any day of the week, and are on submission only. Therefore, there shall be no appearance required or oral argument of motions, unless specifically requested by the court.

Motions brought pursuant to CPLR sections 3211, 3212, or 3213 shall not automatically stay disclosure.

Order to Show Cause: If there is an order to show cause which contains a stay which the parties cannot agree to extend until determination, then all counsel, or pro se parties must appear on the return date.

Failure to appear shall be deemed consent to the continuation or elimination of the stay or temporary restraining order, as requested by the adversary counsel.

Request for Adjournments: Should all parties consent to adjourn a motion, counsel must call the Courtroom Clerk, (571–3520), and request the adjournment, on consent. Only one adjournment, on consent, with the permission of the court, will be permitted. The adjournment shall be no more than thirty days. Any subsequent requests must be approved by the Court.

When the parties cannot agree to adjourn a motion, such contested motion adjournments shall be telephone conferenced with the Law Secretary, (571–2952), at least one day prior to the return date.

Submission of Papers:

All incoming motions, cross-motions, writs, petitions or orders to show cause must be delivered to the Motion Support Office located in the Supreme Court Building, 100 Supreme Court Drive, Room 186, Mineola, New York, for entry and processing. Courtesy copies will be accepted by the Courtroom Clerk located on the 4th floor, and are not required.

All papers (motions, cross-motions, responsive papers, etc.), must be submitted timely. The Court will not consider late papers. All motions, petitions, orders to show cause, and other appropriate requests for relief and replies shall include a self-addressed stamped envelope.

Preliminary Conferences, Compliance Conferences and Certification Conferences

All preliminary conferences will be held in the basement of the courthouse.

All compliance and certification conferences will be held in the courtroom located on the 4th floor, on Wednesdays, at 9:30 A.M. The Court will take the bench for conferences.

Conferences will begin promptly at 9:30 A.M. All attorneys are expected to check in promptly at or before 9:30 A.M. The attorneys shall check in with the Courtroom Clerk. Morever, once counsel checks in with the clerk, they are to remain in the courtroom until the case is called.

Accordingly, counsel is directed to adjust their schedules so as to comply with these directives.

All counsel appearing must be knowledgeable with all the facts, circumstances, history and status of the case. There are no exceptions to this rule for per diem counsel or attorneys of counsel.

Should there be a Trial in progress, compliance and certification conferences will be held in chambers, located on the 4th floor.

The attorneys are advised to call their adversary the day before the scheduled conference to confirm a prompt appearance.

Cases are conferenced in the order in which all attorneys on a matter are checked in. If the case is called and there is no appearance, the Court will take the appropriate action against the nonappearing side, including marking the case off calendar, dismissing an action, dismissing an answer, or setting the matter down for an inquest.

No adjournments of discovery as per Preliminary Conference Order shall take place without court permission. Counsel shall seek court permission before adjourning any deposition date in the Preliminary Conference Order.

Requests for Adjournments

All requests for adjournments of preliminary conferences should be made to the DCM part.

All requests for adjournments of compliance and certification conferences should be made to the Law Secretary, (571–2952), on consent of all parties, prior to 4:00 P.M. the previous day. No adjournments will be granted without permission from the Court. Should the Court give permission to adjourn the conference, the adjournment must be confirmed by letter to the court.

The correspondence shall be faxed to chambers, upon authorization. Copies of the correspondence shall be simultaneously faxed and mailed to all counsel.

Court–Ordered Examinations Before Trial (EBT)

All EBTs scheduled at the compliance or certification conference shall be held at the courthouse.

Non–Compliance with Discovery Orders

If there appears to be non-compliance with discovery orders, the parties should contact the Law

Secretary, (571–2952), by phone before the next scheduled conference date, or as soon as reasonably practical.

Settlements

If an action is settled, discontinued, or otherwise disposed, prior to being placed on this Court's calendar, or the Trial Court's calendar, counsel shall immediately notify chambers by telephone and forward a confirming letter to chambers.

Trial Part Rules

1. *Motions in Limine.* On the first appearance in the Part for trial, any party intending to make a motion in limine shall submit a brief written affirmation setting forth the nature of the application and any supporting statutory or case law. The party shall furnish the Court with an original and two copies and provide counsel for all parties with a copy. There shall be a separate affirmation for each motion in limine.

2. *Premarking Exhibits.* On the first appearance in the Part for trial, each party shall furnish the Court and all other parties with a preliminary list of exhibits which it is his or her intent to offer into evidence. The exhibits shall be pre-marked for identification or, upon consent, into evidence. During opening statements, any party may refer to any pre-marked exhibit which has been admitted into evidence on consent.

3. *Expert Witnesses.* On the first appearance in the Part for trial, and if not otherwise premarked, each party shall, with respect to each expert witness that party intends to call, submit a list identifying with specificity any record, report, photograph, film, computer animation, x-ray, CT scan, MRI, EMG study or similar item or items to which an expert witness is expected to make reference as supporting in whole or in part the opinion he or she will offer.

4. *Requests to Charge.* On the first appearance in the Part for trial, each party shall supply the Court with preliminary requests to charge. Charges from the Pattern Jury Instructions may be identified by number without necessity of reproduction unless a modification of the standard charge is requested in which case the modification is to be highlighted. Each party shall supply an original and three (3) copies to the court and furnish every other party with a copy. The preliminary requests may be supplemented, modified or edited as the trial progresses.

5. *Malpractice "Departures".* In cases involving claims of professional negligence, on the next trial session after a party rests, or such other time as the Court may direct, each party [plaintiff] shall furnish the Court and counsel for all parties with a list of the departures from the standards of good and accepted practice which that party asserts were testified to by its expert witness or witnesses. Where the testimony has been transcribed, page references will be required.

JUSTICE ARTHUR M. DIAMOND

Doc. 1. Hon. Arthur M. Diamond

1) Conferences

Counsel shall appear at 9:30 a.m. for all scheduled conferences. Any counsel who appears for a confer-

ence shall be knowledgeable, and familiar with the case file.

If counsel will be delayed in arrival for a scheduled conference, then counsel shall immediately notify both opposing counsel and the court of the tardiness.

2) Motions

No appearance is required on motions unless an adjournment is not consented to by all the parties.

Appearances are required on all contested Order to Show Causes for withdrawal of counsel.

No oral arguments on motions permitted except as directed by the court.

Motions brought pursuant to CPLR sections 3211, 3212, or 3213 shall not automatically stay disclosure.

3) Temporary Restraining Order

Counsel submitting an order to show cause requesting a temporary restraining order must notify the court to schedule a date and time for submission and oral argument. Notice to opposing party must be given in writing at least 24 hours prior to the scheduled date and time.

4) Adjournments

Motions and conferences cannot be adjourned to a specific date without the consent of all the parties, and the express consent of the court.

5) Settled Actions

If a pending action has been settled, then plaintiff's counsel shall notify chambers by telephone, and in writing that the matter has been settled prior to the next conference date.

6) Submission of Judgments and Motions

Counsel shall not mail motions or judgments directly to chambers. They are to be properly filed with the clerk.

7) Trials

On the first date of trial, counsel shall provide the court with a copy of all pleadings, bill of particulars, CPLR § 3101 (d) notices, proposed jury charges and verdict sheets prior to opening statements. Counsel shall also inform the court of any motions in limine prior to opening statements.

Malpractice Departures: In cases involving claims of professional negligence, on the next trial session after a party rests, or such other time as the Court may direct, each party [plaintiff] shall furnish the court and counsel for all parties with a list of departures from the standards of good and accepted practice which that party asserts were testified to by its expert witness or witnesses. Where the testimony has been transcribed, page references will be required.

8) Communications With Chambers

No ex parte communications shall be permitted with the court. No letters shall be mailed or faxed to chambers without the express permission of the court.

JUSTICE ANGELA G. IANNACCI, PART 16

Rule I. Adjournments

A. Motions and Status Conferences:

1. Adjournments of motions and conferences may be granted if there is consent of all parties **and prior approval of the court**. If all parties do not consent to the adjournment, application shall be made in Court on the day of the conference or the motion.

2. Adjournments of **motions** shall be sought through the courtroom clerk who will advise as to whether the adjournment has been granted.

3. Adjournments of **conferences** shall be sought through chambers. A date certain, consented to by all parties, must be requested at the time the adjournment is sought.

4. Letters confirming adjournments **shall** contain full names of both parties, index number, and shall specify if motion or conference is being adjourned.

5. Adjournments requested because of engagement of counsel must be accompanied by an Affirmation of Engagement in conformity with 22 NYCRR Part 125.

Rule II. Motions

A. Submission of the Motion

1. Motions relating to discovery disputes require appearance of counsel for all parties. All other motions are on submission unless otherwise ordered by the Court.

2. All exhibits must be clearly tabbed; motions not consistent with this rule will be rejected and returned to counsel.

3. No sur-reply affidavit, affirmation, memorandum of law or letter will be accepted or considered by the Court without leave of the Court.

4. Counsel are requested to provide the Court with SELF ADDRESSED STAMPED ENVELOPES with the submitted papers in order to facilitate delivery of the Court's decision.

B. Oral Argument

The Court will determine, after submission, whether oral argument is warranted. Upon such determination, counsel for all parties will be contacted and advised of the new adjourned date for purposes of oral argument.

Rule III. Court Appearances

A. Preliminary and status conferences shall be scheduled for 9:30 a.m. Please check in at 9:30 a.m.

B. Attorneys must check in with Court Officer or Court Clerk. If counsel must also appear before another Judge, they must advise the Part Clerk or Court Officer where they can be reached and note on the sign in sheet.

C. Cases will be conferenced in the order in which **all** attorneys are checked in.

Rule IV. Communication With Chambers

A. In all Communications with chambers by letter, the title of the action, full names of the parties and index number shall be set forth, with copies simultaneously delivered to all counsel. Ex parte communications will be disregarded, except as otherwise provided herein.

B. Copies of correspondence between counsel shall not be sent to the Court. Such copies will be disregarded and not placed in the Court's file.

C. The Court will not accept telefax communications or submissions without prior permission.

Rule V. Sanctions

The Court will not consider a sanctions application unless the moving party first seeks withdrawal or discontinuation of the offending act or action or demands required or necessary action which is refused. Proof of such request must be made a part of the sanctions application.

TRIAL PART RULES

1. Motions in limine—On the first appearance in a Part for trial, any party intending to make a motion *in limine* shall submit a brief written affirmation setting forth the nature of the application and any supporting statutory or case law. The party shall furnish the Court an original and two copies and provide counsel for all parties with a copy. There shall be a separate affirmation for each motion *in limine*.

2. Pre-marking Exhibits—On the first appearance in the Part for trial, each party shall furnish the Court and all other parties with a preliminary list of exhibits which it is his or her intent to offer in evidence. The exhibits shall be pre-marked for identification or, upon consent, into evidence. During opening statements any party may refer to any pre-marked exhibit which has been admitted into evidence on consent.

3. Expert Witnesses—On the first appearance in the Part for trial and if not otherwise pre-marked, each party shall, with respect to each expert witness that party intends to call, submit a list identifying with specificity any record, report, photograph, film, computer animation, x-ray, CT scan, MRI, EMG study or similar item or items to which an expert witness is expected to make reference as supporting in whole or in part the opinion he or she will offer. Where the exhibit is a many paged document such as a hospital record, office record or voluminous (more than 10 pages) business record, counsel shall identify by way of tabs, post-its, page numbering or similar device the particular page or pages to which reference will be made.

4. Requests to Charge—On the first appearance in the Part for trial, each party shall supply the Court with preliminary requests to charge. Charges from the Pattern Jury Instructions may be identified by number without necessity of reproduction unless a modification of the standard charge is requested in which case the modification is to be highlighted. Each party shall supply an original and three (3) copies to the Court and furnish every other party with a copy. The preliminary requests may be supplemented, modified or edited as the trial progresses.

5. Malpractice "Departures"—In cases involving claims of professional negligence, on the next trial session after a party rests or such other time as the Court may direct, each party [plaintiff] shall furnish the Court and counsel for all parties with a list of the departures from the standards of good and accepted practice which that party asserts were testified to by its expert witness or witnesses. Where the testimony has been transcribed, page references will be required.

6. Interpreters—On the first appearance in the Part for trial, any party who intends to call a witness who will require the assistance of an interpreter shall notify the clerk in the Part and specify the language (including dialect, where appropriate).

7. Equipment—On the first appearance in the Part for trial, any party who intends to rely upon the Court to supply equipment for utilizing a video tape recording, an audio tape recording, demonstrative evidence, or the like, shall notify the clerk in the Part.

8. Nassau County Police Officers—On the first appearance in the Part for trial, any party who has issued a subpoena to secure the appearance of a Nassau County police officer shall notify the clerk in the Part so that the clerk may facilitate the officer's appearance through Police Liaison.

Rule VI. Miscellaneous

A. CONFERENCES/TRIAL—If there are any outstanding motions (submitted or pending) at the time of the conference/trial the Law Secretary and/or Judge must be so informed of same that day; the submission date must be provided by counsel. Copies of such motions should be available to the Court at the time of such conference.

B. ATTORNEYS OF RECORD—Attorneys who have appeared in the matter are to make all appearances until they are relieved by the Court or a Consent to Change Attorneys has been filed with Part 23 contemplated, and with the Clerk of the Court.

C. STAFF—The Court functions through the aid and assistance of the courtroom and Chambers staff. They are expected to treat attorneys, litigants and others in a dignified and civil manner; as well they are to be treated in a civil and professional manner.

D. SETTLEMENTS—With respect to actions which have been settled or otherwise discontinued, counsel must comply with 22 NYCRR 202.28 or sanctions may be imposed. Counsel are reminded of their obligations under § 202.28 of the Uniform Rules for Trial Courts to file a stipulation or statement of discontinuance with the part of court to which the matter has been assigned within 20 days of the discontinuance. If a discontinued action is on a trial calendar, a copy of the stipulation or statement shall also be filed with the clerk of the trial part.

JUSTICE RANDY SUE MARBER, PART 18

Rule I. Adjournments

A. Motions and Conferences:

1. Adjournments of motions and conferences may be granted if there is consent of all parties and prior approval of the Court. No adjournments will be granted without the approval of the Court. If all parties do not consent to the adjournment, an application shall be made by conference call, with all counsel, no later than 3:00 p.m. of the day preceding the scheduled conference or the motion. No requests for an adjournment will be entertained without all parties participating in the conference call. Except for applications made in court, upon approval of the adjournment, a letter must immediately be submitted by fax to Chambers confirming same with a copy to all counsel appearing in the matter.

2. Adjournments of motions and conferences may only be sought through Chambers. Potential dates, convenient to all parties must be available at the time the adjournment is sought.

3. Letters confirming adjournments MUST immediately be faxed to Chambers and MUST contain full names of all parties, the index number, and shall specify if a motion and/or a conference is being adjourned.

4. Adjournment requests which are left on the Chamber's Voice Mail shall be disregarded.

5. Adjournments requested because of the actual engagement on trial of counsel must be accompanied by an Affirmation of Engagement in conformity with 22 NYCRR Part 125.

6. No adjournment of discovery as per the Preliminary Conference Order shall take place without prior Court permission. Counsel is advised to seek Court permission before adjourning any deposition date specified in the Preliminary Conference Order to a later date.

B. Preliminary Conference:

1. Preliminary conference adjournments are to be addressed to the DCM Clerk's office and not to Chambers.

Rule II. Motions

A. Pre–Motion Conferences:

1. Prior to the making or filing of any discovery or other non-dispositive motions, counsel for the prospective moving party shall first discuss the issue(s) in question with his or her adversary. If the issue(s) in question cannot be resolved, counsel for the prospective moving party MUST arrange for a conference call to be held with his/her adversary and the Court to discuss the issue(s) involved and the possible resolution thereof. Counsel fully familiar with the matter and with authority to bind their client MUST be available to participate in the conference call.

2. If the matter can be resolved during the conference, an order consistent with such resolution may be issued.

3. This rule does not apply to applications for counsel to be relieved or motions for summary judgment.

B. Submission of the Motion

1. Appearances of all Counsel and Pro se parties are required on all motions and Orders to Show Cause unless otherwise specifically waived by the Court. There are no submitted motions without an appearance in this Part.

2. Courtesy copies should not be submitted, unless requested by the Court.

3. Failure to appear at a calendar call may result in denial of any motion made by the non-appearing party and/or the granting of any motion on default when the opposing party fails to appear.

4. In the event a case is already scheduled for a conference with the Court, counsel should endeavor to make the return date of a motion, if possible, on said date.

5. Counsel must advise the Court, in writing, and as soon as practicable, if any submitted motions have been resolved, withdrawn, or if the motion is moot because the case has been settled.

6. Pursuant to CPLR § 3212(a), a motion for summary judgment shall be made no later than sixty (60) days after the filing of the Note of Issue, except with

leave of court on good cause shown. Any physician affirmations, reports or other medical proof submitted in threshold motions shall contain the original signatures of the physician or medical provider.

7. All exhibits must be clearly tabbed; no exhibits shall be double sided; no mini-scripts are accepted; motions not consistent with this rule will be rejected and returned to counsel.

8. All submissions shall be fully and securely bound and shall have a litigation back attached thereto.

9. When submitting proposed orders or judgments in connection with a motion, the same shall be submitted as a separately bound document. Proposed orders or judgments incorporated within motion papers will be considered exhibits, treated as such, and may be disregarded.

10. All papers must be submitted timely at the time the motion is heard. The Court will not consider late papers absent prior Court approval. No sur-reply affidavit, affirmation, memorandum of law or letter will be accepted or considered by the Court without leave of the Court.

11. Counsel are required to provide the court with SELF–ADDRESSED, STAMPED envelopes with the submitted papers in order to facilitate delivery of the court's decision.

12. Motions brought pursuant to CPLR §§ 3211, 3212 or 3213 shall not automatically stay disclosure.

C. Application for a Stay or Temporary Restraining Order (TRO)

1. If an Order to Show Cause seeking any injunctive relief, including a stay or TRO, is to be submitted, it must comply with Uniform Rule § 202.7 (f). The movant shall first consult with Chambers as to a convenient date and time for counsel to appear with regard to the compliance with Uniform Rule § 202.7 (f).

2. At any conference of the matter, if an Order to Show Cause seeking any injunctive relief, including a stay or TRO, is submitted or pending, counsel shall advise the Court of the pendency of such application, the return date of such Order to Show Cause, the relief sought and whether an immediate hearing is sought.

3. Requests to continue or vacate a stay or TRO beyond the return date of the motion shall be made on the call of the motion calendar. Failure to apply for such extension shall result in the automatic *vacatur* of the stay or TRO, unless the Order to Show Cause provides otherwise.

D. Interim Partial or Full Settlement

If all or part of a submitted motion is settled, a proposed order with notice of settlement (on at least ten [10] days notice) or a signed waiver of settlement shall be submitted with a copy to be conformed and a self-addressed, stamped envelope. Such order shall be accompanied by a letter setting forth the date the motion was submitted, what aspects of the Motion have been settled and what issues remain to be decided. A copy of the stipulation settling such issues shall be forwarded to the Court. If the motion is resolved, in whole or part, on the record, counsel shall obtain such transcript so that same can be "so ordered", unless the Court otherwise directs.

Rule III. Court Appearances

A. Calendar call is at 9:30 am. Please be prompt.

B. Attorneys and "Pro se" litigants must check in with the Court Officer or Part Clerk and complete a sign-in sheet. If counsel must also appear before another Judge, they must advise the Part Clerk or Court Officer where they can be reached. All Counsel and "Pro se" litigants are directed to appear for each and every conference (including preliminary, compliance and certification conferences).

C. All conferences will be held in the order in which all attorneys and/or Pro se litigants have checked in.

D. Counsel who appear in the Part must be fully familiar with the case in regard to which they appear and fully authorized to enter into agreements, both substantive and procedural on behalf of their clients.

E. Failure to appear at the call of any calendar may result in an inquest or dismissal pursuant to 22 NYCRR § 202.27.

F. Counsel are advised to confirm all scheduled appearances with their adversary the day before the appearance date to confirm a prompt appearance.

Rule IV. Communication With Chambers

A. INQUIRIES

1. In all communications with Chambers by letter, the title of the action, full names of the parties and index number shall be set forth, with copies simultaneously delivered to all counsel. Ex parte communications will be disregarded.

2. Copies of correspondence between counsel shall not be sent to the Court. Such copies shall be disregarded and not placed in the Court's file.

3. The Court will not accept telefax communications or submissions without prior permission.

4. The court shall not accept ex parte telephone communications on substantive issues.

5. E-mail correspondence with Chambers staff is not permitted unless prior authorization is obtained.

6. Attorneys shall not call Chambers during the daily lunch hour which is from 1:00 p.m. to 2:00 p.m.

B. SETTLEMENTS

1.   No out of court settlement will be recognized or accepted unless counsel submits a letter, on notice to opposing counsel submitting the executed settlement agreement/stipulation or certifying that such agreement/stipulation has, in fact, been executed.

Rule V.   Sanctions

The Court will not consider a sanctions application unless the moving party first seeks withdrawal or discontinuation of the offending act or action or demands required or necessary action which is refused. Proof of such request must be made a part of the sanctions application.

Rule VI.   Trial Rules

A.   A Note of Issue is to be filed within 90 days after certification, unless otherwise specified in the Certification Order.   Counsel for plaintiff shall pay the requisite fee with the County Clerk and ensure that the Note of Issue is submitted to the Clerk who will then assign a calendar number.

B.   At the first appearance of all cases assigned to this Part for trial, a pre-trial conference will be held. At the conference, the Court shall provide for the submission or scheduling of the following:

1.   *In Limine applications:* Any party intending to make a motion in limine shall submit a brief written affirmation setting forth the nature of the application and any supporting statutory or case law.   The party shall furnish the Court with an original and two (2) copies and provide counsel for all parties with a copy. There shall be a separate affirmation for each motion in limine;

2.   Proof of filing of the Note of Issue;

3.   Pre-trial memoranda providing the Court with cited case law to be considered by the Court.

4.   A courtesy copy of each exhibit intended to be introduced into evidence at trial for the Court and each counsel.   All exhibits shall be tabbed or included in a binder for easy reference;

5.   All trial exhibits, whether the parties stipulate to admit them into evidence to the Court or not, shall be pre-marked by the Court Reporter.   As to those exhibits marked for identification, the Court will address their admissibility *In limine* or during the trial, as may be appropriate;

6.   A list of proposed witnesses for the Court's information;

7.   A list of all expert witnesses with copies of their reports;

8.   Marked pleadings, to be submitted before opening statements;

9.   A statement of stipulated facts.   [Parties are encouraged to stipulate to facts and/or exhibits];

10.   Any written requests for jury instructions. Charges from the Pattern Jury Instructions may be identified by number without necessity of reproduction, unless a modification of the standard charge is requested, in which case the modification is to be highlighted;

11.   Any proposed verdict sheets;

12.   If deposition transcripts are to be utilized, a copy of the witness' deposition transcript should be available to the Court;

13.   Objections should be stated without argument except to simply state the ground therefor, *e.g.,* hearsay, relevance, etc.   If further argument is appropriate, it will be invited by the court;

14.   Trial counsel are responsible for redactions of all evidence;

15.   Trials will be conducted on a continual daily basis until conclusion.   As such, no adjournments or delays during trial will be accepted unless exigent circumstances exist;

16.   Trial counsel are responsible for taking back all exhibits, pleadings, transcripts, etc., at the end of a trial, unless, in the case of non-jury trials the Court reserves its decision.   In all cases, exhibits, pleadings, transcripts, etc. not retrieved within thirty (30) days from the conclusion of a jury trial or within thirty (30) days after the Court renders a decision in a non-jury trial, shall be disposed of.

Rule VII.   Miscellaneous

A.   CONFERENCES/TRIAL—If there are any outstanding motions (submitted or pending) at the time of the conference/trial, the Law Secretary and/or Judge must be so informed of same that day; the submission date must be provided by counsel.   Copies of such motions should be available to the Court at the time of such conference.

B.   ATTORNEYS OF RECORD—Attorneys who have appeared in the matter are to make all appearances until they are relieved by the Court or a fully executed Consent to Change Attorney form has been filed with Part 20 and with the Clerk of the Court.

C.   STAFF—The Court functions through the aid and assistance of the courtroom and Chambers staff. They are expected to treat attorneys, litigants and others in a dignified and civil manner; as well they are to be treated in a civil and professional manner.

JUSTICE VITO M. DESTEFANO, PART 19

Rule I. Adjournments

A. Motions and Status Conferences:

1. Applications to adjourn conferences or motions on consent must be made prior to the conference date or return date of the motion. Applications for adjournments are to be made on the Request for Adjournment Form which can be obtained through chambers. The Request for Adjournment Form is to be filled out by counsel and faxed to chambers. The form requires counsel to provide, among other things, information concerning proposed adjourn dates agreed to by all parties, the date the RJI was purchased, the date preliminary conference was held, the date and nature of the most recent conference, the date the Note of Issue was or is expected to be filed, and the reason for the requested adjournment. If the application is granted, a letter confirming same shall be faxed to chambers. Absent extraordinary circumstances, no request for a consent adjournment will be granted if the application is made later than 2:00 p.m. of the business day prior to the conference or motion return date.

2. Letters confirming adjournments shall state that the court has adjourned the conference or motion on consent of the parties to the specified date, and shall contain the full names of both parties, the index number as well as a notation indicating that **all** parties have been copied.

3. Adjournment requests which are left on the Chamber's Voice Mail shall be disregarded.

4. Adjournments requested because of engagement of counsel must be accompanied by an Affirmation of Engagement in conformity with 22 NYCRR § 125.1, as well as a request for adjournment form.

B. Preliminary Conference:

1. At the preliminary conference, attorney or parties, if not represented, must obtain and review the rules of this part. You are responsible to become familiar with the part rules and to comply with them.

2. Discovery deadlines, Certification Deadlines and Note of Issue deadlines, will be enforced. Deadlines may not be extended absent prior approval by the court.

Rule II. Motions

A. Pre–Motion Conferences:

1. Prior to making or filing any motions, counsel for the moving party **MUST** arrange for a conference call to be held with his/her adversary and the Court to discuss the issues involved and the possible resolution thereof. Counsel fully familiar with the matter and with authority to bind their clients **MUST** be available to participate in the conference.

2. If the matter can be resolved during the conference, an order consistent with such resolution may be issued.

3. This rule does not apply to applications for counsel to be relieved.

B. Submission of the Motion

1. Appearances of all Counsel are required on all motions unless waived by the Court.

2. All exhibits must be clearly tabbed; motions not consistent with this rule will be rejected and returned to counsel.

3. Motions are to be served and filed in conformity with CPLR 2214. In addition, the various branches of the motion as delineated in the Notice of Motion or Order To Show Cause are to be preceded by a number or letter which corresponds to a number or letter in the supporting affirmations and affidavits containing the numbered paragraphs dealing with the particular relief sought.

4. No sur-reply affidavit, affirmation, memorandum of law or letter will be accepted or considered by the Court without leave of the Court.

5. Counsel are requested to provide the court with self-addressed, stamped envelopes with the submitted papers in order to facilitate delivery of the court's decision.

C. Applications for Temporary Injunctive Relief

Applications for temporary injunctive relief must be made in conformity with 22 NYCRR 202.7(f). In addition, the Court generally requires that the party seeking temporary injunctive relief give the opposing side 24 hours notice in advance of presentment of the Order to Show Cause to the court. Notice should be given by telephone, facsimile and/or e-mail, if practicable.

D. Interim Partial or Full Settlement

If all or part of a submitted motion is settled, a proposed order with notice of settlement (on at least 10 days notice), or a signed waiver of settlement, shall be submitted with a copy to be conformed along with a self-addressed, stamped envelope. Such order shall be accompanied by a letter setting forth the date the motion was submitted, what aspects of the Motion have been settled and what issues remain to be decided. A copy of the stipulation settling such issues shall be forwarded to the Court. If the motion is resolved, in whole or part, on the record, counsel shall obtain such transcript so that same can be "so ordered", unless the Court otherwise directs.

Rule III. Court Appearances

A. Generally, calendar call is at 9:30 am. If your case is scheduled for 9:30 A.M. that means your case should be ready to be heard at that time. If your case is scheduled for 9:30 A.M. but not ready to be heard by 10:15 A.M., due to other court appearances or factors beyond your control, absent a prior arrangement with the Court, your case will be heard at a time that the court determines to be convenient. In no way does the foregoing alter or limit any of the options available to the Court in the event of an attorney or litigant's failure to timely appear (22 NYCRR 130–2.1, 202.27).

B. Attorneys and unrepresented litigants must alert the Court Officer or Court Clerk of their presence and complete a sign-in sheet. If counsel must also appear before another Judge, he/she must advise the Part Clerk or Court Officer where he/she can be reached. All counsel and litigants are directed to appear for each and every conference (including preliminary, status and compliance conferences).

C. All conferences will be held in the order in which **all** attorneys have checked in.

Rule IV.   Communication with Chambers

A. In all communications with chambers by letter, the title of the action, full names of the parties and index number shall be set forth, with copies simultaneously delivered to all counsel.

B. Copies of correspondence between counsel shall **not** be sent to the Court. Such copies shall be disregarded and not placed in the Court's file.

C. The Court will not accept telefax communications or submissions without prior permission.

D. No out of court settlement will be recognized or accepted unless counsel submits a letter, on notice to opposing counsel, and, if applicable, the Law Guardian, submitting the executed settlement agreement/stipulation or certifying that such agreement/stipulation has, in fact, been executed.

E. The court shall not accept *ex parte* telephone communications on any substantive issue.

Rule V.   Sanctions

The Court will not consider a sanctions application unless the moving party first seeks withdrawal or discontinuation of the offending act or action or demands required or necessary action which is refused. Proof of such request must be made a part of the sanctions application.

Rule VI.   Trial Rules

Rules applicable to the conduct of trials are attached hereto.

Rule VII.   Miscellaneous

A.   CONFERENCES/TRIAL—If there are any outstanding motions (submitted or pending) at the time of the conference/trial the Law Secretary and/or Judge must be so informed of same that day; the submission date must be provided by counsel. Copies of such motions should be available to the Court at the time of such conference.

B.   ATTORNEYS OF RECORD—Attorneys who have appeared in the matter are to make all appearances until they are relieved by the Court or a Consent to Change Attorneys has been filed with Part 19 and with the Clerk of the Court.

C.   STAFF—The Court functions through the aid and assistance of the courtroom and Chambers staff. They are expected to treat attorneys, litigants and others in a dignified and civil manner. In addition, they are to be treated in a civil and professional manner at all times.

D. In the absence of an emergency, no Order to Show Cause will be heard after 2:00 P.M. All Orders to Show Cause will be heard the next day, at 9:30 A.M.

JUSTICE JEFFREY S. BROWN, PART 21

Rule I.   Adjournments

A.   Motions and Status Conferences:

___ 1. Adjournments of motions and conferences may be granted if there is consent of all parties and prior approval of the court. If all parties do not consent to the adjournment, application shall be made in Court on the day of the conference or motion.

___ 2. Adjournments of motions shall be sought through the courtroom clerk, who will advise as to whether the adjournment has been granted.

3. Adjournments of conferences shall be sought through chambers. A date certain, consented to by all parties, must be requested at the time the adjournment is sought.

4. Letters confirming adjournments shall contain full names of all parties, index number, and shall specify if motion or conference is being adjourned.

5. Adjournments requested because of actual engagement of counsel on trial must be accompanied by an Affirmation of Engagement in conformity with 22 NYCRR Part 125.

6. Adjournment requests which are left on the chamber's voice mail shall be disregarded.

B.   Preliminary Conference

___ 1. Preliminary conference adjournments are to be addressed to the DCM Clerk's office and not to Chambers.

Rule II.   Motions

A.   Submission of Motions

1. All motions relating to DISCOVERY require appearance of counsel and pro se parties on the return date of the motion or order to show cause unless otherwise specifically waived by the court. There are no submitted discovery motions without an appearance in this part. All other motions are done on submission.

2. In the event a case is already scheduled for a conference with the court, counsel should endeavor to make the return date of a motion, if possible, on said date.

3. Motions are to be served and filed in conformity with CPLR § 2214. All motions must be organized in such a manner so that each branch of the motion stated in the notice of motion or order to show cause is preceded by a number or a letter. Said number or letter designation shall be used in the supporting affirmation and affidavits and shall correspond to the number/letter used for each branch as set forth in the notice of motion or order to show cause. Motions not consistent with these rules will be rejected.

4. All exhibits must be clearly tabbed; no exhibits shall be double sided; no miniscripts are accepted. All submissions shall be fully and securely bound and shall have a litigation back attached thereto. Motions not consistent with these rules will be rejected.

5. If all or part of a submitted motion is settled, counsel shall forward the original stipulation of settlement to the court. Such stipulation shall be accompanied by a letter setting forth the date the motion was submitted, what aspects of the motion have been settled and what issues remain to be decided. If the motion is resolved in its entirety, the movant shall indicate same. If the motion is resolved on the record, in whole or in part, movant shall obtain such transcript so that same can be "so-ordered," unless the court directs otherwise.

6. All papers must be submitted in a timely manner. The court will not consider late papers absent prior court approval. No sur-reply affidavit, affirmation, or letter will be accepted or considered without leave of the court.

7. Pursuant to CPLR § 3212(a), a motion for summary judgment shall be made no later than ninety (90) days after the filing of the note of issue, except with leave of court on good cause shown. Any physician affirmations, reports or other medical proof submitted in threshold motions shall contain the original signatures of the physician or medical provider.

8. When submitting proposed orders or judgments in connection with a motion, the same shall be submitted as a separately bound document. Proposed orders or judgments incorporated within the motion papers will be considered as exhibits, treated as such, and may be disregarded.

9. Counsel are required to provide the court with SELF–ADDRESSED, STAMPED ENVELOPES with the submitted papers in order to facilitate delivery of the court's decision.

10. Motions brought pursuant to CPLR §§ 3211, 3212, or 3213 shall not automatically stay disclosure.

B. Oral Argument

The court will determine, after submission, whether oral argument is warranted. Upon such determination, counsel for all parties will be contacted and advised of the new adjourned date for purposes of oral argument.

C. Application for a Stay or Temporary Restraining Order (TRO)

1. If an order to show cause seeking any injunctive relief, including a stay or TRO, is to be submitted, it must comply with Uniform Rule § 202.7(f). The movant shall first consult with chambers as to a convenient time for counsel to appear with regard to the compliance with Uniform Rule § 202.7(f).

2. At any conference of the matter, if an order to show cause seeking any injunctive relief, including a stay or TRO, is submitted or pending, counsel shall advise the court of the pendency of such application, the return date of such order to show cause, the relief sought and whether an immediate hearing is sought.

3. Requests to continue or vacate a stay or TRO beyond the return date of the motion shall be made on the call of the motion calendar. Failure to apply for such extension shall result in the automatic *vacatur* of the stay or TRO, unless the order to show cause provides otherwise.

D. Interim Partial or Full Settlement

If all or part of a submitted motion is settled, a proposed order with notice of settlement (on at least ten [10] days notice) or a signed waiver of settlement shall be submitted with a copy to be conformed and a self-addressed stamped envelope. Such order shall be accompanied by a letter setting forth the date the motion was submitted, what aspects of the motion have been settled and what issues remain to be decided. A copy of the stipulation settling such issues shall be forwarded to the court. If the motion is resolved, in whole or part, on the record, counsel shall obtain such transcript so that same can be "so ordered" unless the court otherwise directs.

Rule III. Court Appearances

A. The court will begin conferencing ready matters at 9:30 a.m. in the order in which all attorneys are checked in. There is no calendar call in this part.

B. Attorneys and "pro se" litigants must check in with the court officer or court clerk and complete the sign-in sheet. If counsel need to appear before another judge, they must advise the part clerk or court officer where they can be reached and note it on the sign-in sheet.

C. All counsel and pro-se litigants are directed to appear for each and every conference unless specifically excused by the court.

D. Counsel who appear in the part must be fully familiar with the case for which they appear and fully authorized to enter into agreements, both substantive and procedural, on behalf of their clients.

E. Counsel are advised to confirm all scheduled appearances with their adversary the day before the appearance date to confirm a prompt appearance.

Rule IV. Communication With Chambers

A. INQUIRES

1. In all communications with chambers by letter, the title of the action, full names of the parties and index number shall be set forth, with copies simultaneously delivered to all counsel. Ex parte communications will be disregarded, except as otherwise provided herein.

2. Copies of correspondence between counsel shall not be sent to the court. Such copies will be disregarded and not placed in the court's file.

3. The court will not accept telefax communications or submissions without prior permission.

4. The court shall not accept ex parte telephone communications on substantive issues.

5. E-mail correspondence with chambers staff is not permitted unless prior authorization is obtained.

6. Attorneys shall not call chambers during the daily lunch hour which is from 1:00 p.m. to 2:00 p.m.

B. SETTLEMENTS

1. No out of court settlement will be recognized or accepted unless counsel submits a letter, on notice to opposing counsel, submitting the executed settlement agreement/stipulation or certifying that such agreement/stipulation has, in fact, been executed.

Rule V. Sanctions

A. The court will not consider a sanctions application unless the moving party first seeks withdrawal or discontinuation of the offending act or action, or demands required or necessary action which is refused. Proof of such request must be made a part of the sanctions application.

Rule VI. Trial Part Rules

A. A note of issue is to be filed within 90 days after certification, unless otherwise specified in the certification order. Counsel for plaintiff shall pay the requisite fee with the County Clerk and ensure that the note of issue is submitted to the clerk who will then assign a calendar number.

B. At the first appearance of all cases assigned to the part for trial, a pre-trial conference will be held. At the conference, the court shall provide for the submission of scheduling of the following:

1. *In limine applications:* Any party intending to make a motion *in limine* shall submit a brief written affirmation setting forth the nature of the application and any supporting statutory or case law. The party shall furnish the court with an original and two (2) copies and provide counsel for all parties with a copy. There shall be a separate affirmation for each motion *in limine*.

2. Proof of filing of the note of issue.

3. Pre-trial memoranda providing the court with cited case law to be considered by the Court.

4. A courtesy copy of each exhibit intended to be introduced into evidence to the court or not, shall be pre-marked by the court reporter. As to those exhibits marked for identification, the court will address their admissibility *in limine* or during the trial, as may be appropriate.

5. All trial exhibits, whether the parties stipulate to admit them into evidence to the court or not, shall be pre-marked by the court reporter. As to those exhibits marked for identification, the court will address their admissibility *in limine* or during the trial, as may be appropriate.

6. A list of proposed witnesses for the court's information.

7. *Expert witnesses*—Each party shall, with respect to each expert witness that party intends to call, submit a list identifying with specificity any record, report, photograph, film, computer animation, x-ray, CT scan, MRI, EMG study or similar item or items to which an expert witness is expected to make reference as supporting in whole or in part the opinion he or she will offer. Where the exhibit is a many-paged document such as a hospital record, office record or voluminous (more than 10 pages) business record, counsel shall identify by way of tabs, Post–Its®, page numbering or similar device, the particular page or pages to which reference will be made.

8. Marked pleadings are to be submitted before opening statements.

9. Parties are encouraged to stipulate to facts and/or exhibits.

10. *Requests to Charge and Verdict Sheets*—Each party shall supply the court with preliminary requests to charge and proposed verdict sheets. Charges from the Pattern Jury Instructions may be identified by number without necessity of reproduction unless a modification of the standard charge is requested, in which case the modification is to be highlighted. Each party shall supply an original and three (3) copies to the court and furnish every other party with a copy. The preliminary requests may be supplemented, modified or edited as the trial progresses.

11. If deposition transcripts are to be utilized, a copy of the witness' deposition transcript should be available to the court.

12. Objections should be stated without argument except to simply state the ground therefor, e.g. hearsay, relevance, etc. If further argument is appropriate, it will be invited by the court.

13. Trial counsel are responsible for redactions of all evidence.

14. Trials will be conducted on a continual daily basis until conclusion. As such, no adjournments or delays during trial will be accepted unless exigent circumstances exist.

15. Trial counsel are responsible for taking back all exhibits, pleadings, transcripts, etc., at the end of a trial, unless, in the case of non-jury trials, the court reserves its decision. In all cases, exhibits, pleadings, transcripts, etc., not retrieved within thirty (30) days after the court renders a decision in a non-jury trial, shall be disposed of.

16. *Malpractice Departures*—In cases involving claims of professional negligence, on the next trial session after a party rests or such other time as the court may direct, each party [plaintiff] shall furnish the court and counsel for all parties with a list of the departures from the standards of good and accepted practice which that party asserts were testified to by its expert witness or witnesses. Where the testimony has been transcribed, page references will be required.

17. *Interpreters*—On the first appearance in the part, any party who will require the assistance of an interpreter shall notify the clerk in the part and specify the language (including dialect, where appropriate).

18. *Equipment*—On the first appearance in the part for trial, any party who intends to rely upon the court to supply equipment for utilizing a video tape recording, an audio tape recording, demonstrative evidence, or the like, shall notify the clerk in the part.

19. *Nassau County Police Officers*—On the first appearance in the part for trial, any party who has issued a subpoena to secure the appearance of a Nassau County Police Officer shall notify the clerk in the part so that the clerk may facilitate the officer's appearance through police liaison.

Rule VII. Miscellaneous

A. CONFERENCES/TRIAL

If there are any outstanding motions (submitted or pending) at the time of the conference/trial, the law secretary and/or judge must be so informed that day and the submission date must be provided by counsel. Copies of such motions should be available to the court at the time of such conference.

B. ATTORNEYS OF RECORD

Attorneys who have appeared in the matter are to make all appearances until they are relieved by the court or a fully executed consent to change attorney has been filed with Part 21and with the clerk of the court.

C. STAFF

The court functions through the aid and assistance of the courtroom and chambers staff. They are expected to treat attorneys, litigants and others in a dignified and civil manner; as well, they are to be treated in a civil and professional manner.

D. SETTLEMENTS

With respect to actions which have been settled or otherwise discontinued, counsel must comply with 22 NYCRR 202.28 or sanctions may be imposed. Counsel are reminded of their obligations under § 202.28 of the Uniform Rules for Trial Courts to file a stipulation or statement of discontinuance with the part of the Court to which the matter has been assigned within 20 days of the discontinuance. If a discontinued action is on a trial calendar, a copy of the stipulation or statement shall also be filed with the clerk of the trial part.

Revised 4.20.11

JUSTICE ROBERT A. BRUNO

Rule I. Adjournments

A. Motions and Status Conferences:

1. Applications to adjourn conferences or motions on consent must be received by Chambers via facsimile by **12:00 noon** on the business day prior to the conference date or return date of the motion. Applications for adjournments MUST be made using the Request for Adjournment Form which can be obtained through chambers or through the OCA website.

The Request for Adjournment Form is to be filled out completely. Incomplete forms or forms received after 12:00 noon on the business day prior to the conference date or return date shall be summarily denied, unless the Court is advised of extraordinary circumstances which will be taken into consideration.

If the application is based on counsel's actual engagement on another matter, an Affirmation of Actual Engagement, in conformity with 22 NYCRR Part 125, must accompany the Request for Adjournment Form.

The Attorney for the Child(ren) shall be notified of all adjournment requests and must, likewise, consent thereto.

If the application is granted, a letter confirming same shall be faxed to chambers, the same day the application is granted.

2. Letters confirming adjournments shall state that the Court has adjourned the conference or motion on consent of the parties to the specified date, and shall contain the full names of both parties, the index number as well as a notation indicating the current date the matter is on the Court's calendar and that all parties have been copied.

3. Adjournment requests which are left on the Chamber's voice mail shall be disregarded.

B. Preliminary Conference:

1. Adjournments of the Preliminary Conference will not be granted absent a compelling reason for same. Counsel are directed to review the provisions of 22 NYCRR § 202.16 (f) concerning conferences.

2. In addition to scheduling a Certification Conference as part of the Preliminary Conference Order, the Court may direct that a pre-trial conference also be held at the time of the Certification Conference in which event, the rules concerning pretrial conferences as hereinafter set forth, shall be applicable.

3. Discovery deadlines, Certification Deadlines and Note of Issue deadlines, will be enforced. Deadlines may not be extended absent prior approval by the Court.

Rule II.　Motions

A. Submission of the Motion

1. Appearances of all Counsel and parties are required on all motion return dates unless specifically waived by the Court.

2. All exhibits must be clearly tabbed; motions not consistent with this rule will be rejected and returned to counsel.

3. Motions are to be served and filed in conformity with CPLR § 2214. All motions must be organized in such a manner so that each branch of the motion stated in the Notice of Motion or Order To Show Cause is preceded by a number or letter. Said number/letter designation shall be used in the supporting affirmations and affidavits and shall correspond to the number/letter used for each branch as set forth in the Notice of Motion or Order To Show Cause.

4. No sur-reply, affidavit, affirmation, memorandum of law or letter will be accepted or considered by the Court without leave of the Court.

5. Counsel shall be fully prepared on the return date of all motions, for oral argument, if the Court requires.

B. Application for a Stay or Temporary Restraining Order

1. Any Order to Show Cause seeking any injunctive relief, including a stay or TRO, must be made in accordance with 22 NYCRR 202.7(f). The moving party shall advise the Court as soon as practicable of counsel's intent to make such application.

2. Requests to continue or vacate a stay or TRO beyond the return date of the motion shall be made on the call of the motion calendar. Failure to apply for such extension shall result in the automatic vacatur of the stay or TRO, unless the Order to Show Cause provides otherwise.

3. An "Emergency" Order to Show Cause requires a special affidavit based upon personal knowledge and affirmation explaining in detail the nature of the emergency. In addition to the foregoing, the movant should be prepared to appear in Court and to make a record before the Court, if the Court requires same.

C. Interim Partial or Full Settlement

If all or part of a submitted motion is settled, counsel shall forward the original stipulation of settlement to the Court. Such stipulation shall be accompanied by a letter setting forth the date the motion was submitted, what aspects of the motion have been settled and what issues remain to be decided. If the motion is resolved in its entirety the movant shall indicate same. If the motion is resolved, in whole or part, on the record, counsel shall obtain such transcript so that same can be "so ordered", unless the Court otherwise directs.

Rule III.　Court Appearances

A. All Court appearances, unless otherwise specified or directed by the Court, shall be scheduled for 9:30 a.m.

B. Attorneys and Pro Se litigants must alert the Court Officer or Court Clerk of their presence and complete a sign-in sheet. If counsel must also appear before another Judge, counsel must advise the Part Clerk or Court Officer where counsel can be reached. All counsel and litigants are directed to appear for each and every conference (including preliminary, status and compliance conferences).

C. All parties and attorneys, are required to appear at all scheduled dates, unless otherwise directed by the Court.

D. All conferences will be held in the order in which all attorneys have checked in.

Rule IV.　Communication with Chambers

A. In all communications with chambers by letter, the title of the action, full names of the parties, date matter is next on the Court's calendar and index number shall be set forth, with copies simultaneously delivered to all counsel. *Ex parte* communications will be disregarded.

B. Copies of correspondence between counsel shall not be sent to the Court. Such copies shall be disregarded and not placed in the Court's file.

C. The Court will not accept telefax communications without prior permission.

D. No out of Court settlement will be recognized or accepted unless counsel submits a letter, on notice to opposing counsel, and, if applicable, the Attorney for the Child(ren), submitting the executed settlement agreement/stipulation or certifying that such agreement/stipulation has, in fact, been executed.

E. The Court shall not accept *ex parte* telephone communications on substantive issues.

Rule V. Sanctions

The Court will not consider a sanctions application unless the moving party first seeks withdrawal or discontinuation of the offending act or action or demands required or necessary action which is refused. Proof of such request must be made a part of the sanctions application.

Rule VI. Trial Rules: Applicable to All Trials and all Hearings

A. A Note of Issue and Certificate of Readiness is to be filed within 30 days after certification unless otherwise instructed by the Court. A statement of Proposed Disposition shall be filed with proof of service along with the Note of Issue. 22 NYCRR § 202.16(h)

B. After a matter has been certified as trial-ready, the Court may set a date for a Pre–Trial Conference. Pre–Trial Conferences will be scheduled approximately 30 days prior to the trial date. Counsel with knowledge of the case and the parties must attend.

There will be no adjournments without the Court's consent. At the Pre–Trial Conference, the Court shall provide for the submission or scheduling of the following to the extent not previously ordered:

1. *In limine* applications must be on notice to all parties returnable at least ten (10) days prior to the first scheduled trial or any hearing date.

2. Annotated Statements of Proposed Disposition in which all of the criteria listed in the statute are provided and counsel's position stated as to each such criteria for both equitable distribution and maintenance issues.

3. Evaluations: In the event there are any valuations of a business interest or increased earning capacity, a cash flow chart shall be submitted by each side, listing counsel's proposal for payment thereof, as well as any other payments claimed due (such as payor's obligations for maintenance, child support, income taxes, etc.).

4. Exhibits: Counsel for the parties shall consult prior to the Pre–Trial conference and shall in good faith attempt to agree upon the exhibits that will be offered into evidence without objection. At the Pre–Trial conference date, each side shall then mark its exhibits into evidence as to those to which no objection has been made. All exhibits not consented to shall be marked for identification only. If the trial exhibits are voluminous, counsel shall consult the clerk of the part for guidance. The court will rule upon the objections to the contested exhibits at the earliest possible time. Exhibits not previously demanded which are to be used solely for credibility or rebuttal need not be pre-marked.

5. Trial Notebook: The parties shall submit trial notebooks two (2) weeks prior to trial or any hearing with all listed exhibits separately and consecutively tabbed [numbers for Plaintiff and letters for Defendant], with the original documents for the witnesses and a copy for the Court. At the conclusion of the trial all exhibits not received into evidence will be removed from notebooks and returned to counsel.

6. A list of proposed witnesses for the Court's information must be submitted at least five (5) business days prior to trial or any hearing, the order in which they will testify and the estimated length of their testimony.

7. A list of all expert witnesses with copies of their reports must be submitted at least five (5) business days prior to trial or any hearing.

8. Marked pleadings, to be submitted before opening statements must be submitted at least five (5) business days prior to trial.

9. Net worth statements, updated and sworn to within thirty [30] days of the trial date or any hearing.

10. A statement of stipulated facts. [Parties are encouraged to stipulate to facts and/or exhibits].

11. All trial exhibits, whether stipulated or contested on admissibility, should be pre-marked by the Court Reporter at least one (1) day prior to trial or any hearing.

12. If deposition transcripts are to be utilized, a copy of the witness' deposition transcript should be available to the Court. Counsel for the parties shall consult prior to trial and shall, in good faith, attempt to agree upon the portions of deposition testimony to be offered into evidence without objection. The parties shall delete from the testimony to be read and questions and answers that are irrelevant to the point for which the deposition testimony is offered. Each party shall prepare a list of deposition testimony to be offered to which no objection been made and, a separate list of deposition testimony as to which objection has been made. At least ten days prior to trial or such other time as the court may set, each party shall submit its list(s) to the Court and other counsel, together with a copy of the portions of the deposition testimony as to which objection has been made. The Court will rule upon the objections at the earliest possible time after consultation with counsel.

13. An accounting of any claimed pendente lite arrears supported by backup documentation.

14. Copies of life insurance polices and medical and dental policies of insurance in effect as of the date of the commencement of the action and as of the present date.

15. A list of issues to be determined by the Court including any pretrial motion issues referred to the trial by the Court.

16. Both sides shall have available at least four (4) copies of all Exhibits which are expected to be introduced into evidence.

17. Both sides shall have available at least four (4) copies of all deposition transcripts and prior statements which are expected to be read into the record or utilized on cross examination at the trial.

18. Both sides shall have available at least four (4) copies of any and all of the following.

(a) relevant orders issued by another court, such as final orders of custody or temporary or permanent orders of protection issued by the Family Court;

(b) any order of this Court that referred issues raised in motion practice to the trial of the action;

(c) any relevant so-ordered stipulation of this Court as well as transcripts of stipulations read into the record in open court during the pendency of the action; and

(d) any properly executed and acknowledged stipulation or agreement relating to material issues in this action.

19. Counsel are urged to stipulate that any issue relating to an award of counsel and expert fees be resolved by the Court, without testimony, upon the submission of affirmations and other appropriate documentation from counsel.

20. Counsel are required to stipulate in writing to any and all relevant material facts that are not and should not be in dispute. If it appears during the course of the trial that no bonafide attempt was undertaken to secure such stipulation, the Court will likely recess and delay the trial until there is compliance.

21. On the date the trial is scheduled, counsel are expected to be prepared to discuss settlement of all unresolved issues and to have complied with each of the trial rules set forth herein.

22. On the day before the scheduled trial or any hearing, counsel are directed to contact the Part Clerk or Chambers to confirm the Court's availability.

23. Objections should be stated without argument except to simply state the ground therefor, e.g., hearsay, relevance, etc. If further argument is appropriate, it will be invited by the Court.

24. Closing Arguments/Summations shall be submitted in writing, consisting of no more than twenty-five (25) pages along with the trial or hearing transcript within thirty (30) days of the conclusion of trial or hearing. Where an excerpt of a witness's testimony is quoted from the record, at the end of the quote, the transcript page number shall be inserted paren-

thetically and keyed to the transcript. Said Summations shall contain the following clearly delineated sections: a) a chronological procedural history of the action, including copies of all relevant orders, written stipulations and transcripts of stipulations placed on the record; b) a recitation of the issues to be determined; c) an in depth summary of the testimony of each witness; d) a summary of the findings of any expert report received in evidence; e) a summary of the exhibits in evidence; f) a detailed recitation of counsel's contentions as to the testimony and exhibits in evidence; and g) application law. The right to submit a Summation shall be deemed waived if not timely submitted to the Court. A copy of each side's and if applicable, the child's or children's Summation shall be served on all other parties simultaneous with filing with the Court. Responses to the Summations are prohibited and will not be considered. Summations shall have a Table of Contents. Failure to provide such Table of Contents may result in the Court not considering such summations.

25. Proposed Judgment and Findings of Fact and Conclusions of Law are to be submitted within thirty (30) days of the conclusion of trial or any hearing.

Rule VII. Miscellaneous

A. CONFERENCES/TRIAL. If there are any outstanding motions (submitted or pending) at the time of the conference/trial the Principal Law Clerk and/or Judge must be so informed of same that day; the submission date must be provided by counsel. Copies of such motions should be available to the Court at the time of such conference.

B. ATTORNEYS OF RECORD. Attorneys who have appeared in the matter are to make all appearances until they are relieved by the Court or a Consent to Change Attorneys has been filed with Part 26 and with the Clerk of the Court.

C. STAFF. The Court functions through the aid and assistance of the courtroom and Chambers staff. They are expected to treat attorneys, litigants and others in a dignified and civil manner, they as well are to be treated in a civil and dignified manner.

D. ATTORNEY FOR THE CHILD(REN). Counsel and the Attorney for the Child(ren) are reminded that the Attorney for the Child(ren) acts in the role of counsel for the child(ren). As such, the Attorney for the Child(ren) are bound by the same ethical and procedural rules as counsel for the parties. Ex-parte communications between the Attorney for the Child(ren) and the Court will not be permitted.

E. Failure to appear at any scheduled call of the calendar or at any conference may result in a default and/or a dismissal of the action (NYCRR § 202.27).

F. All trials and hearings shall continue day-to-day until completed.

G. It is incumbent upon all counsel and parties appearing before this Court to insure they have this

Court's current Part Rules and are in compliance with same.

H. These rules are in addition to the Uniform Rules for New York State Trial Courts and the Local Rules of Court. Failure to comply with any rules or orders of this Court may result in preclusion and/or sanctions without further notice.

Form 1. Request for Adjournment

HON. ROBERT A. BRUNO

REQUEST FOR ADJOURNMENT FORM—Part 24

THIS FORM MUST BE FILLED OUT COMPLETELY
INCOMPLETE FORMS WILL BE DISREGARDED

Case Name: _____ Index # _____

RJI Date: _____ Date Issue Joined: _____ Date PC Held: _____

Date on Calendar: _____ Last Court Appearance: _____

Req'd Adj. Dates(At Least 3): 1) _____ 2) _____ 3) _____

**ALL REQUESTS MUST BE ON CONSENT AND ALL REQUESTED AD-
JOURN DATES MUST BE CONFIRMED WITH YOUR ADVERSARY
AND ATTORNEY FOR THE CHILD, IF APPLICABLE, PRIOR TO MAK-
ING THE REQUEST.**

Nature of Conference: _____

If Motion, Nature of Relief Sought: _____

Reason for Adjournment (Affirmation of Actual Engagement must be attached
if applicable): _____

_____

_____

_____

_____

Discovery Completed (Y/N): ___ Was N/I filed? ___ Date N/I to be filed: ____

Contact Info:

Attorney contacting Court and who attorney represents: _____
Person Making Call: _____ Phone # _____

                                      Fax # _____

Adversary's name: _____ Phone # _____

                                      Fax # _____

ALL REQUESTS MUST BE RECEIVED VIA FAX (516) 571–1600
BEFORE 12:00 P.M. OF THE BUSINESS DAY PRIOR TO
THE CONFERENCE OR MOTION RETURN DATE

PLEASE FAX CONFIRMING LETTER OF DATE OF ADJOURNMENT

PLEASE NOTE:

THERE ARE NEW PRELIMINARY CONFERENCE AND INFORMATION
FORMS THAT ARE REQUIRED TO BE COMPLETED **PRIOR** TO THE
PRELIMINARY CONFERENCE.

FOR YOUR CONVENIENCE, PLEASE VISIT THE NASSAU COUNTY MAT-
RIMONIAL CENTER WEBSITE AT:

http://www.nycourts.gov/courts/10jd/nassau/matrimonial/index.shtml

AND CLICK ON THE "FORMS" TAB,

OR

THE P.C. FORM MAY BE OBTAINED AT:

http://www.nycourts.gov/courts/1   0jd/nassau/matrimonial/forms/PC–OR-
DER–2010.pdf

AND THE INFORMATION FORM MAY BE OBTAINED AT:

http://www.nycourts.gov/courts/1   0jd/nassau/matrimonial/forms/PC–INFO–
SHEET–2010.pdf

PLEASE HAVE THESE FORMS *COMPLETED* AND BE PREPARED TO PROVIDE ALL INFORMATION REQUIRED AT YOUR CONFERENCE WITH THE COURT.

JUSTICE STEVEN M. JAEGER, PART 43

Part 43. Hon. Steven M. Jaeger

Unless otherwise ordered by the Justice in a specific case, matters before the Justice shall be conducted in accordance with the CPLR, the Uniform Civil Rules of the Supreme Court, and the following:

Letters: Except as provided below, communications with chambers shall be by letter, with copies simultaneously delivered to all counsel. Copies of correspondence between counsel shall not be sent to the Court.

Telephone Calls. Except as provided below, telephone calls to chambers are permitted only in emergency situations requiring immediate attention. In such situations only, call chambers at the number listed above.

Faxes. Faxes to chambers are not permitted unless prior authorization is obtained.

Appearances. All appearances shall be made by attorneys with knowledge of the facts and vested with authority to enter into stipulations and/or dispositions which bind their respective clients. The failure to comply with this rule or the failure to appear in timely fashion may subject counsel to one or more of the sanctions authorized by 22 NYCRR § 202.27 and or 22 NYCRR Part 130–2. Attorneys shall comport themselves in accordance with the rules established in 22 NYCRR § 700.4. Attorneys of record must continue to appear for their clients until such time as the court has relieved counsel of that obligation or until a stipulation substituting counsel has been filed with the clerk of the court. See, CPLR § 321. Self-represented litigants shall be subject to the same rules of practice as attorneys appearing in the part.

Preliminary Conferences. Preliminary conferences will be held according to the rules set forth in 22 NYCRR § 202.19 and will be conducted in the Preliminary Conference Part of the Supreme Court Building. The conference will be scheduled by the clerk of the court.

Adjournments of preliminary conferences shall be addressed to the clerk of the Preliminary Conference Part (telephone no. 516–57–3511).

Compliance Conference. The compliance conference date will be set down in the preliminary conference order and must be held no later than 60 days before the date scheduled for the completion of discovery (22 NYCRR § 202.19[b][3]). The conference will be held in the courtroom. Attorneys appearing at the compliance conference must have telephone access to their respective clients and shall be prepared to enter into good faith settlement discussions with the court. Adjournments will be granted only for compelling reasons. In no event shall the compliance conference be held later than the compliance requirement date as set forth in the DCM timetable accompanying the preliminary conference order. To adjourn a compliance conference on consent, call chambers (516–571–2837) not later than 4:00 p.m. the day before the conference. A letter confirming the adjournment must be sent by facsimile (516–571–0161) with a copy to the other side. No compliance conference may be adjourned by phone or stipulation more than once or more than four (4) weeks without permission from the court.

Certification Conference. Pursuant to the rules of the Administrative Judge, a certification conference will be held prior to the filing of a note of issue. The certification conference will be held no later than 90 days before the date fixed for the filing of the note of issue. The conference will be held in the courtroom. Attorneys appearing at the certification conference must have telephone access to their respective clients and shall be prepared to enter into good faith settlement discussions with the court. There shall be no adjournments of certification conferences without the permission of the court.

Pre–Trial Conference. Following the filing of a note of issue and certificate or readiness, a pretrial conference shall be held in accordance with 22 NYCRR § 202.19[c] and § 202.26. Pre-trial conferences shall be held in the calendar control part or in such other courtroom as the Administrative Judge or the Judge presiding in the calendar control part shall direct. Attorneys appearing at the certification conference must have telephone access to their respective clients and shall be prepared to enter into good faith settlement discussions with the court. In the event the action is not settled, a trial date will be established. There shall be no adjournments of pre-trial conferences without the permission of the court.

Motion Practice.

A. *Return date and adjournments.* Motions, orders to show cause, writs and petitions are returnable only on Tuesday, Wednesday or Thursday. To adjourn a motion on consent, call chambers (516-571-2837) not later than 4:00 p.m. the day before the return date of the motion. A letter confirming the adjournment must be sent by facsimile to chambers (516–571–0161) with a copy to the other side. In the event counsel cannot agree to the adjournment of the motion, the court will entertain the application by oral application on the return date of the motion. No motion may be adjourned more than three (3) times, not to exceed a cumulative period of sixty (60) days without permission from the court. The court does not accept adjournments left by message on the chamber's voice mail.

B. *Submission of papers.* All motion papers are to be addressed to and submitted through the Motion Support Office not less than two (2) days prior to the submission date unless permission is otherwise given by the court for a later filing. The court will not accept papers in chambers or in the courtroom. The court will not accept sur-reply papers unless prior authorization has been given by the court. Sur-reply papers submitted in violation of this rule will be disregarded. Do not submit mail or fax papers to the court. They will be discarded. Chambers or courtesy copies are not required nor expected.

C. *Temporary restraining orders.* No temporary restraining order contained in an order to show cause will be extended beyond the initial return date of the motion except upon written stipulation "so ordered" by the court or as otherwise directed by the court. If the parties or counsel cannot agree to the continuation or termination of a temporary restraining order, all counsel and any pro se litigant must appear on the return date of the motion. The failure to appear will be deemed a waiver of the defaulting party's position with respect to the continuation or termination of the TRO.

D. *Cross–Motions.* Submission of a cross-motion with a stated return date that is beyond the return date of the original motion will not serve to adjourn the original motion, although the Court may elect, in its discretion, to adjourn the original motion.

E. *Summary Judgment.* Motions for summary judgment shall be returnable no later than 90 days after the filing of a note of issue.

F. *Proposed Orders.* All motions and cross-motions for dispositive relief submitted for Court consideration must be accompanied, at the time of submission, by a proposed Order. All opposition to any of the aforesaid must contain a proposed Order. Proposed Orders submitted after filing of a motion, Order to Show Cause or opposition must be made on notice to all parties, but do not require formal service.

G. *Memoranda of law required.* Every party in a special proceeding or a motion requesting dispositive relief is required to submit a separate memorandum of law in support of its respective position. Papers are to be submitted through the Motion Support Office. Citations are to be to the official reporters.

H. *Decisions.* Counsel are requested to provide the court with self-addressed postage paid envelopes or their facsimile number for the return of the decision.

Trials.

Jury Trials. A trial conference with the Court shall be held immediately prior to the commencement of all jury trials. At the trial conference, counsel shall supply the Court with marked pleadings, amendments thereto and all bills of particulars served. Counsel shall further provide the Court with a list of proposed jury charges and the contentions of each party and proposed jury verdict sheets. A list of all pre-marked exhibits shall also be provided to the Court and to the stenographer. Counsel shall notify the Court and op-

posing counsel in the conference of any motions in limine and any supporting statutory or case law. Counsel shall notify the Court of their inability to stipulate to the admission of any exhibits to be offered at trial. Counsel shall further advise the Court of the witnesses to be called, and if any be experts, shall further provide the information required by CPLR 3101 (d)(1)(I). The filing of a note of issue is a condition precedent to the commencement of any trial.

Non Jury Trials. Non-jury trials are subject to scheduling upon forty-eight hours notice. A conference with the Court shall proceed the commencement of all non-jury trials at which counsel shall provide the following: 1) A copy of marked pleadings, amendment thereto, bills of particulars; 2) A list of pre-marked exhibits; and identification of those on which counsel could not agree as to their introduction at trial; 3) A list of witnesses and if any be experts, the information required by CPLR 3101(d)(1)(I); and 4) pre-trial memoranda of law. The parties shall be required to provide a transcript of the trial. The filing of a note of issue is a condition precedent to the commencement of any trial.

Miscellaneous Rules.

A. *Ex parte and miscellaneous communications.* The court will not accept any ex parte communications by telephone or letter from counsel or a self-represented litigant. The court will not accept any correspondence between counsel except as may be necessary to confirm any adjournment.

B. *Settlements and other stipulations.* If an action is settled or discontinued or the parties otherwise stipulate to the resolution of an issue in dispute, counsel should advise the court forthwith by sending the court a copy of the stipulation. The original of any stipulation of settlement or discontinuance must be filed with the County Clerk, as the clerk of the court.

C. *Court personnel.* The court functions with the aid and support of the courtroom and chambers personnel. The court and the personnel assigned to the court will treat counsel, litigants and other persons present with dignity and courtesy which is indispensable to the proper administration of justice and the court expects the court personnel to be treated in like manner.

D. *Writs and Contempts.* All applications shall be calendared on the date returnable. Appearance by all parties is mandatory. No adjournments will be granted unless a stipulation consenting to the adjournment, signed by all parties and any alleged contemptor who is not a party, is received in Chambers no later than 1:00 p.m. of the day prior to the return date.

E. *Compromise Applications.* All applications for court approval of a proposed compromise of an infant or other disabled party's claim must be submitted through the Special Term, with proof of service on all remaining parties. Compliance with the provisions of

CPLR 1207, 1208 and 22 NYCRR 202.67 and a proposed distribution of net amounts to be recovered by the disabled plaintiff that is consistent with the provisions of CPLR 1206 is required. The Court will not accept medical reports/affidavits executed more than six months prior to the submission date. The report must indicate whether the injured plaintiff has fully recovered, and if not, the nature and extent of the injuries and the costs of future treatment. Since the Court may direct that notice of the application be given to all persons who possess claims against the proceeds recoverable under the compromise, including those with statutory liens, the names and addresses of all such persons and the amount of their prospective claims must be set forth in the petition. If no person has asserted such a claim, the petition must so state. Once the submissions are complete, an appearance date shall be scheduled by the Court.

F. *Hearings/Inquests.* All hearings and/or inquests emanating from cases in the inventory of IAS Part 43 shall be scheduled by the Court. The filing of a note of issue is a condition precedent to the commencement of any hearing or inquest.

MATRIMONIAL
JUDGES' PART RULES
JUSTICE NORMAN JANOWITZ

Rule I. Adjournments

A. Motions and Status Conferences:

1. Applications to adjourn conferences or motions on consent must be received by Chambers via facsimile by 2:00 p.m. on the business day prior to the conference date or return date of the motion. Applications for adjournments MUST be made using the Request for Adjournment Form which can be obtained through chambers or through the OCA website.

The Request for Adjournment Form is to be filled out completely. Incomplete forms or forms received after 2:00 p.m on the business day prior to the conference date or return date shall be summarily denied, unless the Court is advised of extraordinary circumstances which will be taken into consideration.

If the application is based on counsel's actual engagement on another matter, an Affirmation of Actual Engagement, in conformity with 22 NYCRR Part 125, must accompany the Request for Adjournment Form.

The Attorney for the Child(ren) shall be notified of all adjournment requests and must, likewise, consent thereto.

If the application is granted, a letter confirming same shall be faxed to chambers, the same day the application is granted.

2. Letters confirming adjournments shall state that the Court has adjourned the conference or motion on consent of the parties to the specified date, and shall contain the full names of both parties, the index number as well as a notation indicating the current date the matter is on the Court's calendar and that all parties have been copied.

3. Adjournment requests which are left on the Chamber's voice mail shall be disregarded.

B. Preliminary Conference:

1. Adjournments of the Preliminary Conference will not be granted absent a compelling reason for same. Counsel are directed to review the provisions of 22 NYCRR § 202.16 (f) concerning conferences.

2. In addition to scheduling a Certification Conference as part of the Preliminary Conference Order, the Court may direct that a pre-trial conference also be held at the time of the Certification Conference in which event, the rules concerning pretrial conferences as hereinafter set forth, shall be applicable.

3. Discovery deadlines, Certification Deadlines and Note of Issue deadlines, will be enforced. Deadlines may not be extended absent prior approval by the Court.

Rule II. Motions

A. Pre-Motion Conferences:

1. Prior to making or filing any motions, including applications to be relieved, counsel for the moving party MUST arrange for a conference call to be held with his/her adversary and the Court to discuss the issues involved and the possible resolutions thereof. The Attorney for the Child(ren) shall also be notified and included in such conference calls. Counsel fully familiar with the matter and with authority to bind their clients MUST be available to participate in the conference.

2. If the matter can be resolved during the conference, an order consistent with such resolution may be issued.

3. If the matter cannot be resolved, the Court will set a briefing schedule for the motion which shall be "So Ordered."

B. Submission of the Motion

1. Appearances of all Counsel and parties are required on all motion return dates unless specifically waived by the Court.

2. All exhibits must be clearly tabbed; motions not consistent with this rule will be rejected and returned to counsel.

3. Motions are to be served and filed in conformity with CPLR § 2214. All motions must be organized in such a manner so that each branch of the motion stated in the Notice of Motion or Order To Show Cause is preceded by a number or letter. Said number/letter designation shall be used in the supporting affirmations and affidavits and shall correspond to the number/letter used for each branch as set forth in the Notice of Motion or Order To Show Cause. Motions not consistent with these rules will be rejected.

4. No sur-reply, affidavit, affirmation, memorandum of law or letter will be accepted or considered by the Court without leave of the Court.

5. The Court will determine, after submission, whether oral argument is warranted. Upon such determination, counsel for all parties will be contacted and advised of the new adjourned date for purposes of oral argument.

6. Counsel are requested to provide the Court with SELF-ADDRESSED, STAMPED ENVEL-

OPES with the submitted papers in order to facilitate delivery of the Court's decision.

7. All motions seeking pendente lite relief pursuant to the new mandatory maintenance guidelines effective October 13, 2010 must include a temporary maintenance guidelines worksheet.

C. Application for a Stay or Temporary Restraining Order

1. Any Order to Show Cause seeking any injunctive relief, including a stay or TRO, must be made in accordance with 22 NYCRR 202.7(f). The moving party shall advise the Court as soon as practicable of counsel's intent to make such application.

2. Requests to continue or vacate a stay or TRO beyond the return date of the motion shall be made on the call of the motion calendar. Failure to apply for such extension shall result in the automatic vacatur of the stay or TRO, unless the Order to Show Cause provides otherwise.

3. An "Emergency" Order to Show Cause requires a special affidavit based upon personal knowledge and affirmation explaining in detail the nature of the emergency. In addition to the foregoing, the movant should be prepared to appear in Court and to make a record before the Court, if the Court requires same.

D. Interim Partial or Full Settlement

If all or part of a submitted motion is settled, counsel shall forward the original stipulation of settlement to the Court. Such stipulation shall be accompanied by a letter setting forth the date the motion was submitted, what aspects of the motion have been settled and what issues remain to be decided. If the motion is resolved in its entirety the movant shall indicate same. If the motion is resolved, in whole or part, on the record, counsel shall obtain such transcript so that same can be "so ordered", unless the Court otherwise directs.

Rule III. Court Appearances

A. All Court appearances, unless otherwise specified or directed by the Court, shall be scheduled for 9:30 a.m.

B. Attorneys and Pro Se litigants must alert the Court Officer or Court Clerk of their presence and complete a sign-in sheet. If counsel must also appear before another Judge, counsel must advise the Part Clerk or Court Officer where counsel can be reached. All counsel and litigants are directed to appear for each and every conference (including preliminary, status and compliance conferences).

C. All parties and attorneys, are required to appear at all scheduled dates, unless otherwise directed by the Court.

D. All conferences will be held in the order in which all attorneys and parties have checked in.

Rule IV. Communication with Chambers

A. In all communications with chambers by letter, the title of the action, full names of the parties, date matter is next on the Court's calendar and index number shall be set forth, with copies simultaneously delivered to all counsel. *Ex parte* communications will be disregarded.

B. Copies of correspondence between counsel shall not be sent to the Court. Such copies shall be disregarded and not placed in the Court's file.

C. The Court will not accept telefax communications without prior permission.

D. No out of Court settlement will be recognized or accepted unless counsel submits a letter, on notice to opposing counsel, and, if applicable, the Attorney for the Child(ren), submitting the executed settlement agreement/stipulation or certifying that such agreement/stipulation has, in fact, been executed.

E. The Court shall not accept *ex parte* telephone communications on substantive issues.

Rule V. Sanctions

The Court will not consider a sanctions application unless the moving party first seeks withdrawal or discontinuation of the offending act or action or demands required or necessary action which is refused. Proof of such request must be made a part of the sanctions application.

Rule VI. Trial Rules: Applicable to all Trials and all Hearings

A. A Note of Issue and Certificate of Readiness are to be filed within 30 days after certification unless otherwise instructed by the Court. A statement of Proposed Disposition shall be filed with proof of service along with the Note of Issue. 22 NYCRR § 202.16(h)

B. After a matter has been certified as trial-ready, the Court may set a date for a Pre–Trial Conference. Pre–Trial Conferences will be scheduled approximately 30 days prior to the trial date. Counsel with knowledge of the case and the parties must attend.

There will be no adjournments without the Court's consent. At the Pre–Trial Conference, the Court shall provide for the submission or scheduling of the following to the extent not previously ordered:

1. *In limine* applications must be on notice to all parties returnable at least 10 days prior to the first scheduled trial date.

2. Annotated Statements of Proposed Disposition in which all of the criteria listed in the statute are provided and counsel's position stated as to each such criteria for both equitable distribution and maintenance issues.

3. *Evaluations:* In the event there are any valuations of a business interest or increased earning ca-

pacity, a cash flow chart shall be submitted by each side, listing counsel's proposal for payment thereof, as well as any other payments claimed due (such as payor's obligations for maintenance, child support, income taxes, etc.).

4. *Exhibits:* Counsel for the parties shall consult prior to the Pre–Trial conference and shall in good faith attempt to agree upon the exhibits that will be offered into evidence without objection. At the Pre–Trial conference date, each side shall then mark its exhibits into evidence as to those to which no objection has been made. All exhibits not consented to shall be marked for identification only. If the trial exhibits are voluminous, counsel shall consult the clerk of the part for guidance. The court will rule upon the objections to the contested exhibits at the earliest possible time. Exhibits not previously demanded which are to be used solely for credibility or rebuttal need not be pre-marked.

5. *Trial Notebook:* The parties shall submit trial notebooks two (2) weeks prior to trial with all listed exhibits separately and consecutively tabbed [numbers for Plaintiff and letters for Defendant], with the original documents for the witnesses and a copy for the Court. At the conclusion of the trial all exhibits not received into evidence will be removed from the notebooks and returned to counsel.

6. A list of proposed witnesses for the Court's information must be submitted at least 5 business days prior to trial, the order in which they will testify and the estimated length of their testimony.

7. A list of all expert witnesses with copies of their reports must be submitted at least 5 business days prior to trial.

8. Marked pleadings, to be submitted before opening statements must be submitted at least 5 business days prior to trial.

9. Net worth statements MUST BE updated and sworn to within thirty [30] days of the trial date.

10. A statement of stipulated facts. [Parties are encouraged to stipulate to facts and/or exhibits].

11. All trial exhibits, whether stipulated or contested on admissibility, should be pre-marked by the Court Reporter at least one (1) day prior to trial.

12. If deposition transcripts are to be utilized, a copy of the witness' deposition transcript should be available to the Court. Counsel for the parties shall consult prior to trial and shall, in good faith, attempt to agree upon the portions of deposition testimony to be offered into evidence without objection. The parties shall delete from the testimony to be read the questions and answers that are irrelevant to the point for which the deposition testimony is offered. Each party shall prepare a list of deposition testimony to be offered to which no objection has been made and, a separate list of deposition testimony as to which objections have been made. At least ten days prior to trial

or such other time as the court may set, each party shall submit its list(s) to the Court and other counsel, together with a copy of the portions of the deposition testimony as to which objection has been made. The Court will rule upon the objections at the earliest possible time after consultation with counsel.

13. An accounting of any claimed pendente lite arrears supported by backup documentation.

14. Copies of life insurance polices and medical and dental policies of insurance in effect as of the date of the commencement of the action and as of the present date.

15. A list of issues to be determined by the Court including any pretrial motion issues referred to the trial by the Court.

16. Both sides shall have available at least four (4) copies of all Exhibits which are expected to be introduced into evidence.

17. Both sides shall have available at least four (4) copies of all deposition transcripts and prior statements which are expected to be read into the record or utilized on cross examination at the trial.

18. Both sides shall have available at least four (4) copies of any and all of the following.

   (a) relevant orders issued by another court, such as final orders of custody or temporary or permanent orders of protection issued by the Family Court;

   (b) any order of this Court that referred issues raised in motion practice to the trial of the action;

   (c) any relevant so-ordered stipulation of this Court as well as transcripts of stipulations read into the record in open court during the pendency of the action; and

   (d) any properly executed and acknowledged stipulation or agreement relating to material issues in this action.

19. Counsel are urged to stipulate that any issue relating to an award of counsel and expert fees be resolved by the Court, without testimony, upon the submission of affirmations and other appropriate documentation from counsel.

20. Counsel are required to stipulate in writing to any and all relevant material facts that are not and should not be in dispute. If it appears during the course of the trial that no bonafide attempt was undertaken to secure such stipulation, the Court will likely recess and delay the trial until there is compliance.

21. On the date the trial is scheduled, counsel are expected to be prepared to discuss settlement of all unresolved issues and to have complied with each of the trial rules set forth herein.

22. On the day before the scheduled trial, counsel are directed to contact the Part Clerk or Chambers to confirm the Court's availability.

23. Objections should be stated without argument except to simply state the ground therefor, e.g., hearsay, relevance, etc. If further argument is appropriate, it will be invited by the Court.

24. Closing Arguments/Summations shall be submitted in writing, consisting of no more than 25 pages along with the trial transcript within thirty (30) days of the conclusion of trial. Where an excerpt of a witness's testimony is quoted from the record, at the end of the quote, the transcript page number shall be inserted parenthetically and keyed to the transcript. Said Summations shall contain the following clearly delineated sections: a) a chronological procedural history of the action, including copies of all relevant orders, written stipulations and transcripts of stipulations placed on the record; b) a recitation of the issues to be determined; c) an in depth summary of the testimony of each witness; d) a summary of the findings of any expert report received in evidence; e) a summary of the exhibits in evidence; f) a detailed recitation of counsel's contentions as to the testimony and exhibits in evidence; and g) application law. The right to submit a Summation shall be deemed waived if not timely submitted to the Court. A copy of each side's and if applicable, the child's or children's Summation shall be served on all other parties simultaneous with filing with the Court. Responses to the Summations are prohibited and will not be considered. Summations shall have a Table of Contents. Failure to provide such Table of Contents may result in the Court not considering such summations.

25. Proposed Judgment and Findings of Fact and Conclusions of Law are to be submitted within thirty (30) days of the conclusion of trial.

Rule VII. Miscellaneous

A. CONFERENCES/TRIAL—If there are any outstanding motions (submitted or pending) at the time of the conference/trial the Principal Law Clerk and/or Judge must be so informed of same that day; the submission date must be provided by counsel. Copies of such motions should be available to the Court at the time of such conference.

B. ATTORNEYS OF RECORD—Attorneys who have appeared in the matter are to make all appearances until they are relieved by the Court or a Consent to Change Attorney(s) has been filed with Part 25 and with the Clerk of the Court.

C. STAFF—The Court functions through the aid and assistance of the courtroom and Chambers staff. They are expected to treat attorneys, litigants and others in a dignified and civil manner, they as well are to be treated in a civil and dignified manner.

D. ATTORNEY FOR THE CHILD(REN)—Counsel and the Attorney for the Child(ren) are reminded that the Attorney for the Child(ren) acts in the role of counsel for the child(ren). As such, the Attorney for the Child(ren) are bound by the same ethical and procedural rules as counsel for the parties. Ex-parte communications between the Attorney for the Child(ren) and the Court will not be permitted.

E. Failure to appear at any scheduled call of the calendar or at any conference may result in a default and/or a dismissal of the action (NYCRR § 202.27).

F. All trials and hearings shall continue day-to-day until completed.

G. It is incumbent upon all counsel and parties appearing before this Court to insure they have this Court's current Part Rules and are in compliance with same.

H. These rules are in addition to the Uniform Rules for New York State Trial Courts and the Local Rules of Court. Failure to comply with any rules or orders of this Court may result in preclusion and/or sanctions without further notice.

Form 1. Request for Adjournment

HON. NORMAN JANOWITZ

REQUEST FOR ADJOURNMENT FORM—Part 25

THIS FORM MUST BE FILLED OUT COMPLETELY
INCOMPLETE FORMS WILL BE DISREGARDED

Case Name: _____ Index # _____

RJI Date: _____ Date Issue Joined: _____ Date PC Held: _____

Date on Calendar: _____ Last Court Appearance: _____

Req'd Adj. Dates(At Least 3):   1) _____ 2) _____ 3) _____

ALL REQUESTS MUST BE ON CONSENT AND ALL REQUESTED ADJOURN DATES MUST BE CONFIRMED WITH YOUR ADVERSARY AND ATTORNEY FOR THE CHILD, IF APPLICABLE, PRIOR TO MAKING THE REQUEST.

Nature of Conference: _____

If Motion, Nature of Relief Sought: _____

Reason for Adjournment (Affirmation of Actual Engagement must be attached if applicable):

_____

_____

_____

_____

Discovery Completed (Y/N): ____ Was N/I filed? ____ Date N/ I to be filed: _____

Contact Info:

Attorney contacting Court and who attorney represents: _____

Person Making Call: _____ Phone # _____

                                         Fax # _____

Adversary's name: _____ Phone # _____

                                         Fax # _____

ALL REQUESTS MUST BE RECEIVED VIA FAX (516) 571–0770
BEFORE 12:00 P.M. OF THE BUSINESS DAY PRIOR TO
THE CONFERENCE OR MOTION RETURN DATE

PLEASE FAX CONFIRMING LETTER OF DATE OF ADJOURNMENT

PLEASE NOTE:

THERE ARE NEW PRELIMINARY CONFERENCE AND INFORMATION FORMS THAT ARE REQUIRED TO BE COMPLETED **PRIOR** TO THE PRELIMINARY CONFERENCE.

FOR YOUR CONVENIENCE, PLEASE VISIT THE NASSAU COUNTY MATRIMONIAL CENTER WEBSITE AT:

http://www.nycourts.gov/courts/10jd/nassau/matrimonial/index.shtml

AND CLICK ON THE "FORMS" TAB,

OR

THE P.C. FORM MAY BE OBTAINED AT:

http://www.nycourts.gov/courts/1   0jd/nassau/matrimonial/forms/PC–OR-
DER–2010.pdf

AND THE INFORMATION FORM MAY BE OBTAINED AT:

http://www.nycourts.gov/courts/1   0jd/nassau/matrimonial/forms/PC–INFO–
SHEET–2010.pdf

   **PLEASE HAVE THESE FORMS *COMPLETED* AND BE PREPARED TO
PROVIDE ALL INFORMATION REQUIRED AT YOUR CONFERENCE
WITH THE COURT.**

JUSTICE ANTHONY J. FALANGA

TR 1. Trial Rules

1. A Note of Issue is to be filed within thirty (30) days after certification by counsel for plaintiff.

2. Neither side may prosecute a motion involving discovery issues once the case has been certified for trial without leave of the Court.

3. At least two (2) weeks prior to the scheduled trial date, both sides must exchange and submit to this Part the following:

(a) an up-dated Net Worth Statement/Affidavit, dated within 90 days prior to the date of trial;

(b) the statutory criteria on the attached worksheet regarding maintenance and equitable distribution. The Court will expect these worksheets to be utilized by counsel to facilitate the fact finding process and achieve an expeditious completion of the trial;

(c) in the event there are any evaluations of income producing assets subject to equitable distribution, (business interest, professional practice, enhanced earning capacity, license or degree, etc. involved in the case), then a "cash flow" chart shall be submitted by each side, setting forth counsel's proposal for apportioning the income stream produced by the asset for the payment of a distributive award as well as other obligations such as maintenance, child support, income taxes, interest on payments etc.; and

(d) a list of witnesses each side intends to call at the trial, including expert witnesses. Documentation of compliance with CPLR 3101(d) shall be provided with regard to any expert, other than a court-appointed neutral expert, that a party intends to call at trial.

(e) an accounting of any claimed pendente lite arrears supported by backup documentation.

4. On the date of trial, plaintiff's counsel is to provide the Court with marked pleadings, including pleadings from any proceedings transferred from another court and consolidated with the matrimonial action, such as family offense proceedings transferred from the Family Court (CPLR 4012).

5. Both sides shall have available at least four (4) copies of all Exhibits which are expected to be introduced into evidence.

6. Both sides shall have available at least four (4) copies of all deposition transcripts which are expected to be read into the record or utilized on cross examination at the trial.

7. Both sides shall have available at least four (4) copies of any and all of the following:

(a) relevant orders issued by another court, such as final orders of custody or temporary or permanent orders of protection issued by the Family Court;

(b) any order of this Court that referred issues raised in motion practice to the trial of the action; and

(c) any relevant so-ordered stipulation of this Court read into the record in open court during the pendency of the action.

8. Post Trial Summations will be expected and will be prepared in accordance with the sheet annexed hereto entitled "Post Trial Memos–Summation Rules".

9. Counsel are urged to stipulate that any issue relating to an award of counsel and expert fees be resolved by the Court upon the submission of affirmations and other appropriate documentation from counsel.

10. Counsel are required to stipulate to any and all relevant material facts that are not and should not be in dispute. If it appears during the course of the trial that no bonafide attempt was undertaken to secure such stipulation, the Court will likely recess and delay the trial until there is compliance.

11. On the date the trial is scheduled, counsel are expected to be prepared to discuss settlement of all unresolved issues and to have complied with each of the trial rules set forth herein.

SR 1. Summation Rules

1. At the conclusion of trial, both sides, as well as the law guardian, if any, will be expected to submit a Post Trial Summation with respect to all issues to be decided by the Court. Said Summations shall contain the following clearly delineated sections: a) a chronological procedural history of the action, including copies of all relevant orders, written stipulations and transcripts of stipulations placed on the record; b) a recitation of the issues to be determined; c) an in depth summary of the testimony of each witness; d) a summary of the findings of any expert report received in evidence; e) a summary of the exhibits in evidence; f) a detailed recitation of counsel's contentions as to the testimony and exhibits in evidence relevant to each and every statutory criteria relating to maintenance and equitable distribution; and g) applicable law.

2. Post Trial Summations will be marked as Court Exhibits and shall be part of the record.

3. The date for submission of the Post Trial Summations will be set by the Court after consultation with all counsel. The right to submit a Post Trial Summation shall be deemed waived if not timely submitted to the Court.

4. A copy of each side's Summation shall be served on all other parties simultaneous with filing with the Court.

5. Responses to the Summation are prohibited and will not be considered.

6. The Court is to be provided the original and one copy of each Summation.

7. Summations shall have a Table of Contents. Failure to provide such Table of Contents will result in the Court not considering such summations.

TM 1. Trial Memo

TRIAL MEMO—WORK SHEET

MAINTENANCE CRITERIA

(1) THE INCOME AND PROPERTY OF THE RESPECTIVE PARTIES INCLUDING MARITAL PROPERTY DISTRIBUTED HEREIN—

(2) THE DURATION OF THE MARRIAGE AND THE AGE AND HEALTH OF BOTH PARTIES—

(3) THE PRESENT AND FUTURE EARNING CAPACITY OF BOTH PARTIES—

(4) THE ABILITY OF THE PARTY SEEKING MAINTENANCE TO BECOME SELF–SUPPORTING AND, IF APPLICABLE, THE PERIOD OF TIME AND TRAINING NECESSARY THEREFOR—

(5) REDUCED OR LOST LIFETIME EARNING CAPACITY OF THE PARTY SEEKING MAINTENANCE AS A RESULT OF HAVING FOREGONE OR DELAYED EDUCATION, TRAINING, EMPLOYMENT, OR CAREER OPPORTUNITIES DURING THE MARRIAGE—

(6) THE PRESENCE OF CHILDREN OF THE MARRIAGE IN THE RESPECTIVE HOMES OF THE PARTIES—

(7) THE TAX CONSEQUENCES TO EACH PARTY—

(8) CONTRIBUTIONS AND SERVICES OF THE PARTY SEEKING MAINTENANCE AS A SPOUSE, PARENT, WAGE EARNER AND HOMEMAKER, AND TO THE CAREER OR CAREER POTENTIAL OF THE OTHER PARTY—

(9) THE WASTEFUL DISSIPATION OF MARITAL PROPERTY BY EITHER SPOUSE—

(10) ANY TRANSFER OR ENCUMBRANCE MADE IN CONTEMPLATION OF A MATRIMONIAL ACTION WITHOUT FAIR CONSIDERATION—

(11) ANY OTHER FACTOR WHICH THE COURT SHALL EXPRESSLY FIND TO BE JUST AND PROPER—

TRIAL MEMO—WORK SHEET

EQUITABLE DISTRIBUTION CRITERIA

(1) INCOME AND PROPERTY OF EACH PARTY AT THE TIME OF MARRIAGE AND AT THE TIME OF THE COMMENCEMENT OF THE ACTION—

(2) DURATION OF THE MARRIAGE AND AGE AND HEALTH OF THE PARTIES—

(3) NEED OF CUSTODIAL PARENT TO OCCUPY OR OWN THE MARITAL RESIDENCE—

(4) THE LOSS OF INHERITANCE AND PENSION RIGHTS UPON DISSOLUTION OF THE MARRIAGE AS OF THE DATE OF DISSOLUTION—

(5) ANY AWARD OF MAINTENANCE MADE HEREIN—

(6) ANY EQUITABLE CLAIM TO, INTEREST IN, OR DIRECT OR INDIRECT CONTRIBUTION MADE TO THE ACQUISITION OF SUCH MARITAL PROPERTY BY THE PARTY NOT HAVING TITLE, INCLUDING JOINT EFFORTS OR EXPENDITURES AND CONTRIBUTIONS AND SERVICES AS A SPOUSE, PARENT, WAGE EARNER AND HOMEMAKER AND TO THE CAREER POTENTIAL OF THE OTHER PARTY—

(7) LIQUID OR NON–LIQUID CHARACTER OF ALL MARITAL PROPERTY—

(8) THE PROBABLE FUTURE FINANCIAL CIRCUMSTANCES OF THE PARTIES—

(9) THE IMPOSSIBILITY OR DIFFICULTY OF EVALUATING ANY COMPONENT ASSET OR ANY INTEREST IN A BUSINESS, CORPORATION OR PROFESSION AND THE ECONOMIC DESIRABILITY OF RETAINING SUCH ASSET OR INTEREST INTACT AND FREE FROM ANY CLAIM OR INTERFERENCE BY THE OTHER PARTY—

(10) THE TAX CONSEQUENCES TO EACH PARTY—

(11) THE WASTEFUL DISSIPATION OF AS-
SETS BY EITHER SPOUSE—

(12) ANY TRANSFER OR ENCUMBRANCE
MADE IN CONTEMPLATION OF A MATRIMO-

NIAL ACTION WITHOUT FAIR CONSIDER-
ATION—

(13) ANY OTHER FACTOR—

JUSTICE ROBERT A. ROSS

Rule I. Adjournments

A. Motions and Status Conferences:

1. Adjournments of motions and conferences may
be granted if there is consent of all parties. If all
parties do not consent to the adjournment, application
shall be made by conference call on the day of the
conference or the motion. Except for applications
made in court, upon approval of the adjournment, a
letter must be submitted confirming same with copy
to the client. Law Guardians must be notified of, and
consent to, adjournments on any matters to which
they are assigned.

2. Adjournments of motions shall be sought
through the courtroom clerk who will advise as to
whether the adjournment has been granted.

3. Adjournments of conferences shall be sought
through chambers. A date certain, consented to by
all parties, must be requested at the time the adjournment is sought.

4. Letters confirming adjournments shall contain
full names of both parties, index number, and shall
specify if motion or conference is being adjourned.

5. Adjournment requests which are left on the
Chamber's Voice Mail shall be disregarded.

6. Adjournments requested because of engagement of counsel must be accompanied by an Affirmation of Engagement in conformity with 22 NYCRR
Part 125.

B. Preliminary Conference:

Preliminary conference adjournments will **not** be
granted without a compelling reason for same. Counsel are directed to review the provisions of 22 NYCRR
§ 202.16 (f) concerning conferences.

In addition to scheduling a certification conference
as part of the Preliminary Conference order, the
Court may direct that a pre-trial conference will also
be held at the time of the certification conference in
which event, the rules concerning pre-trial conferences as hereinafter set forth, shall be applicable.

Rule II. Motions

A. Pre–Motion Conferences:

1. Prior to the making or filing of any Motions, the
Counsel for the moving party is urged to communicate
with the Court by telephone or in writing (no more
than two [2] pages) on notice to opposing counsel and,

if appropriate, the Law Guardian, advising as to the
issue(s) in dispute and requesting a conference. If a
cross-motion is contemplated, like notice shall be forwarded to the Court and counsel. Such correspondence shall not be considered by the Court in reaching
its decision.

2. Upon review of the letter application, the Court
may expeditiously schedule a conference with counsel
or the Court may waive the conference requirement
and counsel may proceed with their formal application.
Counsel fully familiar with the matter and with authority to bind their client must be available to participate in the conference.

3. If the matter can be resolved during the conference, an order consistent with such resolution may be
issued.

4. If the matter cannot be resolved, the Court will
set a briefing schedule for the motion which shall be
"So Ordered".

5. This rule does not apply to applications for
counsel to be relieved.

B. Submission of the Motion

1. All motions shall be marked as submitted on the
return date.

2. All exhibits must be clearly tabbed; motions not
consistent with this rule will be rejected and returned
to counsel.

3. No sur-reply affidavit, affirmation, memorandum of law or letter will be accepted or considered by
the Court without leave of the Court.

4. Counsel are requested to provide the court with
self addressed stamped envelopes with the submitted
papers in order to facilitate delivery of the court's
decision.

C. Application for a Stay or Temporary Re-
straining Order (TRO)

1. At any conference of the matter, if an Order to
Show Cause seeking any injunctive relief including a
stay or TRO is submitted or pending, counsel shall
advise the Court of the pendency of such application,
the return date of such Order to Show Cause, the
relief sought and whether an immediate hearing is
sought.

2. Requests to continue or vacate a stay or TRO
beyond the return date of the motion shall be made on
the call of the motion calendar. Failure to apply for

such extension shall result in the automatic vacatur of the stay or TRO, unless the Order to Show Cause provides otherwise.

D.   Interim Partial or Full Settlement

If all or part of a submitted motion is settled, a proposed order with notice of settlement (on at least ten [10] days notice) or a signed waiver of settlement shall be submitted with a copy to be conformed and a self addressed stamped envelope. Such order shall be accompanied by a letter setting forth the date the motion was submitted, what aspects of the Motion have been settled and what issues remain to be decided. A copy of the stipulation settling such issues shall be forwarded to the Court. If the motion is resolved, in whole or part, on the record, counsel shall obtain such transcript so that same can be "so ordered", unless the Court otherwise directs.

Rule III.   Court Appearances

A. Calendar call is 9:30 am. Please be prompt. For preliminary and status conferences, counsel may request that the conference be scheduled for 9:30 a.m., 11:00 a.m. or 2:00 p.m.

B. Attorneys must check in with Court Officer or Court Clerk. If counsel must also appear before another Judge, they must advise the Part Clerk or Court Officer where they can be reached. The litigating parties are required to be present in Court on the day of their preliminary conference and for the compliance/certification conference.

C. Cases will be conferenced in the order in which **all** attorneys are checked in.

Rule IV.   Communication With Chambers

A. In all Communications with chambers by letter, the title of the action, full names of the parties and index number shall be set forth, with copies simultaneously delivered to all counsel. *Ex parte* communications will be disregarded, except as otherwise provided herein.

B. Copies of correspondence between counsel shall not be sent to the Court. Such copies will be disregarded and not placed in the Court's file.

C. The Court will not accept telefax communications or submissions without prior permission.

D. No out of court settlement will be recognized or accepted unless counsel submits a letter on notice to opposing counsel and, if applicable, the law guardian, submitting the executed settlement agreement/stipulation or certifying that such agreement/stipulation has, in fact, been executed.

Rule V.   Sanctions

The Court will not consider a sanctions application unless the moving party first seeks withdrawal or discontinuation of the offending act or action or demands required or necessary action which is refused.

Proof of such request must be made a part of the sanctions application.

Rule VI.   Trial Rules

A Note of Issue is to be filed within 30 days after certification. Counsel for plaintiff shall file and should note that the Nassau County Clerk will not accept a Note of Issue without a Statement Of Proposed Disposition being annexed thereto. Also, appearing at the time of trial or inquest without having filed a Note of Issue may subject counsel to a sanction of up to $250.00 for failure to so file and in addition, the trial or inquest may be delayed while counsel forthwith proceeds to the County Clerk to file same.

After a matter has been certified as trial ready, the Court may set a date for a pre-trial conference. All pre-trial conferences will be scheduled approximately 30 days prior to the trial date. Counsel with knowledge of the case must attend. There will be no adjournments without the court's consent. At the pre-trial conference, the Court shall provide for the submission or scheduling of the following:

1. *In Limine applications* must be on notice to all parties.

2. *Annotated Statement of Proposed Disposition* in which all of the criteria listed in the statute are provided and counsel's position stated as to each such criteria for both equitable distribution and maintenance issues.

3. *Evaluations:* In the event there are any valuations of a business interest or increased earning capacity, then a "cash flow" chart shall be submitted by each side, listing counsel's proposal for payment thereof, as well as any other payments claimed due (such as payor's obligations for maintenance, child support, income taxes, etc.).

4. *Exhibits:* A list of all exhibits for each party indicating whether such exhibits are stipulated to be in evidence or marked for identification. As to those exhibits marked for identification, the Court will address their admissibility *In limine* or during the trial, as may be appropriate. The party offering any exhibit shall provide the original plus three copies, unless a trial notebook is prepared.

5. *Trial Notebook:* If deemed appropriate by the Court, based on the facts and circumstances of the particular case, parties shall submit notebooks with all listed exhibits separately and consecutively tabbed [numbers for Plaintiff and letters for Defendant], with the original documents for the witnesses and a copy for the Court. [To expedite the trial a similarly marked notebook should be provided for the Court.] At the conclusion of the trial all exhibits not received into evidence will be removed from notebooks and returned to counsel.

6. A list of *proposed witnesses* for the Court's information.

7. A list of all *expert witnesses* with copies of their reports.

8. *Marked pleadings*, to be submitted before opening statements.

9. *Net worth statements*, updated within thirty [30] days.

10. *A statement of stipulated facts.* [Parties are encouraged to stipulate to facts and/or exhibits].

11. All *trial exhibits* whether stipulated or contested on admissibility should be pre-marked by the Court Reporter at least one [1] day prior to trial.

12. If *deposition transcript* is to be utilized, a copy of the witness' deposition transcript should be available to the Court.

13. *Objections* should be stated without argument except to simply state the ground therefor, *i.e.*, hearsay, relevance, etc. If further argument is appropriate, it will be invited by the Court.

14. On the day before the scheduled trial, counsel are directed to contact the Part Clerk or chambers to confirm the Court's availability.

15. Pre-trial and post-trial memoranda shall have a table of contents.

Rule VII.   Miscellaneous

A.   Conferences/Trial—If there are any outstanding motions (submitted or pending) at the time of the conference/trial the Law Secretary and/or Judge must be so informed of same that day; the submission date must be provided by counsel. Copies of such motions should be available to the Court at the time of such conference.

B.   Attorneys of Record—Attorneys who have appeared in the matter are to make all appearances until they are relieved by the Court or a Consent to Change Attorneys has been filed with Part and with the Clerk of the Court.

C.   Staff—The Court functions through the aid and assistance of the courtroom and Chambers staff. They are expected to treat attorneys, litigants and others in a dignified and civil manner; as well they are to be treated in a civil and professional manner.

D.   Counsel and the Law Guardian are reminded that the Law Guardian acts in the role of counsel for the child(ren). As such, the Law Guardian is bound by the same ethical and procedural rules as counsel for the parties. *Ex parte* communications between the Law Guardian and the Court will not permitted.

JUSTICE EDWARD A. MARON

Rule I.   Adjournments

A.   Motions and Status Conferences:

1. Any and all applications to adjourn any scheduled date with this Court, including, but not limited to conferences, motions, or submissions of papers, must be ON CONSENT of the opposing party and the Attorney for the Child(ren), if one is assigned, and must be received by Chambers via facsimile by 2:00 p.m. on the business day prior to the scheduled date. All applications for adjournments MUST be made using the Request for Adjournment Form which can be obtained through chambers or through the OCA website. Letter requests will be disregarded.

The Request for Adjournment Form is to be filled out completely. Incomplete forms or forms received after 2:00 p.m. on the business day prior to the return date shall be summarily denied, unless the Court is advised of extraordinary circumstances which will be taken into consideration.

If the application is based on counsel's actual engagement on another matter, an Affirmation of Actual Engagement, in conformity with 22 NYCRR Part 125, must accompany the Request for Adjournment Form. If the application is granted, a letter confirming same shall be faxed to Chambers and copied to the opposing party and the Attorney for the Child(ren), if one is assigned.

2. Letters confirming adjournments shall state that the Court has adjourned the scheduled date on consent of the parties to the specified date, and shall contain the full names of both parties, the index number as well as a notation indicating the current date the matter is on the Court's calendar, and that all parties have been copied.

3. Adjournment requests which are left on the Chamber's voice-mail shall be disregarded.

B.   Preliminary Conference:

1. Adjournments of the Preliminary Conference will not be granted absent a compelling reason for same. Counsel is directed to review the provisions of 22 NYCRR § 202.16 (f) concerning conferences.

2. In addition to scheduling a Certification Conference as part of the Preliminary Conference Order, the Court may direct that a pre-trial conference also be held at the time of the Certification Conference in which event, the rules concerning pretrial conferences as hereinafter set forth, shall be applicable.

3. Discovery deadlines, Certification deadlines and Note of Issue deadlines, will be enforced. Deadlines may not be adjourned or extended without prior approval of the Court, and failure to comply with such deadlines may result in sanctions.

Rule II.   Motions

A.   Pre–Motion Conferences:

1. Prior to making or filing any motions, brought by Notice of Motion or Order to Show Cause, including applications to be relieved, counsel for the moving party MUST arrange for a conference call to be held with his/her adversary and the Court to discuss the issues involved and the possible resolution thereof. The Attorney for the Child(ren) shall also be notified and included in such conference calls. Counsel fully familiar with the matter and with authority to bind their clients MUST be available to participate in the conference call.

2. If the matter can be resolved during the conference call, an order consistent with such resolution may be issued.

B. Submission of Motions

1. Appearances of all Counsel and parties are required on all motion return dates unless specifically waived by the Court.

2. All exhibits must be clearly tabbed; motions not consistent with this rule will be rejected and returned to counsel.

3. Motions are to be served and filed in conformity with CPLR § 2214. All motions must be organized in such a manner so that each branch of the motion stated in the Notice of Motion or Order To Show Cause is preceded by a number or letter. Said number/letter designation shall be used in the supporting affirmations and affidavits and shall correspond to the number/letter used for each branch as set forth in the Notice of Motion or Order To Show Cause.

4. No sur-reply, affidavit, affirmation, memorandum of law or letter will be accepted or considered by the Court without leave of the Court.

5. Counsel shall be fully prepared for oral argument on the return date of all motions.

C. Application for a Stay or Temporary Restraining Order

1. Any Order to Show Cause seeking any injunctive relief, including a stay or temporary restraining order (TRO), must be made in accordance with 22 NYCRR 202.7(f). The moving party shall advise the Court as soon as practicable of counsel's intent to make such application.

2. Requests to continue or vacate a stay or TRO beyond the return date of the motion shall be made on the return date of the motion. Failure to apply for such extension shall result in the automatic vacatur of the stay or TRO, unless the Order to Show Cause provides otherwise.

3. An "Emergency" Order to Show Cause requires a special affidavit based upon personal knowledge and affirmation explaining in detail the nature of the emergency. In addition to the foregoing, the movant should be prepared to appear in Court and to make a record before the Court, if the Court requires same.

D. Interim Partial or Full Settlement

If all or part of a submitted motion is settled, counsel shall forward the original stipulation of settlement to the Court. Such stipulation shall be accompanied by a letter setting forth the date the motion was submitted, what aspects of the motion have been settled and what issues remain to be decided. If the motion is resolved in its entirety the movant shall indicate same. If the motion is resolved, in whole or in part, on the record, counsel shall obtain such transcript so that same can be "so ordered", unless the Court otherwise directs.

Rule III. Court Appearances

A. All Court appearances, unless otherwise specified or directed by the Court, shall be scheduled for 9:30 a.m. Please be prompt.

B. All parties and counsel shall appear at each and every scheduled Court date (including preliminary, status and compliance conferences), unless otherwise directed by the Court.

C. Attorneys and "Pro Se" litigants must alert the Court Officer or Court Clerk of their presence and complete a sign-in sheet. If counsel must also appear before another Judge, counsel must advise the Part Clerk or Court Officer where counsel can be reached.

D. All conferences will be held in the order in which ALL attorneys have checked in with the Part Clerk and completed the sign-in sheet.

Rule IV. Communication with Chambers

A. In all communications with chambers by letter, the title of the action, full names of the parties, the date on which the matter is scheduled on the Court's calendar, and the index number shall be set forth, with copies simultaneously delivered to all counsel. *Ex parte* communications will be discarded.

B. Copies of correspondence between counsel shall not be sent to the Court. Such copies shall be discarded.

C. The Court will not accept telefax submissions without prior permission.

D. No out-of-Court settlement will be recognized or accepted unless counsel submits a letter, on notice to opposing counsel, and, if applicable, the Attorney for the Child(ren), submitting the executed settlement agreement/stipulation or certifying that such agreement/stipulation has, in fact, been executed.

E. The Court shall not accept or participate in any form of *ex parte* communications on substantive issues.

Rule V. Sanctions

The Court will not consider a sanctions application unless the moving party first seeks withdrawal, or discontinuation of the offending act, action, or demands required or necessary action which is refused.

Proof of such request must be made a part of the sanctions application.

Rule VI. Trial Rules

A. A Note of Issue and Certificate of Readiness MUST be filed within 30 days after certification unless otherwise instructed by the Court. A statement of Proposed Disposition shall be filed with proof of service along with the Note of Issue. 22 N.Y.C.R.R. § 202.16 (h).

Neither side may prosecute a motion involving discovery issues once the case has been certified for trial without leave of the Court.

B. After a matter has been certified as ready for trial, the Court may set a date for a pre-trial conference. Pre-trial conferences will be scheduled approximately 30 days prior to the trial date, which shall not be adjourned without the prior consent of the Court. Counsel with knowledge of the case and the parties must attend.

At least three weeks prior to the scheduled date of trial, both sides must exchange and submit to this Part the following:

1. Fully completed worksheets regarding the statutory criteria relating to maintenance and equitable distribution (attached hereto) sworn to by each party. The Court will expect the accuracy of said worksheets to be testified to at trial, and the worksheets to be received in evidence and utilized by counsel to facilitate the fact finding process and achieve an expeditious completion of the trial;

2. An accounting of any claimed pendente lite arrears supported by backup documentation;

Annotated Statements of Proposed Disposition in which all of the criteria listed in the statute are provided and counsel's position stated as to each such criteria for both equitable distribution and maintenance issues;

3. *Evaluations:* In the event there are any evaluations of income producing assets subject to equitable distribution, (business interest, professional practice, enhanced earning capacity, license or degree, etc. involved in the case), then a "cash flow" chart shall be submitted by each side, setting forth counsel's proposal for apportioning the income stream produced by the asset for the payment of a distributive award as well as other obligations such as maintenance, child support, income taxes, interest on payments etc.;

4. *Exhibits:* A list of all exhibits for each party indicating whether such exhibits are stipulated to be in evidence or marked for identification. As to those exhibits marked for identification, the Court will address their admissibility *In limine* or during the trial, as may be appropriate. Both sides shall have available at least four (4) copies of all exhibits which are expected to be introduced into evidence.

5. *Trial Notebooks:* Parties shall submit trial notebooks two (2) weeks prior to trial with all listed exhibits separately and consecutively tabbed [numbers for Plaintiff and letters for Defendant], with the original documents for the witnesses and a copy for the Court. At the conclusion of the trial all exhibits not received into evidence will be removed from notebooks and returned to counsel

6. A list of proposed witnesses, the order in which they will testify and the estimated length of their testimony MUST be submitted at least 5 business days prior to trial.

7. Documentation in compliance with C.P.L.R. 3101(d) shall be provided with regard to any expert, other than a court-appointed neutral expert, that a party intends to call at trial. Such documentation must be submitted at least 5 business days prior to trial.

8. An up-dated Net Worth Affidavit, sworn to within 90 days prior to the date of trial.

9. All trial exhibits, whether stipulated or contested on admissibility, should be pre-marked by the Court Reporter at least one (1) day prior to trial.

10. Both sides shall have available at least four (4) copies of all deposition transcripts and prior statements which are expected to be read into the record or utilized on cross examination at the trial.

11. Counsel for the parties shall consult prior to trial and shall, in good faith, attempt to agree upon the portions of deposition testimony to be offered into evidence without objection. The parties shall delete from the testimony to be read any questions and answers that are irrelevant to the point for which the deposition testimony is offered. Each party shall prepare a list of deposition testimony to be offered to which no objection has been made, and a separate list of deposition testimony to which objection has been made. At least ten days prior to trial or such time as the Court may set, each party shall submit its list(s) to the Court and opposing counsel and Attorney for the Child(ren), if one is appointed, together with a copy of the portions of the deposition testimony as to which objection has been made. The Court will rule upon the objection at the earliest possible time after consultation with counsel.

12. Objections should be stated without argument except to simply state the ground therefor, e.g., hearsay, relevance, etc. If further argument is appropriate, it will be invited by the Court.

13. Closing Arguments and Memoranda of Law shall be submitted in writing within thirty (30) days of the conclusion of trial. Such closing arguments shall parenthetically cite to the trial transcript, shall consist of no more than 25 pages, and must be accompanied by the trial transcript. Such documents shall be prepared in accordance with the Section E of these

rules, entitled "Closing Arguments and Memoranda of Law Rules."

14. Findings of Fact and Conclusions of Law shall be submitted within thirty (30) days of the conclusion of trial.

C. On the day before the scheduled trial, counsel are directed to contact the Part Clerk or Chambers to confirm the Court's availability; and

D. On the scheduled date of trial:

1. Counsel are expected to be prepared to discuss settlement of all unresolved issues and to have complied with each of the trial rules set forth herein

2. Parties are encouraged to submit a statement of stipulated facts and/or exhibits.

Counsel are urged to stipulate that any issue relating to an award of counsel and expert fees be resolved by the Court, without testimony, upon the submission of affirmations and other appropriate documentation from counsel.

If it appears during the course of the trial that no bonafide attempt was undertaken to secure such stipulation, the Court will likely recess and delay the trial until there is compliance.

D. On the scheduled date of trial, both sides must exchange and submit to this Part the following:

1. Marked pleadings, including pleadings from any proceedings transferred from another court and consolidated with the matrimonial action, such as family offense proceedings transferred from the Family Court (CPLR 4012;

2. Copies of life insurance policies and medical and dental policies of insurance in effect as of the date of the commencement of the action and as of the present date;

3. A list of issues to be determined by the Court including any pretrial motion issues referred to the trial by the Court;

4. Copies of any and all of the following:

(a) relevant orders issued by another court, such as final orders of custody or temporary or permanent orders of protection issued by the Family Court;

(b) any order of this Court that referred issues raised in motion practice to the trial of the action;

(c) any relevant so-ordered stipulation of this Court, as well as transcripts of stipulations read into the record in open court during the pendency of the action; and

(d) any properly executed and acknowledged stipulation or agreement relating to material issues in this action.

E. Closing Arguments and Memoranda of Law Rules

1. At the conclusion of the trial, both sides, as well as the Attorney for the Child(ren), if any, will be expected to submit a written Closing Arguments and Memoranda of Law with respect to all issues to be decided by the Court. Said Closing Arguments and Memoranda of Law shall contain the following clearly delineated sections: a) a chronological procedural history of the action, including copies of all relevant orders, written stipulations and transcripts of stipulations placed on the record; b) a recitation of the issues to be determined; c) an in depth summary of the testimony of each witness; d) a summary of the findings of any expert report received in evidence; e) a summary of the exhibits in evidence; f) a detailed recitation of counsel's contentions as to the testimony and exhibits in evidence; and g) applicable law.

2. Closing Arguments and Memoranda of Law will be marked as Court Exhibits and shall be part of the record.

3. The right to submit Closing Arguments and Memoranda of Law shall be deemed waived if not timely submitted to the Court.

4. A copy of each side's Closing Arguments and Memoranda of Law, and, if applicable, the Attorney for the child(ren)'s Closing Arguments and Memoranda of Law shall be served on all other parties simultaneous with filing with the Court.

5. Responses to the Closing Arguments and Memoranda of Law are prohibited and will not be considered.

6. The Court is to be provided the original and one copy of each Closing Arguments and Memorandum of Law.

7. Closing Arguments and Memoranda of Law shall have a Table of Contents. Failure to provide such Table of Contents will result in the Court not considering such summations.

REQUIRED FORMS FOR PRELIMINARY CONFERENCE

PRELIMINARY CONFERENCE ORDER AND INFORMATION FORMS THAT ARE **REQUIRED** TO BE COMPLETED PRIOR TO THE PRELIMINARY CONFERENCE.

• YOU MAY FIND THE PRELIMINARY CONFERENCE ORDER AND THE INFORMATION SHEET AT:

http://www.nycourts.gov/courts/10jd/nassau/matrimonial/index.shtml

UNDER THE "FORMS" SECTION

OR

• THE PRELIMINARY CONFERENCE ORDER MAY BE OBTAINED AT:

http://www.nycourts.gov/courts/ 10jd/nassau/matrimonial/forms/PC-ORDER-2010.pdf

- THE INFORMATION FORM MAY BE OBTAINED AT:

  http://www.nycourts.gov/courts/ 10jd/nassau/matrimonial/forms/PC–INFOSHEET–2010.pdf

  PLEASE HAVE THESE FORMS COMPLETED AND BE PREPARED TO PROVIDE ALL INFORMATION REQUIRED AT YOUR CONFERENCE WITH THE COURT.

***DO NOT COMPLETE SECTION "G" OF THE "NASSAU COUNTY UNIFORM PRELIMINARY CONFERENCE ORDER", ENTITLED "CASE SCHEDULING". THIS SECTION WILL BE COMPLETED BY THE COURT AT THE PRELIMINARY CONFERENCE.

Form 1. Request for Adjournment

HON. EDWARD A. MARON, J.S.C.

REQUEST FOR ADJOURNMENT FORM—Part 22

THIS FORM MUST BE FILLED OUT COMPLETELY
INCOMPLETE FORMS WILL BE SUMMARILY DENIED

ALL REQUESTS MUST BE ON CONSENT AND ALL REQUESTED AD-
JOURN DATES MUST BE CONFIRMED WITH YOUR ADVERSARY
AND ATTORNEY FOR THE CHILD, IF APPLICABLE, PRIOR TO MAK-
ING THE REQUEST.

Case Name: _____ Index No.: _____

Date on Calendar: _____ Action Taken on Last Court Date: _____

Is this request on consent of your adversary and the Attorney for the
Child(ren)? YES / NO

Req'd Adj. Dates (At Least 3): 1) _____ 2) _____ 3) _____

Nature of Appearance:

   P.C. ___ COMPLIANCE ___ CERTIFICATION ___ PRE–TRIAL ___ HEAR-
ING ___ TRIAL ___ MOTION _____

   SUBMISSION OF JUDGMENT PACKAGE _____

Reason for Adjournment (Affirmation of Actual Engagement must be attached
if applicable):

_____
_____
_____

CONTACT INFORMATION

Party making request: PLAINTIFF / DEFENDANT

Attorney contacting Court: _____ Phone No.: (_____) _____ – _____
                                      Fax No.: (_____) _____ – _____

Adversary's Attorney: _____ Phone No.: (_____) _____ – _____
                                      Fax No.: (_____) _____ – _____

Attorney for the Child(ren): _____

ALL REQUESTS MUST BE RECEIVED VIA FAX [(516) 571–5970] BEFORE
2:00 P.M. OF THE BUSINESS DAY PRIOR TO THE CONFERENCE OR
MOTION RETURN DATE A CONFIRMING LETTER, IN FULL COMPLI-
ANCE WITH THIS PART'S RULES MUST BE RECEIVED ON THE
SAME DATE THE ADJOURNMENT IS GRANTED.

COURT NOTICES

Notice 1. General Court Notices

This page contains notices regarding recent changes in law or procedure that effect matrimonial practice in the Nassau County Matrimonial Center. It will also contain any notices regarding court closings during the holiday period.

NEW POSTINGS:

Effective 10/13/10—As part of the "Low Income Support Obligation and Performance Improvement Act", DRL § 236B(7) amended to require that all orders establishing a child support obligation contain a notice regarding the right to apply for a modification of the order if there has been a substantial change in circumstances or the occurrence of additional bases for modification enumerated in the bill. See the notice contained in the Court Notice Section of this site for more information.

Effective 10/12/10—As part of the "Divorce Reform Act of 2010", DRL § 170 is amended to include subdivision 7, a new ground for divorce for irretrievable breakdown of marriage *(commonly called "no fault" divorce)*. See the notice contained in the Court Notice Section of this site for more information.

Effective 10/12/10—DRL § 236 amended to add subdivision 5-a, wherein the court must make awards for temporary maintenance pursuant to the provisions of subdivision 5-a, and must also consider additional factors in DRL § 236B(6) in making awards for final maintenance. See the notice contained in the Court Notice Section of this site for more information.

Effective 1/31/10—"Child Support Modernization Act"—DRL § 240 amended to increase the CSSA income cap on calculations of basic child support obligation from $80,000 to $130,000. See the notice contained in the Court Notice Section of this site for more information.

Effective 10/9/09—DRL § 177 repealed and replaced by DRL § 255—new section still requires notice regarding possible effect of judgment of divorce upon the parties health insurance coverage—but gives court more discretion on whether an agreement complies with the statute. See the notice contained in the Court Notice Section of this site for more information.

Effective 9/1/09—DRL § 236B(2) amended to add subsection b—requires service of a "Notice of Automatic Orders" simultaneous with service of the summons. See the notice contained in the Court Notice Section of this site for more information.

Effective 3/24/09—DRL § 240 amended to add new subdivision 1-a to section 1—requires court to conduct statewide registry searches on custody / visitation cases prior to issuing temporary or permanent orders.

See the notice contained in the Court Notice Section of this site for more information.

Effective 10/30/07—DRL § 177 added—requires both parties to receive notice regarding the possible effect of a judgment of divorce upon their health insurance coverage. See the notice contained in the Court Notice Section of this site for more information.

Effective 6/11/07—Uniform Rule 202.7(f) has been amended to exclude applications for orders of protection. See the notice contained in the Court Notice Section of this site for more information.

Effective 6/11/07—Uniform Rule 202.48(c)(2) has been amended to include a requirement to include a "clearly marked copy" of any counter order or judgment, delineating each proposed change to the order or judgment to which objection is made. See the notice contained in the Court Notice section of this site for more information.

Effective 10/1/06—Uniform Rule 202.7 has been amended to include a subsection (f). This rule change is in regards to applications for Temporary Restraining Orders. See the notice contained in the Court Notice section of this site for more information.

NOTICE: Effective July 14, 2003 the following fee changes concerning Supreme Court matrimonial cases will go into effect:

Index Number (CPLR 8018(a))	$210
Request for Judicial Intervention (CPLR 8020(a))	$95
Note of Issue (CPLR 8020(a))	$30
Demand for Jury Trial (CPLR 8020(c))	$65
Motion / Cross Motion (CPLR 8020(a))	$45
Stipulation of Settlement (CPLR 8020(d))	$35
Voluntary Discontinuance (CPLR 8020(d))	$35
Notice of Appeal (CPLR 8022)	$65

UNCONTESTED DIVORCE PACKETS ARE AVAILABLE AT:

▲ Nassau County Matrimonial Center Clerk's Office
▲ Court Information Center (2nd Floor Supreme Court—Nassau County)
▲ New York State Unified Court System Web Site (*www.nycourts.gov*)
▲ Supreme Court Clerk's Offices throughout the state

* If you are requesting by mail, send in a written request with a self addressed 10 × 13 envelope with approx. $5.00 postage.

Notice 2.   Divorce

DIVORCE RECORDS

Obtaining a certified copy of any signed order or judgment:

The County Clerk is the Clerk of the Supreme Court. All fees are paid to the County Clerk. All original orders and judgments issued by the Supreme Court are filed and entered in the County Clerk's Office.

If you want to obtain a certified copy of any order or judgment on file in your case, you must get it from the County Clerk and pay a fee. You will need the index number, date of the action, and title of the action. Please be advised, that only the parties involved, or an attorney of record can obtain these documents. The fee for a certified copy is $5.00 minimum for the first 4 pages, and $1.25 for each additional page. If the County Clerk does not have the judgment entered as yet, you must find out what transmittal report the judgment was sent on. You can do that by searching on this website.

If you are unable to come in person, the County Clerk will accept a written request, as long as your signature is notarized. If you do not know the index number, a $5.00 search fee is charged for a two year period. This will be in addition to any fee for the certified copy itself. You should provide the year the divorce action was originally filed, not the year it was granted. Please provide a self-addressed stamped envelope for the return of your documents with your request, and send to:

Nassau County Clerk's Office

Records Room 106

240 Old Country Rd.

Mineola, NY 11501

The County Clerk's web page can be found at: www.co.nassau.ny.us/clerk

Notice 3.   Judgment Office Notice

Please take notice that submission of a judgment or order must occur within 60 days of the court directing such submission. Failure to do so may result in the case being deemed abandoned pursuant to Uniform Rule 202.48.

* Judgments and Orders are to be submitted as originals under a legal back which lists the name address and phone number of the submitting party or attorney. CPLR 2101 (d). Submission of fax copies, and illegible photocopies as originals without good cause will not be accepted. Failure to submit papers in this manner may result in rejection by this office.

* Judgments and Orders to be submitted pursuant a decision of the court must include a copy of such decision with the submission. If the decision is rendered on the record, you must submit a copy of the transcript.

* Qualified Domestic Relations Orders to be submitted for signature must include a notice of settlement date or waiver, proof of service, pre-approval by the plan administrator where possible, an affidavit or affirmation detailing plan and participant information, and a copy of the judgment and stipulation which authorizes the QDRO. See the checklist section for details.

* All judgments and orders submitted for signature must be accompanied by a self addressed post card with the name of the case and index number on it. Upon the order or judgment being signed, the date of signature will be put on the card, and mailed out by the County Clerk. This office does not accept telephone inquiries as to status of judgments and orders. You may either appear in person, or send in a written inquiry with a self addressed envelope.

* Any counter-orders or judgments submitted, must include an affirmation or affidavit explaining the need for such submission, and the differences in the submissions. A marked copy of the judgment showing the differences must be submitted pursuant to court rule 202.48 as amended. Failure to do so will result in the rejection of your papers.

* Any request for expedited handling must include an affirmation of emergency, or it will not be considered by the Justice / Referee.

* All stipulations must be in compliance with DRL § 177 — or an addendum will be needed.

PLEASE TAKE NOTICE that the Department of Health requires an original document when filing certificates of dissolution in a matrimonial action. You must use the form provided by the DOH, (form # DOH–2168), amended 5/2000. Photocopies will not be accepted. Forms are available at the Judgment Office, and the County Clerk.

PLEASE TAKE NOTICE that any request for child support must include the requisite advisement regarding Support Collection services (DRL 240). If not contained in your stipulation, a separate Child Support Enforcement Bureau (CSEB) affidavit must be furnished. A copy of the judgment and the affidavit will be forwarded to the CSEB upon signature. Make sure the judgment contains the requisite notice pursuant to DRL 240–c.

Notice 4.   TRO Notice

Procedure for giving notice pursuant to § 202.7 of the Uniform Rules for the Supreme and County Courts

Pursuant to Administrative Order of Hon. Jonathan Lippman, § 202.7 of the Uniform Civil Rules for the Supreme and County Courts were amended, effective October 1, 2006, to add a new subdivision (f), relating to temporary restraining orders.

This rule provides that a party seeking a temporary restraining order ("TRO") must make good faith efforts to notify the party against whom the TRO is sought, of the time, date and place that the application will be made, in a manner sufficient to permit the opposing party an opportunity to appear in response to the application. This notice may be waived by the assigned Justice upon consideration of an affirmation demonstrating that there will be significant prejudice to the party seeking the restraining order by giving such notice.

This rule change pertains to any application brought in a matrimonial action that contains a TRO or stay, (excluding Temporary Orders of Protection- see amendment per administrative order dated June 11, 2007) regardless whether the summons has been served or not prior to the application. Every affirmation or affidavit in support of a TRO must contain language demonstrating "significant prejudice" to the party seeking the restraining order by the giving of prior notice. If the applying party cannot demonstrate "significant prejudice", then the papers will forwarded to chambers of the assigned Justice to await notification of their ruling as to whether argument will be granted prior to the application being considered. The applicant will need to contact chambers as what will be required on their particular application.

Generally, compliance with § 202.7 may be accomplished by providing the opposing parties or their attorneys with a copy of the proposed order, the supporting affidavits/affirmations and exhibits, and a cover letter advising them that the annexed order is being presented to the assigned Justice on a time and date certain which was previously obtained from the chambers of the assigned Justice. Nothing in the new rule precludes the assigned Justice from denying the application in its entirety or from striking the request for the TRO and fixing an expedited return date on the motion for oral argument on the issue.

Notice 5. DRL 255 Notice

DOMESTIC RELATIONS LAW (DRL) § 255 takes effect on Friday, October 9, 2009.

The newly enacted legislation replaces DRL § 177, and requires the court to provide notice to all parties regarding the effect of a signed judgment on a party's health insurance coverage provided by his or her spouse, in an action for divorce, separation, annulment, or to declare the nullity of as a void marriage. On pending cases, chambers will provide the required notice to both sides.

DRL § 255 requires a provision to be included in any stipulation or agreement between the parties which provides for the future coverage of each party or states their understanding of the effect of the divorce judgment upon their health insurance coverage, and the possible availability of COBRA coverage. These requirements may not be waived by the parties.

The court shall require compliance and may grant a 30 day continuance to afford the parties an opportunity to procure their own health insurance coverage.

Note: The "specific" stipulation language as required by DRL § 177, as well as the additional signatures of the parties has been eliminated, and the court will have more discretion as to the conformance of agreements with the statute.

A packet will be available from the Matrimonial Clerk's Office, which contains a form of notice and a form of stipulation on cases where the language is missing from an existing agreement.

Thank you for your cooperation.

Matrimonial Clerk—Nassau County

NOTICE TO PARTIES IN ACTIONS FOR DIVORCE, SEPARATION, ANNULMENT, AND TO DECLARE THE NULLITY OF A VOID MARRIAGE

All parties are hereby given notice, pursuant to Domestic Relations Law Section 255, (DRL § 255) that once a judgment is entered in the action, a person may, or may not, be eligible to be covered under his or her spouse's health insurance plan, depending upon the terms of the plan.

If the parties to an action enter into a Stipulation of Settlement, provisions required by DRL § 255(2) in regards to health insurance coverage should be included in the body of the stipulation, otherwise an addendum will be required.

The provisions of DRL § 255 cannot be waived by the parties or counsel, and pursuant to DRL § 255(2), a 30–day continuance may be granted upon request, to afford the parties an opportunity to procure their own health insurance coverage.

Notice 6. Submission of Counter Judgments

Submission of a counter judgment will not be considered by the Clerk's Office without an affirmation in support which sets forth the reason for the submission, what the specific differences are, and why counsel could not agree on a form of judgment /order prior to submission to the Court.

In addition, pursuant to Administrative Order dated June 11, 2007 (see attached), a marked copy of the counter judgment / order showing the differences is required.

ADMINISTRATIVE ORDER OF THE CHIEF ADMINISTRATIVE JUDGE OF THE COURTS

Pursuant to the authority vested in me, and with the advice and consent of the Administrative Board of the Courts, I hereby amend, effective September 1, 2007, section 202.48(c)(2) of the Uniform Civil Rules for the Supreme and County Courts, relating to the submissions of counter-orders, to read as follows:

§ 202.48. Submission of Orders, Judgments and Decrees for Signature

* * *

(c)(2) Proposed counter-orders or judgments shall be made returnable on the same date and at the same place, and shall be served on all parties by personal service, not less than two days, or by mail, not less than seven days, before the date of settlement. Any proposed counter-order or judgment shall be submitted with a copy clearly marked to delineate each proposed change to the order or judgment to which objection is made.

Notice 7.   Notice of Automatic Orders

Pursuant to Administrative Order of Hon. Ann Pfau dated August 13, 2009, the Uniform Civil Rules for the Supreme and County Courts were amended, effective September 1, 2009, to add a new section (§ 202.16–a) relating to automatic orders in matrimonial actions and proceedings in Supreme Court authorized by § 236(2) of the Domestic Relations Law. The form of automatic orders are to be set forth in a newly established "Appendix F" of the Uniform Rules.

The new section directs that a copy of the automatic orders *(in a notice that substantially conforms to Appendix F)* are to be served simultaneous with the service of the summons.

The automatic orders shall be binding **upon the plaintiff immediately upon filing** of the summons with notice, or summons and verified complaint with the County Clerk, and **upon the defendant immediately upon service** of the automatic orders with the summons.

Any affidavit submitted regarding the service of the summons should contain language that the automatic orders were served simultaneous with the summons.

Copies of the **"Notice of Automatic Orders"** are available at the Matrimonial Clerk's Office and at the Court Information Office in Supreme Court.

REMINDER: This notice must be served simultaneous with the service of the summons. The automatic orders shall be binding on the plaintiff immediately upon filing of the summons, and upon the defendant immediately upon service of the automatic orders with the summons.

APPENDIX F. ___

NOTICE OF AUTOMATIC ORDERS (D.R.L. 236)

PURSUANT TO DOMESTIC RELATIONS LAW § 236 Part B, Section 2, as added by Chapter 72 of the Laws of 2009, both you and your spouse (the parties) are bound by the following AUTOMATIC ORDERS, which shall remain in full force and effect during the pendency of the action unless terminated, modified or amended by further order of the court or upon written agreement between the parties:

(1) Neither party shall sell, transfer, encumber, conceal, assign, remove or in any way dispose of, without the consent of the other party in writing, or by order of the court, any property (including, but not limited to, real estate, personal property, cash accounts, stocks, mutual funds, bank accounts, cars and boats) individually or jointly held by the parties, except in the usual course of business, for customary and usual household expenses or for reasonable attorney's fees in connection with this action.

(2) Neither party shall transfer, encumber, assign, remove, withdraw or in any way dispose of any tax deferred funds, stocks or other assets held in any individual retirement accounts, 401k accounts, profit sharing plans, Keogh accounts, or any other pension or retirement account, and the parties shall further refrain from applying for or requesting the payment of retirement benefits or annuity payments of any kind, without the consent of the other party in writing, or upon further order of the court.

(3) Neither party shall incur unreasonable debts hereafter, including, but not limited to further borrowing against any credit line secured by the family residence, further encumbrancing any assets, or unreasonably using credit cards or cash advances against credit cards, except in the usual course of business or for customary or usual household expenses, or for reasonable attorney's fees in connection with this action.

(4) Neither party shall cause the other party or the children of the marriage to be removed from any existing medical, hospital and dental insurance coverage, and each party shall maintain the existing medical, hospital and dental insurance coverage in full force and effect.

(5) Neither party shall change the beneficiaries of any existing life insurance policies, and each party shall maintain the existing life insurance, automobile insurance, homeowners and renters insurance policies in full force and effect.

Notice 8.   Child Support Modernization Act

The "Child Support Modernization Act" *(Chapter 343 of the Laws of 2009)* makes changes to various sections of the Social Services Law, Family Court Act, and Domestic Relations Law.

As part of this legislation, Section 240 of the Domestic Relations Law will be amended to increase the "combined parental income amount" (the maximum dollar value of parental income, or "cap", to which the Child Support Standards Act (CSSA) percentages must be applied for the calculation of child support) from $80,000 to $130,000.

This amendment will be effective January 31, 2010.

Please be aware that all actions commenced on or after the effective date (as well as any agreements executed after that date) will be controlled by the new legislation. Therefore, all child support language contained in a matrimonial agreement or stipulation should be in compliance with this amendment, as well as the child support language contained in the Findings of Fact and Conclusions of Law.

* * * * * * * * * * *

NOTE: The forms available on the NYS Court web site will be modified to reflect the amendments stated above. If you are utilizing the pre-printed "Uncontested Divorce Packets", you will need to make the changes by hand before submitting to the court.

Notice 9. Records Check Legislation for Custody / Visitation

Commencing June 1, 2009:

▲ all Requests for Preliminary Conference or unassigned Orders to Show Cause with an RJI must be accompanied by a Database Review Information Sheet *(available in the matrimonial clerk's office)* containing pertinent identifying information regarding the litigants and children subject to the divorce action. If there are no children subject to the divorce action, please indicate that on the Information Sheet. (An amended RJI is being promulgated in the near future which will incorporate the required information)

▲ In addition, any other Order to Show Cause or proposed order/judgment containing relief for custody or visitation shall also be submitted with the Information Sheet.

▲ Failure to provide the Information Sheet will result in the return of your submission.

▲ For future submissions—please feel free to pick up copies of the information sheet, make photocopies of a blank form, or create your own with the required information.

Thank you for your cooperation.

Matrimonial Clerk

CHECKLISTS

Checklist 1. Matrimonial Judgments

• All papers to be filed in commencing an action or proceeding (*i.e. summons, complaint, petition*), shall be filed with the County Clerk, which is also the Clerk of the Supreme Court. The County Clerk is located at 240 Old Country Rd., Mineola, NY 11501. All filing fees are to be paid to the County Clerk. The Matrimonial Clerk's Office cannot process any filing fees. *[Please see item # 22 as to the schedule of fees.]*

• When submitting papers to the Matrimonial Clerk's Office, please make sure your index number is reflected on all submitted papers.

• Litigants are advised to utilize the *Uncontested Divorce Packets* when representing themselves in their divorce action, and submitting papers for a judgment of divorce. They are available at the Matrimonial Clerk's Office, or on the Unified Court System website listed above.

• If counsel wishes to utilize the forms contained in the *Uncontested Divorce Packet*, it is requested that all inapplicable information be redacted out of the forms prior to submission, to make for a more professional work product. As always, the use of the *Uncontested Divorce Packet* is not mandatory—if you have a work product that meets the requirements of the statute—it will be accepted for processing.

INQUESTS: Uncontested Divorce

• If you are submitting a case where there is *no agreement* as to the ancillary issues involving child support, custody, visitation, equitable distribution of marital property, etc., and there is no *Family Court Order* as to such issues, the court *may* require that oral testimony be taken at an inquest.

• If there is insufficient documentary proof as to the ancillary issues (i.e. custody, support, property, debts, etc.), and you are seeking an inquest, please submit the following papers:

• *Affirmation or Affidavit requesting inquest, and setting forth reason for request*

• *Request for Judicial Intervention* (with proof of payment and service)

• *Note of Issue* (with proof of payment and service)

• *Pleadings* (summons with notice / summons and complaint with proof of filing with County Clerk)

• *Proof of service of pleadings* (with proof of filing with County Clerk)

• *Self-Addressed stamped envelope* (for notification of inquest date)

• If you feel there is sufficient documentary proof as to the ancillary issues, you may submit the Findings of Fact, Judgment of Divorce, and all other required papers based on relief sought, and proven by detailed affidavits and exhibits. If the court is satisfied with the proof submitted, it may sign the decree without the need for an inquest. If the court is not satisfied, the submitting party will be given an inquest date by the clerk's office as determined by the court.

SUBMISSION OF A JUDGMENT OF DIVORCE:

• **Contested Matrimonial Judgments** - these are divorce judgments issued in cases where there was opposition to the divorce, and the **case was assigned to a judge** for conference or motion. The case either settled after that, or was decided by the court.

• **Uncontested Matrimonial Judgments** - these are divorce judgments issued in cases where either the parties have agreed to the divorce **before** submission to the court, or where there has been a default in appearance by the defendant. **There has been no prior assignment of the case to a judge.**

The following papers are needed when submitting your judgment of divorce for signature by the court: *(not every document is necessary in every case - please see the comments below, and the attached submission chart.)* **Most documents can be used for contested or uncontested submissions, and can be found in the Uncontested Divorce Packet. DO NOT SUBMIT EXTRA COPIES OF YOUR FORMS WITH YOUR ORIGINALS - MAKE SURE YOU KEEP AN EXTRA COPY OF ALL FORMS SUBMITTED.**

1 FINDINGS OF FACT and CONCLUSIONS OF LAW // JUDGMENT OF DIVORCE *(under separate cover)* **with Notice of Settlement and Affidavit of Service** *(Uniform Court Rules 202.48, 5 days personal, 10 days by mail)* **or Waiver of Notice**

a) If a *Family Court Order* is being continued, you must attach a copy of said order, and reference same in the findings and judgment. In addition, the judgment must direct service of a copy of the judgment on the Clerk of the Family Court within 10 days.

b) When child support is an issue, the findings and judgment must contain the *social security numbers* of the *parties* AND *children*. *(if there are no SS#'s - indicate that - do not leave blank)*

c) When child support is an issue, the findings must identify the health plan that will cover the children of the marriage, and the judgment should refer to a separate *Qualified Medical Child Support Order* signed simultaneously with the judgment. *(If there is no health plan, or if it a private insurance, the findings should reflect that as well as the proof)*

d) The findings of fact must contain the required child support findings pursuant to *DRL 240* showing the *net incomes* of the parties, the *child support percentage* to be applied, the *basic obligation* and *pro rata share* of such obligation, the *agreed upon support*, whether it *deviates* from such pro rata obligation, and if so, the *reasons* for such deviation. *(This information must be in conformance with the CSSA language in the settlement agreement or transcript of the court's decision)*

e) If child support is to be paid through the *Support Collection Unit*, the judgment or order directing such support *must* have the required notice on its face pursuant to *DRL 240-c(5)(b)*. It must also have such *method of payment* recited in the findings, and the judgment must reflect the *frequency* of payments, *commencement date* of payments, and *address* of the Support Collection Unit where payments are to be made to: *(Nassau County SCU - NYS Child Support Processing Center, P.O. Box 15363, Albany, NY 12212–5363)*.

f) The findings should state that the parties agreement or addendum to agreement complies with DRL § 255.

2 QUALIFIED MEDICAL SUPPORT ORDER - *(QMSCO)* - *DRL 240(1)* *(must be issued separate from judgment of divorce where child support ordered, and there is an employer provided medical plan to cover the children.)* **with Notice of Settlement and Affidavit of Service** **or Waiver of Notice.**

3 (QUALIFIED) DOMESTIC RELATIONS ORDER *(QDRO)* - *(distribution of retirement benefits)* **with Notice of Settlement** and **Affidavit of Service** or **Waiver**

● *pre-approved by plan administrator, if possible.*

● *if stipulation not specific as to identity of account and other pertinent information, provide affidavit as to those details. (court may require an addendum to the stipulation) (see separate information sheet for submission of a Domestic Relations Order separate from the judgment of divorce.).*

4 ___ **INCOME DEDUCTION ORDER** - *CPLR 5242, DRL 240(1)* **(see adden-dum)** with ___ **Notice of Settlement** and ___ **Affidavit of Service** or ___ **Waiver**.

5 **AFFIRMATION OF REGULARITY** *(Set forth the procedural history of the action as to dates of filing of summons, complaint, service on defendant, appearances, etc.)*

6 **AFFIDAVIT IN LIEU OF TESTIMONY,** *(Affidavit of proof from party getting divorce in their favor)* or **TRANSCRIPT OF INQUEST** *(if testimony done in court on the record)* or **COURT DECISION DIRECTING SUBMISSION OF JUDGMENT.**

 • *Must contain the social security numbers of the parties, and if applicable, the children*

 • *Must contain specific information concerning health plan coverage for the children, if applicable. (If no coverage, proof must indicate such situation)*

 • *Should list the maiden name and other prior surname to be resumed by the wife.*

 • *If action for annulment or divorce based on adultery, provide an affidavit of a corroborating witness in addition to any other proof.*

 • *Must contain information regarding children's address and whereabouts pursuant to DRL § 76-h (contained in plaintiff's affidavit in Uncontested Divorce Packet)*

7 **AFFIDAVIT OF DEFENDANT-** *(signed AFTER the service of the summons)*

 • *Allows defendant to appear in an action and waive the required time frames for submission of a judgment of divorce by plaintiff.*

 • *Can be used to have defendant withdraw a previously interposed answer or neither admit nor deny plaintiff's allegations. (If no coverage, proof must indicate such situation)*

 • *Defendant can waive service of all papers being submitted to the court, or request service and notice of any or all papers.*

 • *May not be needed if defendant's intent is expressed on the record or in an agreement.*

8 **ATTORNEY CERTIFIED COPY OF AGREEMENT,** or **COPY OF STIPULATION PLACED ON RECORD.**

 • *If child support is to be awarded, stipulation MUST contain the required language found in DRL 240 1-b (h) as to the Child Support Standards Act.*

 • *Must be properly acknowledged by the parties (DRL § 236B(3)).*

 • *Note: Must include language regarding future coverage of parties health insurance in compliance with DRL § 255 - if not - an addendum to the agreement is needed.*

 • *Note: Must have fee paid receipt (see #22 for fee schedule)*

9 **REMOVAL OF BARRIERS AFFIDAVIT**—*(DRL 253 (3)—make sure it says that removal of barriers HAS been done)*

 • Needed where the marriage was performed in a religious ceremony. Not required if the parties were married in a civil ceremony.

 • Filed by the party in whose favor the divorce is being granted *(usually the plaintiff)* - UNLESS the divorce is being granted under DRL§ 170(5) or (6)- *conversion of a judgment or agreement of separation.* In such a case, BOTH parties are required to file and serve the affidavit.

 • DRL § 253(3) allows a written waiver by the other party *(usually defendant)* to the filing of this affidavit.

Additional forms where Child Support is an issue:

10 AFFIDAVIT AS TO CHILD SUPPORT ENFORCEMENT SERVICES— *DRL 236B (7)(b)*

• *Must be submitted whenever child support is an issue—provides proof of notice to custodial parent as to availability of Support Collection Unit ("SCU") for collection of payments of child support or combined child support / maintenance.*

• *If custodial parent wants to have payments made to SCU pursuant to agreement or court decision, the affidavit will be used to set up the account with them.*

• *Stipulation can contain the requisite notice, but can be used ONLY if the custodial parent declines such services. Otherwise, the affidavit would be needed for the court to send to Support Collection Unit.*

11 INCOME ITEMIZATION SHEET or CHILD SUPPORT WORKSHEET— *sworn to by submitting parties. Incomes should be reflective of the time the parties settled the action - NOT the time they are submitting the judgment - unless the agreement has been amended.*

12 DIVORCE AND CHILD SUPPORT SUMMARY FORM *(UCS–111)*

13 SUPPORT REGISTRY INFORMATION FORM *(to be submitted on all matters involving child support, or child support and maintenance combined, where payment is to be made* **OTHER THAN** *through the Support Collection Unit)*

14 PROOF OF SERVICE OF CHILD SUPPORT STANDARDS CHART. *(where party is* **unrepresented by counsel,** *and child support is sought)*

Additional forms where the defendant has defaulted in appearance:

15 AFFIDAVIT AS TO MILITARY STATUS OF DEFAULTING PARTY. *(included in plaintiffs' affidavit in Uncontested Matrimonial Packet)*

16 AFFIDAVIT OF SERVICE OF SUMMONS WITH NOTICE/SUMMONS AND COMPLAINT *(together with Notice of Automatic Orders)* **ON DEFENDANT**

• *Provide photo, if necessary, used to ID defendant on service, or other such proof used to identify defendant served.*

17 COPY OF PLEADINGS *(all affidavits of service of initiating pleading should reflect that index number and date of filing were endorsed on the papers when served)*

• *Copy of summons with notice / summons and complaint with proof of filing with County Clerk, together with the receipt for payment of index number. (CPLR 305, 306–a) A stamped copy by the County Clerk is sufficient proof. Provide proof of service of same.*

• *Answer, Counterclaim or Notice of Appearance filed by defendant. Provide proof of service of same.*

18 CERTIFICATE OF DISSOLUTION *(DOH–2168)* — *(include social security numbers - make sure it is signed - County Clerk will not enter judgment without this)*

19 REQUEST FOR JUDICIAL INTERVENTION. *(in duplicate, together with receipt of fee payment and proof of service)*

20 NOTE OF ISSUE *(in duplicate, with receipt of fee payment and proof of service)*

21 SELF ADDRESSED STAMPED POSTCARD — *(used for notification by County Clerk when judgment has been signed — STAPLE or ATTACH to the CERTIFICATE OF DISSOLUTION)*

- OR - check for certified copies with self addressed envelope (see #22 for fee schedule) ** THERE IS NO OTHER METHOD OF NOTIFICATION BY THE CLERK'S OFFICE ON SIGNED JUDGMENTS.*

22 FEES — *(payable to the Nassau County Clerk 240 Old Country Rd. Mineola, NY)*

INDEX NO. $$210.00

RJI $$95.00

NOTE OF ISSUE $$30.00

CERTIFIED COPY $$1.25 per page, $$5.00 minimum charge

STIPULATION OF SETTLEMENT $$35.00

Attachments:

- Addendum concerning Support Collection Unit, Family Court Orders, and Income Deduction Orders.

- Submission Chart for "Settled" Contested Judgments. (Uncontested Matrimonials should utilize the Uncontested Divorce Packet)

ADDENDUM

FAMILY COURT ORDERS: Orders issued by the Family Court in regards to **Child Support, Spousal Support** *(Maintenance)*, **Custody and Visitation,** may be continued by the Supreme Court in a divorce judgment, either by agreement of the parties, or by direction of the Court. The existence of such an order can be helpful to the Court when those issues must be determined. If you have such issues, and you have not yet commenced an action for divorce, you may want to secure a Family Court order as to those issues. The Family Court is located at 1200 Old Country Rd. Westbury, NY 11590.

SUPPORT COLLECTION UNIT: The Support Collection Unit *(Child Support Enforcement Bureau)*, is an arm of the Department of Social Services. They maintain computerized payment records, and provide many services in the collection and enforcement of court ordered support payments *(Child Support or combined Child and Spousal Support)*, whether or not the custodial parent or child is in receipt of public assistance. Such collection and enforcement procedures include, but are not limited to:

- **Immediate income execution**
- **State and Federal Tax Refund Offset**
- **Credit Bureau Reporting**
- **Seizure of Bank Accounts**
- **License suspension**
- **Department of Taxation and Finance collection**
- **Judgments/Liens being filed**
- **Court Enforcement (Contempt proceedings)**

It is suggested that you speak to your local child support enforcement unit for more information. **For correspondence**: *Nassau County SCU, 101 County Seat Dr., Mineola, NY 11501*. **For telephone inquiries**: *Nassau County SCU, Customer Service Unit, 516–571–5671*. A sample copy of the SCU payment instructions is available through the SCU or at the Matrimonial Clerks' Office.

INCOME DEDUCTION ORDERS: The court must issue an income deduction order *(IDO)* where it issues a support order in a case not enforced through a local child support collection unit, and involving someone who earns wages that could be subject to an income deduction order. The court must issue such an order, unless the parties agree to an alternate method of payment, or if the court finds "good cause" not to issue an income deduction order. If the court directs, or if the parties agree to an income deduction order, the form of income deduction order available at the Matrimonial Clerks' Office should be used.

If the income deduction order is for **spousal support (maintenance)** only, you may have the payments go through a state agency **or** have it go direct to the person receiving the money. *Please note that there may be an administrative fee involved with using the state agency.* The agency where payments are to be forwarded is:

Office of Temporary and Disability Assistance

PO Box 15365

Albany, NY 12212–5365

If the income deduction order is for **child support**, or **child and spousal support combined**, insert the name and address of the person who is to receive the monies. This will be a direct payment.

NASSAU COUNTY MATRIMONIAL CENTER

Required documents for submission of a judgment of divorce: <u>**CONTESTED MATRIMONIAL**</u>

Document:	Settled and submitted on written proof:	Settled and submitted on oral proof:
Pleadings (Summons, Complaint, Answer [with counter-claim], Reply) or *Amended* Pleadings with proof of personal service	YES	YES
Affirmation / Affidavit of Regularity	YES	YES
Affidavit of Facts by Plaintiff or (Defendant on counter-claim)	YES	NO - *unless needed to supplement missing information from testimony*
Affidavit of Defendant or (Plaintiff on counterclaim)	YES	NO - *unless needed to supplement missing information from testimony*
Removal of Barriers Affidavit *(DRL § 253)*	YES - *unless marriage was a civil ceremony or filing waived in writing*	YES - *unless marriage was a civil ceremony, filing was waived in writing, or set forth in testimony*
IF CHILD SUPPORT: Child Support Enforcement Bureau Affidavit *(CSEB) - needed by Support Collection Unit [SCU]*	YES - *unless not going through SCU, and stipulation contains required information.*	YES - *unless not going through SCU, and stipulation contains required information.*
IF CHILD SUPPORT: Child Support Worksheet / Itemization Sheet	YES - *unless incomes specifically set forth in stipulation with deductions*	YES - *unless incomes specifically set forth in transcript with deductions.*
Transcript of court testimony / copy of written decision	YES - If written decision after trial	YES - If court's decision was placed on the record
Settlement Agreement	YES - *if applicable*	YES - *if applicable*
Proposed Findings of Fact	YES -*unless complete findings contained in a written decision*	YES
Proposed Judgment of Divorce	YES	YES
IF CHILD SUPPORT: Qualified Medical Child Support Order	YES - *unless no health insurance or private or state subsidized plan*	YES - *unless no health insurance or private or state subsidized plan*
Qualified Domestic Relations Order (QDRO)	*if necessary*	*if necessary*
Income Deduction Order (IDO)	*if necessary*	*if necessary*
Qualified Life Insurance Order (QLIO)	*if necessary*	*if necessary*
Note of Issue *(with proof of payment)*	YES - *unless previously filed*	YES -*unless previously filed*
Certificate of Dissolution DOH 2168- revised 5/2000	YES - *must be original*	YES - *must be original*
IF CHILD SUPPORT: UCS - 111	YES	YES
IF CHILD SUPPORT: State Support Registry Form	YES - *unless SCU payment*	YES - *unless SCU payment*
Part 130 Certification	YES	YES
Postcard *(self-addressed and stamped)*	YES	YES

Checklist 2. Retirement Benefit Orders

SUBMITTING ORDERS TO DISTRIBUTE RETIREMENT BENEFITS

Common forms of these orders include:

- QUALIFIED DOMESTIC RELATION ORDERS (QDRO)
- DOMESTIC RELATIONS ORDERS (DRO)
- COURT ORDERS ACCEPTABLE FOR PROCESSING (COAP)

The type of order needed will depend on the type of benefits and plan you are dealing with. You may want to seek the advice of an attorney or a specialist in preparing these type of orders, as well as the administrator of the particular plan.

PLEASE NOTE THAT EACH PLAN IS DIFFERENT, AND THE COURT CANNOT PROVIDE YOU WITH A FORM OF ORDER.

These orders are generally submitted in one of the following scenarios: *(all require pre-approval by the plan administration — if possible)*

- If the order is submitted **without** a pending action *(i.e., on a separation agreement)*— you must commence an action or proceeding for the court to acquire jurisdiction to issue the order.

- If the order is submitted in a pending action **either prior to judgment, or at the time of submission of the Judgment of Divorce,** you must provide the agreement or court directive which authorizes the issuance of the order.

- If the order is submitted **after the Judgment of Divorce,** you must provide a copy of the Judgment and the agreement or court directive which authorizes the issuance of the order.

NOTE: No matter what scenario the order is submitted under, there are various documents needed and procedures which must be followed in all cases. Failure to follow these directions will result in a rejection of your submission, and a delay in processing the order. The checklist available on this site and at the Clerk's Office contains the requirements for filing.

Checklist 3.   Alternate Service

GENERAL INFORMATION:

Application for Alternative Service of Summons

Service of the *summons with notice or summons and verified complaint* in a matrimonial action is usually done by personally serving (giving) the papers to the defendant. If this cannot be done because the defendant is avoiding service or cannot be located, you may need to make an application for a different way of serving the defendant. You can ask to serve the papers by any method you feel you can reasonably accomplish. The Court though, will make the ultimate decision on what method of service you will use.

Generally, publication of the summons in a newspaper should be a last resort, since it is the method that would be least likely to give notice to defendant. It can also be quite expensive. If there is no other way to serve the defendant, publication may be your only option. In either case, a thorough search must be made of the defendants whereabouts before the Court will consider service by another method.

You must complete your service within 120 days of the commencement of your action *(the date you filed the summons with notice or summons and verified complaint with the County Clerk)*. If you cannot accomplish service in that time, you can apply for more time to serve.

** IT IS SUGGESTED THAT YOU SEEK THE ADVICE OF AN ATTORNEY WHERE PERSONAL SERVICE OF THE DEFENDANT WILL BE A PROBLEM

Common places to conduct search for defendant's whereabouts:

- Post Office
- Board of Elections
- Department of Motor Vehicles
- Telephone Directories
- US Armed Forces (central website and addresses for military branches listed on next page)
- Relatives and friends
- In addition, if you believe the person has left the country, you should check with:
- U.S. Immigration and Naturalization Service as to his/her passport
- the Consulate or Embassy of that country
- friends or relatives in that country to help you locate his or her whereabouts.

Servicemembers' Civil Relief Act (SCRA) Certificates

To obtain certificates of service or non-service under the Servicemembers' Civil Relief Act of 2003 (formerly known as Soldiers' and Sailors' Civil Relief Act of 1940) you can use the public website: https://www.dmdc.osd.mil/scra/owa/home. This website will provide you with the current active military status of an individual. There is no charge for this certificate.

You can also receive certificates from the individual Services by sending your correspondence to the appropriate military office listed below. If other than current status needs to be verified, then you need to send your request direct to the Services listed below. The charge for each SCRA certificate (as of February 21, 2002) is $5.20. Checks should be made payable to "Treasurer of the United States".

ARMY:
Army World Wide Locator Service
Enlisted Records and Evaluation Center
8899 East 56th Street
Indianapolis, IN 46249–5031
NOTE: All requests must be in writing.

NAVY:
Bureau of Naval Personnel
PERS–312E
5720 Integrity Drive
Millington, TN 38055–3120
(901) 874–3388

AIR FORCE:
Air Force Manpower and Personnel Center
ATTN: Air Force Locator/MSIMDL
550 C Street West, Suite 50
Randolph Air Force Base, TX 78150–4752
Locator Service: (210) 652–5775

MARINE CORPS:
Commandant of The Marine Corps
Headquarters, U.S. Marine Corps (MMSB10)
2008 Elliott Road, Suite 201
Quantico, VA 22134–5030
Locator Service: (703) 784–3941–3944

COAST GUARD:
Commander–CGPC-adm3   *$5.20 made payable to US Coast Guard*
US Coast Guard Personnel Command
2100 Second Street SW
Washington DC 20593- 2321
http://www.uscg.mil/hq/cg1/cgpc/adm/adm3/% 1F locator/

Checklist 4. Amending Orders

Order Amending or Resettling a prior Order or Judgment

<u>Resettlement</u>: This is used to correct an error or omission in the original signed order or judgment. It is to be used only in a case like a typographical error. It is not to be used to modify an existing order or judgment because of a change in circumstances (i.e. a new agreement)

<u>Amendment</u>: This is to be used to modify an existing order or judgment because of some sort of change in circumstances - like a new agreement between the parties or a further order by the court. Instead of doing a whole new amended judgment every time you change something - do an order making reference to the specific changes.

In each case, you must:

☐ Have the consent of the other party, *(stipulation between the parties)* or an order of the court authorizing the proposed amendment or resettlement. If not, you must bring on a motion before the court for that relief.

☐ Submit an affidavit detailing the need for the amendment or resettlement.

☐ Submit a copy of the order or judgment you are seeking to amend or resettle.

☐ Provide proof of consent from the other party.

Checklist 5.   Contested Matrimonial Timelines

SUMMONS SERVED

CPLR § 306-b

Within **120** days of filing summons with the County Clerk - unless Court signs an order granting ans extension of time.

RJI FILED

Uniform Rule 202.16(d)

No later than **45** days from service of summons
- or -
No later than **120** days from service of summons if Notice of No Necessity filed by both sides.

NET WORTH STATEMENT

Uniform Rule 202.16 (f) (1) -

Exchanged and filed no later than **10** days prior to the preliminary conference.

See rule for other papers which the Court directs to be exchanged

---

PRELIMINARY CONFERENCE

Uniform Rule 202.16 (f) (1) -

To be held within **45** days of Judge assignment (RJI date).

***Parties must be present and the Judge shall address the parties*

COMPLIANCE CONFERENCE

Uniform Rule 202.16 (f) (3) -

Shall be scheduled unless Court dispenses with it based upon stipulation of compliance filed by parties.

***Parties must be present unless otherwise advised by the Court and the Judge shall address the parties*

DISCOVERY

Uniform Rule 202.16 (f) (2) (iv)

To be completed and Note of Issue filed no later than **6** months from the date of preliminary conference unless otherwise shortened or extended by the Court depending on the circumstances.

** *Certification memorandum required from Judge - file Note w/in time frame set forth in memorandum.*

TRIAL

Uniform Rule 202.16 (f) (3)

To be scheduled for no later than **6** months from the date of preliminary conference.

Checklist 6. Common Filing Mistakes

Common Filing Mistakes in an Uncontested Divorce with no children

Papers which are incomplete and legally insufficient will be rejected by the court and returned to the plaintiff for corrections and/or additional information. Usually, the resulting delay in a granting of the divorce caused by errors and omissions in the forms could have been avoided by a **patient and careful reading of the detailed instructions**. A *statewide survey of court personnel* has shown the following defects to be among the most common reasons upon which papers are rejected:

• **Inconsistencies:** Names, dates, other factual information not consistent throughout the papers.

• **Defendant's Affidavit** (Form A-5) admitting service of the Summons with Notice or the Summons and Verified Complaint **pre-dates the commencement of the action.**

• **Separation Agreement:**

   (a) missing.

   (b) no proof of filing with the county clerk

   (c) not acknowledged in the manner required to entitle a deed to be recorded

• **Proof of Service** of the Summons with Notice or Summons and Complaint **missing or inadequate.** (incomplete/description missing/proof of presence in a foreign country)

• Factual **Affidavit(s)** in support **missing or inadequate** in regard to:

   (a) Residential Requirements (DRL § 230).

   (b) Compliance with DRL § 253 (barriers to remarriage).

   (c) Grounds for divorce. No legal basis for divorce asserted.

   (d) Proof entitling moving party to ancillary relief (financial etc.).

• **Notarization** (missing/expired/ no good)

• **Signing Certification** of papers by the attorney/party missing. (Rule 130.1.–a).

• **Verified Complaint missing** or not verified.

• **Notice of Settlement** or waiver missing.

Checklist 7. Order to Show Cause

If you are submitting an Order to Show Cause ("OSC") to be reviewed by the Clerk's Office, please be aware of the following requirements. Failure to follow the above guidelines may result in either rejection by the Clerk's Office or denial of the motion by the court.

☐ **The OSC must have proof of payment of the motion fee with the County Clerk** (attach recording sheet showing payment)

☐ **All affidavits must be properly notarized.**

☐ **All affidavits/affirmations should be originals** (if not an explanation is required why copies should be accepted).

☐ **All exhibits should be attached which you want the court to consider.**

☐ **All OSC's should have a legal back showing the name, address, phone and fax information of the submitting party or attorney.** (Chambers will fax a conformed copy upon signature—if you want to pick up or have copy mailed to you—please alert the Clerk's Office as to this when submitting your papers)

☐ **If the OSC is the first paper filed in the court on a new case—it requires a signed Request for Judicial Intervention ("RJI")—together with proof of payment of the required fee** (attach County Clerk recording page) **and proof of service on the other side.** (If there is another pending matter or a previously disposed case in Supreme Court that is related—enter the case name and index number in the appropriate area on page two of the RJI).

☐ **If the OSC asks for the payment of maintenance, child support or attorney fees** (*except attorney fees to enforce a prior order pursuant to DRL§ 237 (c) or 238*)—**please be aware that a sworn statement of net worth should be submitted as part of the motion per Uniform Rule 202.16 (k) (2).**

☐ **If the OSC seeks a stay or Temporary Restraining Order ("TRO"), you will need to comply with Uniform Rule 202.7 as to providing prior notice of your application** (*see notice*).

IMPORTANT: IF YOU ARE SEEKING CUSTODY OR VISITATION—YOU MUST COMPLETE A DATABASE REVIEW INFORMATION SHEET WITH YOUR OSC

Matrimonial Clerk

Checklist 8.   Notice of Motion

If you are submitting a motion on notice to be calendared by the Clerk's Office, please be aware of the following requirements.   Failure to follow the above guidelines may result in either rejection by the Clerk's Office or denial of the motion by the court.

☐ **The motion must have a return date for calendaring purposes.**

☐ **The motion must have proof of service—either an affidavit of service or a signed acknowledgment of service** (name must be printed below such signature).

☐ **The motion must have proof of payment of the motion fee with the County Clerk** (attach recording sheet showing payment)

☐ **All affidavits must be properly notarized.**

☐ **All affidavits/affirmations should be originals** (if not an explanation is required why copies should be accepted)

☐ **All exhibits should be attached which you want the court to consider.**

☐ **All motions should have a legal back showing the name, address, phone and fax information of the submitting party or attorney.**

☐ **If the motion is the first paper filed in the court on a new case—it requires a signed Request for Judicial Intervention ("RJI")—together with proof of payment of the required fee** (attach County Clerk recording page) **and proof of service on the other side.**   (If there is another pending matter or a previously disposed case in Supreme Court that is related—enter the case name and index number in the appropriate area on page two of the RJI).

☐ **If the motion asks for the payment of maintenance, child support or attorney fees—please be aware that a sworn statement of net worth should be submitted as part of the motion per Uniform Rule 202.16 (k) (2).**

IMPORTANT: IF YOU ARE SEEKING CUSTODY OR VISITATION—YOU MUST COMPLETE A DATABASE REVIEW INFORMATION SHEET WITH YOUR OSC

Matrimonial Clerk

Checklist 9. Marriage License Waivers

Pursuant to DRL § 13–b, a marriage **may not** be solemnized *(ceremony performed)* within 24 hours of the issuance of a marriage license—**unless** an order is issued by the Court to waive the 24 hour waiting period. Usually, this is only done in emergency circumstances *(i.e. where one of the parties are being shipped out on active military duty forthwith, or some other situation that requires an immediate ceremony)*

- Both petitioners (Husband and Wife—to be) have to be present and produce the marriage license.

- The petition is filled out explaining the need for obtaining the waiver. It is then signed by both petitioners in the presence of the clerk. They are placed under oath as to the contents of the petition, and the clerk signs the petition at the bottom.

- The waiver order is prepared and then the order, petition and license is submitted to a judge for signature.

- If signed, the court seal is placed over the signature of the judge, and the **original** waiver order along with the petition and license is given back to the to the petitioners. A copy is retained for the court's records. The petitioners are to present those documents to the person performing their ceremony, who will then file them with the proper authorities.

MARRIAGE LICENSES & DIVORCE RECORDS

In Nassau County, marriage licenses are issued by the three towns and two cities. Marriage Licenses are maintained by the municipality in which the license was obtained. For a copy, you would go to the same Town Hall in which you originally obtained the license. For example, if you were married in Glen Cove, but you obtained your marriage license in the Town of Hempstead, your license would be available at the Town of Hempstead. The Nassau County Clerk does, however, have a record of marriages beginning with the year 1907 and ending April 29, 1935.

Please note: in order to obtain a copy of a divorce certificate, you must be the husband, wife or attorney of record. Official photo identification such as driver's license or passport must be presented when requesting matrimonial (divorce) files.

Towns & Cities in Nassau County

Town of Oyster Bay:

Unincorporated Communities within the Town of Oyster Bay include: Bethpage; East Norwich; Glen Head; Hicksville; Jericho; Locust Grove; Locust Valley; Massapequa; Old Bethpage; Oyster Bay; Plainedge; Plainview; South Farmingdale; Syosset and Woodbury.

Incorporated Villages using Town of Oyster Bay Registrar: Brookville; Centre Island; Cove Neck; Lattingtown; Laurel Hollow; Matinecock; Mill Neck; Muttontown; Old Brookville; Oyster Bay Cove and Upper Brookville

http://www.oysterbaytown.com

Town Clerk's Office
Town Hall North
54 Audrey Avenue
Oyster Bay, New York 11771
(516) 624–6332

Town of Hempstead

Unincorporated Communities within the Town of Hempstead include: Baldwin; Barnum Island; Bay Park; Bellmore; East Meadow; Elmont; Franklin Square; Garden City Park; Garden City South; Gibson; Green Acres; Harbor Island; Hewlett; Inwood; Lakeview; Levittown; Lido Beach; Meadowmere Park; Merrick; North Bellmore; North Lynbrook; North Merrick, North Valley Stream; North Woodmere; Oceanside; Point Lookout; Roosevelt; Salisbury;

Seaford; South Hempstead; South Valley Stream; Uniondale; Wantagh; West Hempstead and Woodmere.

   Incorporated Villages using Town of Hempstead Registrar: Hewlett Harbor

http://www.townofhempstead.org

Town Clerk's Office
One Washington Street
1st Floor
Hempstead, NY 11550
(516) 489–5000

Town of North Hempstead

   Unincorporated Communities within the Town of North Hempstead include: Albertson; Carle Place; Glenwood Landing; Great Neck Gardens; Greenvale; Harbor Hills; Herricks; Manhasset; Manhasset Hills; New Cassel; North New Hyde Park; Port Washington; Roslyn Heights; Saddle Rock Estates; Searington; Strathmore; University Gardens and Williston Park. Incorporated Villages using Town of North Hempstead Registrar: Baxter Estates; Great Neck; Great Neck Estates; Kensington; Kings Point; Manorhaven; North Hills; Port Washington North; Roslyn Estates; Russell Gardens; Saddle Rock;

http://www.northhempstead.com
Town Clerk's Office
200 Plandome Road
Box 3000
Manhasset, NY 11030
(516) 869–7646

City of Glen Cove

http://www.glencove-li.com
Glen Cove City Hall
9 Glen Street
Glen Cove, NY 11542
(516) 676–3345

City of Long Beach

http://www.longbeachny.org
City Clerk's Office
City Hall Room 307
1 West Chester Street
Long Beach, NY 11561
516–431–1000 Extension 314

Checklist 10. Note of Issue Requirements

- Note of Issue with Certificate of Readiness
- Proof of payment of fee from County Clerk
- Copy of So Ordered Certification Memorandum
- Statement of Proposed Disposition
- Proof of service upon other party or attorney

NOTE: If Note of Issue is being filed on a default for inquest, or on a settled contested matter, please indicate same on the Note of Issue and attach a cover letter.

Checklist 11.   Spelling Errors in Names of Parties

- The spelling of any of the parties' names in any court papers has to match what the County Clerk has on file—which would be the spelling that is found in the summons.

- If it differs in any way (i.e. an error in spelling, an additional middle name or initial, or a suffix like "Jr." or "Sr.")—it will most likely be returned by the County Clerk.

- If the summons is incorrect, you will need to have a stipulation signed to correct and have the Court "so order". This will show the correct spelling as set forth by the parties and will deem any documents corrected. It will also direct the County Clerk to amend her records accordingly.

- Where the defendant defaulted in appearance, an ex parte order can be submitted along with an affidavit explaining the need for the correction. (Attach a copy of the original signed judgment)

FORMS

Form 1. Contested Matrimonial Uniform Information Sheet

A. Information:

(1)   Attorney for Plaintiff   Attorney for Defendant

_____   _____

_____   _____

_____   _____

Phone:_____   Phone:_____

Fax: _____   Fax: _____

(2) Date of Marriage: __ / __ / __; State: _____;

Civil or Religious Ceremony _____;

(3) Name(s) and Date(s) of Birth of Children:

_____   _____

_____   _____

(4) Children reside with: _____;

(5) Parties have been separated since: _____;

(6) Age of plaintiff: __; Plaintiff's date of birth: __ / __ / __.

(7) Age of defendant: __; Defendant's date of birth: __ / __ / __.

(8) Plaintiff's Current Address: _____

Phone #s: Home: _____ Work: _____ Cell: _____;

(9) Defendant's Current Address: _____;

Phone #s: Home: _____ Work: _____ Cell: _____;

(10) Persons residing at Marital Residence: _____;

(11) Plaintiff's Social Security #: _____;

Defendant's Social Security #: _____;

(12) Education of plaintiff: _____; Date(s) plaintiff attained degree(s) _____;

(13) Education of defendant: _____; Date(s) defendant attained degree(s) _____;

(14) Occupation of plaintiff: _____; Monthly gross income: _____;

(15) Occupation of defendant: _____; Monthly gross income: _____;

(16) Income from other sources, i.e., SSDI, dividends, etc. _____;

(17) Employer of plaintiff; if unemployed, so state and set forth date and nature of last employment _____;

(18) Employer of defendant; if unemployed, so state and set forth date and nature of last employment _____;

(19) Marital residence is located at: _____;

(20) Date of purchase: _____; Purchase price: $_____;

Principal balance first mortgage: $_____; equity loan: $_____;

other loans against marital residence: $_____;

Estimated market value: $_____;

(21) Cost of monthly mortgage, equity loan, any other loans against marital residence; homeowners' insurance and real property taxes: $ _____; Title is held by: _____.

(22) Set forth the date of occupancy, cost of rent and utilities for each premises RENTED by a party as a primary residence:

Plaintiff: _____;

Defendant: _____;

(23) Other residences owned by the parties: _____;

(24) Set forth amount paid to date for counsel fees by plaintiff: _____; by defendant: _____;

(25) Set forth source of counsel fees paid: plaintiff: _____; defendant: _____;

(26) Service of Pleadings, Net Worth Statements & Retainer Agreements and Disclosure Required Pursuant to 202.16(f) of the Uniform Rules

The action was commenced on __/ / __;

The Summons was filed on __/ / __ and served on __/ / __;

The Complaint was served on or to be served by: __/ / __;

Issue was or will be joined on: __/ / __;

Reply to Counterclaim, if any, was or will be served on __/ / __;

Wife's Net Worth Statement was or will be filed on __/ / __;

Husband's Net Worth Statement was or will be filed on __/ / __;

A signed copy of Wife's Retainer Agreement was or will be filed on __/ / __;

A signed copy of Husband's Retainer Agreement was or will be filed on __/ / __;

(27) Notice of Necessity Filed: Yes ___ No _____

B. Electronic Discovery

Identify relevant electronic data: _____;

Identify the person(s) in possession of the aforesaid electronic data: _____;

Identify the computer system(s) utilized, the program(s) and manner in which the electronic data is maintained: _____;

Set forth a plan to retain and preserve the electronic data: _____;

Set forth the scope and extent of the data to be produced and the form in which it will be produced: _____;

Set forth the scope of the electronic data review and the review procedures to be undertaken: _____;

Set forth a method to identify and redact privileged electronic data: _____;

Set forth the anticipated cost of data retention, recovery, production and review and the proposed initial allocation of said cost: _____.

Electronic Evidence: For relevant periods relating to the issues in this litigation, each party shall maintain and preserve all electronic files, other data generated by and/or stored on the party's computer system(s) and storage media (i.e., hard disks, floppy disks, backup tapes), or other electronic data. Such items include, but are not limited to, e-mail and other electronic communications, word processing documents, spreadsheets, data bases, calendars, telephone logs, contact manager information, internet usage files, offline storage or information stored on removable media, information contained on laptops or other portable devices and network access information.

Preservation of Records and Electronic Data: EACH PARTY STIPULATES TO MAINTAIN ALL FINANCIAL RECORDS PRESENTLY IN HIS OR HER

POSSESSION OR UNDER HIS OR HER CONTROL, INCLUDING COMPUTER AND OTHER ELECTRONIC FINANCIAL INFORMATION THROUGH THE ENTRY OF A JUDGMENT OF DIVORCE OR OTHER DISPOSITION OF THIS ACTION.
THIS PROVISION SHALL BE INITIALED BY EACH PARTY:

Plaintiff's Initials: _____ Defendant's Initials: _____

   C. Insurance
Identify each life insurance policy on the husband's life in effect as of the date of the commencement of the action and set forth the face value and name of the beneficiary of each policy: _____
_____

Set forth which party paid the premiums on said policies during the marriage and which party will accordingly pay said premiums during the pendency of the action as required by statute: _____
_____

Identify each life insurance policy on the wife's life in effect as of the date of the commencement of the action and set forth the face value and the name of the beneficiary of each policy: _____
_____

Set forth which party paid the premiums on said policies during the marriage and which party will accordingly pay said premiums during the pendency of the action as required by statute: _____
_____

Set forth which party or parties maintained medical insurance as of the date of the commencement of the action and the names of the covered persons:
_____

Set forth which party or parties maintained dental insurance as of the date of the commencement of the action and the names of the covered persons: ___
_____

Set forth which party or parties paid the premiums on said policies during the marriage and which party or parties will accordingly pay said premiums during the pendency of the action as required by statute: _____
_____

Set forth which party or parties paid the premiums for homeowners insurance and/or renters insurance during the marriage and which party or parties will accordingly pay said premiums during the pendency of the action as required by statute: _____
_____

EACH PARTY SHALL ACKNOWLEDGE HE OR SHE MUST COMPLY WITH THE AUTOMATIC STATUTORY RESTRAINTS DRL § 236(B)(2) AND PAY THE PREMIUMS TO MAINTAIN MEDICAL, DENTAL, LIFE, HOMEOWNERS AND RENTERS INSURANCE AS SET FORTH ABOVE. THIS PROVISION SHALL BE INITIALED BY EACH PARTY:

Plaintiff's Initials: _____ Defendant's Initials: _____

   D. Involvement in Other Courts on Related Issues
☐ There are no other actions pending or orders in any other court on related issues.
☐ There is an action pending on related issues in _____ Court.
☐ The following orders are presently in effect on related issues such as custody, support or any family offense, domestic violence and/or Orders of

Protection. Copies of these orders will be provided to this Court by counsel within <u>10</u> days of the date of this Order.

_____

_____

PLAINTIFF	DEFENDANT
PLAINTIFF'S ATTORNEY	DEFENDANT'S ATTORNEY

Form 2.   Uniform Preliminary Conference Order

SUPREME COURT OF THE STATE OF NEW YORK

COUNTY OF NASSAU: IAS PART

---X

Plaintiff

      –against–   **Index No:**

Defendant

---X

NASSAU COUNTY

UNIFORM PRELIMINARY CONFERENCE ORDER

CONTESTED MATRIMONIAL

PRESIDING:

    Justice of the Supreme Court

    The parties and counsel have appeared before this Court on _____, 20 __, at a preliminary conference on this matter held pursuant to 22 NYCRR 202.16(f).

A.   AUTOMATIC STATUTORY RESTRAINTS—DRL § 236(B)(2)

The following automatic statutory orders shall remain in effect during the pendency of this action, unless terminated, modified, or amended by order of the Court upon motion of either party or upon written agreement between the parties duly executed and acknowledged:

(1) Neither party shall sell, transfer, encumber, conceal, assign, remove or in any way dispose of, without the consent of the other party in writing, or by Order of the Court, any property (including, but not limited to, real estate, personal property, cash accounts, stocks, mutual funds, bank accounts, cars and boats) individually or jointly held by the parties, except in the usual course of business, for customary and usual household expenses or for reasonable attorney's fees in connection with this action.

(2) Neither party shall transfer encumber, assign, remove, withdraw or in any way dispose of any tax deferred funds, stocks or other assets held in any individual retirement accounts, 401K accounts, profit sharing plans, Keogh accounts, or any other pension or retirement account, and the parties shall further refrain from applying for or requesting the payment of retirement benefits or annuity payments of any kind, without the consent of the other party in writing, or upon further Order of the Court; except that any party who is already in pay status may continue to receive such payments thereunder.

(3) Neither party shall incur unreasonable debts hereafter, including, but not limited to further borrowing against any credit line secured by the family residence, further encumbrancing any assets, or unreasonably using credit cards or cash advances against credit cards, except in the usual course of business or for customary or usual household expenses, or for reasonable attorney's fees in connection with this action.

(4) Neither party shall cause the other party or the children of the marriage to be removed from any existing medical, hospital and dental insurance coverage, and each party shall maintain the existing medical, hospital and dental insurance coverage in full force and effect.

(5) Neither party shall change the beneficiaries of any existing life insurance policies, and each party shall maintain the existing life insurance, automobile insurance, homeowners and renters insurance policies in full force and effect.

B. ISSUE RESOLUTION:

The parties hereby stipulate, for purposes of trial, that the following issues between them are:

		RESOLVED	UNRESOLVED
(1)	Fault	_____	_____
(2)	Custody	_____	_____
(3)	Visitation/Parental Access	_____	_____
(4)	Child Support	_____	_____
(5)	Maintenance	_____	_____
(6)	Equitable Distribution	_____	_____
(7)	Other	_____	

ALL ISSUES RESOLVED MUST BE CONTAINED IN A STIPULATION PREPARED AT THE PRELIMINARY CONFERENCE OR PLACED UPON THE RECORD AT THE PRELIMINARY CONFERENCE.

The parties and counsel are advised that in the event grounds and/or custody and visitation/parental access have not been resolved by the time of the status conference, the Court will consider an application to bifurcate such issue and schedule a trial for the first available date.

C. *PENDENTE LITE* RELIEF:

Provide the specific details regarding the interim resolution of any of the following issues or state N/A. Resolution will constitute a "so ordered" stipulation.

Resolved

Exclusive Use of Marital Residence   _____

Custody of Children   _____

Parental Access to Children   _____

This temporary Order of Custody and/or Visitation/Parental Access has issued upon the Court's review of records as required by the provisions of DRL§ 240 and FCA§ 651 as amended by Chapter 595 of the Laws of 2008.

Child Support   _____

Educational Expenses   _____

Maintenance   _____

Carrying Charges   _____

Uncovered Health Expenses   _____

Counsel Fees   _____

Expert Fees   _____

Other (specify)   _____

D. RESOURCES AVAILABLE:

Each of the parties may elect to partake in mediation of their dispute, of any issue thereto (valuation, equitable distribution, etc.). A panel of court-approved mediators is available to counsel.

The Model Custody Part/Children Come First Initiative is available to help the parties/counsel formulate and facilitate an interim and/or a permanent parenting plan and/or a permanent order of custody and visitation/parental access. Upon request, the Court will facilitate a meeting between the parties and Vincenzo Renda/Marisa Alleyn of the Model Custody Part to answer all questions and to conduct an intake.

PLAINTIFF	DEFENDANT
PLAINTIFF'S ATTORNEY	DEFENDANT'S ATTORNEY

E. BUSINESS/FINANCIAL RESOURCES:

(1) **Neutral Expert/Business/Practice/License/Degree/Enhanced Earning Capacity** By separate order, the Court will appoint (with consent of the parties)

_____

as a neutral expert to assist the court in evaluating

_____

The cost is to be paid ___ % by the plaintiff and ___ % by the defendant, subject to reallocation at trial.

(2) **Neutral Expert—Real Estate**

By separate order, the Court will appoint (with consent of the parties)

_____

as a neutral expert to assist the court in evaluating

_____

The cost is to be paid ___ % by the plaintiff and ___ % by the defendant, subject to reallocation at trial.

(3) **Neutral Expert/Pension/Deferred Income Assets**

By separate order, the Court will appoint (with consent of the parties)

_____

as a neutral expert to assist the court in evaluating

_____

The cost is to be paid ___ % by the plaintiff and ___ % by the defendant, subject to reallocation at trial.

(4) **Neutral Expert/Other**

By separate order, the Court will appoint (with consent of the parties)

_____

as a neutral expert to assist the court in evaluating

_____

The cost is to be paid ___ % by the plaintiff and ___ % by the defendant, subject to reallocation at trial.

F. PARENTING RESOURCES:

The parties stipulate and the court orders that the parties shall utilize the following parenting resources.

___ MODEL CUSTODY PART/CHILDREN COME FIRST INITIATIVE.

___ P.E.A.C.E. PROGRAM: The parties shall enroll in the next scheduled
Parent Education and Custody Effectiveness Program. Information
regarding upcoming sessions is available at 888–547–3223. Parties
shall provide proof of completion of the program to the court.

___ KIDS PEACE: The following children shall enroll in the Kids Peace
Program: _____. Information regarding upcoming sessions is
available at 516–463–6360. Parties shall provide proof of completion of
the program to the court.

___ COURT MEDIATION: The parties shall meet with the Family Case
Analyst for assistance in arranging parenting time. An appointment
can be made by telephoning 516–571–0772.

___ ATTORNEY FOR THE CHILD(REN): Pursuant to the separate order of
the Court issued simultaneously herewith, the court appoints
_____ as Attorney for the minor child(ren) of the parties, _____.

___ FORENSIC: Pursuant to the separate order of the court issued simultaneously herewith, the court appoints _____ to conduct a forensic examination of the parties, their children and any necessary collateral parties.

G. CASE SCHEDULING:

(1) Discovery Deadlines—to be completed upon consultation with the Court

The Court orders the following discovery deadlines (fill in specific dates for
service or conduct):

	Plaintiff	Defendant
a. Notice for Discovery and Inspection		
Serve By:	_____	_____
Respond By:	_____	_____
b. Interrogatories		
Serve By:	_____	_____
Respond By:	_____	_____

c. If the parties have not heretofore complied with 22 NYCRR 202.16(f)(1),
they shall exchange copies of the following documents on the following dates,
but in no event later than 45 days from the date of this order:

1. Their personal, partnership and closely held corporation's Federal
and State income tax returns for the past three years:
Plaintiff: _/ / Defendant: _/ /

2. Copies of all paycheck stubs for the current year and the last
paycheck stub for the immediately preceding calendar year:
Plaintiff: _/ / Defendant: _/ /

3. All W–2 wage and tax statements, 1099 forms and K–1 forms for any
year in the past three (3) years for which no return was filed:
Plaintiff: _/ / Defendant: _/ /

4. All statements of accounts received during the past three (3) years
from each financial institution in which cash or securities are held:
Plaintiff: _/ / Defendant: _/ /

5. The statements immediately preceding and following the date of
commencement of the matrimonial action pertaining to any policy of life
insurance having cash surrender or dividend value and any deferred compensation plan of any type or nature such as IRAs, pensions, profit-sharing,
Keogh, 401k and other retirement plans:
Plaintiff: _/ / Defendant: _/ /

d. Depositions
  Plaintiffs: at _____ on _/_/_ at _____ am/pm
  Defendant's: at _____ on _/_/_ at _____ am/pm
e. Exchange of Expert Reports
  Plaintiff: _/_/_ Defendant: _/_/_
f. Other _____

_____

g. The parties and counsel shall appear for a status conference on
_____, 20 ___ at ___ a.m./p.m.

h. The parties and counsel shall appear for a compliance/certification
conference to be held on _____, 20 ___ at ___ a.m./p.m. Counsel are
directed to bring to the conference a copy of their Proposed Statement of
Disposition, 22 NYCRR § 202.16(h).

i. The Plaintiff/Defendant shall file a Note of Issue on or before
_____, 20 ___.

j. THE COURT ORDERS THAT THE TRIAL IN THIS MATTER WILL
BE HELD ON:

_____, 20 ___ at ___ a.m. ___ p.m.

These dates may not be adjourned without consent of this Court. Failure
to comply with these dates may result in sanctions, including preclusion.

H. DISCOVERY PROBLEMS:

The parties shall contact the Court immediately if it appears that there are
any problems with the above schedule.

Counsel shall advise the Court in writing of any failure to comply with 22
NYCRR 202.16(f)(1) and the discovery deadlines set forth herein.

I. EXPERT WITNESSES:

At least sixty (60) days prior to the trial date set forth below, each party
shall serve and file with the Court a written report of the expert witness
the party anticipates calling at trial. Any reply report must be served at
least thirty (30) days prior to trial.

THE ABOVE IS HEREBY STIPULATED TO BY THE PARTIES AND
THEIR RESPECTIVE COUNSEL.

_____   _____
PLAINTIFF   DEFENDANT
_____   _____
PLAINTIFF'S ATTORNEY   DEFENDANT'S ATTORNEY

Dated: Mineola, New York   SO ORDERED:

_____, 20 ___

_____
                                            J.S.C.

HEALTH INSURANCE COVERAGE NOTICE

I, _____, fully understand that upon execution of a judgment
of divorce, I may no longer be eligible to be covered under my former spouse's
health insurance plan, depending on the terms of the plan.

Dated: _____, 20 ___ _____

_____

I, _____, fully understand that upon execution of a judgment of divorce, I may no longer be eligible to be covered under my former spouse's health insurance plan, depending on the terms of the plan.

Dated: _____, 20 _____

_____

CLERK'S OFFICE

IR 1. Intake Office Rules

Rules of the Matrimonial Center Clerk's Office (Intake):

Motions/Ex Parte/Preliminary Conference/Notes of Issue

This office handles ex-parte applications, requests for preliminary conference, motions, notes of issue, and incoming submissions on orders and judgments.

NOTE: Do not use the Request for Judicial Intervention contained in the Uncontested Divorce Packet for an application in a Contested Matrimonial.

Orders to Show Cause — ("OSC")

• **Chambers** will conform the signed OSC's by fax. A fax number should be on the legal back upon presentment of the OSC to the Clerk's Intake Office. If the submitting party does not want the OSC conformed by fax, they must inform the Clerk's Intake Office when the OSC is submitted. Please wait 48 hours before inquiring about a presented OSC that has not been received by fax.

• Make sure a certification is in the OSC pursuant to NYCRR 130–1.1–a.

• Make sure the accompanying affidavit or affirmation contains a statement pursuant to CPLR 2217(b)

• Make sure that you comply with Uniform Rule 202.7 (f) in regards to TRO's. See the Court Notice section for the rule.

• If there is a request for expedited handling of the OSC, there must be an affirmation or affidavit of emergency attached to the papers explaining the need for such expedited handling. The attorney, or someone with personal knowledge of the facts shall remain available at the direction of the court until the order has been signed.

• Completed copy of the Registry Information Sheet *(where the relief sought is custody/visitation)*.

Writs of Habeas Corpus

• A new index number and Request for Judicial Intervention with proof of payment, as well as proof of the filing of a copy of the verified petition with the County Clerk is required. The RJI should make reference to any pending or previous matrimonial action, so that it can be referred to the appropriate Justice, if necessary. Signed writs will not be faxed. They will be held in the Intake Office for pickup. The original writ is to be served with a copy of the petition. The court will retain a copy of the writ with the original petition.

• Completed copy of the Registry Information Sheet *(where the relief sought is custody/visitation)*.

Orders of Protection

Applications for a temporary order of protection must include the following:

• an Order to Show Cause with an emergency affidavit

• a completed Family Protection Registry Information Sheet (available in clerk's office)

• an affidavit in support which shall contain the allegations upon which the order of protection is sought as well as information concerning any other orders of protection issued between the parties, where they were issued, and whether they are active or not.

In addition, the applying party must be present in court at the time of the application to give testimony as to the allegations for the order of protection. If the party cannot appear at the time of application, please notify the clerk immediately.

Motions

• All papers submitted to the Court shall have the index number, return date, and name of the assigned Matrimonial Justice on its face. Papers lacking such information may be rejected.

• All motion papers are to be filed with the Matrimonial Intake Office at least five (5) business days before the return date.

• Any motion papers submitted shall be accompanied by a self addressed stamped envelope in order to receive a copy of the courts' decision.

• Adjournments shall be directed to the courtroom clerk for the assigned Matrimonial Justice.

• New cases require an RJI be filed in (2 copies) together with receipt of the fee payment from the County Clerk.

• Completed copy of the Registry Information Sheet *(where the relief sought is custody/visitation)*.

Preliminary Conference

All requests for Preliminary Conference shall be accompanied by:

• 2 copies of a Request for Judicial Intervention ("RJI") with receipt of payment of the statutory fee. (where case is unassigned).

• Proof of Service of RJI and Request for Preliminary Conference.

• Self-Addressed stamped envelope. Court will notify by an order setting conference date.

• Completed copy of the Registry Information Sheet *(where there are children of the marriage subject to custody/visitation)*.

Notes of Issue

Where the court has directed a note of issue to be filed, submit:

• 2 copies of the note of issue/certificate of readiness, together with receipt of payment of the statutory fee, and proof of service.

• Statement of Proposed Disposition (on contested matrimonials)

• Copy of the certification memorandum "so ordered" by the assigned Matrimonial Justice.

NOTE: If seeking a "grounds trial" or inquest, please indicate that on the note of issue. Also, if directed to submit without a statement of proposed disposition or certification memo by the court, please submit a cover letter alerting the clerk's office as to that.

Do not use the Note of Issue contained in the Uncontested Divorce Packet for a Contested Matrimonial

JR 1. Judgment Office Rules

Rules of the Matrimonial Center Clerk's Office:

Judgments and Orders

This office handles judgments and orders to be signed on contested and uncontested cases, as well as processing out-of-court work regarding court decisions and calendars.

Please take notice that submission of a judgment or order must occur within 60 days of the court directing such submission. Failure to do so may result in the case being deemed abandoned pursuant to Uniform Rule 202.48.

Please refer to the Matrimonial Checklists available on this site, and at the Matrimonial Center Clerk's Office.

• Judgments and Orders are to be submitted as originals under a legal back which lists the name address and phone number of the submitting party or attorney. CPLR 2101 (d). Submission of fax copies, and illegible photocopies as originals without good cause will not be accepted. Failure to submit papers in this manner may result in rejection by this office.

• Judgments and Orders to be submitted pursuant a decision of the court must include a copy of such decision with the submission. If the decision is rendered on the record, you must submit a copy of the transcript, unless specifically waived by the court. Indicate such waiver in writing.

• Qualified Domestic Relations Orders to be submitted for signature must include a notice of settlement date or waiver, proof of service, pre-approval by the plan administrator where possible, an affidavit or affirmation detailing the identity of the plan to be distributed, the valuation of the distribution (where the stipulation is not specific), as well as pedigree information concerning the parties and history of the divorce action (addresses, dates of commencement/divorce, etc.) A copy of the judgment and stipulation which authorizes the QDRO must also be submitted. * See checklist available on this site, and at Matrimonial Center Clerk's Office.

• All judgments and orders submitted for signature must be accompanied by a self addressed post card with the name of the case and index number on it. Upon the order or judgment being signed, the date of signature will be put on the card, and mailed out by the County Clerk. To follow up on status, you may either appear in person, send in a written inquiry with a self addressed envelope, or check the transmittal reports available on this site.

• Any counter-orders or judgments submitted, must include an affirmation or affidavit explaining the need for such submission, why a consent submission could not be agreed upon, and the differences in the submissions. By amendment to Uniform Court Rule 202.48, a marked copy of the counter submission showing the proposed changes to the judgment or order being objected to must also be submitted. Failure to do so may result in the rejection of your papers, or your papers not being considered by the Court.

• Any request for expedited handling must include an affirmation of emergency, or it will not be considered by the Justice/Referee.

• Amendments of orders/judgments require either consent or a formal motion for the relief.

• All matrimonial agreements must comply with DRL § 177 (as replaced by DRL § 255) — otherwise an addendum must be executed by the parties. See the notice contained in the Court Notice Section of this site for more information.

PLEASE TAKE NOTICE that the Department of Health requires an original document when filing certificates of dissolution in a matrimonial action. You must use the form provided by the DOH, (form # DOH-2168), amended 5/2000. Photocopies will not be accepted. Forms are available at the Judgment Office, and the County Clerk.

Uncontested Divorce Packets Are Available At:

• Matrimonial Center Clerk's Office

• Court Information Center (2nd floor Supreme Court - Nassau County)

• New York State Unified Court System Web Site (www.nycourts.gov)

• Supreme Court Clerk's Offices throughout the state

* If you are requesting by mail, send in a written request with a self addressed 10 × 13 envelope with approx. $5.00 postage.

MATRIMONIAL ALTERNATIVE DISPUTE RESOLUTION PROGRAM RULES

Rule I. Mission/Purpose Statement

The Matrimonial Alternative Dispute Resolution Program ("MAP") described herein is established to assist the Court, counsel and litigants as they resolve matters. The primary purpose of the process is to recognize, foster and advance the interests of litigants and their children involved in divorce and family litigation. The secondary purpose of the process is to provide a reasonable, cost effective alternative dispute resolution forum for the parties in divorce litigation. The participants are encouraged to take advantage of this unique opportunity with assistance of counsel, while reserving their right to utilize litigation. Mediation shall be provided by mediators appointed to serve on the Court's roster, as described herein.

Rule II. Definitions

(a) Mediation. When the word "mediation" is used herein, it denotes a cooperative process for resolving conflict with the assistance of a trained court-approved, neutral third party, whose role is to facilitate communication, to help define issues, and to assist the parties in identifying and negotiating fair solutions that are mutually agreeable. Fundamental to the mediation process described herein are principles of safety, self determination, procedural informality, privacy, confidentiality, and full disclosure of relevant information between the parties. Mediation under this rule is a means for parties to maintain control of custodial parenting plans or the issues of finances. Parties are encouraged to participate in the mediation process by attempting meaningful negotiation and resolution of the issues brought to mediation.

Mediation under this rule is not to be considered a substitute for independent legal advice. On the contrary, it is to work in direct partnership with the bar and the legal process, by giving the parties the ability to be fully informed of options for resolution of their issues, which would include obtaining legal advice before, during and after the mediation process. It is intended by the promulgation of these rules that mediation is available to resolve issues of custody and visitation as well as issues relating to equitable distribution of matters where values are ascertained in contested matters, or where discovery issues are complex, protracted, or warrant particular oversight.

(b) Capacity. When the word "impairment" is used herein, it means any condition which hinders the ability of a party to negotiate safely and competently, including but not limited to intimidation, substance abuse, mental illness or a cognitive impairment. Pursuant to these rules, the identification of impediments in a case is necessary to determine if mediation should be utilized, and to insure that only parties having a present, undiminished ability to negotiate are referred by the Court under this rule to mediate.

Rule III. Participation

(a) Matters Subject to Participation. The designated Supreme Court Justice may order mediation of any contested action, except matters that are ineligible. Such ineligibility shall include:

1. For mediation:

a. prior or existing domestic violence proceedings between the parties;

b. prior adjudications of guilt or responsibility as a result of an independent criminal or civil proceeding based on domestic or family violence; and

c. pending criminal or civil proceedings based on domestic or family violence.

The designated Supreme Court Justice shall further review information about the financial ability of each party to pay the cost of mediation services. Financial hardship shall be determined on a case by case basis. The cost shall be apportioned subject to review at the time of trial.

3. The parties referred to mediation by the Court shall commence the parent education (Rule 144.3, annexed as "A") program prior to starting mediation or as soon after starting mediation as possible. However, mediation shall not be delayed due to the inability of either party to complete the parent education program.

4. *Discovery.*

a. Mediation

Completion of discovery shall be determined on a case by case basis, but no case should be mediated unless the attorney for each party stipulates that meaningful settlement discussions can be had or the parties agree to mediate the issues of discovery.

5. *First Session.* This mediation process contemplates at least one (1) session of approximately one (1) hour. The parties are required to attend the full session. Following attendance at the initial mediation session, either party may terminate mediation even if mediation is not successful. The parties may agree to continue the mediation process beyond the one (1) session without permission of the Court, at their expense, pursuant to a written retainer agreement between the mediator and the parties.

Rule IV. Appointment and Qualification of Mediators and Neutral Evaluators

(a) List of Approved Persons. For each eligible case, a person approved to provide mediation services or neutral evaluator shall be appointed by the Court from a list of court approved mediators, pursuant to Part 146 of the Rules of the Chief Administrative Judge (annexed hereto as Exhibit II). If the parties have agreed on an approved mediator or neutral evaluator, the Court may make an appointment pursuant to that request.

Rule V. Eligibility Requirement for Mediators and Neutral Evaluators

The Administrative Judge shall maintain and distribute a list of persons approved to provide mediation and/or neutral evaluation services pursuant to 146.3(a) of the Rules of the Chief Administrative Judge. Persons eligible for approval as a mediator and neutral evaluator shall comply with the requirements of Rules 146 (Exhibit II).

(a) Conflicts of Interest and Impartiality. Mediators shall abide by the Standards of Conduct for Family Mediators, as promulgated by AFCC, and shall also adhere to the guidelines and requirements as contained herein.

Rule VI. Duties of the Mediator

(a) Preliminary Responsibilities. Before mediation may begin, the mediator shall:

1. Confirm in an executed agreement the parties' understanding regarding the fee for services, the apportionment of such fee, and any reduced fee arrangements for eligible parties with financial hardship.

2. Advise the parties that the mediator neither represents nor advocates for either party and will not provide therapy or counseling to either party.

3. Advise the parties that either party must have his or her attorney accompany that party to mediation and participate in the mediation process, or, that the attorney waive his/her appearance.

4. Define and describe the process of mediation to the parties, including appropriate procedure when an issue of capacity surfaces after mediation is in progress.

5. Disclose the nature and extent of any existing relationships with the parties or their attorneys and any personal, financial, or other interests that could result in bias or a conflict of interest on the part of the mediator.

(b) Termination without Agreement. Upon termination without agreement, the mediator shall file with the Court a final mediator report stating that the mediation has concluded without disclosing any reasons for the parties' failure to reach agreement.

(c) Completion of Mediation. Unless for good cause shown, cases assigned for mediation shall be completed within thirty (30) days of notification of assignment. If the case cannot be completed within 30 days, the parties may request additional time. The court may consider the length of time that mediation

was pending until completion in making findings, if any, for any delay or extension of the time limitations.

Rule VII. Application of Safeguards in Case of Lack of Capacity

(a) Duty to Assess. While mediation is in progress, the mediator shall assess continuously whether the parties manifest any issues affecting their ability to mediate safely, competently, and promote self determination.

(b) Safety. If an issue affecting safety arises during the course of mediation, the mediator shall adjourn the session to confer with the parties, shall implement appropriate personal safety protocols, shall advise the parties of their right to terminate, and shall terminate mediation when circumstances indicate that protective measures are inadequate to maintain safety and be guided by those provisions as contained in Part XI.

(c) Competency. If an impairment affecting competency or self determination, but not safety, arises during the course of mediation, the mediator shall either:

1. suspend mediation when there is a reasonable likelihood the impaired condition of an affected party is only temporary; or

2. terminate mediation when circumstances indicate an affected party's ability to negotiate cannot be adequately restored.

(d) Effect of Termination. No mediation terminated by the mediator shall proceed further unless ordered by the Court upon motion of a party.

Rule VIII. Confidentiality and Privilege

(a) Confidentiality. Except as otherwise provided, all written and verbal communications made pursuant to a mediation or neutral evaluation session conducted under these rules are confidential and may not be disclosed by the mediator, any other participant, or observer of the mediation except by the parties to their attorneys.

(b) Evidentiary Privilege. Either party's lawyer and the attorney for the children may be present during mediation, which discussions shall be privileged, to the extent provided by law. Clients may waive their right to have their attorney present if so inclined to do so.

Rule IX. Termination of Mediation Generally

(a) Agreements to be Voluntary. Parties shall not be compelled or pressured by a mediator to reach agreement on any issues arising in an action which is subject to mediation by rule or Court order.

(b) Election of Party to Terminate. In cases determined to be eligible after intake, any time after the first joint mediation session a party may elect to terminate the mediation.

(c) Mediator's Authority to Terminate. Termination by a mediator may be based upon reasonable belief that:

1. the parties have reached a final impasse;

2. the willingness or ability of any party to participate meaningfully in mediation is so lacking that an agreement on voluntary terms is unlikely to be reached by prolonging the negotiations; or

3. a disqualifying issue exists and termination is required.

Rule X. Entry of Judgment or Order

(a) Expedited Entry of Judgment. The Supreme Court Part in which the matter is pending shall provide for an expedited process to insure prompt entry of an appropriate judgment or order in cases where agreement has been reached in mediation pursuant to these rules.

Rule XI. Personal Safety Protocols

(a) Personnel Requirements. It is strongly recommended that other staff or nonparticipating persons be available within the physical plant during all mediation sessions. This person or persons should be available to assist with emergency phone matters, to monitor parties' movements, and to assist the mediator in implementing appropriate exit procedures.

Rule XII. Costs and Fees

(a) Hourly Rates. All mediators under this article shall be compensated by the parties at the rate as scheduled by the Court and subject to review by the Court.

Rule XIII. Supreme Court Advisory Committee

(a) The Administrative Judge shall establish an advisory committee known as the Nassau County Matrimonial ADR Advisory Committee, whose membership shall consist of at least twelve (12) persons, including the Supervising Judge of the Matrimonial Parts, 1 Supreme Court Justice, a non-mediator member of the local bar, a practicing attorney-mediator, a practicing mental health professional mediator, a representative of the domestic violence advocacy community, a representative of the Peace Program, the Director of ADR Programs for the Office of Court Administration, and the Chair of the Matrimonial Committee of the Nassau County Bar Association.

(b) The Mediation Advisory Committee shall advise the Administrative Judge in establishing and implementing administrative policy consistent with these rules for the fair and efficient delivery of mediation services including local rules of procedure, standards of conduct for mediators, and systematic review of program performance.

NASSAU COUNTY
MATRIMONIAL MEDIATION PART
INFORMATION
CT. RULE 144.3

§ 144.3   Application of Program

(a) The New York State Parent Education and Awareness Program may apply in any action or proceeding:

1. that affects the interests of children under 18 years of age; and

2. that is brought in Supreme Court or Family Court: (I) to annul a marriage or declare the nullity of a void marriage, (ii) for separation, (iii) for divorce, (iv) to obtain custody of or visitation with minor children, (v) to obtain a modification of a prior order of custody or visitation with minor children, or (vi) where, in the exercise of the court's discretion, a determination is made in a particular matter that attendance by the parents would provide information that would be of benefit to them and their children.

(b) In any action or proceeding to which the Program may apply, the court, in its discretion, may order both parents to attend a parent education and awareness program. The order must direct that both parents attend, not just one parent, but the parties shall not attend the same class session. Such order shall be made as early in the proceeding as practicable.

(c) In determining whether to order parents to attend a parent education and awareness program, a court shall consider all relevant factors bearing upon the parties to the underlying action or proceeding and their children, including, but not limited to, any history, specific allegations or pleadings of domestic violence or other abuse; medical, financial or travel hardship; language barrier; and whether a parent has previously attended parent education. Where there is any history, or there are specific allegations or pleadings, of domestic violence or other abuse involving the parents or their children, the court shall not mandate attendance at the program.

(d) An order to attend a parent education and awareness program shall not delay the expeditious progress of the underlying proceeding.

(e) A parent who is a victim of domestic violence may opt out of attendance by contacting a program administrator.

FORECLOSURE RULES

Doc. 1. General Rules Governing Residential Foreclosure Matters

pursuant to Order of the Foreclosure Part Judge.

The Foreclosure Clerk/*Ex Parte* Clerk is authorized to reject and/or return for corrections any papers submitted to the Court which are not in compliance with the rules set forth herein.

Request for Judicial Intervention (RJI):

1. On or after February 15, 2010, all plaintiffs must file Requests for Judicial Intervention (RJI) on the newly revised form prescribed by the Chief Administrator of the Courts for Settlement Conference in Residential Mortgage Foreclosure Actions. All information requested must be properly and completely set forth on the RJI.

Foreclosure Settlement Conference Rules

1. The parties shall engage in settlement discussions in good faith to reach a mutually agreeable resolution, including a loan modification if possible.

2. Plaintiff's counsel shall appear for the Settlement Conference with all relevant documents including the documents set forth in Rule 202.12–a: current payoff and reinstatement documents; mortgage and note; payment history, workout forms or packet; copies of any recent paperwork regarding reinstatement, settlement offers or loan modification proposals; and an itemization of the amounts needed to cure and pay off the loan.

3. Plaintiff's counsel must appear in the Foreclosure Conference Part with settlement authority and/or a direct contact number where a servicing agent with settlement authority can be reached and participate in settlement discussions before the Court.

4. Defendants should bring the following documents to the conference: current income documentation, including pay stubs and benefits information, list of months expenses; recent mortgage statement, property tax statements and income tax return; loan resolution proposals and any information from previous workout attempts.

5. For cases involving servicing agents who have opted into the Home Affordable Modification Program (HAMP), counsel shall appear in the Foreclosure Conference Part with a status report regarding the outcome of the servicing agents' evaluation for HAMP modification, and specific written justification with supporting details if modification under HAMP was denied.

6. All Foreclosure cases in which the servicing agent as well as the Homeowner has agreed to a trial modification, whether under HAMP or otherwise, will be given a conference date in the Foreclosure Conference Part coincident with the trial modification period.

7. Any agency or representative assisting the Homeowner shall provide copies of all documents, including the completed work-out package, to the homeowner, who should bring them to the Settlement Conference.

8. All parties must appear at the Settlement Conference and any adjourned dates until the action is settled by means of a modification or other agreement. The plaintiff may proceed with the Foreclosure Action once an order has been issued from the Foreclosure Part indicating that the defendant has failed to appear or the Court has determined that the parties would not benefit from further settlement discussions.

9. The Settlement Conference procedures shall be deemed concluded if a settlement has been reached and the plaintiff has filed a Stipulation of Discontinuance or Forbearance Agreement with the County Clerk. In such event, Plaintiff/Counsel must fax a copy of the Stipulation of Discontinuance or Forbearance Agreement to the Foreclosure Clerk at (516) 571–2167.

10. An appearing homeowner shall file a Notice of Appearance in the action indicating the homeowner's name, address, telephone number, and e-mail address on a form provided by the Court, with the Clerk of the Foreclosure Conference Part who shall then forward it for appropriate filing.

11. All counsel appearing for the homeowner shall file a Notice of Appearance in the action indicating the attorney's name, address, telephone number, and e-mail address on a form provided by the Court, together with their representation status, with the Clerk of the Foreclosure Conference Part who shall then forward it for appropriate filing.

Motions/*Ex Parte* Applications:

1. The Foreclosure Clerk/*Ex Parte* Clerk is authorized to reject any papers that are not submitted in accordance with the following:

2. All Motions/*Ex Parte* Applications must be in compliance with the Civil Practice Law and Rules (CPLR). Other than for unrepresented litigants, applications should be indexed with protruding tabs. Motion papers, answering affidavits and reply affidavits must be served on

adversaries in accordance with Civil Practice Law and Rules (CPLR) 2214.

3. Motion papers must be filed with the Court through the Office of the County Clerk or in Room 186 (either receipt of payment or with attorney check only) of the Supreme Court five (5) days or more before the return date of the motion; cross motions shall be filed two (2) days before the return date of the motion.

4. No courtesy copies of motion papers will be accepted by the Court unless specifically directed by the Presiding Judge.

5. Irrespective of the return date indicated in the Notice of Motion, motions will be rescheduled by the Foreclosure Part to a date designated by the Presiding Judge.

6. All motions returnable on or before a Settlement Conference is held will be adjourned to a date subsequent to an order being issued by a Judge, Judicial Hearing Officer or Court Attorney–Referee indicating that Settlement Conference procedures have been completed and the plaintiff may proceed with the action.

7. Applications for surplus money must contain a recognized title search or its equivalent as an exhibit.

8. A proposed Order must be attached to any Order to Show Cause/Motion submitted to the Foreclosure Part. In the event that a proposed order is not submitted, the Order to Show Cause/Motion may be deemed abandoned.

Orders of Reference:

1. Each Order of Reference must have appended thereto, the history of the property by way of a chain of assignment, the date of the assignment, and a reference to the tab where that assignment is located.

2. Within one (1) year after the signing and entry of an Order of Reference, an application for a Judgment of Foreclosure and Sale must be made. Such period of time will be suspended by the filing of a Forbearance or Settlement agreement with the Clerk of the Court. Failure to comply may result in an automatic dismissal of the action.

Auctions/Sales:

1. The Clerk of the Foreclosure Part is authorized to reject any Notice of Sale that does not comply with the following rules:

2. Notices of Sale shall be filed with the Foreclosure Clerk within one (1) year of the entry of the Judgment of Foreclosure and Sale. Permission of the Court must be obtained for any filings made thereafter.

3. A Notice of Sale must be submitted to the Foreclosure Department by facsimile (516) 571–2167 at least ten (10) days prior to the scheduled date of the Auction. A copy of the Notice of Sale must simultaneously be sent to the owner of the equity of redemption at both his/her last known address and the property address. An Affidavit of Service of such Notice shall be presented to the Foreclosure Clerk on or before the Auction/Sale.

4. The property will not be auctioned/sold unless an Affidavit/Affirmation of Compliance is submitted to the Foreclosure Clerk on or before the Auction/Sale. Such Affidavit/Affirmation of Compliance must state that the plaintiff has complied with all Federal and New York State Laws, Rules and Regulations, Executive Orders and any and all other Legislative Orders and Mandates relative to Foreclosure.

5. The Court-appointed referee shall determine the date of the sale which is to be held at the time and place indicated in the Judgement of Foreclosure and Sale and shall notify the plaintiff sufficiently in advance thereof to permit publication of the Notice of Sale in compliance with Real Property Actions and Proceedings Law (RPAPL) 231.

6. It is the plaintiff's responsibility to arrange for publication. The costs of publication may be recouped from the proceeds of the sale.

7. It is the plaintiff's responsibility to notify the Court appointed Referee of any encumbrances in advance of the Auction/Sale date.

8. In the event the plaintiff adjourns or cancels the Auction/Sale, at least five (5) days notice, both written and telephonic must be given to the Court appointed Referee. If such notice is not timely given, the Court appointed Referee may apply to the Foreclosure Part Judge through affirmation seeking additional fees.

9. A legally competent representative of the plaintiff authorized to act on plaintiff's behalf must appear at the Auction/Sale.

Day of Auction Rules

1. The Court appointed Court appointed Referee and all interested parties must be present at the location indicated in the Order of the Court on the published date promptly at 11:30 a.m.

2. The Terms of Sale, including any known encumbrances, must be posted outside of the Courtroom by the plaintiffs no later than 10:45 a.m. on the day of the sale.

3. Court appointed Referees will accept either 1) Cash; or 2) certified or bank check made payable to the Court appointed Referee. No double-endorsed checks will be accepted.

4. A successful bidder must have in his/her possession at the time of the bid the full ten (10%) percent of the sum bid, in cash or certified or bank check to be made payable to the Court appointed Referee.

5. All bidders must have proof of identification and will be required to stand and state their names and addresses on the record at the time the bid is made.

6. No sale will be deemed final until the full ten (10%) percent deposit has been paid to the Court appointed Referee and a contract has been signed, which must be done in the Courthouse immediately following the sale.

7. If a successful bidder fails to immediately pay the deposit and sign the Terms of Sale, the property will be promptly returned to auction the same day.

8. The amount of the successful bid, which will become the "purchase price", will be recorded by the Court Reporter.

9. It is the responsibility of the bidder to acquaint him/herself with the property, any encumbrances thereon, and the Terms of Sale before placing a bid and to be certain that adequate funds are available to make good the bid. The failure of the successful bidder to complete the transaction under the terms bid may result in the bidder's preclusion from bidding at auction for a period of sixty (60) days.

10. An order may be issued by the Judge Presiding at the Foreclosure Part substituting any Court appointed Referee who fails to timely appear on the date of the Auction/Sale.

SUFFOLK COUNTY
SUPREME COURT
JUDGES' PART RULES
JUSTICE JOHN C. BIVONA

Part 2.   Hon. John C. Bivona

Pursuant to and in accordance with **CPLR § 2102** and the Uniform Civil Rules of the Supreme and County Courts **22 NYCRR § 202.5(d)(1)**, it is

ORDERED by the undersigned, as the Presiding Justice of Part 2 of the Supreme Court, County of Suffolk, that the Clerk is hereby authorized and directed to return for correction papers that are deemed defective for failure to comply with the requirements set forth in all applicable statutes, decision law, rules and regulations applicable to the Part; and it is further

ORDERED that the Clerk is hereby authorized to prepare and utilize such forms or checklists, as will reflect the specifications enumerated therein, to be used for the convenience of the attorneys and the parties, in connection with the return of defective papers and such forms and/or checklists are hereby specifically adopted and approved for such use; and it is further

ORDERED that all papers sought to be filed in connection with the matters appearing on the Calendar of Court, Part 2, must comply with all specifications applied by the Clerk.

The foregoing constitutes the Order of this Court.

Dated: April 20, 2010

JUSTICE RALPH T. GAZZILLO

Part 6.   Hon. Ralph T. Gazzillo

Motion Practice

Return Dates/Submissions: All motions made in cases assigned to Judge Gazzillo must be calendared for submission Thursdays. Unless adjourned by the Court, all motions appearing on the Court's Thursday motion calendar shall be marked submitted. Appearances are not required on any motion unless oral argument has been requested and granted. All requests for oral argument must be made in accordance with 22 NYCRR 202.8(d).

Papers

Timely interposition of all papers in accordance with the CPLR is required, as the Court will not consider the merits of any papers, including opposition cross-moving or reply, which have been interposed in an untimely manner. All motion papers must be submitted through Special Term. No courtesy copies are to be submitted unless specifically requested by the court.

Adjournments

Adjournments of motions will be governed by 22 NYCRR 202.8(e). All proposed adjourn dated must fall on a Thursday. All adjournments on consent must be received by Chambers no later than 3:00pm on the day prior to the return date. If the consent of all appearing parties is not obtainable, an oral application for an adjournment on or before the date the motion is returnable must be made by the party seeking the adjournment, upon due notice to all parties.

Settled or Withdrawn Motions

The court is to be advised immediately of the settlement or withdrawal of any motion or any portion of any motion sub judice, and/or the settlement of any underlying case with motions sub judice. The failure to do so will be sanctionable.

Conferences

Scheduling: Conferences shall be calendared for the first and third Thursday of each month.

Appearances: Appearances by person with knowledge of the facts and vested with authority to make binding dispositions are required. Non-appearances will not be countenanced by the Court and may subject the non-appearing party to one or more of the sanctions attendant with defaults. (See, 22 NYCRR 202.27; 22 NYCRR Part 130–2).

Adjournments: All applications whether on consent or over objection must be communicated to Chambers no later than 3:00 pm on the day prior to the scheduled conference/ Any application to the court seeking an adjournment must be done on prior notice to all parties.

Preliminary Conferences: Preliminary conferences will be scheduled by the Court in accordance with 22 NYCRR 202.12 and 202.19 which will be conducted by DCM located in room A 362, 1 Court Street, Riverhead, New York. Counsel for th respective partied are thus directed to appear at 9:30 am on the preliminary conference ready for said conference. All matters, including those raised by pending motion and those contemplated by 22 NYCRR 202.19, shall be undertaken at the preliminary conference.

Compliance Conferences & Pre-trial Conferences: These conferences will be scheduled and conducted in accordance with the provisions of 22 NYCRR 202.19.

Trials

Jury Trials: A trial conference with the Court shall be held immediately prior to the commencement of all jury trials. Thereat, counsel shall supply the Court with marked pleadings, amendments thereto and all bills of particulars served. Counsel shall further provide the Court with a list of proposed jury charges and proposed jury verdict sheets. A list of all pre-marked exhibits shall also be provided to the Court and to the stenographer. Counsel shall advise the Court of the number of witnesses to be called, and if any experts, shall provide the information required by the CPLR 3101(d)(1)(I).

All hospital records and other items in evidence over fifteen (15) pages must be paginated before use in the trial. In all malpractice cases each attorney in anticipation of charge conference and verdict sheet preparation must have the departure and causation testimony located in the trial transcript available for the courts review.

Non Jury Trials: Non–Jury trials will be governed by the same procedures and requirements set forth above for Jury Trials. In addition thereto, for Non–Jury trials, counsel shall submit a proposed order framing the issues to be tried. The parties shall be required to provide a transcript of the trial. The filing of a note of issued is a condition precedent to the commencement of any trial.

Miscellaneous Matters

Contempt Applications: Appearance by all parties is mandatory.

Compromise Applications: All applications for court approval or a proposed compromise of an infant or other disabled party's claim must be submitted through the Special Term, with proof of service on all remaining parties. Compliance with the provisions of CPLR 1207, 1208 and 22 NYCRR 202. 67 and a proposed distribution of net amounts to be recovered by the disabled plaintiff that is consistent with the provisions of CPLR 1206 is required. The Court will not accept medical reports/affidavits executed more than six months prior to the submission date. The report must indicate whether the injured plaintiff has fully recovered, and if not, the nature and extent of the injuries and course of future treatment. Since the Court may direct that notice of the application be given to all persons who possess claims against the proceeds recoverable under the compromise, including those with statutory liens, the names and addresses of all such persons and the amount of their respective claims must be set forth in the petition. If no person has asserted such a claim, the petition must so state. Once the submissions are complete, an appearance date shall be scheduled by the court.

Hearing/Inquests: All hearing and or inquests emanating from cases in the inventory of IAS Part 6 shall be scheduled by the Court. The filing of a note of issue is a condition precedent to the commencement of any hearing or inquest.

Ex Parte Communications with Chambers: Except to the limited extent permitted by these rules and by the rules set forth at 22 NYCRR 100.3 ex parte communications with the Court or any member of its staff by telephone or otherwise, is strictly prohibited. All inquiries regarding the scheduling of conferences or return dates of motions should be directed to the Calendar Department at (631) 852–2355, as direct telephone communication with Chambers is prohibited except for the most exigent circumstances.

Discovery Disputes: With respect to cases already assigned to this Court at the time that a discovery dispute arises, no motion with respect to the dispute shall be made without a prior conference with the Court, which may be obtained by submission of a letter application, not exceeding one (1) page in length.

With respect to cases in which a discovery motion accompanies the Request for Judicial Intervention which leads to the assignment to this Court, no opposition papers shall be served until there has been a prior conference with the Court, which may be obtained by letter application, not exceeding one (1) page in length. The application for a discovery conference may be made by the movant or by the opposing counsel; however, the application must be made within eight (8) days of service of the motion. Counsel must obtain permission from Chambers prior to the submission of a letter application. Failure to request a discovery conference may result in the denial of the motion.

The Court endeavors to resolve discovery disputes promptly, usually by conference, which may be held telephonically or in person. In the event that the dispute is not resolved, the Court will set an expedited briefing schedule. Counsel shall, prior to requesting a conference, meet in person to discuss the issues and endeavor to resolve or limit them, prior to seeking judicial intervention.

Thank you for your courtesies and co-operation.

JUSTICE DANIEL MARTIN

Justice Daniel Martin Part 9. Rules with Respect to Motions

ALL MOTIONS ARE SUBMISSION. MOTIONS SHALL BE MADE RETURNABLE ON TUESDAYS ONLY.

THE PHONE NUMBER AND FAX NUMBER OF YOUR ADVERSARY SHALL BE INCLUDED ON ALL PAPERS SUBMITTED TO THE COURT.

MOTIONS MAY BE ADJOURNED *ON CONSENT* WITH A LETTER INDICATING SAME VIA FACSIMILE TO CHAMBERS AT (631) 852–2834.

JUSTICE PETER FOX COHALAN, PART 24

Rule 1. Motions

All motions in cases assigned to Justice Peter Fox Cohalan in the Supreme Court, Suffolk County, will be scheduled for oral argument by the Court on a Wednesday motion date subsequent to the return date appearing in the notice of motion. Movant will be notified by postcard of the argument date and is required to notify all other parties of the date scheduled by letter with a copy to the Court. All Post Note Motions will be submitted as of the return date and all opposition papers must be submitted as of the return date of the motion unless written consent from all parties has been obtained prior to the return date.

All motions, (except Post Note motions), petitions and orders to show cause must be orally argued before the Court. Where a motion, petition or order to show cause is unopposed, counsel for the moving party shall present to the Court a proposed order or judgment for the relief prayed for therein.

All writs, motions, judgments, orders to show cause, etc., shall be filed with the Clerk's Office and not directly with the Justice. Self-addressed, stamped envelopes firmly stapled inside your blue backs, are to be submitted with all motions, orders to show cause, affirmations, etc. if you wish to be sent a copy of the decision.

If you are unable to appear on the scheduled date, an adjournment should be obtained. Requests for adjournments of motions should be made by contacting our Calendar Clerk, at (631) 852–2355 no later than the day before the scheduled date of the motion. Requests for adjournments that are on consent will be granted. Where there is a problem obtaining consent, contact the Court at (631) 852–2395 at least one day prior to the scheduled motion date.

Rule 2. Certification Conferences

No case may be noticed for trial until a Certification Order has been issued by the Court

Upon completion of all discovery and disclosure proceedings, counsel shall notify the Court, in writing, of the completion of same and shall request a date for a Certification Conference. Counsel shall be notified thereafter, in writing, of the Wednesday date for such conference.

Counsel and/or a pro se litigant must appear on the date for the Certification Conference. At such time, if all discovery has been completed, plaintiff will receive an Order, certifying that the action is ready for trial and plaintiff may serve and file a Note of Issue and Statement of Readiness. Certifications by mail in certain instances may be granted.

Rule 3. Preliminary Conferences (8A)

Upon written request, all parties will be notified of the date and time to appear for a discovery conference. The Court's pre-trial discovery conferences are held on Wednesdays. At that time, an order will be issued stating dates and times concerning all discovery procedures.

Pursuant to new rules adopted by the Office of Court Administration, counsel may avoid the necessity of a personal appearance before the Court if counsel for all sides agree and thereafter obtain and complete a form now designated as a Stipulation of Discovery and "so ordered" by the Court. Absent the completion of that form, appearances are still required.

Requests for Preliminary Conferences can be made by calling our Calendar Clerk, Denise Podlewski at (631) 852–2355. All parties must appear in Supreme Court, 1 Court Street, Riverhead, New York, Courtroom #6 at 9:30 am.

A preliminary conference will only take place upon written request.

Rule 4. Inquests

All inquests shall be scheduled for the dates Justice Cohalan is assigned to Special Term. Such dates for the year 2009 are: Jan. 8 & 30, Feb. 25, Mar. 17, Apr. 9, May 4, June 15, July 8, July 28, Sept. 16, Oct. 15, Nov. 9, Dec. 1 & 16. (Special term dates subject to change without notice).

Rule 5. Infant Compromises

Infant compromise orders should be submitted to the Court through the Clerk's office. Counsel will then be notified of a date for the infant to come to Court. All Infant Compromises are conducted on a Tuesday session of the Court.

No infant compromise order will be signed unless accompanied by an appropriate medical report dated no more than 6 months prior to the date the order is submitted to the Court. The medical report should state that the infant has made a full recovery, or if there is to be a need for further medical treatment, a detailed statement as to the medical treatment that will be required.

Rule 6.   Substitution of Counsel

The party requesting substitution of counsel must file a fully executed Consent to Change Attorneys and/or Substitution of Attorney form. If the foregoing cannot be obtained, application for same must be made to the Court by order to show cause.

Rule 7.   Orders

As previously noted all unopposed motions which have been calendared for a specific date for oral

argument must, by the oral argument date, have an order submitted for signature by Justice Cohalan.

Please be aware that no order will be signed by Justice Peter Fox Cohalan unless his full name is correctly captioned on the order or stipulation.

On any preliminary conference orders, certification orders or stipulations requiring the signatures of an attorney, a firm stamp name is not sufficient. The Justice's rules require a signature of an individual attorney with his name neatly printed below the signature line.

Rule 8.   Inquiries

All inquiries as to case management or calendar status should, in the first instance, be made to the Court's Calendar Clerk, Denise Podlewski at (631) 852–2355 (fax 852–3869). The only inquiries to be made directly to Chambers or the Part should be those involving the exercise of judicial discretion.

JUSTICE ELIZABETH EMERSON, PART 44

Rule 1.   Commercial Division Rules

All parties should familiarize themselves with the Commercial Division Rules, available at http://www.nycourts.gov/courts/comdiv/suffolk.shtml.

Rule 2.   Scheduling

Parties should address questions about scheduling appearances or adjournments to the Part Clerk, at (631) 852–2139.

Please be advised that litigants/counsel must obtain Court permission to adjourn a status conference. Excepting emergencies, such permission must be obtained no later than 2 business days in advance of the scheduled appearance. Counsel must make every effort to obtain consent to an adjournment from all adversaries in the matter and be prepared to communicate that consent to the Court. If counsel is unable to get consent, counsel must send a brief letter to the Court with a copy to all adversaries, explaining the circumstances necessitating the adjournment and the reason consent could not be obtained. Counsel must wait at least 24 hours to allow for the adversary to respond to the request before contacting the Court.

Rule 3.   Mediation

If, at any point, the parties decide that they could benefit from Commercial Division ADR or other mediation, they should write a joint letter to the Court asking to be referred to ADR or such other mediation. In that letter, they should state whether they prefer that discovery continue or be stayed during the mediation process.

Further information on the Court sponsored ADR program can be found at http://www.nycourts.gov/courts/comdiv/suffolk.shtml.

Rule 4.   Motion Practice

After compliance with Rule 14 of the Commercial Division Rules whereby counsel have consulted with one another in a good faith effort to resolve all disputes, the parties may make a written request for a conference with the Court.

Discovery disputes should first be addressed through a court conference prior to the filing of a motion. If the Court is unable to resolve the dispute through a conference, then leave will be given for the parties to file the appropriate motion. The failure to abide by this rule may result in a motion being held in abeyance until the Court has an opportunity to conference the matter.

All papers submitted must include the correct motion sequence number if they refer to a motion, be properly backed, and be filed with Special Term at 1 Court Street, Riverhead, NY 11901. If counsel wishes to receive a copy of the decision, a self-addressed stamped envelope must be provided to the Court.

Rule 19A statements are required for all summary judgment motions.

All dispositive motions require a pre-motion conference with the Court. Counsel must send a letter to the Court, on notice to all adversaries, requesting a pre-motion conference be scheduled.

With respect to Rule 11(d), of the Commercial Division Rules, the presumption is that discovery is

NOT stayed by the filing of a dispositive motion unless otherwise directed.

All citations must include a cite to the official reports.

For all electronically filed motions, a courtesy copy of the papers properly backed, including exhibit tabs must be submitted to chambers.

The Court will notify the parties if oral argument is required after papers in support of and in opposition to the motion have been submitted.

If oral argument is held, at its conclusion the movant is to order the transcript and have a copy sent to the Court. The motion will not be deemed *sub judice* until a transcript has been received.

Rule 5.   Trial Rules

Pre-trial memoranda and briefs are to be submitted in all matters at least 7 business days prior to the start date of trial.

No electronic media devices will be permitted absent express permission from the Court. Requests should be made to the Court in writing, addressed to the Clerk of the Part, and the reasons for the request must be clearly stated.

No adjournments of the trial date will be granted absent exceptional circumstances. All requests must be made in writing to the Court and not by a telephone call to the Clerk of the Part.

All materials used during the trial must be removed within 48 hours of the conclusion of trial. Any materials not timely removed will be discarded.

All trials require full compliance with directives set forth in the Pre-Trial Order. Additionally, if the trial is by jury, counsel will be required to submit a proposed verdict sheet and proposed charges 7 business days prior to trial.

Rule 6.   Communications With the Court

Neither Justice Emerson nor any of the court attorneys assigned to the part will speak to any litigant or counsel *ex parte*. Upon telephoning chambers, counsel must get all parties on the phone before placing the call to the Court.

No party shall send a letter to chambers without first contacting the adversary, trying to resolve the problem and telephoning chambers. With permission of the Court, a party may send correspondence to the Court via fax to (631) 852–3732 or U.S. mail or overnight delivery, but not by more than one method of delivery.

Rule 7.   Appearances

An appearance by an attorney with knowledge of the case and authority to bind the party is required on at all conferences.

Pro se litigants shall be notified of all conferences and Court appearances, and shall be served with all papers.

Rule 8.   Preliminary Conferences

All preliminary conferences will be held on Mondays at 10:00 am at the Differentiated Case Management part located at 1 Court Street, Riverhead unless otherwise directed by the Court.

Rule 9.   Disposition

Counsel must advise Chambers if a case has settled and notify the Court if such a case has any pending motions.

JUSTICE JOSEPH FARNETI, PART 37

Rule 1. Motion Practice: (Except Contempt—see Miscellaneous Matters)

Return Dates/Submissions: All motions made in cases assigned to Justice Farneti shall be calendared for submission on Thursdays. Unless adjourned by the Court or withdrawn by the movant, all motions appearing on the Court's Thursday motion calendar shall be marked submitted.

Papers: Timely interposition of all papers in accordance with the CPLR is required, as the Court will not consider the merits of any papers, including opposition, cross-moving or reply, which appear to have not been interposed in accordance with the CPLR or 22 NYCRR 202.8. The timely submission of memoranda of law is expected in all special proceedings and on motions which include demands for dispositive relief. All motion papers must be submitted through Special Term.

Adjournments: Adjournments of motions are limited to three in number and may not extend the original return date for more than sixty (60) days unless prior permission of the Court is obtained (22 NYCRR 202.8[e]). All proposed adjourn dates must fall on a Thursday. An application for an adjournment of a motion may be made by submission of a written request containing the stipulated consent of counsel for all appearing parties. All stipulations of adjournment must be received by Chambers no later than 2:00 p.m. on the day prior to the return date, and may be forwarded by fax or mail directly to Chambers. The stipulations must indicate the date on which the motion and any cross-motions riding therewith are returnable before the Court; the adjourn date requested (Thursdays only); and the number of prior adjournments granted. A denial of any stipulated adjournment request will be forthwith communicated by telephone or fax by Chambers personnel. If the stipulated consent of all appearing parties is not obtainable, an oral application for an adjournment on the date the motion is returnable before the Court must be made by the party seeking the adjournment, upon due notice to all parties. Interposition of a cross-motion with a return date subsequent to the submission date of the motion-in-chief will not cause an adjournment of the motion-in-chief.

Rule 2.   Conferences

Scheduling: Conferences shall be calendared for any Thursday of each month.

Appearances: Appearances by persons with knowledge of the facts and vested with authority to make binding dispositions are required. Non-appearances will not be countenanced by the Court and may subject the non-appearing party to one or more of the sanctions attendant with defaults (*see* 22 NYCRR 202.27; 22 NYCRR Part 130–2).

Adjournments: Due to the time limitations imposed on various stages of civil cases within the purview of the Comprehensive Civil Justice Program and its cornerstone, the Differentiated Case Management system, adjournments of conferences will not be granted lightly. Applications for adjournments of conferences are governed by the same procedures applicable to adjournments of motions (see above). Appearances are thus required unless the Court has granted an adjournment upon a written request containing the stipulated consent of counsel for all parties received by Chambers no later than 2:00 p.m. of the day preceding the scheduled conference.

Preliminary Conferences: Preliminary conferences will be scheduled by the Court in accordance with 22 NYCRR 202.12 and 202.19(b). All matters, including those raised by pending motions and those contemplated by 22 NYCRR 202.19, shall be undertaken at the preliminary conference.

Compliance Conferences and Pretrial Conferences: These conferences will be scheduled and conducted in accordance with the provisions of 22 NYCRR 202.19.

Rule 3.   Trials

Jury Trials: A trial conference with the Court shall be held immediately prior to the commencement of all jury trials. Thereat, counsel shall supply the Court with marked pleadings, any amendments thereto, and all bills of particulars served. Counsel shall further provide the Court with a list of proposed jury charges, the contentions of each party, and proposed jury verdict sheets. A list of all pre-marked exhibits shall also be provided to the Court and to the stenographer. Counsel shall notify the Court of their inability to stipulate to the admission of any exhibits to be offered at trial. Counsel shall further advise the Court of the witnesses to be called, and if any be experts, shall further provide the information required by CPLR 3101(d)(1)(i).

Non–Jury Trials: Non–Jury trials are subject to scheduling upon forty-eight hours notice. A conference with the Court shall precede the commencement of all non-jury trials at which counsel shall submit the following: (1) a copy of marked pleadings, any amendments thereto, and bills of particulars; (2) a list of pre-marked exhibits, and identification of those on which counsel could not agree as to their introduction at trial; (3) a list of witnesses, and if any be experts, the information required by CPLR 3101(d)(1)(i); (4) pretrial memoranda of law; and (5) a proposed order framing the issues to be tried. The parties shall be required to provide a transcript of the trial. The filing of a note of issue is a condition precedent to the commencement of any trial.

Rule 4.   Miscellaneous Matters

Contempt: All applications shall be calendared on the date returnable. *Appearance by all parties is mandatory.* No adjournments will be granted unless a stipulation consenting to the adjournment, signed by all parties and any alleged contemnor who is not a party, is received in Chambers no later than 2:00 p.m. of the day prior to the return date.

Compromise Applications: All applications for court approval of a proposed compromise of an infant or other disabled party's claim must be submitted through the Special Term, with copies of all pleadings served. Compliance with the provisions of CPLR 1207, 1208 and 22 NYCRR 202.67 and a proposed distribution of the net amounts to be recovered by the disabled plaintiff that is consistent with the provisions of CPLR 1206 is required. The Court will not accept medical reports/affidavits executed more than six months prior to the submission date. The report must indicate whether the injured plaintiff has fully recovered, and if not, the nature and extent of the injuries and the course of future treatment. Since the Court may direct that notice of the application be given to all persons who possess claims against the proceeds recoverable under the compromise, including those with statutory liens, the names and addresses of all such persons and the amounts of their respective claims must be set forth in the petition. If no person has asserted such a claim, the petition must so state. Once the submissions are complete, an appearance date shall be scheduled by the Court with directions for service.

Hearings/Inquests: All hearings and/or inquests emanating from cases in the inventory of IAS Part 37 shall be scheduled by the Court. The filing of a note of issue is a condition precedent to the commencement of any hearing or inquest.

***Ex Parte* Communications With Chambers:** Except to the limited extent permitted by the rules set forth at 22 NYCRR 100.3, ex parte communications with the Court or any member of its staff, by telephone or otherwise, is strictly prohibited. All inquiries regarding the scheduling of conferences or return dates of motions should be directed to the Calendar Department at (631) 852–2350 or Special Term at (631) 852–2400, as direct telephone communication with Chambers is prohibited except for the most exigent circumstances. Authorized communication with Chambers is thus limited to the faxes permitted by these rules, all of which must contain stipulated consents of all other appearing parties or proof that the fax communication was duly served upon all such parties.

Thank you for your courtesies and cooperation.

JUSTICE PETER H. MAYER

Part 17. Hon. Peter H. Mayer

Unless otherwise directed by the Court, the following Rules shall govern practice in Part 17:

Motion Practice: (Except Contempt— See Miscellaneous Matters)

Pre–Motion Conferences: Any party wishing to make a motion (other than those types of motions set forth below) must first schedule a pre-motion conference with the Court and all parties. Such conferences shall be conducted in Chambers on Tuesday afternoons, and shall be scheduled by telephone conference from the prospective movant to Chambers. After obtaining a pre-motion conference date from the Court, the prospective movant shall confirm the conference in writing by fax or mail to Chambers and all parties, and shall provide proof of such written confirmation to the Court at the time of the conference.

All motion papers must include, in the first paragraph of the attorney's affirmation in support, a statement confirming that these pre-motion conference rules have been fully complied with, as well as the date on which the pre-motion conference was held and the parties in attendance at said conference. Noncompliance with the provisions of these Part Rules shall, in the discretion of the Court, result in denial of the motion without prejudice and with leave to resubmit after compliance with these Rules.

A pre-motion conference is not required for the following motions: those filed after the filing of the note of issue; those filed before assignment of the case to this Part; default judgment motions; motions to withdraw as counsel; timely and proper cross-motions; and ex parte motions for orders of reference in foreclosure proceedings.

Return Dates/Submissions: All motions made in cases assigned to Justice Mayer shall be calendared for submission on Tuesdays. Unless adjourned by the Court, all motions appearing on the Court's Tuesday motion calendar shall be marked submitted.

Papers: Timely interposition of all papers in accordance with the CPLR is required, as the Court will not consider the merits of any papers, including opposition, cross-moving or reply, which appear to have been interposed in an untimely or otherwise inappropriate manner. All requests for oral argument must be made in accordance with the 22 NYCRR 202.8(d). The Court may, in its discretion require a hearing or oral argument on any motion. Counsel shall appear at all hearings and oral arguments with complete settlement authority. The timely submission of Memoranda of Law is expected in all special proceedings and on motions which include demands for dispositive relief. All motion papers must be submitted through Special Term. All exhibits, including transcripts, shall be submitted on one-sided paper and in full-sized, noncondensed format. In the event the parties resolve issues which are the subject of a submitted motion, the movant must notify Chambers forthwith by telephone that the motion is withdrawn. Failure to so notify the Court may, in the Court's discretion, result in sanctions pursuant to 22 NYCRR 130–1.1.

Adjournments: Adjournments of motions are limited to three in number and may not extend the original return date for more than sixty days [22 NYCRR 202.8(e)]. All proposed adjourn dates must fall on a Tuesday. An application for an adjournment of a motion may be made by submission of a written request with an attached stipulation executed by counsel for all appearing parties. All stipulations of adjournment must be received by Chambers no later than 1:00 p.m. on the day prior to the return date, and may be forwarded by fax or mail directly to Chambers. The stipulations must indicate the date on which the motion and all cross-motions riding therewith are returnable before the Court, the adjourn date requested [Tuesdays only], and the number of prior adjournments granted. A denial of any stipulated adjournment request will be forthwith communicated by telephone or fax by Chambers personnel. If the stipulated consent of all appearing parties is not obtainable, an oral application for an adjournment on the date the motion is returnable before the Court must be made by the party seeking the adjournment, upon due notice to all parties. Interposition of a cross-motion with a return date subsequent to the submission date of the motion-in-chief will not cause an adjournment of the motion-in-chief.

Conferences:

Scheduling: Conferences shall be calendered for each Tuesday of the month.

Appearances: Appearance shall be made by counsel of record or attorney's acting in an "Of Counsel" capacity. In either case, attorneys must be fully familiar with the facts of the case and have full authority to settle and/or enter appropriate stipulations. Non-appearances will not be countenanced by the Court and may subject the non-appearing party to one or more of the sanctions attendant with defaults (see, 22NYCRR 202.27; 22 NYCRR Part 130–2). Attorneys are directed to bring all prior orders of the Court, including but not limited to Preliminary Conference Orders and additional directives sheets issued by the Court, to all Court conferences.

Adjournments: Due to the time limitations imposed on various stages of civil cases within the purview of the Comprehensive Civil Justice Program and its cornerstone, the Differentiated Case Management system, adjournments of conferences will not be granted lightly. Applications for adjournments of conferences are governed by the same procedures applicable to adjournments of motions [see above]. Appearances are thus required unless the Court has granted an adjournment upon a written request with an attached stipulation executed by counsel for all parties received by Chambers not less than one day prior to the scheduled conference.

Preliminary Conferences: Preliminary conferences will be scheduled by the Court in accordance with 22 NYCRR 202.12 and 202.19. All matters, including those raised by pending motions and those contemplated by 22 NYCRR 202.19, shall be undertaken at the preliminary conference.

Compliance Conferences & Pre–Trial Conferences: These conferences will be scheduled and conducted in accordance with the provisions of 22 NYCRR 202.19.

Trials:

Jury Trials A trial conference with the Court shall be held immediately prior to the commencement of all jury trials. Thereat, counsel shall supply the Court with marked pleadings, amendments thereto and all bills of particulars served. Counsel shall further provide the Court with a list of proposed jury charges and the contentions of each party, all dispositive motions and proposed jury verdict sheets. A list of all premarked exhibits shall also be provided to the Court and to the stenographer. Counsel shall notify the Court of their inability to stipulate to the admission of any exhibits to be offered at trial. Counsel shall further advise the Court of the number of witnesses to be called, and if any be experts, shall further provide the information required by CPLR 3101(d)(1)(1).

Non–Jury Trials: Non-Jury trials are subject to scheduling upon forty-eight hours notice. A trial conference with the Court shall proceed the commencement of all non-jury trials at which counsel shall submit the following: 1) a copy of marked pleadings, amendments thereto, bills of particulars, 2) a list of pre-marked exhibits; and identification of those on which counsel could not agree as to their introduction at trial; 3) a list of witnesses and if any be experts, the information required by CPLR 3101(d)(1)(I); 4) pre-trial memoranda of law; and 5) a proposed order framing the issues to be tried. The parties shall be required to provide to the Court at Chambers a transcript of the trial. The filing of a Note of Issue is a condition precedent to the commencement of any trial.

Foreclosure Proceedings:

Prior to any scheduled conference, the plaintiffs counsel shall review any submitted application(s) and shall appear by a principal of the firm, or by an attorney who has full knowledge of all applicable statutes, case law and Court Rules, as well as any application(s) submitted to the Court, including full authority to dispose of the case and any submitted application(s).

The plaintiff shall bring to each conference all documents necessary for evaluating the potential settlement, modification, or other workout options which may be agreed to, including but not limited to the payment history, an itemization of the amounts needed to cure and pay off the loan, and the mortgage and note; if the plaintiff is not the owner of the mortgage and note, the plaintiff shall provide the name, address and telephone number of the legal owner of the mortgage and note.

In the event any scheduled court conference is adjourned for any reason, the plaintiff shall promptly send, via first class mail, written notice of the adjourn date to the homeowner-defendant(s) at all known addresses (or upon their attorney if represented by counsel), as well as upon all other appearing parties, and shall provide the affidavit(s) of such service to the Court at the time of the subsequent conference, and annex a copy of this Order and the affidavit(s) of service as exhibits to any future applications submitted to the Court.

For all applications submitted to the Court, the moving party(ies) must clearly state, in an initial paragraph of the attorney's affirmation, whether or not the statutorily required foreclosure conference pursuant to CPLR 3408 has been held and, if so, when such conference was conducted and, if not, why no such conference was held.

All proposed orders of reference shall include an ordered paragraph stating, in sum and Substance, that in the discretion of the Court and pursuant to CPLR 8003(a), the Referee shall be paid, upon the filing of his or her report, a fee of $250.00 for the computation stage of the proceedings.

NOTE: For any scheduled court conferences or applications by the parties, if the Court determines that such conferences have been attended, or such applications have been submitted, without proper regard for the applicable statutory and case law, or without regard for the required proofs delineated herein, the Court may, in its discretion, strike the non-compliant party's pleadings or deny such applications with prejudice and/or impose sanctions pursuant to 22 NYCRR§ 130–1, and may deny those costs and attorneys fees attendant with the filing of such future applications.

Miscellaneous Matters:

Contempt: All applications shall be calendared on the date returnable. Appearance by all parties is mandatory. No adjournments will be granted unless a stipulation consenting to the adjournment, signed by all parties and any alleged contemptor who is not a party, is received in Chambers no later than 1:00 p.m. of the day prior to the return date.

Compromise Applications: All applications for Court approval of a proposed compromise of an infant or other disabled party's claim must be submitted through the Special Term, with proof of service on all remaining parties. Compliance with the provisions of CPLR 1207, 1208 and 22 NYCRR 202.67 and a proposed distribution of net amounts to be recovered by the disabled plaintiff that is consistent with the provisions of CPLR 1206 is required. The Court will not accept medical reports/affidavits executed more than six months prior to the submission date. The report must indicate whether the injured plaintiff has fully recovered, and if not, the nature and extent the injuries and course of future treatment. Since the Court may direct that notice of the application be given to all persons who possess claims against the proceeds recoverable under the compromise, including those with statutory liens, the names and addresses of all such persons and the amount of their respective claims must be set forth in the petition. If no person has asserted such a claim, the petition must so state. Once the submissions are complete, an appearance date shall be scheduled by the Court.

Hearings/Inquests: All hearings and or inquests emanating from cases in the inventory of IAS Part 17 shall be scheduled by the Court. The filing of a Note of Issue is a condition precedent to the commencement of any hearing or inquest.

Ex Parte Communications With Chambers: Except to the limited extent permitted by the rules set forth at 22 NYCRR 100.3, ex parte communications with the Court or any member of its staff, by telephone or otherwise, is strictly prohibited. You are advised to avoid unnecessary contact with Court personnel, as they must attend to the paper work and other tasks to which they are assigned during business hours. All inquires regarding the scheduling of conferences or return dates of motions should be directed to the Calendar Department at (631) 852–2350 or Special Term at 852–2407, as direct telephone communication with Chambers is prohibited except for the most exigent circumstances. Authorized communication directly with Chambers is thus limited to those communications permitted by these rules, all of which must contain a stipulation of consent executed by all appearing parties or proof that the communication was duly served upon all such other parties.

JUSTICE JOSEPH C. PASTORESSA

Part 34.   Hon. Joseph C. Pastoressa

Motion Practice:

Return Dates/ Submissions: All motions made in cases assigned to Judge Pastoressa must be calendared for submission on Wednesday's. Unless adjourned by the Court, all motions appearing on the Court's Wednesday motion calendar shall be marked submitted. Appearances are not required on any motion unless oral argument has been requested and granted. All requests for oral argument must be made in accordance with 22 NYCRR 202.8(d).

Papers: Timely interposition of all papers in accordance with the CPLR is required, as the Court will not consider the merits of any papers, including opposition, cross-moving or reply, which have been interposed in an untimely manner. All motion papers must be submitted through Special Term. No courtesy copies are to be submitted.

Adjournments: Adjournments of motions will be governed by 22 NYCRR 202.8 (e). All proposed adjourn dates must fall on a Wednesday. All adjournments on consent must be received by Chambers no later than 3:00 p.m. on the day prior to the return date. If the consent of all appearing parties is not obtainable, an oral application for an adjournment on or before the date the motion is returnable must be made by the party seeking the adjournment, upon due notice to all parties.

Settled or Withdrawn Motions: The court is to be advised immediately of the settlement or withdrawal of any motion or any portion of any motion sub judice, and/or the settlement of any underlying case with motions sub judice. The failure to do so will be sanctionable.

Conferences:

Scheduling: Conferences shall be calendared for the first and third Wednesday of each month.

Appearances: Appearances by persons with knowledge of the facts and vested with authority to make binding dispositions are required. Non-appearances will not be countenanced by the Court and may subject the non-appearing party to one or more of the sanctions attendant with defaults (see, 22 NYCRR 202.27; 22 NYCRR Part 130–2).

Adjournments: All applications whether on consent or over objection must be communicated to Chambers no later than 4:30 p.m. on the day prior to the scheduled conference. Any application to the court seeking an adjournment must be done on prior notice to all parties.

Preliminary Conferences: Preliminary conferences will be scheduled by the Court in accordance with 22 NYCRR 202.12 and 202.19 which will be conducted by DCM located in room A 362, 1 Court Street, Riverhead, New York. Counsel for the respective parties are thus directed to appear at 9:30 a.m. on the preliminary conference ready for said conference. All matters, including those raised by pending motions and those contemplated by 22 NYCRR 202.19, shall be undertaken at the preliminary conference.

Compliance Conferences & Pre-trial Conferences: These conferences will be scheduled and conducted in accordance with the provisions of 22 NYCRR 202.19.

Trials:

Jury Trials: A trial conference with the Court shall be held immediately prior to the commencement of all jury trials. Thereat, counsel shall supply the Court with marked pleadings, amendments thereto and all bills of particulars served. Counsel shall further provide the Court with a list of proposed jury charges and proposed jury verdict sheets. A list of all pre-marked exhibits shall also be provided to the Court and to the stenographer. Counsel shall advise the Court of the number of witnesses to be called, and if any be experts, shall provide the information required by CPLR 3101(d)(1)(l).

All hospital records and other items in evidence over fifteen [15] pages must be paginated before use in the trial. In all malpractice cases each attorney in anticipation of charge conference and verdict sheet preparation must have the departure and causation testimony located in the trial transcript available for the courts review.

Non Jury Trials: Non-Jury trials will be governed by the same procedures and requirements set forth above for Jury Trials. In addition thereto, for non-Jury trials, counsel shall submit a proposed order framing the issues to be tried. The parties shall be required to provide a transcript of the trial. The filing of a note of issue is a condition precedent to the commencement of any trial.

Miscellaneous Matters:

Contempt Applications: Appearance by all parties is mandatory.

Compromise Applications: All applications for court approval of a proposed compromise of an infant or other disabled party's claim must be submitted through the Special Term, with proof of service on all remaining parties. Compliance with the provisions of CPLR 1207, 1208 and 22 NYCRR 202.67 and a proposed distribution of net amounts to be recovered by the disabled plaintiff that is consistent with the provisions of CPLR 1206 is required. The Court will not accept medical reports/affidavits executed more than six months prior to the submission date. The report must indicate whether the injured plaintiff has fully recovered, and if not, the nature and extent of the injuries and course of future treatment. Since the Court may direct that notice of the application be given to all persons who possess claims against the proceeds recoverable under the compromise, including those with statutory liens, the names and addresses of all such persons and the amount of their respective claims must be set forth in the petition. If no person has asserted such a claim, the petition must so state. Once the submissions are complete, an appearance date shall be scheduled by the court.

Hearings/Inquests: All hearing and or inquests emanating from cases in the inventory of IAS Part 34 shall be scheduled by the Court. The filing of a note of issue is a condition precedent to the commencement of any hearing or inquest.

Ex Parte Communications with Chambers: Except to the limited extent permitted by these rules and by the rules set forth at 22 NYCRR 100.3, ex parte communications with the Court or any member of its staff, by telephone or otherwise, is strictly prohibited. All inquiries regarding the scheduling of conferences or return dates of motions should be directed to the Calendar Department at (631) 852-2355, as direct telephone communication with Chambers is prohibited except for the most exigent circumstances.

Thank you for your courtesies and co-operation.

JUSTICE EMILY PINES

Part 23. Hon. Emily Pines

Counsel are expected to be familiar with the Commercial Division Rules and comply therewith. The following information is offered as a guide to the practices followed by this Court:

Scheduling:

All questions about scheduling appearances or adjournments should be addressed to the Court's Secretary, Valarie Genchi, at 631-852-3117. Requests for adjournment of matters appearing on a Tuesday calendar should be made by not later than 3:00 p.m. on

Friday. Requests made after that will likely not be granted. All requests for adjournments must be made with the agreement of opposing counsel and, if approved, continued by letter with copies to all counsel. If consent cannot be obtained, then the requesting counsel must arrange for a conference call with the Court.

Communication with the Court:

1. Counsel may call the Court's Secretary, Valarie Genchi, with respect to the scheduling of appearances and with respect to adjournment applications.

2. Counsel may call Chambers to arrange for a telephone conference with the Court with the Law Secretary, or with Kathryn Coward.

3. Counsel may not contact Chambers on any substantive matter without all opposing counsel on the telephone, except for the purpose of facilitating a conference call.

Motions:

No motion shall be made, except as allowed by Rule 24 of the Commercial Division Rules, without a prior conference with the Court, which conference may be obtained either by conference call or, upon obtaining permission from Chambers, the submittal of a brief letter application, not exceeding 1 page in length. At the conference the Court will set a schedule for making the motion opposing it, and, if applicable, for reply.

Motions are to be returnable on Tuesdays. Motions made returnable at any other time, absent prior permission of the Court, will be adjourned by the Part Clerk to the next available Tuesday.

Adjournments are governed by Rule 16(c) of the Commercial Division Rules.

Motions are submitted without oral argument, unless otherwise directed by the Court.

Reply papers are not permitted, unless: (a) the right of reply is obtained by service of a notice of motion in accordance with CPLR 2214[b]; or (b) expressly permitted by the Court. Counsel may submit supplemental citations as allowed by Rule 18 of the Commercial Division Rules. Sur-reply papers, including papers in support of a cross-motion, are not permitted, absent prior permission of the Court. Any unauthorized papers will not be read and will be discarded.

All papers must comply with the applicable provisions of the CPLR and with Rules 16 and 18 of the Commercial Rules. In addition, the font size of text and footnotes must be no smaller than 12 point. Papers which do not comply may be rejected.

All motions for summary judgment shall be accompanied by a Statement of Undisputed Facts Pursuant to Rule 19–a of the Commercial Rules. A motion for summary judgment which lacks such a statement may be rejected. All opposing papers must include a response to the Statement of Undisputed Facts.

No motion papers will be sealed without a prior, or contemporaneous, application for sealing made pursuant to Part 216 of the Rules of the Chief Administrative Judge.

The Court generally does not stay disclosure pending determination of motions to dismiss or motions for summary judgment (made prior to completion of discovery). All dispositive motions shall be made no more than 60 business days after the filing of the Note of Issue.

Discovery Disputes:

With respect to cases already assigned to this Court at the time that a discovery dispute arises, no motion with respect to the dispute shall be made without a prior conference with the Court, which may be obtained by submission of a letter application, not exceeding one (1) page in length. Counsel must obtain permission from Chambers prior to the submission of such letter application.

With respect to cases in which a discovery motion accompanies the Request for Judicial Intervention which leads to the assignment to this Court, no opposition papers shall be served until there has been a prior conference with the Court, which may be obtained by letter application, not exceeding one (1) page in length. The application for a discovery conference may be made by the movant or by the opposing counsel; however, the application must be made within eight (8) days of service of the motion. Counsel must obtain permission from Chambers prior to the submission of a letter application. Failure to request a discovery conference may result in the denial of the motion.

The Court endeavors to resolve discovery disputes promptly, usually by conference, which may be held telephonically or in person. In the event that the dispute is not resolved, the Court will set an expedited briefing schedule. Counsel shall, prior to requesting a conference, meet in person to discuss the issues and endeavor to resolve or limit them, prior to seeking judicial intervention.

JUSTICE ARTHUR G. PITTS

Part 43. Hon. Arthur G. Pitts

Motion Practice

1. All motions assigned to Justice Pitts shall be made returnable on Thursdays only and shall be marked submitted on said return date unless an adjournment has been granted in accordance with the procedure outlined below. Timely interposition of all papers in accordance with the CPLR is required, as the court will not consider the merits of any papers, including cross motions or replies, which are untimely served.

2. Motion papers shall comply with the form prescribed in 22 NYCRR § 202.8(c). All affidavits and exhibits shall be identified by separately and consecutively numbered or lettered tabs. Legal memoranda must not exceed 15 pages in length, reply memoranda, five pages. Both official and unofficial citations to cases are required. Copies of orders or decisions will

not be furnished unless a self-addressed, stamped envelope is supplied with the motion papers.

3. a. Consistent with 22 NYCRR § 202.8(f), no motion related to disclosure or bills of particulars may be made unless and until a conference has been conducted by this court, notwithstanding that a preliminary or other conference may have been conducted by Justice Pitts or another justice previously assigned the action. The purpose of the conference will be to resolve the dispute between the parties, whether by stipulation or by order of the court. Counsel should be prepared to argue his or her position with regard to the disputed disclosure on the date of the conference. In the event the dispute cannot be resolved, the court may grant permission to make an appropriate motion addressed to the disputed disclosure.

b. Prior to any request for a conference related to disclosure or bills of particulars, however, counsel shall advise the court, in writing and on notice to all adversaries, of the specific items of disclosure or particulars in dispute. This written communication shall contain an affirmation by counsel that there has been a good faith attempt to resolve the dispute without judicial intervention. Opposing counsel shall advise the court, in writing and on notice to all other parties, of their positions with respect to such items or particulars. The court will thereupon address the issues presented either in writing or by telephone conference.

4. a. Requests for adjournments of motions may be obtained, on consent of all parties, by contacting Susan Butler in chambers or the Calendar Clerk for Part 43 at 631–852–3193. Consent to adjourn must be obtained as to any and all motions in chief and cross motions riding therewith. Requests for adjournments on consent will be granted only after verbal approval and upon receipt by chambers and/or the Calendar Clerk of written confirmation of such request (by fax at 631–852–2769 or regular mail received before the date being adjourned) and indicating the consent of all parties thereto.

b. Adjournments are limited to three in number and may not extend the original return date more than 60 days. Application for further adjournments must be made in person before the court on the last submit date given, and in accordance with the procedure prescribed in subdivision (c) below. Such adjournments will be granted by the court only upon good cause shown.

c. Where the consent of all parties cannot be obtained, an application for an adjournment must be made personally before the court on the return date of the motion. Counsel must, upon appearance, affirm that all non-consenting parties received notice that such application would be made to the court. In the event that a non-consenting party fails to appear to oppose the application for an adjournment, the court may entertain a further application for costs against such non-consenting, non-appearing party.

5. An appearance and oral argument shall be required on all motions which seek a preliminary injunction or an extension of a stay or restraining order, unless all parties agree otherwise. An appearance and oral argument shall also be required where a party is seeking emergency relief and/or the immediate intervention of the court, unless all parties agree otherwise. All other motions, including those for summary judgment or dismissal made in the general procedural course of an action or proceeding, are on submission only. Chambers may be contacted in the event counsel has a question concerning the applicability of this rule in a given case.

Conferences

1. In all actions requiring same, there shall be a preliminary conference at which the parties shall enter into a Preliminary Conference Order, which will thereafter be "so-ordered" by the Court, which schedules the disclosure necessary in a given case. The progress of the parties in completing disclosure shall be reported to the court at any and all compliance conferences which are scheduled thereafter. When all disclosure is complete, the parties shall execute a Compliance Conference Order which certifies that all discovery is complete, provides for the filing of the Note of Issue within 30 days of the date thereof, and schedules the pre-trial conference. A copy of the Compliance Conference Order must be filed with the Note of Issue. The subject of such pre-trial conferences shall include settlement of the matter.

2. Adjournments of conferences may be obtained in advance in the same manner as the adjournment of motions, and are subject to the same rules.

3. Counsel appearing for a compliance conference in which disclosure remains incomplete may not obtain an adjournment from the Part Clerk. Counsel must conference the case before the court or the law clerk.

4. No party may file a note of issue and certificate of readiness without first having entered into a Compliance Conference Order certifying that disclosure has been completed and that the case is ready for trial. No order shall be entered certifying a case as ready "subject to" the completion of disclosure at a future date without express permission of the Court.

Miscellaneous

1. *Non-jury trials.*

For all non-jury trials, Justice Pitts requires the entry of a pre-trial order limiting the issues to be determined, to be submitted by the parties for signature. Pre-trial memoranda of law must also be submitted in which both official and unofficial caselaw citations are provided. All trial exhibits must be pre-marked.

2. *Inquests*

All inquests will be scheduled on Thursdays.

3. *Infant's Compromises*

Infant's compromise orders should be submitted to the court through the Clerk's Office. Counsel will then be notified of the date for the infant's appearance before the court. All such appearances will be conducted on Thursdays. No infant's compromise order will be signed unless accompanied by an appropriate medical report dated no earlier than six months prior to the date the order is submitted to the court. The medical report must state that the infant has made a full recovery, or if further medical treatment is required, a detailed statement as to nature and extent of that treatment must be included.

4. *Appearances.*

a. Except in the case of unrepresented litigants, all appearances before the court shall be by an attorney admitted to practice in the State of New York, who must be fully authorized to act on behalf of his/her client.

b. Courtroom personnel and staff are to be treated with courtesy and respect. Disrespectful, uncivil and unprofessional conduct in the courthouse will not be countenanced.

5. *Inquiries.*

All inquiries as to case or calendar status should in the first instance be addressed to the Calendar Clerk for Part 43, at 631–852–3193. The only inquiries which may be made directly to the chambers are those involving the immediate exercise of judicial discretion, or as otherwise permitted by these rules.

JUSTICE JEFFREY ARLEN SPINNER

Part 21. Hon. Jeffrey Arlen Spinner

The following shall comprise the rules of practice and procedure for all matters pending before Supreme Court, Part 21. The intent of these rules is to ensure fair and expeditious handling of all matters that are before the Court for the benefit of both the litigants and their respective attorneys.

Court Staff:

The Court staff includes the Justice, Principal Law Clerk, Confidential Secretary, Senior Court Clerk, Senior Court Officers and Court Reporter. All of these persons constitute a necessary and indispensable part of the Court, and they enable the Court to function fairly and effectively, for the benefit of both litigants and counsel. All members of the staff must be treated with civility, courtesy and respect. Strict adherence to the rules set forth in 22 NYCRR Part 700 ["Decorum"] and 22 NYCRR Part 1200 ["New York State Standards of Civility"] is mandatory. Unprofessional conduct will not be countenanced.

Definitions:

Designated Motion Dates — All motions made in cases assigned to Justice Spinner shall be calendared for submission on either the FIRST or THIRD Wednesday of each month. In the event that the First or

Third Wednesday falls on a legal holiday or a day otherwise pre-empted by the Justice's schedule, then the Designated Motion Date for submission of motions that would have appeared on the calendar for that Wednesday shall be calendared for the next available Wednesday (the SECOND or FOURTH Wednesday of that month, unless same is also an unavailable date).

Parties — For the purposes of these rules, parties shall mean counsel of record and/or *pro se* litigants.

TRO/Stay Return Date — Where a Temporary Restraining Order (TRO) or a stay has been imposed in an Order pending the return date of an application, return date shall mean the date upon which all parties are scheduled to appear for argument thereof, and same shall not be, nor be considered, an adjourn date. In instances where the return date assigned was not an available Designated Motion Date (as defined herein above), and the Court Calendar Department or Chambers therefore administratively carries the return date forward to a proper date, the TRO or stay shall automatically be continued to that rescheduled return date, without the requirement of notice to any party. It is the responsibility of all parties to inquire as to the scheduling or rescheduling of such matters.

GENERAL CIVIL PART RULES

Motion Practice:

Return Dates

Parties are urged to consult with Chambers in advance of scheduling any motion date in order to determine available Designated Motion Dates (as defined herein above). In the event that an application is made returnable on a day other than an available Designated Motion Date, same will be administrative-

ly continued to the Court's next available Designated Motion Date.

Unless an adjournment is granted by the Court (in accordance with these Rules as set forth herein below) all motions appearing on the Court's Designated Motion Date Calendar shall be marked as submitted on that date.

Motion Conferences

Effective September 1, 2009, the Court will no longer convene a mandatory conference on all motions. Instead, after a motion has been submitted it shall be reviewed and, in the event the Court deems a conference necessary, same will be scheduled on a date convenient to the Court, due consideration being given to the availability of the parties.

Appearance of all parties is required at any Motion Conference, and they must be prepared to discuss the matter in an effort to narrow the issues, as well as to explore possible resolution of the case.

Where it is determined by the Court that a discovery motion has been filed cannot be resolved, the matter may be referred to the District Administrative Judge for the appointment of a Referee or Judicial Hearing Officer to supervise discovery.

Post-Note Motion Conferences

All Post-Note of Issue motions must be conferenced with the Court on an available Designated Motion Date. Appearance of all parties is required at all such conferences, prepared to discuss the matter in an effort to narrow the issues, as well as to explore possible resolution of the case.

Adjournments

Adjournments of pending motions must be upon consent of all parties. In accordance with the express provisions of 22 NYCRR § 208.8(e), adjournments may not extend the original return date of the motion beyond sixty days.

All requests for adjournment must be made by stipulation executed by all parties. Said stipulations must contain the full caption of the action, the original return date of the motion and the adjourn date requested (which must be an available Designated Motion Date). Parties are urged to communicate with Chambers prior to submitting such a stipulation. Stipulations must be received by Chambers not later than 4:00 p.m. of the Tuesday immediately preceding the return date, and may be forwarded either by mail or facsimile. In the event that an application for adjournment is denied, such denial will be communicated to all parties by Chambers sufficiently in advance of the scheduled return date.

In the unlikely event that consent of all parties is not forthcoming, the Court will entertain an oral application for adjournment on the date that the motion is returnable. The party seeking adjournment must notify all parties of his or her intent to orally apply for the adjournment. Likewise, where consent for an adjournment is unreasonably withheld, the Court reserves unto itself the right to unilaterally impose an adjournment consistent with the interests of justice to a date convenient to the Court and the parties cooperating in the request for adjournment.

Submission of Papers

All papers must be submitted in accordance with the express provisions of the CPLR. The Court will not consider any papers (opposition, cross-motion, reply, etc.) which appear to have been inappropriately interposed. All motion papers (including motions, opposing papers, affidavits, etc.) must be submitted through the Special Term Clerk's Office, Supreme Court, 1 Court Street, Riverhead, New York 11901. The Court will consider all papers properly submitted on notice and forwarded to Chambers by the Special Term Clerk's Office.

Submission of a cross-motion with a stated return date that is beyond the return date of the original motion will not serve to adjourn the original motion, although the Court may elect, in its discretion, to adjourn the original motion.

All motions and cross-motions submitted for Court consideration must be accompanied, at the time of submission, by a proposed Order. All Orders To Show Cause matters must likewise be submitted with a proposed Order at the time movant's Reply to opposition is filed. All opposition to any of the aforesaid must contain a proposed Order. Proposed Orders submitted after filing of a motion, Order to Show Cause or opposition must be made on notice to all parties, but do not require formal service.

Chambers or courtesy copies of papers are neither expected nor required, and are discouraged.

Oral Argument on Motions

All motions shall decided upon the submission of papers, unless oral argument is specifically requested. Any party may make such a request, which must be done in writing, on notice to all other parties, and received by Chambers not later than seven (7) days before the stated return date. All such requests shall be made in accordance with the provisions of 22 NYCRR § 202.8(d). In the event the Court declines to entertain oral argument, all parties will be notified by Chambers in advance of the return date.

Temporary Restraining Orders & Stays

Where a Temporary Restraining Order ("TRO") or a stay has been imposed pending the return date (as defined herein above) of an application, all parties must appear on the stated return date. The stay or TRO will not continue beyond the stated return date absent further order of the Court, unless the Order imposing said TRO or stay specifically states that it shall remain in effect pending determination of the motion or action.

Where a matter is returnable on a date other than an available Designated Motion Date, it will be administratively carried to the Court's next available proper date. In such event, the return date will be deemed to be the rescheduled date (as per the Definitions herein above), which shall not be deemed to be an adjournment, and the TRO or stay shall continue in effect until that later date.

In the event continuation of a stay or TRO is sought, the requesting party must make application at the call of the calendar. The Court reserves the right to *sua sponte* continue a TRO or stay, if consent is unreasonably withheld under the circumstances or if the interests of justice so dictate.

Calendar Matters:

Scheduling

All conferences (Pre-Trial, Compliance, Certification, Settlement, Post Note of Issue, etc.) and all calendar matters (Hearings, Inquests, Infant Compromises, etc.) shall be initially scheduled for an available Designated Motion Date (as defined herein above). Hearings and Inquests will be scheduled by Chambers in such a manner as to accommodate the schedules of all parties, with consideration given to avoiding unnecessary waiting time and inconvenience to any parties. Motion and/or Status conferences shall also include such considerations, but may be scheduled by the Court for dates other than Designated Motion Dates.

Hearings and Inquests in civil matters assigned to Part 21 shall be scheduled by Chambers. Absent permission of the Court, no inquest may be scheduled unless a Note of Issue has been filed.

Appearances

Attorneys Of Record & *Pro Se* Parties are required to attend all scheduled court appearances unless they have been relieved or otherwise excused by order of the Court or have otherwise been formally substituted.

Preliminary Conferences on matters that are assigned to Part 21 are returnable before, and are handled by, the Differentiated Case Management Part of the Supreme Court, located in Room A362 of the Supreme Court, located at 1 Court Street, Riverhead, New York. The Preliminary Conference Orders shall thereafter submitted to Part 21 for signature.

All other conferences and calendar matters are handled by, and are returnable before, this Court at IAS Part 21, Courtroom 1, Criminal Courts Building, 210 Center Drive, Riverhead, New York.

Appearances are required for all scheduled conferences, and the Court requires the presence of parties with knowledge of the facts of the matter before the Court, who are vested with authority to enter into binding dispositions on behalf of their respective clients. Failure to appear without proper cause may subject the non-appearing party to default or non-suit, as well as potential other sanctions, as provided for by 22 NYCRR § 202.27 and 22 NYCRR §§ 130–1.1 and 130–2.1.

Calendar call commences at 9:30 a.m. Parties are required to check in with the Senior Court Clerk in the Courtroom and indicate their readiness to proceed. If any party is also required to attend proceedings in another Part at the same time, the Senior Court Clerk and adversaries, if any, should be so advised, in order to extend appropriate latitude and courtesy to all parties.

Whenever there are motions pending on a matter that appears on any Conference Calendar, same shall first be discussed with, and reviewed by, Robert De-Gregorio Esq, Principal Law Clerk.

Adjournments

Adjournments of conferences and other calendar matters shall not be granted without good cause and then only for a reasonable period of time. Adjournment applications shall be made in accordance with the procedures set forth under *"Motion Practice"* above.

Trials:

Trials, both jury and non-jury, are assigned to Part 21 on a random basis by the Calendar Control Part of the Supreme Court. The Court will conduct trials on all days, and will continue trials in progress day to day, except that no trial proceedings shall be held on Tuesdays (Foreclosure Conference Calendar Day) and the two Designated Motion Dates per month, which comprise the Court's designated calendar days.

The Court will hold a Trial Conference with parties immediately prior to the commencement of the trial. Parties shall provide the Court with the following items at or before the conference:

(1) a set of marked pleadings and any amendments thereto;

(2) all bills of particulars that have been served;

(3) a list of witnesses for each side;

(4) in the case of any expert witnesses, all of the information mandated by the provisions of CPLR 3101(d)(1)(i); and

(5) a list of pre-marked exhibits.

The Court requires proposed jury charges and a verdict sheet to be submitted by parties immediately in advance of the close of testimony, in order that a Charge Conference be held regarding the same.

At the Trial Conference, the Court will explore the matter with parties and will also discuss settlement of the pending case. Parties must be authorized to negotiate and enter into binding settlements on behalf of their respective clients.

The Court will neither postpone nor adjourn any matter scheduled and ready for trial, absent drastic and emergent circumstances (such as death or hospitalization which affects the parties). In the event that a party fails, without good cause, to proceed on a scheduled trial, appropriate sanctions may be imposed upon the defaulting party, including but not limited to costs and counsel fees in favor of the opposing party and assessment of costs of assembling the petit jury.

Compromise Applications:

All applications for compromise of a claim on behalf of an infant or other incapacitated party must be served upon all parties and submitted through the Special Term Clerk's Office, Supreme Court, 1 Court Street, Riverhead, New York 11901. All such submissions must be in full compliance with 22 NYCRR § 202.67 and CPLR §§ 1206, 1207 and 1208.

Petitions must contain the name, address and attorney (if any) for any statutory or other lienors, together with the amount of their claims, if any. Medical reports must be in the form of an affirmation or affidavit, and must not be dated more than six months prior to the date that the application is submitted to Special Term. Such reports must be fully detailed and indicate the nature and extent of the injuries, whether or not a full recovery has been had and the

nature and extent of future limitations and/or treatment, if any.

In the Order Approving Compromise, counsel shall leave appropriate blanks for the Court to insert the computation and the depository for the infant's funds, as applicable (counsel should not take it upon themselves to designate the depository for the funds, as this is the province of the Court).

Once the submissions have been approved as complete by the Special Term Clerk's Office, the Court will schedule the appearance date. Both the applicant and the infant must be present at the compromise hearing, unless the Court grants an exception due to extreme and extenuating circumstances.

SEX OFFENDER REGISTRATION RE-CLASSIFICATION PART RULES

Justice Spinner also sits as County Court Part 8 which hears the Sex Offender Registration Re-Classification matters pursuant to both Article 6–C of the Correction Law and the authority of *Doe v. Pataki, 3 F.3d 69 (2d. Cir. 2008).*

These matters are calendared for designated Tuesdays at 9:30 a.m. by the Clerk of the County Court. All appearances shall be in Courtroom 1, Criminal Courts Building, 210 Center Drive, Riverhead, New York. Written notification of the date and time of appearance is given by the Court to the involved

parties, whose presence is required, unless waived in writing or as otherwise directed by the Court.

Defendants shall appear with counsel who are prepared to proceed in the matter. In the event that a Defendant is unable to retain counsel, the Court may, after inquiry on the record, assign counsel if the Defendant is otherwise eligible, or may adjourn the matter.

The Court shall require the submission of a Risk Level Assessment Instrument as well as an updated rap sheet.

FORECLOSURE CONFERENCE PROGRAM
FORECLOSURE CONFERENCE PART RULES

Doc. 1. Residential Mortgage Foreclosure Conference Part

Effective January 1, 2009, Justice Spinner will be presiding over a specialized Residential Mortgage Foreclosure Conference Part. In accordance with the provisions of CPLR § 3408, those mortgage loans in foreclosure which are deemed "sub-prime," "high cost" or "non-traditional" (as defined by RPAPL § 1304 and Banking Law § 6–1), and which encumber owner occupied 1-4 family dwellings, shall be referred to this part for conference.

It shall be the obligation of counsel for the foreclosing mortgagee to advise the Court, in writing, as to whether or not the loan in foreclosure falls within the statutory parameters which would require a conference. This reference to the Residential Mortgage Foreclosure Conference Part shall occur prior to the random assignment of the case to an IAS Justice.

In addition, only as to matters already assigned to Justice Spinner (IAS Part 21), upon written application by any mortgagor-defendant, the Court will convene a settlement conference, regardless of the stage to which the action has proceeded and without regard to whether or not the loan falls within the purview of CPLR § 3408.

The purpose of the conference shall be to engage in settlement discussions with regard to the rights, responsibilities and obligations of all parties to the loan transaction. The Court will explore the issues of avoiding the potential loss of the borrower's home, review and evaluation of amicable resolution of the matter, including possible modification and workout of the indebtedness due the lender, and any other purpose deemed necessary and/or appropriate by the Court. Upon the request of the parties, or its own initiative, the Court may adjourn the conference, continue the matter or stay prosecution of the action.

The appearance and/or participation by the Defendant-Mortgagor shall not constitute an appearance in the action nor shall it be deemed to be a waiver, in whole or in part, of any defenses, jurisdictional or otherwise, that the Defendant-Mortgagor may have to the action. Any and all statements made, whether oral or written, and any and all information exchanged at the conference, shall be solely for the purposes of resolution and settlement, and shall not be deemed to be admissions of any party with respect to the underlying action.

Any Defendant who appears *pro se* shall be deemed to have moved to proceed as a poor person and the Court shall determine whether such permission should be granted. The Court may evaluate the matter to determine whether or not counsel should be assigned. In the event that counsel is appointed, the Court will adjourn the conference in order to facilitate the appearance by counsel.

At each scheduled conference Plaintiff shall appear, either in person or by counsel. If appearing by counsel, such attorney shall be vested with authority to negotiate and to enter into a binding settlement and to ultimately dispose of the matter. The failure of Plaintiff and/or counsel to appear at a scheduled conference without good cause shall be dealt with in accordance with the provisions of 22 NYCRR § 130–2.1, and may subject Plaintiff and/or counsel to appropriate remedial action, including but not limited to default, non-suit, dismissal with prejudice and monetary sanctions.

At least three business days prior to the scheduled conference, Plaintiff's counsel shall provide the Court (Chambers) with copies of the foreclosure search, which shall include a copy of the deed vesting title in the mortgagor, the Note and Mortgage and any assignments thereof, the mortgage loan application, the Truth-In-Lending Disclosure Statement, the HUD-I Settlement Statement and the loan payment history. The Defendant-Mortgagor shall bring, to the extent available, copies of all notices received relative to the mortgage loan, a list of all payments made, documents that show monthly income and expenses, as well as any information that may be helpful at the conference.

Conferences will be scheduled by the Court for each Tuesday at 2:30 p.m., Courtroom 1, Criminal Courts Building, 210 Center Drive, Riverhead, New York.

DISTRICT COURT
FORMS

Form 1. Complaint Form and Instructions

SUFFOLK COUNTY DISTRICT COURT
COMPLAINT FORM

COURT DATE   _INDEX NO._

TIME & DISTRICT   _DATE MAILED_

TYPE OR PRINT IN BLACK INK

CHECK ONE TYPE OF CLAIM: SMALL CLAIM   COMMERCIAL CLAIM
CONSUMER TRANSACTION

CHECK ONE SESSION: DAY COURT   NIGHT COURT

PLAINTIFF'S NAME AND ADDRESS	**DEFENDANT'S NAME AND ADDRESS**
If plaintiff is a business you must enter your true business name.	_If defendant is a business you must enter its true business name._
Last Name, First Name or True Business Name	_Last Name, First Name or True Business Name_
Street Address (P.O. Box alone is not acceptable)	_Street Address (P.O. Box alone is not acceptable)_
City, State, ZIP	_City, State, ZIP_
Telephone Number: _____	Telephone Number: _____
Additional Plaintiff Additional Defendant	Additional Plaintiff Additional Defendant
Last Name, First Name or True Business Name	_Last Name, First Name or True Business Name_
Street Address (P.O. Box alone is not acceptable)	_Street Address (P.O. Box alone is not acceptable)_
City, State, ZIP	_City, State, ZIP_
Telephone Number: _____	Telephone Number: _____

If you need to list more than four parties, submit additional pages as needed, and check here: ☐

CHECK ONE CAUSE OF ACTION:

(5) PERSONAL INJURIES
(10) PROPERTY DAMAGE
(15) LOSS OF PERSONAL PROPERTY
(20) GOODS SOLD AND DELIVERED
(25) BREACH OF CONTRACT OR WARRANTY
(35) WORK, LABOR AND SERVICES

(40) MONIES DUE
(50) PAYMENT OF LOAN
(70) REFUND ON DEFECTIVE MERCHANDISE
(80) REFUND ON DEFENDANT'S DEFECTIVE WORK, LABOR AND/OR SERVICES
(85) OTHER CAUSE OF ACTION AS DETAILED BELOW

STATE DETAILS OF YOUR CLAIM:

TOTAL AMOUNT OF DAMAGES: _____

The undersigned acknowledges that he/she has been advised that supporting witnesses, account books, receipts and other documents required to establish the claim herein must be produced at the hearing. The undersigned further certifies to the best of his/her knowledge, the defendant is not in the military service.

If this is a complaint filed as a Commercial Claim (UDCA § 1803-A), the undersigned hereby certifies that no more than five (5) actions or proceedings (including the instant action) pursuant to the commercial claims procedure have been initiated in the courts of this state during the present calendar month.

THIS FORM MUST BE SIGNED IN THE PRESENCE OF A COURT CLERK OR NOTARY

DATED: _____   _____
                                       PLAINTIFF

                                       _____
_____   *AS AUTHORIZED AGENT OF PLAINTIFF*

                                       _____
                                       AS PARENT AND NATURAL GUARDIAN

Instructions for mailing the Small Claims Complaint Form (DC–283)

These instructions are for use with the Suffolk District Court DC–283 Small Claims Complaint Form

USE BLACK INK ONLY!!!

The Maximum You Can Sue For Is $5000

• On the form, request Day Court or Night Court. Night Court is in Ronkonkoma on certain Wednesdays at 6:00 p.m. If you wish day court, choose from the Civil Division Courts and contact them as to which days Small Claims are calendared.

• You are the Plaintiff. Write your last name, first name, street address and telephone number (a Post Office Box alone is not acceptable).

• Write the defendants full name and street address—a PO Box alone is not acceptable. The defendant must reside, work or have a business address within the five western towns of Suffolk County.

• Check only one cause of action. (If you cannot decide, pick #85).

• State briefly the reason why you are suing.

• State the total amount you are suing for.

• Sign and date the form in the presence of a Court Clerk or Notary.

FILING FEES

FEES page for the fee to "SMALL CLAIMS—File an action" [1]

Do not send cash through the mail. Send a money order or check payable to the **CLERK OF THE DISTRICT COURT** for the correct fee.

Please enclose a **SELF–ADDRESSED STAMPED ENVELOPE** if you are mailing the application.

Deliver or mail the form and fee to the Civil Division Courthouse where you want the claim to be heard.

(You must be a New York State based Corporation in order to file in Commercial Claims; see Commercial Claim complaint form instructions)

Commercial Claim Complaint Form Instructions

The maximum you can sue for is $5000.

You must be a New York State-based Corporation in order to file in Commercial Claims.

1. Fill out and mail the demand letter to the defendant. **USE BLACK INK ONLY!** (Do this only if you are suing an individual. You need not do this for another Corporation or Company.)

2. Wait 10 days. If you get no response from defendant after those 10 days, file a COMMERCIAL CLAIM FORM. **USE BLACK INK ONLY!**

3. Sign and notarize the certification (UCS 119/DC-293 form) if you are filing by mail. If filing in person at the court you can sign it in front of a Court Clerk.

4. You are the plaintiff, write your full corporate name and street address - a PO Box is not acceptable.

5. Write the defendants full name and street address - a PO Box alone is not acceptable. The defendant must reside, work or have a business address within the five western towns of Suffolk County.

6. Check only one cause of action. (If you cannot decide, pick #85.)

7. State briefly the reason why you are suing.

8. State the total amount you are suing for.

9. Sign and date the form in the presence of a Court Clerk or Notary.

FILING FEES

FEES page for the fee to "COMMERCIAL CLAIM - File an action" [1]

When are Commercial Claims heard in my District? [2]

Please enclose a self-addressed stamped envelope if mailing the application. Do not send cash by mail. Send a money order or check payable to **Clerk of the District Court.**

Notice To Parties: Small Claims & Commercial Claims Actions

Adjournments

Requests for adjournments must be made in writing to the court with notice of the request given to all parties. Requests may also be made in person on the court date. No requests for adjournments will be accepted by phone. All requests for adjournments are submitted to the judge/arbitrator on the court date for approval. The court does not notify the parties of the new court date if the adjournment request is granted. You must contact the court to ascertain the new date.

Proof of Claim; Defenses to Claim

On the court date you must submit all items necessary to prove the claim or to defend against the claim. Contracts, agreements, receipts, cancelled checks, photographs and other documents should be produced at trial. Property damage may be proven by two itemized written estimates or by one itemized paid bill. Persons having actual knowledge of the facts and circumstances of the claim, or who are experts in a field may be present to testify. Expert witnesses cannot be subpoenaed to testify since most require compensation to appear in court.

Duty to Pay Judgments

Any person, partnership, firm or corporation which is sued in a small or commercial claims court for any cause of action arising out of its business activities, shall pay any judgment rendered against it in its true name or in any name in which it conducts business. "True name" includes the legal name of a natural person and the name under which a partnership, firm or corporation is licensed, registered, incorporated or otherwise authorized to do business. "Conducting business" as used in this section shall include, but not limited to, maintaining signs at business premises or on business vehicles; advertising; entering into contracts; and printing or using sales slips, checks, invoices or receipts. Whenever a judgment has been rendered against a person, partnership, firm or corporation in other than its true name and the judgment has remained unpaid for thirty-five days after receipt by the judgment debtor of notice of its entry, the aggrieved judgment creditor shall be entitled to commence an action in small/commercial claims court against such judgment debtor, notwithstanding the jurisdictional limit of the court, for the sum of the original judgment, costs, reasonable attorney's fees, and one hundred dollars.

Whenever a judgment which relates to activities for which a license is required has been rendered against a business which is licensed by a state or local licensing authority and which remains unpaid for thirty-five days after receipt by the judgment debtor of notice of its entry and the judgment has not been stayed or appealed, the state or local licensing authority shall consider such failure to pay, if deliberate or part of a pattern of similar conduct indicating recklessness, as a basis for the revocation, suspension, conditioning or refusal to grant or renew such license. Nothing herein shall be construed to preempt an authority's existing policy if it is more restrictive.

[1] http://www.nycourts.gov/courts/10jd/suffolk/dist/Fees.shtml#small

[2] http://www.nycourts.gov/courts/10jd/suffolk/dist/civilschedule.shtml#Comm_claim_day

Form 2. Demand Letter for Commercial Claims

Commercial Claim Arising Out of a Consumer Transaction

DEMAND LETTER

TO: _____   Date: _____

Name of Defendant

_____

Address

You have not paid a debt owed to _____, which you incurred on _____. The amount remaining unpaid on the debt is $ _____. Demand is hereby made that this money be paid. Unless payment of this amount is received by the undersigned no later than _____, 20 ___, a lawsuit will be brought against you in the Commercial Claims Part of the Court.

If a lawsuit is brought, you will be notified of the hearing date, and you will be entitled to appear at the hearing and present any defense you may have to this claim.

(If applicable) Our records show that you have made the following payment in partial satisfaction of this debt (fill in dates and amounts paid) _____.

A copy of the original debt instrument - your agreement to pay - is attached. [The names and addresses of the parties to that original debt agreement are _____ (to be completed if claimant was not a party to the original transaction)].

_____

_____

_____

Typed or Printed Name and Address of Claimant

Form 3.   Certification for Commercial Claims

-COMPLETE THIS SECTION FOR COMMERCIAL CLAIM-

ARISING OUT OF A CONSUMER TRANSACTION

* Certification: (NYCCA 1803–A; UCCA 1803–A; UDCA 1803–A)

I hereby certify that I have mailed a demand letter by ordinary first class mail to the party complained against, no less than ten (10) days and no more than one hundred eighty (180) days before I commenced this claim.

I hereby certify, based upon information and belief, that no more than five (5) actions or proceedings (including the instant action or proceeding) pursuant to the commercial claims procedure have been initiated in the courts of this State during the present calendar month.

_____

Signature of Claimant

_____

Signature of Notary/Clerk/

* NOTE: The commercial claims part will not allow your action to proceed if this certification is not made and properly completed.

Form 4. In Person Answer

Index No. _____

DISTRICT COURT OF THE COUNTY OF SUFFOLK

_____ DISTRICT

HELD AT _____

_____

_____

                                            Plaintiff

against

_____

                                       Defendant

ANSWER

Defendant appears this __ day of _____, 20 __ and denies the truth of plaintiff's alleged cause of action.*

_____

_____

_____

_____

_____

                                _____

                                signature of defendant _____

                                signed in the presence of a Court Clerk

                                or Notary

                                _____

VERIFICATION

State of New York,

                   ss.:   Defendant's Address

County of Suffolk

_____, being duly sworn, deposes and says that __ he is the defendant in the within action; that __ he has read the foregoing answer and knows the contents thereof, that the same is true to h __ own knowledge, except as to the matters therein stated to be alleged on information and belief, and that as to those matters __ he believes it to be true.

Sworn to before me, this

__ day of _____, 20 __   _____

_____

Notary   Court Clerk

* Or insert statement of defense as may be made.

907

Form 5. AFFIDAVIT OF PERSONAL SERVICE

STATE OF NEW YORK   }
                                              SS:
COUNTY OF SUFFOLK   }

I, _____, being duly sworn, deposes and says:
            Print your name

I reside at: _____,
                              Insert your complete address

and am over 18 years of age, and not a party to this action.

On the _____ day of_____, 20 _____, at _____ o'clock in the
         insert date   *insert month*   *year*   *hour*

<u>FORENOON   AFTERNOON</u> , I served the within _____
Strike out the inappropriate phrase   Insert the name of the documents served, i.e.,
                                                          the summons, complaint, order, etc.
                                                          Attach a copy of the document to this
                                                          Affidavit of Service

upon _____,known to me to be the defendant
           insert defendant's name here
named therein

by delivering to and leaving with <u>HIM   HER</u>   personally, at _____
                                        Strike out   insert the address where you
                                                                        served the defendant

Town of _____,County of Suffolk, State of New York, a true copy
        Insert Town where you served the defendant
thereof.

Said individual had the following characteristics:

Sex: _____ color of skin: _____ color of hair:_____
approximate age: _____ approximate weight: ____approximate height: _____
other distinguishing characteristics: _____
_____
_____

Sworn to before me on this   _____
                                                       Your Signature

_____ day of _____, 20____
 Day   *Month*   *Year*

_____
      Notary/Clerk of Court

Form 6.   Affidavit of Service (Mail)

DISTRICT COURT, COUNTY OF SUFFOLK
STATE OF NEW YORK

_____

_____   **AFFIDAVIT OF SERVICE**
                Plaintiff

        -against-   Index No: _____

_____   Return Date: _____
                Defendant

_____

I, _____ being over the age of 18, and not a party to this
            Print your name

action, on _____,
            Insert date that the Order to Show Cause was mailed by you by Certified Mail,
                        Return Receipt Requested

mailed a copy of the attached   **ORDER TO SHOW CAUSE   MOTION** by Certified Mail,
                            Strike out the inappropriate document
                                        name
Return Receipt
Requested, to:

        Plaintiff or Plaintiff's Attorney: _____
                    Street Address: _____
                                    _____

                            AND

                                    _____
                        Name: _____
            Street Address: _____
                                    _____

                            For any additional party that also has
                            to be served with the Order or Motion,
                            or the Suffolk County
                            Sheriff who is served to stay the en-
                            forcement of the judgment or warrant.

                            _____
Sworn to before me on this   *Your Signature*
_____ day of _____, 20 ____
   Day   *Month*   *Year*

_____
Notary/Clerk of Court

                            Certified Mailing Receipts are Attached

909

Form 7.   Demand—Trial De Novo

_____ DISTRICT COURT OF THE COUNTY OF SUFFOLK

HELD AT _____

_____
                            Plaintiff

            against   DEMAND FOR TRIAL DE NOVO
                                       Index No. _____

_____
                           Defendant

Please be advised that I am not satisfied with the decision of the arbitrator, and hereby demand a Trial De Novo.

_____

    Signature of _____, Demandant

_____

_____

_____

    Street Address of Demandant

    (a PO Box alone is not acceptable)

THE FEE FOR A TRIAL DE NOVO IS $75.00. This fee must be submitted when this *demand for trial de novo* and affidavit(s) of service are filed. File the *demand*, affidavit(s), and the fee in the Court where the award was filed. The fee may be paid by check or money order made out to the *Clerk of the District Court*.

Such sum shall not be recoverable by the Demandant upon *trial de novo* or in any other proceeding.

Post Arbitration Judgments and **Trial de novo**

After Judgment has been awarded ...

see Frequently asked questions about Judgments [1]

To order the transcript from your arbitration hearing, you must wait thirty-five days from the mailing date of the arbitrator's award (to allow all parties time to request a **trial de novo**). If the award was as the result of the non-appearance of the defendant, we advise that you wait thirty days to allow the defendant time to pay you.

If after the stated time period you have not been served with a **trial de novo** demand or have not received payment, you may request that the District Court Clerk issue you a transcript of judgment to be filed with the Suffolk County Clerk. The request for a transcript must state that you have not received payment, or must state the amount of any partial payment that you have received since the award was granted. Enclose a stamped, self addressed envelope, along with a check or money order payable to THE CLERK OF THE DISTRICT COURT for the proper transcript fee.

When you receive the transcript from the court, it will include instructions on how to proceed.

TRIAL DE NOVO

IF YOU ARE NOT SATISFIED WITH THE DECISION THAT WAS REN-DERED AT THE ARBITRATION HEARING, YOU MAY REQUEST A **TRIAL DE NOVO BY A JUDGE.**

Demand for trial de novo may be made by any party not in default in the court where the action was commenced or, if the action was transferred, the court to which it was transferred, with or without jury. Any party within 35 days after service of the notice of filing of the award with the appropriate court clerk, may serve upon all adverse parties a demand for trial de novo, and file the demand, together with proof of service upon all parties, and the appropriate filing fee, in the Court where the award was filed.

If the Demandant either serves or files a timely demand for trial de novo but neglects through mistake or excusable neglect to do one of those two acts within the time limited, the court where the action was commenced or, if the action was transferred, the court to which it was transferred, may grant an extension of time to correct the omission.

The Demandant shall also concurrently with the filing of the demand, pay to the court clerk where the award was filed, a fee for a trial de novo. Such sum shall not be recoverable by the demandant upon *trial de novo* or in any other proceeding.

The arbitrator shall not be called as a witness nor shall the report or award of the arbitrator be admitted in evidence at the *trial de novo*.

If the judgment upon the trial de novo is not more favorable than the arbitration award in the amount of damages awarded or the type of relief granted to the Demandant, the Demandant shall not recover interest or costs from the time of the award, but shall pay costs to the other party or parties from that time.

1 http://www.courts.state.ny.us/courts/10jd/suffolk/dist/judgmentsFAQ.shtml

Form 8. Notice of Appeal

CIVIL NOTICE OF APPEAL—9TH & 10TH JUDICIAL DISTRICTS

STATE OF NEW YORK
DISTRICT COURT, SUFFOLK COUNTY

——————————————————— X   INDEX NO. ——————

                                 ( )Plaintiff,
——————————————— ( )Petitioner,

                         NOTICE OF APPEAL
     -against-   (CIVIL)

                                ( )Defendant,
——————————————— ( )Respondent.
                                      X

PLEASE TAKE NOTICE that the above-named   ( ) Plaintiff,
                                              ( ) Petitioner,
                                              ( ) Defendant,
                                              ( ) Respondent
hereby appeals to the Appellate Term of the Supreme Court for the Ninth and Tenth Judicial
Districts from the ( ) order ( ) judgment of the:
          District Court, ———— District, County of SUFFOLK,
entered in the office of the Clerk of said court on the __ day of ————, 20 __
and this appeal is taken from: ( ) each and every part thereof.
                          ( ) if only a part thereof, specify what parts of the order or
                          judgment you wish to appeal:

DATED: ——————————

                            Yours,
                      (if self-represented put your own name below)
                     Name: ——————————
                     Address: ——————————
                                    ——————————
                     Telephone no.   ——————————
                     Attorney for Appellant *(if represented by an attorney)*
                     Name: ——————————
                     Address: ——————————
                                    ——————————
                     Telephone no.   ——————————

TO: Opponent or Attorney (if opponent is represented by an attorney)
     Name: ——————————
     Address: ——————————
               ——————————

TO: Appeals Clerk, District Court
     Address: ——————————
               ——————————

Form 9. Affidavit in Support of Motion to Vacate
Default Judgment (Landlord/Tenant)

DISTRICT COURT OF THE COUNTY OF SUFFOLK

_____

_____
Petitioner
    -against-

Affidavit in Support of Motion to Vacate
Default Judgment in Landlord Tenant
Proceeding

_____
Respondent
_____
    Index No. _____

STATE OF NEW YORK }
                }   SS.:
COUNTY OF SUFFOLK }

_____, being duly sworn, deposes and says:

1.   I am the Respondent in the above entitled action.

2.   That I reside at _____.

3.   That this is an action for _____.

4.   That on _____, _____, a default judgment was entered by this court.

5.   That I did not appear/answer because _____
_____
_____

6.   That I have a meritorious defense; specifically [*state the facts which support your defense in as much detail as possible and attach any supporting documentation*]
_____
_____

7.   No previous application for this relief has been made.

WHEREFORE deponent respectfully requests an order vacating the judgment entered on the ___ day of   , ___, or such further relief as may be just and proper.

sign *in the presence of a Notary Public or Court Clerk* = >   _____

                    print name = >   _____ *Respondent*

Sworn to before me this _____ day of _____, 20__.

_____
Notary Public – Court Clerk
affix stamp / seal

Form 10.   Order to Show Cause to Vacate Default Judgment in Landlord Tenant Proceeding

At a Motion Term of the District Court of
the State of New York, County of Suffolk

Present: Hon. _____
Judge of the District Court

_____

_____

Petitioner

-against-

_____

Respondent

Order to Show Cause to Vacate Default

Judgment in Landlord Tenant Proceeding

Index No. _____

Upon the affidavit of _____, Respondent, sworn to on the ___ day of _____, 20___, and upon all prior papers and proceedings,

Let the Petitioner show cause at a Motion Term of this Court to be held at the Courthouse located at _____ on the ___ day of _____, 20___, at 9:30 AM or as soon thereafter as the parties can be heard, why an order should not be entered vacating the default on appearance date and/or the judgment granted in favor of the Petitioner and setting the matter down for trial, and why the Respondent should not have such other and further relief as may be just and proper.

Sufficient reason being presented for the relief requested, it is

Ordered that pending the hearing of this motion, the Sheriff and the Petitioner and all Petitioner's agents are stayed from conducting any proceedings to enforce the judgment, and further it is

Ordered that the Respondent serve a copy of this order on the Petitioner, or Petitioner's attorney if one has been retained, at _____, and the Suffolk County Sheriff at 360 Yaphank Avenue, Yaphank NY 11980 by Personal Delivery by the ___ day of _____, 20___.

All papers the Petitioner desires to submit in opposition to the Respondent's motion must be served on the Respondent and forwarded to the court prior to the hearing date. **Personal appearance** is required and **oral statements** will be considered.

Dated:_____   Enter,

_____   _____

District Court Judge

This order, together with proof of service, must be returned to the Court Clerk's office on or before _____

DC–420.3 (11/08)   A FREE DISTRICT COURT FORM   http://nycourts.gov/suffolkdistrict
no fee may be charged to fill in this form

Form 11. Affidavit in Support of Motion to Vacate a Default Judgment (Civil)

State of New York
County of Suffolk

DISTRICT COURT OF THE COUNTY
OF SUFFOLK HELD AT _____

_____   INDEX NO. _____
Plaintiff

_____
Defendant

_____ being duly sworn, deposes and says:

1. I am the Defendant in the above entitled action.

2. That I reside at _____

3. That this is an action for:

_____

4. That on the __ day of _____, ___, a default judgment was entered by this court.

5. That the Defendant did not appear/answer because: (**STATE REASON**)

_____

6. That your Defendant has a meritorious defense for the following reasons: (**STATE THE FACTS WHICH SUPPORT YOUR DEFENSE IN AS MUCH DETAIL AS POSSIBLE AND ATTACH ANY SUPPORTING DOCUMENTATION THAT YOU MAY HAVE.**)

_____

7. No previous application for this relief has been made.

WHEREFORE, deponent respectfully requests an order vacating the judgment entered on the __ day of _____, ___, or such further relief as may be just and proper.

Sworn to before me
__ **day of** _____, __.

_____

_____, **Defendant**

_____
CLERK/Notary Public, State of New York

Form 12. Order to Show Cause (Civil Judgment)

At a Motion Term of the District
Court of the State of New York,
County of Suffolk

Hon. _____
Judge of the District Court

_____x
Plaintiff
vs

CIVIL
ORDER TO SHOW CAUSE

_____x
Defendant

Index No. _____

Upon the affidavit of _____, sworn to on the ___ day of _____, 20 ___, and upon all prior papers and proceedings,

Let the plaintiff show cause at a Motion Term of this Court to be held at the courthouse located at **District Court of Suffolk County 3105–1 Veterans Memorial Highway, Ronkonkoma, NY 11779** on the ___ day of _____, 20 ___, at 9:30 AM or as soon thereafter as the parties can be heard, why an order should not be entered vacating the default on appearance date and/or the judgment granted in favor of the plaintiff and setting the matter down for trial, and why the defendant should not have such other and further relief as may be just and proper.

Sufficient reason being presented for the relief requested it is,

Ordered, that pending the hearing of this motion, the Sheriff and the plaintiff and all his agents are stayed from conducting any proceedings to enforce the judgment, and further it is

Ordered, that the defendant serve a copy of this order on the plaintiff, or his attorney if one has been retained, at _____, and the **Sheriff of Suffolk County at 360 Yaphank Avenue, Yaphank, New York 11980** by certified mail, return receipt requested by the ___ day of _____, 20 ___.

All papers the plaintiff desires to submit in opposition to the defendant's motion must be forwarded to the court prior to the hearing date. **No personal appearance is required and no oral statements will be considered.**

Order signed at Ronkonkoma, N.Y.

Date _____

THIS ORDER TOGETHER WITH PROOF OF SERVICE MUST BE RETURNED TO THE CLERK'S OFFICE BY _____

Enter,

_____
Hon. Judge of the District Court

SUMMARY JURY TRIAL

Preamble

General Features:

- An SJT is a binding one day jury trial with relaxed rules of evidence

- Medical evidence can be submitted without live medical testimony

- Hi–Low parameters can be stipulated to, i.e., $0/$25k, $50k/$25k, etc.

- No appeal

- No motion practice

- No directed verdicts

- A date certain for trial

- Innovative methods of case presentation to the jury, direct submission to jury of medical records, reports, power point presentations, etc.

- Supreme Court Justice to preside at the trial

General Rules:

- Written stipulation by attorneys to participate which must include a waiver of right to appeal, withdrawal of pending motions and a waiver of right to file motions, including post trial motions

- Pre-marked exhibits, medical records, reports, photos, diagrams, etc. can be submitted directly to jury

- Any evidence, trial notebook, etc. to be submitted to jury must be exchanged 30 days in advance or it is precluded

- Evidentiary hearing held no later than 10 days before trial to hear objections, exchange witness lists and resolve other pre-trial issues, unless a stipulation of compliance is filed with the calendar clerk of the Supreme Court and the SJT Justice is notified.

- Medical records need not be certified or affirmed

- Video live/pre-recorded testimony permitted

General Procedure:

- Abbreviated jury selection

- 10 minute opening and closing statements for each side

- One hour for case presentation and cross examination by each side

A. Nature of the Binding Summary Jury Trial: A summary jury trial is generally a one-day jury trial with relaxed rules of evidence similar to arbitration except that a jury decides factual issues and renders a verdict as a jury would in a traditional trial. The parties may agree on the mode and method of presentation. However, if practical and damages are agreed upon by the parties, the trial will determine liability only. Otherwise, trials will be bifurcated with damages immediately following the liability portion of the trial, in the course of one day. In the absence of agreement of counsel and approved by the trial court, the process and rules that follow shall apply.

Rule 1. Consent of Parties

The signatories to the Transfer Agreement represent that they have the authority of their respective clients and/or insurance carriers to enter into the agreement and such agreement shall be irrevocably binding upon the respective principals.

Rule 2. Stipulation

If the parties agree to a summary jury trial, a written stipulation shall be signed by the attorneys reciting any high/low parameters, agreeing to waive any rights to appeal, agreeing to withdraw any pending motions and agreeing not to file any written motions subsequent to the execution of the written stipulation. The high and low parameters of summary jury trial, if any, shall not be disclosed to the jury.

Rule 3. No Right to Appeal

The parties agree to waive costs and disbursements and further agree to waive the right to appeal from the determination of this matter.

Rule 4. No Motion Practice

The parties shall execute a written stipulation agreeing to withdraw any pending motions filed in the case and agreeing not to file any written motions subsequent to the execution of the written stipulation.

Rule 5. Scheduling

Summary jury trials will be placed on the calendar for trial at the earliest possible date available in the Summary Jury Trial Part, hereinafter referred to as the SJT Part. Once said date is assigned it shall be considered a date certain. Adjournments require permission of the SJT Part Justice.

Rule 6. Pre-trial submissions

a) Any party intending to offer documentary evidence upon trial, including but not limited to accident reports, medical records and lost income records, shall serve copies of such documentary evidence upon all parties not less than 30 days before trial, except that it shall not be necessary to serve any previously exchanged Examination before Trial Transcripts.

b) No later than 10 days before trial the SJT Justice assigned to the case shall conduct an evidentiary hearing at which time objections to any documentary evidence previously submitted as provided for herein shall be determined and witness lists shall be exchanged. If there is no objection at said time, counsel shall so stipulate in writing. The SJT Justice may issue an order of preclusion if either side fails to serve documentary evidence as is required herein.

c) Reference to PJI sections shall be sufficient on requests to charge. Requests to Charge shall be submitted at the evidentiary hearing, together with proposed verdict sheets.

Rule 7. Record

A summary jury trial will be recorded by a court reporter.

Rule 8. Existing Offer and Demand

The parties may stipulate that the pre-trial offer and demand remain unaltered through the binding summary jury trial. Either party may elect to accept the last settlement proposal of the opponent at any time before the verdict is announced by the jury.

Rule 9. Jury Selection

By counsel with strict time limits of the Court and counsel. If the Court or Court Attorney - Referee conducts the voir dire each side shall nonetheless have 10 minutes each to also voir dire the jury. Summary juries shall consist of no less than six jurors and one alternate unless the parties stipulate to fewer jurors. The Court shall allow each side two peremptory challenges.

Rule 10. Time Limits

Each side shall be entitled to a ten minute opening and closing and one hour for presentation of their case. The Court may allot more time to a party to insure full exploration of the issues provided counsel presents a compelling reason to support the request for additional time. Unless the SJT Justice directs otherwise, the court clerk should keep track of the time and remind counsel of the status of allotted time at appropriate intervals.

Rule 11. Rules of Evidence

a) The parties may offer such evidence as is relevant and material to the dispute. Conformity to legal rules of evidence shall not be necessary, subject to the provisions relating to documentary evidence set forth below.

b) Examination before Trial testimony of a party may be offered by any opposing party, however a party shall not be permitted to offer his/her own Examination before Trial testimony except as provided by the CPLR. This section shall apply to video depositions as well.

c) Past and future lost income may be proved by the submission of documentary evidence from the plaintiffs' employer, including but not limited to pay stubs, tax returns, W-2 and/or 1099 forms provided that such amounts may be calculated with a reasonable degree of mathematical certainty based solely upon present income and life expectancy. Any claim of future lost earnings premised upon inflation, lost

opportunity, promotion, career advancement or similar theory shall only be proved by expert testimony or the report of an expert previously exchanged pursuant to these rules.

d) In the event a party wishes to offer the testimony of a non-party witness, such testimony can only be offered through the use of the non-party deposition testimony of such witness taken pursuant to the notice requirements of the CPLR or by producing that witness at trial.

e) None of the foregoing shall be construed to prevent a party from calling witnesses upon trial; live video testimony shall be permitted, however, in the event a party intends to call an expert witness, medical or otherwise, that party must provide written notice to all parties of such witness, along with a copy of that medical expert's narrative report(s), not less than 20 days before trial, in the event of a non-medical expert counsel shall comply with the standard provisions of the CPLR concerning non-medical experts. Failure to comply with this provision shall result in the preclusion of such expert witness at the time of trial.

f) The following shall also be admissible, police reports, the MV104 of any party; medical records including but not limited to hospital records, ambulance records; medical records and/or reports from plaintiff's medical providers, defendant doctor reports inclusive of No Fault medical exam reports; diagnostic test results including but not limited to X-rays, MRI, CT scan, and EMG reports, or any other graphic, numerical, symbolic, or pictorial representation of medical or diagnostic procedure or test of plaintiff, any stipulated evidence shall also be admitted.

g) There shall be no requirement that any record referred to in paragraph "c" or "f" be certified, affirmed or sworn to.

h) Pre-trial evidentiary issues normally determined by the trial judge, such as motions *in limine* and redaction of documentary evidence, shall be determined in conformance with the applicable rules of evidence by the SJT Trial Justice at the evidentiary hearing and in accordance with the rules as provided for in paragraphs 5 and 11 a) through 11 g) herein. Any objections to be raised at said hearing shall be in writing and served on opposing counsel no less than 5 days in advance of said hearing.

i) The SJT Justice shall, where required, issue "So Ordered" subpoenas to secure the attendance of witnesses or the production of documents as may be requested by any party.

Rule 12. Case Presentation

a) Counsel may present summaries of evidence, factual allegations, inferences from discovery. Counsel may use photographs, diagrams, power point presentations, overhead projectors, trial notebooks, all of which can be submitted to the jury, or any other innovative method of presentation. Trial notebooks should be bifurcated in form to allow for presentation of liability and/or damages portion of summary jury trial.

b) Anything which is to be submitted to the jury as part of the presentation of the case must be exchanged with opposing counsel within the conformity of the rules concerning the presentation of case and pre-trial submissions. Counsel shall not refer to or introduce evidence which would not be admissible at trial other than as previously stated. Counsel are encouraged to stipulate to factual and evidentiary matters to the greatest extent possible.

c) No more than two witnesses for each side may be called for direct and cross-examination. On application of a party and upon good cause shown, the court may allow an increase in the number of witnesses. Time spent by counsel on direct and cross examination shall count against their allotted time for presentation of their case unless the court directs otherwise.

d) Counsel by written stipulation, may agree upon the evidence to be submitted.

Rule 13. Jury Verdict

Upon request by the jury, the Court shall give the jury a written copy of the jury charge for use during deliberations. Five out of six jurors must agree on the verdict. The verdict is to be binding as rendered or limited by a high/low stipulation. The jurors may bring into the jury room any trial notebooks, exhibits, presentations, etc. that may have been presented during the trial.

Rule 14. No Directed Verdicts

Parties agree to waive any motions for directed verdicts as well as any motions to set aside the verdict or any judgment rendered by said jury, The Court shall not set aside any verdict or any judgment entered thereon, nor shall it direct the judgment be entered in favor of a party entitled to judgment as a matter of law, nor shall it order a new trial as to any issues where the verdict is alleged to be contrary to the weight of the evidence.

Rule 15. Inconsistent Verdicts

In the case of inconsistent verdicts, the SJT Justice shall question and charge the jury as appropriate to resolve any inconsistency in said verdict.

Rule 16. Infant Plaintiff

In a summary jury trial involving an infant, the Court must approve any high/low parameters prior to trial.

Form 1. Stipulation Form

SUPREME COURT OF THE STATE OF NEW YORK
COUNTY OF SUFFOLK
................................X

	INDEX NO.
Plaintiff(s),	**STIPULATION AND ORDER TO TRANSFER ACTION TO BINDING SUMMARY JURY TRIAL PART**

-against-

Defendant(s).

................................X

[strike that which is inapplicable]

IT IS HEREBY STIPULATED AND AGREED that the parties to this action, by their respective attorneys, voluntarily agree to the transfer of this matter for final disposition to the Summary Jury Trial Part (SJT Part), for a binding summary jury trial, subject to the Rules of the SJT Part. Unless the Court directs otherwise, the Rules of the SJT Part shall govern this action and the conduct of counsel and the parties at the Summary Jury Trial scheduled herein. The signatories to this Agreement represent that they have the authority of their respective clients and/or insurance carriers to enter into this stipulation/order.

IT IS FURTHER STIPULATED AND AGREED THAT a Summary Jury Trial shall be held on the issue(s) of
☐ **liability and damages**
☐ **liability only**
☐ **damages only**

and shall be conducted on _____, at 9:00 a.m., before the SJT Justice. All parties shall be bound by the Summary Jury Trial verdict,

[except that if the verdict is more than _____, the plaintiff will recover _____.]

[except that the parties agree that there is an evaluated amount of damages in the sum of _____ Said evaluation shall be apportioned in accordance with the apportionment of liability as set forth by the jury verdict not to exceed the sum of _____.]

[except that Judgment is capped at _____ (high) and _____ (low).]

IT IS FURTHER STIPULATED AND AGREED that the right to move to set aside the verdict, or to appeal, is waived.

IT IS FURTHER STIPULATED AND AGREED that any pending motions filed with the court in this action are withdrawn and that the parties hereto agree not to file any written motions subsequent to the execution of this Stipulation.

IT IS FURTHER STIPULATED AND AGREED that counsel shall exchange all evidentiary materials to be offered at the trial of this action not later than thirty days prior to the trial date fixed by the terms of this Stipulation and Order.

IT IS FURTHER STIPULATED AND AGREED that an evidentiary hearing shall be held before the SJT Justice on _____, at which time any objections to documentary evidence previously exchanged between the parties shall be addressed by the Court and witness lists shall be exchanged. No appearance shall be necessary on the evidentiary hearing date if, prior thereto, a stipulation is executed between counsel stating that there are no objections to evidentiary materials and that witness lists have been exchanged. Counsel further agree to notify the SJT Justice that said stipulation has been executed and agree to file the original of said stipulation with the calendar clerk of the Supreme Court at 1 Court Street, Riverhead, New York 11901, on or before the evidentiary hearing date.

Attorney for Plaintiff(s)   **Attorney for Defendant(s)**

Print Name: _____   Print Name: _____

Phone Number: _____ Phone Number: _____

E–Mail: _____   E–Mail: _____

Signature: _____   Signature: _____

Attorney for Plaintiff(s)   **Attorney for Defendant(s)**

Print Name: _____   Print Name: _____

Phone Number: _____ Phone Number: _____

E–Mail: _____   E–Mail: _____

Signature: _____   Signature: _____

Dated: _____

SO ORDERED: _____
               J.S.C.

ELEVENTH JUDICIAL DISTRICT — QUEENS COUNTY

Westlaw Electronic Research

These rules may be searched electronically on Westlaw® in the NY–RULES database; updates to these rules may be found on Westlaw in NY–RULESUP-DATES. For search tips and a summary of database content, consult the Westlaw Scope Screens for each database.

CIVIL COMMITMENT/MENTAL HYGIENE

Doc.
1. Civil Commitment/Mental Hygiene

EX PARTE

1. Ex Parte Office

RESIDENTIAL FORECLOSURE

1. Residential Foreclosure Office

MATRIMONIAL OFFICE

1. Matrimonial Office (Divorce)
2. Matrimonial Office Requirements for Filing Uncontested Divorce Papers

MOTION SUPPORT

1. Motion Support Office

SPECIAL ELECTION PART

1. Election Rules

SUBPOENAED RECORDS

1. Subpoenaed Records

SURROGATE'S COURT
LOCAL FORMS

Form
1. Order Extending Preliminary Letters Testamentary
2. Cash Flow Statement
3. Petition to Examine Safe Deposit Box
4. Order to Examine Safe Deposit Box
5. Instruction for Search Order to Examine Apartment or Home
6. Petition to Examine Residence

QUEENS SURROGATE'S DECREES

Decree
1. Decree Granting Probate
2. Application for Preliminary Letters Testamentary
3. Order for Preliminary Letters Testamentary
4. Application for Temporary Letters of Administration
5. Decree Granting Ancillary Probate
6. Order Granting Temporary Letters of Administration
7. Application for Letters of Administration
8. Order Extending Temporary Letters of Administration
9. Bond Affidavit

FEES

Fees
1. Article 24 Court Fees.

QUEENS COUNTY
SUPREME CIVIL TERM
JUDGES' PART RULES
JUSTICE ALLAN B. WEISS

Part 2. Hon. Allan B. Weiss

The motion calendar will be called on WEDNESDAY at 9:30 a.m. A second call will follow shortly thereafter.

All motions are to be submitted, without oral argument except those which are, in any way, discovery related. As to discovery motions, counsel for all parties must appear, prepared to discuss and agree upon a discovery schedule. Counsel for the movant shall notify opposing counsel, in writing, of this requirement and provide the court with a copy on the return date. As to motions brought by Order to Show Cause, the movant must submit the affidavit(s) of service on the return date to the Clerk of Part 2 at the call of the motion calendar.

On the return date, all parties must submit hard courtesy copies of all papers that are electronically filed.

Use of calendar service is permitted to submit papers, and to request consent adjournments. Consent adjournments may also be obtained by stipulation faxed to chambers before the motion return date.

The court requests that the members of the bar make every effort to provide their adversaries and co-counsel with advance notice of all applications.

JUSTICE MARGUERITE A. GRAYS

Part 4. Hon. Marguerite A. Grays

NO TELEPHONE INQUIRIES CONCERNING MOTIONS OR APPLICATIONS MAY BE MADE TO CHAMBERS. All such inquiries must be made to Motion Support (718–298–1009) or to the Ex Parte Office (718–298–1018) or the Clerk of the Part (718–298–1214).

Do not make any inquires via e-mail to the court.

Preliminary Conference

A preliminary conference shall be scheduled (1) automatically by the Court within 45 days after filing a Request for Judicial Intervention, pursuant to 22 NYCRR 202.12(b); or (2) upon filing a written Request for a Preliminary Conference with the Clerk's Office, Room 140, in compliance with 22 NYCRR 202.12(a); or (3) an appropriate notice is filed in malpractice or certiorari cases pursuant to 22 NYCRR 202.56 and 202.60.

All preliminary conferences will be held on Monday at 11:30 a.m. at the Preliminary Conference Part, Room Number 314, of the courthouse, and they are presided over by the court-appointed referee, unless otherwise directed by the Court. Failure to appear at the scheduled preliminary conference may result in discovery being ordered ex-parte or any other appropriate sanction including preclusion or dismissal ordered. Any inquiry pertaining to preliminary conferences shall be made to the Preliminary Conference Part at (718) 298–1046.

Compliance Conference

For all Non-Commercial Division cases, Compliance Conferences shall be held on the date scheduled in the Preliminary Conference Stipulation and Order. Conferences shall be held before Justice Ritholtz in Courtroom 313.

For all Commercial Division cases, Compliance Conferences shall be held on the date scheduled in the Preliminary Conference Stipulation and Order. Conferences shall be held before Justice Grays in Courtroom 66. The call of the calendar will be held at 11:30 a.m.

Motions

Motions are heard on Tuesdays at 9:30 a.m. There are two calls of the calendar. The second call of the calendar will be held at 10:30 a.m.

The moving papers shall be filed in the Motion Support Office at least five business days prior to the scheduled return date in order to be placed on the Part motion calendar for the day noticed. No motion relating to disclosure will be accepted by the Clerk's Office without an affirmation of good faith as required by Uniform Rule 202.7.

The answering papers, including cross-motions, affirmations in opposition and reply affirmations, will be accepted only on the return date in the Part. THE COURT WILL NOT CONSIDER PAPERS SENT TO CHAMBERS OR TO THE PART AFTER SUBMISSION OF THE MOTION NOR CROSS MOTIONS THAT DO NOT HAVE PROOF OF PAYMENT OF THE APPROPRIATE FEE. (CPLR § 8020(a)).

Appearance of counsel and pro se litigants is MANDATORY on all disclosure motions (i.e., Motions to Vacate and Strike Note of Issue, Motions to Strike Pleadings, Motions to Preclude). The motions will be heard for all purposes in the Part on the return date.

On that date, the motion will be conferenced by the Justice or her designee with the expectation that the issues will be resolved by stipulation. Papers will not be accepted from calendar service inasmuch as a personal appearance by counsel and pro se litigants is required.

Appearance of counsel and pro se litigants is also MANDATORY on all Orders To Show Cause, and motions which seek to continue a temporary restraining order or to extend the time to file a note of issue. Papers will not be accepted from calendar service inasmuch as a personal appearance by counsel and pro se litigants is required.

Appearances are not required on any other motions except as set forth above.

Applications for adjournments on consent, or otherwise, will be entertained only at the call of the calendar, and will not be entertained by mail, fax or by telephone. Calendar service or non-attorneys will not be permitted to make applications for adjournments. Applications for an adjournment will be granted as a matter of right for the first time but for no more than three weeks. No further applications will be granted without permission of the Court. Counsel must make every effort to notify their adversaries of their intention to seek an adjournment.

Courtesy copies of moving and answering papers need not be provided.

The Court further directs that any attorney appearing on a case for any purpose MUST be familiar with the case, ready and authorized to resolve any and all issues.

Motion Papers

All motion papers submitted shall be in compliance with Uniform Rule Sec. 202.5, concerning papers filed with the court. In addition to the requirements of Sec. 202.5, all pages are to be numbered and all paragraphs are to be numbered. All exhibits are to be proceeded by a numbered exhibit tab which protrudes from the stack of papers. All submissions are to be securely fastened so as to prevent the papers from separating from each other and becoming lost. FAILURE TO COMPLY WITH THE REQUIREMENTS OF THIS SECTION MAY RESULT IN REJECTION OF THE OFFENDING SUBMISSION.

Any party annexing a deposition transcript in excess of one hundred (100) pages as an exhibit to a motion, shall submit such transcript on a disc, in lieu of paper, with the motion.

Any party who files a motion pursuant to the FBEM System ("filing By Electronic Means") only, shall provide this Court with a courtesy copy of the motion, which shall be submitted to the Part Clerk on the first noticed return date of the motion.

Decisions

Any attorney or pro se litigant desiring a copy of the Court's decision must submit a stamped, self-addressed envelope with the motion papers or at the conclusion of trial.

Trials

All counsel must submit to the court, prior to the commencement of trial, marked pleadings, copy of the bill of particulars, a witness list, exhibit list, proposed jury instruction and a proposed verdict sheet.

Motions *in Limine* - On the first appearance in the Part for trial, any party intending to make a motion *in limine* shall submit a brief written affirmation setting forth the nature of the application and any supporting statutory or case law. The party shall furnish the court with an original and one copy and provide counsel for all parties with a copy.

The trial will be conducted on a continual daily basis until conclusion.

No adjournments or delays during trial will be accepted unless exigent circumstances exist.

Counsel are reminded that for all Commercial Division cases, the parties shall comply with the relevant pre-trial conference and trial rules of 22NYCRR 202.70.

Settlements and Discontinuances

If an action is settled, discontinued or otherwise disposed of, counsel shall immediately inform the court by submission of a copy of the stipulation or a letter directed to the Clerk of the Part. All Stipulations of discontinuances must be accompanied by proof of payment for the appropriate fee. (CPLR § 8020(d)(1))

JUSTICE HOWARD G. LANE

Part 6.   Hon. Howard G. Lane

NO TELEPHONE INQUIRIES CONCERNING MOTIONS OR APPLICATIONS MAY BE MADE TO CHAMBERS. All such inquiries must be made to the Motion Support Office (718–298–1009) or to the Ex Parte Office (718–298–1018) or to the Clerk of the Part (718–298–1210).

Preliminary Conference

A preliminary conference shall be scheduled (1) automatically by the Court within 45 days after filing a Request for Judicial Intervention, pursuant to 22 NYCRR § 202.12(b), or (2) upon filing a written Request for a Preliminary Conference with the Clerk's Office, Room 140, in compliance with 22 NYCRR § 202.12 (a) or an appropriate notice is filed in malpractice or certiorari cases pursuant to 22 NYCRR §§ 202.56 and 202.60.

All preliminary conferences will be held on WEDNESDAYS at 9:30 A.M. at the Preliminary Conference Part, Room 314, of the courthouse, and they are presided over by the court-appointed referee, unless otherwise directed by the Court. Failure to appear at the scheduled preliminary conference may result in discovery being ordered ex parte or any other appropriate sanction including preclusion or dismissal ordered. Any inquiry pertaining to preliminary conferences shall be made to the Preliminary Conference Part at (718) 298–1046.

Compliance Conferences

Compliance conferences shall be held on the date scheduled in the Preliminary Conference Stipulation and Order. Conferences shall be held before Justice Ritholtz in Room 313, of the courthouse.

Motion Practice

The Motion Calendar will be called every TUESDAY at 9:30 A.M. promptly. A second call will follow at 10:00 A.M.

All motions require MANDATORY personal appearance by counsel for all parties. The motions will be heard for all purposes in the Part on the return date. On that date, the motions will be conferenced and/or orally argued at the Court's discretion with the expectation that all discovery issues will be resolved by stipulation. Papers will not be accepted from calendar service inasmuch as a personal appearance by counsel and pro se litigants is required.

Appearance of counsel and pro se litigants is also MANDATORY on all Orders to Show Cause, and motions which seek to continue a temporary restraining order or to extend the time to file a note of issue. Papers will not be accepted from calendar service inasmuch as a personal appearance by counsel and pro se litigants is required.

Discovery motions require inclusion of an affirmation of good faith, setting forth, in detail, the efforts utilized by the moving attorney to obtain discovery prior to requesting judicial intervention. Conclusory statements by the attorney or failure to demonstrate good faith efforts may result in summary denial of the discovery motion.

The Court further directs that any attorney appearing on a case for any purpose MUST be familiar with the case, ready and authorized to resolve any and all issues.

Adjournments

Motions may be adjourned on consent provided a written stipulation of counsel is submitted to the Court prior to the return or adjourn date. All stipulations must contain the signature of the attorney consenting to the adjournment. A form which contains only the name of the firm on a stipulation will not be accepted. Stipulations of adjournments will not be granted on the telephone. Stipulations may be submitted by calendar service or non-attorneys.

The members of the Bar are to make every effort to notify their adversaries and co-counsel of all applications for adjournments in advance. If consent for an adjournment cannot be obtained, an application must be made to Justice Lane by counsel on the return date. Calendar service or non-attorneys will not be permitted to make applications for adjournments.

Absent extenuating circumstances, consent adjournments will be limited to two. Thereafter, attorneys seeking further adjournments MUST APPEAR. No motion shall be adjourned more than the aggregate period of 60 days from the original return date of said motion.

DO NOT TELEPHONE CHAMBERS FOR ADJOURNMENTS.

Motion Papers

All motion papers submitted shall be in compliance with Uniform Rule § 202.5, concerning papers filed with the Court. In addition to the requirements of Section 202.5, all pages are to be numbered and all paragraphs are to be numbered. All exhibits are to be proceeded by a numbered exhibit tab which protrudes from the stack of papers. All submissions are to be securely fastened so as to prevent the papers from separating from each other and becoming lost. Failure to comply with the requirements of this section may result in rejection of the offending submission.

The answering papers, including cross motions, affirmations in opposition and reply affirmations, will be accepted only on the return date in the Part. The court will not consider papers sent to chambers or to the part after submission of the motion or cross motion(s) that do not have proof of payment of the appropriate fee. (CPLR § 8020[a]).

Trials

All counsel must submit to the Court, prior to the commencement of trial, marked pleadings, copy of the bill of particulars, a witness list, exhibit list, proposed jury instruction and a proposed verdict sheet.

Motions *in limine* - On the first appearance in the part for trial, any party intending to make a motion *in limine* shall submit a brief written affirmation setting forth the nature of the application and any supporting statutory or case law. The party shall furnish the court with an original and one copy and provide counsel for all parties with a copy.

The trial will be conducted on a continuous daily basis until conclusion. Tort actions are generally bifurcated. The Court expects that any trial on damages will follow immediately after a verdict finding the defendant liable.

No adjournments or delays during trial will be accepted unless exigent circumstances exist.

A complete copy of the Court's Rules for Trial Counsel will be furnished to trial counsel for the parties prior to trial.

Settlements and Discontinuances

If an action is settled, discontinued or otherwise disposed of, counsel shall immediately inform the court by submission of a copy of the stipulation or a letter directed to the Clerk of the Part. All stipulations of discontinuances must be accompanied by proof of payment for the appropriate fee. (CPLR § 8020[d][1]).

Electronic Filing of Legal Papers

Electronic filing is available for filing legal papers with the Court. Parties interested in electronic filing should read the materials set forth at

https://iapps.courts.state.ny.us/fbem/mainframe.html

and at the Queens County website. The rules and user's manual for electronic filing are available on this website. On the return date, all parties must submit hard copies of any motion/responsive papers that are electronically filed.

JUSTICE VALERIE BRATHWAITE NELSON

Part 7. Hon. Valerie Brathwaite Nelson

NO TELEPHONE INQUIRIES CONCERNING MOTIONS OR APPLICATIONS MAY BE MADE TO CHAMBERS. All such inquiries must be made to Motion Support at (718) 298–1009 or to the Ex Parte Office at (718) 298–1018 or to the Clerk of the Part at (718) 298–1042.

Motions

Motions are heard on Tuesdays. There are two calls of the calendar. The first call of the calendar is at 9:30 a.m. and the second call of the calendar is at 10:30 a.m.

The moving papers shall be filed in the Motion Support Office (Room 140) pursuant to Uniform Rule 202.8(b).

No motion relating to disclosure, discovery or a bill of particulars will be accepted by the Motion Support Office (Room 140) without an affirmation of good faith as required by Uniform Rule 202.7.

The answering papers, including cross-motions, affirmations in opposition and reply affirmations, will be accepted only on the return date in the Part. The Court will not consider papers forwarded to Chambers or to the Part after submission of the motion or cross motion. Additionally, the Court will not consider cross motions unless there exists proof of payment of the appropriate fee (CPLR § 8020(a)).

Appearance of all counsel and pro se litigants is MANDATORY on all DISCLOSURE MOTIONS AND DISCOVERY RELATED MOTIONS including but not limited to Motions to Vacate and Strike Note of Issue, Motions to Strike Pleadings and Motions to Preclude. The motions will be heard for all purposes in the Part on the return date. The Court directs that any attorney appearing on a case for any purpose MUST be familiar with the case, prepared and authorized to resolve any and all issues. On the return date, the motion will be conferenced by the Justice or her designee with the expectation that the issues will be resolved by stipulation. All stipulations must indicate that the motion, and where appropriate the cross-motion, is/are being withdrawn pursuant to the stipulation and must be signed by the attorneys appearing at the calendar call. The name of the firm and the attorney appearing on behalf of the firm are to be printed legibly beneath each signature. Papers will not be accepted from calendar service inasmuch as a personal appearance by counsel and pro se litigants is required.

Appearance of counsel and pro se litigants is also MANDATORY on all Orders To Show Cause and motions which seek to continue a temporary restraining order or to extend the time to file a note of issue. Papers will not be accepted from calendar service inasmuch as a personal appearance by counsel and pro se litigants is required.

Appearances are not required on any other motions except as set forth above.

Applications for adjournments on consent, or otherwise, will be entertained only at the call of the calendar and will not be entertained by mail, fax or by telephone. Calendar service or non-attorneys will not be permitted to make applications for adjournments. Absent unusual or emergency circumstances, applications for an adjournment will be granted for the first time but for no more than three (3) weeks. Opposing papers must be served on all adversaries in hand at least one week prior to the adjourned return date. Reply papers must be served at least one day prior to the adjourned return date. No further applications will be granted without permission of the Court. Counsel must make every effort to notify their adversaries of their intention to seek an adjournment.

Motions marked "FINAL" will be submitted on the return date.

Courtesy copies of moving and answering papers need not be provided to the Court.

Motion Papers

All motion papers submitted shall be in compliance with Uniform Rule 202.5 concerning papers filed with the court. In addition to the requirements of Uniform Rule 202.5, all pages are to be numbered and all paragraphs are to be numbered. All exhibits are to be preceded by a numbered or lettered exhibit tab which protrudes from the stack of papers. All submissions are to be securely fastened so as to prevent the papers from separating from each other and becoming lost. Motion papers, answering affidavits and reply affidavits which are not served in conformity with CPLR § 2214 will not be accepted. FAILURE TO COMPLY WITH THE REQUIREMENTS OF THIS SECTION MAY RESULT IN REJECTION OF THE OFFENDING SUBMISSION.

Trials

All counsel must submit to the Court, prior to the commencement of trial, marked pleadings, a copy of the bill of particulars and a witness list. Proposed jury instructions and proposed verdict sheets will be accepted for consideration if submitted prior to the commencement of testimony, unless otherwise directed by the Court.

Motions in Liminie - On the first appearance in the Part for trial, any party intending to make a Motion in Liminie shall submit a brief written affirmation setting forth the nature of the application and any supporting statutory or case law. The party shall furnish the Court with an original and one copy and provide a copy to counsel for each party.

The trial will be conducted on a continual daily basis until conclusion, unless otherwise directed by the Court.

No adjournments or delays during trial will be accepted unless exigent circumstances exist.

Settlements And Discontinuances

If an action is settled, discontinued or otherwise disposed of, counsel shall immediately inform the Court by submission of a copy of the stipulation or a letter delivered to the Clerk of the Part. All Stipulations of Discontinuances must be accompanied by proof of payment of the appropriate fee, if any (CPLR § 8020(d)(1)).

JUSTICE JAIME A. RIOS

Part 8. Hon. Jaime A. Rios
Article 75 Motions:

1. All petitions or orders to show cause relating to Uninsured/Supplementary Underinsured Automobile

Insurance arbitrations are calendared every Wednesday at 9:30 a.m. promptly. A second calendar call will follow shortly thereafter.

2. Petitions appearing on the calendar for the first time may be adjourned for submission of opposition papers. All petitions must be accompanied by affirmations or affidavits of service.

3. Personal appearance is required; however, calendar service is permitted both to submit papers and to request consent adjournments, which will be limited to two.

4. Adjournments on consent will be allowed upon written stipulation signed by all parties. All stipulations must contain the signature and printed name of the attorney or pro se litigant consenting to the adjournment. A form containing only the name of the firm on a stipulation will not be accepted.

5. All petitions previously appearing on the calendar will be calendared for a framed issue hearing or will be conferenced with the Justice or the Referee.

6. Petitions may be withdrawn by the petitioner without prejudice, with or without consent, at any time.

Orders To Show Cause:

1. Any order to show cause requires the appearance of the parties on the return date. Counsel should be prepared to discuss the merits of their argument at the Court's discretion. The movant shall provide the Court with proof of service.

2. No temporary restraining order contained in an order to show cause will be extended beyond the initial return date of the motion except upon written stipulation executed by all parties which is "so ordered" by the Court or as otherwise directed by the court.

3. If the parties or counsel cannot agree to the continuation or termination of a temporary restraining order, all counsel and any pro se litigant must appear on the return date of the motion. Failure to appear will be deemed a waiver of the defaulting party's position with respect to the continuation or termination of any temporary restraining order contained in the order to show cause.

Other Motions:

1. All motions in mortgage foreclosure proceedings and NYCTL proceedings are calendared on Wednesdays at 11:00 a.m.

2. Appearance is required on all motions.

3. Motions will be heard for all purposes on the return date at which time the Court, in its discretion, will determine whether the motion shall be submitted, adjourned, conferenced or otherwise addressed.

4. All moving papers are to be submitted through the Motion Support Office. All responsive papers are to be filed with the Clerk of the Part on the date of the calendar call. The Court will not accept "supplemental affirmations," "further affirmations," "sur-reply affirmations," or other sur-reply papers unless prior authorization has been given by the Court. Papers submitted in violation of this rule will be disregarded.

5. Motions may be withdrawn by the moving party without prejudice, with or without consent, at any time.

Condemnation Proceedings:

1. All proceedings initiated under the Eminent Domain Procedure Law are calendared every Friday at 9:30 a.m., promptly.

2. Counsel should be prepared to discuss the merits of their argument.

3. Adjournments are at the discretion of the Court.

Article 75 Trials:

1. The Trial Calendar is called every Tuesday and Thursday at 9:30 a.m.

2. Prior to any hearing, the petitioner must file a note of issue. Where the petitioner fails to file a note of issue pursuant to an intermediate order issued in the proceeding, the proceeding is subject to dismissal.

3. On the hearing date, the parties shall be prepared to furnish the court with copies of the pleadings and a stamped copy of the filed note of issue. In addition, on the hearing date the parties shall be prepared to furnish the Court with memoranda of law, cases and/or statutes which support their contentions.

4. Hearings may be held either by the Court or by the Referee where the parties stipulate to allow the Referee to hear and determine on consent.

5. Matters will be tried, to the extent possible, in chronological order as reflected by the date of the Request For Judicial Intervention.

6. Hearings shall not be continued unless permitted by the Court in extenuating circumstances.

7. Proceedings appearing on the trial calendar may be discontinued by the petitioner at any time, pursuant to a stipulation of discontinuance. The petitioner must file the stipulation of discontinuance in advance with the Clerk of Queens County and pay the requisite filing fee.

Other

1. Counsel are not to call chambers to request adjournments. Stipulations of adjournment may be faxed to chambers.

2. Counsel are to make every effort to notify their adversaries and co-counsel of all applications for adjournments in advance.

3. At the motion or trial calendar call, the Court will choose the date for all adjournments. The Court will usually be unable to honor dates chosen by the parties.

4. No adjournments will be granted over the telephone.

JUSTICE PHYLLIS ORLIKOFF FLUG

Part 9. Hon. Phyllis O. Flug

Preliminary Conference

A preliminary conference will take place only after a written request is filed with the Clerk's Office in compliance with Uniform Rule 202.12(a) or upon a specific directive of the Justice. All preliminary conferences are held at Queens Supreme Court, Room 314. Conferences are held on Tuesdays at 9:30 a.m.

Motions:

Motions are heard on Tuesdays at 9:30 a.m. There are two calls of the calendar. The second call will be held following the completion of the first call.

Moving papers shall be filed in the IAS Motion Support Office at least seven (7) business days prior to the scheduled return date in order to be placed on the Part motion calendar for the day noticed.

The answering papers, including cross-motion, affirmations in opposition and reply affirmation, will be accepted only on the return date in the Part.

No motion relating to discovery will be accepted by the Clerk's Office without an affirmation of good faith as required by Uniform Rule 202.7.

No motion relating to discovery shall be made prior to the holding of both a preliminary and compliance conference and proof that such conferences were held shall be attached to the motion.

Appearance of counsel is mandatory on all discovery motions including motions to vacate, motions to strike the note of issue, motions to strike pleadings, motions to compel, and motions to preclude.

All discovery motions shall be heard and conferenced by the Justice or her designee on the return date of the motion and with the expectation that the issues will be resolved by stipulation. Failure of the moving party to appear on the return date or submit a "So-Ordered" Stipulation settling the issues and withdrawing the motion, will result in the motion being marked off the calendar.

Appearances of the parties are also required wherein an application will be made to impose or continue a temporary restraining order or to extend the time to file a note of issue. The Court will not accept a "So-Ordered" Stipulation extending the time to file a note of issue. It must be done by motion practice.

Appearances are not required on any other motions, and oral argument will not be entertained.

Applications for adjournments without consent will only be entertained at the calendar call. Stipulations signed by all parties will be entertained at the calendar call or by fax to be received by Chambers no later than the Friday before the return date at 4:00 p.m.

Initial applications for an adjournment will be granted as a matter of right, but for no more than three weeks. A second application for adjournment may be made in person or by stipulation, but will be granted at the Court's discretion. No further applications will be granted without permission of the court and, even if agreed to be all parties, will be entertained at the calendar call only.

Questions on motions will be entertained after the call of the calendar. Ex parte communications with chambers will not be entertained.

JUSTICE KEVIN J. KERRIGAN

Part 10. Hon. Kevin J. Kerrigan

No telephone inquiries concerning motions or applications shall be made to chambers.

All such inquiries must be made to the Motion Support Office (718-298-1009), the Ex Parte Office (718-298-1018) or the Clerk of Part 10 (718-298-1172).

Preliminary Conferences

A preliminary conference shall be scheduled (1) automatically by the court within 45 days after filing a Request for Judicial Intervention, pursuant to 22 NYCRR 202.12(b), or upon filing a written Request for a Preliminary Conference with the Clerk's Office, Room 140, in compliance with 22 NYCRR 202.12(a) or

an appropriate notice is filed in malpractice or certiorari cases pursuant to 22 NYCRR 202.56 and 202.60.

All preliminary conferences shall be held on TUESDAYS at 11:30 a.m. at the Preliminary Conference Part, Room Number 314 of the courthouse, and they are presided over by the court-appointed referee, unless otherwise directed by the court. Failure to appear at the scheduled preliminary conference may result in discovery being ordered ex-parte or any other appropriate sanction including preclusion or dismissal.

Compliance Conference

Compliance conferences shall be held on the date scheduled in the Preliminary Conference Stipulation and Order. Compliance conferences shall be held before Justice Martin Ritholtz in Room 313.

Any inquiry pertaining to a conference shall be made to the Compliance Conference Part at 718–298–1093.

Trials

All counsel must submit to the court, prior to the commencement of trial, marked pleadings, copy of the bill of particulars, a witness list, proposed jury instructions and a proposed verdict sheet.

Motions *in Limine* - On the first appearance in the Part for trial, any party intending to make a motion *in limine* shall submit a brief written affirmation setting forth the nature of the application and any supporting statutory or case law. The party shall furnish the court with an original and one copy and provide counsel for all parties with a copy.

The trial will be conducted on a continual daily basis until conclusion.

No adjournments or delays during trial will be accepted unless exigent circumstances arise.

Settlements and Discontinuances

If an action is settled, discontinued or otherwise disposed of, counsel shall immediately inform the court by submission of a copy of the stipulation or a letter directed to the Clerk of the Part. All Stipulations of discontinuances must be accompanied by proof of payment for the appropriate fee. (CPLR § 8020(d)(1)).

Any inquiry pertaining to a preliminary conference shall be made to the Preliminary Conference Part at 718–298–1046.

Motion Practice

The motion calendar will be called every Tuesday at 9:30 a.m. promptly. A second calendar call will follow shortly thereafter.

Appearance of counsel and pro se litigants is mandatory on all motions. Mandatory appearance is required by counsel with knowledge of the case and with full authority to settle or enter into binding stipulations on the return date.

On the return date, motions will be conferenced and/or orally argued at the discretion of the court.

Do not call Part 10 or Chambers for adjournments as NO ADJOURNMENTS WILL BE GRANTED BY TELEPHONE.

Motions may be adjourned on consent provided a written stipulation of counsel is submitted to the Court prior to the return or adjourn date. All stipulations must contain the signature of the attorney consenting to the adjournment. A form which contains only the name of the firm on the stipulation will not be accepted. Stipulations must also contain a schedule for exchange of opposition and reply papers occurring prior to the adjourn date. Stipulations may be submitted by calendar service or non-attorneys.

If consent for an adjournment cannot be obtained, an application must be made to Justice Kerrigan by counsel on the return date. Calendar service or non-attorneys will not be permitted to make applications for adjournments.

Under normal circumstances, no motion will be adjourned more than twice. Motions relating to discovery may be adjourned only once.

Answering and reply papers will be accepted only on the return date in the Part. The Court will not consider papers sent to Chambers or the Part after submission. Papers will not be accepted from calendar service if a personal appearance by counsel is required. Courtesy copies of papers are NOT required.

Motion Papers and Ex–Parte Applications

All motions and ex-parte applications submitted shall be in compliance with Uniform Rule § 202.5. In addition to these requirements, all pages and paragraphs must be numbered. All exhibits are to be proceeded by a numbered exhibit tab which protrudes from the stack of papers. All submissions are to be securely fastened so as to prevent the papers from being lost. FAILURE TO COMPLY WITH THE REQUIREMENTS OF THIS SECTION MAY RESULT IN REJECTION OF THE OFFENDING SUBMISSION.

Electronic Filing of Legal Papers

Parties interested in electronic filing should read materials set forth at www.nycourts.gov/efile and the Uniform Rules for Trial Courts §202.5-b.

Where motion/responsive papers, including exhibits and memoranda of law, are filed by electronic means pursuant to Uniform rule §202.5-b, courtesy hard copies of such papers shall be submitted to the Court on the return/adjourned date of the motion. No motion/responsive papers shall be considered unless courtesy hard copies are submitted to the Court on the return/adjourned date of the motion. Each submitted hard copy shall bear a conspicuous notice on the first page thereof that the document has been filed electronically (Uniform rule §202.5-b[d][4]).

The Court's rules concerning motion papers shall apply to courtesy hard copies submitted to the Court. Appearance of counsel is mandatory on all e-filed motions. All other motion practice rules of this part, as well as all rules regarding motion papers and ex-parte applications are applicable to e-filed motions.

Any order, judgment or stipulation that requires the judge's signature shall be submitted in hard copy to the court.

JUSTICE SIDNEY F. STRAUSS

Part 11.   Hon. Sidney F. Strauss

General Rules:

THE COURT WILL NOT ENTERTAIN CONFERENCE CALLS

Use of calendar service is permitted to submit papers including stipulations for adjournments.

Preliminary Conference

Preliminary Conferences for Part 11 will be held on Wednesdays at 11:30 a.m. at the Preliminary Conference Part, Room 314. Any inquiry pertaining to Preliminary Conferences shall be made to the Preliminary Conference part at (718) 298–1046.

Compliance Conference:

Shall be held on the date scheduled in the Preliminary Conference Stipulation and Order and shall be held before the Hon. Justice Ritholtz in courtroom 313. Any inquiry pertaining to Compliance Conferences shall be made to that part at (718) 298–1093.

Motions:

Motions for Part 11 are returnable on Wednesdays at 9:30 a.m. in Courtroom 26. A second call will follow shortly thereafter and will be called continuously until all cases are completed.

Answering papers, including cross-motions, affirmations in opposition and reply affirmations will be accepted only on the return date in the part. Sur-replies will not be considered. Courtesy copies of moving and answering papers need not be provided.

The Movant's failure to appear on a motion will result in the motion being marked off the calendar.

MANDATORY appearance is required by pro se litigants and/or counsel with knowledge of the case and with full authority to settle or enter into binding stipulations on the return date.

Applications for adjournments without consent will only be entertained at the calendar call.

DO NOT CALL CHAMBERS FOR ADJOURNMENTS

Motions may be adjourned on consent provided that the Part is first contacted to ascertain available dates (718–298–1215). Following the selection of a date, a written stipulation shall be faxed to 718–298–1131 at least 24 hours before the return date. All stipulations must contain the signature of the attorney consenting to the adjourn date. Calendar service or non-attorneys (excluding pro-se litigants) will not be permitted to make applications for adjournments. Pro se litigants and/or counsel are to make every effort to notify their adversaries of all applications for adjournments in advance.

Oral argument will granted upon application to the court.

Affirmation of Need: The court may, in its discretion, require an Affirmation of Need prior to the filing of any motion or Order to Show Cause. Such affirmation should indicate why resort to written motion is necessary to obtain the requested relief, the attempts made to settle the matter without resort to written motion and, if applicable, the necessity to calendar a motion on an active case before the next adjourned date. Failure to submit such affirmation will result in the accompanying application being dismissed without prejudice.

Motion Papers:

All motion papers submitted shall be in compliance with Uniform Rule sec. 202.5. In addition, all exhibits are to be preceded by a numbered exhibit tab which protrudes from the stack of papers. All submissions are to be securely fastened so as to prevent papers from separating and becoming lost. FAILURE TO COMPLY WITH THE REQUIREMENTS OF THIS SECTION MAY RESULT IN REJECTION OF THE PAPERS.

The Court will not consider papers handed up after the motion submission date.

Decisions:

Copies of decisions are faxed and/or mailed to the parties and/or their counsel.

Trials:

All counsel MUST submit to the court, prior to the commencement of the trial

1. marked pleadings

2. copy of the bill of particulars

3. A statement, joint if possible, of relevant facts that are not in dispute

4. witness list

5. proposed jury instruction

6. proposed verdict sheet.

Motions in limine - on the first appearance in the part for trial any party intending to make a motion in limine shall submit a brief written affirmation setting forth the nature of the application and any supporting statutory or case law. The party shall furnish the court with an original and provide counsel to all parties with a copy.

No adjournments or delays during trial will be accepted unless exigent circumstances exist.

The trial will be conducted on a continual daily basis until conclusion.

Settlements and Discontinuances:

If an action is settled, discontinued or otherwise disposed of, counsel shall inform the court IMMEDI-ATELY by submission of a copy of the stipulation or a letter directed to the Clerk of the Part.

JUSTICE DENIS J. BUTLER

Part 12. Hon. Denis J. Butler

Preliminary Conference

A preliminary conference shall be scheduled automatically by the Court within forty-five (45) after filing a Request for Judicial Intervention, pursuant to 22 NYCRR 202.12(b); or upon filing a written Request for a Preliminary Conference with the Jamaica Clerk's Office, Room 140, in compliance with 22 NYCRR 202.12(a); or an appropriate notice is filed in malpractice or certiorari cases pursuant to 22 NYCRR 202.56 and 202.60.

All preliminary conferences will be held on Thursdays at 9:30 a.m. at the Preliminary Conference Part, Room 314 at the Jamaica courthouse located at 88–11 Sutphin Blvd., Jamaica, NY, and are presided over by the court-appointed Referee, unless otherwise directed by the Court. Failure to appear at the scheduled preliminary conference may result in discovery being ordered ex-parte or any other appropriate sanction, including preclusion or dismissal ordered. Any inquiry pertaining to preliminary conferences shall be made to the Preliminary Conference Part at (718) 298–1046.

Compliance Conferences

Conferences shall be held before Justice Ritholtz in Room 313 at the Jamaica courthouse.

Compliance conferences shall be held on the date scheduled in the Preliminary Conference Order. Any inquiry pertaining to compliance conferences shall be made to the Compliance Conference Part at 718–298–1093.

Motion Practice

The Motion Calendar for Justice Butler will be called in Courtroom 42 of the Jamaica Supreme Court Courthouse located at 88–11 Sutphin Blvd, Jamaica, NY 11435, every Wednesday at 9:30 AM. PROMPTLY.

MANDATORY APPEARANCE IS REQUIRED by counsel with knowledge of the case and with full authority to settle or enter into binding stipulations on the return date. In the case of e-filed motions, a hard copy must be submitted to the Court on the return date.

On the return date, motions will be conferenced and/or orally argued at the discretion of the Court.

DO NOT CALL CHAMBERS FOR ADJOURNMENTS.

Motions may be adjourned on consent provided a written stipulation of counsel is submitted to the Court on the return date. All stipulations must contain the signature of the attorney consenting to the adjournment. A form which contains only the name of the firm on the stipulation will not be accepted. Stipulations must also contain a schedule for exchange of opposition and reply papers occurring prior to the adjourned date. If consent for an adjournment cannot be obtained, an application must be made to Justice Butler by counsel on the return date. Calendar service or non-attorneys will not be permitted to make applications for adjournment. Counsel are expected to notify their adversaries of their intention to seek an adjournment.

Adjournments will be limited to two, absent extenuating circumstances. The answering papers, including cross motions, affirmations in opposition and reply affirmations, will be accepted only on the return or adjourned date in the Part. The court will not consider papers sent to Chambers or to the Part after full submission of the motion or cross motion(s). Nor will it accept cross-motions that do not have proof of payment of the appropriate fee. (CPLR § 8020[a]).

All motions and ex-parte applications submitted shall be in compliance with Uniform Rule § 202.5. In addition to these requirements, all pages and paragraphs must be numbered. All exhibits are to be preceded by a numbered exhibit tab which protrudes from the stack of papers. All submissions are to be securely fastened so as to prevent the papers from being lost. Failure to comply with the requirements of this section may result in rejection of the non-complying papers.

All inquiries to case or calendar status are to be made to the appropriate clerk's office.

IAS Motion Support Office (718) 298–1009
Ex-Parte Support Office (718) 298–1018

Infant's Compromise Orders

Before submission of an infant's compromise order, counsel shall obtain from the Clerk of Part 12 an infant's compromise checklist to ensure the submission of all necessary information and documentation. Infant's compromise orders sent to chambers without the required completed worksheet will be returned to counsel.

Proof of payment of any appropriate fee is required.

Infant compromise hearings will be scheduled by the Court and the plaintiff will be informed of the hearing date by mail.

Uncontested Matrimonials

Any corrections to a rejected set of matrimonial papers must be submitted to the Part Clerk in person, in the Jamaica Courthouse, Courtroom 42. Do not mail papers to the Court.

This Court takes seriously its duty to protect children in calculating child support. Unsupported deviations from the guidelines will result in rejections and thus slow down the sought-after judgment of divorce. Deviations from child support guidelines must be thoroughly explained in an affidavit of the party, without resorting to conclusory language, and in the attorney's affirmation.

Trials

Plaintiff's counsel shall requisition the file to the Part 12 courtroom immediately after assignment of the case to this Part. Counsel should ascertain the availability of all witnesses and subpoenaed documents. Any special needs, e.g., interpreter, easels, blackboards, shadow boxes, television, subpoenaed material, etc., must be reported to the Court Officer, in advance, so as not to delay the progress of the trial.

All counsel must submit to the Court, prior to the commencement of trial, marked pleadings, a copy of the bill of particulars, a witness list, exhibit list, proposed jury instruction and a proposed jury verdict sheet. Counsel must also know the availability of all witnesses who they intend to call during trial.

With regard to suggested jury charges and a suggested verdict questionnaire, amendments thereto shall be permitted at the final charge conference. Jury charges should be referred to by PJI number and topic. If any changes to the PJI are suggested, then the entire proposed charge should be set forth and the changes should be highlighted. Citations to appropriate statutory or common law authority must be given in support of suggested non-PJI jury charges or suggested PJI modifications.

To the extent any part of a deposition is to be read into evidence (as distinguished from mere use on cross-examination) counsel must, in advance, provide the Court and your adversary with the page and line numbers of all such testimony, so that all objections may be addressed prior to use before the jury.

Pre-trial conferences will be held prior to every trial.

At this conference counsel should be prepared to:

1. Discuss settlement;

2. Advise the Court as to all anticipated disputed issues of law and fact, and provide the Court with copies of all statutory and common law authority upon which counsel will rely;

3. Stipulate to undisputed facts and the admissibility of clearly admissible documents and records;

4. Advise the Court of any anticipated in limine motions or evidentiary objections which counsel intends to make. Motions in limine may be made orally, however they must be supported by a memorandum of law. Any written motions in limine require proof of payment of the appropriate fee. Counsel shall provide the Court and all parties with copies. All prior decisions and orders relevant to any in limine application must be provided to the Court.

5. Advise the Court of any anticipated requests for a jury instruction relating to missing witnesses and/or documents;

6. Advise the Court of any anticipated request for apportionment as to alleged culpable non-parties pursuant to CPLR Article 16.

7. Discuss scheduling and the estimated length of the trial. Counsel should alert the Court as to any anticipated problems regarding the attendance at trial of parties, attorneys or essential witnesses and any other practical problems that the Court should consider in scheduling.

The trial will be conducted on a continual daily basis until its conclusion. No adjournments or delays during trial will be accepted, unless exigent circumstances exist.

Tort actions are generally bifurcated. The Court expects, that any trial on damages will follow immediately after a verdict finding the defendant liable.

The Court encourages trial exhibits be pre-marked for identification and, where possible, that parties stipulate to the admissibility of clearly admissible documents and records.

Counsel should alert the Court, at the pre-trial conference, as to any anticipated problems regarding the attendance at trial of parties, attorneys or essential witnesses and any other practical problems that the Court should consider in scheduling.

Settlements and Discontinuances

If an action is settled, discontinued or otherwise disposed of, counsel shall immediately inform the Court by submission of a copy of the stipulation of settlement or a letter directed to the Clerk of the Part. All stipulations of discontinuances must be accompanied by proof of payment of the appropriate fee. (CPLR § 8020(d)(1).)

JUSTICE PETER J. O'DONOGHUE

Part 13.   Hon. Peter J. O'Donoghue

MEDICAL MALPRACTICE CONFERENCE AND TRIAL RULES

Post Note Cases are assigned to this Part upon filing the Note of Issue. Upon assignment an initial pre-trial conference shall be scheduled. Calendars are published in the New York Law Journal, E–Law and www.nycourts.gov approximately three weeks prior to the initial conference. Follow-up conferences or hearings shall be scheduled at the initial conference.

At All Conferences: Counsel must be fully familiar with the file and have authority to discuss settlement, trial scheduling and any outstanding pre-trial procedural matters including CPLR 3101(d) matters and to make binding stipulations and commitments. All cases shall be conferenced by the Court. At the conference the Court shall also consider the items set forth in 22 NYCRR 202.26(c). Parties shall comply fully with the requirements of 22 NYCRR 202.26(e).

Initial Pre–Trial Conferences:

(a) In order to provide for a meaningful settlement discussion at the initial conference defense counsel at the time of service of the Note of Issue shall notify the defendant and the insurance carrier, if any, of the anticipated date of the conference (approximately one month post-note) and that at least two weeks prior to the initial conference the defense shall be required to indicate to a plaintiff's attorney whether or not the defendant has refused to consent to a settlement or whether or not the defense has an interest in entering into settlement discussions. Any committee meetings or internal consultations required to make such a decision shall be held a sufficient time prior to the conference for a decision to be made at least two weeks prior to the conference. At least two weeks prior to the calendar date for the conference plaintiff's attorney shall initiate a telephone conference with defense counsel. Unless defense counsel states that his or her client has refused to consent to settlement or that the insurance carrier has marked the case "no pay", plaintiff's counsel shall convey a settlement demand at that time. Defense counsel shall discuss this demand with the claims representative prior to the calendar date. The claims representative shall either be present at the conference or available for immediate telephone consultation. If plaintiff is represented by trial counsel without full settlement authority, the attorney of record shall be present or available for immediate telephone consultation.

(b) At the conference plaintiff's counsel shall provide the Court with a courtesy copy of the "Notice of Medical, Dental and Podiatric Malpractice Action" previously served pursuant to 22 NYCRR 202.56 and copies of Preliminary Conference and Compliance Conference orders.

CPLR 3101(d):

Counsel's attention is called to the case of *Thomas v. Alleyne*, (302 A.D.2d 36, 752 N.Y.S.2d 362, Second Dept. December 2002) for the applicable standard for disclosure and protective orders under CPLR 3101(d).

MOTION PRACTICE:

Summary Judgment Motions:

Summary judgment motions shall be made within 120 days after the filing of the Note of Issue. No extensions of time to file a summary judgment motion shall be granted unless "good cause" is shown. Failure to conduct depositions does not constitute "good cause". All motions to restore cases to the active trial calendar will require mandatory appearances.

Motion Calendar:

The motion calendar will be called every Wednesday at 9:30 a.m. promptly. A second call will follow at 10:30 a.m. All (a) Orders to Show Cause and (b) motions relating to (1) any phase of discovery and/or bill of particulars including motions to preclude, strike or restore a case to the Trial Calendar, and/or vacate the Note of Issue; (2) contempt; (3) summary judgment and (4) requesting Article 78 relief requires personal appearance by counsel for all parties. Counsel shall be prepared to discuss and agree upon a discovery schedule. All other motions and applications may be submitted on papers only.

Oral argument will be entertained only in the court's discretion. Whenever a personal appearance is not required use of calendar service is permitted both to submit papers and to request counsel adjournments, which will be limited to two. The Court further directs that any attorney appearing on a case for any purpose must be familiar with the case, ready, and authorized to resolve any and all issues.

ADJOURNMENTS:

Motion Calendar:

The first adjournment on consent will be allowed upon written stipulation. All stipulations must contain the printed name and signature of the attorney consenting to the adjournment. A form which contains only the name of the firm on the stipulation will not be accepted. Thereafter, attorneys seeking a further adjournment must appear. In any event, adjournments will be limited to two absent extenuating circumstances. Do not call the Part or Chambers for adjournments as no adjournments will be granted on the telephone. Use service or mail. The members of the Bar are to make every effort to notify their adversaries and co-counsel of all applications for adjournments in advance.

Conference Calendar:

With respect to conferences scheduled for the first time one adjournment by stipulation shall be permitted.

Trial Calendar:

No adjournments by stipulation on the Medical Malpractice Trial Calendar shall be granted. Requests for an adjournment must be made in person at the call of the calendar.

ON MEDICAL MALPRACTICE CASES THE COURT WILL NOT ACCEPT EX–PARTE COMMUNICATIONS WRITTEN OR ORAL. NO FAX-

ES WILL BE ACCEPTED BY THIS OFFICE AT ANY TIME UNLESS REQUESTED BY THE COURT.

PART 13 - IAS RULES

All telephone inquires concerning matters pending in IAS Part 13, Civil Term of the Supreme Court, County of Queens, Honorable Peter J. O'Donoghue presiding, shall be made directly to the Part at telephone number (718) 298–1123. Contact with chambers shall not be made unless so directed after contacting the Part at the above listed telephone number.

Preliminary Conferences

A preliminary conference shall be scheduled (1) automatically by the Court within 45 days after filing a Request for Judicial Intervention, pursuant to 22 NYCRR 202.12(b), or (2) upon filing a written Request for a Preliminary Conference with the Clerk's Office, Room 140, in compliance with 22 NYCRR 202.12(a) or an appropriate notice is filed in malpractice or certiorari cases pursuant to 22 NYCRR 202.56 and 202.60.

All preliminary conferences will be held on TUESDAYS at 9:30 a.m. at the Preliminary Conference Part, Room 314 of the courthouse, and they are presided over by the court-appointed referee, unless otherwise directed by the Court. Failure to appear at the scheduled preliminary conference may result in discovery being ordered ex-parte or any other appropriate sanction including preclusion or dismissal ordered. Any inquiry pertaining to preliminary conferences shall be made to the Preliminary Conference Part at (718) 298–1046.

Compliance Conferences

Compliance conferences shall be held on the date scheduled in the Preliminary Conference Stipulation and Order. Conferences shall be held before Justice Ritholtz in Room 313.

Motion Practice

The Motion Calendar will be called every Wednesday at 9:30 a.m. promptly. A second call will follow at 10:30 a.m. All (a) Orders to Show Cause and (b) motions relating to (1) any phase of discovery and/or bill of particulars including motions to preclude, strike or restore a case to the Trial Calendar, and/or vacate the Note of Issue; (2) contempt; (3) summary judgment and (4) requesting Article 78 relief requires personal appearance by counsel for all parties. Counsel shall be prepared to discuss and agree upon a discovery schedule. All other motions and applications may be submitted on papers only.

Oral argument will be entertained only in the court's discretion. Whenever a personal appearance is not required use of calendar service is permitted both to submit papers and to request counsel adjournments, which will be limited to two. The first adjournment on consent will be allowed upon written stipulation. All stipulations must contain the printed name and signature of the attorney consenting to the adjournment. A form which contains only the name of the firm on the stipulation will not be accepted. Thereafter, attorneys seeking a further adjournment must appear. In any event, adjournments will be limited to two absent extenuating circumstances. Do not call the Part or Chambers for adjournments as no adjournments will be granted on the telephone. Use service or mail. The members of the Bar are to make every effort to notify their adversaries and co-counsel of all applications for adjournments in advance.

Motion Practice: Summary Judgment Motions: Summary judgment motions shall be made within 120 days after the filing of the Note of Issue. No extensions of time to file a summary judgment motion shall be granted unless "good cause" is shown. Failure to conduct depositions does not constitute "good cause". All motions to restore cases to the active trial calendar will require mandatory appearances.

The Court further directs that any attorney appearing on a case for any purpose must be familiar with the case, ready, and authorized to resolve any and all issues.

ON IAS CASES THE COURT WILL NOT ACCEPT EX–PARTE COMMUNICATIONS WRITTEN OR ORAL. NO FAXES WILL BE ACCEPTED BY THIS OFFICE AT ANY TIME UNLESS REQUESTED BY THE COURT.

JUSTICE DAVID ELLIOT

Part 14. Hon. David Elliot

All inquiries as to case or calendar status are to be made to the appropriate clerk's office.

IAS Motion Support Office (718)

Ex-Parte Support Office (718) 298–1018

Preliminary Conferences

A preliminary conference shall be scheduled (1) automatically by the Court within 45 days after filing a Request for Judicial Intervention, pursuant to 22 NYCRR 202.12(b); or (2) upon filing a written Request for a Preliminary Conference with the Clerk's Office, Room 140, in compliance with 22 NYCRR 202.12(a); or (3) an appropriate notice is filed in malpractice or certiorari cases pursuant to 22 NYCRR 202.56 and 202.60.

All preliminary conferences will be held on Wednesdays at 9:30 A.M. at the Preliminary Conference Part, Room 314, of the courthouse, and they are presided over by the court-appointed referee, unless otherwise directed by the Court. Failure to appear at the scheduled preliminary conference may result in discovery being ordered ex-parte or any other appropriate sanction including preclusion or dismissal ordered. Any inquiry pertaining to preliminary conferences shall be made to the Preliminary Conference Part at (718) 298–1046.

Compliance Conference

Compliance conferences shall be held on the date scheduled in the Preliminary Conference Stipulation and Order. Conferences shall be held before Justice Ritholtz in Room 313.

Motion Practice

The Motion Calendar will be called every TUESDAY at 9:30 A.M. PROMPTLY. A second call will follow at 10:30 A.M. No courtesy copies to chambers are required EXCEPT when papers are filed by e-filing. When papers are filed by e-filing, courtesy copies MUST be delivered to the Part 14 Clerk prior to the submission of the motion to the court for determination.

All motions relating to any phase of discovery including motions to strike or restore a case to the Trial Calendar, require personal appearance by counsel for all parties. Counsel should be prepared to discuss and agree upon a discovery schedule. If the motion has been brought by an Order to Show Cause, all parties MUST appear on the return date. The moving party must appear on all motions relating to actions for foreclosure. All other motions and applications may be submitted on papers only. All exhibits annexed to motion papers shall be preceded by numbered exhibit tabs.

Oral argument will be entertained only in the Court's discretion.

Whenever a personal appearance is not required, use of calendar service is permitted both to submit papers and to request consent adjournments which will be limited to two and will not exceed three weeks each. Adjournments on consent will be allowed upon written stipulation. All stipulations must contain the signature of the attorney consenting to the adjournment. A form bearing only the name of the firm will not be accepted. Thereafter, attorneys seeking a further adjournment MUST APPEAR at the calendar call. Adjournments will be limited to two, absent extenuating circumstances.

Please do not call the Part or Chambers for adjournments as NO adjournments will be granted on the telephone. Use service or mail. The members of the Bar are to make every effort to notify their adversaries and co-counsel of all applications for adjournments in advance.

The Court will not consider papers sent to Chambers or the Part after submission.

The Court further directs that any attorney appearing on a case for any purpose must be familiar with the case, ready and authorized to resolve any and all issues.

Trials

All counsel must submit to the court, prior to the commencement of trial, marked pleadings, a copy of the bill of particulars, a witness list, an exhibit list, proposed jury instructions and a proposed verdict sheet.

Motions *in Limine*—On the first appearance in the Part for trial, any party intending to make a motion *in limine* shall submit a brief written affirmation setting forth the nature of the application and any supporting statutory or case law. The party shall furnish the court with an original and one copy and provide counsel for all parties with a copy.

No adjournments or delays during trial will be accepted unless exigent circumstances exist.

Settlements and Discontinuances

If an action is settled, discontinued or otherwise disposed of, counsel shall immediately inform the court by submission of a copy of the stipulation or a letter directed to the Clerk of the Part. All Stipulations of Discontinuances must be accompanied by proof of payment of the appropriate fee. [CPLR § 802(d)(1)].

JUSTICE JANICE A. TAYLOR

Part 15. Hon. Janice A. Taylor

Absent exigent circumstances, or an emergency, telephones calls will be entertained by chambers only on Mondays or Fridays from 10:00 am until 1:00 pm and 2:00 pm until 4:00 pm. No calls concerning pending matters will be entertained without all attorneys and pro se litigants on a conference call with chambers, other than for scheduling purposes. Letters which require action, or which have not been copied to all parties or their attorneys, if they have one, will not be entertained.

Preliminary Conference

A Preliminary Conference will only take place (1) after written Request for a Preliminary Conference is filed with the Clerk's Office (Room 140) in compliance with Uniform 202.12(a) (or an appropriate notice is filed in malpractice, or certiorari case pursuant to Uniform Rules § 202.56, § 202.16 and § 202.60), or (2) upon a specific directive by Justice JANICE A. TAYLOR. Preliminary conferences in Justice Taylor's cases will be held on Tuesdays before Referee Elizabeth Yablon in the Referee Part.

Orders to Show Cause, Ex Parte Applications

Orders to Show Cause must comply with Uniform Rule 202.7(d) and be brought to the Ex- Part Support Office (Room 140) prior to Judicial review, signature and fixing of a return date. A correct fax number must be listed on the moving papers. Following review and signature or denial by the Justice, a notice to that effect will be faxed to the petitioner or movant. A personal appearance is required for all Orders to Show Cause containing a TRO. Proof of service of Orders to Show Cause and Ex Parte Applications must be submitted on the initial return date set by the Court, and no adjournments for that purpose will be granted.

Motion Procedure

Justice Taylor's regular motion day is TUESDAY. The first call of the calendar is at 9:30 A.M. sharp. The second call is at 10:00 A.M.

Unless otherwise directed by the Justice presiding, all motions shall be made returnable in the Part 15, Courtroom 44 on the above-specified day and time of the week and be subject to the following procedures.

Moving papers, with an affidavit of good faith where required by Uniform Rule 202.7, shall be filed in the IAS Motion Support Office (Room 140) at least five business days prior to the scheduled return date in order to be placed on the Part motion calendar for that day. Do not send, hand-deliver, mail or over-night moving papers to chambers. Motions may be withdrawn, without prejudice, by the moving party, with or without consent, at any time.

Answering papers will be accepted only during the two calendar calls on the return date in Courtroom 44. Do not mail or forward opposition, answering or re-sponsive papers to Chambers. "Supplemental" affir-mations, "further" affirmations, "sur-reply" affirma-tions and "amended" applications will not be accepted or considered. Cross-motions must be timely filed pursuant to the C.P.L.R. along with proof of payment of the statutory motion fee in order to be accepted and considered. Cross-motions will be considered respon-sive in nature. Motions marked "final" will be taken on submission on the "final" return date with all papers which have been received by that date, without further adjournment. No papers will be accepted by chambers or considered by the Court after the motion is marked "submitted" at the calendar call on the return date, unless all parties so stipulate either in writing or by telephone conference.

The motion will be heard for all purposes in the Part on the return date. On that date, the motion will be submitted, adjourned (see below), or conferenced by the Justice, or her designee, or otherwise treated pursuant to the discretion of the Justice. (Ruling on applications will also be made at this time.) Courtesy copies of moving and answering papers need not be provided.

Discovery–Related Motions

(All motions related to discovery, including, but not limited to, motions to compel discovery [C.P.L.R. § 3124], punish for failure to disclose [C.P.L.R. § 3126], strike actions from the calendar for want of discovery or for a protective order [C.P.L.R. § 3103].)

A mandatory appearance on discovery-related mo-tions is required by all parties knowledgeable about the case and fully authorized to settle or enter into binding stipulations. Discovery-related motions will be dismissed for no appearance by the movant, and responsive papers stricken for lack of appearance by the opposing party. Answering papers and consent adjournments will not be accepted from calendar ser-vice in lieu of a personal appearance by counsel. The Court strongly encourages parties to resolve discov-ery-related motions by stipulation, which will then be "so-ordered" by the Court. Unresolved discovery-related motions will be conferenced by the Justice, or her designee, at the completion of the second call of the calendar

Appearances and Adjournments

All other motions, other than discovery-relation mo-tions (see above), will be SUBMITTED for determina-tion, and appearance by counsel or a pro-se litigant is not required. Service will be permitted to answer the calendar on all non-discovery related motions solely for the purpose of submitting papers. Oral argument will be entertained on Orders to Show Cause contain-ing a TRO, and in other extraordinary circumstances, at the discretion of the Justice. Requests for oral argument must be made by stating "Oral Argument Requested" in bold caps above the words "Notice of Motion" in the moving papers.

Consent adjournments will be upon submission of a stipulation, dated, and personally signed by the attor-neys for all parties (print attorney's name below sig-nature). The stipulation should state that the matter is being adjourned "to a date convenient to the Court", and faxed to chambers (718) 520–6442 no latter than 5:00 P.M. on the day prior to the return date. The Court will choose the adjourned date for all adjournments, and cannot honor dates chosen by the parties due to scheduling constraints. If the adjourn-ment is not on consent, it must be on application to the Court on the return date - NO ADJOURN-MENTS, NOT ON CONSENT, SHALL BE PER-MITTED ON ANY MOTION IN AN ACTION UN-LESS DIRECTED BY THE JUSTICE AFTER PERSONAL APPEARANCE AND APPLICATION MADE BY COUNSEL.

Except for threshold motions pursuant to Insurance Law § 5102, in no event shall more than TWO (2) adjournments be granted on motions, neither of which shall be for a period of more than 21 days. Threshold motions pursuant to Insurance Law § 5102 shall be allowed no more than THREE (3) adjournments for a total of six weeks to allow ALL necessary moving papers, cross-motions, opposition papers, and replies to be submitted.

JUSTICE ROBERT L. NAHMAN

Part 16. Hon. Robert L. Nahman

1. No telephone inquiries concerning motions or applications may be made to chambers.

All such inquiries must be made to the Motion Support Office (718–298–1009), the Ex Parte Office (718–298–1018) or the Clerk of Part 16 (718–298–1113).

Preliminary Conferences

A preliminary conference shall be scheduled (1) automatically by the court within 45 days after filing a Request for Judicial Intervention, pursuant to 22 NYCRR 202.12(b), or upon filing a written Request for a Preliminary Conference with the Clerk's Office, Room 140, in compliance with 22 NYCRR 202.12(a) or an appropriate notice is filed in malpractice or certiorari cases pursuant to 22 NYCRR 202.56 and 202.60.

All preliminary conferences shall be held on WEDNESDAYS at 9:30 a.m. at the Preliminary Conference Part, Room 314, of the courthouse, and are presided over by the court-appointed referee, unless otherwise directed by the court. Failure to appear at the scheduled preliminary conference may result in discovery being ordered ex-parte or any other appropriate sanction including preclusion or dismissal.

Any inquiry pertaining to a preliminary conference shall be made to the Preliminary Conference Part at 718–298–1046.

Compliance Conferences

Compliance conferences shall be held on the date scheduled in the Preliminary Conference Stipulation and Order. Compliance conferences shall be held before Justice Martin Ritholtz in Room 313.

Any inquiry pertaining to a conferences conference shall be made to the Compliance Conference Part at 718–298–1093.

Motions

The motion calendar will be called every Tuesday at 9:30 a.m. promptly. A second calendar call will follow shortly thereafter.

Mandatory appearance is required by counsel with knowledge of the case and with full authority to settle or enter into binding stipulations on the return date.

On the return date, motions will be conferenced and/or orally argued at the discretion of the Court.

Do not call Part 16 or Chambers for adjournments as NO ADJOURNMENTS WILL BE GRANTED BY TELEPHONE.

Motions may be adjourned on consent provided a written stipulation of counsel is submitted to the Court prior to the return or adjourn date. All stipulations must contain the signature of the attorney consenting to the adjournment. A form which contains only the name of the firm on the stipulation will not be accepted. Stipulations must also contain a schedule for exchange of opposition and reply papers occurring prior to the adjourn date. Stipulations may be submitted by calendar service or non-attorneys.

If consent for an adjournment can not be obtained, an application must be made to Justice Nahman by counsel on the return date. Calendar service or non-attorneys **will not** be permitted to make applications for adjournments.

Under no circumstances will motions be adjourned more than twice. Motions relating to discovery may be adjourned only once.

Answering and reply papers will be accepted only on the return date in the Part. The Court will not consider papers sent to Chambers or the Part after submission. Papers will not be accepted from calendar service if a personal appearance by counsel is required. Courtesy copies of papers are NOT required.

Motion Papers and Ex–Parte Applications

All motions and ex-parte applications submitted shall be in compliance with Uniform Rule § 202.5. In addition to these requirements, all pages and paragraphs must be numbered. All exhibits are to be proceeded by a numbered exhibit tab which protrudes from the stack of papers. All submissions are to be securely fastened so as to prevent the papers from being lost.

FAILURE TO COMPLY WITH THE REQUIREMENTS OF THIS SECTION MAY RESULT IN REJECTION OF THE OFFENDING SUBMISSION.

Infant's Compromise Orders

Applications for infant's compromise orders will only be accepted when submitted to chambers by mail. Before submission of an infant's compromise order, counsel shall obtain from the Clerk of Part 16 an infant's compromise checklist to ensure the submission of all necessary information and documentation. Infant's compromise orders sent to chambers without the required completed worksheet will be returned to counsel.

JUSTICE ORIN R. KITZES

Part 17.   Hon. Orin R. Kitzes

Preliminary Conference

A preliminary conference shall be scheduled (1) automatically by the court within 45 days after filing a request for Judicial Intervention, pursuant to 22 NYCRR 202.12(b), or (2) upon filing a written Request for a Preliminary Conference with the Clerk's Office (Room 140) in compliance with 22 NYCRR 202.12(a) or an appropriate notice is filed in malpractice or certiorari cases pursuant to 22 NYCRR 202.56 and 202.60.

All Preliminary Conferences will be held on THURSDAYS at 9:30 a.m at the Preliminary Conference Part, Room 307 of the Courthouse, and they are presided over by the court-appointed referee, unless otherwise directed by the court. Failure to appear at the scheduled preliminary conference may result in discovery being ordered ex-parte or any other appropriate sanction including preclusion or dismissal ordered. Contact the Preliminary Conference Part at (718) 298–1046, not chambers.

Compliance Conference

For all Non-Commercial Division cases, Compliance Conferences shall be held on the date scheduled in the Preliminary Conference Stipulation and Order. Conferences shall be held before Justice Ritholtz in Courtroom 313.

For all Commercial Division cases, Compliance Conferences shall be held on the date scheduled in the Preliminary Conference Stipulation and Order. Conferences shall be held before Justice Kitzes in Courtroom 116.

Pre–Trial Conference

Counsel attending the conference must be fully familiar with and authorized to settle, stipulate, and dispose of the action(s).

Motion Practice

The motion calendar will be called every WEDNESDAY at 9:30 a.m. promptly. A second call will follow immediately thereafter. No courtesy copies to chambers are required except in the case of E-filed motions.

All motions and applications are to be submitted on papers only, except those relating to any phases of discovery and/or bills of particulars, including motions to strike or restore a case from trial calendar, which require personal appearance by counsel for all parties. If the application is an Order to Show Cause then all parties MUST appear (movant must submit Affidavit of Service to Part Clerk) on the return date. Counsel should be prepared to discuss and agree upon a discovery schedule.

Oral argument will be entertained only in the Court's discretion.

Use of calendar service is permitted both to submit papers and to request counsel adjournments, which will be limited to two. The first adjournment on consent will be allowed on papers, thereafter attorneys seeking a further adjournment must appear.

Do not call the Part or Chambers for adjournments as NO ADJOURNMENTS WILL BE GRANTED ON THE TELEPHONE. The Court will not consider papers sent to Chambers or to the Part after submission.

The members of the Bar should make every effort to notify their adversaries and co-counsel of all applications for adjournments in advance.

The Court requests that any attorney appearing on a case for any purpose must be familiar with the case, ready and authorized to resolve any and all issues.

Electronic Filing of Legal Papers

Electronic filing is available for filing legal papers with this Court. Parties interested in electronic filing should read the materials set forth at www.nycourts.gov/efile. The rules and User's Manual for electronic filing are available on this web site. Courtesy copies to chambers are required in the case of E-filed motions.

Inquiries

All inquiries as to case or calendar status are to be made to the appropriate Clerk's office.

IAS Motion Support Office (718) 298–1009

Ex Parte Support Office (718) 298–1018

JUSTICE DUANE HART

Part 18.   Hon. Duane Hart

Counsel, with knowledge of the case and with full authority to settle, enter into binding stipulations or try the case, must be present in Court to answer the motion calendar or trial calendar, where applicable. This applies as well to parties representing themselves in a pro se capacity.

Preliminary Conference

A preliminary conference will take place (1) after a written Request for a Preliminary Conference is filed with the Clerk's office (Room 140) in compliance with Uniform Rule 202.12(a) (or an appropriate notice is filed in malpractice matrimonial or certiorari cases pursuant to Uniform Rules Sections 202.56, 202.16 and 202.60), or upon a specific directive of Justice Hart.

Motions:

Initial Motion Procedure (For motions made in unassigned cases)

Moving papers, are to be filed in the clerk's office (Room 140) pursuant to Uniform Rule 202.8(b) and the instructions under the listing for this Court in the New York Law Journal.

No motion relating to disclosure or a bill of particulars will be accepted by the clerk's office (Room 140) without an affirmation of good faith as required by Uniform Rule 202.7.

All initial motions filed and accepted in the clerk's office and assigned to Justice Hart are heard in Part 18 on a rescheduled date. That rescheduled date, which will be on a Wednesday at 9:30 a.m., is specified in the New York Law Journal publication of IAS assignments which appears in the Law Journal on the day after the original return date of the motion, or as soon as practicable thereafter.

The motion appearance requirements in the Part are specified in Subsequent Motion Procedure section below.

Subsequent Motion Procedure (For motions made after assignment of cases)

Regular motion day, Wednesday @ 9:30 A.M.

Unless otherwise directed by Justice Hart, all motions shall be made returnable in the Part, Courtroom 41, on the above specific day and time of the week and subject to the following procedures.

The moving papers, with an affidavit of good faith where required by Uniform Rule 202.7, shall be filed in the IAS Motion Support Office (Room 140) at least 5 business days prior to the scheduled return date in order to be placed on the Part 18 motion calendar for that day.

The answering papers will be accepted only on the return date in the Part.

The motion will be heard for all purposes in the Part on the return date. On that date, the motion will either be orally argued, conference by Justice Hart or his designee, or otherwise treated pursuant to the discretion of the Justice. (Rulings on applications will also be made at this time.) Courtesy copes of moving papers need not be provided.

Mandatory appearance is required for counsel for all parties and pro se litigants on the return date, unless otherwise directed by Justice Hart or his designee. Adjournments may be sought only by application to Justice Hart in open court and not by consent of counsel. Service representatives and non-attorneys will not be permitted to make applications.

Orders to show cause must comply with Uniform Rule 202.7(d) and be brought to the Ex Parte Support Office (Room 140) prior to judicial review, signature and fixing of a return date. Appearance requirements for orders to show cause are the same as listed for all motions.

Prior notice to chambers is not required to bring a motion in IAS Part 18. Counsel shall not call Chambers to check on the status of any motion.

Electronic Filing of Legal Papers

Parties interested in electronic filing should read materials set forth at www.nycourts.gov/efile and the Uniform Rules for Trial Courts § 202.5–b.

Where motion/responsive papers, including exhibits and memoranda of law, are filed by electronic means pursuant to Uniform rule § 202.5–b, courtesy hard copies of such papers shall be submitted to the Court three days prior to the return/adjourned date of the motion. No motion/responsive papers shall be considered unless courtesy hard copies are submitted to the Court three days prior to the return/adjourned date of the motion. Each submitted hard copy shall bear a conspicuous notice on the first page thereof that the document has been filed electronically (Uniform rule § 202.5–b[d][4]).

The Court's rules concerning motion papers shall apply to courtesy hard copies submitted to the Court. All other motion practice rules of this part, as well as all rules regarding motion papers and ex-parte applications are applicable to e-filed motions.

Any order, judgment or stipulation that requires the Justice's signature shall be submitted in hard copy to the court.

Infant's Compromise Orders

Before submission of an Infant's Compromise Order, counsel shall obtain from the Clerk of Part 18 an infant compromise check list to ensure the submission of all necessary information and documentation. Infant's compromise orders sent to chambers without the required completed worksheet will be returned to counsel. Proof of payment of any appropriate fee is required.

Infant Compromise Hearings will be scheduled by the Court, and the plaintiff will be informed of the hearing date by the part.

Trials:

Matters assigned to this Part will be tried, to the extent possible, in chronological order. Trial dates will be set as far in advance as practicable.

Inquiries:

All inquiries as to the case or calendar status shall be made to the appropriate clerk's office. The only inquiries to be made directly to the Chambers or the Part should be those involving the immediate exercise of judicial discretion.

All such inquiries must be made to the Motion Support Office (718–298–1009), the Ex Parte Office

(718–298–1018) or the Clerk of Part 18 (718–298–1110).

JUSTICE BERNICE D. SIEGAL

Part 19. Hon. Bernice D. Siegal
General Rules
Court Appearances of Counsel

Attorneys are directed to appear at 9:30 a.m. sharp for all calendar calls, and at the previously scheduled time for all hearings, either personally or by a representative fully familiar with the case and who is authorized to settle, try, stipulate or dispose of any issue. In the event of actual engagement, as defined in Rule 125.1 of the Court Rules, an affidavit or affirmation must be submitted to the Clerk of the Part prior to the calendar call together with a stipulation signed by opposing counsel setting forth an agreed upon adjourned date. Failure to comply with the foregoing may result in dismissal, inquest or other sanctions. Mandatory appearance of all counsel and pro se litigants is required on all applications made by Order to Show Cause, particularly any applications to impose or continue a temporary restraining order, and all motions involving discovery.

Inquiries

All inquiries as to case or calendar status are, in the first instance, to be made to the appropriate Clerk's Office (see below). The only inquiries to be made directly to Chambers or the Part should be those involving the immediate exercise of judicial discretion.

IAS Motion Support Office: (718) 298–1009

IAS Ex-Parte Support Office: (718) 298–1018

Preliminary Conference

A Preliminary Conference shall be scheduled (1) automatically by the Court within 45 days after filing a Request for Judicial Intervention, pursuant to 22 NYCRR 202.12(b), or (2) upon filing a written Request for a Preliminary Conference with the Clerk's Office, Room 140, in compliance with 22 NYCRR 202.12(a) or an appropriate notice is filed in malpractice or certiorari cases pursuant to 22 NYCRR 202.56 and 202.60.

All Preliminary Conferences will be held on TUESDAYS at 11:30 A.M., at the Preliminary Conference Part, Room 314 of the courthouse, and they are presided over by the court-appointed referee, unless otherwise directed by the Court. Attorneys are required to "sign in" by 11:30 a.m. Counsel attending the conference must be fully familiar with and authorized settle, stipulate or dispose of the proceedings. There shall be no more than one consent adjournment by written stipulation, signed by all parties, and presented to the referee on the date of the scheduled Preliminary conference. Such adjournment shall be for a period of no more than 14 days. Any further adjourn-

ments shall be by application to the referee, in person, upon notice to all other parties. A Preliminary Conference Order will issue setting forth the issues resolved, issues to be determined at trial, a timetable for completion of disclosure proceedings, the compliance conference date, and the date for filing the Note of Issue. No adjournments of any dates of scheduled discovery will be permitted without leave of court. Be further advised that no ex parte application for adjournments will be entertained. Counsel for all parties must appear at all scheduled preliminary conferences and, whether present or not, will be bound by all orders of the court issued in connection therewith. Failure to appear at the scheduled Preliminary Conference may result in discovery being ordered exparte or any other appropriate sanction including preclusion or dismissal. Any inquiry pertaining to Preliminary Conferences shall be made to the Preliminary Conference Part at (718) 298–1046.

Compliance Conference

Compliance Conference shall be held on the date scheduled in the Preliminary Conference Stipulation and Order.

All Compliance Conferences shall be held on WEDNESDAYS at 9:30 A.M. before Justice Martin Ritholtz, Room 313.

Inquiries pertaining to Compliance Conferences shall be made to the Compliance Conference Part at 718–298–1093.

Motions

Motions are heard on WEDNESDAYS at 9:30 A.M. There will be second call of the motion calendar at 10:30 A.M.

In the case of e-filed motions, a hard copy must be submitted to the Court on the return date.

Appearance of counsel and pro se litigants is mandatory on all motions. Mandatory appearance is required by counsel with knowledge of the case and with full authority to settle or enter into binding stipulations on the return date. The motions will be heard for all purposes in the Part on the return date. On that date, the motions will be conferenced and/or orally argued at the Court's discretion with the expectation that all discovery issues will be resolved by stipulation. Papers will not be accepted from calendar service inasmuch as a personal appearance by counsel and pro se litigants is required.

Appearance of counsel and pro se litigants is also MANDATORY on all Orders to Show Cause and motions which seek to continue a temporary restraining order or to extend the time to file a note of issue. Papers will not be accepted from calendar service inasmuch as a personal appearance by counsel and pro se litigants is required.

Discovery motions require inclusion of an affirmation of good faith, setting forth, in detail, the efforts utilized by the moving attorney to obtain discovery prior to requesting judicial intervention. Conclusory statements by the attorney or failure to demonstrate good faith efforts may result in summary denial of the discovery motion.

Absent extenuating circumstances, consent adjournments will be limited to first time only. Thereafter, attorneys seeking further adjournments MUST APPEAR. No motion shall be adjourned more than the aggregate period of 60 days from the original return date of said motion.

The answering papers, including cross motions, affirmations in opposition and reply affirmations, will be accepted only on the return or adjourned date in the Part. The court will not consider papers sent to Chambers or to the Part after full submission of the motion or cross motion(s). Nor will it accept cross-motions that do not have proof of payment of the appropriate fee. (CPLR § 8020[a]).

Applications for adjournment will only be entertained either at the call of the calender in the presence of all parties, or by stipulation, signed by all parties and setting forth the reason(s) for the adjournments request. Such stipulation shall be faxed to chambers at (718) 298–1090 at least 24 hours prior to the calendar call, and followed up by a telephone call to ascertain if the request has been granted. All stipulations must contain the signature of the attorney consenting to the adjournment. A form which contains only the name of the firm on the stipulation will not be accepted. Stipulations must also contain a schedule for exchange of opposition and reply papers occurring prior to the adjourn date. Stipulations may be submitted by calendar service or non-attorneys. In no event shall more than two adjournments be granted, neither of which shall be for a period of more than 21 days, unless good cause is shown. Requests for an adjournment, if a motion has already been adjourned once, must be made in person by an attorney who has authority to settle, stipulate or dispose of all issues raised in the motion papers. Orders to Show Cause may be adjourned by stipulation one time only for no more than two weeks. Counsel must make every effort to notify their adversaries and co-counsel of their intention to seek adjournments, and if possible to obtain consent of all parties.

If consent for an adjournment cannot be obtained, an application must be made to Justice Siegal by counsel on the return date.

Calendar service or non-attorneys will not be permitted to make applications for adjournments.

Under normal circumstances, no motion will be adjourned more than twice. Motions relating to discovery may be adjourned only once.

Answering and reply papers will be accepted only on the return date in the Part. The Court will not consider papers sent to Chambers or the Part after submission. Papers will not be accepted from calendar service if a personal appearance by counsel is required. Courtesy copies of papers are NOT required.

ABSOLUTELY NO ADJOURNMENTS WILL BE GRANTED OVER THE TELEPHONE.

Motions Papers and Ex Parte Applications:

All motion papers submitted shall be in compliance with Uniform Rule Sec. 202.5, concerning papers filed with the court. In addition to the requirements of Sec. 202.5, all pages are to be numbered and all paragraphs are to be numbered. All exhibits are to be proceeded by a numbered exhibit tab which protrudes from the stack of papers. All submissions are to be securely fastened so as to prevent the papers from separating from each other and becoming lost. FAILURE TO COMPLY WITH THE REQUIREMENTS OF THIS SECTION MAY RESULT IN REJECTION OF THE OFFENDING SUBMISSION.

Decisions:

Any attorney or pro se litigant desiring a copy of the Court's decision must submit a stamped, self-addressed envelope with the motion papers or at the conclusion of trial.

Trials

All counsel must submit to the court, prior to the commencement of trial, marked pleadings, copy of the bill of particulars, a witness list, exhibit list, proposed jury instruction and a proposed verdict sheet. If the proposed jury instructions are verbatim from the Pattern Jury Instructions ("PJI"), only PJI numbers are necessary. If a PJI is being modified, exact language must be submitted together with the appropriate authority therefore. In the case of a bench trial, all counsel must submit a witness list, proposed findings of fact and a memorandum of law.

Motions in Limine—On the first appearance in the Part for trial, any party intending to make a motion in limine shall submit a brief written affirmation setting forth the nature of the application and any supporting statutory or case law. The party shall furnish the court with an original and one copy and provide counsel for all parties with a copy.

The trial will be conducted on a continual daily basis until conclusion.

No adjournments or delays during trial will be accepted unless exigent circumstances exist.

Settlements and Discontinuances

If an action is settled, discontinued or otherwise disposed of, counsel shall immediately inform the court by submission of a copy of the stipulation or a letter directed to the Clerk of the Part. Filing a stipulation of discontinuance with the County Clerk does not suffice. All stipulations of discontinuances must be accompanied by proof of payment for the appropriate fee. (CPLR § 8020(d)(1))

Electronic Filing of Legal Papers

Parties interested in electronic filing should read materials set forth at www.nycourts.gov/efile and the Uniform Rules for Trial Courts § 202.5–b.

Where motion/responsive papers, including exhibits and memoranda of law, are filed by electronic means pursuant to Uniform rule § 202.5–b, courtesy hard copies of such papers shall be submitted to the Court on the return/adjourned date of the motion. No motion/responsive papers shall be considered unless courtesy hard copies are submitted to the Court on the return/adjourned date of the motion. Each submitted hard copy shall bear a conspicuous notice on the first page thereof that the document has been filed electronically (Uniform rule § 202.5–b[d][4]).

The Court's rules concerning motion papers shall apply to courtesy hard copies submitted to the Court. Appearance of counsel is mandatory on all e-filed motions. All other motion practice rules of this part, as well as all rules regarding motion papers and ex-parte applications are applicable to e-filed motions.

Any order, judgment or stipulation that requires the Justice's signature shall be submitted in hard copy to the court.

Infant's Compromise Orders

Before submission of an Infant's Compromise Order, counsel shall obtain from the Clerk of Part 19 an infant compromise check list to ensure the submission of all necessary information and documentation. Infant's compromise orders sent to chambers without the required completed worksheet will be returned to counsel. Proof of payment of any appropriate fee is required.

Infant Compromise Hearings will be scheduled by the Court, and the plaintiff will be informed of the hearing date via telephone.

JUSTICE JOSEPH G. GOLIA

Part 21. Hon. Joseph G. Golia

RJI Filings (Tax Certiorari)

All counsel must appear for all calendared matters unless specifically excused.

Counsel must make every effort to notify their adversary of any intention to seek an adjournment, and, if possible, to obtain consent of all parties.

Preliminary Conference (Tax Certiorari)

Counsel for all parties must appear at all scheduled preliminary conferences and, whether present or not, will be bound by all Orders of the Court in connection therewith.

Counsel attending the conference must be fully familiar with and authorized to settle, stipulate or dispose of such actions.

Be further advised that adjournments will not be accepted by telephone.

Motions

The motion calendar will be called every WEDNES-DAY at 9:30 a.m. promptly. A second call will follow shortly thereafter.

All motions relating to any phase of discovery and/or bill of particulars, including motions to strike from or restore a case to the trial calendar, requires

personal appearance by counsel for all parties. Counsel should be prepared to discuss and agree upon a discovery schedule. If the application is an Order to Show Cause, then all parties MUST appear on the return date. All other motions and applications may be submitted on papers only.

Oral argument will be entertained only in the Court's discretion.

Use of calendar service is permitted (except for Orders to Show Cause) both to submit papers and to request counsel adjournments, which will be limited to two. The first adjournment on consent will be allowed on papers. Thereafter, attorneys seeking a further adjournment MUST Appear.

Do not call the Part or Chambers for adjournments as NO ADJOURNMENTS WILL BE GRANTED ON THE TELEPHONE. The Court will not consider papers sent to Chambers or to the Part after submission.

The members of the Bar are to make every effort to notify their adversaries and co-counsel of all applications for adjournments in advance.

The Court further directs that any attorney appearing on a case for any purpose must be familiar with the case, ready, and authorized to resolve any and all issues.

JUSTICE LEE A. MAYERSOHN

Part 22. Hon. Lee A. Mayersohn

Preliminary Conference

A preliminary conference shall be scheduled automatically by the Court within forty-five (45) after filing a Request for Judicial Intervention, pursuant to 22 NYCRR 202.12(b); or upon filing a written Request for a Preliminary Conference with the Jamaica Clerk's Office, Room 140, in compliance with 22 NYCRR 202.12(a); or an appropriate notice is filed in malpractice or certiorari cases pursuant to 22 NYCRR 202.56 and 202.60.

All preliminary conferences will be held on Mondays at 9:30 a.m. at the Preliminary Conference Part, Room 314 at the Jamaica courthouse located at 88–11 Sutphin Blvd., Jamaica, NY, and are presided over by the court-appointed Referee, unless otherwise directed by the Court. Failure to appear at the scheduled preliminary conference may result in discovery being ordered ex-parte or any other appropriate sanction, including preclusion or dismissal ordered. Any inquiry pertaining to preliminary conferences shall be made to the Preliminary Conference Part at (718) 298–1046.

Compliance Conferences

Conferences shall be held before Justice Ritholtz in Room 313 at the Jamaica courthouse.

Compliance conferences shall be held on the date scheduled in the Preliminary Conference Order. Any inquiry pertaining to compliance conferences shall be made to the Compliance Conference Part at 718–298–1093.

Motion Practice

The Motion Calendar for Justice Mayersohn will be called in Courtroom 44A of the Jamaica Supreme Court Courthouse located at 88–11 Sutphin Blvd Jamaica, NY 11101–4335, every Tuesday at 9:30 AM. PROMPTLY.

MANDATORY APPEARANCE IS REQUIRED by counsel with knowledge of the case and with full authority to settle or enter into binding stipulations on the return date. In the case of e-filed motions, a hard copy must be submitted to the Court on the return date.

On the return date, motions will be conferenced and/or orally argued at the discretion of the Court.

DO NOT CALL CHAMBERS FOR ADJOURNMENTS.

Motions may be adjourned on consent provided a written stipulation of counsel is submitted to the Court on the return date. All stipulations must contain the signature of the attorney consenting to the adjournment. A form which contains only the name of the firm on the stipulation will not be accepted.

Stipulations must also contain a schedule for exchange of opposition and reply papers occurring prior to the adjourned date. If consent for an adjournment cannot be obtained, an application must be made to Justice Mayersohn by counsel on the return date. Calendar service or non-attorneys will not be permitted to make applications for adjournment. Counsel are expected to notify their adversaries of their intention to seek an adjournment.

Adjournments will be limited to two, absent extenuating circumstances. The answering papers, including cross motions, affirmations in opposition and reply affirmations, will be accepted only on the return or adjourned date in the Part. The court will not consider papers sent to Chambers or to the Part after full submission of the motion or cross motion(s). Nor will it accept cross-motions that do not have proof of payment of the appropriate fee. (CPLR § 8020[a]).

All motions and ex-parte applications submitted shall be in compliance with Uniform Rule § 202.5. In addition to these requirements, all pages and paragraphs must be numbered. All exhibits are to be preceded by a numbered exhibit tab which protrudes from the stack of papers. All submissions are to be securely fastened so as to prevent the papers from being lost. Failure to comply with the requirements of this section may result in rejection of the non-complying papers.

Copies of decisions on motions will be mailed to attorneys and pro se litigants who provide the Part with a stamped, self-addressed envelope at the time of final submission of their motion. If no stamped, self-addressed envelope is provided, it will be the responsibility of the respective attorneys and pro se litigants to follow up with the appropriate clerk's office to obtain a copy of the decision.

All inquiries to case or calendar status are to be made to the appropriate clerk's office.

IAS Motion Support Office (718) 298–1009
Ex-Parte Support Office (718) 298–1018

Infant's Compromise Orders

Before submission of an infant's compromise order, counsel shall obtain from the Clerk of Part 3 an infant's compromise checklist to ensure the submission of all necessary information and documentation. Infant's compromise orders sent to chambers without the required completed worksheet will be returned to counsel.

Proof of payment of any appropriate fee is required.

Infant compromise hearings will be scheduled by the Court and the plaintiff will be informed of the hearing date by mail.

Uncontested Matrimonials

Any corrections to a rejected set of matrimonial papers must be submitted to the Matrimonial Clerk and NOT directly to chambers.

This Court takes seriously its duty to protect children in calculating child support. Unsupported deviations from the guidelines will result in rejections and thus slow down the sought-after judgment of divorce. Deviations from child support guidelines must be thoroughly explained in an affidavit of the party, without resorting to conclusory language, and in the attorney's affirmation.

Trials

Plaintiff's counsel shall requisition the file to the Part 3 courtroom immediately after assignment of the case to this Part. Counsel should ascertain the availability of all witnesses and subpoenaed documents. Any special needs, e.g., interpreter, easels, blackboards, shadow boxes, television, subpoenaed material, etc., must be reported to the Court Officer, in advance, so as not to delay the progress of the trial.

All counsel must submit to the Court, prior to the commencement of trial, marked pleadings, a copy of the bill of particulars, a witness list, exhibit list, proposed jury instruction and a proposed jury verdict sheet. Counsel must also know the availability of all witnesses who they intend to call during trial.

With regard to suggested jury charges and a suggested verdict questionnaire, amendments thereto shall be permitted at the final charge conference. Jury charges should be referred to by PJI number and topic. If any changes to the PJI are suggested, then the entire proposed charge should be set forth and the changes should be highlighted. Citations to appropriate statutory or common law authority must be given in support of suggested non-PJI jury charges or suggested PJI modifications.

To the extent any part of a deposition is to be read into evidence (as distinguished from mere use on cross-examination) counsel must, in advance, provide the Court and your adversary with the page and line numbers of all such testimony, so that all objections may be addressed prior to use before the jury.

Pre-trial conferences will be held prior to every trial.

At this conference counsel should be prepared to:

1. Discuss settlement;

2. Advise the Court as to all anticipated disputed issues of law and fact, and provide the Court with copies of all statutory and common law authority upon which counsel will rely;

3. Stipulate to undisputed facts and the admissibility of clearly admissible documents and records;

4. Advise the Court of any anticipated in limine motions or evidentiary objections which counsel intends to make. Motions in limine may be made orally,

however they must be supported by a memorandum of law. Any written motions in limine require proof of payment of the appropriate fee. Counsel shall provide the Court and all parties with copies. All prior decisions and orders relevant to any in limine application must be provided to the Court.

5. Advise the Court of any anticipated requests for a jury instruction relating to missing witnesses and/or documents;

6. Advise the Court of any anticipated request for apportionment as to alleged culpable non-parties pursuant to CPLR Article 16.

7. Discuss scheduling and the estimated length of the trial. Counsel should alert the Court as to any anticipated problems regarding the attendance at trial of parties, attorneys or essential witnesses and any other practical problems that the Court should consider in scheduling.

The trial will be conducted on a continual daily basis until its conclusion. No adjournments or delays during trial will be accepted, unless exigent circumstances exist.

Tort actions are generally bifurcated. The Court expects, that any trial on damages will follow immediately after a verdict finding the defendant liable.

The Court encourages trial exhibits be pre-marked for identification and, where possible, that parties stipulate to the admissibility of clearly admissible documents and records.

Counsel should alert the Court, at the pre-trial conference, as to any anticipated problems regarding the attendance at trial of parties, attorneys or essential witnesses and any other practical problems that the Court should consider in scheduling.

Settlements and Discontinuances

If an action is settled, discontinued or otherwise disposed of, counsel shall immediately inform the Court by submission of a copy of the stipulation of settlement or a letter directed to the Clerk of the Part. All stipulations of discontinuances must be accompanied by proof of payment of the appropriate fee. (CPLR § 8020(d)(1).)

Part 22G.   Hon. Lee A. Mayersohn

General Rules:

All counsel must appear for all calendared matters unless specifically excused.

No telephone inquiries concerning motions or applications may be made to chambers.

Telephone call regarding orders and procedures are to be directed to the Guardianship Office at (718) 298-1040.

Any calls regarding legal issues or emergencies may be directed to chambers at (718) 298-1626.

All scheduling and calendar matters shall be brought to the attention of the Clerk of Part 22G at (718) 298–1126.

Except as otherwise provided communications with chambers shall be by letter with the title of the action, index number, and the last date the action appeared on the calendar. Absent exceptional circumstances, ex parte communication shall be disregarded.

Copies of correspondence between counsel should not be sent to the Court as same will not be placed in the Court's file.

Petitions to Appoint a Guardian:

All petitions to appoint a Guardian shall be heard on Mondays, Wednesdays, and Thursdays at 9:30 A.M.

All parties must appear on the return date of a petition to appoint a Guardian.

Applications for adjournments must be on stipulation signed by all parties and the Court evaluator, as well as approved by the Court prior to the date the matter appears on the calendar. Adjournments shall be limited to three (3), and any request thereafter must be made to the Court in person.

No adjournments will be granted by telephone on the date the matter appears on the calendar. Stipulations requesting an adjournment shall be delivered to the clerk two (2) days prior to the return date.

Affidavits of Service for Orders to Show Cause shall be filed in the clerk's office at least two (2) days prior to the return date.

Court Evaluator Reports shall be filed in the clerk's office at least two (2) day prior to the return date.

Motions/Petitions Other Than to Appoint a Guardian:

Motions/Petitions other than to appoint a guardian are heard on Tuesdays at 10:30 A.M.

Adjournments of Motions and/or Petitions other than to Appoint a Guardian, or any other calendered application, shall be made in the same manner as a Petition to Appoint a Guardian except that the number of applications shall not be limited to three (3).

All Motions must be submitted to the Guardianship Clerk's Office at least seven (7) days prior to the return date. Affidavits of Service and a statement that the Affidavit of Service is in conformity with section 81.16(3) of the Mental Hygiene Law must be submitted to the clerk's office.

All requests for expenditures may be submitted to the Court by Application and Order Form with the recommendations of the Court Examiner.

JUSTICE ROGER N. ROSENGARTEN

Part 23.   Hon. Roger N. Rosengarten

All telephone inquires concerning matters pending in IAS Part 23, Civil Term of the Supreme Court, County of Queens, Honorable Roger N. Rosengarten presiding, will be made directly to the Part at telephone number (718) 298–1094. Contact with chambers will not be made unless so directed after contacting the Part at the above listed telephone number. Counsel shall not fax any documents to chambers unless permission has been granted for same.

To confirm whether an ex-parte order or an order to show cause has been processed and sent to chambers call the Ex-Parte Office (718) 298–1018.

To confirm where an order, submitted pursuant to a memorandum decision of the court, has been processed and sent to chambers call the Motion Support Office at (718) 298–1009.

Preliminary Conference

A preliminary conference shall be scheduled (1) automatically by the Court within 45 days after filing a Request for Judicial Intervention, pursuant to 22 NYCRR 202.12(b), or (2) upon filing a written Request for a Preliminary Conference with the Clerk's Office, Room 140, in compliance with 22 NYCRR 202.12(a) or an appropriate notice is filed in malpractice or certiorari cases pursuant to 22 NYCRR 202.56 and 202.60.

All preliminary conferences will be held on WEDNESDAY at 11:30 a.m. at the Preliminary Conference Part, Room 314 of the courthouse, and they are presided over by the court-appointed referee, unless otherwise directed by the Court. Failure to appear at the scheduled preliminary conference may result in discovery being ordered ex-parte or any other appropriate sanction including preclusion or dismissal ordered. Any inquiry pertaining to preliminary conferences shall be made to the Preliminary Conference Part at (718) 298–1046.

Compliance Conferences

Compliance conferences shall be held on the date scheduled in the Preliminary Conference Stipulation and Order. Conferences shall be held before Justice Ritholtz in Room 313. Any inquiry pertaining to compliance conferences shall be made to the Compliance Conference Part at (718) 298–1093. Any question regarding a Note of Issue date given in the Compliance Conference Stipulation and Order shall be addressed to the Compliance Conference Part at (718) 298–1093.

Motion Practice

The Motion Calendar will be called every Wednesday at 9:30 a.m. promptly. A second call will follow at 10:00 a.m.

All motions relating to any phase of discovery and/or bill of particulars; including motions to preclude, strike or restore a case to the Trial Calendar, or to vacate the Note of Issue, require personal appearance by counsel for all parties. Counsel should be prepared to discuss and agree upon a discovery schedule.

All motions to vacate a default judgment require personal appearance by all parties. Petitions to transfer structured settlement rights require the transferor to be present at the calendar call.

All other motions and applications may be submitted on papers only.

Oral argument will be entertained only in the court's discretion. Whenever a personal appearance is not mandated use of calendar service is permitted both to submit papers and to submit stipulations of adjournments, which will be limited to two. The first adjournment on consent will be allowed upon written stipulation. All stipulations must contain the signature of the attorney consenting to the adjournment. A form which contains only the name of the firm on the stipulation will not be accepted. Stipulations must contain a schedule for exchange of opposition and reply papers occurring prior to the adjourned date, or they will otherwise be rejected. Stipulations may be submitted by calendar service or non-attorneys. Thereafter, attorneys seeking a further adjournment must appear. In any event, adjournments will be limited to two absent extenuating circumstances. The members of the Bar are to make every effort to notify their adversaries and co-counsel of all applications for adjournments in advance. The Court further directs that any attorney appearing on a case for any purpose must be familiar with the case, ready, and authorized to resolve any and all issues.

Motions for Summary Judgment must be made within 60 days of the filing of the Note of Issue regardless of any dates set in the Preliminary Conference Order.

Temporary Restraining Orders

Parties seeking a Temporary Restraining Order must notify opposing counsel pursuant to 22 NYCRR 202.7(f) of their intent to present such an Order to Show Cause to the court and present proof of such

notice along with the Order to Show Cause. All such applications shall be made between the hours of 10:00 a.m. to 2:00 p.m.

Trials

All Counsel on cases sent to this Part for must be prepared to immediately select a jury or, if one is already selected, to proceed directly to trial. NO ADJOURNMENTS WILL BE GRANTED ABSENT EXTRAORDINARY CIRCUMSTANCES. Similarly, after a liability verdict in favor of the plaintiff, all counsel must be prepared to proceed immediately to the damages portion of the trial. All witnesses, including doctors and other experts, must be on call and available prior to opening statements on liability, so a meaningful trial schedule can be set. All counsel must submit to the Court, prior to the commencement of the trial, marked pleadings, including a copy of the bill of particulars a proposed witness list, typewritten requests to charge and a typewritten proposed verdict sheet. Further, prior to the commencement of the trial, counsel, with the assistance of the court reporter shall have, wherever possible, pre-marked exhibits and a copy of any deposition transcripts to be read at trial must be provided to the Court, or the party will be precluded reading said testimony.

The Court does not require submission of the "boilerplate" jury charges (e.g., PJI 1:20, Introduction; 1:21. Review principles stated; 1:22, Falsus uno, etc.). Submission of only those charges unique to the case is necessary. If a proposed jury instruction is verbatim from the Pattern Jury Instructions, then only PJI citations are necessary. However, if a PJI instruction is to be modified, or if no PJI charge is available, then counsel must submit a typewritten request of the exact language proposed for the charge, together with any applicable authority. A copy of any case or other authority counsel intends to rely upon at trial, must be provided to the Court and opposing counsel. Departures or contentions to be submitted to the Jury in medical malpractice and other complex cases must be drafted in advance and submitted by counsel.

Counsel are reminded that all requests for interpreters must be made to the Clerk of the Part or to Room 5005 at least 24 hours prior to their required services.

JUSTICE AUGUSTUS C. AGATE

Part 24. Hon. Augustus C. Agate

Preliminary Conference

A preliminary conference shall be scheduled automatically by the Court within forty-five (45) days after filing a Request for Judicial Intervention, pursuant to 22 NYCRR 202.12(b); or upon filing a written Request for a Preliminary Conference with the Clerk's Office, Room 140, in compliance with 22 NYCRR

202.12(a); or an appropriate notice is filed in malpractice or certiorari cases pursuant to 22 NYCRR 202.56 and 202.60.

All preliminary conferences will be held on Thursday at 9:30 a.m. at the Preliminary Conference Part, Room 24A of the courthouse, and they are presided over by the court-appointed referee, unless otherwise directed by the Court. Failure to appear at the scheduled preliminary conference may result in discovery being ordered ex-parte or any other appropriate sanction, including preclusion or dismissal ordered. Any inquiry pertaining to preliminary conferences shall be made to the Preliminary Conference Part at (718) 298–1046.

Compliance Conferences

Compliance conferences shall be held on the date scheduled in the Preliminary Conferences Stipulation and Order. Conferences shall be held before Justice Ritholtz in Room 313. Any inquiry pertaining to compliance conferences shall be made to the Compliance Conference Part at 718–298–1093.

Motion Practice

Beginning September 8, 2009, the Motion Calendar will be called every Tuesday at 9:30 a.m. PROMPTLY. There will be a second call of the calendar at 10:30 a.m.

No courtesy copies of moving and answering are required, EXCEPT FOR E-FILED MOTIONS. Cross Motions, Affirmations In Opposition and Reply Affirmations will only be accepted on the return date in the Part. THE COURT WILL NOT CONSIDER ANY PAPERS SENT TO CHAMBERS OR THE PART AFTER THE TIME OF SUBMISSION.

All motions relating to any phase of discovery and/or Bill of Particulars, including motions to preclude and/or to strike or restore a case to the Trial Calendar, require personal appearance by counsel for all parties on every court date. The movant's failure to appear for a discovery related motion will result in the motion being marked off calendar. If the movant appears but the opponent does not, the matter will be taken in without opposition. Counsel should be familiar with the case and prepared to discuss and agree upon a discovery schedule. If the motion has been brought by an Order to Show Cause and there is a stay or temporary restraining order therein, then all parties MUST APPEAR on the return date. All other motions and applications may be submitted on papers only.

Whenever a personal appearance is not required, use of calendar service is permitted both to submit papers and to request consent adjournments.

Oral argument will be entertained only in the Court's discretion.

Motions may be adjourned on consent by written stipulation of ALL counsel and pro se litigants. The Stipulation can be brought to the Part on the return date or can be faxed to chambers (718–298–1158) no later than 5:00 p.m. on the day prior to the return date.

In the absence of consent to an adjournment, all applications for an adjournment must be made in person on the return date. There will be no more than two (2) adjournments, absent extenuating circumstances. After two (2) adjournments, all further requests for an adjournment must be made in person on the return date.

Please do not call the Part or Chambers for adjournments as NO adjournments will be granted on the telephone. Use service or fax.

All motions and ex-parte applications submitted shall be in compliance with Uniform Rule § 202.5. In addition to these requirements, all pages and paragraphs must be numbered. All exhibits are to be preceded by a numbered exhibit tab which protrudes from the stack of papers. All submissions are to be securely fastened so as to prevent the papers from being lost. Failure to comply with the requirements of this section may result in rejection of the non–complying papers.

Any attorney appearing on a case for any purpose must be familiar with the case, ready and authorized to resolve any and all issues.

Trials

All counsel must submit to the court, prior to the commencement of trial, marked pleadings, copy of the Bill of Particulars, a witness list, exhibit list, proposed jury instruction and a proposed verdict sheet. Counsel must also know the availability of all witnesses who they intend to call during trial.

On the first appearance in the Part for trial, any party intending to make a motion *in limine* shall submit said motion in writing, with an affirmation setting forth the nature of the application and any supporting statutory or case law. The party shall furnish the court with an original and one copy and provide counsel for all parties with a copy.

The trial will be conducted on a continual daily basis until its conclusion. No adjournments or delays during trial will be accepted unless exigent circumstances exist.

Infant's Compromise Orders

Before submission of an infant's compromise order, counsel shall contact the clerk of Part 24 to confirm that all necessary information and documentation has been submitted. If all necessary paperwork is presented, chambers will contact counsel to arrange a date for the infant's compromise order to be reviewed.

All inquiries to case or calendar status are to be made to the appropriate clerk's office.

IAS Motion Support Office (718) 298–1009

Ex–Parte Support Office (718) 298–1018

JUSTICE LAWRENCE V. CULLEN

Part 25. Hon. Lawrence V. Cullen

General Rules:

All counsel must appear for all calendared matters unless specifically excused.

No telephone inquiries concerning motions or applications may be made to chambers.

Motions:

Motions are heard on Tuesdays at 10:00 A.M. prompt. There will only be one (1) call of the calendar.

Mandatory appearance on all motions is required by counsel with knowledge of the case and with full authority to settle or enter into binding stipulations on the return date.

On the return date, motions will be conferenced and/or orally argued at the discretion of the Court.

The moving papers shall be filed in the IAS Motion Support Office at least seven (7) business days prior to the scheduled return date in order to be placed on the Part motion calendar for the day noticed. No motion relating to disclosure will be accepted by the Clerk's Office without an affirmation of good faith as required by Uniform Rule 202.7.

The answering papers, including Cross-Motions, Affirmations in Opposition and Reply Affirmation and Affidavits of Service will be accepted only on the return date in the Part. Do not mail responsive papers nor affidavits of service to chambers.

The Court will not consider papers sent to Chambers or the Part after submission. Papers will not be accepted from calendar service if a personal appearance by counsel is required. Courtesy copies of papers are NOT required except in electronically filed cases.

All inquires to case or calendar status are to be made to the appropriate clerk's office.

IAS Motion Support (718) 298–1009

Ex-Parte Support Office (718) 298–1018

Adjournments:

Do not call Part 25 or Chambers for adjournments as NO ADJOURNMENTS WILL BE GRANTED BY TELEPHONE.

Motions may be adjourned on consent provided a written stipulation of counsel is submitted to the Court on the return date. All stipulations must contain the signature of the attorney consenting to the adjournment. A form which contains only the name of the firm on the stipulation will not be accepted. Stipulations must also contain a schedule for exchange of opposition and reply papers occurring prior to the adjourn date. Stipulations may be submitted by calendar service or non-attorneys.

If consent for an adjournment can not be obtained, an application must be made to Justice Cullen by counsel on the return date. Calendar service or non-attorneys will not be permitted to make application for adjournments.

Motion Papers and Ex-Parte Applications:

All motion papers and ex-parte applications submitted shall be in compliance with Uniform Rule Sec. 202.5 concerning papers filed with the Court. In addition to the requirements of Sec. 202.5, all papers are to be numbered, and all paragraphs are to be numbered. All exhibits are to be preceded by a numbered exhibit tab which protrudes from the stack of papers. All submissions are to be securely fastened so as to prevent the papers from separating from each other and becoming lost. Failure to comply with the requirements of this section may result in rejection of the offending submission.

Trials:

All counsel must submit to the Court, prior to the commencement of trial, marked pleadings, a copy of the bill of particulars, a witness list, an exhibit list, proposed jury instructions and a proposed verdict sheet.

Motions in Limine shall be submitted on the first appearance in the Part for trial. Any party intending to make a Motion in Limine shall submit a brief written affirmation setting forth the nature of the application and any supporting statutory or case law. The party shall furnish the Court with an original and one copy, and provide counsel for all parties with a copy.

No adjournments or delays during trial will be accepted unless exigent circumstances exist.

Settlements and Discontinuances:

If an action is settled, discontinued or otherwise disposed of, counsel shall immediately inform the Court by submission of a copy of the stipulation of settlement or a letter directed to the Clerk of the Part. All Stipulations of Discontinuances must be accompanied by proof of payment of the appropriate fee. (CPLR § 8020[d][1]).

Infant's Compromise Orders:

Before submission of an Infant's Compromise Order, counsel shall obtain from the Clerk of Part 22 an infant compromise check list to ensure the submission of all necessary information and documentation. Infant Compromise Hearings will be scheduled by the Court, and the plaintiff will be informed of the hearing date via telephone.

Electronic Filing of Legal Papers:

Electronic filing is available for filing legal papers with the Court. Parties interested in electronic filing should read the materials set forth at www.nycourts.gov/efile. The rules and user's manual for electronic filing are available on this website.

On the return date, all parties must submit hard courtesy copies of any motion/responsive papers that are electronically filed.

Part 25G.   Hon. Lawrence V. Cullen

General Rules:

All counsel must appear for all calendared matters unless specifically excused.

Telephone calls regarding orders and procedures are to be directed to the Guardianship Office at (718) 298–1040.

Any calls regarding legal issues or emergencies may be directed to chambers at (718) 298–1083.

All scheduling and calendar matters shall be brought to the attention of the Clerk of Part 25G at (718) 298–1005.

Except as otherwise provided communications with chambers shall be by letter with the title of the action, index number, and the last date the action appeared on the calendar. Absent exceptional circumstances, ex parte communication shall be disregarded.

Copies of correspondence between counsel should not be sent to the Court as same will not be placed in the Court's file.

Petitions to Appoint a Guardian:

All petitions to appoint a Guardian shall be heard on Monday, Wednesday, and Thursday at the designated time.

All parties must appear on the return date of a petition to appoint a Guardian.

Affidavits of Service for Orders to Show Cause shall be filed in the clerk's office at least two (2) days prior to the return date.

Court Evaluator Reports shall be filed in the clerk's office at least two (2) day prior to the return date.

Motions/Petitions Other Than to Appoint a Guardian:

Effective Tuesday, November 9, 2010, All Motions/Orders to Show Cause, other than to Appoint a Guardian shall be heard on Tuesdays at 9:30 A.M. prompt.

All Motions must be submitted to the Guardianship Clerk's Office at least seven (7) days prior to the return date. Affidavits of Service and a statement that the Affidavit of Service is in conformity with section 81.16(3) of the Mental Hygiene Law must be submitted to the clerk's office.

All requests for expenditures may be submitted to the Court by Application and Order Form with the recommendations of the Court Examiner.

PROCEDURES FOR ADJOURNMENTS IN PART 25G MATTERS COMMENCED PURSUANT TO ARTICLE 81 OF THE MENTAL HYGIENE LAW

Orders to Show Cause for the Appointment of a Guardian:

Any adjournment sought in an Article 81 proceeding commenced before this Court will be entertained according to the following, which must be sent by facsimile transmission to the Court:

1. The attorney requesting an adjournment must, in writing, identify themselves, who they are representing, the specific nature of the proceeding for which the adjournment is sought, the names of those parties appearing in the matter, and the reason for which the adjournment is being requested;

2. In those matters before the Court pursuant to an initial Order to Show Cause seeking the appointment of a Guardian of the Person and Property, the party requesting the adjournment must clearly and unequivocally state in writing the present status of the alleged incapacitated person, and affirmatively represent to the Court that such person will not suffer any harm or prejudice to their person and property by the requested adjournment.

3. The attorney requesting the adjournment shall state in writing that they have contacted all other parties to the matter, and whether or not there is objection to the request. If said adjournment requested is on consent, then the Court shall be provided with three (3) dates on which all parties shall be available, none of which shall be a Tuesday or a Friday. The Stipulation shall either be delivered to the Clerk, or faxed to chambers at (718) 298–1132 two (2) days prior to the return date.

4. Upon receipt of the foregoing, the Court shall determine whether or not to grant the adjournment and if so, provide a new date via a faxed response to the requesting party only, who shall bear the burden of submitting to the Court a Stipulation of Adjournment executed by all parties. The adjournment will not be granted until receipt of said Stipulation, and failure to do so shall maintain the matter on its original return date.

5. Upon the Court either granting or denying the request for adjournment, the requesting party only, shall bear the burden of advising all parties thereto of the Court's determination.

All Other Motions/Calendared Matters:

1. Applications for adjournments of Motions and/or Petitions, other than those to appoint a guardian, as well as any other calendared matter, must be on Stipulation signed by all parties and the Court Evaluator, as well as approved by the Court prior to the date the matter appears on the calendar.

2. Any such Stipulation requesting an adjournment shall be either delivered to the Clerk, or faxed to chambers at (718) 298–1132, two (2) days prior to the return date. Upon receipt of the foregoing, the Court shall determine whether or not to grant the adjournment.

3. Upon the Court either granting or denying the request for adjournment, the requesting party only, shall bear the burden of advising thereto of the Court's determination.

JUSTICE DARRELL L. GAVRIN

Part 27.   Hon. Darrell L. Gavrin

Preliminary Conference

A preliminary conference shall be scheduled (1) automatically by the Court within 45 days after filing a Request for Judicial Intervention, pursuant to 22 NYCRR § 202.12(b), or (2) upon filing a written Request for a Preliminary Conference with the Clerk's Office, Room 140, in compliance with 22 NYCRR § 202.12(a) or an appropriate notice is filed in malpractice or certiorari cases pursuant to 22 NYCRR §§ 202.56 and 202.60.

All preliminary conferences will be held on MONDAYS at 9:30 A.M. at the Preliminary Conference Part, Room 314, of the courthouse, and they are presided over by the court-appointed referee, unless otherwise directed by the Court. Failure to appear at the scheduled preliminary conference may result in discovery being ordered ex parte or any other appropriate sanction including preclusion or dismissal ordered. Any inquiry pertaining to preliminary conferences shall be made to the Preliminary Conference Part at (718) 298–1046.

Compliance Conferences

Compliance conferences shall be held on the date scheduled in the Preliminary Conference Stipulation and Order. Conferences shall be held before Justice Ritholtz in Room 313, of the courthouse.

Any inquiry pertaining to a compliance conference shall be made to the Compliance Conference Part at 718–298–1093.

Motion Practice

The motion calendar will be called in Courtroom 505 every TUESDAY at 9:30 a.m. promptly. A second call of the calendar will be at 11:00 a.m.

Mandatory appearance is required by COUNSEL with knowledge of the case and with full authority to settle or enter into binding stipulations on the return date.

In the case of e-filed motions, a hard copy must be submitted to the Court on the return date.

On the return date, motions will be conferenced and/or orally argued at the discretion of the Court.

Do not call the Part or Chambers for adjournments as NO ADJOURNMENTS WILL BE GRANTED BY TELEPHONE.

THE COURT WILL NOT CONSIDER ANY LETTERS SENT TO CHAMBERS OR THE PART WITH REGARD TO A CASE.

Motions may be adjourned on consent provided a written stipulation of counsel is submitted to the Court prior to the return or adjourn date. All stipulations must contain the signature of the attorney consenting to the adjournment. A form which contains only the name of the firm on the stipulation will not be accepted. Stipulations must also contain a schedule for exchange of opposition and reply papers occurring prior the adjourn date. Stipulations may be submitted by calendar service or non-attorneys.

If consent for an adjournment cannot be obtained, counsel must make an application to the Court on the return date. Calendar service or non-attorneys will not be permitted to make applications for adjournments. Members of the Bar are to make every effort to notify their adversaries and co-counsel of all applications for adjournments in advance.

Adjournments will be limited to two, absent extenuating circumstances. Motions relating to discovery may be adjourned only once.

Answering and reply papers will be accepted only on the return date in the Part. The Court will not consider papers sent to Chambers or the Part after full submission of the motion or cross-motion(s). Papers will not be accepted from calendar service if a personal appearance by counsel is required. Courtesy copies of papers are NOT required.

Motion Papers and Ex Parte Applications:

All motions and ex parte applications submitted shall be in compliance with Uniform Rule § 202.5. In addition to these requirements, all pages and paragraphs must be numbered. All exhibits annexed to motion papers shall be preceded by numbered exhibit tabs.

FAILURE TO COMPLY WITH THE REQUIRE-MENTS OF THIS SECTION MAY RESULT IN REJECTION OF THE NON-COMPLYING SUBMISSION.

Copies of decisions on motions will only be mailed to attorneys and pro se litigants who provide the Part with a stamped, self-addressed envelope at the time of final submission of their motion. If no stamped, self-addressed envelope is provided, it is the responsibility of the respective attorneys and pro se litigants to follow up with the appropriate clerk's office to obtain a copy of the decision.

All inquiries as to case or calendar status are to be made to the appropriate clerk's office.

IAS Motion Support Office (718) 298–1009

Ex Parte Support Office (718) 298–1018

Trials

All counsel must submit to the Court, prior to the commencement of trial, marked pleadings, a copy of the bill of particulars, a witness list, exhibit list, proposed jury instructions, and a proposed jury verdict sheet. Counsel must also know the availability of all witnesses whom they intend to call during trial.

Motions in limine—On the first appearance in the Part for trial, any party intending to make a motion in limine shall submit a memorandum setting forth the nature of the application including supporting statutory or case law. The party shall furnish the Court with an original and one copy, and provide counsel for all parties with a copy.

The Court encourages trial exhibits be pre-marked for identification and, when possible, that parties stipulate to the admissibility of clearly admissible documents and records.

The trial will be conducted on a continual daily basis until its conclusion. No adjournments or delays during trial will be accepted, unless exigent circumstances exist.

Tort actions are generally bifurcated. The Court expects that any trial on damages will immediately follow a verdict finding the defendant(s) liable.

Settlements and Discontinuances

If an action is settled, discontinued or otherwise disposed of, counsel shall immediately inform the Court by submission of a copy of the stipulation of settlement or a letter directed to the Clerk of the Part. All stipulations of discontinuances must be accompanied by proof of payment of the appropriate fee (CPLR § 8020 [d] [1]).

Infant's Compromise Orders

Before submission of an Infant's Compromise Order, counsel shall obtain from the Clerk of the Part an infant's compromise checklist to ensure the submission of all necessary information and documentation. Infant's compromise orders sent to Chambers without the required completed worksheet will be returned to counsel.

Proof of payment of any appropriate fee is required.

Infant compromise hearings will be scheduled by the Court and the plaintiff will be informed of the hearing date by mail.

Uncontested Matrimonials

Any corrections to a rejected set of matrimonial papers must be submitted to the Matrimonial Clerk and NOT directly to Chambers.

This Court takes seriously its duty to protect children in calculating child support. Unsupported deviations from the guidelines will result in rejections and thus slow down the sought-after judgment of divorce. Deviations from child support guidelines must be thoroughly explained in an affidavit of the party, without resorting to conclusory language, and in the attorney's affirmation.

JUSTICE FREDERICK D. R. SAMPSON

Part 31. Hon. Frederick D. R. Sampson

NO TELEPHONE INQUIRES CONCERNING MOTIONS OR APPLICATIONS MAY BE MADE TO CHAMBERS.

All such inquires must be made to Motion Support (718–298–1009) or to the Ex Parte Office (718–298–1018) or the Clerk of the Part (718–298–1666).

No adjournments will be granted by telephone.

Preliminary Conference

A preliminary conference shall be scheduled automatically by the Court within 45 days after filing a Request for Judicial Intervention, pursuant to 22

NYCRR 202.12; or upon filing a written request for preliminary conference in the Clerk's Office, Room 140, Supreme Court 88–11 Sutphin Blvd. Jamaica, NY, in compliance with 22 NYCRR 202.12 (a); or where an appropriate notice is filed in malpractice or certiorari cases pursuant to 22 NYCRR 202.56 and 202.60.

All preliminary conferences will be held on Monday at 9:30 a.m. at the Preliminary Conference Part, Room 314, of the Jamaica Courthouse located at 88–11 Sutphin Blvd, Jamaica, NY and are presided over by the court-appointed referee, unless otherwise directed by the Court.

Failure to appear at the scheduled preliminary conference may result in discovery being ordered exparte or any other appropriate sanction including preclusion or dismissal. Any inquiry pertaining to preliminary conferences shall be made to the Preliminary Conference Part at (718) 298–1046.

Compliance Conference

The Compliance Conference shall be held on the date scheduled in the Preliminary Conference Stipulation and Order. Conferences shall be held before Justice Ritholz in Room 313 of the Jamaica Courthouse located at 88–11 Sutphin Blvd. Jamaica, NY.

Motions

All motions filed and accepted in the Clerk's Office and assigned to Justice Sampson are to be heard in Part 31 on Thursdays at 11:30 a.m., located at 25–10 Court Square, Long Island City, N.Y. 11101, Courtroom 208. The first calendar call will be held at 11:30 a.m., promptly. A second call will follow immediately thereafter. Matrimonial motions shall be heard on Thursdays at 10:00 a.m.

No motion relating to disclosure will be accepted by the Clerk's Office without an affirmation of good faith as required by Uniform Rule 202.7.

The answering papers, including cross-motions, affirmations in opposition, and reply affirmations, will be accepted only on the return date in the Part.

THE COURT WILL NOT CONSIDER PAPERS SENT TO CHAMBERS OR TO THE PART AFTER SUBMISSION OF THE MOTION, NOR CROSS MOTIONS THAT DO NOT HAVE PROOF OF PAYMENT OF THE APPROPRIATE FEE. (CPLR 8020(a).)

Appearance, of all counsel and pro-se litigants, is MANDATORY on all Motions and Orders to Show Cause. The Motions will be heard for all purposes in the Part on the return date. Any attorney appearing MUST be familiar with the case and authorized to resolve any and all issues. On the return date, the motion will be conferenced with the expectation that the issues will be resolved by stipulation. All stipulations must indicate that the motion(s), and where appropriate, the cross-motion(s) is/are being withdrawn pursuant to the stipulation and must be signed by the attorneys appearing at the calendar call. The name of the attorney appearing on behalf of the firm is to be printed legibly beneath each signature. Papers will not be accepted from calendar service inasmuch as a personal appearance by counsel and/or pro-se litigant is required.

Applications for adjournments either on consent or otherwise will be entertained only at the call of the calendar, and will not be entertained by mail, fax, or telephone. Calendar service or non-attorneys, (except for pro-se Litigants) will not be permitted to make applications for adjournments. No applications will be granted without the permission of the Court. Counsel must notify their adversaries of their intention to seek an adjournment.

Courtesy copies of motions papers need not be provided except as required by the Courts Rules concerning Electronic Filing.

Motion Papers

All motion papers submitted shall be in compliance with Uniform Rule Sec.202.5, concerning papers in the court. In addition to the requirements of Sec.202.5, all pages are to be numbered and all paragraphs are to be numbered. All exhibits are to proceeded by a numbered exhibit tab which protrudes from the stack of papers. All submissions are to be securely fastened so as to prevent the papers from separating from each other and becoming lost.

FAILURE TO COMPLY WITH THE REQUIREMENTS OF THIS SECTION MAY RESULT IN REJECTION OF THE OFFENDING SUBMISSION.

Decisions

Any attorney or pro se litigant desiring a copy of the Court's decision must provide a stamped self-addressed envelope with the motion papers.

Trials

All counsel must submit to the court, prior to the commencement of trial, marked pleadings, a copy of the bill of particulars, a witness list, exhibit list, proposed jury verdict sheet and proposed jury instructions written in the narrative and verbatim as counsel would have the Court to charge.

The trial will be conducted on a continual basis until conclusion.

No adjournments will be permitted unless exigent circumstances exist.

The parties must notify the court of all legal issues and shall furnish the court with copies of the cases and authority relied upon, highlighting in yellow the appropriate portion supporting their positions.

The parties must be present for settlement or discontinuance of any case on trial. There shall be a complete Allocution of the Plaintiff.

Settlements and Discontinuances

If an action is settled, discontinued or otherwise disposed of counsel shall immediately inform the court by submission of a copy of the stipulation or a letter directed to the Clerk of the Part.

All Stipulations of Discontinuance must be accompanied by proof of payment of the appropriate fee. (CPLR 8020(d)(1)).

Electronic Filing

Where motion papers, including exhibits and memorandum of law are filed by electronic means pursuant to uniform rule 202.5–b, courtesy hard copies of such papers must be submitted to the court on the return date of the motion/application. Each submitted copy shall bear a conspicuous notice on the first page thereof that the document has been filed electronically (Uniform rule 202.5–b(d)(4)).

The court's rules concerning motion papers apply to courtesy copies submitted to the court.

All proposed orders to show cause must be submitted to the court in hard copy.

JUSTICE CHARLES J. MARKEY

Part 32.   Hon. Charles J. Markey

Preliminary and Compliance Conference

All preliminary and compliance conferences are held in Jamaica, and not before Justice Markey.

All preliminary conferences of cases assigned to Justice Markey will be held before Court Attorney-Referee Elizabeth Yablon in room 314 of the Jamaica courthouse, on Mondays at 11:30 A.M. The telephone number for the P.C. Part is 718–298–1046.

All compliance conferences of cases assigned to Justice Markey will be held before Justice Ritholtz in room 313 of the Jamaica courthouse on the assigned date in the P.C. order. The telephone number for the Compliance Conference Part is 718–298–1093.

Motions

All motions should be made returnable ONLY on a Thursday, 11:30 am, in Part 32, Room 140, at 25–10 Court Square, Long Island City, NY 11101.

NO adjournments will be granted on the telephone. Applications for adjournments on consent or otherwise will be entertained only at the call of the calendar and will not be entertained by mail, fax, or by telephone. ONLY WITHDRAWALS of motions—not adjournments—may be communicated by Fax to Chambers until 10:30 A.M. of the return date. The fax number to Justice Markey's Chambers is 718–520–7379. Adjournments on consent will be allowed upon written stipulation and are limited to two such adjournments. All adjournment stipulations must contain the signatures of the individual attorneys consenting to the adjournment. Members of the Bar are to make every effort to notify their adversaries and co-counsel of all applications for adjournments in advance.

Where personal appearance is not required under these rules, a lawyer's service may answer the call of the calendar.

The answering papers, including cross-motions, affirmations in opposition and reply affirmations, will be accepted only on the return date in the Part.

THE COURT WILL NOT CONSIDER PAPERS SENT TO CHAMBERS OR TO THE PART AFTER SUBMISSION OF THE MOTION NOR CROSS MOTIONS THAT DO NOT HAVE PROOF OF PAYMENT OF THE APPROPRIATE FEE. (CPLR § 8020(a)).

All motions, except those made by order to show cause and those concerning discovery, are deemed submitted. If the Court requires oral argument on substantive, non-discovery motions, counsel will be alerted.

Personal appearance is required only for orders to show cause and ALL discovery motions. If counsel cannot reach an agreement on a discovery dispute, the Court will hold a conference and make a recommendation which will be set forth in a written order, expeditiously.

On all motions that are "E-filed", Justice Markey requires a hard copy of the complete papers, including all exhibits. If, on the return date of the motion, counsel has failed to provide a hard copy of the motion or responsive papers, the Court will either mark off the motion, or, in the case of opposition papers, consider the motion as unopposed.

All responsive papers are to be submitted on the call of the calendar. Responsive papers cannot be delivered or faxed to Chambers without the express INVITATION by either the Judge or his Law Secretary. Violators will receive such papers returned to them with a notation that they were UNREAD.

Attempts to hinder, thwart, or obstruct discovery or to direct a witness not to answer during an EBT may incur serious sanctions.

Except upon orders to show cause, if time is needed for reply, that should be arranged between counsel before the submission date. Requests for adjournments of motions must be made to the Court and upon consent.

Counsel are reminded that if a case is settled while a motion is under consideration, they have a duty to alert Chambers immediately of such settlement and the withdrawal of the motion, so as to spare the Court the effort of preparing a decision.

The Court will not mail copies of decisions. They will be available either online at WebCivil Supreme or at the County Clerk's Office in Jamaica.

Trials

Requests for Interpreters. Any request for an interpreter for the trial must be clearly and IMMEDIATELY communicated, not only to the Part Clerk, but to the Judge and to the Judge's Law Secretary.

Bifurcated Trials. Tort actions are generally bifurcated. The Court expects, unless advised previously by counsel, that any trial on damages will follow immediately after a verdict finding a defendant liable.

Be Prepared. Prior to jury selection, counsel is cautioned to ascertain the availability of all witnesses and subpoenaed documents. Plaintiff's counsel shall requisition the file and deliver it to the Courtroom as soon as possible after assignment of the case to Part 32. Counsel must advise the Court, Part Clerk, and Court Officer of any special needs, e.g., easels, blackboards, shadow boxes, television, subpoenaed material, etc., in advance, so as not to delay the progress of the trial.

Marked Pleadings Plus: Plaintiff's counsel shall furnish the Court with copies of marked pleadings, the bill of particulars, and a copy of any statutory provisions, including the NYC Administrative Code and the Traffic Regulations of the City of New York, in effect at the time the cause of action arose, upon which either the plaintiff or defendant relies.

In Limine Motions: All oral motions *in limine* must be supported by a written memorandum of law, with citations to cases and treatises of evidence law. In addition, counsel MUST provide the court with photocopies of those cases and pages from evidence law treatises PROVIDED that an exact copy of same is provided to opposing counsel.

In ALL cases involving expert testimony, counsel shall provide the Court with a Glossary of Terms likely to be used during the testimony.

Uncontested Matrimonials

Any corrections to a rejected set of matrimonial papers must be submitted to the Matrimonial Clerk in Jamaica, and NOT directly to Chambers.

This Court takes seriously its duty to protect children in calculating child support. Unsupported deviations from the guidelines will result in rejections and thus delay the sought judgment of divorce. Radical deviations from child support guidelines must be thoroughly explained in an affidavit of a party, without resorting to conclusory language and in an attorney's affirmation. This Court expects counsel and any divorce service to take seriously their roles in reporting incomes honestly and calculating child support pursuant to the guidelines.

JUSTICE JAMES J. GOLIA

Part 33. Hon. James J. Golia

Preliminary Conference

All preliminary conferences will be held on Tuesdays at 9:30 a.m. in the Preliminary Conference Part, Room 314 of the Jamaica courthouse located at 88–11 Sutphin Blvd., Jamaica, NY. Failure to appear at the scheduled preliminary conference may result in discovery being ordered ex-parte or any other appropriate sanction, including preclusion or dismissal ordered. Inquiries pertaining to preliminary conferences shall be made to the Preliminary Conference Part at (718) 298–1046.

Compliance Conference

Compliance conferences shall be held on the date scheduled in the Preliminary Conference Stipulation and Order. Conferences shall be held in Room 313 of the Jamaica courthouse. Inquiries pertaining to compliance conferences shall be made to the Compliance Conference Part at 718–298–1093.

Motions

The Motion Calendar will be called in the Long Island City Supreme Court Courthouse located at 25–10 Court Square, Long Island City, NY 11101–4335, every Thursday at 11:30 AM. PROMPTLY in courtroom B–10. No courtesy copies to chambers are required EXCEPT IN THE CASE OF E-FILED MOTIONS.

Personal appearances are mandatory on all disclosure and discovery related motions and for all orders to show cause. All other motions are deemed submitted and a personal appearance is not required. An attorney appearing on a case for any purpose must be familiar with the case, ready and authorized to resolve any and all issues. Oral argument will be entertained in the Court's discretion. Whenever a personal appearance is not required, use of calendar service is permitted to submit papers and to request consent adjournments.

NO adjournments will be granted on the telephone. Applications for adjournments on consent or otherwise will be entertained only at the call of the calendar and will not be entertained by mail, fax or by telephone. Adjournments on consent will be allowed upon written stipulation and are limited to two such adjournments. All adjournment stipulations must contain the signatures of the individual attorneys consenting to the adjournment. Members of the Bar are to make every effort to notify their adversaries and co-counsel of all applications for adjournments in advance.

Answering papers, including cross motions, affirmations in opposition and reply affirmations, will be accepted only on the return date in the Part.

All motions and ex-parte applications submitted shall be in compliance with Uniform Rule § 202.5. In addition, all pages and paragraphs must be numbered and all exhibits are to be proceeded by a numbered exhibit tab which protrudes from the stack of papers. All submissions are to be securely fastened so as to prevent the papers from being lost. Failure to comply with the requirements of this section may result in rejection of the non-complying papers.

All inquiries to case or calendar status are to be made to the appropriate clerk's office.

IAS Motion Support Office (718) 298–1009

Ex–Parte Support Office (718) 298–1018

Trials

Be Prepared

Plaintiff's counsel shall requisition the file to the Part 33 courtroom immediately after assignment of the case to this part. Counsel should ascertain the availability of all witnesses and subpoenaed documents. Any special needs, e.g., interpreter, easels, blackboards, shadow boxes, television, subpoenaed material, etc., must be reported to the Court Officer, in advance, so as not to delay the progress of the trial.

Marked Pleadings Plus

Plaintiff's counsel shall furnish the Court with copies of marked pleadings, the bill(s) of particulars and a copy of any statutory provisions in effect at the time the cause of action arose upon which any party relies;

Counsel for both parties shall provide to the Court:

a) a chronological summary of all expert reports to be offered into evidence together with a glossary of terms that are used or are expected to be used by the expert witness but are typically unfamiliar to a lay person;

b) a chronological list of all dates relevant to the matter on trial;

c) all reports, depositions and written statements which may be used to either refresh a witness' recollection and/or cross-examine the witness;

d) to the extent any part of a deposition is to be read into evidence (as distinguished from mere use on cross-examination) you must, in advance, provide the Court and your adversary with the page and line number of all such testimony so that all objections can be addressed prior to use before the jury;

e) a list of the names of all witnesses to be called by you and for each such witness the elements of proof to be supplied or addressed by such witness; and

f) suggested jury charges and a suggested verdict questionnaire. Amendments thereto shall be permitted at the final charging conference. Jury charges should be referred to by PJI number and topic. If any changes to the PJI are suggested, then the entire proposed charge should be set forth and the changes should be highlighted. Citations to appropriate statutory or common law authority must be given in support of suggested non–PJI jury charges or suggested PJI modifications.

Pre-trial conferences will be held prior to every trial.

At this conference counsel should be prepared to:

a) Discuss settlement;

b) Advise the Court as to all anticipated disputed issues of law and fact, and provide the Court with copies of all statutory and common law authority upon which counsel will rely;

c) Stipulate to undisputed facts and the admissibility of clearly admissible documents and records;

d) Advise the Court of any anticipated *in limine* motions or evidentiary objections which counsel intends to make. Motions *in limine* may be made orally however must be supported by a memorandum of law. All prior decisions and orders relevant to any *in limine* application must be provided to the Court;

e) Advise the Court of any anticipated requests for a jury instruction relating to missing witnesses and/or documents;

f) Advise the Court of any anticipated request for apportionment as to alleged culpable non-parties pursuant to CPLR Article 16.

g) Discuss scheduling as well as the number of witnesses to be called at trial, and the estimated length of the trial.

Settlements and Discontinuances

If an action is settled, discontinued or otherwise disposed of, counsel shall immediately inform the Court by submission of a copy of the stipulation of settlement or a letter directed to the Clerk of the Part. All stipulations of discontinuances must be accompanied by proof of payment of the appropriate fee. (CPLR § 8020[d][1]).

Infant's Compromise Orders

Before submission of an infant's compromise order, counsel shall obtain from the clerk of Part 33 an infant compromise checklist to ensure the submission of all necessary information and documentation. Infant compromise hearings will be scheduled by the Court and the plaintiff will be informed of the hearing date by mail.

Uncontested Matrimonials

Any corrections to a rejected set of matrimonial papers must be submitted to the Matrimonial Clerk in Jamaica, NOT directly to chambers.

JUSTICE ROBERT J. MCDONALD

Part 34.   Hon. Robert J. McDonald

Preliminary Conference

A preliminary conference shall be scheduled automatically by the Court within forty-five (45) after filing a Request for Judicial Intervention, pursuant to 22 NYCRR 202.12(b); or upon filing a written Request for a Preliminary Conference with the Jamaica Clerk's Office, Room 140, in compliance with 22 NYCRR 202.12(a); or an appropriate notice is filed in malpractice or certiorari cases pursuant to 22 NYCRR 202.56 and 202.60.

Preliminary conferences are held in the Jamaica courthouse not the Long Island City courthouse.

All preliminary conferences will be held on Wednesday at 9:30 a.m. at the Preliminary Conference Part, Room 314 of the Jamaica courthouse located at 88–11 Sutphin Blvd., Jamaica, NY, and they are presided over by the court-appointed referee, unless otherwise directed by the Court. Failure to appear at the scheduled preliminary conference may result in discovery being ordered ex-parte or any other appropriate sanction, including preclusion or dismissal ordered. Any inquiry pertaining to preliminary conferences shall be made to the Preliminary Conference Part at (718) 298–1046.

Compliance Conference

Conferences shall be held before Justice Ritholtz in Room 313 at the Jamaica courthouse, not the Long Island City courthouse.

Compliance conferences shall be held on the date scheduled in the Preliminary Conferences Stipulation and Order. Any inquiry pertaining to compliance conferences shall be made to the Compliance Conference Part at 718–298–1093.

Motion

The Motion Calendar will be called in the Long Island City Supreme Court Courthouse located at 25–10 Court Square, Long Island City, NY 11101–4335, every Thursday at 11:30 AM. PROMPTLY in courtroom 304. No courtesy copies to chambers are required EXCEPT IN THE CASE OF E-FILED MOTIONS. The Court will not accept stipulations to adjourn motions prior to the calendar call.

All motions relating to any phase of discovery and/or Bill of Particulars, including motions to preclude and/or strike or restore to the trial calendar, require a personal appearance by counsel for all parties. Counsel should be familiar with the case and prepared to discuss and agree upon a discovery schedule with the Court. If the Court requires oral argument, counsel will be alerted. If the motion has been brought by an Order to Show Cause and there is a stay or temporary restraining order therein, then all parties MUST APPEAR on the return date. All other motions and applications may be submitted on papers only.

Oral argument is not required and will be entertained only in the Court's discretion. Whenever a personal appearance is not required, use of calendar service is permitted both to submit papers and to request consent adjournments, which will be limited to two. Adjournments on consent will be allowed upon written stipulation. All stipulations must contain the

signature of the attorney consenting to the adjournment. A form bearing only the name of the firm will not be accepted.

Adjournments will be limited to two, absent extenuating circumstances.

The answering papers, including cross motions, affirmations in opposition and reply affirmations, will be accepted only on the return date in the Part. The court will not consider papers sent to chambers or to the part after submission of the motion or cross motion(s) that do not have proof of payment of the appropriate fee. (CPLR § 8020[a]).

The Court further directs that any attorney appearing on a case for any purpose must be familiar with the case, ready and authorized to resolve any and all issues.

All motions and ex-parte applications submitted shall be in compliance with Uniform Rule § 202.5. In addition to these requirements, all pages and paragraphs must be numbered. All exhibits are to be proceeded by a numbered exhibit tab which protrudes from the stack of papers. All submissions are to be securely fastened so as to prevent the papers from being lost. Failure to comply with the requirements of this section may result in rejection of the non-complying papers.

Do not call the Part or Chambers for adjournments. NO adjournments will be granted on the telephone. Use service or mail. The members of the Bar are to make every effort to notify their adversaries and co-counsel of all applications for adjournments in advance.

All inquiries to case or calendar status are to be made to the appropriate clerk's office.

IAS Motion Support Office (718) 298–1009

Ex–Parte Support Office (718) 298–1018

Trials

All counsel must submit to the court, prior to the commencement of trial, marked pleadings, a copy of the Bill of Particulars, a witness list, exhibit list, proposed jury instruction and a proposed verdict sheet. Counsel must also know the availability of all witnesses who they intend to call during trial.

On the first appearance in the Part for trial, any party intending to make a motion *in limine* shall make such motion orally but may submit a memorandum of law in support of the application. The party shall furnish the court with an original and one copy and provide counsel for all parties with a copy. Any written motions *in limine* require proof of payment of the appropriate fee.

The trial will be conducted on a continual daily basis until its conclusion. No adjournments or delays during trial will be accepted unless exigent circumstances exist.

Tort actions are generally bifurcated. The Court expects, unless advised previously by counsel, that any trial on damages will follow immediately after a verdict finding the defendant liable.

Prior to coming to the Part, plaintiff's counsel shall requisition the file from the County Clerk and deliver it to the Part Clerk. Counsel must advise the Court, Part Clerk and Court Officer of any special needs, e.g., interpreters, easels, shadow boxes, television, VCR, etc., in advance, so as not to delay the progress of the trial.

The Court encourages that trial exhibits be pre-marked for identification and, where possible, stipulate to the admissibility of clearly admissible documents and records.

Counsel should alert the Court at the pre-trial conference as to any anticipated problems regarding the attendance at trial of parties, attorneys or essential witnesses and any other practical problems that the Court should consider in scheduling.

Settlements and Discontinuances

If an action is settled, discontinued or otherwise disposed of, counsel shall immediately inform the Court by submission of a copy of the stipulation of settlement or a letter directed to the Clerk of the Part. All stipulations of discontinuances must be accompanied by proof of payment of the appropriate fee. (CPLR § 8020[d][1]).

Infant's Compromise Orders

Before submission of an infant's compromise order, counsel shall obtain from the clerk of Part 34 an infant's compromise checklist to ensure the submission of all necessary information and documentation. Proof of payment of any appropriate fee is required.

Uncontested Matrimonials

Any corrections to a rejected set of matrimonial papers must be submitted to the Matrimonial Clerk in Jamaica, not Long Island City and NOT directly to chambers.

This Court takes seriously its duty to protect children in calculating child support. Unsupported deviations from the guidelines will result in rejections and thus slow down the sought after judgment of divorce. Deviations from child support guidelines must be thoroughly explained in an affidavit of the party, without resorting to conclusory language, and in the attorney's affirmation.

JUSTICE DICCIA PINEDA-KIRWAN

Part 36. Hon. Diccia Pineda–Kirwan

An attorney appearing on a case for any purpose must be familiar with the case, ready and authorized to resolve any and all issues.

Plaintiff's counsel shall requisition the file to the Part 36 courtroom immediately after assignment of the case to this part for trial. Counsel should ascertain the availability of all witnesses and subpoenaed documents. Any special needs, e.g., interpreter, easels, blackboards, shadow boxes, television, subpoenaed, material, etc., must be reported to the Court Officer, in advance, so as not to delay the progress of the trial.

Preliminary Conference

All preliminary conferences will be held on Mondays at 9:30 AM in the Centralized Preliminary Conference Part, Room 314 of the Jamaica courthouse located at 88–11 Sutphin Blvd., Jamaica, NY.

Failure to appear at the scheduled preliminary conference may result in discovery being ordered ex parte or any other appropriate sanction, including preclusion or dismissal ordered. Inquiries pertaining to preliminary conferences shall be made to the Centralized Preliminary Conference Part at (718) 298-1046.

Compliance Conference

Compliance conferences shall be held on the date scheduled in the Preliminary Conference Stipulation and Order.

Conferences shall be held in the Centralized Compliance Conference Part in Room 313 of the Jamaica courthouse. Inquiries pertaining to compliance conferences shall be made to the Centralized Compliance Conference Part at (718) 298–1093.

Motions

The Motion Calendar will be called in the Long Island City Supreme Court Courthouse located at 25-10 Court Square, Long Island City, NY 11101, every Thursday at 11:30 AM PROMPTLY in courtroom 233. Oral arguments will be entertained in the Court's discretion.

PERSONAL APPEARANCES ARE MANDATORY ON ALL MOTIONS AND ORDERS TO SHOW CAUSE.

Discovery related motions are expected to be RESOLVED by the parties. Discovery motions, including motions to strike case from or restore cases to the Trial Calendar, must be in compliance with Uniform Rule 202.7, setting forth IN DETAIL, the efforts made by the moving attorney to obtain discovery prior to requesting judicial intervention. Conclusory statements, a single pro forma letter sent in an attempt to satisfy this requirement, or other failure to demonstrate good faith efforts may result in a summary denial of the motion. All orders to show cause must comply with Uniform Rule 202.7(d). Failure of the moving party to appear will result in the motion being deemed abandoned, and any opposition papers will not be considered.

All motions and ex parte applications submitted shall be in compliance with Uniform Rule § 202.5. In addition, all pages and paragraphs must be numbered and all exhibits are to be proceeded by a numbered exhibit tab which protrudes from the stack of papers. All submissions are to be securely fastened so as to prevent the papers from being lost. Failure to comply with the requirements of this section may result in the rejection of the non-complying papers.

The Court will not consider papers sent to chambers or to the part after submission of the motion or cross motions that do not have proof of payment of the appropriate fee. [CPLR 8020(a)].

If a case is settled while a motion is pending, counsel has a duty to notify the Chambers immediately of the settlement and the withdrawal of the motion, in order to facilitate judicial economy.

E–FILING RULES AND PROTOCOLS

All parties should familiarize themselves with the statewide E-Filing Rules: Uniform Rule §§ 202.5–b and 202.5–bb that are available at www.nycourts.gov/efile. General questions about e-filing should be addressed to the E–Filing Resource Center at (646) 386–3033 or efile@court.state.ny.us.

HARD COPY SUBMISSION

No courtesy copies to chambers are required EXCEPT IN THE CASE OF E-FILED MOTIONS. All hard copy submissions in E-filed cases must bear the Notice of Hard Copy Submission—E–Filed Case required by uniform Rule § 202.5–b9d)(1). If on the return date of the motion, counsel has failed to provide a hard copy of the motion or responsive papers, the Court will either mark off the motion, or, in the case of opposition papers, consider the motion as unopposed.

ADJOURNMENTS

Applications for adjournments on consent or otherwise will be entertained ONLY at the call of the calendar and will NOT be entertained by mail, fax or by telephone. Adjournments on consent will be allowed upon written stipulation and are limited to two adjournments. All adjournment stipulations must contain the signatures of the individual attorneys consenting to the adjournment. Members of the Bar are to make every effort to notify their adversaries and co-counsel of all applications for adjournment in advance. DISCOVERY RELATED MOTIONS WILL NOT BE ADJOURNED.

WITHDRAWALS

WITHDRAWAL of motions—not adjournments— may be communicated by Fax to Chambers with prior notice of same to the adverse party no later than 10:30 AM on the return date of the motion.

ANSWERING PAPERS

Answering papers, including cross motions, affirmations in opposition and reply affirmations, will be accepted only on the return date in the Part. Service requirements under CPLR 2214 and 2215 will be strictly enforced. No sur-reply papers will be considered without express leave of the Court. No papers shall be accepted after a motion is marked submitted.

All copies of decisions will be available either online or at the County Clerk's Office in Jamaica. Counsel should NOT contact Chambers for a copy of a decision rendered. All inquiries to case or calendar status are to be made to the appropriate clerk's office.

IAS Motion Support Office (718) 298–1009

Ex Parte Support Office (718) 298–1018

Matrimonial Office (718) 298–1012

Trials

Marked Pleadings Plus

Plaintiff's counsel shall furnish the Court with copies of marked pleadings, the bill(s) of particulars and a copy of any statutory provisions, including the NYC Administrative Code and the Traffic Regulations of the City of New York, in effect at the time the cause of action arose upon which any party relies;

Counsel for both parties shall provide to the Court:

1. A chronological summary of all expert reports to be offered into evidence together with a glossary of terms that are used or are expected to be used by the expert witness but are typically unfamiliar to a lay person;

2. A chronological list of all dates relevant to the matter on trial;

3. All reports, depositions and written statements which may be used to either refresh a witness' recollection and/or cross-examine the witness;

4. To the extent any part of a deposition is to be read into evidence (as distinguished from mere use on cross-examination) you must, in advance, provide the Court and your adversary with the page and line number of all such testimony so that all objections can be addressed prior to use before the jury;

5. A list of the names of all witnesses to be called by you and for each such witness the elements of proof to be supplied or addressed by such witness; and

6. Suggested jury charges and a suggested verdict questionnaire. Amendments thereto shall be permitted at the final charging conference. Jury charges should be referred to by PJI number and topic. If any changes to the PJI are suggested, then the entire proposed charge should be set forth and the changes should be highlighted. Citations to appropriate statutory or common law authority must be given in sup-

port of suggested non-PJI jury charges or suggested PJI modifications.

Pre-trial conferences will be held prior to every trial.

At this conference counsel should be prepared to:

1. Discuss settlement;

2. Advise the Court as to all anticipated disputed issues of law and fact, and provide the Court with copies of all statutory and common law authority upon which counsel will rely;

3. Stipulate to undisputed facts and the admissibility of clearly admissible documents and records;

4. Advise the Court of any anticipated in limine motions or evidentiary objections which counsel intends to make. Motions in limine may be made orally however must be supported by a memorandum of law, with citations to the relevant statutory and case law relied upon, as well as treatises of evidence law. All prior decisions and orders relevant to any in limine application must be provided to the Court;

5. Advise the Court of any anticipated requests for a jury instruction relating to missing witnesses and/or documents;

6. Advise the Court of any anticipated requests for apportionment as to alleged culpable non-parties pursuant to CPLR Article 16; and

7. Discuss scheduling as well as the number of witnesses to be called at trial, and the estimated length of the trial.

8. Counsel is advised that, pursuant to 22 NYCRR 202.26(e), the court may require parties, representatives of parties, representatives of insurance carriers or persons having an interest in any settlement, including those holding liens on any settlement or verdict, to also attend the conference.

Settlement and Discontinuances

If an action is settled, discontinued or otherwise disposed of, counsel shall immediately inform the Court by submission of a copy of the stipulation of settlement or a letter directed to the Clerk of the Part. All stipulations of discontinuances must be accompanied by proof of payment of the appropriate fee (CPLR § 8020[d][1]).

Infant Compromise Orders

Before submission of an infant's compromise order, counsel shall obtain from the clerk of Part 36 an infant compromise checklist to ensure the submission of all necessary information and documentation. Infant compromise hearings will be scheduled by the Court and the plaintiff's attorney will be informed of the hearing date.

Uncontested Matrimonials

All uncontested matrimonial applications shall contain ALL requisite supporting documentation, which are set forth by the New York State Office of Court Administration on their website.

If an uncontested matrimonial submission is dismissed, counsel may move to restore the matter or recommence the action upon compliance with the court's directives. Those applications must be submitted to the Matrimonial Clerk in Jamaica, NOT directly to chambers.

The Court takes seriously its duty to protect children in calculating child support. Unsupported deviations from the guidelines will result in rejections and thus delay the sought judgment of divorce. Radical deviations from child support guidelines must be thoroughly explained in an affidavit of a party, without resorting to conclusory language and in an attorney's affirmation. This Court expects counsel and any divorce service to take seriously their roles in reporting incomes honestly and calculating child support according to the guidelines.

JUSTICE PAM JACKMAN BROWN

Part 51. Hon. Pam Jackman Brown

Unless otherwise directed by the Court, appearance of counsel and their clients is mandatory on all matrimonial matters including, but not limited to motion calendar calls, preliminary conferences, compliance conferences, pre-trial conferences and all other Court-ordered conferences.

Calendar call is at 9:30 a.m. Second calendar call is at 11:00 A.M., unless the matter is scheduled as a time certain. Please be prompt for all appearances.

Communication with the Court between Court dates is by telephone conference only. If you are unable to obtain the cooperation of opposing counsel or opposing party, pro se, to place a conference call, you may call one of the Law Secretaries and request assistance in setting up a conference call.

Appearances and Adjournments

At the time of calendar call or check in, the Court shall be notified of any Orders of Protection.

Notification for Court Interpreter Services shall be made to the Court as soon as practicable, but not less than 24 hours prior to first court appearance. At time of calendar call or check in, the Court shall be reminded that Court Interpreter Services are needed.

A notice of appearance shall be filed in the Office of the County Clerk and the Matrimonial office with a courtesy copy to Part Clerk.

Two business cards are to be submitted to the Court at the first appearance.

Counsel must notify their adversary of any intention to seek an adjournment, and if possible, to obtain consent of all parties. Adjournments may be sought by telephone conference call with the Law Secretary, Associate Law Secretary, or Part Clerk, to be followed by a written stipulation confirming the date. The stipulation shall be faxed to the Chambers at least one (1) day prior to the scheduled appearance date. All adjournments are subject to final approval by the Judge in advance of a court date and per rules.

All adjournments on the grounds of engagement of counsel shall be granted only in accordance with Part 125 of the Rules of the Chief Administrator of the Courts. Affirmations must be faxed to the Court at least one (1) day prior to the Court appearance. Litigants who are represented by counsel must communicate with the chambers staff through their counsel only.

No calls should be placed to chambers unless at the instruction of the Court.

No ex parte communication with Court.

Minor children are not permitted in the courtroom, except by permission of the Court.

Preliminary Conferences

Preliminary conferences shall be held on Wednesdays. The Calendar call is 9:30 a.m..

Prior to the call of the preliminary conference calendar, counsel and/or pro se litigants will be completing the preliminary conference order.

Pursuant to 22 NYCRR 202.16(d), an RJI shall be filed within forty-five (45) days of the date of service of the summons unless an affidavit of no necessity is filed, in which case, the RJI Shall be filed within 120 days.

Net worth statements with required documents, including parties' recent pay stubs or W-2 and attorney's retainer statement, are to be filed with the Court (10) days prior to the conference date. The appearance of the parties is required at the Preliminary Conference.

Preliminary conferences must be conducted within forty-five (45) after assignment of the action. The Court will not grant adjournments of preliminary conferences beyond the forty-five (45) day period.

Absent submission of a fully completed net worth statement by the moving party, applications for financial relief will be denied without prejudice.

Compliance Conferences

Compliance conferences shall be held on dates as scheduled by the Court. The Calendar call is 9:30 a.m..

Before the call of the compliance conference calendar, counsel and/or pro se litigants will begin completing the compliance conference order.

Failure to comply with discovery or preliminary conference orders shall be brought the Court's attention by conference call to Chambers prior to the compliance conference.

Counsel attending the conference must be fully familiar with and authorized to settle, stipulate or dispose of such actions.

A Note of Issue shall be filed in accordance with the Compliance Conference Order or other order of the Court.

Counsel and their clients must appear at the compliance conference

Matrimonial Motions

Motions shall be heard on Thursdays. The Calendar call is 9:30 a.m.

Motions shall be made returnable only on the part's motion day. All motion papers (including opposition and reply) must state the motion sequence number on the first page. To reduce the need for motion practice, counsel are encouraged to contact the Court by conference call prior to filing a motion.

Oral argument is required on all motions unless dispensed with by the Judge.

The Court does not accept Courtesy copies of motion papers unless by Court's approval.

Pursuant to the CPLR, after argument of an application or submission of a motion, sur-replies, memoranda and letters addressed to the substance of the pending application will not be considered without prior permission of the Court.

If a motion has been brought by Order to Show Cause, the movant must submit the affidavits of service on the return date. Copies of the Family Court petition and any existing orders must be submitted with applications to consolidate.

Any motion pending upon the settlement of the case will be deemed withdrawn unless explicit provision is made for its preservation.

All exhibits shall be clearly marked and tabbed or papers will be rejected and returned to counsel. Any application related to child support shall include a Child Support Standards Act worksheet.

Counsel and parties are required to appear personally on all motions.

Initial post-judgment applications shall be brought by Order to Show Cause. In the event that there is a post-judgment application pending, further application must be made by Notice of Motion or Cross-Motion.

Pretrial Conferences

All attorneys participating in the Pre-Trial conference must be fully familiar with and authorized to settle such action. All counsel must provide the Court with:

1. Pre-proof filing of Note of Issue;

2. Statements of proposed disposition;

3. Updated net worth statements, with the last three (3) years tax returns; and

4. Child support worksheet, if applicable.

In the event that the Matrimonial action remains unresolved at the conclusion of the pre-trial conference, the matter will be set for a firm trial date before this Court or a Judicial Hearing Officer. Once a case has been assigned a trial date, it is presumed ready for trial.

Pursuant to 22 NYCRR 2–216(g), all expert reports are to be exchanged and filed with the Court sixty (60) days before the date set for trial. Reply reports, if any, shall be exchanged no later than thirty (30) days before said date.

Pre-Trial Orders shall be provided to the Court no later than ten (10) days prior to the date of trial, if not previously provided at a pre trial conference.

Trial

Trials and hearings will be held on Mondays, Tuesdays and Fridays. Parties and Children's Attorneys may only use, on their direct case, evidence that is listed on their respective pre-trial exhibit lists and witness who are listed on their respective pre-trial witness lists. Evidence and witnesses not appearing on the pre-trial exhibit and witness list are permitted on cross and rebuttal, where appropriate.

Cases placed on the Trial Calendar with a firm date will not be adjourned unless counsel is actually engaged on trial and provides an affirmation pursuant to Court rules attesting to that fact. Failure to be ready to proceed to trial may result in a judgment of default or dismissal of the action.

Chambers shall be notified by all sides immediately if the action is resolved prior to the scheduled trial date.

Copies of trial memoranda/decisions will be mailed to counsel and self-represented litigants. A self-addressed envelope must be provided to the Court at completion of trial.

Judgments

All judgments shall include a completed copy of the Matrimonial Clerk's Office's contested judgment checklist, indicating all necessary attachments.

After trial, parties and the child's attorney, if any, shall submit post-trial proposed findings of fact and conclusions of law, with copies on computer disk or email attachment in Word Perfect format.

Pursuant to 22 NYCRR 202.48, proposed judgments with proof of service on all parties must be submitted for signature, within sixty (60) days, unless otherwise directed by the Court.

Pursuant to the Domestic Relations Law, the Court will conduct statutory registry checks and advise counsel and parties of all results in writing. If further inquiry is required, the Court may require an appearance by parties and counsel.

Miscellaneous

Parties with unemancipated children should be aware that the Justice may assign the parties to the P.E.A.C.E. program or to consult with Andrew Weinstein, MSW, the Court's Family Counseling and Case Analyst (Tel. # 718–298–1224).

All parties must be properly attired.

Electronic equipment such as beepers, cellular phones, radios, etc., must be turned off while in the Courtroom.

If a party or counsel is required to appear in another Courtroom, they must advise the Court Officer or Clerk of the part where they are going, how they can be reached, or when they will return.

JUSTICE JOSEPH J. ESPOSITO

Part 53.   Hon. Joseph J. Esposito

Appearances and Adjournments:

All parties and attorneys must be present at every appearance unless specifically excused by the court. Calendar call is at 9:30 am unless otherwise instructed by the court. All attorneys and parties appearing pro se must check in with courtroom staff upon entering the courtroom.

1. At time of calendar call or check in, the court shall be notified of any orders of protection.

2. Notification for Court Interpreter Services shall be made to the court as soon as practicable but not less than 24 hours prior to first court appearance. At

time of calendar call or check in the court shall be reminded that court interpreter services are needed.

A notice of appearance shall be filed in the Office of the County Clerk and the Matrimonial Office with a courtesy copy to part clerk.

Two business cards are to be submitted to the court at the first appearance.

Litigants who are represented by counsel should communicate with chambers staff or the court through counsel.

Request for adjournments shall be made in advance by contacting the part clerk in the courtroom. Do not contact chambers concerning adjournments unless instructed to by the part clerk. Do not fax or mail request for adjournment to the court without first contacting the part clerk. After speaking with the part clerk, counsel shall prepare a stipulation including the caption and index number of the case, the appearance date, the adjourn date, and the reason for the adjournment. Faxed stipulations of adjournment will only be accepted if signed by all parties or their attorneys, including the attorney for the child if one has been appointed. The stipulation shall be faxed to chambers at least one (1) day prior to the scheduled appearance date. All adjournments are subject to denial by the Judge.

All adjournments on the grounds of engagement of counsel shall be granted only in accordance with Part 125 of the Rules of the Chief Administrator of the Courts. Affirmation must be faxed to the court at least one (1) day prior to the court appearance.

Preliminary Conference

Preliminary conferences shall be held on Tuesdays unless otherwise directed. The Calendar call is 9:30 am.

Pursuant to 22 NYCRR 202.16(d), an RJI shall be filed within forty-five (45) days of the date of service of the summons unless an affidavit of no necessity is filed, in which case, the RJI shall be filed within 120 days.

Net worth statements with required documents, including parties' recent pay stubs or W–2 and attorney's retainer statement, are to be filed with the court ten (10) days prior to the conference date. The appearance of the parties is required at the Preliminary Conference (22 NYCRR 202.16[F][1]).

Compliance Conference:

Compliance Conferences shall be held on Tuesdays. Calendar call is 9:30 am. Please be prompt. Failure to comply with discovery or preliminary conference orders shall be brought to the court's attention by conference call to chambers prior to the compliance conference.

Motions and Orders to Show Cause:

Motions shall be heard on Wednesdays. Calendar call is at 9:30 am. Motions shall be made returnable only on the part's motion day. When noticed in error the Matrimonial Clerk's Office shall calendar the motion for the part's next available motion day. If the case already has a date scheduled in the future, the motion may be made returnable on that previously assigned date even if it is not a regular scheduled motion day.

Appearance and oral argument are required on all motions.

All cross-motions shall be filed with the County Clerk's office at least two (2) days prior to the return date of the motion. Fees shall be paid and cross-motion and response papers are to be filed with the

Part Clerk two (2) days before the return date of the motion.

No motion papers will be accepted by the court unless all exhibits are properly indicated by protruding tabs.

Any application related to child support shall include a Child Support Standards Act worksheet.

Counsel AND the parties are required to appear on all motions.

The court does not accept courtesy copies of motion papers.

Pursuant to the CPLR, after argument of an application, sur-replies, memoranda and letters addressed to the substance of the pending application will not be considered.

Allegations of fact submitted to the court, including allegations contained in an affidavit or the complaint, must be certified by counsel in the form prescribed by the Chief Administrative Judge.

Copies of the Family Court petition and any existing orders must be submitted with applications to consolidate.

Initial post-judgment applications shall be brought by Order to Show Cause. In the event that there is a post-judgment application pending, further application may be made by Notice of Motion or Cross-Motion.

Ex-Parte Applications:

Any application for temporary injunctive relief shall contain an affirmation demonstrating there will be significant prejudice to the party seeking the restraining order by giving notice. In the absence of a showing of significant prejudice, an affirmation must demonstrate that a good faith effort has been made to notify the party against whom the restraining order is sought in accordance with 22 NYCRR 202.7. This rule does not apply to temporary orders of protection.

Orders of Protection:

Applications for an Ex Parte Order of Protection are heard the same day they are filed.

Counsel are required to have their clients present, unless excused by the court.

Automatic Orders:

Pursuant to Domestic Relations Law § 236 B(2)b, when serving a summons, a copy of the automatic order must also be served and noted in the affidavit of service separately.

Request for Judicial Intervention (RJI):

A request for a preliminary conference shall accompany the RJI and both are to be served on all parties.

Both a copy of the RJI and the request for a Preliminary Conference shall be filed with the Matrimonial Clerk's Office.

Pre–Trial Conferences:

Pre-Trial conferences shall be held on Thursdays. Calendar call is 9:30 am. Please be prompt. At the pretrial conference, counsel shall provide the court with:

1. Pre-proof of filing of Note of Issue;

2. Statements of proposed disposition;

3. updated Networth Statements; and

4. child support worksheet, if applicable.

Counsel shall present all motions in limine at this conference.

Once a case has been assigned a trial date, it is presumed ready for trial.

Adjournment on consent will not be accepted. In the event the action is resolved prior to the court date, counsel are expected to notify chambers immediately.

A Note of Issue shall be filed in accordance with the compliance conference order or other order of the court.

Counsel shall provide the court with statements of proposed disposition, updated net worth statements with the last three (3) years tax returns, and child support worksheets when applicable.

Trials:

All parties must appear at each trial date unless excused by the court.

Chambers shall be notified by all sides immediately if the action is resolved prior to the scheduled trial date.

Pursuant to 22 NYCRR 2–216(g), all experts reports are to be exchanged and filed with the court sixty (60) days before the date set for trial. Reply reports, if any, shall be exchanged no later than thirty (30) days before said date.

The following, if applicable, shall be provided to the court at least one (1) week prior to the date of trial if not previously provided at a pre-trial conference:

1. Marked pleadings;

2. Updated affidavits of net-worth, statements of proposed dispositions and child support worksheets;

3. A witness list and any pre-trial memorandum;

4. Expert reports which were served no later than thirty (30) days before trial;

5. A list of all proposed exhibits;

6. A list of documents, pre-marked by counsel, which counsel may stipulate into evidence.

7. A written copy of any issues or facts to which parties can stipulate before trial; to be read into the record at the commencement of trial.

When presenting a witness with a document to be marked into evidence, a courtesy copy of that document must also be presented to the court.

There will be no adjournments of the trial date without express court permission.

Failure to proceed may result in a judgment of default or dismissal of the action.

Copies of trial memorandum/decisions will be mailed or faxed to counsel and self-represented litigants.

Judgments:

All judgments shall include a completed copy of the Matrimonial Clerk's Office's contested judgment checklist, indicating all necessary attachments.

Pursuant to 22 NYCRR 202.48, proposed judgments with proof of service on all parties must be submitted for signature, within sixty (60) days, unless otherwise directed by the court.

Post Judgment Applications:

If a contested judgment of divorce was signed within 18 months of an application to modify the issue of custody and/or visitation, the application will be heard in the Supreme Court.

JUSTICE JEFFREY D. LEBOWITZ

Part 58.   Hon. Jeffrey D. Lebowitz

Motions:

The Motion Calendar for Justice Lebowitz will be called in Kew Gardens.

MANDATORY APPEARANCE IS REQUIRED by counsel with knowledge of the case and with full authority to settle or enter into binding stipulations on the return date. In the case of e-filed motions, a hard copy must be submitted to the Court on the return date. On the return date, motion will be conferenced and or orally argued at the discretion of the Court.

DO NOT CALL CHAMBERS FOR ADJOURNMENTS

Motions may be adjourned on consent provided a faxed written stipulation of counsel is submitted to the Court at least twenty-four (24) hours before the return date. All stipulations must contain the signature of the attorney consenting to the adjournment. A form which contains only the name of the firm on the stipulation will not be accepted. Stipulations must also contain a schedule for exchange of opposition and reply papers occurring prior to the adjourned date. If consent for an adjournment cannot be obtained, an application must be made to Justice Lebowitz by counsel on the return date. Calendar service or non-attorneys will not be permitted to make applications for adjournments. Counsel are expected to notify their adversaries of their intention to seek an adjournment.

ALL ADJOURNMENTS ON CONSENT MUST BE REQUESTED PRIOR TO THE RETURN DATE. NO APPLICATIONS FOR ADJOURNMENTS ON CONSENT WILL BE ENTERTAINED AT THE CALENDAR CALL.

WHERE CONSENT TO AN ADJOURNMENT IS UNREASONABLY WITHHELD, COURT COSTS WILL BE IMPOSED.

Adjournments will be limited to two, absent extenuating circumstances. The answering papers, including cross motions, affirmations in opposition and reply affirmations contained within the motion schedule will be accepted only on the return or adjourned date in the Part. The court will not consider papers sent to Chambers or to the Part after full submission of the motion or cross motion(s). Nor will it accept cross-motions that do not have proof of payment of the appropriate fee. (CPLR § 8020[a]).

All motions and ex-parte applications submitted shall be in compliance with Uniform Rule § 202.5. All exhibits are to be preceded by a numbered/lettered exhibit tab which protrudes from the stack of papers. All relevant decretal paragraphs or relevant document paragraphs must be highlighted in the exhibits and brought to the Court's attention within the accompanying affidavit or affirmation. All submissions are to be securely fastened so as to prevent the papers from being lost. Failure to comply with the requirements of this section will result in rejection of the noncomplying papers.

Copies of decisions on motions will be mailed to attorneys and pro se litigants who provide the Part with a stamped, self-addressed envelope at the time of final submission of their motion. If no stamped, self-addressed envelope is provided, it will be the responsibility of the respective attorneys and pro se litigants to follow up with the appropriate clerk's office to obtain a copy of the decision.

ALL INQUIRIES TO CASE OR CALENDAR STATUS ARE TO BE MADE TO THE APPROPRIATE CLERK'S OFFICE:

IAS Motion Support Office (718) 298–1009

Ex-Parte Support Office (718) 298–1018

Trial Term Office (718) 298–1015

Trials:

These rules apply to all trials before the Court Plaintiff's counsel shall requisition the file to the Part 58 courtroom immediately after assignment of the case to this Court. Counsel should ascertain the availability of all witnesses and subpoenaed documents. Any special needs, i.e., interpreter, easels, blackboards, shadow boxes, television, subpoenaed

material, etc., must be reported to the Court Officer in advance so as not to delay the progress of the trial.

Motions in Limine: On the first appearance in the Part for trial, any party intending to make a motion in limine shall submit a brief written affirmation setting forth the nature of the application and any supporting statutory or case law. The party shall furnish the Court with an original and one copy and provide counsel for all parties with a copy.

With regard to suggested jury charges and a suggested verdict questionnaire, amendments thereto shall be permitted at the final charge conference. Jury charges should refer to the PJI number and topic. If any changes to the PJI are suggested, then the entire proposed charge should be set forth and the changes should be highlighted. Citations to appropriate statutory or common law authority must be given in support of suggested non-PJI jury charges or suggested PJI modifications.

Not later than prior to selection of the jury, or if already selected prior to opening statement, each counsel shall provide to the other and submit to the Court:

1. marked pleadings in accordance with CPLR Rule 4012;

2. a statement, joint if possible, of the relevant facts that are not in dispute;

3. a list of witnesses whom the party expects to call at trial, stating the address of each witness and the general subject matter as to which each identified witness is expected to testify;

4. a list of all exhibits for each party indicating whether such exhibits are stipulated into evidence or marked for identification. As to those exhibits marked for identification, the Court will address their admissibility In limine or during the trial, as may be appropriate;

5. copies of the exhibits intended to be offered by counsel. Said exhibits are to be pre-marked by the court reporter, with the plaintiff's exhibits numbered sequentially and the defendant's exhibits lettered sequentially;

6. a list of all expert witnesses with copies of their reports;

7. any other information that the Court has determined to be appropriate in the action.

Not later than prior to jury selection, or if a jury is selected prior to opening statement, each counsel shall provide to the other a statement setting forth any objection to the exhibits identified in the list provided by opposing counsel and the specific basis thereof. Any exhibit as to which no objection is identified shall be admitted into evidence on consent. The failure to provide such statement of objections on a timely basis may be deemed to be consent to the admission of all of the exhibits included in the list submitted by the opposing party.

On the day of trial, both sides shall have available at least four (4) copies of all exhibits which are expected to be introduced into evidence.

On the day of trial, both sides shall have available at least four (4) copies of all deposition transcripts which are expected to be read into the record or utilized on cross examination at the trial.

The Court expects counsel to stipulate to as many facts as possible on matters that are not and should not be in dispute. If it appears during the course of the trial that no bonafide attempt was undertaken to secure such stipulation, the Court will likely recess and delay the trial until there is compliance.

Tort Actions are generally bifurcated. The Court expects, and for the convenience of the jurors, that any trial on damages will follow immediately after a verdict finding the defendant liable.

Counsel should alert the Court at the pretrial conference as to any anticipated problem regarding the attendance at trial of the parties, attorney or essential witnesses, and any other practical problems that the Court should consider in scheduling.

No adjournments or delays during trial will be accepted unless exigent circumstances exist.

Settlements and Discontinuances:

If an action is settled, discontinued or otherwise disposed of, counsel shall immediately inform the Court by submission of a copy of the stipulation of settlement or a letter directed to the Clerk of the Part. All stipulations of discontinuance must be accompanied by proof of payment of the appropriate fee. (CPLR §8020(d)(1)).

Electronic Filing of Legal Papers:

Electronic filing is available for filing legal papers with the Court. Parties interested in electronic filing should read the materials set forth at https://iapps. courts.state.ny.us/fbem/mainframe.html and at the Queens County website. The rules and user's manual for electronic filing are available on this website.

On the return date, all parties must submit hard copies of any motion/responsive papers that are electronically filed.

COMPLIANCE, SETTLEMENT AND CONFERENCE PART

Doc. 1. Compliance, Settlement and Conference Part: Hon. Martin E. Ritholtz

All Compliance Conferences are held in a centralized "Compliance, Settlement and Conference Part" (CSCP) in Courtroom 313 before Hon. Martin E. Ritholtz.

The Conferences begin promptly at 9:30 AM. Attorneys must check in with the Court Clerk or Court Officers. Cases are conferenced in the order in which ALL attorneys on a matter are checked in and are actually present in the courtroom. If the case is called and there is no appearance, the Court will take the appropriate action against the non-appearing side, applying such penalties or sanctions as are authorized by the CPLR and Rules of the Chief Administrative Judge. (See *Lopez v. Imperial Delivery*, 282 AD2d 190).

There will be no adjournments of Compliance Conferences whatsoever.

In accordance with 22 NYCRR 202.19(b)(3), the purpose of the Compliance Conference is: (a) to monitor the progress of discovery; (b) to explore potential settlement; and (c) to set a deadline for the filing of the Note of Issue. Consequently, Counsel attending the Conference must be fully familiar with the case, the status of disclosure proceedings, and any settlement negotiations. The attorney MUST be prepared and authorized to enter into binding stipulations regarding disclosure and disposition of the case.

Counsel appearing for the Conference MUST bring the Bill of Particulars and all the previous orders in the case, including the Preliminary Conference Order.

Counsel for Plaintiff in any action involving personal injuries MUST bring proof of plaintiff's injuries, including all medical reports from plaintiff's treating and examining doctors, and all medical and hospital records. Counsel for plaintiff in all other actions MUST bring proof of damages.

In order to aid in settlement negotiations, counsel for Plaintiff MUST be prepared to make a good-faith demand to settle the case, and likewise defense counsel MUST be prepared to make a good-faith offer or indicate why the case is a "no-pay".

If necessary, counsel MUST have the ability to contact the attorney of record, plaintiff, defendant or the assigned insurance adjuster in order to facilitate a potential settlement.

Parties may consent to a Summary Jury Trial (SJT), subject to the Rules of the SJT Part, by execution of a Transfer Stipulation at the Compliance Conference.

Appearance of Counsel is NOT required if a Note of Issue/Certificate of Readiness has been served and filed prior to the date of the Compliance Conference. In such case, however, a copy of the Note of Issue, with the date of filing, must be presented at the call of the conference calendar. It may be presented by any person, including an attorney's service. It may NOT be presented by mail.

The CSCP (Compliance, Settlement and Conference Part) hears motions on Mondays only. NO pre-note motion (including substantive motions) should be presented for calendaring in this Part unless there has been served and filed with the motion papers an affirmation that counsel had contacted Chambers at 718–298–1089, and has held a telephone conference with the court and all parties in a good-faith effort to resolve the issues raised by the motion (see, 22 NYCRR 202.7[a], 202.12[j]). If it appears, after a telephone conference with the Court, that the issues raised by the motion can not be resolved by stipulation, then said motion shall be calendared at the earliest possible date. A strict schedule for the service of moving and opposing papers shall be set. All parties are required to appear at the call of the Motion Calendar, by counsel familiar with the case and prepared and authorized to enter into binding stipulations regarding disclosure.

By direction of the Administrative Judge, all timely motions to vacate notes of issue are returnable in this Part. In order to facilitate the expeditious resolution of such motions by stipulation, Chambers will contact the moving attorney promptly upon receipt of the moving papers to schedule a telephone conference. In lieu of formal motions, counsel are invited to contact Chambers by telephone, within twenty days of the service of the note of issue, whereupon a telephone conference will be scheduled.

Any questions concerning the status of actions assigned to CSCP should be directed to the Differentiated Case Management (DCM) Tracking Coordinators, who may be contacted at (718) 298–1164.

PRELIMINARY CONFERENCE PART

Doc. 2. Preliminary Conference Part: Referee Richard Lazarus

A preliminary conference shall be held within 45 days of the RJI date.

Preliminary conference calendars will be posted Monday through Thursday.

One short adjournment may be granted for good cause.

There will be calls of the calendar at 9:30 A.M. or 11:30 A.M. based upon the part. Please check the PRELIMINARY CONFERENCE SCHEDULE for your time. Prompt attendance is required.

Counsel must appear, be familiar with the case and fully authorized to enter into an agreement, both substantive and procedural on behalf of their clients.

At the conference, inquiry may be made regarding any of the following matters where appropriate:

• Simplification and limitation of factual and legal issues.

• Establishment of a timetable for the completion of all disclosure proceedings.

• Addition of other necessary parties.

• Settlement of the action.

• Any other matters that the court may deem relevant.

Failure to appear may result in the issuance of a court prepared Preliminary Conference Order including a discovery schedule which must be complied with under penalty of sanction (CPLR 3124, 3216).

Centralized Rules for Preliminary
Conference Part Orders

General Rules:

1. The caption, index number, RJI filing date and attorney appearances must be completed.

2. If there is more than one plaintiff and/or defendant in the action, any section which applies to a particular party must specify to which party that section applies.

3. All sections which are inapplicable or NOT completed must be stricken. A notation of n/a is acceptable.

4. Failure to appear at a preliminary conference may result in an ex parte or default order. An adjournment of a P.C. is a courtesy not a right.

5. All sections which require a date by which to comply must be filled in. You must use a specific date certain. Time lines are not acceptable. If you do not fill them in the court may fill in what it deems appropriate.

6. The order must be dated and signed by all appearing parties.

7. Writing on the P.C. order must be legible.

Responses to Sections:

Question # 1 Insurance Coverage: If this section applies to more than one defendant, specify the applicable defendant(s).

Question # 2 Bill of Particulars: Parties must specify which party must serve BP demands and which party must serve a BP.

Question# 3 Medical Records and Authorizations: If employment records or school authorizations are requested, the relevant period must be specified.

Question # 4 Physical Examinations: If an Independent Medical Examination has already been held, indicate same.

Question # 5 Depositions: Make sure the date selected is a weekday. If deposition has already been held please indicate same.

Question # 6 Other Disclosure: The date to comply by must be specified for questions "A", "C", and "D" (DO NOT WRITE "PER C.P.L.R")

Question # 7 and 8 Additional Disclosure Issues: If a demand for is made for compliance with a previously served discovery demand, the provision must indicate: (a) The date of the demand to be complied with, (b) The party to which the discovery demand refers and the specific outstanding items which have not been furnished.

(DO NOT WRITE PLAINTIFF/DEFENDANT TO COMPLY WITH ANY/ALL OUTSTANDING DISCOVERY DEMANDS)

Question # 9 Completion of Disclosure: Insert a date on or before the compliance conference date.

The Attorneys <u>MUST</u> check the court file for the "So Ordered" PC for any changes to the order which the court may have made.

PRETRIAL CONFERENCE PART

Doc. 3. Pretrial Conference Part: Referee Leonard N. Florio

All tort cases (excluding City–Corporation Counsel, Medical Malpractice and Commercial cases) in which a Note of Issue and Certificate of Readiness are filed shall be called in the Pretrial Conference Part (PTCP) four months after said filing.

Prior to the pretrial conference, counsel shall confer in a good faith effort to identify issues not in contention, resolve all disputed questions without need for court intervention, and settle the case. Additionally, counsel shall have knowledge of their schedules and witnesses' schedules in order to permit the fixing of a trial date and a realistic estimate of the trial's length.

Counsel who appear are required to have full and detailed knowledge of all issues related to discovery, together with all orders and/or stipulations related thereto. Failure to appear as required may result in the imposition of sanctions.

The Referee shall report on the trial ready status of the action to the Justice presiding in the Trial Scheduling Part (TSP) who may issue any order deemed appropriate.

TRIAL SCHEDULING PART

Doc. 4. Trial Scheduling Part: Hon. Martin Schulman

Trial Calendar

1. The trial calendar will be called each day of the week commencing at 9:30 a.m., except on Tuesdays, at which time the trial calendar will be called after the motion calendar.

2. Every case on the trial calendar is deemed ready for trial to be sent forthwith to select, unless otherwise annotated CON for conference.

3. Only counsel of record or trial counsel shall appear for a case on the trial calendar. Failure to appear may result in a case being dismissed or set for inquest.

4. No adjournments will be granted on consent or by telephone.

5. Affirmations of actual engagement will not be accepted for any reason if the trial date has been fixed at least two months in advance. The attorneys previously designated as trial counsel must appear for trial on that date. If any attorney previously designated as trial counsel is actually engaged elsewhere, he or she must produce substitute trial counsel. If neither trial counsel nor substitute trial counsel is ready to try the case on the scheduled trial date, the court may impose any sanctions permitted by law. 22 NYCRR 125.1(g).

6. If a jury case is not settled or otherwise disposed, it will be sent to select a jury.

7. If a non-jury case is not settled or otherwise disposed, it will be assigned for trial.

8. All cases will be assigned for trial to the IAS justice, if available. If the IAS justice is unavailable, the case will be sent to the first available justice.

Motion Calendar

1. The motion calendar will be called on Tuesday mornings at 9:30 a.m. in Courtroom 25. There will be no second call of the motion calendar.

2. All motions in Post-Note matters shall be made returnable before the I.A.S. Justice assigned; however, one month prior to the Trial Scheduling Part appearance (not Pretrial Conference appearance) motions shall be made returnable before the Trial Scheduling Justice on a Tuesday.

Discovery Motions

1. Counsel must personally appear and be prepared to discuss and/or orally argue at the call of the motion calendar all discovery motions. If the moving party fails to appear, the motion will be marked off the calendar for non-appearance. If the opposing

party fails to appear, the motion may be granted on default.

2. Discovery motions may not be marked submitted, even on consent of all parties, unless first conferenced by the Court.

3. Counsel must attach to all discovery motions copies of all pleadings and documents as required by the CPLR, including all preliminary conference, compliance conference, discovery orders, as well as stipulations.

4. Motions seeking leave to renew or reargue a prior motion shall include copies of all papers submitted on the prior motion and the order entered thereon.

5. The Court shall mark off of the motion calendar any motion that does not comply with rules 3 and 4 of this section.

Vacate a Stay or Restore to Calendar

1. In order to vacate a stay or restore a case to the trial calendar, counsel must agree, choose a date certain for trial and file a stipulation to that effect, which stipulation shall be signed by all parties and which shall state that all discovery is complete. The stipulation shall be filed with the Clerk in the Trial Scheduling Part.

2. No motion to vacate a stay or restore a case to the trial calendar will be accepted for filing by the Motion Support Office unless accompanied by an affirmation or affidavit of attempts to comply with Rule 1 of this section. The affirmation or affidavit shall be affixed to the face of notice of the motion and all sides must appear on the return date.

3. The Motion Support Office shall reject any motion which does not comply with the requirements of Rule 2 of this section.

COMMERCIAL DIVISION RULES

Doc. 6. Commercial Division Rules

GUIDELINES

The following are guidelines for assignment of cases to Queens County Supreme Court, Commercial Division. These guidelines apply to Request for Judicial Intervention (RJI) filed on commercial cases on or after November 7, 2005.

In general, the Commercial Division of the Queens County Supreme Court will entertain commercial and business disputes in which a party seeks compensatory damages totaling $50,000 or more (exclusive of punitive damages, interests, costs and attorney fees).

A RJI which is marked "Commercial" and is accompanied by a "Commercial Division Certification" will initially be assigned to the Commercial Division. By filing the "Commercial Division Certification", a party gives a brief description of the subject matter of the lawsuit, e.g., "shareholder derivative action" and certifies that he/she believes that the case meets the eligibility requirements set forth below. The certification must be annexed to the RJI at the time of the filing.

Due to caseload considerations, the Commercial Division is empowered to transfer cases out of the Commercial Division which, in its judgment, do not fall within the eligibility requirements set forth below. A Commercial Division Justice may order a transfer notwithstanding that a party has described the case as "commercial" on its RJI.

Consistent with these guidelines, actions and proceedings, which are designated to be eligible for assignment to the Commercial Division, shall be reviewed by the Commercial Division Part to determine whether the matter shall be assigned to or retained in the Commercial Division. The principles set out below will guide the exercise of this authority. Parties should adhere to these principles when designating a case type on the RJI. (See Paragraph D - for documentation which should accompany the RJI).

(A) The monetary threshold of the Commercial Division, exclusive of interest, costs, disbursements and counsel fees, is $50,000.00.

(B) Actions in which the principal claims involve the following will presumptively be retained in the Division, provided that the monetary threshold is met;

(1) Breach of contract or fiduciary duty, fraud, misrepresentation, business tort (e.g., unfair competition) or statutory and /or common law violation arising out of business dealings (e.g., sales of assets or securities, corporate restructuring, partnership, shareholder, joint venture, and other business agreements, trade secrets and restrictive covenants and employment agreements which are not principally claims for discriminatory practices);

(2) Transactions governed by the Uniform Commercial Code (exclusive of those concerning individual co-op units);

(3) Transactions involving commercial real property, including Yellowstone injunctions and excluding actions for the payment of rent only;

(4) Shareholder derivative actions—without consideration of the monetary threshold;

(5) Commercial class actions—without consideration of the monetary threshold;

(6) Commercial bank and financial institution transactions;

(7) Internal affairs of business organizations or liability to third parties or officials thereof;

(8) Environmental insurance coverage litigation;

(9) Commercial insurance coverage litigation (e.g., Directors and Officers and/or Errors and Omissions coverage);

(10) Dissolution or liquidation of corporations, partnerships, limited liability companies, limited liability partnerships and joint ventures—without consideration of the monetary threshold;

(11) Applications to stay or compel arbitration and affirm or disaffirm arbitration awards and related injunctive relief pursuant to CPLR Art. 75 involving any of the foregoing enumerated commercial issues—without consideration for the monetary threshold.

(C) The following will be transferred out of or not retained in the Commercial Division even if the monetary threshold is met;

(1) Suits to collect professional fees;

(2) Cases seeking a declaratory judgment as to insurance coverage for personal injury or property damage;

(3) Residential real estate disputes, including landlord-tenant matters and commercial real estate disputes involving the payment of rent only;

(4) Proceedings to enforce a judgment regardless of the nature of the underlying case;

(5) First-party insurance claims and actions by insurers to collect premiums or rescind non-commercial policies;

(6) Malpractice by attorneys, accountants or actuaries;

(7) Real property foreclosures.

(D) The determination as to whether a case should be retained in the Commercial Division will be made at the Preliminary Conference. In the discretion of the Commercial Division Justice assigned, if a matter does not fall within these guidelines for Commercial Division adjudication, it shall be transferred to a non-commercial part. For this purpose and as an aid to the Court in determining a case's Commercial Division eligibility, counsel shall annex the Commercial Division Attorney's Certification, together with a copy of the pleadings, to any submission accompanying an RJI. Retained cases will remain in the Commercial Division. Counsel who submit a statement justifying Commercial Division designation of special proceeding pursuant hereto shall check the "Other Commercial" box on their RJI; not the "Special Proceedings" box.

(E) An order transferring a matter out of the Commercial Division is an Administrative matter not subject to review or appeal.

(F) If a case is assigned to a non-commercial part because the filing attorney did not designate the case

as "Commercial", any other party to the action may apply for a transfer of the case into the Commercial Division subject to the approval of the Administrative Judge. A case may also be transferred to the Commercial Division on the ground that it is related to one then pending in the Commercial Division.

GENERAL RULES

Rule 1. Appearance by Counsel With Knowledge and Authority.

Counsel who appear in the Commercial Division must be fully familiar with the case in regard to which they appear and fully authorized to enter into agreements, both substantive and procedural, on behalf of their clients. Copies of the pleadings must be brought to each conference. Failure to comply with this rule may be regarded as a default and dealt with appropriately. Counsel must appear on time for all scheduled appearances.

Rule 2. Settlements and Discontinuances.

If an action is settled, discontinued, or otherwise disposed of, counsel shall immediately inform the Court. Attorneys shall also submit a copy of the stipulation with proof of payment of fees and a letter directed to the clerk of the Part. Filing a stipulation with the County Clerk will not suffice to effect a settlement, discontinuance or disposition.

Rule 3. Information on Cases.

Information on future court appearances can be found on the court system's future court appearance site (www.nycourts.gov/ecourts). The Clerk of the Part in question can also provide information about scheduling in the Part (trial, conferences, and arguments on motions). Where circumstance require exceptional notice, it will be furnished directly by Chambers.

Rule 4. Form of Papers.

All papers shall comply with Part 130 of the Rules of the Chief Administrator, CPLR 2101 and 22 NYCRR 202.5(a). The print size of footnotes shall be no smaller than nine-point.

CONFERENCES

Rule 5. Consultation Among Counsel Prior Conferences.

a) Counsel for all parties shall consult prior to a preliminary or compliance conference about (i) resolution of the case, in whole or in part, and (ii) discovery and any other issues to be discussed at the conference. Counsel shall make a good faith effort to reach agreement on these matters in advance of the conference.

b) Prior to the preliminary conference, counsel shall confer with regard to anticipated electronic discovery issues. Such issues shall be addressed with the court at the preliminary conference and shall include but not be limited to (1) implementation of a data preservation plan; (2) identification of relevant data; (3)

the scope, extent and form of production; (4) anticipated cost of data recovery and proposed initial allocation of such cost; (5) disclosure of the programs and manner in which the data is maintained; (6) identification of computer system(s) utilized; (7) identification of the individual(s) responsible for data preservation; (8) confidentiality and privilege issues; and (9) designation of experts.

Rule 6. Preliminary Conferences.

A preliminary conference will be held within forty-five days of the filing of an RJI and shall be held in the centralized Preliminary Conference Part. At the Preliminary Conference, the parties shall bring a copy of the pleadings and complete the Preliminary Conference Order for Commercial Cases. The dates set forth and provisions in the order shall be enforced.

Rule 7. Familiarity With Outstanding Motions.

Counsel must be prepared to discuss any motions that have been submitted and are outstanding at conference appearances and have the authority to make binding stipulations regarding those issues.

Rule 8. Submission of Information.

At any conference, counsel shall be prepared to furnish the court with the following: (i) a complete caption, including the index number; (ii) the name, address, telephone, e-mail address and fax numbers of all counsel; (iii) the dates the action was commenced and issue joined; (iv) a statement as to what motions, if any, are pending and before whom; and (v) copies of any decisions previously rendered in the case.

Rule 9. Discovery Schedule.

The Preliminary Conference will result in the issuance by the court of a Preliminary Conference Order. Where appropriate, the order will contain specific provisions for early means of disposition of the case, such as (i) a schedule of limited-issue discovery in aid of early dispositive motions or settlement and/or (ii) a schedule for dispositive motions before disclosure or after limited-issue disclosure. The order will also contain a comprehensive disclosure schedule, including dates for the completion of impleader and discovery, motion practice, a compliance conference and a date for filing the note of issue.

Rule 10. Compliance Conference.

A Compliance Conference will be held approximately ninety days before the Note of Issue is due, on a Tuesday, in the part of the assigned Commercial Division Justice. The parties shall bring a copy of the pleadings, Preliminary Conference Order and complete a Compliance Conference Order. The dates set forth and the provisions in the order shall be enforced.

Rule 11. Non-Appearance at a Conference.

The failure of counsel to appear for a conference may result in an ex parte discovery order, an order directing dismissal, the striking of an answer and an inquest or direction for judgment, or other appropriate sanction. 22 N.Y.C.R.R. 130–2.1 and 202.27.

Rule 12. Adherence to Discovery Schedule.

Parties shall strictly comply with discovery obligations by the dates set forth in all case scheduling orders. No extensions of such deadlines shall be allowed unless specifically authorized by the court. If any party fails to comply with such order, an appropriate sanction may be imposed against that party pursuant to CPLR 3126 or Part 130 of the Rules of the Chief Administrator.

Rule 13. Disclosure Disputes.

Counsel must consult with one another in a good faith effort to resolve all disputes about disclosure. See N.Y.C.R.R. 202.7. Except as provided in Rule 19 hereof, if counsel are unable to resolve a disclosure dispute in this fashion, the aggrieved party shall contact the Court to arrange a conference as soon as practicable to avoid exceeding the discovery cutoff date. Counsel may request a conference by telephone if, subject to the Commercial Division Justice's discretion, it would be more convenient and efficient than an appearance in court.

MOTIONS

Rule 14. Form of Motion Papers.

The movant shall specify in the notice of motion, order to show cause, and in a concluding section of a memorandum of law, the exact relief sought. Counsel must attach copies of all pleadings and other documents as required by the CPLR and as necessary for an informed decision on the motion. Counsel must always use tabs when submitting papers containing exhibits. Copies must be legible. If a document to be annexed to an affidavit or affirmation is voluminous and only discrete portions are relevant to the motion, counsel may attach excerpts and submit the full exhibit separately. Documents in a foreign language shall be properly translated. CPLR 2101(b). Whenever reliance is placed upon a decision or other authority not readily available to this court, a copy of the case or of pertinent portions of the authority shall be submitted with the motion papers. Motion papers shall comply with Part 130 of the Rules of the Chief Administrator. Papers shall be double spaced and contain print no smaller than ten-point, on 8 ½ × 11 inch paper, bearing margins no smaller than one inch. CPLR 2101; Uniform Rule 202.5(a).

Rule 15. Length of Papers.

Unless otherwise permitted by the court for good cause prior to submission of the motion, briefs or memoranda of law are limited to 25 pages each. Reply memoranda shall be no more than 15 pages and shall not contain any arguments that do not respond or relate to those made in the memoranda in chief. Affidavits and affirmations are limited to 25 pages.

Rule 16. Sur–Reply and Post Submission Papers.

The CPLR does not provide for sur-reply papers. In addition, the presentation of papers or letters to the court after submission or argument of a motion is not permitted. Materials submitted in violation hereof will not be read or considered. Opposing counsel who receive a copy of materials submitted in violation of this rule should not respond in kind.

Rule 17. Orders to Show Cause.

Motions should be brought on by order to show cause only when there is a genuine urgency (e.g., applications for provisional remedies), a stay is requested or a statute mandates so proceeding. Absent permission, reply papers should not be submitted on orders to show cause.

Rule 18. Courtesy Copies.

Courtesy copies should not be submitted unless requested.

Rule 19. Advance Notice of Motions.

(a) Except for motions filed with the RJI, no motion may be made by any party for any relief without a prior conference on the issue raised by the motion. The moving party must advise the court by telephoning chambers of the nature of the relief sort.

(b) The Court will schedule a telephone or court conference with counsel. Counsel fully familiar with the matter and with authority to bind their client must be available to participate in the conference. The unavailability of counsel for the scheduled conference, except for good cause shown, may result in granting of the application without opposition and /or the imposition of sanctions.

(c) If the matter can be resolved during the telephone conference, an order consistent with such resolution may be issued and faxed to counsel, or counsel will be directed to forward a letter confirming the resolution to be "so ordered".

(d) If the matter cannot be resolved, the Court will permit the filing of both moving and opposing papers and render a decision on those papers and on oral argument, if indicated.

(e) On the face of all post–RJI notices of motion and orders to show cause, there shall be an affirmation that there has been compliance with this rule.

(f) Nothing in this rule shall be construed to prevent or limit counsel from making any motion deemed appropriate to best represent a party's interests. However, in order to permit the Court the opportunity to resolve issues before motion practice ensues and to control its calendar, in the context of the discovery and trial schedule, pre-motion conferences in accordance herewith must be held. The failure of counsel to comply with this Rule may result in the motion being marked off the calendar until the Court has an opportunity to conference the matter.

TRIALS

Rule 20. Pretrial Conference.

The Court will set a date and time for pretrial conference. Prior to the conference, counsel shall confer in a good faith effort to identify issues not in contention, resolve all disputed questions without need for Court intervention, and settle the case. At the conference, counsel should be prepared to discuss all matters as to which there is disagreement between the parties, including those identified in Rules 22–25, and the possibility of settlement. At or before the conference, the Court may require the parties to prepare a written stipulation of undisputed facts.

Rule 21. Trial Schedule.

Counsel will be expected to be ready to proceed either to select a jury or to begin presentation of proof on the scheduled date. Once a trial date is set, counsel are to immediately determine the availability of witnesses. Witnesses are to be scheduled so that all trial time is completely utilized. Trials will commence each court day and will proceed on a day-to-day basis on such days as the Court directs. Failure of counsel to attend the trial at the time scheduled will constitute a waiver of the right of that attorney and his or her client to participate in the trial for the period of counsel's absence. With respect to trials scheduled more than 60 days in advance, the actual engagement of trial counsel in another matter will not be recognized as acceptable basis for an adjournment of the trial 22 N.Y.C.R.R. 125.1(g).

Rule 22. Estimated Length of Trial and Witnesses.

At the Pre–Trial Conference or such other time as the Court may set, the parties, after considering the testimony of, and, if necessary, consulting with their witnesses, shall furnish the court with an realistic estimate of the length of trial. Each party shall identify in writing for the court and the other parties the witnesses it intends to call, the order in which they shall testify and the estimated length of their testimony.

Rule 23. Pre–Marking of Exhibits.

Counsel for the parties shall consult prior to trial and shall in good faith attempt to agree upon the exhibits that will be offered into evidence without objection. At the Pre–Trial Conference each side shall then mark its exhibits to which no objection has been made, with plaintiff using numbers for its exhibits and defendant using letters. All exhibits not consented to shall be marked for identification only. At least ten business days prior to trial or such other time as the Court may set, each party shall submit to the court and other counsel a list of the uncontested and contested exhibits and a copy of the latter. If the contested exhibits are exceptionally voluminous, counsel shall consult with the Clerk of the Part for guidance. The court will rule upon objections to the contested exhibits at the earliest possible time after consultation with counsel. Exhibits not previously demanded which are to be used solely for credibility or rebuttal need not be pre-marked.

Rule 24. Identification of Deposition Testimony.

Counsel for the parties shall consult prior to trial and shall in good faith attempt to agree upon the portions of deposition testimony to be offered into evidence without objection. The parties shall delete from the testimony to be read questions and answers that are irrelevant to the point for which the deposition testimony is offered. Each party shall prepare a list of deposition testimony to be offered by it as to which objection has not been made and, identified separately, a list of deposition testimony as to which objection has been made. At least ten days prior to trial or such other time as the court may set, each party shall submit its list to the court and other counsel, together with a copy of the portions of the deposition testimony as to which objection has been made. The court will rule upon the objections at the earliest possible time after consultation with counsel.

Rule 25. Pre-Trial Memoranda, Exhibit Book and Request for Jury Instructions.

(a) Counsel shall submit pre-trial memoranda at the Pre-Trial Conference or such other time as the Court may set. Counsel shall comply with CPLR 2103(e). A single memorandum no longer than 25 pages, with print and margins as set forth in Rule 14, shall be submitted by each side. No memoranda in response shall be submitted.

(b) Counsel shall submit an indexed binder or notebook of trial exhibits for the Court's use. A copy for each attorney on trial and the originals in a like binder or notebook for the witnesses shall be prepared and submitted. Plaintiff's exhibits shall be numerically tabbed and defendant's exhibits shall be tabbed alphabetically.

(c) Where the trial is by jury, counsel shall, on the Pre-Trial Conference date or at such time as the court may set, provide the court with case specific, written requests to charge. Where the requested charge is from the New York Pattern Jury Instructions—Civil and no modifications are necessary, a reference to the PJI number will suffice. Counsel shall also submit proposed jury interrogatories.

Rule 26. Preclusion.

Except for good cause shown, no party shall present the testimony of a witness or exhibits that were not identified as provided in Rules 22–25 and not identified during the course of disclosure in response to a relevant discovery demand of a party or an order of the Court.

SUPREME COURT OF THE STATE OF NEW YORK
COUNTY OF QUEENS

Index No. _____ / _____

Plaintiff(s),

-against-   **COMMERCIAL DIVISION
ATTORNEY'S AFFIRMATION**

Defendant(s).

STATE OF NEW YORK)
) ss:
COUNTY OF QUEENS)

_____, an attorney at law duly licensed to practice in the State of New York, does hereby state under penalty of perjury as provided in CPLR 2106 and certifies pursuant to 22 NYCRR § 130–1.1:

1. Plaintiff's cause(s) of action is/are _____.
2. Plaintiff's claimed relief is _____.
3. Defendant's counterclaim(s) is/are _____
_____
4. Defendant's claimed relief is _____.

Based upon the foregoing, it is respectfully requested that this matter be assigned to the Commercial Division of the Supreme Court, Queens County.

Dated: _____, NY

_____, 20__

PROTOCOL ON COURTHOUSE PROCEDURES
FOR ELECTRONICALLY FILED CASES

Doc. 7. Protocol on Courthouse Procedures for Electronically Filed Cases

Attorneys seeking information about how the court's filing by electronic means system ("E-File") works are advised to consult the User's Manual and FAQ's, both available on-line at the Electronic Filing website (see "E-Courts" at www.nycourts.gov). What follows is an outline of the steps that will be used in e-filed cases to satisfy traditional courthouse requirements for the processing of cases, such as the submission of orders to show cause. The steps outlined here seek, to the maximum extent possible, to integrate e-filing capabilities with normal courthouse procedures in ways that will save attorneys time, trouble and trips to the courthouse while meeting the needs of Justices and the court.

Identifying E-Filed Cases:

All authorized Torts, Commercial and Tax Certiorari cases may be commenced by E-Filing, however all parties must consent for the action to continue as an E-File case.

Cases Converted to E-File:

Cases originally commenced in hard-copy form but later converted to an E-File case, either by stipulation or order will bear a regular index number initially. The County Clerk will issue a new E-File index number

E-File and the Court's Case Management System:

At present, the E-File system is a filing system only. In contrast with the Federal software, it currently is not linked to the court's case management system (CCIS), which serves as the basis for the generation of motion and other calendars. Court staff will enter data in CCIS for E-File cases in the same way as is done with all other cases.

Filing of Papers Generally:

1. *Fees:* Court fees (e.g., RJI fee, motion fee) in E-Filed cases may be paid for on-line using a credit card. Papers may also be filed with the E-File system and the fee may be paid at the County Clerk's Office. In the latter case, the paper is not considered to have been filed until payment of the fee has been tendered (see CPLR 304).

2. *Papers to Be Filed to the System:* All papers to be filed with the court in an E-Filed case shall be filed on-line with the E-File system except as directed by

the court). Papers that attorneys would not ordinarily file with the court in a hard-copy case need not be filed in an E-Filed matter.

3. *Filing With the System First; Deliver Courtesy Hard Copies:* Thereafter: Generally speaking, unless otherwise directed or authorized by the court, counsel should file papers with the E-File system first and thereafter deliver any requested courtesy copy to the Chambers. Filing with the system permits counsel to serve the papers electronically pursuant to Section 202.5-b(f) of the Uniform Rules for the Trial Courts once consent to E-Filing has been filed on-line. Proof of service should be filed on-line.

Requests for Judicial Intervention:

A Request for Judicial Intervention ("RJI") in an E-Filed case shall be submitted via the E-Filing System. When the RJI is approved, filed and paid for on-line, it will be forwarded to the relevant back office for random assignment of the case and processing of the document. In the case of RJIs seeking assignment to the Commercial Division, the filer must submit therewith, as required by the standards for assignment of cases to the Commercial Division (Uniform Rules 202.70(d)(2)), a statement in support of the assignment. Again, all filings in E-File cases should bear the index number with the "E" suffix.

Notice of Medical Malpractice:

Upon the filing of a Notice of Medical Malpractice in an E-Filed case, The Certificate of Merit shall be filed as a separate document. Additionally, the Certificate of Merit must be filed at the time of the filing of the Notice of Medical Malpractice, not at a later time.

Motions/Petitions on Notice:

1. *Motions/Petitions Returnable:* The motions/petitions shall be filed on-line and the fee paid for either on-line by credit card or by the "Pay at the County Clerk's Office" option. As motions and petitions are time sensitive, if opting to pay at the County Clerk's Office payment MUST be made, if filed with a RJI, a minimum of nine business days prior to the applications return date and if filed post RJI, a minimum of five business days prior to the applications return date.

a) RJI Motions/Petitions: Motions/Petitions in actions wherein a Justice has not been assigned and in which an RJI is filed, please check on-line or the Law Journal on the day following the date for which the motion is noticed. The name of the Justice assigned and the date the motion will appear on that Justice's calendar will be listed. All such unassigned applications must be filed a minimum of nine business days prior to the applications return date. Except in Tax Certiorari matters, any Request for Judicial Intervention shall be deemed to include a request for preliminary conference and shall be processed as such. (See 22 NYCRR 202.8(f), 202.12(a) and 202.19).

b) Post RJI Motions/Petitions: Motions/Petitions in actions wherein a Justice has been assigned must be made returnable before the appropriate Justice on their assigned motion day. Applications on notice in assigned cases must be filed a minimum of five business days prior to the return date.

2. *Service:* With regard to service of a motion/petition on notice in an E-Filed action, CPLR 2214(b) and NYCRR 202.5b(f) applies. Proof of service shall be filed on-line.

3. *Exhibits:* It is recommended that, whenever possible, attorneys submitting exhibits to the court on E-File cases make each exhibit a separate attachment to an affidavit/affirmation.

4. *Sequence Number for E-File Motions:* As in a regular case, each motion/proceeding filed on-line in an e-filed case is assigned an identifying motion number (a "Sequence Number," e.g., Seq. No. 006)). The E-File system will prompt the filer to "tag" each new motion with a sequence number, which, of course, should be the next number in chronological order (order of filing with the system) after that of the previous motion as shown on the E-File case docket. In Queens County, cross-motions are not separately numbered, but, like opposition and reply papers, are collected under the sequence number of the motion to which they are addressed, and should be tagged by the filer accordingly.

5. *Cross-Motions and Other Motion Papers to be Filed On-Line:* Cross-motions and opposition and reply papers must be filed on-line. A fee must be paid on cross-motions and may be paid on-line.

6. *Courtesy Hard Copies:* Upon request of chambers, exact hard copies of all papers on E-Filed motions shall be handed in at the call of the calendar. These copies will not be filed with the resulting decision.

7. *Results of E-File Submissions:* The E-File system does not provide notice to counsel of all developments in all cases. Counsel must follow the normal procedures to determine, for instance, whether and when a motion was submitted.

8. *Scanning and Transmission of Decisions:* After the court issues a decision on a motion in a E-File case, it will forward the decision to the County Clerk's office, which will promptly scan it, with County Clerk entry stamp, into the E-File system. The system will immediately transmit notice of this event via e-mail, including a link to the "entered" document, to all parties who have consented on-line in the particular case.

Long Form Orders on Motions:

If the court directs that an order be settled or submitted on a motion in an E-File case, the proposed order and any proposed counter-order shall be filed with the court on-line with proof of service. (If a decision refers to a proceeding on the record, a copy of the transcript must be submitted.) The Motion Support Office will then print out the proposed order and any proposed counter-order and will process the papers in the customary manner. As appropriate, the Clerk may make changes on the proposed order/counter-order by hand. Once a proposed order/counter-order in proper form has been submitted, the Clerk of the back office will forward a hard copy to the Justice for signature. After an order/counter-order has been signed, the County Clerk will scan it, with County Clerk entry stamp, into the E-File system, which will immediately transmit notice of this event via e-mail, including a link to the entered document, to all parties who have consented on-line in the case.

Orders to Show Cause:

1. *Proposed OSC's and Supporting Papers to be Filed On-Line; Alternative Submission by E-Mail:* Proposed orders to show cause and supporting papers in an E-File case must be filed with the system by the applicant. Generally, it is expected that the proposed order and supporting papers will be filed on-line prior to review by the Ex Parte Office. There may, however, be instances in which a party, because of exigent or other circumstances, does not wish to provide advance notice to the adversary of a proposed order by filing it and supporting papers with the E-File system (which will generate an e-mail message to all parties). In those cases, the proposed order to show cause and supporting papers may be submitted to the Ex Parte Office by regular e-mail (i.e., outside the E-File system).

An E-mail box for this office has been established at the following address:

queensexparteef@courts.state.ny.us

In such instances, the applicant must file the proposed order and supporting papers with the E-File system after signature.

2. *Review of Proposed OSC's Will be Done On-Line:* Absent unusual practical difficulties, a proposed order to show cause and supporting papers will be reviewed for form on-line in the Ex Parte Office.

3. *Processing Proposed OSC's:* A proposed order to show cause requires a judicial signature. Thus, after the proposed order to show cause has been transmitted to court and approved for form by the Ex Parte Office and the motion fee has been paid, the Ex Parte Office will print out a hard copy of the proposed

order to show cause and transmit to the appropriate Justice for signature. Further, if a TRO is sought in a Commercial Division case, Rule 20 of the Division's Rules contemplates an appearance by the applicant and requires that the applicant notify the opposing party that an application will be made so as to permit that party to appear and contest the application.

4. *Posting the Signed OSC's to the E-File Sysytem:* In all instances, Chambers will promptly forward to the Motion Support Office the order to show cause as marked up and signed by the Justice. After processing, the Motion Support Office will file the signed order to show cause with the County Clerk. In the event that any supporting papers were not previously posted, counsel will be directed to make such posting.

Marked Pleadings:

All marked pleadings must be E-Filed prior to trial. Upon request, exact hard copies of the marked pleadings shall be provided to the Court.

Procedures Regarding Service On–Line:

1. *Service of Initiating Documents in an Action:* Initiating documents may be served in hard copy pursuant to Article 3 of the CPLR, or in tax certiorari cases, pursuant to the Real Property Tax Law, or by electronic means if the party served agrees to accept such service. A party served by electronic means shall, within 24 hours of service, provide the serving party or attorney with an electronic confirmation that the service has been effected.

2. *Service of Interlocutory Documents*

a.) E-mail address for service: Each party in the action subject to electronic filing that has consented thereto shall identify on an appropriate form an e-mail address at which service of interlocutory documents on that party may be made through notification transmitted by the e-filing Internet site (hereinafter the "e-mail service address"). Each attorney of record and each self represented party shall promptly notify the appropriate clerk in the event he or she changes his or her e-mail service address.

b.) How service is made: Where parties have consented to e-filing, upon the receipt of an interlocutory document by the e-filing Internet site, the site shall automatically transmit electronic notification to all e-mail service addresses. Such notification shall provide the title of the document received, the date received, and the names of those appearing on the list of e-mail service addresses to whom the notification is sent. Each party receiving the notification shall be responsible for the accessing the e-filing Internet site to obtain a copy of the document received. The electronic transmission of the notification shall constitute service of the document on the e-mail service addresses identified therein, except that such service will not be effective if the filing party learns that it did not reach the address of the person to be served. Proof of such service will be recorded on the e-filing Internet site. A party may, however, utilize other service methods permitted by the CPLR provided that, if one of such other methods is used, proof of service shall be filed electronically.

Sealing of Documents:

1. *Sealing—Compliance with Part 216:* In order to seal a paper in an E-File case, a party must proceed in accordance with Part 216 of the Uniform Rules for the Trial Courts.

2. *Secure Documents:* Documents may, however, be designated "secure" by the filing user without an order of the court. The effect of such designation is that the document may be viewed in the E-File system only by the parties to the case who have consented to E-Filing and by the court. The electronic file, however, remains open for public inspection via computer at the courthouse (unless sealed in accordance with Part 216).

3. *Sealing; Procedures:* If a party wishes to file and maintain papers under seal and no sealing order has been issued in the case, the party must, either by motion or on submission to the court of a stipulation, obtain a court order directing the County Clerk to seal the file. The court will conduct a Part 216 analysis in deciding whether to issue such an order. If the motion/stipulation is filed with the E-File system, it will be open to the public until a sealing order is issued. If this creates concern for the parties about the release of confidential information in the meantime, they may wish to consider filing the motion/stipulation as a "secure" document if that is appropriate. Or, the motion/stipulation may be filed with the system but without the attachment of any exhibits that would disclose confidential information. If the file is sealed in whole or in part, the exhibits can be filed with the E-File system after the fact. Or the parties may make a motion or submit a stipulation without filing it to the system until after the court rules on the sealing issue if such filing would disclose confidential information.

4. *Execution of Sealing Order:* If the court issues an order directing the sealing of an E-File in whole or in part, the party seeking the sealing should file with the E-File system a Certificate Requesting Sealing of Document in Electronically-Filed Case,[1] together with a copy of the court's order. This form is available from the E-File website by clicking on the link above. If such a request is properly made, the County Clerk will seal the file or the document(s) in question as directed by the court, both in the E-File system and, if any of the covered documents are found therein, in the hard copy file.

1 http://iapps.courts.state.ny.us/fbem/forms/ certjsealingform_NoCty72707.pdf

5. *Previously Sealed File:* If a case that was previously sealed pursuant to court order is converted to E-File status, counsel for the parties should promptly file with the County Clerk's Office that an order sealing the file was issued. Counsel are advised to contact the Office by e-mail or phone and must submit a copy of the sealing order by posting it to the E-File system. Upon such submission, E-File will be sealed.

Entry and Notice of Entry:

1. *Entry:* Pursuant to the E-File Rules (Section 202.5-b (h)), the Clerk shall file orders electronically and such filing shall constitute entry of the order. The Clerk is required to and will transmit an e-mail message to all filing users on the case notifying that the order has been entered. Such notice does not constitute service of notice of entry by any party.

2. *Notice of Entry:* Notice of entry is served by a party as follows: the party simply transmits electronically to the parties to be served the notification received from the court, along with an express statement that the transmittal constitutes notice of entry.

Judgments and the Judgment Roll:

1. *Entry of Judgment; Procedures:* If the court in an order directs entry of judgment by the County Clerk, the party seeking entry shall submit a proposed judgment with bill of costs, interest calculations and supporting information to the County Clerk, together with a Certificate Requesting Entry of Judgment.[2]

[2] http://iapps.courts.state.ny.us/fbem/forms/certjudg_NoCty 72707 .pdf

These papers should be sent by e-mail outside the FBEM system to the following e-mail box:

qnsjfbem@courts.state.ny.us

The Judgment Clerk will promptly communicate with counsel by e-mail or phone in the event of any difficulties with the submission. Once the judgment is in proper form, it will be printed out by the Judgment Clerk and submitted to the County Clerk for signature. The Judgment Clerk will scan the judgment once signed and post it to the system, along with the supporting information, at which time notification will be sent via e-mail to all consenting users

2. *Default Judgment; Entry by Clerk:* If the plaintiff in an E-File case seeks entry of a default judgment by the Clerk pursuant to CPLR 3215, the attorney should either transmit to the E-File system a proposed Clerk's default judgment with bill of costs, etc. and the Certificate Requesting Entry of Judgment, or forward these documents to the Clerk outside the E-File system to the cited e-mail box. Where the submissions are made to the E-File system, the Judgment Clerk will promptly enter the judgment or will communicate with the filer by phone or e-mail if a problem is detected. If the submission is made to the e-mail box outside, the Judgment Clerk will promptly

communicate with counsel by e-mail or phone advising that the submission is in proper form or pointing out any defects. Once the submission has been approved, the attorney should file on the E-File system the proposed Clerk's default judgment with bill of costs, etc. and Certificate. To enter the judgment the Clerk will print out the judgment from E-File system have it signed, and scan it to the system.

3. *Judgments Signed by Court:* In some instances, the court itself may sign the judgment. Calculation of disbursements, costs and interest will generally be left to the County Clerk by the court. Papers supporting such calculation may be submitted to the County Clerk in the same manner as described above.

4. *Judgment Roll:* Whenever a judgment is to be entered, a judgment roll must be created by counsel or the clerk (CPLR 5017(a)). Counsel shall submit the Certificate Requesting Entry of Judgment and shall identify therein, by title of the paper, number of the paper on the E-File List of Papers Filed, and date filed, all e-filed documents that should form part of the judgment roll. Any documents that were filed in hard-copy form only that are to be included in the judgment roll should be scanned into the system by counsel and included in the Certificate. The County Clerk will post the Certificate on-line once approved and this will constitute the judgment roll.

5. *Entry of Judgment:* Once the County Clerk has taxed costs and disbursements and calculated interest and has in hand a signed judgment, the Clerk will stamp the judgment with the County Clerk file stamp and scan the judgment to the system. This constitutes entry. The County Clerk is required to and will transmit an e-mail message to all filing users on the case notifying that the judgment has been entered. This notice does not constitute service of notice of entry by any party

Notices of Appeal and Appeal Papers:

1. *Notice of Appeal; Payment of Fee:* A notice of appeal shall be filed on-line in an E-File case. The fee therefor must be paid by credit card on-line or by means of the "Pay at the County Clerk's Office" option. In the latter situation, the notice will not be considered "filed" until payment of the fee is tendered to the County Clerk at the office.

2. *Notice of Appeal; Procedures:* The notice shall be filed together with a pre-argument statement and a copy of the judgment or order appealed from. The other parties to the case may be served on-line in the manner described above. Proof of service must also be filed on-line. The County Clerk will print a hard copy of any e-filed notice of appeal and include it in the County Clerk file.

3. *E-File; Appellate Division:* At present, the Appellate Division, Second Department does not handle appeals in E-File cases by electronic means.

Counsel are advised to consult the rules of that court and to confer with the County Clerk.

DHCR PART

Doc. 8. DHCR Part

Effective March 1, 2010, any Article 78 proceeding filed involving the New York State Division of Housing & Community Renewal (DHCR) will be assigned to Judge Timothy J. Dufficy sitting in Room 101, located at 89–17 Sutphin Blvd., Jamaica, NY 11435.

These matters will be called on a Tuesday at 2:15 P.M.

Other than an Order to Show Cause, if the application is filed with a Request for Judicial Intervention, the matter will be administratively rescheduled from the noticed return date to the subsequent week on a Tuesday. Any post Request for Judicial Intervention application MUST be noticed to be heard on a Tuesday at 2:15 P.M., in Room 101, located at 89–17 Sutphin Blvd., Jamaica, NY 11435.

The movant shall be responsible for notifying all parties of any administratively rescheduling.

Mandatory appearance of all counsel and pro se litigants is required. Any requests for an adjournment will only be entertained at the call of the calendar in the presence of all parties, or by stipulation, signed by all parties and faxed in advance to 718–262–7341.

RESIDENTIAL FORECLOSURE PART

Doc. 9. Residential Foreclosure Part

Conference Days:

The Residential Foreclosure Part shall sit Monday thru Friday mornings in Room 42A at 9:30 a.m. and Wednesday and Thursday afternoons in Room 314 at 2:15 p.m. Conferences shall be conducted when all sides have checked in with the Part Clerk.

Part Rules:

These rules apply to those actions that are subject to the foreclosure legislation and/or CPLR 3408.

1. All residential foreclosure actions that are filed must include the following language in the Complaint: Plaintiff must plead whether this action involves a residential, one-to-four family, owner-occupied property upon which the mortgage is considered subprime, high-cost or nontraditional; whether plaintiff has served the homeowner with a 90 day notice as per legislation; and plaintiff must plead that it has a current, valid assignment of the mortgage.

2. Upon filing the affidavit of service of the summons and complaint with the County Clerk, plaintiff must submit a Request for Judicial Intervention for a Settlement Conference in Residential Foreclosure Actions.

3. Pursuant to CPLR 3408, this Part shall conduct a mandatory settlement conference for the purpose of holding settlement discussions pertaining to the relative rights and obligations of the parties under the mortgage loan documents, including, but not limited to: determining whether the parties can reach a mutually agreeable resolution to help the defendant avoid losing his or her home; evaluating the potential for a resolution in which payment schedules or amounts may be modified or other workout options may be agreed to; and for whatever other purposes the court deems appropriate.

4. *Poor Person Applications:* At the initial conference, any defendant appearing pro se shall be deemed to have made a motion to proceed as a poor person, and the court shall determine whether such permission shall be granted. If the court appoints defendant counsel, the court will adjourn the conference to a date certain for appearance of counsel and settlement discussions pursuant to subdivision (a) of CPLR 3408, and otherwise proceed with the conference.

5. *Appearance by the Parties:* At any conference held pursuant to CPLR 3408, the plaintiff, in the absence of written permission of the Part permitting a representative to attend the settlement conference telephonically or by video conference, shall appear in person or by counsel, and if appearing by counsel, such counsel shall be fully authorized to dispose of the case. The defendant shall appear in person or by counsel. If the defendant is appearing pro se, the court shall advise the defendant of the nature of the action and his or her rights and responsibilities as a defendant.

6. Defendant pro se does not waive his or her jurisdictional defenses by appearing at the foreclosure conference. Any and all statements made, whether oral or written, and any and all information exchanged at the conference, shall be solely for the purposes of resolution and settlement and shall not be deemed to be admissions of any party with respect to the underlying action.

7. Plaintiff should attend the conference prepared to discuss the loan amount, default amount, payoff amount, and whether the lender is subject to the Making Homes Affordable Program. Plaintiff may be asked to provide evidence of the status of defendant's

modification paperwork and should have telephone access to its client to address any of the Court's issues. Plaintiff should be aware that a case may be adjourned numerous times at the Court's discretion in order for plaintiff to demonstrate compliance with the above.

8. Defendant homeowner must attend the scheduled required housing counseling meeting. Defendant homeowners are strongly encouraged to go to a housing counseling agency and seek legal representation prior to attending the settlement conference.

9. Defendant must appear at the settlement conference prepared to discuss the following: whether the property is residential, defendant's financial status, the cause of defendant's default in paying the mortgage, and provide documentation to the Court if requested, and to plaintiff to evaluate the possibility of a loan modification

10. *Adjournments:* Either party may request one adjournment of a matter, which will generally be granted by the Court. After the first adjournment, all further requests are in the Court's discretion.

The Part may be contacted via telephone to advise that an action has been settled, discontinued or otherwise disposed of. No adjournments will be granted via telephone.

11. *Applications to Judges:* If a legal issue arises during the foreclosure conference, either party may request a review of said issue by one of the two assigned judges. The party requesting the review must clearly state to the referee the reason for the request and provide the opposing party with an opportunity to respond. The referee will then contact the assigned judges and schedule a hearing on the issue with notice to the parties. However, the assigned judges may decline to hear the issue, if they believe that it is not legal in nature, at which time the referee will issue a ruling on the issue.

12. *Further Proceedings:* If the referee deems that a matter should proceed with litigation, an order will be issued indicating that the matter has not been settled and the parties may proceed with litigation. Any subsequent motions or applications will then be made to the assigned IAS judge and must contain a separate statement from the moving party, affixed to the front of the application, that the action does or does not fit the criteria for inclusion in the Residential Foreclosure Program. Effective May 1, 2009, any application submitted to the Court involving a foreclosure action, where a mandatory settlement conference was held pursuant to CPLR 3408, must also contain a copy of the Residential Foreclosure Conference Order affixed to the front of the application. If a party wishes to obtain information with regard to the status of the case, it may contact the Foreclosure Conference Part or access the computers in the County Clerk's Office.

13. Any questions should be directed to the Foreclosure Conference Part by telephone at 718–298–1092.

CIVIL MOTION RETURN DAY

Doc. 10.   Civil Motion Return Day

MONDAY

RITHOLTZ (CSCP)

TUESDAY

SCHULMAN/WEINSTEIN/TSJ (TSP)

GRAYS (4)

LANE (6)

BRATHWAITE-NELSON (7)

FLUG (9)

KERRIGAN (10)

BUTLER (12)

ELLIOT (14)

TAYLOR (15)

NAHMAN (16)

MAYERSOHN (22)

AGATE (24)

CULLEN (25)

GAVRIN (27)

WEDNESDAY

WEISS (2)

RIOS (8)

STRAUSS (11)

O'DONOGHUE (MDM)

KITZES (17)

HART (18)

SIEGAL (19)

GOLIA, JOSEPH (21)

ROSENGARTEN (23)

THURSDAY

SAMPSON (31)

MARKEY (32)

GOLIA, JAMES (33)

MCDONALD (34)

PINEDA-KIRWAN (36)

CONFERENCE SCHEDULES

Schedule 1. Justices' Preliminary Conference Schedules

88–11 Sutphin Blvd., Room #314

	9:30 a.m.	11:30 a.m.
Mon:	J. Weiss (Part 2) J. Gavrin (Part 27–NYCTA Cases) J. Sampson (Part 31) J. Pineda-Kirwan (Part 36)	J. Grays (Part 4) J. Markey (Part 32)
Tue:	J. Nelson (Part 7) J. Flug (Part 9–City Cases) J. O'Donoghue (MDPC) J. James Golia (Part 33)	J. Kerrigan (Part 10–City Cases) J. Taylor (Part 15) J. Siegal (Part 19)
Wed:	J. Lane (Part 6) J. Elliot (Part 14) J. McDonald (Part 34)	J. Strauss (Part 11) J. Nahman (Part 16) J. Rosengarten (Part 23)
Thu:	J. Butler (Part 12) J. Kitzes (Part 17) J. Hart (Part 18) J. Agate (Part 24)	

Notification to Attorney
Preliminary Conference Procedures

A preliminary conference Shall be held within 45 days of the RJI date. The date of the Preliminary Conference shall appear in the New York Law Journal within one (1) to three (3) weeks of the RJI. Please look for the preliminary conference date in New York Law Journal after Filing an RJI.

Attorneys are also encouraged to use the following link to view future appearances and decisions online:

WebCivil Supreme [1]

*Court calendars for Queens County should be viewed by the court part.

Notes:

1) All Preliminary Conferences scheduled in actions against the City of New York are conducted on Tuesdays in the Supreme Court Building, 88–11 Sutphin Boulevard, Jamaica, New York in Room 314, Before J.H.O. Allan Beldock as Follows:

a. For cases assigned to I.A.S. Part–9 (Justice Flug), Preliminary Conferences will be held at 9:30 a.m.

b. For Cases assigned to I.A.S. Part-10 (Justice Kerrigan), Preliminary Conferences will be held at 11:30 a.m.

2) Preliminary Conferences for cases involving the New York City Transit Authority (but not the City of New York) are conducted on Monday mornings, at 9:30, in the Supreme Court Building, 88–11 Sutphin Blvd., in room #314, before J.H.O. Beldock

3) All Preliminary Conferences are held in the Jamaica Courthouse regardless of the location of the Justice assigned.

[1] http://iapps.courts.state.ny.us/webcivil/FCASMain

ALTERNATIVE DISPUTE RESOLUTION
MATRIMONIAL MEDIATION PILOT PROGRAM

Rule I. Overview

Mediation is a confidential, problem solving process in which a neutral third party—the mediator—helps disputing parties to identify issues, clarify perceptions, and explore options for a mutually acceptable outcome. Mediation often results in faster, less expensive, more durable, and less acrimonious outcomes than might be the case in the normal course of litigation.

The Queens County Supreme Court's Matrimonial Mediation Pilot Program offers parties a free, 90-minute initial session with a Program mediator. Program mediators have significant training and experience in family mediation and in opening paths of communication that enable meaningful dialogue and cooperation. They help divorcing parties to resolve key issues that affect their relationships with their children and the financial well being of all family members. Parties are encouraged, but are not required, to bring their attorneys to the mediation session.

Although parties are not obligated to reach agreement in mediation, the process often concludes with a written agreement, as well as improved communication between the parties. If the parties reach an agreement during mediation, the mediator may assist the parties and their counsel in drafting a written agreement. The written agreement is then returned to the referring Justice for review. Subject to the referring Justice's approval, the agreement will be incorporated in the Court's Order or Judgment of Divorce.

Rule II. Procedures

Supreme Court Justices may refer parties to the Matrimonial Mediation Program or parties on their own may request referral to the Program at any time. Cases involving child abuse or neglect (as defined in Family Court Act § 1012(e) and (f) and Social Services Law § 412) and for which disclosure is required pursuant to Social Services Law § 413, domestic violence, or a severe power imbalance between the parties are not appropriate for mediation and shall be excluded from the Program. Please note that parties may be screened by Court staff or the selected mediator at any time to determine eligibility for participation in the Matrimonial Mediation Program.

To begin the process, the Justice signs an Order of Reference directing parties and their counsel to appear at an initial, free, ninety (90) minute mediation session with a Program mediator from the Matrimonial Mediation Program's Roster of Mediators. The Order of Reference may also contain a control date set by the referring justice for the parties to appear in Court for a conference following the mediation.

Counsel for the parties shall deliver the Order of Reference to Tracy Catapano Fox, Esq., the Matrimonial Mediation Program Coordinator ("Coordinator"), who is located in Administrative Chambers, Room 511, at 88–11 Sutphin Blvd., Jamaica, NY 11435, and who can be reached at 718–298–1100 or tcfox@courts.state.ny.us. The Program Coordinator shall select from the Court's Roster of Mediators the next available mediator, proceeding in alphabetical order.

Within five (5) business days of receiving the Order of Reference, the Program Coordinator shall notify the parties of the assigned mediator and send them a Notice of Confirmation, which shall contain the mediator's name and contact information. The parties are free to select a different mediator, but if they do so, they must notify the Program Coordinator of the substitution in writing within 5 business days. The parties are required to appear at the initial mediation session within twenty (20) days of receiving a Notice of Confirmation.

At least one week before the initial mediation session, parties or their counsel shall send to the mediator a copy of the pleadings, Statements of Net Worth, and any other information necessary for the effective negotiation of the issues involved. The mediator may also request a conference call with the parties' counsel regarding any preliminary matters.

If parties wish to extend the mediation process beyond the initial session, they may schedule additional sessions with the mediator at a per hour rate that shall not exceed $250/hour. Program mediators are strongly encouraged to work on a sliding scale to take into account the parties' financial circumstances. Parties shall complete all scheduled mediation sessions within seventy five (75) days of receiving the Notice of Confirmation.

Within five (5) business days after the mediation's conclusion, which shall occur whenever after the initial 90–minute session one party, both parties, or the mediator decides that the mediation has ended, the mediator shall send a Mediator's Report to counsel and to the Coordinator—but not to the referring Justice—describing the outcome.

The Report shall state (1) the date of the initial session and whether each party and counsel appeared at the initial session; (2) the dates of any subsequent scheduled sessions, but not whether parties appeared; and (3) whether the parties reached partial, complete, or no agreement on the issues. The mediator may attach to the Report any original, signed agreement and return it to the Coordinator.

Once counsel receives a copy of the Mediator Report, counsel shall promptly contact the Part of the assigned Justice to schedule a conference concerning further proceedings in the case. The Program Coordinator shall report to the referring Justice whether the case settled (in whole or in part) but shall not reveal to the referring Justice the selected mediator's identity or disclose other information discussed during the mediation, except as described in Section IX.

Rule III. Role of the Mediator

The mediator's primary role is to help the parties communicate and negotiate. The mediator does not give legal advice, predict likely court outcomes, or force solutions on the parties.

At the initial mediation session, the mediator explains that all communications are confidential (with narrow exceptions outlined below) and will not be disclosed to the Justice hearing the case or in any other judicial or administrative proceeding. The mediator also explains that either party is free at the close of the initial session or at any time thereafter to end the mediation process and return to court.

During the mediation process, all parties are free to discuss the case as they see it and to raise particular issues of concern that they would like to address. The mediator may ask the parties clarifying questions related to the care of their children, parenting time, and allocation of property and income. The mediator then helps the parties to develop and choose options that meet the parties' needs.

At some point in the process, either party, the party's counsel, or the mediator may suggest a caucus. Caucuses are meetings that mediators hold separately with each side in a dispute. During the caucus, the mediator may explore how each party views the dispute and the impact of any proposed solutions. The mediator keeps confidential the information discussed in caucus unless the party permits disclosure.

If the parties reach a written agreement during mediation, the parties are strongly encouraged to submit the agreement to their respective attorneys for review.

Rule IV. The Role of Parties, Counsel, Attorneys for the Child, and Guardians Ad Litem

Experience has demonstrated that party participation—as opposed to exclusive participation by counsel—not only increases the likelihood of settlement, but also improves compliance with any agreed upon terms and enhances the parties' overall satisfaction with the process and outcome. Accordingly, unless exempted by the mediator for good cause shown, the parties must be present during the mediation.

The presence of separate counsel for each party during mediation sessions is encouraged. If counsel for either party is discharged or withdraws for any reason during the mediation process, the case may not proceed in mediation until a substitution occurs unless otherwise ordered by the Court.

Without representation by counsel, parties risk entering into agreements with insufficient knowledge about financial, legal or other issues. If parties decide to participate in mediation without their attorneys present, they are strongly advised to consult counsel before finalizing any agreement.

For those cases in which an attorney for the child has been assigned, mediation may not commence without the child's attorney's present. If the parties and the child's attorney agree to proceed in mediation without the child's attorney, they may do so, unless otherwise ordered by the Court.

Rule V. The Role of the Court

The Program is conducted under Court auspices and pursuant to these rules. Judicial and non judicial staff are encouraged to inform the parties of the Program's existence. If the parties wish to go to mediation but cannot afford it, the Coordinator can assist qualifying parties to find a mediator who will take their case.

The Court welcomes the feedback of parties, counsel, and mediators after the conclusion of the proceedings.

Rule VI. The Roster of Mediators

The Court has assembled a Roster of Mediators. The prerequisites to joining the Roster are as follows:

Training: Completion of at least 60 hours of family mediation training in a training program sponsored or recognized by the New York State Office of Court Administration ("OCA").

Experience: At least four years of family mediation experience, including 250 hours of face to face mediation with clients and a minimum of 25 custody and visitation cases, and any other mediation training or experience deemed appropriate by the Court. Cases involving financial disputes will be referred only to those Program mediators with knowledge of, training in and experience with the financial aspects of divorce.

Continuing Education: Pursuant to Part 146 of the Rules of the Chief Administrative Judge, all mediators must attend at least six hours of additional approved training relevant to their respective practice areas every two years.

See www.nycourts.gov/rules/chiefadmin/146.shtml

Continuing presence on the Court's Roster of Mediators is subject to review by the District Administrative Judge. Mediators may be removed from the Roster at the discretion of the District Administrative Judge in consultation with the NYS Unified Court System's Office of Alternative Dispute Resolution and Court Improvement Programs.

Rule VII. Fees

The Program does not charge or administer fees. Parties referred to mediation pursuant to this Statement of Procedures shall not be required to compensate the mediator for services rendered before or during the initial 90–minute mediation session. Should the parties agree to schedule additional sessions with the mediator, the mediator shall be entitled to compensation for services rendered as follows: compensable services shall consist of time spent conducting any mediation session that follows the initial 90–minute session, and time spent reviewing materials submitted by the parties for purposes of subsequent mediation sessions. The mediator's fee for such services shall not exceed $250.00 per hour. The fee arrangement must be agreed to in writing, and must include the ratio at which the fee will be divided between the parties. The parties must sign this fee agreement before commencing any additional sessions beyond the initial mediation session. Mediators are encouraged to use a sliding scale where appropriate, and shall consult with the Program Coordinator if the parties are unable to pay.

Rule VIII. Immunity

The mediator shall be immune from suit as a result of any conduct or omission during the performance of duties in that capacity to the extent permitted by law.

Rule IX. Confidentiality

Except as set forth below, all oral, written, or other communications made during the course of mediation by any party, mediator or any other person present shall be immune from disclosure in any present or future judicial or administrative proceeding. Similarly, all information generated in or in connection with the mediation—including memoranda, work products or case files of a mediator—shall remain confidential and not be subject to disclosure in any present or future judicial or administrative proceeding. However, mediation will not be used as a shield with respect to otherwise discoverable documents or information produced or occurring prior to or outside the mediation.

Moreover, except as set forth below, nothing about the substance of the mediation, such as the weaknesses or strengths of the parties' cases or the relative willingness of parties to discuss settlement proposals, will be revealed to the referring Justice or any other person by the Mediator or any party or attorney. Nor will any party or lawyer for a party reveal the outcome of the mediation process to the referring Justice or a member of the Justice's staff unless both sides agree to the disclosure.

Notwithstanding these confidentiality provisions, communications and information may be subject to disclosure in any present or future judicial or administrative proceeding in any of the following five circumstances:

1. *Attendance.* Whether the parties and their counsel attended the initial mediation session will be reported to the Program Coordinator who may notify the Court.

2. *Waiver.* Parties to the mediation and the mediator agree in writing to waive confidentiality. The waiver must specify the individual communication(s) or information that will be disclosed, the person or entity to whom the disclosure will be made, and the purpose of the disclosure.

3. *Written Agreement.* A writing signed by all the parties embodying a mediated agreement submitted to the court for review. Additionally, a limited report of the outcome will be sent to the referring Justice. Only those signed, mediated agreements that have become court orders may be admissible in any present or future judicial or administrative proceeding.

4. *Threats of Imminent, Serious Harm.* If communications or information constitute a credible threat of serious and imminent harm, either to the speaker or another person or entity, the appropriate authorities and/or the potential victim may be notified.

5. *Allegations of Child Abuse or Neglect.* The communication or information relates to an allegation of child abuse or neglect as defined in Family Court Act § 1012(e) and (f) and Social Services Law § 412 and for which disclosure is required pursuant to Social Services Law § 413.

Rule X. Child Abuse and Neglect

If an allegation of child abuse or neglect is made by any party during the mediation, the mediator will stop the mediation process and consult with each party individually for the purpose of obtaining as much information about the circumstances as possible. Mediators shall report to the Program Coordinator allegations of child abuse or neglect as defined in Family Court Act § 1012(e) and (f) and Social Services Law § 412, and for which disclosure is required pursuant to Social Services Law § 413.

Rule XI. Domestic Violence/Severe Power Imbalance

When an allegation of domestic violence or severe power imbalance is made by any party during the mediation, the mediator shall safely stop the mediation process, meet with each party individually where appropriate to learn as much as possible about the circumstances, and consult with the Program Coordinator (but not the assigned Justice or members of that Justice's staff) as to whether to resume the mediation process. Allegations of domestic violence will not be disclosed to the referring Justice; instead, victims will be given information regarding their rights in the form prescribed in Family Court Act § 812 (5), and they will receive safety planning information.

Rule XII. Referral to the Program and On-going Litigation

Cases may be referred to mediation, typically at the preliminary conference, on consent of the parties or at any time deemed appropriate by the Justice. A party who attends the initial session complies with the Order of Reference, even if that party ultimately chooses not to proceed with mediation. Parties may move to opt out of the Program for good cause shown.

Referral to mediation will not ordinarily stay the court proceedings in any respect. The "no stay" policy recognizes the special need for prompt action in matrimonial and family proceedings. Full discovery, emergency and pendente lite relief, family dynamics, and the needs of children require ongoing access to the court, as a general rule. However, parties committed to the mediation process who conclude that additional time is required to fully explore the issues pertaining to their case may request an adjournment.

Rule XIII. Avoiding Conflicts of Interest

Before accepting a mediation, a mediator shall make an inquiry that is reasonable under the circumstances to determine whether there are any known facts that a reasonable individual would consider likely to affect the impartiality of the mediator, including a financial or personal interest in the outcome, and an existing or past relationship with a mediation party or foreseeable participant in the mediation. The mediator shall disclose any such known fact to the mediation parties and counsel as soon as possible before accepting a mediation. The mediator is obliged to disclose all potentially disqualifying facts to the parties and, where such facts exist, shall not serve unless the parties consent in writing. If a mediator later learns of any disqualifying fact after accepting a mediation, the mediator shall disclose it as soon as practicable. If unable to function in a fair, impartial and objective manner, the mediator shall seek disqualification.

Rule XIV. Failure to Comply With Order of Reference and These Rules

If a party or counsel refuses to schedule an appearance for an initial mediation session in a timely manner, appear at an initial scheduled session, or otherwise fails to comply with these rules, the Court may impose sanctions, including costs.

CIVIL COMMITMENT/MENTAL HYGIENE

Doc. 1. Civil Commitment/Mental Hygiene

Beginning January 4, 2011, Supreme Court Mental Hygiene hearings will be conducted every Tuesday and Thursday at 10:00 a.m. at the Creedmoor Psychiatric Center located at 80-45 Winchester Blvd., Queens Village, N. Y. The courtroom is located in Building No. 73, on the first floor.

Hon. Martin J. Schulman will preside over the hearings.

EX PARTE

Doc. 1. Ex Parte Office

EMERGENCY ORDERS:

Effective immediately all parties filing "Emergency" Ex–Parte applications must do so in person and must wait in Room 140 while the application is reviewed, processed and returned from Chambers. The application must be accompanied by an "Emergency Affidavit." which does not pray for the underlying relief requested but rather addresses:

1) why the application must be entertained forthwith, and

2) why the application could not have been brought to the court's attention earlier

Requests for Emergency processing will not be entertained unless submitted in person by the requesting attorney.

NOTE OF ISSUE FILING PROCEDURES:

Step 1:

Notes of Issue should be filed and paid for in Room 106 of the County Clerk's Office.

Step 2:

Deposit 1 copy of Note of Issue (with receipt stamp) in the Trial Term basket in Room 140.

** When filing an RJI and Note of Issue together, 1 copy of RJI (with receipt stamp) must also be deposited in the Ex-Parte basket.

When filing a Note of Issue on an action which is disposed, the filing party must attach a copy of an order restoring the action. If there is no restoral order, the Note of Issue cannot be processed

RESIDENTIAL FORECLOSURE

Doc. 1.   Residential Foreclosure Office

The Residential Foreclosure Part shall sit on Tuesdays in Room 3002 before Court–Attorney–Referee Mark Kugelman and on Wednesdays and Thursdays in Room 42A before Court–Attorney–Referee Leonard N. Florio. Conferences shall be conducted when all sides are present, with check in to commence at 9:30 a.m. with the Part Clerk.

Prior to the settlement conference, a housing counseling meeting will be scheduled with Brooklyn Housing & Family Services located at the Queens Supreme Court in Room 25C. Defendant homeowner must attend the scheduled required housing counseling meeting. Defendant homeowners are strongly encouraged to go to a housing counseling agency and seek legal representation prior to attending the settlement conference.

Pursuant to CPLR 3408, this Part shall conduct a mandatory settlement conference for the purpose of holding settlement discussions pertaining to the relative rights and obligations of the parties under the mortgage loan documents, including, but not limited to determining whether the parties can reach a mutually agreeable resolution to help the defendant avoid losing his or her home; evaluating the potential for a resolution in which payment schedules or amounts may be modified or other workout options may be agreed to; and for whatever other purposes the court deems appropriate.

If the referee deems that a matter should proceed with litigation, an order will be issued indicating that the matter has not been settled and the parties may proceed with litigation. Any subsequent motions or applications will then be made to the assigned IAS judge and must contain a separate statement from the moving party, affixed to the front of the application, that the action does or does not fit the criteria for inclusion in the Residential Foreclosure Program. Effective May 1, 2009, any application submitted to the Court involving a foreclosure action, where a mandatory settlement conference was held pursuant to CPLR 3408, must also contain a copy of the Residential Foreclosure Conference Order affixed to the front of the application.

MATRIMONIAL OFFICE

Doc. 1.   Matrimonial Office (Divorce)
PRELIMINARY CONFERENCE

Counsel and Litigants are encouraged to link to the Divorce Resources site, http://www.nycourts.gov/divorce/forms.shtml for forms.

Effective immediately, the Queens Supreme Matrimonial Department shall utilize the Preliminary Conference form listed under "General Forms".

All matrimonial motions must be made returnable for a Monday. Motions must be filed with the matrimonial office at least 5 working days before the return date.

Effective immediately, the filing of all post judgment matrimonial motions and orders to show cause must include:

(a) copy of the judgment;

(b) calendar number of the said matrimonial action;

(c) date of the note of issue.

Additionally, all applications for writs of habeas corpus must indicate, below the present index number, the index number of any previously assigned action and the assigned judge, or state that no other matrimonial actions have been filed.

Notice

All orders to show cause containing an application for the issuance of an Order of Protection will be treated as an emergency and emergency procedures must be followed. The court is required to conduct a hearing before issuance of an order of protection, and the applying party and their attorney, if any, must be present.

Income Deduction Orders Laws of 1994, Ch. 170 Sec. 358–362, 364–366 Section 5242 CPLR

In all Child Support matters, a competent income deduction order must be submitted unless a written alternative agreement is provided.

In accordance with the Family Protection and Domestic violence intervention Act of 1994, an automated statewide registry will be operative effective October 1, 1995. The legislation requires that the registry contain information involving orders of protection and warrants issued statewide in connection with criminal, Family Court and matrimonial cases involving family violence. Effective October 1, 1995, all requests for an order of protection must be submitted with a completed Family Protection Registry information sheet. These forms are available in the matrimonial office, Room 140 in Jamaica.

Doc. 2.   Matrimonial Office Requirements for Filing Uncontested Divorce Papers

Please note that court personnel are prohibited from giving legal advice and are not allowed to fill out the forms for you.

Your papers are accepted subject to review, and, if at any point your papers are found defective, you will be notified by mail. Do not call this office.

Court fees for uncontested note of issue: The usual fee is $125. However, if an RJI fee has been previously paid, the note of issue fee is $30. A postal money order or an attorney's business check are the only acceptable means of payment.

In order to place a matrimonial action on the uncontested calendar, the following papers must be submitted to the Matrimonial Office, Room 140:

1. Three copies of the note of issue form UD–9 with a current printout of the county clerk's minutes (obtained in Room 106).

2. An exact copy of the documents(s) which commenced the action, namely the summons with notice form UD–1 OR summons form UD–1A and verified complaint form UD–2.

3. Proof that the defendant was served. This can be the defendant's affidavit in which (s)he accepts service form UD–7 OR the affidavit of service of the summons form UD–3. The defendant's affidavit or the affidavit of service of the summons must address whether the defendant is a member of the military.

4. Affidavit of regularity form UD–5 AND Part 130 certification UD–12.

5. Affidavit of fact, also known as affidavit of plaintiff form UD–6.

6. A sworn statement as to the removal of barriers to remarriage form UD–4, along with proof of service form UD–4A, if the parties were married by a clergyman, minister or by a leader of the Society for Ethical Culture. (This is not necessary if the parties were married in a civil ceremony, for example, by the city clerk or justice of the peace.)

7. An action for annulment based on fraud or an action for divorce based on adultery must have a corroborating affidavit signed by someone other than the husband or wife.

8. Separate findings of fact with conclusions of law form UD–10 AND separate judgment of divorce form UD–11. If the form from the uncontested divorce package is not used, be sure that these documents

comply with 22 NYCRR–202.50. Appendix B and 202.5, as well as CPLR 2101.

9. A certified copy of the Separation Agreement must be submitted if this is the ground for the divorce, with proof that it was filed with the appropriate county clerk.

10. Original or certified copies of all other stipulations or agreements (signed and acknowledged by both parties) stamped "fee paid" by the County Clerk. (This includes any amendments or addendums.) Note: attorney certifications per CPLR 2105 are acceptable.

11. Original, signed, official, certificate of dissolution form DOH–2168 must be submitted. It must contain social security number information for both parties and the wife's maiden name.

12. A self addressed stamped post card, which will be used to notify you that the judgment has been signed and entered by the county clerk, is mandatory.

If there are children under the age of 21, the following additional documents must be submitted and the following rules apply:

1. Income information pursuant to DRL 240 in the form of a child support worksheet UD–8 is required.

2. When a stipulation addresses child support, it must include a provision stating that the parties have been advised of the child support standards provisions of DRL 240. The stipulation must contain the reason(s) for any deviation from the presumptive amount of child support. See DRL 1(j)1–b(h).

3. Submit copies of any prior orders of custody, visitation and child support of the Family Court or any other court.

4. Qualified Medical Child Support Order UD–8b. See DRL 240 (1)(c).

5. Income deduction order is required (unless the parties stipulate in writing to an alternate payment arrangement OR payments are to be made through the Support Collection Unit).

6. Form UCS–111.

7. Child and Spousal Support Registration form (unless the order will be paid through the Support Collection Unit).

MOTION SUPPORT

Doc. 1. Motion Support Office

RJI Motions and Petitions

All notices of motions or petitions filed with a Request for Judicial Intervention will be administratively rescheduled to the following week before the assigned justice on their motion day.

Please refer to the Web Civil Supreme link to ascertain the rescheduled day.

Post RJI Motions and Petitions

A Motion/Petition on notice in assigned cases must be made returnable before the appropriate Justice on their assigned motion day.

All motions in Post-Note matters shall be made returnable before the I.A.S. Justice assigned; however, one month prior to the Trial Scheduling Part appearance (not Pretrial Conference appearance) motions shall be made returnable before the Trial Scheduling Justice on a Tuesday

Responsive Papers

Motion Support does not process or forward responsive papers including cross motions. Counsel are advised to follow the assigned Judge's rules regarding their submission.

Memorandum Decision

Memorandum decisions are filed with the county clerk awaiting submission of a proposed order or judgment to the Motion Support Office. Counsel are advised to adhere to NYCRR 202.48 regarding the submission or settlement of their proposed order or judgment. Counsel are also asked to attach a copy of the memorandum to their proposed order or judgment.

Submission of Proposed Orders and Judgments With Motions on Notice

Counsel are advised when submitting proposed orders or judgments with motions on notice, to keep proposed orders or proposed judgments separate and apart from the motions papers. Proposed orders or judgments incorporated within the motion papers will be considered exhibits and treated as such.

Counsel are asked not to submit or settle multiple proposed orders or judgments.

Conforming of Orders and Judgments

Court personnel are not authorized to conform copies of orders or judgments. The accuracy of conformed copies rests with counsel. Certified copies may be obtained at the Court Clerk's office for a fee.

Notice of Medical Malpractice

When filing an RJI on a medical malpractice action, after filing and paying for the RJI in Room 106, deposit copy of RJI (with receipt stamp) and Notice of Medical malpractice in the Trial Term basket in Room 140.

Trial Preference

All applications for trial preference must be made via motion through the Motion Support Office.

SPECIAL ELECTION PART

Doc. 1.   Election Rules

Orders to Show Cause to validate or invalidate designating or nominating petitions, shall be returnable before Justice Elliot on Thursday, August 4, 2011 at 9:30 a.m. in Courtroom 25 located at 88-11 Sutphin Blvd., Jamaica, NY 11435.

The calendar must be answered by counsel or the self represented litigant, who must be ready for assignment on the return date. Proof of service of the Order to Show Cause or Notice of Petition, as well as any Answers including proposed Counterclaims, shall be filed with the Clerk of the Part no later than 9:30 a.m, on the initial return date of the proceeding. Failure to serve and file same shall be deemed a waiver and further proof shall be precluded.

Specifications of objections to a designating or nominating petition previously filed and served, pursuant to the Rules of the Board of Elections, need not be filed with the Clerk of the Part.

Specifications of objections, not previously filed and served with the Board of Elections, shall be served upon all opposing parties and filed with the Clerk of the Part no later than 9:30 a.m., on the initial return date of the proceeding. Failure to serve and file same shall be deemed a waiver and further proof shall be precluded.

In any proceeding by an aggrieved candidate to invalidate a designating or nominating petition, a bill of particulars as to specifications of objections shall be served upon all opposing parties and filed with the Clerk of the Part no later than 9:30 a.m., on the initial return date of the proceeding. Failure to serve and file same shall be deemed a waiver and further proof shall be precluded.

In any proceeding alleging a question of residency of a candidate, a complete written offer of proof shall be served upon all opposing parties and filed with the Clerk of the Part no later than 9:30 a.m., on the initial return date of the proceeding. Failure to serve and file same shall be deemed a waiver and further proof shall be precluded.

A complete written offer of proof, in all matters alleging a question of fraud, including a statement as to the number of witnesses expected to be called, the identification of each such witness (by name, address, volume, page and line) and the status of each such witness (i.e., candidate, signatory, subscribing witness, notary public, etc.) shall be served upon all opposing parties and filed with the Clerk of the Part no later than 9:30 a.m., on the initial return date of the proceeding. Failure to serve and file same shall be deemed a waiver and further proof shall be precluded.

SUBPOENAED RECORDS

Doc. 1. Subpoenaed Records

Subpoenaed records may be viewed and copied by a party or their attorney. A delegate of an attorney appearing in the action may only view or copy the records with a signed letter from the attorney giving that specific individual permission to do so. Records must remain in the subpoenaed records room at all times except if they are being removed to the courtroom for trial. Removal of records to the courtroom, at the time of trial, requires a signed judicial authorization.

After disposition of a case, any records remaining in the subpoenaed records room will be destroyed within one week of the date of disposition.

Exceptions:

If a note of issue is vacated, or the case is stricken from the trial calendar, the subpoenaed records will be retained for one year. After this one year period expires, the records will be destroyed.

SURROGATE'S COURT
LOCAL FORMS

Form 1.　Order Extending Preliminary Letters Testamentary

At the Surrogate's Court of
the State of New York, held
in and for the County of
Queens at Jamaica on

PRESENT:
HON. PETER J. KELLY
　　Surrogate

--X

In the Matter of the Probate Proceeding of

**ORDER EXTENDING
PRELIMINARY LETTERS
TESTAMENTARY**

Deceased　　　　File No. _____

--X

The Court having heretofore granted preliminary letters testamentary by order dated _____, and said preliminary letters (having expired) (being due to expire) on _____, and the preliminary executor(s) having filed an application with this Court on _____ requesting that said preliminary letters be extended, and the Court having entertained the application, and being satisfied that justification exists for the extension of said letters, it is

ORDERED that the preliminary letters testamentary heretofore issued to ___ be extended to _____, executor(s), (maintaining in full force and effect a bond with sufficient surety in the sum of $ _____), (the filing of a bond being hereby dispensed with), and said letters shall expire 180 days from date of issuance.

_____
Surrogate

(P15 Pre./4-99)

Form 2. Cash Flow Statement

SURROGATE'S COURT - QUEENS COUNTY

If an application is made for extension of Preliminary or Temporary Letters, this SCHEDULE MUST BE SUBMITTED

Name of Decedent: _____ File # _____

Date of Preliminary or Temporary Letters: _____

   Amount of Assets Collected to Date:

   Collected From (itemize)

   TOTAL COLLECTED: $ _____

Debts Paid: (itemize)

Expenses Paid: (itemize)

Distributions Made: (itemize)

   TOTAL PAID OUT: $ _____

   BALANCE ON HAND: $ _____

Funds are in an Account(s) as follows:

   Name of Depository: _____ _____

   Name of Account: _____ _____

   Type of Account: _____ _____

   Balance in Account: $ _____ $ _____

   Date: _____

Signature of Preliminary/Temporary
Fiduciary

Form 3. Petition to Examine Safe Deposit Box

SURROGATE'S COURT, QUEENS COUNTY   File No. _____

In the Matter of the Application to examine a
Safe Deposit Box of

                                           **Petition to Examine
Safe Deposit Box**

_____ Deceased.

TO THE SURROGATE'S COURT OF THE COUNTY OF QUEENS:

The petition of _____ respectfully shows that he/she is _____ of the deceased, and resides at _____

That the said _____ deceased, died at _____ _____ on _____ a resident of _____ _____, in the County of Queens and State of New York.

That the said deceased has a safe deposit box in the vault of _____ a corporation doing business in the County of Queens and State of New York.

That the names, residence addresses and relationship of the distributees of the decedent are as follows:

Name	Residence	Relationship
_____	_____	_____
_____	_____	_____

Your petitioner believes that said deceased may have left one or more of the following papers or instruments in said safe deposit box, to wit, a will of said deceased, a policy or policies of insurance issued in the name of said decedent and payable to a named beneficiary or beneficiaries and a deed to a burial plot in which said decedent is to be interred.

WHEREFORE your petitioner prays that an order be made permitting the petitioner, or agent of the petitioner, _____ to examine the said safe deposit box in the presence of an officer of said corporation for the purpose of ascertaining if any of said papers or instruments be deposited therein, and if a will of said deceased be found the same be delivered to the clerk of this court; if such policy or policies of insurance be found that they be delivered to the beneficiary or beneficiaries named therein, and if a deed to such burial plot be found that the same be delivered to your petitioner, or agent of the petitioner, and that your petitioner, or agent of the petitioner, be permitted to make a copy of any paper or papers found in said box bearing upon the desire of the said deceased as to the disposal of his/her remains, and your petitioner further prays that; he/she or the agent of your petitioner, be permitted to make an inventory of the contents of said box in order to fix the amount of the bond to be given on an application for letters of administration.

Dated: _____   _____
                                              Petitioner

STATE OF NEW YORK
COUNTY OF _____ }

_____ being duly sworn, says that he/she is the petitioner named in the foregoing petition, that he/she has read the foregoing petition subscribed by him/her and knows the contents thereof; and that the same is true of his/her own knowledge, except as to the matters therein stated to be alleged on information and belief, and that as to those matters he/she believes it to be true.

Sworn to before me this

day of

_____

Petitioner

_____

Notary Public, State of N.Y.

Attorney   _____

Address   _____

              _____

Phone No. (_____) _____—_____

Form 4. Order to Examine Safe Deposit Box

Present
   HON. PETER J. KELLY,
_____
        Surrogate

In the Matter of the Application,

to Examine an Safe Deposit Box of

_____ Deceased.

At a Surrogate's Court held in
and for the County of Queens,
State of New York, at Jamaica,
in said County, on the _____
day of _____, 20 _____

FILE # _____

**Order to Examine Safe
Deposit Box**

Upon reading and filing the petition of _____ verified on the _____ day of _____, 20 _____ the _____ a corporation doing business in the State of New York, is hereby directed to permit said petitioner or agent _____ to examine the safe deposit box of said decedent in the presence of an officer of the corporation, and if a will be found therein, the said corporation is directed forthwith to deliver the same to the Clerk of this Court, or if a policy or policies of insurance in the name of the decedent and payable to a named beneficiary or beneficiaries named therein, the said policy shall be delivered the to the beneficiary or beneficiaries named therein, and if a deed to a burial plot, in which the decedent is to be interred, be found the said corporation is hereby directed to deliver the same to the petitioner, or the agent of the petitioner, and it is further

Directed that the petitioner, or the agent of the petitioner, be permitted to make a copy of any paper or papers found in said box bearing upon the desire of said decedent as to the disposal of his or her remains, and it is further

Directed that the said petitioner, or agent of the petitioner, be permitted to make an inventory of the contents of said safe deposit box.

_____
        SURROGATE

Form 5. Instruction for Search Order
to Examine Apartment or Home

INSTRUCTIONS FOR SEARCH ORDER TO EXAMINE APARTMENT OR HOME (WHICH HAS BEEN SEALED BY POLICE) OF A DECEASED PARTY BEING A RESIDENT OF QUEENS COUNTY

The following items must be submitted:

(1) Petition to examine Apartment or Home (signed and notarized)

(2) Certified Death Certificate (with raised seal)

(If death is more than 30 days)

(3) If Petitioner is Nominated Executor—A copy of the WILL must be submitted.

(4) Order to Examine Apartment or Home (2)

(5) Filing Fee	Petition	$20.00
(2)	Order	12.00
		$32.00

IF YOU ARE PAYING BY CHECK
IT IS TO BE MADE PAY ABLE TO
"CLERK OF THE SURROGATE'S COURT"

Said checks **MUST** BE
NY ATTY. CHECKS or CERTIFIED CHECKS or MONEY ORDER

IF YOU COME IN WITH YOUR PAPERS
WE WILL TAKE CASH

(6) NEED SELF–ADDRESSED ENVELOPE.

Please mail or bring to:

SURROGATE'S COURT

88–11 SUTPHIN BLVD.

ROOM 717

JAMAICA, NY 11435

(7) Please either type the requested information or use black ink pen on the forms.

Form 6. Petition to Examine Residence

<u>SURROGATE'S COURT, QUEENS COUNTY</u>
In the Matter of the Application
to examine a residence of

File No. _____

Petition to Examine Residence

_____ Deceased.

TO THE SURROGATE'S COURT OF THE COUNTY OF QUEENS:

The petition of _____ respectfully shows that he/she is _____ of _____ deceased, and resides at _____.

That the said _____ died at _____ on _____ a resident of _____ in the County of Queens and State of New York.

That the said deceased has a residence at _____ in the County of _____ and State of New York.

That the names, residence addresses and relationship of the distributees of the decedent are as follows:

Name	Residence	Relationship
_____	_____	_____
_____	_____	_____
_____	_____	_____
_____	_____	_____

Your petitioner believes that said deceased may have left one or more of the following papers or instruments in said residence, to wit, a will of said deceased, a policy or policies of insurance issued in the name of said decedent and payable to a named beneficiary or beneficiaries and a deed to a burial plot in which said decedent is to be interred.

WHEREFORE your petitioner prays that an order be made permitting the petitioner, or agent of the petitioner, to examine the said residence accompanied by an officer of the New York City Police Department, for the purpose of ascertaining if any of said papers or instruments be deposited therein, and if a will of said deceased be found the same be delivered to the Clerk of this court; if such policy or policies of insurance be found that they be delivered to the beneficiary or beneficiaries named therein, and if a deed to such burial plot be found that the same be delivered to your petitioner, or agent of the petitioner, and that your petitioner, or agent of the petitioner, be permitted to make a copy of any paper or papers found in said residence bearing upon the desire of the said deceased as to the disposal of his/her remains, and your petitioner further prays that he/she or the agent of the petitioner, be permitted to make an inventory of the contents of said residence in order to fix the amount of the bond to be given on an application for letters of administration.

Dated:

_____
Petitioner

STATE OF NEW YORK,
COUNTY OF _____ }ss.:

_____ being duly sworn, says that he/she is the petitioner named in the foregoing petition, that he/she has read the foregoing petition subscribed by him/her and knows the contents thereof; and the same is true of his/her own knowledge, except as to the matters therein stated to be alleged on information and belief, and that as to those matters he/she believes it to be true.

Sworn to before me this
day of

_____
Petitioner

_____
Notary Public, State of New York

_____
Attorney for Petitioner

QUEENS SURROGATE'S DECREES

Decree 1. Decree Granting Probate

At a Surrogate's Court held in and for the County of Queens, at Jamaica, State of New York in said County on

Present
HON. PETER J. KELLY, Surrogate
Probate Proceeding, Will of

File No. _____

Decree Granting Probate

_____ Deceased.

SATISFACTORY PROOF having been made that jurisdiction has been obtained over all necessary parties and that all necessary notice has been given;

AND _____

the witnesses to said last will bearing date _____

AND _____

the witnesses to said Codicil bearing date _____

having been sworn and examined, their examination having been reduced to writing and filed or their affidavits having been filed, and it appearing that said will (and codicil) was duly executed, and that the Decedent at the time of executing it/them, was in all respects competent to make said will (and codicil), and not under restraint, and the Court being satisfied of the genuineness of the said will (and codicil) and the validity of its/their execution;

IT IS ORDERED, ADJUDGED AND DECREED, that the instrument(s) offered for probate herein be, and the same is (are), admitted to probate as the will (and codicil) of the said _____, deceased, valid to pass real and personal property, and that the said will (and codicil) and this decree be recorded, and that letters

[ ] Testamentary Issue to _____

[ ] Trusteeship Issue to _____

[ ] Administration C.T.A. Issue to _____
upon their qualifying thereunder.

_____
Surrogate

(P–1 -Decree)

998

Decree 2.   Application for Preliminary Letters Testamentary

SURROGATE'S COURT OF THE STATE
OF NEW YORK COUNTY OF QUEENS
---X
PROBATE PROCEEDING, Will of

                                             APPLICATION FOR
                                    PRELIMINARY LETTERS
                                        TESTAMENTARY

a/k/a   (See SCPA 1412)

                          Deceased.   File # _____
---X

1.   The proposed preliminary executor(s) is/are _____ and is/are designated as executor(s) in the Will of the above named decedent dated _____ (together with Codicil(s) dated _____) and duly filed with the court.

2.   The person(s) who would have a right to letters testamentary pursuant to Section 1412.1 is/are: [enter "NONE" or specify name and interest]

_____

3.   Preliminary letters are requested for the following reasons:

_____

_____

4.   Probate is expected to be completed by:

_____

5.   A contest [ ] is [ ] is not expected.

6.   The testamentary assets of decedent's estate are estimated as follows: [describe and state value; annex schedule if space is insufficient]

Personal Property: _____

_____

_____

     Total Personal Property: $ _____

Real Property: _____

_____

_____

     Total Real Property: $ _____

18 months rent, if applicable: _____

_____

_____

     Total of 18 months rent: $ _____

7.   The liabilities of this estate are: _____

_____

_____

8.   By provision in the propounded will, the applicant(s) [is/are] [are not] required to file a bond or other security for the performance of his/her/their duties.

Your applicant(s) respectfully request the issuance to _____ of preliminary letters testamentary upon qualifying.

Dated: _____   _____

                                  Applicant

                                _____

                                Applicant

OATH & DESIGNATION OF PRELIMINARY EXECUTOR

STATE OF NEW YORK   )
COUNTY OF   ) ss.:

I, the undersigned, _____, being duly sworn, say:

1. OATH OF PRELIMINARY EXECUTOR: I am over eighteen (18) years of age and a citizen of the United States; I am an executor named in the Will described in the foregoing petition and will well, faithfully and honestly discharge the duties of preliminary executor and duly account for all money or property which may come into my hands. I am not ineligible to receive letters.

2. DESIGNATION OF CLERK FOR SERVICE OF PROCESS: I hereby designate the Clerk of the Surrogate's Court of Queens County, and his/her successor in office, as a person on whom service of any process issuing from such Surrogate's Court may be made, in like manner and with like effect as if it were served personally upon me whenever I cannot be found and served within the State of New York after due diligence used.

My domicile is: _____

         (Street Address)   (City/Town/Village)   (State)   (Zip)

                  _____

                        (Signature of Petitioner)

                  _____

                        (Print Name)

On _____, 20__, before me personally came _____ to me known to be the person described in and who executed the foregoing instrument. Such person duly swore to such instrument before me and duly acknowledged that he/she executed the same.

_____

Notary Public
Commission Expires:
(Affix Notary Stamp or Seal)
Name of Attorney: _____ Tel. No.: _____
Address of Attorney: _____

NOTE: Each Preliminary Executor must complete a combined Oath & Designation of Preliminary Executor.

CONSENT AND DESIGNATION OF CORPORATE
PRELIMINARY EXECUTOR

STATE OF NEW YORK   )
COUNTY OF   ) ss.:

I, the undersigned, a _____ of

                          (Title)

_____

              (Name of Bank or Trust Company)

a corporation duly qualified to act in a fiduciary capacity without further security, being duly sworn, say:

1. CONSENT: I consent to accept the appointment as Preliminary Executor under the Last Will and Testament of the decedent described in this application and consent to act as such fiduciary.

2. DESIGNATION OF CLERK FOR SERVICE OF PROCESS: I designate the Chief Clerk of the Surrogate's Court of Queens County, and his/her successor in office, as a person on whom service of any process issuing from such Surrogate's Court may be made, in like manner and whenever one of its proper officers cannot be found and served within the State of New York after due diligence used.

_____
(Name of Bank or Trust Company)

BY _____
(Signature)

_____
(Print Name and Title)

On _____, 20___, before me personally came _____, to me known, who duly swore to the foregoing instrument and who did say that he/she resides at _____ and that he/she is a _____ of _____ the corporation/national banking association described in and which executed such instrument, and that he/she signed his/her name thereto by order of the Board of Directors of the corporation.

_____
Notary Public
Commission Expires:
(Affix Notary Stamp or Seal)
Name of Attorney: _____ Tel. No.: _____
Address of Attorney: _____

Decree 3.   Order for Preliminary Letters Testamentary

At the Surrogate's Court of the State of New York held in and for the County of Queens at Jamaica on

PRESENT:
HON. PETER J. KELLY
    Surrogate

--X

In the Matter of the Probate Proceeding of

**ORDER FOR
PRELIMINARY
LETTERS
TESTAMENTARY**

Deceased.

File No. _____

--X

An application by
having been filed on   requesting the issuance of preliminary letters testamentary, and the court having entertained the application, and the application having established the necessity for the issuance of such letters, it is hereby

ORDERED that preliminary letters testamentary issue to   upon duly qualifying according to law, and that the executing and filing of a bond (with sufficient surety in the sum of $ is required) (be dispensed with); and it is further

ORDERED that said preliminary executor shall retain sole custody and control of all the assets of the estate; and it is further

ORDERED that said preliminary executor shall retain custody and preserve all of the papers and records of the deceased and shall make them available for examination and inspection by any person interested in the estate; and it is further

ORDERED that said preliminary letters testamentary shall expire one hundred eighty (180) days after the date of issuance.

                                    _____
                                    Surrogate

Decree 4.   Application for Temporary Letters of Administration

SURROGATE'S COURT OF THE STATE
OF NEW YORK COUNTY OF QUEENS
--X
PROBATE PROCEEDING, Will of

APPLICATION FOR
TEMPORARY LETTERS
OF ADMINISTRATION
(See SCPA 901(1))

a/k/a

Deceased.   File # _____
--X

1.   The proposed temporary administrator(s) is/are _____ and is/are (is/are not) designated in the Will of the above named decedent dated _____ as follows: _____. (together with Codicil(s) dated _____) and duly filed with the court.

2.   The person(s) who would have a right to temporary letters of administration is/are: [enter "NONE" or specify name and interest]

3.   Temporary letters of Administration are requested for the following reasons:

4.   Probate is expected to be completed by: _____

5.   A contest [ ] is [ ] is not expected.

6.   The testamentary assets of decedent's estate are estimated as follows: [describe and state value; annex schedule if space is insufficient]

Personal Property: _____

   Total Personal Property: $ _____
Real Property: _____

   Total Real Property: $ _____
18 months rent, if applicable: _____

   Total of 18 months rent: $ _____

7.   The liabilities of this estate are: _____

8.   By provision in the propounded will, the applicant(s) [is/are] [are not] required to file a bond or other security for the performance of his/her/their duties.

Your applicant(s) respectfully request the issuance to _____ of temporary letters of administration upon qualifying.

Dated: _____   _____
                                         Applicant

                                   _____
                                         Applicant

OATH & DESIGNATION OF TEMPORARY ADMINISTRATOR

STATE OF NEW YORK   )
COUNTY OF   ) ss.:

I, the undersigned, _____, being duly sworn, say:

1. OATH OF TEMPORARY ADMINISTRATOR: I am over eighteen (18) years of age and a citizen of the United States; I am named in the Will described in the foregoing petition and will well, faithfully and honestly discharge the duties of temporary administrator and duly account for all money or property which may come into my hands. I am not ineligible to receive letters.

2. DESIGNATION OF CLERK FOR SERVICE OF PROCESS: I hereby designate the Clerk of the Surrogate's Court of Queens County, and his/her successor in office, as a person on whom service of any process issuing from such Surrogate's Court may be made, in like manner and with like effect as if it were served personally upon me whenever I cannot be found and served within the State of New York after due diligence used.

My domicile is: _____
(Street Address)   (City/Town/Village)   (State)   (Zip)

_____
(Signature of Petitioner)

_____
(Print Name)

On _____, 20__, before me personally came _____ to me known to be the person described in and who executed the foregoing instrument. Such person duly swore to such instrument before me and duly acknowledged that he/she executed the same.

_____
Notary Public
Commission Expires:
(Affix Notary Stamp or Seal)

Name of Attorney: _____ Tel. No.: _____

Address of Attorney: _____

NOTE: Each Temporary Administrator must complete a combined Oath & Designation of Temporary Administrator.

CONSENT AND DESIGNATION OF CORPORATE PRELIMINARY EXECUTOR

STATE OF NEW YORK   )
COUNTY OF   ) ss.:

I, the undersigned, a _____ of
(Title)

_____
(Name of Bank or Trust Company)

a corporation duly qualified to act in a fiduciary capacity without further security, being duly sworn, say:

1. CONSENT: I consent to accept the appointment as Preliminary Executor under the Last Will and Testament of the decedent described in this application and consent to act as such fiduciary.

2. DESIGNATION OF CLERK FOR SERVICE OF PROCESS: I designate the Chief Clerk of the Surrogate's Court of Queens County, and his/her successor in office, as a person on whom service of any process issuing from such Surrogate's Court may be made, in like manner and whenever one of its proper officers cannot be found and served within the State of New York after due diligence used.

_____
(Name of Bank or Trust Company)

BY _____
(Signature)

_____
(Print Name and Title)

On _____, 20___, before me personally came _____, to me known, who duly swore to the foregoing instrument and who did say that he/she resides at _____ and that he/she is a _____ of _____ the corporation/national banking association described in and which executed such instrument, and that he/she signed his/her name thereto by order of the Board of Directors of the corporation.

_____
Notary Public
Commission Expires:
(Affix Notary Stamp or Seal)

Name of Attorney: _____ Tel. No.: _____

Address of Attorney: _____

Decree 5.   Decree Granting Ancillary Probate

At the Surrogate's Court held in and for the County of Queens, at Jamaica, State of New York on

SURROGATES COURT OF THE
STATE OF NEW YORK
COUNTY OF QUEENS

ANCILLARY PROBATE PRO-
CEEDING, WILL OF

**Decree Granting Ancillary
Probate**

a/k/a
a domiciliary of the State of

Deceased.

SCPA ARTICLE 16

File No. _____

A copy of the record of the will of _____
late of the City of _____ and State of _____
deceased, and of the decree admitting such Will to probate in the said State of
_____ (and of letters issued thereon to _____, the
executor/rix in said will), authenticated as prescribed by law, having been filed in
this Court on the _____ day of _____, and the said _____
having therewith presented to and filed in this Court his/her/their verified petition
praying for a decree admitting said Will to ancillary probate in this Court and
awarding to him/her/them (Ancillary Letters Testamentary) (Ancilliary letters of
Administration with the Will Annexed) on said Will and the Surrogate having
ascertained, to his satisfaction, that there are no creditors or persons claiming to be
creditors of the said decedent domiciled within the State of New York, except _____

---

and a citation having been issued to them and to the State Tax Commission, and said
citation having been returned with proof of due service thereof, and no one objecting
to the granting of such letters,

Now, on the motion of the petitioner(s), it is

ORDERED, ADJUDGED AND DECREED that the said Will dated
_____, having been admitted to probate by the State of
_____, being the state of decedent's domicile at death, be and the
same is hereby admitted to ancillary probate in this Court, sufficient to operate on
any property within its terms located in this State, subject to any limitations upon its
operation imposed by the laws of the testator's/rix's domicile in respect of legal
capacity, and it is further

ORDERED, ADJUDGED AND DECREED that said Will, proceedings thereon
and letters be recorded and that (Ancillary Letters Testamentary)(Ancillary Letters
of Administration With the Will Annexed) on said Will of _____
deceased, issue to the said _____ and _____ upon
taking and subscribing the statutory oath and designation; and it further

ORDERED, that no assets are to be removed from the State of New York except
upon notice to the State Tax Commission.

_____
Surrogate

Decree 6. Order Granting Temporary Letters of Administration

At the Surrogate's Court of the State of New York, held in and for the County of Queens, at Jamaica on

PRESENT:
HON. PETER J. KELLY
    Surrogate

---X

In the Matter of the Application for Letters of Temporary Administration, in the

Estate of

Deceased.

---X

ORDER GRANTING
TEMPORARY
ADMINISTRATION

File No.

On reading and filing the application of _____, duly verified on the   day of   , praying for an order awarding Temporary Letters of Administration on the estate of _____, or to such other person or persons who have an equal right thereto, and proving also to the Surrogate the existence of all the jurisdictional facts; And this court being satisfied that it is in the best interest of the estate and a delay will occur in the granting of permanent Letters of Administration and said petitioner is entitled to Temporary Letters of Administration, and is in all respects competent to act as such Temporary Administrator; it is

ORDERED that Temporary Letters of Administration shall issue to the petitioner _____ upon his duly qualifying and posting a bond in the amount of _____; and it is further

ORDERED that said Temporary Letters of Administration shall expire one hundred eighty days (180) after the date of issuance.

_____
SURROGATE

Decree 7. Application for Letters of Administration

At the Surrogate's Court held
in and for the County of
Queens, at Jamaica, State of
New York, in said County, on

Present:
HON. PETER J. KELLY, **Surrogate**

In the Matter of the Application for
Letters of Administration of the
Estate of

FILE No.

Decree

On reading and filing the petition of
duly verified the   day of _____, praying for a decree awarding Letters of
Administration of the estate of the said deceased to
or to such other person or persons who have an equal or prior right thereto, and
proving also to the Surrogate the existence of all the jurisdictional facts.

And this court being satisfied that said petitioner   is entitled to such
Letters of Administration., and is in all respects competent to act as such Administrator, does hereby decree that Letters of Administration of the estate of the said
deceased to be awarded to the said petitioner on the filing the oath of office and
otherwise qualifying as prescribed by statute, and the filing of the bond is hereby
dispensed with.

IT IS FURTHER DECREED that the administrator is hereby restrained from
collecting or receiving any funds or other property of the said decedent in excess of
$ without the further notice of the Surrogate made upon the filing of
satisfactory security.

Surrogate

Decree 8. Order Extending Temporary Letters of Administration

At the Surrogate's Court of the
State of New York, held in and for
the County of Queens at Jamaica on

PRESENT:
HON. PETER J. KELLY
    Surrogate

---X

In the Matter of the Administration
Proceeding of

**ORDER EXTENDING
TEMPORARY LETTERS
OF ADMINISTRATION**
File No. _____

                              Deceased.

---X

The Court having heretofore granted Temporary Letters of Administration by order dated the   , and said Temporary Letters of Administration having expired and the Court being satisfied that justification exists for an extension of said Temporary Letters of Administration, it is

ORDERED that the Temporary Letters of Administration heretofore issued to _____ be extended, maintaining in full force and effect a bond with sufficient surety in the sum of $ _____, and it is

ORDERED that said Temporary Letters of Administration shall expire 180 days from the date of issuance.

                                     _____
                                         Surrogate

Decree 9.   Bond Affidavit

STATE OF NEW YORK
SURROGATE'S COURT, QUEENS
COUNTY

In the Matter of the Application for   **FILE No.**
Letters of Administration of the
Goods, Chattels and Credits which
were of

                                                        Affidavit

                    Deceased.

STATE OF NEW YORK   )
COUNTY OF   ) ss.:

                    being duly sworn, deposes and says that   is
over the age of   years and resides at No.   .

That   is the   of said deceased and the petitioner in the above
entitled proceeding;

Describe In Detail

That the value of all the personal property, wheresoever situated, of which the
said decedent died possessed amounts to   Dollars and consists of

Describe In Detail

That said deceased, at the time of   death, was   seized of real estate
consisting of

THE MARKET value of which is   Dollars,
subject to mortgages in the amount of   held by
and the estimated gross rentals for 18 months is $

That said decedent, at the time of   death was not engaged in business but was
employed as   by
[If Retired State How Long] and that   average earning capacity was   per
week. That decedent was   years of age at the time of   death.

That said decedent left no unpaid bills, debts, or claims, that there are no
executions or judgments against   estate nor was   a principal or surety on any
unpaid or undischarged bond, undertaking or other obligation.

That neither the decedent, nor your deponent, nor any of the distributees herein
were ever recipients of any Federal, State or Municipal Relief.

That the expenses of the last illness of the decedent have been paid in full, and
receipted bills for same are attached hereto.

That the funeral bill of said decedent has been paid in full, and a receipted bill is
attached hereto.

That there are no Federal or State Income or Estate Taxes payable by the estate,
except as follows

Attach
Receipted
Bills

WHEREFORE, your deponent prays, that the filing of a bond by   as administrat be dispensed with

_____
Petitioner

Sworn to before me this
day of

Notary Public, State of New York

_____
Attorney for Petitioner
Office and Post Office Address

_____

Telephone No. _____

SURROGATE'S COURT FEES

Fees 1.   Article 24 Court Fees

§ 2401. Fees in the surrogate's court; general provisions.

1. In the surrogate's court fees for service, filing and other matters shall be as provided in this article to the exclusion of other statutory provisions unless expressly stated to the contrary.

2. The clerk of each surrogate's court shall charge and receive for the services and matters herein set forth the fees indicated in this article which shall be payable in advance.

3. All fees shall be the property of the county unless otherwise provided by law.

4. Unless specifically indicated no fee is chargeable for motions made in a pending proceeding or for ex parte applications.

5. The fees in the surrogate's court of each county of the state shall be the amount specified in the rate column for the service or matter indicated.

§ 2402. Fees; amount of.

1. Probate. Upon filing a petition to commence a proceeding for probate of a will the fee shall be as shown by the following schedule computed initially upon the gross estate passing by will as stated in the petition; provided however that in a proceeding for ancillary probate of a will the fee shall be computed only upon the property within the state passing under such will and provided that in all cases if the value of the estate so passing as subsequently shown by a tax return filed under article twenty six* of the tax law, by a proceeding under such article, by any proceeding in surrogate's court involving such estate, or by such papers or documents in connection with such estate as court rules may require to be filed with the court, exceeds the value originally stated and upon which the fee was paid, then an additional probate fee shall be immediately payable. Such additional fee shall be the difference between the fee based on the value subsequently shown and the fee which was initially paid. In the event that the value of the estate so passing as subsequently shown is less than the value originally stated and upon which the fee was paid, then a refund shall be made which shall be the difference between the fee initially paid and the fee based on the actual value subsequently shown.

The fee paid in a probate or ancillary probate proceeding includes all charges except if probate be contested, fees as required for filing objections, demand for jury trial or for filing note of issue shall be payable.

2. Administration. Upon filing a petition to commence a proceeding for administration in intestacy the fee shall be as shown by the following schedule based initially upon the gross estate passing by intestacy as stated in the petition; provided however that if the value of the estate so passing as subsequently shown by a tax return filed under article twenty-six of the tax law, by a proceeding under such article, by any proceeding in surrogate's court involving such estate, or by such papers or documents in connection with such estate as court rules may require to be filed with the court, exceeds the value originally stated and upon which the fee was paid, then an additional fee shall be immediately payable. Such additional fee shall be the difference between the fee based on the value subsequently shown and the fee which was initially paid. In the event that the value of the estate so passing as subsequently shown is less than the value originally stated and upon which the fee was paid, then a refund shall be made which shall be the difference between the fee initially paid and the fee based on the actual value subsequently shown.

3. Accounting. (a) Upon filing a petition to commence a proceeding for an accounting the fee shall be as shown by the following schedule based on the gross value of assets accounted for including principal and income. Where more than one account is filed under a single petition the fee shall be based separately on the gross value of each separate fund or trust accounted for.

(b) Notwithstanding the provisions of paragraph (a) of this subdivision, upon filing a petition to commence an accounting proceeding for a lifetime trust or upon filing a petition for an accounting in a conservatorship proceeding, the fee shall be the same as that which is payable in the supreme court pursuant to section eight thousand eighteen of the civil practice law and rules.

4. Instruments settling accounts. For filing an instrument which releases and discharges a fiduciary but does not contain any statement of account, no fee shall be charged. For recording any such instrument, the fee shall be six dollars per page or part thereof Upon filing or recording an instrument pursuant to section 2202, the fee shall be as shown by the following schedule based on the gross value of assets accounted for including principal and income, and such fee shall include the filing or recording of such instrument. If separate instruments executed by several beneficiaries release and discharge the same fiduciary or fiduciaries and settle in whole or in the part one and the same account, only a single fee shall be charged for the filing or recording of all such instruments.

5. Decree approving accounts. Upon filing a petition pursuant to section 2203, the fee shall be as shown by the following schedule based on the gross value of assets accounted for including principal and income. In the event no values are shown in the petition and related instruments the fee shall be as

shown by the following schedule based on the estate of the decedent as shown in the estate tax return filed under article 26 of the tax law or a proceeding under such article.

6. Other proceedings. In proceedings not otherwise provided in this act the fee shall be according to the following schedule based on the value of the subject matter.

7. The fee schedule for subdivision 1 through 7 inclusive is as follows:

Value of Estate or Subject Matter	Fee Rate
Less than $10,000	$45.00
10,000 but under 20,000	$75.00
20,000 but under 50,000	$215.00
50,000 but under 100,000	$280.00
100,000 but under 250,000	$420.00
250,000 but under 500,000	$625.00
500,000 and over	$1,250.00

8. (a) For filing a petition to commence the following proceedings, the fee shall be as indicated:

SCPA Fee Rate

SCPA	Fee Rate
607 To punish respondent for contempt	$30.00
711 Suspend, modify, revoke letters or remove a fiduciary other than a custodian or guardian	$75.00
711 Suspend, modify, revoke letters or remove a custodian or guardian	$30.00
715 Application of fiduciary to resign	$30.00
717 Suspend powers-fiduciary in war	$30.00
1401 Compel production of will	$20.00
1420 Construction of will	$75.00
1421 Determination of right of election	$75.00
1502 Appointment of trustee	$45.00
1508 Release against state	$50.00
1703 Appointment of guardian	$20.00
2003 Open safe deposit box	$20.00
2102 Proceedings against a fiduciary	$20.00
2103 Proceedings by fiduciary to discover property	$75.00
2107 Advice and directions	$75.00
2108 Continue business	$45.00
2114 Review corporate trustee compensation	$10.00
2205 Petition to compel fiduciary to account	$30.00
EPTL 7–4.6 Appointment of successor custodian	$20.00

(b) For filing a petition to commence a proceeding for the appointment of a trustee of a lifetime trust or for the appointment of a conservator, the fee shall be the same as that which is payable in the supreme court pursuant to section eight thousand eighteen of the civil practice law and rules.

Court Fees	Fee Rate
9. For filing: (i) a demand for trial by jury in any proceeding, SCPA 502	$150.00
(ii) objections to the probate of a will SCPA 1410	$150.00
(iii) a note of issue in any proceeding	$45.00
(iv) objection or answer in any action or proceeding other than probate	$75.00
(v) a will for safekeeping pursuant to section 2507 of this act except that the court in any county may reduce or dispense with such fee	$45.00
(vi) a bond, including any additional bond: less than $10,000	$20.00
$10,000 and over	$30.00
10. For furnishing a transcript of a decree	$20.00
11. For a certificate of letters evidencing that the appointment of a fiduciary is still in full force and effect	$6.00
12. (a) For making and certifying or comparing and certifying a copy of a will or any paper on file or recorded in his office:	$6.00 pg.
(b) Authenticating the same, additional:	$20.00
13. For searching and certifying to any record for which search is made:	$30.00 for under 25 years
	$90.00 for over 25 years
14. (a) For producing papers, documents, books of record on file in his office under a subpoena duces tccum, for use within the county where the office of the court is situated:	$30.00
(b) For use in any other county, such fee to be paid for each day or part thereof that the messenger is detailed from the office and to be in addition to mileage fee and the necessary expenses of the messenger. The clerk of the court shall not be required to make any collection or return of the money so paid for expenses:	$.30
15. For recording: (a) any instrument, decree or other paper which is required by law to be recorded-	$8.00 per pg. or part $16.00 minimum
(b) for filing an authenticated copy of a foreign will:	$8.00 per page $64 minimum
(c) for taxing bill of costs:	$15.00

S.C.P.A.

16. No fee shall be charged:

(a) for filing objections of a guardian ad litem, or of a respondent in a proceeding brought pursuant to section three hundred eighty-four-b of the social services law

(b) for filing the annual account of a guardian

(c) for any certificate or certified copy of a paper required to be filed with the United States Veterans Administration

(d) for filing a petition in a proceeding for filing an additional bond, to reduce the penalty of a bond or substitute a new bond or discharge any bond when no accounting is required

(e) in respect to the proceedings for the appointment of a fiduciary when the appointment is made solely for the purpose of collecting bounty, arrears of pay, prize money, pension dues or other dues or gratuities due from the federal or state government for services of an infant or of a decedent formerly or now in the military or naval services of the United States or to collect the proceeds of a war risk insurance policy.

(f) to or received from the state of New York or any public agency of the state or any civil subdivision or agency thereof or with respect to a social services official when taking any proceeding with respect to the estate of a person who was a recipient of benefits from social services.

(g) or received for the filing of a petition for an order granting funds for the maintenance or other proper needs of any infant nor for any certificate or any certified copy of the order on such an application.

17. The fee charged herein for the filing of a petition shall include the recording of any decree made in that proceeding which is required by law to be recorded and shall include the recording of any letters required by law to be recorded.

* So in original. Probably should be "twenty-six"

TWELFTH JUDICIAL DISTRICT — BRONX COUNTY

Westlaw Electronic Research

These rules may be searched electronically on Westlaw® in the NY–RULES database; updates to these rules may be found on Westlaw in NY–RULESUP-DATES. For search tips and a summary of database content, consult the Westlaw Scope Screens for each database.

BRONX COUNTY
JUDGES' PART RULES
JUSTICE GEOFFREY D. WRIGHT

Part
IA–1. Hon. Geoffrey D. Wright.

PART IA–2
IA–2. Part 2 — Court Rules.

JUSTICE LARRY SCHACHNER, PART IA–3

Doc.
1. HIPPA Compliance Statement.
2. Rules for Motions, Preliminary Conferences and Compliance Conferences.
3. OSC to Withdraw As Counsel.
4. Settlement Conferences & Trial Assignment.
5. Settlement Conference Justice Larry S. Schachner, Presiding.

JUSTICE HOWARD H. SHERMAN

Part
IA–4. Hon. Howard H. Sherman.

JUSTICE ALISON Y. TUITT

IA–5. Hon. Alison Y. Tuitt.

JUSTICE WILMA GUZMAN

IA–7. Hon. Wilma Guzman.

JUSTICE BETTY OWEN STINSON

IA–8. Hon. Betty Owen Stinson.

JUSTICE LAURA G. DOUGLAS

IA–11. Hon. Laura G. Douglas.

JUSTICE JOHN A. BARONE

IA–12. Hon. John A. Barone.

JUSTICE JULIA I. RODRIGUEZ

IA–18. Hon. Julia I. Rodriguez.

PART IA–21
RULES FOR MOTIONS, CONFERENCES & TRIALS

Rule
1. Orders to Show Cause.
2. Substantive (Non–Discovery) Motions.
3. Discovery Motions.
4. Settlement Conferences and Trial Commencement.

TRIAL RULES FOR TRIAL COUNSEL

Rule
1. Be Prepared.
2. Marked Pleadings Plus.
3. Pre–Marked Exhibits.
4. Assignment Conference.
5. No Communication With Jurors.
6. Check–In.
7. Trial Objections and Arguments.
8. Courtroom Comments and Demeanor.
9. Use of Proposed Exhibits.
10. Examination of Witnesses.
11. Jury Charge & Verdict Sheet.

SETTLEMENT OF CLAIMS BY INFANTS/IMPAIRED PERSONS

A–1. Compliance With Rules and Statutes.
B–1. A Worksheet/Checklist.
C–1. An Ex–Parte Application.
D–1. The Application and Supporting Documents.
E–1. The Hearing.
F–1. Structured Settlements.
G–1. Appendix Form—Structure Broker's Affidavit.

FORMS

Form
1. Worksheet/Checklist for Compromise Applications.
2. Authorization for Release of Health Information Pursuant to HIPAA.
3. Standard Compromise Order.
4. Simple Order for a Structured Settlement.
5. Complex Order for a Structured Settlement.
6. Structure Broker's Affidavit.

JUSTICE NORMA RUIZ

Part
IA–22. Hon. Norma Ruiz.

JUSTICE ALEXANDER W. HUNTER, JR.

IA–23. Hon. Alexander W. Hunter, Jr.

JUSTICE SHARON A. M. AARONS

IA–24. Hon. Sharon A. M. Aaron.

JUSTICE BARRY SALMAN

TT–14. Hon. Barry Salman.

PART IDV

Doc.
1. Part IDV Part Rules.

BRONX COUNTY
JUDGES' PART RULES

JUSTICE GEOFFREY D. WRIGHT

Part IA–1. Hon. Geoffrey D. Wright

Motion Procedure

1. For all motions made in unassigned and assigned cases, moving and responding papers including stipulations and requests for adjournments are to be filed in the clerk's office (Room 103). Papers will not be accepted in Chambers unless requested.

2. All disclosure motions filed and accepted in the clerk's office assigned to Acting Justice Wright will be heard in a PC/CC part, Room 707, on a rescheduled date.

3. All non-disclosure motions filed and accepted as above, will be deemed submitted on the return date subject to the motion procedure. For non-disclosure motions, oral arguments are not required unless directed otherwise.

4. All stipulations and requests for adjournments filed in the clerk's office for all motions will be processed as indicated in the motion procedure printed in the Law Journal.

5. Orders to show cause must comply with Uniform Rule 202.7(d) and be brought to the clerk's office (Room 103) prior to judicial review, signature and fixing of a return date. Appearance requirements for orders to show cause are as indicated in the motion procedure section appearing under 'Court Rules'for Bronx County on this site.

6. Orders to show cause, infant compromises, traverse hearings, and framed issue hearings are heard when the calendar is called.

7. An order to show cause requires appearance of counsel.

8. The order to show cause calendar is held on Mondays, at 9:30 A.M., unless directed otherwise by the Court. Infant compromises, traverse hearings, and framed issue hearings are also heard at this time. Only counsel fully familiar with the file and authorized to make binding concessions, settle, or try the action shall appear at the call of the calendar. Failure to appear at the call of the calendar may result in an inquest or dismissal pursuant to Section 202.27 of the Uniform Civil Rules for the Supreme Court and County Court.

9. A movant shall clearly specify the relief he/she seeks. Counsel shall use tabs when submitting papers containing Exhibits. If a document to be annexed to an affidavit or affirmation is voluminous and only discrete portions are relevant to the motion, Counsel shall highlight the relevant sections of the document.

10. All papers, including stipulations and requests for adjournments, are to be filed in room 103, unless otherwise directed by the Court.

11. A request for an adjournment must be served on all parties in writing, and may be directed to Chambers for consideration. The Court may schedule a conference for scheduling. No adjournment longer than 30 days shall be granted, except for extraordinary circumstances.

12. Stipulations for adjournments must be filed in room 103 if filed prior to the return date. Thereafter, such stipulations may be sent directly to Chambers.

Trials and Hearings

Matters assigned to this Part will be tried, to the extent possible, in chronological order. Counsel must be fully prepared for trial and possess the bill of particulars, marked pleadings, witness list and exhibit list.

Inquiries

All inquiries as to case or calendar status should, in the first instance, be made to the appropriate clerk's office, IAS Motions Support Office Room 103, (718) 618–1310.

The only inquiries to be made directly to Chambers or the Part should be those involving the immediate exercise of judicial discretion.

Revised 3/12/09

PART IA–2

Part IA–2. Part 2 — Court Rules

Unless otherwise indicated, references to Counsel shall apply to both plaintiff's counsel and defendant's counsel.

motion Procedure

Non–Disclosure Motions:

Motions for summary judgment shall be supported by Affidavit(s) made by person(s) having knowledge of the material facts. CPLR 3212(b). Exhibit Tabs shall be used to separate documents annexed as Exhibits. If a document annexed to an affidavit or affirmation is voluminous, all relevant portions shall be highlighted. Papers should be bound in such a way that all printed material is legible, including the page numbers on depositions. Print shall be on only the front side of the page.

Counsel shall include citations to the legal authority (statutes and case law)that is on point. The moving party shall clearly specify the relief requested.

All motion papers, including stipulations, and requests for adjournments, shall be filed in the Clerk's office (Room 103), on, or prior to, the return date, in accordance with the deadlines for acceptance of papers set by the Clerk's office. Non-disclosure Motions filed, and accepted, will be deemed submitted on the return date.

If a request for an adjournment is made after the return date, then Court approval is required. If the party requesting an adjournment after the return date is unable to obtain a Stipulation signed by all parties, then Counsel may make a brief written request for an adjournment, including a showing that he made a good faith effort to obtain a Stipulation signed by all parties, which Counsel shall serve upon all parties.

Courtesy copies of motions filed should not be submitted, unless requested by the Court.

Orders to Show Cause:

Orders to Show Cause must be filed in Room 103; and must comply with Uniform Rule 202.7(d). Appearances are required in the Courtroom, at 9:30 A.M., on the return date, and any adjourned date. Calendars will normally be called on Mondays, except for Holidays. Proof of service of the Order to Show Cause must be filed with the Part 2 Clerk, in the Courtroom, on, or before, the return date. If Movant fails to timely appear, or if proof of service is not filed by the return date: the Order to Show Cause will be denied; and, if the Movant is the Petitioner, the case may be dismissed.

Counsel fully familiar with their file, and authorized to make binding concessions, settle, or try the action, shall appear at the call of the Calendar. Counsel shall bring their complete file, including the bills of particulars and marked pleadings.

Disclosure Motions:

Motions relating to Disclosure will be heard by the Justice presiding in Part Eleven, (not in Part 2).

Inquiries

All Inquiries shall, in the first instance, be made to the Motion Support Office, Room 103, at (718)590–3722; and then, if necessary, to the Clerk for Part 2, in the Courtroom at (718)590–3936. No exparte communications shall be made to Chambers on any substantive matter.

However, all parties (including moving and nonmoving Counsel) are required to immediately inform Chambers if a pending motion is withdrawn, resolved, or otherwise becomes moot, for example, if the case

has settled or has been removed to federal court. A violation of this rule, without good cause shown, will subject Counsel to sanctions.

Trials

1. Counsel shall not commence jury selection without first conferring with the Court. Prior to jury selection, Counsel shall inform the Court of scheduling problems regarding witnesses.

2. At the trial conference, Counsel shall alert the Court regarding the disposition of prior motion(s), and, upon request, provide the Court with a copy of the order(s) deciding prior motion(s).

3. Counsel shall immediately notify the Court Clerk if an interpreter is needed; or if Counsel needs any special devices, such as an easel, blackboard, shadow box, or video equipment.

4. It is Counsel's obligation to ascertain whether subpoenaed documents are in the courtroom.

5. Plaintiff's Counsel shall provide the Court with Marked pleadings (CPLR 4012); and the bill(s) of particulars.

In addition, all Counsel shall provide the Court with:

a. Expert reports, including CPLR 3101(d) responses.

b. Deposition transcript and/or written statements which may be used to either refresh a witness' recollection, or impeach a witness' recollection.

c. Applicable legal authority (statutory and case citations, and a copy of the statutes and cases), which Counsel will reply upon in connection with motions made prior to, or during, trial.

6. Counsel shall stipulate to undisputed facts and admissibility of undisputed documents.

7. Counsel shall promptly alert the Court when attendance at trial, by Counsel or an essential witness, will be delayed.

8. The Court shall be informed of Motions *in limine* before the trial commences; and Counsel shall provide the Court with supporting legal authority.

9. Counsel shall provide the Court with a proposed Verdict Sheet, and jury charge requests, at the commencement of the trial. Amendments shall be provided at least one day prior to the charge conference. In addition, Pattern Jury Instructions shall be referred to by number and topic, and charge requests which modify a PJI charge shall be highlighted. Applicable legal authority (statutory and common law) shall be provided to the Court in support of any non–PJI jury charge or PJI modifications.

At the charge conference, Counsel shall be prepared, and bring a (current) PJI book or a copy of every Jury Charge that any Counsel requests that the Court to charge. Counsel shall also provide the Court with a copy of any statute that Counsel requests be charged.

10. *Courtroom Demeanor:*

a. Derogatory remarks by Counsel will not be tolerated.

b. Counsel shall not interrupt a witness in the middle of an answer, unless the answer is totally unresponsive, in which event Counsel shall seek a ruling from the Court. Counsel must allow the wit-ness to complete his/her answer prior to asking anoth-er question.

c. No party or Counsel shall speak to a Juror, or exchange pleasantries such as "Good Morning". This admonition includes both verbal and non-verbal com-munications.

The failure of Counsel to comply with these rules will subject Counsel, and his/her firm, to sanctions.

Updated March 2006

JUSTICE LARRY SCHACHNER, PART IA–3

Doc. 1. HIPPA Compliance Statement

AUTHORIZATION FOR RELEASE OF HEALTH
INFORMATION PURSUANT TO HIPAA
[This form has been approved by the New York State Department if Health]

Patient Name   Date of Birth   Social Security Number

Patient Address

I, or my authorized representative, request that health information regarding my care and treatment be released as set forth on this form:
In accordance with New York State Law and the Privacy Rule of the Health Insurance Portability and Accountability Act of 1996 (HIPAA), I understand that:

1. This authorization may include disclosure of information relating to **ALCOHOL** and **DRUG ABUSE, MENTAL HEALTH TREAT-MENT,** except psychotherapy notes, and **CONFIDENTIAL HIV * RELATED INFORMATION** only if I place my initials on the appropriate line in Item 9(a). In the event the health information described below includes at y of these types of information, and I initial the line on the box in Item 9(a), I specifically authorize release of such information to the person(s) indicated in Item 8.

2. If I am authorizing the release of HIV–related, alcohol or drug treatment, or mental health treatment information, the recipient is prohibited from redisclosing such information without my authoriza-tion unless permitted to Jo so under federal or state law. I under-stand that I have the tight to request a list of people who may receive or use my HIV–related information without authorization. If I experience discrimination because of the release or disclosure of HIV–related information, I may contact the New York State Division of Human Rights at (212) 480–2493 or the New York City Commission of Human Rights at (212) 306–7450. These agencies are responsible for protecting my rights.

3. I have the right to revoke this authorization at any time by writing to the health care provider listed below. I understand that I may revoke this authorization except to the extent that action has already been taken based on this authorization.

4. I understand that signing this authorization is voluntary. My treatment, payment, enrollment in a health plan, or eligibility for benefits will not be conditioned upon my authorization of this disclo-sure.

5. Information disclosed under this authorization might be redisc-losed by the recipient (except as noted above in Item 2), and this redisclosure may no longer be protected by federal or state law.

6. **THIS AUTHORIZATION DOES NOT AUTHORIZE YOU TO DISCUSS MY HEALTH INFORMATION OR MEDICAL CARE WITH ANYONE OTHER THAN THE ATTORNEY OR GOV-ERNMENTAL AGENCY SPECIFIED IN ITEM 9 (b).**

7. Name and address of health provider or entity to release this information:

8. Name and address of person(s) or category of person to whom this information will be sent:

9(a). Specific information to be released:
☐ Medical Record from (insert date) _____ to (insert date) _____
☐ Entire Medical Record, including patient histories, office notes (except psychotherapy notes), test results, radiology studies, films, referrals, consults, billing records, insurance records, and records sent to you by other health care provid-ers.
☐ Other: _____

Include: (*Indicate by Initialing*)
_____ **Alcohol/Drug Treatment**
_____ **Mental Health Information**
_____ **HIV–Related Information**

Authorization to Discuss Health Information

(b) ☐ By initialing here _____ I authorize _____
Initials   Name of individual health care provider
to discuss my health information with my attorney, or a govern-mental agency, listed here:

(Attorney/First Name or Governmental Agency Name)

10. Reason for release of infor-mation:
☐ At request of individual
☐ Other:

11. Date or event on which this authorization will expire:

12. If not the patient, name of person signing form:

13. Authority to sign on behalf of patient:

All items on this form have been completed and my questions about this form have been answered. In addition, I have been provided a copy of the form.

_____ Date: _____
Signature of patient or repre-sentative authorized by law.

* **Human Immunodeficiency Virus that causes AIDS. The New York State Public Health Law protects information which rea-sonably could identify someone as having HIV symptoms or infection and information regarding a person's contacts.**

Doc. 2. Rules for Motions, Preliminary Con-ferences[1] and Compliance Conferences

(1) Orders to Show Cause:

Orders to show cause are calendared for Thursday morning at 9:30 A.M. Counsel should appear prompt-ly and be prepared to argue their cases.

(2) Submitted (Non–Discovery) Motions:

In accordance with the general rules applicable in Bronx County for civil motions, all non-discovery motions not brought by order to show cause will be submitted without argument.

(3) Discovery Motions:

Attorneys are expected to be present in the courtroom commencing at 9:30 A.M. on Thursdays. Counsel are required to undertake good faith efforts pursuant to Uniform Rule 202.7 (a) to resolve discovery issues. Toward that end, City attorneys are present in the courtroom to conference and resolve by stipulation, if possible, discovery motions. The effort to resolve issues should continue until the call of the calendar at 11:00 A.M. At the call of the calendar, those motions not resolved or adjourned will be conferenced by the court. Discovery motions may not be submitted, even on consent of all parties, unless first conferenced by the Court.

(4) Preliminary Conferences:

Preliminary Conferences are generally handled by counsel in the robing room. Plaintiffs' counsel should fill in the first page of the PC form and place it in a box maintained for that purpose. City attorneys will call PC in the order of appearance by counsel. There is no calendar call for PCs.

(5) Compliance Conferences:

In lieu of a formal motion, parties may make written application to schedule a Discovery Status or Compliance Conference. These conferences are scheduled for Tuesday mornings at 9:30 A.M. Such application shall be forwarded to:

Bronx Supreme Civil
851 Grand Concourse
Bronx, New York 10451
Room 217 DCM Department

Such application shall set forth

1. The case caption, index number and city file #

2. E Mail address for notification

3. Must specify all discovery issues and any other relief being requested.

4. Identify all prior orders addressing discovery issues.

5. The request must be CC d to the

New York City Law Department
100 Church St.
New York, New York 10007

and all other appearing parties.

¹ See the general "Filing Rules" for the 12 Judicial District, Supreme Court.

Doc. 3.   OSC to Withdraw as Counsel

1) The Order to Show Cause must contain the following decretal clause:

"ORDERED, that Plaintiff/Defendant (name) _____ must appear in court, in person on the date and at the place above indicated."

2) Please incorporate the following text into the body of the Order to Show Cause.

NOTICE TO THE PLAINTIFF _____:

YOUR ATTORNEY DOES NOT WANT TO REPRESENT YOU, OR IS PRECLUDED FROM REPRESENTING YOU.

THE COURT WANTS TO PROTECT YOUR RIGHTS, AND TO GIVE YOU AN OPPORTUNITY TO RESPOND TO THE STATEMENT MADE BY YOUR ATTORNEY IN HIS/HER AFFIDAVIT WHICH IS ATTACHED TO THE ORDER TO SHOW CAUSE.

IN ORDER TO FULLY PROTECT YOUR RIGHTS YOU MUST APPEAR IN COURT ON _____. AT THAT TIME YOU MAY OBJECT OR CONSENT TO THE APPLICATION, AND YOU MAY PROVIDE ANY AND ALL INFORMATION WHICH YOU BELIEVE IS IMPORTANT REGARDING THIS APPLICATION.

IF YOUR ATTORNEY IS PERMITTED AND/OR OBLIGATED TO WITHDRAW FROM YOUR CASE, YOU WILL BE REQUIRED TO FIND A NEW ATTORNEY OR REPRESENT YOURSELF.

YOU MUST COMMUNICATE WITH THE COURT IN ORDER TO PROTECT YOUR RIGHTS. IF YOU CAN NOT APPEAR ON THE ABOVE DATE, YOU MAY WRITE TO THE COURT AND ADVISE THE COURT AS TO YOUR WISHES REGARDING THIS CASE, BEING CERTAIN THAT ANY MAIL ADDRESSED TO THE COURT IS RECEIVED ON OR BEFORE THE ABOVE DATE. IN THAT LETTER, PLEASE PROVIDE YOUR TELEPHONE CONTACT INFORMATION IN CASE IT IS NECESSARY FOR THE COURT TO CALL YOU. IF YOU DECIDE TO WRITE TO THE COURT, YOU SHOULD ADDRESS YOUR LETTER AS FOLLOWS:

Hon. Larry S. Schachner
Supreme Court of the State of New York
851 Grand Concourse
Bronx, New York 10451

Sufficient cause appearing therefore, let service of a copy of the within Order, and all the papers upon which it is based, upon the plaintiff and upon defense counsel by regular and certified mail, return receipt requested, on or before the __ day of , 2007, be deemed properly and timely served.

ENTER:

_____ Larry S. Schachner, JSC

Doc. 4. Settlement Conferences and Trial Assignment

Due to the backlog of pending cases in the New York City Part, this Court has adopted revised court rules implementing a calendar system which incorporates a "no adjournment" policy for those cases reached for assignment to a trial part.

The City of New York has assured the Court it will be ready to proceed to trial on approximately five to seven cases each week.

In order to attempt to eliminate the delay in the trial of cases assigned to this Part and to dispose of the pending post note of issue cases in a reasonable fashion within the courts available resources, the following rules have been adopted, effective immediately.

(1) Settlement Conference Information Sheet and Settlement Conferences (3A and 3 Calendars)

(A) Upon the filing of a Note of Issue an initial pre-trial conference will be scheduled. The Court will notify you of the pre-trial conference date. If the Court has not notified you of the conference date within 90 days after filing the Note of Issue contact the Part 3 Clerk. At the initial pre-trial conference counsel will fill out and file a Settlement Conference Information Sheet for the Court's use. Each attorney attending the initial settlement conference must bring a copy of all documents relevant to the issues of liability and damages including but not limited to Big Apple Map, Ambulance Call Report, Emergency Room records, medical records, and photographs, be fully familiar with every aspect of the case, and fully authorized to engage in meaningful settlement negotiations.

(B) For all cases other than "trial ready" cases, the Court will endeavor to schedule several interim settlement conferences before it deems it necessary to provide a "final settlement conference" and a trial date shortly thereafter.

(2) Final Settlement Conference/Special Requirements (3F Calendar)

In a final effort to dispose of the maximum number of cases without the need for a trial, a special "final settlement conference" will be conducted under the following rules:

(A) Only the attorneys of record and/or designated trial counsel may attend these settlement conferences. Attorneys will be bound by all representations made at this conference including those as to trial readiness and the date selected for trial.

(B) Attorneys representing the plaintiff(s) must have evaluated the case prior to the settlement conference date and be prepared to negotiate in good faith to effectuate a reasonable settlement. The City of New York, likewise, shall have evaluated the case prior to the settlement conference date and be prepared to negotiate in good faith to effectuate a reasonable settlement.

(C) Each attorney attending the final settlement conferences must bring a complete file including the marked pleadings, all medical reports and all other documents relating to the issues of liability and damages. Moreover, said counsel must be fully familiar with every aspect of the case and be authorized to settle and/or make binding concessions. In the event the case is not disposed, it shall be scheduled for trial on a date which the Court in its discretion deems appropriate, but in any event, not less than three weeks after said final conference.

(D) The plaintiff must either be present in Court or be available by telephone or cell phone on the final settlement conference date to consent to any settlement order.

(E) Violations of these final conference rules will subject the offending party(s) to the same sanctions, costs and remedies set forth above.

(3) Trial Assignment (3T Calendar)

(A) A minimum of at least seven trial ready cases shall be scheduled for trial on each Monday (or if the Monday is a holiday on the Tuesday following). A call of the "trial ready" calendar shall be made on each Monday promptly at 9:30 A.M., in Room 707, at 851 Grand Concourse, Bronx, New York 10451. Sanctions and/or costs may be imposed on attorneys who are not present upon the call of the trial ready calendar. The Court will endeavor to send all cases to jury selection, beginning with special preference cases, and then by oldest cases as determined by the filing date of the Note of Issue.

(B) Trial counsel for all parties, including the City of New York, must appear and be ready to commence trial and select a jury. On the date scheduled for trial no requests for adjournment by the parties will be granted. Those cases which are not sent out for trial will be deemed ready and passed to the following day or otherwise as directed by the Court.

(C) None of the trial ready cases may be adjourned by stipulation of the parties; and since these trial ready cases are probably the oldest in the City of New York and have already appeared on a final conference calendar, affidavits of engagement and requests for adjournments will not be accepted.

(D) If for any reason the designated trial attorney is not ready to proceed, a new trial attorney must be retained or designated and be present and ready to proceed immediately upon trial assignment.

(E) Failure of a party to be ready to proceed may result in imposition of costs or sanctions; or the striking of the case from the trial calendar; the vacating of the note of issue; or dismissal of the complaint or the striking of the answer, or other remedies, including, but not limited to, those set forth in CPLR 3404 and Uniform Court Rules 202.21 and 202.27. *See, Hood v*

City of NY, 4 Misc 3d 627, 781 NYS2d 431 (Sup. Ct. Bx. Cty.); Chief Administrator's Rules for the Engagement of Counsel, Rule 125(9).

(4) Sanctions and Costs For Lack of Readiness For Trial

(A) *Be Prepared*: Do not wait until the eve of the trial to get prepared. It is counsel's obligation, well before a case is scheduled for trial, to ascertain the availability of all witnesses and the sufficiency of all subpoenaed documents. Counsel should subpoena all required documents in sufficient time to have same available for trial without delay. Subpoenas for medical records must be accompanied by an appropriate HIPPA form. In order to avoid a delay in processing a request for a "court ordered" subpoena for medical records it is strongly suggested that counsel use the HIPPA OCA Official Form No. 960, which can be obtained from the Court website, or from the clerk in Room 103, or from the IA−3 clerk in Room 707.

(B) *Published Notification*: All "trial ready" cases presently pending in IA−3 (i.e. where a final settlement conference has already been held) will be scheduled for trial assignment on a date fixed by the Court without further personal notice to trial counsel. All attorneys are required to monitor the progress of the trial ready calendar by reference to the New York Law Journal, or on the appropriate court web site or by appearance at the office of the Clerk in Room 217.

(C) *Sanctions and Costs*: When a date for trial is fixed the attorneys designated as trial counsel must appear for trial on that date. If any such attorney is actually engaged on trial elsewhere, he or she must provide substitute trial counsel. If neither trial counsel nor substitute trial counsel is ready to try the case on the scheduled date, the Court may impose sanctions or costs permitted by law. [See, *Hood v. City of New York*, 4 Misc. 3rd 627 (Sup. Ct., Bx. Cty.), *Harling v. City of New York*, NYLJ, April 11, 2005 at 19, col 3 (Sup. Ct. Bx. Cty.); Chief Administrator's Uniform Rules for the Engagement of Counsel, Rule 125 (g).

10/6/08

Doc. 5. Settlement Conference Information Sheet

JUSTICE LARRY S. SCHACHNER, PRESIDING

TITLE OF PROCEEDINGS   INDEX # _____

_____   NOTE OF ISSUE DATE ___

                    TYPE OF TORT _____

          vs.

DESCRIPTION OF ACTION AND DAMAGES

OCCURRENCE: DATE: _____ TIME: ___
_____ LOCATION: _____
DESCRIBE OCCURRENCE: _____
_____
_____

DESCRIBE INJURY & TREATMENT: _____
_____
_____

LIENS: _____

DEMAND: _____

OFFER: _____

PLAINTIFF: D.O.B. _____ OCCUPATION: _____

PLAINTIFF: D.O.B. _____ OCCUPATION: _____

ATTORNEYS OF RECORD & TRIAL COUNSEL

COUNSEL FOR PLAINTIFF(S)

1. _____
ATTORNEY OF RECORD FOR _____
OFFICE ADDRESS AND PHONE NUMBER

_____

TRIAL COUNSEL FOR PLAINTIFF NO. 1

_____

2. _____
ATTORNEY OF RECORD FOR _____
OFFICE ADDRESS AND PHONE NUMBER

_____

TRIAL COUNSEL FOR PLAINTIFF NO. 2

_____

3. _____
ATTORNEY OF RECORD FOR _____
OFFICE ADDRESS AND PHONE NUMBER

_____

TRIAL COUNSEL FOR PLAINTIFF NO. 3

_____

COUNSEL FOR DEFENDANT(S)

1. _____
ATTORNEY OF RECORD FOR _____
OFFICE ADDRESS AND PHONE NUMBER

_____

TRIAL COUNSEL FOR DEFENDANT NO. 1

_____

2. _____   3. _____

ATTORNEY OF RECORD FOR _____   ATTORNEY OF RECORD FOR _____
OFFICE ADDRESS AND PHONE NUMBER   OFFICE ADDRESS AND PHONE NUMBER

_____   _____

TRIAL COUNSEL FOR DEFENDANT NO. 2   TRIAL COUNSEL FOR DEFENDANT NO. 3

_____   _____

JUSTICE HOWARD H. SHERMAN

Part IA–4. Hon. Howard H. Sherman

1. Motion Procedure

A. Applicable to Notice of Motion and Order to Show Cause

All papers must comply with CPLR R2101, R2103 and R2214 as well as the applicable provisions of the Court Rules [22 NYCRR Part 202].

Tabs shall be used when submitting exhibits. If an annexed document is voluminous and only discrete portions are relevant, Counsel shall highlight the relevant sections of the document. All cited material shall be viewable without having to remove staples or binding.

Courtesy copies shall not be submitted.

Counsel are advised when submitting proposed orders or judgments to keep proposed orders or proposed judgments separate and apart from motion papers. Proposed orders or judgments incorporated within motion papers will be considered exhibits and treated as such.

Failure to appear at the call of any calendar may result in an inquest or dismissal [22 NYCRR § 202.27].

Counsel must advise the Court in writing as soon as practicable of all motions that have been resolved and/or to be withdrawn.

B. Motions brought by Notice of Motion

Motions are returnable five days a week in the Motion Support Office, Room 103. All opposition and reply papers must be submitted at the Motion Support Office on the return date of the motion. Opposition and reply papers will not be accepted prior to the return date.

All non-disclosure motions will be deemed submitted on the return date and forwarded to Chambers. Stipulations of adjournment compliant with Uniform Rule 202.8(e)(1), submitted in Room 103 on the return or adjourned date of a motion, will be honored and the motion will be adjourned and kept in the Motion Support Office. If a non-stipulated application for adjournment is submitted, the motion and application will be forwarded to Chambers for a ruling. Counsel will be advised of the ruling in writing. Oral applications are not considered.

If oral argument is requested and granted, or directed by the Court, the motion will be adjourned for conference and oral argument in IAS Part 4. Counsel will be advised of the adjourned date in writing.

Disclosure Motions

No motion for substantive relief shall be joined with an application for discovery relief. Discovery related motions are heard by the Judge presiding in IAS Part 11.

Summary Judgment Motions

Pursuant to CPLR R3212(a), a motion for summary judgment shall be made no later than sixty days after the filing of the Note of Issue, except with leave of court on good cause shown.

C. Orders to Show Cause

Orders to Show Cause must comply with Uniform Rule 202.7(d) and be brought to the Motion Support Office from which they are forwarded to Chambers for consideration.

All orders to show cause are returnable on Mondays, except for court holidays, in IAS Part 4 at 9:30 a.m., unless otherwise indicated. Personal appearances are required.

Proof of service must be filed with the Clerk of IAS Part 4 by 9:30 a.m. of the return date. Non-compliance will result in denial of the order to show cause.

Stipulations adjourning an Order to Show Cause shall be filed with the Clerk of IAS Part 4 prior to the call of the calendar.

2. Infant Compromises and other Ex Parte applications

Ex Parte applications are to be submitted to the Motion Support Office. After review of Infant Compromise submissions, Counsel will be notified of the scheduled appearance date by phone.

All proposed infant compromise orders shall contain the following language:

It is further Ordered that the Guardian shall, within thirty days of the deposit of the funds due the infant herein in the above designated bank(s), submit to the Clerk's Office, Room 103, a copy of the Certificate of Deposit issued by said bank.

The attorney's supporting affirmation shall set forth the policy limits of all available insurance.

3. Depositions

Requests for rulings are to be made to the Ex–Parte Justice, not the IAS assigned Justice.

4. Inquiries

All inquiries should be made to the appropriate clerk's office, not chambers.

Motion Support Office: Room 103, (718) 618–1310.

Faxes to chambers are not permitted unless prior authorization is obtained.

E–mails are not permitted unless prior authorization is obtained.

The only inquiries to be made directly to Chambers should be those involving the immediate exercise of judicial discretion.

JUSTICE ALISON Y. TUITT

Part IA–5. Hon. Alison Y. Tuitt

Motion Procedure

1. Moving and responding papers including stipulations and requests for adjournments are to be filed in the clerk's office in Room 103, except that any case that has been marked final in the part itself must seek approval to file an additional adjournment beyond a final marking. (All motions seeking discovery must be directed to the Compliance Conference Part, as no issues of discovery will be entertained by this IAS part).

2. There are NO SUBMITTED MOTIONS IN THIS PART, AND ALL MOTIONS WITHOUT EXCEPTION MUST BE ORALLY ARGUED.

3. Movant's on Motions and Orders to Show Cause that fail to appear for oral argument will be summarily denied for failure to appear. No exceptions.

4. All motions for Summary Judgment must be filed within 120 days of the filing of the Note of Issue. NO EXCEPTIONS.

5. All parties seeking or filing a request for adjournment must insure that such request has been granted prior to the scheduled date in order to avoid a default determination being entered. All request for adjournment must be made in writing, oral applications will not be entertained. No exceptions.

6. If opposition papers have been duly filed in the Clerk's office, courtesy copies need not be provided to the Court.

7. All parties appearing on a motion should have familiarity with the case and the moving papers sufficient to engage in substantive oral argument on the issues raised in the motion papers.

7. As with all matters, Orders to Show Cause must comply with Uniform Rule 202.7(d) and be brought to the clerk's office (Room 103) prior to judicial review,

signature and fixing a return date. Appearance is thus required, no exceptions.

8. A moving parties failure to appear may result in an inquest or dismissal pursuant to Section 202.27 of the Uniform Civil Rules for the Supreme Court and County Court.

Inquiries:

All inquiries as to case or calendar status should, in the first instance, be made to the appropriate clerk's office: IAS Motion Support Office: Room 103

The only inquiries that should be made directly to Chambers or the Part should be those involving the immediate and substantive exercise of judicial discretion.

Trial:

All parties assigned to this part must provide the following:

1. Plaintiff must provide a copy of the pleadings, bills of particular, demands for discovery and corresponding responses, copies of their clients EBT transcript and copies of all their expert 3101(d) exchanges.

2. Defendants must provide copies of their responses to demands for discovery from plaintiff, copies of their clients or witnesses EBT transcripts and copies of their expert 3101(d) exchanges.

3. All parties must raise all pre-trial issues prior to jury selection or openings whichever opportunity is first available to the parties in order that such issue be preserved for appellate purposes.

4. Any pre-trial issues not raised before openings will be deemed WAIVED.

5. All parties must reveal and identify all potential witnesses that may be called during the trial, failure to so reveal or identify will be deemed a voluntary waiver by the party.

JUSTICE WILMA GUZMAN

Part IA-7. Hon. Wilma Guzman

Motion Procedure: Effective January 2, 2010.

There are NO SUBMITTED MOTIONS IN THIS PART, AND ALL MOTIONS WITHOUT EXCEPTION MUST BE ORALLY ARGUED.

Moving and responding papers including stipulations and requests for adjournments are to be filed and with confirmed with Part IAS 7 Clerk. Except that any case that has been marked final in the part itself must seek approval on the record to file an additional adjournment beyond a final marking. (All motions seeking discovery must be directed to the Compliance Conference Part, as no issues of discovery will be entertained by this IAS part 7.)

Movant's on Motions and Orders to Show Cause that fail to appear for oral argument will be summarily denied for failure to appear. No exceptions.

All parties seeking or filling a request for adjournment must insure that such request has been granted prior to the scheduled date in order to avoid a default determination being entered. All request for adjournment must be made in writing, oral applications will not be entertained. No exceptions.

If opposition papers have been duly filed in the Clerk's office, courtesy copies need not be provided to the Court.

All parties appearing on a motion should have familiarity with the case and the moving papers sufficient to engage in substantive oral argument on the issues raised in the motion papers.

As with all matters, Orders to Show Cause must comply with Uniform Rule 202.7(d) and be brought to the Clerk's office (Room 217) prior to judicial review, signature and fixing a return date. Appearance is thus required, no exceptions.

A moving parties failure to appear may result in an Inquest or dismissal pursuant to Section 202.27 of the Uniform Civil Rules for the Supreme Court and County Court.

All papers must comply with CPLR §2101, 2103 and 2214.

Tabs must be used when submitting exhibits with any motion.

All cited material shall be fully viewable without having to remove staples or binding.

All submissions shall be fully and securely bound.

No exhibits shall be double side.

Courtesy copies shall not be submitted unless requested.

When submitting proposed orders or judgments in connection with a motion, the same shall be submitted as a separately bound document. Proposed orders or judgments incorporated within motion papers will be considered exhibits, treated as such, and may be disregarded.

Failure to appear at a calendar call will result in denial of any motion made by the non-appearing party and the granting of any motion on default when the opposing party fails to appear.

Counsel must advise the Court in writing and as soon as practicable if any submitted motions have been resolved, withdrawn, or if the motion is moot because the case has been settled.

This part generally only entertains substantive non-discovery motions. However, this part will entertain motions for pre-action and non-party discovery.

No motion for substantive relief shall be joined with any application for discovery. Discovery related motions are heard by the Judge presiding in the DCM Part, IAS Part 11. In the event that a party makes a discovery cross-motion in response to a substantive motion, the Court shall refer the discovery related application to the DCM Part, IAS Part 11 and upon resolution of the discovery motion, shall resolve the substantive motion.

Effective January 1, 2010, pursuant to CPLR §3212(a), a motion for summary judgment shall be made no later than sixty (60) days after the filing of the Note of Issue, except with leave of court on good cause shown.

No sur-replies shall be considered absent leave of court to interpose the same.

Without exception all motions shall be securely bound and all exhibits submitted in support of any motion shall be one sided. Failure to adhere to this rule shall result in denial of the motion.

Inquiries:

All inquiries as to case or calendar status should, in the first instance, be made to the appropriate clerk's office: IAS Motion Support Office: Room 217.

The only inquiries that should be made directly to Chambers or the Part should be those involving the immediate and substantive exercise of judicial discretion.

Facsimiles to Chambers are not permitted unless prior authorization is obtained.

Attorneys shall not call Chambers or the Court Room during the daily lunch hour which is from 1 PM to 2 PM.[1]

Motions Brought by Notice of Motion:

Motions are returnable (5) days a week in the Motion Support Office.

All opposition and reply papers must be submitted to the Motion Support Office on the return date of the motion, (Oral Argument Date or Notice for motion date by the Court)

All non-disclosure motions are adjourned by Motion Support to the First next available Monday for Oral Argument.

Stipulations of adjournment, compliant with the Uniform Court Rule §202.8(e)(1), submitted to the IAS Part 7 Clerk, prior to the return or adjourned date of a motion, will be adjourned to the next available date to the Court.

Oral applications seeking an adjournment shall be made upon failure to procure prior adjournment on written consent and signed by all parties.

There shall be oral argument and personal appearance is required on all motion brought by notice of Motion, Petition or Order to Show Cause.

All opposition and reply papers submitted prior to the oral argument date shall be submitted to the Motion Support Office. If not, submitted prior to the oral argument date, then copies of the opposition and reply papers shall be brought to the oral argument date.

Trials:

All parties assigned to this part must provide the following:

Be prepared and well organized. Be punctual and professionally attired. Be civil to the Court and to each other.

Plaintiff must provide a copy of the pleadings, bill of particular, demands for discovery and corresponding responses, copies of their clients EBT transcripts and copies of all their expert 3101(d) exchanges.

Defendants must provide copies of their responses to demands for discovery from plaintiff, copies of their client's or witnesses's EBT transcripts and copies of all their expert 3101(d) exchanges.

All parties must raise all pre -trial issues prior to jury selection or openings, or whichever opportunity is first available to the parties, in order that such issues be preserved for appellate purposes.

Any pre -trial issues not raised before openings will be deemed WAIVED.

All parties must reveal and identify all potential witnesses that may be called during the trial; failure to reveal or identify will be deemed a voluntary waiver by the party.

The Court will work with attorneys to resolve scheduling conflicts. However, all scheduling concerns and issues should be promptly discussed during the first conference.

Any special requests, such as interpreters, blackboards, media equipment, shall b e made in advance of commencement of the trial or during the first conference.

There shall be no time limits imposed upon the jury selection process but it is expected that the attorneys will select a jury as expeditiously as possible.

There shall be no time limits imposed upon the jury selection process but it is expected that the attorneys will select a jury as expeditiously as possible.

Parties shall furnish the Court with copies of any statutes that the parties claim are relevant to a particular case.

Parties must provide the Court with copies of all transcripts to be used during the trial prior to their use at trial. Portions of any transcript to be read into evidence on a party's case in chief must be disclosed in advanced and the Court and all parties must be provided with all page and line numbers for the portions to be read.

Parties shall provide the Court copies of all expert exchanges and reports. When the case is first conferenced in the Part, parties shall Alert the Court to all anticipated issues of law and fact and provide the Court with the relevant law applicable to their case.

Stipulate to undisputed facts and the admissibility of clearly admissible documents.

Apprise the Court of any anticipated motions in limine.

Provide the Court with a list of anticipated witnesses.

Provide the Court with any subpoenas it wishes the Court to so-order, provided the same are relevant to the trial at hand.

Motions in Limine should be supported by case law and copies of the same must be provided to the Court prior to the making of such motion.

All trial exhibits must be pre-marked for identification, as well as any records stipulated in evidence.

During the trial no of the attorney, witness, or party shall have any communication with the jurors. All conferences between attorneys and witnesses during trial should be avoided on the 6th floor.

Speaking objections are prohibited. An objection shall be made by standing, saying "objection" and thereafter succinctly stating the basis for the objection. If the objection requires elaboration, parties should request a sidebar.

While opportunity to preserve and make a record may not always be allowed when requested, all attorneys shall ultimately be granted ample opportunity to make a record.

Any item which is sought to be shown to a witness must first shown to opposing counsel.

Due to the Court's motion calendar, there shall be no trials on Monday mornings.

Due to the Court's Mental Hygiene Inventory, there shall be no trials conducted on Tuesdays and on some Fridays.

Motions Brought by Order to Show Cause:

Orders to Show Cause must comply with Uniform Rule 202.7(d) and be brought to the Motion Support Office. Thereafter, they are forwarded, by Motion Support, to Chambers for consideration.

All Orders to Show Cause are returnable on Mondays, except for court holidays, in IAS Part 7 at 10:00 AM, unless otherwise indicated. Personal appearance is required.

Proof of service must be filed with the Clerk of IAS Part 7 by 10:00 AM on the return date. Non-compliance will result in denial of the Order to Show Cause.

Stipulations adjourning an Order to Show Cause shall be filed or facts with the Clerk of IAS Part 7 prior to the call of the calendar. Parties are responsible for confirming the adjournment.

Infant Compromises and Other Ex Parte Applications:

Ex Parte applications are to be submitted to the Motion Support Office. Thereafter, they are forwarded by Motion Support to Chambers for consideration.

After review of Infant Compromise submissions, counsel will be notified when to appear. Counsel shall also be notified of any deficiencies in the papers submitted and shall, when appropriate, be given an opportunity to submit additional information to cure the deficiency.

Hearings are required and are held prior to the approval of any Infant Compromise Order.

The infant and his named guardian must be present on the date scheduled unless a prior waiver of their appearance has been obtained.

All proposed infant compromise orders shall contain the following language:

It is further Ordered that the Guardian shall, within thirty days of the deposit of the funds due the infant herein in the a designated bank(s), submit to the Clerk's Office, Motion Support, a copy of the Certificate of Deposit issued by said bank.

It is at the Court's discretion in which bank the Infant Compromise funds are deposited.

The attorney's supporting affirmation shall set forth the policy limits of all available Insurance.

All infant's Compromise submissions shall comply with C.P.L.R §1207, 1208 and Uniform Rules §202.67.

The Court will not entertain an Infant's Compromise Order where the medical evidence submitted is wholly inappropriate, e.g., a chiropractor rendering an opinion with regard to a wrist fracture, an internist rendering an opinion regarding "psychic trauma", or said opinion or report is more than nine months old.

Mental Hygiene Law Article 81 Proceeding:

Conference and Hearing calendar shall be called at 10:00 AM on Tuesdays.

Since these proceedings are time sensitive, adjournments will be granted only under exigent circumstances and with the prior approval of this Court.

Applications for adjournments must be requested from the Judge or the Principal Law Clerk and thereafter in writing. Written requests for adjournments can be made via letter on notice to all parties and served upon the Court via facsimile. Parties are responsible for confirming the adjournment.

It is expected that the Court Evaluator assigned to any particular proceeding shall fully verse him/herself with his duties and responsibilities and execute the same properly and completely.

Should the AIP request counsel, the Court Evaluator shall notify the Court in writing as soon as practicable and the Court shall appoint counsel pursuant to the Mental Hygiene Law.

Applications for alternate service upon the AIP shall be made by ex-parte Order to be submitted to the Guardianship Office, and shall be accompanied by proof supporting the basis for alternate service.

Applications by the Court Evaluator seeking ta examine AIP's medical records or seeking to have the AIP examined by an independent medical doctor, shall be made pursuant to the Mental Hygiene Law.

The report of the Court Evaluator shall be provided to the Court on the day of the hearing and shall not be published to any other party until the day of the hearing.

All hearings must be conducted in the presence of the AIP pursuant to the Mental Hygiene Law 81.11(c)(2). Accordingly, any discussions regarding the waiver of the AIP's appearance shall be discussed or heard pursuant to the Mental Hygiene Law 81.11(c)(2).

Unless an exception is made, all applications related to Article 81 of the Mental Hygiene aw shall be brought by Order to Show Cause and not by Notice of Motion.

Copies of the Order to Show Cause and Interim decisions will be faxed to the petitioner.

1 Although the number to Chambers has been provided use of said number is subject to limitations set forth herein.

JUSTICE BETTY OWEN STINSON

Part IA-8. Hon. Betty Owen Stinson

Motion Procedure (for submitted motions)

I. Moving and responding papers, including stipulations and for adjournments, are to be filed in the clerk's office (Room 217).

II. All disclosure motions, filed and accepted in the clerk's office, are heard in part IA-11, the PCDM Part, on a rescheduled date (See rule for Part IA-11). All non-disclosure motions filed and accepted as above, will be deemed submitted on the return date subject to the motion procedure.

III. All stipulations and requests for adjournments filed in the clerk's office for all motions will be processed as indicated in the revised motion procedure printed in the Law Journal.

IV. Answering papers will be accepted only on the return date in the clerk's office (Room 217).

V. Courtesy copies of moving and answering papers shall not be provided to the court.

Special Proceedings (OSC & Petitions)

VI. Order to Show Cause must comply with Uniform Rule 202.7(d) and be brought to the clerk's office (Room 103) for judicial review, signature and fixing of a return date. Appearance requirements for orders to show cause are as indicated in the motion procedure appearing in Motion Procedures under "Court Rules" for Bronx County on this site.

VII. Proof of service of all orders to show cause must be filed in the courtroom with the Part clerk on the return date.

Trials (not applicable under present trial assignment system)

Inquiries

All inquiries regarding status should, in the first instance, be made to the clerk's office Room 103 at (718) 618-1310. The only inquires to be made directly to Chambers or the Part should be those involving the immediate exercise of judicial discretion.

Calendars

Order to Show Cause Calendars will be called promptly at 9:30 A.M. Only counsel fully familiar with the file and the application being made will appear at the call of this calendar. Failure of the movant to appear at the call of the calendar will result in denial of the application. Calendar service may not appear or answer an order to show Cause Calendar. The last call of the calendar is at 10:15 a.m.

JUSTICE LAURA G. DOUGLAS

Part IA-11. Hon. Laura G. Douglas

All Preliminary Conferences, Compliance Conferences and discovery applications for Non–City and Non–Matrimonial cases will be conducted in Part 11, Courtroom 711, before Hon. Laura G. Douglas.

All Conferences begin promptly at 9:30am. Only counsel fully familiar with and authorized to stipulate or dispose of the action may appear at the conference. Cases are called in the order in which All attorneys are actually present in the courtroom. When the case is called and there is no appearance, the court will take appropriate action against the non-appearing attorney or non-appearing party, applying such penalties or sanctions as are authorized by the CPLR and the Rules of the Chief Administrative Judge. There will be no adjournments of conferences.

At the preliminary conference, a complete discovery schedule will be set. In instances where the Bill of Particulars has not been served, a complete discovery schedule will be set based on the service date of the Bill of Particulars. Parties must adhere to all dates contained herein relating to the completion of items in the P.C. Order. Counsel will be required to justify, at a hearing before the presiding judge, its failure to adhere to the discovery schedule set forth at the P.C. In the event of non-compliance with any Order, counsel shall contact the Court within five (5) days of the non-compliance for a hearing to determine compliance, or impose cost, sanction and other relief. Counsel may not enter into any adjournments or stipulations without further Order of this Court.

The date for the Compliance Conference will be reflected in the PC order and Counsel will not receive further notification. Counsel may confirm the date of the Compliance Conference on the internet at either "E-Courts" or the "Future Court Appearance System" which are both located on the Unified Court System Web Page at www.courts.state.ny.us.

In accordance with 22 NYCRR 202.19(b)(3), the purpose of the compliance conference is: (a) to monitor the progress of discovery; (b) to explore potential settlement; and (c) to set a deadline for the filing of the Note of Issue. Consequently, Counsel attending the Conference must be fully familiar with the case, the status of disclosure proceedings, and any settlement negotiations. Counsel MUST bring a copy of the Bill of Particulars, medical reports, the Preliminary Conference order and all previous orders in the case and MUST be prepared and authorized to enter into binding stipulations regarding disclosure and disposition of the case.

In lieu of making a motion for discovery, counsel may request a conference for purposes of resolving discovery issues by submitting a written request in room 217, addressed to the Differentiated Case Management Department (DCM). All written requests for an additional conference must fully detail the difficulty encountered in pursuing discovery. If a motion is filed, a discovery conference and the motion will be scheduled for an appearance in this discovery part. An appearance will be required on all motions regardless of any withdrawal or stipulated resolution of the application.

No ex-parte telephone application concerning motions, Preliminary Conferences or Compliance Conferences may be made to Chambers or the courtroom. All normal inquiries are made in the courtroom or in Room 217.

No applications, whether made by letter or by stipulation, submitted by a lawyer's clerical service will be permitted.

CPLR 3211, 3212 and 3213 applications will not stay discovery.

Plaintiff(s) shall file the Note of Issue on the date set forth in the Compliance Conference Order. In cases where there is outstanding discovery, an appropriate Order will be issued by this Court outlining the outstanding discovery and the time frame for compliance by the non-compliant party. It is anticipated that disclosure will not be complete by the time the Note of Issue is to be filed, counsel for plaintiff(s) is directed to request a Status Conference four weeks before the date of filing a Note of issue.

Counsel are further advised that the failure to file the Note of Issue on the date fixed in the compliance Conference Order may result in the service, by the Court upon Plaintiff's(s') Counsel, of a Notice pursuant to CPLR § 3216.

JUSTICE JOHN A. BARONE

Part IA–12. Hon. John A. Barone

1. Motion Practice

The General Rules set forth for motion practice in Supreme Court for the County of the Bronx shall in all instances apply,

Upon assignment to this part additional motions can be made only upon application to and permission from the court. For all such additional motions the relief sought and reasons therefor shall be set forth in a written request for permission to file additional motions.

All counsel appearing on motions must be thoroughly familiar with the case, the previous demands for relief and offers of settlement and must be authorized to settle or try the case within the limits set by the client. All clients must be available by telephone, fax, email, etc., to respond to modified demands or proposed settlements.

2. Trial Rules

Upon assignment to this part for trial, counsel must requisition the file to the courtroom. Counsel must ascertain the availability of all witnesses and subpoenaed documents; additional requests for postponements, subpoenae etc., may be made but will be granted only in the discretion of the court in accordance with the exigencies of the court calendar.

Before trial plaintiff's counsel shall furnish:

1) marked pleadings;

2) statutory provisions specifically relied upon in the pleadings;

3) the bill of particulars;

All counsel shall furnish:

1) expert reports;

2) depositions and written statements which may potentially be used at trial including use in cross-examinations or to refresh a witnesses recollection;

3) any part of a deposition to be read into evidence as part of either party's direct case (not cross-examination);

4) pre-marked exhibits and a list thereof.

In addition, attorneys at pre-trial conference must be prepared to discuss or prepare:

1) all anticipated issues of law with citation to authorities;

2) stipulations to undisputed facts if any;

3) admissions and stipulations of clearly admissible evidence;

4) any anticipated motions *in limine*;

5) scheduling and attendance issues;

6) a witness list;

7) requested jury charges and verdict sheets;

Courtroom demeanor

1) observe the normal professional courtesies;

2) direct all question to the witness and all remarks to the court;

3) make objections as succinctly as possible. Don't make speeches;

4) do not interrupt opposing counsel. Do not interrupt witnesses except to interpose a motion to strike an answer as non-responsive;

5) try to relax. Remember you are officers of the court first and advocates second. Remember that your client's rights are derived from the law

and your duty to your client is paramount except when it clashes with your professional responsibilities or your integrity as a member of the bar. Your clients deserve your best efforts but no more than that. Be proud of your profession and strive to live up to its highest goals. You worked hard to achieve your status as an attorney at law. Never compromise it.

JUSTICE JULIA I. RODRIGUEZ

Part IA–18. Hon. Julia I. Rodriguez

Effective April 30, 2009, all requests for conferences and adjournments must be submitted to the Part Clerk in writing and on notice to all sides setting forth reasons for and/or objections to said request. Requests shall be made in person or by facsimile to (718) 618–3522.

In matters where a Temporary Order of Protection is in place and an adjournment is requested on consent by all parties, the Stipulation of Adjournment must also include whether an extension of the TOP is agreed to by all parties; where the Stipulation fails to address that the TOP will remain in effect, the TOP will be deemed expired as of the date provided in said Order.

Default calendar shall be called ½ hour after the scheduled appearance.

Request for Stays and Temporary Restraining Orders shall be in compliance with 22 NYCRR § 202.7.

Conferences require an appearance by counsel, unless a party does not have counsel, in which case the litigant shall appear *pro se*.

Parties and counsel shall comply with the rules set forth in 22 NYCRR § 202.16 governing matrimonial actions.

Motions must be made on notice to all parties in accordance with CPLR § 2214.

Motion calendars will be called at 9:30 on Tuesdays.

Please be advised that *ex parte* communications will not be entertained.

PART IA–21

RULES FOR MOTIONS, CONFERENCES & TRIALS

Rule 1. Orders to Show Cause

Orders to show cause are calendared for Friday 9:30 AM in Room 810. Attorneys should appear promptly and be prepared to argue their cases.

Rule 2. Substantive (Non–Discovery) Motions

In accordance with the general rules applicable in Bronx County for civil motions, all substantive (non-discovery) motions, except those brought by order to show cause, will be made returnable in Room 217 and submitted without argument, unless otherwise directed by the court.

Rule 3. Discovery Motions

All motions for discovery must also be made returnable in Room 217. However, said motions will be automatically adjourned to a date for appearance and argument before the Justice presiding over Part IA-11 in Room 707.

Rule 4. Settlement Conferences and Trial Commencement

The following rules and forms for cases sent to select a jury or for applications to settle a claim for an infant or impaired person, are separately listed and published on the OCA website for Part IA-21.

A. Trial Rules For Trial Counsel

B. Rules For Settlement of Claim By Infants & Impaired Persons

C. Worksheet For Compromise Application

D. Form - Standard Compromise Order

E. Form - Simple Order For a Structured Settlement

F. Form - Complex Order For a Structured Settlement

G. Form - Sample Broker's Affidavit

H. OCA Official Form - HIPAA Authorization

TRIAL RULES FOR TRIAL COUNSEL

Rule 1. Be Prepared

Prior to jury selection, counsel is cautioned to ascertain the availability of all witnesses and subpoenaed documents. Plaintiff's counsel shall requisition the file to the Courtroom as soon as possible after assignment of the case to this part. If you have non-

English speaking witnesses, or any other special needs, e.g. easels, blackboards, shadow boxes, television, subpoenaed material, etc., it is your responsibility to notify the Court Officer, in advance, so as not to delay the progress of the trial.

Rule 2. Marked Pleadings Plus

Plaintiff's counsel shall furnish the Court with copies of:

A. Marked pleadings as required by CPLR 4012;

B. A copy of any statutory provisions in effect at the time the cause of action arose upon which either the plaintiff or defendant relies;

C. The bill(s) of particulars;

D. All expert reports relevant to the issues;

E. All reports, depositions and written statements which may be used to either refresh a witness' recollection and/or cross-examine the witness.

F. If any part of a deposition is to be read into evidence (as distinguished from mere use on cross-examination) you must, well in advance, provide the Court and your adversary with the page and line number of all such testimony so that all objections can be addressed prior to use before the jury.

Rule 3. Pre–Marked Exhibits

All trial exhibits should be pre-marked for identification, and copies of a list of exhibits must be given to the Court before the trial actually begins. Failure to comply with this rule may result in sanctions, which may include an order precluding the offering of such exhibits at trial. See, *Davis Eckert v. State of New York*, 70 N.Y.2d 633, 518 N.Y.S. 2d 957.

Rule 4. Assignment Conference

At this conference counsel should be prepared:

A. To alert the Court as to all anticipated disputed issues of law and fact, and provide the Court with citations to all statutory and common law authority upon which counsel will rely.

B. To stipulate to undisputed facts and the admissibility of clearly admissible documents and records.

C. To alert the Court to any anticipated *in limine* motions or evidentiary objections which counsel believes will be made during the course of the trial.

D. To provide the Court with a copy of all prior decisions and orders which may be relevant to said *in limine* applications.

E. To discuss scheduling as well as the number of witnesses to be called at trial, and the estimated length of the trial.

F. A list of the names of all witnesses (other than rebuttal witnesses) to be called by you and for each such witness the elements of proof to be supplied (in

the case of plaintiff) or addressed (in the case of defendant) by such witness.

G. To alert the Court as to any anticipated problems regarding the attendance at trial of parties, attorneys or essential witnesses, and any other practical problems which the Court should consider in scheduling.

H. To alert the Court to any anticipated requests for a jury instruction relating to missing witnesses and/or documents.

I. To alert the Court to any anticipated request for apportionment as to alleged culpable non-parties pursuant to CPLR Article 16.

Rule 5. No Communication with Jurors

In order to maintain the appearance of total impartiality, once the jury has been selected no one is to communicate in any form at any time with any juror. This includes both verbal and non-verbal communication, including, without limitation, nods, shrugs and shaking the head. Do not even say "hello" or "good morning".

Rule 6. Check–In

At the start of each day on trial, check in with the clerk of the Court and or the Court Officer so that (s)he will be aware of your presence.

Rule 7. Trial Objections and Arguments

If a lawyer wishes to make an objection, it can be accomplished by standing and saying the word, "objection", and by adding thereto up to three more words so as to state the generic grounds for the objection, such as "hearsay," "bolstering," "leading," or "asked and answered." If you believe further argument is required, ask permission to approach the bench. This request will almost always be granted. Keep in mind that you will always be given the opportunity to make a full record.

Rule 8. Courtroom Comments and Demeanor

All remarks should be directed to the Court. Comments should not be made to opposing counsel. Personal remarks, including name-calling and insults, to or about opposing counsel will not be tolerated. Remember do not try to "talk over" each other; only one person speaks at a time or the record of the proceeding will be incomprehensible. Simple requests (e.g., a request for a document or an exhibit), should be accomplished in a manner which does not disrupt the proceedings or your adversary. If you require a significant discussion with your adversary, such as a possible stipulation, ask for permission to approach the bench. I will grant that request, and you will have a chance to talk to each other outside the presence of the jury. In addition, no grandstanding in the presence of the jury, i.e., making demands, offers or statements that should properly be made outside the presence of the jury.

Rule 9. Use Of Proposed Exhibits

Do not show anything, including an exhibit or proposed exhibit to a witness without first showing it to opposing counsel. If this procedure is claimed to compromise trial strategy, a pre offer ruling outside the presence of the jury should be first obtained.

Rule 10. Examination of Witnesses

Do not approach a witness without permission of the Court. Please allow the witness to complete his/her answer to your question before asking another question. Do not interrupt the witness in the middle of an answer, unless it's totally un-responsive in which event you should seek a ruling from the Court. Direct examination, cross, redirect and re-cross are permitted. However, the Court does not ordinarily permit re-redirect examination of a witness.

Rule 11. Jury Charge and Verdict Sheet

At the commencement of the trial all counsel shall submit suggested jury charges and a suggested verdict questionnaire. Amendments thereto shall be permitted at the final charging conference. If counsel relies on a Pattern Jury Instruction [PJI] without any change thereto, it should be referred to by PJI number and topic only. If any changes to the PJI are suggested, then the entire proposed charge should be set forth and the changes should be highlighted or otherwise called to the Court's attention. Citations to appropriate statutory or common law authority shall be given in support of suggested non–PJI jury charges or suggested PJI modifications. In addition, unless a marshaling of the evidence is waived, Counsel should, at the final charging conference, provide the Court with the proposed facts which counsel believes should be marshaled by the Court; and the respective contentions of the parties.

SETTLEMENT OF CLAIMS BY INFANTS/IMPAIRED PERSONS

Rule A–1. Compliance With Rules and Statutes

These rules are adopted in recognition of the equitable duty of the court to consider infants and impaired persons to be wards of the court and to protect them as such. Thus, in order to zealously safeguard the rights of infants and impaired persons, this court will require strict adherence to its rules and all other applicable laws and rules. Unless there is a waiver for good cause show, a failure to strictly comply will result either in delay and/or denial. Therefore, make certain before you file that all of the affirmations and affidavits are consistent, and that your application fully complies with and provides all information required by these rules as well as Article 12 of the CPLR; Uniform Court Rule 202.67; and Judiciary Law § 474. If a structured settlement is proposed the application must also comply with General Obligations Law, Article 17, §§ 5–1701 et. seq., as well as with Internal Revenue Code §§ 104 and 130.

These rules also require counsel to complete and file a Worksheet/Checklist. The worksheet/checklist and all of the court's rules and forms are available on the OCA Website.[1] The worksheet/checklist and the supporting affidavits and affirmations must each contain the same information and be consistent.

[1] http://www.nycourts.gov/courts/12jd/civil/allforms.shtml#IA3

Rule B–1. A Worksheet/Checklist

On the same day that a compromise application is filed with the Clerk in Room 217, a completed worksheet/checklist must also be delivered to the Clerk. A courtesy copy should be delivered to the Court in Chambers (Room 828). If the worksheet/checklist is not provided to the Court in Chambers, the Court will

not be aware that the application has been filed in Room 217; and it may result in a delay of the delivery of the file to the Court.

As stated above, all information provided in the worksheet/checklist and in the supporting affirmations, affidavits and other supporting papers must be consistent, especially as it relates to the issues of liability, injuries, present complaints and damages. An explanation or statement which is set forth in the worksheet, but not set forth in the supporting affirmations, (or visa versa) will result in a denial.

Rule C–1. An Ex–Parte Application

CPLR 1207 provides, among other things, that a settlement application which is made upon behalf of an infant/impaired person, must be made either by motion in a pending action, or if no action is pending, by special proceeding commenced upon a petition. However, in the County of Bronx, (with one exception) it has always been the rule and practice to process an infant/impaired person's settlement application as an ex-parte proceeding, i.e., the court is presented merely with a proposed order and all supporting documentation, none of which is required to be settled or served upon defendants; and the compromise hearing is conducted in the absence of all other parties. The one exception to this wholly ex-parte procedure is when a structured settlement is proposed. (See below).

Notice of Settlement For Structured Settlements

When a "structured settlement" is being proposed, although the ex-parte procedure is still being utilized, a Notice of Settlement of the Proposed Order is required to be served on all defendants and upon all insurance carriers involved in the transaction. However, only the Notice and Proposed Order need be served; and this should be accomplished only after the hearing has been conducted.

Because of the complexity of such settlements, and the representations and conditions required to be contained in the proposed structured settlement order, the court requires that the defendants and all insurance carriers involved in the structured settlement transaction be served with a Notice of Settlement of the Proposed Order so that they will have an opportunity to object to the proposed order, and be heard before they are bound by its terms. To reiterate: Only the Notice of Settlement and Proposed Order (not the supporting petition or other supporting papers) need be served.

Rule D-1. The Application and Supporting Documents

The application will consist of the following documents:

1. The Proposed Order (Use the court's form)
2. Counsel's Affirmation
3. Petitioner's Affidavit
4. Infant's Affidavit (If over 14)
5. Supporting Medical Proof
6. Other Necessary and/or Helpful Exhibits
7. For Structured Settlements, also include,
   (a) proposed settlement agreement
   (b) proposed assignment agreement
   (c) proposed annuity contract
   (d) proposed guaranty agreement
   (e) the structure settlement broker's affidavit

(1) The Proposed Order.

The court has provided the following form orders on the OCA website, namely: (a) Standard Compromise Order; (b) Simple Order For a Structured Settlement; and (c) Complex Order For a Structured Settlement. Counsel is required to use one of these orders since they contain all of the decretal paragraphs required by the court. Each proposed order can be adapted to fit the circumstances presented; and each of the form orders for structured settlements are accompanied by a set of instructions which will assist counsel and staff to understand and complete the same.

(2) Counsel's Affirmation.

Counsel must provide an affirmation which not only demonstrates full compliance with, and all information required by, CPLR 1208 and UCR 202.67, but also sufficient details concerning the following issues:

(a) *Petitioner's Standing.* Counsel's affirmation must demonstrate that petitioner is a person who is qualified and has standing to bring the application as authorized by CPLR 1207 (See also, Petitioner's Affidavit, below);

(b) *Counsel's Reasons for Recommending the Settlement* (See below);

(c) *Recent and/or Current Complaints of Infant/Impaired Person* (See below);

(d) *Medical Services and Expenses.* Counsel and petitioner must obtain written proof of the total amount of the charges incurred for each doctor, medical provider and hospital in the treatment and care of the said plaintiff, and the amount remaining unpaid for such treatment and care (See, USCR 202.67 [b]);

(e) *All Possible Liens and Claims.* Counsel and petitioner must provide sufficient documentary proof of either the absence or existence of liens against plaintiff's proceeds; obtain an itemized statement for any payments made by a lienor; and provide sufficient details of the efforts made to resolve said liens. Claims for equitable or contractual subrogation or reimbursement by a private medial insurer or employee benefit plan. (ERISA) must be identified; and the reason for paying or not paying or compromising said claim must be explained in detail;

(f) *Other Related Claims and Possible Conflicts.* (See below);

(g) *Fees and Disbursements of Counsel.* Counsel must set forth all services rendered in support of the request for counsel fees; itemize all disbursements, especially those disbursements, if any, which counsel seeks to have reimbursed.

(h) *Retainer Statement Compliance* (See UCR 202.67 (d));

A Fair and Reasonable Settlement. CPLR 1208 (b) (1) requires counsel to provide the "reasons for recommending the settlement." These "reasons" must be set forth in the supporting affirmations and affidavits, as well as in the worksheet/checklist. Moreover, the Court requires that counsel provide a detailed explanation as to why the proposed settlement is fair and reasonable. In that regard, counsel must address the issues of liability and damages and the infant's current complaints, if any. Note: Conclusory assertions (such as "poor liability"; or "full recovery"; or "best interest of the child") without specification and supporting facts, will not be sufficient.

Recent and/or Current Complaints. The issue of the infant/impaired person's recent or current complaints, if any, must also be fully addressed in petitioner's affidavit, as well as in the current medical proof which is provided to the court in support of the application. If plaintiff does have recent or current complaints, the medical proof must provide a prognosis. Counsel is cautioned to make sufficient inquiry in advance so that the court and counsel are not surprised at the hearing concerning the infant/impaired person's recent, intermittent or current complaints.

All Possible Liens. Note: UCR 202.67 (b) requires the court to make provisions for payment of all medical expenses and liens. The court is concerned that if this issue is not properly addressed, the plaintiff may be surprised and held accountable post settlement. It must be noted that a lien may arise by operation of law if public funds were used to pay for the medicals; and that the lien may have to be satisfied from the proceeds of the settlement regardless of the awareness of counsel or petitioner. *See, Gold v. United Health Services Hospitals Inc.,* 95 N.Y. 2d 683 [2001]; *Arkansas Dept. Health and Human Services v. Ahlborn,* 126 S. Ct. 1752, 2006 U.S. Lexus 3455. Note, that if counsel is proposing a settlement for an amount which is less than what would be considered the "full value" for the damages and injuries suffered by plaintiff, it may be necessary to conduct a hearing for the purpose of apportioning the lien. [*See, Lugo Beth Israel Med. Ctr.,* 819 N.Y.S. 2d 892 (Sup Ct. N.Y., 2006).

Other Related Claims and Possible Conflicts. A full identification of all claims made by any person, including a parent or other family member, arising out of the same accident must be provided. If any such other claims exist, counsel for petitioner must provide a copy of the Bill of Particulars and all medical records for all other settling parties so that with full disclosure, the court can determine if the proposed apportionment of the settlement proceeds is "fair and reasonable." [See also CPLR 1208 (a) (8)].

(3) Petitioner's Affidavit.

Petitioner's affidavit must demonstrate that petitioner is one of the persons authorized by CPLR 1207 to make said application; and it must comply with and contain all information required by CPLR 1208 and UCR 202.67; including details concerning the following issues:

(a) Qualification and standing of petitioner to bring the application (See below);

(b) Petitioner's understanding of the proposed settlement (See below);

(c) Recent and/or current complaints, if any of the infant/impaired person (See below);

(d) Medical services rendered, expenses incurred; method of payment; and liens, if any (See below).

Qualification of Petitioner. CPLR 1207 provides that the application may be made by one of the following persons: a guardian of the property; or guardian ad litem of an infant; or a parent having legal custody; or another person having legal custody; or if infant is married, by an adult spouse residing with infant; or a committee of property of a judicially declared incompetent; or a conservator of the property of a conservatee. *Note:* At times a parent may not qualify, for example, when custody has been removed by the Family Court. Also note, that even where a parent has lawful custody a problem can arise, for example, when the lawsuit is commenced by one parent on behalf of the ward and the compromise application is brought not by that parent, but by the other

parent, who was not named as the natural guardian in the underlying claim or action. In such a situation, counsel must also provide, among other things, proof of the authority of the non-party parent to settle or discontinue the loss of services claim.

Petitioner's Understanding of the Settlement. In addition to all of the above, a petitioner must acknowledge an awareness and understanding of all of the reasons given by counsel for recommending the settlement; as well as a full understanding of the proposed apportionment of the settlement proceeds.

Recent and/or Current Complaints. Petitioner must also acknowledge familiarity with all injuries, conditions and complaints, if any, made by the infant/impaired person especially recent and/or current complaints, so that they can be fully addressed at the compromise hearing. At the hearing the following questions will be asked of the petitioner and the infant/impaired person: Does the infant/impaired person have any recent or current pain or limitations? When is the last time any pain or limitations were experienced? How often? Has plaintiff's physical or mental ability or range of motion, or ability to engage in any activities been affected?; and if so, what is the prognosis or plan for the future? (*Note:* Applications have been denied because, although all the supporting papers, including the current medical report, reflect in a conclusory way that the infant has "fully recovered," at the hearing the court discovers otherwise.)

Medical Services, Expenses, Payments and Liens. CPLR 1208 (a) (4) requires that a petitioner provide an itemization of such expenses; and subdivision (a) (7) provides that the affidavit of the petitioner must state whether reimbursement for medical expenses has been received from any source. *Note:* UCR 202.67 (b) goes further than the CPLR. It not only requires petitioner to provide an itemization of the medical expenses but it compels the court to make provision for payment thereof. Thus, petitioner and counsel are cautioned not to be vague. The court must not be left with only mere speculation as to whether there are any unpaid bills or liens. For example, an unsupported statement that "all medical expenses have been paid", or that they have been "paid by Medicaid" will not suffice without documentary proof of payment. In addition, vague statements such as, "I have not been aware of any unpaid liens or bills," also will not suffice. Note: When it is claimed that the medical bills have been paid by "Medicaid", counsel must obtain and submit the HRA client detailed report [CDR] which will assist the court in determining what, if any, bills have been paid by Medicaid, and which if any such payments are related to the occurrence. Only those bills which are related to the occurrence may be claimed as a lien.

(4) Infant's Affidavit and Attendance.

Note that, absent extraordinary circumstances, CPLR 1208 (d) mandates that the attorney, the petitioner and the infant/ incompetent attend the hearing. It has been the longstanding practice in the First Department to require an infant over the age of fourteen to provide a supporting affidavit, and attend the hearing; and thus this court's rules, forms and worksheets also make it mandatory. At the hearing, the court will question the infant/impaired person as to the episode, the injuries sustained and recent or current complaints and limitations, if any; and where appropriate, their understanding of the terms of the settlement. The court will also view the injured area when it can be accomplished without any embarrassment to the plaintiff and others present.

(5) Supporting Medical Proof.

CPLR 1208 (c) states that "if the action or claim is for damages for personal injuries to the infant or incompetent, one or more medical or hospital reports, which need not be verified, shall be included in the supporting papers" [emphasis added]. Note that neither the CPLR nor any other statute or rule requires that said reports and records be verified. The Court's rules and worksheet provide, however, as follows:

"Unless waived by the Court this part of the application must include a recent [not stale] medical record, report or affirmation which provides:

☐ History obtained;

☐ Infant's complaints of pain and/or limitations (past and present);

☐ Treatment rendered;

☐ Details of the examination currently rendered upon which current opinion and conclusion is based;

☐ Diagnosis;

☐ Prognosis, especially if there are any present complaints of pain or limitations;

☐ Opinion, conclusion and recommendations."

While an affirmation is not required, the court does mandate that a recent [not stale] medical record or report be submitted in support of the application. The said record, report or affirmation should provide all of the above information, especially as it relates to recent or current complaints and/or limitations of the infant/incompetent if any. *Note*: If the issue of present or recent complaints and/or limitations is not addressed in the medical proof submitted, the application will probably be denied. In addition, if there are any recent or current complaints and/or limitations, counsel should make sure that the medical proof provides a prognosis so that the Court and the petitioner can make a meaningful determination as to whether the proposed settlement is fair and reasonable. Sparse and conclusory medical reports or affirmations will not be acceptable.

(6) Other Necessary and/or Helpful Exhibits.

When necessary, the application should have as exhibits a copy of all documents (relating to liability

and damages), which would assist the court in arriving at a determination. When such documents are included they should be appropriately identified in the supporting affidavits and affirmations, as well as separated by Exhibit tabs. Note: Additional documents will be necessary when a structured settlement is proposed (See below)

(7) For Structured Settlements—Other Required Exhibits

When a structured settlement is proposed the following additional exhibits are required to be submitted with the application: (a) the proposed settlement agreement; (b) the proposed assignment agreement; (c) the proposed annuity contract; (d) the proposed guaranty agreement; and (e) the affidavit of the Structure Settlement Broker, (See below, Section F, Structured Settlements).

Rule E–1. The Hearing

CPLR 1208 (d) provides that "at the hearing, the moving party or petitioner, the infant or incompetent, and his attorney, shall attend before the court, unless attendance is excused for good cause" (emphasis added]. If attendance at the hearing would create a hardship for any of said persons, the court will consider waiving the appearance and allowing a telephone conference, if appropriate assurance can be made as to the identity of the person who appears by telephone.

Rule F–1. Structured Settlements

(1) Compliance With Rules and Statutes.

These rules for a proposed structured settlement are supplemental to the above rules for the conventional settlement of claims for infants and impaired persons. Because of the multiple benefits achievable (even for modest settlement amounts), structured settlements are highly favored by this Court provided, however, compliance with all applicable statutes and rules, including the mandates of Sections 104 and 130 of the Internal Revenue Code and the New York State Structured Settlement Protection Act (Gen. Obligations Law, Article 17, § 5–1701, et. seq.).

(2) Compliance With the Internal Revenue Code

One of the benefits of a structured settlement is that the full amount of the periodic payments received as physical injury damages is excludable from the claimant's income by law. By comparison, a claimant receiving damages in the form of a lump sum must pay tax on the subsequent earnings from investing that lump sum.

The Internal Revenue Code, in essence, allows settlement funds to be "invested" in an annuity and grow tax free (U.S. Internal Revenue Code §§ 104 and 130) (hereinafter the "Code".) However, it must be noted that the Code does not (without adverse tax consequences) permit a plaintiff to receive (or even constructively receive) settlement funds and then invest same in an annuity. Such a transaction would result in taxable income. By comparison, in the case of a structured settlement, the plaintiff and the defense agree to settle the physical injury claim in exchange for the defendant's promise to make a stream of periodic payments to the plaintiff. Under section 130 of the Code, the defendant or its liability insurance carrier then assigns its periodic payment obligation to an affiliate of a financially strong life insurance company. The assignment company agrees to receive an assignment of defendant's obligation to pay and then acquires an annuity from the life insurer to fund the periodic payments to the plaintiff. Under the Code, the full amount of these periodic payments (including the appreciation in value between the cost of the annuity and the total benefits paid) is tax-free by law to the plaintiff. In other words, the Code allows a defendant or its liability insurance carrier to use the same settlement proceeds to purchase an annuity and, then assign all payments including the growth thereon, to the plaintiff tax free. Therefore, both the settlement proceeds which are used to purchase the annuity, and the interest earned and paid via that annuity, are tax excludable.

It also has been the court's experience that, in addition to the benefit of providing long-term financial security and fully tax-free compensation for the claimant, structured settlements can assist the parties in reaching a settlement by focusing settlement discussions on what damages the plaintiff actually has suffered and how best to match periodic payments to meet those future needs for medical care, living expenses and educational.

The court therefore, mandates that all settling parties, and all insurance carriers involved in the structured settlement transaction, comply fully with requirements of the Internal Revenue Code.

(3) *Ex-Parte* **Application and Notice of Settlement**.

As stated above, the general rule in Bronx County is to process an infant/impaired person's settlement application as an ex-parte application. However, if a structured settlement or a Qualified Settlement Fund (QSF) is being proposed, Notice to the defendants, as provided below, is mandated by these rules.

When a structured settlement is being proposed, although the ex-parte procedure is still utilized, a "Notice of Settlement" of the proposed "Order" is required to be served upon defendants as well as upon all insurance carriers involved in the structured settlement transaction, so that they will have an opportunity to be heard and object before being bound by its terms. Note: This Notice of Settlement and the proposed Order are to be served only after a hearing has been conducted and after the court has tentatively approved the proposed structured settlement. Note further: Only the Notice and proposed Order [not the underlying supporting papers] need be settled and served on the defendants and insurance carriers.

When plaintiff seeks to establish a "Qualified Settlement Fund" (as a prelude to an apportionment of the settlement proceeds and the use of all or a portion of said settlement proceeds for a structured settlement), defendants must be provided with Notice and be served with a copy of the entire application so that they will have an opportunity to join in or object to the application. For the procedures and implementing regulations necessary to establish a "QSF", see below: "(10) Qualified Settlement Fund".

(4) The Proposed Order for a Structured Settlement.

Counsel must use one of the court's two form orders for a structured settlement, each of which are available on the OCA Website. [1] The form orders (simple and complex), which can be adapted to fit the circumstances presented, comport with Internal Revenue Code requirements; contain all of the decretal paragraphs required by the court; and each form is accompanied by a set of helpful instructions. Each form includes vital information concerning the financial aspects of the structured settlement, and an identification of all of the documents and parties necessary to implement the transaction, namely:

THE PARTIES

(a) The Plaintiff/Payee of Annuity

(b) The Defendant/Assignor

(c) The Assignee/Annuity Owner

(d) The Annuity Issuer

(e) The Guarantor

THE IMPLEMENTING DOCUMENTS

(a) The Settlement Agreement

(b) The Assignment Agreement

(c) The Annuity Contract

(d) The Guaranty Agreement

The proposed "order" for a structured settlement must clearly provide a distinction between the "total settlement cost" and the "total settlement payout."

For tax code compliance,[2] the form orders clearly provide the following distinction between "total settlement cost" and "total settlement payout":

___ (a) The Total Settlement Cost, consists of:

___ (i) Up front funds; plus

(ii) Cost to fund annuity;

(b) The Total Settlement Payout, consists of:

(i) Up front funds, plus

(ii) Total of all future periodic payments.

The form orders also require a listing of all annuity payments with an identification of all payments which are guaranteed to be paid regardless of whether plaintiff survives.

(5) Supporting Documents and Additional Requirements.

In addition to the requirements and documents described above for a traditional compromise application, the application for a structured settlement must also include and be supported by:

(a) Counsel's Affirmation (additional requirements, see below);

(b) Petitioner's affidavit (additional acknowledgments, see below);

(c) Affidavit of the Structured Settlement Broker (see below);

(d) The Proposed Settlement Agreement (see below);

(e) The Proposed Assignment Agreement (see below);

(f) The Proposed Annuity Contract (see below);

(g) Proposed Guaranty Agreement (see below)

(6) Counsel's Affirmation.

In addition to compliance with all other requirements for an ordinary compromise application, counsel for the plaintiff, in support of a structured settlement must:

(a) Demonstrate "due diligence" in the selection of an annuity and a structured settlement broker. (See "Due Diligence and Shopping the Best Deal", below);

(b) Demonstrate that the plaintiff has been provided with the disclosure required by General Obligations Law § 5–1702 and § 5–1701(e)

(c) Annex as exhibits [3] a copy of all of the above described proposed implementing structured settlement documents, as well as copies of the alternative and/or other competitive structure proposals from other annuity providers or from other structured settlement brokers, which were considered and rejected.

(7) Petitioner's Affidavit.

Petitioner's affidavit must, among other things, acknowledge receipt of a copy of all of the above documents as well as a copy of counsel's affirmation in support of the proposed structured settlement; and petitioner must acknowledge that all of the above was fully explained by counsel.

Petitioner must further acknowledge receipt of all of the "initial disclosure" required by General Obligations Law § 5–1702, including the advice "to obtain independent professional advice relating to the legal, tax and financial implications of the settlement, including any adverse consequences." It should be noted that § 5–1701(e) of Title 17 of the General Obligations Law [4] provides that:

" 'Independent professional advice' means advice of an attorney, certified public accountant, actuary or other licensed professional adviser:

(i) who is engaged by a claimant or payee to render advice concerning the legal, tax and financial implications of a structured settlement or a transfer of structured settlement payment rights.

(ii) who is not in any manner affiliated with or compensated by the defendant in such settlement or the transferee of such transfer, and

(iii) whose compensation for rendering such advice is not affected by whether a settlement or transfer occurs or does not occur" [emphasis added].

It must be noted that for the purchase of an annuity (as distinguished from a sale or transfer thereof) a structure broker (whether selected by a plaintiff or a defendant) cannot qualify as an "independent professional adviser" under the above definition. Subdivisions (e) (ii) an (e) (iii) disqualify a defendant selected broker; and subdivision (e) (iii) would also disqualify a plaintiff selected broker.

In any event, unless plaintiff receives a prior waiver upon good cause shown, plaintiff is required by this court's rules to obtain a competing proposal from a structure broker who is selected by the plaintiff and who is independent of the defendant and defendant's liability insurance carrier. It should be noted that in some states (e.g. Texas and California) the involvement and use of a structure broker selected by plaintiff is the accepted norm.

(8) Structure Broker's Affidavit.

This court's rules require that an application for approval of a proposed structured settlement must be supported by an affidavit provided by a structure broker. In addition, that affidavit must conform to, and contain all representations and warranties that are set forth in the form affidavit which has been provided by this court and published on the OCA website, above.

In the annuity field the bargaining agents are structured settlement specialists, and are usually referred to as structure brokers. Most defendants and/or their liability insurance companies have their own list of preferred structure brokers and preferred annuity issuers (life insurance companies). In addition, an annuity issuer will generally sell an annuity only through a structure broker that is appointed as an agent for such issuer. The vast majority of structure brokers, however, operate independently, and are not affiliated with any liability insurance company or annuity issuer. Furthermore, most structure brokers have agency relationships with multiple annuity issuers.

The court is advised that structure brokers are listed in a variety of places including lists maintained by bar associations, by trial lawyers associations and structured settlement trade associations. See, for example, the website maintained by the National

Structured Settlement Trade Association (www.nssta.com) which lists such brokers by state.

The structured settlement application, which is being recommended, must be supported by an affidavit provided by the broker who places the annuity. The affidavit must, among other things, include:

(a) a representation that the cost to purchase the proposed annuity was arrived at after a survey of the market of annuity providers in order to confirm and obtain the best value (price/quality) for same.

(b) a full description of all the other annuity plans considered in addition to the one being recommended;

(c) all other warrantees, assurances and affirmations which are set forth in the form sample broker's affidavit, which is published by this court in the above OCA website.

See, Form Affidavit in the Appendix to these Rules.

The following proposed documents, which will implement the recommended structured settlement, must be annexed as exhibits to the application and referred to in the brokers affidavit:

(a) Proposed Settlement Agreement

(b) Proposed Assignment Agreement [5]

(c) Proposed Annuity Contract

(d) Proposed Guaranty Agreement [6]

(e) Rejected and/or Alternative Proposals

(9) Due Diligence and Shopping For the Best Deal.

This court's rules require counsel for plaintiff, in his supporting affirmation to set forth and explain the efforts made to provide the plaintiff with the best and least costly annuity. When conducting such "due diligence", counsel for petitioner should consider the following observations:

(a) *The Cost of the Annuity*

While a fixed annuity is a contractual obligation rather than a traditional investment product, its future payout, and thus its rate of return, is affected mostly by the interest rates prevailing at the time of purchase. Despite the fact that annuity issuers periodically publish a schedule of rates, which set forth the cost to buy various future periodic payments, other variables affect the ultimate quote. First, rates between carriers may differ and, in any event, the published rates for each carrier are periodically adjusted relative to prevailing interest rates. Second, the cost to purchase an annuity may be affected by the sex and life expectancy of the plaintiff. Third, market place competition, rivalry and circumstances,

which effect each annuity issuer, may also play a part in the annuity's return.

When lifetime benefits are part of the proposed annuity, one unknown variable is plaintiff's real life expectancy. For example, when payments which terminate at death are included in the proposed structure, and the plaintiff, due to some injury or condition, has a shorter life expectancy than normal (and is thus given a "rated age"), the cost of the annuity may be less because the annuity issuer may anticipate making fewer payments. In such cases, although the offered annuity may have a large projected payout (if plaintiff lives to a normal life expectancy), the annuity issuer's actuary "calculates" that the actual payout will be truncated by those "payments" which terminate upon death. In any event, as with mortgage rates, market forces and competition between issuers play a role in the proposed cost of the annuity. The court has been informed that it is not uncommon for the costs quoted by different annuity issuers, for the identical proposed annuity benefit to vary by more than 10%.

(b) *Independence of The Structure Broker*

As noted above, the Internal Revenue Code, in essence, prohibits the direct purchase of an annuity by the plaintiff from the settlement funds. The Code mandates (in order to achieve tax excludability) that the claim be settled in exchange for the defendant' promise to make periodic payments. The defendant then assigns its periodic payment obligation to an affiliate of a major life insurance which then acquires and holds an annuity to make those periodic payments to the claimants.[7]

It may appear therefore, that the Code has indirectly provided the settling defendant or its carrier, with a preference in the selection of a structure broker. It should be noted that, although such a defendant selected broker has no fiduciary relationship with or obligation to the plaintiff, this lack of fiduciary obligation does not mean that such a broker cannot provide the best possible annuity advice and plan. In any event, nothing in the Tax Code precludes a plaintiff, from selecting and receiving advice from a structure broker who can act as a fiduciary for plaintiff and who is independent of the settling defendant and its liability insurance carrier. Indeed the recent experience in structured settlements has been that in serious physical injury cases, most often both parties are receiving advice from their own structured settlement brokers. As stated above, in many states the involvement of a broker selected by plaintiff is the accepted norm.

Unless a waiver is obtained upon good cause shown, the court's rules require, among other things, that the plaintiff obtain annuity advice from a structure broker that is independent of the defendant and its liability insurance carrier. This court's chief goal is to make certain that a settling infant or impaired person is being provided with an annuity which is not only personally designed to meet the plaintiff's needs, but also the best value available from a quality and cost evaluation. Although, it is not the purpose of these rules to imply that these goals cannot be achieved by a broker selected by a defendant, plaintiff is required by these rules to obtain advice from an independent plaintiff selected broker if for no other reason but to introduce competition and market forces to the process. Thus, both brokers are required by these rules to survey the annuity market, and the application must provide an explanation why the proposed annuity represents the best value and is most suitable for this claimant.

Obtaining an independent structure broker may not be a useless precaution. Due diligence in the selection of an independent structure broker is required in order to minimize the exposure of the plaintiff to abuses. Although abuses can occur no matter who selects the structure broker,[8] it is hoped by this court, that the fiduciary relationship created by a plaintiff's selection of a broker, and the competition between both brokers, will not only maximize plaintiff's opportunity to get the best annuity, but also minimize, if not eliminate, the plaintiff's exposure to such abuses. Of course, abuses affecting the structured settlement can also take place after an annuity has been purchased. See, for example, footnote No. 4 at page 17 above, dealing with the predatory practices of "factoring" companies that use overbearing tactics to solicit and purchase these annuity payments at a steep discount. Since the sale of a structured settlement may undermine the goal of the court to provide long term financial security to an injured settling party, counsel is advised that when doing due diligence in the selection of a broker, counsel should refrain from engaging the services of any structured settlement broker or company which has an affiliation with any of these factoring companies. This is not meant to imply that, when an annuitant seeks to sell and transfer an annuity, a broker cannot qualify as a "licensed professional adviser", in accordance with § 5-1701(e) of the GOL; nor is it meant to imply that said broker cannot provide good advice on how the annuitant can maximize the purchase price and not fall victim to a predatory factoring company. However, these services, should be provided at the request of the annuitant. In contrast, it would not seem appropriate for a structured settlement broker to provide the names of its client annuitants to such factoring companies for solicitation purposes; and it would certainly seem unethical, if not illegal, for a structured settlement broker to receive a referral fee or any form of compensation from such a company. It must be noted that the "structure broker's affidavit" which is required by this court's rules must contain a representation that said broker does not have any such relationship with a factoring company.

In any event, as stated above, it is not uncommon for costs of an annuity quoted by different annuity issuers, for the identical proposed annuity, to differ by more than 10%. When considerable sums are involved, 10% can be a very considerable savings to a plaintiff; and hopefully the competition between said brokers will result in a benefit for the plaintiff.

(c) *Compensation For The Broker*:

A structure broker is paid a one time commission of 4% for services rendered in connection with the selection and purchase of an annuity. This commission is paid by the annuity issuer. In theory this commission is not deducted from the settlement proceeds, but this cost is certainly taken into consideration by the annuity issuer when it makes an annuity proposal. But, unlike many other types of investment vehicles there are no ongoing management, advisory, or administrative fees under a structured settlement. This can represent a significant cost savings over the decades of pay-out to a permanently disabled infant or minor plaintiff.

In any event, the issue of compensation and/or commissions for structure brokers must be addressed by counsel in the affirmation supporting the application. When more than one broker is involved, a dispute may arise as to which broker is entitled to the commission. Usually these disputes are resolved amicably with a commission sharing agreement. There are times when an amicable agreement cannot be achieved. In such instances the issue should be brought to the court's attention.

If the issue can be resolved amicably by an agreement between the competing brokers, the court will most likely accept the proposed resolution thereof. If there is a dispute a hearing must be held so that the court can review all circumstances concerning the efforts made by each broker in the selection of the recommended annuity. At the hearing each said broker will be required, among other things, to provide testimony as to the financial advice provided and as to the efforts made to obtain the annuity that provides the best value for the particular circumstances for this plaintiff.

(d) *Guaranteed Payments*

Counsel must be aware of, and not confuse the various forms of guarantees which are available and should be provided to a settling plaintiff/annuitant. There are three distinct guarantees. The "guaranteed" payments mentioned in the annuity contract and in the form orders which have been provided by this court, refer to that portion of periodic payments which will not terminate upon the death of infant/impaired person. Upon death, these "guaranteed" payments will be made to the estate of the infant/impaired person, or to the designated beneficiary of said person. These "guaranteed payments" are not to be confused with the guaranty of the annuity contract which is provided by a "guarantor" company.[9] This guarantor company will guarantee the obligation of the assignee company to fulfill its obligation to make the future periodic payments in accordance with the annuity contract. Neither of these guarantees should be confused with the additional guaranty provided by the Life Insurance Company Guaranty Corporation under New York Insurance Law, Article 77.

Under N.Y. Insurance Law, Article 77, the Life Insurance Company Guaranty Corporation of New York provides $500,000 of protection with respect to an annuity in the event an annuity issuer becomes insolvent if the annuity issuer is licensed in New York and the plaintiff is a New York resident. See, N.Y.S. Ins. Dept. O.G.C. Opinion 95–65 (9/24/95); See also N.Y.S. Ins. Dept. O.G.C. Opinion 5–1–96 (May 1, 1996), General Counsel Opinion 2–20–2003 (February 20, 2003). In view of this, where the amount structured is more than $500,000, it may be prudent, but not required by law, to purchase annuities from more than one annuity issuer in order to keep the cost of each annuity below $500,000. The court is informed, however, that purchasing more than one annuity generally results in lower payments to the plaintiff. In any event, if the proposed annuity is to cost more than the above $500,000 maximum guaranteed by Article 77, both counsel and the structure broker must justify any proposed investment in an annuity which does not take full advantage of that added protection.

(e) *Lock–In Quotes and Notices*

Plaintiff's counsel should avoid placing the court in a "catch 22" by locking in an annuity quote before submitting a structured settlement application for approval. Unless the "lock in quote" acknowledges that it is subject to court approval, counsel must seek court approval before agreeing to a lock-in quote or notice! In any event, the said proposal should be brought to the court's attention expeditiously and before there is any change in prevailing interest rates.

The court might consider imposing a penalty or sanction on those who, by violation of this rule, cause an infant or impaired person to be unable to timely survey the market and obtain the annuity that represents the best value available for the particular plaintiff.

(10) Qualified Settlement Fund

This court's rules require full compliance with the Tax Code and its implementing regulations if a "Qualified Settlement Fund" (QSF) is being proposed. The IRC and its implementing regulation, allow a QSF to be established to resolve or satisfy "one or more contested or uncontested claims." (See, IRC § 468B; Treasury Regulation, § 1.468 B–1; see also, Rev. Proc. 93–34, 1993–2 CB 470, 08/10/1993, IRC § (a) 468b; Rev. Rul. 79–313, 1979–2 C.B. #75; Rev. Rul. 79–220, 1979–2 C.B. #74; Rev. Rul. 83–25, 1983–1 C.B. #116). Thus, a QSF is often used to settle class tort actions.

Caveat: Despite the express authority to create a QSF to resolve "one or more" claims,[10] the issue is still uncertain as to whether, in a single plaintiff action, the attempted creation of such a fund would cause the income portion of each periodic annuity payment to be taxable. Most attorneys and judges will not take the risk of utilizing a "qualified settlement fund" for actions or claims involving only one claimant until a definitive ruling is issued by the Internal Revenue Service that such a fund can provide payments that would be fully tax-free damages in the hands of the claimant.

In any event, the establishment of the QSF is initiated by way of a petition to the court for an order allowing its creation. Once the order is signed, the liability insurer pays the settlement amount into the fund, which deposits same into an interest bearing account, and the liability insurer and defendant are released from all further responsibility and liability. Thereafter, attorneys for the plaintiffs have additional time to propose and seek court approval for the appropriate apportionment and use of the settlement funds, and the creation of the appropriate structured settlement. Of course, while the settlement amount is in the "qualified settlement fund", those funds will earn interest that is taxable. However, when the annuity is ultimately purchased via the monies in the QSF, the future periodic payments will be tax free. The court order establishing the fund must completely extinguish the taxpayer's (defendant's) tort liability; and no amounts may be transferred to the fund other than in the form of a qualified payment.

When a QSF is utilized, the structure broker is apparently selected, not by the defendant or its insurance carrier, but by the administrators of the QSF, a majority of whom are independent of the defendant and its liability carrier. However, defendants may have the right to object to the initial establishment of QSF. See, *Continental Casualty Co. et al v. United States of America*, 2006 U.S. Dist. Lexis 90012, 2006 WL 3455055 (N.D. CAL.; 11/29/06) (Court found that it lacked power establish a QSF over defendant's objection).[11] In *Continental* above, the United States District Court, for the Northern District of California, held among other things, that it did not possess the power to establish a QSF over the objection of the defendant, despite a tax regulation which allows for the creation such settlement accounts.

1 http://www.nycourts.gov/courts/12jd/civil/Fallforms.shtml#IA3

2 The "total settlement payout" and the total settlement cost" are different and must be distinguished in order to obtain the tax advantage provided by the Internal Revenue Code. The total settlement cost consists of the up front monies plus the cost to purchase the annuity.

The total settlement payout consists of the up front money plus the total of all future periodic payments.

For example, if the total settlement cost is $1,000,000 ($400,000 up front and $600,000 to fund an annuity) and the annuity will pay a total of $3,000,000 in future periodic payments, the parties and all implementing documents, including the court's order must, in order to comply with the tax code, state that the case is settled (not for the settlement cost of $1,000,000) but for $3,400,000, the total settlement payout.

3 One set of numerically or alphabetically identified exhibits will suffice for the entire application and they can be referred to in the supporting affirmations and affidavits. Do not have separate exhibits within each supporting affirmation and/or affidavit.

4 Title 17 is the General Obligations Law (entitled the "Structured Settlement Protection Act") was enacted by Chapter 537 of the Laws of 2002, in essence, to protect the rights and interests of injured settling litigants from the overbearing and predatory practices of "factoring" companies which vigorously pursue these individuals and entice them with offers to purchase their annuity payments for a "present value" lump sum cash payment less a steep discount and substantial costs. In the memorandum and other correspondence in support of this legislation it is noted, among other things that, by their practices, these unregulated factoring companies "deprive injury victims and their families of the long term financial security their settlements are designed to provide." Among the reforms enacted in Title 17 is a provision that all such sales and transfers must receive prior authorization of the Court.

5 A standard form assignment agreement called a "Uniform Qualified Assignment and Release Agreement," is generally used to implement the transfer of the obligation to make the future payments. However, if a "Uniform Qualified Assignment, Release and Pledge Agreement" is used, the plaintiff receives a security interest in the annuity policy, and thus becomes a "secured creditor" of the assignment company and receives a priority over other creditors in the event of a default or bankruptcy of the assignee.

6 This guaranty is provided by the annuity issuer, a major life insurance company, or by an affiliated insurer of the annuity issuer, which is licensed to issue insurance and annuity products in the State of New York. The annuity issuer must be rated by A.M. Best at no less than A+ + or A+. This guaranty is in addition to the insurance protection provided by New York State Insurance Law. Under N.Y. Ins. Law Article 77, the Life Insurance Company Guaranty Corporation of New York provides $500,000 of protection with respect to a structured settlement annuity in the event an annuity issuer becomes insolvent if the annuity issuer is licensed in New York and the plaintiff is a New York resident. See, N.Y.S. Ins. Dept. O.G.C. Opinion 5–1–96 (May 1, 1996), General Counsel Opinion 2–20–2003 (February 20, 2003). In view of this monetary limitation, where the cost of the annuity is more than $500,000, it may be prudent to purchase annuities from more than one issuer to keep the cost of each annuity below $500,000.

7 In essence, the Code allows the defendant or its liability insurance carrier to arrange for the purchase of the annuity.

8 Any form of a referral fee, rebate or other form of compensation paid by a structure broker (whether plaintiff or defendant selected) to an attorney or to a party or to an insurance carrier that made the referral, would be considered unethical and illegal. See, for example, *Macomber v. Travelers Property And Casualty Corp.*, 261 Conn. 620, 804 A.2d 180 (Conn. Sup Ct., 2002); and also reported on a subsequent appeal at 277 Conn, 617 (Conn. Sup. Ct. 2006); *Lyons v. Medical Malpractice Insurance Association*, 286 A.S.2d 711, 73 N.Y. S.2d 345 (2d Dept., 2001). It must be noted that these actions are still pending and at this stage of each case we are only left with unproven allegations of wrongdoing; and they are included herein only as an example of the type of wrongful conduct this court is seeking to prevent.

In *Macomber*, above (a proposed class action), it was alleged that Travelers Property and Casualty Corp. entered into an illegal arrangement with certain structure brokers pursuant to which the brokers allegedly agreed to rebate a portion of the annuity commission to Travelers. It was alleged further that as a result of the arrangement, Travelers did not expend the full amount that it had represented to each plaintiff as the cost of the annuity. On that first appeal the Connecticut Supreme Court upheld the plaintiffs' right to bring the action by reversing a lower court's dismissal of six of the alleged causes of action which were brought on behalf of the class. However, the Supreme Court directed the lower court to conduct further discovery in order to fully identify the appropriate class. On the second appeal the Supreme Court held, among other things, that by examining only thirty files out of several thousand when it ruled on a motion for class certification, the trial court engaged in a truncated discovery procedure which could not be endorsed. The case was remanded to the trial court for further action and proceedings.

In *Lyons*, above, it was alleged that the liability insurer and its structure broker misrepresented the value of the annuity as $940,000, when the alleged cost was only $410,000! The court denied defendant's motion to dismiss the action stating that "there are questions of fact as to whether the represented present value was a fraudulent, intentional or negligent misrepresentation ..."

9 The "Assignor, The "Assignee", The "Annuity Issuer" and the "Guarrantor"

The defendant (or its insurer), is the "assignor", and they usually assign the obligation to make the periodic payments to an "assignee" company, which is usually a single purpose corporate affiliate of the "annuity issuer". That "assignee" company will then purchase the annuity contract from the "annuity issuer". The following is required by this court's rules:

The "annuity issuer" must be licensed to do business in the State of New York in order for the annuity to be protected by the Life Insurance Company Guaranty Corporation of New York. The annuity issuer must have an A.M. Best Company rating of no less than A+ + or A+, which are the two highest ratings. The ratings of the proposed annuity issuer must be described in the broker's affidavit and must be supported by an appropriate exhibit attached thereto.

The "guarantor" company must guaranty the obligations of the "assignee" company to make the periodic payments. The guarantor is usually the annuity issuer or a substantial affiliated company. If the assignee itself is a substantial company, which is rated A+ + or A+ and it otherwise qualifies for insurance under New York Insurance Law, Article 77, a "guarantor company" may not be necessary.

10 Section 1.468B–1 (c) of the regulations provides, among other things, "that a fund, account, or trust is a qualified settlement fund if: ***(2) it is established to resolve or satisfy one or more contested claims ***" [emphasis added].

11 In the Continental case the parties agreed to an all-inclusive settlement figure of $1.75 million with the expectation that the settlement would include a structure that would be subject to approval by the Center for Medicaid Services. However, the government's proposed structured settlement terms, were objected to by plaintiffs, and the government then took the position that the only alternative was an all cash settlement. The plaintiffs then asked the Court to enter an order establishing a qualified settlement trust presumably to bypass the DOJ requirements and privately create a structured settlement plan. The plaintiffs also sought an order imposing restrictions "on all settlements by the Torts Branch of the United States Department of Justice, Civil Division." As justification for this extraordinary request for relief, the plaintiff's challenged the legality of the government's settlement terms, including DOJ "requirements": that the government select an annuity broker; that the annuities "provide reversionary interests to the government; and that the settlement documents "prohibit the future assignment of the structured settlement payments.

The Court denied the plaintiffs' petition, observing that it was "not in the position to make policy decisions regarding DOJ settlement practices and finds no illegality in any of the requirements." The Court decision summarized and rejected two of the plaintiffs' complaints as follows:

First, plaintiffs argued that an annuity agent selected by the government would have a conflict of interest in violation of Model Rules of Professional Conduct 1.7(a). Unless the annuity agent is a lawyer, however, the model rules are not binding for annuity brokers. Rule 1.8 applies only to lawyers with current clients who have conflicting interests. The court noted that plaintiffs are represented by independent counsel.

Second, plaintiffs argued that any condition prohibiting assignment of the annuity payments would eliminate rights granted by 26 U.S.C. § 5891. The court noted that section 5891 involves tax exemptions for transfers of structured settlement rights and does not establish a statutory right for such transfers; and that plaintiffs are free to contract away any right of assignment; and that the government can seek such a provision.

In response to the plaintiffs' contention that the regulations under IRC§ 468B empower courts to establish qualified settlement funds the decision explained: "This court may not create a qualified settlement account merely because a tax regulations allows the creation of such settlement accounts."

Rule G–1. Appendix Form—Structure Broker's Affidavit

(NAME OF COURT)

-- x

(CASE CAPTION)

_____ an infant, by his/her Parent and Natural Guardian _____; and _____, individually,

Docket No. _____

Plaintiffs,

-against-   STRUCTURE BROKER'S AFFIDAVIT

_____,

Defendants.

-- x

UNDER THE PENALTIES FOR PERJURY, I [Insert Name of Broker], of [Insert Name of Company], acting as structured settlement consultant in the above matter hereby warrant and represent, under oath, having first been duly sworn, the following facts to be true, complete and accurate to the best of my knowledge, information and belief:

1. No rebates, service fees, administrative fees, or other financial consideration of any kind or in any amount has been paid, will be paid or had been promised to be paid to any party, insurer, attorney, guardian or any other person, firm or corporation associated with this case by me or by my above stated company either directly or indirectly, by virtue of the structured settlement or otherwise, relating to this matter.

2. The cost to the defendant(s) and/or casualty insurer(s) of the structured settlement portion of the settlement in this case is $ _____ inclusive of any applicable qualified assignment fee; and this cost to purchase the proposed annuity, was arrived at after a survey of the market of annuity providers in order to confirm and obtain the best value (price/quality) for the periodic payment plan now recommended.

APPENDIX

3. (Insert name of Defendant or Insurer) will make the following future periodic payments to (Name of Annuitant):

[Provide full benefit payment schedule]

4. The obligation of (Name of Defendant or Insurer) to make the above future periodic payments will be

assigned to _____, the Assignee. (Assignee) may fund the obligation assumed by the purchase of an annuity from (Insert name of annuity issuer), an A.M. Best Company rated A+ or A++ insurer. A guarantee letter will be issued by (Insert name of guarantor) to guarantee the performance of said assignee.

5. The Annuity Issuer company above named is licensed to issue insurance and annuity products in the State of New York.

6. The standard industry commission that we are receiving in this case is based on 4% of the premium of $ ___. This commission is paid by (annuity issuer), the life insurer issuing the annuity policy.

[If more than one broker is sharing in the commission, set forth the details supporting same].

7. The annuity being provided in this case is based upon guaranteed non-life contingent payments for the plaintiff, who is presently ___ years of age, having been born on _____. The annuity cost set forth in number two above reflects this non life contingent annuity cost;

Or

The life insurer(s) providing the annuity or annuities in this case has rated the plaintiff, who is presently ___ years of age, having been born on _____, up to age ___ by reason of plaintiff's medical condition. The annuity cost set forth in number two above reflects this rated age with regard to all life contingent annuity benefit payments Period certain only payments and guaranteed lump sum payments are not affected by rated age;

Or

By reason of said plaintiff's non life impairing medical condition, the annuity being provided in this case is based upon a standard age quote for the plaintiff, who is presently years of age _____ having been born on _____. The annuity cost set forth in number two above reflects this standard age rating. Period certain only payments and guaranteed lump sum payments are not affected by a rated age.

8. Medical underwriting is inapplicable in guaranteed non-life contingent cases;

Or

No medical underwriting has taken place or will take place after the agreement to settle has been reached without full disclosure to both plaintiff and defendant. No post settlement medical underwriting has or will take place to secretly reduce the defendant's cost.

9. No present value calculations were provided in this case. All illustrations provided were based on actual cost only.

10. Neither I nor [company name] is an in-house broker of any party or casualty carrier involved in the

settlement; nor am I or said company affiliated with or an "exclusive" broker of any of any party or casualty carrier involved in the settlement.

11. Neither I nor (Insert name of company) will, without the express consent of the plaintiff and the prior written approval of this court:

(a) provide any information about this settlement to any factoring company for any purpose; or

(b) solicit the plaintiff or plaintiff's family on behalf of any factoring company for any purpose, including, but not limited to, the proposed sale of plaintiff's future periodic payments, nor will I or (Insert name of company) participate, assist, promote, or aid in such solicitation by any person, firm, corporation or entity; or

(c) seek or accept any consideration, financial or otherwise, directly or indirectly from a factoring company.

12. The following documents have been annexed as exhibits to the application made to the court for approval of the recommended settlement proposal:

Exhibit A -   Proposed Settlement Agreement
Exhibit B -   Proposed Assignment Agreement
Exhibit C -   Proposed Annuity Contract
Exhibit D -   Proposed Guaranty Agreement
Exhibit E -   Rejected Alternative and/or Competing Proposals.

THIS STRUCTURED SETTLEMENT AFFIDAVIT IS PROVIDED TO THE PARTIES TO THE SETTLEMENT WITHOUT COST AND WITH THE EXPRESS PURPOSE OF INDUCING THE PLAINTIFF(S), THE DEFENDANT(S), AND ALL PARTICIPATING INSURERS TO ENTER INTO AND/OR PARTICIPATE IN FUNDING THE STRUCTURED SETTLEMENT AGREED UPON IN THIS CASE. STATEMENTS SET FORTH HEREIN CONSTITUTE AFFIRMATIVE REPRESENTATIONS AND WARRANTIES BY THE UNDERSIGNED STRUCTURED SETTLEMENT CONSULTANT.

_____

(Insert name of individual) individually and on behalf of [Insert name of company]

Sworn on before me
this ___ day of _____, 2006

Notary
My Commission Expires:

FORMS

Form 1.   Worksheet/Checklist for Compromise Applications

Index No. _____

NAME OF INFANT/IMPAIRED PERSON _____
    Residence: _____
                _____

    Age & D.O.B   _____   Date of Injury _____

    For a Structured Settlement
        Life Expectancy _____ Years   Rated Age (if used) _____

    NAME OF PETITIONER: _____   Relationship _____

        Residence_____   Phone No. _____
        _____

    ATTORNEY OF RECORD FOR PETITIONER: _____

    Address _____   Phone No. _____
        _____   Fax No. _____
                E–Mail Address _____
    _____

    ATTORNEY APPEARING AT HEARING
    Address _____   Phone No. _____
    _____

THE APPLICATION AND ORDER

Read The Rules and Use the Court's Forms

___ Make certain that all information required by law and the court's rules is set forth in the proposed order and in the supporting papers. It is strongly recommended, therefore, that, before filing an application, the court's rules and instructions be read and that the forms provided by this Court on the OCA Website be utilized! This worksheet /checklist only provides an outline for your guidance.

Be Consistent

Make certain that all information in this worksheet is also included in the formal application submitted to the Court, and that the information contained in both the application and worksheet is consistent.

PROPOSED SETTLEMENT COST   ($_____) [1]

[1] For the ordinary settlement the cost to the defendant and the total settlement payout are identical. However, for a structured settlement the "total settlement payout" and the "settlement cost" are different. For a structured settlement, the "total settlement payout" is the sum of all periodic payments (itemized on the next page) plus the up front amounts listed above. For a structured settlement, the "cost" of the settlement to the defendant is the sum of the up front amounts listed above, plus the sum expended to purchase the annuity. For a structured settlement, it is essential, for income tax purposes, that the documents clearly identify and distinguish both amounts.

☐ If a structured settlement is being proposed please provide details on the next page.

☐ If more than one defendant is contributing to the settlement please provide an explanation and an apportionment of the settlement proceeds.

_____
_____
_____

_____

_____

PROPOSED DISTRIBUTION OF SETTLEMENT PROCEEDS

UP FRONT AMOUNTS	Proposed	Allowed
(1) Counsel Fees	$ _____	$ _____
(2) Legal Disbursements	$ _____	$ _____
(3) Other Disbursements	$ _____	$ _____
Doctor _____	$ _____	$ _____
Liens	$ _____	$ _____
Other	$ _____	$ _____
(4) Up Front Cash to Infant	$ _____	$ _____
COST TO FUND ANNUITY	$ _____	$ _____
TOTAL SETTLEMENT COST	$ _____	$ _____

PROPOSED STRUCTURED SETTLEMENT

TOTAL SETTLEMENT PAYOUT
Up-front Amounts $ _____
Total All Periodic Payments $ _____
    TOTAL PAYOUT $ _____

PROPOSED PERIODIC PAYMENTS:

____ Payable as follows:

____ (1) The sum of ($ _____) per month for the life of the plaintiff [increasing by ___ % per year compounded annually], for a guaranteed minimum of ___ years, with the first payment on _____ and the last guaranteed payment on _____; and

(2)	A guaranteed payment of	($ _____) on _____; and	
(3)	A guaranteed payment of	($ _____) on _____; and	
(4)	A guaranteed payment of	($ _____) on _____; and	
(5)	A guaranteed payment of	($ _____) on _____; and	
(6)	A guaranteed payment of	($ _____) on _____; and	
(7)	A guaranteed payment of	($ _____) on _____; ___	
____(8)	Non guaranteed life payments	($ _____; to full life expectancy	

_____

    TOTAL GUARANTEED PAYMENTS $ _____

_____

_____

    TOTAL PERIODIC PAYMENTS $ _____ [2]

[2] This amount should include the total of all proposed periodic payments _i.e._, non-guaranteed life payments to full life expectancy as well as guaranteed payments.

PARTIES TO THE TRANSACTION   NAMES

____(1) Plaintiff/Payee of Annuity   _____

____(2) Defendants/Assignors;   _____

PARTIES TO THE TRANSACTION   NAMES

___(3) Annuity Owner/ Assignee   _____

___(4) Annuity Issuer   _____

___(5) Guarantor ___   _____

ADDITIONAL REQUIRED SETTLEMENT DOCUMENTS

___ ☐ Affidavit of Structure Broker; ☐ Settlement Agreement;

☐ Assignment Agreement; ☐ Annuity Contract; ☐ Guaranty Agreement

THE AFFIRMATION AND AFFIDAVIT OF COUNSEL AND PETITIONER

Retainer No. _____ Date filed _____ [UCR 202.67(d)]

The supporting affidavit by counsel must recite (check those that apply)

☐ that counsel has utilized one of the court's proposed form orders;

☐ that counsel has read and has fully complied with the court's rules for settlement of claims made by infants/impaired persons; and that counsel's affirmation and petitioners affidavit contains all information required by CPLR 1207, 1208 AND UCR 202.67; and for structured settlements, GOL §§ 5–1700 et seq.

☐ that petitioner is qualified and authorized by CPLR 1207 to bring the application;

☐ that all services rendered and details which support the claim for counsel fees and disbursements have been described; [CPLR 1208 (b) and UCR 202.67 (a)],

☐ that all other claims or other circumstances which might possibly result in a conflict of interest, have been identified;

☐ that all medical services rendered, amounts paid, by whom paid, amounts remaining unpaid and possible liens have been identified; and documentation regarding same has been appended to the application;

☐ that counsel has made personal efforts to ascertain if the infant/impaired person currently has, or in the recent past has had, any limitations or complaints of pain which may be related to the injuries sustained in this action.

☐ that petitioner's affidavit contains an acknowledgment of:

☐ the reasons given by counsel for recommending settlement;

☐ the proposed distribution of settlement proceeds; _____

___ ☐ all injuries, conditions sustained by the infant/impaired person plaintiff, as well as the current and/or recent past limitations or complaints of pain if any, made by said plaintiff;

☐ all medical services rendered, amounts paid, by whom paid, amounts remaining unpaid and all possible liens; and

☐ that for structured settlements; that the form structured settlement broker's affidavit and copies of all of the "additional required documents" above have been appended as exhibits; and that counsel's affirmation includes a discussion of the "due diligence" utilized in selection of a structured settlement broker and an annuity.

☐ whether a previous application for the same relief was denied, and if so, an explanation thereof.

If any of the above recitals are not checked off, please explain _____

_____

_____

_____

_____

_____

_____

Check off and/or describe all of the applicable stages of this proceeding which have been completed. ☐ Action commenced; ☐ Discovery completed; ☐ Note of Issue filed; ☐ Jury selected; ☐ Other _____

Provide the history and circumstances giving rise to the action or claim. [§ 1208 (c) (3)]: _____

_____

_____

_____

Provide the nature and extent of injuries and damages sustained and the present (and or recent, past) complaints, conditions and/or limitations of infant/incompetent, if any. [§ 1208 (a) (4)]

_____

_____

_____

Set forth the period of disability and wages lost, if any: [§ 1208 (a) (4)]: _____

_____

_____

Provide the reasons as to why the proposed settlement is fair and reasonable? [§ 1208 (b) (1)]. Please address the issues of liability and damages and insurance coverage issues if any. Caveat: Conclusory assertions (such as "poor liability" or "best interest of child") without elaboration and supporting facts will not be sufficient and will result in a denial:. _____

_____

_____

_____

Provide the name of each hospital and medical facility and each doctor and medical provider that treated the infant or incompetent. Also provide the amounts charged or incurred and the amounts remaining unpaid. [CPLR 1208 (a)4; UCR 202.67(b)].

Name of Provider	Charge [3]	Unpaid
_____	_____	_____
_____	_____	_____
_____	_____	_____
_____	_____	_____
_____	_____	_____

[3] For each medical provider, proof of payment and an invoice must be provided setting forth the charges for each service rendered and the amounts remaining unpaid. When it is claimed that Medicaid made said payments, an HRA "Client Detailed Report" (CDR) must also be provided.

Identify all persons or entities that paid the medical expenses and identify all liens or potential liens that have been or may be filed. Vague Statements such as, "I am not aware of any liens" or "no liens have yet been filed", are not sufficient: _____

Have medical or other expenses been reimbursed from any source, and if so, identify same [§ 1208 (a) (7)]:

Is the loss of service claim being waived and discontinued? _____
(answer)

If being waived, does the proposed order expressly provide for a discontinuance with prejudice of the loss of service claim? _____
(answer)

If the loss of service claim is not being waived, provide the basis for the amounts claimed:

Identify all claims made by others arising out of same occurrence and the proposed terms of the settlement thereof. [§ 1208 (a) (6) and (8)]. In addition, if other claims are being settled provide a copy of the Bill of Particulars and medical records for each claimant so that the Court can make an appropriate comparison and evaluation of the proposed settlement amounts in order to determine if a fair and reasonable apportionment has been provided to the infant/impaired person:

MEDICAL REPORTS, RECORDS OR AFFIRMATION

Unless waived by the Court the application must include a <u>recent</u> [not stale] medical record, report or affirmation which provides:

(1) History obtained;

(2) Infant's complaints of pain and/or limitations (past, recent and <u>present</u>); [4]

(3) Treatment rendered;

(4) Details of the examination recently rendered upon which current opinion and conclusion is based;

(5) Diagnosis;

(6) Prognosis, especially if there are any present or recent limitations or complaints of pain;

(7) Opinion, conclusion and recommendations.

Caveat: If the infant does have any current, or in the recent past has had, any limitations or complaints of pain, a prognosis must be provided!

Does the recent medical report/affirmation, which you have submitted contain all of the above information; and if not, please explain. Caveat: Do not provide a vague explanation.

_____

_____

_____

_____

THE INFANT'S AFFIDAVIT

If the infant is over the age of 14, said infant must provide an affidavit acknowledging all statements made in the other supporting affirmations; and must state whether or not he/she consents to the proposed settlement. In any event, the infant must appear at the hearing unless a waiver is obtained.

THE HEARING

Unless attendance is excused for a good cause the petitioner, the infant and counsel must attend the hearing. [CPLR 1208(d). This hearing will be scheduled only after the court has had an opportunity to review the application as well as this worksheet/checklist.

FOR THE COURT

Documents Reviewed	Dated	Description/Name
☐ The Order;	_____,	_____
☐ Petitioner's Affidavit	_____,	_____
☐ Infant's Affidavit	_____,	_____ D.O.B.
☐ Attorney's Affirmation	_____,	_____
☐ Medical Report/Affidavit	_____,	_____

FOR STRUCTURED SETTLEMENTS;

☐ Structure Broker's Affidavit _____; and the following proposed documents

☐ Settlement Agreement; ☐ Assignment Agreement; ☐ Annuity Contract; and

☐ Guaranty Agreement

OTHER:

_____

_____

_____

COURT'S COMMENTS UPON REVIEW OF THE APPLICATION:

_____

_____
_____
_____
_____

COURTS COMMENTS POST HEARING: _____

_____
_____
_____
_____

4 If the issue of present and/or recent complaints and/or limitations is not addressed in the application, the application will probably be denied. [See, the Court's Procedures and Rules for Settlement of Claims by Infants and Incompetents.]

Form 2. Authorization for Release of Health Information Pursuant to HIPAA

AUTHORIZATION FOR RELEASE OF HEALTH INFORMATION PURSUANT TO HIPAA

[This form has been approved by the New York State Department if Health]

Patient Name	Date of Birth	Social Security Number

| Patient Address | |

I, or my authorized representative, request that health information regarding my care and treatment be released as set forth on this form:

In accordance with New York State Law and the Privacy Rule of the Health Insurance Portability and Accountability Act of 1996(HIPAA), I understand that:

1. This authorization may include disclosure of information relating to **ALCOHOL** and **DRUG ABUSE, MENTAL HEALTH TREATMENT,** except psychotherapy notes, and **CONFIDENTIAL HIV * RELATED INFORMATION** only if I place my initials on the appropriate line in Item 9(a). In the event the health information described below includes at y of these types of information, and I initial the line on the box in Item 9(a), I specifically authorize release of such information to the person(s) indicated in Item 8.

2. If I am authorizing the release of HIV–related, alcohol or drug treatment, or mental health treatment information, the recipient is prohibited from redisclosing such information without my authorization unless permitted to Jo so under federal or state law. I understand that I have the tight to request a list of people who may receive or use my HIV–related information without authorization. If I experience discrimination because of the release or disclosure of HIV–related information, I may contact the New York State Division of Human Rights at (212) 480–2493 or the New York City Commission of Human Rights at (212) 306–7450. These agencies are responsible for protecting my rights.

3. I have the right to revoke this authorization at any time by writing to the health care provider listed below. I understand that I may revoke this authorization except to the extent that action has already been taken based on this authorization.

4. I understand that signing this authorization is voluntary. My treatment, payment, enrollment in a health plan, or eligibility for benefits will not be conditioned upon my authorization of this disclosure.

5. Information disclosed under this authorization might be redisclosed by the recipient (except as noted above in Item 2), and this redisclosure may no longer be protected by federal or state law.

6. **THIS AUTHORIZATION DOES NOT AUTHORIZE YOU TO DISCUSS MY HEALTH INFORMATION OR MEDICAL CARE WITH ANYONE OTHER THAN THE ATTORNEY OR GOVERNMENTAL AGENCY SPECIFIED IN ITEM 9 (b).**

7. Name and address of health provider or entity to release this information:

8. Name and address of person(s) or category of person to whom this information will be sent:

9(a). Specific information to be released:
- ☐ Medical Record from (insert date) _____ to (insert date) _____
- ☐ Entire Medical Record, including patient histories, office notes (except psychotherapy notes), test results, radiology studies, films, referrals, consults, billing records, insurance records, and records sent to you by other health care providers.
- ☐ Other: _____

Include: (*Indicate by Initialing*)
_____ **Alcohol/Drug Treatment**
_____ **Mental Health Information**
_____ **HIV–Related Information**

Authorization to Discuss Health Information

(b) ☐ By initialing here _____ I authorize _____
              Initials   Name of individual health care provider
to discuss my health information with my attorney, or a governmental agency, listed here:

_____
(Attorney/First Name or Governmental Agency Name)

10. Reason for release of information:	11. Date or event on which this authorization will expire:
☐ At request of individual ☐ Other:	
12. If not the patient, name of person signing form:	13. Authority to sign on behalf of patient:

All items on this form have been completed and my questions about this form have been answered. In addition, I have been provided a copy of the form.

_____   Date: _____
Signature of patient or representative authorized by law.

* Human Immunodeficiency Virus that causes AIDS. The New York State Public Health Law
protects information which reasonably could identify someone as having HIV symptoms or infection
and information regarding a person's contacts.

Form 3.   Standard Compromise Order

At an IAS Part ___ of the Supreme
Court of The State of New York, held
in and for the County of Bronx, at the
Courthouse thereof, located at 851
Grand Concourse, on the ___ day of
_____, 200___.

Present: <u>Hon. Paul A. Victor, J.S.C.</u>

_____x   Index No. _____
                                                  Infants Compromise Order

                         Plaintiff(s),

      -against-

                         Defendant(s).

_____x

Upon reading and filing the petition of _____, parent and natural guardian of the infant herein, duly sworn to the ___ day of _____, 200___; the affidavit of _____, the infant plaintiff who is over the age of 14, having been born on _____; the affirmation of _____, attorney(s) for plaintiff(s), dated the ___ day of _____, 200___; the affirmation of _____, M.D. dated the ___ day of _____, 200___; and the aforesaid mother and natural guardian, and the infant plaintiff, and their attorney having appeared before me on the ___ day of _____, 200___; and upon all of the papers, pleadings and proceedings heretofore had herein; and it appearing that the best interests of the infant will be served by approval of this settlement;

NOW, on motion of plaintiffs attorneys, it is

1. ORDERED,[1] that the aforesaid parent and natural guardian of the infant plaintiff, be and hereby is authorized and empowered to settle the action against the defendant(s)for the sum of _____ ($ _____) dollars; and it is further ordered that the aforesaid sum shall be apportioned and paid by defendant(s) as follows:

    (A) The sum of $ _____ shall be paid by the defendant(s) _____ or its/their insurer as hereinafter provided; and

    (B) The sum of $ _____ shall be paid by the defendant(s) _____ or its/their insurer, as hereinafter provided; and

2. ORDERED that the aforesaid defendant, (identified in 1A above) or its/their insurer pay the aforesaid settlement sum as follows:

    (A) The sum of ($ _____) to the order of the above named attorneys for the plaintiff as and for attorneys' fees, inclusive of all disbursements and expenditures made on plaintiff's behalf; and

    (B) The sum of ($ _____) to the order of _____, in full satisfaction of the outstanding lien for services rendered and/or money advanced to said plaintiff; and

    (C) The sum of ($ _____) to the aforesaid parent and natural guardian of the said infant, <u>jointly with</u> an officer of the _____ Bank, located at _____, said funds to be deposited in said Bank and held therein for the sole use and benefit of said infant, subject to the further order of this Court; and

    (D)[2] The sum of ($ _____) to the aforesaid parent and natural guardian of the said infant, <u>jointly with</u> an officer of the _____ Bank, located at _____, said funds to be deposited in said Bank and held therein for the sole use and benefit of said infant, subject to the further order of this Court; and

and it is further

(3) ORDERED that the aforesaid defendant(s), (identified in 1B above) or its/their insurer pay the aforesaid settlement sum as follows:

(A) The sum of ($ _____) to the order of the above named attorney's for the plaintiff as and for attorneys' fees, inclusive of all disbursements and expenditures made on plaintiff's behalf; and

(B) The sum of ($ _____) to the order of _____, in full satisfaction of the outstanding lien for services rendered and/or money advanced to said plaintiff; and

(C) The sum of ($ _____) to the aforesaid parent and natural guardian of the said infant, jointly with an officer of the _____ Bank, located at _____, said funds to be deposited in said Bank and held therein for the sole use and benefit of said infant, subject to the further order of this Court; and

(D) The sum of ($ _____) to the aforesaid parent and natural guardian of the said infant, jointly with an officer of the _____ Bank, located at _____, said funds to be deposited in said Bank and held therein for the sole use and benefit of said infant, subject to the further order of this Court; and

and it is further

(4) ORDERED, that upon full payment of all of the aforesaid amounts, defendant(s) and its (their) insurer(s) shall have no further liability herein; and it is further

(5) ORDERED, that the funds deposited in (each) said Bank shall be held therein for the sole use and benefit of said infant, subject to the further order of this Court.; and it is further

(6) ORDERED, that (each) said Bank shall place these funds in the highest interest bearing time accounts or certificates of deposit, and said certificates and accounts shall be renewed upon maturity, provided, however, the maturity date of such certificates and accounts or any renewal thereof, shall not extend beyond the date of the infant's eighteenth (18th) birthday; and it is further

(7) ORDERED, that the attorney for the plaintiffs shall serve a copy of this Order upon (each) said Bank and shall arrange for the deposit of said funds as expeditiously as is reasonably possible; and it is further

(8) ORDERED, that within thirty (30) days of the deposit of said funds in the above-designated bank(s) the above guardian shall submit to the Clerk's Office, Room 103, a copy of the certificate of deposit(s) issued by said bank(s); and there shall be no right of withdrawal from any of the aforesaid account(s) and certificates of deposit until the infant plaintiff's eighteenth (18th) birthday, except upon further order of this Court, which said Order shall be certified by the Clerk of this Court; and it is further

(9) ORDERED, that in the event that the balance of the aforesaid account(s) and/or certificates exceeds the then prevailing Federal Department Insurance Corporation limits, the officer-trustee of said Bank and the infant's guardian herein are directed to notify the Court so that a further designation of an individual depository may be made in order to keep the balance of each such account and certificate within federally insured limits; and it is further

(10) ORDERED, that (each) Bank shall pay over all monies held in the aforesaid certificates and accounts to the infant plaintiff herein upon demand and without further Court order when the infant reaches the age of eighteen (18) years upon presentation of proper proof and compliance with the Bank rules of withdrawal; and it is further

(11) ORDERED, that each year (or quarterly as the case may be) during the minority of the infant plaintiff, upon presentation to the above named Bank of a duly executed income tax return or other document showing the amount of income or

estimated tax due on behalf of the infant, said Bank shall provide the infant's guardian herein with checks made payable to the Internal Revenue Service and/or State and/or Municipal Taxing Authority to which said income tax is owed by said infant. However, said checks shall be only for such amounts as may be due and payable for that portion of the infant's personal income tax liability attributable to income earned on said accounts [including interest and penalties thereon] as shown on any official bill therefor issued by the taxing authority. Said check and/or checks shall identify the infant and said infants social security number in order to insure that said amounts are being made for the benefit of the infant; and it is further

(12) ORDERED, that said banks be and hereby are authorized without further order of this court to pay out of the infant's bank accounts, reasonable fees for the preparation of any income tax, return or estimated income tax return or accounting that may be required to be filed by or on the infant's behalf. Said fees shall not exceed $ _____ without the further order of the Court; and it is further

(13) ORDERED, that in the event of the death of said infant plaintiff on or prior to the 18th birth date of said infant, all of the aforesaid sums described in (each) said Bank shall be paid to the estate of said infant plaintiff, or to the designated beneficiary of said estate in the same amount and in the same manner as hereinbefore set forth; and it is further

(14) ORDERED, that the cause of action for loss of services and/or medical expenses of the guardian be and the same hereby is dismissed without costs and with prejudice; and it is further

(15) ORDERED, that conditioned upon compliance with the terms of this order, the aforesaid parent and natural guardian of the infant plaintiff, be and hereby is authorized and empowered to execute and deliver a general release and all other instruments necessary to effectuate the settlement herein; and it is further

(16) ORDERED, that if it appears that any government agency may attach a lien to the infant's payment, this Order may be amended to allow the creation of a Supplemental Needs Trust for the benefit of the infant and the Supplemental Needs Trust will be substituted as the payee of the payments.

(17) ORDERED, that the filing of a bond be dispensed within accordance with the applicable provisions of the Civil Practice Law and Rules.

Hon. Paul A. Victor, J.S.C

1 Paragraphs numbered 1, 2 and 3 are designed for settlements where there are two defendants contributing to the settlement. If there are more than, or less than, two defendants, the number of paragraphs and/or sub-paragraphs should be modified to equal the number of contributing defendants. Superfluous paragraphs should be omitted.

2 If the total sum to be received by the infant does not exceed the then prevailing Federal Deposit Insurance Corporation limits, paragraphs 2(D), 3 (C) and 3A(D) can be omitted.

Form 4.   Simple Order for a Structured Settlement

At an IAS Part ___ of the Supreme Court of The State of New York, held in and for the County of Bronx, at the Courthouse thereof, ___ day of _____, 200___.

Present: <u>Hon. Paul A. Victor, J.S.C.</u>

_____x

            Index No:

**COMPROMISE ORDER
FOR A STRUCTURED
SETTLEMENT**

         Plaintiff(s)

-against-

         Defendant(s)

_____x

Upon the application of plaintiff's counsel for judicial approval for a structured settlement, and upon reading and filing of the petition of _____, parent and natural guardian of the infant herein, duly sworn to the ___ day of _____, 20 ___; the affidavit of _____, the infant plaintiff, duly sworn to the ___ day of _____ 200___; the affirmation of _____, attorney for plaintiff(s), dated the ___ day of _____ 200___; the affirmation/report of _____, M.D., dated the ___ day of _____, 200___; the affirmation of _____, a structured settlement broker, dated the ___ day of _____, 200___; and upon all of the exhibits, papers, pleadings and proceedings heretofore had herein, and/or attached hereto; including, without a limitation thereto, the following documents and proposed implementing agreements: Settlement Agreement [Ex. A]; Assignment Agreement [Ex. B]; Annuity Contract [Ex. C]; and Guaranty Agreement [Ex.D]; and such other exhibits as identified in the above supporting affidavits and/or affirmations; and

WHEREAS the plaintiff(s) and the defendant(s) seek judicial approval for a structured settlement and to settle this action for the sums set forth in decretal paragraph 1; and

WHEREAS it is the intention of the parties to comply with all the requirements of section 104 and 130 of the Internal Revenue Code, relating to a structured settlement; and

___ **WHEREAS** plaintiff has been advised to obtain independent professional advice relating to the legal, tax and financial implications of the settlement; and has received all information required by § 5–1702 of the General Obligations Law, including the amounts and due dates of the periodic payments to be made; the amount of the premium payable to the annuity issuer; the nature and amount of any cost that may be deducted from any periodic payments; and the prohibitions against transfer of the periodic payments; and

STRUCTURED SETTLEMENT TOTAL COST

___ **WHEREAS** the plaintiff(s) and the defendant(s) have agreed upon the sum of $ _____ as the total cost of the settlement to defendant(s) (the "Total Settlement Cost"); and

WHEREAS the Total Settlement Cost is comprised of up-front money totaling $ _____, plus $ _____ to fund the purchase of an annuity contract that will make the periodic payments set forth below, and

STRUCTURED SETTLEMENT PAYOUT

WHEREAS, based on plaintiff's normal life expectancy set forth below, it is expected that plaintiff will receive a total settlement payout of $ _____ ("Total Settlement Payout"), consisting of the up-front money totaling $ _____ plus future periodic payments totaling $ _____ (all of which are set forth in decretal paragraph 1); and

WHEREAS, $ _____ of the above total future periodic payments are guaranteed payments (i.e., payments that are payable regardless of whether the plaintiff is alive); and

THE ASSIGNMENT, ANNUITY ISSUER AND GUARANTOR

WHEREAS the defendant(s) propose(s) to assign the liability to make the aforesaid periodic payments to an "assignee" company, which will purchase an annuity contract from the hereinafter described annuity issuer, which is licensed to do business as a life insurance company in the State of New York, and which is rated A++ or A+ by A. M. Best Company; and

WHEREAS said "assignee" company will have its obligation to make said future periodic payments guaranteed by the hereinafter described "guarantor"; and

LIFE EXPECTANCY AND DATE OF BIRTH

WHEREAS the infant plaintiff is now _____ years of age, having been born on _____; and based on normal life expectancy is expected to live to the age of _____ years; and

THE HEARING

WHEREAS the (petitioner/the mother and natural guardian) and the (infant/impaired person) plaintiff and their attorney having appeared before me on the ___ day of _____ 200___; and it appearing that the best interests of the infant will be served by approval of this proposed settlement;.

NOW THEREFORE, it is

1. **ORDERED**, that the plaintiff(s) and the defendant(s) be, and hereby are, authorized and empowered to execute a settlement agreement to settle this action for a total payout consisting of the up-front sum of $ _____, (as apportioned in paragraph 2 (A) below) plus the following periodic payments:

(A) The sum of $ _____ per month for the life of the infant plaintiff [increasing by ___ % per year compounded annually], for a guaranteed minimum of ___ years with the first payment on _____ and the last guaranteed payment on _____; and

(B) A guaranteed payment of $ _____ on _____; and

(C) A guaranteed payment of $ _____ on _____; and

(D) A guaranteed payment of $ _____ on _____; and

(E) A guaranteed payment of $ _____ on _____; and

(F) A guaranteed payment of $ _____ on _____; and

(G) A guaranteed payment of $ _____ on _____; and

(H) A guaranteed payment of $ _____ on _____; and

(I) A guaranteed payment of $ _____ on _____; and

(J) A guaranteed payment of $ _____ on _____; and

(K) A guaranteed payment of $ _____ on _____; and

all of which said periodic payments shall be made payable to (here name the payee); and it is further

2. **ORDERED** that the Total Settlement Cost of $ _____ shall be paid by the defendant(s) within 20 days of the service of this signed order, as follows:

UP–FRONT MONEY

(A)(1) The sum of $ _____ to the order of _____ the attorneys for the plaintiff as and for attorneys fees, inclusive of all disbursements and expenditures made on plaintiff's behalf; and

(2) The sum of $ _____ to the order of said attorneys for plaintiff as and for disbursements and expenditures made on behalf of the plaintiff; and

(3) The sum of $ _____ to the order of _____, in full satisfaction of the outstanding lien for services rendered and/or money advanced to said plaintiff; and

(4) The sum of $ _____ to the order of _____, the parent and natural guardian of the said infant, jointly with an officer of the _____ Bank, located at _____; said funds to be deposited in said Bank and held therein for the sole us and benefit of said infant, subject to the further order of this Court; and

COST OF ANNUITY

(B) The sum of $ _____ to the order of _____ to fund the purchase of a structured settlement annuity which will provide the periodic payments described in paragraph 1 above; and it is further

3. **ORDERED**, that the defendant (the "Assignor"), shall make a qualified assignment under Section 130 of the Internal Revenue Code to _____ (the "Assignee") of the Assignor's obligation to make the periodic payments set forth in Paragraph 1; and it is further

4. **ORDERED**, that aforesaid Assignee shall fund its obligation to make such periodic payments by the purchase of an annuity contract at a cost of $ _____ from _____ (the "Annuity Issuer") which is licensed to do business as a life insurance company in the State of New York, and which is rated _____ by A.M. Best Company; and it is further

5. **ORDERED** that in accordance with the terms of said assignment, the aforesaid Assignee shall be substituted as obligor of such periodic payments for the Assignor, which shall be released from any further obligation to make said periodic payments; and it is further

6. **ORDERED**, that the obligations of the Assignee to make the periodic payments shall be guaranteed by _____ ("Guarantor"); and it is further

7. **ORDERED**, that none of the above described obligors and guarantors, nor the infant, nor his/her guardian, nor any payee may sell, assign, pledge, transfer or encumber the annuity benefits hereinabove described or take any other action to defeat or impair the intent of this Court to provide to the infant plaintiff the payments hereinabove set forth, absent a further order of the Court; and it is further

8. **ORDERED**, that plaintiff's attorney shall serve upon the plaintiff, a copy of this executed order and all supporting papers, as well as a copy of the final and executed structure documents (including the annuity contract, the settlement agreement, the assignment agreement; and the guarantee agreement); and counsel shall file a copy of all of the above with the office of the Clerk for the Court, together with proof of service of same; and it is further

9. **ORDERED**, that aforesaid depository Bank which, pursuant to this Order, receives funds jointly with the parent and natural guardian of the infant, shall place said funds in the highest interest bearing time accounts or certificates of deposit, and said certificates and accounts shall be renewed upon maturity, provided, however, the maturity date of such certificates and accounts or any renewal thereof, shall not extend beyond the date of the infant's eighteenth (18th) birthday; and it is further

10. **ORDERED**, that the attorney for the plaintiffs shall serve a copy of this Order upon said Bank and shall arrange for the deposit of said funds as expeditiously as is reasonably possible; and it is further

11. **ORDERED,** that within thirty (30) days of the deposit of said funds in the above-designated bank(s) the above guardian shall submit to the Office of the Clerk for the Court, a copy of each certificate of deposit(s) issued by said bank(s); and there shall be no right of withdrawal from any of the aforesaid account(s) and certificates of deposit until the infant plaintiff's eighteenth (18th) birthday, except upon further order of this Court, which said Order shall be certified by the Clerk of this Court; and it is further

12. **ORDERED,** that in the event that the amount on deposit at any Bank exceeds the then prevailing Federal Deposit Insurance Corporation limits, the officer-trustee of said Bank and the infant's guardian herein are directed to notify the Court so that a further designation of an additional depository may be made in order to keep the amount within federally insured limits; and it is further

13. **ORDERED,** that said Bank shall pay over all monies held in the aforesaid certificates and accounts to the infant plaintiff herein upon demand and without further Court order when the infant reaches the age of eighteen (18) years upon presentation of proper proof and compliance with the Bank rules of withdrawal; and it is further

14. **ORDERED,** that each year (or quarterly as the case may be) during the minority of the infant plaintiff, upon presentation to the above Bank of a duly executed income tax return or other document showing the amount of income tax or estimated income tax due on behalf of the infant, said Bank shall provide the infant's guardian herein with checks made payable to the Internal Revenue Service and/or State and/or Municipal Taxing Authority to which said income tax is owed by said infant. However, said checks shall be only for the amounts as may be due and payable for that portion of the infant's personal income tax liability attributable to income earned on the accounts maintained pursuant to this Order [including interest and penalties thereon] as shown on any official bill therefor issued by the taxing authority. Said checks shall identify the infant and said infant's social security number in order to insure that said amounts are being made for the benefit of the infant; and it is further

15. **ORDERED,** that the above Bank is hereby authorized without further order of this Court to pay out of the infant's bank accounts, reasonable fees for the preparation of any income tax return or estimated income tax return or accounting that may be required to be filed by or on the infant's behalf. Said fees shall not exceed $ _____ without the further order of the Court; and it is further

16. **ORDERED,** that in the event of the death of said infant plaintiff prior to the date of any guaranteed periodic payment, all sums shall be paid to the estate of said infant plaintiff unless, upon reaching the age of 18, the infant plaintiff has changed his designated beneficiary, in which event said sums shall be paid to said designated beneficiary; and it is further

17. **ORDERED,** that the cause of action for loss of services and/or medical expenses of the guardian be and the same hereby is dismissed without costs and with prejudice; and it is further

18. **ORDERED,** that conditioned upon compliance with the terms of this order, the aforesaid parent and natural guardian of the infant plaintiff, be and hereby is authorized and empowered to execute and deliver a general release and all other instruments necessary to effectuate the settlement herein; and it is further

19. **ORDERED,** that upon the payment of the amounts set forth in paragraph 2 and execution of the settlement agreement and the assignment agreement, defendant and its insurer shall have no further liability herein; and it is further

20. **ORDERED,** that if it appears that any government agency may attach a lien to the infant's payment, this Order may be amended to allow the creation of a Supplemental Needs Trust for the benefit of the infant and the Supplemental Needs Trust will be substituted as the payee of the payments.

21. **ORDERED,** that the filing of a bond be dispensed with in accordance with the applicable provisions of the Civil Practice Law and Rules.

_____
Date   Hon. Paul A. Victor, J.S.C.

INSTRUCTIONS FOR THE SIMPLE ORDER
FOR A STRUCTURED SETTLEMENT

The Court's Rules and Forms

This form is designed for settlements where there is only one defendant (and its insurer) participating in the settlement and in the funding of the purchase of the annuity. If there is a different number of defendants, or more than one annuity is being purchased, the form must be modified accordingly; or the alternate form order (for complex settlements), should be used.

Before completion and submission of the application to settle a claim or action of an infant or impaired person, counsel is cautioned to read the court's rules and to use the court's forms; all of which are available on the OCA website. If counsel has any question, or is unsure of how to proceed, counsel is invited to call Chambers and arrange for an appointment to discuss the matter before an application is filed.

After a hearing has been conducted you will be required to serve a copy of the proposed structured settlement order on all defendants and insurance carriers, with a Notice of Settlement so that they will have an opportunity to be heard and object before being bound by its terms. Note: only the proposed order need be served, not the underlying supporting papers.

Preamble (Whereas) Clause

The terms of the settlement and other relevant information and requirements are outlined in the "Whereas" clauses. Note: This form complies with the requirements of the Internal Revenue Code and explains in its opening "Whereas" clauses, the significant difference between the "Total Settlement Payout" and the "Total Settlement Cost." Decretal Paragraph 1 has been specifically designed to comply with Internal Revenue Code requirements and should not be modified, (except however, to conform it to the specific periodic payments proposed in this application). Note, that when all future periodic payments are guaranteed, the amount set forth in the Whereas Clauses for "future periodic payments" and for "guaranteed periodic payments" will obviously be identical. However, if any of the future periodic payments will terminate upon death, the above amounts will be different. In any event, the whereas clauses can be modified accordingly.

All information set forth in the proposed "Order" must be supported by the underlying affidavits and affirmations as well as in the required exhibits. The proposed implementing structured settlement documents must be appended as exhibits to the application. These exhibits must identify all the necessary parties thereto as well as the annuity payout being proposed.

A structured settlement plan will be approved by the court after a hearing has been conducted. In most instances defendants insist that a structure plan be provided by a structure broker that is selected by defendant and/or its insurer. The Court requires that plaintiff's counsel retain a structure broker before discussing a structured settlement with the defendants, [See, City Part Rules for Settlement of Claims By Infants and Impaired Persons]. Both brokers can be compensated by a splitting of the annuity commission so there is no cost to the plaintiff or the attorney. If there is a dispute regarding commissions, request a hearing and request or subpoena all necessary persons to be present.

The application to settle the claim must be supported by an affidavit by the structure broker whose structure plan is recommended to the court by plaintiff's counsel to be best for the infant/impaired person. This affidavit must conform to the form affidavit provided by this court on the OCA website. After a hearing and review of all submitted plans, and all circumstances leading up to the proposed plan this court will select and approve one of the plans, as well determine the appropriate apportionment of commissions.

Decretal Paragraph No. 1

___ Modify the form to comport with the proposed periodic payments which are described in the underlying documents, but do not otherwise modify the format since this paragraph was designed to comply with Internal Revenue Code requirements.

The Guarantees

The "guaranteed" payments mentioned in this paragraph (as well as in the preamble "Whereas" clauses) refer to that part of periodic payments that will not terminate upon the death of the infant/impaired person. Upon death, these "guaranteed" payments will be made to the estate of the infant/impaired person, or to the designated beneficiary of said person. The "guarantee" mentioned in this paragraph is not to be confused with the guaranty which is provided by a "guarantor" company which will guarantee the obligation of the assignee company to make all of the future periodic payments [See, decretal paragraph No. 6]. Nor should the guarantee mentioned in decretal paragraph 1 be confused with the additional guaranty provided under New York Insurance Law, Article 77.

Under N.Y. Ins. Law Article 77, the Life Insurance Company Guaranty Corporation of New York provides $500,000 of protection with respect to an annuity in the event an annuity issuer becomes insolvent if the annuity issuer is licensed in New York and the plaintiff is a New York resident. See N.Y.S. Ins. Dept. O.G.C. Opinion 95–65 (9/24/95); See also N.Y.S. Ins. Dept. O.G.C. Opinion 5–1–96 (May 1, 1996), General Counsel Opinion 2–20–2003 (February 20, 2003). In view of this, where the amount structured is more than $500,000, it is prudent, but not required by law, to purchase annuities from more than one issuer to keep the cost of each annuity below $500,000. The court is informed, however, that purchasing more than one annuity generally results in lower payments to the plaintiff.

The Payee

At the end of decretal paragraph No. 1, insert the name of the "payee." Here you should insert the name the infant plaintiff individually if payments commence on or after infant's 18th birthday. If payments commence before the 18th birthday or if payments are to an impaired person, provisions must be made for payments to the parent or guardian together with a Bank Officer; or to a guardian appointed pursuant to Article 81 of the Mental Health Law. In cases where an infant or impaired person is receiving, or may in the future receive, needs based governmental benefits, such as Medicaid or Supplemental Security income, Counsel should consider making provision for, and the order should provide for, the creation of a Supplemental Needs Trust to preserve eligibility for such benefits, in which event the trust should be named as the payee in this paragraph.

Decretal Paragraph No. 2

Paragraph (A) sets forth the up-front money to be paid by defendants, to cover the costs for plaintiff's counsel fees, disbursements, liens and up front money to the plaintiff, if any. If other up-front money must be added, the form should be modified accordingly. Paragraph (B) provides for the payment by defendant to fund the purchase of an annuity which will provide the future periodic payments. If this defendant is purchasing more than one annuity, then an additional subparagraph should be added for each payment toward an annuity.

Decretal Paragraphs No. 3 and No. 4

___ The "Assignor', The "Assignee" and The "Annuity Issuer"

The defendant (or its insurer), the "assignor", usually assigns the obligation to make the periodic payments to an "assignee" company, which is usually a shell affiliate of the annuity issuer. That "assignee" company will then purchase the annuity contract from the annuity issuer.

The "annuity issuer" must be licensed to do business in the State of New York, in order for the annuity to be protected by the Life Insurance Company Guaranty

Corporation of New York discussed above, and it should have an A.M. Best Company rating of no less than A++ or A+, which are the two highest ratings. The ratings of the proposed annuity issuer must be described in the broker's affidavit and must be supported by an appropriate exhibit attached thereto.

The "Settlement Agreement" and the "Assignment Agreement"

The "Settlement Agreement" and the "Assignment Agreement" will provide among other things, that the defendant (or its insurer) will assign the obligation to make the future periodic payments to an assignment company which is usually an affiliate of the annuity insurer. In decretal paragraph No.3 that assignment company (the "assignee") must be identified, and in decretal paragraph No. 4, the life insurance company (the "annuity issuer") and its A.M. Best Company rating must be set forth.

The Court's Rules for a structured settlement require a copy of each of the proposed agreements to be submitted as exhibits to the structured settlement broker's affidavit, which is submitted in support of the application to settle the claim or action. There is no standard form of "settlement agreement." However, there are several forms of assignment agreements generally used in structured settlements. The plaintiff should request that the form known as the Uniform Qualified Assignment, Release and Pledge Agreement be used, since it grants the plaintiff a security interest in the annuity. Most annuity issuers will use such a form, if requested. If the annuity issuer does not offer a security interest, then the "Uniform Qualified Assignment and Release Agreement" must be used, and the plaintiff will be a general, unsecured creditor of the Assignee. Please note, that decretal paragraph No.8 of the order requires, among other things that, after all of the documents have been signed, a copy of each must be provided to plaintiff by plaintiff's counsel; and proof of service of same must be filed with the Clerk of the Court.

Decretal Paragraph No. 6

The "Guarantor"

Here insert the name of the "guarantor" company. The obligations of the "assignee" company to make the periodic payments are guaranteed by the annuity issuer or a substantial affiliated company unless the assignee is a substantial company.

Notice of Settlement

After a hearing has been conducted you will be required to serve a copy of the proposed structured settlement order on all defendants and insurance carriers, with a Notice of Settlement so that they will have an opportunity to be heard and object before being bound by its terms. Note: only the proposed order need be served, not the underlying supporting papers.

___ The order will be signed on the "settlement" date, if no issue or objection has been raised by the defendant or the insurance carriers involved in the transaction.

Compliance With Remainder of Decretal Paragraphs

Counsel should carefully read and implement the remainder of the decretal paragraphs after the order has been signed. The order will be signed on the "settlement date" if no issue or objection has been raised by the defendants or the insurance carriers involved in the transaction.

Counsel should take special notice of the obligations imposed by decretal paragraphs No. 8 and 11 which, among other things, require service of the documents on plaintiff, and the filing of the documents with the Clerk for the Court, with proof of compliance.

Form 5. Complex Order for a Structured Settlement

At an IAS Part ___ of the Supreme
Court of The State of New York, held
in and for the County of Bronx, at the
Courthouse thereof, located at 851
Grand Concourse, on the ___ day of
_____, 200___.

Present: Hon. Paul A. Victor, J.S.C.

_____x

                                                Index No. _____

                        Plaintiff(s)   **COMPROMISE ORDER
                                           FOR A STRUCTURED
                                           SETTLEMENT**

        -against-

                        Defendant(s)
_____x

Upon the application of plaintiff's counsel for judicial approval for a structured settlement and upon reading and filing the petition of _____, parent and natural guardian of the infant herein, duly sworn to the ___ day of _____, 200___; the affidavit of _____, the infant plaintiff, duly sworn to the ___ day of _____ 200___; the affirmation of _____, attorney for plaintiff(s), dated the ___ day of _____ 200___; the affirmation report of _____, M.D., dated the ___ day of _____, 200___; the affirmation of _____, a structured settlement broker, dated the ___ day of _____, 200___; and upon all of the exhibits, papers, pleadings and proceedings heretofore had herein, and/or attached hereto; including, without a limitation thereto, the following documents and proposed implementing agreements: Settlement Agreement [Ex.A]; Assignment Agreement [Ex.B]; Annuity Contract [Ex.C]; and Guaranty Agreement [Ex. D]; and such other exhibits as identified in the above supporting affidavits and/or affirmations; and

WHEREAS the plaintiff(s) and the defendant(s) seek judicial approval for a structured settlement and to settle this action for the sums set forth in decretal paragraph 1; and

WHEREAS it is the intention of the parties to comply with all the requirements of section 104 and 130 of the Internal Revenue Code, relating to a structured settlement; and.

WHEREAS plaintiff has been advised to obtain independent professional advice relating to the legal, tax and financial implications of the settlement; and has received all information required by § 5–1702 of the General Obligations Law, including the amounts and due dates of the periodic payments to be made; the amount of the premium payable to the annuity issuer; the nature and amount of any cost that may be deducted from any periodic payments; and the prohibitions against transfer of the periodic payments; and

STRUCTURED SETTLEMENT TOTAL COST

___ **WHEREAS** the plaintiff(s) and the defendant(s) have agreed upon the sum of $ _____ as the total cost of the settlement to defendant(s) (the "Total Settlement Cost"); and

WHEREAS the "Total Settlement Cost" is comprised of up-front money totaling $ _____, plus $ _____ to fund the purchase of an annuity contract that will make the periodic payments set forth below, and

STRUCTURED SETTLEMENT PAYOUT

WHEREAS, based on plaintiff's normal life expectancy set forth below, it is expected that plaintiff will receive a total settlement payout of $ _____ ("Total Settlement Payout"), consisting of the up-front money totaling $ _____ plus future periodic payments totaling $ _____ (all of which are set forth in decretal paragraph 1); and

WHEREAS, $ _____ of the above total future periodic payments are guaranteed payments (i.e., payments that are payable regardless of whether the plaintiff is alive); and

THE ASSIGNMENT, ANNUITY ISSUER AND GUARANTOR

WHEREAS the defendant(s) propose(s) to assign the liability to make the aforesaid periodic payments to an "assignee" company, which will purchase an annuity contract from the hereinafter described annuity issuer, which is licensed to do business as a life insurance company in the State of New York, and which is rated A++ or A+ by A. M. Best Company; and

WHEREAS said "assignee" company will have its obligation to make said future periodic payments guaranteed by the hereinafter described "guarantor"; and

LIFE EXPECTANCY AND DATE OF BIRTH

WHEREAS the infant plaintiff is now _____ years of age, having been born on _____; and based on normal life expectancy is expected to live to the age of _____ years; and

THE HEARING

WHEREAS the (petitioner/the mother and natural guardian) and the (infant/impaired person) plaintiff and their attorney having appeared before me on the ___ day of _____ 200___; and it appearing that the best interests of the infant will be served by approval of this settlement:

NOW THEREFORE, it is

1. **ORDERED**, that the plaintiff(s) and the defendant(s) be, and hereby are, authorized and empowered to execute a settlement agreement to settle this action for a total payout consisting of the up-front money totaling ($ _____), (as hereinafter apportioned in paragraphs 3 and 4 below) plus the following periodic payments:

(A) The sum of ($ _____) per month for the life of the infant plaintiff [increasing by ___ % per year compounded annually], for a guaranteed minimum of _____ years with the first payment on _____ and the last guaranteed payment on _____; and

(B) A guaranteed payment of ($ _____) on _____; and

(C) A guaranteed payment of ($ _____) on _____; and

(D) A guaranteed payment of ($ _____) on _____; and

(E) A guaranteed payment of ($ _____) on _____; and

(F) A guaranteed payment of ($ _____) on _____; and

(G) A guaranteed payment of ($ _____) on _____; and

all of which said periodic payments shall be made payable to (here name the payee); and it is further

2. **ORDERED**, that the Total Settlement Cost of _____ ($ _____) (as further apportioned in paragraphs 3 and 4 below) shall be paid by the defendants, within 20 days of this order, as follows:

(A) The sum of ($ _____) shall be paid by the defendant _____ or its/their insurer and apportioned as hereinafter provided; and

(B) The sum of ($ _____) shall be paid by the defendant _____ or its/their insurer and apportioned as hereinafter provided; and it is further

3. **ORDERED**, that the aforesaid settlement cost to be paid by the defendant(s), identified in paragraph 2(A) above, shall be paid within 20 days of this signed order, as follows:

UP–FRONT MONEY

(A)(1) The sum of ($ _____) to the order of _____ the attorneys for the plaintiff as and for attorneys fees, for services rendered on plaintiff's behalf; and

(2) The sum of $ _____ to the order of said attorneys for plaintiff as and for disbursements and expenditures made on behalf of the plaintiff; and

(3) The sum of ($ _____) to the order of _____, in full satisfaction of the outstanding lien for services rendered and/or money advanced to said plaintiff; and

(4) The sum of ($ _____) to the aforesaid parent and natural guardian of the said infant, jointly with an officer of the _____ Bank, located at _____, said funds to be deposited in said Bank and held therein for the sole use and benefit of said infant, subject to the further order of this Court; and

COST TO FUND ANNUITY

(B)(1) The sum of ($ _____) to the order of _____ to fund the purchase of a structured settlement annuity; and it is further

4. **ORDERED**, that the aforesaid settlement cost to be paid by the defendant(s) identified in paragraph 2(B) above, shall be paid within 20 days of the signed order, as follows:

UP–FRONT MONEY

(A)(1) The sum of ($ _____) to the order of the above named attorneys for the plaintiff as and for attorneys fees, for services rendered on plaintiff's behalf; and

(2) The sum of $ _____ to the order of said attorneys for plaintiff as and for disbursements and expenditures made on behalf of the plaintiff; and

(3) The sum of ($ _____) to the order of _____, in full satisfaction of the outstanding lien for services and/or money advanced to said plaintiff; and

(4) The sum of ($ _____) to the aforesaid parent and natural guardian of the said infant, jointly with an officer of the _____ Bank, located at _____, said funds to be deposited in said Bank and held therein for the sole use and benefit of said infant, subject to the further order of this Court; and it is further

COST TO FUND ANNUITY

(B)(1) The sum of ($ _____) to the order of _____ to fund the purchase of a structured settlement annuity; and it is further

5. ORDERED, that the defendant identified in paragraph 2(A), (the "Assignor") shall make a qualified assignment under Section 130 of the Internal Revenue Code to _____ (the "Assignee") of the Assignor's obligation to make the periodic payments set forth in Paragraph 1; and it is further

6. ORDERED, that aforesaid Assignee shall fund its obligation to make such periodic payments by the purchase of an annuity contract at a cost of ($ _____) from _____ (the "Annuity Issuer"), which is licensed to do business as a life insurance company in the State of New York, and which is rated _____ by A.M. Best Company; and it is further

7. ORDERED that in accordance with the terms of said assignment, the (each) aforesaid Assignee shall be substituted as obligor of such periodic payments for the Assignor, which shall be released from any further obligation to make said periodic payments; and it is further

8. ORDERED, that the obligations of the Assignee to make the periodic payments shall be guaranteed by _____ ("Guarantor"); and it is further

9. ORDERED, that none of the above described obligors and guarantors, nor the infant, nor his/her guardian, nor any payee may sell, assign, pledge, transfer or encumber the annuity benefits hereinabove described or take any other action to defeat or impair the intent of this Court to provide to the infant plaintiff the payments hereinabove set forth, absent a further order of the Court; and it is further

10. ORDERED, that plaintiff's attorney shall serve upon the plaintiff, a copy of this executed order and all supporting papers, as well as a copy of the final and executed structure documents (including the annuity contract, the settlement agreement, the assignment agreement; and the guarantee agreement); and counsel shall file a copy of all of the above with the office of the Clerk for the Court, together with proof of service of same; and it is further

11. ORDERED, that [each] aforesaid depository Bank which, pursuant to this Order, receives funds jointly with the parent and natural guardian of the infant, shall place said funds in the highest interest bearing time accounts or certificates of deposit, and said certificates and accounts shall be renewed upon maturity, provided, however, the maturity date of such certificates and accounts or any renewal thereof, shall not extend beyond the date of the infant's eighteenth (18th) birthday; and it is further

12. ORDERED, that the attorney for the plaintiffs shall serve a copy of this Order upon (each) said Bank and shall arrange for the deposit of said funds as expeditiously as is reasonably possible; and it is further

13. ORDERED, that within thirty (30) days of the deposit of said funds in the above-designated bank(s) the above guardian shall submit to the Office of the Clerk for the Court, a copy of each certificate of deposit(s) issued by said bank(s); and there shall be no right of withdrawal from any of the aforesaid account(s) and certificates of deposit until the infant plaintiff's eighteenth (18th) birthday, except upon further order of this Court, which said Order shall be certified by the Clerk of this Court; and it is further

14. ORDERED, that in the event that the amount on deposit at any Bank exceeds the then prevailing Federal Deposit Insurance Corporation limits, the officer-trustee of said Bank and the infant's guardian herein are directed to notify the Court so that a further designation of an additional depository may be made in order to keep the amount within federally insured limits; and it is further

15. ORDERED, that (each) said Bank shall pay over all monies held in the aforesaid certificates and accounts to the infant plaintiff herein upon demand and without further Court order when the infant reaches the age of eighteen (18) years upon presentation of proper proof and compliance with the Bank rules of withdrawal; and it is further

16. ORDERED, that each year (or quarterly as the case may be) during the minority of the infant plaintiff, upon presentation to the Bank referred to in Paragraph 3(a) hereof of a duly executed income tax return or other document showing the amount of income tax or estimated income tax due on behalf of the infant, said Bank shall provide the infant's guardian herein with checks made payable to the Internal Revenue Service and/or State and/or Municipal Taxing Authority to which said income tax is owed by said infant. However, said checks shall be only for the amounts as may be due and payable for that portion of the infant's personal income tax liability attributable to income earned on the accounts maintained pursuant to this Order [including interest and penalties thereon] as shown on any official bill therefor issued by the taxing authority. Said checks shall

identify the infant and said infant's social security number in order to insure that said amounts are being made for the benefit of the infant; and it is further

17. **ORDERED**, that the Bank referred to in Paragraph 3 (a) is hereby authorized without further order of this Court to pay out of the infPant's bank accounts, reasonable fees for the preparation of any income tax return or estimated income tax return or accounting that may be required to be filed by or on the infant's behalf. Said fees shall not exceed ($ _____) without the further order of the Court; and it is further

18. **ORDERED**, that in the event of the death of said infant plaintiff prior to the date of any guaranteed periodic payment, all sums shall be paid to the estate of said infant plaintiff unless, upon reaching the age of 18, the infant plaintiff has changed his designated beneficiary, in which event said sums shall be paid to said designated beneficiary; and it is further

19. **ORDERED**, that the cause of action for loss of services and/or medical expenses of the guardian be and the same hereby is dismissed without costs and with prejudice; and it is further

20. **ORDERED**, that conditioned upon compliance with the terms of this order, the aforesaid parent and natural guardian of the infant plaintiff, be and hereby is authorized and empowered to execute and deliver a general release and all other instruments necessary to effectuate the settlement herein; and it is further

21. **ORDERED**, that upon the payment of the amounts set forth in decretal paragraphs 1 and 2 above, and execution of the settlement agreement and the assignment agreement, defendant(s) and their insurer(s) shall have no further liability herein; and it is further

22. **ORDERED**, that if it appears that any government agency may attach a lien to the infant's payment, this Order may be amended to allow the creation of a Supplemental Needs Trust for the benefit of the infant and the Supplemental Needs Trust will be substituted as the payee of the payments.

23. **ORDERED**, that the filing of a bond be dispensed with in accordance with the applicable provisions of the Civil Practice Law and Rules.

_____   _____

Date   Hon. Paul A. Victor, J.S.C.

INSTRUCTIONS FOR THE COMPLEX STRUCTURED SETTLEMENT ORDER

The Court's Rules and Forms

This form is designed for settlements where there is more than one defendant (and its insurer), participating in the settlement and in the funding of the purchase of the annuity. If there is a different number of defendants, or more than one annuity is being purchased, the form must be modified accordingly. If only one defendant (and its insurer) is involved in the settlement use the alternate non-complex form order.

Before completion and submission of the application to settle a claim or action of an infant or impaired person, counsel is cautioned to read the court's rules and to use the court's forms; all of which are available on the OCA website. If counsel has any question, or is unsure of how to proceed, counsel is invited to call Chambers and arrange for an appointment to discuss the matter before an application is filed.

After a hearing has been concluded you will be required to serve a copy of the proposed structured settlement order on all defendants and insurance carriers, with a Notice of Settlement so that they will have an opportunity to be heard and object before being bound by its terms. Note: only the proposed Order need be served, not the underlying supporting papers.

Preamble (Whereas) Clause

The terms of the settlement and other relevant information and requirements are outlined in the "Whereas" clauses. Note: This form complies with the requirements of the Internal Revenue Code and explains in its opening "Whereas" clauses, the significant difference between the "Total Settlement Payout" and the "Total Settlement Cost." Decretal Paragraph 1 has been specifically designed to comply with Internal Revenue Code requirements and should not be modified, (except however, to conform it to the specific periodic payments proposed in this application). Note, that when all future periodic payments are guaranteed, the amount set forth in the Whereas Clauses for "future periodic payments" and for "guaranteed periodic payments" will obviously be identical. However, if any of the future periodic payments will terminate upon death, the above amounts will be different. In any event, the whereas clauses can be modified accordingly.

All information set forth in the proposed "Order" must be supported by the underlying affidavits and affirmations as well as in the required exhibits. The proposed implementing documents must be appended as exhibits to the application. These exhibits must identify all the necessary parties thereto as well as the annuity payout being proposed.

A structured settlement plan will be approved by the court after a hearing has been conducted. In most instances defendants insist that a structure plan be provided by a structure broker that is selected by defendant and/or its insurer. The Court requires that plaintiff's counsel retain a structure broker before discussing a structured settlement with the defendants, [See, City Part Rules for Settlement of Claims By Infants and Impaired Persons at pages 16 to 21]. Both brokers can be compensated by a splitting of the annuity commission so there is no cost to the plaintiff or the attorney. If there is a dispute regarding commissions, request a hearing or subpoena all necessary persons to be present.

___ The application to settle the claim must be supported by an affidavit by the structure broker whose structure plan is recommended to the court by plaintiff's counsel to be best for the infant/impaired person. This affidavit must conform to the form affidavit provided by this court on the OCA website. After a hearing and review of all submitted plans, and all circumstances leading up to the proposed plan, the court will select and approve one of the plans as well as the proposed apportionment of commissions..

Decretal Paragraph No. 1

___ Modify the form to comport with the proposed periodic payments which are described in the underlying documents, but do not otherwise modify the format since this paragraph was designed to comply with Internal Revenue Code requirements.

The Guarantees

The "guaranteed" payments mentioned in this paragraph (as well as in the preamble "Whereas" clauses) refer to that part of periodic payments that will not terminate upon the death of the infant/impaired person. Upon death, these "guaranteed" payments will be made to the estate of the infant/impaired person, or to the designated beneficiary of said person. The "guarantee" mentioned in this paragraph is not to be confused with the guaranty which is provided by a "guarantor" company which will guarantee the obligation of the assignee company to make all of the future periodic payments [See, decretal paragraph No. 8]. Nor should the guarantee mentioned in decretal paragraph 1 be confused with the additional guaranty provided under New York Insurance Law, Article 77.

Under N.Y. Ins. Law Article 77, the Life Insurance Company Guaranty Corporation of New York provides $500,000 of protection with respect to an annuity in the event an annuity issuer becomes insolvent if the annuity issuer is licensed in New York and the plaintiff is a New York resident. See N.Y.S. Ins. Dept. O.G.C. Opinion 95–65 (9/24/95); See also N.Y.S. Ins. Dept. O.G.C. Opinion 5–1–96 (May 1, 1996), General Counsel Opinion 2–20–2003 (February 20, 2003). In view of this, where the amount structured is more than $500,000, it is prudent, but not required by law, to purchase annuities from more than one issuer to keep the cost of each annuity below

$500,000. The court is informed, however, that purchasing more than one annuity generally results in lower payments to the plaintiff.

The Payee

At the end of decretal paragraph No. 1, insert the name of the "payee." Here you should insert the name the infant plaintiff individually if payments commence on or after infant's 18th birthday. If payments commence before the 18th birthday or if payments are to an impaired person, provisions must be made for payments to the parent or guardian together with a Bank Officer; or to a guardian appointed pursuant to Article 81 of the Mental Health Law. In cases where an infant or impaired person is receiving, or may in the future receive, needs based governmental benefits, such as Medicaid or Supplemental Security income, Counsel should consider making provision for, and the order should provide for, the creation of a Supplemental Needs Trust to preserve eligibility for such benefits, in which event the trust should be named as the payee in this paragraph.

Decretal Paragraph No. 2

Insert the amount that each defendant is required to pay towards the "Total Settlement Cost." If more than two defendants that are contributing to the settlement, add additional subparagraphs.

Decretal Paragraphs No. 3 And 4

Paragraph (A) in decretal paragraphs 3 and 4 are the up front sums to be paid by defendants, (or their insurers) to cover the plaintiff's counsel fees, disbursements, liens and up front money to the plaintiff, if any. If other up front costs must be added, the form should be modified accordingly. Paragraph (B) in decretal paragraph 3 is for the payment by defendant to fund an annuity which will provide the future periodic payments. If this defendant is purchasing or (contributing to the purchase of) more than one annuity, then an additional subparagraph should be added for each payment toward an annuity. If a second defendant is also contributing to the funding of the annuity and/or funding a separate new annuity a paragraph 4 (B) should be utilized.

Decretal Paragraphs No. 5 and No. 6

The "Assignor, The "Assignee" and The "Annuity Issuer"

The defendant (or its insurer), the "assignor", usually assigns the obligation to make the periodic payments to an "assignee" company, which is usually a shell affiliate of the annuity issuer. That "assignee" company will then purchase the annuity contract from the annuity issuer.

The "annuity issuer" must be licensed to do business in the State of New York, in order for the annuity to be protected by the Life Insurance Company Guaranty Corporation of New York discussed above, and it should have an A.M. Best Company rating of no less than A++ or A+, which are the two highest ratings. The ratings of the proposed annuity issuer must be described in the broker's affidavit and must be supported by an appropriate exhibit attached thereto..

In decretal paragraph No. 5 the assignment company (the "assignee") must be identified, and in decretal Paragraph No. 6, the life insurance company (the "annuity issuer") and its A.M. Best rating must be set forth.

Note: If a second defendant is also purchasing and/or contributing to the funding of an annuity, paragraphs 4,5,6,7 and 8 should be modified accordingly.

The Settlement Agreement and The Assignment Agreement"

The "Settlement Agreement" and the "Assignment Agreement" will provide among other things, that the defendant (or its insurer) will assign the obligation to make the future periodic payments to an assignment company which is usually an affiliate of the annuity insurer. In decretal paragraph No. 5, that assignment company (the "assignee") must be identified, and in decretal paragraph No. 6, the life insurance company (the "annuity issuer") and its A.M. Best Company rating must be set forth.

The Court's Rules for a structured settlement require a copy of each of the proposed agreements to be submitted as exhibits to the structured settlement broker's affidavit, which is submitted in support of the application to settle the claim or action. There is no standard form of "settlement agreement." However, there are several forms of assignment agreements generally used in structured settlements. The plaintiff should request that the form known as the Uniform Qualified Assignment, Release and Pledge Agreement be used, since it grants the plaintiff a security interest in the annuity. Most annuity issuers will use such a form, if requested. If the annuity issuer does not offer a security interest, then the "Uniform Qualified Assignment and Release Agreement" must be used, and the plaintiff will be a general, unsecured creditor of the Assignee. Please note, that decretal paragraph No. 10 of the order requires, among other things that, after all of the documents have been signed, a copy of each must be provided to plaintiff by plaintiff's counsel; and proof of service of same must be filed with the Clerk of the Court.

Decretal Paragraph No. 8

The "Guarantor"

Here insert the name of the "guarantor" company. The obligations of the "assignee" company to make the periodic payments are guaranteed by the annuity insurer or by a substantial affiliated company unless the assignee is a substantial company.

Notice of Settlement

After a hearing has been conducted you will be required to serve a copy of the proposed structured settlement order on all defendants and insurance carriers, with a Notice of Settlement so that they will have an opportunity to be heard and object before being bound by its terms. Note: only the proposed order need be served, not the underlying supporting papers.

The order will be signed on the "settlement" date, if no issue or objection has been raised by the defendant or the insurance carriers involved in the transaction.

Compliance With Remainder Of Decretal Paragraphs

Counsel should carefully read and implement the remainder of the decretal paragraphs after the order has been signed. The order will be signed on the "settlement date" if no issue or objection has been raised by the defendant(s) or the insurance carriers involved in the transaction.

Counsel should take special notice of the obligations imposed by decretal paragraphs No. 10 and 13 which require service of the documents on plaintiff and the filing of documents with the Clerk for the Court, with proof of compliance.

Form 6.   Structure Broker's Affidavit

(NAME OF COURT)
-- x
(CASE CAPTION)

_____ an infant, by his/her Parent
and Natural Guardian _____; and
_____, individually,

Plaintiffs,   Docket No. _____

-against-   STRUCTURE BROKER'S
                                         AFFIDAVIT

Defendants.
-- x

UNDER THE PENALTIES FOR PERJURY, I [Insert Name of Broker], of [Insert Name of Company], acting as structured settlement consultant in the above matter hereby warrant and represent, under oath, having first been duly sworn, the following facts to be true, complete and accurate to the best of my knowledge, information and belief:

1. No rebates, service fees, administrative fees, or other financial consideration of any kind or in any amount has been paid, will be paid or had been promised to be paid to any party, insurer, attorney, guardian or any other person, firm or corporation associated with this case by me or by my above stated company either directly or indirectly, by virtue of the structured settlement or otherwise, relating to this matter.

2. The cost to the defendant(s) and/or casualty insurer(s) of the structured settlement portion of the settlement in this case is $ _____ inclusive of any applicable qualified assignment fee; and this cost to purchase the proposed annuity, was arrived at after a survey of the market of annuity providers in order to confirm and obtain the best value (price/quality) for the periodic payment plan now recommended.

3. (Insert name of Defendant or Insurer) will make the following future periodic payments to (Name of Annuitant):

[Provide full benefit payment schedule]

4. The obligation of (Name of Defendant or Insurer) to make the above future periodic payments will be assigned to _____, the Assignee. (Assignee) may fund the obligation assumed by the purchase of an annuity from (Insert name of annuity issuer), an A.M. Best Company rated A+ or A++ insurer. A guarantee letter will be issued by (Insert name of guarantor) to guarantee the performance of said assignee.

5. The Annuity Issuer company above named, is licensed to issue insurance and annuity products in the State of New York.

6. The standard industry commission that we are receiving in this case is based on 4% of the premium of $ _____. This commission is paid by (annuity issuer), the life insurer issuing the annuity policy.

[If more than one broker is sharing in the commission,
set forth the details supporting same].

7. The annuity being provided in this case is based upon guaranteed non-life contingent payments for the plaintiff, who is presently _____ years of age,

1071

having been born on _____. The annuity cost set forth in number two above reflects this non life contingent annuity cost;

Or

The life insurer(s) providing the annuity or annuities in this case has rated the plaintiff, who is presently _____ years of age, having been born on _____, up to age _____ by reason of plaintiff's medical condition. The annuity cost set forth in number two above reflects this rated age with regard to all life contingent annuity benefit payments Period certain only payments and guaranteed lump sum payments are not affected by rated age;

Or

By reason of said plaintiff's non life impairing medical condition, the annuity being provided in this case is based upon a standard age quote for the plaintiff, who is presently years of age _____ having been born on _____. The annuity cost set forth in number two above reflects this standard age rating. Period certain only payments and guaranteed lump sum payments are not affected by a rated age.

8. Medical underwriting is inapplicable in guaranteed non-life contingent cases;

Or

No medical underwriting has taken place or will take place after the agreement to settle has been reached without full disclosure to both plaintiff and defendant. No post settlement medical underwriting has or will take place to secretly reduce the defendant's cost.

9. No present value calculations were provided in this case. All illustrations provided were based on actual cost only.

10. Neither I nor [company name] is an in-house broker of any party or casualty carrier involved in the settlement; nor am I or said company affiliated with or an "exclusive" broker of any of any party or casualty carrier involved in the settlement.

11. Neither I nor (Insert name of company) will, without the express consent of the plaintiff and the prior written approval of this court:

    (a) provide any information about this settlement to any factoring company for any purpose; or

    (b) solicit the plaintiff or plaintiff's family on behalf of any factoring company for any purpose, including, but not limited to, the proposed sale of plaintiff's future periodic payments, nor will I or (Insert name of company) participate, assist, promote, or aid in such solicitation by any person, firm, corporation or entity; or

    (c) seek or accept any consideration, financial or otherwise, directly or indirectly from a factoring company.

12. The following documents have been annexed as exhibits to the application made to the court for approval of the recommended settlement proposal:

Exhibit A - Proposed Settlement Agreement
Exhibit B - Proposed Assignment Agreement
Exhibit C - Proposed Annuity Contract
Exhibit D - Proposed Guaranty Agreement
Exhibit E - Rejected Alternative and/or Competing Proposals.

THIS STRUCTURED SETTLEMENT AFFIDAVIT IS PROVIDED TO THE PARTIES TO THE SETTLEMENT WITHOUT COST AND WITH THE EXPRESS PURPOSE OF INDUCING THE PLAINTIFF(S), THE DEFENDANT(S), AND ALL PARTICIPATING INSURERS TO ENTER INTO AND/OR PARTICIPATE IN FUNDING THE STRUCTURED SETTLEMENT AGREED UPON IN THIS CASE. STATEMENTS SET FORTH HEREIN CONSTITUTE AFFIRMATIVE REPRESENTATIONS AND WARRANTIES BY THE UNDERSIGNED STRUCTURED SETTLEMENT CONSULTANT.

_____
(Insert name of individual) individually and on behalf of [Insert name of company]

Sworn on before me
this ___ day of _____, 2006

Notary
My Commission Expires:

JUSTICE NORMA RUIZ

Part IA–22. Hon. Norma Ruiz

General Rules

1. *Appearance by Counsel with Knowledge and Authority.* Counsel who appear in the Part must be fully familiar with the case in regard to which they appear and fully authorized to enter into agreements, both substantive and procedural on behalf of their clients. Failure to comply with this rule may be regarded as a default and dealt with appropriately. It is important that counsel be on time for all scheduled appearances.

2. *Settlements and Discontinuance.* If an action is settled, discontinued, or otherwise disposed of, counsel shall immediately inform the Court by submission of a copy of the stipulation or a letter directed to the Clerk of the Part. Filing a stipulation with the County Clerk does not suffice. (See Motion Procedure).

3. *Papers and Fax.* Papers of any sort sent via fax are not accepted unless directed otherwise by the Court.

4. *Information on Cases.* Information on all scheduled court appearances can be obtained from the New York Law Journal. The Part Clerk can also provide information about scheduling of cases (trials, conferences, and arguments of motions) in the Part. Counsel who wish to receive a copy of a decision may submit a stamped, self-addressed envelope with their motion papers.

5. Under NO circumstances will Ex–Parte Communications be accepted.

6. *Stipulations and Adjournments.* The burden is on the parties to inquire as to whether the stipulation was approved by the Court. Information on adjournments can be obtained from the New York Law Journal or the Part Clerk.

7. *Failure to Appear at the Call of any Calendar.* Failure to appear at the call of any calendar may result in an inquest of dismissal pursuant to 22 NYCRR § 202.27.

8. *Papers Will Not be Accepted by Chambers.* All motion papers, as well as stipulations and requests for adjournments are to be filed in room 217.

Motion Procedure

Pursuant to fees schedules effective July 14, 2003, all motions, x-motions, and stipulations of discontinuance must be approved by the Clerks in Room 217 before payment of said fees in Room 118 (County Clerk's Office).

Consistent with the Rules of the Supreme Court, Bronx County, as outlined under Motion Procedure:

1. Oral arguments will be held in IA Part 22, Room 602.

2. Oral arguments and appearance by Counsel with knowledge of the case will be required on ALL motions. NO motion is taken on Submission.

3. Order to Show Cause require the appearance of movant on the return date, regardless of a pro se application.

The Court will not consider discovery requests contained within § 3211 or § 3212 motions. These will be denied, as not appropriately referred to the Part 22 Calendar.

Relief requesting Summary Judgment MAY NOT be brought by Order to Show Cause.

Failure of Counsel with knowledge of the file to appear for oral argument will be considered, by the Court, as a default motion.

Motions may NOT be adjourned more than twice. The Motion Support Clerks will be so informed and advised that requests for further adjournments shall not be forwarded to Chambers. Under no circumstances shall the parties communicate with Chambers with a request for further adjournment beyond the permissible two adjournment exemption. Any request for adjournments beyond the permissible two adjournments shall be referred to the Court's Part Clerk.

Motions may be adjourned on consent in the form of a stipulation. The Court will not consider an Ex Parte communication requesting an adjournment; nor will the Court consider an affirmation which reflects an unsuccessful eleventh hour attempt to obtain a consent adjournment by stipulation.

Requests for adjournments MUST be made in advance, by way of a telephone call to the Part Clerk, before the scheduled appearance. The telephone call shall be made as a conference call with all interested attorneys. The Part Clerk will so inform the parties whether the contemplated adjourn date is suitable for the Court's Calendar. If the Part Clerk allows the adjournment, then service MUST appear with a copy of the stipulation of adjournment on the originally scheduled appearance date. If the stipulation is in the form of a fax, the counsel MUST return on the newly agreed upon adjournment date with an "original" stipulation which clearly reflects original signatures of counsel.

No courtesy copies of papers are to be filed with the Courtroom or Chambers, unless specifically requested by the Court.

Counsel are reminded that the CPLR does not provide for sur-reply papers or allow the presentation of papers or letters to the Court after submission of a motion. Sur-replies, letters, and the responses to such letters addressed to the substance of a submitted motion will not be considered, and are not to be forwarded to either the Part or Chambers.

Trials

Counsel are reminded that pursuant to 22 N.Y.C.R.R. 20216(9), all expert reports are to be exchanged and filed with the Court sixty (60) days before the date set for trial. Reply reports, if any, shall be exchanged and filed no later than thirty (30) days before said date.

Motion in Limine. At the time of assignment to this Part for trial, the parties shall make all motions *in Limine* that require rulings prior to trial, except those not reasonably anticipated in advance. Failure to timely make such motion *in Limine* shall result in the motion being deemed waived. Moreover, counsel shall provide the Court with Memorandum of Law in support of the Motion *in Limine*, with a copy for its adversary.

Trial Rules will be provided to counsel upon the assignment to the Part.

Inquiries

All inquiries as to a case or calendar status should, in the first instance, be made to the appropriate clerk's office (see below). The only inquiries to be made directly to the Part should be those inquiries involving the immediate exercise of judicial discretion.

[IAS Motion Support Office: Room 217, (718) 618-1310]

JUSTICE ALEXANDER W. HUNTER, JR.

Part IA-23. Hon. Alexander W. Hunter, Jr.

Motions

All motion papers, including stipulations and requests for adjournments, shall be filed in the Clerk's Office, Room 217.

All motions filed and accepted will be deemed submitted on the return date, provided all papers are filed on the return date of the motion.

Answering papers will be accepted only on the return date in the Clerk's Office, (Room 217)

Courtesy copies of all motions filed should not be submitted unless requested by the court.

Orders to Show Cause (OTSC) must comply with Uniform Rule 202.7(d) and be submitted to the Clerk's Office, (Room 217) prior to judicial review.

Proof of service of all OTSC must be filed with the IA-23 Part Clerk in courtroom 408 on or before the return date of the OTSC. If proof of service is not timely filed, the OTSC will be removed from the calendar.

The moving party shall clearly specify the relief requested. Counsel, where appropriate, shall use tabs when submitting papers containing several exhibits. If a document annexed to an affidavit or affirmation is voluminous, only relevant portions shall be highlighted.

This Court will not consider sur replies to motions.

Calendars will be called promptly at 9:30 A.M. on Mondays except for holidays falling on Mondays, in which case this calendar will be called on Wednesdays. A second call of the calendar will occur at 10:00 A.M. If both sides do not answer "ready," the motion will be either marked off calendar or deemed submitted on default. Only counsel fully familiar with the file and authorized to make binding concessions, settle or try the action shall appear at the call of the calendar.

Counsel are further advised that they must bring their complete file, including the bill of particulars and marked pleadings to court and have the requisite knowledge of the contents of their file.

Trials

Be prepared and well organized. Be punctual and professionally attired.

Voir dire time limits per side per panel: First round - 30 minutes; each subsequent round: 15 minutes.

Prior to opening statements, submit the parties' marked pleadings, Bills of Particulars, deposition transcripts and in City cases, 50-h hearing minutes. Exhibits can be pre-marked.

In commercial and personal injury cases, voluminous documents such as contracts, leases and medical records, should be paginated for easy reference.

At the charge conference, submit a proposed verdict sheet (on disk and hard copy) and counsel's requests to charge, noting PJI, statute, code and/or regulation sections, the subject of each section and, when warranted, proposed text when marshaling the evidence.

This court works with attorneys on appearance conflicts and scheduling problems.

Lawyers should make trial objections without speeches. When counsel argues a point of law, they should support their position with legal precedent, if it exists.

If counsel cites a case, make sure that it is on point. I have instant access to Westlaw and Lexis and to my Court Attorney Lorraine Martinez via my laptop computer, a constant companion of mine while on the bench.

Put cell phones, beepers and wristwatch alarms on vibrate or silent while in the courtroom.

Please keep "approaching the bench" down to a bare minimum of requests

Article 81 Guardianship Proceedings

Calendars will be called promptly at 9:30 A.M. on Thursdays, except for holidays. If a holiday falls on a Thursday, calendars will be called on the preceding Wednesday. A second call of the calendar will occur at 10:00 A.M. If petitioner fails to answer "ready" at a calendar call, the petitioner will be dismissed without prejudice. If the respondent is represented by counsel who fails to appear, the petition will be adjourned only upon a showing of good cause. Otherwise, the hearing will be conducted.

Since these proceedings are initiated by OTSC, adjournments will be granted only under exigent circumstances and with the prior approval of this court, to be followed by a written stipulation that must be faxed to chambers.

The report of the Court Evaluator must be faxed or e-mailed to the court at least 24 hours before the day and time of the hearing.

Proof of service must be filed with the IA–23 Part Clerk in courtroom 408 on or before the return date. If proof of service is not timely filed, the OTSC will be removed from the calendar.

Non Jury Trial Initiatives Part (NJTIP)

I. *Limitations on Recovery*

Any recovery by the plaintiff(s) is limited to the insurance coverage of the defendant(s). Defendant(s) shall provide coverage information in a separate writing prior to the execution of this agreement. The parties may stipulate to a recovery in an amount less than the insurance coverage, and may also stipulate to a recovery in an amount not less than and not greater than stated parameters, provided that such stipulation is in writing and the greater amount stipulated does not exceed the available insurance coverage. The amount(s) of insurance coverage or stipulated recovery parameters shall not be disclosed by any party to the Judge presiding at the trial of this matter.

II. *No Right to Appeal*

The parties agree to waive costs and disbursements and further agree to waive the right to appeal from the determination of this matter by the presiding Judge. Written Findings of Fact and Conclusions of Law shall not be required. Following the determination, the parties shall not enter judgment but shall instead exchange General Releases and Stipulations of Discontinuance.

III. *Evidentiary Matters*

(a) The NJTIP shall use the following rules of evidence, derived from the American Arbitration As-

sociation Rules for Accident Claims as amended and effective on January 1, 1994.

(1) The parties may officer such evidence as in relevant and material to the dispute. Conformity to legal rules of evidence shall not be necessary, subject to the provisions relating to documentary evidence set forth below. Examination before Trial testimony of a party may be offered by any opposing party, however a party shall not be permitted to offer his/her own Examination before Trial testimony except as provided by the CPLR. In automobile accident cases, a party may offer the Police Report as well as the MV-104 of any party.

(2) The parties may offer medical records, including but not limited to hospital records, treatment records, diagnostic test results and narrative reports in lieu of medical testimony.

(3) Past and future lost income may be proven by the submission of documentary evidence from the plaintiff's employer, including but not limited to pay stubs, tax returns, W-2 and/or 1099 forms, provided that such amounts may be calculated with a reasonable degree of mathematical certainty based solely upon present income and life expectancy. Any claim of future lost earnings premised upon inflation, lost opportunity, promotion, career advancement, or similar theory shall only be proved by expert testimony or the report of an expert previously exchanged pursuant to these rules.

(4) In the event a party wishes to offer the testimony of a non-party eyewitness, such testimony can only be offered by the non-party Examination before Trial testimony of such witness taken pursuant to the notice requirements of the CPLR or by producing that witness at trial.

(5) The Judge shall, where required, issue "So Ordered" subpoenas to secure the attendance of witnesses or the production of documents as may be requested by any party.

(6) Any party intending to offer documentary evidence upon trial, including but not limited to accident reports, medical records and lost income records, shall serve copies of such documentary evidence upon all parties not less than 20 days before trial, except that it shall not be necessary to serve any previously exchanged Examination before Trial Transcripts. Failure to serve such documentary evidence as required shall result in preclusion of that evidence at the time of trial.

(7) None of the foregoing shall be construed to prevent a party from calling witnesses upon trial; however, in the event a party intends to call an expert witness that party must provide written notice to all parties of such witness, along with a copy of that expert's narrative report(s) not less than 20 days before trial. Failure to comply with this provision

shall result in the preclusion of such expert witness at the time of trial.

IV. *Procedural Matters*

(a) The parties agree that all discovery is complete or waived, and the matter is ready for determination.

(b) The signatories to the Transfer Agreement represent that they have the authority of their respective clients and/or insurance carriers into the agreement and such agreement shall be irrevocably binding upon their respective principals.

(c) The signatories may stipulate to apportion liability between the parties, provided such stipulation is in writing or made on the record at the time of trial. If in writing, such stipulated apportionment of liability shall be made known to the presiding Judge at the time of trial.

(d) Pre-trial evidentiary issues normally determined by the trial Judge, such as motions *in limine* and redaction of documentary evidence, shall be determined in conformance with the applicable rules of evidence by a designated Judge upon the application of any party prior to or at the time of trial.

(e) The Trial of any matter transferred to this part shall be scheduled not less than 45 days after the execution of the Transfer Agreement.

(f) Matters involving claims by or on behalf of infants shall not be submitted to the NJTIP.

Inquiries

All inquiries regarding status should, in the first instance, be made to the Motions Support Office Room 217. (718) 618–1310

Inquiries to chambers or the Part should be limited to matters requiring the immediate exercise of judicial discretion.

JUSTICE SHARON A.M. AARONS

Part IA–24. Hon. Sharon A.M. Aaron

PART RULES

Dress Attire—Proper attire for all parties, witnesses and public required. Judge has discretionary power to require proper dress attire in the courtroom. *La Rocca v. Lane*, 37 N.Y.2d 575, 338 N.E.2d 606, 376 N.Y.S.2d 93 (1975); *People v. Rodriguez*, 101 Misc. 2d 536, 424 N.Y.S.2d 600 (Sup. Ct., Kings County 1979); *Close-It Enterprises, Inc. v. Weinberger*, 64 A.D.2d 686, 407 N.Y.S.2d 587 (2nd Dept 1978); *People v. Drucker*, 100 Misc. 2d 91, 418 N.Y.S.2d 744 (Crim. Ct., Queens County 1979); *People v. Lloyd*, 141 A.D.2d 671, 529 N.Y.S.2d 562, 530 N.Y.S.2d 8 (2nd Dept 1988).

Calendars—Will be called promptly at 9:30 a.m. on Mondays (except for holidays falling on Mondays, in which case this calendar will be called on Wednesdays). A second call of the calendar will be at 10:15 a.m. If a party does not appear, the matter will either be denied for failure to appear, marked off the calendar, or deemed submitted on default. 22 NYCRR § 202.27; CPLR § 3215. Only counsel fully familiar with the file and authorized to make binding concessions, settle or try the action shall appear at the call of the calendar. CPLR §§ 3404 and 3216.

Non-attorneys cannot appear on behalf of counsel, it is deemed a non-appearance/default. Attorneys are further advised that they must bring their complete file, including the bill of particulars and marked pleadings to court and have the requisite knowledge of the contents of their file.

1. Motion Procedure

A. Notice of Motion and Order to Show Cause

All papers must comply with CPLR §§ 2101, 2102, 2103, 2211, 2212, 2214 and 2215, as well as the applicable provisions of the Court Rules [22 NYCRR Part 202.27].

1. All motion papers, including stipulations and requests for adjournments, shall be filed in the Clerk's Office, Room 217.

2. All motions filed and accepted will be deemed submitted on the return date, provided all papers are filed by the return date of the motion.

3. Tabs shall be used when submitting exhibits. If an annexed document is voluminous and only discrete portions are relevant, Counsel shall highlight the relevant sections of the document. All cited material shall be viewable without having to remove staples or binding.

4. Courtesy copies shall not be submitted, unless requested by the court.

5. This Court will not consider sur replies to motions.

6. No letters or supplemental papers, affirmations and affidavits are allowed after papers are marked submitted by the Clerk's Office.

7. Counsel are advised when submitting proposed orders or judgments to keep proposed orders or proposed judgements separate and apart from motion papers. Proposed orders or judgments incorporated within motion papers will be considered exhibits and treated as such.

8. Failure to appear at the call of any calendar may result in an inquest or dismissal. 22 NYCRR § 202.27; CPLR § 3215.

9. Counsel must advise the Court in writing as soon as practicable of all motions that have been resolved and/or to be withdrawn.

B. Motions Brought by Notice of Motion

1. *Motions*: Motions are returnable five days a week in the Motion Support Office, Room 217. All opposition and reply papers must be submitted at the Motion Support Office by the return date of the motion. All non-disclosure motions will be deemed submitted on the return date and forwarded to Chambers.

2. *Stipulations of Adjournment*: Only two adjournments by stipulation are allowed. Stipulations must comply with Uniform Rule 202.8(e)(1). Stipulations are to be submitted in Room 217 on the return or adjourned date of the motion. Any other application for adjournment must be in writing and will be forwarded to Chambers for a ruling. Oral applications are not considered. Counsel will be advised of the ruling by publication on the Bronx County website. The Court will not sign a page that has signatures only.

3. *Oral Argument*: If oral argument is requested and granted, or directed by the Court, the motion will be adjourned for conference and oral argument in IAS Part 24. Counsel will be advised of the adjourned date in writing.

4. *Disclosure Motions*: Discovery related motions are heard by the Judge presiding in IAS Part 11. No motion for substantive relief shall be joined with an application for discovery relief. The Court will not consider a discovery request contained within a CPLR § 3211 or CPLR § 3212 motion. These will be denied as not appropriately referred to the Part 11 calendar.

5. *Summary Judgement Motions*: Pursuant to CPLR § 3212(a), a motion for summary judgment shall be made no later than 120 days after the filing of the Note of Issue. No exceptions.

C. Special Proceedings

(Orders to Show Cause (OSC) and Petitions)

1. OSC must comply with Uniform Rule 202.7(d) and be brought to the Motion Support Office (Room 217) prior to judicial review. Reply papers are not allowed.

2. OSC should not be made in lieu of a notice of motion, without the express consent of the Court. CPLR § 2214(a). If done, it will be denied.

3. OSCs are statutorily permitted for the following applications:

a) Temporary restraining order pursuant to CPLR § 6313(a);

b) Motion to withdraw as counsel pursuant to CPLR § 321(b)2; and

c) Motion to vacate default judgment pursuant to CPLR § 5015(a).

4. All OSCs are returnable on Mondays in IAS Part 24 at 9:30 a.m., unless otherwise indicated. OSC will be returnable on the Wednesday in the event the Monday is a Court holiday. **Personal appearance is required.**

5. Proof of service must be filed with the Clerk of IAS Part 24 by 9:30 a.m. on or before the return date of the OSC. Non-compliance will result in removal from the calendar.

6. Stipulations adjourning an OSC shall be filled with the Clerk of IAS Part 24 prior to the call of the calendar.

2. Infant Compromise Orders and Other Ex-Parte Applications

1. Ex-Parte applications are to be submitted to the Motion Support Office, Room 217. Counsel will be notified of the scheduled appearance date by phone after the court has reviewed the Infant Compromise submission.

2. All proposed Infant Compromise orders shall comply with CPLR §§ 1207, 1208 and 22 NYCRR § 202.67 (Supreme Court rule). *See also, Valdimer v. Mount Vernon Hebrew Camps, Inc.*, 9 N.Y.2d 21, 172 N.E.2d 283, 210 N.Y.S.2d 520 (1961); *Naujokas v. H. Frank Carey High School*, 57 Misc. 2d 175, 292 N.Y.S.2d 196 (Sup. Ct. Nassau County 1968), *rev'd on other grounds*, 33 A.D.2d 703, 306 N.Y.S.2d 195 (1969).

3. All proposed infant compromise orders shall contain the following language:

It is further Ordered that the Guardian shall, within thirty days of the deposit of the funds due the infant herein in the above designated bank(s), submit to the Clerk's Office, Room 217, a copy of the Certificate of Deposit issued by said bank.

4. The attorney's supporting affirmation shall set forth the policy limits of all available insurance. All lien waiver letters must be affixed.

3. Depositions

Requests for rulings are to be made to the Ex-Parte Justice, not the IAS assigned Justice.

4. Inquiries/Information on Cases

1. All inquiries should be made to the appropriate Clerk's Office, not chambers.

2. Motion Support Office is located in Room 217; phone number (718) 618–1310.

3. Information on all scheduled Court appearances can be obtained from the NY Law Journal.

4. The Part Clerk can also provide information about rescheduling of cases (trials, conferences, and arguments on motions and OSCs).

5. Faxes to chambers are not permitted unless prior authorization is obtained.

6. E-mails are not permitted unless prior authorization is obtained, and the e-mail must be sent to all other parties at the same time as the court.

7. The only inquiries to be made directly to Chambers should be those involving the immediate exercise of judicial discretion.

8. **Under no circumstances will ex-parte communications be accepted.**

9. Attorneys who wish to receive a copy of a decision may enclose a stamped, self-addressed envelope along with their motion papers. Otherwise, all decisions are available on the Bronx County Clerk's Office website at www.bronxcountyclerkinfo.com/law.

5. Trials

1. *Expert Exchange*: Expert reports are to be exchanged and filed with the court no less than 60 days before the date set for trial.

2. *Pre-trial conference*: At the pre-trial conference attorneys must be prepared to discuss:

1) all anticipated issues of law with citation to authorities with copies for court and all parties;

2) stipulations to undisputed facts if any;

3) admissions and stipulations of clearly admissible evidence;

4) any anticipated motion in limine;

5) scheduling and attendance issues;

6) a witness list; and

7) requested jury charges and verdict sheets.

3. *Trial*: Upon assignment to this part for trial, counsel must requisition the file to the courtroom. Counsel must ascertain the availability of all witnesses and subpoenaed documents. Additional requests for postponements, subpoenas etc., may be made, but will be granted only at the discretion of the court in accordance with the court's calendar.

4. *Before trial plaintiff's counsel shall furnish to the court*:

1) marked pleadings;

2) statutory provisions specifically relied upon in the pleadings;

3) the bill of particulars;

4) depositions and written statements which may potentially be used at trial;

5) any part of a deposition to be read into evidence as part of either party's direct case; and

6) pre-marked exhibits and a list thereof.

5. *Voluminous Documents*: Documents such as contracts, leases and medical records, should be paginated for easy reference.

6. *Motion in Limine*: At the time of assignment to this part for trial, the parties shall make all motions *in limine* that require rulings prior to trial, except those not reasonably anticipated in advance. Failure to timely make such motions *in limine* shall result in the motion being deemed waived. Moreover, counsel shall provide the court with memorandum of law in support of the motions *in limine*, with a copy for all parties.

7. Courtroom Demeanor:

1) observe the normal professional courtesies;

2) direct all questions to the witness and all remarks to the court;

3) no speaking objections, just state the basis;

4) do not interrupt opposing counsel;

5) do not interrupt witnesses except to interpose a motion to strike an answer as non-responsive;

6) put cell phones, beepers, and wristwatch alarms, on vibrate or silent while in the court room; and

7) only attorneys are allowed at counsel table.

8. *At the Charge Conference*:

1) submit the parties proposed verdict sheet (e-mail and hard copy) and counsel's request to charge, noting the PJI; and where applicable, copies of the statute, code and/or regulation; the subject of each section; and when warranted, proposed text when marshaling the evidence; and

2) If the code, statute or regulation has changed since the cause of action arose provide the court with a copy of the applicable statutory authority.

JUSTICE BARRY SALMAN

Part TT-14. Hon. Barry Salman
Motion Procedure

(For all motions made in unassigned and assigned cases).

1. Moving and responding papers including stipulations and requests for adjournments are to be filed in the clerk's office (Room 103).

2. All stipulations and requests for adjournments filed in the clerk's office for all motions will be processed as indicated in the revised motion procedure printed in the Law Journal.

3. The answering papers will be accepted only on the return date in the clerk's (Room 103).

4. Courtesy copies of moving and answering papers need not be provided.

5. Orders to show cause must comply with Uniform Rule 202.7(d) and be brought to the clerk's office (Room 103) prior to judicial review, signature and fixing of a return date. Appearance requirements for orders to show cause are as indicated in the motion procedure appearing in the Law Journal.

Trials

Matters assigned to this Part will be tried, to the extent possible, in chronological order.

Inquiries

All inquiries as to case or calendar status should, in the first instance, be made to the Clerks Office: Room 103, (718) 618–1310. The only inquiries to be made directly to Chambers or the Part should be those involving the immediate exercise of judicial discretion.

Calendars

Calendars will be called promptly at 9:30 A. M. Only counsel fully familiar with the file and authorized to make binding concessions, settle, or try the action shall appear at the call of these calendars.

PART IDV

Doc. 1.   Part IDV Part Rules

Adjournments:

Counsel, their clients and the District Attorney must appear at all scheduled court appearances unless the Court expressly directs otherwise. No adjournments will be granted unless counsel is actually engaged and has submitted an affidavit to that effect, or, upon a showing of exigent circumstances. Affidavits of actual engagement should be submitted to the Court no later than 10 a.m. on the day of the scheduled appearance. Affidavits may be submitted in person or by facsimile at the above number. No adjournments on consent will be accepted.

When the Court grants an adjournment, the party seeking the adjournment must notify the appropriate parties and counsel in all pending matters of the date of the adjournment.

Where the Court has scheduled a civil matter for a time certain and a party or counsel fails to appear and counsel is not actually engaged or has not otherwise secured a Court- approved adjournment, default applications will be entertained within 10 minutes of the scheduled time. In cases of inclement weather, there will be a 15-minute grace period. Counsel in criminal matters before the Court will have their case adjourned if they fail to appear as directed within the above-stated times.

Attorneys who are either late for a scheduled court appearance, hearing and/or trial, or who fail to appear and do not provide an affidavit of engagement in the manner described above, are subject to sanctions.

Conferences:

Counsel must be prepared to discuss all aspects of a matter, including settlement, at any scheduled preliminary, compliance, pre-trial or other scheduled court appearance.

In family court matters, preliminary and compliance conferences are available to counsel upon request in matters where all the litigants are represented by counsel. Such requests may be made by contacting the Court Attorney at the above number in advance of the scheduled court appearance or on the actual date of the scheduled court appearance. All such conferences will be before the Court Attorney with counsel for all the parties. Counsel are encouraged to request conferences where appropriate to expedite the disposition of family court matters.

In matrimonial actions, preliminary conferences must be held within 45 days of the filing of the Request for Judicial Intervention. The RJI must be filed in Supreme Court. When an Order to Show Cause in a matrimonial case is filed prior to the scheduling of a preliminary conference, the Court will hold the preliminary conference on the return date of the Order to Show Cause. Accordingly, counsel are required to appear with their clients on the return date. Counsel are also referred to the Court's separate matrimonial rules.

Pre-trial conferences shall take place in all civil matters. In matrimonial cases counsel or the *pro se* litigants must provide a statement of proposed disposition pursuant to 22 N.Y.C.R.R. 202.16(h), child support worksheet if applicable, an updated net worth statement and proof of filing of the Note of Issue in the Supreme Court.

Motions:

Ex parte applications brought by Order to Show Cause and submitted after 1 p.m. will be placed on the calendar for consideration on the next business day. Oral argument is required on the return date of all Orders to Show Cause as well as proof of service. All Orders to Show Cause in matrimonial cases must first be processed through the ex-parte Motion Part, at Supreme Court. Applicable fees must be paid to the Supreme Court. All other motions must be filed with the IDV clerk in Room 423. Discovery motions in civil matters should not be made without the Court's permission. And where permission is granted, an affirmation of good faith is required.

The Court will not accept, either by facsimile or delivery any papers, for filing.

Subpoenas/Vouchers:

Vouchers and subpoenas will not be signed by the Court while the Court is in session. They may be left in the designated drop-off box in the courtroom. After being signed by the judge they will be left in the designated pick- up box for counsel to retrieve. The Court will reject any subpoenas that are not in accord with CPLR § 2305 (b); and 3120 as amended on September 1, 2003.

PRE–TRIAL PART RULES

Doc. 2. Rules for the Pre–Trial Conference (PT) Part for Settlement Conferences and Trial Commencement

Shortly after the filing of a Note of Issue, counsel for plaintiff must complete and file a "Confidential Settlement Conference Worksheet" which (when completed) will provide the court with all information necessary to conduct a meaningful settlement conference. The worksheet also provides a check-off for the documents which are relevant to the issues of liability and damages.

Each attorney attending the settlement conference must bring a copy of all documents relevant to the issues of liability and damages and be fully familiar with every aspect of the case and be fully authorized to engage in meaningful settlement negotiations.

The worksheet must be filed with the Clerk in Room 810. Copies of the form worksheet can be obtained either on line from OCA Court website or from the Clerk in Room 810.

Caveat:

(1) If the worksheet is not sufficiently completed and filed or if the attorney attending is not prepared, it may result in an adjournment and/or multiple unnecessary appearances.

(2) If the court senses that settlement negotiations are not expeditiously being conducted in good faith, the court pursuant to the Uniform Rules for Trial Courts (22 NYCRR § 202.26[e], "may order parties, representative of parties, representative of insurance carriers [and others] to also attend in person or telephonically at the settlement conference."

(3) Since a note of issue (with a certificate of readiness) has been filed, the court has the discretion to send the case for immediate jury selection and trial; and will do so if settlement negotiations are not expeditiously conducted in good faith.

(4) The Court's "Trial Rules" are published on the OCA website for Part IA–21.

PRE TRIAL WORKSHEET

Doc. 3. Confidential/Settlement Work Sheet

TITLE OF PROCEEDINGS _____
---X

INDEX NO.: _____

vs.

DATE NOTE OF ISSUE FILED: ___

DESCRIBE TORT: _____

---X

THE PARTIES & ATTORNEYS OF RECORD [1]

PLAINTIFF(S)

1. _____
     (Name of Plaintiff)
ATTORNEY OF RECORD
OFFICE ADDRESS AND PHONE NUMBER
_____
_____
_____

DEFENDANT(S)

1. _____
     (Name of Defendant)
ATTORNEY OF RECORD
OFFICE ADDRESS AND PHONE NUMBER
_____
_____

Insurance Carrier _____
Policy Limits _____
Ins. Contact Person _____
Phone No. _____

2. _____
     (Name of Plaintiff)
ATTORNEY OF RECORD
OFFICE ADDRESS AND PHONE NUMBER
_____
_____
_____

2. _____
     (Name of Defendant)
ATTORNEY OF RECORD
OFFICE ADDRESS AND PHONE NUMBER
_____
_____

Insurance Carrier _____
Policy Limits _____
Ins. Contact Person _____

PLAINTIFF(S)   DEFENDANT(S)

                                                Phone No. _____

3. _____   3. _____
        (Name of Plaintiff)   (Name of Defendant)

ATTORNEY OF RECORD   ATTORNEY OF RECORD
OFFICE ADDRESS AND PHONE NUMBER   OFFICE ADDRESS AND PHONE NUMBER
_____   _____
_____   _____
_____   _____

                                                Insurance Carrier _____
                                                Policy Limits _____
                                                Ins. Contact Person _____
                                                Phone No. _____

SUMMARY SHEET

PLAINTIFFS	DOB	OCCUPATION	LOST TIME
1.			
2.			
3.			
4.			

SHORT DESCRIPTION OF TORT ALLEGED: _____

OCCURRENCE DATE: _____ **TIME:** ___ **LOCATION:** _____

PLAINTIFF'S VERSION OF OCCURRENCE: _____
_____
_____
_____
_____
_____

DEFENDANT'S VERSION OF OCCURRENCE: _____
_____
_____
_____
_____

INJURIES AND TREATMENT: _____
_____
_____
_____

PAST AND FUTURE DAMAGES: _____
_____
_____
_____

LIENS: _____

PLAINTIFF(S) DEMANDS: _____
_____

DEFENDANT(S) OFFERS: _____
_____
_____

SETTLEMENT CONFERENCE PROGRESS NOTES

DATE AND ACTION TAKEN: _____
APPEARANCES:

For Plaintiff: _____
For Defendant _____
_____
_____
_____

DATE AND ACTION TAKEN: _____
APPEARANCES:
For Plaintiff: _____
For Defendant _____
_____
_____
_____

DATE AND ACTION TAKEN: _____
APPEARANCES:
For Plaintiff: _____
For Defendant _____
_____
_____
_____
_____
_____

DATE AND ACTION TAKEN: _____
APPEARANCES:
For Plaintiff: _____
For Defendant _____
_____
_____
_____
_____
_____

DATE AND ACTION TAKEN: _____
APPEARANCES:
For Plaintiff: _____
For Defendant _____
_____
_____
_____
_____
_____

DATE AND ACTION TAKEN: _____
APPEARANCES:
For Plaintiff _____
For Defendant _____
_____
_____
_____
_____
_____
_____

DATE AND ACTION TAKEN: _____
APPEARANCES:

For Plaintiff _____

For Defendant _____

_____

_____

_____

_____

_____

_____

DATE AND ACTION TAKEN: _____

APPEARANCES:

For Plaintiff _____

For Defendant _____

_____

_____

_____

_____

_____

_____

DATE AND ACTION TAKEN: _____

APPEARANCES:

For Plaintiff _____

For Defendant _____

_____

_____

_____

DATE AND ACTION TAKEN: _____

APPEARANCES:

For Plaintiff _____

For Defendant _____

_____

_____

_____

_____

DOCUMENTS REQUIRED FOR SETTLEMENT CONFERENCES

YOU MUST BRING TO COURT THE FOLLOWING DOCUMENTS (TO THE EXTENT THEY EXIST). FOR SETTLEMENT PURPOSES IT WOULD BE EXTREMELY HELPFUL TO THE COURT AS WELL AS OF ASSISTANCE TO THE PARTIES, IF THE FOLLOWING DOCUMENTS ARE BROUGHT TO THE COURT ON EACH CONFERENCE DATE.

IF THESE DOCUMENTS ARE NOT PROVIDED THE COURT WILL FIND IT EXTREMELY DIFFICULT TO ASSIST IN A MEANINGFUL SETTLEMENT CONFERENCE.

(1) FOR ALL CASES PROVIDE THE FOLLOWING REPORTS/RECORDS:

DESCRIPTION OF DOCUMENT	EXPLANATION/ COMMENTS
☐ PROOF OF PRIOR NOTICE	_____
☐ NOTICE OF CLAIM	_____
☐ 50-H TRANSCRIPT	_____
☐ EBT'S CONDUCTED	_____
☐ STATEMENTS OBTAINED	_____
☐ PHOTOGRAPHS (NOT PHOTOCOPIES)	
☐ OF LOCATION	_____
☐ OF INJURIES	_____
☐ OTHER DAMAGES	_____

DESCRIPTION OF DOCUMENT   EXPLANATION/
                                       COMMENTS

☐ INCIDENT, ACCIDENT REPORTS   _____
   ☐ BY POLICE   _____
   ☐ BY AGENCY, BOARD OR AUTHORITY   _____
   ☐ BY PLAINTIFF   _____
   ☐ BY DEFENDANT   _____
   ☐ OTHER   _____
☐ HOSPITALIZATIONS AND RECORDS   _____
   ☐ AMBULANCE/EMS   _____
   ☐ EMERGENCY ROOM/TRIAGE   _____
   ☐ RADIOLOGY   _____
   ☐ OPERATIVE   _____
   ☐ OTHER   _____
☐ TREATING DOCTOR(S   _____
☐ PHYSICAL THERAPY   _____
☐ EXPERT(S) -LIABILITY   (PLAINTIFF) _____
                           (DEFENDANT) _____
☐ EXPERT(S) - MEDICAL   (PLAINTIFF) _____
                           (DEFENDANT) _____
☐ PROOF OF ECONOMIC LOSSES   _____
☐ OTHER RELEVANT DOCUMENTS   _____

REQUIRED DOCUMENTS CONTINUED [2]

DESCRIPTION   EXPLANATION/
                                       COMMENTS

(2) FOR TRIP & FALL   _____

   ☐ BIG APPLE MAP   _____
   ☐ WORK ORDERS   _____
   ☐ CONTRACTS, PERMITS, CUT FORMS   _____
   ☐ OTHER DOCUMENTS RELEVANT TO
      NOTICE   _____
(3) FOR PREMISES CLAIMS   _____

   ☐ OWNERSHIP   _____
   ☐ PRIOR COMPLAINTS   _____
   ☐ PHOTOGRAPHS   _____

(4) FOR MOTOR VEHICLE ACCIDENT CLAIMS   _____

   ☐ DMV HEARING TRANSCRIPT   _____
   ☐ PHOTOGRAPHS OF VEHICLE   _____
   ☐ REPAIR BILL AND/OR ESTIMATE   _____

(5) FOR POLICE MISCONDUCT CLAIMS   _____

   ☐ CERTIFICATE OF DISPOSITION   _____
   ☐ ALL RELEVANT POLICE REPORTS   _____
   ☐ PHOTOGRAPHS   _____
   ☐ WITNESS STATEMENTS   _____
   ☐ CRIMINAL COURT COMPLAINT   _____
   ☐ INDICTMENT   _____
   ☐ TRANSCRIPT OF PROCEEDINGS   _____
   ☐ PLAINTIFF'S ARREST/CONVICTION
      RECORD   _____
   ☐ INVOICE FOR LEGAL DEFENSE FEES   _____
   ☐ OTHER ECONOMIC DAMAGES
      INCURRED

(6) FOR PROPERTY DAMAGE CLAIMS   _____

   ☐ PHOTOGRAPHS   _____

DESCRIPTION	EXPLANATION/ COMMENTS
☐ ORIGINAL PURCHASE RECEIPTS	_____
☐ APPRAISALS AND ESTIMATES	_____
☐ INSURANCE AGREEMENTS	_____
☐ OTHER	_____

(7) FOR THIRD PARTY CLAIMS   _____
     ☐ INDEMNITY CONTRACTS   _____
     ☐ ALL APPLICABLE INSURANCE
       POLICIES   _____

[1] ALL PARTIES AND THE ATTORNEYS OF RECORD MUST BE IDENTIFIED ON THIS PAGE. "COVERING" COUNSEL SHALL ONLY BE IDENTIFIED IN THE PROGRESS NOTES, _INFRA_.

[2] PROVIDE A SUPPLEMENTAL SHEET FOR ALL OTHER RELEVANT DOCUMENTS.

FORECLOSURE SETTLEMENT PART RULES

Doc. 4. Foreclosure Settlement Part Rules

1) All parties must appear at the settlement conference until the action is settled by means of a modification or other agreement signed by all parties as well as the IAS judge or the matter is referred to the IAS part.

2) Any and all counsel and/or parties appearing in this Part shall be fully knowledgeable of the facts at the time the case is called, prepared for the conference and fully authorized to resolve all issues.

3) Either side may request one adjournment which will generally be granted. Any subsequent adjournments are solely at the court's discretion and may be granted on conditions the court requires.

4) Plaintiffs and/or their representative shall be prepared to discuss the loan amount, default amount, pay off amount, and any other information concerning loan modification. This includes but is not limited to specific written justification with supporting details if a HAMP modification application was denied.

6) Defendants and/or their representatives shall be prepared to discuss the nature of the property, defendants' financial status and the reason for default. Defendant shall also be prepared to provide documentation needed to evaluate the possibility of a loan modification.

7) Pro Se defendants do not waive any jurisdictional defenses by appearing at the conference. Any and all statements made; oral or written by either party in the context of settlement negotiation and resolution shall not be deemed to be admission in the underlying litigation.

8) Any trial modification entered into is not a final resolution and will result in an adjournment.

9) All parties and counsel are expected to negotiate and attempt to resolve all matters in good faith.

FILING RULES

FILING OF PAPERS IN SUPREME COURT

Doc. 1. Filing of Papers in Supreme Court

All motion papers must be approved by the Motion Support Office, Supreme Court, Civil Term, room 103, before the motion papers are filed and the appropriate fee paid to the County Clerk. Generally, the filing of papers is governed by the Civil Practice Law and Rules (CPLR), and the Uniform Rules for New York State Trial Courts, 22 NYCRR section 202. Any papers filed in court shall comply with: CPLR 105(t), 2101, 8019(b) and (e); and 22 NYCRR sections 202.5, and 130–1.1A.

REQUEST FOR JUDICIAL INTERVENTION

Doc. 2. Request For Judicial Intervention

Generally, the Request For Judicial Intervention, commonly referred to as an "RJI", is required to be filed in any action where the assignment of a Justice is required. The RJI sets forth the information which is entered into the court system's database. It must be completely and accurately filled out. The full caption, as stated on the Summons, must be set forth. Use of terms "et al." and "etc." are not permitted. Only one RJI (revised 1/31/2000) may be filed in each action.

Either a self represented litigant or an attorney must sign the affirmation at the end of the form. Once completed, the RJI must be filed in duplicate. Except in the case of an ex-parte application, the RJI must also be served together with the accompanying application upon all parties.

Proof of accuracy of the index number must accompany the RJI. See 22 NYCRR section 202.6.

Check the Fee Schedule on the menu for any applicable filing fees.

NOTICE OF MOTION

Doc. 3. Notice Of Motion

A Notice of Motion must be served at least eight days, by personal service, nine days by overnight express and thirteen days by mail before the return date (CPLR 2214). Service by mail must be within the state (CPLR 2103 (f)-1). All unassigned motions must be accompanied with a properly filled out RJI and shall be filed in the Motion Support Office, room 103, within five days of service. All motions on actions already assigned to a Justice must be filed at least five business days before the return date.

REQUESTS FOR PRELIMINARY CONFERENCE

Doc. 4. Requests for Preliminary Conference

A party may request a preliminary conference at any time after service of process. The request shall state the title of the action, index number, names, addresses and telephone numbers of all attorneys appearing in the action, and the nature of the action. If the action has not been assigned to a judge, the party shall file a request for judicial intervention (RJI) together with the request for preliminary conference. The request shall be served on all other parties and be filed with the clerk for transmittal to the assigned judge [22 NYCRR] 202.12a. Medical, dental and podiatric malpractice actions: These actions must file a Notice of Malpractice for a preliminary conference to be scheduled [22 NYCRR] 202.56. A Notice of Malpractice must be filed within sixty days after joinder of issue by all defendants named in the complaint or after the time for the a defaulting party to appear, answer or move with respect to the pleading has expired. The form and content must be as contained in [22 NYCRR] 202.56. Such notice shall be filed after the expiration of sixty days only by leave of the court on motion and for good cause shown.

DISCOVERY PART CONFERENCE REQUESTS

Doc. 5. Discovery Part Conference Requests

In lieu of a formal motion, parties may make written application to schedule a Discovery Status or Compliance Conference. Such application shall be forwarded to

Bronx Supreme Civil

851 Grand Concourse

Bronx, New York 10451

Room 217 DCM Department

Such application shall set forth

1. The case caption and index number

2. E Mail address for notification

3. Must specify all discovery issues and any other relief being requested

4. The request must state the courts intervention is necessary to resolve these issues.

5. Identify all prior orders addressing discovery issues.

6. The request must be CCd to all appearing parties.

These applications will be processed by the DCM department.

NOTES OF ISSUE

Doc. 6. Notes of Issue

To put an action on the trial calendar, you must file an original and one copy of the Note of Issue, Certificate of Readiness and Affidavit of service. [22 NYCRR] 202.21b. The note of issue must be filed in the clerk's office within ten days of service. A note of issue can only have one index number and one caption and the caption must be complete (no et. al. or etc. etc.). If one or more actions have been consolidated you should supply the clerk with the order of consolidation showing the consolidated index number and caption. If one or more actions have been joined for trial each action must file a separate note of issue.

SPECIAL PROCEEDINGS

Doc. 7. Special Proceedings

Special proceedings in Supreme Court, Bronx County must be commenced by filing a petition with the County Clerk, Room 118, 851 Grand Concourse. Upon the filing of the petition and payment of appropriate fees, an index number will be assigned. To calendar a Notice of Petition, first serve all papers, using the index number that was assigned, and then bring the Notice of Petition, Petition, Request for Judicial Intervention, printout from the County Clerk and proof of service to Room 217 for approval. If moving by Order to Show Cause, all papers can be brought to Room 217 immediately after filing the petition.

MOTION PROCEDURE

Doc. 8. Motion Procedure

All assigned and unassigned motions will be returnable five (5) days a week in the Civil Branch Clerk's Office, Room 217, at 9:30 A.M. Unassigned motions must be in the Clerk's Office within five (5) days of the date of service of the motion. Assigned motions must be filed in the Clerk's Office not less than five (5) business days prior to the return date of the motion. In accordance with the new civil fee schedule set forth in Article 80 of the C.P.L.R., effective July 14, 2003, all motions, and cross motions must be approved in Room 217 prior to payment of said fees in the County Clerk's Office, Room 118. All answering papers must be submitted to the Clerk's Office on the return date of the motion. Answering papers will not be accepted prior to the return date. Cross motions may be presented for approval on or before the return date, provided that there is a motion already calendared.

All papers served must strictly comply with the time requirements of C.P.L.R. Sections 2101, 2103 and 2214(b). On the return date of the motion all non–City and non–Matrimonial disclosure motions, assigned and unassigned, will be scheduled for appearance in the Preliminary and Compliance Conference Part, IA-11, Room 707. The appearance date shall be no earlier than two weeks from the initial return date of the motion. Non-disclosure motions for IA5, IA7 and IA22 will be adjourned for oral argument to the Monday of the second week following the week of the return date of the motion. All other non-disclosure motions will be deemed submitted on the return date and forwarded to Chambers unless a stipulation of adjournment complying with the requirements of Rule 202.8(e) is submitted, in which event, the motion will be adjourned for the requested date and kept in the Clerk's Office. If a non-stipulated request for adjournment or notice is submitted, the motion and request will be forwarded to Chambers for judicial approval or denial of the request. In either event, the attorney requesting the adjournment will be notified, via telephone, of the granting or denial of the request and instructed to notify his adversary.

If on any submitted non-disclosure motion oral argument is requested and granted, or directed by the Court, the motion shall be adjourned for oral argument before the I.A. Judge on the second Monday following the week of the return date of the motion.

Attorneys will be notified via telephone of the adjourned date.

Calendars of disclosure motions and other motions adjourned for oral argument will be published for the four (4) business days preceding the rescheduled appearance date and on the rescheduled date of the motion. These repetitive publications will serve as the notification of procedure of adjournment of all motions. In addition, two (2) days before the return date of unassigned motions a list of such motions indicating the assigned Justice and the adjourned date of the motion will be published.

All orders to show cause, with the exception of orders to show cause that are returnable in the City Part, the STP Part, the Matrimonial Part and the Preliminary/Compliance Conference Part (IA-11), submitted on or after August 25, 2003, will be returnable on a Monday in the assigned Justice's part and appear on his or her motion calendar. Appearances will be required on orders to show cause.

Counsel/parties must advise the Court in writing on or before the return date of all motions that have been resolved by Counsel/parties themselves and all motions the movant(s) wish to be withdrawn.

See individual Justice's notes for further instructions.

In lieu of contacting the Clerk's Office, counsel and Pro Se litigants may check the Law Journal or see Case Information on the website for motion decisions.

PRELIMINARY CONFERENCES

Doc. 9. Preliminary Conferences

Pursuant to revised sections 202.8 and 202.12 of the Chief Administrator's Uniform Civil Rules for the Supreme and County Courts regarding first disclosure motions or preliminary conferences, appearances will not be required if before the rescheduled date of the motion or the scheduled date of the preliminary conference a "Preliminary Conference Order" in the prescribed form is filed with the Civil Branch Clerk's Office, Room 217. Forms are available in the Clerk's Office and in the DCM Part, Room 707 and most importantly on the Web. Completed forms will be submitted to the court for approval and then filed in the County Clerk's Office. Attorneys and pro se litigants are required to check the final "Preliminary Conference Order" for the date of the compliance conference, if any, and for any additional directives ordered by the Court.

SUMMARY JURY TRIAL PROGRAM (SJT) INFORMATION SHEET

Doc. 10. SUMMARY JURY TRIAL PROGRAM (SJT) INFORMATION SHEET

General Features:

• An SJT is a binding one day jury trial with relaxed rules of evidence

• Medical evidence can be submitted without live medical testimony

• Hi-Low parameters can be stipulated to, i.e. $0/$25k, $50k/$25/k, etc

• No Appeal

• No directed verdicts

• No motions to set aside the verdict

• A date certain for trial

• Innovative methods of case presentation to the jury, direct submission to jury of medical records, reports, power point presentations, etc..

• Supreme Court Judge to preside at the trial

• CLE to be given by Bronx Bar Association

General Rules:

• Written stipulation by attorneys to participate

• Signed waiver of right to appeal and waiver of post trial motions

• Findings of Fact/Conclusions of Law not required

• Judgment not entered, instead releases and stipulations are exchanged

• Pre-marked exhibits, medical records, reports, photos, diagrams, etc. can be submitted directly to jury

• Any evidence, trial notebook, etc. to be submitted to jury must be exchanged 30 days in advance or it is precluded

• Evidentiary hearing held 10 days before trial to resolve objections, redactions and any other pre-trial issues

• Medical records need not be certified or affirmed

• Video live/pre-recorded testimony permitted

• Similar in various respects to the NJI program

General Procedure:

• Abbreviated jury selection

• 10 minute opening and closing for each side

• One hour for case presentation and cross examination by each side

- Modified jury charges
- Record can be waived if all sides agree

SUMMARY JURY TRIAL PROCESS RULES AND PROCEDURES

Doc. 11. Summary Jury Trial Process: Bronx Rules and Procedure

As Amended 9/23/08

A. Nature of the Binding Summary Jury Trial:

A summary jury trial is generally a one-day jury trial with relaxed rules of evidence similar to arbitration except that a jury decides factual issues and renders a verdict as a jury would in a traditional trial. The parties may agree on the mode and method of presentation. In the absence of agreement of counsel and approved by the trial court, the process and rules that follow shall apply.

1. Consent of Parties:

The signatories to the Transfer Agreement represent that they have the authority of their respective clients and/or insurance carriers to enter into the agreement and such agreement shall be irrevocably binding upon their respective principals.

2. Stipulation:

If the parties agree to a summary jury trial, a written stipulation shall be signed by the attorneys reciting any high/low parameters and the agreement waiving any rights to appeal. The high and low parameters of summary jury trial, if any, shall not be disclosed to the jury.

3. No Right to Appeal:

The parties agree to waive costs and disbursements and further agree to waive the right to appeal from the determination of this matter. Written Findings of Fact and Conclusions of Law shall not be required. Following the determination, the parties shall not enter judgment but shall instead exchange General Releases and Stipulations of Discontinuance.

4. Scheduling:

Summary jury trials will be placed on the calendar for trial at the earliest possible date available in the Summary Jury Trial Part. Once said date is assigned it shall be considered a date certain.

5. Pre-trial submissions:

a) Any party intending to offer documentary evidence upon trial, including but not limited to accident reports, medical records and lost income records, shall serve copies of such documentary evidence upon all parties not less than 30 days before trial, except that it shall not be necessary to serve any previously exchanged Examination Before Trial transcripts.

b) No later than 10 days before trial the SJT Judge assigned to the case shall conduct an evidentiary hearing at which time objections to any documentary evidence previously submitted as provided for herein shall be determined and witness lists shall be exchanged. Objections will also be heard concerning live expert testimony at this time otherwise they are waived. If there is no objection at said time, counsel shall so stipulate in writing. Failure to serve such documentary evidence as required shall result in preclusion of that evidence at the time of trial.

c) Reference to PJI sections shall be sufficient on requests to charge. Requests to Charge that deviate from the standard Pattern Jury Instructions should be submitted prior to trial.

6. Record:

A summary jury trial will be recorded by a court reporter unless waived by all parties.

7. Existing Offer and Demand:

The parties may stipulate that the pre-trial offer and demand remain unaltered through the binding summary jury trial. Either party may elect to accept the last settlement proposal of the opponent at any time before the verdict is announced by the jury.

8. Jury Selection:

By counsel with strict time limits or the Court and counsel. If the Court conducts the voir dire each side shall nonetheless have 10 minutes each to also voir dire the jury. Summary juries shall consist of no less than six jurors and one alternate unless the parties stipulate to fewer jurors. The Court shall allow each side two peremptory challenges.

9. Time Limits:

Each side shall be entitled to a ten minute opening and closing and one hour for presentation of its case. The Court may allot more time to a party to insure full exploration of the issues provided counsel presents a compelling reason to support the request for additional time. Unless the Judge directs otherwise, the court clerk should keep track of the time and remind counsel of the status of allotted time at appropriate intervals.

10. Rules of Evidence:

General

a) Parties may offer relevant and material evidence to the dispute. The rules of evidence shall be relaxed subject to any determination at the evidentiary hearing.

Depositions

b) Examination Before Trial testimony of a party may be offered by any opposing party, however a party shall not be permitted to offer his/her own Examination Before Trial testimony except as provided by the CPLR. This section shall apply to video depositions as well.

c) In the event a party wishes to offer the testimony of a non-party eyewitness such testimony can only be offered by the non-party Examination Before Trial testimony of such witness taken pursuant to the notice requirements of the CPLR or by producing that witness at trial.

Loss of Income Documentary Evidence

d) Past and future lost income may be proved by the submission of documentary evidence from the plaintiffs' employer, including but not limited to pay stubs, tax returns, W–2 and/or 1099 forms provided that such amounts may be calculated with a reasonable degree of mathematical certainty based solely upon present income and life expectancy. Any claim of future lost earnings premised upon inflation, lost opportunity, promotion, career advancement, or similar theory shall only be proved by expert testimony or the report of an expert previously exchanged pursuant to these rules.

Live Testimony

e) None of the foregoing shall be construed to prevent a party from calling witnesses upon trial. Live video testimony shall be permitted. In the event a party intends to call an expert witness, medical or otherwise, that party must provide written notice to all parties of such witness, along with a copy of that medical expert's narrative report(s), not less than 20 days before trial. In the event of a non-medical expert counsel shall comply with the standard provisions of the CPLR 3101(d)(1)(i) concerning non-medical experts. Failure to comply with this provision shall result in the preclusion of such expert witness at the time of trial.

Documentary Evidence

f) The following shall also be admissible, Police Reports, the MV104 of any party; medical Records including but not limited to hospital records, ambulance records; medical records and/or reports from plaintiff's medical providers, defendant doctor reports inclusive of No Fault medical exam reports; diagnostic test results including but not limited to X-rays, MRI, CT scan and EMG reports, or any other graphic, numerical, symbolic, or pictorial representation of medical or diagnostic procedure or test of plaintiff. Expert reports, medical or otherwise, shall be admissible providing same was exchanged during the period for pretrial submissions pursuant to Rule 5a. Documentary medical evidence shall not be limited to treating medical providers. Any stipulated evidence shall also be admitted.

g) There shall be no requirement that any record referred to in paragraph "d" or "f" be certified, affirmed or sworn to.

h) Pre-trial evidentiary issues normally determined by the trial Judge, such as motions in limine and redaction of documentary evidence, shall be determined in conformance with the applicable rules of evidence by the SJT Trial Judge at the evidentiary hearing and in accordance with the rules as provided for in paragraphs 5 and 10 a) through 10 g) herein. Any objections to be raised at said hearing shall in writing and served on opposing counsel no less than 5 days in advance of said hearing.

i) The Judge shall, where required, issue "So Ordered" subpoenas to secure the attendance of witnesses or the production of documents as may be requested by any party.

11. Case Presentation:

a) Counsel may present summaries of evidence, factual allegations, inferences from discovery. Counsel may use photographs, diagrams, power point presentations, overhead projectors, trial notebooks all of which can be submitted to the jury, or any other innovative method of presentation.

b) Anything which is to be submitted to the jury as part of the presentation of the case must be exchanged with opposing counsel within the conformity of the rules concerning the presentation of case and pre-trial submissions. Nonetheless counsel shall not refer to or introduce evidence which would not be admissible at trial other than as previously stated. Counsel are encouraged to stipulate to factual and evidentiary matters to the greatest extent possible.

c) No more than two witnesses for each side may be called for direct and cross-examination. On application of a party and good cause shown, the court may allow an increase in the number of witnesses. Plaintiff proceeds first. Plaintiff may be granted a ten (10) minute rebuttal following defendant's presentation. Time spent by counsel on direct and cross examinations counts against their allotted time unless the court directs otherwise.

d) Counsel may stipulate evidence to be submitted.

e) Jurors shall be allowed to take notes upon consent of all parties. Jurors will be permitted to propose questions to be asked of the attorneys. The questions must be presented in writing to the court for approval.

12. Jury Verdict:

Upon by request by the jury, the Court shall give the jury a written copy of the jury charge for use during deliberations. Five out of six jurors must agree on the verdict. The verdict is to be binding as rendered or limited by a high/low stipulation. The jurors may bring into the jury room their notes, any trial notebooks, exhibits, presentations, etc. that may have been presented during the trial.

13. No Directed Verdicts:

Parties agree to waive any motions for directed verdicts as well as any motions to set aside the verdict or any judgment rendered by said jury. The Court shall not set aside any verdict or any judgment entered thereon, nor shall it direct that judgment be entered in favor a party entitled to judgment as a matter of law, nor shall it order a new trial as to any issues where the verdict is alleged to be contrary to the weight of the evidence .

14. Inconsistent Verdicts:

In the case of inconsistent verdicts, the trial judge shall question and charge the jury as appropriate to resolve any inconsistency in said verdict.

15. Infant Plaintiff:

In a summary jury trial involving an infant, the Court must approve any high/low parameters prior to trial.

FILING RULES FOR E-FILED MOTIONS

Doc. 1. Motions on Notice

1) *Motions/Petitions Returnable in Room 217:* A motion on notice or a notice of petition in a New York Supreme Court E-File (hereafter known as NYS-CEF) case, as in others, shall be made returnable in the Motion Support Office (Room 217). The motion must be filed with NYSCEF and the motion fee paid for either via NYSCEF by credit/debit card or by the "Pay at the County Clerk's Office" option. The moving documents must be e-filed no later than eight days prior to the return date.

2) *Calendaring of Motion/Petition and Notice by Court Staff:* After a motion/petition and notice are filed with the NYSCEF system, the Motion Support Office will automatically place the motion/proceeding on the submit calendar in the Motion Support Office (Room 217) for the return date. No appearance or other action by the filing attorney is required in order for the motion to be calendared if the motion fee is paid for via NYSCEF. Motions in e-filed cases (other than tax certiorari cases) appear on the submit calendar for Part IA–23A and IA–6/MM in Room 217 on the return date.

3) *Adjournments on Motions/Petitions in Room 217; Appearance Can Be Avoided:* Motions that have been e-filed may be adjourned in Room 217 if an adjournment complies with the procedures of the Motion Support Office (explained in the "Filing Rules—Motion Procedure" section of the "Courthouse Procedures" link on the website of this court). An adjournment that so complies may be obtained by filing a stipulation of all parties with NYSCEF (designated in the filing menu as a "Stipulation to Adjourn Motion"). The Office will effectuate the adjournment without need for an appearance or any other action by the parties.

4)(a) Working Copies on Motions in Room 217: After papers on motions have been e-filed, working copies thereof, with Confirmation Notice firmly attached as the back page facing out, must be submitted. (Each document or group of documents that is separately bound shall bear a Confirmation Notice.) Working copies lacking the Notice will not be accepted. WORKING COPIES OF MOTION PAPERS MUST BE SUBMITTED NO LATER THAN 5:00 P.M. ON THE RETURN DATE IN THE MOTION SUPPORT OFFICE (ROOM 217) AS EXPLAINED HEREIN.

If an attorney has failed to submit required working copies on or before the return date, the motion will be transmitted as is to the Justice for such action as the Justice finds appropriate. Attorneys may submit working copies on motions by mail or overnight delivery. Any such submission shall be sent in a timely manner to the Motion Support Office (Room 217) and be conspicuously marked on the outside "NYSCEF Matter"; lack of such marking may delay processing.

(b) Working Copies on OSCs Returnable in the Part; Subsequent Papers Handed up in the Part: On orders to show cause that are made returnable in the Part, working copies of e-filed opposition and (if allowed) reply papers (with backs and tabs) must be delivered to the Part. As to all such documents, and any document the court may allow a party to hand up in the courtroom on a motion/petition on notice beyond those previously submitted in Room 217, the attorney must file each document with NYSCEF and thereafter submit in the part a working copy bearing firmly affixed thereto, as the back page facing out, a copy of the related NYSCEF Notice. Documents lacking a copy of the related Notice will not be accepted.

Doc. 2. Orders to Show Cause

1) *Proposed Orders to Show Cause and Supporting Documents to be Filed On–Line:* Except as provided in the following paragraph, proposed orders to show cause and supporting documents in all NYSCEF cases must be submitted by filing with the NYSCEF system; original documents will not be accepted by the Clerk. Counsel must comply with Uniform Rule 202.7(f) regarding notice of the application.

2) *Permissible Submissions in Hard Copy:* If a party seeking a TRO submits an affirmation/affidavit demonstrating significant prejudice from the giving of notice (see Rules 202.7 (f)) seeks to submit documents in an emergency, the proposed order to show cause and supporting documents may be presented to the Legal Support Bureau in hard copy form. The papers must be accompanied by, as the back page facing out, a completed Notice of Hard Copy Submission—E-Filed Case. A proposed order to show cause and supporting documents that must be presented to a Justice outside normal court hours shall be presented in hard copy. In all situations described in this paragraph (other than that of an exempt party), documents submitted in hard copy form must thereafter be e-filed, as set forth below.

3) *Office Review of Submissions Will be Done On–Line:* Absent unusual practical difficulties, a proposed order to show cause and supporting documents that have been filed with NYSCEF will be reviewed on-line by the Legal Support Bureau. If there are problems with the documents, the submitting attorney will be promptly contacted by the back office by e-mail or telephone.

4) *Working Copies:* Except for instances covered by Par. (2) of this section, a working copy of a proposed order to show cause and the supporting documents with Confirmation Notice(s) must be submitted to the Legal Support Bureau.

5) *Hard Copy Service:* In cases in which hard copy service is made of documents that were submitted in hard copy form pursuant to Par. (2) of this section and where no party is served electronically, the filing attorney or party shall, no later than three business days after service, e-file the supporting papers (designating them in the NYSCEF document type drop-down menu on the filing screen as "Supporting Papers to OSC (After Service))," together with proof of hard copy service. Failure to do so will cause the County Clerk file to be incomplete. The Clerk will e-file the signed order to show cause after the deadline for service has passed.

6) *Declination:* If the Justice declines to sign the order to show cause, the Clerk will electronically file the declined order. If the proposed order to show cause and supporting documents were filed with the court in hard copy form, the filing attorney or party (other than an exempt party) shall file the supporting documents with NYSCEF no later than three business days after the filing by the clerk. Failure to do so will cause the County Clerk file to be incomplete.

7) *E–Service of Signed OSC and Supporting Documents:* If the court directs that the signed order to show cause and supporting documents be served electronically, a conformed copy of the signed order should be designated as "Conformed Copy of OSC" in the NYSCEF document type drop-down menu on the filing screen.

SPECIFIC BUREAUS

GUARDIANSHIP

MENTAL HYGIENE LAW ARTICLE 81 MATTERS

Doc. 1.   Accounting and General Assignments

A: Article 81 Matters

Staff within the Guardianship and Fiduciary Support Office (Room 221) process all matters relating to Article 81 of the Mental Hygiene Law. Any interested person (as defined by Section 8106 of the Mental Hygiene Law) of sound mind over the age of 18 has the right to petition the court in the proper jurisdiction for an order directing the appointment of an adult guardian for a person who, because of infirmity, is alleged to be unable to manage his or her affairs or properly to take care of his or her person. At the application stage the allegedly infirm person is known as the Alleged Incapacitated Person ("AIP"). An application may be made to the court by order to show cause or notice of verified petition and supporting papers. Article 81 defines the procedures to be followed. The AIP has various rights and may request the court to appoint legal counsel to represent him or her.

Pursuant to Article 8.10(c) the court shall appoint counsel in the following circumstances unless the court is satisfied that the AIP unless is represented by counsel of his or her own choosing:

1. The person alleged to be incapacitated requests counsel;

2. The person alleged to be incapacitated wishes to contest the petition;

3. The person alleged to be incapacitated does not consent to the authority requested in the petition to move the person alleged to be incapacitated from where that person presently resides to a nursing home or other residential facility as those terms are defined in section two thousand eight hundred one of the public health law, or other similar facility:

4. If the petition alleges that the person is in need of major medical or dental treatment and the person alleged to be incapacitated does not consent;

5. The petition requests the appointment of a temporary guardian pursuant to 81.23 of Article 81;

6. The court determines that a possible conflict may exist between the court evaluator's role and the advocacy needs of the person alleged to be incapacitated:

7. If at any time the court determines that appointment of counsel would be helpful.

If the court appoints counsel under this section, the court may, nevertheless, appoint counsel if the court is not satisfied that the person is capable of making an informed decision regarding the appointment of counsel.

Typically, in the order to show cause the court appoints an individual as a court evaluator to investigate the circumstances of the alleged incapacity and report in writing to the court. Such a person may be an attorney, a physician, a psychologist, an accountant, a social worker, a nurse or any other person properly trained and suitable to perform this task. Under certain circumstances, the court may decide to appoint counsel to protect the interests of the AIP. A hearing is scheduled for no later than 28 days from the filing of the OSC.

At the hearing, evidence is presented on the questions of whether or not the AIP is incapacitated and, if so, what is the best and least restrictive solution to safeguard the AIP and his or her interests. The court will decide these questions expeditiously, often at the conclusion of the hearing on the record, and will often sign a short form decision reciting that the findings required by Article 81 were made on the record. If a guardian is to be appointed, the court will have to set out who the appointee is to be, what role the person will have, any limitations that will constrain the person, and other particulars. The duration of the appointment may be unlimited or for a defined period.

If a Guardian is appointed, he or she will give an oath and receive a commission from the Clerk of the Court. These are included in the form identified above.

After a hearing on the appointment of a Guardian, and after decision on an application to remove a Guardian, for a discharge by reason of the death of the Incapacitated Person ("IP"), or to substitute someone for the original Guardian — perhaps the most common Article 81 matters — the court will order settlement of a judgment in the case of an appointment of a guardian (Click Here) or (ii) an order in the case of the other applications (a judgment already being in existence in those instances). The staff of the Guardianship/ Fiduciary department will review proposed judgments, orders and any counter-orders in these cases, as well as any initial, intermediate, annual or final accountings (Click Here). Counsel should present these to that office. (A final accounting is issued when a guardian has no further role to play, as when all funds have been depleted, the guardian has been replaced, or the IP dies. An interim accounting covers financial transactions for a certain period; when a final accounting is eventually rendered, it will have to cover the period embraced by the interim accounting. An intermediate accounting also covers a defined period, but a later such accounting or a final accounting will only have to pick up and account for the period commencing from the end of the period covered in the intermediate accounting. The Guardian must obtain an order from the court settling and approving all accountings.) In an accounting, the Guardian must show, in detailed schedules, all income, expenses on behalf of the IP, assets, their disposition, and the like. Where there are defects, the staff will communicate with the submitting party and request corrected submissions. When the papers are in final form, the staff will transmit them to Chambers of the Justice assigned.

Article 81 contains educational requirements for guardians and court evaluators. The Association of the Bar of the City of New York and the New York County Lawyers' Association periodically offer classes for such persons and generate a list of those who complete such courses. Those who complete them are certified by the Unified Court System. The schedule of these classes may be obtained by contacting the office of Guardianship & Fiduciary (914) 824–5770 (GFS@courts.state.ny.us) or contacting the guardianship/fiduciary office of Bronx County at (718) 590–4760.

B: Court Rules and the Fiduciary Clerk

In all matters under Article 81 and all other matters involving fiduciaries, certain court rules must be scrupulously followed. The court must be alert to see that required forms are filed in each case. Compliance with these filings is monitored by the Fiduciary Clerk, who is located in Room 148.

Part 36 of the Rules of the Chief Judge applies to appointments of, among others, a guardian, guardian ad litem, court evaluator, and attorney for an AIP, as well as a receiver, referee, and person designated to perform services for a receiver. Section 36.1. Such appointments shall be made from a list established by the Chief Administrative Judge. Section 36.2(b)(1). The Justice may make a designation from outside the list upon a finding of good cause, but in such case must place the basis for the appointment shall be set forth in writing and filed with the Fiduciary Clerk. Section 36.2(b)(2).

Part 36 prohibits, among others, relatives of judges, employees of the Unified Court System, and certain persons connected with a political party or involved in a candidacy for judicial office from being appointed. Section 36.2(c). No receiver or guardian may be appointed as his or her own counsel, nor may a person associated with his or her law firm, absent a compelling reason. Section 36.2(c)(8). The attorney for the AIP shall not be appointed as guardian, or counsel to the guardian, of that person. Section 36.2(c)(9). No court evaluator shall be appointed as guardian for the AIP except under extenuating circumstances that are

set forth in writing and filed with the Fiduciary Clerk. Section 36.2(c)(10).

No person or institution is eligible to receive more than one appointment within a calendar year for which the anticipated compensation to be awarded in any calendar year exceeds $15,000. Section 36.2(d)(1). If a person or entity has been awarded more than an aggregate of $50,000 during any calendar year, the person or entity shall not be eligible for compensated appointments by any court during the next calendar year. Section 36.2(d)(2). These limitations do not apply where the appointment "is necessary to maintain continuity of representation of or service to the same person or entity in further or subsequent proceedings." Section 36.2(d)(4).

All appointees must complete a Notice of Appointment and Certification of Compliance (OCA forms) and submit them within 30 days to the Fiduciary Clerk. Section 36.4(a). Prior to approving compensation of more than $500, the Judge must receive from the Fiduciary Clerk an approval of compensation form endorsed by the Fiduciary Clerk confirming the appointee's compliance with Part 36. The Rules of the Chief Judge prohibit the awarding of fees unless there has been compliance with the fiduciary rules. Section 36.4(b).

If the fees to appointees under Part 36 are $5,000 or more, the Justice must provide a written explanation of the reasons therefor, which is to be filed with the Fiduciary Clerk along with the order approving compensation. Section 36.4(b)(3).

Part 26 of the Rules of the Chief Judge requires that a Justice who has approved compensation of more than $500 shall file with the Office of Court Administration the week after approval a statement of compensation on a form authorized by the Chief Administrative Judge. The appointees covered by Part 26 include guardians, court evaluators and counsel for an incapacitated person, as well as guardians ad litem, referees, counsel and receivers.

All fiduciary forms are prepared by the Guardianship/Fiduciary Office. For access to this sheet and forms. The Rules of Part 36 and Part 26 often lead to confusion on the part of guardians and others. Any inquires as to the need of seeking court approval of an appointment or compensation to an appointee should be directed to the office of Guardianship & Fiduciary (914) 824–5770 (GFS@courts.state.ny.us) or contacting the guardianship/fiduciary office of Bronx County at (718) 590–4760.

The Fiduciary Clerk maintains a database for tracking the filing by appointees of the required fiduciary forms. All original fiduciary forms are mailed to the Office of Court Administration, where a statewide centralized database of reported appointments and approvals of compensation is maintained.

C: Court Examiners

The Guardianship/Fiduciary office is responsible for monitoring the filing of initial and annual accounts by Article 81 guardians and the review of examinations of accounts made by Court Examiners, who are charged by Article 81 with the review of the guardians' accounts for accuracy, propriety, etc. This process is overseen by the Appellate Division, First Department Annual accounts and examinations of accounts are filed in the office. Copies of appointing orders, fee orders and other orders of relevance to the appointment, powers and compensation of the guardian are sent to the us by Justices or their staff. The Guardianship/Fiduciary office staff enter relevant data from these orders, accounts and reports into a comprehensive guardianship database, which is accessible to Justices and court personnel concerned with guardianship matters. The database has the capacity to record and report on all case milestones, appointing orders, fee awards, annual financial summaries and fiduciary compliance.

Court Examiners are attorneys and accountants with expertise in guardianship law and fiduciary accounting who are designated by the Presiding Justice of the Appellate Division to examine reports filed by guardians. The list of Court Examiners is established and maintained by the Appellate Division who supply us with the list of approved court examiners. Upon the submission of a proposed Order and Judgment Appointing a Guardian, the Guardianship / Fiduciary office insert the name and address of the court examiner to be appointed on the particular case. The OCE maintains the list of Court Examiners. Court Examiners are randomly designated in a particular case by the clerks when the Order/Judgment is forwarded to the Judge for determination. The Order and Judgment appointing a guardian details the duties, obligations and powers of the guardian of the person and the powers of the guardian of the property. The guardian must "qualify" immediately after the receipt of the Order and Judgment. To qualify, the guardian must file with the County Clerk a bond (unless waived by the court) and oath and designation of Clerk. Within five days thereafter, a commission must be issued by the County Clerk. The commission is typically prepared by the guardian, his/her attorney or the petitioner's attorney. In some instances, the court may allow a combined Order and Judgment and Commission (see form discussed above). As noted, the guardian must comply with Parts 36 and 26 of the Rules of the Chief Judge and file the requisite fiduciary forms. The guardian should be thoroughly familiar with the terms of the order and should seek clarification when necessary.

Shortly after the guardian's appointment, the Court Examiner will contact the guardian to review the guardian's duties and obligations. The Examiner will typically request a copy of the order of appointment and/or commission, the Court Evaluator's report and other documentation relevant to the guardianship.

The guardian or his/her attorney must serve copies of all reports and applications for fees or other relief on the Examiner. The guardian must cooperate with the Court Examiner at all times. The guardian–Examiner relationship is not intended to be adversarial. However, the Examiner has the power to recommend to the court a reduction in guardian compensation or removal of the guardian when warranted. Pursuant to Section 81.32 of the Mental Hygiene Law, Court Examiners are required to examine and report on initial and annual accounts filed by guardians. The initial reports are filed and reviewed by staff in The Guardianship/Fiduciary office. A copy of the initial report shall be mailed to the court examiner. The law requires the guardian to file an initial report within ninety (90) days of receiving a commission.

The filing of initial report and annual reports is monitored by the Guardianship/Fiduciary office and Court Attorney/Special Referee's who have been assigned the department. The Court Attorney/Special Referee's monitor the timely filing of proposed Orders/Judgments, accounts (initial, annual, final) and any other order directed by a guardianship Judge.

Failure to comply with an order of the court will result in an appearance at a compliance conference before the Court Attorney/Special Referee's. The Court Attorney/Special Referee's will make recommendations to the assigned Judge for removal for failure to comply with court orders. The Court Attorney/Special Referee's mission is to provide assistance guardians and court examiners who have been appointed to oversee the person and property of the incapacitated person.

The initial report must include proof of guardianship education and steps taken to fulfill guardianship requirements. If the guardian has been granted powers with respect to property management, the guardian must include in this report a complete inventory of resources over which the guardian has control, the location of any will, and the plan for management of such property. If the guardian has been granted powers regarding personal needs, the guardian should indicate the dates of visits to the ward, what the guardian has done to provide for the ward's personal needs and a plan for meeting those needs. If the initial report includes any recommendations concerning the need to change any powers authorized by the court, the guardian must apply to the court within ten days of the filing of the report on notice to all persons entitled to notice. The initial report is filed with the Guardianship/Fiduciary office, Room 221. For further information, please see Section 81.30 of the Mental Hygiene Law.

Article 81 requires the guardian to file an annual report with the court by May 31st of each year. The report should be filed with the Guardianship/Fiduciary office, Room 221, and can be submitted any time after January 1st. A copy must be served on the Court Examiner assigned to the guardianship, the IP, the surety and, if the IP is in a nursing home or other rehabilitative facility, the director of the facility and the Mental Hygiene Legal Service.

The first annual report should cover the period beginning on the date the guardian was commissioned and end on December 31st of that year. All subsequent reports must cover the previous calendar year from January 1st through December 31st. The report includes a financial accounting, a social and medical summary and a current medical report from a qualified professional who has evaluated the ward within the three months prior to the filing of the annual report. See Section 81.31 of the Mental Hygiene Law for further information.

The financial section of the annual report should include the following schedules of financial activity: Principal Received; Additional Principal Received; Realized Increases on Sale of Property; Unrealized Increases; Income Received; Disbursements; Realized Losses on Sale of Property; Unrealized Losses; and Account Summary. Some accounts include real and personal property in a separate schedule.

The guardianship training program will provide detailed information on the preparation of the annual account. If needed, additional help should be sought from an attorney, an accountant or the Court Examiner. The Court Examiner will reject the account if it is not in proper form.

The annual account will be reviewed by the Court Examiner and the guardian will be examined under oath concerning financial and personal matters relevant to the guardianship. (Pursuant to a memorandum from the Clerk of the Court, Appellate Division, First Department, that took effect May 5, 1991, in all estates with assets up to $50,000, the examination will be made every two years. In estates with assets of over $50,000, the examination will be made annually.) The examiner will require back-up documentation, such as cancelled checks, brokerage statements, bank statements, bills, invoices, receipts, etc. to audit the account. It is therefore incumbent upon the guardian to maintain accurate records of all financial activity. Additionally, the Examiner will request a copy of any order awarding guardian compensation, attorney and accounting fees, the purchase or sale of real property or any other order pertinent to the guardianship. As

a rule, guardians should not take compensation or pay legal or accounting fees without court authorization.

The Examiner will submit a completed report to the with the Guardianship/Fiduciary office, Room 221. The report will include a proposed order confirming the report, a summary of the guardianship, including the medical and social condition of the IP, and details regarding the appointment of the guardian, a financial summary of the accounting period, a review of all income and disbursements, recommendations for actions to be taken by the guardian, a verified transcript of the guardian's testimony, copies of the order and Judgment appointing the guardian and orders approving fees and commissions and a copy of the guardian's annual account and recent medical evaluation.

The staff of the with the Guardianship/Fiduciary office, Room 221 will review the Examiner's report and proposed order and forward it to the assigned Justice for their determination.

Pursuant to Section 81.33 of the Mental Hygiene Law, a guardian may request permission or be required to file an intermediate or final account.

D: Receivership and Trust Accountings and General Assignments For the Benefit of Creditors

The Guardianship and Fiduciary Support Office handles receivership and trust accountings, and final accounts in general assignments for the benefit of creditors. Likewise, all long form orders disposing of motions to settle such accountings are to be submitted to the Guardianship/Fiduciary office, Room 221. All proposed orders that are requested the establishment of supplemental needs trusts (SNT) are also submitted to this office. This included compromise orders that are also requesting permission to establish an SNT as part of the settlement.

Fiduciaries must pay dose attention not only to the authority granted to them in the order of appointment, but also to the law and rules governing these assignments, appointments, filings, etc. Fiduciaries must comply with the requirements set out in Parts 26 and 36 of the Rules of the Chief Judge and Judiciary Law 35-a. In addition to other authority, receivers should follow CPLR Article 64, CPLR 8004, BCL Article 12, and Uniform Rule 202.52; assignees should follow the Debtor and Creditor Law and Uniform Rule 202.63; and trustees should follow CPLR Article 77 and Uniform Rule 202.53.

GUARDIANSHIP FORMS

Form 1.   Annual Report of Guardian

_____ COURT OF STATE OF NEW YORK
COUNTY OF _____
In the Matter of the Annual Report of

_____,
As Guardian for _____, Index No. _____
An Incapacitated Person.
      Accounting Period: _____ _____ to ____ _____.

General Instructions

1.   All guardians must complete **Sections I and II**

2.   All guardians must attach a copy of the order of appointment.

3.   If you have been appointed guardian for the personal needs of the incapacitated person, please complete **Section III.**

4.   If you have been appointed guardian for the property management of the incapacitated person, please complete **Section IV, the summary and the attached schedules**.

(a) When listing property on a schedule, please be specific. For instance—with bank accounts, list name and address of bank, number of account and balance; with stocks, list number of shares, name of stock, type and value.

(b) Gains or losses should be listed in Schedule B or C, whichever applies. If a schedule does not supply enough space, attach additional sheets with reference to the schedule to which the information applies.

(c) In any schedule, if there is nothing to list, state "NONE".

5.   If the incapacitated person was a resident of New York City at the time of your appointment, file the original annual report in the office of the Clerk of the County in which the incapacitated person last resided before your appointment. If the incapacitated person was not a resident of New York City at the time of your appointment, the original annual report should be filed in the office of the Clerk of the Court which appointed you as guardian.

6.   Send a copy of the annual report to the incapacitated person by mail. If the incapacitated person resides in a facility, hospital, school or alcoholism facility in New York State, a substance abuse program, an adult care facility, a residential health care facility or a general hospital, send a duplicate of the annual report to the chief executive office of the facility and Mental Hygiene Legal Service if the incapacitated person resides in a psychiatric facility:

    Mental Hygiene Legal Service has an office located at:

    Marvin Bernstein

    Director, First Department

    Mental Hygiene Legal Service

    60 Madison Ave.

    New York, New York 10010

Also send a copy of the annual report to the examiner assigned to your case. The name and address of the examiner for your case may be located in the Order and Judgement or from the Guardianship/Fiduciary Dept. of the Supreme Court, Bronx County by calling (718) 618 1330.

SECTION I.   INFORMATION PERTAINING TO THE GUARDIAN (all guardians must complete this section).

1. **REPORT**:

Date of initial report:

Date of last annual report:

Date of this report:

Period covered by this report: _____, ___ through _____, ___. (IN-STRUCTIONS: except for the first and last year of guardianship, the accounting covers the period from January until the end of December of the year preceding the report, or any other period upon order of the court).

2. **GUARDIAN**:

Name:

Address (include mailing address, if different):

Telephone no.:

3. **APPOINTMENT**:

Date of order:

Court:

Name of Judge/Justice:

4. **BOND**:

Bonding company name:

Bonding company address:

Value of bond (If the bonding requirement was waived, so state):

5. **VISITS**: (guardians are required to visit the incapacitated person at least four [4] times a year or more frequently as specified by court order).

Yes ___   No ___

If yes, please provide the date and place of such visits:

Date   Place

If no, please explain:

6. **EARNINGS**:

Have you used or employed the services of the incapacitated person?

Yes ___   No ___

Have any moneys been earned by or received on behalf of the incapacitated person based upon such services?

Yes ___   No ___

If yes, please set forth date, source and amount of moneys earned or derived from such services:

Date   Source   Amount

7. **WILL**:

To your knowledge, has the incapacitated person executed a will?

Yes ___   No ___

If yes, please provide location of the will:

If yes, please provide location of the will:

8. **POWER OF ATTORNEY**:

To your knowledge, has the incapacitated person executed a Power of Attorney?

Yes ___   No ___

If yes, please please provide the name and address of the person with the Power of Attorney:

9. **ADDITIONAL INFORMATION:**

Please provide any additional information which is required by your order of appointment as guardian (In addition to information provided in Sections I, II, III, and IV of this report).

10. **TYPE OF GUARDIANSHIP:**

Have you been granted powers over the personal needs of the incapacitated person?

Yes ___   No ___

If yes, please complete Sections II and III

Have you been granted powers regarding property management of the incapacitated person?

Yes ___   No ___

If yes, please complete Sections II and IV

11. **CHANGE IN POWERS:**

Is there any reason for any alteration of your powers as guardian?

Yes ___   No ___

If yes, please specify change requested:

If you want to change your authorized powers, you must make an application within TEN (10) days of filing this annual report and provide notice to the persons specified in your order of appointment as entitled to such notice. If you fail to comply with this provision, any person entitled to commence a proceeding under this article may petition the court for a change in the powers on notice to you and the persons entitled to such notice as specified in the order of appointment.

SECTION II. INFORMATION PERTAINING TO THE INCAPACITATED PERSON (all guardians must complete this section).

1. **INCAPACITATED PERSON:**

Name:

Address (If residential facility, include name of the Director or person responsible for care):

Telephone no.:

Has there been any substantial change in the incapacitated person's mental or physical condition?

Yes ___   No ___

If yes, please explain:

Has there been any substantial change in the incapacitated person's medication?

If yes, please explain:

2. **EXAMINATION:**

Please state the date and place the incapacitated person was last examined or otherwise seen by a physician and the purpose of such visit:

Date   Physician   Purpose

Please attach a statement by a physician, psychologist, nurse clinician or social worker, or other person who has evaluated or examined the incapacitated person within three (3) months prior to the filing of this report, regarding an evaluation of the incapacitated person's condition and current functional level.

SECTION III. PERSONAL NEEDS

If you have been granted powers with respect to the personal needs of the incapacitated person, please provide the following information:

1. **RESIDENTIAL SETTING:**

Is the current residential setting suitable to the needs of the incapacitated person?

Yes ___   No ___

If no, please explain:

2. TREATMENT:

What professional medical treatment, if any, has been given to the incapacitated person during the preceding year?

Date   Treatment

3. TREATMENT PLAN:

Describe the treatment plan for the coming year for the incapacitated person regarding:

(a) Medical treatment

(b) Dental treatment

(c) Mental health treatment

(d) Additional related services

4. SOCIAL SKILLS:

Please provide information concerning the social condition of the incapacitated person, such as the incapacitated person's social skills and needs and the social and personal services used by the incapacitated person.

SECTION IV.   PROPERTY MANAGEMENT

If you have been granted powers regarding the property management of the incapacitated person, please provide the following information, consistent with your order of appointment, pertaining to your fulfillment of your responsibilities to the incapacitated person to provide for property management:

1. Have you identified, traced and collected assets of the incapacitated person since your appointment?

Yes ___   No ___

If no, please explain:

2. Have all of the incapacitated person's past and current income tax returns and payments been brought up to date?

Yes ___   No ___

If no, please explain:

3. Please complete the following schedules and summary. If you have nothing to list on a schedule, state "NONE".

SCHEDULE A

Assets on Hand at the Beginning of the Accounting Period

Please list all assets of the incapacitated person over which you had sole control as guardian as of the beginning of the accounting period. Do not include in this schedule trust principal in which the incapacitated person has an income interest, property under joint control of any court or real property not transferred to the guardian.

1. **BANK ACCOUNTS AND CASH**—please list the name and address of institutions, account numbers and balance deposited in banks or other financial institutions. Please also list any cash on hand not in bank accounts.

Name of Bank	Acct #	Amount

Name of Bank   Acct #   Amount

_____

_____

_____

_____

_____

_____

_____

_____

_____

_____

_____

_____

_____

_____

_____

_____

_____

_____

_____

                        Total

2. **CORPORATE AND GOVERNMENT SECURITIES (e.g., CORPORATE STOCKS AND BONDS; FEDERAL, STATE OR MUNICIPAL BONDS AND NOTES)**

Name of Securities/Bond   Amount

_____

_____

_____

_____

_____

_____

_____

_____

_____

_____

_____

_____

_____

                        Total

3. **PRESENT OR FUTURE INTERESTS** (e.g., **INTERESTS IN PARTNER-SHIPS, TRUSTS, LITIGATION SETTLEMENT FUNDS OR PENSIONS)**—please list the estimated values of all present and future interests the incapacitated person has in property that has not been transferred to your control.

Names	Acct #	Amount
	Total	

4. **OTHER PERSONAL PROPERTY**—(e.g., **FURNITURE, JEWELRY, ART-WORK)** —please list and describe other personal property and indicate estimated value.

Description of Item	Date of Appraisal	Value
	Total	

5. **REAL PROPERTY**—please describe location and type of real property, type of interest and market value. Please also provide the date of filing of a statement identifying the real property with the County Clerk as required by Mental Hygiene Law § 81.20(a)(6)(vi).

SCHEDULE B

Assets Received During Accounting Period

Please list all principal assets received during the period of this report (show date received, source and amount or value).

Name of Bank/Securities	Account #	Amount

Name of Bank/Securities   Account #   Amount

_____

_____

_____

_____

_____

_____

_____

_____

_____

_____

_____

_____

_____

_____

_____

_____

_____

             Total

SCHEDULE C

Income Received During Accounting Period

Please list all income received during the period from property interests listed in Schedules A and B (show date received, source and amount).

Source of Income   Nature of item   Amount

_____

_____

_____

_____

_____

_____

_____

_____

_____

_____

_____

_____

_____

_____

_____

_____

_____

_____

             Total

SCHEDULE D

Losses Incurred During Accounting Period

Please list all realized losses incurred on principal assets, whether due to sale or liquidation, indicating the asset involved, the date and amount of loss.

Name of Securities	Date of Sale	Amount
	Total	

SCHEDULE E

Moneys Paid Out During Accounting Period

Please list all disbursements, excluding investments, during the period, including date of payment, payee and amount.

Date	Check #	Payee	Purpose	Amount

Date	Check #	Payee	Purpose	Amount

SCHEDULE F

Assets On Hand At End Of The Accounting Period

Please list assets of the type listed in Schedule A on hand at the end of the period and value thereof (see Schedule A for further instructions)

1. **BANK ACCOUNTS AND CASH.**

Name of Bank	Acct #	Amount

Name of Bank   Acct #   Amount

Total

2.   **CORPORATION AND GOVERNMENT SECURITIES.**

Name of Securities/Bond   Amount

Total

3.   **PRESENT OR FUTURE INTERESTS.**

Names   Acct #   Amount

Total

4.   **OTHER PERSONAL PROPERTY.**

Description of Item   Date of Appraisal   Value

Description of Item	Date of Appraisal	Value
	Total	

5. **REAL PROPERTY**

SUMMARY

PART I.

Total beginning balance, as shown on Schedule A, $_____

Total additional assets, as shown on Schedule B, $_____

Total income received during accounting period, as shown on
Schedule C $_____

TOTAL PART I: $_____

PART II.

Total losses during accounting period, as shown on Schedule D $_____

Total moneys paid out during accounting period, as shown on
Schedule E $_____

TOTAL PART II: $_____

BALANCE ON HAND AT END OF ACCOUNTING PERIOD
(Total Part I minus Total Part II) $_____

(This amount should be the same as Schedule F)

VERIFICATION

STATE OF NEW YORK   )
                          ss:

COUNTY OF _____   )

_____, being duly sworn, states that I am the Guardian of the within named incapacitated person and that the attached annual report and schedule(s) are, to the best of my knowledge and belief, a complete and true statement of my activities as such Guardian; receipts and payments on behalf of such incapacitated person; money and other property which has come into my possession or has been received by others pursuant to my order or authority since the date of my appointment or last report; and the value of such property. I do not know of any error or omission in the report or schedule(s) to the prejudice of such incapacitated person.

_____
Guardian

_____

_____

_____
(Your name, address and telephone number)

Sworn to before me this _____ day of _____, 20 ___.

Notary Public

Affidavit of Mailing

I, the undersigned, being sworn, say

On the   day of   , 20

I delivered the within Annual Report of Guardian by mailing a true copy to each person named below at the address indicated:

*List parties and their addresses here

/s/ _____

Print name below signature

Sworn before me on

the _____ day of _____, 20 _____

Notary Public

Form 2. Initial Report

SUPREME COURT OF THE STATE OF NEW YORK   INITIAL REPORT
_____COUNTY

INDEX NO. _____

County   X

In the Matter of

_____

Name of Incapacitated Person

("IP" designates Incapacitated Person in this report)

Please mark appropriate boxes with [X], and type or print all requested information. For more space, please use reverse side of page of question being answered..

_____ X

DATE OF ORDER APPOINTING GUARDIAN: _____

APPOINTING JUDGE: _____

PERSONS FILING THIS REPORT:

What is the status of your educational requirements under MHL § 81.30?   Waived   Completed

☐ ☐

Name	Address

Phone	Relationship

☐ ☐

Name	Address

Phone	Relationship

☐ ☐

Name	Address

Phone	Relationship

☐ ☐

Name	Address

Phone	Relationship

FILING STATUS OF PERSON FILING THIS REPORT:

A. ☐ Sole Guardian of Person   D. ☐ Co–Guardians of Person

B. ☐ Sole Guardian of Property   E. ☐ Co–Guardians of Property

C. ☐ Sole Guardian of Person and Property   F. ☐ Co–Guardians of Person and Property

INCAPACITATED PERSON'S PERSONAL DATA:

1. IP's Age: _____

2. IP resides in:
   a. ☐ Community at: _____
             Address   Phone   Years in residence
      ☐ This address is the IP's own home, which is ☐ rented ☐ owned.
             ☐ The IP lives here alone.

☐ The IP lives here with others: _____

                                                             Name   Relationship

                                                             Name   Relationship

☐ This address is the home of another. _____

                                                             Name   Relationship

b. ☐ Facility: _____

                                      Facility Name   Address

        Phone   FAX   Date Admitted   Name of Social Worker

3. Language of IP: ☐ English   ☐ Spanish   ☐ Other _____

4. Citizenship: ☐ US   ☐ Other _____

PERSONAL NEEDS
(Complete if your filing status is A, C, D or F)

5. Primary Care Physician: _____

                                          Name   Address   Phone

    Frequency of examinations   Date of last examination   Primary Diagnosis

6. Psychiatrist/Psychologist or Other Mental Health Provider:

    Name   Address   Phone

    Frequency of examinations   Date of last examination   Primary Diagnosis

7. Dentist: _____

                  Name   Address   Phone

    Frequency of examinations   Date of last examination

Complete the following ONLY if the IP resides IN THE COMMUNITY.

8. Pharmacy: _____

                  Name   Address   Phone

9. List professionals and service agencies (e.g., geriatric care managers, social workers, home healthcare agencies, social service agencies, "meals on wheels") assisting IP.

Name	Address	Phone	Profession/Service
Name	Address	Phone	Profession/Service
Name	Address	Phone	Profession/Service
Name	Address	Phone	Profession/Service

10. List Day Care Programs or other regularly attended programs for nutrition, rehabilitation, socialization, etc..

Name	Address	Phone	Frequency of Attendance

Name	Address	Phone	Frequency of Attendance

Name	Address	Phone	Frequency of Attendance

Name	Address	Phone	Frequency of Attendance

PROPERTY/FINANCIAL MANAGEMENT

Complete if your filing status is B, C, E or F.
Report all liquid assets, personal property, real property and income you are
AUTHORIZED to take into your possession, management and control, AS
GUARDIAN.

11. Liquid Assets:

a. [   ] Cash Accounts:

Have you changed the title of accounts to your name, *as guardian*?

_____   [   ] Yes   [   ] No
Institution   Acct. Type/Acct. No.   Amount

_____   [   ] Yes   [   ] No
Institution   Acct. Type/Acct. No.   Amount

_____   [   ] Yes   [   ] No
Institution   Acct. Type/Acct. No.   Amount

_____   [   ] Yes   [   ] No
Institution   Acct. Type/Acct. No.   Amount

TOTAL _____

(Accounts in any one institution should not exceed $100,000 in order to avoid the loss
of FDIC coverage.)

b. [   ] Mutual Funds, Securities and Brokerage Accounts:

Have you changed the title of accounts to your name, *as
guardian*?

_____   [   ] Yes   [   ] No
Institution   Acct. Type/Acct. No.   Amount

_____   [   ] Yes   [   ] No
Institution   Acct. Type/Acct. No.   Amount

_____   [   ] Yes   [   ] No
Institution   Acct. Type/Acct. No.   Amount

_____   [   ] Yes   [   ] No
Institution   Acct. Type/Acct. No.   Amount

TOTAL _____

c. [ ] Stocks

Have you changed the title on certificates to your name, *as guardian?*

Corporation	No. of shares	Value	[ ] Yes [ ] No
Corporation	No. of shares	Value	[ ] Yes [ ] No
Corporation	No. of shares	Value	[ ] Yes [ ] No
Corporation	No. of shares	Value	[ ] Yes [ ] No

TOTAL _____

d. [ ] Bonds:

Have you changed the title on bonds to your name, *as guardian?*

Issuing govt./agcy./corp.	Value	[ ] Yes [ ] No
Issuing govt./agcy./corp.	Value	[ ] Yes [ ] No
Issuing govt./agcy./corp.	Value	[ ] Yes [ ] No
Issuing govt./agcy./corp.	Value	[ ] Yes [ ] No

TOTAL _____

e. Other: list any other liquid asset, giving type, location and value:

Have you changed title to these assets to your name, *as guardian*, or not applicable (N/A)?

Type	Location	Value	[ ] Yes [ ] No [ ] N/A
Type	Location	Value	[ ] Yes [ ] No [ ] N/A
Type	Location	Value	[ ] Yes [ ] No [ ] N/A
Type	Location	Value	[ ] Yes [ ] No [ ] N/A

_____

TOTAL   _____

f. **TOTAL VALUE OF LIQUID ASSETS:**

_____

BOX A   _____

12. **Personal Property (e.g., cars, boats, furniture, jewelry, artwork):**

Description	Location	Value
Description	Location	Value
Description	Location	Value
Description	Location	Value
Description	Location	Value
Description	Location	Value
Description	Location	Value
Description	Location	Value

TOTAL VALUE OF PERSONAL PROPERTY:

_____

BOX B   _____

13. **Real Property (e.g., vacant land, residential [including cooperative apartments and condominiums] commercial or income producing property):**

In the letter you received at your appointment, you were instructed about filing the "Statement Identifying Real Property" (Form #3 attached to letter). Attach a copy of form(s) filed for property listed below.

Location	Property Type	Value**			
			[ ] sole [ ] joint [ ] part*** (___ %) ****
Location	Property Type	Value	[ ] sole [ ] joint [ ] part (___ %)
Location	Property Type	Value	[ ] sole [ ] joint [ ] part (___ %)
Location	Property Type	Value	[ ] sole [ ] joint [ ] part (___ %)
Location	Property Type	Value	[ ] sole [ ] joint [ ] part (___ %)

_____ [ ] sole [ ] joint [ ] part (__ %)
Location   Property Type   Value

** Only give value   *** "Part" includes IP's part owner-   **** "%" includes IP's part ownership or
of IP's ownership   ship or mortgage interest. and "%"   mortgage interest. Mortgage % is propor-
share or mortgage   mortgage interest.   tion of debt to total value.

**TOTAL VALUE OF REAL PROP-   BOX C
ERTY:**

ESTATE VALUE

14. TOTAL VALUE OF LIQUID ASSETS, PERSONAL AND REAL PROPERTY:
         (ADD BOXES A, B and C) _____

15. Regular Monthly Income

   a. [ ] Social Security Retirement . . . . $ _____ per month.
   b. [ ] Supplemental Security Income (SSI) . . . . $ _____ per month.
   c. [ ] Social Security Disability (SSD) . . . . $ _____ per month.
   d. [ ] Veterans' Benefits (VA) . . . . $ _____ per month.
   e. [ ] Pension/Retirement Benefits . . . . $ _____ per month.
   f. [ ] Annuity Income . . . . $ _____ per month.
   g   [ ] Rental Income . . . . $ _____ per month.
   h. [ ] Mortgage Interest Income . . . . $ _____ per month.
   i. [Other from list on reverse side . . . . $ _____ per month.
        TOTAL REGULAR MONTHLY INCOME: _____

16. Other Income (report approximate amounts on an annual basis):

   a. [ ] Interest . . . . $ _____
   b. [ ] Dividends . . . . $ _____
   c. [ ] Trust Income . . . . $ _____
   d. [ ] Other from list on reverse side . . . . $ _____
        TOTAL OTHER INCOME: _____

17. [ ] IP is the beneficiary of the following trusts:

Type	Name of Trustee	Trustee's Address/Phone
Type	Name of Trustee	Trustee's Address/Phone
Type	Name of Trustee	Trustee's Address/Phone
Type	Name of Trustee	Trustee's Address/Phone

18. Debt (List all debt over $500):

   a. [ ] Mortgage(s) (Total balance due on all mort-
        gages) . . . . $ _____
   b. [ ] Rent arrears (Total of past due rent) . . . . $_____

1116

c. [   ] Utilities (Total of past due gas, electric, oil, telephone bills) . . . . $ _____

d. [   ] Real Property Taxes (Total of past due real property tax) . . . . $ _____

e. [   ] Hospital/Medical (Total of past due hospital, doctor, lab bills) . . . . $ _____

f. [   ] Income Taxes (Total of federal/state/local income taxes . . . . $ _____

g. [   ] Other from list on reverse side . . . . $ _____

TOTAL DEBT: _____

19. Application has been made for the following government entitlements:

     a. [   ] Social Security Retirement   f. [   ] STAR (relief from property taxes)
     b. [   ] Supplemental Security Income (SSI)   g. [   ] Other (please explain)

     c. [   ] Social Security Disability (SSD   _____

     d. [   ] Medicaid   _____
     e. [   ] HEAP (aid for heating costs)

20. Are any civil judicial proceedings pending or threatened against the IP (e.g., mortgage foreclosure, eviction, debt collection, divorce, immigration proceeding; please explain): _____

_____

_____

_____

_____

_____

21. [   ] Medical/Hospital insurance has been provided for the IP, as follows (please explain):

_____

_____

_____

_____

22. [   ] Homeowner/Renter's insurance has been provided for the IP, as follows (please explain):

_____

_____

_____

23. [   ] Auto insurance has been provided for the IP, as follows (please explain):

_____

_____

_____

24. [   ] Other insurance has been provided for the IP, as follows (please explain):

_____

_____

_____

25. [ ] Safe Deposit Boxes are authorized to be opened and have been located, as follows:

_____   [ ] Opened (inventory attached)
Institution   Address/Phone

_____   [ ] Opened (inventory attached)
Institution   Address/Phone

_____   [ ] Opened (inventory attached)
Institution   Address/Phone

_____   [ ] Opened (inventory attached)
Institution   Address/Phone

26. [ ] Mail is authorized to be collected and opened and arrangements are, as follows (please explain):

_____
_____
_____

27. [ ] Income tax authority has been granted and arrangements to exercise that authority are, as follows (e.g., tax returns filed previously have been located, accountant previously retained to prepare returns has been contacted, IRS FORM 4506 (Request for Copies of Tax Returns) has been filed, IRS FORM 56 (Notice of Fiduciary Relationship) has been filed, IRS FORM SS–4 (Request for Employer Identification Number, if employing persons to assist IP) has been filed, similar state and local forms have been filed; please explain):

_____
_____
_____
_____

The following must be completed by ALL GUARDIANS
DOCUMENTS

28. The following documents have been found (e.g., power of attorney, health care proxy, will); if any document is inconsistent with the powers granted in the guardianship (e.g., power of attorney grants same property management powers as the guardianship of property or health care proxy grants same medical decision making as guardianship of personal needs), application will be made to the court for further instructions; please mark box if fiduciary (e.g., attorney-in-fact, health care agent, executor/trix) has been given NOTICE of guardianship appointment:

_____   [ ] Application to court required
Document Type   Date   Located   [ ] NOTICE given to fiduciary

_____   [ ] Application to court required
Document Type   Date   Located   [ ] NOTICE given to fiduciary

_____   [ ] Application to court required
Document Type   Date   Located   [ ] NOTICE given to fiduciary

_____   [ ] Application to court required
Document Type   Date   Located   [ ] NOTICE given to fiduciary

_____   [ ] Application to court required
Document Type   Date   Located   [ ] NOTICE given to fiduciary

VISITS

29. The frequency of the Guardian/Co–Guardians' visits to the IP and the date of the last visit (Guardians are required to visit at least 4 times per year):

_____
(Frequency (e.g., daily, weekly, monthly, 4 Xs per year)   Date of last visit

CHANGES AND ADDITIONAL POWERS

30. Please report any changes to the IP's personal care and maintenance or management of his/her financial and property affairs currently needed and planned.

_____
_____
_____
_____
_____
_____
_____

31. Do these changes require additional powers or a modification of the powers granted?

DATED:

STATE OF NEW YORK   )
) ss:
COUNTY OF _____   )
            County

I/We, being duly sworn, say, that I am/we are the Guardian/ Co–Guardians for _____ and have executed this Initial Report, which to the best
        Name of IP
of my/our knowledge and belief contains true and accurate information regarding the personal needs and/or property of the Incapacitated Person and all of the activities I/we have undertaken on behalf of the Incapacitated Person. I/we verify that all matters reported herein are known to me/us of my/our own knowledge, except those which are stated upon information and belief.

Sign: _____   Sign:_____

_____   _____
Print Name of Guardian/Co–Guardian of   Print Name of Co–Guardian
[ ] Person [ ] Property [ ] Person & Prop-   [ ] Person [ ] Property [ ] Person &
            erty   Property

Sign: _____

_____
Print Name of Guardian/Co–Guardian
[ ] Person [ ] Property [ ] Person & Prop-
            erty

FILERS & JOINT FILERS   Sworn to before me

All filers may only mark one (1) box   On this _____ day of _____, 20 ___
under their name.
To qualify as joint-filers, the same box   **Affidavit of Mailing**
must be marked under each joint-fil-
er's name.

I, the undersigned, being sworn, say

On the   day of   , 20

I delivered the within Initial Report of Guardian by mailing a true copy to each person named below at the address indicated:

*List parties and their addresses here

_____
Print name below signature

Sworn before me on the
_____ day of _____, 20 _____
           Notary Public

Form 3. Final Report of Guardian

_____ COURT OF STATE OF NEW YORK

COUNTY OF

In the Matter of the Final Report of

_____,

As Guardian for _____, Index No.
An Incapacitated Person /A Former Incapacitated Person.

Accounting Period: ____ ____ to ____ ____.

TO THE SUPREME COURT OF THE STATE OF NEW YORK
COUNTY OF THE BRONX:

I, _____ of _____ being the Guardian of the Person
and/or Property of _____ an incapacitated person/a former incapacitated person, do hereby make, render and file this final account and inventory:

I was appointed as Guardian of the person and/or property of the above named
incapacitated person/former incapacitated person by order of this court dated,
_____, and thereafter, pursuant to said order did file with the
County Clerk of the County of the Bronx a bond with the _____ as
surety thereon, and have continuously acted as such Guardian since the date of my
appointment.

This is the final account of my proceedings as Guardian.

SECTION I   INFORMATION PERTAINING TO THE GUARDIAN
(All guardians must complete this section).

1. **REPORT:**

    Date of last annual report:

    Period covered by this report: ___, ___ through ___, ___ (Instructions: The
    accounting covers the period from the beginning of the guardianship (date of
    appointment) until the end of the reporting period).

2. **GUARDIAN:**

    Name:

    Address (include mailing address, if different):

    Telephone no.:

3. **APPOINTMENT:**

    Date of order:

    Court:

    Name of Judge/Justice:

4. **BOND:**

    Bonding company name:

    Bonding company address:

    Value of bond (If the bonding requirement was waived, so state):

5. **REASON FOR FINAL ACCOUNTING:**

   a.   IP deceased (Attach certified copy of death certificate)
   b.   Assets depleted
   c.   Guardian deceased (Attach certified copy of death certificate)
   d.   Guardian removed
   e.   IP relocated

6. **WILL:**

To your knowledge, has the incapacitated person executed a will?

    Yes ___ No ___

If yes, please provide location of the will:

7. **HEALTH CARE PROXY:**

To your knowledge, has the incapacitated person executed a Health Care Proxy?

    Yes ___ No ___

If yes, please provide the name and address of the person with the Health Care Proxy:

8. **ADDITIONAL INFORMATION:**

Please provide any additional information which is required by your order of appointment as guardian (In addition to information provided in Sections I, II, III, and IV of this report).

9. **TYPE OF GUARDIANSHIP:**

Have you been granted powers over the personal needs of the incapacitated person?

    Yes ___ No ___

If yes, please complete Sections II and III

Have you been granted powers regarding property management of the incapacitated person?

    Yes ___ No ___

If yes, please complete Sections II and IV

SECTION II INFORMATION PERTAINING TO THE INCAPACITATED PERSON

(If IP is deceased, skip Section II and III)

1. **INCAPACITATED PERSON:**

Name:

Address (If residential facility, include name of the Director or person responsible for care):

Telephone no.:

SECTION III PERSONAL NEEDS

If you have been granted powers with respect to the personal needs of the incapacitated person, please provide the following information:

1. **RESIDENTIAL SETTING:**

Is the current residential setting suitable to the needs of the incapacitated person?

    Yes ___ No ___

If no, please explain:

SECTION IV   PROPERTY MANAGEMENT

If you have been granted powers regarding the property management of the incapacitated person, please provide the following information, consistent with your order of appointment, pertaining to your fulfillment of your responsibilities to the incapacitated person to provide for property management:

1. Have you identified, traced and collected assets of the incapacitated person since your appointment?

Yes ___ No ___

If no, please explain:

2. Have all of the incapacitated person's past and current income tax returns and payments been brought up to date?

Yes ___ No ___

If no, please explain:

3. All guardians must attach a copy of the order of appointment.

4. If you have been appointed guardian for the personal needs of the incapacitated person, please complete **Section III.**

5. If you have been appointed guardian for the property management of the incapacitated person, please complete **Section IV, the summary and the attached schedules**.

(a) When listing property on a schedule, please be specific. For instance -with bank accounts, list name and address of bank, number of account and balance; with stocks, list number of shares, name of stock, type and value.

(b) All gains and losses are considered realized for the purpose of this accounting. If a schedule does not supply enough space, attach additional sheets with reference to the schedule to which the information applies.

(c) In any schedule, if there is nothing to list, state "NONE".

SCHEDULE A

Assets on Hand at the Beginning of the Accounting Period

Please list all assets of the incapacitated person over which you had sole control as guardian as of the beginning of the accounting period. Do not include in this schedule trust principal in which the incapacitated person has an income interest, property under joint control of any court or real property not transferred to the guardian.

1. **BANK ACCOUNTS AND CASH** - please list the name and address of institutions, account numbers and balance deposited in banks or other financial institutions. Please also list any cash on hand not in bank accounts.

Name of Bank	Acct #	Amount

Name of Bank	Acct #	Amount
		Total

2. CORPORATE AND GOVERNMENT SECURITIES (e.g., CORPORATE STOCKS AND BONDS; FEDERAL, STATE OR MUNICIPAL BONDS AND NOTES)

Name of Securities/Bond	Amount
	Total

3. PRESENT OR FUTURE INTERESTS (e.g., INTERESTS IN PARTNER-SHIPS, TRUSTS, LITIGATION SETTLEMENT FUNDS OR PENSIONS) -
please list the estimated values of all present and future interests the incapacitated person has in property that has not been transferred to your control.

Names	Acct #	Amount
		Total

4. OTHER PERSONAL PROPERTY - (e.g., FURNITURE, JEWELRY, and ARTWORK) - please list and describe other personal property and indicate estimated value.

Description of Item	Date of Appraisal	Value

Description of Item	Date of Appraisal	Value
	Total	

5. **REAL PROPERTY** - please describe location and type of real property, type of interest and market value. Please also provide the date of filing of a statement identifying the real property with the County Clerk as required by Mental Hygiene Law § 81.20(a)(6)(vi).

SCHEDULE B

Additional Assets Received During Accounting Period

Please list all additional principal assets received during the period of this report (show date received, source and amount or value).

Name of Bank/Securities	Account #	Amount
	Total	

SCHEDULE C

Income Received During Accounting Period

Please list all income received during the period from property interests listed in Schedules A and B (show date received, source and amount).

Source of Income	Nature of item	Amount
		Total

SCHEDULE D

Gains or Losses Incurred During Accounting Period

Please list all realized/unrealized gains and losses incurred on principal assets, whether due to sale or liquidation, indicating the asset involved, the date and amount of gain or loss.

Name of Securities	Date of Sale	Amount
		Total

SCHEDULE E

Monies Paid Out During Accounting Period

Please list all disbursements, excluding investments, during the period, including date of payment, payee and amount.

Name of Payee	Check #	Amount
	Total	

SCHEDULE F

Assets on Hand at End of the Accounting Period

Please list assets of the type listed in Schedule A on hand at the end of the period and value thereof (see Schedule A for further instructions)

1. **BANK ACCOUNTS AND CASH.**

Name of Bank	Acct #	Amount

Name of Bank   Acct #   Amount
                                       Total

2. CORPORATION AND GOVERNMENT SECURITIES.

Name of Securities/Bond   Amount

                                           Total

3. PRESENT OR FUTURE INTERESTS.

Names   Acct #   Amount

                                           Total

4. OTHER PERSONAL PROPERTY.

Description of Item   Date of Appraisal   Value

Description of Item	Date of Appraisal	Value
	Total	

5. REAL PROPERTY.

SUMMARY

PART I.

Total beginning balance, as shown on Schedule A, $_____

Total additional assets, as shown on Schedule B, $_____

Total income received during accounting period, as shown
on Schedule C $_____

TOTAL PART I: $_____

PART II.

Total losses during accounting period, as shown on
Schedule D $_____

Total moneys paid out during accounting period, as shown
on Schedule E $_____

TOTAL PART II: $_____

BALANCE ON HAND AT END OF
ACCOUNTING PERIOD
(Total Part I minus Total Part II) $_____

(This amount should be the same as Schedule F)

VERIFICATION

STATE OF NEW YORK

ss:

COUNTY OF _____

_____, being duly sworn, states that I am the Guardian of the within named incapacitated person/former incapacitated person and that the attached annual report and schedule(s) are, to the best of my knowledge and belief, a complete and true statement of my activities as such Guardian; receipts and payments on behalf of such incapacitated person; money and other property which has come into my possession or has been received by others pursuant to my order or authority since the date of my appointment and the value of such property. I do not know of any error or omission in the report or schedule(s) to the prejudice of such incapacitated person/former incapacitated person.

Guardian

(Your name, address and telephone
number)

Sworn to before me this ___ day
of _____, 20___.

   Notary Public

Form 4.   Ex Parte Application for Approval
of Secondary Appointment

(Mark "X" in appropriate boxes and provide all requested information.)

SUPREME COURT OF THE STATE OF NEW YORK
BRONX COUNTY

--x

Title of Action

_____
_____
_____

--x

EX PARTE APPLICATION
for
APPROVAL OF SECONDARY APPOINTMENT
(Pursuant to 22 NYCRR § 36.1(a)(10)

INDEX NO. _____/_____
_____ *No.*   *Yr.*

APPROVAL of the following SECONDARY APPOINTEE is respectfully requested (attach one page resume):

Name: _____

Address: _____

_____

_____

Phone/FAX/Email _____

___ The secondary appointee will serve as: ☐ COUNSEL   ☐ ACCOUNTANT
☐ APPRAISER   ☐ AUCTIONEER   ☐ REAL ESTATE BROKER   ☐
PROPERTY MANAGER.

The secondary appointee   ☐ is on the list established by the Chief Administrator   of the Courts for the category of appointment   requested.

☐ is NOT on the list established by the Chief
Administrator of the Courts for the category
of appointment requested, but is otherwise qualified for appointment   pursuant to Part 36 of the Rules of the Chief
Judge.

___ The reasons for the request are as follows (If a NON–LIST appointment is
requested, include explanation of good cause for the appointment; if the Guardian or
Receiver requests that he/she, or a person associated with his/her law firm, be
appointed counsel, include an explanation of the compelling reason for the appointment.): _____

_____

_____

_____

_____

_____

_____

DATED: _____

Signature: _____
Print Name: _____

Sworn to before me this ___ day
of _____, 200___.

☐ GUARDIAN   ☐ RECEIVER

1131

Address: _____

_____ Notary Public

Phone _____
FAX _____
Email _____

Form 5.   Article 81 Judgment Sample

At an IAS Part   of the Supreme
Court of the State of New York held
in and for the County of Bronx at the
Courthouse, 851 Grand Concourse
Bronx, New York on the 15th Day of
May 2009.

PRESENT: HON. STEVEN CELONA

         JUSTICE

In the Matter of the application of

DAVID REYNOLDS for the appointment

of a Personal Needs and/or Property

Management Guardian of   ORDER AND JUDGMENT

                                    APPOINTING GUARDIAN

JOHN WILSON   INDEX NO. 90210/93

an Alleged Incapacitated Person

An order having been duly made herein at an IAS Part 4 of this court on the (date of signing of Order To Show Cause), directing that   (list parties whose appearance was directed) show cause why a guardian for personal needs and/or property management should not be appointed for John Oystermann and granting other relief and Mildred Madden having been appointed as court evaluator herein and having duly appeared as same and Larsen E. Cooper having been appointed as counsel for the alleged incapacitated person and having appeared for on behalf of the incapacitated person, and Constance Stewart having appeared for the petitioner and this matter having regularly come on for a hearing on the (date of hearing), and the parties having adduced their proof and it appearing therefrom to the satisfaction of the court by clear and convincing evidence that the alleged incapacitated person is likely to suffer harm because the alleged incapacitated person is unable to provide for personal needs and property management and cannot understand and appreciate the nature and consequences of such inability, and the court having made the findings required by Section 81.15 of the Mental Hygiene Law in a decision made on the record on the (date of Courts decision), and upon all the pleadings and proceedings heretofore had herein, and due deliberation having been had, on motion of Whitelipt and Trembling, attorneys for the petitioner, it is

ORDERED AND ADJUDGED, that John Wilson be and hereby is determined to be a person requiring the appointment of a guardian for personal needs and property management as the court has found that said incapacitated person is likely to suffer harm because of inability to provide for personal needs and property management and is unable adequately to understand and appreciate the nature and consequences of such inability; and it is further

ORDERED AND ADJUDGED, that   of   is hereby appointed guardian for personal needs and property management of John Wilson, upon filing with this court, pursuant to Mental Hygiene Law Section 81.25, a bond in the sum of $ with sufficient sureties, conditioned that the said guardian will in all things faithfully discharge the trust imposed herein, obey all the directions of the court in respect to the trust, make and render a true and just account of all monies and other properties received pursuant to the authority granted herein and the application thereof, and of all acts performed in the administration of the trust imposed herein whenever required to do so by the court, and will file the oath and designation required by section 81.26 of the Mental Hygiene Law;   and it is further

ORDERED AND ADJUDGED, that pursuant to section 81.27 of the Mental Hygiene Law, upon the filing of such oath, bond and designation as required by statute, a commission in due form of law shall be issued by the clerk of the court which shall state 1) the title of the proceeding and the name, address and telephone number of the incapacitated person;   and 2) the name, address, and telephone number of the guardian and the specific powers of such guardian 3) the date when the appointment of the guardian was ordered by the court;   and 4) the date on which the appointment terminates if one has been ordered by the court, **and the commission shall be filed within 15 days of entry of this Order / Judgment,** and it is further

ORDERED AND ADJUDGED, that the attorney for the petitioner shall serve upon the court appointed guardian a copy of this Order and Judgment, assist in the preparation of the commission, oath and designation and obtain, if necessary, the bond, assist the guardian in obtaining the required training and the certified and executed commission from the Clerk of the Court;   and it is further

ORDERED AND ADJUDGED, that the authority of the guardian for property management shall extend to all the property of the incapacitated person, both real and personal, and it is further

ORDERED AND ADJUDGED, that the duration of this guardianship shall be indefinite;   and it is further

ORDERED AND ADJUDGED, that all persons are hereby directed and commanded to deliver to the guardian for property management, upon demand and presentation of a certified copy of the commission, all property of the incapacitated person, of every kind and nature, which may be in their possession or under their control;   and it is further,

ORDERED AND ADJUDGED, that the guardian for property management may, without prior authorization of the court, make reasonable expenditures for the purpose of providing the incapacitated person with necessaries or preserving the property of the incapacitated person, and it is further

ORDERED AND ADJUDGED, that the guardian for property management may, without prior authorization of the court, invest surplus funds in investments eligible by law for the investment of trust funds and may dispose of investments so made and reinvest the proceeds as so authorized.   Except as herein provided, no investment shall be made by the guardian other than pursuant to an order of the court authorizing such investment.   Nothing herein contained shall be deemed to limit the power of the court to approve any investment made without its authorization, or to control the disposition of the property of the incapacitated person or investment or reinvestment of the incapacitated person's funds, or to make a new order respecting investments at any time;   and it is further

ORDERED AND ADJUDGED, that the guardian for property management may not alien, mortgage, lease or otherwise dispose of real property without special direction of the court obtained upon proceedings taken for that purpose as prescribed in Article 17 of the Real Property Actions and Proceedings Law, provided, however that without instituting such proceedings, the guardian for property management may with authorization of the court lease real property for a term not exceeding five years and may, without further authorization of the court, lease a primary residence for the incapacitated person for a term not to exceed three years; and it is further

ORDERED AND ADJUDGED, that the guardian for property management may, without prior authorization of the court, maintain in his or her own name and official title any civil judicial proceeding which the incapacitated person might have maintained were he or she competent;   and it is further

ORDERED AND ADJUDGED, that the guardian may make any secondary appointments without the prior approval of the Court, and that the guardian shall comply with Part 36 of the Rules of the Chief Judge, and it is further (for appointees not subject to Part 36 rules)

OR

ORDERED AND ADJUDGED, that the guardian shall not make any secondary appointments without the prior approval of the Court, and that the guardian shall comply with Part 36 of the Rules of the Chief Judge, and it is further (for appointees subject to Part 36 rules)

ORDERED AND ADJUDGED, that the guardian shall not pay any fees without prior approval of the court, and it is further

ORDERED AND ADJUDGED, that if the incapacitated person has a safe deposit box in any bank, then the guardian be and is hereby directed to take an inventory of the contents of such safe deposit box in the presence of a representative of the surety on the bond (unless the surety waives his presence in writing) and an officer of the bank, and that a list of the contents of such safe deposit shall be certified by all present, and a copy thereof shall be promptly filed by the guardian with the court; and it is further

ORDERED AND ADJUDGED, that pursuant to section 81.36(e) of the Mental Hygiene Law, upon the death of the incapacitated person, the guardian shall have the authority to pay for the reasonable funeral expenses of the incapacitated person; and it is further

ORDERED AND ADJUDGED, that upon the death of the incapacitated person, the guardian shall have the power to pay the bills of the incapacitated person which were incurred prior to the death of the incapacitated person, provided the guardian would otherwise have had the right to pay such bills; and it is further

ORDERED AND ADJUDGED, as it is anticipated that during the pendency of this proceeding, care and treatment for the incapacitated person may be paid for by the New York City Medical Assistance Program, it is ordered that the guardian appointed herein repay the Medicaid Program for funds so expended to the extent that the income and resources of the incapacitated person exceeded the Medicaid eligibility level at the time such assistance was granted, and it is further

ORDERED AND ADJUDGED, that the guardian for property management shall have the authority to pay for the care and maintenance of the incapacitated person in accordance with the following plan: **(If a plan has been formulated and approved)**   and it is further,

ORDERED AND ADJUDGED, that the guardian for property management shall have such authority as may be granted by any statute of the United States of America or the State of New York to a guardian for property management, conservator or committee of the property and the guardian for personal needs shall have such authority as may be granted by any statute of the United States of America or the State of New York to a guardian for personal needs or a committee of the person unless any such statute specifically requires the permission of the court before the exercise of such power granted therein; and it is further

ORDERED AND ADJUDGED, that pursuant to section 81.20 of the Mental Hygiene Law the guardian shall:

(a) exercise only those powers that the guardian is authorized to exercise by order of the court;

(b) exercise the utmost care and diligence when acting on behalf of the incapacitated person;

(c) exhibit the utmost degree of trust, loyalty and fidelity in relation to the incapacitated person;

(d) visit the incapacitated person not less than four times per year;

(e) afford the incapacitated person the greatest amount of independence and self determination with respect to property management and personal needs in light of that person's functional level, understanding and appreciation of his or her functional limitations, and personal wishes, preferences and desires with regard to managing the activities of daily living; and it is further

ORDERED AND ADJUDGED, that pursuant to section 81.20 of the Mental Hygiene Law the guardian shall:

(a) preserve, protect and account for the incapacitated person's property and financial resources faithfully;

(b) determine whether the incapacitated person has a will, determine the location of any will and the appropriate persons to be notified in the event of the death of the incapacitated person and, in the event of the death of the incapacitated person, notify those persons;

(c) at the termination of the appointment, deliver the property of the incapacitated person to the person legally entitled to it;

(d) file with the recording office of the county wherein the incapacitated is possessed of real property, an acknowledged statement to be recorded and indexed under the name of the incapacitated person, identifying the real property possessed by the incapacitated person, and the tax number of the property, and stating the date of adjudication of incapacity of the person regarding property management and the name, address and telephone number of the guardian and the guardian's surety;

(e) perform all other duties required by law; and it is further

ORDERED AND ADJUDGED, that to the extent of the net estate available therefor, the guardian shall provide for the maintenance, support and personal well-being of the incapacitated person and then may, without further Order of the court, provide for the maintenance and support of persons legally dependent upon the incapacitated person; and it is further

with the court; and it is further

ORDERED AND ADJUDGED, that pursuant to Section 81.22 of the Mental Hygiene Law, the guardian for personal needs shall have the authority to make the following decisions concerning the personal needs of the incapacitated persons:

(a) determine who shall provide personal care and assistance to the incapacitated person.

(b) make decisions regarding social environment and other social aspects of the life of the incapacitated person

(c) determine whether the incapacitated person should travel.

(d) determine whether the incapacitated should possess a license to drive

(e) authorize access to or release of confidential records

(f) apply for government and private benefits

(g) consent to or refuse generally accepted routine or major medical or dental treatment provided that the guardian for personal needs shall make treatment decisions consistent with the findings herein and section 81.15 of the Mental Hygiene Law and in accordance with the incapacitated person's, without regard of and respect for the incapacitated person's wishes, including the patient's religious and moral beliefs, or if the incapacitated persons's wishes are not known and cannot be ascertained with reasonable diligence, in accordance with the incapacitated person's best interest, including a consideration of the dignity and uniqueness of every person, the possibility and extent of preserving the incapacitated person's life, the preservation, improvement or restoration of the incapacitated person's health or functioning, the relief of the incapacitated person's suffering, the adverse side effects associated with the treatment, any less intrusive alternative treatments, and such other concerns and values as a reasonable person in the incapacitated person's circumstances would wish to consider

(h) choose the place of abode of the incapacitated person, provided that the choice of abode must be consistent with the findings herein pursuant to Mental Hygiene Law Section 81.15, the existence of and availability of family, friends and social services in the community, the care, comfort and maintenance, and where appropriate, rehabilitation of the incapacitated person, the needs of those with whom the incapacitated person resides; and provided further that based upon the findings made by this court, the guardian for personal needs (shall , shall not) have the authority to place the incapacitated person in a nursing home or residential care facility as those terms are defined in Section 2801 of the Public Health Law without the consent of the incapacitated person; and it is further

ORDERED AND ADJUDGED, that pursuant to Section 81.39 of the Mental Hygiene Law, the guardian shall attend a training program approved by the Chief Administrator of the Courts and obtain proof that the training was completed and furnish proof of such with the Guardianship Clerk; and it is further

ORDERED AND ADJUDGED, that pursuant to section 81.30 of the Mental Hygiene Law, no later than ninety days after the issuance of a commission to the guardian, **the guardian shall file with the Guardianship Department of Bronx Supreme Court, Room 217, an initial report and shall mail a copy to the court examiner assigned herein;** and it is further

ORDERED AND ADJUDGED, the guardian shall file during the month of May of each year with the Guardianship Department of Bronx Supreme Court, Bronx County, the county in which the incapacitated person last resided before the appointment of a guardian, an **annual report** in the form required by Section 81.31 of the Mental Hygiene Law and shall mail a copy of said report to the court examiner assigned herein; and it is further

ORDERED AND ADJUDGED, that if the initial or annual report sets forth any reasons for a change in the powers authorized by the court, the guardian shall make application within ten days of the filing of such report for a change in powers on notice to the persons entitled to such notice, and it is further

ORDERED AND ADJUDGED, that upon the guardian's failure to file the initial report within ninety days after the issuance of the commission, the court examiner shall serve the guardian with a demand letter by certified mail, and upon the guardian's failure to comply, move the court by order to show cause to remove the guardian; and it is further

ORDERED AND ADJUDGED, that the guardian shall notify the Court and the Court Examiner immediately upon any change of address of the guardian or the incapacitated person, and it is further

ORDERED AND ADJUDGED, that in the event of the death of the incapacitated person, the Guardian shall within 20 days of the date of death serve a copy of a Statement of Death on the Court Examiner and upon the Representative of the Estate of the Incapacitated Person stated in the will or Trust Instrument if known, and upon the Public Administrator of the County of the Bronx, and file a copy of this Statement of Death with the Fiduciary Department, Room 221 of this Court, within the same 20 day period, and it is further

ORDERED AND ADJUDGED that in the event of the death of the incapacitated person, the Guardian shall within 150 days of the date of death serve a Statement of Assets and Notice of Claim upon the Representative stated in the Will or Trust Instrument if known, or if there be none, upon the Public Administrator of the County of the Bronx, and file a copy of this Statement of Assets and Notice of Claim with the Fiduciary Department, Room 221 of this Court, within the same 150 day period, and it is further

ORDERED AND ADJUDGED that in the event of the death of the incapacitated person, the Guardian within 150 days of the date of death shall deliver all Guardianship assets, except for property retained by the Guardian to secure any known claim, lien or administrative costs of the Guardianship, to the duly appointed personal representative, or to the Public Administrator or Chief

Fiscal Officer given notice of the filing of the Statement of Death where there is no personal representative, and it is further

ORDERED AND ADJUDGED that in the event of the death of the incapacitated person, the Guardian shall within 150 days of the date of death, unless extended by order of the Court, file the Final Report with the Fiduciary Department, Room 221 of this Court and thereupon proceed to judicially settle the final report with due notice, including notice to the person or entity to whom the property was delivered, and it is further

ORDERED AND ADJUDGED, that the compensation of the guardian shall be at the _____, and it is further

ORDERED AND ADJUDGED, that the guardian shall take no annual commissions/compensation for any year until that year's annual account is filed, reviewed by the Court Examiner, and approved by the court; and it is further

ORDERED AND ADJUDGED, that upon receipt of the commission from the Clerk of the County of th Bronx, the guardian shall make the following disbursements from the funds of the incapacitated person:

(a) To _____ the sum of $ _____ as and for a legal fee for serving as attorney for the Petitioner and $ _____ for disbursements.

(b) To _____ the sum of $ _____ for services rendered as court evaluator.

(c) To _____ the sum of $ _____ for services rendered as attorney for the incapacitated person.

(d) To _____ M.D. the sum of $ _____ for expert services rendered herein; and it is further

ORDERED AND ADJUDGED, that none of the above authorized fees shall be paid until the guardian(s) has filed the bond (if So Ordered), oath and designation and received the commission from the Clerk of th County of the Bronx, and it is further

ORDERED AND ADJUDGED, that pursuant to 81.16(c)(3) of the Mental Hygiene Law notice of all further proceedings with regard to this matter shall be given to: (list names of persons and entities, include examiner and surety, also administrator of facility and NYCHRA/OLA if IP resides in a facility) and it is further

ORDERED AND ADJUDGED, that pursuant to Section 81.16(e) of the Mental Hygiene Law a copy of this order and judgment shall be personally served upon and explained to the incapacitated by the guardian; and it is further

ORDERED AND ADJUDGED, that pursuant to Section 81.38 of the Mental Hygiene Law, _____(if applicable)_____ of _____ is hereby appointed standby guardian for personal needs and property management of the incapacitated person and that upon qualification, the standby guardian for personal needs and property management shall have all the duties, powers and responsibilities of the original guardian for personal needs and property management appointed herein; and it is further

ORDERED AND ADJUDGED, that upon the filing with the court by the standby guardian of a bond, oath and designation, and in addition, upon the filing of an acknowledged statement of resignation signed by the original guardian appointed herein, a certified death certificate of said guardian, or a copy of a judicial order indicating that said guardian has been removed, discharged, suspended, or become incapacitated, the Clerk of the Court shall issue a commission in the due form of law which shall state that it is valid for sixty days from its issuance; and it is further

ORDERED AND ADJUDGED, that _____ of _____, appointed Court Examiner by Order of the Presiding Justice of the Appellate Division, First Department, dated May 11, 1993, is assigned to examine the initial and annual reports of the guardian(s) named herein; and it is further

ORDERED AND ADJUDGED, that the petitioner's attorney herein, within thirty (30) days of the signing of this Order and Judgment, serve upon the Court Examiner a copy of this Order and Judgment together with notice of entry; and it is further

ORDERED AND ADJUDGED, that the said guardian, before taking possession of any personal property valued in excess of the above mentioned bond, file an additional bond to be fixed and approved by a Justice of this court pursuant to Article 81 of the Mental Hygiene Law, and it is further

ORDERED AND ADJUDGED, that any appointee herein shall comply with Part 36 of the Rules of the Chief Judge by filing OCA form 872 with the Fiduciary Clerk in Bronx Supreme Court. Any subsequent affidavit or affirmation of service submitted to this court must contain a statement indicating such compliance and be accompanied by a properly completed 875 and it is further.

ORDERED AND ADJUDGED, that Guardian(s) shall appear for a compliance conference on the   day of   2009 in Room 402 at 9:30 AM and it is further

It is hereby deemed that all service has been properly completed.

ENTER:

_____

J. S. C.

Form 6. Guardianship Oath and Designation Sample

The Supreme Court of the State of New York
County of Bronx _____

In the Matter of the Application of	**Designation of Clerk**
	And
	Consent to Act
Petitioner, For The Appointment Of A Guardian For the Person	**Index No.** _____
and Property of:	
Respondent,	

_____

An Incapacitated Person

_____ residing at _____
New York, the duly appointed guardian of the above named _____
hereby designates the Clerk of the Supreme Court, County of Bronx and his or her
successor in office, as the person upon whom the service of process issuing from said
Court in this proceeding, or any other proceeding, or any other proceeding which
shall effect the person and property management of said _____ may
be made in like manner and with like effect, as if it were personally served on me,
whenever I cannot be found within the State of New York, after due diligence used.

    I FURTHER STATE, that I will faithfully and honestly discharge my duties as
Guardian of the person and property management of _____, a
Person who has been determined to be Incapacitated.

_____

Sworn to before me
on this _____ day of _____, 200___

Form 7.   Commission to Guardianship

The Supreme Court of The State Of New York
County of Bronx

_____

In the Matter Of The Application Of   **COMMISSION TO GUARDIAN**

                                             INDEX NO. _____

                    Petitioner,

For the Appointment Of A Guardian For

An Alleged Incapacitated Person.
_____

TO THE PEOPLE OF THE STATE OF NEW YORK, AND TO ALL WHOM THESE PRESENTS SHALL COME GREETING:

WHEREAS the annexed Order and Judgement of this Court dated _____ appointing _____
residing at _____
as guardian for the (person) and (property) of _____
an incapacitated person, has been entered in this Court on _____.

WHEREAS a bond in the amount of _____, with sufficient sureties was filed in this Court on _____, and

WHEREAS a designation of the Clerk to accept service of process upon such guardian above appointed was filed in this Court on _____.

NOW THEREFORE, KNOW YE THAT WE HAVE GRANTED, GIVEN AND COMMITTED AND DO SO GIVE, GRANT, COMMIT UNTO THE ABOVE NAMED GUARDIAN THE POWERS SET FORTH IN THE ANNEXED ORDER AND JUDGEMENT.

ALL TO WHOM THIS COMMISSION IS PRESENTED ARE COMMANDED TO RESPECT AND RECOGNIZE THE POWERS AND AUTHORITY GRANTED TO THE GUARDIAN IN THE ANNEXED ORDER AND JUDGEMENT.

By the Court this _____ day of
_____, 200___

                                    _____
                                    Clerk of the County of the Bronx

Form 8.　Commission to Co–Guardianship

The Supreme Court of The State Of New York
County of Bronx

_____

In the Matter Of The Application Of　　　**COMMISSION TO CO–GUARDIAN**

　　　　　　　　　　　　　　　　　　INDEX NO. _____

　　　　　　　　　　Petitioner,

For the Appointment Of A Guardian For

An Alleged Incapacitated Person.

_____

TO THE PEOPLE OF THE STATE OF NEW YORK, AND TO ALL WHOM THESE PRESENTS SHALL COME GREETING:

　　WHEREAS the annexed Order and Judgement of this Court dated _____ appointing _____
residing at _____
as co-guardian for the (person) and (property) of _____
an incapacitated person, has been entered in this Court on _____.

　　WHEREAS a bond in the amount of _____, with sufficient sureties was filed in this Court on _____, and

　　WHEREAS a designation of the Clerk to accept service of process upon such co-guardian above appointed was filed in this Court on _____.

　　NOW THEREFORE, KNOW YE THAT WE HAVE GRANTED, GIVEN AND COMMITTED AND DO SO GIVE, GRANT, COMMIT UNTO THE ABOVE NAMED CO–GUARDIAN THE POWERS SET FORTH IN THE ANNEXED ORDER AND JUDGEMENT.

　　ALL TO WHOM THIS COMMISSION IS PRESENTED ARE COMMANDED TO RESPECT AND RECOGNIZE THE POWERS AND AUTHORITY GRANTED TO THE CO–GUARDIAN IN THE ANNEXED ORDER AND JUDGEMENT.

By the Court this _____ day of
_____, 200___

　　　　　　　　　　　　　　　　　　_____
　　　　　　　　　　　　　　　　　　Clerk of the County of the Bronx

LEGAL SUPPORT

Doc. 1. Ex Parte/Orders

Orders to show cause (OSC) and their accompanying papers should be presented at the front desk in Room 217. The petition, affirmation or affidavit must state the result of any prior application for the same relief. The OSC must be double-spaced. Attorneys should comply with any special language or type size requirements called for by applicable statutes.

If an order to show cause is the first paper filed in a case, the OSC should be accompanied by a Request for Judicial Intervention (R.J.I.), if necessary. The attorney should put his fax number in the upper left hand corner of the OSC. If the OSC requests emergency relief, it should be accompanied by an affirmation of emergency.

Motions returnable in Special Trial Part (STP), motions to punish for contempt, and applications for stays or temporary restraining orders must be made by order to show cause. Motions made on "such notice as the court may direct" should be made by order to show cause. The court may grant an order to show cause to be served in lieu of a notice of petition.

Once an OSC has been signed, it will be faxed to the number provided by the attorney. OSC's may also be sent to an e-mail address if one is provided. Unless specifically advised otherwise, an appearance is required for all orders to show cause. Proof of service and any answering or reply papers should be presented to the court at the time the OSC is heard.

Some special requirements are discussed below:

1. Orders to Show Cause for Temporary Restraining Orders (TRO) are subject to Uniform Rule 202.7(f). An application for a TRO must show that the applicant has notified his adversary of the time and place of the application or that giving such notice will result in significant prejudice to the applicant. This rule is also applicable to matrimonial actions.

2. An Order to Show Cause to punish for contempt must comply with Judiciary Law § 756. The Order to Show Cause must contain on its face both a notice and a warning. The notice should state "The purpose of the hearing is to punish the accused for a contempt of court, and that such punishment may consist of fine or imprisonment, or both, according to law". The warning, printed or typewritten in a size equal to at least eight-point bold type, must state:

WARNING: YOUR FAILURE TO APPEAR IN COURT MAY RESULT IN YOUR IMMEDIATE ARREST AND IMPRISONMENT FOR CONTEMPT OF COURT.

1. In matrimonial actions, an Order to Show Cause seeking an Order of protection must contain a Family Protection Registry Information Sheet (FPRIS) as well the addendum to that sheet. Orders to Show Cause seeking child or spousal support must contain a New York State case Registry Filing Form (NYSCRFF). These forms are available on the Unified Court System's own web site.

Doc. 2. Settled Orders

A Judge's decision will often call for a Settled Order. The purpose of the settled order is to give effect to the decision by directing that some action be done and/or that a court official perform some task. For example, a settled order on a decision dismissing a complaint will order that the complaint be dismissed and that the county clerk mark his records accordingly.

A settled order consists of a notice of settlement informing all parties that the proposed order will be presented to the judge who made the decision on a date certain. Next comes the proposed order which will be presented to the judge. This order should conform to the judges decision and should direct the relief granted in the decision. This should be followed by proof of service upon all parties who were noticed with the decision. It is also helpful if a copy of the judge's decision is included along with the other papers. A settled order should always be noticed before the judge who made the decision.

Although an order is usually settled by the party who prevailed on the motion, any party may settle the order. It should be presented to the court within sixty days of the decision. The other parties are entitled to ten days notice where service of the settled order is done by mail, five days if the notice is personally delivered. An attorney who is served with a notice of settlement which he believes does not accurately reflect the decision may settle a counter order. The counter order must be noticed for the same day and must be served not less than seven days if by mail and two days if personally delivered.

Settled orders are usually sent to the judge the day after they noticed for settlement. No appearance is necessary or even contemplated on a settled order. If the decision directs "submit order", then no notice is necessary, and the order will be sent to the judge as soon a practical after it is received. No fees are collected on settled orders.

INFANT COMPROMISE ORDERS

Doc. 3. Infant Compromise Orders

An Infant's compromise Order is an order that settles a cause of action brought on behalf of a minor or a person for whom a legal guardian has been appointed. The order must be accompanied by an affidavit of the parent or guardian and an affirmation of the attorney who is handling the case. If the infant is over fourteen years of age, an infant's consent should also be included. These papers must contain all the information required by CPLR sections 1207 and 1208. Also required is an affirmation by a doctor who has examined the infant within the last six months. This affirmation will contain information on the infant's present condition. After review, the order is sent to the signed judge who will call the attorney to arrange a conference. In all but the most compelling circumstances, the presence of the infant at this conference is required. Compromises of cases assigned to Justice Paul Victor in the city part *must* be accompanied by a worksheet which is available at: http://www.nycourts.gov/courts/12jd/forms/city_part/Worksheet_For_Settlement_Conferences.pdf.

PARTIAL WITHDRAWAL OF INFANT FUNDS

Doc. 4. Partial Withdrawal of Infant Funds

Parents or Legal Guardians who have been awarded funds on behalf of a child may petition the court for a partial withdrawal of those funds for the sole use of the child. The legal Guardian will need to show that the items are necessary, that they are not capable of providing these items for the child. The decision to grant or deny the petition is at the discretion of the judge.

LEGAL SUPPORT FORMS

Form 1.   Family Protection Registry Information Sheet (FPRIS)

Enter "UNK" if data is not available. Do not hold order to collect this information

******ASTERISKED AREAS ARE REQUIRED*****

** Court ORI No: NY0 _ _ _ _ _ J   ** Name of Court: _____
** Order No: 200_ - _ _ _ _ _   ** County: _____
** Docket/Index No: _____   *Court Contact:* Name _____ Tel: _____
** Issuance Date on Order: _____   ** Expiration Date: _____
** *Law Enforcement Agency (Where copy of Order is Filed):* _____ Police Ori: NY _____

**SERVICE OF ORDER:
☐ Police to Serve Order   ☐ Other (later service)   ☐ Order served in Court (Date: _____ Time: _____)
☐ Notification by Mail (Mail date: _____)   ☐ Order Previously Served (Date: _____ no new service to be done)

APPLYING/PROTECTED PARTY (Party Requesting Order)

**Name: (Prefix) ____ (First) ____ (M) ____ (Last) ____ (Seniority) ____ (Suffix)
☐ Child   ☐ Unborn Child   ☐ No First Name
**Date of Birth: ____ **Sex: ☐ Male ☐ Female ☐ Unk   Height: ____ Eye Color: ____
**Race: ☐ White ☐ Black ☐ Other ☐ Unknown   Weight: ____ Hair Color: ____
   ☐ American Indian/Alaskan Native   ☐ Asian/Pacific Islander
** Ethnicity: ☐ Hispanic ☐ Non-Hispanic   Lic Plate # ____ State: ____ Drivers ID: ____ State: ____
Mother's Maiden Name: ____ Soc. Sec. No.: ____ NYSID: ____
Alias or Nickname: (Prefix) ____ (First) ____ (M) ____ (Last) ____ (Seniority) ____ (Suffix)
**Address Information: ** **Confidential? ☐ Yes ☐ No   Type (ie Home, Work) _____
(Street) ____   (Apt) ___ (Floor) ___ (Room) ____
   Mail c/o: _____
(City) ____ (State) ____ (Zip) ____   (County) ____ (Nation) ____
Contact Information: **Confidential? ☐ Yes ☐ No ☐ Outside USA
Phone (home): ____ (work): ____   (other): ____ email: ____ fax: ____

** Is Any Protected Party the Enjoined/Against Party's Intimate Partner, or the Child of either the Protected or Enjoined Party or Both" **   ☐ Yes   ☐ No
** Select the relationship betweenEnjoined/Against Party and Protected Party:
☐ Spouse ☐ Ex-Spouse ☐ Domestic Partner ☐ Child-in-Common ☐ Child of One Party

ENJOINED/AGAINST PARTY (Party Against Whom OrderRuns)

**Name: (Prefix) ____ (First) ____ (M) ____ (Last) ____ (Seniority) ____ (Suffix)
**Date of Birth: ____ **Sex: ☐ Male ☐ Female ☐ Unk   Height: ____ Eye Color: ____
**Race: ☐ White ☐ Black ☐ Other ☐ Unknown   Weight: ____ Hair Color: ____
   ☐ American Indian/Alaskan Native   ☐ Asian/Pacific Islander
** Ethnicity: ☐ Hispanic ☐ Non-Hispanic   Lic Plate # ____ State: ____ Drivers ID: ____ State: ____
Mother's Maiden Name: ____ Soc. Sec. No.: ____ NYSID: ____
Alias or Nickname: (Prefix) ____ (First) ____ (M) ____ (Last) ____ (Seniority) ____ (Suffix)
**Address Information: ** **Confidential? ☐ Yes ☐ No   Type (ie Home, Work) _____
(Street) ____   (Apt) ___ (Floor) ___ (Room) ____
   Mail c/o: _____
(City) ____ (State) ____ (Zip) ____   (County) ____ (Nation) ____
Contact Information: **Confidential? ☐ Yes ☐ No ☐ Outside USA
Phone (home): ____ (work): ____   (other): ____ email: ____ fax: ____

Is Police Caution Advised? If yes, why? _____

Form 2.   Addendum to Family Protection Registry Information Sheet

Use this form for Vacates, Dismisses, Seals, Extensions,
Violations, Warrants and Service.

A copy of the original order of protection is not required.

ASTERISKED AREAS ARE REQUIRED

ORIGINAL ORDER INFORMATION:

COURT ORI No: NY0 _ _ _ _ _ _ J   ****COURT: _____
ORDER NO: 200_ - _ _ _ _ _ _ _   ****COUNTY: _____
**DOCKET/INDEX NO: _____
**Enjoined Party's Name: _____   *Court Contact:*   Name _____
**Applying Party's Name: _____   Tel: _____
Law Enforcement Agency at which Copy of Order is Filed:
   NAME: _____   ****POLICE ORI: NY _____

☐ **ORDER SERVED** Service Date: _____   Time: _____
☐ **ORDER VACATED**   Date: _____   Judge: _____
☐ **CASE DISMISSED *** Date: _____   Judge: _____
☐ **CASE SEALED ***   Date: _____   Judge: _____

☐ ORDER EXTENDED

Date of Extension: _____   ****Judge: _____
**New expiration date: _____

**SERVICE OF EXTENDED ORDER:

☐ **Police to Serve Order**   ☐ **Other** (later service)
☐ **Order served in Court**   (Date: _____   Time: _____
☐ **Notification by Mail**   (Mail date: _____)   ☐ **Order Previously Served** (Date: _____)
                                                (no new service to be done)

☐ VIOLATION

Date of Filing: _____   ****Judge: _____
**Date of Disposition: _____

**Disposition:
   ☐ Dismissed   ☐ Resentence   ☐ Convicted   ☐ New OP
   ☐ Gun license revoked

☐ WARRANT

Issue Date: _____   ****Name: _____
   ☐ Warrant Executed   (date: _____)
   ☐ Return on Warrant (date: _____)
   ☐ Warrant Vacated   (date: _____)

Form 3. New York State Case Registry Filing Form * (NYSCRFF)

For Use With Child Support Orders and Combined Child and Spousal Support Orders Payable To Other Than A Child Support Collection Unit

Name of Court: _____ County Name: _____ Index Number: _____

Child Support
Payor: _____ Social Security #: ____ Date of Birth: _____
        (first)   (last) (middle initial) (Payor)   (Payor)

Child Support
Payee: _____ Social Security #: ____ Date of Birth: _____
        (first)   (last) (middle initial) (Payee)   (Payee)

Child #1 Name: _____ Social Security #: ____ Date of Birth: _____
        (first)   (last) (middle initial) (Child #1)   (Child #1)

Child #2 Name: _____ Social Security #: ____ Date of Birth: _____
        (first)   (last) (middle initial) (Child #2)   (Child #2)

Child #3 Name: _____ Social Security #: ____ Date of Birth: _____
        (first)   (last) (middle initial) (Child #3)   (Child #3)

(If more children, please use additional form.)

FAMILY VIOLENCE INQUIRY

Has a Temporary or Final Order of Protection been granted on behalf of   ☐ yes   ☐ no   ☐ do not know
either party?
    If yes, which party -   ☐ Payor   ☐ Payee

Has a request for confidentiality of address been granted on behalf of either   ☐ yes   ☐ no
party?
    If yes, which party -   ☐ Payor   ☐ Payee

* Social Services Law § 111–b(4)(a) and Domestic Relations Law § 240(5) direct that such orders must be filed with the State Case Registry

Form 4.   Confidential/Settlement Worksheet

TITLE OF PROCEEDINGS 1

--x

V.

--x

INDEX NO.: _____

DATE NOTE OF ISSUE FILED: _____

ESTIMATED LENGTH OF TRIAL: ___2

CASE TYPE: _____

1 IDENTIFY ALL PARTIES IN THE CAPTION.
2 AFTER TRIAL ASSIGNMENT PLEASE PROVIDE AND/OR CERTIFY THAT: THERE ARE NO OUTSTANDING MOTIONS ☐; ALL WITNESSES ARE AVAILABLE ☐; WHETHER AN INTER-PRETER IS NEEDED (YES ___ NO ___) AND IF YES, THE LANGUAGE _____ ☐.

ATTORNEYS OF RECORD & TRIAL COUNSEL[3]

COUNSEL FOR PLAINTIFF(S)

1. _____
ATTORNEY OF RECORD FOR _____
OFFICE ADDRESS AND PHONE NUMBER

_____
_____

TRIAL COUNSEL AND PHONE NUMBER

_____
_____

2. _____
ATTORNEY OF RECORD FOR _____
OFFICE ADDRESS AND PHONE NUMBER

_____
_____

TRIAL COUNSEL AND PHONE NUMBER

_____
_____

3. _____
ATTORNEY OF RECORD FOR _____
OFFICE ADDRESS AND PHONE NUMBER

_____
_____

TRIAL COUNSEL AND PHONE NUMBER

_____

COUNSEL FOR DEFENDANT(S)

1. _____
ATTORNEY OF RECORD FOR _____
OFFICE ADDRESS AND PHONE NUMBER

_____
_____

TRIAL COUNSEL AND PHONE NUMBER

_____
_____

2. _____

ATTORNEY OF RECORD FOR _____
OFFICE ADDRESS AND PHONE NUMBER
_____
_____

TRIAL COUNSEL AND PHONE NUMBER
_____
_____

3. _____
ATTORNEY OF RECORD FOR _____
OFFICE ADDRESS AND PHONE NUMBER
_____
_____

TRIAL COUNSEL AND PHONE NUMBER
_____

3 ONLY ATTORNEYS OF RECORD AND TRIAL COUNSEL MUST BE IDENTIFIED ON THIS PAGE. "COVERING" COUNSEL SHALL ONLY BE IDENTIFIED IN THE PROGRESS NOTES, INFRA.

SUMMARY SHEET[4]

PLAINTIFFS	DOB	OCCUPATION	LOST TIME
1. _____	_____	_____	_____
2. _____	_____	_____	_____
3. _____	_____	_____	_____
4. _____	_____	_____	_____

OCCURRENCE: (PROVIDE PLAINTIFF'S VERSION)

(TYPE OF ACTION)

DATE: _____ TIME: ___ LOCATION: _____
_____
_____
_____
_____

LIABILITY ISSUES AND DEFENDANTS VERSION: _____
_____
_____
_____

INJURIES AND TREATMENT: _____
_____
_____
_____

PAST AND FUTURE DAMAGES: _____
_____
_____

LIENS: _____
PLAINTIFF(S) DEMANDS: _____
_____

DEFENDANT(S) OFFERS: _____

_____

_____

[4] Here provide a <u>simple</u> and short summary only. Provide the details on pages 4 to 9, *infra*.

SETTLEMENT CONFERENCE PROGRESS NOTES[5]

DATE AND ACTION TAKEN: _____
COUNSEL FOR PLAINTIFF: _____

_____

_____

_____

_____

_____

DATE AND ACTION TAKEN: _____
COUNSEL FOR PLAINTIFF: _____

_____

_____

_____

_____

DATE AND ACTION TAKEN: _____
COUNSEL FOR PLAINTIFF; _____

_____

_____

_____

DATE AND ACTION TAKEN: _____
COUNSEL FOR PLAINTIFF; _____

_____

_____

_____

DATE AND ACTION TAKEN: _____
COUNSEL FOR PLAINTIFF; _____

_____

_____

_____

DATE AND ACTION TAKEN: _____
COUNSEL FOR PLAINTIFF; _____

_____

_____

_____

_____

DATE AND ACTION TAKEN: _____

COUNSEL FOR PLAINTIFF; _____

_____

_____

_____

DATE AND ACTION TAKEN: _____

COUNSEL FOR PLAINTIFF; _____

_____

DATE AND ACTION TAKEN: _____

COUNSEL FOR PLAINTIFF: _____

_____

_____

_____

_____

DATE AND ACTION TAKEN: _____

COUNSEL FOR PLAINTIFF: _____

_____

_____

_____

DATE AND ACTION TAKEN: _____

COUNSEL FOR PLAINTIFF; _____

_____

_____

_____

_____

DATE AND ACTION TAKEN: _____

COUNSEL FOR PLAINTIFF; _____

_____

_____

_____

_____

DATE AND ACTION TAKEN: _____

COUNSEL FOR PLAINTIFF; _____

_____

_____

_____

_____

DATE AND ACTION TAKEN: _____

COUNSEL FOR PLAINTIFF; _____

_____

_____

_____

_____

DATE AND ACTION TAKEN: _____

COUNSEL FOR PLAINTIFF; _____

_____

_____

_____

DATE AND ACTION TAKEN: _____

COUNSEL FOR PLAINTIFF; _____

_____

5 For details regarding the occurrence, liability and damages - See pages 4 to 9.

INFORMATION REGARDING THE INCIDENT[6]

OCCURRENCE:

DATE: _____; TIME: _____; WEATHER _____

LOCATION: _____

LIGHTING AND OTHER FACTORS: _____

_____

BRIEF DESCRIPTION OF INCIDENT: (PROVIDE PLAINTIFF'S AND DEFENDANT'S VERSION)

_____

_____

_____

_____

☐ AMBULANCE AT SCENE?; ☐ POLICE AT SCENE?; ☐ OTHER

_____

WITNESSES: (PROVIDE NAME OF EACH WITNESS AND SYNOPSIS OF WITNESSES STATEMENT)

_____

_____

_____

☐ WRITTEN STATEMENT OBTAINED?; ☐ EBT OF WITNESS CONDUCTED?

IDENTIFY ALL PERSONS, DEPARTMENTS AND/OR AGENCIES THAT INVESTIGATED INCIDENT AND STATE WHETHER REPORTS HAVE BEEN PREPARED AND FILED:.

_____

_____

IDENTIFY ALL DISPUTED LEGAL AND FACTUAL ISSUES AND DISPUTES.

_____

_____

_____

6 All information requested herein is confidential and provides the Court with the ability to make a fair evaluation of the settlement value of the case. It is not the intention of the Court to compromise counsel's trial strategy, and counsel is free to decline to provide any and all of other information requested. It is the Court's experience that whenever each side is candid about the strengths and weaknesses of their respective positions, a fair and early settlement is usually achieved. In addition, reliance upon the assumed lack of preparedness of your adversary is usually an illusion that pays no dividends. In any event, your failure to be prepared and/or failure to provide the court with all essential information and documentation, will result in a failed negotiation and a delayed trial! Please help the Court to help you settle this case in an expeditious fashion.

PLAINTIFF'S PERSONAL INFORMATION[7]

NAME: _____; DOB _____; MARITAL STATUS: _____

OCCUPATION AND SALARY: (BOTH AT THE TIME OF INCIDENT AND AT PRESENT)

_____

_____

IDENTIFICATION OF EMPLOYER(S): _____

_____

TIME LOST FROM WORK; AND THE PERIODS THEREOF: _____

_____

TOTAL AMOUNT CLAIMED FOR LOST EARNINGS:

    PAST AMOUNT: $ _____ PERIOD: (FROM) _____ (TO) _____

    FUTURE AMOUNT: $ _____ PERIOD: (FROM) _____ (TO) _____

DESCRIBE ALL LIENS AND/OR COLLATERAL SOURCES:

_____

_____

_____

OTHER RELEVANT FACTORS:

_____

_____

_____

MEDICAL ISSUES

DESCRIPTION, NATURE AND EXTENT OF INJURIES:

_____

_____

_____

AMBULANCE: YES ☐   NO ☐   _____
HOSPITAL: YES ☐   NO ☐   _____
SURGERY: YES ☐   NO ☐   _____

DATE, PLACE AND NATURE OF EACH SURGERY:

_____

_____

_____

FIRST MEDICAL TREATMENT: DATE: _____
1. IDENTIFY HOSPITAL AND/OR MEDICAL PROVIDER: _____

_____

_____

2. DESCRIBE TREATMENT RENDERED: _____

_____

_____

LAST MEDICAL TREATMENT AND REPORT: DATE _____
    1. IDENTIFY HOSPITAL AND/OR MEDICAL PROVIDER: _____

_____

_____

    2. DESCRIBE TREATMENT, COMPLAINTS, FINDINGS AND PROGNO-
SIS:

_____

_____

_____

PRESENT MEDICAL COMPLAINTS AND CONDITIONS: _____

_____

_____

MEDICAL ISSUES CONTINUED

MEDICAL EXPENSES INCURRED TO DATE: $ _____
ESTIMATED FUTURE MEDICAL EXPENSES: $ _____

DESCRIBE THE NATURE OF ALL CLAIMED FUTURE MEDICAL TREAT-
MENT:

_____

_____

_____

HOW WERE ABOVE MEDICAL EXPENSES PAID? _____

HAVE I.M.E.'s BEEN COMPLETED?   ☐ YES ☐ NO
HAVE I.M.E. REPORTS BEEN EXCHANGED?   ☐ YES ☐ NO

DESCRIBE RELEVANT FINDINGS & CONCLUSIONS

_____
_____
_____
_____

IDENTIFY ALL PRIOR AND SUBSEQUENT ACCIDENTS, INJURIES, CLAIMS AND LAWSUITS WHICH MAY BE RELEVANT TO THE MEDICAL ISSUES IN THIS CASE!

_____
_____
_____

LIENS

ARE THERE ANY LIENS?   ☐ YES ☐ NO

PROVIDE THE FOLLOWING WITH REGARD TO EACH LIEN:

LIENOR	AMOUNT	TYPE
_____	_____	_____
_____	_____	_____
_____	_____	_____
_____	_____	_____

DOCUMENTS REQUIRED FOR SETTLEMENT CONFERENCES

YOU MUST BRING TO COURT THE FOLLOWING DOCUMENTS (TO THE EXTENT THEY EXIST). FOR SETTLEMENT PURPOSES IT WOULD BE EXTREMELY HELPFUL TO THE COURT AS WELL AS OF ASSISTANCE TO THE PARTIES, IF THE FOLLOWING DOCUMENTS ARE BROUGHT TO THE COURT ON EACH CONFERENCE DATE.

IF THESE DOCUMENTS ARE NOT PROVIDED THE COURT WILL FIND IT EXTREMELY DIFFICULT TO ASSIST IN A MEANINGFUL SETTLE-MENT CONFERENCE.

(1) FOR ALL CASES PROVIDE THE FOLLOWING REPORTS/RECORDS:

DESCRIPTION OF DOCUMENT	EXPLANATION/COMMENTS
☐ PROOF OF PRIOR NOTICE	_____
☐ NOTICE OF CLAIM	_____
☐ 50-H TRANSCRIPT	_____
☐ EBT'S CONDUCTED	_____
☐ STATEMENTS OBTAINED	_____
☐ PHOTOGRAPHS (NOT PHOTOCOPIES)	
☐ OF LOCATION	_____
☐ OF INJURIES	_____
☐ OTHER DAMAGES	_____
☐ INCIDENT, ACCIDENT REPORTS	_____
☐ BY POLICE	_____
☐ BY AGENCY, BOARD OR AUTHORITY	_____
☐ BY PLAINTIFF	_____
☐ BY DEFENDANT	_____
☐ OTHER	_____

| DESCRIPTION OF DOCUMENT | EXPLANATION/COMMENTS |

☐ HOSPITALIZATIONS AND RECORDS

       ☐ AMBULANCE/EMS
       ☐ EMERGENCY ROOM/TRIAGE
       ☐ RADIOLOGY
       ☐ OPERATIVE
       ☐ OTHER
☐ TREATING DOCTOR(S)
☐ PHYSICAL THERAPY
☐ EXPERT(S) - LIABILITY

                (PLAINTIFF)
                (DEFENDANT)
☐ EXPERT(S) - MEDICAL

                (PLAINTIFF)
                (DEFENDANT)
☐ PROOF OF ECONOMIC LOSSES
☐ OTHER RELEVANT DOCUMENTS

[7] SEPARATE SHEETS MUST BE PROVIDED FOR EACH PLAINTIFF.

REQUIRED DOCUMENTS CONTINUED[8]

| DESCRIPTION | EXPLANATION/COMMENTS |

(2) FOR TRIP & FALL

       ☐ BIG APPLE MAP
       ☐ WORK ORDERS
       ☐ CONTRACTS, PERMITS, CUT
         FORMS
       ☐ OTHER DOCUMENTS
         RELEVANT TO NOTICE

(3) FOR PREMISES CLAIMS

       ☐ OWNERSHIP
       ☐ PRIOR COMPLAINTS
       ☐ PHOTOGRAPHS

(4) FOR MOTOR VEHICLE ACCIDENT
     CLAIMS

       ☐ DMV HEARING TRANSCRIPT
       ☐ PHOTOGRAPHS OF VEHICLE
       ☐ REPAIR BILL AND/OR
         ESTIMATE

(5) FOR POLICE MISCONDUCT CLAIMS

       ☐ CERTIFICATE OF DISPOSITION
       ☐ ALL RELEVANT POLICE
         REPORTS
       ☐ PHOTOGRAPHS
       ☐ WITNESS STATEMENTS
       ☐ CRIMINAL COURT COMPLAINT
       ☐ INDICTMENT
       ☐ TRANSCRIPT OF
         PROCEEDINGS
       ☐ PLAINTIFF'S ARREST/
         CONVICTION RECORD
       ☐ INVOICE FOR LEGAL
         DEFENSE FEES
       ☐ OTHER ECONOMIC DAMAGES IN-
         CURRED

DESCRIPTION   EXPLANATION/COMMENTS

(6) FOR PROPERTY DAMAGE CLAIMS

     ☐ PHOTOGRAPHS   _____
     ☐ ORIGINAL PURCHASE
        RECEIPTS   _____
     ☐ CANCELLED CHECKS   _____
     ☐ APPRAISALS AND ESTIMATES   _____
     ☐ INSURANCE AGREEMENTS   _____
     ☐ OTHER   _____

(7) FOR THIRD PARTY CLAIMS

     ☐ INDEMNITY CONTRACTS   _____
     ☐ ALL APPLICABLE INSURANCE
        POLICIES   _____

8 Provide a supplemental sheet for all other relevant documents.

MATRIMONIAL

CASE MANAGEMENT FLOW CHART

Doc. 1. Matrimonial Case Management Flow Chart

MATRIMONIAL CASE MANAGEMENT FLOW CHART

PRE REQUEST FOR JUDICIAL INTERVENTION ACTIVITY

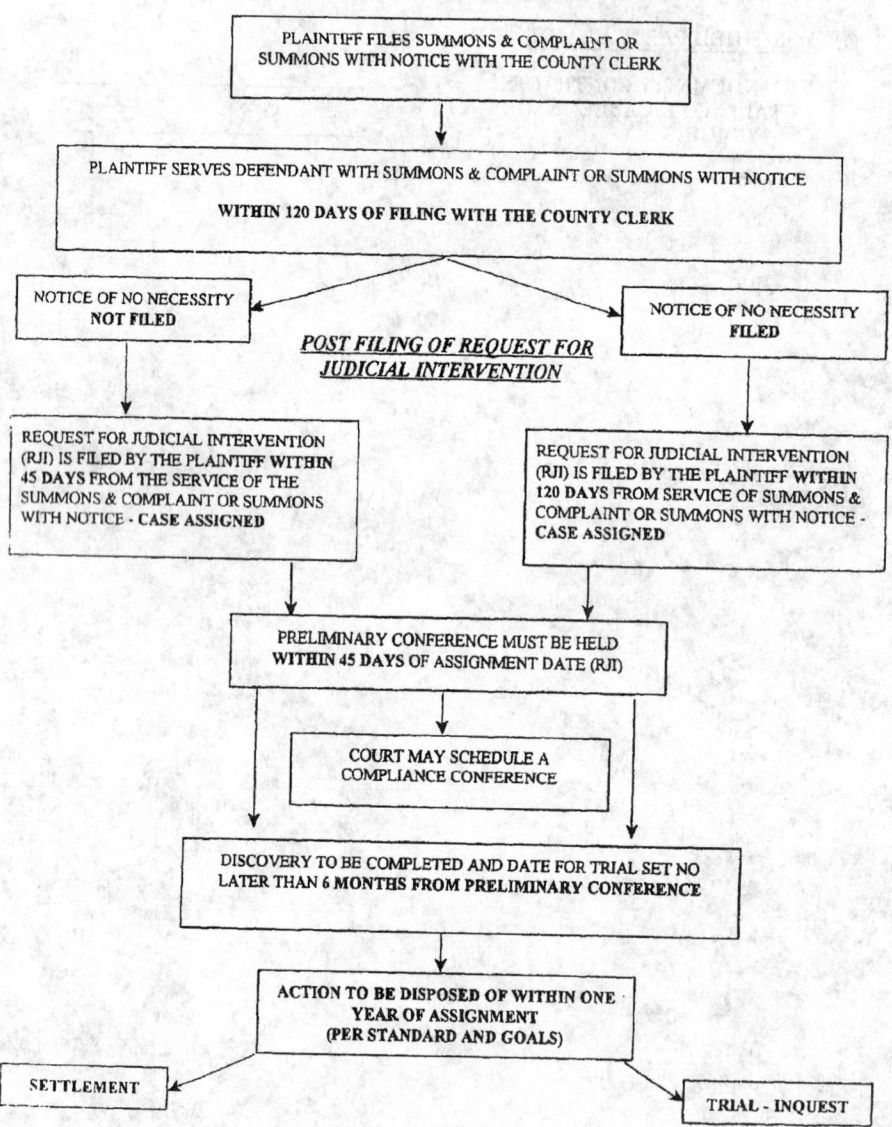

CONTESTED MATRIMONIAL PROCEDURE

Doc. 2.   Contested Matrimonial Procedure

1.   Obtain an Index Number from the County Clerk's Office, Room 118, for a fee of $210.00, and file the Summons with Notice or Summons and Complaint. Obtain a file stamped copy of the Summons with Notice or Summons and Complaint from the County Clerk.

2.   A copy of the Summons with Notice or Summons and Complaint, with the index number and filing date stamped on it, is to be delivered to the defendant personally, or upon application, by court ordered alternate service.

3.   The defendant must be served within 120 days of the purchase of the index number and the filing of the Summons with Notice or Summons and Complaint unless an application for an extension of time to serve is made by the plaintiff's attorney and granted by the court.

4.   Personal service upon the defendant should be made by a person 18 years old or older who is not a party to the action.   No service is to be made on a Sunday.

5.   A Request for Judicial Intervention (R.J.I.) must be filed no later than 45 days from the service of the Summons with Notice or Summons and Complaint unless both parties file a Notice of No Necessity with the court.   If a Notice of No Necessity is filed by both parties, then the R.J.I. must be filed no later than 120 days from the service of the Summons with Notice or Summons and Complaint.

6.   The Request for Judicial Intervention (R.J.I.) filing fee is $95.00.

7.   Once the R.J.I. is filed, a preliminary conference will be scheduled.   The preliminary conference must be held within 45 days of the filing of the R.J.I. Preliminary conferences are usually scheduled by the court within 30 days of the filing of the R.J.I.

8.   The date and time of the conference shall be set forth in a preliminary conference scheduling order which shall be mailed to the attorneys.   The preliminary conference scheduling order will specify the papers that must be exchanged between the parties prior to the preliminary conference, and will specify the time in which such exchange is to take place.

9.   Net Worth Statements must be exchanged between the parties, and filed with the court no later than ten (10) days prior to the preliminary conference. See Uniform Rule 202.16 (f)(1) for a list of other papers that must be exchanged prior to the preliminary conference.   Said papers will also be specified in the courts preliminary conference scheduling order.

10.   The parties must be present at the preliminary conference, and the court shall address them at the conference.

11.   At the close of the conference, the court shall schedule a compliance conference unless the court dispenses with the compliance conference based upon a stipulation of compliance filed by the parties.

12.   The parties must be present at the compliance conference, unless they are excused by the court, and the court shall address them at the conference.

13.   Discovery must be completed and a Note of Issue must be filed within six (6) months from the commencement of the preliminary conference, unless otherwise extended or shortened by the court depending upon the circumstances of the case.

14.   The Note of Issue must be filed within ten (10) days of after it is served. The Note of Issue must be filed in triplicate. The filing fee for a Note of Issue in a contested matrimonial action is $30.00.

15.   A Statement of Proposed Disposition with proof of service must be filed with the Note of Issue.

16.   In accordance with Uniform Rule 202.16(f)(3) a trial is to be scheduled no later than six (6) months from the date of the preliminary conference in a non-complex case.

17.   If the case is settled prior to the filing of the Note of Issue, an inquest will be held and the court will issue an order which allows for the late filing of the Note of Issue, waives the Certificate of Readiness, and dispenses with service.

18.   Once judgment has been granted orally on the record, after trial or inquest, the following documents, in the exact order listed, must be presented personally or by mail to the Matrimonial Clerk's Office, Room 217:

   a.   Three (3) copies of the Note of Issue with $30.00 fee (if not previously filed)

   b.   A copy of the court's short form order permitting the late filing of the Note of Issue and waiving the Certificate of Readiness and service

   c.   Notice of Settlement of Findings of Fact and Conclusions of Law, and Judgment

   d.   Proof of service of Notice of Settlement, Findings of Fact and Conclusions of Law, and Judgment

   e.   Findings of Fact and Conclusions of Law

   f.   Judgment

   g.   Original Certified Transcript — (Secure the name and telephone number of the court stenographer on the day of the inquest or trial.   Call the court stenographer to order the transcript.   The court stenographer will inform you of the fee for the transcript.)

h. Stipulation of parties correcting any errors in the transcripts (if applicable)

i. Affirmation of Lateness with proof of service, if settled more than 60 after inquest or decision after trial

j. Sworn Statement of Removal of Barriers to Remarriage with Proof of Service — (Affidavit must reflect that steps "have been" taken in accordance with D.R.L. 253(3). If grounds are based on Separation Agreement and the defendant appears in the action, the Defendant must also submit a Sworn Statement of Removal of Barriers to Remarriage)

k. Copy of any stipulation entered into between the parties

l. Copy of any Family Court order which is to be continued

m. Summons With Notice or Summons (served with Verified Complaint), with proof of filing

n. Pleadings or copy of pleadings if pleadings were previously filed with court

o. UCS 111 form and Child Support Information Form (Case Registry Form) where a determination of child support has been made

p. Certificate of Dissolution of Marriage — Form DOH 2168

q. Part 130 Certification

r. Two (2) self-addressed, stamped postcards

19. The Notice of Settlement, Findings of Fact and Conclusions of Law, and Judgment must be submitted within 60 days of courts direction to settle on notice.

20. A copy of the Findings of Fact and Conclusions of Law, Judgment, and Notice of Settlement must be served not less than five (5) days before the settlement date if served personally, or not less than ten (10) days before the settlement date if served by mail.

21. Any counter Findings of Fact and Conclusions of Law, and counter Judgment will be made returnable on the same date and place.

22. A copy of any counter papers will be served not less than two (2) days before the settlement date if served personally, or not less than seven (7) days before the settlement date if served by mail.

23. The Notice of Settlement, Findings of Fact and Conclusions of Law, and Judgment must be filed with the matrimonial clerk on or before the return date.

24. The papers will be forwarded by the matrimonial clerk to the court for consideration on the next business day following the settlement date.

25. The Notice of Settlement and proof of service of the Notice of Settlement, Findings of Fact and Conclusions of Law, and Judgment are not required if the other party consents in writing to the form and content of the Findings of Fact and Conclusions of Law, and Judgment.

26. If the papers are acceptable to the court, the Findings of Fact and Conclusions of Law, and Judgment will be signed. Otherwise, further corrections may be required.

27. The divorce is final after the Findings of Fact and Conclusions of Law, and Judgment are signed by the court and entered by the County Clerk. A certified copy of the final signed Judgment may be obtained from the County Clerk's Office, Room 118, for a fee of $8.00 per certified copy.

Contested Matrimonial Checklist

Doc. 3. Contested Matrimonial Checklist

Title of Action: _____ –vs– _____ **Index #:** _____

Once judgment has been granted orally by the court after trial or inquest, the following documents, in the exact order listed, must be presented personally or by mail to the Matrimonial Clerk's Office, Room 217:

___ Note of Issue with $30.00 fee (if not previously filed)

___ A copy of the court's short form order permitting the late filing of the Note of Issue and waiving the Certificate of Readiness and service

___ Notice of Settlement of Findings of Fact and Conclusions of Law, and Judgment

___ Proof of service of Notice of Settlement, Findings of Fact and Conclusions of Law, and Judgment

___ Findings of Fact and Conclusions of Law

___ Judgment

___ Original Certified Transcript

___ Stipulation of parties correcting any errors in transcript (if applicable)

___ Affirmation of Lateness with proof of service, if settled more than 60 days after inquest or decision after trial

___ Sworn Statement of Removal of Barriers to Remarriage with Proof of Service—affidavit must reflect that steps "have been" taken in accordance with DRL 253(3)

(If grounds are based on Separation Agreement and the defendant appears in the action, the Defendant must also submit a Sworn Statement of Removal of Barriers to Remarriage)

___ Copy of any stipulation(s) entered into between the parties. Stipulation must contain DRL § 255

statements or an Addendum containing the DRL § 255 statements must be submitted.

___ Copy of any Family Court order which is to be continued

___ Copy of Summons With Notice <u>or</u> Summons (served with Verified Complaint), with proof of filing

___ Pleadings or copy of pleadings if pleadings were previously filed with court

___ Affidavit regarding social security numbers of parties and children, and prior surname of wife.

___ Special UCS 111–A Form

___ NYS Case Registry Filing Form

___ Certificate of Dissolution of Marriage—Form DOH 2168

___ Part 130 Certification

___ Two (2) self-addressed, stamped envelopes

1. The Findings of Fact and Conclusions of Law, and Judgment must be submitted within 60 days of court's direction to settle on notice.

2. A copy of the Findings of Fact and Conclusions of Law, Judgment and Notice of Settlement must be served not less than five (5) days before settlement date if served personally or not less than ten (10) days before settlement date if served by mail.

3. If child support is to be paid through the Support Collection Unit, the Judgment must contain the Support Collection Unit Notice as required by DRL 240–c(5)(b), and the judgment must reflect that sup-

port be paid through the Support Collection Unit at the following address:

NYS Child Support Processing Center
P.O. Box 15363
Albany, N.Y. 12212–5363

4. Any counter Findings of Fact and Conclusions of Law, and counter Judgment shall be made returnable on same date and place.

5. Any counter Findings of Fact and Conclusions of Law, and counter Judgment shall be submitted with a copy clearly marked to delineate each proposed change to the Findings or Judgment to which objection is made.

6. Copy of counter papers shall be served not less than two (2) days before settlement date if served personally or not less than seven (7) days before settlement date if served by mail.

7. Notice Of Settlement, Findings of Fact and Conclusions of Law, and Judgment must be filed with the Matrimonial Clerk on or before the return date.

8. The papers will be submitted to the court for consideration on the next business day following the settlement date. If the papers are acceptable to the court, Findings of Fact and Conclusions of Law, and Judgment will be signed. Otherwise, further corrections may be required.

9. A certified copy of the final signed Findings of Fact and Conclusions of Law, and Judgment may be obtained from the County Clerk's Office, Room 118, for a fee of $8.00 per certified copy.

Uncontested Matrimonial Procedure

Doc. 4. Uncontested Matrimonial Procedure

1. Obtain an Index Number from the County Clerk's Office, Room 118, for a fee of $210.00, and file the Summons with Notice or Summons and Complaint. Obtain a file stamped copy of the Summons with Notice or Summons and Complaint from the County Clerk.

2. A copy of the Summons with Notice or Summons and Complaint, with the index number and filing date stamped on it, is to be delivered to the defendant personally, or upon application, by court ordered alternate service.

3. The defendant must be served within 120 days of the purchase of the index number and the filing of the Summons with Notice or Summons and Complaint unless an application for an extension of time to serve is made by the plaintiff's attorney and granted by the court.

4. Personal service upon the defendant should be made by a person 18 years old or older who is not a

party to the action. No service is to be made on a Sunday.

5. If the defendant has defaulted, the Note of Issue and all supporting documents may be submitted to the Court after 41 days have elapsed since the service of the Summons with Notice or Summons and Complaint. If the defendant has appeared, consented to the divorce, and waived the statutory period in which to place the case on the calendar, the Note of Issue and all supporting documents may be submitted to the Court immediately. The Note of Issue must be filed within one (1) year of the default.

6. The Note of Issue filing fee is $125.00.

7. After the defendant has defaulted in appearing or answering and 41 days have elapsed since service upon the defendant, or after the defendant has appeared, waived his or her right to answer, and consented to the placement of the action on the calendar, the following documents, in the exact order listed, must be presented personally or by mail to the Matrimonial Clerk's Office, Room 217:

a. Three (3) copies of the Note of Issue with $125.00 fee

b. Summons With Notice or Summons (served with Verified Complaint), with proof of filing

c. Verified Complaint

d. Affidavit of Service or Affidavit of Defendant

e. Sworn Statement of Removal of Barriers to Remarriage with Proof of Service (If grounds are based on a Judgment of Separation or a Separation Agreement and the defendant appears in the action, the Defendant must also submit a Sworn Statement of Removal of Barriers to Remarriage)

f. Affirmation of Regularity

g. Affidavit of Plaintiff

h. Affidavit regarding the military status of the defendant (May is addressed in Affidavit of Plaintiff)

i. Affidavit regarding D.L. 76h information if there are children less than 18 years old (May is addressed in Affidavit of Plaintiff)

j. Corroborating Affidavit of Third Party (Annulment or Adultery Cases Only)

k. Stipulation resolving ancillary issues (Must be acknowledged)

l. Copy of any Family Court order that is to be continued

m. Findings of Fact/Conclusions of Law

n. Judgment of Divorce

o. Part 130 Certification

p. Certificates of Dissolution of Marriage

q. UCS-113 (UCS Divorce and Child Support Summary Form) (If applicable)

r. New York State Case Registry Filing Form (If applicable)

s. Two (2) self-addressed, Stamped Postcards

8. If child support is an issue, the resolution of the issue must be in accordance with the Child Support Standards Act. Before issuing an order of child support, the Court requires either proof of an existing Family Court order of support to be continued, a child support stipulation, or a hearing to determine the issue of support.

9. Uncontested Matrimonial forms, and Child Support Standards Charts are available in the Office of the Self–Represented, Room 121, or online at www. nycourts.gov.

10. On a future date, the papers will be submitted to a Special Referee for consideration. If satisfied as to the proof, the proposed Findings of Fact and Conclusions of Law, and Judgment will be signed. Otherwise, further corrections or a hearing may be required.

11. The divorce is final after the Findings of Fact and Conclusions of Law are signed by the court and entered by the County Clerk. A certified copy of the final signed Judgment may be obtained from the County Clerk's Office, Room 118, for a fee of $8.00 per certified copy.

UNCONTESTED MATRIMONIAL CHECKLIST

Doc. 5.   Uncontested Matrimonial Checklist

Title of Action _____ -vs- _____ Index #_____

Forms listed in **bold** print must be submitted in every case. All packages must be presented in the following order:

☐ Note of Issue with $125.00 fee

☐ Request for Judicial Intervention (RJI) — No fee required.

☐ RJI Addendum (Form 840M)

☐ Notice of Automatic Orders and Notice Concerning Continuation of Health Care Coverage with proof of service

☐ Summons With Notice or Summons (served with Verified Complaint), with proof of filing

☐ Verified Complaint

☐ Affidavit of Service or Affidavit of Defendant

☐ Sworn Statement of Removal of Barriers to Remarriage with Proof of Service

☐ Affirmation of Regularity

☐ Affidavit of Plaintiff

☐ Affidavit regarding military status of defendant (May be addressed in Affidavit of Plaintiff)

☐ Affidavit regarding DRL 76h information if there are children less than 18 years old (May be addressed in Affidavit of Plaintiff)

☐ Corroborating Affidavit of Third Party (Annulment or Adultery Cases Only)

☐ Stipulation resolving ancillary issues. The stipulation must be acknowledged, and mut contain DRL § 255 statements or an Addendum containing the DRL § 255 statements must be submitted. Where there is no stipulation, proof of service of the DRL 255 notice must be submitted.

☐ Copy of any Family Court order that is to be continued

☐ Findings of Fact and Conclusions of Law

☐ Judgment of Divorce

☐ Part 130 Certification

☐ Certificate of Dissolution of Marriage

☐ Special UCS–111A (UCS Divorce and Child Support Summary Form)

☐ New York State Case Registry Filing Form

☐ Two (2) Self–Addressed, Stamped Envelopes

UNCONTESTED DIVORCE FLOW CHART

Doc. 6. Uncontested Divorce Flow Chart

Uncontested Divorce Flow Chart

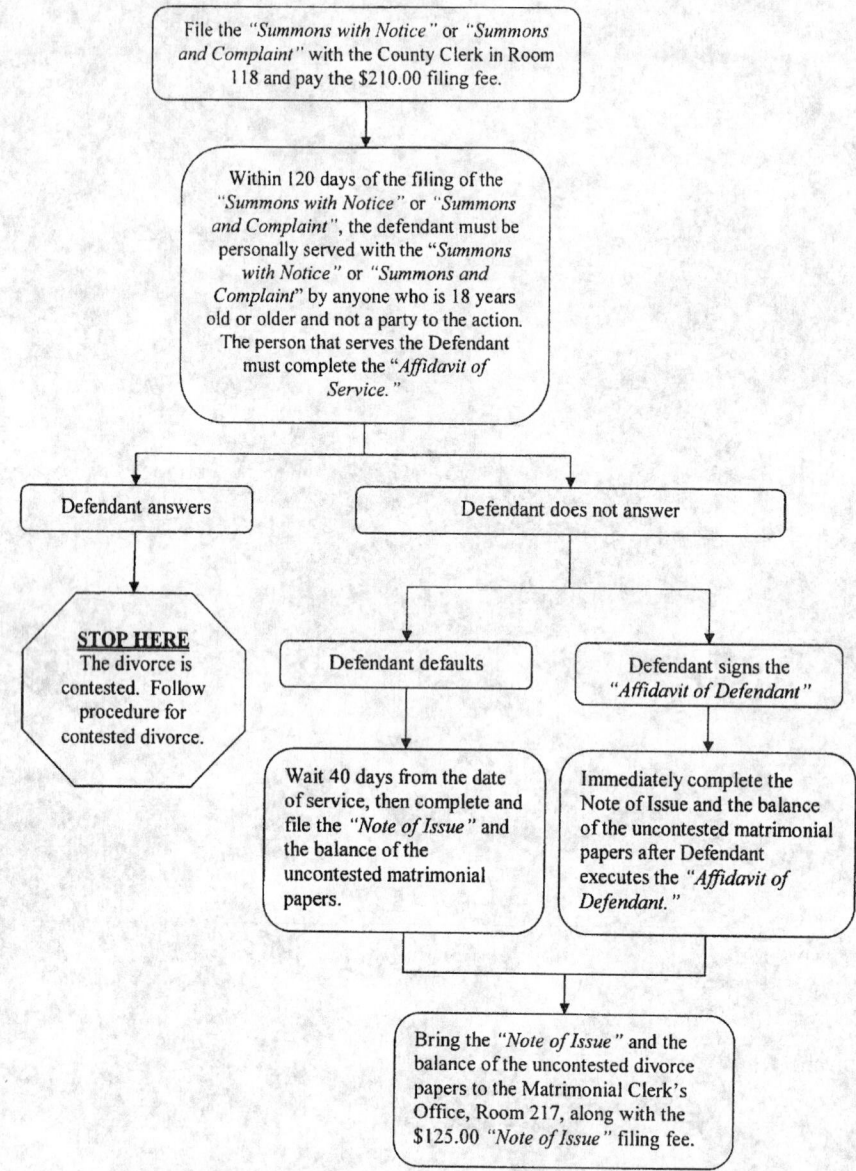

File the *"Summons with Notice"* or *"Summons and Complaint"* with the County Clerk in Room 118 and pay the $210.00 filing fee.

Within 120 days of the filing of the *"Summons with Notice"* or *"Summons and Complaint"*, the defendant must be personally served with the *"Summons with Notice"* or *"Summons and Complaint"* by anyone who is 18 years old or older and not a party to the action. The person that serves the Defendant must complete the *"Affidavit of Service."*

Defendant answers

Defendant does not answer

STOP HERE
The divorce is contested. Follow procedure for contested divorce.

Defendant defaults

Defendant signs the *"Affidavit of Defendant"*

Wait 40 days from the date of service, then complete and file the *"Note of Issue"* and the balance of the uncontested matrimonial papers.

Immediately complete the Note of Issue and the balance of the uncontested matrimonial papers after Defendant executes the *"Affidavit of Defendant."*

Bring the *"Note of Issue"* and the balance of the uncontested divorce papers to the Matrimonial Clerk's Office, Room 217, along with the $125.00 *"Note of Issue"* filing fee.

QDRO Checklist

Doc. 7.   QDRO Checklist

Title of Action _____ —vs— _____
Index # _____

The following documents, in the exact order listed, must be presented personally or by mail to the Matrimonial Clerk's Office, Room 217:

___ $45.00 filing fee — required for each Amended QDRO, DRO or Court Order Acceptable for Processing, otherwise, no filing fee is required. In addition, an affirmation or affidavit detailing the reason for the amendment must be submitted.

___ Notice of Settlement (Refer to instructions for settling Findings of Fact and Judgment)

___ QDRO, DRO or Court Order Acceptable for Processing *

___ The order must contain the following information:

☐ Name and present address of each party

☐ Social security number of each party

☐ Name of plan to which it applies

☐ Name and address of plan administrator

☐ A statement specifying the amount or percentage of the participant's benefits to be paid to the alternate payee by the plan. (Distribution formula)

☐ A statement basically indicating that nothing contained in the Order shall, in any way, require the plan to provide any form, type, or amount of benefit not otherwise provided under the plan

☐ A statement that the Court retains jurisdiction

___ Proof of service of Notice of Settlement and QDRO, DRO or Court Order Acceptable for Processing

___ A copy of the underlying Judgment of Divorce, transcript and stipulation that pertains to the QDRO, DRO or Court Orders Acceptable for Processing, if papers are being submitted after entry of Judgment

___ Part 130 Certification

___ Two (2) self-addressed, stamped postcards

* Pre-approval by plan administrator is suggested.

THIRTEENTH JUDICIAL DISTRICT — RICHMOND COUNTY

Westlaw Electronic Research

These rules may be searched electronically on Westlaw® in the NY–RULES database; updates to these rules may be found on Westlaw in NY–RULESUP-DATES. For search tips and a summary of database content, consult the Westlaw Scope Screens for each database.

RICHMOND COUNTY

SUPREME COURT

UNIFORM CIVIL TERM RULES

Doc.
1. Preliminary Conference.
2. Compliance Conferences.
3. Note of Issue.
4. Motion Requirements.
5. Jury Coordinating Part.

JUDGES' PART RULES

Justice Thomas P. Aliotta.
Justice Joseph J. Maltese.
Justice John A. Fusco.
Justice Judith N. McMahon.
Justice Philip G. Minardo.
Justice Anthony I. Giacobbe.
Justice Catherine M. DiDomenico.
Justice Barbara Panepinto.
Justice Robert J. Collini.

RICHMOND COUNTY
SUPREME COURT

UNIFORM CIVIL TERM RULES

The following uniform rules have been adopted by all Richmond County Supreme Court Justices in order to decrease the complexity of litigation regulations, promote efficiency and expedite the administration of cases. Matrimonial cases shall be governed by the rules for New York State Trial Courts (NYCRR 202.16 *et seq*).

Doc. 1. Preliminary Conference

1. A preliminary conference is mandatory in all cases, whether requested or not, unless a dispositive motion is granted immediately after the case has been assigned to an individual Judge's Part.

2. Upon the filing of a Request for Judicial Intervention (RJI) a case will be assigned to a Justice and a preliminary conference shall be held within forty-five (45) days.

3. During the preliminary conference, a compliance conference date shall be fixed and included within the Preliminary Conference Order.

4. The attorneys who attend the preliminary conference and subsequently the compliance conference, shall have complete knowledge of all the facts and circumstances of the case and have authority to set dates for all discovery proceedings, e.g. scheduled dates for Examinations Before Trial, Independent Medical Examinations and the exchange of all other discovery documents and proceedings.

5. At the time the plaintiff files an RJI requesting a preliminary conference, the bill of particulars must be annexed to that request. If the defendant requests the preliminary conference by the filing of an RJI, the plaintiff shall serve a bill of particulars ten (10) days prior to the preliminary conference.

6. The Preliminary Conference form adopted by the Supreme Court Richmond County shall be utilized in all Parts, except the City Part. The Preliminary Conference Order shall be completed by all parties to the lawsuit.

7. The Preliminary Conference Order shall fix a date wherein all parties are to attend a compliance conference.

8. Matters may not be adjourned, unless specifically authorized by the Court.

9. The Preliminary Conference Order, shall indicate that all impleader actions shall be instituted within a forty-five (45) day period after the completion of examinations before trial. In the event this is not accomplished, any third party action may be severed.

Doc. 2.   Compliance Conferences

1. All parties must attend the compliance conference unless otherwise directed by the court. A party failing to attend may have their pleadings stricken and/or other sanctions imposed. An order certifying that all discovery has been completed shall be issued when the court is satisfied the parties have fully complied with the Preliminary Conference Order and all subsequent Compliance Orders.

Doc. 3.   Note of Issue

1. A Note of Issue may not be filed until a Certification Order has been issued by the court indicating all discovery has been completed. A copy of the Certification Order must be filed with the Note of Issue.

2. A pre-trial conference shall be held within sixty (60) days of the filing of the Note of Issue.

3. If the case cannot be resolved during the pre-trial conference and if a jury demand has been filed, the case will then be adjourned to a specific date in the Jury Coordinating Part (JCP), within three (3) months of the date it has been sent.

Doc. 4.   Motion Requirements

1. All parties must appear when a motion is made.

2. Oral argument is required on all motions unless directed otherwise by the court.

3. Discovery motions shall not be made without leave of court. If such a motion is authorized by the court, the Attorney's Affirmation must state that the court has granted permission for the motion to be made.

4. A motion for summary judgment must be made within sixty (60) days of the filing of the Note of Issue. This date may not be extended by the parties without the approval of the court.

5. The return date of a motion shall not be adjourned without leave of court.

Doc. 5.   Jury Coordinating Part

When a case appears in the Jury Coordinating Part, the following rules apply:

1. Attorneys who are fully familiar with the case must appear and be prepared to select a date for trial.

2. When a case is given a trial date, the attorneys must be prepared to select a jury and try the case on that date.

3. All trial authorizations must be demanded in writing at the time the case first appears on the Jury Coordinating Part calendar. The authorization must be served within thirty (30) days of the demand.

4. All expert disclosures, pursuant to CPLR § 3101(d) must be served by plaintiff forty-five (45) days prior to trial, and by defendants thirty (30) days prior to trial.

JUDGES' PART RULES
JUSTICE THOMAS P. ALIOTTA

City Part 2.   Hon. Thomas P. Aliotta

In addition to the Uniform Rules set forth by the Richmond County Supreme Court, the following rules apply for City Part 2:

MOTIONS

- Check in with Clerk in Courtroom.

- Motions shall be held every other Wednesday in Room 312 at 9:30 A.M. on a designated day.

- No courtesy copies of motion papers are to be filed with Chambers or the Courtroom.

- Oral argument is required on all motions.

- Only attorneys who have full knowledge of the case and authority may appear for oral argument of motions.

- No adjournments without the consent of the Court.

- No discovery motions may be made without prior permission of the Court.

- Any opposition papers to be filed by the Friday before the motion is to be heard.

- Any reply papers to be filed with the Court by the Tuesday before the motion is to he heard.

- Any summary judgment motions that are made after the Note of Issue has been filed must be made within 60 days after the filing of the Note of Issue.

CONFERENCES

- Check in with clerk in the Courtroom

- Conferences arc held every Tuesday in Room 312 at 9:30 A.M.

SETTLEMENT CONFERENCES

- Check in with clerk in the Courtroom.

- Only attorneys who have full knowledge of the case and authority may appear for conference.

PRELIMINARY CONFERENCE RULES

- Preliminary Conferences are to be held within 45 days of the date of the RJI.

- If for any reason the Examinations Board Trial fails to go forward, the Part Clerk is to be notified if the deposition is not RESCHEDULED within 2 weeks of the original scheduled date.

- Independent medical examinations shall be held within 45 days of plaintiff's deposition or pursuant to the Preliminary Conference Order if a shorter time period is so designated.

JUSTICE JOSEPH J. MALTESE

DCM Part 3.   Hon. Joseph J. Maltese

Conferences

(1) Adjournments may be granted on consent, if all counsel agree, by a written stipulation faxed or e-mailed directly to chambers with advance permission of the court.

(2) If all discovery is completed prior to a certification conference, the parties may fax or e-mail a stipulation to court that all discovery is completed in lieu of an appearance. Attorneys will provide their fax numbers and e-mail addresses on the stipulation. The court will fax or e-mail a Certification Order and a new pre-trial/settlement conference date to the attorneys. The Note of Issue shall be filed within 20 days after a Certification Order is issued.

Motions

(1) All motions are returnable in Part DCM 3 at 130 Stuyvesant Place, 3rd Floor, Staten Island, NY 10301 on Fridays at 9:30 a.m. All moving papers, including cross motions, must be filed with the Motion Support Clerk.

(2) *Electronically Filed Cases.* Parties are encouraged to utilize the e-filing system pursuant to the Uniform Rules for New York State Trial Courts § 202.5–b.

(3) *Paper Copies of Motions.* Whether e-filing or paper filing is utilized, attorneys are required to serve a paper copy upon chambers of all motions, cross-motions, opposition, and replies, including memoranda of law and exhibits, before the return date set by the Clerk's Office.

(4) Orders to Show Cause, on DCM 3 cases, shall be brought directly to chambers for review. Fees, as required by law, must be paid to the County Clerk before bringing the OSC to chambers. In any application for temporary injunctive relief to include a stay or a Temporary Restraining Order (TRO), the attorney shall notify the party against whom the TRO or stay is sought, advising of the time, date and place of the application pursuant to the Uniform Rules for New York State Trial Courts § 202.7(f). Call chambers to confirm availability.

(5) Affidavits in support of or in opposition to the motion shall contain factual information only, attested

to by a party or person with actual knowledge of the facts and are limited to 20 pages. Any law shall be cited in a separate memorandum of law and is limited to 20 pages. Any reply is limited to 15 pages. All documents shall be printed in 12 point font and double spaced pursuant to the Uniform Rules for NYS Trial Courts § 202.5(a). All exhibits shall have tabs.

(6) Discovery motions made before a Preliminary Conference (PC) Order is issued will be converted into a PC Order. After a PC Order is issued, counsel must first attempt to resolve discovery disputes. Counsel must request court permission to make a discovery motion after a PC Order has been issued.

(7) All motions will be decided on submission unless the court notifies the attorneys to be prepared for oral argument. Attorneys wishing to have their motions orally argued shall request it in their moving papers. If that request is granted, the court will notify all parties.

(8) *Adjournments.* Any requests for an adjournment of a motion shall be made in writing and be mailed or faxed to 718–720–6403 or e-mailed to jmalfano@nycourts.gov to be received in this court by 5:00 p.m. on the Monday before the Friday return date. Copies of the request for adjournment shall be made to all parties. Stipulations agreeing to the adjournment with proposed adjourned dates in writing is preferred. Any objection to the request for an adjournment shall be faxed or e-mailed to the previously listed fax number or e-mail address by 5:00 p.m. on the Tuesday preceding the Friday return date.

(9) All motions for summary judgment shall be made by the 60th day following the filing of the

Trials Assigned to the Part

(1) *Time to File Expert Witness Disclosure.* The parties shall file a notice of expert witnesses they expect to call at trial, in compliance with CPLR § 3101(d)(i) or (ii), at least 45 days before the date when the case is first listed for trial by the Assignment Judge; or If evidence or expert testimony is intended to contradict or rebut evidence on the same subject matter identified by another party under CPLR § 3101(d)(i) and (ii), the opposing counsel shall file an expert witness disclosure pursuant to CPLR § 3101(d)(i) and (ii) within 15 days after the other party's disclosure, or at least 30 days prior to the first date set for trial by the Assignment Judge.

(2) *Motions in Limine.* Any potential questions on evidence or procedural or substantive law not previously adjudicated shall be made at least 15 days prior to the first date set for trial by the Assignment Judge by way of a written motion in limine. A written memorandum of law with citations is required. Any responding affidavit or cross motion shall be made within 7 days of receipt of the original motion. A motion fee must be paid to the County Clerk prior to submissions of the motion. Copies of the motion with

proof of overnight mail or email or fax service upon opposing counsel shall be filed directly with chambers.

(3) *Frye/Daubert Motions.* Any motion not otherwise covered in a summary judgment motion to preclude an opposing expert witness, an expert witness' opinion or any opposing evidence shall be made at least 15 days before the date first set for trial by the Assignment Judge. All motions are to be filed directly with this chambers after the appropriate fee(s) are paid at the County Clerk. The complete motion is to be filed directly with this trial court that is assigned the case for trial and not with the Assignment Judge. Any Frye/Daubert motion shall contain a written affirmation from an attorney, and an affidavit from an expert witness attesting to why this court should preclude any expert witnesses or any part of their opinions or any evidence with specificity and with supporting data, journal articles or scientific texts attached. Frye/Daubert motions will not be entertained after jury selection, or be re-characterized as an oral Motion in Limine.

(4) *Trial Counsel.* Only trial counsel who are prepared to try the case shall appear in court.

(5) *Marked Pleadings.* Prior to trial, counsel shall furnish to the court marked pleadings pursuant to CPLR § 4012.

(6) *Exhibits.* Counsel shall pre-mark all exhibits in the order which they intend to introduce them at trial. An Exhibits List shall be provided to the court prior to trial (see Court Clerk for the Exhibits List Form). Plaintiffs will number the exhibits and the defendants will letter their exhibits, unless there are more than one defendant, in which case the defendant's name and a sequential letter shall follow it. On the day of trial the exhibits and the list will be given to the court reporter who will officially mark them before trial.

(7) *Numbering Pages.* In any: malpractice action, products liability or commercial matter with voluminous documents, counsel shall number the pages (Bate stamp) of each record sequentially before making copies of same for opposing counsel and the court to ensure that everyone is reading from the same numbered page.

(8) *Witness Lists.* Counsel shall provide to the court a list of potential witnesses or in a medical malpractice case the specialty of the doctor in the order in which they intend to call them at trial. Counsel are strongly urged to disclose the names and specialties of doctors in medical malpractice cases. (See the Court Clerk for the Witness List Form.)

(9) *Proposed Jury Charges and Verdict Sheets.* All proposed jury charges and proposed verdict sheets shall be submitted to the court prior to the close of the plaintiff's case in hardcopy and on a disk or as an attached electronic file by email, to Principal Law Clerk Jeffrey M. Alfano: jmalfano@nycourts.gov.

JUSTICE JOHN A. FUSCO

DCM Part 4.   Hon. John A. Fusco

MOTIONS

Motions are returnable every other Friday. The first call of the calendar is at 9:30 A.M., followed by the second call. Anyone failing to answer the second call of the calendar will have their motion marked off, if they are the movant, or a default will be entered against you, if you are the opponent.

At the call of the calendar, please respond by answering ready or application, as the case may be, and the name of the firm that you represent.

Adjournment of motions are granted only with the court's permission. The court will provide the dates for submission of additional papers and the return date after counsel receives consent for the adjournment from all sides. Counsel may make the request for an adjournment on the Wednesday or Thursday, by stipulation, before the Friday return date only. No ex parte telephone applications for an adjournment will be entertained. No exceptions. Do not call chambers for an adjournment.

Motion papers, answering affidavits and reply affidavits must be served on adversaries as per CPLR § 2214. All Exhibits to Motion papers must have alphabetical tabs.

Moving papers, including cross motions, shall be tiled with the Motion Support Clerk at Room 302, 130 Stuyvesant Place, Staten Island, New York 10301. The movant has the responsibility of ascertaining the return day by contacting the Motion Support Clerk. Courtesy copies are not to be sent to chambers prior to argument without advance permission. Fees must be paid to the County Clerk as required by law.

Summary judgment motions must be made within sixty (60) days of the filing of the Note of Issue.

If the motion seeks relief related to discovery, strict compliance with 22 NYCRR 202.7(C) is required, and prior court approval is required.

Proposed orders to show cause must be brought to the Motion Support Office for review prior to submission to the part.

CONFERENCES

Conferences shall he held every Tuesday, Wednesday and Thursday. The above mentioned rules governing the adjournment of motions apply to the adjournment of conferences.

Adjournments may be granted on consent, if all counsel agree, with permission of the court by written stipulation faxed directly to chambers at (718) 727–4106.

If all discovery is completed prior to a conference the parties may fax a stipulation to court that all discovery is completed in lieu of an appearance. The court will fax a certification order and a new pre-trial settlement conference date to the fax numbers provided in the stipulation confirming that discovery is completed.

TRIALS

(1) *Trial Counsel.* Only trial counsel who are prepared to try the ease shall appear in Court.

(2) *Marked Pleadings.* Prior to trial, counsel shall furnish to the court marked pleadings pursuant to CPLR §4012.

(3) *Exhibits.* Counsel shall pre-mark all exhibits in the order which they intend to introduce them at trial. A list of exhibits shall be provided to the court prior to trial. Plaintiffs will number their exhibits and defendants will letter their exhibits. An exhibit list may be obtained from the court clerk. On the day of the trial the exhibits and the list will be given to the Court reporter who will officially mark them before trial.

(4) In any medical malpractice action, counsel shall number the pages of the medical records sequentially before making copies of same for opposing counsel and the court to facilitate that everyone is reading from the same page.

(5) *Witnesses.* Prior to trial, Counsel shall provide to the court a list of potential witnesses in order in which they intend to call them at trial, including expert witnesses, their expertise, and summary of expected trial testimony.

(6) *Motions in Limine.* Any potential evidentiary question or procedural or substantial law matter not previously adjudicated shall be brought to the court's attention and addressed prior to trial by way of written motion in limine. A written memorandum of law with citations to the Official Reports shall also be required, and shall accompany any such motion. Citations and copies of relevant court decisions and statutes should be furnished to the Court prior commencement of plaintiffs case and when otherwise requested by the Court.

(7) *Depositions.* A copy of counsels intended to be used at trial should be furnished to the Court at the commencement of the trial.

(8) *Proposed Jury Charges and Verdict Sheets.* The parties shall submit proposed jury charges and proposed verdict sheets to the Court in typed or computer generated form, with specific citations to applicable New York Pattern Instructions and any modifications thereto, prior to the commencement of the Court's preliminary instructions to the jury.

INQUIRIES

All inquiries as to case or calendar status should, in the first instance, be made to the Support Office at

718–675–8700. Under no circumstances should telephone inquiries concerning a case status or calendaring be made to chambers. The only inquiries to be made directly to chambers or the Part should be those involving the exercise of judicial discretion.

JUSTICE JUDITH N. McMAHON

DCM Part 5.   Hon. Judith N. McMahon

Conferences

(1) Compliance Conferences and Preliminary Conferences are held every Tuesday and Wednesday in Room 220, in Staten Island Borough Hall, 10 Richmond Terrace, at 9:30 a.m.

(2) Adjournments are granted on consent of the parties. You must call the Court to receive a new adjournment date which date is to be included in the stipulation. A confirmation in stipulation form is to be faxed to Chambers at (718) 876–8086.

Motions

(1) Motions shall be heard every other Tuesday in Room 220, in Staten Island Borough Hall, 10 Richmond Terrace. The calendar call is at 9:30 a.m.

(2) No courtesy copies of motion papers are to be filed with Chambers or the Courtroom unless the motion is e–filed. Courtesy copies of all motion papers are mandatory at the time of filing prior to the motion day only for e–filed cases.

(3) Motion papers, answering affidavits and reply affidavits must be served on adversaries as per CPLR Section 2214.

(4) All motions require appearances and oral arguments.

(5) Adjournments are granted on consent of the parties. You must call the Court to receive a new adjournment date which date is to be included in the stipulation. A confirmation in stipulation form is to be faxed to Chambers at (718) 876–8086.

(6) Summary judgment motions must be made within sixty (60) days of the filing or the note of issue.

(7) Motions to either seek or enforce discovery may not be made without Court approval.

(8) If you are detained, you must call your adversary to inform him/her of the approximate time you will arrive at Court, and then call Chambers at (718) 675–8632 or (718) 675–8630.

Trials

(1) *Marked Pleadings.* Prior to trial, counsel shall furnish marked pleadings pursuant to CPLR Section 4012.

(2) *Exhibits.* Counsel shall pre-mark all exhibits in the order which they intend to introduce them at trial. Plaintiffs will number their exhibits and defendants will letter their exhibits. On the day of trial, the exhibits and the list will be given to the Court reporter who will officially mark them before trial.

(3) *Witnesses.* Prior to trial, counsel shall provide to the Court a list of potential witnesses.

(4) *Motions in Limine.* Any potential evidentiary question or procedural or substantive law matter not previously adjudicated shall be brought to the Court's attention and addressed at the pre-trial conference.

(5) *Depositions.* A copy of depositions intended to be used at trial shall be furnished to the Court at the commencement of trial.

(6) *Proposed Jury Charges and Verdict Sheets.* All proposed jury charges and proposed verdict sheets shall he submitted to the Court at the pre-trial conference.

JUSTICE PHILIP G. MINARDO

DCM Part 6.   Hon. Philip G. Minardo

MOTIONS:

All motions will be heard and orally argued on Thursdays at 9:30 A.M. All answering papers must be filed with the Civil Term Motion Clerk at least five (5) days prior to the appearance date with a duplicate copy submitted directly to chambers at the same time [five (5) days prior to the appearance date]. A duplicate copy of all reply papers must be served directly to chambers at least twenty-four (24) hours prior to the appearance date.

Parties are to refrain from making summary judgment motions until all examinations before trial and other related discovery are completed, and must be made within sixty (60) days after the Note of Issue has been filed. Summary judgment motions will not stay discovery without the court's consent.

Motions to either seek or enforce discovery may not be made without court approval.

ADJOURNMENTS:

All adjournments by stipulation or otherwise require prior court approval. All requests for adjournments of either motions or conferences must be made at least 36 hours prior to the scheduled appearance date.

Stipulations must be faxed to chambers at 718–815–2775 immediately on the day the court approves the adjournment.

CONFERENCES:

Thursday conferences are held at 11:00 A.M. Conference on all other days are held at 9:30 A.M. Attorneys participating in all conferences must be fully familiar with the facts and circumstances of the case.

TRIALS:

COUNSEL SHALL COMPLY WITH THESE RULES WHEN ASSIGNED TO THIS PART FOR TRIAL:

(1) *Prior to trial:* Counsel shall furnish to the court marked pleadings pursuant to CPLR §4012.

(2) *Exhibits:* Counsel shall pre-mark all exhibits in the order in which they intend to introduce them at trial. A list of the exhibits shall be provided to the court prior to trial. Plaintiffs will number their exhibits and defendants will letter their exhibits. An exhibit list may be obtained from the court clerk. On the day of trial, the exhibits and the list will be given to the court reporter who will officially mark them before trial.

(3) *Witnesses:* Prior to trial, counsel shall provide to the court a list of potential witnesses in the order in which they intend to call them at trial, including expert witnesses, their expertise, and summary of expected trial testimony.

(4) *Motions in Limine:* Any potential evidentiary question or procedural or substantive law matter not previously adjudicated shall be brought to the court's attention and addressed prior to trial by way of a written or oral motion in limine. A written memorandum of law with citations to the Official Reports is strongly encouraged; citations and copies of relevant court decisions and statutes should be furnished to the court prior to commencement of plaintiffs case and when otherwise required by the court.

(5) *Depositions:* A copy of depositions intended to be used at trial should be furnished to the court at the commencement of the trial.

(6) *Proposed Jury Charges and Verdict Sheets:* All proposed jury charges and proposed verdict sheets shall be submitted to the court in typed or computer generated form prior to the commencement of the court's preliminary instructions to the jury.

FAILURE TO COMPLY WITH THESE COURT RULES SHALL BE ADDRESSED APPROPRIATELY, INCLUDING THE POSSIBILITY OF PRECLUSION.

JUSTICE ANTHONY I. GIACOBBE

TR Part 9.   Hon. Anthony I. Giacobbe
COUNSEL SHALL COMPLY WITH THESE RULES WHEN ASSIGNED TO THIS PART FOR TRIAL.

(1) *Marked Pleadings.* Prior to trial counsel shall furnish to the Court marked pleadings pursuant to CPLR § 4012.

(2) *Exhibits.* Counsel shall pre-mark all exhibits in the order which they intend to introduce them at trial. A list of the exhibits shall be provided to the Court prior to trial. Plaintiffs will number their exhibits and defendants will letter their exhibits. An exhibit list may be obtained from the court clerk. On the day of trial the exhibits and the list will be given to the Court Reporter who will officially mark them before trial.

(3) *Witnesses.* Prior to trial, Counsel shall provide to the court a list of potential witnesses in order in which they intend to call them at trial, including expert witnesses, their expertise, and summary of expected trial testimony.

(4) *Motions in Limine.* Any potential evidentiary question or procedural or substantive law matter not previously adjudicated shall be brought to the Court's attention and addressed prior to trial by way of a written motion in limine. A written memorandum of law with citations to the Official Reports shall also be required, and shall accompany any such motion. Citations and copies of relevant court decisions and statutes should he furnished to the Court prior to commencement of plaintiff's case and when otherwise requested by the Court.

(5) *Depositions.* A copy of depositions intended to be used at trial should be furnished to the Court at the commencement or the trial.

(6) *Proposed Jury Charges and Verdict Sheets.* The parties shall submit proposed jury charges and proposed verdict sheets to the Court in typed or computer generated form, with specific citations to applicable New York Pattern Instructions and any modifications thereto, prior to the commencement of the Court's preliminary instructions to the jury.

(7) Copies of correspondence exchanged between attorneys and others shall not be sent to the Court unless specifically authorized or requested by the Court.

Failure to comply with these Court Rules shall be addressed appropriately.

JUSTICE CATHERINE M. DiDOMENICO

MP 11 and IDV. Hon. Catherine M. DiDomenico

GENERAL PART RULES

IDV is in session Monday and Tuesday at 18 Richmond Terrace.

MP11 is in session Wednesday, Thursday and Friday at the Homeport Annex, 355 Front Street.

All calendars will be called at 9:30 A.M. in MP11. In IDV, cases will be called when ready or when scheduled.

All adjournments require the prior approval of the Court. However, the Preliminary Conference may be adjourned on consent by written stipulation up to the date that is 45 days from the filing of the RJI. A Compliance Conference may be adjourned once on consent by written stipulation, for up to 60 days, provided the adjourned date is not more than 6 months from the date the RJI was filed. Motions are addressed in the next section of the Rules.

All adjournments on the grounds of engagement of counsel shall be granted only in accordance with Part 125 of the Rules of the chief Administrator of the Courts. Affirmation must be faxed to the Court at least one (1) day prior to the court appearance.

All parties must be present for all appearances and conferences unless a a party is excused by the Court in advance of the court date.

All papers submitted to Part MP11/IDV must include a fax number. Copies of the correspondence between counsel is not to be sent to Chambers.

MOTIONS

Oral argument is required on all motions and orders to show cause.

Counsel are required to file all responsive papers with the Matrimonial Clerk's Office at the Homeport Annex two (2) days before the return date of the motion. All exhibits are to be identified by tabs. Cross motions are to be filed with the Matrimonial Clerk's Office at the Homeport Annex two (2) days prior to the return date.

Motions may be adjourned on consent up to 90 days from the original return date of the motion. Counsel are directed to submit a written stipulation reflecting their counsel which must include several available dates. Further requests for adjournments will require the attorney for the parties to appear personally.

Counsel are reminded that the CPLR does not provide for sur-reply papers or allow the presentation of papers of letters to the court after argument of a motion. Sur-replies, letters and the responses to such letters addressed to the substance of motions will not be considered.

Any allegations of fact submitted to the court, including allegations contained in an affidavit and/or the complaint, must be certified by counsel in the form prescribed by the Chief Administrative Judge.

The Court requests that courtesy copies of all motion papers be delivered to chambers.

ORDERS OF PROTECTION

Ex-parte requests for Orders of Protection must be accompanied by a completed Family Protection Registry Information Sheet and the applicant must be present in Court. Motions to consolidate Family Court actions must contain a complete copy of the Family Court petition and any Family Court Order in effect at the time the motion is made,

EX PARTE APPLICATIONS

Any application for temporary injunctive relief shall contain an affirmation demonstrating there will be significant prejudice to the party seeking the restraining order by giving notice. In the absence of a showing of significant prejudice, an affirmation must demonstrate that a good faith effort has been made to notify the party against whom the restraining order is sought in accordance with 22 NYCRR 202.7. This rule does not apply to temporary orders of protection.

PRELIMINARY CONFERENCE

The Preliminary Conference will be held on a date selected by the Court. The conference must be held within forty-five (45) days of the filing of the RJI. The party seeking judicial intervention is required to notify the opposing party of the Preliminary Conference date. If the opposing party is self-represented, the Court will send out the notification. There will be no adjournments of Preliminary Conferences beyond 45 days from the filing of the RJI without express permission from the Court.

Counsel are reminded that pursuant to 22 N.Y.C.R.R. § 202.16(f)(1), Net Worth Statements are to be filed with the Court ten (10) days prior to the preliminary conference date. They are to be accompanied by the items listed in said section which include the attorneys' retainer statements, the parties recent pay stubs, the end of the year pay stubs for the previous calendar year, as well as W–2 statements, 1099s and K–1 forms.

COMPLIANCE CONFERENCE

Compliance Conference will be held on a date selected by the Court.

The date of the Compliance Conference shall be set at the time of the Preliminary Conference. Counsel should not wait until the date of the Compliance Conference to bring to the Court's attention their adversary's failure to comply with Preliminary Conference directives and/or discovery orders. Such failure must be addressed prior to the Compliance Conference either by motion or conference call to Chambers. Failure to timely comply with Court-Ordered discovery may result in the imposition of sanctions and/or counsel fees.

PRE-TRIAL CONFERENCE

The Note of Issue shall be filed prior to the pre-trial conference and in accordance with the Compliance Order. At the pre-trial conference, counsel will provide the Court with Statements of Proposed Disposition. (See 22 NYCRR § 202.16[h]) updated net worth statements with the last three years of tax returns and a child support worksheet, if applicable, Counsel shall present all motions in limine at this conference.

TRIAL

The Court is to be provided with the following no later than thirty (30) days prior to the first day of trial:

1. Marked pleadings.

2. Updated Statement of Net Worth. Statement or Proposed Disposition and child support worksheet, if not provided at the Pre-trial Conference.

3. A witness list, expert reports not previously filed and any pre-trial memoranda of law.

4. A list of all proposed exhibits.

5. A list of documents which counsel may stipulate into evidence.

6. A written list of any issues or facts to which the parties can stipulate in advance of trial. Said stipulation shall be read into the record at the commencement of trial.

Counsel are reminded that pursuant to N.Y.C.R.R. § 202.16(g) all expert's reports are to be exchanged and filed with the Court sixty days before the date set for trial. Reply reports, if any, shall be exchanged and filed no later than thirty (30) days before said date.

Sanctions and/or costs may be imposed for failure to comply with any Rules set forth herein.

Once a case has been assigned a trial date, it is presumed ready for trial. No consent adjournments will be accepted. Failure to proceed will result in default relief being granted or the action being dismissed. In the event the action is resolved prior to the court date, counsel are expected to notify Chambers immediately.

The Court is to be provided with duplicates of all items marked into evidence.

The Court may direct one or both parties to order the transcript and allocate the costs.

MISCELLANEOUS

All Judgments shall include a completed copy of the Matrimonial Term Clerk Office's contested Judgment checklist indicating all necessary attachments. All judgments must be submitted within 60 days or the action will be deemed abandoned and dismissed. All QDROs must be submitted within 45 days of the signing of the Judgment and must be accompanied by written plan approval.

JUSTICE BARBARA PANEPINTO

MP 12. Hon. Barbara Panepinto

Motions

On Tuesday (Pendente Lite) and Thursday (Post Judgment) and oral argument is required.

Counsel are required to file all responsive papers and Cross Motions with the Matrimonial Support Office two full days before the return date of the motion. All exhibits are to be identified by tabs.

Motions may not be adjourned on consent more than twice and require advance notification to the Court. Further adjournments will require attorneys for the parties to appear personally.

No courtesy copies of papers are to be filed with the Courtroom or Chambers.

Counsel are reminded that the CPLR does not provide for sur-reply papers nor allow submission of papers or letters to the court after argument of a motion. Sur-replies, letters, and responses to such letters addressed to the substance of motions will not be considered.

Any allegations of fact submitted to the Court, including allegations contained in an affidavit and/or the complaint, must be certified by counsel in the form prescribed by the Chief Administrative Judge.

Preliminary Conference

Pursuant to 22 NYCRR 202.16(d), a RJI must be filed within forty-five (45) days of the date of service of the summons unless an affidavit of no necessity is filed, in which event the RJI must be filed within one-hundred-and-twenty (120) days.

Counsel are reminded that pursuant to 22 NYCRR 202.16(f), net worth affidavits are to be exchanged and filed with the Court ten (10) days prior to the conference date. They are to be accompanied by the attorneys' retainer statements and all mandatory attachments pursuant thereto. Both parties must be present at the conference. At this conference a referral may be made to the Parental Education Programs or the Social Worker.

Compliance Conference

The date of the compliance conference shall be set at the time of the preliminary conference. Counsel are directed not to wait until this conference to bring to the Court's attention any failure to comply with discovery orders or preliminary conference directions. Such failure must be addressed prior to the conference either by motion or conference call to Chambers. Both parties are to be present at the compliance conference unless the Court excuses their appearance.

Pre-Trial Conference

The date of the pre-trial conference will be set at the compliance conference. Note of issue shall be filed prior to the pre-trial conference in accordance with the compliance order. At the final pre-trial conference, counsel will provide the Court with statements of proposed disposition, updated net worth statements with the last three years of tax returns and a child support worksheet, if applicable. Counsel shall present all motions in limine at this conference.

Failure to provide these documents or to file a note of issue pursuant to the compliance conference order will result in case being adjourned one week or issues deemed waived.

Trial

One month preceding the trial date the Court is to be provided with the following:

– If grounds are to be tried, marked pleadings.

– If there had been a change in the finances of the parties since the pre-trial conference, updated statement of net worth, proposed disposition and child support worksheet, if applicable.

– A witness list, expert reports not previously filed and any pre-trial memorandum.

Counsel are reminded that pursuant to 22 NYCRR 20216(g), all expert reports are to be exchanged and filed with the Court sixty (60) days before the date set for trial. Reply reports, if any, shall be exchanged and filed no later than thirty (30) days before said date.

– A list of all proposed exhibits.

– A list of documents which counsel may stipulate into evidence, such documents are to be pre-marked by counsel.

– A written copy of any issues or facts to which the parties can stipulate in the advance of trial, said stipulation to be read into the record at the commencement of the trial.

Sanctions including waiver and/or costs may be imposed for failure to comply with any rules set forth herein.

Once a case has been assigned a trial date, it is presumed ready for trial. No consent adjournments will be accepted. Failure to proceed may result in default relief being granted or the action being dismissed. In the event the action is resolved prior to the court date, counsel are expected to notify Chambers immediately.

Copies of decisions and orders will be mailed to all counsel and any self-represented litigants.

Correspondence between counsel is not to be copied to Chambers. Please note if this rule is disregarded, the Court is under no obligation to read or act on same.

JUSTICE ROBERT J. COLLINI

Doc. 1. Hon. Robert J. Collini

Matters Pursuant to Article 9 of the Mental Hygiene Law

NO TELEPHONIC NOR WRITTEN COMMUNICATION CONCERNING ANY APPLICATION, PENDING OR IMPENDING, MAY BE MADE DIRECTLY TO CHAMBERS unless leave is granted by the Court. All applications, correspondence, reports, vouchers from court-appointed experts and other documents must be filed in writing through the Civil Term Support Office (718) 675–8575) and must bear the title of the action, index number, and adjourned date, or as otherwise specified by law or other court rule. Any filing which commences a new action will be provided an index number and appearance date by the Clerk.

All counsel (or pro se party) must inform the Court in writing through Civil Term Support Office if an alleged mentally ill person who is a named party to an action herein has a Guardian appointed under Article 81 of the Mental Hygiene Law. All pleadings and other papers must be served upon the Guardian, in addition to any other necessary parties or persons, and the Guardian must be present for all appearances before the Court unless it directs otherwise.

Orders to Show Cause and Warrant Applications: All proposed Orders to Show Cause, as well as Warrant Applications and Warrant Returns (MHL 9.43) must be initially presented to the Civil Term Support Office before it will be considered in this Part. The moving party on any proposed Order to Show Cause, an applicant for a Warrant, and all parties appearing before the Court on a Warrant Return, will be directed to this Part or an alternate Part based on the Court's availability to consider these emergent applications,

Items marked "courtesy copy" may be forwarded directly to Chambers provided the appropriate party adheres to the preceding rules.

Matters Pursuant to Article 10 of the Mental Hygiene Law

All preceding rules shall be equally applicable to all matters under Article 10 of the Mental Hygiene Law, except that the Criminal Term Support Office (718–675–8760) is substituted for the Civil Term Support Office unless otherwise directed or specified.

It is the responsibility of the Attorney General, not the Court or its staff, to effect the production of incarcerated Respondents. All proposed Orders to Produce and related documents must be filed through the Criminal Term Support Office.

COMMERCIAL DIVISION RULES

Westlaw Electronic Research

These rules may be searched electronically on Westlaw® *in the NY–RULES database; updates to these rules may be found on* Westlaw *in NY–RULESUPDATES. For search tips and a summary of database content, consult the* Westlaw *Scope Screens for each database.*

NEW YORK COUNTY

STATEMENT REGARDING IMPLEMENTATION OF CERTAIN RULES

Doc. 1. Statement of the Administrative Judge

This Statement is issued to inform the Bar about the way in which certain Rules of the Commercial Division (Section 202.70 of the Uniform Rules for the Trial Courts) will, until further notice, be implemented in this county.

1) **Rule 11:** All Justices of the Commercial Division require that, unless otherwise directed in a particular case, the number of interrogatories shall be limited to 25, including subparts.

2) **Rule 16 (a):** On motions to dismiss or for summary judgment pursuant to CPLR 3211, 3212 and 3213 and motions for a preliminary injunction, all memoranda of law shall contain a table of contents and a table of authorities and shall be bound separately from other papers submitted.

3) **Rule 16 (c):** All Justices of the Commercial Division waive the requirement that they be afforded an opportunity to approve adjournments of motions returnable in the Motion Support Office Courtroom (Room 130), provided that the adjournments do not exceed three for a total of no more than 60 days. Adjournments of motions returnable in any Commercial Division Part shall be governed by the procedures of the Part.

4) **Rule 19–a:** All Justices in the New York County Commercial Division require compliance with this Rule.

5) **Rule 27:** All motions *in limine* shall be made by order to show cause returnable in the Part on the date set forth in the Rule.

Dated: June 8, 2007

Jacqueline W. Silbermann
Administrative Judge

Doc. 2. Statement of the Administrative Judge Regarding Implementation of a Rule of the Commercial Division

With regard to implementation of Rule 2 (Settlements and Discontinuances) of the Rules of the Commercial Division (Section 202.70 of the Uniform Rules for the Trial Courts):

At any stage of the litigation, counsel for all parties may request a settlement conference before a Commercial Division Justice. Such request will be granted if it appears that conducting such a conference would be beneficial to the parties and the court and would further the interests of justice.

Dated: June 30, 2010

JUDGES' RULES

JUSTICE EILEEN BRANSTEN

Part 3.   Hon. Eileen Bransten

Practices for Part 3

All documents submitted to the court for review or signature, whether stipulations, orders or letters, must contain, on all pages subsequent to the first, a header bearing the case name, index number and page number out of the total number of pages. For example:

Plaintiff v. Defendant   *Index No.* 600XXX/XX

Communications with the Court

1. Neither Justice Bransten nor any of her court attorneys will speak to any litigant *ex parte.*

2. Unless otherwise provided in the Commercial Division Rules, counsel should contact the Court telephonically between 3:30 and 5:00 p.m.

3. A party seeking an adjournment on any scheduled appearance or court-ordered date, must receive court permission. Adjournments will not be permitted in the absence of a court-authorized stipulation, court order or a conference call with ALL parties on the line.

Requests for adjournments or extensions of time (a) must be made at least 48 hours prior to scheduled appearance or deadline; and (b) the party contacting the court must state: (i) the original date; (ii) the number of previous requests for adjournment or extension; (iii) whether prior requests were granted or denied; (iv) whether ALL other parties consent; and (v) assuming that ALL parties consent, two proposed alternative dates.

4. Inquires regarding appearances may be directed to the Part 3 Clerk, Ms. Lorraine Meletiche, who can be reached at (646) 386–3287 between 9:30 and 12:45 and between 2:15 and 4:30.

Requests for Admission Pro Hac Vice

1. All requests for admission pro hac vice, whether made by motion or stipulation, shall be accompanied

by an affidavit in support from a member of the Bar of the State of New York, an affidavit from the applicant, and a recent certificate of good standing from the applicant.

2. The affidavit of the applicant must advise the court as to the total number of times the applicant has been admitted in New York pro hac vice. The affidavit must also advise the court whether he/she has ever been or is presently subject to a disciplinary proceeding.

Motion Practice

1. With respect to Commercial Division Rule 24(c), counsel is only required to advise the Court prior to making a discovery motion. Before contacting the Court, "counsel must consult with one another in a good faith effort to resolve all disputes about disclosure" (see Rule 14).

2. All courtesy copies submitted in connection with a motion must include the correct motion sequence number, be properly backed and, where necessary, include proper bottom tabs

3. Courtesy copies of all e-filed papers and exhibits for motions returnable in Room 130 must be delivered to Room 130. Courtesy copies of e-filed papers and exhibits related to Orders to Show Cause must be delivered to the courtroom—Room 442. Extra copies of papers will not be accepted.

4. At the conclusion of oral argument, the movant is to order the transcript and have a copy sent to the Court, delivered to the Part 3 Clerk, Room 442. The motion(s) will not be marked submitted for consideration until a transcript has been received.

5. Rule 19–a Statements of Material Facts are required when moving for or opposing summary judgment.

6. Affirmations submitted in support of or in response to dispositive motions must be separate from any memoranda of law submitted in relation to the motion. Affirmations should not include arguments of law.

7. Memoranda of law submitted in support of or in response to dispositive motions must include a Table of Contents and a Table of Authorities.

Confidentiality Order

1. Any order regarding the confidential exchange of information shall be based on the Proposed Stipulation and Order for the Production and Exchange of Confidential Information prepared by a committee of the New York City Bar Association for use in the Commercial Division, available on the Bar Association's website at: htt p://www.nycbar.org/pdf/report/ModelConfidentiality.pdf

2. If the parties believe there is good cause to deviate from the above model, the parties are to call the Part Clerk to schedule a conference to discuss the changes with the Court.

3. The Court will not entertain the sealing of documents without a showing of the nature of the document; reason to seal and "good cause" therefor, pursuant to 22 NYCRR § 216.1. The Court will consider the sealing of documents by stipulation or motion.

Discovery Conferences and Disputes

1. Discovery disputes are to be resolved through a court conference—not through motion practice—unless otherwise directed. If the court is unable to resolve the dispute through a conference, then leave will be given for the parties to file the appropriate motion. The failure to abide by this rule may result in a motion being held in abeyance until the court has an opportunity to conference the matter.

2. Parties are to bring copies of ALL prior discovery orders to each and every court appearance.

Trial Rules

1. No adjournments of the trial date will be granted absent exceptional circumstances. Requests for adjournment must be made in writing to the Court and not by phone call to the Clerk of the Part.

2. At least ten days prior to the start date of the trial the parties are to jointly submit:

(a) A list of witnesses each party expects to call at trial. The witness list must state whether each witness is a fact or an expert witness. If a witness is listed as an "expert," state whether the parties agree or dispute that witness's status as an expert for purposes of the trial.

(b) A list of exhibits that each party may use at trial. The exhibit list must state for each exhibit if that exhibit is agreed to or disputed by the parties as admissible evidence. Exhibits that are agreed to by the parties as admissible evidence will be immediately entered into evidence upon introduction at trial.

3. Pre-trial memorandum briefs are to be submitted in all matters at least seven calendar days prior to the start date of trial.

4. Motions in limine are to be submitted at least seven calendar days prior to the start date of trial.

5. One copy of all exhibits shall be submitted to Part 3 at least seven calendar days prior to the commencement of the trial. The parties should additionally be prepared to hand to the Court one copy of every document that is introduced at trial.

6. If the trial is by jury, counsel will be required to submit proposed jury charges and a proposed verdict sheet. All submissions must be made in hard copy and on disk in WordPerfect 8 format upon the first day of trial.

(a) The Court will accept submissions of proposed opening jury charges for the Court to read to the jury upon the onset of the trial. Proposed opening jury charges must be made in hard copy and on disk in WordPerfect 8 format at least three calendar days prior to the onset of trial.

7. Parties shall provide witness lists, a glossary of names, and any unusual words and any acronyms they anticipate to be using during the trial to the court reporter the morning that the trial is set to begin.

8. Demonstrative evidence is not permitted without first obtaining the permission of the Court.

9. No electronic media devices will be permitted absent express permission from the Court. Requests should be made to the Court in writing and the reasons for the request must be clearly stated.

10. All materials used during the trial must be removed within 48 hours of the conclusion of trial. All materials not timely removed will be discarded.

Additional Trial Rules for Non–Jury Trials in Part Three

1. All direct testimony of a party's own witnesses shall be submitted in affidavit form. During trial, the witness shall swear to the contents of the affidavit, followed by objections to the testimony and cross-examination. Affidavits containing direct testimony shall be exchanged with the adversary and delivered to Part 3 at least seven calendar days prior to the commencement of the trial.

Exception: Counsel need not submit direct testimony in affidavit form if the witness is not within the party's control.

JUSTICE BARBARA R. KAPNICK

Part 39. Hon. Barbara R. Kapnick

Scheduling

Requests for adjournments of conferences and oral arguments of motions shall be made pursuant to stipulation or by conference call at least 24 hours in advance of the scheduled appearance.

Electronic Filing and Courtesy Copies

All cases in Part 39 should be electronically filed through the Court's Filing By Electronic Means (FBEM) system, except those cases involving pro se litigants. All submissions to the Court (including briefs, proposed Orders and Judgments, and letters) should be electronically filed. If hard copies are also submitted to the Court, they should be marked to reflect that they have previously been e-filed with the e-filed document number indicated. For FBEM instructions, contact the Efiling Support Center at (646) 386–3033 or efile@courts.state.ny.us, or see the Commercial Division's website for New York County at: http://www.nycourts.gov/courts/comdiv/newyork.shtml.

Hard Copy Set of Motion Papers

In addition to electronically filing motion papers, a hard copy set of all papers related to any motion must be submitted to the Motion Support Office in Room 119.

Motions for Summary Judgment

Rule 19-a Statements of Material Facts are required when moving for and opposing summary judgment motions.

Mediation

If, at any point, the parties decide that they could benefit from Commercial Division ADR or other mediation, they should write a joint letter to the Court asking to be referred to ADR or such other mediation. In that letter, they should state whether they prefer that discovery continue or be stayed during the mediation process.

Confidentiality Order

Orders regarding the confidential exchange of information should be based on the Proposed Stipulation and Order for the Production and Exchange of Confidential Information, prepared by a committee of the New York City Bar Association for use in the Commercial Division, available on the Bar Association's website at: http://www.nycbar.org/pdf/report/Model Confidentiality.pdf.

Exhibits

At any evidentiary hearing or trial, the parties shall provide the Court with one copy of the exhibit books and any other documents offered into evidence.

JUSTICE MELVIN L. SCHWEITZER

Part 45. Individual Practices Of Justice Melvin L. Schweitzer

1. Commercial Division Rules

All parties should familiarize themselves with the Commercial Division Rules, available at http://www.nyc ourts.gov/courts/comdiv/newyork_rules.shtml

2. Electronic Filing

All cases in Part 45 must be electronically filed through the Court's Filing By Electronic Means (FBEM) system. All submissions to the Court (including briefs, proposed Orders and Judgments, and letters) must be electronically filed. For FBEM instructs, contact the Efiling Support Center at (646) 386–3033 or efile@courts.state.ny.us, or see the Commercial Division's website for New York County at: http://www.nycourts. gov/courts/comdiv/newyork.shtml

3. Scheduling

All scheduling of appearances or adjournments, and questions pertaining to scheduling, must be addressed to our Part Clerk, Steve O'Fee, at (646) 386–3306. Appearances shall be scheduled at either 60 Centre Street, Room 218, or at 26 Broadway, 10th Floor. Court permission is needed to adjourn any scheduled conference. Requests shall be made to Part Clerk Steve O'Fee no later than two (2) business days in advance of the scheduled appearance. Requests submitted after the deadline will be denied absent a showing of good cause.

4. Communications with Chambers

Litigants may communicate with the Court by mail, fax, e-mail or telephone, more specifically as follows:

A. *Written Correspondence.* Hard copies of letters may be mailed or hand delivered to Chambers at 26 Broadway, 10th Floor, New York, NY 10004. All letters concerning a substantive matter also must be electronically filed. Letters may not exceed three pages in length.

B. *Faxes.* Faxes to Chambers (212) 361–8173 are permitted so long as they are followed by a hard copy sent to Chambers. Faxes also must be electronically filed.

C. *E-mail.* Brief e-mail communications with Counsel to Justice Schweitzer, Jay Wilker, will be permitted if initiated by Mr. Wilker. All counsel must be copied on any e-mail sent. If this is not done, the e-mail will be deleted and unread.

D. *Telephone Conferences.* Litigants must call our Part Clerk, Steve O'Fee, at (646) 386–3306 to schedule a telephone conference with Chambers on substantive matters. Such calls generally will be scheduled after 4 p.m. Counsel for all litigants must initiate and be on the call at the time assigned by Mr. O'Fee. Chambers will not communicate with a litigant ex parte.

5. Motion Practice

A. *Motion Sequence Numbers.* Motion sequence numbers shall appear on ALL motion papers; i.e. the notice of motion, memos of law, exhibits, affirmations, settled orders, etc. The numbers shall also appear on all correspondence with Chambers pertaining to the motion.

B. *Questions.* Questions pertaining to motion practice should be addressed in the first instance to the Commercial Division Support Office at (646) 386–3020.

C. *Prior Permission.* No prior permission is required before making a motion except discovery mo-

tions. See ¶ 5D below. Commercial Division Rule 24 letters are not required in Part 45.

D. *Discovery Motions.* Discovery motions may be made only with leave of the Court. Discovery disputes are to be resolved in the first instance through court conference. Adversaries are first to meet and confer in good faith. If they are unable to resolve the dispute, the aggrieved party shall send a letter to the Court describing the issues (no more than three pages in length), after which the Court will schedule the conference. Only if the dispute is incapable of being resolved at the conference will leave be given to file the appropriate motion.

E. *Discovery Not Stayed.* Discovery is not stayed by a dispositive motion unless the Court otherwise directs.

F. *Dispositive Motions; Deadline.* These must be initiated not later than 60 days following the filing of the note of issue.

G. *Motion Submission; Papers.* No additional papers on a motion will be accepted for filing after the papers in support of and in opposition to the motion are filed on the submission date in the Motion Submission Part, Room 130.

H. *Courtesy Copy. As soon as a motion is fully submitted, and not before, a courtesy copy of the motion papers shall be submitted directly to Chambers* (26 Broadway, 10th Floor) in addition to the hard copy which is required to be submitted to the Motion Submission Part in Room 130 on e-filed motions.

I. *Oral Argument.* No oral argument will be heard on the motion submission date. If thereafter the Court determines that oral argument should be heard, the Court will notify the parties. No motion or order to show cause scheduled for oral argument shall be adjourned at the request of the parties unless that request is received by our Part Clerk, Steve O'Fee, no later than two (2) business days prior to the scheduled oral argument.

J. *Transcript.* If oral argument is held, at its conclusion the movant is to order the transcript. The parties are responsible for both e-filing the transcript and submitting a hard copy to Part Clerk Steve O'Fee who, in turn, will submit it to Chambers. The motion will not be deemed sub judice until a transcript has been received in Chambers.

In the event that a party requests a transcript to be "So Ordered" by the Court, the following procedure must be adhered to: the transcript shall be submitted together with an errata sheet correcting all errors in the record, including presumed court errors. If all parties consent to the proposed corrections or agree that no corrections are required, a stipulation to that effect shall accompany the errata sheet or transcript. In the absence of consent, the requesting party shall notice the record for settlement pursuant to CPLR 5525 [c].

6. Discovery

A. *Interrogatories.* Interrogatories are limited to 25 in number unless another limit is specified in the PC Order. This limit also applies to consolidated actions.

B. *Privilege.* If a party objects to a disclosure demand on the ground of privilege, together with its response to the demand the party asserting the privilege shall serve on all other parties a privilege log of the responsive documents that are not being disclosed and a copy of the redacted documents, bate-stamped. The privilege log shall identify all redacted and completely withheld documents by bate-stamp numbers, dates, authors and recipients, and shall state the privileges being asserted. Failure to serve a privilege log and redacted documents with the party's response to a disclosure demand will, absent good cause, be deemed a waiver of the party's objection on the ground of privilege. Following service of a privilege log, the parties shall confer in an attempt to reach agreement on whether the asserted privileges apply. If agreement cannot be reached, the parties shall call the Part Clerk, Steve O'Fee, to schedule a conference.

C. *Confidentiality Orders.* Any order regarding the exchange of confidential information will be based on the Proposed Stipulation and Order for the Production and Exchange of Confidential Information, prepared by a committee of the Association of the Bar of the City of New York for use in the Commercial Division, available at: http://www.nycbar.org/pdf/report/ModelConfidentiality.pdf. If the parties believe there is good cause to depart from this model, they should call the Part Clerk, Steve O'Fee, to schedule a conference.

D. *Sealing.* Documents filed with the court will not be sealed merely on the ground that they are subject to a confidentiality agreement. 22 NYCRR § 216.1. Where a party wishes to seal a submission, the party shall first submit a letter to the Court setting forth good cause for the requested relief. The Court then will conduct a conference in an effort to resolve the matter, i.e. to determine whether "good cause" has been readily demonstrated. In the event the Court is unable to resolve the matter at the conference, it will endeavor to fashion temporary relief until a formal motion is made on which it may rule viz. the question of "good cause."

E. *Electronic Discovery.* Please consult Rule 8 (b) of the Rules of the Commercial Division pertaining to Consultation prior to Preliminary and Compliance Conferences and Rules §§ 202.12 (b) and 202.12 (c) (3) of the Uniform Civil Rules for the Supreme Court pertaining to electronic discovery and the Preliminary Conference. (22 NYCRR)

F. *Expert Disclosure.* No later than thirty days prior to the completion of fact discovery, the parties shall confer on a schedule for expert disclosure, which shall include the identification of experts, the ex-change of expert reports, and depositions of testifying experts—all of which shall be completed no later than four months after completion of fact discovery. In the event that a party withholds consent to this procedure, the parties shall raise the objection as to enhanced expert disclosure and shall request a conference to discuss the objection with the Court. Unless otherwise stipulated or ordered by the Court, expert disclosure must be accompanied by a written report—prepared and signed by the witness—if the witness is one retained or specially employed to provide expert testimony in the case of one whose duties as the party's employee regularly involve giving expert testimony. The report must contain:

(1) a complete statement of all opinions the witness will express and the basis and the reasons for them;

(2) the data or other information considered by the witness in forming them;

(3) any exhibits that will be used to summarize or support them;

(4) the witness's qualifications, including a list of all publications authored in the previous 10 years;

(5) a list of all other cases in which, during the previous four years, the witness testified as an expert at trial or by deposition; and

(6) a statement of the compensation to be paid for the study and testimony in the case.

The note of issue and certificate of readiness may not be filed until completion of expert disclosure, and expert disclosure provided after dates prescribed herein without good cause will be precluded from use at trial.

7. Pre–Trial or Pre–Evidentiary Hearing Conferences

A. *When.* A pre-trial or pre-hearing conference (TPC) will be scheduled to be conducted by the Court's Counsel in Chambers at 26 Broadway approximately two weeks prior to the trial or evidentiary hearing. In the event an evidentiary hearing is to be conducted on an accelerated time schedule (*e.g.* a preliminary injunction evidentiary hearing), the Court will arrange for acceleration of the TPC and its attendant time deadlines pertaining to the matters to be addressed.

B. *Matters to be Addressed.* Attention is directed to the following Commercial Division Rules: Rule 26 (Estimated Length of Trial), Rule 27 (Motions *in Limine*), Rule 28 (Pre–Marking of Exhibits), Rule 29 (Identification of Deposition Testimony), Rule 30(b) (Pre–Trial Conference), Rule 31 (Pre–Trial Memoranda, Exhibit Book and Requests for Jury Instructions), Rule 32 (Scheduling of Witnesses) and Rule 33 (Preclusion). Litigants are directed to address all matters referenced in these rules prior to the TPC (between themselves, where appropriate) and to comply with them so that they come to the TPC prepared to have these matters disposed of in a Pretrial Order. The parties also shall provide the Court with a statement of agreed upon facts and of disputed contentions. With respect to the exhibit binder or book (Rule 32), the Court requires TWO copies for its own use.

C. The TPC will result in the entry of a Pretrial Order, signed by the Court, which will govern the trial or hearing.

8. Non–Jury Trial or Evidentiary Hearings

Unless otherwise ordered, all direct testimony of a party's own witnesses (including expert witnesses) in non-jury trials or evidentiary hearings shall be submitted in affidavit form. At the trial or hearing itself, each witness shall swear to the contents of the affidavit submitted, which shall be followed by the opposing side's objections to the testimony and cross-examination. Affidavits containing direct testimony shall be exchanged between or among adversaries and delivered to Chambers at 26 Broadway at least one week prior to the commencement of the trial or evidentiary hearing (unless this deadline is accelerated by the Court for a hearing conducted on an accelerated time schedule). Counsel need not submit direct testimony in affidavit form if a witness is not within the party's control.

9. Inquest Procedures

A party requesting an inquest shall submit the following information or documents:

A. An affidavit from a person with knowledge of the facts setting forth how damages are computed.

B. Attorney's affirmation setting forth a brief recitation of the facts and the grounds for liability. The affirmation also should discuss the damages incurred by the party.

C. Exhibits should be submitted in support of all requests for damages. For example:

- if the relief is attorneys' fees, the attorney's affirmation should attach the billing statements describing the activity, the identity and title of the person performing the activity, time, date, and billing rate.

- if the relief is for lost profits, financial statements for comparative time periods should be provided.

D. Whenever counsel believes it would assist the Court, affidavits from experts (i.e. accountants, appraisers, etc.) should be submitted.

E. Proof of service must be filed indicating that all papers and exhibits submitted to the Court were served on opposing parties.

F. Proposed findings of fact and a proposed order must be e-filed.

G. Papers in opposition shall follow the format set forth above.

H. For inquests that were not granted on default, no submissions of evidence should be made for causes of action that previously have been dismissed or on which no liability was found.

JUSTICE O. PETER SHERWOOD

Part 49. Practices for Part 49

1. Commercial Division Rules. Parties should be familiar with the Commercial Division Rules (Uniform Rules for the New York State Trial Courts, § 202.70 ["Uniform Rules"]), available at www.nycourts.gov/courts/comdiv/newyork.shtml

2. Note re: Rule 19–a: On all motions for summary judgment, other than a CPLR § 3213 motion, there shall be annexed to the notice of motion a separate, short and concise statement, in numbered paragraphs, of the material facts as to which the moving party contends there is no genuine issue of fact to be tried.

3. Electronic Filing and Courtesy Copies. All cases in Part 49 must be electronically filed through the New York State Courts E–Filing (NYSCEF) system. All submissions (including briefs, proposed Orders and Judgments, and letters) shall be electronically filed. In addition, a hard copy set of all papers related to any motion must be submitted to the Motion Submission Part in Room 130. Do not submit additional courtesy copies. A courtesy copy of every other (i.e. not motion related) e-filed submission

should be delivered by mail or hand-delivery directly to Part 49 together with the e-filing confirmation notice. The E–Filing Rules appear at Uniform Rule § 202.5–bb. See also ¶14G, below. For NYSCEF instructions or assistance, contact the E-filing Resource Center, Room 119M, by telephone (646) 386-3033 or at efile@courts.state.ny.us, or visit the Center's website at: http://www.nycourts.gov/efile

4. Preliminary and Compliance Conferences. Please consult Commercial Division Rules 7–9. Conferences are scheduled on Wednesdays at 9:30 AM. If the parties agree, they may appear at 10:30 AM, provided that a request to delay the time of appearance by one hour is communicated to the Part Clerk on or before the preceding Monday at Noon.

5. Scheduling. All questions about scheduling and adjournments should be addressed to the Part 49 Clerk, (646) 386-4033. Court permission is needed to adjourn any scheduled conference. Requests shall be e-filed no later than two (2) business days in advance of the scheduled appearance, typically by 5:00 p.m. the Friday prior to the court's Wednesday conference day.

Requests submitted after the deadline will be denied absent a showing of good cause.

6. Communicating with the Court. Litigants may communicate with the court by mail or by telephone as follows:

A. *Written correspondence.* Hard copies of letters to Justice Sherwood may be mailed or hand-delivered to Part 49, Room 252, 60 Centre Street, New York, New York 10007. Correspondence may not be faxed without prior permission of the Part Clerk. If the case has been e-filed, all letters concerning a substantive issue (e.g., letter-briefs, discovery disputes) should also be e-filed.

B. *Telephone calls.* Litigants may call the Part Clerk, (646) 386–4033.

Please note: No attorney in Justice Sherwood's chambers will communicate with a litigant ex parte, nor will they assist the litigants in the practice of law, such as by advising as to how to interpret a particular rule or law. If the parties wish to speak with Justice Sherwood or one of his law clerks by telephone, they should first get the other parties on the phone before placing the call to the court. Questions pertaining to motion practice should be addressed to the Commercial Division Support Office, at (646) 386–3020.

7. Transcripts. Unless the court directs otherwise, the movant on any motion shall order the transcript of oral argument. The parties are responsible for both e-filing the transcript and submitting a hard copy to Part 49. The motion will not be deemed *sub judice* until a transcript is received.

8. Mediation. If, at any point, the parties decide that they could benefit from Commercial Division ADR or other mediation, they should write a joint letter to the Court asking that the case be referred. In that letter, they should state whether they prefer that discovery continue or be stayed during the mediation process.

9. Confidentiality Orders. Any order regarding the exchange of confidential information will be based on the Proposed Stipulation and Order for the Production and Exchange of Confidential Information, prepared by a committee of the Association of the Bar of the City of New York for use in the Commercial Division, available at: http://www.nycbar.org/pdf/report/ModelConfidentiality.pdf. If the parties believe there is good cause to depart from this model, they should call the Part Clerk to schedule a conference. Please note that documents filed with the court will not be sealed merely on the ground that they are subject to a confidentiality agreement (*see Mosallem v Berenson*, 76 AD3d 345, 350 [1st Dept 2010]). Where a party wishes to seal a submission, the party shall submit a letter setting forth good cause for the requested relief.

10. Discovery Related Matters

A. *Disclosure Disputes.* Please consult Commercial Division Rules 10–15. If after good faith efforts, counsel are unable to resolve or narrow the issues involving discovery, the aggrieved party shall contact the court by letter or telephone to arrange a conference.

Where a party objects to disclosure on the ground of privilege, its response shall include a log of the documents being withheld and a copy of redacted documents, bates-stamped. The privilege log shall identify all withheld and redacted documents by bates-stamp number; list date, author, and recipients (except where same is disclosed on redacted documents); and state the privilege(s) being asserted. Following service of the privilege log, counsel shall confer and if unable to reach an accommodation, the aggrieved party may contact the court to arrange a conference.

B. **Interrogatories** are limited to 25 in number without subparts unless another limit is specified in the preliminary conference order. This limit applies to consolidated actions as well. Unless otherwise ordered by the court, interrogatories are limited to the following topics: name of witnesses with knowledge of information material and necessary to the subject matter of the action, computation of each category of damage alleged, and the existence, custodian, location and general description of material and necessary documents, including pertinent insurance agreements, and other physical evidence.

C. Unless otherwise directed by the court, discovery is not stayed by a dispositive motion.

D. Except for discovery motions, no prior permission is required before making a motion. Rule 24 letters are NOT required.

E. *Expert Disclosure.* No later than thirty days prior to the completion of fact discovery, the parties shall confer and attempt to agree on a schedule for expert disclosure, including the identification of experts, exchange of reports, and depositions. In the event that a party withholds consent to this procedure, the parties shall consult with the court. Unless otherwise stipulated or ordered by the court, expert disclosure must be accompanied by a written report—prepared and signed by the witness—if the witness is one retained or specially employed to provide expert testimony in the case or one whose duties as the party's employee regularly involve giving expert testimony. The report shall contain:

(1) A complete statement of all opinions the witness will express and the basis for them;

(2) The data or other information considered by the witness in forming them;

(3) Any exhibits that will be used to summarize or support them;

(4) The witness's qualifications, including a list of all publications authored in the previous 10 years;

(5) A list of all other cases in which, during the previous four years, the witness testified as an expert at trial or by deposition; and

(6) A statement of the compensation to be paid for the study and testimony in the case.

11. Consolidation and Change of Caption. All orders on motions or stipulations to consolidate or change captions shall be sent to the Trial Support Office, located in Room 158M. For sample orders visit http://www.nycourts.gov/supctmanh/otherforms.htm

12. Inquest Procedures. A party requesting an inquest shall submit the following information or documents:

A. An affidavit from a person with knowledge of the facts setting forth how damages are computed.

B. Attorney's affirmation setting forth a brief recitation of the facts and the grounds for liability. The affirmation should also discuss the damages incurred by the party.

C. Exhibits should be submitted in support of all requests for damages. For example:

—if the relief is attorneys' fees, the attorney's affirmation should attach the billing statements describing the activity, the identity and title of the person performing the activity, time, date, and billing rate.

—if the relief is for lost profits, financial statements for comparative time periods should be provided.

D. Whenever counsel believes it would assist the court, affidavits from experts (i.e., accountants, appraisers, etc.).

E. Proof of service must be filed indicating that all papers and exhibits submitted to the court were served on opposing parties.

F. Proposed findings of fact and a proposed order should be e-filed.

G. Any additional submissions that will be helpful to the court.

H. Papers in opposition should follow the format set forth above.

I. For inquests that were not granted on default, do not submit evidence on causes of action that have been previously dismissed or on which no liability was found.

13. Exhibits at Trials and Evidentiary Hearings. At any evidentiary hearing or trial, the parties shall provide the court with a copy of the exhibit books and any other documents to be offered in evidence. Exhibits and other documents will be available to be retrieved at Part 49, Room 252, two days after the case/issue is decided and will be discarded if not collected within 14 days.

14. Motion Practice (Please consult Commercial Division Rules 16–24).

A. Motion Sequence Numbers shall appear on motion papers: the notice of motion, memos of law, exhibits, affirmations, settled orders, etc. They shall also appear on all correspondence pertaining to the motion.

B. Questions pertaining to motion practice should be addressed in the first instance to the Commercial Division Support Office at (646) 386–3020.

C. Discovery is not stayed by a dispositive motion unless the court directs otherwise.

D. On a motion brought on by Order to Show Cause, papers shall be served in a manner that results in receipt by 5:00 p.m. on the date specified unless the court directs otherwise.

E. Dispositive Motions (Deadline) shall be initiated not later than 60 days after filing the note of issue.

F. No additional papers on a motion will be accepted for filing after the submission date.

G. *Courtesy Copy, Memoranda, Statements and Proposed Orders on Computer Disk.* On the submission date on any dispositive motion or motion for interim relief, all memoranda of law, statements of undisputed facts and proposed orders shall be submitted in .rtf format on a computer disk along with the hard copies provided for in ¶3, above.

H. *Oral Argument.* No argument will be heard on the motion submission date. If thereafter, the court determines that oral argument should be heard, the court will notify counsel. See ¶7 re: transcript of oral argument.

15. Requests for Admission Pro Hac Vice. All requests for admission *pro hac vice*, whether made by motion or stipulation, shall be accompanied by an affirmation in support from a member of the Bar of the State of New York, an affirmation from the applicant, and a recent certificate of good standing from the applicant. The affirmation must also advise the court whether the applicant has ever been or is presently subject to disciplinary proceedings.

FORM OF PROPOSED ORDER FOR PRO HAC VICE APPLICATIONS

_____, Esq., having applied to this court for admission pro hac vice to represent [plaintiff/defen-

dant] _____ in this action, and said applicant having submitted in support thereof a stipulation of all parties dated, an affirmation, of _____, Esq., a member of the Bar of the State of New York and attorney of record herein for _____, an affirmation of the applicant dated _____, and a Certificate in Good Standing from the jurisdiction in which the applicant was admitted to the practice of law, and the court having reviewed the foregoing submissions and due deliberation having been had, it is now therefore

ORDERED that the motion is granted on consent and _____, Esq. is permitted to appear and to participate in this action on behalf of _____; and it is further

ORDERED that he/she shall at all times be associated herein with counsel who is a member in good standing of the Bar of the State of New York and is attorney of record for the party in question and all pleadings, briefs and other papers filed with the court shall be signed by the attorney of record, who shall be held responsible for such papers and for the conduct of this action; and it is further

ORDERED that, pursuant to Section 520.11 of the Rules of the Court of Appeals and Section 602.2 of the Rules of the Appellate Division, First Department, the attorney hereby admitted pro hac vice shall abide by the standards of professional conduct imposed upon members of the New York Bar, including the Rules of the Courts governing the conduct of attorneys and the Disciplinary Rules of the Code of Professional Responsibility; and it is further

ORDERED that he/she shall be subject to the jurisdiction of the courts of the State of New York with respect to any acts occurring during the course of his/her participation in this matter; and it is further

ORDERED that said counsel shall notify the court immediately of any matter or event in this or any other jurisdiction which affects his/her standing as a member of the Bar.

ENTER:

_____

J.S.C.

JUSTICE CHARLES E. RAMOS

Part 53. Practice Rules

(Revised August 1, 2011)

1. Absent extraordinary circumstances, no motion scheduled for oral argument in Part 53 will be adjourned unless the request for adjournment is received by the Part Clerk no later than noon the day prior to the scheduled argument. Otherwise, only one adjournment is allowed per argument on motion or conference, no matter which side requests it or even if all parties agree.

2. No party shall contact the Part or Chambers to inquire as to whether an order has been signed UNLESS it is an emergency because the order is time sensitive OR it was submitted more than 45 days prior. In the meantime, parties are directed to check SCROLL, E–Filing, E–Courts and the County Clerk's file for orders. If the order is not there, it has not been signed. SCROLL can be accessed here: http://iapps.courts.state.ny.us/iscroll/

3. Motion sequence numbers shall appear on ALL motion papers: the notice of motion, memos of law, exhibits, affirmations, AND settled orders.

4. MOTIONS WILL NOT BE SCHEDULED FOR ORAL ARGUMENT UNTIL PART 53 HAS A COMPLETE SET OF ALL MOTION PAPERS. In light of recent changes in the E-filing office, Part 53 will not schedule newly filed motions for oral argument unless and until all parties to the motion have submitted "Working Copies" in hard copy form to the E–Filing office (SEE Rule #13 regarding E-filing).

5. MOTION PAPERS SHALL NOT BE TAKEN APART subsequent to filing in the Motion Support or E–Filing offices. Each set of motion papers, affidavits and memos of law shall contain the following legend prominently displayed on the face thereof: "By order of Justice Ramos, these motion papers may not be taken apart or otherwise tampered with."

6. Rule 19–A statements (Statements of Undisputed Facts) are required on all summary judgment motions.

7. Memos of Law ARE REQUIRED on ALL motions. Failure to submit separate memos of law (not incorporated into attorney affirmations) may result in the denial of the motion.

8. Dispositive motions must be initiated within 30 days after the filing the Note of Issue.

9. There shall be oral argument on all motions except motions to reargue.

10. Subsequent to each oral argument held on a motion, either party shall request from the court reporter a transcript of the proceedings and promptly provide a copy to the Court, to be delivered to the Part Clerk. The Part Clerk can provide the name and contact information of the court reporter.

11. In the event that a party requests that a transcript be "So Ordered" by the Court, the following procedure must be adhered to: Transcripts shall be submitted together with an errata sheet correcting all errors in the record, including presumed court errors. If all parties consent to the proposed corrections or agree that no corrections are required, a stipulation to

that effect shall accompany the errata sheet or transcript. In the absence of consent, the requesting party shall notice the record for settlement pursuant to CPLR 5525 [c].

12. Proposed Orders submitted in connection with a motion must be settled on NOTICE, contain the motion sequence number, and be sent directly to the Part or Chambers (unless the proposed order is submitted in connection with a default judgment, in which case, the proposed order should be sent to the Commercial Support Office).

13. E–Filing: Please note that as of May 24, 2010, E-filing is mandatory in all commercial cases filed in New York County. For any questions with respect to E-filing rules and procedures, call the E-filing Office at (646) 386–3610. E-filing sample forms and notices are available at: http://www.nycourts.gov/supctmanh/ E–Filing.htm

a. *Opt-out*: If parties are eligible and wish to opt-out from participating in mandatory E-filing, they must file a Notice of Opt–Out (Note: all forms can be found on the E–Filing Website).

b. *Hard Copy Documents*: All documents in mandatory E-filed cases or E-filed cases in which consent has been given must be filed electronically. Any hard-copy documents in E-filed cases, including correspondence and requests for adjournment, that are sent to the Part or to Chambers MUST be E-filed.

c. *Note*: Hard Copy documents SHOULD NOT BE ACCOMPANIED BY A CONFIRMATION NOTICE, as was previously directed. Hard copy documents will be rejected if they are accompanied by a Confirmation Notice as a cover page.

d. *Courtesy Copies (a.k.a. "Working Papers," "Originals," "Duplicate Originals")*:

    i. Counsel shall submit courtesy copies to the E–Filing office ONLY (NOT TO THE PART) pursuant to the E-filing rules, on the return date of the motion (see #4 above). These courtesy copies shall be in the identical form that motion papers in non-E-Filed cases are submitted to the Part 53, and shall include: original signatures, notaries, proofs of service, and all exhibits without redaction.

    ii. Upon the Court's disposition of the motion, ALL original motion papers in an E-filed action will be discarded, UNLESS counsel affixes a legend on the face of the motion papers requesting that they not be discarded. Counsel shall have 30 days from the date of entry of the disposition of the motion to retrieve the original motion papers from Part 53, or they will be discarded.

14. Parties shall use the approved confidentiality agreement and order available at http://www.nycourts. gov/courts/comdiv/newyork.shtml.

15. Part 53 holds telephone conferences everyday after 4 pm. Even if you are in the building on another matter, you shall not appear in person in either chambers or the Part for a scheduled telephone conference. Any party in the case may initiate the call with all parties on the line before contacting the court. A reservation is not necessary. WHEN CONTACTING THE PART OR CHAMBERS, THE PARTIES MUST HAVE THE INDEX NUMBER AVAILABLE.

16. When discovery deadlines are ordered by the Court, service of discovery requests, responses or motions shall be made in hand by 5 pm on the date specified.

17. No party shall send a letter to chambers without first calling the adversary, having a "meet and confer" on the issue, and only when it cannot be resolved, then calling chambers for a conference. With prior permission, a party may send correspondence e-mail at RCE53@courts.state.ny.us, fax at 212–401–9057, hand delivery, U.S. mail or overnight delivery to chambers, but not by more than one method of delivery.

18. Electronic Discovery: After service of demands for discovery, and prior to the deadline for written responses and inspection/production of documents, parties shall confer in good faith in order to identify whether documents sought are computer stored data. Parties shall discuss the associated costs of production, the method and scope of the search to be conducted, and attempt to agree to search terms, and/or sampling. The responding party will produce the information sought in some form of electronic means (i.e. on a disc), unless the parties agree otherwise, and shall be accompanied by an index that identifies the document(s) produced in response to each demand, the electronic file where the document has been stored, and an affidavit, where requested. Any issues relating to electronic disclosure will be raised with the Court at the next compliance conference.

19. Interrogatories are limited to 25 in number unless another limit is specified in the PC order. This limit applies to consolidated actions as well. Unless otherwise ordered by the court, interrogatories are limited to the following topics:

(1) seeking names of witnesses with knowledge of information relevant to the subject matter of the action;

(2) the computation of each category of damages alleged; and

(3) the existence, custodian, location and general description of relevant documents, including pertinent insurance agreements, and other physical evidence, or information of a similar nature.

20. To clarify Rule 11d of the Commercial Division Rules, the presumption is that discovery is not stayed by the filing of a dispositive motion unless otherwise directed by the Court.

21. Except for discovery motions, no prior permission is required before making a motion. Commercial Division Rule 24 letters are NOT required in Part 53.

22. Expert Disclosure: No later than thirty days prior to the completion of fact discovery, the parties shall confer on a schedule for expert disclosure, which shall include the identification of experts, the exchange of expert reports, and depositions. In the event that a party withholds consent to this procedure, the parties shall consult with the Court. Unless otherwise stipulated or ordered by the court, expert disclosure must be accompanied by a written report—prepared and signed by the witness—if the witness is one retained or specially employed to provide expert testimony in the case or one whose duties as the party's employee regularly involve giving expert testimony. The report must contain:

(1) a complete statement of all opinions the witness will express and the basis and the reasons for them;

(2) the data or other information considered by the witness in forming them;

(3) any exhibits that will be used to summarize or support them;

(4) the witness's qualifications, including a list of all publications authored in the previous 10 years;

(5) a list of all other cases in which, during the previous four years, the witness testified as an expert at trial or by deposition; and

(6) a statement of the compensation to be paid for the study and testimony in the case.

23. All attorneys or pro se litigants must provide their contact information to the Trial Support Office, located in Room 158M.

24. All orders on motions or stipulations to consolidate or change captions shall be sent to the Trial Support Office, located in room 158M. Sample orders are available at http ://www.nycourts.gov/supctmanh/other_forms.htm

25. Procedures for Inquests: A party requesting an inquest in Part 53 shall submit the following information or documents to the Court:

A. An affidavit from a person with knowledge of the facts setting forth how damages are computed.

B. Attorney's affirmation setting forth a brief recitation of the facts and the grounds for liability. The affirmation should also discuss the damages incurred by the party.

C. Exhibits should be submitted in support of all requests for damages. For example:

- if the relief is attorneys' fees, the attorney's affirmation should attach the billing statements describing the activity, the identity and title of the person performing the activity, time, date, and billing rate.

- if the relief is for lost profits, financial statements for comparative time periods should be provided.

D. Whenever counsel believes it would assist the Court, affidavits from experts (i.e., accountants, appraisers, etc.) should be submitted.

E. Proof of service must be filed indicating that all papers and exhibits submitted to the Court have been served on opposing parties.

F. A proposed finding of fact and a proposed order for this Court should be submitted, by e-mail at RCE53@courts.state.ny.us.

G. Any additional submissions that will be helpful to the Court should be provided.

H. Papers in opposition should follow the same format as set forth above.

I. For inquests that were not granted on default, do not submit evidence on causes of action that have been previously dismissed or on which no liability was found.

J. Failure to properly document damages will result in the rejection of the inquest.

26. Class Action Settlements: The settlement of class actions pending in Part 53 shall be governed by the following guidelines (when circumstances warrant, exceptions will be made).

A. All notices to members of the proposed class shall be in plain English. A typical member of the class should be able to easily comprehend each notice. Class counsel must draft such notices consistent with their professional obligation to fully disclose to their clients the significance of the information provided.

B. The issue of class certification is not a matter for stipulation between the parties unless prior permission from the Court is obtained, or settlement is without prejudice as provided below in Paragraph 3. Otherwise, a finding that certification of the class is appropriate will be made at an adversarial hearing.

C. The failure to opt out of the class will not result in a release unless a class member accepts the settlement benefit or knew or should have known that a failure to opt out will result in a release. Proof of actual delivery of a pre-approved intelligible notice, written in plain language will suffice. In addition, this Court will approve the terms of a settlement that provides for a portion of the settlement fund to be held in escrow following discontinuance of the class action and pending the expiration of any applicable statute of limitations period, to be used toward any separate, potential claims by those who have not responded or have not opted in. In such event, any unused funds would be released to the original class following expiration of the limitations period. Unless permitted by this Court, the terms of the settlement shall not require the class members to opt out or take other action to preserve an existing right.

D. Where applicable, the procedure to be followed by class members in applying for the settlement benefit shall be simple and shall not require the class member to provide information or documents not required in the first instance to purchase the product or service other than what is reasonably necessary, such as name, address and proof of purchase (if not otherwise determinable from the parties own records). When practicable, the benefit shall be forwarded to the class members in the manner of an account credit or a refund on a product return.

E. A summary of counsel's application for fees, which shall include the basis and justification for the calculation, shall accompany any notice of proposed settlement. This is required without regard to the source of the fee payment. No fee shall be approved unless it bears a reasonable relationship to the benefit actually accepted by the members of the class and is reasonable in light of the risk to counsel of no recovery. Fee calculations may not be based on the potential value of the settlement; rather, fee awards will be awarded in light of the benefits actually received by class members.

F. The Court may appoint independent counsel to represent the proposed class members on the question of class certification, fees to be awarded class counsel or any other issue where the Court is unable to determine the relative strengths of the parties' positions, or if the settlement raises questions about collusion or the ability of plaintiffs' counsel to represent the interests of the class.

G. The Court will not "preliminarily" approve any settlement prior to the hearing on fairness.

H. A member of the proposed class may object orally at the fairness hearing or in writing without the need to notify counsel or to file written objections prior to the hearing.

I. Notwithstanding Paragraph 1 above, a copy of these rules must be appended to each notice to class members.

27. Request for admission pro hac vice, whether made by motion or stipulation, shall be accompanied by a proposed order and an affidavit in support from a member of the Bar of the State of New York and an affidavit of the applicant and a recent certificate of good standing from the applicant. (See the form of Order below).

FORM OF PROPOSED ORDER FOR PRO HAC VICE APPLICATIONS

_____, Esq., having applied to this court for admission pro hac vice to represent [plaintiff/defendant] _____ in this action, and said applicant having submitted in support thereof a stipulation of all parties dated _____, an affidavit of _____, Esq., a member of the Bar of the State of New York and attorney of record herein for _____, an affidavit of the applicant dated

_____, and a Certificate in Good Standing from the jurisdiction in which the applicant was admitted to the practice of law, and the court having reviewed the foregoing submissions and due deliberation having been had, it is now therefore

ORDERED that the motion is granted on consent and _____, Esq. is permitted to appear and to participate in this action on behalf of _____; and it is further

ORDERED that he/she shall at all times be associated herein with counsel who is a member in good standing of the Bar of the State of New York and is attorney of record for the party in question and all pleadings, briefs and other papers filed with the court shall be signed by the attorney of record, who shall be held responsible for such papers and for the conduct of this action; and it is further

ORDERED that, pursuant to Section 520.11 of the Rules of the Court of Appeals and Section 602.2 of the Rules of the Appellate Division, First Department, the attorney hereby admitted pro hac vice shall abide by the standards of professional conduct imposed upon members of the New York Bar, including the Rules of the Courts governing the conduct of attorneys and the Disciplinary Rules of the Code of Professional Responsibility; and it is further

ORDERED that he/she shall be subject to the jurisdiction of the courts of the State of New York with respect to any acts occurring during the course of his/her participation in this matter; and it is further

ORDERED that said counsel shall notify the court immediately of any matter or event in this or any other jurisdiction which affects his/her standing as a member of the Bar.

ENTER:

_____

J.S.C.

(Non–Jury) Additional Trial Rules for Part 53

1. All direct testimony of a party's own witnesses shall be submitted in affidavit form. During trial, the witness shall swear to the contents of the affidavit, followed by objections to the testimony and cross-examination. Affidavits containing direct testimony shall be exchanged with the adversary and delivered to Part 53 at least one week prior to the commencement of the trial.

Exception: Counsel need not submit direct testimony in affidavit form if the witness is not within the party's control.

2. All exhibits shall be submitted to Part 53 at least one week prior to the commencement of the trial. Counsel's assistant shall provide the witness and the court each with a loose copy of the exhibit(s) in question in order to avoid having the witness or the court dealing with exhibit books.

3. Parties shall provide witness lists, a glossary of names, and any unusual words and acronyms they anticipate to be using during the trial to the court reporter the morning that the trial is set to begin.

4. Demonstrative evidence, including charts, graphics, enlarged contract language, and video depositions, are not permitted without first obtaining the permission of the Court.

JUSTICE SHIRLEY WERNER KORNREICH

Part 54. Hon. Shirley Werner Kornreich

1. Commercial Division Rules. All parties should familiarize themselves with the Commercial Division Rules, available at: http://www.nycourts.gov/courts/comdiv/newyork_rules.shtml.

2. Electronic Filing. All cases in Part 54 should be electronically filed through the New York State Courts E-Filing (NYSCEF) system, except those cases involving pro se litigants. All submissions to the Court (including briefs, proposed Orders and Judgments, and letters) should be electronically filed and a courtesy copy of the e-filed document, together with a NYSCEF confirmation, shall be delivered to the court. For NYSCEF instructions, contact the E-filing Support Center at (646) 386–3033 or www.courts.state.ny.us/efile, or see the Commercial Division's website for New York County at: http://www.nycourts.gov/courts/comdiv/newyork.shtml.

3. Scheduling. All questions about scheduling appearances or adjournments should be addressed to the Part Clerk, Celia Rodriguez, at (646) 386–3362.

Please be advised that litigants must obtain Court permission to adjourn a preliminary or status conference. Excepting emergencies, such permission must be obtained no later than 2 business days in advance of the scheduled appearance. In other words, court permission to adjourn a Thursday conference must be secured no later than the close of business on the preceding Monday.

4. Preparation for Preliminary and Compliance Conferences. The parties shall comply with Commercial Division Rule 8 regarding electronic disclosure and shall come to the preliminary conference with proposed search terms and the names of key personnel whose files they wish to search.

5. Communicating with the Court.

a) *Telephone Calls.* Litigants may call the Part Clerk at (646) 386–3362 to schedule a conference with Justice Kornreich and may call Chambers at (646) 386–3363 to schedule a telephone conference with one of her law clerks. Part 54 holds unscheduled telephone conferences every day, but not before 4 pm. If the parties would like to speak by telephone with Justice Kornreich or one of her law clerks, at a scheduled conference call or otherwise, they should first get ALL parties on the phone before placing the call to the court. Please note: no attorney in Justice Kornreich's chambers will communicate with a litigant ex parte, nor will they assist parties in the practice of law, such as by advising how to interpret a rule, law or decision.

b) *Letters.* No party shall send a letter to chambers.

6. Motion Papers: Filing, Courtesy Copies, Form.

a) In addition to electronically filing motion papers, hard copies of all E-filed papers and exhibits for motions returnable in the Motion Support Office, Room 130, must be delivered to Room 130. Extra courtesy copies of papers will not be accepted.

b) Motion sequence numbers shall appear on ALL motion papers: the notice of motion, memos of law, exhibits, affirmations, etc. and settled orders.

c) All exhibits must be separated by exhibit tabs.

c) Unless the papers are bound on the left side, two-sided copies of exhibits are not permitted.

7. Transcripts.

a) Transcripts of oral arguments on motions. At the conclusion of oral argument the movant is to order the transcript and have a copy delivered to the Part 54 Clerk, Room 228, 60 Centre Street, New York, N.Y. 10007.

b) Transcripts to be "So Ordered." In the event that a party requests that a transcript be "So Ordered" by the Court, the following procedure must be adhered to: Transcripts shall be submitted together with an errata sheet correcting all errors in the record, including presumed court errors. If all parties consent to the proposed corrections or agree that no corrections are required, a stipulation to that effect shall accompany the errata sheet or transcript. In the absence of consent, the requesting party shall notice the record for settlement pursuant to CPLR 5525 [c].

8. Summary Judgment Motions.

a) In lieu of filing Commercial Rule 19–a statements with summary judgment motions, the parties shall confer prior to moving for summary judgment and submit with the motion(s) one joint statement of material facts that the parties agree are not in dispute.

b) Summary judgment motions must be served within 60 days of filing the note of issue.

9. Discovery: Service of Papers, Limit on Interrogatories, Stays, Conferences, & Privilege Logs.

a) When discovery deadlines are ordered by the court, service of discovery requests, responses or motions shall be made so as to be received no later than 5 pm on the date specified in the order.

b) Interrogatories are limited to 25, including subparts, unless another limit is specified in the PC order. This limit applies to consolidated actions as well.

c) Discovery is not stayed by a dispositive motion unless otherwise directed by the court.

d) Parties are to bring copies of ALL prior discovery orders to each and every court appearance.

e) If a party objects to a disclosure demand on the ground of privilege, with its response to the demand, the party asserting the privilege shall serve on all other parties a privilege log of the responsive documents that are not being disclosed and a copy of the redacted documents, bate-stamped. The privilege log shall identify all redacted and completely withheld documents by bate-stamp numbers, dates, authors and recipients, and shall state the privileges being asserted. Failure to serve a privilege log and redacted documents with the party's response to a disclosure demand will, absent good cause, be deemed a waiver of the party's objection on the ground of privilege. Following service of a privilege log, the parties shall confer in an attempt to reach agreement on whether the asserted privileges apply. If agreement cannot be reached, the parties shall call the court Clerk to schedule a conference.

10. Contact Information. All attorneys and pro se litigants must provide their contact information to the Trial Support Office, Room 158M at 60 Centre Street, New York, N.Y. 10007, by filing a notice of appearance.

11. Confidentiality Agreements. Parties shall use the approved confidentiality agreement and order available at: http://www.nycourts.gov/courts/comdiv/PDFs/Part54_Confidentiality_Agreement.PDF.

12. Consolidation or Amendment of Captions. All orders on motions or stipulations to consolidate or amend captions shall be served with notice of entry on the Trial Support Office, Room 158M, and the Clerk of the Court.

13. Trials and Evidentiary Hearings. At any evidentiary hearing or trial, prior to the trial date, the parties shall provide the court with a statement of disputed contentions and agreed upon facts.

14. Requests for admission pro hac vice. A request for pro hac vice admission, whether made by motion or stipulation, shall be accompanied by a proposed order and an affidavit in support from a member of the Bar of the State of New York and an affidavit of the applicant and a recent certificate of good standing from the applicant.

JUSTICE BERNARD FRIED

Part 60. Hon. Bernard Fried

Practices in Part 60

Commercial Division Rules

All parties should familiarize themselves with the Commercial Division Rules, available at http://www.nyc ourts.gov/courts/comdiv/newyork_rules.shtml.

Note re: Rule 11: The number of interrogatories, including subparts, shall be limited to 25. *See* Statement of the Administrative Judge Regarding Implementation of Certain Rules of the Commercial Division (June 8, 2007) http://www.nycourts.gov/courts/comdiv/newyork_rules.shtml.

Note re: Rule 14: If, after meeting and conferring in good faith, counsel are unable to resolve a dispute about disclosure, the aggrieved party shall outline the issue in a letter to the Court, on notice to opposing counsel, who will be expected to submit a letter in response. Once letters from all parties have been received, the Court will either schedule a status conference or issue an order directing the parties to take further action. Letters that exceed 3 pages in length (excluding exhibits) will not be accepted.

Note re: Rule 19–a: Any party submitting a motion for summary judgment, other than a CPLR § 3213 motion, shall annex to the notice of motion a separate, short and concise statement, in numbered paragraphs, of the material facts as to which the moving party contends there is no genuine issue to be tried.

Electronic Filing

All cases in Part 60 must be electronically filed through the New York State Courts E–Filing (NYSCEF) system, except cases involving pro se litigants. All submissions to the Court (including briefs, proposed Orders and Judgments, and letters) must be electronically filed.

Attorneys are expected to familiarize themselves with NYSCEF procedures, which are available at the NYSCEF website, https://iapps.courts.state.ny.us/fbem/mainframe.html

Motion Papers and Courtesy Copies

E-filed submissions are NOT printed out by Part 60. It is the litigants' responsibility to ensure that working copies of ALL e-filed documents are received by Part 60 in advance of the relevant appearance date.

To that end, in addition to electronically filing motion papers, litigants must submit a hard copy set of all papers related to any motion to the Motion Support Office in Room 130. All courtesy copies of e-filed documents intended for judicial review must include exhibit tabs and backs. If it appears to the Court that any motion papers have not been timely filed in both electronic and hard copy forms, when the parties appear for their oral argument, that argument may be adjourned.

Working copies of ALL OTHER e-filed submissions should be delivered, by mail or hand-delivery, directly to Part 60, 60 Centre Street, Room 248. Please note that mailed submissions can take up to five business days to reach Part 60. Time-sensitive materials should be hand-delivered.

Working copies may be faxed, but only with the permission of the Court.

Scheduling

Parties should address questions about scheduling appearances or adjournments to the Part Clerk, Vernon Hutchinson, at (646) 386–3310.

Please be advised that litigants must obtain Court permission to adjourn a status conference. Excepting emergencies, such permission must be obtained no later than 2 business days in advance of the scheduled appearance.

Communicating with the Court

Litigants may communicate with the Court by mail or by telephone as follows:

(1) *Written correspondence.*

Letters to Judge Fried must be e-filed, and courtesy copies of same must be mailed or hand-delivered to Part 60, at 60 Centre Street, Room 248. They may be faxed with prior permission from the Part Clerk. Letters may not exceed three pages in length.

As previously noted, mailed submissions may take up to five business days to reach Part 60. Time-sensitive submissions should be hand-delivered or faxed.

(2) *Telephone calls.*

No attorney in Judge Fried's chambers will communicate with a litigant *ex parte* or assist a litigant in the practice of law, such as by advising how to interpret a particular rule or law.

All telephone calls, including scheduled conference calls, shall be directed to the Part, at (646) 386–3310.

Litigants wishing to schedule a conference with Judge Fried or one of his law clerks may do so by calling the Part Clerk, Vernon Hutchinson, at (646) 386–3310.

If the parties would like to speak by telephone with Judge Fried or one of his law clerks, at a scheduled conference call or otherwise, they must get all parties on the phone before placing the call to the Court.

Questions pertaining to motion practice should be addressed to the Commercial Division Support Office, at (646) 386–3020.

Transcripts

If the Court directs the parties to order a transcript from any proceeding in Court, the parties are responsible for both e-filing the transcript and submitting a hard copy of it to Part 60.

Mediation

If, at any point, the parties decide that they could benefit from Commercial Division ADR or other mediation, they may write a joint letter to the Court asking to be referred to ADR or such other mediation. In that letter, they should state whether they prefer that discovery continue or be stayed during the mediation process.

Confidentiality Order

Any order regarding the confidential exchange of information will be based on the Proposed Stipulation and Order for the Production and Exchange of Confidential Information, prepared by a committee of the New York City Bar Association for use in the Commercial Division, available on the Bar Association's website at: http://www.nycbar.org/pdf/report/Model Confidentiality.pdf (the "Model Form").

If the parties believe there is good cause to depart from the Model Form, they should submit their proposed order, along with a brief letter explaining the necessity of their suggested changes.

Exhibits and Other Submissions at Court Proceedings

At any evidentiary hearing or trial, the parties shall provide the Court with two copies of the exhibit books and any other documents offered into evidence. These two copies shall be in addition to any copies provided to a witness.

At any court proceeding, including oral argument on motions, the parties shall be prepared to hand to the Court two copies of every document that they provide to the Court.

STATEMENT IN SUPPORT OF REQUEST FOR ASSIGNMENT

Form 1. Statement in Support of Request for Assignment to Commercial Division

SUPREME COURT OF THE STATE OF NEW YORK

COUNTY OF NEW YORK

--x

Plaintiff/Petitioner,

Index No. _____

- against -

STATEMENT IN SUPPORT OF
REQUEST FOR ASSIGNMENT
TO COMMERCIAL DIVISION

Defendant/Respondent.

--x

_____, counsel for _____, the _____ in this matter, submits this Statement and the accompanying copy of the pleadings, pursuant to Section 202.70 (d) (2) of the Uniform Rules for the Trial Courts, in support of the request of said party for the assignment of this matter to the Commercial Division of this court.

(1) I have reviewed the standards for assignment of cases to the Commercial Division set forth in Section 202.70. This case meets those standards. I therefore request that this case be assigned to the Division.

(2) The sums at issue in this case (exclusive of punitive damages, interest, costs, disbursements, and counsel fees claimed) are equal to or in excess of the monetary threshold of the Division in this county as set out in Subdivision (a) of said Section, or equitable or declaratory relief is sought, in that _____

_____

_____.

(3) This case falls within the standards set out in Subdivision (b) of the Section and does not come within the groups of cases set out in Subdivision (c) that will not be heard in the Division, in that _____

_____

_____.

Dated: _____   _____(Signature)
                           _____, Esq.

                           _____(Firm)
                           _____(Address)

                           _____
                           _____(Phone)
                           _____(Fax)
                           _____(E–Mail)

E–FILING IN THE COMMERCIAL DIVISION

Doc. 1. Mandatory E–Filing Order

ADMINISTRATIVE ORDER OF THE CHIEF ADMINISTRATIVE JUDGE OF THE COURTS

Pursuant to the authority vested in me, and in consultation with the Honorable Luis A. Gonzalez, Presiding Justice of the Appellate Division, First Department, and the Honorable A. Gail Prudenti, Presiding Justice of the Appellate Division, Second Department, I have established programs for the mandatory use of electronic means for the filing and service of documents ("e-filing"), in the manner authorized pursuant to L. 1999, c. 367, as amended by L. 2009, c. 416, and L. 2010, c. 528, in the counties, courts, actions° and circumstances set forth in Appendix A attached hereto. Such programs shall be subject to section 202.5-bb and, as provided therein, section 202.5-b of the Uniform Rules for the New York State Trial Courts.

This order is effective immediately.

Dated: March 1, 2011

APPENDIX A

(March 1, 2011)

County	Authorized Mandatory E–Filing Program Courts	Implemented Mandatory E–Filing Programs (and effective date)
New York	Supreme Court	Commercial actions (5/24/2010)
Westchester	Supreme Court	Commercial actions (2/1/2011) Tort actions (3/1/ 2011)

I. For purposes of the e-filing program, the following definitions, restrictions, and conditions shall apply.[1]

1. "Commercial actions" with threshold amount in controversy requirement. "Commercial actions" shall mean actions which both (a) exceeds the threshold amount in controversy requirement set forth in sec. 2 infra; and (b) address at least one of the following claims or transactions:

(1) in matters arising out of business dealings (including but not limited to sales of assets or securities, corporate restructuring, partnership, shareholder, joint venture, and other business agreements, trade secrets; restrictive covenants; and employment agreements, not including claims that principally involve alleged discriminatory practices), claims of:

(i) breach of contract (with a threshold amount in controversy requirement in New York County and Westchester County only);

(ii) breach of fiduciary duty;

(iii) fraud, misrepresentation, business tort (including but not limited to actions involving claims of unfair competition); and

(iv) statutory and/or common law violation;

(2) transactions governed by the uniform commercial code (exclusive of those concerning individual cooperative or condominium units);

(3) transactions involving commercial real property, including Yellowstone injunctions and excluding actions for the payment of rent only;

(4) business transactions involving or arising out of dealings with commercial banks and other financial institutions;

(5) internal affairs of business organizations;

(6) malpractice by accountants or actuaries;

(7) legal malpractice arising out of representation in commercial matters;

(8) environmental insurance coverage; and

(9) commercial insurance coverage (including but not limited to directors and officers, errors and omissions, and business interruption coverage).

2. Amount in controversy requirement in certain commercial actions. The threshold amount in controversy requirement described in sec. 1(a) supra are as follows, exclusive of punitive damages, interest, costs, disbursements and counsel fees claimed:

    a. New York County: $100,000.00.

    b. Westchester County: $ 100,000.00.

3. "Commercial actions" without threshold amount in controversy requirement. In addition to the actions described in sec. 1 supra, "commercial actions" shall include actions that assert at least one claim arising from the following, without regard to the amount in controversy:

(1) breach of contract (outside New York County and Westchester);

(2) shareholder derivative actions;

(3) commercial class actions;

(4) dissolution of corporations, partnerships, limited liability companies, limited liability partnerships and joint ventures; and

(5) applications to stay or compel arbitration and affirm or disaffirm arbitration awards and related injunctive relief pursuant to article 75 of the civil practice law and rules involving any of the commercial issues enumerated in sec. 1 and this section.

4. Exclusions from commercial actions. "Commercial actions" shall not include:

(1) actions to collect professional fees;

(2) actions seeking a declaratory judgment as to insurance coverage for personal injury or property damage;

(3) residential real estate disputes, including landlord-tenant matters, and commercial real estate disputes involving the payment of rent only;

(4) proceedings to enforce a judgment regardless of the nature of the underlying case;

(5) first-party insurance claims and actions by insurers to collect premiums or rescind non-commercial policies; and

(6) attorney malpractice actions except as otherwise provided in par. 1 above.

5. Tort actions. "Tort actions" are actions that (a) seek only monetary damages; and (b) assert at least one claim (other than a commercial action claim described in pars. 1 and 3 supra, or a claim expressly excluded from commercial actions as described in par. 4 supra) that arises out of or alleges:

(1) a motor vehicle accident, product liability, injury to person or property from tortious conduct, wrongful death, mass tort, and medical, dental or podiatric malpractice;

(2) other professional malpractice;

(3) damages to persons or property from environmental conditions; or

(4) negligence, defamation, intentional infliction of emotional distress or other intentional harm.

6. Commercial and Tort Claims in a Single Action. An action which meets both the definition of "commercial action" and "tort action" shall be treated as a tort action in Westchester County for e-filing purposes.

1 If any definition, restriction or condition set forth in this Administrative Order conflicts with L. 1999, c. 367, as amended by L. 2009, c. 416, and L. 2010, c. 528, or sections 202.5–b and 202.5–bb of the Uniform Rules of the Trial Courts, the statutory provision or Uniform Rule shall apply.

Doc. 2. Protocol on Courthouse Procedures for Electronically Filed Cases (Revised 1/31/11)

[NOTICE TO THE BAR: MANDATORY E-FILING BEGAN IN NEW YORK COUNTY SUPREME COURT IN CERTAIN COMMERCIAL CASES ON MAY 24, 2010]

Attorneys seeking information about how the New York State Courts Electronic Filing System ("NYSCEF") works are advised to consult the *User's Manual* and *FAQ's*, both available at the NYSCEF website (www.nycourts.gov/efile). What follows is an explanation of how traditional courthouse requirements for the processing of cases are applied in e-filed cases. These procedures seek to minimize the need for trips to the courthouse by counsel and inconvenience generally.

A. E–Filed Cases Generally

1) *Cases Commenced via NYSCEF*: Cases that are commenced by filing of the initial papers with the NYSCEF system are identified as e-filed cases by assignment of a special index number (i.e., cases beginning with 650,000 (commercial matters), 250,000 (tax certiorari matters), and 150,000 (tort cases)).

2) *Cases Converted to NYSCEF*: Cases originally commenced in hard-copy form but later converted to NYSCEF status will bear a regular index number initially. However, when a case is converted to that status, court staff will change the case indicator in the court's Civil Case Information System ("CCIS") computer to identify the matter as a NYSCEF case. This action will also add a suffix to the index number in CCIS (e.g., 600136/2005 E). This suffix should be used on all documents filed with the court in e-filed matters.

3) *Mandatory E–Filing*: Certain commercial cases must be commenced by filing with the County Clerk electronically through NYSCEF and all subsequent documents in such cases must be e-filed. Mandatory commercial cases consist of commercial matters of the types set forth in the rules governing mandatory e-filing (Uniform Rule 202.5–bb). See also Chapter 416 of the Laws of 2009 (posted on the "E–Filing" page of this court's website (at www.nycourts.gov/supctmanh)). A summary of the definition is attached hereto. Section 202.5–bb provides for limited exceptions to the mandatory e-filing requirement: commencement in a defined emergency, filing of subsequent documents in a defined emergency, and exemptions from e-filing. An attorney who states in writing in good faith that he or she lacks the equipment or knowledge needed to e-file and who has no staff member or employee under his or her direction who has such knowledge and equipment may opt out of participation in e-filing in a mandatory case by

filing a form with the Clerk. A self-represented party may choose to opt out by filing the same form. The form is posted on the "E–Filing" page on this court's website (at www.nycourts.gov/supctmanh). An attorney may also seek an exemption from the Justice assigned to a mandatory case upon a showing of good cause.

4) *Presumptive E–Filing—Commercial Division Cases and Certain Other Parts*: Commercial Division cases commenced between June 15, 2008 and May 24, 2010 in New York County have been designated as presumptively e-filed matters. All such cases that have not been commenced electronically have been converted by court staff upon filing of the Request for Judicial Intervention ("RJI"). See Notice to the Commercial Division Bar of the Administrative Judge, May 20, 2008 (posted on the "E–Filing" page of this court's website). (The same procedure is followed in commercial and tort cases in General Assignment Parts 12 (Feinman, J.), 35 (Edmead, J.), and 61 (Sherwood, J.)). If parties fail to consent to e-filing in these cases within a reasonable time, the court may convert them back to hard copy cases.

5) *Partially E–Filed Cases*: If one party or more than one but fewer than all consent to e-filing in a consensual case, or if, in a mandatory e-filed case, an attorney or self-represented party obtains an exemption from participating in e-filing, each participating attorney or party shall e-file all interlocutory documents to be filed with the court and such attorneys or parties shall serve one another electronically as provided in the E–Filing Rules. Non-participating parties shall file and serve and be served in hard copy format.

B. Filing of Papers Generally

1) *Mandatory E–Filed Cases; Paper Documents Not Accepted*: All mandatory e-filed cases must be commenced electronically. Unless otherwise provided by the E–Filing Rules or this Protocol, in these cases, the County Clerk will not accept commencement documents in paper form nor will the court accept subsequent documents in that form. If a party wishes to commence a case under seal or to proceed under an anonymous caption, the party should contact the Chief Deputy County Clerk or the Clerk in Charge of Law and Equity of the County Clerk's Office before filing any documents. See "Commencement of Cases" under the "Courthouse Procedures" link on this court's website.

2) *Mandatory E–Filed Cases; Exempt and Emergency Filers*: Any emergency filing made in hard copy in accordance with the Mandatory E–Filing Rules and any document filed with the court in hard copy form by an attorney or self-represented party who has opted out of participation in e-filing in accordance with the Rules must bear, as the back page facing out, a completed Notice of Hard Copy Submis-

sion—E-Filed Case (accessible on the "E-Filing" page of the court's website). Under the Rules, a filer must electronically file the documents initially filed in hard copy form within three business days of an emergency filing. The originals will be discarded after the documents have been processed; failure to e-file as required will therefore lead to an incomplete record.

3) *Consensual E-Filing; Paper Documents Not Accepted*: Unless otherwise provided by the E-Filing Rules or this Protocol, in any case that is subject to e-filing by consent of the parties, all documents required to be filed with the court must be e-filed by consenting parties. Any such document that is submitted in hard copy form will not be accepted by the Clerk.

4) *Index Numbers*: In cases commenced electronically, the County Clerk will issue an index number as soon as possible. In the event that counsel faces exigent circumstances that require the accelerated assignment of an index number, counsel may send a request for such assignment by e-mail to the County Clerk at ccnyef@courts.state.ny.us.

5) *Fees*: Court fees in NYSCEF cases may be paid via NYSCEF by a credit or bank card (Mastercard or Visa). Documents may also be filed with the NYSCEF system and the fee paid at the County Clerk's Office. In the latter case, the document is not considered to have been filed until payment of the fee has been tendered (see CPLR 304). Whenever an attorney uses the latter option, payment must be submitted within three business days. If it is not, the County Clerk will return the document to the filer. When so paying, counsel should alert the County Clerk Cashier (646–386–5932 or 5949) that the case is a NYSCEF matter.

6) *Papers Must Be Filed to the System*: Unless otherwise provided in the Rules or herein, all documents to be filed with the court in a NYSCEF case, including all documents on motions and all letters, must be filed with the NYSCEF system (except where a special exemption is granted (e.g., oversized maps)). Documents that attorneys would not ordinarily file with the court in a hard-copy case need not be filed in a NYSCEF matter.

7) *Working Copies of Documents for Judicial Review*: Unless otherwise directed by the court or as described herein, in all NYSCEF cases in which an RJI has been filed, working copies of e-filed documents that are intended for judicial review must be submitted (except with respect to hard copy emergency or exempt filings in mandatory cases). With the possible exceptions of proposed orders to show cause and supporting documents (see Section G), documents must be filed with the NYSCEF system and any required working copy must be delivered to the court thereafter. The working copies shall include exhibit tabs and backs and, for motion papers, the Motion Sequence Number. In addition, the filer of a working copy of an e-filed document must firmly bind thereto, as the back page facing out, a copy of the Confirmation Notice that was generated by NYSCEF when that document was e-filed. Working copies that are submitted without the related Confirmation Notice will not be accepted. Notwithstanding any references in this Protocol to required working copies, such copies shall not be submitted in e-filed cases in Part 12 (Feinman, J.), Part 35 (Edmead, J.), Part 52 (Kern, J.), and Part 6 (Lobis, J.) unless requested by the court in a particular case.

8) *Discarding of Working Copies*: The official record of a document in an e-filed case is the electronic record of the document stored by the Clerk (Uniform Rule 202.5–b (d) (4)). Working copies are intended only for the use of the Justice and will be discarded after the Justice has finished with them. Thus, in the event that counsel fails to e-file a document, it will not be part of the court record.

9) *Court Will Print Out and Deliver Certain Non-Voluminous Papers for Judicial Review*: To assist counsel, the relevant back office of the court will (after payment via NYSCEF of any related filing fee) print out from the NYSCEF system hard copies of certain non-voluminous documents (i.e., those up to 25 pages long) that are intended for review by a Justice and will deliver them to the relevant back office for processing and transmission to the Justice. No working copy need be delivered by counsel. See, e.g., Section F (proposed long form orders).

10) *Working Copies Not Required of E-Filed Documents Not Intended for Judicial Review*: E-filed documents intended for processing by a back office but not for review by a Justice (e.g., preliminary conference requests, notes of issue) will, after payment of any fee via NYSCEF, be processed by the relevant back office. These papers must be e-filed. Counsel does not need to appear or to submit working copies.

11) *Authorization Form—Filing Agent*: The Rules require that a firm acting as filing agent for an attorney or party to a case must file a form (accessible on the NYSCEF website) whereby the attorney or party authorizes the agent to file on the attorney or party's behalf. Only one such form need be filed for an attorney or party in any specific NYSCEF case.

C. Requests for So-Ordered Stipulations

If an attorney wishes to submit a stipulation to be "so ordered," he or she should file the document with NYSCEF, designating it on the filing menu as a "Proposed Stipulation to be So Ordered." The Clerk will print out a hard copy and forward it to the Justice assigned or transmit the document to the Justice electronically. No appearance by counsel is needed.

D. Requests for Judicial Intervention

1) *Supplement to RJI Required in Certain Hard Copy Cases*: To assist in identification of cases, in any

commercial case or special proceeding involving commercial arbitration or seeking dissolution of a business, the filer of an RJI in hard copy form must file with it a completed Supplement to Request for Judicial Intervention (form available on the "E–Filing" page of this court's website). The papers will not be accepted without the Supplement.

2) *RJI in NYSCEF Cases*: An RJI in a NYSCEF case shall be submitted via NYSCEF. Once filed and paid for via NYSCEF, the RJI and any accompanying document will be forwarded to the relevant back office for random assignment of the case and processing of the document. Counsel need not appear. In the case of RJIs seeking assignment to the Commercial Division, pursuant to Uniform Rule 202.70 (d) (2), the filer must submit therewith a statement in support of the assignment and a copy of the pleadings, which will be forwarded to the assigned Justice for review. If the RJI seeks intervention with regard to a document that is intended for review by a Justice, such as a motion, a working copy of the RJI must be submitted with the working copy of the motion and the NYSCEF Confirmation Notice.

E. Motions on Notice

1) *Motions/Petitions Returnable in Room 130*: A motion on notice or a notice of petition in a NYSCEF case, as in others, shall be made returnable in the Motion Support Office Courtroom (Room 130). The motion must be filed with NYSCEF and the motion fee paid for either via NYSCEF by credit/bank card or by the "Pay at the County Clerk's Office" option. The moving documents must be e-filed no later than eight days prior to the return date.

2) *Calendaring of Motion/Petition and Notice by Court Staff*: After a motion/petition and notice are filed with the NYSCEF system, the Motion Support Office will automatically place the motion/proceeding on the calendar of the Motion Support Office Courtroom (Room 130) for the date fixed; no appearance or other action by the filing attorney is required in order for the motion to be calendared if the motion fee is paid for via NYSCEF. Motions in e-filed cases appear on a separate calendar in the Courtroom.

3) *Adjournments on Motions/Petitions in Room 130; Appearance Can Be Avoided*: Motions that have been e-filed may be adjourned in Room 130 if an adjournment complies with any directives of the assigned Justice and the procedures of the Motion Support Office Courtroom (explained in the "Motions" section of the "Courthouse Procedures" link on the website of this court). An adjournment that so complies may be obtained by filing a stipulation of all parties with NYSCEF (designated in the filing menu as a "Stipulation to Adjourn Motion"). The Office will effectuate the adjournment without need for an appearance or any other action by the parties.

4) (a) *Working Copies on Motions in Room 130*: After papers on motions have been e-filed, working

copies thereof, with Confirmation Notice firmly attached as the back page facing out, must be submitted. (Each document or group of documents that is separately bound shall bear a Confirmation Notice.) Working copies lacking the Notice will not be accepted. WORKING COPIES OF MOTION PAPERS MUST BE SUBMITTED IN THE MOTION SUPPORT OFFICE COURTROOM (ROOM 130) AS EXPLAINED HEREIN. THEY MUST NOT BE DELIVERED TO THE PART OR CHAMBERS; DOING SO WILL CAUSE ADMINISTRATIVE CONFUSION AND POSSIBLE MISPLACEMENT OF PAPERS. Working copies, including copies of the moving papers, will not be accepted in the Motion Support Office (Room 119), but shall be handed up at or before the "call" of the E–Filed Calendar in the Motion Support Office Courtroom (Room 130) on the final return date. Counsel should confer with one another regarding adjournments so that all parties are aware of what the final return date will be. Working copies should not be submitted before that date. Counsel may submit their own working copies on the final return date or agree that one party may submit the copies of all parties at that time. If the Clerk becomes aware that an attorney has failed to submit required working copies on the final return date, the motion may be placed, for one time only, on the three-day calendar to permit submission of those copies. The court will not provide direct notice to the attorney that this has occurred; attorneys should consult the listing in the Law Journal regarding disposition of the Room 130 calendar. If the working copies are not submitted on the three-day calendar, the motion will be transmitted as is to the Justice for such action as the Justice finds appropriate. Attorneys who maintain their office outside the County of New York may submit working copies on motions by mail or overnight delivery. Any such submission shall be sent in a timely manner to the Motion Support Office (Room 119) and be conspicuously marked on the outside "NYSCEF Matter;" lack of such marking may delay processing.

(b) Working Copies on OSCs Returnable in the Part; Subsequent Papers Handed up in the Part: On orders to show cause that are made returnable in the Part, working copies of e-filed opposition and (if allowed) reply papers (with backs and tabs) must be delivered to the Part. As to all such documents, and any document the court may allow a party to hand up in the courtroom on a motion/petition on notice beyond those previously submitted in Room 130, the attorney must file each document with NYSCEF and thereafter submit a working copy bearing firmly affixed thereto, as the back page facing out, a copy of the related NYSCEF Confirmation Notice. Documents lacking a copy of the related Notice will not be accepted.

5) *Exhibits*: Whenever possible, attorneys submitting exhibits in NYSCEF cases should make each

exhibit a separate attachment to an affidavit/affirmation in the system (i.e., they should not be filed as a single PDF).

6) *Notification of Decisions and Orders*: After issuance of a decision and order on a motion in a NYSCEF case, the document will be processed into the NYSCEF system, which constitutes entry (Uniform Rule 202.5–b (h)), as will be reflected in a legend on the document. The NYSCEF system will immediately transmit notice of this event via e-mail, including a link to the entered document, to all participating attorneys and self-represented parties. Such transmittal does not constitute notice of entry. See Section K.

F.   Long Form Orders on Motions

If the court directs that an order be settled or submitted on a motion in a NYSCEF case, the proposed order, with notice of settlement where required, and any proposed counter-order shall be filed with the court via NYSCEF. The relevant back office (the Motion Support Office Order Section (Room 119) or the Commercial Division Support Office (Room 148)) will process the documents in the customary manner. The Clerk of the back office will print out a copy of the documents and, as appropriate, may make changes on the proposed order/counter-order by hand or may contact the submitting attorney by e-mail or telephone. Once a proposed order/counter-order in final form has been arrived at, the Clerk of the back office will forward it in hard copy to the Justice. No appearance by counsel nor working copy is required. After an order/counter-order has been signed, it will be scanned, with County Clerk entry stamp, into the NYSCEF system, which will immediately transmit notice of this event via e-mail, including a link to the entered document, to all participating attorneys and self-represented parties in the case. Such transmittal does not constitute notice of entry. See Section K.

G.   Orders to Show Cause

1) *Proposed Orders to Show Cause and Supporting Documents to be Filed On–Line*: Except as provided in the following paragraph, proposed orders to show cause and supporting documents in all NYSCEF cases must be submitted by filing with the NYSCEF system; original documents will not be accepted by the Clerk. Counsel must comply with Uniform Rule 202.7 (f) regarding notice of the application. See also Commercial Division Rule 20 (Uniform Rule 202.70).

2) *Permissible Submissions in Hard Copy*: If a party seeking a TRO submits an affirmation/affidavit demonstrating significant prejudice from the giving of notice (see Rules 202.7 (f) and Commercial Division Rule 20) or if in accordance with the Rules a party to a mandatory e-filed case is exempt from participation or seeks to submit documents in an emergency, the proposed order to show cause and supporting documents may be presented to the Commercial Division Support Office or the Ex Parte Office in hard copy

form. The papers must be accompanied by, as the back page facing out, a completed Notice of Hard Copy Submission—E-Filed Case. A proposed order to show cause and supporting documents that must be presented to a Justice outside normal court hours shall be presented in hard copy. In all situations described in this paragraph (other than that of an exempt party), documents submitted in hard copy form must thereafter be e-filed, as set forth below.

3) *Office Review of Submissions Will be Done On–Line*: Absent unusual practical difficulties, a proposed order to show cause and supporting documents that have been filed with NYSCEF will be reviewed on-line by the Commercial Division Support Office or by the Ex Parte Office. If there are problems with the documents, the submitting attorney will be promptly contacted by the back office by e-mail or telephone.

4) *Working Copies*: Except for instances covered by Par. (2) of this section, a working copy of a proposed order to show cause and the supporting documents with Confirmation Notice(s) must be submitted to the Commercial Division Support Office or the Ex Parte Office. A second working copy of the proposed order only, to which a Confirmation Notice shall not be attached, shall be submitted simultaneously.

5) *Hard Copy Service*: In cases in which hard copy service is made of documents that were submitted in hard copy form pursuant to Par. (2) of this section and where no party is served electronically, the filing attorney or party shall, no later than three business days after service, e-file the supporting papers (designating them in the NYSCEF document type drop-down menu on the filing screen as "Supporting Papers to OSC (After Service))," together with proof of hard copy service. Failure to do so will cause the County Clerk file to be incomplete. The Clerk will e-file the signed order to show cause after the deadline for service has passed.

6) *Declination*: If the Justice declines to sign the order to show cause, the Clerk will electronically file the declined order. If the proposed order to show cause and supporting documents were filed with the court in hard copy form, the filing attorney or party (other than an exempt party) shall file the supporting documents with NYSCEF no later than three business days after the filing by the clerk. Failure to do so will cause the County Clerk file to be incomplete.

7) *E–Service of Signed OSC and Supporting Documents*: If the court directs that the signed order to show cause and supporting documents be served electronically, a conformed copy of the signed order should be designated as "Conformed Copy of OSC" in the NYSCEF document type drop-down menu on the filing screen.

H.   Procedures Regarding Service On–Line

Pursuant to the NYSCEF Rules, service of interlocutory documents is made by posting a document to the NYSCEF site, which immediately transmits an e-mail notice of the filing, including a link to the document, to all participating counsel and self-represented parties on the case. The Rules also authorize service by other methods permitted by the CPLR. If service by such a method is made, proof of service must be filed with NYSCEF.

I. Service of Orders on the County Clerk and Back Offices

If an order in a NYSCEF case requires that the County Clerk or a back office of the court take action, a copy of the order must be served on the County Clerk or the back office. This may be done by transmitting a copy of the order by e-mail to the appropriate e-mail box. The e-mail addresses are as follows:

County Clerk:
cc-nyef@courts.state.ny.us
Motion Support Office:
mso-nyef@courts.state.ny.us

Trial Support Office:
trialsupport-nyef@ courts.state.ny.us
Special Referee:
spref-nyef@ courts.state.ny.us

J. Secure Documents and Sealing of Documents

1) *Social Security Numbers*: "No person may file any document available for public inspection ... in any court of this state that contains a social security account number of any other person, unless such other person is a dependent child, or has consented to such filing, except as required by federal or state law or regulation, or by court rule." GBL 399–dd (6).

2) *Secure Documents*: Pursuant to the Rules, documents may be designated "secure" by the filing user. The effect of such designation is that the document may be viewed in the NYSCEF system only by counsel and selfrepresented parties to the case who have consented to NYSCEF and by the court and the County Clerk. The electronic file, however, remains open for public inspection via computer at the courthouse (unless sealed in accordance with Part 216 of the Uniform Rules for the Trial Courts).

3) *Sealing; Compliance with Part 216; Procedures*:

(a) Application for Sealing Order: In order to seal a document in a NYSCEF case, a party must proceed in accordance with Part 216 of the Uniform Rules. If a party wishes to file and maintain papers under seal and no sealing order has been issued in the case, the party must, either by motion or on submission to the court of a stipulation, obtain a court order pursuant to Part 216 directing the Clerk to seal the file in whole or in part. If the motion/stipulation is filed with the NYSCEF system, it will be open to the public until a sealing order is issued. Should this create difficulty, the applicant may wish to consider filing the motion/stipulation as a "secure" document if that is appropriate and sufficient. Or counsel may make a motion or submit a stipulation without filing it to the system until

after the court has ruled on the sealing issue or has issued an order temporarily sealing the papers in question. Any such motion or stipulation submitted in hard copy form must bear, as the back page facing out, a Notice of Hard Copy Submission—E-Filed Case and be accompanied by a computer disk containing the papers in PDF format, which the County Clerk will use to e-file the documents after effectuating sealing if directed by the court. Any opposition or reply papers shall likewise be submitted in hard copy form, with said Notice, and be accompanied by a disk containing the documents in PDF format. Each disk shall be identified by the name of the case, the index number, and the name and e-mail address of the attorney submitting it. An attorney or party exempted from e-filing in a mandatory case need not submit a PDF copy.

b) Implementing Sealing Order:

(i) Sealing Existing E–File in Whole or in Part: If the court issues an order directing the sealing of a complete existing NYSCEF file or a document or documents already filed with NYSCEF, the applicant shall file with the NYSCEF system a Notification for Sealing in Electronically–Filed Case (form available on the NYSCEF website), together with a copy of the court's order. No further action by counsel is required. The County Clerk will seal the file or the document(s) in question as directed by the court, both in the NYSCEF system and, if any of the covered documents are found therein, in the hard copy file.

(ii) Sealing Document or Documents Not Yet E–Filed: If the court issues an order directing the sealing of a document that has not yet been e-filed, the document should be presented (unless the court directs otherwise) to the County Clerk in hard copy form with a copy of the court's sealing order and a disk, labeled as indicated above, bearing the document in PDF format.

4) *Previously Sealed File*: If a case that was previously sealed pursuant to court order is converted to NYSCEF status, counsel for the parties should promptly alert the County Clerk's Office (cc-nyef@ courts.state.ny.us or 646–386–5943) that an order sealing the file was issued.

K. Entry and Notice of Entry

Pursuant to the NYSCEF Rules, the Clerk shall file orders electronically and such filing shall constitute entry of the order. An e-mail message will be transmitted to all filing users on the case notifying that the order has been entered. Such notice does not constitute service of notice of entry by any party. Notice of entry is served as follows: a party shall transmit electronically to the parties to be served a notice of entry, a copy of the notification received from the court, and a copy of the order or judgment.

L. Judgments and the Judgment Roll

1) *Entry of Judgment; Procedures*: If the court in an order directs entry of judgment by the County Clerk, the party seeking entry shall submit to the County Clerk a proposed judgment with bill of costs (both of which shall be in one PDF file), and interest calculations and supporting information. It is requested that a legal back be included with these documents since the County Clerk uses the back as the location for stamps affixed upon entry. These documents should be e-filed or may be sent by e-mail outside the NYSCEF system to the following e-mail box: cc-nyef@courts.state.ny.us. The Judgment Clerk will promptly communicate with counsel by e-mail or phone in the event of any difficulties with the submission. Once the judgment is in final form, it will be printed out by the Judgment Clerk and submitted to the County Clerk for signature. When the judgment is signed, the Judgment Clerk will post it to the system, along with the supporting information, at which time notification will be sent via e-mail to all participating parties.

2) *Default Judgment; Entry by Clerk*: If the plaintiff in a NYSCEF case seeks entry of a default judgment by the Clerk pursuant to CPLR 3215, the attorney shall pay the $ 45 motion fee and either transmit to the NYSCEF system a proposed Clerk's default judgment with bill of costs, etc., or forward these documents to the Clerk outside the NYSCEF system (to the e-mail box cc-nyef@courts.state.ny.us). The Clerk will communicate with counsel if any questions or issues arise. Where the submissions are made to NYSCEF, the Judgment Clerk will promptly enter the judgment. If the submission is made to the e-mail box outside NYSCEF, the attorney must file on the NYSCEF system the proposed Clerk's default judgment in final form with bill of costs, etc. To enter the judgment the Clerk will print out the judgment from NYSCEF, have it signed, and scan it to the system.

3) *Judgments Signed by Court*: Where the court signs the judgment, calculation of disbursements, costs and interest will be left to the County Clerk. Papers supporting such calculation may be submitted to the County Clerk in the manner described above.

4) *Entry of Judgment*: Once the County Clerk has taxed costs and disbursements and calculated interest and has in hand a signed judgment, the Clerk will stamp the judgment with the County Clerk file stamp and post the judgment to NYSCEF. This constitutes entry. The Clerk will transmit an e-mail message to all filing users notifying that the judgment has been entered. This notice does not constitute service of notice of entry by any party.

M. Notices of Appeal and Appeal Papers

1) *Notice of Appeal; Payment of Fee*: A notice of appeal shall be filed on-line in a NYSCEF case. The fee therefor must be paid by credit or bank card via NYSCEF or by means of the "Pay at the County Clerk's Office" option. Pursuant to the Rules, in the latter situation the notice will not be considered "filed" until payment of the fee is tendered to the County Clerk at the office. When paying at the Office, the filer must inform the Clerk that the case in question is an e-filed matter. No hard copy should be delivered to the County Clerk's Office.

2) *Notice of Appeal; Procedures*: The notice shall be filed together with a pre-argument statement and a copy of the judgment or order appealed from. The other participating parties to the case may be served via NYSCEF. The County Clerk will print a hard copy of any e-filed notice of appeal and include it in the County Clerk file.

3) *NYSCEF; Appellate Division*: The Appellate Division, First Department does yet not handle appeals in NYSCEF cases by electronic means, although the Court has announced its intention to move toward that goal in the near future. Counsel are advised to consult the rules of that court and to confer with the County Clerk.

ANY ATTORNEY WHO REQUIRES ASSISTANCE IN A NYSCEF CASE IS ENCOURAGED TO CONTACT THE NEW YORK COUNTY E-FILING OFFICE OR THE E-FILING RESOURCE CENTER. COMPUTER EQUIPMENT IS AVAILABLE AT THE COURTHOUSE FOR THE USE OF ATTORNEYS WHO MAY NEED TO MAKE FILINGS IN NYSCEF CASES AND WHO FROM TIME TO TIME ARE UNABLE TO MAKE THE FILINGS FROM THEIR OWN OFFICES.

Dated: January 31, 2011

ELECTRONIC FILING OFFICE
SUPREME COURT, CIVIL BRANCH
NEW YORK COUNTY
60 Centre Street, Room 119
New York, New York 10007
Phone: 646-386-3610
E-Mail: newyorkef@courts.state.ny.us

JEFFREY CARUCCI
STATEWIDE COORDINATOR OF
ELECTRONIC FILING

NEW YORK STATE COURTS
ELECTRONIC FILING
RESOURCE CENTER
60 Centre Street, Room 119 M
New York, New York 10007
646-386-3033
efile@ courts.state.ny.us

EDWARD KVARANTAN
CHRISTOPHER GIBSON
DEPUTY COORDINATORS

Form 1. Notice of Commencement of Action
Subject to Mandatory Electronic Filing

SUPREME COURT OF THE STATE OF NEW YORK
COUNTY OF _____

--x

Plaintiff/Petitioner,

—against—   Index No. _____

Defendant/Respondent.

--x

NOTICE OF COMMENCEMENT OF ACTION SUBJECT
TO MANDATORY ELECTRONIC FILING

PLEASE TAKE NOTICE that the matter captioned above, which has been commenced by filing of the accompanying documents with the County Clerk, is subject to mandatory electronic filing pursuant to Section 202.5–bb of the Uniform Rules for the Trial Courts. This notice is being served as required by Subdivision (b) (3) of that Section.

For information about electronic filing, including access to Section 202. 5–bb, consult the website of the New York State Courts Electronic Filing System ("NYSCEF") at www.nycourts.gov/efile or contact the NYSCEF Resource Center at 646–386–3033 or efile@courts.state.ny.us.

Dated: _____

_____ (Signature)

_____ (Name)

_____ (Firm Name)

_____ (Address)

_____

_____ (Phone)

_____ (E–Mail)

To: _____

          _____

          _____

5/17/10

Form 2.   Notice of Hard Copy Submission—E–Filed Case

SUPREME COURT OF THE STATE OF NEW YORK
COUNTY OF _____

---x

Plaintiff/Petitioner,

Index No. _____

—against—

Defendant/Respondent.

---x

NOTICE OF HARD COPY SUBMISSION—E–FILED CASE

(This Form Must be Annexed to Hard Copy Submissions in E–Filed Cases)

With limited exceptions, all documents in mandatory e-filed cases and e-filed cases in which consent has been given must be filed electronically; all hard copies submitted must be working copies in compliance with the E–Filing Rules. Counsel who seek to submit hard copy original documents in mandatory e-filed cases or cases subject to e-filing in which consent is being withheld must indicate the reason for hard copy submission by initialing in the relevant blank space provided below.

1.   Consensual Cases

____ In this consensual case, I am authorized to and do hereby withhold consent to e-filing on behalf of my client, a party to the case, or, if self-represented, myself.

2.   Mandatory Cases

____ I am exempt from the requirement to e-file because, in accordance with the E–Filing Rules, either I have filed with the court the exemption form required by the Rules or the court has granted my application upon good cause shown.

____ I am authorized to file this document in hard copy in this e-filed case pursuant to an emergency exception and am submitting the affirmation/affidavit required by Uniform Rule 202.5–bb (b) (2) or (c) (3). I understand that I am required by the Rules to, and I shall, e-file these documents within three business days hereafter.

3.   Consensual or Mandatory Case—Sealing Application

____ I am applying for a sealing order and the need to protect sensitive information in the moving papers requires that I submit the papers in hard copy form, as permitted by the Protocol on Electronic Filing.

4.   Proposed Orders to Show Cause

____ As provided by the Protocol on Electronic Filing, I am submitting in hard copy form a proposed order to show cause and supporting papers seeking a TRO, together with an affirmation/affidavit demonstrating that there will be significant prejudice to the applicant from the giving of notice (Uniform Rule 202.7 (f)).

Dated: _____   _____ (Signature)

                            _____ (Name)

                            _____ (Firm Name)

                            _____ (Address)

                            _____

_____ (Phone)

_____ (E–Mail)

9/27/10

Form 3. Notice of Opt–Out From Participation in Action Subject to Mandatory Electronic Filing

SUPREME COURT OF THE STATE OF NEW YORK
COUNTY OF _____
---x

Plaintiff/Petitioner,

Index No. _____

—against—

Defendant/Respondent.
---x

NOTICE OF OPT–OUT FROM PARTICIPATION IN ACTION SUBJECT TO MANDATORY ELECTRONIC FILING

Pursuant to Section 202.5–bb of the Uniform Rules for the Trial Courts, I hereby opt out of participation in electronic filing in this mandatory e-filed case.

For Attorneys:

I certify in good faith that I am unable to participate in mandatory electronic filing of documents in this case on behalf of my client, _____, because [place your initials in the applicable space]:

___I lack [check off the applicable box]:

☐ the necessary computer hardware

☐ a connection to the internet

☐ a scanner or other device by which documents may be converted to an electronic format

___I lack the knowledge regarding operation of computers and/or scanners needed to participate in electronic filing of documents in this case and no employee of mine or of my firm, office or business who is subject to my direction possesses such knowledge.

For Self–Represented Litigants:

I choose not to participate in electronic filing of documents in this case.

Dated: _____   _____ (Signature)

_____ (Name)

_____ (Firm Name)

_____ (Address)

_____

_____ (Phone)

9/27/10

ALTERNATE DISPUTE RESOLUTION

GUIDE

Doc. 1. Guide to the Alternative Dispute Resolution Program

THE COMMERCIAL DIVISION ALTERNATIVE DISPUTE RESOLUTION PROGRAM

The Alternative Dispute Resolution Program of the New York County Commercial Division ("the Program") is governed by rules issued by the Administrative Judge of the Civil Branch of the Supreme Court in the First Judicial District ("the Rules"). This Guide explains the Program's operations. The Rules, the names of the mediators in the Program and biographical information about them, as well as other information, are available on the New York County pages of the Commercial Division's website at www.nycourts.gov/comdiv.

I

ADR IN THE DIVISION—AN OVERVIEW

Alternative dispute resolution ("ADR") refers to a variety of mechanisms for the resolution of legal disputes other than by litigation. ADR offers the possibility of a settlement that is achieved sooner, at less expense, and with less inconvenience and acrimony than would be possible in the normal course of litigation. The principal forms of ADR are the following:

1) Mediation—A process in which a Neutral attempts to facilitate a settlement of a dispute by conferring informally with the parties, jointly and in separate "caucuses,"—and focusing upon practical concerns and needs as well as the merits of each side's position on the issues in the case.

2) Neutral Evaluation—A process in which an expert Neutral receives a presentation about the merits from each side and attempts to evaluate the presentations and predict how a court would decide the matter.

3) Arbitration—A process in which the parties present evidence to a Neutral or panel of Neutrals, who then issue a decision determining the merits of the case. An arbitration may be binding or advisory, depending upon the agreement of the parties. If binding, the decision of the arbitrator(s) ends the case, subject only to circumscribed review pursuant to Article 75 of the Civil Practice Law and Rules.

Commercial cases may be referred to the Program by a Justice of the Division, the Administrative Judge, or a non-Commercial Division Justice who is authorized by the Administrative Judge to make referrals. The Program is mandatory. Volume permitting, cases can also be referred on consent of the parties. Parties ordered into the court-annexed Program may use its resources or pursue ADR through a private service if they prefer. Parties who take part in the Program may choose the form of ADR they wish to pursue. Almost all cases in the Program, though, have been mediations, mediation being the default procedure; for that reason, the ADR process is hereafter referred to as mediation and the neutral assigned as the Mediator. The Program is overseen by the Clerk-in-Charge of the Commercial Division Support Office. Administration of the Program is coordinated by an ADR Coordinator. These and other features of the Program are explained hereafter.

II

INITIATING THE ADR PROCESS

A. THE REFERRAL OF A CASE

Workload permitting, the Program will accept referrals on consent from parties in any eligible case as defined in the Rules. Parties should advise the assigned Justice of their desire to participate in the Program either at a conference or by presentation of a stipulation. After joinder of issue in other cases, any party anxious to proceed to ADR is encouraged to file a Request for Judicial Intervention and a request for a preliminary conference with the Commercial Division Support Office and to raise the ADR question at the conference. The Rules empower the Court, if it determines that ADR might be useful, to order the parties to proceed to ADR. The experience of those who have taken part in the Program confirms that cases that are perceived by the parties to be incapable of settlement and which might not be brought into ADR on a voluntary basis in fact often do settle, to the satisfaction of all concerned.

The Justices will direct ADR at the earliest practical point in a case; as a general rule, the earlier a case is referred, the better. Discovery, of course, is a source of considerable delay in litigation and can cause expense and frustration for litigants. The Court will attempt whenever practicable to promote resolution by ADR before the discovery wheels begin to turn. On the other hand, the Court recognizes that some cases may require focused discovery before they realistically can be resolved by ADR; it may often be possible, though, for that discovery to take place most efficiently and expeditiously under the guidance of the Mediator, on consent of the parties, subject, however, to any disclosure order previously issued by the Justice assigned. The Rules encourage Mediators and parties to pursue just such information exchange. Unless otherwise directed by the assigned Justice in a particular case, discovery will not be stayed during the ADR process.

Whenever a Justice decides to direct ADR, whether on consent of the parties or without it, he or she will sign an Order of Reference.

Litigants whose case is referred to the Program may pursue ADR through the good offices of an outside individual selected by the parties or a private ADR service. In all cases referred to the Program, all deadlines and confidentiality provisions in the Court's Rules will be binding on all parties who proceed to ADR, whether they do so inside or outside the Program. In order to avoid later controversy, other terms of a private retention should be put in writing before the process begins. If the parties elect to proceed to ADR outside the Court, they should so advise the Program Coordinator in the Commercial Division Support Office immediately after the signing of the Order of Reference. The Office will closely monitor the progress of the ADR proceeding to ensure compliance with the Order of Reference.

B. CONFIDENTIALITY AND ETHICAL STANDARDS FOR MEDIATORS

The Rules provide for confidentiality of the ADR process (binding arbitration apart). With narrow exceptions, no use may be made, whether in that case or any other case, of the information generated or communicated in the process by, between, or among the parties, counsel, or the Mediator for any purpose other than resolution of the ADR proceeding. Nothing about the substance of the proceeding (e.g., the nature or the strengths of the parties' cases, statements made by parties, counsel, or the Mediator, whose "fault" it was that the parties could not agree to settle) will be revealed to the assigned Justice by the Mediator or the Program Coordinator. The Mediator will communicate only with the Program Coordinator. The Mediator will only discuss necessary administrative details with the Coordinator and at the end report to the Administration the outcome of the process (success in whole or in part, failure, non-compliance with the Rules). The Program Coordinator will convey that information to the assigned Justice (again, only success, failure, or non-compliance). Thus, if the case remains alive, the parties can be sure that there will be no risk of the Justice's receiving information revealed during the mediation.

The Rules provide that the prospective Mediator shall at the outset make a review for possible conflicts of interest and shall disqualify himself/herself if unable to function in a completely fair, impartial, objective, and disinterested manner. This review shall include a check with respect to subsidiaries of parties and other entities related thereto. The Mediator shall also avoid the appearance of a conflict. The Mediator is obliged to disclose all potentially disqualifying facts to the parties and, where such facts exist, shall not serve unless the parties consent. The Mediator shall adhere to ethical principles set out in the Division's Standards of Conduct for Mediators, which are posted on the website.

C. HOW THE MEDIATION BEGINS

1. *First Steps*

After the Justice signs an Order of Reference, it will usually be delivered to the Coordinator in the Commercial Division Support Office (Room 148) by counsel, who will have been directed to appear there by the Justice. The Coordinator will be able to answer at that time any questions counsel may have. The Coordinator will make available to counsel the Initiation Form (which is posted on the website). If the Justice does not refer counsel to Room 148 in person, the Coordinator will fax to counsel as soon as the Order of Reference reaches the Office a copy of the Order and the Initiation Form.

The Initiation Form requires the parties to provide a description of the case, identifying information about counsel, and a list of entities related to corporate parties so that the Mediator can conduct a conflicts check. If not completed in person in Room 148, the Form must be faxed to the Coordinator within 24 hours of its transmission. It is important that counsel adhere to this deadline, and all others, so that the mediation process can proceed efficiently and quickly.

2. *Selection of the Mediator*

In order to join the Division's Panel of Mediators, a person must have relevant professional experience and training in mediation. Specifically, mediators must be (i) attorneys who have had a minimum of ten years of experience in the practice of commercial law, transactional or in litigation; or (ii) accountants or business professionals with a comparable level of experience. In addition, all such persons must have had the training in mediation techniques and the mediation process required by Part 146 of the Rules of the Chief Administrator, as well as the recent experience required thereby.[1]

Within five business days from completion and submission of the Initiation Form, the Program Coordinator will assign a Mediator to the case. The Coordinator will endeavor to assign Mediators to cases broadly from throughout the Panel. However, the Coordinator will not follow a strict alphabetical approach to assignment. Administrative requirements, including the need to designate a Mediator quickly, limitations on the availability of Mediators to handle a mediation within the relevant deadline under the ADR Rules (45 days), the occasional need to designate a Mediator with special expertise (e.g., in construction law), and similar factors preclude the Coordinator from following a rigid assignment process.

The Coordinator will send to counsel by e-mail within the five-day period the name of a Mediator who has been designated to handle the case. Counsel shall have five business days from such notification within which to choose another Mediator if they wish to do so. Counsel must contact the prospective substitute Mediator directly and make arrangements with that person. This person can be a member of the ADR Panel (biographical information on each Panel member is posted on the New York County Commercial Division webpages (www.nycourts.gov/comdiv)) or someone else, but in either event the mediation must be completed within the 45-day deadline as specified in the Rules. Counsel must notify the Coordinator within the five-day period if a substitute has been designated. Otherwise, the person designated by the Coordinator shall be the Mediator for that case and the 45-day period will have begun effective as of the confirmation date (the date of transmission of confirmation of the designation of a Mediator).

3. *Initial Session; Compensation of Mediator*

All parties are required to appear at the initial mediation session, which shall last for a total of four hours. (If the Mediator directs, the first four hours of the proceeding may be divided into more than one session.) There will be no charge to the parties by the Mediator for the first four hours of the mediation proceeding. Time spent arranging or preparing therefor will not be included in the calculation of the four hours. At the conclusion of the four hours, any party may bring the mediation to an end. If all parties agree to continue, the mediation shall proceed, in accordance with the deadlines set forth in the Rules. If the mediation continues, the parties shall compensate the Mediator for his or her time from that point forward at the rate of $300 per hour. Unless otherwise agreed by the parties, the charge for compensation shall be divided equally among the parties.

III

THE MEDIATION PROCESS

A. BEGINNING THE MEDIATION PROCESS: COMMUNICATING WITH THE MEDIATOR

As soon as a Mediator has been confirmed for a case, counsel shall contact the Mediator. Typically, the Mediator will wish to schedule a conference call with counsel to make all arrangements necessary for the mediation. In order to ensure that the mediation proceeds in accordance with the deadlines set forth in the Rules, it is essential that counsel and the Mediator conduct any necessary preliminary discussions promptly and set an early date for the mediation that will be convenient for all.

The ADR Rules require that each party submit copies of its pleadings and a memorandum (ten pages maximum) directly to the Mediator at least ten days prior to the initial mediation session. This memorandum should include a statement as to the facts and issues that are not in dispute, the party's views about liability and damages, and any opinions the party may have about the terms on which the matter might be resolved. This memorandum shall not be served upon the other side (unless otherwise agreed) nor filed in court, shall be held in confidence by the Mediator,

shall be read by no one else, and shall be destroyed by the Mediator upon completion of the process.

B. DEADLINES

The initial mediation session must take place within 30 days of the Confirmation Date (the—date of notification by the Program Coordinator that a specific Mediator is available and willing to serve in the matter). Further ADR sessions may follow if needed and agreed upon. The entire ADR proceeding shall be completed within 45 days from the Confirmation Date, during which other proceedings in the case (discovery, motion practice, etc.) are usually not stayed. The Rules provide that the mediation may continue for an additional 30 days beyond the 45 days if the parties and the Mediator agree that that would be beneficial. The mediation may continue beyond the 75-day period only if specifically authorized by the Justice assigned.

As noted, the initial mediation session is mandatory. Failure of parties or counsel to respond to communications from the Mediator in a reasonably timely manner, to participate in arrangements for the conference call or the mediation sessions, to appear at a mandatory session, or otherwise to comply with the Rules, will require the Mediator to submit a report so stating to the Program Administration, which will advise the assigned Justice, and this may result in the imposition of sanctions. If at the conclusion of the mandatory four-hour session (or sessions) the ADR process is terminated, no report will be made to the court as to who ended the ADR process unless there has been non-compliance with the Rules.

If a party is represented by counsel, counsel must attend all mediation sessions and must be fully informed about all aspects of the case. In addition, unless exempted by the Mediator for good cause (e.g., residence of a defendant in a foreign country in a matter involving a modest sum), each party must attend all sessions in person or, in cases involving corporations or other entities, by a representative (or more than one if necessary) who is both in possession of all pertinent facts and empowered to settle the case without consultation. The Rules provide that the Mediator may require the presence of an insurance carrier for a party where that is needed for an effective mediation. Experience has demonstrated that the presence of the decision-makers with knowledge of the facts very greatly increases the likelihood of a successful outcome for mediation.

C. FOLLOW-UP ON ADR SESSIONS

The Program Coordinator will closely monitor the ADR process to ensure expedition and compliance with the deadlines. The Mediator and counsel for the parties can expect to receive communications from the Coordinator regarding the status of the case. In all cases in which ADR continues beyond the 45-day period, the Program Administration will very closely monitor progress. Even in the absence of a stay, it is vital that the ADR proceeding, should it ultimately prove unsuccessful, not cause prejudice to any party. The Program Administration will do all it can to ensure that does not occur.

D. REPORT OF THE NEUTRAL

The Mediator will report the outcome of the mediation to the Coordinator. This report is due as soon as possible after the completion of the mediation and in any event within seven days thereof.

The Program Coordinator will report the outcome to the assigned Justice upon receipt of the Mediator's report. If the mediation has succeeded in completely resolving the case, the case will be marked disposed. If the mediation has succeeded only in part or not at all, the parties shall contact the Part of the assigned Justice for a conference concerning further proceedings in the case or other instructions.

IV
WHERE THE MEDIATION DOES NOT PRODUCE A SETTLEMENT

A. BINDING ARBITRATION AFTER MEDIATION

Where a dispute is not resolved in mediation, parties may conclude that it would be in their interests to submit the dispute to binding arbitration before a Program Neutral. The Division will accommodate such parties as follows. Upon the written stipulation of the parties to undergo this procedure, the Division will make a Neutral or panel of Neutrals (a maximum of three), as the parties agree, available to serve as arbitrators for a binding arbitration process. The parties must submit with the stipulation the names of three prospective Neutrals from the Panel for each arbitrator position. If the parties are unable to agree, the Program Coordinator will make the selection.[2] The arbitration shall be completed within 45 days after the selection of the arbitrator(s) is confirmed. An award must be rendered in writing within seven days after the completion of the proceeding. The Neutral shall inform the Program Coordinator of the issuance of the award. Parties who agree to binding arbitration after mediation will be required to pay each Neutral a fee for his/her services as arbitrator. The rate for each arbitrator in these circumstances will be $ 350 per hour, which will cover and apply to time spent reviewing materials in preparation for arbitration hearings, in the hearings themselves, and rendering an award. Even with such a fee, the post-mediation arbitration may prove less expensive than a trial and have other advantages as well. The Program itself will impose no charge upon the parties for this service.

Upon completion of a mediation process in the Program in accordance with the Rules, the parties are free to pursue an arbitration outside the Program if they wish.

B. SECOND MEDIATION

If a reference to the Program does not result in a complete resolution of all outstanding issues, then, as indicated, the case will be remanded to the assigned Justice. Later in the case the Justice may determine that the matter is now likely to settle if returned to mediation and may issue another mandatory Order of Reference, or the parties may consent to a second reference. The parties may choose the same Mediator, if he/she is available. Any such referral shall be directed at as early a point as is practicable. The procedures described above will apply to second referrals (although compensation of the Mediator shall be made from the outset and at a different rate as set forth in the rules).

CONCLUSION

Further information about the ADR Program may be obtained from the Program Coordinator in the Commercial Division Support Office. Comments and suggestions may be sent to the Clerk-in-Charge of the Commercial Division Support Office or the Coordinator.

THE COMMERCIAL DIVISION ALTERNATIVE DISPUTE RESOLUTION PROGRAM

COMMERCIAL DIVISION

Supreme Court, New York County

60 Centre Street, Room 148

New York, New York 10007

Phone: 212–256–7984

Fax: 212–608–4873

EDWARD KVARANTAN

CLERK–IN–CHARGE

MARIS BUCKNER

SENIOR ADR COORDINATOR

SIMONE ABRAMS

ADR COORDINATOR

No. 5: 4/15/11

[1] Neutral evaluators must have completed different training pursuant to Part 146.

[2] The arbitration cannot proceed before the Mediator who conducted the mediation. The reason for this rule is that there otherwise might arise an appearance of unfairness even when parties consent because the Mediator may have received information in an *ex parte* caucus during the mediation process that might unintentionally affect the judgment in the arbitration. Such caucuses have a major role in mediation, but no place in binding arbitration. This limitation does not apply if no *ex parte* information has been received as of the time the choice for arbitration is made.

RULES

Rule 1. Program

The Alternative Dispute Resolution Program ("the Program") of the Commercial Division of the Supreme Court of the State of New York, County of New York, shall be applicable, as hereinafter set forth, to commercial cases referred by Justices of the Commercial Division, the Administrative Judge of the Supreme Court, Civil Branch, New York County ("the Administrative Judge"), and the other Justices of the Supreme Court, New York County upon authorization of the Administrative Judge; and commercial cases referred by consent of the parties to the extent the Program can accommodate them. These Rules shall govern all cases so referred.

Rule 2. Panel; Eligibility Requirements; Redesignation

The Administrative Judge shall establish and maintain a panel of Neutrals ("the Panel"). To be eligible to serve as a Mediator on the Panel, a person shall possess the following qualifications and such others as may hereafter be promulgated. A Mediator must (i) have a minimum of ten years of experience in the practice of commercial law or be an accountant or business professional with a comparable level of experience; (ii) have completed at least the amount and type of training required by Part 146 of the Rules of the Chief Administrator; and (iii) have recent experience mediating commercial cases as mandated by Part 146. A Neutral Evaluator must be an attorney or former Judge who has the background and the training required by Part 146. Anyone who applies to become a member of the Panel thereby agrees and undertakes, if called upon, to serve as a Neutral in three matters annually in the Program. Persons may be added to or removed from the Panel as the Administrative Judge may determine. Neutrals shall be redesignated to serve on the Panel every two years. In order to be redesignated, each Neutral must have satisfied the continuing education requirement of Part 146 and otherwise have served satisfactorily.

Rule 3. Determination of Suitability; Order of Reference

Cases shall be referred to alternative dispute resolution ("ADR") as soon after filing of a Request for Judicial Intervention as is practicable. The suitability of the action for ADR shall be determined by the assigned Justice or the Administrative Judge, after considering the views of the parties insofar as practicable. If the Justice or the Administrative Judge decides to refer a case to the Program or if the parties consent to a referral at a conference or in a written stipulation, the Justice shall issue an Order of Reference requiring that the case proceed to ADR in accordance with these Rules. A case not deemed appropriate for referral at its outset may be referred to the Program later in the discretion of the Justice.

Rule 4. Selection of Neutral; Private ADR Providers

(a) An action referred to the Program shall be assigned to a Neutral chosen from the Panel. The Program Coordinator shall designate the Neutral in the first instance. The Coordinator will endeavor to distribute assignments widely among all active members of the Panel. The Coordinator may, however, depart from this procedure if the nature of the matter in question calls for special expertise on the part of the Neutral, if difficulties are encountered in locating an available Neutral, or for other administrative reasons. Each Neutral contacted will immediately conduct a conflicts check as required by subdivision (d) hereof and advise the Coordinator as to his or her availability. The Coordinator shall inform the parties of the identity of the designated Neutral within five business days from the date on which the Order of Reference reaches the Coordinator. The date of this communication shall constitute the Confirmation Date (except as provided otherwise in subdivision (b)).

(b) Once informed of the identity of the Neutral, the parties shall have five business days within which to select an alternate Neutral from the Panel. The parties shall agree upon the alternate Neutral and contact him or her directly to ensure the Neutral's availability and willingness to handle the matter and that he or she has no conflict. The parties shall inform the Coordinator of the alternate selection within the five-day deadline. The Coordinator may, for good cause, allow the parties an additional five business days within which to make such selection. If the parties designate an alternate Neutral pursuant hereto, the Confirmation Date shall be the date they inform the Coordinator of that selection.

(c) Notwithstanding subdivision (a), the parties may designate as the Neutral a person who is not a member of the Panel or may proceed to ADR through a private ADR provider and in accordance with the rules thereof, but the parties must nevertheless complete the ADR process within the deadlines set forth in these Rules and comply with Rule 6.

(d) Every member of the Panel, and any other person who serves as a Neutral pursuant to this Rule, shall comply with the Standards of Conduct for Mediators of the Commercial Division or, if applicable, the Standards of Conduct for Arbitrators and Neutral Evaluators. In each case, the parties referred to ADR shall identify themselves, including, in the case of corporate parties, their parents, subsidiaries, or affiliates. In order to avoid conflicts of interest, any person tentatively designated to serve as a Neutral in a matter shall, as a condition to confirmation in that role, conduct a review of his or her prior activities, and those of any firm of which he or she is a member or employee, on behalf of, in opposition to, or involving any of the parties or entities related to corporate parties. The Neutral shall decline to serve if he or she would not be able to do so fairly, objectively, impartially, and in accordance with the highest professional standards. The Neutral shall also avoid an appearance of a conflict of interest. In the event that any potentially disqualifying facts are discovered, the Neutral shall fully inform the parties and the Commercial Division's Program Administration of all relevant details. Unless all parties after full disclosure consent to the service of that Neutral, the Neutral shall decline the appointment and another Neutral shall promptly be selected by the Administration.

Rule 5. Compensation of Neutral

(a) The Neutral selected by the Administrator pursuant to Rule 4 (a) shall be compensated by the parties as follows. The Neutral designated as a mediator shall serve in that role at no charge for a total of four hours, regardless of whether such service extends over one mediation session or more than one. Time spent in arranging for the initial session(s) and review of papers in preparation therefor shall not be counted in calculating the four hours. At the conclusion of the four hours, any party may bring the ADR proceeding to an end. If, however, the parties agree to continue, the mediation shall proceed, but the parties shall compensate the mediator for his or her time thereafter at the rate of $ 300 per hour.

(b) If the parties designate an alternate mediator from the Panel pursuant to Rule 4 (b) and that person is available and willing to handle the matter under the circumstances, including at the rate of compensation herein specified, the parties shall compensate the mediator at the rate of $350 per hour commencing from the outset of the initial mediation session.

(c) If the parties agree that the form of ADR to be undertaken shall be arbitration or neutral evaluation, the Neutral shall be compensated at the rate of $300 per hour from the commencement of the initial session.

(d) If the parties and the Neutral agree, the parties may compensate the Neutral at a rate in excess of those specified in this Rule. Any such agreement shall be set forth in writing.

(e) Each party to the ADR proceeding shall pay an equal share of the Neutral's compensation unless otherwise agreed by the parties.

Rule 6. Confidentiality of Mediation and Neutral Evaluation

(a) The ADR proceeding, other than a binding arbitration, shall be confidential and nothing that occurs during the proceeding shall be disclosed outside thereof, except as provided otherwise hereafter.

Therefore, without limitation of the foregoing, none of the following shall be summarized, described, reported, or submitted to the court or revealed to others by the Neutral, the parties, or their counsel: any documents prepared by, or communications made by, parties or their counsel for, during, or in connection with, the ADR proceeding, and any communications made by, or any notes or other writings prepared by, the Neutral for, during, or in connection with the proceeding. No party to the proceeding shall, during the action referred to ADR or in any other legal proceeding, seek to compel production of documents, notes, or other writings prepared for or generated in connection with the ADR proceeding, or the testimony of any other party or the Neutral concerning communications made during the proceeding or any other aspect of the substance of the proceeding, including whether or not the parties agreed to settle the matter. Any settlement, in whole or in part, reached during the ADR proceeding shall be effective only upon execution of a written stipulation signed by all parties affected or their duly authorized agents. The terms of such an agreement shall be kept confidential unless the parties agree otherwise, except that any party thereto may thereafter commence an action for breach of the agreement and may refer to the terms thereof to the extent necessary to prosecute such an action. Documents and information otherwise discoverable under the Civil Practice Law and Rules shall not be shielded from disclosure merely because they are submitted or referred to in the ADR proceeding.

(b) In the event that, notwithstanding subdivision (a) hereof, a party to an action that had or has been referred to the Program attempts in any legal action to compel the testimony of the Neutral concerning the substance of the ADR proceeding, that party shall hold the Neutral harmless against any resulting expenses, including reasonable legal fees incurred by the Neutral or the reasonable value of time spent by the Neutral in representing himself or herself in connection therewith.

(c) Notwithstanding the foregoing:

(i) A Neutral shall disclose to a proper authority information obtained in mediation if required to do so by law or if the Neutral has a reasonable belief that such disclosure will prevent a participant from engaging in an illegal act, including one likely to inflict death or serious physical injury.

(ii) A party or the Program Coordinator may report to a proper authority any unethical conduct engaged in by the Neutral and the Neutral may make such a report with respect to any such conduct engaged in by counsel to a party.

(iii) The parties may include confidential information in a written settlement agreement; the Neutral and the parties may communicate with the Program Coordinator about administrative details of the proceeding, including as provided in Rule 8 (g); the

Program Coordinator may communicate with the assigned Justice in accordance with Rule 8 (h); and the Neutral may make general reference to the fact of services rendered in any action to collect an unpaid fee for services performed under these Rules.

Rule 7. Immunity of the Neutral

Any person designated to serve as Neutral pursuant to these Rules shall be immune from suit based upon any actions engaged in or omissions made while serving in that capacity.

Rule 8. Procedure

(a) Parties referred to the Program are free to choose the form of ADR they wish to undergo. Unless otherwise agreed by the parties, cases shall be mediated.

(b) The issuance of an Order of Reference shall not stay court proceedings in the case unless otherwise directed by the Justice assigned.

(c) The first ADR session shall be conducted no later than 30 days from the Confirmation Date. Immediately after confirmation, all parties shall communicate with one another and the Neutral and take all steps necessary to comply with said deadline. At least ten days before that session, each party shall deliver to the Neutral a copy of its pleadings and a memorandum of not more than ten pages (except as otherwise agreed) setting forth that party's opinions as to the facts and the issues that are not in dispute, contentions as to liability and damages, and suggestions as to how the matter might be resolved. In cases being mediated or undergoing neutral evaluation, this memorandum shall not be filed in court nor, unless otherwise agreed by the parties, served on the adversary, and it shall be destroyed by the Neutral immediately upon completion of the proceeding.

(d) Attendance of the parties is required at the first four hours of the mediation process, whether at a single session or more than one. Unless exempted by the Neutral for good cause, every party must appear at each ADR session in person or, in the case of a corporation, partnership or other business entity, by an official (or more than one if necessary) who is both fully familiar with all pertinent facts and empowered on his or her own to settle the matter. Where necessary to an effective mediation, the Neutral may require the insurance carrier of a party to attend. In addition, counsel for each represented party shall be present at each session. Any attorney who participates in the ADR process shall be fully familiar with the action and authorized to take all steps necessary to a meaningful mediation process.

(e) If the ADR process is successful, the Neutral shall immediately advise the Program Coordinator, and the parties shall forthwith submit a stipulation of discontinuance to the County Clerk (with fee) and transmit a copy to the Part of the Justice assigned.

(f) If after four hours the mediation is terminated without a settlement, the Neutral shall immediately so inform the Program Coordinator.

(g) Notwithstanding the foregoing, if a party or counsel fails to cooperate in making arrangements for the mediation, including making timely communications regarding a conference call or other steps preliminary thereto, fails to appear at any scheduled session, or otherwise fails to comply with these Rules, the Neutral shall advise the Program Coordinator, succinctly specifying the nature of the infraction, and may recommend the imposition of sanctions.

(h) The Program Coordinator may communicate with the assigned Justice about administrative details of the processing of any case referred to the Program by that Justice, but shall not identify the Neutral designated or disclose any substantive aspect of the ADR proceeding. If a proceeding is terminated after four hours without a settlement, the Administration shall not reveal to the Justice which party brought the proceeding to an end. The Administration shall report to the Justice at the conclusion of the proceeding whether the proceeding produced a resolution of the case in whole or in part. The Administration shall also report to the Justice, on an appropriate form, a copy of which shall be forwarded to the parties, any violation of these Rules as indicated by a Neutral pursuant to subdivision (g) of this Rule and any recommendation for sanctions. The Justice may impose sanctions or take such other action as is necessary to ensure respect for the court's Order and these Rules.

Rule 9. Completion of ADR; Report

(a) The ADR process shall be concluded within 45 days from the Confirmation Date. The Neutral shall report the outcome to the Program Administration no later than seven days thereafter.

(b) If the matter has not been entirely resolved within the 45–day period, but the parties and the Neutral believe that it would be beneficial if the ADR process were to continue, the process may go forward for an additional 30 days. However, absent extraordinary circumstances, there shall be no stay of other proceedings in the case. The ADR process shall be completed within 75 days from the Confirmation Date unless the assigned Justice specifically authorizes the process to continue beyond that date.

Rule 10. Arbitration

Parties who choose to proceed to arbitration pursuant to Rule 8 (a) hereof and the Order of Reference shall agree upon appropriate procedures to govern the process to the extent not herein provided. If the parties agree to arbitration, but are unable to agree upon the procedures, the matter shall either be mediated, or, upon consent, arbitrated pursuant to procedures issued by the Program Coordinator. An award shall be issued within the time for a report of the Neutral fixed by Rule 9.

Rule 11. Conversion of Mediation to Binding Arbitration

(a) Mediation may be converted to binding arbitration in the Program upon consent of all parties at any stage in the mediation process.

(b) Any such arbitration must proceed before a different Neutral than the one who presided over the mediation session(s). This subdivision, however, shall not apply if the mediator had not received any material or information from a party *ex parte* by the time an agreement to proceed to arbitration was reached.

(c) As soon as practicable and in any event within five days from conclusion of the mediation proceeding, parties who wish to undergo arbitration pursuant to this Rule shall deliver to the Program Administration a written stipulation submitting the case to arbitration under this Rule and identifying the number of arbitrators agreed upon. There shall be a single arbitrator unless otherwise agreed, in which event there may be a maximum of three. Together with the stipulation the parties shall submit a list identifying the person(s) to serve as arbitrator(s) whom they have chosen or the names of at least three prospective arbitrators from the Panel whom they have agreed upon for each position. If the parties are unable to provide either listing, the Program Coordinator shall select the arbitrator(s). Each arbitrator shall be entitled to a fee as provided in Rule 5 (c).

(d) Any person tentatively selected as an arbitrator shall comply with Rule 4 (d) hereof.

(e) The arbitration shall be completed within 45 days from the date on which the Program Coordinator advises the parties of the confirmation of the selection of the arbitrator(s). The arbitrator(s) shall issue a written award within seven days after completion of the proceeding. This award shall be binding upon the parties.

(f) The parties shall stipulate in advance to all other necessary procedures to govern the arbitration.

Rule 12. Further ADR

After completion of the ADR proceeding, upon request of a party or upon its own initiative, the court, in its discretion, may issue an order directing a second referral to the Program, which shall proceed in accordance with these Rules. In any such case, the parties shall compensate the Neutral as provided in Rule 5(b).

Rule 13. Administration of Program

The Program shall be supervised by the Clerk-in-Charge of the Commercial Division Support Office. The conduct of ADR proceedings shall be coordinated by an Alternative Dispute Resolution Coordinator or Coordinators.

THE COMMERCIAL DIVISION
SUPREME COURT, CIVIL BRANCH NEW YORK COUNTY
COMMERCIAL DIVISION ALTERNATIVE DISPUTE RESOLUTION PROGRAM
Supreme Court, New York County
New York County Courthouse
60 Centre Street, Room 148
New York, New York 10007

Phone: 212–256–7984
Fax: 212–608–4873

FORM

Form 1. ADR Initiation Form

**PLEASE COMPLETE AND FILE WITH ROOM 148 WITHIN THE
FIVE–DAY DEADLINE SET FORTH IN THE RULES.
NO EXTENSIONS OF TIME ALLOWED.**

SUPREME COURT, NY COUNTY
COMMERCIAL DIVISION

---X   Part ____

                  Plaintiff,   Index No.

____

        - against -

              Defendant.   **ADR INITIATION**

FORM

      [FULL CAPTION OR ATTACH COPY]

---X

1) This case was referred to the Alternative Dispute Resolution Program (order of Justice _____ dated _____).

2) The attorneys for the parties herein are as follows:

For Plaintiff: **For Defendant:**

_____   _____

_____   _____

_____   _____

_____   _____

Phone: _____   Phone: _____

Fax: _____   Fax: _____

E–Mail: _____   E–Mail: _____

For Others:

_____   _____

_____   _____

_____   _____

_____   _____

Phone: _____   Phone: _____

Fax: _____   Fax: _____

E–Mail: _____ E–Mail: _____

3) Please briefly describe this case, including, if possible, the damages claimed: _____.

4) In order that the Neutral tentatively selected may run the required conflicts check, counsel for any corporate party must list here or on an attached sheet the names of all corporate parents, subsidiaries or affiliates: _____.

5) This case will be mediated unless otherwise agreed, in which event, identify the procedure selected:

Arbitration _____ Other (Specify): _____

_____

6) Please indicate whether there are in this case:

Motions *sub judice*: Yes ___ No ___   Appeals: Yes ___ No ___

If you indicated yes to either of the foregoing, please contact the ADR Coordinator immediately.

7) By signing below, counsel, on behalf of the parties, certify that they have read and will comply with the ADR Rules of the Commercial Division.

For further information, consult the Commercial Division Internet home page (www.courts.state.ny.us/comdiv) or contact the Division's ADR Program at (212) 256–7984 (Phone) or (212) 608–4873 (Fax).

Counsel for Plaintiff   Counsel for Defendant

Counsel for   Counsel for

This form may be filed by fax (212–748–5312)

(No. 5 5/15/02)

ETHICAL STANDARDS FOR MEDIATORS

Standard I. Self–Determination

A mediator should recognize that mediation is based on the principle of self-determination.

Self-determination is the fundamental principle of mediation. Mediation is built upon the ability and right of the parties to communicate, assess facts, events, and issues, and make choices for themselves, and, if they wish, to reach an agreement, voluntarily and free of coercion.

Ethical Considerations

1. As set forth in Standard VI, a mediator should provide information about the process to the parties. The primary role of the mediator is to foster dialogue and, when desired by the parties, facilitate a voluntary resolution of a dispute. A mediator may identify issues and help parties to communicate and explore options. A mediator should never do anything to undermine an atmosphere of free exchange of views and ideas, or to coerce an agreement.

2. The mediator may facilitate the parties' own engagement in assessment of risks or analysis of legal positions, in private discussions ("the caucus") or in joint sessions, if that will assist the parties to understand options fully. A mediator may also, where appropriate, provide an assessment of the risks associated with litigation or other binding processes.

3. A mediator should encourage balanced discussion and discourage intimidation by either party. A mediator should work to promote each party's understanding of and respect for the perspective, interests, feelings, concerns, and position of each of the other parties, even if they cannot agree.

4. A mediator cannot personally ensure that each party has made a fully informed choice to reach a particular agreement. However, a party in the ADR Program will normally be represented by counsel and the mediator should provide full opportunity to parties and their attorneys to consult with each other and, if necessary, for both to consult with outside professionals.

5. If the mediator discovers an intentional abuse of the process, the mediator may discontinue the process.

Standard II. Impartiality

A mediator should conduct the mediation in an impartial manner.

A mediator should act at all times with the utmost of impartiality and evenhandedness. A mediator should mediate only those matters in which he/she can remain impartial and evenhanded. The mediator should withdraw if unable to do so at any time.

Ethical Considerations

1. A mediator should avoid all conduct that gives the appearance of partiality toward one of the parties. A mediator should avoid favoritism or prejudice based on the parties' background, prominence, personal characteristics, economic importance, performance at the mediation, or any other factors. The quality of the mediation process is enhanced and the reputation of the Program protected when the parties have confidence in the impartiality of the mediator.

2. The principle of impartiality does not prohibit the mediator from engaging in caucuses in accordance with these Standards as part of the mediation process.

Standard III. Conflicts of Interest

A mediator should decline any appointment if acceptance would create a conflict of interest. Before accepting an appointment, a mediator should disclose all potential conflicts of interest. After such disclosure, the mediator may accept the appointment if all parties so request. The mediator should avoid conflicts of interest during and even after the mediation.

A mediator offered an appointment in a case should comply with the ADR Rules regarding conflicts of interest. A mediator should review his/her past or present professional and other relationships, including with attorneys for parties and parents, subsidiaries, and affiliates of corporate parties, and should decline the appointment if the review reveals the existence of a conflict of interest. Consistent with the principle of self-determination by mediating parties, a mediator who contemplates accepting an appointment should disclose to all parties all potential conflicts of interest that could reasonably be seen as raising a question about impartiality. If in doubt, the mediator should err on the side of disclosure. If all parties agree to mediate after such disclosure, the mediator may proceed. If, however, the conflict of interest or potential conflict would cast serious doubt on the integrity of the process or the Program, the mediator should decline the appointment.

A mediator should avoid conflicts of interest during and even after the mediation. Before or during the mediation the mediator should not discuss with any party future retention in any capacity.

Ethical Considerations

1. If, during a mediation, the mediator discovers a conflict, the mediator should notify the Program Administration and counsel. Unless the mediator, the parties, and the Program Administration all give their informed consent to the mediator's continuation and continuation would not cast serious doubt on the integrity of the process or the Program, the mediator should withdraw.

2. A mediator should not recommend the services of particular professionals to assist the parties and

counsel in the mediation unless a request for a recommendation is made jointly by all parties and provided that in so recommending the mediator does not engage in a conflict of interest. A mediator may make reference to professional referral services or associations that maintain rosters of qualified professionals.

Standard IV. Competence

A mediator should mediate only when he/she has the qualifications necessary to satisfy the reasonable expectations of the parties.

In principle, any person may be selected as a mediator, provided that the parties are satisfied with the mediator's qualifications. However, training and experience are necessary for effective mediation. All members of the Roster of Neutrals should comply with the Division's training standards within the deadlines set forth. Parties in the Program are free to utilize mediators not listed in the Roster. Any person who offers to serve as mediator in a case represents that he/she has the training and competency to mediate effectively. If the mediator in fact lacks that ability, due to the complexity or difficulty of the matter or other factors, the mediator should decline the appointment.

Standard V. Confidentiality

A mediator should comply with the ADR Rules regarding confidentiality and should respect the reasonable expectations of the parties on that subject.

The ADR Rules provide for confidentiality in mediation, recognizing that confidentiality is essential to the process. Mediators should at all times comply with these Rules. The parties' expectations of confidentiality generally depend on the Rules and any other rules or law providing for confidentiality, the circumstances of the mediation, and agreements they may make. The parties may provide for additional levels of confidentiality beyond that guaranteed in the Rules and such agreement should be respected. The mediator should not disclose any information that a party, in accordance with the foregoing, reasonably expects to be confidential unless given permission by the confiding party or required by law or authorized by the Rules.

Ethical Considerations

1. At the outset, the mediator should explain to all parties the principle of confidentiality, with regard to both joint sessions and caucuses.

2. If a party conveys to the mediator in a caucus information that the mediator knows or believes the other party to the case does not possess, the mediator should exercise the utmost diligence to prevent revelation of that information to the other party unless the communicating party has specifically agreed to disclosure.

3. A mediator should not disclose confidential information to the Program Administration or the as-

signed Justice, including with regard to the merits of the case, settlement offers, and how the parties acted in the process, except that, as provided in the ADR Rules, the mediator may report violations of the Rules to the Administration.

4. Confidentiality should not be construed to prohibit effective monitoring or evaluation of the Program by the Program Administration. Thus, a mediator may report to the Administration, in general terms, whether the process is continuing and the future schedule for the proceeding. Under appropriate circumstances, the Program Administration may allow researchers access to general statistical data and, with the specific permission of all parties, individual case files, observations of live mediations, and interviews with participants. Similarly, mentors and trainees may observe live mediations, but only with permission of all parties and subject to the ADR Rules on confidentiality.

5. A mediator should not, at any time, use confidential information acquired during the ADR process to gain personal advantage or advantage for others, or to affect adversely the interests of another.

Standard VI. Quality of the Process

A mediator should conduct the mediation fairly, diligently, and in a manner consistent with the principle of self-determination.

A mediator should work to ensure a process of high quality. This requires a commitment by the mediator to fairness, diligence, sensitivity toward the parties, and maintenance of an atmosphere of respect among the parties. The mediator should guarantee that there is adequate and fair opportunity for counsel and each party to participate in discussions. The mediator should observe deadlines and handle his/her responsibilities with diligence and expedition. The parties decide when and under what conditions they will reach an agreement.

Ethical Considerations

1. A mediator should agree to accept an appointment only when able to commit the time and attention essential to a fair and effective process. If the mediator may be too busy with other matters to do so, then the proposed appointment should be declined. If after acceptance of the appointment, circumstances develop that prevent the mediator from serving, the mediator should withdraw. Withdrawal may cause significant inconvenience for the parties; therefore, the mediator should exercise diligence to determine availability in advance of commencement of the proceeding.

2. A mediator should ensure that deadlines set forth in the ADR Rules are adhered to and shall keep the Program Administration informed about the schedule for the process. A mediator should not allow a mediation to be delayed and should consult with the Administration if the process is being delayed.

3. A mediator should treat parties and counsel with sensitivity, civility and respect and should encourage parties and counsel to treat each other in the same way. A mediator should foster cooperation and work to build reasonable trust among the parties in the process. A mediator should provide all counsel and parties with an adequate and fair opportunity to state positions, opinions and interests.

4. The primary purpose of the mediator is to facilitate communication by or among the parties, their development and assessment of options, and a voluntary agreement. A mediator should refrain from providing professional advice and should at all times distinguish between the roles of mediator and adviser. A mediator may, when appropriate, recommend that counsel and parties seek outside professional advice or consider resolving the dispute through arbitration, counseling, neutral evaluation, or other processes. A mediator who at the request of the parties agrees to undertake an additional dispute resolution role in the same matter is governed by other Standards of Conduct.

5. A mediator should explain to all participants at the outset of the process the procedures that will be followed in the process and what the mediator's role will be, including, insofar as practical, the extent to which the mediator will undertake an evaluative function. (Within the ADR field, there are differences of view as to whether, when, and to what degree a mediator may assume an evaluative approach.) The mediator should make reasonable efforts during the process to explain to the parties the mediator's role and these procedures.

6. A mediator should withdraw from a mediation or postpone a session if the mediation is being used to further illegal activity, or if a party or counsel is unable to participate due to physical or mental incapacity. Where authorized by the Rules or required by law a mediator may or shall disclose to appropriate authorities illegal or unprofessional activity being engaged in or threatened by a party to the mediation or counsel.

7. A mediator's behavior should not be distorted by a desire for a high settlement rate.

8. A mediator should be mindful of the needs of persons with disabilities, including but not limited to, obligations under the Americans with Disabilities Act.

Standard VII. Compensation

At the outset of the mediation, the mediator shall explain the rules governing compensation, which are set forth in the ADR Rules. A mediator should not seek compensation in other circumstances.

At present, the Program provides for an initial mandatory mediation session or sessions totaling four hours (excluding time spent in arranging and preparing for the mediation). The Rules also govern compensation paid to a Panel mediator who is selected by the parties as substitute for a mediator designated by the ADR Coordinator. All Panel mediators shall comply with these Rules. The mediator shall explain these rules to the parties and counsel before the mediation begins.

Ethical Considerations

1. A Panel mediator who accepts an appointment should not, directly or indirectly, request from the parties any compensation other than as provided in the ADR Rules.

2. A mediator should not accept a fee or other benefit for referral of a matter to anyone.

3. A mediator who joins the Panel should provide ADR services in accordance with the ADR Rules. Such a mediator should not unreasonably decline to accept appointments upon request of the Program Administration. If the standards of compensation set forth in the Rules are not considered satisfactory by the mediator, he or she shall withdraw from the Panel.

Standard VIII. Obligations to the Mediation Process

Mediators are regarded as knowledgeable about the process of mediation. They should use their expertise to help educate the public about mediation; to make mediation accessible to those who would like to use it; to correct abuses; and to improve their professional skills and abilities. Mediators should cooperate with efforts of court administrators to promote adequate professional skills among those who function as mediators. When serving in the Program, mediators should conduct themselves so as to protect and promote the integrity and standing of the Program.

Dated: June 15, 2008

Hon. Jacqueline W. Silbermann
ADMINISTRATIVE JUDGE

ETHICAL STANDARDS FOR ARBITRATORS AND NEUTRAL EVALUATORS

Standard I. Impartiality

An arbitrator or neutral evaluator should conduct the ADR proceeding in an impartial manner.

An arbitrator or neutral evaluator should act at all times with the utmost impartiality and evenhandedness. An arbitrator or neutral evaluator should handle only those matters in which the neutral can remain impartial and evenhanded. The arbitrator or neutral evaluator should withdraw if unable to do so at any time.

Ethical Considerations

1. An arbitrator or neutral evaluator should avoid all conduct that gives the appearance of partiality toward one of the parties. The quality of the ADR process is enhanced and the reputation of the ADR Programs protected when the parties have confidence in the impartiality of the arbitrator or neutral evaluator.

2. The role of the arbitrator or evaluator is to issue a determination or an evaluation based solely upon the objective facts and merits of the case. An arbitrator or neutral evaluator should avoid partiality or prejudice based on the parties' background, prominence, personal characteristics, economic importance, performance at the ADR proceeding, or any other factors.

Standard II.   Conflicts of Interest

An arbitrator or neutral evaluator should decline any appointment if acceptance would create a conflict of interest. An arbitrator or neutral evaluator who determines to accept an appointment should disclose all potential conflicts of interest. After such disclosure, the neutral may accept the appointment if all parties so request. The arbitrator or neutral evaluator should avoid conflicts of interest during and even after the ADR proceeding.

An arbitrator or neutral evaluator offered an appointment in a case should comply with the ADR Rules regarding conflicts of interest. An arbitrator or neutral evaluator should review his/her past or present professional and other relationships, including those with attorneys for parties and parents, subsidiaries, and affiliates of corporate parties, and should decline the appointment if that review reveals the existence of a conflict of interest. An arbitrator or neutral evaluator who contemplates accepting an appointment should disclose to counsel for all parties all potential conflicts of interest that could reasonably be seen as raising a question about impartiality. If in doubt, the neutral should err on the side of disclosure. If all parties agree to accept that arbitrator or evaluator after such disclosure, the neutral may proceed. If, however, the conflict of interest would cast serious doubt on the integrity of the process or the Programs, the neutral should decline the appointment.

An arbitrator or neutral evaluator should avoid conflicts of interest during and even after the ADR proceeding. Before or during the ADR proceeding, the arbitrator or evaluator should not discuss with any party future retention in any capacity.

Ethical Considerations

1. If, during an arbitration or evaluation, the neutral discovers a conflict, the neutral should notify the Program Administration and counsel for the parties.

Unless the neutral, the parties, and the Program Administration all give their informed consent to the neutral's continuation, and continuation would not cast serious doubt on the integrity of the process or the Program, the neutral should withdraw from the proceeding.

2. An arbitrator or neutral evaluator should not recommend the services of particular professionals to assist the parties and counsel in the ADR proceeding unless a request for a recommendation is made jointly by all parties and provided that in so recommending the neutral does not engage in a conflict of interest. A neutral may make reference to professional referral services or associations that maintain rosters of qualified professionals.

Standard III.   Arbitrators Appointed by One Party

Rules governing court-annexed arbitration may provide that in certain cases each side may select an arbitrator, with the third to be selected jointly by the two or by the Program Administration. An arbitrator chosen by one side only in these cases may, notwithstanding the foregoing Standards, be generally familiar with that party or its counsel and may be a specialist in the same field of law as that counsel. Such relationships shall not require that arbitrator to decline to accept an appointment or to withdraw provided that the arbitrator is able to conduct the arbitration fairly, in good faith, and without bias or prejudice against another party. Except to this extent, these Standards shall apply to arbitrators chosen by one side only.

Standard IV.   Competence

An arbitrator or neutral evaluator should conduct an ADR proceeding only when he/she has the qualifications necessary to satisfy the reasonable expectations of the parties.

In principle, any person may be selected as an arbitrator or neutral evaluator provided that the parties are satisfied with the neutral's qualifications. However, training and experience are necessary for an effective ADR process: Parties in the Programs may be free to utilize neutrals not listed in the rosters of neutrals maintained for the Programs. Any person who offers to serve as an arbitrator or neutral evaluator represents that he/she has the training and competency to handle an arbitration or evaluation effectively. If a neutral in fact lacks that ability, due to the complexity or difficulty of the matter or other factors, the neutral should decline the appointment.

Ethical Considerations

1. All members of the rosters of neutrals should supply the Program Administration with information on their backgrounds and ADR training and experience so that parties will have the information they

need to make a fully informed choice of neutral for their case.

2. A neutral should cooperate with the Program Administration to assist in the determination of whether the neutral is qualified for a particular arbitration or evaluation.

Standard V.   Confidentiality

An arbitrator or neutral evaluator should comply with the ADR Rules regarding confidentiality and should respect the reasonable expectations of the parties on that subject.

Certain ADR Rules provide for confidentiality. Neutrals should at all times comply with these Rules unless otherwise required by law. The parties' expectations of confidentiality generally depend on the Rules and any other rules or law providing for confidentiality, the circumstances of the ADR proceeding, and agreements they may make. The parties may provide for additional levels of confidentiality beyond that guaranteed in the Rules and such agreement should be respected. The arbitrator or neutral evaluator should not disclose any information that a party, in accordance with the foregoing, expects to be confidential unless given permission by the confiding party or unless required by law.

Ethical Considerations

1. At the outset, the arbitrator or neutral evaluator should explain to all parties the principle of confidentiality as set forth in the ADR Rules.

2. A neutral should not disclose confidential information to the Program Administration or the assigned Justice, including with regard to the merits of the case, settlement offers, and how the parties acted in the process, except that, as provided in the ADR Rules, a neutral may report violations of the Rules to the Program Administration.

3. Confidentiality should not be construed to prohibit effective monitoring or evaluation of the Programs by the Program Administration. Under appropriate circumstances, the Program Administration may allow researchers access to general statistical data and, with the specific permission of all parties, individual case files, observations of live proceedings, and interviews with participants. Similarly, mentors and trainees may observe live proceedings, but only with permission of all parties and subject to the ADR Rules on confidentiality.

4. An arbitrator or neutral evaluator should not, at any time, use confidential information acquired during the ADR proceeding to gain personal advantage or advantage for others, or to affect adversely the interests of another.

5. It is improper for an arbitrator or neutral evaluator to disclose the determination or evaluation in advance of its distribution to all parties. In any case in which there are three arbitrators, it is improper for

an arbitrator to reveal to anyone the deliberations of the arbitrators.

Standard VI.   Quality of the Process

An arbitrator or neutral evaluator should conduct the ADR proceeding fairly, diligently, judiciously and in a manner respectful of all parties and the Programs.

An arbitrator or neutral evaluator should work to ensure a process of high quality. This requires a commitment by the arbitrator or neutral evaluator to fairness, high standards of due process, diligence, sensitivity toward the parties, and maintenance of an atmosphere of respect among the parties. The arbitrator or neutral evaluator should provide an adequate and fair opportunity for counsel for each party to prepare for and to make presentations and to challenge those of adversaries. The neutral should determine the matter or issue a recommendation or evaluation upon the basis of the presentations of the parties on the merits. The arbitrator or neutral evaluator should observe deadlines and handle responsibilities with diligence and expedition. The arbitrator or neutral evaluator should be vigilant to ensure that parties do not delay the process. In a non-binding process, the parties decide when and under what conditions they will reach an agreement.

Ethical Considerations

1. A neutral should agree to accept an appointment as arbitrator or neutral evaluator only when able to commit the time and attention essential to a fair and effective process. If the neutral may be too busy with other matters to do these things, then the proposed appointment should be declined. If, after acceptance of the appointment, circumstances develop that prevent the neutral from serving, the neutral should withdraw. Withdrawal may cause significant inconvenience for the parties; therefore, the neutral should exercise diligence to determine availability in advance of commencement of the proceeding.

2. An arbitrator or neutral evaluator should keep the Program Administration informed about the schedule for the process. An arbitrator or neutral evaluator should not allow a proceeding to be unduly delayed and should consult with the Program Administration if delay substantially threatens the process.

3. An arbitrator or neutral evaluator should treat parties and counsel with sensitivity, civility and respect and should encourage parties and counsel to treat each other in the same way. As appropriate to the nature of the ADR proceeding, an arbitrator or neutral evaluator should foster cooperation and work to build reasonable trust among the parties. An arbitrator or neutral evaluator should provide counsel for all parties an adequate and fair opportunity to prepare and to make their presentations.

4. The role of an arbitrator or a neutral evaluator is to make a determination or an evaluation. This

function can be analogized to that of a judge. An arbitrator or neutral evaluator should refrain from providing professional advice and should at all times strive to distinguish between the roles of arbitrator or evaluator and that of adviser. An arbitrator or evaluator may in a proper case recommend that counsel and parties seek outside professional advice.

5. An arbitrator or neutral evaluator should explain to all participants at the outset of the process the procedures that will be followed in the process.

6. In binding arbitration, the arbitrator should not engage in *ex parte* communications about the merits of a case. Discussions may be had with counsel for a party concerning scheduling. However, the arbitrator should promptly inform each other attorney of the discussion and provide that attorney an opportunity to state his/her position on scheduling before making any decision thereon. In addition, the arbitrator may discuss the merits of a case with parties present at a hearing if another party fails to appear after having received due notice. Written or electronic communications from the arbitrator should be sent to counsel for all parties as nearly simultaneously as practicable.

7. An arbitrator or neutral evaluator should withdraw or postpone a session if the ADR proceeding is being used to further illegal activity or if a party or counsel to a party is unable to participate due to physical or mental incapacity.

8. Where the use of more than one ADR procedure is permissible under the ADR Rules and is contemplated by the parties, the neutral should take care at the outset to inform them of the nature of the procedures. It is also incumbent upon a neutral to advise the parties of the transition from one procedure to another.

9. It is not improper for an arbitrator or neutral evaluator to suggest that the parties discuss settlement. If all parties agree, a non-binding arbitration or an evaluation may be converted to a mediation at any stage in the process. The neutral may take part in settlement discussions or assume the role of mediator if the parties wish. An arbitrator/evaluator in a non-binding process who at the request of the parties agrees to undertake an additional dispute resolution role in the same matter may be governed by other Standards of Conduct. In particular, if an arbitrator or evaluator assumes the role of mediator, the neutral should adhere to the Standards of Conduct for Mediators of the Commercial Division.

10. A non-binding process may be converted to a binding arbitration upon consent of all parties and the neutral. If the neutral has received any confidential information *ex parte*, the neutral should permit the parties to designate a different person as arbitrator, as provided in the ADR Rules.

11. In non-binding proceedings in which the parties seek the neutral's assistance in reaching a settlement, the neutral's behavior should not be distorted by a desire for a high settlement rate.

12. If the neutral discovers an intentional abuse of the process, he/she may discontinue the process.

13. The neutral should be mindful of the needs of persons with disabilities, including, but not limited to, obligations, if any, under the Americans with Disabilities Act.

Standard VII. Self–Determination in Cases in Which Settlement is Discussed

In cases of evaluation or non-binding arbitration, the neutral may become involved in efforts to facilitate settlement, as permitted by these Standards. The arbitrator or neutral evaluator in these circumstances, or in cases in which the parties have requested that the process be transformed into mediation, should at all times recognize that settlement must be based on the principle of self-determination. The parties in such cases have the right to communicate, assess facts, events, and issues, and make choices for themselves, and, if they wish, to reach an agreement, voluntarily and free of coercion.

Ethical Considerations

1. A neutral in these situations should provide information about the process to the parties. The neutral may also identify issues and help parties to communicate and explore options. The neutral should never do anything to undermine an atmosphere of free exchange of views and ideas, to impose opinions, or to coerce an agreement. See also the Standards of Conduct for Mediators of the Commercial Division.

2. The neutral should encourage balanced discussion and discourage intimidation by either party. The neutral should work to promote each party's understanding of and respect for the perspective, interests, feelings, concerns, and position of each of the other parties, even if they cannot agree.

3. The neutral cannot personally ensure that each party has made a fully informed choice to reach a particular agreement. However, a party in the ADR Programs will usually be represented by counsel and the neutral should provide full opportunity to parties and their attorneys to consult with each other and, if necessary, for both to consult with outside professionals.

Standard VIII. Compensation

If compensation is permitted under but is not fixed by the ADR Rules, the arbitrator or neutral evaluator should, at the outset, fully disclose and explain the basis of compensation charged to the parties. An arbitrator or neutral evaluator should not seek compensation in other circumstances.

An arbitrator or neutral evaluator should comply with the requirements of the relevant Program as to the minimum necessary commitment of services on a pro bono basis. To the extent that payment for services is permitted by the ADR Rules, the arbitrator or neutral evaluator should comply with those Rules. An arbitrator or neutral evaluator permitted to charge a fee should, before the process begins, refer the parties to the relevant Rules and explain the compensation being sought. Any fee not fixed by the Rules should be reasonable considering, among other things, the dispute resolution service, the type and complexity of the matter, the expertise of the neutral, the time required, and the rates customary in the community. Any agreement as to fees should be in writing and signed by all parties.

Ethical Considerations

1. An arbitrator or neutral evaluator who accepts a pro bono appointment should not, directly or indirectly, request from the parties any compensation as a condition to continuing to perform ADR services in that matter. Such a neutral should not withdraw, terminate the process, or threaten to do so because he/she is not being paid. However, all parties, at their own initiative, may volunteer to compensate a pro bono arbitrator or neutral evaluator and the neutral may accept that compensation if, in the neutral's judgment, the manner in which compensation is offered, the nature of the compensation, and the division of responsibility for such compensation among the parties do not compromise the impartiality of the neutral or the appearance of impartiality.

2. An arbitrator or neutral evaluator who withdraws from an ADR proceeding should return any unearned fee to the parties.

3. A neutral should not accept a fee or any other benefit for referral of a matter to anyone.

4. All discussions of fees should take place in the presence of counsel for all parties, or, if a party is self-represented, in the presence of that party.

5. An arbitrator or neutral evaluator who joins a court-sponsored roster of neutrals should provide ADR services on a pro bono basis to the extent required by the Rules. Such a neutral should not unreasonably decline to accept appointments upon request of the Program Administration.

Standard IX. Obligations to the ADR Process

Arbitrators and neutral evaluators should use their expertise to help educate the public about ADR; to make ADR accessible to those who would like to use it; to correct abuses; and to improve their professional skills and abilities. Arbitrators and neutral evaluators should conduct themselves so as to protect and promote the integrity and standing of the Programs.

Dated: March 1, 2000

Hon. STEPHEN G. CRANE
ADMINISTRATIVE JUDGE

7TH JUDICIAL DISTRICT

GENERAL AND STANDING ORDER

Doc. 1. General and Standing Order

RESPECTING 22 N.Y.C.R.R. § 202.70(g)
(Rules of Practice for the Commercial Division)

Inasmuch as the Administrative Board of the Judicial Conference, and the Chief Administrative Judge of the Courts, have adopted Uniform Rules of Practice for the Commercial Division effective January 17, 2006; and

Inasmuch as predictability and uniformity of practice for all cases is desired, especially within the Commercial Division of a single judicial district; and

Inasmuch as many of the newly promulgated rules provide for the exercise of discretion by the commercial division justice regarding their applicability; it is hereby

ORDERED as follows:

Rule 17 (length of papers): This rule prescribes the length of briefs or memoranda of law, reply memoranda, affidavits and affirmations, "[u]nless otherwise permitted by the court." Henceforth, in all cases, leave is granted in the Seventh Judicial District to file papers in excess of the limits imposed by Rule 17.

Rule 19 (Orders to Show Cause): This rule prohibits the filing of reply papers in connection with motions brought on by order to show cause, "[a]bsent advance permission." Permission is hereby granted in the Seventh Judicial District to file reply papers in connection with motions brought on by order to show cause. Although scheduling of deadlines for submission of reply papers often occurs in the order to show cause itself, such scheduling is not a pre-requisite to the filing of reply papers.

Rule 19-a (Summary Judgment Statements of Material Facts): This rule provides that "the court may direct that there shall be annexed to the notice of motion a separate . . . [Rule 19-a statement]" and that "the papers opposing a motion for summary judgment shall include . . . [a Rule 19-a counterstatement]. In the Seventh Judicial District the court will not direct that motions for summary judgment include a Rule 19-a statement. The filing of a Rule 19-a statement by the moving party does not trigger any obligation on the opposing party to file a counterstatement.

Rule 22 (Oral Argument): Oral argument will be heard in all cases in the Seventh Judicial District unless waived.

SO ORDERED

THOMAS M. VAN STRYDONCK
Administrative Judge
Seventh Judicial District

KENNETH R. FISHER
Justice Supreme Court
Commercial Division

DATED: February 27, 2006

  Rochester, New York

PILOT TAX CERTIORARI PROGRAM

Form 1. Certificate for Assignment of Commercial Tax Certiorari Proceedings to Supreme Court Commercial Division, Seventh Judicial District

1. COMMERCIAL TAX CERTIORARI ASSIGNMENT PROCEDURES

Proceedings commenced to challenge commercial real property tax assessments, as defined herein, shall be assigned in the first instance to the Commercial Division by the Clerk of the Supreme Court, upon the filing of an RJI together with this **Attorney's Certification**. The Certification shall be served upon all parties, and shall set forth the name of the proceeding, the index number and a statement indicating the basis for Commercial Division adjudication. The Certification form appears below.

2. CRITERIA FOR ASSIGNMENT OF COMMERCIAL TAX CERTIORARI PROCEEDINGS TO COMMERCIAL DIVISION

1. The Commercial Division shall hear and determine tax certiorari proceedings in which the principal claim(s) involve commercial real property with an equalized full valuation in excess of one million dollars.

2. The Commercial Division shall hear and determine proceedings where claims relating to two or more parcels are joined in a single petition pursuant to RPTL § 706(2) and the total equalized full valuation of all parcels is equal to or more than one million dollars.

3. The Commercial Division shall also hear and determine proceedings involving real property assessed in accordance with subdivision one of the RPL § 339-y, commenced by a board of managers, acting as agents of one or more condominium unit owners pursuant to subdivision four of such section, provided the total equalized full valuation of all parcels included in the petition is equal to or more than one million dollars.

4. The term "commercial real property" shall included improved or unimproved business, commercial and industrial real property, residential cooperative, condominium and rental property, special franchises and utilities. The Commercial Division may also hear and determine proceedings involving the exemption of improved or unimproved public or private real property under article 4 of the RPTL.

5. The Commercial Division shall not hear proceedings relating to one, two or three family owner-occupied residential structures or unimproved property which is eligible for small claims assessment review pursuant to title one–A of article 7 of the RPTL.

☐ I hereby certify that I have read the Guidelines for Assignment of Commercial Tax Certiorari Proceedings to Commercial Division and I believe that this commercial tax certiorari proceeding should be assigned to the Commercial Division. The equalized full valuation of the subject real property is one million dollars or more.

DATED: _____   Attorney Signature _____

Print Name: _____

Attorney for: _____

Rev. 1/03/2006

8TH JUDICIAL DISTRICT
JUDGES' PART RULES
JUSTICE JOHN A. MICHALEK

Part 26. Hon. John A. Michalek

MOTIONS:

Every Thursday starting on January 13, 2011 in Part 26 at 9:30, 10:00, and 10:30 a.m.

WHEN SCHEDULING OR ADJOURNING MOTIONS—CONTACT THE COURT CLERK WHO WILL ASSIGN A DATE AND TIME.

All moving papers, answering papers, reply papers, memoranda and special term notes of issue to be sent to chambers no later than 48 hours prior to return date. If papers are not timely delivered, motions will be adjourned. Original papers must be supplied to the Court. TROs on notice to other side, if known. TROs in case assigned to other Judge upon approval of IAS judge or his/her law clerk. Motions cannot be adjourned generally, and should only be adjourned upon good cause by informing the law clerk, court clerk or secretary. Orders must be submitted in accordance with the time limits of the CPLR. Motion papers, including cross-motions, must bear the County Clerk's "Paid" stamp pursuant to CPLR § 8020(a). Please do not send motion papers by fax without prior consent of the Court. When E-Filing, a courtesy hard copy of the papers is required. Papers should be submitted to Part 26, 4th Floor of 25 Delaware Avenue.

CONFERENCES:

Preliminary and Pre-trial conferences are scheduled upon court's receipt of RJI or calendar note of issue. Preliminary conferences upon request to Judge's secretary. At first pre-trial, a discovery schedule will be set up by the Court, which will include a trial date. Adjournments granted with consent of parties and by request to Court, with immediate rescheduling.

TRIALS AND REFERENCES:

Adjournments only with the approval of the judge or law clerk. Jury Selection forms and list of witnesses, lay and expert, to be called at trial required one month before jury selection date. Papers for motions in limine required one (1) week prior to commencement of trial. Conference with IAS judge upon completion of jury selection. With respect to Jury Trials, copies of pleadings, requests to charge, proposed verdict sheets, proposed contentions required two (2) weeks prior to the commencement date of trial. If attorneys are making substantial changes to standard PJI format, please submit proposed changes on a Word Perfect formatted disc or CD. Deadline on expert disclosure thirty (30) days before the scheduled jury selection.

With respect to non-jury trials and hearings, pleadings, trial memoranda and marked exhibits must be submitted no later than one week prior to the trial or hearing. Following non-jury trial or hearing, Findings of Fact and Conclusions of Law must be submitted by counsel for all parties.

Orders:

Orders following motion argument should be submitted by the prevailing party. Copy of Decision portion of transcript should be attached to Order and referenced therein if so directed by the Court. Transcript to be obtained by counsel from the Court Reporter. Upon Court's review, execution and granting of the Order, Order may be picked up in the "OUT" basket in Part 26. The Court will not advise via phone when an Order is ready for pickup. Orders will be returned via mail if a self-addressed, stamped envelope is provided to the Court.

TAX CERTIORARI STANDING ORDER

Tax Certiorari Standing Order #1
COMMERCIAL DIVISION
OF THE SUPREME COURT
ERIE COUNTY, STATE OF NEW YORK
STATE OF NEW YORK
SUPREME COURT: COUNTY OF ERIE

IN RE APPLICATIONS ASSIGNED TO THE COMMERCIAL DIVISION, EIGHTH JUDICIAL DISTRICT, UNDER ARTICLE 7 OF THE REAL PROPERTY TAX LAW

STANDING ORDER #1

Pursuant to the pilot program instituted by the Chief Administrative Judge in October 2005, there are pending in the Commercial Division, Eighth Judicial District, numerous proceedings under article 7 of the Real Property Tax Law (hereinafter "tax cert proceedings"), and given that, from the experience of the past three (3) years these matters have been pending in the Commercial Division, the vast majority of these tax cert proceedings settle without motion practice or trial, and with the advice and consent of Administrative Judge of Eighth Judicial District, Hon. Sharon S. Townsend, and the Civil Division Alternative Dispute Resolution Coordinator William Gersten, it is hereby

ORDERED, that tax cert proceedings assigned to the Commercial Division for which a Note of Issue and Certificate of Readiness (hereinafter "NOI") have not been filed may be referred to the Alternative Dispute Resolution Division of Eighth Judicial District (hereinafter "ADR Division") in accordance with the procedures described below for tax cert proceedings assigned to the Commercial Division after the date of this Order; and it is further

ORDERED, that all tax cert proceedings assigned to the Commercial Division after the date of this Order are hereby referred to the ADR Division in accordance with the following procedures:

(A) Unless waived, petitioner shall comply with 22 NYCRR 202.59(b) within thirty (30) days after the first court appearance or conference date in the Commercial Division (subject to extensions of time agreed to by the parties);

(B) Unless waived, the parties shall comply with 22 NYCRR 202.59(c), as applicable, within the time frame set forth therein or unless the Court, upon good cause shown, extends the time for such compli-

ance (and also subject to extensions of time agreed to by the parties);

(C) Tax cert proceedings may be referred back by the ADR Division to the Commercial Division for trial at the discretion of the ADR Division coordinator or upon request of any party; and

(D) Upon receipt of the filed NOI required by 22 NYCRR 202.59(d), the Commercial Division shall schedule the pretrial conference required under 22 NYCRR 202.59(e); and it is further

ORDERED, that the parties in tax cert proceedings are at all times under the jurisdiction of Commercial Division and may seek court-supervised relief with respect to deadlines for disclosure, disclosure disputes or any other matters requiring Court intervention.

Dated: October 1, 2008

HON. JOHN M. CURRAN, J.S.C.

GRANTED:

By: _____

Patricia A. Aiello
Court Clerk

COMMERCIAL DIVISION CERTIFICATION PROGRAM

Form 1. Commercial Division Certification

SUPREME COURT OF THE STATE OF NEW YORK   UCS-840C
                                                                      3/2011

COUNTY OF _____

_____ x   Index No. _____

                                                 RJI No. (if any) _____

                            Plaintiff(s)/Petitioner(s)

-against-   **COMMERCIAL DIVISION**
                                                 Request for Judicial Intervention Addendum

                            Defendant(s)/Respondent(s)
_____ x

COMPLETE WHERE APPLICABLE [add additional pages if needed]:

Plaintiff/Petitioner's cause(s) of action [check all that apply]:

☐ Breach of contract or fiduciary duty, fraud, misrepresentation, business tort (e.g. unfair competition), or statutory and/or common law violation where the breach or violation is alleged to arise out of business dealings (e.g. sales of assets or securities; corporate restructuring; partnership, shareholder, joint venture, and other business agreements; trade secrets; restrictive covenants; and employment agreements not including claims that principally involve alleged discriminatory practices)

☐ Transactions governed by the Uniform Commercial Code (exclusive of those concerning individual cooperative or condominium units)

☐ Transactions involving commercial real property, including Yellowstone injunctions and excluding actions for the payment of rent only

☐ Shareholder derivative actions — without consideration of the monetary threshold

☐ Commercial class actions — without consideration of the monetary threshold

☐ Business transactions involving or arising out of dealings with commercial banks and other financial institutions

☐ Internal affairs of business organizations

☐ Malpractice by accountants or actuaries, and legal malpractice arising out of representation in commercial matters

☐ Environmental insurance coverage

☐ Commercial insurance coverage (e.g. directors and officers, errors and omissions, and business interruption coverage)

☐ Dissolution of corporations, partnerships, limited liability companies, limited liability partnerships and joint ventures — without consideration of the monetary threshold

☐ Applications to stay or compel arbitration and affirm or disaffirm arbitration awards and related injunctive relief pursuant to CPLR Article 75 involving any of the foregoing enumerated commercial issues — without consideration of the monetary threshold

Plaintiff/Petitioner's claim for compensatory damages [exclusive of punitive damages, interest, costs and counsel fees claimed]:

$ _____

Plaintiff/Petitioner's claim for equitable or declaratory relief [brief description]:

_____
| |
| |
| |
| |
| |
| |
_____

Defendant/Respondent's counterclaim(s) [brief description, including claim for monetary relief]:

_____
| |
| |
| |
| |
_____

I REQUEST THAT THIS CASE BE ASSIGNED TO THE COMMERCIAL DIVISION. I CERTIFY THAT THE CASE MEETS THE JURISDICTIONAL REQUIREMENTS OF THE COMMERCIAL DIVISION SET FORTH IN 22 NYCRR § 202.70(a), (b) AND (c).

Dated: _____   _____
                                            SIGNATURE

                                _____
                                        PRINT OR TYPE NAME

ALBANY COUNTY
ASSIGNMENT REQUEST

Form 1. Attorney's Justification For Case Assignment to Commercial Court—Albany County

Index # _____ Dispute Amount $ _____ ($25,000. Plus)

(Note: Matters specifically <u>excluded</u> from the Commercial Division are listed on the back of this form)

1) CONTRACT:

Breach of contract, fraud or misrepresentation actions involving:

___ (a) Purchase or sale of securities.

___ (b) Uniform Commercial Code transactions.

___ (c) Purchase or sale of the assets of a business or merger, consolidation or recapitalization of a business.

___ (d) Providing of goods or services by or to a business entity.

___ (e) Purchase or sale or lease of, or security interest in, commercial real property or personal property.

___ (f) Partnership, shareholder or joint venture agreements.

___ (g) Franchise, distribution or licensing agreements.

2) BUSINESS CORPORATION LAW:

___ (a) Shareholder derivative actions.

___ (b) Actions involving Judicial Dissolution.

___ (c) Actions involving liability and indemnity of corporate directors and officers.

___ (d) Actions involving the internal affairs of corporations, such as voting and inspection rights of shareholders or directors, authorization of corporate acts or interpretations of articles or by-laws.

___ (e) Foreign corporations authorized to do business in the State of New York.

___ (f) Appointment of a Receiver of property of domestic or qualified Foreign corporations.

3) PARTNERSHIP LAW:

___ (a) Property rights of general and limited partners and partnerships.

___ (b) Partnership, general business operation, dissolution and creditors rights.

4) UNIFORM COMMERCIAL CODE:

___ (a) Commercial loans (including failures to make commercial loans), negotiable instruments, letters of credit and bank transactions.

___ (b) Allegations of business torts, including unfair competition, interference with business advantage or contractual relations.

5) OTHER COMMERCIAL MATTERS:

___ (a) Employment agreements or employee incentive or retirement plans (not including qualified retirement plans) in which the business or commercial issues predominate and discharge, modification of foreclosure of mechanics' liens.

___ (b) Declaratory judgment actions and 3rd party indemnification claims versus insurance companies where the underlying cause of action is contract in nature or would otherwise fall within the guidelines set forth herein. (**Note:** Specifically ***not*** *included* are Declaratory Judgment Actions and 3rd party claims relating to fire loss, motor vehicle actions and Tort claims).

___ (c) Commercial Class actions.

___ (d) Opening of default judgments where the underlying cause of action is commercial in nature and would otherwise fall within the monetary and jurisdictional guidelines set forth herein.

___ (e) Actions may involve individuals, as well as business entities, as long as all other criteria are satisfied.

Dated: _____

Submitting Attorney: _____

(Print Name) _____

Revised 10/24/02

MATTERS *SPECIFICALLY EXCLUDED* FROM COMMERCIAL DIVISION:

- Real estate foreclosure actions.
- Proceedings to enforce a judgment.
- Products liability claims, including claims based upon warranty of merchantability and/or fitness for a particular use.
- Declaratory judgment actions involving indemnification claims under insurance policies relating to underlying actions which are not commercial in nature, including, but not limited to, underlying claims for fire loss, motor vehicle actions and tort claims.
- Actions by or against Medicare, Medicaid, or the Department of Social Services.
- Discrimination cases.
- Collection matters involving legal, medical, accounting, architectural fees or other professional fees.

KINGS COUNTY

KINGS COUNTY RULES

GENERAL

Rule 1.   [Application]

The following rules are intended to supplement the Statewide Standards and Rules for the Commercial Division (Uniform Rule § 202.70), which are applicable in Kings County.   Counsel are expected to comply with all Statewide Rules as well as those promulgated herein.

[Adopted effective January 2, 2010.]

Rule 2.   [Monetary Threshold]

The monetary threshold for cases in Kings County Commercial Division has been raised from $50,000.00 to $75,000.00.

[Adopted effective January 2, 2010.]

Rule 3.   [Preliminary Conference Requests]

Any party requesting a preliminary conference must annex a copy of the pleadings to the RJI when the request is filed with the Court.

[Adopted effective January 2, 2010.]

Rule 4.   [Letter Applications; Faxed Communications]

Other than as expressly provided in the Rules of the Commercial Division or upon instruction of the Court, the Court will not accept or entertain letter applications for substantive relief.   Unless directed by the Court, no communications are to be FAXED to Chambers other than Stipulations of Adjournment in compliance with these rules, PC Orders prepared in conformity with Rule 7, or disclosure-related communications pursuant to Rule 18.

[Adopted effective January 2, 2010.]

Rule 5.   [Courtesy Copies]

Courtesy copies should not be provided unless the Court so directs.

[Adopted effective January 2, 2010.]

CONFERENCES

Rule 6.   [Preliminary Conferences]

Preliminary Conferences. All preliminary and compliance conferences will be held on Wednesdays beginning at 9:45 AM unless otherwise directed by the Court. The conference calendar will be called after the first call of the motion calendar.

[Adopted effective January 2, 2010.]

Rule 7.   [Online Preliminary Conference Orders]

Online Preliminary Conference Orders. Preliminary Conference Orders may be entered on consent of the Court and all parties by printing and filling out the Preliminary Conference Form posted on the Kings County Commercial Division website. Following a conference call with the Court, the PC order, executed by all parties, must be faxed to Chambers two (2) business days prior to the date scheduled for the PC conference. Failure to timely comply with the procedural constraints herein will require an appearance on the scheduled date.

[Adopted effective January 2, 2010.]

Rule 8.   [Conferences With Clients]

Prior to appearing for a preliminary conference, counsel should confer with clients so that schedules can be set for discovery.

[Adopted effective January 2, 2010.]

Rule 9.   [Adjournment of Preliminary Conference]

Adjournment of Preliminary Conference. Adjournment of a preliminary conference may be requested by submission of a written stipulation at least two (2) business days prior to the scheduled date. Stipulations must be accompanied by a cover letter explaining the reason for the adjournment. The adjournment of a conference is at the discretion of the Court and may be permitted for good cause shown. No preliminary conference shall be adjourned more than once or for more than thirty (30) days. Fax numbers for all counsel must be provided in the cover letter or the stipulation. Any request for further adjournments will be entertained only under the most compelling circumstances and must be made via a telephone conference call with the Court in which all parties participate.

[Adopted effective January 2, 2010.]

Rule 10. [Adjournment of Other Conferences; Stipulations]

Adjournments of any other conferences are permitted for good cause with the approval of the Court on written stipulation of all parties submitted at least two (2) business days prior to the scheduled date of the conference. Stipulations may be faxed to the Judge's Chambers. Fax numbers may be found on the Kings County Commercial Division website under the Judges' Part and Chambers Information.

[Adopted effective January 2, 2010.]

MOTIONS

Rule 11. [Motion Hearings]

The Court will entertain motions, as scheduled in the New York Law Journal and on ECourts, on Wednesdays unless otherwise directed by the Court. Information on future court appearances is available on E–Courts (www.nycourts.gov/ecourts). All motions require appearances and oral argument. All responsive papers must be filed with the Motion Support Office or the Clerk of the Part at least two (2) business days before the scheduled date of the motion.

[Adopted effective January 2, 2010.]

Rule 12. [Calendar Call]

The first call of the motion calendar will be at 9:45 AM. The second and final call will be held at 10:15 AM.

[Adopted effective January 2, 2010.]

Rule 13. [Appearance By Attorney]

An appearance by an attorney with knowledge of the case and authority to bind the party is required on all motions and conferences.

[Adopted effective January 2, 2010.]

Rule 14. [Argument]

Upon the argument of a dispositive motion the Court will determine whether discovery shall proceed pending decision. As a general rule, discovery is not stayed by the filing of a dispositive motion.

[Adopted effective January 2, 2010.]

Rule 15. [Motions for Summary Judgment]

Motions for Summary Judgement. All summary judgment motions shall be accompanied by a Statement of Material Facts as set forth in the Uniform Rules, § 202.70(g), Rule 19–a.

[Adopted effective January 2, 2010.]

Rule 16. [Supplemental Submissions]

Following argument and reservation of decision by the Court, no supplemental submissions will be ac-cepted by letter or otherwise unless expressly authorized in advance. Uniform Rules, § 202.70(g), Rule 18.

[Adopted effective January 2, 2010.]

Rule 17. [Adjournment of Motions]

Adjournment of Motions. Dispositive motions (made pursuant to CPLR 3211, 3212 or 3213) may be adjourned only with the Court's consent. Non–dispositive motions may be adjourned by written stipulation no more than three times for a total of no more than sixty (60) days unless otherwise directed by the Court. Adjournments must be obtained at least two (2) business days in advance of the return date except in the case of an emergency. Stipulations must be accompanied by a cover letter explaining the reason for the adjournment. Fax numbers for all counsel must be provided in the cover letter or the stipulation.

[Adopted effective January 2, 2010.]

Rule 18. [Disclosure Disputes]

Disclosure Disputes. Parties must comply with the Uniform Rules, § 202.70(g), Rule 14, regarding consultation among counsel prior to contacting the Court. If counsel are unable to resolve a dispute, the party seeking Court intervention shall send a letter to the Court, of no more than two (2) pages, upon notice to all parties, describing the problem and the relief requested. Such letter may be answered within eight (8) days by letter of no more than two (2) pages, also on notice to all parties. The party requesting relief shall then contact Chambers to arrange a conference (preferably by telephone) to resolve such dispute. If no effort is made by counsel to schedule such conference, the Court will infer that the matter has been resolved and will take no action. The Court may order that a motion be made but no discovery motion will be entertained without prior compliance wit this rule.

[Adopted effective January 2, 2010.]

Rule 19. [Papers; Enforcement of Rules]

The Kings County Commercial Division will strictly enforce Uniform Rules, § 202.70(g), Rules 6 and 17 relating to the form and length of papers submitted to the Court. Unless the Court has authorized a longer brief in advance, counsel are advised that briefs and affidavits in excess of 25 and 15 pages as specified in the rules may be rejected.

[Adopted effective January 2, 2010.]

ORDERS TO SHOW CAUSE/TEMPORARY RESTRAINING ORDERS

Rule 20. [Orders to Show Cause]

Orders to Show Cause are argued on the date indicated in the order unless otherwise adjourned with the consent of the court.

[Adopted effective January 2, 2010.]

Rule 21. [Notice of Applications for Temporary Restraining Orders]

Where no affidavit of prejudice has been provided pursuant to Uniform Rules, § 202.70(g)(3), Rule 20, notice of applications for Temporary Restraining Orders (TRO) contained in an Order to Show Cause must be given to opposing counsel, or parties if no attorney has previously appeared, at least six hours in advance of submission to the court and must contain a specific time and date of submission so as to afford an opportunity to appear. Proof of such notice (which may be by attorney's affirmation) must accompany the proposed Order.

[Adopted effective January 2, 2010.]

Rule 22. [Contested Applications; Temporary Restraining Orders; Hearings]

Contested applications for TROs will not be heard after 4:00 PM absent extraordinarily compelling circumstances. [See Uniform Rules, § 202.70(g), Rule 20. Temporary Restraining Orders]

[Adopted effective January 2, 2010.]

TRIALS

Rule 23. [Trial Date]

A firm trial date will be established at a final settlement conference to be held at the conclusion of discovery. The Court may direct the parties to appear at such conference.

[Adopted effective January 2, 2010.]

Rule 24. [Pre-trial Conferences]

At the final settlement conference, a pre-trial conference will be scheduled in compliance with Uniform Rules, § 202.70(g), Rules 25 to 33, to be held following the filing of a Note of Issue and approximately ten (10) days in advance of the trial date. Trial counsel must appear. Pre–marked exhibits, pre-trial memoranda, requests to charge, witness lists, and in-limine applications, which are to be made by letter of no more than two (2) pages, duly served upon all parties and the Court at least eight (8) days in advance of the date of the pre-trial conference, shall be provided at the pre-trial conference as required pursuant to Uniform Rules, § 202.70(g), Rules 25 to 33. Responses to in limine applications, also in letter form of no more than two (2) pages, shall be served at least five (5) days prior to the pre-trial conference. Short and concise pre-trial memoranda are preferred, containing a statement of the facts and issues of the case and the relevant principles of law with citations to controlling authority. Counsel must confer prior to appearance at the pre-trial conference so that exhibits that are not disputed can be identified and stipulated into evidence. Failure to identify an exhibit on the pre-trial list of exhibits may result in preclusion of such exhibit at trial.

[Adopted effective January 2, 2010.]

ALTERNATIVE DISPUTE RESOLUTION

Rule 25. [Mediation Program]

In the interest of expediting prompt resolution of disputes at a minimum expense to the litigants, a mediation program is available through the Kings County Commercial Division. Pursuant to Uniform Rules § 202.70(g) (3), the Court may direct counsel and the parties to participate in non- binding mediation. In Kings County, experienced former jurists, acting as JHOs, are available at no expense to the parties. Alternatively, Kings County has available a roster of trained practitioners willing to accept a referral from the Court for mediation, to whom litigants may be referred. Discovery continues pending mediation unless otherwise ordered by the Court. Counsel are referred to the Rules for Alternative Dispute Resolution for Kings County for more detailed information.

[Adopted effective January 2, 2010.]

DESIGNATION STATEMENT

Form 1. Commercial Division Attorney's Certification

SUPREME COURT OF THE STATE OF NEW YORK
COUNTY OF KINGS

_____

Plaintiff

Index No. _____

COMMERCIAL DIVISION
ATTORNEY'S
CERTIFICATION

Against

Defendant

_____

_____, an attorney duly admitted to practice law before the Courts of the State of New York, hereby affirms the following statements to be true under the penalties of perjury.

1. I am the attorney for the _____ and submit this affirmation in support of assignment of this action to the Commercial Division.

2. This case involves _____

3. I am fully familiar with the facts and pleadings in this action and have reviewed the Rules of the Commercial Division, Kings County, including the Guidelines for the Assignment of Cases to a Commercial Part.

4. I believe that this case complies with the Guidelines for the Assignment of Cases to a Commercial Part and should be assigned to the Commercial Division.

Dated: _____   _____

CASE INFORMATION SHEET

Form 2.　Case Information Sheet

SUPREME COURT OF THE STATE OF NEW YORK
COUNTY OF KINGS

--x

Intake
Date: _____

Plaintiff(s)

-against-

Index No.

_____

Defendant(s)

--x

Plaintiff's Counsel	Address	Phone Number
_____	_____	_____
_____	_____	_____
_____	_____	_____

Defendant's Counsel

_____	_____	_____
_____	_____	_____
_____	_____	_____

Future Adjournments/Comments:

_____
_____
_____
_____
_____
_____
_____
_____
_____
_____
_____
_____
_____
_____
_____
_____

TRANSFER FORM

Form 3.   Transfer Form, Hon. Carolyn E. Demarest

At an IAS term, Commercial Part 2 of the Supreme Court of the State of New York, held in and for the County of Kings, at the Courthouse, at Civic Center, Brooklyn, New York, on the ___ day of _____ 2004.

PRESENT:
    Hon. CAROLYN E. DEMAREST,
            Justice.

--X

                                        Plaintiff,

            - against -

                                                        Index No.

                                        Defendants.

--X

This case has been transferred from the Commercial Part of the Supreme Court Kings County because it does not meet the eligibility requirements as set forth in the Guidelines for Assignment of Cases to the Kings County Supreme Court, Commercial Division.

Specifically, this case:

☐ does not meet the monetary threshold of $50,000 as set forth in the guidelines.

☐ does not fall within the subject matter of cases set forth in the guidelines because _____

☐ is related to another case: Index # _____

☐ This case will be randomly assigned to an IAS Part. Consult the computerized Future Case Appearance System for the date and Part in which the case will be heard.

☐ This case has been assigned to Hon. _____, Part _____ for _____, 2004.

This constitutes the decision and order of the court.

                        ENTER

                    _____
                        J.S.C.

PRELIMINARY CONFERENCE FORM

Form 4. Preliminary Conference Order

COMMERCIAL DIVISION

**PRELIMINARY CONFERENCE ORDER
PURSUANT TO PART 202 OF THE UNIFORM CIVIL RULES
FOR THE SUPREME COURT KINGS COUNTY**

_____   Date _____ 201 _____

Plaintiff(s)

                                                  Index # _____
     –against–

_____ Defendant(s)

Plaintiff _____ is represented by

Firm: _____

Responsible attorney: _____

Address: _____

E-mail: _____

Telephone: _____ Fax: _____

Defendant _____ is represented by

Firm: _____

Responsible Attorney: _____

Address: _____

E-mail: _____

Telephone: _____ Fax: _____

Defendant _____ is represented by

Firm: _____

Responsible Attorney: _____

Address: _____

E-mail: _____

Telephone: _____ Fax: _____

Defendant _____ is represented by

Firm: _____

Responsible Attorney: _____

Address: _____

E-mail: _____

Telephone: _____ Fax: _____

Nature of the Case:

(a) Plaintiff's Claims / Counterclaim Defenses

_____

_____

_____

Amount Demanded: $ _____

(b) Defendant _____'s Claims / Defenses

_____

_____

_____

Amount Demanded: $ _____

Defendant _____'s Claims / Defenses

_____

_____

_____

Amount Demanded: $ _____

Defendant _____'s Claims / Defenses

_____

_____

_____

Amount Demanded: $ _____

Defendant _____'s Claims / Defenses

_____

_____

_____

Amount Demanded: $ _____

IT IS HEREBY ORDERED THAT THIS ACTION IS ASSIGNED TO THE ___ EXPEDITED ___ STANDARD ___ COMPLEX TRACK AND DISCLOSURE SHALL PROCEED AS FOLLOWS:

(1) BILL OF PARTICULARS (See CPLR 3130(1)):

   (a) Demand for a bill of particulars shall be served by _____ on or before

   _____

   (b) Bill of Particulars shall be served by _____ on or before _____

   (c) BILL OF PARTICULARS SERVED:

[ ] Satisfactory

[ ] Unsatisfactory—because:

_____

_____

(2) DOCUMENT PRODUCTION/ DISCOVERY AND INSPECTION:

   (a) All Demands for Discovery and Inspection (CPLR 3120) shall be served not later than ___ days from the date of this Order.

   (b) All responses to Discovery and Inspection demands shall be served not later than ___ days after receipt of the opposing party(ies) demand(s).

   (c) All demands for production of books, documents, records and other writings relevant to the issues in this case shall be deemed to include a demand for production of any photograph(s), audio tape(s), video tape(s), computer disk(s) or program(s) and e-mail. The failure to comply herewith may result in preclusion from the introduction of such evidence.

(3) INTERROGATORIES: Limited to 25 questions per party

(a) Interrogatories shall be served by _____ on or before _____.

(b) Answers to interrogatories shall be served by _____ on or before _____.

---

(4) DEPOSITIONS: To be held as follows:

(Priority shall be in accordance with CPLR 3106 unless otherwise agreed or ordered)

Party	Date	Time	Place

FAILURE TO APPEAR FOR DEPOSITION AS SCHEDULED WILL BE DEEMED A WAIVER. FAILURE TO PRODUCE A SPECIFIED WITNESS FOR DEPOSITION WILL PRECLUDE SUCH WITNESS'S TESTIMONY AT TRIAL ON BEHALF OF THE PARTY FAILING TO PRODUCE. SUCH PARTY MAY ALSO BE DEEMED TO HAVE WAIVED THE DEPOSITION OF THE OPPOSING PARTY.

(5) OTHER DISCLOSURE:

(a) Commissions or letter rogatory (CPLR 3108): Identify and set forth the location of each witness:

(b) Expert disclosure (CPLR 3101[d])

Plaintiff(s) shall provide expert disclosure by _____

Defendant(s) shall provide expert disclosure by _____

(6) PRESERVATION OF ELECTRONIC EVIDENCE:

(a) The term ESI shall include, but not be limited to, e-mails and attachments, voice mail, instant messaging and other electronic communications, word processing documents, text files, hard drive spreadsheets, graphics, audio and video files, databases, calendars, telephone logs, transaction logs, internet usage files, offline storage or information stored on removable media, information contained on laptops or other portable devices and network access information and backup materials, Native Files and the corresponding Metadata which is ordinarily maintained.

(b) Within 10 days of the execution of this PC Order, all signatories hereto shall, in compliance with Rule 8(b) of the Uniform Commercial Division Rules (22 NYCRR 202.70), submit to the Court a copy of the agreed written plan/stipulation for the preservation of ESI related documents, data and tangible things reasonably anticipated to be subject to discovery in this action. Such plan, which may be updated, shall identify the categories of ESI to be preserved, individuals responsible for preservation, maintenance and production of ESI and issues relating to potential costs of maintenance, preservation and production of ESI. In the alternative, counsel may stipulate to limit and/or eliminate the discovery of ESI in whole or part and/or forego or limit the production of information in electronic form. A copy of such stipulation must be submitted to the court within 10 days of this Order.

(c) For the relevant periods relating to the issues in this litigation, each party shall take all reasonable steps (including suspending aspects of ordinary computer processing and/or backup of data that may compromise or destroy ESI) necessary to maintain and preserve such ESI as may be (i) relevant to the parties' claims and/or defenses, or (ii) reasonably calculated to lead to the discovery of admissible evidence, including but not limited to all such ESI data generated by and/or stored on the party's computer system(s) and/or any computer system and storage media (i.e., internal and external hard drives, hard disks, floppy disks, memory sticks, flash drives and backup tapes), under the party's possession, custody and/or control. The failure to comply herewith may result in appropriate sanctions or such other relief as the court may be authorized to impose or award, including but not limited to precluding use of evidence, taking adverse inferences, and/or rendering judgment in whole or part against the offending party(ies).

(d) (i) When ESI is produced, it shall be produced on appropriate electronic media (i.e. CD, DVD or portable hard-drive) in the following format(s), as may be agreed:

____ Digital images endorsed with numbers and confidentiality legends, searchable text and agreed-to metadata fields with regard to the following data:

_____

_____

____ Native Format with metadata intact and, as appropriate under the circumstances, endorsed with numbers and confidentiality legends with regard to the following data:

_____

_____

____ The following format, as agreed by the parties, with regard to the following data:

_____

_____

(ii) In the absence of an agreement by the parties, the court shall direct the manner of production upon application of the party(ies).

(e) Issues with regard to cost shifting shall be brought to the attention of the Court as soon as practicable.

(7) **CONFIDENTIALITY/NON–DISCLOSURE AGREEMENT:**

(a) In the event that there is a need for a Confidentiality/Non–Disclosure Agreement prior to disclosure, the party(ies) demanding same shall prepare and circulate the proposed agreement. If the party(ies) cannot agree as to same, they shall promptly notify the Court. The failure to promptly seek a confidentiality agreement may result in a waiver of same.

(b) _____ anticipates the need for a Confidentiality Agreement as to the following issues: _____

_____

_____

(8) **DISCOVERY—RELATED DISPUTES:**

Issues relating to disclosure shall be resolved between counsel without Court intervention whenever possible. If Court intervention becomes necessary, a conference call may be arranged with the Judge or Law Clerk pursuant to Kings County Commercial Division Rule 18 and <u>must take place</u> prior to any motions being made.

(9) **INSURANCE COVERAGE** (IF APPLICABLE): _____

(10) **IMPLEADER:** Shall be completed on or before _____

(11) **END DATE FOR ALL DISCLOSURE:** _____

(12) **ALTERNATIVE DISPUTE RESOLUTION:**

[ ] Requested

[ ] Declined

(13) **COMPLIANCE CONFERENCE:** Shall be held on _____

(14) **NOTE OF ISSUE:** A note of issue/certificate of readiness shall be filed on or before _____. Failure to file a note of issue by this date may result in the dismissal of this action.

(15) **MOTIONS:** Any dispositive motion(s) shall be made returnable on or before

(16) **FINAL SETTLEMENT CONFERENCE:** A final settlement conference, at which the parties must be present, shall be held on _____

THE DATES SET FORTH HEREIN MAY NOT BE ADJOURNED OR MODIFIED EXCEPT WITH APPROVAL OF THE COURT.

IN THE EVENT OF NON–COMPLIANCE WITH THE TERMS OF THIS ORDER, COSTS OR OTHER SANCTIONS MAY BE IMPOSED, INCLUDING PRECLUSION OF EVIDENCE.

IF A SETTLEMENT IS REACHED, THE COURT SHALL BE PROMPTLY NOTIFIED AND A COURTESY COPY OF THE STIPULATION OF DISCONTINUANCE SHALL BE PROMPTLY FORWARDED TO THE COURT. PLAINTIFF IS RESPONSIBLE FOR FILING THE STIPULATION WITH THE COUNTY CLERK AND SHALL PAY THE FEES UNLESS OTHERWISE AGREED BETWEEN THE PARTIES AS PART OF THE WRITTEN STIPULATION.

ADDITIONAL DIRECTIVES:

**THE PARTIES HAVING APPEARED FOR A PRELIMINARY CONFER-
ENCE ON THIS DATE HAVE REVIEWED THE TERMS AND/OR CONDI-
TIONS OF THIS ORDER AND HEREBY AGREE TO SAME.**

ATTORNEY _____ FOR PLAINTIFF: _____

ATTORNEY _____ FOR DEFENDANT: _____

ATTORNEY _____ FOR DEFENDANT: _____

ATTORNEY _____ FOR DEFENDANT: _____

ATTORNEY _____ FOR DEFENDANT: _____

ATTORNEY _____ FOR DEFENDANT: _____

SO ORDERED:

    Dated: ___ _____ J.S.C.

NASSAU COUNTY

RULES OF THE ALTERNATIVE DISPUTE RESOLUTION PROGRAM

Introduction

Alternative dispute resolution ("ADR") refers to a variety of processes other than litigation that parties use to resolve disputes. ADR offers the possibility of a settlement that is achieved sooner, at less expense, and with less inconvenience and acrimony than would be the case in the normal course of litigation. The principal forms of ADR include arbitration, neutral evaluation and mediation.

The Court will offer mediation as the default ADR option. Mediation is a confidential, informal procedure in which a neutral third party helps disputants negotiate. With the assistance of a mediator, parties identify issues, clarify perceptions and explore options for a mutually acceptable outcome. Although parties are not obligated to settle during mediation, the process frequently concludes with a written agreement.

Mediation is particularly appropriate for the resolution of complex commercial cases. Mediation offers the parties a confidential, structured forum in which to explore practical business concerns and develop tailor-made solutions beyond those that a Judge can often provide. Moreover, a mediator will not impose a solution on the parties or attempt to tell them what to do; if the parties cannot reach agreement, the case will be returned to the referring Justice.

The following Rules shall govern cases sent to mediation by Justices of the Commercial Division and other authorized Justices in Nassau County, as well as cases referred upon consent of the parties. Parties whose cases are the subject of an order of reference are free at the outset to use the services of a private ADR provider of their choosing in lieu of taking part in this court's program. After a case has been submitted to the court's program, parties can terminate the process and proceed to ADR elsewhere.

Rule 1. The Program

The Commercial Division of the Supreme Court of the State of New York, Nassau County, operates the Alternative Dispute Resolution Program ("the Program"). The Program shall be applicable to cases referred by Justices of the Commercial Division, the District Administrative Judge of the Supreme Court, Nassau County ("the Administrative Judge"), and the other Justices of the Supreme Court, Nassau County upon authorization of the Administrative Judge; and commercial cases referred by consent of the parties.

Rule 2. The Roster

(a) The Administrative Judge shall establish and maintain a roster of mediators ("the Roster") who shall possess such qualifications and training as re-

quired by Part 146 of the Rules of the Chief Administrative Judge (see http://www.courts.state.ny.us/rules/chiefadmin/146.shtml).

(b) Every member of the Roster, and any other person who serves as a mediator pursuant to these Rules, shall comply with the Code of Ethical Standards for Mediators of the Commercial Division upon its issuance. Continuing presence on the Roster is subject to review by the Administrative Judge. Mediators may be removed from the Roster at the discretion of the Administrative Judge in consultation with the Unified Court System Office of ADR Programs.

(c) The Roster will be available through the Nassau County Supreme Court or on the Commercial Division website (at http://www.courts.state.ny.us/courts/comdiv/nassau.shtml).

Rule 3. Procedure

(a) Cases shall be referred to mediation as early as is practicable. If the Justice or the Administrative Judge decides to refer a case to the Program or if the parties consent to a referral at a conference or in a written stipulation, the Justice shall issue an Order of Reference requiring that the case proceed to mediation in accordance with these Rules. A case not deemed appropriate for referral at its outset may be referred to the Program later in the discretion of the Justice.

(b) Within five (5) business days from receipt of the Order of Reference, the parties shall confer and select an agreed-upon mediator from the court's roster. During this time, the parties shall also complete and return to the court and selected mediator the Mediation Initiation Form. Copies of the Mediation Initiation Form can be obtained from the Nassau County Supreme Court or on the Commercial Division website (at http://www.courts.state.ny.us/courts/comdiv/nassau.shtml).

(c) If the parties are unable to agree on a mediator, the parties shall within the same five (5) business days from receipt of the Order of Reference, submit to the Court the Mediation Initiation Form with four (4) names from the roster (two names from each party if necessary without indicating who picked which mediator). The Court will select a mediator from among the four (4) names submitted by the parties. Once a mediator is agreed upon or selected by the Court, the parties shall contact the mediator to schedule an initial session. Any mediator selected pursuant to this rule must comply with the conflict check procedures in Rule 8 below.

(d) The parties may agree on a mediator other than one listed on the Court's roster, if they so desire. For a substitution to be made, the parties must contact the other mediator directly, make arrangements for that person to conduct the mediation, and submit a Mediation Initiation Form to both the Court and the selected mediator. Mediators selected from outside the Roster must comply with the deadlines set forth in these Rules and the confidentiality and immunity rules set forth herein as well.

(e) The initial mediation session must be conducted within 45 days from the date of the Order of Reference. This deadline is important and must be met. In the event of any extraordinary difficulties, the mediator shall contact the Court and, if necessary, intervention will occur to expedite the process. The mediator may initially request a conference call with both parties regarding any preliminary matters.

(f) At least one week before the initial session, each party shall deliver to the mediator a memorandum of not more than three pages, (12 point font, doubled spaced) setting forth that party's views as to the nature of the dispute, and suggestions as to how the matter might be resolved. This memorandum shall not be served on the adversary or filed in court, shall be read only by the mediator, and shall be destroyed by the mediator immediately upon completion of the proceeding.

(g) Unless exempted by the mediator for good cause, every party, including counsel must attend the initial mediation session either in person or, in the case of a corporation, partnership or other business entity, by an official (or more than one if necessary) who is both fully familiar with all pertinent facts and authorized to settle the matter. Any attorney who participates in the mediation process shall be fully familiar with the action and authorized to settle.

(h) Parties and their counsel may be referred to mediation for a free four (4) hour initial session. Subject to the mediator's discretion and full disclosure to the parties at the beginning of the initial session, the mediator may apply up to one (1) hour of preparation time toward the initial session, in which case the initial session shall last for no more than three (3) hours. At the conclusion of the initial session, the parties and mediator may (but are not required to) agree to continue the mediation. Mediator compensation for any additional mediation time beyond the initial session is governed by Rule 6, below.

(i) Within seven (7) days after the mediation process has concluded-whether by agreement, or the refusal of one or more parties to continue, the mediator shall complete the Mediation Disposition Form indicating settlement or lack thereof and transmit the Form, along with any written agreement, to the Court. If the mediation process results in a settlement, the parties shall submit an appropriate stipulation to the Part of the Justice assigned.

(k) At the end of an initial session mandated by subdivision (h) of this Rule, any party or the mediator may terminate the mediation process. If the mediation process has been terminated by one party only, the identity of that party shall not be reported.

(l) Notwithstanding the foregoing, if a party or counsel fails to schedule an appearance for a mediation session in a timely manner, appear at any scheduled session or otherwise fail to comply with these Rules, the mediator may advise the Court and the Court may impose sanctions.

Rule 4. Confidentiality

(a) The mediation process shall be confidential. All documents prepared by parties or their counsel and any notes or other writings prepared by the mediator in connection with the proceeding-as well as any communications made by the mediator, parties or their counsel, for, during, or in connection with the mediation process-shall be kept in confidence by the mediator and the parties and shall not be summarized, described, reported or submitted to the court by the mediator or the parties. No party to the mediation process shall, during the action referred to mediation or in any other legal proceeding, seek to compel production of documents, notes or other writings prepared for or generated in connection with the mediation process, or seek to compel the testimony of any other party concerning the substance of the mediation process. Any settlement, in whole or in part, reached during the mediation process shall be effective only upon execution of a written stipulation signed by all parties affected or their duly authorized agents. Such an agreement shall be kept confidential unless the parties agree otherwise, except that any party thereto may thereafter commence an action for breach of this agreement. Documents and information otherwise discoverable under the Civil Practice Law and Rules shall not be shielded from disclosure merely because the documents and information are submitted or referred to in the mediation process (including, without limitation, any documents or information which are directed to be produced pursuant to Rule 7b herein).

(b) No party to an action referred to the Program shall subpoena or otherwise seek to compel the mediator to testify in any legal proceeding concerning the content of the mediation process. In the event that a party to an action that had or has been referred to the Program attempts to compel such testimony, that party shall hold the mediator harmless against any resulting expenses, including reasonable legal fees incurred by the mediator or reasonable sums lost by the mediator in representing himself or herself in connection therewith. However, notwithstanding the foregoing and the provisions of Rule 4 (a), a party or the Court may report to an appropriate disciplinary body any unprofessional conduct engaged in by the mediator and the mediator may do the same with respect to any such conduct engaged in by counsel to a party.

(c) Notwithstanding the foregoing, to the extent necessary, (i) the parties may include confidential information in a written settlement agreement; (ii) the mediator and the parties may communicate with the Court about administrative details of the proceeding; and (iii) the mediator may make general reference to the fact of the services rendered by him or her in any action required to collect an unpaid, authorized fee for services performed under these Rules.

Rule 5. Immunity of the Neutral

Any person designated to serve as a mediator pursuant to these Rules shall be immune from suit based upon any actions engaged in or omissions made while serving in that capacity to the extent permitted by law.

Rule 6. Compensation

Parties shall not be required to compensate the mediator for services rendered during the initial session, or for time spent in preparation for the initial session. Should the parties choose to continue beyond the initial session, mediators shall be compensated at a maximum rate of $300/hour for time spent in mediation, and up to $150/hour for any additional preparation time needed beyond the initial session. All mediator fees and expenses shall be borne equally by the parties unless the court determines otherwise.

Rule 7. Stay of Proceedings

(a) Unless otherwise directed by the Justice assigned, referral to mediation will not stay the court proceedings in any respect.

(b) Parties committed to the mediation process who conclude that additional time is required to fully explore the issues pertaining to their case may request a stay of proceedings. Regardless of whether a stay is granted by the Assigned Justice, if informal exchange of information concerning the case will promote the effectiveness of the mediation process and the parties so agree, the mediator shall make reasonable directives for such exchange consistent with any pre-existing disclosure order of the court and in compliance with the deadlines set forth herein.

(c) If the matter has not been entirely resolved within the 45–day period as provided in these rules (See Rule 3 (e)) but the parties and the mediator believe that it would be beneficial if the mediation process were to continue, the process may go forward. However, the mediation process should be completed within 75 days from the date of the Order of Reference unless the assigned Justice specifically authorizes the process to continue beyond the 75 days.

Rule 8. Conflicts of Interest

In order to avoid conflicts of interest, any person tentatively designated to serve as a mediator shall, as a condition to confirmation in that role, conduct a review of his or her prior activities and those of any firm of which she is a member or employee. The mediator shall disqualify him or herself if the mediator would not be able to participate fairly, objectively, impartially, and in accordance with the highest professional standards. The mediator shall also avoid an appearance of a conflict of interest. In the event that any potentially disqualifying facts should be discovered, the mediator shall fully inform the parties and the Court of all relevant details. Unless all parties after full disclosure consent to the service of that mediator, the mediator shall decline the appointment and another mediator shall promptly be selected by the parties or the Court in a manner consistent with Rule 3 (b). Any such conflicts review shall include a check with regard to all parents, subsidiaries, or affiliates of corporate parties.

Rule 9. Communication with Assigned Justice

The mediator may communicate with the assigned Justice or the assigned Justice's staff about administrative details of the processing of any case referred to the Program by that Justice, but shall not discuss any substantive aspect of the case. Upon termination of the proceeding by a party pursuant these rules, the mediator shall not reveal to the Court which party brought the proceeding to an end. The mediator shall report to the Court at the conclusion of the proceeding whether the proceeding produced a resolution of the case in whole or in part.

Rule 10. Further ADR

(a) While early attempts at mediation may not necessarily result in settlement, follow up attempts at a later date are consistent with the goals of this Program. Accordingly, upon request of a party or upon its own initiative, the Court may in its discretion issue an order directing subsequent referrals to the Program.

(b) Any case subsequently referred shall proceed in accordance with these Rules. For example, the parties shall not compensate the mediator for services rendered during an initial session or for time spent in preparation for an initial session conducted pursuant to a subsequent Order to the Program.

(c) Nothing in this Rule shall prohibit the parties from proceeding to mediation or other ADR, without Order of the court, and at their own expense.

Rule 11. Administration of Program

The Program shall be supervised by the Hon. Anthony Marano, Administrative Judge, Tenth Judicial District—Nassau County.

AFFIRMATION

Form 1. Affirmation

SUPREME COURT OF THE STATE OF NEW YORK
COUNTY OF NASSAU
--X

                  Index No. _____/__

        Plaintiff(s),

  -against-   **AFFIRMATION**

        Defendant(s).
--X

STATE OF NEW YORK   )
) ss:
COUNTY OF NASSAU   )

  _____, an attorney at law duly licensed to practice in the State of New York, does hereby state under penalty of perjury as provided in CPLR 2106 and certifies pursuant to 22 NYCRR § 130–1.1:

 1. Plaintiff's cause(s) of action is/are _____.

 2. Plaintiff's claimed relief is $ _____.

 3. Defendant's counterclaim(s) is/are _____.

 4. Defendant's claimed relief is $ _____.

 Based upon the foregoing, it is respectfully requested that this matter be assigned to the Commercial Division of the Supreme Court, Nassau County.

Dated: _____, NY
    _____, 2001

             _____

            Print Name:

PRELIMINARY CONFERENCE FORM

Form 2. Preliminary Conference Stipulation and Order

SUPREME COURT OF THE STATE OF NEW YORK
COUNTY OF _____
COMMERCIAL DIVISION: IAS PART _____

PRESENT: Hon. _____,
                        Justice.

_____   Index No. _____

                    Plaintiff(s),   **Preliminary Conference**
                                         Stipulation and Order
- against -   (Section 202.8[f] and 202.12
                                         of the Uniform Rules)

                    Defendant(s).
_____

(All items on the form must be completed unless inapplicable.)

It is hereby STIPULATED and ORDERED that disclosure shall proceed as follows:

(1) **Nature of case:**

  (a) Plaintiff's Claims/Counterclaim Defenses

  _____
  _____
  _____

  Amount Demanded $ _____
  (b) Defendant _____'s Claims/Defenses

  _____
  _____
  _____

  Amount Demanded $ _____
  Defendant _____'s Claims/Defenses

  _____
  _____
  _____

  Amount Demanded $ _____
  Defendant _____'s Claims/Defenses

  _____
  _____
  _____

  Amount Demanded $ _____
  Defendant _____'s Claims/Defenses

  _____
  _____
  _____

Amount Demanded $ _____

(Add additional sheets, if needed)

(2) **Insurance Coverage (CPLR 3101[f]):** If not provided, shall be furnished by on or before _____. Not applicable _____.

(3) **Bill of Particulars:** (If relevant)

(a) Demand shall be served on or before _____.

(b) Bill of Particulars shall be served not later than _____ days after receipt of the demand.

(c) All previously served demands shall be responded to on or before _____, 200___.

(4) **Discovery and Inspection:**

(a) All Demands for Discovery and Inspection (CPLR 3120) shall be served not later than ___ days from the date of this Order.

(b) All responses to Discovery and Inspection demands shall be served not later than ___ days after receipt of the opposing party(ies) demand(s).

(c) All demands for production of books, documents, records and other writings relevant to the issues in this case shall be deemed to include a demand for production of any photograph(s), audio tape(s), video tape(s) and Electronically Stored Information ("ESI").

(5) **Depositions:**

(a) Depositions shall be held as follows:

(Priority shall be in accordance with CPLR 3106 unless otherwise agreed or ordered.)

Party	Date	Time	Place

(Add additional sheets, if needed)

(b) Unless otherwise agreed or ordered, if a party fails or refuses to be deposed, he/she may not utilize the deposition of the adverse party(ies) at trial in additional to such other sanctions as may be available (CPLR 3126).

(c) Depositions of non-party witnesses shall not be noticed until the conclusion of all party depositions unless otherwise agreed by all party(ies) or ordered by the Court.

(d) Any disputes with regard to the propriety of questions at a deposition shall be promptly resolved via an application to the Court either in person, if the deposition is conducted in the Courthouse, or via telephone, if the deposition is conducted elsewhere. In the event the Justice presiding or his/her law secretary is not available, such applications shall be addressed to the Justice presiding in Special Term Part II.

(6) **A Compliance Conference** shall be held on _____, 20___.

(7) **Other disclosure:**

(a) Commissions or letters rogatory (CPLR 3108): identify and set forth the location of each witness.

_____

_____

(b) Expert disclosure (CPLR 3101[d]):

1251

Plaintiff(s) shall provide expert disclosure by _____

Defendant(s) shall provide expert disclosure by _____

(c) Interrogatories (CPLR 3130—3133): Each party shall serve no more than 25 interrogatories, inclusive of subdivisions and subparts unless otherwise ordered by the Court.

(8) **End Date for All Disclosure**, other than expert disclosure _____. (Set by Court or Part Clerk)

(9) **Certification Conference** shall be held on _____ 20___. (Set by Court or Part Clerk)

(10) **Motions:**

(a) All dispositive motion(s) (CPLR 3211 and 3212) shall be made on or before _____ 20___. (Not more than 60 days after the Certification Order is granted or conclusion of discovery.)

(b) All other motions, including those for impleader and amendment of pleading(s) shall not be made until compliance with Commercial Division Rule 24.

(11) **Confidentiality/Non–Disclosure Agreement:**

(a) In the event that there is a need for a Confidentiality/Non–Disclosure Agreement prior to disclosure, the party(ies) demanding same shall prepare and circulate the proposed agreement. If the party(ies) cannot agree as to same, they shall promptly notify the Court. The failure to promptly seek a confidentiality agreement may result in a waiver of same.

(b) _____ anticipates the need for a Confidentiality Agreement as to the following issues: _____

_____

_____

_____

(12) **Preservation of Electronic Evidence:**

(a) The term ESI shall include but not be limited to e-mails and attachments, voice mail, instant messaging and other electronic communications, word processing documents, text files, hard drives spreadsheets, graphics, audio and video files, databases, calendars, telephone logs, transaction logs, internet usage files, offline storage or information stored on removable media, information contained on laptops or other portable devices and network access information and backup materials, Native Files and the corresponding Metadata which is ordinarily maintained.

(b) (i) By entering into this Preliminary Conference Stipulation and Order, each signatory hereto represents that, prior to this date, they have complied with Rule 8 of the Uniform Commercial Division Rules (22 NYCRR 202.70) by having met and conferred with regard to all ESI related discovery issues and that they have entered into a preliminary written plan/stipulation for the preservation of ESI related documents, data and tangible things reasonably anticipated to be subject to discovery in this action. Such plan, which may be updated, shall identify the categories of ESI to be preserved, individuals responsible for preservation, maintenance and production of ESI and issues relating to potential costs of maintenance, preservation and production of ESI; or, in the alternative,

(ii) The parties may stipulate to limit and/or eliminate the discovery of ESI in whole or part and/or to forego or limit the production of information in electronic form, as further provided in paragraph 12(d).

(c) For the relevant periods relating to the issues in this litigation, each party shall take all reasonable steps (including suspending aspects of ordinary computer processing and/or backup of data that may compromise or destroy ESI) necessary to maintain and preserve such ESI as may be (i) relevant to the parties' claims and/or defenses, or (ii) reasonably calculated to lead to the discovery of admissible evidence, including but not limited to all such ESI data generated by and/or stored on the party's computer system(s) and/or any computer system and storage media (i.e., internal and external hard drives, hard disks, floppy disks, memory sticks, flash drives and backup tapes), under the party's possession, custody and/or control. The failure to comply herewith may result in appropriate sanctions or such other relief as the court may be authorized to impose or award, including but not limited to precluding use of evidence, taking adverse inferences, and/or rendering judgment in whole or part against the offending party(ies).

(d) (i) When ESI is produced, it shall be produced on appropriate electronic media (i.e. CD, DVD or portable hard-drive) in the following format(s), as may be agreed:

___ TIFF images endorsed with numbers and confidentiality legends, searchable text and agreed-to metadata fields with regard to the following data:

_____;

___ Native Format with metadata intact and, as appropriate under the circumstances, endorsed with numbers and confidentiality legends with regard to the following data:

_____;

___ The following format, as agreed by the parties, with regard to the following data:

_____.

(ii) In the absence of an agreement by the parties, the court shall direct the manner of production upon application of the party(ies).

(e) Issues with regard to cost shifting shall be brought to the attention of the Court as soon as practicable.

(13) **Miscellaneous:**

(a) If the matter settles, the Court shall be promptly notified and a courtesy copy of the Stipulation of Discontinuance shall be promptly forwarded to the Court. Failure to comply with any of these directions may result in the imposition of costs, sanctions or other actions authorized by law.

(b) The failure of any party(ies) to perform any of the requirements contained in this Order shall not excuse any other party(ies) from performing any other requirement contained herein.

(c) Any dates established herein shall not be changed or adjourned without the prior approval of the Court.

(d) Each counsel/party acknowledges receipt of the Commercial Division Rules.

(14) **Trial:**

(a) Plaintiff anticipates his/her/its case on the trial of this matter to be ___ days.

Defendant _____ anticipates the trial of this matter to be ___ days.

Defendant _____ anticipates the trial of this matter to be ___ days. (Add additional sheets, if needed)

(b) The matter is hereby set down for trial on _____ 20___.

(c) All pre-trial filings and submissions (including trial notebooks), jury selection, if appropriate, and marking exhibits pursuant to Rules 28, 29, 31 and 32 (22 NYCRR 202.70) shall be on _____ 20___, at _____ A.M./P.M.

(d) A pre-trial conference of this matter shall be held on _____ 20___, at _____ A.M./P.M.

(15) This Order includes the attached ___ page(s) which is/are incorporated herein by reference.

Attorney for Plaintiff(s)   Name:_____

Address:_____

Telephone:_____ Fax:_____

E-mail:_____

Attorney for Defendant(s)   Name:_____

Address:_____

Telephone:_____ Fax:_____

E-mail:_____

Attorney for Defendant(s)   Name:_____

Address:_____

Telephone:_____ Fax:_____

E-mail:_____

Attorney for Defendant(s)   Name:_____

Address:_____

Telephone:_____ Fax:_____

E-mail:_____

Dated: _____, 20___

SO ORDERED:

_____

_____

J.S.C.

February 1, 2009

MEDIATION INITIATION FORM

Form 3.   Mediation Initiation Form

```
-------------------------------------X        Part ____

              Plaintiff,                      Index No. _____

      -against-
                                              MEDIATION INITIATION FORM

              Defendant,

-------------------------------------X
```

(1) This case was referred to mediation through the Nassau County Commercial Division's ADR Program (order of Justice _____ dated _____).

(2) Pursuant to Rule 3 of the Nassau County Commercial Division ADR Program's Rules, located at http://www.nycourts.gov/courts/comdiv/nassau.shtml, the parties have conferred and **(CHECK APPROPRIATE BOX BELOW)**:

a.   ☐ Selected the following to serve as mediator.

Name	Address	Phone	Email

b.   ☐ Are unable to agree on a mediator and submit the following 4 (four) names from which the Court may assign a mediator.

Name	Name	Name	Name
Address	Address	Address	Address
Phone	Phone	Phone	Phone
Email	Email	Email	Email

(3) For the mediator to run the required conflicts check, counsel for any corporate party must list here or on an attached sheet the names of all corporate parents, subsidiaries or affiliates:

_____

(4) Please indicate whether there are in this case:

Motions *sub judice*: Yes ____ No ____   Appeals: Yes ____ No ____

If you indicated yes to either of the foregoing, please contact the Court immediately.

(5) The attorneys for the parties herein are as follows:

For Plaintiff: For Defendant:

```
_____                         _____
_____                         _____
_____                         _____
Phone: _____                         Phone: _____
E-Mail: _____                         E-Mail: _____
```

(6) This form shall be completed and returned to the Court and the selected mediator **within 5 business days** from receipt of the Order of Reference. This deadline will not be extended. **The initial mediation session must be conducted within 45 days** from the date of the Order of Reference (see Rule 3 (e)). At least one week before the initial session, each party shall deliver to the mediator a memorandum of not more than three pages (see Rule 3(f)).

(7) By signing below, the parties and their Counsel, certify that they have read and will comply with the ADR Rules of the Nassau County Commercial Division. The parties and their Counsel further understand and agree that the mediation process is confidential and that the mediator shall be immune from suit by any of the parties or other participants in this case because of or based upon the mediator's activities as such in this matter to the extent permitted by law. Parties agree that no attorney-client relationship exists between the mediator and the parties, and the mediator shall not provide legal services to the parties during the process.

_____   _____
Counsel for Plaintiff   Counsel for Defendant

Date: _____

ORDER OF REFERENCE TO MEDIATION

Form 4. Order of Reference to Mediation

SUPREME COURT OF THE STATE OF NEW YORK

COMMERCIAL DIVISION—COUNTY OF NASSAU

PRESENT: Hon. _____

Justice

_____X   Index No. _____

Plaintiff,   **ORDER OF REFERENCE TO MEDIATION**

against—

Defendant.

_____X

(1) On CONSENT OF THE PARTIES or by ORDER OF THE COURT (**CIRCLE ONE**) this case is referred to mediation through the ADR Program of the Commercial Division;

(2) The parties shall select a mediator and jointly execute a Mediation Initiation Form, located at http:/ /www.nycourts.gov/courts/comdiv/nassau.shtml within five business days of receipt of this Order.

(3) The parties shall schedule an initial mediation session within 45 days of the date of this Order pursuant to the ADR Program's Rules (available at http://www.nycourts.gov/courts/comdiv/nassau.shtml.)

(4) All proceedings in this action (including motion practice, shall continue during the mediation process except for (depositions), (e-discovery), _____ /shall be stayed during the mediation process (strike non relevant portions).

(5) The parties shall appear for a status conference with the court on _____ at _____ AM/PM.

Dated: _____

_____

J.S.C.

GUIDELINES FOR DISCOVERY OF ELECTRONICALLY STORED INFORMATION ("ESI")

**Commercial Division, Nassau County
Guidelines for Discovery of
Electronically Stored Information ("ESI")** [1]

The purpose of these Guidelines for Discovery of ESI (the "Guidelines") is to:

- Provide efficient discovery of ESI in civil cases;

- Encourage the early assessment and discussion of the costs of preserving, retrieving, reviewing and producing ESI given the nature of the litigation and the amount in controversy;

- Facilitate an early evaluation of the significance of and/or need for ESI in light of the parties' claims or defenses;

- Assist parties in resolving disputes regarding ESI informally and without Court supervision or intervention whenever possible;

- Encourage meaningful discussions and cooperation between parties prior to the Preliminary Conference; and

- Ensure a productive Preliminary Conference by, among other things, identifying terms and issues that will be addressed at the Preliminary Conference and/or in the Preliminary Conference Stipulation and Order.

The Guidelines are intended to be practical suggestions concerning discovery of ESI; they are not intended to be a checklist.

Counsel are encouraged to review the Guidelines at or before the commencement of proceedings.

Eff. 6/1/09

[1] These guidelines, which have been prepared in consultation with members of the bar familiar with current issues and trends in litigation involving ESI, are designed to help practitioners identify at the early stage of a dispute the type and nature of electronically stored information that parties may deem appropriate to preserve and/or produce in litigation — in preparation for a Preliminary Conference under the Commercial Division Uniform Rules. These guidelines substantially rely upon the Suggested Protocol for Discovery of ESI developed by a joint bar-court committee consisting of Chief Magistrate Judge Paul W. Grimm of the United States District Court for the District of Maryland, members of the bar of that court and technical consultants, a copy of which can be found at: www.mdd.uscourts.gov/news/news/ESIProtocol.pdf.

Guideline I.   Definitions

A. As used herein, "ESI" includes, but is not limited to, e-mails and attachments, voice mail, instant messaging and other electronic communications, word processing documents, text files, hard drives, spreadsheets, graphics, audio and video files, databases, calendars, telephone logs, transaction logs, Internet usage files, offline storage or information stored on removable media, information contained on laptops or other portable devices and network access information and backup materials, Native Files and the corresponding Metadata which is ordinarily maintained.

B. As used herein, the term "Metadata" means: (i) information embedded in a Native File that is not ordinarily viewable or printable from the application that generated, edited, or modified such Native File; and (ii) information generated automatically by the operation of a computer or other information technology system when a Native File is created, modified, transmitted, deleted, sent, received or otherwise manipulated by a user of such system. Metadata is a subset of ESI.

C. As used herein, the term "Native File(s)" means ESI in the electronic format of the application in which such ESI was created, viewed and/or modified. Native Files are a subset of ESI.

D. As used herein, the term "Load File" means a file that relates to a set of scanned or electronic images or electronically processed files that indicate where individual pages or files belong together as documents, including attachments, and where each document begins and ends. A Load File may also contain data relevant to the individual documents, such as Metadata, coded data, text, and the like. Load Files must be obtained and provided in prearranged formats to ensure transfer of accurate and usable images and data.[1]

E. As used herein, the term "Static Image(s)" means a representation of ESI produced by converting a Native File into a standard image format capable of being viewed and printed on standard litigation support software. The most common forms of Static Images used in litigation are ESI provided in either Tagged Image File Format (TIFF, or .TIF files) or Portable Document Format (PDF). If Load Files were created in the process of converting Native Files to Static Images, or if Load Files may be created without undue burden or cost, Load Files are typically produced together with Static Images.

[1] The definition of "Load Files" is taken from materials promulgated by the Sedona Conference, whose writings on ESI have had a substantial influence on the development of the law and practices concerning ESI nationwide. Practitioners may find other materials promulgated by the Sedona Conference useful in determining how best to address the challenges their clients face relating to ESI.

Guideline II.   Preliminary Conference

A. Prior to the Preliminary Conference, counsel for the parties should:

1.   review and jointly complete the Preliminary Conference Stipulation and Order, and be familiar with its requirements;

2.   meet and confer in a good faith effort to identify matters concerning ESI not in contention, resolve

disputed questions without need for court intervention and identify issues requiring court approval or intervention, in compliance with Rule 8 of the Uniform Commercial Division Rules; and

3. prepare a written plan/stipulation for the preservation, collection, review and production of ESI, including without limitation, data and tangible things, if any, reasonably anticipated to be subject to discovery in the action, as set forth in the Preliminary Conference Stipulation and Order.

B. Counsel are advised to confer regarding at least the following topics, including and beyond those set forth in Commercial Division Rule 8(b) related to ESI prior to the Preliminary Conference:

1. implementing litigation holds;

a. Courts have held that ESI should be preserved when litigation is reasonably foreseeable. Accordingly, counsel should anticipate that parties and/or the Court will likely expect litigation hold(s) to be in place upon commencement of the action, and no later than the date of the Preliminary Conference. Moreover, counsel should be mindful that some courts have imposed duties upon counsel to take reasonable steps to monitor their clients' implementation of litigation holds and revise or supplement the litigation holds as may be appropriate.

b. Counsel should discuss the scope of each party's litigation hold, including: the categories of potentially discoverable ESI to be segregated and preserved; the claims and defenses as to which ESI is relevant; identification of "key persons" and likely witnesses; the relevant time period for the litigation hold; the types and locations of ESI; how relevant ESI should be preserved; the location and form of maintaining ESI subject to the litigation hold; instructions to be contained in a litigation hold notice regarding preservation of ESI subject to the litigation hold; and whether an "e-discovery" liaison is required for each party.

2. each party's document or record retention policies; and

3. their respective clients' current and relevant past ESI and policies regarding ESI, if any, and become reasonably familiar with same; or alternatively, identify a person familiar with the client's electronic systems who can participate in the Preliminary Conference. Such persons are invited to attend the Preliminary Conference.

C. At the Preliminary Conference, counsel shall be prepared to discuss:

1. all matters concerning ESI as to which there is disagreement between the parties;

2. the anticipated scope of requests for, and objections to, production of ESI;

3. the form of production of ESI and, specifically, but without limitation, whether all ESI will be produced in a single format, or multiple formats, and whether those formats will be Native File, Static Image, and/or other searchable or non-searchable formats;

4. identification, in reasonable detail, of ESI that is or is not reasonably accessible without undue burden or cost, the methods of storing and retrieving ESI that is not reasonably accessible, and the anticipated costs and efforts involved in retrieving such ESI;

5. methods of identifying pages or segments of ESI produced in discovery (i.e. Bates-stamping);

6. the method and manner of redacting information from ESI if only part of the ESI is discoverable, and the exchange of redaction logs;

7. relevant ESI custodians, including such person(s)' name, title and job responsibilities;

8. cost-sharing or cost-shifting, if applicable, for the preservation, retrieval, review and/or production of ESI, including any litigation support database (e.g. Concordance; Summation; etc.);

9. search methodologies or protocols for retrieving or reviewing ESI. For example, some counsel currently use: key word searches, concept searches, "fuzzy search models", probabilistic search models and clustering searches; agreement(s) on search terms; limitations on the fields or document types to be searched; limitations regarding whether back up, archival, legacy or deleted ESI is to be searched; and sampling to develop an objective basis on which to evaluate the likelihood and cost of obtaining responsive ESI;[1]

10. preliminary depositions of information systems personnel, and limits on the scope of such depositions;

11. the need for two-tier or staged discovery of ESI (*e.g.*, an initial search of a key custodian's documents, or a key time-period, only; followed by a broader or different search if necessary). The two-tiered approach is intended to be used when ESI can initially be produced in a manner that is more cost-effective, while reserving the right to request or to oppose additional more comprehensive production in a later stage or stages;

12. the need for any protective orders or confidentiality orders;

13. the need for certified forensic specialists and/or experts to assist with the search for and production of ESI;

14. the protocols to be observed when preparing logs of documents withheld from production, in whole or in part, based on an assertion of (1) attorney client privilege, (2) work product doctrine and/or (3) any other basis for withholding an otherwise responsive document from production; and

15. whether the parties must make reasonable efforts to maintain the data as Native Files in a manner

that preserves the integrity of the files, including but not limited to, the contents of the file and the Metadata related to the file, including the file's creation date and time.

D. Parties are encouraged to exchange information regarding ESI prior to the Preliminary Conference, including but not limited to information regarding network design, types of databases, ESI document retention policies, organizational charts for information systems personnel and inaccessible ESI.

1 Sampling refers to a process by which subsets of ESI are identified and searched for the purpose of developing a factual basis on which to estimate the cost of collecting, reviewing and producing ESI. Examples of ESI samples include, but are not limited to, identified subsets of (*l*) "key" custodians, (2) sources of ESI and (3) time periods.

Guideline III.   Form of Production of ESI

A. ESI shall be produced in the form in which it is ordinarily maintained or in reasonably usable format. The parties shall agree on the format of production prior to the Preliminary Conference.

B. A Producing Party is not required to produce the same ESI in more than one format. However, the parties may agree that ESI will be produced in one format initially (i.e. TIFF format or Static Images) and that some or all of the same ESI will be produced in another format (i.e. with certain Metadata) upon request, if such data is necessary to support the parties' claims or defenses.

C. The Producing Party may not reformat, scrub or alter the ESI to intentionally downgrade the usability of the data.

Guideline IV.   Reasonably Accessible

A. As the term is used herein, ESI is not to be deemed "inaccessible" based solely on its source or type of storage media. Inaccessibility is based on the burden and expense of recovering and producing the ESI and the relative need for the data.

B. No party should object to the discovery of ESI on the basis that it is not reasonably accessible because of undue burden or cost unless the objection has been stated with reasonable particularity, and not in conclusory or boilerplate language. Wherever the term "reasonably accessible" is used in these Guidelines, the party asserting that ESI is not reasonably accessible should be prepared to specify facts that support its contention, including submitting an appropriate and detailed analysis in the form of an affidavit.

Guideline V.   Costs

A. On the issue of whether the Requesting or Producing Party bears the cost of producing ESI, and cost-shifting/cost-sharing, the law in New York is still developing.

B. Several courts in the Commercial Division have addressed the issue, and counsel should consider and

be guided by such case law, including but not limited to:

- *Finkelman v. Klaus*, 17 Misc. 3d 1138(A), 856 N.Y.S.2d 23 (N.Y. Sup. Ct., Nassau Co. Nov. 28, 2007) (Bucaria, J.).

- *Delta Financial Corp. v. Morrison*, 13 Misc.3d 604, 819 N.Y.S.2d 908 (N.Y. Sup. Ct., Nassau Co. Aug. 17, 2006) (Warshawsky, J.).

- *Weiller v. New York Life Ins. Co.*, 6 Misc.3d 1038(A), 800 N.Y.S.2d 359 (N.Y. Sup. Ct., N.Y. Co. Mar. 16, 2005) (Cahn, J.).

- *Lipco Elec. Corp. v. ASG Consulting Corp.*, 4 Misc.3d 1019(A), 798 N.Y.S.2d 345 (N.Y. Sup. Ct., Nassau Co. Aug. 18, 2004) (Austin, J.).

See also:

- *Waltzer v. Tradescape & Co.*, L.L.C., 31 A.D.3d 302, 819 N.Y.S.2d 38 (1st Dep't 2006).

- *Etzion v. Etzion*, 7 Misc. 3d 940, 796 N.Y.S.2d 844 (N.Y. Sup. Ct., Nassau Co. 2005) (Stack, J.).

Guideline VI.   Privilege

Inadvertent or unintentional production of ESI containing information that is subject to the attorney-client privilege, work product protection, or other generally-recognized privilege shall not be deemed a waiver in whole or in part of such privilege if, after learning of such disclosure, the Producing Party promptly gives notice either in writing, or later confirmed in writing, to the Receiving Party or Parties that such information was inadvertently produced and requests that the Receiving Party return the original data. Absent a challenge under this paragraph or during the pendency of any such challenge, or contemplated challenge, the Receiving Party or Parties shall sequester or return all such material, including copies, except as may be necessary to bring a challenge before the Court, to the Producing Party promptly upon receipt of the written notice and request for return. The parties are encouraged to seek an order of the Court to further clarify the protections to be given to inadvertently disclosed privileged materials. Counsel are also reminded of their obligations under Rule 4.4(b) of the New York Rules of Professional Conduct concerning their receipt of documents that appear to have been inadvertently sent to them.

Guideline VII.   Sanctions

A. Sanctions may be imposed against a party and/or its counsel when ESI is demanded, withheld or destroyed in bad faith or with gross negligence, including but not limited to the penalties permitted pursuant to Rule 12 of the Rules of the Commercial Division of the Supreme Court.

B. Sanctions may also be imposed if a party fails to maintain and preserve ESI, as provided in paragraph 12(c) of the Preliminary Conference Stipulation and Order.

ONONDAGA COUNTY
JUDGE'S RULES
JUSTICE DEBORAH KARALUNAS

Rule 1. [Conference Requests]

Requests for a Court conference must be made in writing on notice unless time is of the essence. The requesting party must outline the proposed issue(s) in the written submission. Where time is of the essence (*e.g.*, an issue that arises during an ongoing deposition), a request for a conference may be made by telephone.

Rule 2. [Copies of Motions, Pleadings and Other Documents]

Attorneys must supply the Court with paper copies of all motions, pleadings or other documents that are electronically filed. No other courtesy copies will be accepted.

Rule 3. [Oral Argument]

Oral argument is required on all motions. Absent prior permission of Chambers, all motions must be filed and served a minimum of 28 days before oral argument and opposing papers and any cross-motions must be filed and served a minimum of 14 days before oral argument. Reply papers, if any, and papers in opposition to any cross-motions are due seven days before oral argument.

Rule 4. [Settlement Demand]

Plaintiff must submit a written settlement demand to the defendant(s) at least ten (10) days before the final pre-trial conference. In all cases to be tried by a jury, plaintiff also must submit a copy of the settlement demand to the Court.

Rule 5. [Proposed Order]

Any motion for an order admitting an attorney pro hac vice shall include a proposed order. The proposed order shall include an ordering paragraph reciting 22 NYCRR Sections 520.11(e)(1) & (2) in their entirety.

ATTORNEY STATEMENT IN SUPPORT OF REQUEST FOR ASSIGNMENT

Form 1. Attorney's Statement in Support of Request for Assignment to Commercial Division

STATE OF NEW YORK
SUPREME COURT
COUNTY OF ONONDAGA

Plaintiff(s),

ATTORNEY'S STATEMENT
IN SUPPORT OF REQUEST
FOR ASSIGNMENT TO
COMMERCIAL DIVISION

v.

Index No: _____

Defendant(s),

R.J.I. No: _____

_____, counsel for _____, the _____, in this action, submits this Statement and the accompanying pleadings pursuant to Uniform Rules for the Trial Courts § 202.70(d)(2) in support of the request for assignment of this matter to the Commercial Division of this Court.

1. The **principal claims** in this case are: (check one)

( ) Breach of contract or fiduciary duty, fraud, misrepresentation, business tort (e.g. unfair competition), or statutory and/or common law violation where the breach or violation is alleged to arise out of business dealings (e.g., sales of assets or securities; corporate restructuring; partnership, shareholder, joint venture, and other business agreements; trade secrets; restrictive covenants; and employment agreements not including claims that principally involve alleged discriminatory practices).

( ) Transactions governed by the UCC (exclusive of those concerning individual cooperative or condominium units).

( ) Transactions involving commercial real property, including Yellowstone injunctions and excluding actions for the payment of rent only.

( ) Shareholder derivative actions—without consideration of the monetary threshold.

( ) Commercial class actions—without consideration of the monetary threshold.

( ) Business transactions involving or arising out of dealings with commercial banks and other financial institutions.

( ) Internal affairs of business organizations.

( ) Malpractice by accountants or actuaries, and legal malpractice arising out of representation in commercial matters.

( ) Environmental insurance coverage.

( ) Commercial insurance coverage (e.g. directors and officers, errors and omissions, and business interruption coverage).

( ) Dissolution of corporations, partnerships, limited liability companies, limited liability partnerships and joint ventures—without consideration of the monetary threshold.

( ) Applications to stay or compel arbitration and affirm or disaffirm arbitration awards and related injunctive relief pursuant to CPLR Article 75 involving any of the foregoing enumerated commercial issues—without consideration of the monetary threshold.

2.　The primary relief sought in this case is either equitable or declaratory or, unless otherwise authorized above, the sum at issue (exclusive of punitive damages, interest, costs, disbursements, and counsel fees claimed) **is equal to or in excess of $25,000,** the monetary threshold of the Commercial Division in this County. Identify relief sought: _____.

3.　This is not an action to collect professional fees, obtain a declaratory judgment as to insurance coverage for personal injury or property damage or to enforce a judgment. This is not an action concerning a residential real estate dispute, including landlord-tenant matters, or a commercial real estate dispute involving the payment of rent only. This is not an action for first-party insurance benefits or an action to collect premiums or to rescind a non-commercial insurance policy.

Dated: _____　　　　_____　(Attorney Signature)

　　　　　　　　　　　_____　(Firm Name/Address)

　　　　　　　　　　　_____

　　　　　　　　　　　_____

　　　　　　　　　　　_____　(Phone)
　　　　　　　　　　　_____　(Fax)

STIPULATION AND ORDER

Form 2. Preliminary Conference Stipulation and Order, Hon. Deborah H. Karalunas

SUPREME COURT OF THE STATE OF NEW YORK COUNTY OF ONONDAGA COMMERCIAL DIVISION

PRESIDING JUSTICE:
DEBORAH H. KARALUNAS
_____

                           PRELIMINARY CONFERENCE
                           STIPULATION AND ORDER

           Plaintiff(s),

-v-   Index No.
                            RJI No.

          Defendant(s).
_____

[All items on the form must be completed unless inapplicable.]

(1) **Pertinent Dates:**

(a) Date of Commencement: _____

(b) Date of Joinder: _____

(c) RJI Date: _____

(2) **Nature of Case:**

(a) Plaintiff's Claims: _____

_____

_____

_____

(b) Amount Demanded: _____

(c) Defendant's Defenses and Claims: _____

_____

_____

_____

(d) Amount Demanded: _____

(3) **Attorney's Consultation:**

The parties consulted on _____, 200 ___, in a good faith effort to reach agreement on the issues identified in Uniform Commercial Division Rule 8. Agreement was reached as follows:

(a) Resolution of case _____.

(b) Discovery _____.

(c) ADR _____.

(d) E–discovery _____.

(e) Confidentiality and privilege _____.

(f) Designation of experts _____.

(4) **Early Disposition**:

(a) This case is appropriate for early disposition by:

- ADR (provide type and timing) _____.

- Limited issue discovery in aid of early dispositive motion/settlement _____.

- Dispositive motion will be filed on or before _____.

- Other _____.

(b) This case is not appropriate for early disposition because _____.

It is hereby STIPULATED and ORDERED that disclosure shall proceed as follows:

(5) **Insurance Coverage** shall be furnished on or before _____.

(6) **Bill of Particulars**: Demand for a bill of particulars shall be served on or before _____.

(7) **Interrogatories** shall be served on or before _____.

(8) **Depositions**: Choose (a) or (b)

(a) Deponent	Date & Time	Place
_____	_____	_____
_____	_____	_____
_____	_____	_____
_____	_____	_____
_____	_____	_____

(b) The parties shall set a schedule for depositions. Depositions of all parties shall be completed on or before _____. Depositions of all non-party witnesses are to be completed on or before _____.

(9) **Expert Disclosure**:

(a) Plaintiff(s) shall serve expert disclosure on or before _____ (**no later than 30 days after the filing of the trial note of issue**).

(b) Defendant(s) shall serve expert disclosure on or before _____ (**no later than 30 days after the filing of the trial note of issue**).

Note: Expert disclosure provided after these dates without good cause will be precluded from use at trial.

(10) **Other Disclosure**:

(a) Names and addresses of all witnesses, statements and photographs shall be exchanged by all parties on or before _____.

(b) Demands for discovery and inspection shall be served on or before _____.

(c) Demands for admissions shall be served on or before _____.

(d) Other (specify) _____.

(11) **Confidentiality/Non–Disclosure Agreement**:

(a) _____ anticipates the need for a Confidentiality/Non–Disclosure Agreement as to the following: _____.

Note: In the event that a Confidentiality/Non–Disclosure Agreement is required, the party seeking confidentiality shall promptly prepare and circulate a proposed agreement. The failure to promptly prepare and circulate a proposed agreement may result in a waiver of any claim of confidentiality. See 22 NYCRR § 216.1.

(12) **End Date for All Disclosure**: _____.

Note: On consent parties may modify the specific dates set forth in this discovery stipulation and order provided that all discovery is completed by the discovery cut-off date.

(13) **Impleader** shall be completed on or before _____.

(14) **Motions—Generally**:

(a) Plaintiff(s) intends to make the following motions _____.

(b) Defendant(s) intends to make the following motions _____.

Note: Form of Papers

- The notice of motion or order to show cause shall include a statement of the precise relief sought.

- All dispositive motions must include a copy of the pleadings.

- Exhibit tabs are required.

- If a document to be annexed to an affidavit or affirmation is voluminous and only discrete portions are relevant to the motion, counsel shall attach only the pertinent excerpts and submit the full exhibit separately.

- Memoranda of law shall not exceed 25 pages in length; reply memoranda of law shall not exceed 10 pages in length.

- Sur-replies and post-argument submissions are not allowed without advance express permission of the Court.

(15) **Summary Judgment and Other Dispositive Motions**:

(a) All dispositive motion(s) (including a motion to dismiss or a motion for summary judgment) shall be made no later than the **30th day after filing of the trial note of issue.**

(b) Upon any motion for summary judgment, other than a motion for summary judgment in lieu of a complaint, there shall be annexed to the notice of motion a separate, short and concise statement, in numbered paragraphs, of the material facts as to which the moving party contends there is no genuine issue to be tried.

(c) Papers opposing a motion for summary judgment shall include a correspondingly numbered paragraph responding to each numbered paragraph in the statement of the moving party and, if necessary, additional numbered paragraphs containing a separate short and concise statement of the material facts as to which that party contends that there exists a genuine issue to be tried.

(d) Each numbered paragraph in the statement of material facts required to be served by the moving party will be deemed admitted for purposes of the motion unless specifically controverted by a correspondingly numbered paragraph in the statement required to be served by the opposing party.

(e) Each statement of material fact by the movant or opponent, including each statement controverting any statement of material fact, must be followed by citation to evidence submitted in support of or in opposition to the motion.

(16) **Settlement Conference** will be held on _____ (to be set by the Part Clerk).

(17) **Trial Note of Issue**: Plaintiff(s) shall file a note of issue/certificate of readiness on or before _____.

Note: Trial note of issue must be filed within 12 months of date of filing RJI for a standard case or within 15 months of filing RJI for a complex case.

(18) **Trial:**

(a) Plaintiff(s) anticipates that the trial of this action will take _____ days.

(b) Defendant(s) anticipates that the trial of this action will take _____ days.

(c) A pretrial conference will be held on _____ (to be set by Part Clerk).

(d) The trial of this action will commence on _____.

Note: All pre-trial filings and submissions required by Uniform Commercial Division Rules 27, 28, 29, 31 and 32 (including motions *in limine*, indexed exhibit binder, witness list, identification of deposition testimony (with transcripts), pretrial memorandum, request to charge (with reference to PJI numbers or specific case citations) and jury verdict sheet) shall be filed and exchanged with opposing counsel at least five (5) days before the final pretrial conference.

Failure to comply with any of these deadlines, rules or directives may result in the imposition of costs or sanctions or other action authorized by law.

DATED: _____

_____
Attorney for Plaintiff(s)

_____
Attorney for Defendant(s)

_____
Attorney for Defendant(s)

SO ORDERED: __/__/__

_____
Hon. Deborah H. Karalunas, JSC

QUEENS COUNTY
COMMERCIAL DIVISION ADR RULES

Preamble. Information Guide

Queens Supreme Court encourages the use of alternative dispute resolution ("ADR") methods to encourage the early resolution of matters and avoid protracted litigation. The Commercial Division has devised a program by which cases may be referred to mediation by the assigned commercial judge, the Administrative Judge, or by consent of the parties. Mediation is a confidential and informal process where the parties meet with a trained, neutral third party to identify issues and explore options that may result in a mutually acceptable resolution. Unlike litigation, the neutral third party does not make a determination, but instead assists the parties in creating their own resolution of the issues. While there is no obligation to settle the case through mediation, many cases often result in a written stipulation between the parties. However, if the parties are not able to resolve their dispute through mediation, the matter will proceed before the assigned Justice.

All parties whose cases are sent to the mediation program may choose to use the services of a private ADR practitioner of their own choosing as an alternative to the mediation program. If the parties consent to the use of the court's mediation program, they may later terminate the process and choose to submit their dispute to another ADR program.

The following Rules shall govern all cases sent to the ADR program of the Commercial Division by the Justices assigned to the Commercial Division, the Administrative Judge, or referred upon the consent of the parties.

Rule 1. The Program

The Commercial Division of the Supreme Court of the State of New York, County of Queens, operates the Alternative Dispute Resolution Program ("the Program"). The Program shall apply to cases referred by the Justices assigned to the Commercial Division, the Administrative Judge of Queens Supreme Court, Civil Term, and commercial cases referred by the consent of the parties to the extent that the Program can accommodate them. These Rules shall govern all cases so referred.

Rule 2. Administration of the Program

The Program shall be supervised by the Principal Law Clerk for the Administrative Judge of Queens Supreme Court, Civil Term, who shall act as the Program Administrator. The conduct of ADR proceedings shall be coordinated by the Program Administrator.

Rule 3. The Panel

The Administrative Judge shall establish and maintain a roster of Mediators ("the Roster") who shall serve and be compensated in accordance with the Rules unless the parties stipulate otherwise. (I) In order to be eligible to serve as a Mediator and be included on the Roster, one must have:

a. been admitted to practice law as an attorney in New York State, and;

b. successfully completed a minimum of forty (40) hours of mediation training in an OCA-sponsored or OCA-recognized training program, and must have recent mediation experience per Part 146 of the Rules of the Chief Administrative Judge. http://www.courts.state.ny.us/rules/chiefadmin/146.shtml.

c. any other commercial law or comparable experience deemed appropriate by the Administrative Judge.

d. Mediators shall provide the first, three-hour mediation session free of charge. Mediators shall not charge for time spent preparing for the first initial session.

e. After the first free session, the parties shall compensate the Mediator at a rate of $300 per hour, unless the parties and the Mediator otherwise agree in writing. The Mediator's fees and expenses shall be borne equally by the parties unless otherwise agreed to in writing

f. Every member of the Roster, and any other person who serves as a Mediator pursuant to these Rules, shall comply with the Code of Ethical Standards for Mediators of the Commercial Division.

g. Continuing presence on the Roster is subject to review by the Administrative Judge. Mediators may be removed from the Roster at the discretion of the Administrative Judge in consultation with the New York State Unified Court System's Office of ADR Programs.

h. The Roster will be available through the Program Administrator, located in the Administrative Judge's office in Queens Supreme Court or at http://www.courts.state.ny.us/courts/comdiv/queens.shtml.

Rule 4. Procedure for Submission to the Program

(a) Cases shall be referred to ADR as soon after commencement as practicable. Cases may be sent to the Program by the Commercial Division Justices, the Administrative Judge or by consent of the parties in writing. The assigned Justice shall issue an Order of Reference requiring that the case proceed to ADR in accordance with these Rules. A case not deemed appropriate for referral initially may be later referred to the Program in the discretion of the assigned Commercial Division Justice. Unless otherwise stipulated by the parties, all cases referred to the Program shall be mediated.

(b) The Justice shall submit the Order of Reference to the Program Administrator. Upon receipt of the Order of Reference, the Program Administrator will randomly assign a Mediator chosen from the Roster and contact the Mediator to confirm a date, time, and location upon which to schedule the ADR session. In the alternative, the parties may select another Mediator from the Roster.

(c) Upon assigning a Mediator, the Program Administrator will forward the Order of Reference to the parties and advise the parties of the name and contact information of the Mediator, and the date on which the ADR proceeding will take place. The Program Administrator will also send the ADR Initiation Form to the parties, which requires the names and contact information for all parties and their counsel, and contains additional provisions for confidentiality and immunity for the Mediator.

(d) Within five (5) business days of receiving the Order of Reference, the parties must sign the ADR Initiation Form and return it to the Program Administrator. The parties must also consent to the appointment of the assigned Mediator. If either party does not consent to the assigned Mediator, that party must submit in writing a letter to the Program Administrator explaining the reason for the lack of consent. The Program Administrator will then randomly assign another Mediator to the mediation. If the parties stipulate to a private ADR proceeding, the parties must make their own arrangements for the proceeding. If a private ADR practitioner is chosen, the parties must report to the Program Administrator the name of the Mediator, contact information if not a member of the Roster and the date when the proceeding will be held.

(e) After the Program Administrator receives the ADR Initiation Form, the Program Administrator shall provide the assigned Mediator, the parties and their counsel a Notice of Confirmation and a copy of the ADR Initiation Form.

(f) The initial ADR session must be conducted within forty-five (45) days from the date the Order of Reference was signed. If there is a conflict with the scheduled date of the mediation, the parties and the Mediator shall agree on a convenient date for the initial session without contacting or involving the Program Administrator. However, the new date must fall within the above time frame. The parties and Mediator may also contact each other to resolve any preliminary matters without the intervention of the Program Administrator. In the event of extraordinary circumstances, the Mediator shall contact the Program Ad-

ministrator, who will intervene only if necessary to expedite the process.

(g) At least ten (10) days before the initial ADR session, the Mediator may request the parties provide to the Mediator a copy of the pleadings and a memorandum of not more than ten pages (unless otherwise agreed by the parties and the Mediator) setting forth that party's opinions as to the facts and the issues that are not in dispute, contentions as to liability and damages, and suggestions as to how the matter might be resolved. Except as otherwise agreed, this memorandum shall not be served by the parties on their adversary or be filed in court, shall be read only by the Mediator, and shall be destroyed by the Mediator immediately upon completion of the ADR proceeding. At no time should the parties provide the memorandum to the Program Administrator or the assigned Commercial Division Justice.

(h) Unless the Mediator permits otherwise, every party and counsel must attend the initial ADR session in person. In the case of a corporation, partnership or other business entity, the party may be represented by an official who possesses full knowledge of the facts and issues and authority to resolve the matter. In addition, any participating attorney must be present at every session and also have full knowledge and authority to settle the matter.

(i) At the conclusion of the initial ADR session, any party or the Mediator may opt to terminate the ADR proceeding. In such an instance, the Mediator shall immediately inform the Program Administrator of the termination. If termination is by one party's request, the Mediator must notify the Program Administrator but shall not indicate the identity of that party who chose to terminate the proceeding.

(j) Within ten (10) days after the ADR proceeding has concluded, the Mediator shall complete the ADR Disposition Form indicating resolution or lack thereof and submit the Form, along with any written agreement, to the Program Administrator. If the parties entered into a written stipulation of settlement, the parties shall submit a stipulation of discontinuance to the assigned Commercial Division Justice and file with the County Clerk. If the parties do not resolve the matter, it will be returned to the assigned Justice. However, the Mediator must complete the ADR Disposition Form regardless of the result of the ADR proceeding.

(k) The Program Administrator shall report to the assigned Commercial Division Justice at the conclusion of the proceeding whether the proceeding resulted in a resolution of the case in whole or in part.

(*l*) If a party or counsel to a party fails to appear at a scheduled mediation session, the Mediator shall advise the Program Administrator promptly. Failure to participate may result in the imposition of sanctions.

Rule 5. Confidentiality

(a) The ADR proceeding shall be confidential. All documents prepared by the parties or their counsel and any notes or other writing prepared by the Mediatorl in connection with the proceeding- as well as any communications made by the parties or their counsel for, during or in connection with the ADR proceeding- shall be kept confidential by the Mediatorl and the parties and shall not be summarized, described, reported or submitted to the court by the Mediatorl or the parties. No party to the ADR proceeding shall, during the action referred to ADR or in any other legal proceeding, seek to compel production of documents, notes or the writings prepared for or generated in connection with the ADR proceeding, or seek to compel the testimony of any party concerning the substance of the ADR process. Any settlement, in whole or in part, reached during the ADR proceeding shall be effective only upon execution of a written stipulation signed by all parties affected or their duly authorized agents. Such an agreement shall be kept confidential unless the parties agree otherwise, except that any party thereto may thereafter commence an action for breach of this agreement. Documents and information otherwise discoverable under the Civil Practice Law and Rules shall not be shielded from disclosure merely because the documents and information are submitted or referred to in the ADR proceeding.

(b) No party to an action referred to the Program shall subpoena or otherwise seek to compel the Mediator to testify in any legal proceeding concerning the content of the ADR proceeding. In the event that a party to an action that had or has been referred to the Program attempts to compel such testimony, that party shall hold the Mediator harmless against any resulting expenses, including reasonable legal fees incurred by the Mediator or reasonable sums lost by the Mediator in representing himself or herself in connection therewith. However, notwithstanding the foregoing and the provisions of Rule 5(a), a party or the Program Administrator may report to an appropriate disciplinary body any unprofessional conduct engaged in by the Mediator and the Mediator may do the same with respect to any such conduct engaged in by counsel to a party.

(c) Notwithstanding the foregoing and, to the extent necessary, (i) the parties may include confidential information in a written settlement agreement; (ii) the Mediator and the parties may communicate with the Program Administrator about administrative details of the proceeding; and (iii) the Mediator may make general reference to the fact of the services rendered by him or her in any action required to collect an unpaid, authorized fee for services performed under these Rules.

Rule 6. Immunity of the Mediator; Compensation

Any person designated to serve as Mediator pursuant to these Rules shall be immune from suit based upon any actions engaged in or omissions made while serving in that capacity to the extent permitted by applicable law.

Rule 7. Stay of Proceedings

(a) Unless otherwise directed by the assigned Justice, referral to the ADR program will not stay the court proceedings in any respect.

(b) Parties committed to the mediation process who conclude that additional time is required to fully explore the issues pertaining to their case may request a stay of proceedings. Regardless of whether a stay is granted by the assigned Justice, if informal exchange of information concerning the case will promote the effectiveness of the ADR process and the parties so agree, the Mediator shall make reasonable directives for such exchange consistent with any pre-existing disclosure order of the court and in compliance with the deadlines set forth herein.

(c) If the matter has not been entirely resolved within the 45-day period as provided in these rules but the parties and the Mediator believe that it would be beneficial if the mediation were to continue, the process may continue but shall be completed within 90 days from the date of the Order of Reference. If further time is needed, the parties must seek specific authorization from the assigned Justice to permit the process to continue beyond 90 days.

Rule 8. Conflicts of Interest

In order to avoid conflicts of interest, any person assigned to serve as a Mediator shall, as a condition to confirmation in that role, conduct a review of his or her prior activities and those of any firm of which he or she is a member or employee. The Mediator shall disqualify himself or herself if the Mediator would not be able to participate as a Mediator fairly, objectively, impartially and in accordance with the highest professional standards. The Mediator shall also avoid any appearance of a conflict of interest. In the event that any potentially disqualifying facts should be discovered, the Mediator shall fully inform the parties and the Program Administrator of all relevant details. Unless all parties after full disclosure consent in writing to the service of that Mediator, the Mediator shall decline the appointment and another Mediator shall promptly be randomly assigned by the Program Administrator. Any such conflicts review shall include a check with regard to all parents, subsidiaries or affiliates of corporate parties.

Rule 9. Further ADR

After completion of the initial mediation session, upon request of a party or upon the court's own initiative, the court may in its discretion issue an order directing a second referral to the Program. Any such referral shall be entertained and ordered as early as practicable, and such case shall proceed in accordance with these Rules.

JUDGES' PART RULES

JUSTICE ORIN R. KITZES

Part 17.   Hon. Orin R. Kitzes

Preliminary Conference

A preliminary conference shall be scheduled (1) automatically by the court within 45 days after filing a request for Judicial Intervention, pursuant to 22 NYCRR 202.12(b), or (2) upon filing a written Request for a Preliminary Conference with the Clerk's Office (Room 140) in compliance with 22 NYCRR 202.12(a) or an appropriate notice is filed in malpractice or certiorari cases pursuant to 22 NYCRR 202.56 and 202.60.

All Preliminary Conferences will be held on THURSDAYS at 9:30 a.m at the Preliminary Conference Part, Room 307 of the Courthouse, and they are presided over by the court-appointed referee, unless otherwise directed by the court. Failure to appear at the scheduled preliminary conference may result in discovery being ordered ex-parte or any other appropriate sanction including preclusion or dismissal ordered. Contact the Preliminary Conference Part at (718) 298–1046, not chambers.

Compliance Conference

For all Non-Commercial Division cases, Compliance Conferences shall be held on the date scheduled in the Preliminary Conference Stipulation and Order. Conferences shall be held before Justice Ritholtz in Courtroom 313.

For all Commercial Division cases, Compliance Conferences shall be held on the date scheduled in the Preliminary Conference Stipulation and Order. Conferences shall be held before Justice Kitzes in Courtroom 116.

Pre-Trial Conference

Counsel attending the conference must be fully familiar with and authorized to settle, stipulate, and dispose of the action(s).

Motion Practice

The motion calendar will be called every WEDNESDAY at 9:30 a.m. promptly. A second call will follow immediately thereafter. No courtesy copies to chambers are required EXCEPT IN THE CASE OF E-FILED MOTIONS.

All motions and applications are to be submitted on papers only, except those relating to any phases of discovery and/or bills of particulars, including motions to strike or restore a case from trial calendar, which require personal appearance by counsel for all parties. If the application is an Order to Show Cause then all parties MUST appear (movant must submit Affidavit of Service to Part Clerk) on the return date. Counsel should be prepared to discuss and agree upon a discovery schedule.

Oral argument will be entertained only in the Court's discretion.

Use of calendar service is permitted both to submit papers and to request counsel adjournments, which will be limited to two. The first adjournment on consent will be allowed on papers, thereafter attorneys seeking a further adjournment must appear.

Do not call the Part or Chambers for adjournments as NO ADJOURNMENTS WILL BE GRANTED ON THE TELEPHONE. The Court will not consider papers sent to Chambers or to the Part after submission.

The members of the Bar should make every effort to notify their adversaries and co-counsel of all applications for adjournments in advance.

The Court requests that any attorney appearing on a case for any purpose must be familiar with the case, ready and authorized to resolve any and all issues.

Electronic Filing of Legal Papers

Electronic filing is available for filing legal papers with this Court. Parties interested in electronic filing should read the materials set forth at www.nycourts.gov/efile. The rules and User's Manual for electronic filing are available on this web site. Courtesy copies to chambers are required IN THE CASE OF E-FILED MOTIONS.

Inquiries

All inquiries as to case or calendar status are to be made to the appropriate Clerk's office.

IAS Motion Support Office (718) 298–1009
Ex Parte Support Office (718) 298–1018
Trial Term Office (718) 298–1021

AFFIRMATION IN SUPPORT OF REQUEST FOR ASSIGNMENT

Form 1. Commercial Division Attorney's Affirmation

SUPREME COURT OF THE STATE OF NEW YORK
COUNTY OF QUEENS

	Index No. _____/___
Plaintiff(s),	
-against-	**COMMERCIAL DIVISION**
	ATTORNEY'S AFFIRMATION
Defendant(s).	

STATE OF NEW YORK   )
) ss:
COUNTY OF QUEENS   )

_____, an attorney at law duly licensed to practice in the State of New York, does hereby state under penalty of perjury as provided in CPLR 2106 and certifies pursuant to 22 NYCRR § 130–1.1:

1. Plaintiff's cause(s) of action is/are _____.

2. Plaintiff's claimed relief is _____.

3. Defendant's counterclaim(s) is/are _____.

4. Defendant's claimed relief is _____.

Based upon the foregoing, it is respectfully requested that this matter be assigned to the Commercial Division of the Supreme Court, Queens County.

Dated: _____, NY

_____, 20___

_____

SUFFOLK COUNTY

JUDGES' PART RULES

JUSTICE ELIZABETH EMERSON

Rule 1. Commercial Division Rules

All parties should familiarize themselves with the Commercial Division Rules, available at http://www.nvcourts.gov/courtslcomdiv/suffolk.shtml

Rule 2. Scheduling

Parties should address questions about scheduling appearances or adjournments to the Part Clerk, Rick Pontrelli, at (631) 852–2139.

Please be advised that litigants/counsel must obtain Court permission to adjourn a status conference. Excepting emergencies, such permission must be obtained no later than 2 business days in advance of the scheduled appearance. Counsel must make every effort to obtain consent to an adjournment from an adversaries in the matter and be prepared to communicate that consent to the Court. If counsel is unable to get consent, counsel must send a brief letter to the Court with a copy to all adversaries, explaining the circumstances necessitating the adjournment and the reason consent could not be obtained. Counsel must wait at least 24 hours to allow for the adversary to respond to the request before contacting the Court.

Rule 3. Mediation

If, at any point, the parties decide that they could benefit from Commercial Division ADR or other mediation, they should write a joint letter to the Court asking to be referred to ADR or such other mediation. In that letter, they should state whether they prefer that discovery continue or be stayed during the mediation process.

Further information on the Court sponsored ADR program can be found at http://www.llycourts.gov/courtslcomdiv/suffolk.shtml

Rule 4. Motion Practice

After compliance with Rule 14 of the Commercial Division Rules whereby counsel have consulted with one another in a good faith effort to resolve all disputes, the parties may make a written request for a conference with the Court.

Discovery disputes should first be addressed through a court conference prior to the filing of a motion. If the Court is unable to resolve the dispute through a conference, then leave will be given for the parties to file the appropriate motion. The failure to abide by this rule may result in a motion being held in abeyance until the Court has an opportunity to conference the matter.

All papers submitted must include the correct motion sequence number if they refer to a motion, be properly backed, and be filed with Special Term at 1 Court Street, Riverhead, NY 11901.

Rule 19 A statements are required for all summary judgment motions.

All dispositive motions require a pre-motion conference with the Court. Counsel must send a letter to the Court, on notice to all adversaries, requesting a pre-motion conference be scheduled.

With respect to Rule 11 (d), of the Commercial Division Rules, the presumption is that discovery is NOT stayed by the filing of a dispositive motion unless otherwise directed.

All citations must include a cite to the official reports.

The Court will notify the parties if oral argument is required after papers in support of and in opposition to the motion have been submitted.

If oral argument is held, at its conclusion the movant is to order the transcript and have a copy sent to the Court. The motion will not be deemed sub judice until a transcript has been received.

Rule 5. Trial Rules

Pre-trial memoranda and briefs are to be submitted in all matters at least 7 business days prior to the start date of trial.

No electronic media devices will be permitted absent express permission from the Court. Requests should be made to the Court in writing, addressed to the Clerk of the Part, and the reasons for the request must be clearly stated.

No adjournments of the trial date will be granted absent exceptional circumstances. All requests must be made in writing to the Court and not by a telephone call to the Clerk of the Part.

All materials used during the trial must be removed within 48 hours of the conclusion of trial. Any materials not timely removed will be discarded.

All trials require full compliance with directives set forth in the Pre-Trial Order. Additionally, if the trial is by jury, counsel will be required to submit a proposed verdict sheet and proposed charges 7 business days prior to trial.

Rule 6. Communication with the Court

Neither Justice Emerson nor any of the court attorneys assigned to the part will speak to any litigant or counsel ex parte.

No party shall send a letter to chambers without first contacting the adversary, trying to resolve the problem and telephoning chambers. With permission of the Court, a party may send correspondence to the Court via fax to (631) 852–3732 or U.S. mail or overnight delivery, but not by more than one method of delivery.

JUSTICE EMILY PINES

Preamble. Information Guide

Counsel are expected to be familiar with the Commercial Division Rules and comply therewith. The following information is offered as a guide to the practices followed by this Court.

Rule 1. Scheduling

All questions about scheduling appearances or adjournments should be addressed to the Court's Secretary, Valarie Genchi, at 631–852–3117. Requests for adjournment of matters appearing on a Tuesday calendar should be made by not later than 3:00 p.m. on Friday. Requests made after that will likely not be granted. All requests for adjournments must be made with the agreement of opposing counsel and, if approved, confirmed by letter with copies to all counsel. If consent cannot be obtained, then the requesting counsel must arrange for a conference call with the Court.

Rule 2. Communication with the Court

1. Counsel may call the Court's Secretary, Valarie Genchi, with respect to the scheduling of appearances and with respect to adjournment applications.

2. Counsel may call Chambers to arrange for a telephone conference with the Court with the Law Secretary, or with Kathryn Coward.

3. Counsel may not contact Chambers on any substantive matter without all opposing counsel on the telephone, except for the purpose of facilitating a conference call.

Rule 3. Motions

No motion shall be made, except as allowed by Rule 24 of the Commercial Division Rules, without a prior conference with the Court, which conference may be obtained either by conference call or, upon obtaining permission from Chambers, the submittal of a brief letter application, not exceeding 1 page in length. At the conference the Court will set a schedule for making the motion, opposing it, and, if applicable, for reply.

Motions are to be returnable on Tuesdays. Motions made returnable at any other time, absent prior permission of the Court, will be adjourned by the Part Clerk to the next available Tuesday.

Adjournments are governed by Rule 16(c) of the Commercial Division Rules.

Motions are submitted without oral argument, unless otherwise directed by the Court.

Reply papers are not permitted, unless: (a) the right of reply is obtained by service of a notice of motion in accordance with CPLR 2214[b]; or (b) expressly permitted by the Court. Counsel may submit supplemental citations as allowed by Rule 18 of the Commercial Division Rules. Sur-reply papers, including papers in support of a cross-motion, are not permitted, absent prior permission of the Court. Any unauthorized papers will not be read and will be discarded.

All papers must comply with the applicable provisions of the CPLR and with Rules 16 and 18 of the Commercial Rules. In addition, the font size of text and footnotes must be no smaller than 12 point. Papers which do not comply may be rejected.

All motions for summary judgment shall be accompanied by a Statement of Undisputed Facts Pursuant to Rule 19-a of the Commercial Rules. A motion for summary judgment which lacks such a statement may be rejected. All opposing papers must include a response to the Statement of Undisputed Facts.

No motion papers will be sealed without a prior, or contemporaneous, application for sealing made pursuant to Part 216 of the Rules of the Chief Administrative Judge.

The Court generally does not stay disclosure pending determination of motions to dismiss or motions for summary judgment (made prior to completion of discovery). All dispositive motions shall be made no more than 60 business days after the filing of the Note of Issue.

Rule 4. Discovery Disputes

With respect to cases already assigned to this Court at the time that a discovery dispute arises, no motion with respect to the dispute shall be made without a prior conference with the Court, which may be obtained by submission of a letter application, not exceeding one (1) page in length. Counsel must obtain permission from Chambers prior to the submission of such letter application.

With respect to cases in which a discovery motion accompanies the Request for Judicial Intervention which leads to the assignment to this Court, no opposition papers shall be served until there has been a prior conference with the Court, which may be obtained by letter application, not exceeding one (1) page in length. The application for a discovery conference may be made by the movant or by the opposing counsel; however, the application must be made within eight (8) days of service of the motion. Counsel must obtain permission from Chambers prior to the submission of a letter application. Failure to request a discovery conference may result in the denial of the motion.

The Court endeavors to resolve discovery disputes promptly, usually by conference, which may be held telephonically or in person. In the event that the dispute is not resolved, the Court will set an expedited briefing schedule. Counsel shall, prior to requesting a conference, meet in person to discuss the issues and endeavor to resolve or limit them, prior to seeking judicial intervention.

PRELIMINARY CONFERENCE ORDER

Form 1. Preliminary Conference Stipulation and Order, Hon. Emily Pines

Supreme Court of the State of New York
County of Suffolk
Commercial Division: IAS Part 46

Present: Hon. Emily Pines
             Justice

_____   Index No. _____

                     Plaintiff(s),   **Preliminary Conference**
                                Stipulation and Order
   - against -   (Section 202.8[f] and 202.12
                                 of the Uniform Rules)

                     Defendant(s).
_____

(All items on the form must be completed unless inapplicable.)

It is hereby STIPULATED and ORDERED that disclosure shall proceed as follows:

(1) Nature of case:

(a)

Plaintiff's Claims

_____

_____

Amount Demanded

$ _____

(b)

Defendant's Claims/Defenses

_____

_____

Defendant's Claims/Defenses

_____

_____

Defendant's Claims/Defenses

_____

_____

Defendant's Claims/Defenses

_____

_____

(Add additional sheets, if needed)

(2) Insurance Coverage (CPLR 3101[f]): If not provided, shall be furnished by on or before _____. Not applicable _____.

(3) **Bill of Particulars:** (If relevant) shall be served by _____.

(4) **Discovery and Inspection:**

(a) All Demands for Discovery and Inspection (CPLR 3120) shall be served not later than ___ days from the date of this Order.

(b) All responses to Discovery and Inspection demands shall be served not later than ___ days after receipt of the opposing party(ies) demand(s).

(c) All demands for production of books, documents, records and other writings relevant to the issues in this case shall be deemed to include a demand for production of any photograph(s), audio tape(s), video tape(s), computer disk(s) or program(s) and e-mail. The failure to comply herewith may result in preclusion from the introduction of such evidence.

(5) **Depositions:**

(a) Depositions shall be held as follows:

(Priority shall be in accordance with CPLR 3106 unless otherwise agreed or ordered.)

Party	Date	Time	Place

(Add additional sheets, if needed)

(b) Unless otherwise agreed or ordered, if a party fails or refuses to be deposed, he/she may not utilize the deposition of the adverse party(ies) at trial in additional to such other sanctions as may be available (CPLR 3126).

(c) Depositions of non-party witnesses shall not be noticed until the conclusion of all party depositions unless otherwise agreed by all party(ies) or ordered by the Court.

(d) Any disputes with regard to the propriety of questions at a deposition shall be promptly resolved via an application to the Court either in person, if the deposition is conducted in the Courthouse, or via telephone, if the deposition is conducted elsewhere. In the event the Justice presiding or his/her law secretary is not available, such applications shall be addressed to the Justice presiding in Special Term Part II.

(6) **A Status Conference** shall be held on _____.

(7) **Other disclosure:**

(a) Commissions or letters rogatory (CPLR 3108): identify and set forth the location of each witness.

_____

_____

(b) Expert disclosure (CPLR 3101[d]):

Plaintiff(s) shall provide expert disclosure by _____

Defendant(s) shall provide expert disclosure by _____

(c) Interrogatories (CPLR 3130—3133): Each party shall serve no more than ___ interrogatories, inclusive of subdivisions and subparts.

(8) **End Date for All Disclosure**, other than expert disclosure _____. (Set by Court or Part Clerk)

(9) **Motions:**

(a) All dispositive motion(s) (CPLR 3211 and 3212) shall be made on or before _____. (Not more than 60 days after the Certification Order is granted or conclusion of discovery.)

(b) All other motions, including those for impleader and amendment of pleading(s) shall not be made until compliance with Commercial Division Rule 24.

(10) **Compliance/Certification Conference** shall be held on _____. (Set by Court or Part Clerk)

(11) **Confidentiality/Non–Disclosure Agreement:**

(a) In the event that there is a need for a Confidentiality/Non–Disclosure Agreement prior to disclosure, the party(ies) demanding same shall prepare and circulate the proposed agreement. If the party(ies) cannot agree as to same, they shall promptly notify the Court. The failure to promptly seek a confidentiality agreement may result in a waiver of same.

(b) _____ anticipates the need for a Confidentiality Agreement as to the following issues: _____

_____

_____

_____

(12) **Preservation of Electronic Evidence:**

(a) For the relevant periods relating to the issues in this litigation, each party shall maintain and preserve all electronic files, other data generated by and/or stored on the party's computer system(s) and storage media (i.e. hard disks, floppy disks, backup tapes), or other electronic data. Such items include, but are not limited to, e-mail and other electronic communications, word processing documents, spreadsheets, data bases, calendars, telephone logs, contact manager information, internet usage files, offline storage or information stored on removable media, information contained on laptops or other portable devices and network access information.

(b) When electronically stored documents are produced, they are to be produced in Native Format with MetaData intact and Bates stamped on the CD and/or other media upon which they are produced, in a searchable format, unless the parties agree otherwise.

(13) **Miscellaneous:**

(a) If the matter settles, the Court shall be promptly notified and a courtesy copy of the Stipulation of Discontinuance shall be promptly forwarded to the Court. Failure to comply with any of these directions may result in the imposition of costs, sanctions or other actions authorized by law.

(b) The failure of any party(ies) to perform any of the requirements contained in this Order shall not excuse any other party(ies) from performing any other requirement contained herein.

(c) Any dates established herein shall not be changed or adjourned without the prior approval of the Court.

(d) Each counsel/party acknowledges receipt of the Commercial Division Rules.

(14) **Trial:**

(a) Plaintiff anticipates his/her/its case on the trial of this matter to be ___ days.

Defendant _____ anticipates the trial of this matter to be ___ days.

Defendant _____ anticipates the trial of this matter to be ___ days. (Add additional sheets, if needed)

(b) The matter is hereby set down for trial on _____.

(c) All pre-trial filings and submissions (including trial notebooks), jury selection, if appropriate, and marking exhibits shall be on _____, at _____ A.M./P.M.

(d) A pre-trial conference of this matter shall be held on _____, at _____ A.M./P.M.

(15) This Order includes the attached __ page(s) which is/are incorporated herein by reference.

Attorney for Plaintiff(s) _____

_____

Attorney for Defendant(s) _____

_____

Attorney for Defendant(s) _____

_____

Attorney for Defendant(s) _____

_____

Attorney for Defendant(s) _____

_____

Attorney for Defendant(s) _____

Dated: _____
Riverhead, New York

_____

Emily Pines
J. S. C.

AFFIRMATION IN SUPPORT OF ASSIGNMENT

Form 2. Affirmation

INDEX NO.: _____

SUPREME COURT—STATE OF NEW YORK
COUNTY OF SUFFOLK

---x

Plaintiff,

AFFIRMATION

-against-

Defendant.

---x

_____, an attorney duly admitted to practice law before the Courts of the State of New York, hereby affirms the following statements to be true under the penalties of perjury.

1. I am the attorney for _____ and submit this affirmation in support of the assignment of this action to the Commercial Division.

2. This is an action for (Brief Description of the Action)

_____

_____

_____

_____

3. The amount sought in compensatory damages is $ _____.

4. I am fully familiar with the facts and pleadings in this action and have reviewed the Rules of the Commercial Division, Suffolk County including the guidelines for the assignment of cases to the Commercial Part.

5. I believe that this case complies with the guidelines for the assignment of cases to the Commercial Part and should be assigned to the Commercial Division.

_____

PRELIMINARY CONFERENCE FORM

Form 3. Preliminary Conference Stipulation
and Order, Hon. Elizabeth H. Emerson

SUPREME COURT, COUNTY OF SUFFOLK

COMMERCIAL DIVISION: IAS PART ___

PRESENT: HON._____

JUSTICE

_____   INDEX NO. _____

                 Plaintiff(s),   **Preliminary Conference
Stipulation and Order**
(Section 202.8 [f] and 202.12
of the Uniform Rules)

against

                Defendant(s).

_____

(All items on the form must be completed unless inapplicable.)

(1) Nature of case:

  (a) Plaintiff's Claims/Counterclaim Defenses

_____

_____

_____

  Amount Demanded $ _____

  (b) Defendant _____'s Claims/Defenses

_____

_____

_____

  Amount Demanded $ _____

  Defendant _____'s Claims/Defenses

_____

_____

_____

  Amount Demanded $ _____

  Defendant _____'s Claims/Defenses

_____

_____

_____

  Amount Demanded $ _____

  Defendant _____'s Claims/Defenses

_____

Amount Demanded $ _____

(Add additional sheets, if needed)

It is hereby STIPULATED and ORDERED that disclosure shall proceed as follows:

(2) **Insurance Coverage (CPLR 3101 [f]):** If not provided, shall be furnished by _____ on or before _____. Not Applicable ___.

(3) **Bill of Particulars:** (If relevant)

(a) Demand shall be served on or before _____.

(b) Bill of Particulars shall be served not later than _____ days after receipt of the demand.

(c) All previously served demands shall be responded to on or before _____, 200___.

(4) **Discovery and Inspection:**

(a) All Demands for Discovery and Inspection (CPLR 3120) shall be served not later than ___ days from the date of this Order which shall be on or before _____.

(b) All responses to Discovery and Inspection demands shall be served not later than ___ days after receipt of the opposing party(ies) demand(s).

(c) All previously served demands shall be responded to on or before _____ 200___.

(d) All demands for production of books, documents, records and other writings relevant to the issues in this case shall be deemed to include a demand for production of any photograph(s), audio tape(s), video tape(s) and Electronically Stored Information ("ESI").

To the extent relevant the terms of Annex A are incorporated herein.

(5) **Depositions:**

(a) Depositions shall be held as follows:

(Priority shall be in accordance with CPLR 3106 unless otherwise agreed or ordered)

Party	Date	Time	Place
_____	_____	_____	_____
_____	_____	_____	_____
_____	_____	_____	_____
_____	_____	_____	_____

(Add additional sheets, if needed)

(b) Unless otherwise agreed or **Ordered**, if a party fails or refuses to be deposed, he/she may not utilize the deposition of the adverse party(ies) at trial in additional to such other sanctions as may be available (CPLR 3126).

(c) Depositions of non-party witnesses shall not be noticed until the conclusion of all party depositions unless otherwise agreed by all party(ies) or **Ordered** by the Court.

(d) Any disputes with regard to the propriety of questions at a deposition shall be promptly resolved via an application to the Court either in person, if the deposition is conducted in the Courthouse, or via telephone, if the deposition is conducted elsewhere. In the event the Justice presiding or his/her law secretary is not available, such applications shall be addressed to the Justice presiding in Special Term Justice presiding on that day.

(6) **Other Disclosure:**

(a) Expert disclosure shall be provided pursuant to CPLR 3101[d]

(b) Interrogatories (CPLR 3130-3133): Each party shall serve no more than 25 interrogatories, inclusive of subdivisions and subparts unless otherwise **Ordered** by the Court.

(7) **Preservation of ESI**

Parties shall review Annex A and complete as appropriate. To the extent ESI is relevant to the matters described in this order the provisions set forth on Annex A shall apply.

(8) **Motions:**

(a) All motions shall be made in accordance with the Commercial Division Rules and as appropriate after a pre-motion conference has been completed.

(b) All dispositive motion(s) (CPLR 3211 and 3212) shall also be made pursuant to applicable provisions of the CPLR.

(c) Impleader motion(s) to amend pleadings or to add parties shall be completed on or before _____.

(9) **End Date for All Disclosure**, other than expert disclosure _____. (Set by Court or Part Clerk)

(10) **Certification Conference** shall be held on _____ (set by Court or Part Clerk).

(11) **Status Conference** shall be held on _____ (set by Court or Part Clerk).

(12) **Confidentiality/Nondisclosure Agreement:**

(a) In the event that there is a need for a Confidentiality/Nondisclosure Agreement prior to disclosure, the party(ies) demanding same shall prepare and circulate the proposed agreement. If the party(ies) cannot agree as to same, they shall promptly notify the Court. The failure to promptly seek a confidentiality agreement may result in a waiver of same.

(b) _____ anticipates the need for a Confidentiality Agreement as to the following issues:

_____

_____

_____

(13) **Miscellaneous:**

(a) If the matter settles, the Court shall be promptly notified and a courtesy copy of the Stipulation of Discontinuance shall be promptly forwarded to the Court. Failure to comply with any of these directions may result in the imposition of costs, sanctions or other actions authorized by law.

(b) The failure of any party(ies) to perform any of the requirements contained in this Order shall not excuse any other party(ies) from performing any other requirement contained herein.

(c) Any dates established herein shall not be changed or adjourned without the prior approval of the Court.

(d) Each counsel/party acknowledges that they are familiar with the Commercial Division Rules.

(14) This Order includes the attached ___ page(s) which is/are incorporated herein by reference.

Attorney for Plaintiff(s)   Firm Name:_____

Contact Person:_____

Signature:_____

Address:_____

Telephone:_____ Fax:_____

Attorney for Defendant(s)   Firm Name:_____

Contact Person:_____

Signature:_____

Address:_____

Telephone:_____ Fax:_____

Attorney for Defendant(s)   Firm Name:_____

Contact Person:_____

Signature:_____

Address:_____

Telephone:_____ Fax:_____

Attorney for Defendant(s)   Firm Name:_____

Contact Person:_____

Signature:_____

Address:_____

Telephone:_____ Fax:_____

Dated: _____, 20___

SO ORDERED:

_____

J.S.C.

ANNEX A

RE: _____ v. _____

Index No. _____

SUPREME COURT, SUFFOLK COUNTY

COMMERCIAL DIVISION

PRELIMINARY CONFERENCE ORDER/STIPULATION

ADDITIONAL SHEET

ITEM NO.

_____   _____

_____   _____

_____   _____

_____   _____

_____   _____

_____   _____

_____   _____

_____   _____

——— ———   ————————————————————————
——— ———   ————————————————————————
——— ———   ————————————————————————
——— ———   ————————————————————————
——— ———   ————————————————————————
——— ———   ————————————————————————
——— ———   ————————————————————————
——— ———   ————————————————————————
——— ———   ————————————————————————
——— ———   ————————————————————————
——— ———   ————————————————————————
——— ———   ————————————————————————

PAGE ___ OF ___

ALTERNATIVE DISPUTE RESOLUTION MEDIATION PROGRAM

Protocol I. Overview

Alternative Dispute Resolution ("ADR") refers to a variety of processes other than litigation that parties use to resolve disputes. ADR offers the possibility of a settlement that is achieved sooner, at less expense, and with less inconvenience and acrimony than would be the case in the normal course of litigation. The principal forms of ADR include arbitration, neutral evaluation, and mediation. The Suffolk County Commercial Division will initially focus on mediation.

While there is currently no Court sponsored Arbitration available, parties may choose to proceed to resolve matters with the assistance of a private arbitrator. Parties who choose to proceed to binding arbitration as the initial form of ADR pursuant to an Order of Reference shall agree upon appropriate procedures to govern the process in lieu of the requirements set forth in these rules.

Protocol II. Mediation

Mediation is a confidential, informal procedure in which a neutral third person ("Mediator") helps parties in disagreement, negotiate with each other. Mediation is particularly appropriate for the resolution of complex commercial cases. Mediation offers the parties a confidential, structured forum in which to explore practical business concerns and develop tailor-made solutions beyond those that a Judge can often provide. With the assistance of the Mediator, parties identify issues, clarify perceptions and explore options for mutually acceptable outcomes. Although parties are not obligated to reach an agreement during mediation, the process frequently concludes with a written agreement. A Mediator will not impose a solution on the parties or attempt to tell them what to do. If the parties do not reach agreement, the case continues with the assigned Trial Justice.

In mediation, the goal is to find a mutually acceptable alternative to having a trial Justice make a determination after trial or hearing. Mediation sessions will take place on neutral ground, usually the Mediator's office. A session can be as short as a few hours or continue over the course of several sessions, depending upon the issues. This program shall be applicable to cases referred by Justices of the Commercial Division ("Referring Justice") either upon request of the parties or at the Referring Justices' discretion. Upon such a request the Court shall issue an Order of Reference. The parties and/or counsel will select a Mediator from the Suffolk County ADR Roster of Mediators. The Court shall have the discretion to appoint a Mediator from the Roster in the event that the parties and/or counsel are unable to agree on a Mediator or request same.

All parties will have the opportunity to raise issues of concern and to explain the facts of the dispute as each sees them. The Mediator will ask questions in an effort to identify those issues that each of the parties wants to discuss. The Mediator will not offer an opinion as to the likely Court outcome of any particular issue. Once the Mediator and parties have identified the issues for discussion, the Mediator will assist the parties to work collaboratively to develop and choose options which address these issues.

The Mediator may initiate a caucus. During the caucus, the Mediator will meet separately with each party. The Mediator will not divulge any information discussed in the caucus without first obtaining each party's permission to do so. If the parties agree to resolve any or all issues, their agreement will be reduced to writing and forwarded to the Referring Justice for approval.

Protocol III. The Roster

The Administrative Judge of the 10th Judicial District (Suffolk County) shall establish and maintain a panel of Mediators (the "Roster") who shall possess such qualifications and training as required by Part 146 of the Rules of the Chief Administrative Judge.

Every member of the Roster, and any other person who serves as a Mediator pursuant to these Rules, shall comply with the Code of Ethical Standards for Mediators of the Commercial Division upon its issuance. Continuing presence on the Roster is subject to review by the Administrative Judge. Mediators may be removed from the Roster at the discretion of the Administrative Judge in consultation with the Unified Court System Office of ADR Programs. The Roster will be available on the Commercial Division website at http://www.nycourts.gov/courts/comdiv/suffolk.shtml

Protocol IV. Procedures

Cases shall be referred to Mediation as early as is practicable. Where the parties consent to a referral at a conference or in a written stipulation or by order of the Referring Justice pursuant to Rule 3 of the Rules of Practice for the Commercial Division (202.70 g), the Referring Justice shall issue an Order of Reference requiring that the case proceed to Mediation in accordance with these Rules. Along with the Order of Reference, the Referring Justice shall include the contact information for the mediator appointed by the Court. Within fifteen (15) days of receipt, the parties and/or counsel shall contact the Mediator and obtain from the Mediator a confirmation of their willingness to conduct the Mediation proceeding. If the parties and/or counsel object to the mediator appointed, they must notify the Court within fifteen (15) days or the objection is waived.

The parties and/or counsel shall schedule with the Mediator a time and place for the Mediation proceeding and fill out the Mediation initiation form which requires the names and contact information for all parties and counsel to the case and contains additional provisions for confidentiality and Mediator immunity. This form along with the Confirmation of the Mediator shall be returned to the Referring Justice for approval within 15 days of receipt of the Order of Reference.

The issuance of an Order of Reference shall not stay court proceedings in the case unless otherwise directed by the Referring Justice. In the event the Referring Justice stays the court proceedings, the parties may agree to the informal exchange of information concerning the case if such exchange will promote the effectiveness of the Mediation process. The Mediator shall make reasonable directives for such exchange consistent with any pre-existing disclosure order of the Court and in compliance with the deadlines herein set forth.

Should a conflict arise regarding the scheduled date for the Mediation session, the parties and the Mediator will agree on a convenient date for the initial session without the involvement of the Court. Notwithstanding the above, the initial Mediation session must be conducted within 30 days from the date the Order of Reference was issued. In the event of extraordinary circumstances, the Mediator shall contact the Court which may intervene in order to expedite the process. The Mediator may initially request a conference call with all counsel regarding any preliminary matters.

At least 10 days before the initial session, the Mediator may request that each party deliver to the Mediator a copy of its pleadings and a memorandum of not more than ten pages (except where the parties and the Mediator agree in advance upon a different limit) setting forth that party's opinion as to the facts and the issues that are not in dispute, contentions as to liability and damages, and suggestions as to how the matter might be resolved. This memorandum shall not be served on the adversary or filed in court, shall be read only by the Mediator, and shall be destroyed by the Mediator immediately upon completion of the proceeding.

Unless exempted by the Mediator for good cause, all parties and their respective counsel must attend the Mediation session(s) either in person or, in the case of a corporation, partnership or other business entity, by an official (or more than one if necessary) who is both fully familiar with all pertinent facts and authorized to settle the matter. All attorneys who participate in the Mediation process shall be fully familiar with the action and authorized to settle.

Within seven (7) days after the Mediation process has concluded whether by agreement, or by the refusal of one or more parties to continue, the Mediator shall complete the Mediation Disposition Form and transmit it along with any written agreement, to the Referring Justice. If the Mediation process results in a settlement, the parties shall file a stipulation of discontinuance with Special Term and fax a copy to the Referring Justice.

Notwithstanding the forgoing, if a party or counsel fails to schedule an appearance for a Mediation session in a timely manner, appear at any scheduled session or otherwise comply with these Rules, the Mediator shall advise the Court, as to the nature of the infraction, and may, if deemed appropriate, recommend the imposition of sanctions.

Protocol V. Confidentiality

All communications made—whether in writing, orally, or by other means—during the course of mediation by any party, Mediator, or any other person present, shall not be disclosed, except as noted below. Similarly, information generated in or around the mediation—including memoranda, work products or case files of a Mediator—is confidential and shall not be disclosed, except as noted below. However, mediation may not be used as a shield with respect to discoverable documents and information produced or occurring prior to or outside the confines of mediation.

No party or counsel for a party may reveal the details of the mediation process to the Referring Justice or a member of the his/her staff, except as otherwise provided below. Communications and information may be subject to disclosure in any present or future judicial or administrative proceeding under the following circumstances:

1. Attendance

Information pertaining to whether the parties and their counsel attended the mediation session(s) will be reported to the Referring Justice.

2. Waiver

All parties to the mediation and their attorneys may specifically agree in writing to waive confidentiality with respect to any or all issues.

3. Written Agreement

Agreements signed by all the parties will be submitted to the Court for review.

No party to an action referred to Mediation shall subpoena or otherwise seek to compel the Mediator to testify in any legal proceeding concerning the content of the Mediation proceeding. In the event that a party to an action that had or has been referred to Mediation attempts to compel such testimony, that party shall hold the Mediator harmless against any resulting expenses, including reasonable legal fees incurred by the Mediator or reasonable sums lost by the Mediator in representing himself or herself in connection therewith.

Notwithstanding the foregoing and the provisions of the Confidentiality section above, a party or the Referring Justice may report to an appropriate disciplinary body any unprofessional conduct engaged in by the Mediator and the Mediator may do the same with respect to any such conduct engaged in by counsel to a party.

Protocol VI.   Immunity of the Mediator

Any person designated to serve as Mediator pursuant to these Rules shall be immune from suit based upon any actions engaged in or omissions made while serving in that capacity to the extent permitted by applicable law.

Protocol VII.   Compensation of Mediators

Mediators shall be compensated at the rate of $300 per hour unless the parties and the Mediator agree otherwise in writing, except that Mediators shall not be compensated for the first three (3) hours spent in the Mediation session or for the time spent on the selection and appointment process or in preparation for such Mediation session. The Mediator's fees and expenses shall be borne equally by the parties unless otherwise agreed in writing.

Protocol VIII.   Conflicts of Interest

The Mediator shall disqualify himself or herself in the event that there is an actual conflict of interest or the appearance of a conflict of interest, unless the parties and counsel agree, in writing, after full disclosure, to waive the conflict of interest or the appearance of the conflict of interest.

Protocol IX.   Further Court Participation

In the event that the parties do not reach an agreement during Mediation, the case will return to the Referring Justice. However, nothing set forth herein shall preclude the Referring Justice from participating and/or engaging in further settlement efforts with the parties and/or respective counsel.

ADR Application Form and Instructions

10th JUDICIAL DISTRICT ADR PROGRAM

COURT ROSTER MEDIATOR for SUFFOLK COUNTY COMMERCIAL DIVISION

APPLICATION FORM AND INSTRUCTIONS

The 10th Judicial District Alternative Dispute Resolution (ADR) Program is assembling a Court Roster of mediators for the Suffolk County Commercial Division.

Mediators will not be compensated for the first 3 hours spent in mediation. These first 3 hours may not include time spent in preparing for the mediation session(s). Thereafter, mediators will be paid at an hourly rate of $300.00 per hour for mediation work unless otherwise agreed to by the parties and mediator. Billable time will include actual time spent in mediation session(s). Mediator responsibilities include:

- Coordinating with Court staff;

- Managing cases promptly and efficiently;

- Conducting mediation in accordance with the Model Standard of Conduct for Mediators (www.nycourts.gov/courts/comdiv/PDFs/NYCOUNTY/Attachmet3.pdf);

- Preparing mediation agreements in a format acceptable to the Court;

- Completing a Disposition Report form for submission to the Court;

- Notifying the Court, in writing, if the parties do not participate in the mediation session.

Requirements for roster membership include those qualifications and training as required by Part 146 of the Rules of the Chief Administrative Judge. Applicants must submit this application to the Suffolk County District Administrative Judge's Office. Appointment to the Court Roster is at the discretion of the District Administrative Judge and his or her designee(s), in consultation with the Coordinator of the Unified Court System Office of Alternative Dispute Resolution. Admission will be based on each applicant's training, experience, education, and availability to mediate.

Mediators may be removed from the panel at the discretion of the District Administrative Judge in consultation with the Coordinator of the Unified Court System Office of Alternative Dispute Resolution. To be considered for the Tenth Judicial District Court Roster of Commercial Division Mediators, please complete the enclosed application and return it to:

Suffolk County District Administrative Judge's Office
Attn: Helen Ann Miller
400 Carleton Avenue
Central Islip, New York 11722

Include a copy of your resume or curriculum vitae.

Answer all questions completely.

Inform your references that they may be contacted by the 10th District Administrative Judge's Office.

Sign and date the declaration at the end of the application.

ALTERNATIVE DISPUTE RESOLUTION PROGRAM
SUFFOLK COUNTY COMMERCIAL DIVISION

<u>Court Roster Mediator — Commercial Matters</u>

A. General Information

Name: _____

Address: _____

_____

_____

Phone: _____

Email: _____

Please check one:

☐ I meet the training and experience requirements outlined above and am applying to be included on the Court Roster of Mediators for the Suffolk County Commercial Division.

☐ I do not meet the training requirement; however, I would like my application to be filed and to be informed of further training opportunities.

B. Education

(Please list in reverse chronological order. Attach additional pages if necessary):

School	Graduated?	Major or Type of Course	Degree Earned or Expected date

List any professional licenses you hold:

_____

C. Mediation Training

Please detail all mediation training you have taken (attach additional pages if necessary):

Course	Intstructor(s)	Date of Completion	Total Hours

Attach copies of certificates of completion for the above-referenced trainings. If no certificate is available, the review committee may request relevant syllabus or course materials or other documentation that will enable the committee to determine if the course meets the established requirements.

D. Mediation Experience

How many cases have you mediated in the last five (5) years? ___

Of these, how many involved commercial issues? ___

On a separate sheet, please provide a brief statement (one page) outlining your mediation experience.

Are you able to conduct mediation in a language other than English?

☐   Yes

☐   No

If yes, specify language(s) and level of proficiency:

Answer all questions by placing an X in the appropriate column. If you answer "YES" to any of these questions, provide details on an attached sheet.

Yes   **No**

A) Except for minor traffic offenses and adjudications as youthful offend-er, wayward minor or juvenile delinquent:

    i) Have you ever been convicted of an offense against the law?

    ii) Have you ever forfeited bail or other collateral?

    iii) Do you now have any criminal charges pending against you?

B) Have you ever received a discharge from the Armed Forces that was other than honorable?

C) Have you ever been dismissed from any employment for reasons other than lack of work or funds?

D) Are you currently in violation of a court order in any state for child or spousal support?

I affirm that all statements on this application (including any attached papers) are true.

_____   _____
Signature of Applicant   Date

MEDIATION FORMS

Form 1. Mediation Referral Order

SUPREME COURT, COUNTY OF SUFFOLK
COMMERCIAL DIVISION IAS PART 44/46

PRESENT:

HON. _____
          JUSTICE

_____

                                    INDEX NO. _____

              Plaintiff(s)   MEDIATION REFERRAL
                                           ORDER

against

              Defendant(s)

_____

 The above matter having come on for a conference, and upon consent of the parties and counsel for the parties, said parties and their respective counsel, are hereby directed to:

1. Arrange time to meet with the Mediator for the purpose of resolving their outstanding differences.

2. Comply with the following:

All statements made by the parties in the context of the meeting(s) contemplated herein shall be deemed to be made solely for the purpose of settlement and shall not be disclosed, except for the following:

 a) the parties to the mediation and their attorneys may specifically agree in writing to waive confidentiality with respect to any or all issues;

 b) agreements signed by all the parties and submitted to the Court for review;

 The Trial Court will not ask the Mediator for either a written or oral report with regard to this matter (other than the Mediation Disposition Report). Furthermore, the Mediator shall not be called as a witness by either party or the Court.

 The foregoing constitutes the order of this Court.

_____

                    J.S.C.

Dated: _____
Riverhead, New York

Form 2.   Mediation Initiation Form

MEDIATION INITIATION FORM
SUPREME COURT OF THE STATE OF NEW YORK
COUNTY OF SUFFOLK
COMMERCIAL DIVISION

Referring Justice:

Date:

In the Matter of: Index #:

This case is referred to Mediation with:

INSTRUCTIONS:

This form shall be sent to the selected Mediator accompanied by a Mediation Referral Order signed by the Referring Justice. The selected Mediator shall contact the parties listed below within one (1) week of the above date, and shall arrange for an initial mediation session with all parties and their respective counsel, if indicated, within thirty (30) days of the receipt of this form.

The following individuals have consented to attend a mediation session (the name and contact information of counsel for the respective parties will be provided so they can be present for the mediation):

Client Name: Client Name:

Address: Address:

Tel: Tel:

Counsel: Counsel:

Tel: Tel:

Client Name: Client Name:

Address: Address:

Tel: Tel:

Counsel: Counsel:

Tel: Tel:

Reason for Referral:

The Court will not ask the mediator for either a written or oral report with regard to this matter (other than the Mediation Disposition Report). Furthermore, the mediator shall not be called as a witness by either party or the Court. The mediation process is confidential and voluntary, and discussions had during the course of the mediation session/s will not be disclosed except in instances where:

    a) the parties to the mediation and their attorneys, if applicable, may specifically agree in writing to waive confidentiality with respect to any and all issues; or

    b) an agreement is signed by all the parties and submitted to the Court for review;

Litigants should be aware that no attorney-client relationship exists between the mediator and litigants. Nor may the mediator provide legal services to litigants during the process. The designated or otherwise chosen mediator handling this matter shall be immune from suit by any of the parties or other participants in this case based upon the mediator's activities in this matter. The mediator shall present a waiver for signature by the parties to that end, at the initial mediation session.

The mediator is also responsible for submitting a Disposition Report Form to the Court within seven (7) business days after the conclusion of the mediation process. The Disposition Report Form shall only indicate that a mediation was held, the dates of such mediation and whether or not a settlement was reached.

I confirm that I have read the Suffolk County Commercial Division ADR Protocols, and I confirm my willingness to serve pursuant to such rules.

_____

Date

_____

Signature of acceptance by Mediator

Form 3.   Mediation Disposition Report

SUPREME COURT OF THE STATE OF NEW YORK
COUNTY OF SUFFOLK
COMMERCIAL DIVISION
MEDIATION DISPOSITION REPORT

Date: _____

Case Name: _____

Index No.: _____

To: Hon. _____
                           (Referring Justice)

From: _____
                      (Mediator)

Mediation Held:
   Mediator: _____

   Date(s) Held: _____

Who Participated: _____

Total Length of Mediation _____ (Hrs.) Fees Charged _____

Mediation Outcome: Full agreement _____
                        Written agreement attached

                    Partial agreement_____
                        Written agreement attached

                    No agreement _____

WESTCHESTER COUNTY

PRACTICE GUIDE

Doc. 1. Practice guide to the Commercial Division, Westchester County, Cases Pending Before Hon. Alan D. Scheinkman

Counsel are expected to be familiar with the Commercial Division Rules and comply therewith. The following information is offered as a guide to the practices followed by this Court.

Scheduling:

All questions about scheduling appearances or adjournments should be addressed to the Part Clerk, Maryann Tamberella, at (914) 824-5348. Do not contact Chambers regarding such issues. Requests for adjournment of matters appearing on the weekly Commercial Calendar should be made by not later than 3:00 p.m. on the day before. Requests made after that will likely not be granted. All requests for adjournments must be made with the request of all opposing counsel and, if approved by the Court, confirmed by a signed Stipulation of all counsel. If consent cannot be obtained, then the requesting counsel must either arrange for a conference call with the Court and, if one cannot be timely arranged, then the application must be made at the call of the calendar.

E–Filing Rules and Protocol:

All parties should familiarize themselves with the statewide E-Filing Rules (available at www.nycourts. gov/efile) and the Westchester County E-Filing Protocol (available at http://www.nycourts.gov/courts/9jd/ efile/WestchesterCountyJointProtocols.pdf) and 202.70 of Uniform Civil Rules of the Supreme and County Courts as amended on 7/1/10. General questions about e-filing should be addressed to the E–Filing Resource Center at 646-386-3033 or efile@courts.state.ny.us.

Filing of Papers:

Mandatory e-filing of all Commercial Division actions through the New York State Courts E–Filing system (NYSCEF) is scheduled to begin on February 1, 2011. Submissions to the Court including motion papers, proposed orders, proposed judgments, and letters (after prior permission to send such letters is provided), must be electronically filed. Pre-trial submissions are not to be filed electronically, and shall be delivered to the Court at the Pre-Trial Conference or as the Court may otherwise direct.

Working Copies:

E-filing rules provide that a court may require the submission of "working copies" of any electronically filed documents intended for judicial review. A work-

ing copy is defined as "a hard copy that is an exact copy of a document that is electronically filed."

The Commercial Division, Westchester County, requires that working (courtesy) copies of all papers filed electronically be mailed to Chambers. Pursuant to Uniform Rule 202.5–b(d)(4), the working copy shall bear as a cover page firmly fastened thereto a copy of the confirmation notice received from the NYSCEF site upon the electronic filing of the document. Hard copies not bearing such cover page shall be discarded, unread. All working copies of e-filed documents intended for judicial review must include exhibit tabs and backs.

Working copies of all documents, except stipulations to be so-ordered, are to be mailed or hand delivered so as to be received by Chambers by the return date or notice of settlement date.

WORKING COPIES OF STIPULATIONS TO BE SO-ORDERED (INCLUDING REQUESTS FOR ADJOURNMENT) MUST BE RECEIVED BY CHAMBERS 48 HOURS BEFORE THE EXISTING SCHEDULED DATE. IF THIS CAN NOT BE ACHIEVED, COUNSEL ARE TO CALL OUR PART CLERK AT (914) 824-5348.

Hard Copy Submissions:

Part will reject any hard copy submissions in e-filed cases unless those submissions bear the Cover Sheet for Hard Copy Submission — E–Filed Case required by Uniform Rule § 202.5–b(d)(1). The form is available at www.nycourts.gov/efile.

Communications With the Court:

(a) *Written correspondence*: No written correspondence may be sent to the Court without prior permission. Written correspondence sent by letter, fax or any other means, without permission will not be read and will be discarded.

(b) *Telephone calls*:

1. Counsel may call the Part Clerk with respect to the scheduling of appearances and with respect to adjournment applications.

2. Counsel may call Chambers and/or the Part Clerk to arrange for a telephone conference with the Court or with the Law Secretary.

3. Counsel may not contact Chambers without all opposing counsel on the phone, except for the purpose of facilitating a conference call.

Motions:

No motion shall be made, except as allowed by Rule 24 of the Commercial Division Rules, without a prior conference with the Court, which conference may be obtained either by conference call or, upon obtaining permission from chambers, the submittal of a brief letter application, not exceeding 1 page in length. At the conference, the Court will set a schedule for making the motion, opposing it, and, if applicable, for reply.

Motions are to be returnable on Fridays at 9:30 a.m. Motions made returnable at any other time, absent prior permission of the Court, will be adjourned by the Part Clerk to the next available Friday.

Adjournments are governed by Rule 16(c) of the Commercial Division Rules.

Motions are submitted without oral argument, unless otherwise directed by the Court.

Reply papers are not permitted, unless: (a) the right of reply is obtained by service of a notice of motion in accordance with CPLR 2214[b]; or (b) expressly permitted by the Court. Counsel may submit supplemental citations as allowed by Rule 18 of the Commercial Division Rules. Sur-reply papers, including reply papers in support of a cross-motion, are not permitted, absent prior permission of the Court. Any unauthorized papers will not be read and will be discarded.

All papers must comply with the applicable provisions of the CPLR and with Rules 16 and 18 of the Commercial Division Rules. In addition, the font size of text and footnotes must be no smaller than 12 point. Papers which do not comply may be rejected.

All motions for summary judgment shall be accompanied by a Statement of Undisputed Facts Pursuant to Rule 19-a of the Commercial Division Rules. A motion for summary judgment which lacks such a statement may be rejected. All opposing papers must include a response to the Statement of Undisputed Facts.

All exhibits shall be separately tabbed. In the event that multiple affidavits or affirmations are submitted in support of a motion under the same legal back, each such exhibit shall be accompanied by a clearly discernible side or bottom tab containing the last name of the affiant.

No motion papers will be sealed without a prior, or contemporaneous, application for sealing made pursuant to Part 216 of the Rules of the Chief Administrative Judge.

The Court generally does not stay disclosure pending determination of motions to dismiss or motions for summary judgment (made prior to completion of discovery).

Discovery Disputes:

With respect to cases already assigned to this Court at the time that a discovery dispute arises, no motion with respect to the dispute shall be made without a prior conference with the Court, which may be obtained by submission of a letter application, not exceeding one (1) page in length. Counsel must obtain permission from Chambers prior to the submission of such letter application.

With respect to cases in which a discovery motion accompanies the Request for Judicial Intervention which leads to the assignment to this Court, no opposition papers shall be served until there has been a prior conference with the Court, which may be obtained by letter application, not exceeding one (1) page in length. The application for a discovery conference may be made by the movant or by the opposing counsel; however, the application must be made within eight (8) days of service of the motion. Counsel must obtain permission from Chambers prior the submission of a letter application. Failure to request a discovery conference may result in the denial of the motion.

The Court endeavors to resolve discovery disputes promptly, usually by conference, which may be held telephonically or in person. In the event that the dispute is not resolved, the Court will set an expedited briefing schedule. Counsel shall, prior to requesting a conference, meet in person to discuss the issues and endeavor to resolve or limit them, prior to seeking judicial intervention.

Preliminary Conferences:

Upon receipt of a letter from the Court scheduling a preliminary conference, counsel shall meet in person and shall jointly prepare a brief statement describing the case and the contentions of the parties. In addition, counsel shall jointly complete a proposed Preliminary Conference Order, on the form supplied by the Court (also available on the Court's website).

Counsel are advised that, absent very unusual complexity, the Court will require that discovery be completed within six months of the assignment of the case to the Court. These submissions shall be furnished to the Court not later than 12 p.m. on the day prior to the conference. In the event that the Court does not receive the submissions, the Court will take such action as may be appropriate under the circumstances, including adjournment of the conference, requiring counsel to complete the forms at the conference, or other steps.

Doc. 2. Information, Practices, Rules and Procedures for Commercial Division, Westchester County Cases Pending Before Hon. Gerald E. Loehr

Counsel must be fully familiar with the Uniform Civil Rules for the Supreme Court 22 NYCRR Part 202.

E–Filing Rules and Protocol

All parties should familiarize themselves with the statewide E–Filing Rules (Uniform Rule §§ 202.5–b and 202.5–bb — available at www.nycourts.gov/efile) and the Westchester County E–Filing Protocol available at http://www.courts.state.ny.us/courts/9jd/efile/WestchesterCountyJointProtocols.pdf.

General questions about e-filing should be addressed to the E–Filing Resource Center at 646–386–3033 or efile@courts.state.ny.us.

Specific questions relating to local procedures should be addressed to the Civil Calendar Office (914) 824–5300.

Electronic Filing

All commercial and tort actions in Part 103, Justice Gerald E. Loehr are to be filed through the New York State Courts E–Filing system (NYSCEF). All submissions to the Court, including proposed orders, proposed judgments, and letters, must be electronically filed.

Working Copies

See Uniform Rule § 202.5–b(d)(4).

This Part requires working copies for all electronic submissions.

Working copies shall be delivered to Chambers.

All working copies submitted to this Part must include a copy of the NYSCEF Confirmation

Notice firmly fastened as the [front] cover page of the submission and comply with other requirements set forth in the Westchester County Protocol. Working copies without the Confirmation Notice will not be accepted.

Working copies are to be delivered no later than noon on the first business day following the electronic filing of the document on the NYSCEF site.

Hard Copy Submissions

Part will reject any hard copy submissions in e-filed cases unless those submissions bear the Notice of Hard Copy Submission — E–Filed Case required by Uniform Rule § 202.5–b(d)(1). The form is available at www.nycourts.gov/efile.

Commercial Division Case Rules:

No motion shall be made, except as allowed by Rule 24 of the Commercial Division Rules, without a prior conference with the Court, which conference may be obtained either by conference call or, upon obtaining permission from chambers, the submittal of a brief letter application, not exceeding 1 page in length. At the conference, the Court will set a schedule for making the motion, opposing it, and, if applicable, for reply.

Motions are to be returnable on Fridays at 9:30 a.m. Motions made returnable at any other time, absent prior permission of the Court, will be adjourned by the Part Clerk to the next available Friday.

Adjournments are governed by Rule 16(c) of the Commercial Division Rules.

Motions are submitted without oral argument, unless otherwise directed by the Court.

Reply papers are not permitted, unless: (a) the right of reply is obtained by service of a notice of motion in accordance with CPLR 2214[b]; or (b) expressly permitted by the Court.

Counsel may submit supplemental citations as allowed by Rule 18 of the Commercial Division Rules. Sur-reply papers, including reply papers in support of a cross-motion, are not permitted, absent prior permission of the Court. Any unauthorized papers will not be read and will be discarded.

All papers must comply with the applicable provisions of the CPLR and with Rules 16 and 18 of the Commercial Division Rules. In addition, the font size of text and footnotes must be no smaller than 12 point. Papers which do not comply may be rejected.

All motions for summary judgment shall be accompanied by a Statement of Undisputed Facts Pursuant to Rule 19–a of the Commercial Division Rules. A motion for summary judgment which lacks such a statement may be rejected. All opposing papers must include a response to the Statement of Undisputed Facts.

All exhibits shall be separately tabbed. In the event that multiple affidavits or affirmations are submitted in support of a motion under the same legal back, each such exhibit shall be accompanied by a clearly discernible side or bottom tab containing the last name of the affiant.

No motion papers will be sealed without a prior, or contemporaneous, application for sealing made pursuant to 22 NYCRR § 216.1

The Court generally does not stay disclosure pending determination of motions to dismiss or motions for summary judgment (made prior to completion of discovery).

Discovery Disputes:

With respect to cases already assigned to this Court at the time that a discovery dispute arises, no motion with respect to the dispute shall be made without a prior conference with the Court, which may be obtained by submission of a letter application, not exceeding one (1) page in length. Counsel must obtain permission from Chambers prior to the submission of such letter application.

Counsel are obligated to formulate a discovery plan that states the parties' views and proposals on any issues about disclosure or discovery of electronically stored information, including the form or forms in which it should be produced.

With respect to cases in which a discovery motion accompanies the Request for Judicial Intervention which leads to the assignment to this Court, no opposition papers shall be served until there has been a prior conference with the Court, which may be obtained by letter application, not exceeding one (1) page in length. The application for a discovery conference may be made by the movant or by the opposing counsel; however, the application must be made within eight (8) days of service of the motion. Counsel must obtain permission from Chambers prior the submission of a letter application. Failure to request a discovery conference may result in the denial of the motion.

The Court endeavors to resolve discovery disputes promptly, usually by conference, which may be held telephonically or in person. In the event that the dispute is not resolved, the Court will set an expedited briefing schedule. Counsel shall, prior to requesting a conference, meet in person to discuss the issues and endeavor to resolve or limit them, prior to seeking judicial intervention.

Preliminary Conferences:

Upon receipt of a letter from the Court scheduling a preliminary conference, counsel shall meet in person and shall jointly prepare a brief statement describing the case and the contentions of the parties. In addition, counsel shall jointly complete a proposed Preliminary Conference Order, on the form supplied by the Court (also available on the Court's website). Counsel are advised that, absent very unusual complexity, the Court will require that discovery be completed within six months of the assignment of the case to the Court. These submissions shall be furnished to the Court not later than 12 p.m. on the day prior to the conference. In the event that the Court does not receive the submissions, the Court will take such action as may be appropriate under the circumstances, including adjournment of the conference, requiring counsel to complete the forms at the conference, or other steps.

Commercial Division cases sent to alternate dispute resolution shall proceed in accordance with the Rules Of The Alternate Dispute Resolution Program as promulgated by Justice Alan D. Scheinkman.

For All Cases

Trials

Prior to the commencement of a trial, counsel shall provide the Court with:

a) marked pleadings, and

b) an exhibit list. Material to be used on cross-examination need not be listed. The attorneys are to pre-mark their exhibits. Only those received into evidence will be marked by the reporter.

The reporter is to be provided with an exhibit list.

Requests to charge shall be submitted to the Court as directed. The charge will be drawn from the Pattern Jury Instructions (PJI). A complete list of requested charges is to be submitted.

Unless counsel seek a deviation from the pattern charge or additions to the pattern charge, only the PJI numbers need to be submitted. Where deviations or additions are requested, the full text of such requests must be submitted, together with any supporting legal precedents. All submissions must be served upon opposing counsel.

Verdict sheet— Counsel shall jointly prepare a verdict sheet. The verdict sheet is to be typed and in final form for presentation to the jury. If agreement cannot be reached, then each side shall present a proposed verdict sheet. If it is feasible, such proposals shall also be submitted on a computer disc in a format convertible to Word Perfect 12.0.

Communications with the Court:

(a) *Written correspondence*: No written correspondence may be sent to the Court without prior permission. Written correspondence sent by letter, fax or any other means, without permission will not be read and will be discarded.

(b) *Telephone calls*:

1. Counsel may call the Part Clerk with respect to the scheduling of appearances and with respect to adjournment applications.

2. Counsel may call Chambers and/or the Part Clerk to arrange for a telephone conference with the Court or with the Law Secretary.

3. Counsel may not contact Chambers without all opposing counsel on the phone, except for the purpose of facilitating a conference call.

(c) *Faxes*: Faxes will not be accepted unless it is an emergency and the receipt has been authorized by Chambers.

PRELIMINARY CONFERENCE ORDER

Form 1.   Preliminary Conference Order—Commercial Case

SUPREME COURT OF THE STATE IF NEW YORK
COUNTY OF WESTCHESTER

PRESENT:

Hon. Alan D. Scheinkman
Justice Supreme Court

--X

Plaintiff,	:	**PRELIMINARY CONFERENCE**
		ORDER -COMMERCIAL CASE
-against-	:	Index No.
Defendant.	:	

--X

SCHEINKMAN, J.:

   Counsel having appeared for a preliminary conference on _____, 200___:

Plaintiff: _____

                  Name

                  _____

                  Firm

                  _____

                  Address

                  _____

                  Telephone Number

                  _____

                  Fax

Defendant: _____

                  Name

                  _____

                  Firm

                  _____

                  Address

                  _____

                  Telephone Number

                  _____

                  Fax

and the Court having conducted a preliminary conference in the above-entitled action, it is hereby ORDERED as follows, pursuant to Rule 8 of the Rules of Practice for the Commercial Division:

1. Any Demand for a Bill of Particulars shall be served on or before _____ and any Bill of Particulars shall be served on or before _____.

2. Any Demands for Discovery and Inspection shall be served on or before _____ and all Responses to such Demands shall be served on or before _____.

3. Any Interrogatories shall be served on or before _____ and all Answers to Interrogatories shall be served on or before _____.

4. Any deposition on Oral Questions to be taken of Plaintiff shall be held on or before _____ at _____.

5. Any deposition on Oral Questions to be taken of Defendant shall be held on or before _____ at _____.

6. Any deposition on Oral Questions to be taken of any non parties shall be held on or before _____ at _____.

7. Other Disclosure, including Expert Disclosure, shall be: _____
   _____
   _____
   _____
   _____

8. Electronic Discovery shall be: _____
   _____
   _____
   _____

9. Discovery shall be limited to the following issues: _____
   _____
   _____
   _____

10. Impleader shall be completed on or before _____.

11. All discovery shall be completed by _____ and any discovery not then completed may be considered waived. The failure to provide a document, or to otherwise provide discovery, may result in preclusion.

12. A Trial Readiness Conference will be held on _____ at _____. On this date a Trial Readiness Order will be issued to the Plaintiff to which Plaintiff shall serve and file a Note of Issue and Certificate of Readiness within (10) days of the date of the Trial Readiness Order.

13. Absent an order of the Court to the contrary, the making of any dispositive motion will NOT stay discovery and will NOT result in, or justify, any change or adjustment in the dates set forth hereinabove.

14. THE DATES SET FORTH ABOVE MAY NOT BE ADJOURNED EXCEPT WITH THE PRIOR APPROVAL OF THE COURT.

15. In the event of a discovery dispute, counsel shall comply with Rule 14 of the Rules of Practice in the Commercial Division. In furtherance thereof, in the event that counsel, after good faith consultation, cannot resolve a discovery dispute, counsel shall promptly contact the Court at 914–824–5419 and arrange for either an in-court or telephonic conference. No motion relating to discovery shall be made without the prior permission of the Court. Neither the existence of any discovery dispute nor the making of any discovery motion shall result in, or justify, any change or adjustment in the dates set forth above, unless otherwise permitted by the Court.

16. All motions (including any discovery motions permitted by the Court) shall be governed by Rules 16 through 24 of the Rules of Practice in the Commercial Division. No sur-reply (which includes reply in further support of a cross-motion) or post-submission papers will be considered by the Court, except as authorized by the Court or by Rule 18. All motions shall be made returnable on Fridays. No motion shall, absent the permission of the Court, be made returnable on any other day.

17. Counsel shall not copy the Court on correspondence between them.

18. No document, including correspondence, shall be sent to the Court without prior authorization from Chambers to do so.

19. Absent the express permission of the Court, copies of all papers filed with the Court shall be transmitted to all opposing counsel in such fashion as to be received by counsel prior to, or contemporaneously with, receipt by the Court.

Dated: White Plains, New York

_____
ALAN D. SCHEINKMAN
Supreme Court Justice

CERTIFICATION IN SUPPORT OF ASSIGNMENT

Form 2. Commercial Division Attorney's Certification

SUPREME COURT OF THE STATE OF NEW YORK
COUNTY OF WESTCHESTER
---X

Plaintiff(s)

**COMMERCIAL
DIVISION
ATTORNEY'S
CERTIFICATION**

-against-

Index No.

Defendant(s).
---X

_____, an attorney duly admitted to practice law before the Courts of the State of New York, hereby affirms the following statements to be true under the penalties of perjury:

1. I am the attorney of the _____ and submit this affirmation in support of assignment of this action to the Commercial Division.

2. This case involves the following causes of actions and defenses: _____
_____
_____.

3. This case involves the following amount of money at issue, exclusive of punitive damages, interest, costs, disbursements and counsel fees claimed _____
_____.

4. I am fully familiar with the facts and pleadings in this action and have reviewed the Uniform Rules of the Commercial Division. 22 NYCRR 202.70.

5. I believe that this case complies with the Uniform Rules of the Commercial Division and should be assigned to the Commercial Division.

Dated: _____   _____

RULES OF THE ALTERNATIVE DISPUTE RESOLUTION PROGRAM

Preamble

It is the policy of this Court to encourage the resolution of disputes and the early settlement of pending litigation through voluntary, consensual settlement procedures. The following Rules shall govern cases sent to Alternative Dispute Resolution ("ADR") by the Justice Presiding in the Commercial Division or referred to ADR upon consent of the parties. As indicated hereinafter, parties whose cases are the subject of an Order of Reference are free to use the services of a private ADR provider of their choosing in lieu of taking part in this Court's ADR Program. Further, after a case has been submitted to this Court's program, parties can terminate the process and proceed to ADR elsewhere.

Rule 1. Program

The Commercial Division of the Supreme Court of the State of New York, County of Westchester, operates an Alternative Dispute Resolution Program ("the Program"). Unless otherwise agreed by the parties, cases referred to the Program shall be mediated.

Rule 2. Roster of Mediators

The Administrative Judge shall establish and maintain a Roster of Mediators ("the Roster").

(i) In order to be eligible to serve as a Mediator and be listed on the Roster, a person shall possess the following qualifications and such others as may hereafter be promulgated. A mediator must (a) have a minimum of ten years of experience in the practice of commercial law or be an accountant or business professional with a comparable level of experience; (b) have completed at least the amount and type of training required d by Part 146[1] of the Rules of the Chief Administrator; (c) have recent experience mediating commercial cases as mandated by Part 146; and (d) Comply with the Commercial Division's Standards of Conduct for Mediators.).

(ii) Continuing presence on the Roster is subject to review by the Administrative Judge. Mediators may be removed from the Roster at the discretion of the Administrative Judge in consultation with the Unified Court System Office of ADR Programs.

(iii) The Roster will be available through the Program Administrator, located in Westchester County Supreme Court, or on the Commercial Division website.

Rule 3. Determination of Suitability; Order of Reference; Compensation

At the outset of each case, the Commercial Division Justice shall determine the suitability of the action for mediation. Cases shall be referred to mediation as soon after they have been commenced as is practica-

ble, consistent with the Uniform Rules for NYS Trial Courts, Rules of Practice for the Commercial Division, Section 202.70(g)(3). A case not deemed appropriate for referral at its outset may be referred later to the Program in the discretion of the Commercial Division Justice.

If the Commercial Division Justice orders the parties to mediation or if the parties consent to a referral to the Program, the Commercial Division Justice shall issue an Order of Reference requiring the parties to attend an initial mediation session. The Mediator shall not charge the parties for the first four hours of the initial mediation session. Thereafter, the parties may choose to terminate the mediation or to schedule additional sessions with the Mediator. If the parties choose to continue in mediation beyond the first four hours of the initial session, the parties shall pay the Mediator $300.00 per hour unless the parties and the Mediator agree otherwise in writing.

Rule 4. Selection of Mediator; Private ADR Providers; Conflict of Interest

(i) An action referred to the Program shall be assigned to a Mediator chosen from the Roster. The parties shall be given an opportunity to select the Mediator. If the parties do not submit in writing agreed-upon names of mediators within five business days from notification of the issuance of the Order of Reference, which deadline is not subject to adjournment, or if administrative necessity so requires, the Program Administrator shall select the Mediator.

(ii) Parties may designate as the Mediator a person who is not a member of the Roster or may proceed to ADR using the good offices of a private ADR provider; but in either instance the parties must complete the ADR process within the deadlines set forth in these Rules and comply with Rule 5.

(iii) Every member of the Roster, and any other person who serves as a Mediator pursuant to subdivision (ii) of this Rule, shall comply with the Standards of Conduct for Mediators, promulgated by the Commercial Division of the State of New York.

(iv) To avoid conflicts of interest, any person tentatively designated to serve as a Mediator shall, as a condition to confirmation in that role, conduct a review of his or her prior activities and those of any firm of which he or she is a member or employee. The Mediator shall make disclosures to the parties who may object to the Mediator's ability to serve or the Mediator shall disqualify himself or herself if he or she would not be able to participate as Mediator fairly, objectively, impartially, and in accordance with the highest professional standards. The Mediator shall also avoid an appearance of a conflict of interest. If any potentially disqualifying facts are discovered, the Mediator shall either decline the appointment or shall fully inform the parties and the Commercial Division's Program Administrator of all relevant details. Unless all parties after full disclosure consent to the service of that Mediator, the Mediator shall decline the appointment and another Mediator shall be selected promptly by the Program Administrator. Any such conflicts review shall include a check with regard to all parents, subsidiaries, or affiliates of corporate parties.

Rule 5. Confidentiality

(i) The mediation shall be confidential. All documents prepared by parties or their counsel, and communications made by the parties or their counsel, for, during, or in connection with mediation, and any notes or other writings prepared by the Mediator in connection with the proceeding shall be kept in confidence by the Mediator and the parties. They shall not be summarized, described, reported or submitted to the court by the Mediator or the parties. No party to the mediation shall, during the action referred to mediation or in any other legal proceeding, seek to compel production of documents, notes or other writings prepared for or generated in connection with the mediation, or seek to compel the testimony of any other party or the Mediator concerning the substance of the mediation process. Any settlement, in whole or in part, reached during the mediation shall be effective only upon execution of a written stipulation signed by all parties affected or their duly authorized agents. Such an agreement shall be kept confidential unless the parties agree otherwise, except that any party thereto may thereafter commence an action for breach of the agreement. Documents and information otherwise discoverable under the Civil Practice Law and Rules shall not be shielded from disclosure merely because they are submitted or referred to in the mediation.

(ii) No party to an action referred to the Program shall subpoena or otherwise seek to compel the Mediator to testify in any legal proceeding concerning the content of the mediation. If a party to an action that had or has been referred to the Program attempts to compel such testimony, that party shall hold the Mediator harmless against any resulting expenses, including reasonable legal fees incurred by the Mediator or reasonable sums lost by the Mediator in representing himself or herself in connection therewith. However, notwithstanding the foregoing and the provisions of Rule 5 (i), a party or the Program Administrator may report to an appropriate disciplinary body any unprofessional conduct engaged in by the Mediator, and the Mediator may do the same with respect to any such conduct engaged in by counsel to a party.

(iii) Notwithstanding the foregoing, to the extent necessary, (a) the parties may include confidential information in a written settlement agreement; (b) the Mediator and the parties may communicate with the Program Administrator about administrative details of the proceeding; and (c) the Mediator may make general reference to the fact of the services rendered by him or her in any action required to collect an unpaid, authorized fee for services performed under these Rules.

Rule 6. Immunity of the Mediator

Any person designated to serve as Mediator pursuant to these Rules shall be immune from suit based upon any actions engaged in or omissions made while serving in that capacity to the extent permitted by law.

Rule 7. Procedure

(i) Unless otherwise agreed by the parties, cases referred to the Program shall be mediated.

(ii) Unless otherwise directed by the Commercial Division Justice, all proceedings in this court other than the mediation, including all disclosure proceedings and motion practice, shall not be stayed from the date of the Order of Reference.

(iii) The first mediation session shall be conducted within 30 days from the Confirmation Date. Immediately after confirmation, all parties shall communicate with one another and the Mediator and take all steps necessary to comply with said deadline. The first four hours of the first mediation session shall be offered free of charge.

(iv) Unless otherwise directed by the Mediator, at least ten days before the first mediation session, each party shall deliver to the Mediator a copy of its pleadings. The Mediator may request from each party a memorandum of not more than ten pages (except as otherwise agreed) setting forth each party's opinions as to the facts and the issues that are not in dispute, contentions as to liability and damages, and suggestions as to how the matter might be resolved. Except as otherwise agreed, this memorandum shall not be served on the adversary or filed in court, shall be read only by the Mediator, and shall be destroyed by the Mediator immediately upon completion of the proceeding.

(v) Attendance is required at the first mediation session. The location of each mediation session shall be determined by the Mediator.

(vi) Unless exempted by the Mediator for good cause, every party must appear at each mediation session in person or, in the case of a corporation, partnership or other business entity, by an official (or more than one if necessary) who is both fully familiar with all pertinent facts and empowered on his or her own to settle the matter. In addition, counsel for each represented party shall be present at each session. Any attorney who participates in the mediation shall be fully familiar with the action.

(vii) If the mediation results in a settlement of the case, the Mediator shall immediately advise the Program Administrator, and the parties shall forthwith submit a stipulation of discontinuance to the Commercial Division Justice.

(viii) At the end of the session(s) mandated by subdivision (v) of this Rule, any party or the Mediator may terminate the mediation. In such case the Mediator shall immediately inform the Program Administrator of the termination. If the mediation has been terminated by one party only, the identity of that party shall not be reported.

(ix) Notwithstanding the foregoing, if a party or counsel fails to schedule an appearance for mediation in a timely manner, fails to appear at any scheduled session or otherwise fails to comply with these Rules, the Mediator shall advise the Program Administrator.

(x) Upon termination of the mediation by a party pursuant to subdivision (viii) of this Rule, neither the Mediator nor the parties shall inform the Program Administrator which party brought the mediation to an end. The Program Administrator shall report to the Commercial Division Justice at the conclusion of the mediation whether the mediation produced a resolution of the case in whole or in part. The Program Administrator shall also report to the Commercial Division Justice, on an appropriate form, a copy of which shall be forwarded to the parties, any violation of these Rules as indicated by a Mediator pursuant to subdivision (ix) of this Rule. The Commercial Division Justice may impose sanctions or take such other action as is necessary to ensure compliance with and respect for the court's Order and these Rules.

Rule 8. Compensation of Mediators

(i) Mediators shall be compensated at the rate of $300.00 per hour unless the parties and the Mediator agree otherwise in writing, except that Mediators shall not be compensated for the first four (4) hours spent in required mediation sessions conducted pursuant to Rule 7 of these rules or for time spent on the selection and appointment process.

(ii) The Mediator's fees and expenses shall be borne equally by the parties unless the parties agree otherwise in writing.

Rule 9. Completion of Mediation; Report

The mediation session or sessions shall be concluded within 45 days from the Confirmation Date. The Mediator shall report to the Program Administrator as to success or lack of success no later than seven days thereafter.

Rule 10. Continuation of Mediation After Expiration of the 45–Day Period

If the matter has not been entirely resolved within the 45–day period as provided in Rule 9, but the parties and the Mediator believe that it would be beneficial if the mediation process were to continue, the process may go forward.

Rule 11. Further Mediation

After completion of the mediation, upon request of a party or upon its own initiative, the Commercial Division Justice, in his or her discretion, may issue an order directing a second referral to the Program. Any such referral shall be entertained and ordered as early as practicable. Any case so referred shall proceed in accordance with these Rules.

Rule 12. Administration of Program

The Program shall be supervised and coordinated by the Principal Law Clerk for the Commercial Division Justice, who shall act as the Program Administrator.

Rev. August 2011

THE COMMERCIAL DIVISION
SUPREME COURT–WESTCHESTER COUNTY
WESTCHESTER COUNTY COURTHOUSE
111 DR. MARTIN LUTHER KING, JR. BLVD.
WHITE PLAINS, NEW YORK 10601

Justice Alan D. Scheinkman

Gretchen Walsh
Principal Law Clerk
Phone: (914) 824–5419
Fax: (212) 884–8939

Maryann Tamberella
Part Clerk
(914) 824–5348

[1] Part 146 requires prospective mediators to have successfully completed a minimum of forty (40) hours of training in an OCA-sponsored or OCA-recognized training program, which includes 24 hours of training in basic mediation skills and techniques and 16 hours of training in the specific mediation techniques pertaining to commercial litigation (see Part 146 of the Rules of the Chief Administrator).

COURT OF CLAIMS

Westlaw Electronic Research

These rules may be searched electronically on Westlaw® in the NY–RULES database; updates to these rules may be found on Westlaw in NY–RULESUP-DATES. For search tips and a summary of database content, consult the Westlaw Scope Screens for each database.

JUDGES' RULES

JUSTICE MELVIN SCHWEITZER

Rule 1. Communications with Chambers

A. Letters

Except for routine scheduling and calendar matters, and situations requiring immediate attention, communications with Chambers shall be by letter, sent by regular or express mail, as necessary, addressed to: Judge Melvin L. Schweitzer, 26 Broadway, New York, N.Y. 10004, or delivered by hand to the Court of Claims receptionist on the 10th Floor at 26 Broadway, in an envelope addressed to Chambers. Copies of the letter shall be simultaneously delivered to all counsel in such a manner that opposing counsel will receive it before, or contemporaneously with, the submission to Chambers. Copies of correspondence between counsel shall not be sent to Chambers.

B. Telephone Calls

For routine scheduling and calendar matters, and situations requiring immediate attention, call (212) 361–8170 between 9:00 A.M. and 5:00 P.M.

C. Faxes

Faxes to Chambers are permitted so long as they are followed by a hard copy sent to Chambers, with copies simultaneously delivered to all counsel in such a manner that opposing counsel will receive it before, or contemporaneously with, the submission to Chambers.

D. Requests for Adjournments or Extensions of Time

All requests for adjournments of scheduled Court appearances or of the return date of a motion, or for an extension of time shall be made only after consultation with opposing counsel. The request to Chambers must state (1) the original date, (2) the number of previous requests for adjournment or extension, (3) whether the adversary consents, and, if not, the reasons given by the adversary for refusing to consent, and (4) a proposed new date on which the parties have agreed. See, Disciplinary Rules of the Code of Professional Responsibility, Appendix A, Part III (22 NYCRR Part 1200). A request for an adjournment or an extension of time may be made by letter or telephone call to Chambers. Unless and until notified by Chambers that the requested adjournment or extension of time has been granted, the parties shall adhere to the original schedule.

E. Settlements and Discontinuances.

Pursuant to the provisions of section 20–a of the Court of Claims Act, settlements are by written stipulation approved by the Court and filed with the Chief Clerk at New York State Court of Claims, P.O. Box 7344—Capitol Station, Albany, N.Y. 12224. In the case of a claim brought by an administrator of an estate, or the representative of an infant or incompetent, counsel must submit appropriate documentation as required by the Court. Information that describes the level of substantive detail this Court requires in this regard may be obtained from Chambers upon written request.

Counsel are advised that the Court requires compliance with the provisions of CPLR 3217 governing discontinuance of a claim. In particular, a Court order will be necessary to discontinue a claim brought on behalf of an infant or incompetent or by an administrator of an estate. In the case of an infant or incompetent, counsel must submit an affirmation of counsel and an affidavit of the guardian explaining the reasons why the claim is being discontinued. Information that describes the level of substantive detail this Court requires in this regard may be obtained from Chambers upon written request.

Rule 2. Appearance by Counsel

Counsel appearing at a conference with the Court must be fully familiar with the case; authorized to explore settlement; and able to enter into agreements pertaining to substantive and procedural issues in the case.

Rule 3. Preliminary Conference

A. Counsel will be notified by Chambers of the date set for the Preliminary Conference provided for by Section 206.10 of the Uniform Rules for the Court of Claims. Generally, this will be on the second Tuesday of a month, a discovery conference day.

B. Prior to a Preliminary Conference, counsel for all parties shall confer regarding all discovery and other issues pertaining to matters of case management and shall make a good faith effort to reach agreement on these matters in advance of the conference. Counsel shall come to the Preliminary Confer-

ence fully prepared to report on these consultations and the agreements, if any, that have been reached.

C. If discovery demands have been served prior to the date set for the Preliminary Conference, counsel are encouraged to comply therewith.

D. Counsel appearing at the Preliminary Conference must be fully prepared to discuss any jurisdictional issues raised by the pleadings.

E. The Preliminary Conference will result in the issuance by the Court of a Scheduling Order that will include a schedule for the completion of discovery, a date for filing the note of issue, a date for disclosure of experts, and a date for summary judgment motions.

Rule 4. Motions

A. Motion Days; Filings

i. Motion practice in the Court of Claims is governed by sections 206.8 and 206.9 of the Uniform Rules for the Court of Claims. Motions before this Court are returnable on the second Wednesday of each month. No oral argument on a motion is required or permitted, except where ordered by the Court. If counsel wish to have oral argument, that request should be prominently typed at the top of the Notice of Motion or Cross–Motion, or the Affidavit in Opposition. In the event this Court grants the request, counsel will be contacted with a date and time for oral argument. Unless counsel are so contacted, counsel are to consider the request denied.

ii. Section 206.9(b) of the Uniform Rules for the Court of Claims requires that an original and two copies of motion papers be filed with the Chief Clerk in Albany. Section 206.5–a permits for filing by facsimile transmission. Courtesy copies of motion papers should not be sent to Chambers.

B. Motions Pertaining to Discovery Disputes Pursuant to the provisions of section 206.8 (b) of the Uniform Rules for the Court of Claims, a motion relating to discovery may not be made without first conferring with the Court. Parties who wish to make a discovery motion first must submit a written request to the Court explaining the nature of the dispute and the relief sought. Copies of the request shall simultaneously be delivered to all counsel in such manner that opposing counsel will receive it before or contemporaneously with the submission to Chambers. A conference with the Court or the Judge's Clerk shall be held in an effort to resolve the dispute before such a motion may be made.

C. Summary Judgment Motions; Statements of Material Facts

i. Any party, except a pro se Claimant, filing a motion for summary judgment, or partial summary judgment ("movant") shall submit with that motion a separate, concise statement in numbered paragraphs of the material facts as to which the moving party contends there is no genuine issue to be tried. The statement must contain only one factual assertion in each numbered paragraph. Each factual assertion must be followed by a citation to the portion(s) of the evidentiary record relied upon (for example, "Ms. Jones visited Los Angeles, California on August 3, 2003. Smith Affidavit at ¶ 6; Stone Deposition at page 43").

ii. The party opposing the motion, except a pro se Claimant ("opponent"), must accompany its opposition papers with a response to the movant's statement. The response must contain numbered paragraphs tracking those in the movant's statement, and must address all allegations of the movant's statement, detailing in each paragraph specifically what is admitted, what is disputed, and the basis for any dispute, citing specifically the portion(s) of the evidentiary record relied upon (for example, "Ms. Jones was in New York City at all times during the month of August 2003. Jones Affidavit at ¶ 10; Frank Deposition at pages 62–65"). Lack of relevance is not a valid reason for refusing to agree that a fact is or is not "in dispute." Each assertion must be a factual assertion, not a legal assertion.

iii. Responsive statements by the opponent may go on to make additional factual allegations in additional paragraphs numbered consecutively to follow those of the movant (i.e. do not begin renumbering at 1). If additional factual allegations are made by the opponent in these additional paragraphs, the movant then must file its own separate, concise statement in response to such additional factual allegations.

D. Post–Submission Papers Counsel are reminded that the presentation of papers or letters to the court after submission of a motion is not permitted. Absent express permission in advance, such materials will be returned unread.

Rule 5. Pre–Trial Procedures

A. Trial Preparation Conference (TPC)

i. A Trial Preparation Conference (TPC) will be conducted by this Court's Law Clerk in Chambers approximately two weeks prior to trial. The requirements for the TPC may vary, in the Court's discretion, to suit the type and complexity of the case. Instructions for the conduct of the TPC will be sent to counsel when the TPC and trial are scheduled.

ii. Typically, a TPC will address any matters pertaining to the trial and any information that the Court may deem necessary or desirable for the orderly and efficient administration of the claim including, without limitation:

Pre-marking for identification of exhibits (such exhibits will be returned to the party proffering them until they are presented at trial);

Pre-marking for identification of all excerpts from deposition testimony that each party intends to offer on their case in chief;

Identifying witnesses that each party intends to call on its case in chief, the order in which they will testify and the estimated length of their testimony;

Addressing any evidentiary issues likely to arise at trial;

Discussing the need for pre-trial briefs on any issue;

Arranging for any special requirements, such as an interpreter, audio-visual device, special accessibility, etc.

B. Judicial Subpoenas

Judicial Subpoenas requiring the Court's signature should be submitted to Chambers prior to the date of the TPC so that, if possible, they may be returned signed at the TPC.

C. Expert Disclosure

i. A party who has the burden of proof on a claim, cause of action, or defense shall serve its response to an expert demand pursuant to CPLR 3101(d) on the date ordered by the Court, but in no event less than 30 days before trial.

ii. Any amended or supplemental expert disclosure shall be allowed only with leave of the Court on good cause shown.

ii. Parties are expected to provide *meaningful* compliance with the requirements of CPLR 3101(d) pertaining to the subject matter of expert testimony, the substance of the facts and opinions on which the expert is expected to testify (including the basis and reasons therefore and the information the expert considered in forming the opinions) and the qualifications of the expert.

D. Exploration of Settlement

The Court encourages exploration of settlement at any stage of the litigation, including the pre-trial phase and will arrange for a facilitator for this purpose at the parties' request.

JUSTICE JEREMIAH MORIARTY

Rule 1. Communications with Chambers
Letters.

Except for routine scheduling and calendar matters, and situations requiring immediate attention, communications with Chambers shall be by letter, sent by regular or express mall, as necessary, addressed to: Judge Jeremiah J. Moriarty III, 130 South Elmwood Avenue, Third Floor, Suite 300, Buffalo, New York

14202, or delivered by hand to the receptionist on the 3rd floor, in an envelope addressed to Chambers. Copies of the letter shall be simultaneously delivered to all counsel in such a manner that opposing counsel will receive it before, or contemporaneously with, the submission to Chambers. Copies of correspondence between counsel shall not be sent to Chambers.

Telephone Calls.

For routine scheduling and calendar matters, and situations requiring immediate attention, call (716) 515–4820 between 9:00 A.M. and 5:00 P.M.

Faxes.

Faxes to Chambers are permitted so long as they are followed by a hard copy sent to Chambers, with copies simultaneously delivered to all counsel in such a manner that opposing counsel will receive it before, or contemporaneously with, the submission to Chambers. The fax number is (716) 515–4823.

Rule 2. Requests for Adjournments or Extensions of Time

All requests for adjournments of scheduled Court appearances, return dates of motions, or for an extension of time shall be made only after consultation with opposing counsel. The request to Chambers must indicate whether opposing counsel consents and propose a new date on which the parties have agreed. See, Disciplinary Rules of the Code of Professional Responsibility, Appendix A, Part III (22 NYCRR Part 1200). A request for an adjournment or an extension of time may be made by letter or telephone call to Chambers.

Rule 3. Appearance by Counsel

Counsel appearing at a conference with the Court must be fully familiar with the case, authorized to explore settlement, and able to enter into agreements pertaining to substantive and procedural issues in the case.

Whenever new counsel is substituted or the attorney of record designates trial counsel, written notice of such substitution shall be promptly filed with the Clerk of the Court in Albany and notice given to all parties in compliance with § 206.16 of the Uniform Rules for the Court of Claims.

Rule 4. Preliminary Conference

Counsel will be notified by Chambers of the date set for the Preliminary Conference provided for by § 206.10 of the Uniform Rules for the Court of Claims. Generally, this will be on the fourth Wednesday of a month.

Rule 5. Motions

Motion practice in the Court of Claims is governed by §§ 206.8 and 206.9 of the Uniform Rules for the Court of Claims. Motions before this Court are returnable on the second Wednesday of each month. In compliance with § 206.9 (c) of the Uniform Rules for the Court of Claims, no oral argument on a motion is required or permitted, except where ordered by the Court. If counsel wish to have oral argument, that request shall be prominently typed at the top of the Notice of Motion or Cross–Motion, or the Affidavit in Opposition. In the event this Court grants the request, counsel will be notified of the date and time for oral argument. Unless counsel are so notified, they should consider the request denied.

Section 206.9(b) of the Uniform Rules for the Court of Claims requires that an original and two copies of motion papers be filed with the Clerk of the Court in Albany. Section 206.5–a permits filing by facsimile transmission. Courtesy copies of motion papers should not be sent to Chambers.

Rule 6. Disclosure Motions

Pursuant to § 206.8(b) of the Uniform Rules for the Court of Claims, a motion relating to discovery may not be made without first conferring with the Court. Parties who wish to make a discovery motion must first submit a written request to the Court explaining the nature of the dispute and the relief sought. Copies of the request shall simultaneously be delivered to all counsel in such manner that opposing counsel will receive it before or contemporaneously with the submission to Chambers. A conference with the Court or the Judge's Clerk shall be held in an effort to resolve the dispute before such a motion may be made. If permission to file a disclosure motion is given by the Court, the Notice of Motion must include statement that permission has been granted.

Rule 7. Trial Preparation Conference

A Trial Preparation Conference (TPC) will be conducted by this Court's Law Clerk approximately three weeks prior to trial. The requirements for the TPC may vary, in the Court's discretion, to suit the type and complexity of the case. Instructions for the conduct of the TPC will be sent to counsel when the trial and the TPC are scheduled. Counsel who will try the case are required to be present at this conference.

Typically, a TPC will address any matter pertaining to the trial and the orderly and efficient administration of the claim including, without limitation:

At the TPC each counsel will exchange a written list of all non-opinion witnesses, opinion witnesses and deposition witnesses expected to be called at trial. Counsel should be prepared to discuss the order in which the witnesses will testify and the estimated length of their testimony. With respect to deposition testimony, the Court would prefer that the entire transcript be marked as an Exhibit. Counsel should prepare a list of page and line references when counsel intends to rely on only a portion of a particular deposition transcript.

At the TPC each counsel will exchange a written list of trial Exhibits and be prepared to pre-mark each

Exhibit for identification. The marked Exhibits will be returned to counsel at the conclusion of the TPC.

At the TPC each counsel should be prepared to discuss any evidentiary issues likely to arise at trial, and present copies of any pre-trial briefs, with the original being filed with the Clerk of the Court in Albany.

At the TPC each counsel should be prepared to discuss any special arrangements, such as interpreters, audio-visual equipment, special accessibility, etc.

Rule 8.   Judicial Subpoenas

Counsel are encouraged to issue their own trial subpoenas (CPLR 2302 [a]). Judicial Subpoenas requiring the Court's signature (CPLR 2302 [b] and 2307) should be submitted to Chambers sufficiently in advance so that they may be returned signed to counsel at the TPC.

Rule 9.   Settlements

Pursuant to the provisions of section 20–a of the Court of Claims Act, settlements are by written stipulation approved by the Court and filed with the Clerk of the Court in Albany. In the case of a claim brought by an administrator of an estate, or the representative of an infant or incompetent, counsel must submit appropriate documentation that the administrator or representative is authorized to settle the claim.

The Court encourages the exploration of settlements at any stage of the litigation. Counsel may call Chambers and arrange to meet with my law clerk to discuss this possibility.

Rule 10.   Discontinuances

The Court requires compliance with the provisions of CPLR 3217 governing discontinuance of a claim. In particular, a Court order will be necessary to discontinue a claim brought on behalf of an infant or incompetent or by an administrator of an estate. In the case of an infant or incompetent, counsel must submit an affirmation of counsel and an affidavit of the guardian explaining the reasons why the claim is being discontinued. In the case of an estate, counsel must submit documentation that the administrator is authorized to discontinue the claim.

FORMS

Form 1.   Claim

This form is unofficial and provided primarily for pro se litigants. It should be completed in accordance with the substantive pleading requirements of Court of Claims Act section 11(b).

State of New York
Court of Claims

_____,
_____,

                        Claimant(s)

                v.   **Claim**

_____,
_____,

                        Defendant(s)

1.   The post office address of the claimant (you) is _____.

2.   This claim arises from the acts or omissions of the defendant. Details of said acts or omissions are as follows (be specific): _____

3.   The place where the act(s) took place is (be specific): _____

4.   This claim accrued on the ___ day of _____, ___ at ___ o'clock.

5.   Identify the items of damage or injuries claimed to have been sustained:

_____

6.   **(Check appropriate box):**

☐ This Claim is served and filed within **90 days of accrual.**

OR

☐ **A Notice of Intention to File a Claim was served** on _____, which was within 90 days of accrual.

OR

☐ This is a claim by a correctional facility inmate to recover damages for injury to or loss of personal property and it is served and filed within **120 days of the exhaustion of claimant's administrative remedies.**

By reason of the foregoing, Claimant was damaged in the amount of $ _____, and Claimant demands judgment against the Defendant(s) for said amount.

_____

Claimant

VERIFICATION

STATE OF NEW YORK   ) ss:
COUNTY OF _____   )

_____, being duly sworn, deposes and says that deponent is the Claimant in the within action; that deponent has read the foregoing Claim and knows the contents thereof; that the same is true to deponent's own knowledge, except as to matters therein stated to be alleged upon information and belief, and that as to those matters, deponent believes it to be true.

_____

Sworn to before me this ___ day
of _____, ___.

_____

Notary Public, State of New York

SERVICE AND FILING INSTRUCTIONS

You must serve a copy of the claim in accordance with Court of Claims Act section 11(a) and you must file the original and two copies, with proof of service, and the filing fee of $50.00 or an application for waiver or reduction of the filing fee, with the Clerk of the Court of Claims.

FAILURE TO EFFECT PROPER AND TIMELY SERVICE AND FILING MAY RESULT IN DISMISSAL OF YOUR CLAIM

New York State Court of Claims

Justice Building, P.O. Box 7344

Albany, New York 12224

(518) 432–3411

Form 2.   Affidavit of Service

State of New York
Court of Claims _____

_____,

_____,

Claimant(s)

v.   **Affidavit of Service**

Claim No. _____

_____,

_____,   Assigned Judge:

Defendant(s)   _____

_____

State of New York   )
County of _____)   ss:

_____, being duly sworn, deposes and says:

I am over the age of eighteen (18) years, and on _____, 20 ___, I served a true copy of the attached _____ in the following manner:

(For a Claim):

☐ **by mailing it** in a sealed envelope, **certified mail, return receipt requested,** with postage prepaid, in a post office or official depository of the United States Postal Service within the State of New York, addressed to the last known address of the addressee as follows:

OR

☐ **by delivering it** to the following person(s) at the address(es) indicated below:

(For a Notice of Motion and Supporting Papers):

☐ by mailing them in a sealed envelope, with postage prepaid, in a post office or official depository of the United States Postal Service within the State of New York, addressed to the last known address of the addressee as follows:

_____
(Signature)

Sworn to before me this ___ day
of _____, 2000.

_____
Notary Public

Form 3.   Notice of Motion

State of New York
Court of Claims

_____

_____,

_____,

               Claimant(s)

       V.

_____,

_____,

       Defendant(s)

_____

NOTICE OF MOTION

Claim No. _____

Assigned Judge:

_____

Upon the affidavit of _____, sworn to on _____, 20___, and upon (list additional supporting papers if any):

the (claimant/defendant) will move this court on the ___ day of _____, 20___, for an order (briefly indicate relief requested):

The above-entitled action is for (briefly state nature of action, e.g., personal injury, medical malpractice, etc.).

Dated:

_____ *(print name)*

Attorney for Moving party or party *pro se*

Address:

Phone:

TO: _____ *(print name)*

Attorney for other party or party *pro se*

Address:

Phone:

(The original and two copies of all motion papers, including the notice of motion, supporting affidavits and exhibits, and an affidavit of service, must be filed with the Clerk of the Court — P.O. Box 7344 Capitol Station, Albany, New York 12224 — at least eight days prior to the return date of the motion. Motions should be made returnable any Wednesday. Unless permission for oral argument has been granted, all motions are on submission only — NO COURT APPEARANCE IS REQUIRED OR ALLOWED.)

Please refer to the Uniform Rules for the Court of Claims §§ 206.8 and 206.9

Form 4.   Filing Fee Waiver

State of New York
Court of Claims
_____

_____ ,
                    Claimant,

                                        Affidavit in Support of Application
                                        Pursuant to CPLR 1101 (d)

        v.

                                        Claim No.

The State of New York,
_____ ,

_____
                    Defendant(s).

State of New York   )
) ss:
County of _____)

I, _____, being duly sworn, hereby declare as follows:

1) I am the claimant in this proceeding, I am not an inmate in a federal, state or local correctional facility and I submit this affidavit to support my application for a waiver of the filing fee.

2) I currently receive income from the following sources (check appropriate boxes):

☐ Salary or wages (state employer's name and address and amount of take-home salary or wages:) _____

    ☐ Public assistance (amount): _____

    ☐ Social Security / SSI (amount): _____

    ☐ Other (source and amount): _____

3) In the past twelve months, I have received money from the following sources:

Business, profession or other self-employment	yes	no
Rent payments, interest or dividends	yes	no
Pensions, annuities or life insurance payments	yes	no
Disability or workers' compensation payments	yes	no
Gifts or inheritances	yes	no

(If your answer to any of the above is "yes," list each source of money, the amount received and what you expect to continue to receive) (over):

_____

_____

4) (check appropriate box):
    ☐ I do not own any cash or bank accounts.
    ☐ I own cash and bank accounts with a total value of _____.

5) I own the following property (real estate, bonds, stocks, securities, automobiles or any other property):

    ☐ NONE

    ☐ List property: Value:

    _____   _____

    _____   _____

    _____   _____

6) The following people are dependent on me for their support (list names of dependent(s), your relationship and how much you contribute to their support. If none, write "none."):

_____

_____

_____

7) I have no savings, property, assets or income other than what I have listed above.

8) I am unable to pay the filing fee necessary to prosecute this proceeding.

9) No other person who is able to pay the filing fee has a beneficial interest in the result of this proceeding.

10) The facts of my case are described in my claim and other papers filed with the court.

11) I have made no prior request for this relief in this case.

_____

(signature)

Sworn to before me this ___ day of _____, ___.

_____

Notary Public

Form 5. Filing Fee Reduction

State of New York
Court of Claims

_____

_____,

DIN No. _____, Claimant,

                Affidavit in Support of Application
                Pursuant to CPLR 1101 (f)

    v.

                Claim No.

The State of New York,

_____
              Defendant.

State of New York   )
) ss:
County of _____)

I, _____, being duly sworn, hereby declare as follows:

1) I am the claimant in this proceeding, I am an inmate in a federal, state or local correctional facility (state place of incarceration: _____), and I submit this affidavit to support my application for a reduction of the filing fee.

2) I currently receive income from the following sources, not including correctional facility wages:

_____

_____

3) I own the following valuable property (other than miscellaneous personal property):

☐ NONE

☐ List property: Value:

    _____   _____

    _____   _____

    _____   _____

    _____   _____

4) I have no savings, property, assets or income other than as listed above.

5) I am unable to pay the filing fee necessary to prosecute this proceeding.

6) No other person who is able to pay the filing fee has a beneficial interest in the result of this proceeding.

7) The facts of my case are described in my claim and other papers filed with the court.

8) I have made no other request for this relief in this case.

               _____
                    (signature)

Sworn to before me this ___ day of _____, ___.

_____

Notary Public

AUTHORIZATION

I, _____, inmate number _____, request and authorize the agency holding me in custody to send to the Clerk of the Court of Claims certified copies of the correctional facility trust fund account statement (or the institutional equivalent) for the past six months.

I further request and authorize the agency holding me in custody to deduct the filing fee from my correctional facility trust fund account (or the institutional equivalent) and to disburse those amounts as instructed by the Court of Claims.

This authorization is given in connection with this claim and shall apply to any agency into whose custody I may be transferred.

I UNDERSTAND THAT THE ENTIRE FILING FEE AS DETERMINED BY THE COURT OF CLAIMS WILL BE PAID IN INSTALLMENTS BY AUTOMATIC DEDUCTIONS FROM MY CORRECTIONAL FACILITY TRUST FUND ACCOUNT EVEN IF MY CASE IS DISMISSED.

_____
(signature)

Form 6.   Fax Cover Sheets

New York State Court of Claims - Filing by Fax Cover Sheet

(print form, complete, and fax with paper to be filed)

Date:

Claimant(s):

Claim Number (if any):

Paper Being Filed:

Name and Address of Filing Party or Attorney:

Telephone Number of Filing Party or Attorney:

Fax Number of Filing Party or Attorney:

Total Number of Pages of this Transmission, including Cover Page:

FOR CLAIM FILINGS ONLY

If you are filing a claim, you must either pay the $50.00 filing fee by completing the credit card authorization, or make an application for a waiver or reduction of the filing fee by submitting the appropriate affidavit.

CREDIT CARD AUTHORIZATION

I, _____, authorize the New York State Court of Claims to charge my credit card for the $50.00 filing fee required for filing the above claim.

☐ Master Card

☐ Visa

☐ Discover Card

_____   _____

Cardholder Name   Cardholder Signature

-      _____

Credit Card Number   Expiration Date

FAX to: 866–413–1069 (toll-free)

Form 7. Note of Issue

New York State Court of Claims, _____
District

Claim No. _____

Notice for trial

Filed by attorney for _____
Date claim filed _____
Date claim served _____
Date issue joined _____

Nature of action

Tort: Highway or motor vehicle negligence_____
Medical malpractice_____
Other tort (specify) _____
Appropriation claim _____
Small claim pursuant to article 6 EDPL_____
Public construction contract claim_____
Other contract_____
Other type of action (specify)_____

-against-

Amount demanded $ _____
Other relief _____

Attorney(s) for Claimant(s)
Office and P.O. Address:

Phone No.

Attorney(s) for Defendant(s)
Office and P.O. Address:

Phone No.

Insurance carrier(s):

NOTE: Clerk will not accept this note of issue unless accompanied by a certificate of readiness
and an affidavit of service on opposing counsel.

CERTIFICATE OF READINESS FOR TRIAL

(Items 1–6 must be checked)

		Complete	Waived	Not Required
1.	All pleadings served and filed.	....	....	....
2.	Bill of Particulars served and filed.	....	....	....
3.	Physical examinations completed.	....	....	....
4.	Medical reports filed and exchanged.	....	....	....
5.	Expert reports filed and exchanged.	....	....	....
6.	Discovery proceedings now known to be necessary completed.	....	....	....
7.	There are no outstanding requests for discovery.			
8.	There has been a reasonable opportunity to complete the foregoing proceedings.			
9.	There has been compliance with any order issued pursuant to section 206.10 of this part.			
10.	The action is ready for trial.			

Dated: _____

(Signature) _____

Attorney(s) for: _____

Office and P.O. address: _____

Form 8.   Court Notice Regarding Availability of
Electronic Filing (Court of Claims Cases)

THE STATE OF NEW YORK—COURT OF CLAIMS

_____x

Claimant(s),

-against-   Claim No. _____

Defendant(s).
_____x

COURT NOTICE REGARDING AVAILABILITY OF ELECTRONIC FILING
(COURT OF CLAIMS CASES)

PLEASE TAKE NOTICE that the undersigned party in the case captioned above intends that this matter proceed as an electronically-filed case in the New York State Courts Electronic Filing System ("NYSCEF") in accordance with the procedures described below. Filing and service of papers by electronic means cannot be made by a party nor electronic service be made upon a party unless that party has consented to use of the system. Within ten days after service of this Notice, each party served must indicate whether or not it consents to electronic filing and service through NYSCEF for this case.

General Information

In New York State, actions may be commenced and cases processed by means of the NYSCEF system in claims against the State of New York in the Court of Claims. At present, eligible claims are those brought in the Albany District. Electronic filing is also authorized for tort, commercial, and tax certiorari cases in the Supreme Court in 15 counties, any case type permitted by the Supreme Court in Erie and Broome County Supreme Courts, Surrogate's Court cases in Chautauqua, Erie, Monroe, Queens and Suffolk Counties and no-fault cases in New York City Civil Court.

Electronic filing offers significant benefits for attorneys and litigants, permitting papers to be filed with the court and served in a simple, convenient and expeditious manner. NYSCEF case documents are filed with the court by filing on the NYSCEF Website (www.nycourts.gov/efile), which can be done at any time of the day or night on any day of the week. Documents in Court of Claims cases are deemed filed when received by the NYSCEF server (with payment if required). Service between and among consenting users is effectuated by posting documents with the Website, which immediately sends automatic e-mail notice to all such parties. There is no fee to use the NYSCEF system, whether for filing, service, or consultation of the electronic docket, nor is there a charge to print documents from the docket. Normal filing fees must be paid, but this can be done by credit or debit card on-line. The use of NYSCEF is governed by Sections 206.5 and 206.5–aa of the Uniform Rules for the Court of Claims.

Instructions

1.   Service of this Notice Regarding Availability of Electronic Filing constitutes a statement of intent by the undersigned that the NYSCEF system be used in this case. When an action is being commenced by means of the NYSCEF system, this Notice must accompany service of the initiating papers.

2.   **Within ten days after service of this Notice,** the party served shall file with the court and serve on all parties the Consent to E–Filing, or, if the party does not

wish to consent, a declination of consent. Consent to electronic filing does not constitute an appearance in the action. If the party served is represented by an attorney who has already registered as a NYSCEF Filing User, that attorney may consent electronically on the NYSCEF site. Consent to NYSCEF is required of all current parties to the case in order for it to proceed as a NYSCEF matter, or, if fewer than all parties consent, where permitted by the court, NYSCEF may be used by and between or among consenting parties only.

3. Once parties agree that the case will be subject to NYSCEF, each participating attorney, unless already registered, must **PROMPTLY** complete a Filing User Registration form (see the "Forms" section of the Website) and submit it to the NYSCEF Resource Center (efile@courts.state.ny.us) in order to obtain the confidential Filing User Identification Number and Password necessary to use the system.

4. For additional information about NYSCEF, see the *User's Manual* and *Frequently Asked Questions* on the Website, contact the Court of Claims (518–432–3484) or the NYSCEF Resource Center (646–386–3033 or efile@courts.state.ny.us).

Dated: _____   _____ (Name)
                                   _____ (Firm)
                                   _____ (Address)
                                   _____
                                   _____ (Phone)
                                   _____ (Fax)
                                   _____ (E–Mail)

                    Attorney(s) for _____

Form 9.   Consent to E–Filing Court of Claims Case

THE STATE OF NEW YORK—COURT OF CLAIMS

_____x

                              Claimant(s),   Claim No. _____

-against-

                                                        CONSENT TO E–FILING
                                                        COURT OF CLAIMS CASE*

                              Defendant(s).
_____x

    I, _____, am an attorney for a party or a self-represented party in the above-captioned action, and I consent to the use of the New York State Courts Electronic Filing System ("NYSCEF") in this case. I further consent to be bound by the service and filing provisions of the NYSCEF Rules (Sections 206.5 and 206.5–aa of the Uniform Rules for the Court of Claims) and will comply with the procedures of the NYSCEF system, which are reflected in the _User's Manual_ approved by the Chief Administrator of the Courts and posted on the NYSCEF website.

    Pursuant to the Rules, I have, or will promptly hereafter, set forth in my NYSCEF registration application form an e-mail address that shall constitute the E–Mail Service Address of Record (Primary Address) for the purpose of electronic service of each filing under the Rules.**

_____   _____
Signature   Law Firm Name

                                           _____
_____   Address
Print or Type Name

Attorney for _____
              (Identify party or parties)

                                           _____
                                           Phone

                                           _____
                                           E–Mail

    * Under the Rules, consent of parties is required for filing and service by or upon those parties through NYSCEF. If an attorney has previously registered as a NYSCEF Filing User, the consent may be filed and served by means of the NYSCEF system.

    ** Although under the Rules electronic service is effectuated only through the E–Mail Service Address of Record (Primary Address), additional notice of filings may be obtained through the listing of E–Mail General Addresses of Record. Such addresses may be listed on the registration application and may be recorded in the Profile Section of the NYSCEF system. See www.nycourts.gov/efile.

FILING RULES

Doc. 1.   Fax Filing Instructions

The Court of Claims accepts the filing of papers, including claims, by facsimile transmission. Any papers that are required to be filed with the Clerk of the Court may be filed via fax, provided that the paper does not exceed 50 pages in length. The filed paper should be accompanied by a cover sheet setting forth the following information:

- the nature of the paper being filed
- the claim number (if previously assigned)
- the name and address of the filing party or attorney
- the telephone number of the filing party or attorney
- the fax number that may receive a return transmission
- the total number of pages, including cover sheet, being filed

You may complete online the Fax Cover Sheet (a fillable OmniForm document), print it and use it, or you may use your own cover sheet providing it contains the above information. You may also download the Fax Cover Sheet (PDF), print it, and use it.

If you are filing a Claim, you must either pay the $50.00 required filing fee, by completing the Credit Card Authorization contained on our Fax Cover Sheet (PDF), or submit an application for a waiver of the fee, or an application for a reduction of the fee (for correctional facility inmates).

Please read Court of Claims Rule 206.5–a for complete details on what and how to file and what to expect in return.

The fax number to send papers for filing is 866–413–1069 (toll-free).

Doc. 1.   E–Filing: Filing by Electronic Means

As part of the New York State Courts Electronic Filing System (NYSCEF), certain claims in the Court of Claims may be filed electronically at the NYSCEF web page, subject to the following limitations:

- Only tort claims (claims seeking damages for personal injury or property damage) against the State of New York that accrued in the Court's Albany District—claims accruing in the following counties: Albany, Essex, Rensselaer, Ulster, Clinton, Franklin, Saratoga, Warren, Columbia, Greene, Schenectady or Washington—may be filed electronically.
- All papers must be in Adobe .pdf format to be filed electronically.
- In order to file a document electronically, as an attorney or a self-represented (pro se) litigant, it is necessary to register as a filing user on the NYSCEF page.
- When you file a claim electronically, it will be necessary to pay the $50.00 filing fee via credit card, or in person at the Clerk's office.
- If you file a claim, or any subsequent document, via NYSCEF, DO NOT send courtesy copies to the clerk's office or to judge's chambers unless so directed by the Judge.
- Section 11(a) of the Court of Claims Act provides: "a. (i) The claim shall be filed with the clerk of the court; and, except in the case of a claim for the appropriation by the state of lands, a copy shall be served upon the attorney general within the times hereinbefore provided for filing with the clerk of the court either personally or by certified mail, return receipt requested, or, where authorized by rule of the chief administrator of the courts and upon consent of the attorney general, by facsimile transmission or electronic means, as defined in subdivision (f) of rule twenty-one hundred three of the civil practice law and rules, in such manner as may be provided by rule of court." In any case, an affidavit of service must be filed, electronically, with the court.
- Information and instructions on how to serve the Attorney General electronically may be found at this site.
- You must serve and file, with the claim, a Court Notice Regarding Availability of Electronic Filing. Complete the form and print it out (you will not yet know the claim number) and then serve and file it.
- If you have a pending tort claim in the Albany District and you wish to have that claim be subject to NYSCEF, complete the Court Notice Regarding Availability of Electronic Filing form, serve it on all other parties and file it with the court.
- Use the Consent to E–Filing form.

Please read all of the information on the NYSCEF page for a complete explanation of NYSCEF and instructions on how to proceed.

View the text of Court of Claims Rule 206.5–aa and section 202.5–b of the Rules of the Chief Administrator which together, set forth the procedure for Filing by Electronic means in the Court of Claims.

HOUSING COURT RULES

Westlaw Electronic Research

These rules may be searched electronically on Westlaw® in the NY–RULES database; updates to these rules may be found on Westlaw in NY–RULESUP-DATES. For search tips and a summary of database content, consult the Westlaw Scope Screens for each database.

Form
CIV–LT–47. Affidavit of Service of Judgment With Notice of Entry.

HP's
CIV–LT–66. Instructions for the Service of an in Person (Pro Se) Order to Show Cause and Verified Petition (H.P.).
CIV–LT–61. Inspection Request.

MOTIONS AND ORDERS TO SHOW CAUSE
CIV–LT–65. Instructions for the Service of an in Person (Pro Se) Order to Show Cause and Affidavit in Support.
CIV–LT–13A. Affidavit in Opposition.
CIV–LT–13B. Reply Affidavit.
CIV–LT–19. Affidavit of Service of Order to Show Cause and Affidavit in Support.
CIV–LT–18. Affidavit in Support of an Order for Withdrawal of Funds.
CIV–LT–13. Affidavit in Support of an Order to Show Cause (Generic).
CIV–LT–10. Affidavit in Support of Order to Show Cause to Restore to the Calendar.
CIV–LT–11. Affidavit in Support of Order to Show Cause to Restore to Possession.
CIV–LT–22. Affidavit in Support of an Order to Show Cause to Restore to the Calendar for A Compliance Hearing and for Assessment of Civil Penalties (H.P.).

JUDGES' RULES
NEW YORK COUNTY
JUSTICE TIMMIE ERIN ELSNER
Rule
1. Resolution Part Rules.
2. Trial Part Rules.

JUSTICE CHERYL J. GONZALES
1. Resolution Part Rules.
2. Part Rules.

JUSTICE ARLENE HAHN
1. Resolution Part Rules.
2. Trial Part Rules.

JUSTICE SHELDON HALPRIN
1. Part Rules.

JUSTICE DAVID KAPLAN
1. Resolution Part Rules.
2. Trial Part Rules.

JUSTICE SABRINA KRAUS
1. Resolution Part Rules.

JUSTICE RUBEN ANDRES MARTINO
1. Part Rules.

JUSTICE JEAN SCHNEIDER
1. Resolution Part Rules.
2. Trial Part Rules.

JUSTICE MICHELLE SCHREIBER
1. Resolution Part Rules.
2. Trial Part Rules.

Rule
JUSTICE BRENDA SPEARS
1. Part Rules.

JUSTICE JOHN HENRY STANLEY
1. Resolution Part Rules.

JUSTICE PETER WENDT
1. Resolution Part Rules.
2. Trial Part Rules.

BRONX COUNTY
JUSTICE PAUL ALPERT
1. Resolution Part Rules.
2. Trial Part Rules.

JUSTICE MARIAN C. DOHERTY
1. Resolution Part Rules.
2. Trial Part Rules.

JUSTICE JERALD KLEIN
1. Resolution Part Rules.
2. Trial Part Rules.

JUSTICE LYDIA LAI
1. Resolution Part Rules.
2. Trial Part Rules.

JUSTICE JAYA MADHAVAN
1. Resolution Part Rules.
2. Trial Part Rules.

JUSTICE KEVIN McCLANAHAN
1. Resolution Part Rules.
2. Trial Part Rules.

JUSTICE EARDELL RASHFORD
1. Resolution Part Rules.
2. Trial Part Rules.

JUSTICE JOSE RODRIGUEZ
1. Resolution Part Rules.
2. Trial Part Rules.

JUSTICE ELIZABETH TAO
1. Resolution Part Rules.
2. Trial Part Rules.

JUSTICE LOUIS VILLELLA
1. Resolution Part Rules.
2. Trial Part Rules.

KINGS COUNTY
JUSTICE MARC FINKELSTEIN
1. Part Rules.

JUSTICE ANTHONY J. FIORELLA, JR.
1. Resolution Part Rules.
2. Trial Part Rules.

JUSTICE THOMAS FITZPATRICK
1. Resolution Part Rules.
2. Trial Part Rules.

JUSTICE GEORGE M. HEYMANN
1. Resolution Part Rules.
2. Trial Part Rules.

Rule

JUSTICE INEZ HOYOS

1. Resolution Part Rules.
2. Trial Part Rules.

JUSTICE JOHN S. LANSDEN

1. Resolution Part Rules.
2. Trial Part Rules.

JUSTICE LAURIE LAU

1. Resolution Part Rules.
2. Trial Part Rules.

JUSTICE GARY MARTON

1. Resolution Part Rules.
2. Trial Part Rules.

JUSTICE MARIA MILIN

1. Resolution Part Rules.
2. Trial Part Rules.

JUSTICE ELEONORA OFSHTEIN

1. Part Rules.

JUSTICE BRUCE E. SCHECKOWITZ

1. Resolution Part Rules.
2. HP Part Rules.

JUSTICE MARCIA SIKOWITZ

1. Resolution Part Rules.
2. Trial Part Rules.

Rule

QUEENS COUNTY
JUSTICE GILBERT BADILLO

1. Resolution Part Rules.
2. Trial Part Rules.

JUSTICE RONNI BIRNBAUM

1. Resolution Part Rules.
2. Trial Part Rules.

JUSTICE ANNE KATZ

1. Resolution Part Rules.
2. Trial Part Rules.

JUSTICE ULYSSES B. LEVERETT

1. Resolution Part Rules.
2. Trial Part Rules.

JUSTICE MICHAEL J. PINCKNEY

1. Resolution Part Rules.
2. Trial Part Rules.

JUSTICE MARIA RESSOS

1. Resolution Part Rules.
2. Trial Part Rules.

JUSTICE DEIGHTON WAITHE

1. Resolution Part Rules.
2. Trial Part Rules.

RICHMOND COUNTY
JUSTICE MARINA MUNDY

1. Part Rules.

NONPAYMENT PROCEEDINGS

Doc. 1. Starting a Case

In General

A nonpayment case is brought by the landlord to collect unpaid rent. A tenant may be evicted for non-payment of rent.

If you would like to watch a video on how to bring a nonpayment case in the housing court, go to Collecting Rent [1].

The Demand for Rent

Before the case can be started, the landlord or someone working for the landlord, must demand the overdue rent from the tenant and warn the tenant that if the rent is not paid, the tenant can be evicted. The landlord may tell the tenant this in person or in writing. If the tenant is told in person, the "demand" must be specific and include the months and amount due. For example, the landlord might say, "You owe the rent for June, July and August at $900.00 per month, for a total of $2700.00. Are you going to pay?"

However, If the lease requires that this kind of demand be given in writing, then it must be in writing. If it is in writing, the rent demand must be delivered to the tenant at least three days before the day the court papers are served, unless the lease requires more days.

If you are a landlord with a one or two family house, or a building with fewer than five apartments, or own a coop or condo, the New York State Courts Access to Justice Program has a free DIY (Do-It-Yourself) computer program to help you make a written Rent Demand. Or you can buy a Rent Demand form at a legal stationary store, like Blumberg.

For more information, refer to Rent Demand [2].

Starting the Case

If the tenant does not pay the rent after the demand is made, the landlord may file a nonpayment petition (sometimes called a "dispossess") against the tenant in Housing Court. Landlords who do not have a lawyer, who own a one or two family house, or a building with fewer than five apartments, or own a coop or condo, can use the New York State Courts

Access to Justice Program's free and easy DIY (Do-It-Yourself) Form program to make a nonpayment petition that is ready to print, serve and file to start a case. This program is only for un-regulated housing. There is a fee to start the case.

Or, the landlord may use forms of his or her own, or may buy the following forms at a legal stationary store:

1. Petition

2. Notice of Petition

3. Service copies

4. Postcard

The nonpayment petition must contain:

1) the interest of the petitioner in the premises;

2) the interest of the respondent in the premises and his/her relationship with the petitioner;

3) a description of the premises;

4) the facts upon which the proceeding is based;

5) the relief sought.

The Rules of the Court also require a petitioner to plead whether the building is a multiple dwelling, and if so, that there is a currently effective registration statement on file with the office of code enforcement, the multiple dwelling registration number along with the name and address of the managing agent.

The landlord must fill out the forms (see Requirements for Nonpayment Petitions below) and make photocopies, then bring the forms to the Landlord–Tenant Clerk's Office to the cashier's window to buy an index number. Payment may be made by cash, certified check or money order. Make the money order or certified check payable to the "Clerk of the Civil Court." Go to Locations [3] to find out where to go in your county. Refer to Court Fees [4] to find out the cost of starting the case.

The clerk will stamp the index number on the original forms and will keep the Petition. The clerk will return the Notice of Petition with the index number stamped on the front. The landlord must make sure the tenant receives a copy of the Notice of Petition and the Petition in the manner required by law. Refer to Service of the Notice of Petition and Petition to learn more.

After serving the papers, the landlord must bring back the original Notice of Petition with the notarized affidavit of service on the back filled out. In addition, the landlord must bring in the stamped postcard so that the court can mail it to the tenant. After the tenant answers, the court will mail a postcard to the landlord stating the date, time, and place of the court hearing. To learn more about answering the petition, go to Answering a Case, post. If the tenant does not answer, and the rent is still not paid, the landlord can apply for a default judgment based on the tenant's failure to answer.

Requirements for a Nonpayment Petition

1. The petition must be brought by a person who has a right to recover the property. This may be a landlord, a primary tenant, a roommate who holds a lease in his or her name, an estate, etc.

2. The respondent must be identified. This is done by providing the name of the respondent, although there might be unidentified undertenants who are styled as John and/or Jane Does.

3. The nature of the agreement by which the respondent entered into the tenancy must be provided. This could be a lease or a month to month tenancy, and must have some specificity as to when it began.

4. The amount of rent to be collected as well as the day on which the rent is to be paid.

5. The location of the premises. The petition must be brought in the county where the building is located.

6. There must be a specific allegation as to the rent due. This normally requires that the amounts due for each rental period be specified. If any other money is due, say for taxes as "additional rent," or for late or attorney fees, these must be itemized separately and totaled.

7. There must be an allegation as to the rent demand, either that it was oral, or in writing. If in writing, the demand and an affidavit of service may be submitted to the court.

8. There must be an allegation that the respondent continues to occupy the premises. If the respondent has left the premises, a nonpayment proceeding may not be maintained.

9. There must be a statement that either the premises are not subject to rent regulation, and the reason; or, that the premises are subject to rent regulation, and the kind of rent regulation that applies.

10. The petition must specify whether the premises is a multiple dwelling or not. If it is, the name and address of the managing agent and the multiple dwelling registration must be supplied.

11. There must be a clause specifying the relief requested. This normally must state whether the premises is used by the respondent as a residence or not, the amount of money for which judgment is requested, and the interest date, if interest is sought, as well as a request that the judgment be granted and a warrant of eviction be issued.

12. The petition must be signed by the petitioner.

13. The petition must be verified. The verification may be made by different persons on behalf of the petitioner, or by the petitioner him or herself if a

natural person. The verification must be affirmed or sworn to and notarized.

Going to Court

If you received a postcard from the court with a court date you must appear in the courtroom on that date. You can get Directions if you do not know how to get to the courthouse. Get there early, since you will need to go through a metal detector before entering the courthouse. You should bring all your evidence in support of your claim or defense. The first courtroom you go to is called a "Resolution Part." To learn more about what happens there, refer to the Resolution Part.

1 http://www.courts.state.ny.us/courts/nyc/housing/startingcase.shtml

2 http://www.courts.state.ny.us/courts/nyc/housing/pdfs/improper rentdemand.pdf

3 http://www.courts.state.ny.us/courts/nyc/housing/locations2.shtml

4 http://www.courts.state.ny.us/courts/nyc/housing/fees.shtml

Doc. 2. Answering a Case

Answering: In General

If you have received a petition from the civil court, you must appear and answer within the time period provided for in the notice of petition. If you have received a postcard from the court indicating that papers have been filed asking the court to evict you from your residence, you must also answer. You should bring a copy of the court papers you received, or the postcard from the court, when you come to answer.

If you are an individual, you may answer either orally or in writing. Any individual named as respondent, or any person in possession or claiming possession of the premises, may submit an answer. Your answer should include any legal or equitable defense or explanation that you might have. You may also make a counterclaim in response to a petition at that time.

If you do not answer and appear, the party suing you may be able to enter a possessory judgment and/or a money judgment against you. The petitioner may be able to evict you, as well as garnish your wages or levy on your bank account. If you received a notice from a marshal or a sheriff you may be able to vacate your default and/or stop the eviction. You can learn more about this and other housing court procedures by reading our Legal and Procedural Information sections.

The time to answer the petition and the procedures for answering a nonpayment petition and a holdover petition differ and are set forth below. You should bring a copy of the court papers you received, or the postcard from the court, when you come to answer. The clerk will ask you to show some form of identification.

Answering a Nonpayment Petition

If you are served with a nonpayment petition you must answer within 5 days after you have received the notice of petition. To find out where to answer in your county, refer to Locations [1]. The clerk will set a date for trial between 3 days and 8 days after you answer. You may answer orally or in writing.

To answer orally, you must come to Court and speak to a clerk at the counter who will check off a Landlord/Tenant Answer In Person form based upon what you tell him or her. You should tell the clerk if you are in the military or a dependent of someone in the military. The Answer in Person form contains a list of possible defenses that may or may not apply to you. After the clerk completes this form you will get a duplicate copy of it. Check to make sure that your answer was correctly recorded by the clerk before you leave the counter. If the answer is not correct, tell the clerk. Bring your copy of this form and all court papers to court on the hearing date.

View information on Answering a Notice of Petition And Petition (CIV-LT-92). To read more about the defenses listed on the Answer in Person form, go to the Housing Fact Sheets. If you live in a rent stabilized or NYCHA apartment, you can use the interactive Nonpayment Answer Program to learn about your defenses and help you prepare to answer a nonpayment petition in person. You can also watch a community seminar about Defenses to a Nonpayment Proceeding.

You may answer in writing by using a free Civil Court form, or your own form. You may come to the clerk's office and request a Landlord/Tenant Answer In Writing And Verification form from the clerk at the counter. You will be given two duplicate copies of this form. You may also download the form. You can download the Answer in Writing Instructions.

The procedure for a written answer is more complicated and if not done properly, your answer may be rejected. You must fill out the written answer form and then serve the form on the other side. If you do not prepare your written answer in court, the procedure is slightly different. Go to Serving Your Written Answer for instructions on how to serve the answer correctly. Bring your copy of the answer and all court papers to court on the hearing date.

Answering a Holdover Petition

If you are served with a holdover petition, generally you must answer orally or in writing in the courtroom on the date of the hearing. However, if the petitioner serves the notice of petition at least 8 days prior to the return date, the notice of petition may ask you to answer at least 3 days before the hearing date. To find out where to answer in your county, go to Locations [1].

If you answer orally by coming to the court and speaking to a clerk at the counter, the clerk will indorse your answer on the court file. You should tell the clerk if you are in the military or a dependent of someone in the military. You may also answer in writing by coming to court and asking the clerk for a Landlord/Tenant Answer In Writing And Verification form, or you may submit your own written answer. You may also download the Answer in Writing civil court form. You can download the Answer in Writing Instructions. The procedure for a written answer is more complicated and if not done properly, your answer may be rejected. You must fill out the written answer form and then serve the form on the other side. If you do not prepare your written answer in court, the procedure is slightly different. Continue reading below for instructions on how to serve the answer correctly. Bring your copy of the answer and all court papers to court on the hearing date.

Serving Your Written Answer

After you have completed a written answer, you must serve the petitioner by following the instructions below.

1. Make two copies of the completed written answer.

2. Have someone over the age of 18, who is not a party in this action, mail a copy of the written answer by regular mail to the attorney for the petitioner or to the petitioner directly only if there is no attorney.

3. You may also have someone over the age of 18, who is not a party in the action, personally deliver the written answer to the petitioner's attorney, or the petitioner directly only if there is no attorney.

4. Next you need an affidavit swearing that the written answer was served. Download the free Affidavit of Service civil court form.

5. Prepare an Affidavit of Service for the service on the petitioner and have the person who served the written answer sign the Affidavit of Service in front of a notary.

6. Attach the original Affidavit of Service to the original written answer.

7. For Nonpayment cases, return the written answer and affidavit of service to the Court within five days of receiving the notice of petition.

8. For Holdover cases, if the notice of petition requires you to answer prior to the hearing date, you must return the original of the answer and affidavit of service in the court at least three days before the hearing date. Otherwise, you may bring the written answer to court on the hearing date.

9. Keep a copy for your records and bring all your papers with you when you come to court for the hearing date.

Jury Demand

You can also request that your case be tried before a jury. In a jury trial, the jury, not the judge, makes the decision and a judgment is entered based on the verdict reached by the jury.

If you wish to make a jury demand, you should request a jury trial when you answer the petition. You can tell the clerk and pay the jury demand fee. Go to Court Fees [2] to learn the amount of the fee. If you cannot afford to pay the fee, you may be entitled to have the fee waived. Refer to Poor Person's Relief to learn more.

Keep in mind that the Judge may later decide that you are not entitled to a jury trial because you gave up your right in your lease. Most leases include an agreement to give up a right to a jury trial.

You can also request a jury demand at a later time. However, the judge may deny your request, if you wait too long. For more information on filing a late jury demand, go to Timeliness of Jury Demands to read the Civil Court Directive on the subject.

Inspection Request

If you have a repair problem in your apartment or building, you should ask for an inspection from the clerk or the Judge the first time you are in court or as soon after that as possible. An inspector from the Department of Housing Preservation and Development will come to your home and make a report to the court. The report will help you prove that there are bad conditions that need repair.

If you request an inspection, you may get a date for the inspection and a date to return to court. You will be asked to make a list of the repairs needed. Make sure to include every problem in each room of your apartment and in the public areas of the building. To view a copy of the Tenant's Request for Inspection, make an Inspection Request. If you fail to include a problem or area on the inspection request form, the inspector may refuse to look at it.

On the day of the inspection, it is important that someone be home to let the inspector in. Be sure to show the inspector all of the problems you listed.

Traverse Hearing

If you did not receive a copy of the notice of petition and petition, or you believe that the papers were not served properly, that is a defense to the case and should be included in your answer. Refer to Service of the Notice of Petition and Petition to learn more about the proper way to deliver legal papers. If you raise this defense, the judge may decide to set a date for a hearing, called a traverse hearing, to decide whether the service of the court papers was proper.

At the traverse hearing, the landlord's process server may be asked to tell under oath how he or she served you with the court papers. You will have the right to ask the process server questions, to testify yourself, and to call witnesses to explain that the papers were not delivered properly.

If the judge finds that the service of the papers were not served properly, the case will be dismissed without prejudice. The landlord may start the case over again by giving you a new set of papers. If you receive another set of papers, you must come to court and answer them again.

1 http://www.courts.state.ny.us/courts/nyc/housing/locations2.shtml

2 http://www.courts.state.ny.us/courts/nyc/housing/fees.shtml

Doc. 3. To Proceed as a Poor Person

If you do not have enough money to pay the court costs and fees of the proceeding, you may ask the court to permit you to proceed without having to pay the court costs. These costs include the charges for starting an HP proceeding, filing a petition to be restored to possession, filing a jury demand, and appealing a court ruling.

Your application for "poor person's relief" is made by motion and must be supported by an affidavit which must:

1) set forth the amount and sources of your income, and list your property with its value;

2) state that you are unable to pay the costs, fees and expenses necessary to prosecute or defend the action or proceeding or to maintain or respond to the appeal;

3) indicate the nature of the action or proceeding;

4) provide sufficient facts so that the merit of your claims can be determined;

5) indicate whether any other person would benefit from any award in your case, and if so, whether that person is unable to pay such costs fees and expenses.

You may obtain the affidavit from the court or you may download the civil court form now by clicking on Poor Person's Relief[1]. To find out where to make your application in your county, click on Locations[2].

If the judge approves your application, the judge will sign an order listing which fees and costs you do not have to pay. This order may also contain directions that if you recover any money in your lawsuit, the money shall be paid to the Clerk of the Court which may then recover the fees and costs which you previously could not afford to pay.

If you are starting the case, you may make your application to the court without notifying anyone else. Once your application has been approved the judge may order that a copy of your application and the order granting it be mailed to the New York City Corporation Counsel's office at 100 Church Street, New York, New York 10007. If the case has already begun and you are applying for fees to be waived, you must serve all parties and the New York City Corporation Counsel's office.

1 http://www.courts.state.ny.us/courts/nyc/housing/forms/Poor PersonsRelief.pdf

2 http://www.courts.state.ny.us/courts/nyc/housing/locations2.shtml

Doc. 4. Service of the Notice of Petition and Petition to Start a Nonpayment or Holdover Proceeding

The procedure for service of the papers to start a residential landlord-tenant proceeding is set forth below. For further information on service, you may refer to the Real Property Actions and Proceedings Law section 735.

Who May Serve

1. You may NOT serve the papers yourself.

2. Anyone over the age of 18 years, and NOT A PARTY to the action may serve the papers.

3. If you wish, you may hire a Process Server to serve the papers. See the yellow pages of the phone book to locate one.

When to Serve

Papers may not be served on Sunday. Papers may be served during three time periods:

Non-working hours: 6:00 a.m. — 7:59 a.m.

Working hours: 8:00 a.m. — 6:00 p.m.

Non-working hours: 6:01 p.m. — 10:30 p.m.

How to Serve

A copy of the papers shall be served on the respondent Personally or by Substituted delivery. If neither of those methods can be achieved after a reasonable application, the papers may be served by Conspicuous Place delivery:

a. *Personal delivery:* A copy of the papers may be served by giving it to the respondent in his or her hand. The papers can be handed to the respondent anywhere.

b. *Substituted delivery:* A copy of the papers may be given to any individual who answers the apartment door as long as he or she resides or is employed in the apartment and is of an appropriate age and has appropriate judgment to receive the papers. By the next business day, the server must mail one copy of the papers by regular mail and one copy by certified mail. Keep the certified mail receipts.

c. *Conspicuous Place delivery:* If the server is unsuccessful on the first try to serve the papers either by personal delivery or substituted service, then he or she must make a second attempt during a different time period (see time periods above). For example, if no one is home during working hours, the server can return at 7:30 p.m. during non-working hours. After two unsuccessful attempts have been made to serve the person at home either by personal delivery or substituted service, the server may then use conspicuous place delivery. This is also known as "nail and mail."

This delivery requires that a copy of the papers be affixed to the door of the actual residence of the respondent or be slipped under the entrance door of the apartment. By the next business day, the server must mail one copy of the papers by regular mail and one copy by certified mail to the respondent. Keep the certified mail receipts.

After the summons is served, the person who served the papers must fill out an affidavit of service (see below).

Affidavit of Service

1. After the COPY of the notice of petition and petition has been served, the person who served it shall fill out an Affidavit of Service. You may download the form now by clicking on Affidavit of Service [1], or you may obtain a form from the Court Clerk. The Affidavit of Service shall include a description of the color of skin, hair color, approximate age, approximate weight and height, and other identifying features of the person served.

2. After the Affidavit of Service has been filled out the server shall sign it before a Notary Public, and have it notarized.

3. The completed Affidavit of Service, must be returned to the Clerk's Office within 3 days of the personal delivery or mailing. Make copies of the affidavit of service for your records prior to filing it with the court.

4. You should bring a copy of the papers with you to court on the hearing date.

[1] http://www.courts.state.ny.us/courts/nyc/housing/forms/Poor PersonsRelief.pdf

Doc. 5. Service Under RPAPL Sec. 735

735. Manner of service; filing; when service complete

1. Service of the notice of petition and petition shall be made by personally delivering them to the respondent; or by delivering to and leaving personally with a person of suitable age and discretion who resides or is employed at the property sought to be recovered, a copy of the notice of petition and petition, if upon reasonable application admittance can be obtained and such person found who will receive it; or if admittance cannot be obtained and such person found, by affixing a copy of the notice and petition upon a conspicuous part of the property sought to be recovered or placing a copy under the entrance door of such premises; and in addition, within one day after such delivering to such suitable person or such affixing or placement, by mailing to the respondent both by registered or certified mail and by regular first class mail,

(a) If a natural person, as follows: at the property sought to be recovered, and if such property is not the place of residence of such person and if the petitioner shall have written information of the residence address of such person, at the last residence address as to which the petitioner has such information, or if the

petitioner shall have no such information, but shall have written information of the place of business or employment of such person, to the last business or employment address as to which the petitioner has such information; and

(b) if a corporation, joint-stock or other unincorporated association, as follows: at the property sought to be recovered, and if the principal office or principal place of business of such corporation, joint stock or other unincorporated association is not located on the property sought to be recovered, and if the petitioner shall have written information of the principal office or principal place of business within the state, at the last place as to which petitioner has such information, or if the petitioner shall have no such information but shall have written information of any office or place of business within the state, to any such place as to which the petitioner has such information. Allegations as to such information as may affect the mailing address shall be set forth either in the petition, or in a separate affidavit and filed as part of the proof of service.

2. The notice of petition, or order to show cause, and petition together with proof of service thereof shall be filed with the court or clerk thereof within three days after;

(a) personal delivery to respondent, when service has been made by that means, and such service shall be complete immediately upon such personal delivery; or

(b) mailing to respondent, when service is made by the alternatives above provided, and such service shall be complete upon the filing of proof of service.

Doc. 6. Stopping an Eviction

If you have received a notice from a marshal that you are to be evicted you must come to court as soon as possible. This is a very serious matter, and you must take care of it immediately. If you do not take care of it, the marshal may remove you and your property from the apartment. You can call the marshal's office to find out if the marshal has scheduled your eviction yet. The phone number for the marshal's office is on the notice.

Bring the notice and any other papers that you have received from your landlord, including any rent receipts, to the court. To find out where to go in your county to try to stop or delay your eviction, click on Locations [1].

At the courthouse you will fill out an affidavit in support of an Order to Show Cause. The type of affidavit depends on whether you ever answered or appeared in the case. You will fill out an affidavit explaining why you should not be evicted.

If you never answered a petition and the petitioner obtained a default judgment against you, you will fill out an Affidavit In Support of An Order To Show

Cause to Vacate A Judgment Based Upon Failure To Answer. In the affidavit you will explain the reason you did not answer the petition — for example — you never received a copy of it. You will also explain your defense to the proceeding — for example — you paid all the rent. You can use the free computer program to make your Affidavit in Support of an Order to Show Cause.

If you answered a petition, and a court order or stipulation resulted, or you did not appear in the courtroom and a default judgment was entered, you will fill out an Affidavit in Support of an Order to Show Cause To Vacate A Judgment. If you need more time to pay a judgment or an order, indicate how much time you need and why in the affidavit.

The clerk will send your papers, along with the court file to the judge who handled your case. You may have to wait in the clerk's office or to go to the courtroom where your papers have been sent. The Judge may sign your order to show cause, but may not stop the eviction until the case can be heard. The Judge may also sign the order to show cause, but place conditions, such as paying the rent or bringing proof of funds to pay to court. You must read the order to show cause carefully.

If the judge signs your order to show cause, you must then serve the papers on the other side according to the directions in the order to show cause. You must return to the courthouse on the hearing date with proof of service at the time and in the room designated on the Order to Show Cause.

If the judge declines to sign your order to show cause, or signs it upon conditions that you do not agree with, you may challenge this determination by going to the Appellate Term. You may click on Locations [1] to find the address of the Appellate Term in your county.

[1] http://www.courts.state.ny.us/courts/nyc/housing/locations2.shtml

Doc. 7. Resolution Part

A Resolution Part is a courtroom where the landlord and tenant can discuss their differences before a Judge or Court Attorney to see if an agreement can be reached to settle the dispute. You may also be there for a motion or an order to show cause.

A Resolution Part is presided over by a Judge, who is assisted by two court attorneys, a clerk, and a court officer. The court officer, wearing the uniform, stands in the courtroom to maintain order. The clerk, sitting at a desk at the front of the courtroom, can answer any questions you may have about the calendar or the Judge's rules. The court attorneys, who are lawyers, assist the Judge. In addition, volunteer court representatives are present to assist. The Judge sits on the bench at the front of the Courtroom and hears motions and cases and reviews stipulations and orders to show cause.

Each Resolution Part has its own rules which are posted on the wall and can be obtained from the court clerk. You can also view the Judge's rules at Part Rules. Depending upon the rules of the part, you must either quietly check in with the court clerk or court officer, or listen for your case to be called. If you need an interpreter, you should tell the court clerk.

Your case may have been assigned to one of the Housing Courts specialty Parts depending on the subject matter:

City Part

Coop/Condo Part

New York City Housing Authority Part

Housing Part Proceedings (HP) (proceeding to compel repairs)

When a case is called, the landlord and tenant, or their attorneys will meet with the judge or court attorney to discuss the case. If you are not the named tenant or the named landlord, but are in court on their behalf, you should let the court personnel know. If you are a tenant and your apartment needs repairs, you can ask for an inspection. If you are a landlord and you have completed the repairs, you can ask for an inspection. You may go to Inspection Request [1] to view the civil court form. You will have to come back to Court at a later date if the Judge grants the request for an inspection. You may have an attorney represent you on your case. If you need time to get an attorney or if you need documents that you do not have with you today, or if you have another reason for not being ready, you can ask to come back at a later date. This is called an adjournment. At the landlord's request, the Judge can order the tenant to deposit the future rent if the tenant requests two adjournments or if the case has been in court for more than 30 days.

While you are waiting for the case to be called, you must be quiet. Just as you would want other people to be quiet when your case is being heard, others in the courtroom should receive the same courtesy. If you are approached by the other party or the party's lawyer in your case, you do not have to speak to that person outside the presence of the judge or court attorney. However, you should feel free to step outside the courtroom to speak to the other party or lawyer only if you want to. Every case will be discussed by either the judge or the court attorney before you leave.

There is mediation available in some boroughs as an alternative to having a judge decide your case. In a mediation session, a professionally trained neutral person sits down with the parties, and each party has an opportunity to explain his or her position on the issues in dispute, listen to each other, and work together to reach a mutually acceptable solution. Any agreement reached through mediation will be reviewed by the Court. If you are unable to resolve your case through mediation, your case will be sent back to the Resolution Part. Not all cases are appropriate for mediation. Learn more about mediation at Dispute Resolution Through Mediation. If you wish to have a mediator handle your case either tell the court clerk or say so when you answer the calendar.

When your case is called the judge or court attorney will discuss the case to see if the case can be settled. If after discussing the case, the landlord and tenant agree to a settlement of the case, a document called a Stipulation of Settlement will be written up for the landlord and tenant to read and sign. No one can force anyone to settle a case or sign an agreement. No one should agree to settle a case if they do not agree with the terms of the settlement. The Stipulation of Settlement is a binding agreement between the landlord and tenant. In the Stipulation of Settlement, the landlord and tenant may agree to do certain things by certain dates. If the landlord or tenant fails to follow through on her or his end of the agreement, there may be very serious consequences. It is important that you only make an agreement that you know you can keep and that you agree with.

If, after discussing the case, the landlord and tenant cannot reach an agreement, the case will be referred to another part of the Housing Court, called a Trial Part, for trial. Except, cases assigned to the HP Part remain in the part for trial and do not go to a different Trial Part. The trial may take place that day or it may be scheduled for another date depending on the Court's calendar and on whether the Judge determines that the case is ready for trial. You may learn more about trials at How to Prepare for a Landlord–Tenant Trial.

If you have any questions that have not been answered here, you can learn more about other housing court procedures by reading our Legal and Procedural Information sections. There is also a Public Help Center in the courthouse where you may obtain more information at no cost. Refer to Help Center to learn more and for hours of operation.

[1] http://www.courts.state.ny.us/courts/nyc/housing/forms/ finspection request.pdf

Doc. 8. Restore to Possession

If you think you have been improperly evicted by a marshal based upon a court order or judgment you may seek to be restored to possession. You should come to court as soon as possible. If your landlord has illegally locked you out of your apartment without first going to court and obtaining a judgment of possession and a warrant of eviction, you may also seek to be restored to possession, but you must start a proceeding against your landlord. You may refer to illegal lock-out for more information.

To find out where to go in your county to be restored to possession after eviction by a marshal, go to Locations [1]. At the court, you will fill out an Affidavit In Support Of An Order To Show Cause To Restore To Possession. In your affidavit, you must explain the reasons that entitle you to be put back into your apartment. If you failed to answer a petition or failed to appear in court, you must explain this. If you have defenses to the proceeding, for example, that the rent was paid and you have receipts, you must list your defenses. You should bring all documents in support of your claim. Once you have filled out the Affidavit, the clerk will witness it for you.

The clerk will then submit your Affidavit and an Order to Show Cause to a Judge for review. You may have to wait in the clerk's office or go to the courtroom where your papers have been sent. If your application is signed you will need two or three copies of the Order to Show Cause and Affidavit in Support. You will either be given copies or lent the originals so that you can make the copies yourself. The original Order to Show Cause and Affidavit in Support goes back to the Clerk. You must then serve a copy of the papers on the other side in the manner directed in the order to show cause. The papers should be served by someone over the age of 18, who is not a party in the action. For more information, you can refer to Orders to Show Cause.

You must return to court on the hearing date, which will generally be within one or two days, at the room and time indicated on the order to show cause. You should bring proof of service, a copy of the papers and any other proof of your defenses with you on the hearing date.

If the judge declines to sign your Order to Show Cause or signs it with conditions that you do not agree with, you may challenge this determination by going to the Appellate Term. You may refer to Locations [1] to find the addresses of the Appellate Term in your county.

You can also watch a community seminar discussing what legal and procedural steps to take if you have been evicted from your home called, "What to Do If You've Been Evicted."

[1] http://www.courts.state.ny.us/courts/nyc/housing/locations2.shtml

Doc. 9. Adjournments

In General: Appearance Required

An adjournment may only be granted by the judge presiding at the time of the hearing. You can not call the court clerk for this purpose because the clerk is not permitted to grant adjournments. To get an adjournment, you should appear at the hearing at the appointed time. You will be given an opportunity to explain to the judge your reason for requesting an adjournment. If you know the name of the Judge assigned to your case, you should check the Judge's Part Rules to see if he or she has any requirements that may not be covered in this section. Click on Judge's Rules [1] to check.

Important: Please be aware that upon a second request by a respondent for an adjournment, or if more than 30 days have passed since the case first appeared before the judge, not counting any days due to adjournment requests by the petitioner, the petitioner may ask the judge to order that all the money due from the date of service of the petition be deposited in the court. If this is done, the judge will determine the amount and the respondent will have to make the deposit within five days. If the money is not deposited, the petitioner may get a default judgement against the respondent.

Sending Someone to Request the Adjournment

If it is an emergency and you cannot appear yourself to request the adjournment, but wish to send someone on your behalf, you **must** give that person written authorization to make the request for you. That person **must** bring the written authorization to the court.

The written authorizing statement which allows someone to request an adjournment on your behalf **must** contain the following items:

1. The index number of your case.

2. Your name and your address.

3. A signed statement that you are allowing the person to request an adjournment for you.

4. The name of the person you are sending.

5. The reason you are not appearing yourself to make the request.

The person who comes to court for you must bring this statement and all other papers that you received, and should be able to tell the clerk the reason for the request.

The Judge may deny the request for adjournment. If the request is denied, you will be marked in default, which may be serious. You can learn more about this and other housing court procedures by reading our Legal and Procedural Information sections.

Writing a Letter to Request an Adjournment

In an extreme emergency, where neither you nor anyone else can appear on your behalf, you may write a letter to the court. You must explain your reason for making the request and be sure to include the case number and year of your case, and the scheduled date of the hearing you will not be able to attend.

Address the letter to the appropriate civil court clerk's office. Send a copy of this letter to the other party to the action. If the judge decides to grant your adjournment, you will be notified.

If the request is denied, you will be marked in default, which may be very serious. You can learn more about this and other housing court procedures

by reading our Legal and Procedural Information sections.

   1 http://www.courts.state.ny.us/courts/nyc/housing/judges_profiles.shtml

Doc. 10.   Orders to Show Cause

In General

An Order to Show Cause is a way to present to a judge the reasons why the court should order relief to a party. For example, a tenant who has failed to appear and had a judgment entered against him or her may ask the court to vacate the judgment and restore the case to the calendar; or a landlord may request an order awarding a judgment and warrant of eviction against a tenant who has failed to live up to an agreement to pay rent.

The Order to Show Cause is an alternative to the notice of motion and is different from it, as the Order to Show Cause can shorten the time within which the parties must return to court. It is often used in emergency situations where a stay of the proceedings is required, or if an immediate result is sought. Another significant difference is that a judge must sign an Order to Show Cause. This means that the judge may decline to sign it. A notice of motion will appear on the calendar automatically, and does not need a judge's signature. If you are not sure a judge would sign your order to show cause, if you do not need to appear in court within the motion service time, or if you do not seek interim relief such as a stay before the motion is heard, you may decide to bring a motion instead of an order to show cause.

The Order to Show Cause informs your opposition of what you are seeking from the court and why. It provides the date, time and location where the request will be made. The Order to Show Cause often contains a direction to the parties that they stop some specific activity, like an eviction, until the court hears or decides the motion.

In limited cases an Order to Show Cause can be used to start a case, as an alternative to a notice of petition. Ordinarily an HP case and an illegal lockout are commenced this way.

The requirements for making a motion are standardized and generally more demanding than that for making an Order to Show Cause. Order to Show Cause forms are available at the courthouse, and a judge can set the terms, such as when it will be heard in court, how it will be served on the other side and any conditions or requirements in order to obtain a stay of enforcement of an order or judgment pending the hearing.

The Order to Show Cause must be accompanied by an "Affidavit in Support" and copies of any documents that support the request and would persuade the judge your application should be granted. Copies of all these papers must be served on all the parties in the manner directed on the Order to Show Cause itself. A party served with an Order to Show Cause may prepare papers to oppose the motion. On the hearing date, all parties must come to court and the judge will decide the Order to Show Cause.

If you would like to bring an Order to Show Cause or if you have been served with one and you want to oppose it, continue reading below.

Affidavit in Support

An Order to Show Cause must be supported by an Affidavit. An Affidavit is a sworn statement made before the clerk or notary public which explains to the court why your request should be granted.

The Clerk will give you a free Civil Court form when you come to court, or you may use one of your own, or download a form at Affidavit in Support. To find out where to go in your county to bring an Order to Show Cause, go to Locations. If you missed your court date or didn't answer a petition in a nonpayment or holdover case, you can use the Tenant Affidavit to Vacate a Default Judgment program to make your affidavit in support of your order to show cause.

In the Affidavit in support you should:

1. State the reason you are making your request.

2. State the relevant facts about your case.

3. State whether or not you have ever made the same request before.

4. Attach copies of any relevant documents you are referring to in your Affidavit.

After you have filled out the Affidavit, you must sign it at the bottom in front of the clerk, or in front of a notary, so that it can be attached to the Order to Show Cause and submitted to a Judge.

Submission to the Judge

After the Affidavit is witnessed by the clerk, the clerk will then submit your Affidavit with the Order to Show Cause to a Judge for review. You may have to wait awhile in the clerk's office.

If your application is signed by a Judge, you will need two or three copies of the Order to Show Cause and supporting papers. You will either be given copies or lent the originals so that you can make copies yourself. There are copy machines in the clerk's office, so bring change.

The original Order to Show Cause and Affidavit in Support goes back to the clerk. You must then serve a copy of the papers on the other side in the manner directed in the Order to Show Cause. The Order to Show Cause will often contain a provision requiring service by a specific date. If you are a respondent who has been served with a Marshal's Notice, you will also have to serve a copy of the Order to Show Cause on the Marshal. If your Order to Show Cause contains a provision which stays any eviction until the hearing date, and if you fail to serve the Marshal after

the Judge signs your Order to Show Cause, you might get evicted.

The papers should be served by someone over the age of 18, who is not a party in the action, unless the judge has permitted otherwise. The clerk will give you further instructions, or you may speak with a Housing Court counselor in the Resource Center.

If you are a tenant you may refer to the Instructions for further information on serving papers.

Opposition Papers

If you wish to oppose an order to show cause, you may prepare an Affidavit in Opposition. If you do not submit opposition papers and/or fail to appear in court to oppose the Order to Show Cause, the judge may decide to grant the relief requested based on the information in the Order to Show Cause and your default.

An affidavit is a sworn statement which must be signed in front of a notary public or a court clerk. You may attach copies of any relevant documents to the Affidavit in Opposition. You can download a free Civil Court form by at Affidavit in Opposition, you may use your own form, or obtain one from the clerk or the resource center.

After you have prepared the opposition papers, follow the procedure out lined below:

1. Copies of the opposition papers must be served on all other parties.

2. Opposition papers must be served by a person who is not a party to the action and is eighteen years of age or older.

3. If a party has an attorney, the papers must be served on the attorney. Service of the opposition papers may be made by delivering the papers to the attorney personally, or by mailing the papers to the attorney.

4. After the opposition papers have been served, the person who served the papers must fill out an Affidavit of Service which states how and when the papers were served. The Affidavit of Service must be signed in front of a notary or a court clerk. You may download the free Housing Court form at Affidavit of Service.

5. Make a copy of the Affidavit of Service for your records and attach the original to the copy for the court.

6. Opposition papers can be filed in the courtroom on the date that the Order to Show Cause is heard, or in the clerk's office before that date.

Cross–Motions

If you have been served with an order to show cause and wish to ask the court for relief of your own, you may bring your own Order to Show Cause. Tell the clerk that you want your Order to Show Cause heard on the same day as the Order to Show Cause that is already scheduled to be heard, and if there is enough time, they can be calendared together. You can also schedule a cross-motion for the same day as the Order to Show Cause is noticed to be heard.

Reply Papers

If you have received opposition papers prior to the hearing date of the Order to Show Cause, you may have time to prepare an affidavit in reply. You may go to Reply Affidavit [1] to download a free Civil Court form; you may use a form of your own; or you may obtain one from the clerk or the Housing Court Resource Center. You must serve a copy of the reply affidavit on the other side and bring extra copies and the original, along with proof of service, to the courtroom on the date the Order to Show Cause is to be heard. If you did not have time to prepare reply papers and feel that it is necessary, you can ask the court for an adjournment for time to prepare reply papers. The judge may or may not grant your request.

Appearing in Court

You are required to appear in court on the date the Order to Show Cause is scheduled to be heard. You must appear at the time and place stated in the Order to Show Cause. If you need directions to the courthouse, Directions are available. In general, if you do not appear, and you are the moving party, your Order to Show Cause will be denied; if you do not oppose the motion, the Order to Show Cause may be granted on default. You should give yourself extra time to get to the courtroom since all visitors are required to go through metal detectors at the entrance to the courthouse. You should bring your copies of the papers with you and any papers and affidavits that you have not yet filed with the court.

The courtroom is presided over by a Judge, who is assisted by a court attorney, a clerk and a court officer. The court officer, wearing a uniform, maintains order in the courtroom. The clerk, sitting at a desk at the front of the courtroom, can answer any questions you have about the calendar or the judge's rules. The Judge sits on the bench at the front of the courtroom and hears arguments for and against motions and orders to show cause, reviews stipulations of settlement, and decides request for adjournments. The court attorney assists the Judge and may hold a conference with the parties to see if the order to show cause can be settled.

There is a calendar posted outside the courtroom that lists all the cases that will be called that day. Each case has a number. You should sit quietly in the courtroom and listen for your case to be called. You will have a chance to explain your case to the judge or the judge's court attorney. You always have the right to go before the Judge. You are not required to settle the Order to Show Cause, and you may request a hearing on the record. In that event, the Judge will decide your application.

If you are not ready to discuss the Order to Show Cause on the return date, or you need more time to prepare papers, when the case is called you can ask the court for a postponement or an adjournment of your application. If your case has been adjourned before and marked "final" it means the judge will not allow any further adjournments. For more information, refer to Adjournments.

The other side may want to discuss the Order to Show Cause with you alone to see if you can come to an agreement. If you reach an agreement, you and the other side can write the terms of your agreement into a stipulation. However, you do not have to talk to the other side alone. You can wait until your case is called by the court and the judge will decide.

The Decision on the Order to Show Cause

If you and the other side are unable to agree about the relief being requested, the judge will make a decision on the Order to Show Cause. Sometimes, the judge makes a decision immediately. The judge has 30 days to decide the Order to Show Cause. Some Judges will mail you a copy of the order if you provide a self-addressed stamped envelope. Otherwise, you will have to go to the courthouse to get a copy of the decision. To find out where to go in your county refer to Locations [2].

Depending on the relief sought, the judge's decision may award a judgment to the winning party. When the winning party enters the judgment and serves a copy of the judgment with notice of entry on the losing party, this start's the loser's time to appeal running. To learn more, refer to Serving Notice of Entry.

If you are unhappy with the judge's decision and think that the judge made a legal or factual mistake, you can make a motion to reargue or renew, or file an appeal. The filing of an appeal alone does not stop or stay the execution of a judgment. An appeal requires the posting of an undertaking to stay an eviction.

An appeal must be filed within 30 days from the service of the order appealed from and written notice of entry. If neither side has served a copy of the decision and order with notice of entry, there is no time limitation on the filing of an appeal. For more information about appealing a decision, go to Appeals.

[1] http://www.courts.state.ny.us/courts/nyc/housing/forms/replyaff.pdf

[2] http://www.courts.state.ny.us/courts/nyc/housing/locations2.shtml

Doc. 11. Stipulations and Settlements

In the Resolution Part, Mediation, or even in the Trial Part, the parties, with the assistance of the Judge, the Judge's court attorney, or the court mediator, will discuss the case in an effort to reach a settlement. Most cases in Housing Court are settled, meaning the parties come to an agreement, usually called a "Stipulation of Settlement," which is written down and signed by the parties and the Judge.

When you sign a Stipulation of Settlement, you are making a binding legal agreement that must be followed. Therefore, you must be very careful to read the agreement, understand it, and be certain that you will be able to do everything you have promised. The court attorney can explain any details in the Stipulation of Settlement that you do not understand. If you have any questions or doubts, you have the right to ask to talk to the Judge who must approve your settlement.

What a stipulation provides will depend on what the parties negotiate and the facts of the particular case. For more information about settling a nonpayment or holdover case, click on Tenant's Guide to Housing Court [1], or Landlord's Guide to Housing Court [2].

If decide to sign the stipulation of settlement the judge will speak you to make sure you understand the terms of the settlement. This is called an allocution. If you do not wish to settle the case, you have a right to a trial before a judge.

If you sign an agreement and then you cannot do what you promised - for example, you cannot pay on time or make repairs on time - you should come to court and bring an Order to Show Cause to request more time. If the other side has not done what they are supposed to do in the agreement, you can also come to court and bring an Order to Show Cause to request help from the court. Click on Order to Show Cause [3] if you want to learn more. A Judge will read your Order to Show Cause and decide whether to grant your request.

[1] http://www.courts.state.ny.us/courts/nyc/housing/pdfs/tenantsguide. pdf

[2] http://www.courts.state.ny.us/courts/nyc/housing/pdfs/ Landlord booklet.pdf

[3] http://www.courts.state.ny.us/courts/nyc/housing/osc.shtml

Doc. 12.   Stays Before Entry of Judgment

In General

Any party may seek a stay of a proceeding before a judgment is entered.

A judge may stay proceedings in a case, upon terms that are just, as well as for the reasons that are discussed below.

A landlord or a tenant seeking to obtain an extension of time to comply with an order to pay money, leave the premises, make repairs, or correct mathematical errors, may make an application to the court.

In order to obtain a stay you must come to court and fill out an Order to Show Cause. To read more about this process click on Orders To Show Cause [1]. To find out where to go in your county, click on Locations & Phone Listings [2].

If a judgment has already been entered in your case and you seek a stay, click on Stays after entry of judgment [3].

Stay for Failure to Make Repairs

A tenant may seek a stay of a pending nonpayment proceeding if he/she was constructively evicted, or upon proof that conditions dangerous to life, health or safety exist, as long as the condition was not caused by the tenant. A stay may also be requested if violations have been placed against the premises showing constructive eviction or dangerous conditions. (There must be proper proof that a notice or order to remove the violations has been made by the city department charged with enforcement.) Once violations have been placed, the burden of disproving the condition described by the violation is on the landlord or petitioner.

In order to obtain the stay the tenant must deposit the amount of rent due with the court. The stay may be vacated if such deposit is not made or if the conditions are repaired. During the stay, the court may direct the release of funds on deposit to pay for maintenance of the premises, repairs or utility bills.

Stay Based Upon Utility Shut–Off

A tenant residing in a multiple dwelling may seek a stay of a pending proceeding in the event that utilities are discontinued due to the landlord's failure to pay. The stay shall remain in effect until the landlord pays the amount owed and the utilities are restored to working order.

Stay if Building Where Tenant on Public Assistance Resides has Hazardous Violations

A tenant who receives welfare may seek a stay of entry of judgment in a nonpayment proceeding if there are violations in the building for dangerous conditions. This defense is available only for violations reported by DHPD to DSS. DSS must have withheld the rent from the landlord due to the violations in order for the tenant to assert this defense.

Stay Based Upon Change of Attorneys

There is an automatic stay of a proceeding if the attorney of record of any party dies, becomes incapacitated or is removed, suspended or otherwise disabled at any time before judgment. No further proceedings can be taken against this party without permission from the court. The stay continues until thirty days after notice to appoint another attorney has been served upon the party personally or in a manner directed by the court. If at the end of the stay the party has not replaced his/her attorney, or if he/she decided to continue without an attorney, *pro se*, the proceedings may continue against this party.

Stay Based Upon DHCR Order

In some cases a cause of action or a defense in a proceeding brought in Housing Court may be based upon an order issued by the DHCR. If a landlord or a tenant of a rent-stabilized or rent-controlled apartment files a complaint with the DHCR and disagrees with the resulting order issued by a District Rent Administrator, he/she may bring a Petition for Administrative Review (PAR) at the DHCR. The order may be stayed pending determination of the PAR.

The proper filing of a PAR against a DHCR order, other than an order adjusting, fixing or establishing the legal regulated rent, stays that order until the DHCR Commissioner makes a final determination. Where the DHCR order provides for an adjustment in rent, the retroactive portion of the adjustment, if any, is generally stayed, but not the prospective portion.

The DHCR Commissioner may grant or vacate a stay of its orders under appropriate circumstances, on such terms and conditions as the Commissioner deems appropriate.

1 http://www.courts.state.ny.us/courts/nyc/housing/osc.shtml

2 http://www.courts.state.ny.us/courts/nyc/housing/addresses.shtml

3 http://www.courts.state.ny.us/courts/nyc/housing/   staysafter judg_nonpay.shtml

Doc. 13.   Stays after Entry of Judgment

In General: Stay Of Enforcement Of Judgment Or Order Without Appeal

A tenant who lost at trial and seeks to stay the issuance of the warrant of eviction must apply to the judge who granted the landlord the judgment.

A landlord or a tenant seeking to obtain an extension of time to comply with orders to pay moneys, vacate the premises or make repairs, or to correct mathematical errors may apply to any judge.

The court has general power to stay proceedings in a proper case, upon such terms as may be just, as well as specific powers as discussed below.

In order to obtain a stay you must come to court and fill out an Order to Show Cause. To read more about this process click on Orders To Show Cause [1]. To find out where to go in your county, click on Locations & Phone Listings [2].

To learn about stays of enforcement of judgments when appealing, click on Appeals [3].

After the Tenant has Answered or Appeared

If a tenant has answered, appeared in court and the Judge has awarded a judgment to the landlord, the court cannot stay the issuance of a warrant for more than five days. If more than five days have passed, the court can only stay the issuance or execution of a warrant if the tenant deposits the amount due on the judgment with the clerk or provides documentary evidence (receipts, checks) that the amount has been paid. For further information, you may refer to the Real Property Actions and Proceedings Law section 747–a.

The court has the power in some instances to stay the issuance or execution of a warrant even without a deposit. It will do so in limited circumstances. The court may, however, sign an order to show cause without a stay at any time.

If The Tenant Has Not Answered

If a tenant fails to answer a nonpayment petition within five days from the date of service and petitioner is awarded a judgment on default, a judge may stay the issuance of the warrant for no more than ten days from the date of service of the petition and notice of petition.

Staying Eviction Prior to Issuance of Warrant

A lessee or a tenant in a nonpayment proceeding seeking to stay the issuance of the warrant of eviction may do so by depositing in court the full amount claimed on the petition plus costs and filing fees before a warrant is issued.

A lessee or tenant who has taken the benefit of an insolvency statute or has been adjudicated bankrupt, may obtain a stay of the issuance of a warrant at any time before the warrant of eviction is issued by paying the filing fees for the petition and by depositing an undertaking for the amount directed by the court and continuing to pay the rent as it becomes due.

Stay of Evictions of Persons or Dependents of Persons Serving in the Military

A landlord may not evict a person serving in the military, or his or her spouse, children or other dependents from an apartment, during the period of military service without an application to the court. On such application the court may stay the proceedings for six months, unless the court determines that the respondent's ability to pay rent is not materially affected by the military service.

Under certain circumstances, a person serving in the military or his or her dependents may also seek a stay of an action or proceeding or a stay of the enforcement of a judgment or order.

Automatic Stay After Filing Bankruptcy Petition

When a residential tenant files a bankruptcy petition, an automatic stay prevents the landlord from bringing or continuing a case to obtain possession and from enforcing a judgment obtained before the start of the bankruptcy case. The purpose of the stay is to give the debtor a breathing spell from his creditors.

The automatic stay only applies to proceedings concerning property in which the debtor has an interest at the time the bankruptcy proceeding is commenced, which is when the bankruptcy proceeding is filed.

In landlord/tenant cases the court may determine that the tenant no longer has an interest to protect at the time of filing a bankruptcy petition if the warrant of eviction has already issued. In both the New York State courts and the federal Bankruptcy Court, depending on the facts of the individual cases, the issuance of the warrant of eviction may or may not be a sufficient basis upon which to lift or modify the automatic stay, or to conclude that the bankruptcy petition did not qualify for an automatic stay.

After a tenant files for bankruptcy a landlord may seek to have the stay in Bankruptcy Court vacated, in order to commence or continue an eviction proceeding. The Bankruptcy Court may terminate, modify or condition the stay based upon various factors, including payment of ongoing rent, the condition of the premises and the equities of the case. If the stay in Bankruptcy Court is lifted, the Civil Court will have jurisdiction to hear and decide the eviction proceeding, and the landlord who obtains a judgment and warrant of eviction will be able to enforce a possessory judgment with eviction.

If the tenant's debt, which includes past rent due, is discharged at the conclusion of the bankruptcy proceeding, the landlord may then seek recovery of the premises and eviction of the tenant/debtor. This is because while the debt may have been discharged, it has not been extinguished, and discharge of debt is not equivalent to payment of debt. A discharge only prevents a creditor from proceeding against a debtor on the debt as a personal liability, but does not eliminate any of the other consequences of that debt. Therefore, as long as the landlord does not attempt to obtain a money judgment for a discharged debt, the landlord is free to commence a nonpayment proceeding to recover possession. Thus a landlord may evict the tenant/debtor for his/her failure to pay rent which has been discharged in bankruptcy.

A debtor may voluntarily repay a debt that has been discharged even though the debt can no longer be legally enforced.

To find the Bankruptcy Court in your county, click on Locations [4].

[1] http://www.courts.state.ny.us/courts/nyc/housing/osc.shtml

[2] http://www.courts.state.ny.us/courts/nyc/housing/addresses.shtml

[3] http://www.courts.state.ny.us/courts/nyc/housing/appeals.shtml

[4] http://www.courts.state.ny.us/courts/nyc/housing/locations2.shtml

Doc. 14.   Vacating a Default Judgment

If you have been sued in Housing Court and a judgment has been entered against you because you defaulted, that is, you failed to answer or did not show up to defend yourself, you can seek to have the judgment vacated (thrown out). If you do not, you could be evicted from your home by a marshal as a result of the judgment once the warrant of eviction is issued.

If you are not sure whether a judgment has been entered against you, you can click on Locations [1] and find out where to go in your county to check. If you find that a judgment has not been granted against you, then you should immediately file an answer. If you have already received a notice from a marshal, you should come to court right away.

To vacate a default judgment and obtain a stay of eviction, you should fill out an Order to Show Cause. An Order to Show Cause is a legal paper, signed by the judge, that orders the other side to appear in court and "show cause," that is, give a good reason, why the judgment should not be vacated. You must fill out an Affidavit in Support of the Order To Show Cause explaining the reason you did not go to court, such as, you never received notice of the proceeding, or you were sick; and, you must explain your defenses to the claims against you, such as, you do not owe the rent claimed, or you did not install the dishwasher in the kitchen in violation of the lease. To learn about the procedure, go to Order to Show Cause. If you missed your court date or didn't answer a petition in a nonpayment or holdover case, you can use the Tenant Affidavit to Vacate a Default Judgment program to make your affidavit in support of your order to show cause.

If the judge vacates the default judgment and restores the case to the calendar, you must be ready to prove your side of the case.

[1] http://www.courts.state.ny.us/courts/nyc/housing/locations2.shtml

Doc. 15.   Warrants

A warrant is a document issued by the court based upon a judgment of possession awarded by the court which permits the sheriff or marshal to remove persons from a premises. For information on obtaining a judgment, click on Judgments [1].

A warrant can only be issued to a sheriff or a marshal. After the judgment is awarded, you must contact the marshal so that the marshal can requisition the warrant from the court. For a list of New York City marshals, click on NYC Department of Investigation [2]. The marshal will require the facts of the proceeding, including the index number, the names of the parties, the address of the premises, and a copy of the judgment, or, if it is a judgment based upon the respondent's failure to answer, a letter requesting entry of the judgment. You will also have to pay the marshal a fee. The marshal will submit the papers to the court.

The warrant clerk will review the papers, and if everything is in order, the clerk will issue the warrant to the marshal. If the papers are defective, the clerk will return them to the marshal for correction.

After the marshal receives the warrant, the marshal is then ready to proceed with the eviction. For more information about the eviction, click on Eviction [3].

[1] http://www.courts.state.ny.us/courts/nyc/housing/judgments.shtml

[2] http://www.nyc.gov/html/doi/home.html

[3] http://www.courts.state.ny.us/courts/nyc/housing/eviction.shtml

Doc. 16.   Judgments in Nonpayment Cases

In General

The outcome of a landlord/tenant case is either a judgment, dismissal or discontinuance.

There may be a judgment based upon respondent's failure to appear, or to answer, after trial, by a stipulation of settlement of the parties or by motion.

The final judgment determines the issues raised in the proceeding and establishes the rights and obligations of the parties. The successful party is also awarded the costs and disbursements of the proceeding.

If the petitioner cannot show it is entitled to a judgment, the proceeding may be dismissed with prejudice and cannot be brought again, or dismissed without prejudice and may be brought again. A case can also be discontinued by the petitioner before the respondent has answered, with permission of the respondent or by order of the court.

A respondent's answer may contain a counterclaim, and the court may render a judgment on that counterclaim in favor of the respondent, or the counterclaim may be dismissed or discontinued with or without prejudice, or severed.

If the court awards the petitioner a possessory judgment, then a warrant of eviction may issue. For more information click on Warrants [1].

A final judgment in a nonpayment proceeding generally provides for both a money judgment and a possessory judgment. If the money judgment is timely paid, both the monetary and the possessory judgment are satisfied. If the money judgment is not timely paid, the respondent can be evicted based upon the possessory judgment, and the respondent is still liable to pay the money judgment amount. In some cases the court may also award a non-possessory money judgment, which means that the respondent is responsible for paying the money judgment, but cannot get evicted for not paying it.

The judgment may also contain an award of legal fees to the prevailing party. Generally, each party in a law suit is responsible for its own legal fees, unless there is an agreement or a statute which provides otherwise. If the lease between the parties provides for an award of legal fees to the landlord for the tenant's failure to perform any agreement in the lease, the tenant also has the same right to collect an award of legal fees for his or her attorney. A petitioner may not obtain possession based solely on the tenant's failure to pay legal fees.

Judgment when Respondent Fails to Answer

After a respondent is served he or she may either answer or not answer. If the respondent fails to answer within five days of the service of the notice of petition and petition, the petitioner may, after the respondent's time to answer has expired, ask the court to enter a judgment. This judgment may be for money if the petition and notice of petition were served by in-hand delivery, otherwise, it will be for possession only.

In most cases, the judgment and the warrant are requested at the same time. A petitioner will contact a marshal, and give the marshal a letter addressed to the court requesting that a judgment be entered. In addition, the petitioner must provide the marshal with a current non-military affidavit. For more information, see Non–Military Affidavit below. The marshal will then submit the papers to the court together with a requisition for the issuance of the warrant. For a list of New York City marshals, click on NYC Department of Investigation [2].

When the clerk receives these papers, the clerk will review the papers for legal and procedural sufficiency. If the papers are correct, the clerk will send them to a judge for him or her to review. Ultimately, it is up to the judge to order that the judgment be entered and the warrant issued. For more information on obtaining the warrant in a nonpayment case after the tenant fails to answer, click on Warrants [1].

After the judge signs the judgment, the clerk will issue the warrant to the marshal. The Marshal may then evict the respondent. For more information, click on Eviction [3].

To learn the procedure for vacating the judgment, click on Vacating Judgments [4].

Judgment when Respondent Fails to Appear

If the respondent answers, the clerk will assign the case to a part. On the court date, the respondent may fail to appear. If the respondent fails to appear after the case is called on the calendar the petitioner may ask the judge to enter a judgment against the respondent. This judgment will generally be for money and possession. The judge, or the court attorney, will review the papers for legal and procedural sufficiency. For more information, click on Requirements for a Nonpayment Petition [5]. You will also be required to provide information as to the respondent's military status. If all the papers are in order, the judge will direct that a judgment be entered. The judgment based on respondent's failure to appear will usually have a five-day stay of the issuance of the warrant, and the judge may require that the petitioner serve a copy of the judgment on the respondent. The judgment will normally permit the issuance of a warrant. Most petitioners contact a marshal, provide information and/or a copy of the judgment to the marshal and the marshal then files a request for the issuance of a warrant with the clerk. For more information, click on Warrants [1]. Once the warrant issues, the marshal may evict the respondent. For more information, click on Eviction [3].

To learn the procedure for vacating the judgment, click on Vacating Judgments [4].

Judgment based on Stipulation of Settlement

If both sides appear, the case will be ready to proceed. The vast majority of non-payment cases are settled In conferences which may include the petitioner, the respondent, the attorneys of either party, mediators, court attorneys, and at times even the Judge.

If the case is settled, a stipulation of settlement will be written. For more information, click on Stipulations of Settlement [6]. The stipulation of settlement may provide for the issuance of a judgment and warrant if the respondent fails to comply with the conditions of the stipulation. The stipulation may contain requirements for the petitioner to notify the respondent before the warrant may be issued. The stipulation may require the petitioner to make a motion to the court, either on notice or without notice to the other side, before the warrant can be executed. Whatever, the stipulation requires, the conditions must be complied with before the judgment and/or warrant can be entered or issued.

Once the petitioner has obtained a judgment and warrant of eviction based upon the stipulation of settlement, the marshal can evict the respondent. For more information, click on Eviction [3]. To learn the procedure for vacating the judgment, click on Vacating Judgments [4].

Judgments after Trial

If both parties appear and a settlement cannot be reached, the case will be sent to a Trial Part for trial before a Housing Court Judge. If the petitioner proves his or her case, the Judge will direct that a judgment be entered after the trial. This judgment will generally be for money and possession. If the petitioner fails to prove his or her case, the judge will dismiss the case.

The Judge may not issue his or her decision on the same day that you try the case. This is called "decision reserved." The Judge may send you a copy of the decision in the mail. However, to be certain, you can call or come to court to learn if there has been a decision. To learn where to go in your county, click on Locations [7].

The judgment will normally permit the issuance of a warrant. Most petitioners contact a marshal, provide information and/or a copy of the judgment to the marshal and the marshal then files a request for the issuance of a warrant with the clerk. For more information, click on Warrants [1]. Once the warrant issues, the marshal may then evict the respondent. For more information, click on Eviction [3].

For information about appealing the Judge's decision, click on Appeals [8].

Non–Military Affidavit

In order to obtain a judgment, the petitioner must provide information to the court regarding the respondent's military status. You may be required to file a non-military affidavit setting forth facts as to the basis of the belief that the respondent is not serving in the military, or is not a dependent of someone in military service. This affidavit generally must be less than 30 days old. You may click on Affidavit of Military Investigation [9] to view and/or download a copy of the free Civil Court form. For more information, you may click on Non–Military Affidavit [10] to read the Civil Court Directive on the subject.

1 http://www.courts.state.ny.us/courts/nyc/housing/warrants.shtml

2 http://www.nyc.gov/html/doi/home.html

3 http://www.courts.state.ny.us/courts/nyc/housing/eviction.shtml

4 http://www.courts.state.ny.us/courts/nyc/housing/vacatingjudg.shtml

5 http://www.courts.state.ny.us/courts/nyc/housing/startingcase.shtml#requirements

6 http://www.courts.state.ny.us/courts/nyc/housing/stips.shtml

7 http://www.courts.state.ny.us/courts/nyc/housing/locations2.shtml

8 http://www.courts.state.ny.us/courts/nyc/housing/appeals2.shtml

9 http://www.courts.state.ny.us/courts/nyc/housing/forms/ affmilin-vestigation.pdf

10 http://www.courts.state.ny.us/courts/nyc/housing/directives/LSM/lsm152a.pdf

Doc. 17. Trial

In General

If the parties were unable to reach a settlement in the Resolution Part, the case will be ready to be tried. The case will be assigned to a Trial Part. The court will tell the parties where and when to appear for the trial.

At the trial, the parties each get a chance to present their side of the case, and the judge will make a decision and judgment based on the evidence and arguments presented. The parties must have all their witnesses and evidence ready to present at the trial. If you have a good reason for not being ready to try the case, such as a medical reason, or one of your witnesses is out of town, you can ask the Judge for an adjournment. If this becomes necessary you should notify the other side ahead of time by mail that you are going to ask the court for an adjournment.

A case may still be settled in a Trial Part. A settlement is a voluntary, binding agreement that resolves the differences between the parties to a lawsuit. If the case is settled, there is no trial. For more information about settling a case, click on Stipulations and Settlements [1].

Jury Trials

If the petitioner or respondent has properly filed a jury demand and paid the jury demand fee, the case will be tried before a jury. Jury trials are very infrequent in Housing Court proceedings because most lease contain jury waiver clauses. If the case is tried before a jury, the jury, not the judge, will make the decision and then a judgment will be entered based on the verdict reached by the jury. If the jury is unable to reach a verdict, the Judge will have to declare a mistrial and the case will have to be tried again before a new jury.

A jury trial begins with jury selection. A panel of prospective jurors is called for *voir dire*. The Court will examine the jurors as to their qualifications. A party is entitled to challenge a juror for cause when a prospective juror is not qualified, such as, is not impartial, is related to one of the parties, or will not follow the law. A party is also entitled to a limited number of peremptory challenges. Six jurors, plus alternates, must be selected to hear the case.

After each side presents testimony and evidence, the judge will deliver a charge to the jury, which sets forth the jury's responsibility to decide the facts in light of the applicable rules of law.

Testimony of Witnesses

The petitioner's case is presented first. After being sworn as a witness, the petitioner will tell his or her version of the incident. All relevant papers or other evidence should be presented at this time to be offered in evidence. When the petitioner has finished testifying, the respondent has the right to ask questions. This is called cross-examination. After a party has cross-examined a witness, the other side has the chance to redirect examination of the witness in order to re-question the witness on points covered during the cross-examination. Sometimes the Judge may ask questions to clarify matters. Other witnesses may be presented in support of the petitioner's claims, and they, too can be cross-examined by the respondent and questioned by the Judge.

The respondent may then be sworn and tell his or her side of the story and offer evidence. All papers or other evidence should be presented at this time to be offered in evidence. When the respondent has finished testifying, the petitioner has the right to cross-examine the respondent. After a party has cross-examined a witness, the other side has the chance to redirect examination of the witness in order to re-question the witness on points covered during the cross-examination. Sometimes a Judge may ask questions to clarify matters. Other witnesses may be presented in support of the respondent's claims, and they, too, can be cross-examined by the petitioner and questioned by the Judge. After the presentation of the respondent's case, the petitioner has the right to ask the Judge for an opportunity to present evidence to rebut the respondent's case.

Objections

There is a body of law called "rules of evidence." The purpose of these rules is to make sure that evidence is relevant, reliable and authentic. Because of these rules certain testimony or documents may not be legally admissible. For example, an affidavit is not admissible in evidence because its admission would deprive the other side of the right to question the person who wrote it.

Parties to a lawsuit have a right to object to the introduction of evidence or the way a question is being asked or answered. The proper way to object is to say "objection." The Judge may then ask what the basis for the objection is. If the Judge agrees with the objection, the Judge will say "sustained" and the

evidence will not be admitted. If the Judge disagrees with the objection, the Judge will say "overruled" and the evidence will be admitted.

Trial Decision

When the trial is completed, you may have to wait for the Judge to write a decision. You may contact the court to see if a trial decision has been issued. To find out where to visit or call in your county, click on locations [2].

In a nonpayment or a holdover proceeding, the Judge may award a possessory judgment and/or a money judgment to the winning party. For more information, click on Judgments [3] to read the appropriate section. If you are the losing party, you may want to appeal. You may click on Appeals [4] to learn more.

1 http://www.courts.state.ny.us/courts/nyc/housing/stips.shtml
2 http://www.courts.state.ny.us/courts/nyc/housing/locations2.shtml
3 http://www.courts.state.ny.us/courts/nyc/housing/judgments.shtml
4 http://www.courts.state.ny.us/courts/nyc/housing/appeals2.shtml

Doc. 18. Subpoenas

If you are unable to get a witness to appear voluntarily, or you need records produced in court that are not in your possession, you can ask the court to issue a subpoena. A subpoena is a legal document that commands the person named in it to appear in court to testify or to produce records. For example, DHCR, Buildings Department, HPD or the landlord's employees can be subpoenaed. (An expert witness cannot be compelled to testify by subpoena.)

If you would like to subpoena a witness or documents, you must come to court and fill out the subpoena forms. Click on Locations [1] to find out where to go in your county. After you have filled out the forms, the clerk will present the subpoena to the judge for signature, if necessary. You must then arrange for the service of the subpoena and the payment of a witness fee and, where appropriate, travel expenses for the person subpoenaed. You are responsible for paying these fees. Any person, including a friend or relative, who is 18 years of age or older and who is not a party to the proceeding can serve the subpoena. A party cannot serve a subpoena. For detailed information on how to serve a subpoena, click on Subpoena Instructions [2].

A subpoena can be served any time before the hearing. However, a witness should be given a "reasonable" amount of time before he or she must appear. Generally, it is considered reasonable to serve the subpoena at least 5 days before the hearing date. This will allow the person subpoenaed to prepare the items you request or appear at the hearing.

1 http://www.courts.state.ny.us/courts/nyc/housing/locations2.shtml
2 http://www.courts.state.ny.us/courts/nyc/housing/forms/   instructionsservicesubpoena.pdf

HOLDOVER PROCEEDINGS

Doc. 1. Starting a Case

In General

A holdover case is brought to evict a tenant or a person in the apartment who is not a tenant for reasons other than simple nonpayment of rent. A holdover case is much more complicated than a nonpayment case. A holdover proceeding can have many variations. For example, if the tenant has violated a lease provision, illegally put others in the apartment, has become a nuisance to other tenants, or is staying after a lease has expired, the landlord may bring a holdover case. A roommate who is named on lease can also bring a holdover proceeding to evict a roommate who is not named on the lease from the apartment.

There may or may not be a landlord/tenant relationship, and the petitioner may or may not need to show a good reason why a respondent's occupancy should be terminated. The rights of the parties may be determined by a lease or other agreement, housing laws and regulations and/or the New York State or United States Constitution. A predicate notice may or may not have to be served.

The information given below is very general and there can be a number of differences in individual cases. The help of a lawyer is recommended in holdover cases.

You can go to Landlord's Guide [1] for more information about bringing a proceeding in Housing Court or visit the Civil Court Help Center in your county. You can go to Help Center [2] to learn more.

Predicate Notices

There are many notices that are required by law to be served on the tenant prior to the commencement of a holdover proceeding, depending on the nature of the tenancy and the grounds upon which the proceeding is brought. They include Notices to Quit, Notices to Cure a Substantial Violation of the Lease, Notices of Termination or Notices of Intent Not To Renew a Lease. For example, a 10-day Notice to Quit is for a "squatter" or "licensee." Someone you allowed to stay with you without paying is called a "licensee." A "squatter" is a person who came in without permission and did not pay any rent. The forms can be purchased at a legal stationary store, such as Blumberg.

You must purchase the appropriate predicate notice form and serve it on the tenant in the manner required by law. Different rules for when and how to serve the predicate notices apply in different cases. For example, a 30-day notice must be served on the tenant before the beginning of the next "rental term." A rental term is the time beginning the day the tenant is supposed to pay the rent and ending the day before the next rental payment is due. If you are using the

10-day notice for a licensee or squatter, you can serve it at any time. Once you obtain the correct predicate notice, you should complete the form and make photocopies.

For more information, you can speak to a free Housing Court Counselor in the Civil Court Help Center in your county. To find out where to go, refer to Help Center [2].

Starting a Case

To begin a holdover case, you must purchase the following legal forms, which can be purchased in a legal stationary store, such as Blumberg:

    Notice of Termination

    Petition

    Service Copies

    Notice of Petition

    Postcard

The holdover petition must contain:

1) the interest of the petitioner in the premises;

2) the interest of the respondent in the premises and his/her relationship with the petitioner;

3) a description of the premises;

4) the facts upon which the proceeding is based; and,

5) the relief sought.

The Rules of the Court also require a petitioner to plead whether the building is a multiple dwelling, and if so, that there is a currently effective registration statement on file with the office of code enforcement, and the multiple dwelling registration number along with the name and address of the managing agent.

You must fill out the forms and then bring the forms, including the predicate notice, to the cashier's window, at the Landlord–Tenant Clerk's Office to buy an index number. Payment may be made by cash, certified check or money order. Make the money order or certified check payable to the "Clerk of the Civil Court." Click on Locations [3] to find out where to go in your county. Click on Court Fees [4] to find out the cost of starting the case.

You must choose the court date on the Notice of Petition. A Landlord/Tenant clerk will give you the courtroom number and the assigned time for you to fill out on the papers. The clerk will give you back the Notice of Petition with the index number stamped onto it and the date of the hearing.

The landlord must make sure the tenant receives a copy of the Notice of Petition and the Petition in the manner required by law. The copies of the Petition and Notice of Petition must be served not less than five calendar days and not more than twelve calendar days from the court date. Click on Service of the Notice of Petition and Petition [5] to learn more.

After serving the papers, the landlord must bring back the original Notice of Petition with the notarized affidavit of service on the back filled out. In addition, the landlord must bring in the stamped postcard so that the court can mail it to the tenant.

Going to Court

You should go to court on the date and time stated on the notice of petition. You can click on Directions [3] if you do not know how to get to the courthouse. Get there early, since you will need to go through a metal detector before entering the courthouse. You should bring all your evidence in support of your claim or defense. The first courtroom you go to is called a "Resolution Part." To learn more about what happens there, click on Resolution Part [6], or you may click on Video [7] to watch a video about the Resolution Part.

[1] http://www.courts.state.ny.us/courts/nyc/housing/pdfs/ Landlord booklet.pdf

[2] http://www.courts.state.ny.us/courts/nyc/housing/resourcecenter.shtml

[3] http://www.courts.state.ny.us/courts/nyc/housing/locations2.shtml

[4] http://www.courts.state.ny.us/courts/nyc/housing/fees.shtml

[5] http://www.courts.state.ny.us/courts/nyc/housing/ servicenoticeof petition.shtml

[6] http://www.courts.state.ny.us/courts/nyc/housing/resolutionpart.shtml

[7] http://www.courts.state.ny.us/courts/nyc/housing/resolution video .shtml

Doc. 1a. Starting a Roommate Holdover Case

In General

A roommate holdover case is brought to make a roommate leave the apartment or house that you share. You cannot lock your roommate out of the home you share without a court order.

If you are a renter, to start a roommate holdover case, your roommate must rent from you not the landlord. If your roommate is named on the lease and also rents from the landlord or owner, then you can't start a case in Housing Court. Your roommate is a co-tenant and has the same right to stay in the home as you do. If the police charge your roommate with a crime, like assault or harassment, you may be able to get a Order of Protection from Criminal Court.

To start a roommate case, your roommate must be someone who is supposed to pay you rent to live with you. If your roommate is someone you let live in your home without paying rent, then you can start a "licensee" holdover case, not a roommate holdover. You can visit a Help Center to learn more.

The Notice of Termination

Before you can start a court case to make your roommate leave, you may need to give (serve) your roommate a Notice of Termination. Read the informa-

tion section on Roommate Holdover Termination Notices before continuing below.

Starting the Case

To start a case to make your roommate move out of the home or apartment that you share, you need to fill out a Notice of Petition and a Petition. Use the free DIY (Do-It-Yourself) roommate holdover computer program provided by the NYS Courts Access to Justice Program to make your court papers. The DIY program will help you make your court forms and give you instructions on what to do next.

Once you have used the DIY program, bring your notarized original papers (including the Notice of Termination), your DIY User Survey (if applicable) and your copies to the cashier's window in the Landlord-Tenant Clerk's office to buy an index number. Payment may be made by cash, certified check or money order. Make the money order or certified check payable to the "Clerk of the Civil Court." Go to Locations to find out where to go in your county. Go to Court Fees to find out the cost of filing the Notice of Petition.

You must choose the court date on the Notice of Petition. The court date must be between 5 and 12 days after delivery ("service") of the court papers is "completed." When service is completed depends on how the papers are delivered. Ask the Clerk or go to the Help Center if you do not understand.

A Landlord/Tenant clerk will give you the courtroom number and the assigned time for you to fill out on the papers. The clerk will give you back the Notice of Petition with the index number stamped onto it and the date of the hearing. The Clerk will keep the Petition.

When the Clerk returns the Notice of Petition to you, arrange your copies into three sets for your roommate (and your roommate's roommate, if applicable). The Notice of Petition should be on top, then the Petition with the Notice of Termination and Affidavit of Service of the Notice of Termination for your roommate (and your roommate's roommate, if applicable). Fill in the court date, the courtroom Part, the courtroom number and the time listed on your original Notice of Petition on all of the copies of the Notice of Petition. Fill in the Index No.(Number) on the copies of the Notice of Petition and Petition. In the signature space put /S/ and copy the name of the Clerk of the Court. Keep the original Notice of Petition separate from the copies. Now you are ready to have your server deliver the papers to the your roommate.

You must make sure your roommate receives a copy of the Notice of Petition and the Petition in the manner required by law. The copies of the Petition and Notice of Petition must be served not less than five calendar days and not more than twelve calendar days from the court date. Go to Service of the Notice of Petition and Petition to learn more.

After service of the Notice of Petition and Petition, and the mailings (if necessary) are done, you must bring back the original Notice of Petition and the original Affidavit of service to the Court. Bring stamps for postcards with you. When you return the papers to the court ask the Clerk for a postcard. You must fill it out and put a stamp on it so the Clerk can mail the postcard to your roommate (and roommate's roommate, if applicable). Your roommate will have to answer the Petition in Court.

Going to Court

You must go to the courtroom on the court date. Go to Directions if you do not know how to get to the courthouse. Get there early, because you will need to go through a metal detector before you can go into the courthouse. Bring all the evidence you have to prove your case. The first courtroom you go to is called a "Resolution Part." To learn more about what happens there, go to Resolution Part, or you may watch a Video about the Resolution Part. If you have questions, you can visit a Help Center in any Civil Court.

Doc. 2.   Answering a Case

Answering: In General

If you have received a petition from the civil court, you must appear and answer within the time period provided for in the notice of petition. If you have received a postcard from the court indicating that papers have been filed asking the court to evict you from your residence, you must also answer. You should bring a copy of the court papers you received, or the postcard from the court, when you come to answer.

If you are an individual, you may answer either orally or in writing. Any individual named as respondent, or any person in possession or claiming possession of the premises, may submit an answer. Your answer should include any legal or equitable defense or explanation that you might have. You may also make a counterclaim in response to a petition at that time.

If you do not answer and appear, the party suing you may be able to enter a possessory judgment and/or a money judgment against you. The petitioner may be able to evict you, as well as garnish your wages or levy on your bank account. If you received a notice from a marshal or a sheriff you may be able to vacate your default and/or stop the eviction. You can learn more about this and other housing court procedures by reading our Legal and Procedural Information sections.

The time to answer the petition and the procedures for answering a nonpayment petition and a holdover petition differ and are set forth below. You should bring a copy of the court papers you received, or the postcard from the court, when you come to answer. The clerk will ask you to show some form of identification.

Answering a Nonpayment Petition

If you are served with a nonpayment petition you must answer within 5 days after you have received the notice of petition. To find out where to answer in your county, refer to Locations [1]. The clerk will set a date for trial between 3 days and 8 days after you answer. You may answer orally or in writing.

To answer orally, you must come to Court and speak to a clerk at the counter who will check off a Landlord/Tenant Answer In Person form based upon what you tell him or her. You should tell the clerk if you are in the military or a dependent of someone in the military. The Answer in Person form contains a list of possible defenses that may or may not apply to you. After the clerk completes this form you will get a duplicate copy of it. Check to make sure that your answer was correctly recorded by the clerk before you leave the counter. If the answer is not correct, tell the clerk. Bring your copy of this form and all court papers to court on the hearing date.

View information on Answering a Notice of Petition And Petition (CIV-LT-92). To read more about the defenses listed on the Answer in Person form, go to the Housing Fact Sheets. If you live in a rent stabilized or NYCHA apartment, you can use the interactive Nonpayment Answer Program to learn about your defenses and help you prepare to answer a nonpayment petition in person. You can also watch a community seminar about Defenses to a Nonpayment Proceeding.

You may answer in writing by using a free Civil Court form, or your own form. You may come to the clerk's office and request a Landlord/Tenant Answer In Writing And Verification form from the clerk at the counter. You will be given two duplicate copies of this form. You may also download the form. You can download the Answer in Writing Instructions.

The procedure for a written answer is more complicated and if not done properly, your answer may be rejected. You must fill out the written answer form and then serve the form on the other side. If you do not prepare your written answer in court, the procedure is slightly different. Go to Serving Your Written Answer for instructions on how to serve the answer correctly. Bring your copy of the answer and all court papers to court on the hearing date.

Answering a Holdover Petition

If you are served with a holdover petition, generally you must answer orally or in writing in the courtroom on the date of the hearing. However, if the petitioner serves the notice of petition at least 8 days prior to the return date, the notice of petition may ask you to answer at least 3 days before the hearing date. To find out where to answer in your county, go to Locations [1].

If you answer orally by coming to the court and speaking to a clerk at the counter, the clerk will indorse your answer on the court file. You should tell the clerk if you are in the military or a dependent of someone in the military. You may also answer in writing by coming to court and asking the clerk for a Landlord/Tenant Answer In Writing And Verification form, or you may submit your own written answer. You may also download the Answer in Writing civil court form. You can download the Answer in Writing Instructions. The procedure for a written answer is more complicated and if not done properly, your answer may be rejected. You must fill out the written answer form and then serve the form on the other side. If you do not prepare your written answer in court, the procedure is slightly different. Continue reading below for instructions on how to serve the answer correctly. Bring your copy of the answer and all court papers to court on the hearing date.

Serving Your Written Answer

After you have completed a written answer, you must serve the petitioner by following the instructions below.

1. Make two copies of the completed written answer.

2. Have someone over the age of 18, who is not a party in this action, mail a copy of the written answer by regular mail to the attorney for the petitioner or to the petitioner directly only if there is no attorney.

3. You may also have someone over the age of 18, who is not a party in the action, personally deliver the written answer to the petitioner's attorney, or the petitioner directly only if there is no attorney.

4. Next you need an affidavit swearing that the written answer was served. Download the free Affidavit of Service civil court form.

5. Prepare an Affidavit of Service for the service on the petitioner and have the person who served the written answer sign the Affidavit of Service in front of a notary.

6. Attach the original Affidavit of Service to the original written answer.

7. For Nonpayment cases, return the written answer and affidavit of service to the Court within five days of receiving the notice of petition.

8. For Holdover cases, if the notice of petition requires you to answer prior to the hearing date, you must return the original of the answer and affidavit of service in the court at least three days before the hearing date. Otherwise, you may bring the written answer to court on the hearing date.

9. Keep a copy for your records and bring all your papers with you when you come to court for the hearing date.

Jury Demand

You can also request that your case be tried before a jury. In a jury trial, the jury, not the judge, makes the decision and a judgment is entered based on the verdict reached by the jury.

If you wish to make a jury demand, you should request a jury trial when you answer the petition. You can tell the clerk and pay the jury demand fee. Go to Court Fees [2] to learn the amount of the fee. If you cannot afford to pay the fee, you may be entitled to have the fee waived. Refer to Poor Person's Relief to learn more.

Keep in mind that the Judge may later decide that you are not entitled to a jury trial because you gave up your right in your lease. Most leases include an agreement to give up a right to a jury trial.

You can also request a jury demand at a later time. However, the judge may deny your request, if you wait too long. For more information on filing a late jury demand, go to Timeliness of Jury Demands to read the Civil Court Directive on the subject.

Inspection Request

If you have a repair problem in your apartment or building, you should ask for an inspection from the clerk or the Judge the first time you are in court or as soon after that as possible. An inspector from the Department of Housing Preservation and Development will come to your home and make a report to the court. The report will help you prove that there are bad conditions that need repair.

If you request an inspection, you may get a date for the inspection and a date to return to court. You will be asked to make a list of the repairs needed. Make sure to include every problem in each room of your apartment and in the public areas of the building. To view a copy of the Tenant's Request for Inspection, make an Inspection Request. If you fail to include a problem or area on the inspection request form, the inspector may refuse to look at it.

On the day of the inspection, it is important that someone be home to let the inspector in. Be sure to show the inspector all of the problems you listed.

Traverse Hearing

If you did not receive a copy of the notice of petition and petition, or you believe that the papers were not served properly, that is a defense to the case and should be included in your answer. Refer to Service of the Notice of Petition and Petition to learn more about the proper way to deliver legal papers. If you raise this defense, the judge may decide to set a date for a hearing, called a traverse hearing, to decide whether the service of the court papers was proper.

At the traverse hearing, the landlord's process server may be asked to tell under oath how he or she served you with the court papers. You will have the right to ask the process server questions, to testify yourself, and to call witnesses to explain that the papers were not delivered properly.

If the judge finds that the service of the papers were not served properly, the case will be dismissed without prejudice. The landlord may start the case over again by giving you a new set of papers. If you receive another set of papers, you must come to court and answer them again.

[1] http://www.courts.state.ny.us/courts/nyc/housing/locations2.shtml

[2] http://www.courts.state.ny.us/courts/nyc/housing/fees.shtml

Doc. 3.　Poor Person's Relief

If you do not have enough money to pay the court costs and fees of the proceeding, you may ask the court to permit you to proceed without having to pay the court costs. These costs include the charges for starting an HP proceeding, filing a petition to be restored to possession, filing a jury demand, and appealing a court ruling.

Your application for "poor person's relief" is made by motion and must be supported by an affidavit which must:

1) set forth the amount and sources of your income, and list your property with its value;

2) state that you are unable to pay the costs, fees and expenses necessary to prosecute or defend the action or proceeding or to maintain or respond to the appeal;

3) indicate the nature of the action or proceeding;

4) provide sufficient facts so that the merit of your claims can be determined;

5) indicate whether any other person would benefit from any award in your case, and if so, whether that person is unable to pay such costs fees and expenses.

You may obtain the affidavit from the court or you may download the civil court form now by clicking on Poor Person's Relief[1]. To find out where to make your application in your county, click on Locations[2].

If the judge approves your application, the judge will sign an order listing which fees and costs you do not have to pay. This order may also contain directions that if you recover any money in your lawsuit, the money shall be paid to the Clerk of the Court which may then recover the fees and costs which you previously could not afford to pay.

If you are starting the case, you may make your application to the court without notifying anyone else. Once your application has been approved the judge may order that a copy of your application and the order granting it be mailed to the New York City Corporation Counsel's office at 100 Church Street, New York, New York 10007. If the case has already begun and you are applying for fees to be waived, you must serve all parties and the New York City Corporation Counsel's office.

[1] http://www.courts.state.ny.us/courts/nyc/housing/forms/ PoorPersonsRelief.pdf

[2] http://www.courts.state.ny.us/courts/nyc/housing/locations2.shtml

Doc. 4.　Service of the Notice of Petition and Petition to Start a Nonpayment or Holdover Proceeding

The procedure for service of the papers to start a residential landlord-tenant proceeding is set forth below. For further information on service, you may refer to the Real Property Actions and Proceedings Law section 735.

Who May Serve

1. You may NOT serve the papers yourself.

2. Anyone over the age of 18 years, and NOT A PARTY to the action may serve the papers.

3. If you wish, you may hire a Process Server to serve the papers. See the yellow pages of the phone book to locate one.

When to Serve

Papers may not be served on Sunday. Papers may be served during three time periods:

　　Non-working hours: 6:00 a.m. — 7:59 a.m.

　　Working hours: 8:00 a.m. — 6:00 p.m.

　　Non-working hours: 6:01 p.m. — 10:30 p.m.

How to Serve

A copy of the papers shall be served on the respondent Personally or by Substituted delivery. If neither of those methods can be achieved after a reasonable application, the papers may be served by Conspicuous Place delivery:

a. *Personal delivery:* A copy of the papers may be served by giving it to the respondent in his or her hand. The papers can be handed to the respondent anywhere.

b. *Substituted delivery:* A copy of the papers may be given to any individual who answers the apartment door as long as he or she resides or is employed in the apartment and is of an appropriate age and has appropriate judgment to receive the papers. By the next business day, the server must mail one copy of the papers by regular mail and one copy by certified mail. Keep the certified mail receipts.

c. *Conspicuous Place delivery:* If the server is unsuccessful on the first try to serve the papers either by personal delivery or substituted service, then he or she must make a second attempt during a different time period (see time periods above). For example, if no one is home during working hours, the server can return at 7:30 p.m. during non-working hours. After two unsuccessful attempts have been made to serve the person at home either by personal delivery or substituted service, the server may then use conspicuous place delivery. This is also known as "nail and mail."

This delivery requires that a copy of the papers be affixed to the door of the actual residence of the respondent or be slipped under the entrance door of the apartment. By the next business day, the server must mail one copy of the papers by regular mail and one copy by certified mail to the respondent. Keep the certified mail receipts.

After the summons is served, the person who served the papers must fill out an affidavit of service (see below).

Affidavit of Service

1. After the COPY of the notice of petition and petition has been served, the person who served it shall fill out an Affidavit of Service. You may download the form now by clicking on Affidavit of Service?[1] , or you may obtain a form from the Court Clerk. The Affidavit of Service shall include a description of the color of skin, hair color, approximate age, approximate weight and height, and other identifying features of the person served.

2. After the Affidavit of Service has been filled out the server shall sign it before a Notary Public, and have it notarized.

3. The completed Affidavit of Service, must be returned to the Clerk's Office within 3 days of the personal delivery or mailing. Make copies of the affidavit of service for your records prior to filing it with the court.

4. You should bring a copy of the papers with you to court on the hearing date.

[1] http://www.courts.state.ny.us/courts/nyc/housing/forms.shtml

Doc. 5. RPAPL Sec. 735

735. Manner of service; filing; when service complete

1. Service of the notice of petition and petition shall be made by personally delivering them to the respondent; or by delivering to and leaving personally with a person of suitable age and discretion who resides or is employed at the property sought to be recovered, a copy of the notice of petition and petition, if upon reasonable application admittance can be obtained and such person found who will receive it; or if admittance cannot be obtained and such person found, by affixing a copy of the notice and petition upon a conspicuous part of the property sought to be recovered or placing a copy under the entrance door of such premises; and in addition, within one day after such delivering to such suitable person or such affixing or placement, by mailing to the respondent both by registered or certified mail and by regular first class mail,

(a) if a natural person, as follows: at the property sought to be recovered, and if such property is not the place of residence of such person and if the petitioner shall have written information of the residence address of such person, at the last residence address as to which the petitioner has such information, or if the petitioner shall have no such information, but shall

have written information of the place of business or employment of such person, to the last business or employment address as to which the petitioner has such information; and

(b) if a corporation, joint-stock or other unincorporated association, as follows: at the property sought to be recovered, and if the principal office or principal place of business of such corporation, joint stock or other unincorporated association is not located on the property sought to be recovered, and if the petitioner shall have written information of the principal office or principal place of business within the state, at the last place as to which petitioner has such information, or if the petitioner shall have no such information but shall have written information of any office or place of business within the state, to any such place as to which the petitioner has such information. Allegations as to such information as may affect the mailing address shall be set forth either in the petition, or in a separate affidavit and filed as part of the proof of service.

2. The notice of petition, or order to show cause, and petition together with proof of service thereof shall be filed with the court or clerk thereof within three days after;

(a) personal delivery to respondent, when service has been made by that means, and such service shall be complete immediately upon such personal delivery; or

(b) mailing to respondent, when service is made by the alternatives above provided, and such service shall be complete upon the filing of proof of service.

Doc. 6. Stopping an Eviction

If you have received a notice from a marshal that you are to be evicted you must come to court as soon as possible. This is a very serious matter, and you must take care of it immediately. If you do not take care of it, the marshal may remove you and your property from the apartment. You can call the marshal's office to find out if the marshal has scheduled your eviction yet. The phone number for the marshal's office is on the notice.

Bring the notice and any other papers that you have received from your landlord, including any rent receipts, to the court. To find out where to go in your county to try to stop or delay your eviction, click on Locations [1].

At the courthouse you will fill out an affidavit in support of an Order to Show Cause. The type of affidavit depends on whether you ever answered or appeared in the case. You will fill out an affidavit explaining why you should not be evicted.

If you never answered a petition and the petitioner obtained a default judgment against you, you will fill out an Affidavit In Support of An Order To Show Cause to Vacate A Judgment Based Upon Failure To

Answer. In the affidavit you will explain the reason you did not answer the petition - for example - you never received a copy of it. You will also explain your defense to the proceeding - for example - you paid all the rent. You can use the free DIY (Do-It-Yourself) Form to make your Affidavit in Support of an Order to Show Cause.

If you answered a petition, and a court order or stipulation resulted, or you did not appear in the courtroom and a default judgment was entered, you will fill out an Affidavit in Support of an Order to Show Cause To Vacate A Judgment. If you need more time to pay a judgment or an order, indicate how much time you need and why in the affidavit.

The clerk will send your papers, along with the court file to the judge who handled your case. You may have to wait in the clerk's office or to go to the courtroom where your papers have been sent. The Judge may sign your order to show cause, but may not stop the eviction until the case can be heard. The Judge may also sign the order to show cause, but place conditions, such as paying the rent or bringing proof of funds to pay to court. You must read the order to show cause carefully.

If the judge signs your order to show cause, you must then serve the papers on the other side according to the directions in the order to show cause. You must return to the courthouse on the hearing date with proof of service at the time and in the room designated on the Order to Show Cause.

If the judge declines to sign your order to show cause, or signs it upon conditions that you do not agree with, you may challenge this determination by going to the Appellate Term. You may click on Locations [1] to find the address of the Appellate Term in your county.

[1] http://www.courts.state.ny.us/courts/nyc/housing/locations2.shtml

Doc. 7.   Resolution Part

A Resolution Part is a courtroom where the landlord and tenant can discuss their differences before a Judge or Court Attorney to see if an agreement can be reached to settle the dispute. You may also be there for a motion or an order to show cause.

A Resolution Part is presided over by a Judge, who is assisted by two court attorneys, a clerk, and a court officer. The court officer, wearing the uniform, stands in the courtroom to maintain order. The clerk, sitting at a desk at the front of the courtroom, can answer any questions you may have about the calendar or the Judge's rules. The court attorneys, who are lawyers, assist the Judge. In addition, volunteer court representatives are present to assist. The Judge sits on the bench at the front of the Courtroom and hears motions and cases and reviews stipulations and orders to show cause.

Each Resolution Part has its own rules which are posted on the wall and can be obtained from the court clerk. You can also view the Judge's rules at Part Rules. Depending upon the rules of the part, you must either quietly check in with the court clerk or court officer, or listen for your case to be called. If you need an interpreter, you should tell the court clerk.

Your case may have been assigned to one of the Housing Courts specialty Parts depending on the subject matter:

City Part

Coop/Condo Part

New York City Housing Authority Part

Housing Part Proceedings (HP) (proceeding to compel repairs)

When a case is called, the landlord and tenant, or their attorneys will meet with the judge or court attorney to discuss the case. If you are not the named tenant or the named landlord, but are in court on their behalf, you should let the court personnel know. If you are a tenant and your apartment needs repairs, you can ask for an inspection. If you are a landlord and you have completed the repairs, you can ask for an inspection. You may go to Inspection Request to view the civil court form. You will have to come back to Court at a later date if the Judge grants the request for an inspection. You may have an attorney represent you on your case. If you need time to get an attorney or if you need documents that you do not have with you today, or if you have another reason for not being ready, you can ask to come back at a later date. This is called an adjournment. At the landlord's request, the Judge can order the tenant to deposit the future rent if the tenant requests two adjournments or if the case has been in court for more than 30 days.

While you are waiting for the case to be called, you must be quiet. Just as you would want other people to be quiet when your case is being heard, others in the courtroom should receive the same courtesy. If you are approached by the other party or the party's lawyer in your case, you do not have to speak to that person outside the presence of the judge or court attorney. However, you should feel free to step outside the courtroom to speak to the other party or lawyer only if you want to. Every case will be discussed by either the judge or the court attorney before you leave.

There is mediation available in some boroughs as an alternative to having a judge decide your case. In a mediation session, a professionally trained neutral person sits down with the parties, and each party has an opportunity to explain his or her position on the issues in dispute, listen to each other, and work together to reach a mutually acceptable solution. Any agreement reached through mediation will be reviewed by the Court. If you are unable to resolve your case through mediation, your case will be sent back to the Resolution Part. Not all cases are appropriate for mediation. Learn more about mediation at Dispute Resolution Through Mediation. If you wish to have a mediator handle your case either tell the court clerk or say so when you answer the calendar.

When your case is called the judge or court attorney will discuss the case to see if the case can be settled. If after discussing the case, the landlord and tenant agree to a settlement of the case, a document called a Stipulation of Settlement will be written up for the landlord and tenant to read and sign. No one can force anyone to settle a case or sign an agreement. No one should agree to settle a case if they do not agree with the terms of the settlement. The Stipulation of Settlement is a binding agreement between the landlord and tenant. In the Stipulation of Settlement, the landlord and tenant may agree to do certain things by certain dates. If the landlord or tenant fails to follow through on her or his end of the agreement, there may be very serious consequences. It is important that you only make an agreement that you know you can keep and that you agree with.

If, after discussing the case, the landlord and tenant cannot reach an agreement, the case will be referred to another part of the Housing Court, called a Trial Part, for trial. Except, cases assigned to the HP Part remain in the part for trial and do not go to a different Trial Part. The trial may take place that day or it may be scheduled for another date depending on the Court's calendar and on whether the Judge determines that the case is ready for trial. You may learn more about trials at How to Prepare for a Landlord–Tenant Trial.

If you have any questions that have not been answered here, you can learn more about other housing court procedures by reading our Legal and Procedural Information sections. There is also a Public Help Center in the courthouse where you may obtain more information at no cost. Refer to Help Center to learn more and for hours of operation.

View a video on the Resolution Part.

Doc. 8. Restore to Possession

If you think you have been improperly evicted by a marshal based upon a court order or judgment you may seek to be restored to possession. You should come to court as soon as possible. If your landlord has illegally locked you out of your apartment without first going to court and obtaining a judgment of possession and a warrant of eviction, you may also seek to be restored to possession, but you must start a proceeding against your landlord. You may refer to illegal lock-out for more information.

To find out where to go in your county to be restored to possession after eviction by a marshal, go to Locations[1]. At the court, you will fill out an Affidavit In Support Of An Order To Show Cause To Restore To Possession. In your affidavit, you must

explain the reasons that entitle you to be put back into your apartment. If you failed to answer a petition or failed to appear in court, you must explain this. If you have defenses to the proceeding, for example, that the rent was paid and you have receipts, you must list your defenses. You should bring all documents in support of your claim. Once you have filled out the Affidavit, the clerk will witness it for you.

The clerk will then submit your Affidavit and an Order to Show Cause to a Judge for review. You may have to wait in the clerk's office or go to the courtroom where your papers have been sent. If your application is signed you will need two or three copies of the Order to Show Cause and Affidavit in Support. You will either be given copies or lent the originals so that you can make the copies yourself. The original Order to Show Cause and Affidavit in Support goes back to the Clerk. You must then serve a copy of the papers on the other side in the manner directed in the order to show cause. The papers should be served by someone over the age of 18, who is not a party in the action. For more information, you can refer to Orders to Show Cause.

You must return to court on the hearing date, which will generally be within one or two days, at the room and time indicated on the order to show cause. You should bring proof of service, a copy of the papers and any other proof of your defenses with you on the hearing date.

If the judge declines to sign your Order to Show Cause or signs it with conditions that you do not agree with, you may challenge this determination by going to the Appellate Term. You may refer to Locations[1] to find the addresses of the Appellate Term in your county.

You can also watch a community seminar discussing what legal and procedural steps to take if you have been evicted from your home called, "What to Do If You've Been Evicted."

1 http://www.courts.state.ny.us/courts/nyc/housing/locations2.shtml

Doc. 9. Adjournments

In General: Appearance Required

An adjournment may only be granted by the judge presiding at the time of the hearing. You can not call the court clerk for this purpose because the clerk is not permitted to grant adjournments. To get an adjournment, you should appear at the hearing at the appointed time. You will be given an opportunity to explain to the judge your reason for requesting an adjournment. If you know the name of the Judge assigned to your case, you should check the Judge's Part Rules to see if he or she has any requirements that may not be covered in this section. Click on Judge's Rules[1] to check.

Important: Please be aware that upon a second request by a respondent for an adjournment, or if more than 30 days have passed since the case first appeared before the judge, not counting any days due to adjournment requests by the petitioner, the petitioner may ask the judge to order that all the money due from the date of service of the petition be deposited in the court. If this is done, the judge will determine the amount and the respondent will have to make the deposit within five days. If the money is not deposited, the petitioner may get a default judgement against the respondent.

Sending Someone to Request the Adjournment

If it is an emergency and you cannot appear yourself to request the adjournment, but wish to send someone on your behalf, you **must** give that person written authorization to make the request for you. That person must bring the written authorization to the court.

The written authorizing statement which allows someone to request an adjournment on your behalf **must** contain the following items:

1. The index number of your case.

2. Your name and your address.

3. A signed statement that you are allowing the person to request an adjournment for you.

4. The name of the person you are sending.

5. The reason you are not appearing yourself to make the request.

The person who comes to court for you must bring this statement and all other papers that you received, and should be able to tell the clerk the reason for the request.

The Judge may deny the request for adjournment. If the request is denied, you will be marked in default, which may be serious. You can learn more about this and other housing court procedures by reading our Legal and Procedural Information sections.

Writing a Letter to Request an Adjournment

In an extreme emergency, where neither you nor anyone else can appear on your behalf, you may write a letter to the court. You must explain your reason for making the request and be sure to include the case number and year of your case, and the scheduled date of the hearing you will not be able to attend.

Address the letter to the appropriate civil court clerk's office. Send a copy of this letter to the other party to the action. If the judge decides to grant your adjournment, you will be notified.

If the request is denied, you will be marked in default, which may be very serious. You can learn more about this and other housing court procedures by reading our Legal and Procedural Information sections.

---

1 http://www.courts.state.ny.us/courts/nyc/housing/files.shtml   judges_pro-

Doc. 10.   Order to Show Cause

In General

An Order to Show Cause is a way to present to a judge the reasons why the court should order relief to a party. For example, a tenant who has failed to appear and had a judgment entered against him or her may ask the court to vacate the judgment and restore the case to the calendar; or a landlord may request an order awarding a judgment and warrant of eviction against a tenant who has failed to live up to an agreement to pay rent.

The Order to Show Cause is an alternative to the notice of motion and is different from it, as the Order to Show Cause can shorten the time within which the parties must return to court. It is often used in emergency situations where a stay of the proceedings is required, or if an immediate result is sought. Another significant difference is that a judge must sign an Order to Show Cause. This means that the judge may decline to sign it. A notice of motion will appear on the calendar automatically, and does not need a judge's signature. If you are not sure a judge would sign your order to show cause, if you do not need to appear in court within the motion service time, or if you do not seek interim relief such as a stay before the motion is heard, you may decide to bring a motion instead of an order to show cause.

The Order to Show Cause informs your opposition of what you are seeking from the court and why. It provides the date, time and location where the request will be made. The Order to Show Cause often contains a direction to the parties that they stop some specific activity, like an eviction, until the court hears or decides the motion.

In limited cases an Order to Show Cause can be used to start a case, as an alternative to a notice of petition. Ordinarily an HP case and an illegal lockout are commenced this way.

The requirements for making a motion are standardized and generally more demanding than that for making an Order to Show Cause. Order to Show Cause forms are available at the courthouse, and a judge can set the terms, such as when it will be heard in court, how it will be served on the other side and any conditions or requirements in order to obtain a stay of enforcement of an order or judgment pending the hearing.

The Order to Show Cause must be accompanied by an "Affidavit in Support" and copies of any documents that support the request and would persuade the judge your application should be granted. Copies of all these papers must be served on all the parties in the manner directed on the Order to Show Cause itself. A party served with an Order to Show Cause may prepare papers to oppose the motion. On the hearing date, all parties must come to court and the judge will decide the Order to Show Cause.

If you would like to bring an Order to Show Cause or if you have been served with one and you want to oppose it, continue reading below.

Affidavit in Support

An Order to Show Cause must be supported by an Affidavit. An Affidavit is a sworn statement made before the clerk or notary public which explains to the court why your request should be granted.

The Clerk will give you a free Civil Court form when you come to court, or you may use one of your own, or download a form at Affidavit in Support. To find out where to go in your county to bring an Order to Show Cause, go to Locations. If you missed your court date or didn't answer a petition in a nonpayment or holdover case, you can use the Tenant Affidavit to Vacate a Default Judgment program to make your affidavit in support of your order to show cause.

In the Affidavit in support you should:

1. State the reason you are making your request.

2. State the relevant facts about your case.

3. State whether or not you have ever made the same request before.

4. Attach copies of any relevant documents you are referring to in your Affidavit.

After you have filled out the Affidavit, you must sign it at the bottom in front of the clerk, or in front of a notary, so that it can be attached to the Order to Show Cause and submitted to a Judge.

Submission to the Judge

After the Affidavit is witnessed by the clerk, the clerk will then submit your Affidavit with the Order to Show Cause to a Judge for review. You may have to wait awhile in the clerk's office.

If your application is signed by a Judge, you will need two or three copies of the Order to Show Cause and supporting papers. You will either be given copies or lent the originals so that you can make copies yourself. There are copy machines in the clerk's office, so bring change.

The original Order to Show Cause and Affidavit in Support goes back to the clerk. You must then serve a copy of the papers on the other side in the manner directed in the Order to Show Cause. The Order to Show Cause will often contain a provision requiring service by a specific date. If you are a respondent who has been served with a Marshal's Notice, you will also have to serve a copy of the Order to Show Cause on the Marshal. If your Order to Show Cause contains a provision which stays any eviction until the hearing date, and if you fail to serve the Marshal after the Judge signs your Order to Show Cause, you might get evicted.

The papers should be served by someone over the age of 18, who is not a party in the action, unless the judge has permitted otherwise. The clerk will give you further instructions, or you may speak with a Housing Court counselor in the Help Center.

If you are a tenant you may refer to the Instructions for further information on serving papers.

Opposition Papers

If you wish to oppose an order to show cause, you may prepare an Affidavit in Opposition. If you do not submit opposition papers and/or fail to appear in court to oppose the Order to Show Cause, the judge may decide to grant the relief requested based on the information in the Order to Show Cause and your default.

An affidavit is a sworn statement which must be signed in front of a notary public or a court clerk. You may attach copies of any relevant documents to the Affidavit in Opposition. You can download a free Civil Court form by at Affidavit in Opposition [1], you may use your own form, or obtain one from the clerk or the help center.

After you have prepared the opposition papers, follow the procedure outlined below:

1. Copies of the opposition papers must be served on all other parties.

2. Opposition papers must be served by a person who is not a party to the action and is eighteen years of age or older.

3. If a party has an attorney, the papers must be served on the attorney. Service of the opposition papers may be made by delivering the papers to the attorney personally, or by mailing the papers to the attorney.

4. After the opposition papers have been served, the person who served the papers must fill out an Affidavit of Service which states how and when the papers were served. The Affidavit of Service must be signed in front of a notary or a court clerk. You may download the free Housing Court form at Affidavit of Service.

5. Make a copy of the Affidavit of Service for your records and attach the original to the copy for the court.

6. Opposition papers can be filed in the courtroom on the date that the Order to Show Cause is heard, or in the clerk's office before that date.

Cross–Motions

If you have been served with an order to show cause and wish to ask the court for relief of your own, you may bring your own Order to Show Cause. Tell the clerk that you want your Order to Show Cause heard on the same day as the Order to Show Cause that is already scheduled to be heard, and if there is enough time, they can be calendared together. You can also schedule a cross-motion for the same day as the Order to Show Cause is noticed to be heard.

Reply Papers

If you have received opposition papers prior to the hearing date of the Order to Show Cause, you may have time to prepare an affidavit in reply. You may go to Reply Affidavit [2] to download a free Civil Court form; you may use a form of your own; or you may obtain one from the clerk or the Housing Court Resource Center. You must serve a copy of the reply affidavit on the other side and bring extra copies and the original, along with proof of service, to the courtroom on the date the Order to Show Cause is to be heard. If you did not have time to prepare reply papers and feel that it is necessary, you can ask the court for an adjournment for time to prepare reply papers. The judge may or may not grant your request.

Appearing in Court

You are required to appear in court on the date the Order to Show Cause is scheduled to be heard. You must appear at the time and place stated in the Order to Show Cause. If you need directions to the courthouse, Directions are available. In general, if you do not appear, and you are the moving party, your Order to Show Cause will be denied; if you do not oppose the motion, the Order to Show Cause may be granted on default. You should give yourself extra time to get to the courtroom since all visitors are required to go through metal detectors at the entrance to the courthouse. You should bring your copies of the papers with you and any papers and affidavits that you have not yet filed with the court.

The courtroom is presided over by a Judge, who is assisted by a court attorney, a clerk and a court officer. The court officer, wearing a uniform, maintains order in the courtroom. The clerk, sitting at a desk at the front of the courtroom, can answer any questions you have about the calendar or the judge's rules. The Judge sits on the bench at the front of the courtroom and hears arguments for and against motions and orders to show cause, reviews stipulations of settlement, and decides request for adjournments. The court attorney assists the Judge and may hold a conference with the parties to see if the order to show cause can be settled.

There is a calendar posted outside the courtroom that lists all the cases that will be called that day. Each case has a number. You should sit quietly in the courtroom and listen for your case to be called. You will have a chance to explain your case to the judge or the judge's court attorney. You always have the right to go before the Judge. You are not required to settle the Order to Show Cause, and you may request a hearing on the record. In that event, the Judge will decide your application.

If you are not ready to discuss the Order to Show Cause on the return date, or you need more time to prepare papers, when the case is called you can ask the court for a postponement or an adjournment of your application. If your case has been adjourned

before and marked "final" it means the judge will not allow any further adjournments. For more information, refer to Adjournments.

The other side may want to discuss the Order to Show Cause with you alone to see if you can come to an agreement. If you reach an agreement, you and the other side can write the terms of your agreement into a stipulation. However, you do not have to talk to the other side alone. You can wait until your case is called by the court and the judge will decide.

The Decision on the Order to Show Cause

If you and the other side are unable to agree about the relief being requested, the judge will make a decision on the Order to Show Cause. Sometimes, the judge makes a decision immediately. The judge has 30 days to decide the Order to Show Cause. Some Judges will mail you a copy of the order if you provide a self-addressed stamped envelope. Otherwise, you will have to go to the courthouse to get a copy of the decision. To find out where to go in your county refer to Locations [3].

Depending on the relief sought, the judge's decision may award a judgment to the winning party. When the winning party enters the judgment and serves a copy of the judgment with notice of entry on the losing party, this start's the loser's time to appeal running. To learn more, refer to Serving Notice of Entry [4].

If you are unhappy with the judge's decision and think that the judge made a legal or factual mistake, you can make a motion to reargue or renew, or file an appeal. The filing of an appeal alone does not stop or stay the execution of a judgment. An appeal requires the posting of an undertaking to stay an eviction.

An appeal must be filed within 30 days from the service of the order appealed from and written notice of entry. If neither side has served a copy of the decision and order with notice of entry, there is no time limitation on the filing of an appeal. For more information about appealing a decision, go to Appeals. [5]

---

[1] http://www.courts.state.ny.us/courts/nyc/housing/forms/ affinopposition.pdf

[2] http://www.courts.state.ny.us/courts/nyc/housing/forms/replyaff.pdf

[3] http://www.courts.state.ny.us/courts/nyc/housing/locations2.shtml

[4] http://www.courts.state.ny.us/courts/nyc/housing/ servingnoe.shtml

[5] http://www.courts.state.ny.us/courts/nyc/housing/appeals2.shtml

Doc. 11.   Stipulations and Settlements

In the Resolution Part, Mediation, or even in the Trial Part, the parties, with the assistance of the Judge, the Judge's court attorney, or the court mediator, will discuss the case in an effort to reach a settlement. Most cases in Housing Court are settled, meaning the parties come to an agreement, usually called a "Stipulation of Settlement," which is written down and signed by the parties and the Judge.

When you sign a Stipulation of Settlement, you are making a binding legal agreement that must be followed. Therefore, you must be very careful to read the agreement, understand it, and be certain that you will be able to do everything you have promised. The court attorney can explain any details in the Stipulation of Settlement that you do not understand. If you have any questions or doubts, you have the right to ask to talk to the Judge who must approve your settlement.

What a stipulation provides will depend on what the parties negotiate and the facts of the particular case. For more information about settling a nonpayment or holdover case, click on Tenant's Guide to Housing Court [1], or Landlord's Guide to Housing Court [2].

If decide to sign the stipulation of settlement the judge will speak you to make sure you understand the terms of the settlement. This is called an allocution. If you do not wish to settle the case, you have a right to a trial before a judge.

If you sign an agreement and then you cannot do what you promised - for example, you cannot pay on time or make repairs on time - you should come to court and bring an Order to Show Cause to request more time. If the other side has not done what they are supposed to do in the agreement, you can also come to court and bring an Order to Show Cause to request help from the court. Click on Order to Show Cause [3] if you want to learn more. A Judge will read your Order to Show Cause and decide whether to grant your request.

1 http://www.courts.state.ny.us/courts/nyc/housing/pdfs/ tenants guide.pdf

2 http://www.courts.state.ny.us/courts/nyc/housing/pdfs/ Landlord booklet.pdf

3 http://www.courts.state.ny.us/courts/nyc/housing/osc.shtml

Doc. 12. Judgments in Holdover Cases

In General

The outcome of a landlord/tenant case is either a judgment, dismissal or discontinuance.

There may be a judgment based upon respondent's default, after trial, by a stipulation of settlement of the parties or by motion.

The final judgment determines the issues raised in the proceeding and establishes the rights and obligations of the parties. The successful party is also awarded the costs and disbursements of the proceeding.

If the petitioner cannot show it is entitled to a judgment, the proceeding may be dismissed with prejudice and cannot be brought again, or dismissed without prejudice and may be brought again. A case can also be discontinued by the petitioner before the respondent has answered, with permission of the respondent or by order of the court.

A respondent's answer may contain a counterclaim, and the court may render a judgment on that counterclaim in favor of the respondent, or the counterclaim may be dismissed or discontinued with or without prejudice, or severed.

If the court awards the petitioner a possessory judgment, then a warrant of eviction may issue.

The judgment may include rent due, and if no rent is due while the respondent is in possession, the fair value of use and occupancy of the premises.

The judgment may also contain an award of legal fees to the winning party. Generally, each party in a law suit is responsible for its own legal fees, unless there is an agreement or a statute which provides otherwise. If the lease between the parties provides for an award of legal fees to the landlord for the tenant's failure to perform any agreement in the lease, the tenant also has the same right to collect an award of legal fees for his or her attorney.

Judgment when Respondent Fails to Answer or Appear

If a respondent fails to answer or appear in court, the petitioner is entitled to seek a default judgment. Unlike a nonpayment proceeding, the Judge will hold an inquest for the petitioner to prove his or her claims. The court will tell you when and where the inquest will take place, it may or may not be conducted in the Resolution Part. At the inquest, the petitioner will also be required to provide information as to the respondent's military status.

If the petitioner proves his or her case, the judge will direct that a judgment be entered. A final judgment in a holdover proceeding provides for a possessory judgment and may also provide for a money judgment. If the money judgment is not timely paid, the respondent can be evicted. Even if the money judgment is paid, or if there is no money judgment, the respondent can be evicted if there is a possessory judgment. The judge may require that the petitioner serve a copy of the judgment on the respondent. The judgment will normally permit the issuance of a warrant. Most petitioners contact a marshal, provide information and/or a copy of the judgment to the marshal and the marshal then files a request for the issuance of a warrant with the clerk. Once the warrant issues, the marshal may evict the respondent.

Learn the procedure for vacating the judgment.[1]

Judgment based on Stipulation of Settlement

If both sides appear, the case will be ready to proceed. A large number of holdover cases are settled in conferences which may include the petitioner, the respondent, the attorneys of either party, mediators, court attorneys, and at times even the Judge.

If the case is settled, a stipulation of settlement will be written. The stipulation of settlement may provide for the issuance of a judgment and warrant if the respondent fails to comply with the conditions of the stipulation. The stipulation may contain requirements for the petitioner to notify the respondent before the warrant may be issued. The stipulation may require the petitioner to make a motion to the court, either on notice or without notice to the other side, before the warrant can be executed. Whatever, the stipulation requires, the conditions must be complied with before the judgment and/or warrant can be entered or issued.

Once the petitioner has obtained a judgment and warrant of eviction based upon the stipulation of settlement, the marshal can evict the respondent.

Learn the procedure for vacating the judgment.[1]

Judgments after Trial

If both parties appear and a settlement cannot be reached, the case will be sent to a Trial Part for trial before a Housing Court Judge. If the petitioner proves his or her case, the Judge will direct that a judgment be entered after the trial. The judgment will be a possessory judgment. The judgment may also include rent due, and if no rent is due while the respondent is in possession, the fair value of use and occupancy of the premises. If the petitioner fails to prove his or her case, the judge will dismiss the case.

The Judge may not issue his or her decision on the same day that you try the case. This is called "decision reserved." The Judge may send you a copy of the decision in the mail. However, to be certain, you can call or come to court to learn if there has been a decision. (Learn where to go in your county.)[2].

The judgment will normally permit the issuance of a warrant. If the proceeding is based upon a claim that the respondent has breached a provision of the lease, the court will stay the issuance of the warrant for 10 days, during which time the respondent may correct the breach and avoid eviction.

Most petitioners contact a marshal, provide information and/or a copy of the judgment to the marshal and the marshal then files a request for the issuance of a warrant with the clerk. Once the warrant issues, the marshal may then evict the respondent.

Information about appealing the Judge's decision.[3]

Non–Military Affidavit

In order to obtain a judgment, the petitioner must provide information to the court regarding the respondent's military status. You may be required to file a non-military affidavit setting forth facts as to the basis of the belief that the respondent is not serving in the military, or is not a dependent of someone in military service. This affidavit generally must be less than 30 days old. You may view and/or download a copy of the Affidavit of Military Investigation, a free Civil Court form. For more information, refer to the Non–

Military Affidavit to read the Civil Court Directive on the subject.

[1] www.courts.state.ny.us/courts/nyc/housing/vacatingjudg.shtml
[2] http://www.courts.state.ny.us/courts/nyc/housing/locations2.shtml
[3] www.courts.state.ny.us/courts/nyc/housing/appeals.shtml

Doc. 13.   Stays Before Entry of Judgment

In General

Any party may seek a stay of a proceeding before a judgment is entered.

A judge may stay proceedings in a case, upon terms that are just, as well as for the reasons that are discussed below.

A landlord or a tenant seeking to obtain an extension of time to comply with an order to pay money, leave the premises, make repairs, or correct mathematical errors, may make an application to the court.

In order to obtain a stay you must come to court and fill out an Order to Show Cause. To read more about this process click on Orders To Show Cause [1]. To find out where to go in your county, click on Locations & Phone Listings [2].

If a judgment has already been entered in your case and you seek a stay, click on Stays after entry of judgment [3].

Stay for Failure to Make Repairs

A tenant may seek a stay of a pending nonpayment proceeding if he/she was constructively evicted, or upon proof that conditions dangerous to life, health or safety exist, as long as the condition was not caused by the tenant. A stay may also be requested if violations have been placed against the premises showing constructive eviction or dangerous conditions. (There must be proper proof that a notice or order to remove the violations has been made by the city department charged with enforcement.) Once violations have been placed, the burden of disproving the condition described by the violation is on the landlord or petitioner.

In order to obtain the stay the tenant must deposit the amount of rent due with the court. The stay may be vacated if such deposit is not made or if the conditions are repaired. During the stay, the court may direct the release of funds on deposit to pay for maintenance of the premises, repairs or utility bills.

Stay Based Upon Utility Shut–Off

A tenant residing in a multiple dwelling may seek a stay of a pending proceeding in the event that utilities are discontinued due to the landlord's failure to pay. The stay shall remain in effect until the landlord pays the amount owed and the utilities are restored to working order.

Stay if Building Where Tenant on Public Assistance Resides has Hazardous Violations

A tenant who receives welfare may seek a stay of entry of judgment in a nonpayment proceeding if there are violations in the building for dangerous conditions. This defense is available only for violations reported by DHPD to DSS. DSS must have withheld the rent from the landlord due to the violations in order for the tenant to assert this defense.

Stay Based Upon Change of Attorneys

There is an automatic stay of a proceeding if the attorney of record of any party dies, becomes incapacitated or is removed, suspended or otherwise disabled at any time before judgment. No further proceedings can be taken against this party without permission from the court. The stay continues until thirty days after notice to appoint another attorney has been served upon the party personally or in a manner directed by the court. If at the end of the stay the party has not replaced his/her attorney, or if he/she decided to continue without an attorney, pro se, the proceedings may continue against this party.

Stay Based Upon DHCR Order

In some cases a cause of action or a defense in a proceeding brought in Housing Court may be based upon an order issued by the DHCR. If a landlord or a tenant of a rent-stabilized or rent-controlled apartment files a complaint with the DHCR and disagrees with the resulting order issued by a District Rent Administrator, he/she may bring a Petition for Administrative Review (PAR) at the DHCR. The order may be stayed pending determination of the PAR.

The proper filing of a PAR against a DHCR order, other than an order adjusting, fixing or establishing the legal regulated rent, stays that order until the DHCR Commissioner makes a final determination. Where the DHCR order provides for an adjustment in rent, the retroactive portion of the adjustment, if any, is generally stayed, but not the prospective portion.

The DHCR Commissioner may grant or vacate a stay of its orders under appropriate circumstances, on such terms and conditions as the Commissioner deems appropriate.

1 http://www.courts.state.ny.us/courts/nyc/housing/definitions.shtml#osc

2 http://www.courts.state.ny.us/courts/nyc/housing/addresses.shtml

3 http://www.courts.state.ny.us/courts/nyc/housing/staysafterjudg_nonpay.shtml

Doc. 14. Stays After Entry of Judgment in a Holdover Proceeding

In General: Stay Of Enforcement Of Judgment Or Order Without Appeal

A tenant who lost at trial and seeks to stay the issuance of the warrant of eviction must apply to the judge who granted the landlord the judgment.

A landlord or a tenant seeking to obtain an extension of time to comply with orders to pay moneys, vacate the premises or make repairs, or to correct mathematical errors may be determined by any judge.

The court has the general power to stay proceedings in a proper case upon such terms as may be just, as well as specific powers as discussed below.

In order to obtain a stay you can come to court and fill out an Order to Show Cause. To read more about this process click on Orders To Show Cause [1]. To find out where to go in your county, click on Locations [2].

To learn about stays of enforcement of judgments when appealing, click on Appeals [3].

Obtaining a Maximum Six–Month Stay

A tenant who is the losing party in a holdover proceeding may ask the court for a stay of up to six months to relocate. The tenant must show he/she cannot find similar housing after a good faith, reasonable effort, or that extreme hardship to the tenant or his/her family would result without the stay. Such a stay is conditioned upon payment as the court shall direct for use and occupancy. Although the court has the discretion to grant a stay of up to six months, the tenant may get less time.

This six-month stay is not available where the landlord demonstrates he or she desires in good faith to demolish the building, intends to construct a new building and such plans have been duly filed and approved. The stay is also not available where the landlord claimed that the tenant is objectionable and has been found objectionable.

To learn more about the law which gives the judge the discretion to grant a stay after judgment of up to six months, click on Real Property Actions and Proceedings Law section 753.

Breach Of The Lease

The court will stay issuance of the warrant of eviction for ten days for a tenant or lessee who lost a holdover proceeding based upon a claim of breach of the lease. During that time the tenant or lessee may correct such breach.

Automatic Stay After Filing Bankruptcy Petition

When a residential tenant files a bankruptcy petition, an automatic stay prevents the landlord from bringing or continuing a case to obtain possession and from enforcing a judgment obtained before the commencement of the bankruptcy case. The purpose of the stay is to give the debtor a breathing spell from his creditors.

The automatic stay only applies to proceedings concerning property in which the debtor has an interest at the time the bankruptcy proceeding is filed.

In landlord/tenant cases the court may determine that the tenant no longer has an interest to protect at the time of filing a bankruptcy petition if the warrant of eviction has already issued. In both the New York State courts and the federal Bankruptcy Court, depending on the facts of the individual cases, the issuance of the warrant of eviction may or may not be a sufficient basis upon which to lift or modify the automatic stay, or to conclude that the bankruptcy petition did not qualify for an automatic stay.

After a tenant files for bankruptcy a landlord may seek to have the stay in Bankruptcy Court vacated in order to commence or continue an eviction proceeding. The Bankruptcy Court may terminate, modify or condition such stay based upon various factors, including payment of ongoing rent, the condition of the premises and the equities of the case. If the stay in Bankruptcy Court is lifted, the Civil Court will have jurisdiction to hear and decide the eviction proceeding, and the landlord who obtains a judgment and warrant of eviction will be able to evict the tenant.

If the tenant's debt, which includes past rent due, is discharged at the conclusion of the bankruptcy proceeding, the landlord may then seek recovery of the premises and eviction of the tenant/debtor. This is because while the debt may have been discharged, it has not been extinguished, and discharge of debt is not equivalent to payment of debt. A discharge only prevents a creditor from proceeding against a debtor on the debt as a personal liability, but does not eliminate any of the other consequences of that debt. Therefore, as long as the landlord does not attempt to obtain a money judgment for a discharged debt, the landlord is free to commence a nonpayment proceeding to recover possession. Thus a landlord may evict the tenant/debtor for his/her failure to pay rent which has been discharged in bankruptcy.

A debtor may voluntarily repay a debt that has been discharged even though the debt can no longer be legally enforced.

To find the Bankruptcy Court in your county, click on Locations [2].

[1] http://www.courts.state.ny.us/courts/nyc/housing/definitions.shtml#osc

[2] http://www.courts.state.ny.us/courts/nyc/housing/addresses.shtml

[3] http://www.courts.state.ny.us/courts/nyc/housing/appeals.shtml

Doc. 15.   Vacating a Default Judgment

If you have been sued in Housing Court and a judgment has been entered against you because you defaulted, that is, you failed to answer or did not show up to defend yourself, you can seek to have the judgment vacated (thrown out). If you do not, you could be evicted from your home by a marshal as a result of the judgment once the warrant of eviction is issued.

If you are not sure whether a judgment has been entered against you, you can click on Locations [1] and find out where to go in your county to check. If you find that a judgment has not been granted against you, then you should immediately file an answer. If you have already received a notice from a marshal, you should come to court right away.

To vacate a default judgment and obtain a stay of eviction, you should fill out an Order to Show Cause. An Order to Show Cause is a legal paper, signed by the judge, that orders the other side to appear in court and "show cause," that is, give a good reason, why the judgment should not be vacated. You must fill out an Affidavit in Support of the Order To Show Cause explaining the reason you did not go to court, such as, you never received notice of the proceeding, or you were sick; and, you must explain your defenses to the claims against you, such as, you do not owe the rent claimed, or you did not install the dishwasher in the kitchen in violation of the lease. To learn about the procedure, go to Order to Show Cause. If you missed your court date or didn't answer a petition in a nonpayment or holdover case, you can use the Tenant Affidavit to Vacate a Default Judgment program to make your affidavit in support of your order to show cause.

If the judge vacates the default judgment and restores the case to the calendar, you must be ready to prove your side of the case.

[1] http://www.courts.state.ny.us/courts/nyc/housing/addresses.shtml

Doc. 16.   Warrants

A warrant is a document issued by the court based upon a judgment of possession awarded by the court which permits the sheriff or marshal to remove persons from a premises. For information on obtaining a judgment, click on Judgments [1].

A warrant can only be issued to a sheriff or a marshal. After the judgment is awarded, you must contact the marshal so that the marshal can requisition the warrant from the court. For a list of New York City marshals, click on NYC Department of Investigation [2]. The marshal will require the facts of the proceeding, including the index number, the names of the parties, the address of the premises, and a copy of the judgment, or, if it is a judgment based upon the respondent's failure to answer, a letter requesting entry of the judgment. You will also have to pay the marshal a fee. The marshal will submit the papers to the court.

The warrant clerk will review the papers, and if everything is in order, the clerk will issue the warrant to the marshal. If the papers are defective, the clerk will return them to the marshal for correction.

After the marshal receives the warrant, the marshal is then ready to proceed with the eviction. For more information about the eviction, click on Eviction [3].

[1] http://www.courts.state.ny.us/courts/nyc/housing/judgments.shtml

[2] http://www.nyc.gov/html/doi/home.html

[3] http://www.courts.state.ny.us/courts/nyc/housing/eviction.shtml

Doc. 17.   Trial

In General

If the parties were unable to reach a settlement in the Resolution Part, the case will be ready to be tried.

The case will be assigned to a Trial Part. The court will tell the parties where and when to appear for the trial.

At the trial, the parties each get a chance to present their side of the case, and the judge will make a decision and judgment based on the evidence and arguments presented. The parties must have all their witnesses and evidence ready to present at the trial. If you have a good reason for not being ready to try the case, such as a medical reason, or one of your witnesses is out of town, you can ask the Judge for an adjournment. If this becomes necessary you should notify the other side ahead of time by mail that you are going to ask the court for an adjournment.

A case may still be settled in a Trial Part. A settlement is a voluntary, binding agreement that resolves the differences between the parties to a lawsuit. If the case is settled, there is no trial. For more information about settling a case, click on Stipulations and Settlements [1].

Jury Trials

If the petitioner or respondent has properly filed a jury demand and paid the jury demand fee, the case will be tried before a jury. Jury trials are very infrequent in Housing Court proceedings. If the case is tried before a jury, the jury, not the judge, will make the decision and then a judgment will be entered based on the verdict reached by the jury. If the jury is unable to reach a verdict, the Judge will have to declare a mistrial and the case will have to be tried again before a new jury.

A jury trial begins with jury selection. A panel of prospective jurors is called for voir dire. The Court will examine the jurors as to their qualifications. A party is entitled to challenge a juror for cause when a prospective juror is not qualified, such as, is not impartial, is related to one of the parties, or will not follow the law. A party is also entitled to a limited number of peremptory challenges. Six jurors, plus alternates, must be selected to hear the case.

After each side presents testimony and evidence, the judge will deliver a charge to the jury, which sets forth the jury's responsibility to decide the facts in light of the applicable rules of law.

Testimony of Witnesses

The petitioner's case is presented first. After being sworn as a witness, the petitioner will tell his or her version of the incident. All relevant papers or other evidence should be presented at this time to be offered in evidence. When the petitioner has finished testifying, the respondent has the right to ask questions. This is called cross-examination. After a party has cross-examined a witness, the other side has the chance to redirect examination of the witness in order to re-question the witness on points covered during the cross-examination. Sometimes the Judge may ask

questions to clarify matters. Other witnesses may be presented in support of the petitioner's claims, and they, too can be cross-examined by the respondent and questioned by the Judge.

The respondent may then be sworn and tell his or her side of the story and offer evidence. All papers or other evidence should be presented at this time to be offered in evidence. When the respondent has finished testifying, the petitioner has the right to cross-examine the respondent. After a party has cross-examined a witness, the other side has the chance to redirect examination of the witness in order to re-question the witness on points covered during the cross-examination. Sometimes a Judge may ask questions to clarify matters. Other witnesses may be presented in support of the respondent's claims, and they, too, can be cross-examined by the petitioner and questioned by the Judge. After the presentation of the respondent's case, the petitioner has the right to ask the Judge for an opportunity to present evidence to rebut the respondent's case.

Objections

There is a body of law called "rules of evidence." The purpose of these rules is to make sure that evidence is relevant, reliable and authentic. Because of these rules certain testimony or documents may not be legally admissible. For example, an affidavit is not admissible in evidence because its admission would deprive the other side of the right to question the person who wrote it.

Parties to a lawsuit have a right to object to the introduction of evidence or the way a question is being asked or answered. The proper way to object is to say "objection." The Judge may then ask what the basis for the objection is. If the Judge agrees with the objection, the Judge will say "sustained" and the evidence will not be admitted. If the Judge disagrees with the objection, the Judge will say "overruled" and the evidence will be admitted.

Trial Decision

When the trial is completed, you may have to wait for the Judge to write a decision. You may contact the court to see if a trial decision has been issued. To find out where to visit or call in your county, click on locations [2].

In a nonpayment or a holdover proceeding, the Judge may award a possessory judgment and/or a money judgment to the winning party. For more information, click on Judgments [3] to read the appropriate section. If you are the losing party, you may want to appeal. You may click on Appeals [4] to learn more.

1 http://www.courts.state.ny.us/courts/nyc/housing/stips.shtml
2 http://www.courts.state.ny.us/courts/nyc/housing/addresses.shtml
3 http://www.courts.state.ny.us/courts/nyc/housing/judgments.shtml
4 http://www.courts.state.ny.us/courts/nyc/housing/appeals.shtml

Doc. 18. Subpoenas

If you are unable to get a witness to appear voluntarily, or you need records produced in court that are not in your possession, you can ask the court to issue a subpoena. A subpoena is a legal document that commands the person named in it to appear in court to testify or to produce records. For example, DHCR, Buildings Department, HPD or the landlord's employees can be subpoenaed. (An expert witness cannot be compelled to testify by subpoena.)

If you would like to subpoena a witness or documents, you must come to court and fill out the subpoena forms. Click on Locations [1] to find out where to go in your county. After you have filled out the forms, the clerk will present the subpoena to the judge for signature, if necessary. You must then arrange for the service of the subpoena and the payment of a witness fee and, where appropriate, travel expenses for the person subpoenaed. You are responsible for paying these fees. Any person, including a friend or relative, who is 18 years of age or older and who is not a party to the proceeding can serve the subpoena. A party cannot serve a subpoena. For detailed information on how to serve a subpoena, click on Subpoena Instructions [2].

A subpoena can be served any time before the hearing. However, a witness should be given a "reasonable" amount of time before he or she must appear. Generally, it is considered reasonable to serve the subpoena at least 5 days before the hearing date. This will allow the person subpoenaed to prepare the items you request or appear at the hearing.

[1] http://www.courts.state.ny.us/courts/nyc/housing/addresses.shtml

[2] http://www.courts.state.ny.us/courts/nyc/housing/forms/ instructionsservicesubpoena.pdf

HP CASES

Doc. 1. Emergency Access and Repairs

Landlords

You may not begin a proceeding in Housing Court either by ex parte application or by Order to Show Cause solely to obtain access to a tenant's apartment for the purpose of correcting a violation or making a repair, even if the violation or repair is an emergency. For more information, you can read the Civil Court Directive on the subject of Access Orders.

If you are a landlord or owner and emergency repairs are urgently needed to prevent damage to the property or to prevent injury to persons, then you have a right to enter the apartment without advance notice to the tenant. For example, you would have the right to enter the apartment if there was smoke, water or gas coming out of the tenant's apartment.

In non-emergency situations, you have a right to enter the property to make necessary repairs at reasonable hours with reasonable notice. A tenant is required to give you reasonable access to perform repairs, make improvements, or for the purpose of an inspection. A tenant's refusal to let you in can be grounds to bring an eviction proceeding. To learn how to start a holdover case by serving a notice of petition and petition, go to Starting A Case.

Tenants

If you need emergency repairs due to conditions in your home which threaten life, health or safety, you may come to court and start a case against your landlord to obtain repairs. This case is called a HP proceeding. If the judge believes the condition is an emergency, you will get a hearing date within approximately one week of your request. After the hearing, the Judge will issue an order to correct directing the landlord to make repairs.

Tenants with emergency conditions, such as no heat, can also call 311 for emergency assistance, 24 hours a day, 7 days a week. For hearing impaired, call ITY (212) 863-5504. You may also click on HPD for more information.

To learn how to start a case against your landlord to obtain emergency repairs, click on Starting a HP Proceeding. Be sure to tell the Housing Part clerk that it is urgent that the conditions be repaired.

Doc. 2. Cold Weather Heat Requirements

October 1st — May 31st

During the Day between 6 a.m. — 10 p.m:

If it is below 55° outside, then it must be at least 68° inside.

At Night between 10 p.m. — 6 a.m.:

If it is below 40° outside, then it must be at least 55° inside.

Tenants without heat can call 311 for emergency assistance, 24 hours a day, 7 days a week. For hearing impaired, call ITY (212) 863-5504. You may also click on HPD for more information.

You may also click on HP proceeding to learn more about starting a proceeding to obtain repairs.

Doc. 3. Poor Person's Relief

If you do not have enough money to pay the court costs and fees of the proceeding, you may ask the court to permit you to proceed without having to pay the court costs. These costs include the charges for starting an HP proceeding, filing a petition to be restored to possession, filing a jury demand, and appealing a court ruling.

Your application for "poor person's relief" is made by motion and must be supported by an affidavit which must:

1) set forth the amount and sources of your income, and list your property with its value;

2) state that you are unable to pay the costs, fees and expenses necessary to prosecute or defend the action or proceeding or to maintain or respond to the appeal;

3) indicate the nature of the action or proceeding;

4) provide sufficient facts so that the merit of your claims can be determined;

5) indicate whether any other person would benefit from any award in your case, and if so, whether that person is unable to pay such costs fees and expenses.

You may obtain the affidavit from the court or you may download the civil court form now by clicking on Poor Person's Relief [1]. To find out where to make your application in your county, click on Locations [2].

If the judge approves your application, the judge will sign an order listing which fees and costs you do not have to pay. This order may also contain directions that if you recover any money in your lawsuit, the money shall be paid to the Clerk of the Court which may then recover the fees and costs which you previously could not afford to pay.

If you are starting the case, you may make your application to the court without notifying anyone else. Once your application has been approved the judge may order that a copy of your application and the order granting it be mailed to the New York City Corporation Counsel's office at 100 Church Street, New York, New York 10007. If the case has already begun and you are applying for fees to be waived, you must serve all parties and the New York City Corporation Counsel's office.

1 http://www.courts.state.ny.us/courts/nyc/housing/forms/ PoorPersonsRelief.pdf

2 http://www.courts.state.ny.us/courts/nyc/housing/addresses.shtml

Doc. 4. Starting an HP Case

If you have conditions or violations in your home which need to be repaired, including lack of heat and hot water or lack of other services, or have other emergency conditions, you may begin a proceeding against the landlord to force the landlord to make repairs and correct building violations. This is called a HP proceeding.

Before you do this, you should contact the landlord and let the landlord know that the conditions exist, that you want them repaired, and that you will go to court unless the repairs are made, If you write to the landlord, keep a copy of the letter so that you can bring it to court.

After you have contacted the landlord, and if the conditions are still not repaired, you may come to court in the county in which your apartment is located, to begin a HP proceeding against your landlord. To find out where to go in your county, click on Locations [1]. When you come to court be sure to bring the name and address of the landlord, or the managing agent, or both. The clerk will give you forms to fill out called an "Order to Show Cause Directing the Correction of Violations (HP Action)," and a "Verified Petition in Support of an Order to Show Cause Directing the Correction of Violation." In your petition you should list all the conditions in need of repair in each room of the apartment and public areas. You may also request an inspection of the conditions from the Department of Housing Preservation and Development by filling out a Tenant's Request For Inspection. You may click on Inspection Request [2] if you wish to download this form now. If you are seeking emergency repairs, you may not be able to have an inspection prior to the hearing date.

You must submit your signed and completed forms to the HP clerk along with payment of the court fee. The fee must be paid by cash, certified check, money order or bank check. Personal checks will not be accepted. You may click on Court Fees [3] to find out the cost of the fee. If you cannot afford to pay the court fee to start this case, you may apply to proceed as a poor person. For more information, click on Poor Person's Relief [4]. After you pay the fee to the cashier in the clerk's office you will be given an index number. If the HP Judge has approved your application to proceed as a poor person, you will be given a free index number.

The clerk will notarize your petition, and your application to proceed as a poor person if also submitted. The clerk will also assign an inspection date if you requested one. Your papers will be given to the HP Judge, who will review and sign your application, if appropriate. The clerk of the HP part will then assign a hearing date and a date by which you must serve these papers.

After obtaining the signed Order To Show Cause and the Petition from the clerk, you must then have the papers served on the respondent and the Department of Housing Preservation and Development (HPD) (and the New York City Corporation Counsel's Office if you are proceeding as a poor person). Check the Order to Show Cause for the directions as to how and by when the papers must be served. It may direct that the papers be served by certified mail, return receipt requested. The HP clerk will give you envelopes for service of these papers. Once you have served the papers you must fill out an Affidavit of Service. You may obtain this form from the clerk, or you may click on Affidavit of Service [5] to download the appropriate form now. Proof of service may be filed with the HP clerk before the court date, or with the clerk in the courtroom on the date of the hearing. The HP clerk will file the original of the petition with the court and give you a copy of the papers. For more information as to how to serve the Order to Show Cause and Verified Petition, go to Instructions.

Bring your copy of the papers with you to court on the hearing date, as well as any other records you think are important to your case.

To watch an instructional video on HP proceedings, go to Getting Repairs & Services.

1 http://www.courts.state.ny.us/courts/nyc/housing/addresses.shtml

2 http://www.courts.state.ny.us/courts/nyc/housing/forms/ inspection request.pdf

3 http://www.courts.state.ny.us/courts/nyc/housing/fees.shtml

4 http://www.courts.state.ny.us/courts/nyc/housing/forms/ PoorPersonsRelief.pdf

5 http://www.courts.state.ny.us/courts/nyc/housing/forms.shtml

Doc. 5. Appearing on an HP Case: Tenant Initiated Action

In General

The law requires that an owner maintain adequate services, and to keep a building and apartment in good repair. An inspector may be sent out by DHPD to see if the owner is providing essential services such as heat, hot water, or extermination, and is making repairs such as leaky faucets, faulty electrical outlets or peeling paint and plaster. If an inspector goes out to a premises and finds that the owner is not maintaining the building and apartment, the inspector will place violations against the building.

A tenant/petitioner may request that an inspector be sent out when bringing an HP case, or in the courtroom. However, an inspection report is not necessary for an HP case. A tenant can also prove the existence of conditions through photographs and testimony. If an inspector does go out and places a violation against the building, the violation can be classified in three different ways:

"A" violations are nonhazardous and must be corrected within 90 days.

"B" violations are hazardous and must be corrected within 30 days.

"C" violations are immediately hazardous and must be corrected within 24 hours.

Respondent/Owner's Answer or Appearance

If you are the respondent or owner and have been served with an order to show cause starting an HP case against you, you must appear in court on the date and time stated in the order to show cause. When your case is called, you will have a chance to raise before the judge any affirmative defenses you have.

Your possible defenses may include:

- lack of jurisdiction
- that petitioners lack standing to maintain the proceeding because they have no lawful right of possession
- that the conditions alleged do not constitute a violation of the Housing Maintenance Code or other laws relating to housing standards
- economic infeasibility.

In defense of your liability for civil penalties you may show:

- you timely corrected the violation and filed a certificate of compliance, or
- that the violation did not exist at the time the notice of violation was served.

In mitigation of your liability you may show that:

- although you quickly tried to correct the violation, you could not complete it in time due to technical difficulties
- you were unable to obtain necessary materials, funds or labor, or gain access
- you made a diligent and prompt application to get a permit or a license necessary to correct the violation, but you were unsuccessful
- the violation was caused by the act or negligence, neglect or abuse of another not in your employ or subject to your direction.

Courtroom Procedure

After the papers are served on the respondent and DHPD, all the parties are to appear in the HP part on the court date. Please check the calendar posted outside the courtroom to be sure that the case is scheduled for that day. If it is not listed, tell the clerk immediately. If it is listed, follow the check-in procedure. Find out who the DHPD attorney is and let him or her know who you are. The DHPD attorney appears on behalf of the City of New York, since you have sued it along with your landlord, and generally shares common interests with you. However, this attorney is not your attorney.

Settling an HP Action

Most of the conferences on HP cases are mediated by the attorney from DHPD. However, if there is a problem or if for some reason you are dissatisfied, the judge or his or her court attorney are also available. Most conferences lead to a settlement or an order to correct. In a stipulation of settlement the respondent will generally agree to make repairs in a short period of time. If the respondent requires more time, the stipulation may provide for an order to correct, which will allow the respondent the statutory time to make the repairs. It is always better to specify the days, the times, and the repairs that are to be done.

After the stipulation or order to correct is written, usually by the attorney for DHPD, all parties should review it to be sure that they understand what is to happen. The stipulation will also be reviewed by the court attorney and ultimately by the judge, who will 'so order' it. It is also important to understand that in an HP case the issue is the maintenance of the building. Other common landlord/tenant issues, such as payment of rent or breaches of a lease will not be discussed.

Inspections

In most cases the petitioner will be able to get an inspection scheduled at the time that the action is filed. This inspection will be carried out between the time that the action is filed and the court date. You can ask the clerk about this procedure or you can click on Inspection Request [1] for more information. If no inspection can be scheduled, or if there is no one home to allow the inspector access, the inspection may be requested in the courtroom.

If there is a disagreement as to the existence or severity of repair, any party may ask for an inspection in the courtroom. This will result in the case being adjourned so that an inspector can visit the apartment. The inspection form must be filled out properly so that the inspector can know what he or she is to look for.

Inquest

If the respondent/landlord fails to come to court, the attorney for DHPD will request an inquest. In the inquest the judge will take testimony from the petitioner, look at any inspection reports, etc., then may direct an 'order to correct.' The order to correct will be prepared by the DHPD staff in the HP part. It will be signed by the judge and will direct that work be done (violations be cured) by the respondent and will be served on the respondent by DHPD.

Trial

If the case can not be settled, the parties may have to go before the judge for a trial. In an HP case, the issue to be tried is the existence of violations and the respondent's failure to correct them. The petitioner's case can be proven by supplying evidence relating to the existence of violations. This can be done by a report from an inspector, by testimony from the petitioner and from other witnesses, by introducing pictures into evidence showing the violation, etc. A respondent may defend by showing that the repairs were corrected, do not exist, or were caused by the respondent or someone under her or his control, or that the tenant does not cooperate with the respondent to get the violations corrected. This is explained more fully in Respondent/owner's answer and appearance. At the end of the trial the judge will weigh the evidence and, if appropriate, direct an order to correct.

Post-appearance Proceedings

Both a so-ordered stipulation and an order to correct can form the basis for further proceedings. If the repairs are completed and the petitioner is satisfied, the case is finished. If the repairs are not completed, or are completed improperly, the petitioner may return to the clerk's office, explain what happened, and ask that the case be restored to the calendar for a finding of non-compliance with the judge's order. The clerk will supply the required forms and instructions. If the respondent has failed to correct the violations that he or she agreed to repair in a stipulation, the petitioner may seek an order to correct on the return to court. If there already was an order to correct, the respondent may seek an application for contempt. A motion to punish for contempt requests that the respondent be fined, jailed, or both for his or her failure to comply with a judge's order. The DHPD attorney will assist the petitioner with this process. Contempt is a 'last-resort' measure, and should only be utilized sparingly. In addition to that, it is difficult process which must be done correctly. In general, repairs can be secured without contempt proceedings, but in extreme cases this remedy is available. For more information, click on Contempt and Penalties [2].

[1] http://www.courts.state.ny.us/courts/nyc/housing/forms/ inspection request.pdf

[2] http://www.courts.state.ny.us/courts/nyc/housing/contempt.shtml

Doc. 6. Appearing on an HP Case: DHPD Initiated Action

In General

The law requires that an owner maintain adequate services, and to keep a building and apartment in good repair. An inspector may be sent out by DHPD to see if the owner is providing essential services such as heat, hot water, or extermination, and is making repairs such as leaky faucets, faulty electrical outlets or peeling paint and plaster. If an inspector goes out to a premises and finds that the owner is not maintaining the building and apartment, the inspector will place violations against the building.

If an inspector does go out and places a violation against the building, the violation can be classified in three different ways:

"A" violations are nonhazardous and must be corrected within 90 days.

"B" violations are hazardous and must be corrected within 30 days.

"C" violations are immediately hazardous and must be corrected within 24 hours.

Respondent/Owner's Answer or Appearance

If you are the respondent or owner and have been served with an order to show cause starting an HP case against you, you must appear in court on the date and time stated in the order to show cause. When your case is called, you will have a chance to raise before the judge any affirmative defenses you have.

Your possible defenses may include:

• lack of jurisdiction

• that the conditions alleged do not constitute a violation of the Housing Maintenance Code or other laws relating to housing standards

• economic infeasibility.

In defense of your liability for civil penalties you may show:

• you timely corrected the violation and filed a certificate of compliance, or

• that the violation did not exist at the time the notice of violation was served.

In mitigation of your liability you may show that:

• although you quickly tried to correct the violation, you could not complete it in time due to technical difficulties

• you were unable to obtain necessary materials, funds or labor, or gain access

• you made a diligent and prompt application to get a permit or a license necessary to correct the violation, but you were unsuccessful

• the violation was caused by the act or negligence, neglect or abuse of another not in your employ or subject to your direction.

Courtroom Procedure

Inspectors from DHPD visit buildings either on requests by tenants or as part of the regular inspection cycles. After an inspector finds a violation of the Housing Maintenance Code, he or she will record it, report it to DHPD, and DHPD will inform the landlord by sending him or her a Notice of Violation. This notice allows a certain amount of time, depending on the type of violation for the landlord to correct the violation and certify that it has been corrected to DHPD. If the landlord corrects the violation and so certifies to DHPD in a timely manner, the violation will be deemed corrected. If the landlord does not correct the violation, or corrects it but fails to certify the correction to DHPD, DHPD may sue the landlord for the failure to correct, for the failure to certify the correction, or for late certification. The suit may be over one, several, or building-wide violations. DHPD also sues over lack or insufficient heat and hot water.

When the landlord is sued by DHPD, the case is normally begun by the filing and service of a notice of petition and petitions, or sometimes by order to show cause and petition. Section 110 of the Civil Court Act specifies who may be served in this kind of case. The Order to Show Cause or notice of petition will specify a date for the landlord to appear in court. If the landlord appears, an attorney from DHPD will try to negotiate a settlement. When the case is settled the first time, the stipulation will normally provide for an order to correct with and may provide for a payment of money. If the violations are not corrected, and the respondent is brought back to court, DHPD will normally require money penalties as part of any further settlement. If the respondent does not agree to a settlement, a trial must be held.

Trial

In the trial, the DHPD will have to show that a violation was placed, that a notice of violation was served on the landlord, managing agent, etc., and that the certificate of correction was not filed in a timely manner. In defense of the claims by DHPD, the respondent may introduce evidence showing his or her lack of responsibility as set forth in Respondent/Owners Answer or Appearance.

Inquest

If the respondent fails to appear, the attorney for DHPD will request an inquest. In this inquest DHPD will have to show that the violation was placed, the notice of violation was served, the petition and notice were served, there was no certification of correction, and the specific time and class of each violation.

Judgment

After an inquest or a trial, if the petitioner proves his or her case, the court may order a judgment for money and an order to correct. The paperwork will be prepared for the judge to sign, and a copy of the judgment will be served on the respondent. The order to correct will serve as the basis for future contempt proceedings, and the judgment will be executed against the respondent.

Doc. 7. Resolution Part

A Resolution Part is a courtroom where the landlord and tenant can discuss their differences before a Judge or Court Attorney to see if an agreement can be reached to settle the dispute. You may also be there for a motion or an order to show cause.

A Resolution Part is presided over by a Judge, who is assisted by two court attorneys, a clerk, and a court officer. The court officer, wearing the uniform, stands in the courtroom to maintain order. The clerk, sitting at a desk at the front of the courtroom, can answer any questions you may have about the calendar or the Judge's rules. The court attorneys, who are lawyers, assist the Judge. In addition, volunteer court representatives are present to assist. The Judge sits on the bench at the front of the Courtroom and hears motions and cases and reviews stipulations and orders to show cause.

Each Resolution Part has its own rules which are posted on the wall and can be obtained from the court clerk. You can also view the Judge's rules at Part Rules. Depending upon the rules of the part, you must either quietly check in with the court clerk or court officer, or listen for your case to be called. If you need an interpreter, you should tell the court clerk.

Your case may have been assigned to one of the Housing Courts specialty Parts depending on the subject matter:

City Part

Coop/Condo Part

New York City Housing Authority Part

Housing Part Proceedings (HP) (proceeding to compel repairs)

When a case is called, the landlord and tenant, or their attorneys will meet with the judge or court attorney to discuss the case. If you are not the named tenant or the named landlord, but are in court on their behalf, you should let the court personnel know. If you are a tenant and your apartment needs repairs, you can ask for an inspection. If you are a landlord and you have completed the repairs, you can ask for an inspection. You may go to Inspection Request [1] to view the civil court form. You will have to come back to Court at a later date if the Judge grants the request for an Inspection. You may have an attorney represent you on your case. If you need time to get an attorney or if you need documents that you do not have with you today, or if you have another reason for not being ready, you can ask to come back at a later date. This is called an adjournment. At the landlord's request, the Judge can order the tenant to deposit the future rent if the tenant requests two adjournments or if the case has been in court for more than 30 days.

While you are waiting for the case to be called, you must be quiet. Just as you would want other people to be quiet when your case is being heard, others in the courtroom should receive the same courtesy. If you are approached by the other party or the party's lawyer in your case, you do not have to speak to that person outside the presence of the judge or court attorney. However, you should feel free to step outside the courtroom to speak to the other party or lawyer only if you want to. Every case will be discussed by either the judge or the court attorney before you leave.

There is mediation available in some boroughs as an alternative to having a judge decide your case. In a mediation session, a professionally trained neutral person sits down with the parties, and each party has an opportunity to explain his or her position on the issues in dispute, listen to each other, and work together to reach a mutually acceptable solution. Any agreement reached through mediation will be reviewed by the Court. If you are unable to resolve your case through mediation, your case will be sent back to the Resolution Part. Not all cases are appropriate for mediation. Learn more about mediation at Dispute Resolution Through Mediation [2]. If you wish to have a mediator handle your case either tell the court clerk or say so when you answer the calendar.

When your case is called the judge or court attorney will discuss the case to see if the case can be settled. If after discussing the case, the landlord and tenant agree to a settlement of the case, a document called a Stipulation of Settlement will be written up for the landlord and tenant to read and sign. No one can force anyone to settle a case or sign an agreement. No one should agree to settle a case if they do not agree with the terms of the settlement. The Stipulation of Settlement is a binding agreement between the landlord and tenant. In the Stipulation of Settlement, the landlord and tenant may agree to do certain things by certain dates. If the landlord or tenant fails to follow through on her or his end of the agreement, there may be very serious consequences. It is important that you only make an agreement that you know you can keep and that you agree with.

If, after discussing the case, the landlord and tenant cannot reach an agreement, the case will be referred to another part of the Housing Court, called a Trial Part, for trial. Except, cases assigned to the HP Part remain in the part for trial and do not go to a different Trial Part. The trial may take place that day or it may be scheduled for another date depending on the Court's calendar and on whether the Judge determines that the case is ready for trial. You may learn more about trials at How to Prepare for a Landlord–Tenant Trial.

If you have any questions that have not been answered here, you can learn more about other housing court procedures by reading our Legal and Procedural Information sections. There is also a Public Help Center in the courthouse where you may obtain more information at no cost. Refer to Help Center to learn more and for hours of operation.

View a video on the Resolution Part.

[1] http://www.courts.state.ny.us/courts/nyc/housing/forms/ inspection request.pdf

[2] http://www.courts.state.ny.us/courts/nyc/civil/pdfs/mediation.pdf

Doc. 8. Adjournments

In General: Appearance Required

An adjournment may only be granted by the judge presiding at the time of the hearing. You can not call the court clerk for this purpose because the clerk is not permitted to grant adjournments. To get an adjournment, you should appear at the hearing at the appointed time. You will be given an opportunity to explain to the judge your reason for requesting an adjournment. If you know the name of the Judge assigned to your case, you should check the Judge's Part Rules to see if he or she has any requirements that may not be covered in this section. Click on Judge's Rules [1] to check.

Important: Please be aware that upon a second request by a respondent for an adjournment, or if more than 30 days have passed since the case first appeared before the judge, not counting any days due to adjournment requests by the petitioner, the petitioner may ask the judge to order that all the money due from the date of service of the petition be deposited in the court. If this is done, the judge will determine the amount and the respondent will have to make the deposit within five days. If the money is not deposited, the petitioner may get a default judgement against the respondent.

Sending Someone to Request the Adjournment

If it is an emergency and you cannot appear yourself to request the adjournment, but wish to send someone on your behalf, you must give that person written authorization to make the request for you. That person must bring the written authorization to the court.

The written authorizing statement which allows someone to request an adjournment on your behalf must contain the following items:

1. The index number of your case.

2. Your name and your address.

3. A signed statement that you are allowing the person to request an adjournment for you.

4. The name of the person you are sending.

5. The reason you are not appearing yourself to make the request.

The person who comes to court for you **must** bring this statement and all other papers that you received, and should be able to tell the clerk the reason for the request.

The Judge may deny the request for adjournment. If the request is denied, you will be marked in default, which may be serious. You can learn more about this and other housing court procedures by reading our Legal and Procedural Information sections.

Writing a Letter to Request an Adjournment

In an extreme emergency, where neither you nor anyone else can appear on your behalf, you may write a letter to the court. You must explain your reason for making the request and be sure to include the case number and year of your case, and the scheduled date of the hearing you will not be able to attend.

Address the letter to the appropriate civil court clerk's office. Send a copy of this letter to the other party to the action. If the judge decides to grant your adjournment, you will be notified.

If the request is denied, you will be marked in default, which may be very serious. You can learn more about this and other housing court procedures by reading our Legal and Procedural Information sections.

1 http://www.courts.state.ny.us/courts/nyc/housing/ judges_profiles.shtml

Doc. 9. Order to Show Cause

In General

An Order to Show Cause is a way to present to a judge the reasons why the court should order relief to a party. For example, a tenant who has failed to appear and had a judgment entered against him or her may ask the court to vacate the judgment and restore the case to the calendar; or a landlord may request an order awarding a judgment and warrant of eviction against a tenant who has failed to live up to an agreement to pay rent.

The Order to Show Cause is an alternative to the notice of motion and is different from it, as the Order to Show Cause can shorten the time within which the parties must return to court. It is often used in emergency situations where a stay of the proceedings is required, or if an immediate result is sought. Another significant difference is that a judge must sign an Order to Show Cause. This means that the judge may decline to sign it. A notice of motion will appear on the calendar automatically, and does not need a judge's signature. If you are not sure a judge would sign your order to show cause, if you do not need to appear in court within the motion service time, or if you do not seek interim relief such as a stay before the motion is heard, you may decide to bring a motion instead of an order to show cause.

The Order to Show Cause informs your opposition of what you are seeking from the court and why. It provides the date, time and location where the request will be made. The Order to Show Cause often contains a direction to the parties that they stop some specific activity, like an eviction, until the court hears or decides the motion.

In limited cases an Order to Show Cause can be used to start a case, as an alternative to a notice of petition. Ordinarily an HP case and an illegal lockout are commenced this way.

The requirements for making a motion are standardized and generally more demanding than that for making an Order to Show Cause. Order to Show Cause forms are available at the courthouse, and a judge can set the terms, such as when it will be heard in court, how it will be served on the other side and any conditions or requirements in order to obtain a

stay of enforcement of an order or judgment pending the hearing.

The Order to Show Cause must be accompanied by an "Affidavit in Support" and copies of any documents that support the request and would persuade the judge your application should be granted. Copies of all these papers must be served on all the parties in the manner directed on the Order to Show Cause itself. A party served with an Order to Show Cause may prepare papers to oppose the motion. On the hearing date, all parties must come to court and the judge will decide the Order to Show Cause.

If you would like to bring an Order to Show Cause or if you have been served with one and you want to oppose it, continue reading below.

Affidavit in Support

An Order to Show Cause must be supported by an Affidavit. An Affidavit is a sworn statement made before the clerk or notary public which explains to the court why your request should be granted.

The Clerk will give you a free Civil Court form when you come to court, or you may use one of your own, or download a form at Affidavit in Support. To find out where to go in your county to bring an Order to Show Cause, go to Locations. If you missed your court date or didn't answer a petition in a nonpayment or holdover case, you can use the Tenant Affidavit to Vacate a Default Judgment program to make your affidavit in support of your order to show cause.

In the Affidavit in support you should:

1. State the reason you are making your request.

2. State the relevant facts about your case.

3. State whether or not you have ever made the same request before.

4. Attach copies of any relevant documents you are referring to in your Affidavit.

After you have filled out the Affidavit, you must sign it at the bottom in front of the clerk, or in front of a notary, so that it can be attached to the Order to Show Cause and submitted to a Judge.

Submission to the Judge

After the Affidavit is witnessed by the clerk, the clerk will then submit your Affidavit with the Order to Show Cause to a Judge for review. You may have to wait awhile in the clerk's office.

If your application is signed by a Judge, you will need two or three copies of the Order to Show Cause and supporting papers. You will either be given copies or lent the originals so that you can make copies yourself. There are copy machines in the clerk's office, so bring change.

The original Order to Show Cause and Affidavit in Support goes back to the clerk. You must then serve a copy of the papers on the other side in the manner directed in the Order to Show Cause. The Order to Show Cause will often contain a provision requiring service by a specific date. If you are a respondent who has been served with a Marshal's Notice, you will also have to serve a copy of the Order to Show Cause on the Marshal. If your Order to Show Cause contains a provision which stays any eviction until the hearing date, and if you fail to serve the Marshal after the Judge signs your Order to Show Cause, you might get evicted.

The papers should be served by someone over the age of 18, who is not a party in the action, unless the judge has permitted otherwise. The clerk will give you further instructions, or you may speak with a Housing Court counselor in the Help Center.

If you are a tenant you may refer to the Instructions [1] for further information on serving papers.

Opposition Papers

If you wish to oppose an order to show cause, you may prepare an Affidavit in Opposition. If you do not submit opposition papers and/or fail to appear in court to oppose the Order to Show Cause, the judge may decide to grant the relief requested based on the information in the Order to Show Cause and your default.

An affidavit is a sworn statement which must be signed in front of a notary public or a court clerk. You may attach copies of any relevant documents to the Affidavit in Opposition. You can download a free Civil Court form by at Affidavit in Opposition [2], you may use your own form, or obtain one from the clerk or the help center.

After you have prepared the opposition papers, follow the procedure outlined below:

1. Copies of the opposition papers must be served on all other parties.

2. Opposition papers must be served by a person who is not a party to the action and is eighteen years of age or older.

3. If a party has an attorney, the papers must be served on the attorney. Service of the opposition papers may be made by delivering the papers to the attorney personally, or by mailing the papers to the attorney.

4. After the opposition papers have been served, the person who served the papers must fill out an Affidavit of Service which states how and when the papers were served. The Affidavit of Service must be signed in front of a notary or a court clerk. You may download the free Housing Court form at Affidavit of Service [3].

5. Make a copy of the Affidavit of Service for your records and attach the original to the copy for the court.

6. Opposition papers can be filed in the courtroom on the date that the Order to Show Cause is heard, or in the clerk's office before that date.

Cross–Motions

If you have been served with an order to show cause and wish to ask the court for relief of your own, you may bring your own Order to Show Cause. Tell the clerk that you want your Order to Show Cause heard on the same day as the Order to Show Cause that is already scheduled to be heard, and if there is enough time, they can be calendared together. You can also schedule a cross-motion for the same day as the Order to Show Cause is noticed to be heard.

Reply Papers

If you have received opposition papers prior to the hearing date of the Order to Show Cause, you may have time to prepare an affidavit in reply. You may go to Reply Affidavit [4] to download a free Civil Court form; you may use a form of your own; or you may obtain one from the clerk or the Housing Court Help Center. You must serve a copy of the reply affidavit on the other side and bring extra copies and the original, along with proof of service, to the courtroom on the date the Order to Show Cause is to be heard. If you did not have time to prepare reply papers and feel that it is necessary, you can ask the court for an adjournment for time to prepare reply papers. The judge may or may not grant your request.

Appearing in Court

You are required to appear in court on the date the Order to Show Cause is scheduled to be heard. You must appear at the time and place stated in the Order to Show Cause. If you need directions to the courthouse, Directions are available. In general, if you do not appear, and you are the moving party, your Order to Show Cause will be denied; if you do not oppose the motion, the Order to Show Cause may be granted on default. You should give yourself extra time to get to the courtroom since all visitors are required to go through metal detectors at the entrance to the courthouse. You should bring your copies of the papers with you and any papers and affidavits that you have not yet filed with the court.

The courtroom is presided over by a Judge, who is assisted by a court attorney, a clerk and a court officer. The court officer, wearing a uniform, maintains order in the courtroom. The clerk, sitting at a desk at the front of the courtroom, can answer any questions you have about the calendar or the judge's rules. The Judge sits on the bench at the front of the courtroom and hears arguments for and against motions and orders to show cause, reviews stipulations of settlement, and decides request for adjournments. The court attorney assists the Judge and may hold a conference with the parties to see if the order to show cause can be settled.

There is a calendar posted outside the courtroom that lists all the cases that will be called that day. Each case has a number. You should sit quietly in the courtroom and listen for your case to be called. You will have a chance to explain your case to the judge or the judge's court attorney. You always have the right to go before the Judge. You are not required to settle the Order to Show Cause, and you may request a hearing on the record. In that event, the Judge will decide your application.

If you are not ready to discuss the Order to Show Cause on the return date, or you need more time to prepare papers, when the case is called you can ask the court for a postponement or an adjournment of your application. If your case has been adjourned before and marked "final" it means the judge will not allow any further adjournments. For more information, refer to Adjournments.

The other side may want to discuss the Order to Show Cause with you alone to see if you can come to an agreement. If you reach an agreement, you and the other side can write the terms of your agreement into a stipulation. However, you do not have to talk to the other side alone. You can wait until your case is called by the court and the judge will decide.

The Decision on the Order to Show Cause

If you and the other side are unable to agree about the relief being requested, the judge will make a decision on the Order to Show Cause. Sometimes, the judge makes a decision immediately. The judge has 30 days to decide the Order to Show Cause. Some Judges will mail you a copy of the order if you provide a self-addressed stamped envelope. Otherwise, you will have to go to the courthouse to get a copy of the decision. To find out where to go in your county refer to Locations [5].

Depending on the relief sought, the judge's decision may award a judgment to the winning party. When the winning party enters the judgment and serves a copy of the judgment with notice of entry on the losing party, this start's the loser's time to appeal running. To learn more, refer to Serving Notice of Entry [6].

If you are unhappy with the judge's decision and think that the judge made a legal or factual mistake, you can make a motion to reargue or renew, or file an appeal. The filing of an appeal alone does not stop or stay the execution of a judgment. An appeal requires the posting of an undertaking to stay an eviction.

An appeal must be filed within 30 days from the service of the order appealed from and written notice of entry. If neither side has served a copy of the decision and order with notice of entry, there is no time limitation on the filing of an appeal. For more information about appealing a decision, go to Appeals.

1 http://www.courts.state.ny.us/courts/nyc/housing/forms/ oscinstructions.pdf

2 http://www.courts.state.ny.us/courts/nyc/housing/forms/ affinopposition.pdf

3 http://www.courts.state.ny.us/courts/nyc/housing/ forms.shtml#affsofservice

4 http://www.courts.state.ny.us/courts/nyc/housing/forms/replyaff.pdf

5 http://www.courts.state.ny.us/courts/nyc/housing/locations2.shtml

6 http://www.courts.state.ny.us/courts/nyc/housing/servingnoe.shtml

Doc. 10.   Stipulations and Settlements

In the Resolution Part, Mediation, or even in the Trial Part, the parties, with the assistance of the Judge, the Judge's court attorney, or the court mediator, will discuss the case in an effort to reach a settlement. Most cases in Housing Court are settled, meaning the parties come to an agreement, usually called a "Stipulation of Settlement," which is written down and signed by the parties and the Judge.

When you sign a Stipulation of Settlement, you are making a binding legal agreement that must be followed. Therefore, you must be very careful to read the agreement, understand it, and be certain that you will be able to do everything you have promised. The court attorney can explain any details in the Stipulation of Settlement that you do not understand. If you have any questions or doubts, you have the right to ask to talk to the Judge who must approve your settlement.

What a stipulation provides will depend on what the parties negotiate and the facts of the particular case. For more information about settling a nonpayment or holdover case, click on Tenant's Guide to Housing Court [1], or Landlord's Guide to Housing Court [2].

If decide to sign the stipulation of settlement the judge will speak you to make sure you understand the terms of the settlement. This is called an allocution. If you do not wish to settle the case, you have a right to a trial before a judge.

If you sign an agreement and then you cannot do what you promised - for example, you cannot pay on time or make repairs on time - you should come to court and bring an Order to Show Cause to request more time. If the other side has not done what they are supposed to do in the agreement, you can also come to court and bring an Order to Show Cause to request help from the court. Click on Order to Show Cause [3] if you want to learn more. A Judge will read your Order to Show Cause and decide whether to grant your request.

1 http://www.courts.state.ny.us/courts/nyc/housing/pdfs/   tenants guide.pdf

2 http://www.courts.state.ny.us/courts/nyc/housing/pdfs/   Landlord booklet.pdf

3 http://www.courts.state.ny.us/courts/nyc/housing/osc.shtml

Doc. 11.   Vacating A Default Judgment

If you have been sued in an HP proceeding and a judgment has been entered against you because you defaulted, that is, you failed to answer or did not show up to defend yourself, you can seek to have the judgment vacated (thrown out). If you are not sure whether a judgment has been entered against you, you can click on Locations [1] and find out where to go in your county to check.

To vacate a default judgment, you should fill out an Order to Show Cause. An Order to Show Cause is a legal paper, signed by the judge, that orders the other side to appear in court and "show cause," that is, give a good reason, why the judgment should not be vacated. You must fill out an Affidavit in Support of the Order To Show Cause explaining the reason you did not go to court, such as, you never received notice of the proceeding, or you were sick; and, you must explain your defenses to the claims against you, such as, the apartment does not need any repairs. To learn about the procedure, click on Order to Show Cause [2].

If the judge vacates the default judgment and restores the case to the calendar, you must be ready to prove your side of the case.

[1] http://www.courts.state.ny.us/courts/nyc/housing/locations2.shtml

[2] http://www.courts.state.ny.us/courts/nyc/housing/osc.shtml

Doc. 12.   Contempt and Penalties

In General

A landlord who fails to carry out a court order to make repairs and/or restore services, may be subject to civil penalties and fines, liens, and civil or criminal contempt.

Civil Penalties

If the respondent/landlord fails to correct the conditions or violations as required by an order to correct, the petitioner/tenant or the New York City Department of Housing Preservation and Development (HPD) can restore the case to the calendar by order to show cause for a compliance hearing and assessment of civil penalties. The court form used to restore the HP case to the calendar may be obtained by going to the clerk's office in your county. Click on Locations[1] to find where to go in your county. For more information, click on Orders to Show Cause.[2]

Penalties imposed for violations of the Housing Maintenance Code are payable only to HPD.

Upon respondent/landlord's failure to correct conditions and/or violations, the court can assess the following penalties per day:

— $10.00—$50.00 for each "A"(nonhazardous) violation;

— $25.00—$110.00 for each "B" (hazardous) violation;

— $50.00 for each "C" (immediately hazardous) violation in a multiple dwelling containing five or fewer dwellings.

— $50.00—150.00, plus $125.00 for each "C" (immediately hazardous) violation occurring in a multiple dwelling containing more than five dwelling units.

Failure to provide heat and hot water when legally required can also result in the imposition of a penalty of $250.00 per day. To learn more about when a landlord must supply heat click on Cold Weather Heat Requirements. Hot water must be supplied at all times at a constant minimum of 120 degrees between the hours of 6 a.m. and midnight. A penalty of a minimum of $1,000.00, plus $25.00 per day for each day the violation continues, will be imposed for failure to keep the system which provides heat and hot water free of devices which impede its ability to meet its minimum requirements.

Liens

Any judgment in favor of HPD against a respondent/landlord becomes a lien against the property once the judgment is entered and a transcript of judgment is filed in the county clerk's office. HPD may seize the rents if the judgment remains unpaid. If the total amount of the lien equals or exceeds $5,000.00, HPD may secure an order appointing the HPD Commissioner as a receiver of the premises for purposes of taking rent, until the judgment is satisfied.

Contempt Proceedings

If the respondent/landlord fails to comply with the court order to cure the conditions and/or violations, the petitioner/tenant or HPD can also seek to punish the respondent with civil contempt and/or criminal contempt of court. In a contempt proceeding, the court may punish the landlord with fines and/or imprisonment.

The affidavit used to bring an order to show cause to punish the landlord for contempt and for civil penalties in an HP case may be obtained by going to the clerk's office in your county. Click on Locations[1] to find the clerk's office in your county. Click on Orders to Show Cause[2] to learn more.

[1] http://www.nycourts.gov/courts/nyc/housing/locations2.shtml

[2] http://www.nycourts.gov/courts/nyc/housing/osc.shtml

Doc. 13.   Subpoenas

If you are unable to get a witness to appear voluntarily, or you need records produced in court that are not in your possession, you can ask the court to issue a subpoena. A subpoena is a legal document that commands the person named in it to appear in court to testify or to produce records. For example, DHCR, Buildings Department, HPD or the landlord's employees can be subpoenaed. (An expert witness cannot be compelled to testify by subpoena.)

If you would like to subpoena a witness or documents, you must come to court and fill out the subpoena forms. Click on Locations [1] to find out where to go in your county. After you have filled out the forms, the clerk will present the subpoena to the judge for signature, if necessary. You must then arrange for the service of the subpoena and the payment of a witness fee and, where appropriate, travel expenses for the person subpoenaed. You are responsible for paying these fees. Any person, including a friend or relative, who is 18 years of age or older and who is not a party to the proceeding can serve the subpoena. A party cannot serve a subpoena. For detailed information on how to serve a subpoena, click on Subpoena Instructions [2].

A subpoena can be served any time before the hearing. However, a witness should be given a "reasonable" amount of time before he or she must appear. Generally, it is considered reasonable to serve the subpoena at least 5 days before the hearing date. This will allow the person subpoenaed to prepare the items you request or appear at the hearing.

[1] http://www.courts.state.ny.us/courts/nyc/housing/locations2.shtml

[2] http://www.courts.state.ny.us/courts/nyc/housing/forms/ instructionsservicesubpoena.pdf

UNLAWFUL EVICTION

Doc. 1.   Illegal Lock-outs

If you have legally occupied an apartment for at least 30 days (with or without a lease), you may not be evicted without a court order awarding a judgment of possession and warrant of eviction against you. This is a violation of the "illegal eviction law" and is a misdemeanor. You may click on unlawful eviction [1] to review the law.

If you have been forcibly or unlawfully locked out of your apartment without court order you should first call or visit your local police department for assistance. If the police are unable to help, you may start a proceeding in the Housing Court to be "restored to possession," which means put back in the apartment. You must come to court immediately and start a case called an "illegal lockout."

It is not an illegal lock-out if you have been evicted by a marshal based upon a court order or judgment. However, you may still seek to be put back in the apartment. Click on Restore to Possession [2] for information on how to proceed.

If you have been illegally locked-out of your apartment, click on Locations [3] to find out where to go in your county to be restored to possession. At the courthouse you will fill out a petition in support of an Order to Show Cause. In your affidavit, you must show that you have been wrongfully put out of your apartment. It is helpful to bring documentation, such as, a lease, rent receipts, utility bills and mail addressed to you at the apartment. The clerk will witness your completed petition, assign a hearing date and submit the papers to a judge.

If the judge signs your order to show cause, you must pay a court fee to the cashier to obtain an index number. The fee must be paid by cash, certified check, money order or bank check. Personal checks will not be accepted. You may click on Court Fees [4] to find out the cost of issuing the petition. If you cannot afford to pay the fee you may apply to proceed as a poor person. For more information, click on Poor Person's Relief [5].

You must serve your petition in the manner directed in the order to show cause. You must return to court on the hearing date, which will generally be within one or two days, at the room and time indicated. Bring your copy of the papers, proof of service, and any other proof with you on the hearing date.

1 www.courts.state.ny.us/courts/nyc/housing/unlawfuleviction.shtml

2 http://www.courts.state.ny.us/courts/nyc/housing/restoration.shtml

3 http://www.courts.state.ny.us/courts/nyc/housing/locations2.shtml

4 http://www.courts.state.ny.us/courts/nyc/housing/fees.shtml

5 http://www.courts.state.ny.us/courts/nyc/housing/poorrelief.shtml

Doc. 2.   Illegal Eviction Law

NYC Administrative Code § 26–521.   Unlawful eviction.

a. It shall be unlawful for any person to evict or attempt to evict an occupant of a dwelling unit who has lawfully occupied the dwelling unit for thirty consecutive days or longer or who has entered into a lease with respect to such dwelling unit or has made a request for a lease for such dwelling unit pursuant to the hotel stabilization provisions of the rent stabilization law except to the extent permitted by law pursuant to a warrant of eviction or other order of a court of competent jurisdiction or a governmental vacate order by:

(1) using or threatening the use of force to induce the occupant to vacate the dwelling unit; or

(2) engaging in a course of conduct which interferes with or is intended to interfere with or disturb the comfort, repose, peace or quiet of such occupant in the use or occupancy of the dwelling unit, to induce the occupant to vacate the dwelling unit including, but not limited to, the interruption or discontinuance of essential services; or

(3) engaging or threatening to engage in any other conduct which prevents or is intended to prevent such occupant from the lawful occupancy of such dwelling unit or to induce the occupant to vacate the dwelling unit including, but not limited to, removing the occupant's possessions from the dwelling unit, removing the door at the entrance to the dwelling unit; removing, plugging or otherwise rendering the lock on such entrance door inoperable; or changing the lock on such entrance door without supplying the occupant with a key.

b. It shall be unlawful for an owner of a dwelling unit to fail to take all reasonable and necessary action to restore to occupancy an occupant of a dwelling unit who either vacates, has been removed from or is otherwise prevented from occupying a dwelling unit as the result of any of the acts or omissions prescribed in subdivision a of this section and to provide to such occupant a dwelling unit within such dwelling suitable for occupancy, after being requested to do so by such occupant or the representative of such occupant, if such owner either committed such unlawful acts or omissions or knew or had reason to know of such unlawful acts or omissions, or if such acts or omissions occurred within seven days prior to such request.

Doc. 3.   Poor Person's Relief

If you do not have enough money to pay the court costs and fees of the proceeding, you may ask the court to permit you to proceed without having to pay the court costs. These costs include the charges for starting an HP proceeding, filing a petition to be restored to possession, filing a jury demand, and appealing a court ruling.

Your application for "poor person's relief" is made by motion and must be supported by an affidavit which must:

1) set forth the amount and sources of your income, and list your property with its value;

2) state that you are unable to pay the costs, fees and expenses necessary to prosecute or defend the action or proceeding or to maintain or respond to the appeal;

3) indicate the nature of the action or proceeding;

4) provide sufficient facts so that the merit of your claims can be determined;

5) indicate whether any other person would benefit from any award in your case, and if so, whether that person is unable to pay such costs fees and expenses.

You may obtain the affidavit from the court or you may download the civil court form now by clicking on Poor Person's Relief [1]. To find out where to make your application in your county, click on Locations [2].

If the judge approves your application, the judge will sign an order listing which fees and costs you do not have to pay. This order may also contain directions that if you recover any money in your lawsuit, the money shall be paid to the Clerk of the Court which may then recover the fees and costs which you previously could not afford to pay.

If you are starting the case, you may make your application to the court without notifying anyone else. Once your application has been approved the judge may order that a copy of your application and the order granting it be mailed to the New York City Corporation Counsel's office at 100 Church Street, New York, New York 10007. If the case has already begun and you are applying for fees to be waived, you must serve all parties and the New York City Corporation Counsel's office.

[1] http://www.courts.state.ny.us/courts/nyc/housing/poorrelief.shtml

[2] http://www.courts.state.ny.us/courts/nyc/housing/locations2.shtml

Doc. 4. Adjournments

In General: Appearance Required

An adjournment may only be granted by the judge presiding at the time of the hearing. You can not call the court clerk for this purpose because the clerk is not permitted to grant adjournments. To get an adjournment, you should appear at the hearing at the appointed time. You will be given an opportunity to explain to the judge your reason for requesting an adjournment. If you know the name of the Judge assigned to your case, you should check the Judge's Part Rules to see if he or she has any requirements that may not be covered in this section. Click on Judge's Rules [1] to check.

Important: Please be aware that upon a second request by a respondent for an adjournment, or if more than 30 days have passed since the case first appeared before the judge, not counting any days due to adjournment requests by the petitioner, the petitioner may ask the judge to order that all the money due from the date of service of the petition be deposited in the court. If this is done, the judge will determine the amount and the respondent will have to make the deposit within five days. If the money is not deposited, the petitioner may get a default judgement against the respondent.

Sending Someone to Request the Adjournment

If it is an emergency and you cannot appear yourself to request the adjournment, but wish to send someone on your behalf, you must give that person written authorization to make the request for you. That person must bring the written authorization to the court.

The written authorizing statement which allows someone to request an adjournment on your behalf **must** contain the following items:

1. The index number of your case.

2. Your name and your address.

3. A signed statement that you are allowing the person to request an adjournment for you.

4. The name of the person you are sending.

5. The reason you are not appearing yourself to make the request.

The person who comes to court for you **must** bring this statement and all other papers that you received, and should be able to tell the clerk the reason for the request.

The Judge may deny the request for adjournment. If the request is denied, you will be marked in default, which may be serious. You can learn more about this and other housing court procedures by reading our Legal and Procedural Information sections.

Writing a Letter to Request an Adjournment

In an extreme emergency, where neither you nor anyone else can appear on your behalf, you may write a letter to the court. You must explain your reason for making the request and be sure to include the case number and year of your case, and the scheduled date of the hearing you will not be able to attend.

Address the letter to the appropriate civil court clerk's office. Send a copy of this letter to the other party to the action. If the judge decides to grant your adjournment, you will be notified.

If the request is denied, you will be marked in default, which may be very serious. You can learn more about this and other housing court procedures by reading our Legal and Procedural Information sections.

1 http://www.courts.state.ny.us/courts/nyc/housing/judges_profiles. shtml

Doc. 5. Order to Show Cause

In General

An Order to Show Cause is a way to present to a judge the reasons why the court should order relief to a party. For example, a tenant who has failed to appear and had a judgment entered against him or her may ask the court to vacate the judgment and restore the case to the calendar; or a landlord may request an order awarding a judgment and warrant of eviction against a tenant who has failed to live up to an agreement to pay rent.

The Order to Show Cause is an alternative to the notice of motion and is different from it, as the Order to Show Cause can shorten the time within which the parties must return to court. It is often used in emergency situations where a stay of the proceedings is required, or if an immediate result is sought. Another significant difference is that a judge must sign an Order to Show Cause. This means that the judge may decline to sign it. A notice of motion will appear on the calendar automatically, and does not need a judge's signature. If you are not sure a judge would sign your order to show cause, if you do not need to appear in court within the motion service time, or if you do not seek interim relief such as a stay before the motion is heard, you may decide to bring a motion instead of an order to show cause.

The Order to Show Cause informs your opposition of what you are seeking from the court and why. It provides the date, time and location where the request will be made. The Order to Show Cause often contains a direction to the parties that they stop some specific activity, like an eviction, until the court hears or decides the motion.

In limited cases an Order to Show Cause can be used to start a case, as an alternative to a notice of petition. Ordinarily an HP case and an illegal lockout are commenced this way.

The requirements for making a motion are standardized and generally more demanding than that for making an Order to Show Cause. Order to Show Cause forms are available at the courthouse, and a judge can set the terms, such as when it will be heard in court, how it will be served on the other side and any conditions or requirements in order to obtain a stay of enforcement of an order or judgment pending the hearing.

The Order to Show Cause must be accompanied by an "Affidavit in Support" and copies of any documents that support the request and would persuade the judge your application should be granted. Copies of all these papers must be served on all the parties in the manner directed on the Order to Show Cause

itself. A party served with an Order to Show Cause may prepare papers to oppose the motion. On the hearing date, all parties must come to court and the judge will decide the Order to Show Cause.

If you would like to bring an Order to Show Cause or if you have been served with one and you want to oppose it, continue reading below.

Affidavit in Support

An Order to Show Cause must be supported by an Affidavit. An Affidavit is a sworn statement made before the clerk or notary public which explains to the court why your request should be granted.

The Clerk will give you a free Civil Court form when you come to court, or you may use one of your own, or download a form at Affidavit in Support. To find out where to go in your county to bring an Order to Show Cause, go to Locations. If you missed your court date or didn't answer a petition in a nonpayment or holdover case, you can use the Tenant Affidavit to Vacate a Default Judgment program to make your affidavit in support of your order to show cause.

In the Affidavit in support you should:

1. State the reason you are making your request.

2. State the relevant facts about your case.

3. State whether or not you have ever made the same request before.

4. Attach copies of any relevant documents you are referring to in your Affidavit.

After you have filled out the Affidavit, you must sign it at the bottom in front of the clerk, or in front of a notary, so that it can be attached to the Order to Show Cause and submitted to a Judge.

Submission to the Judge

After the Affidavit is witnessed by the clerk, the clerk will then submit your Affidavit with the Order to Show Cause to a Judge for review. You may have to wait awhile in the clerk's office.

If your application is signed by a Judge, you will need two or three copies of the Order to Show Cause and supporting papers. You will either be given copies or lent the originals so that you can make copies yourself. There are copy machines in the clerk's office, so bring change.

The original Order to Show Cause and Affidavit in Support goes back to the clerk. You must then serve a copy of the papers on the other side in the manner directed in the Order to Show Cause. The Order to Show Cause will often contain a provision requiring service by a specific date. If you are a respondent who has been served with a Marshal's Notice, you will also have to serve a copy of the Order to Show Cause on the Marshal. If your Order to Show Cause contains a provision which stays any eviction until the hearing date, and if you fail to serve the Marshal after the Judge signs your Order to Show Cause, you might get evicted.

The papers should be served by someone over the age of 18, who is not a party in the action, unless the judge has permitted otherwise. The clerk will give you further instructions, or you may speak with a Housing Court counselor in the Help Center.

If you are a tenant you may refer to the Instructions [1] for further information on serving papers.

Opposition Papers

If you wish to oppose an order to show cause, you may prepare an Affidavit in Opposition. If you do not submit opposition papers and/or fail to appear in court to oppose the Order to Show Cause, the judge may decide to grant the relief requested based on the information in the Order to Show Cause and your default.

An affidavit is a sworn statement which must be signed in front of a notary public or a court clerk. You may attach copies of any relevant documents to the Affidavit in Opposition. You can download a free Civil Court form by at Affidavit in Opposition [2], you may use your own form, or obtain one from the clerk or the help center.

After you have prepared the opposition papers, follow the procedure outlined below:

1. Copies of the opposition papers must be served on all other parties.

2. Opposition papers must be served by a person who is not a party to the action and is eighteen years of age or older.

3. If a party has an attorney, the papers must be served on the attorney. Service of the opposition papers may be made by delivering the papers to the attorney personally, or by mailing the papers to the attorney.

4. After the opposition papers have been served, the person who served the papers must fill out an Affidavit of Service which states how and when the papers were served. The Affidavit of Service must be signed in front of a notary or a court clerk. You may download the free Housing Court form at Affidavit of Service [3].

5. Make a copy of the Affidavit of Service for your records and attach the original to the copy for the court.

6. Opposition papers can be filed in the courtroom on the date that the Order to Show Cause is heard, or in the clerk's office before that date.

Cross–Motions

If you have been served with an order to show cause and wish to ask the court for relief of your own, you may bring your own Order to Show Cause. Tell the clerk that you want your Order to Show Cause heard on the same day as the Order to Show Cause

that is already scheduled to be heard, and if there is enough time, they can be calendared together. You can also schedule a cross-motion for the same day as the Order to Show Cause is noticed to be heard.

Reply Papers

If you have received opposition papers prior to the hearing date of the Order to Show Cause, you may have time to prepare an affidavit in reply. You may go to Reply Affidavit [4] to download a free Civil Court form; you may use a form of your own; or you may obtain one from the clerk or the Housing Court Help Center. You must serve a copy of the reply affidavit on the other side and bring extra copies and the original, along with proof of service, to the courtroom on the date the Order to Show Cause is to be heard. If you did not have time to prepare reply papers and feel that it is necessary, you can ask the court for an adjournment for time to prepare reply papers. The judge may or may not grant your request.

Appearing in Court

You are required to appear in court on the date the Order to Show Cause is scheduled to be heard. You must appear at the time and place stated in the Order to Show Cause. If you need directions to the courthouse, Directions are available. In general, if you do not appear, and you are the moving party, your Order to Show Cause will be denied; if you do not oppose the motion, the Order to Show Cause may be granted on default. You should give yourself extra time to get to the courtroom since all visitors are required to go through metal detectors at the entrance to the courthouse. You should bring your copies of the papers with you and any papers and affidavits that you have not yet filed with the court.

The courtroom is presided over by a Judge, who is assisted by a court attorney, a clerk and a court officer. The court officer, wearing a uniform, maintains order in the courtroom. The clerk, sitting at a desk at the front of the courtroom, can answer any questions you have about the calendar or the judge's rules. The Judge sits on the bench at the front of the courtroom and hears arguments for and against motions and orders to show cause, reviews stipulations of settlement, and decides request for adjournments. The court attorney assists the Judge and may hold a conference with the parties to see if the order to show cause can be settled.

There is a calendar posted outside the courtroom that lists all the cases that will be called that day. Each case has a number. You should sit quietly in the courtroom and listen for your case to be called. You will have a chance to explain your case to the judge or the judge's court attorney. You always have the right to go before the Judge. You are not required to settle the Order to Show Cause, and you may request a hearing on the record. In that event, the Judge will decide your application.

If you are not ready to discuss the Order to Show Cause on the return date, or you need more time to prepare papers, when the case is called you can ask the court for a postponement or an adjournment of your application. If your case has been adjourned before and marked "final" it means the judge will not allow any further adjournments. For more information, refer to Adjournments.

The other side may want to discuss the Order to Show Cause with you alone to see if you can come to an agreement. If you reach an agreement, you and the other side can write the terms of your agreement into a stipulation. However, you do not have to talk to the other side alone. You can wait until your case is called by the court and the judge will decide.

The Decision on the Order to Show Cause

If you and the other side are unable to agree about the relief being requested, the judge will make a decision on the Order to Show Cause. Sometimes, the judge makes a decision immediately. The judge has 30 days to decide the Order to Show Cause. Some Judges will mail you a copy of the order if you provide a self-addressed stamped envelope. Otherwise, you will have to go to the courthouse to get a copy of the decision. To find out where to go in your county refer to Locations [5].

Depending on the relief sought, the judge's decision may award a judgment to the winning party. When the winning party enters the judgment and serves a copy of the judgment with notice of entry on the losing party, this start's the loser's time to appeal running. To learn more, refer to Serving Notice of Entry [6].

If you are unhappy with the judge's decision and think that the judge made a legal or factual mistake, you can make a motion to reargue or renew, or file an appeal. The filing of an appeal alone does not stop or stay the execution of a judgment. An appeal requires the posting of an undertaking to stay an eviction.

An appeal must be filed within 30 days from the service of the order appealed from and written notice of entry. If neither side has served a copy of the decision and order with notice of entry, there is no time limitation on the filing of an appeal. For more information about appealing a decision, go to Appeals.

[1] http://www.courts.state.ny.us/courts/nyc/housing/forms/ oscinstructions.pdf

[2] http://www.courts.state.ny.us/courts/nyc/housing/forms/ affinopposition.pdf

[3] http://www.courts.state.ny.us/courts/nyc/housing/ forms.shtml#affsofservice

[4] http://www.courts.state.ny.us/courts/nyc/housing/forms/replyaff.pdf

[5] http://www.courts.state.ny.us/courts/nyc/housing/locations2.shtml

[6] http://www.courts.state.ny.us/courts/nyc/housing/servingnoe.shtml

Doc. 6. Stipulations and Settlements

In the Resolution Part, Mediation, or even in the Trial Part, the parties, with the assistance of the Judge, the Judge's court attorney, or the court mediator, will discuss the case in an effort to reach a settlement. Most cases in Housing Court are settled, meaning the parties come to an agreement, usually called a "Stipulation of Settlement," which is written down and signed by the parties and the Judge.

When you sign a Stipulation of Settlement, you are making a binding legal agreement that must be followed. Therefore, you must be very careful to read the agreement, understand it, and be certain that you will be able to do everything you have promised. The court attorney can explain any details in the Stipulation of Settlement that you do not understand. If you have any questions or doubts, you have the right to ask to talk to the Judge who must approve your settlement.

What a stipulation provides will depend on what the parties negotiate and the facts of the particular case. For more information about settling a nonpayment or holdover case, click on Tenant's Guide to Housing Court [1], or Landlord's Guide to Housing Court [2].

If decide to sign the stipulation of settlement the judge will speak you to make sure you understand the terms of the settlement. This is called an allocution. If you do not wish to settle the case, you have a right to a trial before a judge.

If you sign an agreement and then you cannot do what you promised - for example, you cannot pay on time or make repairs on time - you should come to court and bring an Order to Show Cause to request more time. If the other side has not done what they are supposed to do in the agreement, you can also come to court and bring an Order to Show Cause to request help from the court. Click on Order to Show Cause [3] if you want to learn more. A Judge will read your Order to Show Cause and decide whether to grant your request.

[1] http://www.courts.state.ny.us/courts/nyc/housing/pdfs/ tenantsguide.pdf

[2] http://www.courts.state.ny.us/courts/nyc/housing/pdfs/ Landlordbooklet.pdf

[3] http://www.courts.state.ny.us/courts/nyc/housing/osc.shtml

APPEALS

Doc. 1. Appeals

In General

An appeal cannot be taken from anything other than a written order or judgment made by a judge. Where matters have been settled by mutual agreement of the parties, through mediation, by ex parte order, or on default, no appeal is possible. In such cases, you must first bring a motion or order to show cause to vacate the settlement, the default judgment or the ex parte order. The order which grants or denies your motion or order to show cause is then appealable. You should consult an attorney regarding any legal remedies you may have.

The appeal process may be costly. In order to submit an appeal you will have to provide a copy of the transcript of the hearing, which may be transcribed from a tape recording machine or from the notes of a court reporter. The fee may be based upon the length of the transcript which must be prepared. It is suggested that you obtain an estimate of the cost of preparing a typewritten transcript of the minutes of the trial. You may also wish to listen to the tapes before having them transcribed. You may consider the information useful in determining whether or not to appeal. You may also qualify for Poor Person's Relief which would pay for the cost of the appeal. To find out where in your county to contact the court reporter, obtain a transcript of the tape recording of your hearing and/or apply for poor person's relief go to Locations [1].

A notice of appeal must be filed within 30 days from the service of the judgment or order appealed from, with written notice of its entry. If a copy of the judgment or order is not served, there are no time limitations on the filing of the appeal. Go to Serving "Notice of Entry" [2] to learn more.

A party served with a notice of appeal may take a cross-appeal within ten days after service of appellant's notice of appeal or motion papers, or within the original 30-day time period, whichever is later.

An appeal does not mean a new trial or the presenting of new evidence. Rather, it is a review of the relevant portions of the court file and the relevant portions of the transcript of the trial minutes by the judges of the Appellate Term of the State Supreme Court.

Stay of Enforcement of Judgment or Order Pending Appeal

In general, an appeal does not stop or stay the execution of a judgment. If there is a possessory judgment against you and you want to stop it while your appeal is being decided, you must follow the instructions in this section.

A stay is available to anyone facing an eviction who provides the required undertaking, that is, the deposit of an amount of money equal to the judgment amount, or another amount set by the court. The undertaking is required for protection in case any harm is committed against the property during the months that the appeal is being decided

In order to obtain a stay:

1. You must serve a notice of appeal on the other side.

2. You must apply to the trial court which rendered the judgment or order to set the amount of the undertaking. You may do so by order to show cause. The court will set the undertaking, which may include payment of use and occupancy in installments as it becomes due while the appeal is pending.

3. After the trial court sets the amount of the undertaking you must then deposit that amount with the clerk of the New York City Civil Court in your county. You may be required to continue to deposit use and occupancy as it becomes due while the appeal is pending.

4. The automatic stay is not effective until the notice of appeal is served, the court has set the undertaking and the appellant has paid the undertaking.

The appellant may also apply directly to the Appellate Term for a limited stay, or to vacate, limit or modify a stay imposed by the trial court. If a stay is granted, it may be based upon conditions determined within the discretion of the Appellate Term. It is likely that the amount the court will require to be deposited with the Civil Court as an undertaking will be the entire judgment amount awarded by the trial court.

If a respondent disagrees with the imposition of a stay, the respondent can challenge the stay at the court where the appeal is pending. That court has the power to vacate, limit or modify any stay imposed. The respondent must show that the appeal is without merit, was brought in bad faith or solely to delay, that the stay will cause an undue burden or hardship, or that the appellant failed to comply with the court's order requiring an undertaking.

Any New York State or political subdivision of the State, such as the New York City Housing Authority, can also obtain an automatic stay. For example, the Housing Authority or the City of New York can obtain an automatic stay if it appeals an order to correct violations or to perform repairs in an HP case, or an order in favor of a respondent in an eviction proceeding.

If you are interested in appealing a Housing Court judgment or order, which consists of filing a notice of appeal and perfecting the appeal, continue reading the procedure set forth below.

Filing of Notice of Appeal

The form required to appeal may be downloaded for free by going to Notice of Appeal [3] or you may obtain the form from the Appeals Clerk in your county.

Fill out the Notice of Appeal then make two copies. Have someone who is over the age of 18 and not a party serve a copy on the opponent. (If the opponent has an attorney, the attorney must be served). Such service may be by mail or in person. The server must fill out an affidavit of service form. Go to Affidavit of Service [4] to obtain the appropriate free civil court form.

The original Notice of Appeal with the Affidavit of Service must be filed with the Civil Court, and the fee paid. To find out the cost of the fee go to Court Fees [5]. If you do not have enough money to pay the fee, you may ask the court to waive the fees. To learn how to apply for a waiver of the filing fee, go to Poor Person's Relief [6]. To find out where to file the Notice of Appeal in your county, go to Locations [1].

The remaining copy should be retained by you for your records.

Obtaining the Transcript of Trial

The appellant must order and pay for a transcript of the minutes of the trial from a transcribing service if the proceedings were recorded by a digital recording system, or from the court reporter if one was present in the courtroom.

For the Record System (FTR)

There is a digital recording system in the courtroom that records all the proceedings before the Judge. To obtain a transcript of your hearing follow the steps below:

1. You must requisition the audio record in order to create a transcript. To do so you will need to know the index number of the case, the Part and the day(s) and time(s) that you were in court.

2. After you have that information and are ready to request the record, go to Locations [1] and check the section on "Tape Recording Transcription" to find out where to go in your county.

3. To listen to, get a copy of or to request that the record be transcribed, you will be asked to fill out a Civil Court "Request for Audio Record" form. On this form you will indicate the caption and index number of the case, the name of the judge, the part and room, the date(s) and time(s) of trial, and your name address and telephone number. This form must be signed and dated. If you wish to have the record transcribed at this point, you will need to add the

name of the transcription company (see number 5 below).

4. Court personnel will contact the person whose name and telephone number are listed on the form. You may return to court to listen to the record and/or obtain a copy of the record on a CD. You may also obtain a copy of the record, on an audio file, that can be emailed to a web address. You may wish to do this before having the record transcribed because the information may be useful in determining whether or not to appeal.

5. If you wish to have the record transcribed, you must select an Authorized Transcription Company from the list of Electronic Recorder Transcription Services. These companies are not employed by the court system and they set their own rates. You may obtain a copy of this list from the Audio Records Office (ARO).

6. The name of the Authorized Transcription Company must be added to the Request for Audio Records form.

7. The ARO will arrange for the transfer of the record to the transcribing company.

8. You will make your own arrangements with the transcription company as to payment and delivery of the transcript.

9. If you have requested a copy of the record on a CD, the court will contact the person named on the form to pick up the CDs when they are ready.

Court Reporter

If you requested that a court reporter be present at your hearing and the minutes of the proceeding were recorded by a court reporter you must follow the procedure below to obtain a transcript:

1. You must contact the court reporter's office. Go to Locations [1] to find out where to go in your county. You will need the date of the hearing and the name of the Judge.

2. The court reporter will provide an estimate of the cost of preparing the transcript. If you order a transcript a deposit of part or all of the estimated cost may be required.

3. You will make your own arrangements with the court reporter as to payment and delivery of the transcript.

Poor Person's Relief to Obtain the Transcript

You must pay for the cost of preparing the transcript, unless you have obtained Poor Person's Relief. If you believe that you may qualify for a waiver of costs and fees, go to Poor Person's Relief [6] to learn more. When filing for poor person's relief you must provide in your affidavit in support of your request an estimate of the cost of preparing the transcript. You may obtain this from either the court reporter or the

Tape Recording Transcription office. Go to Locations to find where to go in your county.

Procedure for Making Proposed Amendments

If you find that there are mistakes in the transcript because the transcriber did not correctly type what was said in the courtroom, you must suggest corrections to the transcript within 15 days after receiving the transcript by following the procedure below. Any proposed changes will later be decided by the Judge.

1. The appellant should read the transcript.

2. If there is an error in the transcript, the appellant should make a note of the page and line number.

3. After the whole transcript has been reviewed, the appellant should list each error by page and line number along with proposed amendments on a page entitled "Proposed Amendments and Objections."

4. The appellant should then make a copy of the proposed amendments and objections list, and attach it to the transcript. It must then be served on the respondent by following the procedure below.

Serving the Transcript

A Notice of Transmittal of Transcript, a copy of the transcript and the copy of the proposed amendments and objections, must then be served on the respondent by someone over 18 years of age and not a party. You may download the form required to send the transcript to the respondent by going to Notice of Transmittal of Transcript [7], or you may obtain the forms from the appeals clerk in your county.

The respondent shall make any proposed amendments or objections and serve them on the appellant or his/her attorney within 15 days. After the 15 day period has expired, the appellant may "settle" the transcript (see below) whether or not the respondent has served objections.

Settlement of the Transcript

The transcript must be "settled" by the Judge who heard the case, or by agreement of the parties. In this Instance the word "settled" is used to mean that the transcript of the minutes of the trial and the proposed amendments and objections will be examined or reviewed for accuracy and finalized by the court. You may go to Notice of Settlement of Transcript [7] to download the form you need or you may obtain the form from the appeals clerk in your county.

The Notice of Settlement of Transcript form is intended to notify the opposing party or his/her attorney of the date on which the judge will settle the transcript. You need not appear in Court on that day. The opposing party or his/her attorney must be given at least four days advanced notice (nine days if service of the Notice of Settlement is by mail) of the scheduled date of such settlement. The person who serves the Notice of Settlement must fill out an Affidavit of Service, which must be notarized.

The Notice of Settlement of Transcript form is to be filled out in triplicate and distributed as follows:

Copy 1, the original, along with the transcript of the minutes of the trial (with the objections and/or proposed corrections, if any) is to be submitted to the Appeals Clerk before the day of settlement. The Appeals Clerk will provide all the papers to the trial judge on the day of settlement along with the Affidavit of Service.

Copy 2, must be "served" on the opposing party or his/her attorney by someone over 18 years of age and not a party to the action, notifying him/her of the date on which the judge will settle the transcript.

Copy 3, should be retained by you as your record.

The Appellate Term

After the transcript is settled, the Appeals Clerk will prepare a Clerk's Return on Appeal and submit it to the Appellate Term with the transcript, Notice of Appeal, court record and any other related papers.

You must perfect (complete the filing of) your appeal with the Appellate Term of the Supreme Court in accordance with their rules, regulations and instructions. To find out where the Appellate Term is in your county, go to Locations [1].

1 http://www.courts.state.ny.us/courts/nyc/housing/locations2.shtml

2 http://www.courts.state.ny.us/courts/nyc/housing/servingnoe.shtml

3 http://www.courts.state.ny.us/courts/nyc/housing/forms/ noticeofappeal.pdf

4 http://www.courts.state.ny.us/courts/nyc/housing/ forms.shtml#affsofservice

5 http://www.courts.state.ny.us/courts/nyc/housing/fees.shtml

6 http://www.courts.state.ny.us/courts/nyc/housing/poorrelief.shtml

7 http://www.courts.state.ny.us/courts/nyc/housing/forms/ transmittaloftranscript.pdf

Doc. 2. Poor Person's Relief

If you do not have enough money to pay the court costs and fees of the proceeding, you may ask the court to permit you to proceed without having to pay the court costs. These costs include the charges for starting an HP proceeding, filing a petition to be restored to possession, filing a jury demand, and appealing a court ruling.

Your application for "poor person's relief" is made by motion and must be supported by an affidavit which must:

1) set forth the amount and sources of your income, and list your property with its value;

2) state that you are unable to pay the costs, fees and expenses necessary to prosecute or defend the action or proceeding or to maintain or respond to the appeal;

3) indicate the nature of the action or proceeding;

4) provide sufficient facts so that the merit of your claims can be determined;

5) indicate whether any other person would benefit from any award in your case, and if so, whether that person is unable to pay such costs fees and expenses.

You may obtain the affidavit from the court or you may download the civil court form now by clicking on Poor Person's Relief [1]. To find out where to make your application in your county, click on Locations [2].

If the judge approves your application, the judge will sign an order listing which fees and costs you do not have to pay. This order may also contain directions that if you recover any money in your lawsuit, the money shall be paid to the Clerk of the Court which may then recover the fees and costs which you previously could not afford to pay.

If you are starting the case, you may make your application to the court without notifying anyone else. Once your application has been approved the judge may order that a copy of your application and the order granting it be mailed to the New York City Corporation Counsel's office at 100 Church Street, New York, New York 10007. If the case has already begun and you are applying for fees to be waived, you must serve all parties and the New York City Corporation Counsel's office.

[1] http://www.courts.state.ny.us/courts/nyc/housing/poorrelief.shtml
[2] http://www.courts.state.ny.us/courts/nyc/housing/locations2.shtml

FORMS

GENERAL

CIV–GP–15. Poor Person's Relief

Civil Court of the City of New York
County of
     Part
In the Matter of the Application of

to prosecute as a poor person against

Index Number

AFFIDAVIT IN SUPPORT OF
AN APPLICATION TO
PROCEED AS A POOR PERSON
AND TO WAIVE COURT FEES

State of New York, County of   ss:
            , being duly sworn, deposes and says:

  PRINT YOUR NAME

1. I am the party named as _____ in the above titled action.

2. I reside at _____

3. I seek to proceed in the above titled action.

4. I have a good and meritorious cause of action in that

_____

_____

5. I request that an Order be granted:

☐ waiving any and all statutory fees for the defense or prosecution of the action,

☐ waiving the fee for the filing of a Notice of Appeal

☐ other (Specify) _____

6. I make this application based on CPLR § 1101. I do not have, nor am I able to obtain, the funds needed to pay the court fees. I will be unable to proceed unless the Order is granted.

7. I am/am not a recipient of Public Assistance from the Department of Social Services of the City of New York.

8. I have no income other than the sum of $ _____ per _____ from

_____

9. I own no property of any kind except necessary personal wearing apparel and

[Indicate other property and the value of such property]

10. No other person is beneficially interested in the recovery sought.

11. ☐ a) I have not made a previous application for this or similar relief.

  ☐ b) I have made previous application(s) for this or similar relief, but I am making this further application because _____

_____

       Sign your name

       _____

Print your address

_____

Sworn to before me this   day of   20

Signature of Court Employee and Title

Telephone Number

CIV–GP–15–i(Revised 5/04)

FREE HOUSING COURT FORM

No fee may be charged to fill in this form.

Form can be found at: http://www.nycourts.gov/courts/nyc/housing/forms.shtml.

CIV–LT–106. Affidavit of Military Investigation

CIVIL COURT OF THE CITY OF NEW YORK
County _____ Part: _____   Index No. L&T: _____

Petitioner(s),

AFFIDAVIT OF
MILITARY
INVESTIGATION

-against-

Respondent(s).

STATE OF NEW YORK   )
COUNTY OF _____) ss.:

_____, being duly sworn
(Name)

deposes and says:

I am over 18 years of age and am not a party to this action.

I reside at _____

In compliance with the Service members Civil Relief Act, I believe that the respondent,_____ is not

(Name of Respondent)

currently in the military service, nor is he or she a dependent on someone in the military service, based upon the following:

_____

_____

_____

_____ (Sign Name)

_____ (Print Name)

Sworn to before me this
___ day of _____ 20_____

_____

Notary Public

CIV–LT–106(4/05)

FREE HOUSING COURT FORM

No fee may be charged to fill in this form.

Form can be found at: http://www.nycourts.gov/courts/nyc/housing/forms.shtml.

CIV–LT–105.　Notice of Entry

Civil Court of the City of New York
County of _____Housing Part ___

L&T Index Number _____

Petitioner(s),

-against-

NOTICE OF ENTRY

Respondent(s),

_____

　　Please take notice that the within is a true copy of a(n)
(DECISION/ORDER) (JUDGMENT) duly entered in the Landlord/Tenant office of
　　　　　(choose one)
the Clerk of the Civil Court of the City of New York, County of _____ on the
___ day of _____ 20___

Dated: _____

_____　Signature:　x _____

_____　Print Name:　_____

_____　Address:　_____

_____　　　　　　_____

CIV–LT–105 (9/04)–i

FREE HOUSING COURT FORM
No fee may be charged to fill in this form.
Form can be found at: http://www.nycourts.gov/courts/nyc/housing/forms.shtml.

CIV–GP–63.   Instructions for Service of Subpoena

Subpoena available

There are three kinds of Subpoena,

I. *Subpoena To Testify. (Ad Testificandum)*

Requires **a person** to come to the Court to testify as a witness.

II. *Subpoena For Records. (Duces Tecum)*

Requires **documents, papers, writing, etc.** to be brought to the Court.

III. *Information Subpoena.*

Requires the **information** be provided to the person requesting it.

Methods of Service

A *Subpoena to Testify* or a *Subpoena for Records* is **generally** served on an individual* by personal (in hand) delivery. [*For service on a corporation or on a partnership, see the Clerk.]

For service on an individual, under certain circumstances it may be appropriate to use an **alternate method** of service such as "Substituted Service" or "Conspicuous Service."

"Substituted Service" is the personal service of the Subpoena on someone other than the person who is being subpoenaed (the witness) at the actual place of business or place of residence of the witness. The server must then mail a copy of the Subpoena to the witness by first class mail to the actual place of business or place of residence of the witness. Mark the envelop "Personal and Confidential."

"Conspicuous Service" is the service of the Subpoena by leaving it at the residence or place of business of the witness. Prior to leaving the Subpoena, the server must make at least two attempts. If no one is found on either attempt, on the third try the Subpoena may be affixed to the door with adhesive tape, and a copy must be mailed to the residence of the witness by first class mail. Mark the envelope "Personal and Confidential."

An *Information Subpoena* is **generally** served by Certified or Registered Mail, Return Receipt Requested, or it may **alternatively** be served by personal delivery or by using the "Substituted Service" or "Conspicuous Service" method.

Who May Serve a Subpoena

Anyone NOT A PARTY to the action, who is over the age of 18, and not a Police Officer, may serve the Subpoena.

CIV–GP–63(Revised 5/04)

Proof of Service

The person who serves the *Subpoena to Testify* or the *Subpoena for Records* must fill out an Affidavit of Service and have it notarized.

Procedure

The person who is going to serve the Subpoena must:

1) Find the person to be served.

2) Show that person the *original* Subpoena.

3) Give that person a *copy* of the Subpoena.

4) Fill out the Affidavit of Service on back of the *original*.

5) Retain the Affidavit of Service for further procedures if the person fails to comply with the Subpoena.

6) A copy of a Subpoena for Records (*Duces Tecum*) must also be served either 'in hand' or by mail on each party who has appeared in the action so that it is received by them promptly after service on the witness.

For an *Information Subpoena* follow the above procedure, *or*

1) Place a copy of the Subpoena, together with an original and copy of the questions to be answered in an envelope addressed to the witness.

2) Include a self-addressed, stampede envelope for use by the witness returning the answered questions to you.

3) Mail the envelope to the witness by Certified or Registered Mail, Return Receipt Requested.

Fees for Service

When served with a *Subpoena to Testify* or a *Subpoena for Records*, the witness must be paid a witness fee of $15.00 per day. If the witness is served outside the City of New York s/he shall also be paid 23 cents per mile to the place of attendance, from the place where s/he was served, and return. The fee must be paid a reasonable amount of time *before* the scheduled date. Nonpayment of the witness fee voids the duty to appear.

NOTE: A subpoena for records must also be served on all parties to the action following CPLR § 2303.

Location

A subpoena from the Civil Court of the City of New York may be served only within the City of New York or in Nassau County or Westchester County, Service anywhere else may only be done if permitted by a Judge.

Restrictions

General

A Subpoena may be served on a Sunday.

A City or State agency or a public library may be subpoenaed only by order of the court.

Time

Any witness must be served a "reasonable" amount of time prior to the date of appearance. It is suggested that service be *at least 5 days before* the date of the hearing.

A City or State agency or a public library *must* be served *at least 24 hours prior* to the time of appearance.

CIV–GP–63–*i* (Revised 5/04)

CIV–LT–90.   Request for Audio Record

THE CIVIL COURT OF THE Index #LT/SC _____
CITY OF NEW YORK

___ COUNTY OF _____ Control Number: _____ /20 ___

REQUEST FOR AUDIO RECORD

☐ Transcribe ☐ Listen
Copy (☐ FTR ☐ Audio)

	Initials	Date
Processed by		
Audio Picked Up		
Audio E–mailed		
Transcript Received		
Req. Recv. By Email		

vs.

_____

NAME OF JUDGE: _____

DATE OF TRIAL	**TIME OF TRIAL**	**PART AND ROOM #**
_____	_____	_____
_____	_____	_____
_____	_____	_____
_____	_____	_____
_____	_____	_____

REQUEST MADE BY:

**REQUESTED TRANSCRIPTION
COMPANY**

NAME _____
ADDRESS _____   SEE AUTHORIZED TRANSCRIPTION
_____   COMPANY LIST

PHONE #: ( ) _____   _____ ___ / ___ / ___
                                        Signature   Date

E–MAIL ADDRESS _____

CIV–LT–90 (Revised 12/06) (3-ply)

FREE HOUSING COURT FORM
No fee may be charged to fill in this form.

Form can be found at: http://www.nycourts.gov/courts/nyc/housing/forms.shtml.

CIV–LT–100.   Request for Warrant

CITY MARSHAL   ADDRESS

BADGE #

FAX   (   ) _____   PHONE   (   ) _____

INDEX NUMBER _____   MARSHAL'S DOCKET # _____

      PETITIONER(S)   RESPONDENT(S)

_____   _____

_____   _____

_____   _____

_____   _____

ADDRESS   _____

For Marshal's use only

_____   ☐ N/P   ☐ RIES   ☐ A/T

_____   ☐ H/O   ☐ DEF   ☐ COM

_____

COMMENTS   _____

                  _____

                  _____

DATE _____   SIGNATURE _____

CIV–LT–100 (Revised 9/06)

FREE HOUSING COURT FORM
No fee may be charged to fill in this form.

Form can be found at: http://www.nycourts.gov/courts/nyc/housing/forms.shtml.

ANSWERING

CIV–LT–91a. Answer in Writing

CIVIL COURT OF THE CITY OF
NEW YORK
County of

Housing Part

Index No.:

Petitioner(s),

**LANDLORD/TENANT ANSWER
IN WRITING AND
VERIFICATION**

*Respondent must serve a copy of
this answer on Petitioner and file
the original with proof of service.*

-against-

Respondent(s)

(Attorney for the) Petitioner

I _____, am the Respondent in this proceeding. As my answer to
the allegation(s) made in the Petition, I offer the following:

☐ General Denial

☐ _____

_____

_____

_____

_____

Counterclaim: $ _____ Reason: _____

_____

Date   Respondent's Signature

                                  Respondent's Address

Respondent's Telephone No. .... City, State, Zip Code ....

VERIFICATION

State of New York, County of _____ ss:

_____, being duly sworn, deposes and says: I am the respondent in
this proceeding. I have read the Answer in Writing and know the contents thereof
to be true to my own knowledge, except as to those matters stated on information
and belief, and as to those matters I believe them to be true.

Sworn to before me this   day of   20   Signature of Respondent

                                                         For Court Use Only
                                                         Initial Calendar Date
_____   Both Sides Notified
Signature of Court Employee and Title, or
Notary Public

CIV–LT–91–a–i (February 2004)

FREE HOUSING COURT FORM
No fee may be charged to fill in this form.
Form can be found at: http://www.nycourts.gov/courts/nyc/housing/forms.shtml.

CIV–LT–91b. Answer in Writing and Verification

CIVIL COURT OF THE CITY OF
NEW YORK
County of   Index No.:
     Housing Part

                                 ANSWER IN WRITING
                                     AND
           Petitioner(s),   **VERIFICATION**
     -against-   *Respondent is to have a copy*
                            of this answer served on Pe-
                            titioner or Attorney for Peti-
                                tioner:

           Respondent(s)

I, _____ am the ☐ Respondent **or** ☐ Claiming possession in this proceeding.

As my answer to the allegation(s) made in the Petition, I offer the following:

Initial each numbered statement below that applies

SERVICE

1.   ___I did not receive a copy of the Petition and Notice of Petition.
2.   ___I received the Petition and Notice of Petition, but service was not correct as required by law.

PARTIES

3.   ___The respondent is indicated improperly, by the wrong name, or is not indicated on the Petition and Notice of Petition.
4.   ___The Petitioner is not the Landlord or Owner of the building.

RENT

5.   ___I was not asked, either orally or in writing, to pay the rent before I received the Petition and Notice of Petition.
6.   ___I tried to pay the rent, but the Petitioner refused to accept it.
7.   ___The monthly rent being requested is not the legal rent or the amount on the current lease.
8.   ___The Petitioner owes money to the Respondent because of a rent overcharge.
9.   ___The rent, or a portion of the rent, has already been paid to the Petitioner.

APARTMENT

10.   ___There are conditions in the apartment which need to be repaired and/or services which the Petitioner has not provided.
11.   ___The Respondent receives Public Assistance and there are Housing Code violations in the apartment or the building.
12.   ___The apartment is an illegal apartment.

OTHER

13.   ___Laches.   14. ___ General Denial.
15.   ___Respondent/Person claiming possession is in the military service or is a dependant of someone in the military service.
16.   ___Other/Counterclaim _____

A copy of this Answer must be served on (Attorney for) petitioner, then the original with Affidavit of Service is to be filed in the court. See Answer in Writing Instructions.

VERIFICATION

State of New York, County of _____ ss:

_____, being duly sworn, deposes and says: I am the respondent/person claiming possession in this proceeding. I have read the Answer in Writing and know the contents thereof to be true to my own knowledge, except as to those matters stated on information and belief, and as to those matters I believe them to be true.

Sworn to before me this ___ day of ____, 20 ___.

_____   _____
               Notary   Signature of Respondent/
                                         Person claiming posses-
                                         sion

This case is scheduled to appear on the calendar as follows:

Date: _____ Part: _____ Room: _____ Time: _____ Both sides notified _____

CIV–LT–91b Answer in Writing and reverse (September 2007)

FREE HOUSING COURT FORM

No fee may be charged to fill in this form.

Form can be found at: http://www.nycourts.gov/courts/nyc/housing/forms.shtml.

CIVIL COURT OF THE CITY OF CITY OF NEW YORK

Housing Part

   TO:

CIV–LT–69.   Answer in Writing Instructions

Only the Respondent or a person having rights to possession can Answer the petition.

You will receive an *Answer in Writing (CIV–LT–91b)* form (4 copies), an *Affidavit of Service by Mail* (CIV–GP–11) form and the *Answer in Writing Instructions* (CIV–LT-69).

You must complete the *Answer in Writing* form.

The form must be notarized or verified by a court employee.

One copy of the completed answer must be served on the petitioner or if the petitioner is represented by an attorney, it must be served on the attorney:

Have someone over the age of 18, who is not a party in this action, mail a copy of the written answer by regular first class mail to the attorney for the petitioner or to the petitioner directly <u>only</u> if there is no attorney.

The original (with attached 2 copies) of the *Answer in Writing* form with the completed *Affidavit of Service by mail* CIV–GP–11 must be filed with the court:

For Holdover cases, if the notice of petition requires you to answer prior to the hearing date, you must return the original of the answer and affidavit of service in the court at least three days before the hearing date. Otherwise, you may bring the written answer to court on the hearing date noted on the petition.

For Nonpayment cases, return the written answer and affidavit of service to the Court within five days of receiving the notice of petition.

Upon filing the Answer to a Nonpayment Petition, the clerk will schedule the case before a judge and give you a copy of the *Answer in Writing*.

On the scheduled date you should arrive at the courthouse at least one half hour before the above scheduled time, to allow time to be processed through the metal detectors. Bring all your papers with you when you come to court for the hearing date.

An Affidavit of Unavailability (CIV–LT-107) should be used by persons who are homebound, incarcerated or otherwise unable to appear in court.

If a settlement is not reached on the above scheduled date the case may be sent to a trial-ready part for a trial.

The Clerk Cannot Change the Scheduled Date or Time.

FOR ASSISTANCE VISIT A RESOURCE CENTER IN THE COURTHOUSE OR THE COURT'S WEBSITE: <u>www.nycourts.gov/courts/nyc/housing/index.shtml</u>.

CIV–LT–69 (4/07)

CIV–LT–92. Information on Answering
a Notice of Petition and Petition

(EVICTION/DISPOSSESS PAPERS for NON–PAYMENT of RENT)

If you are in court for a "Non–Payment" case, because the Landlord claims you owe rent, you have the right to tell the Court the reason(s) why the rent may not be owed. Below are some reasons, called defenses, which the Court can consider in deciding how much rent you may owe to your Landlord. Tell the Clerk any reason(s) which you believe you are able to prove to the Judge. You may go to the Resource Center if you need more information to help you answer in your case.

SERVICE

1. I did not receive a copy of the Petition and Notice of Petition (Eviction papers/Dispossess).

2. I did not receive the court papers correctly as required by law. *(See a Housing Court Counselor (Pro–Se Attorney) or seek legal advice if you think you did not receive the eviction papers properly.)*

PARTIES

3. My name is not correct or is missing from the court papers.

4. The Petitioner is not the Landlord or Owner of the building.

RENT

5. I was not asked, either orally or in writing, to pay the rent before the Landlord started this proceeding.

6. I tried to pay the rent, but the Landlord refused to accept it.

7. The monthly rent being requested is not the legal rent or the amount on the current lease.

8. The Landlord owes money to me because of a rent overcharge.

9. The rent, or a portion of the rent, has already been paid to the Landlord.

APARTMENT

10. There are conditions in the apartment/building which need to be repaired and/or services which the Landlord has not provided.

11. I receive Public Assistance and there are Housing Code violations in the apartment or building.

12. The apartment is an illegal apartment.

OTHER

13. Laches: the petition comes as a surprise, the landlord knew for a long time that I owed the rent and waited too long to bring me to court. This delay has caused me harm.

14. I am not certain the petition is correct.

15. I am in the military /dependant on someone in the military.

16. Other Answer
 (Please tell the Clerk any other reason(s) why you believe you do not owe your Landlord some or all of the rent or tell the clerk if you wish to file a counter claim)

CIV–LT–92 (Revised, November 2009)

APPEALS

CIV–GP–67A. Notice of Appeal

Civil Court of the City of New York
County of
      Part   Index Number

    Claimant(s)/Plaintiff(s)/Petitioner(s),   NOTICE OF APPEAL

    -against-

              Defendant(s)/Respondent(s)

   PLEASE TAKE NOTICE that the Appellant, _____
hereby appeals to the Appellate Term of the Supreme Court, First/Second
                                            Strike one
Department, from the Order/Judgment by the Hon. _____
                Strike one
Judge of the Civil/Housing Court of the City of New York, entered in the
          Strike one

office of the Clerk of said Court on
every part thereof.   , and from each and

Dated: Appellant's Signature:

                                    Appellant's Name:

To: Address:

                                    Appellant's Phone:

CIV–GP–67A (Revised October, 2003)

CIV–GP–42. Notice of Transmittal of Transcript

Civil Court of the City of New York
County of

Index Number

Claimant(s)/Plaintiff(s)/Petitioner(s)
-against-

NOTICE OF TRANSMITTAL
OF TRANSCRIPT

Defendant(s)/Respondent(s)

TO: _____

The enclosed transcript is being forwarded to you, the appellee, following Section 1704 of the Civil Court Act together with a copy of the proposed amendments.

Within fifteen (15) days of service you shall make any proposed amendments or objections to the transcript and serve them on the appellant.

The amendments or objections are to be made by referring to the page and line number in the transcript and specifying the change. For example, if the transcript says that the time that an incident occurred was 3:30 P.M. when the testimony given at the trial was 2:30 P.M., label a piece of paper Proposed Amendments and Objections, list the page, the line number and the proposed amendment.

You must return a copy of the proposed amendments to the appellant. Be sure to serve the proposed amendments on the appellant within fifteen (15) days.

After the appellant receives the transcript he/she will set a date for settlement. At that time the transcript and the proposed amendments will be submitted to the judge. You need not appear in Court on that day.

Any further proceedings will take place in the Appellate Term of the Supreme Court.

Dated: Signature:
                                           Appellant

                                Address:

CIV–GP–42–i (Revised 4/04)

FREE HOUSING COURT FORM

No fee may be charged to fill in this form.

Form can be found at: http://www.nycourts.gov/courts/nyc/housing/forms.shtml.

CIV–GP–42A. Notice of Settlement of Transcript

Civil Court of the City of New York
County of

Index Number

                    Petitioner,   NOTICE OF SETTLEMENT
-against-   OF TRANSCRIPT

                    Respondent.

To the Appeals Clerk, Civil Court, City of New York, County of _____ and to
_____ Respondent.

The above captioned case is to be settled before the Hon. _____
on _____ 20___.

I have attached my list of objections/corrections to this Notice.

___ The respondent has provided a list of objections/corrections, and that list is attached.

___ The respondent has <u>not</u> provided a list of objections/corrections.

(Initial the appropriate section above)

Dated: _____

                    _____   Signature

                    _____

                    _____   Address

                    _____

CIV–GP–42A–i(Revised 4/04)

FREE HOUSING COURT FORM
No fee may be charged to fill in this form.
Form can be found at: http://www.nycourts.gov/courts/nyc/housing/forms.shtml.

AFFIDAVITS OF SERVICE

CIV–GP–11.   Affidavit of Service by Mail

CIVIL COURT OF THE CITY OF NEW YORK
COUNTY OF   :PART   Index No.:

            Petitioner,   AFFIDAVIT OF SERVICE
                                     BY MAIL

      -against-

           Respondent.

STATE OF NEW YORK
COUNTY OF _____ ss:

_____ being duly sworn, deposes and says:
I am over 18 years of age and not a party to this action. On _____
I served _____
upon _____, the _____ in this proceeding, by mailing a true
copy of the attached papers, enclosed and properly sealed in a postpaid envelope,
which I deposited in an official depository under the exclusive care and custody of
the United States Postal Services within the State of New York addressed to
_____ the _____
at: _____

                               Signature: _____

Sworn to before me this ___ day of _____ 20___

_____
Notary Public or Court Employee
CIV–GP–11 (March 2001)–1

CIV–RCF–57. Affidavit of Personal Service

CIVIL COURT OF THE CITY OF NEW YORK
COUNTY: PART

Index No.

AFFIDAVIT OF PERSONAL
SERVICE

Petitioner,

- against -

Respondent.

STATE OF NEW YORK
COUNTY OF

_____ being duly sworn deposes and says:

I reside at _____

I am not a licensed process server, nor have I served more than five legal documents during the past year. At _____ AM/PM, on _____ in the County of _____ in the City of New York I served the annexed _____ in this matter upon _____ known to me to be the _____ by personally delivering a true copy to him/her at the following address:

_____

Description of Individual Served in Person

Sex: _____ Color of Skin: _____ Color of Hair: _____

Approximate Age: _____ Approximate Weight: _____ Approximate Height: _____

_____
Signature

Sworn to before me this ___ day of _____ 20___

_____
Notary Public or Court Employee

CIV–RCF–57–i (10/01)

FREE HOUSING COURT FORM

No fee may be charged to fill in this form.

Form can be found at: http://www.nycourts.gov/courts/nyc/housing/forms.shtml.

CIV–RCF–62.   Service Other Than by Personal Delivery

State of New York

County of _____   ss: SERVICE OTHER THAN BY
                                            PERSONAL DELIVERY

___ being duly sworn, deposes and says, that I
am over 18 years of age and have not served more than 5 papers during the past
year. I reside at

The property sought to be recovered is _____

I was unable to serve _____ tenant by personal delivery on _____
day of 20__ at ___ o'clock. I served the within _____

Substituted   by gaining admittance to said property and delivering to and leaving
Service   copy thereof personally with   a person
                of suitable age and discretion, who was willing to receive same and
                who-resided-was employed at said property.

Conspicuous   By placing a copy thereof under the entrance door
Place Service   By affixing a copy thereof upon a conspicuous part, to wit: -entrance
                door of said property; I was unable to gain admittance threat or to find
                a person of suitable age and discretion willing to receive same.
                I attempted personal service on   day of   20   at   am/pm.
                My second attempt was made on   day of   20   at   am/pm.

Mailing   and within 1 day thereafter, on   day of   20   I mailed a copy
                 thereof enclosed in a post-paid properly addressed wrapper to tenant
                at the property sought to be recovered which is tenant's residence or
                corporate tenant's principal office or principal place of business by
                registered certified mail,

                And an additional copy No.

**use either
(a) or (b)
if applicable**   (a) which is individual tenant's last-residence address-place of business
                or employment address.
                (b) which is corporate tenant's last known principal office or principal
                place of business within the state by depositing the same in -a post
                office- official depository under the exclusive care and custody of the
                United States Postal Service within the state.

Sworn to me before on   day of 20
                                                     Signature

Notary Public

CIV–RCF–62–i (I0/01)

FREE HOUSING COURT FORM
No fee may be charged to fill in this form.

Form can be found at: http://www.nycourts.gov/courts/nyc/housing/forms.shtml.

CIV–LT–47. Affidavit of Service of Judgment with Notice of Entry

Civil Court of the City of New York
County of   Housing Part   L&T Index Number

                            Petitioner(s),   AFFIDAVIT OF SERVICE
                                                    OF JUDGMENT WITH
-against-   NOTICE OF ENTRY

                            Respondent(s),

State of New York
County of   ss:

_____, being duly sworn, deposes and says:
     (Print Name of Deponent)

1) I am over the age of 18 and not a party to this action.

2) On the ___ day of _____ 20___ I served a copy of the attached Judgment
with Notice of Entry on:

_____
                            (Name)
by putting it in a stamped envelope and mailing it to:

_____
                           (Address)

_____
                        (City, State, Zip)

                                   _____   *(Signature of Depo-*
                                               nent)*

Sworn to before me this ___ day
of _____ 20___

_____
     (Notary Public)
CIV–LT–47 (9/04)–i

FREE HOUSING COURT FORM
No fee may be charged to fill in this form.
Form can be found at: http://www.nycourts.gov/courts/nyc/housing/forms.shtml.

HP's

CIV–LT–66. Instructions for the Service of an In Person (Pro Se) Order to Show Cause and Verified Petition (H.P.)

1. Once a Judge has signed an Order to *Show* Cause (OSC) you will either be given copies or be lent the originals and be told to make three copies.

2. The Clerk will keep the original Verified Petition and the Order to *Show* Cause, and will give you the copies. The copies are to be served (delivered) as follows:

   a. The first set of copies goes to the landlord.

   b. The second set of copies goes to the Department of Housing Preservation and Development (DHPD)

   c. The third set of copies is your set.

3. The first set of copies of the Order to *Show* Cause and the Verified Petition must be served on the landlord as directed.

   You may serve the Order to *Show* Cause and the Verified Petition by:

   a. giving them to the respondent/landlord in person;

   ### OR, IF PERMITTED BY THE JUDGE

   b. mailing them to the respondent/landlord by Certified Mail, Return Receipt Requested.

4. You must also mail the second set of copies of both the Order to *Show* Cause and the Verified Petition, by Certified Mail, Return Receipt Requested, to:

   Department of Housing Preservation and Development

   Housing Litigation Bureau

   100 Gold Street

   New York, NY 10038

5. You must fill out an Affidavit *of* Service *of* Order to Show Cause and Verified Petition (CIV–LT-25), attach the Certified Mail receipt(s) to it, and sign it in front of either a Notary Public or the Clerk. You must bring the Affidavit *of* Service, with the receipt(s) attached, to the court on the date of the hearing.

6. Normally an inspection of your apartment will be scheduled by the Clerk. In some counties you will have to contact the inspector yourself. Ask the Clerk.

Come to Court at 9:30 A.M. in _____ in Room _____

DON'T BE LATE!

Be sure to bring: 1) Order to Show Cause

2) Verified Petition

3) Affidavit(s) of Service with Certified Mail Receipt(s) attached.

CIV–LT–66–i (Revised 3/04)

FREE HOUSING COURT FORM

No fee may be charged to fill in this form.

Form can be found at: http://www.nycourts.gov/courts/nyc/housing/forms.shtml.

CIV–LT–61. Inspection Request

Department of
**Housing Preservation and Development
Division of Code Enforcement**
(Form A–B)

**TENANT'S REQUEST FOR
INSPECTION**

Tenant's Name:

Tenant's Address:

Apt. No.   Floor:

Tenant's Phone #"s: Home:( )

                       Work:( )

Civil Court Index No: LT/HP
County of

Housing Part: Room

The case of

vs.

will appear on the Court Calendar on:
                   at   AM/PM

Is there a child under the age of 6
residing in this apartment?
Yes ☐ No ☐

If yes, please provide name and age or
date of birth for each child.

Name   **Age/Date of Birth**

You may gain access by contacting: _____

TENANT'S ALLEGATION OF VIOLATIONS				**DIVISION OF CODE ENFORCEMENT** Inspector's No: Date:
Apt. No. (Or Public Area)	Which Room?		Condition(s) -Be Specific	Signature REPORT
	1.			
	2.			
	3.			
	4.			
	5.			
	6.			
	7.			
	8.			
	9.			
	10.			

In connection with the above mentioned case in the Civil Court of the City of New York, I, the tenant of the apartment referred to, wish to call the Court's attention to the conditions listed above which I allege are violations, and request that an inspection of the property be made to verify my allegations.

Date of Request: Tenant's Signature:

INSPECTION DATE	**INSPECTION TIME**
An inspector will come to inspect these conditions on:	☐ 10 AM — 2 PM ☐ 2 PM — 6 PM ☐ 5 PM — 9 PM ☐ **Weekend** 10 AM — 3 PM ☐ **Staten Island** 10 AM — 2 PM

CIV–LT–61(9/06)(Replaces A&B)

FREE HOUSING COURT FORM

No fee may be charged to fill in this form.

Form can be found at: http://www.nycourts.gov/courts/nyc/housing/forms.shtml.

MOTIONS AND ORDERS TO SHOW CAUSE

CIV-LT-65. Instructions for the Service of an In Person (Pro Se) Order to Show Cause and Affidavit in Support

1. Once a Judge has signed an Order to Show Cause (OSC) you will either be given copies or be lent the originals and be told to make two or three copies.

2. The Clerk will keep the original Affidavit in Support and the Order to Show Cause, and will give you the copies. The copies are to be served (delivered) as follows:

   a. The first set of copies goes to the landlord. If the landlord has an attorney, then the copies go to the attorney and not to the landlord.

   b. The second set of copies goes to the Marshal, if there is one in your case.

   c. The third set of copies is your set.

3. Serve (deliver) the first set of copies to the landlord's attorney (or to the landlord) personally. The papers must be served by the date indicated in the Order. Ask the person receiving the copies to sign the back of the third copy, acknowledging receipt.

If the person refuses to sign, leave the copes with him/her and write out a statement on the back of the third copy explaining what happened, or complete the appropriate sections of "Affidavit of Service of Order to Show Cause and Affidavit in Support" (CIV-LT-19) given to you by the Clerk. Sign the form and have your signature notarized or witnessed by the Clerk. Be sure to tell the Clerk about this on the date of the hearing.

4. If there is a Marshal on your case, serve the second set of copies by delivering them to the Marshal's office. Someone there will sign the back of the third set of copies, acknowledging service.

5. You must bring the third set of copies to the Court on the date of the hearing as they are your proof of service. If the Judge permitted served by Certified Mail, Return Receipt Requested, be sure to attach the receipt(s) to the third copy.

6. If the Judge ordered a deposit of money, it must be brought to the Clerk by the date indicated in the Order. You must provide the exact amount required. Such payment should be in a certified check, bank teller's check or money order made payable to the "NYC Department of Finance." Cash will only be accepted under special circumstances. Failure to make the deposit may result in the denial of your Order to Show Cause.

Come to Court at _____ on _____ in Room _____

DON'T BE LATE!

Be sure to bring:

1) Order to Show Cause

2) Affidavit in Support

3) Affidavit(s) of Service, if any, with Certified Mail Receipt(s) attached.

CIV-LT-65-i(Revised 9/04)

FREE HOUSING COURT FORM

No fee may be charged to fill in this form.

Form can be found at: http://www.nycourts.gov/courts/nyc/housing/forms.shtml.

CIV–LT–13A.   Affidavit in Opposition

CIVIL COURT OF THE CITY OF
NEW YORK
COUNTY OF   PART

            Petitioner,   AFFIDAVIT
                              IN OPPOSITION

    -against-   Index No. L&T:

            Respondent.

STATE OF NEW YORK
COUNTY OF _____ ss.:
_____, being duly sworn, hereby deposes and says:

_____

_____

_____

_____

_____

_____

_____

_____

_____

_____

_____

_____

_____

_____

_____

  WHEREFORE, THE UNDERSIGNED RESPECTFULLY REQUESTS THE
WITHIN MOTION BE DENIED.

_____
Signature
Sworn to before me this ___ day of _____ 20___

_____
Notary Public/Court Employee
  CIV–LT–13A–i

FREE HOUSING COURT FORM
No fee may be charged to fill in this form.
Form can be found at: http://www.nycourts.gov/courts/nyc/housing/forms.shtml.

1411

CIV–LT–13B. Reply Affidavit

CIVIL COURT OF THE CITY OF
NEW YORK
COUNTY OF   PART

                   Petitioner,   REPLY AFFIDAVIT

-against-

                                         Index No. L&T:

                   Respondent.

STATE OF NEW YORK
COUNTY OF _____ ss.:

_____, being duly sworn, hereby deposes and says:

_____

_____

_____

_____

_____

_____

_____

_____

_____

_____

_____

_____

_____

_____

_____

_____

_____

_____

_____

_____

_____

   WHEREFORE, THE UNDERSIGNED RESPECTFULLY REQUESTS THE WITHIN MOTION BE GRANTED.

_____
Signature

Sworn to before me this ___ day of _____ 20___

_____
Notary Public/Court Employee
   CIV–LT–1313–i

FREE HOUSING COURT FORM
No fee may be charged to fill in this form.
Form can be found at: http://www.nycourts.gov/courts/nyc/housing/forms.shtml.

CIV–LT–19. Affidavit of Service of Order to Show Cause and Affidavit in Support

CIVIL COURT OF THE CITY OF
NEW YORK
COUNTY OF   PART   Index No. LT:

AFFIDAVIT OF SERVICE OF
ORDER TO SHOW CAUSE AND
AFFIDAVIT IN SUPPORT (LT)

Petitioner(s),

-against-

Address: _____

Respondent(s).   Apt.

State of New York,
County of _____ ss.:

_____, being duly sworn, deposes and says:

(Print your name)

I am over 18 years of age and _____ this action. At ___ AM/PM on
_____, I served the annexed ORDER TO SHOW CAUSE and AFFIDAVIT
IN SUPPORT in this matter on:

1.

(Name(s) of Person(s) Served)

Known to me to be the Petitioner(s) by

☐ a) Delivering a true copy to him/her/them at the following address:
_____
_____

☐ b) Delivering a true copy to his/her/their attorney(s) or managing agent(s) at
the following address:
_____
_____
_____

Description of Individual Served in Person:

Sex:	Color of Skin:	Color of Hair:
Approximate Age:	Approximate Weight:	Approximate Height:

☐ c) Mailing a copy, properly sealed and enclosed in a post-paid wrapper by
Certified Mail, Return Receipt Requested, in a Post Office of the United States
Postal Service within the State of New York, addressed to the petitioner (or his/her
registered managing agent) at the address registered with the Department of
Housing Preservation and Development.

AND ALSO SERVED ON THEM ON

2. Marshall _____ by:

☐ a) Delivering a copy to _____, a person in the Marshall's
office.

Description of Individual Served in Person:

Sex:	Color of Skin:	Color of Hair:
Approximate Age:	Approximate Weight:	Approximate Height:

☐ b) Mailing a copy, properly sealed and enclosed in a post-paid wrapper by
Certified Mail, Return Receipt Requested, in a Post Office of the United States
Postal Service within the State of New York, addressed to:

Marshall

_____

_____

_____

Sworn to before me this ____ day of _____ 20___

_____

(Signature of Respondent)

_____

(Signature of Court Employee and Title)

CIV–LT–19 (Revised 12/04)

FREE HOUSING COURT FORM

No fee may be charged to fill in this form.

Form can be found at: http://www.nycourts.gov/courts/nyc/housing/forms.shtml.

CIV–LT–18. Affidavit in Support of an
Order for Withdrawal of Funds

CIVIL COURT OF THE CITY OF
NEW YORK
COUNTY OF   PART   Index No.LT:

                                    AFFIDAVIT IN SUPPORT OF
          Petitioner(s),   AN ORDER FOR
                                    WITHDRAWAL OF FUNDS
     -against-

                                    Address:
          Respondent(s).
                                              Apt.

State of New York,
County of _____ ss.:

_____, being duly sworn, deposes and says:
     (Print your name)

1. I reside at _____

2. There is now on deposit in the above-entitled action with the Department of Finance of the City of New York the sum of $ _____, as evidenced by the attached Certificate of Deposit.

3. I further state that I am the person entitled to receive this deposit for the following reason(s):

_____

4. I, therefore, request that an Order be entered directing the Department of Finance of the City of New York to pay this deposit, with interest to the date of payment, less any lawful commissions.

5. a) ☐ I have not made previous application for this or similar relief.

   b) ☐ I have made previous application for this or similar relief, but I am making this further application because:

_____

_____

Sworn to before me this ____ day of _____ 20___

                         _____ (Signature of Respon-
                         dent)

_____
     (Signature of Court Employee and Title)

CIV–LT–18 (Revised 12/04)
FREE HOUSING COURT FORM
No fee may be charged to fill in this form.
Form can be found at: http://www.nycourts.gov/courts/nyc/housing/forms.shtml.

CIV–LT–13. Affidavit in Support of an Order to Show Cause (Generic)

CIVIL COURT OF THE CITY   Index No. LT:
OF NEW YORK
COUNTY OF   PART

                                  AFFIDAVIT IN SUPPORT OF
                                  ORDER TO SHOW CAUSE
                   Petitioner(s),   GENERIC

                               For
-against-   (Relief Requested)
                               Address:
                  Respondent(s).

                                                   Apt.

State of New York,
County of _____ ss.:

                                  , being duly sworn, deposes and says:
            (Print your name)

         Tenant's Initials

1.   a) I am the party named as (petitioner)(respondent) in the
PARTY   entitled proceeding.
                 b) I am the   of the party named as (petitioner)
                 (respondent) in this proceeding.

2.   I request that:
REQUEST

3.   I have a good defense/claim because:
DEFENSE
CLAIM

4.   I have a good excuse/reason because:
EXCUSE/
REASON

5.   a) I have not had a previous order to show cause regarding this
PRIOR   index number.
ORDER

                 b) I have had a previous order to show cause regarding this
                 index number, but I
                 am making this further application because:

Sworn to before me this ____ day of _____, 20___

                                   _____ (Signature of Respon-
                                   dent)

_____
(Signature of Court Employee and Title)

CIV–LT–13 (Revised 12/04)

FREE HOUSING COURT FORM

No fee may be charged to fill in this form.

Form can be found at: http://www.nycourts.gov/courts/nyc/housing/forms.shtml.

CIV–LT–10. Affidavit in Support of Order to Show Cause to Restore to the Calendar

CIVIL COURT OF THE CITY
OF NEW YORK
COUNTY OF   PART   Index No.LT:

                                                      AFFIDAVIT IN SUPPORT OF
             Petitioner(s),   ORDER TO SHOW CAUSE
                                      To Restore to the Calendar
     -against-

                                       Address:
             Respondent(s).

                                                        Apt.

State of New York,
County of _____ ss.:

                                    , being duly sworn, deposes and says:
        (Print your name)

                         Tenant's Initials

1.
PARTY
                 a) I am the (petitioner/respondent) in the above summary
                   proceeding.
                 b) I am the person claiming possession to these premises
                   and am the
                                   of the tenant named above.

2.
TRIAL
              On the Date of Trial

                 a) a stipulation (a written agreement) was made between
                   landlord and tenant.
                 b) a trial was held before Judge
                 c) Other:

3.
REASON FOR
APPLICATION
             I make this application to Restore the Case to the Calendar
               because:

4.
REQUEST
             I request that the case be restored to the calendar and that I be
             granted permission to serve these papers in person.

5.
PRIOR ORDER
                 a) I have not had a previous order to show cause regard-
                   ing this index number.
                 b) I have had a previous order to show cause regarding
                   this index number, but I am making this further
                   application because:

6.
PRIOR CASES
             The same landlord and tenant have been in Housing Court before.
             Earlier Index Number(s):

Sworn to before me this ____ day of _____, 20____

                                         _____ (Signature of Respon-
                                         dent)

_____

(Signature of Court Employee and Title)

CIV–LT–10 (Revised 12/04)

FREE HOUSING COURT FORM

No fee may be charged to fill in this form.

Form can be found at: http://www.nycourts.gov/courts/nyc/housing/forms.shtml.

CIV–LT–11.   Affidavit in Support of Order to Show Cause to Restore to Possession

Civil Court of the City of New York
County of

Part

[Please Press Hard]

Index Number

Petitioner,

-against-

Respondent.

AFFIDAVIT IN SUPPORT OF AN ORDER TO SHOW CAUSE
To Restore to Possession

Address:

Apt. #

State of New York,
County of _____ ss.:

_____ being duly sworn, deposes and says:
(Print your name)

<u>Tenant's
Initials</u>

1. Party
a) I am the tenant named as respondent in the above summary proceeding.
b) I am the person claiming possession of these premises and am the
                                                of the tenant named above.

2. Service and Answer
a) I received the Notice of Petition and Petition in this proceeding, filed my answer in the Clerk's Office and received a date for trial.
b) I received a Holdover Notice of Petition and Petition and the date had already passed.

3. Excuse
On the Date of Trial before Judge
a) a Judgment was entered against me by default for my *failure to appear*. My reason for not appearing in Court on the date scheduled for **(Trial) (Motion)** is:

b) a Judgment was entered **(after trial) (after stipulation) but (I) (the Landlord)** *failed to comply* with the Order ofthe Court because:

4. Claim and Defense
I allege that I have a good defense to my being evicted from the subject premises.

5. Request
Respondent requests that an Order be entered awarding and restoring the respondent to possession of the subject premises and the issuance of a warrant of eviction forthwith, granting permission to serve these papers in person, and such other relief as this Court deems proper.

6. Prior Order
a) I **have not** had a previous Order to Show Cause regarding this index number.
b) I **have** had a previous Order to Show Cause regarding this index number but I am making this further application because:

Sworn to before me this ____ day of _____, 20__

_____ *Signature of Respondent*

_____
Signature of Court Employee and Title

CIV–LT–11 (Replaces CIV–LT–11B) (Revised 4/04)

FREE HOUSING COURT FORM

No fee may be charged to fill in this form.

Form can be found at: http://www.nycourts.gov/courts/nyc/housing/forms.shtml.

CIV–LT–22. Affidavit in Support of an Order to Show Cause to Restore to the Calendar for a Compliance Hearing and for Assessment of Civil Penalties (H.P.)

Civil Court of the City of New York
County of
       Housing Part

Index Number

                   Petitioner,
-against-

**AFFIDAVIT IN SUPPORT OF AN
ORDER TO SHOW CAUSE
To Restore to the Calendar for
a Compliance Hearing and for
Assessment of Civil Penalties
(H.P.)**

Address:
          Respondent(s), and
The Dept. of Housing Preservation
and Development

       (Address of Petitioner)
            Apt.#

State of New York,
County of _____ ss:

_____ being duly sworn, deposes and says:

1. **PARTY:** I am the _____ in the above proceeding.
       (Petitioner/a [relative/friend/etc.] of the Petitioner)

2. **HISTORY:** An Order of the Court directing the correction of violations was made, or a stipulation between the parties was entered into, on _____

3. **FACTS:** The following violations / conditions have not been corrected:

1)   4)   7)

2)   5)   8)

3)   6)   9)

TENANT'S
INITIALS

4. **PRIOR
ORDER**

I **have not** requested a prior Order to Show Cause for a Compliance Hearing in this case.
I **have** requested a prior Order to Show Cause for a Compliance Hearing in this case but I am making this further application because

5. **REQUESTS:** I respectfully request that:

— this case be restored to the calendar for a Compliance Hearing and assessment of civil penalties (fine) against my landlord since violations have not been corrected pursuant to the Court's Order.

— because I am appearing *in person*, without an attorney or process server, permission be granted to serve these papers myself, by Certified Mail, Return Receipt Requested.

— the attached Order be signed.

Sworn to before me this ___ day of _____ 20___

_____ Signature of Petitioner

_____
Signature of Court Employee and Title, or Notary Public

CIV–LT–22 (Revised 4/04) (4ply)

FREE HOUSING COURT FORM

No fee may be charged to fill in this form.

Form can be found at: http://www.nycourts.gov/courts/nyc/housing/forms.shtml.

JUDGES' RULES

NEW YORK COUNTY

JUSTICE TIMMIE ERIN ELSNER

Elsner 1. Resolution Part Rules

1. All parties or their attorneys are to sign in with the Clerk upon entering the Part. There will be no roll or calendar call.

2. Service or a representative of a party, other than an attorney, may not answer in the part on behalf of a party to request an adjournment nor may they appear before the Court in any matter scheduled for trial or hearing. Where a matter is scheduled for a motion, service may appear in order to request an adjournment.

3. Defaults on matters scheduled for 9:30 A.M. will be taken at 10:30 A.M. At that time, court personnel will call those matters for which only one party answered. In the event the absent party does not respond, a default will be taken against them.

4. Parties may not adjourn proceedings by stipulation in matters scheduled for trial. Applications for adjournments of continuing trials must be made before the Court. An application for adjournment of a trial will be granted only if an emergency has arisen which prevents either counsel, a litigant, or a witness from appearing in court.

5. The Court will allow two stipulated adjournments of motions pending before the Court. Thereafter, the parties must appear before the Judge in order to request additional time.

6. Attorneys must appear with their clients on all matters referred for trial from Part X. Agents appearing on behalf of a petitioner must have authority to enter into a stipulation of settlement and to participate in meaningful negotiations.

7. A default judgment will be entered against any party who does not appear in the part for trial within one half hour and after referral of the matter from Part X.

Elsner 2. Trial Part Rules

1. All parties or their attorneys are required to check in with the Court Officer upon entering the part. There will be no role or calendar call. Neither attorneys nor parties are permitted to "call out" for the other side. Only court personnel may call out in the courtroom.

2. Service may not answer in the part on behalf of a party to request an adjournment nor may they appear before the Court in any matter scheduled for trial or hearing. A representative of a party, other than an attorney, may not answer or appear on behalf of any party without written authority from said party.

3. All parties and their attorneys are required to appear in this part within fifteen minutes of the proceeding's referral from Part X. Witnesses on call at the time of the referral are to be present within thirty minutes after the attorneys check into the part. Defaults on matters referred from Part X will be taken fifteen minutes after the file is received in this part.

4. All proceedings shall be conferenced by the Court between the parties and counsel before a trial will be conducted. If the parties are discussing settlement of the proceeding, they must appear before the Court and inform the Court of same. The parties shall inform the Court of the status of the settlement discussions within thirty minutes thereof.

5. Defaults on matters scheduled in this part for 9:30 a.m. will be taken at 10:00 am. At that time, court personnel will call those matters for which only one party checked in or answered. In the event the party who has not checked in or answered does not respond to court personnel, a default will be taken against them.

6. Parties may not adjourn trials or hearings by stipulation. An application to the Court must be made. Adjournments will only be granted where an emergency has arisen which prevents either counsel, a litigant or a witness from appearing in court. All stipulated adjournments where one side is pro se must be reduced to writing and reviewed by the Court.

7. Every stipulation of settlement in a nonpayment proceeding must provide a breakdown of the arrears alleged owed. If the tenant intends to seek assistance from DSS, said breakdown shall contain a listing of the actual months for which the tenant or agency failed to pay rent. A "first in first out" breakdown will not be accepted.

8. Every stipulation of settlement where repairs are an issue shall contain a list of the repairs allegedly required or a statement that no repairs are needed.

9. The parties must provide a submission schedule to the Court upon adjourning any motion. The Court will allow one stipulated adjournment of any pending motion. Thereafter, the parties must appear before the judge to request any additional adjournments. Unless a motion is returnable by order to show cause, all papers must be submitted to the Court one (1) business day prior to the date the motion is scheduled

to be heard so they may be reviewed by Court prior to oral argument.

JUSTICE CHERYL J. GONZALES

Gonzales 1. Resolution Rules

1. All parties are to check in with their calendar number with the officer/clerk upon entering the courtroom.

2. Anyone who is not represented by a lawyer can request a conference with the judge's court attorney.

3. The default calendars will be called as follows:

9:30 a.m. calendar at 11:00 a.m.

11:00 a.m. calendar at 12:30 p.m.

2:00 p.m. calendar at 3:00 p.m.

4. All requests for adjournments and discontinuances must be in writing and must state the reason for the adjournment or discontinuance. Discontinued non-payments must include the period through which all rent has been paid.

5. Proposed stipulations of settlement must be legible, and must submitted to the clerk for review by the court attorney and/ or judge. Parties must remain in the courtroom or advise the clerk where they can be located. Failure to remain or be located may result in a dismissal, default, or adjournment at the court's discretion.

6. The court will have a status call on all cases where both parties checked in. If such parties do not return to the Part to resolve their matters by 11:30 a.m. for 9:30 a.m. cases, 12:45 p.m. for 11:00 a.m. cases, or 3:30 p.m. for 2:00 p.m. cases, the matters will be defaulted, dismissed or adjourned, at the discretion of the court, unless explanation of such absence is advanced.

7. Parties or attorneys who return to the Part after 12:30 p.m. should not expect a matter to be heard prior to the prompt closing of the Part at 1:00 p.m.

8. Stipulations in non-payment proceedings must contain a rent breakdown, and a statement of conditions in the apartment. Tenants must be given a landlord generated rent breakdown that clearly shows the rent arrears and any other charges.

Gonzales 2. Part Rules

1. All litigants and attorneys are required to check in with the Court Officer/Clerk before the default calendar call and provide the calendar number of the case which is on the calendar posted in the display case outside the courtroom.

2. There will be a default calendar call at 10:30AM. Requests to vacate calendar defaults will be heard only if all parties are present.

3. All notices of appearance, withdrawals, substitutions or discharges must be submitted in proper form. Attorneys are obligated to ensure that a current notice of appearance is on file with the court.

4. All requests for adjournments and discontinuances must be submitted to the Court Attorney or the Judge for review. The reason for the request must also be stated.

5. Cases must be conferenced with the HPD staff; the court attorney's assistance may also be requested. If no resolution is reached, any party may request a conference with the judge. All parties must remain in the courtroom and be available for the conference.

6. Proposed stipulations of settlement and consent order to correct must be legible and shall be submitted to the Court Officer or Clerk for review by the Court Attorney or the Judge. All stipulations and orders to correct must have access dates and indicate that workers must arrive no later than noon, and include a completion date for the repairs.

7. **9:30AM cases** - if petitioner does not check in by the time of the default calendar call the case may be dismissed. If respondent fails to check in by the time of the default calendar call an order may be entered after an inquest is held. If a party checks in and fails to return by noon, the other side may request that Clerk put the case before the Judge for a default, dismissal or adjournment in the discretion of the Court.

8. **2:15 p.m. trials/hearings** - if a party fails to appear by 3:00 p.m., the Court in its discretion may Conduct an inquest, dismiss or adjourn the matter.

JUSTICE ARLENE HAHN

Hahn 1. Resolution Part Rules

1. All parties must report to the court officer or court clerk upon entering the courtroom.

2. All attorneys must file a written Notice of Appearance. It shall be the obligation of the attorney to

insure that a current Notice of Appearance is on file with the court.

3. All proposed stipulations shall be submitted to the court clerk or officer for review by the court attorney and judge. Pending such review, the parties

shall remain available or be subject to rejection of the stipulation, default, dismissal or adjournment.

4. In all proceedings involving repairs, alleged conditions shall be included in the stipulation, as well as access dates, arrival by noon and completion dates.

5. In proceedings where rent is an issue, petitioner shall provide a current, detailed accounting of monies billed and received.

6. All discontinuances and adjournments shall be reviewed by the court attorney and/or judge.

7. Conferences

(a) Any party or attorney may request a conference with the Court or a Court Attorney by notifying court personnel.

(b) The Court or the Court Attorneys shall conference all cases in which settlement cannot be reached. If after conference settlement is still not reached, the case shall be sent to a trial part or adjourned and marked final for trial, at the Court's discretion.

8. Defaults shall be taken as follows: 9:30 A.M calendar at 10:30 A.M 11:00 A.M calendar at 12:00 P.M 2:00 P.M calendar at 3:00 P.M.

9. If a party does not check in by the above times, the clerk shall put the case before the judge for a default or dismissal. If a party checks in, but fails to return by the stated default time, the other side may ask the clerk to put the case before the judge for a default, dismissal or adjournment, at the discretion of the court.

10. Upon application, cases on the 9:30 calendar for trial will be dismissed or defaulted where a party or their attorney has not checked in by 10:00 a.m.

Hahn 2.   Trial Part Rules

1. All parties or their attorneys are to check in with the clerk upon entering the part. There will be no roll or calendar call. Cases will be placed before

the judge or a court attorney for conference when both sides have appeared.

2. Service or a representative may check in with the Part for their respective cases.

3. All requests for adjournments and discontinuances will be reviewed by the court attorney or by application to the judge.

4. All attorneys must have a notice of appearance filed or appropriate papers on the cases they are appearing on.

5. If attorneys are appearing of counsel, they must submit a notice of appearance for the record.

6. 9:30 a.m. cases will be called for default at 10:30 a.m.

7. 11:00 a.m. cases will be called for default at 12:00 noon.

8. The status of all 9:30 a.m. and 11:00 a.m. cases must be reported to the court by 12:00 p.m.

9. 2:00 p.m. cases will be defaulted at 3:30 p.m. All morning cases not previously disposed of will be called at 12:00 p.m. Dismissals and defaults may be taken or adjournments may be granted on this call at the court's discretion whether or not the parties have previously checked in with the clerk. It is not necessary to be in the courtroom when defaults are called if the litigant has signed in. But all cases must be complete by the appropriate time indicated or status given to the court.

10. Once a stipulation is given to the clerk or court attorney in the part for review and allocution, it is the responsibility of the attorney to be sure the stipulation has been accepted and so ordered by the judge. Failure to return to the court within a reasonable time may result in the stipulation being rejected and the case adjourned or dismissed at the discretion of the court.

JUSTICE SHELDON HALPRIN

Halprin 1.   Part Rules

Check In:

Upon entering the part, all litigants and attorneys are to check in with the Clerk or Court Officer.

Discontinuances & Adjournments:

Any request for an adjournment or discontinuance shall be reviewed by the Court Attorney, Judge or Court Clerk.

Conferences:

Where a party requests a conference by the Judge, all parties and attorneys shall remain in the part unless otherwise directed by the Court.

Stipulations:

Proposed stipulations shall be submitted to the Clerk or Court Officer for review by the Court Attorney and/or Judge. Pending review by the Court Attorney or Judge, the parties shall remain available or be subject to default, or an adjournment of the case, at the court's discretion.

Defaults:

9:30 a.m. Calendar:

(a) There will be a calendar call at 11:00 a.m. of all cases scheduled for 9:30 a.m. Dismissals and defaults will be taken at that time.

(b) All cases not previously disposed of will be called at 12:30 p.m. Dismissals and defaults may be taken or adjournments granted on this call at the court's discretion, whether or not the parties have previously checked in with the clerk.

2:00 p.m. Calendar:

(c) Applications for defaults of cases on the 2:00 p.m. calendar will be entered at 3:00 p.m.

Trials/Hearings:

(d) Parties and attorneys in cases scheduled for trial or hearing are expected to arrive in the Part promptly at the assigned time. Dismissals and defaults in cases scheduled for trial or hearing will be taken 30 minutes after the scheduled time.

JUSTICE DAVID KAPLAN

Kaplan 1. Resolution Part Rules

I. Check In

All parties must check in with the Court Personnel upon arrival. Any party may request a conference with the court by notifying court personnel. No party is required to leave the courtroom to discuss a case.

II. Appearances

All attorneys must file a written Notice of Appearance. It shall be the obligation of the attorney appearing to ensure that such notice is on file with the Court; absent such notice the Court will not accept a stipulation.

III. Defaults

A default is entered by the clerk only after the file is endorsed by the court.

(a) For 9:30 AM cases: parties that have not checked in by 10:30 AM will be held in default for failure to appear; if a party has checked in by 10:30 AM but does not return by 11:30 AM to address the case, the Court will dismiss, default, or adjourn the case, at it's discretion.

(b) For 11:00 AM cases: parties that have not checked in by 12:00 noon will be held in default for failure to appear; if a party has checked in by 12:00 but does not return by 12:30 PM to address the case, the Court will dismiss, default, or adjourn the case, at it's discretion.

(c) For 2:00 PM cases: parties that have not checked in by 3:00 PM will be held in default for failure to appear; if a party has checked in by 3:00 PM but does not return by 3:30 PM to address the case, the Court will dismiss, default, or adjourn the case, at it's discretion.

IV. Applications/Adjournments

All applications for adjournments must be in writing stating the reason for the adjournment and the party being charged for the adjournment. The application must be submitted to the court for approval; parties must remain available to the court until the application is reviewed.

V. Stipulations

(a) Proposed stipulations of settlement shall be submitted to the Court Officer or Clerk for review by the Court Attorney and/or Judge. Pending such review,

the parties must remain available or be subject to rejection of the stipulation, default, dismissal or adjournment. If a party is required to appear in another courtroom, they must advise the Officer/Clerk where they are going and when they will return.

(b) In all nonpayment cases petitioners must provide a breakdown with a zero balance; a deed and assignment of rent must be available where appropriate. If there is a disputed amount, parties must agree upon a date when that disputed amount must be addressed or restored.

(c) If repairs are at issue, a list of alleged repairs, access times and dates, and completion dates must be included. If attorneys fees or other fees are requested petitioner must have a copy of the lease allowing such fees.

VI. Discontinuances

(a) All discontinuances must be memorialized in a stipulation indicating the reason for the discontinuance and whether the discontinuance is with or without prejudice.

(b) A stipulation discontinuing a nonpayment proceeding where the respondent has alleged conditions or repairs as a defense shall also designate whether repairs are necessary, and if so, a list of the repairs as well as access and completion dates.

VII. Motions

All motions must be argued and may not be submitted on consent without first being heard by the Judge. Parties should be prepared to resolve issues by stipulation if possible, particularly in discovery motions, and be prepared to argue the motion when all papers are before the court.

These rules are subject to modification by the Court.

Kaplan 2. Trial Part Rules

I. The Part opens promptly at 9:30 a.m. and 2:00 p.m. (unless there is an extended morning session necessitating a delayed opening in the afternoon).

II. There is no roll/calendar call. Parties are to check in with the Court Clerk or Court Officer.

III. Defaults may be taken after 10:00 a.m. for scheduled trials. Defaults may be taken on cases referred from Part X if both parties fail to check in within 30 minutes of the referral.

IV. The Court Attorney or Judge will conference the case before commencing the trial. If the matter cannot be resolved the trial will commence immediately.

V. The Court will not accept adjournments over the telephone.

VI. The above rules are subject to modification in the discretion of the Court.

JUSTICE SABRINA B. KRAUS

Kraus 1. Resolution Part Rules

1. All parties or their attorneys must check in with the Court Officer upon entering the part.

2. Where one or both sides have not checked in, cases on the 9:30 a.m. calendar may be subject to default and/or dismissal as of 10:30 a.m., cases on the 11:00 a.m. calendar may be subject to default or dismissal as of 12:00 p.m., and cases on the 2:00 p.m. calendar may be subject to default or dismissal as of 3:00 p.m.

3. All attorneys, including those who appear of counsel, must file a notice of appearance in any case in which they appear. If an attorney is appearing of counsel, she should note the extent of the appearance.

4. Stipulations must be legible. All signatories to a stipulation must print their name clearly underneath their signature.

5. All consent adjournments must be in writing, and should specify the reason for the adjournment. Any adjournments, beyond the first time the case is on, may only be had by leave of court. Any adjournments of motions, should provide for service of any opposition papers, reply papers and cross-motions, prior to the adjourned date.

6. All discontinuances of cases, and withdrawals of motions must be in writing, and should state whether the discontinuance or withdrawal is with prejudice, and if not, the reason why not.

7. Parties and attorneys in cases scheduled for a trial or hearing, which are to be sent to the expediter, must appear at 9:30 a.m. to be sent to Part X. In such matters, the court may entertain applications for default or dismissal as of 10:00 a.m.

8. Hearings and inquests may be held in the resolution part, as necessary, and subject to the court's availability. Such hearings or inquests will be scheduled for 2:30 p.m. and subject to default or dismissal as of 2:45 p.m.

9. Generally, other than where a party is represented by counsel, the court will not so-order stipulations where an individual purports to be signing on behalf of, or with authority for, a party, who is a natural person. Similarly, the court will not so-order stipulations where an individual executing the stipulation is not a party to the proceeding. The forgoing may be subject to exception where the individual shows a documented legal basis to be entitled to execute the stipulation (i.e. attorney-in-fact, Article 81 Guardian, etc.).

10. The submission of a stipulation to be so-ordered and/or allocuted is deemed to be consent for court to proceed with the case, in the absence of the attorney, and make such orders or modifications as may be necessary and appropriate. Similarly, any case which an attorney requests be marked for conference or argument requires that the attorney remain in the Court room until the case is called. If the attorney is not present when a case is called the court may proceed in the attorney's absence.

JUSTICE RUBEN ANDRES MARTINO

Martino 1. Part Rules
Check in:

All litigants and attorneys are to check in with the Clerk at the time the case is noticed to be heard.
Stipulations:

Proposed stipulations shall be submitted to the Clerk or Court Officer for review by the Court Attorney and Judge. Pending review by the Court Attorney or Judge, the parties and the attorneys shall remain available or be subject to default or dismissal.
Defaults:

9:30 a.m. cases: Defaults or dismissals shall occur at 11:00 a.m.

2:15 p.m. cases: Defaults or dismissals shall occur at 3:00 p.m. The Court strongly suggests that new cases be settled per stipulation with a right to restore for a judgment. Repairs, if any, should be included in the agreement with access and completion dates.

If a case or proceeding is not completed by the time cases are called for default, any party not present shall be subject to default or adjournment regardless of having checked in earlier with the Clerk.

JUSTICE JEAN SCHNEIDER

Schneider 1.   Resolution Part Rules

1.   All parties and attorneys must check in with court personnel upon arrival in the Part. Cases scheduled for 9:30 a.m. will be dismissed or defaulted if the party or attorney has not checked in by 10:30 am. Cases scheduled for 11:00 a.m. will be dismissed or defaulted at 12:00 noon. Cases scheduled for 2:00 p.m. will be dismissed or defaulted at 3:00 p.m.

2.   All cases on the 9:30 a.m. and 11:00 a.m. calendars that have not previously been disposed of may be called by the court at 12:30 p.m. and dismissed, defaulted, or adjourned at the court's discretion if the parties or attorneys are not present, whether or not the parties have checked in. Parties or attorneys whose cases have not been disposed of at that time and who do not plan to remain in the courtroom must specifically advise the court of the status of the case and the whereabouts of the party or attorney prior to that time. Cases on the 2:00 p.m. calendar may similarly be called and dismissed, defaulted, or adjourned if not disposed of by 4:00 p.m.

3.   Parties and attorneys with applications for adjournments should notify court personnel at the time of check-in. The court will hear applications as soon as both sides are present. No adjournment time will be charged for purposes of RPAPL Section 745(2) unless noted by the court at the time the adjournment is granted.

4.   Any party or attorney may request a conference with the court or with a court attorney, or may indicate readiness to argue a motion by notifying court personnel. Parties and attorneys who have requested a conference or argument are expected to remain in the courtroom until the case is called.

5.   All proposed stipulations of settlement must be submitted for review by the court. Parties must remain in the courthouse and available to the part until a proposed stipulation has been reviewed and "so ordered." Failure to remain available until a stipulation has been reviewed may result in a dismissal or default or in adjournment of the case, at the court's discretion.

6.   All motions must be argued. The court will not take any motions on submission.

7.   Parties and attorneys may not call out names in the courtroom. Any party or attorney who wishes to learn if his or her adversary is present may ask court personnel for assistance. Court personnel will advise litigants that they may have a conference with a court attorney or the court.

Schneider 2.   Trial Part Rules

1.   Cases scheduled for 9:30 a.m. will be dismissed or defaulted if parties and/or attorneys are not in the courtroom and ready to proceed at 10:30 am. There is no check-in procedure. Cases scheduled for 2:15 p.m. will be dismissed or defaulted at 3:00 p.m.

2.   All motions must be argued. The court will not take any motion on submission.

3.   All cases referred to this Part for trial will be tried from day to day until completed.

4.   No case may be adjourned in this Part except by application to the Court. Adjournments in the Part will be granted only in exceptional circumstances.

JUSTICE MICHELLE SCHREIBER

Schreiber 1.   Resolution Part Rules

1.   All parties must check in with the Court Personnel upon arrival. Any party may request a conference with the court by notifying court personnel. No party is required to leave the courtroom to discuss a case.

2.   **Defaults:** a default is entered by the clerk only after the file is endorsed by the court. 9:30 AM cases: parties that have not checked in by 11:00 AM will be held in default for failure to appear; if a party has checked in by 11:00 AM but does not return by 11:30 AM to address the case, that party will also be held in default.

11:00 AM cases: parties that have not checked in by 12:00 noon will be held in default for failure to appear; if a party has checked in by 12:00 but does not return by 12:30 PM to address the case, that party will also be held in default.

2:00 PM cases: parties that have not checked in by 3:00 PM will be held in default for failure to appear; if a party has checked in by 3:00 PM but does not return by 3:30 PM to address the case, that party will also be held in default. Please note that these times will be adjusted back by 15 minutes if there is a protracted morning session.

3.   **Notice of Appearance:** all attorneys must file a written Notice of Appearance. It shall be the obligation of the attorney appearing to ensure that such notice is on file with the Court; absent such notice the Court will not accept a stipulation.

4.   **Adjournments:** all applications for adjournments must be in writing stating the reason for the adjournment and the party being charged for the adjournment. The application must be submitted to the court for approval; parties must remain available to the court until the application is reviewed.

5. Stipulations: proposed stipulations of settlement shall be submitted to the Court Officer or Clerk for review by the Court Attorney and/or Judge. Pending such review, the parties must remain available or be subject to rejection of the stipulation, default, dismissal or adjournment. If a party is required to appear in another courtroom, they must advise the Officer/Clerk where they are going and when they will return. In all nonpayment cases petitioners must provide a breakdown with a zero balance; a deed and assignment of rent must be available where appropriate. If there is a disputed amount, parties must agree upon a date when that disputed amount must be addressed or restored. If repairs are at issue, a list of alleged repairs, access times and dates, and completion dates must be included. If attorneys fees or other fees are requested petitioner must have a copy of the lease allowing such fees.

6. Discontinuances: all discontinuances must be memorialized in a stipulation indicating the reason for the discontinuance and whether the discontinuance is with or without prejudice. A stipulation discontinuing a nonpayment proceeding shall also designate whether repairs are necessary, and if so, a list of the repairs as well as access and completion dates.

7. Motions: all motions must be argued and may not be submitted on consent without first being heard by the Judge. Parties should be prepared to resolve issues by stipulation if possible, particularly in discovery motions, and be prepared to argue the motion when all papers are before the court.

8. Inquests: inquests will be conducted in the Part at 3:00 PM. Petitioner must be prepared to submit evidence of nonmilitary status before a default judgment will be entered.

9. NYCHA cases: in addition to the above, in order to avoid a default the Housing Assistant (HA) must check in prior to the default times noted in paragraph two; applications for adjournments due to the unavailability of the HA must be made timely. All stipulations must indicate whether there are any other proceedings pending, and if so, dispositions on those proceedings must be included. Prior to entry of a default judgment in nonpayment cases, the HA must provide proof that the petition has not been satisfied. If a holdover proceeding is scheduled for inquest on more than two occasions and NYCHA is not prepared the matter will be dismissed or marked off calendar in the discretion of the court.

These rules are subject to modification by the Court.

Schreiber 2. Trial Part Rules

1. The Part opens promptly at 9:30 a.m. and 2:00 p.m. (unless there is an extended morning session necessitating a delayed opening in the afternoon).

2. There is no roll/calendar call. Parties are to check in with the Court Clerk or Court Officer.

3. Defaults may be taken after 10:00 a.m. for scheduled trials. Defaults may be taken on cases referred from Part X if both parties fail to check in within 30 minutes of the referral.

4. The Court Attorney or Judge will conference the case before commencing the trial. If the matter cannot be resolved the trial will commence immediately.

5. The Court will not accept adjournments over the telephone.

6. The above rules are subject to modification in the discretion of the Court.

JUSTICE BRENDA SPEARS

Spears 1. Part Rules

1. All parties must check in with the Part Clerk.

2. When a party is represented by an attorney, a paralegal or lawyer's service may check in for the party. All stipulations must be signed by the party's attorney.

3. Except for matters marked as "Final" for trial, defaults will be called by the Clerk at 11:00 a.m. for the 9:30 a.m. calendar and at 3:00 p.m. for the 2:00 p.m. calendar.

4. Matters adjourned and marked "Final" for trial will be called by the Part by 10:30 am. Defaults will be entered with respect to cases set down for trial at 10:30 am.

5. With respect to a matter where the parties have checked in, but the matter remains unattended to by 12:30 p.m. (for the 9:30 a.m. calendar) or 3:30 p.m. (for the 2:00 p.m. calendar) said matter shall be resolved solely on the documents before the court.

6. All adjournments or other scheduling adjustments shall be in person in the Part. No adjournments will be granted by telephone.

7. All matters marked off the calendar may be restored only by motion, unless the proceeding was marked off the calendar by stipulation and said stipulation permitted the subsequent restoration of the proceeding by stipulation. The original stipulation must be included as an exhibit to the restoration stipulation.

8. All stipulations must contain a current rent breakdown.

JUSTICE JOHN HENRY STANLEY

Stanley 1. Resolution Part Rules

1. Upon arrival, you must inform the court you are here. Please find the calendar number for your case on the court calendar located outside the courtroom door. Then, go to the court officer=s desk located inside the courtroom and inform the officer of the calendar number. Then, you may take a seat in the courtroom.

2. Parties will be defaulted as follows:

9:30 a.m. calendar at 11:00 a.m.

11:00 a.m. calendar at 12:00 p.m.

2:15 p.m. calendar at 3:00 p.m.

3. All adjournments and discontinuances must be in writing stating the reason for the adjournment or discontinuance. Stipulations discontinuing non-payment proceedings must state the period through which all rent has been paid.

4. Proposed stipulations of settlement must be submitted to the court for review. Attorneys who leave the part before review of a stipulation must advise the clerk in which part they can be located.

Failure to remain in the courtroom may result in a dismissal, default, or adjournment at the court's discretion.

5. There will be a status call on all cases where both parties have appeared. If such parties do not return to the part to resolve their matters by 11:30 a.m. for 9:30 a.m. cases, 12:30 p.m. for 11:00 a.m. cases, or 3:15 p.m. for 2:00 p.m. cases, the matters can be defaulted, dismissed or adjourned at the discretion of the court.

6. Parties who return to the part after 12:30 p.m. cannot expect to have their matter addressed by the court prior to the closing of the Part at 1:00 p.m.

7. Stipulations in non-payment proceedings must contain a rent breakdown and a statement as to whether there are conditions to be corrected in the premises. All stipulations with alleged repairs must include access dates and completion dates.

8. Any non-payment stipulation of settlement containing a dispute over amounts owed must contain a date certain by which the matter is to be resolved.

JUSTICE PETER WENDT

Wendt 1. Resolution Part Rules

1. A serious attempt to settle all matters will be made by the Court and the Court Attorneys before proceedings are sent out for trial. However, litigants and attorneys assigned to the Part will be expected to be ready to proceed to trial at the time the case is called, unless a good reason for postponement of the matter is presented.

2. There are three calendars — 9:30 am, 11:00 am and 2:00 pm. Cases and motions on the 9:30 calendar will be subject to default, dismissal or denial for non-appearance at 10:30 am. 11:00 am cases will be subject to default or dismissal at 11:30 am. Cases on for 2:00 pm will be subject to default or dismissal at 3:00 pm. Litigants and attorneys will be expected to arrive at the time their case is noticed to be heard. Proceedings on the Part calendars will be subject to dismissal, default orders or denial for non-appearance when they are called, if one or the other or both parties fail to appear.

3. Adjourned cases set for times other than 9:30 am will be called at the time they are scheduled. Litigants who fail to appear for such matters at the scheduled time will be subject to default order, dismissal, or denial of their motion.

4. All motions, including orders to show cause, should be made returnable at 9:30 am.

5. All proposed stipulations where one or both parties are unrepresented by counsel **must** be reviewed and explained by the Court Attorney or the Judge before they are signed by the unrepresented litigant.

6. Counsel **must** appear for a party who is represented by an attorney.

7. Corporations may not appear without counsel. (See CPLR 321[a]).

Wendt 2. Trial Part Rules

1. Cases are assigned to the part by the Expediter for trial, not for any other purpose. Therefore, litigants and their attorneys assigned to this part for trial will be expected to be ready to proceed to trial immediately at the time of assignment to the part.

2. There will be one roll call at 9:45 A.M.. Motions and all other matters returnable at 9:30 A.M. will be subject to dismissal, denial for non-appearance or default orders at the roll call.

3. Adjourned cases set for times other than 9:30 A.M. will be called at the time they are scheduled. Litigants who fail to appear for such matters at the scheduled time will be subject to default orders or dismissal.

4. Counsel **must** appear for a party who is represented by an attorney. Corporations may not appear without counsel. (See CPLR 321 [a]).

BRONX COUNTY

JUSTICE PAUL ALPERT

Alpert 1. Resolution Part Rules

(1) Part E is the New York City Housing Authority (NYCHA) part. NYCHA cases are heard in Part E on Tuesdays, Wednesdays and Fridays. There is a calendar call in Part E on NYCHA days at 9:45 a.m. for the 9:30 a.m. calendar and 2:15 p.m. for the 2:00 p.m. calendar. All parties **must** be present for the calendar call. There is no calendar call in Part E on Mondays or Thursdays. On those dates all parties or their attorneys are to sign in with the court officer upon entering the part.

(2) Defaults on matters appearing on the 9:30 a.m. calendar will be taken at 11:00 a.m. Defaults on matters appearing on the 11:00 a.m. calendar will be taken at 12:00 p.m. Defaults on matter appearing on the 2:00 p.m. calendar will be taken at 3:00 p.m. Holdover defaults **must** be scheduled for inquest.

(3) Parties and attorneys should check on the status of their cases periodically with court personnel and advise accordingly on the status of their cases. Open cases are subject to default or dismissal regardless of whether the parties have checked in, where the court is unable to ascertain the whereabouts of parties or attorneys and the status of a case.

(4) Adjournments on consent shall be submitted by stipulation by both sides. Parties **must** first check with court personnel to confirm the availability of an adjourn date. Where the time is not explicitly charged to either side in the stipulation of adjournment, neither side shall be deemed charged. The court shall entertain all applications for adjournments where the parties cannot consent. The court shall also entertain adjournment requests, where the court determines that the number of consent adjournments has been excessive. In such instances, the parties **must** provide sufficient basis for an additional adjournment. If the court determines there is no basis for an additional adjournment, the case shall either be marked off calendar or referred to Part X for trial, at the discretion of the Judge.

(5) If a matter has been adjourned for the sole purpose of allowing the parties to be ready for trial assignment to Part X, the parties must be present no later than 10:00 a.m. on the adjourned date.

(6) All motions for non–NYCHA cases should, to the extent possible, be noticed on Monday or Thursday. The court will not accept any sur-reply's or accept any submissions after the motion has been heard. If a case has been adjourned for trial in Part X, the court will not entertain any dispositive motion if the return date is made the same as the date set for trial.

Alpert 2. Trial Part Rules

(1) All parties or their counsel **must** check in with the court officer or clerk upon entering the Part.

(2) There will be no calendar or roll call.

(3) All litigants or their counsel should then check in with the Court Officer. All litigants will conference the case with the Court Attorney assigned to the part. If the Court Attorney cannot resolve the case, the Court will commence the trail immediately.

(4) The Court does not accept adjournments over the phone. All requests for adjournments will be dealt with by the Court. Stipulations for adjournments will not be accepted unless a party or counsel is present in Court

JUSTICE MARIAN C. DOHERTY

Doherty 1. Resolution Part Rules

1. All parties or their attorneys are to check in with the clerk upon entering the courtroom. You must provide the clerk with your calendar number and advise the clerk if you wish an adjournment for any reason.

2. All applications for adjournments will be heard by the court when both sides are present.

3. If you are not represented by counsel, you do not have to speak with the other side without the court attorney or judge being present.

4. Defaults will be taken as follows:

9:30 a.m. calendar at 11:00 a.m.

11:00 a.m. calendar at 12:30 p.m.
2:00 p.m. calendar at 3:00 p.m.

5. Service or a representative of a party other than an attorney may answer in the part on behalf of a party to request an adjournment.

6. Proposed stipulations of settlement must be submitted to the clerk for review by the court. Parties must remain in the courtroom or advise the clerk in which part they can be located. Failure to remain or be located may result in a dismissal, default, or adjournment at the court's discretion.

7. Any non-party who appears for more than an application to adjourn must have written notarized authorization to act on that party's behalf.

8. All parties checking in as required by the afore-mentioned rules and thereafter leaving the courtroom, and upon failure to return to resolve their respective matters by 11:30 a.m. for 9:30 a.m. cases, 12:45 p.m. for 11:00 a.m. cases, or 3:30 p.m. for 2:00 p.m. cases will either be defaulted or dismissed unless explanation of such absence is advanced.

9. Stipulations in non-payment proceedings must recite amount due, monthly rent and a rent breakdown applying payments to the month in which they are made.

Doherty 2. Trial Part Rules

Part D is a trial part pursuant to the Housing Court Initiative. Parties assigned to this part are presumed ready for trial with all necessary documents and witnesses available. If a trial is continued or adjourned for any reason, defaults or dismissals will be taken if a party has not appeared within 30 minutes of the scheduled time. Orders to Show Cause are returnable at 9:30 a.m. Defaults, dismissals and/or inquests on an alleged illegal lockouts will be determined at 10:15 a.m.

JUSTICE JERALD KLEIN

Klein 1. Resolution Part Rules

1. Assigned trial times will be enforced.

2. Motions are to be calendared for 9:30 am.

3. Parties or attorneys may check in with the Clerk.

4. Defaults and dismissals will be entertained beginning at 10:30 am.

Klein 2. Trial Part Rules

1. There will be a roll/calendar call at 9:45 am. All parties must answer the roll/calendar call. Parties arriving after the roll/calendar call has been completed must check in with the Clerk upon entering the Part and give the Clerk their calendar number which is on the calendar posted outside the courtroom.

2. All attorneys must file a written Notice of Appearance. It shall be the obligation of the attorney appearing to ensure that a current Notice of Appearance is on file with the Court.

3. All requests for adjournments and discontinuances must be submitted to the Court Attorney or the Judge for review. These requests will be considered immediately after the roll/calendar call; all parties should remain in the courtroom until after the application is heard.

4. HP cases must be conferenced initially with the HPD staff; assistance from the Court Attorney may be requested. In the event the conferences do not conclude in a resolution of the case, any party may request a conference with the Judge. All parties

must remain in the courtroom and be available for the conference.

5. Proposed stipulations of settlement shall be submitted to the Court Officer or Clerk for review by the Court Attorney or the Judge. Pending such review, the parties shall remain available or be subject to rejection of the stipulation, default, dismissal or adjournment. If a party is required to appear in another courtroom, they must advise the Court Officer or the Clerk of the part where they are going and when they will return. All stipulations and orders to correct in HP actions must have access dates, indicate that workers must arrive by no later than noon, and include a completion date for the repairs.

6. All motions must be conferenced by the Court Attorney or Judge. No motion shall be submitted without argument before the Judge.

7. 9:30 a.m. cases - if a party does not check in by 11:00 am the Clerk will put the case before the Judge for default or dismissal. If a party checks in at the roll/calendar call but fails to return by 11:30 am, the other side may ask the Clerk to put the case before the Judge for a default, dismissal or adjournment in the discretion of the Court.

8. 2:15 p.m. trials/hearings - if a party fails to appear by 2:45 p.m. for a matter scheduled for a trial or hearing, the Court in its discretion may conduct an inquest, dismiss or adjourn the matter.

THESE RULES ARE SUBJECT
TO MODIFICATION BY
THE COURT.

JUSTICE LYDIA LAI

Lai 1. Resolution Part Rules
Check In Procedure

All parties must check in with the court officer. Parties shall indicate to the court officer the calendar number of their case as it appears on the wall outside the courtroom.

When a party is represented by counsel, only counsel may argue or conference a case.

Defaults

Parties scheduled to appear at 9:30 a.m. will be held in default upon failure to appear by 10:30 a.m.

Parties scheduled to appear at 11:00 a.m. will be held in default upon failure to appear by 12 noon.

Parties scheduled to appear at 2:00 p.m. will be held in default upon failure to appear by 3:00 p.m.

If a party appears timely, but leaves and does not reappear within 30 minutes of the default period, the court may enter a default, mark the proceeding off-calendar or adjourn the case at the discretion of the court.

Defaults in holdover proceedings must be scheduled for inquest. Nonmilitary affidavits are required for all inquests.

Adjournments

Adjournments may be granted upon approval of the court for good cause.

Stipulations

Proposed stipulations of settlement must be submitted to the court officer or clerk for review by the court attorney and/or Judge.

Motions

The court requires oral argument on all motions.

Lai 2. Trial Part Rules

Check In Procedure

All parties must check in with the court officer.

Defaults

All parties must be ready to proceed to trial at the time they are assigned to the Part.

Parties scheduled to appear at 9:30 a.m. will be held in default upon failure to appear by 10:00 a.m.

Parties scheduled to appear at 2:15 p.m. will be held in default upon failure to appear by 3:00 p.m.

Parties who fail to appear at the scheduled time will be subject to default, dismissal or other appropriate relief.

Adjournments

Adjournments may be granted upon approval of the court for good cause only.

Motions

The court requires oral argument on all motions.

JUSTICE JAYA MADHAVAN

Madhavan 1. Resolution Part Rules

1. Check In

(a) All parties, their attorneys or service must check in with court personnel upon entering the part.

2. Appearances

(a) All attorneys must file a written notice of appearance. The Court will reject any stipulation signed by an attorney who has not filed such notice.

(b) Only parties and attorneys fully authorized to settle a matter may appear before the Court.

3. Defaults

(a) Cases scheduled for 9:30 a.m. will be dismissed or defaulted where a party or their attorney has not checked in by 11:00 a.m. Cases scheduled for 2:00 p.m. will be dismissed or defaulted at 3:00 p.m.

(b) Cases that appear on the 9:30 calendar for trial, inquest or a hearing will be dismissed or defaulted where a party or their attorney has not checked in by 10:00 a.m.

(c) Where all parties or their attorneys have checked in, but the case remains unattended to by 12:30 p.m. (for cases on the 9:30 a.m. calendar) or 3:00 p.m. (for cases on the 2:00 p.m. calendar), the Court shall dismiss or default or adjourn the case, at its discretion.

(d) Parties or their attorneys cannot return to the Part after 12:30 p.m. and expect their cases to be heard. The Part closes promptly at 1:00 p.m. and resumes at 2:00 p.m.

4. Conferences

(a) Any party or attorney may request a conference with the Court or a Court Attorney by notifying court personnel.

(b) The Court or the Court Attorneys shall conference all cases in which a settlement cannot be reached. If after conference settlement is still not reached, the case shall be sent to a trial part or adjourned and marked final for trial, at the Court's discretion.

5. Stipulations

(a) All stipulations of settlement in nonpayment proceedings must contain a clear rent breakdown applying payments to the months in which they are made. The petitioner may refer to a printed breakdown provided that a copy of the same is given to the respondent and/or made available to the Court for review.

(b) All stipulations of settlement must state whether repairs are at issue. Alleged conditions requiring repair must be specifically listed in the stipulation, access dates provided and a completion date set unless special circumstances dictate otherwise.

(c) All stipulations of settlement must be submitted for review and allocution by the Court. Parties or their attorneys must be available to the part until a proposed stipulation has been reviewed and "so ordered." Failure to remain available until a stipulation has been reviewed may result in a dismissal or a default or an adjournment of the case, at the Court's discretion.

6. Adjournments

(a) All requests for adjournments and discontinuances must be in writing and state the reason for the adjournment or discontinuance. The application must then be submitted to the Court for approval.

Madhavan 2. Trial Part Rules

1. Parties assigned to this part are presumed ready for trial with all necessary documents and witnesses available.

2. All parties, their attorneys or service must check in with court personnel upon entering the part.

3. Cases scheduled for 9:30 a.m. in this part will be dismissed or defaulted where a party or their attorney has not checked in by 10:00 a.m. Cases scheduled for 2:00 p.m. in this part will be dismissed or defaulted at 2:30 p.m. Cases otherwise assigned to this part will be dismissed or defaulted where a party or their attorney fails to check in within 15 minutes of the case being sent to this part.

4. No case may be adjourned except by application to the Court. Adjournments will be granted only in exceptional circumstances.

5. The Court shall conference all cases between the parties and their counsel before a trial is conducted.

6. Cases shall be tried from day to day unless special circumstances dictate otherwise.

JUSTICE KEVIN McCLANAHAN

McClanahan 1. Resolution Part Rules

1. All parties or their counsel must check in with the Clerk or the Court Officer upon entering the Part.

2. Counsel who appear must be fully familiar with the case in regard to which they appear, be ready for trial and/or fully authorized to enter into agreements, both substantive and procedural, on behalf of their clients. Failure to comply with this rule will be regarded as a default and dealt with appropriately. It is important that counsel be on time for all scheduled appearances.

3. There are three (3) calendars called in this Part: 9:30 am, 11:00 a.m. and 2:00 p.m.

4. Cases on the 9:30 a.m. calendar shall be called for default at 11:00 am; cases on the 11:00 a.m. calendar shall be called for default at Noon; cases on the 2:00 p.m. calendar shall be called for default at 3:00 p.m.

5. All requests for adjournments and discontinuances must be submitted to the Court Attorney for review. These requests will be considered immediately after the roll/calendar call; all parties should remain in the courtroom until after the application is heard. Stipulations for adjournments will not be accepted unless a party or counsel is present in court.

6. If a case is settled, discontinued, or otherwise disposed of, counsel shall immediately inform the Court by submission of the stipulation directed to the Clerk of the Part.

7. Unless otherwise directed by the Court, a stipulation or notice of motion is required to restore to the trial calendar all cases that have been "marked off".

8. All parties and/or counsel may conference a matter with the Court Attorney or the Court. Cases will be conferenced or placed before the Court when both sides have appeared. In the event the case cannot be settled, it will be scheduled for trial.

9. In nonpayment proceedings, all stipulations shall contain the monthly rent, an itemized rent breakdown of arrears and a payment schedule, if applicable. Alleged conditions requiring repair shall be specifically listed in the stipulation, access dates provided and a completion date set.

10. All self-represented litigants must appear in court for allocution of stipulations. Stipulations will be thoroughly reviewed and explained to all self-represented litigants prior to being "so-ordered" by the Court.

11. Pursuant to CPLR 2302(b), Subpoenas Duces Tecum will only be signed if the face thereof includes the case's index number, the trial date and will not be signed more than 30 days prior to the scheduled trial.

12. Service of motions pursuant to CPLR 2214 is encouraged and CPLR 406 service is discouraged. All motions must be orally argued. The Court requires written opposition to all motions. This does not permit submission schedules.

13. All motions must be conferenced by the Court Attorney or Judge. Parties should be prepared to resolve issues by stipulation if possible, particularly in discovery motions, and be prepared to argue the motion when all papers are before the Court.

McClanahan 2. Trial Part Rules

1. Parties or their counsel must sign in with the Clerk or court officer upon entering the Part.

2. Motions and all other matters returnable in this part at 9:30 a.m. will be subject to dismissal, denial for non-appearance or default at 10:00 am.

3. This is a trial ready part. Cases are assigned to the Part by the Expediter for trial, not for any other purpose. Therefore, litigants and their attor-

neys assigned to this part for trial will be expected to be ready to proceed to trial immediately at the time of assignment to the Part.

4. Adjourned cases set for times other than 9:30 a.m. will be called at the time they are scheduled. Litigants who fail to appear for such matters at the scheduled time will be subject to default orders or dismissal within 30 minutes following the scheduled starting time.

5. Counsel must appear for a party who is represented by an attorney. Corporations may not appear without counsel (see CPLR 321[a]).

6. The case is called inside and outside the courtroom. If the respondent does not appear, a final judgment is entered against the respondent. If the petitioner fails to appear, the petition is dismissed. In a holdover proceeding, if the respondent fails to appear, the judge holds an inquest; if the petitioner fails to appear, the petition is dismissed. If the respondent fails to appear on the return date of his/her Order to Show Cause, it will be denied; if the petitioner fails to appear on the return date, any relief requested by the respondent can be granted.

JUSTICE EARDELL RASHFORD

Rashford 1. Resolution Part Rules

1. Calendar calls

(a) All parties and attorneys must check in with the clerk upon arrival in the Part. There will be a calendar call of all cases in which both parties have not previously checked in at 11:00 am. Dismissals and defaults will be taken on this calendar call.

(b) All cases not previously disposed of will be called at 12:30 pm. Dismissals and defaults may be taken or adjournments granted on this call at the court's discretion, whether or not the parties have previously checked in with the clerk.

2. Conferences

Cases will be called for conference when all parties are present in the courtroom and ready to proceed. Any party may request a conference with the court or with the court attorney by notifying the clerk. Parties and attorneys who have requested a conference are expected to remain in the courtroom until the case is called.

3. Stipulations

Proposed stipulations of settlement must be submitted to the clerk for review by the court. Parties must remain in the courthouse until a proposed stipulation has been reviewed and approved. Failure to remain until a stipulation has been reviewed and approved may result in a dismissal or default or in an adjournment of the case, at the court's discretion.

4. Trials/Hearings

Parties and attorneys in cases scheduled for trial or hearing are expected to arrive in the part promptly at the assigned time. Dismissals and defaults in cases schedule for trial or hearing will be taken 15 minutes after the scheduled time.

Rashford 2.   Trial Part Rules

This Part will serve as a Trial Part pursuant to the Housing Court Initiative. Parties assigned to this Part for trial are presumed ready for trial with all the necessary documents and witnesses available. There will be no roll calls or calendar calls. Parties must appear in the Part within 30 minutes of transfer by the expediter. Defaults and/or dismissals will be entered if any party fails to appear within 30 minutes after the Part receives the case for Trial. Matters that are not ready for trial will at the court's discretion be either dismissed or returned to the Resolution Part from which the matter was transferred. If a matter is settled pursuant to a stipulation prior the commencement of the trial, the matter shall be transferred back to the Resolution Part.

JUSTICE JOSE RODRIGUEZ

Rodriguez 1.   Resolution Part Rules

1. All parties or their attorneys are to check in with the court officer upon arrival.

2. Calendar calls will be held at the following times. Only those cases where one or both parties has not checked in will be called. Defaults and dismissals will be entered.

10:30 a.m. all cases scheduled for 9:30 a.m. will be called

11:45 a.m. all cases scheduled for 11:00 a.m. will be called

2:45 p.m. all cases scheduled for 2:00 p.m. will be called

3. Cases where both sides have checked in and are marked "ready" will be held for a reasonable period of time to allow the parties an opportunity to discuss a resolution of the case. The court will dispose of those cases, in a manner deemed appropriate, where attorneys or parties check in but fail to return to conference or otherwise resolve their cases within a reasonable period of time.

3. Applications for adjournments will be heard immediately following the calendar calls. If you have an

application please inform the court officer or court clerk upon arrival or at the calendar call.

4. On nonpayment proceedings or motions in which a party has defaulted, attorneys must provide the court information regarding the status of their defaults. Failure to provide the information prior to 1:00 p.m. for morning cases or 3:30 p.m. for afternoon cases will result in dismissals and/or denials of the petitions or motions.

5. In holdover proceedings where respondents have failed to appear, please inform the court if you are ready for inquest or require an application for an adjournment.

Rodriguez 2. Trial Part Rules

1. All parties or their attorneys are to check in with the court officer upon arrival.

2. Calendar calls will be held at 9:45 a.m. for cases scheduled for trial or hearing. A second call shall be held at 11:00 a.m. for motions and any other matter pending before the Court.

3. Applications for adjournments on cases from the expediter will be referred back to the resolution part from which the matter was transferred.

4. Cases referred by the expediter for trial shall be held for twenty minutes to allow the parties and their attorneys time to appear prepared to proceed. The court will dispose of those cases, in a manner deemed appropriate, where a party has failed to appear.

5. Applications for adjournments will be heard immediately following the calendar calls.

6. On nonpayment proceedings in which a respondent has defaulted, attorneys or pro se petitioners are required to inform the Court of the status of the default and if the amounts alleged remain unpaid.

JUSTICE ELIZABETH TAO

Tao 1. Resolution Part Rules

1. Check In

Upon arrival in the courtroom, all parties must check in with the Clerk or Court Officer. After checking in parties must remain available and/or accessible for resolution of the matter within the default deadline or the proceeding shall be dismissed, defaulted or adjourned at the Court's discretion.

2. Defaults

Parties scheduled to appear at 9:30 a.m. will be held in default upon failure to appear by 10:45 a.m. Parties scheduled for a trial or hearing at 9:30 a.m. will be held in default upon failure to be ready to proceed or upon failure to appear by 10:00 a.m. Parties scheduled to appear at 11:00 a.m. will be held in default upon failure to appear by 12:00 p.m. Parties scheduled to appear at 2:00 p.m. will be held in default upon failure to appear by 3:00 p.m.

3. Discontinuances and Adjournments

All requests for discontinuances or adjournments must be made on the return date and must be reviewed by the judge or a court attorney; the parties should not leave until after such review. Where possible, the requests should be reduced to a writing, preferably in the form of a stipulation signed by the parties, and should give a reason for the discontinuance or adjournment.

4. Stipulations

All stipulations shall be submitted for review by the judge or a court attorney. The parties must remain available for such review.

5. Conferences

In those cases where the parties are unable or unwilling to reach a settlement agreement, the matter shall be submitted promptly for review by the judge or a court attorney. Both sides shall remain available for the case to be called.

6. Court Room Decorum

There shall be no talking, eating, reading or use of any electronic devices in the courtroom.

Tao 2. Trial Part Rules

1. This a trial part pursuant to the Housing Court Initiative. Parties assigned to this part are presumed ready for trial with all necessary documents and witnesses available.

2. Cases shall be tried from day-to-day unless good cause is shown to adjourn the matter to nonconsecutive dates.

3. If a trial is continued or adjourned for any reason, defaults or dismissals will be taken if a party has not appeared within 30 minutes of the scheduled time.

4. Orders to Show Cause are returnable at 9:30 am. Defaults, dismissals and/or inquests on alleged illegal lockouts will be determined at 10:15 am.

JUSTICE LOUIS VILLELLA

Villella 1. Resolution Part Rules

Check In Procedure

All parties must check in with the court clerk or court officer. Parties shall indicate to the court clerk or court officer the calendar number of their case as it appears on the wall outside the courtroom.

When a party is represented by counsel, only counsel may argue or conference a case.

Defaults

Parties scheduled to appear at 9:30 a.m. will be held in default upon failure to appear by 11:00 a.m.

Parties scheduled to appear at 11:00 a.m. will be held in default upon failure to appear by 12 noon.

Parties scheduled to appear at 2:00 p.m. will be held in default upon failure to appear by 3:00 p.m.

If a party appears timely, but leaves and does not reappear within 30 minutes of the default period, the court may enter a default, or adjourn the case at the discretion of the court.

Defaults in holdover proceedings must be scheduled for inquest. Nonmilitary affidavits are required for all inquests.

Adjournments

Adjournments may be granted upon approval of the court for good cause.

Stipulations

Proposed stipulations of settlement must be submitted to the court clerk or court officer for review by the court attorney and/or Judge.

Motions

The court requires oral argument on all motions.

Villella 2. Trial Part Rules

Check In Procedure

All parties must check in with the court clerk or court officer.

Defaults

All parties must be ready to proceed to trial at the time they are assigned to the Part.

Parties scheduled to appear at 9:30 a.m. will be held in default upon failure to appear by 10:00 a.m.

Parties scheduled to appear at 2:15 p.m. will be held in default upon failure to appear by 3:00 p.m.

Parties who fail to appear at the scheduled time will be subject to default, dismissal or other appropriate relief.

Adjournments

Adjournments may be granted upon approval of the court for good cause only.

Motions

The court requires oral argument on all motions.

KINGS COUNTY

JUSTICE MARC FINKELSTEIN

Finkelstein 1.   Part Rules

Part S is a Trial Part. Cases are heard during the day on Wednesdays, Thursdays and Fridays only. There are no roll calls or calendar calls. Unless otherwise specified by the Court, adjourned cases and orders to show cause and motions are scheduled at 9:30 am. Upon arrival, all individuals with cases are to check in with the Court Officer by giving the calendar number (the calendar is posted on the bulletin board immediately outside the courtroom with the calendar number highlighted), whether the appearance is for the landlord or tenant and whether there is an attorney on the case. For cases where both sides have not checked in, defaults, dismissals and other dispositions will be considered at approximately 10:45 am. Where attorneys or parties check in but fail to return to conference or otherwise resolve their cases within a reasonable period of time, the Court will consider appropriate disposition.

Cases assigned to the Part S by the Expediter (Part X) for hearing, trial or inquest are expected to be ready to promptly proceed. The rule that the parties shall have 20 minutes after assignment by the Expediter to appear in the part for trial will be enforced.

Part N is a Trial and Resolution Part. Cases are heard on Tuesday and Thursday nights only. Cases are heard beginning at 6:00 p.m. or earlier if the part is open. Only cases where neither party has a lawyer and scheduled for night court in Part N. If an attorney does appear, it will be the Court's discretion whether to hear the matter that evening, adjourn it to another evening, or reschedule it to day court. At each appearance before the Court, the parties should be prepared both to conference their case, and if the case is not settled, to have a trial conducted by the Court.

When applicable, a notice of appearance, withdrawal, substitution or discharge of attorney is to be submitted on a proper form. There are no automatic adjournments or discontinuances. The Court will hear all such requests and will require a stated reason for the adjournment or discontinuance. If a case is "put up" for conference or allocution of a stipulation, the parties and attorneys are expected to remain in the part unless otherwise directed by the Court. In all cases, the parties and attorneys shall periodically inform the court staff as to the progress of their case and remain available for the case to be called.

All stipulations will be allocated by the Court. They must be legible. Non-payment stipulations shall contain either an accurate and proper breakdown or make specific reference to a breakdown being provided. Stipulations shall contain a list of alleged repairs, access dates for inspection and repair (unless the parties must indicate "access dates to be arranged") and a final completion date, or a statement that no repairs are alleged or needed. The Court strongly prefers that if a "disputed amount clause" is to be contained in a stipulation, the stipulation provide a date for the landlord and tenant to meet to attempt to resolve the dispute, and if it cannot be resolved, the case must be restored to the Court's calendar by a reasonable date, failing which the disputed amount is deemed waived.

Dignity, order, decorum, respect and consideration are indispensable to the fair, equal and proper administration of justice. Therefore, the Court will insist that counsel, parties, witnesses and spectators conduct themselves appropriately while in or around the courtroom/courthouse.

JUSTICE ANTHONY J. FIORELLA, JR.

Fiorella 1.   Resolution Part Rules

Check in:

Upon entering the part, all litigants and attorneys are to check in with the clerk or court officer.

Discontinuances and Adjournments:

Any request for an adjournment or discontinuance shall be reviewed by the court attorney or judge. Service or a representative of a party other than an attorney may answer in the part on behalf of a party to request an adjournment.

Stipulations:

All stipulations shall be submitted for review by the judge or court attorney. The parties must remain available for such review. Stipulations in non-payment proceedings must recite amount due, monthly rent and a rent breakdown applying payments to the month in which they are made.

Conferences:

In those cases where the parties are unable or unwilling to reach a settlement agreement, the matter shall be submitted promptly for review by the judge or a court attorney. Both sides shall remain available for the case to be called.

Defaults:

9:30 a.m. cases: Parties to cases scheduled at 9:30 a.m. will be held in default upon failure to appear by 11:00 am.

11:00 a.m. cases: Parties to cases scheduled at 11:00 a.m. will be held in default upon failure to appear by 12:00 p.m.

2:00 p.m. cases: Parties to cases that are scheduled for 2:00 p.m. will be held in default upon failure to appear by 3:00 p.m.

Fiorella 2.   Trial Part Rules

Part D is a trial part pursuant to the Housing Court Initiative. Parties assigned to this part are presumed ready for trial with all necessary documents and witnesses available. If a trial is continued or adjourned for any reason, defaults or dismissals will be taken if a party has not appeared within 30 minutes of the scheduled time. Orders to Show Cause are returnable at 9:30 a.m. Defaults, dismissals and/or inquests on alleged illegal lockouts will be determined at 10:30 a.m.

JUSTICE THOMAS FITZPATRICK

Fitzpatrick 1.   Resolution Part Rules

1. Unless a calendar call is being conducted, all parties must report to the Court Officer or Court Clerk upon entering the courtroom.

2. Parties that are scheduled to appear at 9:30 a.m. will be held in default upon failure to appear by 11:00 am; parties that are scheduled to appear at 11:00 a.m. will be held in default upon failure to appear by 12:00 noon; parties that are scheduled to appear at 2:00 p.m. will be held in default upon failure to appear by 3:00 p.m.. Holdover defaults shall be scheduled for inquest.

Where a case has been previously scheduled for a trial or hearing, a party may ask for a default against a non-appearing party one half hour after the scheduled time to appear.

3. After checking in parties must resolve the matter within the default deadline, or be available inside or immediately outside the courtroom, or be subject to default or adjournment within the Court's discretion.

4. Proposed stipulations of settlement shall be submitted to the Court Officer or Clerk for review by a Court Attorney or Judge. Pending such review, the parties shall remain available or be subject to rejection of the stipulation, default, dismissal or adjournment. In Non–Payment proceedings, the Petitioner shall provide to respondent a detailed rent history showing actual charges and payments on a month by month basis back to a zero balance, or the Court shall not enter judgment.

5. Adjournments on consent shall be submitted by stipulation signed by both sides. Where the reason for the adjournment is not explicitly stated in the stipulation of adjournment, neither side shall be charged with the time. All stipulations to adjourn require the Court's consent, or the parties shall be subject to default.

6. Oral argument is required on all motions, unless the Court permits submission without argument.

Fitzpatrick 2.   Trial Part Rules

1. If petitioner is not ready to proceed after transfer of the case from Part X, the proceeding will be dismissed pursuant to CPLR Section 3215(a).

2. If respondent is not ready to proceed after transfer of the case from Part X, a default will be taken or an inquest will be conducted pursuant to CPLR Section 3215(a).

3. All parties or their attorneys must check in with the clerk or court officer upon entering the Part.

4. Cases on the 9:30 a.m. calendar shall be defaulted at 10:30 a.m. where one or both sides have not checked in.

5. If a trial cannot be completed on the date it was transferred to the Trial Part, it will continue day to day until completion, unless otherwise specified by the court.

JUSTICE GEORGE M. HEYMANN

Heymann 1.   Resolution Part Rules

1. Although there are no formal roll calls or calendar calls, all parties are requested to sign in with the clerk.

2. When all parties to a case are present and have prepared a stipulation for review or require a conference before the court, the court clerk will put the case before the court or assign it to one of the court attorneys. No party shall place any case before the court without requesting permission from the court clerk or officer.

3. Service may request an adjournment from the clerk but may not appear before the court. Parties may adjourn proceedings by stipulation or on verbal consent to a date and time convenient to the parties and the court, after clearing the date with the clerk of

the part. The court file will contain a notation that such adjournment is on consent. Stipulations between represented and unrepresented parties must contain a statement the "period covered by the adjournment is not chargeable to either side pursuant to the provisions of RPAPL section 745(2)." Two-attorney stipulations need not contain such provision. All other applications for adjournments must be made before the court.

4. Anyone, other than an attorney, who appears on behalf of a party must have written/notarized authorization to enter into a stipulation or to argue before the court.

5. Defaults on matters scheduled for 9:30 a.m. will be called at 11:30 a.m.; matters scheduled for 11:00 a.m. will be defaulted at 12:00 noon; and matters scheduled for 2:15 p.m. will be defaulted at 3:30 p.m.

6. Any party (or their attorney/representative) who leaves the court without notifying the clerk or officer and is not present when the court recesses for lunch is subject to having the proceeding dismissed, the motion denied, or the matter adjourned at the court's discretion.

Heymann 2. Trial Part Rules

If designated a trial part pursuant to the Housing Court Initiative, parties whose cases are assigned to the Part will be presumed ready for trial with all necessary witnesses and documents and must appear within 15 minutes after the court file is transferred to the Part. Once a trial has commenced it will continue until completion. If it is necessary to adjourn the matter for any reason, defaults or dismissals will be taken if a party has not appeared within 30 minutes of the scheduled time. Orders to Show Cause are returnable at 9:30 a.m. Defaults, dismissals and inquests on all other matters not scheduled for trial will be taken at 10:15 a.m.

JUSTICE INEZ HOYOS

Hoyos 1. Resolution Part Rules

1. Cases on the 9:30 a.m. calendar shall be called for default at 11:00 am; cases on the 11:00 a.m. calendar shall be called for default at noon; cases on the 2:00 p.m. calendar shall be called for default at 3:00 p.m.

2. The Court has the discretion to issue a default or adjourn a if after the initial check in, if party fails to return to the courtroom to deal with the matter in a timely fashion.

3. All parties or their counsel must check in with the Court Officer upon entering the Part.

4. All parties and/or counsel may conference a matter with the Court Attorney or the Court. In the event the case cannot be settled, it will be scheduled for trial.

5. All motions must be conferenced with the Court Attorney or Judge. Parties should be prepared to resolve issues by stipulations, particularly in discovery motions. All motions must be orally argued before taken on submission.

6. In nonpayment proceedings, all stipulations shall contain the monthly rent, an itemized rent breakdown of arrears and a payment schedule if applicable. If repairs are needed, the stipulation shall contain the listed items to be repaired, access times and dates and the completion date of the repairs.

Hoyos 2. Trial Part Rules

1. Case scheduled for 9:30 a.m. will be dismissed or defaulted if parties and/or attorneys are not in the courtroom and ready to proceed at 10:30 am. Cases scheduled for 2:00 p.m. will be dismissed or defaulted by 3:00 p.m. Cases scheduled for trial at any other hour will be dismissed or defaulted after one hour of scheduled time if parties and/or attorneys are not in the courtroom and ready to proceed.

2. All parties and their attorneys are required to appear in this part within thirty minutes of the proceeding's referral from Part X. Dismissals or defaults on matters referred Part X will be taken thirty minutes after the file is received in this part.

3. All proceedings shall be conferenced by the Court between the parties and counsel before a trial will be conducted. If the parties are discussing settlement of the proceeding, they must appear before the Court and inform the Court of the status of the settlement discussions within thirty minutes.

4. All motions must be argued before the Court prior to being taken on submission.

5. All adjournments must be approved by the Court.

6. This is a trial ready part, all parties are expected to be ready for trial.

JUSTICE JOHN S. LANSDEN

Lansden 1. Resolution Part Rules

1. All parties or their attorneys are required to check in with the Court Officer upon entering the part. There will be no role or calendar call. Neither Attorneys nor parties are permitted to "call out" for the other side. Only court personnel may "call out" in the courtroom.

2. Service may not answer in the part on behalf of a party to request an adjournment nor may they appear before the Court in any matter scheduled for trial or hearing. A representative of a party, other than an attorney, may not answer or appear on behalf of any party without written authority from said party.

3. Every stipulation of settlement in a nonpayment proceeding must provide a breakdown of the arrears alleged owed. If the tenant intends to seek assistance from DSS, said breakdown shall contain a listing of the actual months for which the tenant or agency failed to pay rent. A "first in first out" breakdown will not be accepted.

4. All proceedings shall be conferenced by the Court between the parties and counsel before a court conference will be conducted. If the parties are discussing settlement of the proceeding, they must appear before the Court and inform the Court of same. The parties shall inform the Court of the status of the settlement discussions within thirty minutes thereof.

5. Defaults on matters scheduled in the Part for 9:30 a.m. will be taken at 10:30 a.m. At that time, Court personnel will call those matters for which only one party checked in or answered. In the event the party who has not checked in or answered does not respond to Court personnel, a default will be taken against them. All cases on for 9:30 a.m. must, if not resolved, provide the court with a status update no later than 12:30 or the case will be subject to dismissal/default.

6. The Parties must provide a submission schedule to the Court upon adjourning any motion. The Court will allow one stipulated adjournment of any pending motion. Thereafter, the parties must appear before the judge to request any additional adjournments. Unless a motion is returnable by order to show cause, all papers must be submitted to the Court one (1) business day prior to the date the motion is scheduled to be heard so they may be reviewed by the Court prior to oral argument.

7. Every stipulation of settlement where repairs are an issue shall contain a list of the repairs alleged required or a statement that no repairs are needed.

Lansden 2. Trial Part Rules

1. All parties or their attorneys are required to check in with the Court Officer upon entering the part. Neither Attorneys nor parties are permitted to "call out" for the other side. Only court personnel may call out in the courtroom.

2. Service may not answer in the part on behalf of a party to request an adjournment nor may they appear before the Court in any matter scheduled for trial or hearing. A representative of a party, other than an attorney, may not answer or appear on behalf of any party without written authority from said party.

3. All parties and their attorneys are required to appear in this Part within fifteen minutes of the proceeding's referral from Part X being sent from Part X. Witnesses on call at the time of the referral are to be present within thirty minutes after the attorneys check into the Part. Defaults will be taken fifteen minutes after the file is received in this Part.

4. All proceedings shall be conferenced by the Court between the parties and counsel before a trial will be conducted. If the parties are discussing settlement of the proceeding, they must appear before the Court and inform the Court of same. The parties shall inform the Court of the status of the settlement discussions within thirty minutes thereof.

5. Defaults on matters scheduled in this Part for 9:30 a.m. will be taken at 10:00 a.m. At that time, Court personnel will call those matters for which only one party checked in or answered. In the event the party who has not checked in or answered does not respond to Court personnel, a default will be taken against them.

6. Parties may not adjourn trials or hearings by stipulation. An application to the Court must be made. Adjournments will only be granted where an emergency has arisen which prevents either counsel, a litigant or a witness from appearing in Court.

7. Every stipulation of settlement in a nonpayment proceeding must provide a breakdown of the arrears alleged owed. If the tenant intends to seek assistance from DSS, said breakdown shall contain a listing of the actual months for which the tenant or agency failed to pay rent. A "first in first out" breakdown will not be accepted.

8. Every stipulation of settlement where repairs are an issue shall contain a list of the repairs alleged required or a statement that no repairs are needed.

JUSTICE LAURIE LAU

Lau 1. Resolution Part Rules

Roll Call: There is no roll call.

Calendar Call: There is no calendar call.

Check-in Procedure: Check in with the Officer.

Defaults: Defaults on the 9:30 a.m. calendar are taken at 10:30 a.m.

Defaults on the 11:00 a.m. calendar are taken at noon.

Defaults on the 2:00 p.m. calendar are taken at 3 p.m.

Inquest defaults are taken at 10:30 a.m.

Default Procedure: The proceeding is called inside and outside of the courtroom. If a respondent does not appear in a nonpayment proceeding, a default judgment is entered against the respondent. If a respondent does not appear in a holdover proceeding, an inquest is held. If a petitioner does not appear in a holdover or nonpayment proceeding, or on any motion or order to show cause, the petition is dismissed or any relief requested by a respondent can be granted. If a respondent does not appear on his or her order to show cause it will be denied. If a respondent does not appear on a petitioner's proper motion, petitioner's motion will be granted on default.

Lau 2. Trial Part Rules

1. There is no roll call.

2. Check in with the officer. Unrepresented parties check in on their own behalf; attorneys or a member of the attorney's firm check in on behalf of their client(s).

3. There is no calendar call.

4. Defaults are taken at 10:30 a.m. for motions and orders to show cause. Defaults on hearings and trials scheduled by the Court shall be taken at 9:45 am.

5. **Default Procedure:** The case is called inside and outside the courtroom. If respondent does not appear, a final judgment is entered against the respondent. If petitioner fails to appear, the petition is dismissed. In a holdover proceeding, if respondent fails to appear, the judge holds an inquest; if petitioner fails to appear, the petition is dismissed. If respondent fails to appear on the return date of his/her Order to Show Cause, it will be denied; if petitioner fails to appear on the return date, any relief requested by the respondent can be granted.

JUSTICE GARY MARTON

Marton 1. Resolution Part Rules

One: Mandatory Check–in

When the courtroom is opened, tenants, landlords, and their lawyers **must** check in with the Court Clerk or Court Officer. Beepers, cell phones, and tape and CD players **must** be turned off or they will be confiscated. Eating and drinking are prohibited.

Two: Defaults and Roll Calls

One hour after the scheduled appearance time, the Court Clerk will call the roll of cases. You **must** answer when your case is called. Defaults, dismissals, adjournments, and other relief will be granted for cases scheduled as follows:

9:30 A.M. cases at 10:30 A.M.;

11:00 A.M. cases at 12:00 noon; and

2:00 P.M. cases at 3:00 P.M.

EXCEPTION AT 9:45 A.M. FOR TRIALS AND HEARINGS: Cases that have been adjourned for trial or hearing will be called at 9:45 A.M. Lawyers and parties who are not present at that time may be defaulted, or their cases may be marked off, dismissed, adjourned, or sent out for trial or hearing.

EXCEPTION AT NOON: Landlords, tenants, and their lawyers are expected to work diligently to resolve their cases. Beginning at 12:00 noon, the Court may call and then dismiss, mark off, or adjourn any case, or default any absent party, whether or not the party has previously checked in with the Court Clerk or Court Officer, if the case has not yet been conferenced, argued, or resolved by stipulation.

Three: Stipulations (and Other Agreements)

(A) Stipulations must be easy to read.

(B) Stipulations shall be submitted for review by the Court Attorney. Pending review by the Court Attorney, the parties and their lawyers shall remain available or be subject to default, adjournment, or dismissal.

(C) Stipulations shall state whether repairs are necessary. If repairs are necessary, they shall be itemized, and access and completion dates shall be specified. If repairs are not necessary, the stipulation shall so state.

(D) Stipulations shall include a breakdown of rent arrears.

(E) Stipulations may not include a "disputed amount" provision unless either (i) the disputed amount is subject to a "finality" provision or (ii) the stipulation states a good reason for the omission of a "finality" provision. A "finality" provision is one which provides that the dispute must be resolved or restored to the Court's calendar by a date certain, failing which the disputed amount is waived.

(F) Once again, stipulations must be easy to read.

Four: Questions If you have questions, ask the Court Officer.

Marton 2.   Trial Part Rules

Mandatory Check–in:

All parties and their lawyers **must** check in with the Court Clerk or Court Officer. If you do not speak English, tell the Court Officer which language you speak so that the Court can call for an interpreter. Beepers, cell phones, and tape and CD players must be turned off or they will be confiscated. Eating and drinking are prohibited.

Defaults and Roll Calls:

One hour after the scheduled appearance time, the Court Clerk will call the roll of cases. You **must** answer when your case has been called. Defaults, dismissals, and ex parte relief will be granted for cases scheduled as follows:

- 9:30 a.m. cases at 10:30 a.m.

- 11:00 a.m. cases at 12:00 noon

- 2:00 p.m. cases at 3:00 p.m.

EXCEPTION AT 10:00 AM FOR TRIALS AND HEARINGS: Cases that have been adjourned for trial or hearing will be called at 10:00 am. Lawyers and parties who are not present at that time may be defaulted, or their cases may be marked off, dismissed, adjourned, or sent out for trial or hearing.

EXCEPTION AT NOON: Landlords, tenants, and their lawyers are expected to work diligently to resolve their cases. Beginning at 12:00 noon, the Court may call and then dismiss, mark off, or adjourn any case, or default any absent party, whether or not the party has previously checked in with the Court Clerk or Court Officer, if the case has not yet been conferenced, argued, or resolved by stipulation.

Stipulations (and Other Agreements):

a) Stipulations must be easily legible.

b) Stipulations shall be submitted for review by the Court Attorney. Pending review by the Court Attorney, the parties and their lawyers shall remain available or be subject to default, adjournment, or dismissal.

c) Stipulations shall state whether repairs are necessary. If repairs are necessary, they shall be itemized; access and completion dates shall be specified.

d) Stipulations shall include a breakdown of rent arrears.

e) Stipulations may not include a "disputed amount" provision unless either (i) the disputed amount is subject to a "finality" provision or (ii) the stipulation states a good reason for the omission of a "finality" provision. A "finality" provision is one which provides that the dispute must be resolved or restored to the Court's calendar by a date certain, failing which the disputed amount is waived.

f) Once again, stipulations must be easily legible.

Questions:

If you have questions, ask the Court Officer.

JUSTICE MARIA MILIN

Milin 1.   Resolution Part Rules

1. Upon arrival in the Courtroom, all parties must check in with a part staff member (usually the Court Clerk or the Court Officer).

2. **9:30 a.m. cases** - parties for cases that are scheduled for 9:30 a.m. will be held in default upon failure to appear by 11:00 am.

3. **11:00 a.m. cases** - parties to cases that are scheduled for 11:00 a.m. will be held in default upon failure to appear by 12:00 p.m.

4. **2:00 p.m. cases** - parties to cases that are scheduled for 2:00 p.m. will be held in default upon failure to appear by 3:00 p.m.

These guidelines are subject to modification at the discretion of the Court.

Milin 2.   Trial Part Rules

1. Upon arrival in the Courtroom, all parties must check in with a staff member in the Part (usually the Court Clerk or Court Officer).

2. **9:30 a.m. cases:** Parties that are scheduled to appear for 9:30 a.m. will be held in default upon failure to appear by 10:00 a.m.

3. **2:00 p.m. cases:** Parties that are scheduled to appear for 2:00 p.m. cases will be held in default upon failure to appear by 3:00 p.m.

4. After a case is referred from Part X, the parties have 30 minutes to appear in the Part ready to proceed or the matter will be dismissed or the party defaulted.

5. These guidelines are subject to modification at the discretion of the Court.

JUSTICE ELEONORA OFSHTEIN

Ofshtein 1. Part Rules

I. Check In/Appearances:

1. All parties/attorneys must timely check in with the Part Clerk.

2. It is the responsibility of the party/attorney to verify the disposition of cases on a daily basis.

II. Defaults:

1. A default calendar will be called at the following times, circumstances permitting:

(A) 11:00 a.m. for cases on the 9:30 a.m. calendar;

(B) 3:00 p.m. for cases on the 2:00 p.m. calendar.

2. If a party/attorney has not checked in after the default calendar is called, the case will be disposed of in the Court's discretion.

3. If a party/attorney fails to return to the Part within a reasonable time after checking in or submitting a stipulation, the case will be disposed of in the Court's discretion.

4. All applications for a default judgment must be made to the Court or the case will be disposed of in the Court's discretion.

III. Adjournments/Discontinuances/Motions:

1. Adjournments/Discontinuances are not automatic and are subject to the approval of the Court. All such applications must be made in writing or orally before the Court and must state the reason.

2. Motions may not be submitted without oral argument unless permitted by the Court.

IV. Inquests:

1. Inquests are not held the first time a case appears on the calendar. Rather, the case is adjourned and the court mails a postcard to respondent.

2. Petitioners must be prepared to submit competent evidence of the non-military status of all non-answering respondents before a judgment is entered after Inquest.

V. Conferences/Stipulations:

1. Any party/attorney may request a conference by notifying court personnel.

2. All stipulations must be legible and comprehensible.

3. Where rent/use and occupancy are at issue, a detailed rent history must be provided and issues of repairs, if any, addressed including alleged conditions, access dates and a completion date.

4. All stipulations of settlement must be submitted for review, allocution and approval by the Court.

5. Parties/attorneys must remain available to the Court to address any issues that may arise during the allocution of a stipulation. If a party/attorney is not available to the Court within a reasonable period of time after allocution, the case will be disposed of in the Court's discretion.

6. All stipulations where a party has a guardian ad litem (GAL) will be reviewed by the Court and may not be labeled "Two Attorney." All GALs must be available to the Court for such review.

These rules are subject to modification by the Court. (3/08)

JUSTICE BRUCE E. SCHECKOWITZ

Scheckowitz 1. Resolution Part Rules

1. **Check-in Procedure:** There will be no roll call or calendar call in the Part. All litigants are expected to check in with court personnel. Frequent announcements will be made in the courtroom advising litigants to check in on their respective case.

The Resolution Part will permit all of the following to check in on a case: attorneys, represented parties, pro se litigants, individuals with authority to appear, law office clerks and paralegals and calendar service.

2. **Defaults:** Defaults and dismissals will be taken by the court at the following times:

i) 10:30 A.M. for cases on the 9:30 A.M. calendar;

ii) 12:00 P.M. for cases on the 11:00 A.M. calendar;

and iii) 3:00 P.M. for cases on the 2:00 P.M. calendar.

All cases will be called by court personnel in the courtroom at these respective times prior to default or dismissal by the court.

3. **Adjournments:** All adjournments which are on the consent of the parties shall be memorialized in stipulations which designate the time and date. Parties are advised to consult with court personnel before selecting the date for the adjournment.

Court approval shall be required for all adjournments.

Parties are encouraged to adjourn all cases for 9:30 A.M. However, proceedings will be scheduled on the 2:00 P.M. calendar upon demonstration of special circumstances.

Stipulations adjourning the proceedings shall state the reason for seeking the adjournment. The stipulation should also state that the adjournment is to be marked for trial or hearing on the return date, where appropriate.

4. Cases scheduled for trial/hearing: Where a case was previously adjourned for trial or hearing, both sides are expected to appear in the Part at 9:30 A.M. on the return date. At that time, the case will be sent to the Court Expediter for immediate referral to a trial part, provided both sides are ready to proceed. Where one party is not ready or does not appear by 10:00 A.M., the court will entertain the appropriate application for dismissal, default or inquest.

Scheckowitz 2.   HP Part Rules

1. Calendar Call/Sign–In Procedure: There will be a formal calendar call of the HP Part morning (9:30 a.m.) calendar at 10:30 a.m. and of the afternoon (2:00 p.m.) calendar at 3:00 p.m. All litigants are expected to be checked in with court personnel. The purpose of the calendar call is to provide litigants with a final check-in before designating the status of each case. Proceedings will be designated for application, conference, inquest, hearing, trial, and dismissal. Frequent announcements will be made in the courtroom advising litigants to check in on their respective case(s). An informal "roll call" will also be conducted at 10:00 a.m.; this is merely a status check to ascertain which parties are present.

The HP Part will permit all of the following to check in on a case: attorneys, represented parties, pro se litigants, individuals with authority to appear, law office clerks and paralegals and calendar service.

Practitioners and litigants who have other matters scheduled in the court house are not required to be present in the court room for the 10:30 a.m. and 3:00 p.m. calendar calls so long as they have already checked in on their respective case(s). However, such individuals are advised that the court will entertain ex parte applications for appropriate relief after a reasonable period of time has passed where one party has not returned to the HP Part after check-in.

Attorneys are also expected to file a notice of appearance at the time they check in, if a notice of appearance has not already been filed with the Clerk.

2. Default/Dismissal Timetable: Defaults and dismissals will be entered by the court during the 10:30 a.m. and 3:00 p.m. calendar calls. Inquests will be conducted at the conclusion of the calendar calls.

3. Adjournments: All adjournments which are on the consent of the parties shall be memorialized in stipulations which designate the time and date. Parties are advised to consult with court personnel before selecting the date for the adjournment.

Court approval shall be required for all adjournments.

Parties are encouraged to adjourn all cases for 9:30 a.m. However, proceedings will be scheduled on the 2:00 p.m. calendar upon demonstration of special circumstances.

Stipulations adjourning the proceedings shall state the reason for seeking the adjournment. Stipulation should also identify whether the proceeding is being adjourned for trial or hearing on the return date, as appropriate.

4. Cases Scheduled for Trial/Hearing: Where a case was previously adjourned for trial or hearing, both sides are expected to appear in the HP Part on the return date at the scheduled time of 9:30 a.m. or 2:00 p.m. Where one party is not ready or does not appear by 10:30 a.m. or 2:30 p.m., the court will entertain the appropriate application for dismissal, default or inquest.

JUSTICE MARCIA SIKOWITZ

Sikowitz 1.   Resolution Part Rules

1. 11:00 a.m. default call for all 9:30 a.m. cases where one or more parties have not checked in.

2. 12:00 noon default call for 11:00 a.m. cases where one or more parties have not checked in.

3. 3:00 p.m. default call for all 2:00 p.m. cases where one or more parties have not checked in.

ALL STIPULATIONS SETTLING NONPAYMENT CASES ON FOR THE FIRST TIME MUST INCLUDE A RENT BREAKDOWN.

Sikowitz 2.   Trial Part Rules

1. Defaults will be called at 11:00 am.

2. Parties have 20 minutes to appear in the Part after a case has been sent from the Expeditor or else the non-appearing parties are in default.

QUEENS COUNTY
JUSTICE GILBERT BADILLO

Badillo 1. Resolution Part Rules

1. Upon entering the part, all litigants and attorneys are to check-in with the Clerk.

2. Any request for an adjournment or discontinuance shall be reviewed by the Court Attorney or Judge.

3. All attorneys must file a written Notice of Appearance. It shall be the obligation of the attorney appearing to ensure that a current Notice of Appearance is on file with the Court.

3. HP cases must be conferenced initially with HPD staff; assistance from the Court Attorney may be requested. In the event the conference does not conclude in a resolution of the case, any party may request a conference with the Judge. All parties must remain in the courtroom and be available for the conference.

4. Where parties are referred to Part Q from the expeditor they are presumed ready for trial with all witnesses and documents necessary to proceed. The Court will not entertain applications for adjournments. All applications will be referred back to the Resolution Part for disposition. Further, once a trial is commenced it will continue until completion. If it exceeds more than one day, the parties are expected to resume the trial the following business day. Any continuances are solely at the discretion of the Court.

5. Defaults on any adjourned trials, orders to show cause or illegal lockouts will be entertained 30 minutes after the time noted for appearing in Court.

6. Defaults on 9:30 HP cases will be at 11:00. If a party checks in at the calendar call but fails to return by 11:30 A.M., the other side may ask the Clerk to put the case before the Judge for a default, dismissal or adjournment in the discretion of the Court.

7. The 2:15 P.M. trials/hearings - if a party fails to appear by 2:45 P.M. for a matter scheduled for a trial or hearing, the Court in its discretion may conduct an inquest, dismiss, default or adjourn the matter.

These rules are subject to modification by the Court.

Badillo 2. Trial Part Rules

1. Upon entering the part, all litigants and attorneys are to check-in with the Clerk.

2. Any request for an adjournment or discontinuance shall be reviewed by the Court Attorney or Judge.

3. All attorneys must file a written Notice of Appearance. It shall be the obligation of the attorney appearing to ensure that a current Notice of Appearance is on file with the Court.

4. HP cases must be conferenced initially with HPD staff; assistance from the Court Attorney may be requested. In the event the conference does not conclude in a resolution of the case, any party may request a conference with the Judge. All parties must remain in the courtroom and be available for the conference.

5. Where parties are referred this part from the expeditor they are presumed ready for trial with all witnesses and documents necessary to proceed. The Court will not entertain applications for adjournments. All applications will be referred back to the Resolution Part for disposition. Further, once a trial is commenced it will continue until completion. If it exceeds more than one day, the parties are expected to resume the trial the following business day. Any continuances are solely at the discretion of the Court.

6. Defaults on any adjourned trials, orders to show cause or illegal lockouts will be entertained 30 minutes after the time noted for appearing in Court.

7. Defaults on 9:30 a.m. HP cases will be at 11:00 am. If a party checks in at the calendar call but fails to return by 11:30 am, the other side may ask the Clerk to put the case before the Judge for a default, dismissal or adjournment in the discretion of the Court.

8. The 2:15 p.m. trials/hearings - if a party fails to appear by 2:45 p.m. for a matter scheduled for a trial or hearing, the Court in its discretion may conduct an inquest, dismiss, default or adjourn the matter.

These rules are subject to modification by the Court.

JUSTICE RONNI BIRNBAUM

Birnbaum 1. Resolution Part Rules

1. All parties must check in with the Court Officer at the desk.

2. Defaults for 9:30 AM are taken at 10:30 AM. Defaults for 11:00 A.M. cases are taken at 12:00 Noon.

Defaults for 2:00 P.M. are taken at 3:00 PM.

3. All non-payment stipulations should contain an accurate breakdown of rental arrears.

4. Any repair issues should be addressed in stipulations, with access dates and completion dates.

Birnbaum 2. Trial Part Rules

1. All parties must check in with court officer upon entering the part.

2. All parties must be ready to proceed. There are no applications for adjournments in the trial part.

In the event a trial is not finished in one day, it will continue to the next day until it is completed.

3. Counsel who appear must be fully familiar with the case and be ready for trial and/or fully authorized to enter into a settlement agreement.

JUSTICE ANNE KATZ

Katz 1. Resolution Part Rules

1. Upon entering the Courtroom, all parties and/or their respective lawyers are to check in with the Clerk of the Part. There is no calendar or roll call.

2. Defaults are taken one hour after the matter is noticed to be heard.

3. With respect to a nonpayment proceeding where the respondent fails to appear, a Judgment will be granted in favor of the petitioner and against the respondent for the amount sought on the petition. Where the petitioner fails to appear, the proceeding will be dismissed. With respect to a holdover proceeding where the respondent fails to appear, the Court will adjourn the proceeding for an Inquest. The Court will send the respondent a postcard notifying the respondent of the adjourned date, time and place. On the adjourned date if the respondent fails to appear the Court will conduct the Inquest. If the respondent appears the Court will conference the

proceeding and if a settlement is not possible, send the matter out for trial. If the petitioner fails to appear the proceeding will be dismissed.

4. Oral argument is required on all motions.

Katz 2. Trial Part Rules

1. This is a Trial Part pursuant to the Housing Court Initiative. When parties are sent to this part from the expeditor they are presumed ready for trial with all witnesses and documents necessary to proceed. The Court will entertain no applications for adjournments. Applications for adjournments will be referred back to the Resolution Part for disposition.

2. Trials are presumed to continue day-to-day until conclusion.

3. Defaults on any adjourned trials, orders to show cause or illegal lockouts will be entertained 30 minutes after the time noted for appearing in Court.

JUSTICE ULYSSES B. LEVERETT

Leverett 1. Resolution Part Rules

1. There is no roll or calendar call for 9:30 am, 11:00 am, or 2:00 p.m. All parties or their attorneys must check in with the part clerk upon entering the courtroom. You must provide the clerk with your calendar number and advise the clerk if your case is scheduled for trial.

2. All requests for adjournments and discontinuances must be submitted to a court attorney for review or by application to the judge. Stipulations for adjournments will not be accepted unless a party or counsel is present in court.

3. All settlement stipulations where any party is not represented by counsel must be reviewed by a court attorney. Parties must remain in the courtroom or advise the clerk in which part they can be located. Failure to return to the court within a reasonable time may result in dismissal, default, or adjournment at the court's discretion.

4. Defaults will be taken at the following times: 9:30 a.m. calendar at 11:00 a.m., 11:00 a.m. calendar at 12:30 p.m., and 2:00 p.m. calendar at 3:30 p.m.

5. In nonpayment proceedings, all stipulations must contain an itemized rent/maintenance breakdown of arrears and a payment schedule, if applicable.

Leverett 2. Trial Part Rules

1. All cases marked ready for trial must be trial ready; all witnesses must be immediately available.

2. There is no roll or calendar call for 9:30 A.M., 11:00 A.M. or 2:00 P.M. cases. All parties or their attorneys are to check in with the part clerk upon entering the courtroom. You must provide the clerk with your calendar number and advise the clerk if your case is scheduled for trial.

3. All litigants will conference with the Court Attorney assigned to the part. If the Court Attorney is unable to resolve the matter, the Court will commence the hearing or trial immediately.

4. All settlement stipulations where any party is not represented by counsel must be reviewed by a court attorney. Parties must remain in the courtroom or advise the clerk in which part they can be located. Failure to return to the court within a reasonable time may result in dismissal, default or adjournment at the court's discretion.

5. Defaults will be taken at the following times: 9:30 A.M. calendar at 11:00 A.M., 11:00 A.M. calendar at 12:30 P.M. and 2:00 P.M. calendar at 3:30 P.M.

JUSTICE MICHAEL J. PINCKNEY

Pinckney 1.   Resolution Part Rules

Calendar Check in Procedure

All parties or their attorneys are to check in with the court officer upon arrival by giving the officer the calendar number (the calendar is posted outside the courtroom) and name of the case. Parties should inform the court officer whether counsel represents them.

Attorneys checking in are to give the officer their names and the name of the office they represent. If attorneys have to leave the courtroom, they should inform the court officer how they can be reached.

If neither party has an attorney, the matter will be conferenced with the court attorney once both parties are present.

If a matter is marked for trial/hearing, all parties and their attorneys should check in by 9:45 AM. If an attorney checks in on a case marked for trial or hearing and leaves the room without requesting an application for an adjournment, the proceeding will be sent to the expediter once all parties have checked in.

If a party or attorney has an application for an adjournment, the parties should inform the court officer upon checking in and stay in the courtroom, as applications will be called immediately.

Default Call

Calendar calls will be held at the following times only for those cases where either one or both parties have failed to check in. Defaults and dismissals will be noted at that time.

For cases scheduled for 9:30 AM, the default call will be at 11:00 AM.

For cases scheduled for 11:00 AM, the default call will be at 11:45 AM.

For cases scheduled for 2:00 PM, the default call will be at 3:00 PM.

Orders to Show Cause/Motions

If a party requests oral argument on a motion/order to show cause, the Court will hear oral argument at the Court's discretion, depending on such factors as the time of morning an argument is requested and the caseload for the Part. Attorneys should not assume that the Court will hear argument on a motion/order to show cause at any time the request is made. If the Court declines to hear oral argument on the return date of a motion, the matter may be taken on submission if fully briefed. If not fully briefed, an application for a briefing schedule should be made. If oral argument is still requested, the Court will set a date and time for argument.

If a briefing schedule is established, the attorneys should file their papers in this part so that the Court may review them prior to the return date set for oral argument.

Adjournments

Applications for a trial date and a briefing schedule for an argument on a motion must be made to the Court. Only the Court can establish a date for trial, to be done only after it is convinced that the matter can not be resolved.

Morning Cases

If a case scheduled for 9:30 AM or 11:00 AM has not been resolved by 1:00 PM (either by stipulation, adjournment or decision/submission on a motion) the Court in its discretion may dispose of the matter at that time in an appropriate manner. Attorneys should be present before 1:00 PM to inform the Court of the status of the case, including attempts made to settle. If attorneys are not present by 1:00 PM, the defaulting party risks dismissal or entry of a default judgment.

Pinckney 2.   Trial Part Rules

Upon transfer to this Trial Part, the parties are expected to be ready for trial immediately with all witnesses/documents present.

Unless otherwise directed by the Court, upon commencement the trial will continue that day until completion, and if necessary will resume the following day. All parties and their attorneys should be prepared to proceed accordingly.

The Court will conference the case prior to the start of trial. If the parties have an extensive number of exhibits to be introduced, the Court may require pre-marking by the party (petitioner in number sequence, respondent in letter sequence), courtesy copies for the opposing party and a negotiation of a stipulation to the introduction of as many exhibits as possible.

If the trial is adjourned, the parties and their attorneys are expected to appear on the adjourned date at the time set by the Court. Since another trial may be scheduled at a different time on that date, it is extremely important that the parties be timely. If the parties or their attorneys are not present on time, a dismissal/default may be summarily entered.

JUSTICE MARIA RESSOS

Ressos 1.   Resolution Part Rules

1. All parties or their attorneys are to check in with the Clerk or Court Officer by 11:00 a.m. for cases appearing on the 9:30 a.m. calendar; 12:00 p.m. for cases appearing on the 11:00 a.m. calendar; and 2:00 p.m. for cases appearing on the 2:00 p.m. calendar.

2. All cases adjourned for referral to the Expediter for trial/hearing or those matters adjourned for a hearing in the Part will be called promptly at 9:45 am. Both parties and counsel must be present and ready to proceed or the case may be dismissed/defaulted or adjourned by the Court. Paralegals may **not** appear.

Matters shall be referred to the Judge or Court Attorney once both sides have appeared and checked in.

3. A professional answering service or a party's representative, although not an attorney, may answer in the Part on behalf of the party for the sole purpose of requesting an adjournment. Only an attorney or party of record may appear for all other purposes, including the discontinuance of a proceeding or withdrawal of a motion.

Defaults

4. Defaults shall be taken against any party that fails to check in or answer at 11:00 a.m. for 9:30 a.m. cases (other than cases specifically marked for trial/hearing); 12:00 p.m. for 11:00 a.m. cases; and 3:00 p.m. for 2:00 p.m. cases.

Parties who have checked in with the Clerk need not be present when matters are called for default, unless they have an application regarding the form of relief sought from the Court.

5. All cases from the 9:30 a.m. and 11:00 a.m. calendars, where both parties checked in, but which have not been disposed of by 12:00 noon, will be called at that time. At 12:00 noon, dismissals and defaults may be taken or adjournments may be granted at the Court's discretion, whether or not the parties have previously checked in with the Clerk. All cases from the 2:00 p.m. calendar must be disposed of by 3:15 p.m. Any case that has not been disposed of will be called at 3:15 p.m. and dismissals/defaults may be

taken or adjournments may be granted at the Court's discretion.

6. All consent adjournments must be in writing. The Court will permit one stipulated adjournment on consent, thereafter any adjournment(s) must be by leave of the Court. The stipulation must specify the reason(s) for the adjournment.

7. All discontinuances of cases and withdrawals of motions must be in writing.

8. Once a stipulation is given to the Clerk or Court Attorney in the Part for review and allocution, it is the responsibility of the attorney(s) to be sure that the stipulation has been accepted and so ordered by the Court. Failure to return to the Court within an acceptable time (i.e. by the 12:00 p.m. final call for all morning cases and by 3:15 p.m. final call on the afternoon cases) may result in the stipulation being rejected and the case being adjourned or dismissed at the discretion of the Court.

9. ALL stipulations must contain a rent breakdown and address any repair issues.

10. All parties appearing in the Court must be appropriately dressed at all times. Shorts, tube tops, halter tops, hats, sunglasses and headsets are not permitted. Electronic equipment such as cell phones, beepers, etc. must be turned off while in the Courtroom. If they go off, they will be taken by the Court Officer. Parties must exercise civility, at all times, when in the Court.

Ressos 2.   Trial Part Rules

1. Parties are presumed to be ready for trial.

2. Parties or their counsel must sign in with the Clerk upon entering the Part.

3. Calendar service or representatives may sign in on behalf of a party, but may not appear in the Part for any other reason.

4. There will be no calendar or roll calls.

5. Defaults for scheduled trials or hearings may take place 20 minutes following the scheduled starting time.

JUSTICE DEIGHTON WAITHE

Waithe 1.   Resolution Part Rules

Rules of the Resolution Part are subject to change, adjustment or modification, as may be warranted, in the discretion of the court.

1. The Resolution Part will be available to hear all cases on its calendar promptly at 9:30 and 11:00 A.M.

and at 2:15 P.M. or as otherwise directed by the court or agreed by the parties, with leave of court.

2. Cases on the 9:30 calendar will be subject to dismissal/default upon failure to appear by 11:00 A.M., upon application of the appearing party. Cases scheduled for the 11:00 A.M. calendar will be subject to dismissal/default upon failure to appear by 12:30 P.M.,

upon application of the appearing party. Cases on the 2:00 P.M. calendar will be subject to dismissal/default upon failure to appear by 3:30 P.M., upon application of the appearing party.

3. If neither party appears at the appointed time, the case will be held until 4:00 P.M. at which time the court will call the case and enter a default upon failure of both parties to appear, or adjourn the matter as may be warranted.

4. All parties or counsel, must check in with the court officer or clerk upon entering the court room. There will be no formal calendar call.

5. It shall be the responsibility of each attorney to file a current notice of appearance with the court as necessary and be fully authorized to engage in settlement discussion on behalf of the client, to resolution.

6. Applications for adjournment must first be submitted to the Court Attorney for initial review relative to propriety and availability. The court reserves the right to deny any application for adjournment, notwithstanding prior agreement between the parties. Therefore, attorneys should not presume the court will sanction "two attorney" stipulations left without the court's knowledge. No adjournments, on matters pending before the court, will be granted telephonically except upon exigent circumstances, and only via three way communication with the court and the applicant's adversary. If the parties cannot agree on a date, the court's calendar will be controlling.

7. Determinations as to the "trial-readiness" of each case will be made by the court after appropriate conference and consideration. No case will be sent out for trial simply because the attorneys believe they have reached an impasse.

8. Cases resolved outside of court by settlement, discontinuance, or otherwise must be disposed of by way of written stipulation presented to the clerk of the part for submission to the court for approval.

9. Stipulations must be reviewed by the court and will be thoroughly explained to all self-represented litigants before they are "so-ordered". Therefore, all self-represented litigants must be present in the court room for formal allocution. Although Petitioner's counsel need not be present for the allocution, counsel must remain available and subject to "call" in the event the self represented litigant has questions or wishes to disavow or nullify the proposed agreement. Failure of Respondent to be present for the allocution or counsel to appear on call, may result in rejection of the stipulation, default, dismissal or adjournment. Whenever repairs are at issue, the stipulation must include a list of the alleged conditions or violations with specific dates for access and a provision that Respondent may restore the case to the court's calendar for appropriate relief in the event of default. All monies due under the stipulation must be broken down by month.

10. The court will not accept submission on any motion without prior oral argument.

Waithe 2.   Trial Part Rules

1. The Trial Part will be available to hear "trial-ready" cases promptly at 9:30 A.M. and at 2:15 P.M. or as otherwise directed by the court or agreed by the parties with leave of court.

2. Cases on the 9:30 trial calendar will be subject to dismissal/default upon failure to appear by 11 A.M. and upon application of the appearing party.

3. If neither party appears at the appointed time, the case will be held until 4:00 P.M. at which time the court will call the case and enter a default upon failure of both parties to appear, or adjourn the matter as may be warranted.

4. All parties, or counsel, must check in with the court officer or clerk upon entering the court room. It shall be the responsibility of each attorney to file a current notice of appearance with the court as necessary and be ready to proceed to trial and/or be fully authorized to engage in settlement discussion on behalf of the client, to resolution.

5. Since cases referred to the trial part should be ready for trial upon arrival, applications for adjournment will not be liberally granted. No adjournments, on matters pending before the court, will be granted telephonically except upon exigent circumstances, and only via three way communication with the court and the applicant's adversary. However, mutual agreements to adjourn may be forwarded to the court by facsimile copy so long as the document is signed by all parties concerned.

6. Notwithstanding the presumed trial readiness of each case, the court reserves the right to re-conference the matter prior to commencing trial. In the event the case cannot be settled, the parties must be prepared to go immediately to trial.

7. Cases resolved outside of court by settlement, discontinuance, or otherwise must be disposed of by way of written stipulation submitted to the court, court officer or clerk when available in the part.

8. Stipulations must be reviewed by the court and thoroughly explained to all self-represented litigants before they are "so-ordered". Therefore, all self-represented litigants must be present in the court room for formal allocution. Although Petitioner's counsel need not be present for the allocution, counsel must remain available and subject to "call" in the event the self represented litigant has questions or wishes to disavow or nullify the proposed agreement.

9. The court will not accept submission on any motion without prior oral argument.

10. The rules of the Trial Part are subject to change or adjustment as may be warranted in the discretion of the court.

RICHMOND COUNTY
JUSTICE MARINA MUNDY

Mundy 1. Part Rules

— This is an all purpose part.

— There will be a 10:30 a.m. default call for all cases scheduled for 9:30 am.

— If a case is marked for Trial the parties are expected to be ready to proceed on that date.

COURT DIRECTORY

GENERAL INFORMATION
1–800–COURTNY or 1–800–268–7869
www.courts.state.ny.us
www.nycourts.gov
TDD: (212) 428–2990

STATE-WIDE ADMINISTRATIVE OFFICES AND ASSOCIATIONS

Office of Court Administration
4 Empire State Plaza, Suite 2001
Albany, NY 12223–1450
Tel. (518) 474–3828
Fax. (518) 473–5514
     or
25 Beaver Street - Rm. 852
New York, NY 10004
Tel. (212) 428–2700

New York State CLE Board
25 Beaver Street, Room 888
New York, NY 10004
Tel. (212) 428–2105
Tel. 1–877–697–4253
www.nycourts.gov/attorneys/cle

Community Dispute Resolution Centers Program
New York State Unified Court System
98 Niver Street
Cohoes, NY 12047–4712
Tel. (518) 238–4351
Fax. (518) 238–2951
www.nycourts.gov/ip/adr/cdrc.shtml

Commission on Judicial Conduct
61 Broadway, Suite 1200
New York, NY 10006
Tel. (646) 386–4800
Fax. (646) 458–0037
     or
Corning Tower, Suite 2301
Empire State Plaza
Albany, NY 12223
Tel. (518) 453–4600
Fax. (518) 486-1850
     or
400 Andrews Street
Rochester, NY 14604
Tel. (585) 784–4141
Fax. (585) 232–7834
www.scjc.state.ny.us/

New York State Board of Law Examiners
Corporate Plaza – Building 3
254 Washington Avenue Extension
Albany, NY 12203–5195
Tel. (518) 452–8700
Fax. (518) 452–5729
www.nybarexam.org

OCA – Attorney Registration Unit
25 Beaver Street, Room 840
New York, NY 10004
Tel. (212) 428–2800
Fax. (212) 428–2804
Email: attyreg@nycourts.gov
www.nycourts.gov/attorneys/registration/

Lawyers' Fund for Client Protection
119 Washington Avenue
Albany, NY 12210
Tel. (518) 434–1935 or (800) 442–FUND
Fax: (518) 434-5641
Email: info@nylawfund.org
www.nylawfund.org

New York State Bar Association
1 Elk Street
Albany, NY 12207–1096
Tel. (518) 463–3200
Fax. (518) 487-5517
www.nysba.org

Department of State
One Commerce Plaza
99 Washington Ave,
Albany, NY 12231–0001
Tel. (518) 474–4752
Fax. (518) 474–4597
Email: info@dos.state.ny.us
www.dos.state.ny.us
     or
123 William Street
New York, NY 10038–3804
Tel. (212) 417–5800
Fax. (212) 417–2383

COURT DIRECTORY

New York State Department of State
Division of Corporations, State Records, and Uniform
    Commercial Code
One Commerce Plaza
99 Washington Avenue
Suite 600
Albany, NY 12231–0001
Email: corporations@dos.state.ny.us
Corporations—General Information:
Tel. (518) 473–2492
Fax. (518) 474–1418
State Records:
Tel. (518) 474–4770
Uniform Commercial Code:
Tel. (518) 474–4763
Fax. (518) 474–4478

Department of Family Assistance

www.dfa.state.ny.us

Office of Children and Family Services
General information Tel. (518) 473–7793
Abandoned Infant Protection Act Tel. (866) 505-SAFE
    (7233)
Adoption and other children's programs Tel. (800) 345–
    KIDS (5437)
Adult Protective Services Tel. (800) 342-3009 (dial 6)
Child abuse hotline Tel. (800) 342–3720
Child care complaint line Tel. (800) 732–5207
Domestic Violence Hotline (English) Tel. (800) 942–
    6906
Domestic Violence Hotline (Spanish) Tel. (800) 942–
    6908
www.ocfs.state.ny.us/main/

Office of Temporary and Disability Assistance
40 North Pearl Street
Albany, NY 12243
Tel. (518) 473–1090

COURT OF APPEALS
Court of Appeals Hall
20 Eagle Street
Albany, NY 12207–1095
Tel. (518) 455–7700
www.courts.state.ny.us/ctapps/

APPELLATE DIVISIONS
First Department
27 Madison Avenue
New York, NY 10010
Tel. (212) 340–0400
www.courts.state.ny.us/courts/ad1

CD-2

Second Department
45 Monroe Place
Brooklyn, NY 11201
Tel. (718) 875–1300
www.courts.state.ny.us/courts/ad2

Third Department
Empire State Plaza
State Street, Room 511
Albany, NY 12223
Mailing Address:
P.O. Box 7288, Capitol Station
Albany, NY 12224–0288
Tel. (518) 471–4777
Fax. (518) 471–4750
www.nycourts.gov/ad3

Fourth Department
M. Dolores Denman Courthouse
50 East Avenue
Rochester, NY 14604
Tel. (585) 530–3100
www.nycourts.gov/ad4

COURT OF CLAIMS

www.nyscourtofclaims.state.ny.us

Clerk of the Court of Claims
P.O. Box 7344
Capitol Station
Albany, NY 12224
Tel. (518) 432–3411
Fax. (866) 413–1069
Email: rdecatal@courts.state.ny.us

26 Broadway
New York, NY 10004
Tel. (212) 361-8100

State Office Building
44 Hawley Street
Binghamton, NY 13901–4418
Tel. (607) 721–8623
Fax. (607) 721–8621

State Office Building
130 South Elmwood Avenue
Suite 300
Buffalo, NY 14202
Tel. (716) 515–4810

COURT DIRECTORY

State Office Building, 3rd Floor
Veterans Memorial Highway
Hauppauge, NY 11788
Tel. (631) 952–6542
Fax. (631) 952–6727

Supreme Court Building
100 Supreme Court Drive
Mineola, NY 11501
Tel. (516) 571–3883

500 Court Exchange Building
144 Exchange Boulevard
Rochester, NY 14614–2108
Tel. (585) 325–4500
Fax. (585) 262–5715

65 South Broadway
Saratoga Springs, NY 12866
Tel. (518) 583–5330

205 South Salina Street
Syracuse, NY 13202
Tel. (315) 466–7151
Fax. (315) 466–7154

State Office Building
207 E. Genessee Street
Utica, NY 13501
Tel. (315) 793–2601
Fax. (315) 793–2606

140 Grand Street
White Plains, NY 10601
Tel. (914) 289–2310
Fax. (914) 289–2313

ALBANY COUNTY
[3rd Judicial District, 3rd Judicial Department]
www.nycourts.gov/courts/3jd

Supreme Court
Albany County Courthouse
16 Eagle Street, Room 102
Albany, NY 12207
Tel. (518) 285–8989
Fax. (518) 487–5020

County Court
Albany County Courthouse
6 Lodge Street
Albany, NY 12207
Tel. (518) 285–8777
Fax. (518) 436–3986

Family Court
30 Clinton Avenue
Albany, NY 12207
Tel. (518) 285–8600
Fax. (518) 462–4248

Surrogate's Court
Albany County Family Court Building
30 Clinton Avenue
Albany, NY 12207
Tel. (518) 462–0194
Fax. (518) 487–5087

Albany City Court–Civil Part
Albany City Hall, Room 209
24 Eagle Street
Albany, NY 12207
(518) 453–4640
Fax. (518) 434–5034

Albany City Court–Traffic Part
Albany City Hall, Basement
24 Eagle Street
Albany, NY 12207
(518) 453–4630
Fax. (518) 434–5084

Albany City Court–Criminal Part
Public Safety Building
1 Morton Avenue
Albany, NY 12202
Tel. (518) 462–6714
Fax. (518) 462–8778

Cohoes City Court
City Hall, Room 219
97 Mohawk Street
P.O. Box 678
Cohoes, NY 12047
Tel. (518) 233–2133 x 219
Fax. (518) 233–8202

Watervliet City Court
City Hall
2 Fifteenth Street
Watervliet, NY 12189
Tel. (518) 270–3803
Fax. (518) 270–3812

Frances Bergan Law Library
Albany County Courthouse, Room 316
16 Eagle Street
Albany, NY 12207
Tel. (518) 285–6183

COURT DIRECTORY

Sheriff
Albany County Court House
16 Eagle Street
Albany, NY 12207
Tel. (518) 487–5440
Fax. (518) 487–5037

ALLEGANY COUNTY

[8th Judicial District, 4th Judicial Department]

Supreme Court
Allegany County Courthouse
7 Court Street
Belmont, NY 14813–1084
Tel. (585) 268–5800
Fax. (585) 268–7090

County Court
Allegany County Courthouse
7 Court Street
Belmont, NY 14813–1084
Tel. (585) 268–5800
Fax. (585) 268–7090

Family Court
Allegany County Courthouse
7 Court Street
Belmont, NY 14813–1084
Tel. (585) 268–5816
Fax. (585) 268–7090

Surrogate's Court
Allegany County Courthouse
7 Court Street
Belmont, NY 14813–1084
Tel. (585) 268–5815
Fax. (585) 268–7090

Allegany County Law Library
Allegany County Courthouse
7 Court Street
Belmont, NY 14813–1084
Tel. (716) 268–5813

Sheriff
4884 State Route 19
Belmont, NY 14813
Tel. (585) 268–9200
Fax. (585) 268-9475
Email: Tompkiw@alleganyco.com
CD-4

BRONX COUNTY

[12th Judicial District, 1st Judicial Department]

Supreme Court
851 Grand Concourse
Bronx, NY 10451
Tel. (718) 618–1200

Family Court
900 Sheridan Avenue
Bronx, NY 10451
Tel. (718) 618–2098
Fax. (718) 590–2681
www.courts.state.ny.us/famhome.htm

Surrogate's Court
851 Grand Concourse
Bronx, NY 10451
Tel. (718) 618–2300

Civil Court of the City of New York
Bronx County Branch
851 Grand Concourse
Bronx, NY 10451–2988
Tel. (718) 618–1200

Criminal Court of the City of New York
Bronx County Branch
215 East 161st Street
Bronx, NY 10451
Tel. (718) 618–3100
Fax. (718) 618–3585

Bronx County Housing Court
1118 Grand Concourse
Bronx, NY 10456
Tel. (718) 466–3000
Fax. (718) 466–3006

Bronx County Law Library
851 Grand Concourse, Room 817
Bronx, NY 10451
Tel. (718) 618–3710

Sheriff
3030 Third Ave.
Bronx, NY 10455
Tel. (718) 993–3880
Fax. (718) 993–3116

COURT DIRECTORY

BROOME COUNTY

[6th Judicial District, 3rd Judicial Department]

Supreme Court
Broome County Courthouse
92 Court St., P.O. Box 1766
Binghamton, NY 13902–1766
Tel. (607) 778–2448
Fax. (607) 778–6426

County Court
Family and County Court Building
65 Hawley St., P.O. Box 1766
Binghamton, NY 13901
Tel. (607) 778–2156
Fax. (607) 778–2439

Family Court
Family and County Court Building
65 Hawley Street
Binghamton, NY 13902–1766
Tel. (607) 778–2156
Fax. (607) 778–2439

Surrogate's Court
Broome County Courthouse
92 Court St.
Binghamton, NY 13901
Tel. (607) 778–2111
Fax. (607) 778–2308

Binghamton City Court
City Hall, Governmental Plaza
38 Hawley Street, 5th Floor
Binghamton, NY 13901
Tel. (607) 772–7006
Fax. (607) 772–7041

Binghamton County Law Library
Broome County Courthouse
92 Court Street, Room 107
Binghamton, NY 13901
Tel. (607) 778–2119
Fax. (607) 772–8331

Sheriff
155 Lt. Van Winkle Drive
Binghamton, NY 13905
Tel. (607) 778–1911
Fax. (607) 778-2100
Email: bcsheriff@co.broome.ny.us

CATTARAUGUS COUNTY

[8th Judicial District, 4th Judicial Department]

Supreme Court
303 Court Street
Little Valley, NY 14755
Tel. (716) 938–9111
Fax. (716) 938–9328
or
Supreme Court
One Leo Moss Drive
Olean, NY 14760
Tel. (716) 373–8035
Fax. (716) 373–0449

County Court
303 Court Street
Little Valley, NY 14755
Tel. (716) 938–9111
Fax. (716) 938–6413

Family Court
One Leo Moss Drive
Suite 1140
Olean, NY 14760–1152
Tel. (716) 373–8035
Fax. (716) 373–0449

Surrogate's Court
303 Court Street
Little Valley, NY 14755
Tel. (716) 938–2327
Fax. (716) 938–6983
or
Surrogate's Court
One Leo Moss Drive
Olean, NY 14760
Tel. (716) 373–8043
Fax. (716) 373–0449

Olean City Court
Municipal Building
101 East State Street
P.O. Box 631
Olean, NY 14760–0631
Tel. (716) 376–5621
Fax. (716) 376–5623

Salamanca City Court
225 Wildwood Avenue
Salamanca, NY 14779
Tel. (716) 945–4153
Fax. (716) 945–2362

COURT DIRECTORY

Cattaraugus County Law Library
303 Court Street
Little Valley, NY 14755–1028
Tel. (716) 938–9111 ext. 326

Sheriff
301 Court Street
Little Valley, NY 14755–1090
Tel. (716) 938–9191 or (800) 443–3403
Fax. (716) 938–6552
Email: dbjohn@cattco.org
www.sheriff.cattco.org

CAYUGA COUNTY

[7th Judicial District, 4th Judicial Department]

Supreme Court
Cayuga County Courthouse
153 Genesee Street
Auburn, NY 13021
Tel. (315) 255–4320
Fax. (315) 255–4322

County Court
Cayuga County Courthouse
153 Genesee Street
Auburn, NY 13021
Tel. (315) 255–4320
Fax. (315) 255–4322

Family Court
Cayuga County Courthouse
Old Historic Post Office Building
157 Genesee Street, 2nd Floor
Auburn, NY 13021–3476
Tel. (315) 255–4306
Fax. (315) 255–4312

Surrogate's Court
Cayuga County Courthouse
153 Genesee Street
Auburn, NY 13021
Tel. (315) 255–1570
Fax. (315) 255–4324

Auburn City Court
157 Genesee Street
Auburn, NY 13021
Tel. (315) 253–1570
Fax. (315) 253–1085

CD-6

New York Cayuga County Law Library
Court House Building
152 Genesee Street
Auburn, NY 13021
Tel. (315) 255–4310
Fax. (315) 255–4322

Sheriff
7445 County House Road
P.O. Box 518
Auburn, NY 13021
Tel. (315) 253–1222
Fax. (315) 253–4575
Email: sheriff@cayugacounty.us

CHAUTAUQUA COUNTY

[8th Judicial District, 4th Judicial Department]

Supreme Court
Chautauqua County Courthouse
1 North Erie Street
P.O. Box 292
Mayville, NY 14757–0292
Tel. (716) 753–4266
Fax. (716) 753–4993

County Court
Chautauqua County Courthouse
1 North Erie Street
P.O. Box 292
Mayville, NY 14757–0292
Tel. (716) 753–4000

Family Court
2 Academy Street, Suite 5,
Mayville, NY 14757–0149
Tel. (716) 753–4351
Fax. (716) 753–4350

Surrogate's Court
Gerace Office Building
Courthouse - PO Box C
Mayville, NY 14757
Tel. (716) 753–4339
Fax. (716) 753–4600

Dunkirk City Court
City Hall
342 Central Avenue
Dunkirk, NY 14048–2122
Tel. (716) 366–2055
Fax. (716) 366–3622

COURT DIRECTORY

Jamestown City Court
Municipal Building
200 East Third Street
Jamestown, NY 14701–5494
Tel. (716) 483–7561
Tel. (716) 483–7562
Fax. (716) 483–7519

Chautauqua County Law Library
Chautauqua County Courthouse
1 North Erie Street
Mayville, NY 14757–0292
Tel. (716) 753–7111

Sheriff
15 East Chautauqua Street
P.O. Box 128
Mayville, NY 14757–0128
Tel. (716) 753–4900
Fax. (716) 753–4969
Email: jg@sheriff.us
www.sheriff.us/

CHEMUNG COUNTY
[6th Judicial District, 3rd Judicial Department]

Supreme Court
Hazlett Building
203–205 Lake Street
Elmira, NY 14901
Tel. (607) 737–2084
Fax. (607) 732–8879

County Court
Chemung County Courthouse
Hazlett Building
203–205 Lake Street
Elmira, NY 14902–0588
Tel. (607) 737–2940
Fax. (607) 732–3343

Family Court
Justice Building
203–209 William Street
P.O. Box 588
Elmira, NY 14901
Tel. (607) 737–2902 or 737–2903
Fax. (607) 737–2898

Surrogate's Court
224 Lake Street
P.O. Box 588
Elmira, NY 14901
Tel. (607) 737–2873
Fax. (607) 737–2874

Elmira City Court
317 East Church Street, Suite 3
Elmira, NY 14901
Tel. (607) 737–5681
Fax. (607) 737–5820

Chemung County Law Library
Hazlett Building
203–205 Lake Street, 1st Floor,
Elmira, NY 14901
Tel. (607) 737–2983
Fax. (607) 733–9863

Sheriff
203 William Street
P.O. Box 588
Elmira, NY 14902–0588
Tel. (607) 737–2987
Fax. (607) 737–2931
Email: cmoss@co.chemung.ny.us

CHENANGO COUNTY
[6th Judicial District, 3rd Judicial Department]

Supreme Court
County Office Building
5 Court Street
Norwich, NY 13815
Tel. (607) 337–1457
Fax. (607) 337–1835

County Court
County Office Building
5 Court Street
Norwich, NY 13815–1676
Tel. (607) 337–1457
Fax. (607) 337–1835

Family Court
County Office Building
5 Court Street
Norwich, NY 13815
Tel. (607) 337–1820
Fax. (607) 337–1835

Surrogate's Court
County Office Building
5 Court Street
Norwich, NY 13815
Tel. (607) 337–1827
Fax. (607) 337–1834

COURT DIRECTORY

Norwich City Court
One Court Plaza
Norwich, NY 13815
Tel. (607) 334–1224
Fax. (607) 334–8494

Chenango County Law Library
David L. Follett Library
5–9 West Main Street, 2nd Floor
Norwich, NY 13815
Tel. (607) 334–9463
Fax. (607) 334–9236

Sheriff
279 County Route 46
Norwich, NY 13815–1698
Tel. (607) 337–1857
Fax. (607) 336–1568
www.chenangosheriff.us

CLINTON COUNTY
[4th Judicial District, 3rd Judicial Department]

Supreme Court
137 Margaret Street, Third Floor
Plattsburgh, NY 12901–2990
Tel. (518) 565–4715
Fax. (518) 565–4708

County Court
137 Margaret Street, Third Floor
Plattsburgh, NY 12901–2990
Tel. (518) 565–4715
Fax. (518) 565–4708

Family Court
137 Margaret Street , Third Floor
Suite 311
Plattsburgh, NY 12901–2964
Tel. (518) 565–4658
Fax. (518) 565–4688

Surrogate's Court
137 Margaret Street , Third Floor
Plattsburgh, NY 12901
Tel. (518) 565–4630
Fax. (518) 565–4769

Plattsburgh City Court
24 U.S. Oval
Plattsburgh, NY 12903
Tel. (518) 563–7870
Fax. (518) 563–3124

CD-8

Clinton County Law Library
72 Clinton Street
Plattsburgh, NY 12901
Tel. (518) 565–4808
Fax. (518) 562–1193

Sheriff
25 McCarthy Drive
Plattsburgh, NY 12901–6203
Tel. (518) 565–4330
Fax. (518) 565–4333

COLUMBIA COUNTY
[3rd Judicial District, 3rd Judicial Department]

Supreme Court
Columbia County Courthouse
401 Union Street
Hudson, NY 12534
Tel. (518) 828–7858
Fax. (518) 828–1603

County Court
Columbia County Courthouse
401 Union Street
Hudson, NY 12534
Tel. (518) 828–7858
Fax. (518) 828–1603

Family Court
Columbia County Courthouse
401 Union Street
Hudson, NY 12534
Tel. (518) 828–0315
Fax. (518) 828–1603

Surrogate's Court
Columbia County Courthouse
401 Union Street
Hudson, NY 12534
Tel. (518) 828–0414
Fax. (518) 828–1603

Hudson City Court
427-429 Warren Street
Hudson, NY 12534
Tel. (518) 828–3100
Fax. (518) 828–3628

Columbia County Law Library
Supreme Court Courthouse
401 Union Street
Hudson, NY 12534
Tel. (518) 828–3206
Fax. (518) 828–2101

COURT DIRECTORY

Sheriff
85 Industrial Tract
Hudson, NY 12534
Tel. (518) 828–0601
Fax. (518) 828–9088

CORTLAND COUNTY
[6th Judicial District, 3rd Judicial Department]

Supreme Court
Cortland County Courthouse
46 Greenbush Street, Suite 301
Cortland, NY 13045
Tel. (607) 753–5013
Fax. (607) 756–3409

County Court
Cortland County Courthouse
46 Greenbush Street, Suite 301
Cortland, NY 13045
Tel. (607) 753–5013
Fax. (607) 756–3409

Family Court
Cortland County Courthouse
46 Greenbush Street, Suite 301
Cortland, NY 13045
Tel. (607) 753–5353
Fax. (607) 756–3409

Surrogate's Court
Cortland County Courthouse
46 Greenbush Street, Suite 301
Cortland, NY 13045
Tel. (607) 753–5355
Fax. (607) 756–3409

Cortland City Court
25 Court Street
Cortland, NY 13045
Tel. (607) 428–5420
Fax. (607) 428–5435

Cortland County Law Library
Cortland County Courthouse
46 Greenbush Street
Cortland, NY 13045
Tel. (607) 753–5011
Fax. (607) 756–3409

Sheriff
54 Greenbush Street
Cortland, NY 13045
Tel. (607) 758–5599
Fax. (607) 753–6649

DELAWARE COUNTY
[6th Judicial District, 3rd Judicial Department]

Supreme Court
Delaware County Courthouse
3 Court Street
Delhi, NY 13753
Tel. (607) 746–2131
Fax. (607) 746–3253

County Court
Delaware County Courthouse
3 Court Street
Delhi, NY 13753
Tel. (607) 746–2131
Fax. (607) 746–3253

Family Court
Delaware County Courthouse
3 Court Street
Delhi, NY 13753
Tel. (607) 746–2298
Fax. (607) 746–2288

Surrogate's Court
Delaware County Courthouse
3 Court Street
Delhi, NY 13753
Tel. (607) 746–2126
Fax. (607) 746–3253

Delaware County Law Library
Delaware County Courthouse
3 Court Street
Delhi, NY 13753
Tel. (607) 746–3959
Fax. (607) 746–8198

Sheriff
280 Phoebe Lane, Suite 1
Delhi, NY 13753
Tel. (607) 746–2336
Fax. (607) 746–2632

DUTCHESS COUNTY
[9th Judicial District, 2nd Judicial Department]

Supreme Court
Dutchess County Courthouse
10 Market Street
Poughkeepsie, NY 12601
Tel. (845) 486–2285
Fax. (845) 486–2697

COURT DIRECTORY

County Court
Dutchess County Courthouse
10 Market Street
Poughkeepsie, NY 12601
Tel. (845) 486–2260
Fax. (845) 473–5403

Family Court
50 Market Street
Poughkeepsie, NY 12601–3204
Tel. (845) 486–2500
Fax. (845) 486–2510

Surrogate's Court
Dutchess County Courthouse
10 Market Street
Poughkeepsie, NY 12601
Tel. (845) 486–2235
Fax. (845) 486–2234

Beacon City Court
1 Municipal Plaza, Suite 2
Beacon, NY 12508
Tel. (845) 838–5030
Fax. (845) 838–5041

Poughkeepsie City Court
62 Civic Center Plaza
P.O. Box 300
Poughkeepsie, NY 12601
Tel. (845) 483–8200
Fax. (845) 451–4094

Dutchess County Law Library
50 Market Street
Poughkeepsie, NY 12601
Tel. (845) 486–2215

Sheriff
150 North Hamilton Street
Poughkeepsie, NY 12601
Tel. (845) 486–3800
Fax. (845) 486–3927

ERIE COUNTY
[8th Judicial District, 4th Judicial Department]

Supreme Court
Erie County Court Building
25 Delaware Avenue
Buffalo, NY 14202
Tel. (716) 845–9300
Fax. (716) 851–3293

CD-10

Supreme Court
Erie County Hall
92 Franklin Street
Buffalo, NY 14202
Tel. (716) 845–2560
Fax. (716) 853–3741

Supreme Court
Buffalo City Court Building
50 Delaware Avenue
Buffalo, NY 14202

Supreme Court
Eagle Street Office Building
77 West Eagle Street
Buffalo, NY 14202

County Court
Erie County Court Building
25 Delaware Avenue
Buffalo, NY 14202
Tel. (716) 845–9300
Fax. (716) 851–3293

Family Court
One Niagara Plaza
Buffalo, NY 14202
Tel. (716) 845–7400
Fax. (716) 858–8432

Surrogate's Court
Erie County Hall
92 Franklin Street
Buffalo, NY 14202
Tel. (716) 845–2560
Fax. (716) 853–3741

Buffalo City Court
50 Delaware Avenue
Buffalo, NY 14202
Tel. (716) 845–2600
Fax. (716) 847–8257

Lackawanna City Court
714 Ridge Road
Lackawanna, NY 14218
Tel. (716) 827–6486
Fax. (716) 825–1874

Tonawanda City Court
200 Niagara Street
Tonawanda, NY 14150
Tel. (716) 845–2160
Fax. (716) 693–1612

Erie County Law Library
77 West Eagle Street
Buffalo, NY 14202
Tel. (716) 845–9400
Fax. (716) 852–3454

Sheriff
10 Delaware Avenue
Buffalo, NY 14202
Tel. (716) 858–7608
Fax. (716) 858–7680
www.erie.gov/sheriff

ESSEX COUNTY
[4th Judicial District, 3rd Judicial Department]

Supreme Court
Essex County Courthouse
7559 Court Street
P.O. Box 217
Elizabethtown, NY 12932
Tel. (518) 873–3371
Fax. (518) 873–3376

County Court
Essex County Courthouse
7559 Court Street
P.O. Box 217
Elizabethtown, NY 12932
Tel. (518) 873–3375
Fax. (518) 873–3376

Family Court
Essex County Courthouse
7559 Court Street
Elizabethtown, NY 12932
Tel. (518) 873–3320
Fax. (518) 873–3626

Surrogate's Court
Essex County Courthouse
7559 Court Street
P.O. Box 505
Elizabethtown, NY 12932
Tel. (518) 873–3384
Fax. (518) 873–3731

Essex County Court Law Library
Essex County Courthouse
7559 Court Street
P.O. Box 217
Elizabethtown, NY 12932
Tel. (518) 873–3377
Fax. (518) 873–3376

Sheriff
702 Stowersville Road
P.O. Box 68
Lewis, NY 12950
Tel. (518) 873–6321
Fax. (518) 873–3340

FRANKLIN COUNTY
[4th Judicial District, 3rd Judicial Department]

Supreme Court
Franklin County Courthouse
355 West Main Street, Suite 3223
Malone, NY 12953–1817
Tel. (518) 481–1817
Fax. (518) 481–5456

County Court
Franklin County Courthouse
355 West Main Street, Suite 3223
Malone, NY 12953–1817
Tel. (518) 481–1817
Fax. (518) 481–5456

Family Court
Franklin County Courthouse
355 West Main Street, Suite 3223
Malone, NY 12953–1817
Tel. (518) 481–1742
Fax. (518) 481–5453

Surrogate's Court
Franklin County Courthouse
355 West Main Street, Suite 3223
Malone, NY 12953–1817
Tel. (518) 481–1736
Fax. (518) 481–1443

Franklin County Court Law Library
Franklin County Courthouse
63 West Main Street
Malone, NY 12953–1817
Tel. (518) 481–1732

Sheriff
45 Bare Hill Road
Malone, NY 12953
Tel. (518) 483–3304
Fax. (518) 483–3205

FULTON COUNTY
[4th Judicial District, 3rd Judicial Department]

COURT DIRECTORY

Supreme Court
Fulton County Office Building
223 West Main Street
Johnstown, NY 12095
Tel. (518) 736–5539
Fax. (518) 762–5078

County Court
Fulton County Office Building
223 West Main Street
Johnstown, NY 12095
Tel. (518) 736–5539
Fax. (518) 762–5078

Family Court
11 North William Street
Johnstown, NY 12095–2116
Tel. (518) 762–3840
Fax. (518) 762–9540

Surrogate's Court
Fulton County Office Building
223 West Main Street
Johnstown, NY 12095
Tel. (518) 736–5695
Fax. (518) 762–6372

Gloversville City Court
City Hall
3 Frontage Road
Gloversville, NY 12078
Tel. (518) 773–4527
Fax. (518) 773–4599

Johnstown City Court
33–41 East Main Street, Suite 105
Johnstown, NY 12095
Tel. (518) 762–0007
Fax. (518) 762–2720

Fulton County Court Law Library
Fulton County Office Building
223 West Main Street
Johnstown, NY 12095
Tel. (518) 762–0685
Fax. (518) 762–6372

Sheriff
2712 State Highway 29
Johnstown, NY 12095
Tel. (518) 736–2100
Fax. (518) 736–2126

CD-12

GENESEE COUNTY
[8th Judicial District, 4th Judicial Department]

Supreme Court
Genesee County Courts Facility
1 West Main Street
Batavia, NY 14020–2019
Tel. (585) 344–2310
Fax. (585) 344–8517

Commissioner of Jurors

Tel. (585) 344–2550 Ext. 2223
Fax. (585) 343–4244

County Court
Genesee County Courts Facility
1 West Main Street
Batavia, NY 14020–2019
Tel. (585) 344–2310
Fax. (585) 344–8517

Commissioner of Jurors

Tel. (585) 344–2550 Ext. 2223
Fax. (585) 343–4244

Family Court
Genesee County Courts Facility
1 West Main Street
Batavia, NY 14020–2019
Tel. (585) 344–2228
Fax. (585) 344–8520

Surrogate's Court
Genesee County Courts Facility
1 West Main Street
Batavia, NY 14020–2019
Tel. (585) 344–2237
Fax. (585) 344–8517

Batavia City Court
Genesee County Courts Facility
1 West Main Street
Batavia, NY 14020–2019
Tel. (585) 344–2417
Fax. (585) 344–8556
Email: lgiambro@courts.state.ny.us

Genesee County Law Library
Genesee County Courts Facility
1 West Main Street
Batavia, NY 14020–2019
Tel. (585) 344–2550 ext. 2224
Fax. (585) 344–8517

COURT DIRECTORY

Sheriff
165 Park Road
Batavia, NY 14020
Tel. (585) 345–3000
Fax. (585) 344–3102
Email: sheriff@co.genesee.ny.us

GREENE COUNTY
[3rd Judicial District, 3rd Judicial Department]

Supreme Court
Greene County Courthouse
320 Main Street,
Catskill, NY 12414–1825
Tel. (518) 444–8760
Fax. (518) 943–0247

County Court
Greene County Courthouse
320 Main Street,
Catskill, NY 12414–1816
Tel. (518) 444–8760
Fax. (518) 943–0247

Family Court
Greene County Courthouse
320 Main Street,
Catskill, NY 12414–1816
Tel. (518) 444–8780
Fax. (518) 943–1864
Email: bvanderm@courts.state.ny.us

Surrogate's Court
Greene County Courthouse
320 Main Street,
Catskill, NY 12414–1825
Tel. (518) 444–8750
Fax. (518) 943–5811

Greene County Law Library
Greene County Courthouse
320 Main Street
Catskill, NY 12414
Tel. (518) 943–3130

Sheriff
80 Bridge Street
P.O. Box 231
Catskill, NY 12414
Tel. (518) 943–3300
Fax. (518) 943–6832
Email: sheriff@discovergreene.com

HAMILTON COUNTY
[4th Judicial District, 3rd Judicial Department]

Supreme Court
[Sessions held in Fulton County]
County Clerk's Office
P.O. Box 204
Lake Pleasant, NY 12108
Tel. (518) 548–7111
Fax. (518) 548–9740

Chief Clerk's Office
79 White Birch Lane
P.O. Box 780
Indian Lake, NY 12842–0780

County Court
Hamilton County Courthouse
Route 8
Lake Pleasant, NY 12108
Tel. (518) 648–5411
Fax. (518) 648–6286
Mailing address:
Court Chambers
P.O. Box 780
Indian Lake, NY 12842

Family Court
Hamilton County Courthouse
Route 8
Lake Pleasant, NY 12108
Tel. (518) 648–5411
Fax. (518) 648–6286
Mailing address:
Court Chambers
P.O. Box 780
Indian Lake, NY 12842

Surrogate's Court
Hamilton County Courthouse
Route 8
Lake Pleasant, NY 12108
Tel. (518) 648–5411
Fax. (518) 648–6286
Mailing address:
Court Chambers
P.O. Box 780
Indian Lake, NY 12842

Hamilton County Court Law Library
Hamilton County Courthouse
Route 8
P.O. Box 780
Lake Pleasant, NY 12108
Tel. (518) 648–5411
Fax. (518) 648–6286
Mailing address:
Court Chambers
P.O. Box 780
Indian Lake, NY 12842

COURT DIRECTORY

Sheriff
South Shore Road
P.O. Box 210
Lake Pleasant, NY 12108
Tel. (518) 548–3113
Fax. (518) 548–5704

HERKIMER COUNTY

[5th Judicial District, 4th Judicial Department]

Supreme Court
Herkimer County Office & Court Facility
301 North Washington Street
Fifth Floor, Suite 5550
Herkimer, NY 13350
Civil Tel. (315) 867–1209
Crim. Tel. (315) 867–1282
Fax. (315) 866–1802

County Court
Herkimer County Office & Court Facility
301 North Washington Street
Fifth Floor, Suite 5550
Herkimer, NY 13350
Civil Tel. (315) 867–1209
Crim. Tel. (315) 867–1282
Fax. (315) 866–1802

Family Court
Herkimer County Office & Court Facility
301 North Washington Street, 4th Floor
P.O. Box 749
Herkimer, NY 13350
Tel. (315) 867–1139
Fax. (315) 867–1369

Surrogate's Court
Herkimer County Office & Court Facility
301 North Washington Street
Fifth Floor, Suite 5550
Herkimer, NY 13350
Tel. (315) 867–1170
Fax. (315) 866–1802

Little Falls City Court
Little Falls City Hall
659 East Main Street
Little Falls, NY 13365
Tel. (315) 823–1690
Fax. (315) 823–1623

Herkimer County Law Library
320 North Washington Street
Suite 5511
Herkimer, NY 13350
Tel. (315) 867–1172
Fax. (315) 866–7991

Sheriff
320 North Main Street
Herkimer, NY 13350–2922
Tel. (315) 867–1167
Fax. (315) 867–1354

JEFFERSON COUNTY

[5th Judicial District, 4th Judicial Department]

Supreme Court
Dulles State Office Building
317 Washington Street, 10th Fl.
Watertown, NY 13601
Tel. (315) 785–7906
Fax. (315) 785–7909

County Court
Jefferson County Court Complex
163 Arsenal Street
2nd Floor
Watertown, NY 13601
Tel. (315) 785–3044
Fax. (315) 786–7409

Family Court
Jefferson County Court Complex
163 Arsenal Street
2nd Floor
Watertown, NY 13601
Tel. (315) 785–3001
Fax. (315) 785–3198

Surrogate's Court
Jefferson County Court Complex
163 Arsenal Street
3rd Floor
Watertown, NY 13601
Tel. (315) 785–3019
Fax. (315) 785–5194

Watertown City Court
Municipal Building
245 Washington Street
1st Floor
Watertown, NY 13601
Tel. (315) 785–7785
Fax. (315) 785–7856

COURT DIRECTORY

Jefferson County Law Library
Jefferson County Courthouse
163 Arsenal Street
2nd Floor
Watertown, NY 13601
Tel. (315) 785–3064
Fax. (315) 785–3330

Sheriff
753 Waterman Drive
Watertown, NY 13601
Tel. (315) 786–2660
Fax. (315) 786–2684

KINGS COUNTY
[2nd Judicial District, 2nd Judicial Department]

Supreme Court (Criminal)
320 Jay Street
Brooklyn, NY 11201
Tel. (347) 296–1076
      or
Supreme Court (Civil)
360 Adams Street
Brooklyn, NY 11201
Tel. (718) 675–7699

Family Court
330 Jay Street
Brooklyn, NY 11201
Tel. (347) 401–9600
Fax. (347) 401–9609
www.courts.state.ny.us/famhome.htm

Surrogate's Court
2 Johnson Street
Brooklyn, NY 11201
Tel. (347) 404–9700
Fax. (718) 643–6237

Civil Court of the City of New York
Kings County Branch
141 Livingston Street
Brooklyn, NY 11201
General (212) 791–6000
Civil (347) 404–9123
Housing: (347) 404–9201
Small claims: (347) 404–9021

Criminal Court of the City of New York
Kings County Branch
120 Schermerhorn Street
Brooklyn, NY 11201
Tel: (646) 386–4500
Fax. (718) 643–7733

Kings County Housing Court
141 Livingston Street
Brooklyn, NY 11201
Tel. (347) 404–9201

Kings County Law Library
360 Adams Street, Room 349
Brooklyn, NY 11201
Tel. (347) 296–1144
Fax. (718) 643–2412

Sheriff
210 Joralemon Street, Room 911
Brooklyn, NY 11201–3745
Tel. (718) 802-3543

LEWIS COUNTY
[5th Judicial District, 4th Judicial Department]

Supreme Court
Lewis County Courthouse
7660 State Street
Lowville, NY 13367
Tel. (315) 376–5347
Fax. (315) 376–5398

County Court
Lewis County Courthouse
7660 N. State Street
2nd Floor
Lowville, NY 13367–1396
Tel. (315) 376–5366
Fax. (315) 376–4145

Family Court
Lewis County Courthouse
7660 State Street
Lowville, NY 13367
Tel. (315) 376–5345
Fax. (315) 376–5189

Surrogate's Court
Lewis County Courthouse
7660 State Street
Lowville, NY 13367
Tel. (315) 376–5344
Fax. (315) 376–1647

Lewis County Law Library
Lewis County Courthouse
7660 State Street
Lowville, NY 13367–1396
Tel. (315) 376–5383 or
(315) 376-5317
Fax. (315) 376–1674

COURT DIRECTORY

Sheriff
Outer Stowe Street
P.O. Box 233
Lowville, NY 13367
Tel. (315) 376–3511
Fax. (315) 376–5232

LIVINGSTON COUNTY
[7th Judicial District, 4th Judicial Department]
www.courts.state.ny.us/courts/7jd/

Supreme Court
Livingston County Courthouse
2 Court Street
Geneseo, NY 14454–1030
Tel. (585) 243–7060
Fax. (585) 243–7067

County Court
Livingston County Courthouse
2 Court Street
Geneseo, NY 14454–1030
Tel. (585) 243–7060
Fax. (585) 243–7067

Family Court
Livingston County Courthouse
2 Court Street
Geneseo, NY 14454–1030
Tel. (585) 243–7070
Fax. (585) 243–7076

Surrogate's Court
Livingston County Courthouse
2 Court Street
Geneseo, NY 14454–1030
Tel. (585) 243–7095
Fax. (585) 243–7583

Livingston County Law Library
24 Center Street
Geneseo, NY 14454
Tel. (585) 243–0440

Sheriff
4 Court Street
Geneseo, NY 14454
Tel. (585) 243–7100
Fax. (585) 243–7926

MADISON COUNTY
[6th Judicial District, 3rd Judicial Department]
CD-16

Supreme Court
Madison County Courthouse
138 North Court Street
Wampsville, NY 13163
Tel. (315) 366–2267
Fax. (315) 366–2539

County Court
Madison County Courthouse
138 North Court Street
Wampsville, NY 13163
Tel. (315) 366–2266
Fax. (315) 366–2539

Family Court
Madison County Courthouse
138 North Court Street
Wampsville, NY 13163
Tel. (315) 366–2291
Fax. (315) 366–2828

Surrogate's Court
Madison County Courthouse
138 North Court Street
Wampsville, NY 13163
Tel. (315) 366–2392
Fax. (315) 366–2539

Oneida City Court
109 North Main Street
Oneida, NY 13421
Tel. (315) 363–1310
Fax. (315) 363–3230

Oneida Public Library
220 Broad Street
Oneida, NY 13421
Tel. (315) 363–3050
Fax. (607) 772–8331

Sheriff
North Court Street
P.O. Box 16
Wampsville, NY 13163
Tel. (315) 366–2318
Fax. (315) 366–2286
Email: sheriff@co.madison.ny.us

MONROE COUNTY
[7th Judicial District, 4th Judicial Department]
www.courts.state.ny.us/courts/7jd/

COURT DIRECTORY

Supreme Court
Hall of Justice, Room 545
99 Exchange Blvd.
Rochester, NY 14614–2185
Supreme & County Courts (585) 428–2020
Chief Clerk (585) 428–5001
Fax. (585) 428–2190

County Court
Hall of Justice, Room 545
99 Exchange Blvd.
Rochester, NY 14614–2185
Chief Clerk Tel. (585) 428–5001
Civil Tel. (585) 428–2020
Fax. (585) 428–2190

Family Court
Hall of Justice, Room 361
99 Exchange Blvd.
Rochester, NY 14614–2187
Tel. (585) 428–5429
Fax. (585) 428–2597

Surrogate's Court
Hall of Justice, Room 541
99 Exchange Blvd.
Rochester, NY 14614–2186
Tel. (585) 428–5200
Fax. (585) 428–2650

Rochester City Court
Civil Branch
Hall of Justice, Room 6
99 Exchange Blvd.
Rochester, NY 14614–2199
Civil Tel. (585) 428–2444
Civil Fax. (585) 428–2588
Criminal Branch
123 Public Safety Building
Rochester, NY 14614
Crim. Tel. (585) 428–2447
Crim. Fax. (585) 428–2732

Monroe County Law Library
Hall of Justice, Room 525
99 Exchange Blvd.
Rochester, NY 14614
Tel. (585) 428–1854
Fax. (585) 428–3182

Sheriff
130 South Plymouth Avenue
Rochester, NY 14614
Tel. (585) 753–4178
Fax. (585) 753–4524

MONTGOMERY COUNTY
[4th Judicial District, 3rd Judicial Department]

Supreme Court
Montgomery County Courthouse
58 Broadway
P.O. Box 1500
Fonda, NY 12068–1500
Tel. (518) 853–4516
Fax. (518) 853–3596

County Court
Montgomery County Courthouse
58 Broadway
P.O. Box 1500
Fonda, NY 12068–1500
Tel. (518) 853–4516
Fax. (518) 853–3596

Family Court
Montgomery County Courthouse
58 Broadway
P.O. Box 1500
Fonda, NY 12068–1500
Tel. (518) 853–8133
Fax. (518) 853–8148

Surrogate's Court
Montgomery County Courthouse
58 Broadway
P.O. Box 1500
Fonda, NY 12068–1500
Tel. (518) 853–8108
Fax. (518) 853–8230

Amsterdam City Court
One Guy Park Avenue Extension
Public Safety Building, Room 208
Amsterdam, NY 12010
Tel. (518) 842–9510
Fax. (518) 843–8474

Montgomery County Court Law Library
Montgomery County Courthouse
58 Broadway
P.O. Box 1500
Fonda, NY 12068–1500

Sheriff
200 Clark Drive
P.O. Box 432
Fultonville, NY 12072–0432
Tel. (518) 853–5500
Fax. (518) 853–4096

COURT DIRECTORY

COURT DIRECTORY

Appellate Term
60 Centre Street
New York, NY 10007
Tel. (646) 386-3040

Family Court
60 Lafayette Street
New York, NY 10013
Tel. (646) 386–5206
Fax. (212) 374–4567
www.nycourts.gov/courts/nyc/family/

Surrogate's Court
31 Chambers Street
New York, NY 10007
Tel. (646) 386–5000
Fax. (212) 374–3250

Civil Court of the City of New York
New York County Branch
111 Centre Street
New York, NY 10013–4390
Tel. (646) 386–5700
Tel. (646) 386–5600
Fax. (212) 374–8053

Criminal Court of the City of New York
100 Centre Street
New York, NY 10013
Tel. (646) 386–4500
Fax. (212) 374–5293

New York County Housing Court
111 Centre Street
New York, NY 10013
Tel. (646) 386–5700
Small Claims (646) 386–5480

NY County Supreme Civil Law Library
80 Centre Street, Room 468
New York, NY 10013
Tel. (646) 386–3715
Fax. (212) 374–8159

Sheriff
31 Chambers Street, 6th Floor
New York, NY 10017
Tel. (212) 788–8731
Fax. (212) 766–9666

NIAGARA COUNTY
[8th Judicial District, 4th Judicial Department]

Supreme Court
Civic Building
775 3rd Street
Niagara Falls, NY 14302–1710
Tel. (716) 278–1800
Fax. (716) 278–1809
Email: mflorian@courts.state.ny.us

County Court
Niagara County Courthouse
175 Hawley Street
Lockport, NY 14094
Tel. (716) 439–7148
Fax. (716) 439–7157
Email: afarnold@courts.state.ny.us

Family Court
Niagara County Courthouse
175 Hawley Street
Lockport, NY 14094
Tel. (716) 439–7172
Fax. (716) 439–7170

Surrogate's Court
Niagara County Courthouse
175 Hawley Street
Lockport, NY 14094
Tel. (716) 439–7130
Fax. (716) 439–7319

Lockport City Court
1 Locks Plaza
Lockport, NY 14094–3694
Civil Tel. (716) 439–6660, ext. 502
Crim. Tel. (716) 439–6660, ext. 501
Traffic Tel. (716) 439–6660, ext. 503
Treatment Tel. (716) 439–6660, ext. 504
Fax. (716) 439–6684

Niagara Falls City Court
Niagara Falls Municipal Complex
1925 Main Street
Niagara Falls, NY 14305
Civil Tel. (716) 278–9860
Criminal Tel. (716) 278–9800
Traffic Tel. (716) 278–9840
Fax. (716) 278–9809
Email: mfarbo@courts.state.ny.us

North Tonawanda City Court
City Hall
216 Payne Avenue
North Tonawanda, NY 14120
Tel. (716) 693–1010
Fax. (716) 743–1754

Niagara County Library
Niagara County Courthouse
175 Hawley Street
Lockport, NY 14094
Tel. (716) 439–7148

Sheriff
5526 Niagara Street Extension
P.O. Box 496
Lockport, NY 14095–0496
Tel. (716) 438–3393
Fax. (716) 438–3302

ONEIDA COUNTY

[5th Judicial District, 4th Judicial Department]

Supreme Court
Oneida County Courthouse, 4th Floor
200 Elizabeth Street
Utica, NY 13501
Tel. (315) 266–4200
Fax. (315) 798–6436
    or
Supreme Court
NYS Office Building
207 Genesee Street
Utica, NY 13501
Tel. (315) 793–2184
Fax. (315) 793–2217
    or
Supreme Court
Oneida County Courthouse
302 North James St.
Rome, NY 13440

Oneida County Court
Oneida County Courthouse, 4th Floor
200 Elizabeth Street
Utica, NY 13501
Tel. (315) 798–5889
Fax. (315) 798–6047

Oneida County Family Court
Oneida County Courthouse
200 Elizabeth Street, 1st Floor
Utica, NY 13501
Tel. (315) 266–4444
Fax. (315) 798–6404
    or
301 West Dominick Street
Rome, NY 13440
Tel. (315) 266–4500
Fax. (315) 336–3828

CD-20

Surrogate's Court
Oneida County Office Building
800 Park Avenue, 8th Floor
Utica, NY 13501
Tel. (315) 266–4550
Rome Off. Tel. (315) 266–4309
Fax. (315) 797–9237

Rome City Court
100 West Court Street
Rome, NY 13440
Tel. (315) 337–6440
Fax. (315) 338–0343

Sherrill City Court
373 Sherrill Road
Sherrill, NY 13461
Tel. (315) 363–0996
Fax. (315) 363–1176

Utica City Court
411 Oriskany Street West
Utica, NY 13502
Civil Tel. (315) 724–8157
Fax. (315) 792–8038
Crim. Tel. (315) 724–8227
Fax. (315) 724–0762
Traffic Tel. (315) 724–8158
Fax. (315) 792–0762

Oneida County Law Library
Oneida County Courthouse
235 Elizabeth Street
Utica, NY 13501
Tel. (315) 798–5703
Fax. (315) 798–6470

Sheriff
6065 Judd Road
Oriskany, NY 13424–4218
Tel. (315) 765–2222
Fax. (315) 765–2205

ONONDAGA COUNTY
[5th Judicial District, 4th Judicial Department]

Supreme Court
Onondaga County Courthouse
401 Montgomery Street
Syracuse, NY 13202
Civil Division
Tel. (315) 671–1030
Fax. (315) 671–1176
Criminal Division
Tel. (315) 671–1020
Fax. (315) 671–1191

COURT DIRECTORY

County Court
Onondaga County Courthouse
505 South State Street
Syracuse, NY 13202–2104
Tel. (315) 671–1020
Fax. (315) 671-1191

Family Court
Onondaga County Courthouse
401 Montgomery Street
Syracuse, NY 13202
Tel. (315) 671–2000
Fax. (315) 671-1163

Surrogate's Court
Onondaga County Courthouse
401 Montgomery Street
Syracuse, NY 13202
Tel. (315) 671–2100
Fax. (315) 671-1162

Syracuse City Court
505 South State Street
Syracuse, NY 13202–2104
Crim. Tel. (315) 671–2760
Crim. Fax. (315) 671–2744
Civil Tel. (315) 671–2782
Civil Fax. (315) 671–2741
Traffic Tel. (315) 671–2770
Traffic Fax. (315) 671–2743

Onondaga County Law Library
Onondaga County Courthouse
401 Montgomery Street
Syracuse, NY 13202
Tel. (315) 671–1150
Fax. (315) 671–1160

Sheriff
407 South State Street
Syracuse, NY 13202
Tel. (315) 435–3044
Fax. (315) 435–2942

ONTARIO COUNTY
[7th Judicial District, 4th Judicial Department]
www.courts.state.ny.us/courts/7jd/

Supreme Court
Ontario County Courthouse
27 North Main Street
Canandaigua, NY 14424
Tel. (585) 396–4239
Fax. (585) 396–4576

County Court
Ontario County Courthouse
27 North Main Street
Canandaigua, NY 14424
Tel. (585) 396–4239
Fax. (585) 396–4576

Family Court
Ontario County Courthouse
27 North Main Street
Canandaigua, NY 14424
Tel. (585) 396–4272
Fax. (585) 396–4576
Email: ontariofamilycourt@courts.state.ny.us

Surrogate's Court
Ontario County Courthouse
27 North Main Street
Canandaigua, NY 14424
Tel. (585) 396–4055
Fax. (585) 396–4576
Email: dcrudele@courts.state.ny.us

Canandaigua City Court
2 North Main Street
Canandaigua, NY 14424
Tel. (585) 396–5011
Fax. (585) 396–5012
Email: lschutz@courts.state.ny.us

Geneva City Court
255 Exchange Street
Geneva, NY 14456
Tel. (315) 789–6560
Fax. (315) 781–2802
Email: jguard@courts.state.ny.us

Ontario County Law Library
Finger Lakes Community College
4355 Lakeshore Drive
Canandaigua, NY 14424
Tel. (585) 394–3500, ext. 7371

Sheriff
74 Ontario Street
Canandaigua, NY 14424
Tel. (585) 394–4560
Fax. (585) 396–4844

ORANGE COUNTY
[9th Judicial District, 2nd Judicial Department]

Supreme Court
285 Main Street
Goshen, NY 10924
Tel. (845) 291–3111
Fax. (845) 291–2595

County Court
285 Main Street
Goshen, NY 10924
Tel. (845) 291–3111
Fax. (845) 291–2595

Family Court
285 Main Street
Goshen, NY 10924
Tel. (845) 291–3030
Fax. (845) 291–3054

Surrogate's Court
30 Park Place
Goshen, NY 10924
Tel. (845) 291–2193
Fax. (845) 291–2196

Middletown City Court
2 James Street
Middletown, NY 10940
Tel. (845) 346–4050
Fax. (845) 343–5737

Newburgh City Court
300 Broadway
Newburgh, NY 12550
Tel. (845) 565–3208
Fax. (845) 483–8100

Port Jervis City Court
20 Hammond Street
Port Jervis, NY 12771
Tel. (845) 858–4034
Fax. (845) 858–9883

Orange County Law Library
Orange County Government Center
255–275 Main Street
Goshen, NY 10924
Tel. (845) 297–3138
Fax. (212) 401–9144

Sheriff
110 Wells Farm Road
Goshen, NY 10924–6740
Tel. (845) 291–4033
Fax. (845) 294–1590

ORLEANS COUNTY
[8th Judicial District, 4th Judicial Department]

Supreme Court
1 South Main Street
Suite 3,
Albion, NY 14411–1497
Tel. (585) 589–5458
Fax. (585) 589–0632

County Court
1 South Main Street
Suite 3,
Albion, NY 14411–1497
Tel. (585) 589–5458
Fax. (585) 589–0632

Family Court
1 South Main Street
Suite 3,
Albion, NY 14411–1497
Tel. (585) 589–4457
Fax. (585) 589–0632
Email: mwashak@courts.state.ny.us

Surrogate's Court
1 South Main Street
Suite 3,
Albion, NY 14411–1497
Tel. (585) 589–4457
Fax. (585) 589–0632
Email: dberry@courts.state.ny.us

Orleans County Law Library
Orleans County Court
County Building
Albion, NY 14411–1497
Tel. (716) 589–4457

Sheriff
13925 State Route 31, Suite 400
Albion, NY 14411–9386
Tel. (585) 590–4142
Fax. (585) 590–4178
Email: ocsher@orleansny.com

OSWEGO COUNTY
[5th Judicial District, 4th Judicial Department]

Supreme Court
Oswego County Courthouse
25 East Oneida Street
Oswego, NY 13126
Tel. (315) 349–3280
Fax. (315) 349–8513

COURT DIRECTORY

County Court
25 East Oneida Street
Oswego, NY 13126
Tel. (315) 349–3277
Fax. (315) 349–8513

Family Court
Oswego County Public Safety Center
39 Churchill Road
Oswego, NY 13126
Tel. (315) 349–3350
Fax. (315) 349–3457

Surrogate's Court
Oswego County Courthouse
25 East Oneida Street
Oswego, NY 13126
Tel. (315) 349–3295
Fax. (315) 349–8514

Fulton City Court
Municipal Building
141 South First Street
2nd Floor
Fulton, NY 13069
Tel. (315) 593–8400
Fax. (315) 592–3415

Oswego City Court
Conway Municipal Building
20 West Oneida Street
Oswego, NY 13126
Tel. (315) 343–0415
Fax. (315) 343–0531

Oswego County Law Library
Oswego County Courthouse
25 East Oneida Street
Oswego, NY 13126
Tel. (315) 349–3297
Fax. (315) 349–3273

Sheriff
Oswego County Public Safety Center
39 Churchill Road
Oswego, NY 13126
Tel. (315) 349–3307
Fax. (315) 349–3483
Email: sheriff@oswegocounty.com

OTSEGO COUNTY
[6th Judicial District, 3rd Judicial Department]

Supreme Court
Otsego County Office Building
197 Main Street
Cooperstown, NY 13326
Tel. (607) 547–4364
Fax. (607) 547–7567

County Court
Otsego County Office Building
197 Main Street
Cooperstown, NY 13326
Tel. (607) 547–4364
Fax. (607) 547–7567

Family Court
Otsego County Office Building
197 Main Street
Cooperstown, NY 13326
Tel. (607) 547–4264
Fax. (607) 547–6412

Surrogate's Court
Otsego County Office Building
197 Main Street
Cooperstown, NY 13326
Tel. (607) 547–4213
Fax. (607) 547–7566

Oneonta City Court
Public Safety Building
81 Main Street
Oneonta, NY 13820
Tel. (607) 432–4480
Fax. (607) 432–2328

Otsego County Law Library
Otsego County Office Building
197 Main Street
Cooperstown, NY 13326–1129
Tel. (607) 547–5425
Fax. (607) 547–6109

Sheriff
172 County Highway 33 West
Cooperstown, NY 13326
Tel. (607) 547–4271
Fax. (607) 547–6413

PUTNAM COUNTY
[9th Judicial District, 2nd Judicial Department]

COURT DIRECTORY

Supreme Court
20 County Center
Carmel, NY 10512
Tel. (845) 208–7830
Fax. (845) 228–9611

County Court
20 County Center
Carmel, NY 10512
Tel. (845) 208–7830
Fax. (845) 228–9611

Family Court
20 County Center
Carmel, NY 10512
Tel. (845) 208–7805
Fax. (845) 228–9614

Surrogate's Court
44 Gleneida Avenue
Carmel, NY 10512
Tel. (845) 208–7860
Fax. (845) 228–5761

Putnam County Law Library
Putnam County Office Building
20 County Center
Carmel, NY 10512
Tel. (845) 208–7804
Fax. (845) 225–4395

Sheriff
3 County Center
Carmel, NY 10512
Tel. (845) 225–4300
Fax. (845) 225–4399

QUEENS COUNTY
[11th Judicial District, 2nd Judicial Department]
www.courts.state.ny.us/courts/11jd/

Supreme Court (Civil Term)
88–11 Sutphin Boulevard, Suite 2
Jamaica, NY 11435
Tel. (718) 298–1000
Fax. (718) 520–2204
   or
(Criminal Term)
125–01 Queens Boulevard
Kew Gardens, NY 11415
Tel. (718) 298–1000
Fax. (718) 520–2494
   or
Civil Court
89–17 Sutphin Blvd.
Jamaica, NY 11435
Tel. (718) 262–7100
Fax. (718) 262–7107
Criminal Court
125–01 Queens Blvd.
Kew Gardens, NY 11415
Tel. (212) 374–5880
Fax. (718) 520–4712

Family Court
151–20 Jamaica Avenue
Jamaica, NY 11432
Tel. (718) 298–0197
Fax. (718) 297–2826
www.nycourts.gov/courts/nyc/family

Surrogate's Court
88–11 Sutphin Boulevard, 7th Floor
Jamaica, NY 11435
Tel. (718) 298–0500

Queens County Housing Court
89–17 Sutphin Boulevard
Jamaica, NY 11435
Tel. (646) 386–5750
www.courts.state.ny.us/courts/nyc/housing

Queens County Law Library
Queens County General Courthouse
88–11 Sutphin Boulevard, Room 65
Jamaica, NY 11435
Tel. (718) 298–1206
Fax. (718) 520–3589
Email: law_library_queens@courts.state.ny.us
www.nycourts.gov/library/queens/

Sheriff
144–06 94th Avenue
Jamaica, NY 11435
Tel. (718) 298–7550
Fax. (718) 298–7470

COURT DIRECTORY

RENSSELAER COUNTY
[3rd Judicial District, 3rd Judicial Department]

Supreme Court
80 Second Street
Troy, NY 12180–4098
Tel. (518) 285–5025
Fax. (518) 270–3714

County Court
80 Second Street
Troy, NY 12180–4098
Tel. (518) 285–5025
Fax. (518) 270–3714

Family Court
1504 Fifth Avenue
Troy, NY 12180–4107
Tel. (518) 270–3761
Fax. (518) 272–6573
Email: pbeeler@courts.state.ny.us

Surrogate's Court
80 Second Street
Troy, NY 12180–4098
Tel. (518) 270–3724
Fax. (518) 272–5452

Rensselaer City Court
62 Washington St.
Rensselaer, NY 12144
Tel. (518) 453–4680

Troy City Court – Civil
51 State Street, 3rd Floor
Troy, NY 12180
Tel. (518) 273–2434

Troy City Court – Criminal and Traffic
51 State Street, 2nd Floor
Troy, NY 12180
Tel. (518) 271–1602
Tel. (518) 274–2816

Rensselaer County Law Library
Courthouse
80 Second Street Annex
Troy, NY 12180
Tel. (518) 285–6183
Fax. (518) 274–0590

Sheriff
4000 Main Street
Troy, NY 12180
Tel. (518) 270–5448
Fax. (518) 270–5447

RICHMOND COUNTY
[13th Judicial District, 2nd Judicial Department]
www.nycourts.gov/courts/2jd/richmond.shtml

Supreme Court (Civil)
18 Richmond Terrace
Staten Island, NY 10301
Tel. (718) 675–8700
Fax. (718) 390–5435
        or
355 Front Street
Staten Island, NY 10304
Tel. (718) 876–6411

Supreme Court (Criminal)
18 Richmond Terrace
Staten Island, NY 10301
Tel. (718) 390–5280
Fax. (718) 390–5435

Family Court
100 Richmond Terrace
Staten Island, NY 10301
Tel. (718) 390–5460/5461
Fax. (718) 390–5247
www.courts.state.ny.us/famhome.htm

Surrogate's Court
18 Richmond Terrace
Staten Island, NY 10301
Tel. (718) 675–8500

Civil Court of the City of New York
Richmond County Branch
927 Castleton Avenue
Staten Island, NY 10310
General Info: (212) 791–6000
Civil Tel. (718) 390–5417
Small claims: (718) 390–5421
Fax. (718) 390–8108

Criminal Court of the City of New York
Richmond County Branch
67 Targee Street
Staten Island, NY 10304
Tel. (212) 374–5880
Fax. (718) 390–8405

Richmond County Housing Court
927 Castleton Avenue
Staten Island, NY 10310
Tel. (718) 675–8452

Richmond County Law Library
Supreme Court Building
18 Richmond Terrace
Staten Island, NY 10301
Tel. (718) 390–5291
Fax. (718) 390–5230
Email: bagnese@courts.state.ny.us

Sheriff
350 Saint Marks Avenue
Staten Island, NY 10301
Tel. (718) 815–8407
Fax. (718) 815–8412

ROCKLAND COUNTY

[9th Judicial District, 2nd Judicial Department]

Supreme Court
Rockland County Courthouse
1 South Main Street
New City, NY 10956
Tel. (845) 638–5393
Fax. (845) 638–5312

County Court
Rockland County Courthouse
1 South Main Street
New City, NY 10956
Tel. (845) 638–5393
Fax. (845) 638–5312

Family Court
Rockland County Courthouse
1 South Main Street
New City, NY 10956
Tel. (845) 638–5300
Fax. (845) 638–5319

Surrogate's Court
Rockland County Courthouse
1 South Main Street
New City, NY 10956
Tel. (845) 638–5330
Fax. (845) 638–5632

Rockland County Law Library
Rockland County Courthouse
1 South Main Street
Suite 235
New City, NY 10956–3551
Tel. (845) 638–5396
Fax. (212) 401–9143

Sheriff
55 New Hempstead Road
New City, NY 10956
Tel. (845) 638–5400
Fax. (845) 638–5035

ST. LAWRENCE COUNTY
[4th Judicial District, 3rd Judicial Department]
www.nycourts.gov/courts/4jd/stlawrence/

Supreme Court
St. Lawrence County Courthouse
48 Court Street
Canton, NY 13617–1194
Tel. (315) 379–2219
Fax. (315) 379–2423

County Court
48 Court Street
Canton, NY 13617–1194
Tel. (315) 379–2219
Fax. (315) 379–2423

Family Court
48 Court Street
Canton, NY 13617–1194
Tel. (315) 379–2410
Fax. (315) 386–3197

Surrogate's Court
48 Court Street
Canton, NY 13617–1194
Tel. (315) 379–2217
Fax. (315) 379–2372

Ogdensburg City Court
330 Ford Street
Ogdensburg, NY 13669
Tel. (315) 393–3941
Fax. (315) 393–6839

St. Lawrence County Supreme Court Law Library
St. Lawrence County Courthouse
48 Court Street
Canton, NY 13617–1194
Tel. (315) 379–2279
Fax. (315) 379–2424
Email: tlomaki@courts.state.ny.us

Sheriff
48 Court Street
Canton, NY 13617
Tel. (315) 379–2430
Fax. (315) 379–0335

COURT DIRECTORY

SARATOGA COUNTY
[4th Judicial District, 3rd Judicial Department]

Supreme Court
Municipal Center
Building 3
30 McMaster Street
Ballston Spa, NY 12020
Tel. (518) 885–2224
Fax. (518) 884–4758

County Court
Municipal Center
Building 3
30 McMaster Street
Ballston Spa, NY 12020
Tel. (518) 885–2224
Fax. (518) 884–4758

Family Court
Saratoga County Municipal Center
Building 2
35 West High Street
Ballston Spa, NY 12020
Tel. (518) 884–9207
Fax. (518) 884–9094

Surrogate's Court
Municipal Center
Building 3
30 McMaster Street
Ballston Spa, NY 12020
Tel. (518) 884–4722
Fax. (518) 884–4774

Saratoga Springs City Court
474 Broadway, Suite 3
Saratoga Springs, NY 12866
Tel. (518) 581–1797
Fax. (518) 584–3097

Mechanicville City Court
36 North Main Street
Mechanicville, NY 12118
Tel. (518) 664–9876
Fax. (518) 664–8606

Saratoga County Supreme Court Law Library
City Hall, 3rd Floor
Suite 10
474 Broadway
Saratoga Springs, NY 12866
Tel. (518) 584–4862
Fax. (518) 581–0966

Sheriff
6010 County Farm Road
Ballston Spa, NY 12020–2207
Tel. (518) 885–6761
Fax. (518) 885–2253

SCHENECTADY COUNTY
[4th Judicial District, 3rd Judicial Department]

Supreme Court
Schenectady County Courthouse
612 State Street
Schenectady, NY 12305
Tel. (518) 285–8401
Fax. (518) 388–4520

County Court
Schenectady County Courthouse
612 State Street
Schenectady, NY 12305
Tel. (518) 285–8401
Fax. (518) 388–4520

Family Court
Schenectady County Office Building
620 State Street
Schenectady, NY 12305
Tel. (518) 285–8435
Fax. (518) 393–1565

Surrogate's Court
Schenectady County Courthouse
612 State Street
Schenectady, NY 12305
Tel. (518) 285–8455
Fax. (518) 377–6378

Schenectady City Court (Civil Division)
City Hall
105 Jay Street, Room 214-215
Schenectady, NY 12305
Tel. (518) 382–5077
Fax. (518) 382–5080

Schenectady City Court (Criminal Division)
531 Liberty Street
Schenectady, NY 12305
Tel. (518) 382–5239
Fax. (518) 382–5241

Schenectady County Supreme Court Law Library
612 State Street
Schenectady, NY 12305–2114
Tel. (518) 285–8518
Fax. (518) 377–5909

COURT DIRECTORY

Sheriff
320 Veeder Avenue
Schenectady, NY 12307
Tel. (518) 388–4300
Fax. (518) 388–4593

SCHOHARIE COUNTY
[3rd Judicial District, 3rd Judicial Department]

Supreme Court
Schoharie County Courthouse
290 Main Street
P.O. Box 669
Schoharie, NY 12157
Tel. (518) 295–8342
Fax. (518) 295–7226

County Court
Schoharie County Courthouse
290 Main Street
P.O. Box 669
Schoharie, NY 12157
Tel. (518) 295–8342
Fax. (518) 295–7226

Family Court
Schoharie County Courthouse
290 Main Street
P.O. Box 669
Schoharie, NY 12157–0669
Tel. (518) 295–8383
Fax. (518) 295–8451

Surrogate's Court
Schoharie County Courthouse
290 Main Street
P.O. Box 669
Schoharie, NY 12157–0669
Tel. (518) 295–8387
Fax. (518) 295–8451

Schoharie County Law Library
Schoharie County Courthouse
290 Main Street
Schoharie, NY 12157–0447
Tel. (518) 295–7900
Fax. (518) 295–8451

Sheriff
157 Depot Lane
P.O. Box 689
Schoharie, NY 12157
Tel. (518) 295–7066
Fax. (518) 295–7094

SCHUYLER COUNTY
[6th Judicial District, 3rd Judicial Department]

Supreme Court
Schuyler County Courthouse
105 Ninth Street, Unit 35
Watkins Glen, NY 14891
Tel. (607) 535–7760
Fax. (607) 535–4918

County Court
Schuyler County Courthouse
105 Ninth Street, Unit 35
Watkins Glen, NY 14891
Tel. (607) 535–7015
Fax. (607) 535–4918

Family Court
Schuyler County Courthouse
105 Ninth Street, Unit 35
Watkins Glen, NY 14891
Tel. (607) 535–7015
Fax. (607) 535–4918

Surrogate's Court
Schuyler County Courthouse
105 Ninth Street, Unit 35
Watkins Glen, NY 14891
Tel. (607) 535–7144
Fax. (607) 535–4918

Watkins Glen Public Library
610 South Decatur Street
Watkins Glen, NY 14891
Tel. (607) 535–2346
Fax. (607) 535–7338

Sheriff
106 Tenth Street
Watkins Glen, NY 14891
Tel. (607) 535–8222
Fax. (607) 535–8216

SENECA COUNTY
[7th Judicial District, 4th Judicial Department]
www.courts.state.ny.us/courts/7jd

Supreme Court
48 West Williams Street
Waterloo, NY 13165
Tel. (315) 539–7021
Fax. (315) 539–7929
Email: eyoung@courts.state.ny.us

COURT DIRECTORY

County Court
48 West Williams Street
Waterloo, NY 13165
Tel. (315) 539–7021
Fax. (315) 539–7929

Family Court
48 West Williams Street
Waterloo, NY 13165
Tel. (315) 539–4917
Fax. (315) 539–4225
Email: cbrown@courts.state.ny.us

Surrogate's Court
48 West Williams Street
Waterloo, NY 13165
Tel. (315) 539–7531
Fax. (315) 539–3267

Seneca County Law Library
47 Cayuga Street
Seneca Falls, NY 13148
Tel. (315) 568–8265

Sheriff
6150 State Route 96
Romulus, NY 14541
Tel. (315) 220–3200
Fax. (315) 220–3478

STEUBEN COUNTY
[7th Judicial District, 4th Judicial Department]
www.courts.state.ny.us/courts/7jd/steuben/

Supreme Court
Steuben County Courthouse
3 East Pulteney Square
Bath, NY 14810–1575
Tel. (607) 776–7879
Fax. (607) 776–5226

County Court
Steuben County Courthouse
3 East Pulteney Square
Bath, NY 14810–1575
Tel. (607) 776–7879
Fax. (607) 776–5226

Family Court
Steuben County Courthouse
3 East Pulteney Square
Bath, NY 14810–1575
Tel. (607) 776–9631
Fax. (607) 776–7857

Surrogate's Court
Steuben County Courthouse
3 East Pulteney Square
Bath, NY 14810
Tel. (607) 776–7126
Fax. (607) 776–4987

Corning City Court
12 Civic Center Plaza
Corning, NY 14830–2884
Tel. (607) 936–4111
Fax. (607) 936–0519

Hornell City Court
82 Main St.
P.O. Box 627
Hornell, NY 14843–0627
Tel. (607) 324–7531
Fax. (607) 324–6325
Email: lbeltz@courts.state.ny.us

Steuben County Supreme Court Law Library
3 East Pulteney Square
Bath, NY 14810–1557
Tel. (607) 664–2099
Fax. (607) 776–7715

Sheriff
7007 Rumsey Street Extension
Bath, NY 14810–7827
Tel. (607) 776–7009
Fax. (607) 776–4271

SUFFOLK COUNTY
[10th Judicial District, 2nd Judicial Department]

Supreme Court
400 Carleton Avenue
Central Islip, NY 11722
Tel. (631) 853–6162
Fax. (631) 853–5835
or
210 Center Drive
Riverhead, NY 11901
Tel. (631) 852–2586
Fax. (631) 852–2340
or
One Court Street
Riverhead, NY 11901
Tel. (631) 852–3750

COURT DIRECTORY

County Court
Arthur M. Cromarty Court Complex
210 Center Drive
Riverhead, NY 11901
Tel. (631) 852–1431
Fax. (631) 852–2568

Family Court
John P. Cohalan, Jr., Courthouse
400 Carleton Avenue
Central Islip, NY 11722–9076
Tel. (631) 853–4289
Fax. (631) 853–4283
                or
Family Court
Millbrook Office Campus
889 East Main Street
Suite 308
Riverhead, NY 11901
Tel. (631) 852–3905
Fax. (631) 852–2851

Surrogate's Court
County Center Building
320 Center Drive
Riverhead, NY 11901
Tel. (631) 852–1746
Fax. (631) 852–1777

District Court—Chief Clerk's Office
John P. Cohalan, Jr. Courthouse
400 Carleton Avenue
Room D255
Central Islip, NY 11722
Tel. (631) 853–7500
Fax. (631) 853–4505

District Court—Criminal Division: Main Office
Cohalan Court Complex
400 Carleton Avenue
Room D220
Central Islip, NY 11722
Tel. (631) 853–7500

1st District Court—Civil
3105 Veterans Memorial Highway
Ronkonkoma, NY 11779
Tel. (631) 854–9676
Fax. (631) 854–9681

2nd District Court
30 East Hoffman Ave
Lindenhurst, NY 11757
Tel. (631) 854–1121
Fax. (631) 854–1127
CD-30

3rd District Court
1850 New York Avenue
Huntington Station, NY 11746
Tel. (631) 854–4545
Fax. (631) 854–4549

4th District Court
North County Complex, Bldg. #C158
Veterans Memorial Highway
Hauppauge, NY 11787
Tel. (631) 853–5408
Fax. (631) 853–5951

5th District Court
3105 Veterans Memorial Highway
Ronkonkoma, NY 11779
Tel. (631) 854–9676
Fax. (631) 854–9681

6th District Court
150 West Main Street
Patchogue, NY 11772
Tel. (631) 854–1440
Fax. (631) 854–1444

Suffolk County Supreme Court Law Library
Cohalan Court Complex
400 Carleton Avenue
Central Islip, NY 11702
Tel. (516) 853–7530
Fax. (516) 853–7533
                or
Suffolk County Law Library
Arthur M. Cromarty Court Complex
1st Floor
210 Center Drive
Riverhead, NY 11901–3312
Tel. (631) 852–2419

Sheriff
100 Center Drive
Riverhead, NY 11901–3307
Tel. (631) 852–2200
Fax. (631) 852–1898

SULLIVAN COUNTY
[3rd Judicial District, 3rd Judicial Department]

Supreme Court
Sullivan County Courthouse
414 Broadway
Monticello, NY 12701
Tel. (845) 794–4066
Fax. (845) 791–6170

COURT DIRECTORY

County Court
Sullivan County Courthouse
414 Broadway
Monticello, NY 12701
Tel. (845) 794–4066
Fax. (845) 791–6170
Email: elilley@courts.state.ny.us

Family Court
Sullivan County Government Center
100 North Street
Monticello, NY 12701
Tel. (845) 807–0650
Fax. (845) 794–0199

Surrogate's Court
County Government Center
100 North Street
Monticello, NY 12701
Tel. (845) 807–0690
Fax. (845) 794–0310

Sullivan County Law Library
Sullivan County Courthouse
441 Broadway
Monticello, NY 12701
Tel. (845) 794–1547
Fax. (845) 794–6170

Sheriff
4 Bushnell Avenue
Monticello, NY 12701–1304
Tel. (845) 794–7100
Fax. (845) 794–0810

TIOGA COUNTY
[6th Judicial District, 3rd Judicial Department]

Supreme Court
16 Court Street
Courthouse Square
Owego, NY 13827
Tel. (607) 778–2201
Fax. (607) 778–2398

County Court
16 Court Street
P.O. Box 307
Owego, NY 13827
Tel. (607) 687–0338
Fax. (607) 687–5680

Family Court
Court Annex Building
20 Court Street
P.O. Box 10
Owego, NY 13827
Tel. (607) 687–1730
Fax. (607) 687–3240

Surrogate's Court
Court Annex Building
20 Court Street
Owego, NY 13827
Tel. (607) 687–1303
Fax. (607) 687–3240

Tioga County Law Library
18 East Street
Waverly, NY 14892
Tel. (607) 565–9341

Sheriff
Tioga County Public Safety Building
103 Corporate Drive
Owego, NY 13827–3249
Tel. (607) 687–1010
Fax. (607) 687–6755

TOMPKINS COUNTY
[6th Judicial District, 3rd Judicial Department]
www.courts.state.ny.us/courts/6jd/tompkins/

Supreme Court
Tompkins County Courthouse
320 North Tioga Street
P.O. Box 70
Ithaca, NY 14851–0070
Tel. (607) 272–0466
Fax. (607) 256–0301

County Court
Tompkins County Courthouse
320 North Tioga Street
P.O. Box 70
Ithaca, NY 14851–0070
Tel. (607) 272–0466
Fax. (607) 256–0301

Family Court
Tompkins County Courthouse
320 North Tioga Street
P.O. Box 70
Ithaca, NY 14851–0070
Tel. (607) 277–1517
Fax. (607) 277–5027

COURT DIRECTORY

Surrogate's Court
Tompkins County Courthouse
320 North Tioga Street
Ithaca, NY 14851–0070
Tel. (607) 277–0622
Fax. (607) 256–2572

Ithaca City Court
118 East Clinton Street
Ithaca, NY 14850–5689
Tel. (607) 273–2263
Fax. (607) 277–3702

Tompkins County Law Library
Tompkins County Courthouse
P.O. Box 70
320 North Tioga Street
Ithaca, NY 14850
Tel. (607) 272–0045
Fax. (607) 272–3276

Sheriff
779 Warren Road
Ithaca, NY 14850–1255
Tel. (607) 257–1345
Fax. (607) 266–5436

ULSTER COUNTY
[3rd Judicial District, 3rd Judicial Department]

Supreme Court
Ulster County Courthouse
285 Wall Street
Kingston, NY 12401–3817
Tel. (845) 340–3377
Fax. (845) 340–3387

County Court
Ulster County Courthouse
285 Wall Street
Kingston, NY 12401-3817
Tel. (845) 340–3377
Fax. (845) 340–3387

Family Court
16 Lucas Avenue
Kingston, NY 12401–3708
Tel. (845) 340–3600
Fax. (845) 340–3626

Surrogate's Court
240 Fair Street
Kingston, NY 12401–3806
Tel. (845) 340–3348
Fax. (845) 340–3352

CD-32

Kingston City Court
1 Garraghan Drive
Kingston, NY 12401–6065
Tel. (845) 338–2974
Fax. (845) 338–1443

Ulster County Supreme Court Law Library
285 Wall Street
Kingston, NY 12401
Tel. (845) 340–3053
Fax. (845) 340–3773

Sheriff
380 Boulevard
Kingston, NY 12401
Tel. (845) 340–3590
Fax. (845) 331–2810

WARREN COUNTY
[4th Judicial District, 3rd Judicial Department]

Supreme Court
Warren County Municipal Center
1340 State Route 9
Lake George, NY 12845
Tel. (518) 761–6431
Fax. (518) 761–6253

County Court
Warren County Municipal Center
1340 State Route 9
Lake George, NY 12845
Tel. (518) 761–6431
Fax. (518) 791–6253

Family Court
Warren County Municipal Center
1340 State Route 9
Lake George, NY 12845
Tel. (518) 761–6500
Fax. (518) 761–6230

Surrogate's Court
Warren County Municipal Center
1340 State Route 9
Lake George, NY 12845
Tel. (518) 761–6514
Fax. (518) 761–6511

Glens Falls City Court
City Hall
42 Ridge Street, 3rd Floor
Glens Falls, NY 12801
Tel. (518) 798–4714
Fax. (518) 798–0137

Warren County Supreme Court Law Library
Warren County Municipal Center
1340 State Route 9
Lake George, NY 12845
Tel. (518) 761–6442
Fax. (518) 761–6586

Sheriff
1400 State Route 9
Lake George, NY 12845–3434
Tel. (518) 743–2500
Fax. (518) 743–2519

WASHINGTON COUNTY
[4th Judicial District, 3rd Judicial Department]

Supreme Court
383 Broadway
Fort Edward, NY 12828–1015
Tel. (518) 746–2521
Fax. (518) 746–2519

County Court
383 Broadway
Fort Edward, NY 12828–1015
Tel. (518) 746–2521
Fax. (518) 746–2519

Family Court
383 Broadway
Fort Edward, NY 12828–1015
Tel. (518) 746–2501
Fax. (518) 746–2503

Surrogate's Court
383 Broadway
Fort Edward, NY 12828–1015
Tel. (518) 746–2545
Fax. (518) 746–2547

Washington County Law Library
383 Broadway
Fort Edward, NY 12828–1015
Tel. (518) 746–2521

Sheriff
399 Broadway
Fort Edward, NY 12828–1021
Tel. (518) 746–2475
Fax. (518) 746–2398

WAYNE COUNTY
[7th Judicial District, 4th Judicial Department]

Supreme Court
Wayne County Hall of Justice
54 Broad Street, Suite 106
Lyons, NY 14489
Tel. (315) 946–5459
Fax. (315) 946–5456

County Court
Wayne County Hall of Justice
54 Broad Street, Suite 106
Lyons, NY 14489
Tel. (315) 946–5459
Fax. (315) 946–5456

Family Court
Wayne County Hall of Justice
54 Broad Street, Suite 106
Lyons, NY 14489
Tel. (315) 946–5420
Fax. (315) 946–5456

Surrogate's Court
Wayne County Hall of Justice
54 Broad Street, Suite 106
Lyons, NY 14489
Tel. (315) 946–5430
Fax. (315) 946–5433

Wayne County Law Library
122 Broad Street
Lyons, NY 14489
Tel. (315) 946–9262

Sheriff
7368 Route 31
Lyons, NY 14489
Tel. (315) 946–9711
Fax. (315) 946–5811

WESTCHESTER COUNTY
[9th Judicial District, 2nd Judicial Department]
www.courts.state.ny.us/courts/9jd/westchester/

Supreme Court
111 Dr. Martin Luther King, Jr. Boulevard
White Plains, NY 10601
Tel. (914) 824–5300/5400
Fax. (914) 995–3427

COURT DIRECTORY

County Court
111 Dr. Martin Luther King, Jr. Boulevard
White Plains, NY 10601
Tel. (914) 824–5300/5400
Fax. (914) 995–3427

Family Court (New Rochelle)
420 North Avenue
New Rochelle, NY 10801
Tel. (914) 813–6590
Fax. (914) 813–5580

Family Court (White Plains)
Westchester County Courthouse
111 Dr. Martin Luther King, Jr. Boulevard
White Plains, NY 10601
Tel. (914) 824–5500
Fax. (914) 995–4468

Family Court (Yonkers)
53 South Broadway
Yonkers, NY 10701
Tel. (914) 831–6555
Fax. (914) 231–3016

Surrogate's Court
111 Dr. Martin Luther King Jr. Blvd.
White Plains, NY 10601
Tel. (914) 824–5656
Fax. (914) 995–3728

Mount Vernon City Court
2 Roosevelt Square North
Mount Vernon, NY 10550–2060
Tel. (914) 831–6440
Fax. (914) 699–1230

New Rochelle City Court
475 North Avenue
New Rochelle, NY 10801
Tel. (914) 654–2207
Fax. (914) 654–0344

Peekskill City Court
2 Nelson Avenue
Peekskill, NY 10566
Tel. (914) 831–6480
Fax. (914) 736–1889

Rye City Court
21 McCullough Place
Rye, NY 10580
Tel. (914) 831–6400
Fax. (914) 967–4354

White Plains City Court
77 South Lexington Avenue
White Plains, NY 10601
Tel. (914) 824–5675
Fax. (914) 422–6058

Yonkers City Court
100 South Broadway
Yonkers, NY 10701
Tel. (914) 831–6450
Fax. (914) 377–6395

Westchester County Law Library
111 Dr. Martin Luther King, Jr. Boulevard
White Plains, NY 10601
Tel. (914) 824–5660

Sheriff
Department of Public Safety
Saw Mill River Parkway
Hawthorne, NY 10532–1027
Tel. (914) 741–4400

WYOMING COUNTY

[8th Judicial District, 4th Judicial Department]

Supreme Court
147 North Main Street
Warsaw, NY 14569
Tel. (585) 786–3148
Fax. (585) 786–2818

County Court
147 North Main Street
Warsaw, NY 14569
Tel. (585) 786–2253
Fax. (585) 786–2818

Family Court
147 North Main Street
Warsaw, NY 14569
Tel. (585) 786–3148
Fax. (585) 786–3800

Surrogate's Court
147 North Main Street
Warsaw, NY 14569
Tel. (585) 786–3148
Fax. (585) 786–3800

Wyoming County Law Library
Wyoming County Courthouse
143 North Main Street
Warsaw, NY 14569–1199
Tel. (585) 786–3148
Fax. (585) 786–3800

Sheriff
151 North Main Street
Warsaw, NY 14569–1123
Tel. (585) 786–8989
Fax: (585) 786–8961
Email: fheimann@wyomingco.net

YATES COUNTY
[7th Judicial District, 4th Judicial Department]
www.courts.state.ny.us/courts/7jd/

Supreme Court
Yates County Courthouse
415 Liberty Street
Penn Yan, NY 14527
Tel. (315) 536–5126
Fax. (315) 536–5190

County Court
Yates County Courthouse
415 Liberty Street
Penn Yan, NY 14527
Tel. (315) 536–5126
Fax. (315) 536–5190

Family Court
415 Liberty Street
Penn Yan, NY 14527
Tel. (315) 536–5127
Fax. (315) 536–5190

Surrogate's Court
415 Liberty Street
Penn Yan, NY 14527
Tel. (315) 536–5130
Fax. (315) 536–5190

Yates County Law Library
214 Main Street
Penn Yan, NY 14527
Tel. (315) 536–6114

Sheriff
227 Main Street
Penn Yan, NY 14527–1720
Tel. (315) 536–4438
Fax. (315) 536–5191

NEW YORK LOCAL CIVIL RULES

ISBN 978-0-314-94055-1

9 780314 940551